2009

INGENIX®

Educational ICD-9-CM Volumes 1, 2, & 3 and HCPCS Level II

First Printing — December 2008
Made in the USA

ISBN 978-1-60151-131-7

PUBLISHER'S NOTICE

All codes, indexes, and other material in the ICD-9-CM are compiled from official ICD-9-CM codes and instructions as well as the Medicare regulations and manuals issued or authorized by the Centers for Medicare and Medicaid Services. The code book is designed to provide accurate and authoritative information in regard to the subject covered, and every reasonable effort has been made to ensure the accuracy of the information within these pages. However, the ultimate responsibility for correct coding lies with the provider of services.

Ingenix, its employees, agents and staff make no representation, warranty or guarantee that this compilation of codes and narratives is error-free or that the use of this code book will prevent differences of opinion or disputes with Medicare or other third-party payers as to the codes that are accepted or the amounts that will be paid to providers for services, and will bear no responsibilty or liability for the results or consequences of the use of this code book.

CODE UPDATE INFORMATION

We are committed to providing you with the code update information you need to code accurately and to be in compliance with HIPAA regulations. In case of adoption of additional ICD-9-CM code changes effective April 1, 2009, Ingenix will provide these code changes to you at no additional cost! Just check back at **http://www.shopingenix.com/productalerts** to review the latest information concerning any new changes.

In case of HCPCS Level II code changes. Just check back at **http:\\www.shopingenix.com/productalerts** and look for the HCPCS Level II update file.

Contents

Preface

Providers are required by law under the Health Insurance Portability and Accountability Act of 1996 (HIPAA) to document and report healthcare services provided to Medicare beneficiares using standard code sets. The standard code set for documenting and reporting diagnoses and reasons for health care encounters in all setting's is ICD-9-CM. For acute care hospital admissions, ICD-9-CM is required for documenting and reporting procedures and services. The HCPCS (Healthcare Common Procedure Coding System) Level II code set is the standard code set for reporting medical services and supplies.

Educational ICD-9-CM Volumes 1, 2, &3 and HCPCS Level II has been designed with the coder in mind. All volumes of the most recent official government versions have been combined into one book.

Our technical experts have drawn upon their extensive hands-on experience to enhance the government's book with valuable features essential to correct coding and reimbursement. Additional coding information and self-test are designed to enhance the learning experience. This coding resource is designed to function not only as a training tool, but also as a professional guide to both ICD-9-CM and HCPCS Level II code sets.

As you review the content, you'll find the following:

- ICD-9-CM official guidelines for coding and reporting, published by the U.S. Department of Health and Human Services and approved by the cooperating parties (American Hospital Association (AHA), American Health Information Management Association (AHIMA), Centers for Medicare and Medicaid Services (formerly known as Health Care Financing Administration) and National Center for Health Statisics (NCHS))
- All the official ICD-9-CM codes
- Symbols that alert coders to codes requiring a fourth- or fifth-digit assignment
- An explanation of the basic ICD-9-CM coding conventions
- The 10 steps to Correct Coding feature
- All official HCPCS Level II code and descriptions
- Medicare rules indicated by color coding and icons
- Enhanced index to HCPCS Level II
- Medicare manual references
- HCPCS modifiers
- Enhanced table of drugs and chemicals

Please review "How to Use ICD-9-CM for Hospitals (Volumes 1, 2 & 3)" in this section to learn about the features that will help you assign and report correct codes, ensuring appropriate reimbursement.

Use of Official Sources

The ICD-9-CM for Hospitals contains the official U.S. Department of Health and Human Services, Ninth Revision, Sixth Edition ICD-9-CM codes, effective for the current year.

Technical Editors

Wendy Gabbert, CPC, CPC-H, PCS, FCS, *Clinical/Technical Editor, Ingenix*
Ms. Gabbert has more than 25 years of experience in the health care field. She has extensive background in CPT/HCPCS and ICD-9-CM coding. She served several years as a coding consultant. Her areas of expertise include physician and hospital CPT coding assessments, chargemaster reviews, and the outpatient prospective payment system (OPPS). She is a member of the American Academy of Professional Coders and American College of Medical Coding Specialists.

Anita C. Hart, RHIA, CCS, CCS-P, *Product Manager, Ingenix*
Ms. Hart's experience includes conducting and publishing research in clinical medicine and human genetics for Yale University, Massachusetts General Hospital, and Massachusetts Institute of Technology. In addition, Ms. Hart has supervised medical records management, health information management, coding and reimbursement, and worker's compensation issues as the office manager for a physical therapy rehabilitation clinic. Ms. Hart is an expert in physician and facility coding, reimbursement systems, and compliance issues. Ms. Hart has developed and has served as technical consultant for numerous other publications for hospital and physician practices. Currrently, Ms. Hart is the Product Manager and Technical Editor for the ICD-9-CM and ICD-10-CM/PCS product lines.

Melinda S. Stegman, MBA, CCS, *Clinical/Technical Editor, Ingenix*
Ms. Stegman has 27 years of experience in the HIM profession and has been responsible for managing the clinical aspects of the HSS/Ingenix HIM Consulting practice in the Washington, DC area office. Her areas of specialization include training on inpatient and DRG coding, outpatient coding, and Ambulatory Payment Classifications (APCs) for HIM professionals, software developers, and other clients; developing an outpatient billing/coding compliance tool for a major accounting firm; and managing HIM consulting practices. Ms. Stegman is a regular contributing author for *Advance for Health Information Management Professionals* and for the *Journal of Health Care Compliance*. She has performed coding assessments and educational sessions throughout the country. Ms. Stegman is credentialed by the American Health Information Management Association (AHIMA) as a Certified Coding Specialist (CCS) and holds a Master of Business Administration degree with a concentration in health care management from the University of New Mexico – Albuquerque.

Beth Ford, RHIT, CCS, *Clinical/Technical Editor, Ingenix*
Ms. Ford is a clinical/technical editor for Ingenix. She has extensive background in both physician and facility ICD-9-CM and CPT/HCPCS coding. Ms. Ford has served as a coding specialist, coding manager, coding trainer/educator and coding consultant, as well as a health information management director. She is an active member of the American Heath Information Management Association (AHIMA).

In addition to the editors, the following people have contributed to this book:

Stacy Perry, Manager, Desktop Publishing Manager
Tracy Betzler, Desktop Publishing Specialist
Hope Dunn, Desktop Publishing Specialist
Toni Stewart, Desktop Publishing Specialist
Kate Holden, Editor

Introduction

History and Future of ICD-9

The International Classification of Diseases, Ninth Revision, Clinical Modification (ICD-9-CM) is based on the official version of the World Health Organization's Ninth Revision, International Classification of Diseases (ICD-9). ICD-9 classifies morbidity and mortality information for statistical purposes, and for the indexing of hospital records by disease and operations, for data storage and retrieval.

This modification of ICD-9 supplants the Eighth Revision International Classification of Diseases, Adapted for Use in the United States (ICDA-8) and the Hospital Adaptation of ICDA (H-ICDA).

The concept of extending the International Classification of Diseases for use in hospital indexing was originally developed in response to a need for a more efficient basis for storage and retrieval of diagnostic data. In 1950, the U.S. Public Health Service and the Veterans Administration began independent tests of the International Classification of Diseases for hospital indexing purposes. The following year, the Columbia Presbyterian Medical Center in New York City adopted the International Classification of Diseases, Sixth Revision, with some modifications for use in its medical record department. A few years later, the Commission on Professional and Hospital Activities (CPHA) in Ann Arbor, Mich., adopted the International Classification of Diseases with similar modifications for use in hospitals participating in the Professional Activity Study.

The problem of adapting ICD for indexing hospital records was taken up by the U.S. National Committee on Vital and Health Statistics through its subcommittee on hospital statistics. The subcommittee reviewed the modifications made by the various users of ICD and proposed that uniform changes be made. This was done by a small working party.

In view of the growing interest in the use of the International Classification of Diseases for hospital indexing, a study was undertaken in 1956 by the American Hospital Association and the American Medical Record Association (then the American Association of Medical Record Librarians) of the relative efficiencies of coding systems for diagnostic indexing. This study indicated the International Classification of Diseases provided a suitable and efficient framework for indexing hospital records. The major users of the International Classification of Diseases for hospital indexing purposes then consolidated their experiences, and an adaptation was first published in December 1959. A revision was issued in 1962 and the first "Classification of Operations and Treatments" was included.

In 1966, the international conference for revising the International Classification of Diseases noted the eighth revision of ICD had been constructed with hospital indexing in mind and considered the revised classification suitable, in itself, for hospital use in some countries. However, it was recognized that the basic classification might provide inadequate detail for diagnostic indexing in other countries. A group of consultants was asked to study the eighth revision of ICD (ICD-8) for applicability to various users in the United States. This group recommended that further detail be provided for coding of hospital and morbidity data. The American Hospital Association was requested to develop the needed adaptation proposals. This was done by an advisory committee (the Advisory Committee to the Central Office on ICDA). In 1968 the United States Public Health Service published the product, Eighth Revision International Classification of Diseases, Adapted for Use in the United States. This became commonly known as ICDA-8, and beginning in 1968 it served as the basis for coding diagnostic data for both official morbidity and mortality statistics in the United States.

In 1968, the CPHA published the Hospital Adaptation of ICDA (H-ICDA) based on both the original ICD-8 and ICDA-8. In 1973, CPHA published a revision of H-ICDA, referred to as H-ICDA-2. Hospitals throughout the United States were divided in their use of these classifications until January 1979, when ICD-9-CM was made the single classification intended primarily for use in the United States, replacing these earlier related, but somewhat dissimilar, classifications.

Physicians have been required by law to submit diagnosis codes for Medicare reimbursement since the passage of the Medicare Catastrophic Coverage Act of 1988. This act requires physician offices to include the appropriate diagnosis codes when billing for services provided to Medicare beneficiaries on or after April 1, 1989. The Centers for Medicare and Medicaid Services (formerly known as Health Care Financing Administration) designated ICD-9-CM as the coding system physicians must use.

In 1993 the World Health Organization published the newest version of International Classification of Diseases, Tenth Revision, ICD-10. This version contains the greatest number of changes in the history of ICD. There are more codes (5,500 more than ICD-9) to allow more specific reporting of diseases and newly recognized conditions. ICD-10 consists of three volumes; Tabular List (volume I), instructions (volume 2) and the Alphabetic Index (volume 3). It contains 21 chapters including two supplementary ones. The codes are alphanumeric (A00–T98, V01–Y98 and Z00–Z99). Currently ICD-10 is being used in some European countries with implementation expected in the year 2011 in the United States.

ICD-9-CM Background

In February 1977, a steering committee was convened by the National Center for Health Statistics to provide advice and counsel in developing a clinical modification of ICD-9. The organizations represented on the steering committee included the following:

- American Association of Health Data Systems
- American Hospital Association
- American Medical Record Association
- Association for Health Records
- Council on Clinical Classifications
- Centers for Medicare and Medicaid Services, Department of Health and Human Services
- WHO Center for Classification of Diseases for North America, sponsored by the National Center for Health Statistics, Department of Health and Human Services

The Council on Clinical Classifications was sponsored by the following:

- American Academy of Pediatrics
- American College of Obstetricians and Gynecologists
- American College of Physicians
- American College of Surgeons
- American Psychiatric Association
- Commission on Professional and Hospital Activities

The steering committee met periodically in 1977. Clinical guidance and technical input were provided by task forces on classification from the Council on Clinical Classification's sponsoring organizations.

ICD-9-CM is a clinical modification of the World Health Organization's ICD-9. The term "clinical" is used to emphasize the modification's intent: to serve as a useful tool to classify morbidity data for indexing medical records, medical care review, and ambulatory and other medical care programs, as well as for basic health statistics. To describe the clinical picture of the patient, the codes must be more precise than those needed only for statistical groupings and trend analysis.

Characteristics of ICD-9-CM

ICD-9-CM far exceeds its predecessors in the number of codes provided. The disease classification has been expanded to include health-related conditions and to provide greater specificity at the fifth-digit level of detail. These fifth digits are not optional; they are intended for use in recording the information substantiated in the clinical record.

Volume I (Tabular List) of ICD-9-CM contains four appendices:

Appendix A:	Morphology of Neoplasms
Appendix B:	Deleted Effective October 1, 2004
Appendix C:	Classification of Drugs by American Hospital Formulary Service List Number and Their ICD-9-CM Equivalents
Appendix D:	Classification of Industrial Accidents According to Agency
Appendix E:	List of Three-Digit Categories

These appendices are included as a reference to provide further information about the patient's clinical picture, to further define a diagnostic statement, to aid in classifying new drugs or to reference three-digit categories.

Volume 2 (Alphabetic Index) of ICD-9-CM contains many diagnostic terms that do not appear in Volume I since the index includes most diagnostic terms currently in use.

Volume 3 (Procedure Index and Procedure Tabular) of ICD-9-CM contains codes for operations and procedures. The format for the tabular is the same as Volume 1 disease tabular, except the codes consist of two digits with one or two digits following the decimal point. Conventions in the index follow Volume 2 conventions except some subterms appear immediately below the main term rather than following alphabetizing rules.

The Disease Classification

ICD-9-CM is totally compatible with its parent system, ICD-9, thus meeting the need for comparability of morbidity and mortality statistics at the international level. A few fourth-digit codes were created in existing three-digit rubrics only when the necessary detail could not be accommodated by the use of a fifth-digit subclassification. To ensure that each rubric of ICD-9-CM collapses back to its ICD-9 counterpart the following specifications governed the ICD-9-CM disease classification:

Specifications for the Tabular List:

1. Three-digit rubrics and their contents are unchanged from ICD-9.
2. The sequence of three-digit rubrics is unchanged from ICD-9.
3. Three-digit rubrics are not added to the main body of the classification.
4. Unsubdivided three-digit rubrics are subdivided where necessary to
   - add clinical detail
   - isolate terms for clinical accuracy.
5. The modification in ICD-9-CM is accomplished by adding a fifth digit to existing ICD-9 rubrics, except as noted under #7 below.
6. The optional dual classification in ICD-9 is modified.
   - Duplicate rubrics are deleted:
     - four-digit manifestation categories duplicating etiology entries
     - manifestation inclusion terms duplicating etiology entries
   - Manifestations of disease are identified, to the extent possible, by creating five-digit codes in the etiology rubrics.
   - When the manifestation of a disease cannot be included in the etiology rubrics, provision for its identification is made by retaining the ICD-9 rubrics used for classifying manifestations of disease.
7. The format of ICD-9-CM is revised from that used in ICD-9.
   - American spelling of medical terms is used.
   - Inclusion terms are indented beneath the titles of codes.
   - Codes not to be used for primary tabulation of disease are printed in italics with the notation, "code first underlying disease."

Specifications for the Alphabetic Index:

1. The format of the Alphabetic Index follows that of ICD-9.
2. When two codes are required to indicate etiology and manifestation, the manifestation code appears in brackets (e.g., diabetic cataract 250.5 *[366.41]*).

The ICD-9-CM Coordination and Maintenance Committee

The four cooperating parties involved in maintaining the ICD-9-CM classification system include representatives of the American Hospital Association (AHA), the Centers for Medicare and Medicaid Services (CMS), the National Center for Health Statistics (NCHS), and the American Health Information Management Association (AHIMA).

Proposals for changes to the ICD-9-CM classification system are submitted and discussed in two open forum meetings held in March and September of each year at the Headquarters of the Centers for Medicare and Medicaid Services, Baltimore, Maryland. Comments received during and after the meetings are then discussed by the Committee. A notice of the new codes and code revisions approved by the Committee are published in the Federal Register as part of the proposed and final rule for the changes to the inpatient prospective payment system. The complete official document of changes to the classification system is released as the Addenda for the International Classification of Diseases, Ninth Revision, Clinical Modification, Sixth Edition, Volumes 1, 2 and 3.ICD-9-CM for Hospitals is based on the official version of the International Classification of Diseases, Ninth Revision, Clinical Modification, Sixth Edition, issued by the U.S. Department of Health and Human Services. Annual code changes are implemented by the government and are effective Oct. 1 and valid through Sept. 30 of the following year.

Schedule of official ICD-9-CM Update

To comply with the provisions of the Medicare Prescription Drug, Improvement and Modernization Act of 2003, the Centers for Medicare and Medicaid Services (CMS) is required to update the ICD-9-CM code set for both diagnoses and procedures on a semi-annual basis (October 1 and April 1). This provision was enacted to capture new services and technology that will be considered for add-on payments under the Inpatient Prospective Payment System (PPS) or the capture data on emergent diseases.

How to Use the ICD-9-CM for Hospitals (Volumes 1, 2 & 3)

This code book is totally compatible with its parent system, ICD-9, thus meeting the need for comparability of morbidity and mortality statistics at the international level.

This book is consistent with the content of the government's version of ICD-9-CM. However, to accommodate the coder's approach to coding, the Alphabetic Index has been placed before the Tabular List in both the disease and procedure classifications. This allows the user to locate the correct codes in a logical, natural manner by locating the term in the index, then confirming the accuracy of the code in the Tabular List.

Steps to Correct Coding

1. Look up the main term in the Alphabetic Index and scan the subterm entries as appropriate. Follow any cross-references such as "*see*" and "*see also*." Do not code from the Alphabetic Index without verifying the accuracy of the code in the Tabular List.
2. Locate the code in the numerically arranged Tabular List.
3. Observe the punctuation, footnotes, cross-references, color-coded prompts and other conventions described in the 'Conventions' section.
4. To determine the appropriateness of the code selection, read all instructional material:
   - "includes" and "*excludes*" notes
   - "see," "*see also*" and "*see category*" cross-references
   - "use additional code" and "*code first underlying disease*" instructions
   - "code also" and "*omit code*" notes
   - fourth- and fifth-digit requirements
   - CC exclusions
5. Consult definitions, relevant illustrations, CC exclusions, color coding and reimbursement prompts, the check fourth- and fifth-digit, age and sex symbols. Refer to the color/symbol legend at the bottom of each page for symbols. Refer to the list of footnotes that is included in the "Additional Conventions" section of this book for a full explanation of a footnote associated with a code.
6. Consult the official ICD-9-CM guidelines for coding and reporting, and refer to the AHA's *Coding Clinic for ICD-9-CM* for coding guidelines governing the use of specific codes.
7. Confirm and transcribe the correct code.

Organization

Introduction

The introductory material in this book includes the history and future of ICD-9-CM as well as an overview of the classification system.

Official ICD-9-CM Conventions

This section provides a full explanation of all the official footnotes, symbols, instructional notes, and conventions found in the official government version.

Coding Guidelines

Included in this book are the official ICD-9-CM coding guidelines as approved by the four cooperating parties of the ICD-9-CM Coordination and Maintenance Committee. Failure to comply with the official coding guidelines may result in denied or delayed claims.

Disease Classification: Alphabetic Index to Diseases

The Alphabetic Index to Diseases is separated by tabs labeled with the letters of the alphabet, contains diagnostic terms for illnesses, injuries and reasons for encounters with health care professionals. The Table of Drugs and Chemicals is easily located with the tab in this section.

The warning statement at the bottom of every page of the index, Subterms under main terms may continue to next column or page, is a reminder to always check for additional subterms before making final selection.

Disease Classification: Tabular List of Diseases

The Tabular List of Diseases arranges the ICD-9-CM codes and descriptors numerically. QuickFlip color tabs divide this section into chapters, identified by the code range on the tab.

The Tabular List includes two supplementary classifications:

- V Codes—Supplementary Classification of Factors Influencing Health Status and Contact with Health Services (V01–V89)
- E Codes—Supplementary Classification of External Causes of Injury and Poisoning (E800–E999)

ICD-9-CM includes four official appendixes.

- Appendix A — Morphology of Neoplasms
- Appendix B: — Deleted Effective October 1, 2004
- Appendix C — Classification of Drugs by AHFS List
- Appendix D — Classification of Industrial Accidents According to Agency
- Appendix E — List of Three-digit Categories

These appendices are included as a reference to provide further information about the patient's circumstances, help further define a diagnostic statement, maintain a tumor registry and aid in classifying new drugs.

Procedure Classification: Alphabetic Index to Procedures

The Alphabetic Index to Procedures lists common surgical and procedural terminology.

The warning statement at the bottom of every page of the index, Subterms under main terms may continue to next column or page, is a reminder to always check for additional subterms before making final selection.

Procedure Classification: Tabular List of Procedures

The Tabular List of Procedures numerically arranges the procedure codes and their descriptors.

ICD-9-CM Official Conventions

ICD-9-CM Footnotes, Symbols, Instructional Notes and Conventions

This ICD-9-CM for Hospitals preserves all the footnotes, symbols, instructional notes and conventions found in the government's official version. Accurate coding depends upon understanding the meaning of these elements.

The following appear in the disease Tabular List, unless otherwise noted.

ICD-9-CM Conventions Used in the Tabular List

In addition to the symbols and footnotes above, the ICD-9-CM disease tabular has certain abbreviations, punctuation, symbols and other conventions. Our ICD-9-CM for Hospitals preserves these conventions. Proper use of the conventions will lead to efficient and accurate coding.

Abbreviations

NEC Not elsewhere classifiable
This abbreviation is used when the ICD-9-CM system does not provide a code specific for the patient's condition.

NOS Not otherwise specified
This abbreviation is the equivalent of 'unspecified' and is used only when the coder lacks the information necessary to code to a more specific four-digit subcategory.

[ ] Brackets enclose synonyms, alternative terminology or explanatory phrases.

Brackets that appear beneath a code indicate the fifth digits that are considered valid fifth digits for the code. This convention is applied for those instances in ICD-9-CM where not all common fifth digits are considered valid for each subcategory within a category.

[ ] Slanted brackets that appear in the Alphabetic Indexes indicate mandatory multiple coding. Both codes must be assigned to fully describe the condition and are sequenced in the order listed.

( ) Parentheses enclose supplementary words, called nonessential modifiers, that may be present in the narrative description of a disease without affecting the code assignment.

: Colons are used in the Tabular List after an incomplete term that needs one or more of the modifiers that follow in order to make it assignable to a given category.

} Braces enclose a series of terms, each of which is modified by the statement appearing to the right of the brace.

Other Conventions

Boldface Boldface type is used for all codes and titles in the Tabular List.

Italicized Italicized type is used for all exclusion notes and to identify codes that should not be used for describing the primary diagnosis.

Instructional Notes Used in the Tabular

These notes appear only in the Tabular List of Diseases:

Includes: An includes note further defines or clarifies the content of the chapter, subchapter, category, sub-category or subclassification.

Excludes: Terms following the word "Excludes" are not classified to the chapter, subchapter, category, subcategory or specific subclassification code under which it is found. The note also may provide the location of the excluded diagnosis. Excludes notes are italicized.

Use additional code:

This instruction signals the coder that an additional code should be used if the information is available to provide a more complete picture of that diagnosis.

There are coding circumstances outside of the etiology/ manifestation convention when multiple coding for a single condition is required. The 'Use additional code' note will be found under the associated condition code in the tabular. In the index, the multiple coding requirement is indicated by the use of the slanted bracket. The two codes are to be sequenced as listed in the index. For example, retinal arterisosclerosis must be coded using two codes sequenced as listed in the index.

Code first underlying disease:

The "Code first underlying disease" instructional note found under certain codes is a sequencing rule. Most often this sequencing rule applies to the etiology/manifestation convention and is found under at the manifestation code. The manifestation code may never be used alone or as a primary diagnosis (i.e., sequenced first). The instructional note, the code and its descriptor appear in italics in the Tabular List.

Not all codes with a 'Code first underlying disease' instructional note are part of the etiology/manifestation convention. The 'Code first' note will appear, but the title of the code and the instructional note are not in italics. These codes may be reported alone or as the secondary diagnosis. For example, disseminated chorioretinitis may be reported as a principal diagnosis. However, if the underlying condition that caused disseminated chorioretinitis is known, such as tuberculous disseminated chorioretinitis, two codes are required and sequenced as listed in the index.

Code, if applicable, any causal condition first:

A code with this note indicates that this code may be assigned as a principal diagnosis when the causal condition is unknown or not applicable. If a causal condition is known, then the code for that condition should be sequenced as the principal or first-listed diagnosis.

Instructional Notes Used in the Index

Omit code:

"Omit code" is used to instruct the coder that no code is to be assigned. When this instruction is found in the Alphabetic Index to Diseases the medical term should not be coded as a diagnosis.

When used in Volume 3, '*omit code*' is meant to indicate procedures that do not merit separate code assignments, such as minor procedures preformed in conjunction with more extensive procedures or procedures that represent an operative approach.

See Condition:

The "*see* condition" note found in the Alphabetic Index to Disease instructs the coder to refer to a main term for the condition. This note will follow index terms that are nouns for anatomical sites or adjectival forms of disease term.

Morphology Codes

For each neoplastic disease listed in the index, a morphology code is provided that identifies histological type and behavior.

The histology is identified by the first four digits and the behavior is identified by the digit following the slash. Appendix A of Volume 1 contains a listing of morphology codes. This appendix is helpful when the pathology report identifies the neoplasm by using an M code. The coder may refer to Appendix A to determine the nomenclature of the neoplasm that will be the main term to search in the Index.

Additional Conventions

Additional Digits Required

✓3rd symbol indicates that the code requires a third digit.

✓4th This symbol indicates that the code requires a fourth digit.

✓5th This symbol indicates that a code requires a fifth digit.

☑ This symbol found only in the Alphabetic Index sections and the Table of Drugs and Chemicals indicates that an additional digit is required. Referring to the tabular section is essential to locate the appropriate additional digit.

Definitions

DEF: This symbol indicates a definition of disease or procedure term. The definition will appear in blue type in the Disease and Procedure Tabular Lists.

Color Coding

Manifestation Code

These codes will appear in italic type as well as with a blue color bar over the code title. A manifestation code is not allowed to be reported as a primary diagnosis because each describes a manifestation of some other underlying disease, not the disease itself. This is referred to as mandatory multiple coding of etiology and manifestation. Code the underlying disease first. A 'Code first underlying disease' instructional note will appear with underlying disease codes identified. In the Alphabetic Index these codes are listed as the secondary code in slanted bracket with the code for the underlying disease listed first. Medicare code edit

Other Notations

Alphabetic Indexes

▽ **Subterms under main terms may continue to next column or page.**

This warning statement is a reminder to always check for additional subterms and information that may continue onto the next page or column before making a final selection.

Coding Guidelines

Effective October 1, 2008
Narrative changes appear in bold text. Items underlined have been moved within the guidelines since October 1, 2007. The guidelines include the updated V Code Table.

The Centers for Medicare and Medicaid Services (CMS) and the National Center for Health Statistics (NCHS), two departments within the U.S. Federal Government's Department of Health and Human Services (DHHS) provide the following guidelines for coding and reporting using the International Classification of Diseases, 9th Revision, Clinical Modification (ICD-9-CM). These guidelines should be used as a companion document to the official version of the ICD-9CM as published on CD-ROM by the U.S. Government Printing Office (GPO).

These guidelines have been approved by the four organizations that make up the Cooperating Parties for the ICD-9-CM: the American Hospital Association (AHA), the American Health Information Management Association (AHIMA), CMS, and NCHS. These guidelines are included on the official government version of the ICD-9-CM, and also appear in "*Coding Clinic for ICD-9-CM*" published by the AHA.

These guidelines are a set of rules that have been developed to accompany and complement the official conventions and instructions provided within the ICD-9-CM itself. These guidelines are based on the coding and sequencing instructions in Volumes I, II and III of ICD-9-CM, but provide additional instruction. Adherence to these guidelines when assigning ICD-9-CM diagnosis and procedure codes is required under the Health Insurance Portability and Accountability Act (HIPAA). The diagnosis codes (Volumes 1-2) have been adopted under HIPAA for all healthcare settings. Volume 3 procedure codes have been adopted for inpatient procedures reported by hospitals. A joint effort between the healthcare provider and the coder is essential to achieve complete and accurate documentation, code assignment, and reporting of diagnoses and procedures. These guidelines have been developed to assist both the healthcare provider and the coder in identifying those diagnoses and procedures that are to be reported. The importance of consistent, complete documentation in the medical record cannot be overemphasized. Without such documentation accurate coding cannot be achieved. The entire record should be reviewed to determine the specific reason for the encounter and the conditions treated.

The term encounter is used for all settings, including hospital admissions. In the context of these guidelines, the term provider is used throughout the guidelines to mean physician or any qualified health care practitioner who is legally accountable for establishing the patient's diagnosis. Only this set of guidelines, approved by the Cooperating Parties, is official.

The guidelines are organized into sections. Section I includes the structure and conventions of the classification and general guidelines that apply to the entire classification, and chapter-specific guidelines that correspond to the chapters as they are arranged in the classification. Section II includes guidelines for selection of principal diagnosis for non-outpatient settings. Section III includes guidelines for reporting additional diagnoses in non-outpatient settings. Section IV is for outpatient coding and reporting.

Section I. Conventions, general coding guidelines and chapter specific guidelines

A. Conventions for the ICD-9-CM
   1. Format:
   2. Abbreviations
      a. Index abbreviations
      b. Tabular abbreviations
   3. Punctuation
   4. Includes and Excludes Notes and Inclusion terms
   5. Other and Unspecified codes
      a. "Other" codes
      b. "Unspecified" codes
   6. Etiology/manifestation convention ("code first", "use additional code" and "in diseases classified elsewhere" notes)
   7. "And"
   8. "With"
   9. "See" and "See Also"
B. General Coding Guidelines
   1. Use of Both Alphabetic Index and Tabular List
   2. Locate each term in the Alphabetic Index
   3. Level of Detail in Coding
   4. Code or codes from 001.0 through **V89**
   5. Selection of codes 001.0 through 999.9
   6. Signs and symptoms
   7. Conditions that are an integral part of a disease process
   8. Conditions that are not an integral part of a disease process
   9. Multiple coding for a single condition
   10. Acute and Chronic Conditions
   11. Combination Code
   12. Late Effects
   13. Impending or Threatened Condition
   14. Reporting Same Diagnosis Code More than Once
   15. Admissions/Encounters for Rehabilitation
   16. Documentation for BMI and Pressure Ulcer Stages
C. Chapter-Specific Coding Guidelines
   1. Chapter 1: Infectious and Parasitic Diseases (001-139)
      a. Human Immunodeficiency Virus (HIV) Infections
      b. Septicemia, Systemic Inflammatory Response Syndrome (SIRS), Sepsis, Severe Sepsis and Septic Shock
      c. Methicillin Resistant *Staphylococcus aureus* (MRSA) Conditions
   2. Chapter 2: Neoplasms (140-239)
      a. Treatment directed at the malignancy
      b. Treatment of secondary site
      c. Coding and sequencing of complications
      d. Primary malignancy previously excised
      e. Admissions/Encounters involving chemotherapy, immunotherapy and radiation therapy
      f. Admission/encounter to determine extent of malignancy
      g. Symptoms, signs, and ill-defined conditions listed in Chapter 16 associated with neoplasms
      h. Admission/encounter for pain control/management
      i. Malignant neoplasm associated with transplanted organ
   3. Chapter 3: Endocrine, Nutritional, and Metabolic Diseases and Immunity Disorders (240-279)
      a. Diabetes mellitus
   4. Chapter 4: Diseases of Blood and Blood Forming Organs (280-289)
      a. Anemia of chronic disease
   5. Chapter 5: Mental Disorders (290-319)
      Reserved for future guideline expansion
   6. Chapter 6: Diseases of Nervous System and Sense Organs (320-389)
      a. Pain - Category 338
   7. Chapter 7: Diseases of Circulatory System (390-459)
      a. Hypertension
      b. Cerebral infarction/stroke/cerebrovascular accident (CVA)
      c. Postoperative cerebrovascular accident
      d. Late Effects of Cerebrovascular Disease
      e. Acute myocardial infarction (AMI)
   8. Chapter 8: Diseases of Respiratory System (460-519)
      a. Chronic Obstructive Pulmonary Disease [COPD] and Asthma
      b. Chronic Obstructive Pulmonary Disease [COPD] and Bronchitis
      c. Acute Respiratory Failure
      d. Influenza due to identified avian influenza virus (avian influenza)
   9. Chapter 9: Diseases of Digestive System (520-579)
      Reserved for future guideline expansion
   10. Chapter 10: Diseases of Genitourinary System (580-629)
      a. Chronic kidney disease
   11. Chapter 11: Complications of Pregnancy, Childbirth, and the Puerperium **(630-679)**
      a. General Rules for Obstetric Cases
      b. Selection of OB Principal or First-listed Diagnosis
      c. Fetal Conditions Affecting the Management of the Mother
      d. HIV Infection in Pregnancy, Childbirth and the Puerperium
      e. Current Conditions Complicating Pregnancy
      f. Diabetes mellitus in pregnancy
      g. Gestational diabetes
      h. Normal Delivery, Code 650
      i. The Postpartum and Peripartum Periods
      j. Code 677, Late effect of complication of pregnancy
      k. Abortions
   12. Chapter 12: Diseases Skin and Subcutaneous Tissue (680-709)
      a. Pressure ulcer stage codes

13. Chapter 13: Diseases of Musculoskeletal and Connective Tissue (710-739)
    a. Coding of Pathologic Fractures
14. Chapter 14: Congenital Anomalies (740-759)
    a. Codes in categories 740-759, Congenital Anomalies
15. Chapter 15: Newborn (Perinatal) Guidelines (760-779)
    a. General Perinatal Rules
    b. Use of codes V30-V39
    c. Newborn transfers
    d. Use of category V29
    e. Use of other V codes on perinatal records
    f. Maternal Causes of Perinatal Morbidity
    g. Congenital Anomalies in Newborns
    h. Coding Additional Perinatal Diagnoses
    i. Prematurity and Fetal Growth Retardation
    j. Newborn sepsis
16. Chapter 16: Signs, Symptoms and Ill-Defined Conditions (780-799)
    Reserved for future guideline expansion
17. Chapter 17: Injury and Poisoning (800-999)
    a. Coding of Injuries
    b. Coding of Traumatic Fractures
    c. Coding of Burns
    d. Coding of Debridement of Wound, Infection, or Burn
    e. Adverse Effects, Poisoning and Toxic Effects
    f. Complications of care
    g. SIRS due to Non-infectious Process
18. Classification of Factors Influencing Health Status and Contact with Health Service (Supplemental V01-**V89**)
    a. Introduction
    b. V codes use in any healthcare setting
    c. V Codes indicate a reason for an encounter
    d. Categories of V Codes
    e. V Code Table
19. Supplemental Classification of External Causes of Injury and Poisoning (E-codes, E800-E999)
    a. General E Code Coding Guidelines
    b. Place of Occurrence Guideline
    c. Adverse Effects of Drugs, Medicinal and Biological Substances Guidelines
    d. Multiple Cause E Code Coding Guidelines
    e. Child and Adult Abuse Guideline
    f. Unknown or Suspected Intent Guideline
    g. Undetermined Cause
    h. Late Effects of External Cause Guidelines
    i. Misadventures and Complications of Care Guidelines
    j. Terrorism Guidelines

Section II. Selection of Principal Diagnosis

A. Codes for symptoms, signs, and ill-defined conditions
B. Two or more interrelated conditions, each potentially meeting the definition for principal diagnosis
C. Two or more diagnoses that equally meet the definition for principal diagnosis
D. Two or more comparative or contrasting conditions
E. A symptom(s) followed by contrasting/comparative diagnoses
F. Original treatment plan not carried out
G. Complications of surgery and other medical care
H. Uncertain Diagnosis
I. Admission from Observation Unit
   1. Admission Following Medical Observation
   2. Admission Following Post-Operative Observation
J. Admission from Outpatient Surgery

Section III. Reporting Additional Diagnoses

A. Previous conditions
B. Abnormal findings
C. Uncertain Diagnosis

Section IV. Diagnostic Coding and Reporting Guidelines for Outpatient Services

A. Selection of first-listed condition
   1. Outpatient Surgery
   2. Observation Stay
B. Codes from 001.0 through **V89.09**
C. Accurate reporting of ICD-9-CM diagnosis codes
D. Selection of codes 001.0 through 999.9
E. Codes that describe symptoms and signs
F. Encounters for circumstances other than a disease or injury
G. Level of Detail in Coding
   1. ICD-9-CM codes with 3, 4, or 5 digits
   2. Use of full number of digits required for a code
H. ICD-9-CM code for the diagnosis, condition, problem, or other reason for encounter/visit
I. Uncertain diagnosis
J. Chronic diseases
K. Code all documented conditions that coexist
L. Patients receiving diagnostic services only
M. Patients receiving therapeutic services only
N. Patients receiving preoperative evaluations only
O. Ambulatory surgery
P. Routine outpatient prenatal visits

Appendix I: Present on Admission Reporting Guidelines

Section I. Conventions, General Coding Guidelines and Chapter Specific Guidelines

The conventions, general guidelines and chapter-specific guidelines are applicable to all health care settings unless otherwise indicated.

A. Conventions for the ICD-9-CM

The conventions for the ICD-9-CM are the general rules for use of the classification independent of the guidelines. These conventions are incorporated within the index and tabular of the ICD-9-CM as instructional notes. The conventions are as follows:

1. Format:

The ICD-9-CM uses an indented format for ease in reference

2. Abbreviations

a. Index abbreviations

NEC "Not elsewhere classifiable"
This abbreviation in the index represents "other specified" when a specific code is not available for a condition the index directs the coder to the "other specified" code in the tabular.

b. Tabular abbreviations

NEC "Not elsewhere classifiable"
This abbreviation in the tabular represents "other specified". When a specific code is not available for a condition the tabular includes an NEC entry under a code to identify the code as the "other specified" code.
(See Section I.A.5.a. "Other" codes").

NOS "Not otherwise specified"
This abbreviation is the equivalent of unspecified.
(See Section I.A.5.b., "Unspecified" codes)

3. Punctuation

[ ] Brackets are used in the tabular list to enclose synonyms, alternative wording or explanatory phrases. Brackets are used in the index to identify manifestation codes.
(See Section I.A.6. "Etiology/manifestations")

( ) Parentheses are used in both the index and tabular to enclose supplementary words that may be present or absent in the statement of a disease or procedure without affecting the code number to which it is assigned. The terms within the parentheses are referred to as nonessential modifiers.

: Colons are used in the Tabular list after an incomplete term which needs one or more of the modifiers following the colon to make it assignable to a given category.

4. Includes and Excludes Notes and Inclusion terms

Includes: This note appears immediately under a three-digit code title to further define, or give examples of, the content of the category.

Excludes: An excludes note under a code indicates that the terms excluded from the code are to be coded elsewhere. In some cases the codes for the excluded terms should not be used in conjunction with the code from which it is excluded. An example of this is a congenital condition excluded from an acquired form of the same condition. The congenital and acquired codes should not be used together. In other cases, the excluded terms may be used together with an excluded code. An example of this is when fractures of different bones are coded to different codes. Both codes may be used together if both types of fractures are present.

Inclusion terms: List of terms is included under certain four and five digit codes. These terms are the conditions for which that code number is to be used. The terms may be synonyms of the code title, or, in the case of "other specified" codes, the terms are a list of the various conditions assigned to that code. The inclusion terms are not necessarily exhaustive. Additional terms found only in the index may also be assigned to a code.

5. **Other and Unspecified codes**

a. **"Other" codes**

Codes titled "other" or "other specified" (usually a code with a 4th digit 8 or fifth-digit 9 for diagnosis codes) are for use when the information in the medical record provides detail for which a specific code does not exist. Index entries with NEC in the line designate "other" codes in the tabular. These index entries represent specific disease entities for which no specific code exists so the term is included within an "other" code.

b. **"Unspecified" codes**

Codes (usually a code with a 4th digit 9 or 5th digit 0 for diagnosis codes) titled "unspecified" are for use when the information in the medical record is insufficient to assign a more specific code.

6. **Etiology/manifestation convention ("Code first," "Use additional code" and "In diseases classified elsewhere" notes)**

Certain conditions have both an underlying etiology and multiple body system manifestations due to the underlying etiology. For such conditions, the ICD-9-CM has a coding convention that requires the underlying condition be sequenced first followed by the manifestation. Wherever such a combination exists, there is a "Use additional code" note at the etiology code, and a "Code first" note at the manifestation code. These instructional notes indicate the proper sequencing order of the codes, etiology followed by manifestation.

In most cases the manifestation codes will have in the code title, "In diseases classified elsewhere." Codes with this title are a component of the etiology/ manifestation convention. The code title indicates that it is a manifestation code. "In diseases classified elsewhere" codes are never permitted to be used as first listed or principal diagnosis codes. They must be used in conjunction with an underlying condition code and they must be listed following the underlying condition.

There are manifestation codes that do not have "In diseases classified elsewhere" in the title. For such codes a "Use additional code" note will still be present and the rules for sequencing apply.

In addition to the notes in the tabular, these conditions also have a specific index entry structure. In the index both conditions are listed together with the etiology code first followed by the manifestation codes in brackets. The code in brackets is always to be sequenced second.

The most commonly used etiology/manifestation combinations are the codes for Diabetes mellitus, category 250. For each code under category 250 there is a use additional code note for the manifestation that is specific for that particular diabetic manifestation. Should a patient have more than one manifestation of diabetes, more than one code from category 250 may be used with as many manifestation codes as are needed to fully describe the patient's complete diabetic condition. The category 250 diabetes codes should be sequenced first, followed by the manifestation codes.

"Code first" and "Use additional code" notes are also used as sequencing rules in the classification for certain codes that are not part of an etiology/ manifestation combination.

See - Section I.B.9. "Multiple coding for a single condition."

7. **"And"**

The word "and" should be interpreted to mean either "and" or "or" when it appears in a title.

8. **"With"**

The word "with" in the alphabetic index is sequenced immediately following the main term, not in alphabetical order.

9. **"See" and "See Also"**

The "see" instruction following a main term in the index indicates that another term should be referenced. It is necessary to go to the main term referenced with the "see" note to locate the correct code.

A "see also" instruction following a main term in the index instructs that there is another main term that may also be referenced that may provide additional index entries that may be useful. It is not necessary to follow the "see also" note when the original main term provides the necessary code.

B. **General Coding Guidelines**

1. **Use of Both Alphabetic Index and Tabular List** Use both the Alphabetic Index and the Tabular List when locating and assigning a code. Reliance on only the Alphabetic Index or the Tabular List leads to errors in code assignments and less specificity in code selection.

2. **Locate each term in the Alphabetic Index**

Locate each term in the Alphabetic Index and verify the code selected in the Tabular List. Read and be guided by instructional notations that appear in both the Alphabetic Index and the Tabular List.

3. **Level of Detail in Coding**

Diagnosis and procedure codes are to be used at their highest number of digits available.

ICD-9-CM diagnosis codes are composed of codes with 3, 4, or 5 digits. Codes with three digits are included in ICD-9-CM as the heading of a category of codes that may be further subdivided by the use of fourth and/or fifth-digits, which provide greater detail.

A three-digit code is to be used only if it is not further subdivided. Where fourth-digit subcategories and/or fifth-digit subclassifications are provided, they must be assigned. A code is invalid if it has not been coded to the full number of digits required for that code. For example, Acute myocardial infarction, code 410, has fourth-digits that describe the location of the infarction (e.g., 410.2, Of inferolateral wall), and fifth-digits that identify the episode of care. It would be incorrect to report a code in category 410 without a fourth and fifth-digit.

ICD-9-CM Volume 3 procedure codes are composed of codes with either 3 or 4 digits. Codes with two digits are included in ICD-9-CM as the heading of a category of codes that may be further subdivided by the use of third and/or fourth-digits, which provide greater detail.

4. **Code or codes from 001.0 through V89.09**

The appropriate code or codes from 001.0 through **V89.09** must be used to identify diagnoses, symptoms, conditions, problems, complaints or other reason(s) for the encounter/visit.

5. **Selection of codes 001.0 through 999.9**

The selection of codes 001.0 through 999.9 will frequently be used to describe the reason for the admission/encounter. These codes are from the section of ICD-9-CM for the classification of diseases and injuries (e.g., infectious and parasitic diseases; neoplasms; symptoms, signs, and ill-defined conditions, etc.).

6. **Signs and symptoms**

Codes that describe symptoms and signs, as opposed to diagnoses, are acceptable for reporting purposes when a related definitive diagnosis has not been established (confirmed) by the provider. Chapter 16 of ICD-9-CM, Symptoms, Signs, and Ill-Defined conditions (codes 780.0 - 799.9) contain many, but not all codes for symptoms.

7. **Conditions that are an integral part of a disease process**

Signs and symptoms that are **associated routinely with a** disease process should not be assigned as additional codes, unless otherwise instructed by the classification.

8. **Conditions that are not an integral part of a disease process**

Additional signs and symptoms that may not be associated routinely with a disease process should be coded when present.

9. **Multiple coding for a single condition**

In addition to the etiology/manifestation convention that requires two codes to fully describe a single condition that affects multiple body systems, there are other single conditions that also require more than one code. "Use additional code" notes are found in the tabular at codes that are not part of an etiology/manifestation pair where a secondary code is useful to fully describe a condition. The sequencing rule is the same as the etiology/manifestation pair - , "Use additional code" indicates that a secondary code should be added.

For example, for infections that are not included in chapter 1, a secondary code from category 041, Bacterial infection in conditions classified elsewhere and of unspecified site, may be required to identify the bacterial organism causing the infection. A "Use additional code" note will normally be found at the infectious disease code, indicating a need for the organism code to be added as a secondary code.

"Code first" notes are also under certain codes that are not specifically manifestation codes but may be due to an underlying cause. When a "Code first" note is present and an underlying condition is present the underlying condition should be sequenced first.

"Code, if applicable, any causal condition first", notes indicate that this code may be assigned as a principal diagnosis when the causal condition is unknown or not applicable. If a causal condition is known, then the code for that condition should be sequenced as the principal or first-listed diagnosis.

Multiple codes may be needed for late effects, complication codes and obstetric codes to more fully describe a condition. See the specific guidelines for these conditions for further instruction.

10. Acute and Chronic Conditions

If the same condition is described as both acute (subacute) and chronic, and separate subentries exist in the Alphabetic Index at the same indentation level, code both and sequence the acute (subacute) code first.

11. Combination Code

A combination code is a single code used to classify:

- Two diagnoses, or
- A diagnosis with an associated secondary process (manifestation)
- A diagnosis with an associated complication

Combination codes are identified by referring to subterm entries in the Alphabetic Index and by reading the inclusion and exclusion notes in the Tabular List.

Assign only the combination code when that code fully identifies the diagnostic conditions involved or when the Alphabetic Index so directs. Multiple coding should not be used when the classification provides a combination code that clearly identifies all of the elements documented in the diagnosis. When the combination code lacks necessary specificity in describing the manifestation or complication, an additional code should be used as a secondary code.

12. Late Effects

A late effect is the residual effect (condition produced) after the acute phase of an illness or injury has terminated. There is no time limit on when a late effect code can be used. The residual may be apparent early, such as in cerebrovascular accident cases, or it may occur months or years later, such as that due to a previous injury. Coding of late effects generally requires two codes sequenced in the following order: The condition or nature of the late effect is sequenced first. The late effect code is sequenced second.

An exception to the above guidelines are those instances where the code for late effect is followed by a manifestation code identified in the Tabular List and title, or the late effect code has been expanded (at the fourth and fifth-digit levels) to include the manifestation(s). The code for the acute phase of an illness or injury that led to the late effect is never used with a code for the late effect.

13. Impending or Threatened Condition

Code any condition described at the time of discharge as "impending" or "threatened" as follows:

If it did occur, code as confirmed diagnosis. If it did not occur, reference the Alphabetic Index to determine if the condition has a subentry term for "impending" or "threatened" and also reference main term entries for "Impending" and for "Threatened." If the subterms are listed, assign the given code. If the subterms are not listed, code the existing underlying condition(s) and not the condition described as impending or threatened.

14. Reporting Same Diagnosis Code More than Once

Each unique ICD-9-CM diagnosis code may be reported only once for an encounter. This applies to bilateral conditions or two different conditions classified to the same ICD-9-CM diagnosis code.

15. Admissions/Encounters for Rehabilitation

When the purpose for the admission/encounter is rehabilitation, sequence the appropriate V code from category V57, Care involving use of rehabilitation procedures, as the principal/first-listed diagnosis. The code for the condition for which the service is being performed should be reported as an additional diagnosis.

Only one code from category V57 is required. Code V57.89, Other specified rehabilitation procedures, should be assigned if more than one type of rehabilitation is performed during a single encounter. A procedure code should be reported to identify each type of rehabilitation therapy actually performed.

16. Documentation for BMI and Pressure Ulcer Stages

For the Body Mass Index (BMI) and pressure ulcer stage codes, code assignment may be based on medical record documentation from clinicians who are not the patient's provider (i.e., physician or other qualified healthcare practitioner legally accountable for establishing the patient's diagnosis), since this information is typically documented by other clinicians involved in the care of the patient (e.g., a dietitian often documents the BMI and nurses often documents the pressure ulcer stages). However, the associated diagnosis (such as overweight, obesity, or pressure ulcer) must be documented by the patient's provider. If there is conflicting medical record documentation, either from the same clinician or different clinicians, the patient's attending provider should be queried for clarification.

The BMI and pressure ulcer stage codes should only be reported as secondary diagnoses. As with all other secondary diagnosis codes, the BMI and pressure ulcer stage codes should only be assigned when they meet the definition of a reportable additional diagnosis (see Section III, Reporting Additional Diagnoses).

C. Chapter-Specific Coding Guidelines

In addition to general coding guidelines, there are guidelines for specific diagnoses and/or conditions in the classification. Unless otherwise indicated, these guidelines apply to all health care settings. Please refer to Section II for guidelines on the selection of principal diagnosis.

1. Chapter 1: Infectious and Parasitic Diseases (001-139)

a. Human Immunodeficiency Virus (HIV) Infections

1) Code only confirmed cases

Code only confirmed cases of HIV infection/illness. This is an exception to the hospital inpatient guideline Section II, H.

In this context, "confirmation" does not require documentation of positive serology or culture for HIV; the provider's diagnostic statement that the patient is HIV positive, or has an HIV-related illness is sufficient.

2) Selection and sequencing of HIV codes

(a) Patient admitted for HIV-related condition

If a patient is admitted for an HIV-related condition, the principal diagnosis should be 042, followed by additional diagnosis codes for all reported HIV-related conditions.

(b) Patient with HIV disease admitted for unrelated condition

If a patient with HIV disease is admitted for an unrelated condition (such as a traumatic injury), the code for the unrelated condition (e.g., the nature of injury code) should be the principal diagnosis. Other diagnoses would be 042 followed by additional diagnosis codes for all reported HIV-related conditions.

(c) Whether the patient is newly diagnosed

Whether the patient is newly diagnosed or has had previous admissions/encounters for HIV conditions is irrelevant to the sequencing decision.

(d) Asymptomatic human immunodeficiency virus

V08 Asymptomatic human immunodeficiency virus [HIV] infection, is to be applied when the patient without any documentation of symptoms is listed as being "HIV positive," "known HIV," "HIV test positive," or similar terminology. Do not use this code if the term "AIDS" is used or if the patient is treated for any HIV-related illness or is described as having any condition(s) resulting from his/her HIV positive status; use 042 in these cases.

(e) Patients with inconclusive HIV serology

Patients with inconclusive HIV serology, but no definitive diagnosis or manifestations of the illness, may be assigned code 795.71, Inconclusive serologic test for Human Immunodeficiency Virus [HIV].

(f) Previously diagnosed HIV-related illness

Patients with any known prior diagnosis of an HIV-related illness should be coded to 042. Once a patient has developed an HIV-related illness, the patient should always be assigned code 042 on every subsequent admission/encounter. Patients previously diagnosed with any HIV illness (042) should never be assigned to 795.71 or V08.

(g) HIV Infection in Pregnancy, Childbirth and the Puerperium

During pregnancy, childbirth or the puerperium, a patient admitted (or presenting for a health care encounter) because of an HIV-related illness should receive a principal diagnosis code of 647.6X, Other specified infectious and parasitic diseases in the mother classifiable elsewhere, but complicating the pregnancy, childbirth or the puerperium, followed by 042 and the code(s) for the HIV-related illness(es). Codes from Chapter 15 always take sequencing priority.

Patients with asymptomatic HIV infection status admitted (or presenting for a health care encounter) during pregnancy, childbirth, or the puerperium should receive codes of 647.6X and V08.

(h) Encounters for testing for HIV

If a patient is being seen to determine his/her HIV status, use code V73.89, Screening for other specified viral disease. Use code V69.8, Other problems related to lifestyle, as a secondary code if an asymptomatic patient is in a known high risk group for HIV. Should a patient with signs or symptoms or illness, or a confirmed HIV related diagnosis be tested for HIV, code the signs and symptoms or the diagnosis. An additional counseling code V65.44 may be used if counseling is provided during the encounter for the test.

When a patient returns to be informed of his/her HIV test results use code V65.44, HIV counseling, if the results of the test are negative.

If the results are positive but the patient is asymptomatic use code V08, Asymptomatic HIV infection. If the results are positive and the patient is symptomatic use code 042, HIV infection, with codes for the HIV related symptoms or diagnosis. The HIV counseling code may also be used if counseling is provided for patients with positive test results.

b. Septicemia, Systemic Inflammatory Response Syndrome (SIRS), Sepsis, Severe Sepsis, and Septic Shock

1) SIRS, Septicemia, and Sepsis

(a) The terms *septicemia* and *sepsis* are often used interchangeably by providers, however they are not considered synonymous terms. The following descriptions are provided for reference but do not preclude querying the provider for clarification about terms used in the documentation:

(i) Septicemia generally refers to a systemic disease associated with the presence of pathological microorganisms or toxins in the blood, which can include bacteria, viruses, fungi or other organisms.

(ii) Systemic inflammatory response syndrome (SIRS) generally refers to the systemic response to infection, trauma/burns, or other insult (such as cancer) with symptoms including fever, tachycardia, tachypnea, and leukocytosis.

(iii) Sepsis generally refers to SIRS due to infection.

(iv) Severe sepsis generally refers to sepsis with associated acute organ dysfunction.

(b) The coding of SIRS, sepsis and severe sepsis

The coding of SIRS, sepsis and severe sepsis requires a minimum of 2 codes: a code for the underlying cause (such as infection or trauma) and a code from subcategory 995.9 Systemic inflammatory response syndrome (SIRS).

(i) The code for the underlying cause (such as infection or trauma) must be sequenced before the code from subcategory 995.9 Systemic inflammatory response syndrome (SIRS).

(ii) Sepsis and severe sepsis require a code for the systemic infection (038.xx, 112.5, etc.) and either code 995.91, Sepsis, or 995.92, Severe sepsis. If the causal organism is not documented, assign code 038.9, Unspecified septicemia.

(iii) Severe sepsis requires additional code(s) for the associated acute organ dysfunction(s).

(iv) If a patient has sepsis with multiple organ dysfunctions, follow the instructions for coding severe sepsis.

(v) Either the term sepsis or SIRS must be documented to assign a code from subcategory 995.9.

(vi) See Section I.C.17.g), Injury and poisoning, for information regarding systemic inflammatory response syndrome (SIRS) due to trauma/burns and other non-infectious processes.

(c) Due to the complex nature of sepsis and severe sepsis, some cases may require querying the provider prior to assignment of the codes.

2) Sequencing sepsis and severe sepsis

(a) Sepsis and severe sepsis as principal diagnosis

If sepsis or severe sepsis is present on admission, and meets the definition of principal diagnosis, the systemic infection code (e.g., 038.xx, 112.5, etc) should be assigned as the principal diagnosis, followed by code 995.91, Sepsis, or 995.92, Severe sepsis, as required by the sequencing rules in the Tabular List. Codes from subcategory 995.9 can never be assigned as a principal diagnosis. A code should also be assigned for any localized infection, if present.

If the sepsis or severe sepsis is due to a postprocedural infection, see Section I.C.10 for guidelines related to sepsis due to postprocedural infection.

(b) Sepsis and severe sepsis as secondary diagnoses

When sepsis or severe sepsis develops during the encounter (it was not present on admission), the systemic infection code and code 995.91 or 995.92 should be assigned as secondary diagnoses.

(c) Documentation unclear as to whether sepsis or severe sepsis is present on admission

Sepsis or severe sepsis may be present on admission but the diagnosis may not be confirmed until sometime after admission. If the documentation is not clear whether the sepsis or severe sepsis was present on admission, the provider should be queried.

3) Sepsis/SIRS with Localized Infection

If the reason for admission is both sepsis, severe sepsis, or SIRS and a localized infection, such as pneumonia or cellulitis, a code for the systemic infection (038.xx, 112.5, etc) should be assigned first, then code 995.91 or 995.92, followed by the code for the localized infection. If the patient is admitted with a localized infection, such as pneumonia, and sepsis/SIRS doesn't develop until after admission, see guideline I.C.1.b.2.b).

If the localized infection is postprocedural, *see Section I.C.10 for guidelines related to sepsis due to postprocedural infection.*

Note: The term urosepsis is a nonspecific term. If that is the only term documented then only code 599.0 should be assigned based on the default for the term in the ICD-9-CM index, in addition to the code for the causal organism if known.

4) Bacterial Sepsis and Septicemia

In most cases, it will be a code from category 038, Septicemia, that will be used in conjunction with a code from subcategory 995.9 such as the following:

(a) Streptococcal sepsis

If the documentation in the record states streptococcal sepsis, codes 038.0, Streptococcal septicemia, and code 995.91 should be used, in that sequence.

(b) Streptococcal septicemia

If the documentation states streptococcal septicemia, only code 038.0 should be assigned, however, the provider should be queried whether the patient has sepsis, an infection with SIRS.

5) **Acute organ dysfunction that is not clearly associated with the sepsis**
If a patient has sepsis and an acute organ dysfunction, but the medical record documentation indicates that the acute organ dysfunction is related to a medical condition other than the sepsis, do not assign code 995.92, Severe sepsis. An acute organ dysfunction must be associated with the sepsis in order to assign the severe sepsis code. If the documentation is not clear as to whether an acute organ dysfunction is related to the sepsis or another medical condition, query the provider.

6) **Septic shock**

(a) **Sequencing of septic shock**
Septic shock generally refers to circulatory failure associated with severe sepsis, and, therefore, it represents a type of acute organ dysfunction.

For all cases of septic shock, the code for the systemic infection should be sequenced first, followed by codes 995.92 and 785.52. Any additional codes for other acute organ dysfunctions should also be assigned. As noted in the sequencing instructions in the Tabular List, the code for septic shock cannot be assigned as a principal diagnosis.

(b) **Septic Shock without documentation of severe sepsis**
Septic shock indicates the presence of severe sepsis.

Code 995.92, Severe sepsis, must be assigned with code 785.52, Septic shock, even if the term severe sepsis is not documented in the record. The "Use additional code" note and the "Code first" note in the tabular support this guideline.

7) **Sepsis and septic shock complicating abortion and pregnancy**
Sepsis and septic shock complicating abortion, ectopic pregnancy, and molar pregnancy are classified to category codes in Chapter 11 (630-639).
See section I.C.11.

8) **Negative or inconclusive blood cultures**
Negative or inconclusive blood cultures do not preclude a diagnosis of septicemia or sepsis in patients with clinical evidence of the condition, however, the provider should be queried.

9) **Newborn sepsis**
See Section I.C.15.j for information on the coding of newborn sepsis.

10) **Sepsis due to a postprocedural infection**

(a) **Documentation of causal relationship**
As with all postprocedural complications, code assignment is based on the provider's documentation of the relationship between the infection and the procedure.

(b) **Sepsis due to postprocedural infection**
In cases of postprocedural sepsis, the complication code, such as code 998.59, Other postoperative infection, or 674.3x, Other complications of obstetrical surgical wounds should be coded first followed by the appropriate sepsis codes (systemic infection code and either code 995.91or 995.92). An additional code(s) for any acute organ dysfunction should also be assigned for cases of severe sepsis.

11) **External cause of injury codes with SIRS**
Refer to Section I.C.19.a.7 for instruction on the use of external cause of injury codes with codes for SIRS resulting from trauma.

12) **Sepsis and severe sepsis associated with noninfectious process**
In some cases, a non-infectious process, such as trauma, may lead to an infection which can result in sepsis or severe sepsis. If sepsis or severe sepsis is documented as associated with a non-infectious condition, such as a burn or serious injury, and this condition meets the definition for principal diagnosis, the code for the noninfectious condition should be sequenced first, followed by the code for the systemic infection and either code 995.91, Sepsis, or 995.92, Severe sepsis. Additional codes for any associated acute organ dysfunction(s) should also be assigned for cases of severe sepsis. If the sepsis or severe sepsis meets the definition of principal diagnosis, the systemic infection and sepsis codes should be sequenced before the non-infectious condition. When both the associated non-infectious condition and the sepsis or severe sepsis meet the definition of principal diagnosis, either may be assigned as principal diagnosis.

See Section I.C.1.b.2) (a) for guidelines pertaining to sepsis or severe sepsis as the principal diagnosis.

Only one code from subcategory 995.9 should be assigned. Therefore, when a non-infectious condition leads to an infection resulting in sepsis or severe sepsis, assign either code 995.91 or 995.92. Do not additionally assign code 995.93, Systemic inflammatory response syndrome due to non-infectious process without acute organ dysfunction, or 995.94, Systemic inflammatory response syndrome with acute organ dysfunction.

See Section I.C.17.g for information on the coding of SIRS due to trauma/burns or other non-infectious disease processes.

c. **Methicillin Resistant *Staphylococcus aureus* (MRSA) Conditions**

1) **Selection and sequencing of MRSA codes**

(a) **Combination codes for MRSA infection**
When a patient is diagnosed with an infection that is due to methicillin resistant *Staphylococcus aureus* (MRSA), and that infection has a combination code that includes the causal organism (e.g., septicemia, pneumonia) assign the appropriate code for the condition (e.g., code 038.12, Methicillin resistant *Staphylococcus aureus* septicemia or code 482.42, Methicillin resistant pneumonia due to *Staphylococcus aureus*). Do not assign code 041.12, Methicillin resistant *Staphylococcus aureus*, as an additional code because the code includes the type of infection and the MRSA organism. Do not assign a code from subcategory V09.0, Infection with microorganisms resistant to penicillins, as an additional diagnosis.

See Section C.1.b.1 for instructions on coding and sequencing of septicemia.

(b) **Other codes for MRSA infection**
When there is documentation of a current infection (e.g., wound infection, stitch abscess, urinary tract infection) due to MRSA, and that infection does not have a combination code that includes the causal organism, select the appropriate code to identify the condition along with code 041.12, Methicillin resistant *Staphylococcus aureus*, for the MRSA infection. Do not assign a code from subcategory V09.0, Infection with microorganisms resistant to penicillins.

(c) **Methicillin susceptible *Staphylococcus aureus* (MSSA) and MRSA colonization**
The condition or state of being colonized or carrying MSSA or MRSA is called colonization or carriage, while an individual person is described as being colonized or being a carrier. Colonization means that MSSA or MSRA is present on or in the body without necessarily causing illness. A positive MRSA colonization test might be documented by the provider as "MRSA screen positive" or "MRSA nasal swab positive".

Assign code V02.54, Carrier or suspected carrier, Methicillin resistant *Staphylococcus aureus*, for patients documented as having MRSA colonization. Assign code V02.53, Carrier or suspected carrier, Methicillin

susceptible *Staphylococcus aureus*, for patient documented as having MSSA colonization. Colonization is not necessarily indicative of a disease process or as the cause of a specific condition the patient may have unless documented as such by the provider.

Code V02.59, Other specified bacterial diseases, should be assigned for other types of staphylococcal colonization (e.g., *S. epidermidis, S. saprophyticus*). Code V02.59 should not be assigned for colonization with any type of *Staphylococcus aureus* (MRSA, MSSA).

(d) **MRSA colonization and infection**
If a patient is documented as having both MRSA colonization and infection during a hospital admission, code V02.54, Carrier or suspected carrier, Methicillin resistant *Staphylococcus aureus*, and a code for the MRSA infection may both be assigned.

2. **Chapter 2: Neoplasms (140-239)**

General guidelines

Chapter 2 of the ICD-9-CM contains the codes for most benign and all malignant neoplasms. Certain benign neoplasms, such as prostatic adenomas, may be found in the specific body system chapters. To properly code a neoplasm it is necessary to determine from the record if the neoplasm is benign, in-situ, malignant, or of uncertain histologic behavior. If malignant, any secondary (metastatic) sites should also be determined.

The neoplasm table in the Alphabetic Index should be referenced first. However, if the histological term is documented, that term should be referenced first, rather than going immediately to the Neoplasm Table, in order to determine which column in the Neoplasm Table is appropriate. For example, if the documentation indicates "adenoma," refer to the term in the Alphabetic Index to review the entries under this term and the instructional note to "see also neoplasm, by site, benign." The table provides the proper code based on the type of neoplasm and the site. It is important to select the proper column in the table that corresponds to the type of neoplasm. The tabular should then be referenced to verify that the correct code has been selected from the table and that a more specific site code does not exist.

See Section I. C. 18.d.4. for information regarding V codes for genetic susceptibility to cancer.

a. **Treatment directed at the malignancy**
If the treatment is directed at the malignancy, designate the malignancy as the principal diagnosis.

The only exception to this guideline is if a patient admission/encounter is solely for the administration of chemotherapy, immunotherapy or radiation therapy, assign the appropriate V58.x code as the first-listed or principal diagnosis, and the diagnosis or problem for which the service is being performed as a secondary diagnosis.

b. **Treatment of secondary site**
When a patient is admitted because of a primary neoplasm with metastasis and treatment is directed toward the secondary site only, the secondary neoplasm is designated as the principal diagnosis even though the primary malignancy is still present.

c. **Coding and sequencing of complications**
Coding and sequencing of complications associated with the malignancies or with the therapy thereof are subject to the following guidelines:

1) **Anemia associated with malignancy**
When admission/encounter is for management of an anemia associated with the malignancy, and the treatment is only for anemia, the appropriate anemia code (such as code 285.22, Anemia in neoplastic disease) is designated as the principal diagnosis and is followed by the appropriate code(s) for the malignancy.

Code 285.22 may also be used as a secondary code if the patient suffers from anemia and is being treated for the malignancy.

2) **Anemia associated with chemotherapy, immunotherapy and radiation therapy**
When the admission/encounter is for management of an anemia associated with chemotherapy, immunotherapy or radiotherapy and the only treatment is for the anemia, the anemia is sequenced first followed by code E933.1. The appropriate neoplasm code should be assigned as an additional code.

3) **Management of dehydration due to the malignancy**
When the admission/encounter is for management of dehydration due to the malignancy or the therapy, or a combination of both, and only the dehydration is being treated (intravenous rehydration), the dehydration is sequenced first, followed by the code(s) for the malignancy.

4) **Treatment of a complication resulting from a surgical procedure**
When the admission/encounter is for treatment of a complication resulting from a surgical procedure, designate the complication as the principal or first-listed diagnosis if treatment is directed at resolving the complication.

d. **Primary malignancy previously excised**
When a primary malignancy has been previously excised or eradicated from its site and there is no further treatment directed to that site and there is no evidence of any existing primary malignancy, a code from category V10, Personal history of malignant neoplasm, should be used to indicate the former site of the malignancy. Any mention of extension, invasion, or metastasis to another site is coded as a secondary malignant neoplasm to that site. The secondary site may be the principal or first-listed with the V10 code used as a secondary code.

e. **Admissions/Encounters involving chemotherapy, immunotherapy and radiation therapy**

1) **Episode of care involves surgical removal of neoplasm**
When an episode of care involves the surgical removal of a neoplasm, primary or secondary site, followed by adjunct chemotherapy or radiation treatment during the same episode of care, the neoplasm code should be assigned as principal or first-listed diagnosis, using codes in the 140-198 series or where appropriate in the 200-203 series.

2) **Patient admission/encounter solely for administration of chemotherapy, immunotherapy and radiation therapy**
If a patient admission/encounter is solely for the administration of chemotherapy, immunotherapy or radiation therapy assign code V58.0, Encounter for radiation therapy, or V58.11, Encounter for antineoplastic chemotherapy, or V58.12, Encounter for antineoplastic immunotherapy as the first-listed or principal diagnosis. If a patient receives more than one of these therapies during the same admission more than one of these codes may be assigned, in any sequence.

The malignancy for which the therapy is being administered should be assigned as a secondary diagnosis.

3) **Patient admitted for radiotherapy/chemotherapy and immunotherapy and develops complications**
When a patient is admitted for the purpose of radiotherapy, immunotherapy or chemotherapy and develops complications such as uncontrolled nausea and vomiting or dehydration, the principal or first-listed diagnosis is V58.0, Encounter for radiotherapy, or V58.11, Encounter for antineoplastic chemotherapy, or V58.12, Encounter for antineoplastic immunotherapy followed by any codes for the complications.

f. **Admission/encounter to determine extent of malignancy**
When the reason for admission/encounter is to determine the extent of the malignancy, or for a procedure such as paracentesis or thoracentesis, the primary malignancy or appropriate metastatic site is designated as the principal or first-listed diagnosis, even though chemotherapy or radiotherapy is administered.

g. **Symptoms, signs, and ill-defined conditions listed in Chapter 16 associated with neoplasms**
Symptoms, signs, and ill-defined conditions listed in Chapter 16 characteristic of, or associated with, an existing primary or secondary site malignancy cannot be used to replace the malignancy as principal or first-listed diagnosis, regardless of the number of admissions or encounters for treatment and care of the neoplasm.

See section I.C.18.d.14, Encounter for prophylactic organ removal.

h. Admission/encounter for pain control/management

See Section I.C.6.a.5 for information on coding admission/encounter for pain control/management.

i. Malignant neoplasm associated with transplanted organ

A malignant neoplasm of a transplanted organ should be coded as a transplant complication. Assign first the appropriate code from subcategory 996.8, Complications of transplanted organ, followed by code 199.2, Malignant neoplasm associated with transplanted organ. Use an additional code for the specific malignancy.

3. Chapter 3: Endocrine, Nutritional, and Metabolic Diseases and Immunity Disorders (240-279)

a. Diabetes mellitus

Codes under category 250, Diabetes mellitus, identify complications/manifestations associated with diabetes mellitus. A fifth-digit is required for all category 250 codes to identify the type of diabetes mellitus and whether the diabetes is controlled or uncontrolled.

See I.C.3.a.7 for secondary diabetes

1) Fifth-digits for category 250:

The following are the fifth-digits for the codes under category 250:

0 type II or unspecified type, not stated as uncontrolled

1 type I, [juvenile type], not stated as uncontrolled

2 type II or unspecified type, uncontrolled

3 type I, [juvenile type], uncontrolled

The age of a patient is not the sole determining factor, though most type I diabetics develop the condition before reaching puberty. For this reason type I diabetes mellitus is also referred to as juvenile diabetes.

2) Type of diabetes mellitus not documented

If the type of diabetes mellitus is not documented in the medical record the default is type II.

3) Diabetes mellitus and the use of insulin

All type I diabetics must use insulin to replace what their bodies do not produce. However, the use of insulin does not mean that a patient is a type I diabetic. Some patients with type II diabetes mellitus are unable to control their blood sugar through diet and oral medication alone and do require insulin.

If the documentation in a medical record does not indicate the type of diabetes but does indicate that the patient uses insulin, the appropriate fifth-digit for type II must be used. For type II patients who routinely use insulin, code V58.67, Long-term (current) use of insulin, should also be assigned to indicate that the patient uses insulin. Code V58.67 should not be assigned if insulin is given temporarily to bring a type II patient's blood sugar under control during an encounter.

4) Assigning and sequencing diabetes codes and associated conditions

When assigning codes for diabetes and its associated conditions, the code(s) from category 250 must be sequenced before the codes for the associated conditions. The diabetes codes and the secondary codes that correspond to them are paired codes that follow the etiology/manifestation convention of the classification *(See Section I.A.6., Etiology/manifestation convention).* Assign as many codes from category 250 as needed to identify all of the associated conditions that the patient has. The corresponding secondary codes are listed under each of the diabetes codes.

(a) Diabetic retinopathy/diabetic macular edema

Diabetic macular edema, code 362.07, is only present with diabetic retinopathy. Another code from subcategory 362.0, Diabetic retinopathy, must be used with code 362.07. Codes under subcategory 362.0 are diabetes manifestation codes, so they must be used following the appropriate diabetes code.

5) Diabetes mellitus in pregnancy and gestational diabetes

(a) For diabetes mellitus complicating pregnancy, *see Section I.C.11.f., Diabetes mellitus in pregnancy.*

(b) For gestational diabetes, *see Section I.C.11, g., Gestational diabetes.*

6) Insulin pump malfunction

(a) Underdose of insulin due insulin pump failure

An underdose of insulin due to an insulin pump failure should be assigned 996.57, Mechanical complication due to insulin pump, as the principal or first listed code, followed by the appropriate diabetes mellitus code based on documentation.

(b) Overdose of insulin due to insulin pump failure

The principal or first listed code for an encounter due to an insulin pump malfunction resulting in an overdose of insulin, should also be 996.57, Mechanical complication due to insulin pump, followed by code 962.3, Poisoning by insulins and antidiabetic agents, and the appropriate diabetes mellitus code based on documentation.

7) Secondary Diabetes Mellitus

Codes under category 249, Secondary diabetes mellitus, identify complications/manifestations associated with secondary diabetes mellitus. Secondary diabetes is always caused by another condition or event (e.g., cystic fibrosis, malignant neoplasm of pancreas, pancreatectomy, adverse effect of drug, or poisoning).

(a) Fifth-digits for category 249:

A fifth-digit is required for all category 249 codes to identify whether the diabetes is controlled or uncontrolled.

(b) Secondary diabetes mellitus and the use of insulin

For patients who routinely use insulin, code V58.67, Long-term (current) use of insulin, should also be assigned. Code V58.67 should not be assigned if insulin is given temporarily to bring a patient's blood sugar under control during an encounter.

(c) Assigning and sequencing secondary diabetes codes and associated conditions

When assigning codes for secondary diabetes and its associated conditions (e.g. renal manifestations), the code(s) from category 249 must be sequenced before the codes for the associated conditions. The secondary diabetes codes and the diabetic manifestation codes that correspond to them are paired codes that follow the etiology/manifestation convention of the classification. Assign as many codes from category 249 as needed to identify all of the associated conditions that the patient has. The corresponding codes for the associated conditions are listed under each of the secondary diabetes codes. For example, secondary diabetes with diabetic nephrosis is assigned to code 249.40, followed by 581.81.

(d) Assigning and sequencing secondary diabetes codes and its causes

The sequencing of the secondary diabetes codes in relationship to codes for the cause of the diabetes is based on the reason for the encounter, applicable ICD-9-CM sequencing conventions, and chapter-specific guidelines.

If a patient is seen for treatment of the secondary diabetes or one of its associated conditions, a code from category 249 is sequenced as the principal or first-listed diagnosis, with the cause of the secondary diabetes (e.g. cystic fibrosis) sequenced as an additional diagnosis.

If, however, the patient is seen for the treatment of the condition causing the secondary diabetes (e.g., malignant neoplasm of pancreas), the code for the cause of the secondary diabetes should be sequenced as the principal or first-listed diagnosis followed by a code from category 249.

(i) Secondary diabetes mellitus due to pancreatectomy

For postpancreatectomy diabetes mellitus (lack of insulin due to the surgical removal of all or part of the pancreas), assign code 251.3, Postsurgical hypoinsulinemia. A code from subcategory 249 should not be assigned for secondary diabetes mellitus due to

pancreatectomy. Code also any diabetic manifestations (e.g. diabetic nephrosis 581.81).

(ii) Secondary diabetes due to drugs
Secondary diabetes may be caused by an adverse effect of correctly administered medications, poisoning or late effect of poisoning.
See section I.C.17.e for coding of adverse effects and poisoning, and section I.C.19 for E code reporting.

4. Chapter 4: Diseases of Blood and Blood Forming Organs (280-289)

a. Anemia of chronic disease
Subcategory 285.2, Anemia in chronic illness, has codes for anemia in chronic kidney disease, code 285.21; anemia in neoplastic disease, code 285.22; and anemia in other chronic illness, code 285.29. These codes can be used as the principal/first listed code if the reason for the encounter is to treat the anemia. They may also be used as secondary codes if treatment of the anemia is a component of an encounter, but not the primary reason for the encounter. When using a code from subcategory 285 it is also necessary to use the code for the chronic condition causing the anemia.

1) Anemia in chronic kidney disease
When assigning code 285.21, Anemia in chronic kidney disease, it is also necessary to assign a code from category 585, Chronic kidney disease, to indicate the stage of chronic kidney disease.
See I.C.10.a. Chronic kidney disease (CKD).

2) Anemia in neoplastic disease
When assigning code 285.22, Anemia in neoplastic disease, it is also necessary to assign the neoplasm code that is responsible for the anemia. Code 285.22 is for use for anemia that is due to the malignancy, not for anemia due to antineoplastic chemotherapy drugs, which is an adverse effect.
See I.C.2.c.1 Anemia associated with malignancy. See I.C.2.c.2 Anemia associated with chemotherapy, immunotherapy and radiation therapy. See I.C.17.e.1. Adverse effects.

5. Chapter 5: Mental Disorders (290-319)
Reserved for future guideline expansion

6. Chapter 6: Diseases of Nervous System and Sense Organs (320-389)

a. Pain - Category 338

1) General coding information
Codes in category 338 may be used in conjunction with codes from other categories and chapters to provide more detail about acute or chronic pain and neoplasm- related pain, unless otherwise indicated below.
If the pain is not specified as acute or chronic, do not assign codes from category 338, except for post-thoracotomy pain, postoperative pain, neoplasm related pain, or central pain syndrome.
A code from subcategories 338.1 and 338.2 should not be assigned if the underlying (definitive) diagnosis is known, unless the reason for the encounter is pain control/ management and not management of the underlying condition.

(a) Category 338 codes as principal or first-listed diagnosis
Category 338 codes are acceptable as principal diagnosis or the first-listed code:

- When pain control or pain management is the reason for the admission/encounter (e.g., a patient with displaced intervertebral disc, nerve impingement and severe back pain presents for injection of steroid into the spinal canal). The underlying cause of the pain should be reported as an additional diagnosis, if known.
- When an admission or encounter is for a procedure aimed at treating the underlying condition (e.g., spinal fusion, kyphoplasty), a code for the underlying condition (e.g., vertebral fracture, spinal stenosis) should be assigned as the principal diagnosis. No code from category 338 should be assigned.
- When a patient is admitted for the insertion of a neurostimulator for pain control, assign the appropriate pain code as the principal or first listed diagnosis. When an admission or encounter is for a procedure aimed at treating the underlying condition and a neurostimulator is inserted for pain control during the same admission/encounter, a code for the underlying condition should be assigned as the principal diagnosis and the appropriate pain code should be assigned as a secondary diagnosis.

(b) Use of category 338 codes in conjunction with site specific pain codes

(i) Assigning category 338 codes and site-specific pain codes
Codes from category 338 may be used in conjunction with codes that identify the site of pain (including codes from chapter 16) if the category 338 code provides additional information. For example, if the code describes the site of the pain, but does not fully describe whether the pain is acute or chronic, then both codes should be assigned.

(ii) Sequencing of category 338 codes with site-specific pain codes
The sequencing of category 338 codes with site-specific pain codes (including chapter 16 codes), is dependent on the circumstances of the encounter/admission as follows:

- If the encounter is for pain control or pain management, assign the code from category 338 followed by the code identifying the specific site of pain (e.g., encounter for pain management for acute neck pain from trauma is assigned code 338.11, Acute pain due to trauma, followed by code 723.1, Cervicalgia, to identify the site of pain).
- If the encounter is for any other reason except pain control or pain management, and a related definitive diagnosis has not been established (confirmed) by the provider, assign the code for the specific site of pain first, followed by the appropriate code from category 338.

2) Pain due to devices, implants and grafts
Pain associated with devices, implants or grafts left in a surgical site (for example painful hip prosthesis) is assigned to the appropriate code(s) found in Chapter 17, Injury and Poisoning. Use additional code(s) from category 338 to identify acute or chronic pain due to presence of the device, implant or graft (338.18- 338.19 or 338.28-338.29).

3) Postoperative pain
Post-thoracotomy pain and other postoperative pain are classified to subcategories 338.1 and 338.2, depending on whether the pain is acute or chronic. The default for post-thoracotomy and other postoperative pain not specified as acute or chronic is the code for the acute form.
Routine or expected postoperative pain immediately after surgery should not be coded.

(a) Postoperative pain not associated with specific postoperative complication
Postoperative pain not associated with a specific postoperative complication is assigned to the appropriate postoperative pain code in category 338.

(b) Postoperative pain associated with specific postoperative complication
Postoperative pain associated with a specific postoperative complication (such as painful wire sutures) is assigned to the appropriate code(s) found in Chapter 17, Injury and Poisoning. If appropriate, use additional code(s) from category 338 to identify acute or chronic pain (338.18 or 338.28). If pain control/management is the reason for the encounter, a code from category 338 should be assigned as the principal or first-listed diagnosis in accordance with *Section I.C.6.a.1.a above.*

(c) **Postoperative pain as principal or first-listed diagnosis**
Postoperative pain may be reported as the principal or first-listed diagnosis when the stated reason for the admission/encounter is documented as postoperative pain control/management.

(d) **Postoperative pain as secondary diagnosis**
Postoperative pain may be reported as a secondary diagnosis code when a patient presents for outpatient surgery and develops an unusual or inordinate amount of postoperative pain.

The provider's documentation should be used to guide the coding of postoperative pain, as well as *Section III. Reporting Additional Diagnoses* and *Section IV. Diagnostic Coding and Reporting in the Outpatient Setting.*

See Section II.I.2 for information on sequencing of diagnoses for patients admitted to hospital inpatient care following post-operative observation.

See Section II.J for information on sequencing of diagnoses for patients admitted to hospital inpatient care from outpatient surgery.

See Section IV.A.2 for information on sequencing of diagnoses for patients admitted for observation.

4) **Chronic pain**
Chronic pain is classified to subcategory 338.2. There is no time frame defining when pain becomes chronic pain. The provider's documentation should be used to guide use of these codes.

5) **Neoplasm related pain**
Code 338.3 is assigned to pain documented as being related, associated or due to cancer, primary or secondary malignancy, or tumor. This code is assigned regardless of whether the pain is acute or chronic.

This code may be assigned as the principal or first-listed code when the stated reason for the admission/encounter is documented as pain control/pain management. The underlying neoplasm should be reported as an additional diagnosis.

When the reason for the admission/encounter is management of the neoplasm and the pain associated with the neoplasm is also documented, code 338.3 may be assigned as an additional diagnosis.

See Section I.C.2 for instructions on the sequencing of neoplasms for all other stated reasons for the admission/encounter (except for pain control/pain management).

6) **Chronic pain syndrome**
This condition is different than the term "chronic pain," and therefore this code should only be used when the provider has specifically documented this condition.

7. **Chapter 7: Diseases of Circulatory System (390-459)**

a. **Hypertension**
Hypertension Table
The Hypertension Table, found under the main term, "Hypertension," in the Alphabetic Index, contains a complete listing of all conditions due to or associated with hypertension and classifies them according to malignant, benign, and unspecified.

1) **Hypertension, essential, or NOS**
Assign hypertension (arterial) (essential) (primary) (systemic) (NOS) to category code 401 with the appropriate fourth-digit to indicate malignant (.0), benign (.1), or unspecified (.9). Do not use either .0 malignant or .1 benign unless medical record documentation supports such a designation.

2) **Hypertension with heart disease**
Heart conditions (425.8, 429.0-429.3, 429.8, 429.9) are assigned to a code from category 402 when a causal relationship is stated (due to hypertension) or implied (hypertensive). Use an additional code from category 428 to identify the type of heart failure in those patients with heart failure. More than one code from category 428 may be assigned if the patient has systolic or diastolic failure and congestive heart failure.

The same heart conditions (425.8, 429.0-429.3, 429.8, 429.9) with hypertension, but without a stated causal relationship, are coded separately. Sequence according to the circumstances of the admission/encounter.

3) **Hypertensive chronic kidney disease**
Assign codes from category 403, Hypertensive chronic kidney disease, when conditions classified to categories 585-587 are present. Unlike hypertension with heart disease, ICD-9-CM presumes a cause-and-effect relationship and classifies chronic kidney disease (CKD) with hypertension as hypertensive chronic kidney disease.

Fifth-digits for category 403 should be assigned as follows:

- 0 with CKD stage I through stage IV, or unspecified.
- 1 with CKD stage V or end stage renal disease.

The appropriate code from category 585, Chronic kidney disease, should be used as a secondary code with a code from category 403 to identify the stage of chronic kidney disease.

See Section I.C.10.a for information on the coding of chronic kidney disease.

4) **Hypertensive heart and chronic kidney disease**
Assign codes from combination category 404, Hypertensive heart and chronic kidney disease, when both hypertensive kidney disease and hypertensive heart disease are stated in the diagnosis. Assume a relationship between the hypertension and the chronic kidney disease, whether or not the condition is so designated. Assign an additional code from category 428, to identify the type of heart failure. More than one code from category 428 may be assigned if the patient has systolic or diastolic failure and congestive heart failure.

Fifth-digits for category 404 should be assigned as follows:

- 0 without heart failure and with chronic kidney disease (CKD) stage I through stage IV, or unspecified
- 1 with heart failure and with CKD stage I through stage IV, or unspecified
- 2 without heart failure and with CKD stage V or end stage renal disease
- 3 with heart failure and with CKD stage V or end stage renal disease

The appropriate code from category 585, Chronic kidney disease, should be used as a secondary code with a code from category 404 to identify the stage of kidney disease.

See Section I.C.10.a for information on the coding of chronic kidney disease.

5) **Hypertensive cerebrovascular disease**
First assign codes from 430-438, Cerebrovascular disease, then the appropriate hypertension code from categories 401-405.

6) **Hypertensive retinopathy**
Two codes are necessary to identify the condition. First assign the code from subcategory 362.11, Hypertensive retinopathy, then the appropriate code from categories 401-405 to indicate the type of hypertension.

7) **Hypertension, secondary**
Two codes are required: one to identify the underlying etiology and one from category 405 to identify the hypertension. Sequencing of codes is determined by the reason for admission/encounter.

8) **Hypertension, transient**
Assign code 796.2, Elevated blood pressure reading without diagnosis of hypertension, unless patient has an established diagnosis of hypertension. Assign code 642.3x for transient hypertension of pregnancy.

9) **Hypertension, controlled**
Assign appropriate code from categories 401-405. This diagnostic statement usually refers to an existing state of hypertension under control by therapy.

10) **Hypertension, uncontrolled**
Uncontrolled hypertension may refer to untreated hypertension or hypertension not responding to current therapeutic regimen. In either case, assign the

appropriate code from categories 401-405 to designate the stage and type of hypertension. Code to the type of hypertension.

11) **Elevated blood pressure**
For a statement of elevated blood pressure without further specificity, assign code 796.2, Elevated blood pressure reading without diagnosis of hypertension, rather than a code from category 401.

b. **Cerebral infarction/stroke/cerebrovascular accident (CVA)**
The terms stroke and CVA are often used interchangeably to refer to a cerebral infarction. The terms stroke, CVA, and cerebral infarction NOS are all indexed to the default code 434.91, Cerebral artery occlusion, unspecified, with infarction. Code 436, Acute, but ill-defined, cerebrovascular disease, should not be used when the documentation states stroke or CVA.
See Section I.C.18.d.3 for information on coding status post administration of tPA in a different facility within the last 24 hours.

c. **Postoperative cerebrovascular accident**
A cerebrovascular hemorrhage or infarction that occurs as a result of medical intervention is coded to 997.02, Iatrogenic cerebrovascular infarction or hemorrhage. Medical record documentation should clearly specify the cause- and-effect relationship between the medical intervention and the cerebrovascular accident in order to assign this code. A secondary code from the code range 430-432 or from a code from subcategories 433 or 434 with a fifth-digit of "1" should also be used to identify the type of hemorrhage or infarct.
This guideline conforms to the use additional code note instruction at category 997. Code 436, Acute, but ill-defined, cerebrovascular disease, should not be used as a secondary code with code 997.02.

d. **Late Effects of cerebrovascular disease**

1) **Category 438, late effects of cerebrovascular disease**
Category 438 is used to indicate conditions classifiable to categories 430-437 as the causes of late effects (neurologic deficits), themselves classified elsewhere. These "late effects" include neurologic deficits that persist after initial onset of conditions classifiable to 430-437. The neurologic deficits caused by cerebrovascular disease may be present from the onset or may arise at any time after the onset of the condition classifiable to 430-437.

2) **Codes from category 438 with codes from 430-437**
Codes from category 438 may be assigned on a health care record with codes from 430-437, if the patient has a current cerebrovascular accident (CVA) and deficits from an old CVA.

3) **Code V12.54**
Assign code V12.54, Transient ischemic attack (TIA), and cerebral infarction without residual deficits (and not a code from category 438) as an additional code for history of cerebrovascular disease when no neurologic deficits are present.

e. **Acute myocardial infarction (AMI)**

1) **ST elevation myocardial infarction (STEMI) and non ST elevation myocardial infarction (NSTEMI)**
The ICD-9-CM codes for acute myocardial infarction (AMI) identify the site, such as anterolateral wall or true posterior wall. Subcategories 410.0-410.6 and 410.8 are used for ST elevation myocardial infarction (STEMI). Subcategory 410.7, Subendocardial infarction, is used for non ST elevation myocardial infarction (NSTEMI) and nontransmural MIs.

2) **Acute myocardial infarction, unspecified**
Subcategory 410.9 is the default for the unspecified term acute myocardial infarction. If only STEMI or transmural MI without the site is documented, query the provider as to the site, or assign a code from subcategory 410.9.

3) **AMI documented as nontransmural or subendocardial but site provided**
If an AMI is documented as nontransmural or subendocardial, but the site is provided, it is still coded as a subendocardial AMI. If NSTEMI evolves to STEMI, assign the STEMI code. If STEMI converts to NSTEMI due to thrombolytic therapy, it is still coded as STEMI.
See Section I.C.18.d.3 for information on coding status post administration of tPA in a different facility within the last 24 hours.

8. **Chapter 8: Diseases of Respiratory System (460-519)**
See I.C.17.f. for ventilator-associated pneumonia.

a. **Chronic obstructive pulmonary disease [COPD] and asthma**

1) **Conditions that comprise COPD and asthma**
The conditions that comprise COPD are obstructive chronic bronchitis, subcategory 491.2, and emphysema, category 492. All asthma codes are under category 493, Asthma. Code 496, Chronic airway obstruction, not elsewhere classified, is a nonspecific code that should only be used when the documentation in a medical record does not specify the type of COPD being treated.

2) **Acute exacerbation of chronic obstructive bronchitis and asthma**
The codes for chronic obstructive bronchitis and asthma distinguish between uncomplicated cases and those in acute exacerbation. An acute exacerbation is a worsening or a decompensation of a chronic condition. An acute exacerbation is not equivalent to an infection superimposed on a chronic condition, though an exacerbation may be triggered by an infection.

3) **Overlapping nature of the conditions that comprise COPD and asthma**
Due to the overlapping nature of the conditions that make up COPD and asthma, there are many variations in the way these conditions are documented. Code selection must be based on the terms as documented. When selecting the correct code for the documented type of COPD and asthma, it is essential to first review the index, and then verify the code in the tabular list. There are many instructional notes under the different COPD subcategories and codes. It is important that all such notes be reviewed to assure correct code assignment.

4) **Acute exacerbation of asthma and status asthmaticus**
An acute exacerbation of asthma is an increased severity of the asthma symptoms, such as wheezing and shortness of breath. Status asthmaticus refers to a patient's failure to respond to therapy administered during an asthmatic episode and is a life threatening complication that requires emergency care. If status asthmaticus is documented by the provider with any type of COPD or with acute bronchitis, the status asthmaticus should be sequenced first. It supersedes any type of COPD including that with acute exacerbation or acute bronchitis. It is inappropriate to assign an asthma code with 5th digit 2, with acute exacerbation, together with an asthma code with 5th digit 1, with status asthmatics. Only the 5th digit 1 should be assigned.

b. **Chronic obstructive pulmonary disease [COPD] and bronchitis**

1) **Acute bronchitis with COPD**
Acute bronchitis, code 466.0, is due to an infectious organism. When acute bronchitis is documented with COPD, code 491.22, Obstructive chronic bronchitis with acute bronchitis, should be assigned. It is not necessary to also assign code 466.0. If a medical record documents acute bronchitis with COPD with acute exacerbation, only code 491.22 should be assigned. The acute bronchitis included in code 491.22 supersedes the acute exacerbation. If a medical record documents COPD with acute exacerbation without mention of acute bronchitis, only code 491.21 should be assigned.

c. **Acute Respiratory Failure**

1) **Acute respiratory failure as principal diagnosis**
Code 518.81, Acute respiratory failure, may be assigned as a principal diagnosis when it is the condition established after study to be chiefly responsible for occasioning the admission to the hospital, and the selection is supported by the Alphabetic Index and Tabular List. However, chapter-specific coding guidelines (such as obstetrics, poisoning, HIV, newborn) that provide sequencing direction take precedence.

2) **Acute respiratory failure as secondary diagnosis**
Respiratory failure may be listed as a secondary diagnosis if it occurs after admission, or if it is present on admission, but does not meet the definition of principal diagnosis.

3) **Sequencing of acute respiratory failure and another acute condition**
When a patient is admitted with respiratory failure and another acute condition, (e.g., myocardial infarction, cerebrovascular accident, **aspiration pneumonia**), the principal diagnosis will not be the same in every situation. **This applies whether the other acute condition is a respiratory or nonrespiratory condition.** Selection of the principal diagnosis will be dependent on the circumstances of admission. If both the respiratory failure and the other acute condition are equally responsible for occasioning the admission to the hospital, and there are no chapter-specific sequencing rules, the guideline regarding two or more diagnoses that equally meet the definition for principal diagnosis *(Section II, C.)* may be applied in these situations.
If the documentation is not clear as to whether acute respiratory failure and another condition are equally responsible for occasioning the admission, query the provider for clarification.

d. **Influenza due to identified avian influenza virus (avian influenza)**
Code only confirmed cases of avian influenza. This is an exception to the hospital inpatient guideline Section II, H. (Uncertain Diagnosis).
In this context, "confirmation" does not require documentation of positive laboratory testing specific for avian influenza. However, coding should be based on the provider's diagnostic statement that the patient has avian influenza.
If the provider records "suspected or possible or probable avian influenza," the appropriate influenza code from category 487 should be assigned. Code 488, Influenza due to identified avian influenza virus, should not be assigned.

9. **Chapter 9: Diseases of Digestive System (520-579)**
Reserved for future guideline expansion

10. **Chapter 10: Diseases of Genitourinary System (580-629)**

a. **Chronic kidney disease**

1) **Stages of chronic kidney disease (CKD)**
The ICD-9-CM classifies CKD based on severity. The severity of CKD is designated by stages I-V. Stage II, code 585.2, equates to mild CKD; stage III, code 585.3, equates to moderate CKD; and stage IV, code 585.4, equates to severe CKD. Code 585.6, End stage renal disease (ESRD), is assigned when the provider has documented end-stage-renal disease (ESRD).
If both a stage of CKD and ESRD are documented, assign code 585.6 only.

2) **Chronic kidney disease and kidney transplant status**
Patients who have undergone kidney transplant may still have some form of CKD, because the kidney transplant may not fully restore kidney function. Therefore, the presence of CKD alone does not constitute a transplant complication. Assign the appropriate 585 code for the patient's stage of CKD and code V42.0. If a transplant complication such as failure or rejection is documented, see section I.C.17.f.1.b for information on coding complications of a kidney transplant. If the documentation is unclear as to whether the patient has a complication of the transplant, query the provider.

3) **Chronic kidney disease with other conditions**
Patients with CKD may also suffer from other serious conditions, most commonly diabetes mellitus and hypertension. The sequencing of the CKD code in relationship to codes for other contributing conditions is based on the conventions in the tabular list.
See I.C.3.a.4 for sequencing instructions for diabetes.
See I.C.4.a.1 for anemia in CKD.
See I.C.7.a.3 for hypertensive chronic kidney disease.
See I.C.17.f.1.b, Kidney transplant complications, for instructions on coding of documented rejection or failure.

11. **Chapter 11: Complications of Pregnancy, Childbirth, and the Puerperium (630-679)**

a. **General Rules for Obstetric Cases**

1) **Codes from chapter 11 and sequencing priority**
Obstetric cases require codes from chapter 11, codes in the range 630-679, Complications of Pregnancy, Childbirth, and the Puerperium. Chapter 11 codes have sequencing priority over codes from other chapters. Additional codes from other chapters may be used in conjunction with chapter 11 codes to further specify conditions. Should the provider document that the pregnancy is incidental to the encounter, then code V22.2 should be used in place of any chapter 11 codes. It is the provider's responsibility to state that the condition being treated is not affecting the pregnancy.

2) **Chapter 11 codes used only on the maternal record**
Chapter 11 codes are to be used only on the maternal record, never on the record of the newborn.

3) **Chapter 11 fifth-digits**
Categories 640-648, 651-676 have required fifth-digits, which indicate whether the encounter is antepartum, postpartum and whether a delivery has also occurred.

4) **Fifth-digits, appropriate for each code**
The fifth-digits, which are appropriate for each code number, are listed in brackets under each code. The fifth-digits on each code should all be consistent with each other. That is, should a delivery occur all of the fifth-digits should indicate the delivery.

b. **Selection of OB Principal or First-listed Diagnosis**

1) **Routine outpatient prenatal visits**
For routine outpatient prenatal visits when no complications are present codes V22.0, Supervision of normal first pregnancy, and V22.1, Supervision of other normal pregnancy, should be used as the first-listed diagnoses. These codes should not be used in conjunction with chapter 11 codes.

2) **Prenatal outpatient visits for high-risk patients**
For prenatal outpatient visits for patients with high-risk pregnancies, a code from category V23, Supervision of high-risk pregnancy, should be used as the first-listed diagnosis. Secondary chapter 11 codes may be used in conjunction with these codes if appropriate.

3) **Episodes when no delivery occurs**
In episodes when no delivery occurs, the principal diagnosis should correspond to the principal complication of the pregnancy, which necessitated the encounter. Should more than one complication exist, all of which are treated or monitored, any of the complications codes may be sequenced first.

4) **When a delivery occurs**
When a delivery occurs, the principal diagnosis should correspond to the main circumstances or complication of the delivery. In cases of cesarean delivery, the selection of the principal diagnosis should correspond to the reason the cesarean delivery was performed unless the reason for admission/encounter was unrelated to the condition resulting in the cesarean delivery.

5) **Outcome of delivery**
An outcome of delivery code, V27.0-V27.9, should be included on every maternal record when a delivery has occurred. These codes are not to be used on subsequent records or on the newborn record.

c. **Fetal conditions affecting the management of the mother**

1) **Codes from category 655**
Known or suspected fetal abnormality affecting management of the mother, and category 656, Other fetal and placental problems affecting the management of the mother, are assigned only when the fetal condition is actually responsible for modifying the management of the mother, i.e., by requiring diagnostic studies, additional observation, special care, or termination of pregnancy. The fact that the fetal condition exists does not justify assigning a code from this series to the mother's record.
See I.C.18.d. for suspected maternal and fetal conditions not found

2) **In utero surgery**
In cases when surgery is performed on the fetus, a diagnosis code from category 655, Known or suspected fetal abnormalities affecting management of the mother, should be assigned identifying the fetal condition. Procedure code 75.36, Correction of fetal defect, should be assigned on the hospital inpatient record.
No code from Chapter 15, the perinatal codes, should be used on the mother's record to identify fetal conditions. Surgery performed in utero on a fetus is still to be coded as an obstetric encounter.

d. HIV infection in pregnancy, childbirth and the puerperium
During pregnancy, childbirth or the puerperium, a patient admitted because of an HIV-related illness should receive a principal diagnosis of 647.6X, Other specified infectious and parasitic diseases in the mother classifiable elsewhere, but complicating the pregnancy, childbirth or the puerperium, followed by 042 and the code(s) for the HIV-related illness(es).
Patients with asymptomatic HIV infection status admitted during pregnancy, childbirth, or the puerperium should receive codes of 647.6X and V08.

e. Current conditions complicating pregnancy
Assign a code from subcategory 648.x for patients that have current conditions when the condition affects the management of the pregnancy, childbirth, or the puerperium. Use additional secondary codes from other chapters to identify the conditions, as appropriate.

f. Diabetes mellitus in pregnancy
Diabetes mellitus is a significant complicating factor in pregnancy. Pregnant women who are diabetic should be assigned code 648.0x, Diabetes mellitus complicating pregnancy, and a secondary code from category 250, Diabetes mellitus, **or category 249, Secondary diabetes** to identify the type of diabetes.
Code V58.67, Long-term (current) use of insulin, should also be assigned if the diabetes mellitus is being treated with insulin.

g. Gestational diabetes
Gestational diabetes can occur during the second and third trimester of pregnancy in women who were not diabetic prior to pregnancy. Gestational diabetes can cause complications in the pregnancy similar to those of pre-existing diabetes mellitus. It also puts the woman at greater risk of developing diabetes after the pregnancy. Gestational diabetes is coded to 648.8x, Abnormal glucose tolerance. Codes 648.0x and 648.8x should never be used together on the same record.
Code V58.67, Long-term (current) use of insulin, should also be assigned if the gestational diabetes is being treated with insulin.

h. Normal delivery, Code 650

1) Normal delivery
Code 650 is for use in cases when a woman is admitted for a full-term normal delivery and delivers a single, healthy infant without any complications antepartum, during the delivery, or postpartum during the delivery episode. Code 650 is always a principal diagnosis. It is not to be used if any other code from chapter 11 is needed to describe a current complication of the antenatal, delivery, or perinatal period. Additional codes from other chapters may be used with code 650 if they are not related to or are in any way complicating the pregnancy.

2) Normal delivery with resolved antepartum complication
Code 650 may be used if the patient had a complication at some point during her pregnancy, but the complication is not present at the time of the admission for delivery.

3) V27.0, Single liveborn, outcome of delivery
V27.0, Single liveborn, is the only outcome of delivery code appropriate for use with 650.

i. The postpartum and peripartum periods

1) Postpartum and peripartum periods
The postpartum period begins immediately after delivery and continues for six weeks following delivery. The peripartum period is defined as the last month of pregnancy to five months postpartum.

2) Postpartum complication
A postpartum complication is any complication occurring within the six-week period.

3) Pregnancy-related complications after 6 week period
Chapter 11 codes may also be used to describe pregnancy-related complications after the six-week period should the provider document that a condition is pregnancy related.

4) Postpartum complications occurring during the same admission as delivery
Postpartum complications that occur during the same admission as the delivery are identified with a fifth-digit of "2." Subsequent admissions/encounters for postpartum complications should be identified with a fifth-digit of "4."

5) Admission for routine postpartum care following delivery outside hospital
When the mother delivers outside the hospital prior to admission and is admitted for routine postpartum care and no complications are noted, code V24.0, Postpartum care and examination immediately after delivery, should be assigned as the principal diagnosis.

6) Admission following delivery outside hospital with postpartum conditions
A delivery diagnosis code should not be used for a woman who has delivered prior to admission to the hospital. Any postpartum conditions and/or postpartum procedures should be coded.

j. Code 677, Late effect of complication of pregnancy

1) Code 677
Code 677, Late effect of complication of pregnancy, childbirth, and the puerperium is for use in those cases when an initial complication of a pregnancy develops a sequelae requiring care or treatment at a future date.

2) After the initial postpartum period
This code may be used at any time after the initial postpartum period.

3) Sequencing of Code 677
This code, like all late effect codes, is to be sequenced following the code describing the sequelae of the complication.

k. Abortions

1) Fifth-digits required for abortion categories
Fifth-digits are required for abortion categories 634-637. Fifth-digit 1, incomplete, indicates that all of the products of conception have not been expelled from the uterus. fifth-digit 2, complete, indicates that all products of conception have been expelled from the uterus prior to the episode of care.

2) Code from categories 640-648 and 651-659
A code from categories 640-648 and 651-659 may be used as additional codes with an abortion code to indicate the complication leading to the abortion.
Fifth-digit 3 is assigned with codes from these categories when used with an abortion code because the other fifth-digits will not apply. Codes from the 660-669 series are not to be used for complications of abortion.

3) Code 639 for complications
Code 639 is to be used for all complications following abortion. Code 639 cannot be assigned with codes from categories 634-638.

4) Abortion with liveborn fetus
When an attempted termination of pregnancy results in a liveborn fetus assign code 644.21, Early onset of delivery, with an appropriate code from category V27, Outcome of Delivery. The procedure code for the attempted termination of pregnancy should also be assigned.

5) Retained products of conception following an abortion
Subsequent admissions for retained products of conception following a spontaneous or legally induced abortion are assigned the appropriate code from category 634, Spontaneous abortion, or 635 Legally induced abortion, with a fifth-digit of "1" (incomplete). This advice is appropriate even when the patient was discharged previously with a discharge diagnosis of complete abortion.

12. Chapter 12: Diseases of Skin and Subcutaneous Tissue (680-709)

a. Pressure ulcer stage codes

1) Pressure ulcer stages
Two codes are needed to completely describe a pressure ulcer: A code from subcategory 707.0, Pressure ulcer, to identify the site of the pressure ulcer and a code from subcategory 707.2, Pressure ulcer stages.
The codes in subcategory 707.2, Pressure ulcer stages, are to be used as an additional diagnosis with a code(s) from subcategory 707.0, Pressure Ulcer. Codes from 707.2, Pressure ulcer stages, may not be assigned as a principal or first-listed diagnosis. The pressure ulcer stage codes should only be used with pressure ulcers and not with other types of ulcers (e.g., stasis ulcer).

The ICD-9-CM classifies pressure ulcer stages based on severity, which is designated by stages I-IV and unstageable.

2) **Unstageable pressure ulcers**
Assignment of code 707.25, Pressure ulcer, unstageable, should be based on the clinical documentation. Code 707.25 is used for pressure ulcers whose stage cannot be clinically determined (e.g., the ulcer is covered by eschar or has been treated with a skin or muscle graft) and pressure ulcers that are documented as deep tissue injury but not documented as due to trauma. This code should not be confused with code 707.20, Pressure ulcer, stage unspecified. Code 707.20 should be assigned when there is no documentation regarding the stage of the pressure ulcer.

3) **Documented pressure ulcer stage**
Assignment of the pressure ulcer stage code should be guided by clinical documentation of the stage or documentation of the terms found in the index. For clinical terms describing the stage that are not found in the index, and there is no documentation of the stage, the provider should be queried.

4) **Bilateral pressure ulcers with same stage**
When a patient has bilateral pressure ulcers (e.g., both buttocks) and both pressure ulcers are documented as being the same stage, only the code for the site and one code for the stage should be reported.

5) **Bilateral pressure ulcers with different stages**
When a patient has bilateral pressure ulcers at the same site (e.g., both buttocks) and each pressure ulcer is documented as being at a different stage, assign one code for the site and the appropriate codes for the pressure ulcer stage.

6) **Multiple pressure ulcers of different sites and stages**
When a patient has multiple pressure ulcers at different sites (e.g., buttock, heel, shoulder) and each pressure ulcer is documented as being at different stages (e.g., stage 3 and stage 4), assign the appropriate codes for each different site and a code for each different pressure ulcer stage.

7) **Patients admitted with pressure ulcers documented as healed**
No code is assigned if the documentation states that the pressure ulcer is completely healed.

8) **Patients admitted with pressure ulcers documented as healing**
Pressure ulcers described as healing should be assigned the appropriate pressure ulcer stage code based on the documentation in the medical record. If the documentation does not provide information about the stage of the healing pressure ulcer, assign code 707.20, Pressure ulcer stage, unspecified.
If the documentation is unclear as to whether the patient has a current (new) pressure ulcer or if the patient is being treated for a healing pressure ulcer, query the provider.

9) **Patient admitted with pressure ulcer evolving into another stage during the admission**
If a patient is admitted with a pressure ulcer at one stage and it progresses to a higher stage, assign the code for highest stage reported for that site.

13. **Chapter 13: Diseases of Musculoskeletal and Connective Tissue (710-739)**

a. **Coding of pathologic fractures**

1) **Acute fractures vs. aftercare**
Pathologic fractures are reported using subcategory 733.1, when the fracture is newly diagnosed. Subcategory 733.1 may be used while the patient is receiving active treatment for the fracture. Examples of active treatment are: surgical treatment, emergency department encounter, evaluation and treatment by a new physician.
Fractures are coded using the aftercare codes (subcategories V54.0, V54.2, V54.8 or V54.9) for encounters after the patient has completed active treatment of the fracture and is receiving routine care for the fracture during the healing or recovery phase. Examples of fracture aftercare are: cast change or removal, removal of external or internal fixation device, medication adjustment, and follow up visits following fracture treatment.
Care for complications of surgical treatment for fracture repairs during the healing or recovery phase should be coded with the appropriate complication codes.
Care of complications of fractures, such as malunion and nonunion, should be reported with the appropriate codes.
See Section I. C. 17.b for information on the coding of traumatic fractures.

14. **Chapter 14: Congenital Anomalies (740-759)**

a. **Codes in categories 740-759, congenital anomalies**
Assign an appropriate code(s) from categories 740-759, Congenital Anomalies, when an anomaly is documented. A congenital anomaly may be the principal/first listed diagnosis on a record or a secondary diagnosis.
When a congenital anomaly does not have a unique code assignment, assign additional code(s) for any manifestations that may be present.
When the code assignment specifically identifies the congenital anomaly, manifestations that are an inherent component of the anomaly should not be coded separately. Additional codes should be assigned for manifestations that are not an inherent component.
Codes from Chapter 14 may be used throughout the life of the patient. If a congenital anomaly has been corrected, a personal history code should be used to identify the history of the anomaly. Although present at birth, a congenital anomaly may not be identified until later in life. Whenever the condition is diagnosed by the physician, it is appropriate to assign a code from codes 740-759.
For the birth admission, the appropriate code from category V30, Liveborn infants, according to type of birth should be sequenced as the principal diagnosis, followed by any congenital anomaly codes, 740-759.

15. **Chapter 15: Newborn (Perinatal) Guidelines (760-779)**
For coding and reporting purposes the perinatal period is defined as before birth through the 28th day following birth. The following guidelines are provided for reporting purposes. Hospitals may record other diagnoses as needed for internal data use.

a. **General perinatal rules**

1) **Chapter 15 Codes**
They are <u>never</u> for use on the maternal record. Codes from Chapter 11, the obstetric chapter, are never permitted on the newborn record. Chapter 15 code may be used throughout the life of the patient if the condition is still present.

2) **Sequencing of perinatal codes**
Generally, codes from Chapter 15 should be sequenced as the principal/first-listed diagnosis on the newborn record, with the exception of the appropriate V30 code for the birth episode, followed by codes from any other chapter that provide additional detail. The "use additional code" note at the beginning of the chapter supports this guideline. If the index does not provide a specific code for a perinatal condition, assign code 779.89, Other specified conditions originating in the perinatal period, followed by the code from another chapter that specifies the condition. Codes for signs and symptoms may be assigned when a definitive diagnosis has not been established.

3) **Birth process or community acquired conditions**
If a newborn has a condition that may be either due to the birth process or community acquired and the documentation does not indicate which it is, the default is due to the birth process and the code from Chapter 15 should be used. If the condition is community-acquired, a code from Chapter 15 should not be assigned.

4) **Code all clinically significant conditions**
All clinically significant conditions noted on routine newborn examination should be coded. A condition is clinically significant if it requires:
- clinical evaluation; or
- therapeutic treatment; or
- diagnostic procedures; or
- extended length of hospital stay; or
- increased nursing care and/or monitoring; or
- has implications for future health care needs

Note: The perinatal guidelines listed above are the same as the general coding guidelines for "additional diagnoses", except for the final point regarding implications for future health care needs. Codes should be assigned for conditions that have been specified by the provider as having implications for future health care needs. Codes from the perinatal chapter should not be assigned unless the provider has established a definitive diagnosis.

b. **Use of codes V30-V39**
When coding the birth of an infant, assign a code from categories V30-V39, according to the type of birth. A code from this series is assigned as a principal diagnosis, and assigned only once to a newborn at the time of birth.

c. **Newborn transfers**
If the newborn is transferred to another institution, the V30 series is not used at the receiving hospital.

d. **Use of category V29**

1) **Assigning a code from category V29**
Assign a code from category V29, Observation and evaluation of newborns and infants for suspected conditions not found, to identify those instances when a healthy newborn is evaluated for a suspected condition that is determined after study not to be present. Do not use a code from category V29 when the patient has identified signs or symptoms of a suspected problem; in such cases, code the sign or symptom.
A code from category V29 may also be assigned as a principal code for readmissions or encounters when the V30 code no longer applies. Codes from category V29 are for use only for healthy newborns and infants for which no condition after study is found to be present.

2) **V29 code on a birth record**
A V29 code is to be used as a secondary code after the V30, Outcome of delivery, code.

e. **Use of other V codes on perinatal records**
V codes other than V30 and V29 may be assigned on a perinatal or newborn record code. The codes may be used as a principal or first-listed diagnosis for specific types of encounters or for readmissions or encounters when the V30 code no longer applies.
See Section I.C.18 for information regarding the assignment of V codes.

f. **Maternal causes of perinatal morbidity**
Codes from categories 760-763, Maternal causes of perinatal morbidity and mortality, are assigned only when the maternal condition has actually affected the fetus or newborn. The fact that the mother has an associated medical condition or experiences some complication of pregnancy, labor or delivery does not justify the routine assignment of codes from these categories to the newborn record.

g. **Congenital anomalies in newborns**
For the birth admission, the appropriate code from category V30, Liveborn infants according to type of birth, should be used, followed by any congenital anomaly codes, categories 740-759. Use additional secondary codes from other chapters to specify conditions associated with the anomaly, if applicable.
Also, see Section I.C.14 for information on the coding of congenital anomalies.

h. **Coding additional perinatal diagnoses**

1) **Assigning codes for conditions that require treatment**
Assign codes for conditions that require treatment or further investigation, prolong the length of stay, or require resource utilization.

2) **Codes for conditions specified as having implications for future health care needs**
Assign codes for conditions that have been specified by the provider as having implications for future health care needs.
Note: This guideline should not be used for adult patients.

3) **Codes for newborn conditions originating in the perinatal period**
Assign a code for newborn conditions originating in the perinatal period (categories 760-779), as well as complications arising during the current episode of care classified in other chapters, only if the diagnoses have been documented by the responsible provider at the time of transfer or discharge as having affected the fetus or newborn.

i. **Prematurity and fetal growth retardation**
Providers utilize different criteria in determining prematurity. A code for prematurity should not be assigned unless it is documented. The 5th digit assignment for codes from category 764 and subcategories 765.0 and 765.1 should be based on the recorded birth weight and estimated gestational age.
A code from subcategory 765.2, Weeks of gestation, should be assigned as an additional code with category 764 and codes from 765.0 and 765.1 to specify weeks of gestation as documented by the provider in the record.

j. **Newborn sepsis**
Code 771.81, Septicemia [sepsis] of newborn, should be assigned with a secondary code from category 041, Bacterial infections in conditions classified elsewhere and of unspecified site, to identify the organism. It is not necessary to use a code from subcategory 995.9, Systemic inflammatory response syndrome (SIRS), on a newborn record. **Do not assign code 995.91, Sepsis, as code 771.81 describes the sepsis. If applicable, use additional codes to identify severe sepsis (995.92) and any associated acute organ dysfunction.**

16. **Chapter 16: Signs, Symptoms and Ill-Defined Conditions (780-799)**
Reserved for future guideline expansion

17. **Chapter 17: Injury and Poisoning (800-999)**

a. **Coding of injuries**
When coding injuries, assign separate codes for each injury unless a combination code is provided, in which case the combination code is assigned. Multiple injury codes are provided in ICD-9-CM, but should not be assigned unless information for a more specific code is not available. These codes are not to be used for normal, healing surgical wounds or to identify complications of surgical wounds.
The code for the most serious injury, as determined by the provider and the focus of treatment, is sequenced first.

1) **Superficial injuries**
Superficial injuries such as abrasions or contusions are not coded when associated with more severe injuries of the same site.

2) **Primary injury with damage to nerves/blood vessels**
When a primary injury results in minor damage to peripheral nerves or blood vessels, the primary injury is sequenced first with additional code(s) from categories 950-957, Injury to nerves and spinal cord, and/or 900-904, Injury to blood vessels. When the primary injury is to the blood vessels or nerves, that injury should be sequenced first.

b. **Coding of traumatic fractures**
The principles of multiple coding of injuries should be followed in coding fractures. Fractures of specified sites are coded individually by site in accordance with both the provisions within categories 800-829 and the level of detail furnished by medical record content. Combination categories for multiple fractures are provided for use when there is insufficient detail in the medical record (such as trauma cases transferred to another hospital), when the reporting form limits the number of codes that can be used in reporting pertinent clinical data, or when there is insufficient specificity at the fourth-digit or fifth-digit level. More specific guidelines are as follows:

1) **Acute fractures vs. aftercare**
Traumatic fractures are coded using the acute fracture codes (800-829) while the patient is receiving active treatment for the fracture. Examples of active treatment are: surgical treatment, emergency department encounter, and evaluation and treatment by a new physician.
Fractures are coded using the aftercare codes (subcategories V54.0, V54.1, V54.8, or V54.9) for encounters after the patient has completed active treatment of the fracture and is receiving routine care for the fracture during the healing or recovery phase. Examples of fracture aftercare are: cast change or removal, removal of external or internal fixation device, medication adjustment, and follow up visits following fracture treatment.

Care for complications of surgical treatment for fracture repairs during the healing or recovery phase should be coded with the appropriate complication codes.

Care of complications of fractures, such as malunion and nonunion, should be reported with the appropriate codes.

Pathologic fractures are not coded in the 800-829 range, but instead are assigned to subcategory 733.1. *See Section I.C.13.a for additional information.*

2) **Multiple fractures of same limb**
Multiple fractures of same limb classifiable to the same three-digit or four-digit category are coded to that category.

3) **Multiple unilateral or bilateral fractures of same bone**
Multiple unilateral or bilateral fractures of same bone(s) but classified to different fourth-digit subdivisions (bone part) within the same three-digit category are coded individually by site.

4) **Multiple fracture categories 819 and 828**
Multiple fracture categories 819 and 828 classify bilateral fractures of both upper limbs (819) and both lower limbs (828), but without any detail at the fourth-digit level other than open and closed type of fractures.

5) **Multiple fractures sequencing**
Multiple fractures are sequenced in accordance with the severity of the fracture. The provider should be asked to list the fracture diagnoses in the order of severity.

c. **Coding of burns**
Current burns (940-948) are classified by depth, extent and by agent (E code). Burns are classified by depth as first degree (erythema), second degree (blistering), and third degree (full-thickness involvement).

1) **Sequencing of burn and related condition codes**
Sequence first the code that reflects the highest degree of burn when more than one burn is present.

a. When the reason for the admission or encounter is for treatment of external multiple burns, sequence first the code that reflects the burn of the highest degree.

b. When a patient has both internal and external burns, the circumstances of admission govern the selection of the principal diagnosis or first-listed diagnosis.

c. When a patient is admitted for burn injuries and other related conditions such as smoke inhalation and/or respiratory failure, the circumstances of admission govern the selection of the principal or first-listed diagnosis.

2) **Burns of the same local site**
Classify burns of the same local site (three-digit category level, 940-947) but of different degrees to the subcategory identifying the highest degree recorded in the diagnosis.

3) **Non-healing burns**
Non-healing burns are coded as acute burns.

Necrosis of burned skin should be coded as a non-healed burn.

4) **Code 958.3, posttraumatic wound infection**
Assign code 958.3, Posttraumatic wound infection, not elsewhere classified, as an additional code for any documented infected burn site.

5) **Assign separate codes for each burn site**
When coding burns, assign separate codes for each burn site. Category 946 Burns of Multiple specified sites, should only be used if the location of the burns are not documented.

Category 949, Burn, unspecified, is extremely vague and should rarely be used.

6) **Assign codes from category 948, burns**
Burns classified according to extent of body surface involved, when the site of the burn is not specified or when there is a need for additional data. It is advisable to use category 948 as additional coding when needed to provide data for evaluating burn mortality, such as that needed by burn units. It is also advisable to use category 948 as an additional code for reporting purposes when there is mention of a third-degree burn involving 20 percent or more of the body surface.

In assigning a code from category 948:

Fourth-digit codes are used to identify the percentage of total body surface involved in a burn (all degree).

Fifth-digits are assigned to identify the percentage of body surface involved in third-degree burn.

Fifth-digit zero (0) is assigned when less than 10 percent or when no body surface is involved in a third-degree burn.

Category 948 is based on the classic "rule of nines" in estimating body surface involved: head and neck are assigned nine percent, each arm nine percent, each leg 18 percent, the anterior trunk 18 percent, posterior trunk 18 percent, and genitalia one percent. Providers may change these percentage assignments where necessary to accommodate infants and children who have proportionately larger heads than adults and patients who have large buttocks, thighs, or abdomen that involve burns.

7) **Encounters for treatment of late effects of burns**
Encounters for the treatment of the late effects of burns (i.e., scars or joint contractures) should be coded to the residual condition (sequelae) followed by the appropriate late effect code (906.5-906.9). A late effect E code may also be used, if desired.

8) **Sequelae with a late effect code and current burn**
When appropriate, both a sequelae with a late effect code, and a current burn code may be assigned on the same record (when both a current burn and sequelae of an old burn exist).

d. **Coding of debridement of wound, infection, or burn**
Excisional debridement involves surgical removal or cutting away, as opposed to a mechanical (brushing, scrubbing, washing) debridement.

For coding purposes, excisional debridement is assigned to code 86.22.

Nonexcisional debridement is assigned to code 86.28.

e. **Adverse effects, poisoning and toxic effects**
The properties of certain drugs, medicinal and biological substances or combinations of such substances, may cause toxic reactions. The occurrence of drug toxicity is classified in ICD-9-CM as follows:

1) **Adverse effect**
When the drug was correctly prescribed and properly administered, code the reaction plus the appropriate code from the E930-E949 series. Codes from the E930-E949 series must be used to identify the causative substance for an adverse effect of drug, medicinal and biological substances, correctly prescribed and properly administered. The effect, such as tachycardia, delirium, gastrointestinal hemorrhaging, vomiting, hypokalemia, hepatitis, renal failure, or respiratory failure, is coded and followed by the appropriate code from the E930-E949 series.

Adverse effects of therapeutic substances correctly prescribed and properly administered (toxicity, synergistic reaction, side effect, and idiosyncratic reaction) may be due to (1) differences among patients, such as age, sex, disease, and genetic factors, and (2) drug-related factors, such as type of drug, route of administration, duration of therapy, dosage, and bioavailability.

2) **Poisoning**

(a) **Error was made in drug prescription**
Errors made in drug prescription or in the administration of the drug by provider, nurse, patient, or other person, use the appropriate poisoning code from the 960-979 series.

(b) **Overdose of a drug intentionally taken**
If an overdose of a drug was intentionally taken or administered and resulted in drug toxicity, it would be coded as a poisoning (960-979 series).

(c) **Nonprescribed drug taken with correctly prescribed and properly administered drug**
If a nonprescribed drug or medicinal agent was taken in combination with a correctly prescribed and properly administered drug, any drug toxicity or other reaction resulting from the interaction of the two drugs would be classified as a poisoning.

(d) **Sequencing of poisoning**
When a reaction results from the interaction of a drug(s) and alcohol, this would be classified as poisoning.

(e) **Sequencing of poisoning**
When coding a poisoning or reaction to the improper use of a medication (e.g., wrong dose, wrong substance, wrong route of administration) the poisoning code is sequenced first, followed by a code for the manifestation. If there is also a diagnosis of drug abuse or dependence to the substance, the abuse or dependence is coded as an additional code.

See Section I.C.3.a.6.b. if poisoning is the result of insulin pump malfunctions and Section I.C.19 for general use of E-codes.

3) **Toxic effects**

(a) **Toxic effect codes**
When a harmful substance is ingested or comes in contact with a person, this is classified as a toxic effect. The toxic effect codes are in categories 980-989.

(b) **Sequencing toxic effect codes**
A toxic effect code should be sequenced first, followed by the code(s) that identify the result of the toxic effect.

(c) **External cause codes for toxic effects**
An external cause code from categories E860-E869 for accidental exposure, codes E950.6 or E950.7 for intentional self-harm, category E962 for assault, or categories E980-E982, for undetermined, should also be assigned to indicate intent.

f. **Complications of care**

1) **Complications of care**

(a) **Documentation of complications of care**
As with all procedural or postprocedural complications, code assignment is based on the provider's documentation of the relationship between the condition and the procedure.

2) **Transplant complications**

(a) **Transplant complications other than kidney**
Codes under subcategory 996.8, Complications of transplanted organ, are for use for both complications and rejection of transplanted organs. A transplant complication code is only assigned if the complication affects the function of the transplanted organ. Two codes are required to fully describe a transplant complication, the appropriate code from subcategory 996.8 and a secondary code that identifies the complication.

Pre-existing conditions or conditions that develop after the transplant are not coded as complications unless they affect the function of the transplanted organs.

See I.C.18.d.3) for transplant organ removal status

See I.C.2.i for malignant neoplasm associated with transplanted organ.

(b) **Chronic kidney disease and kidney transplant complications**
Patients who have undergone kidney transplant may still have some form of chronic kidney disease (CKD) because the kidney transplant may not fully restore kidney function. Code 996.81 should be assigned for documented complications of a kidney transplant, such as transplant failure **or rejection or other transplant complication**. Code 996.81 should not be assigned for post kidney transplant patients who have chronic kidney (CKD) unless a transplant complication such as transplant failure or rejection is documented. If the documentation is unclear as to whether the patient has a complication of the transplant, query the provider.

For patients with CKD following a kidney transplant, but who do not have a complication such as failure or rejection, see section I.C.10.a.2, *Chronic kidney disease and kidney transplant status.*

3) **Ventilator associated pneumonia**

(a) **Documentation of Ventilator associated Pneumonia**
As with all procedural or postprocedural complications, code assignment is based on the provider's documentation of the relationship between the condition and the procedure.

Code 997.31, Ventilator associated pneumonia, should be assigned only when the provider has documented ventilator associated pneumonia (VAP). An additional code to identify the organism (e.g., Pseudomonas aeruginosa, code 041.7) should also be assigned. Do not assign an additional code from categories 480-484 to identify the type of pneumonia.

Code 997.31 should not be assigned for cases where the patient has pneumonia and is on a mechanical ventilator but the provider has not specifically stated that the pneumonia is ventilator-associated pneumonia.

If the documentation is unclear as to whether the patient has a pneumonia that is a complication attributable to the mechanical ventilator, query the provider.

(b) **Patient admitted with pneumonia and develops VAP**
A patient may be admitted with one type of pneumonia (e.g., code 481, Pneumococcal pneumonia) and subsequently develop VAP. In this instance, the principal diagnosis would be the appropriate code from categories 480-484 for the pneumonia diagnosed at the time of admission. Code 997.31, Ventilator associated pneumonia, would be assigned as an additional diagnosis when the provider has also documented the presence of ventilator associated pneumonia.

g. **SIRS due to non-infectious process**
The systemic inflammatory response syndrome (SIRS) can develop as a result of certain non-infectious disease processes, such as trauma, malignant neoplasm, or pancreatitis. When SIRS is documented with a noninfectious condition, and no subsequent infection is documented, the code for the underlying condition, such as an injury, should be assigned, followed by code 995.93, Systemic inflammatory response syndrome due to noninfectious process without acute organ dysfunction, or 995.94, Systemic inflammatory response syndrome due to non-infectious process with acute organ dysfunction. If an acute organ dysfunction is documented, the appropriate code(s) for the associated acute organ dysfunction(s) should be assigned in addition to code 995.94. If acute organ dysfunction is documented, but it cannot be determined if the acute organ dysfunction is associated with SIRS or due to another condition (e.g., directly due to the trauma), the provider should be queried.

When the non-infectious condition has led to an infection that results in SIRS, *see Section I.C.1.b.***12** *for the guideline for sepsis and severe sepsis associated with a non-infectious process.*

18. **Classification of Factors Influencing Health Status and Contact with Health Service (Supplemental V01-V89)**

Note: The chapter specific guidelines provide additional information about the use of V codes for specified encounters.

a. **Introduction**
ICD-9-CM provides codes to deal with encounters for circumstances other than a disease or injury. The Supplementary Classification of Factors Influencing Health Status and Contact with Health Services (V01.0 - V89.09) is provided to deal with occasions when circumstances other than a disease or injury (codes 001-**V89.09**) are recorded as a diagnosis or problem.

There are four primary circumstances for the use of V codes:

1) A person who is not currently sick encounters the health services for some specific reason, such as to act as an organ donor, to receive prophylactic care, such as inoculations or health screenings, or to receive counseling on health related issues.

2) A person with a resolving disease or injury, or a chronic, long-term condition requiring continuous care, encounters the health care system for specific aftercare of that disease or injury (e.g., dialysis for renal disease; chemotherapy for malignancy; cast change). A

diagnosis/symptom code should be used whenever a current, acute, diagnosis is being treated or a sign or symptom is being studied.

3) Circumstances or problems influence a person's health status but are not in themselves a current illness or injury.

4) Newborns, to indicate birth status

b. **V codes use in any healthcare setting**

V codes are for use in any healthcare setting. V codes may be used as either a first listed (principal diagnosis code in the inpatient setting) or secondary code, depending on the circumstances of the encounter. Certain V codes may only be used as first listed, others only as secondary codes.

See Section I.C.18.e, V Code Table.

c. **V Codes indicate a reason for an encounter**

They are not procedure codes. A corresponding procedure code must accompany a V code to describe the procedure performed.

d. **Categories of V codes**

1) **Contact/exposure**

Category V01 indicates contact with or exposure to communicable diseases. These codes are for patients who do not show any sign or symptom of a disease but have been exposed to it by close personal contact with an infected individual or are in an area where a disease is epidemic. These codes may be used as a first listed code to explain an encounter for testing, or, more commonly, as a secondary code to identify a potential risk.

2) **Inoculations and vaccinations**

Categories V03-V06 are for encounters for inoculations and vaccinations. They indicate that a patient is being seen to receive a prophylactic inoculation against a disease. The injection itself must be represented by the appropriate procedure code. A code from V03-V06 may be used as a secondary code if the inoculation is given as a routine part of preventive health care, such as a well-baby visit.

3) **Status**

Status codes indicate that a patient is either a carrier of a disease or has the sequelae or residual of a past disease or condition. This includes such things as the presence of prosthetic or mechanical devices resulting from past treatment. A status code is informative, because the status may affect the course of treatment and its outcome. A status code is distinct from a history code. The history code indicates that the patient no longer has the condition.

A status code should not be used with a diagnosis code from one of the body system chapters, if the diagnosis code includes the information provided by the status code. For example, code V42.1, Heart transplant status, should not be used with code 996.83, Complications of transplanted heart. The status code does not provide additional information. The complication code indicates that the patient is a heart transplant patient.

The status V codes/categories are:

V02 Carrier or suspected carrier of infectious diseases

Carrier status indicates that a person harbors the specific organisms of a disease without manifest symptoms and is capable of transmitting the infection.

V07.5X Prophylactic use of agents affecting estrogen receptors and estrogen level

This code indicates when a patient is receiving a drug that affects estrogen receptors and estrogen levels for prevention of cancer.

V08 Asymptomatic HIV infection status

This code indicates that a patient has tested positive for HIV but has manifested no signs or symptoms of the disease.

V09 Infection with drug-resistant microorganisms

This category indicates that a patient has an infection that is resistant to drug treatment. Sequence the infection code first.

V21 Constitutional states in development

V22.2 Pregnant state, incidental

This code is a secondary code only for use when the pregnancy is in no way complicating the reason for visit. Otherwise, a code from the obstetric chapter is required.

V26.5x Sterilization status

V42 Organ or tissue replaced by transplant

V43 Organ or tissue replaced by other means

V44 Artificial opening status

V45 Other postsurgical states

Assign code V45.87, Transplant organ removal status, to indicate that a transplanted organ has been previously removed. This code should not be assigned for the encounter in which the transplanted organ is removed. The complication necessitating removal of the transplant organ should be assigned for that encounter.

See section I.C17.f.2. for information on the coding of organ transplant complications.

Assign code V45.88, Status post administration of tPA (rtPA) in a different facility within the last 24 hours prior to admission to the current facility, as a secondary diagnosis when a patient is received by transfer into a facility and documentation indicates they were administered tissue plasminogen activator (tPA) within the last 24 hours prior to admission to the current facility.

This guideline applies even if the patient is still receiving the tPA at the time they are received into the current facility.

The appropriate code for the condition for which the tPA was administered (such as cerebrovascular disease or myocardial infarction) should be assigned first.

Code V45.88 is only applicable to the receiving facility record and not to the transferring facility record.

V46 Other dependence on machines

V49.6 Upper limb amputation status

V49.7 Lower limb amputation status

Note: Categories V42-V46, and subcategories V49.6, V49.7 are for use only if there are no complications or malfunctions of the organ or tissue replaced, the amputation site or the equipment on which the patient is dependent.

V49.81 Postmenopausal status

V49.82 Dental sealant status

V49.83 Awaiting organ transplant status

V58.6**x** Long-term (current) drug use

Codes from this subcategory indicate a patient's continuous use of a prescribed drug (including such things as aspirin therapy) for the long-term treatment of a condition or for prophylactic use. It is not for use for patients who have addictions to drugs. **This subcategory is not for use of medications for detoxification or maintenance programs to prevent withdrawal symptoms in patients with drug dependence (e.g., methadone maintenance for opiate dependence). Assign the appropriate code for the drug dependence instead.**

Assign a code from subcategory V58.6, Long-term (current) drug use, if the patient is receiving a medication for an extended period as a prophylactic measure (such as for the prevention of deep vein thrombosis) or as treatment of a chronic condition (such as arthritis) or a disease requiring a lengthy course of treatment (such as cancer). Do not assign a code from subcategory V58.6 for medication being administered for a brief period of time to treat an acute illness or injury (such as a course of antibiotics to treat acute bronchitis).

V83 Genetic carrier status
Genetic carrier status indicates that a person carries a gene, associated with a particular disease, which may be passed to offspring who may develop that disease. The person does not have the disease and is not at risk of developing the disease.

V84 Genetic susceptibility status
Genetic susceptibility indicates that a person has a gene that increases the risk of that person developing the disease.

Codes from category V84, Genetic susceptibility to disease, should not be used as principal or first-listed codes. If the patient has the condition to which he/she is susceptible, and that condition is the reason for the encounter, the code for the current condition should be sequenced first. If the patient is being seen for follow-up after completed treatment for this condition, and the condition no longer exists, a follow-up code should be sequenced first, followed by the appropriate personal history and genetic susceptibility codes. If the purpose of the encounter is genetic counseling associated with procreative management, a code from subcategory V26.3, Genetic counseling and testing, should be assigned as the first-listed code, followed by a code from category V84. Additional codes should be assigned for any applicable family or personal history.

See Section I.C. 18.d.14 for information on prophylactic organ removal due to a genetic susceptibility.

V86 Estrogen receptor status

V88 Acquired absence of other organs and tissue

4) History (of)

There are two types of history V codes, personal and family. Personal history codes explain a patient's past medical condition that no longer exists and is not receiving any treatment, but that has the potential for recurrence, and therefore may require continued monitoring. The exceptions to this general rule are category V14, Personal history of allergy to medicinal agents, and subcategory V15.0, Allergy, other than to medicinal agents. A person who has had an allergic episode to a substance or food in the past should always be considered allergic to the substance.

Family history codes are for use when a patient has a family member(s) who has had a particular disease that causes the patient to be at higher risk of also contracting the disease.

Personal history codes may be used in conjunction with follow-up codes and family history codes may be used in conjunction with screening codes to explain the need for a test or procedure. History codes are also acceptable on any medical record regardless of the reason for visit. A history of an illness, even if no longer present, is important information that may alter the type of treatment ordered.

The history V code categories are:

V10 Personal history of malignant neoplasm
V12 Personal history of certain other diseases
V13 Personal history of other diseases
Except: V13.4, Personal history of arthritis, and V13.6, Personal history of congenital malformations. These conditions are life-long so are not true history codes.
V14 Personal history of allergy to medicinal agents
V15 Other personal history presenting hazards to health
Except: V15.7, Personal history of contraception.
V16 Family history of malignant neoplasm
V17 Family history of certain chronic disabling diseases
V18 Family history of certain other specific diseases
V19 Family history of other conditions
V87 Other specified personal exposures and history presenting hazards to health

5) Screening

Screening is the testing for disease or disease precursors in seemingly well individuals so that early detection and treatment can be provided for those who test positive for the disease. Screenings that are recommended for many subgroups in a population include: routine mammograms for women over 40, a fecal occult blood test for everyone over 50, an amniocentesis to rule out a fetal anomaly for pregnant women over 35, because the incidence of breast cancer and colon cancer in these subgroups is higher than in the general population, as is the incidence of Down's syndrome in older mothers.

The testing of a person to rule out or confirm a suspected diagnosis because the patient has some sign or symptom is a diagnostic examination, not a screening. In these cases, the sign or symptom is used to explain the reason for the test.

A screening code may be a first listed code if the reason for the visit is specifically the screening exam. It may also be used as an additional code if the screening is done during an office visit for other health problems. A screening code is not necessary if the screening is inherent to a routine examination, such as a pap smear done during a routine pelvic examination.

Should a condition be discovered during the screening then the code for the condition may be assigned as an additional diagnosis.

The V code indicates that a screening exam is planned. A procedure code is required to confirm that the screening was performed.

The screening V code categories:

V28 Antenatal screening
V73-V82 Special screening examinations

6) Observation

There are **three** observation V code categories. They are for use in very limited circumstances when a person is being observed for a suspected condition that is ruled out. The observation codes are not for use if an injury or illness or any signs or symptoms related to the suspected condition are present. In such cases the diagnosis/symptom code is used with the corresponding E code to identify any external cause.

The observation codes are to be used as principal diagnosis only. The only exception to this is when the principal diagnosis is required to be a code from the V30, Live born infant, category. Then the V29 observation code is sequenced after the V30 code. Additional codes may be used in addition to the observation code but only if they are unrelated to the suspected condition being observed.

Codes from subcategory V89.0, Suspected maternal and fetal conditions not found, may either be used as a first listed or as an additional code assignment depending on the case. They are for use in very limited circumstances on a maternal record when an encounter is for a suspected maternal or fetal condition that is ruled out during that encounter (for example, a maternal or fetal condition may be suspected due to an abnormal test result). These codes should not be used when the condition is confirmed. In those cases, the confirmed condition should be coded. In addition, these codes are not for use if an illness or any signs or symptoms related to the suspected condition or problem are present. In such cases the diagnosis/symptom code is used.

Additional codes may be used in addition to the code from subcategory V89.0, but only if they are unrelated to the suspected condition being evaluated.

Codes from subcategory V89.0 may not be used for encounters for antenatal screening of mother. ***See Section I.C.18.d., Screening).***

For encounters for suspected fetal condition that are inconclusive following testing and evaluation, assign the appropriate code from category 655, 656, 657 or 658.

The observation V code categories:

V29 Observation and evaluation of newborns for suspected condition not found
For the birth encounter, a code from category V30 should be sequenced before the V29 code.

V71 Observation and evaluation for suspected condition not found

V89 Suspected maternal and fetal conditions not found

7) Aftercare

Aftercare visit codes cover situations when the initial treatment of a disease or injury has been performed and the patient requires continued care during the healing or recovery phase, or for the long-term consequences of the disease. The aftercare V code should not be used if treatment is directed at a current, acute disease or injury. The diagnosis code is to be used in these cases. Exceptions to this rule are codes V58.0, Radiotherapy, and codes from subcategory V58.1, Encounter for chemotherapy and immunotherapy for neoplastic conditions. These codes are to be first listed, followed by the diagnosis code when a patient's encounter is solely to receive radiation therapy or chemotherapy for the treatment of a neoplasm. Should a patient receive both chemotherapy and radiation therapy during the same encounter code V58.0 and V58.1 may be used together on a record with either one being sequenced first.

The aftercare codes are generally first listed to explain the specific reason for the encounter. An aftercare code may be used as an additional code when some type of aftercare is provided in addition to the reason for admission and no diagnosis code is applicable. An example of this would be the closure of a colostomy during an encounter for treatment of another condition.

Aftercare codes should be used in conjunction with any other aftercare codes or other diagnosis codes to provide better detail on the specifics of an aftercare encounter visit, unless otherwise directed by the classification. The sequencing of multiple aftercare codes is discretionary.

Certain aftercare V code categories need a secondary diagnosis code to describe the resolving condition or sequelae, for others, the condition is inherent in the code title.

Additional V code aftercare category terms include, fitting and adjustment, and attention to artificial openings.

Status V codes may be used with aftercare V codes to indicate the nature of the aftercare. For example code V45.81, Aortocoronary bypass status, may be used with code V58.73, Aftercare following surgery of the circulatory system, NEC, to indicate the surgery for which the aftercare is being performed. Also, a transplant status code may be used following code V58.44, Aftercare following organ transplant, to identify the organ transplanted. A status code should not be used when the aftercare code indicates the type of status, such as using V55.0, Attention to tracheostomy with V44.0, Tracheostomy status.

See Section I. B.16 Admissions/Encounter for Rehabilitation

The aftercare V category/codes:

V51.0 Encounter for breast reconstruction following mastectomy

V52 Fitting and adjustment of prosthetic device and implant

V53 Fitting and adjustment of other device

V54 Other orthopedic aftercare

V55 Attention to artificial openings

V56 Encounter for dialysis and dialysis catheter care

V57 Care involving the use of rehabilitation procedures

V58.0 Radiotherapy

V58.11 Encounter for antineoplastic chemotherapy

V58.12 Encounter for antineoplastic immunotherapy

V58.3x Attention to dressings and sutures

V58.41 Encounter for planned post-operative wound closure

V58.42 Aftercare, surgery, neoplasm

V58.43 Aftercare, surgery, trauma

V58.44 Aftercare involving organ transplant

V58.49 Other specified aftercare following surgery

V58.7x Aftercare following surgery

V58.81 Fitting and adjustment of vascular catheter

V58.82 Fitting and adjustment of non-vascular catheter

V58.83 Monitoring therapeutic drug

V58.89 Other specified aftercare

8) Follow-up

The follow-up codes are used to explain continuing surveillance following completed treatment of a disease, condition, or injury. They imply that the condition has been fully treated and no longer exists. They should not be confused with aftercare codes that explain current treatment for a healing condition or its sequelae. Follow-up codes may be used in conjunction with history codes to provide the full picture of the healed condition and its treatment. The follow-up code is sequenced first, followed by the history code.

A follow-up code may be used to explain repeated visits. Should a condition be found to have recurred on the follow-up visit, then the diagnosis code should be used in place of the follow-up code.

The follow-up V code categories:

V24 Postpartum care and evaluation

V67 Follow-up examination

9) Donor

Category V59 is the donor codes. They are used for living individuals who are donating blood or other body tissue. These codes are only for individuals donating for others, not for self donations. They are not for use to identify cadaveric donations.

10) Counseling

Counseling V codes are used when a patient or family member receives assistance in the aftermath of an illness or injury, or when support is required in coping with family or social problems. They are not necessary for use in conjunction with a diagnosis code when the counseling component of care is
considered integral to standard treatment.

The counseling V categories/codes:

V25.0 General counseling and advice for contraceptive management

V26.3 Genetic counseling

V26.4 General counseling and advice for procreative management

V61.**X** Other family circumstances

V65.1 Person consulted on behalf of another person

V65.3 Dietary surveillance and counseling

V65.4 Other counseling, not elsewhere classified

11) Obstetrics and related conditions

See Section I.C.11., the Obstetrics guidelines for further instruction on the use of these codes.

V codes for pregnancy are for use in those circumstances when none of the problems or complications included in the codes from the Obstetrics chapter exist (a routine prenatal visit or postpartum care). Codes V22.0, Supervision of normal first pregnancy, and V22.1, Supervision of other normal pregnancy, are always first listed and are not to be used with any other code from the OB chapter.

The outcome of delivery, category V27, should be included on all maternal delivery records. It is always a secondary code.

V codes for family planning (contraceptive) or procreative management and counseling should be included on an obstetric record either during the pregnancy or the postpartum stage, if applicable.

Obstetrics and related conditions V code categories:

V22 Normal pregnancy

V23 Supervision of high-risk pregnancy
Except: V23.2, Pregnancy with history of abortion. Code 646.3, Habitual aborter, from the OB chapter is required to indicate a history of abortion during a pregnancy.

V24 Postpartum care and evaluation

V25 Encounter for contraceptive management
Except V25.0x
(See Section I.C.18.d.11, Counseling)

V26 Procreative management
Except V26.5x, Sterilization status, V26.3 and V26.4
(See Section I.C.18.d.11., Counseling)
V27 Outcome of delivery
V28 Antenatal screening
(See Section I.C.18.d.6., Screening)

12) Newborn, infant and child

See Section I.C.15, the Newborn guidelines for further instruction on the use of these codes.

Newborn V code categories:

V20 Health supervision of infant or child
V29 Observation and evaluation of newborns for suspected condition not found
(See Section I.C.18.d.7, Observation)
V30-V39 Liveborn infant according to type of birth

13) Routine and administrative examinations

The V codes allow for the description of encounters for routine examinations, such as, a general check-up, or, examinations for administrative purposes, such as, a pre-employment physical. The codes are not to be used if the examination is for diagnosis of a suspected condition or for treatment purposes. In such cases the diagnosis code is used. During a routine exam, should a diagnosis or condition be discovered, it should be coded as an additional code. Pre-existing and chronic conditions and history codes may also be included as additional codes as long as the examination is for administrative purposes and not focused on any particular condition.

Pre-operative examination V codes are for use only in those situations when a patient is being cleared for surgery and no treatment is given.

The V codes categories/code for routine and administrative examinations:

V20.2 Routine infant or child health check
Any injections given should have a corresponding procedure code.
V70 General medical examination
V72 Special investigations and examinations
Codes V72.5 and V72.6 may be used if the reason for the patient encounter is for routine laboratory/radiology testing in the absence of any signs, symptoms, or associated diagnosis. If routine testing is performed during the same encounter as a test to evaluate a sign, symptom, or diagnosis, it is appropriate to assign both the V code and the code describing the reason for the non-routine test.

14) Miscellaneous V codes

The miscellaneous V codes capture a number of other health care encounters that do not fall into one of the other categories. Certain of these codes identify the reason for the encounter, others are for use as additional codes that provide useful information on circumstances that may affect a patient's care and treatment.

Prophylactic organ removal

For encounters specifically for prophylactic removal of breasts, ovaries, or another organ due to a genetic susceptibility to cancer or a family history of cancer, the principal or first listed code should be a code from subcategory V50.4, Prophylactic organ removal, followed by the appropriate genetic susceptibility code and the appropriate family history code.

If the patient has a malignancy of one site and is having prophylactic removal at another site to prevent either a new primary malignancy or metastatic disease, a code for the malignancy should also be assigned in addition to a code from subcategory V50.4. A V50.4 code should not be assigned if the patient is having organ removal for treatment of a malignancy, such as the removal of the testes for the treatment of prostate cancer.

Miscellaneous V code categories/codes:

V07 Need for isolation and other prophylactic measures
Except V07.5, Prophylactic use of agents affecting estrogen receptors and estrogen levels
V50 Elective surgery for purposes other than remedying health states
V58.5 Orthodontics
V60 Housing, household, and economic circumstances
V62 Other psychosocial circumstances
V63 Unavailability of other medical facilities for care
V64 Persons encountering health services for specific procedures, not carried out
V66 Convalescence and palliative care
V68 Encounters for administrative purposes
V69 Problems related to lifestyle
V85 Body Mass Index

15) Nonspecific V codes

Certain V codes are so non-specific, or potentially redundant with other codes in the classification, that there can be little justification for their use in the inpatient setting. Their use in the outpatient setting should be limited to those instances when there is no further documentation to permit more precise coding. Otherwise, any sign or symptom or any other reason for visit that is captured in another code should be used.

Nonspecific V code categories/codes:

V11 Personal history of mental disorder A code from the mental disorders chapter, with an in remission fifth-digit, should be used.
V13.4 Personal history of arthritis
V13.6 Personal history of congenital malformations
V15.7 Personal history of contraception
V23.2 Pregnancy with history of abortion
V40 Mental and behavioral problems
V41 Problems with special senses and other special functions
V47 Other problems with internal organs
V48 Problems with head, neck, and trunk
V49 Problems with limbs and other problems
Exception:
V49.6 Upper limb amputation status
V49.7 Lower limb amputation status
V49.81 Postmenopausal status
V49.82 Dental sealant status
V49.83 Awaiting organ transplant status
V51.**8** **Other a**ftercare involving the use of plastic surgery
V58.2 Blood transfusion, without reported diagnosis
V58.9 Unspecified aftercare
See Section IV.K. and Section IV.L. of the Outpatient guidelines.

V CODE TABLE

October 1, 2008 (FY2009)

Items in bold indicate a new entry or change from the October 2007 table. Items underlined have been moved within the table since October 2007.

The following V code table contains columns for 1st listed, 1st or additional, additional only, and non-specific. Each code or category is listed on the left hand column and the allowable sequencing of the code or codes within the category is noted under the appropriate column.

As indicated by the footnote in the "1st Dx Only" column, the V codes designated as first-listed only are generally intended to be limited for use as a first-listed only diagnosis, but may be reported as an additional diagnosis in those situations when the patient has more than one encounter on a single day and the codes for the multiple encounters are combined, or when there is more than one V code that meets the definition of principal diagnosis (e.g., a patient is admitted to home healthcare for both aftercare and rehabilitation and they equally meet the definition of principal diagnosis). The V codes designated as first-listed only should not be reported if they do not meet the definition of principal or first-listed diagnosis.

See Section II and Section IV.A for information on selection of principal and first-listed diagnosis.

See Section II.C for information on two or more diagnoses that equally meet the definition for principal diagnosis.

Code(s)	Description	1st Dx Only[1]	1st or Add'l Dx[2]	Add'l Dx Only[3]	Non-Specific Diagnosis[4]
V01.X	Contact with or exposure to communicable diseases		X		
V02.X	Carrier or suspected carrier of infectious diseases		X		
V03.X	Need for prophylactic vaccination and inoculation against bacterial diseases		X		
V04.X	Need for prophylactic vaccination and inoculation against certain diseases		X		
V05.X	Need for prophylactic vaccination and inoculation against single diseases		X		
V06.X	Need for prophylactic vaccination and inoculation against combinations of diseases		X		
V07.0	**Isolation**		**X**		
V07.1	**Desensitization to allergens**		**X**		
V07.2	**Prophylactic immunotherapy**		**X**		
V07.3X	**Other prophylactic chemotherapy**		**X**		
V07.4	**Hormone replacement therapy (postmenopausal)**			**X**	
V07.5X	**Prophylactic use of agents affecting estrogen receptors and estrogen levels**			**X**	
V07.8	**Other specified prophylactic measure**		**X**		
V07.9	**Unspecified prophylactic measure**				**X**
V08	Asymptomatic HIV infection status		X		
V09.X	Infection with drug resistant organisms			X	
V10.X	Personal history of malignant neoplasm		X		
V11.X	Personal history of mental disorder				X
V12.X	Personal history of certain other diseases		X		
V13.0X	Personal history of other disorders of urinary system		X		
V13.1	Personal history of trophoblastic disease		X		
V13.2X	Personal history of other genital system and obstetric disorders		X		
V13.3	Personal history of diseases of skin and subcutaneous tissue		X		
V13.4	Personal history of arthritis				X
V13.5**X**	Personal history of other musculoskeletal disorders		X		
V13.61	Personal history of hypospadias			X	
V13.69	Personal history of congenital malformations				X
V13.7	Personal history of perinatal problems		X		
V13.8	Personal history of other specified diseases		X		
V13.9	Personal history of unspecified disease				X
V14.X	Personal history of allergy to medicinal agents			X	
V15.0X	Personal history of allergy, other than to medicinal agents			X	
V15.1	Personal history of surgery to heart and great vessels			X	
V15.2X	**Personal history of surgery to other organs**			**X**	
V15.3	Personal history of irradiation			X	
V15.4X	Personal history of psychological trauma			X	
V15.5X	Personal history of injury			X	
V15.6	Personal history of poisoning			X	
V15.7	Personal history of contraception				X
V15.81	Personal history of noncompliance with medical treatment			X	
V15.82	Personal history of tobacco use			X	
V15.84	Personal history of exposure to asbestos			X	
V15.85	Personal history of exposure to potentially hazardous body fluids			X	
V15.86	Personal history of exposure to lead			X	
V15.87	Personal history of extracorporeal membrane oxygenation [ECMO]			X	
V15.88	History of fall		X		
V15.89	Other specified personal history presenting hazards to health			X	
V16.X	Family history of malignant neoplasm		X		
V17.X	Family history of certain chronic disabling diseases		X		
V18.X	Family history of certain other specific conditions		X		
V19.X	Family history of other conditions		X		
V20.X	Health supervision of infant or child	X			
V21.X	Constitutional states in development			X	
V22.0	Supervision of normal first pregnancy	X			
V22.1	Supervision of other normal pregnancy	X			
V22.2	Pregnancy state, incidental			X	
V23.X	Supervision of high-risk pregnancy		X		

1. Generally for use as first listed only but may be used as additional if patient has more than one encounter on one day or there is more than one reason for the encounter
2. These codes may be used as first listed or additional codes
3. These codes are only for use as additional codes
4. These codes are primarily for use in the nonacute setting and should be limited to encounters for which no sign or symptom or reason for visit is documented in the record. Their use may be as either a first listed or additional code.

Code(s)	Description	1st Dx Only[1]	1st or Add'l Dx[2]	Add'l Dx Only[3]	Non-Specific Diagnosis[4]
V24.X	Postpartum care and examination	X			
V25.X	Encounter for contraceptive management		X		
V26.0	Tuboplasty or vasoplasty after previous sterilization		X		
V26.1	Artificial insemination		X		
V26.2X	Procreative management investigation and testing		X		
V26.3X	Procreative management, genetic counseling and testing		X		
V26.4X	Procreative management, genetic counseling and advice		X		
V26.5X	Procreative management, sterilization status			X	
V26.81	Encounter for assisted reproductive fertility procedure cycle	X			
V26.89	Other specified procreative management		X		
V26.9	Unspecified procreative management		X		
V27.X	Outcome of delivery			X	
V28.X	Encounter for antenatal screening of mother		X		
V29.X	Observation and evaluation of newborns for suspected condition not found		X		
V30.X	Single liveborn	X			
V31.X	Twin, mate liveborn	X			
V32.X	Twin, mate stillborn	X			
V33.X	Twin, unspecified	X			
V34.X	Other multiple, mates all liveborn	X			
V35.X	Other multiple, mates all stillborn	X			
V36.X	Other multiple, mates live- and stillborn	X			
V37.X	Other multiple, unspecified	X			
V39.X	Unspecified	X			
V40.X	Mental and behavioral problems				X
V41.X	Problems with special senses and other special functions				X
V42.X	Organ or tissue replaced by transplant			X	
V43.0	Organ or tissue replaced by other means, eye globe			X	
V43.1	Organ or tissue replaced by other means, lens			X	
V43.21	Organ or tissue replaced by other means, heart assist device			X	
V43.22	Fully implantable artificial heart status		X		
V43.3	Organ or tissue replaced by other means, heart valve			X	
V43.4	Organ or tissue replaced by other means, blood vessel			X	
V43.5	Organ or tissue replaced by other means, bladder			X	
V43.6X	Organ or tissue replaced by other means, joint			X	
V43.7	Organ or tissue replaced by other means, limb			X	
V43.8X	Other organ or tissue replaced by other means			X	
V44.X	Artificial opening status			X	
V45.0X	Cardiac device in situ			X	
V45.1**X**	Renal dialysis status			X	
V45.2	Presence of cerebrospinal fluid drainage device			X	
V45.3	Intestinal bypass or anastomosis status			X	
V45.4	Arthrodesis status			X	
V45.5X	Presence of contraceptive device			X	
V45.6X	States following surgery of eye and adnexa			X	
V45.7X	Acquired absence of organ		X		
V45.8X	Other postprocedural status			X	
V46.0	Other dependence on machines, aspirator			X	
V46.11	Dependence on respiratory, status			X	
V46.12	Encounter for respirator dependence during power failure	X			
V46.13	Encounter for weaning from respirator [ventilator]	X			
V46.14	Mechanical complication of respirator [ventilator]		X		
V46.2	Other dependence on machines, supplemental oxygen			X	
V46.3	**Wheelchair dependence**			**X**	
V46.8	Other dependence on other enabling machines			X	
V46.9	Unspecified machine dependence				X
V47.X	Other problems with internal organs				X
V48.X	Problems with head, neck and trunk				X
V49.0	Deficiencies of limbs				X

1. Generally for use as first listed only but may be used as additional if patient has more than one encounter on one day or there is more than one reason for the encounter
2. These codes may be used as first listed or additional codes
3. These codes are only for use as additional codes
4. These codes are primarily for use in the nonacute setting and should be limited to encounters for which no sign or symptom or reason for visit is documented in the record. Their use may be as either a first listed or additional code.

Code(s)	Description	1st Dx Only[1]	1st or Add'l Dx[2]	Add'l Dx Only[3]	Non-Specific Diagnosis[4]
V49.1	Mechanical problems with limbs				X
V49.2	Motor problems with limbs				X
V49.3	Sensory problems with limbs				X
V49.4	Disfigurements of limbs				X
V49.5	Other problems with limbs				X
V49.6X	Upper limb amputation status		X		
V49.7X	Lower limb amputation status		X		
V49.81	Asymptomatic postmenopausal status (age-related) (natural)		X		
V49.82	Dental sealant status			X	
V49.83	Awaiting organ transplant status			X	
V49.84	Bed confinement status		X		
V49.85	Dual sensory impairment			X	
V49.89	Other specified conditions influencing health status		X		
V49.9	Unspecified condition influencing health status				X
V50.X	Elective surgery for purposes other than remedying health states		X		
V51.0	**Encounter for breast reconstruction following mastectomy**	**X**			
V51.8	**Other aftercare involving the use of plastic surgery**				**X**
V52.X	Fitting and adjustment of prosthetic device and implant		X		
V53.X	Fitting and adjustment of other device		X		
V54.X	Other orthopedic aftercare		X		
V55.X	Attention to artificial openings		X		
V56.0	Extracorporeal dialysis	X			
V56.1	Encounter for fitting and adjustment of extracorporeal dialysis catheter		X		
V56.2	Encounter for fitting and adjustment of peritoneal dialysis catheter		X		
V56.3X	Encounter for adequacy testing for dialysis		X		
V56.8	Encounter for other dialysis and dialysis catheter care		X		
V57.X	Care involving use of rehabilitation procedures	X			
V58.0	Radiotherapy	X			
V58.11	Encounter for antineoplastic chemotherapy	X			
V58.12	Encounter for antineoplastic immunotherapy	X			
V58.2	Blood transfusion without reported diagnosis				X
V58.3X	Attention to dressings and sutures		X		
V58.4X	Other aftercare following surgery		X		
V58.5	Encounter for orthodontics				X
V58.6X	Long term (current) drug use			X	
V58.7X	Aftercare following surgery to specified body systems, not elsewhere classified		X		
V58.8X	Other specified procedures and aftercare		X		
V58.9	Unspecified aftercare				X
V59.X	Donors	X			
V60.X	Housing, household, and economic circumstances			X	
V61.X	Other family circumstances		X		
V62.X	Other psychosocial circumstances			X	
V63.X	Unavailability of other medical facilities for care		X		
V64.X	Persons encountering health services for specified procedure, not carried out			X	
V65.X	Other persons seeking consultation without complaint or sickness		X		
V66.0	Convalescence and palliative care following surgery	X			
V66.1	Convalescence and palliative care following radiotherapy	X			
V66.2	Convalescence and palliative care following chemotherapy	X			
V66.3	Convalescence and palliative care following psychotherapy and other treatment for mental disorder	X			
V66.4	Convalescence and palliative care following treatment of fracture	X			
V66.5	Convalescence and palliative care following other treatment	X			
V66.6	Convalescence and palliative care following combined treatment	X			
V66.7	Encounter for palliative care			X	
V66.9	Unspecified convalescence	X			
V67.X	Follow-up examination		X		
V68.X	Encounters for administrative purposes	X			
V69.X	Problems related to lifestyle		X		
V70.0	Routine general medical examination at a health care facility	X			

1. Generally for use as first listed only but may be used as additional if patient has more than one encounter on one day or there is more than one reason for the encounter
2. These codes may be used as first listed or additional codes
3. These codes are only for use as additional codes
4. These codes are primarily for use in the nonacute setting and should be limited to encounters for which no sign or symptom or reason for visit is documented in the record. Their use may be as either a first listed or additional code.

Code(s)	Description	1st Dx Only[1]	1st or Add'l Dx[2]	Add'l Dx Only[3]	Non-Specific Diagnosis[4]
V70.1	General psychiatric examination, requested by the authority	X			
V70.2	General psychiatric examination, other and unspecified	X			
V70.3	Other medical examination for administrative purposes	X			
V70.4	Examination for medicolegal reasons	X			
V70.5	Health examination of defined subpopulations	X			
V70.6	Health examination in population surveys	X			
V70.7	Examination of participant in clinical trial		X		
V70.8	Other specified general medical examinations	X			
V70.9	Unspecified general medical examination	X			
V71.X	Observation and evaluation for suspected conditions not found	X			
V72.0	Examination of eyes and vision		X		
V72.1X	Examination of ears and hearing		X		
V72.2	Dental examination		X		
V72.3X	Gynecological examination		X		
V72.4X	Pregnancy examination or test		X		
V72.5	Radiological examination, NEC		X		
V72.6	Laboratory examination		X		
V72.7	Diagnostic skin and sensitization tests		X		
V72.81	Preoperative cardiovascular examination		X		
V72.82	Preoperative respiratory examination		X		
V72.83	Other specified preoperative examination		X		
V72.84	Preoperative examination, unspecified		X		
V72.85	Other specified examination		X		
V72.86	Encounter for blood typing		X		
V72.9	Unspecified examination				X
V73.X	Special screening examination for viral and chlamydial diseases		X		
V74.X	Special screening examination for bacterial and spirochetal diseases		X		
V75.X	Special screening examination for other infectious diseases		X		
V76.X	Special screening examination for malignant neoplasms		X		
V77.X	Special screening examination for endocrine, nutritional, metabolic and immunity disorders		X		
V78.X	Special screening examination for disorders of blood and blood-forming organs		X		
V79.X	Special screening examination for mental disorders and developmental handicaps		X		
V80.X	Special screening examination for neurological, eye, and ear diseases		X		
V81.X	Special screening examination for cardiovascular, respiratory, and genitourinary diseases		X		
V82.X	Special screening examination for other conditions		X		
V83.X	Genetic carrier status		X		
V84.X	Genetic susceptibility to disease			X	
V85	Body mass index			X	
V86	Estrogen receptor status			X	
V87.0X	**Contact with and (suspected) exposure to hazardous metals**		**X**		
V87.1X	**Contact with and (suspected) exposure to hazardous aromatic compounds**		**X**		
V87.2	**Contact with and (suspected) exposure to other potentially hazardous chemicals**		**X**		
V87.3X	**Contact with and (suspected) exposure to other potentially hazardous substances**		**X**		
V87.4X	**Personal history of drug therapy**			**X**	
V88.0X	**Acquired absence of cervix and uterus**			**X**	
V89.0X	**Suspected maternal and fetal anomalies not found**		**X**		

1. Generally for use as first listed only but may be used as additional if patient has more than one encounter on one day or there is more than one reason for the encounter
2. These codes may be used as first listed or additional codes
3. These codes are only for use as additional codes
4. These codes are primarily for use in the nonacute setting and should be limited to encounters for which no sign or symptom or reason for visit is documented in the record. Their use may be as either a first listed or additional code.

19. Supplemental Classification of External Causes of Injury and Poisoning (E codes, E800-E999)

Introduction: These guidelines are provided for those who are currently collecting E codes in order that there will be standardization in the process. If your institution plans to begin collecting E codes, these guidelines are to be applied. The use of E codes is supplemental to the application of ICD-9-CM diagnosis codes. E codes are never to be recorded as principal diagnoses (first-listed in non-inpatient setting) and are not required for reporting to CMS.

External causes of injury and poisoning codes (E codes) are intended to provide data for injury research and evaluation of injury prevention strategies. E codes capture how the injury or poisoning happened (cause), the intent (unintentional or accidental; or intentional, such as suicide or assault), and the place where the event occurred.

Some major categories of E codes include:

- transport accidents
- poisoning and adverse effects of drugs, medicinal substances and biologicals

- accidental falls
- accidents caused by fire and flames
- accidents due to natural and environmental factors
- late effects of accidents, assaults or self injury
- assaults or purposely inflicted injury
- suicide or self inflicted injury

These guidelines apply for the coding and collection of E codes from records in hospitals, outpatient clinics, emergency departments, other ambulatory care settings and provider offices, and nonacute care settings, except when other specific guidelines apply.

a. **General E code coding guidelines**

1) **Used with any code in the range of 001-V89**
An E code may be used with any code in the range of 001-**V89**, which indicates an injury, poisoning, or adverse effect due to an external cause.

2) **Assign the appropriate E code for all initial treatments**
Assign the appropriate E code for the initial encounter of an injury, poisoning, or adverse effect of drugs, not for subsequent treatment.
External cause of injury codes (E-codes) may be assigned while the acute fracture codes are still applicable.
See Section I.C.17.b.1 for coding of acute fractures.

3) **Use the full range of E codes**
Use the full range of E codes to completely describe the cause, the intent and the place of occurrence, if applicable, for all injuries, poisonings, and adverse effects of drugs.

4) **Assign as many E codes as necessary**
Assign as many E codes as necessary to fully explain each cause. If only one E code can be recorded, assign the E code most related to the principal diagnosis.

5) **The selection of the appropriate E code**
The selection of the appropriate E code is guided by the Index to External Causes, which is located after the alphabetical index to diseases and by Inclusion and Exclusion notes in the Tabular List.

6) **E code can never be a principal diagnosis**
An E code can never be a principal (first listed) diagnosis.

7) **External cause code(s) with systemic inflammatory response syndrome (SIRS)**
An external cause code is not appropriate with a code from subcategory 995.9, unless the patient also has an injury, poisoning, or adverse effect of drugs.

b. **Place of occurrence guideline**
Use an additional code from category E849 to indicate the Place of Occurrence for injuries and poisonings. The Place of Occurrence describes the place where the event occurred and not the patient's activity at the time of the event.
Do not use E849.9 if the place of occurrence is not stated.

c. **Adverse effects of drugs, medicinal and biological substances guidelines**

1) **Do not code directly from the Table of Drugs**
Do not code directly from the Table of Drugs and Chemicals. Always refer back to the Tabular List.

2) **Use as many codes as necessary to describe**
Use as many codes as necessary to describe completely all drugs, medicinal or biological substances.

3) **If the same E code would describe the causative agent**
If the same E code would describe the causative agent for more than one adverse reaction, assign the code only once.

4) **If two or more drugs, medicinal or biological substances**
If two or more drugs, medicinal or biological substances are reported, code each individually unless the combination code is listed in the Table of Drugs and Chemicals. In that case, assign the E code for the combination.

5) **When a reaction results from the interaction of a drug(s)**
When a reaction results from the interaction of a drug(s) and alcohol, use poisoning codes and E codes for both.

6) **If the reporting format limits the number of E codes**
If the reporting format limits the number of E codes that can be used in reporting clinical data, code the one most related to the principal diagnosis. Include at least one from each category (cause, intent, place) if possible.
If there are different fourth-digit codes in the same three digit category, use the code for "Other specified" of that category. If there is no "Other specified" code in that category, use the appropriate "Unspecified" code in that category.
If the codes are in different three digit categories, assign the appropriate E code for other multiple drugs and medicinal substances.

7) **Codes from the E930-E949 series**
Codes from the E930-E949 series must be used to identify the causative substance for an adverse effect of drug, medicinal and biological substances, correctly prescribed and properly administered. The effect, such as tachycardia, delirium, gastrointestinal hemorrhaging, vomiting, hypokalemia, hepatitis, renal failure, or respiratory failure, is coded and followed by the appropriate code from the E930-E949 series.

d. **Multiple cause E code coding guidelines**
If two or more events cause separate injuries, an E code should be assigned for each cause. The first listed E code will be selected in the following order:
E codes for child and adult abuse take priority over all other E codes.
See Section I.C.19.e., Child and Adult abuse guidelines.
E codes for terrorism events take priority over all other E codes except child and adult abuse.
E codes for cataclysmic events take priority over all other E codes except child and adult abuse and terrorism.
E codes for transport accidents take priority over all other E codes except cataclysmic events and child and adult abuse and terrorism.
The first-listed E code should correspond to the cause of the most serious diagnosis due to an assault, accident, or self-harm, following the order of hierarchy listed above.

e. **Child and adult abuse guideline**

1) **Intentional injury**
When the cause of an injury or neglect is intentional child or adult abuse, the first listed E code should be assigned from categories E960-E968, Homicide and injury purposely inflicted by other persons, (except category E967). An E code from category E967, Child and adult battering and other maltreatment, should be added as an additional code to identify the perpetrator, if known.

2) **Accidental intent**
In cases of neglect when the intent is determined to be accidental E code E904.0, Abandonment or neglect of infant and helpless person, should be the first listed E code.

f. **Unknown or suspected intent guideline**

1) **If the intent (accident, self-harm, assault) of the cause of an injury or poisoning is unknown**
If the intent (accident, self-harm, assault) of the cause of an injury or poisoning is unknown or unspecified, code the intent as undetermined E980-E989.

2) **If the intent (accident, self-harm, assault) of the cause of an injury or poisoning is questionable**
If the intent (accident, self-harm, assault) of the cause of an injury or poisoning is questionable, probable or suspected, code the intent as undetermined E980-E989.

g. **Undetermined cause**
When the intent of an injury or poisoning is known, but the cause is unknown, use codes: E928.9, Unspecified accident, E958.9, Suicide and self-inflicted injury by unspecified means, and E968.9, Assault by unspecified means.
These E codes should rarely be used, as the documentation in the medical record, in both the inpatient outpatient and other settings, should normally provide sufficient detail to determine the cause of the injury.

h. **Late effects of external cause guidelines**

1) **Late effect E codes**
Late effect E codes exist for injuries and poisonings but not for adverse effects of drugs, misadventures and surgical complications.

2) **Late effect E codes (E929, E959, E969, E977, E989, or E999.1)**
A late effect E code (E929, E959, E969, E977, E989, or

E999.1) should be used with any report of a late effect or sequela resulting from a previous injury or poisoning (905-909).

3) **Late effect E code with a related current injury**
A late effect E code should never be used with a related current nature of injury code.

4) **Use of late effect E codes for subsequent visits**
Use a late effect E code for subsequent visits when a late effect of the initial injury or poisoning is being treated. There is no late effect E code for adverse effects of drugs. Do not use a late effect E code for subsequent visits for follow-up care (e.g., to assess healing, to receive rehabilitative therapy) of the injury or poisoning when no late effect of the injury has been documented.

i. **Misadventures and complications of care guidelines**

1) **Code range E870-E876**
Assign a code in the range of E870-E876 if misadventures are stated by the provider.

2) **Code range E878-E879**
Assign a code in the range of E878-E879 if the provider attributes an abnormal reaction or later complication to a surgical or medical procedure, but does not mention misadventure at the time of the procedure as the cause of the reaction.

j. **Terrorism guidelines**

1) **Cause of injury identified by the Federal Government (FBI) as terrorism**
When the cause of an injury is identified by the Federal Government (FBI) as terrorism, the first-listed E-code should be a code from category E979, Terrorism. The definition of terrorism employed by the FBI is found at the inclusion note at E979. The terrorism E-code is the only E-code that should be assigned. Additional E codes from the assault categories should not be assigned.

2) **Cause of an injury is suspected to be the result of terrorism**
When the cause of an injury is suspected to be the result of terrorism a code from category E979 should not be assigned. Assign a code in the range of E codes based circumstances on the documentation of intent and mechanism.

3) **Code E979.9, Terrorism, secondary effects**
Assign code E979.9, Terrorism, secondary effects, for conditions occurring subsequent to the terrorist event. This code should not be assigned for conditions that are due to the initial terrorist act.

4) **Statistical tabulation of terrorism codes**
For statistical purposes these codes will be tabulated within the category for assault, expanding the current category from E960-E969 to include E979 and E999.1.

SECTION II. SELECTION OF PRINCIPAL DIAGNOSIS

The circumstances of inpatient admission always govern the selection of principal diagnosis. The principal diagnosis is defined in the Uniform Hospital Discharge Data Set (UHDDS) as "that condition established after study to be chiefly responsible for occasioning the admission of the patient to the hospital for care."

The UHDDS definitions are used by hospitals to report inpatient data elements in a standardized manner. These data elements and their definitions can be found in the July 31, 1985, Federal Register (Vol. 50, No, 147), pp. 31038-40.

Since that time the application of the UHDDS definitions has been expanded to include all non-outpatient settings (acute care, short term, long term care and psychiatric hospitals; home health agencies; rehab facilities; nursing homes, etc).

In determining principal diagnosis the coding conventions in the ICD-9-CM, Volumes I and II take precedence over these official coding guidelines.

(See Section I.A., Conventions for the ICD-9-CM)

The importance of consistent, complete documentation in the medical record cannot be overemphasized. Without such documentation the application of all coding guidelines is a difficult, if not impossible, task.

A. **Codes for symptoms, signs, and ill-defined conditions**
Codes for symptoms, signs, and ill-defined conditions from Chapter 16 are not to be used as principal diagnosis when a related definitive diagnosis has been established.

B. **Two or more interrelated conditions, each potentially meeting the definition for principal diagnosis**
When there are two or more interrelated conditions (such as diseases in the same ICD-9-CM chapter or manifestations characteristically associated with a certain disease) potentially meeting the definition of principal diagnosis, either condition may be sequenced first, unless the circumstances of the admission, the therapy provided, the Tabular List, or the Alphabetic Index indicate otherwise.

C. **Two or more diagnoses that equally meet the definition for principal diagnosis**
In the unusual instance when two or more diagnoses equally meet the criteria for principal diagnosis as determined by the circumstances of admission, diagnostic workup and/or therapy provided, and the Alphabetic Index, Tabular List, or another coding guidelines does not provide sequencing direction, any one of the diagnoses may be sequenced first.

D. **Two or more comparative or contrasting conditions**
In those rare instances when two or more contrasting or comparative diagnoses are documented as "either/or" (or similar terminology), they are coded as if the diagnoses were confirmed and the diagnoses are sequenced according to the circumstances of the admission. If no further determination can be made as to which diagnosis should be principal, either diagnosis may be sequenced first.

E. **A symptom(s) followed by contrasting/comparative diagnoses**
When a symptom(s) is followed by contrasting/comparative diagnoses, the symptom code is sequenced first. All the contrasting/comparative diagnoses should be coded as additional diagnoses.

F. **Original treatment plan not carried out**
Sequence as the principal diagnosis the condition, which after study occasioned the admission to the hospital, even though treatment may not have been carried out due to unforeseen circumstances.

G. **Complications of surgery and other medical care**
When the admission is for treatment of a complication resulting from surgery or other medical care, the complication code is sequenced as the principal diagnosis. If the complication is classified to the 996-999 series and the code lacks the necessary specificity in describing the complication, an additional code for the specific complication should be assigned.

H. **Uncertain diagnosis**
If the diagnosis documented at the time of discharge is qualified as "probable", "suspected", "likely", "questionable", "possible", or "still to be ruled out", or other similar terms indicating uncertainty, code the condition as if it existed or was established. The bases for these guidelines are the diagnostic workup, arrangements for further workup or observation, and initial therapeutic approach that correspond most closely with the established diagnosis.
Note: This guideline is applicable only to inpatient admissions to short-term, acute, long-term care and psychiatric hospitals.

I. **Admission from observation unit**

1. **Admission following medical observation**
When a patient is admitted to an observation unit for a medical condition, which either worsens or does not improve, and is subsequently admitted as an inpatient of the same hospital for this same medical condition, the principal diagnosis would be the medical condition which led to the hospital admission.

2. **Admission following post-operative observation**
When a patient is admitted to an observation unit to monitor a condition (or complication) that develops following outpatient surgery, and then is subsequently admitted as an inpatient of the same hospital, hospitals should apply the Uniform Hospital Discharge Data Set (UHDDS) definition of principal diagnosis as "that condition established after study to be chiefly responsible for occasioning the admission of the patient to the hospital for care."

J. **Admission from outpatient surgery**
When a patient receives surgery in the hospital's outpatient surgery department and is subsequently admitted for continuing inpatient care at the same hospital, the following guidelines should be followed in selecting the principal diagnosis for the inpatient admission:

- If the reason for the inpatient admission is a complication, assign the complication as the principal diagnosis.
- If no complication, or other condition, is documented as the reason for the inpatient admission, assign the reason for the outpatient surgery as the principal diagnosis.
- If the reason for the inpatient admission is another condition unrelated to the surgery, assign the unrelated condition as the principal diagnosis.

Section III. Reporting Additional Diagnoses

GENERAL RULES FOR OTHER (ADDITIONAL) DIAGNOSES

For reporting purposes the definition for "other diagnoses" is interpreted as additional conditions that affect patient care in terms of requiring:

clinical evaluation; or
therapeutic treatment; or
diagnostic procedures; or
extended length of hospital stay; or
increased nursing care and/or monitoring.

The UHDDS item #11-b defines Other Diagnoses as "all conditions that coexist at the time of admission, that develop subsequently, or that affect the treatment received and/or the length of stay. Diagnoses that relate to an earlier episode which have no bearing on the current hospital stay are to be excluded." UHDDS definitions apply to inpatients in acute care, short-term, long term care and psychiatric hospital setting. The UHDDS definitions are used by acute care short-term hospitals to report inpatient data elements in a standardized manner. These data elements and their definitions can be found in the July 31, 1985, Federal Register (Vol. 50, No, 147), pp. 31038-40.

Since that time the application of the UHDDS definitions has been expanded to include all non-outpatient settings (acute care, short term, long term care and psychiatric hospitals; home health agencies; rehab facilities; nursing homes, etc).

The following guidelines are to be applied in designating "other diagnoses" when neither the Alphabetic Index nor the Tabular List in ICD-9-CM provide direction. The listing of the diagnoses in the patient record is the responsibility of the attending provider.

A. Previous conditions

If the provider has included a diagnosis in the final diagnostic statement, such as the discharge summary or the face sheet, it should ordinarily be coded. Some providers include in the diagnostic statement resolved conditions or diagnoses and status-post procedures from previous admission that have no bearing on the current stay. Such conditions are not to be reported and are coded only if required by hospital policy.

However, history codes (V10-V19) may be used as secondary codes if the historical condition or family history has an impact on current care or influences treatment.

B. Abnormal findings

Abnormal findings (laboratory, x-ray, pathologic, and other diagnostic results) are not coded and reported unless the provider indicates their clinical significance. If the findings are outside the normal range and the attending provider has ordered other tests to evaluate the condition or prescribed treatment, it is appropriate to ask the provider whether the abnormal finding should be added.

Please note: This differs from the coding practices in the outpatient setting for coding encounters for diagnostic tests that have been interpreted by a provider.

C. Uncertain diagnosis

If the diagnosis documented at the time of discharge is qualified as "probable", "suspected", "likely", "questionable", "possible", or "still to be ruled out" or other similar terms indicating uncertainty, code the condition as if it existed or was established. The bases for these guidelines are the diagnostic workup, arrangements for further workup or observation, and initial therapeutic approach that correspond most closely with the established diagnosis.

Note: This guideline is applicable only to inpatient admissions to short-term, acute, long-term care and psychiatric hospitals.

Section IV. Diagnostic Coding and Reporting Guidelines for Outpatient Services

These coding guidelines for outpatient diagnoses have been approved for use by hospitals/ providers in coding and reporting hospital-based outpatient services and provider-based office visits.

Information about the use of certain abbreviations, punctuation, symbols, and other conventions used in the ICD-9-CM Tabular List (code numbers and titles), can be found in Section IA of these guidelines, under "Conventions Used in the Tabular List." Information about the correct sequence to use in finding a code is also described in Section I.

The terms encounter and visit are often used interchangeably in describing outpatient service contacts and, therefore, appear together in these guidelines without distinguishing one from the other.

Though the conventions and general guidelines apply to all settings, coding guidelines for outpatient and provider reporting of diagnoses will vary in a number of instances from those for inpatient diagnoses, recognizing that:

The Uniform Hospital Discharge Data Set (UHDDS) definition of principal diagnosis applies only to inpatients in acute, short-term, long-term care and psychiatric hospitals.

Coding guidelines for inconclusive diagnoses (probable, suspected, rule out, etc.) were developed for inpatient reporting and do not apply to outpatients.

A. Selection of first-listed condition

In the outpatient setting, the term first-listed diagnosis is used in lieu of principal diagnosis.

In determining the first-listed diagnosis the coding conventions of ICD-9-CM, as well as the general and disease specific guidelines take precedence over the outpatient guidelines.

Diagnoses often are not established at the time of the initial encounter/visit. It may take two or more visits before the diagnosis is confirmed.

The most critical rule involves beginning the search for the correct code assignment through the Alphabetic Index. Never begin searching initially in the Tabular List as this will lead to coding errors.

1. Outpatient surgery

When a patient presents for outpatient surgery, code the reason for the surgery as the first-listed diagnosis (reason for the encounter), even if the surgery is not performed due to a contraindication.

2. Observation stay

When a patient is admitted for observation for a medical condition, assign a code for the medical condition as the first-listed diagnosis.

When a patient presents for outpatient surgery and develops complications requiring admission to observation, code the reason for the surgery as the first reported diagnosis (reason for the encounter), followed by codes for the complications as secondary diagnoses.

B. Codes from 001.0 through V89

The appropriate code or codes from 001.0 through **V89** must be used to identify diagnoses, symptoms, conditions, problems, complaints, or other reason(s) for the encounter/visit.

C. Accurate reporting of ICD-9-CM diagnosis codes

For accurate reporting of ICD-9-CM diagnosis codes, the documentation should describe the patient's condition, using terminology which includes specific diagnoses as well as symptoms, problems, or reasons for the encounter. There are ICD-9-CM codes to describe all of these.

D. Selection of codes 001.0 through 999.9

The selection of codes 001.0 through 999.9 will frequently be used to describe the reason for the encounter. These codes are from the section of ICD-9-CM for the classification of diseases and injuries (e.g. infectious and parasitic diseases; neoplasms; symptoms, signs, and ill-defined conditions, etc.).

E. Codes that describe symptoms and signs

Codes that describe symptoms and signs, as opposed to diagnoses, are acceptable for reporting purposes when a diagnosis has not been established (confirmed) by the provider. Chapter 16 of ICD-9-CM, Symptoms, Signs, and Ill-defined conditions (codes 780.0-799.9) contain many, but not all codes for symptoms.

F. Encounters for circumstances other than a disease or injury

ICD-9-CM provides codes to deal with encounters for circumstances other than a disease or injury. The Supplementary Classification of factors Influencing Health Status and Contact with Health Services (V01.0-**V89**) is provided to deal with occasions when circumstances other than a disease or injury are recorded as diagnosis or problems.
See Section I.C. 18 for information on V-codes

G. Level of detail in coding

1. ICD-9-CM codes with 3, 4, or 5 digits

ICD-9-CM is composed of codes with either 3, 4, or 5 digits. Codes with three digits are included in ICD-9-CM as the heading of a category of codes that may be further subdivided by the use of fourth and/or fifth-digits, which provide greater specificity.

2. Use of full number of digits required for a code

A three-digit code is to be used only if it is not further subdivided. Where fourth-digit subcategories and/or fifth-digit subclassifications are provided, they must be assigned. A code is invalid if it has not been coded to the full number of digits required for that code.

See also discussion under Section I.b.3., General Coding Guidelines, Level of Detail in Coding.

H. ICD-9-CM code for the diagnosis, condition, problem, or other reason for encounter/visit

List first the ICD-9-CM code for the diagnosis, condition, problem, or other reason for encounter/visit shown in the medical record to be chiefly responsible for the services provided. List additional codes that describe any coexisting conditions. In some cases the first-listed diagnosis may be a symptom when a diagnosis has not been established (confirmed) by the physician.

I. Uncertain diagnosis

Do not code diagnoses documented as "probable", "suspected," "questionable," "rule out," or "working diagnosis" or other similar terms indicating uncertainty. Rather, code the condition(s) to the highest degree of certainty for that encounter/visit, such as symptoms, signs, abnormal test results, or other reason for the visit.

Please note: This differs from the coding practices used by short-term, acute care, long-term care and psychiatric hospitals.

J. Chronic diseases

Chronic diseases treated on an ongoing basis may be coded and reported as many times as the patient receives treatment and care for the condition(s)

K. Code all documented conditions that coexist

Code all documented conditions that coexist at the time of the encounter/visit, and require or affect patient care treatment or management. Do not code conditions that were previously treated and no longer exist. However, history codes (V10-V19) may be used as secondary codes if the historical condition or family history has an impact on current care or influences treatment.

L. Patients receiving diagnostic services only

For patients receiving diagnostic services only during an encounter/visit, sequence first the diagnosis, condition, problem, or other reason for encounter/visit shown in the medical record to be chiefly responsible for the outpatient services provided during the encounter/visit. Codes for other diagnoses (e.g., chronic conditions) may be sequenced as additional diagnoses.

For encounters for routine laboratory/radiology testing in the absence of any signs, symptoms, or associated diagnosis, assign V72.5 and V72.6. If routine testing is performed during the same encounter as a test to evaluate a sign, symptom, or diagnosis, it is appropriate to assign both the V code and the code describing the reason for the non-routine test.

For outpatient encounters for diagnostic tests that have been interpreted by a physician, and the final report is available at the time of coding, code any confirmed or definitive diagnosis(es) documented in the interpretation. Do not code related signs and symptoms as additional diagnoses.

Please note: This differs from the coding practice in the hospital inpatient setting regarding abnormal findings on test results.

M. Patients receiving therapeutic services only

For patients receiving therapeutic services only during an encounter/visit, sequence first the diagnosis, condition, problem, or other reason for encounter/visit shown in the medical record to be chiefly responsible for the outpatient services provided during the encounter/visit. Codes for other diagnoses (e.g., chronic conditions) may be sequenced as additional diagnoses.

The only exception to this rule is that when the primary reason for the admission/encounter is chemotherapy, radiation therapy, or rehabilitation, the appropriate V code for the service is listed first, and the diagnosis or problem for which the service is being performed listed second.

N. Patients receiving preoperative evaluations only

For patients receiving preoperative evaluations only, sequence first a code from category V72.8, Other specified examinations, to describe the pre-op consultations. Assign a code for the condition to describe the reason for the surgery as an additional diagnosis. Code also any findings related to the pre-op evaluation.

O. Ambulatory surgery

For ambulatory surgery, code the diagnosis for which the surgery was performed. If the postoperative diagnosis is known to be different from the preoperative diagnosis at the time the diagnosis is confirmed, select the postoperative diagnosis for coding, since it is the most definitive.

P. Routine outpatient prenatal visits

For routine outpatient prenatal visits when no complications are present, codes V22.0, Supervision of normal first pregnancy, or V22.1, Supervision of other normal pregnancy, should be used as the principal diagnosis. These codes should not be used in conjunction with chapter 11 codes.

Appendix I. Present on Admission Reporting Guidelines

Introduction

These guidelines are to be used as a supplement to the *ICD-9-CM Official Guidelines for Coding and Reporting* to facilitate the assignment of the Present on Admission (POA) indicator for each diagnosis and external cause of injury code reported on claim forms (UB-04 and 837 Institutional).

These guidelines are not intended to replace any guidelines in the main body of the *ICD-9-CM Official Guidelines for Coding and Reporting.* The POA guidelines are not intended to provide guidance on when a condition should be coded, but rather, how to apply the POA indicator to the final set of diagnosis codes that have been assigned in accordance with Sections I, II, and III of the official coding guidelines. Subsequent to the assignment of the ICD-9-CM codes, the POA indicator should then be assigned to those conditions that have been coded.

As stated in the Introduction to the ICD-9-CM Official Guidelines for Coding and Reporting, a joint effort between the healthcare provider and the coder is essential to achieve complete and accurate documentation, code assignment, and reporting of diagnoses and procedures. The importance of consistent, complete documentation in the medical record cannot be overemphasized. Medical record documentation from any provider involved in the care and treatment of the patient may be used to support the determination of whether a condition was present on admission or not. In the context of the official coding guidelines, the term "provider" means a physician or any qualified healthcare practitioner who is legally accountable for establishing the patient's diagnosis.

These guidelines are not a substitute for the provider's clinical judgment as to the determination of whether a condition was/was not present on admission. The provider should be queried regarding issues related to the linking of signs/symptoms, timing of test results, and the timing of findings.

General Reporting Requirements

All claims involving inpatient admissions to general acute care hospitals or other facilities that are subject to a law or regulation mandating collection of present on admission information.

Present on admission is defined as present at the time the order for inpatient admission occurs -- conditions that develop during an outpatient encounter, including emergency department, observation, or outpatient surgery, are considered as present on admission.

POA indicator is assigned to principal and secondary diagnoses (as defined in Section II of the Official Guidelines for Coding and Reporting) and the external cause of injury codes.

Issues related to inconsistent, missing, conflicting or unclear documentation must still be resolved by the provider.

If a condition would not be coded and reported based on UHDDS definitions and current official coding guidelines, then the POA indicator would not be reported.

Reporting Options

Y - Yes

N - No

U - Unknown

W – Clinically undetermined

Unreported/Not used **(or "1" for Medicare usage)** – (Exempt from POA reporting)

For more specific instructions on Medicare POA indicator reporting options, refer to http://www.cms.hhs.gov/HospitalAcqCond/02_Statute_Regulations_Program_Instructions.asp#TopOfPage

Reporting Definitions

Y = present at the time of inpatient admission

N = not present at the time of inpatient admission

U = documentation is insufficient to determine if condition is present on admission

W = provider is unable to clinically determine whether condition was present on admission or not

Timeframe for POA Identification and Documentation

There is no required timeframe as to when a provider (per the definition of "provider" used in these guidelines) must identify or document a condition to be present on admission. In some clinical situations, it may not be possible for a provider to make a definitive diagnosis (or a condition may not be recognized or reported by the patient) for a period of time after admission. In some cases it may be several days before the provider arrives at a definitive diagnosis. This does not mean that the condition was not present on admission. Determination of whether the condition was present on admission or not will be based on the applicable POA guideline as identified in this document, or on the provider's best clinical judgment.

If at the time of code assignment the documentation is unclear as to whether a condition was present on admission or not, it is appropriate to query the provider for clarification.

Assigning the POA Indicator

Condition is on the "Exempt from Reporting" list Leave the "present on admission" field blank if the condition is on the list of ICD-9-CM codes for which this field is not applicable. This is the only circumstance in which the field may be left blank.

POA explicitly documented

Assign Y for any condition the provider explicitly documents as being present on admission.

Assign N for any condition the provider explicitly documents as not present at the time of admission.

Conditions diagnosed prior to inpatient admission

Assign "Y" for conditions that were diagnosed prior to admission (example: hypertension, diabetes mellitus, asthma)

Conditions diagnosed during the admission but clearly present before admission

Assign "Y" for conditions diagnosed during the admission that were clearly present but not diagnosed until after admission occurred.

Diagnoses subsequently confirmed after admission are considered present on admission if at the time of admission they are documented as suspected, possible, rule out, differential diagnosis, or constitute an underlying cause of a symptom that is present at the time of admission.

Condition develops during outpatient encounter prior to inpatient admission

Assign Y for any condition that develops during an outpatient encounter prior to a written order for inpatient admission.

Documentation does not indicate whether condition was present on admission

Assign "U" when the medical record documentation is unclear as to whether the condition was present on admission. "U" should not be routinely assigned and used only in very limited circumstances. Coders are encouraged to query the providers when the documentation is unclear.

Documentation states that it cannot be determined whether the condition was or was not present on admission

Assign "W" when the medical record documentation indicates that it cannot be clinically determined whether or not the condition was present on admission.

Chronic condition with acute exacerbation during the admission

If the code is a combination code that identifies both the chronic condition and the acute exacerbation, see POA guidelines pertaining to combination codes.

If the combination code only identifies the chronic condition and not the acute exacerbation (e.g., acute exacerbation of CHF), assign "Y."

Conditions documented as possible, probable, suspected, or rule out at the time of discharge

If the final diagnosis contains a possible, probable, suspected, or rule out diagnosis, and this diagnosis was suspected at the time of inpatient admission, assign "Y."

If the final diagnosis contains a possible, probable, suspected, or rule out diagnosis, and this diagnosis was based on symptoms or clinical findings that were not present on admission, assign "N".

Conditions documented as impending or threatened at the time of discharge

If the final diagnosis contains an impending or threatened diagnosis, and this diagnosis is based on symptoms or clinical findings that were present on admission, assign "Y".

If the final diagnosis contains an impending or threatened diagnosis, and this diagnosis is based on symptoms or clinical findings that were not present on admission, assign "N".

Acute and chronic conditions

Assign "Y" for acute conditions that are present at time of admission and N for acute conditions that are not present at time of admission.

Assign "Y" for chronic conditions, even though the condition may not be diagnosed until after admission.

If a single code identifies both an acute and chronic condition, see the POA guidelines for combination codes.

Combination codes

Assign "N" if any part of the combination code was not present on admission (e.g., obstructive chronic bronchitis with acute exacerbation and the exacerbation was not present on admission; gastric ulcer that does not start bleeding until after admission; asthma patient develops status asthmaticus after admission)

Assign "Y" if all parts of the combination code were present on admission (e.g., patient with diabetic nephropathy is admitted with uncontrolled diabetes)

If the final diagnosis includes comparative or contrasting diagnoses, and both were present, or suspected, at the time of admission, assign "Y".

For infection codes that include the causal organism, assign "Y" if the infection (or signs of the infection) was present on admission, even though the culture results may not be known until after admission (e.g., patient is admitted with pneumonia and the provider documents pseudomonas as the causal organism a few days later).

Same Diagnosis Code for Two or More Conditions

When the same ICD-9-CM diagnosis code applies to two or more conditions during the same encounter (e.g. bilateral condition, or two separate conditions classified to the same ICD-9-CM diagnosis code):

Assign "Y" if all conditions represented by the single ICD-9-CM code were present on admission (e.g. bilateral fracture of the same bone, same site, and both fractures were present on admission)

Assign "N" if any of the conditions represented by the single ICD-9-CM code was not present on admission (e.g. dehydration with hyponatremia is assigned to code 276.1, but only one of these conditions was present on admission).

Obstetrical conditions

Whether or not the patient delivers during the current hospitalization does not affect assignment of the POA indicator. The determining factor for POA assignment is whether the pregnancy complication or obstetrical condition described by the code was present at the time of admission or not.

If the pregnancy complication or obstetrical condition was present on admission (e.g., patient admitted in preterm labor), assign "Y".

If the pregnancy complication or obstetrical condition was not present on admission (e.g., 2nd degree laceration during delivery, postpartum hemorrhage that occurred during current hospitalization, fetal distress develops after admission), assign "N".

If the obstetrical code includes more than one diagnosis and any of the diagnoses identified by the code were not present on admission (e.g., Code 642.7, Pre-eclampsia or eclampsia superimposed on preexisting hypertension) assign "N".

If the obstetrical code includes information that is not a diagnosis, do not consider that information in the POA determination. Example, code 652.1x, Breech or other malpresentation successfully converted to cephalic presentation, should be reported as present on admission if the fetus was breech on admission but was converted to cephalic presentation after admission. Since the conversion to cephalic presentation does not represent a diagnosis, the fact that the conversion occurred after admission has no bearing on the POA determination.

Perinatal conditions

Newborns are not considered to be admitted until after birth. Therefore, any condition present at birth or that developed in utero is considered present at admission and should be assigned "Y". This includes conditions that occur during delivery (e.g., injury during delivery, meconium aspiration, exposure to streptococcus B in the vaginal canal).

Congenital conditions and anomalies

Assign "Y" for congenital conditions and anomalies. Congenital conditions are always considered present on admission.

External cause of injury codes

Assign "Y" for any E code representing an external cause of injury or poisoning that occurred prior to inpatient admission (e.g., patient fell out of bed at home, patient fell out of bed in emergency room prior to admission)

Assign "N" for any E code representing an external cause of injury or poisoning that occurred during inpatient hospitalization (e.g., patient fell out of hospital bed during hospital stay, patient experienced an adverse reaction to a medication administered after inpatient admission)

Categories and Codes Exempt from Diagnosis Present on Admission Requirement

Note: "Diagnosis present on admission" for these code categories are exempt because they represent circumstances regarding the healthcare encounter or factors influencing health status that do not

represent a current disease or injury or are always present on admission

137-139 Late effects of infectious and parasitic diseases
268.1 Rickets, late effect
326 Late effects of intracranial abscess or pyogenic infection
412 Old myocardial infarction
438 Late effects of cerebrovascular disease
650 Normal delivery
660.7 Failed forceps or vacuum extractor, unspecified
677 Late effect of complication of pregnancy, childbirth, and the puerperium
905-909 Late effects of injuries, poisonings, toxic effects, and other external causes
V02 Carrier or suspected carrier of infectious diseases
V03 Need for prophylactic vaccination and inoculation against bacterial diseases
V04 Need for prophylactic vaccination and inoculation against certain viral diseases
V05 Need for other prophylactic vaccination and inoculation against single diseases
V06 Need for prophylactic vaccination and inoculation against combinations of diseases
V07 Need for isolation and other prophylactic measures
V10 Personal history of malignant neoplasm
V11 Personal history of mental disorder
V12 Personal history of certain other diseases
V13 Personal history of other diseases
V14 Personal history of allergy to medicinal agents
V15.01-V15.09 Other personal history, Allergy, other than to medicinal agents
V15.1 Other personal history, Surgery to heart and great vessels
V15.2 Other personal history, Surgery to other major organs
V15.3 Other personal history, Irradiation
V15.4 Other personal history, Psychological trauma
V15.5 Other personal history, Injury
V15.6 Other personal history, Poisoning
V15.7 Other personal history, Contraception
V15.81 Other personal history, Noncompliance with medical treatment
V15.82 Other personal history, History of tobacco use
V15.88 Other personal history, History of fall
V15.89 Other personal history, Other
V15.9 Unspecified personal history presenting hazards to health
V16 Family history of malignant neoplasm
V17 Family history of certain chronic disabling diseases
V18 Family history of certain other specific conditions
V19 Family history of other conditions
V20 Health supervision of infant or child
V21 Constitutional states in development
V22 Normal pregnancy
V23 Supervision of high-risk pregnancy
V24 Postpartum care and examination
V25 Encounter for contraceptive management
V26 Procreative management
V27 Outcome of delivery
V28 Antenatal screening
V29 Observation and evaluation of newborns for suspected condition not found
V30-V39 Liveborn infants according to type of birth
V42 Organ or tissue replaced by transplant
V43 Organ or tissue replaced by other means
V44 Artificial opening status
V45 Other postprocedural states
V46 Other dependence on machines
V49.60-V49.77 Upper and lower limb amputation status
V49.81-V49.84 Other specified conditions influencing health status
V50 Elective surgery for purposes other than remedying health states
V51 Aftercare involving the use of plastic surgery
V52 Fitting and adjustment of prosthetic device and implant
V53 Fitting and adjustment of other device
V54 Other orthopedic aftercare
V55 Attention to artificial openings
V56 Encounter for dialysis and dialysis catheter care
V57 Care involving use of rehabilitation procedures
V58 Encounter for other and unspecified procedures and aftercare
V59 Donors
V60 Housing, household, and economic circumstances
V61 Other family circumstances
V62 Other psychosocial circumstances
V64 Persons encountering health services for specific procedures, not carried out
V65 Other persons seeking consultation
V66 Convalescence and palliative care
V67 Follow-up examination
V68 Encounters for administrative purposes
V69 Problems related to lifestyle
V70 General medical examination
V71 Observation and evaluation for suspected condition not found
V72 Special investigations and examinations
V73 Special screening examination for viral and chlamydial diseases
V74 Special screening examination for bacterial and spirochetal diseases
V75 Special screening examination for other infectious diseases
V76 Special screening for malignant neoplasms
V77 Special screening for endocrine, nutritional, metabolic, and immunity disorders
V78 Special screening for disorders of blood and blood-forming organs
V79 Special screening for mental disorders and developmental handicaps
V80 Special screening for neurological, eye, and ear diseases
V81 Special screening for cardiovascular, respiratory, and genitourinary diseases
V82 Special screening for other conditions
V83 Genetic carrier status
V84 Genetic susceptibility to disease
V85 Body Mass Index
V86 Estrogen receptor status
V87.4 Personal history of drug therapy
V88 Acquired absence of cervix and uterus
V89 Suspected maternal and fetal conditions not found
E800-E807 Railway accidents
E810-E819 Motor vehicle traffic accidents
E820-E825 Motor vehicle nontraffic accidents E826-E829, Other road vehicle accidents
E830-E838 Water transport accidents
E840-E845 Air and space transport accidents
E846-E848 Vehicle accidents not elsewhere classifiable
E849.0-E849.6 Place of occurrence
E849.8-E849.9 Place of occurrence
E883.1 Accidental fall into well
E883.2 Accidental fall into storm drain or manhole
E884.0 Fall from playground equipment
E884.1 Fall from cliff
E885.0 Fall from (nonmotorized) scooter
E885.1 Fall from roller skates
E885.2 Fall from skateboard
E885.3 Fall from skis
E885.4 Fall from snowboard
E886.0 Fall on same level from collision, pushing, or shoving, by or with other person, In sports
E890.0-E890.9 Conflagration in private dwelling
E893.0 Accident caused by ignition of clothing, from controlled fire in private dwelling
E893.2 Accident caused by ignition of clothing, from controlled fire not in building or structure
E894 Ignition of highly inflammable material
E895 Accident caused by controlled fire in private dwelling
E897 Accident caused by controlled fire not in building or structure
E898.0-E898.1 Accident caused by other specified fire and flames
E917.0 Striking against or struck accidentally by objects or persons, in sports without subsequent fall
E917.1 Striking against or struck accidentally by objects or persons, caused by a crowd, by collective fear or panic without subsequent fall
E917.2 Striking against or struck accidentally by objects or persons, in running water without subsequent fall
E917.5 Striking against or struck accidentally by objects or persons, object in sports with subsequent fall
E917.6 Striking against or struck accidentally by objects or persons, caused by a crowd, by collective fear or panic with subsequent fall
E919.0-E919.1 Accidents caused by machinery

E919.3-E919.9	Accidents caused by machinery
E921.0-E921.9	Accident caused by explosion of pressure vessel
E922.0-E922.9	Accident caused by firearm and air gun missile
E924.1	Caustic and corrosive substances
E926.2	Visible and ultraviolet light sources
E928.0-E928.8	Other and unspecified environmental and accidental causes
E929.0-E929.9	Late effects of accidental injury
E959	Late effects of self-inflicted injury
E970-E978	Legal intervention
E979	Terrorism
E981.0-E981.8	Poisoning by gases in domestic use, undetermined whether accidentally or purposely inflicted
E982.0-E982.9	Poisoning by other gases, undetermined whether accidentally or purposely inflicted
E985.0-E985.7	Injury by firearms, air guns and explosives, undetermined whether accidentally or purposely inflicted
E987.0	Falling from high place, undetermined whether accidentally or purposely inflicted, residential premises
E987.2	Falling from high place, undetermined whether accidentally or purposely inflicted, natural sites
E989	Late effects of injury, undetermined whether accidentally or purposely inflicted
E990-E999	Injury resulting from operations of war

POA Examples

General Medical Surgical

1. Patient is admitted for diagnostic work-up for cachexia. The final diagnosis is malignant neoplasm of lung with metastasis.
   Assign "Y" on the POA field for the malignant neoplasm. The malignant neoplasm was clearly present on admission, although it was not diagnosed until after the admission occurred.
2. A patient undergoes outpatient surgery. During the recovery period, the patient develops atrial fibrillation and the patient is subsequently admitted to the hospital as an inpatient.
   Assign "Y" on the POA field for the atrial fibrillation since it developed prior to a written order for inpatient admission.
3. A patient is treated in observation and while in Observation, the patient falls out of bed and breaks a hip. The patient is subsequently admitted as an inpatient to treat the hip fracture.
   Assign "Y" on the POA field for the hip fracture since it developed prior to a written order for inpatient admission.
4. A patient with known congestive heart failure is admitted to the hospital after he develops decompensated congestive heart failure.
   Assign "Y" on the POA field for the congestive heart failure. The ICD-9-CM code identifies the chronic condition and does not specify the acute exacerbation.
5. A patient undergoes inpatient surgery. After surgery, the patient develops fever and is treated aggressively. The physician's final diagnosis documents "possible postoperative infection following surgery."
   Assign "N" on the POA field for the postoperative infection since final diagnoses that contain the terms "possible", "probable", "suspected" or "rule out" and that are based on symptoms or clinical findings that were not present on admission should be reported as "N".
6. A patient with severe cough and difficulty breathing was diagnosed during his hospitalization to have lung cancer.
   Assign "Y" on the POA field for the lung cancer. Even though the cancer was not diagnosed until after admission, it is a chronic condition that was clearly present before the patient's admission.
7. A patient is admitted to the hospital for a coronary artery bypass surgery. Postoperatively he developed a pulmonary embolism.
   Assign "N" on the POA field for the pulmonary embolism. This is an acute condition that was not present on admission.
8. A patient is admitted with a known history of coronary atherosclerosis, status post myocardial infarction five years ago is now admitted for treatment of impending myocardial infarction. The final diagnosis is documented as "impending myocardial infarction."
   Assign "Y" to the impending myocardial infarction because the condition is present on admission.
9. A patient with diabetes mellitus developed uncontrolled diabetes on day 3 of the hospitalization.
   Assign "N" to the diabetes code because the "uncontrolled" component of the code was not present on admission.
10. A patient is admitted with high fever and pneumonia. The patient rapidly deteriorates and becomes septic. The discharge diagnosis lists sepsis and pneumonia. The documentation is unclear as to whether the sepsis was present on admission or developed shortly after admission.
    Query the physician as to whether the sepsis was present on admission, developed shortly after admission, or it cannot be clinically determined as to whether it was present on admission or not.
11. A patient is admitted for repair of an abdominal aneurysm. However, the aneurysm ruptures after hospital admission.
    Assign "N" for the ruptured abdominal aneurysm. Although the aneurysm was present on admission, the "ruptured" component of the code description did not occur until after admission.
12. A patient with viral hepatitis B progresses to hepatic coma after admission.
    Assign "N" for the viral hepatitis B with hepatic coma because part of the code description did not develop until after admission.
13. A patient with a history of varicose veins and ulceration of the left lower extremity strikes the area against the side of his hospital bed during an inpatient hospitalization. It bleeds profusely. The final diagnosis lists varicose veins with ulcer and hemorrhage.
    Assign "Y" for the varicose veins with ulcer. Although the hemorrhage occurred after admission, the code description for varicose veins with ulcer does not mention hemorrhage.
14. The nursing initial assessment upon admission documents the presence of a decubitus ulcer. There is no mention of the decubitus ulcer in the physician documentation until several days after admission.
    Query the physician as to whether the decubitus ulcer was present on admission, or developed after admission. Both diagnosis code assignment and determination of whether a condition was present on admission must be based on provider documentation in the medical record (per the definition of "provider" found at the beginning of these POA guidelines and in the introductory section of the ICD-9-CM Official Guidelines for Coding and Reporting). If it cannot be determined from the provider documentation whether or not a condition was present on admission, the provider should be queried.
15. **A urine culture is obtained on admission. The provider documents urinary tract infection when the culture results become available a few days later.**
    Assign "Y" to the urinary tract infection since the diagnosis is based on test results from a specimen obtained on admission. It may not be possible for a provider to make a definitive diagnosis for a period of time after admission. There is no required timeframe as to when a provider must identify or document a condition to be present on admission.
16. **A patient tested positive for Methicillin resistant Staphylococcus (MRSA) on routine nasal culture on admission to the hospital. During the hospitalization, he underwent insertion of a central venous catheter and later developed an infection and was diagnosed with MRSA sepsis due to central venous catheter infection.**
    Assign "Y" to the positive MRSA colonization. Assign "N" for the MRSA sepsis due to central venous catheter infection since the patient did not have a MRSA infection at the time of admission.

Obstetrics

1. A female patient was admitted to the hospital and underwent a normal delivery.
   Leave the "present on admission" (POA) field blank. Code 650, Normal delivery, is on the "exempt from reporting" list.
2. Patient admitted in late pregnancy due to excessive vomiting and dehydration. During admission patient goes into premature labor
   Assign "Y" for the excessive vomiting and the dehydration.
   Assign "N" for the premature labor
3. Patient admitted in active labor. During the stay, a breast abscess is noted when mother attempted to breast feed. Provider is unable to determine whether the abscess was present on admission
   Assign "W" for the breast abscess.
4. Patient admitted in active labor. After 12 hours of labor it is noted that the infant is in fetal distress and a Cesarean section is performed
   Assign "N" for the fetal distress.
5. **Pregnant female was admitted in labor and fetal nuchal cord entanglement was diagnosed. Physician is queried, but is unable to determine whether the cord entanglement was present on admission or not.**
   Assign "W" for the fetal nuchal cord entanglement.

Newborn

1. A single liveborn infant was delivered in the hospital via Cesarean section. The physician documented fetal bradycardia during labor in the final diagnosis in the newborn record.
   Assign " Y" because the bradycardia developed prior to the newborn admission (birth).
2. A newborn developed diarrhea which was believed to be due to the hospital baby formula.
   Assign " N" because the diarrhea developed after admission.
3. **A newborn born in the hospital, birth complicated by nuchal cord entanglement.**
   Assign "Y" for the nuchal cord entanglement on the baby's record. Any condition that is present at birth or that developed in utero is considered present at admission, including conditions that occur during delivery.

10 Steps to Outpatient Correct Coding

Follow the 10 steps below to correctly code encounters for healthcare services.

Step 1: Identify the reason for the visit or encounter (i.e., a sign, symptom, diagnosis and/or condition).

The medical record documentation should accurately reflect the patient's condition, using terminology that includes specific diagnoses and symptoms, or clearly states the reasons for the encounter.

Choosing the main term that best describes the reason chiefly responsible for the service provided is the most important step in coding. If symptoms are present and documented, but a definitive diagnosis has not yet been determined, code the symptoms. **Do not code conditions that are referred to as "rule out," "suspected," "probable" or "questionable."** Diagnoses often are not established at the time of the initial encounter/visit. Two or more visits may be necessary to establish the diagnosis. Code only what is documented in the available records and only to the highest degree of certainty known at the time of the patient's visit.

Step 2: After selecting the reason for the encounter, always consult the Alphabetic Index, Volume 2, before verifying code selection in the Tabular section.

The most critical rule is to begin the code selection process in the *Alphabetic Index.* Never turn first to the Tabular List (Volume 1). The Index provides cross references, essential and non-essential modifiers, and inclusion terms not found in the Tabular List. To prevent coding errors, always use both the Alphabetic Index and the Tabular List when locating and assigning a code. Always verify the code found in the Alphabetic Index in the Tabular List. First, the Index does not include the important instructional notes found in the Tabular. Second, the advantage of a classification system is that like items are grouped together. A quick scan of the Tabular might provide coding options for the coder that would have been missed.

Step 3: Locate the main term entry.

The Alphabetic Index is a listing of conditions. Conditions may be expressed as nouns or eponyms, with critical use of adjectives. Some conditions have multiple entries under synonyms. Reasons for encounters may be located under general terms such as admission, encounter, and examination. Other general terms such as history of or status post are used to locate factors influencing health.

Step 4: Read and interpret any notes listed with the main term or the subterm.

Notes such as common fifth-digit references and cross references are identified by italicized type. Always check any cross-references to ensure that all alternative terms are researched.

Step 5: Review entries for modifiers.

Nonessential modifiers are the terms located within parentheses following the main term entry. These parenthetical terms are supplementary words or explanatory information that may either be present or absent in the diagnostic statement and do not affect code selection. The subterms listed under the main term are essential modifiers that do affect coding assignment. Each line of indent represents a more specific code entry.

Step 6: Interpret abbreviations, cross-references, fifth digits, and brackets.

The cross-references used are "see," "see category" and "see also" which indicate alternative term choices for code searches. The abbreviation NEC may follow main terms or subterms. NEC (not elsewhere classified) indicates that there is no specific code for the condition even though the medical documentation may be very specific. Is a fifth digit required? You MUST refer to the Tabular List to discover the correct code. Italicized brackets [ ] enclose a second code that must be used along with the code immediately preceding it, with the bracketed code sequenced as the secondary code. This is a mandatory multiple code situation. Both the underlying condition and the manifestation (code in the slanted bracket) must be reported.

Step 7: Choose a potential code and locate it in the Tabular List.

The coder must follow any Includes, Excludes notes, and other instructional notes, such as "Code first" and "Use additional code," listed in the Tabular for the chapter, category, subcategory, and subclassification level of code selection which direct the coder to use a different or additional code.

Any codes in the Tabular range, 001.0 through 999.9, may be used to identify the diagnostic reason for the encounter. The Tabular encompasses many codes describing disease and injury classifications (e.g., infectious and parasitic diseases, neoplasms, symptoms, signs and ill-defined conditions, etc.).

Codes that describe symptoms and signs, as opposed to definitive diagnoses, should be used for reporting purposes when an established diagnosis has not been made (confirmed) by the physician. Chapter 16 of the ICD-9-CM code book, "Symptoms, Signs, and Ill-Defined Conditions" (codes 780.01-799.9) contains many, but not all, codes for symptoms.

ICD-9-CM classifies encounters with health care providers for circumstances other than a disease or injury using codes in the Supplementary Classification of Factors Influencing Health Status and Contact with Health Services (V01.0-V89.09). There are many occasions when circumstances other than a disease or injury are recorded as chiefly responsible for the encounter.

Step 8: Determine whether the code is at the highest level of specificity.

A code is invalid if it has not been coded to the full number of digits (greatest level of specificity) required. A three-digit code is to be used only if the category is not further subdivided. Assign four-digit codes (subcategory codes) only if there are no five-digit codes for that category. Assign five-digit codes (fifth-digit subclassification codes) for those categories mandating the use of five digits.

Step 9: Assign the code.

Having reviewed all relevant information concerning the possible code choices, assign the code that most completely describes the condition.

Repeat steps one through nine for all additional documented conditions that meet the following criteria:

- Conditions that currently exist at the time of the visit
- Conditions that require or affect patient care, treatment or management.

Step 10: Sequence codes correctly

Sequencing is defined as the order in which the codes are listed on the claim. List first the ICD-9-CM code for the diagnosis, condition, problem or other reason for the encounter/visit, which is shown in the medical record to be chiefly responsible for the services provided. List additional codes that describe any coexisting conditions. Follow the official coding guidelines (See Section IV Diagnostic Coding and reporting Guidelines for Outpatient Services) concerning proper sequencing of codes.

Coding Examples

Diagnosis: Anorexia

- Step 1: The reason for the encounter was the condition, anorexia.
- Step 2. Consult the Index to Diseases.
- Step 3: Locate the main term "Anorexia," which indicates a code of
- Step 4: There are no italicized instructional notes to interpret.
- Step 5: Note that there are two possible subterms (essential modifiers), "hysterical" and "nervosa," neither of which is documented in this instance and therefore cannot be used in code

selection. The code listed next to the main term is called the default code selection.

- Step 6: There are no abbreviations, cross-references, fifth-digit notations, or brackets.
- Step 7: Turn to code 783.0 in the Tabular List and read the instructional notes. In this case the "Excludes" note indicates that anorexia determined to be of non-organic origin should be coded to Chapter 5. The diagnostic statement does not indicate non-organic origin.
- Step 8: There is no further division of the category past the fourth digit subcategory. Therefore, the subcategory code level is the highest level of specificity.
- Step 9: The default code, 783.0 is the correct code selection.
- Step 10: Since anorexia is listed as the chief reason for the healthcare encounter, the primary or principal diagnosis is 783.0.

Diagnosis: Acute bronchitis due to staphylococcus

- Step 1: The reason for the encounter was the condition, acute bronchitis due to staphylococcus.
- Step 2. Consult the Index to Diseases.
- Step 3: Locate the main term "Bronchitis."
- Step 4: There are no italicized instructional notes to interpret.
- Step 5: Review entries for modifiers. Since "acute" is not listed as a nonessential modifier, read past the "with" modifier until you find the subterm "acute or subacute" with code 466.0. Continue to search to see if the subterm "due to" appears under "acute or subacute". The subterm "due to" is present; there is no entry for staphylococcus.
- Step 6: There are no abbreviations, cross-references, fifth digit notations, or brackets.
- Step 7: Since there are no more appropriate subterms, turn to code 466.0 in the Tabular List. The Includes note under category 466.0 does refer to possible infective organism, but not to staphylococcus specifically. The note does include acute bronchitis. However, at the beginning of chapter 8, "Diseases of the Respiratory System," you will notice the "use additional code" note that tells you to assign a code to identify the infectious organism. This instructional note applies to the entire chapter.
- Step 8: There is no further division of the category past the fourth digit subcategory. Therefore, the subcategory code level is the highest level of specificity.
- • Step 9: Assign code 466.0.

Repeat steps 1-9 for any additional code assignments.

- Step 1: The reason for the encounter was the condition, acute bronchitis due to staphylococcus.
- Step 2. Consult the Index to Diseases.
- Step 3: Locate the main term Staphylococcus, staphylococcal.
- Step 4: The italicized instructional notes states see condition. Locate the main term "Infection, infected, infective".
- Step 5: Review entries for modifiers. Locate the subterm "staphylococcal NEC," where you will find code 041.10 referenced.
- Step 6: The abbreviation NEC indicates that a review of the medical record may be necessary to determine if there is documentation concerning the specific type of staphylococcus.
- Step 7: Verify code 041.10 in the Tabular List. The code title is Staphylococcus, unspecified. If there is additional information identifying the organism as aureus methicillin resistant, or other, assign the appropriate code, 041.11, 041.12, or 041.19. Otherwise, assign code 041.10, Staphylococcus, unspecified, as an additional code.
- Step 8: There is no further division of the category past the fifth-digit subclassification level. Therefore, the subclassification code level is the highest level of specificity. The final code assignment would be 041.10.
- Step 9: Assign code 041.10.
- Step 10: Sequence codes as directed by the instructional note for category 466. Code first 466.0 and assign code 041.10 as additional.

Diagnosis: Traveler's diarrhea

- Step 1: The reason for the encounter was the condition, Traveler's diarrhea.
- Step 2. Consult the Index to Diseases.
- Step 3: Locate the main term "Diarrhea" in the Alphabetic Index.
- Step 4: There are no italicized instructional notes to interpret.
- Step 5: Review entries for modifiers. Note that the nonessential modifiers (in parentheses) after the main term do not include the term "Traveler's," which means that the coder should search the subterms for the term "Traveler's." The subterm "Traveler's" has a possible code selection, 009.2, and suggests the subterm "due to specified organism NEC 008.8." The diagnostic statement does not include the infectious agent; therefore, code 008.8 does not apply.
- Step 6: There are no abbreviations, cross-references, fifth-digit notations, or brackets.
- Step 7: Locate code 009.2 in the Tabular List and read all instructional notes under the main category and subcategories. The Includes notes does not list the term "Traveler's" under code 009.2. As instructed by the Alphabetic Index, you should code the condition to 009.2. The ICD-9-CM code book implies that "Traveler's diarrhea" is the same as infectious diarrhea when it is not attributed to any specified infectious agent.
- Step 8: There is no further division of the category past the fourth-digit subcategory level. Therefore, the subcategory code level is the highest level of specificity. The final code assignment would be 009.2.
- Step 9: Assign code 009.2.
- Step 10: Since infectious diarrhea is listed as the chief reason for the healthcare encounter, the primary or principal diagnosis is 009.2.

Diagnosis: Ingrown toenail, infected

- Step 1: The reason for the encounter was the condition, infected ingrown toenail.
- Step 2. Consult the Index to Diseases.
- Step 3: First you must decide what the searchable main term should be. Reminder: search for condition, not anatomical site. The Alphabetic Index helps you determine the main term. Refer to "toenail" in the Alphabetic Index; the closest match is "Toe," which includes the instruction "see condition." Locate the main term "Infection" in the Alphabetic Index. The subterm toe has a subterm "nail" which refers the coder to category 681, Cellulitis and abscess of finger and toe. This does not indicate the condition ingrown toenail. The main term, therefore, is "Ingrown." A review of the Alphabetic Index takes you to "Ingrowing."
- Step 4: There are no italicized instructional notes to interpret.
- Step 5: Review the subterms. The subterm "nail" appears and lists nonessential modifiers (in parentheses) as "finger," "toe" and "infected." These nonessential modifiers complete the diagnostic statement.
- Step 6: There are no abbreviations, cross-references, fifth-digit notations, or brackets.
- Step 7: Verify code 703.0 in the Tabular List Before assigning the code, review all instructional notes under category 703 and under code 703.0. The note, "Excludes: infection, nail NOS (681.9)," can be ignored because the diagnostic statement specifies the infection is due to the ingrowing nail.
- Step 8: Therefore, the subcategory code level is the highest level of specificity. The final code assignment would be 703.0.
- Step 9: The correct code choice is 703.0, Ingrowing nail with infection.
- Step 10: Since infectious infected ingrown toenail is listed as the chief reason for the healthcare encounter, the primary or principal diagnosis is 703.0.

ICD-9-CM Self Test

Part I ICD-9-CM Diagnosis

1. A 55-year-old woman is brought to the emergency department by family members after developing symptoms that include high fever, confusion, muscle weakness, and severe headaches. Family members inform the staff that she recently returned from a visit to relatives in Colorado where she spent time outdoors camping. Family members are now concerned since the patient had made a remark about the number of bug bites she suffered while camping there. A blood sample is drawn and the physician also performs a spinal tap. Laboratory tests confirm the presence of the West Nile virus in both samples and the physician admits the patient with a diagnosis of encephalomyelitis due to West Nile virus infection.

2. A health care worker presents with symptoms of jaundice, nausea, and dark urine. The doctor orders an HCV enzyme linked immunosorbent assay blood test, which returns positive and is later confirmed by a recombinant immunoblot assay. The health care worker is diagnosed with acute hepatitis C and the decision to begin therapy with interferon and/or ribavarin is deferred until a quantitative HCV polymerase chain reaction test can be done to determine the titer level and the genotype of the C virus.

3. A 28 year-old patient presents for evaluation exhibits prominent psychiatric/behavioral symptoms painful distortion of sense of touch, ataxia and a non-diagnostic diffusely abnormal electroencephalogram. The physician makes a clinical determination of variant Creutzfeldt-Jakob disease (vCJD) with behavioral disturbances.

4. A patient with eczema was treated for fever and diffuse rash over 80 percent of the body associated with exposure to a family member who was recently vaccinated for smallpox.

5. A 34-year-old female presents post-assessment and treatment of associated glandular conditions by her endocrinologist. Family history is positive for MEN syndrome of similar type, with one ancestor's demise attributed to complications of thyroid cancer. Diagnosis is consistent with bilateral medullary carcinoma, secondary hypertension, and hyperparathyroidism diagnosed as multiple endocrine neoplasia (MEN) syndrome, Type IIA. The tumor is localized in the upper central lobe of the thyroid. The patient will be admitted for total substernal thyroidectomy.

6. A 2-year-old female is brought to the urgent care center by her mother, who says the child has been running intermittent fevers over the past three days. She also reports that she was appearing somewhat sluggish earlier in the day. Upon examination, the child is currently afebrile and is alert and playful. CBC, however, reveals bandemia. She will be referred to her primary care pediatrician for further workup to rule out bacterial infection.

7. The husband of a young mother of three observed her suddenly falling asleep for no apparent reason while feeding the youngest child. She appeared to be in a state of unconsciousness for several minutes. Alarmed, the husband was checking for heart beat and pulse, and instructing the older child to call 911, when the wife suddenly became alert. The wife behaved as if she had just simply awakened from sleep. After reporting this episode to her physician, who found no other underlying reason for these episodes to occur, the physician asked the patient to keep a sleep diary for two weeks. The diary indicated that episodes of sudden uncontrollable sleepiness occurred again and again during the daytime. The physician then ordered a multiple sleep latency test (MSLT). The result indicated a diagnosis of narcolepsy.

8. A 16-year-old girl came to the physician's office with her outer ear severely abscessed and the surrounding tissue beginning to show signs of vascular compromise. Recently, she had multiple ear piercings around her ear that did not heal properly. She tried a topical antiseptic, but the condition worsened. A culture was taken that revealed a *Pseudomonas aeruginosa* infection. The physician recommended that she be hospitalized for care including drain insertion, wound debridement, and intravenous antibiotic therapy of amikacin sulfate. A diagnosis of chondritis of the pinna with *Pseudomonas aeruginosa* infection was established.

9. A patient is admitted to an acute care hospital experiencing sudden numbness or weakness of the left arm, sudden confusion, loss of balance and coordination, and a severe headache. CT scan indicates an occlusion and the patient is given a course of tPA. The patient is discharged a few days later with all symptoms resolved prior to release from the hospital. Final physician diagnosis of cerebrovascular accident is documented.

10. A 45-year-old woman, noted to be about 30 pounds overweight, who recently returned from India via a long plane journey presents to her physician's office complaining of pain and tenderness in her right leg. The physician notes swelling and redness developing in the lower half of her upper thigh. Since deep vein thrombosis is suspected, with a greater risk of developing pulmonary embolism, the physician orders a Doppler ultrasound and venography. A thrombus in the femoral vein is confirmed. She is admitted, the leg is held in elevated position, and the administration of intravenous heparin is initiated.

11. A patient presents with flushing, diarrhea, and fibrosis of the tricuspid valve. Urinalysis results indicate high level 5-HIAA (5-hydroxyindoleacetic acid), a degradation product of serotonin. After localization of a tumor and biopsy, diagnosis of malignant carcinoma of the rectum was established.

12. An adult male, age 67, with mild form of COPD was admitted to the hospital with a fever, productive cough, and signs of bronchial obstruction,, such as wheezing and dyspnea on exertion. The patient was in obvious distress. Sputum cultures exhibited normal flora. The physician ruled out pneumonia. The physician determined that the patient was experiencing an acute bronchitis in addition to the chronic bronchitis. The patient was provided an Albuterol inhaler to relieve the bronchospasms and IV hydration.

13. A 19-year-old boy presents to his dentist for his semiannual oral exam after the recent removal of his orthodontic braces. The dentist discovers initial decay and white spots on the buccal smooth surface of his lower canines where the edge of the metal braces had been secured to the teeth for the last two years. He is advised to practice good brushing habits and informed that the initial decay will progress very slowly and not require filling for a while yet.

14. A 45-year-old man with irregular brushing habits comes to the dentist having noticed that some of his teeth are appearing much longer and he is experiencing some bleeding from gums when brushing. The dentist notes that the gums are receding above his maxillary canines and premolars but does not note redness or swelling. The dentist educates the patient about the possible dangerous progression of bacterial infection and gingivitis when the gums have begun to recede and informs the patient that at this stage, he has minimal gingival recession.

15. A patient post liver transplant currently on glucocorticoid immunosuppressant drug therapy develops mononucleosis-like illness with lymphadenopathy. Laryngeal examination revealed hypopharyngeal and supraglottic mucosal hyperplasia. Immunostaining of laryngeal biopsy was positive for latent membrane protein-1 (LMP1). A diagnosis of post transplant lymphoproliferative disorder (PTLD) was established.

16. A 29-year-old female presents in premature labor at 35 weeks for delivery of twin pregnancy, with spontaneous rupture of membranes post-onset of labor. Fetal lung maturity has been assessed, and the twins are determined ready for delivery. The pregnancy has been complicated by moderate pre-eclampsia and threatened premature labor. The patient was mildly pre-eclamptic on admission. At 12 weeks' gestation, the patient underwent an elective fetal reduction procedure to sustain pregnancy. Two viable twin males were delivered without complication via spontaneous vaginal delivery, with episiotomy.

17. A patient is admitted with diabetic neuropathy due to secondary diabetes from chronic therapeutic adrenocorticosteroid use.

18. A 47-year-old male presents with recent history is significant for a 12 lb weight gain over this past year, and a total 22 lb weight gain during the past five years. The patient states that he injured his back last year and has had to limit his physical activity due to the injury. He has not made dietary modifications accordingly. Physical exam reveals no acute injury. The patient complains of intermittent recurrent low back pain bilaterally; but worse on the right. BP is slightly elevated at 144/100, cholesterol is elevated at 272. Height 72 inches, weight 205 lbs; BMI 27.9. Diagnoses on exam are borderline HTN, hypercholesterolemia, and overweight. Antihypertensive cholesterol medications have been discussed with the patient; however, he is urged to manage his diet and resume an exercise program.

19. A 7-year-old patient was admitted for observation one week status post flu-like illness. Parents have noted unexplained bruising, nosebleeds, and change in energy level. Lab values are normal with the exception of decreased platelet and low red blood cell count. Bone marrow testing has ruled out underlying diagnoses. Physician documents Evans' syndrome.

20. A type II diabetic patient presents with blurring of vision. Upon eye exam, multiple vascular hemorrhages and areas of ischemic changes were noted bilaterally in multiple quadrants of the retina consistent with severe nonproliferative diabetic retinopathy with retinal edema. No revascularizations were noted on this exam.

21. A 62-year-old male with longstanding hypertensive renal disease is admitted with progressive exacerbation of renal symptoms with indicative BUN and creatinine compromise. Management is focused on assessment of renal function and control of underlying hypertensive disease. GFR is assessed at 22, and the nephrologist elects to initiate dialysis. The patient is diagnosed with Stage IV chronic kidney disease and imminent renal failure.

22. A 55-year-old man diagnosed with Lou Gehrig's disease experienced rapid progression of the muscle weakness and paralysis and opted for placement of an esophagostomy for tube feeding. The patient now presents with an infected esophagostomy site. The physician documentation confirms septicemia due to *Staphylococcus aureus*.

23. An otherwise healthy 55-year-old woman was admitted with a recent history of flu-like syndrome with fever, chills, cough, and myalgia. On admission, she had dyspnea, nonproductive cough, and rales in both lungs. Diagnostic imaging showed diffuse alveolar infiltration of both lungs, without pleural effusion. Sputum cultures were obtained on admission and empirical antibiotic treatment was initiated with Vancomycin due to suspected bacterial pneumonia. Due to her progressive respiratory failure, mechanical ventilation was initiated on day two. Sputum cultures identified *S. aureus* with an antimicrobial drug resistance profile.

24. A 37-year-old woman who gave birth one year ago is experiencing sensations of bladder fullness, incomplete emptying after urination, and urine leakage or incontinence upon changing position. Upon physical examination, the physician notes bulging in the anterior vaginal wall, some loss of normal vaginal rugae, but the lateral vaginal sulcus is intact. The physician documents a diagnosis of central defect cystocele with overflow incontinence.

25. Patient with obstructive mediastinal lymphoma presents with progressive dyspnea. Diagnostic imaging and pleurocentesis confirms malignant pleural effusion.

26. A patient with a long-standing history of irritable bowel-like symptoms presents for outpatient endoscopic examination and biopsy, which reveals colitis with an abnormal concentration of eosinophils in the colon. The physician documents eosinophilic colitis.

27. A patient is admitted with high fever, nausea, and vomiting. The site of a recently placed PICC-line is slightly reddened and sore. The catheter is cultured and removed. Etiology of symptoms is determined to be PICC-line associated *Staphylococcus aureus* septicemia. The patient is treated with IV antibiotics.

28. A patient presents for local infection characterized by swelling, tenderness, and erythema at the upper extremity injection site following hepatitis B vaccination.

29. An HIV-positive male presents for anal Papanicolaou smear, which is positive for histologically-confirmed anal intraepithelial neoplasia (AIN I).

30. An 87-year-old man with uncomplicated vascular dementia has been bedridden for months and is now discovered to have a stage III decubitus ulcer appearing over the ischial area of the right buttock, affecting the subcutaneous layer, which are beginning to necrose and appearing with craterization. Appropriate wound debridement and protective dressing is carried out.

31. A patient develops signs and symptoms of acute respiratory distress, pulmonary edema, and hypotension within 2 hours of receiving a transfusion for a chronic anemia. Upon admission, labs revealed an increased white blood cell (WBC) count. Clinical presentation was felt to be consistent with TRALI. Investigation has been initiated into the blood products in question. Of primary importance is stopping of the offending transfusion. The patient responded positively to treatment with continuous positive airway pressure and added oxygen and hemodynamic support with no sequelae.

32. A 6-year old patient presents with erythema multiform minor due to amoxicillin prescribed for otitis media. The patient has approximately 13 percent body surface exfoliation, primarily on limbs.

33. This 4-year-old female presents for ophthalmologic evaluation. The mother reports squinting and avoidance of light, and has noticed at times that the child seems unaware of people or objects in the periphery. Direct examination reveals bilateral optic nerves to be underdeveloped. The ophthalmologist documents a diagnosis of optic nerve hypoplasia. Further testing will be undertaken to determine the degree of impairment.

34. A 45-year-old female presents with low-back pain, leg weakness, sensory symptoms, and sphincter involvement. She has had multiple exacerbations of shingles over the years, and a lower back rash appeared three weeks ago. MRI revealed no mass lesion outside or within the spinal cord, and presumptive diagnosis was made of herpes zoster myelitis. The patient was placed on corticosteroids.

35. A patient presents to the emergency room with dermatitis, conjunctivitis, and pharyngitis. The patient is an avid swimmer who persisted with his morning workout in the bay, despite red tide warnings. Due to the absence of ™cold symptoms½ and onset associated with exposure, diagnosis is consistent with effects of red tide.

PART II ICD-9-CM Procedure Coding

1. Prior to a cardiac stenting procedure, the interventional cardiologist uses a fiber-optic, catheter-based near-infrared intravascular spectroscopy system to assess coronary plaques in the coronary vessels in order to determine whether a drug eluting or metal stent is the most appropriate type of stent. The final diagnosis is arteriosclerotic heart disease due to lipid rich plaque.

2. A 63-year-old male is hospitalized for sepsis due to septicemia from a gram negative bacteria. In the last 48 hours, he developed acute respiratory failure and is now noted to be in septic shock. He was placed on mechanical ventilators, with a heart rate of over 90 beats/min, a fever of 103 Fahrenheit, and severe hypotension. In an attempt to restore hemodynamic stability and control hypotension, the patient is also given fluid resuscitation with hypertonic saline and IV infusion of norepinephrine

3. 63-year-old man was admitted to the hospital with a history of eight hours of chest pain associated with nausea, diaphoresis, and dyspnea. His electrocardiogram revealed 4-5 mm ST-segment elevation in the inferior leads with reciprocal ST-depression. Oxygen, aspirin, and morphine were administered. 50 mg tPA was administered per the Global Utilization of Streptokinase and Tissue Plasminogen Activator for Occluded Coronary Arteries (GUSTO) trial protocol and

eptifibatide was also initiated. The patient was intubated, stabilized, and brought to the O.R. for PTCA with drug-eluting stent insertion. Diagnostic left heart cardiac catheterization indicated the left anterior descending branch of the main coronary artery to have a major obstruction. PTCA with drug-eluting stent insertion was performed. IVUS was used to visualize the lumen of the descending branch, determine the patency of the vessel prior to insertion of the stent. After stent placement, IVUS was used to determine if the stent was positioned fully against the wall of the artery.

4. An 81-year-old man fell from the front steps of his home. He has a fracture of the right femur neck at the head and requires total hip replacement. The surgeon uses CT-based preoperative planning and navigational tools to precisely measure pelvic position on the O.R. table and the acetabular alignment of the implant.

5. A 70-year-old white male with arteriosclerosis of the carotid artery is diagnosed with stenosis or occlusion of the carotid artery. The patient is admitted for carotid artery atherectomy and insertion of non-drug-eluting stent. This is done now in an attempt to reduce his risk of cerebrovascular accident. The patient undergoes percutaneous angioplasty with tPA infusion of the area in question within the carotid artery before a non-drug-eluting stent deployment is carried out with cerebral protection from a thrombus or emboli also being used.

6. A patient is admitted with severe emphysema and undergoes bronchoscopy to determine the most appropriate treatment (e.g., endobronchial valve therapy or lung volume reduction surgery). The physician views the airway using a bronchoscope that is inserted through the oral cavity and advanced past the larynx to inspect the bronchus. The physician also assesses the patient's intrapulmonary air flow using intrapulmonary balloon catheters inserted into diseased portions of the lung during the bronchoscopy.

7. A 45-year-old male with loud snoring suffers from fatigue, irritability, and high blood pressure. Previous overnight exam in the sleep lab helped determine that he has severe obstructive sleep apnea. He presents at the hospital for a scheduled uvulopalatopharygealplasty with the implantation of a palatal implant to remain in the soft palate.

8. Seventy six year-old male patient with congestive heart failure due to malignant hypertension is admitted for the implantation of the DeBakey axial flow ventricular assist device (VAD).

9. The physician repairs an umbilical hernia in a 5-year-old patient. The physician makes an umbilical incision and the laparoscope is placed through the umbilical port. Additional trocars are placed through small incisions in the lower abdomen. The hernia sac is identified and reduced and mesh is placed to reinforce the defect.

10. A 40-year-old female with a 3 inch discrepancy in the length of her legs has walked for years with specially made platform shoes that equalize her shorter leg and keep her hips aligned. In childhood, she suffered a fracture of the right femur that developed a bone infection. This interference with the natural growth opportunity of the bone resulted in one leg being shorter than the other. She has previously refused to undergo limb lengthening with the external frame device method and has opted now to have the internal limb lengthening device implanted to gradually elongate her short leg with distraction.

11. A patient is admitted for surgical removal and treatment of malignant neoplasm of the breast. Immediately after lumpectomy for removal of the tumor, the radiation oncologist delivers a specialized high dose of focal radiation directly to the tumor bed while normal tissues are protected.

12. A patient with metastatic, overlapping brain tumors is taken to the interventional radiology suite. After an infusion of Mannitol into the carotid artery, chemotherapy is infused into the same artery.

13. A 9-year-old patient with cerebral palsy reports to the operating suite for surgical correction of congenital planovalgus flat foot deformity. Subtalar arthroereisis is performed with implant of a Vitallium staple across the lateral subtalar joint.

14. A closed fracture reduction with external fixation of the proximal tibial plateau is performed in the operating suite. A Sheffield ring external fixation device is affixed with the assistance of tensioned Kirchner wires. Adequate alignment confirmed radiologically.

15. The physician repairs a defect in a vertebral disc after a lumbar discectomy for degenerative disc disease. Sutures are fastened to the vertebral disc and a mesh device is positioned adjacent to the defect. Tension is applied to the sutures, which are then attached to hold the mesh adjacent the defect.

16. A patient with cancer throughout the colon is admitted for treatment. The physician makes an abdominal incision, removes the entire colon and rectum, strips the mucosa from the distal rectum, and performs an anastomosis between the terminal ileum and anus.

17. A patient with chronic liver disease undergoes a liver biopsy. Using imaging guidance, the radiologist inserts a catheter into the jugular vein in the neck and directs it into the primary vein in the liver. A small biopsy needle is then inserted through the tube and into the liver to obtain a sample of tissue.

18. This 75-year-old male was admitted through the emergency room with slurred speech and unilateral weakness, which has worsened in severity over the past five hours. MRI and CT revealed acute ischemic cerebral thrombosis.

    Once the location of the stroke-inducing thrombus was identified using angiography, the balloon guide catheter was inserted employing standard catheterization techniques via a femoral artery approach. Under x-ray guidance, the catheter was maneuvered to the carotid artery. A guidewire and the microcatheter were deployed through the balloon guide catheter and then placed just beyond the clot in the appropriate intracranial artery. The retriever device was deployed in order to engage and ensnare the thrombus. Upon capture of the thrombus, the balloon guide catheter was inflated to momentarily halt forward flow during this maneuver. The thrombus was pulled into the balloon guide catheter and completely out of the body. The balloon was then deflated, and blood flow was restored. The patient was taken to the floor in stable condition.

19. A 75-year-old active female who is fourteen years status post total hip replacement with ceramic-on-polyethylene bearing surface complains of increasing pain and inflammation. Radiographic studies reveal wear of the articular bearing surface of the prosthetic joint, necessitating revision of the acetabular component. This was carried out without complications.

20. A 47-year-old male with coronary atherosclerosis was taken to the angioplasty suite where percutaneous transluminal coronary angioplasty (PTCA) was performed on lesions in the left anterior descending artery (LAD) main branch and the diagonal and the circumflex/obtuse marginal bifurcation. A drug-eluting stent in the main branch of the LAD and angioplasty with two additional stents were placed in the branch vessels of the circumflex and obtuse marginal bifurcation of this vessel utilizing a crush technique.

Answer Key can be found in the back of the book.

A

- **AAT** (alpha-1 antitrypsin) deficiency 273.4
- **AAV (disease) (illness) (infection)** — *see* Human immunodeficiency virus (disease) (illness) (infection)
- **Abactio** — *see* Abortion, induced
- **Abactus venter** — *see* Abortion, induced
- **Abarognosis** 781.99
- **Abasia** (-astasia) 307.9
  - atactica 781.3
  - choreic 781.3
  - hysterical 300.11
  - paroxysmal trepidant 781.3
  - spastic 781.3
  - trembling 781.3
  - trepidans 781.3
- **Abderhalden-Kaufmann-Lignac syndrome** (cystinosis) 270.0
- **Abdomen, abdominal** — *see also* condition
  - accordion 306.4
  - acute 789.0 ☑
  - angina 557.1
  - burst 868.00
  - convulsive equivalent (*see also* Epilepsy) 345.5 ☑
  - heart 746.87
  - muscle deficiency syndrome 756.79
  - obstipum 756.79
- **Abdominalgia** 789.0 ☑
  - periodic 277.31
- **Abduction contracture, hip or other joint** — *see* Contraction, joint
- **Abercrombie's syndrome** (amyloid degeneration) 277.39
- **Aberrant** (congenital) — *see also* Malposition, congenital
  - adrenal gland 759.1
  - blood vessel NEC 747.60
    - arteriovenous NEC 747.60
    - cerebrovascular 747.81
    - gastrointestinal 747.61
    - lower limb 747.64
    - renal 747.62
    - spinal 747.82
    - upper limb 747.63
  - breast 757.6
  - endocrine gland NEC 759.2
  - gastrointestinal vessel (peripheral) 747.61
  - hepatic duct 751.69
  - lower limb vessel (peripheral) 747.64
  - pancreas 751.7
  - parathyroid gland 759.2
  - peripheral vascular vessel NEC 747.60
  - pituitary gland (pharyngeal) 759.2
  - renal blood vessel 747.62
  - sebaceous glands, mucous membrane, mouth 750.26
  - spinal vessel 747.82
  - spleen 759.0
  - testis (descent) 752.51
  - thymus gland 759.2
  - thyroid gland 759.2
  - upper limb vessel (peripheral) 747.63
- **Aberratio**
  - lactis 757.6
  - testis 752.51
- **Aberration** — *see also* Anomaly
  - chromosome — *see* Anomaly, chromosome(s)
  - distantial 368.9
  - mental (*see also* Disorder, mental, nonpsychotic) 300.9
- **Abetalipoproteinemia** 272.5
- **Abionarce** 780.79
- **Abiotrophy** 799.89
- **Ablatio**
  - placentae — *see* Placenta, ablatio
  - retinae (*see also* Detachment, retina) 361.9
- **Ablation**
  - pituitary (gland) (with hypofunction) 253.7
  - placenta — *see* Placenta, ablatio
- **Ablation** — *continued*
  - uterus 621.8
- **Ablepharia, ablepharon, ablephary** 743.62
- **Ablepsia** — *see* Blindness
- **Ablepsy** — *see* Blindness
- **Ablutomania** 300.3
- **Abnormal, abnormality, abnormalities** — *see also* Anomaly
  - acid-base balance 276.4
    - fetus or newborn — *see* Distress, fetal
  - adaptation curve, dark 368.63
  - alveolar ridge 525.9
  - amnion 658.9 ☑
    - affecting fetus or newborn 762.9
  - anatomical relationship NEC 759.9
  - apertures, congenital, diaphragm 756.6
  - auditory perception NEC 388.40
  - autosomes NEC 758.5
    - 13 758.1
    - 18 758.2
    - 21 or 22 758.0
    - D_1 758.1
    - E_3 758.2
    - G 758.0
  - ballistocardiogram 794.39
  - basal metabolic rate (BMR) 794.7
  - biosynthesis, testicular androgen 257.2
  - blood level (of)
    - cobalt 790.6
    - copper 790.6
    - iron 790.6
    - lead 790.6
    - lithium 790.6
    - magnesium 790.6
    - mineral 790.6
    - zinc 790.6
  - blood pressure
    - elevated (without diagnosis of hypertension) 796.2
    - low (*see also* Hypotension) 458.9
      - reading (incidental) (isolated) (nonspecific) 796.3
  - blood sugar 790.29
  - bowel sounds 787.5
  - breathing behavior — *see* Respiration
  - caloric test 794.19
  - cervix (acquired) NEC 622.9
    - congenital 752.40
    - in pregnancy or childbirth 654.6 ☑
      - causing obstructed labor 660.2 ☑
        - affecting fetus or newborn 763.1
  - chemistry, blood NEC 790.6
  - chest sounds 786.7
  - chorion 658.9 ☑
    - affecting fetus or newborn 762.9
  - chromosomal NEC 758.89
    - analysis, nonspecific result 795.2
    - autosomes (*see also* Abnormal, autosomes NEC) 758.5
    - fetal, (suspected) affecting management of pregnancy 655.1 ☑
    - sex 758.81
  - clinical findings NEC 796.4
  - communication — *see* Fistula
  - configuration of pupils 379.49
  - coronary
    - artery 746.85
    - vein 746.9
  - cortisol-binding globulin 255.8
  - course, Eustachian tube 744.24
  - creatinine clearance 794.4
  - dentofacial NEC 524.9
    - functional 524.50
    - specified type NEC 524.89
  - development, developmental NEC 759.9
    - bone 756.9
    - central nervous system 742.9
  - direction, teeth 524.30
- **Abnormal, abnormality, abnormalities** — *see also* Anomaly — *continued*
  - Dynia (*see also* Defect, coagulation) 286.9
  - Ebstein 746.2
  - echocardiogram 793.2
  - echoencephalogram 794.01
  - echogram NEC — *see* Findings, abnormal, structure
  - electrocardiogram (ECG) (EKG) 794.31
  - electroencephalogram (EEG) 794.02
  - electromyogram (EMG) 794.17
    - ocular 794.14
  - electro-oculogram (EOG) 794.12
  - electroretinogram (ERG) 794.11
  - erythrocytes 289.9
    - congenital, with perinatal jaundice 282.9 *[774.0]*
  - Eustachian valve 746.9
  - excitability under minor stress 301.9
  - fat distribution 782.9
  - feces 787.7
  - fetal heart rate — *see* Distress, fetal
  - fetus NEC
    - affecting management of pregnancy — *see* Pregnancy, management affected by, fetal
    - causing disproportion 653.7 ☑
      - affecting fetus or newborn 763.1
      - causing obstructed labor 660.1 ☑
        - affecting fetus or newborn 763.1
  - findings without manifest disease — *see* Findings, abnormal
  - fluid
    - amniotic 792.3
    - cerebrospinal 792.0
    - peritoneal 792.9
    - pleural 792.9
    - synovial 792.9
    - vaginal 792.9
  - forces of labor NEC 661.9 ☑
    - affecting fetus or newborn 763.7
  - form, teeth 520.2
  - function studies
    - auditory 794.15
    - bladder 794.9
    - brain 794.00
    - cardiovascular 794.30
    - endocrine NEC 794.6
    - kidney 794.4
    - liver 794.8
    - nervous system
      - central 794.00
      - peripheral 794.19
    - oculomotor 794.14
    - pancreas 794.9
    - placenta 794.9
    - pulmonary 794.2
    - retina 794.11
    - special senses 794.19
    - spleen 794.9
    - thyroid 794.5
    - vestibular 794.16
  - gait 781.2
    - hysterical 300.11
  - gastrin secretion 251.5
  - globulin
    - cortisol-binding 255.8
    - thyroid-binding 246.8
  - glucagon secretion 251.4
  - glucose 790.29
    - in pregnancy, childbirth, or puerperium 648.8 ☑
      - fetus or newborn 775.0
    - non-fasting 790.29
  - gravitational (G) forces or states 994.9
  - hair NEC 704.2
  - hard tissue formation in pulp 522.3
  - head movement 781.0
- **Abnormal, abnormality, abnormalities** — *see also* Anomaly — *continued*
  - heart
    - rate
      - fetus, affecting liveborn infant
        - before the onset of labor 763.81
        - during labor 763.82
        - unspecified as to time of onset 763.83
      - intrauterine
        - before the onset of labor 763.81
        - during labor 763.82
        - unspecified as to time of onset 763.83
      - newborn
        - before the onset of labor 763.81
        - during labor 763.82
        - unspecified as to time of onset 763.83
    - shadow 793.2
    - sounds NEC 785.3
  - hemoglobin (*see also* Disease, hemoglobin) 282.7
    - trait — *see* Trait, hemoglobin, abnormal
  - hemorrhage, uterus — *see* Hemorrhage, uterus
  - histology NEC 795.4
  - increase
    - in
      - appetite 783.6
      - development 783.9
  - involuntary movement 781.0
  - jaw closure 524.51
  - karyotype 795.2
  - knee jerk 796.1
  - labor NEC 661.9 ☑
    - affecting fetus or newborn 763.7
  - laboratory findings — *see* Findings, abnormal
  - length, organ or site, congenital — *see* Distortion
  - liver function test 790.6
  - loss of height 781.91
  - loss of weight 783.21
  - lung shadow 793.1
  - mammogram 793.80
    - calcification 793.89
    - calculus 793.89
    - microcalcification 793.81
  - Mantoux test 795.5
  - membranes (fetal)
    - affecting fetus or newborn 762.9
    - complicating pregnancy 658.8 ☑
  - menstruation — *see* Menstruation
  - metabolism (*see also* condition) 783.9
  - movement 781.0
    - disorder NEC 333.90
      - sleep related, unspecified 780.58
      - specified NEC 333.99
    - head 781.0
    - involuntary 781.0
    - specified type NEC 333.99
  - muscle contraction, localized 728.85
  - myoglobin (Aberdeen) (Annapolis) 289.9
  - narrowness, eyelid 743.62
  - optokinetic response 379.57
  - organs or tissues of pelvis NEC
    - in pregnancy or childbirth 654.9 ☑
      - affecting fetus or newborn 763.89
      - causing obstructed labor 660.2 ☑
        - affecting fetus or newborn 763.1
  - origin — *see* Malposition, congenital
  - palmar creases 757.2
  - Papanicolaou (smear)
    - anus 796.70

Note — Use the following fifth-digit subclassification with categories 634–637:

0 unspecified
1 incomplete
2 complete

- **Abortion** — *continued*
  - failed — *continued*
    - with — *continued*
      - specified complication NEC 638.7
      - toxemia 638.3
      - unspecified complication(s) 638.8
      - urinary tract infection 638.7
  - fetal indication — *see* Abortion, legal
  - fetus 779.6
  - following threatened abortion — *see* Abortion, by type
  - habitual or recurrent (care during pregnancy) 646.3 ☑
    - with current abortion (*see also* Abortion, spontaneous) 634.9 ☑
      - affecting fetus or newborn 761.8
    - without current pregnancy 629.81
  - homicidal — *see* Abortion, illegal
  - illegal 636.9 ☑
    - with
      - damage to pelvic organ (laceration) (rupture) (tear) 636.2 ☑
      - embolism (air) (amniotic fluid) (blood clot) (pulmonary) (pyemic) (septic) (soap) 636.6 ☑
      - genital tract and pelvic infection 636.0 ☑
      - hemorrhage, delayed or excessive 636.1 ☑
      - metabolic disorder 636.4 ☑
      - renal failure 636.3 ☑
      - sepsis (genital tract) (pelvic organ) 636.0 ☑
        - urinary tract 636.7 ☑
      - shock (postoperative) (septic) 636.5 ☑
      - specified complication NEC 636.7 ☑
      - toxemia 636.3 ☑
      - unspecified complication(s) 636.8 ☑
      - urinary tract infection 636.7 ☑
    - fetus 779.6
  - induced 637.9 ☑
    - illegal — *see* Abortion, illegal
    - legal indications — *see* Abortion, legal
    - medical indications — *see* Abortion, legal
    - therapeutic — *see* Abortion, legal
  - late — *see* Abortion, spontaneous
  - legal (legal indication) (medical indication) (under medical supervision) 635.9 ☑
    - with
      - damage to pelvic organ (laceration) (rupture) (tear) 635.2 ☑
      - embolism (air) (amniotic fluid) (blood clot) (pulmonary) (pyemic) (septic) (soap) 635.6 ☑
      - genital tract and pelvic infection 635.0 ☑
      - hemorrhage, delayed or excessive 635.1 ☑
      - metabolic disorder 635.4 ☑
      - renal failure (acute) 635.3 ☑
      - sepsis (genital tract) (pelvic organ) 635.0 ☑
        - urinary tract 635.7 ☑
      - shock (postoperative) (septic) 635.5 ☑
      - specified complication NEC 635.7 ☑
      - toxemia 635.3 ☑
      - unspecified complication(s) 635.8 ☑
      - urinary tract infection 635.7 ☑
    - fetus 779.6

- **Abortion** — *continued*
  - medical indication — *see* Abortion, legal
  - mental hygiene problem — *see* Abortion, legal
  - missed 632
  - operative — *see* Abortion, legal
  - psychiatric indication — *see* Abortion, legal
  - recurrent — *see* Abortion, spontaneous
  - self-induced — *see* Abortion, illegal
  - septic — *see* Abortion, by type, with sepsis
  - spontaneous 634.9 ☑
    - with
      - damage to pelvic organ (laceration) (rupture) (tear) 634.2 ☑
      - embolism (air) (amniotic fluid) (blood clot) (pulmonary) (pyemic) (septic) (soap) 634.6 ☑
      - genital tract and pelvic infection 634.0 ☑
      - hemorrhage, delayed or excessive 634.1 ☑
      - metabolic disorder 634.4 ☑
      - renal failure 634.3 ☑
      - sepsis (genital tract) (pelvic organ) 634.0 ☑
        - urinary tract 634.7 ☑
      - shock (postoperative) (septic) 634.5 ☑
      - specified complication NEC 634.7 ☑
      - toxemia 634.3 ☑
      - unspecified complication(s) 634.8 ☑
      - urinary tract infection 634.7 ☑
    - fetus 761.8
    - threatened 640.0 ☑
      - affecting fetus or newborn 762.1
  - surgical — *see* Abortion, legal
  - therapeutic — *see* Abortion, legal
  - threatened 640.0 ☑
    - affecting fetus or newborn 762.1
  - tubal — *see* Pregnancy, tubal
  - voluntary — *see* Abortion, legal
- **Abortus fever** 023.9
- **Aboulomania** 301.6
- **Abrachia** 755.20
- **Abrachiatism** 755.20
- **Abrachiocephalia** 759.89
- **Abrachiocephalus** 759.89
- **Abrami's disease** (acquired hemolytic jaundice) 283.9
- **Abramov-Fiedler myocarditis** (acute isolated myocarditis) 422.91
- **Abrasion** — *see also* Injury, superficial, by site
  - cornea 918.1
  - dental 521.20
    - extending into
      - dentine 521.22
      - pulp 521.23
    - generalized 521.25
    - limited to enamel 521.21
    - localized 521.24
  - teeth, tooth (dentifrice) (habitual) (hard tissues) (occupational) (ritual) (traditional) (wedge defect) (*see also* Abrasion, dental) 521.20
- **Abrikossov's tumor** (M9580/0) — *see also* Neoplasm, connective tissue, benign
  - malignant (M9580/3) — *see* Neoplasm, connective tissue, malignant
- **Abrism** 988.8
- **Abruption, placenta** — *see* Placenta, abruptio
- **Abruptio placentae** — *see* Placenta, abruptio

- **Abscess** (acute) (chronic) (infectional) (lymphangitic) (metastatic) (multiple) (pyogenic) (septic) (with lymphangitis) — *see also* Cellulitis 682.9
  - abdomen, abdominal
    - cavity 567.22
    - wall 682.2
  - abdominopelvic 567.22
  - accessory sinus (chronic) (*see also* Sinusitis) 473.9
  - adrenal (capsule) (gland) 255.8
  - alveolar 522.5
    - with sinus 522.7
  - amebic 006.3
    - bladder 006.8
    - brain (with liver or lung abscess) 006.5
    - liver (without mention of brain or lung abscess) 006.3
      - with
        - brain abscess (and lung abscess) 006.5
        - lung abscess 006.4
    - lung (with liver abscess) 006.4
      - with brain abscess 006.5
    - seminal vesicle 006.8
    - specified site NEC 006.8
    - spleen 006.8
  - anaerobic 040.0
  - ankle 682.6
  - anorectal 566
  - antecubital space 682.3
  - antrum (chronic) (Highmore) (*see also* Sinusitis, maxillary) 473.0
  - anus 566
  - apical (tooth) 522.5
    - with sinus (alveolar) 522.7
  - appendix 540.1
  - areola (acute) (chronic) (nonpuerperal) 611.0
    - puerperal, postpartum 675.1 ☑
  - arm (any part, above wrist) 682.3
  - artery (wall) 447.2
  - atheromatous 447.2
  - auditory canal (external) 380.10
  - auricle (ear) (staphylococcal) (streptococcal) 380.10
  - axilla, axillary (region) 682.3
    - lymph gland or node 683
  - back (any part) 682.2
  - Bartholin's gland 616.3
    - with
      - abortion — *see* Abortion, by type, with sepsis
      - ectopic pregnancy (*see also* categories 633.0–633.9) 639.0
      - molar pregnancy (*see also* categories 630–632) 639.0
    - complicating pregnancy or puerperium 646.6 ☑
    - following
      - abortion 639.0
      - ectopic or molar pregnancy 639.0
  - bartholinian 616.3
  - Bezold's 383.01
  - bile, biliary, duct or tract (*see also* Cholecystitis) 576.8
  - bilharziasis 120.1
  - bladder (wall) 595.89
    - amebic 006.8
  - bone (subperiosteal) (*see also* Osteomyelitis) 730.0 ☑
    - accessory sinus (chronic) (*see also* Sinusitis) 473.9
    - acute 730.0 ☑
    - chronic or old 730.1 ☑
    - jaw (lower) (upper) 526.4
    - mastoid — *see* Mastoiditis, acute
    - petrous (*see also* Petrositis) 383.20
    - spinal (tuberculous) (*see also* Tuberculosis) 015.0 ☑ *[730.88]*
      - nontuberculous 730.08
  - bowel 569.5

- **Abscess** — *see also* Cellulitis — *continued*
  - brain (any part) 324.0
    - amebic (with liver or lung abscess) 006.5
    - cystic 324.0
    - late effect — *see* category 326
    - otogenic 324.0
    - tuberculous (*see also* Tuberculosis) 013.3 ☑
  - breast (acute) (chronic) (nonpuerperal) 611.0
    - newborn 771.5
    - puerperal, postpartum 675.1 ☑
    - tuberculous (*see also* Tuberculosis) 017.9 ☑
  - broad ligament (chronic) (*see also* Disease, pelvis, inflammatory) 614.4
    - acute 614.3
  - Brodie's (chronic) (localized) (*see also* Osteomyelitis) 730.1 ☑
  - bronchus 519.19
  - buccal cavity 528.3
  - bulbourethral gland 597.0
  - bursa 727.89
    - pharyngeal 478.29
  - buttock 682.5
  - canaliculus, breast 611.0
  - canthus 372.20
  - cartilage 733.99
  - cecum 569.5
    - with appendicitis 540.1
  - cerebellum, cerebellar 324.0
    - late effect — *see* category 326
  - cerebral (embolic) 324.0
    - late effect — *see* category 326
  - cervical (neck region) 682.1
    - lymph gland or node 683
    - stump (*see also* Cervicitis) 616.0
  - cervix (stump) (uteri) (*see also* Cervicitis) 616.0
  - cheek, external 682.0
    - inner 528.3
  - chest 510.9
    - with fistula 510.0
    - wall 682.2
  - chin 682.0
  - choroid 363.00
  - ciliary body 364.3
  - circumtonsillar 475
  - cold (tuberculous) (*see also* Tuberculosis, abscess)
    - articular — *see* Tuberculosis, joint
  - colon (wall) 569.5
  - colostomy or enterostomy 569.61
  - conjunctiva 372.00
  - connective tissue NEC 682.9
  - cornea 370.55
    - with ulcer 370.00
  - corpus
    - cavernosum 607.2
    - luteum (*see also* Salpingo-oophoritis) 614.2
  - Cowper's gland 597.0
  - cranium 324.0
  - cul-de-sac (Douglas') (posterior) (*see also* Disease, pelvis, inflammatory) 614.4
    - acute 614.3
  - dental 522.5
    - with sinus (alveolar) 522.7
  - dentoalveolar 522.5
    - with sinus (alveolar) 522.7
  - diaphragm, diaphragmatic 567.22
  - digit NEC 681.9
  - Douglas' cul-de-sac or pouch (*see also* Disease, pelvis, inflammatory) 614.4
    - acute 614.3
  - Dubois' 090.5
  - ductless gland 259.8
  - ear
    - acute 382.00
    - external 380.10
    - inner 386.30

- **Abscess** — *see also* Cellulitis — *continued*
  - peritoneum, peritoneal — *continued*
    - with — *continued*
      - molar pregnancy (*see also* categories 630–632) 639.0
    - following
      - abortion 639.0
      - ectopic or molar pregnancy 639.0
    - pelvic, female (*see also* Disease, pelvis, inflammatory) 614.4
      - acute 614.3
    - postoperative 998.59
    - puerperal, postpartum, childbirth 670.0 ☑
    - tuberculous (*see also* Tuberculosis) 014.0 ☑
  - peritonsillar 475
  - perityphlic 540.1
  - periureteral 593.89
  - periurethral 597.0
    - gonococcal (acute) 098.0
      - chronic or duration of 2 months or over 098.2
  - periuterine (*see also* Disease, pelvis, inflammatory) 614.4
    - acute 614.3
  - perivesical 595.89
  - pernicious NEC 682.9
  - petrous bone — *see* Petrositis
  - phagedenic NEC 682.9
    - chancroid 099.0
  - pharynx, pharyngeal (lateral) 478.29
  - phlegmonous NEC 682.9
  - pilonidal 685.0
  - pituitary (gland) 253.8
  - pleura 510.9
    - with fistula 510.0
  - popliteal 682.6
  - postanal 566
  - postcecal 540.1
  - postlaryngeal 478.79
  - postnasal 478.19
  - postpharyngeal 478.24
  - posttonsillar 475
  - posttyphoid 002.0
  - Pott's (*see also* Tuberculosis) 015.0 ☑ *[730.88]*
  - pouch of Douglas (chronic) (*see also* Disease, pelvis, inflammatory) 614.4
  - premammary — *see* Abscess, breast
  - prepatellar 682.6
  - prostate (*see also* Prostatitis) 601.2
    - gonococcal (acute) 098.12
      - chronic or duration of 2 months or over 098.32
  - psoas 567.31
    - nontuberculous 728.89
    - tuberculous (*see also* Tuberculosis) 015.0 ☑ *[730.88]*
  - pterygopalatine fossa 682.8
  - pubis 682.2
  - puerperal — *see* Puerperal, abscess, by site
  - pulmonary — *see* Abscess, lung
  - pulp, pulpal (dental) 522.0
    - finger 681.01
    - toe 681.10
  - pyemic — *see* Septicemia
  - pyloric valve 535.0 ☑
  - rectovaginal septum 569.5
  - rectovesical 595.89
  - rectum 566
  - regional NEC 682.9
  - renal (*see also* Abscess, kidney) 590.2
  - retina 363.00
  - retrobulbar 376.01
  - retrocecal 567.22
  - retrolaryngeal 478.79
  - retromammary — *see* Abscess, breast
  - retroperineal 682.2
  - retroperitoneal 567.38
    - postprocedural 998.59
  - retropharyngeal 478.24
    - tuberculous (*see also* Tuberculosis) 012.8 ☑
  - retrorectal 566
  - retrouterine (*see also* Disease, pelvis, inflammatory) 614.4
    - acute 614.3
  - retrovesical 595.89
  - root, tooth 522.5
    - with sinus (alveolar) 522.7
  - round ligament (*see also* Disease, pelvis, inflammatory) 614.4
    - acute 614.3
  - rupture (spontaneous) NEC 682.9
  - sacrum (tuberculous) (*see also* Tuberculosis) 015.0 ☑ *[730.88]*
    - nontuberculous 730.08
  - salivary duct or gland 527.3
  - scalp (any part) 682.8
  - scapular 730.01
  - sclera 379.09
  - scrofulous (*see also* Tuberculosis) 017.2 ☑
  - scrotum 608.4
  - seminal vesicle 608.0
    - amebic 006.8
  - septal, dental 522.5
    - with sinus (alveolar) 522.7
  - septum (nasal) 478.19
  - serous (*see also* Periostitis) 730.3 ☑
  - shoulder 682.3
  - side 682.2
  - sigmoid 569.5
  - sinus (accessory) (chronic) (nasal) (*see also* Sinusitis) 473.9
    - intracranial venous (any) 324.0
      - late effect — *see* category 326
  - Skene's duct or gland 597.0
  - skin NEC 682.9
    - tuberculous (primary) (*see also* Tuberculosis) 017.0 ☑
  - sloughing NEC 682.9
  - specified site NEC 682.8
    - amebic 006.8
  - spermatic cord 608.4
  - sphenoidal (sinus) (*see also* Sinusitis, sphenoidal) 473.3
  - spinal
    - cord (any part) (staphylococcal) 324.1
      - tuberculous (*see also* Tuberculosis) 013.5 ☑
    - epidural 324.1
  - spine (column) (tuberculous) (*see also* Tuberculosis) 015.0 ☑ *[730.88]*
    - nontuberculous 730.08
  - spleen 289.59
    - amebic 006.8
  - staphylococcal NEC 682.9
  - stitch 998.59
  - stomach (wall) 535.0 ☑
  - strumous (tuberculous) (*see also* Tuberculosis) 017.2 ☑
  - subarachnoid 324.9
    - brain 324.0
    - cerebral 324.0
    - late effect — *see* category 326
    - spinal cord 324.1
  - subareolar (*see also* Abscess, breast)
    - puerperal, postpartum 675.1 ☑
  - subcecal 540.1
  - subcutaneous NEC 682.9
  - subdiaphragmatic 567.22
  - subdorsal 682.2
  - subdural 324.9
    - brain 324.0
    - late effect — *see* category 326
    - spinal cord 324.1
  - subgaleal 682.8
  - subhepatic 567.22
  - sublingual 528.3
    - gland 527.3
  - submammary — *see* Abscess, breast
  - submandibular (region) (space) (triangle) 682.0
    - gland 527.3
  - submaxillary (region) 682.0
    - gland 527.3
  - submental (pyogenic) 682.0
    - gland 527.3
  - subpectoral 682.2
  - subperiosteal — *see* Abscess, bone
  - subperitoneal 567.22
  - subphrenic (*see also* Abscess, peritoneum) 567.22
    - postoperative 998.59
  - subscapular 682.2
  - subungual 681.9
  - suburethral 597.0
  - sudoriparous 705.89
  - suppurative NEC 682.9
  - supraclavicular (fossa) 682.3
  - suprahepatic 567.22
  - suprapelvic (*see also* Disease, pelvis, inflammatory) 614.4
    - acute 614.3
  - suprapubic 682.2
  - suprarenal (capsule) (gland) 255.8
  - sweat gland 705.89
  - syphilitic 095.8
  - teeth, tooth (root) 522.5
    - with sinus (alveolar) 522.7
    - supporting structures NEC 523.30
  - temple 682.0
  - temporal region 682.0
  - temporosphenoidal 324.0
    - late effect — *see* category 326
  - tendon (sheath) 727.89
  - testicle — *see* Orchitis
  - thecal 728.89
  - thigh (acquired) 682.6
  - thorax 510.9
    - with fistula 510.0
  - throat 478.29
  - thumb (intrathecal) (periosteal) (subcutaneous) (subcuticular) 681.00
  - thymus (gland) 254.1
  - thyroid (gland) 245.0
  - toe (any) (intrathecal) (periosteal) (subcutaneous) (subcuticular) 681.10
  - tongue (staphylococcal) 529.0
  - tonsil(s) (lingual) 475
  - tonsillopharyngeal 475
  - tooth, teeth (root) 522.5
    - with sinus (alveolar) 522.7
    - supporting structure NEC 523.30
  - trachea 478.9
  - trunk 682.2
  - tubal (*see also* Salpingo-oophoritis) 614.2
  - tuberculous — *see* Tuberculosis, abscess
  - tubo-ovarian (*see also* Salpingo-oophoritis) 614.2
  - tunica vaginalis 608.4
  - umbilicus NEC 682.2
    - newborn 771.4
  - upper arm 682.3
  - upper respiratory 478.9
  - urachus 682.2
  - urethra (gland) 597.0
  - urinary 597.0
  - uterus, uterine (wall) (*see also* Endometritis) 615.9
    - ligament (*see also* Disease, pelvis, inflammatory) 614.4
      - acute 614.3
    - neck (*see also* Cervicitis) 616.0
  - uvula 528.3
  - vagina (wall) (*see also* Vaginitis) 616.10
  - vaginorectal (*see also* Vaginitis) 616.10
  - vas deferens 608.4
  - vermiform appendix 540.1
  - vertebra (column) (tuberculous) (*see also* Tuberculosis) 015.0 ☑ *[730.88]*
    - nontuberculous 730.0 ☑
  - vesical 595.89
  - vesicouterine pouch (*see also* Disease, pelvis, inflammatory) 614.4
  - vitreous (humor) (pneumococcal) 360.04
  - vocal cord 478.5
  - von Bezold's 383.01
  - vulva 616.4
    - complicating pregnancy, childbirth, or puerperium 646.6 ☑
  - vulvovaginal gland (*see also* Vaginitis) 616.3
  - web-space 682.4
  - wrist 682.4
- **Absence** (organ or part) (complete or partial)
  - acoustic nerve 742.8
  - adrenal (gland) (congenital) 759.1
    - acquired V45.79
  - albumin (blood) 273.8
  - alimentary tract (complete) (congenital) (partial) 751.8
    - lower 751.5
    - upper 750.8
  - alpha-fucosidase 271.8
  - alveolar process (acquired) 525.8
    - congenital 750.26
  - anus, anal (canal) (congenital) 751.2
  - aorta (congenital) 747.22
  - aortic valve (congenital) 746.89
  - appendix, congenital 751.2
  - arm (acquired) V49.60
    - above elbow V49.66
    - below elbow V49.65
    - congenital (*see also* Deformity, reduction, upper limb) 755.20
      - lower — *see* Absence, forearm, congenital
      - upper (complete) (partial) (with absence of distal elements, incomplete) 755.24
        - with
          - complete absence of distal elements 755.21
          - forearm (incomplete) 755.23
  - artery (congenital) (peripheral) NEC (*see also* Anomaly, peripheral vascular system) 747.60
    - brain 747.81
    - cerebral 747.81
    - coronary 746.85
    - pulmonary 747.3
    - umbilical 747.5
  - atrial septum 745.69
  - auditory canal (congenital) (external) 744.01
  - auricle (ear) (with stenosis or atresia of auditory canal), congenital 744.01
  - bile, biliary duct (common) or passage (congenital) 751.61
  - bladder (acquired) V45.74
    - congenital 753.8
  - bone (congenital) NEC 756.9
    - marrow 284.9
      - acquired (secondary) 284.89
      - congenital 284.09
      - hereditary 284.09
      - idiopathic 284.9
    - skull 756.0
  - bowel sounds 787.5
  - brain 740.0
    - specified part 742.2
  - breast(s) (acquired) V45.71
    - congenital 757.6
  - broad ligament (congenital) 752.19
  - bronchus (congenital) 748.3
  - calvarium, calvaria (skull) 756.0

Index

Absence — Absence

Absence — *continued*
- radius, congenital — *continued*
  - with
    - complete absence of distal elements 755.21
    - ulna 755.25
      - with
        - complete absence of distal elements 755.21
        - humerus (incomplete) 755.23
- ray, congenital 755.4
  - lower limb (complete) (partial) (*see also* Deformity, reduction, lower limb) 755.38
    - meaning all rays 755.31
    - transverse 755.31
  - upper limb (complete) (partial) (*see also* Deformity, reduction, upper limb) 755.28
    - meaning all rays 755.21
    - transverse 755.21
- rectum (congenital) 751.2
  - acquired V45.79
- red cell 284.9
  - acquired (secondary) 284.81
  - congenital 284.01
  - hereditary 284.01
  - idiopathic 284.9
- respiratory organ (congenital) NEC 748.9
- rib (acquired) 738.3
  - congenital 756.3
- roof of orbit (congenital) 742.0
- round ligament (congenital) 752.89
- sacrum, congenital 756.13
- salivary gland(s) (congenital) 750.21
- scapula 755.59
- scrotum, congenital 752.89
- seminal tract or duct (congenital) 752.89
  - acquired V45.77
- septum (congenital) (*see also* Imperfect, closure, septum)
  - atrial 745.69
    - and ventricular 745.7
  - between aorta and pulmonary artery 745.0
  - ventricular 745.3
    - and atrial 745.7
- sex chromosomes 758.81
- shoulder girdle, congenital (complete) (partial) 755.59
- skin (congenital) 757.39
- skull bone 756.0
  - with
    - anencephalus 740.0
    - encephalocele 742.0
    - hydrocephalus 742.3
      - with spina bifida (*see also* Spina bifida) 741.0 ☑
    - microcephalus 742.1
- spermatic cord (congenital) 752.89
- spinal cord 742.59
- spine, congenital 756.13
- spleen (congenital) 759.0
  - acquired V45.79
- sternum, congenital 756.3
- stomach (acquired) (partial) (postoperative) V45.75
  - with postgastric surgery syndrome 564.2
  - congenital 750.7
- submaxillary gland(s) (congenital) 750.21
- superior vena cava (congenital) 747.49
- tarsal(s), congenital (complete) (partial) (with absence of distal elements, incomplete) (*see also* Deformity, reduction, lower limb) 755.38
- teeth, tooth (congenital) 520.0
  - with abnormal spacing 524.30
  - acquired 525.10
    - with malocclusion 524.30
    - due to
      - caries 525.13

Absence — *continued*
- teeth, tooth — *continued*
  - acquired — *continued*
    - due to — *continued*
      - extraction 525.10
      - periodontal disease 525.12
      - trauma 525.11
- tendon (congenital) 756.81
- testis (congenital) 752.89
  - acquired V45.77
- thigh (acquired) 736.89
- thumb (acquired) V49.61
  - congenital 755.29
- thymus gland (congenital) 759.2
- thyroid (gland) (surgical) 246.8
  - with hypothyroidism 244.0
  - cartilage, congenital 748.3
  - congenital 243
- tibia, congenital (complete) (partial) (with absence of distal elements, incomplete) (*see also* Deformity, reduction, lower limb) 755.36
  - with
    - complete absence of distal elements 755.31
    - fibula 755.35
      - with
        - complete absence of distal elements 755.31
        - femur (incomplete) 755.33
          - with complete absence of distal elements 755.31
- toe (acquired) V49.72
  - congenital (complete) (partial) 755.39
    - meaning all toes 755.31
    - transverse 755.31
  - great V49.71
- tongue (congenital) 750.11
- tooth, teeth (congenital) 520.0
  - with abnormal spacing 524.30
  - acquired 525.10
    - with malocclusion 524.30
    - due to
      - caries 525.13
      - extraction 525.10
      - periodontal disease 525.12
      - trauma 525.11
- trachea (cartilage) (congenital) (rings) 748.3
- transverse aortic arch (congenital) 747.21
- tricuspid valve 746.1
- ulna, congenital (complete) (partial) (with absence of distal elements, incomplete) (*see also* Deformity, reduction, upper limb) 755.27
  - with
    - complete absence of distal elements 755.21
    - radius 755.25
      - with
        - complete absence of distal elements 755.21
        - humerus (incomplete) 755.23
- umbilical artery (congenital) 747.5
- ureter (congenital) 753.4
  - acquired V45.74
- urethra, congenital 753.8
  - acquired V45.74
- urinary system, part NEC, congenital 753.8
  - acquired V45.74
- uterus (acquired) V88.01
  - with remaining cervical stump V88.02
  - and cervix V88.01
  - congenital 752.3
- uvula (congenital) 750.26
- vagina, congenital 752.49
  - acquired V45.77
- vas deferens (congenital) 752.89
  - acquired V45.77

Absence — *continued*
- vein (congenital) (peripheral) NEC (*see also* Anomaly, peripheral vascular system) 747.60
  - brain 747.81
  - great 747.49
  - portal 747.49
  - pulmonary 747.49
- vena cava (congenital) (inferior) (superior) 747.49
- ventral horn cell 742.59
- ventricular septum 745.3
- vermis of cerebellum 742.2
- vertebra, congenital 756.13
- vulva, congenital 752.49

Absentia epileptica — *see also* Epilepsy 345.0 ☑

Absinthemia — *see also* Dependence 304.6 ☑

Absinthism — *see also* Dependence 304.6 ☑

Absorbent system disease 459.89

Absorption
- alcohol, through placenta or breast milk 760.71
- antibiotics, through placenta or breast milk 760.74
- anticonvulsants, through placenta or breast milk 760.77
- antifungals, through placenta or breast milk 760.74
- anti-infective, through placenta or breast milk 760.74
- antimetabolics, through placenta or breast milk 760.78
- chemical NEC 989.9
  - specified chemical or substance — *see* Table of Drugs and Chemicals
  - through placenta or breast milk (fetus or newborn) 760.70
    - alcohol 760.71
    - anticonvulsants 760.77
    - antifungals 760.74
    - anti-infective agents 760.74
    - antimetabolics 760.78
    - cocaine 760.75
    - "crack" 760.75
    - diethylstilbestrol [DES] 760.76
    - hallucinogenic agents 760.73
    - medicinal agents NEC 760.79
    - narcotics 760.72
    - obstetric anesthetic or analgesic drug 763.5
    - specified agent NEC 760.79
    - suspected, affecting management of pregnancy 655.5 ☑
- cocaine, through placenta or breast milk 760.75
- drug NEC (*see also* Reaction, drug)
  - through placenta or breast milk (fetus or newborn) 760.70
    - alcohol 760.71
    - anticonvulsants 760.77
    - antifungals 760.74
    - anti-infective agents 760.74
    - antimetabolics 760.78
    - cocaine 760.75
    - "crack" 760.75
    - diethylstilbestrol [DES] 760.76
    - hallucinogenic agents 760.73
    - medicinal agents NEC 760.79
    - narcotics 760.72
    - obstetric anesthetic or analgesic drug 763.5
    - specified agent NEC 760.79
    - suspected, affecting management of pregnancy 655.5 ☑
- fat, disturbance 579.8
- hallucinogenic agents, through placenta or breast milk 760.73
- immune sera, through placenta or breast milk 760.79
- lactose defect 271.3

Absorption — *continued*
- medicinal agents NEC, through placenta or breast milk 760.79
- narcotics, through placenta or breast milk 760.72
- noxious substance — *see* Absorption, chemical
- protein, disturbance 579.8
- pus or septic, general — *see* Septicemia
- quinine, through placenta or breast milk 760.74
- toxic substance — *see* Absorption, chemical
- uremic — *see* Uremia

Abstinence symptoms or syndrome
- alcohol 291.81
- drug 292.0

Abt-Letterer-Siwe syndrome (acute histiocytosis X) (M9722/3) 202.5 ☑

Abulia 799.89

Abulomania 301.6

Abuse
- adult 995.80
  - emotional 995.82
  - multiple forms 995.85
  - neglect (nutritional) 995.84
  - physical 995.81
  - psychological 995.82
  - sexual 995.83
- alcohol — *see* also Alcoholism 305.0 ☑
  - dependent 303.9 ☑
  - non-dependent 305.0 ☑
- child 995.50
  - counseling
    - perpetrator
      - non-parent V62.83
      - parent V61.22
    - victim V61.21
  - emotional 995.51
  - multiple forms 995.59
  - neglect (nutritional) 995.52
  - physical 995.54
    - shaken infant syndrome 995.55
  - psychological 995.51
  - sexual 995.53
- drugs, nondependent 305.9 ☑

> *Note — Use the following fifth-digit subclassification with the following codes: 305.0, 305.2–305.9:*
>
> 0 *unspecified*
>
> 1 *continuous*
>
> 2 *episodic*
>
> 3 *in remission*

  - amphetamine type 305.7 ☑
  - antidepressants 305.8 ☑
  - anxiolytic 305.4 ☑
  - barbiturates 305.4 ☑
  - caffeine 305.9 ☑
  - cannabis 305.2 ☑
  - cocaine type 305.6 ☑
  - hallucinogens 305.3 ☑
  - hashish 305.2 ☑
  - hypnotic 305.4 ☑
  - inhalant 305.9 ☑
  - LSD 305.3 ☑
  - marijuana 305.2 ☑
  - mixed 305.9 ☑
  - morphine type 305.5 ☑
  - opioid type 305.5 ☑
  - phencyclidine (PCP) 305.9 ☑
  - sedative 305.4 ☑
  - specified NEC 305.9 ☑
  - tranquilizers 305.4 ☑
- spouse 995.80
- tobacco 305.1

Acalcerosis 275.40

Acalcicosis 275.40

Acalculia 784.69
- developmental 315.1

Acanthocheilonemiasis 125.4

Acanthocytosis 272.5

Acanthokeratodermia 701.1

Acantholysis 701.8
- bullosa 757.39

Acanthoma (benign) (M8070/0) — *see also* Neoplasm, by site, benign
- malignant (M8070/3) — *see* Neoplasm, by site, malignant

Acanthosis (acquired) (nigricans) 701.2
- adult 701.2
- benign (congenital) 757.39
- congenital 757.39
- glycogenic
  - esophagus 530.89
- juvenile 701.2
- tongue 529.8

Acanthrocytosis 272.5

Acapnia 276.3

Acarbia 276.2

Acardia 759.89

Acardiacus amorphus 759.89

Acardiotrophia 429.1

Acardius 759.89

Acariasis 133.9
- sarcoptic 133.0

Acaridiasis 133.9

Acarinosis 133.9

Acariosis 133.9

Acarodermatitis 133.9
- urticarioides 133.9

Acarophobia 300.29

Acatalasemia 277.89

Acatalasia 277.89

Acatamathesia 784.69

Acataphasia 784.5

Acathisia 781.0
- due to drugs 333.99

Acceleration, accelerated
- atrioventricular conduction 426.7
- idioventricular rhythm 427.89

Accessory (congenital)
- adrenal gland 759.1
- anus 751.5
- appendix 751.5
- atrioventricular conduction 426.7
- auditory ossicles 744.04
- auricle (ear) 744.1
- autosome(s) NEC 758.5
  - 21 or 22 758.0
- biliary duct or passage 751.69
- bladder 753.8
- blood vessels (peripheral) (congenital) NEC (*see also* Anomaly, peripheral vascular system) 747.60
  - cerebral 747.81
  - coronary 746.85
- bone NEC 756.9
  - foot 755.67
- breast tissue, axilla 757.6
- carpal bones 755.56
- cecum 751.5
- cervix 752.49
- chromosome(s) NEC 758.5
  - 13-15 758.1
  - 16-18 758.2
  - 21 or 22 758.0
  - autosome(s) NEC 758.5
  - D_1 758.1
  - E_3 758.2
  - G 758.0
  - sex 758.81
- coronary artery 746.85
- cusp(s), heart valve NEC 746.89
  - pulmonary 746.09
- cystic duct 751.69
- digits 755.00
- ear (auricle) (lobe) 744.1
- endocrine gland NEC 759.2
- external os 752.49
- eyelid 743.62
- eye muscle 743.69
- face bone(s) 756.0
- fallopian tube (fimbria) (ostium) 752.19
- fingers 755.01
- foreskin 605
- frontonasal process 756.0
- gallbladder 751.69
- genital organ(s)
  - female 752.89
    - external 752.49
    - internal NEC 752.89
  - male NEC 752.89
    - penis 752.69
- genitourinary organs NEC 752.89
- heart 746.89
  - valve NEC 746.89
    - pulmonary 746.09
- hepatic ducts 751.69
- hymen 752.49
- intestine (large) (small) 751.5
- kidney 753.3
- lacrimal canal 743.65
- leaflet, heart valve NEC 746.89
  - pulmonary 746.09
- ligament, broad 752.19
- liver (duct) 751.69
- lobule (ear) 744.1
- lung (lobe) 748.69
- muscle 756.82
- navicular of carpus 755.56
- nervous system, part NEC 742.8
- nipple 757.6
- nose 748.1
- organ or site NEC — *see* Anomaly, specified type NEC
- ovary 752.0
- oviduct 752.19
- pancreas 751.7
- parathyroid gland 759.2
- parotid gland (and duct) 750.22
- pituitary gland 759.2
- placental lobe — *see* Placenta, abnormal
- preauricular appendage 744.1
- prepuce 605
- renal arteries (multiple) 747.62
- rib 756.3
  - cervical 756.2
- roots (teeth) 520.2
- salivary gland 750.22
- sesamoids 755.8
- sinus — *see* condition
- skin tags 757.39
- spleen 759.0
- sternum 756.3
- submaxillary gland 750.22
- tarsal bones 755.67
- teeth, tooth 520.1
  - causing crowding 524.31
- tendon 756.89
- thumb 755.01
- thymus gland 759.2
- thyroid gland 759.2
- toes 755.02
- tongue 750.13
- tragus 744.1
- ureter 753.4
- urethra 753.8
- urinary organ or tract NEC 753.8
- uterus 752.2
- vagina 752.49
- valve, heart NEC 746.89
  - pulmonary 746.09
- vertebra 756.19
- vocal cords 748.3
- vulva 752.49

Accident, accidental — *see also* condition
- birth NEC 767.9
- cardiovascular (*see also* Disease, cardiovascular) 429.2
- cerebral (*see also* Disease, cerebrovascular, acute) 434.91
- cerebrovascular (current) (CVA) (*see also* Disease, cerebrovascular, acute) 434.91
  - aborted 434.91
  - embolic 434.11
  - healed or old V12.54
  - hemorrhagic — *see* Hemorrhage, brain
  - impending 435.9
  - ischemic 434.91
  - late effect — *see* Late effect(s) (of) cerebrovascular disease
  - postoperative 997.02
  - thrombotic 434.01
- coronary (*see also* Infarct, myocardium) 410.9 ☑
- craniovascular (*see also* Disease, cerebrovascular, acute) 436
- during pregnancy, to mother, affecting fetus or newborn 760.5
- heart, cardiac (*see also* Infarct, myocardium) 410.9 ☑
- intrauterine 779.89
- vascular — *see* Disease, cerebrovascular, acute

Accommodation
- disorder of 367.51
  - drug-induced 367.89
  - toxic 367.89
- insufficiency of 367.4
- paralysis of 367.51
  - hysterical 300.11
- spasm of 367.53

Accouchement — *see* Delivery

Accreta placenta (without hemorrhage) 667.0 ☑
- with hemorrhage 666.0 ☑

Accretio cordis (nonrheumatic) 423.1

Accretions on teeth 523.6

Accumulation secretion, prostate 602.8

Acephalia, acephalism, acephaly 740.0

Acephalic 740.0

Acephalobrachia 759.89

Acephalocardia 759.89

Acephalocardius 759.89

Acephalochiria 759.89

Acephalochirus 759.89

Acephalogaster 759.89

Acephalostomus 759.89

Acephalothorax 759.89

Acephalus 740.0

Acetonemia 790.6
- diabetic 250.1 ☑
  - due to secondary diabetes 249.1 ☑

Acetonglycosuria 982.8

Acetonuria 791.6

Achalasia 530.0
- cardia 530.0
- digestive organs congenital NEC 751.8
- esophagus 530.0
- pelvirectal 751.3
- psychogenic 306.4
- pylorus 750.5
- sphincteral NEC 564.89

Achard-Thiers syndrome (adrenogenital) 255.2

Ache(s) — *see* Pain

Acheilia 750.26

Acheiria 755.21

Achillobursitis 726.71

Achillodynia 726.71

Achlorhydria, achlorhydric 536.0
- anemia 280.9
- diarrhea 536.0
- neurogenic 536.0
- postvagotomy 564.2
- psychogenic 306.4
- secondary to vagotomy 564.2

Achloroblepsia 368.52

Achloropsia 368.52

Acholia 575.8

Acholuric jaundice (familial) (splenomegalic) — *see also* Spherocytosis 282.0
- acquired 283.9

Achondroplasia 756.4

Achrestic anemia 281.8

Achroacytosis, lacrimal gland 375.00
- tuberculous (*see also* Tuberculosis) 017.3 ☑

Achroma, cutis 709.00

Achromate (congenital) 368.54

Achromatopia 368.54

Achromatopsia (congenital) 368.54

Achromia
- congenital 270.2
- parasitica 111.0
- unguium 703.8

Achylia
- gastrica 536.8
  - neurogenic 536.3
  - psychogenic 306.4
- pancreatica 577.1

Achylosis 536.8

Acid
- burn (*see also* Burn, by site)
  - from swallowing acid — *see* Burn, internal organs
- deficiency
  - amide nicotinic 265.2
  - amino 270.9
  - ascorbic 267
  - folic 266.2
  - nicotinic (amide) 265.2
  - pantothenic 266.2
- intoxication 276.2
- peptic disease 536.8
- stomach 536.8
  - psychogenic 306.4

Acidemia 276.2
- arginosuccinic 270.6
- fetal
  - affecting management of pregnancy 656.3 ☑
  - before onset of labor, in liveborn infant 768.2
  - during labor and delivery in liveborn infant 768.3
  - intrauterine 656.3 ☑
  - unspecified as to time of onset, in liveborn infant 768.4
- newborn 775.81
- pipecolic 270.7

Acidity, gastric (high) (low) 536.8
- psychogenic 306.4

Acidocytopenia 288.59

Acidocytosis 288.3

Acidopenia 288.59

Acidosis 276.2
- diabetic 250.1 ☑
  - due to secondary diabetes 249.1 ☑
- fetal, affecting management of pregnancy 756.8 ☑
- fetal, affecting newborn 775.81
- kidney tubular 588.89
  - newborn 775.81
- lactic 276.2
- metabolic NEC 276.2
  - with respiratory acidosis 276.4
    - of newborn 775.81
  - late, of newborn 775.7
- newborn 775.81
- renal
  - hyperchloremic 588.89
  - tubular (distal) (proximal) 588.89
- respiratory 276.2
  - complicated by
    - metabolic acidosis 276.4
      - of newborn 775.81
    - metabolic alkalosis 276.4

Aciduria 791.9
- arginosuccinic 270.6
- beta-aminoisobutyric (BAIB) 277.2
- glutaric
  - type I 270.7
  - type II (type IIA, IIB, IIC) 277.85
  - type III 277.86
- glycolic 271.8
- methylmalonic 270.3
  - with glycinemia 270.7
- organic 270.9

Aciduria — *continued*
  orotic (congenital) (hereditary) (pyrimidine deficiency) 281.4
Acladiosis 111.8
  skin 111.8
Aclasis
  diaphyseal 756.4
  tarsoepiphyseal 756.59
Acleistocardia 745.5
Aclusion 524.4
Acmesthesia 782.0
Acne (pustular) (vulgaris) 706.1
  agminata (*see also* Tuberculosis) 017.0 ☑
  artificialis 706.1
  atrophica 706.0
  cachecticorum (Hebra) 706.1
  conglobata 706.1
  conjunctiva 706.1
  cystic 706.1
  decalvans 704.09
  erythematosa 695.3
  eyelid 706.1
  frontalis 706.0
  indurata 706.1
  keloid 706.1
  lupoid 706.0
  necrotic, necrotica 706.0
    miliaris 704.8
  neonatal 706.1
  nodular 706.1
  occupational 706.1
  papulosa 706.1
  rodens 706.0
  rosacea 695.3
  scorbutica 267
  scrofulosorum (Bazin) (*see also* Tuberculosis) 017.0 ☑
  summer 692.72
  tropical 706.1
  varioliformis 706.0
Acneiform drug eruptions 692.3
Acnitis (primary) — *see also* Tuberculosis 017.0 ☑
Acomia 704.00
Acontractile bladder 344.61
Aconuresis — *see also* Incontinence 788.30
Acosta's disease 993.2
Acousma 780.1
Acoustic — *see* condition
Acousticophobia 300.29
Acquired — *see* condition
Acquired immune deficiency syndrome — *see* Human immunodeficiency virus (disease) (illness) (infection)
Acquired immunodeficiency syndrome — *see* Human immunodeficiency virus (disease) (illness) (infection)
Acragnosis 781.99
Acrania 740.0
Acroagnosis 781.99
Acroasphyxia, chronic 443.89
Acrobrachycephaly 756.0
Acrobystiolith 608.89
Acrobystitis 607.2
Acrocephalopolysyndactyly 755.55
Acrocephalosyndactyly 755.55
Acrocephaly 756.0
Acrochondrohyperplasia 759.82
Acrocyanosis 443.89
  newborn 770.83
    meaning transient blue hands and feet — *omit code*
Acrodermatitis 686.8
  atrophicans (chronica) 701.8
  continua (Hallopeau) 696.1
  enteropathica 686.8
  Hallopeau's 696.1
  perstans 696.1
  pustulosa continua 696.1
  recalcitrant pustular 696.1
Acrodynia 985.0
Acrodysplasia 755.55
Acrohyperhidrosis — *see also* Hyperhidrosis 780.8
Acrokeratosis verruciformis 757.39
Acromastitis 611.0
Acromegaly, acromegalia (skin) 253.0
Acromelalgia 443.82
Acromicria, acromikria 756.59
Acronyx 703.0
Acropachyderma 757.39
Acropachy, thyroid — *see also* Thyrotoxicosis 242.9 ☑
Acroparesthesia 443.89
  simple (Schultz's type) 443.89
  vasomotor (Nothnagel's type) 443.89
Acropathy thyroid — *see also* Thyrotoxicosis 242.9 ☑
Acrophobia 300.29
Acroposthitis 607.2
Acroscleriasis — *see also* Scleroderma 710.1
Acroscleroderma — *see also* Scleroderma 710.1
Acrosclerosis — *see also* Scleroderma 710.1
Acrosphacelus 785.4
Acrosphenosyndactylia 755.55
Acrospiroma, eccrine (M8402/0) — *see* Neoplasm, skin, benign
Acrostealgia 732.9
Acrosyndactyly — *see also* Syndactylism 755.10
Acrotrophodynia 991.4
Actinic — *see also* condition
  cheilitis (due to sun) 692.72
    chronic NEC 692.74
    due to radiation, except from sun 692.82
  conjunctivitis 370.24
  dermatitis (due to sun) (*see also* Dermatitis, actinic) 692.70
    due to
      roentgen rays or radioactive substance 692.82
      ultraviolet radiation, except from sun 692.82
    sun NEC 692.70
  elastosis solare 692.74
  granuloma 692.73
  keratitis 370.24
  ophthalmia 370.24
  reticuloid 692.73
Actinobacillosis, general 027.8
Actinobacillus
  lignieresii 027.8
  mallei 024
  muris 026.1
Actinocutitis NEC — *see also* Dermatitis, actinic 692.70
Actinodermatitis NEC — *see also* Dermatitis, actinic 692.70
Actinomyces
  israelii (infection) — *see* Actinomycosis
  muris-ratti (infection) 026.1
Actinomycosis, actinomycotic 039.9
  with
    pneumonia 039.1
  abdominal 039.2
  cervicofacial 039.3
  cutaneous 039.0
  pulmonary 039.1
  specified site NEC 039.8
  thoracic 039.1
Actinoneuritis 357.89
Action, heart
  disorder 427.9
    postoperative 997.1
  irregular 427.9
    postoperative 997.1
    psychogenic 306.2
Active — *see* condition
Activity decrease, functional 780.99
Acute — *see also* condition
  abdomen NEC 789.0 ☑
  gallbladder (*see also* Cholecystitis, acute) 575.0
Acyanoblepsia 368.53
Acyanopsia 368.53
Acystia 753.8
Acystinervia — *see* Neurogenic, bladder
Acystineuria — *see* Neurogenic, bladder
Adactylia, adactyly (congenital) 755.4
  lower limb (complete) (intercalary) (partial) (terminal) (*see also* Deformity, reduction, lower limb) 755.39
    meaning all digits (complete) (partial) 755.31
    transverse (complete) (partial) 755.31
  upper limb (complete) (intercalary) (partial) (terminal) (*see also* Deformity, reduction, upper limb) 755.29
    meaning all digits (complete) (partial) 755.21
    transverse (complete) (partial) 755.21
Adair-Dighton syndrome (brittle bones and blue sclera, deafness) 756.51
Adamantinoblastoma (M9310/0) — *see* Ameloblastoma
Adamantinoma (M9310/0) — *see* Ameloblastoma
Adamantoblastoma (M9310/0) — *see* Ameloblastoma
Adams-Stokes (-Morgagni) disease or syndrome (syncope with heart block) 426.9
Adaptation reaction — *see also* Reaction, adjustment 309.9
Addiction — *see also* Dependence
  absinthe 304.6 ☑
  alcoholic (ethyl) (methyl) (wood) 303.9 ☑
    complicating pregnancy, childbirth, or puerperium 648.4 ☑
      affecting fetus or newborn 760.71
    suspected damage to fetus affecting management of pregnancy 655.4 ☑
  drug (*see also* Dependence) 304.9 ☑
  ethyl alcohol 303.9 ☑
  heroin 304.0 ☑
  hospital 301.51
  methyl alcohol 303.9 ☑
  methylated spirit 303.9 ☑
  morphine (-like substances) 304.0 ☑
  nicotine 305.1
  opium 304.0 ☑
  tobacco 305.1
  wine 303.9 ☑
Addison's
  anemia (pernicious) 281.0
  disease (bronze) (primary adrenal insufficiency) 255.41
    tuberculous (*see also* Tuberculosis) 017.6 ☑
  keloid (morphea) 701.0
  melanoderma (adrenal cortical hypofunction) 255.41
Addison-Biermer anemia (pernicious) 281.0
Addison-Gull disease — *see* Xanthoma
Addisonian crisis or melanosis (acute adrenocortical insufficiency) 255.41
Additional — *see also* Accessory
  chromosome(s) 758.5
    13-15 758.1
    16-18 758.2
    21 758.0
    autosome(s) NEC 758.5
    sex 758.81
Adduction contracture, hip or other joint — *see* Contraction, joint
ADEM (acute disseminated encephalomyelitis) (postinfectious) 136.9 *[323.61]*
  infectious 136.9 *[323.61]*
  noninfectious 323.81
Adenasthenia gastrica 536.0
Aden fever 061
Adenitis — *see also* Lymphadenitis 289.3
Adenitis — *see also* Lymphadenitis — *continued*
  acute, unspecified site 683
    epidemic infectious 075
  axillary 289.3
    acute 683
    chronic or subacute 289.1
  Bartholin's gland 616.89
  bulbourethral gland (*see also* Urethritis) 597.89
  cervical 289.3
    acute 683
    chronic or subacute 289.1
  chancroid (Ducrey's bacillus) 099.0
  chronic (any lymph node, except mesenteric) 289.1
    mesenteric 289.2
  Cowper's gland (*see also* Urethritis) 597.89
  epidemic, acute 075
  gangrenous 683
  gonorrheal NEC 098.89
  groin 289.3
    acute 683
    chronic or subacute 289.1
  infectious 075
  inguinal (region) 289.3
    acute 683
    chronic or subacute 289.1
  lymph gland or node, except mesenteric 289.3
    acute 683
    chronic or subacute 289.1
    mesenteric (acute) (chronic) (nonspecific) (subacute) 289.2
  mesenteric (acute) (chronic) (nonspecific) (subacute) 289.2
    due to Pasteurella multocida (P. septica) 027.2
  parotid gland (suppurative) 527.2
  phlegmonous 683
  salivary duct or gland (any) (recurring) (suppurative) 527.2
  scrofulous (*see also* Tuberculosis) 017.2 ☑
  septic 289.3
  Skene's duct or gland (*see also* Urethritis) 597.89
  strumous, tuberculous (*see also* Tuberculosis) 017.2 ☑
  subacute, unspecified site 289.1
  sublingual gland (suppurative) 527.2
  submandibular gland (suppurative) 527.2
  submaxillary gland (suppurative) 527.2
  suppurative 683
  tuberculous — *see* Tuberculosis, lymph gland
  urethral gland (*see also* Urethritis) 597.89
  venereal NEC 099.8
  Wharton's duct (suppurative) 527.2
Adenoacanthoma (M8570/3) — *see* Neoplasm, by site, malignant
Adenoameloblastoma (M9300/0) 213.1
  upper jaw (bone) 213.0

- **Adenocarcinoma** (M8140/3) — *see also* Neoplasm, by site, malignant

> *Note — The list of adjectival modifiers below is not exhaustive. A description of adenocarcinoma that does not appear in this list should be coded in the same manner as carcinoma with that description. Thus, "mixed acidophil-basophil adenocarcinoma," should be coded in the same manner as "mixed acidophil-basophil carcinoma," which appears in the list under "Carcinoma."*
>
> *Except where otherwise indicated, the morphological varieties of adenocarcinoma in the list below should be coded by site as for "Neoplasm, malignant."*

  - with
    - apocrine metaplasia (M8573/3)
    - cartilaginous (and osseous) metaplasia (M8571/3)
    - osseous (and cartilaginous) metaplasia (M8571/3)
    - spindle cell metaplasia (M8572/3)
    - squamous metaplasia (M8570/3)
  - acidophil (M8280/3)
    - specified site — *see* Neoplasm, by site, malignant
    - unspecified site 194.3
  - acinar (M8550/3)
  - acinic cell (M8550/3)
  - adrenal cortical (M8370/3) 194.0
  - alveolar (M8251/3)
    - and
      - epidermoid carcinoma, mixed (M8560/3)
      - squamous cell carcinoma, mixed (M8560/3)
  - apocrine (M8401/3)
    - breast — *see* Neoplasm, breast, malignant
    - specified site NEC — *see* Neoplasm, skin, malignant
    - unspecified site 173.9
  - basophil (M8300/3)
    - specified site — *see* Neoplasm, by site, malignant
    - unspecified site 194.3
  - bile duct type (M8160/3)
    - liver 155.1
    - specified site NEC — *see* Neoplasm, by site, malignant
    - unspecified site 155.1
  - bronchiolar (M8250/3) — *see* Neoplasm, lung, malignant
  - ceruminous (M8420/3) 173.2
  - chromophobe (M8270/3)
    - specified site — *see* Neoplasm, by site, malignant
    - unspecified site 194.3
  - clear cell (mesonephroid type) (M8310/3)
  - colloid (M8480/3)
  - cylindroid type (M8200/3)
  - diffuse type (M8145/3)
    - specified site — *see* Neoplasm, by site, malignant
    - unspecified site 151.9
  - duct (infiltrating) (M8500/3)
    - with Paget's disease (M8541/3) — *see* Neoplasm, breast, malignant
    - specified site — *see* Neoplasm, by site, malignant
    - unspecified site 174.9
  - embryonal (M9070/3)
  - endometrioid (M8380/3) — *see* Neoplasm, by site, malignant
  - eosinophil (M8280/3)
    - specified site — *see* Neoplasm, by site, malignant
    - unspecified site 194.3
  - follicular (M8330/3)
    - and papillary (M8340/3) 193
    - moderately differentiated type (M8332/3) 193
    - pure follicle type (M8331/3) 193
    - specified site — *see* Neoplasm, by site, malignant
    - trabecular type (M8332/3) 193
    - unspecified type 193
    - well differentiated type (M8331/3) 193
  - gelatinous (M8480/3)
  - granular cell (M8320/3)
  - Hürthle cell (M8290/3) 193
  - in
    - adenomatous
      - polyp (M8210/3)
      - polyposis coli (M8220/3) 153.9
    - polypoid adenoma (M8210/3)
    - tubular adenoma (M8210/3)
    - villous adenoma (M8261/3)
  - infiltrating duct (M8500/3)
    - with Paget's disease (M8541/3) — *see* Neoplasm, breast, malignant
    - specified site — *see* Neoplasm, by site, malignant
    - unspecified site 174.9
  - inflammatory (M8530/3)
    - specified site — *see* Neoplasm, by site, malignant
    - unspecified site 174.9
  - in situ (M8140/2) — *see* Neoplasm, by site, in situ
  - intestinal type (M8144/3)
    - specified site — *see* Neoplasm, by site, malignant
    - unspecified site 151.9
  - intraductal (noninfiltrating) (M8500/2)
    - papillary (M8503/2)
      - specified site — *see* Neoplasm, by site, in situ
      - unspecified site 233.0
    - specified site — *see* Neoplasm, by site, in situ
    - unspecified site 233.0
  - islet cell (M8150/3)
    - and exocrine, mixed (M8154/3)
      - specified site — *see* Neoplasm, by site, malignant
      - unspecified site 157.9
    - pancreas 157.4
    - specified site NEC — *see* Neoplasm, by site, malignant
    - unspecified site 157.4
  - lobular (M8520/3)
    - specified site — *see* Neoplasm, by site, malignant
    - unspecified site 174.9
  - medullary (M8510/3)
  - mesonephric (M9110/3)
  - mixed cell (M8323/3)
  - mucinous (M8480/3)
  - mucin-producing (M8481/3)
  - mucoid (M8480/3) (*see also* Neoplasm, by site, malignant)
    - cell (M8300/3)
      - specified site — *see* Neoplasm, by site, malignant
      - unspecified site 194.3
  - nonencapsulated sclerosing (M8350/3) 193
  - oncocytic (M8290/3)
  - oxyphilic (M8290/3)
  - papillary (M8260/3)
    - and follicular (M8340/3) 193
    - intraductal (noninfiltrating) (M8503/2)
      - specified site — *see* Neoplasm, by site, in situ
      - unspecified site 233.0
    - serous (M8460/3)
      - specified site — *see* Neoplasm, by site, malignant
      - unspecified site 183.0
  - papillocystic (M8450/3)
    - specified site — *see* Neoplasm, by site, malignant
    - unspecified site 183.0
  - pseudomucinous (M8470/3)
    - specified site — *see* Neoplasm, by site, malignant
    - unspecified site 183.0
  - renal cell (M8312/3) 189.0
  - sebaceous (M8410/3)
  - serous (M8441/3) (*see also* Neoplasm, by site, malignant)
    - papillary
      - specified site — *see* Neoplasm, by site, malignant
      - unspecified site 183.0
  - signet ring cell (M8490/3)
  - superficial spreading (M8143/3)
  - sweat gland (M8400/3) — *see* Neoplasm, skin, malignant
  - trabecular (M8190/3)
  - tubular (M8211/3)
  - villous (M8262/3)
  - water-clear cell (M8322/3) 194.1
- **Adenofibroma** (M9013/0)
  - clear cell (M8313/0) — *see* Neoplasm, by site, benign
  - endometrioid (M8381/0) 220
    - borderline malignancy (M8381/1) 236.2
    - malignant (M8381/3) 183.0
  - mucinous (M9015/0)
    - specified site — *see* Neoplasm, by site, benign
    - unspecified site 220
  - prostate 600.20
    - with
      - other lower urinary tract symptoms (LUTS) 600.21
      - urinary
        - obstruction 600.21
        - retention 600.21
  - serous (M9014/0)
    - specified site — *see* Neoplasm, by site, benign
    - unspecified site 220
  - specified site — *see* Neoplasm, by site, benign
  - unspecified site 220
- **Adenofibrosis**
  - breast 610.2
  - endometrioid 617.0
- **Adenoiditis** 474.01
  - acute 463
  - chronic 474.01
    - with chronic tonsillitis 474.02
- **Adenoids** (congenital) (of nasal fossa) 474.9
  - hypertrophy 474.12
  - vegetations 474.2
- **Adenolipomatosis** (symmetrical) 272.8
- **Adenolymphoma** (M8561/0)
  - specified site — *see* Neoplasm, by site, benign
  - unspecified 210.2
- **Adenomatosis** (M8220/0)
  - endocrine (multiple) (M8360/1)
    - single specified site — *see* Neoplasm, by site, uncertain behavior
    - two or more specified sites 237.4
    - unspecified site 237.4
  - erosive of nipple (M8506/0) 217
  - pluriendocrine — *see* Adenomatosis, endocrine
  - pulmonary (M8250/1) 235.7
    - malignant (M8250/3) — *see* Neoplasm, lung, malignant
  - specified site — *see* Neoplasm, by site, benign
  - unspecified site 211.3
- **Adenomatous**
  - cyst, thyroid (gland) — *see* Goiter, nodular
  - goiter (nontoxic) (*see also* Goiter, nodular) 241.9
    - toxic or with hyperthyroidism 242.3 ☑
- **Adenoma** (sessile) (M8140/0) — *see* also Neoplasm, by site, benign

> *Note — Except where otherwise indicated, the morphological varieties of adenoma in the list below should be coded by site as for "Neoplasm, benign."*

  - acidophil (M8280/0)
    - specified site — *see* Neoplasm, by site, benign
    - unspecified site 227.3
  - acinar (cell) (M8550/0)
  - acinic cell (M8550/0)
  - adrenal (cortex) (cortical) (functioning) (M8370/0) 227.0
    - clear cell type (M8373/0) 227.0
    - compact cell type (M8371/0) 227.0
    - glomerulosa cell type (M8374/0) 227.0
    - heavily pigmented variant (M8372/0) 227.0
    - mixed cell type (M8375/0) 227.0
  - alpha cell (M8152/0)
    - pancreas 211.7
    - specified site NEC — *see* Neoplasm, by site, benign
    - unspecified site 211.7
  - alveolar (M8251/0)
  - apocrine (M8401/0)
    - breast 217
    - specified site NEC — *see* Neoplasm, skin, benign
    - unspecified site 216.9
  - basal cell (M8147/0)
  - basophil (M8300/0)
    - specified site — *see* Neoplasm, by site, benign
    - unspecified site 227.3
  - beta cell (M8151/0)
    - pancreas 211.7
    - specified site NEC — *see* Neoplasm, by site, benign
    - unspecified site 211.7
  - bile duct (M8160/0) 211.5
  - black (M8372/0) 227.0
  - bronchial (M8140/1) 235.7
    - carcinoid type (M8240/3) — *see* Neoplasm, lung, malignant
    - cylindroid type (M8200/3) — *see* Neoplasm, lung, malignant
  - ceruminous (M8420/0) 216.2
  - chief cell (M8321/0) 227.1
  - chromophobe (M8270/0)
    - specified site — *see* Neoplasm, by site, benign
    - unspecified site 227.3
  - clear cell (M8310/0)
  - colloid (M8334/0)
    - specified site — *see* Neoplasm, by site, benign
    - unspecified site 226
  - cylindroid type, bronchus (M8200/3) — *see* Neoplasm, lung, malignant
  - duct (M8503/0)
  - embryonal (M8191/0)
  - endocrine, multiple (M8360/1)
    - single specified site — *see* Neoplasm, by site, uncertain behavior
    - two or more specified sites 237.4
    - unspecified site 237.4
  - endometrioid (M8380/0) (*see also* Neoplasm, by site, benign)
    - borderline malignancy (M8380/1) — *see* Neoplasm, by site, uncertain behavior
  - eosinophil (M8280/0)
    - specified site — *see* Neoplasm, by site, benign
    - unspecified site 227.3

Adenoma — *see* also Neoplasm, by site, benign — *continued*
fetal (M8333/0)
specified site — *see* Neoplasm, by site, benign
unspecified site 226
follicular (M8330/0)
specified site — *see* Neoplasm, by site, benign
unspecified site 226
hepatocellular (M8170/0) 211.5
Hürthle cell (M8290/0) 226
intracystic papillary (M8504/0)
islet cell (functioning) (M8150/0)
pancreas 211.7
specified site NEC — *see* Neoplasm, by site, benign
unspecified site 211.7
liver cell (M8170/0) 211.5
macrofollicular (M8334/0)
specified site NEC — *see* Neoplasm, by site, benign
unspecified site 226
malignant, malignum (M8140/3) — *see* Neoplasm, by site, malignant
mesonephric (M9110/0)
microfollicular (M8333/0)
specified site — *see* Neoplasm, by site, benign
unspecified site 226
mixed cell (M8323/0)
monomorphic (M8146/0)
mucinous (M8480/0)
mucoid cell (M8300/0)
specified site — *see* Neoplasm, by site, benign
unspecified site 227.3
multiple endocrine (M8360/1)
single specified site — *see* Neoplasm, by site, uncertain behavior
two or more specified sites 237.4
unspecified site 237.4
nipple (M8506/0) 217
oncocytic (M8290/0)
oxyphilic (M8290/0)
papillary (M8260/0) (*see also* Neoplasm, by site, benign)
intracystic (M8504/0)
papillotubular (M8263/0)
Pick's tubular (M8640/0)
specified site — *see* Neoplasm, by site, benign
unspecified site
female 220
male 222.0
pleomorphic (M8940/0)
polypoid (M8210/0)
prostate (benign) 600.20
with
other lower urinary tract symptoms (LUTS) 600.21
urinary
obstruction 600.21
retention 600.21
rete cell 222.0
sebaceous, sebaceum (gland) (senile) (M8410/0) (*see also* Neoplasm, skin, benign)
disseminata 759.5
Sertoli cell (M8640/0)
specified site — *see* Neoplasm, by site, benign
unspecified site
female 220
male 222.0
skin appendage (M8390/0) — *see* Neoplasm, skin, benign
sudoriferous gland (M8400/0) — *see* Neoplasm, skin, benign
sweat gland or duct (M8400/0) — *see* Neoplasm, skin, benign
testicular (M8640/0)
specified site — *see* Neoplasm, by site, benign

Adenoma — *see* also Neoplasm, by site, benign — *continued*
testicular — *continued*
unspecified site
female 220
male 222.0
thyroid 226
trabecular (M8190/0)
tubular (M8211/0) (*see also* Neoplasm, by site, benign)
papillary (M8460/3)
Pick's (M8640/0)
specified site — *see* Neoplasm, by site, benign
unspecified site
female 220
male 222.0
tubulovillous (M8263/0)
villoglandular (M8263/0)
villous (M8261/1) — *see* Neoplasm, by site, uncertain behavior
water-clear cell (M8322/0) 227.1
wolffian duct (M9110/0)
Adenomyoma (M8932/0) — *see also* Neoplasm, by site, benign
prostate 600.20
with
other lower urinary tract symptoms (LUTS) 600.21
urinary
obstruction 600.21
retention 600.21
Adenomyometritis 617.0
Adenomyosis (uterus) (internal) 617.0
Adenopathy (lymph gland) 785.6
inguinal 785.6
mediastinal 785.6
mesentery 785.6
syphilitic (secondary) 091.4
tracheobronchial 785.6
tuberculous (*see also* Tuberculosis) 012.1 ☑
primary, progressive 010.8 ☑
tuberculous (*see also* Tuberculosis, lymph gland) 017.2 ☑
tracheobronchial 012.1 ☑
primary, progressive 010.8 ☑
Adenopharyngitis 462
Adenophlegmon 683
Adenosalpingitis 614.1
Adenosarcoma (M8960/3) 189.0
Adenosclerosis 289.3
Adenosis
breast (sclerosing) 610.2
vagina, congenital 752.49
Adentia (complete) (partial) — *see also* Absence, teeth 520.0
Adherent
labium (minus) 624.4
pericardium (nonrheumatic) 423.1
rheumatic 393
placenta 667.0 ☑
with hemorrhage 666.0 ☑
prepuce 605
scar (skin) NEC 709.2
tendon in scar 709.2
Adhesion(s), adhesive (postinfectional) (postoperative)
abdominal (wall) (*see also* Adhesions, peritoneum) 568.0
amnion to fetus 658.8 ☑
affecting fetus or newborn 762.8
appendix 543.9
arachnoiditis — *see* Meningitis
auditory tube (Eustachian) 381.89
bands (*see also* Adhesions, peritoneum)
cervix 622.3
uterus 621.5
bile duct (any) 576.8
bladder (sphincter) 596.8
bowel (*see also* Adhesions, peritoneum) 568.0
cardiac 423.1
rheumatic 398.99

Adhesion(s), adhesive — *continued*
cecum (*see also* Adhesions, peritoneum) 568.0
cervicovaginal 622.3
congenital 752.49
postpartal 674.8 ☑
old 622.3
cervix 622.3
clitoris 624.4
colon (*see also* Adhesions, peritoneum) 568.0
common duct 576.8
congenital (*see also* Anomaly, specified type NEC)
fingers (*see also* Syndactylism, fingers) 755.11
labium (majus) (minus) 752.49
omental, anomalous 751.4
ovary 752.0
peritoneal 751.4
toes (*see also* Syndactylism, toes) 755.13
tongue (to gum or roof of mouth) 750.12
conjunctiva (acquired) (localized) 372.62
congenital 743.63
extensive 372.63
cornea — *see* Opacity, cornea
cystic duct 575.8
diaphragm (*see also* Adhesions, peritoneum) 568.0
due to foreign body — *see* Foreign body
duodenum (*see also* Adhesions, peritoneum) 568.0
with obstruction 537.3
ear, middle — *see* Adhesions, middle ear
epididymis 608.89
epidural — *see* Adhesions, meninges
epiglottis 478.79
Eustachian tube 381.89
eyelid 374.46
postoperative 997.99
surgically created V45.69
gallbladder (*see also* Disease, gallbladder) 575.8
globe 360.89
heart 423.1
rheumatic 398.99
ileocecal (coil) (*see also* Adhesions, peritoneum) 568.0
ileum (*see also* Adhesions, peritoneum) 568.0
intestine (postoperative) (*see also* Adhesions, peritoneum) 568.0
with obstruction 560.81
with hernia (*see also* Hernia, by site, with obstruction)
gangrenous — *see* Hernia, by site, with gangrene
intra-abdominal (*see also* Adhesions, peritoneum) 568.0
iris 364.70
to corneal graft 996.79
joint (*see also* Ankylosis) 718.5 ☑
kidney 593.89
labium (majus) (minus), congenital 752.49
liver 572.8
lung 511.0
mediastinum 519.3
meninges 349.2
cerebral (any) 349.2
congenital 742.4
congenital 742.8
spinal (any) 349.2
congenital 742.59
tuberculous (cerebral) (spinal) (*see also* Tuberculosis, meninges) 013.0 ☑
mesenteric (*see also* Adhesions, peritoneum) 568.0
middle ear (fibrous) 385.10
drum head 385.19

Adhesion(s), adhesive — *continued*
middle ear — *continued*
drum head — *continued*
to
incus 385.11
promontorium 385.13
stapes 385.12
specified NEC 385.19
nasal (septum) (to turbinates) 478.19
nerve NEC 355.9
spinal 355.9
root 724.9
cervical NEC 723.4
lumbar NEC 724.4
lumbosacral 724.4
thoracic 724.4
ocular muscle 378.60
omentum (*see also* Adhesions, peritoneum) 568.0
organ or site, congenital NEC — *see* Anomaly, specified type NEC
ovary 614.6
congenital (to cecum, kidney, or omentum) 752.0
parauterine 614.6
parovarian 614.6
pelvic (peritoneal)
female (postoperative) (postinfection) 614.6
male (postoperative) (postinfection) (*see also* Adhesions, peritoneum) 568.0
postpartal (old) 614.6
tuberculous (*see also* Tuberculosis) 016.9 ☑
penis to scrotum (congenital) 752.69
periappendiceal (*see also* Adhesions, peritoneum) 568.0
pericardium (nonrheumatic) 423.1
rheumatic 393
tuberculous (*see also* Tuberculosis) 017.9 ☑ *[420.0]*
pericholecystic 575.8
perigastric (*see also* Adhesions, peritoneum) 568.0
periovarian 614.6
periprostatic 602.8
perirectal (*see also* Adhesions, peritoneum) 568.0
perirenal 593.89
peritoneum, peritoneal (fibrous) (postoperative) 568.0
with obstruction (intestinal) 560.81
with hernia (*see also* Hernia, by site, with obstruction)
gangrenous — *see* Hernia, by site, with gangrene
duodenum 537.3
congenital 751.4
female (postoperative) (postinfective) 614.6
pelvic, female 614.6
pelvic, male 568.0
postpartal, pelvic 614.6
to uterus 614.6
peritubal 614.6
periureteral 593.89
periuterine 621.5
perivesical 596.8
perivesicular (seminal vesicle) 608.89
pleura, pleuritic 511.0
tuberculous (*see also* Tuberculosis, pleura) 012.0 ☑
pleuropericardial 511.0
postoperative (gastrointestinal tract) (*see also* Adhesions, peritoneum) 568.0
eyelid 997.99
surgically created V45.69
pelvic female 614.9
pelvic male 568.0
urethra 598.2
postpartal, old 624.4
preputial, prepuce 605
pulmonary 511.0

Admission — *continued*
for — *continued*
counseling (*see also* Counseling) — *continued*
genetic V26.33
gonorrhea V65.45
HIV V65.44
human immunodeficiency virus V65.44
injury prevention V65.43
insulin pump training V65.46
natural family planning
procreative V26.41
to avoid pregnancy V25.04
procreative management V26.49
using natural family planning V26.41
sexually transmitted disease NEC V65.45
HIV V65.44
specified reason NEC V65.49
substance use and abuse V65.42
syphilis V65.45
victim of abuse
child V61.21
partner or spouse V61.11
desensitization to allergens V07.1
dialysis V56.0
catheter
fitting and adjustment
extracorporeal V56.1
peritoneal V56.2
removal or replacement
extracorporeal V56.1
peritoneal V56.2
extracorporeal (renal) V56.0
peritoneal V56.8
renal V56.0
dietary surveillance and counseling V65.3
drug monitoring, therapeutic V58.83
ear piercing V50.3
elective surgery V50.9
breast
augmentation or reduction V50.1
reconstruction following mastectomy V51.0
removal, prophylactic V50.41
circumcision, ritual or routine (in absence of medical indication) V50.2
cosmetic NEC V50.1
breast reconstruction following mastectomy V51.0
following healed injury or operation V51.8
ear piercing V50.3
face-lift V50.1
hair transplant V50.0
plastic
breast reconstruction following mastectomy V51.0
cosmetic NEC V50.1
following healed injury or operation V51.8
prophylactic organ removal V50.49
breast V50.41
ovary V50.42
repair of scarred tissue (following healed injury or operation) V51.8
specified type NEC V50.8
end-of-life care V66.7
examination (*see also* Examination) V70.9
administrative purpose NEC V70.3
adoption V70.3
allergy V72.7
at health care facility V70.0
athletic team V70.3
camp V70.3

Admission — *continued*
for — *continued*
examination (*see also* Examination) — *continued*
cardiovascular, preoperative V72.81
clinical research investigation (control) (participant) V70.7
dental V72.2
developmental testing (child) (infant) V20.2
donor (potential) V70.8
driver's license V70.3
ear V72.19
employment V70.5
eye V72.0
follow-up (routine) — *see* Examination, follow-up
for admission to
old age home V70.3
school V70.3
general V70.9
specified reason NEC V70.8
gynecological V72.31
health supervision (child) (infant) V20.2
hearing V72.19
following failed hearing screening V72.11
immigration V70.3
infant, routine V20.2
insurance certification V70.3
laboratory V72.6
marriage license V70.3
medical (general) (*see also* Examination, medical) V70.9
medicolegal reasons V70.4
naturalization V70.3
pelvic (annual) (periodic) V72.31
postpartum checkup V24.2
pregnancy (possible) (unconfirmed) V72.40
negative result V72.41
positive result V72.42
preoperative V72.84
cardiovascular V72.81
respiratory V72.82
specified NEC V72.83
preprocedural V72.84
cardiovascular V72.81
general physical V72.83
respiratory V72.82
specified NEC V72.83
prison V70.3
psychiatric (general) V70.2
requested by authority V70.1
radiological NEC V72.5
respiratory, preoperative V72.82
school V70.3
screening — *see* Screening
skin hypersensitivity V72.7
specified type NEC V72.85
sport competition V70.3
vision V72.0
well baby and child care V20.2
exercise therapy V57.1
face-lift, cosmetic reason V50.1
fitting (of)
artificial
arm (complete) (partial) V52.0
eye V52.2
leg (complete) (partial) V52.1
biliary drainage tube V58.82
brain neuropacemaker V53.02
breast V52.4
implant V52.4
prosthesis V52.4
cardiac pacemaker V53.31
catheter
non-vascular V58.82
vascular V58.81
cerebral ventricle (communicating) shunt V53.01
chest tube V58.82

Admission — *continued*
for — *continued*
fitting — *continued*
colostomy belt V55.2
contact lenses V53.1
cystostomy device V53.6
dental prosthesis V52.3
device, unspecified type V53.90
abdominal V53.5
cerebral ventricle (communicating) shunt V53.01
insulin pump V53.91
intrauterine contraceptive V25.1
nervous system V53.09
orthodontic V53.4
other device V53.99
prosthetic V52.9
breast V52.4
dental V52.3
eye V52.2
special senses V53.09
substitution
auditory V53.09
nervous system V53.09
visual V53.09
diaphragm (contraceptive) V25.02
fistula (sinus tract) drainage tube V58.82
growth rod V54.02
hearing aid V53.2
ileostomy device V55.2
intestinal appliance or device NEC V53.5
intrauterine contraceptive device V25.1
neuropacemaker (brain) (peripheral nerve) (spinal cord) V53.02
orthodontic device V53.4
orthopedic (device) V53.7
brace V53.7
cast V53.7
shoes V53.7
pacemaker
brain V53.02
cardiac V53.31
carotid sinus V53.39
spinal cord V53.02
pleural drainage tube V58.82
portacath V58.81
prosthesis V52.9
arm (complete) (partial) V52.0
breast V52.4
dental V52.3
eye V52.2
leg (complete) (partial) V52.1
specified type NEC V52.8
spectacles V53.1
wheelchair V53.8
follow-up examination (routine) (following) V67.9
cancer chemotherapy V67.2
chemotherapy V67.2
high-risk medication NEC V67.51
injury NEC V67.59
psychiatric V67.3
psychotherapy V67.3
radiotherapy V67.1
specified surgery NEC V67.09
surgery V67.00
vaginal pap smear V67.01
treatment (for) V67.9
combined V67.6
fracture V67.4
involving high-risk medication NEC V67.51
mental disorder V67.3
specified NEC V67.59
hair transplant, for cosmetic reason V50.0
health advice, education, or instruction V65.4 ☑

Admission — *continued*
for — *continued*
hearing conservation and treatment V72.12
hormone replacement therapy (postmenopausal) V07.4
hospice care V66.7
immunotherapy, antineoplastic V58.12
insertion (of)
subdermal implantable contraceptive V25.5
insulin pump titration V53.91
insulin pump training V65.46
intrauterine device
insertion V25.1
management V25.42
investigation to determine further disposition V63.8
in vitro fertilization cycle V26.81
isolation V07.0
issue of
disability examination certificate V68.01
medical certificate NEC V68.09
repeat prescription NEC V68.1
contraceptive device NEC V25.49
kidney dialysis V56.0
lengthening of growth rod V54.02
mental health evaluation V70.2
requested by authority V70.1
natural family planning counseling and advice
procreative V26.41
to avoid pregnancy V25.04
nonmedical reason NEC V68.89
nursing care evaluation V63.8
observation (without need for further medical care) (*see also* Observation) V71.9
accident V71.4
alleged rape or seduction V71.5
criminal assault V71.6
following accident V71.4
at work V71.3
foreign body ingestion V71.89
growth and development variations, childhood V21.0
inflicted injury NEC V71.6
ingestion of deleterious agent or foreign body V71.89
injury V71.6
malignant neoplasm V71.1
mental disorder V71.09
newborn — *see* Observation, suspected, condition, newborn
rape V71.5
specified NEC V71.89
suspected
abuse V71.81
accident V71.4
at work V71.3
benign neoplasm V71.89
cardiovascular V71.7
disorder V71.9
exposure
anthrax V71.82
biological agent NEC V71.83
SARS V71.83
heart V71.7
inflicted injury NEC V71.6
malignant neoplasm V71.1
maternal and fetal problem not found
amniotic cavity and membrane V89.01
cervical shortening V89.05
fetal anomaly V89.03
fetal growth V89.04
oligohydramnios V89.01
other specified NEC V89.09

- **Admission** — *continued*
  - for — *continued*
    - vaccination, prophylactic — *continued*
      - typhoid alone — *continued*
        - with diphtheria-tetanus-pertussis (TAB + DTP) V06.2
      - typhoid-paratyphoid alone (TAB) V03.1
      - typhus V05.8
      - varicella (chicken pox) V05.4
      - viral encephalitis, arthropod-borne V05.0
      - viral hepatitis V05.3
      - yellow fever V04.4
    - vasectomy V25.2
    - vasoplasty for previous sterilization V26.0
    - vision examination V72.0
    - vocational therapy V57.22
    - waiting period for admission to other facility V63.2
      - undergoing social agency investigation V63.8
    - well baby and child care V20.2
    - x-ray of chest
      - for suspected tuberculosis V71.2
      - routine V72.5
- **Adnexitis** (suppurative) — *see also* Salpingo-oophoritis 614.2
- **Adolescence** NEC V21.2
- **Adoption**
  - agency referral V68.89
  - examination V70.3
  - held for V68.89
- **Adrenal gland** — *see* condition
- **Adrenalism** 255.9
  - tuberculous (*see also* Tuberculosis) 017.6 ☑
- **Adrenalitis, adrenitis** 255.8
  - meningococcal hemorrhagic 036.3
- **Adrenarche, precocious** 259.1
- **Adrenocortical syndrome** 255.2
- **Adrenogenital syndrome** (acquired) (congenital) 255.2
  - iatrogenic, fetus or newborn 760.79
- **Adrenoleukodystrophy** 277.86
  - neonatal 277.86
  - x-linked 277.86
- **Adrenomyeloneuropathy** 277.86
- **Adventitious bursa** — *see* Bursitis
- **Adynamia** (episodica) (hereditary) (periodic) 359.3
- **Adynamic**
  - ileus or intestine (*see also* Ileus) 560.1
  - ureter 753.22
- **Aeration lung, imperfect, newborn** 770.5
- **Aerobullosis** 993.3
- **Aerocele** — *see* Embolism, air
- **Aerodermectasia**
  - subcutaneous (traumatic) 958.7
    - surgical 998.81
  - surgical 998.81
- **Aerodontalgia** 993.2
- **Aeroembolism** 993.3
- **Aerogenes capsulatus infection** — *see also* Gangrene, gas 040.0
- **Aero-otitis media** 993.0
- **Aerophagy, aerophagia** 306.4
  - psychogenic 306.4
- **Aerosinusitis** 993.1
- **Aerotitis** 993.0
- **Affection, affections** — *see also* Disease
  - sacroiliac (joint), old 724.6
  - shoulder region NEC 726.2
- **Afibrinogenemia** 286.3
  - acquired 286.6
  - congenital 286.3
  - postpartum 666.3 ☑
- **African**
  - sleeping sickness 086.5
  - tick fever 087.1
  - trypanosomiasis 086.5
- **African** — *continued*
  - trypanosomiasis — *continued*
    - Gambian 086.3
    - Rhodesian 086.4
- **Aftercare** V58.9
  - amputation stump V54.89
  - artificial openings — *see* Attention to, artificial, opening
  - blood transfusion without reported diagnosis V58.2
  - breathing exercise V57.0
  - cardiac device V53.39
    - defibrillator, automatic implantable V53.32
    - pacemaker V53.31
      - carotid sinus V53.39
  - carotid sinus pacemaker V53.39
  - cerebral ventricle (communicating) shunt V53.01
  - chemotherapy session (adjunctive) (maintenance) V58.11
  - defibrillator, automatic implantable cardiac V53.32
  - exercise (remedial) (therapeutic) V57.1
    - breathing V57.0
  - extracorporeal dialysis (intermittent) (treatment) V56.0
  - following surgery NEC V58.49
    - for
      - injury V58.43
      - neoplasm V58.42
      - organ transplant V58.44
      - trauma V58.43
    - joint replacement V54.81
    - of
      - circulatory system V58.73
      - digestive system V58.75
      - genital organs V58.76
      - genitourinary system V58.76
      - musculoskeletal system V58.78
      - nervous system V58.72
      - oral cavity V58.75
      - respiratory system V58.74
      - sense organs V58.71
      - skin V58.77
      - subcutaneous tissue V58.77
      - teeth V58.75
      - urinary system V58.76
    - spinal — *see* Aftercare, following surgery, of, specified body system
    - wound closure, planned V58.41
  - fracture V54.9
    - healing V54.89
      - pathologic
        - ankle V54.29
        - arm V54.20
          - lower V54.22
          - upper V54.21
        - finger V54.29
        - foot V54.29
        - hand V54.29
        - hip V54.23
        - leg V54.24
          - lower V54.26
          - upper V54.25
        - pelvis V54.29
        - specified site NEC V54.29
        - toe(s) V54.29
        - vertebrae V54.27
        - wrist V54.29
      - traumatic
        - ankle V54.19
        - arm V54.10
          - lower V54.12
          - upper V54.11
        - finger V54.19
        - foot V54.19
        - hand V54.19
        - hip V54.13
        - leg V54.14
          - lower V54.16
          - upper V54.15
        - pelvis V54.19
        - specified site NEC V54.19
        - toe(s) V54.19
- **Aftercare** — *continued*
  - fracture — *continued*
    - healing — *continued*
      - traumatic — *continued*
        - vertebrae V54.17
        - wrist V54.19
    - removal of
      - external fixation device V54.89
      - internal fixation device V54.01
    - specified care NEC V54.89
  - gait training V57.1
    - for use of artificial limb(s) V57.81
  - internal fixation device V54.09
  - involving
    - dialysis (intermittent) (treatment)
      - extracorporeal V56.0
      - peritoneal V56.8
      - renal V56.0
    - gait training V57.1
      - for use of artificial limb(s) V57.81
    - growth rod
      - adjustment V54.02
      - lengthening V54.02
    - internal fixation device V54.09
    - orthoptic training V57.4
    - orthotic training V57.81
    - radiotherapy session V58.0
    - removal of
      - drains V58.49
      - dressings
        - wound V58.30
          - nonsurgical V58.30
          - surgical V58.31
      - fixation device
        - external V54.89
        - internal V54.01
      - fracture plate V54.01
      - nonsurgical wound dressing V58.30
      - pins V54.01
      - plaster cast V54.89
      - rods V54.01
      - screws V58.32
      - staples V58.32
      - surgical wound dressings V58.31
      - sutures V58.32
      - traction device, external V54.89
      - wound packing V58.30
        - nonsurgical V58.30
        - surgical V58.31
  - neuropacemaker (brain) (peripheral nerve) (spinal cord) V53.02
  - occupational therapy V57.21
  - orthodontic V58.5
  - orthopedic V54.9
    - change of external fixation or traction device V54.89
    - following joint replacement V54.81
    - internal fixation device V54.09
    - removal of fixation device
      - external V54.89
      - internal V54.01
    - specified care NEC V54.89
  - orthoptic training V57.4
  - orthotic training V57.81
  - pacemaker
    - brain V53.02
    - cardiac V53.31
    - carotid sinus V53.39
    - peripheral nerve V53.02
    - spinal cord V53.02
  - peritoneal dialysis (intermittent) (treatment) V56.8
  - physical therapy NEC V57.1
    - breathing exercises V57.0
  - radiotherapy session V58.0
  - rehabilitation procedure V57.9
    - breathing exercises V57.0
    - multiple types V57.89
    - occupational V57.21
    - orthoptic V57.4
    - orthotic V57.81
    - physical therapy NEC V57.1
    - remedial exercises V57.1
- **Aftercare** — *continued*
  - rehabilitation procedure — *continued*
    - specified type NEC V57.89
    - speech V57.3
    - therapeutic exercises V57.1
    - vocational V57.22
  - renal dialysis (intermittent) (treatment) V56.0
  - specified type NEC V58.89
    - removal of non-vascular catheter V58.82
    - removal of vascular catheter V58.81
  - speech therapy V57.3
  - stump, amputation V54.89
  - vocational rehabilitation V57.22
- **After-cataract** 366.50
  - obscuring vision 366.53
  - specified type, not obscuring vision 366.52
- **Agalactia** 676.4 ☑
- **Agammaglobulinemia** 279.00
  - with lymphopenia 279.2
  - acquired (primary) (secondary) 279.06
  - Bruton's X-linked 279.04
  - infantile sex-linked (Bruton's) (congenital) 279.04
  - Swiss-type 279.2
- **Aganglionosis** (bowel) (colon) 751.3
- **Age** (old) — *see also* Senile 797
- **Agenesis** — *see also* Absence, by site, congenital
  - acoustic nerve 742.8
  - adrenal (gland) 759.1
  - alimentary tract (complete) (partial) NEC 751.8
    - lower 751.2
    - upper 750.8
  - anus, anal (canal) 751.2
  - aorta 747.22
  - appendix 751.2
  - arm (complete) (partial) (*see also* Deformity, reduction, upper limb) 755.20
  - artery (peripheral) NEC (*see also* Anomaly, peripheral vascular system) 747.60
    - brain 747.81
    - coronary 746.85
    - pulmonary 747.3
    - umbilical 747.5
  - auditory (canal) (external) 744.01
  - auricle (ear) 744.01
  - bile, biliary duct or passage 751.61
  - bone NEC 756.9
  - brain 740.0
    - specified part 742.2
  - breast 757.6
  - bronchus 748.3
  - canaliculus lacrimalis 743.65
  - carpus NEC (*see also* Deformity, reduction, upper limb) 755.28
  - cartilage 756.9
  - cecum 751.2
  - cerebellum 742.2
  - cervix 752.49
  - chin 744.89
  - cilia 743.63
  - circulatory system, part NEC 747.89
  - clavicle 755.51
  - clitoris 752.49
  - coccyx 756.13
  - colon 751.2
  - corpus callosum 742.2
  - cricoid cartilage 748.3
  - diaphragm (with hernia) 756.6
  - digestive organ(s) or tract (complete) (partial) NEC 751.8
    - lower 751.2
    - upper 750.8
  - ductus arteriosus 747.89
  - duodenum 751.1
  - ear NEC 744.09
    - auricle 744.01
    - lobe 744.21

- **Agenesis** — *see also* Absence, by site, congenital — *continued*
  - ejaculatory duct 752.89
  - endocrine (gland) NEC 759.2
  - epiglottis 748.3
  - esophagus 750.3
  - Eustachian tube 744.24
  - extrinsic muscle, eye 743.69
  - eye 743.00
    - adnexa 743.69
  - eyelid (fold) 743.62
  - face
    - bones NEC 756.0
    - specified part NEC 744.89
  - fallopian tube 752.19
  - femur NEC (*see also* Absence, femur, congenital) 755.34
  - fibula NEC (*see also* Absence, fibula, congenital) 755.37
  - finger NEC (*see also* Absence, finger, congenital) 755.29
  - foot (complete) (*see also* Deformity, reduction, lower limb) 755.31
  - gallbladder 751.69
  - gastric 750.8
  - genitalia, genital (organ)
    - female 752.89
      - external 752.49
      - internal NEC 752.89
    - male 752.89
      - penis 752.69
  - glottis 748.3
  - gonadal 758.6
  - hair 757.4
  - hand (complete) (*see also* Deformity, reduction, upper limb) 755.21
  - heart 746.89
    - valve NEC 746.89
      - aortic 746.89
      - mitral 746.89
      - pulmonary 746.01
  - hepatic 751.69
  - humerus NEC (*see also* Absence, humerus, congenital) 755.24
  - hymen 752.49
  - ileum 751.1
  - incus 744.04
  - intestine (small) 751.1
    - large 751.2
  - iris (dilator fibers) 743.45
  - jaw 524.09
  - jejunum 751.1
  - kidney(s) (partial) (unilateral) 753.0
  - labium (majus) (minus) 752.49
  - labyrinth, membranous 744.05
  - lacrimal apparatus (congenital) 743.65
  - larynx 748.3
  - leg NEC (*see also* Deformity, reduction, lower limb) 755.30
  - lens 743.35
  - limb (complete) (partial) (*see also* Deformity, reduction) 755.4
    - lower NEC 755.30
    - upper 755.20
  - lip 750.26
  - liver 751.69
  - lung (bilateral) (fissures) (lobe) (unilateral) 748.5
  - mandible 524.09
  - maxilla 524.09
  - metacarpus NEC 755.28
  - metatarsus NEC 755.38
  - muscle (any) 756.81
  - musculoskeletal system NEC 756.9
  - nail(s) 757.5
  - neck, part 744.89
  - nerve 742.8
  - nervous system, part NEC 742.8
  - nipple 757.6
  - nose 748.1
  - nuclear 742.8
  - organ
    - of Corti 744.05
    - or site not listed — *see* Anomaly, specified type NEC
  - osseous meatus (ear) 744.03

- **Agenesis** — *see also* Absence, by site, congenital — *continued*
  - ovary 752.0
  - oviduct 752.19
  - pancreas 751.7
  - parathyroid (gland) 759.2
  - patella 755.64
  - pelvic girdle (complete) (partial) 755.69
  - penis 752.69
  - pericardium 746.89
  - perineal body 756.81
  - pituitary (gland) 759.2
  - prostate 752.89
  - pulmonary
    - artery 747.3
    - trunk 747.3
    - vein 747.49
  - punctum lacrimale 743.65
  - radioulnar NEC (*see also* Absence, forearm, congenital) 755.25
  - radius NEC (*see also* Absence, radius, congenital) 755.26
  - rectum 751.2
  - renal 753.0
  - respiratory organ NEC 748.9
  - rib 756.3
  - roof of orbit 742.0
  - round ligament 752.89
  - sacrum 756.13
  - salivary gland 750.21
  - scapula 755.59
  - scrotum 752.89
  - seminal duct or tract 752.89
  - septum
    - atrial 745.69
    - between aorta and pulmonary artery 745.0
    - ventricular 745.3
  - shoulder girdle (complete) (partial) 755.59
  - skull (bone) 756.0
    - with
      - anencephalus 740.0
      - encephalocele 742.0
      - hydrocephalus 742.3
        - with spina bifida (*see also* Spina bifida) 741.0 ☑
      - microcephalus 742.1
  - spermatic cord 752.89
  - spinal cord 742.59
  - spine 756.13
    - lumbar 756.13
      - isthmus 756.11
      - pars articularis 756.11
  - spleen 759.0
  - sternum 756.3
  - stomach 750.7
  - tarsus NEC 755.38
  - tendon 756.81
  - testicular 752.89
  - testis 752.89
  - thymus (gland) 759.2
  - thyroid (gland) 243
    - cartilage 748.3
  - tibia NEC (*see also* Absence, tibia, congenital) 755.36
  - tibiofibular NEC 755.35
  - toe (complete) (partial) (*see also* Absence, toe, congenital) 755.39
  - tongue 750.11
  - trachea (cartilage) 748.3
  - ulna NEC (*see also* Absence, ulna, congenital) 755.27
  - ureter 753.4
  - urethra 753.8
  - urinary tract NEC 753.8
  - uterus 752.3
  - uvula 750.26
  - vagina 752.49
  - vas deferens 752.89
  - vein(s) (peripheral) NEC (*see also* Anomaly, peripheral vascular system) 747.60
    - brain 747.81
    - great 747.49
    - portal 747.49

- **Agenesis** — *see also* Absence, by site, congenital — *continued*
  - vein(s) (*see also* Anomaly, peripheral vascular system) — *continued*
    - pulmonary 747.49
  - vena cava (inferior) (superior) 747.49
  - vermis of cerebellum 742.2
  - vertebra 756.13
    - lumbar 756.13
      - isthmus 756.11
      - pars articularis 756.11
  - vulva 752.49
- **Ageusia** — *see also* Disturbance, sensation 781.1
- **Aggressiveness** 301.3
- **Aggressive outburst** — *see also* Disturbance, conduct 312.0 ☑
  - in children or adolescents 313.9
- **Aging skin** 701.8
- **Agitated** — *see* condition
- **Agitation** 307.9
  - catatonic (*see also* Schizophrenia) 295.2 ☑
- **Aglossia** (congenital) 750.11
- **Aglycogenosis** 271.0
- **Agnail** (finger) (with lymphangitis) 681.02
- **Agnosia** (body image) (tactile) 784.69
  - verbal 784.69
    - auditory 784.69
      - secondary to organic lesion 784.69
    - developmental 315.8
      - secondary to organic lesion 784.69
  - visual 368.16
    - object 368.16
- **Agoraphobia** 300.22
  - with panic disorder 300.21
- **Agrammatism** 784.69
- **Agranulocytopenia** — *see also* Agranulocytosis 288.09
- **Agranulocytosis** (angina) 288.09
  - chronic 288.09
  - cyclical 288.02
  - genetic 288.01
  - infantile 288.01
  - periodic 288.02
  - pernicious 288.09
- **Agraphia** (absolute) 784.69
  - with alexia 784.61
  - developmental 315.39
- **Agrypnia** — *see also* Insomnia 780.52
- **Ague** — *see also* Malaria 084.6
  - brass-founders' 985.8
  - dumb 084.6
  - tertian 084.1
- **Agyria** 742.2
- **Ahumada-del Castillo syndrome** (nonpuerperal galactorrhea and amenorrhea) 253.1
- **AIDS** 042
- **AIDS-associated retrovirus** (disease) (illness) 042
  - infection — *see* Human immunodeficiency virus, infection
- **AIDS-associated virus** (disease) (illness) 042
  - infection — *see* Human immunodeficiency virus, infection
- **AIDS-like disease** (illness) (syndrome) 042
- **AIDS-related complex** 042
- **AIDS-related conditions** 042
- **AIDS-related virus** (disease) (illness) 042
  - infection — *see* Human immunodeficiency virus, infection
- **AIDS virus** (disease) (illness) 042
  - infection — *see* Human immunodeficiency virus, infection
- **Ailment, heart** — *see* Disease, heart
- **Ailurophobia** 300.29
- **Ainhum** (disease) 136.0
- **AIN I** [anal intraepithelial neoplasia I] (histologically confirmed) 569.44
- **AIN II** [anal intraepithelial neoplasia II] (histologically confirmed) 569.44
- **AIN III** [anal intraepithelial neoplasia III] 230.6
  - anal canal 230.5
- **Air**
  - anterior mediastinum 518.1
  - compressed, disease 993.3
  - embolism (any site) (artery) (cerebral) 958.0
    - with
      - abortion — *see* Abortion, by type, with embolism
      - ectopic pregnancy (*see also* categories 633.0–633.9) 639.6
      - molar pregnancy (*see also* categories 630–632) 639.6
    - due to implanted device — *see* Complications, due to (presence of) any device, implant, or graft classified to 996.0–996.5 NEC
    - following
      - abortion 639.6
      - ectopic or molar pregnancy 639.6
      - infusion, perfusion, or transfusion 999.1
    - in pregnancy, childbirth, or puerperium 673.0 ☑
    - traumatic 958.0
  - hunger 786.09
    - psychogenic 306.1
  - leak (lung) (pulmonary) (thorax) 512.8
    - iatrogenic 512.1
    - postoperative 512.1
  - rarefied, effects of — *see* Effect, adverse, high altitude
  - sickness 994.6
- **Airplane sickness** 994.6
- **Akathisia, acathisia** 781.0
  - due to drugs 333.99
  - neuroleptic-induced acute 333.99
- **Akinesia algeria** 352.6
- **Akiyami** 100.89
- **Akureyri disease** (epidemic neuromyasthenia) 049.8
- **Alacrima** (congenital) 743.65
- **Alactasia** (hereditary) 271.3
- **Alagille syndrome** 759.89
- **Alalia** 784.3
  - developmental 315.31
    - receptive-expressive 315.32
  - secondary to organic lesion 784.3
- **Alaninemia** 270.8
- **Alastrim** 050.1
- **Albarrán's disease** (colibacilluria) 791.9
- **Albers-Schönberg's disease** (marble bones) 756.52
- **Albert's disease** 726.71
- **Albinism, albino** (choroid) (cutaneous) (eye) (generalized) (isolated) (ocular) (oculocutaneous) (partial) 270.2
- **Albinismus** 270.2
- **Albright (-Martin) (-Bantam) disease** (pseudohypoparathyroidism) 275.49
- **Albright (-McCune) (-Sternberg) syndrome** (osteitis fibrosa disseminata) 756.59
- **Albuminous** — *see* condition
- **Albuminuria, albuminuric** (acute) (chronic) (subacute) 791.0
  - Bence-Jones 791.0
  - cardiac 785.9
  - complicating pregnancy, childbirth, or puerperium 646.2 ☑
    - with hypertension — *see* Toxemia, of pregnancy
    - affecting fetus or newborn 760.1
  - cyclic 593.6
  - gestational 646.2 ☑
  - gravidarum 646.2 ☑
    - with hypertension — *see* Toxemia, of pregnancy
    - affecting fetus or newborn 760.1
  - heart 785.9

- **Albuminuria, albuminuric** — *continued*
  - idiopathic 593.6
  - orthostatic 593.6
  - postural 593.6
  - pre-eclamptic (mild) 642.4 ☑
    - affecting fetus or newborn 760.0
    - severe 642.5 ☑
      - affecting fetus or newborn 760.0
  - recurrent physiologic 593.6
  - scarlatinal 034.1
- **Albumosuria** 791.0
  - Bence-Jones 791.0
  - myelopathic (M9730/3) 203.0 ☑
- **Alcaptonuria** 270.2
- **Alcohol, alcoholic**
  - abstinence 291.81
  - acute intoxication 305.0 ☑
    - with dependence 303.0 ☑
  - addiction (*see also* Alcoholism) 303.9 ☑
    - maternal
      - with suspected fetal damage affecting management of pregnancy 655.4 ☑
      - affecting fetus or newborn 760.71
  - amnestic disorder, persisting 291.1
  - anxiety 291.89
  - brain syndrome, chronic 291.2
  - cardiopathy 425.5
  - chronic (*see also* Alcoholism) 303.9 ☑
  - cirrhosis (liver) 571.2
  - delirium 291.0
    - acute 291.0
    - chronic 291.1
    - tremens 291.0
    - withdrawal 291.0
  - dementia NEC 291.2
  - deterioration 291.2
  - drunkenness (simple) 305.0 ☑
  - hallucinosis (acute) 291.3
  - induced
    - circadian rhythm sleep disorder 291.82
    - hypersomnia 291.82
    - insomnia 291.82
    - mental disorder 291.9
      - anxiety 291.89
      - mood 291.89
      - sexual 291.89
      - sleep 291.82
      - specified type 291.89
    - parasomnia 291.82
    - persisting
      - amnestic disorder 291.1
      - dementia 291.2
    - psychotic disorder
      - with
        - delusions 291.5
        - hallucinations 291.3
    - sleep disorder 291.82
  - insanity 291.9
  - intoxication (acute) 305.0 ☑
    - with dependence 303.0 ☑
    - pathological 291.4
  - jealousy 291.5
  - Korsakoff's, Korsakov's, Korsakow's 291.1
  - liver NEC 571.3
    - acute 571.1
    - chronic 571.2
  - mania (acute) (chronic) 291.9
  - mood 291.89
  - paranoia 291.5
  - paranoid (type) psychosis 291.5
  - pellagra 265.2
  - poisoning, accidental (acute) NEC 980.9
    - specified type of alcohol — *see* Table of Drugs and Chemicals
  - psychosis (*see also* Psychosis, alcoholic) 291.9
    - Korsakoff's, Korsakov's, Korsakow's 291.1
    - polyneuritic 291.1
- **Alcohol, alcoholic** — *continued*
  - psychosis (*see also* Psychosis, alcoholic) — *continued*
    - polyneuritic — *continued*
      - with
        - delusions 291.5
        - hallucinations 291.3
  - related disorder 291.9
  - withdrawal symptoms, syndrome NEC 291.81
    - delirium 291.0
    - hallucinosis 291.3
- **Alcoholism** 303.9 ☑

Note — Use the following fifth-digit subclassification with category 303:

0 unspecified
1 continuous
2 episodic
3 in remission

  - with psychosis (*see also* Psychosis, alcoholic) 291.9
  - acute 303.0 ☑
  - chronic 303.9 ☑
    - with psychosis 291.9
  - complicating pregnancy, childbirth, or puerperium 648.4 ☑
    - affecting fetus or newborn 760.71
  - history V11.3
  - Korsakoff's, Korsakov's, Korsakow's 291.1
  - suspected damage to fetus affecting management of pregnancy 655.4 ☑
- **Alder's anomaly or syndrome** (leukocyte granulation anomaly) 288.2
- **Alder-Reilly anomaly** (leukocyte granulation) 288.2
- **Aldosteronism** (primary) 255.10
  - congenital 255.10
  - familial type I 255.11
  - glucocorticoid-remediable 255.11
  - secondary 255.14
- **Aldosteronoma** (M8370/1) 237.2
- **Aldrich (-Wiskott) syndrome** (eczema-thrombocytopenia) 279.12
- **Aleppo boil** 085.1
- **Aleukemic** — *see* condition
- **Aleukia**
  - congenital 288.09
  - hemorrhagica 284.9
    - acquired (secondary) 284.89
    - congenital 284.09
    - idiopathic 284.9
  - splenica 289.4
- **Alexia** (congenital) (developmental) 315.01
  - secondary to organic lesion 784.61
- **Algoneurodystrophy** 733.7
- **Algophobia** 300.29
- **Alibert-Bazin disease** (M9700/3) 202.1 ☑
- **Alibert's disease** (mycosis fungoides) (M9700/3) 202.1 ☑
- **Alice in Wonderland syndrome** 293.89
- **Alienation, mental** — *see also* Psychosis 298.9
- **Alkalemia** 276.3
- **Alkalosis** 276.3
  - metabolic 276.3
    - with respiratory acidosis 276.4
  - respiratory 276.3
- **Alkaptonuria** 270.2
- **Allen-Masters syndrome** 620.6
- **Allergic bronchopulmonary aspergillosis** 518.6
- **Allergy, allergic** (reaction) 995.3
  - air-borne substance — *see* also Fever, hay 477.9
    - specified allergen NEC 477.8
  - alveolitis (extrinsic) 495.9
    - due to
      - Aspergillus clavatus 495.4
      - cryptostroma corticale 495.6
- **Allergy, allergic** — *continued*
  - alveolitis — *continued*
    - due to — *continued*
      - organisms (fungal, thermophilic actinomycete, other) growing in ventilation (air conditioning systems) 495.7
    - specified type NEC 495.8
  - anaphylactic shock 999.4
    - due to food — *see* Anaphylactic shock, due to, food
  - angioneurotic edema 995.1
  - animal (cat) (dog) (epidermal) 477.8
    - dander 477.2
    - hair 477.2
  - arthritis (*see also* Arthritis, allergic) 716.2 ☑
  - asthma — *see* Asthma
  - bee sting (anaphylactic shock) 989.5
  - biological — *see* Allergy, drug
  - bronchial asthma — *see* Asthma
  - conjunctivitis (eczematous) 372.14
  - dander, animal (cat) (dog) 477.2
  - dandruff 477.8
  - dermatitis (venenata) — *see* Dermatitis
  - diathesis V15.09
  - drug, medicinal substance, and biological (any) (correct medicinal substance properly administered) (external) (internal) 995.27
    - wrong substance given or taken NEC 977.9
      - specified drug or substance — *see* Table of Drugs and Chemicals
  - dust (house) (stock) 477.8
  - eczema — *see* Eczema
  - endophthalmitis 360.19
  - epidermal (animal) 477.8
  - existing dental restorative material 525.66
  - feathers 477.8
  - food (any) (ingested) 693.1
    - atopic 691.8
    - in contact with skin 692.5
  - gastritis 535.4 ☑
  - gastroenteritis 558.3
  - gastrointestinal 558.3
  - grain 477.0
  - grass (pollen) 477.0
    - asthma (*see also* Asthma) 493.0 ☑
    - hay fever 477.0
  - hair, animal (cat) (dog) 477.2
  - hay fever (grass) (pollen) (ragweed) (tree) (*see also* Fever, hay) 477.9
  - history (of) V15.09
    - to
      - eggs V15.03
      - food additives V15.05
      - insect bite V15.06
      - latex V15.07
      - milk products V15.02
      - nuts V15.05
        - peanuts V15.01
      - radiographic dye V15.08
      - seafood V15.04
      - specified food NEC V15.05
      - spider bite V15.06
  - horse serum — see Allergy, serum
  - inhalant 477.9
    - dust 477.8
    - pollen 477.0
    - specified allergen other than pollen 477.8
  - kapok 477.8
  - medicine — *see* Allergy, drug
  - migraine 339.00
  - milk protein 558.3
  - pannus 370.62
  - pneumonia 518.3
  - pollen (any) (hay fever) 477.0
    - asthma (*see also* Asthma) 493.0 ☑
  - primrose 477.0
- **Allergy, allergic** — *continued*
  - primula 477.0
  - purpura 287.0
  - ragweed (pollen) (Senecio jacobae) 477.0
    - asthma (*see also* Asthma) 493.0 ☑
    - hay fever 477.0
  - respiratory (*see also* Allergy, inhalant) 477.9
    - due to
      - drug — *see* Allergy, drug
      - food — *see* Allergy, food
  - rhinitis (*see also* Fever, hay) 477.9
    - due to food 477.1
  - rose 477.0
  - Senecio jacobae 477.0
  - serum (prophylactic) (therapeutic) 999.5
    - anaphylactic shock 999.4
  - shock (anaphylactic) (due to adverse effect of correct medicinal substance properly administered) 995.0
    - food — *see* Anaphylactic shock, due to, food
    - from serum or immunization 999.5
      - anaphylactic 999.4
  - sinusitis (*see also* Fever, hay) 477.9
  - skin reaction 692.9
    - specified substance — *see* Dermatitis, due to
  - tree (any) (hay fever) (pollen) 477.0
    - asthma (*see also* Asthma) 493.0 ☑
  - upper respiratory (*see also* Fever, hay) 477.9
  - urethritis 597.89
  - urticaria 708.0
  - vaccine — *see* Allergy, serum
- **Allescheriosis** 117.6
- **Alligator skin disease** (ichthyosis congenita) 757.1
  - acquired 701.1
- **Allocheiria, allochiria** — *see also* Disturbance, sensation 782.0
- **Almeida's disease** (Brazilian blastomycosis) 116.1
- **Alopecia** (atrophicans) (pregnancy) (premature) (senile) 704.00
  - adnata 757.4
  - areata 704.01
  - celsi 704.01
  - cicatrisata 704.09
  - circumscripta 704.01
  - congenital, congenitalis 757.4
  - disseminata 704.01
  - effluvium (telogen) 704.02
  - febrile 704.09
  - generalisata 704.09
  - hereditaria 704.09
  - marginalis 704.01
  - mucinosa 704.09
  - postinfectional 704.09
  - seborrheica 704.09
  - specific 091.82
  - syphilitic (secondary) 091.82
  - telogen effluvium 704.02
  - totalis 704.09
  - toxica 704.09
  - universalis 704.09
  - x-ray 704.09
- **Alpers' disease** 330.8
- **Alpha-lipoproteinemia** 272.4
- **Alpha thalassemia** 282.49
- **Alphos** 696.1
- **Alpine sickness** 993.2
- **Alport's syndrome** (hereditary hematuria-nephropathy-deafness) 759.89
- **Alteration** (of), altered
  - awareness 780.09
    - transient 780.02
  - consciousness 780.09
    - persistent vegetative state 780.03
    - transient 780.02
  - mental status 780.97
    - amnesia (retrograde) 780.93
    - memory loss 780.93

- **Alternaria** (infection) 118
- **Alternating** — *see* condition
- **Altitude, high** (effects) — *see* Effect, adverse, high altitude
- **Aluminosis** (of lung) 503
- **Alvarez syndrome** (transient cerebral ischemia) 435.9
- **Alveolar capillary block syndrome** 516.3
- **Alveolitis**
  - allergic (extrinsic) 495.9
    - due to organisms (fungal, thermophilic actinomycete, other) growing in ventilation (air conditioning systems) 495.7
    - specified type NEC 495.8
  - due to
    - Aspergillus clavatus 495.4
    - Cryptostroma corticale 495.6
  - fibrosing (chronic) (cryptogenic) (lung) 516.3
    - idiopathic 516.3
    - rheumatoid 714.81
  - jaw 526.5
  - sicca dolorosa 526.5
- **Alveolus, alveolar** — *see* condition
- **Alymphocytosis** (pure) 279.2
- **Alymphoplasia, thymic** 279.2
- **Alzheimer's**
  - dementia (senile)
    - with behavioral disturbance 331.0 *[294.11]*
    - without behavioral disturbance 331.0 *[294.10]*
  - disease or sclerosis 331.0
    - with dementia — *see* Alzheimer's, dementia
- **Amastia** — *see also* Absence, breast 611.89
- **Amaurosis** (acquired) (congenital) — *see also* Blindness 369.00
  - fugax 362.34
  - hysterical 300.11
  - Leber's (congenital) 362.76
  - tobacco 377.34
  - uremic — *see* Uremia
- **Amaurotic familial idiocy** (infantile) (juvenile) (late) 330.1
- **Ambisexual** 752.7
- **Amblyopia** (acquired) (congenital) (partial) 368.00
  - color 368.59
    - acquired 368.55
  - deprivation 368.02
  - ex anopsia 368.00
  - hysterical 300.11
  - nocturnal 368.60
    - vitamin A deficiency 264.5
  - refractive 368.03
  - strabismic 368.01
  - suppression 368.01
  - tobacco 377.34
  - toxic NEC 377.34
  - uremic — *see* Uremia
- **Ameba, amebic** (histolytica) — *see also* Amebiasis
  - abscess 006.3
    - bladder 006.8
    - brain (with liver and lung abscess) 006.5
    - liver 006.3
      - with
        - brain abscess (and lung abscess) 006.5
        - lung abscess 006.4
    - lung (with liver abscess) 006.4
      - with brain abscess 006.5
    - seminal vesicle 006.8
    - spleen 006.8
  - carrier (suspected of) V02.2
  - meningoencephalitis
    - due to Naegleria (gruberi) 136.29
    - primary 136.29
- **Amebiasis** NEC 006.9
- **Amebiasis** — *continued*
  - with
    - brain abscess (with liver or lung abscess) 006.5
    - liver abscess (without mention of brain or lung abscess) 006.3
    - lung abscess (with liver abscess) 006.4
      - with brain abscess 006.5
  - acute 006.0
  - bladder 006.8
  - chronic 006.1
  - cutaneous 006.6
  - cutis 006.6
  - due to organism other than Entamoeba histolytica 007.8
  - hepatic (*see also* Abscess, liver, amebic) 006.3
  - nondysenteric 006.2
  - seminal vesicle 006.8
  - specified
    - organism NEC 007.8
    - site NEC 006.8
- **Ameboma** 006.8
- **Amelia** 755.4
  - lower limb 755.31
  - upper limb 755.21
- **Ameloblastoma** (M9310/0) 213.1
  - jaw (bone) (lower) 213.1
    - upper 213.0
  - long bones (M9261/3) — *see* Neoplasm, bone, malignant
  - malignant (M9310/3) 170.1
    - jaw (bone) (lower) 170.1
      - upper 170.0
  - mandible 213.1
  - tibial (M9261/3) 170.7
- **Amelogenesis imperfecta** 520.5
  - nonhereditaria (segmentalis) 520.4
- **Amenorrhea** (primary) (secondary) 626.0
  - due to ovarian dysfunction 256.8
  - hyperhormonal 256.8
- **Amentia** — *see also* Retardation, mental 319
  - Meynert's (nonalcoholic) 294.0
    - alcoholic 291.1
  - nevoid 759.6
- **American**
  - leishmaniasis 085.5
  - mountain tick fever 066.1
  - trypanosomiasis — *see* Trypanosomiasis, American
- **Ametropia** — *see also* Disorder, accommodation 367.9
- **Amianthosis** 501
- **Amimia** 784.69
- **Amino acid**
  - deficiency 270.9
    - anemia 281.4
  - metabolic disorder (*see also* Disorder, amino acid) 270.9
- **Aminoaciduria** 270.9
  - imidazole 270.5
- **Amnesia** (retrograde) 780.93
  - auditory 784.69
    - developmental 315.31
    - secondary to organic lesion 784.69
  - dissociative 300.12
  - hysterical or dissociative type 300.12
  - psychogenic 300.12
  - transient global 437.7
- **Amnestic** (confabulatory) **syndrome** 294.0
  - alcohol-induced persisting 291.1
  - drug-induced persisting 292.83
  - posttraumatic 294.0
- **Amniocentesis screening** (for) V28.2
  - alphafetoprotein level, raised V28.1
  - chromosomal anomalies V28.0
- **Amnion, amniotic** — *see also* condition
  - nodosum 658.8 ☑
- **Amnionitis** (complicating pregnancy) 658.4 ☑
  - affecting fetus or newborn 762.7
- **Amoral trends** 301.7
- **Amotio retinae** — *see also* Detachment, retina 361.9
- **Ampulla**
  - lower esophagus 530.89
  - phrenic 530.89
- **Amputation**
  - any part of fetus, to facilitate delivery 763.89
  - cervix (supravaginal) (uteri) 622.8
    - in pregnancy or childbirth 654.6 ☑
      - affecting fetus or newborn 763.89
  - clitoris — *see* Wound, open, clitoris
  - congenital
    - lower limb 755.31
    - upper limb 755.21
  - neuroma (traumatic) (*see also* Injury, nerve, by site)
    - surgical complication (late) 997.61
  - penis — *see* Amputation, traumatic, penis
  - status (without complication) — *see* Absence, by site, acquired
  - stump (surgical) (posttraumatic)
    - abnormal, painful, or with complication (late) 997.60
    - healed or old NEC (*see also* Absence, by site, acquired)
      - lower V49.70
      - upper V49.60
  - traumatic (complete) (partial)

Note — "Complicated" includes traumatic amputation with delayed healing, delayed treatment, foreign body, or infection.

    - arm 887.4
      - at or above elbow 887.2
        - complicated 887.3
      - below elbow 887.0
        - complicated 887.1
      - both (bilateral) (any level(s)) 887.6
        - complicated 887.7
      - complicated 887.5
    - finger(s) (one or both hands) 886.0
      - with thumb(s) 885.0
        - complicated 885.1
      - complicated 886.1
    - foot (except toe(s) only) 896.0
      - and other leg 897.6
        - complicated 897.7
      - both (bilateral) 896.2
        - complicated 896.3
      - complicated 896.1
      - toe(s) only (one or both feet) 895.0
        - complicated 895.1
    - genital organ(s) (external) NEC 878.8
      - complicated 878.9
    - hand (except finger(s) only) 887.0
      - and other arm 887.6
        - complicated 887.7
      - both (bilateral) 887.6
        - complicated 887.7
      - complicated 887.1
      - finger(s) (one or both hands) 886.0
        - with thumb(s) 885.0
          - complicated 885.1
        - complicated 886.1
      - thumb(s) (with fingers of either hand) 885.0
        - complicated 885.1
    - head 874.9
    - late effect — *see* Late, effects (of), amputation
    - leg 897.4
      - and other foot 897.6
        - complicated 897.7
      - at or above knee 897.2
        - complicated 897.3
      - below knee 897.0
        - complicated 897.1
      - both (bilateral) 897.6
        - complicated 897.7
- **Amputation** — *continued*
  - traumatic — *continued*
    - leg — *continued*
      - complicated 897.5
    - lower limb(s) except toe(s) — *see* Amputation, traumatic, leg
    - nose — *see* Wound, open, nose
    - penis 878.0
      - complicated 878.1
    - sites other than limbs — *see* Wound, open, by site
    - thumb(s) (with finger(s) of either hand) 885.0
      - complicated 885.1
    - toe(s) (one or both feet) 895.0
      - complicated 895.1
    - upper limb(s) — *see* Amputation, traumatic, arm
- **Amputee** (bilateral) (old) — *see also* Absence, by site, acquired V49.70
- **Amusia** 784.69
  - developmental 315.39
  - secondary to organic lesion 784.69
- **Amyelencephalus** 740.0
- **Amyelia** 742.59
- **Amygdalitis** — *see* Tonsillitis
- **Amygdalolith** 474.8
- **Amyloid disease or degeneration** 277.30
  - heart 277.39 *[425.7]*
- **Amyloidosis** (familial) (general) (generalized) (genetic) (primary) 277.30
  - with lung involvement 277.39 *[517.8]*
  - cardiac, hereditary 277.39
  - heart 277.39 *[425.7]*
  - nephropathic 277.39 *[583.81]*
  - neuropathic (Portuguese) (Swiss) 277.39 *[357.4]*
  - pulmonary 277.39 *[517.8]*
  - secondary 277.39
  - systemic, inherited 277.39
- **Amylopectinosis** (brancher enzyme deficiency) 271.0
- **Amylophagia** 307.52
- **Amyoplasia, congenita** 756.89
- **Amyotonia** 728.2
  - congenita 358.8
- **Amyotrophia, amyotrophy, amyotrophic** 728.2
  - congenita 756.89
  - diabetic 250.6 ☑ *[353.5]*
    - due to secondary diabetes 249.6 ☑ *[353.5]*
  - lateral sclerosis (syndrome) 335.20
  - neuralgic 353.5
  - sclerosis (lateral) 335.20
  - spinal progressive 335.21
- **Anacidity, gastric** 536.0
  - psychogenic 306.4
- **Anaerosis of newborn** 770.88
- **Analbuminemia** 273.8
- **Analgesia** — *see also* Anesthesia 782.0
- **Analphalipoproteinemia** 272.5
- **Anaphylactic shock or reaction** (correct substance properly administered) 995.0
  - due to
    - food 995.60
      - additives 995.66
      - crustaceans 995.62
      - eggs 995.68
      - fish 995.65
      - fruits 995.63
      - milk products 995.67
      - nuts (tree) 995.64
      - peanuts 995.61
      - seeds 995.64
      - specified NEC 995.69
      - tree nuts 995.64
      - vegetables 995.63
    - immunization 999.4
    - overdose or wrong substance given or taken 977.9
      - specified drug — *see* Table of Drugs and Chemicals
    - serum 999.4

Anesthesia, anesthetic — *continued*
- complication or reaction — *continued*
  - due to — *continued*
    - overdose or wrong substance given — *continued*
      - specified anesthetic — *see* Table of Drugs and Chemicals
- cornea 371.81
- death from
  - correct substance properly administered 995.4
  - during delivery 668.9 ☑
  - overdose or wrong substance given 968.4
  - specified anesthetic — *see* Table of Drugs and Chemicals
- eye 371.81
- functional 300.11
- hyperesthetic, thalamic 338.0
- hysterical 300.11
- local skin lesion 782.0
- olfactory 781.1
- sexual (psychogenic) 302.72
- shock
  - due to
    - correct substance properly administered 995.4
    - overdose or wrong substance given 968.4
    - specified anesthetic — *see* Table of Drugs and Chemicals
- skin 782.0
- tactile 782.0
- testicular 608.9
- thermal 782.0

Anetoderma (maculosum) 701.3

Aneuploidy NEC 758.5

Aneurin deficiency 265.1

Aneurysm (anastomotic) (artery) (cirsoid) (diffuse) (false) (fusiform) (multiple) (ruptured) (saccular) (varicose) 442.9
- abdominal (aorta) 441.4
  - ruptured 441.3
  - syphilitic 093.0
- aorta, aortic (nonsyphilitic) 441.9
  - abdominal 441.4
    - dissecting 441.02
    - ruptured 441.3
    - syphilitic 093.0
  - arch 441.2
    - ruptured 441.1
  - arteriosclerotic NEC 441.9
    - ruptured 441.5
  - ascending 441.2
    - ruptured 441.1
  - congenital 747.29
  - descending 441.9
    - abdominal 441.4
      - ruptured 441.3
    - ruptured 441.5
    - thoracic 441.2
      - ruptured 441.1
  - dissecting 441.00
    - abdominal 441.02
    - thoracic 441.01
    - thoracoabdominal 441.03
  - due to coarctation (aorta) 747.10
  - ruptured 441.5
  - sinus, right 747.29
  - syphilitic 093.0
  - thoracoabdominal 441.7
    - ruptured 441.6
  - thorax, thoracic (arch) (nonsyphilitic) 441.2
    - dissecting 441.01
    - ruptured 441.1
    - syphilitic 093.0
  - transverse 441.2
    - ruptured 441.1
  - valve (heart) (*see also* Endocarditis, aortic) 424.1
- arteriosclerotic NEC 442.9
  - cerebral 437.3

Aneurysm — *continued*
- arteriosclerotic — *continued*
  - cerebral — *continued*
    - ruptured (*see also* Hemorrhage, subarachnoid) 430
- arteriovenous (congenital) (peripheral) NEC (*see also* Anomaly, arteriovenous) 747.60
  - acquired NEC 447.0
    - brain 437.3
      - ruptured (*see also* Hemorrhage, subarachnoid) 430
    - coronary 414.11
    - pulmonary 417.0
  - brain (cerebral) 747.81
    - ruptured (*see also* Hemorrhage, subarachnoid) 430
  - coronary 746.85
  - pulmonary 747.3
  - retina 743.58
  - specified site NEC 747.89
    - acquired 447.0
  - traumatic (*see also* Injury, blood vessel, by site) 904.9
- basal — *see* Aneurysm, brain
- berry (congenital) (ruptured) (*see also* Hemorrhage, subarachnoid) 430
- brain 437.3
  - arteriosclerotic 437.3
    - ruptured (*see also* Hemorrhage, subarachnoid) 430
  - arteriovenous 747.81
    - acquired 437.3
      - ruptured (*see also* Hemorrhage, subarachnoid) 430
    - ruptured (*see also* Hemorrhage, subarachnoid) 430
  - berry (congenital) (ruptured) (*see also* Hemorrhage, subarachnoid) 430
  - congenital 747.81
    - ruptured (*see also* Hemorrhage, subarachnoid) 430
  - meninges 437.3
    - ruptured (*see also* Hemorrhage, subarachnoid) 430
  - miliary (congenital) (ruptured) (*see also* Hemorrhage, subarachnoid) 430
  - mycotic 421.0
    - ruptured (*see also* Hemorrhage, subarachnoid) 430
  - nonruptured 437.3
  - ruptured (*see also* Hemorrhage, subarachnoid) 430
    - syphilitic 094.87
  - syphilitic (hemorrhage) 094.87
  - traumatic — *see* Injury, intracranial
- cardiac (false) (*see also* Aneurysm, heart) 414.10
- carotid artery (common) (external) 442.81
  - internal (intracranial portion) 437.3
    - extracranial portion 442.81
    - ruptured into brain (*see also* Hemorrhage, subarachnoid) 430
  - syphilitic 093.89
    - intracranial 094.87
- cavernous sinus (*see also* Aneurysm, brain) 437.3
  - arteriovenous 747.81
    - ruptured (*see also* Hemorrhage, subarachnoid) 430
  - congenital 747.81
    - ruptured (*see also* Hemorrhage, subarachnoid) 430
- celiac 442.84
- central nervous system, syphilitic 094.89
- cerebral — *see* Aneurysm, brain
- chest — *see* Aneurysm, thorax

Aneurysm — *continued*
- circle of Willis (*see also* Aneurysm, brain) 437.3
  - congenital 747.81
    - ruptured (*see also* Hemorrhage, subarachnoid) 430
  - ruptured (*see also* Hemorrhage, subarachnoid) 430
- common iliac artery 442.2
- congenital (peripheral) NEC 747.60
  - brain 747.81
    - ruptured (*see also* Hemorrhage, subarachnoid) 430
  - cerebral — *see* Aneurysm, brain, congenital
  - coronary 746.85
  - gastrointestinal 747.61
  - lower limb 747.64
  - pulmonary 747.3
  - renal 747.62
  - retina 743.58
  - specified site NEC 747.89
  - spinal 747.82
  - upper limb 747.63
- conjunctiva 372.74
- conus arteriosus (*see also* Aneurysm, heart) 414.10
- coronary (arteriosclerotic) (artery) (vein) (*see also* Aneurysm, heart) 414.11
  - arteriovenous 746.85
  - congenital 746.85
  - syphilitic 093.89
- cylindrical 441.9
  - ruptured 441.5
  - syphilitic 093.9
- dissecting 442.9
  - aorta 441.00
    - abdominal 441.02
    - thoracic 441.01
    - thoracoabdominal 441.03
  - syphilitic 093.9
- ductus arteriosus 747.0
- embolic — *see* Embolism, artery
- endocardial, infective (any valve) 421.0
- femoral 442.3
- gastroduodenal 442.84
- gastroepiploic 442.84
- heart (chronic or with a stated duration of over 8 weeks) (infectional) (wall) 414.10
  - acute or with a stated duration of 8 weeks or less (*see also* Infarct, myocardium) 410.9 ☑
  - congenital 746.89
  - valve — *see* Endocarditis
- hepatic 442.84
- iliac (common) 442.2
- infective (any valve) 421.0
- innominate (nonsyphilitic) 442.89
  - syphilitic 093.89
- interauricular septum (*see also* Aneurysm, heart) 414.10
- interventricular septum (*see also* Aneurysm, heart) 414.10
- intracranial — *see* Aneurysm, brain
- intrathoracic (nonsyphilitic) 441.2
  - ruptured 441.1
  - syphilitic 093.0
- jugular vein 453.8
- lower extremity 442.3
- lung (pulmonary artery) 417.1
- malignant 093.9
- mediastinal (nonsyphilitic) 442.89
  - syphilitic 093.89
- miliary (congenital) (ruptured) (*see also* Hemorrhage, subarachnoid) 430
- mitral (heart) (valve) 424.0
- mural (arteriovenous) (heart) (*see also* Aneurysm, heart) 414.10
- mycotic, any site 421.0
  - without endocarditis — *see* Aneurysm by site
  - ruptured, brain (*see also* Hemorrhage, subarachnoid) 430

Aneurysm — *continued*
- myocardium (*see also* Aneurysm, heart) 414.10
- neck 442.81
- pancreaticoduodenal 442.84
- patent ductus arteriosus 747.0
- peripheral NEC 442.89
  - congenital NEC (*see also* Aneurysm, congenital) 747.60
- popliteal 442.3
- pulmonary 417.1
  - arteriovenous 747.3
    - acquired 417.0
  - syphilitic 093.89
  - valve (heart) (*see also* Endocarditis, pulmonary) 424.3
- racemose 442.9
  - congenital (peripheral) NEC 747.60
- radial 442.0
- Rasmussen's (*see also* Tuberculosis) 011.2 ☑
- renal 442.1
- retinal (acquired) 362.17
  - congenital 743.58
  - diabetic 250.5 ☑ *[362.01]*
    - due to secondary diabetes 249.5 ☑ *[362.01]*
- sinus, aortic (of Valsalva) 747.29
- specified site NEC 442.89
- spinal (cord) 442.89
  - congenital 747.82
  - syphilitic (hemorrhage) 094.89
- spleen, splenic 442.83
- subclavian 442.82
  - syphilitic 093.89
- superior mesenteric 442.84
- syphilitic 093.9
  - aorta 093.0
  - central nervous system 094.89
  - congenital 090.5
  - spine, spinal 094.89
- thoracoabdominal 441.7
  - ruptured 441.6
- thorax, thoracic (arch) (nonsyphilitic) 441.2
  - dissecting 441.01
  - ruptured 441.1
  - syphilitic 093.0
- traumatic (complication) (early) — *see* Injury, blood vessel, by site
- tricuspid (heart) (valve) — *see* Endocarditis, tricuspid
- ulnar 442.0
- upper extremity 442.0
- valve, valvular — *see* Endocarditis
- venous 456.8
  - congenital NEC (*see also* Aneurysm, congenital) 747.60
- ventricle (arteriovenous) (*see also* Aneurysm, heart) 414.10
- visceral artery NEC 442.84

Angiectasis 459.89

Angiectopia 459.9

Angiitis 447.6
- allergic granulomatous 446.4
- hypersensitivity 446.20
  - Goodpasture's syndrome 446.21
  - specified NEC 446.29
- necrotizing 446.0
- Wegener's (necrotizing respiratory granulomatosis) 446.4

Angina (attack) (cardiac) (chest) (effort) (heart) (pectoris) (syndrome) (vasomotor) 413.9
- abdominal 557.1
- accelerated 411.1
- agranulocytic 288.03
- aphthous 074.0
- catarrhal 462
- crescendo 411.1
- croupous 464.4
- cruris 443.9

Angina — *continued*
  cruris — *continued*
    due to atherosclerosis NEC (*see also* Arteriosclerosis, extremities) 440.20
  decubitus 413.0
  diphtheritic (membranous) 032.0
  erysipelatous 034.0
  erythematous 462
  exudative, chronic 476.0
  faucium 478.29
  gangrenous 462
    diphtheritic 032.0
  infectious 462
  initial 411.1
  intestinal 557.1
  ludovici 528.3
  Ludwig's 528.3
  malignant 462
    diphtheritic 032.0
  membranous 464.4
    diphtheritic 032.0
  mesenteric 557.1
  monocytic 075
  nocturnal 413.0
  phlegmonous 475
    diphtheritic 032.0
  preinfarctional 411.1
  Prinzmetal's 413.1
  progressive 411.1
  pseudomembranous 101
  psychogenic 306.2
  pultaceous, diphtheritic 032.0
  scarlatinal 034.1
  septic 034.0
  simple 462
  stable NEC 413.9
  staphylococcal 462
  streptococcal 034.0
  stridulous, diphtheritic 032.3
  syphilitic 093.9
    congenital 090.5
  tonsil 475
  trachealis 464.4
  unstable 411.1
  variant 413.1
  Vincent's 101
Angioblastoma (M9161/1) — *see* Neoplasm, connective tissue, uncertain behavior
Angiocholecystitis — *see also* Cholecystitis, acute 575.0
Angiocholitis — *see also* Cholecystitis, acute 576.1
Angiodysgensis spinalis 336.1
Angiodysplasia (intestinalis) (intestine) 569.84
  with hemorrhage 569.85
  duodenum 537.82
    with hemorrhage 537.83
  stomach 537.82
    with hemorrhage 537.83
Angioedema (allergic) (any site) (with urticaria) 995.1
  hereditary 277.6
Angioendothelioma (M9130/1) — *see* also Neoplasm, by site, uncertain behavior
  benign (M9130/0) (*see also* Hemangioma, by site) 228.00
  bone (M9260/3) — *see* Neoplasm, bone, malignant
    Ewing's (M9260/3) — *see* Neoplasm, bone, malignant
  nervous system (M9130/0) 228.09
Angiofibroma (M9160/0) — *see also* Neoplasm, by site, benign
  juvenile (M9160/0) 210.7
    specified site — *see* Neoplasm, by site, benign
    unspecified site 210.7
Angiohemophilia (A) (B) 286.4
Angioid streaks (choroid) (retina) 363.43
Angiokeratoma (M9141/0) — *see also* Neoplasm, skin, benign
  corporis diffusum 272.7
Angiokeratosis
  diffuse 272.7
Angioleiomyoma (M8894/0) — *see* Neoplasm, connective tissue, benign
Angioleucitis 683
Angiolipoma (M8861/0) — *see also* Lipoma, by site 214.9
  infiltrating (M8861/1) — *see* Neoplasm, connective tissue, uncertain behavior
Angioma (M9120/0) — *see also* Hemangioma, by site 228.00
  capillary 448.1
  hemorrhagicum hereditaria 448.0
  malignant (M9120/3) — *see* Neoplasm, connective tissue, malignant
  pigmentosum et atrophicum 757.33
  placenta — *see* Placenta, abnormal
  plexiform (M9131/0) — *see* Hemangioma, by site
  senile 448.1
  serpiginosum 709.1
  spider 448.1
  stellate 448.1
Angiomatosis 757.32
  bacillary 083.8
  corporis diffusum universale 272.7
  cutaneocerebral 759.6
  encephalocutaneous 759.6
  encephalofacial 759.6
  encephalotrigeminal 759.6
  hemorrhagic familial 448.0
  hereditary familial 448.0
  heredofamilial 448.0
  meningo-oculofacial 759.6
  multiple sites 228.09
  neuro-oculocutaneous 759.6
  retina (Hippel's disease) 759.6
  retinocerebellosa 759.6
  retinocerebral 759.6
  systemic 228.09
Angiomyolipoma (M8860/0)
  specified site — *see* Neoplasm, connective tissue, benign
  unspecified site 223.0
Angiomyoliposarcoma (M8860/3) — *see* Neoplasm, connective tissue, malignant
Angiomyoma (M8894/0) — *see* Neoplasm, connective tissue, benign
Angiomyosarcoma (M8894/3) — *see* Neoplasm, connective tissue, malignant
Angioneurosis 306.2
Angioneurotic edema (allergic) (any site) (with urticaria) 995.1
  hereditary 277.6
Angiopathia, angiopathy 459.9
  diabetic (peripheral) 250.7 ☑ *[443.81]*
    due to secondary diabetes 249.7 ☑ *[443.81]*
  peripheral 443.9
    diabetic 250.7 ☑ *[443.81]*
      due to secondary diabetes 249.7 ☑ *[443.81]*
    specified type NEC 443.89
  retinae syphilitica 093.89
  retinalis (juvenilis) 362.18
    background 362.10
    diabetic 250.5 ☑ *[362.01]*
      due to secondary diabetes 249.5 ☑ *[362.01]*
    proliferative 362.29
    tuberculous (*see also* Tuberculosis) 017.3 ☑ *[362.18]*
Angiosarcoma (M9120/3) — *see* Neoplasm, connective tissue, malignant
Angiosclerosis — *see* Arteriosclerosis
Angioscotoma, enlarged 368.42
Angiospasm 443.9
  brachial plexus 353.0
  cerebral 435.9
  cervical plexus 353.2
Angiospasm — *continued*
  nerve
    arm 354.9
      axillary 353.0
      median 354.1
      ulnar 354.2
    autonomic (*see also* Neuropathy, peripheral, autonomic) 337.9
    axillary 353.0
    leg 355.8
      plantar 355.6
    lower extremity — *see* Angiospasm, nerve, leg
    median 354.1
    peripheral NEC 355.9
    spinal NEC 355.9
    sympathetic (*see also* Neuropathy, peripheral, autonomic) 337.9
    ulnar 354.2
    upper extremity — *see* Angiospasm, nerve, arm
  peripheral NEC 443.9
  traumatic 443.9
    foot 443.9
    leg 443.9
  vessel 443.9
Angiospastic disease or edema 443.9
Angle's
  class I 524.21
  class II 524.22
  class III 524.23
Anguillulosis 127.2
Angulation
  cecum (*see also* Obstruction, intestine) 560.9
  coccyx (acquired) 738.6
    congenital 756.19
  femur (acquired) 736.39
    congenital 755.69
  intestine (large) (small) (*see also* Obstruction, intestine) 560.9
  sacrum (acquired) 738.5
    congenital 756.19
  sigmoid (flexure) (*see also* Obstruction, intestine) 560.9
  spine (*see also* Curvature, spine) 737.9
  tibia (acquired) 736.89
    congenital 755.69
  ureter 593.3
  wrist (acquired) 736.09
    congenital 755.59
Angulus infectiosus 686.8
Anhedonia 780.99
Anhidrosis (lid) (neurogenic) (thermogenic) 705.0
Anhydration 276.51
  with
    hypernatremia 276.0
    hyponatremia 276.1
Anhydremia 276.52
  with
    hypernatremia 276.0
    hyponatremia 276.1
Anidrosis 705.0
Aniridia (congenital) 743.45
Anisakiasis (infection) (infestation) 127.1
Anisakis larva infestation 127.1
Aniseikonia 367.32
Anisocoria (pupil) 379.41
  congenital 743.46
Anisocytosis 790.09
Anisometropia (congenital) 367.31
Ankle — *see* condition
Ankyloblepharon (acquired) (eyelid) 374.46
  filiforme (adnatum) (congenital) 743.62
  total 743.62
Ankylodactly — *see also* Syndactylism 755.10
Ankyloglossia 750.0
Ankylosis (fibrous) (osseous) 718.50
  ankle 718.57
  any joint, produced by surgical fusion V45.4
Ankylosis — *continued*
  cricoarytenoid (cartilage) (joint) (larynx) 478.79
  dental 521.6
  ear ossicle NEC 385.22
    malleus 385.21
  elbow 718.52
  finger 718.54
  hip 718.55
  incostapedial joint (infectional) 385.22
  joint, produced by surgical fusion NEC V45.4
  knee 718.56
  lumbosacral (joint) 724.6
  malleus 385.21
  multiple sites 718.59
  postoperative (status) V45.4
  sacroiliac (joint) 724.6
  shoulder 718.51
  specified site NEC 718.58
  spine NEC 724.9
  surgical V45.4
  teeth, tooth (hard tissues) 521.6
  temporomandibular joint 524.61
  wrist 718.53
Ankylostoma — *see* Ancylostoma
Ankylostomiasis (intestinal) — *see* Ancylostomiasis
Ankylurethria — *see also* Stricture, urethra 598.9
Annular — *see also* condition
  detachment, cervix 622.8
  organ or site, congenital NEC — *see* Distortion
  pancreas (congenital) 751.7
Anodontia (complete) (partial) (vera) 520.0
  with abnormal spacing 524.30
  acquired 525.10
    causing malocclusion 524.30
    due to
      caries 525.13
      extraction 525.10
      periodontal disease 525.12
      trauma 525.11
Anomaly, anomalous (congenital) (unspecified type) 759.9
  abdomen 759.9
  abdominal wall 756.70
  acoustic nerve 742.9
  adrenal (gland) 759.1
  Alder (-Reilly) (leukocyte granulation) 288.2
  alimentary tract 751.9
    lower 751.5
    specified type NEC 751.8
    upper (any part, except tongue) 750.9
      tongue 750.10
        specified type NEC 750.19
  alveolar 524.70
    ridge (process) 525.8
    specified NEC 524.79
  ankle (joint) 755.69
  anus, anal (canal) 751.5
  aorta, aortic 747.20
    arch 747.21
    coarctation (postductal) (preductal) 747.10
    cusp or valve NEC 746.9
    septum 745.0
    specified type NEC 747.29
  aorticopulmonary septum 745.0
  apertures, diaphragm 756.6
  appendix 751.5
  aqueduct of Sylvius 742.3
    with spina bifida (*see also* Spina bifida) 741.0 ☑
  arm 755.50
    reduction (*see also* Deformity, reduction, upper limb) 755.20
  arteriovenous (congenital) (peripheral) NEC 747.60
    brain 747.81
    cerebral 747.81
    coronary 746.85

Anomaly, anomalous — *continued*
- peripheral vascular system — *continued*
  - spinal 747.82
  - upper limb 747.63
- Peter's 743.44
- pharynx 750.9
  - branchial cleft 744.41
  - specified type NEC 750.29
- Pierre Robin 756.0
- pigmentation 709.00
  - congenital 757.33
  - specified NEC 709.09
- pituitary (gland) 759.2
- pleural folds 748.8
- portal vein 747.40
- position tooth, teeth 524.30
  - crowding 524.31
  - displacement 524.30
    - horizontal 524.33
    - vertical 524.34
  - distance
    - interocclusal
      - excessive 524.37
      - insufficient 524.36
  - excessive spacing 524.32
  - rotation 524.35
  - specified NEC 524.39
- preauricular sinus 744.46
- prepuce 752.9
- prostate 752.9
- pulmonary 748.60
  - artery 747.3
  - circulation 747.3
  - specified type NEC 748.69
  - valve 746.00
    - atresia 746.01
    - insufficiency 746.09
    - specified type NEC 746.09
    - stenosis 746.02
      - infundibular 746.83
      - subvalvular 746.83
  - vein 747.40
  - venous
    - connection 747.49
      - partial 747.42
      - total 747.41
    - return 747.49
      - partial 747.42
      - total (TAPVR) (complete) (subdiaphragmatic) (supradiaphragmatic) 747.41
- pupil 743.9
- pylorus 750.9
  - hypertrophy 750.5
  - stenosis 750.5
- rachitic, fetal 756.4
- radius 755.50
- rectovaginal (septum) 752.40
- rectum 751.5
- refraction 367.9
- renal 753.9
  - vessel 747.62
- respiratory system 748.9
  - specified type NEC 748.8
- rib 756.3
  - cervical 756.2
- Rieger's 743.44
- rings, trachea 748.3
- rotation (*see also* Malrotation)
  - hip or thigh (*see also* Subluxation, congenital, hip) 754.32
- round ligament 752.9
- sacroiliac (joint) 755.69
- sacrum 756.10
- saddle
  - back 754.2
  - nose 754.0
    - syphilitic 090.5
- salivary gland or duct 750.9
  - specified type NEC 750.26
- scapula 755.50
- sclera 743.9
  - specified type NEC 743.47
- scrotum 752.9

Anomaly, anomalous — *continued*
- sebaceous gland 757.9
- seminal duct or tract 752.9
- sense organs 742.9
  - specified type NEC 742.8
- septum
  - heart — *see* Anomaly, heart, septum
  - nasal 748.1
- sex chromosomes NEC (*see also* Anomaly, chromosomes) 758.81
- shoulder (girdle) (joint) 755.50
  - specified type NEC 755.59
- sigmoid (flexure) 751.5
- sinus of Valsalva 747.29
- site NEC 759.9
- skeleton generalized NEC 756.50
- skin (appendage) 757.9
  - specified type NEC 757.39
- skull (bone) 756.0
  - with
    - anencephalus 740.0
    - encephalocele 742.0
    - hydrocephalus 742.3
      - with spina bifida (*see also* Spina bifida) 741.0 ☑
    - microcephalus 742.1
- specified type NEC
  - adrenal (gland) 759.1
  - alimentary tract (complete) (partial) 751.8
    - lower 751.5
    - upper 750.8
  - ankle 755.69
  - anus, anal (canal) 751.5
  - aorta, aortic 747.29
    - arch 747.21
  - appendix 751.5
  - arm 755.59
  - artery (peripheral) NEC (*see also* Anomaly, peripheral vascular system) 747.60
    - brain 747.81
    - coronary 746.85
    - eye 743.58
    - pulmonary 747.3
    - retinal 743.58
    - umbilical 747.5
  - auditory canal 744.29
    - causing impairment of hearing 744.02
  - bile duct or passage 751.69
  - bladder 753.8
    - neck 753.8
  - bone(s) 756.9
    - arm 755.59
    - face 756.0
    - leg 755.69
    - pelvic girdle 755.69
    - shoulder girdle 755.59
    - skull 756.0
      - with
        - anencephalus 740.0
        - encephalocele 742.0
        - hydrocephalus 742.3
          - with spina bifida (*see also* Spina bifida) 741.0 ☑
        - microcephalus 742.1
  - brain 742.4
  - breast 757.6
  - broad ligament 752.19
  - bronchus 748.3
  - canal of Nuck 752.89
  - cardiac septal closure 745.8
  - carpus 755.59
  - cartilaginous 756.9
  - cecum 751.5
  - cervix 752.49
  - chest (wall) 756.3
  - chin 744.89
  - ciliary body 743.46
  - circulatory system 747.89
  - clavicle 755.51
  - clitoris 752.49
  - coccyx 756.19

Anomaly, anomalous — *continued*
- specified type — *continued*
  - colon 751.5
  - common duct 751.69
  - connective tissue 756.89
  - cricoid cartilage 748.3
  - cystic duct 751.69
  - diaphragm 756.6
  - digestive organ(s) or tract 751.8
    - lower 751.5
    - upper 750.8
  - duodenum 751.5
  - ear 744.29
    - auricle 744.29
      - causing impairment of hearing 744.02
    - causing impairment of hearing 744.09
    - inner (causing impairment of hearing) 744.05
    - middle, except ossicles 744.03
      - ossicles 744.04
  - ejaculatory duct 752.89
  - endocrine 759.2
  - epiglottis 748.3
  - esophagus 750.4
  - Eustachian tube 744.24
  - eye 743.8
    - lid 743.63
    - muscle 743.69
  - face 744.89
    - bone(s) 756.0
  - fallopian tube 752.19
  - fascia 756.89
  - femur 755.69
  - fibula 755.69
  - finger 755.59
  - foot 755.67
  - fovea centralis 743.55
  - gallbladder 751.69
  - Gartner's duct 752.89
  - gastrointestinal tract 751.8
  - genitalia, genital organ(s)
    - female 752.89
      - external 752.49
      - internal NEC 752.89
    - male 752.89
      - penis 752.69
      - scrotal transposition 752.81
  - genitourinary tract NEC 752.89
  - glottis 748.3
  - hair 757.4
  - hand 755.59
  - heart 746.89
    - valve NEC 746.89
      - pulmonary 746.09
  - hepatic duct 751.69
  - hydatid of Morgagni 752.89
  - hymen 752.49
  - integument 757.8
  - intestine (large) (small) 751.5
    - fixational type 751.4
  - iris 743.46
  - jejunum 751.5
  - joint 755.8
  - kidney 753.3
  - knee 755.64
  - labium (majus) (minus) 752.49
  - labyrinth, membranous 744.05
  - larynx 748.3
  - leg 755.69
  - lens 743.39
  - limb, except reduction deformity 755.8
    - lower 755.69
      - reduction deformity (*see also* Deformity, reduction, lower limb) 755.30
    - upper 755.59
      - reduction deformity (*see also* Deformity, reduction, upper limb) 755.20
  - lip 750.26
  - liver 751.69
  - lung (fissure) (lobe) 748.69
  - meatus urinarius 753.8

Anomaly, anomalous — *continued*
- specified type — *continued*
  - metacarpus 755.59
  - mouth 750.26
  - muscle 756.89
    - eye 743.69
  - musculoskeletal system, except limbs 756.9
  - nail 757.5
  - neck 744.89
  - nerve 742.8
    - acoustic 742.8
    - optic 742.8
  - nervous system 742.8
  - nipple 757.6
  - nose 748.1
  - organ NEC 759.89
    - of Corti 744.05
  - osseous meatus (ear) 744.03
  - ovary 752.0
  - oviduct 752.19
  - pancreas 751.7
  - parathyroid 759.2
  - patella 755.64
  - pelvic girdle 755.69
  - penis 752.69
  - pericardium 746.89
  - peripheral vascular system NEC (*see also* Anomaly, peripheral vascular system) 747.60
  - pharynx 750.29
  - pituitary 759.2
  - prostate 752.89
  - radius 755.59
  - rectum 751.5
  - respiratory system 748.8
  - rib 756.3
  - round ligament 752.89
  - sacrum 756.19
  - salivary duct or gland 750.26
  - scapula 755.59
  - sclera 743.47
  - scrotum 752.89
    - transposition 752.81
  - seminal duct or tract 752.89
  - shoulder girdle 755.59
  - site NEC 759.89
  - skin 757.39
  - skull (bone(s)) 756.0
    - with
      - anencephalus 740.0
      - encephalocele 742.0
      - hydrocephalus 742.3
        - with spina bifida (*see also* Spina bifida) 741.0 ☑
      - microcephalus 742.1
  - specified organ or site NEC 759.89
  - spermatic cord 752.89
  - spinal cord 742.59
  - spine 756.19
  - spleen 759.0
  - sternum 756.3
  - stomach 750.7
  - tarsus 755.67
  - tendon 756.89
  - testis 752.89
  - thorax (wall) 756.3
  - thymus 759.2
  - thyroid (gland) 759.2
    - cartilage 748.3
  - tibia 755.69
  - toe 755.66
  - tongue 750.19
  - trachea (cartilage) 748.3
  - ulna 755.59
  - urachus 753.7
  - ureter 753.4
    - obstructive 753.29
  - urethra 753.8
    - obstructive 753.6
  - urinary tract 753.8
  - uterus 752.3
  - uvula 750.26
  - vagina 752.49

Anomaly, anomalous — *continued*
  specified type — *continued*
    vascular NEC (*see also* Anomaly, peripheral vascular system) 747.60
      brain 747.81
    vas deferens 752.89
    vein(s) (peripheral) NEC (*see also* Anomaly, peripheral vascular system) 747.60
      brain 747.81
      great 747.49
      portal 747.49
      pulmonary 747.49
    vena cava (inferior) (superior) 747.49
    vertebra 756.19
    vulva 752.49
  spermatic cord 752.9
  spine, spinal 756.10
    column 756.10
    cord 742.9
      meningocele (*see also* Spina bifida) 741.9 ☑
      specified type NEC 742.59
      spina bifida (*see also* Spina bifida) 741.9 ☑
      vessel 747.82
    meninges 742.59
    nerve root 742.9
  spleen 759.0
  Sprengel's 755.52
  sternum 756.3
  stomach 750.9
    specified type NEC 750.7
  submaxillary gland 750.9
  superior vena cava 747.40
  talipes — *see* Talipes
  tarsus 755.67
    with complete absence of distal elements 755.31
  teeth, tooth NEC 520.9
    position 524.30
      crowding 524.31
      displacement 524.30
        horizontal 524.33
        vertical 524.34
      distance
        interocclusal
          excessive 524.37
          insufficient 524.36
      excessive spacing 524.32
      rotation 524.35
      specified NEC 524.39
    spacing 524.30
  tendon 756.9
    specified type NEC 756.89
  termination
    coronary artery 746.85
  testis 752.9
  thebesian valve 746.9
  thigh 755.60
    flexion (*see also* Subluxation, congenital, hip) 754.32
  thorax (wall) 756.3
  throat 750.9
  thumb 755.50
    supernumerary 755.01
  thymus gland 759.2
  thyroid (gland) 759.2
    cartilage 748.3
  tibia 755.60
    saber 090.5
  toe 755.66
    supernumerary 755.02
    webbed (*see also* Syndactylism, toes) 755.13
  tongue 750.10
    specified type NEC 750.19
  trachea, tracheal 748.3
    cartilage 748.3
    rings 748.3
  tragus 744.3
  transverse aortic arch 747.21
  trichromata 368.59
  trichromatopsia 368.59

Anomaly, anomalous — *continued*
  tricuspid (leaflet) (valve) 746.9
    atresia 746.1
    Ebstein's 746.2
    specified type NEC 746.89
    stenosis 746.1
  trunk 759.9
  Uhl's (hypoplasia of myocardium, right ventricle) 746.84
  ulna 755.50
  umbilicus 759.9
    artery 747.5
  union, trachea with larynx 748.3
  unspecified site 759.9
  upper extremity 755.50
    vessel 747.63
  urachus 753.7
    specified type NEC 753.7
  ureter 753.9
    obstructive 753.20
    specified type NEC 753.4
      obstructive 753.29
  urethra (valve) 753.9
    obstructive 753.6
    specified type NEC 753.8
  urinary tract or system (any part, except urachus) 753.9
    specified type NEC 753.8
    urachus 753.7
  uterus 752.3
    with only one functioning horn 752.3
    in pregnancy or childbirth 654.0 ☑
      affecting fetus or newborn 763.89
      causing obstructed labor 660.2 ☑
        affecting fetus or newborn 763.1
  uvula 750.9
  vagina 752.40
  valleculae 748.3
  valve (heart) NEC 746.9
    formation, ureter 753.29
    pulmonary 746.00
    specified type NEC 746.89
  vascular NEC (*see also* Anomaly, peripheral vascular system) 747.60
    ring 747.21
  vas deferens 752.9
  vein(s) (peripheral) NEC (*see also* Anomaly, peripheral vascular system) 747.60
    brain 747.81
    cerebral 747.81
    coronary 746.89
    great 747.40
      specified type NEC 747.49
    portal 747.40
    pulmonary 747.40
    retina 743.9
  vena cava (inferior) (superior) 747.40
  venous — *see* Anomaly, vein
  venous return (pulmonary) 747.49
    partial 747.42
    total 747.41
  ventricle, ventricular (heart) 746.9
    bands 746.9
    folds 746.9
    septa 745.4
  vertebra 756.10
  vesicourethral orifice 753.9
  vessels NEC (*see also* Anomaly, peripheral vascular system) 747.60
    optic papilla 743.9
  vitelline duct 751.0
  vitreous humor 743.9
    specified type NEC 743.51
  vulva 752.40
  wrist (joint) 755.50
Anomia 784.69
Anonychia 757.5
  acquired 703.8
Anophthalmos, anophthalmus (clinical) (congenital) (globe) 743.00

Anophthalmos, anophthalmus — *continued*
  acquired V45.78
Anopsia (altitudinal) (quadrant) 368.46
Anorchia 752.89
Anorchism, anorchidism 752.89
Anorexia 783.0
  hysterical 300.11
  nervosa 307.1
Anosmia — *see also* Disturbance, sensation 781.1
  hysterical 300.11
  postinfectional 478.9
  psychogenic 306.7
  traumatic 951.8
Anosognosia 780.99
Anosphrasia 781.1
Anosteoplasia 756.50
Anotia 744.09
Anovulatory cycle 628.0
Anoxemia 799.02
  newborn 770.88
Anoxia 799.02
  altitude 993.2
  cerebral 348.1
    with
      abortion — *see* Abortion, by type, with specified complication NEC
      ectopic pregnancy (*see also* categories 633.0–633.9) 639.8
      molar pregnancy (*see also* categories 630–632) 639.8
    complicating
      delivery (cesarean) (instrumental) 669.4 ☑
      ectopic or molar pregnancy 639.8
      obstetric anesthesia or sedation 668.2 ☑
    during or resulting from a procedure 997.01
    following
      abortion 639.8
      ectopic or molar pregnancy 639.8
    newborn (*see also* Distress, fetal, liveborn infant) 770.88
  due to drowning 994.1
  fetal, affecting newborn 770.88
  heart — *see* Insufficiency, coronary
  high altitude 993.2
  intrauterine
    fetal death (before onset of labor) 768.0
      during labor 768.1
    liveborn infant — *see* Distress, fetal, liveborn infant
  myocardial — *see* Insufficiency, coronary
  newborn 768.9
    mild or moderate 768.6
    severe 768.5
  pathological 799.02
Anteflexion — *see* Anteversion
Antenatal
  care, normal pregnancy V22.1
    first V22.0
  sampling
    chorionic villus V28.89
  screening of mother (for) V28.9
    based on amniocentesis NEC V28.2
      chromosomal anomalies V28.0
      raised alphafetoprotein levels V28.1
    chromosomal anomalies V28.0
    fetal growth retardation using ulatrasonics V28.4
    genomic V28.89
    isoimmunization V28.5
    malformations using ulatrasonics V28.3
    proteomic V28.89
    raised alphafetoprotein levels in amniotic fluid V28.1

Antenatal — *continued*
  screening of mother — *continued*
    risk
      pre-term labor V28.82
    specified condition NEC V28.89
    Streptococcus B V28.6
  survey
    fetal anatomic V28.81
  testing
    nuchal translucency V28.89
Antepartum — *see* condition
Anterior — *see also* condition
  spinal artery compression syndrome 721.1
Antero-occlusion 524.24
Anteversion
  cervix — *see* Anteversion, uterus
  femur (neck), congenital 755.63
  uterus, uterine (cervix) (postinfectional) (postpartal, old) 621.6
    congenital 752.3
    in pregnancy or childbirth 654.4 ☑
      affecting fetus or newborn 763.89
      causing obstructed labor 660.2 ☑
        affecting fetus or newborn 763.1
Anthracosilicosis (occupational) 500
Anthracosis (lung) (occupational) 500
  lingua 529.3
Anthrax 022.9
  with pneumonia 022.1 *[484.5]*
  colitis 022.2
  cutaneous 022.0
  gastrointestinal 022.2
  intestinal 022.2
  pulmonary 022.1
  respiratory 022.1
  septicemia 022.3
  specified manifestation NEC 022.8
Anthropoid pelvis 755.69
  with disproportion (fetopelvic) 653.2 ☑
    affecting fetus or newborn 763.1
    causing obstructed labor 660.1 ☑
      affecting fetus or newborn 763.1
Anthropophobia 300.29
Antibioma, breast 611.0
Antibodies
  maternal (blood group) (*see also* Incompatibility) 656.2 ☑
    anti-D, cord blood 656.1 ☑
      fetus or newborn 773.0
Antibody deficiency syndrome
  agammaglobulinemic 279.00
  congenital 279.04
  hypogammaglobulinemic 279.00
Anticoagulant, circulating — *see also* Circulating anticoagulants 286.5
Antimongolism syndrome 758.39
Antimonial cholera 985.4
Antisocial personality 301.7
Antithrombinemia — *see also* Circulating anticoagulants 286.5
Antithromboplastinemia — *see also* Circulating anticoagulants 286.5
Antithromboplastinogenemia — *see also* Circulating anticoagulants 286.5
Antitoxin complication or reaction — *see* Complications, vaccination
Anton (-Babinski) syndrome (hemiasomatognosia) 307.9
Antritis (chronic) 473.0
  maxilla 473.0
    acute 461.0
  stomach 535.4 ☑
Antrum, antral — *see* condition
Anuria 788.5
  with
    abortion — *see* Abortion, by type, with renal failure
    ectopic pregnancy (*see also* categories 633.0–633.9) 639.3
    molar pregnancy (*see also* categories 630–632) 639.3

Anuria — *continued*
calculus (impacted) (recurrent) 592.9
kidney 592.0
ureter 592.1
congenital 753.3
due to a procedure 997.5
following
abortion 639.3
ectopic or molar pregnancy 639.3
newborn 753.3
postrenal 593.4
puerperal, postpartum, childbirth 669.3 ☑
specified as due to a procedure 997.5
sulfonamide
correct substance properly administered 788.5
overdose or wrong substance given or taken 961.0
traumatic (following crushing) 958.5
Anus, anal — *see also* condition
high risk human papillomavirus (HPV) DNA test positive 796.75
low risk human papillomavirus (HPV) DNA test positive 796.79
Anusitis 569.49
Anxiety (neurosis) (reaction) (state) 300.00
alcohol-induced 291.89
depression 300.4
drug-induced 292.89
due to or associated with physical condition 293.84
generalized 300.02
hysteria 300.20
in
acute stress reaction 308.0
transient adjustment reaction 309.24
panic type 300.01
separation, abnormal 309.21
syndrome (organic) (transient) 293.84
Aorta, aortic — *see* condition
Aortectasia 441.9
Aortitis (nonsyphilitic) 447.6
arteriosclerotic 440.0
calcific 447.6
Döhle-Heller 093.1
luetic 093.1
rheumatic (*see also* Endocarditis, acute, rheumatic) 391.1
rheumatoid — *see* Arthritis, rheumatoid
specific 093.1
syphilitic 093.1
congenital 090.5
Apathetic thyroid storm — *see also* Thyrotoxicosis 242.9 ☑
Apepsia 536.8
achlorhydric 536.0
psychogenic 306.4
Aperistalsis, esophagus 530.0
Apert-Gallais syndrome (adrenogenital) 255.2
Apertognathia 524.20
Apert's syndrome (acrocephalosyndactyly) 755.55
Aphagia 787.20
psychogenic 307.1
Aphakia (acquired) (bilateral) (postoperative) (unilateral) 379.31
congenital 743.35
Aphalangia (congenital) 755.4
lower limb (complete) (intercalary) (partial) (terminal) 755.39
meaning all digits (complete) (partial) 755.31
transverse 755.31
upper limb (complete) (intercalary) (partial) (terminal) 755.29
meaning all digits (complete) (partial) 755.21
transverse 755.21
Aphasia (amnestic) (ataxic) (auditory) (Broca's) (choreatic) (classic) (expressive) (global) (ideational) (ideokinetic) (ideomotor) (jargon) (motor) (nominal) (receptive) (semantic) (sensory) (syntactic) (verbal) (visual) (Wernicke's) 784.3
developmental 315.31
syphilis, tertiary 094.89
uremic — *see* Uremia
Aphemia 784.3
uremic — *see* Uremia
Aphonia 784.41
clericorum 784.49
hysterical 300.11
organic 784.41
psychogenic 306.1
Aphthae, aphthous — *see also* condition
Bednar's 528.2
cachectic 529.0
epizootic 078.4
fever 078.4
oral 528.2
stomatitis 528.2
thrush 112.0
ulcer (oral) (recurrent) 528.2
genital organ(s) NEC
female 616.50
male 608.89
larynx 478.79
Apical — *see* condition
Apical ballooning syndrome 429.83
Aplasia — *see also* Agenesis
alveolar process (acquired) 525.8
congenital 750.26
aorta (congenital) 747.22
aortic valve (congenital) 746.89
axialis extracorticalis (congenital) 330.0
bone marrow (myeloid) 284.9
acquired (secondary) 284.89
congenital 284.01
idiopathic 284.9
brain 740.0
specified part 742.2
breast 757.6
bronchus 748.3
cementum 520.4
cerebellar 742.2
congenital (pure) red cell 284.01
corpus callosum 742.2
erythrocyte 284.81
congenital 284.01
extracortical axial 330.0
eye (congenital) 743.00
fovea centralis (congenital) 743.55
germinal (cell) 606.0
iris 743.45
labyrinth, membranous 744.05
limb (congenital) 755.4
lower NEC 755.30
upper NEC 755.20
lung (bilateral) (congenital) (unilateral) 748.5
nervous system NEC 742.8
nuclear 742.8
ovary 752.0
Pelizaeus-Merzbacher 330.0
prostate (congenital) 752.89
red cell (with thymoma) (adult) 284.81
acquired (secondary) 284.81
congenital 284.01
hereditary 284.01
of infants 284.01
primary 284.01
pure 284.01
round ligament (congenital) 752.89
salivary gland 750.21
skin (congenital) 757.39
spinal cord 742.59
spleen 759.0
testis (congenital) 752.89
thymic, with immunodeficiency 279.2
thyroid 243
uterus 752.3
ventral horn cell 742.59
Apleuria 756.3
Apnea, apneic (spells) 786.03
newborn, neonatorum 770.81
essential 770.81
obstructive 770.82
primary 770.81
sleep 770.81
specified NEC 770.82
psychogenic 306.1
sleep, unspecified 780.57
with
hypersomnia, unspecified 780.53
hyposomnia, unspecified 780.51
insomnia, unspecified 780.51
sleep disturbance 780.57
central, in conditions classified elsewhere 327.27
obstructive (adult) (pediatric) 327.23
organic 327.20
other 327.29
primary central 327.21
Apneumatosis newborn 770.4
Apodia 755.31
Aponeurosis 726.90
Apophysitis (bone) — *see also* Osteochondrosis 732.9
calcaneus 732.5
juvenile 732.6
Apoplectiform convulsions — *see also* Disease, cerebrovascular, acute 436
Apoplexia, apoplexy, apoplectic — *see also* Disease, cerebrovascular, acute 436
abdominal 569.89
adrenal 036.3
attack 436
basilar (*see also* Disease, cerebrovascular, acute) 436
brain (*see also* Disease, cerebrovascular, acute) 436
bulbar (*see also* Disease, cerebrovascular, acute) 436
capillary (*see also* Disease, cerebrovascular, acute) 436
cardiac (*see also* Infarct, myocardium) 410.9 ☑
cerebral (*see also* Disease, cerebrovascular, acute) 436
chorea (*see also* Disease, cerebrovascular, acute) 436
congestive (*see also* Disease, cerebrovascular, acute) 436
newborn 767.4
embolic (*see also* Embolism, brain) 434.1 ☑
fetus 767.0
fit (*see also* Disease, cerebrovascular, acute) 436
healed or old V12.54
heart (auricle) (ventricle) (*see also* Infarct, myocardium) 410.9 ☑
heat 992.0
hemiplegia (*see also* Disease, cerebrovascular, acute) 436
hemorrhagic (stroke) (*see also* Hemorrhage, brain) 432.9
ingravescent (*see also* Disease, cerebrovascular, acute) 436
late effect — *see* Late effect(s) (of) cerebrovascular disease
lung — *see* Embolism, pulmonary
meninges, hemorrhagic (*see also* Hemorrhage, subarachnoid) 430
neonatorum 767.0
newborn 767.0
pancreatitis 577.0
placenta 641.2 ☑
progressive (*see also* Disease, cerebrovascular, acute) 436
pulmonary (artery) (vein) — *see* Embolism, pulmonary
sanguineous (*see also* Disease, cerebrovascular, acute) 436
Apoplexia, apoplexy, apoplectic — *see also* Disease, cerebrovascular, acute — *continued*
seizure (*see also* Disease, cerebrovascular, acute) 436
serous (*see also* Disease, cerebrovascular, acute) 436
spleen 289.59
stroke (*see also* Disease, cerebrovascular, acute) 436
thrombotic (*see also* Thrombosis, brain) 434.0 ☑
uremic — *see* Uremia
uteroplacental 641.2 ☑
Appendage
fallopian tube (cyst of Morgagni) 752.11
intestine (epiploic) 751.5
preauricular 744.1
testicular (organ of Morgagni) 752.89
Appendicitis 541
with
perforation, peritonitis (generalized), or rupture 540.0
with peritoneal abscess 540.1
peritoneal abscess 540.1
acute (catarrhal) (fulminating) (gangrenous) (inflammatory) (obstructive) (retrocecal) (suppurative) 540.9
with
perforation, peritonitis, or rupture 540.0
with peritoneal abscess 540.1
peritoneal abscess 540.1
amebic 006.8
chronic (recurrent) 542
exacerbation — *see* Appendicitis, acute
fulminating — *see* Appendicitis, acute
gangrenous — *see* Appendicitis, acute
healed (obliterative) 542
interval 542
neurogenic 542
obstructive 542
pneumococcal 541
recurrent 542
relapsing 542
retrocecal 541
subacute (adhesive) 542
subsiding 542
suppurative — *see* Appendicitis, acute
tuberculous (*see also* Tuberculosis) 014.8 ☑
Appendiclausis 543.9
Appendicolithiasis 543.9
Appendicopathia oxyurica 127.4
Appendix, appendicular — *see also* condition
Morgagni (male) 752.89
fallopian tube 752.11
Appetite
depraved 307.52
excessive 783.6
psychogenic 307.51
lack or loss (*see also* Anorexia) 783.0
nonorganic origin 307.59
perverted 307.52
hysterical 300.11
Apprehension, apprehensiveness (abnormal) (state) 300.00
specified type NEC 300.09
Approximal wear 521.10
Apraxia (classic) (ideational) (ideokinetic) (ideomotor) (motor) 784.69
oculomotor, congenital 379.51
verbal 784.69
Aptyalism 527.7
Aqueous misdirection 365.83
Arabicum elephantiasis — *see also* Infestation, filarial 125.9
Arachnidism 989.5
Arachnitis — *see* Meningitis
Arachnodactyly 759.82
Arachnoidism 989.5

Arachnoiditis (acute) (adhesive) (basic) (brain) (cerebrospinal) (chiasmal) (chronic) (spinal) — *see also* Meningitis 322.9
- meningococcal (chronic) 036.0
- syphilitic 094.2
- tuberculous (*see also* Tuberculosis, meninges) 013.0 ☑

Araneism 989.5
Arboencephalitis, Australian 062.4
Arborization block (heart) 426.6
Arbor virus, arbovirus (infection) NEC 066.9
ARC 042
Arches — *see* condition
Arcuatus uterus 752.3
Arcus (cornea)
- juvenilis 743.43
  - interfering with vision 743.42
- senilis 371.41

Arc-welders' lung 503
Arc-welders' syndrome (photokeratitis) 370.24
Areflexia 796.1
Areola — *see* condition
Argentaffinoma (M8241/1) — *see* also Neoplasm, by site, uncertain behavior
- benign (M8241/0) — *see* Neoplasm, by site, benign
- malignant (M8241/3) — *see* Neoplasm, by site, malignant
- syndrome 259.2

Argentinian hemorrhagic fever 078.7
Arginosuccinicaciduria 270.6
Argonz-Del Castillo syndrome (nonpuerperal galactorrhea and amenorrhea) 253.1
Argyll-Robertson phenomenon, pupil, or syndrome (syphilitic) 094.89
- atypical 379.45
- nonluetic 379.45
- nonsyphilitic 379.45
- reversed 379.45

Argyria, argyriasis NEC 985.8
- conjunctiva 372.55
- cornea 371.16
- from drug or medicinal agent
  - correct substance properly administered 709.09
  - overdose or wrong substance given or taken 961.2

Arhinencephaly 742.2
Arias-Stella phenomenon 621.30
Ariboflavinosis 266.0
Arizona enteritis 008.1
Arm — *see* condition
Armenian disease 277.31
Arnold-Chiari obstruction or syndrome — *see also* Spina bifida 741.0 ☑
- type I 348.4
- type II (*see also* Spina bifida) 741.0 ☑
- type III 742.0
- type IV 742.2

Arousals
- confusional 327.41

Arrest, arrested
- active phase of labor 661.1 ☑
  - affecting fetus or newborn 763.7
- any plane in pelvis
  - complicating delivery 660.1 ☑
    - affecting fetus or newborn 763.1
- bone marrow (*see also* Anemia, aplastic) 284.9
- cardiac 427.5
  - with
    - abortion — *see* Abortion, by type, with specified complication NEC
    - ectopic pregnancy (*see also* categories 633.0–633.9) 639.8
    - molar pregnancy (*see also* categories 630–632) 639.8

Arrest, arrested — *continued*
- cardiac — *continued*
  - complicating
    - anesthesia
      - correct substance properly administered 427.5
      - obstetric 668.1 ☑
      - overdose or wrong substance given 968.4
      - specified anesthetic — *see* Table of Drugs and Chemicals
    - delivery (cesarean) (instrumental) 669.4 ☑
    - ectopic or molar pregnancy 639.8
    - surgery (nontherapeutic) (therapeutic) 997.1
  - fetus or newborn 779.85
  - following
    - abortion 639.8
    - ectopic or molar pregnancy 639.8
  - personal history, successfully resuscitated V12.53
  - postoperative (immediate) 997.1
    - long-term effect of cardiac surgery 429.4
- cardiorespiratory (*see also* Arrest, cardiac) 427.5
- deep transverse 660.3 ☑
  - affecting fetus or newborn 763.1
- development or growth
  - bone 733.91
  - child 783.40
  - fetus 764.9 ☑
    - affecting management of pregnancy 656.5 ☑
  - tracheal rings 748.3
- epiphyseal 733.91
- granulopoiesis 288.09
- heart — *see* Arrest, cardiac
- respiratory 799.1
  - newborn 770.87
- sinus 426.6
- transverse (deep) 660.3 ☑
  - affecting fetus or newborn 763.1

Arrhenoblastoma (M8630/1)
- benign (M8630/0)
  - specified site — *see* Neoplasm, by site, benign
  - unspecified site
    - female 220
    - male 222.0
- malignant (M8630/3)
  - specified site — *see* Neoplasm, by site, malignant
  - unspecified site
    - female 183.0
    - male 186.9
- specified site — *see* Neoplasm, by site, uncertain behavior
- unspecified site
  - female 236.2
  - male 236.4

Arrhinencephaly 742.2
- due to
  - trisomy 13 (13-15) 758.1
  - trisomy 18 (16-18) 758.2

Arrhythmia (auricle) (cardiac) (cordis) (gallop rhythm) (juvenile) (nodal) (reflex) (sinus) (supraventricular) (transitory) (ventricle) 427.9
- bigeminal rhythm 427.89
- block 426.9
- bradycardia 427.89
- contractions, premature 427.60
- coronary sinus 427.89
- ectopic 427.89
- extrasystolic 427.60
- postoperative 997.1
- psychogenic 306.2
- vagal 780.2

Arrillaga-Ayerza syndrome (pulmonary artery sclerosis with pulmonary hypertension) 416.0

Arsenical
- dermatitis 692.4
- keratosis 692.4
- pigmentation 985.1
  - from drug or medicinal agent
    - correct substance properly administered 709.09
    - overdose or wrong substance given or taken 961.1

Arsenism 985.1
- from drug or medicinal agent
  - correct substance properly administered 692.4
  - overdose or wrong substance given or taken 961.1

Arterial — *see* condition
Arteriectasis 447.8
Arteriofibrosis — *see* Arteriosclerosis
Arteriolar sclerosis — *see* Arteriosclerosis
Arteriolith — *see* Arteriosclerosis
Arteriolitis 447.6
- necrotizing, kidney 447.5
- renal — *see* Hypertension, kidney

Arteriolosclerosis — *see* Arteriosclerosis
Arterionephrosclerosis — *see also* Hypertension, kidney 403.90
Arteriopathy 447.9
Arteriosclerosis, arteriosclerotic (artery) (deformans) (diffuse) (disease) (endarteritis) (general) (obliterans) (obliterative) (occlusive) (senile) (with calcification) 440.9
- with
  - gangrene 440.24
  - psychosis (*see also* Psychosis, arteriosclerotic) 290.40
  - ulceration 440.23
- aorta 440.0
- arteries of extremities — *see* Arteriosclerosis, extremities
- basilar (artery) (*see also* Occlusion, artery, basilar) 433.0 ☑
- brain 437.0
- bypass graft
  - coronary artery 414.05
    - autologous artery (gastroepiploic) (internal mammary) 414.04
    - autologous vein 414.02
    - nonautologous biological 414.03
    - of transplanted heart 414.07
  - extremity 440.30
    - autologous vein 440.31
    - nonautologous biological 440.32
- cardiac — *see* Arteriosclerosis, coronary
- cardiopathy — *see* Arteriosclerosis, coronary
- cardiorenal (*see also* Hypertension, cardiorenal) 404.90
- cardiovascular (*see also* Disease, cardiovascular) 429.2
- carotid (artery) (common) (internal) (*see also* Occlusion, artery, carotid) 433.1 ☑
- central nervous system 437.0
- cerebral 437.0
  - late effect — *see* Late effect(s) (of) cerebrovascular disease
- cerebrospinal 437.0
- cerebrovascular 437.0
- coronary (artery) 414.00
  - due to lipid rich plaque 414.3
  - graft — *see* Arteriosclerosis, bypass graft
  - native artery 414.01
    - of transplanted heart 414.06
- extremities (native artery) NEC 440.20
  - bypass graft 440.30
    - autologous vein 440.31
    - nonautologous biological 440.32
  - claudication (intermittent) 440.21
    - and
      - gangrene 440.24
      - rest pain 440.22

Arteriosclerosis, arteriosclerotic — *continued*
- extremities — *continued*
  - claudication — *continued*
    - and — *continued*
      - rest pain — *continued*
        - and
          - gangrene 440.24
          - ulceration 440.23
            - and gangrene 440.24
      - ulceration 440.23
        - and gangrene 440.24
  - gangrene 440.24
  - rest pain 440.22
    - and
      - gangrene 440.24
      - ulceration 440.23
        - and gangrene 440.24
  - specified site NEC 440.29
  - ulceration 440.23
    - and gangrene 440.24
- heart (disease) (*see also* Arteriosclerosis, coronary)
  - valve 424.99
    - aortic 424.1
    - mitral 424.0
    - pulmonary 424.3
    - tricuspid 424.2
- kidney (*see also* Hypertension, kidney) 403.90
- labyrinth, labyrinthine 388.00
- medial NEC (*see also* Arteriosclerosis, extremities) 440.20
- mesentery (artery) 557.1
- Mönckeberg's (*see also* Arteriosclerosis, extremities) 440.20
- myocarditis 429.0
- nephrosclerosis (*see also* Hypertension, kidney) 403.90
- peripheral (of extremities) — *see* Arteriosclerosis, extremities
- precerebral 433.9 ☑
  - specified artery NEC 433.8 ☑
- pulmonary (idiopathic) 416.0
- renal (*see also* Hypertension, kidney) 403.90
  - arterioles (*see also* Hypertension, kidney) 403.90
  - artery 440.1
- retinal (vascular) 440.8 *[362.13]*
- specified artery NEC 440.8
  - with gangrene 440.8 *[785.4]*
- spinal (cord) 437.0
- vertebral (artery) (*see also* Occlusion, artery, vertebral) 433.2 ☑

Arteriospasm 443.9
Arteriovenous — *see* condition
Arteritis 447.6
- allergic (*see also* Angiitis, hypersensitivity) 446.20
- aorta (nonsyphilitic) 447.6
  - syphilitic 093.1
- aortic arch 446.7
- brachiocephalica 446.7
- brain 437.4
  - syphilitic 094.89
- branchial 446.7
- cerebral 437.4
  - late effect — *see* Late effect(s) (of) cerebrovascular disease
  - syphilitic 094.89
- coronary (artery) (*see also* Arteriosclerosis, coronary)
  - rheumatic 391.9
    - chronic 398.99
  - syphilitic 093.89
- cranial (left) (right) 446.5
- deformans — *see* Arteriosclerosis
- giant cell 446.5
- necrosing or necrotizing 446.0
- nodosa 446.0
- obliterans (*see also* Arteriosclerosis)
  - subclaviocarotica 446.7
- pulmonary 417.8
- retina 362.18

Arteritis — *continued*
rheumatic — *see* Fever, rheumatic
senile — *see* Arteriosclerosis
suppurative 447.2
syphilitic (general) 093.89
brain 094.89
coronary 093.89
spinal 094.89
temporal 446.5
young female, syndrome 446.7
Artery, arterial — *see* condition
Arthralgia — *see also* Pain, joint 719.4 ☑
allergic (*see also* Pain, joint) 719.4 ☑
in caisson disease 993.3
psychogenic 307.89
rubella 056.71
Salmonella 003.23
temporomandibular joint 524.62
Arthritis, arthritic (acute) (chronic) (subacute) 716.9 ☑
meaning Osteoarthritis — *see* Osteoarthrosis

Note — Use the following fifth-digit subclassification with categories 711–712, 715–716:

0	*site unspecified*
1	*shoulder region*
2	*upper arm*
3	*forearm*
4	*hand*
5	*pelvic region and thigh*
6	*lower leg*
7	*ankle and foot*
8	*other specified sites*
9	*multiple sites*

allergic 716.2 ☑
ankylosing (crippling) (spine) 720.0
sites other than spine 716.9 ☑
atrophic 714.0
spine 720.9
back (*see also* Arthritis, spine) 721.90
Bechterew's (ankylosing spondylitis) 720.0
blennorrhagic 098.50
cervical, cervicodorsal (*see also* Spondylosis, cervical) 721.0
Charcôt's 094.0 *[713.5]*
diabetic 250.6 ☑ *[713.5]*
due to secondary diabetes 249.6 ☑ *[713.5]*
syringomyelic 336.0 *[713.5]*
tabetic 094.0 *[713.5]*
chylous (*see also* Filariasis) 125.9 *[711.7]* ☑
climacteric NEC 716.3 ☑
coccyx 721.8
cricoarytenoid 478.79
crystal (-induced) — *see* Arthritis, due to crystals
deformans (*see also* Osteoarthrosis) 715.9 ☑
spine 721.90
with myelopathy 721.91
degenerative (*see also* Osteoarthrosis) 715.9 ☑
idiopathic 715.09
polyarticular 715.09
spine 721.90
with myelopathy 721.91
dermatoarthritis, lipoid 272.8 *[713.0]*
due to or associated with
acromegaly 253.0 *[713.0]*
actinomycosis 039.8 *[711.4]* ☑
amyloidosis 277.39 *[713.7]*
bacterial disease NEC 040.89 *[711.4]* ☑
Behçet's syndrome 136.1 *[711.2]* ☑
blastomycosis 116.0 *[711.6]* ☑
brucellosis (*see also* Brucellosis) 023.9 *[711.4]* ☑

Arthritis, arthritic — *continued*
due to or associated with — *continued*
caisson disease 993.3
coccidioidomycosis 114.3 *[711.6]* ☑
coliform (Escherichia coli) 711.0 ☑
colitis, ulcerative (*see also* Colitis, ulcerative) 556.9 *[713.1]*
cowpox 051.01 *[711.5]* ☑
crystals (*see also* Gout)
dicalcium phosphate 275.49 *[712.1]* ☑
pyrophosphate 275.49 *[712.2]* ☑
specified NEC 275.49 *[712.8]* ☑
dermatoarthritis, lipoid 272.8 *[713.0]*
dermatological disorder NEC 709.9 *[713.3]*
diabetes 250.6 ☑ *[713.5]*
due to secondary diabetes 249.6 ☑ *[713.5]*
diphtheria 032.89 *[711.4]* ☑
dracontiasis 125.7 *[711.7]* ☑
dysentery 009.0 *[711.3]* ☑
endocrine disorder NEC 259.9 *[713.0]*
enteritis NEC 009.1 *[711.3]* ☑
infectious (*see also* Enteritis, infectious) 009.0 *[711.3]* ☑
specified organism NEC 008.8 *[711.3]* ☑
regional (*see also* Enteritis, regional) 555.9 *[713.1]*
specified organism NEC 008.8 *[711.3]* ☑
epiphyseal slip, nontraumatic (old) 716.8 ☑
erysipelas 035 *[711.4]* ☑
erythema
epidemic 026.1
multiforme 695.10 *[713.3]*
nodosum 695.2 *[713.3]*
Escherichia coli 711.0 ☑
filariasis NEC 125.9 *[711.7]* ☑
gastrointestinal condition NEC 569.9 *[713.1]*
glanders 024 *[711.4]* ☑
Gonococcus 098.50
gout 274.0
helminthiasis NEC 128.9 *[711.7]* ☑
hematological disorder NEC 289.9 *[713.2]*
hemochromatosis 275.0 *[713.0]*
hemoglobinopathy NEC (*see also* Disease, hemoglobin) 282.7 *[713.2]*
hemophilia (*see also* Hemophilia) 286.0 *[713.2]*
Hemophilus influenzae (H. influenzae) 711.0 ☑
Henoch (-Schönlein) purpura 287.0 *[713.6]*
H. influenzae 711.0 ☑
histoplasmosis NEC (*see also* Histoplasmosis) 115.99 *[711.6]* ☑
human parvovirus 079.83 *[711.5]* ☑
hyperparathyroidism 252.00 *[713.0]*
hypersensitivity reaction NEC 995.3 *[713.6]*
hypogammaglobulinemia (*see also* Hypogamma-globulinemia) 279.00 *[713.0]*
hypothyroidism NEC 244.9 *[713.0]*
infection (*see also* Arthritis, infectious) 711.9 ☑
infectious disease NEC 136.9 *[711.8]* ☑
leprosy (*see also* Leprosy) 030.9 *[711.4]* ☑
leukemia NEC (M9800/3) 208.9 *[713.2]*

Arthritis, arthritic — *continued*
due to or associated with — *continued*
lipoid dermatoarthritis 272.8 *[713.0]*
Lyme disease 088.81 *[711.8]* ☑
Mediterranean fever, familial 277.31 *[713.7]*
meningococcal infection 036.82
metabolic disorder NEC 277.9 *[713.0]*
multiple myelomatosis (M9730/3) 203.0 *[713.2]*
mumps 072.79 *[711.5]* ☑
mycobacteria 031.8 *[711.4]* ☑
mycosis NEC 117.9 *[711.6]* ☑
neurological disorder NEC 349.9 *[713.5]*
ochronosis 270.2 *[713.0]*
O'Nyong Nyong 066.3 *[711.5]* ☑
parasitic disease NEC 136.9 *[711.8]* ☑
paratyphoid fever (*see also* Fever, paratyphoid) 002.9 *[711.3]* ☑
parvovirus B19 079.83 *[711.5]* ☑
Pneumococcus 711.0 ☑
poliomyelitis (*see also* Poliomyelitis) 045.9 ☑ *[711.5]* ☑
Pseudomonas 711.0 ☑
psoriasis 696.0
pyogenic organism (E. coli) (H. influenzae) (Pseudomonas) (Streptococcus) 711.0 ☑
rat-bite fever 026.1 *[711.4]* ☑
regional enteritis (*see also* Enteritis, regional) 555.9 *[713.1]*
Reiter's disease 099.3 *[711.1]* ☑
respiratory disorder NEC 519.9 *[713.4]*
reticulosis, malignant (M9720/3) 202.3 *[713.2]*
rubella 056.71
salmonellosis 003.23
sarcoidosis 135 *[713.7]*
serum sickness 999.5 *[713.6]*
Staphylococcus 711.0 ☑
Streptococcus 711.0 ☑
syphilis (*see also* Syphilis) 094.0 *[711.4]* ☑
syringomyelia 336.0 *[713.5]*
thalassemia 282.49 *[713.2]*
tuberculosis (*see also* Tuberculosis, arthritis) 015.9 ☑ *[711.4]* ☑
typhoid fever 002.0 *[711.3]* ☑
ulcerative colitis (*see also* Colitis, ulcerative) 556.9 *[713.1]*
urethritis
nongonococcal (*see also* Urethritis, nongonococcal) 099.40 *[711.1]* ☑
nonspecific (*see also* Urethritis, nongonococcal) 099.40 *[711.1]* ☑
Reiter's 099.3
viral disease NEC 079.99 *[711.5]* ☑
erythema epidemic 026.1
gonococcal 098.50
gouty (acute) 274.0
hypertrophic (*see also* Osteoarthrosis) 715.9 ☑
spine 721.90
with myelopathy 721.91
idiopathic, blennorrheal 099.3
in caisson disease 993.3 *[713.8]*
infectious or infective (acute) (chronic) (subacute) NEC 711.9 ☑
nonpyogenic 711.9 ☑
spine 720.9
inflammatory NEC 714.9
juvenile rheumatoid (chronic) (polyarticular) 714.30
acute 714.31
monoarticular 714.33
pauciarticular 714.32
lumbar (*see also* Spondylosis, lumbar) 721.3

Arthritis, arthritic — *continued*
meningococcal 036.82
menopausal NEC 716.3 ☑
migratory — *see* Fever, rheumatic
neuropathic (Charcôt's) 094.0 *[713.5]*
diabetic 250.6 ☑ *[713.5]*
due to secondary diabetes 249.6 ☑ *[713.5]*
nonsyphilitic NEC 349.9 *[713.5]*
syringomyelic 336.0 *[713.5]*
tabetic 094.0 *[713.5]*
nodosa (*see also* Osteoarthrosis) 715.9 ☑
spine 721.90
with myelopathy 721.91
nonpyogenic NEC 716.9 ☑
spine 721.90
with myelopathy 721.91
ochronotic 270.2 *[713.0]*
palindromic (see also Rheumatism, palindromic) 719.3 ☑
pneumococcal 711.0 ☑
postdysenteric 009.0 *[711.3]* ☑
postrheumatic, chronic (Jaccoud's) 714.4
primary progressive 714.0
spine 720.9
proliferative 714.0
spine 720.0
psoriatic 696.0
purulent 711.0 ☑
pyogenic or pyemic 711.0 ☑
rheumatic 714.0
acute or subacute — *see* Fever, rheumatic
chronic 714.0
spine 720.9
rheumatoid (nodular) 714.0
with
splenoadenomegaly and leukopenia 714.1
visceral or systemic involvement 714.2
aortitis 714.89
carditis 714.2
heart disease 714.2
juvenile (chronic) (polyarticular) 714.30
acute 714.31
monoarticular 714.33
pauciarticular 714.32
spine 720.0
rubella 056.71
sacral, sacroiliac, sacrococcygeal (*see also* Spondylosis, sacral) 721.3
scorbutic 267
senile or senescent (*see also* Osteoarthrosis) 715.9 ☑
spine 721.90
with myelopathy 721.91
septic 711.0 ☑
serum (nontherapeutic) (therapeutic) 999.5 *[713.6]*
specified form NEC 716.8 ☑
spine 721.90
with myelopathy 721.91
atrophic 720.9
degenerative 721.90
with myelopathy 721.91
hypertrophic (with deformity) 721.90
with myelopathy 721.91
infectious or infective NEC 720.9
Marie-Strümpell 720.0
nonpyogenic 721.90
with myelopathy 721.91
pyogenic 720.9
rheumatoid 720.0
traumatic (old) 721.7
tuberculous (*see also* Tuberculosis) 015.0 ☑ *[720.81]*
staphylococcal 711.0 ☑
streptococcal 711.0 ☑
suppurative 711.0 ☑
syphilitic 094.0 *[713.5]*
congenital 090.49 *[713.5]*

- **Aspiration** — *continued*
  - newborn — *continued*
    - blood — *continued*
      - with
        - pneumonia 770.16
        - pneumonitis 770.16
        - respiratory symptoms 770.16
  - pneumonia 507.0
    - fetus or newborn 770.18
      - meconium 770.12
  - pneumonitis 507.0
    - fetus or newborn 770.18
      - meconium 770.12
    - obstetric 668.0 ☑
  - postnatal stomach contents 770.85
    - with
      - pneumonia 770.86
      - pneumonitis 770.86
      - respiratory symptoms 770.86
  - syndrome of newborn (massive) 770.18
    - meconium 770.12
  - vernix caseosa 770.12
- **Asplenia** 759.0
  - with mesocardia 746.87
- **Assam fever** 085.0
- **Assimilation, pelvis**
  - with disproportion 653.2 ☑
    - affecting fetus or newborn 763.1
    - causing obstructed labor 660.1 ☑
      - affecting fetus or newborn 763.1
- **Assmann's focus** — *see also* Tuberculosis 011.0 ☑
- **Astasia** (-abasia) 307.9
  - hysterical 300.11
- **Asteatosis** 706.8
  - cutis 706.8
- **Astereognosis** 780.99
- **Asterixis** 781.3
  - in liver disease 572.8
- **Asteroid hyalitis** 379.22
- **Asthenia, asthenic** 780.79
  - cardiac (*see also* Failure, heart) 428.9
    - psychogenic 306.2
  - cardiovascular (*see also* Failure, heart) 428.9
    - psychogenic 306.2
  - heart (*see also* Failure, heart) 428.9
    - psychogenic 306.2
  - hysterical 300.11
  - myocardial (*see also* Failure, heart) 428.9
    - psychogenic 306.2
  - nervous 300.5
  - neurocirculatory 306.2
  - neurotic 300.5
  - psychogenic 300.5
  - psychoneurotic 300.5
  - psychophysiologic 300.5
  - reaction, psychoneurotic 300.5
  - senile 797
  - Stiller's 780.79
  - tropical anhidrotic 705.1
- **Asthenopia** 368.13
  - accommodative 367.4
  - hysterical (muscular) 300.11
  - psychogenic 306.7
- **Asthenospermia** 792.2
- **Asthma, asthmatic** (bronchial) (catarrh) (spasmodic) 493.9 ☑

> *Note — Use the following fifth-digit subclassification with category 493:*
>
> 0 *without mention of status asthmaticus or acute exacerbation or unspecified*
>
> 1 *with status asthmaticus*
>
> 2 *with acute exacerbation*

- with
  - chronic obstructive pulmonary disease (COPD) 493.2 ☑
  - hay fever 493.0 ☑
  - rhinitis, allergic 493.0 ☑
- allergic 493.9 ☑

- **Asthma, asthmatic** — *continued*
  - allergic — *continued*
    - stated cause (external allergen) 493.0 ☑
  - atopic 493.0 ☑
  - cardiac (*see also* Failure, ventricular, left) 428.1
  - cardiobronchial (*see also* Failure, ventricular, left) 428.1
  - cardiorenal (*see also* Hypertension, cardiorenal) 404.90
  - childhood 493.0 ☑
  - Colliers' 500
  - cough variant 493.82
  - croup 493.9 ☑
  - detergent 507.8
  - due to
    - detergent 507.8
    - inhalation of fumes 506.3
    - internal immunological process 493.0 ☑
  - endogenous (intrinsic) 493.1 ☑
  - eosinophilic 518.3
  - exercise induced bronchospasm 493.81
  - exogenous (cosmetics) (dander or dust) (drugs) (dust) (feathers) (food) (hay) (platinum) (pollen) 493.0 ☑
  - extrinsic 493.0 ☑
  - grinders' 502
  - hay 493.0 ☑
  - heart (*see also* Failure, ventricular, left) 428.1
  - IgE 493.0 ☑
  - infective 493.1 ☑
  - intrinsic 493.1 ☑
  - Kopp's 254.8
  - late-onset 493.1 ☑
  - meat-wrappers' 506.9
  - Millar's (laryngismus stridulus) 478.75
  - millstone makers' 502
  - miners' 500
  - Monday morning 504
  - New Orleans (epidemic) 493.0 ☑
  - platinum 493.0 ☑
  - pneumoconiotic (occupational) NEC 505
  - potters' 502
  - psychogenic 316 *[493.9]* ☑
  - pulmonary eosinophilic 518.3
  - red cedar 495.8
  - Rostan's (*see also* Failure, ventricular, left) 428.1
  - sandblasters' 502
  - sequoiosis 495.8
  - stonemasons' 502
  - thymic 254.8
  - tuberculous (*see also* Tuberculosis, pulmonary) 011.9 ☑
  - Wichmann's (laryngismus stridulus) 478.75
  - wood 495.8
- **Astigmatism** (compound) (congenital) 367.20
  - irregular 367.22
  - regular 367.21
- **Astroblastoma** (M9430/3)
  - nose 748.1
  - specified site — *see* Neoplasm, by site, malignant
  - unspecified site 191.9
- **Astrocytoma** (cystic) (M9400/3)
  - anaplastic type (M9401/3)
    - specified site — *see* Neoplasm, by site, malignant
    - unspecified site 191.9
  - fibrillary (M9420/3)
    - specified site — *see* Neoplasm, by site, malignant
    - unspecified site 191.9
  - fibrous (M9420/3)
    - specified site — *see* Neoplasm, by site, malignant
    - unspecified site 191.9

- **Astrocytoma** — *continued*
  - gemistocytic (M9411/3)
    - specified site — *see* Neoplasm, by site, malignant
    - unspecified site 191.9
  - juvenile (M9421/3)
    - specified site — *see* Neoplasm, by site, malignant
    - unspecified site 191.9
  - nose 748.1
  - pilocytic (M9421/3)
    - specified site — *see* Neoplasm, by site, malignant
    - unspecified site 191.9
  - piloid (M9421/3)
    - specified site — *see* Neoplasm, by site, malignant
    - unspecified site 191.9
  - protoplasmic (M9410/3)
    - specified site — *see* Neoplasm, by site, malignant
    - unspecified site 191.9
  - specified site — *see* Neoplasm, by site, malignant
  - subependymal (M9383/1) 237.5
    - giant cell (M9384/1) 237.5
  - unspecified site 191.9
- **Astroglioma** (M9400/3)
  - nose 748.1
  - specified site — *see* Neoplasm, by site, malignant
  - unspecified site 191.9
- **Asymbolia** 784.60
- **Asymmetrical breathing** 786.09
- **Asymmetry** — *see also* Distortion
  - breast, between native and reconstructed 612.1
  - chest 786.9
  - face 754.0
  - jaw NEC 524.12
    - maxillary 524.11
  - pelvis with disproportion 653.0 ☑
    - affecting fetus or newborn 763.1
    - causing obstructed labor 660.1 ☑
      - affecting fetus or newborn 763.1
- **Asynergia** 781.3
- **Asynergy** 781.3
  - ventricular 429.89
- **Asystole** (heart) — *see also* Arrest, cardiac 427.5
- **Ataxia, ataxy, ataxic** 781.3
  - acute 781.3
  - brain 331.89
  - cerebellar 334.3
    - hereditary (Marie's) 334.2
    - in
      - alcoholism 303.9 ☑ *[334.4]*
      - myxedema (*see also* Myxedema) 244.9 *[334.4]*
      - neoplastic disease NEC 239.9 *[334.4]*
  - cerebral 331.89
  - family, familial 334.2
    - cerebral (Marie's) 334.2
    - spinal (Friedreich's) 334.0
  - Friedreich's (heredofamilial) (spinal) 334.0
  - frontal lobe 781.3
  - gait 781.2
    - hysterical 300.11
  - general 781.3
  - hereditary NEC 334.2
    - cerebellar 334.2
    - spastic 334.1
    - spinal 334.0
  - heredofamilial (Marie's) 334.2
  - hysterical 300.11
  - locomotor (progressive) 094.0
    - diabetic 250.6 ☑ *[337.1]*
      - due to secondary diabetes 249.6 ☑ *[337.1]*
  - Marie's (cerebellar) (heredofamilial) 334.2
  - nonorganic origin 307.9
  - partial 094.0
  - postchickenpox 052.7

- **Ataxia, ataxy, ataxic** — *continued*
  - progressive locomotor 094.0
  - psychogenic 307.9
  - Sanger-Brown's 334.2
  - spastic 094.0
    - hereditary 334.1
    - syphilitic 094.0
  - spinal
    - hereditary 334.0
    - progressive locomotor 094.0
  - telangiectasia 334.8
- **Ataxia-telangiectasia** 334.8
- **Atelectasis** (absorption collapse) (complete) (compression) (massive) (partial) (postinfective) (pressure collapse) (pulmonary) (relaxation) 518.0
  - newborn (congenital) (partial) 770.5
    - primary 770.4
  - primary 770.4
  - tuberculous (*see also* Tuberculosis, pulmonary) 011.9 ☑
- **Ateleiosis, ateliosis** 253.3
- **Atelia** — *see* Distortion
- **Ateliosis** 253.3
- **Atelocardia** 746.9
- **Atelomyelia** 742.59
- **Athelia** 757.6
- **Atheroembolism**
  - extremity
    - lower 445.02
    - upper 445.01
  - kidney 445.81
  - specified site NEC 445.89
- **Atheroma, atheromatous** — *see also* Arteriosclerosis 440.9
  - aorta, aortic 440.0
    - valve (*see also* Endocarditis, aortic) 424.1
  - artery — *see* Arteriosclerosis
  - basilar (artery) (*see also* Occlusion, artery, basilar) 433.0 ☑
  - carotid (artery) (common) (internal) (*see also* Occlusion, artery, carotid) 433.1 ☑
  - cerebral (arteries) 437.0
  - coronary (artery) — *see* Arteriosclerosis, coronary
  - degeneration — *see* Arteriosclerosis
  - heart, cardiac — *see* Arteriosclerosis, coronary
  - mitral (valve) 424.0
  - myocardium, myocardial — *see* Arteriosclerosis, coronary
  - pulmonary valve (heart) (*see also* Endocarditis, pulmonary) 424.3
  - skin 706.2
  - tricuspid (heart) (valve) 424.2
  - valve, valvular — *see* Endocarditis
  - vertebral (artery) (*see also* Occlusion, artery, vertebral) 433.2 ☑
- **Atheromatosis** — *see also* Arteriosclerosis
  - arterial, congenital 272.8
- **Atherosclerosis** — *see* Arteriosclerosis
- **Athetosis** (acquired) 781.0
  - bilateral 333.79
  - congenital (bilateral) 333.6
  - double 333.71
  - unilateral 781.0
- **Athlete's**
  - foot 110.4
  - heart 429.3
- **Athletic team examination** V70.3
- **Athrepsia** 261
- **Athyrea** (acquired) — *see also* Hypothyroidism 244.9
  - congenital 243
- **Athyreosis** (congenital) 243
  - acquired — *see* Hypothyroidism
- **Athyroidism** (acquired) — *see also* Hypothyroidism 244.9
  - congenital 243
- **Atmospheric pyrexia** 992.0
- **Atonia, atony, atonic**
  - abdominal wall 728.2

Attention to — *continued*
- sutures V58.32
- tracheostomy V55.0
- ureterostomy V55.6
- urethrostomy V55.6

Attrition
- gum (*see also* Recession, gingival) 523.20
- teeth (hard tissues) 521.10
  - excessive 521.10
    - extending into
      - dentine 521.12
      - pulp 521.13
    - generalized 521.15
    - limited to enamel 521.11
    - localized 521.14

Atypical — *see also* condition
- cells
  - endocervical 795.00
  - endometrial 795.00
  - glandular
    - anus 796.70
    - cervical 795.00
    - vaginal 795.10
- distribution, vessel (congenital) (peripheral) NEC 747.60
- endometrium 621.9
- kidney 593.89

Atypism, cervix 622.10
Audible tinnitus — *see also* Tinnitus 388.30
Auditory — *see* condition
Audry's syndrome (acropachyderma) 757.39
Aujeszky's disease 078.89
Aura
- jacksonian (*see also* Epilepsy) 345.5 ☑
- persistent migraine 346.5 ☑
  - with cerebral infarction 346.6 ☑
  - without cerebral infarction 346.5 ☑

Aurantiasis, cutis 278.3
Auricle, auricular — *see* condition
Auriculotemporal syndrome 350.8
Australian
- Q fever 083.0
- X disease 062.4

Autism, autistic (child) (infantile) 299.0 ☑
Autodigestion 799.89
Autoerythrocyte sensitization 287.2
Autographism 708.3
Autoimmune
- cold sensitivity 283.0
- disease NEC 279.4
- hemolytic anemia 283.0
- thyroiditis 245.2

Autoinfection, septic — *see* Septicemia
Autointoxication 799.89
Automatism 348.8
- epileptic (*see also* Epilepsy) 345.4 ☑
- paroxysmal, idiopathic (*see also* Epilepsy) 345.4 ☑

Autonomic, autonomous
- bladder 596.54
  - neurogenic 596.54
    - with cauda equina 344.61
- dysreflexia 337.3
- faciocephalalgia (*see also* Neuropathy, peripheral, autonomic) 337.9
- hysterical seizure 300.11
- imbalance (*see also* Neuropathy, peripheral, autonomic) 337.9

Autophony 388.40
Autosensitivity, erythrocyte 287.2
Autotopagnosia 780.99
Autotoxemia 799.89
Autumn — *see* condition
Avellis' syndrome 344.89
Aviators
- disease or sickness (*see also* Effect, adverse, high altitude) 993.2
- ear 993.0
- effort syndrome 306.2

Avitaminosis (multiple NEC) — *see also* Deficiency, vitamin 269.2
- A 264.9

Avitaminosis — *see also* Deficiency, vitamin — *continued*
- B 266.9
  - with
    - beriberi 265.0
    - pellagra 265.2
- B_1 265.1
- B_2 266.0
- B_6 266.1
- B_{12} 266.2
- C (with scurvy) 267
- D 268.9
  - with
    - osteomalacia 268.2
    - rickets 268.0
- E 269.1
- G 266.0
- H 269.1
- K 269.0
- multiple 269.2
- nicotinic acid 265.2
- P 269.1

Avulsion (traumatic) 879.8
- blood vessel — *see* Injury, blood vessel, by site
- cartilage (*see also* Dislocation, by site)
  - knee, current (*see also* Tear, meniscus) 836.2
  - symphyseal (inner), complicating delivery 665.6 ☑
- complicated 879.9
- diaphragm — *see* Injury, internal, diaphragm
- ear — *see* Wound, open, ear
- epiphysis of bone — *see* Fracture, by site
- external site other than limb — *see* Wound, open, by site
- eye 871.3
- fingernail — *see* Wound, open, finger
- fracture — *see* Fracture, by site
- genital organs, external — *see* Wound, open, genital organs
- head (intracranial) NEC (*see also* Injury, intracranial, with open intracranial wound)
  - complete 874.9
  - external site NEC 873.8
    - complicated 873.9
- internal organ or site — *see* Injury, internal, by site
- joint (*see also* Dislocation, by site)
  - capsule — *see* Sprain, by site
- ligament — *see* Sprain, by site
- limb (*see also* Amputation, traumatic, by site)
  - skin and subcutaneous tissue — *see* Wound, open, by site
- muscle — *see* Sprain, by site
- nerve (root) — *see* Injury, nerve, by site
- scalp — *see* Wound, open, scalp
- skin and subcutaneous tissue — *see* Wound, open, by site
- symphyseal cartilage (inner), complicating delivery 665.6 ☑
- tendon (*see also* Sprain, by site)
  - with open wound — *see* Wound, open, by site
- toenail — *see* Wound, open, toe(s)
- tooth 873.63
  - complicated 873.73

Awaiting organ transplant status V49.83
Awareness of heart beat 785.1
Axe grinders' disease 502
Axenfeld's anomaly or syndrome 743.44
Axilla, axillary — *see also* condition
- breast 757.6

Axonotmesis — *see* Injury, nerve, by site
Ayala's disease 756.89
Ayerza's disease or syndrome (pulmonary artery sclerosis with pulmonary hypertension) 416.0
Azoospermia 606.0
Azorean disease (of the nervous system) 334.8
Azotemia 790.6
- meaning uremia (*see also* Uremia) 586

Aztec ear 744.29
Azygos lobe, lung (fissure) 748.69

B

Baader's syndrome (erythema multiforme exudativum) 695.19
Baastrup's syndrome 721.5
Babesiasis 088.82
Babesiosis 088.82
Babington's disease (familial hemorrhagic telangiectasia) 448.0
Babinski-Fröhlich syndrome (adiposogenital dystrophy) 253.8
Babinski-Nageotte syndrome 344.89
Babinski's syndrome (cardiovascular syphilis) 093.89
Bacillary — *see* condition
Bacilluria 791.9
- asymptomatic, in pregnancy or puerperium 646.5 ☑
- tuberculous (*see also* Tuberculosis) 016.9 ☑

Bacillus — *see also* Infection, bacillus
- abortus infection 023.1
- anthracis infection 022.9
- coli
  - infection 041.4
    - generalized 038.42
    - intestinal 008.00
  - pyemia 038.42
  - septicemia 038.42
- Flexner's 004.1
- fusiformis infestation 101
- mallei infection 024
- Shiga's 004.0
- suipestifer infection (*see also* Infection, Salmonella) 003.9

Back — *see* condition
Backache (postural) 724.5
- psychogenic 307.89
- sacroiliac 724.6

Backflow (pyelovenous) — *see also* Disease, renal 593.9
Backknee — *see also* Genu, recurvatum 736.5
Bacteremia 790.7
- newborn 771.83

Bacteria
- in blood (*see also* Bacteremia) 790.7
- in urine (*see also* Bacteriuria) 599.0

Bacterial — *see* condition
Bactericholia — *see also* Cholecystitis, acute 575.0
Bacterid, bacteride (Andrews' pustular) 686.8
Bacteriuria, bacteruria 791.9
- with
  - urinary tract infection 599.0
- asymptomatic 791.9
  - in pregnancy or puerperium 646.5 ☑
    - affecting fetus or newborn 760.1

Bad
- breath 784.99
- heart — *see* Disease, heart
- trip (*see also* Abuse, drugs, nondependent) 305.3 ☑

Baehr-Schiffrin disease (thrombotic thrombocytopenic purpura) 446.6
Baelz's disease (cheilitis glandularis apostematosa) 528.5
Baerensprung's disease (eczema marginatum) 110.3
Bagassosis (occupational) 495.1
Baghdad boil 085.1
Bagratuni's syndrome (temporal arteritis) 446.5
Baker's
- cyst (knee) 727.51
  - tuberculous (*see also* Tuberculosis) 015.2 ☑

Baker's — *continued*
- itch 692.89

Bakwin-Krida syndrome (craniometaphyseal dysplasia) 756.89
Balanitis (circinata) (gangraenosa) (infectious) (vulgaris) 607.1
- amebic 006.8
- candidal 112.2
- chlamydial 099.53
- due to Ducrey's bacillus 099.0
- erosiva circinata et gangraenosa 607.1
- gangrenous 607.1
- gonococcal (acute) 098.0
  - chronic or duration of 2 months or over 098.2
- nongonococcal 607.1
- phagedenic 607.1
- venereal NEC 099.8
- xerotica obliterans 607.81

Balanoposthitis 607.1
- chlamydial 099.53
- gonococcal (acute) 098.0
  - chronic or duration of 2 months or over 098.2
- ulcerative NEC 099.8

Balanorrhagia — *see* Balanitis
Balantidiasis 007.0
Balantidiosis 007.0
Balbuties, balbutio 307.0
Bald
- patches on scalp 704.00
- tongue 529.4

Baldness — *see also* Alopecia 704.00
Balfour's disease (chloroma) 205.3 ☑
Balint's syndrome (psychic paralysis of visual fixation) 368.16
Balkan grippe 083.0
Ball
- food 938
- hair 938

Ballantyne (-Runge) syndrome (postmaturity) 766.22
Balloon disease — *see also* Effect, adverse, high altitude 993.2
Ballooning posterior leaflet syndrome 424.0
Baló's disease or concentric sclerosis 341.1
Bamberger's disease (hypertrophic pulmonary osteoarthropathy) 731.2
Bamberger-Marie disease (hypertrophic pulmonary osteoarthropathy) 731.2
Bamboo spine 720.0
Bancroft's filariasis 125.0
Band(s)
- adhesive (*see also* Adhesions, peritoneum) 568.0
- amniotic 658.8 ☑
  - affecting fetus or newborn 762.8
- anomalous or congenital (*see also* Anomaly, specified type NEC)
  - atrial 746.9
  - heart 746.9
  - intestine 751.4
  - omentum 751.4
  - ventricular 746.9
- cervix 622.3
- gallbladder (congenital) 751.69
- intestinal (adhesive) (*see also* Adhesions, peritoneum) 568.0
  - congenital 751.4
- obstructive (*see also* Obstruction, intestine) 560.81
- periappendiceal (congenital) 751.4
- peritoneal (adhesive) (*see also* Adhesions, peritoneum) 568.0
  - with intestinal obstruction 560.81
  - congenital 751.4
- uterus 621.5
- vagina 623.2

Bandemia (without diagnosis of specific infection) 288.66
Bandl's ring (contraction)
- complicating delivery 661.4 ☑
  - affecting fetus or newborn 763.7

Bang's disease (Brucella abortus) 023.1

Bangkok hemorrhagic fever 065.4

Bannister's disease 995.1

Bantam-Albright-Martin disease (pseudohypoparathyroidism) 275.49

Banti's disease or syndrome (with cirrhosis) (with portal hypertension) — *see* Cirrhosis, liver

Bar
- calcaneocuboid 755.67
- calcaneonavicular 755.67
- cubonavicular 755.67
- prostate 600.90
  - with
    - other lower urinary tract symptoms (LUTS) 600.91
    - urinary
      - obstruction 600.91
      - retention 600.91
- talocalcaneal 755.67

Baragnosis 780.99

Barasheh, barashek 266.2

Barcoo disease or rot — *see also* Ulcer, skin 707.9

Bard-Pic syndrome (carcinoma, head of pancreas) 157.0

Bärensprung's disease (eczema marginatum) 110.3

Baritosis 503

Barium lung disease 503

Barlow (-Möller) disease or syndrome (meaning infantile scurvy) 267

Barlow's syndrome (meaning mitral valve prolapse) 424.0

Barodontalgia 993.2

Baron Münchausen syndrome 301.51

Barosinusitis 993.1

Barotitis 993.0

Barotrauma 993.2
- odontalgia 993.2
- otitic 993.0
- sinus 993.1

Barraquer's disease or syndrome (progressive lipodystrophy) 272.6

Barré-Guillain syndrome 357.0

Barrel chest 738.3

Barré-Liéou syndrome (posterior cervical sympathetic) 723.2

Barrett's esophagus 530.85

Barrett's syndrome or ulcer (chronic peptic ulcer of esophagus) 530.85

Bársony-Polgár syndrome (corkscrew esophagus) 530.5

Bársony-Teschendorf syndrome (corkscrew esophagus) 530.5

Bartholin's
- adenitis (*see also* Bartholinitis) 616.89
- gland — *see* condition

Bartholinitis (suppurating) 616.89
- gonococcal (acute) 098.0
  - chronic or duration of 2 months or over 098.2

Barth syndrome 759.89

Bartonellosis 088.0

Bartter's syndrome (secondary hyperaldosteronism with juxtaglomerular hyperplasia) 255.13

Basal — *see* condition

Basan's (hidrotic) **ectodermal dysplasia** 757.31

Baseball finger 842.13

Basedow's disease or syndrome (exophthalmic goiter) 242.0 ☑

Basic — *see* condition

Basilar — *see* condition

Bason's (hidrotic) **ectodermal dysplasia** 757.31

Basopenia 288.59

Basophilia 288.65

Basophilism (corticoadrenal) (Cushing's) (pituitary) (thymic) 255.0

Bassen-Kornzweig syndrome (abetalipoproteinemia) 272.5

Bat ear 744.29

Bateman's
- disease 078.0
- purpura (senile) 287.2

Bathing cramp 994.1

Bathophobia 300.23

Batten's disease, retina 330.1 *[362.71]*

Batten-Mayou disease 330.1 *[362.71]*

Batten-Steinert syndrome 359.21

Battered
- adult (syndrome) 995.81
- baby or child (syndrome) 995.54
- spouse (syndrome) 995.81

Battey mycobacterium infection 031.0

Battledore placenta — *see* Placenta, abnormal

Battle exhaustion — *see also* Reaction, stress, acute 308.9

Baumgarten-Cruveilhier (cirrhosis) **disease, or syndrome** 571.5

Bauxite
- fibrosis (of lung) 503
- workers' disease 503

Bayle's disease (dementia paralytica) 094.1

Bazin's disease (primary) — *see also* Tuberculosis 017.1 ☑

Beach ear 380.12

Beaded hair (congenital) 757.4

Beals syndrome 759.82

Beard's disease (neurasthenia) 300.5

Bearn-Kunkel (-Slater) syndrome (lupoid hepatitis) 571.49

Beat
- elbow 727.2
- hand 727.2
- knee 727.2

Beats
- ectopic 427.60
- escaped, heart 427.60
  - postoperative 997.1
- premature (nodal) 427.60
  - atrial 427.61
  - auricular 427.61
  - postoperative 997.1
  - specified type NEC 427.69
  - supraventricular 427.61
  - ventricular 427.69

Beau's
- disease or syndrome (*see also* Degeneration, myocardial) 429.1
- lines (transverse furrows on fingernails) 703.8

Bechterew's disease (ankylosing spondylitis) 720.0

Bechterew-Strümpell-Marie syndrome (ankylosing spondylitis) 720.0

Becker's
- disease
  - idiopathic mural endomyocardial disease 425.2
  - myotonia congenita, recessive form 359.22
- dystrophy 359.22

Beck's syndrome (anterior spinal artery occlusion) 433.8 ☑

Beckwith (-Wiedemann) syndrome 759.89

Bedbugs bite(s) — *see* Injury, superficial, by site

Bedclothes, asphyxiation or suffocation by 994.7

Bed confinement status V49.84

Bednar's aphthae 528.2

Bedsore (*see also* Ulcer, pressure) 707.00
- with gangrene 707.00 *[785.4]*

Bedwetting — *see also* Enuresis 788.36

Beer-drinkers' heart (disease) 425.5

Bee sting (with allergic or anaphylactic shock) 989.5

Begbie's disease (exophthalmic goiter) 242.0 ☑

Behavior disorder, disturbance — *see also* Disturbance, conduct
- antisocial, without manifest psychiatric disorder
  - adolescent V71.02
  - adult V71.01
  - child V71.02

Behavior disorder, disturbance — *see also* Disturbance, conduct — *continued*
- dyssocial, without manifest psychiatric disorder
  - adolescent V71.02
  - adult V71.01
  - child V71.02
- high risk — *see* Problem

Behçet's syndrome 136.1

Behr's disease 362.50

Beigel's disease or morbus (white piedra) 111.2

Bejel 104.0

Bekhterev's disease (ankylosing spondylitis) 720.0

Bekhterev-Strümpell-Marie syndrome (ankylosing spondylitis) 720.0

Belching — *see also* Eructation 787.3

Bell's
- disease (*see also* Psychosis, affective) 296.0 ☑
- mania (*see also* Psychosis, affective) 296.0 ☑
- palsy, paralysis 351.0
  - infant 767.5
  - newborn 767.5
  - syphilitic 094.89
- spasm 351.0

Bence-Jones albuminuria, albuminosuria, or proteinuria 791.0

Bends 993.3

Benedikt's syndrome (paralysis) 344.89

Benign — *see also* condition
- cellular changes, cervix 795.09
- prostate
  - with
    - other lower urinary tract symptoms (LUTS) 600.21
    - urinary
      - obstruction 600.21
      - retention 600.21
  - hyperplasia 600.20
  - neoplasm 222.2

Bennett's
- disease (leukemia) 208.9 ☑
- fracture (closed) 815.01
  - open 815.11

Benson's disease 379.22

Bent
- back (hysterical) 300.11
- nose 738.0
  - congenital 754.0

Bereavement V62.82
- as adjustment reaction 309.0

Bergeron's disease (hysteroepilepsy) 300.11

Berger's paresthesia (lower limb) 782.0

Beriberi (acute) (atrophic) (chronic) (dry) (subacute) (wet) 265.0
- with polyneuropathy 265.0 *[357.4]*
- heart (disease) 265.0 *[425.7]*
- leprosy 030.1
- neuritis 265.0 *[357.4]*

Berlin's disease or edema (traumatic) 921.3

Berloque dermatitis 692.72

Bernard-Horner syndrome — *see also* Neuropathy, peripheral, autonomic 337.9

Bernard-Sergent syndrome (acute adrenocortical insufficiency) 255.41

Bernard-Soulier disease or thrombopathy 287.1

Bernhardt's disease or paresthesia 355.1

Bernhardt-Roth disease or syndrome (paresthesia) 355.1

Bernheim's syndrome — *see also* Failure, heart 428.0

Bertielliasis 123.8

Bertolotti's syndrome (sacralization of fifth lumbar vertebra) 756.15

Berylliosis (acute) (chronic) (lung) (occupational) 503

Besnier's
- lupus pernio 135
- prurigo (atopic dermatitis) (infantile eczema) 691.8

Besnier-Boeck disease or sarcoid 135

Besnier-Boeck-Schaumann disease (sarcoidosis) 135

Best's disease 362.76

Bestiality 302.1

Beta-adrenergic hyperdynamic circulatory state 429.82

Beta-aminoisobutyric aciduria 277.2

Beta-mercaptolactate-cysteine disulfiduria 270.0

Beta thalassemia (major) (minor) (mixed) 282.49

Beurmann's disease (sporotrichosis) 117.1

Bezoar 938
- intestine 936
- stomach 935.2

Bezold's abscess — *see also* Mastoiditis 383.01

Bianchi's syndrome (aphasia-apraxia-alexia) 784.69

Bicornuate or bicornis uterus 752.3
- in pregnancy or childbirth 654.0 ☑
  - with obstructed labor 660.2 ☑
    - affecting fetus or newborn 763.1
  - affecting fetus or newborn 763.89

Bicuspid aortic valve 746.4

Biedl-Bardet syndrome 759.89

Bielschowsky's disease 330.1

Bielschowsky-Jansky
- amaurotic familial idiocy 330.1
- disease 330.1

Biemond's syndrome (obesity, polydactyly, and mental retardation) 759.89

Biermer's anemia or disease (pernicious anemia) 281.0

Biett's disease 695.4

Bifid (congenital) — *see also* Imperfect, closure
- apex, heart 746.89
- clitoris 752.49
- epiglottis 748.3
- kidney 753.3
- nose 748.1
- patella 755.64
- scrotum 752.89
- toe 755.66
- tongue 750.13
- ureter 753.4
- uterus 752.3
- uvula 749.02
  - with cleft lip (*see also* Cleft, palate, with cleft lip) 749.20

Biforis uterus (suprasimplex) 752.3

Bifurcation (congenital) — *see also* Imperfect, closure
- gallbladder 751.69
- kidney pelvis 753.3
- renal pelvis 753.3
- rib 756.3
- tongue 750.13
- trachea 748.3
- ureter 753.4
- urethra 753.8
- uvula 749.02
  - with cleft lip (*see also* Cleft, palate, with cleft lip) 749.20
- vertebra 756.19

Bigeminal pulse 427.89

Bigeminy 427.89

Big spleen syndrome 289.4

Bilateral — *see* condition

Bile duct — *see* condition

Bile pigments in urine 791.4

Bilharziasis — *see also* Schistosomiasis 120.9
- chyluria 120.0
- cutaneous 120.3
- galacturia 120.0
- hematochyluria 120.0
- intestinal 120.1
- lipemia 120.9

- **Bilharziasis** — *see also* Schistosomiasis — *continued*
  - lipuria 120.0
  - Oriental 120.2
  - piarhemia 120.9
  - pulmonary 120.2
  - tropical hematuria 120.0
  - vesical 120.0
- **Biliary** — *see* condition
- **Bilious** (attack) — *see also* Vomiting
  - fever, hemoglobinuric 084.8
- **Bilirubinuria** 791.4
- **Biliuria** 791.4
- **Billroth's disease**
  - meningocele (*see also* Spina bifida) 741.9 ☑
- **Bilobate placenta** — *see* Placenta, abnormal
- **Bilocular**
  - heart 745.7
  - stomach 536.8
- **Bing-Horton syndrome** (histamine cephalgia) 339.00
- **Binswanger's disease or dementia** 290.12
- **Biörck (-Thorson) syndrome** (malignant carcinoid) 259.2
- **Biparta, bipartite** — *see also* Imperfect, closure
  - carpal scaphoid 755.59
  - patella 755.64
  - placenta — *see* Placenta, abnormal
  - vagina 752.49
- **Bird**
  - face 756.0
  - fanciers' lung or disease 495.2
- **Bird's disease** (oxaluria) 271.8
- **Birth**
  - abnormal fetus or newborn 763.9
  - accident, fetus or newborn — *see* Birth, injury
  - complications in mother — *see* Delivery, complicated
  - compression during NEC 767.9
  - defect — *see* Anomaly
  - delayed, fetus 763.9
  - difficult NEC, affecting fetus or newborn 763.9
  - dry, affecting fetus or newborn 761.1
  - forced, NEC, affecting fetus or newborn 763.89
  - forceps, affecting fetus or newborn 763.2
  - hematoma of sternomastoid 767.8
  - immature 765.1 ☑
    - extremely 765.0 ☑
  - inattention, after or at 995.52
  - induced, affecting fetus or newborn 763.89
  - infant — *see* Newborn
  - injury NEC 767.9
    - adrenal gland 767.8
    - basal ganglia 767.0
    - brachial plexus (paralysis) 767.6
    - brain (compression) (pressure) 767.0
    - cerebellum 767.0
    - cerebral hemorrhage 767.0
    - conjunctiva 767.8
    - eye 767.8
    - fracture
      - bone, any except clavicle or spine 767.3
      - clavicle 767.2
      - femur 767.3
      - humerus 767.3
      - long bone 767.3
      - radius and ulna 767.3
      - skeleton NEC 767.3
      - skull 767.3
      - spine 767.4
      - tibia and fibula 767.3
    - hematoma 767.8
      - liver (subcapsular) 767.8
      - mastoid 767.8
      - skull 767.19
- **Birth** — *continued*
  - injury — *continued*
    - hematoma — *continued*
      - sternomastoid 767.8
      - testes 767.8
      - vulva 767.8
    - intracranial (edema) 767.0
    - laceration
      - brain 767.0
      - by scalpel 767.8
      - peripheral nerve 767.7
    - liver 767.8
    - meninges
      - brain 767.0
      - spinal cord 767.4
    - nerves (cranial, peripheral) 767.7
      - brachial plexus 767.6
      - facial 767.5
    - paralysis 767.7
      - brachial plexus 767.6
      - Erb (-Duchenne) 767.6
      - facial nerve 767.5
      - Klumpke (-Déjérine) 767.6
      - radial nerve 767.6
      - spinal (cord) (hemorrhage) (laceration) (rupture) 767.4
    - rupture
      - intracranial 767.0
      - liver 767.8
      - spinal cord 767.4
      - spleen 767.8
      - viscera 767.8
    - scalp 767.19
    - scalpel wound 767.8
    - skeleton NEC 767.3
    - specified NEC 767.8
    - spinal cord 767.4
    - spleen 767.8
    - subdural hemorrhage 767.0
    - tentorial, tear 767.0
    - testes 767.8
    - vulva 767.8
  - instrumental, NEC, affecting fetus or newborn 763.2
  - lack of care, after or at 995.52
  - multiple
    - affected by maternal complications of pregnancy 761.5
    - healthy liveborn — *see* Newborn, multiple
  - neglect, after or at 995.52
  - newborn — *see* Newborn
  - palsy or paralysis NEC 767.7
  - precipitate, fetus or newborn 763.6
  - premature (infant) 765.1 ☑
  - prolonged, affecting fetus or newborn 763.9
  - retarded, fetus or newborn 763.9
  - shock, newborn 779.89
  - strangulation or suffocation
    - due to aspiration of clear amniotic fluid 770.13
      - with respiratory symptoms 770.14
    - mechanical 767.8
  - trauma NEC 767.9
  - triplet
    - affected by maternal complications of pregnancy 761.5
    - healthy liveborn — *see* Newborn, multiple
  - twin
    - affected by maternal complications of pregnancy 761.5
    - healthy liveborn — *see* Newborn, twin
  - ventouse, affecting fetus or newborn 763.3
- **Birthmark** 757.32
- **Birt-Hogg-Dube syndrome** 759.89
- **Bisalbuminemia** 273.8
- **Biskra button** 085.1
- **Bite(s)**
  - with intact skin surface — *see* Contusion
  - animal — *see* Wound, open, by site
- **Bite(s)** — *continued*
  - animal — *see* Wound, open, by site — *continued*
    - intact skin surface — *see* Contusion
  - bedbug — *see* Injury, superficial, by site
  - centipede 989.5
  - chigger 133.8
  - fire ant 989.5
  - flea — *see* Injury, superficial, by site
  - human (open wound) (*see also* Wound, open, by site)
    - intact skin surface — *see* Contusion
  - insect
    - nonvenomous — *see* Injury, superficial, by site
    - venomous 989.5
  - mad dog (death from) 071
  - open
    - anterior 524.24
    - posterior 524.25
  - poisonous 989.5
  - red bug 133.8
  - reptile 989.5
    - nonvenomous — *see* Wound, open, by site
  - snake 989.5
    - nonvenomous — *see* Wound, open, by site
  - spider (venomous) 989.5
    - nonvenomous — *see* Injury, superficial, by site
  - venomous 989.5
- **Biting**
  - cheek or lip 528.9
  - nail 307.9
- **Black**
  - death 020.9
  - eye NEC 921.0
  - hairy tongue 529.3
  - heel 924.20
  - lung disease 500
  - palm 923.20
- **Blackfan-Diamond anemia or syndrome** (congenital hypoplastic anemia) 284.01
- **Blackhead** 706.1
- **Blackout** 780.2
- **Blackwater fever** 084.8
- **Bladder** — *see* condition
- **Blast**
  - blindness 921.3
  - concussion — *see* Blast, injury
  - injury 869.0
    - with open wound into cavity 869.1
    - abdomen or thorax — *see* Injury, internal, by site
    - brain (*see also* Concussion, brain) 850.9
      - with skull fracture — *see* Fracture, skull
    - ear (acoustic nerve trauma) 951.5
      - with perforation, tympanic membrane — *see* Wound, open, ear, drum
    - lung (*see also* Injury, internal, lung) 861.20
    - otitic (explosive) 388.11
- **Blastomycosis, blastomycotic** (chronic) (cutaneous) (disseminated) (lung) (pulmonary) (systemic) 116.0
  - Brazilian 116.1
  - European 117.5
  - keloidal 116.2
  - North American 116.0
  - primary pulmonary 116.0
  - South American 116.1
- **Bleb(s)** 709.8
  - emphysematous (bullous) (diffuse) (lung) (ruptured) (solitary) 492.0
  - filtering, eye (postglaucoma) (status) V45.69
    - with complication 997.99
- **Bleb(s)** — *continued*
  - filtering, eye — *continued*
    - postcataract extraction (complication) 997.99
  - lung (ruptured) 492.0
    - congenital 770.5
  - subpleural (emphysematous) 492.0
- **Bleeder** (familial) (hereditary) — *see also* Defect, coagulation 286.9
  - nonfamilial 286.9
- **Bleeding** — *see also* Hemorrhage 459.0
  - anal 569.3
  - anovulatory 628.0
  - atonic, following delivery 666.1 ☑
  - capillary 448.9
  - due to subinvolution 621.1
    - puerperal 666.2 ☑
  - ear 388.69
  - excessive, associated with menopausal onset 627.0
  - familial (*see also* Defect, coagulation) 286.9
  - following intercourse 626.7
  - gastrointestinal 578.9
  - gums 523.8
  - hemorrhoids — *see* Hemorrhoids, bleeding
  - intermenstrual
    - irregular 626.6
    - regular 626.5
  - intraoperative 998.11
  - irregular NEC 626.4
  - menopausal 627.0
  - mouth 528.9
  - nipple 611.79
  - nose 784.7
  - ovulation 626.5
  - postclimacteric 627.1
  - postcoital 626.7
  - postmenopausal 627.1
    - following induced menopause 627.4
  - postoperative 998.11
  - preclimacteric 627.0
  - puberty 626.3
    - excessive, with onset of menstrual periods 626.3
  - rectum, rectal 569.3
  - tendencies (*see also* Defect, coagulation) 286.9
  - throat 784.8
  - umbilical stump 772.3
  - umbilicus 789.9
  - unrelated to menstrual cycle 626.6
  - uterus, uterine 626.9
    - climacteric 627.0
    - dysfunctional 626.8
    - functional 626.8
    - unrelated to menstrual cycle 626.6
  - vagina, vaginal 623.8
    - functional 626.8
  - vicarious 625.8
- **Blennorrhagia, blennorrhagic** — *see* Blennorrhea
- **Blennorrhea** (acute) 098.0
  - adultorum 098.40
  - alveolaris 523.40
  - chronic or duration of 2 months or over 098.2
  - gonococcal (neonatorum) 098.40
  - inclusion (neonatal) (newborn) 771.6
  - neonatorum 098.40
- **Blepharelosis** — *see also* Entropion 374.00
- **Blepharitis** (eyelid) 373.00
  - angularis 373.01
  - ciliaris 373.00
    - with ulcer 373.01
  - marginal 373.00
    - with ulcer 373.01
  - scrofulous (*see also* Tuberculosis) 017.3 ☑ *[373.00]*
  - squamous 373.02
  - ulcerative 373.01
- **Blepharochalasis** 374.34
  - congenital 743.62

- **Blood** — *continued*
  - pressure
    - decreased, due to shock following injury 958.4
    - fluctuating 796.4
    - high (*see also* Hypertension) 401.9
      - incidental reading (isolated) (nonspecific), without diagnosis of hypertension 796.2
    - low (*see also* Hypotension) 458.9
      - incidental reading (isolated) (nonspecific), without diagnosis of hypotension 796.3
  - spitting (*see also* Hemoptysis) 786.3
  - staining cornea 371.12
  - transfusion
    - without reported diagnosis V58.2
    - donor V59.01
      - stem cells V59.02
    - reaction or complication — *see* Complications, transfusion
  - tumor — *see* Hematoma
  - vessel rupture — *see* Hemorrhage
  - vomiting (*see also* Hematemesis) 578.0
- **Blood-forming organ disease** 289.9
- **Bloodgood's disease** 610.1
- **Bloodshot eye** 379.93
- **Bloom (-Machacek) (-Torre) syndrome** 757.39
- **Blotch, palpebral** 372.55
- **Blount-Barber syndrome** (tibia vara) 732.4
- **Blount's disease** (tibia vara) 732.4
- **Blue**
  - baby 746.9
  - bloater 491.20
    - with
      - acute bronchitis 491.22
      - exacerbation (acute) 491.21
  - diaper syndrome 270.0
  - disease 746.9
  - dome cyst 610.0
  - drum syndrome 381.02
  - sclera 743.47
    - with fragility of bone and deafness 756.51
  - toe syndrome 445.02
- **Blueness** — *see also* Cyanosis 782.5
- **Blurring, visual** 368.8
- **Blushing** (abnormal) (excessive) 782.62
- **BMI** (body mass index)
  - adult
    - 25.0-25.9 V85.21
    - 26.0-26.9 V85.22
    - 27.0-27.9 V85.23
    - 28.0-28.9 V85.24
    - 29.0-29.9 V85.25
    - 30.0-30.9 V85.30
    - 31.0-31.9 V85.31
    - 32.0-32.9 V85.32
    - 33.0-33.9 V85.33
    - 34.0-34.9 V85.34
    - 35.0-35.9 V85.35
    - 36.0-36.9 V85.36
    - 37.0-37.9 V85.37
    - 38.0-38.9 V85.38
    - 39.0-39.9 V85.39
    - 40 and over V85.4
    - between 19-24 V85.1
    - less than 19 V85.0
  - pediatric
    - 5th percentile to less than 85th percentile for age V85.52
    - 85th percentile to less than 95th percentile for age V85.53
    - greater than or equal to 95th percentile for age V85.54
    - less than 5th percentile for age V85.51
- **Boarder, hospital** V65.0
  - infant V65.0
- **Bockhart's impetigo** (superficial folliculitis) 704.8
- **Bodechtel-Guttmann disease** (subacute sclerosing panencephalitis) 046.2
- **Boder-Sedgwick syndrome** (ataxia-telangiectasia) 334.8
- **Body, bodies**
  - Aschoff (*see also* Myocarditis, rheumatic) 398.0
  - asteroid, vitreous 379.22
  - choroid, colloid (degenerative) 362.57
    - hereditary 362.77
  - cytoid (retina) 362.82
  - drusen (retina) (*see also* Drusen) 362.57
    - optic disc 377.21
  - fibrin, pleura 511.0
  - foreign — *see* Foreign body
  - Hassall-Henle 371.41
  - loose
    - joint (*see also* Loose, body, joint) 718.1 ☑
      - knee 717.6
    - knee 717.6
    - sheath, tendon 727.82
  - Mallory's 034.1
  - mass index (BMI)
    - adult
      - 25.0-25.9 V85.21
      - 26.0-26.9 V85.22
      - 27.0-27.9 V85.23
      - 28.0-28.9 V85.24
      - 29.0-29.9 V85.25
      - 30.0-30.9 V85.30
      - 31.0-31.9 V85.31
      - 32.0-32.9 V85.32
      - 33.0-33.9 V85.33
      - 34.0-34.9 V85.34
      - 36.0-36.9 V85.36
      - 37.0-37.9 V85.37
      - 38.0-38.9 V85.38
      - 39.0-39.9 V85.39
      - 40 and over V85.4
      - between 19-24 V85.1
      - less than 19 V85.0
    - pediatric
      - 5th percentile to less than 85th percentile for age V85.52
      - 85th percentile to less than 95th percentile for age V85.53
      - greater than or equal to 95th percentile for age V85.54
      - less than 5th percentile for age V85.51
  - Mooser 081.0
  - Negri 071
  - rice (joint) (*see also* Loose, body, joint) 718.1 ☑
    - knee 717.6
  - rocking 307.3
- **Boeck's**
  - disease (sarcoidosis) 135
  - lupoid (miliary) 135
  - sarcoid 135
- **Boerhaave's syndrome** (spontaneous esophageal rupture) 530.4
- **Boggy**
  - cervix 622.8
  - uterus 621.8
- **Boil** — *see also* Carbuncle 680.9
  - abdominal wall 680.2
  - Aleppo 085.1
  - ankle 680.6
  - anus 680.5
  - arm (any part, above wrist) 680.3
  - auditory canal, external 680.0
  - axilla 680.3
  - back (any part) 680.2
  - Baghdad 085.1
  - breast 680.2
  - buttock 680.5
  - chest wall 680.2
  - corpus cavernosum 607.2
  - Delhi 085.1
  - ear (any part) 680.0
  - eyelid 373.13
  - face (any part, except eye) 680.0
- **Boil** — *see also* Carbuncle — *continued*
  - finger (any) 680.4
  - flank 680.2
  - foot (any part) 680.7
  - forearm 680.3
  - Gafsa 085.1
  - genital organ, male 608.4
  - gluteal (region) 680.5
  - groin 680.2
  - hand (any part) 680.4
  - head (any part, except face) 680.8
  - heel 680.7
  - hip 680.6
  - knee 680.6
  - labia 616.4
  - lacrimal (*see also* Dacryocystitis) 375.30
    - gland (*see also* Dacryoadenitis) 375.00
    - passages (duct) (sac) (*see also* Dacryocystitis) 375.30
  - leg, any part, except foot 680.6
  - multiple sites 680.9
  - natal 085.1
  - neck 680.1
  - nose (external) (septum) 680.0
  - orbit, orbital 376.01
  - partes posteriores 680.5
  - pectoral region 680.2
  - penis 607.2
  - perineum 680.2
  - pinna 680.0
  - scalp (any part) 680.8
  - scrotum 608.4
  - seminal vesicle 608.0
  - shoulder 680.3
  - skin NEC 680.9
  - specified site NEC 680.8
  - spermatic cord 608.4
  - temple (region) 680.0
  - testis 608.4
  - thigh 680.6
  - thumb 680.4
  - toe (any) 680.7
  - tropical 085.1
  - trunk 680.2
  - tunica vaginalis 608.4
  - umbilicus 680.2
  - upper arm 680.3
  - vas deferens 608.4
  - vulva 616.4
  - wrist 680.4
- **Bold hives** — *see also* Urticaria 708.9
- **Bolivian hemorrhagic fever** 078.7
- **Bombé, iris** 364.74
- **Bomford-Rhoads anemia** (refractory) 238.72
- **Bone** — *see* condition
- **Bonnevie-Ullrich syndrome** 758.6
- **Bonnier's syndrome** 386.19
- **Bonvale Dam fever** 780.79
- **Bony block of joint** 718.80
  - ankle 718.87
  - elbow 718.82
  - foot 718.87
  - hand 718.84
  - hip 718.85
  - knee 718.86
  - multiple sites 718.89
  - pelvic region 718.85
  - shoulder (region) 718.81
  - specified site NEC 718.88
  - wrist 718.83
- **BOOP** (bronchiolitis obliterans organized pneumonia) 516.8
- **Borderline**
  - intellectual functioning V62.89
  - osteopenia 733.90
  - pelvis 653.1 ☑
    - with obstruction during labor 660.1 ☑
      - affecting fetus or newborn 763.1
  - psychosis (*see also* Schizophrenia) 295.5 ☑
- **Borderline** — *continued*
  - psychosis (*see also* Schizophrenia) — *continued*
    - of childhood (*see also* Psychosis, childhood) 299.8 ☑
    - schizophrenia (*see also* Schizophrenia) 295.5 ☑
- **Borna disease** 062.9
- **Bornholm disease** (epidemic pleurodynia) 074.1
- **Borrelia vincentii** (mouth) (pharynx) (tonsils) 101
- **Bostock's catarrh** — *see also* Fever, hay 477.9
- **Boston exanthem** 048
- **Botalli, ductus** (patent) (persistent) 747.0
- **Bothriocephalus latus infestation** 123.4
- **Botulism** 005.1
  - food poisoning 005.1
  - infant 040.41
  - non-foodborne 040.42
  - wound 040.42
- **Bouba** — *see also* Yaws 102.9
- **Bouffée délirante** 298.3
- **Bouillaud's disease or syndrome** (rheumatic heart disease) 391.9
- **Bourneville's disease** (tuberous sclerosis) 759.5
- **Boutonneuse fever** 082.1
- **Boutonniere**
  - deformity (finger) 736.21
  - hand (intrinsic) 736.21
- **Bouveret (-Hoffmann) disease or syndrome** (paroxysmal tachycardia) 427.2
- **Bovine heart** — *see* Hypertrophy, cardiac
- **Bowel** — *see* condition
- **Bowen's**
  - dermatosis (precancerous) (M8081/2) — *see* Neoplasm, skin, in situ
  - disease (M8081/2) — *see* Neoplasm, skin, in situ
  - epithelioma (M8081/2) — *see* Neoplasm, skin, in situ
  - type
    - epidermoid carcinoma in situ (M8081/2) — *see* Neoplasm, skin, in situ
    - intraepidermal squamous cell carcinoma (M8081/2) — *see* Neoplasm, skin, in situ
- **Bowing**
  - femur 736.89
    - congenital 754.42
  - fibula 736.89
    - congenital 754.43
  - forearm 736.09
    - away from midline (cubitus valgus) 736.01
    - toward midline (cubitus varus) 736.02
  - leg(s), long bones, congenital 754.44
  - radius 736.09
    - away from midline (cubitus valgus) 736.01
    - toward midline (cubitus varus) 736.02
  - tibia 736.89
    - congenital 754.43
- **Bowleg(s)** 736.42
  - congenital 754.44
  - rachitic 268.1
- **Boyd's dysentery** 004.2
- **Brachial** — *see* condition
- **Brachman-de Lange syndrome** (Amsterdam dwarf, mental retardation, and brachycephaly) 759.89
- **Brachycardia** 427.89
- **Brachycephaly** 756.0
- **Brachymorphism and ectopia lentis** 759.89
- **Bradley's disease** (epidemic vomiting) 078.82
- **Bradycardia** 427.89

Bradycardia — *continued*
- chronic (sinus) 427.81
- newborn 779.81
- nodal 427.89
- postoperative 997.1
- reflex 337.09
- sinoatrial 427.89
  - with paroxysmal tachyarrhythmia or tachycardia 427.81
  - chronic 427.81
- sinus 427.89
  - with paroxysmal tachyarrhythmia or tachycardia 427.81
  - chronic 427.81
  - persistent 427.81
  - severe 427.81
- tachycardia syndrome 427.81
- vagal 427.89

Bradypnea 786.09

Brailsford's disease 732.3
- radial head 732.3
- tarsal scaphoid 732.5

Brailsford-Morquio disease or syndrome (mucopolysaccharidosis IV) 277.5

Brain — *see also* condition
- death 348.8
- syndrome (acute) (chronic) (nonpsychotic) (organic) (with neurotic reaction) (with behavioral reaction) (*see also* Syndrome, brain) 310.9
  - with
    - presenile brain disease 290.10
    - psychosis, psychotic reaction (*see also* Psychosis, organic) 294.9
  - congenital (*see also* Retardation, mental) 319

Branched-chain amino-acid disease 270.3

Branchial — *see* condition

Brandt's syndrome (acrodermatitis enteropathica) 686.8

Brash (water) 787.1

Brass-founders' ague 985.8

Bravais-Jacksonian epilepsy — *see also* Epilepsy 345.5 ☑

Braxton Hicks contractions 644.1 ☑

Braziers' disease 985.8

Brazilian
- blastomycosis 116.1
- leishmaniasis 085.5

BRBPR (bright red blood per rectum) 569.3

Break
- cardiorenal — *see* Hypertension, cardiorenal
- retina (*see also* Defect, retina) 361.30

Breakbone fever 061

Breakdown
- device, implant, or graft — *see* Complications, mechanical
- nervous (*see also* Disorder, mental, nonpsychotic) 300.9
- perineum 674.2 ☑

Breast — *see also* condition
- buds 259.1
  - in newborn 779.89
- dense — *omit code*
- nodule 793.89

Breast feeding difficulties 676.8 ☑

Breath
- foul 784.99
- holder, child 312.81
- holding spells 786.9
- shortness 786.05

Breathing
- asymmetrical 786.09
- bronchial 786.09
- exercises V57.0
- labored 786.09
- mouth 784.99
  - causing malocclusion 524.59
- periodic 786.09
  - high altitude 327.22

Breathing — *continued*
- tic 307.20

Breathlessness 786.09

Breda's disease — *see also* Yaws 102.9

Breech
- delivery, affecting fetus or newborn 763.0
- extraction, affecting fetus or newborn 763.0
- presentation (buttocks) (complete) (frank) 652.2 ☑
  - with successful version 652.1 ☑
  - before labor, affecting fetus or newborn 761.7
  - during labor, affecting fetus or newborn 763.0

Breisky's disease (kraurosis vulvae) 624.09

Brennemann's syndrome (acute mesenteric lymphadenitis) 289.2

Brenner's
- tumor (benign) (M9000/0) 220
  - borderline malignancy (M9000/1) 236.2
  - malignant (M9000/3) 183.0
  - proliferating (M9000/1) 236.2

Bretonneau's disease (diphtheritic malignant angina) 032.0

Breus' mole 631

Brevicollis 756.16

Bricklayers' itch 692.89

Brickmakers' anemia 126.9

Bridge
- myocardial 746.85

Bright's
- blindness — *see* Uremia
- disease (*see also* Nephritis) 583.9
  - arteriosclerotic (*see also* Hypertension, kidney) 403.90

Bright red blood per rectum (BRBPR) 569.3

Brill's disease (recrudescent typhus) 081.1
- flea-borne 081.0
- louse-borne 081.1

Brill-Symmers disease (follicular lymphoma) (M9690/3) 202.0 ☑

Brill-Zinsser disease (recrudescent typhus) 081.1

Brinton's disease (linitis plastica) (M8142/3) 151.9

Brion-Kayser disease — *see also* Fever, paratyphoid 002.9

Briquet's disorder or syndrome 300.81

Brissaud's
- infantilism (infantile myxedema) 244.9
- motor-verbal tic 307.23

Brissaud-Meige syndrome (infantile myxedema) 244.9

Brittle
- bones (congenital) 756.51
- nails 703.8
  - congenital 757.5

Broad — *see also* condition
- beta disease 272.2
- ligament laceration syndrome 620.6

Brock's syndrome (atelectasis due to enlarged lymph nodes) 518.0

Brocq's disease 691.8
- atopic (diffuse) neurodermatitis 691.8
- lichen simplex chronicus 698.3
- parakeratosis psoriasiformis 696.2
- parapsoriasis 696.2

Brocq-Duhring disease (dermatitis herpetiformis) 694.0

Brodie's
- abscess (localized) (chronic) (*see also* Osteomyelitis) 730.1 ☑
- disease (joint) (*see also* Osteomyelitis) 730.1 ☑

Broken
- arches 734
  - congenital 755.67
- back — *see* Fracture, vertebra, by site
- bone — *see* Fracture, by site
- compensation — *see* Disease, heart

Broken — *continued*
- heart syndrome 429.83
- implant or internal device — *see* listing under Complications, mechanical
- neck — *see* Fracture, vertebra, cervical
- nose 802.0
  - open 802.1
- tooth, teeth 873.63
  - complicated 873.73

Bromhidrosis 705.89

Bromidism, bromism
- acute 967.3
  - correct substance properly administered 349.82
  - overdose or wrong substance given or taken 967.3
- chronic (*see also* Dependence) 304.1 ☑

Bromidrosiphobia 300.23

Bromidrosis 705.89

Bronchi, bronchial — *see* condition

Bronchiectasis (cylindrical) (diffuse) (fusiform) (localized) (moniliform) (postinfectious) (recurrent) (saccular) 494.0
- with acute exacerbation 494.1
- congenital 748.61
- tuberculosis (*see also* Tuberculosis) 011.5 ☑

Bronchiolectasis — *see* Bronchiectasis

Bronchiolitis (acute) (infectious) (subacute) 466.19
- with
  - bronchospasm or obstruction 466.19
  - influenza, flu, or grippe 487.1
- catarrhal (acute) (subacute) 466.19
- chemical 506.0
  - chronic 506.4
- chronic (obliterative) 491.8
- due to external agent — *see* Bronchitis, acute, due to
- fibrosa obliterans 491.8
- influenzal 487.1
- obliterans 491.8
  - with organizing pneumonia (BOOP) 516.8
  - status post lung transplant 996.84
- obliterative (chronic) (diffuse) (subacute) 491.8
  - due to fumes or vapors 506.4
- respiratory syncytial virus 466.11
- vesicular — *see* Pneumonia, bronchopneumonia

Bronchitis (diffuse) (hypostatic) (infectious) (inflammatory) (simple) 490
- with
  - emphysema — *see* Emphysema
  - influenza, flu, or grippe 487.1
  - obstruction airway, chronic 491.20
    - with
      - acute bronchitis 491.22
      - exacerbation (acute) 491.21
  - tracheitis 490
    - acute or subacute 466.0
      - with bronchospasm or obstruction 466.0
    - chronic 491.8
- acute or subacute 466.0
  - with
    - bronchiectasis 494.1
    - bronchospasm 466.0
    - obstruction 466.0
    - tracheitis 466.0
  - chemical (due to fumes or vapors) 506.0
  - due to
    - fumes or vapors 506.0
    - radiation 508.8
- allergic (acute) (*see also* Asthma) 493.9 ☑
- arachidic 934.1
- aspiration 507.0
  - due to fumes or vapors 506.0
- asthmatic (acute) 493.90

Bronchitis — *continued*
- asthmatic — *continued*
  - with
    - acute exacerbation 493.92
    - status asthmaticus 493.91
  - chronic 493.2 ☑
- capillary 466.19
  - with bronchospasm or obstruction 466.19
  - chronic 491.8
- caseous (*see also* Tuberculosis) 011.3 ☑
- Castellani's 104.8
- catarrhal 490
  - acute — *see* Bronchitis, acute
  - chronic 491.0
- chemical (acute) (subacute) 506.0
  - chronic 506.4
  - due to fumes or vapors (acute) (subacute) 506.0
    - chronic 506.4
- chronic 491.9
  - with
    - tracheitis (chronic) 491.8
  - asthmatic 493.2 ☑
  - catarrhal 491.0
  - chemical (due to fumes and vapors) 506.4
  - due to
    - fumes or vapors (chemical) (inhalation) 506.4
    - radiation 508.8
    - tobacco smoking 491.0
  - mucopurulent 491.1
  - obstructive 491.20
    - with
      - acute bronchitis 491.22
      - exacerbation (acute) 491.21
  - purulent 491.1
  - simple 491.0
  - specified type NEC 491.8
- croupous 466.0
  - with bronchospasm or obstruction 466.0
  - due to fumes or vapors 506.0
- emphysematous 491.20
  - with
    - acute bronchitis 491.22
    - exacerbation (acute) 491.21
- exudative 466.0
- fetid (chronic) (recurrent) 491.1
- fibrinous, acute or subacute 466.0
  - with bronchospasm or obstruction 466.0
- grippal 487.1
- influenzal 487.1
- membranous, acute or subacute 466.0
  - with bronchospasm or obstruction 466.0
- moulders' 502
- mucopurulent (chronic) (recurrent) 491.1
  - acute or subacute 466.0
- obliterans 491.8
- obstructive (chronic) 491.20
  - with
    - acute bronchitis 491.22
    - exacerbation (acute) 491.21
- pituitous 491.1
- plastic (inflammatory) 466.0
- pneumococcal, acute or subacute 466.0
  - with bronchospasm or obstruction 466.0
- pseudomembranous 466.0
- purulent (chronic) (recurrent) 491.1
  - acute or subacute 466.0
    - with bronchospasm or obstruction 466.0
- putrid 491.1
- scrofulous (*see also* Tuberculosis) 011.3 ☑
- senile 491.9
- septic, acute or subacute 466.0

Bronchitis — *continued*
septic, acute or subacute — *continued*
with bronchospasm or obstruction 466.0
smokers' 491.0
spirochetal 104.8
suffocative, acute or subacute 466.0
summer (*see also* Asthma) 493.9 ☑
suppurative (chronic) 491.1
acute or subacute 466.0
tuberculous (*see also* Tuberculosis) 011.3 ☑
ulcerative 491.8
Vincent's 101
Vincent's 101
viral, acute or subacute 466.0
Bronchoalveolitis 485
Bronchoaspergillosis 117.3
Bronchocele
meaning
dilatation of bronchus 519.19
goiter 240.9
Bronchogenic carcinoma 162.9
Bronchohemisporosis 117.9
Broncholithiasis 518.89
tuberculous (*see also* Tuberculosis) 011.3 ☑
Bronchomalacia 748.3
Bronchomoniliasis 112.89
Bronchomycosis 112.89
Bronchonocardiosis 039.1
Bronchopleuropneumonia — *see* Pneumonia, broncho-
Bronchopneumonia — *see* Pneumonia, broncho-
Bronchopneumonitis — *see* Pneumonia, broncho-
Bronchopulmonary — *see* condition
Bronchopulmonitis — *see* Pneumonia, broncho-
Bronchorrhagia 786.3
newborn 770.3
tuberculous (*see also* Tuberculosis) 011.3 ☑
Bronchorrhea (chronic) (purulent) 491.0
acute 466.0
Bronchospasm 519.11
with
asthma — *see* Asthma
bronchiolitis, acute 466.19
due to respiratory syncytial virus 466.11
bronchitis — *see* Bronchitis
chronic obstructive pulmonary disease (COPD) 496
emphysema — *see* Emphysema
due to external agent — *see* Condition, respiratory, acute, due to
acute 519.11
exercise induced 493.81
Bronchospirochetosis 104.8
Bronchostenosis 519.19
Bronchus — *see* condition
Bronze, bronzed
diabetes 275.0
disease (Addison's) (skin) 255.41
tuberculous (*see also* Tuberculosis) 017.6 ☑
Brooke's disease or tumor (M8100/0) — *see* Neoplasm, skin, benign
Brown enamel of teeth (hereditary) 520.5
Brown-Séquard's paralysis (syndrome) 344.89
Brown's tendon sheath syndrome 378.61
Brow presentation complicating delivery 652.4 ☑
Brucella, brucellosis (infection) 023.9
abortus 023.1
canis 023.3
dermatitis, skin 023.9
melitensis 023.0
mixed 023.8
Brucella, brucellosis — *continued*
suis 023.2
Bruck-de Lange disease or syndrome (Amsterdam dwarf, mental retardation, and brachycephaly) 759.89
Bruck's disease 733.99
Brugada syndrome 746.89
Brug's filariasis 125.1
Brugsch's syndrome (acropachyderma) 757.39
Bruhl's disease (splenic anemia with fever) 285.8
Bruise (skin surface intact) — *see also* Contusion
with
fracture — *see* Fracture, by site
open wound — *see* Wound, open, by site
internal organ (abdomen, chest, or pelvis) — *see* Injury, internal, by site
umbilical cord 663.6 ☑
affecting fetus or newborn 762.6
Bruit 785.9
arterial (abdominal) (carotid) 785.9
supraclavicular 785.9
Brushburn — *see* Injury, superficial, by site
Bruton's X-linked agammaglobulinemia 279.04
Bruxism 306.8
sleep related 327.53
Bubbly lung syndrome 770.7
Bubo 289.3
blennorrhagic 098.89
chancroidal 099.0
climatic 099.1
due to Hemophilus ducreyi 099.0
gonococcal 098.89
indolent NEC 099.8
inguinal NEC 099.8
chancroidal 099.0
climatic 099.1
due to H. ducreyi 099.0
scrofulous (*see also* Tuberculosis) 017.2 ☑
soft chancre 099.0
suppurating 683
syphilitic 091.0
congenital 090.0
tropical 099.1
venereal NEC 099.8
virulent 099.0
Bubonic plague 020.0
Bubonocele — *see* Hernia, inguinal
Buccal — *see* condition
Buchanan's disease (juvenile osteochondrosis of iliac crest) 732.1
Buchem's syndrome (hyperostosis corticalis) 733.3
Buchman's disease (osteochondrosis, juvenile) 732.1
Bucket handle fracture (semilunar cartilage) — *see also* Tear, meniscus 836.2
Budd-Chiari syndrome (hepatic vein thrombosis) 453.0
Budgerigar-fanciers' disease or lung 495.2
Büdinger-Ludloff-Läwen disease 717.89
Buds
breast 259.1
in newborn 779.89
Buerger's disease (thromboangiitis obliterans) 443.1
Bulbar — *see* condition
Bulbus cordis 745.9
persistent (in left ventricle) 745.8
Bulging fontanels (congenital) 756.0
Bulimia 783.6
nervosa 307.51
nonorganic origin 307.51
Bulky uterus 621.2
Bulla(e) 709.8
lung (emphysematous) (solitary) 492.0
Bullet wound — *see also* Wound, open, by site
fracture — *see* Fracture, by site, open
internal organ (abdomen, chest, or pelvis) — *see* Injury, internal, by site, with open wound
intracranial — *see* Laceration, brain, with open wound
Bullis fever 082.8
Bullying — *see also* Disturbance, conduct 312.0 ☑
Bundle
branch block (complete) (false) (incomplete) 426.50
bilateral 426.53
left (*see also* Block, bundle branch, left) 426.3
hemiblock 426.2
right (*see also* Block, bundle branch, right) 426.4
of His — *see* condition
of Kent syndrome (anomalous atrioventricular excitation) 426.7
Bungpagga 040.81
Bunion 727.1
Bunionette 727.1
Bunyamwera fever 066.3
Buphthalmia, buphthalmos (congenital) 743.20
associated with
keratoglobus, congenital 743.22
megalocornea 743.22
ocular anomalies NEC 743.22
isolated 743.21
simple 743.21
Bürger-Grütz disease or syndrome (essential familial hyperlipemia) 272.3
Buried roots 525.3
Burke's syndrome 577.8
Burkitt's
tumor (M9750/3) 200.2 ☑
type malignant, lymphoma, lymphoblastic, or undifferentiated (M9750/3) 200.2 ☑
Burn (acid) (cathode ray) (caustic) (chemical) (electric heating appliance) (electricity) (fire) (flame) (hot liquid or object) (irradiation) (lime) (radiation) (steam) (thermal) (x-ray) 949.0

Note — Use the following fifth-digit subclassification with category 948 to indicate the percent of body surface with third degree burn:

0	*Less than 10% or unspecified*
1	*10–19%*
2	*20–29%*
3	*30–39%*
4	*40–49%*
5	*50–59%*
6	*60–69%*
7	*70–79%*
8	*80–89%*
9	*90% or more of body surface*

with
blisters — *see* Burn, by site, second degree
erythema — *see* Burn, by site, first degree
skin loss (epidermal) (*see also* Burn, by site, second degree)
full thickness (*see also* Burn, by site, third degree)
with necrosis of underlying tissues — *see* Burn, by site, third degree, deep
first degree — *see* Burn, by site, first degree
second degree — *see* Burn, by site, second degree
Burn — *continued*
third degree — *see* Burn, by site, third degree
deep — *see* Burn, by site, third degree, deep
abdomen, abdominal (muscle) (wall) 942.03
with
trunk — *see* Burn, trunk, multiple sites
first degree 942.13
second degree 942.23
third degree 942.33
deep 942.43
with loss of body part 942.53
ankle 945.03
with
lower limb(s) — *see* Burn, leg, multiple sites
first degree 945.13
second degree 945.23
third degree 945.33
deep 945.43
with loss of body part 945.53
anus — *see* Burn, trunk, specified site NEC
arm(s) 943.00
first degree 943.10
second degree 943.20
third degree 943.30
deep 943.40
with loss of body part 943.50
lower — *see* Burn, forearm(s)
multiple sites, except hand(s) or wrist(s) 943.09
first degree 943.19
second degree 943.29
third degree 943.39
deep 943.49
with loss of body part 943.59
upper 943.03
first degree 943.13
second degree 943.23
third degree 943.33
deep 943.43
with loss of body part 943.53
auditory canal (external) — *see* Burn, ear
auricle (ear) — *see* Burn, ear
axilla 943.04
with
upper limb(s), except hand(s) or wrist(s) — *see* Burn, arm(s), multiple sites
first degree 943.14
second degree 943.24
third degree 943.34
deep 943.44
with loss of body part 943.54
back 942.04
with
trunk — *see* Burn, trunk, multiple sites
first degree 942.14
second degree 942.24
third degree 942.34
deep 942.44
with loss of body part 942.54
biceps
brachii — *see* Burn, arm(s), upper
femoris — *see* Burn, thigh
breast(s) 942.01
with
trunk — *see* Burn, trunk, multiple sites
first degree 942.11
second degree 942.21
third degree 942.31
deep 942.41
with loss of body part 942.51
brow — *see* Burn, forehead
buttock(s) — *see* Burn, back
canthus (eye) 940.1
chemical 940.0

Index

Bronchitis — Burn

- **Burn** — *continued*
  - nose — *continued*
    - first degree 941.15
    - second degree 941.25
    - third degree 941.35
      - deep 941.45
        - with loss of body part 941.55
  - occipital region — *see* Burn, scalp
  - orbit region 940.1
    - chemical 940.0
  - oronasopharynx 947.0
  - palate 947.0
  - palm(s) 944.05
    - with
      - hand(s) and wrist(s) — *see* Burn, hand(s), multiple sites
    - first degree 944.15
    - second degree 944.25
    - third degree 944.35
      - deep 944.45
        - with loss of a body part 944.55
  - parietal region — *see* Burn, scalp
  - penis — *see* Burn, genitourinary organs, external
  - perineum — *see* Burn, genitourinary organs, external
  - periocular area 940.1
    - chemical 940.0
  - pharynx 947.0
  - pleura 947.1
  - popliteal space — *see* Burn, knee
  - prepuce — *see* Burn, genitourinary organs, external
  - pubic region — *see* Burn, genitourinary organs, external
  - pudenda — *see* Burn, genitourinary organs, external
  - rectum 947.3
  - sac, lacrimal 940.1
    - chemical 940.0
  - sacral region — *see* Burn, back
  - salivary (ducts) (glands) 947.0
  - scalp 941.06
    - with
      - face or neck — *see* Burn, head, multiple sites
    - first degree 941.16
    - second degree 941.26
    - third degree 941.36
      - deep 941.46
        - with loss of body part 941.56
  - scapular region 943.06
    - with
      - upper limb(s), except hand(s) or wrist(s) — *see* Burn, arm(s), multiple sites
    - first degree 943.16
    - second degree 943.26
    - third degree 943.36
      - deep 943.46
        - with loss of body part 943.56
  - sclera — *see* Burn, eyeball
  - scrotum — *see* Burn, genitourinary organs, external
  - septum, nasal — *see* Burn, nose
  - shoulder(s) 943.05
    - with
      - hand(s) and wrist(s) — *see* Burn, multiple, specified sites
      - upper limb(s), except hand(s) or wrist(s) — *see* Burn, arm(s), multiple sites
    - first degree 943.15
    - second degree 943.25
    - third degree 943.35
      - deep 943.45
        - with loss of body part 943.55
  - skin NEC (*see also* Burn, unspecified) 949.0
  - skull — *see* Burn, head
  - small intestine 947.3
  - sternal region — *see* Burn, chest wall
  - stomach 947.3
- **Burn** — *continued*
  - subconjunctival — *see* Burn, conjunctiva
  - subcutaneous — *see* Burn, by site, third degree
  - submaxillary region — *see* Burn, head
  - submental region — *see* Burn, chin
  - sun — *see* Sunburn
  - supraclavicular fossa — *see* Burn, neck
  - supraorbital — *see* Burn, forehead
  - temple — *see* Burn, scalp
  - temporal region — *see* Burn, scalp
  - testicle — *see* Burn, genitourinary organs, external
  - testis — *see* Burn, genitourinary organs, external
  - thigh 945.06
    - with
      - lower limb(s) — *see* Burn, leg, multiple sites
    - first degree 945.16
    - second degree 945.26
    - third degree 945.36
      - deep 945.46
        - with loss of body part 945.56
  - thorax (external) — *see* Burn, chest wall
  - throat 947.0
  - thumb(s) (nail) (subungual) 944.02
    - with
      - finger(s) — *see* Burn, finger, with other sites, thumb
      - hand(s) and wrist(s) — *see* Burn, hand(s), multiple sites
    - first degree 944.12
    - second degree 944.22
    - third degree 944.32
      - deep 944.42
        - with loss of body part 944.52
  - toe (nail) (subungual) 945.01
    - with
      - lower limb(s) — *see* Burn, leg, multiple sites
    - first degree 945.11
    - second degree 945.21
    - third degree 945.31
      - deep 945.41
        - with loss of body part 945.51
  - tongue 947.0
  - tonsil 947.0
  - trachea 947.1
  - trunk 942.00
    - first degree 942.10
    - second degree 942.20
    - third degree 942.30
      - deep 942.40
        - with loss of body part 942.50
    - multiple sites 942.09
      - first degree 942.19
      - second degree 942.29
      - third degree 942.39
        - deep 942.49
          - with loss of body part 942.59
    - specified site NEC 942.09
      - first degree 942.19
      - second degree 942.29
      - third degree 942.39
        - deep 942.49
          - with loss of body part 942.59
  - tunica vaginalis — *see* Burn, genitourinary organs, external
  - tympanic membrane — *see* Burn, ear
  - tympanum — *see* Burn, ear
  - ultraviolet 692.82
  - unspecified site (multiple) 949.0
    - with extent of body surface involved specified
      - less than 10 percent 948.0 ☑
      - 10-19 percent 948.1 ☑
      - 20-29 percent 948.2 ☑
      - 30-39 percent 948.3 ☑
      - 40-49 percent 948.4 ☑
- **Burn** — *continued*
  - unspecified site — *continued*
    - with extent of body surface involved specified — *continued*
      - 50-59 percent 948.5 ☑
      - 60-69 percent 948.6 ☑
      - 70-79 percent 948.7 ☑
      - 80-89 percent 948.8 ☑
      - 90 percent or more 948.9 ☑
    - first degree 949.1
    - second degree 949.2
    - third degree 949.3
      - deep 949.4
        - with loss of body part 949.5
  - uterus 947.4
  - uvula 947.0
  - vagina 947.4
  - vulva — *see* Burn, genitourinary organs, external
  - wrist(s) 944.07
    - with
      - hand(s) — *see* Burn, hand(s), multiple sites
    - first degree 944.17
    - second degree 944.27
    - third degree 944.37
      - deep 944.47
        - with loss of body part 944.57
- **Burnett's syndrome** (milk-alkali) 275.42
- **Burnier's syndrome** (hypophyseal dwarfism) 253.3
- **Burning**
  - feet syndrome 266.2
  - sensation (*see also* Disturbance, sensation) 782.0
  - tongue 529.6
- **Burns' disease** (osteochondrosis, lower ulna) 732.3
- **Bursa** — *see also* condition
  - pharynx 478.29
- **Bursitis** NEC 727.3
  - Achilles tendon 726.71
  - adhesive 726.90
    - shoulder 726.0
  - ankle 726.79
  - buttock 726.5
  - calcaneal 726.79
  - collateral ligament
    - fibular 726.63
    - tibial 726.62
  - Duplay's 726.2
  - elbow 726.33
  - finger 726.8
  - foot 726.79
  - gonococcal 098.52
  - hand 726.4
  - hip 726.5
  - infrapatellar 726.69
  - ischiogluteal 726.5
  - knee 726.60
  - occupational NEC 727.2
  - olecranon 726.33
  - pes anserinus 726.61
  - pharyngeal 478.29
  - popliteal 727.51
  - prepatellar 726.65
  - radiohumeral 727.3
  - scapulohumeral 726.19
    - adhesive 726.0
  - shoulder 726.10
    - adhesive 726.0
  - subacromial 726.19
    - adhesive 726.0
  - subcoracoid 726.19
  - subdeltoid 726.19
    - adhesive 726.0
  - subpatellar 726.69
  - syphilitic 095.7
  - Thornwaldt's, Tornwaldt's (pharyngeal) 478.29
  - toe 726.79
  - trochanteric area 726.5
  - wrist 726.4
- **Burst stitches or sutures** (complication of surgery) (external) (*see also* Dehiscence) 998.32
- **Burst stitches or sutures** (*see also* Dehiscence) — *continued*
  - internal 998.31
- **Buruli ulcer** 031.1
- **Bury's disease** (erythema elevatum diutinum) 695.89
- **Buschke's disease or scleredema** (adultorum) 710.1
- **Busquet's disease** (osteoperiostitis) — *see also* Osteomyelitis 730.1 ☑
- **Busse-Buschke disease** (cryptococcosis) 117.5
- **Buttock** — *see* condition
- **Button**
  - Biskra 085.1
  - Delhi 085.1
  - oriental 085.1
- **Buttonhole hand** (intrinsic) 736.21
- **Bwamba fever** (encephalitis) 066.3
- **Byssinosis** (occupational) 504
- **Bywaters' syndrome** 958.5

C

- **Cacergasia** 300.9
- **Cachexia** 799.4
  - cancerous (*see also* Neoplasm, by site, malignant) 799.4
  - cardiac — *see* Disease, heart
  - dehydration 276.51
    - with
      - hypernatremia 276.0
      - hyponatremia 276.1
  - due to malnutrition 799.4
  - exophthalmic 242.0 ☑
  - heart — *see* Disease, heart
  - hypophyseal 253.2
  - hypopituitary 253.2
  - lead 984.9
    - specified type of lead — *see* Table of Drugs and Chemicals
  - malaria 084.9
  - malignant (*see also* Neoplasm, by site, malignant) 799.4
  - marsh 084.9
  - nervous 300.5
  - old age 797
  - pachydermic — *see* Hypothyroidism
  - paludal 084.9
  - pituitary (postpartum) 253.2
  - renal (*see also* Disease, renal) 593.9
  - saturnine 984.9
    - specified type of lead — *see* Table of Drugs and Chemicals
  - senile 797
  - Simmonds' (pituitary cachexia) 253.2
  - splenica 289.59
  - strumipriva (*see also* Hypothyroidism) 244.9
  - tuberculous NEC (*see also* Tuberculosis) 011.9 ☑
- **Café au lait spots** 709.09
- **Caffey's disease or syndrome** (infantile cortical hyperostosis) 756.59
- **Caisson disease** 993.3
- **Caked breast** (puerperal, postpartum) 676.2 ☑
- **Cake kidney** 753.3
- **Calabar swelling** 125.2
- **Calcaneal spur** 726.73
- **Calcaneoapophysitis** 732.5
- **Calcaneonavicular bar** 755.67
- **Calcareous** — *see* condition
- **Calcicosis** (occupational) 502
- **Calciferol** (vitamin D) **deficiency** 268.9
  - with
    - osteomalacia 268.2
    - rickets (*see also* Rickets) 268.0
- **Calcification**
  - adrenal (capsule) (gland) 255.41
    - tuberculous (*see also* Tuberculosis) 017.6 ☑
  - aorta 440.0
  - artery (annular) — *see* Arteriosclerosis
  - auricle (ear) 380.89
  - bladder 596.8
    - due to S. hematobium 120.0

Note — Except where otherwise indicated, the morphological varieties of carcinoma in the list below should be coded by site as for "Neoplasm, malignant."

Carcinoma — *see also* Neoplasm, by site, malignant — *continued*
  lobular — *continued*
    non-infiltrating — *continued*
      unspecified site 233.0
    specified site — *see* Neoplasm, by site, malignant
    unspecified site 174.9
  lymphoepithelial (M8082/3)
  medullary (M8510/3)
    with
      amyloid stroma (M8511/3)
        specified site — *see* Neoplasm, by site, malignant
        unspecified site 193
      lymphoid stroma (M8512/3)
        specified site — *see* Neoplasm, by site, malignant
        unspecified site 174.9
  mesometanephric (M9110/3)
  mesonephric (M9110/3)
  metastatic (M8010/6) — *see* Metastasis, cancer
  metatypical (M8095/3) — *see* Neoplasm, skin, malignant
  morphea type basal cell (M8092/3) — *see* Neoplasm, skin, malignant
  mucinous (M8480/3)
  mucin-producing (M8481/3)
  mucin-secreting (M8481/3)
  mucoepidermoid (M8430/3)
  mucoid (M8480/3)
    cell (M8300/3)
      specified site — *see* Neoplasm, by site, malignant
      unspecified site 194.3
  mucous (M8480/3)
  neuroendocrine
    high grade (M8240/3) 209.30
    malignant poorly differentiated (M8240/3) 209.30
  nonencapsulated sclerosing (M8350/3) 193
  noninfiltrating
    intracystic (M8504/2) — *see* Neoplasm, by site, in situ
    intraductal (M8500/2)
      papillary (M8503/2)
        specified site — *see* Neoplasm, by site, in situ
        unspecified site 233.0
      specified site — *see* Neoplasm, by site, in situ
      unspecified site 233.0
    lobular (M8520/2)
      specified site — *see* Neoplasm, by site, in situ
      unspecified site 233.0
  oat cell (M8042/3)
    specified site — *see* Neoplasm, by site, malignant
    unspecified site 162.9
  odontogenic (M9270/3) 170.1
    upper jaw (bone) 170.0
  onocytic (M8290/3)
  oxyphilic (M8290/3)
  papillary (M8050/3)
    and follicular (mixed) (M8340/3) 193
    epidermoid (M8052/3)
    intraductal (noninfiltrating) (M8503/2)
      specified site — *see* Neoplasm, by site, in situ
      unspecified site 233.0
    serous (M8460/3)
      specified site — *see* Neoplasm, by site, malignant
      surface (M8461/3)
        specified site — *see* Neoplasm, by site, malignant
        unspecified site 183.0
      unspecified site 183.0

Carcinoma — *see also* Neoplasm, by site, malignant — *continued*
  papillary — *continued*
    squamous cell (M8052/3)
    transitional cell (M8130/3)
  papillocystic (M8450/3)
    specified site — *see* Neoplasm, by site, malignant
    unspecified site 183.0
  parafollicular cell (M8510/3)
    specified site — *see* Neoplasm, by site, malignant
    unspecified site 193
  pleomorphic (M8022/3)
  polygonal cell (M8034/3)
  prickle cell (M8070/3)
  pseudoglandular, squamous cell (M8075/3)
  pseudomucinous (M8470/3)
    specified site — *see* Neoplasm, by site, malignant
    unspecified site 183.0
  pseudosarcomatous (M8033/3)
  regaud type (M8082/3) — *see* Neoplasm, nasopharynx, malignant
  renal cell (M8312/3) 189.0
  reserve cell (M8041/3)
  round cell (M8041/3)
  Schmincke (M8082/3) — *see* Neoplasm, nasopharynx, malignant
  Schneiderian (M8121/3)
    specified site — *see* Neoplasm, by site, malignant
    unspecified site 160.0
  scirrhous (M8141/3)
  sebaceous (M8410/3) — *see* Neoplasm, skin, malignant
  secondary (M8010/6) — *see* Neoplasm, by site, malignant, secondary
  secretory, breast (M8502/3) — *see* Neoplasm, breast, malignant
  serous (M8441/3)
    papillary (M8460/3)
      specified site — *see* Neoplasm, by site, malignant
      unspecified site 183.0
    surface, papillary (M8461/3)
      specified site — *see* Neoplasm, by site, malignant
      unspecified site 183.0
  Sertoli cell (M8640/3)
    specified site — *see* Neoplasm, by site, malignant
    unspecified site 186.9
  signet ring cell (M8490/3)
    metastatic (M8490/6) — *see* Neoplasm, by site, secondary
  simplex (M8231/3)
  skin appendage (M8390/3) — *see* Neoplasm, skin, malignant
  small cell (M8041/3)
    fusiform cell type (M8043/3)
    squamous cell, non-keratinizing type (M8073/3)
  solid (M8230/3)
    with amyloid stroma (M8511/3)
      specified site — *see* Neoplasm, by site, malignant
      unspecified site 193
  spheroidal cell (M8035/3)
  spindle cell (M8032/3)
    and giant cell (M8030/3)
  spinous cell (M8070/3)
  squamous (cell) (M8070/3)
    adenoid type (M8075/3)
    and adenocarcinoma, mixed (M8560/3)
    intraepidermal, Bowen's type — *see* Neoplasm, skin, in situ

Carcinoma — *see also* Neoplasm, by site, malignant — *continued*
  squamous — *continued*
    keratinizing type (large cell) (M8071/3)
    large cell, non-keratinizing type (M8072/3)
    microinvasive (M8076/3)
      specified site — *see* Neoplasm, by site, malignant
      unspecified site 180.9
    non-keratinizing type (M8072/3)
    papillary (M8052/3)
    pseudoglandular (M8075/3)
    small cell, non-keratinizing type (M8073/3)
    spindle cell type (M8074/3)
    verrucous (M8051/3)
  superficial spreading (M8143/3)
  sweat gland (M8400/3) — *see* Neoplasm, skin, malignant
  theca cell (M8600/3) 183.0
  thymic (M8580/3) 164.0
  trabecular (M8190/3)
  transitional (cell) (M8120/3)
    papillary (M8130/3)
    spindle cell type (M8122/3)
  tubular (M8211/3)
  undifferentiated type (M8020/3)
  urothelial (M8120/3)
  ventriculi 151.9
  verrucous (epidermoid) (squamous cell) (M8051/3)
  villous (M8262/3)
  water-clear cell (M8322/3) 194.1
  wolffian duct (M9110/3)
Carcinosarcoma (M8980/3) — *see also* Neoplasm, by site, malignant
  embryonal type (M8981/3) — *see* Neoplasm, by site, malignant
Cardiac — *see also* condition
  death — *see* Disease, heart
  device
    defibrillator, automatic implantable V45.02
    in situ NEC V45.00
    pacemaker
      cardiac
        fitting or adjustment V53.31
        in situ V45.01
      carotid sinus
        fitting or adjustment V53.39
        in situ V45.09
  pacemaker — *see* Cardiac, device, pacemaker
  tamponade 423.3
Cardia, cardial — *see* condition
Cardialgia — *see also* Pain, precordial 786.51
Cardiectasis — *see* Hypertrophy, cardiac
Cardiochalasia 530.81
Cardiomalacia — *see also* Degeneration, myocardial 429.1
Cardiomegalia glycogenica diffusa 271.0
Cardiomegaly — *see also* Hypertrophy, cardiac 429.3
  congenital 746.89
  glycogen 271.0
  hypertensive (*see also* Hypertension, heart) 402.90
  idiopathic 429.3
Cardiomyoliposis — *see also* Degeneration, myocardial 429.1
Cardiomyopathy (congestive) (constrictive) (familial) (infiltrative) (obstructive) (restrictive) (sporadic) 425.4
  alcoholic 425.5
  amyloid 277.39 *[425.7]*
  beriberi 265.0 *[425.7]*
  cobalt-beer 425.5
  congenital 425.3
  due to
    amyloidosis 277.39 *[425.7]*
    beriberi 265.0 *[425.7]*
    cardiac glycogenosis 271.0 *[425.7]*

Cardiomyopathy — *continued*
  due to — *continued*
    Chagas' disease 086.0
    Friedreich's ataxia 334.0 *[425.8]*
    hypertension — *see* Hypertension, with, heart involvement
    mucopolysaccharidosis 277.5 *[425.7]*
    myotonia atrophica 359.21 *[425.8]*
    progressive muscular dystrophy 359.1 *[425.8]*
    sarcoidosis 135 *[425.8]*
  glycogen storage 271.0 *[425.7]*
  hypertensive — *see* Hypertension, with, heart involvement
  hypertrophic
    nonobstructive 425.4
    obstructive 425.1
      congenital 746.84
  idiopathic (concentric) 425.4
  in
    Chagas' disease 086.0
    sarcoidosis 135 *[425.8]*
  ischemic 414.8
  metabolic NEC 277.9 *[425.7]*
    amyloid 277.39 *[425.7]*
    thyrotoxic (*see also* Thyrotoxicosis) 242.9 ☑ *[425.7]*
    thyrotoxicosis (*see also* Thyrotoxicosis) 242.9 ☑ *[425.7]*
  newborn 425.4
    congenital 425.3
  nutritional 269.9 *[425.7]*
    beriberi 265.0 *[425.7]*
  obscure of Africa 425.2
  peripartum 674.5 ☑
  postpartum 674.5 ☑
  primary 425.4
  secondary 425.9
  stress inuced 429.83
  takotsubo 429.83
  thyrotoxic (*see also* Thyrotoxicosis) 242.9 ☑ *[425.7]*
  toxic NEC 425.9
  tuberculous (*see also* Tuberculosis) 017.9 ☑ *[425.8]*
Cardionephritis — *see* Hypertension, cardiorenal
Cardionephropathy — *see* Hypertension, cardiorenal
Cardionephrosis — *see* Hypertension, cardiorenal
Cardioneurosis 306.2
Cardiopathia nigra 416.0
Cardiopathy — *see also* Disease, heart 429.9
  hypertensive (*see also* Hypertension, heart) 402.90
  idiopathic 425.4
  mucopolysaccharidosis 277.5 *[425.7]*
Cardiopericarditis — *see also* Pericarditis 423.9
Cardiophobia 300.29
Cardioptosis 746.87
Cardiorenal — *see* condition
Cardiorrhexis — *see also* Infarct, myocardium 410.9 ☑
Cardiosclerosis — *see* Arteriosclerosis, coronary
Cardiosis — *see* Disease, heart
Cardiospasm (esophagus) (reflex) (stomach) 530.0
  congenital 750.7
Cardiostenosis — *see* Disease, heart
Cardiosymphysis 423.1
Cardiothyrotoxicosis — *see* Hyperthyroidism
Cardiovascular — *see* condition
Carditis (acute) (bacterial) (chronic) (subacute) 429.89
  Coxsackie 074.20
  hypertensive (*see also* Hypertension, heart) 402.90
  meningococcal 036.40
  rheumatic — *see* Disease, heart, rheumatic

- **Carditis** — *continued*
  - rheumatoid 714.2
- **Care** (of)
  - child (routine) V20.1
  - convalescent following V66.9
    - chemotherapy V66.2
    - medical NEC V66.5
    - psychotherapy V66.3
    - radiotherapy V66.1
    - surgery V66.0
    - surgical NEC V66.0
    - treatment (for) V66.5
      - combined V66.6
      - fracture V66.4
      - mental disorder NEC V66.3
      - specified type NEC V66.5
  - end-of-life V66.7
  - family member (handicapped) (sick)
    - creating problem for family V61.49
    - provided away from home for holiday relief V60.5
    - unavailable, due to
      - absence (person rendering care) (sufferer) V60.4
      - inability (any reason) of person rendering care V60.4
  - holiday relief V60.5
  - hospice V66.7
  - lack of (at or after birth) (infant) (child) 995.52
    - adult 995.84
  - lactation of mother V24.1
  - palliative V66.7
  - postpartum
    - immediately after delivery V24.0
    - routine follow-up V24.2
  - prenatal V22.1
    - first pregnancy V22.0
    - high-risk pregnancy V23.9
      - specified problem NEC V23.89
  - terminal V66.7
  - unavailable, due to
    - absence of person rendering care V60.4
    - inability (any reason) of person rendering care V60.4
  - well baby V20.1
- **Caries** (bone) — *see also* Tuberculosis, bone 015.9 ☑ *[730.8]* ☑
  - arrested 521.04
  - cementum 521.03
  - cerebrospinal (tuberculous) 015.0 ☑ *[730.88]*
  - dental (acute) (chronic) (incipient) (infected) 521.00
    - with pulp exposure 521.03
    - extending to
      - dentine 521.02
      - pulp 521.03
    - other specified NEC 521.09
    - pit and fissure 521.06
    - primary
      - pit and fissure origin 521.06
      - root surface 521.08
      - smooth surface origin 521.07
    - root surface 521.08
    - smooth surface 521.07
  - dentin (acute) (chronic) 521.02
  - enamel (acute) (chronic) (incipient) 521.01
  - external meatus 380.89
  - hip (*see also* Tuberculosis) 015.1 ☑ *[730.85]*
  - initial 521.01
  - knee 015.2 ☑ *[730.86]*
  - labyrinth 386.8
  - limb NEC 015.7 ☑ *[730.88]*
  - mastoid (chronic) (process) 383.1
  - middle ear 385.89
  - nose 015.7 ☑ *[730.88]*
  - orbit 015.7 ☑ *[730.88]*
  - ossicle 385.24
  - petrous bone 383.20
  - sacrum (tuberculous) 015.0 ☑ *[730.88]*
- **Caries** — *see also* Tuberculosis, bone — *continued*
  - spine, spinal (column) (tuberculous) 015.0 ☑ *[730.88]*
  - syphilitic 095.5
    - congenital 090.0 *[730.8]* ☑
  - teeth (internal) 521.00
    - initial 521.01
  - vertebra (column) (tuberculous) 015.0 ☑ *[730.88]*
- **Carini's syndrome** (ichthyosis congenita) 757.1
- **Carious teeth** 521.00
- **Carneous mole** 631
- **Carnosinemia** 270.5
- **Carotid body or sinus syndrome** 337.01
- **Carotidynia** 337.01
- **Carotinemia** (dietary) 278.3
- **Carotinosis** (cutis) (skin) 278.3
- **Carpal tunnel syndrome** 354.0
- **Carpenter's syndrome** 759.89
- **Carpopedal spasm** — *see also* Tetany 781.7
- **Carpoptosis** 736.05
- **Carrier** (suspected) **of**
  - amebiasis V02.2
  - bacterial disease (meningococcal, staphylococcal) NEC V02.59
  - cholera V02.0
  - cystic fibrosis gene V83.81
  - defective gene V83.89
  - diphtheria V02.4
  - dysentery (bacillary) V02.3
    - amebic V02.2
  - Endamoeba histolytica V02.2
  - gastrointestinal pathogens NEC V02.3
  - genetic defect V83.89
  - gonorrhea V02.7
  - group B streptococcus V02.51
  - HAA (hepatitis Australian-antigen) V02.61
  - hemophilia A (asymptomatic) V83.01
    - symptomatic V83.02
  - hepatitis V02.60
    - Australian-antigen (HAA) V02.61
    - B V02.61
    - C V02.62
    - serum V02.61
    - specified type NEC V02.69
    - viral V02.60
  - infective organism NEC V02.9
  - malaria V02.9
  - paratyphoid V02.3
  - Salmonella V02.3
    - typhosa V02.1
  - serum hepatitis V02.61
  - Shigella V02.3
  - Staphylococcus NEC V02.59
    - methicillin
      - resistant Staphylococcus aureus V02.54
      - susceptible Staphylococcus aureus V02.53
  - Streptococcus NEC V02.52
    - group B V02.51
  - typhoid V02.1
  - venereal disease NEC V02.8
- **Carrión's disease** (Bartonellosis) 088.0
- **Car sickness** 994.6
- **Carter's**
  - relapsing fever (Asiatic) 087.0
- **Cartilage** — *see* condition
- **Caruncle** (inflamed)
  - abscess, lacrimal (*see also* Dacryocystitis) 375.30
  - conjunctiva 372.00
    - acute 372.00
  - eyelid 373.00
  - labium (majus) (minus) 616.89
  - lacrimal 375.30
  - urethra (benign) 599.3
  - vagina (wall) 616.89
- **Cascade stomach** 537.6
- **Caseation lymphatic gland** — *see also* Tuberculosis 017.2 ☑
- **Caseous**
  - bronchitis — *see* Tuberculosis, pulmonary
  - meningitis 013.0 ☑
  - pneumonia — *see* Tuberculosis, pulmonary
- **Cassidy (-Scholte) syndrome** (malignant carcinoid) 259.2
- **Castellani's bronchitis** 104.8
- **Castleman's tumor or lymphoma** (mediastinal lymph node hyperplasia) 785.6
- **Castration, traumatic** 878.2
  - complicated 878.3
- **Casts in urine** 791.7
- **Catalepsy** 300.11
  - catatonic (acute) (*see also* Schizophrenia) 295.2 ☑
  - hysterical 300.11
  - schizophrenic (*see also* Schizophrenia) 295.2 ☑
- **Cataphasia** 307.0
- **Cataplexy** (idiopathic) — *see* Narcolepsy
- **Cataract** (anterior cortical) (anterior polar) (black) (capsular) (central) (cortical) (hypermature) (immature) (incipient) (mature) 366.9
  - anterior
    - and posterior axial embryonal 743.33
    - pyramidal 743.31
    - subcapsular polar
      - infantile, juvenile, or presenile 366.01
      - senile 366.13
  - associated with
    - calcinosis 275.40 *[366.42]*
    - craniofacial dysostosis 756.0 *[366.44]*
    - galactosemia 271.1 *[366.44]*
    - hypoparathyroidism 252.1 *[366.42]*
    - myotonic disorders 359.21 *[366.43]*
    - neovascularization 366.33
  - blue dot 743.39
  - cerulean 743.39
  - complicated NEC 366.30
  - congenital 743.30
    - capsular or subcapsular 743.31
    - cortical 743.32
    - nuclear 743.33
    - specified type NEC 743.39
    - total or subtotal 743.34
    - zonular 743.32
  - coronary (congenital) 743.39
    - acquired 366.12
  - cupuliform 366.14
  - diabetic 250.5 ☑ *[366.41]*
    - due to secondary diabetes 249.5 ☑ *[366.41]*
  - drug-induced 366.45
  - due to
    - chalcosis 360.24 *[366.34]*
    - chronic choroiditis (*see also* Choroiditis) 363.20 *[366.32]*
    - degenerative myopia 360.21 *[366.34]*
    - glaucoma (*see also* Glaucoma) 365.9 *[366.31]*
    - infection, intraocular NEC 366.32
    - inflammatory ocular disorder NEC 366.32
    - iridocyclitis, chronic 364.10 *[366.33]*
    - pigmentary retinal dystrophy 362.74 *[366.34]*
    - radiation 366.46
  - electric 366.46
  - glassblowers' 366.46
  - heat ray 366.46
  - heterochromic 366.33
  - in eye disease NEC 366.30
  - infantile (*see also* Cataract, juvenile) 366.00
  - intumescent 366.12
  - irradiational 366.46
  - juvenile 366.00
- **Cataract** — *continued*
  - juvenile — *continued*
    - anterior subcapsular polar 366.01
    - combined forms 366.09
    - cortical 366.03
    - lamellar 366.03
    - nuclear 366.04
    - posterior subcapsular polar 366.02
    - specified NEC 366.09
    - zonular 366.03
  - lamellar 743.32
    - infantile, juvenile, or presenile 366.03
  - morgagnian 366.18
  - myotonic 359.21 *[366.43]*
  - myxedema 244.9 *[366.44]*
  - nuclear 366.16
  - posterior, polar (capsular) 743.31
    - infantile, juvenile, or presenile 366.02
    - senile 366.14
  - presenile (*see also* Cataract, juvenile) 366.00
  - punctate
    - acquired 366.12
    - congenital 743.39
  - secondary (membrane) 366.50
    - obscuring vision 366.53
    - specified type, not obscuring vision 366.52
  - senile 366.10
    - anterior subcapsular polar 366.13
    - combined forms 366.19
    - cortical 366.15
    - hypermature 366.18
    - immature 366.12
    - incipient 366.12
    - mature 366.17
    - nuclear 366.16
    - posterior subcapsular polar 366.14
    - specified NEC 366.19
    - total or subtotal 366.17
  - snowflake 250.5 ☑ *[366.41]*
    - due to secondary diabetes 249.5 ☑ *[366.41]*
  - specified NEC 366.8
  - subtotal (senile) 366.17
    - congenital 743.34
  - sunflower 360.24 *[366.34]*
  - tetanic NEC 252.1 *[366.42]*
  - total (mature) (senile) 366.17
    - congenital 743.34
    - localized 366.21
    - traumatic 366.22
  - toxic 366.45
  - traumatic 366.20
    - partially resolved 366.23
    - total 366.22
  - zonular (perinuclear) 743.32
    - infantile, juvenile, or presenile 366.03
- **Cataracta** 366.10
  - brunescens 366.16
  - cerulea 743.39
  - complicata 366.30
  - congenita 743.30
  - coralliformis 743.39
  - coronaria (congenital) 743.39
    - acquired 366.12
  - diabetic 250.5 ☑ *[366.41]*
    - due to secondary diabetes 249.5 ☑ *[366.41]*
  - floriformis 360.24 *[366.34]*
  - membranacea
    - accreta 366.50
    - congenita 743.39
  - nigra 366.16
- **Catarrh, catarrhal** (inflammation) — *see also* condition 460
  - acute 460
  - asthma, asthmatic (*see also* Asthma) 493.9 ☑
  - Bostock's (*see also* Fever, hay) 477.9
  - bowel — *see* Enteritis
  - bronchial 490
    - acute 466.0

Index
Cervical — Cheyne-Stokes respiration

Note — for malignant change occurring in a neoplasm, use the appropriate M code with behavior digit /3 e.g., malignant change in uterine fibroid — M8890/3. For malignant change occurring in a nonneoplastic condition (e.g., gastric ulcer) use the M code M8000/3.

- **Chiari's**
  - disease or syndrome (hepatic vein thrombosis) 453.0
  - malformation
    - type I 348.4
    - type II (*see also* Spina bifida) 741.0 ☑
    - type III 742.0
    - type IV 742.2
  - network 746.89
- **Chiari-Frommel syndrome** 676.6 ☑
- **Chicago disease** (North American blastomycosis) 116.0
- **Chickenpox** — *see also* Varicella 052.9
  - exposure to V01.71
  - vaccination and inoculation (prophylactic) V05.4
- **Chiclero ulcer** 085.4
- **Chiggers** 133.8
- **Chignon** 111.2
  - fetus or newborn (from vacuum extraction) 767.19
- **Chigoe disease** 134.1
- **Chikungunya fever** 066.3
- **Chilaiditi's syndrome** (subphrenic displacement, colon) 751.4
- **Chilblains** 991.5
  - lupus 991.5
- **Child**
  - behavior causing concern V61.20
- **Childbed fever** 670.0 ☑
- **Childbirth** — *see also* Delivery
  - puerperal complications — *see* Puerperal
- **Childhood, period of rapid growth** V21.0
- **Chill(s)** 780.64
  - with fever 780.60
  - without fever 780.64
  - congestive 780.99
    - in malarial regions 084.6
  - septic — *see* Septicemia
  - urethral 599.84
- **Chilomastigiasis** 007.8
- **Chin** — *see* condition
- **Chinese dysentery** 004.9
- **Chiropractic dislocation** — *see also* Lesion, nonallopathic, by site 739.9
- **Chitral fever** 066.0
- **Chlamydia, chlamydial** — *see* condition
- **Chloasma** 709.09
  - cachecticorum 709.09
  - eyelid 374.52
    - congenital 757.33
    - hyperthyroid 242.0 ☑
  - gravidarum 646.8 ☑
  - idiopathic 709.09
  - skin 709.09
  - symptomatic 709.09
- **Chloroma** (M9930/3) 205.3 ☑
- **Chlorosis** 280.9
  - Egyptian (*see also* Ancylostomiasis) 126.9
  - miners' (*see also* Ancylostomiasis) 126.9
- **Chlorotic anemia** 280.9
- **Chocolate cyst** (ovary) 617.1
- **Choked**
  - disk or disc — *see* Papilledema
  - on food, phlegm, or vomitus NEC (*see also* Asphyxia, food) 933.1
  - phlegm 933.1
  - while vomiting NEC (*see also* Asphyxia, food) 933.1
- **Chokes** (resulting from bends) 993.3
- **Choking sensation** 784.99
- **Cholangiectasis** — *see also* Disease, gallbladder 575.8
- **Cholangiocarcinoma** (M8160/3)
  - and hepatocellular carcinoma, combined (M8180/3) 155.0
  - liver 155.1
  - specified site NEC — *see* Neoplasm, by site, malignant
  - unspecified site 155.1
- **Cholangiohepatitis** 575.8
- **Cholangiohepatitis** — *continued*
  - due to fluke infestation 121.1
- **Cholangiohepatoma** (M8180/3) 155.0
- **Cholangiolitis** (acute) (chronic) (extrahepatic) (gangrenous) 576.1
  - intrahepatic 575.8
  - paratyphoidal (*see also* Fever, paratyphoid) 002.9
  - typhoidal 002.0
- **Cholangioma** (M8160/0) 211.5
  - malignant — *see* Cholangiocarcinoma
- **Cholangitis** (acute) (ascending) (catarrhal) (chronic) (infective) (malignant) (primary) (recurrent) (sclerosing) (secondary) (stenosing) (suppurative) 576.1
  - chronic nonsuppurative destructive 571.6
  - nonsuppurative destructive (chronic) 571.6
- **Cholecystdocholithiasis** — *see* Choledocholithiasis
- **Cholecystitis** 575.10
  - with
    - calculus, stones in
      - bile duct (common) (hepatic) — *see* Choledocholithiasis
      - gallbladder — *see* Cholelithiasis
  - acute 575.0
  - acute and chronic 575.12
  - chronic 575.11
  - emphysematous (acute) (*see also* Cholecystitis, acute) 575.0
  - gangrenous (*see also* Cholecystitis, acute) 575.0
  - paratyphoidal, current (*see also* Fever, paratyphoid) 002.9
  - suppurative (*see also* Cholecystitis, acute) 575.0
  - typhoidal 002.0
- **Choledochitis** (suppurative) 576.1
- **Choledocholith** — *see* Choledocholithiasis
- **Choledocholithiasis** 574.5 ☑

> *Note — Use the following fifth-digit subclassification with category 574:*
>
> 0 *without mention of obstruction*
>
> 1 *with obstruction*

  - with
    - cholecystitis 574.4 ☑
      - acute 574.3 ☑
      - chronic 574.4 ☑
    - cholelithiasis 574.9 ☑
      - with
        - cholecystitis 574.7 ☑
          - acute 574.6 ☑
            - and chronic 574.8 ☑
          - chronic 574.7 ☑
- **Cholelithiasis** (impacted) (multiple) 574.2 ☑

> *Note — Use the following fifth-digit subclassification with category 574:*
>
> 0 *without mention of obstruction*
>
> 1 *with obstruction*

  - with
    - cholecystitis 574.1 ☑
      - acute 574.0 ☑
      - chronic 574.1 ☑
    - choledocholithiasis 574.9 ☑
      - with
        - cholecystitis 574.7 ☑
          - acute 574.6 ☑
            - and chronic 574.8 ☑
          - chronic cholecystitis 574.7 ☑
- **Cholemia** — *see also* Jaundice 782.4
  - familial 277.4
  - Gilbert's (familial nonhemolytic) 277.4
- **Cholemic gallstone** — *see* Cholelithiasis
- **Choleperitoneum, choleperitonitis** — *see also* Disease, gallbladder 567.81
- **Cholera** (algid) (Asiatic) (asphyctic) (epidemic) (gravis) (Indian) (malignant) (morbus) (pestilential) (spasmodic) 001.9
  - antimonial 985.4
  - carrier (suspected) of V02.0
  - classical 001.0
  - contact V01.0
  - due to
    - Vibrio
      - cholerae (Inaba, Ogawa, Hikojima serotypes) 001.0
        - El Tor 001.1
  - El Tor 001.1
  - exposure to V01.0
  - vaccination, prophylactic (against) V03.0
- **Cholerine** — *see also* Cholera 001.9
- **Cholestasis** 576.8
  - due to total parenteral nutrition (TPN) 573.8
- **Cholesteatoma** (ear) 385.30
  - attic (primary) 385.31
  - diffuse 385.35
  - external ear (canal) 380.21
  - marginal (middle ear) 385.32
    - with involvement of mastoid cavity 385.33
    - secondary (with middle ear involvement) 385.33
  - mastoid cavity 385.30
  - middle ear (secondary) 385.32
    - with involvement of mastoid cavity 385.33
  - postmastoidectomy cavity (recurrent) 383.32
  - primary 385.31
  - recurrent, postmastoidectomy cavity 383.32
  - secondary (middle ear) 385.32
    - with involvement of mastoid cavity 385.33
- **Cholesteatosis** (middle ear) — *see also* Cholesteatoma 385.30
  - diffuse 385.35
- **Cholesteremia** 272.0
- **Cholesterin**
  - granuloma, middle ear 385.82
  - in vitreous 379.22
- **Cholesterol**
  - deposit
    - retina 362.82
    - vitreous 379.22
  - elevated (high) 272.0
    - with elevated (high) triglycerides 272.2
  - imbibition of gallbladder (*see also* Disease, gallbladder) 575.6
- **Cholesterolemia** 272.0
  - essential 272.0
  - familial 272.0
  - hereditary 272.0
- **Cholesterosis, cholesterolosis** (gallbladder) 575.6
  - with
    - cholecystitis — *see* Cholecystitis
    - cholelithiasis — *see* Cholelithiasis
  - middle ear (*see also* Cholesteatoma) 385.30
- **Cholocolic fistula** — *see also* Fistula, gallbladder 575.5
- **Choluria** 791.4
- **Chondritis** (purulent) 733.99
  - auricle 380.03
  - costal 733.6
    - Tietze's 733.6
  - patella, posttraumatic 717.7
  - pinna 380.03
  - posttraumatica patellae 717.7
  - tuberculous (active) (*see also* Tuberculosis) 015.9 ☑
    - intervertebral 015.0 ☑ *[730.88]*
- **Chondroangiopathia calcarea seu punctate** 756.59
- **Chondroblastoma** (M9230/0) — *see also* Neoplasm, bone, benign
- **Chondroblastoma** — *see also* Neoplasm, bone, benign — *continued*
  - malignant (M9230/3) — *see* Neoplasm, bone, malignant
- **Chondrocalcinosis** (articular) (crystal deposition) (dihydrate) — *see also* Arthritis, due to, crystals 275.49 *[712.3]* ☑
  - due to
    - calcium pyrophosphate 275.49 *[712.2]* ☑
    - dicalcium phosphate crystals 275.49 *[712.1]* ☑
    - pyrophosphate crystals 275.49 *[712.2]* ☑
- **Chondrodermatitis nodularis helicis** 380.00
- **Chondrodysplasia** 756.4
  - angiomatose 756.4
  - calcificans congenita 756.59
  - epiphysialis punctata 756.59
  - hereditary deforming 756.4
  - rhizomelic punctata 277.86
- **Chondrodystrophia** (fetalis) 756.4
  - calcarea 756.4
  - calcificans congenita 756.59
  - fetalis hypoplastica 756.59
  - hypoplastica calcinosa 756.59
  - punctata 756.59
  - tarda 277.5
- **Chondrodystrophy** (familial) (hypoplastic) 756.4
  - myotonic (congenital) 359.23
- **Chondroectodermal dysplasia** 756.55
- **Chondrolysis** 733.99
- **Chondroma** (M9220/0) — *see also* Neoplasm cartilage, benign
  - juxtacortical (M9221/0) — *see* Neoplasm, bone, benign
  - periosteal (M9221/0) — *see* Neoplasm, bone, benign
- **Chondromalacia** 733.92
  - epiglottis (congenital) 748.3
  - generalized 733.92
  - knee 717.7
  - larynx (congenital) 748.3
  - localized, except patella 733.92
  - patella, patellae 717.7
  - systemic 733.92
  - tibial plateau 733.92
  - trachea (congenital) 748.3
- **Chondromatosis** (M9220/1) — *see* Neoplasm, cartilage, uncertain behavior
- **Chondromyxosarcoma** (M9220/3) — *see* Neoplasm, cartilage, malignant
- **Chondro-osteodysplasia** (Morquio-Brailsford type) 277.5
- **Chondro-osteodystrophy** 277.5
- **Chondro-osteoma** (M9210/0) — *see* Neoplasm, bone, benign
- **Chondropathia tuberosa** 733.6
- **Chondrosarcoma** (M9220/3) — *see also* Neoplasm, cartilage, malignant
  - juxtacortical (M9221/3) — *see* Neoplasm, bone, malignant
  - mesenchymal (M9240/3) — *see* Neoplasm, connective tissue, malignant
- **Chordae tendineae rupture** (chronic) 429.5
- **Chordee** (nonvenereal) 607.89
  - congenital 752.63
  - gonococcal 098.2
- **Chorditis** (fibrinous) (nodosa) (tuberosa) 478.5
- **Chordoma** (M9370/3) — *see* Neoplasm, by site, malignant
- **Chorea** (gravis) (minor) (spasmodic) 333.5
  - with
    - heart involvement — *see* Chorea with rheumatic heart disease

Chorea — *continued*
- with — *continued*
  - rheumatic heart disease (chronic, inactive, or quiescent) (conditions classifiable to 393–398) (*see* rheumatic heart condition involved)
    - active or acute (conditions classifiable to 391) 392.0
- acute — *see* Chorea, Sydenham's
- apoplectic (*see also* Disease, cerebrovascular, acute) 436
- chronic 333.4
- electric 049.8
- gravidarum — *see* Eclampsia, pregnancy
- habit 307.22
- hereditary 333.4
- Huntington's 333.4
- posthemiplegic 344.89
- pregnancy — *see* Eclampsia, pregnancy
- progressive 333.4
  - chronic 333.4
  - hereditary 333.4
- rheumatic (chronic) 392.9
  - with heart disease or involvement — *see* Chorea, with rheumatic heart disease
- senile 333.5
- Sydenham's 392.9
  - with heart involvement — *see* Chorea, with rheumatic heart disease
  - nonrheumatic 333.5
- variabilis 307.23

Choreoathetosis (paroxysmal) 333.5

Chorioadenoma (destruens) (M9100/1) 236.1

Chorioamnionitis 658.4 ☑
- affecting fetus or newborn 762.7

Chorioangioma (M9120/0) 219.8

Choriocarcinoma (M9100/3)
- combined with
  - embryonal carcinoma (M9101/3) — *see* Neoplasm, by site, malignant
  - teratoma (M9101/3) — *see* Neoplasm, by site, malignant
- specified site — *see* Neoplasm, by site, malignant
- unspecified site
  - female 181
  - male 186.9

Chorioencephalitis, lymphocytic (acute) (serous) 049.0

Chorioepithelioma (M9100/3) — *see* Choriocarcinoma

Choriomeningitis (acute) (benign) (lymphocytic) (serous) 049.0

Chorionepithelioma (M9100/3) — *see* Choriocarcinoma

Chorionitis — *see also* Scleroderma 710.1

Chorioretinitis 363.20
- disseminated 363.10
  - generalized 363.13
  - in
    - neurosyphilis 094.83
    - secondary syphilis 091.51
  - peripheral 363.12
  - posterior pole 363.11
  - tuberculous (*see also* Tuberculosis) 017.3 ☑ *[363.13]*
- due to
  - histoplasmosis (*see also* Histoplasmosis) 115.92
  - toxoplasmosis (acquired) 130.2
    - congenital (active) 771.2
- focal 363.00
  - juxtapapillary 363.01
  - peripheral 363.04
  - posterior pole NEC 363.03
- juxtapapillaris, juxtapapillary 363.01
- progressive myopia (degeneration) 360.21

Chorioretinitis — *continued*
- syphilitic (secondary) 091.51
  - congenital (early) 090.0 *[363.13]*
    - late 090.5 *[363.13]*
  - late 095.8 *[363.13]*
- tuberculous (*see also* Tuberculosis) 017.3 ☑ *[363.13]*

Choristoma — *see* Neoplasm, by site, benign

Choroid — *see* condition

Choroideremia, choroidermia (initial stage) (late stage) (partial or total atrophy) 363.55

Choroiditis — *see also* Chorioretinitis 363.20
- leprous 030.9 *[363.13]*
- senile guttate 363.41
- sympathetic 360.11
- syphilitic (secondary) 091.51
  - congenital (early) 090.0 *[363.13]*
    - late 090.5 *[363.13]*
  - late 095.8 *[363.13]*
- Tay's 363.41
- tuberculous (*see also* Tuberculosis) 017.3 ☑ *[363.13]*

Choroidopathy NEC 363.9
- degenerative (*see also* Degeneration, choroid) 363.40
- hereditary (*see also* Dystrophy, choroid) 363.50
- specified type NEC 363.8

Choroidoretinitis — *see* Chorioretinitis

Choroidosis, central serous 362.41

Choroidretinopathy, serous 362.41

Christian's syndrome (chronic histiocytosis X) 277.89

Christian-Weber disease (nodular nonsuppurative panniculitis) 729.30

Christmas disease 286.1

Chromaffinoma (M8700/0) — *see also* Neoplasm, by site, benign
- malignant (M8700/3) — *see* Neoplasm, by site, malignant

Chromatopsia 368.59

Chromhidrosis, chromidrosis 705.89

Chromoblastomycosis 117.2

Chromomycosis 117.2

Chromophytosis 111.0

Chromotrichomycosis 111.8

Chronic — *see* condition

Churg-Strauss syndrome 446.4

Chyle cyst, mesentery 457.8

Chylocele (nonfilarial) 457.8
- filarial (*see also* Infestation, filarial) 125.9
- tunica vaginalis (nonfilarial) 608.84
  - filarial (*see also* Infestation, filarial) 125.9

Chylomicronemia (fasting) (with hyperprebetalipoproteinemia) 272.3

Chylopericardium (acute) 420.90

Chylothorax (nonfilarial) 457.8
- filarial (*see also* Infestation, filarial) 125.9

Chylous
- ascites 457.8
- cyst of peritoneum 457.8
- hydrocele 603.9
- hydrothorax (nonfilarial) 457.8
  - filarial (*see also* Infestation, filarial) 125.9

Chyluria 791.1
- bilharziasis 120.0
- due to
  - Brugia (malayi) 125.1
  - Wuchereria (bancrofti) 125.0
    - malayi 125.1
- filarial (*see also* Infestation, filarial) 125.9
- filariasis (*see also* Infestation, filarial) 125.9
- nonfilarial 791.1

Cicatricial (deformity) — *see* Cicatrix

Cicatrix (adherent) (contracted) (painful) (vicious) 709.2
- adenoid 474.8

Cicatrix — *continued*
- alveolar process 525.8
- anus 569.49
- auricle 380.89
- bile duct (*see also* Disease, biliary) 576.8
- bladder 596.8
- bone 733.99
- brain 348.8
- cervix (postoperative) (postpartal) 622.3
  - in pregnancy or childbirth 654.6 ☑
    - causing obstructed labor 660.2 ☑
- chorioretinal 363.30
  - disseminated 363.35
  - macular 363.32
  - peripheral 363.34
  - posterior pole NEC 363.33
- choroid — *see* Cicatrix, chorioretinal
- common duct (*see also* Disease, biliary) 576.8
- congenital 757.39
- conjunctiva 372.64
- cornea 371.00
  - tuberculous (*see also* Tuberculosis) 017.3 ☑ *[371.05]*
- duodenum (bulb) 537.3
- esophagus 530.3
- eyelid 374.46
  - with
    - ectropion — *see* Ectropion
    - entropion — *see* Entropion
- hypopharynx 478.29
- knee, semilunar cartilage 717.5
- lacrimal
  - canaliculi 375.53
  - duct
    - acquired 375.56
    - neonatal 375.55
  - punctum 375.52
  - sac 375.54
- larynx 478.79
- limbus (cystoid) 372.64
- lung 518.89
- macular 363.32
  - disseminated 363.35
  - peripheral 363.34
- middle ear 385.89
- mouth 528.9
- muscle 728.89
- nasolacrimal duct
  - acquired 375.56
  - neonatal 375.55
- nasopharynx 478.29
- palate (soft) 528.9
- penis 607.89
- prostate 602.8
- rectum 569.49
- retina 363.30
  - disseminated 363.35
  - macular 363.32
  - peripheral 363.34
  - posterior pole NEC 363.33
- semilunar cartilage — *see* Derangement, meniscus
- seminal vesicle 608.89
- skin 709.2
  - infected 686.8
  - postinfectional 709.2
  - tuberculous (*see also* Tuberculosis) 017.0 ☑
- specified site NEC 709.2
- throat 478.29
- tongue 529.8
- tonsil (and adenoid) 474.8
- trachea 478.9
- tuberculous NEC (*see also* Tuberculosis) 011.9 ☑
- ureter 593.89
- urethra 599.84
- uterus 621.8
- vagina 623.4
  - in pregnancy or childbirth 654.7 ☑
    - causing obstructed labor 660.2 ☑

Cicatrix — *continued*
- vocal cord 478.5
- wrist, constricting (annular) 709.2

CIDP (chronic inflammatory demyelinating polyneuropathy) 357.81

CIN I [cervical intraepithelial neoplasia I] 622.11

CIN II [cervical intraepithelial neoplasia II] 622.12

CIN III [cervical intraepithelial neoplasia III] 233.1

Cinchonism
- correct substance properly administered 386.9
- overdose or wrong substance given or taken 961.4

Circine herpes 110.5

Circle of Willis — *see* condition

Circular — *see also* condition
- hymen 752.49

Circulating anticoagulants 286.5
- following childbirth 666.3 ☑
- postpartum 666.3 ☑

Circulation
- collateral (venous), any site 459.89
- defective 459.9
  - congenital 747.9
  - lower extremity 459.89
- embryonic 747.9
- failure 799.89
  - fetus or newborn 779.89
  - peripheral 785.59
- fetal, persistent 747.83
- heart, incomplete 747.9

Circulatory system — *see* condition

Circulus senilis 371.41

Circumcision
- in absence of medical indication V50.2
- ritual V50.2
- routine V50.2
- status (post), female 629.20

Circumscribed — *see* condition

Circumvallata placenta — *see* Placenta, abnormal

Cirrhosis, cirrhotic 571.5
- with alcoholism 571.2
- alcoholic (liver) 571.2
- atrophic (of liver) — *see* Cirrhosis, portal
- Baumgarten-Cruveilhier 571.5
- biliary (cholangiolitic) (cholangitic) (cholestatic) (extrahepatic) (hypertrophic) (intrahepatic) (nonobstructive) (obstructive) (pericholangiolitic) (posthepatic) (primary) (secondary) (xanthomatous) 571.6
  - due to
    - clonorchiasis 121.1
    - flukes 121.3
- brain 331.9
- capsular — *see* Cirrhosis, portal
- cardiac 571.5
  - alcoholic 571.2
- central (liver) — *see* Cirrhosis, liver
- Charcôt's 571.6
- cholangiolitic — *see* Cirrhosis, biliary
- cholangitic — *see* Cirrhosis, biliary
- cholestatic — *see* Cirrhosis, biliary
- clitoris (hypertrophic) 624.2
- coarsely nodular 571.5
- congestive (liver) — *see* Cirrhosis, cardiac
- Cruveilhier-Baumgarten 571.5
- cryptogenic (of liver) 571.5
  - alcoholic 571.2
- dietary (*see also* Cirrhosis, portal) 571.5
- due to
  - bronzed diabetes 275.0
  - congestive hepatomegaly — *see* Cirrhosis, cardiac
  - cystic fibrosis 277.00
  - hemochromatosis 275.0
  - hepatolenticular degeneration 275.1

Coloenteritis — *see* Enteritis
Colon — *see* condition
Colonization
- MRSA (methicillin resistant Staphylococcus aureus) V02.54
- MSSA (methicillin susceptible Staphylococcus aureus) V02.53

Coloptosis 569.89
Color
- amblyopia NEC 368.59
  - acquired 368.55
- blindness NEC (congenital) 368.59
  - acquired 368.55

Colostomy
- attention to V55.3
- fitting or adjustment V55.3
- malfunctioning 569.62
- status V44.3

Colpitis — *see also* Vaginitis 616.10
Colpocele 618.6
Colpocystitis — *see also* Vaginitis 616.10
Colporrhexis 665.4 ☑
Colpospasm 625.1
Column, spinal, vertebral — *see* condition
Coma 780.01
- apoplectic (*see also* Disease, cerebrovascular, acute) 436
- diabetic (with ketoacidosis) 250.3 ☑
  - due to secondary diabetes 249.3 ☑
  - hyperosmolar 250.2 ☑
    - due to secondary diabetes 249.2 ☑
- eclamptic (*see also* Eclampsia) 780.39
- epileptic 345.3
- hepatic 572.2
- hyperglycemic 250.3 ☑
  - due to secondary diabetes 249.3 ☑
- hyperosmolar (diabetic) (nonketotic) 250.2 ☑
  - due to secondary diabetes 249.2 ☑
- hypoglycemic 251.0
  - diabetic 250.3 ☑
    - due to secondary diabetes 249.3 ☑
- insulin 250.3 ☑
  - due to secondary diabetes 249.3 ☑
  - hyperosmolar 250.2 ☑
    - due to secondary diabetes 249.2 ☑
  - non-diabetic 251.0
  - organic hyperinsulinism 251.0
- Kussmaul's (diabetic) 250.3 ☑
  - due to secondary diabetes 249.3 ☑
- liver 572.2
- newborn 779.2
- prediabetic 250.2 ☑
  - due to secondary diabetes 249.2 ☑
- uremic — *see* Uremia

Combat fatigue — *see also* Reaction, stress, acute 308.9
Combined — *see* condition
Comedo 706.1
Comedocarcinoma (M8501/3) — *see also* Neoplasm, breast, malignant
- noninfiltrating (M8501/2)
  - specified site — *see* Neoplasm, by site, in situ
  - unspecified site 233.0

Comedomastitis 610.4
Comedones 706.1
- lanugo 757.4

Comma bacillus, carrier (suspected) of V02.3
Comminuted fracture — *see* Fracture, by site
Common
- aortopulmonary trunk 745.0
- atrioventricular canal (defect) 745.69
- atrium 745.69
- cold (head) 460
  - vaccination, prophylactic (against) V04.7
- truncus (arteriosus) 745.0
- ventricle 745.3

Commotio (current)
- cerebri (*see also* Concussion, brain) 850.9
  - with skull fracture — *see* Fracture, skull, by site
- retinae 921.3
- spinalis — *see* Injury, spinal, by site

Commotion (current)
- brain (without skull fracture) (*see also* Concussion, brain) 850.9
  - with skull fracture — *see* Fracture, skull, by site
- spinal cord — *see* Injury, spinal, by site

Communication
- abnormal (*see also* Fistula)
  - between
    - base of aorta and pulmonary artery 745.0
    - left ventricle and right atrium 745.4
    - pericardial sac and pleural sac 748.8
    - pulmonary artery and pulmonary vein 747.3
  - congenital, between uterus and anterior abdominal wall 752.3
    - bladder 752.3
    - intestine 752.3
    - rectum 752.3
- left ventricular — right atrial 745.4
- pulmonary artery — pulmonary vein 747.3

Compartment syndrome — *see* Syndrome, compartment
Compensation
- broken — *see* Failure, heart
- failure — *see* Failure, heart
- neurosis, psychoneurosis 300.11

Complaint — *see also* Disease
- bowel, functional 564.9
  - psychogenic 306.4
- intestine, functional 564.9
  - psychogenic 306.4
- kidney (*see also* Disease, renal) 593.9
- liver 573.9
- miners' 500

Complete — *see* condition
Complex
- cardiorenal (*see also* Hypertension, cardiorenal) 404.90
- castration 300.9
- Costen's 524.60
- ego-dystonic homosexuality 302.0
- Eisenmenger's (ventricular septal defect) 745.4
- homosexual, ego-dystonic 302.0
- hypersexual 302.89
- inferiority 301.9
- jumped process
  - spine — *see* Dislocation, vertebra
- primary, tuberculosis (*see also* Tuberculosis) 010.0 ☑
- regional pain syndrome 355.9
  - type I 337.20
    - lower limb 337.22
    - specified site NEC 337.29
    - upper limb 337.21
  - type II
    - lower limb 355.71
    - upper limb 354.4
- Taussig-Bing (transposition, aorta and overriding pulmonary artery) 745.11

Complications
- abortion NEC — *see* categories 634-639 ☑
- accidental puncture or laceration during a procedure 998.2
- amniocentesis, fetal 679.1 ☑
- amputation stump (late) (surgical) 997.60
  - traumatic — *see* Amputation, traumatic

Complications — *continued*
- anastomosis (and bypass) (*see also* Complications, due to (presence of) any device, implant, or graft classified to 996.0–996.5 NEC)
  - hemorrhage NEC 998.11
  - intestinal (internal) NEC 997.4
    - involving urinary tract 997.5
  - mechanical — *see* Complications, mechanical, graft
  - urinary tract (involving intestinal tract) 997.5
- anesthesia, anesthetic NEC (*see also* Anesthesia, complication) 995.22
  - in labor and delivery 668.9 ☑
    - affecting fetus or newborn 763.5
    - cardiac 668.1 ☑
    - central nervous system 668.2 ☑
    - pulmonary 668.0 ☑
    - specified type NEC 668.8 ☑
- aortocoronary (bypass) graft 996.03
  - atherosclerosis — *see* Arteriosclerosis, coronary
  - embolism 996.72
  - occlusion NEC 996.72
  - thrombus 996.72
- arthroplasty (*see also* Complications, prosthetic joint) 996.49
- artificial opening
  - cecostomy 569.60
  - colostomy 569.60
  - cystostomy 997.5
  - enterostomy 569.60
  - esophagostomy 530.87
    - infection 530.86
    - mechanical 530.87
  - gastrostomy 536.40
  - ileostomy 569.60
  - jejunostomy 569.60
  - nephrostomy 997.5
  - tracheostomy 519.00
  - ureterostomy 997.5
  - urethrostomy 997.5
- bariatric surgery 997.4
- bile duct implant (prosthetic) NEC 996.79
  - infection or inflammation 996.69
  - mechanical 996.59
- bleeding (intraoperative) (postoperative) 998.11
- blood vessel graft 996.1
  - aortocoronary 996.03
    - atherosclerosis — *see* Arteriosclerosis, coronary
    - embolism 996.72
    - occlusion NEC 996.72
    - thrombus 996.72
  - atherosclerosis — *see* Arteriosclerosis, extremities
  - embolism 996.74
  - occlusion NEC 996.74
  - thrombus 996.74
- bone growth stimulator NEC 996.78
  - infection or inflammation 996.67
- bone marrow transplant 996.85
- breast implant (prosthetic) NEC 996.79
  - infection or inflammation 996.69
  - mechanical 996.54
- bypass (*see also* Complications, anastomosis)
  - aortocoronary 996.03
    - atherosclerosis — *see* Arteriosclerosis, coronary
    - embolism 996.72
    - occlusion NEC 996.72
    - thrombus 996.72
  - carotid artery 996.1
    - atherosclerosis — *see* Arteriosclerosis, extremities
    - embolism 996.74
    - occlusion NEC 996.74
    - thrombus 996.74
- cardiac (*see also* Disease, heart) 429.9

Complications — *continued*
- cardiac (*see also* Disease, heart) — *continued*
  - device, implant, or graft NEC 996.72
    - infection or inflammation 996.61
    - long-term effect 429.4
    - mechanical (*see also* Complications, mechanical, by type) 996.00
    - valve prosthesis 996.71
      - infection or inflammation 996.61
  - postoperative NEC 997.1
    - long-term effect 429.4
- cardiorenal (*see also* Hypertension, cardiorenal) 404.90
- carotid artery bypass graft 996.1
  - atherosclerosis — *see* Arteriosclerosis, extremities
  - embolism 996.74
  - occlusion NEC 996.74
  - thrombus 996.74
- cataract fragments in eye 998.82
- catheter device NEC (*see also* Complications, due to (presence of) any device, implant, or graft classified to 996.0–996.5 NEC)
  - mechanical — *see* Complications, mechanical, catheter
- cecostomy 569.60
- cesarean section wound 674.3 ☑
- chemotherapy (antineoplastic) 995.29
- chin implant (prosthetic) NEC 996.79
  - infection or inflammation 996.69
  - mechanical 996.59
- colostomy (enterostomy) 569.60
  - specified type NEC 569.69
- contraceptive device, intrauterine NEC 996.76
  - infection 996.65
  - inflammation 996.65
  - mechanical 996.32
- cord (umbilical) — *see* Complications, umbilical cord
- cornea
  - due to
    - contact lens 371.82
- coronary (artery) bypass (graft) NEC 996.03
  - atherosclerosis — *see* Arteriosclerosis, coronary
  - embolism 996.72
  - infection or inflammation 996.61
  - mechanical 996.03
  - occlusion NEC 996.72
  - specified type NEC 996.72
  - thrombus 996.72
- cystostomy 997.5
- delivery 669.9 ☑
  - procedure (instrumental) (manual) (surgical) 669.4 ☑
  - specified type NEC 669.8 ☑
- dialysis (hemodialysis) (peritoneal) (renal) NEC 999.9
  - catheter NEC (*see also* Complications, due to (presence of) any device, implant, or graft classified to 996.0–996.5 NEC)
    - infection or inflammation 996.62
      - peritoneal 996.68
    - mechanical 996.1
      - peritoneal 996.56
- drug NEC 995.29
- due to (presence of) any device, implant, or graft classified to 996.0–996.5 NEC 996.70
  - with infection or inflammation — *see* Complications, infection or inflammation, due to (presence of) any device, implant, or graft classified to 996.0–996.5 NEC

Complications — *continued*
- mechanical — *continued*
  - graft — *continued*
    - nervous system 996.2
    - organ (immune or nonimmune cause) 996.80
      - heart 996.83
      - intestines 996.87
      - kidney 996.81
      - liver 996.82
      - lung 996.84
      - pancreas 996.86
      - specified NEC 996.89
    - orthopedic, internal 996.49
    - peripheral nerve 996.2
    - prosthetic NEC 996.59
    - skin 996.52
      - artificial 996.55
    - specified NEC 996.59
    - tendon 996.49
    - tissue NEC 996.52
    - tooth 996.59
    - ureter, without mention of resection 996.39
    - vascular 996.1
  - heart valve prosthesis 996.02
    - long-term effect 429.4
  - implant NEC 996.59
    - cardiac 996.00
      - automatic implantable defibrillator 996.04
      - long-term effect 429.4
      - specified NEC 996.09
    - electrode NEC 996.59
      - brain 996.2
      - cardiac 996.01
      - spinal column 996.2
    - genitourinary 996.30
    - nervous system 996.2
    - orthopedic, internal 996.49
    - prosthetic NEC 996.59
      - in
        - bile duct 996.59
        - breast 996.54
        - chin 996.59
        - eye
          - ocular lens 996.53
          - orbital globe 996.59
    - vascular 996.1
  - insulin pump 996.57
  - nonabsorbable surgical material 996.59
  - pacemaker NEC 996.59
    - brain 996.2
    - cardiac 996.01
    - nerve (phrenic) 996.2
  - patch — *see* Complications, mechanical, graft
  - prosthesis NEC 996.59
    - bile duct 996.59
    - breast 996.54
    - chin 996.59
    - ocular lens 996.53
    - reconstruction, vas deferens 996.39
  - reimplant NEC 996.59
    - extremity (*see also* Complications, reattached, extremity) 996.90
    - organ (*see also* Complications, transplant, organ, by site) 996.80
  - repair — *see* Complications, mechanical, graft
  - respirator [ventilator] V46.14
  - shunt NEC 996.59
    - arteriovenous, surgically created 996.1
    - ventricular (communicating) 996.2
  - stent NEC 996.59
  - tracheostomy 519.02
  - vas deferens reconstruction 996.39
  - ventilator [respirator] V46.14
- medical care NEC 999.9
  - cardiac NEC 997.1

Complications — *continued*
- medical care — *continued*
  - gastrointestinal NEC 997.4
  - nervous system NEC 997.00
  - peripheral vascular NEC 997.2
  - respiratory NEC 997.39
  - urinary NEC 997.5
  - vascular
    - mesenteric artery 997.71
    - other vessels 997.79
    - peripheral vessels 997.2
    - renal artery 997.72
- nephrostomy 997.5
- nervous system
  - device, implant, or graft NEC 349.1
    - mechanical 996.2
  - postoperative NEC 997.00
- obstetric 669.9 ☑
  - procedure (instrumental) (manual) (surgical) 669.4 ☑
  - specified NEC 669.8 ☑
  - surgical wound 674.3 ☑
- ocular lens implant NEC 996.79
  - infection or inflammation 996.69
  - mechanical 996.53
- organ transplant — *see* Complications, transplant, organ, by site
- orthopedic device, implant, or graft
  - internal (fixation) (nail) (plate) (rod) NEC 996.78
    - infection or inflammation 996.67
    - joint prosthesis 996.77
      - infection or inflammation 996.66
    - mechanical 996.40
- pacemaker (cardiac) 996.72
  - infection or inflammation 996.61
  - mechanical 996.01
- pancreas transplant (immune or nonimmune cause) 996.86
- perfusion NEC 999.9
- perineal repair (obstetrical) 674.3 ☑
  - disruption 674.2 ☑
- pessary (uterus) (vagina) — *see* Complications, contraceptive device
- phototherapy 990
- postcystoscopic 997.5
- postmastoidectomy NEC 383.30
- postoperative — *see* Complications, surgical procedures
- pregnancy NEC 646.9 ☑
  - affecting fetus or newborn 761.9
- prosthetic device, internal (*see also* Complications, due to (presence of) any device, implant or graft classified to 996.0–996.5 NEC)
  - mechanical NEC (*see also* Complications, mechanical) 996.59
- puerperium NEC (*see also* Puerperal) 674.9 ☑
- puncture, spinal 349.0
- pyelogram 997.5
- radiation 990
- radiotherapy 990
- reattached
  - body part, except extremity 996.99
  - extremity (infection) (rejection) 996.90
    - arm(s) 996.94
    - digit(s) (hand) 996.93
      - foot 996.95
    - finger(s) 996.93
    - foot 996.95
    - forearm 996.91
    - hand 996.92
    - leg 996.96
    - lower NEC 996.96
    - toe(s) 996.95
    - upper NEC 996.94
- reimplant NEC (*see also* Complications, due to (presence of) any device, implant, or graft classified to 996.0–996.5 NEC)
  - bone marrow 996.85

Complications — *continued*
- reimplant (*see also* Complications, due to any device, implant, or graft classified to 996.0–996.5) — *continued*
  - extremity (*see also* Complications, reattached, extremity) 996.90
    - due to infection 996.90
  - mechanical — *see* Complications, mechanical, reimplant
  - organ (immune or nonimmune cause) (partial) (total) (*see also* Complications, transplant, organ, by site) 996.80
- renal allograft 996.81
- renal dialysis — *see* Complications, dialysis
- respirator [ventilator], mechanical V46.14
- respiratory 519.9
  - device, implant or graft NEC 996.79
    - infection or inflammation 996.69
    - mechanical 996.59
  - distress syndrome, adult, following trauma or surgery 518.5
  - insufficiency, acute, postoperative 518.5
  - postoperative NEC 997.39
  - therapy NEC 999.9
- sedation during labor and delivery 668.9 ☑
  - affecting fetus or newborn 763.5
  - cardiac 668.1 ☑
  - central nervous system 668.2 ☑
  - pulmonary 668.0 ☑
  - specified type NEC 668.8 ☑
- seroma (intraoperative) (postoperative) (noninfected) 998.13
  - infected 998.51
- shunt (*see also* Complications, due to (presence of) any device, implant, or graft classified to 996.0–996.5 NEC)
  - mechanical — *see* Complications, mechanical, shunt
- specified body system NEC
  - device, implant, or graft — *see* Complications, due to (presence of) any device, implant, or graft classified to 996.0–996.5 NEC
  - postoperative NEC 997.99
- spinal puncture or tap 349.0
- stomach banding 997.4
- stomach stapling 997.4
- stoma, external
  - gastrointestinal tract
    - colostomy 569.60
    - enterostomy 569.60
    - esophagostomy 530.87
      - infection 530.86
      - mechanical 530.87
    - gastrostomy 536.40
  - urinary tract 997.5
- surgical procedures 998.9
  - accidental puncture or laceration 998.2
  - amputation stump (late) 997.60
  - anastomosis — *see* Complications, anastomosis
  - burst stitches or sutures (external) (*see also* Dehiscence) 998.32
    - internal 998.31
  - cardiac 997.1
    - long-term effect following cardiac surgery 429.4
  - cataract fragments in eye 998.82
  - catheter device — *see* Complications, catheter device
  - cecostomy malfunction 569.62
  - colostomy malfunction 569.62
  - cystostomy malfunction 997.5
  - dehiscence (of incision) (external) (*see also* Dehiscence) 998.32

Complications — *continued*
- surgical procedures — *continued*
  - dehiscence (*see also* Dehiscence) — *continued*
    - internal 998.31
  - dialysis NEC (*see also* Complications, dialysis) 999.9
  - disruption (*see also* Dehiscence)
    - anastomosis (internal) — *see* Complications, mechanical, graft
    - internal suture (line) 998.31
    - wound (external) 998.32
      - internal 998.31
  - dumping syndrome (postgastrectomy) 564.2
  - elephantiasis or lymphedema 997.99
    - postmastectomy 457.0
  - emphysema (surgical) 998.81
  - enterostomy malfunction 569.62
  - esophagostomy malfunction 530.87
  - evisceration 998.32
  - fistula (persistent postoperative) 998.6
  - foreign body inadvertently left in wound (sponge) (suture) (swab) 998.4
  - from nonabsorbable surgical material (Dacron) (mesh) (permanent suture) (reinforcing) (Teflon) — *see* Complications, due to (presence of) any device, implant, or graft classified to 996.0–996.5 NEC
  - gastrointestinal NEC 997.4
  - gastrostomy malfunction 536.42
  - hematoma 998.12
  - hemorrhage 998.11
  - ileostomy malfunction 569.62
  - internal prosthetic device NEC (*see also* Complications, internal device) 996.70
    - hemolytic anemia 283.19
    - infection or inflammation 996.60
    - malfunction — *see* Complications, mechanical
    - mechanical complication — *see* Complications, mechanical
    - thrombus 996.70
  - jejunostomy malfunction 569.62
  - nervous system NEC 997.00
  - obstruction, internal anastomosis — *see* Complications, mechanical, graft
  - other body system NEC 997.99
  - peripheral vascular NEC 997.2
  - postcardiotomy syndrome 429.4
  - postcholecystectomy syndrome 576.0
  - postcommissurotomy syndrome 429.4
  - postgastrectomy dumping syndrome 564.2
  - postmastectomy lymphedema syndrome 457.0
  - postmastoidectomy 383.30
    - cholesteatoma, recurrent 383.32
    - cyst, mucosal 383.31
    - granulation 383.33
    - inflammation, chronic 383.33
  - postvagotomy syndrome 564.2
  - postvalvulotomy syndrome 429.4
  - reattached extremity (infection) (rejection) (*see also* Complications, reattached, extremity) 996.90
  - respiratory NEC 997.39
  - seroma 998.13
  - shock (endotoxic) (hypovolemic) (septic) 998.0

Complications — *continued*
- surgical procedures — *continued*
  - shunt, prosthetic (thrombus) (*see also* Complications, due to (presence of) any device, implant, or graft classified to 996.0–996.5 NEC)
    - hemolytic anemia 283.19
  - specified complication NEC 998.89
  - stitch abscess 998.59
  - transplant — *see* Complications, graft
  - ureterostomy malfunction 997.5
  - urethrostomy malfunction 997.5
  - urinary NEC 997.5
  - vascular
    - mesenteric artery 997.71
    - other vessels 997.79
    - peripheral vessels 997.2
    - renal artery 997.72
  - wound infection 998.59
- therapeutic misadventure NEC 999.9
  - surgical treatment 998.9
- tracheostomy 519.00
- transfusion (blood) (lymphocytes) (plasma) NEC 999.89
  - acute lung injury (TRALI) 518.7
  - atrophy, liver, yellow, subacute (within 8 months of administration) — *see* Hepatitis, viral
  - bone marrow 996.85
  - embolism
    - air 999.1
    - thrombus 999.2
  - hemolysis NEC 999.89
    - bone marrow 996.85
  - hepatitis (serum) (type B) (within 8 months after administration) — *see* Hepatitis, viral
  - incompatibility reaction (ABO) (blood group) 999.6
    - Rh (factor) 999.7
  - infection 999.39
  - jaundice (serum) (within 8 months after administration) — *see* Hepatitis, viral
  - sepsis 999.39
  - shock or reaction NEC 999.89
    - bone marrow 996.85
  - subacute yellow atrophy of liver (within 8 months after administration) — *see* Hepatitis, viral
  - thromboembolism 999.2
- transplant NEC (*see also* Complications, due to (presence of) any device, implant, or graft classified to 996.0–996.5 NEC)
  - bone marrow 996.85
  - organ (immune or nonimmune cause) (partial) (total) 996.80
    - bone marrow 996.85
    - heart 996.83
    - intestines 996.87
    - kidney 996.81
    - liver 996.82
    - lung 996.84
    - pancreas 996.86
    - specified NEC 996.89
- trauma NEC (early) 958.8
- ultrasound therapy NEC 999.9
- umbilical cord
  - affecting fetus or newborn 762.6
  - complicating delivery 663.9 ☑
    - affecting fetus or newborn 762.6
    - specified type NEC 663.8 ☑
- urethral catheter NEC 996.76
  - infection or inflammation 996.64
  - mechanical 996.31
- urinary, postoperative NEC 997.5
- vaccination 999.9
  - anaphylaxis NEC 999.4
  - cellulitis 999.39
  - encephalitis or encephalomyelitis 323.51

Complications — *continued*
- vaccination — *continued*
  - hepatitis (serum) (type B) (within 8 months after administration) — *see* Hepatitis, viral
  - infection (general) (local) NEC 999.39
  - jaundice (serum) (within 8 months after administration) — *see* Hepatitis, viral
  - meningitis 997.09 *[321.8]*
  - myelitis 323.52
  - protein sickness 999.5
  - reaction (allergic) 999.5
    - Herxheimer's 995.0
    - serum 999.5
  - sepsis 999.39
  - serum intoxication, sickness, rash, or other serum reaction NEC 999.5
  - shock (allergic) (anaphylactic) 999.4
  - subacute yellow atrophy of liver (within 8 months after administration) — *see* Hepatitis, viral
  - vaccinia (generalized) 999.0
    - localized 999.39
- vascular
  - device, implant, or graft NEC 996.74
    - infection or inflammation 996.62
    - mechanical NEC 996.1
      - cardiac (*see also* Complications, mechanical, by type) 996.00
  - following infusion, perfusion, or transfusion 999.2
  - postoperative NEC 997.2
    - mesenteric artery 997.71
    - other vessels 997.79
    - peripheral vessels 997.2
    - renal artery 997.72
- ventilation therapy NEC 999.9
- ventilator [respirator], mechanical V46.14

Compound presentation, complicating delivery 652.8 ☑
- causing obstructed labor 660.0 ☑

Compressed air disease 993.3

Compression
- with injury — *see* specific injury
- arm NEC 354.9
- artery 447.1
  - celiac, syndrome 447.4
- brachial plexus 353.0
- brain (stem) 348.4
  - due to
    - contusion, brain — *see* Contusion, brain
    - injury NEC (*see also* Hemorrhage, brain, traumatic)
      - birth — *see* Birth, injury, brain
    - laceration, brain — *see* Laceration, brain
  - osteopathic 739.0
- bronchus 519.19
- by cicatrix — *see* Cicatrix
- cardiac 423.9
- cauda equina 344.60
  - with neurogenic bladder 344.61
- celiac (artery) (axis) 447.4
- cerebral — *see* Compression, brain
- cervical plexus 353.2
- cord (umbilical) — *see* Compression, umbilical cord
- cranial nerve 352.9
  - second 377.49
  - third (partial) 378.51
    - total 378.52
  - fourth 378.53
  - fifth 350.8
  - sixth 378.54
  - seventh 351.8

Compression — *continued*
- divers' squeeze 993.3
- duodenum (external) (*see also* Obstruction, duodenum) 537.3
- during birth 767.9
- esophagus 530.3
  - congenital, external 750.3
- Eustachian tube 381.63
- facies (congenital) 754.0
- fracture — *see* Fracture, by site
- heart — *see* Disease, heart
- intestine (*see also* Obstruction, intestine) 560.9
  - with hernia — *see* Hernia, by site, with obstruction
- laryngeal nerve, recurrent 478.79
- leg NEC 355.8
- lower extremity NEC 355.8
- lumbosacral plexus 353.1
- lung 518.89
- lymphatic vessel 457.1
- medulla — *see* Compression, brain
- nerve NEC (*see also* Disorder, nerve)
  - arm NEC 354.9
  - autonomic nervous system (*see also* Neuropathy, peripheral, autonomic) 337.9
  - axillary 353.0
  - cranial NEC 352.9
  - due to displacement of intervertebral disc 722.2
    - with myelopathy 722.70
    - cervical 722.0
      - with myelopathy 722.71
    - lumbar, lumbosacral 722.10
      - with myelopathy 722.73
    - thoracic, thoracolumbar 722.11
      - with myelopathy 722.72
  - iliohypogastric 355.79
  - ilioinguinal 355.79
  - leg NEC 355.8
  - lower extremity NEC 355.8
  - median (in carpal tunnel) 354.0
  - obturator 355.79
  - optic 377.49
  - plantar 355.6
  - posterior tibial (in tarsal tunnel) 355.5
  - root (by scar tissue) NEC 724.9
    - cervical NEC 723.4
    - lumbar NEC 724.4
    - lumbosacral 724.4
    - thoracic 724.4
  - saphenous 355.79
  - sciatic (acute) 355.0
  - sympathetic 337.9
  - traumatic — *see* Injury, nerve
  - ulnar 354.2
  - upper extremity NEC 354.9
- peripheral — *see* Compression, nerve
- spinal (cord) (old or nontraumatic) 336.9
  - by displacement of intervertebral disc — *see* Displacement, intervertebral disc
  - nerve
    - root NEC 724.9
      - postoperative 722.80
        - cervical region 722.81
        - lumbar region 722.83
        - thoracic region 722.82
      - traumatic — *see* Injury, nerve, spinal
    - traumatic — *see* Injury, nerve, spinal
  - spondylogenic 721.91
    - cervical 721.1
    - lumbar, lumbosacral 721.42
    - thoracic 721.41
  - traumatic (*see also* Injury, spinal, by site)
    - with fracture, vertebra — *see* Fracture, vertebra, by site, with spinal cord injury

Compression — *continued*
- spondylogenic — *see* Compression, spinal cord, spondylogenic
- subcostal nerve (syndrome) 354.8
- sympathetic nerve NEC 337.9
- syndrome 958.5
- thorax 512.8
  - iatrogenic 512.1
  - postoperative 512.1
- trachea 519.19
  - congenital 748.3
- ulnar nerve (by scar tissue) 354.2
- umbilical cord
  - affecting fetus or newborn 762.5
    - cord prolapsed 762.4
  - complicating delivery 663.2 ☑
    - cord around neck 663.1 ☑
    - cord prolapsed 663.0 ☑
- upper extremity NEC 354.9
- ureter 593.3
- urethra — *see* Stricture, urethra
- vein 459.2
- vena cava (inferior) (superior) 459.2
- vertebral NEC — *see* Compression, spinal (cord)

Compulsion, compulsive
- eating 307.51
- neurosis (obsessive) 300.3
- personality 301.4
- states (mixed) 300.3
- swearing 300.3
  - in Gilles de la Tourette's syndrome 307.23
- tics and spasms 307.22
- water drinking NEC (syndrome) 307.9

Concato's disease (pericardial polyserositis) 423.2
- peritoneal 568.82
- pleural — *see* Pleurisy

Concavity, chest wall 738.3

Concealed
- hemorrhage NEC 459.0
- penis 752.65

Concentric fading 368.12

Concern (normal) **about sick person in family** V61.49

Concrescence (teeth) 520.2

Concretio cordis 423.1
- rheumatic 393

Concretion — *see also* Calculus
- appendicular 543.9
- canaliculus 375.57
- clitoris 624.8
- conjunctiva 372.54
- eyelid 374.56
- intestine (impaction) (obstruction) 560.39
- lacrimal (passages) 375.57
- prepuce (male) 605
  - female (clitoris) 624.8
- salivary gland (any) 527.5
- seminal vesicle 608.89
- stomach 537.89
- tonsil 474.8

Concussion (current) 850.9
- with
  - loss of consciousness 850.5
    - brief (less than one hour)
      - 30 minutes or less 850.11
      - 31-59 minutes 850.12
    - moderate (1-24 hours) 850.2
    - prolonged (more than 24 hours) (with complete recovery) (with return to pre-existing conscious level) 850.3
    - without return to pre-existing conscious level 850.4
  - mental confusion or disorientation (without loss of consciousness) 850.0
    - with loss of consciousness — *see* Concussion, with, loss of consciousness
- without loss of consciousness 850.0

Concussion — *continued*
- blast (air) (hydraulic) (immersion) (underwater) 869.0
  - with open wound into cavity 869.1
  - abdomen or thorax — *see* Injury, internal, by site
  - brain — *see* Concussion, brain
  - ear (acoustic nerve trauma) 951.5
    - with perforation, tympanic membrane — *see* Wound, open, ear drum
  - thorax — *see* Injury, internal, intrathoracic organs NEC
- brain or cerebral (without skull fracture) 850.9
  - with
    - loss of consciousness 850.5
      - brief (less than one hour)
        - 30 minutes or less 850.11
        - 31-59 minutes 850.12
      - moderate (1-24 hours) 850.2
      - prolonged (more than 24 hours) (with complete recovery) (with return to pre-existing conscious level) 850.3
        - without return to pre-existing conscious level 850.4
    - mental confusion or disorientation (without loss of consciousness) 850.0
      - with loss of consciousness — *see* Concussion, brain, with, loss of consciousness
    - skull fracture — *see* Fracture, skull, by site
  - without loss of consciousness 850.0
- cauda equina 952.4
- cerebral — *see* Concussion, brain
- conus medullaris (spine) 952.4
- hydraulic — *see* Concussion, blast
- internal organs — *see* Injury, internal, by site
- labyrinth — *see* Injury, intracranial
- ocular 921.3
- osseous labyrinth — *see* Injury, intracranial
- spinal (cord) (*see also* Injury, spinal, by site)
  - due to
    - broken
      - back — *see* Fracture, vertebra, by site, with spinal cord injury
      - neck — *see* Fracture, vertebra, cervical, with spinal cord injury
    - fracture, fracture dislocation, or compression fracture of spine or vertebra — *see* Fracture, vertebra, by site, with spinal cord injury
- syndrome 310.2
- underwater blast — *see* Concussion, blast

Condition — *see also* Disease
- fetal hematologic 678.0 ☑
- psychiatric 298.9
- respiratory NEC 519.9
  - acute or subacute NEC 519.9
    - due to
      - external agent 508.9
        - specified type NEC 508.8
      - fumes or vapors (chemical) (inhalation) 506.3
      - radiation 508.0
  - chronic NEC 519.9
    - due to
      - external agent 508.9
        - specified type NEC 508.8
      - fumes or vapors (chemical) (inhalation) 506.4

Condition — *see also* Disease — *continued*
- respiratory — *continued*
  - chronic — *continued*
    - due to — *continued*
      - radiation 508.1
  - due to
    - external agent 508.9
      - specified type NEC 508.8
    - fumes or vapors (chemical) (inhalation) 506.9

Conduct disturbance — *see also* Disturbance, conduct 312.9
- adjustment reaction 309.3
- hyperkinetic 314.2

Condyloma NEC 078.11
- acuminatum 078.11
- gonorrheal 098.0
- latum 091.3
- syphilitic 091.3
  - congenital 090.0
- venereal, syphilitic 091.3

Confinement — *see* Delivery

Conflagration — *see also* Burn, by site
- asphyxia (by inhalation of smoke, gases, fumes, or vapors) 987.9
  - specified agent — *see* Table of Drugs and Chemicals

Conflict
- family V61.9
  - specified circumstance NEC V61.8
- interpersonal NEC V62.81
- marital V61.10
  - involving
    - divorce V61.03
    - estrangement V61.09
- parent-child V61.20
- partner V61.10

Confluent — *see* condition

Confusional arousals 327.41

Confusion, confused (mental) (state) — *see also* State, confusional 298.9
- acute 293.0
- epileptic 293.0
- postoperative 293.9
- psychogenic 298.2
- reactive (from emotional stress, psychological trauma) 298.2
- subacute 293.1

Congelation 991.9

Congenital — *see also* condition
- aortic septum 747.29
- generalized fibromatosis (CGF) 759.89
- intrinsic factor deficiency 281.0
- malformation — *see* Anomaly

Congestion, congestive
- asphyxia, newborn 768.9
- bladder 596.8
- bowel 569.89
- brain (*see also* Disease, cerebrovascular NEC) 437.8
  - malarial 084.9
- breast 611.79
- bronchi 519.19
- bronchial tube 519.19
- catarrhal 472.0
- cerebral — *see* Congestion, brain
- cerebrospinal — *see* Congestion, brain
- chest 786.9
- chill 780.99
  - malarial (*see also* Malaria) 084.6
- circulatory NEC 459.9
- conjunctiva 372.71
- due to disturbance of circulation 459.9
- duodenum 537.3
- enteritis — *see* Enteritis
- eye 372.71
- fibrosis syndrome (pelvic) 625.5
- gastroenteritis — *see* Enteritis
- general 799.89
- glottis 476.0
- heart (*see also* Failure, heart) 428.0
- hepatic 573.0
- hypostatic (lung) 514
- intestine 569.89

Congestion, congestive — *continued*
- intracranial — *see* Congestion, brain
- kidney 593.89
- labyrinth 386.50
- larynx 476.0
- liver 573.0
- lung 786.9
  - active or acute (*see also* Pneumonia) 486
    - congenital 770.0
  - chronic 514
  - hypostatic 514
  - idiopathic, acute 518.5
  - passive 514
- malaria, malarial (brain) (fever) (*see also* Malaria) 084.6
- medulla — *see* Congestion, brain
- nasal 478.19
- nose 478.19
- orbit, orbital 376.33
  - inflammatory (chronic) 376.10
    - acute 376.00
- ovary 620.8
- pancreas 577.8
- pelvic, female 625.5
- pleural 511.0
- prostate (active) 602.1
- pulmonary — *see* Congestion, lung
- renal 593.89
- retina 362.89
- seminal vesicle 608.89
- spinal cord 336.1
- spleen 289.51
  - chronic 289.51
- stomach 537.89
- trachea 464.11
- urethra 599.84
- uterus 625.5
  - with subinvolution 621.1
- viscera 799.89

Congestive — *see* Congestion

Conical
- cervix 622.6
- cornea 371.60
- teeth 520.2

Conjoined twins 759.4
- causing disproportion (fetopelvic) 678.1 ☑
- fetal 678.1 ☑

Conjugal maladjustment V61.10
- involving
  - divorce V61.03
  - estrangement V61.09

Conjunctiva — *see* condition

Conjunctivitis (exposure) (infectious) (nondiphtheritic) (pneumococcal) (pustular) (staphylococcal) (streptococcal) NEC 372.30
- actinic 370.24
- acute 372.00
  - atopic 372.05
  - contagious 372.03
  - follicular 372.02
  - hemorrhagic (viral) 077.4
- adenoviral (acute) 077.3
- allergic (chronic) 372.14
  - with hay fever 372.05
- anaphylactic 372.05
- angular 372.03
- Apollo (viral) 077.4
- atopic 372.05
- blennorrhagic (neonatorum) 098.40
- catarrhal 372.03
- chemical 372.01
  - allergic 372.05
  - meaning corrosion — *see* Burn, conjunctiva
- chlamydial 077.98
  - due to
    - Chlamydia trachomatis — *see* Trachoma
    - paratrachoma 077.0
- chronic 372.10
  - allergic 372.14
  - follicular 372.12
  - simple 372.11

Conjunctivitis — *continued*
- chronic — *continued*
  - specified type NEC 372.14
  - vernal 372.13
- diphtheritic 032.81
- due to
  - dust 372.05
  - enterovirus type 70 077.4
  - erythema multiforme 695.10 *[372.33]*
  - filariasis (*see also* Filariasis) 125.9 *[372.15]*
  - mucocutaneous
    - disease NEC 372.33
    - leishmaniasis 085.5 *[372.15]*
  - Reiter's disease 099.3 *[372.33]*
  - syphilis 095.8 *[372.10]*
  - toxoplasmosis (acquired) 130.1
    - congenital (active) 771.2
  - trachoma — *see* Trachoma
- dust 372.05
- eczematous 370.31
- epidemic 077.1
  - hemorrhagic 077.4
- follicular (acute) 372.02
  - adenoviral (acute) 077.3
  - chronic 372.12
- glare 370.24
- gonococcal (neonatorum) 098.40
- granular (trachomatous) 076.1
  - late effect 139.1
- hemorrhagic (acute) (epidemic) 077.4
- herpetic (simplex) 054.43
  - zoster 053.21
- inclusion 077.0
- infantile 771.6
- influenzal 372.03
- Koch-Weeks 372.03
- light 372.05
- medicamentosa 372.05
- membranous 372.04
- meningococcic 036.89
- Morax-Axenfeld 372.02
- mucopurulent NEC 372.03
- neonatal 771.6
  - gonococcal 098.40
- Newcastle's 077.8
- nodosa 360.14
- of Beal 077.3
- parasitic 372.15
  - filariasis (*see also* Filariasis) 125.9 *[372.15]*
  - mucocutaneous leishmaniasis 085.5 *[372.15]*
- Parinaud's 372.02
- petrificans 372.39
- phlyctenular 370.31
- pseudomembranous 372.04
  - diphtheritic 032.81
- purulent 372.03
- Reiter's 099.3 *[372.33]*
- rosacea 695.3 *[372.31]*
- serous 372.01
  - viral 077.99
- simple chronic 372.11
- specified NEC 372.39
- sunlamp 372.04
- swimming pool 077.0
- trachomatous (follicular) 076.1
  - acute 076.0
  - late effect 139.1
- traumatic NEC 372.39
- tuberculous (*see also* Tuberculosis) 017.3 ☑ *[370.31]*
- tularemic 021.3
- tularensis 021.3
- vernal 372.13
  - limbar 372.13 *[370.32]*
- viral 077.99
  - acute hemorrhagic 077.4
  - specified NEC 077.8

Conjunctivochalasis 372.81

Conjunctoblepharitis — *see* Conjunctivitis

Connective tissue — *see* condition

Contraction, contracture, contracted — *continued*
- rectum, rectal — *continued*
  - psychogenic 306.4
- ring (Bandl's) 661.4 ☑
  - affecting fetus or newborn 763.7
- scar — *see* Cicatrix
- sigmoid (*see also* Obstruction, intestine) 560.9
- socket, eye 372.64
- spine (*see also* Curvature, spine) 737.9
- stomach 536.8
  - hourglass 536.8
    - congenital 750.7
  - psychogenic 306.4
- tendon (sheath) (*see also* Short, tendon) 727.81
- toe 735.8
- ureterovesical orifice (postinfectional) 593.3
- urethra 599.84
- uterus 621.8
  - abnormal 661.9 ☑
    - affecting fetus or newborn 763.7
  - clonic, hourglass or tetanic 661.4 ☑
    - affecting fetus or newborn 763.7
  - dyscoordinate 661.4 ☑
    - affecting fetus or newborn 763.7
  - hourglass 661.4 ☑
    - affecting fetus or newborn 763.7
  - hypotonic NEC 661.2 ☑
    - affecting fetus or newborn 763.7
  - incoordinate 661.4 ☑
    - affecting fetus or newborn 763.7
  - inefficient or poor 661.2 ☑
    - affecting fetus or newborn 763.7
  - irregular 661.2 ☑
    - affecting fetus or newborn 763.7
  - tetanic 661.4 ☑
    - affecting fetus or newborn 763.7
- vagina (outlet) 623.2
- vesical 596.8
  - neck or urethral orifice 596.0
- visual field, generalized 368.45
- Volkmann's (ischemic) 958.6

Contusion (skin surface intact) 924.9
- with
  - crush injury — *see* Crush
  - dislocation — *see* Dislocation, by site
  - fracture — *see* Fracture, by site
  - internal injury (*see also* Injury, internal, by site)
    - heart — *see* Contusion, cardiac
    - kidney — *see* Contusion, kidney
    - liver — *see* Contusion, liver
    - lung — *see* Contusion, lung
    - spleen — *see* Contusion, spleen
  - intracranial injury — *see* Injury, intracranial
  - nerve injury — *see* Injury, nerve
  - open wound — *see* Wound, open, by site
- abdomen, abdominal (muscle) (wall) 922.2
  - organ(s) NEC 868.00
- adnexa, eye NEC 921.9
- ankle 924.21
  - with other parts of foot 924.20
- arm 923.9
  - lower (with elbow) 923.10
  - upper 923.03
    - with shoulder or axillary region 923.09
- auditory canal (external) (meatus) (and other part(s) of neck, scalp, or face, except eye) 920
- auricle, ear (and other part(s) of neck, scalp, or face except eye) 920
- axilla 923.02
  - with shoulder or upper arm 923.09
- back 922.31
- bone NEC 924.9

Contusion — *continued*
- brain (cerebral) (membrane) (with hemorrhage) 851.8 ☑

> *Note — Use the following fifth-digit subclassification with categories 851–854:*
>
> 0 *unspecified state of consciousness*
>
> 1 *with no loss of consciousness*
>
> 2 *with brief [less than one hour] loss of consciousness*
>
> 3 *with moderate [1–24 hours] loss of consciousness*
>
> 4 *with prolonged [more than 24 hours] loss of consciousness and return to pre-existing conscious level*
>
> 5 *with prolonged [more than 24 hours] loss of consciousness, without return to pre-existing conscious level*
>
> *Use fifth-digit 5 to designate when a patient is unconscious and dies before regaining consciousness, regardless of the duration of the loss of consciousness*
>
> 6 *with loss of consciousness of unspecified duration*
>
> 9 *with concussion, unspecified*

  - with
    - open intracranial wound 851.9 ☑
    - skull fracture — *see* Fracture, skull, by site
  - cerebellum 851.4 ☑
    - with open intracranial wound 851.5 ☑
  - cortex 851.0 ☑
    - with open intracranial wound 851.1 ☑
  - occipital lobe 851.4 ☑
    - with open intracranial wound 851.5 ☑
  - stem 851.4 ☑
    - with open intracranial wound 851.5 ☑
- breast 922.0
- brow (and other part(s) of neck, scalp, or face, except eye) 920
- buttock 922.32
- canthus 921.1
- cardiac 861.01
  - with open wound into thorax 861.11
- cauda equina (spine) 952.4
- cerebellum — *see* Contusion, brain, cerebellum
- cerebral — *see* Contusion, brain
- cheek(s) (and other part(s) of neck, scalp, or face, except eye) 920
- chest (wall) 922.1
- chin (and other part(s) of neck, scalp, or face, except eye) 920
- clitoris 922.4
- conjunctiva 921.1
- conus medullaris (spine) 952.4
- cornea 921.3
- corpus cavernosum 922.4
- cortex (brain) (cerebral) — *see* Contusion, brain, cortex
- costal region 922.1
- ear (and other part(s) of neck, scalp, or face except eye) 920
- elbow 923.11
  - with forearm 923.10
- epididymis 922.4
- epigastric region 922.2
- eye NEC 921.9
- eyeball 921.3
- eyelid(s) (and periocular area) 921.1
- face (and neck, or scalp, any part, except eye) 920

Contusion — *continued*
- femoral triangle 922.2
- fetus or newborn 772.6
- finger(s) (nail) (subungual) 923.3
- flank 922.2
- foot (with ankle) (excluding toe(s)) 924.20
- forearm (and elbow) 923.10
- forehead (and other part(s) of neck, scalp, or face, except eye) 920
- genital organs, external 922.4
- globe (eye) 921.3
- groin 922.2
- gum(s) (and other part(s) of neck, scalp, or face, except eye) 920
- hand(s) (except fingers alone) 923.20
- head (any part, except eye) (and face) (and neck) 920
- heart — *see* Contusion, cardiac
- heel 924.20
- hip 924.01
  - with thigh 924.00
- iliac region 922.2
- inguinal region 922.2
- internal organs (abdomen, chest, or pelvis) NEC — *see* Injury, internal, by site
- interscapular region 922.33
- iris (eye) 921.3
- kidney 866.01
  - with open wound into cavity 866.11
- knee 924.11
  - with lower leg 924.10
- labium (majus) (minus) 922.4
- lacrimal apparatus, gland, or sac 921.1
- larynx (and other part(s) of neck, scalp, or face, except eye) 920
- late effect — *see* Late, effects (of), contusion
- leg 924.5
  - lower (with knee) 924.10
- lens 921.3
- lingual (and other part(s) of neck, scalp, or face, except eye) 920
- lip(s) (and other part(s) of neck, scalp, or face, except eye) 920
- liver 864.01
  - with
    - laceration — *see* Laceration, liver
    - open wound into cavity 864.11
- lower extremity 924.5
  - multiple sites 924.4
- lumbar region 922.31
- lung 861.21
  - with open wound into thorax 861.31
- malar region (and other part(s) of neck, scalp, or face, except eye) 920
- mandibular joint (and other part(s) of neck, scalp, or face, except eye) 920
- mastoid region (and other part(s) of neck, scalp, or face, except eye) 920
- membrane, brain — *see* Contusion, brain
- midthoracic region 922.1
- mouth (and other part(s) of neck, scalp, or face, except eye) 920
- multiple sites (not classifiable to same three-digit category) 924.8
  - lower limb 924.4
  - trunk 922.8
  - upper limb 923.8
- muscle NEC 924.9
- myocardium — *see* Contusion, cardiac
- nasal (septum) (and other part(s) of neck, scalp, or face, except eye) 920
- neck (and scalp or face, any part, except eye) 920
- nerve — *see* Injury, nerve, by site

Contusion — *continued*
- nose (and other part(s) of neck, scalp, or face, except eye) 920
- occipital region (scalp) (and neck or face, except eye) 920
  - lobe — *see* Contusion, brain, occipital lobe
- orbit (region) (tissues) 921.2
- palate (soft) (and other part(s) of neck, scalp, or face, except eye) 920
- parietal region (scalp) (and neck, or face, except eye) 920
  - lobe — *see* Contusion, brain
- penis 922.4
- pericardium — *see* Contusion, cardiac
- perineum 922.4
- periocular area 921.1
- pharynx (and other part(s) of neck, scalp, or face, except eye) 920
- popliteal space (*see also* Contusion, knee) 924.11
- prepuce 922.4
- pubic region 922.4
- pudenda 922.4
- pulmonary — *see* Contusion, lung
- quadriceps femoralis 924.00
- rib cage 922.1
- sacral region 922.32
- salivary ducts or glands (and other part(s) of neck, scalp, or face, except eye) 920
- scalp (and neck, or face any part, except eye) 920
- scapular region 923.01
  - with shoulder or upper arm 923.09
- sclera (eye) 921.3
- scrotum 922.4
- shoulder 923.00
  - with upper arm or axillar regions 923.09
- skin NEC 924.9
- skull 920
- spermatic cord 922.4
- spinal cord (*see also* Injury, spinal, by site)
  - cauda equina 952.4
  - conus medullaris 952.4
- spleen 865.01
  - with open wound into cavity 865.11
- sternal region 922.1
- stomach — *see* Injury, internal, stomach
- subconjunctival 921.1
- subcutaneous NEC 924.9
- submaxillary region (and other part(s) of neck, scalp, or face, except eye) 920
- submental region (and other part(s) of neck, scalp, or face, except eye) 920
- subperiosteal NEC 924.9
- supraclavicular fossa (and other part(s) of neck, scalp, or face, except eye) 920
- supraorbital (and other part(s) of neck, scalp, or face, except eye) 920
- temple (region) (and other part(s) of neck, scalp, or face, except eye) 920
- testis 922.4
- thigh (and hip) 924.00
- thorax 922.1
  - organ — *see* Injury, internal, intrathoracic
- throat (and other part(s) of neck, scalp, or face, except eye) 920
- thumb(s) (nail) (subungual) 923.3
- toe(s) (nail) (subungual) 924.3
- tongue (and other part(s) of neck, scalp, or face, except eye) 920
- trunk 922.9
  - multiple sites 922.8
  - specified site — *see* Contusion, by site
- tunica vaginalis 922.4

Cramp(s) — *continued*
  colic 789.0 ☑
    psychogenic 306.4
  due to immersion 994.1
  extremity (lower) (upper) NEC 729.82
  fireman 992.2
  heat 992.2
  hysterical 300.11
  immersion 994.1
  intestinal 789.0 ☑
    psychogenic 306.4
  linotypist's 300.89
    organic 333.84
  muscle (extremity) (general) 729.82
    due to immersion 994.1
    hysterical 300.11
  occupational (hand) 300.89
    organic 333.84
  psychogenic 307.89
  salt depletion 276.1
  sleep related leg 327.52
  stoker 992.2
  stomach 789.0 ☑
  telegraphers' 300.89
    organic 333.84
  typists' 300.89
    organic 333.84
  uterus 625.8
    menstrual 625.3
  writers' 333.84
    organic 333.84
    psychogenic 300.89
Cranial — *see* condition
Cranioclasis, fetal 763.89
Craniocleidodysostosis 755.59
Craniofenestria (skull) 756.0
Craniolacunia (skull) 756.0
Craniopagus 759.4
Craniopathy, metabolic 733.3
Craniopharyngeal — *see* condition
Craniopharyngioma (M9350/1) 237.0
Craniorachischisis (totalis) 740.1
Cranioschisis 756.0
Craniostenosis 756.0
Craniosynostosis 756.0
Craniotabes (cause unknown) 733.3
  rachitic 268.1
  syphilitic 090.5
Craniotomy, fetal 763.89
Cranium — *see* condition
Craw-craw 125.3
CRBSI (catheter-related bloodstream infection) 999.31
Creaking joint 719.60
  ankle 719.67
  elbow 719.62
  foot 719.67
  hand 719.64
  hip 719.65
  knee 719.66
  multiple sites 719.69
  pelvic region 719.65
  shoulder (region) 719.61
  specified site NEC 719.68
  wrist 719.63
Creeping
  eruption 126.9
  palsy 335.21
  paralysis 335.21
Crenated tongue 529.8
Creotoxism 005.9
Crepitus
  caput 756.0
  joint 719.60
    ankle 719.67
    elbow 719.62
    foot 719.67
    hand 719.64
    hip 719.65
    knee 719.66
    multiple sites 719.69
    pelvic region 719.65
    shoulder (region) 719.61
    specified site NEC 719.68
    wrist 719.63
Crescent or conus choroid, congenital 743.57
Cretin, cretinism (athyrotic) (congenital) (endemic) (metabolic) (nongoitrous) (sporadic) 243
  goitrous (sporadic) 246.1
  pelvis (dwarf type) (male type) 243
    with disproportion (fetopelvic) 653.1 ☑
      affecting fetus or newborn 763.1
      causing obstructed labor 660.1 ☑
        affecting fetus or newborn 763.1
  pituitary 253.3
Cretinoid degeneration 243
Creutzfeldt-Jakob disease (CJD) (syndrome) 046.19
  with dementia
    with behavioral disturbance 046.19 *[294.11]*
    without behavioral disturbance 046.19 *[294.10]*
  familial 046.19
  iatrogenic 046.19
  specified NEC 046.19
  sporadic 046.19
  variant (vCJD) 046.11
    with dementia
      with behavioral disturbance 046.11 *[294.11]*
      without behavioral disturbance 046.11 *[294.10]*
Crib death 798.0
Cribriform hymen 752.49
Cri-du-chat syndrome 758.31
Crigler-Najjar disease or syndrome (congenital hyperbilirubinemia) 277.4
Crimean hemorrhagic fever 065.0
Criminalism 301.7
Crisis
  abdomen 789.0 ☑
  addisonian (acute adrenocortical insufficiency) 255.41
  adrenal (cortical) 255.41
  asthmatic — *see* Asthma
  brain, cerebral (*see also* Disease, cerebrovascular, acute) 436
  celiac 579.0
  Dietl's 593.4
  emotional NEC 309.29
    acute reaction to stress 308.0
    adjustment reaction 309.9
    specific to childhood or adolescence 313.9
  gastric (tabetic) 094.0
  glaucomatocyclitic 364.22
  heart (*see also* Failure, heart) 428.9
  hypertensive — *see* Hypertension
  nitritoid
    correct substance properly administered 458.29
    overdose or wrong substance given or taken 961.1
  oculogyric 378.87
    psychogenic 306.7
  Pel's 094.0
  psychosexual identity 302.6
  rectum 094.0
  renal 593.81
  sickle cell 282.62
  stomach (tabetic) 094.0
  tabetic 094.0
  thyroid (*see also* Thyrotoxicosis) 242.9 ☑
  thyrotoxic (*see also* Thyrotoxicosis) 242.9 ☑
  vascular — *see* Disease, cerebrovascular, acute
Crocq's disease (acrocyanosis) 443.89
Crohn's disease — *see also* Enteritis, regional 555.9
Cronkhite-Canada syndrome 211.3
Crooked septum, nasal 470
Cross
  birth (of fetus) complicating delivery 652.3 ☑
    with successful version 652.1 ☑
    causing obstructed labor 660.0 ☑
  bite, anterior or posterior 524.27
  eye (*see also* Esotropia) 378.00
Crossed ectopia of kidney 753.3
Crossfoot 754.50
Croup, croupous (acute) (angina) (catarrhal) (infective) (inflammatory) (laryngeal) (membranous) (nondiphtheritic) (pseudomembranous) 464.4
  asthmatic (*see also* Asthma) 493.9 ☑
  bronchial 466.0
  diphtheritic (membranous) 032.3
  false 478.75
  spasmodic 478.75
    diphtheritic 032.3
  stridulous 478.75
    diphtheritic 032.3
Crouzon's disease (craniofacial dysostosis) 756.0
Crowding, teeth 524.31
CRST syndrome (cutaneous systemic sclerosis) 710.1
Cruchet's disease (encephalitis lethargica) 049.8
Cruelty in children — *see also* Disturbance, conduct 312.9
Crural ulcer — *see also* Ulcer, lower extremity 707.10
Crush, crushed, crushing (injury) 929.9
  abdomen 926.19
    internal — *see* Injury, internal, abdomen
  ankle 928.21
    with other parts of foot 928.20
  arm 927.9
    lower (and elbow) 927.10
    upper 927.03
      with shoulder or axillary region 927.09
  axilla 927.02
    with shoulder or upper arm 927.09
  back 926.11
  breast 926.19
  buttock 926.12
  cheek 925.1
  chest — *see* Injury, internal, chest
  ear 925.1
  elbow 927.11
    with forearm 927.10
  face 925.1
  finger(s) 927.3
    with hand(s) 927.20
      and wrist(s) 927.21
  flank 926.19
  foot, excluding toe(s) alone (with ankle) 928.20
  forearm (and elbow) 927.10
  genitalia, external (female) (male) 926.0
    internal — *see* Injury, internal, genital organ NEC
  hand, except finger(s) alone (and wrist) 927.20
  head — *see* Fracture, skull, by site
  heel 928.20
  hip 928.01
    with thigh 928.00
  internal organ (abdomen, chest, or pelvis) — *see* Injury, internal, by site
  knee 928.11
    with leg, lower 928.10
  labium (majus) (minus) 926.0
  larynx 925.2
  late effect — *see* Late, effects (of), crushing
  leg 928.9
    lower 928.10
      and knee 928.11
    upper 928.00
Crush, crushed, crushing — *continued*
  limb
    lower 928.9
      multiple sites 928.8
    upper 927.9
      multiple sites 927.8
  multiple sites NEC 929.0
  neck 925.2
  nerve — *see* Injury, nerve, by site
  nose 802.0
    open 802.1
  penis 926.0
  pharynx 925.2
  scalp 925.1
  scapular region 927.01
    with shoulder or upper arm 927.09
  scrotum 926.0
  shoulder 927.00
    with upper arm or axillary region 927.09
  skull or cranium — *see* Fracture, skull, by site
  spinal cord — *see* Injury, spinal, by site
  syndrome (complication of trauma) 958.5
  testis 926.0
  thigh (with hip) 928.00
  throat 925.2
  thumb(s) (and fingers) 927.3
  toe(s) 928.3
    with foot 928.20
      and ankle 928.21
  tonsil 925.2
  trunk 926.9
    chest — *see* Injury, internal, intrathoracic organs NEC
    internal organ — *see* Injury, internal, by site
    multiple sites 926.8
    specified site NEC 926.19
  vulva 926.0
  wrist 927.21
    with hand(s), except fingers alone 927.20
Crusta lactea 690.11
Crusts 782.8
Crutch paralysis 953.4
Cruveilhier-Baumgarten cirrhosis, disease, or syndrome 571.5
Cruveilhier's disease 335.21
Cruz-Chagas disease — *see also* Trypanosomiasis 086.2
Crying
  constant, continuous
    adolescent 780.95
    adult 780.95
    baby 780.92
    child 780.95
    infant 780.92
    newborn 780.92
  excessive
    adolescent 780.95
    adult 780.95
    baby 780.92
    child 780.95
    infant 780.92
    newborn 780.92
Cryofibrinogenemia 273.2
Cryoglobulinemia (mixed) 273.2
Crypt (anal) (rectal) 569.49
Cryptitis (anal) (rectal) 569.49
Cryptococcosis (European) (pulmonary) (systemic) 117.5
Cryptococcus 117.5
  epidermicus 117.5
  neoformans, infection by 117.5
Cryptopapillitis (anus) 569.49
Cryptophthalmos (eyelid) 743.06
Cryptorchid, cryptorchism, cryptorchidism 752.51
Cryptosporidiosis 007.4
Cryptotia 744.29

Crystallopathy
- calcium pyrophosphate (*see also* Arthritis) 275.49 *[712.2]* ☑
- dicalcium phosphate (*see also* Arthritis) 275.49 *[712.1]* ☑
- gouty 274.0
- pyrophosphate NEC (*see also* Arthritis) 275.49 *[712.2]* ☑
- uric acid 274.0

Crystalluria 791.9

Csillag's disease (lichen sclerosis et atrophicus) 701.0

Cuban itch 050.1

Cubitus
- valgus (acquired) 736.01
  - congenital 755.59
  - late effect of rickets 268.1
- varus (acquired) 736.02
  - congenital 755.59
  - late effect of rickets 268.1

Cultural deprivation V62.4

Cupping of optic disc 377.14

Curling esophagus 530.5

Curling's ulcer — *see* Ulcer, duodenum

Curschmann (-Batten) (-Steinert) disease or syndrome 359.21

Curvature
- organ or site, congenital NEC — *see* Distortion
- penis (lateral) 752.69
- Pott's (spinal) (*see also* Tuberculosis) 015.0 ☑ *[737.43]*
- radius, idiopathic, progressive (congenital) 755.54
- spine (acquired) (angular) (idiopathic) (incorrect) (postural) 737.9
  - congenital 754.2
  - due to or associated with
    - Charcôt-Marie-Tooth disease 356.1 *[737.40]*
    - mucopolysaccharidosis 277.5 *[737.40]*
    - neurofibromatosis 237.71 *[737.40]*
    - osteitis
      - deformans 731.0 *[737.40]*
      - fibrosa cystica 252.01 *[737.40]*
    - osteoporosis (*see also* Osteoporosis) 733.00 *[737.40]*
    - poliomyelitis (*see also* Poliomyelitis) 138 *[737.40]*
    - tuberculosis (Pott's curvature) (*see also* Tuberculosis) 015.0 ☑ *[737.43]*
  - kyphoscoliotic (*see also* Kyphoscoliosis) 737.30
  - kyphotic (*see also* Kyphosis) 737.10
  - late effect of rickets 268.1 *[737.40]*
  - Pott's 015.0 ☑ *[737.40]*
  - scoliotic (*see also* Scoliosis) 737.30
  - specified NEC 737.8
  - tuberculous 015.0 ☑ *[737.40]*

Cushing's
- basophilism, disease, or syndrome (iatrogenic) (idiopathic) (pituitary basophilism) (pituitary dependent) 255.0
- ulcer — *see* Ulcer, peptic

Cushingoid due to steroid therapy
- correct substance properly administered 255.0
- overdose or wrong substance given or taken 962.0

Cut (external) — *see* Wound, open, by site

Cutaneous — *see also* condition
- hemorrhage 782.7
- horn (cheek) (eyelid) (mouth) 702.8
- larva migrans 126.9

Cutis — *see also* condition
- hyperelastic 756.83
  - acquired 701.8
- laxa 756.83
  - senilis 701.8

Cutis — *see also* condition — *continued*
- marmorata 782.61
- osteosis 709.3
- pendula 756.83
  - acquired 701.8
- rhomboidalis nuchae 701.8
- verticis gyrata 757.39
  - acquired 701.8

Cyanopathy, newborn 770.83

Cyanosis 782.5
- autotoxic 289.7
- common atrioventricular canal 745.69
- congenital 770.83
- conjunctiva 372.71
- due to
  - endocardial cushion defect 745.60
  - nonclosure, foramen botalli 745.5
  - patent foramen botalli 745.5
  - persistent foramen ovale 745.5
- enterogenous 289.7
- fetus or newborn 770.83
- ostium primum defect 745.61
- paroxysmal digital 443.0
- retina, retinal 362.10

Cycle
- anovulatory 628.0
- menstrual, irregular 626.4

Cyclencephaly 759.89

Cyclical vomiting 536.2
- associated with migraine 346.2 ☑
- psychogenic 306.4

Cyclitic membrane 364.74

Cyclitis — *see also* Iridocyclitis 364.3
- acute 364.00
  - primary 364.01
  - recurrent 364.02
- chronic 364.10
  - in
    - sarcoidosis 135 *[364.11]*
    - tuberculosis (*see also* Tuberculosis) 017.3 ☑ *[364.11]*
- Fuchs' heterochromic 364.21
- granulomatous 364.10
- lens induced 364.23
- nongranulomatous 364.00
- posterior 363.21
- primary 364.01
- recurrent 364.02
- secondary (noninfectious) 364.04
  - infectious 364.03
- subacute 364.00
  - primary 364.01
  - recurrent 364.02

Cyclokeratitis — *see* Keratitis

Cyclophoria 378.44

Cyclopia, cyclops 759.89

Cycloplegia 367.51

Cyclospasm 367.53

Cyclosporiasis 007.5

Cyclothymia 301.13

Cyclothymic personality 301.13

Cyclotropia 378.33

Cyesis — *see* Pregnancy

Cylindroma (M8200/3) — *see also* Neoplasm, by site, malignant
- eccrine dermal (M8200/0) — *see* Neoplasm, skin, benign
- skin (M8200/0) — *see* Neoplasm, skin, benign

Cylindruria 791.7

Cyllosoma 759.89

Cynanche
- diphtheritic 032.3
- tonsillaris 475

Cynorexia 783.6

Cyphosis — *see* Kyphosis

Cyprus fever — *see also* Brucellosis 023.9

Cyriax's syndrome (slipping rib) 733.99

Cyst (mucus) (retention) (serous) (simple)

> *Note — In general, cysts are not neoplastic and are classified to the appropriate category for disease of the specified anatomical site. This generalization does not apply to certain types of cysts which are neoplastic in nature, for example, dermoid, nor does it apply to cysts of certain structures, for example, branchial cleft, which are classified as developmental anomalies.*
>
> *The following listing includes some of the most frequently reported sites of cysts as well as qualifiers which indicate the type of cyst. The latter qualifiers usually are not repeated under the anatomical sites. Since the code assignment for a given site may vary depending upon the type of cyst, the coder should refer to the listings under the specified type of cyst before consideration is given to the site.*

- accessory, fallopian tube 752.11
- adenoid (infected) 474.8
- adrenal gland 255.8
  - congenital 759.1
- air, lung 518.89
- allantoic 753.7
- alveolar process (jaw bone) 526.2
- amnion, amniotic 658.8 ☑
- anterior chamber (eye) 364.60
  - exudative 364.62
  - implantation (surgical) (traumatic) 364.61
  - parasitic 360.13
- anterior nasopalatine 526.1
- antrum 478.19
- anus 569.49
- apical (periodontal) (tooth) 522.8
- appendix 543.9
- arachnoid, brain 348.0
- arytenoid 478.79
- auricle 706.2
- Baker's (knee) 727.51
  - tuberculous (*see also* Tuberculosis) 015.2 ☑
- Bartholin's gland or duct 616.2
- bile duct (*see also* Disease, biliary) 576.8
- bladder (multiple) (trigone) 596.8
- Blessig's 362.62
- blood, endocardial (*see also* Endocarditis) 424.90
- blue dome 610.0
- bone (local) 733.20
  - aneurysmal 733.22
  - jaw 526.2
    - developmental (odontogenic) 526.0
    - fissural 526.1
    - latent 526.89
  - solitary 733.21
  - unicameral 733.21
- brain 348.0
  - congenital 742.4
  - hydatid (*see also* Echinococcus) 122.9
  - third ventricle (colloid) 742.4
- branchial (cleft) 744.42
- branchiogenic 744.42
- breast (benign) (blue dome) (pedunculated) (solitary) (traumatic) 610.0
  - involution 610.4
  - sebaceous 610.8
- broad ligament (benign) 620.8
  - embryonic 752.11
- bronchogenic (mediastinal) (sequestration) 518.89
  - congenital 748.4
- buccal 528.4
- bulbourethral gland (Cowper's) 599.89
- bursa, bursal 727.49
  - pharyngeal 478.26

Cyst — *continued*
- calcifying odontogenic (M9301/0) 213.1
  - upper jaw (bone) 213.0
- canal of Nuck (acquired) (serous) 629.1
  - congenital 752.41
- canthus 372.75
- carcinomatous (M8010/3) — *see* Neoplasm, by site, malignant
- cartilage (joint) — *see* Derangement, joint
- cauda equina 336.8
- cavum septi pellucidi NEC 348.0
- celomic (pericardium) 746.89
- cerebellopontine (angle) — *see* Cyst, brain
- cerebellum — *see* Cyst, brain
- cerebral — *see* Cyst, brain
- cervical lateral 744.42
- cervix 622.8
  - embryonal 752.41
  - nabothian (gland) 616.0
- chamber, anterior (eye) 364.60
  - exudative 364.62
  - implantation (surgical) (traumatic) 364.61
  - parasitic 360.13
- chiasmal, optic NEC (*see also* Lesion, chiasmal) 377.54
- chocolate (ovary) 617.1
- choledochal (congenital) 751.69
  - acquired 576.8
- choledochus 751.69
- chorion 658.8 ☑
- choroid plexus 348.0
- chyle, mesentery 457.8
- ciliary body 364.60
  - exudative 364.64
  - implantation 364.61
  - primary 364.63
- clitoris 624.8
- coccyx (*see also* Cyst, bone) 733.20
- colloid
  - third ventricle (brain) 742.4
  - thyroid gland — *see* Goiter
- colon 569.89
- common (bile) duct (*see also* Disease, biliary) 576.8
- congenital NEC 759.89
  - adrenal glands 759.1
  - epiglottis 748.3
  - esophagus 750.4
  - fallopian tube 752.11
  - kidney 753.10
    - multiple 753.19
    - single 753.11
  - larynx 748.3
  - liver 751.62
  - lung 748.4
  - mediastinum 748.8
  - ovary 752.0
  - oviduct 752.11
  - pancreas 751.7
  - periurethral (tissue) 753.8
  - prepuce NEC 752.69
    - penis 752.69
  - sublingual 750.26
  - submaxillary gland 750.26
  - thymus (gland) 759.2
  - tongue 750.19
  - ureterovesical orifice 753.4
  - vulva 752.41
- conjunctiva 372.75
- cornea 371.23
- corpora quadrigemina 348.0
- corpus
  - albicans (ovary) 620.2
  - luteum (ruptured) 620.1
- Cowper's gland (benign) (infected) 599.89
- cranial meninges 348.0
- craniobuccal pouch 253.8
- craniopharyngeal pouch 253.8
- cystic duct (*see also* Disease, gallbladder) 575.8

Cyst — *continued*
primordial (jaw) 526.0
prostate 600.3
pseudomucinous (ovary) (M8470/0) 220
pudenda (sweat glands) 624.8
pupillary, miotic 364.55
sebaceous 624.8
radicular (residual) 522.8
radiculodental 522.8
ranular 527.6
Rathke's pouch 253.8
rectum (epithelium) (mucous) 569.49
renal — *see* Cyst, kidney
residual (radicular) 522.8
retention (ovary) 620.2
retina 361.19
macular 362.54
parasitic 360.13
primary 361.13
secondary 361.14
retroperitoneal 568.89
sacrococcygeal (dermoid) 685.1
with abscess 685.0
salivary gland or duct 527.6
mucous extravasation or retention 527.6
Sampson's 617.1
sclera 379.19
scrotum (sebaceous) 706.2
sweat glands 706.2
sebaceous (duct) (gland) 706.2
breast 610.8
eyelid 374.84
genital organ NEC
female 629.89
male 608.89
scrotum 706.2
semilunar cartilage (knee) (multiple) 717.5
seminal vesicle 608.89
serous (ovary) 620.2
sinus (antral) (ethmoidal) (frontal) (maxillary) (nasal) (sphenoidal) 478.19
Skene's gland 599.89
skin (epidermal) (epidermoid, inclusion) (epithelial) (inclusion) (retention) (sebaceous) 706.2
breast 610.8
eyelid 374.84
genital organ NEC
female 629.89
male 608.89
neoplastic 216.3
scrotum 706.2
sweat gland or duct 705.89
solitary
bone 733.21
kidney 593.2
spermatic cord 608.89
sphenoid sinus 478.19
spinal meninges 349.2
spine (*see also* Cyst, bone) 733.20
spleen NEC 289.59
congenital 759.0
hydatid (*see also* Echinococcus) 122.9
spring water (pericardium) 746.89
subarachnoid 348.0
intrasellar 793.0
subdural (cerebral) 348.0
spinal cord 349.2
sublingual gland 527.6
mucous extravasation or retention 527.6
submaxillary gland 527.6
mucous extravasation or retention 527.6
suburethral 599.89
suprarenal gland 255.8
suprasellar — *see* Cyst, brain
sweat gland or duct 705.89
sympathetic nervous system 337.9
synovial 727.40
popliteal space 727.51

Cyst — *continued*
Tarlov's 355.9
tarsal 373.2
tendon (sheath) 727.42
testis 608.89
theca-lutein (ovary) 620.2
Thornwaldt's, Tornwaldt's 478.26
thymus (gland) 254.8
thyroglossal (duct) (infected) (persistent) 759.2
thyroid (gland) 246.2
adenomatous — *see* Goiter, nodular
colloid (*see also* Goiter) 240.9
thyrolingual duct (infected) (persistent) 759.2
tongue (mucous) 529.8
tonsil 474.8
tooth (dental root) 522.8
tubo-ovarian 620.8
inflammatory 614.1
tunica vaginalis 608.89
turbinate (nose) (*see also* Cyst, bone) 733.20
Tyson's gland (benign) (infected) 607.89
umbilicus 759.89
urachus 753.7
ureter 593.89
ureterovesical orifice 593.89
congenital 753.4
urethra 599.84
urethral gland (Cowper's) 599.89
uterine
ligament 620.8
embryonic 752.11
tube 620.8
uterus (body) (corpus) (recurrent) 621.8
embryonal 752.3
utricle (ear) 386.8
prostatic 599.89
utriculus masculinus 599.89
vagina, vaginal (squamous cell) (wall) 623.8
embryonal 752.41
implantation 623.8
inclusion 623.8
vallecula, vallecular 478.79
ventricle, neuroepithelial 348.0
verumontanum 599.89
vesical (orifice) 596.8
vitreous humor 379.29
vulva (sweat glands) 624.8
congenital 752.41
implantation 624.8
inclusion 624.8
sebaceous gland 624.8
vulvovaginal gland 624.8
wolffian 752.89
Cystadenocarcinoma (M8440/3) — *see also* Neoplasm, by site, malignant
bile duct type (M8161/3) 155.1
endometrioid (M8380/3) — *see* Neoplasm, by site, malignant
mucinous (M8470/3)
papillary (M8471/3)
specified site — *see* Neoplasm, by site, malignant
unspecified site 183.0
specified site — *see* Neoplasm, by site, malignant
unspecified site 183.0
papillary (M8450/3)
mucinous (M8471/3)
specified site — *see* Neoplasm, by site, malignant
unspecified site 183.0
pseudomucinous (M8471/3)
specified site — *see* Neoplasm, by site, malignant
unspecified site 183.0
serous (M8460/3)
specified site — *see* Neoplasm, by site, malignant
unspecified site 183.0

Cystadenocarcinoma — *see also* Neoplasm, by site, malignant — *continued*
papillary — *continued*
specified site — *see* Neoplasm, by site, malignant
unspecified site 183.0
pseudomucinous (M8470/3)
papillary (M8471/3)
specified site — *see* Neoplasm, by site, malignant
unspecified site 183.0
specified site — *see* Neoplasm, by site, malignant
unspecified site 183.0
serous (M8441/3)
papillary (M8460/3)
specified site — *see* Neoplasm, by site, malignant
unspecified site 183.0
specified site — *see* Neoplasm, by site, malignant
unspecified site 183.0
Cystadenofibroma (M9013/0)
clear cell (M8313/0) — *see* Neoplasm, by site, benign
endometrioid (M8381/0) 220
borderline malignancy (M8381/1) 236.2
malignant (M8381/3) 183.0
mucinous (M9015/0)
specified site — *see* Neoplasm, by site, benign
unspecified site 220
serous (M9014/0)
specified site — *see* Neoplasm, by site, benign
unspecified site 220
specified site — *see* Neoplasm, by site, benign
unspecified site 220
Cystadenoma (M8440/0) — *see also* Neoplasm, by site, benign
bile duct (M8161/0) 211.5
endometrioid (M8380/0) (*see also* Neoplasm, by site, benign)
borderline malignancy (M8380/1) — *see* Neoplasm, by site, uncertain behavior
malignant (M8440/3) — *see* Neoplasm, by site, malignant
mucinous (M8470/0)
borderline malignancy (M8470/1)
specified site — *see* Neoplasm, uncertain behavior
unspecified site 236.2
papillary (M8471/0)
borderline malignancy (M8471/1)
specified site — *see* Neoplasm, by site, uncertain behavior
unspecified site 236.2
specified site — *see* Neoplasm, by site, benign
unspecified site 220
specified site — *see* Neoplasm, by site, benign
unspecified site 220
papillary (M8450/0)
borderline malignancy (M8450/1)
specified site — *see* Neoplasm, by site, uncertain behavior
unspecified site 236.2
lymphomatosum (M8561/0) 210.2
mucinous (M8471/0)
borderline malignancy (M8471/1)
specified site — *see* Neoplasm, by site, uncertain behavior
unspecified site 236.2
specified site — *see* Neoplasm, by site, benign
unspecified site 220

Cystadenoma — *see also* Neoplasm, by site, benign — *continued*
papillary — *continued*
pseudomucinous (M8471/0)
borderline malignancy (M8471/1)
specified site — *see* Neoplasm, by site, uncertain behavior
unspecified site 236.2
specified site — *see* Neoplasm, by site, benign
unspecified site 220
serous (M8460/0)
borderline malignancy (M8460/1)
specified site — *see* Neoplasm, by site, uncertain behavior
unspecified site 236.2
specified site — *see* Neoplasm, by site, benign
unspecified site 220
specified site — *see* Neoplasm, by site, benign
unspecified site 220
pseudomucinous (M8470/0)
borderline malignancy (M8470/1)
specified site — *see* Neoplasm, by site, uncertain behavior
unspecified site 236.2
papillary (M8471/0)
borderline malignancy (M8471/1)
specified site — *see* Neoplasm, by site, uncertain behavior
unspecified site 236.2
specified site — *see* Neoplasm, by site, benign
unspecified site 220
specified site — *see* Neoplasm, by site, benign
unspecified site 220
serous (M8441/0)
borderline malignancy (M8441/1)
specified site — *see* Neoplasm, by site, uncertain behavior
unspecified site 236.2
papillary (M8460/0)
borderline malignancy (M8460/1)
specified site — *see* Neoplasm, by site, uncertain behavior
unspecified site 236.2
specified site — *see* Neoplasm, by site, benign
unspecified site 220
specified site — *see* Neoplasm, by site, benign
unspecified site 220
thyroid 226
Cystathioninemia 270.4
Cystathioninuria 270.4
Cystic — *see also* condition
breast, chronic 610.1
corpora lutea 620.1
degeneration, congenital
brain 742.4
kidney (*see also* Cystic, disease, kidney) 753.10
disease
breast, chronic 610.1
kidney, congenital 753.10
medullary 753.16
multiple 753.19
polycystic — *see* Polycystic, kidney
single 753.11
specified NEC 753.19
liver, congenital 751.62
lung 518.89
congenital 748.4

Cystic — *see also* condition — *continued*
disease — *continued*
pancreas, congenital 751.7
semilunar cartilage 717.5
duct — *see* condition
eyeball, congenital 743.03
fibrosis (pancreas) 277.00
with
manifestations
gastrointestinal 277.03
pulmonary 277.02
specified NEC 277.09
meconium ileus 277.01
pulmonary exacerbation 277.02
hygroma (M9173/0) 228.1
kidney, congenital 753.10
medullary 753.16
multiple 753.19
polycystic — *see* Polycystic, kidney
single 753.11
specified NEC 753.19
liver, congenital 751.62
lung 518.89
congenital 748.4
mass — *see* Cyst
mastitis, chronic 610.1
ovary 620.2
pancreas, congenital 751.7
Cysticerciasis 123.1
Cysticercosis (mammary) (subretinal) 123.1
Cysticercus 123.1
cellulosae infestation 123.1
Cystinosis (malignant) 270.0
Cystinuria 270.0
Cystitis (bacillary) (colli) (diffuse) (exudative) (hemorrhagic) (purulent) (recurrent) (septic) (suppurative) (ulcerative) 595.9
with
abortion — *see* Abortion, by type, with urinary tract infection
ectopic pregnancy (*see also* categories 633.0–633.9) 639.8
Cystitis — *continued*
with — *continued*
fibrosis 595.1
leukoplakia 595.1
malakoplakia 595.1
metaplasia 595.1
molar pregnancy (*see also* categories 630–632) 639.8
actinomycotic 039.8 *[595.4]*
acute 595.0
of trigone 595.3
allergic 595.89
amebic 006.8 *[595.4]*
bilharzial 120.9 *[595.4]*
blennorrhagic (acute) 098.11
chronic or duration of 2 months or more 098.31
bullous 595.89
calculous 594.1
chlamydial 099.53
chronic 595.2
interstitial 595.1
of trigone 595.3
complicating pregnancy, childbirth, or puerperium 646.6 ☑
affecting fetus or newborn 760.1
cystic(a) 595.81
diphtheritic 032.84
echinococcal
granulosus 122.3 *[595.4]*
multilocularis 122.6 *[595.4]*
emphysematous 595.89
encysted 595.81
follicular 595.3
following
abortion 639.8
ectopic or molar pregnancy 639.8
gangrenous 595.89
glandularis 595.89
gonococcal (acute) 098.11
chronic or duration of 2 months or more 098.31
incrusted 595.89
interstitial 595.1
irradiation 595.82
Cystitis — *continued*
irritation 595.89
malignant 595.89
monilial 112.2
of trigone 595.3
panmural 595.1
polyposa 595.89
prostatic 601.3
radiation 595.82
Reiter's (abacterial) 099.3
specified NEC 595.89
subacute 595.2
submucous 595.1
syphilitic 095.8
trichomoniasis 131.09
tuberculous (*see also* Tuberculosis) 016.1 ☑
ulcerative 595.1
Cystocele
female (without uterine prolapse) 618.01
with uterine prolapse 618.4
complete 618.3
incomplete 618.2
lateral 618.02
midline 618.01
paravaginal 618.02
in pregnancy or childbirth 654.4 ☑
affecting fetus or newborn 763.89
causing obstructed labor 660.2 ☑
affecting fetus or newborn 763.1
male 596.8
Cystoid
cicatrix limbus 372.64
degeneration macula 362.53
Cystolithiasis 594.1
Cystoma (M8440/0) — *see also* Neoplasm, by site, benign
endometrial, ovary 617.1
mucinous (M8470/0)
specified site — *see* Neoplasm, by site, benign
unspecified site 220
Cystoma — *see also* Neoplasm, by site, benign — *continued*
serous (M8441/0)
specified site — *see* Neoplasm, by site, benign
unspecified site 220
simple (ovary) 620.2
Cystoplegia 596.53
Cystoptosis 596.8
Cystopyelitis — *see also* Pyelitis 590.80
Cystorrhagia 596.8
Cystosarcoma phyllodes (M9020/1) 238.3
benign (M9020/0) 217
malignant (M9020/3) — *see* Neoplasm, breast, malignant
Cystostomy status V44.50
with complication 997.5
appendico-vesicostomy V44.52
cutaneous-vesicostomy V44.51
specified type NEC V44.59
Cystourethritis — *see also* Urethritis 597.89
Cystourethrocele — *see also* Cystocele
female (without uterine prolapse) 618.09
with uterine prolapse 618.4
complete 618.3
incomplete 618.2
male 596.8
Cytomegalic inclusion disease 078.5
congenital 771.1
Cytomycosis, reticuloendothelial — *see also* Histoplasmosis, American 115.00
Cytopenia 289.9
refractory
with
multilineage dysplasia (RCMD) 238.72
and ringed sideroblasts (RCMD-RS) 238.72

D

- **Daae (-Finsen) disease** (epidemic pleurodynia) 074.1
- **Dabney's grip** 074.1
- **Da Costa's syndrome** (neurocirculatory asthenia) 306.2
- **Dacryoadenitis, dacryadenitis** 375.00
  - acute 375.01
  - chronic 375.02
- **Dacryocystitis** 375.30
  - acute 375.32
  - chronic 375.42
  - neonatal 771.6
  - phlegmonous 375.33
  - syphilitic 095.8
    - congenital 090.0
  - trachomatous, active 076.1
    - late effect 139.1
  - tuberculous (*see also* Tuberculosis) 017.3 ☑
- **Dacryocystoblenorrhea** 375.42
- **Dacryocystocele** 375.43
- **Dacryolith, dacryolithiasis** 375.57
- **Dacryoma** 375.43
- **Dacryopericystitis** (acute) (subacute) 375.32
  - chronic 375.42
- **Dacryops** 375.11
- **Dacryosialadenopathy, atrophic** 710.2
- **Dacryostenosis** 375.56
  - congenital 743.65
- **Dactylitis**
  - bone (*see also* Osteomyelitis) 730.2 ☑
  - sickle-cell 282.62
    - Hb-C 282.64
    - Hb-SS 282.62
    - specified NEC 282.69
  - syphilitic 095.5
  - tuberculous (*see also* Tuberculosis) 015.5 ☑
- **Dactylolysis spontanea** 136.0
- **Dactylosymphysis** — *see also* Syndactylism 755.10
- **Damage**
  - arteriosclerotic — *see* Arteriosclerosis
  - brain 348.9
    - anoxic, hypoxic 348.1
      - during or resulting from a procedure 997.01
    - ischemic, in newborn 768.7
    - child NEC 343.9
    - due to birth injury 767.0
    - minimal (child) (*see also* Hyperkinesia) 314.9
    - newborn 767.0
  - cardiac (*see also* Disease, heart)
  - cardiorenal (vascular) (*see also* Hypertension, cardiorenal) 404.90
  - central nervous system — *see* Damage, brain
  - cerebral NEC — *see* Damage, brain
  - coccyx, complicating delivery 665.6 ☑
  - coronary (*see also* Ischemia, heart) 414.9
  - eye, birth injury 767.8
  - heart (*see also* Disease, heart)
    - valve — *see* Endocarditis
  - hypothalamus NEC 348.9
  - liver 571.9
    - alcoholic 571.3
  - medication 995.20
  - myocardium (*see also* Degeneration, myocardial) 429.1
  - pelvic
    - joint or ligament, during delivery 665.6 ☑
    - organ NEC
      - with
        - abortion — *see* Abortion, by type, with damage to pelvic organs
        - ectopic pregnancy (*see also* categories 633.0–633.9) 639.2

Damage — *continued*
  - pelvic — *continued*
    - organ — *continued*
      - with — *continued*
        - molar pregnancy (*see also* categories 630–632) 639.2
      - during delivery 665.5 ☑
      - following
        - abortion 639.2
        - ectopic or molar pregnancy 639.2
  - renal (*see also* Disease, renal) 593.9
  - skin, solar 692.79
    - acute 692.72
    - chronic 692.74
  - subendocardium, subendocardial (*see also* Degeneration, myocardial) 429.1
  - vascular 459.9
- **Dameshek's syndrome** (erythroblastic anemia) 282.49
- **Dana-Putnam syndrome** (subacute combined sclerosis with pernicious anemia) 281.0 *[336.2]*
- **Danbolt (-Closs) syndrome** (acrodermatitis enteropathica) 686.8
- **Dandruff** 690.18
- **Dandy fever** 061
- **Dandy-Walker deformity or syndrome** (atresia, foramen of Magendie) 742.3
  - with spina bifida (*see also* Spina bifida) 741.0 ☑
- **Dangle foot** 736.79
- **Danielssen's disease** (anesthetic leprosy) 030.1
- **Danlos' syndrome** 756.83
- **Darier's disease** (congenital) (keratosis follicularis) 757.39
  - due to vitamin A deficiency 264.8
  - meaning erythema annulare centrifugum 695.0
- **Darier-Roussy sarcoid** 135
- **Darling's**
  - disease (*see also* Histoplasmosis, American) 115.00
  - histoplasmosis (*see also* Histoplasmosis, American) 115.00
- **Dartre** 054.9
- **Darwin's tubercle** 744.29
- **Davidson's anemia** (refractory) 284.9
- **Davies-Colley syndrome** (slipping rib) 733.99
- **Davies' disease** 425.0
- **Dawson's encephalitis** 046.2
- **Day blindness** — *see also* Blindness, day 368.60
- **Dead**
  - fetus
    - retained (in utero) 656.4 ☑
      - early pregnancy (death before 22 completed weeks gestation) 632
      - late (death after 22 completed weeks gestation) 656.4 ☑
    - syndrome 641.3 ☑
  - labyrinth 386.50
  - ovum, retained 631
- **Deaf and dumb** NEC 389.7
- **Deaf mutism** (acquired) (congenital) NEC 389.7
  - endemic 243
  - hysterical 300.11
  - syphilitic, congenital 090.0
- **Deafness** (acquired) (complete) (congenital) (hereditary) (middle ear) (partial) 389.9
  - with
    - blindness V49.85
    - blue sclera and fragility of bone 756.51
  - auditory fatigue 389.9
  - aviation 993.0
    - nerve injury 951.5
  - boilermakers' 951.5

Deafness — *continued*
  - central 389.14
    - with conductive hearing loss 389.20
      - bilateral 389.22
      - unilateral 389.21
  - conductive (air) 389.00
    - with sensorineural hearing loss 389.20
      - bilateral 389.22
      - unilateral 389.21
    - bilateral 389.06
    - combined types 389.08
    - external ear 389.01
    - inner ear 389.04
    - middle ear 389.03
    - multiple types 389.08
    - tympanic membrane 389.02
    - unilateral 389.05
  - emotional (complete) 300.11
  - functional (complete) 300.11
  - high frequency 389.8
  - hysterical (complete) 300.11
  - injury 951.5
  - low frequency 389.8
  - mental 784.69
  - mixed conductive and sensorineural 389.20
    - bilateral 389.22
    - unilateral 389.21
  - nerve
    - with conductive hearing loss 389.20
      - bilateral 389.22
      - unilateral 389.21
    - bilateral 389.12
    - unilateral 389.13
  - neural
    - with conductive hearing loss 389.20
      - bilateral 389.22
      - unilateral 389.21
    - bilateral 389.12
    - unilateral 389.13
  - noise-induced 388.12
    - nerve injury 951.5
  - nonspeaking 389.7
  - perceptive 389.10
    - with conductive hearing loss 389.20
      - bilateral 389.22
      - unilateral 389.21
    - central 389.14
    - neural
      - bilateral 389.12
      - unilateral 389.13
    - sensorineural 389.10
      - asymmetrical 389.16
      - bilateral 389.18
      - unilateral 389.15
    - sensory
      - bilateral 389.11
      - unilateral 389.17
  - psychogenic (complete) 306.7
  - sensorineural (*see also* Deafness, perceptive) 389.10
    - asymmetrical 389.16
    - bilateral 389.18
    - unilateral 389.15
  - sensory
    - with conductive hearing loss 389.20
      - bilateral 389.22
      - unilateral 389.21
    - bilateral 389.11
    - unilateral 389.17
  - specified type NEC 389.8
  - sudden NEC 388.2
  - syphilitic 094.89
  - transient ischemic 388.02
  - transmission — *see* Deafness, conductive
  - traumatic 951.5
  - word (secondary to organic lesion) 784.69
    - developmental 315.31
- **Death**
  - after delivery (cause not stated) (sudden) 674.9 ☑
  - anesthetic
    - due to
      - correct substance properly administered 995.4
      - overdose or wrong substance given 968.4
        - specified anesthetic — *see* Table of Drugs and Chemicals
    - during delivery 668.9 ☑
  - brain 348.8
  - cardiac (sudden) (SCD) — code to underlying condition
    - family history of V17.41
    - personal history of, successfully resuscitated V12.53
  - cause unknown 798.2
  - cot (infant) 798.0
  - crib (infant) 798.0
  - fetus, fetal (cause not stated) (intrauterine) 779.9
    - early, with retention (before 22 completed weeks gestation) 632
    - from asphyxia or anoxia (before labor) 768.0
      - during labor 768.1
    - late, affecting management of pregnancy (after 22 completed weeks gestation) 656.4 ☑
  - from pregnancy NEC 646.9 ☑
  - instantaneous 798.1
  - intrauterine (*see also* Death, fetus) 779.9
    - complicating pregnancy 656.4 ☑
  - maternal, affecting fetus or newborn 761.6
  - neonatal NEC 779.9
  - sudden (cause unknown) 798.1
    - cardiac (SCD)
      - family history of V17.41
      - personal history of, successfully resuscitated V12.53
    - during delivery 669.9 ☑
      - under anesthesia NEC 668.9 ☑
    - infant, syndrome (SIDS) 798.0
    - puerperal, during puerperium 674.9 ☑
  - unattended (cause unknown) 798.9
  - under anesthesia NEC
    - due to
      - correct substance properly administered 995.4
      - overdose or wrong substance given 968.4
        - specified anesthetic — *see* Table of Drugs and Chemicals
    - during delivery 668.9 ☑
  - violent 798.1
- **de Beurmann-Gougerot disease** (sporotrichosis) 117.1
- **Debility** (general) (infantile) (postinfectional) 799.3
  - with nutritional difficulty 269.9
  - congenital or neonatal NEC 779.9
  - nervous 300.5
  - old age 797
  - senile 797
- **Débove's disease** (splenomegaly) 789.2
- **Decalcification**
  - bone (*see also* Osteoporosis) 733.00
  - teeth 521.89
- **Decapitation** 874.9
  - fetal (to facilitate delivery) 763.89
- **Decapsulation, kidney** 593.89
- **Decay**
  - dental 521.00
  - senile 797
  - tooth, teeth 521.00
- **Decensus, uterus** — *see* Prolapse, uterus

- **Deciduitis** (acute)
  - with
    - abortion — *see* Abortion, by type, with sepsis
    - ectopic pregnancy (*see also* categories 633.0–633.9) 639.0
    - molar pregnancy (*see also* categories 630–632) 639.0
  - affecting fetus or newborn 760.8
  - following
    - abortion 639.0
    - ectopic or molar pregnancy 639.0
  - in pregnancy 646.6 ☑
  - puerperal, postpartum 670.0 ☑
- **Deciduoma malignum** (M9100/3) 181
- **Deciduous tooth** (retained) 520.6
- **Decline** (general) — *see also* Debility 799.3
- **Decompensation**
  - cardiac (acute) (chronic) (*see also* Disease, heart) 429.9
    - failure — *see* Failure, heart
  - cardiorenal (*see also* Hypertension, cardiorenal) 404.90
  - cardiovascular (*see also* Disease, cardiovascular) 429.2
  - heart (*see also* Disease, heart) 429.9
    - failure — *see* Failure, heart
  - hepatic 572.2
  - myocardial (acute) (chronic) (*see also* Disease, heart) 429.9
    - failure — *see* Failure, heart
  - respiratory 519.9
- **Decompression sickness** 993.3
- **Decrease, decreased**
  - blood
    - platelets (*see also* Thrombocytopenia) 287.5
    - pressure 796.3
      - due to shock following
        - injury 958.4
        - operation 998.0
    - white cell count 288.50
      - specified NEC 288.59
  - cardiac reserve — *see* Disease, heart
  - estrogen 256.39
    - postablative 256.2
  - fetal movements 655.7 ☑
  - fragility of erythrocytes 289.89
  - function
    - adrenal (cortex) 255.41
      - medulla 255.5
    - ovary in hypopituitarism 253.4
    - parenchyma of pancreas 577.8
    - pituitary (gland) (lobe) (anterior) 253.2
      - posterior (lobe) 253.8
  - functional activity 780.99
  - glucose 790.29
  - haptoglobin (serum) NEC 273.8
  - leukocytes 288.50
  - libido 799.81
  - lymphocytes 288.51
  - platelets (*see also* Thrombocytopenia) 287.5
  - pulse pressure 785.9
  - respiration due to shock following injury 958.4
  - sexual desire 799.81
  - tear secretion NEC 375.15
  - tolerance
    - fat 579.8
    - salt and water 276.9
  - vision NEC 369.9
  - white blood cell count 288.50
- **Decubital gangrene** — *see also* Ulcer, pressure 707.00 *[785.4]*
- **Decubiti** — *see also* Ulcer, pressure 707.00
- **Decubitus** (ulcer) — *see also* Ulcer, pressure 707.00
  - with gangrene 707.00 *[785.4]*
  - ankle 707.06
  - back
    - lower 707.03
    - upper 707.02
- **Decubitus** — *see also* Ulcer, pressure — *continued*
  - buttock 707.05
  - elbow 707.01
  - head 707.09
  - heel 707.07
  - hip 707.04
  - other site 707.09
  - sacrum 707.03
  - shoulder blades 707.02
- **Deepening acetabulum** 718.85
- **Defect, defective** 759.9
  - 3-beta-hydroxysteroid dehydrogenase 255.2
  - 11-hydroxylase 255.2
  - 21-hydroxylase 255.2
  - abdominal wall, congenital 756.70
  - aorticopulmonary septum 745.0
  - aortic septal 745.0
  - atrial septal (ostium secundum type) 745.5
    - acquired 429.71
    - ostium primum type 745.61
    - sinus venosus 745.8
  - atrioventricular
    - canal 745.69
    - septum 745.4
      - acquired 429.71
  - atrium secundum 745.5
    - acquired 429.71
  - auricular septal 745.5
    - acquired 429.71
  - bilirubin excretion 277.4
  - biosynthesis, testicular androgen 257.2
  - bridge 525.60
  - bulbar septum 745.0
  - butanol-insoluble iodide 246.1
  - chromosome — *see* Anomaly, chromosome
  - circulation (acquired) 459.9
    - congenital 747.9
    - newborn 747.9
  - clotting NEC (*see also* Defect, coagulation) 286.9
  - coagulation (factor) (*see also* Deficiency, coagulation factor) 286.9
    - with
      - abortion — *see* Abortion, by type, with hemorrhage
      - ectopic pregnancy (*see also* categories 634–638) 639.1
      - molar pregnancy (*see also* categories 630–632) 639.1
    - acquired (any) 286.7
    - antepartum or intrapartum 641.3 ☑
      - affecting fetus or newborn 762.1
    - causing hemorrhage of pregnancy or delivery 641.3 ☑
    - complicating pregnancy, childbirth, or puerperium 649.3 ☑
    - due to
      - liver disease 286.7
      - vitamin K deficiency 286.7
    - newborn, transient 776.3
    - postpartum 666.3 ☑
    - specified type NEC 286.9
  - conduction (heart) 426.9
    - bone (*see also* Deafness, conductive) 389.00
  - congenital, organ or site NEC (*see also* Anomaly)
    - circulation 747.9
    - Descemet's membrane 743.9
      - specified type NEC 743.49
    - diaphragm 756.6
    - ectodermal 757.9
    - esophagus 750.9
    - pulmonic cusps — *see* Anomaly, heart valve
    - respiratory system 748.9
      - specified type NEC 748.8
  - crown 525.60
  - cushion endocardial 745.60
  - dental restoration 525.60
- **Defect, defective** — *continued*
  - dentin (hereditary) 520.5
  - Descemet's membrane (congenital) 743.9
    - acquired 371.30
    - specific type NEC 743.49
  - deutan 368.52
  - developmental (*see also* Anomaly, by site)
    - cauda equina 742.59
    - left ventricle 746.9
      - with atresia or hypoplasia of aortic orifice or valve, with hypoplasia of ascending aorta 746.7
      - in hypoplastic left heart syndrome 746.7
    - testis 752.9
    - vessel 747.9
  - diaphragm
    - with elevation, eventration, or hernia — *see* Hernia, diaphragm
    - congenital 756.6
      - with elevation, eventration, or hernia 756.6
      - gross (with elevation, eventration, or hernia) 756.6
  - ectodermal, congenital 757.9
  - Eisenmenger's (ventricular septal defect) 745.4
  - endocardial cushion 745.60
    - specified type NEC 745.69
  - esophagus, congenital 750.9
  - extensor retinaculum 728.9
  - fibrin polymerization (*see also* Defect, coagulation) 286.3
  - filling
    - biliary tract 793.3
    - bladder 793.5
    - dental 525.60
    - gallbladder 793.3
    - kidney 793.5
    - stomach 793.4
    - ureter 793.5
  - fossa ovalis 745.5
  - gene, carrier (suspected) of V83.89
  - Gerbode 745.4
  - glaucomatous, without elevated tension 365.89
  - Hageman (factor) (*see also* Defect, coagulation) 286.3
  - hearing (*see also* Deafness) 389.9
  - high grade 317
  - homogentisic acid 270.2
  - interatrial septal 745.5
    - acquired 429.71
  - interauricular septal 745.5
    - acquired 429.71
  - interventricular septal 745.4
    - with pulmonary stenosis or atresia, dextraposition of aorta, and hypertrophy of right ventricle 745.2
    - acquired 429.71
    - in tetralogy of Fallot 745.2
  - iodide trapping 246.1
  - iodotyrosine dehalogenase 246.1
  - kynureninase 270.2
  - learning, specific 315.2
  - major osseous 731.3
  - mental (*see also* Retardation, mental) 319
  - osseous, major 731.3
  - osteochondral NEC 738.8
  - ostium
    - primum 745.61
    - secundum 745.5
  - pericardium 746.89
  - peroxidase-binding 246.1
  - placental blood supply — *see* Placenta, insufficiency
  - platelet (qualitative) 287.1
    - constitutional 286.4
  - postural, spine 737.9
  - protan 368.51
  - pulmonic cusps, congenital 746.00
- **Defect, defective** — *continued*
  - renal pelvis 753.9
    - obstructive 753.29
    - specified type NEC 753.3
  - respiratory system, congenital 748.9
    - specified type NEC 748.8
  - retina, retinal 361.30
    - with detachment (*see also* Detachment, retina, with retinal defect) 361.00
    - multiple 361.33
      - with detachment 361.02
    - nerve fiber bundle 362.85
    - single 361.30
      - with detachment 361.01
  - septal (closure) (heart) NEC 745.9
    - acquired 429.71
    - atrial 745.5
    - specified type NEC 745.8
  - speech NEC 784.5
    - developmental 315.39
    - secondary to organic lesion 784.5
  - Taussig-Bing (transposition, aorta and overriding pulmonary artery) 745.11
  - teeth, wedge 521.20
  - thyroid hormone synthesis 246.1
  - tritan 368.53
  - ureter 753.9
    - obstructive 753.29
  - vascular (acquired) (local) 459.9
    - congenital (peripheral) NEC 747.60
      - gastrointestinal 747.61
      - lower limb 747.64
      - renal 747.62
      - specified NEC 747.69
      - spinal 747.82
      - upper limb 747.63
  - ventricular septal 745.4
    - with pulmonary stenosis or atresia, dextraposition of aorta, and hypertrophy of right ventricle 745.2
    - acquired 429.71
    - atrioventricular canal type 745.69
    - between infundibulum and anterior portion 745.4
    - in tetralogy of Fallot 745.2
    - isolated anterior 745.4
  - vision NEC 369.9
  - visual field 368.40
    - arcuate 368.43
    - heteronymous, bilateral 368.47
    - homonymous, bilateral 368.46
    - localized NEC 368.44
    - nasal step 368.44
    - peripheral 368.44
    - sector 368.43
  - voice 784.40
  - wedge, teeth (abrasion) 521.20
- **Defeminization syndrome** 255.2
- **Deferentitis** 608.4
  - gonorrheal (acute) 098.14
    - chronic or duration of 2 months or over 098.34
- **Defibrination syndrome** — *see also* Fibrinolysis 286.6
- **Deficiency, deficient**
  - 3-beta-hydroxysteroid dehydrogenase 255.2
  - 6-phosphogluconic dehydrogenase (anemia) 282.2
  - 11-beta-hydroxylase 255.2
  - 17-alpha-hydroxylase 255.2
  - 18-hydroxysteroid dehydrogenase 255.2
  - 20-alpha-hydroxylase 255.2
  - 21-hydroxylase 255.2
  - AAT (alpha-1 antitrypsin) 273.4
  - abdominal muscle syndrome 756.79
  - accelerator globulin (Ac G) (blood) (*see also* Defect, coagulation) 286.3
  - AC globulin (congenital) (*see also* Defect, coagulation) 286.3
    - acquired 286.7

Deformity — *continued*
- vena cava (inferior) (superior) (congenital) 747.40
- vertebra — *see* Deformity, spine
- vesicourethral orifice (acquired) 596.8
  - congenital NEC 753.9
    - specified type NEC 753.8
- vessels of optic papilla (congenital) 743.9
- visual field (contraction) 368.45
- vitreous humor (congenital) 743.9
  - acquired 379.29
- vulva (congenital) 752.40
  - acquired 624.8
- wrist (joint) (acquired) 736.00
  - congenital 755.50
  - contraction 718.43
  - valgus 736.03
    - congenital 755.59
  - varus 736.04
    - congenital 755.59

Degeneration, degenerative
- adrenal (capsule) (gland) 255.8
  - with hypofunction 255.41
  - fatty 255.8
  - hyaline 255.8
  - infectional 255.8
  - lardaceous 277.39
- amyloid (any site) (general) 277.39
- anterior cornua, spinal cord 336.8
- anterior labral 840.8
- aorta, aortic 440.0
  - fatty 447.8
  - valve (heart) (*see also* Endocarditis, aortic) 424.1
- arteriovascular — *see* Arteriosclerosis
- artery, arterial (atheromatous) (calcareous) (*see also* Arteriosclerosis)
  - amyloid 277.39
  - lardaceous 277.39
  - medial NEC (*see also* Arteriosclerosis, extremities) 440.20
- articular cartilage NEC (*see also* Disorder, cartilage, articular) 718.0 ☑
  - elbow 718.02
  - knee 717.5
  - patella 717.7
  - shoulder 718.01
  - spine (*see also* Spondylosis) 721.90
- atheromatous — *see* Arteriosclerosis
- bacony (any site) 277.39
- basal nuclei or ganglia NEC 333.0
- bone 733.90
- brachial plexus 353.0
- brain (cortical) (progressive) 331.9
  - arteriosclerotic 437.0
  - childhood 330.9
    - specified type NEC 330.8
  - congenital 742.4
  - cystic 348.0
    - congenital 742.4
  - familial NEC 331.89
  - grey matter 330.8
  - heredofamilial NEC 331.89
  - in
    - alcoholism 303.9 ☑ *[331.7]*
    - beriberi 265.0 *[331.7]*
    - cerebrovascular disease 437.9 *[331.7]*
    - congenital hydrocephalus 742.3 *[331.7]*
      - with spina bifida (*see also* Spina bifida) 741.0 ☑ *[331.7]*
    - Fabry's disease 272.7 *[330.2]*
    - Gaucher's disease 272.7 *[330.2]*
    - Hunter's disease or syndrome 277.5 *[330.3]*
    - lipidosis
      - cerebral 330.1
      - generalized 272.7 *[330.2]*
    - mucopolysaccharidosis 277.5 *[330.3]*
    - myxedema (*see also* Myxedema) 244.9 *[331.7]*

Degeneration, degenerative — *continued*
- brain — *continued*
  - in — *continued*
    - neoplastic disease NEC (M8000/1) 239.9 *[331.7]*
    - Niemann-Pick disease 272.7 *[330.2]*
    - sphingolipidosis 272.7 *[330.2]*
    - vitamin B_{12} deficiency 266.2 *[331.7]*
  - motor centers 331.89
  - senile 331.2
  - specified type NEC 331.89
- breast — *see* Disease, breast
- Bruch's membrane 363.40
- bundle of His 426.50
  - left 426.3
  - right 426.4
- calcareous NEC 275.49
- capillaries 448.9
  - amyloid 277.39
  - fatty 448.9
  - lardaceous 277.39
- cardiac (brown) (calcareous) (fatty) (fibrous) (hyaline) (mural) (muscular) (pigmentary) (senile) (with arteriosclerosis) (*see also* Degeneration, myocardial) 429.1
  - valve, valvular — *see* Endocarditis
- cardiorenal (*see also* Hypertension, cardiorenal) 404.90
- cardiovascular (*see also* Disease, cardiovascular) 429.2
  - renal (*see also* Hypertension, cardiorenal) 404.90
- cartilage (joint) — *see* Derangement, joint
- cerebellar NEC 334.9
  - primary (hereditary) (sporadic) 334.2
- cerebral — *see* Degeneration, brain
- cerebromacular 330.1
- cerebrovascular 437.1
  - due to hypertension 437.2
  - late effect — *see* Late effect(s) (of) cerebrovascular disease
- cervical plexus 353.2
- cervix 622.8
  - due to radiation (intended effect) 622.8
    - adverse effect or misadventure 622.8
- changes, spine or vertebra (*see also* Spondylosis) 721.90
- chitinous 277.39
- chorioretinal 363.40
  - congenital 743.53
  - hereditary 363.50
- choroid (colloid) (drusen) 363.40
  - hereditary 363.50
  - senile 363.41
    - diffuse secondary 363.42
- cochlear 386.8
- collateral ligament (knee) (medial) 717.82
  - lateral 717.81
- combined (spinal cord) (subacute) 266.2 *[336.2]*
  - with anemia (pernicious) 281.0 *[336.2]*
    - due to dietary deficiency 281.1 *[336.2]*
  - due to vitamin B_{12} deficiency anemia (dietary) 281.1 *[336.2]*
- conjunctiva 372.50
  - amyloid 277.39 *[372.50]*
- cornea 371.40
  - calcerous 371.44
  - familial (hereditary) (*see also* Dystrophy, cornea) 371.50
    - macular 371.55
    - reticular 371.54
  - hyaline (of old scars) 371.41
  - marginal (Terrien's) 371.48
  - mosaic (shagreen) 371.41

Degeneration, degenerative — *continued*
- cornea — *continued*
  - nodular 371.46
  - peripheral 371.48
  - senile 371.41
- cortical (cerebellar) (parenchymatous) 334.2
  - alcoholic 303.9 ☑ *[334.4]*
  - diffuse, due to arteriopathy 437.0
- corticostriatal-spinal 334.8
- cretinoid 243
- cruciate ligament (knee) (posterior) 717.84
  - anterior 717.83
- cutis 709.3
  - amyloid 277.39
- dental pulp 522.2
- disc disease — *see* Degeneration, intervertebral disc
- dorsolateral (spinal cord) — *see* Degeneration, combined
- endocardial 424.90
- extrapyramidal NEC 333.90
- eye NEC 360.40
  - macular (*see also* Degeneration, macula) 362.50
    - congenital 362.75
    - hereditary 362.76
- fatty (diffuse) (general) 272.8
  - liver 571.8
    - alcoholic 571.0
  - localized site — *see* Degeneration, by site, fatty
  - placenta — *see* Placenta, abnormal
- globe (eye) NEC 360.40
  - macular — *see* Degeneration, macula
- grey matter 330.8
- heart (brown) (calcareous) (fatty) (fibrous) (hyaline) (mural) (muscular) (pigmentary) (senile) (with arteriosclerosis) (*see also* Degeneration, myocardial) 429.1
  - amyloid 277.39 *[425.7]*
  - atheromatous — *see* Arteriosclerosis, coronary
  - gouty 274.82
  - hypertensive (*see also* Hypertension, heart) 402.90
  - ischemic 414.9
  - valve, valvular — *see* Endocarditis
- hepatolenticular (Wilson's) 275.1
- hepatorenal 572.4
- heredofamilial
  - brain NEC 331.89
  - spinal cord NEC 336.8
- hyaline (diffuse) (generalized) 728.9
  - localized (*see also* Degeneration, by site)
    - cornea 371.41
    - keratitis 371.41
- hypertensive vascular — *see* Hypertension
- infrapatellar fat pad 729.31
- internal semilunar cartilage 717.3
- intervertebral disc 722.6
  - with myelopathy 722.70
  - cervical, cervicothoracic 722.4
    - with myelopathy 722.71
  - lumbar, lumbosacral 722.52
    - with myelopathy 722.73
  - thoracic, thoracolumbar 722.51
    - with myelopathy 722.72
- intestine 569.89
  - amyloid 277.39
  - lardaceous 277.39
- iris (generalized) (*see also* Atrophy, iris) 364.59
  - pigmentary 364.53
  - pupillary margin 364.54
- ischemic — *see* Ischemia
- joint disease (*see also* Osteoarthrosis) 715.9 ☑
  - multiple sites 715.09
  - spine (*see also* Spondylosis) 721.90

Degeneration, degenerative — *continued*
- kidney (*see also* Sclerosis, renal) 587
  - amyloid 277.39 *[583.81]*
  - cyst, cystic (multiple) (solitary) 593.2
    - congenital (*see also* Cystic, disease, kidney) 753.10
  - fatty 593.89
  - fibrocystic (congenital) 753.19
  - lardaceous 277.39 *[583.81]*
  - polycystic (congenital) 753.12
    - adult type (APKD) 753.13
    - autosomal dominant 753.13
    - autosomal recessive 753.14
    - childhood type (CPKD) 753.14
    - infantile type 753.14
  - waxy 277.39 *[583.81]*
- Kuhnt-Junius (retina) 362.52
- labyrinth, osseous 386.8
- lacrimal passages, cystic 375.12
- lardaceous (any site) 277.39
- lateral column (posterior), spinal cord (*see also* Degeneration, combined) 266.2 *[336.2]*
- lattice 362.63
- lens 366.9
  - infantile, juvenile, or presenile 366.00
  - senile 366.10
- lenticular (familial) (progressive) (Wilson's) (with cirrhosis of liver) 275.1
  - striate artery 437.0
- lethal ball, prosthetic heart valve 996.02
- ligament
  - collateral (knee) (medial) 717.82
    - lateral 717.81
  - cruciate (knee) (posterior) 717.84
    - anterior 717.83
- liver (diffuse) 572.8
  - amyloid 277.39
  - congenital (cystic) 751.62
  - cystic 572.8
    - congenital 751.62
  - fatty 571.8
    - alcoholic 571.0
  - hypertrophic 572.8
  - lardaceous 277.39
  - parenchymatous, acute or subacute (*see also* Necrosis, liver) 570
  - pigmentary 572.8
  - toxic (acute) 573.8
  - waxy 277.39
- lung 518.89
- lymph gland 289.3
  - hyaline 289.3
  - lardaceous 277.39
- macula (acquired) (senile) 362.50
  - atrophic 362.51
  - Best's 362.76
  - congenital 362.75
  - cystic 362.54
  - cystoid 362.53
  - disciform 362.52
  - dry 362.51
  - exudative 362.52
  - familial pseudoinflammatory 362.77
  - hereditary 362.76
  - hole 362.54
  - juvenile (Stargardt's) 362.75
  - nonexudative 362.51
  - pseudohole 362.54
  - wet 362.52
- medullary — *see* Degeneration, brain
- membranous labyrinth, congenital (causing impairment of hearing) 744.05
- meniscus — *see* Derangement, joint
- microcystoid 362.62
- mitral — *see* Insufficiency, mitral
- Mönckeberg's (*see also* Arteriosclerosis, extremities) 440.20

Delirium, delirious — *continued*
- manic, maniacal (acute) (*see also* Psychosis, affective) 296.0 ☑
  - recurrent episode 296.1 ☑
  - single episode 296.0 ☑
- puerperal 293.9
- senile 290.3
- subacute (psychotic) 293.1
- thyroid (*see also* Thyrotoxicosis) 242.9 ☑
- traumatic (*see also* Injury, intracranial)
  - with
    - lesion, spinal cord — *see* Injury, spinal, by site
    - shock, spinal — *see* Injury, spinal, by site
- tremens (impending) 291.0
- uremic — *see* Uremia
- withdrawal
  - alcoholic (acute) 291.0
    - chronic 291.1
  - drug 292.0

Delivery

> *Note — Use the following fifth-digit subclassification with categories 640–649, 651–676:*
>
> 0 *unspecified as to episode of care*
>
> 1 *delivered, with or without mention of antepartum condition*
>
> 2 *delivered, with mention of postpartum complication*
>
> 3 *antepartum condition or complication*
>
> 4 *postpartum condition or complication*

- breech (assisted) (buttocks) (complete) (frank) (spontaneous) 652.2 ☑
  - affecting fetus or newborn 763.0
  - extraction NEC 669.6 ☑
- cesarean (for) 669.7 ☑
  - abnormal
    - cervix 654.6 ☑
    - pelvic organs or tissues 654.9 ☑
    - pelvis (bony) (major) NEC 653.0 ☑
    - presentation or position 652.9 ☑
      - in multiple gestation 652.6 ☑
    - size, fetus 653.5 ☑
    - soft parts (of pelvis) 654.9 ☑
    - uterus, congenital 654.0 ☑
    - vagina 654.7 ☑
    - vulva 654.8 ☑
  - abruptio placentae 641.2 ☑
  - acromion presentation 652.8 ☑
  - affecting fetus or newborn 763.4
  - anteversion, cervix or uterus 654.4 ☑
  - atony, uterus 661.2 ☑
    - with hemorrhage 666.1 ☑
  - bicornis or bicornuate uterus 654.0 ☑
  - breech presentation (buttocks) (complete) (frank) 652.2 ☑
  - brow presentation 652.4 ☑
  - cephalopelvic disproportion (normally formed fetus) 653.4 ☑
  - chin presentation 652.4 ☑
  - cicatrix of cervix 654.6 ☑
  - contracted pelvis (general) 653.1 ☑
    - inlet 653.2 ☑
    - outlet 653.3 ☑
  - cord presentation or prolapse 663.0 ☑
  - cystocele 654.4 ☑
  - deformity (acquired) (congenital)
    - pelvic organs or tissues NEC 654.9 ☑
    - pelvis (bony) NEC 653.0 ☑
  - displacement, uterus NEC 654.4 ☑
  - disproportion NEC 653.9 ☑

Delivery — *continued*
- cesarean — *continued*
  - distress
    - fetal 656.8 ☑
    - maternal 669.0 ☑
  - eclampsia 642.6 ☑
  - face presentation 652.4 ☑
  - failed
    - forceps 660.7 ☑
    - trial of labor NEC 660.6 ☑
    - vacuum extraction 660.7 ☑
    - ventouse 660.7 ☑
  - fetal deformity 653.7 ☑
  - fetal-maternal hemorrhage 656.0 ☑
  - fetus, fetal
    - distress 656.8 ☑
    - prematurity 656.8 ☑
  - fibroid (tumor) (uterus) 654.1 ☑
  - footling 652.8 ☑
    - with successful version 652.1 ☑
  - hemorrhage (antepartum) (intrapartum) NEC 641.9 ☑
  - hydrocephalic fetus 653.6 ☑
  - incarceration of uterus 654.3 ☑
  - incoordinate uterine action 661.4 ☑
  - inertia, uterus 661.2 ☑
    - primary 661.0 ☑
    - secondary 661.1 ☑
  - lateroversion, uterus or cervix 654.4 ☑
  - mal lie 652.9 ☑
  - malposition
    - fetus 652.9 ☑
      - in multiple gestation 652.6 ☑
    - pelvic organs or tissues NEC 654.9 ☑
    - uterus NEC or cervix 654.4 ☑
  - malpresentation NEC 652.9 ☑
    - in multiple gestation 652.6 ☑
  - maternal
    - diabetes mellitus (conditions classifiable to 249 and 250) 648.0 ☑
    - heart disease NEC 648.6 ☑
  - meconium in liquor 656.8 ☑
    - staining only 792.3
  - oblique presentation 652.3 ☑
  - oversize fetus 653.5 ☑
  - pelvic tumor NEC 654.9 ☑
  - placental insufficiency 656.5 ☑
  - placenta previa 641.0 ☑
    - with hemorrhage 641.1 ☑
  - poor dilation, cervix 661.0 ☑
  - pre-eclampsia 642.4 ☑
    - severe 642.5 ☑
  - previous
    - cesarean delivery, section 654.2 ☑
    - surgery (to)
      - cervix 654.6 ☑
      - gynecological NEC 654.9 ☑
      - rectum 654.8 ☑
      - uterus NEC 654.9 ☑
        - previous cesarean delivery, section 654.2 ☑
      - vagina 654.7 ☑
  - prolapse
    - arm or hand 652.7 ☑
    - uterus 654.4 ☑
  - prolonged labor 662.1 ☑
  - rectocele 654.4 ☑
  - retroversion, uterus or cervix 654.3 ☑
  - rigid
    - cervix 654.6 ☑
    - pelvic floor 654.4 ☑
    - perineum 654.8 ☑
    - vagina 654.7 ☑
    - vulva 654.8 ☑
  - sacculation, pregnant uterus 654.4 ☑

Delivery — *continued*
- cesarean — *continued*
  - scar(s)
    - cervix 654.6 ☑
    - cesarean delivery, section 654.2 ☑
    - uterus NEC 654.9 ☑
      - due to previous cesarean delivery, section 654.2 ☑
  - Shirodkar suture in situ 654.5 ☑
  - shoulder presentation 652.8 ☑
  - stenosis or stricture, cervix 654.6 ☑
  - transverse presentation or lie 652.3 ☑
  - tumor, pelvic organs or tissues NEC 654.4 ☑
  - umbilical cord presentation or prolapse 663.0 ☑
- completely normal case — *see* category 650
- complicated (by) NEC 669.9 ☑
  - abdominal tumor, fetal 653.7 ☑
    - causing obstructed labor 660.1 ☑
  - abnormal, abnormality of
    - cervix 654.6 ☑
      - causing obstructed labor 660.2 ☑
    - forces of labor 661.9 ☑
    - formation of uterus 654.0 ☑
    - pelvic organs or tissues 654.9 ☑
      - causing obstructed labor 660.2 ☑
    - pelvis (bony) (major) NEC 653.0 ☑
      - causing obstructed labor 660.1 ☑
    - presentation or position NEC 652.9 ☑
      - causing obstructed labor 660.0 ☑
    - size, fetus 653.5 ☑
      - causing obstructed labor 660.1 ☑
    - soft parts (of pelvis) 654.9 ☑
      - causing obstructed labor 660.2 ☑
    - uterine contractions NEC 661.9 ☑
    - uterus (formation) 654.0 ☑
      - causing obstructed labor 660.2 ☑
    - vagina 654.7 ☑
      - causing obstructed labor 660.2 ☑
  - abnormally formed uterus (any type) (congenital) 654.0 ☑
    - causing obstructed labor 660.2 ☑
  - acromion presentation 652.8 ☑
    - causing obstructed labor 660.0 ☑
  - adherent placenta 667.0 ☑
    - with hemorrhage 666.0 ☑
  - adhesions, uterus (to abdominal wall) 654.4 ☑
  - advanced maternal age NEC 659.6 ☑
    - multigravida 659.6 ☑
    - primigravida 659.5 ☑
  - air embolism 673.0 ☑
  - amnionitis 658.4 ☑
  - amniotic fluid embolism 673.1 ☑
  - anesthetic death 668.9 ☑
  - annular detachment, cervix 665.3 ☑
  - antepartum hemorrhage — *see* Delivery, complicated, hemorrhage
  - anteversion, cervix or uterus 654.4 ☑
    - causing obstructed labor 660.2 ☑
  - apoplexy 674.0 ☑

Delivery — *continued*
- complicated — *continued*
  - apoplexy — *continued*
    - placenta 641.2 ☑
  - arrested active phase 661.1 ☑
  - asymmetrical pelvis bone 653.0 ☑
    - causing obstructed labor 660.1 ☑
  - atony, uterus with hemorrhage (hypotonic) (inertia) 666.1 ☑
    - hypertonic 661.4 ☑
  - Bandl's ring 661.4 ☑
  - battledore placenta — *see* Placenta, abnormal
  - bicornis or bicornuate uterus 654.0 ☑
    - causing obstructed labor 660.2 ☑
  - birth injury to mother NEC 665.9 ☑
  - bleeding (*see also* Delivery, complicated, hemorrhage) 641.9 ☑
  - breech presentation (assisted) (buttocks) (complete) (frank) (spontaneous) 652.2 ☑
    - with successful version 652.1 ☑
  - brow presentation 652.4 ☑
  - cephalopelvic disproportion (normally formed fetus) 653.4 ☑
    - causing obstructed labor 660.1 ☑
  - cerebral hemorrhage 674.0 ☑
  - cervical dystocia 661.2 ☑
  - chin presentation 652.4 ☑
    - causing obstructed labor 660.0 ☑
  - cicatrix
    - cervix 654.6 ☑
      - causing obstructed labor 660.2 ☑
    - vagina 654.7 ☑
      - causing obstructed labor 660.2 ☑
  - coagulation defect 649.3 ☑
  - colporrhexis 665.4 ☑
    - with perineal laceration 664.0 ☑
  - compound presentation 652.8 ☑
    - causing obstructed labor 660.0 ☑
  - compression of cord (umbilical) 663.2 ☑
    - around neck 663.1 ☑
    - cord prolapsed 663.0 ☑
  - contraction, contracted pelvis 653.1 ☑
    - causing obstructed labor 660.1 ☑
    - general 653.1 ☑
      - causing obstructed labor 660.1 ☑
    - inlet 653.2 ☑
      - causing obstructed labor 660.1 ☑
    - midpelvic 653.8 ☑
      - causing obstructed labor 660.1 ☑
    - midplane 653.8 ☑
      - causing obstructed labor 660.1 ☑
    - outlet 653.3 ☑
      - causing obstructed labor 660.1 ☑
  - contraction ring 661.4 ☑
  - cord (umbilical) 663.9 ☑
    - around neck, tightly or with compression 663.1 ☑
      - without compression 663.3 ☑
    - bruising 663.6 ☑
    - complication NEC 663.9 ☑
      - specified type NEC 663.8 ☑
    - compression NEC 663.2 ☑
    - entanglement NEC 663.3 ☑
      - with compression 663.2 ☑
    - forelying 663.0 ☑

- **Delivery** — *continued*
  - complicated — *continued*
    - tumor
      - abdominal, fetal 653.7 ☑
        - causing obstructed labor 660.1 ☑
      - pelvic organs or tissues NEC 654.9 ☑
        - causing obstructed labor 660.2 ☑
    - umbilical cord (*see also* Delivery, complicated, cord) 663.9 ☑
      - around neck tightly, or with compression 663.1 ☑
      - entanglement NEC 663.3 ☑
        - with compression 663.2 ☑
      - prolapse (complete) (occult) (partial) 663.0 ☑
    - unstable lie 652.0 ☑
      - causing obstructed labor 660.0 ☑
    - uterine
      - inertia (*see also* Delivery, complicated, inertia, uterus) 661.2 ☑
      - spasm 661.4 ☑
    - vasa previa 663.5 ☑
    - velamentous insertion of cord 663.8 ☑
    - young maternal age 659.8 ☑
  - delayed NEC 662.1 ☑
    - following rupture of membranes (spontaneous) 658.2 ☑
      - artificial 658.3 ☑
    - second twin, triplet, etc. 662.3 ☑
  - difficult NEC 669.9 ☑
    - previous, affecting management of pregnancy or childbirth V23.49
    - specified type NEC 669.8 ☑
  - early onset (spontaneous) 644.2 ☑
  - footling 652.8 ☑
    - with successful version 652.1 ☑
  - forceps NEC 669.5 ☑
    - affecting fetus or newborn 763.2
  - missed (at or near term) 656.4 ☑
  - multiple gestation NEC 651.9 ☑
    - with fetal loss and retention of one or more fetus(es) 651.6 ☑
    - following (elective) fetal reduction 651.7 ☑
    - specified type NEC 651.8 ☑
      - with fetal loss and retention of one or more fetus(es) 651.6 ☑
      - following (elective) fetal reduction 651.7 ☑
  - nonviable infant 656.4 ☑
  - normal — *see* category 650
  - precipitate 661.3 ☑
    - affecting fetus or newborn 763.6
  - premature NEC (before 37 completed weeks gestation) 644.2 ☑
    - previous, affecting management of pregnancy V23.41
  - quadruplet NEC 651.2 ☑
    - with fetal loss and retention of one or more fetus(es) 651.5 ☑
    - following (elective) fetal reduction 651.7 ☑
  - quintuplet NEC 651.8 ☑
    - with fetal loss and retention of one or more fetus(es) 651.6 ☑
    - following (elective) fetal reduction 651.7 ☑
  - sextuplet NEC 651.8 ☑
    - with fetal loss and retention of one or more fetus(es) 651.6 ☑
    - following (elective) fetal reduction 651.7 ☑
  - specified complication NEC 669.8 ☑
  - stillbirth (near term) NEC 656.4 ☑
    - early (before 22 completed weeks gestation) 632

- **Delivery** — *continued*
  - term pregnancy (live birth) NEC — *see* category 650
    - stillbirth NEC 656.4 ☑
  - threatened premature 644.2 ☑
  - triplets NEC 651.1 ☑
    - with fetal loss and retention of one or more fetus(es) 651.4 ☑
    - delayed delivery (one or more mates) 662.3 ☑
    - following (elective) fetal reduction 651.7 ☑
    - locked mates 660.5 ☑
  - twins NEC 651.0 ☑
    - with fetal loss and retention of one fetus 651.3 ☑
    - delayed delivery (one or more mates) 662.3 ☑
    - locked mates 660.5 ☑
  - uncomplicated — *see* category 650
  - vacuum extractor NEC 669.5 ☑
    - affecting fetus or newborn 763.3
  - ventouse NEC 669.5 ☑
    - affecting fetus or newborn 763.3
- **Dellen, cornea** 371.41
- **Delusions** (paranoid) 297.9
  - grandiose 297.1
  - parasitosis 300.29
  - systematized 297.1
- **Dementia** 294.8
  - alcohol-induced persisting (*see also* Psychosis, alcoholic) 291.2
  - Alzheimer's — *see* Alzheimer's, dementia
  - arteriosclerotic (simple type) (uncomplicated) 290.40
    - with
      - acute confusional state 290.41
      - delirium 290.41
      - delusions 290.42
      - depressed mood 290.43
    - depressed type 290.43
    - paranoid type 290.42
  - Binswanger's 290.12
  - catatonic (acute) (*see also* Schizophrenia) 295.2 ☑
  - congenital (*see also* Retardation, mental) 319
  - degenerative 290.9
    - presenile-onset — *see* Dementia, presenile
    - senile-onset — *see* Dementia, senile
  - developmental (*see also* Schizophrenia) 295.9 ☑
  - dialysis 294.8
    - transient 293.9
  - drug-induced persisting (*see also* Psychosis, drug) 292.82
  - due to or associated with condition(s) classified elsewhere
    - Alzheimer's
      - with behavioral disturbance 331.0 *[294.11]*
      - without behavioral disturbance 331.0 *[294.10]*
    - cerebral lipidoses
      - with behavioral disturbance 330.1 *[294.11]*
      - without behavioral disturbance 330.1 *[294.10]*
    - epilepsy
      - with behavioral disturbance 345.9 ☑ *[294.11]*
      - without behavioral disturbance 345.9 ☑ *[294.10]*
    - hepatolenticular degeneration
      - with behavioral disturbance 275.1 *[294.11]*
      - without behavioral disturbance 275.1 *[294.10]*
    - HIV
      - with behavioral disturbance 042 *[294.11]*
      - without behavioral disturbance 042 *[294.10]*

- **Dementia** — *continued*
  - due to or associated with condition(s) classified elsewhere — *continued*
    - Huntington's chorea
      - with behavioral disturbance 333.4 *[294.11]*
      - without behavioral disturbance 333.4 *[294.10]*
    - Jakob-Creutzfeldt disease (CJD)
      - with behavioral disturbance 046.19 *[294.11]*
      - without behavioral disturbance 046.19 *[294.10]*
      - variant (vCJD) 046.11
        - with dementia
          - with behavioral disturbance 046.11 *[294.11]*
          - without behavioral disburbance 046.11 *[294.10]*
    - Lewy bodies
      - with behavioral disturbance 331.82 *[294.11]*
      - without behavioral disturbance 331.82 *[294.10]*
    - multiple sclerosis
      - with behavioral disturbance 340 *[294.11]*
      - without behavioral disturbance 340 *[294.10]*
    - neurosyphilis
      - with behavioral disturbance 094.9 *[294.11]*
      - without behavioral disturbance 094.9 *[294.10]*
    - Parkinsonism
      - with behavioral disturbance 331.82 *[294.11]*
      - without behavioral disturbance 331.82 *[294.10]*
    - Pelizaeus-Merzbacher disease
      - with behavioral disturbance 333.0 *[294.11]*
      - without behavioral disturbance 333.0 *[294.10]*
    - Pick's disease
      - with behavioral disturbance 331.11 *[294.11]*
      - without behavioral disturbance 331.11 *[294.10]*
    - polyarteritis nodosa
      - with behavioral disturbance 446.0 *[294.11]*
      - without behavioral disturbance 446.0 *[294.10]*
    - syphilis
      - with behavioral disturbance 094.1 *[294.11]*
      - without behavioral disturbance 094.1 *[294.10]*
    - Wilson's disease
      - with behavioral disturbance 275.1 *[294.11]*
      - without behavioral disturbance 275.1 *[294.10]*
  - frontal 331.19
    - with behavioral disturbance 331.19 *[294.11]*
    - without behavioral disturbance 331.19 *[294.10]*
  - frontotemporal 331.19
    - with behavioral disturbance 331.19 *[294.11]*
    - without behavioral disturbance 331.19 *[294.10]*
  - hebephrenic (acute) 295.1 ☑
  - Heller's (infantile psychosis) (*see also* Psychosis, childhood) 299.1 ☑
  - idiopathic 290.9
    - presenile-onset — *see* Dementia, presenile
    - senile-onset — *see* Dementia, senile

- **Dementia** — *continued*
  - in
    - arteriosclerotic brain disease 290.40
    - senility 290.0
  - induced by drug 292.82
  - infantile, infantilia (*see also* Psychosis, childhood) 299.0 ☑
  - Lewy body 331.82
    - with behavioral disturbance 331.82 *[294.11]*
    - without behavioral disturbance 331.82 *[294.10]*
  - multi-infarct (cerebrovascular) (*see also* Dementia, arteriosclerotic) 290.40
  - old age 290.0
  - paralytica, paralytic 094.1
    - juvenilis 090.40
    - syphilitic 094.1
      - congenital 090.40
    - tabetic form 094.1
  - paranoid (*see also* Schizophrenia) 295.3 ☑
  - paraphrenic (*see also* Schizophrenia) 295.3 ☑
  - paretic 094.1
  - praecox (*see also* Schizophrenia) 295.9 ☑
  - presenile 290.10
    - with
      - acute confusional state 290.11
      - delirium 290.11
      - delusional features 290.12
      - depressive features 290.13
    - depressed type 290.13
    - paranoid type 290.12
    - simple type 290.10
    - uncomplicated 290.10
  - primary (acute) (*see also* Schizophrenia) 295.0 ☑
  - progressive, syphilitic 094.1
  - puerperal — *see* Psychosis, puerperal
  - schizophrenic (*see also* Schizophrenia) 295.9 ☑
  - senile 290.0
    - with
      - acute confusional state 290.3
      - delirium 290.3
      - delusional features 290.20
      - depressive features 290.21
    - depressed type 290.21
    - exhaustion 290.0
    - paranoid type 290.20
  - simple type (acute) (*see also* Schizophrenia) 295.0 ☑
  - simplex (acute) (*see also* Schizophrenia) 295.0 ☑
  - syphilitic 094.1
  - uremic — *see* Uremia
  - vascular 290.40
    - with
      - delirium 290.41
      - delusions 290.42
      - depressed mood 290.43
- **Demerol dependence** — *see also* Dependence 304.0 ☑
- **Demineralization, ankle** — *see also* Osteoporosis 733.00
- **Demodex folliculorum** (infestation) 133.8
- **de Morgan's spots** (senile angiomas) 448.1
- **Demyelinating**
  - polyneuritis, chronic inflammatory 357.81
- **Demyelination, demyelinization**
  - central nervous system 341.9
    - specified NEC 341.8
  - corpus callosum (central) 341.8
  - global 340
- **Dengue** (fever) 061
  - sandfly 061
  - vaccination, prophylactic (against) V05.1
  - virus hemorrhagic fever 065.4

Dens
  evaginatus 520.2
  in dente 520.2
  invaginatus 520.2
Dense
  breast(s) — *omit code*
Density
  increased, bone (disseminated) (generalized) (spotted) 733.99
  lung (nodular) 518.89
Dental — *see also* condition
  examination only V72.2
Dentia praecox 520.6
Denticles (in pulp) 522.2
Dentigerous cyst 526.0
Dentin
  irregular (in pulp) 522.3
  opalescent 520.5
  secondary (in pulp) 522.3
  sensitive 521.89
Dentinogenesis imperfecta 520.5
Dentinoma (M9271/0) 213.1
  upper jaw (bone) 213.0
Dentition 520.7
  abnormal 520.6
  anomaly 520.6
  delayed 520.6
  difficult 520.7
  disorder of 520.6
  precocious 520.6
  retarded 520.6
Denture sore (mouth) 528.9
Dependence

Note — Use the following fifth-digit subclassification with category 304:
0 unspecified
1 continuous
2 episodic
3 in remission

  with
    withdrawal symptoms
      alcohol 291.81
      drug 292.0
  14-hydroxy-dihydromorphinone 304.0 ☑
  absinthe 304.6 ☑
  acemorphan 304.0 ☑
  acetanilid(e) 304.6 ☑
  acetophenetidin 304.6 ☑
  acetorphine 304.0 ☑
  acetyldihydrocodeine 304.0 ☑
  acetyldihydrocodeinone 304.0 ☑
  Adalin 304.1 ☑
  Afghanistan black 304.3 ☑
  agrypnal 304.1 ☑
  alcohol, alcoholic (ethyl) (methyl) (wood) 303.9 ☑
    maternal, with suspected fetal damage affecting management of pregnancy 655.4 ☑
  allobarbitone 304.1 ☑
  allonal 304.1 ☑
  allylisopropylacetylurea 304.1 ☑
  alphaprodine (hydrochloride) 304.0 ☑
  Alurate 304.1 ☑
  Alvodine 304.0 ☑
  amethocaine 304.6 ☑
  amidone 304.0 ☑
  amidopyrine 304.6 ☑
  aminopyrine 304.6 ☑
  amobarbital 304.1 ☑
  amphetamine(s) (type) (drugs classifiable to 969.7) 304.4 ☑
  amylene hydrate 304.6 ☑
  amylobarbitone 304.1 ☑
  amylocaine 304.6 ☑
  Amytal (sodium) 304.1 ☑
  analgesic (drug) NEC 304.6 ☑
    synthetic with morphine-like effect 304.0 ☑
  anesthetic (agent) (drug) (gas) (general) (local) NEC 304.6 ☑
  Angel dust 304.6 ☑

Dependence — *continued*
  anileridine 304.0 ☑
  antipyrine 304.6 ☑
  anxiolytic 304.1 ☑
  aprobarbital 304.1 ☑
  aprobarbitone 304.1 ☑
  atropine 304.6 ☑
  Avertin (bromide) 304.6 ☑
  barbenyl 304.1 ☑
  barbital(s) 304.1 ☑
  barbitone 304.1 ☑
  barbiturate(s) (compounds) (drugs classifiable to 967.0) 304.1 ☑
  barbituric acid (and compounds) 304.1 ☑
  benzedrine 304.4 ☑
  benzylmorphine 304.0 ☑
  Beta-chlor 304.1 ☑
  bhang 304.3 ☑
  blue velvet 304.0 ☑
  Brevital 304.1 ☑
  bromal (hydrate) 304.1 ☑
  bromide(s) NEC 304.1 ☑
  bromine compounds NEC 304.1 ☑
  bromisovalum 304.1 ☑
  bromoform 304.1 ☑
  Bromo-seltzer 304.1 ☑
  bromural 304.1 ☑
  butabarbital (sodium) 304.1 ☑
  butabarpal 304.1 ☑
  butallylonal 304.1 ☑
  butethal 304.1 ☑
  buthalitone (sodium) 304.1 ☑
  Butisol 304.1 ☑
  butobarbitone 304.1 ☑
  butyl chloral (hydrate) 304.1 ☑
  caffeine 304.4 ☑
  cannabis (indica) (sativa) (resin) (derivatives) (type) 304.3 ☑
  carbamazepine 304.6 ☑
  Carbrital 304.1 ☑
  carbromal 304.1 ☑
  carisoprodol 304.6 ☑
  Catha (edulis) 304.4 ☑
  chloral (betaine) (hydrate) 304.1 ☑
  chloralamide 304.1 ☑
  chloralformamide 304.1 ☑
  chloralose 304.1 ☑
  chlordiazepoxide 304.1 ☑
  Chloretone 304.1 ☑
  chlorobutanol 304.1 ☑
  chlorodyne 304.1 ☑
  chloroform 304.6 ☑
  Cliradon 304.0 ☑
  coca (leaf) and derivatives 304.2 ☑
  cocaine 304.2 ☑
    hydrochloride 304.2 ☑
    salt (any) 304.2 ☑
  codeine 304.0 ☑
  combination of drugs (excluding morphine or opioid type drug) NEC 304.8 ☑
    morphine or opioid type drug with any other drug 304.7 ☑
  croton-chloral 304.1 ☑
  cyclobarbital 304.1 ☑
  cyclobarbitone 304.1 ☑
  dagga 304.3 ☑
  Delvinal 304.1 ☑
  Demerol 304.0 ☑
  desocodeine 304.0 ☑
  desomorphine 304.0 ☑
  desoxyephedrine 304.4 ☑
  DET 304.5 ☑
  dexamphetamine 304.4 ☑
  dexedrine 304.4 ☑
  dextromethorphan 304.0 ☑
  dextromoramide 304.0 ☑
  dextronorpseudoephedrine 304.4 ☑
  dextrorphan 304.0 ☑
  diacetylmorphine 304.0 ☑
  Dial 304.1 ☑
  diallylbarbituric acid 304.1 ☑
  diamorphine 304.0 ☑

Dependence — *continued*
  diazepam 304.1 ☑
  dibucaine 304.6 ☑
  dichloroethane 304.6 ☑
  diethyl barbituric acid 304.1 ☑
  diethylsulfone-diethylmethane 304.1 ☑
  difencloxazine 304.0 ☑
  dihydrocodeine 304.0 ☑
  dihydrocodeinone 304.0 ☑
  dihydrohydroxycodeinone 304.0 ☑
  dihydroisocodeine 304.0 ☑
  dihydromorphine 304.0 ☑
  dihydromorphinone 304.0 ☑
  dihydroxcodeinone 304.0 ☑
  Dilaudid 304.0 ☑
  dimenhydrinate 304.6 ☑
  dimethylmeperidine 304.0 ☑
  dimethyltriptamine 304.5 ☑
  Dionin 304.0 ☑
  diphenoxylate 304.6 ☑
  dipipanone 304.0 ☑
  d-lysergic acid diethylamide 304.5 ☑
  DMT 304.5 ☑
  Dolophine 304.0 ☑
  DOM 304.2 ☑
  Doriden 304.1 ☑
  dormiral 304.1 ☑
  Dormison 304.1 ☑
  Dromoran 304.0 ☑
  drug NEC 304.9 ☑
    analgesic NEC 304.6 ☑
    combination (excluding morphine or opioid type drug) NEC 304.8 ☑
      morphine or opioid type drug with any other drug 304.7 ☑
    complicating pregnancy, childbirth, or puerperium 648.3 ☑
      affecting fetus or newborn 779.5
    hallucinogenic 304.5 ☑
    hypnotic NEC 304.1 ☑
    narcotic NEC 304.9 ☑
    psychostimulant NEC 304.4 ☑
    sedative 304.1 ☑
    soporific NEC 304.1 ☑
    specified type NEC 304.6 ☑
    suspected damage to fetus affecting management of pregnancy 655.5 ☑
    synthetic, with morphine-like effect 304.0 ☑
    tranquilizing 304.1 ☑
  duboisine 304.6 ☑
  ectylurea 304.1 ☑
  Endocaine 304.6 ☑
  Equanil 304.1 ☑
  Eskabarb 304.1 ☑
  ethchlorvynol 304.1 ☑
  ether (ethyl) (liquid) (vapor) (vinyl) 304.6 ☑
  ethidene 304.6 ☑
  ethinamate 304.1 ☑
  ethoheptazine 304.6 ☑
  ethyl
    alcohol 303.9 ☑
    bromide 304.6 ☑
    carbamate 304.6 ☑
    chloride 304.6 ☑
    morphine 304.0 ☑
  ethylene (gas) 304.6 ☑
    dichloride 304.6 ☑
  ethylidene chloride 304.6 ☑
  etilfen 304.1 ☑
  etorphine 304.0 ☑
  etoval 304.1 ☑
  eucodal 304.0 ☑
  euneryl 304.1 ☑
  Evipal 304.1 ☑
  Evipan 304.1 ☑
  fentanyl 304.0 ☑
  ganja 304.3 ☑
  gardenal 304.1 ☑

Dependence — *continued*
  gardenpanyl 304.1 ☑
  gelsemine 304.6 ☑
  Gelsemium 304.6 ☑
  Gemonil 304.1 ☑
  glucochloral 304.1 ☑
  glue (airplane) (sniffing) 304.6 ☑
  glutethimide 304.1 ☑
  hallucinogenics 304.5 ☑
  hashish 304.3 ☑
  headache powder NEC 304.6 ☑
  Heavenly Blue 304.5 ☑
  hedonal 304.1 ☑
  hemp 304.3 ☑
  heptabarbital 304.1 ☑
  Heptalgin 304.0 ☑
  heptobarbitone 304.1 ☑
  heroin 304.0 ☑
    salt (any) 304.0 ☑
  hexethal (sodium) 304.1 ☑
  hexobarbital 304.1 ☑
  Hycodan 304.0 ☑
  hydrocodone 304.0 ☑
  hydromorphinol 304.0 ☑
  hydromorphinone 304.0 ☑
  hydromorphone 304.0 ☑
  hydroxycodeine 304.0 ☑
  hypnotic NEC 304.1 ☑
  Indian hemp 304.3 ☑
  inhalant 304.6 ☑
  intranarcon 304.1 ☑
  Kemithal 304.1 ☑
  ketobemidone 304.0 ☑
  khat 304.4 ☑
  kif 304.3 ☑
  Lactuca (virosa) extract 304.1 ☑
  lactucarium 304.1 ☑
  laudanum 304.0 ☑
  Lebanese red 304.3 ☑
  Leritine 304.0 ☑
  lettuce opium 304.1 ☑
  Levanil 304.1 ☑
  Levo-Dromoran 304.0 ☑
  levo-iso-methadone 304.0 ☑
  levorphanol 304.0 ☑
  Librium 304.1 ☑
  Lomotil 304.6 ☑
  Lotusate 304.1 ☑
  LSD (-25) (and derivatives) 304.5 ☑
  Luminal 304.1 ☑
  lysergic acid 304.5 ☑
    amide 304.5 ☑
  maconha 304.3 ☑
  magic mushroom 304.5 ☑
  marihuana 304.3 ☑
  MDA (methylene dioxyamphetamine) 304.4 ☑
  Mebaral 304.1 ☑
  Medinal 304.1 ☑
  Medomin 304.1 ☑
  megahallucinogenics 304.5 ☑
  meperidine 304.0 ☑
  mephobarbital 304.1 ☑
  meprobamate 304.1 ☑
  mescaline 304.5 ☑
  methadone 304.0 ☑
  methamphetamine(s) 304.4 ☑
  methaqualone 304.1 ☑
  metharbital 304.1 ☑
  methitural 304.1 ☑
  methobarbitone 304.1 ☑
  methohexital 304.1 ☑
  methopholine 304.6 ☑
  methyl
    alcohol 303.9 ☑
    bromide 304.6 ☑
    morphine 304.0 ☑
    sulfonal 304.1 ☑
  methylaparafynol 304.1 ☑
  methylated spirit 303.9 ☑
  methylbutinol 304.6 ☑
  methyldihydromorphinone 304.0 ☑
  methylene
    chloride 304.6 ☑

Index
Dens — Dependence

Deprivation — *continued*
- emotional — *continued*
  - affecting
    - adult 995.82
    - infant or child 995.51
- food 994.2
  - specific substance NEC 269.8
- protein (familial) (kwashiorkor) 260
- sleep V69.4
- social V62.4
  - affecting
    - adult 995.82
    - infant or child 995.51
- symptoms, syndrome
  - alcohol 291.81
  - drug 292.0
- vitamins (*see also* Deficiency, vitamin) 269.2
- water 994.3

de Quervain's
- disease (tendon sheath) 727.04
- syndrome 259.51
- thyroiditis (subacute granulomatous thyroiditis) 245.1

Derangement
- ankle (internal) 718.97
  - current injury (*see also* Dislocation, ankle) 837.0
  - recurrent 718.37
- cartilage (articular) NEC (*see also* Disorder, cartilage, articular) 718.0 ☑
  - knee 717.9
    - recurrent 718.36
  - recurrent 718.3 ☑
- collateral ligament (knee) (medial) (tibial) 717.82
  - current injury 844.1
    - lateral (fibular) 844.0
  - lateral (fibular) 717.81
    - current injury 844.0
- cruciate ligament (knee) (posterior) 717.84
  - anterior 717.83
    - current injury 844.2
  - current injury 844.2
- elbow (internal) 718.92
  - current injury (*see also* Dislocation, elbow) 832.00
  - recurrent 718.32
- gastrointestinal 536.9
- heart — *see* Disease, heart
- hip (joint) (internal) (old) 718.95
  - current injury (*see also* Dislocation, hip) 835.00
  - recurrent 718.35
- intervertebral disc — *see* Displacement, intervertebral disc
- joint (internal) 718.90
  - ankle 718.97
  - current injury (*see also* Dislocation, by site)
    - knee, meniscus or cartilage (*see also* Tear, meniscus) 836.2
  - elbow 718.92
  - foot 718.97
  - hand 718.94
  - hip 718.95
  - knee 717.9
  - multiple sites 718.99
  - pelvic region 718.95
  - recurrent 718.30
    - ankle 718.37
    - elbow 718.32
    - foot 718.37
    - hand 718.34
    - hip 718.35
    - knee 718.36
    - multiple sites 718.39
    - pelvic region 718.35
    - shoulder (region) 718.31
    - specified site NEC 718.38
    - temporomandibular (old) 524.69
    - wrist 718.33
  - shoulder (region) 718.91

Derangement — *continued*
- joint — *continued*
  - specified site NEC 718.98
  - spine NEC 724.9
  - temporomandibular 524.69
  - wrist 718.93
- knee (cartilage) (internal) 717.9
  - current injury (*see also* Tear, meniscus) 836.2
  - ligament 717.89
    - capsular 717.85
    - collateral — *see* Derangement, collateral ligament
    - cruciate — *see* Derangement, cruciate ligament
    - specified NEC 717.85
  - recurrent 718.36
- low back NEC 724.9
- meniscus NEC (knee) 717.5
  - current injury (*see also* Tear, meniscus) 836.2
  - lateral 717.40
    - anterior horn 717.42
    - posterior horn 717.43
    - specified NEC 717.49
  - medial 717.3
    - anterior horn 717.1
    - posterior horn 717.2
  - recurrent 718.3 ☑
  - site other than knee — *see* Disorder, cartilage, articular
- mental (*see also* Psychosis) 298.9
- rotator cuff (recurrent) (tear) 726.10
  - current 840.4
- sacroiliac (old) 724.6
  - current — *see* Dislocation, sacroiliac
- semilunar cartilage (knee) 717.5
  - current injury 836.2
    - lateral 836.1
    - medial 836.0
  - recurrent 718.3 ☑
- shoulder (internal) 718.91
  - current injury (*see also* Dislocation, shoulder) 831.00
  - recurrent 718.31
- spine (recurrent) NEC 724.9
  - current — *see* Dislocation, spine
- temporomandibular (internal) (joint) (old) 524.69
  - current — *see* Dislocation, jaw

Dercum's disease or syndrome (adiposis dolorosa) 272.8

Derealization (neurotic) 300.6

Dermal — *see* condition

Dermaphytid — *see* Dermatophytosis

Dermatergosis — *see* Dermatitis

Dermatitis (allergic) (contact) (occupational) (venenata) 692.9
- ab igne 692.82
- acneiform 692.9
- actinic (due to sun) 692.70
  - acute 692.72
  - chronic NEC 692.74
  - other than from sun NEC 692.82
- ambustionis
  - due to
    - burn or scald — *see* Burn, by site
    - sunburn (*see also* Sunburn) 692.71
- amebic 006.6
- ammonia 691.0
- anaphylactoid NEC 692.9
- arsenical 692.4
- artefacta 698.4
  - psychogenic 316 *[698.4]*
- asthmatic 691.8
- atopic (allergic) (intrinsic) 691.8
  - psychogenic 316 *[691.8]*
- atrophicans 701.8
  - diffusa 701.8
  - maculosa 701.3
- berlock, berloque 692.72
- blastomycetic 116.0
- blister beetle 692.89

Dermatitis — *continued*
- Brucella NEC 023.9
- bullosa 694.9
  - striata pratensis 692.6
- bullous 694.9
  - mucosynechial, atrophic 694.60
    - with ocular involvement 694.61
  - seasonal 694.8
- calorica
  - due to
    - burn or scald — *see* Burn, by site
    - cold 692.89
    - sunburn (*see also* Sunburn) 692.71
- caterpillar 692.89
- cercarial 120.3
- combustionis
  - due to
    - burn or scald — *see* Burn, by site
    - sunburn (*see also* Sunburn) 692.71
- congelationis 991.5
- contusiformis 695.2
- diabetic 250.8 ☑
- diaper 691.0
- diphtheritica 032.85
- due to
  - acetone 692.2
  - acids 692.4
  - adhesive plaster 692.4
  - alcohol (skin contact) (substances classifiable to 980.0–980.9) 692.4
    - taken internally 693.8
  - alkalis 692.4
  - allergy NEC 692.9
  - ammonia (household) (liquid) 692.4
  - animal
    - dander (cat) (dog) 692.84
    - hair (cat) (dog) 692.84
  - arnica 692.3
  - arsenic 692.4
    - taken internally 693.8
  - blister beetle 692.89
  - cantharides 692.3
  - carbon disulphide 692.2
  - caterpillar 692.89
  - caustics 692.4
  - cereal (ingested) 693.1
    - contact with skin 692.5
  - chemical(s) NEC 692.4
    - internal 693.8
    - irritant NEC 692.4
    - taken internally 693.8
  - chlorocompounds 692.2
  - coffee (ingested) 693.1
    - contact with skin 692.5
  - cold weather 692.89
  - cosmetics 692.81
  - cyclohexanes 692.2
  - dander, animal (cat) (dog) 692.84
  - deodorant 692.81
  - detergents 692.0
  - dichromate 692.4
  - drugs and medicinals (correct substance properly administered) (internal use) 693.0
    - external (in contact with skin) 692.3
      - wrong substance given or taken 976.9
        - specified substance — *see* Table of Drugs and Chemicals
    - wrong substance given or taken 977.9
      - specified substance — *see* Table of Drugs and Chemicals
  - dyes 692.89
    - hair 692.89
  - epidermophytosis — *see* Dermatophytosis
  - esters 692.2

Dermatitis — *continued*
- due to — *continued*
  - external irritant NEC 692.9
    - specified agent NEC 692.89
  - eye shadow 692.81
  - fish (ingested) 693.1
    - contact with skin 692.5
  - flour (ingested) 693.1
    - contact with skin 692.5
  - food (ingested) 693.1
    - in contact with skin 692.5
  - fruit (ingested) 693.1
    - contact with skin 692.5
  - fungicides 692.3
  - furs 692.84
  - glycols 692.2
  - greases NEC 692.1
  - hair, animal (cat) (dog) 692.84
  - hair dyes 692.89
  - hot
    - objects and materials — *see* Burn, by site
    - weather or places 692.89
  - hydrocarbons 692.2
  - infrared rays, except from sun 692.82
    - solar NEC (*see also* Dermatitis, due to, sun) 692.70
  - ingested substance 693.9
    - drugs and medicinals (*see also* Dermatitis, due to, drugs and medicinals) 693.0
    - food 693.1
    - specified substance NEC 693.8
  - ingestion or injection of chemical 693.8
    - drug (correct substance properly administered) 693.0
    - wrong substance given or taken 977.9
      - specified substance — *see* Table of Drugs and Chemicals
  - insecticides 692.4
  - internal agent 693.9
    - drugs and medicinals (*see also* Dermatitis, due to, drugs and medicinals) 693.0
    - food (ingested) 693.1
      - in contact with skin 692.5
    - specified agent NEC 693.8
  - iodine 692.3
  - iodoform 692.3
  - irradiation 692.82
  - jewelry 692.83
  - keratolytics 692.3
  - ketones 692.2
  - lacquer tree (Rhus verniciflua) 692.6
  - light (sun) NEC (*see also* Dermatitis, due to, sun) 692.70
    - other 692.82
  - low temperature 692.89
  - mascara 692.81
  - meat (ingested) 693.1
    - contact with skin 692.5
  - mercury, mercurials 692.3
  - metals 692.83
  - milk (ingested) 693.1
    - contact with skin 692.5
  - Neomycin 692.3
  - nylon 692.4
  - oils NEC 692.1
  - paint solvent 692.2
  - pediculocides 692.3
  - petroleum products (substances classifiable to 981) 692.4
  - phenol 692.3
  - photosensitiveness, photosensitivity (sun) 692.72
    - other light 692.82
  - plants NEC 692.6
  - plasters, medicated (any) 692.3
  - plastic 692.4
  - poison
    - ivy (Rhus toxicodendron) 692.6

Destruction — *continued*
rectal sphincter 569.49
septum (nasal) 478.19
tuberculous NEC (*see also* Tuberculosis) 011.9 ☑
tympanic membrane 384.82
tympanum 385.89
vertebral disc — *see* Degeneration, intervertebral disc
Destructiveness — *see also* Disturbance, conduct 312.9
adjustment reaction 309.3
Detachment
cartilage (*see also* Sprain, by site)
knee — *see* Tear, meniscus
cervix, annular 622.8
complicating delivery 665.3 ☑
choroid (old) (postinfectional) (simple) (spontaneous) 363.70
hemorrhagic 363.72
serous 363.71
knee, medial meniscus (old) 717.3
current injury 836.0
ligament — *see* Sprain, by site
placenta (premature) — *see* Placenta, separation
retina (recent) 361.9
with retinal defect (rhegmatogenous) 361.00
giant tear 361.03
multiple 361.02
partial
with
giant tear 361.03
multiple defects 361.02
retinal dialysis (juvenile) 361.04
single defect 361.01
retinal dialysis (juvenile) 361.04
single 361.01
subtotal 361.05
total 361.05
delimited (old) (partial) 361.06
old
delimited 361.06
partial 361.06
total or subtotal 361.07
pigment epithelium (RPE) (serous) 362.42
exudative 362.42
hemorrhagic 362.43
rhegmatogenous (*see also* Detachment, retina, with retinal defect) 361.00
serous (without retinal defect) 361.2
specified type NEC 361.89
traction (with vitreoretinal organization) 361.81
vitreous humor 379.21
Detergent asthma 507.8
Deterioration
epileptic
with behavioral disturbance 345.9 ☑ *[294.11]*
without behavioral disturbance 345.9 ☑ *[294.10]*
heart, cardiac (*see also* Degeneration, myocardial) 429.1
mental (*see also* Psychosis) 298.9
myocardium, myocardial (*see also* Degeneration, myocardial) 429.1
senile (simple) 797
transplanted organ — *see* Complications, transplant, organ, by site
de Toni-Fanconi syndrome (cystinosis) 270.0
Deuteranomaly 368.52
Deuteranopia (anomalous trichromat) (complete) (incomplete) 368.52
Deutschländer's disease — *see* Fracture, foot
Development
abnormal, bone 756.9
arrested 783.40
bone 733.91

Development — *continued*
arrested — *continued*
child 783.40
due to malnutrition (protein-calorie) 263.2
fetus or newborn 764.9 ☑
tracheal rings (congenital) 748.3
defective, congenital (*see also* Anomaly)
cauda equina 742.59
left ventricle 746.9
with atresia or hypoplasia of aortic orifice or valve with hypoplasia of ascending aorta 746.7
in hypoplastic left heart syndrome 746.7
delayed (*see also* Delay, development) 783.40
arithmetical skills 315.1
language (skills) 315.31
and speech due to hearing loss 315.34
expressive 315.31
mixed receptive-expressive 315.32
learning skill, specified NEC 315.2
mixed skills 315.5
motor coordination 315.4
reading 315.00
specified
learning skill NEC 315.2
type NEC, except learning 315.8
speech 315.39
and language due to hearing loss 315.34
associated with hyperkinesia 314.1
phonological 315.39
spelling 315.09
written expression 315.2
imperfect, congenital (*see also* Anomaly)
heart 746.9
lungs 748.60
improper (fetus or newborn) 764.9 ☑
incomplete (fetus or newborn) 764.9 ☑
affecting management of pregnancy 656.5 ☑
bronchial tree 748.3
organ or site not listed — *see* Hypoplasia
respiratory system 748.9
sexual, precocious NEC 259.1
tardy, mental (*see also* Retardation, mental) 319
Developmental — *see* condition
Devergie's disease (pityriasis rubra pilaris) 696.4
Deviation
conjugate (eye) 378.87
palsy 378.81
spasm, spastic 378.82
esophagus 530.89
eye, skew 378.87
mandible, opening and closing 524.53
midline (jaw) (teeth) 524.29
specified site NEC — *see* Malposition
occlusal plane 524.76
organ or site, congenital NEC — *see* Malposition, congenital
septum (acquired) (nasal) 470
congenital 754.0
sexual 302.9
bestiality 302.1
coprophilia 302.89
ego-dystonic
homosexuality 302.0
lesbianism 302.0
erotomania 302.89
Clérambault's 297.8
exhibitionism (sexual) 302.4
fetishism 302.81
transvestic 302.3
frotteurism 302.89

Deviation — *continued*
sexual — *continued*
homosexuality, ego-dystonic 302.0
pedophilic 302.2
lesbianism, ego-dystonic 302.0
masochism 302.83
narcissism 302.89
necrophilia 302.89
nymphomania 302.89
pederosis 302.2
pedophilia 302.2
sadism 302.84
sadomasochism 302.84
satyriasis 302.89
specified type NEC 302.89
transvestic fetishism 302.3
transvestism 302.3
voyeurism 302.82
zoophilia (erotica) 302.1
teeth, midline 524.29
trachea 519.19
ureter (congenital) 753.4
Devic's disease 341.0
Device
cerebral ventricle (communicating) in situ V45.2
contraceptive — *see* Contraceptive, device
drainage, cerebrospinal fluid V45.2
Devil's
grip 074.1
pinches (purpura simplex) 287.2
Devitalized tooth 522.9
Devonshire colic 984.9
specified type of lead — *see* Table of Drugs and Chemicals
Dextraposition, aorta 747.21
with ventricular septal defect, pulmonary stenosis or atresia, and hypertrophy of right ventricle 745.2
in tetralogy of Fallot 745.2
Dextratransposition, aorta 745.11
Dextrinosis, limit (debrancher enzyme deficiency) 271.0
Dextrocardia (corrected) (false) (isolated) (secondary) (true) 746.87
with
complete transposition of viscera 759.3
situs inversus 759.3
Dextroversion, kidney (left) 753.3
Dhobie itch 110.3
Diabetes, diabetic (brittle) (congenital) (familial) (mellitus) (poorly controlled) (severe) (slight) (without complication) 250.0 ☑

Note — Use the following fifth-digit subclassification with category 250:

0 type II or unspecified type, not stated as uncontrolled

Fifth-digit 0 is for use for type II patients, even if the patient requires insulin

1 type I [juvenile type], not stated as uncontrolled

2 type II or unspecified type, uncontrolled

Fifth-digit 2 is for use for type II patients, even if the patient requires insulin

3 type I [juvenile type], uncontrolled

with
coma (with ketoacidosis) 250.3 ☑
due to secondary diabetes 249.3 ☑
hyperosmolar (nonketotic) 250.2 ☑
due to secondary diabetes 249.2 ☑
complication NEC 250.9 ☑

Diabetes, diabetic — *continued*
with — *continued*
complication — *continued*
due to secondary diabetes 249.9 ☑
specified NEC 250.8 ☑
due to secondary diabetes 249.8 ☑
gangrene 250.7 ☑ *[785.4]*
due to secondary diabetes 249.7 ☑ *[785.4]*
hyperglycemia — code to Diabetes, by type, with 5th digit for not stated as uncontrolled
hyperosmolarity 250.2 ☑
due to secondary diabetes 249.2 ☑
ketosis, ketoacidosis 250.1 ☑
due to secondary diabetes 249.1 ☑
osteomyelitis 250.8 ☑ *[731.8]*
due to secondary diabetes 249.8 ☑ *[731.8]*
specified manifestations NEC 250.8 ☑
due to secondary diabetes 249.8 ☑
acetonemia 250.1 ☑
due to secondary diabetes 249.1 ☑
acidosis 250.1 ☑
due to secondary diabetes 249.1 ☑
amyotrophy 250.6 ☑ *[353.5]*
due to secondary diabetes 249.6 ☑ *[353.5]*
angiopathy, peripheral 250.7 ☑ *[443.81]*
due to secondary diabetes 249.7 ☑ *[443.81]*
asymptomatic 790.29
autonomic neuropathy (peripheral) 250.6 ☑ *[337.1]*
due to secondary diabetes 249.6 ☑ *[337.1]*
bone change 250.8 ☑ *[731.8]*
due to secondary diabetes 249.8 ☑ *[731.8]*
bronze, bronzed 275.0
cataract 250.5 ☑ *[366.41]*
due to secondary diabetes 249.5 ☑ *[366.41]*
chemical induced — *see* Diabetes, secondary
complicating pregnancy, childbirth, or puerperium 648.0 ☑
coma (with ketoacidosis) 250.3 ☑
due to secondary diabetes 249.3 ☑
hyperglycemic 250.3 ☑
due to secondary diabetes 249.3 ☑
hyperosmolar (nonketotic) 250.2 ☑
due to secondary diabetes 249.2 ☑
hypoglycemic 250.3 ☑
due to secondary diabetes 249.3 ☑
insulin 250.3 ☑
due to secondary diabetes 249.3 ☑
complicating pregnancy, childbirth, or puerperium (maternal) (conditions classifiable to 249 and 250) 648.0 ☑
affecting fetus or newborn 775.0
complication NEC 250.9 ☑
due to secondary diabetes 249.9 ☑
specified NEC 250.8 ☑
due to secondary diabetes 249.8 ☑
dorsal sclerosis 250.6 ☑ *[340]*
due to secondary diabetes 249.6 ☑ *[340]*
drug-induced — *see also* Diabetes, secondary

Dialysis — *continued*
peritoneal — *continued*
status only V45.11
renal V56.0
status only V45.11
specified type NEC V56.8
Diamond-Blackfan anemia or syndrome (congenital hypoplastic anemia) 284.01
Diamond-Gardener syndrome (autoerythrocyte sensitization) 287.2
Diaper rash 691.0
Diaphoresis (excessive) NEC — *see also* Hyperhidrosis) 780.8
Diaphragm — *see* condition
Diaphragmalgia 786.52
Diaphragmitis 519.4
Diaphyseal aclasis 756.4
Diaphysitis 733.99
Diarrhea, diarrheal (acute) (autumn) (bilious) (bloody) (catarrhal) (choleraic) (chronic) (gravis) (green) (infantile) (lienteric) (noninfectious) (presumed noninfectious) (putrefactive) (secondary) (sporadic) (summer) (symptomatic) (thermic) 787.91
achlorhydric 536.0
allergic 558.3
amebic (*see also* Amebiasis) 006.9
with abscess — *see* Abscess, amebic
acute 006.0
chronic 006.1
nondysenteric 006.2
bacillary — *see* Dysentery, bacillary
bacterial NEC 008.5
balantidial 007.0
bile salt-induced 579.8
cachectic NEC 787.91
chilomastix 007.8
choleriformis 001.1
coccidial 007.2
Cochin-China 579.1
anguilluliasis 127.2
psilosis 579.1
Dientamoeba 007.8
dietetic 787.91
due to
achylia gastrica 536.8
Aerobacter aerogenes 008.2
Bacillus coli — *see* Enteritis, E. coli
bacteria NEC 008.5
bile salts 579.8
Capillaria
hepatica 128.8
philippinensis 127.5
Clostridium perfringens (C) (F) 008.46
Enterobacter aerogenes 008.2
enterococci 008.49
Escherichia coli — *see* Enteritis, E. coli
Giardia lamblia 007.1
Heterophyes heterophyes 121.6
irritating foods 787.91
Metagonimus yokogawai 121.5
Necator americanus 126.1
Paracolobactrum arizonae 008.1
Paracolon bacillus NEC 008.47
Arizona 008.1
Proteus (bacillus) (mirabilis) (Morganii) 008.3
Pseudomonas aeruginosa 008.42
S. japonicum 120.2
specified organism NEC 008.8
bacterial 008.49
viral NEC 008.69
Staphylococcus 008.41
Streptococcus 008.49
anaerobic 008.46
Strongyloides stercoralis 127.2
Trichuris trichiuria 127.3
virus NEC (*see also* Enteritis, viral) 008.69
dysenteric 009.2

Diarrhea, diarrheal — *continued*
dysenteric — *continued*
due to specified organism NEC 008.8
dyspeptic 787.91
endemic 009.3
due to specified organism NEC 008.8
epidemic 009.2
due to specified organism NEC 008.8
fermentative 787.91
flagellate 007.9
Flexner's (ulcerative) 004.1
functional 564.5
following gastrointestinal surgery 564.4
psychogenic 306.4
giardial 007.1
Giardia lamblia 007.1
hill 579.1
hyperperistalsis (nervous) 306.4
infectious 009.2
due to specified organism NEC 008.8
presumed 009.3
inflammatory 787.91
due to specified organism NEC 008.8
malarial (*see also* Malaria) 084.6
mite 133.8
mycotic 117.9
nervous 306.4
neurogenic 564.5
parenteral NEC 009.2
postgastrectomy 564.4
postvagotomy 564.4
prostaglandin induced 579.8
protozoal NEC 007.9
psychogenic 306.4
septic 009.2
due to specified organism NEC 008.8
specified organism NEC 008.8
bacterial 008.49
viral NEC 008.69
Staphylococcus 008.41
Streptococcus 008.49
anaerobic 008.46
toxic 558.2
travelers' 009.2
due to specified organism NEC 008.8
trichomonal 007.3
tropical 579.1
tuberculous 014.8 ☑
ulcerative (chronic) (*see also* Colitis, ulcerative) 556.9
viral (*see also* Enteritis, viral) 008.8
zymotic NEC 009.2
Diastasis
cranial bones 733.99
congenital 756.0
joint (traumatic) — *see* Dislocation, by site
muscle 728.84
congenital 756.89
recti (abdomen) 728.84
complicating delivery 665.8 ☑
congenital 756.79
Diastema, teeth, tooth 524.30
Diastematomyelia 742.51
Diataxia, cerebral, infantile 343.0
Diathesis
allergic V15.09
bleeding (familial) 287.9
cystine (familial) 270.0
gouty 274.9
hemorrhagic (familial) 287.9
newborn NEC 776.0
oxalic 271.8
scrofulous (*see also* Tuberculosis) 017.2 ☑
spasmophilic (*see also* Tetany) 781.7
ulcer 536.9
uric acid 274.9

Diaz's disease or osteochondrosis 732.5
Dibothriocephaliasis 123.4
larval 123.5
Dibothriocephalus (infection) (infestation) (latus) 123.4
larval 123.5
Dicephalus 759.4
Dichotomy, teeth 520.2
Dichromat, dichromata (congenital) 368.59
Dichromatopsia (congenital) 368.59
Dichuchwa 104.0
Dicroceliasis 121.8
Didelphys, didelphic — *see also* Double uterus 752.2
Didymitis — *see also* Epididymitis 604.90
Died — *see also* Death
without
medical attention (cause unknown) 798.9
sign of disease 798.2
Dientamoeba diarrhea 007.8
Dietary
inadequacy or deficiency 269.9
surveillance and counseling V65.3
Dietl's crisis 593.4
Dieulafoy lesion (hemorrhagic)
of
duodenum 537.84
esophagus 530.82
intestine 569.86
stomach 537.84
Difficult
birth, affecting fetus or newborn 763.9
delivery NEC 669.9 ☑
Difficulty
feeding 783.3
adult 783.3
breast 676.8 ☑
child 783.3
elderly 783.3
infant 783.3
newborn 779.3
nonorganic (infant) NEC 307.59
mechanical, gastroduodenal stoma 537.89
reading 315.00
specific, spelling 315.09
swallowing (*see also* Dysphagia) 787.20
walking 719.7
Diffuse — *see* condition
Diffused ganglion 727.42
Di George's syndrome (thymic hypoplasia) 279.11
Digestive — *see* condition
Di Guglielmo's disease or syndrome (M9841/3) 207.0 ☑
Diktyoma (M9051/3) — *see* Neoplasm, by site, malignant
Dilaceration, tooth 520.4
Dilatation
anus 564.89
venule — *see* Hemorrhoids
aorta (focal) (general) (*see also* Aneurysm, aorta) 441.9
congenital 747.29
infectional 093.0
ruptured 441.5
syphilitic 093.0
appendix (cystic) 543.9
artery 447.8
bile duct (common) (cystic) (congenital) 751.69
acquired 576.8
bladder (sphincter) 596.8
congenital 753.8
in pregnancy or childbirth 654.4 ☑
causing obstructed labor 660.2 ☑
affecting fetus or newborn 763.1
blood vessel 459.89
bronchus, bronchi 494.0

Dilatation — *continued*
bronchus, bronchi — *continued*
with acute exacerbation 494.1
calyx (due to obstruction) 593.89
capillaries 448.9
cardiac (acute) (chronic) (*see also* Hypertrophy, cardiac) 429.3
congenital 746.89
valve NEC 746.89
pulmonary 746.09
hypertensive (*see also* Hypertension, heart) 402.90
cavum septi pellucidi 742.4
cecum 564.89
psychogenic 306.4
cervix (uteri) (*see also* Incompetency, cervix)
incomplete, poor, slow
affecting fetus or newborn 763.7
complicating delivery 661.0 ☑
affecting fetus or newborn 763.7
colon 564.7
congenital 751.3
due to mechanical obstruction 560.89
psychogenic 306.4
common bile duct (congenital) 751.69
acquired 576.8
with calculus, choledocholithiasis, or stones — *see* Choledocholithiasis
cystic duct 751.69
acquired (any bile duct) 575.8
duct, mammary 610.4
duodenum 564.89
esophagus 530.89
congenital 750.4
due to
achalasia 530.0
cardiospasm 530.0
Eustachian tube, congenital 744.24
fontanel 756.0
gallbladder 575.8
congenital 751.69
gastric 536.8
acute 536.1
psychogenic 306.4
heart (acute) (chronic) (*see also* Hypertrophy, cardiac) 429.3
congenital 746.89
hypertensive (*see also* Hypertension, heart) 402.90
valve (*see also* Endocarditis)
congenital 746.89
ileum 564.89
psychogenic 306.4
inguinal rings — *see* Hernia, inguinal
jejunum 564.89
psychogenic 306.4
kidney (calyx) (collecting structures) (cystic) (parenchyma) (pelvis) 593.89
lacrimal passages 375.69
lymphatic vessel 457.1
mammary duct 610.4
Meckel's diverticulum (congenital) 751.0
meningeal vessels, congenital 742.8
myocardium (acute) (chronic) (*see also* Hypertrophy, cardiac) 429.3
organ or site, congenital NEC — *see* Distortion
pancreatic duct 577.8
pelvis, kidney 593.89
pericardium — *see* Pericarditis
pharynx 478.29
prostate 602.8
pulmonary
artery (idiopathic) 417.8
congenital 747.3
valve, congenital 746.09
pupil 379.43
rectum 564.89
renal 593.89

- **Dilatation** — *continued*
  - saccule vestibularis, congenital 744.05
  - salivary gland (duct) 527.8
  - sphincter ani 564.89
  - stomach 536.8
    - acute 536.1
    - psychogenic 306.4
  - submaxillary duct 527.8
  - trachea, congenital 748.3
  - ureter (idiopathic) 593.89
    - congenital 753.20
    - due to obstruction 593.5
  - urethra (acquired) 599.84
  - vasomotor 443.9
  - vein 459.89
  - ventricular, ventricle (acute) (chronic) (*see also* Hypertrophy, cardiac) 429.3
    - cerebral, congenital 742.4
    - hypertensive (*see also* Hypertension, heart) 402.90
  - venule 459.89
    - anus — *see* Hemorrhoids
  - vesical orifice 596.8
- **Dilated, dilation** — *see* Dilatation
- **Diminished**
  - hearing (acuity) (*see also* Deafness) 389.9
  - pulse pressure 785.9
  - vision NEC 369.9
  - vital capacity 794.2
- **Diminuta taenia** 123.6
- **Diminution, sense or sensation** (cold) (heat) (tactile) (vibratory) — *see also* Disturbance, sensation 782.0
- **Dimitri-Sturge-Weber disease** (encephalocutaneous angiomatosis) 759.6
- **Dimple**
  - parasacral 685.1
    - with abscess 685.0
  - pilonidal 685.1
    - with abscess 685.0
  - postanal 685.1
    - with abscess 685.0
- **Dioctophyma renale** (infection) (infestation) 128.8
- **Dipetalonemiasis** 125.4
- **Diphallus** 752.69
- **Diphtheria, diphtheritic** (gangrenous) (hemorrhagic) 032.9
  - carrier (suspected) of V02.4
  - cutaneous 032.85
  - cystitis 032.84
  - faucial 032.0
  - infection of wound 032.85
  - inoculation (anti) (not sick) V03.5
  - laryngeal 032.3
  - myocarditis 032.82
  - nasal anterior 032.2
  - nasopharyngeal 032.1
  - neurological complication 032.89
  - peritonitis 032.83
  - specified site NEC 032.89
- **Diphyllobothriasis** (intestine) 123.4
  - larval 123.5
- **Diplacusis** 388.41
- **Diplegia** (upper limbs) 344.2
  - brain or cerebral 437.8
  - congenital 343.0
  - facial 351.0
    - congenital 352.6
  - infantile or congenital (cerebral) (spastic) (spinal) 343.0
  - lower limbs 344.1
  - syphilitic, congenital 090.49
- **Diplococcus, diplococcal** — *see* condition
- **Diplomyelia** 742.59
- **Diplopia** 368.2
  - refractive 368.15
- **Dipsomania** — *see also* Alcoholism 303.9 ☑
  - with psychosis (*see also* Psychosis, alcoholic) 291.9
- **Dipylidiasis** 123.8
  - intestine 123.8
- **Direction, teeth, abnormal** 524.30
- **Dirt-eating child** 307.52
- **Disability**
  - heart — *see* Disease, heart
  - learning NEC 315.2
  - special spelling 315.09
- **Disarticulation** — *see also* Derangement, joint 718.9 ☑
  - meaning
    - amputation
      - status — *see* Absence, by site
      - traumatic — *see* Amputation, traumatic
    - dislocation, traumatic or congenital — *see* Dislocation
- **Disaster, cerebrovascular** — *see also* Disease, cerebrovascular, acute 436
- **Discharge**
  - anal NEC 787.99
  - breast (female) (male) 611.79
  - conjunctiva 372.89
  - continued locomotor idiopathic (*see also* Epilepsy) 345.5 ☑
  - diencephalic autonomic idiopathic (*see also* Epilepsy) 345.5 ☑
  - ear 388.60
    - blood 388.69
    - cerebrospinal fluid 388.61
  - excessive urine 788.42
  - eye 379.93
  - nasal 478.19
  - nipple 611.79
  - patterned motor idiopathic (*see also* Epilepsy) 345.5 ☑
  - penile 788.7
  - postnasal — *see* Sinusitis
  - sinus, from mediastinum 510.0
  - umbilicus 789.9
  - urethral 788.7
    - bloody 599.84
  - vaginal 623.5
- **Discitis** 722.90
  - cervical, cervicothoracic 722.91
  - lumbar, lumbosacral 722.93
  - thoracic, thoracolumbar 722.92
- **Discogenic syndrome** — *see* Displacement, intervertebral disc
- **Discoid**
  - kidney 753.3
  - meniscus, congenital 717.5
  - semilunar cartilage 717.5
- **Discoloration**
  - mouth 528.9
  - nails 703.8
  - teeth 521.7
    - due to
      - drugs 521.7
      - metals (copper) (silver) 521.7
      - pulpal bleeding 521.7
    - during formation 520.8
    - extrinsic 523.6
    - intrinsic posteruptive 521.7
- **Discomfort**
  - chest 786.59
  - visual 368.13
- **Discomycosis** — *see* Actinomycosis
- **Discontinuity, ossicles, ossicular chain** 385.23
- **Discrepancy**
  - centric occlusion
    - maximum intercuspation 524.55
    - of teeth 524.55
  - leg length (acquired) 736.81
    - congenital 755.30
  - uterine size-date 649.6 ☑
- **Discrimination**
  - political V62.4
  - racial V62.4
  - religious V62.4
  - sex V62.4
- **Disease, diseased** — *see also* Syndrome
  - Abrami's (acquired hemolytic jaundice) 283.9
  - absorbent system 459.89
  - accumulation — *see* Thesaurismosis
  - acid-peptic 536.8
  - Acosta's 993.2
  - Adams-Stokes (-Morgagni) (syncope with heart block) 426.9
  - Addison's (bronze) (primary adrenal insufficiency) 255.41
    - anemia (pernicious) 281.0
    - tuberculous (*see also* Tuberculosis) 017.6 ☑
  - Addison-Gull — *see* Xanthoma
  - adenoids (and tonsils) (chronic) 474.9
  - adrenal (gland) (capsule) (cortex) 255.9
    - hyperfunction 255.3
    - hypofunction 255.41
    - specified type NEC 255.8
  - ainhum (dactylolysis spontanea) 136.0
  - akamushi (scrub typhus) 081.2
  - Akureyri (epidemic neuromyasthenia) 049.8
  - Albarrán's (colibacilluria) 791.9
  - Albers-Schönberg's (marble bones) 756.52
  - Albert's 726.71
  - Albright (-Martin) (-Bantam) 275.49
  - Alibert's (mycosis fungoides) (M9700/3) 202.1 ☑
  - Alibert-Bazin (M9700/3) 202.1 ☑
  - alimentary canal 569.9
  - alligator skin (ichthyosis congenita) 757.1
    - acquired 701.1
  - Almeida's (Brazilian blastomycosis) 116.1
  - Alpers' 330.8
  - alpine 993.2
  - altitude 993.2
  - alveoli, teeth 525.9
  - Alzheimer's — *see* Alzheimer's
  - amyloid (any site) 277.30
  - anarthritic rheumatoid 446.5
  - Anders' (adiposis tuberosa simplex) 272.8
  - Andersen's (glycogenosis IV) 271.0
  - Anderson's (angiokeratoma corporis diffusum) 272.7
  - Andes 993.2
  - Andrews' (bacterid) 686.8
  - angiospastic, angiospasmodic 443.9
    - cerebral 435.9
      - with transient neurologic deficit 435.9
    - vein 459.89
  - anterior
    - chamber 364.9
    - horn cell 335.9
      - specified type NEC 335.8
  - antral (chronic) 473.0
    - acute 461.0
  - anus NEC 569.49
  - aorta (nonsyphilitic) 447.9
    - syphilitic NEC 093.89
  - aortic (heart) (valve) (*see also* Endocarditis, aortic) 424.1
  - apollo 077.4
  - aponeurosis 726.90
  - appendix 543.9
  - aqueous (chamber) 364.9
  - arc-welders' lung 503
  - Armenian 277.31
  - Arnold-Chiari (*see also* Spina bifida) 741.0 ☑
  - arterial 447.9
    - occlusive (*see also* Occlusion, by site) 444.22
      - with embolus or thrombus — *see* Occlusion, by site
      - due to stricture or stenosis 447.1
    - specified type NEC 447.8
  - arteriocardiorenal (*see also* Hypertension, cardiorenal) 404.90
- **Disease, diseased** — *see also* Syndrome — *continued*
  - arteriolar (generalized) (obliterative) 447.9
    - specified type NEC 447.8
  - arteriorenal — *see* Hypertension, kidney
  - arteriosclerotic (*see also* Arteriosclerosis)
    - cardiovascular 429.2
    - coronary — *see* Arteriosclerosis, coronary
    - heart — *see* Arteriosclerosis, coronary
    - vascular — *see* Arteriosclerosis
  - artery 447.9
    - cerebral 437.9
    - coronary — *see* Arteriosclerosis, coronary
    - specified type NEC 447.8
  - arthropod-borne NEC 088.9
    - specified type NEC 088.89
  - Asboe-Hansen's (incontinentia pigmenti) 757.33
  - atticoantral, chronic (with posterior or superior marginal perforation of ear drum) 382.2
  - auditory canal, ear 380.9
  - Aujeszky's 078.89
  - auricle, ear NEC 380.30
  - Australian X 062.4
  - autoimmune NEC 279.4
    - hemolytic (cold type) (warm type) 283.0
    - parathyroid 252.1
    - thyroid 245.2
  - aviators' (*see also* Effect, adverse, high altitude) 993.2
  - ax(e)-grinders' 502
  - Ayala's 756.89
  - Ayerza's (pulmonary artery sclerosis with pulmonary hypertension) 416.0
  - Azorean (of the nervous system) 334.8
  - Babington's (familial hemorrhagic telangiectasia) 448.0
  - back bone NEC 733.90
  - bacterial NEC 040.89
    - zoonotic NEC 027.9
      - specified type NEC 027.8
  - Baehr-Schiffrin (thrombotic thrombocytopenic purpura) 446.6
  - Baelz's (cheilitis glandularis apostematosa) 528.5
  - Baerensprung's (eczema marginatum) 110.3
  - Balfour's (chloroma) 205.3 ☑
  - balloon (*see also* Effect, adverse, high altitude) 993.2
  - Baló's 341.1
  - Bamberger (-Marie) (hypertrophic pulmonary osteoarthropathy) 731.2
  - Bang's (Brucella abortus) 023.1
  - Bannister's 995.1
  - Banti's (with cirrhosis) (with portal hypertension) — *see* Cirrhosis, liver
  - Barcoo (*see also* Ulcer, skin) 707.9
  - barium lung 503
  - Barlow (-Möller) (infantile scurvy) 267
  - barometer makers' 985.0
  - Barraquer (-Simons) (progressive lipodystrophy) 272.6
  - basal ganglia 333.90
    - degenerative NEC 333.0
    - specified NEC 333.89
  - Basedow's (exophthalmic goiter) 242.0 ☑
  - basement membrane NEC 583.89
    - with
      - pulmonary hemorrhage (Goodpasture's syndrome) 446.21 *[583.81]*
  - Bateman's 078.0
    - purpura (senile) 287.2

Disease, diseased — *see also* Syndrome — *continued*
hemoglobin — *continued*
D — *continued*
with other abnormal hemoglobin NEC 282.7
Hb-S (without crisis) 282.68
with crisis 282.69
sickle-cell (without crisis) 282.68
with crisis 282.69
thalassemia 282.49
E (Hb-E) 282.7
with other abnormal hemoglobin NEC 282.7
Hb-S (without crisis) 282.68
with crisis 282.69
sickle-cell (without crisis) 282.68
with crisis 282.69
thalassemia 282.49
elliptocytosis 282.7
F (Hb-F) 282.7
G (Hb-G) 282.7
H (Hb-H) 282.49
hereditary persistence, fetal (HPFH) ("Swiss variety") 282.7
high fetal gene 282.7
I thalassemia 282.49
M 289.7
S (*see also* Disease, sickle-cell, Hb-S)
thalassemia (without crisis) 282.41
with
crisis 282.42
vaso-occlusive pain 282.42
spherocytosis 282.7
unstable, hemolytic 282.7
Zurich (Hb-Zurich) 282.7
hemolytic (fetus) (newborn) 773.2
autoimmune (cold type) (warm type) 283.0
due to or with
incompatibility
ABO (blood group) 773.1
blood (group) (Duffy) (Kell) (Kidd) (Lewis) (M) (S) NEC 773.2
Rh (blood group) (factor) 773.0
Rh negative mother 773.0
unstable hemoglobin 282.7
hemorrhagic 287.9
newborn 776.0
Henoch (-Schönlein) (purpura nervosa) 287.0
hepatic — *see* Disease, liver
hepatolenticular 275.1
heredodegenerative NEC
brain 331.89
spinal cord 336.8
Hers' (glycogenosis VI) 271.0
Herter (-Gee) (-Heubner) (nontropical sprue) 579.0
Herxheimer's (diffuse idiopathic cutaneous atrophy) 701.8
Heubner's 094.89
Heubner-Herter (nontropical sprue) 579.0
high fetal gene or hemoglobin thalassemia 282.49
Hildenbrand's (typhus) 081.9
hip (joint) NEC 719.95
congenital 755.63
suppurative 711.05
tuberculous (*see also* Tuberculosis) 015.1 ☑ *[730.85]*
Hippel's (retinocerebral angiomatosis) 759.6
Hirschfeld's (acute diabetes mellitus) (*see also* Diabetes) 250.0 ☑
due to secondary diabetes 249.0 ☑
Hirschsprung's (congenital megacolon) 751.3

Disease, diseased — *see also* Syndrome — *continued*
His (-Werner) (trench fever) 083.1
HIV 042
Hodgkin's (M9650/3) 201.9 ☑

Note — Use the following fifth-digit subclassification with category 201:

0	*unspecified site*
1	*lymph nodes of head, face, and neck*
2	*intrathoracic lymph nodes*
3	*intra-abdominal lymph nodes*
4	*lymph nodes of axilla and upper limb*
5	*lymph nodes of inguinal region and lower limb*
6	*intrapelvic lymph nodes*
7	*spleen*
8	*lymph nodes of multiple sites*

lymphocytic
depletion (M9653/3) 201.7 ☑
diffuse fibrosis (M9654/3) 201.7 ☑
reticular type (M9655/3) 201.7 ☑
predominance (M9651/3) 201.4 ☑
lymphocytic-histiocytic predominance (M9651/3) 201.4 ☑
mixed cellularity (M9652/3) 201.6 ☑
nodular sclerosis (M9656/3) 201.5 ☑
cellular phase (M9657/3) 201.5 ☑
Hodgson's 441.9
ruptured 441.5
Hoffa (-Kastert) (liposynovitis prepatellaris) 272.8
Holla (*see also* Spherocytosis) 282.0
homozygous-Hb-S 282.61
hoof and mouth 078.4
hookworm (*see also* Ancylostomiasis) 126.9
Horton's (temporal arteritis) 446.5
host-versus-graft (immune or nonimmune cause) 279.50
HPFH (hereditary persistence of fetal hemoglobin) ("Swiss variety") 282.7
Huchard's disease (continued arterial hypertension) 401.9
Huguier's (uterine fibroma) 218.9
human immunodeficiency (virus) 042
hunger 251.1
Hunt's
dyssynergia cerebellaris myoclonica 334.2
herpetic geniculate ganglionitis 053.11
Huntington's 333.4
Huppert's (multiple myeloma) (M9730/3) 203.0 ☑
Hurler's (mucopolysaccharidosis I) 277.5
Hutchinson-Boeck (sarcoidosis) 135
Hutchinson-Gilford (progeria) 259.8
Hutchinson's, meaning
angioma serpiginosum 709.1
cheiropompholyx 705.81
prurigo estivalis 692.72
hyaline (diffuse) (generalized) 728.9
membrane (lung) (newborn) 769
hydatid (*see also* Echinococcus) 122.9
Hyde's (prurigo nodularis) 698.3
hyperkinetic (*see also* Hyperkinesia) 314.9
heart 429.82
hypertensive (*see also* Hypertension) 401.9
hypophysis 253.9

Disease, diseased — *see also* Syndrome — *continued*
hypophysis — *continued*
hyperfunction 253.1
hypofunction 253.2
Iceland (epidemic neuromyasthenia) 049.8
I cell 272.7
ill-defined 799.89
immunologic NEC 279.9
immunoproliferative 203.8 ☑
inclusion 078.5
salivary gland 078.5
infancy, early NEC 779.9
infective NEC 136.9
inguinal gland 289.9
internal semilunar cartilage, cystic 717.5
intervertebral disc 722.90
with myelopathy 722.70
cervical, cervicothoracic 722.91
with myelopathy 722.71
lumbar, lumbosacral 722.93
with myelopathy 722.73
thoracic, thoracolumbar 722.92
with myelopathy 722.72
intestine 569.9
functional 564.9
congenital 751.3
psychogenic 306.4
lardaceous 277.39
organic 569.9
protozoal NEC 007.9
iris 364.9
specified NEC 364.89
iron
metabolism 275.0
storage 275.0
Isambert's (*see also* Tuberculosis, larynx) 012.3 ☑
Iselin's (osteochondrosis, fifth metatarsal) 732.5
island (scrub typhus) 081.2
itai-itai 985.5
Jadassohn's (maculopapular erythroderma) 696.2
Jadassohn-Pellizari's (anetoderma) 701.3
Jakob-Creutzfeldt (CJD) 046.19
with dementia
with behavioral disturbance 046.19 *[294.11]*
without behavioral disturbance 046.19 *[294.10]*
familial 046.19
iatrogenic 046.19
specified NEC 046.19
sporadic 046.19
variant (vCJD) 046.11
with dementia
with behavioral disturbance 046.11 *[294.11]*
without behavioral disturbance 046.11 *[294.10]*
Jaksch (-Luzet) (pseudoleukemia infantum) 285.8
Janet's 300.89
Jansky-Bielschowsky 330.1
jaw NEC 526.9
fibrocystic 526.2
Jensen's 363.05
Jeune's (asphyxiating thoracic dystrophy) 756.4
jigger 134.1
Johnson-Stevens (erythema multiforme exudativum) 695.13
joint NEC 719.9 ☑
ankle 719.97
Charcôt 094.0 *[713.5]*
degenerative (*see also* Osteoarthrosis) 715.9 ☑
multiple 715.09
spine (*see also* Spondylosis) 721.90
elbow 719.92
foot 719.97

Disease, diseased — *see also* Syndrome — *continued*
joint — *continued*
hand 719.94
hip 719.95
hypertrophic (chronic) (degenerative) (*see also* Osteoarthrosis) 715.9 ☑
spine (*see also* Spondylosis) 721.90
knee 719.96
Luschka 721.90
multiple sites 719.99
pelvic region 719.95
sacroiliac 724.6
shoulder (region) 719.91
specified site NEC 719.98
spine NEC 724.9
pseudarthrosis following fusion 733.82
sacroiliac 724.6
wrist 719.93
Jourdain's (acute gingivitis) 523.00
Jüngling's (sarcoidosis) 135
Kahler (-Bozzolo) (multiple myeloma) (M9730/3) 203.0 ☑
Kalischer's 759.6
Kaposi's 757.33
lichen ruber 697.8
acuminatus 696.4
moniliformis 697.8
xeroderma pigmentosum 757.33
Kaschin-Beck (endemic polyarthritis) 716.00
ankle 716.07
arm 716.02
lower (and wrist) 716.03
upper (and elbow) 716.02
foot (and ankle) 716.07
forearm (and wrist) 716.03
hand 716.04
leg 716.06
lower 716.06
upper 716.05
multiple sites 716.09
pelvic region (hip) (thigh) 716.05
shoulder region 716.01
specified site NEC 716.08
Katayama 120.2
Kawasaki 446.1
Kedani (scrub typhus) 081.2
kidney (functional) (pelvis) (*see also* Disease, renal) 593.9
chronic 585.9
requiring chronic dialysis 585.6
stage
I 585.1
II (mild) 585.2
III (moderate) 585.3
IV (severe) 585.4
V 585.5
cystic (congenital) 753.10
multiple 753.19
single 753.11
specified NEC 753.19
fibrocystic (congenital) 753.19
in gout 274.10
polycystic (congenital) 753.12
adult type (APKD) 753.13
autosomal dominant 753.13
autosomal recessive 753.14
childhood type (CPKD) 753.14
infantile type 753.14
Kienböck's (carpal lunate) (wrist) 732.3
Kimmelstiel (-Wilson) (intercapillary glomerulosclerosis) 250.4 ☑ *[581.81]*
due to secondary diabetes 249.4 ☑ *[581.81]*
Kinnier Wilson's (hepatolenticular degeneration) 275.1
kissing 075
Kleb's (*see also* Nephritis) 583.9
Klinger's 446.4
Klippel's 723.8

- **Disease, diseased** — *see also* Syndrome — *continued*
  - Pollitzer's (hidradenitis suppurativa) 705.83
  - polycystic (congenital) 759.89
    - congenital 748.4
    - kidney or renal 753.12
      - adult type (APKD) 753.13
      - autosomal dominant 753.13
      - autosomal recessive 753.14
      - childhood type (CPKD) 753.14
      - infantile type 753.14
    - liver or hepatic 751.62
    - lung or pulmonary 518.89
    - ovary, ovaries 256.4
    - spleen 759.0
  - Pompe's (glycogenosis II) 271.0
  - Poncet's (tuberculous rheumatism) (*see also* Tuberculosis) 015.9 ☑
  - Posada-Wernicke 114.9
  - Potain's (pulmonary edema) 514
  - Pott's (*see also* Tuberculosis) 015.0 ☑ *[730.88]*
    - osteomyelitis 015.0 ☑ *[730.88]*
    - paraplegia 015.0 ☑ *[730.88]*
    - spinal curvature 015.0 ☑ *[737.43]*
    - spondylitis 015.0 ☑ *[720.81]*
  - Potter's 753.0
  - Poulet's 714.2
  - pregnancy NEC (*see also* Pregnancy) 646.9 ☑
  - Preiser's (osteoporosis) 733.09
  - Pringle's (tuberous sclerosis) 759.5
  - Profichet's 729.90
  - prostate 602.9
    - specified type NEC 602.8
  - protozoal NEC 136.8
    - intestine, intestinal NEC 007.9
  - pseudo-Hurler's (mucolipidosis III) 272.7
  - psychiatric (*see also* Psychosis) 298.9
  - psychotic (*see also* Psychosis) 298.9
  - Puente's (simple glandular cheilitis) 528.5
  - puerperal NEC (*see also* Puerperal) 674.9 ☑
  - pulmonary (*see also* Disease, lung)
    - amyloid 277.39 *[517.8]*
    - artery 417.9
    - circulation, circulatory 417.9
      - specified NEC 417.8
    - diffuse obstructive (chronic) 496
      - with
        - acute bronchitis 491.22
        - asthma (chronic) (obstructive) 493.2 ☑
        - exacerbation NEC (acute) 491.21
    - heart (chronic) 416.9
      - specified NEC 416.8
    - hypertensive (vascular) 416.0
      - cardiovascular 416.0
    - obstructive diffuse (chronic) 496
      - with
        - acute bronchitis 491.22
        - asthma (chronic) (obstructive) 493.2 ☑
        - bronchitis (chronic) 491.20
          - with
            - exacerbation (acute) 491.21
        - acute 491.22
          - exacerbation NEC (acute) 491.21
      - decompensated 491.21
        - with exacerbation 491.21
    - valve (*see also* Endocarditis, pulmonary) 424.3
  - pulp (dental) NEC 522.9
  - pulseless 446.7
  - Putnam's (subacute combined sclerosis with pernicious anemia) 281.0 *[336.2]*
  - Pyle (-Cohn) (craniometaphyseal dysplasia) 756.89
  - pyramidal tract 333.90
  - Quervain's
    - tendon sheath 727.04
    - thyroid (subacute granulomatous thyroiditis) 245.1
  - Quincke's — *see* Edema, angioneurotic
  - Quinquaud (acne decalvans) 704.09
  - rag sorters' 022.1
  - Raynaud's (paroxysmal digital cyanosis) 443.0
  - reactive airway — *see* Asthma
  - Recklinghausen's (M9540/1) 237.71
    - bone (osteitis fibrosa cystica) 252.01
  - Recklinghausen-Applebaum (hemochromatosis) 275.0
  - Reclus' (cystic) 610.1
  - rectum NEC 569.49
  - Refsum's (heredopathia atactica polyneuritiformis) 356.3
  - Reichmann's (gastrosuccorrhea) 536.8
  - Reimann's (periodic) 277.31
  - Reiter's 099.3
  - renal (functional) (pelvis) (*see also* Disease, kidney) 593.9
    - with
      - edema (*see also* Nephrosis) 581.9
      - exudative nephritis 583.89
      - lesion of interstitial nephritis 583.89
      - stated generalized cause — *see* Nephritis
    - acute 593.9
    - basement membrane NEC 583.89
      - with
        - pulmonary hemorrhage (Goodpasture's syndrome) 446.21 *[583.81]*
    - chronic (*see also* Disease, kidney, chronic) 585.9
    - complicating pregnancy or puerperium NEC 646.2 ☑
      - with hypertension — *see* Toxemia, of pregnancy
      - affecting fetus or newborn 760.1
    - cystic, congenital (*see also* Cystic, disease, kidney) 753.10
    - diabetic 250.4 ☑ *[583.81]*
      - due to secondary diabetes 249.4 ☑ *[581.81]*
    - due to
      - amyloidosis 277.39 *[583.81]*
      - diabetes mellitus 250.4 ☑ *[583.81]*
        - due to secondary diabetes 249.4 ☑ *[581.81]*
      - systemic lupus erythematosis 710.0 *[583.81]*
    - end-stage 585.6
    - exudative 583.89
    - fibrocystic (congenital) 753.19
    - gonococcal 098.19 *[583.81]*
    - gouty 274.10
    - hypertensive (*see also* Hypertension, kidney) 403.90
    - immune complex NEC 583.89
    - interstitial (diffuse) (focal) 583.89
    - lupus 710.0 *[583.81]*
    - maternal, affecting fetus or newborn 760.1
      - hypertensive 760.0
    - phosphate-losing (tubular) 588.0
    - polycystic (congenital) 753.12
      - adult type (APKD) 753.13
      - autosomal dominant 753.13
      - autosomal recessive 753.14
      - childhood type (CPKD) 753.14
      - infantile type 753.14
    - specified lesion or cause NEC (*see also* Glomerulonephritis) 583.89
    - subacute 581.9
    - syphilitic 095.4
    - tuberculous (*see also* Tuberculosis) 016.0 ☑ *[583.81]*
    - tubular (*see also* Nephrosis, tubular) 584.5
  - Rendu-Osler-Weber (familial hemorrhagic telangiectasia) 448.0
  - renovascular (arteriosclerotic) (*see also* Hypertension, kidney) 403.90
  - respiratory (tract) 519.9
    - acute or subacute (upper) NEC 465.9
      - due to fumes or vapors 506.3
      - multiple sites NEC 465.8
      - noninfectious 478.9
      - streptococcal 034.0
    - chronic 519.9
      - arising in the perinatal period 770.7
      - due to fumes or vapors 506.4
    - due to
      - aspiration of liquids or solids 508.9
      - external agents NEC 508.9
        - specified NEC 508.8
      - fumes or vapors 506.9
        - acute or subacute NEC 506.3
        - chronic 506.4
    - fetus or newborn NEC 770.9
    - obstructive 496
    - specified type NEC 519.8
    - upper (acute) (infectious) NEC 465.9
      - multiple sites NEC 465.8
      - noninfectious NEC 478.9
      - streptococcal 034.0
  - retina, retinal NEC 362.9
    - Batten's or Batten-Mayou 330.1 *[362.71]*
    - degeneration 362.89
    - vascular lesion 362.17
  - rheumatic (*see also* Arthritis) 716.8 ☑
    - heart — *see* Disease, heart, rheumatic
  - rheumatoid (heart) — *see* Arthritis, rheumatoid
  - rickettsial NEC 083.9
    - specified type NEC 083.8
  - Riedel's (ligneous thyroiditis) 245.3
  - Riga (-Fede) (cachectic aphthae) 529.0
  - Riggs' (compound periodontitis) 523.40
  - Ritter's 695.81
  - Rivalta's (cervicofacial actinomycosis) 039.3
  - Robles' (onchocerciasis) 125.3 *[360.13]*
  - Roger's (congenital interventricular septal defect) 745.4
  - Rokitansky's (*see also* Necrosis, liver) 570
  - Romberg's 349.89
  - Rosenthal's (factor XI deficiency) 286.2
  - Rossbach's (hyperchlorhydria) 536.8
    - psychogenic 306.4
  - Roth (-Bernhardt) 355.1
  - Runeberg's (progressive pernicious anemia) 281.0
  - Rust's (tuberculous spondylitis) (*see also* Tuberculosis) 015.0 ☑ *[720.81]*
  - Rustitskii's (multiple myeloma) (M9730/3) 203.0 ☑
  - Ruysch's (Hirschsprung's disease) 751.3
  - Sachs (-Tay) 330.1
  - sacroiliac NEC 724.6
  - salivary gland or duct NEC 527.9
    - inclusion 078.5
      - streptococcal 034.0
    - virus 078.5
  - Sander's (paranoia) 297.1
  - Sandhoff's 330.1
  - sandworm 126.9
  - Savill's (epidemic exfoliative dermatitis) 695.89
  - Schamberg's (progressive pigmentary dermatosis) 709.09
  - Schaumann's (sarcoidosis) 135
  - Schenck's (sporotrichosis) 117.1
  - Scheuermann's (osteochondrosis) 732.0
  - Schilder (-Flatau) 341.1
  - Schimmelbusch's 610.1
  - Schlatter-Osgood 732.4
  - Schlatter's tibia (tubercle) 732.4
  - Schmorl's 722.30
    - cervical 722.39
    - lumbar, lumbosacral 722.32
    - specified region NEC 722.39
    - thoracic, thoracolumbar 722.31
  - Scholz's 330.0
  - Schönlein (-Henoch) (purpura rheumatica) 287.0
  - Schottmüller's (*see also* Fever, paratyphoid) 002.9
  - Schüller-Christian (chronic histiocytosis X) 277.89
  - Schultz's (agranulocytosis) 288.09
  - Schwalbe-Ziehen-Oppenheimer 333.6
  - Schwartz-Jampel 359.23
  - Schweninger-Buzzi (macular atrophy) 701.3
  - sclera 379.19
  - scrofulous (*see also* Tuberculosis) 017.2 ☑
  - scrotum 608.9
  - sebaceous glands NEC 706.9
  - Secretan's (posttraumatic edema) 782.3
  - semilunar cartilage, cystic 717.5
  - seminal vesicle 608.9
  - Senear-Usher (pemphigus erythematosus) 694.4
  - serum NEC 999.5
  - Sever's (osteochondrosis calcaneum) 732.5
  - sexually transmitted — *see* Disease, venereal
  - Sézary's (reticulosis) (M9701/3) 202.2 ☑
  - Shaver's (bauxite pneumoconiosis) 503
  - Sheehan's (postpartum pituitary necrosis) 253.2
  - shimamushi (scrub typhus) 081.2
  - shipyard 077.1
  - sickle cell 282.60
    - with
      - crisis 282.62
      - Hb-S disease 282.61
      - other abnormal hemoglobin (Hb-D) (Hb-E) (Hb-G) (Hb-J) (Hb-K) (Hb-O) (Hb-P) (high fetal gene) (without crisis) 282.68
        - with crisis 282.69
    - elliptocytosis 282.60
    - Hb-C (without crisis) 282.63
      - with
        - crisis 282.64
        - vaso-occlusive pain 282.64
    - Hb-S 282.61
      - with
        - crisis 282.62
        - Hb-C (without crisis) 282.63
          - with
            - crisis 282.64
            - vaso-occlusive pain 282.64
        - other abnormal hemoglobin (Hb-D) (Hb-E) (Hb-G) (Hb-J) (Hb-K) (Hb-O) (Hb-P) (high fetal gene) (without crisis) 282.68
          - with crisis 282.69
    - spherocytosis 282.60
    - thalassemia (without crisis) 282.41

Disease, diseased — *see also* Syndrome — *continued*
  virus — *continued*
    maternal
      with fetal damage affecting management of pregnancy 655.3 ☑
    nonarthropod-borne NEC 078.89
      central nervous system NEC 049.9
        specified NEC 049.8
    vaccination, prophylactic (against) V04.89
  vitreous 379.29
  vocal cords NEC 478.5
  Vogt's (Cecile) 333.71
  Vogt-Spielmeyer 330.1
  Volhard-Fahr (malignant nephrosclerosis) 403.00
  Volkmann's
    acquired 958.6
  von Bechterew's (ankylosing spondylitis) 720.0
  von Economo's (encephalitis lethargica) 049.8
  von Eulenburg's (congenital paramyotonia) 359.29
  von Gierke's (glycogenosis I) 271.0
  von Graefe's 378.72
  von Hippel's (retinocerebral angiomatosis) 759.6
  von Hippel-Lindau (angiomatosis retinocerebellosa) 759.6
  von Jaksch's (pseudoleukemia infantum) 285.8
  von Recklinghausen's (M9540/1) 237.71
    bone (osteitis fibrosa cystica) 252.01
  von Recklinghausen-Applebaum (hemochromatosis) 275.0
  von Willebrand (-Jürgens) (angiohemophilia) 286.4
  von Zambusch's (lichen sclerosus et atrophicus) 701.0
  Voorhoeve's (dyschondroplasia) 756.4
  Vrolik's (osteogenesis imperfecta) 756.51
  vulva
    inflammatory 616.10
    noninflammatory 624.9
      specified NEC 624.8
  Wagner's (colloid milium) 709.3
  Waldenström's (osteochondrosis capital femoral) 732.1
  Wallgren's (obstruction of splenic vein with collateral circulation) 459.89
  Wardrop's (with lymphangitis) 681.9
    finger 681.02
    toe 681.11
  Wassilieff's (leptospiral jaundice) 100.0
  wasting NEC 799.4
    due to malnutrition 261
    paralysis 335.21
  Waterhouse-Friderichsen 036.3
  waxy (any site) 277.39
  Weber-Christian (nodular nonsuppurative panniculitis) 729.30
  Wegner's (syphilitic osteochondritis) 090.0
  Weil's (leptospiral jaundice) 100.0
    of lung 100.0
  Weir Mitchell's (erythromelalgia) 443.82
  Werdnig-Hoffmann 335.0
  Werlhof's (*see also* Purpura, thrombocytopenic) 287.39
  Wermer's 258.01
  Werner's (progeria adultorum) 259.8
  Werner-His (trench fever) 083.1
  Werner-Schultz (agranulocytosis) 288.09
  Wernicke's (superior hemorrhagic polioencephalitis) 265.1

Disease, diseased — *see also* Syndrome — *continued*
  Wernicke-Posadas 114.9
  Whipple's (intestinal lipodystrophy) 040.2
  whipworm 127.3
  White's (congenital) (keratosis follicularis) 757.39
  white
    blood cell 288.9
      specified NEC 288.8
    spot 701.0
  Whitmore's (melioidosis) 025
  Widal-Abrami (acquired hemolytic jaundice) 283.9
  Wilkie's 557.1
  Wilkinson-Sneddon (subcorneal pustular dermatosis) 694.1
  Willis' (diabetes mellitus) (*see also* Diabetes) 250.0 ☑
    due to secondary diabetes 249.0 ☑
  Wilson's (hepatolenticular degeneration) 275.1
  Wilson-Brocq (dermatitis exfoliativa) 695.89
  winter vomiting 078.82
  Wise's 696.2
  Wohlfart-Kugelberg-Welander 335.11
  Woillez's (acute idiopathic pulmonary congestion) 518.5
  Wolman's (primary familial xanthomatosis) 272.7
  wool-sorters' 022.1
  Zagari's (xerostomia) 527.7
  Zahorsky's (exanthem subitum) 058.10
  Ziehen-Oppenheim 333.6
  zoonotic, bacterial NEC 027.9
    specified type NEC 027.8
Disfigurement (due to scar) 709.2
  head V48.6
  limb V49.4
  neck V48.7
  trunk V48.7
Disgerminoma — *see* Dysgerminoma
Disinsertion, retina 361.04
Disintegration, complete, of the body 799.89
  traumatic 869.1
Disk kidney 753.3
Dislocatable hip, congenital — *see also* Dislocation, hip, congenital 754.30
Dislocation (articulation) (closed) (displacement) (simple) (subluxation) 839.8

Note — "Closed" includes simple, complete, partial, uncomplicated, and unspecified dislocation.

"Open" includes dislocation specified as infected or compound and dislocation with foreign body.

"Chronic," "habitual," "old," or "recurrent" dislocations should be coded as indicated under the entry "Dislocation, recurrent," and "pathological" as indicated under the entry "Dislocation, pathological."

For late effect of dislocation see Late, effect, dislocation.

  with fracture — *see* Fracture, by site
  acromioclavicular (joint) (closed) 831.04
    open 831.14
  anatomical site (closed)
    specified NEC 839.69
      open 839.79
    unspecified or ill-defined 839.8
      open 839.9
  ankle (scaphoid bone) (closed) 837.0
    open 837.1
  arm (closed) 839.8
    open 839.9
  astragalus (closed) 837.0
    open 837.1

Dislocation — *continued*
  atlanto-axial (closed) 839.01
    open 839.11
  atlas (closed) 839.01
    open 839.11
  axis (closed) 839.02
    open 839.12
  back (closed) 839.8
    open 839.9
  Bell-Daly 723.8
  breast bone (closed) 839.61
    open 839.71
  capsule, joint — *see* Dislocation, by site
  carpal (bone) — *see* Dislocation, wrist
  carpometacarpal (joint) (closed) 833.04
    open 833.14
  cartilage (joint) (*see also* Dislocation, by site)
    knee — *see* Tear, meniscus
  cervical, cervicodorsal, or cervicothoracic (spine) (vertebra) — *see* Dislocation, vertebra, cervical
  chiropractic (*see also* Lesion, nonallopathic) 739.9
  chondrocostal — *see* Dislocation, costochondral
  chronic — *see* Dislocation, recurrent
  clavicle (closed) 831.04
    open 831.14
  coccyx (closed) 839.41
    open 839.51
  collar bone (closed) 831.04
    open 831.14
  compound (open) NEC 839.9
  congenital NEC 755.8
    hip (*see also* Dislocation, hip, congenital) 754.30
    lens 743.37
    rib 756.3
    sacroiliac 755.69
    spine NEC 756.19
    vertebra 756.19
  coracoid (closed) 831.09
    open 831.19
  costal cartilage (closed) 839.69
    open 839.79
  costochondral (closed) 839.69
    open 839.79
  cricoarytenoid articulation (closed) 839.69
    open 839.79
  cricothyroid (cartilage) articulation (closed) 839.69
    open 839.79
  dorsal vertebrae (closed) 839.21
    open 839.31
  ear ossicle 385.23
  elbow (closed) 832.00
    anterior (closed) 832.01
      open 832.11
    congenital 754.89
    divergent (closed) 832.09
      open 832.19
    lateral (closed) 832.04
      open 832.14
    medial (closed) 832.03
      open 832.13
    open 832.10
    posterior (closed) 832.02
      open 832.12
    recurrent 718.32
    specified type NEC 832.09
      open 832.19
  eye 360.81
    lateral 376.36
  eyeball 360.81
    lateral 376.36
  femur
    distal end (closed) 836.50
      anterior 836.52
        open 836.62
      lateral 836.54
        open 836.64
      medial 836.53
        open 836.63

Dislocation — *continued*
  femur — *continued*
    distal end — *continued*
      open 836.60
      posterior 836.51
        open 836.61
    proximal end (closed) 835.00
      anterior (pubic) 835.03
        open 835.13
      obturator 835.02
        open 835.12
      open 835.10
      posterior 835.01
        open 835.11
  fibula
    distal end (closed) 837.0
      open 837.1
    proximal end (closed) 836.59
      open 836.69
  finger(s) (phalanx) (thumb) (closed) 834.00
    interphalangeal (joint) 834.02
      open 834.12
    metacarpal (bone), distal end 834.01
      open 834.11
    metacarpophalangeal (joint) 834.01
      open 834.11
    open 834.10
    recurrent 718.34
  foot (closed) 838.00
    open 838.10
    recurrent 718.37
  forearm (closed) 839.8
    open 839.9
  fracture — *see* Fracture, by site
  glenoid (closed) 831.09
    open 831.19
  habitual — *see* Dislocation, recurrent
  hand (closed) 839.8
    open 839.9
  hip (closed) 835.00
    anterior 835.03
      obturator 835.02
        open 835.12
      open 835.13
    congenital (unilateral) 754.30
      with subluxation of other hip 754.35
      bilateral 754.31
    developmental 718.75
    open 835.10
    posterior 835.01
      open 835.11
    recurrent 718.35
  humerus (closed) 831.00
    distal end (*see also* Dislocation, elbow) 832.00
    open 831.10
    proximal end (closed) 831.00
      anterior (subclavicular) (subcoracoid) (subglenoid) (closed) 831.01
        open 831.11
      inferior (closed) 831.03
        open 831.13
      open 831.10
      posterior (closed) 831.02
        open 831.12
  implant — *see* Complications, mechanical
  incus 385.23
  infracoracoid (closed) 831.01
    open 831.11
  innominate (pubic junction) (sacral junction) (closed) 839.69
    acetabulum (*see also* Dislocation, hip) 835.00
    open 839.79
  interphalangeal (joint)
    finger or hand (closed) 834.02
      open 834.12
    foot or toe (closed) 838.06
      open 838.16
  jaw (cartilage) (meniscus) (closed) 830.0

Index

Disobedience, hostile — Disorder

- **Disorder** — *see also* Disease — *continued*
  - female sexual arousal 302.72
  - fluid NEC 276.9
  - gastric (functional) 536.9
    - motility 536.8
    - psychogenic 306.4
    - secretion 536.8
  - gastrointestinal (functional) NEC 536.9
    - newborn (neonatal) 777.9
      - specified NEC 777.8
    - psychogenic 306.4
  - gender (child) 302.6
    - adult 302.85
  - gender identity (childhood) 302.6
    - adolescents 302.85
    - adults (-life) 302.85
  - genitourinary system, psychogenic 306.50
  - globe 360.9
    - degenerative 360.20
      - specified NEC 360.29
    - specified type NEC 360.89
  - hearing (*see also* Deafness)
    - conductive type (air) (*see also* Deafness, conductive) 389.00
    - mixed conductive and sensorineural 389.20
      - bilateral 389.22
      - unilateral 389.21
    - nerve
      - bilateral 389.12
      - unilateral 389.13
    - perceptive (*see also* Deafness, perceptive) 389.10
    - sensorineural type NEC (*see also* Deafness, sensorineural 389.10
  - heart action 427.9
    - postoperative 997.1
  - hematological, transient neonatal 776.9
    - specified type NEC 776.8
  - hematopoietic organs 289.9
  - hemorrhagic NEC 287.9
    - due to intrinsic circulating anticoagulants 286.5
    - specified type NEC 287.8
  - hemostasis (*see also* Defect, coagulation) 286.9
  - homosexual conflict 302.0
  - hypomanic (chronic) 301.11
  - identity
    - childhood and adolescence 313.82
      - gender 302.6
  - immune mechanism (immunity) 279.9
    - single complement (C1-C9) 279.8
    - specified type NEC 279.8
  - impulse control (*see also* Disturbance, conduct, compulsive) 312.30
  - infant sialic acid storage 271.8
  - integument, fetus or newborn 778.9
    - specified type NEC 778.8
  - interactional psychotic (childhood) (*see also* Psychosis, childhood) 299.1 ☑
  - intermittent explosive 312.34
  - intervertebral disc 722.90
    - cervical, cervicothoracic 722.91
    - lumbar, lumbosacral 722.93
    - thoracic, thoracolumbar 722.92
  - intestinal 569.9
    - functional NEC 564.9
      - congenital 751.3
      - postoperative 564.4
    - psychogenic 306.4
  - introverted, of childhood and adolescence 313.22
  - involuntary emotional expression (IEED) 310.8
  - iris 364.9
    - specified NEC 364.89
  - iron, metabolism 275.0
  - isolated explosive 312.35
  - joint NEC 719.90

- **Disorder** — *see also* Disease — *continued*
  - joint — *continued*
    - ankle 719.97
    - elbow 719.92
    - foot 719.97
    - hand 719.94
    - hip 719.95
    - knee 719.96
    - multiple sites 719.99
    - pelvic region 719.95
    - psychogenic 306.0
    - shoulder (region) 719.91
    - specified site NEC 719.98
    - temporomandibular 524.60
      - sounds on opening or closing 524.64
      - specified NEC 524.69
    - wrist 719.93
  - kidney 593.9
    - functional 588.9
      - specified NEC 588.89
  - labyrinth, labyrinthine 386.9
    - specified type NEC 386.8
  - lactation 676.9 ☑
  - language (developmental) (expressive) 315.31
    - mixed receptive-expressive 315.32
  - learning 315.9
  - ligament 728.9
  - ligamentous attachments, peripheral (*see also* Enthesopathy)
    - spine 720.1
  - limb NEC 729.90
    - psychogenic 306.0
  - lipid
    - metabolism, congenital 272.9
    - storage 272.7
  - lipoprotein deficiency (familial) 272.5
  - low back NEC 724.9
    - psychogenic 306.0
  - lumbosacral
    - plexus 353.1
    - root (nerve) NEC 353.4
  - lymphoproliferative (chronic) NEC (M9970/1) 238.79
    - post-transplant (PTLD) 238.77
  - major depressive (*see also* Psychosis, affective) 296.2 ☑
    - recurrent episode 296.3 ☑
    - single episode 296.2 ☑
  - male erectile 607.84
    - nonorganic origin 302.72
  - manic (*see also* Psychosis, affective) 296.0 ☑
    - atypical 296.81
  - mathematics 315.1
  - meniscus NEC (*see also* Disorder, cartilage, articular) 718.0 ☑
  - menopausal 627.9
    - specified NEC 627.8
  - menstrual 626.9
    - psychogenic 306.52
    - specified NEC 626.8
  - mental (nonpsychotic) 300.9
    - affecting management of pregnancy, childbirth, or puerperium 648.4 ☑
    - drug-induced 292.9
      - hallucinogen persisting perception 292.89
      - specified type NEC 292.89
    - due to or associated with
      - alcoholism 291.9
      - drug consumption NEC 292.9
        - specified type NEC 292.89
      - physical condition NEC 293.9
    - induced by drug 292.9
      - specified type NEC 292.89
    - neurotic (*see also* Neurosis) 300.9
    - of infancy, childhood or adolescence 313.9
    - persistent
      - other
        - due to conditions classified elsewhere 294.8

- **Disorder** — *see also* Disease — *continued*
  - mental — *continued*
    - persistent — *continued*
      - unspecified
        - due to conditions classified elsewhere 294.9
    - presenile 310.1
      - psychotic NEC 290.10
    - previous, affecting management of pregnancy V23.89
    - psychoneurotic (*see also* Neurosis) 300.9
    - psychotic (*see also* Psychosis) 298.9
      - brief 298.8
      - senile 290.20
    - specific, following organic brain damage 310.9
      - cognitive or personality change of other type 310.1
      - frontal lobe syndrome 310.0
      - postconcussional syndrome 310.2
      - specified type NEC 310.8
    - transient
      - in conditions classified elsewhere 293.9
  - metabolism NEC 277.9
    - with
      - abortion — *see* Abortion, by type, with metabolic disorder
      - ectopic pregnancy (*see also* categories 633.0–633.9) 639.4
      - molar pregnancy (*see also* categories 630–632) 639.4
    - alkaptonuria 270.2
    - amino acid (*see also* Disorder, amino acid) 270.9
      - specified type NEC 270.8
    - ammonia 270.6
    - arginine 270.6
    - argininosuccinic acid 270.6
    - basal 794.7
    - bilirubin 277.4
    - calcium 275.40
    - carbohydrate 271.9
      - specified type NEC 271.8
    - cholesterol 272.9
    - citrulline 270.6
    - copper 275.1
    - corticosteroid 255.2
    - cystine storage 270.0
    - cystinuria 270.0
    - fat 272.9
    - fatty acid oxidation 277.85
    - following
      - abortion 639.4
      - ectopic or molar pregnancy 639.4
    - fructosemia 271.2
    - fructosuria 271.2
    - fucosidosis 271.8
    - galactose-1-phosphate uridyl transferase 271.1
    - glutamine 270.7
    - glycine 270.7
    - glycogen storage NEC 271.0
      - hepatorenal 271.0
    - hemochromatosis 275.0
    - in labor and delivery 669.0 ☑
    - iron 275.0
    - lactose 271.3
    - lipid 272.9
      - specified type NEC 272.8
      - storage 272.7
    - lipoprotein (*see also* Hyperlipemia deficiency (familial)) 272.5
    - lysine 270.7
    - magnesium 275.2
    - mannosidosis 271.8
    - mineral 275.9
      - specified type NEC 275.8
    - mitochondrial 277.87

- **Disorder** — *see also* Disease — *continued*
  - metabolism — *continued*
    - mucopolysaccharide 277.5
    - nitrogen 270.9
    - ornithine 270.6
    - oxalosis 271.8
    - pentosuria 271.8
    - phenylketonuria 270.1
    - phosphate 275.3
    - phosphorous 275.3
    - plasma protein 273.9
      - specified type NEC 273.8
    - porphyrin 277.1
    - purine 277.2
    - pyrimidine 277.2
    - serine 270.7
    - sodium 276.9
    - specified type NEC 277.89
    - steroid 255.2
    - threonine 270.7
    - urea cycle 270.6
    - xylose 271.8
  - micturition NEC 788.69
    - psychogenic 306.53
  - misery and unhappiness, of childhood and adolescence 313.1
  - mitochondrial metabolism 277.87
  - mitral valve 424.0
  - mood (*see also* Disorder, bipolar) 296.90
    - episodic 296.90
      - specified NEC 296.99
    - in conditions classified elsewhere 293.83
  - motor tic 307.20
    - chronic 307.22
    - transient (childhood) 307.21
  - movement NEC 333.90
    - hysterical 300.11
    - medication-induced 333.90
    - periodic limb 327.51
    - sleep related, unspecified 780.58
      - other organic 327.59
    - specified type NEC 333.99
    - stereotypic 307.3
  - mucopolysaccharide 277.5
  - muscle 728.9
    - psychogenic 306.0
    - specified type NEC 728.3
  - muscular attachments, peripheral (*see also* Enthesopathy)
    - spine 720.1
  - musculoskeletal system NEC 729.90
    - psychogenic 306.0
  - myeloproliferative (chronic) NEC (M9960/1) 238.79
  - myoneural 358.9
    - due to lead 358.2
    - specified type NEC 358.8
    - toxic 358.2
  - myotonic 359.29
  - neck region NEC 723.9
  - nerve 349.9
    - abducens NEC 378.54
    - accessory 352.4
    - acoustic 388.5
    - auditory 388.5
    - auriculotemporal 350.8
    - axillary 353.0
    - cerebral — *see* Disorder, nerve, cranial
    - cranial 352.9
      - first 352.0
      - second 377.49
      - third
        - partial 378.51
        - total 378.52
      - fourth 378.53
      - fifth 350.9
      - sixth 378.54
      - seventh NEC 351.9
      - eighth 388.5
      - ninth 352.2
      - tenth 352.3
      - eleventh 352.4

Disorder — *see also* Disease — *continued*
  retina 362.9
    specified type NEC 362.89
  rumination 307.53
  sacroiliac joint NEC 724.6
  sacrum 724.6
  schizo-affective (*see also* Schizophrenia) 295.7 ☑
  schizoid, childhood or adolescence 313.22
  schizophreniform 295.4 ☑
  schizotypal personality 301.22
  secretion, thyrocalcitonin 246.0
  seizure 345.9 ☑
    recurrent 345.9 ☑
      epileptic — *see* Epilepsy
  semantic pragmatic 315.39
    with autism 299.0 ☑
  sense of smell 781.1
    psychogenic 306.7
  separation anxiety 309.21
  sexual (*see also* Deviation, sexual) 302.9
    aversion 302.79
    desire, hypoactive 302.71
    function, psychogenic 302.70
  shyness, of childhood and adolescence 313.21
  single complement (C1-C9) 279.8
  skin NEC 709.9
    fetus or newborn 778.9
      specified type 778.8
    psychogenic (allergic) (eczematous) (pruritic) 306.3
    specified type NEC 709.8
    vascular 709.1
  sleep 780.50
    with apnea — *see* Apnea, sleep
    alcohol induced 291.82
    arousal 307.46
      confusional 327.41
    circadian rhythm 327.30
      advanced sleep phase type 327.32
      alcohol induced 291.82
      delayed sleep phase type 327.31
      drug induced 292.85
      free running type 327.34
      in conditions classified elsewhere 327.37
      irregular sleep-wake type 327.33
      jet lag type 327.35
      other 327.39
      shift work type 327.36
    drug induced 292.85
    initiation or maintenance (*see also* Insomnia) 780.52
      nonorganic origin (transient) 307.41
        persistent 307.42
    nonorganic origin 307.40
      specified type NEC 307.49
    organic specified type NEC 327.8
    periodic limb movement 327.51
    specified NEC 780.59
    wake
      cycle — *see* Disorder, sleep, circadian rhythm
      schedule — *see* Disorer, sleep, circadian rhythm
  social, of childhood and adolescence 313.22
  soft tissue 729.90
    specified type NEC 729.99
  somatization 300.81
  somatoform (atypical) (undifferentiated) 300.82
    severe 300.81
    specified type NEC 300.89
  speech NEC 784.5
    nonorganic origin 307.9
  spine NEC 724.9
    ligamentous or muscular attachments, peripheral 720.1

Disorder — *see also* Disease — *continued*
  steroid metabolism NEC 255.2
  stomach (functional) (*see also* Disorder, gastric) 536.9
    psychogenic 306.4
  storage, iron 275.0
  stress (*see also* Reaction, stress, acute) 308.3
    posttraumatic
      acute 309.81
      brief 309.81
      chronic 309.81
  substitution 300.11
  suspected — *see* Observation
  synovium 727.9
  temperature regulation, fetus or newborn 778.4
  temporomandibular joint NEC 524.60
    sounds on opening or closing 524.64
    specified NEC 524.69
  tendon 727.9
    shoulder region 726.10
  thoracic root (nerve) NEC 353.3
  thyrocalcitonin secretion 246.0
  thyroid (gland) NEC 246.9
    specified type NEC 246.8
  tic 307.20
    chronic (motor or vocal) 307.22
    motor-verbal 307.23
    organic origin 333.1
    transient (of childhood) 307.21
  tooth NEC 525.9
    development NEC 520.9
      specified type NEC 520.8
    eruption 520.6
    specified type NEC 525.8
  Tourette's 307.23
  transport, carbohydrate 271.9
    specified type NEC 271.8
  tubular, phosphate-losing 588.0
  tympanic membrane 384.9
  unaggressive, unsocialized (*see also* Disturbance, conduct) 312.1 ☑
  undersocialized, unsocialized (*see also* Disturbance, conduct)
    aggressive (type) 312.0 ☑
    unaggressive (type) 312.1 ☑
  vision, visual NEC 368.9
    binocular NEC 368.30
    cortex 377.73
      associated with
        inflammatory disorders 377.73
        neoplasms 377.71
        vascular disorders 377.72
    pathway NEC 377.63
      associated with
        inflammatory disorders 377.63
        neoplasms 377.61
        vascular disorders 377.62
  vocal tic
    chronic 307.22
  wakefulness (*see also* Hypersomnia) 780.54
    nonorganic origin (transient) 307.43
      persistent 307.44
  written expression 315.2
Disorganized globe 360.29
Displacement, displaced

Note — For acquired displacement of bones, cartilage, joints, tendons, due to injury, see also Dislocation.

Displacements at ages under one year should be considered congenital, provided there is no indication the condition was acquired after birth.

  acquired traumatic of bone, cartilage, joint, tendon NEC (without fracture) (*see also* Dislocation) 839.8

Displacement, displaced — *continued*
  acquired traumatic of bone, cartilage, joint, tendon (*see also* Dislocation) — *continued*
    with fracture — *see* Fracture, by site
  adrenal gland (congenital) 759.1
  alveolus and teeth, vertical 524.75
  appendix, retrocecal (congenital) 751.5
  auricle (congenital) 744.29
  bladder (acquired) 596.8
    congenital 753.8
  brachial plexus (congenital) 742.8
  brain stem, caudal 742.4
  canaliculus lacrimalis 743.65
  cardia, through esophageal hiatus 750.6
  cerebellum, caudal 742.4
  cervix — *see* Displacement, uterus
  colon (congenital) 751.4
  device, implant, or graft — *see* Complications, mechanical
  epithelium
    columnar of cervix 622.10
    cuboidal, beyond limits of external os (uterus) 752.49
  esophageal mucosa into cardia of stomach, congenital 750.4
  esophagus (acquired) 530.89
    congenital 750.4
  eyeball (acquired) (old) 376.36
    congenital 743.8
    current injury 871.3
    lateral 376.36
  fallopian tube (acquired) 620.4
    congenital 752.19
    opening (congenital) 752.19
  gallbladder (congenital) 751.69
  gastric mucosa 750.7
    into
      duodenum 750.7
      esophagus 750.7
      Meckel's diverticulum, congenital 750.7
  globe (acquired) (lateral) (old) 376.36
    current injury 871.3
  graft
    artificial skin graft 996.55
    decellularized allodermis graft 996.55
  heart (congenital) 746.87
    acquired 429.89
  hymen (congenital) (upward) 752.49
  internal prosthesis NEC — *see* Complications, mechanical
  intervertebral disc (with neuritis, radiculitis, sciatica, or other pain) 722.2
    with myelopathy 722.70
    cervical, cervicodorsal, cervicothoracic 722.0
      with myelopathy 722.71
      due to major trauma — *see* Dislocation, vertebra, cervical
    due to trauma — *see* Dislocation, vertebra
    lumbar, lumbosacral 722.10
      with myelopathy 722.73
      due to major trauma — *see* Dislocation, vertebra, lumbar
    thoracic, thoracolumbar 722.11
      with myelopathy 722.72
      due to major trauma — *see* Dislocation, vertebra, thoracic
  intrauterine device 996.32
  kidney (acquired) 593.0
    congenital 753.3
  lacrimal apparatus or duct (congenital) 743.65
  macula (congenital) 743.55
  Meckel's diverticulum (congenital) 751.0

Displacement, displaced — *continued*
  nail (congenital) 757.5
    acquired 703.8
  opening of Wharton's duct in mouth 750.26
  organ or site, congenital NEC — *see* Malposition, congenital
  ovary (acquired) 620.4
    congenital 752.0
    free in peritoneal cavity (congenital) 752.0
    into hernial sac 620.4
  oviduct (acquired) 620.4
    congenital 752.19
  parathyroid (gland) 252.8
  parotid gland (congenital) 750.26
  punctum lacrimale (congenital) 743.65
  sacroiliac (congenital) (joint) 755.69
    current injury — *see* Dislocation, sacroiliac
    old 724.6
  spine (congenital) 756.19
  spleen, congenital 759.0
  stomach (congenital) 750.7
    acquired 537.89
  subglenoid (closed) 831.01
  sublingual duct (congenital) 750.26
  teeth, tooth 524.30
    horizontal 524.33
    vertical 524.34
  tongue (congenital) (downward) 750.19
  trachea (congenital) 748.3
  ureter or ureteric opening or orifice (congenital) 753.4
  uterine opening of oviducts or fallopian tubes 752.19
  uterus, uterine (*see also* Malposition, uterus) 621.6
    congenital 752.3
  ventricular septum 746.89
    with rudimentary ventricle 746.89
  xyphoid bone (process) 738.3
Disproportion 653.9 ☑
  affecting fetus or newborn 763.1
  breast, reconstructed 612.1
    between native and reconstructed 612.1
  caused by
    conjoined twins 678.1 ☑
    contraction, pelvis (general) 653.1 ☑
      inlet 653.2 ☑
      midpelvic 653.8 ☑
      midplane 653.8 ☑
      outlet 653.3 ☑
    fetal
      ascites 653.7 ☑
      hydrocephalus 653.6 ☑
      hydrops 653.7 ☑
      meningomyelocele 653.7 ☑
      sacral teratoma 653.7 ☑
      tumor 653.7 ☑
    hydrocephalic fetus 653.6 ☑
    pelvis, pelvic, abnormality (bony) NEC 653.0 ☑
    unusually large fetus 653.5 ☑
  causing obstructed labor 660.1 ☑
  cephalopelvic, normally formed fetus 653.4 ☑
    causing obstructed labor 660.1 ☑
  fetal NEC 653.5 ☑
    causing obstructed labor 660.1 ☑
  fetopelvic, normally formed fetus 653.4 ☑
    causing obstructed labor 660.1 ☑
  mixed maternal and fetal origin, normally formed fetus 653.4 ☑
  pelvis, pelvic (bony) NEC 653.1 ☑
    causing obstructed labor 660.1 ☑
  specified type NEC 653.8 ☑
Disruption
  cesarean wound 674.1 ☑
  family V61.09

- **Disruption** — *continued*
  - family — *continued*
    - due to
      - child in
        - care of non-parental family member V61.06
        - foster care V61.06
        - welfare custody V61.05
      - divorce V61.03
      - estrangement V61.09
        - parent-child V61.04
      - family member
        - on military deployment V61.01
        - return from military deployment V61.02
      - legal separation V61.03
  - gastrointestinal anastomosis 997.4
  - ligament(s) (*see also* Sprain)
    - knee
      - current injury — *see* Dislocation, knee
      - old 717.89
        - capsular 717.85
        - collateral (medial) 717.82
          - lateral 717.81
        - cruciate (posterior) 717.84
          - anterior 717.83
        - specified site NEC 717.85
  - marital V61.10
    - involving
      - divorce V61.03
      - estrangement V61.09
  - operation wound (external) (*see also* Dehiscence) 998.32
    - internal 998.31
  - organ transplant, anastomosis site — *see* Complications, transplant, organ, by site
  - ossicles, ossicular chain 385.23
    - traumatic — *see* Fracture, skull, base
  - parenchyma
    - liver (hepatic) — *see* Laceration, liver, major
    - spleen — *see* Laceration, spleen, parenchyma, massive
  - phase-shift, of 24-hour sleep-wake cycle, unspecified 780.55
    - nonorganic origin 307.45
  - sleep-wake cycle (24-hour), unspecified 780.55
    - circadian rhythm 327.33
    - nonorganic origin 307.45
  - suture line (external) (*see also* Dehiscence) 998.32
    - internal 998.31
  - wound 998.30
    - cesarean operation 674.1 ☑
    - episiotomy 674.2 ☑
    - operation (surgical) 998.32
      - cesarean 674.1 ☑
      - internal 998.31
    - perineal (obstetric) 674.2 ☑
    - uterine 674.1 ☑
- **Disruptio uteri** — *see also* Rupture, uterus
  - complicating delivery — *see* Delivery, complicated, rupture, uterus
- **Dissatisfaction with**
  - employment V62.29
  - school environment V62.3
- **Dissecting** — *see* condition
- **Dissection**
  - aorta 441.00
    - abdominal 441.02
    - thoracic 441.01
    - thoracoabdominal 441.03
  - artery, arterial
    - carotid 443.21
    - coronary 414.12
    - iliac 443.22
    - renal 443.23
    - specified NEC 443.29
    - vertebral 443.24
  - vascular 459.9
- **Dissection** — *continued*
  - wound — *see* Wound, open, by site
- **Disseminated** — *see* condition
- **Dissociated personality** NEC 300.15
- **Dissociation**
  - auriculoventricular or atrioventricular (any degree) (AV) 426.89
    - with heart block 426.0
  - interference 426.89
  - isorhythmic 426.89
  - rhythm
    - atrioventricular (AV) 426.89
    - interference 426.89
- **Dissociative**
  - identity disorder 300.14
  - reaction NEC 300.15
- **Dissolution, vertebra** — *see also* Osteoporosis 733.00
- **Distention**
  - abdomen (gaseous) 787.3
  - bladder 596.8
  - cecum 569.89
  - colon 569.89
  - gallbladder 575.8
  - gaseous (abdomen) 787.3
  - intestine 569.89
  - kidney 593.89
  - liver 573.9
  - seminal vesicle 608.89
  - stomach 536.8
    - acute 536.1
    - psychogenic 306.4
  - ureter 593.5
  - uterus 621.8
- **Distichia, distichiasis** (eyelid) 743.63
- **Distoma hepaticum infestation** 121.3
- **Distomiasis** 121.9
  - bile passages 121.3
    - due to Clonorchis sinensis 121.1
  - hemic 120.9
  - hepatic (liver) 121.3
    - due to Clonorchis sinensis (clonorchiasis) 121.1
  - intestinal 121.4
  - liver 121.3
    - due to Clonorchis sinensis 121.1
  - lung 121.2
  - pulmonary 121.2
- **Distomolar** (fourth molar) 520.1
  - causing crowding 524.31
- **Disto-occlusion** (division I) (division II) 524.22
- **Distortion** (congenital)
  - adrenal (gland) 759.1
  - ankle (joint) 755.69
  - anus 751.5
  - aorta 747.29
  - appendix 751.5
  - arm 755.59
  - artery (peripheral) NEC (*see also* Distortion, peripheral vascular system) 747.60
    - cerebral 747.81
    - coronary 746.85
    - pulmonary 747.3
    - retinal 743.58
    - umbilical 747.5
  - auditory canal 744.29
    - causing impairment of hearing 744.02
  - bile duct or passage 751.69
  - bladder 753.8
  - brain 742.4
  - bronchus 748.3
  - cecum 751.5
  - cervix (uteri) 752.49
  - chest (wall) 756.3
  - clavicle 755.51
  - clitoris 752.49
  - coccyx 756.19
  - colon 751.5
  - common duct 751.69
  - cornea 743.41
  - cricoid cartilage 748.3
  - cystic duct 751.69
  - duodenum 751.5
- **Distortion** — *continued*
  - ear 744.29
    - auricle 744.29
      - causing impairment of hearing 744.02
    - causing impairment of hearing 744.09
    - external 744.29
      - causing impairment of hearing 744.02
    - inner 744.05
    - middle, except ossicles 744.03
      - ossicles 744.04
    - ossicles 744.04
  - endocrine (gland) NEC 759.2
  - epiglottis 748.3
  - Eustachian tube 744.24
  - eye 743.8
    - adnexa 743.69
  - face bone(s) 756.0
  - fallopian tube 752.19
  - femur 755.69
  - fibula 755.69
  - finger(s) 755.59
  - foot 755.67
  - gallbladder 751.69
  - genitalia, genital organ(s)
    - female 752.89
      - external 752.49
      - internal NEC 752.89
    - male 752.89
      - penis 752.69
  - glottis 748.3
  - gyri 742.4
  - hand bone(s) 755.59
  - heart (auricle) (ventricle) 746.89
    - valve (cusp) 746.89
  - hepatic duct 751.69
  - humerus 755.59
  - hymen 752.49
  - ileum 751.5
  - intestine (large) (small) 751.5
    - with anomalous adhesions, fixation or malrotation 751.4
  - jaw NEC 524.89
  - jejunum 751.5
  - kidney 753.3
  - knee (joint) 755.64
  - labium (majus) (minus) 752.49
  - larynx 748.3
  - leg 755.69
  - lens 743.36
  - liver 751.69
  - lumbar spine 756.19
    - with disproportion (fetopelvic) 653.0 ☑
      - affecting fetus or newborn 763.1
      - causing obstructed labor 660.1 ☑
  - lumbosacral (joint) (region) 756.19
  - lung (fissures) (lobe) 748.69
  - nerve 742.8
  - nose 748.1
  - organ
    - of Corti 744.05
    - of site not listed — *see* Anomaly, specified type NEC
  - ossicles, ear 744.04
  - ovary 752.0
  - oviduct 752.19
  - pancreas 751.7
  - parathyroid (gland) 759.2
  - patella 755.64
  - peripheral vascular system NEC 747.60
    - gastrointestinal 747.61
    - lower limb 747.64
    - renal 747.62
    - spinal 747.82
    - upper limb 747.63
  - pituitary (gland) 759.2
  - radius 755.59
  - rectum 751.5
  - rib 756.3
  - sacroiliac joint 755.69
  - sacrum 756.19
- **Distortion** — *continued*
  - scapula 755.59
  - shoulder girdle 755.59
  - site not listed — *see* Anomaly, specified type NEC
  - skull bone(s) 756.0
    - with
      - anencephalus 740.0
      - encephalocele 742.0
      - hydrocephalus 742.3
        - with spina bifida (*see also* Spina bifida) 741.0 ☑
      - microcephalus 742.1
  - spinal cord 742.59
  - spine 756.19
  - spleen 759.0
  - sternum 756.3
  - thorax (wall) 756.3
  - thymus (gland) 759.2
  - thyroid (gland) 759.2
    - cartilage 748.3
  - tibia 755.69
  - toe(s) 755.66
  - tongue 750.19
  - trachea (cartilage) 748.3
  - ulna 755.59
  - ureter 753.4
    - causing obstruction 753.20
  - urethra 753.8
    - causing obstruction 753.6
  - uterus 752.3
  - vagina 752.49
  - vein (peripheral) NEC (*see also* Distortion, peripheral vascular system) 747.60
    - great 747.49
    - portal 747.49
    - pulmonary 747.49
  - vena cava (inferior) (superior) 747.49
  - vertebra 756.19
  - visual NEC 368.15
    - shape or size 368.14
  - vulva 752.49
  - wrist (bones) (joint) 755.59
- **Distress**
  - abdomen 789.0 ☑
  - colon 564.9
  - emotional V40.9
  - epigastric 789.0 ☑
  - fetal (syndrome) 768.4
    - affecting management of pregnancy or childbirth 656.8 ☑
    - liveborn infant 768.4
      - first noted
        - before onset of labor 768.2
        - during labor and delivery 768.3
    - stillborn infant (death before onset of labor) 768.0
      - death during labor 768.1
  - gastrointestinal (functional) 536.9
    - psychogenic 306.4
  - intestinal (functional) NEC 564.9
    - psychogenic 306.4
  - intrauterine — *see* Distress, fetal
  - leg 729.5
  - maternal 669.0 ☑
  - mental V40.9
  - respiratory 786.09
    - acute (adult) 518.82
    - adult syndrome (following shock, surgery, or trauma) 518.5
      - specified NEC 518.82
    - fetus or newborn 770.89
    - syndrome (idiopathic) (newborn) 769
  - stomach 536.9
    - psychogenic 306.4
- **Distribution vessel, atypical** NEC 747.60
  - coronary artery 746.85
  - spinal 747.82
- **Districhiasis** 704.2
- **Disturbance** — *see also* Disease
  - absorption NEC 579.9
    - calcium 269.3

- **Disturbance** — *see also* Disease — *continued*
  - absorption — *continued*
    - carbohydrate 579.8
    - fat 579.8
    - protein 579.8
    - specified type NEC 579.8
    - vitamin (*see also* Deficiency, vitamin) 269.2
  - acid-base equilibrium 276.9
  - activity and attention, simple, with hyperkinesis 314.01
  - amino acid (metabolic) (*see also* Disorder, amino acid) 270.9
    - imidazole 270.5
    - maple syrup (urine) disease 270.3
    - transport 270.0
  - assimilation, food 579.9
  - attention, simple 314.00
    - with hyperactivity 314.01
  - auditory, nerve, except deafness 388.5
  - behavior (*see also* Disturbance, conduct) 312.9
  - blood clotting (hypoproteinemia) (mechanism) (*see also* Defect, coagulation) 286.9
  - central nervous system NEC 349.9
  - cerebral nerve NEC 352.9
  - circulatory 459.9
  - conduct 312.9

> *Note — Use the following fifth-digit subclassification with categories 312.0–312.2:*
>
> *0 unspecified*
>
> *1 mild*
>
> *2 moderate*
>
> *3 severe*

    - adjustment reaction 309.3
    - adolescent onset type 312.82
    - childhood onset type 312.81
    - compulsive 312.30
      - intermittent explosive disorder 312.34
      - isolated explosive disorder 312.35
      - kleptomania 312.32
      - pathological gambling 312.31
      - pyromania 312.33
    - hyperkinetic 314.2
    - intermittent explosive 312.34
    - isolated explosive 312.35
    - mixed with emotions 312.4
    - socialized (type) 312.20
      - aggressive 312.23
      - unaggressive 312.21
    - specified type NEC 312.89
    - undersocialized, unsocialized
      - aggressive (type) 312.0 ☑
      - unaggressive (type) 312.1 ☑
  - coordination 781.3
  - cranial nerve NEC 352.9
  - deep sensibility — *see* Disturbance, sensation
  - digestive 536.9
    - psychogenic 306.4
  - electrolyte — *see* Imbalance, electrolyte
  - emotions specific to childhood or adolescence 313.9
    - with
      - academic underachievement 313.83
      - anxiety and fearfulness 313.0
      - elective mutism 313.23
      - identity disorder 313.82
      - jealousy 313.3
      - misery and unhappiness 313.1
      - oppositional defiant disorder 313.81
      - overanxiousness 313.0
      - sensitivity 313.21
      - shyness 313.21
      - social withdrawal 313.22
      - withdrawal reaction 313.22

- **Disturbance** — *see also* Disease — *continued*
  - emotions specific to childhood or adolescence — *continued*
    - involving relationship problems 313.3
    - mixed 313.89
    - specified type NEC 313.89
  - endocrine (gland) 259.9
    - neonatal, transitory 775.9
      - specified NEC 775.89
  - equilibrium 780.4
  - feeding (elderly) (infant) 783.3
    - newborn 779.3
    - nonorganic origin NEC 307.59
    - psychogenic NEC 307.59
  - fructose metabolism 271.2
  - gait 781.2
    - hysterical 300.11
  - gastric (functional) 536.9
    - motility 536.8
    - psychogenic 306.4
    - secretion 536.8
  - gastrointestinal (functional) 536.9
    - psychogenic 306.4
  - habit, child 307.9
  - hearing, except deafness 388.40
  - heart, functional (conditions classifiable to 426, 427, 428)
    - due to presence of (cardiac) prosthesis 429.4
    - postoperative (immediate) 997.1
      - long-term effect of cardiac surgery 429.4
    - psychogenic 306.2
  - hormone 259.9
  - innervation uterus, sympathetic, parasympathetic 621.8
  - keratinization NEC
    - gingiva 523.10
    - lip 528.5
    - oral (mucosa) (soft tissue) 528.79
      - residual ridge mucosa
        - excessive 528.72
        - minimal 528.71
    - tongue 528.79
  - labyrinth, labyrinthine (vestibule) 386.9
  - learning, specific NEC 315.2
  - memory (*see also* Amnesia) 780.93
    - mild, following organic brain damage 310.8
  - mental (*see also* Disorder, mental) 300.9
    - associated with diseases classified elsewhere 316
  - metabolism (acquired) (congenital) (*see also* Disorder, metabolism) 277.9
    - with
      - abortion — *see* Abortion, by type, with metabolic disorder
      - ectopic pregnancy (*see also* categories 633.0–633.9) 639.4
      - molar pregnancy (*see also* categories 630–632) 639.4
    - amino acid (*see also* Disorder, amino acid) 270.9
      - aromatic NEC 270.2
      - branched-chain 270.3
      - specified type NEC 270.8
      - straight-chain NEC 270.7
      - sulfur-bearing 270.4
      - transport 270.0
    - ammonia 270.6
    - arginine 270.6
    - argininosuccinic acid 270.6
    - carbohydrate NEC 271.9
    - cholesterol 272.9
    - citrulline 270.6
    - cystathionine 270.4
    - fat 272.9
    - following
      - abortion 639.4

- **Disturbance** — *see also* Disease — *continued*
  - metabolism (*see also* Disorder, metabolism) — *continued*
    - following — *continued*
      - ectopic or molar pregnancy 639.4
    - general 277.9
      - carbohydrate 271.9
      - iron 275.0
      - phosphate 275.3
      - sodium 276.9
    - glutamine 270.7
    - glycine 270.7
    - histidine 270.5
    - homocystine 270.4
    - in labor or delivery 669.0 ☑
    - iron 275.0
    - isoleucine 270.3
    - leucine 270.3
    - lipoid 272.9
      - specified type NEC 272.8
    - lysine 270.7
    - methionine 270.4
    - neonatal, transitory 775.9
      - specified type NEC 775.89
    - nitrogen 788.99
    - ornithine 270.6
    - phosphate 275.3
    - phosphatides 272.7
    - serine 270.7
    - sodium NEC 276.9
    - threonine 270.7
    - tryptophan 270.2
    - tyrosine 270.2
    - urea cycle 270.6
    - valine 270.3
  - motor 796.1
  - nervous functional 799.2
  - neuromuscular mechanism (eye) due to syphilis 094.84
  - nutritional 269.9
    - nail 703.8
  - ocular motion 378.87
    - psychogenic 306.7
  - oculogyric 378.87
    - psychogenic 306.7
  - oculomotor NEC 378.87
    - psychogenic 306.7
  - olfactory nerve 781.1
  - optic nerve NEC 377.49
  - oral epithelium, including tongue 528.79
    - residual ridge mucosa
      - excessive 528.72
      - minimal 528.71
  - personality (pattern) (trait) (*see also* Disorder, personality) 301.9
    - following organic brain damage 310.1
  - polyglandular 258.9
  - psychomotor 307.9
  - pupillary 379.49
  - reflex 796.1
  - rhythm, heart 427.9
    - postoperative (immediate) 997.1
      - long-term effect of cardiac surgery 429.4
    - psychogenic 306.2
  - salivary secretion 527.7
  - sensation (cold) (heat) (localization) (tactile discrimination localization) (texture) (vibratory) NEC 782.0
    - hysterical 300.11
    - skin 782.0
    - smell 781.1
    - taste 781.1
  - sensory (*see also* Disturbance, sensation) 782.0
    - innervation 782.0
  - situational (transient) (*see also* Reaction, adjustment) 309.9
    - acute 308.3
  - sleep 780.50
    - with apnea — *see* Apnea, sleep

- **Disturbance** — *see also* Disease — *continued*
  - sleep — *continued*
    - initiation or maintenance (*see also* Insomnia) 780.52
      - nonorganic origin 307.41
    - nonorganic origin 307.40
      - specified type NEC 307.49
    - specified NEC 780.59
      - nonorganic origin 307.49
    - wakefulness (*see also* Hypersomnia) 780.54
      - nonorganic origin 307.43
  - sociopathic 301.7
  - speech NEC 784.5
    - developmental 315.39
      - associated with hyperkinesis 314.1
    - secondary to organic lesion 784.5
  - stomach (functional) (*see also* Disturbance, gastric) 536.9
  - sympathetic (nerve) (*see also* Neuropathy, peripheral, autonomic) 337.9
  - temperature sense 782.0
    - hysterical 300.11
  - tooth
    - eruption 520.6
    - formation 520.4
    - structure, hereditary NEC 520.5
  - touch (*see also* Disturbance, sensation) 782.0
  - vascular 459.9
    - arteriosclerotic — *see* Arteriosclerosis
  - vasomotor 443.9
  - vasospastic 443.9
  - vestibular labyrinth 386.9
  - vision, visual NEC 368.9
    - psychophysical 368.16
    - specified NEC 368.8
    - subjective 368.10
  - voice 784.40
  - wakefulness (initiation or maintenance) (*see also* Hypersomnia) 780.54
    - nonorganic origin 307.43
- **Disulfiduria, beta-mercaptolactate-cysteine** 270.0
- **Disuse atrophy, bone** 733.7
- **Ditthomska syndrome** 307.81
- **Diuresis** 788.42
- **Divers'**
  - palsy or paralysis 993.3
  - squeeze 993.3
- **Diverticula, diverticulosis, diverticulum** (acute) (multiple) (perforated) (ruptured) 562.10
  - with diverticulitis 562.11
  - aorta (Kommerell's) 747.21
  - appendix (noninflammatory) 543.9
  - bladder (acquired) (sphincter) 596.3
    - congenital 753.8
  - broad ligament 620.8
  - bronchus (congenital) 748.3
    - acquired 494.0
      - with acute exacerbation 494.1
  - calyx, calyceal (kidney) 593.89
  - cardia (stomach) 537.1
  - cecum 562.10
    - with
      - diverticulitis 562.11
        - with hemorrhage 562.13
      - hemorrhage 562.12
    - congenital 751.5
  - colon (acquired) 562.10
    - with
      - diverticulitis 562.11
        - with hemorrhage 562.13
      - hemorrhage 562.12
    - congenital 751.5
  - duodenum 562.00
    - with
      - diverticulitis 562.01
        - with hemorrhage 562.03
      - hemorrhage 562.02

- **Dysfibrinogenemia** (congenital) — *see also* Defect, coagulation 286.3
- **Dysfunction**
  - adrenal (cortical) 255.9
    - hyperfunction 255.3
    - hypofunction 255.41
  - associated with sleep stages or arousal from sleep 780.56
    - nonorganic origin 307.47
  - bladder NEC 596.59
  - bleeding, uterus 626.8
  - brain, minimal (*see also* Hyperkinesia) 314.9
  - cerebral 348.30
  - colon 564.9
    - psychogenic 306.4
  - colostomy or enterostomy 569.62
  - cystic duct 575.8
  - diastolic 429.9
    - with heart failure — *see* Failure, heart
    - due to
      - cardiomyopathy — *see* Cardiomyopathy
      - hypertension — *see* Hypertension, heart
  - endocrine NEC 259.9
  - endometrium 621.8
  - enteric stoma 569.62
  - enterostomy 569.62
  - erectile 607.84
    - nonorganic origin 302.72
  - esophagostomy 530.87
  - Eustachian tube 381.81
  - gallbladder 575.8
  - gastrointestinal 536.9
  - gland, glandular NEC 259.9
  - heart 427.9
    - postoperative (immediate) 997.1
      - long-term effect of cardiac surgery 429.4
  - hemoglobin 289.89
  - hepatic 573.9
  - hepatocellular NEC 573.9
  - hypophysis 253.9
    - hyperfunction 253.1
    - hypofunction 253.2
    - posterior lobe 253.6
      - hypofunction 253.5
  - kidney (*see also* Disease, renal) 593.9
  - labyrinthine 386.50
    - specified NEC 386.58
  - liver 573.9
    - constitutional 277.4
  - minimal brain (child) (*see also* Hyperkinesia) 314.9
  - ovary, ovarian 256.9
    - hyperfunction 256.1
      - estrogen 256.0
    - hypofunction 256.39
      - postablative 256.2
    - postablative 256.2
    - specified NEC 256.8
  - papillary muscle 429.81
    - with myocardial infarction 410.8 ☑
  - parathyroid 252.8
    - hyperfunction 252.00
    - hypofunction 252.1
  - pineal gland 259.8
  - pituitary (gland) 253.9
    - hyperfunction 253.1
    - hypofunction 253.2
    - posterior 253.6
      - hypofunction 253.5
  - placental — *see* Placenta, insufficiency
  - platelets (blood) 287.1
  - polyglandular 258.9
    - specified NEC 258.8
  - psychosexual 302.70
    - with
      - dyspareunia (functional) (psychogenic) 302.76
      - frigidity 302.72
      - impotence 302.72
      - inhibition
        - orgasm
          - female 302.73
          - male 302.74
        - sexual
          - desire 302.71
          - excitement 302.72
      - premature ejaculation 302.75
      - sexual aversion 302.79
      - specified disorder NEC 302.79
      - vaginismus 306.51
  - pylorus 537.9
  - rectum 564.9
    - psychogenic 306.4
  - segmental (*see also* Dysfunction, somatic) 739.9
  - senile 797
  - sexual 302.70
  - sinoatrial node 427.81
  - somatic 739.9
    - abdomen 739.9
    - acromioclavicular 739.7
    - cervical 739.1
    - cervicothoracic 739.1
    - costochondral 739.8
    - costovertebral 739.8
    - extremities
      - lower 739.6
      - upper 739.7
    - head 739.0
    - hip 739.5
    - lumbar, lumbosacral 739.3
    - occipitocervical 739.0
    - pelvic 739.5
    - pubic 739.5
    - rib cage 739.8
    - sacral 739.4
    - sacrococcygeal 739.4
    - sacroiliac 739.4
    - specified site NEC 739.9
    - sternochondral 739.8
    - sternoclavicular 739.7
    - temporomandibular 739.0
    - thoracic, thoracolumbar 739.2
  - stomach 536.9
    - psychogenic 306.4
  - suprarenal 255.9
    - hyperfunction 255.3
    - hypofunction 255.41
  - symbolic NEC 784.60
    - specified type NEC 784.69
  - systolic 429.9
    - with heart failure — *see* Failure, heart
  - temporomandibular (joint) (joint-pain-syndrome) NEC 524.60
    - sounds on opening or closing 524.64
    - specified NEC 524.69
  - testicular 257.9
    - hyperfunction 257.0
    - hypofunction 257.2
    - specified type NEC 257.8
  - thymus 254.9
  - thyroid 246.9
    - complicating pregnancy, childbirth, or puerperium 648.1 ☑
    - hyperfunction — *see* Hyperthyroidism
    - hypofunction — *see* Hypothyroidism
  - uterus, complicating delivery 661.9 ☑
    - affecting fetus or newborn 763.7
    - hypertonic 661.4 ☑
    - hypotonic 661.2 ☑
      - primary 661.0 ☑
      - secondary 661.1 ☑
  - velopharyngeal (acquired) 528.9
    - congenital 750.29
  - ventricular 429.9
    - with congestive heart failure (*see also* Failure, heart) 428.0
    - due to
      - cardiomyopathy — *see* Cardiomyopathy
      - hypertension — *see* Hypertension, heart
    - left, reversible following sudden emotional stress 429.83
  - vesicourethral NEC 596.59
  - vestibular 386.50
    - specified type NEC 386.58
- **Dysgammaglobulinemia** 279.06
- **Dysgenesis**
  - gonadal (due to chromosomal anomaly) 758.6
    - pure 752.7
  - kidney(s) 753.0
  - ovarian 758.6
  - renal 753.0
  - reticular 279.2
  - seminiferous tubules 758.6
  - tidal platelet 287.31
- **Dysgerminoma** (M9060/3)
  - specified site — *see* Neoplasm, by site, malignant
  - unspecified site
    - female 183.0
    - male 186.9
- **Dysgeusia** 781.1
- **Dysgraphia** 781.3
- **Dyshidrosis** 705.81
- **Dysidrosis** 705.81
- **Dysinsulinism** 251.8
- **Dyskaryotic cervical smear** 795.09
- **Dyskeratosis** — *see also* Keratosis 701.1
  - bullosa hereditaria 757.39
  - cervix 622.10
  - congenital 757.39
  - follicularis 757.39
    - vitamin A deficiency 264.8
  - gingiva 523.8
  - oral soft tissue NEC 528.79
  - tongue 528.79
  - uterus NEC 621.8
- **Dyskinesia** 781.3
  - biliary 575.8
  - esophagus 530.5
  - hysterical 300.11
  - intestinal 564.89
  - neuroleptic-induced tardive 333.85
  - nonorganic origin 307.9
  - orofacial 333.82
    - due to drugs 333.85
  - psychogenic 307.9
  - subacute, due to drugs 333.85
  - tardive (oral) 333.85
- **Dyslalia** 784.5
  - developmental 315.39
- **Dyslexia** 784.61
  - developmental 315.02
  - secondary to organic lesion 784.61
- **Dyslipidemia** 272.4
- **Dysmaturity** — *see also* Immaturity 765.1 ☑
  - lung 770.4
  - pulmonary 770.4
- **Dysmenorrhea** (essential) (exfoliative) (functional) (intrinsic) (membranous) (primary) (secondary) 625.3
  - psychogenic 306.52
- **Dysmetabolic syndrome X** 277.7
- **Dysmetria** 781.3
- **Dysmorodystrophia mesodermalis congenita** 759.82
- **Dysnomia** 784.3
- **Dysorexia** 783.0
  - hysterical 300.11
- **Dysostosis**
  - cleidocranial, cleidocranialis 755.59
  - craniofacial 756.0
  - Fairbank's (idiopathic familial generalized osteophytosis) 756.50
  - mandibularis 756.0
  - mandibulofacial, incomplete 756.0
  - multiplex 277.5
  - orodigitofacial 759.89
- **Dyspareunia** (female) 625.0
  - male 608.89
  - psychogenic 302.76
- **Dyspepsia** (allergic) (congenital) (fermentative) (flatulent) (functional) (gastric) (gastrointestinal) (neurogenic) (occupational) (reflex) 536.8
  - acid 536.8
  - atonic 536.3
    - psychogenic 306.4
  - diarrhea 787.91
    - psychogenic 306.4
  - intestinal 564.89
    - psychogenic 306.4
  - nervous 306.4
  - neurotic 306.4
  - psychogenic 306.4
- **Dysphagia** 787.20
  - cervical 787.29
  - functional 300.11
  - hysterical 300.11
  - nervous 300.11
  - neurogenic 787.29
  - oral phase 787.21
  - oropharyngeal phase 787.22
  - pharyngeal phase 787.23
  - pharyngoesophageal phase 787.24
  - psychogenic 306.4
  - sideropenic 280.8
  - spastica 530.5
  - specified NEC 787.29
- **Dysphagocytosis, congenital** 288.1
- **Dysphasia** 784.5
- **Dysphonia** 784.49
  - clericorum 784.49
  - functional 300.11
  - hysterical 300.11
  - psychogenic 306.1
  - spastica 478.79
- **Dyspigmentation** — *see also* Pigmentation
  - eyelid (acquired) 374.52
- **Dyspituitarism** 253.9
  - hyperfunction 253.1
  - hypofunction 253.2
  - posterior lobe 253.6
- **Dysplasia** — *see also* Anomaly
  - anus 569.44
    - intraepithelial neoplasia I [AIN I] (histologically confirmed) 569.44
    - intraepithelial neoplasia II [AIN II] (histologically confirmed) 569.44
    - intraepithelial neoplasia III [AIN III] 230.6
      - anal canal 230.5
    - mild (histologically confirmed) 569.44
    - moderate (histologically confirmed) 569.44
    - severe 230.6
      - anal canal 230.5
  - artery
    - fibromuscular NEC 447.8
      - carotid 447.8
      - renal 447.3
  - bladder 596.8
  - bone (fibrous) NEC 733.29
    - diaphyseal, progressive 756.59
    - jaw 526.89
    - monostotic 733.29
    - polyostotic 756.54
    - solitary 733.29
  - brain 742.9
  - bronchopulmonary, fetus or newborn 770.7
  - cervix (uteri) 622.10
    - cervical intraepithelial neoplasia I [CIN I] 622.11
    - cervical intraepithelial neoplasia II [CIN II] 622.12
    - cervical intraepithelial neoplasia III [CIN III] 233.1

- **Dysplasia** — *see also* Anomaly — *continued*
  - cervix — *continued*
    - CIN I 622.11
    - CIN II 622.12
    - CIN III 233.1
    - mild 622.11
    - moderate 622.12
    - severe 233.1
  - chondroectodermal 756.55
  - chondromatose 756.4
  - colon 211.3
  - craniocarpotarsal 759.89
  - craniometaphyseal 756.89
  - dentinal 520.5
  - diaphyseal, progressive 756.59
  - ectodermal (anhidrotic) (Bason) (Clouston's) (congenital) (Feinmesser) (hereditary) (hidrotic) (Marshall) (Robinson's) 757.31
  - epiphysealis 756.9
    - multiplex 756.56
    - punctata 756.59
  - epiphysis 756.9
    - multiple 756.56
  - epithelial
    - epiglottis 478.79
    - uterine cervix 622.10
  - erythroid NEC 289.89
  - eye (*see also* Microphthalmos) 743.10
  - familial metaphyseal 756.89
  - fibromuscular, artery NEC 447.8
    - carotid 447.8
    - renal 447.3
  - fibrous
    - bone NEC 733.29
    - diaphyseal, progressive 756.59
    - jaw 526.89
    - monostotic 733.29
    - polyostotic 756.54
    - solitary 733.29
  - high-grade, focal — *see* Neoplasm, by site, benign
  - hip (congenital) 755.63
    - with dislocation (*see also* Dislocation, hip, congenital) 754.30
  - hypohidrotic ectodermal 757.31
  - joint 755.8
  - kidney 753.15
  - leg 755.69
  - linguofacialis 759.89
  - lung 748.5
  - macular 743.55
  - mammary (benign) (gland) 610.9
    - cystic 610.1
    - specified type NEC 610.8
  - metaphyseal 756.9
    - familial 756.89
  - monostotic fibrous 733.29
  - muscle 756.89
  - myeloid NEC 289.89
  - nervous system (general) 742.9
  - neuroectodermal 759.6
  - oculoauriculovertebral 756.0
  - oculodentodigital 759.89
  - olfactogenital 253.4
  - osteo-onycho-arthro (hereditary) 756.89
  - periosteum 733.99
  - polyostotic fibrous 756.54
  - progressive diaphyseal 756.59
  - prostate 602.3
    - intraepithelial neoplasia I [PIN I] 602.3
    - intraepithelial neoplasia II [PIN II] 602.3
    - intraepithelial neoplasia III [PIN III] 233.4
  - renal 753.15
  - renofacialis 753.0
  - retinal NEC 743.56
  - retrolental (*see also* Retinopathy of prematurity) 362.21
  - skin 709.8
  - spinal cord 742.9
  - thymic, with immunodeficiency 279.2
  - vagina 623.0
    - mild 623.0
    - moderate 623.0
    - severe 233.31
  - vocal cord 478.5
  - vulva 624.8
    - intraepithelial neoplasia I [VIN I] 624.01
    - intraepithelial neoplasia II [VIN II] 624.02
    - intraepithelial neoplasia III [VIN III] 233.32
    - mild 624.01
    - moderate 624.02
    - severe 233.32
    - VIN I 624.01
    - VIN II 624.02
    - VIN III 233.32
- **Dyspnea** (nocturnal) (paroxysmal) 786.09
  - asthmatic (bronchial) (*see also* Asthma) 493.9 ☑
    - with bronchitis (*see also* Asthma) 493.9 ☑
      - chronic 493.2 ☑
    - cardiac (*see also* Failure, ventricular, left) 428.1
  - cardiac (*see also* Failure, ventricular, left) 428.1
  - functional 300.11
  - hyperventilation 786.01
  - hysterical 300.11
  - Monday morning 504
  - newborn 770.89
  - psychogenic 306.1
  - uremic — *see* Uremia
- **Dyspraxia** 781.3
  - syndrome 315.4
- **Dysproteinemia** 273.8
  - transient with copper deficiency 281.4
- **Dysprothrombinemia** (constitutional) — *see also* Defect, coagulation 286.3
- **Dysreflexia, autonomic** 337.3
- **Dysrhythmia**
  - cardiac 427.9
    - postoperative (immediate) 997.1
      - long-term effect of cardiac surgery 429.4
    - specified type NEC 427.89
  - cerebral or cortical 348.30
- **Dyssecretosis, mucoserous** 710.2
- **Dyssocial reaction, without manifest psychiatric disorder**
  - adolescent V71.02
  - adult V71.01
  - child V71.02
- **Dyssomnia** NEC 780.56
  - nonorganic origin 307.47
- **Dyssplenism** 289.4
- **Dyssynergia**
  - biliary (*see also* Disease, biliary) 576.8
  - cerebellaris myoclonica 334.2
  - detrusor sphincter (bladder) 596.55
  - ventricular 429.89
- **Dystasia, hereditary areflexic** 334.3
- **Dysthymia** 300.4
- **Dysthymic disorder** 300.4
- **Dysthyroidism** 246.9
- **Dystocia** 660.9 ☑
  - affecting fetus or newborn 763.1
  - cervical 661.2 ☑
    - affecting fetus or newborn 763.7
  - contraction ring 661.4 ☑
    - affecting fetus or newborn 763.7
  - fetal 660.9 ☑
    - abnormal size 653.5 ☑
    - affecting fetus or newborn 763.1
    - deformity 653.7 ☑
  - maternal 660.9 ☑
    - affecting fetus or newborn 763.1
  - positional 660.0 ☑
    - affecting fetus or newborn 763.1
  - shoulder (girdle) 660.4 ☑
    - affecting fetus or newborn 763.1
  - uterine NEC 661.4 ☑
- **Dystocia** — *continued*
  - uterine — *continued*
    - affecting fetus or newborn 763.7
- **Dystonia**
  - acute
    - due to drugs 333.72
    - neuroleptic-induced acute 333.72
  - deformans progressiva 333.6
  - lenticularis 333.6
  - musculorum deformans 333.6
  - torsion (idiopathic) 333.6
    - acquired 333.79
    - fragments (of) 333.89
    - genetic 333.6
    - symptomatic 333.79
- **Dystonic**
  - movements 781.0
- **Dystopia kidney** 753.3
- **Dystrophia myotonica** 359.2 ☑
- **Dystrophy, dystrophia** 783.9
  - adiposogenital 253.8
  - asphyxiating thoracic 756.4
  - Becker's type 359.22
  - brevicollis 756.16
  - Bruch's membrane 362.77
  - cervical (sympathetic) NEC 337.09
  - chondro-osseus with punctate epiphyseal dysplasia 756.59
  - choroid (hereditary) 363.50
    - central (areolar) (partial) 363.53
      - total (gyrate) 363.54
    - circinate 363.53
    - circumpapillary (partial) 363.51
      - total 363.52
    - diffuse
      - partial 363.56
      - total 363.57
    - generalized
      - partial 363.56
      - total 363.57
    - gyrate
      - central 363.54
      - generalized 363.57
    - helicoid 363.52
    - peripapillary — *see* Dystrophy, choroid, circumpapillary
    - serpiginous 363.54
  - cornea (hereditary) 371.50
    - anterior NEC 371.52
    - Cogan's 371.52
    - combined 371.57
    - crystalline 371.56
    - endothelial (Fuchs') 371.57
    - epithelial 371.50
      - juvenile 371.51
      - microscopic cystic 371.52
    - granular 371.53
    - lattice 371.54
    - macular 371.55
    - marginal (Terrien's) 371.48
    - Meesman's 371.51
    - microscopic cystic (epithelial) 371.52
    - nodular, Salzmann's 371.46
    - polymorphous 371.58
    - posterior NEC 371.58
    - ring-like 371.52
    - Salzmann's nodular 371.46
    - stromal NEC 371.56
  - dermatochondrocorneal 371.50
  - Duchenne's 359.1
  - due to malnutrition 263.9
  - Erb's 359.1
  - familial
    - hyperplastic periosteal 756.59
    - osseous 277.5
  - foveal 362.77
  - Fuchs', cornea 371.57
  - Gowers' muscular 359.1
  - hair 704.2
  - hereditary, progressive muscular 359.1
  - hypogenital, with diabetic tendency 759.81
  - Landouzy-Déjérine 359.1
  - Leyden-Möbius 359.1
- **Dystrophy, dystrophia** — *continued*
  - mesodermalis congenita 759.82
  - muscular 359.1
    - congenital (hereditary) 359.0
      - myotonic 359.22
    - distal 359.1
    - Duchenne's 359.1
    - Erb's 359.1
    - fascioscapulohumeral 359.1
    - Gowers' 359.1
    - hereditary (progressive) 359.1
    - Landouzy-Déjérine 359.1
    - limb-girdle 359.1
    - myotonic 359.21
    - progressive (hereditary) 359.1
      - Charcôt-Marie-Tooth 356.1
    - pseudohypertrophic (infantile) 359.1
  - myocardium, myocardial (*see also* Degeneration, myocardial) 429.1
  - myotonic 359.21
  - myotonica 359.21
  - nail 703.8
    - congenital 757.5
  - neurovascular (traumatic) (*see also* Neuropathy, peripheral, autonomic) 337.9
  - nutritional 263.9
  - ocular 359.1
  - oculocerebrorenal 270.8
  - oculopharyngeal 359.1
  - ovarian 620.8
  - papillary (and pigmentary) 701.1
  - pelvicrural atrophic 359.1
  - pigmentary (*see also* Acanthosis) 701.2
  - pituitary (gland) 253.8
  - polyglandular 258.8
  - posttraumatic sympathetic — *see* Dystrophy, sympathetic
  - progressive ophthalmoplegic 359.1
  - reflex neuromuscular — *see* Dystrophy, sympathetic
  - retina, retinal (hereditary) 362.70
    - albipunctate 362.74
    - Bruch's membrane 362.77
    - cone, progressive 362.75
    - hyaline 362.77
    - in
      - Bassen-Kornzweig syndrome 272.5 *[362.72]*
      - cerebroretinal lipidosis 330.1 *[362.71]*
      - Refsum's disease 356.3 *[362.72]*
      - systemic lipidosis 272.7 *[362.71]*
    - juvenile (Stargardt's) 362.75
    - pigmentary 362.74
    - pigment epithelium 362.76
    - progressive cone (-rod) 362.75
    - pseudoinflammatory foveal 362.77
    - rod, progressive 362.75
    - sensory 362.75
    - vitelliform 362.76
  - Salzmann's nodular 371.46
  - scapuloperoneal 359.1
  - skin NEC 709.9
  - sympathetic (posttraumatic) (reflex) 337.20
    - lower limb 337.22
    - specified site NEC 337.29
    - upper limb 337.21
  - tapetoretinal NEC 362.74
  - thoracic asphyxiating 756.4
  - unguium 703.8
    - congenital 757.5
  - vitreoretinal (primary) 362.73
    - secondary 362.66
  - vulva 624.09
- **Dysuria** 788.1
  - psychogenic 306.53

E

- **Eagle-Barrett syndrome** 756.71
- **Eales' disease** (syndrome) 362.18
- **Ear** — *see also* condition
  - ache 388.70

Ear — *see also* condition — *continued*
ache — *continued*
otogenic 388.71
referred 388.72
lop 744.29
piercing V50.3
swimmers' acute 380.12
tank 380.12
tropical 111.8 *[380.15]*
wax 380.4
Earache 388.70
otogenic 388.71
referred 388.72
Early satiety 780.94
Eaton-Lambert syndrome — *see also* Neoplasm, by site, malignant 199.1 *[358.1]*
Eberth's disease (typhoid fever) 002.0
Ebstein's
anomaly or syndrome (downward displacement, tricuspid valve into right ventricle) 746.2
disease (diabetes) 250.4 ☑ *[581.81]*
due to secondary diabetes 249.4 ☑ *[581.81]*
Eccentro-osteochondrodysplasia 277.5
Ecchondroma (M9210/0) — *see* Neoplasm, bone, benign
Ecchondrosis (M9210/1) 238.0
Ecchordosis physaliphora 756.0
Ecchymosis (multiple) 459.89
conjunctiva 372.72
eye (traumatic) 921.0
eyelids (traumatic) 921.1
newborn 772.6
spontaneous 782.7
traumatic — *see* Contusion
Echinococciasis — *see* Echinococcus
Echinococcosis — *see* Echinococcus
Echinococcus (infection) 122.9
granulosus 122.4
liver 122.0
lung 122.1
orbit 122.3 *[376.13]*
specified site NEC 122.3
thyroid 122.2
liver NEC 122.8
granulosus 122.0
multilocularis 122.5
lung NEC 122.9
granulosus 122.1
multilocularis 122.6
multilocularis 122.7
liver 122.5
specified site NEC 122.6
orbit 122.9 *[376.13]*
granulosus 122.3 *[376.13]*
multilocularis 122.6 *[376.13]*
specified site NEC 122.9
granulosus 122.3
multilocularis 122.6 *[376.13]*
thyroid NEC 122.9
granulosus 122.2
multilocularis 122.6
Echinorhynchiasis 127.7
Echinostomiasis 121.8
Echolalia 784.69
ECHO virus infection NEC 079.1
Eclampsia, eclamptic (coma) (convulsions) (delirium) 780.39
female, child-bearing age NEC — *see* Eclampsia, pregnancy
gravidarum — *see* Eclampsia, pregnancy
male 780.39
not associated with pregnancy or childbirth 780.39
pregnancy, childbirth, or puerperium 642.6 ☑
with pre-existing hypertension 642.7 ☑
affecting fetus or newborn 760.0
uremic 586
Eclipse blindness (total) 363.31
Economic circumstance affecting care V60.9
Economic circumstance affecting care — *continued*
specified type NEC V60.8
Economo's disease (encephalitis lethargica) 049.8
Ectasia, ectasis
aorta (*see also* Aneurysm, aorta) 441.9
ruptured 441.5
breast 610.4
capillary 448.9
cornea (marginal) (postinfectional) 371.71
duct (mammary) 610.4
gastric antral vascular (GAVE) 537.82
with hemorrhage 537.83
without hemorrhage 537.82
kidney 593.89
mammary duct (gland) 610.4
papillary 448.9
renal 593.89
salivary gland (duct) 527.8
scar, cornea 371.71
sclera 379.11
Ecthyma 686.8
contagiosum 051.2
gangrenosum 686.09
infectiosum 051.2
Ectocardia 746.87
Ectodermal dysplasia, congenital 757.31
Ectodermosis erosiva pluriorificialis 695.19
Ectopic, ectopia (congenital) 759.89
abdominal viscera 751.8
due to defect in anterior abdominal wall 756.79
ACTH syndrome 255.0
adrenal gland 759.1
anus 751.5
auricular beats 427.61
beats 427.60
bladder 753.5
bone and cartilage in lung 748.69
brain 742.4
breast tissue 757.6
cardiac 746.87
cerebral 742.4
cordis 746.87
endometrium 617.9
gallbladder 751.69
gastric mucosa 750.7
gestation — *see* Pregnancy, ectopic
heart 746.87
hormone secretion NEC 259.3
hyperparathyroidism 259.3
kidney (crossed) (intrathoracic) (pelvis) 753.3
in pregnancy or childbirth 654.4 ☑
causing obstructed labor 660.2 ☑
lens 743.37
lentis 743.37
mole — *see* Pregnancy, ectopic
organ or site NEC — *see* Malposition, congenital
ovary 752.0
pancreas, pancreatic tissue 751.7
pregnancy — *see* Pregnancy, ectopic
pupil 364.75
renal 753.3
sebaceous glands of mouth 750.26
secretion
ACTH 255.0
adrenal hormone 259.3
adrenalin 259.3
adrenocorticotropin 255.0
antidiuretic hormone (ADH) 259.3
epinephrine 259.3
hormone NEC 259.3
norepinephrine 259.3
pituitary (posterior) 259.3
spleen 759.0
testis 752.51
thyroid 759.2
ureter 753.4
ventricular beats 427.69
Ectopic, ectopia — *continued*
vesicae 753.5
Ectrodactyly 755.4
finger (*see also* Absence, finger, congenital) 755.29
toe (*see also* Absence, toe, congenital) 755.39
Ectromelia 755.4
lower limb 755.30
upper limb 755.20
Ectropion 374.10
anus 569.49
cervix 622.0
with mention of cervicitis 616.0
cicatricial 374.14
congenital 743.62
eyelid 374.10
cicatricial 374.14
congenital 743.62
mechanical 374.12
paralytic 374.12
senile 374.11
spastic 374.13
iris (pigment epithelium) 364.54
lip (congenital) 750.26
acquired 528.5
mechanical 374.12
paralytic 374.12
rectum 569.49
senile 374.11
spastic 374.13
urethra 599.84
uvea 364.54
Eczema (acute) (allergic) (chronic) (erythematous) (fissum) (occupational) (rubrum) (squamous) 692.9
asteatotic 706.8
atopic 691.8
contact NEC 692.9
dermatitis NEC 692.9
due to specified cause — *see* Dermatitis, due to
dyshidrotic 705.81
external ear 380.22
flexural 691.8
gouty 274.89
herpeticum 054.0
hypertrophicum 701.8
hypostatic — *see* Varicose, vein
impetiginous 684
infantile (acute) (chronic) (due to any substance) (intertriginous) (seborrheic) 690.12
intertriginous NEC 692.9
infantile 690.12
intrinsic 691.8
lichenified NEC 692.9
marginatum 110.3
nummular 692.9
pustular 686.8
seborrheic 690.18
infantile 690.12
solare 692.72
stasis (lower extremity) 454.1
ulcerated 454.2
vaccination, vaccinatum 999.0
varicose (lower extremity) — *see* Varicose, vein
verrucosum callosum 698.3
Eczematoid, exudative 691.8
Eddowes' syndrome (brittle bones and blue sclera) 756.51
Edema, edematous 782.3
with nephritis (*see also* Nephrosis) 581.9
allergic 995.1
angioneurotic (allergic) (any site) (with urticaria) 995.1
hereditary 277.6
angiospastic 443.9
Berlin's (traumatic) 921.3
brain 348.5
due to birth injury 767.8
fetus or newborn 767.8
cardiac (*see also* Failure, heart) 428.0
Edema, edematous — *continued*
cardiovascular (*see also* Failure, heart) 428.0
cerebral — *see* Edema, brain
cerebrospinal vessel — *see* Edema, brain
cervix (acute) (uteri) 622.8
puerperal, postpartum 674.8 ☑
chronic hereditary 757.0
circumscribed, acute 995.1
hereditary 277.6
complicating pregnancy (gestational) 646.1 ☑
with hypertension — *see* Toxemia, of pregnancy
conjunctiva 372.73
connective tissue 782.3
cornea 371.20
due to contact lenses 371.24
idiopathic 371.21
secondary 371.22
cystoid macular 362.53
due to
lymphatic obstruction — *see* Edema, lymphatic
salt retention 276.0
epiglottis — *see* Edema, glottis
essential, acute 995.1
hereditary 277.6
extremities, lower — *see* Edema, legs
eyelid NEC 374.82
familial, hereditary (legs) 757.0
famine 262
fetus or newborn 778.5
genital organs
female 629.89
male 608.86
gestational 646.1 ☑
with hypertension — *see* Toxemia, of pregnancy
glottis, glottic, glottides (obstructive) (passive) 478.6
allergic 995.1
hereditary 277.6
due to external agent — *see* Condition, respiratory, acute, due to specified agent
heart (*see also* Failure, heart) 428.0
newborn 779.89
heat 992.7
hereditary (legs) 757.0
inanition 262
infectious 782.3
intracranial 348.5
due to injury at birth 767.8
iris 364.89
joint (*see also* Effusion, joint) 719.0 ☑
larynx (*see also* Edema, glottis) 478.6
legs 782.3
due to venous obstruction 459.2
hereditary 757.0
localized 782.3
due to venous obstruction 459.2
lower extremity 459.2
lower extremities — *see* Edema, legs
lung 514
acute 518.4
with heart disease or failure (*see also* Failure, ventricular, left) 428.1
congestive 428.0
chemical (due to fumes or vapors) 506.1
due to
external agent(s) NEC 508.9
specified NEC 508.8
fumes and vapors (chemical) (inhalation) 506.1
radiation 508.0
chemical (acute) 506.1
chronic 506.4
chronic 514
chemical (due to fumes or vapors) 506.4
due to
external agent(s) NEC 508.9

Ehrlichiosis — *continued*
  specified type NEC 082.49
Eichstedt's disease (pityriasis versicolor) 111.0
Eisenmenger's complex or syndrome (ventricular septal defect) 745.4
Ejaculation, semen
  painful 608.89
    psychogenic 306.59
  premature 302.75
  retrograde 608.87
Ekbom syndrome (restless legs) 333.94
Ekman's syndrome (brittle bones and blue sclera) 756.51
Elastic skin 756.83
  acquired 701.8
Elastofibroma (M8820/0) — *see* Neoplasm, connective tissue, benign
Elastoidosis
  cutanea nodularis 701.8
  cutis cystica et comedonica 701.8
Elastoma 757.39
  juvenile 757.39
  Miescher's (elastosis perforans serpiginosa) 701.1
Elastomyofibrosis 425.3
Elastosis 701.8
  atrophicans 701.8
  perforans serpiginosa 701.1
  reactive perforating 701.1
  senilis 701.8
  solar (actinic) 692.74
Elbow — *see* condition
Electric
  current, electricity, effects (concussion) (fatal) (nonfatal) (shock) 994.8
    burn — *see* Burn, by site
  feet (foot) syndrome 266.2
  shock from electroshock gun (taser) 994.8
Electrocution 994.8
Electrolyte imbalance 276.9
  with
    abortion — *see* Abortion, by type, with metabolic disorder
    ectopic pregnancy (*see also* categories 633.0–633.9) 639.4
    hyperemesis gravidarum (before 22 completed weeks gestation) 643.1 ☑
    molar pregnancy (*see also* categories 630–632) 639.4
  following
    abortion 639.4
    ectopic or molar pregnancy 639.4
Elephantiasis (nonfilarial) 457.1
  arabicum (*see also* Infestation, filarial) 125.9
  congenita hereditaria 757.0
  congenital (any site) 757.0
  due to
    Brugia (malayi) 125.1
    mastectomy operation 457.0
    Wuchereria (bancrofti) 125.0
      malayi 125.1
  eyelid 374.83
  filarial (*see also* Infestation, filarial) 125.9
  filariensis (*see also* Infestation, filarial) 125.9
  gingival 523.8
  glandular 457.1
  graecorum 030.9
  lymphangiectatic 457.1
  lymphatic vessel 457.1
    due to mastectomy operation 457.0
  neuromatosa 237.71
  postmastectomy 457.0
  scrotum 457.1
  streptococcal 457.1
  surgical 997.99
    postmastectomy 457.0
  telangiectodes 457.1
  vulva (nonfilarial) 624.8
Elephant man syndrome 237.71
Elevated — *see* Elevation
Elevation
  17-ketosteroids 791.9
  acid phosphatase 790.5
  alkaline phosphatase 790.5
  amylase 790.5
  antibody titers 795.79
  basal metabolic rate (BMR) 794.7
  blood pressure (*see also* Hypertension) 401.9
    reading (incidental) (isolated) (nonspecific), no diagnosis of hypertension 796.2
  blood sugar 790.29
  body temperature (of unknown origin) (*see also* Pyrexia) 780.60
  cancer antigen 125 [CA 125] 795.82
  carcinoembryonic antigen [CEA] 795.81
  cholesterol 272.0
    with high triglycerides 272.2
  conjugate, eye 378.81
  C-reactive protein (CRP) 790.95
  CRP (C-reactive protein) 790.95
  diaphragm, congenital 756.6
  glucose
    fasting 790.21
    tolerance test 790.22
  immunoglobulin level 795.79
  indolacetic acid 791.9
  lactic acid dehydrogenase (LDH) level 790.4
  leukocytes 288.60
  lipase 790.5
  lipoprotein a level 272.8
  liver function test (LFT) 790.6
    alkaline phosphatase 790.5
    aminotransferase 790.4
    bilirubin 782.4
    hepatic enzyme NEC 790.5
    lactate dehydrogenase 790.4
  lymphocytes 288.61
  prostate specific antigen (PSA) 790.93
  renin 790.99
    in hypertension (*see also* Hypertension, renovascular) 405.91
  Rh titer 999.7
  scapula, congenital 755.52
  sedimentation rate 790.1
  SGOT 790.4
  SGPT 790.4
  transaminase 790.4
  triglycerides 272.1
    with high cholesterol 272.2
  vanillylmandelic acid 791.9
  venous pressure 459.89
  VMA 791.9
  white blood cell count 288.60
    specified NEC 288.69
Elliptocytosis (congenital) (hereditary) 282.1
  Hb-C (disease) 282.7
  hemoglobin disease 282.7
  sickle-cell (disease) 282.60
    trait 282.5
Ellison-Zollinger syndrome (gastric hypersecretion with pancreatic islet cell tumor) 251.5
Ellis-van Creveld disease or syndrome (chondroectodermal dysplasia) 756.55
Elongation, elongated (congenital) — *see also* Distortion
  bone 756.9
  cervix (uteri) 752.49
    acquired 622.6
    hypertrophic 622.6
  colon 751.5
  common bile duct 751.69
  cystic duct 751.69
  frenulum, penis 752.69
  labia minora, acquired 624.8
  ligamentum patellae 756.89
  petiolus (epiglottidis) 748.3
  styloid bone (process) 733.99
  tooth, teeth 520.2
Elongation, elongated — *see also* Distortion — *continued*
  uvula 750.26
    acquired 528.9
Elschnig bodies or pearls 366.51
El Tor cholera 001.1
Emaciation (due to malnutrition) 261
Emancipation disorder 309.22
Embadomoniasis 007.8
Embarrassment heart, cardiac — *see* Disease, heart
Embedded tooth, teeth 520.6
  root only 525.3
Embolic — *see* condition
Embolism 444.9
  with
    abortion — *see* Abortion, by type, with embolism
    ectopic pregnancy (*see also* categories 633.0–633.9) 639.6
    molar pregnancy (*see also* categories 630–632) 639.6
  air (any site) 958.0
    with
      abortion — *see* Abortion, by type, with embolism
      ectopic pregnancy (*see also* categories 633.0–633.9) 639.6
      molar pregnancy (*see also* categories 630–632) 639.6
    due to implanted device — *see* Complications, due to (presence of) any device, implant, or graft classified to 996.0–996.5 NEC
    following
      abortion 639.6
      ectopic or molar pregnancy 639.6
      infusion, perfusion, or transfusion 999.1
    in pregnancy, childbirth, or puerperium 673.0 ☑
    traumatic 958.0
  amniotic fluid (pulmonary) 673.1 ☑
    with
      abortion — *see* Abortion, by type, with embolism
      ectopic pregnancy (*see also* categories 633.0–633.9) 639.6
      molar pregnancy (*see also* categories 630–632) 639.6
    following
      abortion 639.6
      ectopic or molar pregnancy 639.6
  aorta, aortic 444.1
    abdominal 444.0
    bifurcation 444.0
    saddle 444.0
    thoracic 444.1
  artery 444.9
    auditory, internal 433.8 ☑
    basilar (*see also* Occlusion, artery, basilar) 433.0 ☑
    bladder 444.89
    carotid (common) (internal) (*see also* Occlusion, artery, carotid) 433.1 ☑
    cerebellar (anterior inferior) (posterior inferior) (superior) 433.8 ☑
    cerebral (*see also* Embolism, brain) 434.1 ☑
    choroidal (anterior) 433.8 ☑
    communicating posterior 433.8 ☑
    coronary (*see also* Infarct, myocardium) 410.9 ☑
      without myocardial infarction 411.81
    extremity 444.22
      lower 444.22
      upper 444.21
    hypophyseal 433.8 ☑
Embolism — *continued*
  artery — *continued*
    mesenteric (with gangrene) 557.0
    ophthalmic (*see also* Occlusion, retina) 362.30
    peripheral 444.22
    pontine 433.8 ☑
    precerebral NEC — *see* Occlusion, artery, precerebral
    pulmonary — *see* Embolism, pulmonary
    pyemic 449
      pulmonary 415.12
    renal 593.81
    retinal (*see also* Occlusion, retina) 362.30
    septic 449
      pulmonary 415.12
    specified site NEC 444.89
    vertebral (*see also* Occlusion, artery, vertebral) 433.2 ☑
  auditory, internal 433.8 ☑
  basilar (artery) (*see also* Occlusion, artery, basilar) 433.0 ☑
  birth, mother — *see* Embolism, obstetrical
  blood-clot
    with
      abortion — *see* Abortion, by type, with embolism
      ectopic pregnancy (*see also* categories 633.0–633.9) 639.6
      molar pregnancy (*see also* categories 630–632) 639.6
    following
      abortion 639.6
      ectopic or molar pregnancy 639.6
    in pregnancy, childbirth, or puerperium 673.2 ☑
  brain 434.1 ☑
    with
      abortion — *see* Abortion, by type, with embolism
      ectopic pregnancy (*see also* categories 633.0–633.9) 639.6
      molar pregnancy (*see also* categories 630–632) 639.6
    following
      abortion 639.6
      ectopic or molar pregnancy 639.6
    late effect — *see* Late effect(s) (of) cerebrovascular disease
    puerperal, postpartum, childbirth 674.0 ☑
  capillary 448.9
  cardiac (*see also* Infarct, myocardium) 410.9 ☑
  carotid (artery) (common) (internal) (*see also* Occlusion, artery, carotid) 433.1 ☑
  cavernous sinus (venous) — *see* Embolism, intracranial venous sinus
  cerebral (*see also* Embolism, brain) 434.1 ☑
  cholesterol — *see* Atheroembolism
  choroidal (anterior) (artery) 433.8 ☑
  coronary (artery or vein) (systemic) (*see also* Infarct, myocardium) 410.9 ☑
    without myocardial infarction 411.81
  due to (presence of) any device, implant, or graft classifiable to 996.0–996.5 — *see* Complications, due to (presence of) any device, implant, or graft classified to 996.0–996.5 NEC
  encephalomalacia (*see also* Embolism, brain) 434.1 ☑
  extremities 444.22
    lower 444.22

Embolism — *continued*
  extremities — *continued*
    upper 444.21
  eye 362.30
  fat (cerebral) (pulmonary) (systemic) 958.1
    with
      abortion — *see* Abortion, by type, with embolism
      ectopic pregnancy (*see also* categories 633.0–633.9) 639.6
      molar pregnancy (*see also* categories 630–632) 639.6
    complicating delivery or puerperium 673.8 ☑
    following
      abortion 639.6
      ectopic or molar pregnancy 639.6
    in pregnancy, childbirth, or the puerperium 673.8 ☑
  femoral (artery) 444.22
    vein 453.8
      deep 453.41
  following
    abortion 639.6
    ectopic or molar pregnancy 639.6
    infusion, perfusion, or transfusion
      air 999.1
      thrombus 999.2
  heart (fatty) (*see also* Infarct, myocardium) 410.9 ☑
  hepatic (vein) 453.0
  iliac (artery) 444.81
  iliofemoral 444.81
  in pregnancy, childbirth, or puerperium (pulmonary) — *see* Embolism, obstetrical
  intestine (artery) (vein) (with gangrene) 557.0
  intracranial (*see also* Embolism, brain) 434.1 ☑
    venous sinus (any) 325
      late effect — *see* category 326
      nonpyogenic 437.6
        in pregnancy or puerperium 671.5 ☑
  kidney (artery) 593.81
  lateral sinus (venous) — *see* Embolism, intracranial venous sinus
  longitudinal sinus (venous) — *see* Embolism, intracranial venous sinus
  lower extremity 444.22
  lung (massive) — *see* Embolism, pulmonary
  meninges (*see also* Embolism, brain) 434.1 ☑
  mesenteric (artery) (with gangrene) 557.0
  multiple NEC 444.9
  obstetrical (pulmonary) 673.2 ☑
    air 673.0 ☑
    amniotic fluid (pulmonary) 673.1 ☑
    blood-clot 673.2 ☑
    cardiac 674.8 ☑
    fat 673.8 ☑
    heart 674.8 ☑
    pyemic 673.3 ☑
    septic 673.3 ☑
    specified NEC 674.8 ☑
  ophthalmic (*see also* Occlusion, retina) 362.30
  paradoxical NEC 444.9
  penis 607.82
  peripheral arteries NEC 444.22
    lower 444.22
    upper 444.21
  pituitary 253.8
  popliteal (artery) 444.22
  portal (vein) 452
  postoperative NEC 997.2
    cerebral 997.02
    mesenteric artery 997.71

Embolism — *continued*
  postoperative — *continued*
    other vessels 997.79
    peripheral vascular 997.2
    pulmonary 415.11
      septic 415.11
    renal artery 997.72
  precerebral artery (*see also* Occlusion, artery, precerebral) 433.9 ☑
  puerperal — *see* Embolism, obstetrical
  pulmonary (artery) (vein) 415.19
    with
      abortion — *see* Abortion, by type, with embolism
      ectopic pregnancy (*see also* categories 633.0–633.9) 639.6
      molar pregnancy (*see also* categories 630–632) 639.6
    following
      abortion 639.6
      ectopic or molar pregnancy 639.6
    iatrogenic 415.11
    in pregnancy, childbirth, or puerperium — *see* Embolism, obstetrical
    postoperative 415.11
    septic 415.12
  pyemic (multiple) (*see also* Septicemia) 415.12
    with
      abortion — *see* Abortion, by type, with embolism
      ectopic pregnancy (*see also* categories 633.0–633.9) 639.6
      molar pregnancy (*see also* categories 630–632) 639.6
    Aerobacter aerogenes 415.12
    enteric gram-negative bacilli 415.12
    Enterobacter aerogenes 415.12
    Escherichia coli 415.12
    following
      abortion 639.6
      ectopic or molar pregnancy 639.6
    Hemophilus influenzae 415.12
    pneumococcal 415.12
    Proteus vulgaris 415.12
    Pseudomonas (aeruginosa) 415.12
    puerperal, postpartum, childbirth (any organism) 673.3 ☑
    Serratia 415.12
    specified organism NEC 415.12
    staphylococcal 415.12
      aureus 415.12
      specified organism NEC 415.12
    streptococcal 415.12
  renal (artery) 593.81
    vein 453.3
  retina, retinal (*see also* Occlusion, retina) 362.30
  saddle (aorta) 444.0
  septic 415.12
    arterial 449
  septicemic — *see* Embolism, pyemic
  sinus — *see* Embolism, intracranial venous sinus
  soap
    with
      abortion — *see* Abortion, by type, with embolism
      ectopic pregnancy (*see also* categories 633.0–633.9) 639.6
      molar pregnancy (*see also* categories 630–632) 639.6
    following
      abortion 639.6
      ectopic or molar pregnancy 639.6
  spinal cord (nonpyogenic) 336.1
    in pregnancy or puerperium 671.5 ☑

Embolism — *continued*
  spinal cord — *continued*
    pyogenic origin 324.1
      late effect — *see* category 326
  spleen, splenic (artery) 444.89
  thrombus (thromboembolism) following infusion, perfusion, or transfusion 999.2
  upper extremity 444.21
  vein 453.9
    with inflammation or phlebitis — *see* Thrombophlebitis
    cerebral (*see also* Embolism, brain) 434.1 ☑
    coronary (*see also* Infarct, myocardium) 410.9 ☑
      without myocardial infarction 411.81
    hepatic 453.0
    lower extremity 453.8
      deep 453.40
        calf 453.42
        distal (lower leg) 453.42
        femoral 453.41
        iliac 453.41
        lower leg 453.42
        peroneal 453.42
        popliteal 453.41
        proximal (upper leg) 453.41
        thigh 453.41
        tibial 453.42
    mesenteric (with gangrene) 557.0
    portal 452
    pulmonary — *see* Embolism, pulmonary
    renal 453.3
    specified NEC 453.8
      with inflammation or phlebitis — *see* Thrombophlebitis
  vena cava (inferior) (superior) 453.2
  vessels of brain (*see also* Embolism, brain) 434.1 ☑
Embolization — *see* **Embolism**
Embolus — *see* Embolism
Embryoma (M9080/1) — *see also* Neoplasm, by site, uncertain behavior
  benign (M9080/0) — *see* Neoplasm, by site, benign
  kidney (M8960/3) 189.0
  liver (M8970/3) 155.0
  malignant (M9080/3) (*see also* Neoplasm, by site, malignant)
    kidney (M8960/3) 189.0
    liver (M8970/3) 155.0
    testis (M9070/3) 186.9
      undescended 186.0
  testis (M9070/3) 186.9
    undescended 186.0
Embryonic
  circulation 747.9
  heart 747.9
  vas deferens 752.89
Embryopathia NEC 759.9
Embryotomy, fetal 763.89
Embryotoxon 743.43
  interfering with vision 743.42
Emesis — *see also* Vomiting
  gravidarum — *see* Hyperemesis, gravidarum
Emissions, nocturnal (semen) 608.89
Emotional
  crisis — *see* Crisis, emotional
  disorder (*see also* Disorder, mental) 300.9
  instability (excessive) 301.3
  overlay — *see* Reaction, adjustment
  upset 300.9
Emotionality, pathological 301.3
Emotogenic disease — *see also* Disorder, psychogenic 306.9

Emphysema (atrophic) (centriacinar) (centrilobular) (chronic) (diffuse) (essential) (hypertrophic) (interlobular) (lung) (obstructive) (panlobular) (paracicatricial) (paracinar) (postural) (pulmonary) (senile) (subpleural) (traction) (unilateral) (unilobular) (vesicular) 492.8
  with bronchitis
    chronic 491.20
      with
        acute bronchitis 491.22
        exacerbation (acute) 491.21
  bullous (giant) 492.0
  cellular tissue 958.7
    surgical 998.81
  compensatory 518.2
  congenital 770.2
  conjunctiva 372.89
  connective tissue 958.7
    surgical 998.81
  due to fumes or vapors 506.4
  eye 376.89
  eyelid 374.85
    surgical 998.81
    traumatic 958.7
  fetus or newborn (interstitial) (mediastinal) (unilobular) 770.2
  heart 416.9
  interstitial 518.1
    congenital 770.2
    fetus or newborn 770.2
  laminated tissue 958.7
    surgical 998.81
  mediastinal 518.1
    fetus or newborn 770.2
  newborn (interstitial) (mediastinal) (unilobular) 770.2
  obstructive diffuse with fibrosis 492.8
  orbit 376.89
  subcutaneous 958.7
    due to trauma 958.7
    nontraumatic 518.1
    surgical 998.81
  surgical 998.81
  thymus (gland) (congenital) 254.8
  traumatic 958.7
  tuberculous (*see also* Tuberculosis, pulmonary) 011.9 ☑
Employment examination (certification) V70.5
Empty sella (turcica) syndrome 253.8
Empyema (chest) (diaphragmatic) (double) (encapsulated) (general) (interlobar) (lung) (medial) (necessitatis) (perforating chest wall) (pleura) (pneumococcal) (residual) (sacculated) (streptococcal) (supradiaphragmatic) 510.9
  with fistula 510.0
  accessory sinus (chronic) (*see also* Sinusitis) 473.9
  acute 510.9
    with fistula 510.0
  antrum (chronic) (*see also* Sinusitis, maxillary) 473.0
  brain (any part) (*see also* Abscess, brain) 324.0
  ethmoidal (sinus) (chronic) (*see also* Sinusitis, ethmoidal) 473.2
  extradural (*see also* Abscess, extradural) 324.9
  frontal (sinus) (chronic) (*see also* Sinusitis, frontal) 473.1
  gallbladder (*see also* Cholecystitis, acute) 575.0
  mastoid (process) (acute) (*see also* Mastoiditis, acute) 383.00
  maxilla, maxillary 526.4
    sinus (chronic) (*see also* Sinusitis, maxillary) 473.0
  nasal sinus (chronic) (*see also* Sinusitis) 473.9
  sinus (accessory) (nasal) (*see also* Sinusitis) 473.9

Endometritis — *continued*
  blennorrhagic — *continued*
    chronic or duration of 2 months or over 098.36
  cervix, cervical (*see also* Cervicitis) 616.0
    hyperplastic 616.0
  chronic 615.1
  complicating pregnancy 670 ☑
    affecting fetus or newborn 760.8
  decidual 615.9
  following
    abortion 639.0
    ectopic or molar pregnancy 639.0
  gonorrheal (acute) 098.16
    chronic or duration of 2 months or over 098.36
  hyperplastic (*see also* Hyperplasia, endometrium) 621.30
    cervix 616.0
  polypoid — *see* Endometritis, hyperplastic
  puerperal, postpartum, childbirth 670.0 ☑
  senile (atrophic) 615.9
  subacute 615.0
  tuberculous (*see also* Tuberculosis) 016.7 ☑
Endometrium — *see* condition
Endomyocardiopathy, South African 425.2
Endomyocarditis — *see* Endocarditis
Endomyofibrosis 425.0
Endomyometritis — *see also* Endometritis 615.9
Endopericarditis — *see* Endocarditis
Endoperineuritis — *see* Disorder, nerve
Endophlebitis — *see also* Phlebitis 451.9
  leg 451.2
    deep (vessels) 451.19
    superficial (vessels) 451.0
  portal (vein) 572.1
  retina 362.18
  specified site NEC 451.89
  syphilitic 093.89
Endophthalmia — *see also* Endophthalmitis 360.00
  gonorrheal 098.42
Endophthalmitis (globe) (infective) (metastatic) (purulent) (subacute) 360.00
  acute 360.01
  bleb associated 379.63
  chronic 360.03
  parasitic 360.13
  phacoanaphylactic 360.19
  specified type NEC 360.19
  sympathetic 360.11
Endosalpingioma (M9111/1) 236.2
Endosalpingiosis 629.89
Endosteitis — *see* Osteomyelitis
Endothelioma, bone (M9260/3) — *see* Neoplasm, bone, malignant
Endotheliosis 287.8
  hemorrhagic infectional 287.8
Endotoxemia — code to condition
Endotoxic shock 785.52
Endotrachelitis — *see also* Cervicitis 616.0
Enema rash 692.89
Engelmann's disease (diaphyseal sclerosis) 756.9
Engel-von Recklinghausen disease or syndrome (osteitis fibrosa cystica) 252.01
English disease — *see also* Rickets 268.0
Engman's disease (infectious eczematoid dermatitis) 690.8
Engorgement
  breast 611.79
    newborn 778.7
    puerperal, postpartum 676.2 ☑
  liver 573.9
  lung 514
  pulmonary 514
Engorgement — *continued*
  retina, venous 362.37
  stomach 536.8
  venous, retina 362.37
Enlargement, enlarged — *see also* Hypertrophy
  abdomen 789.3 ☑
  adenoids 474.12
    and tonsils 474.10
  alveolar process or ridge 525.8
  apertures of diaphragm (congenital) 756.6
  blind spot, visual field 368.42
  gingival 523.8
  heart, cardiac (*see also* Hypertrophy, cardiac) 429.3
  lacrimal gland, chronic 375.03
  liver (*see also* Hypertrophy, liver) 789.1
  lymph gland or node 785.6
  orbit 376.46
  organ or site, congenital NEC — *see* Anomaly, specified type NEC
  parathyroid (gland) 252.01
  pituitary fossa 793.0
  prostate (simple) (soft) 600.00
    with
      other lower urinary tract symptoms (LUTS) 600.01
      urinary
        obstruction 600.01
        retention 600.01
  sella turcica 793.0
  spleen (*see also* Splenomegaly) 789.2
    congenital 759.0
  thymus (congenital) (gland) 254.0
  thyroid (gland) (*see also* Goiter) 240.9
  tongue 529.8
  tonsils 474.11
    and adenoids 474.10
  uterus 621.2
Enophthalmos 376.50
  due to
    atrophy of orbital tissue 376.51
    surgery 376.52
    trauma 376.52
Enostosis 526.89
Entamebiasis — *see* Amebiasis
Entamebic — *see* Amebiasis
Entanglement, umbilical cord(s) 663.3 ☑
  with compression 663.2 ☑
  affecting fetus or newborn 762.5
  around neck with compression 663.1 ☑
  twins in monoamniotic sac 663.2 ☑
Enteralgia 789.0 ☑
Enteric — *see* condition
Enteritis (acute) (catarrhal) (choleraic) (chronic) (congestive) (diarrheal) (exudative) (follicular) (hemorrhagic) (infantile) (lienteric) (noninfectious) (perforative) (phlegmonous) (presumed noninfectious) (pseudomembranous) 558.9
  adaptive 564.9
  aertrycke infection 003.0
  allergic 558.3
  amebic (*see also* Amebiasis) 006.9
    with abscess — *see* Abscess, amebic
    acute 006.0
      with abscess — *see* Abscess, amebic
      nondysenteric 006.2
    chronic 006.1
      with abscess — *see* Abscess, amebic
      nondysenteric 006.2
    nondysenteric 006.2
  anaerobic (cocci) (gram-negative) (gram-positive) (mixed) NEC 008.46
  bacillary NEC 004.9
  bacterial NEC 008.5
    specified NEC 008.49
Enteritis — *continued*
  Bacteroides (fragilis) (melaninogeniscus) (oralis) 008.46
  Butyrivibrio (fibriosolvens) 008.46
  Campylobacter 008.43
  Candida 112.85
  Chilomastix 007.8
  choleriformis 001.1
  chronic 558.9
    ulcerative (*see also* Colitis, ulcerative) 556.9
  cicatrizing (chronic) 555.0
  Clostridium
    botulinum 005.1
    difficile 008.45
    haemolyticum 008.46
    novyi 008.46
    perfringens (C) (F) 008.46
    specified type NEC 008.46
  coccidial 007.2
  dietetic 558.9
  due to
    achylia gastrica 536.8
    adenovirus 008.62
    Aerobacter aerogenes 008.2
    anaerobes (*see also* Enteritis, anaerobic) 008.46
    Arizona (bacillus) 008.1
    astrovirus 008.66
    Bacillus coli — *see* Enteritis, E. coli
    bacteria NEC 008.5
      specified NEC 008.49
    Bacteroides (*see also* Enteritis, Bacteroides) 008.46
    Butyrivibrio (fibriosolvens) 008.46
    Calcivirus 008.65
    Camplyobacter 008.43
    Clostridium — *see* Enteritis, Clostridium
    Cockle agent 008.64
    Coxsackie (virus) 008.67
    Ditchling agent 008.64
    ECHO virus 008.67
    Enterobacter aerogenes 008.2
    enterococci 008.49
    enterovirus NEC 008.67
    Escherichia coli — *see* Enteritis, E. coli
    Eubacterium 008.46
    Fusobacterium (nucleatum) 008.46
    gram-negative bacteria NEC 008.47
      anaerobic NEC 008.46
    Hawaii agent 008.63
    irritating foods 558.9
    Klebsiella aerogenes 008.47
    Marin County agent 008.66
    Montgomery County agent 008.63
    Norwalk-like agent 008.63
    Norwalk virus 008.63
    Otofuke agent 008.63
    Paracolobactrum arizonae 008.1
    paracolon bacillus NEC 008.47
      Arizona 008.1
    Paramatta agent 008.64
    Peptococcus 008.46
    Peptostreptococcus 008.46
    Proprionibacterium 008.46
    Proteus (bacillus) (mirabilis) (morganii) 008.3
    Pseudomonas aeruginosa 008.42
    Rotavirus 008.61
    Sapporo agent 008.63
    small round virus (SRV) NEC 008.64
      featureless NEC 008.63
      structured NEC 008.63
    Snow Mountain (SM) agent 008.63
    specified
      bacteria NEC 008.49
      organism, nonbacterial NEC 008.8
      virus NEC 008.69
    Staphylococcus 008.41
    Streptococcus 008.49
      anaerobic 008.46
    Taunton agent 008.63
Enteritis — *continued*
  due to — *continued*
    Torovirus 008.69
    Treponema 008.46
    Veillonella 008.46
    virus 008.8
      specified type NEC 008.69
    Wollan (W) agent 008.64
    Yersinia enterocolitica 008.44
  dysentery — *see* Dysentery
  E. coli 008.00
    enterohemorrhagic 008.04
    enteroinvasive 008.03
    enteropathogenic 008.01
    enterotoxigenic 008.02
    specified type NEC 008.09
  el tor 001.1
  embadomonial 007.8
  eosinophilic 558.41
  epidemic 009.0
  Eubacterium 008.46
  fermentative 558.9
  fulminant 557.0
  Fusobacterium (nucleatum) 008.46
  gangrenous (*see also* Enteritis, due to, by organism) 009.0
  giardial 007.1
  gram-negative bacteria NEC 008.47
    anaerobic NEC 008.46
  infectious NEC (*see also* Enteritis, due to, by organism) 009.0
    presumed 009.1
  influenzal 487.8
  ischemic 557.9
    acute 557.0
    chronic 557.1
    due to mesenteric artery insufficiency 557.1
  membranous 564.9
  mucous 564.9
  myxomembranous 564.9
  necrotic (*see also* Enteritis, due to, by organism) 009.0
  necroticans 005.2
  necrotizing of fetus or newborn (*see also* Enterocolitis, necrotizing, newborn) 777.50
  neurogenic 564.9
  newborn 777.8
    necrotizing (*see also* Enterocolitis, necrotizing, newborn) 777.50
  parasitic NEC 129
  paratyphoid (fever) (*see also* Fever, paratyphoid) 002.9
  Peptococcus 008.46
  Peptostreptococcus 008.46
  Proprionibacterium 008.46
  protozoal NEC 007.9
  radiation 558.1
  regional (of) 555.9
    intestine
      large (bowel, colon, or rectum) 555.1
        with small intestine 555.2
      small (duodenum, ileum, or jejunum) 555.0
        with large intestine 555.2
  Salmonella infection 003.0
  salmonellosis 003.0
  segmental (*see also* Enteritis, regional) 555.9
  septic (*see also* Enteritis, due to, by organism) 009.0
  Shigella 004.9
  simple 558.9
  spasmodic 564.9
  spastic 564.9
  staphylococcal 008.41
    due to food 005.0
  streptococcal 008.49
    anaerobic 008.46
  toxic 558.2
  Treponema (denticola) (macrodentium) 008.46
  trichomonal 007.3

Epilepsy, epileptic — *continued*
tonic (-clonic) 345.1 ☑
traumatic (injury unspecified) 907.0
injury specified — *see* Late, effect (of) specified injury
twilight 293.0
uncinate (gyrus) 345.4 ☑
Unverricht (-Lundborg) (familial myoclonic) 333.2
visceral 345.5 ☑
visual 345.5 ☑
Epileptiform
convulsions 780.39
seizure 780.39
Epiloia 759.5
Epimenorrhea 626.2
Epipharyngitis — *see also* Nasopharyngitis 460
Epiphora 375.20
due to
excess lacrimation 375.21
insufficient drainage 375.22
Epiphyseal arrest 733.91
femoral head 732.2
Epiphyseolysis, epiphysiolysis — *see also* Osteochondrosis 732.9
Epiphysitis — *see also* Osteochondrosis 732.9
juvenile 732.6
marginal (Scheuermann's) 732.0
os calcis 732.5
syphilitic (congenital) 090.0
vertebral (Scheuermann's) 732.0
Epiplocele — *see also* Hernia 553.9
Epiploitis — *see also* Peritonitis 567.9
Epiplosarcomphalocele — *see also* Hernia, umbilicus 553.1
Episcleritis 379.00
gouty 274.89 *[379.09]*
nodular 379.02
periodica fugax 379.01
angioneurotic — *see* Edema, angioneurotic
specified NEC 379.09
staphylococcal 379.00
suppurative 379.00
syphilitic 095.0
tuberculous (*see also* Tuberculosis) 017.3 ☑ *[379.09]*
Episode
brain (*see also* Disease, cerebrovascular, acute) 436
cerebral (*see also* Disease, cerebrovascular, acute) 436
depersonalization (in neurotic state) 300.6
hyporesponsive 780.09
psychotic (*see also* Psychosis) 298.9
organic, transient 293.9
schizophrenic (acute) NEC (*see also* Schizophrenia) 295.4 ☑
Epispadias
female 753.8
male 752.62
Episplenitis 289.59
Epistaxis (multiple) 784.7
hereditary 448.0
vicarious menstruation 625.8
Epithelioma (malignant) (M8011/3) — *see also* Neoplasm, by site, malignant
adenoides cysticum (M8100/0) — *see* Neoplasm, skin, benign
basal cell (M8090/3) — *see* Neoplasm, skin, malignant
benign (M8011/0) — *see* Neoplasm, by site, benign
Bowen's (M8081/2) — *see* Neoplasm, skin, in situ
calcifying (benign) (Malherbe's) (M8110/0) — *see* Neoplasm, skin, benign
external site — *see* Neoplasm, skin, malignant
intraepidermal, Jadassohn (M8096/0) — *see* Neoplasm, skin, benign
Epithelioma — *see also* Neoplasm, by site, malignant — *continued*
squamous cell (M8070/3) — *see* Neoplasm, by site, malignant
Epitheliopathy
pigment, retina 363.15
posterior multifocal placoid (acute) 363.15
Epithelium, epithelial — *see* condition
Epituberculosis (allergic) (with atelectasis) — *see also* Tuberculosis 010.8 ☑
Eponychia 757.5
Epstein's
nephrosis or syndrome (*see also* Nephrosis) 581.9
pearl (mouth) 528.4
Epstein-Barr infection (viral) 075
chronic 780.79 *[139.8]*
Epulis (giant cell) (gingiva) 523.8
Equinia 024
Equinovarus (congenital) 754.51
acquired 736.71
Equivalent
convulsive (abdominal) (*see also* Epilepsy) 345.5 ☑
epileptic (psychic) (*see also* Epilepsy) 345.5 ☑
Erb's
disease 359.1
palsy, paralysis (birth) (brachial) (newborn) 767.6
spinal (spastic) syphilitic 094.89
pseudohypertrophic muscular dystrophy 359.1
Erb-Goldflam disease or syndrome 358.00
Erb (-Duchenne) paralysis (birth injury) (newborn) 767.6
Erdheim's syndrome (acromegalic macrospondylitis) 253.0
Erection, painful (persistent) 607.3
Ergosterol deficiency (vitamin D) 268.9
with
osteomalacia 268.2
rickets (*see also* Rickets) 268.0
Ergotism (ergotized grain) 988.2
from ergot used as drug (migraine therapy)
correct substance properly administered 349.82
overdose or wrong substance given or taken 975.0
Erichsen's disease (railway spine) 300.16
Erlacher-Blount syndrome (tibia vara) 732.4
Erosio interdigitalis blastomycetica 112.3
Erosion
arteriosclerotic plaque — *see* Arteriosclerosis, by site
artery NEC 447.2
without rupture 447.8
bone 733.99
bronchus 519.19
cartilage (joint) 733.99
cervix (uteri) (acquired) (chronic) (congenital) 622.0
with mention of cervicitis 616.0
cornea (recurrent) (*see also* Keratitis) 371.42
traumatic 918.1
dental (idiopathic) (occupational) 521.30
extending into
dentine 521.32
pulp 521.33
generalized 521.35
limited to enamel 521.31
localized 521.34
duodenum, postpyloric — *see* Ulcer, duodenum
esophagus 530.89
gastric 535.4 ☑
intestine 569.89
Erosion — *continued*
lymphatic vessel 457.8
pylorus, pyloric (ulcer) 535.4 ☑
sclera 379.16
spine, aneurysmal 094.89
spleen 289.59
stomach 535.4 ☑
teeth (idiopathic) (occupational) (*see also* Erosion, dental) 521.30
due to
medicine 521.30
persistent vomiting 521.30
urethra 599.84
uterus 621.8
vertebra 733.99
Erotomania 302.89
Clérambault's 297.8
Error
in diet 269.9
refractive 367.9
astigmatism (*see also* Astigmatism) 367.20
drug-induced 367.89
hypermetropia 367.0
hyperopia 367.0
myopia 367.1
presbyopia 367.4
toxic 367.89
Eructation 787.3
nervous 306.4
psychogenic 306.4
Eruption
creeping 126.9
drug — *see* Dermatitis, due to, drug
Hutchinson, summer 692.72
Kaposi's varicelliform 054.0
napkin (psoriasiform) 691.0
polymorphous
light (sun) 692.72
other source 692.82
psoriasiform, napkin 691.0
recalcitrant pustular 694.8
ringed 695.89
skin (*see also* Dermatitis) 782.1
creeping (meaning hookworm) 126.9
due to
chemical(s) NEC 692.4
internal use 693.8
drug — *see* Dermatitis, due to, drug
prophylactic inoculation or vaccination against disease — *see* Dermatitis, due to, vaccine
smallpox vaccination NEC — *see* Dermatitis, due to, vaccine
erysipeloid 027.1
feigned 698.4
Hutchinson, summer 692.72
Kaposi's, varicelliform 054.0
vaccinia 999.0
lichenoid, axilla 698.3
polymorphous, due to light 692.72
toxic NEC 695.0
vesicular 709.8
teeth, tooth
accelerated 520.6
delayed 520.6
difficult 520.6
disturbance of 520.6
in abnormal sequence 520.6
incomplete 520.6
late 520.6
natal 520.6
neonatal 520.6
obstructed 520.6
partial 520.6
persistent primary 520.6
premature 520.6
prenatal 520.6
vesicular 709.8
Erysipelas (gangrenous) (infantile) (newborn) (phlegmonous) (suppurative) 035
Erysipelas — *continued*
external ear 035 *[380.13]*
puerperal, postpartum, childbirth 670.0 ☑
Erysipelatoid (Rosenbach's) 027.1
Erysipeloid (Rosenbach's) 027.1
Erythema, erythematous (generalized) 695.9
ab igne — *see* Burn, by site, first degree
annulare (centrifugum) (rheumaticum) 695.0
arthriticum epidemicum 026.1
brucellum (*see also* Brucellosis) 023.9
bullosum 695.19
caloricum — *see* Burn, by site, first degree
chronicum migrans 088.81
circinatum 695.19
diaper 691.0
due to
chemical (contact) NEC 692.4
internal 693.8
drug (internal use) 693.0
contact 692.3
elevatum diutinum 695.89
endemic 265.2
epidemic, arthritic 026.1
figuratum perstans 695.0
gluteal 691.0
gyratum (perstans) (repens) 695.19
heat — *see* Burn, by site, first degree
ichthyosiforme congenitum 757.1
induratum (primary) (scrofulosorum) (*see also* Tuberculosis) 017.1 ☑
nontuberculous 695.2
infantum febrile 057.8
infectional NEC 695.9
infectiosum 057.0
inflammation NEC 695.9
intertrigo 695.89
iris 695.10
lupus (discoid) (localized) (*see also* Lupus, erythematosus) 695.4
marginatum 695.0
rheumaticum — *see* Fever, rheumatic
medicamentosum — *see* Dermatitis, due to, drug
migrans 529.1
chronicum 088.81
multiforme 695.10
bullosum 695.19
conjunctiva 695.19
exudativum (Hebra) 695.19
major 695.12
minor 695.11
pemphigoides 694.5
napkin 691.0
neonatorum 778.8
nodosum 695.2
tuberculous (*see also* Tuberculosis) 017.1 ☑
nummular, nummulare 695.19
palmar 695.0
palmaris hereditarium 695.0
pernio 991.5
perstans solare 692.72
rash, newborn 778.8
scarlatiniform (exfoliative) (recurrent) 695.0
simplex marginatum 057.8
solare (*see also* Sunburn) 692.71
streptogenes 696.5
toxic, toxicum NEC 695.0
newborn 778.8
tuberculous (primary) (*see also* Tuberculosis) 017.0 ☑
venenatum 695.0
Erythematosus — *see* condition
Erythematous — *see* condition
Erythermalgia (primary) 443.82
Erythralgia 443.82
Erythrasma 039.0
Erythredema 985.0
polyneuritica 985.0

- **Examination** — *continued*
  - postpartum
    - immediately after delivery V24.0
    - routine follow-up V24.2
  - pregnancy (unconfirmed) (possible) V72.40
    - negative result V72.41
    - positive result V72.42
  - prenatal V22.1
    - first pregnancy V22.0
    - high-risk pregnancy V23.9
      - specified problem NEC V23.89
  - preoperative V72.84
    - cardiovascular V72.81
    - respiratory V72.82
    - specified NEC V72.83
  - preprocedural V72.84
    - cardiovascular V72.81
    - general physical V72.83
    - respiratory V72.82
    - specified NEC V72.83
  - psychiatric V70.2
    - follow-up not needing further care V67.3
    - requested by authority V70.1
  - radiological NEC V72.5
  - respiratory preoperative V72.82
  - screening — *see* Screening
  - sensitization V72.7
  - skin V72.7
    - hypersensitivity V72.7
  - special V72.9
  - specified type or reason NEC V72.85
    - preoperative V72.83
      - specified NEC V72.83
  - teeth V72.2
  - vaginal Papanicolaou smear V76.47
    - following hysterectomy for malignant condition V67.01
  - victim or culprit following
    - alleged rape or seduction V71.5
    - inflicted injury NEC V71.6
  - vision V72.0
  - well baby V20.2
- **Exanthem, exanthema** — *see also* Rash 782.1
  - Boston 048
  - epidemic, with meningitis 048
  - lichenoid psoriasiform 696.2
  - subitum 058.10
    - due to
      - human herpesvirus 6 058.11
      - human herpesvirus 7 058.12
  - viral, virus NEC 057.9
    - specified type NEC 057.8
- **Excess, excessive, excessively**
  - alcohol level in blood 790.3
  - carbohydrate tissue, localized 278.1
  - carotene (dietary) 278.3
  - cold 991.9
    - specified effect NEC 991.8
  - convergence 378.84
  - crying 780.95
    - of
      - adolescent 780.95
      - adult 780.95
      - baby 780.92
      - child 780.95
      - infant (baby) 780.92
      - newborn 780.92
  - development, breast 611.1
  - diaphoresis (*see also* Hyperhidrosis) 780.8
  - distance, interarch 524.28
  - divergence 378.85
  - drinking (alcohol) NEC (*see also* Abuse, drugs, nondependent) 305.0 ☑
    - continual (*see also* Alcoholism) 303.9 ☑
    - habitual (*see also* Alcoholism) 303.9 ☑
  - eating 783.6
  - eyelid fold (congenital) 743.62
  - fat 278.02
- **Excess, excessive, excessively** — *continued*
  - fat — *continued*
    - in heart (*see also* Degeneration, myocardial) 429.1
    - tissue, localized 278.1
  - foreskin 605
  - gas 787.3
  - gastrin 251.5
  - glucagon 251.4
  - heat (*see also* Heat) 992.9
  - horizontal
    - overjet 524.26
    - overlap 524.26
  - interarch distance 524.28
  - intermaxillary vertical dimension 524.37
  - interocclusal distance of teeth 524.37
  - large
    - colon 564.7
      - congenital 751.3
    - fetus or infant 766.0
      - with obstructed labor 660.1 ☑
      - affecting management of pregnancy 656.6 ☑
      - causing disproportion 653.5 ☑
    - newborn (weight of 4500 grams or more) 766.0
    - organ or site, congenital NEC — *see* Anomaly, specified type NEC
  - lid fold (congenital) 743.62
  - long
    - colon 751.5
    - organ or site, congenital NEC — *see* Anomaly, specified type NEC
    - umbilical cord (entangled)
      - affecting fetus or newborn 762.5
      - in pregnancy or childbirth 663.3 ☑
        - with compression 663.2 ☑
  - menstruation 626.2
  - number of teeth 520.1
    - causing crowding 524.31
  - nutrients (dietary) NEC 783.6
  - potassium (K) 276.7
  - salivation (*see also* Ptyalism) 527.7
  - secretion (*see also* Hypersecretion)
    - milk 676.6 ☑
    - sputum 786.4
    - sweat (*see also* Hyperhidrosis) 780.8
  - short
    - organ or site, congenital NEC — *see* Anomaly, specified type NEC
    - umbilical cord
      - affecting fetus or newborn 762.6
      - in pregnancy or childbirth 663.4 ☑
  - skin NEC 701.9
    - eyelid 743.62
      - acquired 374.30
  - sodium (Na) 276.0
  - spacing of teeth 524.32
  - sputum 786.4
  - sweating (*see also* Hyperhidrosis) 780.8
  - tearing (ducts) (eye) (*see also* Epiphora) 375.20
  - thirst 783.5
    - due to deprivation of water 994.3
  - tissue in reconstructed breast 612.0
  - tuberosity 524.07
  - vitamin
    - A (dietary) 278.2
      - administered as drug (chronic) (prolonged excessive intake) 278.2
        - reaction to sudden overdose 963.5
    - D (dietary) 278.4
      - administered as drug (chronic) (prolonged excessive intake) 278.4
- **Excess, excessive, excessively** — *continued*
  - vitamin — *continued*
    - D — *continued*
      - administered as drug — *continued*
        - reaction to sudden overdose 963.5
  - weight 278.02
    - gain 783.1
      - of pregnancy 646.1 ☑
    - loss 783.21
- **Excitability, abnormal, under minor stress** 309.29
- **Excitation**
  - catatonic (*see also* Schizophrenia) 295.2 ☑
  - psychogenic 298.1
  - reactive (from emotional stress, psychological trauma) 298.1
- **Excitement**
  - manic (*see also* Psychosis, affective) 296.0 ☑
    - recurrent episode 296.1 ☑
    - single episode 296.0 ☑
  - mental, reactive (from emotional stress, psychological trauma) 298.1
  - state, reactive (from emotional stress, psychological trauma) 298.1
- **Excluded pupils** 364.76
- **Excoriation** (traumatic) — *see also* Injury, superficial, by site 919.8
  - neurotic 698.4
- **Excyclophoria** 378.44
- **Excyclotropia** 378.33
- **Exencephalus, exencephaly** 742.0
- **Exercise**
  - breathing V57.0
  - remedial NEC V57.1
  - therapeutic NEC V57.1
- **Exfoliation**
  - skin
    - due to erythematous condition 695.50
      - involving (percent of body surface)
        - less than 10 percent 695.50
        - 10-19 percent 695.51
        - 20-29 percent 695.52
        - 30-39 percent 695.53
        - 40-49 percent 695.54
        - 50-59 percent 695.55
        - 60-69 percent 695.56
        - 70-79 percent 695.57
        - 80-89 percent 695.58
        - 90 percent or more 695.59
  - teeth
    - due to systemic causes 525.0
- **Exfoliative** — *see also* condition
  - dermatitis 695.89
- **Exhaustion, exhaustive** (physical NEC) 780.79
  - battle (*see also* Reaction, stress, acute) 308.9
  - cardiac (*see also* Failure, heart) 428.9
  - delirium (*see also* Reaction, stress, acute) 308.9
  - due to
    - cold 991.8
    - excessive exertion 994.5
    - exposure 994.4
    - overexertion 994.5
  - fetus or newborn 779.89
  - heart (*see also* Failure, heart) 428.9
  - heat 992.5
    - due to
      - salt depletion 992.4
      - water depletion 992.3
  - manic (*see also* Psychosis, affective) 296.0 ☑
    - recurrent episode 296.1 ☑
    - single episode 296.0 ☑
  - maternal, complicating delivery 669.8 ☑
    - affecting fetus or newborn 763.89
- **Exhaustion, exhaustive** — *continued*
  - mental 300.5
  - myocardium, myocardial (*see also* Failure, heart) 428.9
  - nervous 300.5
  - old age 797
  - postinfectional NEC 780.79
  - psychogenic 300.5
  - psychosis (*see also* Reaction, stress, acute) 308.9
  - senile 797
    - dementia 290.0
- **Exhibitionism** (sexual) 302.4
- **Exomphalos** 756.79
- **Exophoria** 378.42
  - convergence, insufficiency 378.83
  - divergence, excess 378.85
- **Exophthalmic**
  - cachexia 242.0 ☑
  - goiter 242.0 ☑
  - ophthalmoplegia 242.0 ☑ *[376.22]*
- **Exophthalmos** 376.30
  - congenital 743.66
  - constant 376.31
  - endocrine NEC 259.9 *[376.22]*
  - hyperthyroidism 242.0 ☑ *[376.21]*
  - intermittent NEC 376.34
  - malignant 242.0 ☑ *[376.21]*
  - pulsating 376.35
    - endocrine NEC 259.9 *[376.22]*
  - thyrotoxic 242.0 ☑ *[376.21]*
- **Exostosis** 726.91
  - cartilaginous (M9210/0) — *see* Neoplasm, bone, benign
  - congenital 756.4
  - ear canal, external 380.81
  - gonococcal 098.89
  - hip 726.5
  - intracranial 733.3
  - jaw (bone) 526.81
  - luxurians 728.11
  - multiple (cancellous) (congenital) (hereditary) 756.4
  - nasal bones 726.91
  - orbit, orbital 376.42
  - osteocartilaginous (M9210/0) — *see* Neoplasm, bone, benign
  - spine 721.8
    - with spondylosis — *see* Spondylosis
  - syphilitic 095.5
  - wrist 726.4
- **Exotropia** 378.10
  - alternating 378.15
    - with
      - A pattern 378.16
      - specified noncomitancy NEC 378.18
      - V pattern 378.17
      - X pattern 378.18
      - Y pattern 378.18
    - intermittent 378.24
  - intermittent 378.20
    - alternating 378.24
    - monocular 378.23
  - monocular 378.11
    - with
      - A pattern 378.12
      - specified noncomitancy NEC 378.14
      - V pattern 378.13
      - X pattern 378.14
      - Y pattern 378.14
    - intermittent 378.23
- **Explanation of**
  - investigation finding V65.4 ☑
  - medication V65.4 ☑
- **Exposure** 994.9
  - cold 991.9
    - specified effect NEC 991.8
  - effects of 994.9
  - exhaustion due to 994.4
  - to
    - AIDS virus V01.79
    - anthrax V01.81

- **Exposure** — *continued*
  - to — *continued*
    - aromatic
      - amines V87.11
      - dyes V87.19
    - arsenic V87.01
    - asbestos V15.84
    - benzene V87.12
    - body fluids (hazardous) V15.85
    - cholera V01.0
    - chromium compounds V87.09
    - communicable disease V01.9
      - specified type NEC V01.89
    - dyes V87.2
      - aromatic V87.19
    - Escherichia coli (E. coli) V01.83
    - German measles V01.4
    - gonorrhea V01.6
    - hazardous
      - aromatic compounds NEC V87.19
      - body fluids V15.85
      - chemicals NEC V87.2
      - metals V87.09
      - substances V87.39
    - HIV V01.79
    - human immunodeficiency virus V01.79
    - lead V15.86
    - meningococcus V01.84
    - mold V87.31
    - nickel dust V87.09
    - parasitic disease V01.89
    - poliomyelitis V01.2
    - polycyclic aromatic hydrocarbons V87.19
    - potentially hazardous body fluids V15.85
    - rabies V01.5
    - rubella V01.4
    - SARS-associated coronavirus V01.82
    - smallpox V01.3
    - syphilis V01.6
    - tuberculosis V01.1
    - varicella V01.71
    - venereal disease V01.6
    - viral disease NEC V01.79
      - varicella V01.71
- **Exsanguination, fetal** 772.0
- **Exstrophy**
  - abdominal content 751.8
  - bladder (urinary) 753.5
- **Extensive** — *see* condition
- **Extra** — *see also* Accessory
  - rib 756.3
    - cervical 756.2
- **Extraction**
  - with hook 763.89
  - breech NEC 669.6 ☑
    - affecting fetus or newborn 763.0
  - cataract postsurgical V45.61
  - manual NEC 669.8 ☑
    - affecting fetus or newborn 763.89
- **Extrasystole** 427.60
  - atrial 427.61
  - postoperative 997.1
  - ventricular 427.69
- **Extrauterine gestation or pregnancy** — *see* Pregnancy, ectopic
- **Extravasation**
  - blood 459.0
    - lower extremity 459.0
  - chemotherapy, vesicant 999.81
  - chyle into mesentery 457.8
  - pelvicalyceal 593.4
  - pyelosinus 593.4
  - urine 788.8
    - from ureter 788.8
  - vesicant
    - agent NEC 998.82
    - chemotherapy 998.81
- **Extremity** — *see* condition
- **Extrophy** — *see* Exstrophy
- **Extroversion**
  - bladder 753.5
- **Extroversion** — *continued*
  - uterus 618.1
    - complicating delivery 665.2 ☑
      - affecting fetus or newborn 763.89
    - postpartal (old) 618.1
- **Extruded tooth** 524.34
- **Extrusion**
  - alveolus and teeth 524.75
  - breast implant (prosthetic) 996.54
  - device, implant, or graft — *see* Complications, mechanical
  - eye implant (ball) (globe) 996.59
  - intervertebral disc — *see* Displacement, intervertebral disc
  - lacrimal gland 375.43
  - mesh (reinforcing) 996.59
  - ocular lens implant 996.53
  - prosthetic device NEC — *see* Complications, mechanical
  - vitreous 379.26
- **Exudate, pleura** — *see* Effusion, pleura
- **Exudates, retina** 362.82
- **Exudative** — *see* condition
- **Eye, eyeball, eyelid** — *see* condition
- **Eyestrain** 368.13
- **Eyeworm disease of Africa** 125.2

F

- **Faber's anemia or syndrome** (achlorhydric anemia) 280.9
- **Fabry's disease** (angiokeratoma corporis diffusum) 272.7
- **Face, facial** — *see* condition
- **Facet of cornea** 371.44
- **Faciocephalalgia, autonomic** — *see also* Neuropathy, peripheral, autonomic 337.9
- **Facioscapulohumeral myopathy** 359.1
- **Factitious disorder, illness** — *see* Illness, factitious
- **Factor**
  - deficiency — *see* Deficiency, factor
  - psychic, associated with diseases classified elsewhere 316
  - risk — *see* Problem
- **Fahr-Volhard disease** (malignant nephrosclerosis) 403.00
- **Failure, failed**
  - adenohypophyseal 253.2
  - attempted abortion (legal) (*see also* Abortion, failed) 638.9
  - bone marrow (anemia) 284.9
    - acquired (secondary) 284.89
    - congenital 284.09
    - idiopathic 284.9
  - cardiac (*see also* Failure, heart) 428.9
    - newborn 779.89
  - cardiorenal (chronic) 428.9
    - hypertensive (*see also* Hypertension, cardiorenal) 404.93
  - cardiorespiratory 799.1
    - specified during or due to a procedure 997.1
      - long-term effect of cardiac surgery 429.4
  - cardiovascular (chronic) 428.9
  - cerebrovascular 437.8
  - cervical dilatation in labor 661.0 ☑
    - affecting fetus or newborn 763.7
  - circulation, circulatory 799.89
    - fetus or newborn 779.89
    - peripheral 785.50
  - compensation — *see* Disease, heart
  - congestive (*see also* Failure, heart) 428.0
  - coronary (*see also* Insufficiency, coronary) 411.89
  - dental implant 525.79
    - due to
      - infection 525.71
      - lack of attached gingiva 525.72
      - occlusal trauma (caused by poor prosthetic design) 525.72
      - parafunctional habits 525.72
- **Failure, failed** — *continued*
  - dental implant — *continued*
    - due to — *continued*
      - periodontal infection (peri-implantitis) 525.72
      - poor oral hygiene 525.72
      - unintentional loading 525.71
    - endosseous NEC 525.79
    - mechanical 525.73
    - osseointegration 525.71
      - due to
        - complications of systemic disease 525.71
        - poor bone quality 525.71
        - premature loading 525.71
      - following intentional prosthetic loading 525.72
      - iatrogenic 525.71
      - prior to intentional prosthetic loading 525.71
    - post-osseointegration
      - biological 525.72
        - iatrogenic 525.72
      - due to complications of systemic disease 525.72
      - mechanical 525.73
    - pre-integration 525.71
    - pre-osseointegration 525.71
  - dental prosthesis causing loss of dental implant 525.73
  - dental restoration
    - marginal integrity 525.61
    - periodontal anatomical integrity 525.65
  - descent of head (at term) 652.5 ☑
    - affecting fetus or newborn 763.1
    - in labor 660.0 ☑
      - affecting fetus or newborn 763.1
  - device, implant, or graft — *see* Complications, mechanical
  - engagement of head NEC 652.5 ☑
    - in labor 660.0 ☑
  - extrarenal 788.99
  - fetal head to enter pelvic brim 652.5 ☑
    - affecting fetus or newborn 763.1
    - in labor 660.0 ☑
      - affecting fetus or newborn 763.1
  - forceps NEC 660.7 ☑
    - affecting fetus or newborn 763.1
  - fusion (joint) (spinal) 996.49
  - growth in childhood 783.43
  - heart (acute) (sudden) 428.9
    - with
      - abortion — *see* Abortion, by type, with specified complication NEC
      - acute pulmonary edema (*see also* Failure, ventricular, left) 428.1
        - with congestion (*see also* Failure, heart) 428.0
      - decompensation (*see also* Failure, heart) 428.0
      - dilation — *see* Disease, heart
      - ectopic pregnancy (*see also* categories 633.0–633.9) 639.8
      - molar pregnancy (*see also* categories 630–632) 639.8
    - arteriosclerotic 440.9
    - combined left-right sided 428.0
    - combined systolic and diastolic 428.40
      - acute 428.41
      - acute on chronic 428.43
      - chronic 428.42
    - compensated (*see also* Failure, heart) 428.0
    - complicating
      - abortion — *see* Abortion, by type, with specified complication NEC
      - delivery (cesarean) (instrumental) 669.4 ☑
- **Failure, failed** — *continued*
  - heart — *continued*
    - complicating — *continued*
      - ectopic pregnancy (*see also* categories 633.0–633.9) 639.8
      - molar pregnancy (*see also* categories 630–632) 639.8
      - obstetric anesthesia or sedation 668.1 ☑
      - surgery 997.1
    - congestive (compensated) (decompensated) (*see also* Failure, heart) 428.0
      - with rheumatic fever (conditions classifiable to 390)
        - active 391.8
        - inactive or quiescent (with chorea) 398.91
      - fetus or newborn 779.89
      - hypertensive (*see also* Hypertension, heart) 402.91
        - with renal disease (*see also* Hypertension, cardiorenal) 404.91
          - with renal failure 404.93
        - benign 402.11
        - malignant 402.01
      - rheumatic (chronic) (inactive) (with chorea) 398.91
        - active or acute 391.8
          - with chorea (Sydenham's) 392.0
    - decompensated (*see also* Failure, heart) 428.0
    - degenerative (*see also* Degeneration, myocardial) 429.1
    - diastolic 428.30
      - acute 428.31
      - acute on chronic 428.33
      - chronic 428.32
    - due to presence of (cardiac) prosthesis 429.4
    - fetus or newborn 779.89
    - following
      - abortion 639.8
      - cardiac surgery 429.4
      - ectopic or molar pregnancy 639.8
    - high output NEC 428.9
    - hypertensive (*see also* Hypertension, heart) 402.91
      - with renal disease (*see also* Hypertension, cardiorenal) 404.91
        - with renal failure 404.93
      - benign 402.11
      - malignant 402.01
    - left (ventricular) (*see also* Failure, ventricular, left) 428.1
      - with right-sided failure (see also Failure, heart) 428.0
    - low output (syndrome) NEC 428.9
    - organic — *see* Disease, heart
    - postoperative (immediate) 997.1
      - long term effect of cardiac surgery 429.4
    - rheumatic (chronic) (congestive) (inactive) 398.91
    - right (secondary to left heart failure, conditions classifiable to 428.1) (ventricular) (*see also* Failure, heart) 428.0
    - senile 797
    - specified during or due to a procedure 997.1
      - long-term effect of cardiac surgery 429.4
    - systolic 428.20
      - acute 428.21
      - acute on chronic 428.23
      - chronic 428.22
    - thyrotoxic (*see also* Thyrotoxicosis) 242.9 ☑ *[425.7]*
    - valvular — *see* Endocarditis
  - hepatic 572.8

Failure, failed — *continued*
  hepatic — *continued*
    acute 570
    due to a procedure 997.4
  hepatorenal 572.4
  hypertensive heart (*see also* Hypertension, heart) 402.91
    benign 402.11
    malignant 402.01
  induction (of labor) 659.1 ☑
    abortion (legal) (*see also* Abortion, failed) 638.9
    affecting fetus or newborn 763.89
    by oxytocic drugs 659.1 ☑
    instrumental 659.0 ☑
    mechanical 659.0 ☑
    medical 659.1 ☑
    surgical 659.0 ☑
  initial alveolar expansion, newborn 770.4
  involution, thymus (gland) 254.8
  kidney — *see* Failure, renal
  lactation 676.4 ☑
  Leydig's cell, adult 257.2
  liver 572.8
    acute 570
  medullary 799.89
  mitral — *see* Endocarditis, mitral
  myocardium, myocardial (*see also* Failure, heart) 428.9
    chronic (*see also* Failure, heart) 428.0
    congestive (*see also* Failure, heart) 428.0
  ovarian (primary) 256.39
    iatrogenic 256.2
    postablative 256.2
    postirradiation 256.2
    postsurgical 256.2
  ovulation 628.0
  prerenal 788.99
  renal 586
    with
      abortion — *see* Abortion, by type, with renal failure
      ectopic pregnancy (*see also* categories 633.0–633.9) 639.3
      edema (*see also* Nephrosis) 581.9
      hypertension (*see also* Hypertension, kidney) 403.91
      hypertensive heart disease (conditions classifiable to 402) 404.92
        with heart failure 404.93
        benign 404.12
          with heart failure 404.13
        malignant 404.02
          with heart failure 404.03
      molar pregnancy (*see also* categories 630–632) 639.3
      tubular necrosis (acute) 584.5
    acute 584.9
      with lesion of
        necrosis
          cortical (renal) 584.6
          medullary (renal) (papillary) 584.7
          tubular 584.5
        specified pathology NEC 584.8
    chronic 585.9
      hypertensive or with hypertension (*see also* Hypertension, kidney) 403.91
    due to a procedure 997.5
    following
      abortion 639.3
      crushing 958.5
      ectopic or molar pregnancy 639.3
      labor and delivery (acute) 669.3 ☑
    hypertensive (*see also* Hypertension, kidney) 403.91

Failure, failed — *continued*
  renal — *continued*
    puerperal, postpartum 669.3 ☑
  respiration, respiratory 518.81
    acute 518.81
    acute and chronic 518.84
    center 348.8
      newborn 770.84
    chronic 518.83
    due to trauma, surgery or shock 518.5
    newborn 770.84
  rotation
    cecum 751.4
    colon 751.4
    intestine 751.4
    kidney 753.3
  segmentation (*see also* Fusion)
    fingers (*see also* Syndactylism, fingers) 755.11
    toes (*see also* Syndactylism, toes) 755.13
  seminiferous tubule, adult 257.2
  senile (general) 797
    with psychosis 290.20
  testis, primary (seminal) 257.2
  to progress 661.2 ☑
  to thrive
    adult 783.7
    child 783.41
  transplant 996.80
    bone marrow 996.85
    organ (immune or nonimmune cause) 996.80
      bone marrow 996.85
      heart 996.83
      intestines 996.87
      kidney 996.81
      liver 996.82
      lung 996.84
      pancreas 996.86
      specified NEC 996.89
    skin 996.52
      artificial 996.55
      decellularized allodermis 996.55
      temporary allograft or pigskin graft — omit code
  trial of labor NEC 660.6 ☑
    affecting fetus or newborn 763.1
  tubal ligation 998.89
  urinary 586
  vacuum extraction
    abortion — *see* Abortion, failed
    delivery NEC 660.7 ☑
      affecting fetus or newborn 763.1
  vasectomy 998.89
  ventouse NEC 660.7 ☑
    affecting fetus or newborn 763.1
  ventricular (*see also* Failure, heart) 428.9
    left 428.1
      with rheumatic fever (conditions classifiable to 390)
        active 391.8
          with chorea 392.0
        inactive or quiescent (with chorea) 398.91
      hypertensive (*see also* Hypertension, heart) 402.91
        benign 402.11
        malignant 402.01
      rheumatic (chronic) (inactive) (with chorea) 398.91
        active or acute 391.8
          with chorea 392.0
    right (*see also* Failure, heart) 428.0
  vital centers, fetus or newborn 779.89
  weight gain in childhood 783.41
Fainting (fit) (spell) 780.2
Falciform hymen 752.49
Fallen arches 734
Falling, any organ or part — *see* Prolapse
Fall, maternal, affecting fetus or newborn 760.5

Fallopian
  insufflation
    fertility testing V26.21
    following sterilization reversal V26.22
  tube — *see* condition
Fallot's
  pentalogy 745.2
  tetrad or tetralogy 745.2
  triad or trilogy 746.09
Fallout, radioactive (adverse effect) NEC 990
False — *see also* condition
  bundle branch block 426.50
  bursa 727.89
  croup 478.75
  joint 733.82
  labor (pains) 644.1 ☑
  opening, urinary, male 752.69
  passage, urethra (prostatic) 599.4
  positive
    serological test for syphilis 795.6
    Wassermann reaction 795.6
  pregnancy 300.11
Family, familial — *see also* condition
  affected by
    family member
      currently on deployment (military) V61.01
      returned from deployment (military) (current or past conflict) V61.02
  disruption (*see also* Disruption, family) V61.09
  estrangement V61.09
  hemophagocytic
    lymphohistiocytosis 288.4
    reticulosis 288.4
  Li-Fraumeni (syndrome) V84.01
  planning advice V25.09
    natural
      procreative V26.41
      to avoid pregnancy V25.04
  problem V61.9
    specified circumstance NEC V61.8
  retinoblastoma (syndrome) 190.5
Famine 994.2
  edema 262
Fanconi's anemia (congenital pancytopenia) 284.09
Fanconi (-de Toni) (-Debré) syndrome (cystinosis) 270.0
Farber (-Uzman) syndrome or disease (disseminated lipogranulomatosis) 272.8
Farcin 024
Farcy 024
Farmers'
  lung 495.0
  skin 692.74
Farsightedness 367.0
Fascia — *see* condition
Fasciculation 781.0
Fasciculitis optica 377.32
Fasciitis 729.4
  eosinophilic 728.89
  necrotizing 728.86
  nodular 728.79
  perirenal 593.4
  plantar 728.71
  pseudosarcomatous 728.79
  traumatic (old) NEC 728.79
    current — *see* Sprain, by site
Fasciola hepatica infestation 121.3
Fascioliasis 121.3
Fasciolopsiasis (small intestine) 121.4
Fasciolopsis (small intestine) 121.4
Fast pulse 785.0
Fat
  embolism (cerebral) (pulmonary) (systemic) 958.1
    with
      abortion — *see* Abortion, by type, with embolism

Fat — *continued*
  embolism — *continued*
    with — *continued*
      ectopic pregnancy (*see also* categories 633.0–633.9) 639.6
      molar pregnancy (*see also* categories 630–632) 639.6
    complicating delivery or puerperium 673.8 ☑
    following
      abortion 639.6
      ectopic or molar pregnancy 639.6
    in pregnancy, childbirth, or the puerperium 673.8 ☑
  excessive 278.02
    in heart (*see also* Degeneration, myocardial) 429.1
  general 278.02
  hernia, herniation 729.30
    eyelid 374.34
    knee 729.31
    orbit 374.34
    retro-orbital 374.34
    retropatellar 729.31
    specified site NEC 729.39
  indigestion 579.8
  in stool 792.1
  localized (pad) 278.1
    heart (*see also* Degeneration, myocardial) 429.1
    knee 729.31
    retropatellar 729.31
  necrosis (*see also* Fatty, degeneration)
    breast (aseptic) (segmental) 611.3
    mesentery 567.82
    omentum 567.82
    peritoneum 567.82
  pad 278.1
Fatal familial insomnia (FFI) 046.72
Fatal syncope 798.1
Fatigue 780.79
  auditory deafness (*see also* Deafness) 389.9
  chronic, syndrome 780.71
  combat (*see also* Reaction, stress, acute) 308.9
  during pregnancy 646.8 ☑
  general 780.79
    psychogenic 300.5
  heat (transient) 992.6
  muscle 729.89
  myocardium (*see also* Failure, heart) 428.9
  nervous 300.5
  neurosis 300.5
  operational 300.89
  postural 729.89
  posture 729.89
  psychogenic (general) 300.5
  senile 797
  syndrome NEC 300.5
    chronic 780.71
  undue 780.79
  voice 784.49
Fatness 278.02
Fatty — *see also* condition
  apron 278.1
  degeneration (diffuse) (general) NEC 272.8
    localized — *see* Degeneration, by site, fatty
    placenta — *see* Placenta, abnormal
  heart (enlarged) (*see also* Degeneration, myocardial) 429.1
  infiltration (diffuse) (general) (*see also* Degeneration, by site, fatty) 272.8
    heart (enlarged) (*see also* Degeneration, myocardial) 429.1
  liver 571.8
    alcoholic 571.0
  necrosis — *see* Degeneration, fatty
  phanerosis 272.8
Fauces — *see* condition

Fibroma (M8810/0) — *see also* Neoplasm, connective tissue, benign
  ameloblastic (M9330/0) 213.1
    upper jaw (bone) 213.0
  bone (nonossifying) 733.99
    ossifying (M9262/0) — *see* Neoplasm, bone, benign
  cementifying (M9274/0) — *see* Neoplasm, bone, benign
  chondromyxoid (M9241/0) — *see* Neoplasm, bone, benign
  desmoplastic (M8823/1) — *see* Neoplasm, connective tissue, uncertain behavior
  facial (M8813/0) — *see* Neoplasm, connective tissue, benign
  invasive (M8821/1) — *see* Neoplasm, connective tissue, uncertain behavior
  molle (M8851/0) (*see also* Lipoma, by site) 214.9
  myxoid (M8811/0) — *see* Neoplasm, connective tissue, benign
  nasopharynx, nasopharyngeal (juvenile) (M9160/0) 210.7
  nonosteogenic (nonossifying) — *see* Dysplasia, fibrous
  odontogenic (M9321/0) 213.1
    upper jaw (bone) 213.0
  ossifying (M9262/0) — *see* Neoplasm, bone, benign
  periosteal (M8812/0) — *see* Neoplasm, bone, benign
  prostate 600.20
    with
      other lower urinary tract symptoms (LUTS) 600.21
      urinary
        obstruction 600.21
        retention 600.21
  soft (M8851/0) (*see also* Lipoma, by site) 214.9
Fibromatosis 728.79
  abdominal (M8822/1) — *see* Neoplasm, connective tissue, uncertain behavior
  aggressive (M8821/1) — *see* Neoplasm, connective tissue, uncertain behavior
  congenital generalized (CGF) 759.89
  Dupuytren's 728.6
  gingival 523.8
  plantar fascia 728.71
  proliferative 728.79
  pseudosarcomatous (proliferative) (subcutaneous) 728.79
  subcutaneous pseudosarcomatous (proliferative) 728.79
Fibromyalgia 729.1
Fibromyoma (M8890/0) — *see also* Neoplasm, connective tissue, benign
  uterus (corpus) (*see also* Leiomyoma, uterus) 218.9
    in pregnancy or childbirth 654.1 ☑
      affecting fetus or newborn 763.89
      causing obstructed labor 660.2 ☑
        affecting fetus or newborn 763.1
Fibromyositis — *see also* Myositis 729.1
  scapulohumeral 726.2
Fibromyxolipoma (M8852/0) — *see also* Lipoma, by site 214.9
Fibromyxoma (M8811/0) — *see* Neoplasm, connective tissue, benign
Fibromyxosarcoma (M8811/3) — *see* Neoplasm, connective tissue, malignant
Fibro-odontoma, ameloblastic (M9290/0) 213.1
  upper jaw (bone) 213.0
Fibro-osteoma (M9262/0) — *see* Neoplasm, bone, benign
Fibroplasia, retrolental (*see also* Retinopathy of prematurity) 362.21
Fibropurulent — *see* condition
Fibrosarcoma (M8810/3) — *see also* Neoplasm, connective tissue, malignant
  ameloblastic (M9330/3) 170.1
    upper jaw (bone) 170.0
  congenital (M8814/3) — *see* Neoplasm, connective tissue, malignant
  fascial (M8813/3) — *see* Neoplasm, connective tissue, malignant
  infantile (M8814/3) — *see* Neoplasm, connective tissue, malignant
  odontogenic (M9330/3) 170.1
    upper jaw (bone) 170.0
  periosteal (M8812/3) — *see* Neoplasm, bone, malignant
Fibrosclerosis
  breast 610.3
  corpora cavernosa (penis) 607.89
  familial multifocal NEC 710.8
  multifocal (idiopathic) NEC 710.8
  penis (corpora cavernosa) 607.89
Fibrosis, fibrotic
  adrenal (gland) 255.8
  alveolar (diffuse) 516.3
  amnion 658.8 ☑
  anal papillae 569.49
  anus 569.49
  appendix, appendiceal, noninflammatory 543.9
  arteriocapillary — *see* Arteriosclerosis
  bauxite (of lung) 503
  biliary 576.8
    due to Clonorchis sinensis 121.1
  bladder 596.8
    interstitial 595.1
    localized submucosal 595.1
    panmural 595.1
  bone, diffuse 756.59
  breast 610.3
  capillary (*see also* Arteriosclerosis)
    lung (chronic) (*see also* Fibrosis, lung) 515
  cardiac (*see also* Myocarditis) 429.0
  cervix 622.8
  chorion 658.8 ☑
  corpus cavernosum 607.89
  cystic (of pancreas) 277.00
    with
      manifestations
        gastrointestinal 277.03
        pulmonary 277.02
        specified NEC 277.09
      meconium ileus 277.01
      pulmonary exacerbation 277.02
  due to (presence of) any device, implant, or graft — *see* Complications, due to (presence of) any device, implant, or graft classified to 996.0–996.5 NEC
  ejaculatory duct 608.89
  endocardium (*see also* Endocarditis) 424.90
  endomyocardial (African) 425.0
  epididymis 608.89
  eye muscle 378.62
  graphite (of lung) 503
  heart (*see also* Myocarditis) 429.0
  hepatic (*see also* Cirrhosis, liver)
    due to Clonorchis sinensis 121.1
  hepatolienal — *see* Cirrhosis, liver
  hepatosplenic — *see* Cirrhosis, liver
  infrapatellar fat pad 729.31
  interstitial pulmonary, newborn 770.7
  intrascrotal 608.89
  kidney (*see also* Sclerosis, renal) 587
  liver — *see* Cirrhosis, liver
  lung (atrophic) (capillary) (chronic) (confluent) (massive) (perialveolar) (peribronchial) 515
    with
      anthracosilicosis (occupational) 500
      anthracosis (occupational) 500
      asbestosis (occupational) 501
      bagassosis (occupational) 495.1
      bauxite 503
      berylliosis (occupational) 503
      byssinosis (occupational) 504
      calcicosis (occupational) 502
      chalicosis (occupational) 502
      dust reticulation (occupational) 504
      farmers' lung 495.0
      gannister disease (occupational) 502
      graphite 503
      pneumonoconiosis (occupational) 505
      pneumosiderosis (occupational) 503
      siderosis (occupational) 503
      silicosis (occupational) 502
      tuberculosis (*see also* Tuberculosis) 011.4 ☑
    diffuse (idiopathic) (interstitial) 516.3
    due to
      bauxite 503
      fumes or vapors (chemical) (inhalation) 506.4
      graphite 503
    following radiation 508.1
    postinflammatory 515
    silicotic (massive) (occupational) 502
    tuberculous (*see also* Tuberculosis) 011.4 ☑
  lymphatic gland 289.3
  median bar 600.90
    with
      other lower urinary tract symptoms (LUTS) 600.91
      urinary
        obstruction 600.91
        retention 600.91
  mediastinum (idiopathic) 519.3
  meninges 349.2
  muscle NEC 728.2
    iatrogenic (from injection) 999.9
  myocardium, myocardial (*see also* Myocarditis) 429.0
  oral submucous 528.8
  ovary 620.8
  oviduct 620.8
  pancreas 577.8
    cystic 277.00
      with
        manifestations
          gastrointestinal 277.03
          pulmonary 277.02
          specified NEC 277.09
        meconium ileus 277.01
        pulmonary exacerbation 277.02
  penis 607.89
  periappendiceal 543.9
  periarticular (*see also* Ankylosis) 718.5 ☑
  pericardium 423.1
  perineum, in pregnancy or childbirth 654.8 ☑
    affecting fetus or newborn 763.89
    causing obstructed labor 660.2 ☑
      affecting fetus or newborn 763.1
  perineural NEC 355.9
    foot 355.6
  periureteral 593.89
  placenta — *see* Placenta, abnormal
  pleura 511.0
  popliteal fat pad 729.31
  preretinal 362.56
  prostate (chronic) 600.90
    with
      other lower urinary tract symptoms (LUTS) 600.91
      urinary
        obstruction 600.91
        retention 600.91
  pulmonary (chronic) (*see also* Fibrosis, lung) 515
    alveolar capillary block 516.3
    interstitial
      diffuse (idiopathic) 516.3
      newborn 770.7
  radiation — *see* Effect, adverse, radiation
  rectal sphincter 569.49
  retroperitoneal, idiopathic 593.4
  sclerosing mesenteric (idiopathic) 567.82
  scrotum 608.89
  seminal vesicle 608.89
  senile 797
  skin NEC 709.2
  spermatic cord 608.89
  spleen 289.59
    bilharzial (*see also* Schistosomiasis) 120.9
  subepidermal nodular (M8832/0) — *see* Neoplasm, skin, benign
  submucous NEC 709.2
    oral 528.8
    tongue 528.8
  syncytium — *see* Placenta, abnormal
  testis 608.89
    chronic, due to syphilis 095.8
  thymus (gland) 254.8
  tunica vaginalis 608.89
  ureter 593.89
  urethra 599.84
  uterus (nonneoplastic) 621.8
    bilharzial (*see also* Schistosomiasis) 120.9
    neoplastic (*see also* Leiomyoma, uterus) 218.9
  vagina 623.8
  valve, heart (*see also* Endocarditis) 424.90
  vas deferens 608.89
  vein 459.89
    lower extremities 459.89
  vesical 595.1
Fibrositis (periarticular) (rheumatoid) 729.0
  humeroscapular region 726.2
  nodular, chronic
    Jaccoud's 714.4
    rheumatoid 714.4
  ossificans 728.11
  scapulohumeral 726.2
Fibrothorax 511.0
Fibrotic — *see* Fibrosis
Fibrous — *see* condition
Fibroxanthoma (M8831/0) — *see also* Neoplasm, connective tissue, benign
  atypical (M8831/1) — *see* Neoplasm, connective tissue, uncertain behavior
  malignant (M8831/3) — *see* Neoplasm, connective tissue, malignant
Fibroxanthosarcoma (M8831/3) — *see* Neoplasm, connective tissue, malignant
Fiedler's
  disease (leptospiral jaundice) 100.0
  myocarditis or syndrome (acute isolated myocarditis) 422.91
Fiessinger-Leroy (-Reiter) syndrome 099.3
Fiessinger-Rendu syndrome (erythema muliforme exudativum) 695.19
Fifth disease (eruptive) 057.0
  venereal 099.1
Filaria, filarial — *see* Infestation, filarial
Filariasis — *see also* Infestation, filarial 125.9

- **Filariasis** — *see also* Infestation, filarial — *continued*
  - bancroftian 125.0
  - Brug's 125.1
  - due to
    - bancrofti 125.0
    - Brugia (Wuchereria) (malayi) 125.1
    - Loa loa 125.2
    - malayi 125.1
    - organism NEC 125.6
    - Wuchereria (bancrofti) 125.0
      - malayi 125.1
  - Malayan 125.1
  - ozzardi 125.5
  - specified type NEC 125.6
- **Filatoff's, Filatov's, Filatow's disease** (infectious mononucleosis) 075
- **File-cutters' disease** 984.9
  - specified type of lead — *see* Table of Drugs and Chemicals
- **Filling defect**
  - biliary tract 793.3
  - bladder 793.5
  - duodenum 793.4
  - gallbladder 793.3
  - gastrointestinal tract 793.4
  - intestine 793.4
  - kidney 793.5
  - stomach 793.4
  - ureter 793.5
- **Filtering bleb, eye** (postglaucoma) (status) V45.69
  - with complication or rupture 997.99
  - postcataract extraction (complication) 997.99
- **Fimbrial cyst** (congenital) 752.11
- **Fimbriated hymen** 752.49
- **Financial problem affecting care** V60.2
- **Findings, abnormal, without diagnosis** (examination) (laboratory test) 796.4
  - 17-ketosteroids, elevated 791.9
  - acetonuria 791.6
  - acid phosphatase 790.5
  - albumin-globulin ratio 790.99
  - albuminuria 791.0
  - alcohol in blood 790.3
  - alkaline phosphatase 790.5
  - amniotic fluid 792.3
  - amylase 790.5
  - anisocytosis 790.09
  - antenatal screening 796.5
  - anthrax, positive 795.31
  - antibody titers, elevated 795.79
  - anticardiolipin antibody 795.79
  - antigen-antibody reaction 795.79
  - antiphospholipid antibody 795.79
  - bacteriuria 791.9
  - ballistocardiogram 794.39
  - bicarbonate 276.9
  - bile in urine 791.4
  - bilirubin 277.4
  - bleeding time (prolonged) 790.92
  - blood culture, positive 790.7
  - blood gas level (arterial) 790.91
  - blood sugar level 790.29
    - high 790.29
      - fasting glucose 790.21
      - glucose tolerance test 790.22
    - low 251.2
  - calcium 275.40
  - cancer antigen 125 [CA 125] 795.82
  - carbonate 276.9
  - carcinoembryonic antigen [CEA] 795.81
  - casts, urine 791.7
  - catecholamines 791.9
  - cells, urine 791.7
  - cerebrospinal fluid (color) (content) (pressure) 792.0
  - cervical
    - high risk human papillomavirus (HPV) DNA test positive 795.05

Findings, abnormal, without diagnosis — *continued*

  - cervical — *continued*
    - low risk human papillomavirus (HPV) DNA test positive 795.09
  - chloride 276.9
  - cholesterol 272.9
    - high 272.0
      - with high triglycerides 272.2
  - chromosome analysis 795.2
  - chyluria 791.1
  - circulation time 794.39
  - cloudy dialysis effluent 792.5
  - cloudy urine 791.9
  - coagulation study 790.92
  - cobalt, blood 790.6
  - color of urine (unusual) NEC 791.9
  - copper, blood 790.6
  - C-reactive protein (CRP) 790.95
  - creatinine clearance 794.4
  - crystals, urine 791.9
  - culture, positive NEC 795.39
    - blood 790.7
      - HIV V08
      - human immunodeficiency virus V08
    - nose 795.39
      - Staphylococcus — *see* Carrier (suspected) of, Staphylococcus
    - skin lesion NEC 795.39
    - spinal fluid 792.0
    - sputum 795.39
    - stool 792.1
    - throat 795.39
    - urine 791.9
    - viral
      - human immunodeficiency V08
    - wound 795.39
  - echocardiogram 793.2
  - echoencephalogram 794.01
  - echogram NEC — *see* Findings, abnormal, structure
  - electrocardiogram (ECG) (EKG) 794.31
  - electroencephalogram (EEG) 794.02
  - electrolyte level, urinary 791.9
  - electromyogram (EMG) 794.17
    - ocular 794.14
  - electro-oculogram (EOG) 794.12
  - electroretinogram (ERG) 794.11
  - enzymes, serum NEC 790.5
  - fibrinogen titer coagulation study 790.92
  - filling defect — *see* Filling defect
  - function study NEC 794.9
    - auditory 794.15
    - bladder 794.9
    - brain 794.00
    - cardiac 794.30
    - endocrine NEC 794.6
      - thyroid 794.5
    - kidney 794.4
    - liver 794.8
    - nervous system
      - central 794.00
      - peripheral 794.19
    - oculomotor 794.14
    - pancreas 794.9
    - placenta 794.9
    - pulmonary 794.2
    - retina 794.11
    - special senses 794.19
    - spleen 794.9
    - vestibular 794.16
  - gallbladder, nonvisualization 793.3
  - glucose 790.29
    - elevated
      - fasting 790.21
      - tolerance test 790.22
  - glycosuria 791.5
  - heart
    - shadow 793.2
    - sounds 785.3
  - hematinuria 791.2

Findings, abnormal, without diagnosis — *continued*

  - hematocrit
    - drop (precipitous) 790.01
    - elevated 282.7
    - low 285.9
  - hematologic NEC 790.99
  - hematuria 599.70
  - hemoglobin
    - elevated 282.7
    - low 285.9
  - hemoglobinuria 791.2
  - histological NEC 795.4
  - hormones 259.9
  - immunoglobulins, elevated 795.79
  - indolacetic acid, elevated 791.9
  - iron 790.6
  - karyotype 795.2
  - ketonuria 791.6
  - lactic acid dehydrogenase (LDH) 790.4
  - lead 790.6
  - lipase 790.5
  - lipids NEC 272.9
  - lithium, blood 790.6
  - liver function test 790.6
  - lung field (coin lesion) (shadow) 793.1
  - magnesium, blood 790.6
  - mammogram 793.80
    - calcification 793.89
    - calculus 793.89
    - microcalcification 793.81
  - mediastinal shift 793.2
  - melanin, urine 791.9
  - microbiologic NEC 795.39
  - mineral, blood NEC 790.6
  - myoglobinuria 791.3
  - nasal swab, anthrax 795.31
  - neonatal screening 796.6
  - nitrogen derivatives, blood 790.6
  - nonvisualization of gallbladder 793.3
  - nose culture, positive 795.39
  - odor of urine (unusual) NEC 791.9
  - oxygen saturation 790.91
  - Papanicolaou (smear) 796.9
    - anus 796.70
      - with
        - atypical squamous cells
          - cannot exclude high grade squamous intraepithelial lesion (ASC-H) 796.72
          - of undetermined significance (ASC-US) 796.71
        - cytologic evidence of malignancy 796.76
        - high grade squamous intraepithelial lesion (HGSIL) 796.74
        - low grade squamous intraepithelial lesion (LGSIL) 796.73
      - glandular 796.70
      - specified finding NEC 796.79
    - cervix 795.00
      - with
        - atypical squamous cells
          - cannot exclude high grade squamous intraepithelial lesion (ASC-H) 795.02
          - of undetermined significance (ASC-US) 795.01
        - cytologic evidence of malignancy 795.06
        - high grade squamous intraepithelial lesion (HGSIL) 795.04
        - low grade squamous intraepithelial lesion (LGSIL) 795.03
      - dyskaryotic 795.09
      - nonspecific finding NEC 795.09
    - other site 796.9
    - vagina 795.10

Findings, abnormal, without diagnosis — *continued*

  - Papanicolaou — *continued*
    - vagina — *continued*
      - with
        - atypical squamous cells
          - cannot exclude high grade squamous intraepithelial lesion (ASC-H) 795.12
          - of undetermined significance (ASC-US) 795.11
        - cytologic evidence of malignancy 795.16
        - high grade squamous intraepithelial lesion (HGSIL) 795.14
        - low grade squamous intraepithelial lesion (LGSIL) 795.13
      - glandular 795.10
      - specified NEC 795.19
  - peritoneal fluid 792.9
  - phonocardiogram 794.39
  - phosphorus 275.3
  - pleural fluid 792.9
  - pneumoencephalogram 793.0
  - PO_2-oxygen ratio 790.91
  - poikilocytosis 790.09
  - potassium
    - deficiency 276.8
    - excess 276.7
  - PPD 795.5
  - prostate specific antigen (PSA) 790.93
  - protein, serum NEC 790.99
  - proteinuria 791.0
  - prothrombin time (partial) (prolonged) (PT) (PTT) 790.92
  - pyuria 791.9
  - radiologic (x-ray) 793.99
    - abdomen 793.6
    - biliary tract 793.3
    - breast 793.89
      - abnormal mammogram NOS 793.80
      - mammographic
        - calcification 793.89
        - calculus 793.89
        - microcalcification 793.81
    - gastrointestinal tract 793.4
    - genitourinary organs 793.5
    - head 793.0
    - image test inconclusive due to excess body fat 793.91
    - intrathoracic organs NEC 793.2
    - lung 793.1
    - musculoskeletal 793.7
    - placenta 793.99
    - retroperitoneum 793.6
    - skin 793.99
    - skull 793.0
    - subcutaneous tissue 793.99
  - red blood cell 790.09
    - count 790.09
    - morphology 790.09
    - sickling 790.09
    - volume 790.09
  - saliva 792.4
  - scan NEC 794.9
    - bladder 794.9
    - bone 794.9
    - brain 794.09
    - kidney 794.4
    - liver 794.8
    - lung 794.2
    - pancreas 794.9
    - placental 794.9
    - spleen 794.9
    - thyroid 794.5
  - sedimentation rate, elevated 790.1
  - semen 792.2
  - serological (for)
    - human immunodeficiency virus (HIV)
      - inconclusive 795.71

- **Fitting** — *continued*
  - device, unspecified type — *continued*
    - insulin pump V53.91
    - intrauterine contraceptive V25.1
    - nervous system V53.09
    - orthodontic V53.4
    - orthoptic V53.1
    - other device V53.99
    - prosthetic V52.9
      - breast V52.4
      - dental V52.3
      - eye V52.2
      - specified type NEC V52.8
    - special senses V53.09
    - substitution
      - auditory V53.09
      - nervous system V53.09
      - visual V53.09
    - urinary V53.6
  - diaphragm (contraceptive) V25.02
  - glasses (reading) V53.1
  - growth rod V54.02
  - hearing aid V53.2
  - ileostomy device V53.5
  - intestinal appliance or device NEC V53.5
  - intrauterine contraceptive device V25.1
  - neuropacemaker (brain) (peripheral nerve) (spinal cord) V53.02
  - orthodontic device V53.4
  - orthopedic (device) V53.7
    - brace V53.7
    - cast V53.7
    - corset V53.7
    - shoes V53.7
  - pacemaker (cardiac) V53.31
    - brain V53.02
    - carotid sinus V53.39
    - peripheral nerve V53.02
    - spinal cord V53.02
  - prosthesis V52.9
    - arm (complete) (partial) V52.0
    - breast V52.4
      - implant exchange (different material) (different size) V52.4
    - dental V52.3
    - eye V52.2
    - leg (complete) (partial) V52.1
    - specified type NEC V52.8
  - spectacles V53.1
  - wheelchair V53.8
- **Fitz-Hugh and Curtis syndrome** 098.86
  - due to
    - Chlamydia trachomatis 099.56
    - Neisseria gonorrhoeae (gonococcal peritonitis) 098.86
- **Fitz's syndrome** (acute hemorrhagic pancreatitis) 577.0
- **Fixation**
  - joint — *see* Ankylosis
  - larynx 478.79
  - pupil 364.76
  - stapes 385.22
    - deafness (*see also* Deafness, conductive) 389.04
  - uterus (acquired) — *see* Malposition, uterus
  - vocal cord 478.5
- **Flaccid** — *see also* condition
  - foot 736.79
  - forearm 736.09
  - palate, congenital 750.26
- **Flail**
  - chest 807.4
    - newborn 767.3
  - joint (paralytic) 718.80
    - ankle 718.87
    - elbow 718.82
    - foot 718.87
    - hand 718.84
    - hip 718.85
    - knee 718.86
    - multiple sites 718.89
- **Flail** — *continued*
  - joint — *continued*
    - pelvic region 718.85
    - shoulder (region) 718.81
    - specified site NEC 718.88
    - wrist 718.83
- **Flajani (-Basedow) syndrome or disease** (exophthalmic goiter) 242.0 ☑
- **Flap, liver** 572.8
- **Flare, anterior chamber** (aqueous) (eye) 364.04
- **Flashback phenomena** (drug) (hallucinogenic) 292.89
- **Flat**
  - chamber (anterior) (eye) 360.34
  - chest, congenital 754.89
  - electroencephalogram (EEG) 348.8
  - foot (acquired) (fixed type) (painful) (postural) (spastic) 734
    - congenital 754.61
      - rocker bottom 754.61
      - vertical talus 754.61
    - rachitic 268.1
    - rocker bottom (congenital) 754.61
    - vertical talus, congenital 754.61
  - organ or site, congenital NEC — *see* Anomaly, specified type NEC
  - pelvis 738.6
    - with disproportion (fetopelvic) 653.2 ☑
      - affecting fetus or newborn 763.1
      - causing obstructed labor 660.1 ☑
        - affecting fetus or newborn 763.1
    - congenital 755.69
- **Flatau-Schilder disease** 341.1
- **Flattening**
  - head, femur 736.39
  - hip 736.39
  - lip (congenital) 744.89
  - nose (congenital) 754.0
    - acquired 738.0
- **Flatulence** 787.3
- **Flatus** 787.3
  - vaginalis 629.89
- **Flax dressers' disease** 504
- **Flea bite** — *see* Injury, superficial, by site
- **Fleischer (-Kayser) ring** (corneal pigmentation) 275.1 *[371.14]*
- **Fleischner's disease** 732.3
- **Fleshy mole** 631
- **Flexibilitas cerea** — *see also* Catalepsy 300.11
- **Flexion**
  - cervix — *see* Flexion, uterus
  - contracture, joint (*see also* Contraction, joint) 718.4 ☑
  - deformity, joint (*see also* Contraction, joint) 736.9
    - hip, congenital (*see also* Subluxation, congenital, hip) 754.32
  - uterus (*see also* Malposition, uterus) 621.6
- **Flexner's**
  - bacillus 004.1
  - diarrhea (ulcerative) 004.1
  - dysentery 004.1
- **Flexner-Boyd dysentery** 004.2
- **Flexure** — *see* condition
- **Floater, vitreous** 379.24
- **Floating**
  - cartilage (joint) (*see also* Disorder, cartilage, articular) 718.0 ☑
    - knee 717.6
  - gallbladder (congenital) 751.69
  - kidney 593.0
    - congenital 753.3
  - liver (congenital) 751.69
  - rib 756.3
  - spleen 289.59
- **Flooding** 626.2
- **Floor** — *see* condition
- **Floppy**
  - infant NEC 781.99
- **Floppy** — *continued*
  - iris syndrome 364.81
  - valve syndrome (mitral) 424.0
- **Flu** — *see also* Influenza
  - gastric NEC 008.8
- **Fluctuating blood pressure** 796.4
- **Fluid**
  - abdomen 789.59
  - chest (*see also* Pleurisy, with effusion) 511.9
  - heart (*see also* Failure, heart) 428.0
  - joint (*see also* Effusion, joint) 719.0 ☑
  - loss (acute) 276.50
    - with
      - hypernatremia 276.0
      - hyponatremia 276.1
  - lung (*see also* Edema, lung)
    - encysted 511.89
  - peritoneal cavity 789.59
    - malignant 789.51
  - pleural cavity (*see also* Pleurisy, with effusion) 511.9
  - retention 276.6
- **Flukes** NEC — *see also* Infestation, fluke 121.9
  - blood NEC (*see also* Infestation, Schistosoma) 120.9
  - liver 121.3
- **Fluor** (albus) (vaginalis) 623.5
  - trichomonal (Trichomonas vaginalis) 131.00
- **Fluorosis** (dental) (chronic) 520.3
- **Flushing** 782.62
  - menopausal 627.2
- **Flush syndrome** 259.2
- **Flutter**
  - atrial or auricular 427.32
  - heart (ventricular) 427.42
    - atrial 427.32
  - impure 427.32
  - postoperative 997.1
  - ventricular 427.42
- **Flux** (bloody) (serosanguineous) 009.0
- **Focal** — *see* condition
- **Fochier's abscess** — *see* Abscess, by site
- **Focus, Assmann's** — *see also* Tuberculosis 011.0 ☑
- **Fogo selvagem** 694.4
- **Foix-Alajouanine syndrome** 336.1
- **Folds, anomalous** — *see also* Anomaly, specified type NEC
  - Bowman's membrane 371.31
  - Descemet's membrane 371.32
  - epicanthic 743.63
  - heart 746.89
  - posterior segment of eye, congenital 743.54
- **Folie à deux** 297.3
- **Follicle**
  - cervix (nabothian) (ruptured) 616.0
  - graafian, ruptured, with hemorrhage 620.0
  - nabothian 616.0
- **Folliclis** (primary) — *see also* Tuberculosis 017.0 ☑
- **Follicular** — *see also* condition
  - cyst (atretic) 620.0
- **Folliculitis** 704.8
  - abscedens et suffodiens 704.8
  - decalvans 704.09
  - gonorrheal (acute) 098.0
    - chronic or duration of 2 months or more 098.2
  - keloid, keloidalis 706.1
  - pustular 704.8
  - ulerythematosa reticulata 701.8
- **Folliculosis, conjunctival** 372.02
- **Følling's disease** (phenylketonuria) 270.1
- **Follow-up** (examination) (routine) (following) V67.9
  - cancer chemotherapy V67.2
  - chemotherapy V67.2
  - fracture V67.4
  - high-risk medication V67.51
  - injury NEC V67.59
- **Follow-up** — *continued*
  - postpartum
    - immediately after delivery V24.0
    - routine V24.2
  - psychiatric V67.3
  - psychotherapy V67.3
  - radiotherapy V67.1
  - specified condition NEC V67.59
  - specified surgery NEC V67.09
  - surgery V67.00
    - vaginal pap smear V67.01
  - treatment V67.9
    - combined NEC V67.6
    - fracture V67.4
    - involving high-risk medication NEC V67.51
    - mental disorder V67.3
    - specified NEC V67.59
- **Fong's syndrome** (hereditary osteoonychodysplasia) 756.89
- **Food**
  - allergy 693.1
  - anaphylactic shock — *see* Anaphylactic shock, due to, food
  - asphyxia (from aspiration or inhalation) (*see also* Asphyxia, food) 933.1
  - choked on (*see also* Asphyxia, food) 933.1
  - deprivation 994.2
    - specified kind of food NEC 269.8
  - intoxication (*see also* Poisoning, food) 005.9
  - lack of 994.2
  - poisoning (*see also* Poisoning, food) 005.9
  - refusal or rejection NEC 307.59
  - strangulation or suffocation (*see also* Asphyxia, food) 933.1
  - toxemia (*see also* Poisoning, food) 005.9
- **Foot** — *see also* condition
  - and mouth disease 078.4
  - process disease 581.3
- **Foramen ovale** (nonclosure) (patent) (persistent) 745.5
- **Forbes-Albright syndrome** (nonpuerperal amenorrhea and lactation associated with pituitary tumor) 253.1
- **Forbes'(glycogen storage) disease** 271.0
- **Forced birth or delivery** NEC 669.8 ☑
  - affecting fetus or newborn NEC 763.89
- **Forceps**
  - delivery NEC 669.5 ☑
    - affecting fetus or newborn 763.2
- **Fordyce's disease** (ectopic sebaceous glands) (mouth) 750.26
- **Fordyce-Fox disease** (apocrine miliaria) 705.82
- **Forearm** — *see* condition
- **Foreign body**

> *Note — For foreign body with open wound, or other injury, see Wound, open, or the type of injury specified.*

  - accidentally left during a procedure 998.4
  - anterior chamber (eye) 871.6
    - magnetic 871.5
      - retained or old 360.51
    - retained or old 360.61
  - ciliary body (eye) 871.6
    - magnetic 871.5
      - retained or old 360.52
    - retained or old 360.62
  - entering through orifice (current) (old)
    - accessory sinus 932
    - air passage (upper) 933.0
      - lower 934.8
    - alimentary canal 938
    - alveolar process 935.0
    - antrum (Highmore) 932
    - anus 937
    - appendix 936

Foreign body — *continued*
  entering through orifice — *continued*
    asphyxia due to (*see also* Asphyxia, food) 933.1
    auditory canal 931
    auricle 931
    bladder 939.0
    bronchioles 934.8
    bronchus (main) 934.1
    buccal cavity 935.0
    canthus (inner) 930.1
    cecum 936
    cervix (canal) uterine 939.1
    coil, ileocecal 936
    colon 936
    conjunctiva 930.1
    conjunctival sac 930.1
    cornea 930.0
    digestive organ or tract NEC 938
    duodenum 936
    ear (external) 931
    esophagus 935.1
    eye (external) 930.9
      combined sites 930.8
      intraocular — *see* Foreign body, by site
      specified site NEC 930.8
    eyeball 930.8
      intraocular — *see* Foreign body, intraocular
    eyelid 930.1
      retained or old 374.86
    frontal sinus 932
    gastrointestinal tract 938
    genitourinary tract 939.9
    globe 930.8
      penetrating 871.6
        magnetic 871.5
          retained or old 360.50
        retained or old 360.60
    gum 935.0
    Highmore's antrum 932
    hypopharynx 933.0
    ileocecal coil 936
    ileum 936
    inspiration (of) 933.1
    intestine (large) (small) 936
    lacrimal apparatus, duct, gland, or sac 930.2
    larynx 933.1
    lung 934.8
    maxillary sinus 932
    mouth 935.0
    nasal sinus 932
    nasopharynx 933.0
    nose (passage) 932
    nostril 932
    oral cavity 935.0
    palate 935.0
    penis 939.3
    pharynx 933.0
    pyriform sinus 933.0
    rectosigmoid 937
      junction 937
    rectum 937
    respiratory tract 934.9
      specified part NEC 934.8
    sclera 930.1
    sinus 932
      accessory 932
      frontal 932
      maxillary 932
      nasal 932
      pyriform 933.0
    small intestine 936
    stomach (hairball) 935.2
    suffocation by (*see also* Asphyxia, food) 933.1
    swallowed 938
      tongue 933.0
    tear ducts or glands 930.2
    throat 933.0
    tongue 935.0
      swallowed 933.0
    tonsil, tonsillar 933.0

Foreign body — *continued*
  entering through orifice — *continued*
    tonsil, tonsillar — *continued*
      fossa 933.0
    trachea 934.0
    ureter 939.0
    urethra 939.0
    uterus (any part) 939.1
    vagina 939.2
    vulva 939.2
    wind pipe 934.0
  feeling of, in throat 784.99
  granuloma (old) 728.82
    bone 733.99
    in operative wound (inadvertently left) 998.4
      due to surgical material intentionally left — *see* Complications, due to (presence of) any device, implant, or graft classified to 996.0–996.5 NEC
    muscle 728.82
    skin 709.4
    soft tissue 709.4
    subcutaneous tissue 709.4
  in
    bone (residual) 733.99
    open wound — *see* Wound, open, by site complicated
    soft tissue (residual) 729.6
  inadvertently left in operation wound (causing adhesions, obstruction, or perforation) 998.4
  ingestion, ingested NEC 938
  inhalation or inspiration (*see also* Asphyxia, food) 933.1
  internal organ, not entering through an orifice — *see* Injury, internal, by site, with open wound
  intraocular (nonmagnetic) 871.6
    combined sites 871.6
      magnetic 871.5
        retained or old 360.59
      retained or old 360.69
    magnetic 871.5
      retained or old 360.50
    retained or old 360.60
    specified site NEC 871.6
      magnetic 871.5
        retained or old 360.59
      retained or old 360.69
  iris (nonmagnetic) 871.6
    magnetic 871.5
      retained or old 360.52
    retained or old 360.62
  lens (nonmagnetic) 871.6
    magnetic 871.5
      retained or old 360.53
    retained or old 360.63
  lid, eye 930.1
  ocular muscle 870.4
    retained or old 376.6
  old or residual
    bone 733.99
    eyelid 374.86
    middle ear 385.83
    muscle 729.6
      ocular 376.6
    retrobulbar 376.6
    skin 729.6
      with granuloma 709.4
    soft tissue 729.6
      with granuloma 709.4
    subcutaneous tissue 729.6
      with granuloma 709.4
  operation wound, left accidentally 998.4
  orbit 870.4
    retained or old 376.6
  posterior wall, eye 871.6
    magnetic 871.5
      retained or old 360.55
    retained or old 360.65
  respiratory tree 934.9

Foreign body — *continued*
  respiratory tree — *continued*
    specified site NEC 934.8
  retained (old) (nonmagnetic) (in)
    anterior chamber (eye) 360.61
      magnetic 360.51
    ciliary body 360.62
      magnetic 360.52
    eyelid 374.86
    globe 360.60
      magnetic 360.50
    intraocular 360.60
      magnetic 360.50
      specified site NEC 360.69
        magnetic 360.59
    iris 360.62
      magnetic 360.52
    lens 360.63
      magnetic 360.53
    muscle 729.6
    orbit 376.6
    posterior wall of globe 360.65
      magnetic 360.55
    retina 360.65
      magnetic 360.55
    retrobulbar 376.6
    skin 729.6
      with granuloma 709.4
    soft tissue 729.6
      with granuloma 709.4
    subcutaneous tissue 729.6
      with granuloma 709.4
    vitreous 360.64
      magnetic 360.54
  retina 871.6
    magnetic 871.5
      retained or old 360.55
    retained or old 360.65
  superficial, without major open wound (*see also* Injury, superficial, by site) 919.6
  swallowed NEC 938
  throat, feeling of 784.99
  vitreous (humor) 871.6
    magnetic 871.5
      retained or old 360.54
    retained or old 360.64

Forking, aqueduct of Sylvius 742.3
  with spina bifida (*see also* Spina bifida) 741.0 ☑

Formation
  bone in scar tissue (skin) 709.3
  connective tissue in vitreous 379.25
  Elschnig pearls (postcataract extraction) 366.51
  hyaline in cornea 371.49
  sequestrum in bone (due to infection) (*see also* Osteomyelitis) 730.1 ☑
  valve
    colon, congenital 751.5
    ureter (congenital) 753.29

Formication 782.0

Fort Bragg fever 100.89

Fossa — *see also* condition
  pyriform — *see* condition

Foster-Kennedy syndrome 377.04

Fothergill's
  disease, meaning scarlatina anginosa 034.1
  neuralgia (*see also* Neuralgia, trigeminal) 350.1

Foul breath 784.99

Found dead (cause unknown) 798.9

Foundling V20.0

Fournier's disease (idiopathic gangrene) 608.83

Fourth
  cranial nerve — *see* condition
  disease 057.8
  molar 520.1

Foville's syndrome 344.89

Fox's
  disease (apocrine miliaria) 705.82
  impetigo (contagiosa) 684

Fox-Fordyce disease (apocrine miliaria) 705.82

Fracture (abduction) (adduction) (avulsion) (compression) (crush) (dislocation) (oblique) (separation) (closed) 829.0

Note — For fracture of any of the following sites with fracture of other bones — see Fracture, multiple.

"Closed" includes the following descriptions of fractures, with or without delayed healing, unless they are specified as open or compound:

comminuted	*linear*
depressed	*simple*
elevated	*slipped epiphysis*
fissured	*spiral*
greenstick	*unspecified*
impacted	

"Open" includes the following descriptions of fractures, with or without delayed healing:

compound	*puncture*
infected	*with foreign body*
missile	

For late effect of fracture, see Late, effect, fracture, by site.

  with
    internal injuries in same region (conditions classifiable to 860–869) (*see also* Injury, internal, by site)
      pelvic region — *see* Fracture, pelvis
  acetabulum (with visceral injury) (closed) 808.0
    open 808.1
  acromion (process) (closed) 811.01
    open 811.11
  alveolus (closed) 802.8
    open 802.9
  ankle (malleolus) (closed) 824.8
    bimalleolar (Dupuytren's) (Pott's) 824.4
      open 824.5
    bone 825.21
      open 825.31
    lateral malleolus only (fibular) 824.2
      open 824.3
    medial malleolus only (tibial) 824.0
      open 824.1
    open 824.9
    pathologic 733.16
    talus 825.21
      open 825.31
    trimalleolar 824.6
      open 824.7
  antrum — *see* Fracture, skull, base
  arm (closed) 818.0
    and leg(s) (any bones) 828.0
      open 828.1
    both (any bones) (with rib(s)) (with sternum) 819.0
      open 819.1
    lower 813.80
      open 813.90
    open 818.1
    upper — *see* Fracture, humerus
  astragalus (closed) 825.21
    open 825.31
  atlas — *see* Fracture, vertebra, cervical, first
  axis — *see* Fracture, vertebra, cervical, second
  back — *see* Fracture, vertebra, by site
  Barton's — *see* Fracture, radius, lower end
  basal (skull) — *see* Fracture, skull, base
  Bennett's (closed) 815.01

Note — Multiple fractures of sites classifiable to the same three- or four-digit category are coded to that category, except for sites classifiable to 810–818 or 820–827 in different limbs.

Multiple fractures of sites classifiable to different fourth-digit subdivisions within the same three-digit category should be dealt with according to coding rules.

Multiple fractures of sites classifiable to different three-digit categories (identifiable from the listing under "Fracture"), and of sites classifiable to 810–818 or 820–827 in different limbs should be coded according to the following list, which should be referred to in the following priority order: skull or face bones, pelvis or vertebral column, legs, arms.

Note — Use the following fifth-digit subclassification with categories 800, 801, 803, and 804:

0 *unspecified state of consciousness*

1 *with no loss of consciousness*

2 *with brief [less than one hour] loss of consciousness*

3 *with moderate [1–24 hours] loss of consciousness*

4 *with prolonged [more than 24 hours] loss of consciousness and return to pre-existing conscious level*

5 *with prolonged [more than 24 hours] loss of consciousness, without return to pre-existing conscious level*

Use fifth-digit 5 to designate when a patient is unconscious and dies before regaining consciousness, regardless of the duration of the loss of consciousness

6 *with loss of consciousness of unspecified duration*

9 *with concussion, unspecified*

- **Fracture** — *continued*
  - multiple — *continued*
    - skull, specified or unspecified bones, or face bone(s) with any other bone(s) — *continued*
      - open — *continued*
        - with — *continued*
          - extradural hemorrhage 804.7 ☑
          - hemorrhage (intracranial) NEC 804.8 ☑
          - intracranial injury NEC 804.9 ☑
          - laceration, cerebral 804.6 ☑
          - subarachnoid hemorrhage 804.7 ☑
          - subdural hemorrhage 804.7 ☑
    - vertebral column with other bones, except skull or face bones (sites classifiable to 805 or 806 with sites classifiable to 807–808 or 810–829) (closed) 809.0
      - open 809.1
  - nasal (bone(s)) (closed) 802.0
    - open 802.1
    - sinus — *see* Fracture, skull, base
  - navicular
    - carpal (wrist) (closed) 814.01
      - open 814.11
    - tarsal (ankle) (closed) 825.22
      - open 825.32
  - neck — *see* Fracture, vertebra, cervical
  - neural arch — *see* Fracture, vertebra, by site
  - nonunion 733.82
  - nose, nasal, (bone) (septum) (closed) 802.0
    - open 802.1
  - occiput — *see* Fracture, skull, base
  - odontoid process — *see* Fracture, vertebra, cervical
  - olecranon (process) (ulna) (closed) 813.01
    - open 813.11
  - open 829.1
  - orbit, orbital (bone) (region) (closed) 802.8
    - floor (blow-out) 802.6
      - open 802.7
    - open 802.9
    - roof — *see* Fracture, skull, base
    - specified part NEC 802.8
      - open 802.9
  - os
    - calcis (closed) 825.0
      - open 825.1
    - magnum (closed) 814.07
      - open 814.17
    - pubis (with visceral injury) (closed) 808.2
      - open 808.3
    - triquetrum (closed) 814.03
      - open 814.13
  - osseous
    - auditory meatus — *see* Fracture, skull, base
    - labyrinth — *see* Fracture, skull, base
  - ossicles, auditory (incus) (malleus) (stapes) — *see* Fracture, skull, base
  - osteoporotic — *see* Fracture, pathologic
  - palate (closed) 802.8
    - open 802.9
  - paratrooper — *see* Fracture, tibia, lower end
  - parietal bone — *see* Fracture, skull, vault
  - parry — *see* Fracture, Monteggia's
  - patella (closed) 822.0

- **Fracture** — *continued*
  - patella — *continued*
    - open 822.1
  - pathologic (cause unknown) 733.10
    - ankle 733.16
    - femur (neck) 733.14
      - specified NEC 733.15
    - fibula 733.16
    - hip 733.14
    - humerus 733.11
    - radius (distal) 733.12
    - specified site NEC 733.19
    - tibia 733.16
    - ulna 733.12
    - vertebrae (collapse) 733.13
    - wrist 733.12
  - pedicle (of vertebral arch) — *see* Fracture, vertebra, by site
  - pelvis, pelvic (bone(s)) (with visceral injury) (closed) 808.8
    - multiple (with disruption of pelvic circle) 808.43
      - open 808.53
    - open 808.9
    - rim (closed) 808.49
      - open 808.59
  - peritrochanteric (closed) 820.20
    - open 820.30
  - phalanx, phalanges, of one
    - foot (closed) 826.0
      - with bone(s) of same lower limb 827.0
        - open 827.1
      - open 826.1
    - hand (closed) 816.00
      - with metacarpal bone(s) of same hand 817.0
        - open 817.1
      - distal 816.02
        - open 816.12
      - middle 816.01
        - open 816.11
      - multiple sites NEC 816.03
        - open 816.13
      - open 816.10
      - proximal 816.01
        - open 816.11
  - pisiform (closed) 814.04
    - open 814.14
  - pond — *see* Fracture, skull, vault
  - Pott's (closed) 824.4
    - open 824.5
  - prosthetic device, internal — *see* Complications, mechanical
  - pubis (with visceral injury) (closed) 808.2
    - open 808.3
  - Quervain's (closed) 814.01
    - open 814.11
  - radius (alone) (closed) 813.81
    - with ulna NEC 813.83
      - open 813.93
    - distal end — *see* Fracture, radius, lower end
    - epiphysis
      - lower — *see* Fracture, radius, lower end
      - upper — *see* Fracture, radius, upper end
    - head — *see* Fracture, radius, upper end
    - lower end or extremity (distal end) (lower epiphysis) 813.42
      - with ulna (lower end) 813.44
        - open 813.54
      - open 813.52
      - torus 813.45
    - neck — *see* Fracture, radius, upper end
    - open NEC 813.91
    - pathologic 733.12
    - proximal end — *see* Fracture, radius, upper end
    - shaft (closed) 813.21
      - with ulna (shaft) 813.23
        - open 813.33

- **Fracture** — *continued*
  - radius — *continued*
    - shaft — *continued*
      - open 813.31
    - upper end 813.07
      - with ulna (upper end) 813.08
        - open 813.18
      - epiphysis 813.05
        - open 813.15
      - head 813.05
        - open 813.15
      - multiple sites 813.07
        - open 813.17
      - neck 813.06
        - open 813.16
      - open 813.17
      - specified site NEC 813.07
        - open 813.17
  - ramus
    - inferior or superior (with visceral injury) (closed) 808.2
      - open 808.3
    - ischium — *see* Fracture, ischium
    - mandible 802.24
      - open 802.34
  - rib(s) (closed) 807.0 ☑

> *Note — Use the following fifth-digit subclassification with categories 807.0–807.1:*
>
> 0 *rib(s), unspecified*
> 1 *one rib*
> 2 *two ribs*
> 3 *three ribs*
> 4 *four ribs*
> 5 *five ribs*
> 6 *six ribs*
> 7 *seven ribs*
> 8 *eight or more ribs*
> 9 *multiple ribs, unspecified*

  - with flail chest (open) 807.4
  - open 807.1 ☑
- root, tooth 873.63
  - complicated 873.73
- sacrum — *see* Fracture, vertebra, sacrum
- scaphoid
  - ankle (closed) 825.22
    - open 825.32
  - wrist (closed) 814.01
    - open 814.11
- scapula (closed) 811.00
  - acromial, acromion (process) 811.01
    - open 811.11
  - body 811.09
    - open 811.19
  - coracoid process 811.02
    - open 811.12
  - glenoid (cavity) (fossa) 811.03
    - open 811.13
  - neck 811.03
    - open 811.13
  - open 811.10
- semilunar
  - bone, wrist (closed) 814.02
    - open 814.12
  - cartilage (interior) (knee) — *see* Tear, meniscus
- sesamoid bone — *see* Fracture, by site
- Shepherd's (closed) 825.21
  - open 825.31
- shoulder (*see also* Fracture, humerus, upper end)
  - blade — *see* Fracture, scapula
- silverfork — *see* Fracture, radius, lower end
- sinus (ethmoid) (frontal) (maxillary) (nasal) (sphenoidal) — *see* Fracture, skull, base
- Skillern's — *see* Fracture, radius, shaft

- **Fracture** — *continued*
  - skull (multiple NEC) (with face bones) (closed) 803.0 ☑

> *Note — Use the following fifth-digit subclassification with categories 800, 801, 803, and 804:*
>
> 0 *unspecified state of consciousness*
> 1 *with no loss of consciousness*
> 2 *with brief [less than one hour] loss of consciousness*
> 3 *with moderate [1-24 hours] loss of consciousness*
> 4 *with prolonged [more than 24 hours] loss of consciousness and return to pre-existing conscious level*
> 5 *with prolonged [more than 24 hours] loss of consciousness, without return to pre-existing conscious level*
>
> *Use fifth-digit 5 to designate when a patient is unconscious and dies before regaining consciousness, regardless of the duration of the loss of consciousness*
>
> 6 *with loss of consciousness of unspecified duration*
> 9 *with concussion, unspecified*

  - with
    - contusion, cerebral 803.1 ☑
    - epidural hemorrhage 803.2 ☑
    - extradural hemorrhage 803.2 ☑
    - hemorrhage (intracranial) NEC 803.3 ☑
    - intracranial injury NEC 803.4 ☑
    - laceration, cerebral 803.1 ☑
    - other bones — *see* Fracture, multiple, skull
    - subarachnoid hemorrhage 803.2 ☑
    - subdural hemorrhage 803.2 ☑
  - base (antrum) (ethmoid bone) (fossa) (internal ear) (nasal sinus) (occiput) (sphenoid) (temporal bone) (closed) 801.0 ☑
    - with
      - contusion, cerebral 801.1 ☑
      - epidural hemorrhage 801.2 ☑
      - extradural hemorrhage 801.2 ☑
      - hemorrhage (intracranial) NEC 801.3 ☑
      - intracranial injury NEC 801.4 ☑
      - laceration, cerebral 801.1 ☑
      - subarachnoid hemorrhage 801.2 ☑
      - subdural hemorrhage 801.2 ☑
    - open 801.5 ☑
      - with
        - contusion, cerebral 801.6 ☑
        - epidural hemorrhage 801.7 ☑
        - extradural hemorrhage 801.7 ☑
        - hemorrhage (intracranial) NEC 801.8 ☑
        - intracranial injury NEC 801.9 ☑

Note — Use the following fifth-digit subclassification with categories 806.0–806.3:

C_1–C_4 or unspecified level and D_1–D_6 (T_1–T_6) or unspecified level with

- 0 *unspecified spinal cord injury*
- 1 *complete lesion of cord*
- 2 *anterior cord syndrome*
- 3 *central cord syndrome*
- 4 *specified injury NEC*

C_5–C_7 level and D_7–D_{12} level with:

- 5 *unspecified spinal cord injury*
- 6 *complete lesion of cord*
- 7 *anterior cord syndrome*
- 8 *central cord syndrome*
- 9 *specified injury NEC*

Index

Fracture — Fracture

Fusion, fused — *continued*
limb 755.8
lower 755.69
upper 755.59
lobe, lung 748.5
lumbosacral (acquired) 724.6
congenital 756.15
surgical V45.4
nares (anterior) (posterior) 748.0
nose, nasal 748.0
nostril(s) 748.0
organ or site NEC — *see* Anomaly, specified type NEC

Fusion, fused — *continued*
ossicles 756.9
auditory 744.04
pulmonary valve segment 746.02
pulmonic cusps 746.02
ribs 756.3
sacroiliac (acquired) (joint) 724.6
congenital 755.69
surgical V45.4
skull, imperfect 756.0
spine (acquired) 724.9
arthrodesis status V45.4
congenital (vertebra) 756.15

Fusion, fused — *continued*
spine — *continued*
postoperative status V45.4
sublingual duct with submaxillary duct at opening in mouth 750.26
talonavicular (bar) 755.67
teeth, tooth 520.2
testes 752.89
toes (*see also* Syndactylism, toes) 755.13
trachea and esophagus 750.3
twins 759.4

Fusion, fused — *continued*
urethral-hymenal 599.89
vagina 752.49
valve cusps — *see* Fusion, cusps, heart valve
ventricles, heart 745.4
vertebra (arch) — *see* Fusion, spine
vulva 752.49
Fusospirillosis (mouth) (tongue) (tonsil) 101
Fussy infant (baby) 780.91

G

Note — Use the following fifth-digit subclassification for category 535:

0 without mention of hemorrhage

1 with hemorrhage

- **Gastritis** — *continued*
  - subacute 535.0 ☑
  - superficial 535.4 ☑
  - suppurative 535.0 ☑
  - toxic 535.4 ☑
  - tuberculous (*see also* Tuberculosis) 017.9 ☑
- **Gastrocarcinoma** (M8010/3) 151.9
- **Gastrocolic** — *see* condition
- **Gastrocolitis** — *see* Enteritis
- **Gastrodisciasis** 121.8
- **Gastroduodenitis** — *see also* Gastritis 535.5 ☑
  - catarrhal 535.0 ☑
  - infectional 535.0 ☑
  - virus, viral 008.8
    - specified type NEC 008.69
- **Gastrodynia** 536.8
- **Gastroenteritis** (acute) (catarrhal) (congestive) (hemorrhagic) (noninfectious) — *see also* Enteritis 558.9
  - aertrycke infection 003.0
  - allergic 558.3
  - chronic 558.9
    - ulcerative (*see also* Colitis, ulcerative) 556.9
  - dietetic 558.9
  - due to
    - antineoplastic chemotherapy 558.9
    - food poisoning (*see also* Poisoning, food) 005.9
    - radiation 558.1
  - eosinophilic 558.41
  - epidemic 009.0
  - functional 558.9
  - infectious (*see also* Enteritis, due to, by organism) 009.0
    - presumed 009.1
  - salmonella 003.0
  - septic (*see also* Enteritis, due to, by organism) 009.0
  - toxic 558.2
  - tuberculous (*see also* Tuberculosis) 014.8 ☑
  - ulcerative (*see also* Colitis, ulcerative) 556.9
  - viral NEC 008.8
    - specified type NEC 008.69
  - zymotic 009.0
- **Gastroenterocolitis** — *see* Enteritis
- **Gastroenteropathy, protein-losing** 579.8
- **Gastroenteroptosis** 569.89
- **Gastroesophageal laceration-hemorrhage syndrome** 530.7
- **Gastroesophagitis** 530.19
- **Gastrohepatitis** — *see also* Gastritis 535.5 ☑
- **Gastrointestinal** — *see* condition
- **Gastrojejunal** — *see* condition
- **Gastrojejunitis** — *see also* Gastritis 535.5 ☑
- **Gastrojejunocolic** — *see* condition
- **Gastroliths** 537.89
- **Gastromalacia** 537.89
- **Gastroparalysis** 536.3
  - diabetic 250.6 ☑ *[536.3]*
    - due to secondary diabetes 249.6 ☑ *[536.3]*
- **Gastroparesis** 536.3
  - diabetic 250.6 ☑ *[536.3]*
    - due to secondary diabetes 249.6 ☑ *[536.3]*
- **Gastropathy** 537.9
  - congestive portal 537.89
  - erythematous 535.5 ☑
  - exudative 579.8
  - portal hypertensive 537.89
- **Gastroptosis** 537.5
- **Gastrorrhagia** 578.0
- **Gastrorrhea** 536.8
  - psychogenic 306.4
- **Gastroschisis** (congenital) 756.79
  - acquired 569.89
- **Gastrospasm** (neurogenic) (reflex) 536.8
  - neurotic 306.4
- **Gastrospasm** — *continued*
  - psychogenic 306.4
- **Gastrostaxis** 578.0
- **Gastrostenosis** 537.89
- **Gastrostomy**
  - attention to V55.1
  - complication 536.40
    - specified type 536.49
  - infection 536.41
  - malfunctioning 536.42
  - status V44.1
- **Gastrosuccorrhea** (continuous) (intermittent) 536.8
  - neurotic 306.4
  - psychogenic 306.4
- **Gaucher's**
  - disease (adult) (cerebroside lipidosis) (infantile) 272.7
  - hepatomegaly 272.7
  - splenomegaly (cerebroside lipidosis) 272.7
- **GAVE** (gastric antral vascular ectasia) 537.82
  - with hemorrhage 537.83
  - without hemorrhage 537.82
- **Gayet's disease** (superior hemorrhagic polioencephalitis) 265.1
- **Gayet-Wernicke's syndrome** (superior hemorrhagic polioencephalitis) 265.1
- **Gee (-Herter) (-Heubner) (-Thaysen) disease or syndrome** (nontropical sprue) 579.0
- **Gélineau's syndrome** — *see also* Narcolepsy 347.00
- **Gemination, teeth** 520.2
- **Gemistocytoma** (M9411/3)
  - specified site — *see* Neoplasm, by site, malignant
  - unspecified site 191.9
- **General, generalized** — *see* condtion
- **Genetic**
  - susceptibility to
    - MEN (multiple endocrine neoplasia) V84.81
    - neoplasia
      - multiple endocrine [MEN] V84.81
    - neoplasm
      - malignant, of
        - breast V84.01
        - endometrium V84.04
        - other V84.09
        - ovary V84.02
        - prostate V84.03
    - specified disease NEC V84.89
- **Genital** — *see* condition
  - warts 078.11
- **Genito-anorectal syndrome** 099.1
- **Genitourinary system** — *see* condition
- **Genu**
  - congenital 755.64
  - extrorsum (acquired) 736.42
    - congenital 755.64
    - late effects of rickets 268.1
  - introrsum (acquired) 736.41
    - congenital 755.64
    - late effects of rickets 268.1
  - rachitic (old) 268.1
  - recurvatum (acquired) 736.5
    - congenital 754.40
      - with dislocation of knee 754.41
    - late effects of rickets 268.1
  - valgum (acquired) (knock-knee) 736.41
    - congenital 755.64
    - late effects of rickets 268.1
  - varum (acquired) (bowleg) 736.42
    - congenital 755.64
    - late effect of rickets 268.1
- **Geographic tongue** 529.1
- **Geophagia** 307.52
- **Geotrichosis** 117.9
  - intestine 117.9
  - lung 117.9
  - mouth 117.9
- **Gephyrophobia** 300.29
- **Gerbode defect** 745.4
- **GERD** (gastroesophageal reflux disease) 530.81
- **Gerhardt's**
  - disease (erythromelalgia) 443.82
  - syndrome (vocal cord paralysis) 478.30
- **Gerlier's disease** (epidemic vertigo) 078.81
- **German measles** 056.9
  - exposure to V01.4
- **Germinoblastoma** (diffuse) (M9614/3) 202.8 ☑
  - follicular (M9692/3) 202.0 ☑
- **Germinoma** (M9064/3) — *see* Neoplasm, by site, malignant
- **Gerontoxon** 371.41
- **Gerstmann-Sträussler-Scheinker syndrome** (GSS) 046.71
- **Gerstmann's syndrome** (finger agnosia) 784.69
- **Gestation** (period) — *see also* Pregnancy
  - ectopic NEC (*see also* Pregnancy, ectopic) 633.90
    - with intrauterine pregnancy 633.91
- **Gestational proteinuria** 646.2 ☑
  - with hypertension — *see* Toxemia, of pregnancy
- **Ghon tubercle primary infection** — *see also* Tuberculosis 010.0 ☑
- **Ghost**
  - teeth 520.4
  - vessels, cornea 370.64
- **Ghoul hand** 102.3
- **Gianotti Crosti syndrome** 057.8
  - due to known virus — *see* Infection, virus
  - due to unknown virus 057.8
- **Giant**
  - cell
    - epulis 523.8
    - peripheral (gingiva) 523.8
    - tumor, tendon sheath 727.02
  - colon (congenital) 751.3
  - esophagus (congenital) 750.4
  - kidney 753.3
  - urticaria 995.1
    - hereditary 277.6
- **Giardia lamblia infestation** 007.1
- **Giardiasis** 007.1
- **Gibert's disease** (pityriasis rosea) 696.3
- **Gibraltar fever** — *see* Brucellosis
- **Giddiness** 780.4
  - hysterical 300.11
  - psychogenic 306.9
- **Gierke's disease** (glycogenosis I) 271.0
- **Gigantism** (cerebral) (hypophyseal) (pituitary) 253.0
- **Gilbert's disease or cholemia** (familial nonhemolytic jaundice) 277.4
- **Gilchrist's disease** (North American blastomycosis) 116.0
- **Gilford (-Hutchinson) disease or syndrome** (progeria) 259.8
- **Gilles de la Tourette's disease** (motor-verbal tic) 307.23
- **Gillespie's syndrome** (dysplasia oculodentodigitalis) 759.89
- **Gingivitis** 523.10
  - acute 523.00
    - necrotizing 101
    - non-plaque induced 523.01
    - plaque induced 523.00
  - catarrhal 523.00
  - chronic 523.10
    - non-plaque induced 523.11
  - desquamative 523.10
  - expulsiva 523.40
  - hyperplastic 523.10
  - marginal, simple 523.10
  - necrotizing, acute 101
  - non-plaque induced 523.11
  - pellagrous 265.2
  - plaque induced 523.10
  - ulcerative 523.10
- **Gingivitis** — *continued*
  - ulcerative — *continued*
    - acute necrotizing 101
  - Vincent's 101
- **Gingivoglossitis** 529.0
- **Gingivopericementitis** 523.40
- **Gingivosis** 523.10
- **Gingivostomatitis** 523.10
  - herpetic 054.2
- **Giovannini's disease** 117.9
- **GISA** (glycopeptide intermediate staphylococcus aureus) V09.8 ☑
- **Glanders** 024
- **Gland, glandular** — *see* condition
- **Glanzmann (-Naegeli) disease or thrombasthenia** 287.1
- **Glassblowers' disease** 527.1
- **Glaucoma** (capsular) (inflammatory) (noninflammatory) (primary) 365.9
  - with increased episcleral venous pressure 365.82
  - absolute 360.42
  - acute 365.22
    - narrow angle 365.22
    - secondary 365.60
  - angle closure 365.20
    - acute 365.22
    - chronic 365.23
    - intermittent 365.21
    - interval 365.21
    - residual stage 365.24
    - subacute 365.21
  - borderline 365.00
  - chronic 365.11
    - noncongestive 365.11
    - open angle 365.11
    - simple 365.11
  - closed angle — *see* Glaucoma, angle closure
  - congenital 743.20
    - associated with other eye anomalies 743.22
    - simple 743.21
  - congestive — *see* Glaucoma, narrow angle
  - corticosteroid-induced (glaucomatous stage) 365.31
    - residual stage 365.32
  - hemorrhagic 365.60
  - hypersecretion 365.81
  - infantile 365.14
    - congenital 743.20
      - associated with other eye anomalies 743.22
      - simple 743.21
  - in or with
    - aniridia 365.42
    - Axenfeld's anomaly 365.41
    - congenital syndromes NEC 759.89 *[365.44]*
    - disorder of lens NEC 365.59
    - iris
      - anomalies NEC 365.42
      - atrophy, essential 365.42
      - bombé 365.61
    - microcornea 365.43
    - neurofibromatosis 237.71 *[365.44]*
    - ocular
      - cysts NEC 365.64
      - disorders NEC 365.60
      - trauma 365.65
      - tumors NEC 365.64
    - pupillary block or seclusion 365.61
    - Rieger's anomaly or syndrome 365.41
    - seclusion of pupil 365.61
    - Sturge-Weber (-Dimitri) syndrome 759.6 *[365.44]*
    - systemic syndrome NEC 365.44
    - tumor of globe 365.64
    - vascular disorders NEC 365.63
  - juvenile 365.14
  - low tension 365.12
  - malignant 365.83
  - narrow angle (primary) 365.20
    - acute 365.22

Glycogenosis — *see also* Disease, glycogen storage 271.0
- cardiac 271.0 *[425.7]*
- Cori, types I-VII 271.0
- diabetic, secondary 250.8 ☑ *[259.8]*
  - due to secondary diabetes 249.8 ☑ *[259.8]*
- diffuse (with hepatic cirrhosis) 271.0
- generalized 271.0
- glucose-6-phosphatase deficiency 271.0
- hepatophosphorylase deficiency 271.0
- hepatorenal 271.0
- myophosphorylase deficiency 271.0

Glycopenia 251.2

Glycopeptide
- intermediate staphylococcus aureus (GISA) V09.8 ☑
- resistant
  - enterococcus V09.8 ☑
  - staphylococcus aureus (GRSA) V09.8 ☑

Glycoprolinuria 270.8

Glycosuria 791.5
- renal 271.4

Gnathostoma (spinigerum) (infection) (infestation) 128.1
- wandering swellings from 128.1

Gnathostomiasis 128.1

Goiter (adolescent) (colloid) (diffuse) (dipping) (due to iodine deficiency) (endemic) (euthyroid) (heart) (hyperplastic) (internal) (intrathoracic) (juvenile) (mixed type) (nonendemic) (parenchymatous) (plunging) (sporadic) (subclavicular) (substernal) 240.9
- with
  - hyperthyroidism (recurrent) (*see also* Goiter, toxic) 242.0 ☑
  - thyrotoxicosis (*see also* Goiter, toxic) 242.0 ☑
- adenomatous (*see also* Goiter, nodular) 241.9
- cancerous (M8000/3) 193
- complicating pregnancy, childbirth, or puerperium 648.1 ☑
- congenital 246.1
- cystic (*see also* Goiter, nodular) 241.9
- due to enzyme defect in synthesis of thyroid hormone (butane-insoluble iodine) (coupling) (deiodinase) (iodide trapping or organification) (iodotyrosine dehalogenase) (peroxidase) 246.1
- dyshormonogenic 246.1
- exophthalmic (*see also* Goiter, toxic) 242.0 ☑
- familial (with deaf-mutism) 243
- fibrous 245.3
- lingual 759.2
- lymphadenoid 245.2
- malignant (M8000/3) 193
- multinodular (nontoxic) 241.1
  - toxic or with hyperthyroidism (*see also* Goiter, toxic) 242.2 ☑
- nodular (nontoxic) 241.9
  - with
    - hyperthyroidism (*see also* Goiter, toxic) 242.3 ☑
    - thyrotoxicosis (*see also* Goiter, toxic) 242.3 ☑
  - endemic 241.9
  - exophthalmic (diffuse) (*see also* Goiter, toxic) 242.0 ☑
  - multinodular (nontoxic) 241.1
  - sporadic 241.9
  - toxic (*see also* Goiter, toxic) 242.3 ☑
  - uninodular (nontoxic) 241.0
- nontoxic (nodular) 241.9
  - multinodular 241.1
  - uninodular 241.0
- pulsating (*see also* Goiter, toxic) 242.0 ☑
- simple 240.0

Goiter — *continued*
- toxic 242.0 ☑

> *Note — Use the following fifth-digit subclassification with category 242:*
>
> 0 *without mention of thyrotoxic crisis or storm*
>
> 1 *with mention of thyrotoxic crisis or storm*

  - adenomatous 242.3 ☑
    - multinodular 242.2 ☑
    - uninodular 242.1 ☑
  - multinodular 242.2 ☑
  - nodular 242.3 ☑
    - multinodular 242.2 ☑
    - uninodular 242.1 ☑
  - uninodular 242.1 ☑
- uninodular (nontoxic) 241.0
  - toxic or with hyperthyroidism (*see also* Goiter, toxic) 242.1 ☑

Goldberg (-Maxwell) (-Morris) syndrome (testicular feminization) 259.51

Goldblatt's
- hypertension 440.1
- kidney 440.1

Goldenhar's syndrome (oculoauriculovertebral dysplasia) 756.0

Goldflam-Erb disease or syndrome 358.00

Goldscheider's disease (epidermolysis bullosa) 757.39

Goldstein's disease (familial hemorrhagic telangiectasia) 448.0

Golfer's elbow 726.32

Goltz-Gorlin syndrome (dermal hypoplasia) 757.39

Gonadoblastoma (M9073/1)
- specified site — *see* Neoplasm, by site uncertain behavior
- unspecified site
  - female 236.2
  - male 236.4

Gonecystitis — *see also* Vesiculitis 608.0

Gongylonemiasis 125.6
- mouth 125.6

Goniosynechiae 364.73

Gonococcemia 098.89

Gonococcus, gonococcal (disease) (infection) — *see also* condition 098.0
- anus 098.7
- bursa 098.52
- chronic NEC 098.2
- complicating pregnancy, childbirth, or puerperium 647.1 ☑
  - affecting fetus or newborn 760.2
- conjunctiva, conjunctivitis (neonatorum) 098.40
- dermatosis 098.89
- endocardium 098.84
- epididymo-orchitis 098.13
  - chronic or duration of 2 months or over 098.33
- eye (newborn) 098.40
- fallopian tube (chronic) 098.37
  - acute 098.17
- genitourinary (acute) (organ) (system) (tract) (*see also* Gonorrhea) 098.0
  - lower 098.0
    - chronic 098.2
  - upper 098.10
    - chronic 098.30
- heart NEC 098.85
- joint 098.50
- keratoderma 098.81
- keratosis (blennorrhagica) 098.81
- lymphatic (gland) (node) 098.89
- meninges 098.82
- orchitis (acute) 098.13
  - chronic or duration of 2 months or over 098.33
- pelvis (acute) 098.19
  - chronic or duration of 2 months or over 098.39

Gonococcus, gonococcal — *see also* condition — *continued*
- pericarditis 098.83
- peritonitis 098.86
- pharyngitis 098.6
- pharynx 098.6
- proctitis 098.7
- pyosalpinx (chronic) 098.37
  - acute 098.17
- rectum 098.7
- septicemia 098.89
- skin 098.89
- specified site NEC 098.89
- synovitis 098.51
- tendon sheath 098.51
- throat 098.6
- urethra (acute) 098.0
  - chronic or duration of 2 months or over 098.2
- vulva (acute) 098.0
  - chronic or duration of 2 months or over 098.2

Gonocytoma (M9073/1)
- specified site — *see* Neoplasm, by site, uncertain behavior
- unspecified site
  - female 236.2
  - male 236.4

Gonorrhea 098.0
- acute 098.0
- Bartholin's gland (acute) 098.0
  - chronic or duration of 2 months or over 098.2
- bladder (acute) 098.11
  - chronic or duration of 2 months or over 098.31
- carrier (suspected of) V02.7
- cervix (acute) 098.15
  - chronic or duration of 2 months or over 098.35
- chronic 098.2
- complicating pregnancy, childbirth, or puerperium 647.1 ☑
  - affecting fetus or newborn 760.2
- conjunctiva, conjunctivitis (neonatorum) 098.40
- contact V01.6
- Cowper's gland (acute) 098.0
  - chronic or duration of 2 months or over 098.2
- duration of two months or over 098.2
- exposure to V01.6
- fallopian tube (chronic) 098.37
  - acute 098.17
- genitourinary (acute) (organ) (system) (tract) 098.0
  - chronic 098.2
  - duration of two months or over 098.2
- kidney (acute) 098.19
  - chronic or duration of 2 months or over 098.39
- ovary (acute) 098.19
  - chronic or duration of 2 months or over 098.39
- pelvis (acute) 098.19
  - chronic or duration of 2 months or over 098.39
- penis (acute) 098.0
  - chronic or duration of 2 months or over 098.2
- prostate (acute) 098.12
  - chronic or duration of 2 months or over 098.32
- seminal vesicle (acute) 098.14
  - chronic or duration of 2 months or over 098.34
- specified site NEC — *see* Gonococcus
- spermatic cord (acute) 098.14
  - chronic or duration of 2 months or over 098.34
- urethra (acute) 098.0
  - chronic or duration of 2 months or over 098.2
- vagina (acute) 098.0

Gonorrhea — *continued*
- vagina — *continued*
  - chronic or duration of 2 months or over 098.2
- vas deferens (acute) 098.14
  - chronic or duration of 2 months or over 098.34
- vulva (acute) 098.0
  - chronic or duration of 2 months or over 098.2

Goodpasture's syndrome (pneumorenal) 446.21

Good's syndrome 279.06

Gopalan's syndrome (burning feet) 266.2

Gordon's disease (exudative enteropathy) 579.8

Gorlin-Chaudhry-Moss syndrome 759.89

Gougerot-Blum syndrome (pigmented purpuric lichenoid dermatitis) 709.1

Gougerot-Carteaud disease or syndrome (confluent reticulate papillomatosis) 701.8

Gougerot-Hailey-Hailey disease (benign familial chronic pemphigus) 757.39

Gougerot (-Houwer) -Sjögren syndrome (keratoconjunctivitis sicca) 710.2

Gougerot's syndrome (trisymptomatic) 709.1

Gouley's syndrome (constrictive pericarditis) 423.2

Goundou 102.6

Gout, gouty 274.9
- with specified manifestations NEC 274.89
- arthritis (acute) 274.0
- arthropathy 274.0
- degeneration, heart 274.82
- diathesis 274.9
- eczema 274.89
- episcleritis 274.89 *[379.09]*
- external ear (tophus) 274.81
- glomerulonephritis 274.10
- iritis 274.89 *[364.11]*
- joint 274.0
- kidney 274.10
- lead 984.9
  - specified type of lead — *see* Table of Drugs and Chemicals
- nephritis 274.10
- neuritis 274.89 *[357.4]*
- phlebitis 274.89 *[451.9]*
- rheumatic 714.0
- saturnine 984.9
  - specified type of lead — *see* Table of Drugs and Chemicals
- spondylitis 274.0
- synovitis 274.0
- syphilitic 095.8
- tophi 274.0
  - ear 274.81
  - heart 274.82
  - specified site NEC 274.82

Gowers'
- muscular dystrophy 359.1
- syndrome (vasovagal attack) 780.2

Gowers-Paton-Kennedy syndrome 377.04

Gradenigo's syndrome 383.02

Graft-versus-host disease 279.50
- bone marrow 996.85
- due to organ transplant NEC — *see* Complications, transplant, organ

Graham Steell's murmur (pulmonic regurgitation) — *see also* Endocarditis, pulmonary 424.3

Grain-handlers' disease or lung 495.8

Grain mite (itch) 133.8

Grand
- mal (idiopathic) (*see also* Epilepsy) 345.1 ☑
  - hysteria of Charcôt 300.11
  - nonrecurrent or isolated 780.39

H

- **Habit, habituation**
  - chorea 307.22
  - disturbance, child 307.9
  - drug (*see also* Dependence) 304.9 ☑
  - laxative (*see also* Abuse, drugs, nondependent) 305.9 ☑
  - spasm 307.20
    - chronic 307.22
    - transient (of childhood) 307.21
  - tic 307.20
    - chronic 307.22
    - transient (of childhood) 307.21
  - use of
    - nonprescribed drugs (*see also* Abuse, drugs, nondependent) 305.9 ☑
    - patent medicines (*see also* Abuse, drugs, nondependent) 305.9 ☑
  - vomiting 536.2
- **Hadfield-Clarke syndrome** (pancreatic infantilism) 577.8
- **Haff disease** 985.1
- **Hageman factor defect, deficiency, or disease** — *see also* Defect, coagulation 286.3
- **Haglund's disease** (osteochondrosis os tibiale externum) 732.5
- **Haglund-Läwen-Fründ syndrome** 717.89
- **Hagner's disease** (hypertrophic pulmonary osteoarthropathy) 731.2
- **Hag teeth, tooth** 524.39
- **Hailey-Hailey disease** (benign familial chronic pemphigus) 757.39
- **Hair** — *see also* condition
  - plucking 307.9
- **Hairball in stomach** 935.2
- **Hairy black tongue** 529.3
- **Half vertebra** 756.14
- **Halitosis** 784.99
- **Hallermann-Streiff syndrome** 756.0
- **Hallervorden-Spatz disease or syndrome** 333.0
- **Hallopeau's**
  - acrodermatitis (continua) 696.1
  - disease (lichen sclerosis et atrophicus) 701.0
- **Hallucination** (auditory) (gustatory) (olfactory) (tactile) 780.1
  - alcohol-induced 291.3
  - drug-induced 292.12
  - visual 368.16
- **Hallucinosis** 298.9
  - alcohol-induced (acute) 291.3
  - drug-induced 292.12
- **Hallus** — *see* Hallux
- **Hallux** 735.9
  - limitus 735.8
  - malleus (acquired) 735.3
  - rigidus (acquired) 735.2
    - congenital 755.66
    - late effects of rickets 268.1
  - valgus (acquired) 735.0
    - congenital 755.66
  - varus (acquired) 735.1
    - congenital 755.66
- **Halo, visual** 368.15
- **Hamartoblastoma** 759.6
- **Hamartoma** 759.6
  - epithelial (gingival), odontogenic, central, or peripheral (M9321/0) 213.1
    - upper jaw (bone) 213.0
  - vascular 757.32
- **Hamartosis, hamartoses** NEC 759.6
- **Hamman's disease or syndrome** (spontaneous mediastinal emphysema) 518.1
- **Hamman-Rich syndrome** (diffuse interstitial pulmonary fibrosis) 516.3
- **Hammer toe** (acquired) 735.4
  - congenital 755.66
  - late effects of rickets 268.1
- **Hand** — *see* condition
- **Hand-foot syndrome** 693.0
- **Hand-Schüller-Christian disease or syndrome** (chronic histiocytosis x) 277.89
- **Hanging** (asphyxia) (strangulation) (suffocation) 994.7
- **Hangnail** (finger) (with lymphangitis) 681.02
- **Hangover** (alcohol) — *see also* Abuse, drugs, nondependent 305.0 ☑
- **Hanot-Chauffard (-Troisier) syndrome** (bronze diabetes) 275.0
- **Hanot's cirrhosis or disease** — *see* Cirrhosis, biliary
- **Hansen's disease** (leprosy) 030.9
  - benign form 030.1
  - malignant form 030.0
- **Harada's disease or syndrome** 363.22
- **Hard chancre** 091.0
- **Hardening**
  - artery — *see* Arteriosclerosis
  - brain 348.8
  - liver 571.8
- **Hard firm prostate** 600.10
  - with
    - urinary
      - obstruction 600.11
      - retention 600.11
- **Harelip** — *see also* Cleft, lip 749.10
- **Hare's syndrome** (M8010/3) (carcinoma, pulmonary apex) 162.3
- **Harkavy's syndrome** 446.0
- **Harlequin** (fetus) 757.1
  - color change syndrome 779.89
- **Harley's disease** (intermittent hemoglobinuria) 283.2
- **Harris'**
  - lines 733.91
  - syndrome (organic hyperinsulinism) 251.1
- **Hart's disease or syndrome** (pellagra-cerebellar ataxia-renal aminoaciduria) 270.0
- **Hartmann's pouch** (abnormal sacculation of gallbladder neck) 575.8
  - of intestine V44.3
    - attention to V55.3
- **Hartnup disease** (pellagra-cerebellar ataxia-renal aminoaciduria) 270.0
- **Harvester lung** 495.0
- **Hashimoto's disease or struma** (struma lymphomatosa) 245.2
- **Hassall-Henle bodies** (corneal warts) 371.41
- **Haut mal** — *see also* Epilepsy 345.1 ☑
- **Haverhill fever** 026.1
- **Hawaiian wood rose dependence** 304.5 ☑
- **Hawkins' keloid** 701.4
- **Hay**
  - asthma (*see also* Asthma) 493.0 ☑
  - fever (allergic) (with rhinitis) 477.9
    - with asthma (bronchial) (*see also* Asthma) 493.0 ☑
    - allergic, due to grass, pollen, ragweed, or tree 477.0
    - conjunctivitis 372.05
    - due to
      - dander, animal (cat) (dog) 477.2
      - dust 477.8
      - fowl 477.8
      - hair, animal (cat) (dog) 477.2
      - pollen 477.0
      - specified allergen other than pollen 477.8
- **Hayem-Faber syndrome** (achlorhydric anemia) 280.9
- **Hayem-Widal syndrome** (acquired hemolytic jaundice) 283.9
- **Haygarth's nodosities** 715.04
- **Hazard-Crile tumor** (M8350/3) 193
- **Hb** (abnormal)
  - disease — *see* Disease, hemoglobin
  - trait — *see* Trait
- **H disease** 270.0
- **Head** — *see also* condition
  - banging 307.3
- **Headache** 784.0
  - allergic 339.00
  - associated with sexual activity 339.82
  - cluster 339.00
    - chronic 339.02
    - episodic 339.01
  - daily
    - chronic 784.0
    - new persistent (NPDH) 339.42
  - drug induced 339.3
  - due to
    - loss, spinal fluid 349.0
    - lumbar puncture 349.0
    - saddle block 349.0
  - emotional 307.81
  - histamine 339.00
  - hypnic 339.81
  - lumbar puncture 349.0
  - medication overuse 339.3
  - menopausal 627.2
  - menstrual 346.4 ☑
  - migraine 346.9 ☑
  - nasal septum 784.0
  - nonorganic origin 307.81
  - orgasmic 339.82
  - postspinal 349.0
  - post-traumatic 339.20
    - acute 339.21
    - chronic 339.22
  - premenstrual 346.4 ☑
  - preorgasmic 339.82
  - primary
    - cough 339.83
    - exertional 339.84
    - stabbing 339.85
    - thunderclap 339.43
  - psychogenic 307.81
  - psychophysiologic 307.81
  - rebound 339.3
  - short lasting unilateral neuralgiform with conjunctival injection and tearing (SUNCT) 339.05
  - sick 346.9 ☑
  - spinal 349.0
    - complicating labor and delivery 668.8 ☑
    - postpartum 668.8 ☑
  - spinal fluid loss 349.0
  - syndrome
    - cluster 339.00
    - complicated NEC 339.44
    - periodic in child or adolescent 346.2 ☑
    - specified NEC 339.89
  - tension 307.81
    - type 339.10
      - chronic 339.12
      - episodic 339.11
  - vascular 784.0
    - migraine type 346.9 ☑
  - vasomotor 346.9 ☑
- **Health**
  - advice V65.4 ☑
  - audit V70.0
  - checkup V70.0
  - education V65.4 ☑
  - hazard (*see also* History of) V15.9
    - falling V15.88
    - specified cause NEC V15.89
  - instruction V65.4 ☑
  - services provided because (of)
    - boarding school residence V60.6
    - holiday relief for person providing home care V60.5
    - inadequate
      - housing V60.1
      - resources V60.2
    - lack of housing V60.0
    - no care available in home V60.4
    - person living alone V60.3
    - poverty V60.3
    - residence in institution V60.6
    - specified cause NEC V60.8
    - vacation relief for person providing home care V60.5
- **Healthy**
  - donor (*see also* Donor) V59.9
  - infant or child
    - accompanying sick mother V65.0
    - receiving care V20.1
  - person
    - accompanying sick relative V65.0
    - admitted for sterilization V25.2
    - receiving prophylactic inoculation or vaccination (*see also* Vaccination, prophylactic) V05.9
- **Hearing**
  - conservation and treatment V72.12
  - examination V72.19
    - following failed hearing screening V72.11
- **Heart** — *see* condition
- **Heartburn** 787.1
  - psychogenic 306.4
- **Heat** (effects) 992.9
  - apoplexy 992.0
  - burn (*see also* Burn, by site)
    - from sun (*see also* Sunburn) 692.71
  - collapse 992.1
  - cramps 992.2
  - dermatitis or eczema 692.89
  - edema 992.7
  - erythema — *see* Burn, by site
  - excessive 992.9
    - specified effect NEC 992.8
  - exhaustion 992.5
    - anhydrotic 992.3
    - due to
      - salt (and water) depletion 992.4
      - water depletion 992.3
  - fatigue (transient) 992.6
  - fever 992.0
  - hyperpyrexia 992.0
  - prickly 705.1
  - prostration — *see* Heat, exhaustion
  - pyrexia 992.0
  - rash 705.1
  - specified effect NEC 992.8
  - stroke 992.0
  - sunburn (*see also* Sunburn) 692.71
  - syncope 992.1
- **Heavy-chain disease** 273.2
- **Heavy-for-dates** (fetus or infant) 766.1
  - 4500 grams or more 766.0
  - exceptionally 766.0
- **Hebephrenia, hebephrenic** (acute) — *see also* Schizophrenia 295.1 ☑
  - dementia (praecox) (*see also* Schizophrenia) 295.1 ☑
  - schizophrenia (*see also* Schizophrenia) 295.1 ☑
- **Heberden's**
  - disease or nodes 715.04
  - syndrome (angina pectoris) 413.9
- **Hebra's disease**
  - dermatitis exfoliativa 695.89
  - erythema multiforme exudativum 695.19
  - pityriasis 695.89
    - maculata et circinata 696.3
    - rubra 695.89
      - pilaris 696.4
  - prurigo 698.2
- **Hebra, nose** 040.1
- **Hedinger's syndrome** (malignant carcinoid) 259.2
- **Heel** — *see* condition
- **Heerfordt's disease or syndrome** (uveoparotitis) 135
- **Hegglin's anomaly or syndrome** 288.2
- **Heidenhain's disease** 290.10
  - with dementia 290.10
- **Heilmeyer-Schöner disease** (M9842/3) 207.1 ☑
- **Heine-Medin disease** — *see also* Poliomyelitis 045.9 ☑
- **Heinz-body anemia, congenital** 282.7
- **Heller's disease or syndrome** (infantile psychosis) — *see also* Psychosis, childhood 299.1 ☑

H.E.L.L.P 642.5 ☑
Helminthiasis — *see also* Infestation, by specific parasite 128.9
Ancylostoma (*see also* Ancylostoma) 126.9
intestinal 127.9
mixed types (types classifiable to more than one of the categories 120.0–127.7) 127.8
specified type 127.7
mixed types (intestinal) (types classifiable to more than one of the categories 120.0–127.7) 127.8
Necator americanus 126.1
specified type NEC 128.8
Trichinella 124
Heloma 700
Hemangioblastoma (M9161/1) — *see also* Neoplasm, connective tissue, uncertain behavior
malignant (M9161/3) — *see* Neoplasm, connective tissue, malignant
Hemangioblastomatosis, cerebelloretinal 759.6
Hemangioendothelioma (M9130/1) — *see also* Neoplasm, by site, uncertain behavior
benign (M9130/0) 228.00
bone (diffuse) (M9130/3) — *see* Neoplasm, bone, malignant
malignant (M9130/3) — *see* Neoplasm, connective tissue, malignant
nervous system (M9130/0) 228.09
Hemangioendotheliosarcoma (M9130/3) — *see* Neoplasm, connective tissue, malignant
Hemangiofibroma (M9160/0) — *see* Neoplasm, by site, benign
Hemangiolipoma (M8861/0) — *see* Lipoma
Hemangioma (M9120/0) 228.00
arteriovenous (M9123/0) — *see* Hemangioma, by site
brain 228.02
capillary (M9131/0) — *see* Hemangioma, by site
cavernous (M9121/0) — *see* Hemangioma, by site
central nervous system NEC 228.09
choroid 228.09
heart 228.09
infantile (M9131/0) — *see* Hemangioma, by site
intra-abdominal structures 228.04
intracranial structures 228.02
intramuscular (M9132/0) — *see* Hemangioma, by site
iris 228.09
juvenile (M9131/0) — *see* Hemangioma, by site
malignant (M9120/3) — *see* Neoplasm, connective tissue, malignant
meninges 228.09
brain 228.02
spinal cord 228.09
peritoneum 228.04
placenta — *see* Placenta, abnormal
plexiform (M9131/0) — *see* Hemangioma, by site
racemose (M9123/0) — *see* Hemangioma, by site
retina 228.03
retroperitoneal tissue 228.04
sclerosing (M8832/0) — *see* Neoplasm, skin, benign
simplex (M9131/0) — *see* Hemangioma, by site
skin and subcutaneous tissue 228.01
specified site NEC 228.09
spinal cord 228.09
venous (M9122/0) — *see* Hemangioma, by site

Hemangioma — *continued*
verrucous keratotic (M9142/0) — *see* Hemangioma, by site
Hemangiomatosis (systemic) 757.32
involving single site — *see* Hemangioma
Hemangiopericytoma (M9150/1) — *see also* Neoplasm, connective tissue, uncertain behavior
benign (M9150/0) — *see* Neoplasm, connective tissue, benign
malignant (M9150/3) — *see* Neoplasm, connective tissue, malignant
Hemangiosarcoma (M9120/3) — *see* Neoplasm, connective tissue, malignant
Hemarthrosis (nontraumatic) 719.10
ankle 719.17
elbow 719.12
foot 719.17
hand 719.14
hip 719.15
knee 719.16
multiple sites 719.19
pelvic region 719.15
shoulder (region) 719.11
specified site NEC 719.18
traumatic — *see* Sprain, by site
wrist 719.13
Hematemesis 578.0
with ulcer — *see* Ulcer, by site, with hemorrhage
due to S. japonicum 120.2
Goldstein's (familial hemorrhagic telangiectasia) 448.0
newborn 772.4
due to swallowed maternal blood 777.3
Hematidrosis 705.89
Hematinuria — *see also* Hemoglobinuria 791.2
malarial 084.8
paroxysmal 283.2
Hematite miners' lung 503
Hematobilia 576.8
Hematocele (congenital) (diffuse) (idiopathic) 608.83
broad ligament 620.7
canal of Nuck 629.0
cord, male 608.83
fallopian tube 620.8
female NEC 629.0
ischiorectal 569.89
male NEC 608.83
ovary 629.0
pelvis, pelvic
female 629.0
with ectopic pregnancy (*see also* Pregnancy, ectopic) 633.90
with intrauterine pregnancy 633.91
male 608.83
periuterine 629.0
retrouterine 629.0
scrotum 608.83
spermatic cord (diffuse) 608.83
testis 608.84
traumatic — *see* Injury, internal, pelvis
tunica vaginalis 608.83
uterine ligament 629.0
uterus 621.4
vagina 623.6
vulva 624.5
Hematocephalus 742.4
Hematochezia — *see also* Melena 578.1
Hematochyluria — *see also* Infestation, filarial 125.9
Hematocolpos 626.8
Hematocornea 371.12
Hematogenous — *see* condition

Hematoma (skin surface intact) (traumatic) — *see also* Contusion

Note — Hematomas are coded according to origin and the nature and site of the hematoma or the accompanying injury. Hematomas of unspecified origin are coded as injuries of the sites involved, except:

(a) hematomas of genital organs which are coded as diseases of the organ involved unless they complicate pregnancy or delivery

(b) hematomas of the eye which are coded as diseases of the eye.

For late effect of hematoma classifiable to 920–924 see Late, effect, contusion

with
crush injury — *see* Crush
fracture — *see* Fracture, by site
injury of internal organs (*see also* Injury, internal, by site)
kidney — *see* Hematoma, kidney traumatic
liver — *see* Hematoma, liver, traumatic
spleen — *see* Hematoma, spleen
nerve injury — *see* Injury, nerve
open wound — *see* Wound, open, by site
skin surface intact — *see* Contusion
abdomen (wall) — *see* Contusion, abdomen
amnion 658.8 ☑
aorta, dissecting 441.00
abdominal 441.02
thoracic 441.01
thoracoabdominal 441.03
arterial (complicating trauma) 904.9
specified site — *see* Injury, blood vessel, by site
auricle (ear) 380.31
birth injury 767.8
skull 767.19
brain (traumatic) 853.0 ☑

Note — Use the following fifth-digit subclassification with categories 851–854:

0 unspecified state of consciousness

1 with no loss of consciousness

2 with brief [less than one hour] loss of consciousness

3 with moderate [1–24 hours] loss of consciousness

4 with prolonged [more than 24 hours] loss of consciousness and return to pre–existing conscious level

5 with prolonged [more than 24 hours] loss of consciousness, without return to pre–existing conscious level

Use fifth-digit 5 to designate when a patient is unconscious and dies before regaining consciousness, regardless of the duration of the loss of consciousness

6 with loss of consciousness of unspecified duration

9 with concussion, unspecified

with
cerebral
contusion — *see* Contusion, brain
laceration — *see* Laceration, brain
open intracranial wound 853.1 ☑

Hematoma — *see also* Contusion — *continued*
brain — *continued*
with — *continued*
skull fracture — *see* Fracture, skull, by site
extradural or epidural 852.4 ☑
with open intracranial wound 852.5 ☑
fetus or newborn 767.0
nontraumatic 432.0
fetus or newborn NEC 767.0
nontraumatic (*see also* Hemorrhage, brain) 431
epidural or extradural 432.0
newborn NEC 772.8
subarachnoid, arachnoid, or meningeal (*see also* Hemorrhage, subarachnoid) 430
subdural (*see also* Hemorrhage, subdural) 432.1
subarachnoid, arachnoid, or meningeal 852.0 ☑
with open intracranial wound 852.1 ☑
fetus or newborn 772.2
nontraumatic (*see also* Hemorrhage, subarachnoid) 430
subdural 852.2 ☑
with open intracranial wound 852.3 ☑
fetus or newborn (localized) 767.0
nontraumatic (*see also* Hemorrhage, subdural) 432.1
breast (nontraumatic) 611.89
broad ligament (nontraumatic) 620.7
complicating delivery 665.7 ☑
traumatic — *see* Injury, internal, broad ligament
calcified NEC 959.9
capitis 920
due to birth injury 767.19
newborn 767.19
cerebral — *see* Hematoma, brain
cesarean section wound 674.3 ☑
chorion — *see* Placenta, abnormal
complicating delivery (perineum) (vulva) 664.5 ☑
pelvic 665.7 ☑
vagina 665.7 ☑
corpus
cavernosum (nontraumatic) 607.82
luteum (nontraumatic) (ruptured) 620.1
dura (mater) — *see* Hematoma, brain, subdural
epididymis (nontraumatic) 608.83
epidural (traumatic) (*see also* Hematoma, brain, extradural)
spinal — *see* Injury, spinal, by site
episiotomy 674.3 ☑
external ear 380.31
extradural (*see also* Hematoma, brain, extradural)
fetus or newborn 767.0
nontraumatic 432.0
fetus or newborn 767.0
fallopian tube 620.8
genital organ (nontraumatic)
female NEC 629.89
male NEC 608.83
traumatic (external site) 922.4
internal — *see* Injury, internal, genital organ
graafian follicle (ruptured) 620.0
internal organs (abdomen, chest, or pelvis) (*see also* Injury, internal, by site)
kidney — *see* Hematoma, kidney, traumatic
liver — *see* Hematoma, liver, traumatic
spleen — *see* Hematoma, spleen
intracranial — *see* Hematoma, brain

Hematoma — *see also* Contusion — *continued*
kidney, cystic 593.81
traumatic 866.01
with open wound into cavity 866.11
labia (nontraumatic) 624.5
lingual (and other parts of neck, scalp, or face, except eye) 920
liver (subcapsular) 573.8
birth injury 767.8
fetus or newborn 767.8
traumatic NEC 864.01
with
laceration — *see* Laceration, liver
open wound into cavity 864.11
mediastinum — *see* Injury, internal, mediastinum
meninges, meningeal (brain) (*see also* Hematoma, brain, subarachnoid)
spinal — *see* Injury, spinal, by site
mesosalpinx (nontraumatic) 620.8
traumatic — *see* Injury, internal, pelvis
muscle (traumatic) — *see* Contusion, by site
nontraumatic 729.92
nasal (septum) (and other part(s) of neck, scalp, or face, except eye) 920
obstetrical surgical wound 674.3 ☑
orbit, orbital (nontraumatic) 376.32
traumatic 921.2
ovary (corpus luteum) (nontraumatic) 620.1
traumatic — *see* Injury, internal, ovary
pelvis (female) (nontraumatic) 629.89
complicating delivery 665.7 ☑
male 608.83
traumatic (*see also* Injury, internal, pelvis)
specified organ NEC (*see also* Injury, internal, pelvis) 867.6
penis (nontraumatic) 607.82
pericranial (and neck, or face any part, except eye) 920
due to injury at birth 767.19
perineal wound (obstetrical) 674.3 ☑
complicating delivery 664.5 ☑
perirenal, cystic 593.81
pinna 380.31
placenta — *see* Placenta, abnormal
postoperative 998.12
retroperitoneal (nontraumatic) 568.81
traumatic — *see* Injury, internal, retroperitoneum
retropubic, male 568.81
scalp (and neck, or face any part, except eye) 920
fetus or newborn 767.19
scrotum (nontraumatic) 608.83
traumatic 922.4
seminal vesicle (nontraumatic) 608.83
traumatic — *see* Injury, internal, seminal, vesicle
soft tissue 729.92
spermatic cord (*see also* Injury, internal, spermatic cord)
nontraumatic 608.83
spinal (cord) (meninges) (*see also* Injury, spinal, by site)
fetus or newborn 767.4
nontraumatic 336.1
spleen 865.01
with
laceration — *see* Laceration, spleen
open wound into cavity 865.11
sternocleidomastoid, birth injury 767.8
sternomastoid, birth injury 767.8

Hematoma — *see also* Contusion — *continued*
subarachnoid (*see also* Hematoma, brain, subarachnoid)
fetus or newborn 772.2
nontraumatic (*see also* Hemorrhage, subarachnoid) 430
newborn 772.2
subdural (*see also* Hematoma, brain, subdural)
fetus or newborn (localized) 767.0
nontraumatic (*see also* Hemorrhage, subdural) 432.1
subperiosteal (syndrome) 267
traumatic — *see* Hematoma, by site
superficial, fetus or newborn 772.6
syncytium — *see* Placenta, abnormal
testis (nontraumatic) 608.83
birth injury 767.8
traumatic 922.4
tunica vaginalis (nontraumatic) 608.83
umbilical cord 663.6 ☑
affecting fetus or newborn 762.6
uterine ligament (nontraumatic) 620.7
traumatic — *see* Injury, internal, pelvis
uterus 621.4
traumatic — *see* Injury, internal, pelvis
vagina (nontraumatic) (ruptured) 623.6
complicating delivery 665.7 ☑
traumatic 922.4
vas deferens (nontraumatic) 608.83
traumatic — *see* Injury, internal, vas deferens
vitreous 379.23
vocal cord 920
vulva (nontraumatic) 624.5
complicating delivery 664.5 ☑
fetus or newborn 767.8
traumatic 922.4
Hematometra 621.4
Hematomyelia 336.1
with fracture of vertebra (*see also* Fracture, vertebra, by site, with spinal cord injury) 806.8
fetus or newborn 767.4
Hematomyelitis 323.9
late effect — *see* category 326
Hematoperitoneum — *see also* Hemoperitoneum 568.81
Hematopneumothorax — *see also* Hemothorax 511.89
Hematopoiesis, cyclic 288.02
Hematoporphyria (acquired) (congenital) 277.1
Hematoporphyrinuria (acquired) (congenital) 277.1
Hematorachis, hematorrhachis 336.1
fetus or newborn 767.4
Hematosalpinx 620.8
with
ectopic pregnancy (*see also* categories 633.0–633.9) 639.2
infectional (*see also* Salpingo-oophoritis) 614.2
molar pregnancy (*see also* categories 630–632) 639.2
Hematospermia 608.82
Hematothorax — *see also* Hemothorax 511.89
Hematotympanum 381.03
Hematuria (benign) (essential) (idiopathic) 599.70
due to S. hematobium 120.0
endemic 120.0
gross 599.71
intermittent 599.70
malarial 084.8
microscopic 599.72
paroxysmal 599.70

Hematuria — *continued*
sulfonamide
correct substance properly administered 599.70
overdose or wrong substance given or taken 961.0
tropical (bilharziasis) 120.0
tuberculous (*see also* Tuberculosis) 016.9 ☑
Hematuric bilious fever 084.8
Hemeralopia 368.10
Hemiabiotrophy 799.89
Hemi-akinesia 781.8
Hemianalgesia — *see also* Disturbance, sensation 782.0
Hemianencephaly 740.0
Hemianesthesia — *see also* Disturbance, sensation 782.0
Hemianopia, hemianopsia (altitudinal) (homonymous) 368.46
binasal 368.47
bitemporal 368.47
heteronymous 368.47
syphilitic 095.8
Hemiasomatognosia 307.9
Hemiathetosis 781.0
Hemiatrophy 799.89
cerebellar 334.8
face 349.89
progressive 349.89
fascia 728.9
leg 728.2
tongue 529.8
Hemiballism (us) 333.5
Hemiblock (cardiac) (heart) (left) 426.2
Hemicardia 746.89
Hemicephalus, hemicephaly 740.0
Hemichorea 333.5
Hemicrania 346.9 ☑
congenital malformation 740.0
continua 339.41
paroxysmal 339.03
chronic 339.04
episodic 339.03
Hemidystrophy — *see* Hemiatrophy
Hemiectromelia 755.4
Hemihypalgesia — *see also* Disturbance, sensation 782.0
Hemihypertrophy (congenital) 759.89
cranial 756.0
Hemihypesthesia — *see also* Disturbance, sensation 782.0
Hemi-inattention 781.8
Hemimelia 755.4
lower limb 755.30
paraxial (complete) (incomplete) (intercalary) (terminal) 755.32
fibula 755.37
tibia 755.36
transverse (complete) (partial) 755.31
upper limb 755.20
paraxial (complete) (incomplete) (intercalary) (terminal) 755.22
radial 755.26
ulnar 755.27
transverse (complete) (partial) 755.21
Hemiparalysis — *see also* Hemiplegia 342.9 ☑
Hemiparesis — *see also* Hemiplegia 342.9 ☑
Hemiparesthesia — *see also* Disturbance, sensation 782.0
Hemiplegia 342.9 ☑
acute (*see also* Disease, cerebrovascular, acute) 436
alternans facialis 344.89
apoplectic (*see also* Disease, cerebrovascular, acute) 436
late effect or residual
affecting
dominant side 438.21
nondominant side 438.22

Hemiplegia — *continued*
apoplectic (*see also* Disease, cerebrovascular, acute) — *continued*
late effect or residual — *continued*
affecting — *continued*
unspecified side 438.20
arteriosclerotic 437.0
late effect or residual
affecting
dominant side 438.21
nondominant side 438.22
unspecified side 438.20
ascending (spinal) NEC 344.89
attack (*see also* Disease, cerebrovascular, acute) 436
brain, cerebral (current episode) 437.8
congenital 343.1
cerebral — *see* Hemiplegia, brain
congenital (cerebral) (spastic) (spinal) 343.1
conversion neurosis (hysterical) 300.11
cortical — *see* Hemiplegia, brain
due to
arteriosclerosis 437.0
late effect or residual
affecting
dominant side 438.21
nondominant side 438.22
unspecified side 438.20
cerebrovascular lesion (*see also* Disease, cerebrovascular, acute) 436
late effect
affecting
dominant side 438.21
nondominant side 438.22
unspecified side 438.20
embolic (current) (*see also* Embolism, brain) 434.1 ☑
late effect
affecting
dominant side 438.21
nondominant side 438.22
unspecified side 438.20
flaccid 342.0 ☑
hypertensive (current episode) 437.8
infantile (postnatal) 343.4
late effect
birth injury, intracranial or spinal 343.4
cerebrovascular lesion — *see* Late effect(s) (of) cerebrovascular disease
viral encephalitis 139.0
middle alternating NEC 344.89
newborn NEC 767.0
seizure (current episode) (*see also* Disease, cerebrovascular, acute) 436
spastic 342.1 ☑
congenital or infantile 343.1
specified NEC 342.8 ☑
thrombotic (current) (*see also* Thrombosis, brain) 434.0 ☑
late effect — *see* Late effect(s) (of) cerebrovascular disease
Hemisection, spinal cord — *see* Fracture, vertebra, by site, with spinal cord injury
Hemispasm 781.0
facial 781.0
Hemispatial neglect 781.8
Hemisporosis 117.9
Hemitremor 781.0
Hemivertebra 756.14
Hemobilia 576.8
Hemocholecyst 575.8
Hemochromatosis (acquired) (diabetic) (hereditary) (liver) (myocardium) (primary idiopathic) (secondary) 275.0
with refractory anemia 238.72
Hemodialysis V56.0

Hemoglobin — *see also* condition
  abnormal (disease) — *see* Disease, hemoglobin
  AS genotype 282.5
  fetal, hereditary persistence 282.7
  high-oxygen-affinity 289.0
  low NEC 285.9
  S (Hb-S), heterozygous 282.5
Hemoglobinemia 283.2
  due to blood transfusion NEC 999.89
    bone marrow 996.85
  paroxysmal 283.2
Hemoglobinopathy (mixed) — *see also* Disease, hemoglobin 282.7
  with thalassemia 282.49
  sickle-cell 282.60
    with thalassemia (without crisis) 282.41
      with
        crisis 282.42
        vaso-occlusive pain 282.42
Hemoglobinuria, hemoglobinuric 791.2
  with anemia, hemolytic, acquired (chronic) NEC 283.2
  cold (agglutinin) (paroxysmal) (with Raynaud's syndrome) 283.2
  due to
    exertion 283.2
    hemolysis (from external causes) NEC 283.2
  exercise 283.2
  fever (malaria) 084.8
  infantile 791.2
  intermittent 283.2
  malarial 084.8
  march 283.2
  nocturnal (paroxysmal) 283.2
  paroxysmal (cold) (nocturnal) 283.2
Hemolymphangioma (M9175/0) 228.1
Hemolysis
  fetal — *see* Jaundice, fetus or newborn
  intravascular (disseminated) NEC 286.6
    with
      abortion — *see* Abortion, by type, with hemorrhage, delayed or excessive
      ectopic pregnancy (*see also* categories 633.0–633.9) 639.1
      hemorrhage of pregnancy 641.3 ☑
        affecting fetus or newborn 762.1
      molar pregnancy (*see also* categories 630–632) 639.1
    acute 283.2
    following
      abortion 639.1
      ectopic or molar pregnancy 639.1
  neonatal — *see* Jaundice, fetus or newborn
  transfusion NEC 999.89
    bone marrow 996.85
Hemolytic — *see also* condition
  anemia — *see* Anemia, hemolytic
  uremic syndrome 283.11
Hemometra 621.4
Hemopericardium (with effusion) 423.0
  newborn 772.8
  traumatic (*see also* Hemothorax, traumatic) 860.2
    with open wound into thorax 860.3
Hemoperitoneum 568.81
  infectional (*see also* Peritonitis) 567.29
  traumatic — *see* Injury, internal, peritoneum
Hemophagocytic syndrome 288.4
  infection-associated 288.4
Hemophilia (familial) (hereditary) 286.0
  A 286.0
    carrier (asymptomatic) V83.01
      symptomatic V83.02
  acquired 286.5
Hemophilia — *continued*
  B (Leyden) 286.1
  C 286.2
  calcipriva (*see also* Fibrinolysis) 286.7
  classical 286.0
  nonfamilial 286.7
  secondary 286.5
  vascular 286.4
Hemophilus influenzae NEC 041.5
  arachnoiditis (basic) (brain) (spinal) 320.0
    late effect — *see* category 326
  bronchopneumonia 482.2
  cerebral ventriculitis 320.0
    late effect — *see* category 326
  cerebrospinal inflammation 320.0
    late effect — *see* category 326
  infection NEC 041.5
  leptomeningitis 320.0
    late effect — *see* category 326
  meningitis (cerebral) (cerebrospinal) (spinal) 320.0
    late effect — *see* category 326
  meningomyelitis 320.0
    late effect — *see* category 326
  pachymeningitis (adhesive) (fibrous) (hemorrhagic) (hypertrophic) (spinal) 320.0
    late effect — *see* category 326
  pneumonia (broncho-) 482.2
Hemophthalmos 360.43
Hemopneumothorax — *see also* Hemothorax 511.89
  traumatic 860.4
    with open wound into thorax 860.5
Hemoptysis 786.3
  due to Paragonimus (westermani) 121.2
  newborn 770.3
  tuberculous (*see also* Tuberculosis, pulmonary) 011.9 ☑
Hemorrhage, hemorrhagic (nontraumatic) 459.0
  abdomen 459.0
  accidental (antepartum) 641.2 ☑
    affecting fetus or newborn 762.1
  adenoid 474.8
  adrenal (capsule) (gland) (medulla) 255.41
    newborn 772.5
  after labor — *see* Hemorrhage, postpartum
  alveolar
    lung, newborn 770.3
    process 525.8
  alveolus 525.8
  amputation stump (surgical) 998.11
    secondary, delayed 997.69
  anemia (chronic) 280.0
    acute 285.1
  antepartum — *see* Hemorrhage, pregnancy
  anus (sphincter) 569.3
  apoplexy (stroke) 432.9
  arachnoid — *see* Hemorrhage, subarachnoid
  artery NEC 459.0
    brain (*see also* Hemorrhage, brain) 431
    middle meningeal — *see* Hemorrhage, subarachnoid
  basilar (ganglion) (*see also* Hemorrhage, brain) 431
  bladder 596.8
  blood dyscrasia 289.9
  bowel 578.9
    newborn 772.4
  brain (miliary) (nontraumatic) 431
    with
      birth injury 767.0
    arachnoid — *see* Hemorrhage, subarachnoid
    due to
      birth injury 767.0
Hemorrhage, hemorrhagic — *continued*
  brain — *continued*
    due to — *continued*
      rupture of aneurysm (congenital) (*see also* Hemorrhage, subarachnoid) 430
        mycotic 431
      syphilis 094.89
    epidural or extradural — *see* Hemorrhage, extradural
    fetus or newborn (anoxic) (hypoxic) (due to birth trauma) (nontraumatic) 767.0
      intraventricular 772.10
        grade I 772.11
        grade II 772.12*
        grade III 772.13
        grade IV 772.14
    iatrogenic 997.02
    postoperative 997.02
    puerperal, postpartum, childbirth 674.0 ☑
    stem 431
    subarachnoid, arachnoid, or meningeal — *see* Hemorrhage, subarachnoid
    subdural — *see* Hemorrhage, subdural
    traumatic NEC 853.0 ☑

> *Note — Use the following fifth-digit subclassification with categories 851–854:*
>
> 0 *unspecified state of consciousness*
>
> 1 *with no loss of consciousness*
>
> 2 *with brief [less than one hour] loss of consciousness*
>
> 3 *with moderate [1–24 hours] loss of consciousness*
>
> 4 *with prolonged [more than 24 hours] loss of consciousness and return to pre-existing conscious level*
>
> 5 *with prolonged [more than 24 hours] loss of consciousness, without return to pre-existing conscious level*
>
> *Use fifth-digit 5 to designate when a patient is unconscious and dies before regaining consciousness, regardless of the duration of the loss of consciousness*
>
> 6 *with loss of consciousness of unspecified duration*
>
> 9 *with concussion, unspecified*

      with
        cerebral
          contusion — *see* Contusion, brain
          laceration — *see* Laceration, brain
        open intracranial wound 853.1 ☑
        skull fracture — *see* Fracture, skull, by site
      extradural or epidural 852.4 ☑
        with open intracranial wound 852.5 ☑
      subarachnoid 852.0 ☑
        with open intracranial wound 852.1 ☑
      subdural 852.2 ☑
        with open intracranial wound 852.3 ☑
  breast 611.79
  bronchial tube — *see* Hemorrhage, lung
  bronchopulmonary — *see* Hemorrhage, lung
  bronchus (cause unknown) (*see also* Hemorrhage, lung) 786.3
Hemorrhage, hemorrhagic — *continued*
  bulbar (*see also* Hemorrhage, brain) 431
  bursa 727.89
  capillary 448.9
    primary 287.8
  capsular — *see* Hemorrhage, brain
  cardiovascular 429.89
  cecum 578.9
  cephalic (*see also* Hemorrhage, brain) 431
  cerebellar (*see also* Hemorrhage, brain) 431
  cerebellum (*see also* Hemorrhage, brain) 431
  cerebral (*see also* Hemorrhage, brain) 431
    fetus or newborn (anoxic) (traumatic) 767.0
  cerebromeningeal (*see also* Hemorrhage, brain) 431
  cerebrospinal (*see also* Hemorrhage, brain) 431
  cerebrovascular accident — *see* Hemorrhage, brain
  cerebrum (*see also* Hemorrhage, brain) 431
  cervix (stump) (uteri) 622.8
  cesarean section wound 674.3 ☑
  chamber, anterior (eye) 364.41
  childbirth — *see* Hemorrhage, complicating, delivery
  choroid 363.61
    expulsive 363.62
  ciliary body 364.41
  cochlea 386.8
  colon — *see* Hemorrhage, intestine
  complicating
    delivery 641.9 ☑
      affecting fetus or newborn 762.1
      associated with
        afibrinogenemia 641.3 ☑
          affecting fetus or newborn 763.89
        coagulation defect 641.3 ☑
          affecting fetus or newborn 763.89
        hyperfibrinolysis 641.3 ☑
          affecting fetus or newborn 763.89
        hypofibrinogenemia 641.3 ☑
          affecting fetus or newborn 763.89
      due to
        low-lying placenta 641.1 ☑
          affecting fetus or newborn 762.0
        placenta previa 641.1 ☑
          affecting fetus or newborn 762.0
        premature separation of placenta 641.2 ☑
          affecting fetus or newborn 762.1
        retained
          placenta 666.0 ☑
          secundines 666.2 ☑
        trauma 641.8 ☑
          affecting fetus or newborn 763.89
        uterine leiomyoma 641.8 ☑
          affecting fetus or newborn 763.89
    surgical procedure 998.11
  complication(s)
    of dental implant placement 525.71
  concealed NEC 459.0
  congenital 772.9
  conjunctiva 372.72
    newborn 772.8
  cord, newborn 772.0
    slipped ligature 772.3
    stump 772.3
  corpus luteum (ruptured) 620.1

Hemorrhage, hemorrhagic — *continued*
  cortical (*see also* Hemorrhage, brain) 431
  cranial 432.9
  cutaneous 782.7
    newborn 772.6
  cystitis — *see* Cystitis
  cyst, pancreas 577.2
  delayed
    with
      abortion — *see* Abortion, by type, with hemorrhage, delayed or excessive
      ectopic pregnancy (*see also* categories 633.0–633.9) 639.1
      molar pregnancy (*see also* categories 630–632) 639.1
    following
      abortion 639.1
      ectopic or molar pregnancy 639.1
    postpartum 666.2 ☑
  diathesis (familial) 287.9
    newborn 776.0
  disease 287.9
    newborn 776.0
    specified type NEC 287.8
  disorder 287.9
    due to intrinsic circulating anticoagulants 286.5
    specified type NEC 287.8
  due to
    any device, implant or graft (presence of) classifiable to 996.0–996.5 — *see* Complications, due to (presence of) any device, implant, or graft classified to 996.0–996.5NEC
    intrinsic circulating anticoagulant 286.5
  duodenum, duodenal 537.89
    ulcer — *see* Ulcer, duodenum, with hemorrhage
  dura mater — *see* Hemorrhage, subdural
  endotracheal — *see* Hemorrhage, lung
  epicranial subaponeurotic (massive) 767.11
  epidural — *see* Hemorrhage, extradural
  episiotomy 674.3 ☑
  esophagus 530.82
    varix (*see also* Varix, esophagus, bleeding) 456.0
  excessive
    with
      abortion — *see* Abortion, by type, with hemorrhage, delayed or excessive
      ectopic pregnancy (*see also* categories 633.0–633.9) 639.1
      molar pregnancy (*see also* categories 630–632) 639.1
    following
      abortion 639.1
      ectopic or molar pregnancy 639.1
  external 459.0
  extradural (traumatic) (*see also* Hemorrhage, brain, traumatic, extradural)
    birth injury 767.0
    fetus or newborn (anoxic) (traumatic) 767.0
    nontraumatic 432.0
  eye 360.43
    chamber (anterior) (aqueous) 364.41
    fundus 362.81
  eyelid 374.81
  fallopian tube 620.8
  fetomaternal 772.0

Hemorrhage, hemorrhagic — *continued*
  fetomaternal — *continued*
    affecting management of pregnancy or puerperium 656.0 ☑
  fetus, fetal 772.0
    from
      cut end of co-twin's cord 772.0
      placenta 772.0
      ruptured cord 772.0
      vasa previa 772.0
    into
      co-twin 772.0
      mother's circulation 772.0
        affecting management of pregnancy or puerperium 656.0 ☑
  fever (*see also* Fever, hemorrhagic) 065.9
    with renal syndrome 078.6
    arthropod-borne NEC 065.9
    Bangkok 065.4
    Crimean 065.0
    dengue virus 065.4
    epidemic 078.6
    Junin virus 078.7
    Korean 078.6
    Machupo virus 078.7
    mite-borne 065.8
    mosquito-borne 065.4
    Philippine 065.4
    Russian (Yaroslav) 078.6
    Singapore 065.4
    southeast Asia 065.4
    Thailand 065.4
    tick-borne NEC 065.3
  fibrinogenolysis (*see also* Fibrinolysis) 286.6
  fibrinolytic (acquired) (*see also* Fibrinolysis) 286.6
  fontanel 767.19
  from tracheostomy stoma 519.09
  fundus, eye 362.81
  funis
    affecting fetus or newborn 772.0
    complicating delivery 663.8 ☑
  gastric (*see also* Hemorrhage, stomach) 578.9
  gastroenteric 578.9
    newborn 772.4
  gastrointestinal (tract) 578.9
    newborn 772.4
  genitourinary (tract) NEC 599.89
  gingiva 523.8
  globe 360.43
  gravidarum — *see* Hemorrhage, pregnancy
  gum 523.8
  heart 429.89
  hypopharyngeal (throat) 784.8
  intermenstrual 626.6
    irregular 626.6
    regular 626.5
  internal (organs) 459.0
    capsule (*see also* Hemorrhage, brain) 431
    ear 386.8
    newborn 772.8
  intestine 578.9
    congenital 772.4
    newborn 772.4
  into
    bladder wall 596.7
    bursa 727.89
    corpus luysii (*see also* Hemorrhage, brain) 431
  intra-abdominal 459.0
    during or following surgery 998.11
  intra-alveolar, newborn (lung) 770.3
  intracerebral (*see also* Hemorrhage, brain) 431
  intracranial NEC 432.9
    puerperal, postpartum, childbirth 674.0 ☑
    traumatic — *see* Hemorrhage, brain, traumatic

Hemorrhage, hemorrhagic — *continued*
  intramedullary NEC 336.1
  intraocular 360.43
  intraoperative 998.11
  intrapartum — *see* Hemorrhage, complicating, delivery
  intrapelvic
    female 629.89
    male 459.0
  intraperitoneal 459.0
  intrapontine (*see also* Hemorrhage, brain) 431
  intrauterine 621.4
    complicating delivery — *see* Hemorrhage, complicating, delivery
    in pregnancy or childbirth — *see* Hemorrhage, pregnancy
    postpartum (*see also* Hemorrhage, postpartum) 666.1 ☑
  intraventricular (*see also* Hemorrhage, brain) 431
    fetus or newborn (anoxic) (traumatic) 772.10
      grade I 772.11
      grade II 772.12
      grade III 772.13
      grade IV 772.14
  intravesical 596.7
  iris (postinfectional) (postinflammatory) (toxic) 364.41
  joint (nontraumatic) 719.10
    ankle 719.17
    elbow 719.12
    foot 719.17
    forearm 719.13
    hand 719.14
    hip 719.15
    knee 719.16
    lower leg 719.16
    multiple sites 719.19
    pelvic region 719.15
    shoulder (region) 719.11
    specified site NEC 719.18
    thigh 719.15
    upper arm 719.12
    wrist 719.13
  kidney 593.81
  knee (joint) 719.16
  labyrinth 386.8
  leg NEC 459.0
  lenticular striate artery (*see also* Hemorrhage, brain) 431
  ligature, vessel 998.11
  liver 573.8
  lower extremity NEC 459.0
  lung 786.3
    newborn 770.3
    tuberculous (*see also* Tuberculosis, pulmonary) 011.9 ☑
  malaria 084.8
  marginal sinus 641.2 ☑
  massive subaponeurotic, birth injury 767.11
  maternal, affecting fetus or newborn 762.1
  mediastinum 786.3
  medulla (*see also* Hemorrhage, brain) 431
  membrane (brain) (*see also* Hemorrhage, subarachnoid) 430
    spinal cord — *see* Hemorrhage, spinal cord
  meninges, meningeal (brain) (middle) (*see also* Hemorrhage, subarachnoid) 430
    spinal cord — *see* Hemorrhage, spinal cord
  mesentery 568.81
  metritis 626.8
  midbrain (*see also* Hemorrhage, brain) 431
  mole 631
  mouth 528.9
  mucous membrane NEC 459.0
    newborn 772.8

Hemorrhage, hemorrhagic — *continued*
  muscle 728.89
  nail (subungual) 703.8
  nasal turbinate 784.7
    newborn 772.8
  nasopharynx 478.29
  navel, newborn 772.3
  newborn 772.9
    adrenal 772.5
    alveolar (lung) 770.3
    brain (anoxic) (hypoxic) (due to birth trauma) 767.0
    cerebral (anoxic) (hypoxic) (due to birth trauma) 767.0
    conjunctiva 772.8
    cutaneous 772.6
    diathesis 776.0
    due to vitamin K deficiency 776.0
    epicranial subaponeurotic (massive) 767.11
    gastrointestinal 772.4
    internal (organs) 772.8
    intestines 772.4
    intra-alveolar (lung) 770.3
    intracranial (from any perinatal cause) 767.0
    intraventricular (from any perinatal cause) 772.10
      grade I 772.11
      grade II 772.12
      grade III 772.13
      grade IV 772.14
    lung 770.3
    pulmonary (massive) 770.3
    spinal cord, traumatic 767.4
    stomach 772.4
    subaponeurotic (massive) 767.11
    subarachnoid (from any perinatal cause) 772.2
    subconjunctival 772.8
    subgaleal 767.11
    umbilicus 772.0
      slipped ligature 772.3
      vasa previa 772.0
  nipple 611.79
  nose 784.7
    newborn 772.8
  obstetrical surgical wound 674.3 ☑
  omentum 568.89
    newborn 772.4
  optic nerve (sheath) 377.42
  orbit 376.32
  ovary 620.1
  oviduct 620.8
  pancreas 577.8
  parathyroid (gland) (spontaneous) 252.8
  parturition — *see* Hemorrhage, complicating, delivery
  penis 607.82
  pericardium, pericarditis 423.0
  perineal wound (obstetrical) 674.3 ☑
  peritoneum, peritoneal 459.0
  peritonsillar tissue 474.8
    after operation on tonsils 998.11
    due to infection 475
  petechial 782.7
  pituitary (gland) 253.8
  placenta NEC 641.9 ☑
    affecting fetus or newborn 762.1
    from surgical or instrumental damage 641.8 ☑
      affecting fetus or newborn 762.1
    previa 641.1 ☑
      affecting fetus or newborn 762.0
  pleura — *see* Hemorrhage, lung
  polioencephalitis, superior 265.1
  polymyositis — *see* Polymyositis
  pons (*see also* Hemorrhage, brain) 431
  pontine (*see also* Hemorrhage, brain) 431
  popliteal 459.0
  postcoital 626.7
  postextraction (dental) 998.11
  postmenopausal 627.1

Hepatitis — *continued*
  fibrous (chronic) 571.49
    acute 570
  from injection, inoculation, or transfusion (blood) (other substance) (plasma) (serum) (onset within 8 months after administration) — *see* Hepatitis, viral
  fulminant (viral) (*see also* Hepatitis, viral) 070.9
    with hepatic coma 070.6
    type A 070.1
      with hepatic coma 070.0
    type B — *see* Hepatitis, viral, type B
  giant cell (neonatal) 774.4
  hemorrhagic 573.8
  history of
    B V12.09
    C V12.09
  homologous serum — *see* Hepatitis, viral
  hypertrophic (chronic) 571.49
    acute 570
  infectious, infective (acute) (chronic) (subacute) 070.1
    with hepatic coma 070.0
  inoculation — *see* Hepatitis, viral
  interstitial (chronic) 571.49
    acute 570
  lupoid 571.49
  malarial 084.9 *[573.2]*
  malignant (*see also* Necrosis, liver) 570
  neonatal (toxic) 774.4
  newborn 774.4
  parenchymatous (acute) (*see also* Necrosis, liver) 570
  peliosis 573.3
  persistent, chronic 571.41
  plasma cell 571.49
  postimmunization — *see* Hepatitis, viral
  postnecrotic 571.49
  posttransfusion — *see* Hepatitis, viral
  recurrent 571.49
  septic 573.3
  serum — *see* Hepatitis, viral
    carrier (suspected of) V02.61
  subacute (*see also* Necrosis, liver) 570
  suppurative (diffuse) 572.0
  syphilitic (late) 095.3
    congenital (early) 090.0 *[573.2]*
      late 090.5 *[573.2]*
    secondary 091.62
  toxic (noninfectious) 573.3
    fetus or newborn 774.4
  tuberculous (*see also* Tuberculosis) 017.9 ☑
  viral (acute) (anicteric) (cholangiolitic) (cholestatic) (chronic) (subacute) 070.9
    with hepatic coma 070.6
    AU-SH type virus — *see* Hepatitis, viral, type B
    Australian antigen — *see* Hepatitis, viral, type B
    B-antigen — *see* Hepatitis, viral, type B
    Coxsackie 074.8 *[573.1]*
    cytomegalic inclusion 078.5 *[573.1]*
    IH (virus) — *see* Hepatitis, viral, type A
    infectious hepatitis virus — *see* Hepatitis, viral, type A
    serum hepatitis virus — *see* Hepatitis, viral, type B
    SH — *see* Hepatitis, viral, type B
    specified type NEC 070.59
      with hepatic coma 070.49
    type A 070.1
      with hepatic coma 070.0
    type B (acute) 070.30
      with
        hepatic coma 070.20

Hepatitis — *continued*
  viral — *continued*
    type B — *continued*
      with — *continued*
        hepatic coma — *continued*
          with hepatitis delta 070.21
        hepatitis delta 070.31
          with hepatic coma 070.21
      carrier status V02.61
      chronic 070.32
        with
          hepatic coma 070.22
            with hepatitis delta 070.23
          hepatitis delta 070.33
            with hepatic coma 070.23
    type C
      acute 070.51
        with hepatic coma 070.41
      carrier status V02.62
      chronic 070.54
        with hepatic coma 070.44
      in remission 070.54
      unspecified 070.70
        with hepatic coma 070.71
    type delta (with hepatitis B carrier state) 070.52
      with
        active hepatitis B disease — *see* Hepatitis, viral, type B
        hepatic coma 070.42
    type E 070.53
      with hepatic coma 070.43
    vaccination and inoculation (prophylactic) V05.3
  Waldenström's (lupoid hepatitis) 571.49
Hepatization, lung (acute) — *see also* Pneumonia, lobar
  chronic (*see also* Fibrosis, lung) 515
Hepatoblastoma (M8970/3) 155.0
Hepatocarcinoma (M8170/3) 155.0
Hepatocholangiocarcinoma (M8180/3) 155.0
Hepatocholangioma, benign (M8180/0) 211.5
Hepatocholangitis 573.8
Hepatocystitis — *see also* Cholecystitis 575.10
Hepatodystrophy 570
Hepatolenticular degeneration 275.1
Hepatolithiasis — *see* Choledocholithiasis
Hepatoma (malignant) (M8170/3) 155.0
  benign (M8170/0) 211.5
  congenital (M8970/3) 155.0
  embryonal (M8970/3) 155.0
Hepatomegalia glycogenica diffusa 271.0
Hepatomegaly — *see also* Hypertrophy, liver 789.1
  congenital 751.69
    syphilitic 090.0
  due to Clonorchis sinensis 121.1
  Gaucher's 272.7
  syphilitic (congenital) 090.0
Hepatoptosis 573.8
Hepatorrhexis 573.8
Hepatosis, toxic 573.8
Hepatosplenomegaly 571.8
  due to S. japonicum 120.2
  hyperlipemic (Bürger-Grutz type) 272.3
Herald patch 696.3
Hereditary — *see* condition
Heredodegeneration 330.9
  macular 362.70
Heredopathia atactica polyneuritiformis 356.3
Heredosyphilis — *see also* Syphilis, congenital 090.9
Hermaphroditism (true) 752.7

Hermaphroditism — *continued*
  with specified chromosomal anomaly — *see* Anomaly, chromosomes, sex
Hernia, hernial (acquired) (recurrent) 553.9
  with
    gangrene (obstructed) NEC 551.9
    obstruction NEC 552.9
      and gangrene 551.9
  abdomen (wall) — *see* Hernia, ventral
  abdominal, specified site NEC 553.8
    with
      gangrene (obstructed) 551.8
      obstruction 552.8
        and gangrene 551.8
  appendix 553.8
    with
      gangrene (obstructed) 551.8
      obstruction 552.8
        and gangrene 551.8
  bilateral (inguinal) — *see* Hernia, inguinal
  bladder (sphincter)
    congenital (female) (male) 756.71
    female (*see also* Cystocele, female) 618.01
    male 596.8
  brain 348.4
    congenital 742.0
  broad ligament 553.8
  cartilage, vertebral — *see* Displacement, intervertebral disc
  cerebral 348.4
    congenital 742.0
    endaural 742.0
  ciliary body 364.89
    traumatic 871.1
  colic 553.9
    with
      gangrene (obstructed) 551.9
      obstruction 552.9
        and gangrene 551.9
  colon 553.9
    with
      gangrene (obstructed) 551.9
      obstruction 552.9
        and gangrene 551.9
  colostomy (stoma) 569.69
  Cooper's (retroperitoneal) 553.8
    with
      gangrene (obstructed) 551.8
      obstruction 552.8
        and gangrene 551.8
  crural — *see* Hernia, femoral
  diaphragm, diaphragmatic 553.3
    with
      gangrene (obstructed) 551.3
      obstruction 552.3
        and gangrene 551.3
    congenital 756.6
    due to gross defect of diaphragm 756.6
    traumatic 862.0
      with open wound into cavity 862.1
  direct (inguinal) — *see* Hernia, inguinal
  disc, intervertebral — *see* Displacement, intervertebral disc
  diverticulum, intestine 553.9
    with
      gangrene (obstructed) 551.9
      obstruction 552.9
        and gangrene 551.9
  double (inguinal) — *see* Hernia, inguinal
  due to adhesion with obstruction 560.81
  duodenojejunal 553.8
    with
      gangrene (obstructed) 551.8
      obstruction 552.8
        and gangrene 551.8
  en glissade — *see* Hernia, inguinal
  enterostomy (stoma) 569.69

Hernia, hernial — *continued*
  epigastric 553.29
    with
      gangrene (obstruction) 551.29
      obstruction 552.29
        and gangrene 551.29
    recurrent 553.21
      with
        gangrene (obstructed) 551.21
        obstruction 552.21
          and gangrene 551.21
  esophageal hiatus (sliding) 553.3
    with
      gangrene (obstructed) 551.3
      obstruction 552.3
        and gangrene 551.3
    congenital 750.6
  external (inguinal) — *see* Hernia, inguinal
  fallopian tube 620.4
  fascia 728.89
  fat 729.30
    eyelid 374.34
    orbital 374.34
    pad 729.30
      eye, eyelid 374.34
      knee 729.31
      orbit 374.34
      popliteal (space) 729.31
      specified site NEC 729.39
  femoral (unilateral) 553.00
    with
      gangrene (obstructed) 551.00
      obstruction 552.00
        with gangrene 551.00
    bilateral 553.02
      gangrenous (obstructed) 551.02
      obstructed 552.02
        with gangrene 551.02
      recurrent 553.03
        gangrenous (obstructed) 551.03
        obstructed 552.03
          with gangrene 551.03
    recurrent (unilateral) 553.01
      bilateral 553.03
        gangrenous (obstructed) 551.03
        obstructed 552.03
          with gangrene 551.01
      gangrenous (obstructed) 551.01
      obstructed 552.01
        with gangrene 551.01
  foramen
    Bochdalek 553.3
      with
        gangrene (obstructed) 551.3
        obstruction 552.3
          and gangrene 551.3
      congenital 756.6
    magnum 348.4
    Morgagni, Morgagnian 553.3
      with
        gangrene 551.3
        obstruction 552.3
          and gangrene 551.3
      congenital 756.6
  funicular (umbilical) 553.1
    with
      gangrene (obstructed) 551.1
      obstruction 552.1
        and gangrene 551.1
    spermatic cord — *see* Hernia, inguinal
  gangrenous — *see* Hernia, by site, with gangrene
  gastrointestinal tract 553.9
    with
      gangrene (obstructed) 551.9
      obstruction 552.9
        and gangrene 551.9
  gluteal — *see* Hernia, femoral
  Gruber's (internal mesogastric) 553.8
    with
      gangrene (obstructed) 551.8
      obstruction 552.8

Herpes, herpetic — *continued*
- keratitis — *continued*
  - interstitial — *continued*
    - zoster 053.21
- keratoconjunctivitis (simplex) 054.43
  - zoster 053.21
- labialis 054.9
  - meningococcal 036.89
- lip 054.9
- meningitis (simplex) 054.72
  - zoster 053.0
- ophthalmicus (zoster) 053.20
  - simplex 054.40
- otitis externa (zoster) 053.71
  - simplex 054.73
- penis 054.13
- perianal 054.10
- pharyngitis 054.79
- progenitalis 054.10
- scrotum 054.19
- septicemia 054.5
- simplex 054.9
  - complicated 054.8
    - ophthalmic 054.40
      - specified NEC 054.49
    - specified NEC 054.79
  - congenital 771.2
  - external ear 054.73
  - keratitis 054.43
    - dendritic 054.42
  - meningitis 054.72
  - myelitis 054.74
  - neuritis 054.79
  - specified complication NEC 054.79
    - ophthalmic 054.49
  - visceral 054.71
- stomatitis 054.2
- tonsurans 110.0
  - maculosus (of Hebra) 696.3
- visceral 054.71
- vulva 054.12
- vulvovaginitis 054.11
- whitlow 054.6
- zoster 053.9
  - auricularis 053.71
  - complicated 053.8
    - specified NEC 053.79
  - conjunctiva 053.21
  - cornea 053.21
  - ear 053.71
  - eye 053.29
  - geniculate 053.11
  - keratitis 053.21
    - interstitial 053.21
  - myelitis 053.14
  - neuritis 053.10
  - ophthalmicus(a) 053.20
  - oticus 053.71
  - otitis externa 053.71
  - specified complication NEC 053.79
  - specified site NEC 053.9
- zosteriform, intermediate type 053.9

Herrick's
- anemia (hemoglobin S disease) 282.61
- syndrome (hemoglobin S disease) 282.61

Hers' disease (glycogenosis VI) 271.0
Herter (-Gee) disease or syndrome (nontropical sprue) 579.0
Herter's infantilism (nontropical sprue) 579.0
Herxheimer's disease (diffuse idiopathic cutaneous atrophy) 701.8
Herxheimer's reaction 995.0
Hesitancy, urinary 788.64
Hesselbach's hernia — *see* Hernia, Hesselbach's
Heterochromia (congenital) 743.46
- acquired 364.53
- cataract 366.33
- cyclitis 364.21
- hair 704.3
- iritis 364.21
- retained metallic foreign body 360.62
  - magnetic 360.52
- uveitis 364.21

Heterophoria 378.40
- alternating 378.45
- vertical 378.43

Heterophyes, small intestine 121.6
Heterophyiasis 121.6
Heteropsia 368.8
Heterotopia, heterotopic — *see also* Malposition, congenital
- cerebralis 742.4
- pancreas, pancreatic 751.7
- spinalis 742.59

Heterotropia 378.30
- intermittent 378.20
  - vertical 378.31
- vertical (constant) (intermittent) 378.31

Heubner's disease 094.89
Heubner-Herter disease or syndrome (nontropical sprue) 579.0
Hexadactylism 755.0 ☑
Heyd's syndrome (hepatorenal) 572.4
HGSIL (high grade squamous intraepithelial lesion) (cytologic finding) (Pap smear finding)
- anus 796.74
- cervix 795.04
  - biopsy finding — code to CIN II or CIN III
- vagina 795.14

Hibernoma (M8880/0) — *see* Lipoma
Hiccough 786.8
- epidemic 078.89
- psychogenic 306.1

Hiccup — *see also* Hiccough 786.8
Hicks (-Braxton) contractures 644.1 ☑
Hidden penis 752.65
Hidradenitis (axillaris) (suppurative) 705.83
Hidradenoma (nodular) (M8400/0) — *see also* Neoplasm, skin, benign
- clear cell (M8402/0) — *see* Neoplasm, skin, benign
- papillary (M8405/0) — *see* Neoplasm, skin, benign

Hidrocystoma (M8404/0) — *see* Neoplasm, skin, benign
HIE (hypoxic-ischemic encephalopathy) 768.7
High
- A_2 anemia 282.49
- altitude effects 993.2
  - anoxia 993.2
  - on
    - ears 993.0
    - sinuses 993.1
  - polycythemia 289.0
- arch
  - foot 755.67
  - palate 750.26
- artery (arterial) tension (*see also* Hypertension) 401.9
  - without diagnosis of hypertension 796.2
- basal metabolic rate (BMR) 794.7
- blood pressure (*see also* Hypertension) 401.9
  - incidental reading (isolated) (nonspecific), no diagnosis of hypertension 796.2
- cholesterol 272.0
  - with high triglycerides 272.2
- compliance bladder 596.4
- diaphragm (congenital) 756.6
- frequency deafness (congenital) (regional) 389.8
- head at term 652.5 ☑
  - affecting fetus or newborn 763.1
- output failure (cardiac) (*see also* Failure, heart) 428.9
- oxygen-affinity hemoglobin 289.0
- palate 750.26
- risk
  - behavior — *see* Problem
  - family situation V61.9
    - specified circumstance NEC V61.8

High — *continued*
- risk — *continued*
  - human papillomavirus (HPV) DNA test positive
    - anal 796.75
    - cervical 795.05
    - vaginal 795.15
  - individual NEC V62.89
  - infant NEC V20.1
  - patient taking drugs (prescribed) V67.51
    - nonprescribed (*see also* Abuse, drugs, nondependent) 305.9 ☑
  - pregnancy V23.9
    - inadequate prenatal care V23.7
    - specified problem NEC V23.89
- temperature (of unknown origin) (*see also* Pyrexia) 780.60
- thoracic rib 756.3
- triglycerides 272.1
  - with high cholesterol 272.2

Hildenbrand's disease (typhus) 081.9
Hilger's syndrome 337.09
Hill diarrhea 579.1
Hilliard's lupus — *see also* Tuberculosis 017.0 ☑
Hilum — *see* condition
Hip — *see* condition
Hippel's disease (retinocerebral angiomatosis) 759.6
Hippus 379.49
Hirschfeld's disease (acute diabetes mellitus) — *see also* Diabetes 250.0 ☑
- due to secondary diabetes 249.0 ☑

Hirschsprung's disease or megacolon (congenital) 751.3
Hirsuties — *see also* Hypertrichosis 704.1
Hirsutism — *see also* Hypertrichosis 704.1
Hirudiniasis (external) (internal) 134.2
Hiss-Russell dysentery 004.1
Histamine cephalgia 339.00
Histidinemia 270.5
Histidinuria 270.5
Histiocytic syndromes 288.4
Histiocytoma (M8832/0) — *see also* Neoplasm, skin, benign
- fibrous (M8830/0) (*see also* Neoplasm, skin, benign)
  - atypical (M8830/1) — *see* Neoplasm, connective tissue, uncertain behavior
  - malignant (M8830/3) — *see* Neoplasm, connective tissue, malignant

Histiocytosis (acute) (chronic) (subacute) 277.89
- acute differentiated progressive (M9722/3) 202.5 ☑
- cholesterol 277.89
- essential 277.89
- lipid, lipoid (essential) 272.7
- lipochrome (familial) 288.1
- malignant (M9720/3) 202.3 ☑
- X (chronic) 277.89
  - acute (progressive) (M9722/3) 202.5 ☑

Histoplasmosis 115.90
- with
  - endocarditis 115.94
  - meningitis 115.91
  - pericarditis 115.93
  - pneumonia 115.95
  - retinitis 115.92
  - specified manifestation NEC 115.99
- African (due to Histoplasma duboisii) 115.10
  - with
    - endocarditis 115.14
    - meningitis 115.11
    - pericarditis 115.13
    - pneumonia 115.15

Histoplasmosis — *continued*
- African — *continued*
  - with — *continued*
    - retinitis 115.12
    - specified manifestation NEC 115.19
- American (due to Histoplasma capsulatum) 115.00
  - with
    - endocarditis 115.04
    - meningitis 115.01
    - pericarditis 115.03
    - pneumonia 115.05
    - retinitis 115.02
    - specified manifestation NEC 115.09
- Darling's — *see* Histoplasmosis, American
- large form (*see also* Histoplasmosis, African) 115.10
- lung 115.05
- small form (*see also* Histoplasmosis, American) 115.00

History (personal) of
- abuse
  - emotional V15.42
  - neglect V15.42
  - physical V15.41
  - sexual V15.41
- affective psychosis V11.1
- alcoholism V11.3
  - specified as drinking problem (*see also* Abuse, drugs, nondependent) 305.0 ☑
- allergy to
  - analgesic agent NEC V14.6
  - anesthetic NEC V14.4
  - antibiotic agent NEC V14.1
    - penicillin V14.0
  - anti-infective agent NEC V14.3
  - diathesis V15.09
  - drug V14.9
    - specified type NEC V14.8
  - eggs V15.03
  - food additives V15.05
  - insect bite V15.06
  - latex V15.07
  - medicinal agents V14.9
    - specified type NEC V14.8
  - milk products V15.02
  - narcotic agent NEC V14.5
  - nuts V15.05
    - peanuts V15.01
  - penicillin V14.0
  - radiographic dye V15.08
  - seafood V15.04
  - serum V14.7
  - specified food NEC V15.05
  - specified nonmedicinal agents NEC V15.09
  - spider bite V15.06
  - sulfa V14.2
  - sulfonamides V14.2
  - therapeutic agent NEC V15.09
  - vaccine V14.7
- anemia V12.3
- arrest, sudden cardiac V12.53
- arthritis V13.4
- attack, transient ischemic (TIA) V12.54
- benign neoplasm of brain V12.41
- blood disease V12.3
- calculi, urinary V13.01
- cardiovascular disease V12.50
  - myocardial infarction 412
- chemotherapy, antineoplastic V87.41
- child abuse V15.41
- cigarette smoking V15.82
- circulatory system disease V12.50
  - myocardial infarction 412
- congenital malformation V13.69
- contraception V15.7
- death, sudden, successfully resuscitated V12.53

History of — *continued*
  malignant neoplasm — *continued*
    oropharynx V10.02
    ovary V10.43
    pancreas V10.09
    parathyroid V10.88
    penis V10.49
    pharynx V10.02
    pineal V10.88
    pituitary V10.88
    placenta V10.44
    pleura V10.29
    prostate V10.46
    rectosigmoid junction V10.06
    rectum V10.06
    renal pelvis V10.53
    respiratory organs NEC V10.20
    salivary gland V10.02
    skin V10.83
      melanoma V10.82
    small intestine NEC V10.09
    soft tissue NEC V10.89
    specified site NEC V10.89
    stomach V10.04
    testis V10.47
    thymus V10.29
    thyroid V10.87
    tongue V10.01
    trachea V10.12
    ureter V10.59
    urethra V10.59
    urinary organ V10.50
    uterine adnexa V10.44
    uterus V10.42
    vagina V10.44
    vulva V10.44
  manic-depressive psychosis V11.1
  meningitis V12.42
  mental disorder V11.9
    affective type V11.1
    manic-depressive V11.1
    neurosis V11.2
    schizophrenia V11.0
    specified type NEC V11.8
  metabolic disorder V12.2
  methicillin resistant Staphylococcus aureus (MRSA) V12.04
  MRSA (methicillin resistant Staphylococcus aureus) V12.04
  musculoskeletal disorder NEC V13.59
  myocardial infarction 412
  neglect (emotional) V15.42
  nephrotic syndrome V13.03
  nervous system disorder V12.40
    specified type NEC V12.49
  neurosis V11.2
  noncompliance with medical treatment V15.81
  nutritional deficiency V12.1
  obstetric disorder V13.29
    affecting management of current pregnancy V23.49
      pre-term labor V23.41
    pre-term labor V13.21
  parasitic disease V12.00
    specified NEC V12.09
  perinatal problems V13.7
    low birth weight (*see also* Status, low birth weight) V21.30
  physical abuse V15.41
  poisoning V15.6
  poliomyelitis V12.02
  polyps, colonic V12.72
  poor obstetric V13.29
    affecting management of current pregnancy V23.49
      pre-term labor V23.41
    pre-term labor V13.21
  prolonged reversible ischemic neurologic deficit (PRIND) V12.54
  psychiatric disorder V11.9
    affective type V11.1
    manic-depressive V11.1
    neurosis V11.2
    schizophrenia V11.0
    specified type NEC V11.8

History of — *continued*
  psychological trauma V15.49
    emotional abuse V15.42
    neglect V15.42
    physical abuse V15.41
    rape V15.41
  psychoneurosis V11.2
  radiation therapy V15.3
  rape V15.41
  respiratory system disease V12.60
    pneumonia V12.61
    specified NEC V12.69
  reticulosarcoma V10.71
  return from military deployment V62.22
  reversible ischemic neurologic deficit (RIND) V12.54
  schizophrenia V11.0
  skin disease V13.3
  smoking (tobacco) V15.82
  stroke without residual deficits V12.54
  subcutaneous tissue disease V13.3
  sudden
    cardiac
      arrest V12.53
      death (successfully resuscitated) V12.53
  surgery to
    great vessels V15.1
    heart V15.1
    in utero
      during pregnancy V15.21
      while a fetus V15.22
    organs NEC V15.29
  syndrome, nephrotic V13.03
  therapy
    antineoplastic drug V87.41
    drug NEC V87.49
    monoclonal drug V87.42
  thrombophlebitis V12.52
  thrombosis V12.51
  tobacco use V15.82
  trophoblastic disease V13.1
    affecting management of pregnancy V23.1
  tuberculosis V12.01
  ulcer, peptic V12.71
  urinary system disorder V13.00
    calculi V13.01
    infection V13.02
    nephrotic syndrome V13.03
    specified NEC V13.09
His-Werner disease (trench fever) 083.1
HIT (heparin-induced thrombocytopenia) 289.84
Hives (bold) — *see also* Urticaria 708.9
HIV infection (disease) (illness) — *see* Human immunodeficiency virus (disease) (illness) (infection)
Hoarseness 784.49
Hobnail liver — *see* Cirrhosis, portal
Hobo, hoboism V60.0
Hodgkin's
  disease (M9650/3) 201.9 ☑
    lymphocytic
      depletion (M9653/3) 201.7 ☑
        diffuse fibrosis (M9654/3) 201.7 ☑
        reticular type (M9655/3) 201.7 ☑
      predominance (M9651/3) 201.4 ☑
    lymphocytic-histiocytic predominance (M9651/3) 201.4 ☑
    mixed cellularity (M9652/3) 201.6 ☑
    nodular sclerosis (M9656/3) 201.5 ☑
      cellular phase (M9657/3) 201.5 ☑
  granuloma (M9661/3) 201.1 ☑
  lymphogranulomatosis (M9650/3) 201.9 ☑
  lymphoma (M9650/3) 201.9 ☑
  lymphosarcoma (M9650/3) 201.9 ☑
  paragranuloma (M9660/3) 201.0 ☑

Hodgkin's — *continued*
  sarcoma (M9662/3) 201.2 ☑
Hodgson's disease (aneurysmal dilatation of aorta) 441.9
  ruptured 441.5
Hodi-potsy 111.0
Hoffa (-Kastert) disease or syndrome (liposynovitis prepatellaris) 272.8
Hoffmann-Bouveret syndrome (paroxysmal tachycardia) 427.2
Hoffman's syndrome 244.9 *[359.5]*
Hole
  macula 362.54
  optic disc, crater-like 377.22
  retina (macula) 362.54
    round 361.31
      with detachment 361.01
Holla disease — *see also* Spherocytosis 282.0
Holländer-Simons syndrome (progressive lipodystrophy) 272.6
Hollow foot (congenital) 754.71
  acquired 736.73
Holmes' syndrome (visual disorientation) 368.16
Holoprosencephaly 742.2
  due to
    trisomy 13 758.1
    trisomy 18 758.2
Holthouse's hernia — *see* Hernia, inguinal
Homesickness 309.89
Homocystinemia 270.4
Homocystinuria 270.4
Homologous serum jaundice (prophylactic) (therapeutic) — *see* Hepatitis, viral
Homosexuality — omit code
  ego-dystonic 302.0
  pedophilic 302.2
  problems with 302.0
Homozygous Hb-S disease 282.61
Honeycomb lung 518.89
  congenital 748.4
Hong Kong ear 117.3
HOOD (hereditary osteo-onychodysplasia) 756.89
Hooded
  clitoris 752.49
  penis 752.69
Hookworm (anemia) (disease) (infestation) — *see* Ancylostomiasis
Hoppe-Goldflam syndrome 358.00
Hordeolum (external) (eyelid) 373.11
  internal 373.12
Horn
  cutaneous 702.8
    cheek 702.8
    eyelid 702.8
    penis 702.8
  iliac 756.89
  nail 703.8
    congenital 757.5
  papillary 700
Horner's
  syndrome (*see also* Neuropathy, peripheral, autonomic) 337.9
    traumatic 954.0
  teeth 520.4
Horseshoe kidney (congenital) 753.3
Horton's
  disease (temporal arteritis) 446.5
  headache or neuralgia 339.00
Hospice care V66.7
Hospitalism (in children) NEC 309.83
Hourglass contraction, contracture
  bladder 596.8
  gallbladder 575.2
    congenital 751.69
  stomach 536.8
    congenital 750.7
    psychogenic 306.4
  uterus 661.4 ☑
    affecting fetus or newborn 763.7
Household circumstance affecting care V60.9

Household circumstance affecting care — *continued*
  specified type NEC V60.8
Housemaid's knee 727.2
Housing circumstance affecting care V60.9
  specified type NEC V60.8
HTLV-I infection 079.51
HTLV-II infection 079.52
HTLV-III/LAV (disease) (illness) (infection) — *see* Human immunodeficiency virus (disease) (illness) (infection)
HTLV-III (disease) (illness) (infection) — *see* Human immunodeficiency virus (disease) (illness) (infection)
Huchard's disease (continued arterial hypertension) 401.9
Hudson-Stähli lines 371.11
Huguier's disease (uterine fibroma) 218.9
Human bite (open wound) — see also Wound, open, by site
  intact skin surface — *see* Contusion
Human immunodeficiency virus (disease) (illness) 042
  infection V08
    with symptoms, symptomatic 042
Human immunodeficiency virus-2 infection 079.53
Human immunovirus (disease) (illness) (infection) — *see* Human immunodeficiency virus (disease) (illness) (infection)
Human papillomavirus 079.4
  high risk, DNA test positive
    anal 796.75
    cervical 795.05
    vaginal 795.15
  low risk, DNA test positive
    anal 796.79
    cervical 795.09
    vaginal 795.19
Human parvovirus 079.83
Human T-cell lymphotrophic virus-I infection 079.51
Human T-cell lymphotrophic virus-II infection 079.52
Human T-cell lymphotrophic virus-III (disease) (illness) (infection) — *see* Human immunodeficiency virus (disease) (illness) (infection)
Humpback (acquired) 737.9
  congenital 756.19
Hum, venous — omit code
Hunchback (acquired) 737.9
  congenital 756.19
Hunger 994.2
  air, psychogenic 306.1
  disease 251.1
Hungry bone syndrome 275.5
Hunner's ulcer — *see also* Cystitis 595.1
Hunt's
  neuralgia 053.11
  syndrome (herpetic geniculate ganglionitis) 053.11
    dyssynergia cerebellaris myoclonica 334.2
Hunter's glossitis 529.4
Hunterian chancre 091.0
Hunter (-Hurler) syndrome (mucopolysaccharidosis II) 277.5
Huntington's
  chorea 333.4
  disease 333.4
Huppert's disease (multiple myeloma) (M9730/3) 203.0 ☑
Hurler (-Hunter) disease or syndrome (mucopolysaccharidosis II) 277.5
Hürthle cell
  adenocarcinoma (M8290/3) 193
  adenoma (M8290/0) 226
  carcinoma (M8290/3) 193
  tumor (M8290/0) 226

Hypercalcemia, hypercalcemic — *continued*
nephropathy 588.89
Hypercalcinuria 275.40
Hypercapnia 786.09
with mixed acid-based disorder 276.4
fetal, affecting newborn 770.89
Hypercarotinemia 278.3
Hypercementosis 521.5
Hyperchloremia 276.9
Hyperchlorhydria 536.8
neurotic 306.4
psychogenic 306.4
Hypercholesterinemia — *see* Hypercholesterolemia
Hypercholesterolemia 272.0
with hyperglyceridemia, endogenous 272.2
essential 272.0
familial 272.0
hereditary 272.0
primary 272.0
pure 272.0
Hypercholesterolosis 272.0
Hyperchylia gastrica 536.8
psychogenic 306.4
Hyperchylomicronemia (familial) (with hyperbetalipoproteinemia) 272.3
Hypercoagulation syndrome (primary) 289.81
secondary 289.82
Hypercorticosteronism
correct substance properly administered 255.3
overdose or wrong substance given or taken 962.0
Hypercortisonism
correct substance properly administered 255.3
overdose or wrong substance given or taken 962.0
Hyperdynamic beta-adrenergic state or syndrome (circulatory) 429.82
Hyperekplexia 759.89
Hyperelectrolytemia 276.9
Hyperemesis 536.2
arising during pregnancy — *see* Hyperemesis, gravidarum
gravidarum (mild) (before 22 completed weeks gestation) 643.0 ☑
with
carbohydrate depletion 643.1 ☑
dehydration 643.1 ☑
electrolyte imbalance 643.1 ☑
metabolic disturbance 643.1 ☑
affecting fetus or newborn 761.8
severe (with metabolic disturbance) 643.1 ☑
psychogenic 306.4
Hyperemia (acute) 780.99
anal mucosa 569.49
bladder 596.7
cerebral 437.8
conjunctiva 372.71
ear, internal, acute 386.30
enteric 564.89
eye 372.71
eyelid (active) (passive) 374.82
intestine 564.89
iris 364.41
kidney 593.81
labyrinth 386.30
liver (active) (passive) 573.8
lung 514
ovary 620.8
passive 780.99
pulmonary 514
renal 593.81
retina 362.89
spleen 289.59
stomach 537.89
Hyperesthesia (body surface) — *see also* Disturbance, sensation 782.0
larynx (reflex) 478.79
hysterical 300.11
pharynx (reflex) 478.29
Hyperestrinism 256.0
Hyperestrogenism 256.0
Hyperestrogenosis 256.0
Hyperexplexia 759.89
Hyperextension, joint 718.80
ankle 718.87
elbow 718.82
foot 718.87
hand 718.84
hip 718.85
knee 718.86
multiple sites 718.89
pelvic region 718.85
shoulder (region) 718.81
specified site NEC 718.88
wrist 718.83
Hyperfibrinolysis — *see* Fibrinolysis
Hyperfolliculinism 256.0
Hyperfructosemia 271.2
Hyperfunction
adrenal (cortex) 255.3
androgenic, acquired benign 255.3
medulla 255.6
virilism 255.2
corticoadrenal NEC 255.3
labyrinth — *see* Hyperactive, labyrinth
medulloadrenal 255.6
ovary 256.1
estrogen 256.0
pancreas 577.8
parathyroid (gland) 252.00
pituitary (anterior) (gland) (lobe) 253.1
testicular 257.0
Hypergammaglobulinemia 289.89
monoclonal, benign (BMH) 273.1
polyclonal 273.0
Waldenström's 273.0
Hyperglobulinemia 273.8
Hyperglycemia 790.29
maternal
affecting fetus or newborn 775.0
manifest diabetes in infant 775.1
postpancreatectomy (complete) (partial) 251.3
Hyperglyceridemia 272.1
endogenous 272.1
essential 272.1
familial 272.1
hereditary 272.1
mixed 272.3
pure 272.1
Hyperglycinemia 270.7
Hypergonadism
ovarian 256.1
testicular (infantile) (primary) 257.0
Hyperheparinemia — *see also* Circulating anticoagulants 286.5
Hyperhidrosis, hyperidrosis 705.21
axilla 705.21
face 705.21
focal (localized) 705.21
primary 705.21
axilla 705.21
face 705.21
palms 705.21
soles 705.21
secondary 705.22
axilla 705.22
face 705.22
palms 705.22
soles 705.22
generalized 780.8
palms 705.21
psychogenic 306.3
secondary 780.8
soles 705.21
Hyperhistidinemia 270.5
Hyperinsulinism (ectopic) (functional) (organic) NEC 251.1
iatrogenic 251.0
reactive 251.2
spontaneous 251.2
therapeutic misadventure (from administration of insulin) 962.3
Hyperiodemia 276.9
Hyperirritability (cerebral), in newborn 779.1
Hyperkalemia 276.7
Hyperkeratosis — *see also* Keratosis 701.1
cervix 622.2
congenital 757.39
cornea 371.89
due to yaws (early) (late) (palmar or plantar) 102.3
eccentrica 757.39
figurata centrifuga atrophica 757.39
follicularis 757.39
in cutem penetrans 701.1
limbic (cornea) 371.89
palmoplantaris climacterica 701.1
pinta (carate) 103.1
senile (with pruritus) 702.0
tongue 528.79
universalis congenita 757.1
vagina 623.1
vocal cord 478.5
vulva 624.09
Hyperkinesia, hyperkinetic (disease) (reaction) (syndrome) 314.9
with
attention deficit — *see* Disorder, attention deficit
conduct disorder 314.2
developmental delay 314.1
simple disturbance of activity and attention 314.01
specified manifestation NEC 314.8
heart (disease) 429.82
of childhood or adolescence NEC 314.9
Hyperlacrimation — *see also* Epiphora 375.20
Hyperlipemia — *see also* Hyperlipidemia 272.4
Hyperlipidemia 272.4
carbohydrate-induced 272.1
combined 272.4
endogenous 272.1
exogenous 272.3
fat-induced 272.3
group
A 272.0
B 272.1
C 272.2
D 272.3
mixed 272.2
specified type NEC 272.4
Hyperlipidosis 272.7
hereditary 272.7
Hyperlipoproteinemia (acquired) (essential) (familial) (hereditary) (primary) (secondary) 272.4
Fredrickson type
I 272.3
IIa 272.0
IIb 272.2
III 272.2
IV 272.1
V 272.3
low-density-lipoid-type (LDL) 272.0
very-low-density-lipoid-type (VLDL) 272.1
Hyperlucent lung, unilateral 492.8
Hyperluteinization 256.1
Hyperlysinemia 270.7
Hypermagnesemia 275.2
neonatal 775.5
Hypermaturity (fetus or newborn)
post-term infant 766.21
prolonged gestation infant 766.22
Hypermenorrhea 626.2
Hypermetabolism 794.7
Hypermethioninemia 270.4
Hypermetropia (congenital) 367.0
Hypermobility
cecum 564.9
coccyx 724.71
colon 564.9
psychogenic 306.4
ileum 564.89
Hypermobility — *continued*
joint (acquired) 718.80
ankle 718.87
elbow 718.82
foot 718.87
hand 718.84
hip 718.85
knee 718.86
multiple sites 718.89
pelvic region 718.85
shoulder (region) 718.81
specified site NEC 718.88
wrist 718.83
kidney, congenital 753.3
meniscus (knee) 717.5
scapula 718.81
stomach 536.8
psychogenic 306.4
syndrome 728.5
testis, congenital 752.52
urethral 599.81
Hypermotility
gastrointestinal 536.8
intestine 564.9
psychogenic 306.4
stomach 536.8
Hypernasality 784.49
Hypernatremia 276.0
with water depletion 276.0
Hypernephroma (M8312/3) 189.0
Hyperopia 367.0
Hyperorexia 783.6
Hyperornithinemia 270.6
Hyperosmia — *see also* Disturbance, sensation 781.1
Hyperosmolality 276.0
Hyperosteogenesis 733.99
Hyperostosis 733.99
calvarial 733.3
cortical 733.3
infantile 756.59
frontal, internal of skull 733.3
interna frontalis 733.3
monomelic 733.99
skull 733.3
congenital 756.0
vertebral 721.8
with spondylosis — *see* Spondylosis
ankylosing 721.6
Hyperovarianism 256.1
Hyperovarism, hyperovaria 256.1
Hyperoxaluria (primary) 271.8
Hyperoxia 987.8
Hyperparathyroidism 252.00
ectopic 259.3
other 252.08
primary 252.01
secondary (of renal origin) 588.81
non-renal 252.02
tertiary 252.08
Hyperpathia — *see also* Disturbance, sensation 782.0
psychogenic 307.80
Hyperperistalsis 787.4
psychogenic 306.4
Hyperpermeability, capillary 448.9
Hyperphagia 783.6
Hyperphenylalaninemia 270.1
Hyperphoria 378.40
alternating 378.45
Hyperphosphatemia 275.3
Hyperpiesia — *see also* Hypertension 401.9
Hyperpiesis — *see also* Hypertension 401.9
Hyperpigmentation — *see* Pigmentation
Hyperpinealism 259.8
Hyperpipecolatemia 270.7
Hyperpituitarism 253.1
Hyperplasia, hyperplastic
adenoids (lymphoid tissue) 474.12
and tonsils 474.10
adrenal (capsule) (cortex) (gland) 255.8
with
sexual precocity (male) 255.2

Hyperplasia, hyperplastic — *continued*
  adrenal — *continued*
    with — *continued*
      virilism, adrenal 255.2
      virilization (female) 255.2
    congenital 255.2
    due to excess ACTH (ectopic) (pituitary) 255.0
    medulla 255.8
  alpha cells (pancreatic)
    with
      gastrin excess 251.5
      glucagon excess 251.4
  appendix (lymphoid) 543.0
  artery, fibromuscular NEC 447.8
    carotid 447.8
    renal 447.3
  bone 733.99
    marrow 289.9
  breast (*see also* Hypertrophy, breast) 611.1
  carotid artery 447.8
  cementation, cementum (teeth) (tooth) 521.5
  cervical gland 785.6
  cervix (uteri) 622.10
    basal cell 622.10
    congenital 752.49
    endometrium 622.10
    polypoid 622.10
  chin 524.05
  clitoris, congenital 752.49
  dentin 521.5
  endocervicitis 616.0
  endometrium, endometrial (adenomatous) (atypical) (cystic) (glandular) (polypoid) (uterus) 621.30
    with atypia 621.33
    without atypia
      complex 621.32
      simple 621.31
    cervix 622.10
  epithelial 709.8
    focal, oral, including tongue 528.79
    mouth (focal) 528.79
    nipple 611.89
    skin 709.8
    tongue (focal) 528.79
    vaginal wall 623.0
  erythroid 289.9
  fascialis ossificans (progressiva) 728.11
  fibromuscular, artery NEC 447.8
    carotid 447.8
    renal 447.3
  genital
    female 629.89
    male 608.89
  gingiva 523.8
  glandularis
    cystica uteri 621.30
    endometrium (uterus) 621.30
    interstitialis uteri 621.30
  granulocytic 288.69
  gum 523.8
  hymen, congenital 752.49
  islands of Langerhans 251.1
  islet cell (pancreatic) 251.9
    alpha cells
      with excess
        gastrin 251.5
        glucagon 251.4
    beta cells 251.1
  juxtaglomerular (complex) (kidney) 593.89
  kidney (congenital) 753.3
  liver (congenital) 751.69
  lymph node (gland) 785.6
  lymphoid (diffuse) (nodular) 785.6
    appendix 543.0
    intestine 569.89
  mandibular 524.02
    alveolar 524.72
    unilateral condylar 526.89
  Marchand multiple nodular (liver) — *see* Cirrhosis, postnecrotic
  maxillary 524.01
    alveolar 524.71
  medulla, adrenal 255.8
  myometrium, myometrial 621.2
  nose (lymphoid) (polypoid) 478.19
  oral soft tissue (inflammatory) (irritative) (mucosa) NEC 528.9
    gingiva 523.8
    tongue 529.8
  organ or site, congenital NEC — *see* Anomaly, specified type NEC
  ovary 620.8
  palate, papillary 528.9
  pancreatic islet cells 251.9
    alpha
      with excess
        gastrin 251.5
        glucagon 251.4
    beta 251.1
  parathyroid (gland) 252.01
  persistent, vitreous (primary) 743.51
  pharynx (lymphoid) 478.29
  prostate 600.90
    with
      other lower urinary tract symptoms (LUTS) 600.91
      urinary
        obstruction 600.91
        retention 600.91
    adenofibromatous 600.20
      with
        other lower urinary tract symptoms (LUTS) 600.21
        urinary
          obstruction 600.21
          retention 600.21
    nodular 600.10
      with
        urinary
          obstruction 600.11
          retention 600.11
  renal artery (fibromuscular) 447.3
  reticuloendothelial (cell) 289.9
  salivary gland (any) 527.1
  Schimmelbusch's 610.1
  suprarenal (capsule) (gland) 255.8
  thymus (gland) (persistent) 254.0
  thyroid (*see also* Goiter) 240.9
    primary 242.0 ☑
    secondary 242.2 ☑
  tonsil (lymphoid tissue) 474.11
    and adenoids 474.10
  urethrovaginal 599.89
  uterus, uterine (myometrium) 621.2
    endometrium (*see also* Hyperplasia, endometrium) 621.30
  vitreous (humor), primary persistent 743.51
  vulva 624.3
  zygoma 738.11
Hyperpnea — *see also* Hyperventilation 786.01
Hyperpotassemia 276.7
Hyperprebetalipoproteinemia 272.1
  with chylomicronemia 272.3
  familial 272.1
Hyperprolactinemia 253.1
Hyperprolinemia 270.8
Hyperproteinemia 273.8
Hyperprothrombinemia 289.89
Hyperpselaphesia 782.0
Hyperpyrexia 780.60
  heat (effects of) 992.0
  malarial (*see also* Malaria) 084.6
  malignant, due to anesthetic 995.86
  rheumatic — *see* Fever, rheumatic
  unknown origin (*see also* Pyrexia) 780.60
Hyperreactor, vascular 780.2
Hyperreflexia 796.1
  bladder, autonomic 596.54
    with cauda equina 344.61
  detrusor 344.61
Hypersalivation — *see also* Ptyalism 527.7
Hypersarcosinemia 270.8
Hypersecretion
  ACTH 255.3
  androgens (ovarian) 256.1
  calcitonin 246.0
  corticoadrenal 255.3
  cortisol 255.0
  estrogen 256.0
  gastric 536.8
    psychogenic 306.4
  gastrin 251.5
  glucagon 251.4
  hormone
    ACTH 255.3
    anterior pituitary 253.1
    growth NEC 253.0
    ovarian androgen 256.1
    testicular 257.0
    thyroid stimulating 242.8 ☑
  insulin — *see* Hyperinsulinism
  lacrimal glands (*see also* Epiphora) 375.20
  medulloadrenal 255.6
  milk 676.6 ☑
  ovarian androgens 256.1
  pituitary (anterior) 253.1
  salivary gland (any) 527.7
  testicular hormones 257.0
  thyrocalcitonin 246.0
  upper respiratory 478.9
Hypersegmentation, hereditary 288.2
  eosinophils 288.2
  neutrophil nuclei 288.2
Hypersensitive, hypersensitiveness, hypersensitivity — *see also* Allergy
  angiitis 446.20
    specified NEC 446.29
  carotid sinus 337.01
  colon 564.9
    psychogenic 306.4
  DNA (deoxyribonucleic acid) NEC 287.2
  drug (*see also* Allergy, drug) 995.27
  esophagus 530.89
  insect bites — *see* Injury, superficial, by site
  labyrinth 386.58
  pain (*see also* Disturbance, sensation) 782.0
  pneumonitis NEC 495.9
  reaction (*see also* Allergy) 995.3
    upper respiratory tract NEC 478.8
  stomach (allergic) (nonallergic) 536.8
    psychogenic 306.4
Hypersomatotropism (classic) 253.0
Hypersomnia, unspecified 780.54
  with sleep apnea, unspecified 780.53
  alcohol induced 291.82
  drug induced 292.85
  due to
    medical condition classified elsewhere 327.14
    mental disorder 327.15
  idiopathic
    with long sleep time 327.11
    without long sleep time 327.12
  menstrual related 327.13
  nonorganic origin 307.43
    persistent (primary) 307.44
    transient 307.43
  organic 327.10
    other 327.19
  primary 307.44
  recurrent 327.13
Hypersplenia 289.4
Hypersplenism 289.4
Hypersteatosis 706.3
Hyperstimulation, ovarian 256.1
Hypersuprarenalism 255.3
Hypersusceptibility — *see* Allergy
Hyper-TBG-nemia 246.8
Hypertelorism 756.0
  orbit, orbital 376.41

	Malignant	Benign	Unspecified
Hypertension, hypertensive (arterial) (arteriolar) (crisis) (degeneration) (disease) (essential) (fluctuating) (idiopathic) (intermittent) (labile) (low renin) (orthostatic) (paroxysmal) (primary) (systemic) (uncontrolled) (vascular)	401.0	401.1	401.9
with			
chronic kidney disease			
stage I through stage IV, or unspecified	403.00	403.10	403.90
stage V or end stage renal disese	403.01	403.11	403.91
heart involvement (conditions classifiable to 429.0–429.3, 429.8, 429.9 due to hypertension) (*see also* Hypertension, heart)	402.00	402.10	402.90
with kidney involvement — *see* Hypertension, cardiorenal			
renal involvement (only conditions classifiable to 585, 586, 587) (excludes conditions classifiable to 584) (*see also* Hypertension, kidney)	403.00	403.10	403.90
with heart involvement — *see* Hypertension, cardiorenal			
failure (and sclerosis) (*see also* Hypertension, kidney)	403.01	403.11	403.91
sclerosis without failure (*see also* Hypertension, kidney)	403.00	403.10	403.90
accelerated (*see also* Hypertension, by type, malignant))	401.0	—	—
antepartum — *see* Hypertension, complicating pregnancy, childbirth, or the puerperium			
cardiorenal (disease)	404.00	404.10	404.90
with			
chronic kidney disease			
stage I through stage IV, or unspecified	404.00	404.10	404.90
and heart failure	404.01	404.11	404.91
stage V or end stage renal disease	404.02	404.12	404.92
and heart failure	404.03	404.13	404.93
heart failure	404.01	404.11	404.91
and chronic kidney disease	404.01	404.11	404.91
stage I through stage IV or unspecified	404.01	404.11	404.91
stave V or end stage renal disease	404.03	404.13	404.93
cardiovascular disease (arteriosclerotic) (sclerotic)	402.00	402.10	402.90
with			
heart failure	402.01	402.11	402.91
renal involvement (conditions classifiable to 403) (*see also* Hypertension, cardiorenal)	404.00	404.10	404.90
cardiovascular renal (disease) (sclerosis) (*see also* Hypertension, cardiorenal)	404.00	404.10	404.90
cerebrovascular disease NEC	437.2	437.2	437.2
complicating pregnancy, childbirth, or the puerperium	642.2 ☑	642.0 ☑	642.9 ☑
with			
albuminuria (and edema) (mild)	—	—	642.4 ☑
severe	—	—	642.5 ☑
chronic kidney disesae	642.2 ☑	642.2 ☑	642.2 ☑
and heart disease	642.2 ☑	642.2 ☑	642.2 ☑
edema (mild)	—	—	642.4 ☑
severe	—	—	642.5 ☑
heart disease	642.2 ☑	642.2 ☑	642.2 ☑
and chronic kidney disease	642.2 ☑	642.2 ☑	642.2 ☑
renal disease	642.2 ☑	642.2 ☑	642.2 ☑
and heart disease	642.2 ☑	642.2 ☑	642.2 ☑
chronic	642.2 ☑	642.0 ☑	642.0 ☑
with pre-eclampsia or eclampsia	642.7 ☑	642.7 ☑	642.7 ☑
fetus or newborn	760.0	760.0	760.0
essential	—	642.0 ☑	642.0 ☑
with pre-eclampsia or eclampsia	—	642.7 ☑	642.7 ☑
fetus or newborn	760.0	760.0	760.0
fetus or newborn	760.0	760.0	760.0
gestational	—	—	642.3 ☑
pre-existing	642.2 ☑	642.0 ☑	642.0 ☑
with pre-eclampsia or eclampsia	642.7 ☑	642.7 ☑	642.7 ☑
fetus or newborn	760.0	760.0	760.0
secondary to renal disease	642.1 ☑	642.1 ☑	642.1 ☑
with pre-eclampsia or eclampsia	642.7 ☑	642.7 ☑	642.7 ☑
fetus or newborn	760.0	760.0	760.0
transient	—	—	642.3 ☑
due to			
aldosteronism, primary	405.09	405.19	405.99
brain tumor	405.09	405.19	405.99
bulbar poliomyelitis	405.09	405.19	405.99
calculus			
kidney	405.09	405.19	405.99
ureter	405.09	405.19	405.99
coarctation, aorta	405.09	405.19	405.99
Cushing's disease	405.09	405.19	405.99
glomerulosclerosis (*see also* Hypertension, kidney)	403.00	403.10	403.90
periarteritis nodosa	405.09	405.19	405.99
pheochromocytoma	405.09	405.19	405.99
polycystic kidney(s)	405.09	405.19	405.99
polycythemia	405.09	405.19	405.99
porphyria	405.09	405.19	405.99
pyelonephritis	405.09	405.19	405.99
renal (artery)			

	Malignant	Benign	Unspecified
Hypertension, hypertensive — *continued*			
due to — *continued*			
renal — *continued*			
aneurysm	405.01	405.11	405.91
anomaly	405.01	405.11	405.91
embolism	405.01	405.11	405.91
fibromuscular hyperplasia	405.01	405.11	405.91
occlusion	405.01	405.11	405.91
stenosis	405.01	405.11	405.91
thrombosis	405.01	405.11	405.91
encephalopathy	437.2	437.2	437.2
gestational (transient) NEC	—	—	642.3 ☑
Goldblatt's	440.1	440.1	440.1
heart (disease) (conditions classifiable to 429.0–429.3, 429.8, 429.9 due to hypertension)	402.00	402.10	402.90
with heart failure	402.01	402.11	402.91
hypertensive kidney disease (conditions classifiable to 403) (*see also* Hypertension, cardiorenal)	404.00	404.10	404.90
renal sclerosis (*see also* Hypertension, cardiorenal)	404.00	404.10	404.90
intracranial, benign	—	348.2	—
intraocular	—	—	365.04
kidney	403.00	403.10	403.90
with			
chronic kidney disease			
stage I through stage IV, or unspecified	403.00	403.10	403.90
stage V or end stage renal disese	403.01	403.11	403.91
heart involvement (conditions classifiable to 429.0–429.3, 429.8, 429.9 due to hypertension) (*see also* Hypertension, cardiorenal)	404.00	404.10	404.90
hypertensive heart (disease) (conditions classifiable to 402) (*see also* Hypertension, cardiorenal)	404.00	404.10	404.90
lesser circulation	—	—	416.0
necrotizing	401.0	—	—
ocular	—	—	365.04
pancreatic duct — code to underlying condition			
with			
chronic pancreatitis	—	—	577.1
portal (due to chronic liver disease)	—	—	572.3
postoperative	—	—	997.91
psychogenic	—	—	306.2
puerperal, postpartum — *see* Hypertension, complicating pregnancy, childbirth, or the puerperium			
pulmonary (artery)	—	—	416.8
with cor pulmonale (chronic)	—	—	416.8
acute	—	—	415.0
idiopathic	—	—	416.0
primary	—	—	416.0
of newborn	—	—	747.83
secondary	—	—	416.8
renal (disease) (*see also* Hypertension, kidney)	403.00	403.10	403.90
renovascular NEC	405.01	405.11	405.91
secondary NEC	405.09	405.19	405.99
due to			
aldosteronism, primary	405.09	405.19	405.99
brain tumor	405.09	405.19	405.99
bulbar poliomyelitis	405.09	405.19	405.99
calculus			
kidney	405.09	405.19	405.99
ureter	405.09	405.19	405.99
coarctation, aorta	405.09	405.19	405.99
Cushing's disease	405.09	405.19	405.99
glomerulosclerosis (*see also* Hypertension, kidney)	403.00	403.10	403.90
periarteritis nodosa	405.09	405.19	405.99
pheochromocytoma	405.09	405.19	405.99
polycystic kidney(s)	405.09	405.19	405.99
polycythemia	405.09	405.19	405.99
porphyria	405.09	405.19	405.99
pyelonephritis	405.09	405.19	405.99
renal (artery)			
aneurysm	405.01	405.11	405.91
anomaly	405.01	405.11	405.91
embolism	405.01	405.11	405.91
fibromuscular hyperplasia	405.01	405.11	405.91
occlusion	405.01	405.11	405.91
stenosis	405.01	405.11	405.91
thrombosis	405.01	405.11	405.91
transient	—	—	796.2
of pregnancy	—	—	642.3 ☑
vascular degeneration	401.0	401.1	401.9
venous, chronic (asymptomatic) (idiopathic)	—	—	459.30
with			
complication, NEC	—	—	459.39
inflammation	—	—	459.32
with ulcer	—	—	459.33

Hyperthecosis, ovary 256.8
Hyperthermia (of unknown origin) — *see also* Pyrexia 780.60
malignant (due to anesthesia) 995.86
newborn 778.4
Hyperthymergasia — *see also* Psychosis, affective 296.0 ☑
reactive (from emotional stress, psychological trauma) 298.1
recurrent episode 296.1 ☑
single episode 296.0 ☑
Hyperthymism 254.8
Hyperthyroid (recurrent) — *see* Hyperthyroidism
Hyperthyroidism (latent) (preadult) (recurrent) (without goiter) 242.9 ☑

> *Note — Use the following fifth-digit subclassification with category 242:*
>
> 0 *without mention of thyrotoxic crisis or storm*
>
> 1 *with mention of thyrotoxic crisis or storm*

with
goiter (diffuse) 242.0 ☑
adenomatous 242.3 ☑
multinodular 242.2 ☑
uninodular 242.1 ☑
nodular 242.3 ☑
multinodular 242.2 ☑
uninodular 242.1 ☑
thyroid nodule 242.1 ☑
complicating pregnancy, childbirth, or puerperium 648.1 ☑
neonatal (transient) 775.3
Hypertonia — *see* Hypertonicity
Hypertonicity
bladder 596.51
fetus or newborn 779.89
gastrointestinal (tract) 536.8
infancy 779.89
due to electrolyte imbalance 779.89
muscle 728.85
stomach 536.8
psychogenic 306.4
uterus, uterine (contractions) 661.4 ☑
affecting fetus or newborn 763.7
Hypertony — *see* Hypertonicity
Hypertransaminemia 790.4
Hypertrichosis 704.1
congenital 757.4
eyelid 374.54
lanuginosa 757.4
acquired 704.1
Hypertriglyceridemia, essential 272.1
Hypertrophy, hypertrophic
adenoids (infectional) 474.12
and tonsils (faucial) (infective) (lingual) (lymphoid) 474.10
adrenal 255.8
alveolar process or ridge 525.8
anal papillae 569.49
apocrine gland 705.82
artery NEC 447.8
carotid 447.8
congenital (peripheral) NEC 747.60
gastrointestinal 747.61
lower limb 747.64
renal 747.62
specified NEC 747.69
spinal 747.82
upper limb 747.63
renal 447.3
arthritis (chronic) (*see also* Osteoarthrosis) 715.9 ☑
spine (*see also* Spondylosis) 721.90
arytenoid 478.79
asymmetrical (heart) 429.9
auricular — *see* Hypertrophy, cardiac
Bartholin's gland 624.8
bile duct 576.8
bladder (sphincter) (trigone) 596.8
blind spot, visual field 368.42
bone 733.99
brain 348.8

Hypertrophy, hypertrophic — *continued*
breast 611.1
cystic 610.1
fetus or newborn 778.7
fibrocystic 610.1
massive pubertal 611.1
puerperal, postpartum 676.3 ☑
senile (parenchymatous) 611.1
cardiac (chronic) (idiopathic) 429.3
with
rheumatic fever (conditions classifiable to 390)
active 391.8
with chorea 392.0
inactive or quiescent (with chorea) 398.99
congenital NEC 746.89
fatty (*see also* Degeneration, myocardial) 429.1
hypertensive (*see also* Hypertension, heart) 402.90
rheumatic (with chorea) 398.99
active or acute 391.8
with chorea 392.0
valve (*see also* Endocarditis) 424.90
congenital NEC 746.89
cartilage 733.99
cecum 569.89
cervix (uteri) 622.6
congenital 752.49
elongation 622.6
clitoris (cirrhotic) 624.2
congenital 752.49
colon 569.89
congenital 751.3
conjunctiva, lymphoid 372.73
cornea 371.89
corpora cavernosa 607.89
duodenum 537.89
endometrium (uterus) (*see also* Hyperplasia, endometrium) 621.30
cervix 622.6
epididymis 608.89
esophageal hiatus (congenital) 756.6
with hernia — *see* Hernia, diaphragm
eyelid 374.30
falx, skull 733.99
fat pad 729.30
infrapatellar 729.31
knee 729.31
orbital 374.34
popliteal 729.31
prepatellar 729.31
retropatellar 729.31
specified site NEC 729.39
foot (congenital) 755.67
frenum, frenulum (tongue) 529.8
linguae 529.8
lip 528.5
gallbladder or cystic duct 575.8
gastric mucosa 535.2 ☑
gingiva 523.8
gland, glandular (general) NEC 785.6
gum (mucous membrane) 523.8
heart (idiopathic) (*see also* Hypertrophy, cardiac)
valve (*see also* Endocarditis)
congenital NEC 746.89
hemifacial 754.0
hepatic — *see* Hypertrophy, liver
hiatus (esophageal) 756.6
hilus gland 785.6
hymen, congenital 752.49
ileum 569.89
infrapatellar fat pad 729.31
intestine 569.89
jejunum 569.89
kidney (compensatory) 593.1
congenital 753.3
labial frenulum 528.5
labium (majus) (minus) 624.3
lacrimal gland, chronic 375.03
ligament 728.9

Hypertrophy, hypertrophic — *continued*
ligament — *continued*
spinal 724.8
linguae frenulum 529.8
lingual tonsil (infectional) 474.11
lip (frenum) 528.5
congenital 744.81
liver 789.1
acute 573.8
cirrhotic — *see* Cirrhosis, liver
congenital 751.69
fatty — *see* Fatty, liver
lymph gland 785.6
tuberculous — *see* Tuberculosis, lymph gland
mammary gland — *see* Hypertrophy, breast
maxillary frenulum 528.5
Meckel's diverticulum (congenital) 751.0
medial meniscus, acquired 717.3
median bar 600.90
with
other lower urinary tract symptoms (LUTS) 600.91
urinary
obstruction 600.91
retention 600.91
mediastinum 519.3
meibomian gland 373.2
meniscus, knee, congenital 755.64
metatarsal head 733.99
metatarsus 733.99
mouth 528.9
mucous membrane
alveolar process 523.8
nose 478.19
turbinate (nasal) 478.0
muscle 728.9
muscular coat, artery NEC 447.8
carotid 447.8
renal 447.3
myocardium (*see also* Hypertrophy, cardiac) 429.3
idiopathic 425.4
myometrium 621.2
nail 703.8
congenital 757.5
nasal 478.19
alae 478.19
bone 738.0
cartilage 478.19
mucous membrane (septum) 478.19
sinus (*see also* Sinusitis) 473.9
turbinate 478.0
nasopharynx, lymphoid (infectional) (tissue) (wall) 478.29
neck, uterus 622.6
nipple 611.1
normal aperture diaphragm (congenital) 756.6
nose (*see also* Hypertrophy, nasal) 478.19
orbit 376.46
organ or site, congenital NEC — *see* Anomaly, specified type NEC
osteoarthropathy (pulmonary) 731.2
ovary 620.8
palate (hard) 526.89
soft 528.9
pancreas (congenital) 751.7
papillae
anal 569.49
tongue 529.3
parathyroid (gland) 252.01
parotid gland 527.1
penis 607.89
phallus 607.89
female (clitoris) 624.2
pharyngeal tonsil 474.12
pharyngitis 472.1
pharynx 478.29
lymphoid (infectional) (tissue) (wall) 478.29

Hypertrophy, hypertrophic — *continued*
pituitary (fossa) (gland) 253.8
popliteal fat pad 729.31
preauricular (lymph) gland (Hampstead) 785.6
prepuce (congenital) 605
female 624.2
prostate (asymptomatic) (early) (recurrent) 600.90
with
other lower urinary tract symptlms (LUTS) 600.91
urinary
obstruction 600.91
retention 600.91
adenofibromatous 600.20
with
other lower urinary tract symptoms (LUTS) 600.21
urinary
obstruction 600.21
retention 600.21
benign 600.00
with
other lower urinary tract symptoms (LUTS) 600.01
urinary
obstruction 600.01
retention 600.01
congenital 752.89
pseudoedematous hypodermal 757.0
pseudomuscular 359.1
pylorus (muscle) (sphincter) 537.0
congenital 750.5
infantile 750.5
rectal sphincter 569.49
rectum 569.49
renal 593.1
rhinitis (turbinate) 472.0
salivary duct or gland 527.1
congenital 750.26
scaphoid (tarsal) 733.99
scar 701.4
scrotum 608.89
sella turcica 253.8
seminal vesicle 608.89
sigmoid 569.89
skin condition NEC 701.9
spermatic cord 608.89
spinal ligament 724.8
spleen — *see* Splenomegaly
spondylitis (spine) (*see also* Spondylosis) 721.90
stomach 537.89
subaortic stenosis (idiopathic) 425.1
sublingual gland 527.1
congenital 750.26
submaxillary gland 527.1
suprarenal (gland) 255.8
tendon 727.9
testis 608.89
congenital 752.89
thymic, thymus (congenital) (gland) 254.0
thyroid (gland) (*see also* Goiter) 240.9
primary 242.0 ☑
secondary 242.2 ☑
toe (congenital) 755.65
acquired 735.8
tongue 529.8
congenital 750.15
frenum 529.8
papillae (foliate) 529.3
tonsil (faucial) (infective) (lingual) (lymphoid) 474.11
with
adenoiditis 474.01
tonsillitis 474.00
and adenoiditis 474.02
and adenoids 474.10
tunica vaginalis 608.89
turbinate (mucous membrane) 478.0
ureter 593.89

Hypertrophy, hypertrophic — *continued*
urethra 599.84
uterus 621.2
puerperal, postpartum 674.8 ☑
uvula 528.9
vagina 623.8
vas deferens 608.89
vein 459.89
ventricle, ventricular (heart) (left) (right) (*see also* Hypertrophy, cardiac)
congenital 746.89
due to hypertension (left) (right) (*see also* Hypertension, heart) 402.90
benign 402.10
malignant 402.00
right with ventricular septal defect, pulmonary stenosis or atresia, and dextraposition of aorta 745.2
verumontanum 599.89
vesical 596.8
vocal cord 478.5
vulva 624.3
stasis (nonfilarial) 624.3
Hypertropia (intermittent) (periodic) 378.31
Hypertyrosinemia 270.2
Hyperuricemia 790.6
Hypervalinemia 270.3
Hyperventilation (tetany) 786.01
hysterical 300.11
psychogenic 306.1
syndrome 306.1
Hyperviscidosis 277.00
Hyperviscosity (of serum) (syndrome) NEC 273.3
polycythemic 289.0
sclerocythemic 282.8
Hypervitaminosis (dietary) NEC 278.8
A (dietary) 278.2
D (dietary) 278.4
from excessive administration or use of vitamin preparations (chronic) 278.8
reaction to sudden overdose 963.5
vitamin A 278.2
reaction to sudden overdose 963.5
vitamin D 278.4
reaction to sudden overdose 963.5
vitamin K
correct substance properly administered 278.8
overdose or wrong substance given or taken 964.3
Hypervolemia 276.6
Hypesthesia — *see also* Disturbance, sensation 782.0
cornea 371.81
Hyphema (anterior chamber) (ciliary body) (iris) 364.41
traumatic 921.3
Hyphemia — *see* Hyphema
Hypoacidity, gastric 536.8
psychogenic 306.4
Hypoactive labyrinth (function) — *see* Hypofunction, labyrinth
Hypoadrenalism 255.41
tuberculous (*see also* Tuberculosis) 017.6 ☑
Hypoadrenocorticism 255.41
pituitary 253.4
Hypoalbuminemia 273.8
Hypoaldosteronism 255.42
Hypoalphalipoproteinemia 272.5
Hypobarism 993.2
Hypobaropathy 993.2
Hypobetalipoproteinemia (familial) 272.5
Hypocalcemia 275.41
cow's milk 775.4
dietary 269.3
Hypocalcemia — *continued*
neonatal 775.4
phosphate-loading 775.4
Hypocalcification, teeth 520.4
Hypochloremia 276.9
Hypochlorhydria 536.8
neurotic 306.4
psychogenic 306.4
Hypocholesteremia 272.5
Hypochondria (reaction) 300.7
Hypochondriac 300.7
Hypochondriasis 300.7
Hypochromasia blood cells 280.9
Hypochromic anemia 280.9
due to blood loss (chronic) 280.0
acute 285.1
microcytic 280.9
Hypocoagulability — *see also* Defect, coagulation 286.9
Hypocomplementemia 279.8
Hypocythemia (progressive) 284.9
Hypodontia — *see also* Anodontia 520.0
Hypoeosinophilia 288.59
Hypoesthesia — *see also* Disturbance, sensation 782.0
cornea 371.81
tactile 782.0
Hypoestrinism 256.39
Hypoestrogenism 256.39
Hypoferremia 280.9
due to blood loss (chronic) 280.0
Hypofertility
female 628.9
male 606.1
Hypofibrinogenemia 286.3
acquired 286.6
congenital 286.3
Hypofunction
adrenal (gland) 255.41
cortex 255.41
medulla 255.5
specified NEC 255.5
cerebral 331.9
corticoadrenal NEC 255.41
intestinal 564.89
labyrinth (unilateral) 386.53
with loss of labyrinthine reactivity 386.55
bilateral 386.54
with loss of labyrinthine reactivity 386.56
Leydig cell 257.2
ovary 256.39
postablative 256.2
pituitary (anterior) (gland) (lobe) 253.2
posterior 253.5
testicular 257.2
iatrogenic 257.1
postablative 257.1
postirradiation 257.1
postsurgical 257.1
Hypogammaglobulinemia 279.00
acquired primary 279.06
non-sex-linked, congenital 279.06
sporadic 279.06
transient of infancy 279.09
Hypogenitalism (congenital) (female) (male) 752.89
penis 752.69
Hypoglycemia (spontaneous) 251.2
coma 251.0
diabetic 250.3 ☑
due to secondary diabetes 249.3 ☑
diabetic 250.8 ☑
due to secondary diabetes 249.8 ☑
due to insulin 251.0
therapeutic misadventure 962.3
familial (idiopathic) 251.2
following gastrointestinal surgery 579.3
infantile (idiopathic) 251.2
in infant of diabetic mother 775.0
leucine-induced 270.3
neonatal 775.6
reactive 251.2
Hypoglycemia — *continued*
specified NEC 251.1
Hypoglycemic shock 251.0
diabetic 250.8 ☑
due to secondary diabetes 249.8 ☑
due to insulin 251.0
functional (syndrome) 251.1
Hypogonadism
female 256.39
gonadotrophic (isolated) 253.4
hypogonadotropic (isolated) (with anosmia) 253.4
isolated 253.4
male 257.2
hereditary familial (Reifenstein's syndrome) 259.52
ovarian (primary) 256.39
pituitary (secondary) 253.4
testicular (primary) (secondary) 257.2
Hypohidrosis 705.0
Hypohidrotic ectodermal dysplasia 757.31
Hypoidrosis 705.0
Hypoinsulinemia, postsurgical 251.3
postpancreatectomy (complete) (partial) 251.3
Hypokalemia 276.8
Hypokinesia 780.99
Hypoleukia splenica 289.4
Hypoleukocytosis 288.50
Hypolipidemia 272.5
Hypolipoproteinemia 272.5
Hypomagnesemia 275.2
neonatal 775.4
Hypomania, hypomanic reaction — *see also* Psychosis, affective 296.0 ☑
recurrent episode 296.1 ☑
single episode 296.0 ☑
Hypomastia (congenital) 611.82
Hypomenorrhea 626.1
Hypometabolism 783.9
Hypomotility
gastrointestinal tract 536.8
psychogenic 306.4
intestine 564.89
psychogenic 306.4
stomach 536.8
psychogenic 306.4
Hyponasality 784.49
Hyponatremia 276.1
Hypo-ovarianism 256.39
Hypo-ovarism 256.39
Hypoparathyroidism (idiopathic) (surgically induced) 252.1
neonatal 775.4
Hypopharyngitis 462
Hypophoria 378.40
Hypophosphatasia 275.3
Hypophosphatemia (acquired) (congenital) (familial) 275.3
renal 275.3
Hypophyseal, hypophysis — *see also* condition
dwarfism 253.3
gigantism 253.0
syndrome 253.8
Hypophyseothalamic syndrome 253.8
Hypopiesis — *see* Hypotension
Hypopigmentation 709.00
eyelid 374.53
Hypopinealism 259.8
Hypopituitarism (juvenile) (syndrome) 253.2
due to
hormone therapy 253.7
hypophysectomy 253.7
radiotherapy 253.7
postablative 253.7
postpartum hemorrhage 253.2
Hypoplasia, hypoplasis 759.89
adrenal (gland) 759.1
alimentary tract 751.8
lower 751.2
upper 750.8
anus, anal (canal) 751.2
aorta 747.22
Hypoplasia, hypoplasis — *continued*
aortic
arch (tubular) 747.10
orifice or valve with hypoplasia of ascending aorta and defective development of left ventricle (with mitral valve atresia) 746.7
appendix 751.2
areola 757.6
arm (*see also* Absence, arm, congenital) 755.20
artery (congenital) (peripheral) 747.60
brain 747.81
cerebral 747.81
coronary 746.85
gastrointestinal 747.61
lower limb 747.64
pulmonary 747.3
renal 747.62
retinal 743.58
specified NEC 747.69
spinal 747.82
umbilical 747.5
upper limb 747.63
auditory canal 744.29
causing impairment of hearing 744.02
biliary duct (common) or passage 751.61
bladder 753.8
bone NEC 756.9
face 756.0
malar 756.0
mandible 524.04
alveolar 524.74
marrow 284.9
acquired (secondary) 284.89
congenital 284.09
idiopathic 284.9
maxilla 524.03
alveolar 524.73
skull (*see also* Hypoplasia, skull) 756.0
brain 742.1
gyri 742.2
specified part 742.2
breast (areola) 611.82
bronchus (tree) 748.3
cardiac 746.89
valve — *see* Hypoplasia, heart, valve
vein 746.89
carpus (*see also* Absence, carpal, congenital) 755.28
cartilaginous 756.9
cecum 751.2
cementum 520.4
hereditary 520.5
cephalic 742.1
cerebellum 742.2
cervix (uteri) 752.49
chin 524.06
clavicle 755.51
coccyx 756.19
colon 751.2
corpus callosum 742.2
cricoid cartilage 748.3
dermal, focal (Goltz) 757.39
digestive organ(s) or tract NEC 751.8
lower 751.2
upper 750.8
ear 744.29
auricle 744.23
lobe 744.29
middle, except ossicles 744.03
ossicles 744.04
ossicles 744.04
enamel of teeth (neonatal) (postnatal) (prenatal) 520.4
hereditary 520.5
endocrine (gland) NEC 759.2
endometrium 621.8
epididymis 752.89
epiglottis 748.3
erythroid, congenital 284.01

Hypoplasia, hypoplasis — *continued*
  erythropoietic, chronic acquired 284.81
  esophagus 750.3
  Eustachian tube 744.24
  eye (*see also* Microphthalmos) 743.10
    lid 743.62
  face 744.89
    bone(s) 756.0
  fallopian tube 752.19
  femur (*see also* Absence, femur, congenital) 755.34
  fibula (*see also* Absence, fibula, congenital) 755.37
  finger (*see also* Absence, finger, congenital) 755.29
  focal dermal 757.39
  foot 755.31
  gallbladder 751.69
  genitalia, genital organ(s)
    female 752.89
      external 752.49
      internal NEC 752.89
    in adiposogenital dystrophy 253.8
    male 752.89
      penis 752.69
  glottis 748.3
  hair 757.4
  hand 755.21
  heart 746.89
    left (complex) (syndrome) 746.7
    valve NEC 746.89
      pulmonary 746.01
  humerus (*see also* Absence, humerus, congenital) 755.24
  hymen 752.49
  intestine (small) 751.1
    large 751.2
  iris 743.46
  jaw 524.09
  kidney(s) 753.0
  labium (majus) (minus) 752.49
  labyrinth, membranous 744.05
  lacrimal duct (apparatus) 743.65
  larynx 748.3
  leg (*see also* Absence, limb, congenital, lower) 755.30
  limb 755.4
    lower (*see also* Absence, limb, congenital, lower) 755.30
    upper (*see also* Absence, limb, congenital, upper) 755.20
  liver 751.69
  lung (lobe) 748.5
  mammary (areolar) 611.82
  mandibular 524.04
    alveolar 524.74
    unilateral condylar 526.89
  maxillary 524.03
    alveolar 524.73
  medullary 284.9
  megakaryocytic 287.30
  metacarpus (*see also* Absence, metacarpal, congenital) 755.28
  metatarsus (*see also* Absence, metatarsal, congenital) 755.38
  muscle 756.89
    eye 743.69
  myocardium (congenital) (Uhl's anomaly) 746.84
  nail(s) 757.5
  nasolacrimal duct 743.65
  nervous system NEC 742.8
  neural 742.8
  nose, nasal 748.1
  ophthalmic (*see also* Microphthalmos) 743.10
  optic nerve 377.43
  organ
    of Corti 744.05
    or site NEC — *see* Anomaly, by site
  osseous meatus (ear) 744.03
  ovary 752.0
  oviduct 752.19

Hypoplasia, hypoplasis — *continued*
  pancreas 751.7
  parathyroid (gland) 759.2
  parotid gland 750.26
  patella 755.64
  pelvis, pelvic girdle 755.69
  penis 752.69
  peripheral vascular system (congenital) NEC 747.60
    gastrointestinal 747.61
    lower limb 747.64
    renal 747.62
    specified NEC 747.69
    spinal 747.82
    upper limb 747.63
  pituitary (gland) 759.2
  pulmonary 748.5
    arteriovenous 747.3
    artery 747.3
    valve 746.01
  punctum lacrimale 743.65
  radioulnar (*see also* Absence, radius, congenital, with ulna) 755.25
  radius (*see also* Absence, radius, congenital) 755.26
  rectum 751.2
  respiratory system NEC 748.9
  rib 756.3
  sacrum 756.19
  scapula 755.59
  shoulder girdle 755.59
  skin 757.39
  skull (bone) 756.0
    with
      anencephalus 740.0
      encephalocele 742.0
      hydrocephalus 742.3
        with spina bifida (*see also* Spina bifida) 741.0 ☑
      microcephalus 742.1
  spinal (cord) (ventral horn cell) 742.59
    vessel 747.82
  spine 756.19
  spleen 759.0
  sternum 756.3
  tarsus (*see also* Absence, tarsal, congenital) 755.38
  testis, testicle 752.89
  thymus (gland) 279.11
  thyroid (gland) 243
    cartilage 748.3
  tibiofibular (*see also* Absence, tibia, congenital, with fibula) 755.35
  toe (*see also* Absence, toe, congenital) 755.39
  tongue 750.16
  trachea (cartilage) (rings) 748.3
  Turner's (tooth) 520.4
  ulna (*see also* Absence, ulna, congenital) 755.27
  umbilical artery 747.5
  ureter 753.29
  uterus 752.3
  vagina 752.49
  vascular (peripheral) NEC (*see also* Hypoplasia, peripheral vascular system) 747.60
    brain 747.81
  vein(s) (peripheral) NEC (*see also* Hypoplasia, peripheral vascular system) 747.60
    brain 747.81
    cardiac 746.89
    great 747.49
    portal 747.49
    pulmonary 747.49
  vena cava (inferior) (superior) 747.49
  vertebra 756.19
  vulva 752.49
  zonule (ciliary) 743.39
  zygoma 738.12
Hypopotassemia 276.8
Hypoproaccelerinemia — *see also* Defect, coagulation 286.3
Hypoproconvertinemia (congenital) — *see also* Defect, coagulation 286.3
Hypoproteinemia (essential) (hypermetabolic) (idiopathic) 273.8
Hypoproteinosis 260
Hypoprothrombinemia (congenital) (hereditary) (idiopathic) — *see also* Defect, coagulation 286.3
  acquired 286.7
  newborn 776.3
Hypopselaphesia 782.0
Hypopyon (anterior chamber) (eye) 364.05
  iritis 364.05
  ulcer (cornea) 370.04
Hypopyrexia 780.99
Hyporeflex 796.1
Hyporeninemia, extreme 790.99
  in primary aldosteronism 255.10
Hyporesponsive episode 780.09
Hyposecretion
  ACTH 253.4
  ovary 256.39
    postablative 256.2
  salivary gland (any) 527.7
Hyposegmentation of neutrophils, hereditary 288.2
Hyposiderinemia 280.9
Hyposmolality 276.1
  syndrome 276.1
Hyposomatotropism 253.3
Hyposomnia, unspecified — *see also* Insomnia 780.52
  with sleep apnea, unspecified 780.51
Hypospadias (male) 752.61
  female 753.8
Hypospermatogenesis 606.1
Hyposphagma 372.72
Hyposplenism 289.59
Hypostasis, pulmonary 514
Hypostatic — *see* condition
Hyposthenuria 593.89
Hyposuprarenalism 255.41
Hypo-TBG-nemia 246.8
Hypotension (arterial) (constitutional) 458.9
  chronic 458.1
  iatrogenic 458.29
  maternal, syndrome (following labor and delivery) 669.2 ☑
  of hemodialysis 458.21
  orthostatic (chronic) 458.0
    dysautonomic-dyskinetic syndrome 333.0
  permanent idiopathic 458.1
  postoperative 458.29
  postural 458.0
  specified type NEC 458.8
  transient 796.3
Hypothermia (accidental) 991.6
  anesthetic 995.89
  associated with low environmental temperature 991.6
  newborn NEC 778.3
  not associated with low environmental temperature 780.65
Hypothymergasia — *see also* Psychosis, affective 296.2 ☑
  recurrent episode 296.3 ☑
  single episode 296.2 ☑
Hypothyroidism (acquired) 244.9
  complicating pregnancy, childbirth, or puerperium 648.1 ☑
  congenital 243
  due to
    ablation 244.1
      radioactive iodine 244.1
      surgical 244.0
    iodine (administration) (ingestion) 244.2
      radioactive 244.1
    irradiation therapy 244.1
    p-aminosalicylic acid (PAS) 244.3

Hypothyroidism — *continued*
  due to — *continued*
    phenylbutazone 244.3
    resorcinol 244.3
    specified cause NEC 244.8
    surgery 244.0
  goitrous (sporadic) 246.1
  iatrogenic NEC 244.3
  iodine 244.2
  pituitary 244.8
  postablative NEC 244.1
  postsurgical 244.0
  primary 244.9
  secondary NEC 244.8
  specified cause NEC 244.8
  sporadic goitrous 246.1
Hypotonia, hypotonicity, hypotony 781.3
  benign congenital 358.8
  bladder 596.4
  congenital 779.89
    benign 358.8
  eye 360.30
    due to
      fistula 360.32
      ocular disorder NEC 360.33
    following loss of aqueous or vitreous 360.33
    primary 360.31
  infantile muscular (benign) 359.0
  muscle 728.9
  uterus, uterine (contractions) — *see* Inertia, uterus
Hypotrichosis 704.09
  congenital 757.4
  lid (congenital) 757.4
    acquired 374.55
  postinfectional NEC 704.09
Hypotropia 378.32
Hypoventilation 786.09
  congenital central alveolar syndrome 327.25
  idiopathic sleep related nonobstructive alveolar 327.24
  sleep related, in conditions classifiable elsewhere 327.26
Hypovitaminosis — *see also* Deficiency, vitamin 269.2
Hypovolemia 276.52
  surgical shock 998.0
  traumatic (shock) 958.4
Hypoxemia — *see also* Anoxia 799.02
  sleep related, in conditions classifiable elsewhere 327.26
Hypoxia — *see also* Anoxia 799.02
  cerebral 348.1
    during or resulting from a procedure 997.01
    newborn 770.88
      mild or moderate 768.6
      severe 768.5
  fetal, affecting newborn 770.88
  intrauterine — *see* Distress, fetal
  myocardial (*see also* Insufficiency, coronary) 411.89
    arteriosclerotic — *see* Arteriosclerosis, coronary
  newborn 770.88
  sleep related 327.24
Hypoxic-ischemic encephalopathy (HIE) 768.7
Hypsarrhythmia — *see also* Epilepsy 345.6 ☑
Hysteralgia, pregnant uterus 646.8 ☑
Hysteria, hysterical 300.10
  anxiety 300.20
  Charcôt's gland 300.11
  conversion (any manifestation) 300.11
  dissociative type NEC 300.15
  psychosis, acute 298.1
Hysteroepilepsy 300.11
Hysterotomy, affecting fetus or newborn 763.89

I

Iatrogenic syndrome of excess cortisol 255.0
Iceland disease (epidemic neuromyasthenia) 049.8
Ichthyosis (congenita) 757.1
acquired 701.1
fetalis gravior 757.1
follicularis 757.1
hystrix 757.39
lamellar 757.1
lingual 528.6
palmaris and plantaris 757.39
simplex 757.1
vera 757.1
vulgaris 757.1
Ichthyotoxism 988.0
bacterial (*see also* Poisoning, food) 005.9
Icteroanemia, hemolytic (acquired) 283.9
congenital (*see also* Spherocytosis) 282.0
Icterus — *see also* Jaundice 782.4
catarrhal — *see* Icterus, infectious
conjunctiva 782.4
newborn 774.6
epidemic — *see* Icterus, infectious
febrilis — *see* Icterus, infectious
fetus or newborn — *see* Jaundice, fetus or newborn
gravis (*see also* Necrosis, liver) 570
complicating pregnancy 646.7 ☑
affecting fetus or newborn 760.8
fetus or newborn NEC 773.0
obstetrical 646.7 ☑
affecting fetus or newborn 760.8
hematogenous (acquired) 283.9
hemolytic (acquired) 283.9
congenital (*see also* Spherocytosis) 282.0
hemorrhagic (acute) 100.0
leptospiral 100.0
newborn 776.0
spirochetal 100.0
infectious 070.1
with hepatic coma 070.0
leptospiral 100.0
spirochetal 100.0
intermittens juvenilis 277.4
malignant (*see also* Necrosis, liver) 570
neonatorum (*see also* Jaundice, fetus or newborn) 774.6
pernicious (*see also* Necrosis, liver) 570
spirochetal 100.0
Ictus solaris, solis 992.0
Ideation
suicidal V62.84
Identity disorder 313.82
dissociative 300.14
gender role (child) 302.6
adult 302.85
psychosexual (child) 302.6
adult 302.85
Idioglossia 307.9
Idiopathic — *see* condition
Idiosyncrasy — *see also* Allergy 995.3
drug, medicinal substance, and biological — *see* Allergy, drug
Idiot, idiocy (congenital) 318.2
amaurotic (Bielschowsky) (-Jansky) (family) (infantile (late)) (juvenile (late)) (Vogt-Spielmeyer) 330.1
microcephalic 742.1
Mongolian 758.0
oxycephalic 756.0
Id reaction (due to bacteria) 692.89
IEED (involuntary emotional expression disorder) 310.8
IFIS (intraoperative floppy iris syndrome) 364.81
IgE asthma 493.0 ☑
Ileitis (chronic) — *see also* Enteritis 558.9
Ileitis — *see also* Enteritis — *continued*
infectious 009.0
noninfectious 558.9
regional (ulcerative) 555.0
with large intestine 555.2
segmental 555.0
with large intestine 555.2
terminal (ulcerative) 555.0
with large intestine 555.2
Ileocolitis — *see also* Enteritis 558.9
infectious 009.0
regional 555.2
ulcerative 556.1
Ileostomy status V44.2
with complication 569.60
Ileotyphus 002.0
Ileum — *see* condition
Ileus (adynamic) (bowel) (colon) (inhibitory) (intestine) (neurogenic) (paralytic) 560.1
arteriomesenteric duodenal 537.2
due to gallstone (in intestine) 560.31
duodenal, chronic 537.2
following gastrointestinal surgery 997.4
gallstone 560.31
mechanical (*see also* Obstruction, intestine) 560.9
meconium 777.1
due to cystic fibrosis 277.01
myxedema 564.89
postoperative 997.4
transitory, newborn 777.4
Iliac — *see* condition
Iliotibial band friction syndrome 728.89
Illegitimacy V61.6
Ill, louping 063.1
Illness — *see also* Disease
factitious 300.19
with
combined psychological and physical signs and symptoms 300.19
predominantly
physical signs and symptoms 300.19
psychological symptoms 300.16
chronic (with physical symptoms) 301.51
heart — *see* Disease, heart
manic-depressive (*see also* Psychosis, affective) 296.80
mental (*see also* Disorder, mental) 300.9
Imbalance 781.2
autonomic (*see also* Neuropathy, peripheral, autonomic) 337.9
electrolyte 276.9
with
abortion — *see* Abortion, by type, with metabolic disorder
ectopic pregnancy (*see also* categories 633.0–633.9) 639.4
hyperemesis gravidarum (before 22 completed weeks gestation) 643.1 ☑
molar pregnancy (*see also* categories 630–632) 639.4
following
abortion 639.4
ectopic or molar pregnancy 639.4
neonatal, transitory NEC 775.5
endocrine 259.9
eye muscle NEC 378.9
heterophoria — *see* Heterophoria
glomerulotubular NEC 593.89
hormone 259.9
hysterical (*see also* Hysteria) 300.10
labyrinth NEC 386.50
posture 729.90
Imbalance — *continued*
sympathetic (*see also* Neuropathy, peripheral, autonomic) 337.9
Imbecile, imbecility 318.0
moral 301.7
old age 290.9
senile 290.9
specified IQ — *see* IQ
unspecified IQ 318.0
Imbedding, intrauterine device 996.32
Imbibition, cholesterol (gallbladder) 575.6
Imerslund (-Gräsbeck) syndrome (anemia due to familial selective vitamin B_{12} malabsorption) 281.1
Iminoacidopathy 270.8
Iminoglycinuria, familial 270.8
Immature — *see also* Immaturity
personality 301.89
Immaturity 765.1 ☑
extreme 765.0 ☑
fetus or infant light-for-dates — *see* Light-for-dates
lung, fetus or newborn 770.4
organ or site NEC — *see* Hypoplasia
pulmonary, fetus or newborn 770.4
reaction 301.89
sexual (female) (male) 259.0
Immersion 994.1
foot 991.4
hand 991.4
Immobile, immobility
complete
due to severe physical disability or frailty 780.72
intestine 564.89
joint — *see* Ankylosis
syndrome (paraplegic) 728.3
Immunization
ABO
affecting management of pregnancy 656.2 ☑
fetus or newborn 773.1
complication — *see* Complications, vaccination
Rh factor
affecting management of pregnancy 656.1 ☑
fetus or newborn 773.0
from transfusion 999.7
Immunodeficiency 279.3
with
adenosine-deaminase deficiency 279.2
defect, predominant
B-cell 279.00
T-cell 279.10
hyperimmunoglobulinemia 279.2
lymphopenia, hereditary 279.2
thrombocytopenia and eczema 279.12
thymic
aplasia 279.2
dysplasia 279.2
autosomal recessive, Swiss-type 279.2
common variable 279.06
severe combined (SCID) 279.2
to Rh factor
affecting management of pregnancy 656.1 ☑
fetus or newborn 773.0
X-linked, with increased IgM 279.05
Immunotherapy, prophylactic V07.2
antineoplastic V58.12
Impaction, impacted
bowel, colon, rectum 560.30
with hernia (*see also* Hernia, by site, with obstruction)
gangrenous — *see* Hernia, by site, with gangrene
by
calculus 560.39
gallstone 560.31
fecal 560.39
specified type NEC 560.39
calculus — *see* Calculus
Impaction, impacted — *continued*
cerumen (ear) (external) 380.4
cuspid 520.6
dental 520.6
fecal, feces 560.39
with hernia (*see also* Hernia, by site, with obstruction)
gangrenous — *see* Hernia, by site, with gangrene
fracture — *see* Fracture, by site
gallbladder — *see* Cholelithiasis
gallstone(s) — *see* Cholelithiasis
in intestine (any part) 560.31
intestine(s) 560.30
with hernia (*see also* Hernia, by site, with obstruction)
gangrenous — *see* Hernia, by site, with gangrene
by
calculus 560.39
gallstone 560.31
fecal 560.39
specified type NEC 560.39
intrauterine device (IUD) 996.32
molar 520.6
shoulder 660.4 ☑
affecting fetus or newborn 763.1
tooth, teeth 520.6
turbinate 733.99
Impaired, impairment (function)
arm V49.1
movement, involving
musculoskeletal system V49.1
nervous system V49.2
auditory discrimination 388.43
back V48.3
body (entire) V49.89
cognitive, mild, so stated 331.83
combined visual hearing V49.85
dual sensory V49.85
glucose
fasting 790.21
tolerance test (oral) 790.22
hearing (*see also* Deafness) 389.9
combined with visual impairment V49.85
heart — *see* Disease, heart
kidney (*see also* Disease, renal) 593.9
disorder resulting from 588.9
specified NEC 588.89
leg V49.1
movement, involving
musculoskeletal system V49.1
nervous system V49.2
limb V49.1
movement, involving
musculoskeletal system V49.1
nervous system V49.2
liver 573.8
mastication 524.9
mild cognitive, so stated 331.83
mobility
ear ossicles NEC 385.22
incostapedial joint 385.22
malleus 385.21
myocardium, myocardial (*see also* Insufficiency, myocardial) 428.0
neuromusculoskeletal NEC V49.89
back V48.3
head V48.2
limb V49.2
neck V48.3
spine V48.3
trunk V48.3
rectal sphincter 787.99
renal (*see also* Disease, renal) 593.9
disorder resulting from 588.9
specified NEC 588.89
spine V48.3
vision NEC 369.9
both eyes NEC 369.3
combined with hearing impairment V49.85
moderate 369.74
both eyes 369.25

Inadequate, inadequacy — *continued*
pulmonary — *continued*
ventilation, newborn 770.89
respiration 786.09
newborn 770.89
sample
cytology
anal 796.78
cervical 795.08
vaginal 795.18
social 301.6
Inanition 263.9
with edema 262
due to
deprivation of food 994.2
malnutrition 263.9
fever 780.60
Inappropriate secretion
ACTH 255.0
antidiuretic hormone (ADH) (excessive) 253.6
deficiency 253.5
ectopic hormone NEC 259.3
pituitary (posterior) 253.6
Inattention after or at birth 995.52
Inborn errors of metabolism — *see* Disorder, metabolism
Incarceration, incarcerated
bubonocele (*see also* Hernia, inguinal, with obstruction)
gangrenous — *see* Hernia, inguinal, with gangrene
colon (by hernia) (*see also* Hernia, by site with obstruction)
gangrenous — *see* Hernia, by site, with gangrene
enterocele 552.9
gangrenous 551.9
epigastrocele 552.29
gangrenous 551.29
epiplocele 552.9
gangrenous 551.9
exomphalos 552.1
gangrenous 551.1
fallopian tube 620.8
hernia (*see also* Hernia, by site, with obstruction)
gangrenous — *see* Hernia, by site, with gangrene
iris, in wound 871.1
lens, in wound 871.1
merocele (*see also* Hernia, femoral, with obstruction) 552.00
omentum (by hernia) (*see also* Hernia, by site, with obstruction)
gangrenous — *see* Hernia, by site, with gangrene
omphalocele 756.79
rupture (meaning hernia) (*see also* Hernia, by site, with obstruction) 552.9
gangrenous (*see also* Hernia, by site, with gangrene) 551.9
sarcoepiplocele 552.9
gangrenous 551.9
sarcoepiplomphalocele 552.1
with gangrene 551.1
uterus 621.8
gravid 654.3 ☑
causing obstructed labor 660.2 ☑
affecting fetus or newborn 763.1
Incident, cerebrovascular — *see also* Disease, cerebrovascular, acute 436
Incineration (entire body) (from fire, conflagration, electricity, or lightning) — *see* Burn, multiple, specified sites
Incised wound
external — *see* Wound, open, by site
internal organs (abdomen, chest, or pelvis) — *see* Injury, internal, by site, with open wound
Incision, incisional
hernia — *see* Hernia, incisional
surgical, complication — *see* Complications, surgical procedures
traumatic
external — *see* Wound, open, by site
internal organs (abdomen, chest, or pelvis) — *see* Injury, internal, by site, with open wound
Inclusion
azurophilic leukocytic 288.2
blennorrhea (neonatal) (newborn) 771.6
cyst — *see* Cyst, skin
gallbladder in liver (congenital) 751.69
Incompatibility
ABO
affecting management of pregnancy 656.2 ☑
fetus or newborn 773.1
infusion or transfusion reaction 999.6
blood (group) (Duffy) (E) (K(ell)) (Kidd) (Lewis) (M) (N) (P) (S) NEC
affecting management of pregnancy 656.2 ☑
fetus or newborn 773.2
infusion or transfusion reaction 999.6
contour of existing restoration of tooth with oral health 525.65
marital V61.10
involving
divorce V61.03
estrangement V61.09
Rh (blood group) (factor)
affecting management of pregnancy 656.1 ☑
fetus or newborn 773.0
infusion or transfusion reaction 999.7
Rhesus — *see* Incompatibility, Rh
Incompetency, incompetence, incompetent
annular
aortic (valve) (*see also* Insufficiency, aortic) 424.1
mitral (valve) (*see also* Insufficiency, mitral) 424.0
pulmonary valve (heart) (*see also* Endocarditis, pulmonary) 424.3
aortic (valve) (*see also* Insufficiency, aortic) 424.1
syphilitic 093.22
cardiac (orifice) 530.0
valve — *see* Endocarditis
cervix, cervical (os) 622.5
in pregnancy 654.5 ☑
affecting fetus or newborn 761.0
chronotropic 426.89
with
autonomic dysfunction 337.9
ischemic heart disease 414.9
left ventricular dysfunction 429.89
sinus node dysfunction 427.81
esophagogastric (junction) (sphincter) 530.0
heart valve, congenital 746.89
mitral (valve) — *see* Insufficiency, mitral
papillary muscle (heart) 429.81
pelvic fundus
pubocervical tissue 618.81
rectovaginal tissue 618.82
pulmonary valve (heart) (*see also* Endocarditis, pulmonary) 424.3
congenital 746.09
tricuspid (annular) (rheumatic) (valve) (*see also* Endocarditis, tricuspid) 397.0
valvular — *see* Endocarditis
vein, venous (saphenous) (varicose) (*see also* Varicose, vein) 454.9
Incompetency, incompetence, incompetent — *continued*
velopharyngeal (closure)
acquired 528.9
congenital 750.29
Incomplete — *see also* condition
bladder emptying 788.21
expansion lungs (newborn) 770.5
gestation (liveborn) — *see* Immaturity
rotation — *see* Malrotation
Incontinence 788.30
without sensory awareness 788.34
anal sphincter 787.6
continuous leakage 788.37
feces 787.6
due to hysteria 300.11
nonorganic origin 307.7
hysterical 300.11
mixed (male) (female) (urge and stress) 788.33
overflow 788.38
paradoxical 788.39
rectal 787.6
specified NEC 788.39
stress (female) 625.6
male NEC 788.32
urethral sphincter 599.84
urge 788.31
and stress (male) (female) 788.33
urine 788.30
active 788.30
due to
cognitive impairment 788.91
immobility 788.91
severe physical disability 788.91
functional 788.91
male 788.30
stress 788.32
and urge 788.33
neurogenic 788.39
nonorganic origin 307.6
stress (female) 625.6
male NEC 788.32
urge 788.31
and stress 788.33
Incontinentia pigmenti 757.33
Incoordinate
uterus (action) (contractions) 661.4 ☑
affecting fetus or newborn 763.7
Incoordination
esophageal-pharyngeal (newborn) 787.24
muscular 781.3
papillary muscle 429.81
Increase, increased
abnormal, in development 783.9
androgens (ovarian) 256.1
anticoagulants (antithrombin) (anti-VIIIa) (anti-IXa) (anti-Xa) (anti-XIa) 286.5
postpartum 666.3 ☑
cold sense (*see also* Disturbance, sensation) 782.0
estrogen 256.0
function
adrenal (cortex) 255.3
medulla 255.6
pituitary (anterior) (gland) (lobe) 253.1
posterior 253.6
heat sense (*see also* Disturbance, sensation) 782.0
intracranial pressure 781.99
injury at birth 767.8
light reflex of retina 362.13
permeability, capillary 448.9
pressure
intracranial 781.99
injury at birth 767.8
intraocular 365.00
pulsations 785.9
pulse pressure 785.9
sphericity, lens 743.36
splenic activity 289.4
venous pressure 459.89
portal 572.3
Incrustation, cornea, lead or zinc 930.0
Incyclophoria 378.44
Incyclotropia 378.33
Indeterminate sex 752.7
India rubber skin 756.83
Indicanuria 270.2
Indigestion (bilious) (functional) 536.8
acid 536.8
catarrhal 536.8
due to decomposed food NEC 005.9
fat 579.8
nervous 306.4
psychogenic 306.4
Indirect — *see* condition
Indolent bubo NEC 099.8
Induced
abortion — *see* Abortion, induced
birth, affecting fetus or newborn 763.89
delivery — *see* Delivery
labor — *see* Delivery
Induration, indurated
brain 348.8
breast (fibrous) 611.79
puerperal, postpartum 676.3 ☑
broad ligament 620.8
chancre 091.0
anus 091.1
congenital 090.0
extragenital NEC 091.2
corpora cavernosa (penis) (plastic) 607.89
liver (chronic) 573.8
acute 573.8
lung (black) (brown) (chronic) (fibroid) (*see also* Fibrosis, lung) 515
essential brown 275.0 *[516.1]*
penile 607.89
phlebitic — *see* Phlebitis
skin 782.8
stomach 537.89
Induratio penis plastica 607.89
Industrial — *see* condition
Inebriety — *see also* Abuse, drugs, nondependent 305.0 ☑
Inefficiency
kidney (*see also* Disease, renal) 593.9
thyroid (acquired) (gland) 244.9
Inelasticity, skin 782.8
Inequality, leg (acquired) (length) 736.81
congenital 755.30
Inertia
bladder 596.4
neurogenic 596.54
with cauda equina syndrome 344.61
stomach 536.8
psychogenic 306.4
uterus, uterine 661.2 ☑
affecting fetus or newborn 763.7
primary 661.0 ☑
secondary 661.1 ☑
vesical 596.4
neurogenic 596.54
with cauda equina 344.61
Infant — *see also* condition
excessive crying of 780.92
fussy (baby) 780.91
held for adoption V68.89
newborn — *see* Newborn
post-term (gestation period over 40 completed weeks to 42 completed weeks) 766.21
prolonged gestation of (period over 42 completed weeks) 766.22
syndrome of diabetic mother 775.0
"Infant Hercules" syndrome 255.2
Infantile — *see also* condition
genitalia, genitals 259.0
in pregnancy or childbirth NEC 654.4 ☑
affecting fetus or newborn 763.89
causing obstructed labor 660.2 ☑

Infantile — *see also* condition — *continued*
- genitalia, genitals — *continued*
  - in pregnancy or childbirth — *continued*
    - causing obstructed labor — *continued*
      - affecting fetus or newborn 763.1
- heart 746.9
- kidney 753.3
- lack of care 995.52
- macula degeneration 362.75
- melanodontia 521.05
- os, uterus (*see also* Infantile, genitalia) 259.0
- pelvis 738.6
  - with disproportion (fetopelvic) 653.1 ☑
    - affecting fetus or newborn 763.1
    - causing obstructed labor 660.1 ☑
      - affecting fetus or newborn 763.1
- penis 259.0
- testis 257.2
- uterus (*see also* Infantile, genitalia) 259.0
- vulva 752.49

Infantilism 259.9
- with dwarfism (hypophyseal) 253.3
- Brissaud's (infantile myxedema) 244.9
- celiac 579.0
- Herter's (nontropical sprue) 579.0
- hypophyseal 253.3
- hypothalamic (with obesity) 253.8
- idiopathic 259.9
- intestinal 579.0
- pancreatic 577.8
- pituitary 253.3
- renal 588.0
- sexual (with obesity) 259.0

Infants, healthy liveborn — *see* Newborn

Infarct, infarction
- adrenal (capsule) (gland) 255.41
- amnion 658.8 ☑
- anterior (with contiguous portion of intraventricular septum) NEC (*see also* Infarct, myocardium) 410.1 ☑
- appendices epiploicae 557.0
- bowel 557.0
- brain (stem) 434.91
  - embolic (*see also* Embolism, brain) 434.11
  - healed or old without residuals V12.54
  - iatrogenic 997.02
  - lacunar 434.91
  - late effect — *see* Late effect(s) (of) cerebrovascular disease
  - postoperative 997.02
  - puerperal, postpartum, childbirth 674.0 ☑
  - thrombotic (*see also* Thrombosis, brain) 434.01
- breast 611.89
- Brewer's (kidney) 593.81
- cardiac (*see also* Infarct, myocardium) 410.9 ☑
- cerebellar (*see also* Infarct, brain) 434.91
  - embolic (*see also* Embolism, brain) 434.11
- cerebral (*see also* Infarct, brain) 434.91
  - aborted 434.91
  - embolic (*see also* Embolism, brain) 434.11
  - thrombotic (*see also* Infarct, brain) 434.01
- chorion 658.8 ☑
- colon (acute) (agnogenic) (embolic) (hemorrhagic) (nonocclusive) (nonthrombotic) (occlusive) (segmental) (thrombotic) (with gangrene) 557.0
- coronary artery (*see also* Infarct, myocardium) 410.9 ☑
- cortical 434.91
- embolic (*see also* Embolism) 444.9
- fallopian tube 620.8
- gallbladder 575.8
- heart (*see also* Infarct, myocardium) 410.9 ☑
- hepatic 573.4
- hypophysis (anterior lobe) 253.8
- impending (myocardium) 411.1
- intestine (acute) (agnogenic) (embolic) (hemorrhagic) (nonocclusive) (nonthrombotic) (occlusive) (thrombotic) (with gangrene) 557.0
- kidney 593.81
- lacunar 434.91
- liver 573.4
- lung (embolic) (thrombotic) 415.19
  - with
    - abortion — *see* Abortion, by type, with, embolism
    - ectopic pregnancy (*see also* categories 633.0–633.9) 639.6
    - molar pregnancy (*see also* categories 630–632) 639.6
  - following
    - abortion 639.6
    - ectopic or molar pregnancy 639.6
  - iatrogenic 415.11
  - in pregnancy, childbirth, or puerperium — *see* Embolism, obstetrical
  - postoperative 415.11
  - septic 415.12
- lymph node or vessel 457.8
- medullary (brain) — *see* Infarct, brain
- meibomian gland (eyelid) 374.85
- mesentery, mesenteric (embolic) (thrombotic) (with gangrene) 557.0
- midbrain — *see* Infarct, brain
- myocardium, myocardial (acute or with a stated duration of 8 weeks or less) (with hypertension) 410.9 ☑

> Note — *Use the following fifth-digit subclassification with category 410:*
>
> *0 episode unspecified*
>
> *1 initial episode*
>
> *2 subsequent episode without recurrence*

  - with symptoms after 8 weeks from date of infarction 414.8
  - anterior (wall) (with contiguous portion of intraventricular septum) NEC 410.1 ☑
  - anteroapical (with contiguous portion of intraventricular septum) 410.1 ☑
  - anterolateral (wall) 410.0 ☑
  - anteroseptal (with contiguous portion of intraventricular septum) 410.1 ☑
  - apical-lateral 410.5 ☑
  - atrial 410.8 ☑
  - basal-lateral 410.5 ☑
  - chronic (with symptoms after 8 weeks from date of infarction) 414.8
  - diagnosed on ECG, but presenting no symptoms 412
  - diaphragmatic wall (with contiguous portion of intraventricular septum) 410.4 ☑
  - healed or old, currently presenting no symptoms 412
  - high lateral 410.5 ☑
  - impending 411.1
  - inferior (wall) (with contiguous portion of intraventricular septum) 410.4 ☑
  - inferolateral (wall) 410.2 ☑
  - inferoposterior wall 410.3 ☑
  - intraoperative 997.1
  - lateral wall 410.5 ☑
  - non-Q wave 410.7 ☑
  - non-ST elevation (NSTEMI)
  - nontransmural 410.7 ☑
  - papillary muscle 410.8 ☑
  - past (diagnosed on ECG or other special investigation, but currently presenting no symptoms) 412
    - with symptoms NEC 414.8
  - posterior (strictly) (true) (wall) 410.6 ☑
  - posterobasal 410.6 ☑
  - posteroinferior 410.3 ☑
  - posterolateral 410.5 ☑
  - postprocedural 997.1
  - previous, currently presenting no symptoms 412
  - Q wave (*see also* Infarct, myocardium, by site) 410.9 ☑
  - septal 410.8 ☑
  - specified site NEC 410.8 ☑
  - ST elevation (STEMI) 410.9 ☑
    - anterior (wall) 410.1 ☑
    - anterolateral (wall) 410.0 ☑
    - inferior (wall) 410.4 ☑
    - inferolateral (wall) 410.2 ☑
    - inferoposterior wall 410.3 ☑
    - lateral wall 410.5 ☑
    - posterior (strictly) (true) (wall) 410.6 ☑
    - specified site NEC 410.8 ☑
  - subendocardial 410.7 ☑
  - syphilitic 093.82
- non-ST elevation myocardial infarction (NSTEMI) 410.7 ☑
- nontransmural 410.7 ☑
- omentum 557.0
- ovary 620.8
- pancreas 577.8
- papillary muscle (*see also* Infarct, myocardium) 410.8 ☑
- parathyroid gland 252.8
- pituitary (gland) 253.8
- placenta (complicating pregnancy) 656.7 ☑
  - affecting fetus or newborn 762.2
- pontine — *see* Infarct, brain
- posterior NEC (*see also* Infarct, myocardium) 410.6 ☑
- prostate 602.8
- pulmonary (artery) (hemorrhagic) (vein) 415.19
  - with
    - abortion — *see* Abortion, by type, with embolism
    - ectopic pregnancy (*see also* categories 633.0–633.9) 639.6
    - molar pregnancy (*see also* categories 630–632) 639.6
  - following
    - abortion 639.6
    - ectopic or molar pregnancy 639.6
  - iatrogenic 415.11
  - in pregnancy, childbirth, or puerperium — *see* Embolism, obstetrical
  - postoperative 415.11
  - septic 415.12
- renal 593.81
  - embolic or thrombotic 593.81
- retina, retinal 362.84
  - with occlusion — *see* Occlusion, retina
- spinal (acute) (cord) (embolic) (nonembolic) 336.1
- spleen 289.59
  - embolic or thrombotic 444.89
- subchorionic — *see* Infarct, placenta
- subendocardial (*see also* Infarct, myocardium) 410.7 ☑
- suprarenal (capsule) (gland) 255.41
- syncytium — *see* Infarct, placenta
- testis 608.83
- thrombotic (*see also* Thrombosis) 453.9
  - artery, arterial — *see* Embolism
- thyroid (gland) 246.3
- ventricle (heart) (*see also* Infarct, myocardium) 410.9 ☑

Infecting — *see* condition

Infection, infected, infective (opportunistic) 136.9
- with lymphangitis — *see* Lymphangitis
- abortion — *see* Abortion, by type, with, sepsis
- abscess (skin) — *see* Abscess, by site
- Absidia 117.7
- acanthamoeba 136.21
- Acanthocheilonema (perstans) 125.4
  - streptocerca 125.6
- accessory sinus (chronic) (*see also* Sinusitis) 473.9
- Achorion — *see* Dermatophytosis
- Acremonium falciforme 117.4
- acromioclavicular (joint) 711.91
- actinobacillus
  - lignieresii 027.8
  - mallei 024
  - muris 026.1
- actinomadura — *see* Actinomycosis
- Actinomyces (israelii) (*see also* Actinomycosis)
  - muris-ratti 026.1
- Actinomycetales (actinomadura) (Actinomyces) (Nocardia) (Streptomyces) — *see* Actinomycosis
- actinomycotic NEC (*see also* Actinomycosis) 039.9
- adenoid (chronic) 474.01
  - acute 463
  - and tonsil (chronic) 474.02
    - acute or subacute 463
- adenovirus NEC 079.0
  - in diseases classified elsewhere — *see* category 079 ☑
  - unspecified nature or site 079.0
- Aerobacter aerogenes NEC 041.85
  - enteritis 008.2
- aerogenes capsulatus (*see also* Gangrene, gas) 040.0
- aertrycke (*see also* Infection, Salmonella) 003.9
- ajellomyces dermatitidis 116.0
- alimentary canal NEC (*see also* Enteritis, due to, by organism) 009.0
- Allescheria boydii 117.6
- Alternaria 118
- alveolus, alveolar (process) (pulpal origin) 522.4
- ameba, amebic (histolytica) (*see also* Amebiasis) 006.9
  - acute 006.0
  - chronic 006.1
  - free-living 136.29
  - hartmanni 007.8
  - specified
    - site NEC 006.8
    - type NEC 007.8
- amniotic fluid or cavity 658.4 ☑
  - affecting fetus or newborn 762.7
- anaerobes (cocci) (gram-negative) (gram-positive) (mixed) NEC 041.84

Infection, infected, infective — *continued*

- anal canal 569.49
- Ancylostoma braziliense 126.2
- Angiostrongylus cantonensis 128.8
- anisakiasis 127.1
- Anisakis larva 127.1
- anthrax (*see also* Anthrax) 022.9
- antrum (chronic) (*see also* Sinusitis, maxillary) 473.0
- anus (papillae) (sphincter) 569.49
- arbor virus NEC 066.9
- arbovirus NEC 066.9
- argentophil-rod 027.0
- Ascaris lumbricoides 127.0
- ascomycetes 117.4
- Aspergillus (flavus) (fumigatus) (terreus) 117.3
- atypical
  - acid-fast (bacilli) (*see also* Mycobacterium, atypical) 031.9
  - mycobacteria (*see also* Mycobacterium, atypical) 031.9
- auditory meatus (circumscribed) (diffuse) (external) (*see also* Otitis, externa) 380.10
- auricle (ear) (*see also* Otitis, externa) 380.10
- axillary gland 683
- Babesiasis 088.82
- Babesiosis 088.82
- Bacillus NEC 041.89
  - abortus 023.1
  - anthracis (*see also* Anthrax) 022.9
  - cereus (food poisoning) 005.89
  - coli — *see* Infection, Escherichia coli
  - coliform NEC 041.85
  - Ducrey's (any location) 099.0
  - Flexner's 004.1
  - Friedländer's NEC 041.3
  - fusiformis 101
  - gas (gangrene) (*see also* Gangrene, gas) 040.0
  - mallei 024
  - melitensis 023.0
  - paratyphoid, paratyphosus 002.9
    - A 002.1
    - B 002.2
    - C 002.3
  - Schmorl's 040.3
  - Shiga 004.0
  - suipestifer (*see also* Infection, Salmonella) 003.9
  - swimming pool 031.1
  - typhosa 002.0
  - welchii (*see also* Gangrene, gas) 040.0
  - Whitmore's 025
- bacterial NEC 041.9
  - specified NEC 041.89
    - anaerobic NEC 041.84
    - gram-negative NEC 041.85
      - anaerobic NEC 041.84
- Bacterium
  - paratyphosum 002.9
    - A 002.1
    - B 002.2
    - C 002.3
  - typhosum 002.0
- Bacteroides (fragilis) (melaninogenicus) (oralis) NEC 041.82
- balantidium coli 007.0
- Bartholin's gland 616.89
- Basidiobolus 117.7
- Bedsonia 079.98
  - specified NEC 079.88
- bile duct 576.1
- bladder (*see also* Cystitis) 595.9
- Blastomyces, blastomycotic 116.0
  - brasiliensis 116.1
  - dermatitidis 116.0
  - European 117.5
  - loboi 116.2
  - North American 116.0
  - South American 116.1
- bleb
  - postprocedural 379.60
    - stage 1 379.61
    - stage 2 379.62
    - stage 3 379.63
- blood stream — *see also* Septicemia
  - catheter-related (CRBSI) 999.31
- bone 730.9 ☑
  - specified — *see* Osteomyelitis
- Bordetella 033.9
  - bronchiseptica 033.8
  - parapertussis 033.1
  - pertussis 033.0
- Borrelia
  - bergdorfi 088.81
  - vincentii (mouth) (pharynx) (tonsil) 101
- bovine stomatitis 059.11
- brain (*see also* Encephalitis) 323.9
  - late effect — *see* category 326
  - membranes (*see also* Meningitis) 322.9
  - septic 324.0
    - late effect — *see* category 326
    - meninges (*see also* Meningitis) 320.9
- branchial cyst 744.42
- breast 611.0
  - puerperal, postpartum 675.2 ☑
    - with nipple 675.9 ☑
      - specified type NEC 675.8 ☑
    - nonpurulent 675.2 ☑
    - purulent 675.1 ☑
- bronchus (*see also* Bronchitis) 490
  - fungus NEC 117.9
- Brucella 023.9
  - abortus 023.1
  - canis 023.3
  - melitensis 023.0
  - mixed 023.8
  - suis 023.2
- Brugia (Wuchereria) malayi 125.1
- bursa — *see* Bursitis
- buttocks (skin) 686.9
- Candida (albicans) (tropicalis) (*see also* Candidiasis) 112.9
  - congenital 771.7
- Candiru 136.8
- Capillaria
  - hepatica 128.8
  - philippinensis 127.5
- cartilage 733.99
- catheter-related bloodstream (CRBSI) 999.31
- cat liver fluke 121.0
- cellulitis — *see* Cellulitis, by site
- Cephalosporum falciforme 117.4
- Cercomonas hominis (intestinal) 007.3
- cerebrospinal (*see also* Meningitis) 322.9
  - late effect — *see* category 326
- cervical gland 683
- cervix (*see also* Cervicitis) 616.0
- cesarean section wound 674.3 ☑
- Chilomastix (intestinal) 007.8
- Chlamydia 079.98
  - specified NEC 079.88
- cholera (*see also* Cholera) 001.9
- chorionic plate 658.8 ☑
- Cladosporium
  - bantianum 117.8
  - carrionii 117.2
  - mansoni 111.1
  - trichoides 117.8
  - wernecki 111.1
- Clonorchis (sinensis) (liver) 121.1
- Clostridium (haemolyticum) (novyi) NEC 041.84
  - botulinum 005.1
  - histolyticum (*see also* Gangrene, gas) 040.0
  - oedematiens (*see also* Gangrene, gas) 040.0
  - perfringens 041.83

Infection, infected, infective — *continued*

- Clostridium — *continued*
  - perfringens — *continued*
    - due to food 005.2
  - septicum (*see also* Gangrene, gas) 040.0
  - sordellii (*see also* Gangrene, gas) 040.0
  - welchii (*see also* Gangrene, gas) 040.0
    - due to food 005.2
- Coccidioides (immitis) (*see also* Coccidioidomycosis) 114.9
- coccus NEC 041.89
- colon (*see also* Enteritis, due to, by organism) 009.0
  - bacillus — *see* Infection, Escherichia coli
- colostomy or enterostomy 569.61
- common duct 576.1
- complicating pregnancy, childbirth, or puerperium NEC 647.9 ☑
  - affecting fetus or newborn 760.2
- Condiobolus 117.7
- congenital NEC 771.89
  - Candida albicans 771.7
  - chronic 771.2
  - cytomegalovirus 771.1
  - hepatitis, viral 771.2
  - herpes simplex 771.2
  - listeriosis 771.2
  - malaria 771.2
  - poliomyelitis 771.2
  - rubella 771.0
  - toxoplasmosis 771.2
  - tuberculosis 771.2
  - urinary (tract) 771.82
  - vaccinia 771.2
- coronavirus 079.89
  - SARS-associated 079.82
- corpus luteum (*see also* Salpingo-oophoritis) 614.2
- Corynebacterium diphtheriae — *see* Diphtheria
- cotia virus 059.8
- Coxsackie (*see also* Coxsackie) 079.2
  - endocardium 074.22
  - heart NEC 074.20
  - in diseases classified elsewhere — *see* category 079 ☑
  - meninges 047.0
  - myocardium 074.23
  - pericardium 074.21
  - pharynx 074.0
  - specified disease NEC 074.8
  - unspecified nature or site 079.2
- Cryptococcus neoformans 117.5
- Cryptosporidia 007.4
- Cunninghamella 117.7
- cyst — *see* Cyst
- Cysticercus cellulosae 123.1
- cytomegalovirus 078.5
  - congenital 771.1
- dental (pulpal origin) 522.4
- deuteromycetes 117.4
- Dicrocoelium dendriticum 121.8
- Dipetalonema (perstans) 125.4
  - streptocerca 125.6
- diphtherial — *see* Diphtheria
- Diphyllobothrium (adult) (latum) (pacificum) 123.4
  - larval 123.5
- Diplogonoporus (grandis) 123.8
- Dipylidium (caninum) 123.8
- Dirofilaria 125.6
- dog tapeworm 123.8
- Dracunculus medinensis 125.7
- Dreschlera 118
  - hawaiiensis 117.8
- Ducrey's bacillus (any site) 099.0
- due to or resulting from
  - central venous catheter 999.31

Infection, infected, infective — *continued*

- due to or resulting from — *continued*
  - device, implant, or graft (any) (presence of) — *see* Complications, infection and inflammation, due to (presence of) any device, implant, or graft classified to 996.0–996.5 NEC
  - injection, inoculation, infusion, transfusion, or vaccination (prophylactic) (therapeutic) 999.39
  - injury NEC — *see* Wound, open, by site, complicated
  - surgery 998.59
- duodenum 535.6 ☑
- ear (*see also* Otitis)
  - external (*see also* Otitis, externa) 380.10
  - inner (*see also* Labyrinthitis) 386.30
  - middle — *see* Otitis, media
- Eaton's agent NEC 041.81
- Eberthella typhosa 002.0
- Ebola 078.89
- echinococcosis 122.9
- Echinococcus (*see also* Echinococcus) 122.9
- Echinostoma 121.8
- ECHO virus 079.1
  - in diseases classified elsewhere — *see* category 079 ☑
  - unspecified nature or site 079.1
- Ehrlichiosis 082.40
  - chaffeensis 082.41
  - specified type NEC 082.49
- Endamoeba — *see* Infection, ameba
- endocardium (*see also* Endocarditis) 421.0
- endocervix (*see also* Cervicitis) 616.0
- Entamoeba — *see* Infection, ameba
- enteric (*see also* Enteritis, due to, by organism) 009.0
- Enterobacter aerogenes NEC 041.85
- Enterobacter sakazakii 041.85
- Enterobius vermicularis 127.4
- enterococcus NEC 041.04
- enterovirus NEC 079.89
  - central nervous system NEC 048
  - enteritis 008.67
  - meningitis 047.9
- Entomophthora 117.7
- Epidermophyton — *see* Dermatophytosis
- epidermophytosis — *see* Dermatophytosis
- episiotomy 674.3 ☑
- Epstein-Barr virus 075
  - chronic 780.79 *[139.8]*
- erysipeloid 027.1
- Erysipelothrix (insidiosa) (rhusiopathiae) 027.1
- erythema infectiosum 057.0
- Escherichia coli NEC 041.4
  - enteritis — *see* Enteritis, E. coli
  - generalized 038.42
  - intestinal — *see* Enteritis, E. coli
- esophagostomy 530.86
- ethmoidal (chronic) (sinus) (*see also* Sinusitis, ethmoidal) 473.2
- Eubacterium 041.84
- Eustachian tube (ear) 381.50
  - acute 381.51
  - chronic 381.52
- exanthema subitum (*see also* Exanthem subitum) 058.10
- external auditory canal (meatus) (*see also* Otitis, externa) 380.10
- eye NEC 360.00
- eyelid 373.9
  - specified NEC 373.8
- fallopian tube (*see also* Salpingo-oophoritis) 614.2

Infection, infected, infective — *continued*
- fascia 728.89
- Fasciola
  - gigantica 121.3
  - hepatica 121.3
- Fasciolopsis (buski) 121.4
- fetus (intra-amniotic) — *see* Infection, congenital
- filarial — *see* Infestation, filarial
- finger (skin) 686.9
  - abscess (with lymphangitis) 681.00
    - pulp 681.01
  - cellulitis (with lymphangitis) 681.00
  - distal closed space (with lymphangitis) 681.00
  - nail 681.02
    - fungus 110.1
- fish tapeworm 123.4
  - larval 123.5
- flagellate, intestinal 007.9
- fluke — *see* Infestation, fluke
- focal
  - teeth (pulpal origin) 522.4
  - tonsils 474.00
    - and adenoids 474.02
- Fonsecaea
  - compactum 117.2
  - pedrosoi 117.2
- food (*see also* Poisoning, food) 005.9
- foot (skin) 686.9
  - fungus 110.4
- Francisella tularensis (*see also* Tularemia) 021.9
- frontal sinus (chronic) (*see also* Sinusitis, frontal) 473.1
- fungus NEC 117.9
  - beard 110.0
  - body 110.5
  - dermatiacious NEC 117.8
  - foot 110.4
  - groin 110.3
  - hand 110.2
  - nail 110.1
  - pathogenic to compromised host only 118
  - perianal (area) 110.3
  - scalp 110.0
  - scrotum 110.8
  - skin 111.9
    - foot 110.4
    - hand 110.2
  - toenails 110.1
  - trachea 117.9
- Fusarium 118
- Fusobacterium 041.84
- gallbladder (*see also* Cholecystitis, acute) 575.0
- Gardnerella vaginalis 041.89
- gas bacillus (*see also* Gas, gangrene) 040.0
- gastric (*see also* Gastritis) 535.5 ☑
- Gastrodiscoides hominis 121.8
- gastroenteric (*see also* Enteritis, due to, by organism) 009.0
- gastrointestinal (*see also* Enteritis, due to, by organism) 009.0
- gastrostomy 536.41
- generalized NEC (*see also* Septicemia) 038.9
- genital organ or tract NEC
  - female 614.9
    - with
      - abortion — *see* Abortion, by type, with sepsis
      - ectopic pregnancy (*see also* categories 633.0–633.9) 639.0
      - molar pregnancy (*see also* categories 630–632) 639.0
    - complicating pregnancy 646.6 ☑
      - affecting fetus or newborn 760.8

Infection, infected, infective — *continued*
- genital organ or tract — *continued*
  - female — *continued*
    - following
      - abortion 639.0
      - ectopic or molar pregnancy 639.0
    - puerperal, postpartum, childbirth 670.0 ☑
      - minor or localized 646.6 ☑
        - affecting fetus or newborn 760.8
  - male 608.4
- genitourinary tract NEC 599.0
- Ghon tubercle, primary (*see also* Tuberculosis) 010.0 ☑
- Giardia lamblia 007.1
- gingival (chronic) 523.10
  - acute 523.00
  - Vincent's 101
- glanders 024
- Glenosporopsis amazonica 116.2
- Gnathostoma spinigerum 128.1
- Gongylonema 125.6
- gonococcal NEC (*see also* Gonococcus) 098.0
- gram-negative bacilli NEC 041.85
  - anaerobic 041.84
- guinea worm 125.7
- gum (*see also* Infection, gingival) 523.10
- Hantavirus 079.81
- heart 429.89
- Helicobacter pylori (H. pylori) 041.86
- helminths NEC 128.9
  - intestinal 127.9
    - mixed (types classifiable to more than one category in 120.0–127.7) 127.8
    - specified type NEC 127.7
  - specified type NEC 128.8
- Hemophilus influenzae NEC 041.5
  - generalized 038.41
- herpes (simplex) (*see also* Herpes, simplex) 054.9
  - congenital 771.2
  - zoster (*see also* Herpes, zoster) 053.9
    - eye NEC 053.29
- Heterophyes heterophyes 121.6
- Histoplasma (*see also* Histoplasmosis) 115.90
  - capsulatum (*see also* Histoplasmosis, American) 115.00
  - duboisii (*see also* Histoplasmosis, African) 115.10
- HIV V08
  - with symptoms, symptomatic 042
- hookworm (*see also* Ancylostomiasis) 126.9
- human herpesvirus NEC 058.89
- human herpesvirus 6 058.81
- human herpesvirus 7 058.82
- human herpesvirus 8 058.89
- human immunodeficiency virus V08
  - with symptoms, symptomatic 042
- human papillomavirus 079.4
- hydrocele 603.1
- hydronephrosis 591
- Hymenolepis 123.6
- hypopharynx 478.29
- inguinal glands 683
  - due to soft chancre 099.0
- intestine, intestinal (*see also* Enteritis, due to, by organism) 009.0
- intrauterine (*see also* Endometritis) 615.9
  - complicating delivery 646.6 ☑
- isospora belli or hominis 007.2
- Japanese B encephalitis 062.0
- jaw (bone) (acute) (chronic) (lower) (subacute) (upper) 526.4
- joint — *see* Arthritis, infectious or infective

Infection, infected, infective — *continued*
- Kaposi's sarcoma-associated herpesvirus 058.89
- kidney (cortex) (hematogenous) 590.9
  - with
    - abortion — *see* Abortion, by type, with urinary tract infection
    - calculus 592.0
    - ectopic pregnancy (*see also* categories 633.0–633.9) 639.8
    - molar pregnancy (*see also* categories 630–632) 639.8
  - complicating pregnancy or puerperium 646.6 ☑
    - affecting fetus or newborn 760.1
  - following
    - abortion 639.8
    - ectopic or molar pregnancy 639.8
  - pelvis and ureter 590.3
- Klebsiella pneumoniae NEC 041.3
- knee (skin) NEC 686.9
  - joint — *see* Arthritis, infectious
- Koch's (*see also* Tuberculosis, pulmonary) 011.9 ☑
- labia (majora) (minora) (*see also* Vulvitis) 616.10
- lacrimal
  - gland (*see also* Dacryoadenitis) 375.00
  - passages (duct) (sac) (*see also* Dacryocystitis) 375.30
- larynx NEC 478.79
- leg (skin) NEC 686.9
- Leishmania (*see also* Leishmaniasis) 085.9
  - braziliensis 085.5
  - donovani 085.0
  - ethiopica 085.3
  - furunculosa 085.1
  - infantum 085.0
  - mexicana 085.4
  - tropica (minor) 085.1
    - major 085.2
- Leptosphaeria senegalensis 117.4
- leptospira (*see also* Leptospirosis) 100.9
  - Australis 100.89
  - Bataviae 100.89
  - pyrogenes 100.89
  - specified type NEC 100.89
- leptospirochetal NEC (*see also* Leptospirosis) 100.9
- Leptothrix — *see* Actinomycosis
- Listeria monocytogenes (listeriosis) 027.0
  - congenital 771.2
- liver fluke — *see* Infestation, fluke, liver
- Loa loa 125.2
  - eyelid 125.2 *[373.6]*
- Loboa loboi 116.2
- local, skin (staphylococcal) (streptococcal) NEC 686.9
  - abscess — *see* Abscess, by site
  - cellulitis — *see* Cellulitis, by site
  - ulcer (*see also* Ulcer, skin) 707.9
- Loefflerella
  - mallei 024
  - whitmori 025
- lung 518.89
  - atypical Mycobacterium 031.0
    - tuberculous (*see also* Tuberculosis, pulmonary) 011.9 ☑
  - basilar 518.89
  - chronic 518.89
  - fungus NEC 117.9
  - spirochetal 104.8
  - virus — *see* Pneumonia, virus
- lymph gland (axillary) (cervical) (inguinal) 683
  - mesenteric 289.2

Infection, infected, infective — *continued*
- lymphoid tissue, base of tongue or posterior pharynx, NEC 474.00
- madurella
  - grisea 117.4
  - mycetomii 117.4
- major
  - with
    - abortion — *see* Abortion, by type, with sepsis
    - ectopic pregnancy (*see also* categories 633.0–633.9) 639.0
    - molar pregnancy (*see also* categories 630–632) 639.0
  - following
    - abortion 639.0
    - ectopic or molar pregnancy 639.0
  - puerperal, postpartum, childbirth 670.0 ☑
- Malassezia furfur 111.0
- Malleomyces
  - mallei 024
  - pseudomallei 025
- mammary gland 611.0
  - puerperal, postpartum 675.2 ☑
- Mansonella (ozzardi) 125.5
- mastoid (suppurative) — *see* Mastoiditis
- maxilla, maxillary 526.4
  - sinus (chronic) (*see also* Sinusitis, maxillary) 473.0
- mediastinum 519.2
- medina 125.7
- meibomian
  - cyst 373.12
  - gland 373.12
- melioidosis 025
- meninges (*see also* Meningitis) 320.9
- meningococcal (*see also* condition) 036.9
  - brain 036.1
  - cerebrospinal 036.0
  - endocardium 036.42
  - generalized 036.2
  - meninges 036.0
  - meningococcemia 036.2
  - specified site NEC 036.89
- mesenteric lymph nodes or glands NEC 289.2
- Metagonimus 121.5
- metatarsophalangeal 711.97
- methicillin
  - resistant Staphylococcus aureus (MRSA) 041.12
  - susceptible Staphylococcus aureus (MSSA) 041.11
- microorganism resistant to drugs — *see* Resistance (to), drugs by microorganisms
- Microsporidia 136.8
- microsporum, microsporic — *see* Dermatophytosis
- Mima polymorpha NEC 041.85
- mixed flora NEC 041.89
- Monilia (*see also* Candidiasis) 112.9
  - neonatal 771.7
- monkeypox 059.01
- Monosporium apiospermum 117.6
- mouth (focus) NEC 528.9
  - parasitic 136.9
- MRSA (methicillin resistant Staphylococcus aureus) 041.12
- MSSA (methicillin susceptible Staphylococcus aureus) 041.11
- Mucor 117.7
- muscle NEC 728.89
- mycelium NEC 117.9
- mycetoma
  - actinomycotic NEC (*see also* Actinomycosis) 039.9
  - mycotic NEC 117.4
- Mycobacterium, mycobacterial (*see also* Mycobacterium) 031.9

Infection, infected, infective — *continued*
- staphylococcal — *continued*
  - septicemia — *continued*
    - MRSA (methicillin resistant Staphylococcus aureus) 038.12
    - MSSA (methicillin susceptible Staphylococcus aureus) 038.11
    - specified organism NEC 038.19
  - specified NEC 041.19
- steatoma 706.2
- Stellantchasmus falcatus 121.6
- Streptobacillus moniliformis 026.1
- streptococcal NEC 041.00
  - generalized (purulent) 038.0
  - Group
    - A 041.01
    - B 041.02
    - C 041.03
    - D [enterococcus] 041.04
    - G 041.05
  - pneumonia — *see* Pneumonia, streptococcal
  - septicemia 038.0
  - sore throat 034.0
  - specified NEC 041.09
- Streptomyces — *see* Actinomycosis
- streptotrichosis — *see* Actinomycosis
- Strongyloides (stercoralis) 127.2
- stump (amputation) (posttraumatic) (surgical) 997.62
  - traumatic — *see* Amputation, traumatic, by site, complicated
- subcutaneous tissue, local NEC 686.9
- submaxillary region 528.9
- suipestifer (*see also* Infection, Salmonella) 003.9
- swimming pool bacillus 031.1
- syphilitic — *see* Syphilis
- systemic — *see* Septicemia
- Taenia — *see* Infestation, Taenia
- Taeniarhynchus saginatus 123.2
- tanapox 059.21
- tapeworm — *see* Infestation, tapeworm
- tendon (sheath) 727.89
- Ternidens diminutus 127.7
- testis (*see also* Orchitis) 604.90
- thigh (skin) 686.9
- threadworm 127.4
- throat 478.29
  - pneumococcal 462
  - staphylococcal 462
  - streptococcal 034.0
  - viral NEC (*see also* Pharyngitis) 462
- thumb (skin) 686.9
  - abscess (with lymphangitis) 681.00
    - pulp 681.01
  - cellulitis (with lymphangitis) 681.00
  - nail 681.02
- thyroglossal duct 529.8
- toe (skin) 686.9
  - abscess (with lymphangitis) 681.10
  - cellulitis (with lymphangitis) 681.10
  - nail 681.11
    - fungus 110.1
- tongue NEC 529.0
  - parasitic 112.0
- tonsil (faucial) (lingual) (pharyngeal) 474.00
  - acute or subacute 463
  - and adenoid 474.02
  - tag 474.00
- tooth, teeth 522.4
  - periapical (pulpal origin) 522.4
  - peridental 523.30
  - periodontal 523.31
  - pulp 522.0
  - socket 526.5

Infection, infected, infective — *continued*
- TORCH — *see* Infection, congenital NEC
  - without active infection 760.2
- Torula histolytica 117.5
- Toxocara (cani) (cati) (felis) 128.0
- Toxoplasma gondii (*see also* Toxoplasmosis) 130.9
- trachea, chronic 491.8
  - fungus 117.9
- traumatic NEC 958.3
- trematode NEC 121.9
- trench fever 083.1
- Treponema
  - denticola 041.84
  - macrodenticum 041.84
  - pallidum (*see also* Syphilis) 097.9
- Trichinella (spiralis) 124
- Trichomonas 131.9
  - bladder 131.09
  - cervix 131.09
  - hominis 007.3
  - intestine 007.3
  - prostate 131.03
  - specified site NEC 131.8
  - urethra 131.02
  - urogenitalis 131.00
  - vagina 131.01
  - vulva 131.01
- Trichophyton, trichophytid — *see* Dermatophytosis
- Trichosporon (beigelii) cutaneum 111.2
- Trichostrongylus 127.6
- Trichuris (trichiuria) 127.3
- Trombicula (irritans) 133.8
- Trypanosoma (*see also* Trypanosomiasis) 086.9
  - cruzi 086.2
- tubal (*see also* Salpingo-oophoritis) 614.2
- tuberculous NEC (*see also* Tuberculosis) 011.9 ☑
- tubo-ovarian (*see also* Salpingo-oophoritis) 614.2
- tunica vaginalis 608.4
- tympanic membrane — *see* Myringitis
- typhoid (abortive) (ambulant) (bacillus) 002.0
- typhus 081.9
  - flea-borne (endemic) 081.0
  - louse-borne (epidemic) 080
  - mite-borne 081.2
  - recrudescent 081.1
  - tick-borne 082.9
    - African 082.1
    - North Asian 082.2
- umbilicus (septic) 686.9
  - newborn NEC 771.4
- ureter 593.89
- urethra (*see also* Urethritis) 597.80
- urinary (tract) NEC 599.0
  - with
    - abortion — *see* Abortion, by type, with urinary tract infection
    - ectopic pregnancy (*see also* categories 633.0–633.9) 639.8
    - molar pregnancy (*see also* categories 630–632) 639.8
  - candidal 112.2
  - complicating pregnancy, childbirth, or puerperium 646.6 ☑
    - affecting fetus or newborn 760.1
    - asymptomatic 646.5 ☑
      - affecting fetus or newborn 760.1
  - diplococcal (acute) 098.0
    - chronic 098.2
  - due to Trichomonas (vaginalis) 131.00
    - following
      - abortion 639.8

Infection, infected, infective — *continued*
- urinary — *continued*
  - due to Trichomonas — *continued*
    - following — *continued*
      - ectopic or molar pregnancy 639.8
    - gonococcal (acute) 098.0
      - chronic or duration of 2 months or over 098.2
  - newborn 771.82
  - trichomonal 131.00
  - tuberculous (*see also* Tuberculosis) 016.3 ☑
  - uterus, uterine (*see also* Endometritis) 615.9
  - utriculus masculinus NEC 597.89
  - vaccination 999.39
  - vagina (granulation tissue) (wall) (*see also* Vaginitis) 616.10
  - varicella 052.9
  - varicose veins — *see* Varicose, veins
  - variola 050.9
    - major 050.0
    - minor 050.1
  - vas deferens NEC 608.4
  - Veillonella 041.84
  - verumontanum 597.89
  - vesical (*see also* Cystitis) 595.9
  - Vibrio
    - cholerae 001.0
      - El Tor 001.1
    - parahaemolyticus (food poisoning) 005.4
    - vulnificus 041.85
  - Vincent's (gums) (mouth) (tonsil) 101
- vaccination 999.39
- virus, viral 079.99
  - adenovirus
    - in diseases classified elsewhere — *see* category 079 ☑
    - unspecified nature or site 079.0
  - central nervous system NEC 049.9
    - enterovirus 048
      - meningitis 047.9
        - specified type NEC 047.8
    - slow virus 046.9
    - specified condition NEC 046.8
  - chest 519.8
  - conjunctivitis 077.99
    - specified type NEC 077.8
  - coronavirus 079.89
    - SARS-associated 079.82
  - Coxsackie (*see also* Infection, Coxsackie) 079.2
  - Ebola 065.8
  - ECHO
    - in diseases classified elsewhere — *see* category 079 ☑
    - unspecified nature or site 079.1
  - encephalitis 049.9
    - arthropod-borne NEC 064
    - tick-borne 063.9
      - specified type NEC 063.8
  - enteritis NEC (*see also* Enteritis, viral) 008.8
  - exanthem NEC 057.9
  - Hantavirus 079.81
  - human papilloma 079.4
  - in diseases classified elsewhere — *see* category 079 ☑
  - intestine (*see also* Enteritis, viral) 008.8
  - lung — *see* Pneumonia, viral
  - respiratory syncytial (RSV) 079.6
  - retrovirus 079.50
  - rhinovirus
    - in diseases classified elsewhere — *see* category 079 ☑
    - unspecified nature or site 079.3
  - salivary gland disease 078.5
  - slow 046.9
    - specified condition NEC 046.8

Infection, infected, infective — *continued*
- virus, viral — *continued*
  - specified type NEC 079.89
    - in diseases classified elsewhere — *see* category 079 ☑
  - unspecified nature or site 079.99
  - warts 078.10
    - specified NEC 078.19
  - yaba monkey tumor 059.22
- vulva (*see also* Vulvitis) 616.10
- whipworm 127.3
- Whitmore's bacillus 025
- wound (local) (posttraumatic) NEC 958.3
  - with
    - dislocation — *see* Dislocation, by site, open
    - fracture — *see* Fracture, by site, open
    - open wound — *see* Wound, open, by site, complicated
  - postoperative 998.59
  - surgical 998.59
- Wuchereria 125.0
  - bancrofti 125.0
  - malayi 125.1
- yaba monkey tumor virus 059.22
- yatapoxvirus 059.20
- yaws — *see* Yaws
- yeast (*see also* Candidiasis) 112.9
- yellow fever (*see also* Fever, yellow) 060.9
- Yersinia pestis (*see also* Plague) 020.9
- Zeis' gland 373.12
- zoonotic bacterial NEC 027.9
- Zopfia senegalensis 117.4

Infective, infectious — *see* condition

Inferiority complex 301.9
- constitutional psychopathic 301.9

Infertility
- female 628.9
  - age related 628.8
  - associated with
    - adhesions, peritubal 614.6 *[628.2]*
    - anomaly
      - cervical mucus 628.4
      - congenital
        - cervix 628.4
        - fallopian tube 628.2
        - uterus 628.3
        - vagina 628.4
    - anovulation 628.0
    - dysmucorrhea 628.4
    - endometritis, tuberculous (*see also* Tuberculosis) 016.7 ☑ *[628.3]*
    - Stein-Leventhal syndrome 256.4 *[628.0]*
  - due to
    - adiposogenital dystrophy 253.8 *[628.1]*
    - anterior pituitary disorder NEC 253.4 *[628.1]*
      - hyperfunction 253.1 *[628.1]*
    - cervical anomaly 628.4
    - fallopian tube anomaly 628.2
    - ovarian failure 256.39 *[628.0]*
    - Stein-Leventhal syndrome 256.4 *[628.0]*
    - uterine anomaly 628.3
    - vaginal anomaly 628.4
  - nonimplantation 628.3
  - origin
    - cervical 628.4
    - pituitary-hypothalamus NEC 253.8 *[628.1]*
      - anterior pituitary NEC 253.4 *[628.1]*
        - hyperfunction NEC 253.1 *[628.1]*
      - dwarfism 253.3 *[628.1]*
      - panhypopituitarism 253.2 *[628.1]*
    - specified NEC 628.8

Infiltrate, infiltration — *continued*
- heart, cardiac
  - fatty (*see also* Degeneration, myocardial) 429.1
  - glycogenic 271.0 *[425.7]*
- inflammatory in vitreous 379.29
- kidney (*see also* Disease, renal) 593.9
- leukemic (M9800/3) — *see* Leukemia
- liver 573.8
  - fatty — *see* Fatty, liver
  - glycogen (*see also* Disease, glycogen storage) 271.0
- lung (*see also* Infiltrate, pulmonary) 518.3
  - eosinophilic 518.3
  - x-ray finding only 793.1
- lymphatic (*see also* Leukemia, lymphatic) 204.9 ☑
  - gland, pigmentary 289.3
- muscle, fatty 728.9
- myelogenous (*see also* Leukemia, myeloid) 205.9 ☑
- myocardium, myocardial
  - fatty (*see also* Degeneration, myocardial) 429.1
  - glycogenic 271.0 *[425.7]*
- pulmonary 518.3
  - with
    - eosinophilia 518.3
    - pneumonia — *see* Pneumonia, by type
  - x-ray finding only 793.1
- Ranke's primary (*see also* Tuberculosis) 010.0 ☑
- skin, lymphocytic (benign) 709.8
- thymus (gland) (fatty) 254.8
- urine 788.8
- vesicant
  - agent NEC 998.82
  - chemotherapy 998.81
- vitreous humor 379.29

Infirmity 799.89
- senile 797

Inflammation, inflamed, inflammatory (with exudation)
- abducens (nerve) 378.54
- accessory sinus (chronic) (*see also* Sinusitis) 473.9
- adrenal (gland) 255.8
- alimentary canal — *see* Enteritis
- alveoli (teeth) 526.5
  - scorbutic 267
- amnion — *see* Amnionitis
- anal canal 569.49
- antrum (chronic) (*see also* Sinusitis, maxillary) 473.0
- anus 569.49
- appendix (*see also* Appendicitis) 541
- arachnoid — *see* Meningitis
- areola 611.0
  - puerperal, postpartum 675.0 ☑
- areolar tissue NEC 686.9
- artery — *see* Arteritis
- auditory meatus (external) (*see also* Otitis, externa) 380.10
- Bartholin's gland 616.89
- bile duct or passage 576.1
- bladder (*see also* Cystitis) 595.9
- bleb
  - postprocedural 379.60
    - stage 1 379.61
    - stage 2 379.62
    - stage 3 379.63
- bone — *see* Osteomyelitis
- bowel (*see also* Enteritis) 558.9
- brain (*see also* Encephalitis) 323.9
  - late effect — *see* category 326
  - membrane — *see* Meningitis
- breast 611.0
  - puerperal, postpartum 675.2 ☑
- broad ligament (*see also* Disease, pelvis, inflammatory) 614.4
  - acute 614.3
- bronchus — *see* Bronchitis
- bursa — *see* Bursitis

Inflammation, inflamed, inflammatory — *continued*
- capsule
  - liver 573.3
  - spleen 289.59
- catarrhal (*see also* Catarrh) 460
  - vagina 616.10
- cecum (*see also* Appendicitis) 541
- cerebral (*see also* Encephalitis) 323.9
  - late effect — *see* category 326
  - membrane — *see* Meningitis
- cerebrospinal (*see also* Meningitis) 322.9
  - late effect — *see* category 326
  - meningococcal 036.0
  - tuberculous (*see also* Tuberculosis) 013.6 ☑
- cervix (uteri) (*see also* Cervicitis) 616.0
- chest 519.9
- choroid NEC (*see also* Choroiditis) 363.20
- cicatrix (tissue) — *see* Cicatrix
- colon (*see also* Enteritis) 558.9
  - granulomatous 555.1
  - newborn 558.9
- connective tissue (diffuse) NEC 728.9
- cornea (*see also* Keratitis) 370.9
  - with ulcer (*see also* Ulcer, cornea) 370.00
- corpora cavernosa (penis) 607.2
- cranial nerve — *see* Disorder, nerve, cranial
- diarrhea — *see* Diarrhea
- disc (intervertebral) (space) 722.90
  - cervical, cervicothoracic 722.91
  - lumbar, lumbosacral 722.93
  - thoracic, thoracolumbar 722.92
- Douglas' cul-de-sac or pouch (chronic) (*see also* Disease, pelvis, inflammatory) 614.4
  - acute 614.3
- due to (presence of) any device, implant, or graft classifiable to 996.0–996.5 — *see* Complications, infection and inflammation, due to (presence of) any device, implant, or graft classified to 996.0–996.5 NEC
- duodenum 535.6 ☑
- dura mater — *see* Meningitis
- ear (*see also* Otitis)
  - external (*see also* Otitis, externa) 380.10
  - inner (*see also* Labyrinthitis) 386.30
  - middle — *see* Otitis media
- esophagus 530.10
- ethmoidal (chronic) (sinus) (*see also* Sinusitis, ethmoidal) 473.2
- Eustachian tube (catarrhal) 381.50
  - acute 381.51
  - chronic 381.52
- extrarectal 569.49
- eye 379.99
- eyelid 373.9
  - specified NEC 373.8
- fallopian tube (*see also* Salpingo-oophoritis) 614.2
- fascia 728.9
- fetal membranes (acute) 658.4 ☑
  - affecting fetus or newborn 762.7
- follicular, pharynx 472.1
- frontal (chronic) (sinus) (*see also* Sinusitis, frontal) 473.1
- gallbladder (*see also* Cholecystitis, acute) 575.0
- gall duct (*see also* Cholecystitis) 575.10
- gastrointestinal (*see also* Enteritis) 558.9
- genital organ (diffuse) (internal)
  - female 614.9
    - with
      - abortion — *see* Abortion, by type, with sepsis

Inflammation, inflamed, inflammatory — *continued*
- genital organ — *continued*
  - female — *continued*
    - with — *continued*
      - ectopic pregnancy (*see also* categories 633.0–633.9) 639.0
      - molar pregnancy (*see also* categories 630–632) 639.0
    - complicating pregnancy, childbirth, or puerperium 646.6 ☑
      - affecting fetus or newborn 760.8
    - following
      - abortion 639.0
      - ectopic or molar pregnancy 639.0
  - male 608.4
- gland (lymph) (*see also* Lymphadenitis) 289.3
- glottis (*see also* Laryngitis) 464.00
  - with obstruction 464.01
- granular, pharynx 472.1
- gum 523.10
- heart (*see also* Carditis) 429.89
- hepatic duct 576.8
- hernial sac — *see* Hernia, by site
- ileum (*see also* Enteritis) 558.9
  - terminal or regional 555.0
    - with large intestine 555.2
- intervertebral disc 722.90
  - cervical, cervicothoracic 722.91
  - lumbar, lumbosacral 722.93
  - thoracic, thoracolumbar 722.92
- intestine (*see also* Enteritis) 558.9
- jaw (acute) (bone) (chronic) (lower) (suppurative) (upper) 526.4
- jejunum — *see* Enteritis
- joint NEC (*see also* Arthritis) 716.9 ☑
  - sacroiliac 720.2
- kidney (*see also* Nephritis) 583.9
- knee (joint) 716.66
  - tuberculous (active) (*see also* Tuberculosis) 015.2 ☑
- labium (majus) (minus) (*see also* Vulvitis) 616.10
- lacrimal
  - gland (*see also* Dacryoadenitis) 375.00
  - passages (duct) (sac) (*see also* Dacryocystitis) 375.30
- larynx (*see also* Laryngitis) 464.00
  - with obstruction 464.01
  - diphtheritic 032.3
- leg NEC 686.9
- lip 528.5
- liver (capsule) (*see also* Hepatitis) 573.3
  - acute 570
  - chronic 571.40
  - suppurative 572.0
- lung (acute) (*see also* Pneumonia) 486
  - chronic (interstitial) 518.89
- lymphatic vessel (*see also* Lymphangitis) 457.2
- lymph node or gland (*see also* Lymphadenitis) 289.3
- mammary gland 611.0
  - puerperal, postpartum 675.2 ☑
- maxilla, maxillary 526.4
  - sinus (chronic) (*see also* Sinusitis, maxillary) 473.0
- membranes of brain or spinal cord — *see* Meningitis
- meninges — *see* Meningitis
- mouth 528.00
- muscle 728.9
- myocardium (*see also* Myocarditis) 429.0
- nasal sinus (chronic) (*see also* Sinusitis) 473.9
- nasopharynx — *see* Nasopharyngitis
- navel 686.9

Inflammation, inflamed, inflammatory — *continued*
- navel — *continued*
  - newborn NEC 771.4
- nerve NEC 729.2
- nipple 611.0
  - puerperal, postpartum 675.0 ☑
- nose 478.19
  - suppurative 472.0
- oculomotor nerve 378.51
- optic nerve 377.30
- orbit (chronic) 376.10
  - acute 376.00
  - chronic 376.10
- ovary (*see also* Salpingo-oophoritis) 614.2
- oviduct (*see also* Salpingo-oophoritis) 614.2
- pancreas — *see* Pancreatitis
- parametrium (chronic) (*see also* Disease, pelvis, inflammatory) 614.4
  - acute 614.3
- parotid region 686.9
  - gland 527.2
- pelvis, female (*see also* Disease, pelvis, inflammatory) 614.9
- penis (corpora cavernosa) 607.2
- perianal 569.49
- pericardium (*see also* Pericarditis) 423.9
- perineum (female) (male) 686.9
- perirectal 569.49
- peritoneum (*see also* Peritonitis) 567.9
- periuterine (*see also* Disease, pelvis, inflammatory) 614.9
- perivesical (*see also* Cystitis) 595.9
- petrous bone (*see also* Petrositis) 383.20
- pharynx (*see also* Pharyngitis) 462
  - follicular 472.1
  - granular 472.1
- pia mater — *see* Meningitis
- pleura — *see* Pleurisy
- postmastoidectomy cavity 383.30
  - chronic 383.33
- prostate (*see also* Prostatitis) 601.9
- rectosigmoid — *see* Rectosigmoiditis
- rectum (*see also* Proctitis) 569.49
- respiratory, upper (*see also* Infection, respiratory, upper) 465.9
  - chronic, due to external agent — *see* Condition, respiratory, chronic, due to, external agent
  - due to
    - fumes or vapors (chemical) (inhalation) 506.2
    - radiation 508.1
- retina (*see also* Retinitis) 363.20
- retrocecal (*see also* Appendicitis) 541
- retroperitoneal (*see also* Peritonitis) 567.9
- salivary duct or gland (any) (suppurative) 527.2
- scorbutic, alveoli, teeth 267
- scrotum 608.4
- sigmoid — *see* Enteritis
- sinus (*see also* Sinusitis) 473.9
- Skene's duct or gland (*see also* Urethritis) 597.89
- skin 686.9
- spermatic cord 608.4
- sphenoidal (sinus) (*see also* Sinusitis, sphenoidal) 473.3
- spinal
  - cord (*see also* Encephalitis) 323.9
    - late effect — *see* category 326
  - membrane — *see* Meningitis
  - nerve — *see* Disorder, nerve
- spine (*see also* Spondylitis) 720.9
- spleen (capsule) 289.59
- stomach — *see* Gastritis
- stricture, rectum 569.49
- subcutaneous tissue NEC 686.9
- suprarenal (gland) 255.8

- **Injury** — *continued*
  - blood vessel — *continued*
    - saphenous — *continued*
      - vein (greater) (lesser) 904.3
    - splenic
      - artery 902.23
      - vein 902.34
    - subclavian
      - artery 901.1
      - vein 901.3
    - suprarenal 902.49
    - thoracic 901.9
      - multiple 901.83
      - specified NEC 901.89
    - tibial 904.50
      - artery 904.50
        - anterior 904.51
        - posterior 904.53
      - vein 904.50
        - anterior 904.52
        - posterior 904.54
    - ulnar (artery) (vein) 903.3
    - uterine 902.59
      - artery 902.55
      - vein 902.56
    - vena cava
      - inferior 902.10
        - specified branches NEC 902.19
      - superior 901.2
  - brachial plexus 953.4
    - newborn 767.6
  - brain NEC (*see also* Injury, intracranial) 854.0 ☑
  - breast 959.19
  - broad ligament — *see* Injury, internal, broad ligament
  - bronchus, bronchi — *see* Injury, internal, bronchus
  - brow 959.09
  - buttock 959.19
  - canthus, eye 921.1
  - cathode ray 990
  - cauda equina 952.4
    - with fracture, vertebra — *see* Fracture, vertebra, sacrum
  - cavernous sinus (*see also* Injury, intracranial) 854.0 ☑
  - cecum — *see* Injury, internal, cecum
  - celiac ganglion or plexus 954.1
  - cerebellum (*see also* Injury, intracranial) 854.0 ☑
  - cervix (uteri) — *see* Injury, internal, cervix
  - cheek 959.09
  - chest (*see also* Injury, internal, chest)
    - wall 959.11
  - childbirth (*see also* Birth, injury)
    - maternal NEC 665.9 ☑
  - chin 959.09
  - choroid (eye) 921.3
  - clitoris 959.14
  - coccyx 959.19
    - complicating delivery 665.6 ☑
  - colon — *see* Injury, internal, colon
  - common duct — *see* Injury, internal, common duct
  - conjunctiva 921.1
    - superficial 918.2
  - cord
    - spermatic — *see* Injury, internal, spermatic cord
    - spinal — *see* Injury, spinal, by site
  - cornea 921.3
    - abrasion 918.1
      - due to contact lens 371.82
    - penetrating — *see* Injury, eyeball, penetrating
    - superficial 918.1
      - due to contact lens 371.82
  - cortex (cerebral) (*see also* Injury, intracranial) 854.0 ☑
    - visual 950.3
  - costal region 959.11
  - costochondral 959.11

- **Injury** — *continued*
  - cranial
    - bones — *see* Fracture, skull, by site
    - cavity (*see also* Injury, intracranial) 854.0 ☑
    - nerve — *see* Injury, nerve, cranial
  - crushing — *see* Crush
  - cutaneous sensory nerve
    - lower limb 956.4
    - upper limb 955.5
  - deep tissue — *see* Contusion, by site
    - meaning pressure ulcer 707.25
  - delivery (*see also* Birth, injury)
    - maternal NEC 665.9 ☑
  - Descemet's membrane — *see* Injury, eyeball, penetrating
  - diaphragm — *see* Injury, internal, diaphragm
  - diffuse axonal — *see* Injury, intracranial
  - duodenum — *see* Injury, internal, duodenum
  - ear (auricle) (canal) (drum) (external) 959.09
  - elbow (and forearm) (and wrist) 959.3
  - epididymis 959.14
  - epigastric region 959.12
  - epiglottis 959.09
  - epiphyseal, current — *see* Fracture, by site
  - esophagus — *see* Injury, internal, esophagus
  - Eustachian tube 959.09
  - extremity (lower) (upper) NEC 959.8
  - eye 921.9
    - penetrating eyeball — *see* Injury, eyeball, penetrating
    - superficial 918.9
  - eyeball 921.3
    - penetrating 871.7
      - with
        - partial loss (of intraocular tissue) 871.2
        - prolapse or exposure (of intraocular tissue) 871.1
      - without prolapse 871.0
      - foreign body (nonmagnetic) 871.6
        - magnetic 871.5
    - superficial 918.9
  - eyebrow 959.09
  - eyelid(s) 921.1
    - laceration — *see* Laceration, eyelid
    - superficial 918.0
  - face (and neck) 959.09
  - fallopian tube — *see* Injury, internal, fallopian tube
  - finger(s) (nail) 959.5
  - flank 959.19
  - foot (and ankle) (and knee) (and leg, except thigh) 959.7
  - forceps NEC 767.9
    - scalp 767.19
  - forearm (and elbow) (and wrist) 959.3
  - forehead 959.09
  - gallbladder — *see* Injury, internal, gallbladder
  - gasserian ganglion 951.2
  - gastrointestinal tract — *see* Injury, internal, gastrointestinal tract
  - genital organ(s)
    - with
      - abortion — *see* Abortion, by type, with, damage to pelvic organs
      - ectopic pregnancy (*see also* categories 633.0–633.9) 639.2
      - molar pregnancy (*see also* categories 630–632) 639.2
    - external 959.14
      - fracture of corpus cavernosum penis 959.13
    - following
      - abortion 639.2

- **Injury** — *continued*
  - genital organ(s) — *continued*
    - following — *continued*
      - ectopic or molar pregnancy 639.2
    - internal — *see* Injury, internal, genital organs
    - obstetrical trauma NEC 665.9 ☑
      - affecting fetus or newborn 763.89
  - gland
    - lacrimal 921.1
      - laceration 870.8
    - parathyroid 959.09
    - salivary 959.09
    - thyroid 959.09
  - globe (eye) (*see also* Injury, eyeball) 921.3
  - grease gun — *see* Wound, open, by site, complicated
  - groin 959.19
  - gum 959.09
  - hand(s) (except fingers) 959.4
  - head NEC 959.01
    - with
      - loss of consciousness 850.5
      - skull fracture — *see* Fracture, skull, by site
  - heart — *see* Injury, internal, heart
  - heel 959.7
  - hip (and thigh) 959.6
  - hymen 959.14
  - hyperextension (cervical) (vertebra) 847.0
  - ileum — *see* Injury, internal, ileum
  - iliac region 959.19
  - infrared rays NEC 990
  - instrumental (during surgery) 998.2
    - birth injury — *see* Birth, injury
    - nonsurgical (*see also* Injury, by site) 959.9
    - obstetrical 665.9 ☑
      - affecting fetus or newborn 763.89
      - bladder 665.5 ☑
      - cervix 665.3 ☑
      - high vaginal 665.4 ☑
      - perineal NEC 664.9 ☑
      - urethra 665.5 ☑
      - uterus 665.5 ☑
  - internal 869.0

> *Note — For injury of internal organ(s) by foreign body entering through a natural orifice (e.g., inhaled, ingested, or swallowed) — see Foreign body, entering through orifice.*
>
> *For internal injury of any of the following sites with internal injury of any other of the sites — see Injury, internal, multiple.*

-
  -
    - with
      - fracture
        - pelvis — *see* Fracture, pelvis
        - specified site, except pelvis — *see* Injury, internal, by site
      - open wound into cavity 869.1
    - abdomen, abdominal (viscera) NEC 868.00
      - with
        - fracture, pelvis — *see* Fracture, pelvis
        - open wound into cavity 868.10
      - specified site NEC 868.09
        - with open wound into cavity 868.19
    - adrenal (gland) 868.01
      - with open wound into cavity 868.11
    - aorta (thoracic) 901.0
      - abdominal 902.0
    - appendix 863.85
      - with open wound into cavity 863.95

- **Injury** — *continued*
  - internal — *continued*
    - bile duct 868.02
      - with open wound into cavity 868.12
    - bladder (sphincter) 867.0
      - with
        - abortion — *see* Abortion, by type, with damage to pelvic organs
        - ectopic pregnancy (*see also* categories 633.0–633.9) 639.2
        - molar pregnancy (*see also* categories 630–632) 639.2
        - open wound into cavity 867.1
      - following
        - abortion 639.2
        - ectopic or molar pregnancy 639.2
      - obstetrical trauma 665.5 ☑
        - affecting fetus or newborn 763.89
    - blood vessel — *see* Injury, blood vessel, by site
    - broad ligament 867.6
      - with open wound into cavity 867.7
    - bronchus, bronchi 862.21
      - with open wound into cavity 862.31
    - cecum 863.89
      - with open wound into cavity 863.99
    - cervix (uteri) 867.4
      - with
        - abortion — *see* Abortion, by type, with damage to pelvic organs
        - ectopic pregnancy (*see also* categories 633.0–633.9) 639.2
        - molar pregnancy (*see also* categories 630–632) 639.2
        - open wound into cavity 867.5
      - following
        - abortion 639.2
        - ectopic or molar pregnancy 639.2
      - obstetrical trauma 665.3 ☑
        - affecting fetus or newborn 763.89
    - chest (*see also* Injury, internal, intrathoracic organs) 862.8
      - with open wound into cavity 862.9
    - colon 863.40
      - with
        - open wound into cavity 863.50
        - rectum 863.46
          - with open wound into cavity 863.56
      - ascending (right) 863.41
        - with open wound into cavity 863.51
      - descending (left) 863.43
        - with open wound into cavity 863.53
      - multiple sites 863.46
        - with open wound into cavity 863.56
      - sigmoid 863.44
        - with open wound into cavity 863.54
      - specified site NEC 863.49
        - with open wound into cavity 863.59
      - transverse 863.42
        - with open wound into cavity 863.52
    - common duct 868.02
      - with open wound into cavity 868.12

Injury — *continued*
internal — *continued*
vas deferens — *continued*
with open wound into cavity 867.7
vesical (sphincter) 867.0
with open wound into cavity 867.1
viscera (abdominal) (*see also* Injury, internal, multiple) 868.00
with
fracture, pelvis — *see* Fracture, pelvis
open wound into cavity 868.10
thoracic NEC (*see also* Injury, internal, intrathoracic organs) 862.8
with open wound into cavity 862.9
interscapular region 959.19
intervertebral disc 959.19
intestine — *see* Injury, internal, intestine
intra-abdominal (organs) NEC — *see* Injury, internal, intra-abdominal
intracranial 854.0 ☑

Note — Use the following fifth-digit subclassification with categories 851–854:

0	*unspecified state of consciousness*
1	*with no loss of consciousness*
2	*with brief [less than one hour] loss of consciousness*
3	*with moderate [1–24 hours] loss of consciousness*
4	*with prolonged [more than 24 hours] loss of consciousness and return to pre–existing conscious level*
5	*with prolonged [more than 24 hours] loss of consciousness, without return to pre–existing conscious level*

Use fifth-digit 5 to designate when a patient is unconscious and dies before regaining consciousness, regardless of the duration of the loss of consciousness

6	*with loss of consciousness of unspecified duration*
9	*with concussion, unspecified*

with
open intracranial wound 854.1 ☑
skull fracture — *see* Fracture, skull, by site
contusion 851.8 ☑
with open intracranial wound 851.9 ☑
brain stem 851.4 ☑
with open intracranial wound 851.5 ☑
cerebellum 851.4 ☑
with open intracranial wound 851.5 ☑
cortex (cerebral) 851.0 ☑
with open intracranial wound 851.2 ☑
hematoma — *see* Injury, intracranial, hemorrhage
hemorrhage 853.0 ☑
with
laceration — *see* Injury, intracranial, laceration
open intracranial wound 853.1 ☑
extradural 852.4 ☑
with open intracranial wound 852.5 ☑

Injury — *continued*
intracranial — *continued*
hemorrhage — *continued*
subarachnoid 852.0 ☑
with open intracranial wound 852.1 ☑
subdural 852.2 ☑
with open intracranial wound 852.3 ☑
laceration 851.8 ☑
with open intracranial wound 851.9 ☑
brain stem 851.6 ☑
with open intracranial wound 851.7 ☑
cerebellum 851.6 ☑
with open intracranial wound 851.7 ☑
cortex (cerebral) 851.2 ☑
with open intracranial wound 851.3 ☑
intraocular — *see* Injury, eyeball, penetrating
intrathoracic organs (multiple) — *see* Injury, internal, intrathoracic organs
intrauterine — *see* Injury, internal, intrauterine
iris 921.3
penetrating — *see* Injury, eyeball, penetrating
jaw 959.09
jejunum — *see* Injury, internal, jejunum
joint NEC 959.9
old or residual 718.80
ankle 718.87
elbow 718.82
foot 718.87
hand 718.84
hip 718.85
knee 718.86
multiple sites 718.89
pelvic region 718.85
shoulder (region) 718.81
specified site NEC 718.88
wrist 718.83
kidney — *see* Injury, internal, kidney
acute (nontraumatic) 584.9
knee (and ankle) (and foot) (and leg, except thigh) 959.7
labium (majus) (minus) 959.14
labyrinth, ear 959.09
lacrimal apparatus, gland, or sac 921.1
laceration 870.8
larynx 959.09
late effect — *see* Late, effects (of), injury
leg, except thigh (and ankle) (and foot) (and knee) 959.7
upper or thigh 959.6
lens, eye 921.3
penetrating — *see* Injury, eyeball, penetrating
lid, eye — *see* Injury, eyelid
lip 959.09
liver — *see* Injury, internal, liver
lobe, parietal — *see* Injury, intracranial
lumbar (region) 959.19
plexus 953.5
lumbosacral (region) 959.19
plexus 953.5
lung — *see* Injury, internal, lung
malar region 959.09
mastoid region 959.09
maternal, during pregnancy, affecting fetus or newborn 760.5
maxilla 959.09
mediastinum — *see* Injury, internal, mediastinum
membrane
brain (*see also* Injury, intracranial) 854.0 ☑
tympanic 959.09

Injury — *continued*
meningeal artery — *see* Hemorrhage, brain, traumatic, subarachnoid
meninges (cerebral) — *see* Injury, intracranial
mesenteric
artery — *see* Injury, blood vessel, mesenteric, artery
plexus, inferior 954.1
vein — *see* Injury, blood vessel, mesenteric, vein
mesentery — *see* Injury, internal, mesentery
mesosalpinx — *see* Injury, internal, mesosalpinx
middle ear 959.09
midthoracic region 959.11
mouth 959.09
multiple (sites not classifiable to the same four–digit category in 959.0–959.7) 959.8
internal 869.0
with open wound into cavity 869.1
musculocutaneous nerve 955.4
nail
finger 959.5
toe 959.7
nasal (septum) (sinus) 959.09
nasopharynx 959.09
neck (and face) 959.09
nerve 957.9
abducens 951.3
abducent 951.3
accessory 951.6
acoustic 951.5
ankle and foot 956.9
anterior crural, femoral 956.1
arm (*see also* Injury, nerve, upper limb) 955.9
auditory 951.5
axillary 955.0
brachial plexus 953.4
cervical sympathetic 954.0
cranial 951.9
first or olfactory 951.8
second or optic 950.0
third or oculomotor 951.0
fourth or trochlear 951.1
fifth or trigeminal 951.2
sixth or abducens 951.3
seventh or facial 951.4
eighth, acoustic, or auditory 951.5
ninth or glossopharyngeal 951.8
tenth, pneumogastric, or vagus 951.8
eleventh or accessory 951.6
twelfth or hypoglossal 951.7
newborn 767.7
cutaneous sensory
lower limb 956.4
upper limb 955.5
digital (finger) 955.6
toe 956.5
facial 951.4
newborn 767.5
femoral 956.1
finger 955.9
foot and ankle 956.9
forearm 955.9
glossopharyngeal 951.8
hand and wrist 955.9
head and neck, superficial 957.0
hypoglossal 951.7
involving several parts of body 957.8
leg (*see also* Injury, nerve, lower limb) 956.9
lower limb 956.9
multiple 956.8
specified site NEC 956.5
lumbar plexus 953.5
lumbosacral plexus 953.5
median 955.1
forearm 955.1

Injury — *continued*
nerve — *continued*
median — *continued*
wrist and hand 955.1
multiple (in several parts of body) (sites not classifiable to the same three-digit category) 957.8
musculocutaneous 955.4
musculospiral 955.3
upper arm 955.3
oculomotor 951.0
olfactory 951.8
optic 950.0
pelvic girdle 956.9
multiple sites 956.8
specified site NEC 956.5
peripheral 957.9
multiple (in several regions) (sites not classifiable to the same three-digit category) 957.8
specified site NEC 957.1
peroneal 956.3
ankle and foot 956.3
lower leg 956.3
plantar 956.5
plexus 957.9
celiac 954.1
mesenteric, inferior 954.1
spinal 953.9
brachial 953.4
lumbosacral 953.5
multiple sites 953.8
sympathetic NEC 954.1
pneumogastric 951.8
radial 955.3
wrist and hand 955.3
sacral plexus 953.5
sciatic 956.0
thigh 956.0
shoulder girdle 955.9
multiple 955.8
specified site NEC 955.7
specified site NEC 957.1
spinal 953.9
plexus — *see* Injury, nerve, plexus, spinal
root 953.9
cervical 953.0
dorsal 953.1
lumbar 953.2
multiple sites 953.8
sacral 953.3
splanchnic 954.1
sympathetic NEC 954.1
cervical 954.0
thigh 956.9
tibial 956.5
ankle and foot 956.2
lower leg 956.5
posterior 956.2
toe 956.9
trigeminal 951.2
trochlear 951.1
trunk, excluding shoulder and pelvic girdles 954.9
specified site NEC 954.8
sympathetic NEC 954.1
ulnar 955.2
forearm 955.2
wrist (and hand) 955.2
upper limb 955.9
multiple 955.8
specified site NEC 955.7
vagus 951.8
wrist and hand 955.9
nervous system, diffuse 957.8
nose (septum) 959.09
obstetrical NEC 665.9 ☑
affecting fetus or newborn 763.89
occipital (region) (scalp) 959.09
lobe (*see also* Injury, intracranial) 854.0 ☑
optic 950.9
chiasm 950.1

- **Injury** — *continued*
  - optic — *continued*
    - cortex 950.3
    - nerve 950.0
    - pathways 950.2
  - orbit, orbital (region) 921.2
    - penetrating 870.3
      - with foreign body 870.4
  - ovary — *see* Injury, internal, ovary
  - paint-gun — *see* Wound, open, by site, complicated
  - palate (soft) 959.09
  - pancreas — *see* Injury, internal, pancreas
  - parathyroid (gland) 959.09
  - parietal (region) (scalp) 959.09
    - lobe — *see* Injury, intracranial
  - pelvic
    - floor 959.19
      - complicating delivery 664.1 ☑
        - affecting fetus or newborn 763.89
    - joint or ligament, complicating delivery 665.6 ☑
      - affecting fetus or newborn 763.89
    - organs (*see also* Injury, internal, pelvis)
      - with
        - abortion — *see* Abortion, by type, with damage to pelvic organs
        - ectopic pregnancy (*see also* categories 633.0–633.9) 639.2
        - molar pregnancy (*see also* categories 633.0–633.9) 639.2
      - following
        - abortion 639.2
        - ectopic or molar pregnancy 639.2
      - obstetrical trauma 665.5 ☑
        - affecting fetus or newborn 763.89
  - pelvis 959.19
  - penis 959.14
    - fracture of corpus cavernosum 959.13
  - perineum 959.14
  - peritoneum — *see* Injury, internal, peritoneum
  - periurethral tissue
    - with
      - abortion — *see* Abortion, by type, with damage to pelvic organs
      - ectopic pregnancy (*see also* categories 633.0–633.9) 639.2
      - molar pregnancy (*see also* categories 630–632) 639.2
    - complicating delivery 665.5 ☑
      - affecting fetus or newborn 763.89
    - following
      - abortion 639.2
      - ectopic or molar pregnancy 639.2
  - phalanges
    - foot 959.7
    - hand 959.5
  - pharynx 959.09
  - pleura — *see* Injury, internal, pleura
  - popliteal space 959.7
  - post-cardiac surgery (syndrome) 429.4
  - prepuce 959.14
  - prostate — *see* Injury, internal, prostate
  - pubic region 959.19
  - pudenda 959.14
  - radiation NEC 990
  - radioactive substance or radium NEC 990
  - rectovaginal septum 959.14
  - rectum — *see* Injury, internal, rectum
  - retina 921.3
    - penetrating — *see* Injury, eyeball, penetrating
  - retroperitoneal — *see* Injury, internal, retroperitoneum
  - roentgen rays NEC 990
  - round ligament — *see* Injury, internal, round ligament
  - sacral (region) 959.19
    - plexus 953.5
  - sacroiliac ligament NEC 959.19
  - sacrum 959.19
  - salivary ducts or glands 959.09
  - scalp 959.09
    - due to birth trauma 767.19
    - fetus or newborn 767.19
  - scapular region 959.2
  - sclera 921.3
    - penetrating — *see* Injury, eyeball, penetrating
    - superficial 918.2
  - scrotum 959.14
  - seminal vesicle — *see* Injury, internal, seminal vesicle
  - shoulder (and upper arm) 959.2
  - sinus
    - cavernous (*see also* Injury, intracranial) 854.0 ☑
    - nasal 959.09
  - skeleton NEC, birth injury 767.3
  - skin NEC 959.9
  - skull — *see* Fracture, skull, by site
  - soft tissue (of external sites) (severe) — *see* Wound, open, by site
  - specified site NEC 959.8
  - spermatic cord — *see* Injury, internal, spermatic cord
  - spinal (cord) 952.9
    - with fracture, vertebra — *see* Fracture, vertebra, by site, with spinal cord injury
    - cervical (C_1-C_4) 952.00
      - with
        - anterior cord syndrome 952.02
        - central cord syndrome 952.03
        - complete lesion of cord 952.01
        - incomplete lesion NEC 952.04
        - posterior cord syndrome 952.04
      - C_5-C_7 level 952.05
        - with
          - anterior cord syndrome 952.07
          - central cord syndrome 952.08
          - complete lesion of cord 952.06
          - incomplete lesion NEC 952.09
          - posterior cord syndrome 952.09
        - specified type NEC 952.09
      - specified type NEC 952.04
    - dorsal (D_1-D_6) (T_1-T_6) (thoracic) 952.10
      - with
        - anterior cord syndrome 952.12
        - central cord syndrome 952.13
        - complete lesion of cord 952.11
        - incomplete lesion NEC 952.14
        - posterior cord syndrome 952.14
      - D_7-D_{12} level (T_7-T_{12}) 952.15
        - with
          - anterior cord syndrome 952.17
- **Injury** — *continued*
  - spinal — *continued*
    - dorsal — *continued*
      - D_7-D_{12} level — *continued*
        - with — *continued*
          - central cord syndrome 952.18
          - complete lesion of cord 952.16
          - incomplete lesion NEC 952.19
          - posterior cord syndrome 952.19
        - specified type NEC 952.19
      - specified type NEC 952.14
    - lumbar 952.2
    - multiple sites 952.8
    - nerve (root) NEC — *see* Injury, nerve, spinal, root
    - plexus 953.9
      - brachial 953.4
      - lumbosacral 953.5
      - multiple sites 953.8
    - sacral 952.3
    - thoracic (*see also* Injury, spinal, dorsal) 952.10
  - spleen — *see* Injury, internal, spleen
  - stellate ganglion 954.1
  - sternal region 959.11
  - stomach — *see* Injury, internal, stomach
  - subconjunctival 921.1
  - subcutaneous 959.9
  - subdural — *see* Injury, intracranial
  - submaxillary region 959.09
  - submental region 959.09
  - subungual
    - fingers 959.5
    - toes 959.7
  - superficial 919 ☑

Note — Use the following fourth-digit subdivisions with categories 910–919:

- 0 *Abrasion or friction burn without mention of infection*
- 1 *Abrasion or friction burn, infected*
- 2 *Blister without mention of infection*
- 3 *Blister, infected*
- 4 *Insect bite, nonvenomous, without mention of infection*
- 5 *Insect bite, nonvenomous, infected*
- 6 *Superficial foreign body (splinter) without major open wound and without mention of infection*
- 7 *Superficial foreign body (splinter) without major open wound, infected*
- 8 *Other and unspecified superficial injury without mention of infection*
- 9 *Other and unspecified superficial injury, infected*

For late effects of superficial injury, see category 906.2.

- abdomen, abdominal (muscle) (wall) (and other part(s) of trunk) 911 ☑
- ankle (and hip, knee, leg, or thigh) 916 ☑
- anus (and other part(s) of trunk) 911 ☑
- arm 913 ☑
  - upper (and shoulder) 912 ☑
- auditory canal (external) (meatus) (and other part(s) of face, neck, or scalp, except eye) 910 ☑
- axilla (and upper arm) 912 ☑
- back (and other part(s) of trunk) 911 ☑
- **Injury** — *continued*
  - superficial — *continued*
    - breast (and other part(s) of trunk) 911 ☑
    - brow (and other part(s) of face, neck, or scalp, except eye) 910 ☑
    - buttock (and other part(s) of trunk) 911 ☑
    - canthus, eye 918.0
    - cheek(s) (and other part(s) of face, neck, or scalp, except eye) 910 ☑
    - chest wall (and other part(s) of trunk) 911 ☑
    - chin (and other part(s) of face, neck, or scalp, except eye) 910 ☑
    - clitoris (and other part(s) of trunk) 911 ☑
    - conjunctiva 918.2
    - cornea 918.1
      - due to contact lens 371.82
    - costal region (and other part(s) of trunk) 911 ☑
    - ear(s) (auricle) (canal) (drum) (external) (and other part(s) of face, neck, or scalp, except eye) 910 ☑
    - elbow (and forearm) (and wrist) 913 ☑
    - epididymis (and other part(s) of trunk) 911 ☑
    - epigastric region (and other part(s) of trunk) 911 ☑
    - epiglottis (and other part(s) of face, neck, or scalp, except eye) 910 ☑
    - eye(s) (and adnexa) NEC 918.9
    - eyelid(s) (and periocular area) 918.0
    - face (any part(s), except eye) (and neck or scalp) 910 ☑
    - finger(s) (nail) (any) 915 ☑
    - flank (and other part(s) of trunk) 911 ☑
    - foot (phalanges) (and toe(s)) 917 ☑
    - forearm (and elbow) (and wrist) 913 ☑
    - forehead (and other part(s) of face, neck, or scalp, except eye) 910 ☑
    - globe (eye) 918.9
    - groin (and other part(s) of trunk) 911 ☑
    - gum(s) (and other part(s) of face, neck, or scalp, except eye) 910 ☑
    - hand(s) (except fingers alone) 914 ☑
    - head (and other part(s) of face, neck, or scalp, except eye) 910 ☑
    - heel (and foot or toe) 917 ☑
    - hip (and ankle, knee, leg, or thigh) 916 ☑
    - iliac region (and other part(s) of trunk) 911 ☑
    - interscapular region (and other part(s) of trunk) 911 ☑
    - iris 918.9
    - knee (and ankle, hip, leg, or thigh) 916 ☑
    - labium (majus) (minus) (and other part(s) of trunk) 911 ☑
    - lacrimal (apparatus) (gland) (sac) 918.0
    - leg (lower) (upper) (and ankle, hip, knee, or thigh) 916 ☑
    - lip(s) (and other part(s) of face, neck, or scalp, except eye) 910 ☑
    - lower extremity (except foot) 916 ☑
    - lumbar region (and other part(s) of trunk) 911 ☑

- **Injury** — *continued*
  - superficial — *continued*
    - malar region (and other part(s) of face, neck, or scalp, except eye) 910 ☑
    - mastoid region (and other part(s) of face, neck, or scalp, except eye) 910 ☑
    - midthoracic region (and other part(s) of trunk) 911 ☑
    - mouth (and other part(s) of face, neck, or scalp, except eye) 910 ☑
    - multiple sites (not classifiable to the same three-digit category) 919 ☑
    - nasal (septum) (and other part(s) of face, neck, or scalp, except eye) 910 ☑
    - neck (and face or scalp, any part(s), except eye) 910 ☑
    - nose (septum) (and other part(s) of face, neck, or scalp, except eye) 910 ☑
    - occipital region (and other part(s) of face, neck, or scalp, except eye) 910 ☑
    - orbital region 918.0
    - palate (soft) (and other part(s) of face, neck, or scalp, except eye) 910 ☑
    - parietal region (and other part(s) of face, neck, or scalp, except eye) 910 ☑
    - penis (and other part(s) of trunk) 911 ☑
    - perineum (and other part(s) of trunk) 911 ☑
    - periocular area 918.0
    - pharynx (and other part(s) of face, neck, or scalp, except eye) 910 ☑
    - popliteal space (and ankle, hip, leg, or thigh) 916 ☑
    - prepuce (and other part(s) of trunk) 911 ☑
    - pubic region (and other part(s) of trunk) 911 ☑
    - pudenda (and other part(s) of trunk) 911 ☑
    - sacral region (and other part(s) of trunk) 911 ☑
    - salivary (ducts) (glands) (and other part(s) of face, neck, or scalp, except eye) 910 ☑
    - scalp (and other part(s) of face or neck, except eye) 910 ☑
    - scapular region (and upper arm) 912 ☑
    - sclera 918.2
    - scrotum (and other part(s) of trunk) 911 ☑
    - shoulder (and upper arm) 912 ☑
    - skin NEC 919 ☑
    - specified site(s) NEC 919 ☑
    - sternal region (and other part(s) of trunk) 911 ☑
    - subconjunctival 918.2
    - subcutaneous NEC 919 ☑
    - submaxillary region (and other part(s) of face, neck, or scalp, except eye) 910 ☑
    - submental region (and other part(s) of face, neck, or scalp, except eye) 910 ☑
    - supraclavicular fossa (and other part(s) of face, neck, or scalp, except eye) 910 ☑
    - supraorbital 918.0
    - temple (and other part(s) of face, neck, or scalp, except eye) 910 ☑
    - temporal region (and other part(s) of face, neck, or scalp, except eye) 910 ☑

- **Injury** — *continued*
  - superficial — *continued*
    - testis (and other part(s) of trunk) 911 ☑
    - thigh (and ankle, hip, knee, or leg) 916 ☑
    - thorax, thoracic (external) (and other part(s) of trunk) 911 ☑
    - throat (and other part(s) of face, neck, or scalp, except eye) 910 ☑
    - thumb(s) (nail) 915 ☑
    - toe(s) (nail) (subungual) (and foot) 917 ☑
    - tongue (and other part(s) of face, neck, or scalp, except eye) 910 ☑
    - tooth, teeth (*see also* Abrasion, dental) 521.20
    - trunk (any part(s)) 911 ☑
    - tunica vaginalis 959.14
    - tympanum, tympanic membrane (and other part(s) of face, neck, or scalp, except eye) 910 ☑
    - upper extremity NEC 913 ☑
    - uvula (and other part(s) of face, neck, or scalp, except eye) 910 ☑
    - vagina (and other part(s) of trunk) 911 ☑
    - vulva (and other part(s) of trunk) 911 ☑
    - wrist (and elbow) (and forearm) 913 ☑
  - supraclavicular fossa 959.19
  - supraorbital 959.09
  - surgical complication (external or internal site) 998.2
  - symphysis pubis 959.19
    - complicating delivery 665.6 ☑
      - affecting fetus or newborn 763.89
  - temple 959.09
  - temporal region 959.09
  - testis 959.14
  - thigh (and hip) 959.6
  - thorax, thoracic (external) 959.11
    - cavity — *see* Injury, internal, thorax
    - internal — *see* Injury, internal, intrathoracic organs
  - throat 959.09
  - thumb(s) (nail) 959.5
  - thymus — *see* Injury, internal, thymus
  - thyroid (gland) 959.09
  - toe (nail) (any) 959.7
  - tongue 959.09
  - tonsil 959.09
  - tooth NEC 873.63
    - complicated 873.73
  - trachea — *see* Injury, internal, trachea
  - trunk 959.19
  - tunica vaginalis 959.14
  - tympanum, tympanic membrane 959.09
  - ultraviolet rays NEC 990
  - ureter — *see* Injury, internal, ureter
  - urethra (sphincter) — *see* Injury, internal, urethra
  - uterus — *see* Injury, internal, uterus
  - uvula 959.09
  - vagina 959.14
  - vascular — *see* Injury, blood vessel
  - vas deferens — *see* Injury, internal, vas deferens
  - vein (*see also* Injury, blood vessel, by site) 904.9
  - vena cava
    - inferior 902.10
    - superior 901.2
  - vesical (sphincter) — *see* Injury, internal, vesical

- **Injury** — *continued*
  - viscera (abdominal) — *see* Injury, internal, viscera
    - with fracture, pelvis — *see* Fracture, pelvis
  - visual 950.9
    - cortex 950.3
  - vitreous (humor) 871.2
  - vulva 959.14
  - whiplash (cervical spine) 847.0
  - wringer — *see* Crush, by site
  - wrist (and elbow) (and forearm) 959.3
  - x-ray NEC 990
- **Inoculation** — *see also* Vaccination
  - complication or reaction — *see* Complication, vaccination
- **INPH** (idiopathic normal pressure hydrocephalus) 331.5
- **Insanity, insane** — *see also* Psychosis 298.9
  - adolescent (*see also* Schizophrenia) 295.9 ☑
  - alternating (*see also* Psychosis, affective, circular) 296.7
  - confusional 298.9
    - acute 293.0
    - subacute 293.1
  - delusional 298.9
  - paralysis, general 094.1
    - progressive 094.1
  - paresis, general 094.1
  - senile 290.20
- **Insect**
  - bite — *see* Injury, superficial, by site
  - venomous, poisoning by 989.5
- **Insemination, artificial** V26.1
- **Insensitivity**
  - adrenocorticotropin hormone (ACTH) 255.41
  - androgen 259.50
    - complete 259.51
    - partial 259.52
- **Insertion**
  - cord (umbilical) lateral or velamentous 663.8 ☑
    - affecting fetus or newborn 762.6
  - intrauterine contraceptive device V25.1
  - placenta, vicious — *see* Placenta, previa
  - subdermal implantable contraceptive V25.5
  - velamentous, umbilical cord 663.8 ☑
    - affecting fetus or newborn 762.6
- **Insolation** 992.0
  - meaning sunstroke 992.0
- **Insomnia, unspecified** 780.52
  - with sleep apnea, unspecified 780.51
  - adjustment 307.41
  - alcohol induced 291.82
  - behavioral, of childhood V69.5
  - drug induced 292.85
  - due to
    - medical condition classified elsewhere 327.01
    - mental disorder 327.02
  - fatal familial (FFI) 046.72
  - idiopathic 307.42
  - nonorganic origin 307.41
    - persistent (primary) 307.42
    - transient 307.41
  - organic 327.00
    - other 327.09
  - paradoxical 307.42
  - primary 307.42
  - psychophysiological 307.42
  - subjective complaint 307.49
- **Inspiration**
  - food or foreign body (*see also* Asphyxia, food or foreign body) 933.1
  - mucus (*see also* Asphyxia, mucus) 933.1
- **Inspissated bile syndrome, newborn** 774.4
- **Instability**
  - detrusor 596.59

- **Instability** — *continued*
  - emotional (excessive) 301.3
  - joint (posttraumatic) 718.80
    - ankle 718.87
    - elbow 718.82
    - foot 718.87
    - hand 718.84
    - hip 718.85
    - knee 718.86
    - lumbosacral 724.6
    - multiple sites 718.89
    - pelvic region 718.85
    - sacroiliac 724.6
    - shoulder (region) 718.81
    - specified site NEC 718.88
    - wrist 718.83
  - lumbosacral 724.6
  - nervous 301.89
  - personality (emotional) 301.59
  - thyroid, paroxysmal 242.9 ☑
  - urethral 599.83
  - vasomotor 780.2
- **Insufficiency, insufficient**
  - accommodation 367.4
  - adrenal (gland) (acute) (chronic) 255.41
    - medulla 255.5
    - primary 255.41
    - specified site NEC 255.5
  - adrenocortical 255.41
  - anterior (occlusal) guidance 524.54
  - anus 569.49
  - aortic (valve) 424.1
    - with
      - mitral (valve) disease 396.1
        - insufficiency, incompetence, or regurgitation 396.3
        - stenosis or obstruction 396.1
      - stenosis or obstruction 424.1
        - with mitral (valve) disease 396.8
    - congenital 746.4
    - rheumatic 395.1
      - with
        - mitral (valve) disease 396.1
          - insufficiency, incompetence, or regurgitation 396.3
          - stenosis or obstruction 396.1
        - stenosis or obstruction 395.2
          - with mitral (valve) disease 396.8
    - specified cause NEC 424.1
    - syphilitic 093.22
  - arterial 447.1
    - basilar artery 435.0
    - carotid artery 435.8
    - cerebral 437.1
    - coronary (acute or subacute) 411.89
    - mesenteric 557.1
    - peripheral 443.9
    - precerebral 435.9
    - vertebral artery 435.1
    - vertebrobasilar 435.3
  - arteriovenous 459.9
  - basilar artery 435.0
  - biliary 575.8
  - cardiac (*see also* Insufficiency, myocardial) 428.0
    - complicating surgery 997.1
    - due to presence of (cardiac) prosthesis 429.4
    - postoperative 997.1
      - long-term effect of cardiac surgery 429.4
    - specified during or due to a procedure 997.1
      - long-term effect of cardiac surgery 429.4
  - cardiorenal (*see also* Hypertension, cardiorenal) 404.90
  - cardiovascular (*see also* Disease, cardiovascular) 429.2

J

Jaccoud's nodular fibrositis, chronic (Jaccoud's syndrome) 714.4
Jackson's
- membrane 751.4
- paralysis or syndrome 344.89
- veil 751.4

Jacksonian
- epilepsy (*see also* Epilepsy) 345.5 ☑
- seizures (focal) (*see also* Epilepsy) 345.5 ☑

Jacob's ulcer (M8090/3) — *see* Neoplasm, skin, malignant, by site
Jacquet's dermatitis (diaper dermatitis) 691.0
Jadassohn's
- blue nevus (M8780/0) — *see* Neoplasm, skin, benign
- disease (maculopapular erythroderma) 696.2
- intraepidermal epithelioma (M8096/0) — *see* Neoplasm, skin, benign

Jadassohn-Lewandowski syndrome (pachyonychia congenita) 757.5
Jadassohn-Pellizari's disease (anetoderma) 701.3
Jadassohn-Tièche nevus (M8780/0) — *see* Neoplasm, skin, benign
Jaffe-Lichtenstein (-Uehlinger) syndrome 252.01
Jahnke's syndrome (encephalocutaneous angiomatosis) 759.6
Jakob-Creutzfeldt disease (CJD) (syndrome) 046.19
- with dementia
  - with behavioral disturbance 046.19 *[294.11]*
  - without behavioral disturbance 046.19 *[294.10]*
- familial 046.19
- iatrogenic 046.19
- specified NEC 046.19
- sporadic 046.19
- variant (vCJD) 046.11
  - with dementia
    - with behavioral disturbance 046.11 *[294.11]*
    - without behavioral disturbance 046.11 *[294.10]*

Jaksch (-Luzet) disease or syndrome (pseudoleukemia infantum) 285.8
Jamaican
- neuropathy 349.82
- paraplegic tropical ataxic-spastic syndrome 349.82

Janet's disease (psychasthenia) 300.89
Janiceps 759.4
Jansky-Bielschowsky amaurotic familial idiocy 330.1
Japanese
- B type encephalitis 062.0
- river fever 081.2
- seven-day fever 100.89

Jaundice (yellow) 782.4
- acholuric (familial) (splenomegalic) (*see also* Spherocytosis) 282.0
  - acquired 283.9
- breast milk 774.39
- catarrhal (acute) 070.1
  - with hepatic coma 070.0
  - chronic 571.9
  - epidemic — *see* Jaundice, epidemic
- cholestatic (benign) 782.4
- chronic idiopathic 277.4
- epidemic (catarrhal) 070.1
  - with hepatic coma 070.0
  - leptospiral 100.0
  - spirochetal 100.0
- febrile (acute) 070.1
  - with hepatic coma 070.0
  - leptospiral 100.0
  - spirochetal 100.0
- fetus or newborn 774.6

Jaundice — *continued*
- fetus or newborn — *continued*
  - due to or associated with
    - ABO
    - absence or deficiency of enzyme system for bilirubin conjugation (congenital) 774.39
    - antibodies 773.1
    - blood group incompatibility NEC 773.2
    - breast milk inhibitors to conjugation 774.39
      - associated with preterm delivery 774.2
    - bruising 774.1
    - Crigler-Najjar syndrome 277.4 *[774.31]*
    - delayed conjugation 774.30
      - associated with preterm delivery 774.2
      - development 774.39
    - drugs or toxins transmitted from mother 774.1
    - G-6-PD deficiency 282.2 *[774.0]*
    - galactosemia 271.1 *[774.5]*
    - Gilbert's syndrome 277.4 *[774.31]*
    - hepatocellular damage 774.4
    - hereditary hemolytic anemia (*see also* Anemia, hemolytic) 282.9 *[774.0]*
    - hypothyroidism, congenital 243 *[774.31]*
    - incompatibility, maternal/fetal NEC 773.2
    - incompatibility, maternal/fetal 773.1
    - infection 774.1
    - inspissated bile syndrome 774.4
    - isoimmunization NEC 773.2
    - isoimmunization 773.1
    - mucoviscidosis 277.01 *[774.5]*
    - obliteration of bile duct, congenital 751.61 *[774.5]*
    - polycythemia 774.1
    - preterm delivery 774.2
    - red cell defect 282.9 *[774.0]*
    - Rh
      - antibodies 773.0
      - incompatibility, maternal/fetal 773.0
      - isoimmunization 773.0
    - spherocytosis (congenital) 282.0 *[774.0]*
    - swallowed maternal blood 774.1
  - physiological NEC 774.6
- from injection, inoculation, infusion, or transfusion (blood) (plasma) (serum) (other substance) (onset within 8 months after administration) — *see* Hepatitis, viral
- Gilbert's (familial nonhemolytic) 277.4
- hematogenous 283.9
- hemolytic (acquired) 283.9
  - congenital (*see also* Spherocytosis) 282.0
- hemorrhagic (acute) 100.0
  - leptospiral 100.0
  - newborn 776.0
  - spirochetal 100.0
- hepatocellular 573.8
- homologous (serum) — *see* Hepatitis, viral
- idiopathic, chronic 277.4
- infectious (acute) (subacute) 070.1
  - with hepatic coma 070.0
  - leptospiral 100.0
  - spirochetal 100.0
- leptospiral 100.0
- malignant (*see also* Necrosis, liver) 570
- newborn (physiological) (*see also* Jaundice, fetus or newborn) 774.6
- nonhemolytic, congenital familial (Gilbert's) 277.4

Jaundice — *continued*
- nuclear, newborn (*see also* Kernicterus of newborn) 774.7
- obstructive NEC (*see also* Obstruction, biliary) 576.8
- postimmunization — *see* Hepatitis, viral
- posttransfusion — *see* Hepatitis, viral
- regurgitation (*see also* Obstruction, biliary) 576.8
- serum (homologous) (prophylactic) (therapeutic) — *see* Hepatitis, viral
- spirochetal (hemorrhagic) 100.0
- symptomatic 782.4
  - newborn 774.6

Jaw — *see* condition
Jaw-blinking 374.43
- congenital 742.8

Jaw-winking phenomenon or syndrome 742.8
Jealousy
- alcoholic 291.5
- childhood 313.3
- sibling 313.3

Jejunitis — *see also* Enteritis 558.9
Jejunostomy status V44.4
Jejunum, jejunal — *see* condition
Jensen's disease 363.05
Jericho boil 085.1
Jerks, myoclonic 333.2
Jervell-Lange-Nielsen syndrome 426.82
Jeune's disease or syndrome (asphyxiating thoracic dystrophy) 756.4
Jigger disease 134.1
Job's syndrome (chronic granulomatous disease) 288.1
Jod-Basedow phenomenon 242.8 ☑
Johnson-Stevens disease (erythema multiforme exudativum) 695.13
Joint — *see also* condition
- Charcôt's 094.0 *[713.5]*
- false 733.82
- flail — *see* Flail, joint
- mice — *see* Loose, body, joint, by site
- sinus to bone 730.9 ☑
- von Gies' 095.8

Jordan's anomaly or syndrome 288.2
Josephs-Diamond-Blackfan anemia (congenital hypoplastic) 284.01
Joubert syndrome 759.89
Jumpers' knee 727.2
Jungle yellow fever 060.0
Jüngling's disease (sarcoidosis) 135
Junin virus hemorrhagic fever 078.7
Juvenile — *see also* condition
- delinquent 312.9
  - group (*see also* Disturbance, conduct) 312.2 ☑
  - neurotic 312.4

K

Kabuki syndrome 759.89
Kahler (-Bozzolo) disease (multiple myeloma) (M9730/3) 203.0 ☑
Kakergasia 300.9
Kakke 265.0
Kala-azar (Indian) (infantile) (Mediterranean) (Sudanese) 085.0
Kalischer's syndrome (encephalocutaneous angiomatosis) 759.6
Kallmann's syndrome (hypogonadotropic hypogonadism with anosmia) 253.4
Kanner's syndrome (autism) — *see also* Psychosis, childhood 299.0 ☑
Kaolinosis 502
Kaposi's
- disease 757.33
  - lichen ruber 696.4
    - acuminatus 696.4
    - moniliformis 697.8
  - xeroderma pigmentosum 757.33
- sarcoma (M9140/3) 176.9
  - adipose tissue 176.1
  - aponeurosis 176.1

Kaposi's — *continued*
- sarcoma — *continued*
  - artery 176.1
  - associated herpesvirus infection 058.89
  - blood vessel 176.1
  - bursa 176.1
  - connective tissue 176.1
  - external genitalia 176.8
  - fascia 176.1
  - fatty tissue 176.1
  - fibrous tissue 176.1
  - gastrointestinal tract NEC 176.3
  - ligament 176.1
  - lung 176.4
  - lymph
    - gland(s) 176.5
    - node(s) 176.5
  - lymphatic(s) NEC 176.1
  - muscle (skeletal) 176.1
  - oral cavity NEC 176.8
  - palate 176.2
  - scrotum 176.8
  - skin 176.0
  - soft tissue 176.1
  - specified site NEC 176.8
  - subcutaneous tissue 176.1
  - synovia 176.1
  - tendon (sheath) 176.1
  - vein 176.1
  - vessel 176.1
  - viscera NEC 176.9
  - vulva 176.8
- varicelliform eruption 054.0
  - vaccinia 999.0

Kartagener's syndrome or triad (sinusitis, bronchiectasis, situs inversus) 759.3
Kasabach-Merritt syndrome (capillary hemangioma associated with thrombocytopenic purpura) 287.39
Kaschin-Beck disease (endemic polyarthritis) — *see* Disease, Kaschin-Beck
Kast's syndrome (dyschondroplasia with hemangiomas) 756.4
Katatonia — *see* Catatonia
Katayama disease or fever 120.2
Kathisophobia 781.0
Kawasaki disease 446.1
Kayser-Fleischer ring (cornea) (pseudosclerosis) 275.1 *[371.14]*
Kaznelson's syndrome (congenital hypoplastic anemia) 284.01
Kearns-Sayre syndrome 277.87
Kedani fever 081.2
Kelis 701.4
Kelly (-Patterson) syndrome (sideropenic dysphagia) 280.8
Keloid, cheloid 701.4
- Addison's (morphea) 701.0
- cornea 371.00
- Hawkins' 701.4
- scar 701.4

Keloma 701.4
Kenya fever 082.1
Keratectasia 371.71
- congenital 743.41

Keratinization NEC
- alveolar ridge mucosa
  - excessive 528.72
  - minimal 528.71

Keratitis (nodular) (nonulcerative) (simple) (zonular) NEC 370.9
- with ulceration (*see also* Ulcer, cornea) 370.00
- actinic 370.24
- arborescens 054.42
- areolar 370.22
- bullosa 370.8
- deep — *see* Keratitis, interstitial
- dendritic(a) 054.42
- desiccation 370.34
- diffuse interstitial 370.52
- disciform(is) 054.43
  - varicella 052.7 *[370.44]*

- **Kuhnt-Junius degeneration or disease** 362.52
- **Kulchitsky's cell carcinoma** (carcinoid tumor of intestine) 259.2
- **Kümmell's disease or spondylitis** 721.7
- **Kundrat's disease** (lymphosarcoma) 200.1 ☑
- **Kunekune** — *see* Dermatophytosis
- **Kunkel syndrome** (lupoid hepatitis) 571.49
- **Kupffer cell sarcoma** (M9124/3) 155.0
- **Kuru** 046.0
- **Kussmaul's**
  - coma (diabetic) 250.3 ☑
    - due to secondary diabetes 249.3 ☑
  - disease (polyarteritis nodosa) 446.0
  - respiration (air hunger) 786.09
- **Kwashiorkor** (marasmus type) 260
- **Kyasanur Forest disease** 065.2
- **Kyphoscoliosis, kyphoscoliotic** (acquired) — *see also* Scoliosis 737.30
  - congenital 756.19
  - due to radiation 737.33
  - heart (disease) 416.1
  - idiopathic 737.30
    - infantile
      - progressive 737.32
      - resolving 737.31
  - late effect of rickets 268.1 *[737.43]*
  - specified NEC 737.39
  - thoracogenic 737.34
  - tuberculous (*see also* Tuberculosis) 015.0 ☑ *[737.43]*
- **Kyphosis, kyphotic** (acquired) (postural) 737.10
  - adolescent postural 737.0
  - congenital 756.19
  - dorsalis juvenilis 732.0
  - due to or associated with
    - Charcôt-Marie-Tooth disease 356.1 *[737.41]*
    - mucopolysaccharidosis 277.5 *[737.41]*
    - neurofibromatosis 237.71 *[737.41]*
    - osteitis
      - deformans 731.0 *[737.41]*
      - fibrosa cystica 252.01 *[737.41]*
    - osteoporosis (*see also* Osteoporosis) 733.0 ☑ *[737.41]*
    - poliomyelitis (*see also* Poliomyelitis) 138 *[737.41]*
    - radiation 737.11
    - tuberculosis (*see also* Tuberculosis) 015.0 ☑ *[737.41]*
  - Kümmell's 721.7
  - late effect of rickets 268.1 *[737.41]*
  - Morquio-Brailsford type (spinal) 277.5 *[737.41]*
  - pelvis 738.6
  - postlaminectomy 737.12
  - specified cause NEC 737.19
  - syphilitic, congenital 090.5 *[737.41]*
  - tuberculous (*see also* Tuberculosis) 015.0 ☑ *[737.41]*
- **Kyrle's disease** (hyperkeratosis follicularis in cutem penetrans) 701.1

L

- **Labia, labium** — *see* condition
- **Labiated hymen** 752.49
- **Labile**
  - blood pressure 796.2
  - emotions, emotionality 301.3
  - vasomotor system 443.9
- **Labioglossal paralysis** 335.22
- **Labium leporinum** — *see also* Cleft, lip 749.10
- **Labor** — *see also* Delivery
  - with complications — *see* Delivery, complicated
  - abnormal NEC 661.9 ☑
    - affecting fetus or newborn 763.7
  - arrested active phase 661.1 ☑
    - affecting fetus or newborn 763.7
  - desultory 661.2 ☑
    - affecting fetus or newborn 763.7
  - dyscoordinate 661.4 ☑
    - affecting fetus or newborn 763.7
  - early onset (22-36 weeks gestation) 644.2 ☑
  - failed
    - induction 659.1 ☑
      - mechanical 659.0 ☑
      - medical 659.1 ☑
      - surgical 659.0 ☑
    - trial (vaginal delivery) 660.6 ☑
  - false 644.1 ☑
  - forced or induced, affecting fetus or newborn 763.89
  - hypertonic 661.4 ☑
    - affecting fetus or newborn 763.7
  - hypotonic 661.2 ☑
    - affecting fetus or newborn 763.7
    - primary 661.0 ☑
      - affecting fetus or newborn 763.7
    - secondary 661.1 ☑
      - affecting fetus or newborn 763.7
  - incoordinate 661.4 ☑
    - affecting fetus or newborn 763.7
  - irregular 661.2 ☑
    - affecting fetus or newborn 763.7
  - long — *see* Labor, prolonged
  - missed (at or near term) 656.4 ☑
  - obstructed NEC 660.9 ☑
    - affecting fetus or newborn 763.1
    - due to female genital mutilation 660.8 ☑
    - specified cause NEC 660.8 ☑
      - affecting fetus or newborn 763.1
  - pains, spurious 644.1 ☑
  - precipitate 661.3 ☑
    - affecting fetus or newborn 763.6
  - premature 644.2 ☑
    - threatened 644.0 ☑
  - prolonged or protracted 662.1 ☑
    - first stage 662.0 ☑
      - affecting fetus or newborn 763.89
    - second stage 662.2 ☑
      - affecting fetus or newborn 763.89
    - affecting fetus or newborn 763.89
  - threatened NEC 644.1 ☑
  - undelivered 644.1 ☑
- **Labored breathing** — *see also* Hyperventilation 786.09
- **Labyrinthitis** (inner ear) (destructive) (latent) 386.30
  - circumscribed 386.32
  - diffuse 386.31
  - focal 386.32
  - purulent 386.33
  - serous 386.31
  - suppurative 386.33
  - syphilitic 095.8
  - toxic 386.34
  - viral 386.35
- **Laceration** — *see also* Wound, open, by site
  - accidental, complicating surgery 998.2
  - Achilles tendon 845.09
    - with open wound 892.2
  - anus (sphincter) 879.6
    - with
      - abortion — *see* Abortion, by type, with damage to pelvic organs
      - ectopic pregnancy (*see also* categories 633.0–633.9) 639.2
      - molar pregnancy (*see also* categories 630–632) 639.2
    - complicated 879.7
    - complicating delivery (healed) (old) 654.8 ☑
      - with laceration of anal or rectal mucosa 664.3 ☑
      - not associated with third-degree perineal laceration 664.6 ☑
    - following
      - abortion 639.2
      - ectopic or molar pregnancy 639.2
    - nontraumatic, nonpuerperal (healed) (old) 569.43
  - bladder (urinary)
    - with
      - abortion — *see* Abortion, by type, with damage to pelvic organs
      - ectopic pregnancy (*see also* categories 633.0–633.9) 639.2
      - molar pregnancy (*see also* categories 630–632) 639.2
    - following
      - abortion 639.2
      - ectopic or molar pregnancy 639.2
    - obstetrical trauma 665.5 ☑
  - blood vessel — *see* Injury, blood vessel, by site
  - bowel
    - with
      - abortion — *see* Abortion, by type, with damage to pelvic organs
      - ectopic pregnancy (*see also* categories 633.0–633.9) 639.2
      - molar pregnancy (*see also* categories 630–632) 639.2
    - following
      - abortion 639.2
      - ectopic or molar pregnancy 639.2
    - obstetrical trauma 665.5 ☑
  - brain (cerebral) (membrane) (with hemorrhage) 851.8 ☑

> *Note — Use the following fifth-digit subclassification with categories 851–854:*
>
> 0 *unspecified state of consciousness*
>
> 1 *with no loss of consciousness*
>
> 2 *with brief [less than one hour] loss of consciousness*
>
> 3 *with moderate [1–24 hours] loss of consciousness*
>
> 4 *with prolonged [more than 24 hours] loss of consciousness and return to pre-existing conscious level*
>
> 5 *with prolonged [more than 24 hours] loss of consciousness, without return to pre-existing conscious level*
>
> *Use fifth-digit 5 to designate when a patient is unconscious and dies before regaining consciousness, regardless of the duration of the loss of consciousness*
>
> 6 *with loss of consciousness of unspecified duration*
>
> 9 *with concussion, unspecified*

    - with
      - open intracranial wound 851.9 ☑
      - skull fracture — *see* Fracture, skull, by site
    - cerebellum 851.6 ☑
      - with open intracranial wound 851.7 ☑
    - cortex 851.2 ☑
      - with open intracranial wound 851.3 ☑
    - during birth 767.0
    - stem 851.6 ☑
      - with open intracranial wound 851.7 ☑
  - broad ligament
    - with
      - abortion — *see* Abortion, by type, with damage to pelvic organs
      - ectopic pregnancy (*see also* categories 633.0–633.9) 639.2
      - molar pregnancy (*see also* categories 630–632) 639.2
    - following
      - abortion 639.2
      - ectopic or molar pregnancy 639.2
    - nontraumatic 620.6
    - obstetrical trauma 665.6 ☑
    - syndrome (nontraumatic) 620.6
  - capsule, joint — *see* Sprain, by site
  - cardiac — *see* Laceration, heart
  - causing eversion of cervix uteri (old) 622.0
  - central, complicating delivery 664.4 ☑
  - cerebellum — *see* Laceration, brain, cerebellum
  - cerebral (*see also* Laceration, brain)
    - during birth 767.0
  - cervix (uteri)
    - with
      - abortion — *see* Abortion, by type, with damage to pelvic organs
      - ectopic pregnancy (*see also* categories 633.0–633.9) 639.2
      - molar pregnancy (*see also* categories 630–632) 639.2
    - following
      - abortion 639.2
      - ectopic or molar pregnancy 639.2
    - nonpuerperal, nontraumatic 622.3
    - obstetrical trauma (current) 665.3 ☑
    - old (postpartal) 622.3
    - traumatic — *see* Injury, internal, cervix
  - chordae heart 429.5
  - complicated 879.9
  - cornea — *see* Laceration, eyeball
    - superficial 918.1
  - cortex (cerebral) — *see* Laceration, brain, cortex
  - esophagus 530.89
  - eye(s) — *see* Laceration, ocular
  - eyeball NEC 871.4
    - with prolapse or exposure of intraocular tissue 871.1
    - penetrating — *see* Penetrating wound, eyeball
    - specified as without prolapse of intraocular tissue 871.0
  - eyelid NEC 870.8
    - full thickness 870.1
      - involving lacrimal passages 870.2
    - skin (and periocular area) 870.0
      - penetrating — *see* Penetrating wound, orbit
  - fourchette
    - with
      - abortion — *see* Abortion, by type, with damage to pelvic organs
      - ectopic pregnancy (*see also* categories 633.0–633.9) 639.2

Laceration — *see also* Wound, open, by site — *continued*
vulva — *continued*
with — *continued*
molar pregnancy (*see also* categories 630–632) 639.2
complicating delivery 664.0 ☑
following
abortion 639.2
ectopic or molar pregnancy 639.2
nonpuerperal, nontraumatic 624.4
old (postpartal) 624.4
Lachrymal — *see* condition
Lachrymonasal duct — *see* condition
Lack of
adequate intermaxillary vertical dimension 524.36
appetite (*see also* Anorexia) 783.0
care
in home V60.4
of adult 995.84
of infant (at or after birth) 995.52
coordination 781.3
development (*see also* Hypoplasia)
physiological in childhood 783.40
education V62.3
energy 780.79
financial resources V60.2
food 994.2
in environment V60.8
growth in childhood 783.43
heating V60.1
housing (permanent) (temporary) V60.0
adequate V60.1
material resources V60.2
medical attention 799.89
memory (*see also* Amnesia) 780.93
mild, following organic brain damage 310.1
ovulation 628.0
person able to render necessary care V60.4
physical exercise V69.0
physiologic development in childhood 783.40
posterior occlusal support 524.57
prenatal care in current pregnancy V23.7
shelter V60.0
sleep V69.4
water 994.3
Lacrimal — *see* condition
Lacrimation, abnormal — *see also* Epiphora 375.20
Lacrimonasal duct — *see* condition
Lactation, lactating (breast) (puerperal) (postpartum)
defective 676.4 ☑
disorder 676.9 ☑
specified type NEC 676.8 ☑
excessive 676.6 ☑
failed 676.4 ☑
mastitis NEC 675.2 ☑
mother (care and/or examination) V24.1
nonpuerperal 611.6
suppressed 676.5 ☑
Lacticemia 271.3
excessive 276.2
Lactosuria 271.3
Lacunar skull 756.0
Laennec's cirrhosis (alcoholic) 571.2
nonalcoholic 571.5
Lafora's disease 333.2
Lagleyze-von Hippel disease (retinocerebral angiomatosis) 759.6
Lag, lid (nervous) 374.41
Lagophthalmos (eyelid) (nervous) 374.20
cicatricial 374.23
keratitis (*see also* Keratitis) 370.34
mechanical 374.22
paralytic 374.21
La grippe — *see* Influenza
Lahore sore 085.1
Lakes, venous (cerebral) 437.8
Laki-Lorand factor deficiency — *see also* Defect, coagulation 286.3
Lalling 307.9
Lambliasis 007.1
Lame back 724.5
Lancereaux's diabetes (diabetes mellitus with marked emaciation) 250.8 ☑ *[261]*
due to secondary diabetes 249.8 ☑ *[261]*
Landau-Kleffner syndrome 345.8 ☑
Landouzy-Déjérine dystrophy (fascioscapulohumeral atrophy) 359.1
Landry's disease or paralysis 357.0
Landry-Guillain-Barré syndrome 357.0
Lane's
band 751.4
disease 569.89
kink (*see also* Obstruction, intestine) 560.9
Langdon Down's syndrome (mongolism) 758.0
Language abolition 784.69
Lanugo (persistent) 757.4
Laparoscopic surgical procedure converted to open procedure V64.41
Lardaceous
degeneration (any site) 277.39
disease 277.39
kidney 277.39 *[583.81]*
liver 277.39
Large
baby (regardless of gestational age) 766.1
exceptionally (weight of 4500 grams or more) 766.0
of diabetic mother 775.0
ear 744.22
fetus (*see also* Oversize, fetus)
causing disproportion 653.5 ☑
with obstructed labor 660.1 ☑
for dates
fetus or newborn (regardless of gestational age) 766.1
affecting management of pregnancy 656.6 ☑
exceptionally (weight of 4500 grams or more) 766.0
physiological cup 743.57
stature 783.9
waxy liver 277.39
white kidney — *see* Nephrosis
Larsen-Johansson disease (juvenile osteopathia patellae) 732.4
Larsen's syndrome (flattened facies and multiple congenital dislocations) 755.8
Larva migrans
cutaneous NEC 126.9
ancylostoma 126.9
of Diptera in vitreous 128.0
visceral NEC 128.0
Laryngeal — *see also* condition 786.2
syncope 786.2
Laryngismus (acute) (infectious) (stridulous) 478.75
congenital 748.3
diphtheritic 032.3
Laryngitis (acute) (edematous) (fibrinous) (gangrenous) (infective) (infiltrative) (malignant) (membranous) (phlegmonous) (pneumococcal) (pseudomembranous) (septic) (subglottic) (suppurative) (ulcerative) (viral) 464.00
with
influenza, flu, or grippe 487.1
obstruction 464.01
tracheitis (*see also* Laryngotracheitis) 464.20
with obstruction 464.21
acute 464.20
with obstruction 464.21
chronic 476.1
atrophic 476.0
Laryngitis — *continued*
Borrelia vincentii 101
catarrhal 476.0
chronic 476.0
with tracheitis (chronic) 476.1
due to external agent — *see* Condition, respiratory, chronic, due to
diphtheritic (membranous) 032.3
due to external agent — *see* Inflammation, respiratory, upper, due to
Hemophilus influenzae 464.00
with obstruction 464.01
H. influenzae 464.00
with obstruction 464.01
hypertrophic 476.0
influenzal 487.1
pachydermic 478.79
sicca 476.0
spasmodic 478.75
acute 464.00
with obstruction 464.01
streptococcal 034.0
stridulous 478.75
syphilitic 095.8
congenital 090.5
tuberculous (*see also* Tuberculosis, larynx) 012.3 ☑
Vincent's 101
Laryngocele (congenital) (ventricular) 748.3
Laryngofissure 478.79
congenital 748.3
Laryngomalacia (congenital) 748.3
Laryngopharyngitis (acute) 465.0
chronic 478.9
due to external agent — *see* Condition, respiratory, chronic, due to
due to external agent — *see* Inflammation, respiratory, upper, due to
septic 034.0
Laryngoplegia — *see also* Paralysis, vocal cord 478.30
Laryngoptosis 478.79
Laryngospasm 478.75
due to external agent — *see* Condition, respiratory, acute, due to
Laryngostenosis 478.74
congenital 748.3
Laryngotracheitis (acute) (infectional) (viral) — *see also* Laryngitis 464.20
with obstruction 464.21
atrophic 476.1
Borrelia vincenti 101
catarrhal 476.1
chronic 476.1
due to external agent — *see* Condition, respiratory, chronic, due to
diphtheritic (membranous) 032.3
due to external agent — *see* Inflammation, respiratory, upper, due to
H. influenzae 464.20
with obstruction 464.21
hypertrophic 476.1
influenzal 487.1
pachydermic 478.75
sicca 476.1
spasmodic 478.75
acute 464.20
with obstruction 464.21
streptococcal 034.0
stridulous 478.75
syphilitic 095.8
congenital 090.5
tuberculous (*see also* Tuberculosis, larynx) 012.3 ☑
Vincent's 101
Laryngotracheobronchitis — *see also* Bronchitis 490
acute 466.0
chronic 491.8
viral 466.0
Laryngotracheobronchopneumonitis — *see* Pneumonia, broncho-
Larynx, laryngeal — *see* condition
Lasègue's disease (persecution mania) 297.9
Lassa fever 078.89
Lassitude — *see also* Weakness 780.79
Late — *see also* condition
effect(s) (of) (*see also* condition)
abscess
intracranial or intraspinal (conditions classifiable to 324) — *see* category 326
adverse effect of drug, medicinal or biological substance 909.5
allergic reaction 909.9
amputation
postoperative (late) 997.60
traumatic (injury classifiable to 885–887 and 895–897) 905.9
burn (injury classifiable to 948–949) 906.9
extremities NEC (injury classifiable to 943 or 945) 906.7
hand or wrist (injury classifiable to 944) 906.6
eye (injury classifiable to 940) 906.5
face, head, and neck (injury classifiable to 941) 906.5
specified site NEC (injury classifiable to 942 and 946–947) 906.8
cerebrovascular disease (conditions classifiable to 430–437) 438.9
with
alterations of sensations 438.6
aphasia 438.11
apraxia 438.81
ataxia 438.84
cognitive deficits 438.0
disturbances of vision 438.7
dysphagia 438.82
dysphasia 438.12
facial droop 438.83
facial weakness 438.83
hemiplegia/hemiparesis
affecting
dominant side 438.21
nondominant side 438.22
unspecified side 438.20
monoplegia of lower limb
affecting
dominant side 438.41
nondominant side 438.42
unspecified side 438.40
monoplegia of upper limb
affecting
dominant side 438.31
nondominant side 438.32
unspecified side 438.30
paralytic syndrome NEC
affecting
bilateral 438.53
dominant side 438.51
nondominant side 438.52
unspecified side 438.50
speech and language deficit 438.10
specified type NEC 438.19
vertigo 438.85
specified type NEC 438.89
childbirth complication(s) 677
complication(s) of
childbirth 677
delivery 677
pregnancy 677

- **Leydig cell** — *continued*
  - carcinoma — *continued*
    - unspecified site
      - female 183.0
      - male 186.9
  - tumor (M8650/1)
    - benign (M8650/0)
      - specified site — *see* Neoplasm, by site, benign
      - unspecified site
        - female 220
        - male 222.0
    - malignant (M8650/3)
      - specified site — *see* Neoplasm, by site, malignant
      - unspecified site
        - female 183.0
        - male 186.9
    - specified site — *see* Neoplasm, by site, uncertain behavior
    - unspecified site
      - female 236.2
      - male 236.4
- **Leydig-Sertoli cell tumor** (M8631/0)
  - specified site — *see* Neoplasm, by site, benign
  - unspecified site
    - female 220
    - male 222.0
- **LGSIL** (low grade squamous intraepithelial lesion)
  - anus 796.73
  - cervix 795.03
  - vagina 795.13
- **Liar, pathologic** 301.7
- **Libman-Sacks disease or syndrome** 710.0 *[424.91]*
- **Lice** (infestation) 132.9
  - body (pediculus corporis) 132.1
  - crab 132.2
  - head (pediculus capitis) 132.0
  - mixed (classifiable to more than one of the categories 132.0–132.2) 132.3
  - pubic (pediculus pubis) 132.2
- **Lichen** 697.9
  - albus 701.0
  - annularis 695.89
  - atrophicus 701.0
  - corneus obtusus 698.3
  - myxedematous 701.8
  - nitidus 697.1
  - pilaris 757.39
    - acquired 701.1
  - planopilaris 697.0
  - planus (acute) (chronicus) (hypertrophic) (verrucous) 697.0
    - morphoeicus 701.0
    - sclerosus (et atrophicus) 701.0
  - ruber 696.4
    - acuminatus 696.4
    - moniliformis 697.8
    - obtusus corneus 698.3
    - of Wilson 697.0
    - planus 697.0
  - sclerosus (et atrophicus) 701.0
  - scrofulosus (primary) (*see also* Tuberculosis) 017.0 ☑
  - simplex (Vidal's) 698.3
    - chronicus 698.3
    - circumscriptus 698.3
  - spinulosus 757.39
    - mycotic 117.9
  - striata 697.8
  - urticatus 698.2
- **Lichenification** 698.3
  - nodular 698.3
- **Lichenoides tuberculosis** (primary) — *see also* Tuberculosis 017.0 ☑
- **Lichtheim's disease or syndrome** (subacute combined sclerosis with pernicious anemia) 281.0 *[336.2]*
- **Lien migrans** 289.59
- **Lientery** — *see also* Diarrhea 787.91
  - infectious 009.2
- **Life circumstance problem** NEC V62.89
- **Li-Fraumeni cancer syndrome** V84.01
- **Ligament** — *see* condition
- **Light-for-dates** (infant) 764.0 ☑
  - with signs of fetal malnutrition 764.1 ☑
  - affecting management of pregnancy 656.5 ☑
- **Light-headedness** 780.4
- **Lightning** (effects) (shock) (stroke) (struck by) 994.0
  - burn — *see* Burn, by site
  - foot 266.2
- **Lightwood's disease or syndrome** (renal tubular acidosis) 588.89
- **Lignac's disease** (cystinosis) 270.0
- **Lignac (-Fanconi) syndrome** (cystinosis) 270.0
- **Lignac (-de Toni) (-Fanconi) (-Debré) syndrome** (cystinosis) 270.0
- **Ligneous thyroiditis** 245.3
- **Likoff's syndrome** (angina in menopausal women) 413.9
- **Limb** — *see* condition
- **Limitation of joint motion** — *see also* Stiffness, joint 719.5 ☑
  - sacroiliac 724.6
- **Limit dextrinosis** 271.0
- **Limited**
  - cardiac reserve — *see* Disease, heart
  - duction, eye NEC 378.63
  - mandibular range of motion 524.52
- **Lindau (-von Hippel) disease** (angiomatosis retinocerebellosa) 759.6
- **Lindau's disease** (retinocerebral angiomatosis) 759.6
- **Linea corneae senilis** 371.41
- **Lines**
  - Beau's (transverse furrows on fingernails) 703.8
  - Harris' 733.91
  - Hudson-Stähli 371.11
  - Stähli's 371.11
- **Lingua**
  - geographical 529.1
  - nigra (villosa) 529.3
  - plicata 529.5
    - congenital 750.13
  - tylosis 528.6
- **Lingual** (tongue) — *see* also condition
  - thyroid 759.2
- **Linitis** (gastric) 535.4 ☑
  - plastica (M8142/3) 151.9
- **Lioderma essentialis** (cum melanosis et telangiectasia) 757.33
- **Lip** — *see also* condition
  - biting 528.9
- **Lipalgia** 272.8
- **Lipedema** — *see* Edema
- **Lipemia** — *see also* Hyperlipidemia 272.4
  - retina, retinalis 272.3
- **Lipidosis** 272.7
  - cephalin 272.7
  - cerebral (infantile) (juvenile) (late) 330.1
  - cerebroretinal 330.1 *[362.71]*
  - cerebroside 272.7
  - cerebrospinal 272.7
  - chemically-induced 272.7
  - cholesterol 272.7
  - diabetic 250.8 ☑ *[272.7]*
    - due to secondary diabetes 249.8 ☑ *[272.7]*
  - dystopic (hereditary) 272.7
  - glycolipid 272.7
  - hepatosplenomegalic 272.3
  - hereditary, dystopic 272.7
  - sulfatide 330.0
- **Lipoadenoma** (M8324/0) — *see* Neoplasm, by site, benign
- **Lipoblastoma** (M8881/0) — *see* Lipoma, by site
- **Lipoblastomatosis** (M8881/0) — *see* Lipoma, by site
- **Lipochondrodystrophy** 277.5
- **Lipochrome histiocytosis** (familial) 288.1
- **Lipodystrophia progressiva** 272.6
- **Lipodystrophy** (progressive) 272.6
  - insulin 272.6
  - intestinal 040.2
  - mesenteric 567.82
- **Lipofibroma** (M8851/0) — *see* Lipoma, by site
- **Lipoglycoproteinosis** 272.8
- **Lipogranuloma, sclerosing** 709.8
- **Lipogranulomatosis** (disseminated) 272.8
  - kidney 272.8
- **Lipoid** — *see also* condition
  - histiocytosis 272.7
    - essential 272.7
  - nephrosis (*see also* Nephrosis) 581.3
  - proteinosis of Urbach 272.8
- **Lipoidemia** — *see also* Hyperlipidemia 272.4
- **Lipoidosis** — *see also* Lipidosis 272.7
- **Lipoma** (M8850/0) 214.9
  - breast (skin) 214.1
  - face 214.0
  - fetal (M8881/0) (*see also* Lipoma, by site)
    - fat cell (M8880/0) — *see* Lipoma, by site
  - infiltrating (M8856/0) — *see* Lipoma, by site
  - intra-abdominal 214.3
  - intramuscular (M8856/0) — *see* Lipoma, by site
  - intrathoracic 214.2
  - kidney 214.3
  - mediastinum 214.2
  - muscle 214.8
  - peritoneum 214.3
  - retroperitoneum 214.3
  - skin 214.1
    - face 214.0
  - spermatic cord 214.4
  - spindle cell (M8857/0) — *see* Lipoma, by site
  - stomach 214.3
  - subcutaneous tissue 214.1
    - face 214.0
  - thymus 214.2
  - thyroid gland 214.2
- **Lipomatosis** (dolorosa) 272.8
  - epidural 214.8
  - fetal (M8881/0) — *see* Lipoma, by site
  - Launois-Bensaude's 272.8
- **Lipomyohemangioma** (M8860/0)
  - specified site — *see* Neoplasm, connective tissue, benign
  - unspecified site 223.0
- **Lipomyoma** (M8860/0)
  - specified site — *see* Neoplasm, connective tissue, benign
  - unspecified site 223.0
- **Lipomyxoma** (M8852/0) — *see* Lipoma, by site
- **Lipomyxosarcoma** (M8852/3) — *see* Neoplasm, connective tissue, malignant
- **Lipophagocytosis** 289.89
- **Lipoproteinemia** (alpha) 272.4
  - broad-beta 272.2
  - floating-beta 272.2
  - hyper-pre-beta 272.1
- **Lipoproteinosis** (Rössle-Urbach-Wiethe) 272.8
- **Liposarcoma** (M8850/3) — *see also* Neoplasm, connective tissue, malignant
  - differentiated type (M8851/3) — *see* Neoplasm, connective tissue, malignant
  - embryonal (M8852/3) — *see* Neoplasm, connective tissue, malignant
  - mixed type (M8855/3) — *see* Neoplasm, connective tissue, malignant
  - myxoid (M8852/3) — *see* Neoplasm, connective tissue, malignant
- **Liposarcoma** — *see also* Neoplasm, connective tissue, malignant — *continued*
  - pleomorphic (M8854/3) — *see* Neoplasm, connective tissue, malignant
  - round cell (M8853/3) — *see* Neoplasm, connective tissue, malignant
  - well differentiated type (M8851/3) — *see* Neoplasm, connective tissue, malignant
- **Liposynovitis prepatellaris** 272.8
- **Lipping**
  - cervix 622.0
  - spine (*see also* Spondylosis) 721.90
  - vertebra (*see also* Spondylosis) 721.90
- **Lip pits** (mucus), congenital 750.25
- **Lipschütz disease or ulcer** 616.50
- **Lipuria** 791.1
  - bilharziasis 120.0
- **Liquefaction, vitreous humor** 379.21
- **Lisping** 307.9
- **Lissauer's paralysis** 094.1
- **Lissencephalia, lissencephaly** 742.2
- **Listerellose** 027.0
- **Listeriose** 027.0
- **Listeriosis** 027.0
  - congenital 771.2
  - fetal 771.2
  - suspected fetal damage affecting management of pregnancy 655.4 ☑
- **Listlessness** 780.79
- **Lithemia** 790.6
- **Lithiasis** — *see also* Calculus
  - hepatic (duct) — *see* Choledocholithiasis
  - urinary 592.9
- **Lithopedion** 779.9
  - affecting management of pregnancy 656.8 ☑
- **Lithosis** (occupational) 502
  - with tuberculosis — *see* Tuberculosis, pulmonary
- **Lithuria** 791.9
- **Litigation** V62.5
- **Little**
  - league elbow 718.82
  - stroke syndrome 435.9
- **Little's disease** — *see* Palsy, cerebral
- **Littre's**
  - gland — *see* condition
  - hernia — *see* Hernia, Littre's
- **Littritis** — *see also* Urethritis 597.89
- **Livedo** 782.61
  - annularis 782.61
  - racemose 782.61
  - reticularis 782.61
- **Live flesh** 781.0
- **Liver** — *see also* condition
  - donor V59.6
- **Livida, asphyxia**
  - newborn 768.6
- **Living**
  - alone V60.3
    - with handicapped person V60.4
- **Lloyd's syndrome** 258.1
- **Loa loa** 125.2
- **Loasis** 125.2
- **Lobe, lobar** — *see* condition
- **Lobo's disease or blastomycosis** 116.2
- **Lobomycosis** 116.2
- **Lobotomy syndrome** 310.0
- **Lobstein's disease** (brittle bones and blue sclera) 756.51
- **Lobster-claw hand** 755.58
- **Lobulation** (congenital) — *see also* Anomaly, specified type NEC, by site
  - kidney, fetal 753.3
  - liver, abnormal 751.69
  - spleen 759.0
- **Lobule, lobular** — *see* condition
- **Local, localized** — *see* condition

- **Locked bowel or intestine** — *see also* Obstruction, intestine 560.9
- **Locked-in state** 344.81
- **Locked twins** 660.5 ☑
  - affecting fetus or newborn 763.1
- **Locking**
  - joint (*see also* Derangement, joint) 718.90
  - knee 717.9
- **Lockjaw** — *see also* Tetanus 037
- **Locomotor ataxia** (progressive) 094.0
- **Löffler's**
  - endocarditis 421.0
  - eosinophilia or syndrome 518.3
  - pneumonia 518.3
  - syndrome (eosinophilic pneumonitis) 518.3
- **Löfgren's syndrome** (sarcoidosis) 135
- **Loiasis** 125.2
  - eyelid 125.2 *[373.6]*
- **Loneliness** V62.89
- **Lone star fever** 082.8
- **Longitudinal stripes or grooves, nails** 703.8
  - congenital 757.5
- **Long labor** 662.1 ☑
  - affecting fetus or newborn 763.89
  - first stage 662.0 ☑
  - second stage 662.2 ☑
- **Long-term** (current) **drug use** V58.69
  - antibiotics V58.62
  - anticoagulants V58.61
  - anti-inflammatories, non-steroidal (NSAID) V58.64
  - antiplatelets/antithrombotics V58.63
  - aspirin V58.66
  - high-risk medications NEC V58.69
  - insulin V58.67
  - methadone V58.69
  - opiate analgesic V58.69
  - pain killers V58.69
    - anti-inflammatories, non-steroidal (NSAID) V58.64
    - aspirin V58.66
  - steroids V58.65
  - tamoxifen V07.51
- **Loop**
  - intestine (*see also* Volvulus) 560.2
  - intrascleral nerve 379.29
  - vascular on papilla (optic) 743.57
- **Loose** — *see also* condition
  - body
    - in tendon sheath 727.82
    - joint 718.10
      - ankle 718.17
      - elbow 718.12
      - foot 718.17
      - hand 718.14
      - hip 718.15
      - knee 717.6
      - multiple sites 718.19
      - pelvic region 718.15
      - prosthetic implant — *see* Complications, mechanical
      - shoulder (region) 718.11
      - specified site NEC 718.18
      - wrist 718.13
  - cartilage (joint) (*see also* Loose, body, joint) 718.1 ☑
    - knee 717.6
  - facet (vertebral) 724.9
  - prosthetic implant — *see* Complications, mechanical
  - sesamoid, joint (*see also* Loose, body, joint) 718.1 ☑
  - tooth, teeth 525.8
- **Loosening epiphysis** 732.9
- **Looser (-Debray) -Milkman syndrome** (osteomalacia with pseudofractures) 268.2
- **Lop ear** (deformity) 744.29
- **Lorain's disease or syndrome** (pituitary dwarfism) 253.3
- **Lorain-Levi syndrome** (pituitary dwarfism) 253.3
- **Lordosis** (acquired) (postural) 737.20
- **Lordosis** — *continued*
  - congenital 754.2
  - due to or associated with
    - Charcôt-Marie-Tooth disease 356.1 *[737.42]*
    - mucopolysaccharidosis 277.5 *[737.42]*
    - neurofibromatosis 237.71 *[737.42]*
    - osteitis
      - deformans 731.0 *[737.42]*
      - fibrosa cystica 252.01 *[737.42]*
    - osteoporosis (*see also* Osteoporosis) 733.00 *[737.42]*
    - poliomyelitis (*see also* Poliomyelitis) 138 *[737.42]*
    - tuberculosis (*see also* Tuberculosis) 015.0 ☑ *[737.42]*
  - late effect of rickets 268.1 *[737.42]*
  - postlaminectomy 737.21
  - postsurgical NEC 737.22
  - rachitic 268.1 *[737.42]*
  - specified NEC 737.29
  - tuberculous (*see also* Tuberculosis) 015.0 ☑ *[737.42]*
- **Loss**
  - appetite 783.0
    - hysterical 300.11
    - nonorganic origin 307.59
    - psychogenic 307.59
  - blood — *see* Hemorrhage
  - central vision 368.41
  - consciousness 780.09
    - transient 780.2
  - control, sphincter, rectum 787.6
    - nonorganic origin 307.7
  - ear ossicle, partial 385.24
  - elasticity, skin 782.8
  - extremity or member, traumatic, current — *see* Amputation, traumatic
  - fluid (acute) 276.50
    - with
      - hypernatremia 276.0
      - hyponatremia 276.1
    - fetus or newborn 775.5
  - hair 704.00
  - hearing (*see also* Deafness)
    - central 389.14
    - conductive (air) 389.00
      - with sensorineural hearing loss 389.20
        - bilateral 389.22
        - unilateral 389.21
      - bilateral 389.06
      - combined types 389.08
      - external ear 389.01
      - inner ear 389.04
      - middle ear 389.03
      - multiple types 389.08
      - tympanic membrane 389.02
      - unilateral 389.05
    - mixed conductive and sensorineural 389.20
      - bilateral 389.22
      - unilateral 389.21
    - mixed type 389.20
      - bilateral 389.22
      - unilateral 389.21
    - nerve
      - bilateral 389.12
      - unilateral 389.13
    - neural
      - bilateral 389.12
      - unilateral 389.13
    - noise-induced 388.12
    - perceptive NEC (*see also* Loss, hearing, sensorineural) 389.10
    - sensorineural 389.10
      - with conductive hearing loss 389.20
        - bilateral 389.22
        - unilateral 389.21
      - asymmetrical 389.16
      - bilateral 389.18
      - central 389.14
- **Loss** — *continued*
  - hearing (*see also* Deafness) — *continued*
    - sensorineural — *continued*
      - neural 389.12
        - bilateral 389.12
        - unilateral 389.13
      - sensory
        - bilateral 389.11
        - unilateral 389.17
      - unilateral 389.15
    - sensory
      - bilateral 389.11
      - unilateral 389.17
    - specified type NEC 389.8
    - sudden NEC 388.2
  - height 781.91
  - labyrinthine reactivity (unilateral) 386.55
    - bilateral 386.56
  - memory (*see also* Amnesia) 780.93
    - mild, following organic brain damage 310.1
  - mind (*see also* Psychosis) 298.9
  - occlusal vertical dimension 524.37
  - organ or part — *see* Absence, by site, acquired
  - sensation 782.0
  - sense of
    - smell (*see also* Disturbance, sensation) 781.1
    - taste (*see also* Disturbance, sensation) 781.1
    - touch (*see also* Disturbance, sensation) 781.1
  - sight (acquired) (complete) (congenital) — *see* Blindness
  - spinal fluid
    - headache 349.0
  - substance of
    - bone (*see also* Osteoporosis) 733.00
    - cartilage 733.99
      - ear 380.32
    - vitreous (humor) 379.26
  - tooth, teeth
    - acquired 525.10
      - due to
        - caries 525.13
        - extraction 525.10
        - periodontal disease 525.12
        - specified NEC 525.19
        - trauma 525.11
  - vision, visual (*see also* Blindness) 369.9
    - both eyes (*see also* Blindness, both eyes) 369.3
    - complete (*see also* Blindness, both eyes) 369.00
    - one eye 369.8
    - sudden 368.11
    - transient 368.12
  - vitreous 379.26
  - voice (*see also* Aphonia) 784.41
  - weight (cause unknown) 783.21
- **Lou Gehrig's disease** 335.20
- **Louis-Bar syndrome** (ataxia-telangiectasia) 334.8
- **Louping ill** 063.1
- **Lousiness** — *see* Lice
- **Low**
  - back syndrome 724.2
  - basal metabolic rate (BMR) 794.7
  - birthweight 765.1 ☑
    - extreme (less than 1000 grams) 765.0 ☑
    - for gestational age 764.0 ☑
    - status (*see also* Status, low birth weight) V21.30
  - bladder compliance 596.52
  - blood pressure (*see also* Hypotension) 458.9
    - reading (incidental) (isolated) (nonspecific) 796.3
  - cardiac reserve — *see* Disease, heart
  - compliance bladder 596.52
- **Low** — *continued*
  - frequency deafness — *see* Disorder, hearing
  - function (*see also* Hypofunction)
    - kidney (*see also* Disease, renal) 593.9
    - liver 573.9
  - hemoglobin 285.9
  - implantation, placenta — *see* Placenta, previa
  - insertion, placenta — *see* Placenta, previa
  - lying
    - kidney 593.0
    - organ or site, congenital — *see* Malposition, congenital
    - placenta — *see* Placenta, previa
  - output syndrome (cardiac) (*see also* Failure, heart) 428.9
  - platelets (blood) (*see also* Thrombocytopenia) 287.5
  - reserve, kidney (*see also* Disease, renal) 593.9
  - risk
    - human papillomavirus (HPA) DNA test positive
      - anal 796.79
      - cervical 795.09
      - vaginal 795.19
  - salt syndrome 593.9
  - tension glaucoma 365.12
  - vision 369.9
    - both eyes 369.20
    - one eye 369.70
- **Lower extremity** — *see* condition
- **Lowe (-Terrey-MacLachlan) syndrome** (oculocerebrorenal dystrophy) 270.8
- **Lown (-Ganong) -Levine syndrome** (short P-R interval, normal QRS complex, and paroxysmal supraventricular tachycardia) 426.81
- **LSD reaction** — *see also* Abuse, drugs, nondependent 305.3 ☑
- **L-shaped kidney** 753.3
- **Lucas-Championnière disease** (fibrinous bronchitis) 466.0
- **Lucey-Driscoll syndrome** (jaundice due to delayed conjugation) 774.30
- **Ludwig's**
  - angina 528.3
  - disease (submaxillary cellulitis) 528.3
- **Lues** (venerea), **luetic** — *see* Syphilis
- **Luetscher's syndrome** (dehydration) 276.51
- **Lumbago** 724.2
  - due to displacement, intervertebral disc 722.10
- **Lumbalgia** 724.2
  - due to displacement, intervertebral disc 722.10
- **Lumbar** — *see* condition
- **Lumbarization, vertebra** 756.15
- **Lumbermen's itch** 133.8
- **Lump** — *see also* Mass
  - abdominal 789.3 ☑
  - breast 611.72
  - chest 786.6
  - epigastric 789.3 ☑
  - head 784.2
  - kidney 753.3
  - liver 789.1
  - lung 786.6
  - mediastinal 786.6
  - neck 784.2
  - nose or sinus 784.2
  - pelvic 789.3 ☑
  - skin 782.2
  - substernal 786.6
  - throat 784.2
  - umbilicus 789.3 ☑
- **Lunacy** — *see also* Psychosis 298.9
- **Lunatomalacia** 732.3
- **Lung** — *see also* condition
  - donor V59.8

Note — Use the following fifth-digit subclassification with categories 200–202:

0	*unspecified site, extranodal and solid organ sites*
1	*lymph nodes of head, face, and neck*
2	*intrathoracic lymph nodes*
3	*intra-abdominal lymph nodes*
4	*lymph nodes of axilla and upper limb*
5	*lymph nodes of inguinal region and lower limb*
6	*intrapelvic lymph nodes*
7	*spleen*
8	*lymph nodes of multiple sites*

Lymphoma — *continued*
  follicular — *continued*
    mixed (cell type) (lymphocytic-histiocytic) (small cell and large cell) (M9691/3) 202.0 ☑
  germinocytic (M9622/3) 202.8 ☑
  giant, follicular or follicle (M9690/3) 202.0 ☑
  histiocytic (diffuse) (M9640/3) 200.0 ☑
    nodular (M9642/3) 200.0 ☑
    pleomorphic cell type (M9641/3) 200.0 ☑
  Hodgkin's (M9650/3) (*see also* Disease, Hodgkin's) 201.9 ☑
  immunoblastic (type) (M9612/3) 200.8 ☑
  large cell (M9640/3) 200.7 ☑
    anaplastic 200.6 ☑
    nodular (M9642/3) 200.0 ☑
    pleomorphic cell type (M9641/3) 200.0 ☑
  lymphoblastic (diffuse) (M9630/3) 200.1 ☑
    Burkitt's type (M9750/3) 200.2 ☑
    convoluted cell type (M9602/3) 202.8 ☑
  lymphocytic (cell type) (diffuse) (M9620/3) 200.1 ☑
    with plasmacytoid differentiation, diffuse (M9611/3) 200.8 ☑
    intermediate differentiation (diffuse) (M9621/3) 200.1 ☑
      follicular (M9694/3) 202.0 ☑
      nodular (M9694/3) 202.0 ☑
    nodular (M9690/3) 202.0 ☑
    poorly differentiated (diffuse) (M9630/3) 200.1 ☑
      follicular (M9696/3) 202.0 ☑
      nodular (M9696/3) 202.0 ☑
    well differentiated (diffuse) (M9620/3) 200.1 ☑
      follicular (M9693/3) 202.0 ☑
      nodular (M9693/3) 202.0 ☑
  lymphocytic-histiocytic, mixed (diffuse) (M9613/3) 200.8 ☑
    follicular (M9691/3) 202.0 ☑
    nodular (M9691/3) 202.0 ☑
  lymphoplasmacytoid type (M9611/3) 200.8 ☑
  lymphosarcoma type (M9610/3) 200.1 ☑
  macrofollicular (M9690/3) 202.0 ☑
  mantle cell 200.4 ☑
  marginal zone 200.3 ☑
    extranodal B-cell 200.3 ☑
    nodal B-cell 200.3 ☑
    splenic B-cell 200.3 ☑
  mixed cell type (diffuse) (M9613/3) 200.8 ☑
    follicular (M9691/3) 202.0 ☑
    nodular (M9691/3) 202.0 ☑
  nodular (M9690/3) 202.0 ☑
    histiocytic (M9642/3) 200.0 ☑
    lymphocytic (M9690/3) 202.0 ☑
      intermediate differentiation (M9694/3) 202.0 ☑
      poorly differentiated (M9696/3) 202.0 ☑
    mixed (cell type) (lymphocytic-histiocytic) (small cell and large cell) (M9691/3) 202.0 ☑
  non-Hodgkin's type NEC (M9591/3) 202.8 ☑
  peripheral T-cell 202.7 ☑
  primary central nervous system 200.5 ☑
  reticulum cell (type) (M9640/3) 200.0 ☑
  small cell and large cell, mixed (diffuse) (M9613/3) 200.8 ☑
    follicular (M9691/3) 202.0 ☑
    nodular (9691/3) 202.0 ☑
  stem cell (type) (M9601/3) 202.8 ☑
  T-cell 202.1 ☑

Lymphoma — *continued*
  T-cell — *continued*
    peripheral 202.7 ☑
  undifferentiated (cell type) (non-Burkitt's) (M9600/3) 202.8 ☑
    Burkitt's type (M9750/3) 200.2 ☑
Lymphomatosis (M9590/3) — *see also* Lymphoma
  granulomatous 099.1
Lymphopathia
  venereum 099.1
  veneris 099.1
Lymphopenia 288.51
  familial 279.2
Lymphoreticulosis, benign (of inoculation) 078.3
Lymphorrhea 457.8
Lymphosarcoma (M9610/3) 200.1 ☑
  diffuse (M9610/3) 200.1 ☑
    with plasmacytoid differentiation (M9611/3) 200.8 ☑
    lymphoplasmacytic (M9611/3) 200.8 ☑
  follicular (giant) (M9690/3) 202.0 ☑
    lymphoblastic (M9696/3) 202.0 ☑
    lymphocytic, intermediate differentiation (M9694/3) 202.0 ☑
    mixed cell type (M9691/3) 202.0 ☑
  giant follicular (M9690/3) 202.0 ☑
  Hodgkin's (M9650/3) 201.9 ☑
  immunoblastic (M9612/3) 200.8 ☑
  lymphoblastic (diffuse) (M9630/3) 200.1 ☑
    follicular (M9696/3) 202.0 ☑
    nodular (M9696/3) 202.0 ☑
  lymphocytic (diffuse) (M9620/3) 200.1 ☑
    intermediate differentiation (diffuse) (M9621/3) 200.1 ☑
      follicular (M9694/3) 202.0 ☑
      nodular (M9694/3) 202.0 ☑
  mixed cell type (diffuse) (M9613/3) 200.8 ☑
    follicular (M9691/3) 202.0 ☑
    nodular (M9691/3) 202.0 ☑
  nodular (M9690/3) 202.0 ☑
    lymphoblastic (M9696/3) 202.0 ☑
    lymphocytic, intermediate differentiation (M9694/3) 202.0 ☑
    mixed cell type (M9691/3) 202.0 ☑
  prolymphocytic (M9631/3) 200.1 ☑
  reticulum cell (M9640/3) 200.0 ☑
Lymphostasis 457.8
Lypemania — *see also* Melancholia 296.2 ☑
Lyssa 071

M

Macacus ear 744.29
Maceration
  fetus (cause not stated) 779.9
  wet feet, tropical (syndrome) 991.4
Machado-Joseph disease 334.8
Machupo virus hemorrhagic fever 078.7
Macleod's syndrome (abnormal transradiancy, one lung) 492.8
Macrocephalia, macrocephaly 756.0
Macrocheilia (congenital) 744.81
Macrochilia (congenital) 744.81
Macrocolon (congenital) 751.3
Macrocornea 743.41
  associated with buphthalmos 743.22
Macrocytic — *see* condition
Macrocytosis 289.89
Macrodactylia, macrodactylism (fingers) (thumbs) 755.57
  toes 755.65
Macrodontia 520.2
Macroencephaly 742.4
Macrogenia 524.05
Macrogenitosomia (female) (male) (praecox) 255.2
Macrogingivae 523.8
Macroglobulinemia (essential) (idiopathic) (monoclonal) (primary) (syndrome) (Waldenström's) 273.3
Macroglossia (congenital) 750.15
  acquired 529.8
Macrognathia, macrognathism (congenital) 524.00
  mandibular 524.02
    alveolar 524.72
  maxillary 524.01
    alveolar 524.71
Macrogyria (congenital) 742.4
Macrohydrocephalus — *see also* Hydrocephalus 331.4
Macromastia — *see also* Hypertrophy, breast 611.1
Macrophage activation syndrome 288.4
Macropsia 368.14
Macrosigmoid 564.7
  congenital 751.3
Macrospondylitis, acromegalic 253.0
Macrostomia (congenital) 744.83
Macrotia (external ear) (congenital) 744.22
Macula
  cornea, corneal
    congenital 743.43
      interfering with vision 743.42
    interfering with central vision 371.03
    not interfering with central vision 371.02
  degeneration (*see also* Degeneration, macula) 362.50
    hereditary (*see also* Dystrophy, retina) 362.70
  edema, cystoid 362.53
Maculae ceruleae 132.1
Macules and papules 709.8
Maculopathy, toxic 362.55
Madarosis 374.55
Madelung's
  deformity (radius) 755.54
  disease (lipomatosis) 272.8
  lipomatosis 272.8
Madness — *see also* Psychosis 298.9
  myxedema (acute) 293.0
    subacute 293.1
Madura
  disease (actinomycotic) 039.9
    mycotic 117.4
  foot (actinomycotic) 039.4
    mycotic 117.4
Maduromycosis (actinomycotic) 039.9
  mycotic 117.4
Maffucci's syndrome (dyschondroplasia with hemangiomas) 756.4
Magenblase syndrome 306.4
Main en griffe (acquired) 736.06
  congenital 755.59
Maintenance
  chemotherapy regimen or treatment V58.11
  dialysis regimen or treatment
    extracorporeal (renal) V56.0
    peritoneal V56.8
    renal V56.0
  drug therapy or regimen
    chemotherapy, antineoplastic V58.11
    immunotherapy, antineoplastic V58.12
  external fixation NEC V54.89
  radiotherapy V58.0
  traction NEC V54.89
Majocchi's
  disease (purpura annularis telangiectodes) 709.1
  granuloma 110.6
Major — *see* condition
Mal
  cerebral (idiopathic) (*see also* Epilepsy) 345.9 ☑
  comital (*see also* Epilepsy) 345.9 ☑
  de los pintos (*see also* Pinta) 103.9
  de Meleda 757.39

Mal — *continued*
  de mer 994.6
  lie — *see* Presentation, fetal
  perforant (*see also* Ulcer, lower extremity) 707.15
Malabar itch 110.9
  beard 110.0
  foot 110.4
  scalp 110.0
Malabsorption 579.9
  calcium 579.8
  carbohydrate 579.8
  disaccharide 271.3
  drug-induced 579.8
  due to bacterial overgrowth 579.8
  fat 579.8
  folate, congenital 281.2
  galactose 271.1
  glucose-galactose (congenital) 271.3
  intestinal 579.9
  isomaltose 271.3
  lactose (hereditary) 271.3
  methionine 270.4
  monosaccharide 271.8
  postgastrectomy 579.3
  postsurgical 579.3
  protein 579.8
  sucrose (-isomaltose) (congenital) 271.3
  syndrome 579.9
    postgastrectomy 579.3
    postsurgical 579.3
Malacia, bone 268.2
  juvenile (*see also* Rickets) 268.0
  Kienböck's (juvenile) (lunate) (wrist) 732.3
    adult 732.8
Malacoplakia
  bladder 596.8
  colon 569.89
  pelvis (kidney) 593.89
  ureter 593.89
  urethra 599.84
Malacosteon 268.2
  juvenile (*see also* Rickets) 268.0
Maladaptation — *see* Maladjustment
Maladie de Roger 745.4
Maladjustment
  conjugal V61.10
    involving
      divorce V61.03
      estrangement V61.09
  educational V62.3
  family V61.9
    specified circumstance NEC V61.8
  marital V61.10
    involving
      divorce V61.03
      estrangement V61.09
  occupational V62.29
    current military deployment status V62.21
  simple, adult (*see also* Reaction, adjustment) 309.9
  situational acute (*see also* Reaction, adjustment) 309.9
  social V62.4
Malaise 780.79
Malakoplakia — *see* Malacoplakia
Malaria, malarial (fever) 084.6
  algid 084.9
  any type, with
    algid malaria 084.9
    blackwater fever 084.8
    fever
      blackwater 084.8
      hemoglobinuric (bilious) 084.8
    hemoglobinuria, malarial 084.8
    hepatitis 084.9 *[573.2]*
    nephrosis 084.9 *[581.81]*
    pernicious complication NEC 084.9
      cardiac 084.9
      cerebral 084.9
  cardiac 084.9
  carrier (suspected) of V02.9
  cerebral 084.9

Malposition — *continued*
congenital — *continued*
vein(s) (peripheral) NEC (*see also* Malposition, congenital, peripheral vascular system) 747.60
great 747.49
portal 747.49
pulmonary 747.49
vena cava (inferior) (superior) 747.49
device, implant, or graft — *see* Complications, mechanical
fetus NEC (*see also* Presentation, fetal) 652.9 ☑
with successful version 652.1 ☑
affecting fetus or newborn 763.1
before labor, affecting fetus or newborn 761.7
causing obstructed labor 660.0 ☑
in multiple gestation (one fetus or more) 652.6 ☑
with locking 660.5 ☑
causing obstructed labor 660.0 ☑
gallbladder (*see also* Disease, gallbladder) 575.8
gastrointestinal tract 569.89
congenital 751.8
heart (*see also* Malposition, congenital, heart) 746.87
intestine 569.89
congenital 751.5
pelvic organs or tissues
in pregnancy or childbirth 654.4 ☑
affecting fetus or newborn 763.89
causing obstructed labor 660.2 ☑
affecting fetus or newborn 763.1
placenta — *see* Placenta, previa
stomach 537.89
congenital 750.7
tooth, teeth 524.30
with impaction 520.6
uterus (acquired) (acute) (adherent) (any degree) (asymptomatic) (postinfectional) (postpartal, old) 621.6
anteflexion or anteversion (*see also* Anteversion, uterus) 621.6
congenital 752.3
flexion 621.6
lateral (*see also* Lateroversion, uterus) 621.6
in pregnancy or childbirth 654.4 ☑
affecting fetus or newborn 763.89
causing obstructed labor 660.2 ☑
affecting fetus or newborn 763.1
inversion 621.6
lateral (flexion) (version) (*see also* Lateroversion, uterus) 621.6
lateroflexion (*see also* Lateroversion, uterus) 621.6
lateroversion (*see also* Lateroversion, uterus) 621.6
retroflexion or retroversion (*see also* Retroversion, uterus) 621.6
Malposture 729.90
Malpresentation, fetus — *see also* Presentation, fetal 652.9 ☑
Malrotation
cecum 751.4
colon 751.4
intestine 751.4
kidney 753.3
MALT (mucosa associated lymphoid tissue) 200.3 ☑
Malta fever — *see also* Brucellosis 023.9
Maltosuria 271.3
Maltreatment (of)
adult 995.80
emotional 995.82
multiple forms 995.85
neglect (nutritional) 995.84
physical 995.81
psychological 995.82
sexual 995.83
child 995.50
emotional 995.51
multiple forms 995.59
neglect (nutritional) 995.52
physical 995.54
shaken infant syndrome 995.55
psychological 995.51
sexual 995.53
spouse (*see also* Maltreatment, adult) 995.80
Malt workers' lung 495.4
Malum coxae senilis 715.25
Malunion, fracture 733.81
Mammillitis — *see also* Mastitis 611.0
puerperal, postpartum 675.2 ☑
Mammitis — *see also* Mastitis 611.0
puerperal, postpartum 675.2 ☑
Mammographic
calcification 793.89
calculus 793.89
microcalcification 793.81
Mammoplasia 611.1
Management
contraceptive V25.9
specified type NEC V25.8
procreative V26.9
specified type NEC V26.89
Mangled NEC — *see also* nature and site of injury 959.9
Mania (monopolar) — *see also* Psychosis, affective 296.0 ☑
alcoholic (acute) (chronic) 291.9
Bell's — *see* Mania, chronic
chronic 296.0 ☑
recurrent episode 296.1 ☑
single episode 296.0 ☑
compulsive 300.3
delirious (acute) 296.0 ☑
recurrent episode 296.1 ☑
single episode 296.0 ☑
epileptic (*see also* Epilepsy) 345.4 ☑
hysterical 300.10
inhibited 296.89
puerperal (after delivery) 296.0 ☑
recurrent episode 296.1 ☑
single episode 296.0 ☑
recurrent episode 296.1 ☑
senile 290.8
single episode 296.0 ☑
stupor 296.89
stuporous 296.89
unproductive 296.89
Manic-depressive insanity, psychosis, reaction, or syndrome — *see also* Psychosis, affective 296.80
circular (alternating) 296.7
currently
depressed 296.5 ☑
episode unspecified 296.7
hypomanic, previously depressed 296.4 ☑
manic 296.4 ☑
mixed 296.6 ☑
depressed (type), depressive 296.2 ☑
atypical 296.82
recurrent episode 296.3 ☑
single episode 296.2 ☑
hypomanic 296.0 ☑
recurrent episode 296.1 ☑
single episode 296.0 ☑
manic 296.0 ☑
atypical 296.81
recurrent episode 296.1 ☑
single episode 296.0 ☑
mixed NEC 296.89
perplexed 296.89
stuporous 296.89
Manifestations, rheumatoid
lungs 714.81
pannus — *see* Arthritis, rheumatoid
subcutaneous nodules — *see* Arthritis, rheumatoid
Mankowsky's syndrome (familial dysplastic osteopathy) 731.2
Mannoheptulosuria 271.8
Mannosidosis 271.8
Manson's
disease (schistosomiasis) 120.1
pyosis (pemphigus contagiosus) 684
schistosomiasis 120.1
Mansonellosis 125.5
Manual — *see* condition
Maple bark disease 495.6
Maple bark-strippers' lung 495.6
Maple syrup (urine) disease or syndrome 270.3
Marable's syndrome (celiac artery compression) 447.4
Marasmus 261
brain 331.9
due to malnutrition 261
intestinal 569.89
nutritional 261
senile 797
tuberculous NEC (*see also* Tuberculosis) 011.9 ☑
Marble
bones 756.52
skin 782.61
Marburg disease (virus) 078.89
March
foot 733.94
hemoglobinuria 283.2
Marchand multiple nodular hyperplasia (liver) 571.5
Marchesani (-Weill) syndrome (brachymorphism and ectopia lentis) 759.89
Marchiafava (-Bignami) disease or syndrome 341.8
Marchiafava-Micheli syndrome (paroxysmal nocturnal hemoglobinuria) 283.2
Marcus Gunn's syndrome (jaw-winking syndrome) 742.8
Marfan's
congenital syphilis 090.49
disease 090.49
syndrome (arachnodactyly) 759.82
meaning congenital syphilis 090.49
with luxation of lens 090.49 *[379.32]*
Marginal
implantation, placenta — *see* Placenta, previa
placenta — *see* Placenta, previa
sinus (hemorrhage) (rupture) 641.2 ☑
affecting fetus or newborn 762.1
Marie's
cerebellar ataxia 334.2
syndrome (acromegaly) 253.0
Marie-Bamberger disease or syndrome (hypertrophic) (pulmonary) (secondary) 731.2
idiopathic (acropachyderma) 757.39
primary (acropachyderma) 757.39
Marie-Charcôt-Tooth neuropathic atrophy, muscle 356.1
Marie-Strümpell arthritis or disease (ankylosing spondylitis) 720.0
Marihuana, marijuana
abuse (*see also* Abuse, drugs, nondependent) 305.2 ☑
dependence (*see also* Dependence) 304.3 ☑
Marion's disease (bladder neck obstruction) 596.0
Marital conflict V61.10
Mark
port wine 757.32
raspberry 757.32
strawberry 757.32
stretch 701.3
Mark — *continued*
tattoo 709.09
Maroteaux-Lamy syndrome (mucopolysaccharidosis VI) 277.5
Marriage license examination V70.3
Marrow (bone)
arrest 284.9
megakaryocytic 287.30
poor function 289.9
Marseilles fever 082.1
Marshall's (hidrotic) **ectodermal dysplasia** 757.31
Marsh's disease (exophthalmic goiter) 242.0 ☑
Marsh fever — *see also* Malaria 084.6
Martin-Albright syndrome (pseudohypoparathyroidism) 275.49
Martin's disease 715.27
Martorell-Fabre syndrome (pulseless disease) 446.7
Masculinization, female , with adrenal hyperplasia 255.2
Masculinovoblastoma (M8670/0) 220
Masochism 302.83
Masons' lung 502
Mass
abdominal 789.3 ☑
anus 787.99
bone 733.90
breast 611.72
cheek 784.2
chest 786.6
cystic — *see* Cyst
ear 388.8
epigastric 789.3 ☑
eye 379.92
female genital organ 625.8
gum 784.2
head 784.2
intracranial 784.2
joint 719.60
ankle 719.67
elbow 719.62
foot 719.67
hand 719.64
hip 719.65
knee 719.66
multiple sites 719.69
pelvic region 719.65
shoulder (region) 719.61
specified site NEC 719.68
wrist 719.63
kidney (*see also* Disease, kidney) 593.9
lung 786.6
lymph node 785.6
malignant (M8000/3) — *see* Neoplasm, by site, malignant
mediastinal 786.6
mouth 784.2
muscle (limb) 729.89
neck 784.2
nose or sinus 784.2
palate 784.2
pelvis, pelvic 789.3 ☑
penis 607.89
perineum 625.8
rectum 787.99
scrotum 608.89
skin 782.2
specified organ NEC — *see* Disease of specified organ or site
splenic 789.2
substernal 786.6
thyroid (*see also* Goiter) 240.9
superficial (localized) 782.2
testes 608.89
throat 784.2
tongue 784.2
umbilicus 789.3 ☑
uterus 625.8
vagina 625.8
vulva 625.8
Massive — *see* condition
Mastalgia 611.71
psychogenic 307.89

Mast cell
  disease 757.33
    systemic (M9741/3) 202.6 ☑
  leukemia (M9900/3) 207.8 ☑
  sarcoma (M9742/3) 202.6 ☑
  tumor (M9740/1) 238.5
    malignant (M9740/3) 202.6 ☑
Masters-Allen syndrome 620.6
Mastitis (acute) (adolescent) (diffuse) (interstitial) (lobular) (nonpuerperal) (nonsuppurative) (parenchymatous) (phlegmonous) (simple) (subacute) (suppurative) 611.0
  chronic (cystic) (fibrocystic) 610.1
  cystic 610.1
    Schimmelbusch's type 610.1
  fibrocystic 610.1
  infective 611.0
  lactational 675.2 ☑
  lymphangitis 611.0
  neonatal (noninfective) 778.7
    infective 771.5
  periductal 610.4
  plasma cell 610.4
  puerperalis 675.2 ☑
  puerperal, postpartum, (interstitial) (nonpurulent) (parenchymatous) 675.2 ☑
    purulent 675.1 ☑
    stagnation 676.2 ☑
  retromammary 611.0
    puerperal, postpartum 675.1 ☑
  submammary 611.0
    puerperal, postpartum 675.1 ☑
Mastocytoma (M9740/1) 238.5
  malignant (M9740/3) 202.6 ☑
Mastocytosis 757.33
  malignant (M9741/3) 202.6 ☑
  systemic (M9741/3) 202.6 ☑
Mastodynia 611.71
  psychogenic 307.89
Mastoid — *see* condition
Mastoidalgia — *see also* Otalgia 388.70
Mastoiditis (coalescent) (hemorrhagic) (pneumococcal) (streptococcal) (suppurative) 383.9
  acute or subacute 383.00
    with
      Gradenigo's syndrome 383.02
      petrositis 383.02
      specified complication NEC 383.02
      subperiosteal abscess 383.01
  chronic (necrotic) (recurrent) 383.1
  tuberculous (*see also* Tuberculosis) 015.6 ☑
Mastopathy, mastopathia 611.9
  chronica cystica 610.1
  diffuse cystic 610.1
  estrogenic 611.89
  ovarian origin 611.89
Mastoplasia 611.1
Masturbation 307.9
Maternal condition, affecting fetus or newborn
  acute yellow atrophy of liver 760.8
  albuminuria 760.1
  anesthesia or analgesia 763.5
  blood loss 762.1
  chorioamnionitis 762.7
  circulatory disease, chronic (conditions classifiable to 390–459, 745–747) 760.3
  congenital heart disease (conditions classifiable to 745–746) 760.3
  cortical necrosis of kidney 760.1
  death 761.6
  diabetes mellitus 775.0
    manifest diabetes in the infant 775.1
  disease NEC 760.9
    circulatory system, chronic (conditions classifiable to 390–459, 745–747) 760.3
Maternal condition, affecting fetus or newborn — *continued*
  disease — *continued*
    genitourinary system (conditions classifiable to 580–599) 760.1
    respiratory (conditions classifiable to 490–519, 748) 760.3
  eclampsia 760.0
  hemorrhage NEC 762.1
  hepatitis acute, malignant, or subacute 760.8
  hyperemesis (gravidarum) 761.8
  hypertension (arising during pregnancy) (conditions classifiable to 642) 760.0
  infection
    disease classifiable to 001-136 ☑, 760.2
    genital tract NEC 760.8
    urinary tract 760.1
  influenza 760.2
    manifest influenza in the infant 771.2
  injury (conditions classifiable to 800–996) 760.5
  malaria 760.2
    manifest malaria in infant or fetus 771.2
  malnutrition 760.4
  necrosis of liver 760.8
  nephritis (conditions classifiable to 580–583) 760.1
  nephrosis (conditions classifiable to 581) 760.1
  noxious substance transmitted via breast milk or placenta 760.70
    alcohol 760.71
    anticonvulsants 760.77
    antifungals 760.74
    anti-infective agents 760.74
    antimetabolics 760.78
    cocaine 760.75
    "crack" 760.75
    diethylstilbestrol [DES] 760.76
    hallucinogenic agents 760.73
    medicinal agents NEC 760.79
    narcotics 760.72
    obstetric anesthetic or analgesic drug 760.72
    specified agent NEC 760.79
  nutritional disorder (conditions classifiable to 260–269) 760.4
  operation unrelated to current delivery (*see also* Newborn, affected by) 760.64
  pre-eclampsia 760.0
  pyelitis or pyelonephritis, arising during pregnancy (conditions classifiable to 590) 760.1
  renal disease or failure 760.1
  respiratory disease, chronic (conditions classifiable to 490–519, 748) 760.3
  rheumatic heart disease (chronic) (conditions classifiable to 393–398) 760.3
  rubella (conditions classifiable to 056) 760.2
    manifest rubella in the infant or fetus 771.0
  surgery unrelated to current delivery (*see also* Newborn, affected by) 760.64
    to uterus or pelvic organs 760.64
  syphilis (conditions classifiable to 090–097) 760.2
    manifest syphilis in the infant or fetus 090.0
  thrombophlebitis 760.3
  toxemia (of pregnancy) 760.0
    pre-eclamptic 760.0
  toxoplasmosis (conditions classifiable to 130) 760.2
    manifest toxoplasmosis in the infant or fetus 771.2
Maternal condition, affecting fetus or newborn — *continued*
  transmission of chemical substance through the placenta 760.70
    alcohol 760.71
    anticonvulsants 760.77
    antifungals 760.74
    anti-infective 760.74
    antimetabolics 760.78
    cocaine 760.75
    "crack" 760.75
    diethylstilbestrol [DES] 760.76
    hallucinogenic agents 760.73
    narcotics 760.72
    specified substance NEC 760.79
  uremia 760.1
  urinary tract conditions (conditions classifiable to 580–599) 760.1
  vomiting (pernicious) (persistent) (vicious) 761.8
Maternity — *see* Delivery
Matheiu's disease (leptospiral jaundice) 100.0
Mauclaire's disease or osteochondrosis 732.3
Maxcy's disease 081.0
Maxilla, maxillary — *see* condition
May (-Hegglin) anomaly or syndrome 288.2
Mayaro fever 066.3
Mazoplasia 610.8
MBD (minimal brain dysfunction), child — *see also* Hyperkinesia 314.9
MCAD (medium chain acyl CoA dehydrogenase deficiency) 277.85
McArdle (-Schmid-Pearson) disease or syndrome (glycogenosis V) 271.0
McCune-Albright syndrome (osteitis fibrosa disseminata) 756.59
MCLS (mucocutaneous lymph node syndrome) 446.1
McQuarrie's syndrome (idiopathic familial hypoglycemia) 251.2
Measles (black) (hemorrhagic) (suppressed) 055.9
  with
    encephalitis 055.0
    keratitis 055.71
    keratoconjunctivitis 055.71
    otitis media 055.2
    pneumonia 055.1
  complication 055.8
    specified type NEC 055.79
  encephalitis 055.0
  French 056.9
  German 056.9
  keratitis 055.71
  keratoconjunctivitis 055.71
  liberty 056.9
  otitis media 055.2
  pneumonia 055.1
  specified complications NEC 055.79
  vaccination, prophylactic (against) V04.2
Meatitis, urethral — *see also* Urethritis 597.89
Meat poisoning — *see* Poisoning, food
Meatus, meatal — *see* condition
Meat-wrappers' asthma 506.9
Meckel's
  diverticulitis 751.0
  diverticulum (displaced) (hypertrophic) 751.0
Meconium
  aspiration 770.11
    with
      pneumonia 770.12
      pneumonitis 770.12
      respiratory symptoms 770.12
    below vocal cords 770.11
      with respiratory symptoms 770.12
    syndrome 770.12
  delayed passage in newborn 777.1
  ileus 777.1
    due to cystic fibrosis 277.01
Meconium — *continued*
  in liquor 792.3
    noted during delivery 656.8 ☑
  insufflation 770.11
    with respiratory symptoms 770.12
  obstruction
    fetus or newborn 777.1
      in mucoviscidosis 277.01
  passage of 792.3
    noted during delivery 763.84
  peritonitis 777.6
  plug syndrome (newborn) NEC 777.1
  staining 779.84
Median — *see also* condition
  arcuate ligament syndrome 447.4
  bar (prostate) 600.90
    with
      other lower urinary tract symptoms (LUTS) 600.91
      urinary
        obstruction 600.91
        retention 600.91
  rhomboid glossitis 529.2
  vesical orifice 600.90
    with
      other lower urinary tract symptoms (LUTS) 600.91
      urinary
        obstruction 600.91
        retention 600.91
Mediastinal shift 793.2
Mediastinitis (acute) (chronic) 519.2
  actinomycotic 039.8
  syphilitic 095.8
  tuberculous (*see also* Tuberculosis) 012.8 ☑
Mediastinopericarditis — *see also* Pericarditis 423.9
  acute 420.90
  chronic 423.8
    rheumatic 393
  rheumatic, chronic 393
Mediastinum, mediastinal — *see* condition
Medical services provided for — *see* Health, services provided because (of)
Medicine poisoning (by overdose) (wrong substance given or taken in error) 977.9
  specified drug or substance — *see* Table of Drugs and Chemicals
Medin's disease (poliomyelitis) 045.9 ☑
Mediterranean
  anemia (with other hemoglobinopathy) 282.49
  disease or syndrome (hemipathic) 282.49
  fever (*see also* Brucellosis) 023.9
    familial 277.31
  kala-azar 085.0
  leishmaniasis 085.0
  tick fever 082.1
Medulla — *see* condition
Medullary
  cystic kidney 753.16
  sponge kidney 753.17
Medullated fibers
  optic (nerve) 743.57
  retina 362.85
Medulloblastoma (M9470/3)
  desmoplastic (M9471/3) 191.6
  specified site — *see* Neoplasm, by site, malignant
  unspecified site 191.6
Medulloepithelioma (M9501/3) — *see also* Neoplasm, by site, malignant
  teratoid (M9502/3) — *see* Neoplasm, by site, malignant
Medullomyoblastoma (M9472/3)
  specified site — *see* Neoplasm, by site, malignant
  unspecified site 191.6
Meekeren-Ehlers-Danlos syndrome 756.83
Megacaryocytic — *see* condition

Megacolon (acquired) (functional) (not Hirschsprung's disease) 564.7
aganglionic 751.3
congenital, congenitum 751.3
Hirschsprung's (disease) 751.3
psychogenic 306.4
toxic (*see also* Colitis, ulcerative) 556.9
Megaduodenum 537.3
Megaesophagus (functional) 530.0
congenital 750.4
Megakaryocytic — *see* condition
Megalencephaly 742.4
Megalerythema (epidermicum) (infectiosum) 057.0
Megalia, cutis et ossium 757.39
Megaloappendix 751.5
Megalocephalus, megalocephaly NEC 756.0
Megalocornea 743.41
associated with buphthalmos 743.22
Megalocytic anemia 281.9
Megalodactylia (fingers) (thumbs) 755.57
toes 755.65
Megaloduodenum 751.5
Megaloesophagus (functional) 530.0
congenital 750.4
Megalogastria (congenital) 750.7
Megalomania 307.9
Megalophthalmos 743.8
Megalopsia 368.14
Megalosplenia — *see also* Splenomegaly 789.2
Megaloureter 593.89
congenital 753.22
Megarectum 569.49
Megasigmoid 564.7
congenital 751.3
Megaureter 593.89
congenital 753.22
Megrim 346.9 ☑
Meibomian
cyst 373.2
infected 373.12
gland — *see* condition
infarct (eyelid) 374.85
stye 373.11
Meibomitis 373.12
Meige
-Milroy disease (chronic hereditary edema) 757.0
syndrome (blepharospasm-oromandibular dystonia) 333.82
Melalgia, nutritional 266.2
Melancholia — *see also* Psychosis, affective 296.90
climacteric 296.2 ☑
recurrent episode 296.3 ☑
single episode 296.2 ☑
hypochondriac 300.7
intermittent 296.2 ☑
recurrent episode 296.3 ☑
single episode 296.2 ☑
involutional 296.2 ☑
recurrent episode 296.3 ☑
single episode 296.2 ☑
menopausal 296.2 ☑
recurrent episode 296.3 ☑
single episode 296.2 ☑
puerperal 296.2 ☑
reactive (from emotional stress, psychological trauma) 298.0
recurrent 296.3 ☑
senile 290.21
stuporous 296.2 ☑
recurrent episode 296.3 ☑
single episode 296.2 ☑
Melanemia 275.0
Melanoameloblastoma (M9363/0) — *see* Neoplasm, bone, benign
Melanoblastoma (M8720/3) — *see* Melanoma
Melanoblastosis
Block-Sulzberger 757.33
cutis linearis sive systematisata 757.33
Melanocarcinoma (M8720/3) — *see* Melanoma
Melanocytoma, eyeball (M8726/0) 224.0
Melanoderma, melanodermia 709.09
Addison's (primary adrenal insufficiency) 255.41
Melanodontia, infantile 521.05
Melanodontoclasia 521.05
Melanoepithelioma (M8720/3) — *see* Melanoma
Melanoma (malignant) (M8720/3) 172.9

Note — Except where otherwise indicated, the morphological varieties of melanoma in the list below should be coded by site as for "Melanoma (malignant)". Internal sites should be coded to malignant neoplasm of those sites.

abdominal wall 172.5
ala nasi 172.3
amelanotic (M8730/3) — *see* Melanoma, by site
ankle 172.7
anus, anal 154.3
canal 154.2
arm 172.6
auditory canal (external) 172.2
auricle (ear) 172.2
auricular canal (external) 172.2
axilla 172.5
axillary fold 172.5
back 172.5
balloon cell (M8722/3) — *see* Melanoma, by site
benign (M8720/0) — *see* Neoplasm, skin, benign
breast (female) (male) 172.5
brow 172.3
buttock 172.5
canthus (eye) 172.1
cheek (external) 172.3
chest wall 172.5
chin 172.3
choroid 190.6
conjunctiva 190.3
ear (external) 172.2
epithelioid cell (M8771/3) (*see also* Melanoma, by site)
and spindle cell, mixed (M8775/3) — *see* Melanoma, by site
external meatus (ear) 172.2
eye 190.9
eyebrow 172.3
eyelid (lower) (upper) 172.1
face NEC 172.3
female genital organ (external) NEC 184.4
finger 172.6
flank 172.5
foot 172.7
forearm 172.6
forehead 172.3
foreskin 187.1
gluteal region 172.5
groin 172.5
hand 172.6
heel 172.7
helix 172.2
hip 172.7
in
giant pigmented nevus (M8761/3) — *see* Melanoma, by site
Hutchinson's melanotic freckle (M8742/3) — *see* Melanoma, by site
junctional nevus (M8740/3) — *see* Melanoma, by site
precancerous melanosis (M8741/3) — *see* Melanoma, by site
in situ — *see* Melanoma, by site
skin 172.9
interscapular region 172.5
iris 190.0
jaw 172.3
juvenile (M8770/0) — *see* Neoplasm, skin, benign
Melanoma — *continued*
knee 172.7
labium
majus 184.1
minus 184.2
lacrimal gland 190.2
leg 172.7
lip (lower) (upper) 172.0
liver 197.7
lower limb NEC 172.7
male genital organ (external) NEC 187.9
meatus, acoustic (external) 172.2
meibomian gland 172.1
metastatic
of or from specified site — *see* Melanoma, by site
site not of skin — *see* Neoplasm, by site, malignant, secondary
to specified site — *see* Neoplasm, by site, malignant, secondary
unspecified site 172.9
nail 172.9
finger 172.6
toe 172.7
neck 172.4
nodular (M8721/3) — *see* Melanoma, by site
nose, external 172.3
orbit 190.1
penis 187.4
perianal skin 172.5
perineum 172.5
pinna 172.2
popliteal (fossa) (space) 172.7
prepuce 187.1
pubes 172.5
pudendum 184.4
retina 190.5
scalp 172.4
scrotum 187.7
septum nasal (skin) 172.3
shoulder 172.6
skin NEC 172.8
in situ 172.9
spindle cell (M8772/3) (*see also* Melanoma, by site)
type A (M8773/3) 190.0
type B (M8774/3) 190.0
submammary fold 172.5
superficial spreading (M8743/3) — *see* Melanoma, by site
temple 172.3
thigh 172.7
toe 172.7
trunk NEC 172.5
umbilicus 172.5
upper limb NEC 172.6
vagina vault 184.0
vulva 184.4
Melanoplakia 528.9
Melanosarcoma (M8720/3) — *see also* Melanoma
epithelioid cell (M8771/3) — *see* Melanoma
Melanosis 709.09
addisonian (primary adrenal insufficiency) 255.41
tuberculous (*see also* Tuberculosis) 017.6 ☑
adrenal 255.41
colon 569.89
conjunctiva 372.55
congenital 743.49
corii degenerativa 757.33
cornea (presenile) (senile) 371.12
congenital 743.43
interfering with vision 743.42
eye 372.55
congenital 743.49
jute spinners' 709.09
lenticularis progressiva 757.33
liver 573.8
precancerous (M8741/2) (*see also* Neoplasm, skin, in situ)
Melanosis — *continued*
precancerous (*see also* Neoplasm, skin, in situ) — *continued*
malignant melanoma in (M8741/3) — *see* Melanoma
prenatal 743.43
interfering with vision 743.42
Riehl's 709.09
sclera 379.19
congenital 743.47
suprarenal 255.41
tar 709.09
toxic 709.09
Melanuria 791.9
Melasma 709.09
adrenal (gland) 255.41
suprarenal (gland) 255.41
MELAS syndrome (mitochondrial encephalopathy, lactic acidosis and stroke-like episodes) 277.87
Melena 578.1
due to
swallowed maternal blood 777.3
ulcer — *see* Ulcer, by site, with hemorrhage
newborn 772.4
due to swallowed maternal blood 777.3
Meleney's
gangrene (cutaneous) 686.09
ulcer (chronic undermining) 686.09
Melioidosis 025
Melitensis, febris 023.0
Melitococcosis 023.0
Melkersson (-Rosenthal) syndrome 351.8
Mellitus, diabetes — *see* Diabetes
Melorheostosis (bone) (leri) 733.99
Meloschisis 744.83
Melotia 744.29
Membrana
capsularis lentis posterior 743.39
epipapillaris 743.57
Membranacea placenta — *see* Placenta, abnormal
Membranaceous uterus 621.8
Membrane, membranous — *see also* condition
folds, congenital — *see* Web
Jackson's 751.4
over face (causing asphyxia), fetus or newborn 768.9
premature rupture — *see* Rupture, membranes, premature
pupillary 364.74
persistent 743.46
retained (complicating delivery) (with hemorrhage) 666.2 ☑
without hemorrhage 667.1 ☑
secondary (eye) 366.50
unruptured (causing asphyxia) 768.9
vitreous humor 379.25
Membranitis, fetal 658.4 ☑
affecting fetus or newborn 762.7
Memory disturbance, loss or lack — *see also* Amnesia 780.93
mild, following organic brain damage 310.1
MEN (multiple endocrine neoplasia) (syndromes)
type I 258.01
type IIA 258.02
type IIB 258.03
Menadione (vitamin K) **deficiency** 269.0
Menarche, precocious 259.1
Mendacity, pathologic 301.7
Mendelson's syndrome (resulting from a procedure) 997.39
obstetric 668.0 ☑
Mende's syndrome (ptosis-epicanthus) 270.2
Ménétrier's disease or syndrome (hypertrophic gastritis) 535.2 ☑
Ménière's disease, syndrome, or vertigo 386.00
cochlear 386.02

Ménière's disease, syndrome, or vertigo — *continued*
- cochleovestibular 386.01
- inactive 386.04
- in remission 386.04
- vestibular 386.03

Meninges, meningeal — *see* condition

Meningioma (M9530/0) — *see also* Neoplasm, meninges, benign
- angioblastic (M9535/0) — *see* Neoplasm, meninges, benign
- angiomatous (M9534/0) — *see* Neoplasm, meninges, benign
- endotheliomatous (M9531/0) — *see* Neoplasm, meninges, benign
- fibroblastic (M9532/0) — *see* Neoplasm, meninges, benign
- fibrous (M9532/0) — *see* Neoplasm, meninges, benign
- hemangioblastic (M9535/0) — *see* Neoplasm, meninges, benign
- hemangiopericytic (M9536/0) — *see* Neoplasm, meninges, benign
- malignant (M9530/3) — *see* Neoplasm, meninges, malignant
- meningiothelial (M9531/0) — *see* Neoplasm, meninges, benign
- meningotheliomatous (M9531/0) — *see* Neoplasm, meninges, benign
- mixed (M9537/0) — *see* Neoplasm, meninges, benign
- multiple (M9530/1) 237.6
- papillary (M9538/1) 237.6
- psammomatous (M9533/0) — *see* Neoplasm, meninges, benign
- syncytial (M9531/0) — *see* Neoplasm, meninges, benign
- transitional (M9537/0) — *see* Neoplasm, meninges, benign

Meningiomatosis (diffuse) (M9530/1) 237.6

Meningism — *see also* Meningismus 781.6

Meningismus (infectional) (pneumococcal) 781.6
- due to serum or vaccine 997.09 *[321.8]*
- influenzal NEC 487.8

Meningitis (basal) (basic) (basilar) (brain) (cerebral) (cervical) (congestive) (diffuse) (hemorrhagic) (infantile) (membranous) (metastatic) (nonspecific) (pontine) (progressive) (simple) (spinal) (subacute) (sympathetica) (toxic) 322.9
- abacterial NEC (*see also* Meningitis, aseptic) 047.9
- actinomycotic 039.8 *[320.7]*
- adenoviral 049.1
- Aerobacter aerogenes 320.82
- anaerobes (cocci) (gram-negative) (gram-positive) (mixed) (NEC) 320.81
- arbovirus NEC 066.9 *[321.2]*
  - specified type NEC 066.8 *[321.2]*
- aseptic (acute) NEC 047.9
  - adenovirus 049.1
  - Coxsackie virus 047.0
  - due to
    - adenovirus 049.1
    - Coxsackie virus 047.0
    - ECHO virus 047.1
    - enterovirus 047.9
    - mumps 072.1
    - poliovirus (*see also* Poliomyelitis) 045.2 ☑ *[321.2]*
  - ECHO virus 047.1
  - herpes (simplex) virus 054.72
    - zoster 053.0
  - leptospiral 100.81
  - lymphocytic choriomeningitis 049.0
  - noninfective 322.0
- Bacillus pyocyaneus 320.89
- bacterial NEC 320.9
  - anaerobic 320.81
  - gram-negative 320.82
    - anaerobic 320.81
  - Bacteroides (fragilis) (oralis) (melaninogenicus) 320.81
- cancerous (M8000/6) 198.4
- candidal 112.83
- carcinomatous (M8010/6) 198.4
- caseous (*see also* Tuberculosis, meninges) 013.0 ☑
- cerebrospinal (acute) (chronic) (diplococcal) (endemic) (epidemic) (fulminant) (infectious) (malignant) (meningococcal) (sporadic) 036.0
  - carrier (suspected) of V02.59
- chronic NEC 322.2
- clear cerebrospinal fluid NEC 322.0
- Clostridium (haemolyticum) (novyi) NEC 320.81
- coccidioidomycosis 114.2
- Coxsackie virus 047.0
- cryptococcal 117.5 *[321.0]*
- diplococcal 036.0
  - gram-negative 036.0
  - gram-positive 320.1
- Diplococcus pneumoniae 320.1
- due to
  - actinomycosis 039.8 *[320.7]*
  - adenovirus 049.1
  - coccidiomycosis 114.2
  - enterovirus 047.9
    - specified NEC 047.8
  - histoplasmosis (*see also* Histoplasmosis) 115.91
  - Listerosis 027.0 *[320.7]*
  - Lyme disease 088.81 *[320.7]*
  - moniliasis 112.83
  - mumps 072.1
  - neurosyphilis 094.2
  - nonbacterial organisms NEC 321.8
  - oidiomycosis 112.83
  - poliovirus (*see also* Poliomyelitis) 045.2 ☑ *[321.2]*
  - preventive immunization, inoculation, or vaccination 997.09 *[321.8]*
  - sarcoidosis 135 *[321.4]*
  - sporotrichosis 117.1 *[321.1]*
  - syphilis 094.2
    - acute 091.81
    - congenital 090.42
    - secondary 091.81
  - trypanosomiasis (*see also* Trypanosomiasis) 086.9 *[321.3]*
  - whooping cough 033.9 *[320.7]*
- ECHO virus 047.1
- E. coli 320.82
- endothelial-leukocytic, benign, recurrent 047.9
- Enterobacter aerogenes 320.82
- enteroviral 047.9
  - specified type NEC 047.8
- enterovirus 047.9
  - specified NEC 047.8
- eosinophilic 322.1
- epidemic NEC 036.0
- Escherichia coli (E. coli) 320.82
- Eubacterium 320.81
- fibrinopurulent NEC 320.9
  - specified type NEC 320.89
- Friedländer (bacillus) 320.82
- fungal NEC 117.9 *[321.1]*
- Fusobacterium 320.81
- gonococcal 098.82
- gram-negative bacteria NEC 320.82
  - anaerobic 320.81
  - cocci 036.0
    - specified NEC 320.82
- gram-negative cocci NEC 036.0
  - specified NEC 320.82
- gram-positive cocci NEC 320.9
- herpes (simplex) virus 054.72
  - zoster 053.0
- H. influenzae 320.0
- infectious NEC 320.9
- influenzal 320.0
- Klebsiella pneumoniae 320.82
- late effect — *see* Late, effect, meningitis
- leptospiral (aseptic) 100.81
- Listerella (monocytogenes) 027.0 *[320.7]*
- Listeria monocytogenes 027.0 *[320.7]*
- lymphocytic (acute) (benign) (serous) 049.0
  - choriomeningitis virus 049.0
- meningococcal (chronic) 036.0
- Mima polymorpha 320.82
- Mollaret's 047.9
- monilial 112.83
- mumps (virus) 072.1
- mycotic NEC 117.9 *[321.1]*
- Neisseria 036.0
- neurosyphilis 094.2
- nonbacterial NEC (*see also* Meningitis, aseptic) 047.9
- nonpyogenic NEC 322.0
- oidiomycosis 112.83
- ossificans 349.2
- Peptococcus 320.81
- Peptostreptococcus 320.81
- pneumococcal 320.1
- poliovirus (*see also* Poliomyelitis) 045.2 ☑ *[321.2]*
- Proprionibacterium 320.81
- Proteus morganii 320.82
- Pseudomonas (aeruginosa) (pyocyaneus) 320.82
- purulent NEC 320.9
  - specified organism NEC 320.89
- pyogenic NEC 320.9
  - specified organism NEC 320.89
- Salmonella 003.21
- septic NEC 320.9
  - specified organism NEC 320.89
- serosa circumscripta NEC 322.0
- serous NEC (*see also* Meningitis, aseptic) 047.9
  - lymphocytic 049.0
  - syndrome 348.2
- Serratia (marcescens) 320.82
- specified organism NEC 320.89
- sporadic cerebrospinal 036.0
- sporotrichosis 117.1 *[321.1]*
- staphylococcal 320.3
- sterile 997.09
- streptococcal (acute) 320.2
- suppurative 320.9
  - specified organism NEC 320.89
- syphilitic 094.2
  - acute 091.81
  - congenital 090.42
  - secondary 091.81
- torula 117.5 *[321.0]*
- traumatic (complication of injury) 958.8
- Treponema (denticola) (macrodenticum) 320.81
- trypanosomiasis 086.1 *[321.3]*
- tuberculous (*see also* Tuberculosis, meninges) 013.0 ☑
- typhoid 002.0 *[320.7]*
- Veillonella 320.81
- Vibrio vulnificus 320.82
- viral, virus NEC (*see also* Meningitis, aseptic) 047.9
- Wallgren's (*see also* Meningitis, aseptic) 047.9

Meningocele (congenital) (spinal) — *see also* Spina bifida 741.9 ☑
- acquired (traumatic) 349.2
- cerebral 742.0
- cranial 742.0

Meningocerebritis — *see* Meningoencephalitis

Meningococcemia (acute) (chronic) 036.2

Meningococcus, meningococcal — *see also* condition 036.9
- adrenalitis, hemorrhagic 036.3
- carditis 036.40
- carrier (suspected) of V02.59
- cerebrospinal fever 036.0
- encephalitis 036.1
- endocarditis 036.42
- exposure to V01.84
- infection NEC 036.9
- meningitis (cerebrospinal) 036.0
- myocarditis 036.43
- optic neuritis 036.81
- pericarditis 036.41
- septicemia (chronic) 036.2

Meningoencephalitis — *see also* Encephalitis 323.9
- acute NEC 048
- bacterial, purulent, pyogenic, or septic — *see* Meningitis
- chronic NEC 094.1
- diffuse NEC 094.1
- diphasic 063.2
- due to
  - actinomycosis 039.8 *[320.7]*
  - blastomycosis NEC (*see also* Blastomycosis) 116.0 *[323.41]*
  - free-living amebae 136.29
  - Listeria monocytogenes 027.0 *[320.7]*
  - Lyme disease 088.81 *[320.7]*
  - mumps 072.2
  - Naegleria (amebae) (gruberi) (organisms) 136.29
  - rubella 056.01
  - sporotrichosis 117.1 *[321.1]*
  - toxoplasmosis (acquired) 130.0
    - congenital (active) 771.2 *[323.41]*
  - Trypanosoma 086.1 *[323.2]*
- epidemic 036.0
- herpes 054.3
- herpetic 054.3
- H. influenzae 320.0
- infectious (acute) 048
- influenzal 320.0
- late effect — *see* category 326
- Listeria monocytogenes 027.0 *[320.7]*
- lymphocytic (serous) 049.0
- mumps 072.2
- parasitic NEC 123.9 *[323.41]*
- pneumococcal 320.1
- primary amebic 136.29
- rubella 056.01
- serous 048
  - lymphocytic 049.0
- specific 094.2
- staphylococcal 320.3
- streptococcal 320.2
- syphilitic 094.2
- toxic NEC 989.9 *[323.71]*
  - due to
    - carbon tetrachloride (vapor) 987.8 *[323.71]*
    - hydroxyquinoline derivatives poisoning 961.3 *[323.71]*
    - lead 984.9 *[323.71]*
    - mercury 985.0 *[323.71]*
    - thallium 985.8 *[323.71]*
- toxoplasmosis (acquired) 130.0
- trypanosomic 086.1 *[323.2]*
- tuberculous (*see also* Tuberculosis, meninges) 013.0 ☑
- virus NEC 048

Meningoencephalocele 742.0
- syphilitic 094.89
  - congenital 090.49

Meningoencephalomyelitis — *see also* Meningoencephalitis 323.9
- acute NEC 048
  - disseminated (postinfectious) 136.9 *[323.61]*
    - postimmunization or postvaccination 323.51
- due to
  - actinomycosis 039.8 *[320.7]*

Meningoencephalomyelitis — *see also* Meningoencephalitis — *continued*
due to — *continued*
torula 117.5 *[323.41]*
toxoplasma or toxoplasmosis (acquired) 130.0
congenital (active) 771.2 *[323.41]*
late effect — *see* category 326
Meningoencephalomyelopathy — *see also* Meningoencephalomyelitis 349.9
Meningoencephalopathy — *see also* Meningoencephalitis 348.39
Meningoencephalopoliomyelitis — *see also* Poliomyelitis, bulbar 045.0 ☑
late effect 138
Meningomyelitis — *see also* Meningoencephalitis 323.9
blastomycotic NEC (*see also* Blastomycosis) 116.0 *[323.41]*
due to
actinomycosis 039.8 *[320.7]*
blastomycosis (*see also* Blastomycosis) 116.0 *[323.41]*
Meningococcus 036.0
sporotrichosis 117.1 *[323.41]*
torula 117.5 *[323.41]*
late effect — *see* category 326
lethargic 049.8
meningococcal 036.0
syphilitic 094.2
tuberculous (*see also* Tuberculosis, meninges) 013.0 ☑
Meningomyelocele — *see also* Spina bifida 741.9 ☑
syphilitic 094.89
Meningomyeloneuritis — *see* Meningoencephalitis
Meningoradiculitis — *see* Meningitis
Meningovascular — *see* condition
Meniscocytosis 282.60
Menkes' syndrome — *see* Syndrome, Menkes'
Menolipsis 626.0
Menometrorrhagia 626.2
Menopause, menopausal (symptoms) (syndrome) 627.2
arthritis (any site) NEC 716.3 ☑
artificial 627.4
bleeding 627.0
crisis 627.2
depression (*see also* Psychosis, affective) 296.2 ☑
agitated 296.2 ☑
recurrent episode 296.3 ☑
single episode 296.2 ☑
psychotic 296.2 ☑
recurrent episode 296.3 ☑
single episode 296.2 ☑
recurrent episode 296.3 ☑
single episode 296.2 ☑
melancholia (*see also* Psychosis, affective) 296.2 ☑
recurrent episode 296.3 ☑
single episode 296.2 ☑
paranoid state 297.2
paraphrenia 297.2
postsurgical 627.4
premature 256.31
postirradiation 256.2
postsurgical 256.2
psychoneurosis 627.2
psychosis NEC 298.8
surgical 627.4
toxic polyarthritis NEC 716.39
Menorrhagia (primary) 626.2
climacteric 627.0
menopausal 627.0
postclimacteric 627.1
postmenopausal 627.1
preclimacteric 627.0
premenopausal 627.0
puberty (menses retained) 626.3
Menorrhalgia 625.3
Menoschesis 626.8
Menostaxis 626.2
Menses, retention 626.8
Menstrual — *see also* Menstruation
cycle, irregular 626.4
disorders NEC 626.9
extraction V25.3
fluid, retained 626.8
molimen 625.4
period, normal V65.5
regulation V25.3
Menstruation
absent 626.0
anovulatory 628.0
delayed 626.8
difficult 625.3
disorder 626.9
psychogenic 306.52
specified NEC 626.8
during pregnancy 640.8 ☑
excessive 626.2
frequent 626.2
infrequent 626.1
irregular 626.4
latent 626.8
membranous 626.8
painful (primary) (secondary) 625.3
psychogenic 306.52
passage of clots 626.2
precocious 626.8
protracted 626.8
retained 626.8
retrograde 626.8
scanty 626.1
suppression 626.8
vicarious (nasal) 625.8
Mentagra — *see also* Sycosis 704.8
Mental — *see also* condition
deficiency (*see also* Retardation, mental) 319
deterioration (*see also* Psychosis) 298.9
disorder (*see also* Disorder, mental) 300.9
exhaustion 300.5
insufficiency (congenital) (*see also* Retardation, mental) 319
observation without need for further medical care NEC V71.09
retardation (*see also* Retardation, mental) 319
subnormality (*see also* Retardation, mental) 319
mild 317
moderate 318.0
profound 318.2
severe 318.1
upset (*see also* Disorder, mental) 300.9
Meralgia paresthetica 355.1
Mercurial — *see* condition
Mercurialism NEC 985.0
Merergasia 300.9
Merkel cell tumor — *see* Neoplasm, by site, malignant
Merocele — *see also* Hernia, femoral 553.00
Meromelia 755.4
lower limb 755.30
intercalary 755.32
femur 755.34
tibiofibular (complete) (incomplete) 755.33
fibula 755.37
metatarsal(s) 755.38
tarsal(s) 755.38
tibia 755.36
tibiofibular 755.35
terminal (complete) (partial) (transverse) 755.31
longitudinal 755.32
metatarsal(s) 755.38
phalange(s) 755.39
tarsal(s) 755.38
transverse 755.31
upper limb 755.20
Meromelia — *continued*
upper limb — *continued*
intercalary 755.22
carpal(s) 755.28
humeral 755.24
radioulnar (complete) (incomplete) 755.23
metacarpal(s) 755.28
phalange(s) 755.29
radial 755.26
radioulnar 755.25
ulnar 755.27
terminal (complete) (partial) (transverse) 755.21
longitudinal 755.22
carpal(s) 755.28
metacarpal(s) 755.28
phalange(s) 755.29
transverse 755.21
Merosmia 781.1
MERRF syndrome (myoclonus with epilepsy and with ragged red fibers) 277.87
Merycism — *see also* Vomiting
psychogenic 307.53
Merzbacher-Pelizaeus disease 330.0
Mesaortitis — *see* Aortitis
Mesarteritis — *see* Arteritis
Mesencephalitis — *see also* Encephalitis 323.9
late effect — *see* category 326
Mesenchymoma (M8990/1) — *see also* Neoplasm, connective tissue, uncertain behavior
benign (M8990/0) — *see* Neoplasm, connective tissue, benign
malignant (M8990/3) — *see* Neoplasm, connective tissue, malignant
Mesenteritis
retractile 567.82
sclerosing 567.82
Mesentery, mesenteric — *see* condition
Mesiodens, mesiodentes 520.1
causing crowding 524.31
Mesio-occlusion 524.23
Mesocardia (with asplenia) 746.87
Mesocolon — *see* condition
Mesonephroma (malignant) (M9110/3) — *see also* Neoplasm, by site, malignant
benign (M9110/0) — *see* Neoplasm, by site, benign
Mesophlebitis — *see* Phlebitis
Mesostromal dysgenesis 743.51
Mesothelioma (malignant) (M9050/3) — *see also* Neoplasm, by site, malignant
benign (M9050/0) — *see* Neoplasm, by site, benign
biphasic type (M9053/3) (*see also* Neoplasm, by site, malignant)
benign (M9053/0) — *see* Neoplasm, by site, benign
epithelioid (M9052/3) (*see also* Neoplasm, by site, malignant)
benign (M9052/0) — *see* Neoplasm, by site, benign
fibrous (M9051/3) (*see also* Neoplasm, by site, malignant)
benign (M9051/0) — *see* Neoplasm, by site, benign
Metabolic syndrome 277.7
Metabolism disorder 277.9
specified type NEC 277.89
Metagonimiasis 121.5
Metagonimus infestation (small intestine) 121.5
Metal
pigmentation (skin) 709.00
polishers' disease 502
Metalliferous miners' lung 503
Metamorphopsia 368.14
Metaplasia
bone, in skin 709.3
breast 611.89
Metaplasia — *continued*
cervix — *omit code*
endometrium (squamous) 621.8
esophagus 530.85
intestinal, of gastric mucosa 537.89
kidney (pelvis) (squamous) (*see also* Disease, renal) 593.89
myelogenous 289.89
myeloid 289.89
agnogenic 238.76
megakaryocytic 238.76
spleen 289.59
squamous cell
amnion 658.8 ☑
bladder 596.8
cervix — *see* condition
trachea 519.19
tracheobronchial tree 519.19
uterus 621.8
cervix — *see* condition
Metastasis, metastatic
abscess — *see* Abscess
calcification 275.40
cancer, neoplasm, or disease
from specified site (M8000/3) — *see* Neoplasm, by site, malignant
to specified site (M8000/6) — *see* Neoplasm, by site, secondary
deposits (in) (M8000/6) — *see* Neoplasm, by site, secondary
pneumonia 038.8 *[484.8]*
spread (to) (M8000/6) — *see* Neoplasm, by site, secondary
Metatarsalgia 726.70
anterior 355.6
due to Freiberg's disease 732.5
Morton's 355.6
Metatarsus, metatarsal — *see also* condition
abductus valgus (congenital) 754.60
adductus varus (congenital) 754.53
primus varus 754.52
valgus (adductus) (congenital) 754.60
varus (abductus) (congenital) 754.53
primus 754.52
Methadone use 304.00
Methemoglobinemia 289.7
acquired (with sulfhemoglobinemia) 289.7
congenital 289.7
enzymatic 289.7
Hb-M disease 289.7
hereditary 289.7
toxic 289.7
Methemoglobinuria — *see also* Hemoglobinuria 791.2
Methicillin
resistant staphyloccocus aureus (MRSA) 041.12
colonization V02.54
personal history of V12.04
susceptible staphylococcus aureus (MSSA) 041.11
colonization V02.53
Methioninemia 270.4
Metritis (catarrhal) (septic) (suppurative) — *see also* Endometritis 615.9
blennorrhagic 098.16
chronic or duration of 2 months or over 098.36
cervical (*see also* Cervicitis) 616.0
gonococcal 098.16
chronic or duration of 2 months or over 098.36
hemorrhagic 626.8
puerperal, postpartum, childbirth 670.0 ☑
tuberculous (*see also* Tuberculosis) 016.7 ☑
Metropathia hemorrhagica 626.8
Metroperitonitis — *see also* Peritonitis, pelvic, female 614.5
Metrorrhagia 626.6
arising during pregnancy — *see* Hemorrhage, pregnancy

Mobile, mobility — *continued*
organ or site, congenital NEC — *see* Malposition, congenital
spleen 289.59
Mobitz heart block (atrioventricular) 426.10
type I (Wenckebach's) 426.13
type II 426.12
Möbius'
disease 346.2 ☑
syndrome
congenital oculofacial paralysis 352.6
ophthalmoplegic migraine 346.2 ☑
Moeller(-Barlow) disease (infantile scurvy) 267
glossitis 529.4
Mohr's syndrome (types I and II) 759.89
Mola destruens (M9100/1) 236.1
Molarization, premolars 520.2
Molar pregnancy 631
hydatidiform (delivered) (undelivered) 630
Molding, head (during birth) — *omit code*
Mold(s) in vitreous 117.9
Mole (pigmented) (M8720/0) — *see also* Neoplasm, skin, benign
blood 631
Breus' 631
cancerous (M8720/3) — *see* Melanoma
carneous 631
destructive (M9100/1) 236.1
ectopic — *see* Pregnancy, ectopic
fleshy 631
hemorrhagic 631
hydatid, hydatidiform (benign) (complicating pregnancy) (delivered) (undelivered) (*see also* Hydatidiform mole) 630
invasive (M9100/1) 236.1
malignant (M9100/1) 236.1
previous, affecting management of pregnancy V23.1
invasive (hydatidiform) (M9100/1) 236.1
malignant
meaning
malignant hydatidiform mole (9100/1) 236.1
melanoma (M8720/3) — *see* Melanoma
nonpigmented (M8730/0) — *see* Neoplasm, skin, benign
pregnancy NEC 631
skin (M8720/0) — *see* Neoplasm, skin, benign
tubal — *see* Pregnancy, tubal
vesicular (*see also* Hydatidiform mole) 630
Molimen, molimina (menstrual) 625.4
Mollaret's meningitis 047.9
Mollities (cerebellar) (cerebral) 437.8
ossium 268.2
Molluscum
contagiosum 078.0
epitheliale 078.0
fibrosum (M8851/0) — *see* Lipoma, by site
pendulum (M8851/0) — *see* Lipoma, by site
Mönckeberg's arteriosclerosis, degeneration, disease, or sclerosis — *see also* Arteriosclerosis, extremities 440.20
Monday fever 504
Monday morning dyspnea or asthma 504
Mondini's malformation (cochlea) 744.05
Mondor's disease (thrombophlebitis of breast) 451.89
Mongolian, mongolianism, mongolism, mongoloid 758.0
spot 757.33
Monilethrix (congenital) 757.4
Monilia infestation — *see* Candidiasis
Moniliasis — *see also* Candidiasis
neonatal 771.7
vulvovaginitis 112.1
Monkeypox 059.01
Monoarthritis 716.60
ankle 716.67
arm 716.62
lower (and wrist) 716.63
upper (and elbow) 716.62
foot (and ankle) 716.67
forearm (and wrist) 716.63
hand 716.64
leg 716.66
lower 716.66
upper 716.65
pelvic region (hip) (thigh) 716.65
shoulder (region) 716.61
specified site NEC 716.68
Monoblastic — *see* condition
Monochromatism (cone) (rod) 368.54
Monocytic — *see* condition
Monocytopenia 288.59
Monocytosis (symptomatic) 288.63
Monofixation syndrome 378.34
Monomania — *see also* Psychosis 298.9
Mononeuritis 355.9
cranial nerve — *see* Disorder, nerve, cranial
femoral nerve 355.2
lateral
cutaneous nerve of thigh 355.1
popliteal nerve 355.3
lower limb 355.8
specified nerve NEC 355.79
medial popliteal nerve 355.4
median nerve 354.1
multiplex 354.5
plantar nerve 355.6
posterior tibial nerve 355.5
radial nerve 354.3
sciatic nerve 355.0
ulnar nerve 354.2
upper limb 354.9
specified nerve NEC 354.8
vestibular 388.5
Mononeuropathy — *see also* Mononeuritis 355.9
diabetic NEC 250.6 ☑ *[355.9]*
due to secondary diabetes 249.6 ☑ *[355.9]*
lower limb 250.6 ☑ *[355.8]*
due to secondary diabetes 249.6 ☑ *[355.8]*
upper limb 250.6 ☑ *[354.9]*
due to secondary diabetes 249.6 ☑ *[354.9]*
iliohypogastric nerve 355.79
ilioinguinal nerve 355.79
obturator nerve 355.79
saphenous nerve 355.79
Mononucleosis, infectious 075
with hepatitis 075 *[573.1]*
Monoplegia 344.5
brain (current episode) (*see also* Paralysis, brain) 437.8
fetus or newborn 767.8
cerebral (current episode) (*see also* Paralysis, brain) 437.8
congenital or infantile (cerebral) (spastic) (spinal) 343.3
embolic (current) (*see also* Embolism, brain) 434.1 ☑
late effect — *see* Late effect(s) (of) cerebrovascular disease
infantile (cerebral) (spastic) (spinal) 343.3
lower limb 344.30
affecting
dominant side 344.31
nondominant side 344.32
due to late effect of cerebrovascular accident — *see* Late effect(s) (of) cerebrovascular accident
newborn 767.8
psychogenic 306.0
Monoplegia — *continued*
psychogenic — *continued*
specified as conversion reaction 300.11
thrombotic (current) (*see also* Thrombosis, brain) 434.0 ☑
late effect — *see* Late effect(s) (of) cerebrovascular disease
transient 781.4
upper limb 344.40
affecting
dominant side 344.41
nondominant side 344.42
due to late effect of cerebrovascular accident — *see* Late effect(s) (of) cerebrovascular accident
Monorchism, monorchidism 752.89
Monteggia's fracture (closed) 813.03
open 813.13
Mood swings
brief compensatory 296.99
rebound 296.99
Mooren's ulcer (cornea) 370.07
Moore's syndrome — *see also* Epilepsy 345.5 ☑
Mooser bodies 081.0
Mooser-Neill reaction 081.0
Moral
deficiency 301.7
imbecility 301.7
Morax-Axenfeld conjunctivitis 372.03
Morbilli — *see also* Measles 055.9
Morbus
anglicus, anglorum 268.0
Beigel 111.2
caducus (*see also* Epilepsy) 345.9 ☑
caeruleus 746.89
celiacus 579.0
comitialis (see also Epilepsy) 345.9 ☑
cordis (*see also* Disease, heart)
valvulorum — *see* Endocarditis
coxae 719.95
tuberculous (*see also* Tuberculosis) 015.1 ☑
hemorrhagicus neonatorum 776.0
maculosus neonatorum 772.6
renum 593.0
senilis (*see also* Osteoarthrosis) 715.9 ☑
Morel-Kraepelin disease — *see also* Schizophrenia 295.9 ☑
Morel-Moore syndrome (hyperostosis frontalis interna) 733.3
Morel-Morgagni syndrome (hyperostosis frontalis interna) 733.3
Morgagni
cyst, organ, hydatid, or appendage 752.89
fallopian tube 752.11
disease or syndrome (hyperostosis frontalis interna) 733.3
Morgagni-Adams-Stokes syndrome (syncope with heart block) 426.9
Morgagni-Stewart-Morel syndrome (hyperostosis frontalis interna) 733.3
Moria — *see also* Psychosis 298.9
Morning sickness 643.0 ☑
Moron 317
Morphea (guttate) (linear) 701.0
Morphine dependence — *see also* Dependence 304.0 ☑
Morphinism — *see also* Dependence 304.0 ☑
Morphinomania — *see also* Dependence 304.0 ☑
Morphoea 701.0
Morquio (-Brailsford) (-Ullrich) disease or syndrome (mucopolysaccharidosis IV) 277.5
kyphosis 277.5
Morris syndrome (testicular feminization) 259.51
Morsus humanus (open wound) — *see also* Wound, open, by site
skin surface intact — *see* Contusion
Mortification (dry) (moist) — *see also* Gangrene 785.4
Morton's
disease 355.6
foot 355.6
metatarsalgia (syndrome) 355.6
neuralgia 355.6
neuroma 355.6
syndrome (metatarsalgia) (neuralgia) 355.6
toe 355.6
Morvan's disease 336.0
Mosaicism, mosaic (chromosomal) 758.9
autosomal 758.5
sex 758.81
Moschcowitz's syndrome (thrombotic thrombocytopenic purpura) 446.6
Mother yaw 102.0
Motion sickness (from travel, any vehicle) (from roundabouts or swings) 994.6
Mottled teeth (enamel) (endemic) (nonendemic) 520.3
Mottling enamel (endemic) (nonendemic) (teeth) 520.3
Mouchet's disease 732.5
Mould(s) (in vitreous) 117.9
Moulders'
bronchitis 502
tuberculosis (*see also* Tuberculosis) 011.4 ☑
Mounier-Kuhn syndrome 748.3
with
acute exacerbation 494.1
bronchiectasis 494.0
with (acute) exacerbation 494.1
acquired 519.19
with bronchiectasis 494.0
with (acute) exacerbation 494.1
Mountain
fever — *see* Fever, mountain
sickness 993.2
with polycythemia, acquired 289.0
acute 289.0
tick fever 066.1
Mouse, joint — *see also* Loose, body, joint 718.1 ☑
knee 717.6
Mouth — *see* condition
Movable
coccyx 724.71
kidney (*see also* Disease, renal) 593.0
congenital 753.3
organ or site, congenital NEC — *see* Malposition, congenital
spleen 289.59
Movement
abnormal (dystonic) (involuntary) 781.0
decreased fetal 655.7 ☑
paradoxical facial 374.43
Moya Moya disease 437.5
Mozart's ear 744.29
MRSA (methicillin-resistant staphylococcus aureus) 041.12
colonization V02.54
personal history of V12.04
MSSA (methicillin susceptible staphylococcus aureus) 041.11
colonization V02.53
Mucha's disease (acute parapsoriasis varioliformis) 696.2
Mucha-Haberman syndrome (acute parapsoriasis varioliformis) 696.2
Mu-chain disease 273.2
Mucinosis (cutaneous) (papular) 701.8
Mucocele
appendix 543.9
buccal cavity 528.9
gallbladder (*see also* Disease, gallbladder) 575.3
lacrimal sac 375.43
orbit (eye) 376.81
salivary gland (any) 527.6
sinus (accessory) (nasal) 478.19

- **Mucocele** — *continued*
  - turbinate (bone) (middle) (nasal) 478.19
  - uterus 621.8
- **Mucocutaneous lymph node syndrome** (acute) (febrile) (infantile) 446.1
- **Mucoenteritis** 564.9
- **Mucolipidosis I, II, III** 272.7
- **Mucopolysaccharidosis** (types 1-6) 277.5
  - cardiopathy 277.5 *[425.7]*
- **Mucormycosis** (lung) 117.7
- **Mucosa associated lymphoid tissue** (MALT) 200.3 ☑
- **Mucositis** — *see also* Inflammation, by site 528.00
  - cervix (ulcerative) 616.81
  - due to
    - antineoplastic therapy (ulcerative) 528.01
    - other drugs (ulcerative) 528.02
    - specified NEC 528.09
  - gastrointestinal (ulcerative) 538
  - nasal (ulcerative) 478.11
  - necroticans agranulocytica (*see also* Agranulocytosis) 288.09
  - ulcerative 528.00
  - vagina (ulcerative) 616.81
  - vulva (ulcerative) 616.81
- **Mucous** — *see also* condition
  - patches (syphilitic) 091.3
    - congenital 090.0
- **Mucoviscidosis** 277.00
  - with meconium obstruction 277.01
- **Mucus**
  - asphyxia or suffocation (*see also* Asphyxia, mucus) 933.1
    - newborn 770.18
  - in stool 792.1
  - plug (*see also* Asphyxia, mucus) 933.1
    - aspiration, of newborn 770.17
    - tracheobronchial 519.19
      - newborn 770.18
- **Muguet** 112.0
- **Mulberry molars** 090.5
- **Müllerian mixed tumor** (M8950/3) — *see* Neoplasm, by site, malignant
- **Multicystic kidney** 753.19
- **Multilobed placenta** — *see* Placenta, abnormal
- **Multinodular prostate** 600.10
  - with
    - urinary
      - obstruction 600.11
      - retention 600.11
- **Multiparity** V61.5
  - affecting
    - fetus or newborn 763.89
    - management of
      - labor and delivery 659.4 ☑
      - pregnancy V23.3
  - requiring contraceptive management (*see also* Contraception) V25.9
- **Multipartita placenta** — *see* Placenta, abnormal
- **Multiple, multiplex** — *see also* condition
  - birth
    - affecting fetus or newborn 761.5
    - healthy liveborn — *see* Newborn, multiple
  - digits (congenital) 755.00
    - fingers 755.01
    - toes 755.02
  - organ or site NEC — *see* Accessory
  - personality 300.14
  - renal arteries 747.62
- **Mumps** 072.9
  - with complication 072.8
    - specified type NEC 072.79
  - encephalitis 072.2
  - hepatitis 072.71
  - meningitis (aseptic) 072.1
  - meningoencephalitis 072.2
  - oophoritis 072.79
  - orchitis 072.0
  - pancreatitis 072.3
- **Mumps** — *continued*
  - polyneuropathy 072.72
  - vaccination, prophylactic (against) V04.6
- **Mumu** — *see also* Infestation, filarial 125.9
- **Münchausen syndrome** 301.51
- **Münchmeyer's disease or syndrome** (exostosis luxurians) 728.11
- **Mural** — *see* condition
- **Murmur** (cardiac) (heart) (nonorganic) (organic) 785.2
  - abdominal 787.5
  - aortic (valve) (*see also* Endocarditis, aortic) 424.1
  - benign — *omit code*
  - cardiorespiratory 785.2
  - diastolic — *see* condition
  - Flint (*see also* Endocarditis, aortic) 424.1
  - functional — *omit code*
  - Graham Steell (pulmonic regurgitation) (*see also* Endocarditis, pulmonary) 424.3
  - innocent — *omit code*
  - insignificant — *omit code*
  - midsystolic 785.2
  - mitral (valve) — *see* Stenosis, mitral
  - physiologic — *see* condition
  - presystolic, mitral — *see* Insufficiency, mitral
  - pulmonic (valve) (*see also* Endocarditis, pulmonary) 424.3
  - Still's (vibratory) — *omit code*
  - systolic (valvular) — *see* condition
  - tricuspid (valve) — *see* Endocarditis, tricuspid
  - undiagnosed 785.2
  - valvular — *see* condition
  - vibratory — *omit code*
- **Murri's disease** (intermittent hemoglobinuria) 283.2
- **Muscae volitantes** 379.24
- **Muscle, muscular** — *see* condition
- **Musculoneuralgia** 729.1
- **Mushrooming hip** 718.95
- **Mushroom workers' (pickers') lung** 495.5
- **Mutation**
  - factor V leiden 289.81
  - prothrombin gene 289.81
- **Mutism** — *see also* Aphasia 784.3
  - akinetic 784.3
  - deaf (acquired) (congenital) 389.7
  - hysterical 300.11
  - selective (elective) 313.23
    - adjustment reaction 309.83
- **Myà's disease** (congenital dilation, colon) 751.3
- **Myalgia** (intercostal) 729.1
  - eosinophilia syndrome 710.5
  - epidemic 074.1
    - cervical 078.89
  - psychogenic 307.89
  - traumatic NEC 959.9
- **Myasthenia** 358.00
  - cordis — *see* Failure, heart
  - gravis 358.00
    - with exacerbation (acute) 358.01
    - in crisis 358.01
    - neonatal 775.2
    - pseudoparalytica 358.00
  - stomach 536.8
    - psychogenic 306.4
  - syndrome
    - in
      - botulism 005.1 *[358.1]*
      - diabetes mellitus 250.6 ☑ *[358.1]*
        - due to secondary diabetes 249.6 ☑ *[358.1]*
      - hypothyroidism (*see also* Hypothyroidism) 244.9 *[358.1]*
      - malignant neoplasm NEC 199.1 *[358.1]*
- **Myasthenia** — *continued*
  - syndrome — *continued*
    - in — *continued*
      - pernicious anemia 281.0 *[358.1]*
      - thyrotoxicosis (*see also* Thyrotoxicosis) 242.9 ☑ *[358.1]*
- **Myasthenic** 728.87
- **Mycelium infection** NEC 117.9
- **Mycetismus** 988.1
- **Mycetoma** (actinomycotic) 039.9
  - bone 039.8
    - mycotic 117.4
  - foot 039.4
    - mycotic 117.4
  - madurae 039.9
    - mycotic 117.4
  - maduromycotic 039.9
    - mycotic 117.4
  - mycotic 117.4
  - nocardial 039.9
- **Mycobacteriosis** — *see* Mycobacterium
- **Mycobacterium, mycobacterial** (infection) 031.9
  - acid-fast (bacilli) 031.9
  - anonymous (*see also* Mycobacterium, atypical) 031.9
  - atypical (acid-fast bacilli) 031.9
    - cutaneous 031.1
    - pulmonary 031.0
      - tuberculous (*see also* Tuberculosis, pulmonary) 011.9 ☑
    - specified site NEC 031.8
  - avium 031.0
    - intracellulare complex bacteremia (MAC) 031.2
  - balnei 031.1
  - Battey 031.0
  - cutaneous 031.1
  - disseminated 031.2
    - avium-intracellulare complex (DMAC) 031.2
  - fortuitum 031.0
  - intracellulare (battey bacillus) 031.0
  - kakerifu 031.8
  - kansasii 031.0
  - kasongo 031.8
  - leprae — *see* Leprosy
  - luciflavum 031.0
  - marinum 031.1
  - pulmonary 031.0
    - tuberculous (*see also* Tuberculosis, pulmonary) 011.9 ☑
  - scrofulaceum 031.1
  - tuberculosis (human, bovine) (*see also* Tuberculosis)
    - avian type 031.0
  - ulcerans 031.1
  - xenopi 031.0
- **Mycosis, mycotic** 117.9
  - cutaneous NEC 111.9
  - ear 111.8 *[380.15]*
  - fungoides (M9700/3) 202.1 ☑
  - mouth 112.0
  - pharynx 117.9
  - skin NEC 111.9
  - stomatitis 112.0
  - systemic NEC 117.9
  - tonsil 117.9
  - vagina, vaginitis 112.1
- **Mydriasis** (persistent) (pupil) 379.43
- **Myelatelia** 742.59
- **Myelinoclasis, perivascular**, acute (postinfectious) NEC 136.9 *[323.61]*
  - postimmunization or postvaccinal 323.51
- **Myelinosis, central pontine** 341.8
- **Myelitis** (ascending) (cerebellar) (childhood) (chronic) (descending) (diffuse) (disseminated) (pressure) (progressive) (spinal cord) (subacute) — *see also* Encephalitis 323.9
  - acute (transverse) 341.20
    - idiopathic 341.22
    - in conditions classified elsewhere 341.21
- **Myelitis** — *see also* Encephalitis — *continued*
  - due to
    - infection classified elsewhere 136.9 *[323.42]*
    - specified cause NEC 323.82
    - vaccination (any) 323.52
    - viral diseases classified elsewhere 323.02
  - herpes simplex 054.74
  - herpes zoster 053.14
  - late effect — *see* category 326
  - optic neuritis in 341.0
  - postchickenpox 052.2
  - postimmunization 323.52
  - postinfectious 136.9 *[323.63]*
  - postvaccinal 323.52
  - postvaricella 052.2
  - syphilitic (transverse) 094.89
  - toxic 989.9 *[323.72]*
  - transverse 323.82
    - acute 341.20
      - idiopathic 341.22
      - in conditions classified elsewhere 341.21
    - idiopathic 341.22
  - tuberculous (*see also* Tuberculosis) 013.6 ☑
  - virus 049.9
- **Myeloblastic** — *see* condition
- **Myelocele** — *see also* Spina bifida 741.9 ☑
  - with hydrocephalus 741.0 ☑
- **Myelocystocele** — *see also* Spina bifida 741.9 ☑
- **Myelocytic** — *see* condition
- **Myelocytoma** 205.1 ☑
- **Myelodysplasia** (spinal cord) 742.59
  - meaning myelodysplastic syndrome — *see* Syndrome, myelodysplastic
- **Myeloencephalitis** — *see* Encephalitis
- **Myelofibrosis** 289.83
  - with myeloid metaplasia 238.76
  - idiopathic (chronic) 238.76
  - megakaryocytic 238.79
  - primary 238.76
  - secondary 289.83
- **Myelogenous** — *see* condition
- **Myeloid** — *see* condition
- **Myelokathexis** 288.09
- **Myeloleukodystrophy** 330.0
- **Myelolipoma** (M8870/0) — *see* Neoplasm, by site, benign
- **Myeloma** (multiple) (plasma cell) (plasmacytic) (M9730/3) 203.0 ☑
  - monostotic (M9731/1) 238.6
  - solitary (M9731/1) 238.6
- **Myelomalacia** 336.8
- **Myelomata, multiple** (M9730/3) 203.0 ☑
- **Myelomatosis** (M9730/3) 203.0 ☑
- **Myelomeningitis** — *see* Meningoencephalitis
- **Myelomeningocele** (spinal cord) — *see also* Spina bifida 741.9 ☑
  - fetal, causing fetopelvic disproportion 653.7 ☑
- **Myelo-osteo-musculodysplasia** hereditaria 756.89
- **Myelopathic** — *see* condition
- **Myelopathy** (spinal cord) 336.9
  - cervical 721.1
  - diabetic 250.6 ☑ *[336.3]*
    - due to secondary diabetes 249.6 ☑ *[336.3]*
  - drug-induced 336.8
  - due to or with
    - carbon tetrachloride 987.8 *[323.72]*
    - degeneration or displacement, intervertebral disc 722.70
      - cervical, cervicothoracic 722.71
      - lumbar, lumbosacral 722.73
      - thoracic, thoracolumbar 722.72
    - hydroxyquinoline derivatives 961.3 *[323.72]*

Myelopathy — *continued*
  due to or with — *continued*
    infection — *see* Encephalitis
    intervertebral disc disorder 722.70
      cervical, cervicothoracic 722.71
      lumbar, lumbosacral 722.73
      thoracic, thoracolumbar 722.72
    lead 984.9 *[323.72]*
    mercury 985.0 *[323.72]*
    neoplastic disease (*see also* Neoplasm, by site) 239.9 *[336.3]*
    pernicious anemia 281.0 *[336.3]*
    spondylosis 721.91
      cervical 721.1
      lumbar, lumbosacral 721.42
      thoracic 721.41
    thallium 985.8 *[323.72]*
  lumbar, lumbosacral 721.42
  necrotic (subacute) 336.1
  radiation-induced 336.8
  spondylogenic NEC 721.91
    cervical 721.1
    lumbar, lumbosacral 721.42
    thoracic 721.41
  thoracic 721.41
  toxic NEC 989.9 *[323.72]*
  transverse (*see also* Myelitis) 323.82
  vascular 336.1
Myelophthisis 284.2
Myeloproliferative disease (M9960/1) 238.79
Myeloradiculitis — *see also* Polyneuropathy 357.0
Myeloradiculodysplasia (spinal) 742.59
Myelosarcoma (M9930/3) 205.3 ☑
Myelosclerosis 289.89
  with myeloid metaplasia (M9961/1) 238.76
  disseminated, of nervous system 340
  megakaryocytic (M9961/1) 238.79
Myelosis (M9860/3) — *see also* Leukemia, myeloid 205.9 ☑
  acute (M9861/3) 205.0 ☑
  aleukemic (M9864/3) 205.8 ☑
  chronic (M9863/3) 205.1 ☑
  erythremic (M9840/3) 207.0 ☑
    acute (M9841/3) 207.0 ☑
  megakaryocytic (M9920/3) 207.2 ☑
  nonleukemic (chronic) 288.8
  subacute (M9862/3) 205.2 ☑
Myesthenia — *see* Myasthenia
Myiasis (cavernous) 134.0
  orbit 134.0 *[376.13]*
Myoadenoma, prostate 600.20
  with
    other lower urinary tract symptoms (LUTS) 600.21
    urinary
      obstruction 600.21
      retention 600.21
Myoblastoma
  granular cell (M9580/0) (*see also* Neoplasm, connective tissue, benign)
    malignant (M9580/3) — *see* Neoplasm, connective tissue, malignant
  tongue (M9580/0) 210.1
Myocardial — *see* condition
Myocardiopathy (congestive) (constrictive) (familial) (hypertrophic nonobstructive) (idiopathic) (infiltrative) (obstructive) (primary) (restrictive) (sporadic) 425.4
  alcoholic 425.5
  amyloid 277.39 *[425.7]*
  beriberi 265.0 *[425.7]*
  cobalt-beer 425.5
  due to
    amyloidosis 277.39 *[425.7]*
    beriberi 265.0 *[425.7]*
    cardiac glycogenosis 271.0 *[425.7]*
    Chagas' disease 086.0
    Friedreich's ataxia 334.0 *[425.8]*
    influenza 487.8 *[425.8]*

Myocardiopathy — *continued*
  due to — *continued*
    mucopolysaccharidosis 277.5 *[425.7]*
    myotonia atrophica 359.21 *[425.8]*
    progressive muscular dystrophy 359.1 *[425.8]*
    sarcoidosis 135 *[425.8]*
  glycogen storage 271.0 *[425.7]*
  hypertrophic obstructive 425.1
  metabolic NEC 277.9 *[425.7]*
  nutritional 269.9 *[425.7]*
  obscure (African) 425.2
  peripartum 674.5 ☑
  postpartum 674.5 ☑
  secondary 425.9
  thyrotoxic (*see also* Thyrotoxicosis) 242.9 ☑ *[425.7]*
  toxic NEC 425.9
Myocarditis (fibroid) (interstitial) (old) (progressive) (senile) (with arteriosclerosis) 429.0
  with
    rheumatic fever (conditions classifiable to 390) 398.0
      active (*see also* Myocarditis, acute, rheumatic) 391.2
      inactive or quiescent (with chorea) 398.0
  active (nonrheumatic) 422.90
    rheumatic 391.2
      with chorea (acute) (rheumatic) (Sydenham's) 392.0
  acute or subacute (interstitial) 422.90
    due to Streptococcus (beta-hemolytic) 391.2
    idiopathic 422.91
    rheumatic 391.2
      with chorea (acute) (rheumatic) (Sydenham's) 392.0
    specified type NEC 422.99
  aseptic of newborn 074.23
  bacterial (acute) 422.92
  chagasic 086.0
  chronic (interstitial) 429.0
  congenital 746.89
  constrictive 425.4
  Coxsackie (virus) 074.23
  diphtheritic 032.82
  due to or in
    Coxsackie (virus) 074.23
    diphtheria 032.82
    epidemic louse-borne typhus 080 *[422.0]*
    influenza 487.8 *[422.0]*
    Lyme disease 088.81 *[422.0]*
    scarlet fever 034.1 *[422.0]*
    toxoplasmosis (acquired) 130.3
    tuberculosis (*see also* Tuberculosis) 017.9 ☑ *[422.0]*
    typhoid 002.0 *[422.0]*
    typhus NEC 081.9 *[422.0]*
  eosinophilic 422.91
  epidemic of newborn 074.23
  Fiedler's (acute) (isolated) (subacute) 422.91
  giant cell (acute) (subacute) 422.91
  gonococcal 098.85
  granulomatous (idiopathic) (isolated) (nonspecific) 422.91
  hypertensive (*see also* Hypertension, heart) 402.90
  idiopathic 422.91
    granulomatous 422.91
  infective 422.92
  influenzal 487.8 *[422.0]*
  isolated (diffuse) (granulomatous) 422.91
  malignant 422.99
  meningococcal 036.43
  nonrheumatic, active 422.90
  parenchymatous 422.90
  pneumococcal (acute) (subacute) 422.92
  rheumatic (chronic) (inactive) (with chorea) 398.0

Myocarditis — *continued*
  rheumatic — *continued*
    active or acute 391.2
      with chorea (acute) (rheumatic) (Sydenham's) 392.0
  septic 422.92
  specific (giant cell) (productive) 422.91
  staphylococcal (acute) (subacute) 422.92
  suppurative 422.92
  syphilitic (chronic) 093.82
  toxic 422.93
    rheumatic (*see also* Myocarditis, acute rheumatic) 391.2
  tuberculous (*see also* Tuberculosis) 017.9 ☑ *[422.0]*
  typhoid 002.0 *[422.0]*
  valvular — *see* Endocarditis
  viral, except Coxsackie 422.91
    Coxsackie 074.23
    of newborn (Coxsackie) 074.23
Myocardium, myocardial — *see* condition
Myocardosis — *see also* Cardiomyopathy 425.4
Myoclonia (essential) 333.2
  epileptica 333.2
  Friedrich's 333.2
  massive 333.2
Myoclonic
  epilepsy, familial (progressive) 333.2
  jerks 333.2
Myoclonus (familial essential) (multifocal) (simplex) 333.2
  with epilepsy and with ragged red fibers (MERRF syndrome) 277.87
  facial 351.8
  massive (infantile) 333.2
  pharyngeal 478.29
Myodiastasis 728.84
Myoendocarditis — *see also* Endocarditis
  acute or subacute 421.9
Myoepithelioma (M8982/0) — *see* Neoplasm, by site, benign
Myofascitis (acute) 729.1
  low back 724.2
Myofibroma (M8890/0) — *see also* Neoplasm, connective tissue, benign
  uterus (cervix) (corpus) (*see also* Leiomyoma) 218.9
Myofibromatosis
  infantile 759.89
Myofibrosis 728.2
  heart (*see also* Myocarditis) 429.0
  humeroscapular region 726.2
  scapulohumeral 726.2
Myofibrositis — *see also* Myositis 729.1
  scapulohumeral 726.2
Myogelosis (occupational) 728.89
Myoglobinuria 791.3
Myoglobulinuria, primary 791.3
Myokymia — *see also* Myoclonus
  facial 351.8
Myolipoma (M8860/0)
  specified site — *see* Neoplasm, connective tissue, benign
  unspecified site 223.0
Myoma (M8895/0) — *see also* Neoplasm, connective tissue, benign
  cervix (stump) (uterus) (*see also* Leiomyoma) 218.9
  malignant (M8895/3) — *see* Neoplasm, connective tissue, malignant
  prostate 600.20
    with
      other lower urinary tract symptoms (LUTS) 600.21
      urinary
        obstruction 600.21
        retention 600.21
  uterus (cervix) (corpus) (*see also* Leiomyoma) 218.9
    in pregnancy or childbirth 654.1 ☑

Myoma — *see also* Neoplasm, connective tissue, benign — *continued*
  uterus (*see also* Leiomyoma) — *continued*
    in pregnancy or childbirth — *continued*
      affecting fetus or newborn 763.89
      causing obstructed labor 660.2 ☑
        affecting fetus or newborn 763.1
Myomalacia 728.9
  cordis, heart (*see also* Degeneration, myocardial) 429.1
Myometritis — *see also* Endometritis 615.9
Myometrium — *see* condition
Myonecrosis, clostridial 040.0
Myopathy 359.9
  alcoholic 359.4
  amyloid 277.39 *[359.6]*
  benign, congenital 359.0
  central core 359.0
  centronuclear 359.0
  congenital (benign) 359.0
  critical illness 359.81
  distal 359.1
  due to drugs 359.4
  endocrine 259.9 *[359.5]*
    specified type NEC 259.8 *[359.5]*
  extraocular muscles 376.82
  facioscapulohumeral 359.1
  in
    Addison's disease 255.41 *[359.5]*
    amyloidosis 277.39 *[359.6]*
    cretinism 243 *[359.5]*
    Cushing's syndrome 255.0 *[359.5]*
    disseminated lupus erythematosus 710.0 *[359.6]*
    giant cell arteritis 446.5 *[359.6]*
    hyperadrenocorticism NEC 255.3 *[359.5]*
    hyperparathyroidism 252.01 *[359.5]*
    hypopituitarism 253.2 *[359.5]*
    hypothyroidism (*see also* Hypothyroidism) 244.9 *[359.5]*
    malignant neoplasm NEC (M8000/3) 199.1 *[359.6]*
    myxedema (*see also* Myxedema) 244.9 *[359.5]*
    polyarteritis nodosa 446.0 *[359.6]*
    rheumatoid arthritis 714.0 *[359.6]*
    sarcoidosis 135 *[359.6]*
    scleroderma 710.1 *[359.6]*
    Sjögren's disease 710.2 *[359.6]*
    thyrotoxicosis (*see also* Thyrotoxicosis) 242.9 ☑ *[359.5]*
  inflammatory 359.89
  intensive care (ICU) 359.81
  limb-girdle 359.1
  myotubular 359.0
  necrotizing, acute 359.81
  nemaline 359.0
  ocular 359.1
  oculopharyngeal 359.1
  of critical illness 359.81
  primary 359.89
  progressive NEC 359.89
  proximal myotonic (PROMM) 359.21
  quadriplegic, acute 359.81
  rod body 359.0
  scapulohumeral 359.1
  specified type NEC 359.89
  toxic 359.4
Myopericarditis — *see also* Pericarditis 423.9
Myopia (axial) (congenital) (increased curvature or refraction, nucleus of lens) 367.1
  degenerative, malignant 360.21
  malignant 360.21
  progressive high (degenerative) 360.21

- **Myosarcoma** (M8895/3) — *see* Neoplasm, connective tissue, malignant
- **Myosis** (persistent) 379.42
  - stromal (endolymphatic) (M8931/1) 236.0
- **Myositis** 729.1
  - clostridial 040.0
  - due to posture 729.1
  - epidemic 074.1
  - fibrosa or fibrous (chronic) 728.2
    - Volkmann's (complicating trauma) 958.6
  - infective 728.0
  - interstitial 728.81
  - multiple — *see* Polymyositis
  - occupational 729.1
  - orbital, chronic 376.12
  - ossificans 728.12
    - circumscribed 728.12
    - progressive 728.11
    - traumatic 728.12
  - progressive fibrosing 728.11
  - purulent 728.0
  - rheumatic 729.1
  - rheumatoid 729.1
  - suppurative 728.0
  - syphilitic 095.6
  - traumatic (old) 729.1
- **Myospasia impulsiva** 307.23
- **Myotonia** (acquisita) (intermittens) 728.85
  - atrophica 359.21
  - congenita 359.22
    - acetazolamide responsive 359.22
    - dominant form 359.22
    - recessive form 359.22
  - drug-induced 359.24
  - dystrophica 359.21
  - fluctuans 359.29
  - levior 359.29
  - permanens 359.29
- **Myotonic pupil** 379.46
- **Myriapodiasis** 134.1
- **Myringitis**
  - with otitis media — *see* Otitis media
  - acute 384.00
    - specified type NEC 384.09
  - bullosa hemorrhagica 384.01
  - bullous 384.01
  - chronic 384.1
- **Mysophobia** 300.29
- **Mytilotoxism** 988.0
- **Myxadenitis labialis** 528.5
- **Myxedema** (adult) (idiocy) (infantile) (juvenile) (thyroid gland) — *see also* Hypothyroidism 244.9
  - circumscribed 242.9 ☑
  - congenital 243
  - cutis 701.8
  - localized (pretibial) 242.9 ☑
  - madness (acute) 293.0
    - subacute 293.1
  - papular 701.8
  - pituitary 244.8
  - postpartum 674.8 ☑
  - pretibial 242.9 ☑
  - primary 244.9
- **Myxochondrosarcoma** (M9220/3) — *see* Neoplasm, cartilage, malignant
- **Myxofibroma** (M8811/0) — *see also* Neoplasm, connective tissue, benign
  - odontogenic (M9320/0) 213.1
    - upper jaw (bone) 213.0
- **Myxofibrosarcoma** (M8811/3) — *see* Neoplasm, connective tissue, malignant
- **Myxolipoma** (M8852/0) — *see also* Lipoma, by site 214.9
- **Myxoliposarcoma** (M8852/3) — *see* Neoplasm, connective tissue, malignant
- **Myxoma** (M8840/0) — *see also* Neoplasm, connective tissue, benign
  - odontogenic (M9320/0) 213.1
    - upper jaw (bone) 213.0
- **Myxosarcoma** (M8840/3) — *see* Neoplasm, connective tissue, malignant

N

- **Naegeli's**
  - disease (hereditary hemorrhagic thrombasthenia) 287.1
  - leukemia, monocytic (M9863/3) 205.1 ☑
  - syndrome (incontinentia pigmenti) 757.33
- **Naffziger's syndrome** 353.0
- **Naga sore** — *see also* Ulcer, skin 707.9
- **Nägele's pelvis** 738.6
  - with disproportion (fetopelvic) 653.0 ☑
    - affecting fetus or newborn 763.1
    - causing obstructed labor 660.1 ☑
      - affecting fetus or newborn 763.1
- **Nager-de Reynier syndrome** (dysostosis mandibularis) 756.0
- **Nail** — *see also* condition
  - biting 307.9
  - patella syndrome (hereditary osteoonychodysplasia) 756.89
- **Nanism, nanosomia** — *see also* Dwarfism 259.4
  - hypophyseal 253.3
  - pituitary 253.3
  - renis, renalis 588.0
- **Nanukayami** 100.89
- **Napkin rash** 691.0
- **Narcissism** 301.81
- **Narcolepsy** 347.00
  - with cataplexy 347.01
  - in conditions classified elsewhere 347.10
    - with cataplexy 347.11
- **Narcosis**
  - carbon dioxide (respiratory) 786.09
  - due to drug
    - correct substance properly administered 780.09
    - overdose or wrong substance given or taken 977.9
      - specified drug — *see* Table of Drugs and Chemicals
- **Narcotism (chronic)** — *see also* Dependence 304.9 ☑
  - acute
    - correct substance properly administered 349.82
    - overdose or wrong substance given or taken 967.8
      - specified drug — *see* Table of Drugs and Chemicals
- **NARP** (ataxia and retinitis pigmentosa) 277.87
- **Narrow**
  - anterior chamber angle 365.02
  - pelvis (inlet) (outlet) — *see* Contraction, pelvis
- **Narrowing**
  - artery NEC 447.1
    - auditory, internal 433.8 ☑
    - basilar 433.0 ☑
      - with other precerebral artery 433.3 ☑
      - bilateral 433.3 ☑
    - carotid 433.1 ☑
      - with other precerebral artery 433.3 ☑
      - bilateral 433.3 ☑
    - cerebellar 433.8 ☑
    - choroidal 433.8 ☑
    - communicating posterior 433.8 ☑
    - coronary (*see also* Arteriosclerosis, coronary)
      - congenital 746.85
        - due to syphilis 090.5
    - hypophyseal 433.8 ☑
    - pontine 433.8 ☑
    - precerebral NEC 433.9 ☑
      - multiple or bilateral 433.3 ☑
      - specified NEC 433.8 ☑
    - vertebral 433.2 ☑
      - with other precerebral artery 433.3 ☑
      - bilateral 433.3 ☑
  - auditory canal (external) (*see also* Stricture, ear canal, acquired) 380.50
  - cerebral arteries 437.0
  - cicatricial — *see* Cicatrix
  - congenital — *see* Anomaly, congenital
  - coronary artery — *see* Narrowing, artery, coronary
  - ear, middle 385.22
  - Eustachian tube (*see also* Obstruction, Eustachian tube) 381.60
  - eyelid 374.46
    - congenital 743.62
  - intervertebral disc or space NEC — *see* Degeneration, intervertebral disc
  - joint space, hip 719.85
  - larynx 478.74
  - lids 374.46
    - congenital 743.62
  - mesenteric artery (with gangrene) 557.0
  - palate 524.89
  - palpebral fissure 374.46
  - retinal artery 362.13
  - ureter 593.3
  - urethra (*see also* Stricture, urethra) 598.9
- **Narrowness, abnormal, eyelid** 743.62
- **Nasal** — *see* condition
- **Nasolacrimal** — *see* condition
- **Nasopharyngeal** — *see also* condition
  - bursa 478.29
  - pituitary gland 759.2
  - torticollis 723.5
- **Nasopharyngitis** (acute) (infective) (subacute) 460
  - chronic 472.2
    - due to external agent — *see* Condition, respiratory, chronic, due to
  - due to external agent — *see* Condition, respiratory, due to
  - septic 034.0
  - streptococcal 034.0
  - suppurative (chronic) 472.2
  - ulcerative (chronic) 472.2
- **Nasopharynx, nasopharyngeal** — *see* condition
- **Natal tooth, teeth** 520.6
- **Nausea** — *see also* Vomiting 787.02
  - with vomiting 787.01
  - epidemic 078.82
  - gravidarum — *see* Hyperemesis, gravidarum
  - marina 994.6
- **Navel** — *see* condition
- **Neapolitan fever** — *see also* Brucellosis 023.9
- **Near drowning** 994.1
- **Nearsightedness** 367.1
- **Near-syncope** 780.2
- **Nebécourt's syndrome** 253.3
- **Nebula, cornea** (eye) 371.01
  - congenital 743.43
    - interfering with vision 743.42
- **Necator americanus infestation** 126.1
- **Necatoriasis** 126.1
- **Neck** — *see* condition
- **Necrencephalus** — *see also* Softening, brain 437.8
- **Necrobacillosis** 040.3
- **Necrobiosis** 799.89
  - brain or cerebral (*see also* Softening, brain) 437.8
  - lipoidica 709.3
    - diabeticorum 250.8 ☑ *[709.3]*
      - due to secondary diabetes 249.8 ☑ *[709.3]*
- **Necrodermolysis** 695.15
- **Necrolysis, toxic epidermal** 695.15
  - due to drug
    - correct substance properly administered 695.15
    - overdose or wrong substance given or taken 977.9
      - specified drug — *see* Table of Drugs and Chemicals
  - Stevens-Johnson syndrome overlap (SJS-TEN overlap syndrome) 695.14
- **Necrophilia** 302.89
- **Necrosis, necrotic**
  - adrenal (capsule) (gland) 255.8
  - antrum, nasal sinus 478.19
  - aorta (hyaline) (*see also* Aneurysm, aorta) 441.9
    - cystic medial 441.00
      - abdominal 441.02
      - thoracic 441.01
      - thoracoabdominal 441.03
    - ruptured 441.5
  - arteritis 446.0
  - artery 447.5
  - aseptic, bone 733.40
    - femur (head) (neck) 733.42
      - medial condyle 733.43
    - humoral head 733.41
    - jaw 733.45
    - medial femoral condyle 733.43
    - specific site NEC 733.49
    - talus 733.44
  - avascular, bone NEC (*see also* Necrosis, aseptic, bone) 733.40
  - bladder (aseptic) (sphincter) 596.8
  - bone (*see also* Osteomyelitis) 730.1 ☑
    - acute 730.0 ☑
    - aseptic or avascular 733.40
      - femur (head) (neck) 733.42
        - medial condyle 733.43
      - humoral head 733.41
      - jaw 733.45
      - medial femoral condyle 733.43
      - specified site NEC 733.49
      - talus 733.44
    - ethmoid 478.19
    - ischemic 733.40
    - jaw 526.4
      - asceptic 733.45
    - marrow 289.89
    - Paget's (osteitis deformans) 731.0
    - tuberculous — *see* Tuberculosis, bone
  - brain (softening) (*see also* Softening, brain) 437.8
  - breast (aseptic) (fat) (segmental) 611.3
  - bronchus, bronchi 519.19
  - central nervous system NEC (*see also* Softening, brain) 437.8
  - cerebellar (*see also* Softening, brain) 437.8
  - cerebral (softening) (*see also* Softening, brain) 437.8
  - cerebrospinal (softening) (*see also* Softening, brain) 437.8
  - colon 557.0
  - cornea (*see also* Keratitis) 371.40
  - cortical, kidney 583.6
  - cystic medial (aorta) 441.00
    - abdominal 441.02
    - thoracic 441.01
    - thoracoabdominal 441.03
  - dental 521.09
    - pulp 522.1
  - due to swallowing corrosive substance — *see* Burn, by site
  - ear (ossicle) 385.24
  - esophagus 530.89
  - ethmoid (bone) 478.19
  - eyelid 374.50

Necrosis, necrotic — *continued*
fat, fatty (generalized) (*see also* Degeneration, fatty) 272.8
abdominal wall 567.82
breast (aseptic) (segmental) 611.3
intestine 569.89
localized — *see* Degeneration, by site, fatty
mesentery 567.82
omentum 567.82
pancreas 577.8
peritoneum 567.82
skin (subcutaneous) 709.3
newborn 778.1
femur (aseptic) (avascular) 733.42
head 733.42
medial condyle 733.43
neck 733.42
gallbladder (*see also* Cholecystitis, acute) 575.0
gangrenous 785.4
gastric 537.89
glottis 478.79
heart (myocardium) — *see* Infarct, myocardium
hepatic (*see also* Necrosis, liver) 570
hip (aseptic) (avascular) 733.42
intestine (acute) (hemorrhagic) (massive) 557.0
ischemic 785.4
jaw 526.4
asceptic 733.45
kidney (bilateral) 583.9
acute 584.9
cortical 583.6
acute 584.6
with
abortion — *see* Abortion, by type, with renal failure
ectopic pregnancy (*see also* categories 633.0–633.9) 639.3
molar pregnancy (*see also* categories 630–632) 639.3
complicating pregnancy 646.2 ☑
affecting fetus or newborn 760.1
following labor and delivery 669.3 ☑
medullary (papillary) (*see also* Pyelitis) 590.80
in
acute renal failure 584.7
nephritis, nephropathy 583.7
papillary (*see also* Pyelitis) 590.80

Necrosis, necrotic — *continued*
kidney — *continued*
papillary (*see also* Pyelitis) — *continued*
in
acute renal failure 584.7
nephritis, nephropathy 583.7
tubular 584.5
with
abortion — *see* Abortion, by type, with renal failure
ectopic pregnancy (*see also* categories 633.0–633.9) 639.3
molar pregnancy (*see also* categories 630–632) 639.3
complicating
abortion 639.3
ectopic or molar pregnancy 639.3
pregnancy 646.2 ☑
affecting fetus or newborn 760.1
following labor and delivery 669.3 ☑
traumatic 958.5
larynx 478.79
liver (acute) (congenital) (diffuse) (massive) (subacute) 570
with
abortion — *see* Abortion, by type, with specified complication NEC
ectopic pregnancy (*see also* categories 633.0–633.9) 639.8
molar pregnancy (*see also* categories 630–632) 639.8
complicating pregnancy 646.7 ☑
affecting fetus or newborn 760.8
following
abortion 639.8
ectopic or molar pregnancy 639.8
obstetrical 646.7 ☑
postabortal 639.8
puerperal, postpartum 674.8 ☑
toxic 573.3
lung 513.0
lymphatic gland 683
mammary gland 611.3
mastoid (chronic) 383.1
mesentery 557.0
fat 567.82
mitral valve — *see* Insufficiency, mitral

Necrosis, necrotic — *continued*
myocardium, myocardial — *see* Infarct, myocardium
nose (septum) 478.19
omentum 557.0
with mesenteric infarction 557.0
fat 567.82
orbit, orbital 376.10
ossicles, ear (aseptic) 385.24
ovary (*see also* Salpingo-oophoritis) 614.2
pancreas (aseptic) (duct) (fat) 577.8
acute 577.0
infective 577.0
papillary, kidney (*see also* Pyelitis) 590.80
perineum 624.8
peritoneum 557.0
with mesenteric infarction 557.0
fat 567.82
pharynx 462
in granulocytopenia 288.09
phosphorus 983.9
pituitary (gland) (postpartum) (Sheehan) 253.2
placenta (*see also* Placenta, abnormal) 656.7 ☑
pneumonia 513.0
pulmonary 513.0
pulp (dental) 522.1
pylorus 537.89
radiation — *see* Necrosis, by site
radium — *see* Necrosis, by site
renal — *see* Necrosis, kidney
sclera 379.19
scrotum 608.89
skin or subcutaneous tissue 709.8
due to burn — see Burn, by site
gangrenous 785.4
spine, spinal (column) 730.18
acute 730.18
cord 336.1
spleen 289.59
stomach 537.89
stomatitis 528.1
subcutaneous fat 709.3
fetus or newborn 778.1
subendocardial — *see* Infarct, myocardium
suprarenal (capsule) (gland) 255.8
teeth, tooth 521.09
testis 608.89
thymus (gland) 254.8
tonsil 474.8
trachea 519.19
tuberculous NEC — *see* Tuberculosis
tubular (acute) (anoxic) (toxic) 584.5
due to a procedure 997.5

Necrosis, necrotic — *continued*
umbilical cord, affecting fetus or newborn 762.6
vagina 623.8
vertebra (lumbar) 730.18
acute 730.18
tuberculous (*see also* Tuberculosis) 015.0 ☑ *[730.8]* ☑
vesical (aseptic) (bladder) 596.8
vulva 624.8
x-ray — *see* Necrosis, by site
Necrospermia 606.0
Necrotizing angiitis 446.0
Negativism 301.7
Neglect (child) (newborn) NEC 995.52
adult 995.84
after or at birth 995.52
hemispatial 781.8
left-sided 781.8
sensory 781.8
visuospatial 781.8
Negri bodies 071
Neill-Dingwall syndrome (microcephaly and dwarfism) 759.89
Neisserian infection NEC — *see* Gonococcus
Nematodiasis NEC — *see also* Infestation, Nematode 127.9
ancylostoma (*see also* Ancylostomiasis) 126.9
Neoformans cryptococcus infection 117.5
Neonatal — *see also* condition
adrenoleukodystrophy 277.86
teeth, tooth 520.6
Neonatorum — *see* condition
Neoplasia
anal intraepithelial I [AIN I] (histologically confirmed) 569.44
anal intraepithelial II [AIN II] (histologically confirmed) 569.44
anal intraepithelial III [AIN III] 230.6
anal canal 230.5
multiple endocrine [MEN]
type I 258.01
type IIA 258.02
type IIB 258.03
vaginal intraepithelial I [VAIN I] 623.0
vaginal intraepithelial II [VAIN II] 623.0
vaginal intraepithelial III [VAIN III] 233.31
vulvular intraepithelial I [VIN I] 624.01
vulvular intraepithelial II [VIN II] 624.02
vulvular intraepithelial III [VIN III] 233.32

	Malignant					
	Primary	Secondary	Ca in situ	Benign	Uncertain Behavior	Unspecified
Neoplasm, neoplastic	199.1	199.1	234.9	229.9	238.9	239.9

Notes — 1. The list below gives the code numbers for neoplasms by anatomical site. For each site there are six possible code numbers according to whether the neoplasm in question is malignant, benign, in situ, of uncertain behavior, or of unspecified nature. The description of the neoplasm will often indicate which of the six columns is appropriate; e.g., malignant melanoma of skin, benign fibroadenoma of breast, carcinoma in situ of cervix uteri.

Where such descriptors are not present, the remainder of the Index should be consulted where guidance is given to the appropriate column for each morphological (histological) variety listed; e.g., Mesonephroma — see Neoplasm, malignant; Embryoma — see also Neoplasm, uncertain behavior; Disease, Bowen's — see Neoplasm, skin, in situ. However, the guidance in the Index can be overridden if one of the descriptors mentioned above is present; e.g., malignant adenoma of colon is coded to 153.9 and not to 211.3 as the adjective "malignant" overrides the Index entry "Adenoma — see also Neoplasm, benign."

*2. Sites marked with the sign * (e.g., face NEC*) should be classified to malignant neoplasm of skin of these sites if the variety of neoplasm is a squamous cell carcinoma or an epidermoid carcinoma, and to benign neoplasm of skin of these sites if the variety of neoplasm is a papilloma (any type).*

	Primary	Secondary	Ca in situ	Benign	Uncertain Behavior	Unspecified
abdomen, abdominal	195.2	198.89	234.8	229.8	238.8	239.8
cavity	195.2	198.89	234.8	229.8	238.8	239.8
organ	195.2	198.89	234.8	229.8	238.8	239.8
viscera	195.2	198.89	234.8	229.8	238.8	239.8
wall	173.5	198.2	232.5	216.5	238.2	239.2
connective tissue	171.5	198.89	—	215.5	238.1	239.2
abdominopelvic	195.8	198.89	234.8	229.8	238.8	239.8
accessory sinus — *see* Neoplasm, sinus						
acoustic nerve	192.0	198.4	—	225.1	237.9	239.7
acromion (process)	170.4	198.5	—	213.4	238.0	239.2
adenoid (pharynx) (tissue)	147.1	198.89	230.0	210.7	235.1	239.0
adipose tissue (*see also* Neoplasm, connective tissue)	171.9	198.89	—	215.9	238.1	239.2
adnexa (uterine)	183.9	198.82	233.39	221.8	236.3	239.5
adrenal (cortex) (gland) (medulla)	194.0	198.7	234.8	227.0	237.2	239.7
ala nasi (external)	173.3	198.2	232.3	216.3	238.2	239.2
alimentary canal or tract NEC	159.9	197.8	230.9	211.9	235.5	239.0
alveolar	143.9	198.89	230.0	210.4	235.1	239.0
mucosa	143.9	198.89	230.0	210.4	235.1	239.0
lower	143.1	198.89	230.0	210.4	235.1	239.0
upper	143.0	198.89	230.0	210.4	235.1	239.0
ridge or process	170.1	198.5	—	213.1	238.0	239.2
carcinoma	143.9	—	—	—	—	—
lower	143.1	—	—	—	—	—
upper	143.0	—	—	—	—	—
lower	170.1	198.5	—	213.1	238.0	239.2
mucosa	143.9	198.89	230.0	210.4	235.1	239.0
lower	143.1	198.89	230.0	210.4	235.1	239.0
upper	143.0	198.89	230.0	210.4	235.1	239.0
upper	170.0	198.5	—	213.0	238.0	239.2
sulcus	145.1	198.89	230.0	210.4	235.1	239.0
alveolus	143.9	198.89	230.0	210.4	235.1	239.0
lower	143.1	198.89	230.0	210.4	235.1	239.0
upper	143.0	198.89	230.0	210.4	235.1	239.0
ampulla of Vater	156.2	197.8	230.8	211.5	235.3	239.0
ankle NEC*	195.5	198.89	232.7	229.8	238.8	239.8
anorectum, anorectal (junction)	154.8	197.5	230.7	211.4	235.2	239.0
antecubital fossa or space*	195.4	198.89	232.6	229.8	238.8	239.8
antrum (Highmore) (maxillary)	160.2	197.3	231.8	212.0	235.9	239.1
pyloric	151.2	197.8	230.2	211.1	235.2	239.0
tympanicum	160.1	197.3	231.8	212.0	235.9	239.1
anus, anal	154.3	197.5	230.6	211.4	235.5	239.0
canal	154.2	197.5	230.5	211.4	235.5	239.0
contiguous sites with rectosigmoid junction or rectum	154.8	—	—	—	—	—
margin	173.5	198.2	232.5	216.5	238.2	239.2
skin	173.5	198.2	232.5	216.5	238.2	239.2
sphincter	154.2	197.5	230.5	211.4	235.5	239.0
aorta (thoracic)	171.4	198.89	—	215.4	238.1	239.2
Neoplasm, neoplastic — *continued*						
aorta — *continued*						
abdominal	171.5	198.89	—	215.5	238.1	239.2
aortic body	194.6	198.89	—	227.6	237.3	239.7
aponeurosis	171.9	198.89	—	215.9	238.1	239.2
palmar	171.2	198.89	—	215.2	238.1	239.2
plantar	171.3	198.89	—	215.3	238.1	239.2
appendix	153.5	197.5	230.3	211.3	235.2	239.0
arachnoid (cerebral)	192.1	198.4	—	225.2	237.6	239.7
spinal	192.3	198.4	—	225.4	237.6	239.7
areola (female)	174.0	198.81	233.0	217	238.3	239.3
male	175.0	198.81	233.0	217	238.3	239.3
arm NEC*	195.4	198.89	232.6	229.8	238.8	239.8
artery — *see* Neoplasm, connective tissue						
aryepiglottic fold	148.2	198.89	230.0	210.8	235.1	239.0
hypopharyngeal aspect	148.2	198.89	230.0	210.8	235.1	239.0
laryngeal aspect	161.1	197.3	231.0	212.1	235.6	239.1
marginal zone	148.2	198.89	230.0	210.8	235.1	239.0
arytenoid (cartilage)	161.3	197.3	231.0	212.1	235.6	239.1
fold — *see* Neoplasm, aryepiglottic						
associated with transplanted organ	199.2	—	—	—	—	—
atlas	170.2	198.5	—	213.2	238.0	239.2
atrium, cardiac	164.1	198.89	—	212.7	238.8	239.8
auditory						
canal (external) (skin)	173.2	198.2	232.2	216.2	238.2	239.2
internal	160.1	197.3	231.8	212.0	235.9	239.1
nerve	192.0	198.4	—	225.1	237.9	239.7
tube	160.1	197.3	231.8	212.0	235.9	239.1
Eustachian	160.1	197.3	231.8	212.0	235.9	239.1
opening	147.2	198.89	230.0	210.7	235.1	239.0
auricle, ear	173.2	198.2	232.2	216.2	238.2	239.2
cartilage	171.0	198.89	—	215.0	238.1	239.2
auricular canal (external)	173.2	198.2	232.2	216.2	238.2	239.2
internal	160.1	197.3	231.8	212.0	235.9	239.1
autonomic nerve or nervous system NEC	171.9	198.89	—	215.9	238.1	239.2
axilla, axillary	195.1	198.89	234.8	229.8	238.8	239.8
fold	173.5	198.2	232.5	216.5	238.2	239.2
back NEC*	195.8	198.89	232.5	229.8	238.8	239.8
Bartholin's gland	184.1	198.82	233.32	221.2	236.3	239.5
basal ganglia	191.0	198.3	—	225.0	237.5	239.6
basis pedunculi	191.7	198.3	—	225.0	237.5	239.6
bile or biliary (tract)	156.9	197.8	230.8	211.5	235.3	239.0
canaliculi (biliferi) (intrahepatic)	155.1	197.8	230.8	211.5	235.3	239.0
canals, interlobular	155.1	197.8	230.8	211.5	235.3	239.0
contiguous sites	156.8	—	—	—	—	—
duct or passage (common) (cystic) (extrahepatic)	156.1	197.8	230.8	211.5	235.3	239.0
contiguous sites with gallbladder	156.8	—	—	—	—	—
interlobular	155.1	197.8	230.8	211.5	235.3	239.0
intrahepatic	155.1	197.8	230.8	211.5	235.3	239.0
and extrahepatic	156.9	197.8	230.8	211.5	235.3	239.0
bladder (urinary)	188.9	198.1	233.7	223.3	236.7	239.4
contiguous sites	188.8	—	—	—	—	—
dome	188.1	198.1	233.7	223.3	236.7	239.4
neck	188.5	198.1	233.7	223.3	236.7	239.4
orifice	188.9	198.1	233.7	223.3	236.7	239.4
ureteric	188.6	198.1	233.7	223.3	236.7	239.4
urethral	188.5	198.1	233.7	223.3	236.7	239.4
sphincter	188.8	198.1	233.7	223.3	236.7	239.4
trigone	188.0	198.1	233.7	223.3	236.7	239.4
urachus	188.7	—	233.7	223.3	236.7	239.4
wall	188.9	198.1	233.7	223.3	236.7	239.4
anterior	188.3	198.1	233.7	223.3	236.7	239.4
lateral	188.2	198.1	233.7	223.3	236.7	239.4
posterior	188.4	198.1	233.7	223.3	236.7	239.4

	Malignant					
	Primary	Secondary	Ca in situ	Benign	Uncertain Behavior	Unspecified
Neoplasm, neoplastic — *continued*						
blood vessel — *see* Neoplasm, connective tissue						
bone (periosteum)	170.9	198.5	—	213.9	238.0	239.2

Note — Carcinomas and adenocarcinomas, of any type other than intraosseous or odontogenic, of the sites listed under "Neoplasm, bone" should be considered as constituting metastatic spread from an unspecified primary site and coded to 198.5 for morbidity coding.

	Primary	Secondary	Ca in situ	Benign	Uncertain Behavior	Unspecified
acetabulum	170.6	198.5	—	213.6	238.0	239.2
acromion (process)	170.4	198.5	—	213.4	238.0	239.2
ankle	170.8	198.5	—	213.8	238.0	239.2
arm NEC	170.4	198.5	—	213.4	238.0	239.2
astragalus	170.8	198.5	—	213.8	238.0	239.2
atlas	170.2	198.5	—	213.2	238.0	239.2
axis	170.2	198.5	—	213.2	238.0	239.2
back NEC	170.2	198.5	—	213.2	238.0	239.2
calcaneus	170.8	198.5	—	213.8	238.0	239.2
calvarium	170.0	198.5	—	213.0	238.0	239.2
carpus (any)	170.5	198.5	—	213.5	238.0	239.2
cartilage NEC	170.9	198.5	—	213.9	238.0	239.2
clavicle	170.3	198.5	—	213.3	238.0	239.2
clivus	170.0	198.5	—	213.0	238.0	239.2
coccygeal vertebra	170.6	198.5	—	213.6	238.0	239.2
coccyx	170.6	198.5	—	213.6	238.0	239.2
costal cartilage	170.3	198.5	—	213.3	238.0	239.2
costovertebral joint	170.3	198.5	—	213.3	238.0	239.2
cranial	170.0	198.5	—	213.0	238.0	239.2
cuboid	170.8	198.5	—	213.8	238.0	239.2
cuneiform	170.9	198.5	—	213.9	238.0	239.2
ankle	170.8	198.5	—	213.8	238.0	239.2
wrist	170.5	198.5	—	213.5	238.0	239.2
digital	170.9	198.5	—	213.9	238.0	239.2
finger	170.5	198.5	—	213.5	238.0	239.2
toe	170.8	198.5	—	213.8	238.0	239.2
elbow	170.4	198.5	—	213.4	238.0	239.2
ethmoid (labyrinth)	170.0	198.5	—	213.0	238.0	239.2
face	170.0	198.5	—	213.0	238.0	239.2
lower jaw	170.1	198.5	—	213.1	238.0	239.2
femur (any part)	170.7	198.5	—	213.7	238.0	239.2
fibula (any part)	170.7	198.5	—	213.7	238.0	239.2
finger (any)	170.5	198.5	—	213.5	238.0	239.2
foot	170.8	198.5	—	213.8	238.0	239.2
forearm	170.4	198.5	—	213.4	238.0	239.2
frontal	170.0	198.5	—	213.0	238.0	239.2
hand	170.5	198.5	—	213.5	238.0	239.2
heel	170.8	198.5	—	213.8	238.0	239.2
hip	170.6	198.5	—	213.6	238.0	239.2
humerus (any part)	170.4	198.5	—	213.4	238.0	239.2
hyoid	170.0	198.5	—	213.0	238.0	239.2
ilium	170.6	198.5	—	213.6	238.0	239.2
innominate	170.6	198.5	—	213.6	238.0	239.2
intervertebral cartilage or disc	170.2	198.5	—	213.2	238.0	239.2
ischium	170.6	198.5	—	213.6	238.0	239.2
jaw (lower)	170.1	198.5	—	213.1	238.0	239.2
upper	170.0	198.5	—	213.0	238.0	239.2
knee	170.7	198.5	—	213.7	238.0	239.2
leg NEC	170.7	198.5	—	213.7	238.0	239.2
limb NEC	170.9	198.5	—	213.9	238.0	239.2
lower (long bones)	170.7	198.5	—	213.7	238.0	239.2
short bones	170.8	198.5	—	213.8	238.0	239.2
upper (long bones)	170.4	198.5	—	213.4	238.0	239.2
short bones	170.5	198.5	—	213.5	238.0	239.2
long	170.9	198.5	—	213.9	238.0	239.2
lower limbs NEC	170.7	198.5	—	213.7	238.0	239.2
upper limbs NEC	170.4	198.5	—	213.4	238.0	239.2
malar	170.0	198.5	—	213.0	238.0	239.2
mandible	170.1	198.5	—	213.1	238.0	239.2
marrow NEC	202.9 ☑	198.5	—	—	—	238.79
mastoid	170.0	198.5	—	213.0	238.0	239.2
maxilla, maxillary (superior)	170.0	198.5	—	213.0	238.0	239.2
inferior	170.1	198.5	—	213.1	238.0	239.2
metacarpus (any)	170.5	198.5	—	213.5	238.0	239.2
Neoplasm, neoplastic — *continued*						
bone — *continued*						
metatarsus (any)	170.8	198.5	—	213.8	238.0	239.2
navicular (ankle)	170.8	198.5	—	213.8	238.0	239.2
hand	170.5	198.5	—	213.5	238.0	239.2
nose, nasal	170.0	198.5	—	213.0	238.0	239.2
occipital	170.0	198.5	—	213.0	238.0	239.2
orbit	170.0	198.5	—	213.0	238.0	239.2
parietal	170.0	198.5	—	213.0	238.0	239.2
patella	170.8	198.5	—	213.8	238.0	239.2
pelvic	170.6	198.5	—	213.6	238.0	239.2
phalanges	170.9	198.5	—	213.9	238.0	239.2
foot	170.8	198.5	—	213.8	238.0	239.2
hand	170.5	198.5	—	213.5	238.0	239.2
pubic	170.6	198.5	—	213.6	238.0	239.2
radius (any part)	170.4	198.5	—	213.4	238.0	239.2
rib	170.3	198.5	—	213.3	238.0	239.2
sacral vertebra	170.6	198.5	—	213.6	238.0	239.2
sacrum	170.6	198.5	—	213.6	238.0	239.2
scaphoid (of hand)	170.5	198.5	—	213.5	238.0	239.2
of ankle	170.8	198.5	—	213.8	238.0	239.2
scapula (any part)	170.4	198.5	—	213.4	238.0	239.2
sella turcica	170.0	198.5	—	213.0	238.0	239.2
short	170.9	198.5	—	213.9	238.0	239.2
lower limb	170.8	198.5	—	213.8	238.0	239.2
upper limb	170.5	198.5	—	213.5	238.0	239.2
shoulder	170.4	198.5	—	213.4	238.0	239.2
skeleton, skeletal NEC	170.9	198.5	—	213.9	238.0	239.2
skull	170.0	198.5	—	213.0	238.0	239.2
sphenoid	170.0	198.5	—	213.0	238.0	239.2
spine, spinal (column)	170.2	198.5	—	213.2	238.0	239.2
coccyx	170.6	198.5	—	213.6	238.0	239.2
sacrum	170.6	198.5	—	213.6	238.0	239.2
sternum	170.3	198.5	—	213.3	238.0	239.2
tarsus (any)	170.8	198.5	—	213.8	238.0	239.2
temporal	170.0	198.5	—	213.0	238.0	239.2
thumb	170.5	198.5	—	213.5	238.0	239.2
tibia (any part)	170.7	198.5	—	213.7	238.0	239.2
toe (any)	170.8	198.5	—	213.8	238.0	239.2
trapezium	170.5	198.5	—	213.5	238.0	239.2
trapezoid	170.5	198.5	—	213.5	238.0	239.2
turbinate	170.0	198.5	—	213.0	238.0	239.2
ulna (any part)	170.4	198.5	—	213.4	238.0	239.2
unciform	170.5	198.5	—	213.5	238.0	239.2
vertebra (column)	170.2	198.5	—	213.2	238.0	239.2
coccyx	170.6	198.5	—	213.6	238.0	239.2
sacrum	170.6	198.5	—	213.6	238.0	239.2
vomer	170.0	198.5	—	213.0	238.0	239.2
wrist	170.5	198.5	—	213.5	238.0	239.2
xiphoid process	170.3	198.5	—	213.3	238.0	239.2
zygomatic	170.0	198.5	—	213.0	238.0	239.2
book-leaf (mouth)	145.8	198.89	230.0	210.4	235.1	239.0
bowel — *see* Neoplasm, intestine						
brachial plexus	171.2	198.89	—	215.2	238.1	239.2
brain NEC	191.9	198.3	—	225.0	237.5	239.6
basal ganglia	191.0	198.3	—	225.0	237.5	239.6
cerebellopontine angle	191.6	198.3	—	225.0	237.5	239.6
cerebellum NOS	191.6	198.3	—	225.0	237.5	239.6
cerebrum	191.0	198.3	—	225.0	237.5	239.6
choroid plexus	191.5	198.3	—	225.0	237.5	239.6
contiguous sites	191.8	—	—	—	—	—
corpus callosum	191.8	198.3	—	225.0	237.5	239.6
corpus striatum	191.0	198.3	—	225.0	237.5	239.6
cortex (cerebral)	191.0	198.3	—	225.0	237.5	239.6
frontal lobe	191.1	198.3	—	225.0	237.5	239.6
globus pallidus	191.0	198.3	—	225.0	237.5	239.6
hippocampus	191.2	198.3	—	225.0	237.5	239.6
hypothalamus	191.0	198.3	—	225.0	237.5	239.6
internal capsule	191.0	198.3	—	225.0	237.5	239.6
medulla oblongata	191.7	198.3	—	225.0	237.5	239.6
meninges	192.1	198.4	—	225.2	237.6	239.7
midbrain	191.7	198.3	—	225.0	237.5	239.6
occipital lobe	191.4	198.3	—	225.0	237.5	239.6
parietal lobe	191.3	198.3	—	225.0	237.5	239.6

	Malignant					
	Primary	Secondary	Ca in situ	Benign	Uncertain Behavior	Unspecified
Neoplasm, neoplastic — *continued*						
brain — *continued*						
peduncle	191.7	198.3	—	225.0	237.5	239.6
pons	191.7	198.3	—	225.0	237.5	239.6
stem	191.7	198.3	—	225.0	237.5	239.6
tapetum	191.8	198.3	—	225.0	237.5	239.6
temporal lobe	191.2	198.3	—	225.0	237.5	239.6
thalamus	191.0	198.3	—	225.0	237.5	239.6
uncus	191.2	198.3	—	225.0	237.5	239.6
ventricle (floor)	191.5	198.3	—	225.0	237.5	239.6
branchial (cleft) (vestiges)	146.8	198.89	230.0	210.6	235.1	239.0
breast (connective tissue) (female) (glandular tissue) (soft parts)	174.9	198.81	233.0	217	238.3	239.3
areola	174.0	198.81	233.0	217	238.3	239.3
male	175.0	198.81	233.0	217	238.3	239.3
axillary tail	174.6	198.81	233.0	217	238.3	239.3
central portion	174.1	198.81	233.0	217	238.3	239.3
contiguous sites	174.8	—	—	—	—	—
ectopic sites	174.8	198.81	233.0	217	238.3	239.3
inner	174.8	198.81	233.0	217	238.3	239.3
lower	174.8	198.81	233.0	217	238.3	239.3
lower-inner quadrant	174.3	198.81	233.0	217	238.3	239.3
lower-outer quadrant	174.5	198.81	233.0	217	238.3	239.3
male	175.9	198.81	233.0	217	238.3	239.3
areola	175.0	198.81	233.0	217	238.3	239.3
ectopic tissue	175.9	198.81	233.0	217	238.3	239.3
nipple	175.0	198.81	233.0	217	238.3	239.3
mastectomy site (skin)	173.5	198.2	—	—	—	—
specified as breast tissue	174.8	198.81	—	—	—	—
midline	174.8	198.81	233.0	217	238.3	239.3
nipple	174.0	198.81	233.0	217	238.3	239.3
male	175.0	198.81	233.0	217	238.3	239.3
outer	174.8	198.81	233.0	217	238.3	239.3
skin	173.5	198.2	232.5	216.5	238.2	239.2
tail (axillary)	174.6	198.81	233.0	217	238.3	239.3
upper	174.8	198.81	233.0	217	238.3	239.3
upper-inner quadrant	174.2	198.81	233.0	217	238.3	239.3
upper-outer quadrant	174.4	198.81	233.0	217	238.3	239.3
broad ligament	183.3	198.82	233.39	221.0	236.3	239.5
bronchiogenic, bronchogenic (lung)	162.9	197.0	231.2	212.3	235.7	239.1
bronchiole	162.9	197.0	231.2	212.3	235.7	239.1
bronchus	162.9	197.0	231.2	212.3	235.7	239.1
carina	162.2	197.0	231.2	212.3	235.7	239.1
contiguous sites with lung or trachea	162.8	—	—	—	—	—
lower lobe of lung	162.5	197.0	231.2	212.3	235.7	239.1
main	162.2	197.0	231.2	212.3	235.7	239.1
middle lobe of lung	162.4	197.0	231.2	212.3	235.7	239.1
upper lobe of lung	162.3	197.0	231.2	212.3	235.7	239.1
brow	173.3	198.2	232.3	216.3	238.2	239.2
buccal (cavity)	145.9	198.89	230.0	210.4	235.1	239.0
commissure	145.0	198.89	230.0	210.4	235.1	239.0
groove (lower) (upper)	145.1	198.89	230.0	210.4	235.1	239.0
mucosa	145.0	198.89	230.0	210.4	235.1	239.0
sulcus (lower) (upper)	145.1	198.89	230.0	210.4	235.1	239.0
bulbourethral gland	189.3	198.1	233.9	223.81	236.99	239.5
bursa — *see* Neoplasm, connective tissue						
buttock NEC*	195.3	198.89	232.5	229.8	238.8	239.8
calf*	195.5	198.89	232.7	229.8	238.8	239.8
calvarium	170.0	198.5	—	213.0	238.0	239.2
calyx, renal	189.1	198.0	233.9	223.1	236.91	239.5
canal						
anal	154.2	197.5	230.5	211.4	235.5	239.0
auditory (external)	173.2	198.2	232.2	216.2	238.2	239.2
auricular (external)	173.2	198.2	232.2	216.2	238.2	239.2

	Malignant					
	Primary	Secondary	Ca in situ	Benign	Uncertain Behavior	Unspecified
Neoplasm, neoplastic — *continued*						
canaliculi, biliary (biliferi) (intrahepatic)	155.1	197.8	230.8	211.5	235.3	239.0
canthus (eye) (inner) (outer)	173.1	198.2	232.1	216.1	238.2	239.2
capillary — *see* Neoplasm, connective tissue						
caput coli	153.4	197.5	230.3	211.3	235.2	239.0
cardia (gastric)	151.0	197.8	230.2	211.1	235.2	239.0
cardiac orifice (stomach)	151.0	197.8	230.2	211.1	235.2	239.0
cardio-esophageal junction	151.0	197.8	230.2	211.1	235.2	239.0
cardio-esophagus	151.0	197.8	230.2	211.1	235.2	239.0
carina (bronchus)	162.2	197.0	231.2	212.3	235.7	239.1
carotid (artery)	171.0	198.89	—	215.0	238.1	239.2
body	194.5	198.89	—	227.5	237.3	239.7
carpus (any bone)	170.5	198.5	—	213.5	238.0	239.2
cartilage (articular) (joint) NEC (*see also* Neoplasm, bone)	170.9	198.5	—	213.9	238.0	239.2
arytenoid	161.3	197.3	231.0	212.1	235.6	239.1
auricular	171.0	198.89	—	215.0	238.1	239.2
bronchi	162.2	197.3	—	212.3	235.7	239.1
connective tissue — *see* Neoplasm, connective tissue						
costal	170.3	198.5	—	213.3	238.0	239.2
cricoid	161.3	197.3	231.0	212.1	235.6	239.1
cuneiform	161.3	197.3	231.0	212.1	235.6	239.1
ear (external)	171.0	198.89	—	215.0	238.1	239.2
ensiform	170.3	198.5	—	213.3	238.0	239.2
epiglottis	161.1	197.3	231.0	212.1	235.6	239.1
anterior surface	146.4	198.89	230.0	210.6	235.1	239.0
eyelid	171.0	198.89	—	215.0	238.1	239.2
intervertebral	170.2	198.5	—	213.2	238.0	239.2
larynx, laryngeal	161.3	197.3	231.0	212.1	235.6	239.1
nose, nasal	160.0	197.3	231.8	212.0	235.9	239.1
pinna	171.0	198.89	—	215.0	238.1	239.2
rib	170.3	198.5	—	213.3	238.0	239.2
semilunar (knee)	170.7	198.5	—	213.7	238.0	239.2
thyroid	161.3	197.3	231.0	212.1	235.6	239.1
trachea	162.0	197.3	231.1	212.2	235.7	239.1
cauda equina	192.2	198.3	—	225.3	237.5	239.7
cavity						
buccal	145.9	198.89	230.0	210.4	235.1	239.0
nasal	160.0	197.3	231.8	212.0	235.9	239.1
oral	145.9	198.89	230.0	210.4	235.1	239.0
peritoneal	158.9	197.6	—	211.8	235.4	239.0
tympanic	160.1	197.3	231.8	212.0	235.9	239.1
cecum	153.4	197.5	230.3	211.3	235.2	239.0
central						
nervous system — *see* Neoplasm, nervous system						
white matter	191.0	198.3	—	225.0	237.5	239.6
cerebellopontine (angle)	191.6	198.3	—	225.0	237.5	239.6
cerebellum, cerebellar	191.6	198.3	—	225.0	237.5	239.6
cerebrum, cerebral (cortex) (hemisphere) (white matter)	191.0	198.3	—	225.0	237.5	239.6
meninges	192.1	198.4	—	225.2	237.6	239.7
peduncle	191.7	198.3	—	225.0	237.5	239.6
ventricle (any)	191.5	198.3	—	225.0	237.5	239.6
cervical region	195.0	198.89	234.8	229.8	238.8	239.8
cervix (cervical) (uteri) (uterus)	180.9	198.82	233.1	219.0	236.0	239.5
canal	180.0	198.82	233.1	219.0	236.0	239.5
contiguous sites	180.8	—	—	—	—	—
endocervix (canal) (gland)	180.0	198.82	233.1	219.0	236.0	239.5
exocervix	180.1	198.82	233.1	219.0	236.0	239.5
external os	180.1	198.82	233.1	219.0	236.0	239.5
internal os	180.0	198.82	233.1	219.0	236.0	239.5
nabothian gland	180.0	198.82	233.1	219.0	236.0	239.5

	Malignant					
	Primary	Secondary	Ca in situ	Benign	Uncertain Behavior	Unspecified
Neoplasm, neoplastic — *continued*						
cervix — *continued*						
squamocolumnar junction	180.8	198.82	233.1	219.0	236.0	239.5
stump	180.8	198.82	233.1	219.0	236.0	239.5
cheek	195.0	198.89	234.8	229.8	238.8	239.8
external	173.3	198.2	232.3	216.3	238.2	239.2
inner aspect	145.0	198.89	230.0	210.4	235.1	239.0
internal	145.0	198.89	230.0	210.4	235.1	239.0
mucosa	145.0	198.89	230.0	210.4	235.1	239.0
chest (wall) NEC	195.1	198.89	234.8	229.8	238.8	239.8
chiasma opticum	192.0	198.4	—	225.1	237.9	239.7
chin	173.3	198.2	232.3	216.3	238.2	239.2
choana	147.3	198.89	230.0	210.7	235.1	239.0
cholangiole	155.1	197.8	230.8	211.5	235.3	239.0
choledochal duct	156.1	197.8	230.8	211.5	235.3	239.0
choroid	190.6	198.4	234.0	224.6	238.8	239.8
plexus	191.5	198.3	—	225.0	237.5	239.6
ciliary body	190.0	198.4	234.0	224.0	238.8	239.8
clavicle	170.3	198.5	—	213.3	238.0	239.2
clitoris	184.3	198.82	233.32	221.2	236.3	239.5
clivus	170.0	198.5	—	213.0	238.0	239.2
cloacogenic zone	154.8	197.5	230.7	211.4	235.5	239.0
coccygeal						
body or glomus	194.6	198.89	—	227.6	237.3	239.7
vertebra	170.6	198.5	—	213.6	238.0	239.2
coccyx	170.6	198.5	—	213.6	238.0	239.2
colon (*see also* Neoplasm, intestine, large) and rectum	154.0	197.5	230.4	211.4	235.2	239.0
columnella	173.3	198.2	232.3	216.3	238.2	239.2
column, spinal — *see* Neoplasm, spine						
commissure						
labial, lip	140.6	198.89	230.0	210.4	235.1	239.0
laryngeal	161.0	197.3	231.0	212.1	235.6	239.1
common (bile) duct	156.1	197.8	230.8	211.5	235.3	239.0
concha	173.2	198.2	232.2	216.2	238.2	239.2
nose	160.0	197.3	231.8	212.0	235.9	239.1
conjunctiva	190.3	198.4	234.0	224.3	238.8	239.8
connective tissue NEC	171.9	198.89	—	215.9	238.1	239.2

Note — For neoplasms of connective tissue (blood vessel, bursa, fascia, ligament, muscle, peripheral nerves, sympathetic and parasympathetic nerves and ganglia, synovia, tendon, etc.) or of morphological types that indicate connective tissue, code according to the list under "Neoplasm, connective tissue"; for sites that do not appear in this list, code to neoplasm of that site; e.g.,

liposarcoma, shoulder 171.2

leiomyosarcoma, stomach 151.9

neurofibroma, chest wall 215.4

Morphological types that indicate connective tissue appear in the proper place in the alphabetic index with the instruction "see Neoplasm, connective tissue..."

	Primary	Secondary	Ca in situ	Benign	Uncertain Behavior	Unspecified
abdomen	171.5	198.89	—	215.5	238.1	239.2
abdominal wall	171.5	198.89	—	215.5	238.1	239.2
ankle	171.3	198.89	—	215.3	238.1	239.2
antecubital fossa or space	171.2	198.89	—	215.2	238.1	239.2
arm	171.2	198.89	—	215.2	238.1	239.2
auricle (ear)	171.0	198.89	—	215.0	238.1	239.2
axilla	171.4	198.89	—	215.4	238.1	239.2
back	171.7	198.89	—	215.7	238.1	239.2
breast (female) (*see also* Neoplasm, breast)	174.9	198.81	233.0	217	238.3	239.3
male	175.9	198.81	233.0	217	238.3	239.3
buttock	171.6	198.89	—	215.6	238.1	239.2
calf	171.3	198.89	—	215.3	238.1	239.2
cervical region	171.0	198.89	—	215.0	238.1	239.2
cheek	171.0	198.89	—	215.0	238.1	239.2
chest (wall)	171.4	198.89	—	215.4	238.1	239.2
chin	171.0	198.89	—	215.0	238.1	239.2
contiguous sites	171.8	—	—	—	—	—
diaphragm	171.4	198.89	—	215.4	238.1	239.2
ear (external)	171.0	198.89	—	215.0	238.1	239.2
elbow	171.2	198.89	—	215.2	238.1	239.2

	Malignant					
	Primary	Secondary	Ca in situ	Benign	Uncertain Behavior	Unspecified
Neoplasm, neoplastic — *continued*						
connective tissue — *continued*						
extrarectal	171.6	198.89	—	215.6	238.1	239.2
extremity	171.8	198.89	—	215.8	238.1	239.2
lower	171.3	198.89	—	215.3	238.1	239.2
upper	171.2	198.89	—	215.2	238.1	239.2
eyelid	171.0	198.89	—	215.0	238.1	239.2
face	171.0	198.89	—	215.0	238.1	239.2
finger	171.2	198.89	—	215.2	238.1	239.2
flank	171.7	198.89	—	215.7	238.1	239.2
foot	171.3	198.89	—	215.3	238.1	239.2
forearm	171.2	198.89	—	215.2	238.1	239.2
forehead	171.0	198.89	—	215.0	238.1	239.2
gastric	171.5	198.89	—	215.5	238.1	—
gastrointestinal	171.5	198.89	—	215.5	238.1	—
gluteal region	171.6	198.89	—	215.6	238.1	239.2
great vessels NEC	171.4	198.89	—	215.4	238.1	239.2
groin	171.6	198.89	—	215.6	238.1	239.2
hand	171.2	198.89	—	215.2	238.1	239.2
head	171.0	198.89	—	215.0	238.1	239.2
heel	171.3	198.89	—	215.3	238.1	239.2
hip	171.3	198.89	—	215.3	238.1	239.2
hypochondrium	171.5	198.89	—	215.5	238.1	239.2
iliopsoas muscle	171.6	198.89	—	215.5	238.1	239.2
infraclavicular region	171.4	198.89	—	215.4	238.1	239.2
inguinal (canal) (region)	171.6	198.89	—	215.6	238.1	239.2
intestine	171.5	198.89	—	215.5	238.1	—
intrathoracic	171.4	198.89	—	215.4	238.1	239.2
ischorectal fossa	171.6	198.89	—	215.6	238.1	239.2
jaw	143.9	198.89	230.0	210.4	235.1	239.0
knee	171.3	198.89	—	215.3	238.1	239.2
leg	171.3	198.89	—	215.3	238.1	239.2
limb NEC	171.9	198.89	—	215.8	238.1	239.2
lower	171.3	198.89	—	215.3	238.1	239.2
upper	171.2	198.89	—	215.2	238.1	239.2
nates	171.6	198.89	—	215.6	238.1	239.2
neck	171.0	198.89	—	215.0	238.1	239.2
orbit	190.1	198.4	234.0	224.1	238.8	239.8
pararectal	171.6	198.89	—	215.6	238.1	239.2
para-urethral	171.6	198.89	—	215.6	238.1	239.2
paravaginal	171.6	198.89	—	215.6	238.1	239.2
pelvis (floor)	171.6	198.89	—	215.6	238.1	239.2
pelvo-abdominal	171.8	198.89	—	215.8	238.1	239.2
perineum	171.6	198.89	—	215.6	238.1	239.2
perirectal (tissue)	171.6	198.89	—	215.6	238.1	239.2
periurethral (tissue)	171.6	198.89	—	215.6	238.1	239.2
popliteal fossa or space	171.3	198.89	—	215.3	238.1	239.2
presacral	171.6	198.89	—	215.6	238.1	239.2
psoas muscle	171.5	198.89	—	215.5	238.1	239.2
pterygoid fossa	171.0	198.89	—	215.0	238.1	239.2
rectovaginal septum or wall	171.6	198.89	—	215.6	238.1	239.2
rectovesical	171.6	198.89	—	215.6	238.1	239.2
retroperitoneum	158.0	197.6	—	211.8	235.4	239.0
sacrococcygeal region	171.6	198.89	—	215.6	238.1	239.2
scalp	171.0	198.89	—	215.0	238.1	239.2
scapular region	171.4	198.89	—	215.4	238.1	239.2
shoulder	171.2	198.89	—	215.2	238.1	239.2
skin (dermis) NEC	173.9	198.2	232.9	216.9	238.2	239.2
stomach	171.5	198.89	—	215.5	238.1	—
submental	171.0	198.89	—	215.0	238.1	239.2
supraclavicular region	171.0	198.89	—	215.0	238.1	239.2
temple	171.0	198.89	—	215.0	238.1	239.2
temporal region	171.0	198.89	—	215.0	238.1	239.2
thigh	171.3	198.89	—	215.3	238.1	239.2
thoracic (duct) (wall)	171.4	198.89	—	215.4	238.1	239.2
thorax	171.4	198.89	—	215.4	238.1	239.2
thumb	171.2	198.89	—	215.2	238.1	239.2
toe	171.3	198.89	—	215.3	238.1	239.2
trunk	171.7	198.89	—	215.7	238.1	239.2
umbilicus	171.5	198.89	—	215.5	238.1	239.2

	Malignant					
	Primary	Secondary	Ca in situ	Benign	Uncertain Behavior	Unspecified
Neoplasm, neoplastic — *continued*						
connective tissue — *continued*						
vesicorectal	171.6	198.89	—	215.6	238.1	239.2
wrist	171.2	198.89	—	215.2	238.1	239.2
conus medullaris	192.2	198.3	—	225.3	237.5	239.7
cord (true) (vocal)	161.0	197.3	231.0	212.1	235.6	239.1
false	161.1	197.3	231.0	212.1	235.6	239.1
spermatic	187.6	198.82	233.6	222.8	236.6	239.5
spinal (cervical) (lumbar) (thoracic)	192.2	198.3	—	225.3	237.5	239.7
cornea (limbus)	190.4	198.4	234.0	224.4	238.8	239.8
corpus						
albicans	183.0	198.6	233.39	220	236.2	239.5
callosum, brain	191.8	198.3	—	225.0	237.5	239.6
cavernosum	187.3	198.82	233.5	222.1	236.6	239.5
gastric	151.4	197.8	230.2	211.1	235.2	239.0
penis	187.3	198.82	233.5	222.1	236.6	239.5
striatum, cerebrum	191.0	198.3	—	225.0	237.5	239.6
uteri	182.0	198.82	233.2	219.1	236.0	239.5
isthmus	182.1	198.82	233.2	219.1	236.0	239.5
cortex						
adrenal	194.0	198.7	234.8	227.0	237.2	239.7
cerebral	191.0	198.3	—	225.0	237.5	239.6
costal cartilage	170.3	198.5	—	213.3	238.0	239.2
costovertebral joint	170.3	198.5	—	213.3	238.0	239.2
Cowper's gland	189.3	198.1	233.9	223.81	236.99	239.5
cranial (fossa, any)	191.9	198.3	—	225.0	237.5	239.6
meninges	192.1	198.4	—	225.2	237.6	239.7
nerve (any)	192.0	198.4	—	225.1	237.9	239.7
craniobuccal pouch	194.3	198.89	234.8	227.3	237.0	239.7
craniopharyngeal (duct) (pouch)	194.3	198.89	234.8	227.3	237.0	239.7
cricoid	148.0	198.89	230.0	210.8	235.1	239.0
cartilage	161.3	197.3	231.0	212.1	235.6	239.1
cricopharynx	148.0	198.89	230.0	210.8	235.1	239.0
crypt of Morgagni	154.8	197.5	230.7	211.4	235.2	239.0
crystalline lens	190.0	198.4	234.0	224.0	238.8	239.8
cul-de-sac (Douglas')	158.8	197.6	—	211.8	235.4	239.0
cuneiform cartilage	161.3	197.3	231.0	212.1	235.6	239.1
cutaneous — *see* Neoplasm, skin						
cutis — *see* Neoplasm, skin						
cystic (bile) duct (common)	156.1	197.8	230.8	211.5	235.3	239.0
dermis — *see* Neoplasm, skin						
diaphragm	171.4	198.89	—	215.4	238.1	239.2
digestive organs, system, tube, or tract NEC	159.9	197.8	230.9	211.9	235.5	239.0
contiguous sites with peritoneum	159.8	—	—	—	—	—
disc, intervertebral	170.2	198.5	—	213.2	238.0	239.2
disease, generalized	199.0	199.0	234.9	229.9	238.9	199.0
disseminated	199.0	199.0	234.9	229.9	238.9	199.0
Douglas' cul-de-sac or pouch	158.8	197.6	—	211.8	235.4	239.0
duodenojejunal junction	152.8	197.4	230.7	211.2	235.2	239.0
duodenum	152.0	197.4	230.7	211.2	235.2	239.0
dura (cranial) (mater)	192.1	198.4	—	225.2	237.6	239.7
cerebral	192.1	198.4	—	225.2	237.6	239.7
spinal	192.3	198.4	—	225.4	237.6	239.7
ear (external)	173.2	198.2	232.2	216.2	238.2	239.2
auricle or auris	173.2	198.2	232.2	216.2	238.2	239.2
canal, external	173.2	198.2	232.2	216.2	238.2	239.2
cartilage	171.0	198.89	—	215.0	238.1	239.2
external meatus	173.2	198.2	232.2	216.2	238.2	239.2
inner	160.1	197.3	231.8	212.0	235.9	239.8
lobule	173.2	198.2	232.2	216.2	238.2	239.2
middle	160.1	197.3	231.8	212.0	235.9	239.8
contiguous sites with accessory sinuses or nasal cavities	160.8	—	—	—	—	—
skin	173.2	198.2	232.2	216.2	238.2	239.2
earlobe	173.2	198.2	232.2	216.2	238.2	239.2
ejaculatory duct	187.8	198.82	233.6	222.8	236.6	239.5
elbow NEC*	195.4	198.89	232.6	229.8	238.8	239.8
endocardium	164.1	198.89	—	212.7	238.8	239.8
endocervix (canal) (gland)	180.0	198.82	233.1	219.0	236.0	239.5
endocrine gland NEC	194.9	198.89	—	227.9	237.4	239.7
pluriglandular NEC	194.8	198.89	234.8	227.8	237.4	239.7
endometrium (gland) (stroma)	182.0	198.82	233.2	219.1	236.0	239.5
ensiform cartilage	170.3	198.5	—	213.3	238.0	239.2
enteric — *see* Neoplasm, intestine						
ependyma (brain)	191.5	198.3	—	225.0	237.5	239.6
epicardium	164.1	198.89	—	212.7	238.8	239.8
epididymis	187.5	198.82	233.6	222.3	236.6	239.5
epidural	192.9	198.4	—	225.9	237.9	239.7
epiglottis	161.1	197.3	231.0	212.1	235.6	239.1
anterior aspect or surface	146.4	198.89	230.0	210.6	235.1	239.0
cartilage	161.3	197.3	231.0	212.1	235.6	239.1
free border (margin)	146.4	198.89	230.0	210.6	235.1	239.0
junctional region	146.5	198.89	230.0	210.6	235.1	239.0
posterior (laryngeal) surface	161.1	197.3	231.0	212.1	235.6	239.1
suprahyoid portion	161.1	197.3	231.0	212.1	235.6	239.1
esophagogastric junction	151.0	197.8	230.2	211.1	235.2	239.0
esophagus	150.9	197.8	230.1	211.0	235.5	239.0
abdominal	150.2	197.8	230.1	211.0	235.5	239.0
cervical	150.0	197.8	230.1	211.0	235.5	239.0
contiguous sites	150.8	—	—	—	—	—
distal (third)	150.5	197.8	230.1	211.0	235.5	239.0
lower (third)	150.5	197.8	230.1	211.0	235.5	239.0
middle (third)	150.4	197.8	230.1	211.0	235.5	239.0
proximal (third)	150.3	197.8	230.1	211.0	235.5	239.0
specified part NEC	150.8	197.8	230.1	211.0	235.5	239.0
thoracic	150.1	197.8	230.1	211.0	235.5	239.0
upper (third)	150.3	197.8	230.1	211.0	235.5	239.0
ethmoid (sinus)	160.3	197.3	231.8	212.0	235.9	239.1
bone or labyrinth	170.0	198.5	—	213.0	238.0	239.2
Eustachian tube	160.1	197.3	231.8	212.0	235.9	239.1
exocervix	180.1	198.82	233.1	219.0	236.0	239.5
external						
meatus (ear)	173.2	198.2	232.2	216.2	238.2	239.2
os, cervix uteri	180.1	198.82	233.1	219.0	236.0	239.5
extradural	192.9	198.4	—	225.9	237.9	239.7
extrahepatic (bile) duct	156.1	197.8	230.8	211.5	235.3	239.0
contiguous sites with gallbladder	156.8	—	—	—	—	—
extraocular muscle	190.1	198.4	234.0	224.1	238.8	239.8
extrarectal	195.3	198.89	234.8	229.8	238.8	239.8
extremity*	195.8	198.89	232.8	229.8	238.8	239.8
lower*	195.5	198.89	232.7	229.8	238.8	239.8
upper*	195.4	198.89	232.6	229.8	238.8	239.8
eye NEC	190.9	198.4	234.0	224.9	238.8	239.8
contiguous sites	190.8	—	—	—	—	—
specified sites NEC	190.8	198.4	234.0	224.8	238.8	239.8
eyeball	190.0	198.4	234.0	224.0	238.8	239.8
eyebrow	173.3	198.2	232.3	216.3	238.2	239.2
eyelid (lower) (skin) (upper)	173.1	198.2	232.1	216.1	238.2	239.2
cartilage	171.0	198.89	—	215.0	238.1	239.2
face NEC*	195.0	198.89	232.3	229.8	238.8	239.8
fallopian tube (accessory)	183.2	198.82	233.39	221.0	236.3	239.5
falx (cerebelli) (cerebri)	192.1	198.4	—	225.2	237.6	239.7
fascia (*see also* Neoplasm, connective tissue)						
palmar	171.2	198.89	—	215.2	238.1	239.2
plantar	171.3	198.89	—	215.3	238.1	239.2
fatty tissue — *see* Neoplasm, connective tissue						
fauces, faucial NEC	146.9	198.89	230.0	210.6	235.1	239.0

	Malignant					
	Primary	Secondary	Ca in situ	Benign	Uncertain Behavior	Unspecified
Neoplasm, neoplastic — *continued*						
fauces, faucial — *continued*						
pillars	146.2	198.89	230.0	210.6	235.1	239.0
tonsil	146.0	198.89	230.0	210.5	235.1	239.0
femur (any part)	170.7	198.5	—	213.7	238.0	239.2
fetal membrane	181	198.82	233.2	219.8	236.1	239.5
fibrous tissue — *see* Neoplasm, connective tissue						
fibula (any part)	170.7	198.5	—	213.7	238.0	239.2
filum terminale	192.2	198.3	—	225.3	237.5	239.7
finger NEC*	195.4	198.89	232.6	229.8	238.8	239.8
flank NEC*	195.8	198.89	232.5	229.8	238.8	239.8
follicle, nabothian	180.0	198.82	233.1	219.0	236.0	239.5
foot NEC*	195.5	198.89	232.7	229.8	238.8	239.8
forearm NEC*	195.4	198.89	232.6	229.8	238.8	239.8
forehead (skin)	173.3	198.2	232.3	216.3	238.2	239.2
foreskin	187.1	198.82	233.5	222.1	236.6	239.5
fornix						
pharyngeal	147.3	198.89	230.0	210.7	235.1	239.0
vagina	184.0	198.82	233.31	221.1	236.3	239.5
fossa (of)						
anterior (cranial)	191.9	198.3	—	225.0	237.5	239.6
cranial	191.9	198.3	—	225.0	237.5	239.6
ischiorectal	195.3	198.89	234.8	229.8	238.8	239.8
middle (cranial)	191.9	198.3	—	225.0	237.5	239.6
pituitary	194.3	198.89	234.8	227.3	237.0	239.7
posterior (cranial)	191.9	198.3	—	225.0	237.5	239.6
pterygoid	171.0	198.89	—	215.0	238.1	239.2
pyriform	148.1	198.89	230.0	210.8	235.1	239.0
Rosenmüller	147.2	198.89	230.0	210.7	235.1	239.0
tonsillar	146.1	198.89	230.0	210.6	235.1	239.0
fourchette	184.4	198.82	233.32	221.2	236.3	239.5
frenulum						
labii — *see* Neoplasm, lip, internal						
linguae	141.3	198.89	230.0	210.1	235.1	239.0
frontal						
bone	170.0	198.5	—	213.0	238.0	239.2
lobe, brain	191.1	198.3	—	225.0	237.5	239.6
meninges	192.1	198.4	—	225.2	237.6	239.7
pole	191.1	198.3	—	225.0	237.5	239.6
sinus	160.4	197.3	231.8	212.0	235.9	239.1
fundus						
stomach	151.3	197.8	230.2	211.1	235.2	239.0
uterus	182.0	198.82	233.2	219.1	236.0	239.5
gallbladder	156.0	197.8	230.8	211.5	235.3	239.0
contiguous sites with extrahepatic bile ducts	156.8	—	—	—	—	—
gall duct (extrahepatic)	156.1	197.8	230.8	211.5	235.3	239.0
intrahepatic	155.1	197.8	230.8	211.5	235.3	239.0
ganglia (*see also* Neoplasm, connective tissue)	171.9	198.89	—	215.9	238.1	239.2
basal	191.0	198.3	—	225.0	237.5	239.6
ganglion (*see also* Neoplasm, connective tissue)	171.9	198.89	—	215.9	238.1	239.2
cranial nerve	192.0	198.4	—	225.1	237.9	239.7
Gartner's duct	184.0	198.82	233.31	221.1	236.3	239.5
gastric — *see* Neoplasm, stomach						
gastrocolic	159.8	197.8	230.9	211.9	235.5	239.0
gastroesophageal junction	151.0	197.8	230.2	211.1	235.2	239.0
gastrointestinal (tract) NEC	159.9	197.8	230.9	211.9	235.5	239.0
generalized	199.0	199.0	234.9	229.9	238.9	199.0
genital organ or tract						
female NEC	184.9	198.82	233.39	221.9	236.3	239.5
contiguous sites	184.8	—	—	—	—	—
specified site NEC	184.8	198.82	233.39	221.8	236.3	239.5
male NEC	187.9	198.82	233.6	222.9	236.6	239.5
contiguous sites	187.8	—	—	—	—	—
Neoplasm, neoplastic — *continued*						
genital organ or tract — *continued*						
male — *continued*						
specified site NEC	187.8	198.82	233.6	222.8	236.6	239.5
genitourinary tract						
female	184.9	198.82	233.39	221.9	236.3	239.5
male	187.9	198.82	233.6	222.9	236.6	239.5
gingiva (alveolar) (marginal)	143.9	198.89	230.0	210.4	235.1	239.0
lower	143.1	198.89	230.0	210.4	235.1	239.0
mandibular	143.1	198.89	230.0	210.4	235.1	239.0
maxillary	143.0	198.89	230.0	210.4	235.1	239.0
upper	143.0	198.89	230.0	210.4	235.1	239.0
gland, glandular (lymphatic) (system) (*see also* Neoplasm, lymph gland)						
endocrine NEC	194.9	198.89	—	227.9	237.4	239.7
salivary — *see* Neoplasm, salivary, gland						
glans penis	187.2	198.82	233.5	222.1	236.6	239.5
globus pallidus	191.0	198.3	—	225.0	237.5	239.6
glomus						
coccygeal	194.6	198.89	—	227.6	237.3	239.7
jugularis	194.6	198.89	—	227.6	237.3	239.7
glosso-epiglottic fold(s)	146.4	198.89	230.0	210.6	235.1	239.0
glossopalatine fold	146.2	198.89	230.0	210.6	235.1	239.0
glossopharyngeal sulcus	146.1	198.89	230.0	210.6	235.1	239.0
glottis	161.0	197.3	231.0	212.1	235.6	239.1
gluteal region*	195.3	198.89	232.5	229.8	238.8	239.8
great vessels NEC	171.4	198.89	—	215.4	238.1	239.2
groin NEC	195.3	198.89	232.5	229.8	238.8	239.8
gum	143.9	198.89	230.0	210.4	235.1	239.0
contiguous sites	143.8	—	—	—	—	—
lower	143.1	198.89	230.0	210.4	235.1	239.0
upper	143.0	198.89	230.0	210.4	235.1	239.0
hand NEC*	195.4	198.89	232.6	229.8	238.8	239.8
head NEC*	195.0	198.89	232.4	229.8	238.8	239.8
heart	164.1	198.89	—	212.7	238.8	239.8
contiguous sites with mediastinum or thymus	164.8	—	—	—	—	—
heel NEC*	195.5	198.89	232.7	229.8	238.8	239.8
helix	173.2	198.2	232.2	216.2	238.2	239.2
hematopoietic, hemopoietic tissue NEC	202.8 ☑	198.89	—	—	—	238.79
hemisphere, cerebral	191.0	198.3	—	225.0	237.5	239.6
hemorrhoidal zone	154.2	197.5	230.5	211.4	235.5	239.0
hepatic	155.2	197.7	230.8	211.5	235.3	239.0
duct (bile)	156.1	197.8	230.8	211.5	235.3	239.0
flexure (colon)	153.0	197.5	230.3	211.3	235.2	239.0
primary	155.0	—	—	—	—	—
hilus of lung	162.2	197.0	231.2	212.3	235.7	239.1
hip NEC*	195.5	198.89	232.7	229.8	238.8	239.8
hippocampus, brain	191.2	198.3	—	225.0	237.5	239.6
humerus (any part)	170.4	198.5	—	213.4	238.0	239.2
hymen	184.0	198.82	233.31	221.1	236.3	239.5
hypopharynx, hypopharyngeal NEC	148.9	198.89	230.0	210.8	235.1	239.0
contiguous sites	148.8	—	—	—	—	—
postcricoid region	148.0	198.89	230.0	210.8	235.1	239.0
posterior wall	148.3	198.89	230.0	210.8	235.1	239.0
pyriform fossa (sinus)	148.1	198.89	230.0	210.8	235.1	239.0
specified site NEC	148.8	198.89	230.0	210.8	235.1	239.0
wall	148.9	198.89	230.0	210.8	235.1	239.0
posterior	148.3	198.89	230.0	210.8	235.1	239.0
hypophysis	194.3	198.89	234.8	227.3	237.0	239.7
hypothalamus	191.0	198.3	—	225.0	237.5	239.6
ileocecum, ileocecal (coil) (junction) (valve)	153.4	197.5	230.3	211.3	235.2	239.0
ileum	152.2	197.4	230.7	211.2	235.2	239.0

	Malignant					
	Primary	Secondary	Ca in situ	Benign	Uncertain Behavior	Unspecified
Neoplasm, neoplastic — *continued*						
ilium	170.6	198.5	—	213.6	238.0	239.2
immunoproliferative NEC	203.8 ☑	—	—	—	—	—
infraclavicular (region)*	195.1	198.89	232.5	229.8	238.8	239.8
inguinal (region)*	195.3	198.89	232.5	229.8	238.8	239.8
insula	191.0	198.3	—	225.0	237.5	239.6
insular tissue (pancreas)	157.4	197.8	230.9	211.7	235.5	239.0
brain	191.0	198.3	—	225.0	237.5	239.6
interarytenoid fold	148.2	198.89	230.0	210.8	235.1	239.0
hypopharyngeal aspect	148.2	198.89	230.0	210.8	235.1	239.0
laryngeal aspect	161.1	197.3	231.0	212.1	235.6	239.1
marginal zone	148.2	198.89	230.0	210.8	235.1	239.0
interdental papillae	143.9	198.89	230.0	210.4	235.1	239.0
lower	143.1	198.89	230.0	210.4	235.1	239.0
upper	143.0	198.89	230.0	210.4	235.1	239.0
internal						
capsule	191.0	198.3	—	225.0	237.5	239.6
os (cervix)	180.0	198.82	233.1	219.0	236.0	239.5
intervertebral cartilage or disc	170.2	198.5	—	213.2	238.0	239.2
intestine, intestinal	159.0	197.8	230.7	211.9	235.2	239.0
large	153.9	197.5	230.3	211.3	235.2	239.0
appendix	153.5	197.5	230.3	211.3	235.2	239.0
caput coli	153.4	197.5	230.3	211.3	235.2	239.0
cecum	153.4	197.5	230.3	211.3	235.2	239.0
colon	153.9	197.5	230.3	211.3	235.2	239.0
and rectum	154.0	197.5	230.4	211.4	235.2	239.0
ascending	153.6	197.5	230.3	211.3	235.2	239.0
caput	153.4	197.5	230.3	211.3	235.2	239.0
contiguous sites	153.8	—	—	—	—	—
descending	153.2	197.5	230.3	211.3	235.2	239.0
distal	153.2	197.5	230.3	211.3	235.2	239.0
left	153.2	197.5	230.3	211.3	235.2	239.0
pelvic	153.3	197.5	230.3	211.3	235.2	239.0
right	153.6	197.5	230.3	211.3	235.2	239.0
sigmoid (flexure)	153.3	197.5	230.3	211.3	235.2	239.0
transverse	153.1	197.5	230.3	211.3	235.2	239.0
contiguous sites	153.8	—	—	—	—	—
hepatic flexure	153.0	197.5	230.3	211.3	235.2	239.0
ileocecum, ileocecal (coil) (valve)	153.4	197.5	230.3	211.3	235.2	239.0
sigmoid flexure (lower) (upper)	153.3	197.5	230.3	211.3	235.2	239.0
splenic flexure	153.7	197.5	230.3	211.3	235.2	239.0
small	152.9	197.4	230.7	211.2	235.2	239.0
contiguous sites	152.8	—	—	—	—	—
duodenum	152.0	197.4	230.7	211.2	235.2	239.0
ileum	152.2	197.4	230.7	211.2	235.2	239.0
jejunum	152.1	197.4	230.7	211.2	235.2	239.0
tract NEC	159.0	197.8	230.7	211.9	235.2	239.0
intra-abdominal	195.2	198.89	234.8	229.8	238.8	239.8
intracranial NEC	191.9	198.3	—	225.0	237.5	239.6
intrahepatic (bile) duct	155.1	197.8	230.8	211.5	235.3	239.0
intraocular	190.0	198.4	234.0	224.0	238.8	239.8
intraorbital	190.1	198.4	234.0	224.1	238.8	239.8
intrasellar	194.3	198.89	234.8	227.3	237.0	239.7
intrathoracic (cavity) (organs NEC)	195.1	198.89	234.8	229.8	238.8	239.8
contiguous sites with respiratory organs	165.8	—	—	—	—	—
iris	190.0	198.4	234.0	224.0	238.8	239.8
ischiorectal (fossa)	195.3	198.89	234.8	229.8	238.8	239.8
ischium	170.6	198.5	—	213.6	238.0	239.2
island of Reil	191.0	198.3	—	225.0	237.5	239.6
islands or islets of Langerhans	157.4	197.8	230.9	211.7	235.5	239.0
isthmus uteri	182.1	198.82	233.2	219.1	236.0	239.5
jaw	195.0	198.89	234.8	229.8	238.8	239.8
bone	170.1	198.5	—	213.1	238.0	239.2
carcinoma	143.9	—	—	—	—	—

	Malignant					
	Primary	Secondary	Ca in situ	Benign	Uncertain Behavior	Unspecified
Neoplasm, neoplastic — *continued*						
jaw — *continued*						
bone — *continued*						
carcinoma — *continued*						
lower	143.1	—	—	—	—	—
upper	143.0	—	—	—	—	—
lower	170.1	198.5	—	213.1	238.0	239.2
upper	170.0	198.5	—	213.0	238.0	239.2
carcinoma (any type) (lower) (upper)	195.0	—	—	—	—	—
skin	173.3	198.2	232.3	216.3	238.2	239.2
soft tissues	143.9	198.89	230.0	210.4	235.1	239.0
lower	143.1	198.89	230.0	210.4	235.1	239.0
upper	143.0	198.89	230.0	210.4	235.1	239.0
jejunum	152.1	197.4	230.7	211.2	235.2	239.0
joint NEC (*see also* Neoplasm, bone)	170.9	198.5	—	213.9	238.0	239.2
acromioclavicular	170.4	198.5	—	213.4	238.0	239.2
bursa or synovial membrane — *see* Neoplasm, connective tissue						
costovertebral	170.3	198.5	—	213.3	238.0	239.2
sternocostal	170.3	198.5	—	213.3	238.0	239.2
temporomandibular	170.1	198.5	—	213.1	238.0	239.2
junction						
anorectal	154.8	197.5	230.7	211.4	235.5	239.0
cardioesophageal	151.0	197.8	230.2	211.1	235.2	239.0
esophagogastric	151.0	197.8	230.2	211.1	235.2	239.0
gastroesophageal	151.0	197.8	230.2	211.1	235.2	239.0
hard and soft palate	145.5	198.89	230.0	210.4	235.1	239.0
ileocecal	153.4	197.5	230.3	211.3	235.2	239.0
pelvirectal	154.0	197.5	230.4	211.4	235.2	239.0
pelviureteric	189.1	198.0	233.9	223.1	236.91	239.5
rectosigmoid	154.0	197.5	230.4	211.4	235.2	239.0
squamocolumnar, of cervix	180.8	198.82	233.1	219.0	236.0	239.5
kidney (parenchyma)	189.0	198.0	233.9	223.0	236.91	239.5
calyx	189.1	198.0	233.9	223.1	236.91	239.5
hilus	189.1	198.0	233.9	223.1	236.91	239.5
pelvis	189.1	198.0	233.9	223.1	236.91	239.5
knee NEC*	195.5	198.89	232.7	229.8	238.8	239.8
labia (skin)	184.4	198.82	233.32	221.2	236.3	239.5
majora	184.1	198.82	233.32	221.2	236.3	239.5
minora	184.2	198.82	233.32	221.2	236.3	239.5
labial (*see also* Neoplasm, lip)						
sulcus (lower) (upper)	145.1	198.89	230.0	210.4	235.1	239.0
labium (skin)	184.4	198.82	233.32	221.2	236.3	239.5
majus	184.1	198.82	233.32	221.2	236.3	239.5
minus	184.2	198.82	233.32	221.2	236.3	239.5
lacrimal						
canaliculi	190.7	198.4	234.0	224.7	238.8	239.8
duct (nasal)	190.7	198.4	234.0	224.7	238.8	239.8
gland	190.2	198.4	234.0	224.2	238.8	239.8
punctum	190.7	198.4	234.0	224.7	238.8	239.8
sac	190.7	198.4	234.0	224.7	238.8	239.8
Langerhans, islands or islets	157.4	197.8	230.9	211.7	235.5	239.0
laryngopharynx	148.9	198.89	230.0	210.8	235.1	239.0
larynx, laryngeal NEC	161.9	197.3	231.0	212.1	235.6	239.1
aryepiglottic fold	161.1	197.3	231.0	212.1	235.6	239.1
cartilage (arytenoid) (cricoid) (cuneiform) (thyroid)	161.3	197.3	231.0	212.1	235.6	239.1
commissure (anterior) (posterior)	161.0	197.3	231.0	212.1	235.6	239.1
contiguous sites	161.8	—	—	—	—	—
extrinsic NEC	161.1	197.3	231.0	212.1	235.6	239.1
meaning hypopharynx	148.9	198.89	230.0	210.8	235.1	239.0
interarytenoid fold	161.1	197.3	231.0	212.1	235.6	239.1
intrinsic	161.0	197.3	231.0	212.1	235.6	239.1
ventricular band	161.1	197.3	231.0	212.1	235.6	239.1
leg NEC*	195.5	198.89	232.7	229.8	238.8	239.8
lens, crystalline	190.0	198.4	234.0	224.0	238.8	239.8

	Malignant					
	Primary	Secondary	Ca in situ	Benign	Uncertain Behavior	Unspecified
Neoplasm, neoplastic — *continued*						
lid (lower) (upper)	173.1	198.2	232.1	216.1	238.2	239.2
ligament (*see also* Neoplasm, connective tissue)						
broad	183.3	198.82	233.39	221.0	236.3	239.5
Mackenrodt's	183.8	198.82	233.39	221.8	236.3	239.5
non-uterine — *see* Neoplasm, connective tissue						
round	183.5	198.82	—	221.0	236.3	239.5
sacro-uterine	183.4	198.82	—	221.0	236.3	239.5
uterine	183.4	198.82	—	221.0	236.3	239.5
utero-ovarian	183.8	198.82	233.39	221.8	236.3	239.5
uterosacral	183.4	198.82	—	221.0	236.3	239.5
limb*	195.8	198.89	232.8	229.8	238.8	239.8
lower*	195.5	198.89	232.7	229.8	238.8	239.8
upper*	195.4	198.89	232.6	229.8	238.8	239.8
limbus of cornea	190.4	198.4	234.0	224.4	238.8	239.8
lingual NEC (*see also* Neoplasm, tongue)	141.9	198.89	230.0	210.1	235.1	239.0
lingula, lung	162.3	197.0	231.2	212.3	235.7	239.1
lip (external) (lipstick area) (vermillion border)	140.9	198.89	230.0	210.0	235.1	239.0
buccal aspect — *see* Neoplasm, lip, internal						
commissure	140.6	198.89	230.0	210.4	235.1	239.0
contiguous sites	140.8	—	—	—	—	—
with oral cavity or pharynx	149.8	—	—	—	—	—
frenulum — *see* Neoplasm, lip, internal						
inner aspect — *see* Neoplasm, lip, internal						
internal (buccal) (frenulum) (mucosa) (oral)	140.5	198.89	230.0	210.0	235.1	239.0
lower	140.4	198.89	230.0	210.0	235.1	239.0
upper	140.3	198.89	230.0	210.0	235.1	239.0
lower	140.1	198.89	230.0	210.0	235.1	239.0
internal (buccal) (frenulum) (mucosa) (oral)	140.4	198.89	230.0	210.0	235.1	239.0
mucosa — *see* Neoplasm, lip, internal						
oral aspect — *see* Neoplasm, lip, internal						
skin (commissure) (lower) (upper)	173.0	198.2	232.0	216.0	238.2	239.2
upper	140.0	198.89	230.0	210.0	235.1	239.0
internal (buccal) (frenulum) (mucosa) (oral)	140.3	198.89	230.0	210.0	235.1	239.0
liver	155.2	197.7	230.8	211.5	235.3	239.0
primary	155.0	—	—	—	—	—
lobe						
azygos	162.3	197.0	231.2	212.3	235.7	239.1
frontal	191.1	198.3	—	225.0	237.5	239.6
lower	162.5	197.0	231.2	212.3	235.7	239.1
middle	162.4	197.0	231.2	212.3	235.7	239.1
occipital	191.4	198.3	—	225.0	237.5	239.6
parietal	191.3	198.3	—	225.0	237.5	239.6
temporal	191.2	198.3	—	225.0	237.5	239.6
upper	162.3	197.0	231.2	212.3	235.7	239.1
lumbosacral plexus	171.6	198.4	—	215.6	238.1	239.2
lung	162.9	197.0	231.2	212.3	235.7	239.1
azygos lobe	162.3	197.0	231.2	212.3	235.7	239.1
carina	162.2	197.0	231.2	212.3	235.7	239.1
Neoplasm, neoplastic — *continued*						
lung — *continued*						
contiguous sites with bronchus or trachea	162.8	—	—	—	—	—
hilus	162.2	197.0	231.2	212.3	235.7	239.1
lingula	162.3	197.0	231.2	212.3	235.7	239.1
lobe NEC	162.9	197.0	231.2	212.3	235.7	239.1
lower lobe	162.5	197.0	231.2	212.3	235.7	239.1
main bronchus	162.2	197.0	231.2	212.3	235.7	239.1
middle lobe	162.4	197.0	231.2	212.3	235.7	239.1
upper lobe	162.3	197.0	231.2	212.3	235.7	239.1
lymph, lymphatic						
channel NEC (*see also* Neoplasm, connective tissue)	171.9	198.89	—	215.9	238.1	239.2
gland (secondary)	—	196.9	—	229.0	238.8	239.8
abdominal	—	196.2	—	229.0	238.8	239.8
aortic	—	196.2	—	229.0	238.8	239.8
arm	—	196.3	—	229.0	238.8	239.8
auricular (anterior) (posterior)	—	196.0	—	229.0	238.8	239.8
axilla, axillary	—	196.3	—	229.0	238.8	239.8
brachial	—	196.3	—	229.0	238.8	239.8
bronchial	—	196.1	—	229.0	238.8	239.8
bronchopulmonary	—	196.1	—	229.0	238.8	239.8
celiac	—	196.2	—	229.0	238.8	239.8
cervical	—	196.0	—	229.0	238.8	239.8
cervicofacial	—	196.0	—	229.0	238.8	239.8
Cloquet	—	196.5	—	229.0	238.8	239.8
colic	—	196.2	—	229.0	238.8	239.8
common duct	—	196.2	—	229.0	238.8	239.8
cubital	—	196.3	—	229.0	238.8	239.8
diaphragmatic	—	196.1	—	229.0	238.8	239.8
epigastric, inferior	—	196.6	—	229.0	238.8	239.8
epitrochlear	—	196.3	—	229.0	238.8	239.8
esophageal	—	196.1	—	229.0	238.8	239.8
face	—	196.0	—	229.0	238.8	239.8
femoral	—	196.5	—	229.0	238.8	239.8
gastric	—	196.2	—	229.0	238.8	239.8
groin	—	196.5	—	229.0	238.8	239.8
head	—	196.0	—	229.0	238.8	239.8
hepatic	—	196.2	—	229.0	238.8	239.8
hilar (pulmonary)	—	196.1	—	229.0	238.8	239.8
splenic	—	196.2	—	229.0	238.8	239.8
hypogastric	—	196.6	—	229.0	238.8	239.8
ileocolic	—	196.2	—	229.0	238.8	239.8
iliac	—	196.6	—	229.0	238.8	239.8
infraclavicular	—	196.3	—	229.0	238.8	239.8
inguina, inguinal	—	196.5	—	229.0	238.8	239.8
innominate	—	196.1	—	229.0	238.8	239.8
intercostal	—	196.1	—	229.0	238.8	239.8
intestinal	—	196.2	—	229.0	238.8	239.8
intra-abdominal	—	196.2	—	229.0	238.8	239.8
intrapelvic	—	196.6	—	229.0	238.8	239.8
intrathoracic	—	196.1	—	229.0	238.8	239.9
jugular	—	196.0	—	229.0	238.8	239.8
leg	—	196.5	—	229.0	238.8	239.8
limb						
lower	—	196.5	—	229.0	238.8	239.8
upper	—	196.3	—	229.0	238.8	239.8
lower limb	—	196.5	—	229.0	238.8	238.9
lumbar	—	196.2	—	229.0	238.8	239.8
mandibular	—	196.0	—	229.0	238.8	239.8
mediastinal	—	196.1	—	229.0	238.8	239.8
mesenteric (inferior) (superior)	—	196.2	—	229.0	238.8	239.8
midcolic	—	196.2	—	229.0	238.8	239.8
multiple sites in categories 196.0–196.6	—	196.8	—	229.0	238.8	239.8
neck	—	196.0	—	229.0	238.8	239.8
obturator	—	196.6	—	229.0	238.8	239.8
occipital	—	196.0	—	229.0	238.8	239.8
pancreatic	—	196.2	—	229.0	238.8	239.8
para-aortic	—	196.2	—	229.0	238.8	239.8

	Malignant					
	Primary	Secondary	Ca in situ	Benign	Uncertain Behavior	Unspecified
Neoplasm, neoplastic — *continued*						
lymph, lymphatic — *continued*						
gland — *continued*						
paracervical	—	196.6	—	229.0	238.8	239.8
parametrial	—	196.6	—	229.0	238.8	239.8
parasternal	—	196.1	—	229.0	238.8	239.8
parotid	—	196.0	—	229.0	238.8	239.8
pectoral	—	196.3	—	229.0	238.8	239.8
pelvic	—	196.6	—	229.0	238.8	239.8
peri-aortic	—	196.2	—	229.0	238.8	239.8
peripancreatic	—	196.2	—	229.0	238.8	239.8
popliteal	—	196.5	—	229.0	238.8	239.8
porta hepatis	—	196.2	—	229.0	238.8	239.8
portal	—	196.2	—	229.0	238.8	239.8
preauricular	—	196.0	—	229.0	238.8	239.8
prelaryngeal	—	196.0	—	229.0	238.8	239.8
presymphysial	—	196.6	—	229.0	238.8	239.8
pretracheal	—	196.0	—	229.0	238.8	239.8
primary (any site) NEC	202.9 ☑	—	—	—	—	—
pulmonary (hiler)	—	196.1	—	229.0	238.8	239.8
pyloric	—	196.2	—	229.0	238.8	239.8
retroperitoneal	—	196.2	—	229.0	238.8	239.8
retropharyngeal	—	196.0	—	229.0	238.8	239.8
Rosenmüller's	—	196.5	—	229.0	238.8	239.8
sacral	—	196.6	—	229.0	238.8	239.8
scalene	—	196.0	—	229.0	238.8	239.8
site NEC	—	196.9	—	229.0	238.8	239.8
splenic (hilar)	—	196.2	—	229.0	238.8	239.8
subclavicular	—	196.3	—	229.0	238.8	239.8
subinguinal	—	196.5	—	229.0	238.8	239.8
sublingual	—	196.0	—	229.0	238.8	239.8
submandibular	—	196.0	—	229.0	238.8	239.8
submaxillary	—	196.0	—	229.0	238.8	239.8
submental	—	196.0	—	229.0	238.8	239.8
subscapular	—	196.3	—	229.0	238.8	239.8
supraclavicular	—	196.0	—	229.0	238.8	239.8
thoracic	—	196.1	—	229.0	238.8	239.8
tibial	—	196.5	—	229.0	238.8	239.8
tracheal	—	196.1	—	229.0	238.8	239.8
tracheobronchial	—	196.1	—	229.0	238.8	239.8
upper limb	—	196.3	—	229.0	238.8	239.8
Virchow's	—	196.0	—	229.0	238.8	239.8
node (*see also* Neoplasm, lymph gland)						
primary NEC	202.9 ☑	—	—	—	—	—
vessel (*see also* Neoplasm, connective tissue)	171.9	198.89	—	215.9	238.1	239.2
Mackenrodt's ligament	183.8	198.82	233.39	221.8	236.3	239.5
malar	170.0	198.5	—	213.0	238.0	239.2
region — *see* Neoplasm, cheek						
mammary gland — *see* Neoplasm, breast						
mandible	170.1	198.5	—	213.1	238.0	239.2
alveolar						
mucosa	143.1	198.89	230.0	210.4	235.1	239.0
mucose	143.1	198.89	230.0	210.4	235.1	239.0
ridge or process	170.1	198.5	—	213.1	238.0	239.2
carcinoma	143.1	—	—	—	—	—
carcinoma	143.1	—	—	—	—	—
marrow (bone) NEC	202.9 ☑	198.5	—	—	—	238.79
mastectomy site (skin)	173.5	198.2	—	—	—	—
specified as breast tissue	174.8	198.81	—	—	—	—
mastoid (air cells) (antrum) (cavity)	160.1	197.3	231.8	212.0	235.9	239.1
bone or process	170.0	198.5	—	213.0	238.0	239.2
maxilla, maxillary (superior)	170.0	198.5	—	213.0	238.0	239.2
alveolar						
mucosa	143.0	198.89	230.0	210.4	235.1	239.0
ridge or process	170.0	198.5	—	213.0	238.0	239.2

	Malignant					
	Primary	Secondary	Ca in situ	Benign	Uncertain Behavior	Unspecified
Neoplasm, neoplastic — *continued*						
maxilla, maxillary — *continued*						
alveolar — *continued*						
ridge or process — *continued*						
carcinoma	143.0	—	—	—	—	—
antrum	160.2	197.3	231.8	212.0	235.9	239.1
carcinoma	143.0	—	—	—	—	—
inferior — *see* Neoplasm, mandible						
sinus	160.2	197.3	231.8	212.0	235.9	239.1
meatus						
external (ear)	173.2	198.2	232.2	216.2	238.2	239.2
Meckel's diverticulum	152.3	197.4	230.7	211.2	235.2	239.0
mediastinum, mediastinal	164.9	197.1	—	212.5	235.8	239.8
anterior	164.2	197.1	—	212.5	235.8	239.8
contiguous sites with heart and thymus	164.8	—	—	—	—	—
posterior	164.3	197.1	—	212.5	235.8	239.8
medulla						
adrenal	194.0	198.7	234.8	227.0	237.2	239.7
oblongata	191.7	198.3	—	225.0	237.5	239.6
meibomian gland	173.1	198.2	232.1	216.1	238.2	239.2
meninges (brain) (cerebral) (cranial) (intracranial)	192.1	198.4	—	225.2	237.6	239.7
spinal (cord)	192.3	198.4	—	225.4	237.6	239.7
meniscus, knee joint (lateral) (medial)	170.7	198.5	—	213.7	238.0	239.2
mesentery, mesenteric	158.8	197.6	—	211.8	235.4	239.0
mesoappendix	158.8	197.6	—	211.8	235.4	239.0
mesocolon	158.8	197.6	—	211.8	235.4	239.0
mesopharynx — *see* Neoplasm, oropharynx						
mesosalpinx	183.3	198.82	233.39	221.0	236.3	239.5
mesovarium	183.3	198.82	233.39	221.0	236.3	239.5
metacarpus (any bone)	170.5	198.5	—	213.5	238.0	239.2
metastatic NEC (*see also* Neoplasm, by site, secondary)	—	199.1	—	—	—	—
metatarsus (any bone)	170.8	198.5	—	213.8	238.0	239.2
midbrain	191.7	198.3	—	225.0	237.5	239.6
milk duct — *see* Neoplasm, breast						
mons						
pubis	184.4	198.82	233.32	221.2	236.3	239.5
veneris	184.4	198.82	233.32	221.2	236.3	239.5
motor tract	192.9	198.4	—	225.9	237.9	239.7
brain	191.9	198.3	—	225.0	237.5	239.6
spinal	192.2	198.3	—	225.3	237.5	239.7
mouth	145.9	198.89	230.0	210.4	235.1	239.0
contiguous sites	145.8	—	—	—	—	—
floor	144.9	198.89	230.0	210.3	235.1	239.0
anterior portion	144.0	198.89	230.0	210.3	235.1	239.0
contiguous sites	144.8	—	—	—	—	—
lateral portion	144.1	198.89	230.0	210.3	235.1	239.0
roof	145.5	198.89	230.0	210.4	235.1	239.0
specified part NEC	145.8	198.89	230.0	210.4	235.1	239.0
vestibule	145.1	198.89	230.0	210.4	235.1	239.0
mucosa						
alveolar (ridge or process)	143.9	198.89	230.0	210.4	235.1	239.0
lower	143.1	198.89	230.0	210.4	235.1	239.0
upper	143.0	198.89	230.0	210.4	235.1	239.0
buccal	145.0	198.89	230.0	210.4	235.1	239.0
cheek	145.0	198.89	230.0	210.4	235.1	239.0
lip — *see* Neoplasm, lip, internal						
nasal	160.0	197.3	231.8	212.0	235.9	239.1
oral	145.0	198.89	230.0	210.4	235.1	239.0
Müllerian duct						
female	184.8	198.82	233.39	221.8	236.3	239.5
male	187.8	198.82	233.6	222.8	236.6	239.5

	Malignant					
	Primary	Secondary	Ca in situ	Benign	Uncertain Behavior	Unspecified
Neoplasm, neoplastic — *continued*						
multiple sites NEC	199.0	199.0	234.9	229.9	238.9	199.0
muscle (*see also* Neoplasm, connective tissue)						
extraocular	190.1	198.4	234.0	224.1	238.8	239.8
myocardium	164.1	198.89	—	212.7	238.8	239.8
myometrium	182.0	198.82	233.2	219.1	236.0	239.5
myopericardium	164.1	198.89	—	212.7	238.8	239.8
nabothian gland (follicle)	180.0	198.82	233.1	219.0	236.0	239.5
nail	173.9	198.2	232.9	216.9	238.2	239.2
finger	173.6	198.2	232.6	216.6	238.2	239.2
toe	173.7	198.2	232.7	216.7	238.2	239.2
nares, naris (anterior) (posterior)	160.0	197.3	231.8	212.0	235.9	239.1
nasal — *see* Neoplasm, nose						
nasolabial groove	173.3	198.2	232.3	216.3	238.2	239.2
nasolacrimal duct	190.7	198.4	234.0	224.7	238.8	239.8
nasopharynx, nasopharyngeal	147.9	198.89	230.0	210.7	235.1	239.0
contiguous sites	147.8	—	—	—	—	—
floor	147.3	198.89	230.0	210.7	235.1	239.0
roof	147.0	198.89	230.0	210.7	235.1	239.0
specified site NEC	147.8	198.89	230.0	210.7	235.1	239.0
wall	147.9	198.89	230.0	210.7	235.1	239.0
anterior	147.3	198.89	230.0	210.7	235.1	239.0
lateral	147.2	198.89	230.0	210.7	235.1	239.0
posterior	147.1	198.89	230.0	210.7	235.1	239.0
superior	147.0	198.89	230.0	210.7	235.1	239.0
nates	173.5	198.2	232.5	216.5	238.2	239.2
neck NEC*	195.0	198.89	234.8	229.8	238.8	239.8
nerve (autonomic) (ganglion) (parasympathetic) (peripheral) (sympathetic) (*see also* Neoplasm, connective tissue)						
abducens	192.0	198.4	—	225.1	237.9	239.7
accessory (spinal)	192.0	198.4	—	225.1	237.9	239.7
acoustic	192.0	198.4	—	225.1	237.9	239.7
auditory	192.0	198.4	—	225.1	237.9	239.7
brachial	171.2	198.89	—	215.2	238.1	239.2
cranial (any)	192.0	198.4	—	225.1	237.9	239.7
facial	192.0	198.4	—	225.1	237.9	239.7
femoral	171.3	198.89	—	215.3	238.1	239.2
glossopharyngeal	192.0	198.4	—	225.1	237.9	239.7
hypoglossal	192.0	198.4	—	225.1	237.9	239.7
intercostal	171.4	198.89	—	215.4	238.1	239.2
lumbar	171.7	198.89	—	215.7	238.1	239.2
median	171.2	198.89	—	215.2	238.1	239.2
obturator	171.3	198.89	—	215.3	238.1	239.2
oculomotor	192.0	198.4	—	225.1	237.9	239.7
olfactory	192.0	198.4	—	225.1	237.9	239.7
optic	192.0	198.4	—	225.1	237.9	239.7
peripheral NEC	171.9	198.89	—	215.9	238.1	239.2
radial	171.2	198.89	—	215.2	238.1	239.2
sacral	171.6	198.89	—	215.6	238.1	239.2
sciatic	171.3	198.89	—	215.3	238.1	239.2
spinal NEC	171.9	198.89	—	215.9	238.1	239.2
trigeminal	192.0	198.4	—	225.1	237.9	239.7
trochlear	192.0	198.4	—	225.1	237.9	239.7
ulnar	171.2	198.89	—	215.2	238.1	239.2
vagus	192.0	198.4	—	225.1	237.9	239.7
nervous system (central) NEC	192.9	198.4	—	225.9	237.9	239.7
autonomic NEC	171.9	198.89	—	215.9	238.1	239.2
brain (*see also* Neoplasm, brain)						
membrane or meninges	192.1	198.4	—	225.2	237.6	239.7
contiguous sites	192.8	—	—	—	—	—
parasympathetic NEC	171.9	198.89	—	215.9	238.1	239.2
sympathetic NEC	171.9	198.89	—	215.9	238.1	239.2
nipple (female)	174.0	198.81	233.0	217	238.3	239.3
male	175.0	198.81	233.0	217	238.3	239.3
nose, nasal	195.0	198.89	234.8	229.8	238.8	239.8

	Malignant					
	Primary	Secondary	Ca in situ	Benign	Uncertain Behavior	Unspecified
Neoplasm, neoplastic — *continued*						
nose, nasal — *continued*						
ala (external)	173.3	198.2	232.3	216.3	238.2	239.2
bone	170.0	198.5	—	213.0	238.0	239.2
cartilage	160.0	197.3	231.8	212.0	235.9	239.1
cavity	160.0	197.3	231.8	212.0	235.9	239.1
contiguous sites with accessory sinuses or middle ear	160.8	—	—	—	—	—
choana	147.3	198.89	230.0	210.7	235.1	239.0
external (skin)	173.3	198.2	232.3	216.3	238.2	239.2
fossa	160.0	197.3	231.8	212.0	235.9	239.1
internal	160.0	197.3	231.8	212.0	235.9	239.1
mucosa	160.0	197.3	231.8	212.0	235.9	239.1
septum	160.0	197.3	231.8	212.0	235.9	239.1
posterior margin	147.3	198.89	230.0	210.7	235.1	239.0
sinus — *see* Neoplasm, sinus						
skin	173.3	198.2	232.3	216.3	238.2	239.2
turbinate (mucosa)	160.0	197.3	231.8	212.0	235.9	239.1
bone	170.0	198.5	—	213.0	238.0	239.2
vestibule	160.0	197.3	231.8	212.0	235.9	239.1
nostril	160.0	197.3	231.8	212.0	235.9	239.1
nucleus pulposus	170.2	198.5	—	213.2	238.0	239.2
occipital						
bone	170.0	198.5	—	213.0	238.0	239.2
lobe or pole, brain	191.4	198.3	—	225.0	237.5	239.6
odontogenic — *see* Neoplasm, jaw bone						
oesophagus — *see* Neoplasm, esophagus						
olfactory nerve or bulb	192.0	198.4	—	225.1	237.9	239.7
olive (brain)	191.7	198.3	—	225.0	237.5	239.6
omentum	158.8	197.6	—	211.8	235.4	239.0
operculum (brain)	191.0	198.3	—	225.0	237.5	239.6
optic nerve, chiasm, or tract	192.0	198.4	—	225.1	237.9	239.7
oral (cavity)	145.9	198.89	230.0	210.4	235.1	239.0
contiguous sites with lip or pharynx	149.8	—	—	—	—	—
ill-defined	149.9	198.89	230.0	210.4	235.1	239.0
mucosa	145.9	198.89	230.0	210.4	235.1	239.0
orbit	190.1	198.4	234.0	224.1	238.8	239.8
bone	170.0	198.5	—	213.0	238.0	239.2
eye	190.1	198.4	234.0	224.1	238.8	239.8
soft parts	190.1	198.4	234.0	224.1	238.8	239.8
organ of Zuckerkandl	194.6	198.89	—	227.6	237.3	239.7
oropharynx	146.9	198.89	230.0	210.6	235.1	239.0
branchial cleft (vestige)	146.8	198.89	230.0	210.6	235.1	239.0
contiguous sites	146.8	—	—	—	—	—
junctional region	146.5	198.89	230.0	210.6	235.1	239.0
lateral wall	146.6	198.89	230.0	210.6	235.1	239.0
pillars of fauces	146.2	198.89	230.0	210.6	235.1	239.0
posterior wall	146.7	198.89	230.0	210.6	235.1	239.0
specified part NEC	146.8	198.89	230.0	210.6	235.1	239.0
vallecula	146.3	198.89	230.0	210.6	235.1	239.0
os						
external	180.1	198.82	233.1	219.0	236.0	239.5
internal	180.0	198.82	233.1	219.0	236.0	239.5
ovary	183.0	198.6	233.39	220	236.2	239.5
oviduct	183.2	198.82	233.39	221.0	236.3	239.5
palate	145.5	198.89	230.0	210.4	235.1	239.0
hard	145.2	198.89	230.0	210.4	235.1	239.0
junction of hard and soft palate	145.5	198.89	230.0	210.4	235.1	239.0
soft	145.3	198.89	230.0	210.4	235.1	239.0
nasopharyngeal surface	147.3	198.89	230.0	210.7	235.1	239.0
posterior surface	147.3	198.89	230.0	210.7	235.1	239.0
superior surface	147.3	198.89	230.0	210.7	235.1	239.0
palatoglossal arch	146.2	198.89	230.0	210.6	235.1	239.0
palatopharyngeal arch	146.2	198.89	230.0	210.6	235.1	239.0
pallium	191.0	198.3	—	225.0	237.5	239.6
palpebra	173.1	198.2	232.1	216.1	238.2	239.2

	Malignant					
	Primary	Secondary	Ca in situ	Benign	Uncertain Behavior	Unspecified
Neoplasm, neoplastic — *continued*						
pancreas	157.9	197.8	230.9	211.6	235.5	239.0
body	157.1	197.8	230.9	211.6	235.5	239.0
contiguous sites	157.8	—	—	—	—	—
duct (of Santorini) (of Wirsung)	157.3	197.8	230.9	211.6	235.5	239.0
ectopic tissue	157.8	197.8	230.9	211.6	235.5	239.0
head	157.0	197.8	230.9	211.6	235.5	239.0
islet cells	157.4	197.8	230.9	211.7	235.5	239.0
neck	157.8	197.8	230.9	211.6	235.5	239.0
tail	157.2	197.8	230.9	211.6	235.5	239.0
para-aortic body	194.6	198.89	—	227.6	237.3	239.7
paraganglion NEC	194.6	198.89	—	227.6	237.3	239.7
parametrium	183.4	198.82	—	221.0	236.3	239.5
paranephric	158.0	197.6	—	211.8	235.4	239.0
pararectal	195.3	198.89	—	229.8	238.8	239.8
parasagittal (region)	195.0	198.89	234.8	229.8	238.8	239.8
parasellar	192.9	198.4	—	225.9	237.9	239.7
parathyroid (gland)	194.1	198.89	234.8	227.1	237.4	239.7
paraurethral	195.3	198.89	—	229.8	238.8	239.8
gland	189.4	198.1	233.9	223.89	236.99	239.5
paravaginal	195.3	198.89	—	229.8	238.8	239.8
parenchyma, kidney	189.0	198.0	233.9	223.0	236.91	239.5
parietal						
bone	170.0	198.5	—	213.0	238.0	239.2
lobe, brain	191.3	198.3	—	225.0	237.5	239.6
paroophoron	183.3	198.82	233.39	221.0	236.3	239.5
parotid (duct) (gland)	142.0	198.89	230.0	210.2	235.0	239.0
parovarium	183.3	198.82	233.39	221.0	236.3	239.5
patella	170.8	198.5	—	213.8	238.0	239.2
peduncle, cerebral	191.7	198.3	—	225.0	237.5	239.6
pelvirectal junction	154.0	197.5	230.4	211.4	235.2	239.0
pelvis, pelvic	195.3	198.89	234.8	229.8	238.8	239.8
bone	170.6	198.5	—	213.6	238.0	239.2
floor	195.3	198.89	234.8	229.8	238.8	239.8
renal	189.1	198.0	233.9	223.1	236.91	239.5
viscera	195.3	198.89	234.8	229.8	238.8	239.8
wall	195.3	198.89	234.8	229.8	238.8	239.8
pelvo-abdominal	195.8	198.89	234.8	229.8	238.8	239.8
penis	187.4	198.82	233.5	222.1	236.6	239.5
body	187.3	198.82	233.5	222.1	236.6	239.5
corpus (cavernosum)	187.3	198.82	233.5	222.1	236.6	239.5
glans	187.2	198.82	233.5	222.1	236.6	239.5
skin NEC	187.4	198.82	233.5	222.1	236.6	239.5
periadrenal (tissue)	158.0	197.6	—	211.8	235.4	239.0
perianal (skin)	173.5	198.2	232.5	216.5	238.2	239.2
pericardium	164.1	198.89	—	212.7	238.8	239.8
perinephric	158.0	197.6	—	211.8	235.4	239.0
perineum	195.3	198.89	234.8	229.8	238.8	239.8
periodontal tissue NEC	143.9	198.89	230.0	210.4	235.1	239.0
periosteum — *see* Neoplasm, bone						
peripancreatic	158.0	197.6	—	211.8	235.4	239.0
peripheral nerve NEC	171.9	198.89	—	215.9	238.1	239.2
perirectal (tissue)	195.3	198.89	—	229.8	238.8	239.8
perirenal (tissue)	158.0	197.6	—	211.8	235.4	239.0
peritoneum, peritoneal (cavity)	158.9	197.6	—	211.8	235.4	239.0
contiguous sites	158.8	—	—	—	—	—
with digestive organs	159.8	—	—	—	—	—
parietal	158.8	197.6	—	211.8	235.4	239.0
pelvic	158.8	197.6	—	211.8	235.4	239.0
specified part NEC	158.8	197.6	—	211.8	235.4	239.0
peritonsillar (tissue)	195.0	198.89	234.8	229.8	238.8	239.8
periurethral tissue	195.3	198.89	—	229.8	238.8	239.8
phalanges	170.9	198.5	—	213.9	238.0	239.2
foot	170.8	198.5	—	213.8	238.0	239.2
hand	170.5	198.5	—	213.5	238.0	239.2
pharynx, pharyngeal	149.0	198.89	230.0	210.9	235.1	239.0
bursa	147.1	198.89	230.0	210.7	235.1	239.0
fornix	147.3	198.89	230.0	210.7	235.1	239.0
recess	147.2	198.89	230.0	210.7	235.1	239.0
region	149.0	198.89	230.0	210.9	235.1	239.0
tonsil	147.1	198.89	230.0	210.7	235.1	239.0

	Malignant					
	Primary	Secondary	Ca in situ	Benign	Uncertain Behavior	Unspecified
Neoplasm, neoplastic — *continued*						
pharynx, pharyngeal — *continued*						
wall (lateral) (posterior)	149.0	198.89	230.0	210.9	235.1	239.0
pia mater (cerebral) (cranial)	192.1	198.4	—	225.2	237.6	239.7
spinal	192.3	198.4	—	225.4	237.6	239.7
pillars of fauces	146.2	198.89	230.0	210.6	235.1	239.0
pineal (body) (gland)	194.4	198.89	234.8	227.4	237.1	239.7
pinna (ear) NEC	173.2	198.2	232.2	216.2	238.2	239.2
cartilage	171.0	198.89	—	215.0	238.1	239.2
piriform fossa or sinus	148.1	198.89	230.0	210.8	235.1	239.0
pituitary (body) (fossa) (gland) (lobe)	194.3	198.89	234.8	227.3	237.0	239.7
placenta	181	198.82	233.2	219.8	236.1	239.5
pleura, pleural (cavity)	163.9	197.2	—	212.4	235.8	239.1
contiguous sites	163.8	—	—	—	—	—
parietal	163.0	197.2	—	212.4	235.8	239.1
visceral	163.1	197.2	—	212.4	235.8	239.1
plexus						
brachial	171.2	198.89	—	215.2	238.1	239.2
cervical	171.0	198.89	—	215.0	238.1	239.2
choroid	191.5	198.3	—	225.0	237.5	239.6
lumbosacral	171.6	198.89	—	215.6	238.1	239.2
sacral	171.6	198.89	—	215.6	238.1	239.2
pluri-endocrine	194.8	198.89	234.8	227.8	237.4	239.7
pole						
frontal	191.1	198.3	—	225.0	237.5	239.6
occipital	191.4	198.3	—	225.0	237.5	239.6
pons (varolii)	191.7	198.3	—	225.0	237.5	239.6
popliteal fossa or space*	195.5	198.89	234.8	229.8	238.8	239.8
postcricoid (region)	148.0	198.89	230.0	210.8	235.1	239.0
posterior fossa (cranial)	191.9	198.3	—	225.0	237.5	239.6
postnasal space	147.9	198.89	230.0	210.7	235.1	239.0
prepuce	187.1	198.82	233.5	222.1	236.6	239.5
prepylorus	151.1	197.8	230.2	211.1	235.2	239.0
presacral (region)	195.3	198.89	—	229.8	238.8	239.8
prostate (gland)	185	198.82	233.4	222.2	236.5	239.5
utricle	189.3	198.1	233.9	223.81	236.99	239.5
pterygoid fossa	171.0	198.89	—	215.0	238.1	239.2
pubic bone	170.6	198.5	—	213.6	238.0	239.2
pudenda, pudendum (female)	184.4	198.82	233.32	221.2	236.3	239.5
pulmonary	162.9	197.0	231.2	212.3	235.7	239.1
putamen	191.0	198.3	—	225.0	237.5	239.6
pyloric						
antrum	151.2	197.8	230.2	211.1	235.2	239.0
canal	151.1	197.8	230.2	211.1	235.2	239.0
pylorus	151.1	197.8	230.2	211.1	235.2	239.0
pyramid (brain)	191.7	198.3	—	225.0	237.5	239.6
pyriform fossa or sinus	148.1	198.89	230.0	210.8	235.1	239.0
radius (any part)	170.4	198.5	—	213.4	238.0	239.2
Rathke's pouch	194.3	198.89	234.8	227.3	237.0	239.7
rectosigmoid (colon) (junction)	154.0	197.5	230.4	211.4	235.2	239.0
contiguous sites with anus or rectum	154.8	—	—	—	—	—
rectouterine pouch	158.8	197.6	—	211.8	235.4	239.0
rectovaginal septum or wall	195.3	198.89	234.8	229.8	238.8	239.8
rectovesical septum	195.3	198.89	234.8	229.8	238.8	239.8
rectum (ampulla)	154.1	197.5	230.4	211.4	235.2	239.0
and colon	154.0	197.5	230.4	211.4	235.2	239.0
contiguous sites with anus or rectosigmoid junction	154.8	—	—	—	—	—
renal	189.0	198.0	233.9	223.0	236.91	239.5
calyx	189.1	198.0	233.9	223.1	236.91	239.5
hilus	189.1	198.0	233.9	223.1	236.91	239.5
parenchyma	189.0	198.0	233.9	223.0	236.91	239.5
pelvis	189.1	198.0	233.9	223.1	236.91	239.5
respiratory						

	Malignant					
	Primary	Secondary	Ca in situ	Benign	Uncertain Behavior	Unspecified
Neoplasm, neoplastic — *continued*						
respiratory — *continued*						
organs or system NEC	165.9	197.3	231.9	212.9	235.9	239.1
contiguous sites with intrathoracic organs	165.8	—	—	—	—	—
specified sites NEC	165.8	197.3	231.8	212.8	235.9	239.1
tract NEC	165.9	197.3	231.9	212.9	235.9	239.1
upper	165.0	197.3	231.9	212.9	235.9	239.1
retina	190.5	198.4	234.0	224.5	238.8	239.8
retrobulbar	190.1	198.4	—	224.1	238.8	239.8
retrocecal	158.0	197.6	—	211.8	235.4	239.0
retromolar (area) (triangle) (trigone)	145.6	198.89	230.0	210.4	235.1	239.0
retro-orbital	195.0	198.89	234.8	229.8	238.8	239.8
retroperitoneal (space) (tissue)	158.0	197.6	—	211.8	235.4	239.0
contiguous sites	158.8	—	—	—	—	—
retroperitoneum	158.0	197.6	—	211.8	235.4	239.0
contiguous sites	158.8	—	—	—	—	—
retropharyngeal	149.0	198.89	230.0	210.9	235.1	239.0
retrovesical (septum)	195.3	198.89	234.8	229.8	238.8	239.8
rhinencephalon	191.0	198.3	—	225.0	237.5	239.6
rib	170.3	198.5	—	213.3	238.0	239.2
Rosenmüller's fossa	147.2	198.89	230.0	210.7	235.1	239.0
round ligament	183.5	198.82	—	221.0	236.3	239.5
sacrococcyx, sacrococcygeal	170.6	198.5	—	213.6	238.0	239.2
region	195.3	198.89	234.8	229.8	238.8	239.8
sacrouterine ligament	183.4	198.82	—	221.0	236.3	239.5
sacrum, sacral (vertebra)	170.6	198.5	—	213.6	238.0	239.2
salivary gland or duct (major)	142.9	198.89	230.0	210.2	235.0	239.0
contiguous sites	142.8	—	—	—	—	—
minor NEC	145.9	198.89	230.0	210.4	235.1	239.0
parotid	142.0	198.89	230.0	210.2	235.0	239.0
pluriglandular	142.8	198.89	—	210.2	235.0	239.0
sublingual	142.2	198.89	230.0	210.2	235.0	239.0
submandibular	142.1	198.89	230.0	210.2	235.0	239.0
submaxillary	142.1	198.89	230.0	210.2	235.0	239.0
salpinx (uterine)	183.2	198.82	233.39	221.0	236.3	239.5
Santorini's duct	157.3	197.8	230.9	211.6	235.5	239.0
scalp	173.4	198.2	232.4	216.4	238.2	239.2
scapula (any part)	170.4	198.5	—	213.4	238.0	239.2
scapular region	195.1	198.89	234.8	229.8	238.8	239.8
scar NEC (*see also* Neoplasm, skin)	173.9	198.2	232.9	216.9	238.2	239.2
sciatic nerve	171.3	198.89	—	215.3	238.1	239.2
sclera	190.0	198.4	234.0	224.0	238.8	239.8
scrotum (skin)	187.7	198.82	—	222.4	236.6	239.5
sebaceous gland — *see* Neoplasm, skin						
sella turcica	194.3	198.89	234.8	227.3	237.0	239.7
bone	170.0	198.5	—	213.0	238.0	239.2
semilunar cartilage (knee)	170.7	198.5	—	213.7	238.0	239.2
seminal vesicle	187.8	198.82	233.6	222.8	236.6	239.5
septum						
nasal	160.0	197.3	231.8	212.0	235.9	239.1
posterior margin	147.3	198.89	230.0	210.7	235.1	239.0
rectovaginal	195.3	198.89	234.8	229.8	238.8	239.8
rectovesical	195.3	198.89	234.8	229.8	238.8	239.8
urethrovaginal	184.9	198.82	233.39	221.9	236.3	239.5
vesicovaginal	184.9	198.82	233.39	221.9	236.3	239.5
shoulder NEC*	195.4	198.89	232.6	229.8	238.8	239.8
sigmoid flexure (lower) (upper)	153.3	197.5	230.3	211.3	235.2	239.0
sinus (accessory)	160.9	197.3	231.8	212.0	235.9	239.1
bone (any)	170.0	198.5	—	213.0	238.0	239.2
contiguous sites with middle ear or nasal cavities	160.8	—	—	—	—	—
ethmoidal	160.3	197.3	231.8	212.0	235.9	239.1
frontal	160.4	197.3	231.8	212.0	235.9	239.1
maxillary	160.2	197.3	231.8	212.0	235.9	239.1

	Malignant					
	Primary	Secondary	Ca in situ	Benign	Uncertain Behavior	Unspecified
Neoplasm, neoplastic — *continued*						
sinus — *continued*						
nasal, paranasal NEC	160.9	197.3	231.8	212.0	235.9	239.1
pyriform	148.1	198.89	230.0	210.8	235.1	239.0
sphenoidal	160.5	197.3	231.8	212.0	235.9	239.1
skeleton, skeletal NEC	170.9	198.5	—	213.9	238.0	239.2
Skene's gland	189.4	198.1	233.9	223.89	236.99	239.5
skin NEC	173.9	198.2	232.9	216.9	238.2	239.2
abdominal wall	173.5	198.2	232.5	216.5	238.2	239.2
ala nasi	173.3	198.2	232.3	216.3	238.2	239.2
ankle	173.7	198.2	232.7	216.7	238.2	239.2
antecubital space	173.6	198.2	232.6	216.6	238.2	239.2
anus	173.5	198.2	232.5	216.5	238.2	239.2
arm	173.6	198.2	232.6	216.6	238.2	239.2
auditory canal (external)	173.2	198.2	232.2	216.2	238.2	239.2
auricle (ear)	173.2	198.2	232.2	216.2	238.2	239.2
auricular canal (external)	173.2	198.2	232.2	216.2	238.2	239.2
axilla, axillary fold	173.5	198.2	232.5	216.5	238.2	239.2
back	173.5	198.2	232.5	216.5	238.2	239.2
breast	173.5	198.2	232.5	216.5	238.2	239.2
brow	173.3	198.2	232.3	216.3	238.2	239.2
buttock	173.5	198.2	232.5	216.5	238.2	239.2
calf	173.7	198.2	232.7	216.7	238.2	239.2
canthus (eye) (inner) (outer)	173.1	198.2	232.1	216.1	238.2	239.2
cervical region	173.4	198.2	232.4	216.4	238.2	239.2
cheek (external)	173.3	198.2	232.3	216.3	238.2	239.2
chest (wall)	173.5	198.2	232.5	216.5	238.2	239.2
chin	173.3	198.2	232.3	216.3	238.2	239.2
clavicular area	173.5	198.2	232.5	216.5	238.2	239.2
clitoris	184.3	198.82	233.32	221.2	236.3	239.5
columnella	173.3	198.2	232.3	216.3	238.2	239.2
concha	173.2	198.2	232.2	216.2	238.2	239.2
contiguous sites	173.8	—	—	—	—	—
ear (external)	173.2	198.2	232.2	216.2	238.2	239.2
elbow	173.6	198.2	232.6	216.6	238.2	239.2
eyebrow	173.3	198.2	232.3	216.3	238.2	239.2
eyelid	173.1	198.2	232.1	—	238.2	239.2
face NEC	173.3	198.2	232.3	216.3	238.2	239.2
female genital organs (external)	184.4	198.82	233.30	221.2	236.3	239.5
clitoris	184.3	198.82	233.32	221.2	236.3	239.5
labium NEC	184.4	198.82	233.32	221.2	236.3	239.5
majus	184.1	198.82	233.32	221.2	236.3	239.5
minus	184.2	198.82	233.32	221.2	236.3	239.5
pudendum	184.4	198.82	233.32	221.2	236.3	239.5
vulva	184.4	198.82	233.32	221.2	236.3	239.5
finger	173.6	198.2	232.6	216.6	238.2	239.2
flank	173.5	198.2	232.5	216.5	238.2	239.2
foot	173.7	198.2	232.7	216.7	238.2	239.2
forearm	173.6	198.2	232.6	216.6	238.2	239.2
forehead	173.3	198.2	232.3	216.3	238.2	239.2
glabella	173.3	198.2	232.3	216.3	238.2	239.2
gluteal region	173.5	198.2	232.5	216.5	238.2	239.2
groin	173.5	198.2	232.5	216.5	238.2	239.2
hand	173.6	198.2	232.6	216.6	238.2	239.2
head NEC	173.4	198.2	232.4	216.4	238.2	239.2
heel	173.7	198.2	232.7	216.7	238.2	239.2
helix	173.2	198.2	—	216.2	238.2	239.2
hip	173.7	198.2	232.7	216.7	238.2	239.2
infraclavicular region	173.5	198.2	232.5	216.5	238.2	239.2
inguinal region	173.5	198.2	232.5	216.5	238.2	239.2
jaw	173.3	198.2	232.3	216.3	238.2	239.2
knee	173.7	198.2	232.7	216.7	238.2	239.2
labia						
majora	184.1	198.82	233.32	221.2	236.3	239.5
minora	184.2	198.82	233.32	221.2	236.3	239.5
leg	173.7	198.2	232.7	216.7	238.2	239.2
lid (lower) (upper)	—	198.2	232.1	216.1	238.2	239.2
limb NEC	173.9	198.2	232.9	216.9	238.2	239.5
lower	173.7	198.2	232.7	216.7	238.2	239.2
upper	173.6	198.2	232.6	216.6	238.2	239.2
lip (lower) (upper)	173.0	198.2	232.0	216.0	238.2	239.2

	Malignant					
	Primary	Secondary	Ca in situ	Benign	Uncertain Behavior	Unspecified
Neoplasm, neoplastic — *continued*						
skin — *continued*						
male genital organs	187.9	198.82	233.6	222.9	236.6	239.5
penis	187.4	198.82	233.5	222.1	236.6	239.5
prepuce	187.1	198.82	233.5	222.1	236.6	239.5
scrotum	187.7	198.82	233.6	222.4	236.6	239.5
mastectomy site	173.5	198.2	—	—	—	—
specified as breast tissue	174.8	198.81	—	—	—	—
meatus, acoustic (external)	173.2	198.2	232.2	216.2	238.2	239.2
nates	173.5	198.2	232.5	216.5	238.2	239.0
neck	173.4	198.2	232.4	216.4	238.2	239.2
nose (external)	173.3	198.2	232.3	216.3	238.2	239.2
palm	173.6	198.2	232.6	216.6	238.2	239.2
palpebra	173.1	198.2	232.1	216.1	238.2	239.2
penis NEC	187.4	198.82	233.5	222.1	236.6	239.5
perianal	173.5	198.2	232.5	216.5	238.2	239.2
perineum	173.5	198.2	232.5	216.5	238.2	239.2
pinna	173.2	198.2	232.2	216.2	238.2	239.2
plantar	173.7	198.2	232.7	216.7	238.2	239.2
popliteal fossa or space	173.7	198.2	232.7	216.7	238.2	239.2
prepuce	187.1	198.82	233.5	222.1	236.6	239.5
pubes	173.5	198.2	232.5	216.5	238.2	239.2
sacrococcygeal region	173.5	198.2	232.5	216.5	238.2	239.2
scalp	173.4	198.2	232.4	216.4	238.2	239.2
scapular region	173.5	198.2	232.5	216.5	238.2	239.2
scrotum	187.7	198.82	233.6	222.4	236.6	239.5
shoulder	173.6	198.2	232.6	216.6	238.2	239.2
sole (foot)	173.7	198.2	232.7	216.7	238.2	239.2
specified sites NEC	173.8	198.2	232.8	216.8	232.8	239.2
submammary fold	173.5	198.2	232.5	216.5	238.2	239.2
supraclavicular region	173.4	198.2	232.4	216.4	238.2	239.2
temple	173.3	198.2	232.3	216.3	238.2	239.2
thigh	173.7	198.2	232.7	216.7	238.2	239.2
thoracic wall	173.5	198.2	232.5	216.5	238.2	239.2
thumb	173.6	198.2	232.6	216.6	238.2	239.2
toe	173.7	198.2	232.7	216.7	238.2	239.2
tragus	173.2	198.2	232.2	216.2	238.2	239.2
trunk	173.5	198.2	232.5	216.5	238.2	239.2
umbilicus	173.5	198.2	232.5	216.5	238.2	239.2
vulva	184.4	198.82	233.32	221.2	236.3	239.5
wrist	173.6	198.2	232.6	216.6	238.2	239.2
skull	170.0	198.5	—	213.0	238.0	239.2
soft parts or tissues — *see* Neoplasm, connective tissue						
specified site NEC	195.8	198.89	234.8	229.8	238.8	239.8
specified site — *see* Neoplasm, skin						
spermatic cord	187.6	198.82	233.6	222.8	236.6	239.5
sphenoid	160.5	197.3	231.8	212.0	235.9	239.1
bone	170.0	198.5	—	213.0	238.0	239.2
sinus	160.5	197.3	231.8	212.0	235.9	239.1
sphincter						
anal	154.2	197.5	230.5	211.4	235.5	239.0
of Oddi	156.1	197.8	230.8	211.5	235.3	239.0
spine, spinal (column)	170.2	198.5	—	213.2	238.0	239.2
bulb	191.7	198.3	—	225.0	237.5	239.6
coccyx	170.6	198.5	—	213.6	238.0	239.2
cord (cervical) (lumbar) (sacral) (thoracic)	192.2	198.3	—	225.3	237.5	239.7
dura mater	192.3	198.4	—	225.4	237.6	239.7
lumbosacral	170.2	198.5	—	213.2	238.0	239.2
membrane	192.3	198.4	—	225.4	237.6	239.7
meninges	192.3	198.4	—	225.4	237.6	239.7
nerve (root)	171.9	198.89	—	215.9	238.1	239.2
pia mater	192.3	198.4	—	225.4	237.6	239.7
root	171.9	198.89	—	215.9	238.1	239.2
sacrum	170.6	198.5	—	213.6	238.0	239.2
spleen, splenic NEC	159.1	197.8	230.9	211.9	235.5	239.0
flexure (colon)	153.7	197.5	230.3	211.3	235.2	239.0
stem, brain	191.7	198.3	—	225.0	237.5	239.6
Stensen's duct	142.0	198.89	230.0	210.2	235.0	239.0
Neoplasm, neoplastic — *continued*						
sternum	170.3	198.5	—	213.3	238.0	239.2
stomach	151.9	197.8	230.2	211.1	235.2	239.0
antrum (pyloric)	151.2	197.8	230.2	211.1	235.2	239.0
body	151.4	197.8	230.2	211.1	235.2	239.0
cardia	151.0	197.8	230.2	211.1	235.2	239.0
cardiac orifice	151.0	197.8	230.2	211.1	235.2	239.0
contiguous sites	151.8	—	—	—	—	—
corpus	151.4	197.8	230.2	211.1	235.2	239.0
fundus	151.3	197.8	230.2	211.1	235.2	239.0
greater curvature NEC	151.6	197.8	230.2	211.1	235.2	239.0
lesser curvature NEC	151.5	197.8	230.2	211.1	235.2	239.0
prepylorus	151.1	197.8	230.2	211.1	235.2	239.0
pylorus	151.1	197.8	230.2	211.1	235.2	239.0
wall NEC	151.9	197.8	230.2	211.1	235.2	239.0
anterior NEC	151.8	197.8	230.2	211.1	235.2	239.0
posterior NEC	151.8	197.8	230.2	211.1	235.2	239.0
stroma, endometrial	182.0	198.82	233.2	219.1	236.0	239.5
stump, cervical	180.8	198.82	233.1	219.0	236.0	239.5
subcutaneous (nodule) (tissue) NEC — *see* Neoplasm, connective tissue						
subdural	192.1	198.4	—	225.2	237.6	239.7
subglottis, subglottic	161.2	197.3	231.0	212.1	235.6	239.1
sublingual	144.9	198.89	230.0	210.3	235.1	239.0
gland or duct	142.2	198.89	230.0	210.2	235.0	239.0
submandibular gland	142.1	198.89	230.0	210.2	235.0	239.0
submaxillary gland or duct	142.1	198.89	230.0	210.2	235.0	239.0
submental	195.0	198.89	234.8	229.8	238.8	239.8
subpleural	162.9	197.0	—	212.3	235.7	239.1
substernal	164.2	197.1	—	212.5	235.8	239.8
sudoriferous, sudoriparous gland, site unspecified	173.9	198.2	232.9	216.9	238.2	239.2
specified site — *see* Neoplasm, skin						
supraclavicular region	195.0	198.89	234.8	229.8	238.8	239.8
supraglottis	161.1	197.3	231.0	212.1	235.6	239.1
suprarenal (capsule) (cortex) (gland) (medulla)	194.0	198.7	234.8	227.0	237.2	239.7
suprasellar (region)	191.9	198.3	—	225.0	237.5	239.6
sweat gland (apocrine) (eccrine), site unspecified	173.9	198.2	232.9	216.9	238.2	239.2
sympathetic nerve or nervous system NEC	171.9	198.89	—	215.9	238.1	239.2
symphysis pubis	170.6	198.5	—	213.6	238.0	239.2
synovial membrane — *see* Neoplasm, connective tissue						
tapetum, brain	191.8	198.3	—	225.0	237.5	239.6
tarsus (any bone)	170.8	198.5	—	213.8	238.0	239.2
temple (skin)	173.3	198.2	232.3	216.3	238.2	239.2
temporal						
bone	170.0	198.5	—	213.0	238.0	239.2
lobe or pole	191.2	198.3	—	225.0	237.5	239.6
region	195.0	198.89	234.8	229.8	238.8	239.8
skin	173.3	198.2	232.3	216.3	238.2	239.2
tendon (sheath) — *see* Neoplasm, connective tissue						
tentorium (cerebelli)	192.1	198.4	—	225.2	237.6	239.7
testis, testes (descended) (scrotal)	186.9	198.82	233.6	222.0	236.4	239.5
ectopic	186.0	198.82	233.6	222.0	236.4	239.5
retained	186.0	198.82	233.6	222.0	236.4	239.5
undescended	186.0	198.82	233.6	222.0	236.4	239.5
thalamus	191.0	198.3	—	225.0	237.5	239.6
thigh NEC*	195.5	198.89	234.8	229.8	238.8	239.8
thorax, thoracic (cavity) (organs NEC)	195.1	198.89	234.8	229.8	238.8	239.8
duct	171.4	198.89	—	215.4	238.1	239.2
wall NEC	195.1	198.89	234.8	229.8	238.8	239.8

	Malignant					
	Primary	Secondary	Ca in situ	Benign	Uncertain Behavior	Unspecified
Neoplasm, neoplastic — *continued*						
throat	149.0	198.89	230.0	210.9	235.1	239.0
thumb NEC*	195.4	198.89	232.6	229.8	238.8	239.8
thymus (gland)	164.0	198.89	—	212.6	235.8	239.8
contiguous sites with heart and mediastinum	164.8	—	—	—	—	—
thyroglossal duct	193	198.89	234.8	226	237.4	239.7
thyroid (gland)	193	198.89	234.8	226	237.4	239.7
cartilage	161.3	197.3	231.0	212.1	235.6	239.1
tibia (any part)	170.7	198.5	—	213.7	238.0	239.2
toe NEC*	195.5	198.89	232.7	229.8	238.8	239.8
tongue	141.9	198.89	230.0	210.1	235.1	239.0
anterior (two-thirds) NEC	141.4	198.89	230.0	210.1	235.1	239.0
dorsal surface	141.1	198.89	230.0	210.1	235.1	239.0
ventral surface	141.3	198.89	230.0	210.1	235.1	239.0
base (dorsal surface)	141.0	198.89	230.0	210.1	235.1	239.0
border (lateral)	141.2	198.89	230.0	210.1	235.1	239.0
contiguous sites	141.8	—	—	—	—	—
dorsal surface NEC	141.1	198.89	230.0	210.1	235.1	239.0
fixed part NEC	141.0	198.89	230.0	210.1	235.1	239.0
foreamen cecum	141.1	198.89	230.0	210.1	235.1	239.0
frenulum linguae	141.3	198.89	230.0	210.1	235.1	239.0
junctional zone	141.5	198.89	230.0	210.1	235.1	239.0
margin (lateral)	141.2	198.89	230.0	210.1	235.1	239.0
midline NEC	141.1	198.89	230.0	210.1	235.1	239.0
mobile part NEC	141.4	198.89	230.0	210.1	235.1	239.0
posterior (third)	141.0	198.89	230.0	210.1	235.1	239.0
root	141.0	198.89	230.0	210.1	235.1	239.0
surface (dorsal)	141.1	198.89	230.0	210.1	235.1	239.0
base	141.0	198.89	230.0	210.1	235.1	239.0
ventral	141.3	198.89	230.0	210.1	235.1	239.0
tip	141.2	198.89	230.0	210.1	235.1	239.0
tonsil	141.6	198.89	230.0	210.1	235.1	239.0
tonsil	146.0	198.89	230.0	210.5	235.1	239.0
fauces, faucial	146.0	198.89	230.0	210.5	235.1	239.0
lingual	141.6	198.89	230.0	210.1	235.1	239.0
palatine	146.0	198.89	230.0	210.5	235.1	239.0
pharyngeal	147.1	198.89	230.0	210.7	235.1	239.0
pillar (anterior) (posterior)	146.2	198.89	230.0	210.6	235.1	239.0
tonsillar fossa	146.1	198.89	230.0	210.6	235.1	239.0
tooth socket NEC	143.9	198.89	230.0	210.4	235.1	239.0
trachea (cartilage) (mucosa)	162.0	197.3	231.1	212.2	235.7	239.1
contiguous sites with bronchus or lung	162.8	—	—	—	—	—
tracheobronchial	162.8	197.3	231.1	212.2	235.7	239.1
contiguous sites with lung	162.8	—	—	—	—	—
tragus	173.2	198.2	232.2	216.2	238.2	239.2
trunk NEC*	195.8	198.89	232.5	229.8	238.8	239.8
tubo-ovarian	183.8	198.82	233.39	221.8	236.3	239.5
tunica vaginalis	187.8	198.82	233.6	222.8	236.6	239.5
turbinate (bone)	170.0	198.5	—	213.0	238.0	239.2
nasal	160.0	197.3	231.8	212.0	235.9	239.1
tympanic cavity	160.1	197.3	231.8	212.0	235.9	239.1
ulna (any part)	170.4	198.5	—	213.4	238.0	239.2
umbilicus, umbilical	173.5	198.2	232.5	216.5	238.2	239.2
uncus, brain	191.2	198.3	—	225.0	237.5	239.6
unknown site or unspecified	199.1	199.1	234.9	229.9	238.9	239.9
urachus	188.7	198.1	233.7	223.3	236.7	239.4
ureter-bladder junction	188.6	198.1	233.7	223.3	236.7	239.4
ureter, ureteral	189.2	198.1	233.9	223.2	236.91	239.5
orifice (bladder)	188.6	198.1	233.7	223.3	236.7	239.4
urethra, urethral (gland)	189.3	198.1	233.9	223.81	236.99	239.5
orifice, internal	188.5	198.1	233.7	223.3	236.7	239.4
urethrovaginal (septum)	184.9	198.82	233.39	221.9	236.3	239.5
urinary organ or system NEC	189.9	198.1	233.9	223.9	236.99	239.5
Neoplasm, neoplastic — *continued*						
urinary organ or system — *continued*						
bladder — *see* Neoplasm, bladder						
contiguous sites	189.8	—	—	—	—	—
specified sites NEC	189.8	198.1	233.9	223.89	236.99	239.5
utero-ovarian	183.8	198.82	233.39	221.8	236.3	239.5
ligament	183.3	198.82	—	221.0	236.3	239.5
uterosacral ligament	183.4	198.82	—	221.0	236.3	239.5
uterus, uteri, uterine	179	198.82	233.2	219.9	236.0	239.5
adnexa NEC	183.9	198.82	233.39	221.8	236.3	239.5
contiguous sites	183.8	—	—	—	—	—
body	182.0	198.82	233.2	219.1	236.0	239.5
contiguous sites	182.8	—	—	—	—	—
cervix	180.9	198.82	233.1	219.0	236.0	239.5
cornu	182.0	198.82	233.2	219.1	236.0	239.5
corpus	182.0	198.82	233.2	219.1	236.0	239.5
endocervix (canal) (gland)	180.0	198.82	233.1	219.0	236.0	239.5
endometrium	182.0	198.82	233.2	219.1	236.0	239.5
exocervix	180.1	198.82	233.1	219.0	236.0	239.5
external os	180.1	198.82	233.1	219.0	236.0	239.5
fundus	182.0	198.82	233.2	219.1	236.0	239.5
internal os	180.0	198.82	233.1	219.0	236.0	239.5
isthmus	182.1	198.82	233.2	219.1	236.0	239.5
ligament	183.4	198.82	—	221.0	236.3	239.5
broad	183.3	198.82	233.39	221.0	236.3	239.5
round	183.5	198.82	—	221.0	236.3	239.5
lower segment	182.1	198.82	233.2	219.1	236.0	239.5
myometrium	182.0	198.82	233.2	219.1	236.0	239.5
squamocolumnar junction	180.8	198.82	233.1	219.0	236.0	239.5
tube	183.2	198.82	233.39	221.0	236.3	239.5
utricle, prostatic	189.3	198.1	233.9	223.81	236.99	239.5
uveal tract	190.0	198.4	234.0	224.0	238.8	239.8
uvula	145.4	198.89	230.0	210.4	235.1	239.0
vagina, vaginal (fornix) (vault) (wall)	184.0	198.82	233.31	221.1	236.3	239.5
vaginovesical	184.9	198.82	233.39	221.9	236.3	239.5
septum	184.9	198.82	233.39	221.9	236.3	239.5
vallecula (epiglottis)	146.3	198.89	230.0	210.6	235.1	239.0
vascular — *see* Neoplasm, connective tissue						
vas deferens	187.6	198.82	233.6	222.8	236.6	239.5
Vater's ampulla	156.2	197.8	230.8	211.5	235.3	239.0
vein, venous — *see* Neoplasm, connective tissue						
vena cava (abdominal) (inferior)	171.5	198.89	—	215.5	238.1	239.2
superior	171.4	198.89	—	215.4	238.1	239.2
ventricle (cerebral) (floor) (fourth) (lateral) (third)	191.5	198.3	—	225.0	237.5	239.6
cardiac (left) (right)	164.1	198.89	—	212.7	238.8	239.8
ventricular band of larynx	161.1	197.3	231.0	212.1	235.6	239.1
ventriculus — see Neoplasm, stomach						
vermillion border — *see* Neoplasm, lip						
vermis, cerebellum	191.6	198.3	—	225.0	237.5	239.6
vertebra (column)	170.2	198.5	—	213.2	238.0	239.2
coccyx	170.6	198.5	—	213.6	238.0	239.2
sacrum	170.6	198.5	—	213.6	238.0	239.2
vesical — *see* Neoplasm, bladder						
vesicle, seminal	187.8	198.82	233.6	222.8	236.6	239.5
vesicocervical tissue	184.9	198.82	233.39	221.9	236.3	239.5
vesicorectal	195.3	198.89	234.8	229.8	238.8	239.8
vesicovaginal	184.9	198.82	233.39	221.9	236.3	239.5
septum	184.9	198.82	233.39	221.9	236.3	239.5
vessel (blood) — *see* Neoplasm, connective tissue						
vestibular gland, greater	184.1	198.82	233.32	221.2	236.3	239.5

	Malignant					
	Primary	Secondary	Ca in situ	Benign	Uncertain Behavior	Unspecified
Neoplasm, neoplastic — *continued*						
vestibule						
mouth	145.1	198.89	230.0	210.4	235.1	239.0
nose	160.0	197.3	231.8	212.0	235.9	239.1
Virchow's gland	—	196.0	—	229.0	238.8	239.8
viscera NEC	195.8	198.89	234.8	229.8	238.8	239.8
vocal cords (true)	161.0	197.3	231.0	212.1	235.6	239.1
false	161.1	197.3	231.0	212.1	235.6	239.1
vomer	170.0	198.5	—	213.0	238.0	239.2
vulva	184.4	198.82	233.32	221.2	236.3	239.5
vulvovaginal gland	184.4	198.82	233.32	221.2	236.3	239.5
Waldeyer's ring	149.1	198.89	230.0	210.9	235.1	239.0
Wharton's duct	142.1	198.89	230.0	210.2	235.0	239.0
white matter (central) (cerebral)	191.0	198.3	—	225.0	237.5	239.6
windpipe	162.0	197.3	231.1	212.2	235.7	239.1
Wirsung's duct	157.3	197.8	230.9	211.6	235.5	239.0
wolffian (body) (duct)						
female	184.8	198.82	233.39	221.8	236.3	239.5
male	187.8	198.82	233.6	222.8	236.6	239.5
womb — *see* Neoplasm, uterus						
wrist NEC*	195.4	198.89	232.6	229.8	238.8	239.8
xiphoid process	170.3	198.5	—	213.3	238.0	239.2
Zuckerkandl's organ	194.6	198.89	—	227.6	237.3	239.7

Neovascularization
- choroid 362.16
- ciliary body 364.42
- cornea 370.60
  - deep 370.63
  - localized 370.61
- iris 364.42
- retina 362.16
- subretinal 362.16

Nephralgia 788.0

Nephritis, nephritic (albuminuric) (azotemic) (congenital) (degenerative) (diffuse) (disseminated) (epithelial) (familial) (focal) (granulomatous) (hemorrhagic) (infantile) (nonsuppurative, excretory) (uremic) 583.9
- with
  - edema — *see* Nephrosis
  - lesion of
    - glomerulonephritis
      - hypocomplementemic persistent 583.2
        - with nephrotic syndrome 581.2
        - chronic 582.2
      - lobular 583.2
        - with nephrotic syndrome 581.2
        - chronic 582.2
      - membranoproliferative 583.2
        - with nephrotic syndrome 581.2
        - chronic 582.2
      - membranous 583.1
        - with nephrotic syndrome 581.1
        - chronic 582.1
      - mesangiocapillary 583.2
        - with nephrotic syndrome 581.2
        - chronic 582.2
      - mixed membranous and proliferative 583.2
        - with nephrotic syndrome 581.2
        - chronic 582.2
      - proliferative (diffuse) 583.0
        - with nephrotic syndrome 581.0
        - acute 580.0
        - chronic 582.0
      - rapidly progressive 583.4
        - acute 580.4
        - chronic 582.4
    - interstitial nephritis (diffuse) (focal) 583.89
      - with nephrotic syndrome 581.89
      - acute 580.89
      - chronic 582.89
    - necrotizing glomerulitis 583.4
      - acute 580.4
      - chronic 582.4
    - renal necrosis 583.9
      - cortical 583.6
      - medullary 583.7
    - specified pathology NEC 583.89
      - with nephrotic syndrome 581.89
      - acute 580.89
      - chronic 582.89
  - necrosis, renal 583.9
    - cortical 583.6
    - medullary (papillary) 583.7
  - nephrotic syndrome (*see also* Nephrosis) 581.9
  - papillary necrosis 583.7
  - specified pathology NEC 583.89
- acute 580.9
  - extracapillary with epithelial crescents 580.4
  - hypertensive (*see also* Hypertension, kidney) 403.90
  - necrotizing 580.4
  - poststreptococcal 580.0

Nephritis, nephritic — *continued*
- acute — *continued*
  - proliferative (diffuse) 580.0
  - rapidly progressive 580.4
  - specified pathology NEC 580.89
- amyloid 277.39 *[583.81]*
  - chronic 277.39 *[582.81]*
- arteriolar (*see also* Hypertension, kidney) 403.90
- arteriosclerotic (*see also* Hypertension, kidney) 403.90
- ascending (*see also* Pyelitis) 590.80
- atrophic 582.9
- basement membrane NEC 583.89
  - with
    - pulmonary hemorrhage (Goodpasture's syndrome) 446.21 *[583.81]*
- calculous, calculus 592.0
- cardiac (*see also* Hypertension, kidney) 403.90
- cardiovascular (*see also* Hypertension, kidney) 403.90
- chronic 582.9
  - arteriosclerotic (*see also* Hypertension, kidney) 403.90
  - hypertensive (*see also* Hypertension, kidney) 403.90
- cirrhotic (*see also* Sclerosis, renal) 587
- complicating pregnancy, childbirth, or puerperium 646.2 ☑
  - with hypertension 642.1 ☑
    - affecting fetus or newborn 760.0
  - affecting fetus or newborn 760.1
- croupous 580.9
- desquamative — *see* Nephrosis
- due to
  - amyloidosis 277.39 *[583.81]*
    - chronic 277.39 *[582.81]*
  - arteriosclerosis (*see also* Hypertension, kidney) 403.90
  - diabetes mellitus 250.4 ☑ *[583.81]*
    - with nephrotic syndrome 250.4 ☑ *[581.81]*
      - due to secondary diabetes 249.4 ☑ *[581.81]*
    - due to secondary diabetes 249.4 ☑ *[583.81]*
  - diphtheria 032.89 *[580.81]*
  - gonococcal infection (acute) 098.19 *[583.81]*
    - chronic or duration of 2 months or over 098.39 *[583.81]*
  - gout 274.10
  - infectious hepatitis 070.9 *[580.81]*
  - mumps 072.79 *[580.81]*
  - specified kidney pathology NEC 583.89
    - acute 580.89
    - chronic 582.89
  - streptotrichosis 039.8 *[583.81]*
  - subacute bacterial endocarditis 421.0 *[580.81]*
  - systemic lupus erythematosus 710.0 *[583.81]*
    - chronic 710.0 *[582.81]*
  - typhoid fever 002.0 *[580.81]*
- endothelial 582.2
- end stage (chronic) (terminal) NEC 585.6
- epimembranous 581.1
- exudative 583.89
  - with nephrotic syndrome 581.89
  - acute 580.89
  - chronic 582.89
- gonococcal (acute) 098.19 *[583.81]*
  - chronic or duration of 2 months or over 098.39 *[583.81]*
- gouty 274.10
- hereditary (Alport's syndrome) 759.89
- hydremic — *see* Nephrosis
- hypertensive (*see also* Hypertension, kidney) 403.90
- hypocomplementemic persistent 583.2
  - with nephrotic syndrome 581.2
  - chronic 582.2

Nephritis, nephritic — *continued*
- immune complex NEC 583.89
- infective (*see also* Pyelitis) 590.80
- interstitial (diffuse) (focal) 583.89
  - with nephrotic syndrome 581.89
  - acute 580.89
  - chronic 582.89
- latent or quiescent — *see* Nephritis, chronic
- lead 984.9
  - specified type of lead — *see* Table of Drugs and Chemicals
- lobular 583.2
  - with nephrotic syndrome 581.2
  - chronic 582.2
- lupus 710.0 *[583.81]*
  - acute 710.0 *[580.81]*
  - chronic 710.0 *[582.81]*
- membranoproliferative 583.2
  - with nephrotic syndrome 581.2
  - chronic 582.2
- membranous 583.1
  - with nephrotic syndrome 581.1
  - chronic 582.1
- mesangiocapillary 583.2
  - with nephrotic syndrome 581.2
  - chronic 582.2
- minimal change 581.3
- mixed membranous and proliferative 583.2
  - with nephrotic syndrome 581.2
  - chronic 582.2
- necrotic, necrotizing 583.4
  - acute 580.4
  - chronic 582.4
- nephrotic — *see* Nephrosis
- old — *see* Nephritis, chronic
- parenchymatous 581.89
- polycystic 753.12
  - adult type (APKD) 753.13
  - autosomal dominant 753.13
  - autosomal recessive 753.14
  - childhood type (CPKD) 753.14
  - infantile type 753.14
- poststreptococcal 580.0
- pregnancy — *see* Nephritis, complicating pregnancy
- proliferative 583.0
  - with nephrotic syndrome 581.0
  - acute 580.0
  - chronic 582.0
- purulent (*see also* Pyelitis) 590.80
- rapidly progressive 583.4
  - acute 580.4
  - chronic 582.4
- salt-losing or salt-wasting (*see also* Disease, renal) 593.9
- saturnine 984.9
  - specified type of lead — *see* Table of Drugs and Chemicals
- septic (*see also* Pyelitis) 590.80
- specified pathology NEC 583.89
  - acute 580.89
  - chronic 582.89
- staphylococcal (*see also* Pyelitis) 590.80
- streptotrichosis 039.8 *[583.81]*
- subacute (*see also* Nephrosis) 581.9
- suppurative (*see also* Pyelitis) 590.80
- syphilitic (late) 095.4
  - congenital 090.5 *[583.81]*
  - early 091.69 *[583.81]*
- terminal (chronic) (end-stage) NEC 585.6
- toxic — *see* Nephritis, acute
- tubal, tubular — *see* Nephrosis, tubular
- tuberculous (*see also* Tuberculosis) 016.0 ☑ *[583.81]*
- type II (Ellis) — *see* Nephrosis
- vascular — *see* Hypertension, kidney
- war 580.9

Nephroblastoma (M8960/3) 189.0
- epithelial (M8961/3) 189.0
- mesenchymal (M8962/3) 189.0

Nephrocalcinosis 275.49

Nephrocystitis, pustular — *see also* Pyelitis 590.80

Nephrolithiasis (congenital) (pelvis) (recurrent) 592.0
- uric acid 274.11

Nephroma (M8960/3) 189.0
- mesoblastic (M8960/1) 236.9 ☑

Nephronephritis — *see also* Nephrosis 581.9

Nephronopthisis 753.16

Nephropathy — *see also* Nephritis 583.9
- with
  - exudative nephritis 583.89
  - interstitial nephritis (diffuse) (focal) 583.89
  - medullary necrosis 583.7
  - necrosis 583.9
    - cortical 583.6
    - medullary or papillary 583.7
  - papillary necrosis 583.7
  - specified lesion or cause NEC 583.89
- analgesic 583.89
  - with medullary necrosis, acute 584.7
- arteriolar (*see also* Hypertension, kidney) 403.90
- arteriosclerotic (*see also* Hypertension, kidney) 403.90
- complicating pregnancy 646.2 ☑
- diabetic 250.4 ☑ *[583.81]*
  - due to secondary diabetes 249.4 ☑ *[581.81]*
- gouty 274.10
  - specified type NEC 274.19
- hereditary amyloid 277.31
- hypercalcemic 588.89
- hypertensive (*see also* Hypertension, kidney) 403.90
- hypokalemic (vacuolar) 588.89
- IgA 583.9
- obstructive 593.89
  - congenital 753.20
- phenacetin 584.7
- phosphate-losing 588.0
- potassium depletion 588.89
- proliferative (*see also* Nephritis, proliferative) 583.0
- protein-losing 588.89
- salt-losing or salt-wasting (*see also* Disease, renal) 593.9
- sickle-cell (*see also* Disease, sickle-cell) 282.60 *[583.81]*
- toxic 584.5
- vasomotor 584.5
- water-losing 588.89

Nephroptosis — *see also* Disease, renal 593.0
- congenital (displaced) 753.3

Nephropyosis — *see also* Abscess, kidney 590.2

Nephrorrhagia 593.81

Nephrosclerosis (arteriolar) (arteriosclerotic) (chronic) (hyaline) — *see also* Hypertension, kidney 403.90
- gouty 274.10
- hyperplastic (arteriolar) (*see also* Hypertension, kidney) 403.90
- senile (*see also* Sclerosis, renal) 587

Nephrosis, nephrotic (Epstein's) (syndrome) 581.9
- with
  - lesion of
    - focal glomerulosclerosis 581.1
    - glomerulonephritis
      - endothelial 581.2
      - hypocomplementemic persistent 581.2
      - lobular 581.2
      - membranoproliferative 581.2
      - membranous 581.1
      - mesangiocapillary 581.2
      - minimal change 581.3
      - mixed membranous and proliferative 581.2
      - proliferative 581.0

Nephrosis, nephrotic — *continued*
  with — *continued*
    lesion of — *continued*
      segmental hyalinosis 581.1
      specified pathology NEC 581.89
  acute — *see* Nephrosis, tubular
  anoxic — *see* Nephrosis, tubular
  arteriosclerotic (*see also* Hypertension, kidney) 403.90
  chemical — *see* Nephrosis, tubular
  cholemic 572.4
  complicating pregnancy, childbirth, or puerperium — *see* Nephritis, complicating pregnancy
  diabetic 250.4 ☑ *[581.81]*
    due to secondary diabetes 249.4 ☑ *[581.81]*
  Finnish type (congenital) 759.89
  hemoglobinuric — *see* Nephrosis, tubular
  in
    amyloidosis 277.39 *[581.81]*
    diabetes mellitus 250.4 ☑ *[581.81]*
      due to secondary diabetes 249.4 ☑ *[581.81]*
    epidemic hemorrhagic fever 078.6
    malaria 084.9 *[581.81]*
    polyarteritis 446.0 *[581.81]*
    systemic lupus erythematosus 710.0 *[581.81]*
  ischemic — *see* Nephrosis, tubular
  lipoid 581.3
  lower nephron — *see* Nephrosis, tubular
  lupoid 710.0 *[581.81]*
  lupus 710.0 *[581.81]*
  malarial 084.9 *[581.81]*
  minimal change 581.3
  necrotizing — *see* Nephrosis, tubular
  osmotic (sucrose) 588.89
  polyarteritic 446.0 *[581.81]*
  radiation 581.9
  specified lesion or cause NEC 581.89
  syphilitic 095.4
  toxic — *see* Nephrosis, tubular
  tubular (acute) 584.5
    due to a procedure 997.5
    radiation 581.9
Nephrosonephritis hemorrhagic (endemic) 078.6
Nephrostomy status V44.6
  with complication 997.5
Nerve — *see* condition
Nerves 799.2
Nervous — *see also* condition 799.2
  breakdown 300.9
  heart 306.2
  stomach 306.4
  tension 799.2
Nervousness 799.2
Nesidioblastoma (M8150/0)
  pancreas 211.7
  specified site NEC — *see* Neoplasm, by site, benign
  unspecified site 211.7
Netherton's syndrome (ichthyosiform erythroderma) 757.1
Nettle rash 708.8
Nettleship's disease (urticaria pigmentosa) 757.33
Neumann's disease (pemphigus vegetans) 694.4
Neuralgia, neuralgic (acute) — *see also* Neuritis 729.2
  accessory (nerve) 352.4
  acoustic (nerve) 388.5
  ankle 355.8
  anterior crural 355.8
  anus 787.99
  arm 723.4
  auditory (nerve) 388.5
  axilla 353.0
  bladder 788.1
  brachial 723.4
  brain — *see* Disorder, nerve, cranial
  broad ligament 625.9

Neuralgia, neuralgic — *see also* Neuritis — *continued*
  cerebral — *see* Disorder, nerve, cranial
  ciliary 339.00
  cranial nerve (*see also* Disorder, nerve, cranial)
    fifth or trigeminal (*see also* Neuralgia, trigeminal) 350.1
  ear 388.71
    middle 352.1
  facial 351.8
  finger 354.9
  flank 355.8
  foot 355.8
  forearm 354.9
  Fothergill's (*see also* Neuralgia, trigeminal) 350.1
    postherpetic 053.12
  glossopharyngeal (nerve) 352.1
  groin 355.8
  hand 354.9
  heel 355.8
  Horton's 339.00
  Hunt's 053.11
  hypoglossal (nerve) 352.5
  iliac region 355.8
  infraorbital (*see also* Neuralgia, trigeminal) 350.1
  inguinal 355.8
  intercostal (nerve) 353.8
    postherpetic 053.19
  jaw 352.1
  kidney 788.0
  knee 355.8
  loin 355.8
  malarial (*see also* Malaria) 084.6
  mastoid 385.89
  maxilla 352.1
  median thenar 354.1
  metatarsal 355.6
  middle ear 352.1
  migrainous 339.00
  Morton's 355.6
  nerve, cranial — *see* Disorder, nerve, cranial
  nose 352.0
  occipital 723.8
  olfactory (nerve) 352.0
  ophthalmic 377.30
    postherpetic 053.19
  optic (nerve) 377.30
  penis 607.9
  perineum 355.8
  pleura 511.0
  postherpetic NEC 053.19
    geniculate ganglion 053.11
    ophthalmic 053.19
    trifacial 053.12
    trigeminal 053.12
  pubic region 355.8
  radial (nerve) 723.4
  rectum 787.99
  sacroiliac joint 724.3
  sciatic (nerve) 724.3
  scrotum 608.9
  seminal vesicle 608.9
  shoulder 354.9
  Sluder's 337.09
  specified nerve NEC — *see* Disorder, nerve
  spermatic cord 608.9
  sphenopalatine (ganglion) 337.09
  subscapular (nerve) 723.4
  suprascapular (nerve) 723.4
  testis 608.89
  thenar (median) 354.1
  thigh 355.8
  tongue 352.5
  trifacial (nerve) (*see also* Neuralgia, trigeminal) 350.1
  trigeminal (nerve) 350.1
    postherpetic 053.12
  tympanic plexus 388.71
  ulnar (nerve) 723.4
  vagus (nerve) 352.3

Neuralgia, neuralgic — *see also* Neuritis — *continued*
  wrist 354.9
  writers' 300.89
    organic 333.84
Neurapraxia — *see* Injury, nerve, by site
Neurasthenia 300.5
  cardiac 306.2
  gastric 306.4
  heart 306.2
  postfebrile 780.79
  postviral 780.79
Neurilemmoma (M9560/0) — *see also* Neoplasm, connective tissue, benign
  acoustic (nerve) 225.1
  malignant (M9560/3) (*see also* Neoplasm, connective tissue, malignant)
    acoustic (nerve) 192.0
Neurilemmosarcoma (M9560/3) — *see* Neoplasm, connective tissue, malignant
Neurilemoma — *see* Neurilemmoma
Neurinoma (M9560/0) — *see* Neurilemmoma
Neurinomatosis (M9560/1) — *see also* Neoplasm, connective tissue, uncertain behavior
  centralis 759.5
Neuritis — *see also* Neuralgia 729.2
  abducens (nerve) 378.54
  accessory (nerve) 352.4
  acoustic (nerve) 388.5
    syphilitic 094.86
  alcoholic 357.5
    with psychosis 291.1
  amyloid, any site 277.39 *[357.4]*
  anterior crural 355.8
  arising during pregnancy 646.4 ☑
  arm 723.4
  ascending 355.2
  auditory (nerve) 388.5
  brachial (nerve) NEC 723.4
    due to displacement, intervertebral disc 722.0
  cervical 723.4
  chest (wall) 353.8
  costal region 353.8
  cranial nerve (*see also* Disorder, nerve, cranial)
    first or olfactory 352.0
    second or optic 377.30
    third or oculomotor 378.52
    fourth or trochlear 378.53
    fifth or trigeminal (*see also* Neuralgia, trigeminal) 350.1
    sixth or abducens 378.54
    seventh or facial 351.8
      newborn 767.5
    eighth or acoustic 388.5
    ninth or glossopharyngeal 352.1
    tenth or vagus 352.3
    eleventh or accessory 352.4
    twelfth or hypoglossal 352.5
  Déjérine-Sottas 356.0
  diabetic 250.6 ☑ *[357.2]*
    due to secondary diabetes 249.6 ☑ *[357.2]*
  diphtheritic 032.89 *[357.4]*
  due to
    beriberi 265.0 *[357.4]*
    displacement, prolapse, protrusion, or rupture of intervertebral disc 722.2
      cervical 722.0
      lumbar, lumbosacral 722.10
      thoracic, thoracolumbar 722.11
    herniation, nucleus pulposus 722.2
      cervical 722.0
      lumbar, lumbosacral 722.10
      thoracic, thoracolumbar 722.11
  endemic 265.0 *[357.4]*
  facial (nerve) 351.8
    newborn 767.5

Neuritis — *see also* Neuralgia — *continued*
  general — *see* Polyneuropathy
  geniculate ganglion 351.1
    due to herpes 053.11
  glossopharyngeal (nerve) 352.1
  gouty 274.89 *[357.4]*
  hypoglossal (nerve) 352.5
  ilioinguinal (nerve) 355.8
  in diseases classified elsewhere — *see* Polyneuropathy, in
  infectious (multiple) 357.0
  intercostal (nerve) 353.8
  interstitial hypertrophic progressive NEC 356.9
  leg 355.8
  lumbosacral NEC 724.4
  median (nerve) 354.1
    thenar 354.1
  multiple (acute) (infective) 356.9
    endemic 265.0 *[357.4]*
  multiplex endemica 265.0 *[357.4]*
  nerve root (*see also* Radiculitis) 729.2
  oculomotor (nerve) 378.52
  olfactory (nerve) 352.0
  optic (nerve) 377.30
    in myelitis 341.0
    meningococcal 036.81
  pelvic 355.8
  peripheral (nerve) (*see also* Neuropathy, peripheral)
    complicating pregnancy or puerperium 646.4 ☑
    specified nerve NEC — *see* Mononeuritis
  pneumogastric (nerve) 352.3
  postchickenpox 052.7
  postherpetic 053.19
  progressive hypertrophic interstitial NEC 356.9
  puerperal, postpartum 646.4 ☑
  radial (nerve) 723.4
  retrobulbar 377.32
    syphilitic 094.85
  rheumatic (chronic) 729.2
  sacral region 355.8
  sciatic (nerve) 724.3
    due to displacement of intervertebral disc 722.10
  serum 999.5
  specified nerve NEC — *see* Disorder, nerve
  spinal (nerve) 355.9
    root (*see also* Radiculitis) 729.2
  subscapular (nerve) 723.4
  suprascapular (nerve) 723.4
  syphilitic 095.8
  thenar (median) 354.1
  thoracic NEC 724.4
  toxic NEC 357.7
  trochlear (nerve) 378.53
  ulnar (nerve) 723.4
  vagus (nerve) 352.3
Neuroangiomatosis, encephalofacial 759.6
Neuroastrocytoma (M9505/1) — *see* Neoplasm, by site, uncertain behavior
Neuro-avitaminosis 269.2
Neuroblastoma (M9500/3)
  olfactory (M9522/3) 160.0
  specified site — *see* Neoplasm, by site, malignant
  unspecified site 194.0
Neurochorioretinitis — *see also* Chorioretinitis 363.20
Neurocirculatory asthenia 306.2
Neurocytoma (M9506/0) — *see* Neoplasm, by site, benign
Neurodermatitis (circumscribed) (circumscripta) (local) 698.3
  atopic 691.8
  diffuse (Brocq) 691.8
  disseminated 691.8
  nodulosa 698.3

- **Neuroencephalomyelopathy, optic** 341.0
- **Neuroendocrine tumor** — *see* Tumor, neuroendocrine
- **Neuroepithelioma** (M9503/3) — *see also* Neoplasm, by site, malignant
  - olfactory (M9521/3) 160.0
- **Neurofibroma** (M9540/0) — *see also* Neoplasm, connective tissue, benign
  - melanotic (M9541/0) — *see* Neoplasm, connective tissue, benign
  - multiple (M9540/1) 237.70
    - type 1 237.71
    - type 2 237.72
  - plexiform (M9550/0) — *see* Neoplasm, connective tissue, benign
- **Neurofibromatosis** (multiple) (M9540/1) 237.70
  - acoustic 237.72
  - malignant (M9540/3) — *see* Neoplasm, connective tissue, malignant
  - type 1 237.71
  - type 2 237.72
  - von Recklinghausen's 237.71
- **Neurofibrosarcoma** (M9540/3) — *see* Neoplasm, connective tissue, malignant
- **Neurogenic** — *see also* condition
  - bladder (atonic) (automatic) (autonomic) (flaccid) (hypertonic) (hypotonic) (inertia) (infranuclear) (irritable) (motor) (nonreflex) (nuclear) (paralysis) (reflex) (sensory) (spastic) (supranuclear) (uninhibited) 596.54
    - with cauda equina syndrome 344.61
  - bowel 564.81
  - heart 306.2
- **Neuroglioma (M9505/1)** — *see* Neoplasm, by site, uncertain behavior
- **Neurolabyrinthitis** (of Dix and Hallpike) 386.12
- **Neurolathyrism** 988.2
- **Neuroleprosy** 030.1
- **Neuroleptic malignant syndrome** 333.92
- **Neurolipomatosis** 272.8
- **Neuroma** (M9570/0) — *see also* Neoplasm, connective tissue, benign
  - acoustic (nerve) (M9560/0) 225.1
  - amputation (traumatic) (*see also* Injury, nerve, by site)
    - surgical complication (late) 997.61
  - appendix 211.3
  - auditory nerve 225.1
  - digital 355.6
    - toe 355.6
  - interdigital (toe) 355.6
  - intermetatarsal 355.6
  - Morton's 355.6
  - multiple 237.70
    - type 1 237.71
    - type 2 237.72
  - nonneoplastic 355.9
    - arm NEC 354.9
    - leg NEC 355.8
    - lower extremity NEC 355.8
    - specified site NEC — *see* Mononeuritis, by site
    - upper extremity NEC 354.9
  - optic (nerve) 225.1
  - plantar 355.6
  - plexiform (M9550/0) — *see* Neoplasm, connective tissue, benign
  - surgical (nonneoplastic) 355.9
    - arm NEC 354.9
    - leg NEC 355.8
    - lower extremity NEC 355.8
    - upper extremity NEC 354.9
  - traumatic (*see also* Injury, nerve, by site)
    - old — *see* Neuroma, nonneoplastic
- **Neuromyalgia** 729.1
- **Neuromyasthenia** (epidemic) 049.8
- **Neuromyelitis** 341.8
  - ascending 357.0
  - optica 341.0
- **Neuromyopathy** NEC 358.9
- **Neuromyositis** 729.1
- **Neuronevus** (M8725/0) — *see* Neoplasm, skin, benign
- **Neuronitis** 357.0
  - ascending (acute) 355.2
  - vestibular 386.12
- **Neuroparalytic** — *see* condition
- **Neuropathy, neuropathic** — *see also* Disorder, nerve 355.9
  - acute motor 357.82
  - alcoholic 357.5
    - with psychosis 291.1
  - arm NEC 354.9
  - ataxia and retinitis pigmentosa (NARP syndrome) 277.87
  - autonomic (peripheral) — *see* Neuropathy, peripheral, autonomic
  - axillary nerve 353.0
  - brachial plexus 353.0
  - cervical plexus 353.2
  - chronic
    - progressive segmentally demyelinating 357.89
    - relapsing demyelinating 357.89
  - congenital sensory 356.2
  - Déjérine-Sottas 356.0
  - diabetic 250.6 ☑ *[357.2]*
    - due to secondary diabetes 249.6 ☑ *[357.2]*
  - entrapment 355.9
    - iliohypogastric nerve 355.79
    - ilioinguinal nerve 355.79
    - lateral cutaneous nerve of thigh 355.1
    - median nerve 354.0
    - obturator nerve 355.79
    - peroneal nerve 355.3
    - posterior tibial nerve 355.5
    - saphenous nerve 355.79
    - ulnar nerve 354.2
  - facial nerve 351.9
  - hereditary 356.9
    - peripheral 356.0
    - sensory (radicular) 356.2
  - hypertrophic
    - Charcôt-Marie-Tooth 356.1
    - Déjérine-Sottas 356.0
    - interstitial 356.9
    - Refsum 356.3
  - intercostal nerve 354.8
  - ischemic — *see* Disorder, nerve
  - Jamaican (ginger) 357.7
  - leg NEC 355.8
  - lower extremity NEC 355.8
  - lumbar plexus 353.1
  - median nerve 354.1
  - motor
    - acute 357.82
  - multiple (acute) (chronic) (*see also* Polyneuropathy) 356.9
  - optic 377.39
    - ischemic 377.41
    - nutritional 377.33
    - toxic 377.34
  - peripheral (nerve) (*see also* Polyneuropathy) 356.9
    - arm NEC 354.9
    - autonomic 337.9
      - amyloid 277.39 *[337.1]*
      - idiopathic 337.00
      - in
        - amyloidosis 277.39 *[337.1]*
        - diabetes (mellitus) 250.6 ☑ *[337.1]*
          - due to secondary diabetes 249.6 ☑ *[337.1]*
        - diseases classified elsewhere 337.1
        - gout 274.89 *[337.1]*
        - hyperthyroidism 242.9 ☑ *[337.1]*
- **Neuropathy, neuropathic** — *see also* Disorder, nerve — *continued*
  - peripheral (*see also* Polyneuropathy) — *continued*
    - due to
      - antitetanus serum 357.6
      - arsenic 357.7
      - drugs 357.6
      - lead 357.7
      - organophosphate compounds 357.7
      - toxic agent NEC 357.7
    - hereditary 356.0
    - idiopathic 356.9
      - progressive 356.4
      - specified type NEC 356.8
    - in diseases classified elsewhere — *see* Polyneuropathy, in
    - leg NEC 355.8
    - lower extremity NEC 355.8
    - upper extremity NEC 354.9
  - plantar nerves 355.6
  - progressive hypertrophic interstitial 356.9
  - radicular NEC 729.2
    - brachial 723.4
    - cervical NEC 723.4
    - hereditary sensory 356.2
    - lumbar 724.4
    - lumbosacral 724.4
    - thoracic NEC 724.4
  - sacral plexus 353.1
  - sciatic 355.0
  - spinal nerve NEC 355.9
    - root (*see also* Radiculitis) 729.2
  - toxic 357.7
  - trigeminal sensory 350.8
  - ulnar nerve 354.2
  - upper extremity NEC 354.9
  - uremic 585.9 *[357.4]*
  - vitamin B_{12} 266.2 *[357.4]*
    - with anemia (pernicious) 281.0 *[357.4]*
      - due to dietary deficiency 281.1 *[357.4]*
- **Neurophthisis** — *see also* Disorder, nerve
  - diabetic 250.6 ☑ *[357.2]*
    - due to secondary diabetes 249.6 ☑ *[357.2]*
  - peripheral 356.9
- **Neuropraxia** — *see* Injury, nerve
- **Neuroretinitis** 363.05
  - syphilitic 094.85
- **Neurosarcoma** (M9540/3) — *see* Neoplasm, connective tissue, malignant
- **Neurosclerosis** — *see* Disorder, nerve
- **Neurosis, neurotic** 300.9
  - accident 300.16
  - anancastic, anankastic 300.3
  - anxiety (state) 300.00
    - generalized 300.02
    - panic type 300.01
  - asthenic 300.5
  - bladder 306.53
  - cardiac (reflex) 306.2
  - cardiovascular 306.2
  - climacteric, unspecified type 627.2
  - colon 306.4
  - compensation 300.16
  - compulsive, compulsion 300.3
  - conversion 300.11
  - craft 300.89
  - cutaneous 306.3
  - depersonalization 300.6
  - depressive (reaction) (type) 300.4
  - endocrine 306.6
  - environmental 300.89
  - fatigue 300.5
  - functional (*see also* Disorder, psychosomatic) 306.9
  - gastric 306.4
  - gastrointestinal 306.4
  - genitourinary 306.50
  - heart 306.2
- **Neurosis, neurotic** — *continued*
  - hypochondriacal 300.7
  - hysterical 300.10
    - conversion type 300.11
    - dissociative type 300.15
  - impulsive 300.3
  - incoordination 306.0
    - larynx 306.1
    - vocal cord 306.1
  - intestine 306.4
  - larynx 306.1
    - hysterical 300.11
    - sensory 306.1
  - menopause, unspecified type 627.2
  - mixed NEC 300.89
  - musculoskeletal 306.0
  - obsessional 300.3
    - phobia 300.3
  - obsessive-compulsive 300.3
  - occupational 300.89
  - ocular 306.7
  - oral 307.0
  - organ (*see also* Disorder, psychosomatic) 306.9
  - pharynx 306.1
  - phobic 300.20
  - posttraumatic (acute) (situational) 309.81
    - chronic 309.81
  - psychasthenic (type) 300.89
  - railroad 300.16
  - rectum 306.4
  - respiratory 306.1
  - rumination 306.4
  - senile 300.89
  - sexual 302.70
  - situational 300.89
  - specified type NEC 300.89
  - state 300.9
    - with depersonalization episode 300.6
  - stomach 306.4
  - vasomotor 306.2
  - visceral 306.4
  - war 300.16
- **Neurospongioblastosis diffusa** 759.5
- **Neurosyphilis** (arrested) (early) (inactive) (late) (latent) (recurrent) 094.9
  - with ataxia (cerebellar) (locomotor) (spastic) (spinal) 094.0
  - acute meningitis 094.2
  - aneurysm 094.89
  - arachnoid (adhesive) 094.2
  - arteritis (any artery) 094.89
  - asymptomatic 094.3
  - congenital 090.40
  - dura (mater) 094.89
  - general paresis 094.1
  - gumma 094.9
  - hemorrhagic 094.9
  - juvenile (asymptomatic) (meningeal) 090.40
  - leptomeninges (aseptic) 094.2
  - meningeal 094.2
  - meninges (adhesive) 094.2
  - meningovascular (diffuse) 094.2
  - optic atrophy 094.84
  - parenchymatous (degenerative) 094.1
  - paresis (*see also* Paresis, general) 094.1
  - paretic (*see also* Paresis, general) 094.1
  - relapse 094.9
  - remission in (sustained) 094.9
  - serological 094.3
  - specified nature or site NEC 094.89
  - tabes (dorsalis) 094.0
    - juvenile 090.40
  - tabetic 094.0
    - juvenile 090.40
  - taboparesis 094.1
    - juvenile 090.40
  - thrombosis 094.89
  - vascular 094.89
- **Neurotic** — *see also* Neurosis 300.9
  - excoriation 698.4

- **Neurotic** — *see also* Neurosis — *continued*
  - excoriation — *continued*
    - psychogenic 306.3
- **Neurotmesis** — *see* Injury, nerve, by site
- **Neurotoxemia** — *see* Toxemia
- **Neutro-occlusion** 524.21
- **Neutropenia, neutropenic** (idiopathic) (pernicious) (primary) 288.00
  - chronic 288.09
    - hypoplastic 288.09
  - congenital (nontransient) 288.01
  - cyclic 288.02
  - drug induced 288.03
  - due to infection 288.04
  - fever 288.00
  - genetic 288.01
  - immune 288.09
  - infantile 288.01
  - malignant 288.09
  - neonatal, transitory (isoimmune) (maternal transfer) 776.7
  - periodic 288.02
  - splenic 289.53
  - splenomegaly 289.53
  - toxic 288.09
- **Neutrophilia, hereditary giant** 288.2
- **Nevocarcinoma** (M8720/3) — *see* Melanoma
- **Nevus** (M8720/0) — *see also* Neoplasm, skin, benign

Note — Except where otherwise indicated, varieties of nevus in the list below that are followed by a morphology code number (M----/0) should be coded by site as for "Neoplasm, skin, benign."

  - acanthotic 702.8
  - achromic (M8730/0)
  - amelanotic (M8730/0)
  - anemic, anemicus 709.09
  - angiomatous (M9120/0) (*see also* Hemangioma) 228.00
  - araneus 448.1
  - avasculosus 709.09
  - balloon cell (M8722/0)
  - bathing trunk (M8761/1) 238.2
  - blue (M8780/0)
    - cellular (M8790/0)
    - giant (M8790/0)
    - Jadassohn's (M8780/0)
    - malignant (M8780/3) — *see* Melanoma
  - capillary (M9131/0) (*see also* Hemangioma) 228.00
  - cavernous (M9121/0) (*see also* Hemangioma) 228.00
  - cellular (M8720/0)
    - blue (M8790/0)
  - comedonicus 757.33
  - compound (M8760/0)
  - conjunctiva (M8720/0) 224.3
  - dermal (M8750/0)
    - and epidermal (M8760/0)
  - epithelioid cell (and spindle cell) (M8770/0)
  - flammeus 757.32
    - osteohypertrophic 759.89
  - hairy (M8720/0)
  - halo (M8723/0)
  - hemangiomatous (M9120/0) (*see also* Hemangioma) 228.00
  - intradermal (M8750/0)
  - intraepidermal (M8740/0)
  - involuting (M8724/0)
  - Jadassohn's (blue) (M8780/0)
  - junction, junctional (M8740/0)
    - malignant melanoma in (M8740/3) — *see* Melanoma
  - juvenile (M8770/0)
  - lymphatic (M9170/0) 228.1
  - magnocellular (M8726/0)
    - specified site — *see* Neoplasm, by site, benign
    - unspecified site 224.0
  - malignant (M8720/3) — *see* Melanoma
- **Nevus** — *see also* Neoplasm, skin, benign — *continued*
  - meaning hemangioma (M9120/0) (*see also* Hemangioma) 228.00
  - melanotic (pigmented) (M8720/0)
  - multiplex 759.5
  - nonneoplastic 448.1
  - nonpigmented (M8730/0)
  - nonvascular (M8720/0)
  - oral mucosa, white sponge 750.26
  - osteohypertrophic, flammeus 759.89
  - papillaris (M8720/0)
  - papillomatosus (M8720/0)
  - pigmented (M8720/0)
    - giant (M8761/1) (*see also* Neoplasm, skin, uncertain behavior)
      - malignant melanoma in (M8761/3) — *see* Melanoma
  - systematicus 757.33
  - pilosus (M8720/0)
  - port wine 757.32
  - sanguineous 757.32
  - sebaceous (senile) 702.8
  - senile 448.1
  - spider 448.1
  - spindle cell (and epithelioid cell) (M8770/0)
  - stellar 448.1
  - strawberry 757.32
  - syringocystadenomatous papilliferous (M8406/0)
  - unius lateris 757.33
  - Unna's 757.32
  - vascular 757.32
  - verrucous 757.33
  - white sponge (oral mucosa) 750.26
- **Newborn** (infant) (liveborn)
  - affected by
    - amniocentesis 760.61
    - maternal abuse of drugs (gestational) (via placenta) (via breast milk) (*see also* Noxious, substances transmitted through placenta or breast milk (affecting fetus or newborn)) 760.70
      - methamphetamine(s) 760.72
    - procedure
      - amniocentesis 760.61
      - in utero NEC 760.62
      - surgical on mother
        - during pregnancy NEC 760.63
        - previous not associated with pregnancy 760.64
  - apnea 770.81
    - obstructive 770.82
    - specified NEC 770.82
  - breast buds 779.89
  - cardiomyopathy 425.4
    - congenital 425.3
  - convulsion 779.0
  - electrolyte imbalance NEC (transitory) 775.5
  - fever (environmentally-induced) 778.4
  - gestation
    - 24 completed weeks 765.22
    - 25-26 completed weeks 765.23
    - 27-28 completed weeks 765.24
    - 29-30 completed weeks 765.25
    - 31-32 completed weeks 765.26
    - 33-34 completed weeks 765.27
    - 35-36 completed weeks 765.28
    - 37 or more completed weeks 765.29
    - less than 24 completed weeks 765.21
    - unspecified completed weeks 765.20
  - infection 771.89
    - candida 771.7
    - mastitis 771.5
    - specified NEC 771.89
    - urinary tract 771.82
- **Newborn** — *continued*
  - mastitis 771.5
  - multiple NEC
    - born in hospital (without mention of cesarean delivery or section) V37.00
      - with cesarean delivery or section V37.01
    - born outside hospital
      - hospitalized V37.1
      - not hospitalized V37.2
  - mates all liveborn
    - born in hospital (without mention of cesarean delivery or section) V34.00
      - with cesarean delivery or section V34.01
    - born outside hospital
      - hospitalized V34.1
      - not hospitalized V34.2
  - mates all stillborn
    - born in hospital (without mention of cesarean delivery or section) V35.00
      - with cesarean delivery or section V35.01
    - born outside hospital
      - hospitalized V35.1
      - not hospitalized V35.2
  - mates liveborn and stillborn
    - born in hospital (without mention of cesarean delivery or section) V36.00
      - with cesarean delivery or section V36.01
    - born outside hospital
      - hospitalized V36.1
      - not hospitalized V36.2
  - omphalitis 771.4
  - seizure 779.0
  - sepsis 771.81
  - single
    - born in hospital (without mention of cesarean delivery or section) V30.00
      - with cesarean delivery or section V30.01
    - born outside hospital
      - hospitalized V30.1
      - not hospitalized V30.2
  - specified condition NEC 779.89
  - twin NEC
    - born in hospital (without mention of cesarean delivery or section) V33.00
      - with cesarean delivery or section V33.01
    - born outside hospital
      - hospitalized V33.1
      - not hospitalized V33.2
  - mate liveborn
    - born in hospital V31.0 ☑
    - born outside hospital
      - hospitalized V31.1
      - not hospitalized V31.2
  - mate stillborn
    - born in hospital V32.0 ☑
    - born outside hospital
      - hospitalized V32.1
      - not hospitalized V32.2
  - unspecified as to single or multiple birth
    - born in hospital (without mention of cesarean delivery or section) V39.00
      - with cesarean delivery or section V39.01
    - born outside hospital
      - hospitalized V39.1
      - not hospitalized V39.2
- **Newcastle's conjunctivitis or disease** 077.8
- **Nezelof's syndrome** (pure alymphocytosis) 279.13
- **Niacin** (amide) **deficiency** 265.2
- **Nicolas-Durand-Favre disease** (climatic bubo) 099.1
- **Nicolas-Favre disease** (climatic bubo) 099.1
- **Nicotinic acid** (amide) **deficiency** 265.2
- **Niemann-Pick disease** (lipid histiocytosis) (splenomegaly) 272.7
- **Night**
  - blindness (*see also* Blindness, night) 368.60
    - congenital 368.61
    - vitamin A deficiency 264.5
  - cramps 729.82
  - sweats 780.8
  - terrors, child 307.46
- **Nightmare** 307.47
  - REM-sleep type 307.47
- **Nipple** — *see* condition
- **Nisbet's chancre** 099.0
- **Nishimoto (-Takeuchi) disease** 437.5
- **Nitritoid crisis or reaction** — *see* Crisis, nitritoid
- **Nitrogen retention, extrarenal** 788.99
- **Nitrosohemoglobinemia** 289.89
- **Njovera** 104.0
- **No**
  - diagnosis 799.9
  - disease (found) V71.9
  - room at the inn V65.0
- **Nocardiasis** — *see* Nocardiosis
- **Nocardiosis** 039.9
  - with pneumonia 039.1
  - lung 039.1
  - specified type NEC 039.8
- **Nocturia** 788.43
  - psychogenic 306.53
- **Nocturnal** — *see also* condition
  - dyspnea (paroxysmal) 786.09
  - emissions 608.89
  - enuresis 788.36
    - psychogenic 307.6
  - frequency (micturition) 788.43
    - psychogenic 306.53
- **Nodal rhythm disorder** 427.89
- **Nodding of head** 781.0
- **Node(s)** — *see also* Nodule(s)
  - Heberden's 715.04
  - larynx 478.79
  - lymph — *see* condition
  - milkers' 051.1
  - Osler's 421.0
  - rheumatic 729.89
  - Schmorl's 722.30
    - lumbar, lumbosacral 722.32
    - specified region NEC 722.39
    - thoracic, thoracolumbar 722.31
  - singers' 478.5
  - skin NEC 782.2
  - tuberculous — *see* Tuberculosis, lymph gland
  - vocal cords 478.5
- **Nodosities, Haygarth's** 715.04
- **Nodule(s), nodular**
  - actinomycotic (*see also* Actinomycosis) 039.9
  - arthritic — *see* Arthritis, nodosa
  - breast 793.89
  - cutaneous 782.2
  - Haygarth's 715.04
  - inflammatory — *see* Inflammation
  - juxta-articular 102.7
    - syphilitic 095.7
    - yaws 102.7
  - larynx 478.79
  - lung, solitary 518.89
    - emphysematous 492.8
  - milkers' 051.1
  - prostate 600.10
    - with
      - urinary
        - obstruction 600.11
        - retention 600.11
  - retrocardiac 785.9
  - rheumatic 729.89
  - rheumatoid — *see* Arthritis, rheumatoid

O

- **Oasthouse urine disease** 270.2
- **Obermeyer's relapsing fever** (European) 087.0
- **Obesity** (constitutional) (exogenous) (familial) (nutritional) (simple) 278.00
  - adrenal 255.8
  - complicating pregnancy, childbirth, or puerperium 649.1 ☑
  - due to hyperalimentation 278.00
  - endocrine NEC 259.9
  - endogenous 259.9
  - Fröhlich's (adiposogenital dystrophy) 253.8
  - glandular NEC 259.9
  - hypothyroid (*see also* Hypothyroidism) 244.9
  - morbid 278.01
  - of pregnancy 649.1 ☑
  - pituitary 253.8
  - severe 278.01
  - thyroid (*see also* Hypothyroidism) 244.9
- **Oblique** — *see also* condition
  - lie before labor, affecting fetus or newborn 761.7
- **Obliquity, pelvis** 738.6
- **Obliteration**
  - abdominal aorta 446.7
  - appendix (lumen) 543.9
  - artery 447.1
  - ascending aorta 446.7
  - bile ducts 576.8
    - with calculus, choledocholithiasis, or stones — *see* Choledocholithiasis
    - congenital 751.61
      - jaundice from 751.61 *[774.5]*
  - common duct 576.8
    - with calculus, choledocholithiasis, or stones — *see* Choledocholithiasis
    - congenital 751.61
  - cystic duct 575.8
    - with calculus, choledocholithiasis, or stones — *see* Choledocholithiasis
  - disease, arteriolar 447.1
  - endometrium 621.8
  - eye, anterior chamber 360.34
  - fallopian tube 628.2
  - lymphatic vessel 457.1
    - postmastectomy 457.0
  - organ or site, congenital NEC — *see* Atresia
  - placental blood vessels — *see* Placenta, abnormal
  - supra-aortic branches 446.7
  - ureter 593.89
  - urethra 599.84
  - vein 459.9
  - vestibule (oral) 525.8
- **Observation** (for) V71.9
  - without need for further medical care V71.9
  - accident NEC V71.4
    - at work V71.3
  - criminal assault V71.6
  - deleterious agent ingestion V71.89
  - disease V71.9
    - cardiovascular V71.7
    - heart V71.7
    - mental V71.09
    - specified condition NEC V71.89
  - foreign body ingestion V71.89
  - growth and development variations V21.8
  - injuries (accidental) V71.4
    - inflicted NEC V71.6
      - during alleged rape or seduction V71.5
  - malignant neoplasm, suspected V71.1
  - postpartum
    - immediately after delivery V24.0
    - routine follow-up V24.2

Observation — *continued*
  - pregnancy
    - high-risk V23.9
      - specified problem NEC V23.89
    - normal (without complication) V22.1
      - with nonobstetric complication V22.2
      - first V22.0
  - rape or seduction, alleged V71.5
    - injury during V71.5
  - suicide attempt, alleged V71.89
  - suspected (undiagnosed) (unproven)
    - abuse V71.81
    - cardiovascular disease V71.7
    - child or wife battering victim V71.6
    - concussion (cerebral) V71.6
    - condition NEC V71.89
      - infant — *see* Observation, suspected, condition, newborn
      - maternal and fetal
        - amniotic cavity and membrane problem V89.01
        - cervical shortening V89.05
        - fetal anomaly V89.03
        - fetal growth problem V89.04
        - oligohydramnios V89.01
        - other specified problem NEC V89.09
        - placental problem V89.02
        - polyhydramnios V89.01
      - newborn V29.9
        - cardiovascular disease V29.8
        - congenital anomaly V29.8
        - genetic V29.3
        - infectious V29.0
        - ingestion foreign object V29.8
        - injury V29.8
        - metabolic V29.3
        - neoplasm V29.8
        - neurological V29.1
        - poison, poisoning V29.8
        - respiratory V29.2
        - specified NEC V29.8
    - exposure
      - anthrax V71.82
      - biologic agent NEC V71.83
      - SARS V71.83
    - infectious disease not requiring isolation V71.89
    - malignant neoplasm V71.1
    - mental disorder V71.09
    - neglect V71.81
    - neoplasm
      - benign V71.89
      - malignant V71.1
    - specified condition NEC V71.89
    - tuberculosis V71.2
  - tuberculosis, suspected V71.2
- **Obsession, obsessional** 300.3
  - ideas and mental images 300.3
  - impulses 300.3
  - neurosis 300.3
  - phobia 300.3
  - psychasthenia 300.3
  - ruminations 300.3
  - state 300.3
  - syndrome 300.3
- **Obsessive-compulsive** 300.3
  - neurosis 300.3
  - personality 301.4
  - reaction 300.3
- **Obstetrical trauma** NEC (complicating delivery) 665.9 ☑
  - with
    - abortion — *see* Abortion, by type, with damage to pelvic organs
    - ectopic pregnancy (*see also* categories 633.0–633.9) 639.2
    - molar pregnancy (*see also* categories 630–632) 639.2
  - affecting fetus or newborn 763.89
  - following
    - abortion 639.2

Obstetrical trauma — *continued*
  - following — *continued*
    - ectopic or molar pregnancy 639.2
- **Obstipation** — *see also* Constipation 564.00
  - psychogenic 306.4
- **Obstruction, obstructed, obstructive**
  - airway NEC 519.8
    - with
      - allergic alveolitis NEC 495.9
      - asthma NEC (*see also* Asthma) 493.9 ☑
      - bronchiectasis 494.0
        - with acute exacerbation 494.1
      - bronchitis (chronic) (*see also* Bronchitis, with, obstruction) 491.20
      - emphysema NEC 492.8
    - chronic 496
      - with
        - allergic alveolitis NEC 495.5
        - asthma NEC (*see also* Asthma) 493.2 ☑
        - bronchiectasis 494.0
          - with acute exacerbation 494.1
        - bronchitis (chronic) (*see also* Bronchitis, with, obstruction) 491.20
        - emphysema NEC 492.8
    - due to
      - bronchospasm 519.11
      - foreign body 934.9
      - inhalation of fumes or vapors 506.9
      - laryngospasm 478.75
  - alimentary canal (*see also* Obstruction, intestine) 560.9
  - ampulla of Vater 576.2
    - with calculus, cholelithiasis, or stones — *see* Choledocholithiasis
  - aortic (heart) (valve) (*see also* Stenosis, aortic) 424.1
    - rheumatic (*see also* Stenosis, aortic, rheumatic) 395.0
  - aortoiliac 444.0
  - aqueduct of Sylvius 331.4
    - congenital 742.3
      - with spina bifida (*see also* Spina bifida) 741.0 ☑
  - Arnold-Chiari (*see also* Spina bifida) 741.0 ☑
  - artery (*see also* Embolism, artery) 444.9
    - basilar (complete) (partial) (*see also* Occlusion, artery, basilar) 433.0 ☑
    - carotid (complete) (partial) (*see also* Occlusion, artery, carotid) 433.1 ☑
    - precerebral — *see* Occlusion, artery, precerebral NEC
    - retinal (central) (*see also* Occlusion, retina) 362.30
    - vertebral (complete) (partial) (*see also* Occlusion, artery, vertebral) 433.2 ☑
  - asthma (chronic) (with obstructive pulmonary disease) 493.2 ☑
  - band (intestinal) 560.81
  - bile duct or passage (*see also* Obstruction, biliary) 576.2
    - congenital 751.61
      - jaundice from 751.61 *[774.5]*
  - biliary (duct) (tract) 576.2
    - with calculus 574.51
      - with cholecystitis (chronic) 574.41
        - acute 574.31
    - congenital 751.61
      - jaundice from 751.61 *[774.5]*
    - gallbladder 575.2
      - with calculus 574.21

Obstruction, obstructed, obstructive — *continued*
  - biliary — *continued*
    - gallbladder — *continued*
      - with calculus — *continued*
        - with cholecystitis (chronic) 574.11
          - acute 574.01
  - bladder neck (acquired) 596.0
    - congenital 753.6
  - bowel (*see also* Obstruction, intestine) 560.9
  - bronchus 519.19
  - canal, ear (*see also* Stricture, ear canal, acquired) 380.50
  - cardia 537.89
  - caval veins (inferior) (superior) 459.2
  - cecum (*see also* Obstruction, intestine) 560.9
  - circulatory 459.9
  - colon (*see also* Obstruction, intestine) 560.9
    - sympathicotonic 560.89
  - common duct (*see also* Obstruction, biliary) 576.2
    - congenital 751.61
  - coronary (artery) (heart) (*see also* Arteriosclerosis, coronary)
    - acute (*see also* Infarct, myocardium) 410.9 ☑
      - without myocardial infarction 411.81
  - cystic duct (*see also* Obstruction, gallbladder) 575.2
    - congenital 751.61
  - device, implant, or graft — *see* Complications, due to (presence of) any device, implant, or graft classified to 996.0–996.5 NEC
  - due to foreign body accidentally left in operation wound 998.4
  - duodenum 537.3
    - congenital 751.1
    - due to
      - compression NEC 537.3
      - cyst 537.3
      - intrinsic lesion or disease NEC 537.3
      - scarring 537.3
      - torsion 537.3
      - ulcer 532.91
      - volvulus 537.3
  - ejaculatory duct 608.89
  - endocardium 424.90
    - arteriosclerotic 424.99
    - specified cause, except rheumatic 424.99
  - esophagus 530.3
  - eustachian tube (complete) (partial) 381.60
    - cartilaginous
      - extrinsic 381.63
      - intrinsic 381.62
    - due to
      - cholesteatoma 381.61
      - osseous lesion NEC 381.61
      - polyp 381.61
    - osseous 381.61
  - fallopian tube (bilateral) 628.2
  - fecal 560.39
    - with hernia (*see also* Hernia, by site, with obstruction)
      - gangrenous — *see* Hernia, by site, with gangrene
  - foramen of Monro (congenital) 742.3
    - with spina bifida (*see also* Spina bifida) 741.0 ☑
  - foreign body — *see* Foreign body
  - gallbladder 575.2
    - with calculus, cholelithiasis, or stones 574.21
      - with cholecystitis (chronic) 574.11
        - acute 574.01
    - congenital 751.69
      - jaundice from 751.69 *[774.5]*

Obstruction, obstructed, obstructive — *continued*
- gastric outlet 537.0
- gastrointestinal (*see also* Obstruction, intestine) 560.9
- glottis 478.79
- hepatic 573.8
  - duct (*see also* Obstruction, biliary) 576.2
    - congenital 751.61
- icterus (*see also* Obstruction, biliary) 576.8
  - congenital 751.61
- ileocecal coil (*see also* Obstruction, intestine) 560.9
- ileum (*see also* Obstruction, intestine) 560.9
- iliofemoral (artery) 444.81
- internal anastomosis — *see* Complications, mechanical, graft
- intestine (mechanical) (neurogenic) (paroxysmal) (postinfectional) (reflex) 560.9
  - with
    - adhesions (intestinal) (peritoneal) 560.81
    - hernia (*see also* Hernia, by site, with obstruction)
      - gangrenous — *see* Hernia, by site, with gangrene
  - adynamic (*see also* Ileus) 560.1
  - by gallstone 560.31
  - congenital or infantile (small) 751.1
    - large 751.2
  - due to
    - Ascaris lumbricoides 127.0
    - mural thickening 560.89
    - procedure 997.4
      - involving urinary tract 997.5
  - impaction 560.39
  - infantile — *see* Obstruction, intestine, congenital
  - newborn
    - due to
      - fecaliths 777.1
      - inspissated milk 777.2
      - meconium (plug) 777.1
        - in mucoviscidosis 277.01
    - transitory 777.4
  - specified cause NEC 560.89
  - transitory, newborn 777.4
  - volvulus 560.2
- intracardiac ball valve prosthesis 996.02
- jaundice (*see also* Obstruction, biliary) 576.8
  - congenital 751.61
- jejunum (*see also* Obstruction, intestine) 560.9
- kidney 593.89
- labor 660.9 ☑
  - affecting fetus or newborn 763.1
  - by
    - bony pelvis (conditions classifiable to 653.0–653.9) 660.1 ☑
    - deep transverse arrest 660.3 ☑
    - impacted shoulder 660.4 ☑
    - locked twins 660.5 ☑
    - malposition (fetus) (conditions classifiable to 652.0–652.9) 660.0 ☑
      - head during labor 660.3 ☑
    - persistent occipitoposterior position 660.3 ☑
    - soft tissue, pelvic (conditions classifiable to 654.0–654.9) 660.2 ☑
- lacrimal
  - canaliculi 375.53
  - congenital 743.65
  - punctum 375.52
  - sac 375.54
- lacrimonasal duct 375.56
  - congenital 743.65
  - neonatal 375.55
- lacteal, with steatorrhea 579.2
- laryngitis (*see also* Laryngitis) 464.01
- larynx 478.79
  - congenital 748.3
- liver 573.8
  - cirrhotic (*see also* Cirrhosis, liver) 571.5
- lung 518.89
  - with
    - asthma — *see* Asthma
    - bronchitis (chronic) 491.20
    - emphysema NEC 492.8
  - airway, chronic 496
  - chronic NEC 496
    - with
      - asthma (chronic) (obstructive) 493.2 ☑
  - disease, chronic 496
    - with
      - asthma (chronic) (obstructive) 493.2 ☑
  - emphysematous 492.8
- lymphatic 457.1
- meconium
  - fetus or newborn 777.1
    - in mucoviscidosis 277.01
  - newborn due to fecaliths 777.1
- mediastinum 519.3
- mitral (rheumatic) — *see* Stenosis, mitral
- nasal 478.19
  - duct 375.56
    - neonatal 375.55
  - sinus — *see* Sinusitis
- nasolacrimal duct 375.56
  - congenital 743.65
  - neonatal 375.55
- nasopharynx 478.29
- nose 478.19
- organ or site, congenital NEC — *see* Atresia
- pancreatic duct 577.8
- parotid gland 527.8
- pelviureteral junction (*see also* Obstruction, ureter) 593.4
- pharynx 478.29
- portal (circulation) (vein) 452
- prostate 600.90
  - with
    - other lower urinary tract symptoms (LUTS) 600.91
    - urinary
      - obstruction 600.91
      - retention 600.91
  - valve (urinary) 596.0
- pulmonary
  - valve (heart) (*see also* Endocarditis, pulmonary) 424.3
  - vein, isolated 747.49
- pyemic — *see* Septicemia
- pylorus (acquired) 537.0
  - congenital 750.5
  - infantile 750.5
- rectosigmoid (*see also* Obstruction, intestine) 560.9
- rectum 569.49
- renal 593.89
- respiratory 519.8
  - chronic 496
- retinal (artery) (vein) (central) (*see also* Occlusion, retina) 362.30
- salivary duct (any) 527.8
  - with calculus 527.5
- sigmoid (*see also* Obstruction, intestine) 560.9
- sinus (accessory) (nasal) (*see also* Sinusitis) 473.9
- Stensen's duct 527.8
- stomach 537.89
  - acute 536.1
  - congenital 750.7
- submaxillary gland 527.8
  - with calculus 527.5
- thoracic duct 457.1
- thrombotic — *see* Thrombosis
- tooth eruption 520.6
- trachea 519.19
- tracheostomy airway 519.09
- tricuspid — *see* Endocarditis, tricuspid
- upper respiratory, congenital 748.8
- ureter (functional) 593.4
  - congenital 753.20
  - due to calculus 592.1
- ureteropelvic junction, congenital 753.21
- ureterovesical junction, congenital 753.22
- urethra 599.60
  - congenital 753.6
- urinary (moderate) 599.60
  - organ or tract (lower) 599.60
    - due to
      - benign prostatic hypertrophy (BPH) - see category 600
    - specified NEC 599.69
      - due to
        - benign prostatic hypertrophy (BPH) — see category 600
  - prostatic valve 596.0
- uropathy 599.60
- uterus 621.8
- vagina 623.2
- valvular — *see* Endocarditis
- vascular graft or shunt 996.1
  - atherosclerosis — *see* Arteriosclerosis, coronary
  - embolism 996.74
  - occlusion NEC 996.74
  - thrombus 996.74
- vein, venous 459.2
  - caval (inferior) (superior) 459.2
  - thrombotic — *see* Thrombosis
- vena cava (inferior) (superior) 459.2
- ventricular shunt 996.2
- vesical 596.0
- vesicourethral orifice 596.0
- vessel NEC 459.9

Obturator — *see* condition

Occlusal
- plane deviation 524.76
- wear, teeth 521.10

Occlusion
- anus 569.49
  - congenital 751.2
  - infantile 751.2
- aortoiliac (chronic) 444.0
- aqueduct of Sylvius 331.4
  - congenital 742.3
    - with spina bifida (*see also* Spina bifida) 741.0 ☑
- arteries of extremities, lower 444.22
  - without thrombus or embolus (*see also* Arteriosclerosis, extremities) 440.20
  - due to stricture or stenosis 447.1
  - upper 444.21
    - without thrombus or embolus (*see also* Arteriosclerosis, extremities) 440.20
    - due to stricture or stenosis 447.1
- artery NEC (*see also* Embolism, artery) 444.9
  - auditory, internal 433.8 ☑
  - basilar 433.0 ☑
    - with other precerebral artery 433.3 ☑
    - bilateral 433.3 ☑
  - brain or cerebral (*see also* Infarct, brain) 434.9 ☑
  - carotid 433.1 ☑
    - with other precerebral artery 433.3 ☑
    - bilateral 433.3 ☑

Occlusion — *continued*
- artery (*see also* Embolism, artery) — *continued*
  - cerebellar (anterior inferior) (posterior inferior) (superior) 433.8 ☑
  - cerebral (*see also* Infarct, brain) 434.9 ☑
  - choroidal (anterior) 433.8 ☑
  - chronic total
    - coronary 414.2
    - extremity(ies) 440.4
  - communicating posterior 433.8 ☑
  - complete
    - coronary 414.2
    - extremity(ies) 440.4
  - coronary (thrombotic) (*see also* Infarct, myocardium) 410.9 ☑
    - acute 410.9 ☑
      - without myocardial infarction 411.81
    - chronic total 414.2
    - complete 414.2
    - healed or old 412
    - total 414.2
  - extremity(ies)
    - chronic total 440.4
    - complete 440.4
    - total 440.4
  - hypophyseal 433.8 ☑
  - iliac (artery) 444.81
  - mesenteric (embolic) (thrombotic) (with gangrene) 557.0
  - pontine 433.8 ☑
  - precerebral NEC 433.9 ☑
    - late effect — *see* Late effect(s) (of) cerebrovascular disease
    - multiple or bilateral 433.3 ☑
    - puerperal, postpartum, childbirth 674.0 ☑
    - specified NEC 433.8 ☑
  - renal 593.81
  - retinal — *see* Occlusion, retina, artery
  - spinal 433.8 ☑
  - vertebral 433.2 ☑
    - with other precerebral artery 433.3 ☑
    - bilateral 433.3 ☑
- basilar (artery) — *see* Occlusion, artery, basilar
- bile duct (any) (*see also* Obstruction, biliary) 576.2
- bowel (*see also* Obstruction, intestine) 560.9
- brain (artery) (vascular) (*see also* Infarct, brain) 434.9 ☑
- breast (duct) 611.89
- carotid (artery) (common) (internal) — *see* Occlusion, artery, carotid
- cerebellar (anterior inferior) (artery) (posterior inferior) (superior) 433.8 ☑
- cerebral (artery) (*see also* Infarct, brain) 434.9 ☑
- cerebrovascular (*see also* Infarct, brain) 434.9 ☑
  - diffuse 437.0
- cervical canal (*see also* Stricture, cervix) 622.4
  - by falciparum malaria 084.0
- cervix (uteri) (*see also* Stricture, cervix) 622.4
- choanal 748.0
- choroidal (artery) 433.8 ☑
- colon (*see also* Obstruction, intestine) 560.9
- communicating posterior artery 433.8 ☑
- coronary (artery) (thrombotic) (*see also* Infarct, myocardium) 410.9 ☑
  - without myocardial infarction 411.81
  - acute 410.9 ☑

- **Operculum, retina** — *continued*
  - with detachment 361.01
- **Ophiasis** 704.01
- **Ophthalmia** — *see also* Conjunctivitis 372.30
  - actinic rays 370.24
  - allergic (acute) 372.05
    - chronic 372.14
  - blennorrhagic (neonatorum) 098.40
  - catarrhal 372.03
  - diphtheritic 032.81
  - Egyptian 076.1
  - electric, electrica 370.24
  - gonococcal (neonatorum) 098.40
  - metastatic 360.11
  - migraine 346.8 ☑
  - neonatorum, newborn 771.6
    - gonococcal 098.40
  - nodosa 360.14
  - phlyctenular 370.31
    - with ulcer (*see also* Ulcer, cornea) 370.00
  - sympathetic 360.11
- **Ophthalmitis** — *see* Ophthalmia
- **Ophthalmocele** (congenital) 743.66
- **Ophthalmoneuromyelitis** 341.0
- **Ophthalmopathy, infiltrative with thyrotoxicosis** 242.0 ☑
- **Ophthalmoplegia** — *see also* Strabismus 378.9
  - anterior internuclear 378.86
  - ataxia-areflexia syndrome 357.0
  - bilateral 378.9
  - diabetic 250.5 ☑ *[378.86]*
    - due to secondary diabetes 249.5 ☑ *[378.86]*
  - exophthalmic 242.0 ☑ *[376.22]*
  - external 378.55
    - progressive 378.72
    - total 378.56
  - internal (complete) (total) 367.52
  - internuclear 378.86
  - migraine 346.2 ☑
  - painful 378.55
  - Parinaud's 378.81
  - progressive external 378.72
  - supranuclear, progressive 333.0
  - total (external) 378.56
    - internal 367.52
  - unilateral 378.9
- **Opisthognathism** 524.00
- **Opisthorchiasis** (felineus) (tenuicollis) (viverrini) 121.0
- **Opisthotonos, opisthotonus** 781.0
- **Opitz's disease** (congestive splenomegaly) 289.51
- **Opiumism** — *see also* Dependence 304.0 ☑
- **Oppenheim's disease** 358.8
- **Oppenheim-Urbach disease or syndrome** (necrobiosis lipoidica diabeticorum) 250.8 ☑ *[709.3]*
  - due to secondary diabetes 249.8 ☑ *[709.3]*
- **Opsoclonia** 379.59
- **Optic nerve** — *see* condition
- **Orbit** — *see* condition
- **Orchioblastoma** (M9071/3) 186.9
- **Orchitis** (nonspecific) (septic) 604.90
  - with abscess 604.0
  - blennorrhagic (acute) 098.13
    - chronic or duration of 2 months or over 098.33
  - diphtheritic 032.89 *[604.91]*
  - filarial 125.9 *[604.91]*
  - gangrenous 604.99
  - gonococcal (acute) 098.13
    - chronic or duration of 2 months or over 098.33
  - mumps 072.0
  - parotidea 072.0
  - suppurative 604.99
  - syphilitic 095.8 *[604.91]*
  - tuberculous (*see also* Tuberculosis) 016.5 ☑ *[608.81]*
- **Orf** 051.2
- **Organic** — *see also* condition
  - heart — *see* Disease, heart
  - insufficiency 799.89
- **Oriental**
  - bilharziasis 120.2
  - schistosomiasis 120.2
  - sore 085.1
- **Orientation**
  - ego-dystonic sexual 302.0
- **Orifice** — *see* condition
- **Origin, both great vessels from right ventricle** 745.11
- **Ormond's disease or syndrome** 593.4
- **Ornithosis** 073.9
  - with
    - complication 073.8
      - specified NEC 073.7
    - pneumonia 073.0
    - pneumonitis (lobular) 073.0
- **Orodigitofacial dysostosis** 759.89
- **Oropouche fever** 066.3
- **Orotaciduria, oroticaciduria** (congenital) (hereditary) (pyrimidine deficiency) 281.4
- **Oroya fever** 088.0
- **Orthodontics** V58.5
  - adjustment V53.4
  - aftercare V58.5
  - fitting V53.4
- **Orthopnea** 786.02
- **Orthoptic training** V57.4
- **Osgood-Schlatter**
  - disease 732.4
  - osteochondrosis 732.4
- **Osler's**
  - disease (M9950/1) (polycythemia vera) 238.4
  - nodes 421.0
- **Osler-Rendu disease** (familial hemorrhagic telangiectasia) 448.0
- **Osler-Vaquez disease** (M9950/1) (polycythemia vera) 238.4
- **Osler-Weber-Rendu syndrome** (familial hemorrhagic telangiectasia) 448.0
- **Osmidrosis** 705.89
- **Osseous** — *see* condition
- **Ossification**
  - artery — *see* Arteriosclerosis
  - auricle (ear) 380.39
  - bronchus 519.19
  - cardiac (*see also* Degeneration, myocardial) 429.1
  - cartilage (senile) 733.99
  - coronary (artery) — *see* Arteriosclerosis, coronary
  - diaphragm 728.10
  - ear 380.39
    - middle (*see also* Otosclerosis) 387.9
  - falx cerebri 349.2
  - fascia 728.10
  - fontanel
    - defective or delayed 756.0
    - premature 756.0
  - heart (*see also* Degeneration, myocardial) 429.1
    - valve — *see* Endocarditis
  - larynx 478.79
  - ligament
    - posterior longitudinal 724.8
      - cervical 723.7
  - meninges (cerebral) 349.2
    - spinal 336.8
  - multiple, eccentric centers 733.99
  - muscle 728.10
    - heterotopic, postoperative 728.13
  - myocardium, myocardial (*see also* Degeneration, myocardial) 429.1
  - penis 607.81
  - periarticular 728.89
  - sclera 379.16
  - tendon 727.82
  - trachea 519.19
  - tympanic membrane (*see also* Tympanosclerosis) 385.00
  - vitreous (humor) 360.44
- **Osteitis** — *see also* Osteomyelitis 730.2 ☑
  - acute 730.0 ☑
  - alveolar 526.5
  - chronic 730.1 ☑
  - condensans (ilii) 733.5
  - deformans (Paget's) 731.0
    - due to or associated with malignant neoplasm (*see also* Neoplasm, bone, malignant) 170.9 *[731.1]*
  - due to yaws 102.6
  - fibrosa NEC 733.29
    - cystica (generalisata) 252.01
    - disseminata 756.59
    - osteoplastica 252.01
  - fragilitans 756.51
  - Garré's (sclerosing) 730.1 ☑
  - infectious (acute) (subacute) 730.0 ☑
    - chronic or old 730.1 ☑
  - jaw (acute) (chronic) (lower) (neonatal) (suppurative) (upper) 526.4
  - parathyroid 252.01
  - petrous bone (*see also* Petrositis) 383.20
  - pubis 733.5
  - sclerotic, nonsuppurative 730.1 ☑
  - syphilitic 095.5
  - tuberculosa
    - cystica (of Jüngling) 135
    - multiplex cystoides 135
- **Osteoarthritica spondylitis** (spine) — *see also* Spondylosis 721.90
- **Osteoarthritis** — *see also* Osteoarthrosis 715.9 ☑
  - distal interphalangeal 715.9 ☑
  - hyperplastic 731.2
  - interspinalis (*see also* Spondylosis) 721.90
  - spine, spinal NEC (*see also* Spondylosis) 721.90
- **Osteoarthropathy** — *see also* Osteoarthrosis 715.9 ☑
  - chronic idiopathic hypertrophic 757.39
  - familial idiopathic 757.39
  - hypertrophic pulmonary 731.2
    - secondary 731.2
  - idiopathic hypertrophic 757.39
  - primary hypertrophic 731.2
  - pulmonary hypertrophic 731.2
  - secondary hypertrophic 731.2
- **Osteoarthrosis** (degenerative) (hypertrophic) (rheumatoid) 715.9 ☑

> *Note — Use the following fifth-digit subclassification with category 715:*
>
> | | |
> |---|---|
> | 0 | *site unspecified* |
> | 1 | *shoulder region* |
> | 2 | *upper arm* |
> | 3 | *forearm* |
> | 4 | *hand* |
> | 5 | *pelvic region and thigh* |
> | 6 | *lower leg* |
> | 7 | *ankle and foot* |
> | 8 | *other specified sites except spine* |
> | 9 | *multiple sites* |

  - Deformans alkaptonurica 270.2
  - generalized 715.09
  - juvenilis (Köhler's) 732.5
  - localized 715.3 ☑
    - idiopathic 715.1 ☑
    - primary 715.1 ☑
    - secondary 715.2 ☑
  - multiple sites, not specified as generalized 715.89
  - polyarticular 715.09
  - spine (*see also* Spondylosis) 721.90
  - temporomandibular joint 524.69
- **Osteoblastoma** (M9200/0) — *see* Neoplasm, bone, benign
- **Osteochondritis** — *see also* Osteochondrosis 732.9
  - dissecans 732.7
    - hip 732.7
  - ischiopubica 732.1
  - multiple 756.59
  - syphilitic (congenital) 090.0
- **Osteochondrodermodysplasia** 756.59
- **Osteochondrodystrophy** 277.5
  - deformans 277.5
  - familial 277.5
  - fetalis 756.4
- **Osteochondrolysis** 732.7
- **Osteochondroma** (M9210/0) — *see also* Neoplasm, bone, benign
  - multiple, congenital 756.4
- **Osteochondromatosis** (M9210/1) 238.0
  - synovial 727.82
- **Osteochondromyxosarcoma** (M9180/3) — *see* Neoplasm, bone, malignant
- **Osteochondropathy** NEC 732.9
- **Osteochondrosarcoma** (M9180/3) — *see* Neoplasm, bone, malignant
- **Osteochondrosis** 732.9
  - acetabulum 732.1
  - adult spine 732.8
  - astragalus 732.5
  - Blount's 732.4
  - Buchanan's (juvenile osteochondrosis of iliac crest) 732.1
  - Buchman's (juvenile osteochondrosis) 732.1
  - Burns' 732.3
  - calcaneus 732.5
  - capitular epiphysis (femur) 732.1
  - carpal
    - lunate (wrist) 732.3
    - scaphoid 732.3
  - coxae juvenilis 732.1
  - deformans juvenilis (coxae) (hip) 732.1
    - Scheuermann's 732.0
    - spine 732.0
    - tibia 732.4
    - vertebra 732.0
  - Diaz's (astragalus) 732.5
  - dissecans (knee) (shoulder) 732.7
  - femoral capital epiphysis 732.1
  - femur (head) (juvenile) 732.1
  - foot (juvenile) 732.5
  - Freiberg's (disease) (second metatarsal) 732.5
  - Haas' 732.3
  - Haglund's (os tibiale externum) 732.5
  - hand (juvenile) 732.3
  - head of
    - femur 732.1
    - humerus (juvenile) 732.3
  - hip (juvenile) 732.1
  - humerus (juvenile) 732.3
  - iliac crest (juvenile) 732.1
  - ilium (juvenile) 732.1
  - ischiopubic synchondrosis 732.1
  - Iselin's (osteochondrosis fifth metatarsal) 732.5
  - juvenile, juvenilis 732.6
    - arm 732.3
    - capital femoral epiphysis 732.1
    - capitellum humeri 732.3
    - capitular epiphysis 732.1
    - carpal scaphoid 732.3
    - clavicle, sternal epiphysis 732.6
    - coxae 732.1
    - deformans 732.1
    - foot 732.5
    - hand 732.3
    - hip and pelvis 732.1
    - lower extremity, except foot 732.4
    - lunate, wrist 732.3
    - medial cuneiform bone 732.5
    - metatarsal (head) 732.5
    - metatarsophalangeal 732.5
    - navicular, ankle 732.5
    - patella 732.4
    - primary patellar center (of Köhler) 732.4
    - specified site NEC 732.6

- **Osteochondrosis** — *continued*
  - juvenile, juvenilis — *continued*
    - spine 732.0
    - tarsal scaphoid 732.5
    - tibia (epiphysis) (tuberosity) 732.4
    - upper extremity 732.3
    - vertebra (body) (Calvé) 732.0
      - epiphyseal plates (of Scheuermann) 732.0
  - Kienböck's (disease) 732.3
  - Köhler's (disease) (navicular, ankle) 732.5
    - patellar 732.4
    - tarsal navicular 732.5
  - Legg-Calvé-Perthes (disease) 732.1
  - lower extremity (juvenile) 732.4
  - lunate bone 732.3
  - Mauclaire's 732.3
  - metacarpal heads (of Mauclaire) 732.3
  - metatarsal (fifth) (head) (second) 732.5
  - navicular, ankle 732.5
  - os calcis 732.5
  - Osgood-Schlatter 732.4
  - os tibiale externum 732.5
  - Panner's 732.3
  - patella (juvenile) 732.4
  - patellar center
    - primary (of Köhler) 732.4
    - secondary (of Sinding-Larsen) 732.4
  - pelvis (juvenile) 732.1
  - Pierson's 732.1
  - radial head (juvenile) 732.3
  - Scheuermann's 732.0
  - Sever's (calcaneum) 732.5
  - Sinding-Larsen (secondary patellar center) 732.4
  - spine (juvenile) 732.0
    - adult 732.8
  - symphysis pubis (of Pierson) (juvenile) 732.1
  - syphilitic (congenital) 090.0
  - tarsal (navicular) (scaphoid) 732.5
  - tibia (proximal) (tubercle) 732.4
  - tuberculous — *see* Tuberculosis, bone
  - ulna 732.3
  - upper extremity (juvenile) 732.3
  - van Neck's (juvenile osteochondrosis) 732.1
  - vertebral (juvenile) 732.0
    - adult 732.8
- **Osteoclastoma** (M9250/1) 238.0
  - malignant (M9250/3) — *see* Neoplasm, bone, malignant
- **Osteocopic pain** 733.90
- **Osteodynia** 733.90
- **Osteodystrophy**
  - azotemic 588.0
  - chronica deformans hypertrophica 731.0
  - congenital 756.50
    - specified type NEC 756.59
  - deformans 731.0
  - fibrosa localisata 731.0
  - parathyroid 252.01
  - renal 588.0
- **Osteofibroma** (M9262/0) — *see* Neoplasm, bone, benign
- **Osteofibrosarcoma** (M9182/3) — *see* Neoplasm, bone, malignant
- **Osteogenesis imperfecta** 756.51
- **Osteogenic** — *see* condition
- **Osteoma** (M9180/0) — *see also* Neoplasm, bone, benign
  - osteoid (M9191/0) (*see also* Neoplasm, bone, benign)
    - giant (M9200/0) — *see* Neoplasm, bone, benign
- **Osteomalacia** 268.2
  - chronica deformans hypertrophica 731.0
  - due to vitamin D deficiency 268.2
  - infantile (*see also* Rickets) 268.0
  - juvenile (*see also* Rickets) 268.0
  - pelvis 268.2
  - vitamin D-resistant 275.3
- **Osteomalacic bone** 268.2
- **Osteomalacosis** 268.2
- **Osteomyelitis** (general) (infective) (localized) (neonatal) (purulent) (pyogenic) (septic) (staphylococcal) (streptococcal) (suppurative) (with periostitis) 730.2 ☑

> *Note — Use the following fifth-digit subclassification with category 730:*
>
> *0 site unspecified*
> *1 shoulder region*
> *2 upper arm*
> *3 forearm*
> *4 hand*
> *5 pelvic region and thigh*
> *6 lower leg*
> *7 ankle and foot*
> *8 other specified sites*
> *9 multiple sites*

  - acute or subacute 730.0 ☑
  - chronic or old 730.1 ☑
  - due to or associated with
    - diabetes mellitus 250.8 ☑ *[731.8]*
      - due to secondary diabetes 249.8 ☑ *[731.8]*
    - tuberculosis (*see also* Tuberculosis, bone) 015.9 ☑ *[730.8]* ☑
      - limb bones 015.5 ☑ *[730.8]* ☑
      - specified bones NEC 015.7 ☑ *[730.8]* ☑
      - spine 015.0 ☑ *[730.8]* ☑
    - typhoid 002.0 *[730.8]* ☑
  - Garré's 730.1 ☑
  - jaw (acute) (chronic) (lower) (neonatal) (suppurative) (upper) 526.4
  - nonsuppurating 730.1 ☑
  - orbital 376.03
  - petrous bone (*see also* Petrositis) 383.20
  - Salmonella 003.24
  - sclerosing, nonsuppurative 730.1 ☑
  - sicca 730.1 ☑
  - syphilitic 095.5
    - congenital 090.0 *[730.8]* ☑
  - tuberculous — *see* Tuberculosis, bone
  - typhoid 002.0 *[730.8]* ☑
- **Osteomyelofibrosis** 289.89
- **Osteomyelosclerosis** 289.89
- **Osteonecrosis** 733.40
  - meaning osteomyelitis 730.1 ☑
- **Osteo-onycho-arthro dysplasia** 756.89
- **Osteo-onychodysplasia, hereditary** 756.89
- **Osteopathia**
  - condensans disseminata 756.53
  - hyperostotica multiplex infantilis 756.59
  - hypertrophica toxica 731.2
  - striata 756.4
- **Osteopathy resulting from poliomyelitis** — *see also* Poliomyelitis 045.9 ☑ *[730.7]* ☑
  - familial dysplastic 731.2
- **Osteopecilia** 756.53
- **Osteopenia** 733.90
  - borderline 733.90
- **Osteoperiostitis** — *see also* Osteomyelitis 730.2 ☑
  - ossificans toxica 731.2
  - toxica ossificans 731.2
- **Osteopetrosis** (familial) 756.52
- **Osteophyte** — *see* Exostosis
- **Osteophytosis** — *see* Exostosis
- **Osteopoikilosis** 756.53
- **Osteoporosis** (generalized) 733.00
  - circumscripta 731.0
  - disuse 733.03
  - drug-induced 733.09
  - idiopathic 733.02
  - postmenopausal 733.01
  - posttraumatic 733.7
  - screening V82.81
  - senile 733.01
  - specified type NEC 733.09
- **Osteoporosis-osteomalacia syndrome** 268.2
- **Osteopsathyrosis** 756.51
- **Osteoradionecrosis, jaw** 526.89
- **Osteosarcoma** (M9180/3) — *see also* Neoplasm, bone, malignant
  - chondroblastic (M9181/3) — *see* Neoplasm, bone, malignant
  - fibroblastic (M9182/3) — *see* Neoplasm, bone, malignant
  - in Paget's disease of bone (M9184/3) — *see* Neoplasm, bone, malignant
  - juxtacortical (M9190/3) — *see* Neoplasm, bone, malignant
  - parosteal (M9190/3) — *see* Neoplasm, bone, malignant
  - telangiectatic (M9183/3) — *see* Neoplasm, bone, malignant
- **Osteosclerosis** 756.52
  - fragilis (generalisata) 756.52
- **Osteosclerotic anemia** 289.89
- **Osteosis**
  - acromegaloid 757.39
  - cutis 709.3
  - parathyroid 252.01
  - renal fibrocystic 588.0
- **Österreicher-Turner syndrome** 756.89
- **Ostium**
  - atrioventriculare commune 745.69
  - primum (arteriosum) (defect) (persistent) 745.61
  - secundum (arteriosum) (defect) (patent) (persistent) 745.5
- **Ostrum-Furst syndrome** 756.59
- **Os, uterus** — *see* condition
- **Otalgia** 388.70
  - otogenic 388.71
  - referred 388.72
- **Othematoma** 380.31
- **Otitic hydrocephalus** 348.2
- **Otitis** 382.9
  - with effusion 381.4
    - purulent 382.4
    - secretory 381.4
    - serous 381.4
    - suppurative 382.4
  - acute 382.9
  - adhesive (*see also* Adhesions, middle ear) 385.10
  - chronic 382.9
    - with effusion 381.3
    - mucoid, mucous (simple) 381.20
    - purulent 382.3
    - secretory 381.3
    - serous 381.10
    - suppurative 382.3
  - diffuse parasitic 136.8
  - externa (acute) (diffuse) (hemorrhagica) 380.10
    - actinic 380.22
    - candidal 112.82
    - chemical 380.22
    - chronic 380.23
      - mycotic — *see* Otitis, externa, mycotic
      - specified type NEC 380.23
    - circumscribed 380.10
    - contact 380.22
    - due to
      - erysipelas 035 *[380.13]*
      - impetigo 684 *[380.13]*
      - seborrheic dermatitis 690.10 *[380.13]*
    - eczematoid 380.22
    - furuncular 680.0 *[380.13]*
    - infective 380.10
      - chronic 380.16
    - malignant 380.14
    - mycotic (chronic) 380.15
- **Otitis** — *continued*
  - externa — *continued*
    - mycotic — *continued*
      - due to
        - aspergillosis 117.3 *[380.15]*
        - moniliasis 112.82
        - otomycosis 111.8 *[380.15]*
    - reactive 380.22
    - specified type NEC 380.22
    - tropical 111.8 *[380.15]*
  - insidiosa (*see also* Otosclerosis) 387.9
  - interna (*see also* Labyrinthitis) 386.30
  - media (hemorrhagic) (staphylococcal) (streptococcal) 382.9
    - acute 382.9
      - with effusion 381.00
      - allergic 381.04
        - mucoid 381.05
        - sanguineous 381.06
        - serous 381.04
      - catarrhal 381.00
      - exudative 381.00
      - mucoid 381.02
        - allergic 381.05
      - necrotizing 382.00
        - with spontaneous rupture of ear drum 382.01
        - in
          - influenza 487.8 *[382.02]*
          - measles 055.2
          - scarlet fever 034.1 *[382.02]*
      - nonsuppurative 381.00
      - purulent 382.00
        - with spontaneous rupture of ear drum 382.01
      - sanguineous 381.03
        - allergic 381.06
      - secretory 381.01
      - seromucinous 381.02
      - serous 381.01
        - allergic 381.04
      - suppurative 382.00
        - with spontaneous rupture of ear drum 382.01
        - due to
          - influenza 487.8 *[382.02]*
          - scarlet fever 034.1 *[382.02]*
      - transudative 381.00
    - adhesive (*see also* Adhesions, middle ear) 385.10
    - allergic 381.4
      - acute 381.04
        - mucoid 381.05
        - sanguineous 381.06
        - serous 381.04
      - chronic 381.3
    - catarrhal 381.4
      - acute 381.00
      - chronic (simple) 381.10
    - chronic 382.9
      - with effusion 381.3
      - adhesive (*see also* Adhesions, middle ear) 385.10
      - allergic 381.3
      - atticoantral, suppurative (with posterior or superior marginal perforation of ear drum) 382.2
      - benign suppurative (with anterior perforation of ear drum) 382.1
      - catarrhal 381.10
      - exudative 381.3
      - mucinous 381.20
      - mucoid, mucous (simple) 381.20
      - mucosanguineous 381.29
      - nonsuppurative 381.3
      - purulent 382.3
      - secretory 381.3
      - seromucinous 381.3
      - serosanguineous 381.19
      - serous (simple) 381.10
      - suppurative 382.3

P

Note — Except where otherwise indicated, the morphological varieties of papilloma in the list below should be coded by site as for "Neoplasm, benign."

Paralysis, paralytic — *continued*
arm 344.40
affecting
dominant side 344.41
nondominant side 344.42
both 344.2
hysterical 300.11
late effect — *see* Late effect(s) (of) cerebrovascular disease
psychogenic 306.0
transient 781.4
traumatic NEC (*see also* Injury, nerve, upper limb) 955.9
arteriosclerotic (current episode) 437.0
late effect — *see* Late effect(s) (of) cerebrovascular disease
ascending (spinal), acute 357.0
associated, nuclear 344.89
asthenic bulbar 358.00
ataxic NEC 334.9
general 094.1
athetoid 333.71
atrophic 356.9
infantile, acute (*see also* Poliomyelitis, with paralysis) 045.1 ☑
muscle NEC 355.9
progressive 335.21
spinal (acute) (*see also* Poliomyelitis, with paralysis) 045.1 ☑
attack (*see also* Disease, cerebrovascular, acute) 436
axillary 353.0
Babinski-Nageotte's 344.89
Bell's 351.0
newborn 767.5
Benedikt's 344.89
birth (injury) 767.7
brain 767.0
intracranial 767.0
spinal cord 767.4
bladder (sphincter) 596.53
neurogenic 596.54
with cauda equina syndrome 344.61
puerperal, postpartum, childbirth 665.5 ☑
sensory 596.54
with cauda equina 344.61
spastic 596.54
with cauda equina 344.61
bowel, colon, or intestine (*see also* Ileus) 560.1
brachial plexus 353.0
due to birth injury 767.6
newborn 767.6
brain
congenital — *see* Palsy, cerebral
current episode 437.8
diplegia 344.2
hemiplegia 342.9 ☑
late effect — *see* Late effect(s) (of) cerebrovascular disease
infantile — *see* Palsy, cerebral
late effect — *see* Late effect(s) (of) cerebrovascular disease
monoplegia (*see also* Monoplegia)
late effect — *see* Late effect(s) (of) cerebrovascular disease
paraplegia 344.1
quadriplegia — *see* Quadriplegia
syphilitic, congenital 090.49
triplegia 344.89
bronchi 519.19
Brown-Séquard's 344.89
bulbar (chronic) (progressive) 335.22
infantile (*see also* Poliomyelitis, bulbar) 045.0 ☑
poliomyelitic (*see also* Poliomyelitis, bulbar) 045.0 ☑
pseudo 335.23
supranuclear 344.89
bulbospinal 358.00
cardiac (*see also* Failure, heart) 428.9

Paralysis, paralytic — *continued*
cerebral
current episode 437.8
spastic, infantile — *see* Palsy, cerebral
cerebrocerebellar 437.8
diplegic infantile 343.0
cervical
plexus 353.2
sympathetic NEC 337.09
Céstan-Chenais 344.89
Charcôt-Marie-Tooth type 356.1
childhood — *see* Palsy, cerebral
Clark's 343.9
colon (*see also* Ileus) 560.1
compressed air 993.3
compression
arm NEC 354.9
cerebral — *see* Paralysis, brain
leg NEC 355.8
lower extremity NEC 355.8
upper extremity NEC 354.9
congenital (cerebral) (spastic) (spinal) — *see* Palsy, cerebral
conjugate movement (of eye) 378.81
cortical (nuclear) (supranuclear) 378.81
convergence 378.83
cordis (*see also* Failure, heart) 428.9
cortical (*see also* Paralysis, brain) 437.8
cranial or cerebral nerve (*see also* Disorder, nerve, cranial) 352.9
creeping 335.21
crossed leg 344.89
crutch 953.4
deglutition 784.99
hysterical 300.11
dementia 094.1
descending (spinal) NEC 335.9
diaphragm (flaccid) 519.4
due to accidental section of phrenic nerve during procedure 998.2
digestive organs NEC 564.89
diplegic — *see* Diplegia
divergence (nuclear) 378.85
divers' 993.3
Duchenne's 335.22
due to intracranial or spinal birth injury — *see* Palsy, cerebral
embolic (current episode) (*see also* Embolism, brain) 434.1 ☑
late effect — *see* Late effect(s) (of) cerebrovascular disease
enteric (*see also* Ileus) 560.1
with hernia — *see* Hernia, by site, with obstruction
Erb (-Duchenne) (birth) (newborn) 767.6
Erb's syphilitic spastic spinal 094.89
esophagus 530.89
essential, infancy (*see also* Poliomyelitis) 045.9 ☑
extremity
lower — *see* Paralysis, leg
spastic (hereditary) 343.3
noncongenital or noninfantile 344.1
transient (cause unknown) 781.4
upper — *see* Paralysis, arm
eye muscle (extrinsic) 378.55
intrinsic 367.51
facial (nerve) 351.0
birth injury 767.5
congenital 767.5
following operation NEC 998.2
newborn 767.5
familial 359.3
periodic 359.3
spastic 334.1
fauces 478.29
finger NEC 354.9
foot NEC 355.8
gait 781.2
gastric nerve 352.3

Paralysis, paralytic — *continued*
gaze 378.81
general 094.1
ataxic 094.1
insane 094.1
juvenile 090.40
progressive 094.1
tabetic 094.1
glossopharyngeal (nerve) 352.2
glottis (*see also* Paralysis, vocal cord) 478.30
gluteal 353.4
Gubler (-Millard) 344.89
hand 354.9
hysterical 300.11
psychogenic 306.0
heart (*see also* Failure, heart) 428.9
hemifacial, progressive 349.89
hemiplegic — *see* Hemiplegia
hyperkalemic periodic (familial) 359.3
hypertensive (current episode) 437.8
hypoglossal (nerve) 352.5
hypokalemic periodic 359.3
Hyrtl's sphincter (rectum) 569.49
hysterical 300.11
ileus (*see also* Ileus) 560.1
infantile (*see also* Poliomyelitis) 045.9 ☑
atrophic acute 045.1 ☑
bulbar 045.0 ☑
cerebral — *see* Palsy, cerebral
paralytic 045.1 ☑
progressive acute 045.9 ☑
spastic — *see* Palsy, cerebral
spinal 045.9 ☑
infective (*see also* Poliomyelitis) 045.9 ☑
inferior nuclear 344.9
insane, general or progressive 094.1
internuclear 378.86
interosseous 355.9
intestine (*see also* Ileus) 560.1
intracranial (current episode) (*see also* Paralysis, brain) 437.8
due to birth injury 767.0
iris 379.49
due to diphtheria (toxin) 032.81 *[379.49]*
ischemic, Volkmann's (complicating trauma) 958.6
isolated sleep, recurrent
Jackson's 344.89
jake 357.7
Jamaica ginger (jake) 357.7
juvenile general 090.40
Klumpke (-Déjérine) (birth) (newborn) 767.6
labioglossal (laryngeal) (pharyngeal) 335.22
Landry's 357.0
laryngeal nerve (recurrent) (superior) (*see also* Paralysis, vocal cord) 478.30
larynx (*see also* Paralysis, vocal cord) 478.30
due to diphtheria (toxin) 032.3
late effect
due to
birth injury, brain or spinal (cord) — *see* Palsy, cerebral
edema, brain or cerebral — *see* Paralysis, brain
lesion
late effect — *see* Late effect(s) (of) cerebrovascular disease
spinal (cord) — *see* Paralysis, spinal
lateral 335.24
lead 984.9
specified type of lead — *see* Table of Drugs and Chemicals
left side — *see* Hemiplegia
leg 344.30

Paralysis, paralytic — *continued*
leg — *continued*
affecting
dominant side 344.31
nondominant side 344.32
both (*see also* Paraplegia) 344.1
crossed 344.89
hysterical 300.11
psychogenic 306.0
transient or transitory 781.4
traumatic NEC (*see also* Injury, nerve, lower limb) 956.9
levator palpebrae superioris 374.31
limb NEC 344.5
all four — *see* Quadriplegia
quadriplegia — *see* Quadriplegia
lip 528.5
Lissauer's 094.1
local 355.9
lower limb (*see also* Paralysis, leg)
both (*see also* Paraplegia) 344.1
lung 518.89
newborn 770.89
median nerve 354.1
medullary (tegmental) 344.89
mesencephalic NEC 344.89
tegmental 344.89
middle alternating 344.89
Millard-Gubler-Foville 344.89
monoplegic — *see* Monoplegia
motor NEC 344.9
cerebral — *see* Paralysis, brain
spinal — *see* Paralysis, spinal
multiple
cerebral — *see* Paralysis, brain
spinal — *see* Paralysis, spinal
muscle (flaccid) 359.9
due to nerve lesion NEC 355.9
eye (extrinsic) 378.55
intrinsic 367.51
oblique 378.51
iris sphincter 364.89
ischemic (complicating trauma) (Volkmann's) 958.6
pseudohypertrophic 359.1
muscular (atrophic) 359.9
progressive 335.21
musculocutaneous nerve 354.9
musculospiral 354.9
nerve (*see also* Disorder, nerve)
third or oculomotor (partial) 378.51
total 378.52
fourth or trochlear 378.53
sixth or abducens 378.54
seventh or facial 351.0
birth injury 767.5
due to
injection NEC 999.9
operation NEC 997.09
newborn 767.5
accessory 352.4
auditory 388.5
birth injury 767.7
cranial or cerebral (*see also* Disorder, nerve, cranial) 352.9
facial 351.0
birth injury 767.5
newborn 767.5
laryngeal (*see also* Paralysis, vocal cord) 478.30
newborn 767.7
phrenic 354.8
newborn 767.7
radial 354.3
birth injury 767.6
newborn 767.6
syphilitic 094.89
traumatic NEC (*see also* Injury, nerve, by site) 957.9
trigeminal 350.9
ulnar 354.2
newborn NEC 767.0
normokalemic periodic 359.3
obstetrical, newborn 767.7
ocular 378.9
oculofacial, congenital 352.6

- **Pericarditis** — *continued*
  - acute — *continued*
    - benign 420.91
    - hemorrhagic 420.90
    - idiopathic 420.91
    - infective 420.90
    - nonspecific 420.91
    - rheumatic 391.0
      - with chorea (acute) (rheumatic) (Sydenham's) 392.0
    - sicca 420.90
    - viral 420.91
  - adhesive or adherent (external) (internal) 423.1
    - acute — *see* Pericarditis, acute
    - rheumatic (external) (internal) 393
  - amebic 006.8 *[420.0]*
  - bacterial (acute) (subacute) (with serous or seropurulent effusion) 420.99
  - calcareous 423.2
  - cholesterol (chronic) 423.8
    - acute 420.90
  - chronic (nonrheumatic) 423.8
    - rheumatic 393
  - constrictive 423.2
  - Coxsackie 074.21
  - due to
    - actinomycosis 039.8 *[420.0]*
    - amebiasis 006.8 *[420.0]*
    - Coxsackie (virus) 074.21
    - histoplasmosis (*see also* Histoplasmosis) 115.93
    - nocardiosis 039.8 *[420.0]*
    - tuberculosis (*see also* Tuberculosis) 017.9 ☑ *[420.0]*
  - fibrinocaseous (*see also* Tuberculosis) 017.9 ☑ *[420.0]*
  - fibrinopurulent 420.99
  - fibrinous — *see* Pericarditis, rheumatic
  - fibropurulent 420.99
  - fibrous 423.1
  - gonococcal 098.83
  - hemorrhagic 423.0
  - idiopathic (acute) 420.91
  - infective (acute) 420.90
  - meningococcal 036.41
  - neoplastic (chronic) 423.8
    - acute 420.90
  - nonspecific 420.91
  - obliterans, obliterating 423.1
  - plastic 423.1
  - pneumococcal (acute) 420.99
  - postinfarction 411.0
  - purulent (acute) 420.99
  - rheumatic (active) (acute) (with effusion) (with pneumonia) 391.0
    - with chorea (acute) (rheumatic) (Sydenham's) 392.0
    - chronic or inactive (with chorea) 393
  - septic (acute) 420.99
  - serofibrinous — *see* Pericarditis, rheumatic
  - staphylococcal (acute) 420.99
  - streptococcal (acute) 420.99
  - suppurative (acute) 420.99
  - syphilitic 093.81
  - tuberculous (acute) (chronic) (*see also* Tuberculosis) 017.9 ☑ *[420.0]*
  - uremic 585.9 *[420.0]*
  - viral (acute) 420.91
- **Pericardium, pericardial** — *see* condition
- **Pericellulitis** — *see also* Cellulitis 682.9
- **Pericementitis** 523.40
  - acute 523.30
  - chronic (suppurative) 523.40
- **Pericholecystitis** — *see also* Cholecystitis 575.10
- **Perichondritis**
  - auricle 380.00
    - acute 380.01
    - chronic 380.02
  - bronchus 491.9
- **Perichondritis** — *continued*
  - ear (external) 380.00
    - acute 380.01
    - chronic 380.02
  - larynx 478.71
    - syphilitic 095.8
    - typhoid 002.0 *[478.71]*
  - nose 478.19
  - pinna 380.00
    - acute 380.01
    - chronic 380.02
  - trachea 478.9
- **Periclasia** 523.5
- **Pericolitis** 569.89
- **Pericoronitis** (chronic) 523.40
  - acute 523.33
- **Pericystitis** — *see also* Cystitis 595.9
- **Pericytoma** (M9150/1) — *see also* Neoplasm, connective tissue, uncertain behavior
  - benign (M9150/0) — *see* Neoplasm, connective tissue, benign
  - malignant (M9150/3) — *see* Neoplasm, connective tissue, malignant
- **Peridacryocystitis, acute** 375.32
- **Peridiverticulitis** — *see also* Diverticulitis 562.11
- **Periduodenitis** 535.6 ☑
- **Periendocarditis** — *see also* Endocarditis 424.90
  - acute or subacute 421.9
- **Periepididymitis** — *see also* Epididymitis 604.90
- **Perifolliculitis** (abscedens) 704.8
  - capitis, abscedens et suffodiens 704.8
  - dissecting, scalp 704.8
  - scalp 704.8
  - superficial pustular 704.8
- **Perigastritis** (acute) 535.0 ☑
- **Perigastrojejunitis** (acute) 535.0 ☑
- **Perihepatitis** (acute) 573.3
  - chlamydial 099.56
  - gonococcal 098.86
- **Peri-ileitis** (subacute) 569.89
- **Perilabyrinthitis** (acute) — *see* Labyrinthitis
- **Perimeningitis** — *see* Meningitis
- **Perimetritis** — *see also* Endometritis 615.9
- **Perimetrosalpingitis** — *see also* Salpingo-oophoritis 614.2
- **Perineocele** 618.05
- **Perinephric** — *see* condition
- **Perinephritic** — *see* condition
- **Perinephritis** — *see also* Infection, kidney 590.9
  - purulent (*see also* Abscess, kidney) 590.2
- **Perineum, perineal** — *see* condition
- **Perineuritis** NEC 729.2
- **Periodic** — *see also* condition
  - disease (familial) 277.31
  - edema 995.1
    - hereditary 277.6
  - fever 277.31
  - headache syndromes in child or adolescent 346.2 ☑
  - limb movement disorder 327.51
  - paralysis (familial) 359.3
  - peritonitis 277.31
  - polyserositis 277.31
  - somnolence (*see also* Narcolepsy) 347.00
- **Periodontal**
  - cyst 522.8
  - pocket 523.8
- **Periodontitis** (chronic) (complex) (compound) (simplex) 523.40
  - acute 523.33
  - aggressive 523.30
    - generalized 523.32
    - localized 523.31
  - apical 522.6
    - acute (pulpal origin) 522.4
  - generalized 523.42
- **Periodontitis** — *continued*
  - localized 523.41
- **Periodontoclasia** 523.5
- **Periodontosis** 523.5
- **Periods** — *see also* Menstruation
  - heavy 626.2
  - irregular 626.4
- **Perionychia** (with lymphangitis) 681.9
  - finger 681.02
  - toe 681.11
- **Perioophoritis** — *see also* Salpingo-oophoritis 614.2
- **Periorchitis** — *see also* Orchitis 604.90
- **Periosteum, periosteal** — *see* condition
- **Periostitis** (circumscribed) (diffuse) (infective) 730.3 ☑

> *Note — Use the following fifth-digit subclassification with category 730:*
>
> *0 site unspecified*
> *1 shoulder region*
> *2 upper arm*
> *3 forearm*
> *4 hand*
> *5 pelvic region and thigh*
> *6 lower leg*
> *7 ankle and foot*
> *8 other specified sites*
> *9 multiple sites*

  - with osteomyelitis (*see also* Osteomyelitis) 730.2 ☑
    - acute or subacute 730.0 ☑
    - chronic or old 730.1 ☑
  - albuminosa, albuminosus 730.3 ☑
  - alveolar 526.5
  - alveolodental 526.5
  - dental 526.5
  - gonorrheal 098.89
  - hyperplastica, generalized 731.2
  - jaw (lower) (upper) 526.4
  - monomelic 733.99
  - orbital 376.02
  - syphilitic 095.5
    - congenital 090.0 *[730.8]* ☑
    - secondary 091.61
  - tuberculous (*see also* Tuberculosis, bone) 015.9 ☑ *[730.8]* ☑
  - yaws (early) (hypertrophic) (late) 102.6
- **Periostosis** — *see also* Periostitis 730.3 ☑
  - with osteomyelitis (*see also* Osteomyelitis) 730.2 ☑
    - acute or subacute 730.0 ☑
    - chronic or old 730.1 ☑
  - hyperplastic 756.59
- **Peripartum cardiomyopathy** 674.5 ☑
- **Periphlebitis** — *see also* Phlebitis 451.9
  - lower extremity 451.2
    - deep (vessels) 451.19
    - superficial (vessels) 451.0
  - portal 572.1
  - retina 362.18
  - superficial (vessels) 451.0
  - tuberculous (*see also* Tuberculosis) 017.9 ☑
    - retina 017.3 ☑ *[362.18]*
- **Peripneumonia** — *see* Pneumonia
- **Periproctitis** 569.49
- **Periprostatitis** — *see also* Prostatitis 601.9
- **Perirectal** — *see* condition
- **Perirenal** — *see* condition
- **Perisalpingitis** — *see also* Salpingo-oophoritis 614.2
- **Perisigmoiditis** 569.89
- **Perisplenitis** (infectional) 289.59
- **Perispondylitis** — *see* Spondylitis
- **Peristalsis reversed or visible** 787.4
- **Peritendinitis** — *see also* Tenosynovitis 726.90
  - adhesive (shoulder) 726.0
- **Perithelioma** (M9150/1) — *see* Pericytoma
- **Peritoneum, peritoneal** — *see also* condition
  - equilibration test V56.32
- **Peritonitis** (acute) (adhesive) (fibrinous) (hemorrhagic) (idiopathic) (localized) (perforative) (primary) (with adhesions) (with effusion) 567.9
  - with or following
    - abortion — *see* Abortion, by type, with sepsis
    - abscess 567.21
    - appendicitis 540.0
      - with peritoneal abscess 540.1
    - ectopic pregnancy (*see also* categories 633.0–633.9) 639.0
    - molar pregnancy (*see also* categories 630–632) 639.0
  - aseptic 998.7
  - bacterial 567.29
    - spontaneous 567.23
  - bile, biliary 567.81
  - chemical 998.7
  - chlamydial 099.56
  - chronic proliferative 567.89
  - congenital NEC 777.6
  - diaphragmatic 567.22
  - diffuse NEC 567.29
  - diphtheritic 032.83
  - disseminated NEC 567.29
  - due to
    - bile 567.81
    - foreign
      - body or object accidentally left during a procedure (instrument) (sponge) (swab) 998.4
      - substance accidentally left during a procedure (chemical) (powder) (talc) 998.7
    - talc 998.7
    - urine 567.89
  - fibrinopurulent 567.29
  - fibrinous 567.29
  - fibrocaseous (*see also* Tuberculosis) 014.0 ☑
  - fibropurulent 567.29
  - general, generalized (acute) 567.21
  - gonococcal 098.86
  - in infective disease NEC 136.9 *[567.0]*
  - meconium (newborn) 777.6
  - pancreatic 577.8
  - paroxysmal, benign 277.31
  - pelvic
    - female (acute) 614.5
      - chronic NEC 614.7
        - with adhesions 614.6
      - puerperal, postpartum, childbirth 670.0 ☑
    - male (acute) 567.21
  - periodic (familial) 277.31
  - phlegmonous 567.29
  - pneumococcal 567.1
  - postabortal 639.0
  - proliferative, chronic 567.89
  - puerperal, postpartum, childbirth 670.0 ☑
  - purulent 567.29
  - septic 567.29
  - spontaneous bacterial 567.23
  - staphylococcal 567.29
  - streptococcal 567.29
  - subdiaphragmatic 567.29
  - subphrenic 567.29
  - suppurative 567.29
  - syphilitic 095.2
    - congenital 090.0 *[567.0]*
  - talc 998.7
  - tuberculous (*see also* Tuberculosis) 014.0 ☑
  - urine 567.89
- **Peritonsillar** — *see* condition
- **Peritonsillitis** 475
- **Perityphlitis** — *see also* Appendicitis 541

Periureteritis 593.89
Periurethral — *see* condition
Periurethritis (gangrenous) 597.89
Periuterine — *see* condition
Perivaginitis — *see also* Vaginitis 616.10
Perivasculitis, retinal 362.18
Perivasitis (chronic) 608.4
Periventricular leukomalacia 779.7
Perivesiculitis (seminal) — *see also* Vesiculitis 608.0
Perlèche 686.8
  due to
    moniliasis 112.0
    riboflavin deficiency 266.0
Pernicious — *see* condition
Pernio, perniosis 991.5
Persecution
  delusion 297.9
  social V62.4
Perseveration (tonic) 784.69
Persistence, persistent (congenital) 759.89
  anal membrane 751.2
  arteria stapedia 744.04
  atrioventricular canal 745.69
  bloody ejaculate 792.2
  branchial cleft 744.41
  bulbus cordis in left ventricle 745.8
  canal of Cloquet 743.51
  capsule (opaque) 743.51
  cilioretinal artery or vein 743.51
  cloaca 751.5
  communication — *see* Fistula, congenital
  convolutions
    aortic arch 747.21
    fallopian tube 752.19
    oviduct 752.19
    uterine tube 752.19
  double aortic arch 747.21
  ductus
    arteriosus 747.0
    Botalli 747.0
  fetal
    circulation 747.83
    form of cervix (uteri) 752.49
    hemoglobin (hereditary) ("Swiss variety") 282.7
    pulmonary hypertension 747.83
  foramen
    Botalli 745.5
    ovale 745.5
  Gartner's duct 752.41
  hemoglobin, fetal (hereditary) (HPFH) 282.7
  hyaloid
    artery (generally incomplete) 743.51
    system 743.51
  hymen (tag)
    in pregnancy or childbirth 654.8 ☑
      causing obstructed labor 660.2 ☑
  lanugo 757.4
  left
    posterior cardinal vein 747.49
    root with right arch of aorta 747.21
    superior vena cava 747.49
  Meckel's diverticulum 751.0
  mesonephric duct 752.89
    fallopian tube 752.11
  mucosal disease (middle ear) (with posterior or superior marginal perforation of ear drum) 382.2
  nail(s), anomalous 757.5
  occiput, anterior or posterior 660.3 ☑
    fetus or newborn 763.1
  omphalomesenteric duct 751.0
  organ or site NEC — *see* Anomaly, specified type NEC
  ostium
    atrioventriculare commune 745.69
    primum 745.61
    secundum 745.5
  ovarian rests in fallopian tube 752.19

Persistence, persistent — *continued*
  pancreatic tissue in intestinal tract 751.5
  primary (deciduous)
    teeth 520.6
    vitreous hyperplasia 743.51
  pulmonary hypertension 747.83
  pupillary membrane 743.46
    iris 743.46
  Rhesus (Rh) titer 999.7
  right aortic arch 747.21
  sinus
    urogenitalis 752.89
    venosus with imperfect incorporation in right auricle 747.49
  thymus (gland) 254.8
    hyperplasia 254.0
  thyroglossal duct 759.2
  thyrolingual duct 759.2
  truncus arteriosus or communis 745.0
  tunica vasculosa lentis 743.39
  umbilical sinus 753.7
  urachus 753.7
  vegetative state 780.03
  vitelline duct 751.0
  wolffian duct 752.89
Person (with)
  admitted for clinical research, as participant or control subject V70.7
  affected by
    family member
      currently on deployment (military) V61.01
      returned from deployment (military) (current or past conflict) V61.02
  awaiting admission to adequate facility elsewhere V63.2
    undergoing social agency investigation V63.8
  concern (normal) about sick person in family V61.49
  consulting on behalf of another V65.19
    pediatric pre-birth visit for expectant mother V65.11
  currently deployed in theater or in support of military war, peacekeeping and humanitarian operations V62.21
  feared
    complaint in whom no diagnosis was made V65.5
    condition not demonstrated V65.5
  feigning illness V65.2
  healthy, accompanying sick person V65.0
  history of military war, peacekeeping and humanitarian deployment (current or past conflict) V62.22
  living (in)
    without
      adequate
        financial resources V60.2
        housing (heating) (space) V60.1
      housing (permanent) (temporary) V60.0
      material resources V60.2
      person able to render necessary care V60.4
      shelter V60.0
    alone V60.3
    boarding school V60.6
    residence remote from hospital or medical care facility V63.0
    residential institution V60.6
  medical services in home not available V63.1
  on waiting list V63.2
    undergoing social agency investigation V63.8
  sick or handicapped in family V61.49
  "worried well" V65.5

Personality
  affective 301.10
  aggressive 301.3
  amoral 301.7
  anancastic, anankastic 301.4
  antisocial 301.7
  asocial 301.7
  asthenic 301.6
  avoidant 301.82
  borderline 301.83
  change 310.1
  compulsive 301.4
  cycloid 301.13
  cyclothymic 301.13
  dependent 301.6
  depressive (chronic) 301.12
  disorder, disturbance NEC 301.9
    with
      antisocial disturbance 301.7
      pattern disturbance NEC 301.9
      sociopathic disturbance 301.7
      trait disturbance 301.9
  dual 300.14
  dyssocial 301.7
  eccentric 301.89
    "haltlose" type 301.89
  emotionally unstable 301.59
  epileptoid 301.3
  explosive 301.3
  fanatic 301.0
  histrionic 301.50
  hyperthymic 301.11
  hypomanic 301.11
  hypothymic 301.12
  hysterical 301.50
  immature 301.89
  inadequate 301.6
  labile 301.59
  masochistic 301.89
  morally defective 301.7
  multiple 300.14
  narcissistic 301.81
  obsessional 301.4
  obsessive-compulsive 301.4
  overconscientious 301.4
  paranoid 301.0
  passive (-dependent) 301.6
  passive-aggressive 301.84
  pathologic NEC 301.9
  pattern defect or disturbance 301.9
  pseudosocial 301.7
  psychoinfantile 301.59
  psychoneurotic NEC 301.89
  psychopathic 301.9
    with
      amoral trend 301.7
      antisocial trend 301.7
      asocial trend 301.7
      pathologic sexuality (*see also* Deviation, sexual) 302.9
    mixed types 301.9
  schizoid 301.20
  type A 301.4
  unstable (emotional) 301.59
Perthes' disease (capital femoral osteochondrosis) 732.1
Pertussis — *see also* Whooping cough 033.9
  vaccination, prophylactic (against) V03.6
Peruvian wart 088.0
Perversion, perverted
  appetite 307.52
    hysterical 300.11
  function
    pineal gland 259.8
    pituitary gland 253.9
      anterior lobe
        deficient 253.2
        excessive 253.1
      posterior lobe 253.6
    placenta — *see* Placenta, abnormal
  sense of smell or taste 781.1
    psychogenic 306.7
  sexual (*see also* Deviation, sexual) 302.9

Pervious, congenital — *see also* Imperfect, closure
  ductus arteriosus 747.0
Pes (congenital) — *see also* Talipes 754.70
  abductus (congenital) 754.60
    acquired 736.79
  acquired NEC 736.79
    planus 734
  adductus (congenital) 754.79
    acquired 736.79
  cavus 754.71
    acquired 736.73
  planovalgus (congenital) 754.69
    acquired 736.79
  planus (acquired) (any degree) 734
    congenital 754.61
    rachitic 268.1
  valgus (congenital) 754.61
    acquired 736.79
  varus (congenital) 754.50
    acquired 736.79
Pest — *see also* Plague 020.9
Pestis — *see also* Plague 020.9
  bubonica 020.0
  fulminans 020.0
  minor 020.8
  pneumonica — *see* Plague, pneumonic
Petechial
  fever 036.0
  typhus 081.9
Petechia, petechiae 782.7
  fetus or newborn 772.6
Petges-Cléjat or Petges-Clégat syndrome (poikilodermatomyositis) 710.3
Petit's
  disease (*see also* Hernia, lumbar) 553.8
Petit mal (idiopathic) — *see also* Epilepsy 345.0 ☑
  status 345.2
Petrellidosis 117.6
Petrositis 383.20
  acute 383.21
  chronic 383.22
Peutz-Jeghers disease or syndrome 759.6
Peyronie's disease 607.85
Pfeiffer's disease 075
Phacentocele 379.32
  traumatic 921.3
Phacoanaphylaxis 360.19
Phacocele (old) 379.32
  traumatic 921.3
Phaehyphomycosis 117.8
Phagedena (dry) (moist) — *see also* Gangrene 785.4
  arteriosclerotic 440.24
  geometric 686.09
  penis 607.89
  senile 440.2 ☑ *[785.4]*
  sloughing 785.4
  tropical (*see also* Ulcer, skin) 707.9
  vulva 616.50
Phagedenic — *see also* condition
  abscess (*see also* Abscess)
    chancroid 099.0
  bubo NEC 099.8
  chancre 099.0
  ulcer (tropical) (*see also* Ulcer, skin) 707.9
Phagomania 307.52
Phakoma 362.89
Phantom limb (syndrome) 353.6
Pharyngeal — *see also* condition
  arch remnant 744.41
  pouch syndrome 279.11
Pharyngitis (acute) (catarrhal) (gangrenous) (infective) (malignant) (membranous) (phlegmonous) (pneumococcal) (pseudomembranous) (simple) (staphylococcal) (subacute) (suppurative) (ulcerative) (viral) 462
  with influenza, flu, or grippe 487.1

Pharyngitis — *continued*
  aphthous 074.0
  atrophic 472.1
  chlamydial 099.51
  chronic 472.1
  Coxsackie virus 074.0
  diphtheritic (membranous) 032.0
  follicular 472.1
  fusospirochetal 101
  gonococcal 098.6
  granular (chronic) 472.1
  herpetic 054.79
  hypertrophic 472.1
  infectional, chronic 472.1
  influenzal 487.1
  lymphonodular, acute 074.8
  septic 034.0
  streptococcal 034.0
  tuberculous (*see also* Tuberculosis) 012.8 ☑
  vesicular 074.0
Pharyngoconjunctival fever 077.2
Pharyngoconjunctivitis, viral 077.2
Pharyngolaryngitis (acute) 465.0
  chronic 478.9
  septic 034.0
Pharyngoplegia 478.29
Pharyngotonsillitis 465.8
  tuberculous 012.8 ☑
Pharyngotracheitis (acute) 465.8
  chronic 478.9
Pharynx, pharyngeal — *see* condition
Phase of life problem NEC V62.89
Phenomenon
  Arthus' 995.21
  flashback (drug) 292.89
  jaw-winking 742.8
  Jod-Basedow 242.8 ☑
  L. E. cell 710.0
  lupus erythematosus cell 710.0
  Pelger-Huët (hereditary hyposegmentation) 288.2
  Raynaud's (paroxysmal digital cyanosis) (secondary) 443.0
  Reilly's (*see also* Neuropathy, peripheral, autonomic) 337.9
  vasomotor 780.2
  vasospastic 443.9
  vasovagal 780.2
  Wenckebach's, heart block (second degree) 426.13
Phenylketonuria (PKU) 270.1
Phenylpyruvicaciduria 270.1
Pheochromoblastoma (M8700/3)
  specified site — *see* Neoplasm, by site, malignant
  unspecified site 194.0
Pheochromocytoma (M8700/0)
  malignant (M8700/3)
    specified site — *see* Neoplasm, by site, malignant
    unspecified site 194.0
  specified site — *see* Neoplasm, by site, benign
  unspecified site 227.0
Phimosis (congenital) 605
  chancroidal 099.0
  due to infection 605
Phlebectasia — *see also* Varicose, vein 454.9
  congenital NEC 747.60
  esophagus (*see also* Varix, esophagus) 456.1
    with hemorrhage (*see also* Varix, esophagus, bleeding) 456.0
Phlebitis (infective) (pyemic) (septic) (suppurative) 451.9
  antecubital vein 451.82
  arm NEC 451.84
    axillary vein 451.89
    basilic vein 451.82
    deep 451.83
    superficial 451.82
  axillary vein 451.89
  basilic vein 451.82
  blue 451.9

Phlebitis — *continued*
  brachial vein 451.83
  breast, superficial 451.89
  cavernous (venous) sinus — *see* Phlebitis, intracranial sinus
  cephalic vein 451.82
  cerebral (venous) sinus — *see* Phlebitis, intracranial sinus
  chest wall, superficial 451.89
  complicating pregnancy or puerperium 671.9 ☑
    affecting fetus or newborn 760.3
  cranial (venous) sinus — *see* Phlebitis, intracranial sinus
  deep (vessels) 451.19
    femoral vein 451.11
    specified vessel NEC 451.19
  due to implanted device — *see* Complications, due to (presence of) any device, implant, or graft classified to 996.0–996.5 NEC
  during or resulting from a procedure 997.2
  femoral vein (deep) (superficial) 451.11
  femoropopliteal 451.19
  following infusion, perfusion, or transfusion 999.2
  gouty 274.89 *[451.9]*
  hepatic veins 451.89
  iliac vein 451.81
  iliofemoral 451.11
  intracranial sinus (any) (venous) 325
    late effect — *see* category 326
    nonpyogenic 437.6
      in pregnancy or puerperium 671.5 ☑
  jugular vein 451.89
  lateral (venous) sinus — *see* Phlebitis, intracranial sinus
  leg 451.2
    deep (vessels) 451.19
      femoral vein 451.11
      specified vessel NEC 451.19
    superficial (vessels) 451.0
      femoral vein 451.11
  longitudinal sinus — *see* Phlebitis, intracranial sinus
  lower extremity 451.2
    deep (vessels) 451.19
      femoral vein 451.11
      specified vessel NEC 451.19
    migrans, migrating (superficial) 453.1
    superficial (vessels) 451.0
      femoral vein 451.11
  pelvic
    with
      abortion — *see* Abortion, by type, with sepsis
      ectopic pregnancy (*see also* categories 633.0–633.9) 639.0
      molar pregnancy (*see also* categories 630–632) 639.0
    following
      abortion 639.0
      ectopic or molar pregnancy 639.0
    puerperal, postpartum 671.4 ☑
  popliteal vein 451.19
  portal (vein) 572.1
  postoperative 997.2
  pregnancy 671.9 ☑
    deep 671.3 ☑
    specified type NEC 671.5 ☑
    superficial 671.2 ☑
  puerperal, postpartum, childbirth 671.9 ☑
    deep 671.4 ☑
    lower extremities 671.2 ☑
    pelvis 671.4 ☑
    specified site NEC 671.5 ☑
    superficial 671.2 ☑
  radial vein 451.83
  retina 362.18
  saphenous (great) (long) 451.0

Phlebitis — *continued*
  saphenous — *continued*
    accessory or small 451.0
  sinus (meninges) — *see* Phlebitis, intracranial sinus
  specified site NEC 451.89
  subclavian vein 451.89
  syphilitic 093.89
  tibial vein 451.19
  ulcer, ulcerative 451.9
    leg 451.2
      deep (vessels) 451.19
        femoral vein 451.11
        specified vessel NEC 451.19
      superficial (vessels) 451.0
        femoral vein 451.11
    lower extremity 451.2
      deep (vessels) 451.19
        femoral vein 451.11
        specified vessel NEC 451.19
      superficial (vessels) 451.0
  ulnar vein 451.83
  umbilicus 451.89
  upper extremity (*see also* Phlebitis, arm)
    deep (veins) 451.83
      brachial vein 451.83
      radial vein 451.83
      ulnar vein 451.83
    superficial (veins) 451.82
      antecubital vein 451.82
      basilica vein 451.82
      cephalic vein 451.82
  uterus (septic) (*see also* Endometritis) 615.9
  varicose (leg) (lower extremity) (*see also* Varicose, vein) 454.1
Phlebofibrosis 459.89
Phleboliths 459.89
Phlebosclerosis 459.89
Phlebothrombosis — *see* Thrombosis
Phlebotomus fever 066.0
Phlegmasia
  alba dolens (deep vessels) 451.19
    complicating pregnancy 671.3 ☑
    nonpuerperal 451.19
    puerperal, postpartum, childbirth 671.4 ☑
  cerulea dolens 451.19
Phlegm, choked on 933.1
Phlegmon — *see also* Abscess 682.9
  erysipelatous (*see also* Erysipelas) 035
  iliac 682.2
    fossa 540.1
  throat 478.29
Phlegmonous — *see* condition
Phlyctenulosis (allergic) (keratoconjunctivitis) (nontuberculous) 370.31
  cornea 370.31
    with ulcer (*see also* Ulcer, cornea) 370.00
  tuberculous (*see also* Tuberculosis) 017.3 ☑ *[370.31]*
Phobia, phobic (reaction) 300.20
  animal 300.29
  isolated NEC 300.29
  obsessional 300.3
  simple NEC 300.29
  social 300.23
  specified NEC 300.29
  state 300.20
Phocas' disease 610.1
Phocomelia 755.4
  lower limb 755.32
    complete 755.33
    distal 755.35
    proximal 755.34
  upper limb 755.22
    complete 755.23
    distal 755.25
    proximal 755.24
Phoria — *see also* Heterophoria 378.40
Phosphate-losing tubular disorder 588.0
Phosphatemia 275.3
Phosphaturia 275.3

Photoallergic response 692.72
Photocoproporphyria 277.1
Photodermatitis (sun) 692.72
  light other than sun 692.82
Photokeratitis 370.24
Photo-ophthalmia 370.24
Photophobia 368.13
Photopsia 368.15
Photoretinitis 363.31
Photoretinopathy 363.31
Photosensitiveness (sun) 692.72
  light other than sun 692.82
Photosensitization (skin) (sun) 692.72
  light other than sun 692.82
Phototoxic response 692.72
Phrenitis 323.9
Phrynoderma 264.8
Phthiriasis (pubis) (any site) 132.2
  with any infestation classifiable to 132.0, 132.1, 132.3
Phthirus infestation — *see* Phthiriasis
Phthisis — *see also* Tuberculosis 011.9 ☑
  bulbi (infectional) 360.41
  colliers' 011.4 ☑
  cornea 371.05
  eyeball (due to infection) 360.41
  millstone makers' 011.4 ☑
  miners' 011.4 ☑
  potters' 011.4 ☑
  sandblasters' 011.4 ☑
  stonemasons' 011.4 ☑
Phycomycosis 117.7
Physalopteriasis 127.7
Physical therapy NEC V57.1
  breathing exercises V57.0
Physiological cup, optic papilla
  borderline, glaucoma suspect 365.00
  enlarged 377.14
  glaucomatous 377.14
Phytobezoar 938
  intestine 936
  stomach 935.2
Pian — *see also* Yaws 102.9
Pianoma 102.1
Piarhemia, piarrhemia — *see also* Hyperlipemia 272.4
  bilharziasis 120.9
Pica 307.52
  hysterical 300.11
Pick's
  cerebral atrophy 331.11
    with dementia
      with behavioral disturbance 331.11 *[294.11]*
      without behavioral disturbance 331.11 *[294.10]*
  disease
    brain 331.11
      dementia in
        with behavioral disturbance 331.11 *[294.11]*
        without behavioral disturbance 331.11 *[294.10]*
    lipid histiocytosis 272.7
    liver (pericardial pseudocirrhosis of liver) 423.2
    pericardium (pericardial pseudocirrhosis of liver) 423.2
    polyserositis (pericardial pseudocirrhosis of liver) 423.2
  syndrome
    heart (pericardial pseudocirrhosis of liver) 423.2
    liver (pericardial pseudocirrhosis of liver) 423.2
  tubular adenoma (M8640/0)
    specified site — *see* Neoplasm, by site, benign
    unspecified site
      female 220
      male 222.0
Pick-Herxheimer syndrome (diffuse idiopathic cutaneous atrophy) 701.8
Pick-Niemann disease (lipid histiocytosis) 272.7

Pleurisy (acute) (adhesive) (chronic) (costal) (diaphragmatic) (double) (dry) (fetid) (fibrinous) (fibrous) (interlobar) (latent) (lung) (old) (plastic) (primary) (residual) (sicca) (sterile) (subacute) (unresolved) (with adherent pleura) 511.0
- with
  - effusion (without mention of cause) 511.9
    - bacterial, nontuberculous 511.1
    - nontuberculous NEC 511.9
      - bacterial 511.1
    - pneumococcal 511.1
    - specified type NEC 511.89
    - staphylococcal 511.1
    - streptococcal 511.1
    - tuberculous (*see also* Tuberculosis, pleura) 012.0 ☑
      - primary, progressive 010.1 ☑
  - influenza, flu, or grippe 487.1
  - tuberculosis — *see* Pleurisy, tuberculous
- encysted 511.89
- exudative (*see also* Pleurisy, with effusion) 511.9
  - bacterial, nontuberculous 511.1
- fibrinopurulent 510.9
  - with fistula 510.0
- fibropurulent 510.9
  - with fistula 510.0
- hemorrhagic 511.89
- influenzal 487.1
- pneumococcal 511.0
  - with effusion 511.1
- purulent 510.9
  - with fistula 510.0
- septic 510.9
  - with fistula 510.0
- serofibrinous (*see also* Pleurisy, with effusion) 511.9
  - bacterial, nontuberculous 511.1
- seropurulent 510.9
  - with fistula 510.0
- serous (*see also* Pleurisy, with effusion) 511.9
  - bacterial, nontuberculous 511.1
- staphylococcal 511.0
  - with effusion 511.1
- streptococcal 511.0
  - with effusion 511.1
- suppurative 510.9
  - with fistula 510.0
- traumatic (post) (current) 862.29
  - with open wound into cavity 862.39
- tuberculous (with effusion) (*see also* Tuberculosis, pleura) 012.0 ☑
  - primary, progressive 010.1 ☑

Pleuritis sicca — *see* Pleurisy

Pleurobronchopneumonia — *see also* Pneumonia, broncho- 485

Pleurodynia 786.52
- epidemic 074.1
- viral 074.1

Pleurohepatitis 573.8

Pleuropericarditis — *see also* Pericarditis 423.9
- acute 420.90

Pleuropneumonia (acute) (bilateral) (double) (septic) — *see also* Pneumonia 486
- chronic (*see also* Fibrosis, lung) 515

Pleurorrhea — *see also* Hydrothorax 511.89

Plexitis, brachial 353.0

Plica
- knee 727.83
- polonica 132.0
- syndrome 727.83
- tonsil 474.8

Plicae dysphonia ventricularis 784.49

Plicated tongue 529.5
- congenital 750.13

Plug
- bronchus NEC 519.19

Plug — *continued*
- meconium (newborn) NEC 777.1
- mucus — *see* Mucus, plug

Plumbism 984.9
- specified type of lead — *see* Table of Drugs and Chemicals

Plummer's disease (toxic nodular goiter) 242.3 ☑

Plummer-Vinson syndrome (sideropenic dysphagia) 280.8

Pluricarential syndrome of infancy 260

Plurideficiency syndrome of infancy 260

Plus (and minus) hand (intrinsic) 736.09

PMDD (premenstrual dysphoric disorder) 625.4

PMS 625.4

Pneumathemia — see Air, embolism, by type

Pneumatic drill or hammer disease 994.9

Pneumatocele (lung) 518.89
- intracranial 348.8
- tension 492.0

Pneumatosis
- cystoides intestinalis 569.89
- peritonei 568.89
- pulmonum 492.8

Pneumaturia 599.84

Pneumoblastoma (M8981/3) — *see* Neoplasm, lung, malignant

Pneumocephalus 348.8

Pneumococcemia 038.2

Pneumococcus, pneumococcal — *see* condition

Pneumoconiosis (due to) (inhalation of) 505
- aluminum 503
- asbestos 501
- bagasse 495.1
- bauxite 503
- beryllium 503
- carbon electrode makers' 503
- coal
  - miners' (simple) 500
  - workers' (simple) 500
- cotton dust 504
- diatomite fibrosis 502
- dust NEC 504
  - inorganic 503
  - lime 502
  - marble 502
  - organic NEC 504
- fumes or vapors (from silo) 506.9
- graphite 503
- hard metal 503
- mica 502
- moldy hay 495.0
- rheumatoid 714.81
- silica NEC 502
  - and carbon 500
- silicate NEC 502
- talc 502

Pneumocystis carinii pneumonia 136.3

Pneumocystis jiroveci pneumonia 136.3

Pneumocystosis 136.3
- with pneumonia 136.3

Pneumoenteritis 025

Pneumohemopericardium — *see also* Pericarditis 423.9

Pneumohemothorax — *see also* Hemothorax 511.89
- traumatic 860.4
  - with open wound into thorax 860.5

Pneumohydropericardium — *see also* Pericarditis 423.9

Pneumohydrothorax — *see also* Hydrothorax 511.89

Pneumomediastinum 518.1
- congenital 770.2
- fetus or newborn 770.2

Pneumomycosis 117.9

Pneumonia (acute) (Alpenstich) (benign) (bilateral) (brain) (cerebral) (circumscribed) (congestive) (creeping) (delayed resolution) (double) (epidemic) (fever) (flash) (fulminant) (fungoid) (granulomatous) (hemorrhagic) (incipient) (infantile) (infectious) (infiltration) (insular) (intermittent) (latent) (lobe) (migratory) (newborn) (organized) (overwhelming) (primary) (progressive) (pseudolobar) (purulent) (resolved) (secondary) (senile) (septic) (suppurative) (terminal) (true) (unresolved) (vesicular) 486
- with influenza, flu, or grippe 487.0
- adenoviral 480.0
- adynamic 514
- alba 090.0
- allergic 518.3
- alveolar — *see* Pneumonia, lobar
- anaerobes 482.81
- anthrax 022.1 *[484.5]*
- apex, apical — *see* Pneumonia, lobar
- ascaris 127.0 *[484.8]*
- aspiration 507.0
  - due to
    - aspiration of microorganisms
      - bacterial 482.9
        - specified type NEC 482.89
      - specified organism NEC 483.8
        - bacterial NEC 482.89
      - viral 480.9
        - specified type NEC 480.8
    - food (regurgitated) 507.0
    - gastric secretions 507.0
    - milk 507.0
    - oils, essences 507.1
    - solids, liquids NEC 507.8
    - vomitus 507.0
  - fetal 770.18
    - due to
      - blood 770.16
      - clear amniotic fluid 770.14
      - meconium 770.12
      - postnatal stomach contents 770.86
  - newborn 770.18
    - due to
      - blood 770.16
      - clear amniotic fluid 770.14
      - meconium 770.12
      - postnatal stomach contents 770.86
- asthenic 514
- atypical (disseminated) (focal) (primary) 486
  - with influenza 487.0
- bacillus 482.9
  - specified type NEC 482.89
- bacterial 482.9
  - specified type NEC 482.89
- Bacteroides (fragilis) (oralis) (melaninogenicus) 482.81
- basal, basic, basilar — *see* Pneumonia, lobar
- bronchiolitis obliterans organized (BOOP) 516.8
- broncho-, bronchial (confluent) (croupous) (diffuse) (disseminated) (hemorrhagic) (involving lobes) (lobar) (terminal) 485
  - with influenza 487.0
  - allergic 518.3
  - aspiration (*see also* Pneumonia, aspiration) 507.0
  - bacterial 482.9
    - specified type NEC 482.89
  - capillary 466.19
    - with bronchospasm or obstruction 466.19
  - chronic (*see also* Fibrosis, lung) 515
  - congenital (infective) 770.0
  - diplococcal 481

Pneumonia — *continued*
- broncho-, bronchial — *continued*
  - Eaton's agent 483.0
  - Escherichia coli (E. coli) 482.82
  - Friedländer's bacillus 482.0
  - Hemophilus influenzae 482.2
  - hiberno-vernal 083.0 *[484.8]*
  - hypostatic 514
  - influenzal 487.0
  - inhalation (*see also* Pneumonia, aspiration) 507.0
    - due to fumes or vapors (chemical) 506.0
  - Klebsiella 482.0
  - lipid 507.1
    - endogenous 516.8
  - Mycoplasma (pneumoniae) 483.0
  - ornithosis 073.0
  - pleuropneumonia-like organisms (PPLO) 483.0
  - pneumococcal 481
  - Proteus 482.83
  - Pseudomonas 482.1
  - specified organism NEC 483.8
    - bacterial NEC 482.89
  - staphylococcal 482.40
    - aureus 482.41
      - methicillin
        - resistant (MRSA) 482.42
        - susceptible (MSSA) 482.41
    - specified type NEC 482.49
  - streptococcal — *see* Pneumonia, streptococcal
  - typhoid 002.0 *[484.8]*
  - viral, virus (*see also* Pneumonia, viral) 480.9
- Butyrivibrio (fibriosolvens) 482.81
- Candida 112.4
- capillary 466.19
  - with bronchospasm or obstruction 466.19
- caseous (*see also* Tuberculosis) 011.6 ☑
- catarrhal — *see* Pneumonia, broncho-
- central — *see* Pneumonia, lobar
- Chlamydia, chlamydial 483.1
  - pneumoniae 483.1
  - psittaci 073.0
  - specified type NEC 483.1
  - trachomatis 483.1
- cholesterol 516.8
- chronic (*see also* Fibrosis, lung) 515
- cirrhotic (chronic) (*see also* Fibrosis, lung) 515
- Clostridium (haemolyticum) (novyi) NEC 482.81
- confluent — *see* Pneumonia, broncho-
- congenital (infective) 770.0
  - aspiration 770.18
- croupous — *see* Pneumonia, lobar
- cytomegalic inclusion 078.5 *[484.1]*
- deglutition (*see also* Pneumonia, aspiration) 507.0
- desquamative interstitial 516.8
- diffuse — *see* Pneumonia, broncho-
- diplococcal, diplococcus (broncho-) (lobar) 481
- disseminated (focal) — *see* Pneumonia, broncho-
- due to
  - adenovirus 480.0
  - anaerobes 482.81
  - Bacterium anitratum 482.83
  - Chlamydia, chlamydial 483.1
    - pneumoniae 483.1
    - psittaci 073.0
    - specified type NEC 483.1
    - trachomatis 483.1
  - coccidioidomycosis 114.0
  - Diplococcus (pneumoniae) 481
  - Eaton's agent 483.0
  - Escherichia coli (E. coli) 482.82
  - Friedländer's bacillus 482.0
  - fumes or vapors (chemical) (inhalation) 506.0

Pneumosiderosis (occupational) 503
Pneumothorax (acute) (chronic) 512.8
congenital 770.2
due to operative injury of chest wall or lung 512.1
accidental puncture or laceration 512.1
fetus or newborn 770.2
iatrogenic 512.1
postoperative 512.1
spontaneous 512.8
fetus or newborn 770.2
tension 512.0
sucking 512.8
iatrogenic 512.1
postoperative 512.1
tense valvular, infectional 512.0
tension 512.0
iatrogenic 512.1
postoperative 512.1
spontaneous 512.0
traumatic 860.0
with
hemothorax 860.4
with open wound into thorax 860.5
open wound into thorax 860.1
tuberculous (*see also* Tuberculosis) 011.7 ☑
Pocket(s)
endocardial (*see also* Endocarditis) 424.90
periodontal 523.8
Podagra 274.9
Podencephalus 759.89
Poikilocytosis 790.09
Poikiloderma 709.09
Civatte's 709.09
congenital 757.33
vasculare atrophicans 696.2
Poikilodermatomyositis 710.3
Pointed ear 744.29
Poise imperfect 729.90
Poisoned — *see* Poisoning
Poisoning (acute) — *see also* Table of Drugs and Chemicals
Bacillus, B.
aertrycke (*see also* Infection, Salmonella) 003.9
botulinus 005.1
cholerae (suis) (*see also* Infection, Salmonella) 003.9
paratyphosus (*see also* Infection, Salmonella) 003.9
suipestifer (*see also* Infection, Salmonella) 003.9
bacterial toxins NEC 005.9
berries, noxious 988.2
blood (general) — *see* Septicemia
botulism 005.1
bread, moldy, mouldy — *see* Poisoning, food
Ciguatera 988.0
damaged meat — *see* Poisoning, food
death-cap (Amanita phalloides) (Amanita verna) 988.1
decomposed food — *see* Poisoning, food
diseased food — *see* Poisoning, food
drug — *see* Table of Drugs and Chemicals
epidemic, fish, meat, or other food — *see* Poisoning, food
fava bean 282.2
fish (bacterial) (*see also* Poisoning, food)
noxious 988.0
food (acute) (bacterial) (diseased) (infected) NEC 005.9
due to
bacillus
aertrycke (*see also* Poisoning, food, due to Salmonella) 003.9
botulinus 005.1
cereus 005.89

Poisoning — *see also* Table of Drugs and Chemicals — *continued*
food — *continued*
due to — *continued*
bacillus — *continued*
choleraesuis (*see also* Poisoning, food, due to Salmonella) 003.9
paratyphosus (*see also* Poisoning, food, due to Salmonella) 003.9
suipestifer (*see also* Poisoning, food, due to Salmonella) 003.9
Clostridium 005.3
botulinum 005.1
perfringens 005.2
welchii 005.2
Salmonella (aertrycke) (callinarum) (choleraesuis) (enteritidis) (paratyphi) (suipestifer) 003.9
with
gastroenteritis 003.0
localized infection(s) (*see also* Infection, Salmonella) 003.20
septicemia 003.1
specified manifestation NEC 003.8
specified bacterium NEC 005.89
Staphylococcus 005.0
Streptococcus 005.89
Vibrio parahaemolyticus 005.4
Vibrio vulnificus 005.81
noxious or naturally toxic 988.0
berries 988.2
fish 988.0
mushroom 988.1
plants NEC 988.2
ice cream — *see* Poisoning, food
ichthyotoxism (bacterial) 005.9
kreotoxism, food 005.9
malarial — *see* Malaria
meat — *see* Poisoning, food
mushroom (noxious) 988.1
mussel (*see also* Poisoning, food)
noxious 988.0
noxious foodstuffs (*see also* Poisoning, food, noxious) 988.9
specified type NEC 988.8
plants, noxious 988.2
pork (*see also* Poisoning, food)
specified NEC 988.8
Trichinosis 124
ptomaine — *see* Poisoning, food
putrefaction, food — *see* Poisoning, food
radiation 508.0
Salmonella (*see also* Infection, Salmonella) 003.9
sausage (*see also* Poisoning, food)
Trichinosis 124
saxitoxin 988.0
shellfish (*see also* Poisoning, food)
noxious (amnesic) (azaspiracid) (diarrheic) (neurotoxic) (paralytic) 988.0
Staphylococcus, food 005.0
toxic, from disease NEC 799.89
truffles — *see* Poisoning, food
uremic — *see* Uremia
uric acid 274.9
water 276.6
Poison ivy, oak, sumac or other plant dermatitis 692.6
Poker spine 720.0
Policeman's disease 729.2
Polioencephalitis (acute) (bulbar) — *see also* Poliomyelitis, bulbar 045.0 ☑
inferior 335.22
influenzal 487.8
superior hemorrhagic (acute) (Wernicke's) 265.1
Wernicke's (superior hemorrhagic) 265.1

Polioencephalomyelitis (acute) (anterior) (bulbar) — *see also* Polioencephalitis 045.0 ☑
Polioencephalopathy, superior hemorrhagic 265.1
with
beriberi 265.0
pellagra 265.2
Poliomeningoencephalitis — *see* Meningoencephalitis
Poliomyelitis (acute) (anterior) (epidemic) 045.9 ☑

Note — Use the following fifth-digit subclassification with category 045:

0	*poliovirus, unspecified type*
1	*poliovirus, type I*
2	*poliovirus, type II*
3	*poliovirus, type III*

with
paralysis 045.1 ☑
bulbar 045.0 ☑
abortive 045.2 ☑
ascending 045.9 ☑
progressive 045.9 ☑
bulbar 045.0 ☑
cerebral 045.0 ☑
chronic 335.21
congenital 771.2
contact V01.2
deformities 138
exposure to V01.2
late effect 138
nonepidemic 045.9 ☑
nonparalytic 045.2 ☑
old with deformity 138
posterior, acute 053.19
residual 138
sequelae 138
spinal, acute 045.9 ☑
syphilitic (chronic) 094.89
vaccination, prophylactic (against) V04.0
Poliosis (eyebrow) (eyelashes) 704.3
circumscripta (congenital) 757.4
acquired 704.3
congenital 757.4
Pollakiuria 788.41
psychogenic 306.53
Pollinosis 477.0
Pollitzer's disease (hidradenitis suppurativa) 705.83
Polyadenitis — *see also* Adenitis 289.3
malignant 020.0
Polyalgia 729.99
Polyangiitis (essential) 446.0
Polyarteritis (nodosa) (renal) 446.0
Polyarthralgia 719.49
psychogenic 306.0
Polyarthritis, polyarthropathy NEC 716.59
due to or associated with other specified conditions — *see* Arthritis, due to or associated with
endemic (*see also* Disease, Kaschin-Beck) 716.0 ☑
inflammatory 714.9
specified type NEC 714.89
juvenile (chronic) 714.30
acute 714.31
migratory — *see* Fever, rheumatic
rheumatic 714.0
fever (acute) — *see* Fever, rheumatic
Polycarential syndrome of infancy 260
Polychondritis (atrophic) (chronic) (relapsing) 733.99
Polycoria 743.46
Polycystic (congenital) (disease) 759.89
degeneration, kidney — *see* Polycystic, kidney
kidney (congenital) 753.12
adult type (APKD) 753.13
autosomal dominant 753.13

Polycystic — *continued*
kidney — *continued*
autosomal recessive 753.14
childhood type (CPKD) 753.14
infantile type 753.14
liver 751.62
lung 518.89
congenital 748.4
ovary, ovaries 256.4
spleen 759.0
Polycythemia (primary) (rubra) (vera) (M9950/1) 238.4
acquired 289.0
benign 289.0
familial 289.6
due to
donor twin 776.4
fall in plasma volume 289.0
high altitude 289.0
maternal-fetal transfusion 776.4
stress 289.0
emotional 289.0
erythropoietin 289.0
familial (benign) 289.6
Gaisböck's (hypertonica) 289.0
high altitude 289.0
hypertonica 289.0
hypoxemic 289.0
neonatorum 776.4
nephrogenous 289.0
relative 289.0
secondary 289.0
spurious 289.0
stress 289.0
Polycytosis cryptogenica 289.0
Polydactylism, polydactyly 755.00
fingers 755.01
toes 755.02
Polydipsia 783.5
Polydystrophic oligophrenia 277.5
Polyembryoma (M9072/3) — *see* Neoplasm, by site, malignant
Polygalactia 676.6 ☑
Polyglandular
deficiency 258.9
dyscrasia 258.9
dysfunction 258.9
syndrome 258.8
Polyhydramnios — *see also* Hydramnios 657.0 ☑
Polymastia 757.6
Polymenorrhea 626.2
Polymicrogyria 742.2
Polymyalgia 725
arteritica 446.5
rheumatica 725
Polymyositis (acute) (chronic) (hemorrhagic) 710.4
with involvement of
lung 710.4 *[517.8]*
skin 710.3
ossificans (generalisata) (progressiva) 728.19
Wagner's (dermatomyositis) 710.3
Polyneuritis, polyneuritic — *see also* Polyneuropathy 356.9
alcoholic 357.5
with psychosis 291.1
cranialis 352.6
demyelinating, chronic inflammatory (CIDP) 357.81
diabetic 250.6 ☑ *[357.2]*
due to secondary diabetes 249.6 ☑ *[357.2]*
due to lack of vitamin NEC 269.2 *[357.4]*
endemic 265.0 *[357.4]*
erythredema 985.0
febrile 357.0
hereditary ataxic 356.3
idiopathic, acute 357.0
infective (acute) 357.0
nutritional 269.9 *[357.4]*
postinfectious 357.0
Polyneuropathy (peripheral) 356.9
alcoholic 357.5

Note — Use the following fifth-digit subclassification with categories 640–649, 651–676:

0	*unspecified as to episode of care*
1	*delivered, with or without mention of antepartum condition*
2	*delivered, with mention of postpartum complication*
3	*antepartum condition or complication*
4	*postpartum condition or complication*

Pregnancy — *continued*
- complicated — *continued*
  - disorders of liver 646.7 ☑
  - displacement, uterus NEC 654.4 ☑
  - disproportion — *see* Disproportion
  - double uterus 654.0 ☑
  - drug dependence (conditions classifiable to 304) 648.3 ☑
  - dysplasia, cervix 654.6 ☑
  - early onset of delivery (spontaneous) 644.2 ☑
  - eclampsia, eclamptic (coma) (convulsions) (delirium) (nephritis) (uremia) 642.6 ☑
    - with pre-existing hypertension 642.7 ☑
  - edema 646.1 ☑
    - with hypertension — *see* Toxemia, of pregnancy
  - effusion, amniotic fluid 658.1 ☑
    - delayed delivery following 658.2 ☑
  - embolism
    - air 673.0 ☑
    - amniotic fluid 673.1 ☑
    - blood-clot 673.2 ☑
    - cerebral 674.0 ☑
    - pulmonary NEC 673.2 ☑
    - pyemic 673.3 ☑
    - septic 673.3 ☑
  - emesis (gravidarum) — *see* Pregnancy, complicated, vomiting
  - endometritis (conditions classifiable to 615.0–615.9) 670 ☑
    - decidual 646.6 ☑
  - epilepsy 649.4 ☑
  - excessive weight gain NEC 646.1 ☑
  - face presentation 652.4 ☑
  - failure, fetal head to enter pelvic brim 652.5 ☑
  - false labor (pains) 644.1 ☑
  - fatigue 646.8 ☑
  - fatty metamorphosis of liver 646.7 ☑
  - female genital mutilation 648.9 ☑
  - fetal
    - conjoined twins 678.1 ☑
    - death (near term) 656.4 ☑
      - early (before 22 completed weeks gestation) 632
    - deformity 653.7 ☑
    - distress 656.8 ☑
    - reduction of multiple fetuses reduced to single fetus 651.7 ☑
  - fibroid (tumor) (uterus) 654.1 ☑
  - footling presentation 652.8 ☑
    - with successful version 652.1 ☑
  - gallbladder disease 646.8 ☑
  - gastric banding status 649.2 ☑
  - gastric bypass status for obesity
  - goiter 648.1 ☑
  - gonococcal infection (conditions classifiable to 098) 647.1 ☑
  - gonorrhea (conditions classifiable to 098) 647.1 ☑
  - hemorrhage 641.9 ☑
    - accidental 641.2 ☑
    - before 22 completed weeks gestation NEC 640.9 ☑
    - cerebrovascular 674.0 ☑
    - due to
      - afibrinogenemia or other coagulation defect (conditions classifiable to 286.0–286.9) 641.3 ☑
      - leiomyoma, uterine 641.8 ☑
      - marginal sinus (rupture) 641.2 ☑
      - premature separation, placenta 641.2 ☑
      - trauma 641.8 ☑
    - early (before 22 completed weeks gestation) 640.9 ☑
    - threatened abortion 640.0 ☑

Pregnancy — *continued*
- complicated — *continued*
  - hemorrhage — *continued*
    - unavoidable 641.1 ☑
  - hepatitis (acute) (malignant) (subacute) 646.7 ☑
    - viral 647.6 ☑
  - herniation of uterus 654.4 ☑
  - high head at term 652.5 ☑
  - hydatidiform mole (delivered) (undelivered) 630
  - hydramnios 657.0 ☑
  - hydrocephalic fetus 653.6 ☑
  - hydrops amnii 657.0 ☑
  - hydrorrhea 658.1 ☑
  - hyperemesis (gravidarum) — *see* Hyperemesis, gravidarum
  - hypertension — *see* Hypertension, complicating pregnancy
  - hypertensive
    - chronic kidney disease 642.2 ☑
    - heart and chronic kidney disease 642.2 ☑
    - heart and renal disease 642.2 ☑
    - heart disease 642.2 ☑
    - renal disease 642.2 ☑
  - hypertensive heart and chronic kidney disease 642.2 ☑
  - hyperthyroidism 648.1 ☑
  - hypothyroidism 648.1 ☑
  - hysteralgia 646.8 ☑
  - icterus gravis 646.7 ☑
  - incarceration, uterus 654.3 ☑
  - incompetent cervix (os) 654.5 ☑
  - infection 647.9 ☑
    - amniotic fluid 658.4 ☑
    - bladder 646.6 ☑
    - genital organ (conditions classifiable to 614.0–614.5, 614.7–614.9, 615) 646.6 ☑
    - kidney (conditions classifiable to 590.0–590.9) 646.6 ☑
    - urinary (tract) 646.6 ☑
      - asymptomatic 646.5 ☑
  - infective and parasitic diseases NEC 647.8 ☑
  - inflammation
    - bladder 646.6 ☑
    - genital organ (conditions classifiable to 614.0–614.5, 614.7–614.9, 615) 646.6 ☑
    - urinary tract NEC 646.6 ☑
  - insufficient weight gain 646.8 ☑
  - intrauterine fetal death (near term) NEC 656.4 ☑
    - early (before 22 completed weeks' gestation) 632
  - malaria (conditions classifiable to 084) 647.4 ☑
  - malformation, uterus (congenital) 654.0 ☑
  - malnutrition (conditions classifiable to 260–269) 648.9 ☑
  - malposition
    - fetus — *see* Pregnancy, complicated, malpresentation
    - uterus or cervix 654.4 ☑
  - malpresentation 652.9 ☑
    - with successful version 652.1 ☑
    - in multiple gestation 652.6 ☑
    - specified type NEC 652.8 ☑
  - marginal sinus hemorrhage or rupture 641.2 ☑
  - maternal drug abuse 648.4 ☑
  - maternal obesity syndrome 646.1 ☑
  - menstruation 640.8 ☑
  - mental disorders (conditions classifiable to 290–303, 305.0, 305.2-305.9, 306–316, 317–319) 648.4 ☑
  - mentum presentation 652.4 ☑

Pregnancy — *continued*
- complicated — *continued*
  - missed
    - abortion 632
    - delivery (at or near term) 656.4 ☑
    - labor (at or near term) 656.4 ☑
  - necrosis
    - genital organ or tract (conditions classifiable to 614.0–614.5, 614.7–614.9, 615) 646.6 ☑
    - liver (conditions classifiable to 570) 646.7 ☑
    - renal, cortical 646.2 ☑
  - nephritis or nephrosis (conditions classifiable to 580–589) 646.2 ☑
    - with hypertension 642.1 ☑
  - nephropathy NEC 646.2 ☑
  - neuritis (peripheral) 646.4 ☑
  - nutritional deficiency (conditions classifiable to 260–269) 648.9 ☑
  - obesity 649.1 ☑
    - surgery status 649.2 ☑
  - oblique lie or presentation 652.3 ☑
    - with successful version 652.1 ☑
  - obstetrical trauma NEC 665.9 ☑
  - oligohydramnios NEC 658.0 ☑
  - onset of contractions before 37 weeks 644.0 ☑
  - oversize fetus 653.5 ☑
  - papyraceous fetus 646.0 ☑
  - patent cervix 654.5 ☑
  - pelvic inflammatory disease (conditions classifiable to 614.0–614.5, 614.7–614.9, 615) 646.6 ☑
  - pelvic peritoneal adhesion 648.9 ☑
  - placenta, placental
    - abnormality 656.7 ☑
    - abruptio or ablatio 641.2 ☑
    - detachment 641.2 ☑
    - disease 656.7 ☑
    - infarct 656.7 ☑
    - low implantation 641.1 ☑
      - without hemorrhage 641.0 ☑
    - malformation 656.7 ☑
    - malposition 641.1 ☑
      - without hemorrhage 641.0 ☑
    - marginal sinus hemorrhage 641.2 ☑
    - previa 641.1 ☑
      - without hemorrhage 641.0 ☑
    - separation (premature) (undelivered) 641.2 ☑
  - placentitis 658.4 ☑
  - polyhydramnios 657.0 ☑
  - postmaturity
    - post-term 645.1 ☑
    - prolonged 645.2 ☑
  - prediabetes 648.8 ☑
  - pre-eclampsia (mild) 642.4 ☑
    - severe 642.5 ☑
    - superimposed on pre-existing hypertensive disease 642.7 ☑
  - premature rupture of membranes 658.1 ☑
    - with delayed delivery 658.2 ☑
  - previous
    - infertility V23.0
    - in utero procedure during previous pregnancy V23.86
    - nonobstetric condition V23.89
    - poor obstetrical history V23.49
    - premature delivery V23.41
    - trophoblastic disease (conditions classifiable to 630) V23.1
  - prolapse, uterus 654.4 ☑
  - proteinuria (gestational) 646.2 ☑

Pregnancy — *continued*
- complicated — *continued*
  - proteinuria — *continued*
    - with hypertension — *see* Toxemia, of pregnancy
  - pruritus (neurogenic) 646.8 ☑
  - psychosis or psychoneurosis 648.4 ☑
  - ptyalism 646.8 ☑
  - pyelitis (conditions classifiable to 590.0–590.9) 646.6 ☑
  - renal disease or failure NEC 646.2 ☑
    - with secondary hypertension 642.1 ☑
    - hypertensive 642.2 ☑
  - retention, retained dead ovum 631
  - retroversion, uterus 654.3 ☑
  - Rh immunization, incompatibility, or sensitization 656.1 ☑
  - rubella (conditions classifiable to 056) 647.5 ☑
  - rupture
    - amnion (premature) 658.1 ☑
      - with delayed delivery 658.2 ☑
    - marginal sinus (hemorrhage) 641.2 ☑
    - membranes (premature) 658.1 ☑
      - with delayed delivery 658.2 ☑
    - uterus (before onset of labor) 665.0 ☑
  - salivation (excessive) 646.8 ☑
  - salpingo-oophoritis (conditions classifiable to 614.0–614.2) 646.6 ☑
  - septicemia (conditions classifiable to 038.0–038.9) 647.8 ☑
    - postpartum 670.0 ☑
    - puerperal 670.0 ☑
  - smoking 649.0 ☑
  - spasms, uterus (abnormal) 646.8 ☑
  - specified condition NEC 646.8 ☑
  - spotting 649.5 ☑
  - spurious labor pains 644.1 ☑
  - status post
    - bariatric surgery 649.2 ☑
    - gastric banding 649.2 ☑
    - gastric bypass for obesity 649.2 ☑
    - obesity surgery 649.2 ☑
  - superfecundation 651.9 ☑
  - superfetation 651.9 ☑
  - syphilis (conditions classifiable to 090–097) 647.0 ☑
  - threatened
    - abortion 640.0 ☑
    - premature delivery 644.2 ☑
    - premature labor 644.0 ☑
  - thrombophlebitis (superficial) 671.2 ☑
    - deep 671.3 ☑
  - thrombosis 671.9 ☑
    - venous (superficial) 671.2 ☑
      - deep 671.3 ☑
  - thyroid dysfunction (conditions classifiable to 240–246) 648.1 ☑
  - thyroiditis 648.1 ☑
  - thyrotoxicosis 648.1 ☑
  - tobacco use disorder 649.0 ☑
  - torsion of uterus 654.4 ☑
  - toxemia — *see* Toxemia, of pregnancy
  - transverse lie or presentation 652.3 ☑
    - with successful version 652.1 ☑
  - trauma 648.9 ☑
    - obstetrical 665.9 ☑
  - tuberculosis (conditions classifiable to 010–018) 647.3 ☑

Pregnancy — *continued*
  complicated — *continued*
    tumor
      cervix 654.6 ☑
      ovary 654.4 ☑
      pelvic organs or tissue NEC 654.4 ☑
      uterus (body) 654.1 ☑
        cervix 654.6 ☑
      vagina 654.7 ☑
      vulva 654.8 ☑
    unstable lie 652.0 ☑
    uremia — *see* Pregnancy, complicated, renal disease
    urethritis 646.6 ☑
    vaginitis or vulvitis (conditions classifiable to 616.1) 646.6 ☑
    varicose
      placental vessels 656.7 ☑
      veins (legs) 671.0 ☑
        perineum 671.1 ☑
        vulva 671.1 ☑
    varicosity, labia or vulva 671.1 ☑
    venereal disease NEC (conditions classifiable to 099) 647.2 ☑
    viral disease NEC (conditions classifiable to 042, 050–055, 057–079, 795.05, 795.15, 796.75) 647.6 ☑
    vomiting (incoercible) (pernicious) (persistent) (uncontrollable) (vicious) 643.9 ☑
      due to organic disease or other cause 643.8 ☑
      early — *see* Hyperemesis, gravidarum
      late (after 22 completed weeks gestation) 643.2 ☑
    young maternal age 659.8 ☑
  complications NEC 646.9 ☑
  cornual 633.80
    with intrauterine pregnancy 633.81
    affecting fetus or newborn 761.4
  death, maternal NEC 646.9 ☑
  delivered — *see* Delivery
  ectopic (ruptured) NEC 633.90
    with intrauterine pregnancy 633.91
    abdominal — *see* Pregnancy, abdominal
    affecting fetus or newborn 761.4
    combined (extrauterine and intrauterine) — *see* Pregnancy, cornual
    ovarian — *see* Pregnancy, ovarian
    specified type NEC 633.80
      with intrauterine pregnancy 633.81
      affecting fetus or newborn 761.4
    tubal — *see* Pregnancy, tubal
  examination, pregnancy
    negative result V72.41
    not confirmed V72.40
    positive result V72.42
  extrauterine — *see* Pregnancy, ectopic
  fallopian — *see* Pregnancy, tubal
  false 300.11
    labor (pains) 644.1 ☑
  fatigue 646.8 ☑
  illegitimate V61.6
  incidental finding V22.2
  in double uterus 654.0 ☑
  interstitial — *see* Pregnancy, cornual
  intraligamentous — *see* Pregnancy, cornual
  intramural — *see* Pregnancy, cornual
  intraperitoneal — *see* Pregnancy, abdominal
  isthmian — *see* Pregnancy, tubal
  management affected by
    abnormal, abnormality
      fetus (suspected) 655.9 ☑
        specified NEC 655.8 ☑
      placenta 656.7 ☑
    advanced maternal age NEC 659.6 ☑

Pregnancy — *continued*
  management affected by — *continued*
    advanced maternal age — *continued*
      multigravida 659.6 ☑
      primigravida 659.5 ☑
    antibodies (maternal)
      anti-c 656.1 ☑
      anti-d 656.1 ☑
      anti-e 656.1 ☑
      blood group (ABO) 656.2 ☑
        Rh(esus) 656.1 ☑
    appendicitis 648.9 ☑
    bariatric surgery status 649.2 ☑
    coagulation defect 649.3 ☑
    elderly multigravida 659.6 ☑
    elderly primigravida 659.5 ☑
    epilepsy 649.4 ☑
    fetal (suspected)
      abnormality 655.9 ☑
        abdominal 655.8 ☑
        acid-base balance 656.8 ☑
        cardiovascular 655.8 ☑
        facial 655.8 ☑
        gastrointestinal 655.8 ☑
        gentourinary 655.8 ☑
        heart rate or rhythm 659.7 ☑
        limb 655.8 ☑
        specified NEC 655.8 ☑
      acidemia 656.3 ☑
      anencephaly 655.0 ☑
      aneuploidy 655.1 ☑
      bradycardia 659.7 ☑
      central nervous system malformation 655.0 ☑
      chromosomal abnormalities (conditions classifiable to 758.0–758.9) 655.1 ☑
      damage from
        drugs 655.5 ☑
          obstetric, anesthetic, or sedative 655.5 ☑
        environmental toxins 655.8 ☑
        intrauterine contraceptive device 655.8 ☑
        maternal
          alcohol addiction 655.4 ☑
          disease NEC 655.4 ☑
          drug use 655.5 ☑
          listeriosis 655.4 ☑
          rubella 655.3 ☑
          toxoplasmosis 655.4 ☑
          viral infection 655.3 ☑
        radiation 655.6 ☑
      death (near term) 656.4 ☑
        early (before 22 completed weeks' gestation) 632
      distress 656.8 ☑
      excessive growth 656.6 ☑
      fetal-maternal hemorrhage 656.0 ☑
      growth retardation 656.5 ☑
      hereditary disease 655.2 ☑
      hereditary disease in family (possibly) affecting fetus 655.2 ☑
      hydrocephalus 655.0 ☑
      incompatibility, blood groups (ABO) 656.2 ☑
      intrauterine death 656.4 ☑
      poor growth 656.5 ☑
      Rh(esus) 656.1 ☑
      spina bifida (with myelomeningocele) 655.0 ☑
    gastric banding status 649.2 ☑
    gastric bypass status for obesity 649.2 ☑
    insufficient prenatal care V23.7
    intrauterine death 656.4 ☑
    isoimmunization (ABO) 656.2 ☑
      Rh(esus) 656.1 ☑

Pregnancy — *continued*
  management affected by — *continued*
    large-for-dates fetus 656.6 ☑
    light-for-dates fetus 656.5 ☑
    meconium in liquor 656.8 ☑
    mental disorder (conditions classifiable to 290–303, 305.0, 305.2–305.9, 306–316, 317–319) 648.4 ☑
    multiparity (grand) 659.4 ☑
    obesity 649.1 ☑
      surgery status 649.2 ☑
    poor obstetric history V23.49
      pre-term labor V23.41
    postmaturity
      post-term 645.1 ☑
      prolonged 645.2 ☑
    post-term pregnancy 645.1 ☑
    previous
      abortion V23.2
        habitual 646.3 ☑
      cesarean delivery 654.2 ☑
      difficult delivery V23.49
      forceps delivery V23.49
      habitual abortions 646.3 ☑
      hemorrhage, antepartum or postpartum V23.49
      hydatidiform mole V23.1
      infertility V23.0
      in utero procedure during previous pregnancy V23.86
      malignancy NEC V23.89
      nonobstetrical conditions V23.8 ☑
      premature delivery V23.41
      trophoblastic disease (conditions in 630) V23.1
      vesicular mole V23.1
    prolonged pregnancy 645.2 ☑
    small-for-dates fetus 656.5 ☑
    smoking 649.0 ☑
    spotting 649.5 ☑
    suspected conditions not found
      amniotic cavity and membrane problem V89.01
      cervical shortening V89.05
      fetal anomaly V89.03
      fetal growth problem V89.04
      oligohydramnios V89.01
      other specified problem NEC V89.09
      placental problem V89.02
      polyhydramnios V89.01
    tobacco use disorder 649.0 ☑
    young maternal age 659.8 ☑
  maternal death NEC 646.9 ☑
  mesometric (mural) — *see* Pregnancy, cornual
  molar 631
    hydatidiform (*see also* Hydatidiform mole) 630
      previous, affecting management of pregnancy V23.1
    previous, affecting management of pregnancy V23.49
  multiple NEC 651.9 ☑
    with fetal loss and retention of one or more fetus(es) 651.6 ☑
    affecting fetus or newborn 761.5
    following (elective) fetal reduction 651.7 ☑
    specified type NEC 651.8 ☑
      with fetal loss and retention of one or more fetus(es) 651.6 ☑
      following (elective) fetal reduction 651.7 ☑
  mural — *see* Pregnancy, cornual
  observation NEC V22.1
    first pregnancy V22.0
    high-risk V23.9
      specified problem NEC V23.89
  ovarian 633.20
    with intrauterine pregnancy 633.21
    affecting fetus or newborn 761.4

Pregnancy — *continued*
  possible, not (yet) confirmed V72.40
  postmature
    post-term 645.1 ☑
    prolonged 645.2 ☑
  post-term 645.1 ☑
  prenatal care only V22.1
    first pregnancy V22.0
    high-risk V23.9
      specified problem NEC V23.89
  prolonged 645.2 ☑
  quadruplet NEC 651.2 ☑
    with fetal loss and retention of one or more fetus(es) 651.5 ☑
    affecting fetus or newborn 761.5
    following (elective) fetal reduction 651.7 ☑
  quintuplet NEC 651.8 ☑
    with fetal loss and retention of one or more fetus(es) 651.6 ☑
    affecting fetus or newborn 761.5
    following (elective) fetal reduction 651.7 ☑
  resulting from
    assisted reproductive technology V23.85
    in vitro fertilization V23.85
  sextuplet NEC 651.8 ☑
    with fetal loss and retention of one or more fetus(es) 651.6 ☑
    affecting fetus or newborn 761.5
    following (elective) fetal reduction 651.7 ☑
  spurious 300.11
  superfecundation NEC 651.9 ☑
    with fetal loss and retention of one or more fetus(es) 651.6 ☑
    following (elective) fetal reduction 651.7 ☑
  superfetation NEC 651.9 ☑
    with fetal loss and retention of one or more fetus(es) 651.6 ☑
    following (elective) fetal reduction 651.7 ☑
  supervision (of) (for) (*see also* Pregnancy, management affected by)
    elderly
      multigravida V23.82
      primigravida V23.81
    high-risk V23.9
      insufficient prenatal care V23.7
      specified problem NEC V23.89
    multiparity V23.3
    normal NEC V22.1
      first V22.0
    poor
      obstetric history V23.49
        pre-term labor V23.41
      reproductive history V23.5
    previous
      abortion V23.2
      hydatidiform mole V23.1
      infertility V23.0
      neonatal death V23.5
      stillbirth V23.5
      trophoblastic disease V23.1
      vesicular mole V23.1
    specified problem NEC V23.89
    young
      multigravida V23.84
      primigravida V23.83
  triplet NEC 651.1 ☑
    with fetal loss and retention of one or more fetus(es) 651.4 ☑
    affecting fetus or newborn 761.5
    following (elective) fetal reduction 651.7 ☑
  tubal (with rupture) 633.10
    with intrauterine pregnancy 633.11
    affecting fetus or newborn 761.4
  twin NEC 651.0 ☑
    with fetal loss and retention of one fetus 651.3 ☑
    affecting fetus or newborn 761.5
    conjoined 678.1 ☑

Problem — *continued*
- placenta, affecting management of pregnancy — *continued*
  - specified type NEC 656.8 ☑
- poverty V60.2
- presence of sick or handicapped person in family or household V61.49
- psychiatric 300.9
- psychosocial V62.9
  - specified type NEC V62.89
- relational NEC V62.81
- relationship, childhood 313.3
- religious or spiritual belief
  - other than medical care V62.89
  - regarding medical care V62.6
- self-damaging behavior V69.8
- sexual
  - behavior, high-risk V69.2
  - function NEC V41.7
- sibling
  - relational V61.8
  - relationship V61.8
- sight V41.0
- sleep disorder, child 307.40
- sleep, lack of V69.4
- smell V41.5
- speech V40.1
- spite reaction, child (*see also* Disturbance, conduct) 312.0 ☑
- spoiled child reaction (*see also* Disturbance, conduct) 312.1 ☑
- swallowing V41.6
- tantrum, child (*see also* Disturbance, conduct) 312.1 ☑
- taste V41.5
- thumb sucking, child 307.9
- tic (child) 307.21
- trunk V48.9
  - deficiency V48.1
  - disfigurement V48.7
  - mechanical V48.3
  - motor V48.3
  - movement V48.3
  - sensory V48.5
  - specified condition NEC V48.8
- unemployment V62.0
- urinary NEC V47.4
- voice production V41.4

Procedure (surgical) **not done** NEC V64.3
- because of
  - contraindication V64.1
  - patient's decision V64.2
    - for reasons of conscience or religion V62.6
  - specified reason NEC V64.3

Procidentia
- anus (sphincter) 569.1
- rectum (sphincter) 569.1
- stomach 537.89
- uteri 618.1

Proctalgia 569.42
- fugax 564.6
- spasmodic 564.6
  - psychogenic 307.89

Proctitis 569.49
- amebic 006.8
- chlamydial 099.52
- gonococcal 098.7
- granulomatous 555.1
- idiopathic 556.2
  - with ulcerative sigmoiditis 556.3
- tuberculous (*see also* Tuberculosis) 014.8 ☑
- ulcerative (chronic) (nonspecific) 556.2
  - with ulcerative sigmoiditis 556.3

Proctocele
- female (without uterine prolapse) 618.04
  - with uterine prolapse 618.4
    - complete 618.3
    - incomplete 618.2
- male 569.49

Proctocolitis, idiopathic 556.2
- with ulcerative sigmoiditis 556.3

Proctoptosis 569.1

Proctosigmoiditis 569.89
- ulcerative (chronic) 556.3

Proctospasm 564.6
- psychogenic 306.4

Prodromal-AIDS — *see* Human immunodeficiency virus (disease) (illness) (infection)

Profichet's disease or syndrome 729.90

Progeria (adultorum) (syndrome) 259.8

Prognathism (mandibular) (maxillary) 524.00

Progonoma (melanotic) (M9363/0) — *see* Neoplasm, by site, benign

Progressive — *see* condition

Prolapse, prolapsed
- anus, anal (canal) (sphincter) 569.1
- arm or hand, complicating delivery 652.7 ☑
  - causing obstructed labor 660.0 ☑
    - affecting fetus or newborn 763.1
  - fetus or newborn 763.1
- bladder (acquired) (mucosa) (sphincter)
  - congenital (female) (male) 756.71
  - female (*see also* Cystocele, female) 618.01
  - male 596.8
- breast implant (prosthetic) 996.54
- cecostomy 569.69
- cecum 569.89
- cervix, cervical (hypertrophied) 618.1
  - anterior lip, obstructing labor 660.2 ☑
    - affecting fetus or newborn 763.1
  - congenital 752.49
  - postpartal (old) 618.1
  - stump 618.84
- ciliary body 871.1
- colon (pedunculated) 569.89
- colostomy 569.69
- conjunctiva 372.73
- cord — *see* Prolapse, umbilical cord
- disc (intervertebral) — *see* Displacement, intervertebral disc
- duodenum 537.89
- eye implant (orbital) 996.59
  - lens (ocular) 996.53
- fallopian tube 620.4
- fetal extremity, complicating delivery 652.8 ☑
  - causing obstructed labor 660.0 ☑
  - fetus or newborn 763.1
- funis — *see* Prolapse, umbilical cord
- gastric (mucosa) 537.89
- genital, female 618.9
  - specified NEC 618.89
- globe 360.81
- ileostomy bud 569.69
- intervertebral disc — *see* Displacement, intervertebral disc
- intestine (small) 569.89
- iris 364.89
  - traumatic 871.1
- kidney (*see also* Disease, renal) 593.0
  - congenital 753.3
- laryngeal muscles or ventricle 478.79
- leg, complicating delivery 652.8 ☑
  - causing obstructed labor 660.0 ☑
  - fetus or newborn 763.1
- liver 573.8
- meatus urinarius 599.5
- mitral valve 424.0
- ocular lens implant 996.53
- organ or site, congenital NEC — *see* Malposition, congenital
- ovary 620.4
- pelvic (floor), female 618.89
- perineum, female 618.89
- pregnant uterus 654.4 ☑
- rectum (mucosa) (sphincter) 569.1
  - due to Trichuris trichiuria 127.3
- spleen 289.59
- stomach 537.89
- umbilical cord
  - affecting fetus or newborn 762.4

Prolapse, prolapsed — *continued*
- umbilical cord — *continued*
  - complicating delivery 663.0 ☑
- ureter 593.89
  - with obstruction 593.4
- ureterovesical orifice 593.89
- urethra (acquired) (infected) (mucosa) 599.5
  - congenital 753.8
- uterovaginal 618.4
  - complete 618.3
  - incomplete 618.2
  - specified NEC 618.89
- uterus (first degree) (second degree) (third degree) (complete) (without vaginal wall prolapse) 618.1
  - with mention of vaginal wall prolapse — *see* Prolapse, uterovaginal
  - congenital 752.3
  - in pregnancy or childbirth 654.4 ☑
    - affecting fetus or newborn 763.1
    - causing obstructed labor 660.2 ☑
      - affecting fetus or newborn 763.1
  - postpartal (old) 618.1
- uveal 871.1
- vagina (anterior) (posterior) (vault) (wall) (without uterine prolapse) 618.00
  - with uterine prolapse 618.4
    - complete 618.3
    - incomplete 618.2
  - paravaginal 618.02
  - posthysterectomy 618.5
  - specified NEC 618.09
- vitreous (humor) 379.26
  - traumatic 871.1
- womb — *see* Prolapse, uterus

Prolapsus, female 618.9

Proliferative — *see* condition

Prolinemia 270.8

Prolinuria 270.8

Prolonged, prolongation
- bleeding time (*see also* Defect, coagulation) 790.92
  - "idiopathic" (in von Willebrand's disease) 286.4
- coagulation time (*see also* Defect, coagulation) 790.92
- gestation syndrome 766.22
- labor 662.1 ☑
  - affecting fetus or newborn 763.89
  - first stage 662.0 ☑
  - second stage 662.2 ☑
- pregnancy 645.2 ☑
- PR interval 426.11
- prothrombin time (*see also* Defect, coagulation) 790.92
- QT interval 794.31
  - syndrome 426.82
- rupture of membranes (24 hours or more prior to onset of labor) 658.2 ☑
- uterine contractions in labor 661.4 ☑
  - affecting fetus or newborn 763.7

Prominauris 744.29

Prominence
- auricle (ear) (congenital) 744.29
  - acquired 380.32
- ischial spine or sacral promontory
  - with disproportion (fetopelvic) 653.3 ☑
    - affecting fetus or newborn 763.1
    - causing obstructed labor 660.1 ☑
      - affecting fetus or newborn 763.1
- nose (congenital) 748.1
  - acquired 738.0

PROMM (proximal myotonic myotonia) 359.21

Pronation
- ankle 736.79
- foot 736.79

Pronation — *continued*
- foot — *continued*
  - congenital 755.67

Prophylactic
- administration of
  - agents affecting estrogen receptors and estrogen levels NEC V07.59
  - anastrozole (Arimidex) V07.52
  - antibiotics V58.62
  - antitoxin, any V07.2
  - antivenin V07.2
  - aromatase inhibitors V07.52
  - chemotherapeutic agent NEC V07.39
    - fluoride V07.31
  - diphtheria antitoxin V07.2
  - drug V07.39
  - estrogen receptor downregulators V07.59
  - exemestar (Aromasin) V07.52
  - fulvestrant (Faslodex) V07.59
  - gamma globulin V07.2
  - gonadotropin-releasing hormone (GnRH) agonist V07.59
  - goserelin acetate (Zoladex) V07.59
  - immune sera (gamma globulin) V07.2
  - letrozole (Femara) V07.52
  - leuprolide acetate (leuprorelin) (Lupron) V07.59
  - megestrol acetate (Megace) V07.59
  - raloxifene (Evista) V07.51
  - RhoGAM V07.2
  - selective estrogen receptor modulators (SERMs) V07.51
  - tamoxifen (Nolvadex) V07.51
  - tetanus antitoxin V07.2
  - toremifene (Fareston) V07.51
- chemotherapy NEC V07.39
  - fluoride V07.31
- hormone replacement (postmenopausal) V07.4
- immunotherapy V07.2
- measure V07.9
  - specified type NEC V07.8
- medication V07.39
- postmenopausal hormone replacement V07.4
- sterilization V25.2

Proptosis (ocular) — *see also* Exophthalmos 376.30
- thyroid 242.0 ☑

Propulsion
- eyeball 360.81

Prosecution, anxiety concerning V62.5

Prosopagnosia 368.16

Prostate, prostatic — *see* condition

Prostatism 600.90
- with
  - other lower urinary tract symptoms (LUTS) 600.91
  - urinary
    - obstruction 600.91
    - retention 600.91

Prostatitis (congestive) (suppurative) 601.9
- acute 601.0
- cavitary 601.8
- chlamydial 099.54
- chronic 601.1
- diverticular 601.8
- due to Trichomonas (vaginalis) 131.03
- fibrous 600.90
  - with
    - other lower urinary tract symptoms (LUTS) 600.91
    - urinary
      - obstruction 600.91
      - retention 600.91
- gonococcal (acute) 098.12
  - chronic or duration of 2 months or over 098.32
- granulomatous 601.8
- hypertrophic 600.00

Prostatitis — *continued*
hypertrophic — *continued*
with
other lower urinary tract symptoms (LUTS) 600.01
urinary
obstruction 600.01
retention 600.01
specified type NEC 601.8
subacute 601.1
trichomonal 131.03
tuberculous (*see also* Tuberculosis) 016.5 ☑ *[601.4]*
Prostatocystitis 601.3
Prostatorrhea 602.8
Prostatoseminovesiculitis, trichomonal 131.03
Prostration 780.79
heat 992.5
anhydrotic 992.3
due to
salt (and water) depletion 992.4
water depletion 992.3
nervous 300.5
newborn 779.89
senile 797
Protanomaly 368.51
Protanopia (anomalous trichromat) (complete) (incomplete) 368.51
Protection (against) (from) — *see* Prophylactic
Protein
deficiency 260
malnutrition 260
sickness (prophylactic) (therapeutic) 999.5
Proteinemia 790.99
Proteinosis
alveolar, lung or pulmonary 516.0
lipid 272.8
lipoid (of Urbach) 272.8
Proteinuria — *see also* Albuminuria 791.0
Bence-Jones NEC 791.0
gestational 646.2 ☑
with hypertension — *see* Toxemia, of pregnancy
orthostatic 593.6
postural 593.6
Proteolysis, pathologic 286.6
Protocoproporphyria 277.1
Protoporphyria (erythrohepatic) (erythropoietic) 277.1
Protrusio acetabuli 718.65
Protrusion
acetabulum (into pelvis) 718.65
device, implant, or graft — *see* Complications, mechanical
ear, congenital 744.29
intervertebral disc — *see* Displacement, intervertebral disc
nucleus pulposus — *see* Displacement, intervertebral disc
Proud flesh 701.5
Prune belly (syndrome) 756.71
Prurigo (ferox) (gravis) (Hebra's) (hebrae) (mitis) (simplex) 698.2
agria 698.3
asthma syndrome 691.8
Besnier's (atopic dermatitis) (infantile eczema) 691.8
eczematodes allergicum 691.8
estivalis (Hutchinson's) 692.72
Hutchinson's 692.72
nodularis 698.3
psychogenic 306.3
Pruritus, pruritic 698.9
ani 698.0
psychogenic 306.3
conditions NEC 698.9
psychogenic 306.3
due to Onchocerca volvulus 125.3
ear 698.9
essential 698.9
genital organ(s) 698.1
psychogenic 306.3
Pruritus, pruritic — *continued*
gravidarum 646.8 ☑
hiemalis 698.8
neurogenic (any site) 306.3
perianal 698.0
psychogenic (any site) 306.3
scrotum 698.1
psychogenic 306.3
senile, senilis 698.8
Trichomonas 131.9
vulva, vulvae 698.1
psychogenic 306.3
Psammocarcinoma (M8140/3) — *see* Neoplasm, by site, malignant
Pseudarthrosis, pseudoarthrosis (bone) 733.82
joint following fusion V45.4
Pseudoacanthosis
nigricans 701.8
Pseudoaneurysm — *see* Aneurysm
Pseudoangina (pectoris) — *see* Angina
Pseudoangioma 452
Pseudo-Argyll-Robertson pupil 379.45
Pseudoarteriosus 747.89
Pseudoarthrosis — *see* Pseudarthrosis
Pseudoataxia 799.89
Pseudobulbar affect (PBA) 310.8
Pseudobursa 727.89
Pseudocholera 025
Pseudochromidrosis 705.89
Pseudocirrhosis, liver, pericardial 423.2
Pseudocoarctation 747.21
Pseudocowpox 051.1
Pseudocoxalgia 732.1
Pseudocroup 478.75
Pseudocyesis 300.11
Pseudocyst
lung 518.89
pancreas 577.2
retina 361.19
Pseudodementia 300.16
Pseudoelephantiasis neuroarthritica 757.0
Pseudoemphysema 518.89
Pseudoencephalitis
superior (acute) hemorrhagic 265.1
Pseudoerosion cervix, congenital 752.49
Pseudoexfoliation, lens capsule 366.11
Pseudofracture (idiopathic) (multiple) (spontaneous) (symmetrical) 268.2
Pseudoglanders 025
Pseudoglioma 360.44
Pseudogout — *see* Chondrocalcinosis
Pseudohallucination 780.1
Pseudohemianesthesia 782.0
Pseudohemophilia (Bernuth's) (hereditary) (typeB) 286.4
type A 287.8
vascular 287.8
Pseudohermaphroditism 752.7
with chromosomal anomaly — *see* Anomaly, chromosomal
adrenal 255.2
female (without adrenocortical disorder) 752.7
with adrenocortical disorder 255.2
adrenal 255.2
male (without gonadal disorder) 752.7
with
adrenocortical disorder 255.2
cleft scrotum 752.7
feminizing testis 259.51
gonadal disorder 257.9
adrenal 255.2
Pseudohole, macula 362.54
Pseudo-Hurler's disease (mucolipidosis III) 272.7
Pseudohydrocephalus 348.2
Pseudohypertrophic muscular dystrophy (Erb's) 359.1
Pseudohypertrophy, muscle 359.1
Pseudohypoparathyroidism 275.49
Pseudoinfluenza 487.1
Pseudoinsomnia 307.49
Pseudoleukemia 288.8
infantile 285.8
Pseudomembranous — *see* condition
Pseudomeningocele (cerebral) (infective) 349.2
postprocedural 997.01
spinal 349.2
Pseudomenstruation 626.8
Pseudomucinous
cyst (ovary) (M8470/0) 220
peritoneum 568.89
Pseudomyeloma 273.1
Pseudomyxoma peritonei (M8480/6) 197.6
Pseudoneuritis optic (nerve) 377.24
papilla 377.24
congenital 743.57
Pseudoneuroma — *see* Injury, nerve, by site
Pseudo-obstruction
intestine (chronic) (idiopathic) (intermittent secondary) (primary) 564.89
acute 560.89
Pseudopapilledema 377.24
Pseudoparalysis
arm or leg 781.4
atonic, congenital 358.8
Pseudopelade 704.09
Pseudophakia V43.1
Pseudopolycythemia 289.0
Pseudopolyposis, colon 556.4
Pseudoporencephaly 348.0
Pseudopseudohypoparathyroidism 275.49
Pseudopsychosis 300.16
Pseudopterygium 372.52
Pseudoptosis (eyelid) 374.34
Pseudorabies 078.89
Pseudoretinitis, pigmentosa 362.65
Pseudorickets 588.0
senile (Pozzi's) 731.0
Pseudorubella 057.8
Pseudoscarlatina 057.8
Pseudosclerema 778.1
Pseudosclerosis (brain)
Jakob's 046.19
of Westphal (-Strümpell) (hepatolenticular degeneration) 275.1
spastic 046.19
with dementia
with behavioral disturbance 046.19 *[294.11]*
without behavioral disturbance 046.19 *[294.10]*
Pseudoseizure 780.39
non-psychiatric 780.39
psychiatric 300.11
Pseudotabes 799.89
diabetic 250.6 ☑ *[337.1]*
due to secondary diabetes 249.6 ☑ *[337.1]*
Pseudotetanus — *see also* Convulsions 780.39
Pseudotetany 781.7
hysterical 300.11
Pseudothalassemia 285.0
Pseudotrichinosis 710.3
Pseudotruncus arteriosus 747.29
Pseudotuberculosis, pasteurella (infection) 027.2
Pseudotumor
cerebri 348.2
orbit (inflammatory) 376.11
Pseudo-Turner's syndrome 759.89
Pseudoxanthoma elasticum 757.39
Psilosis (sprue) (tropical) 579.1
Monilia 112.89
nontropical 579.0
not sprue 704.00
Psittacosis 073.9
Psoitis 728.89
Psora NEC 696.1
Psoriasis 696.1
any type, except arthropathic 696.1
arthritic, arthropathic 696.0
Psoriasis — *continued*
buccal 528.6
flexural 696.1
follicularis 696.1
guttate 696.1
inverse 696.1
mouth 528.6
nummularis 696.1
psychogenic 316 *[696.1]*
punctata 696.1
pustular 696.1
rupioides 696.1
vulgaris 696.1
Psorospermiasis 136.4
Psorospermosis 136.4
follicularis (vegetans) 757.39
Psychalgia 307.80
Psychasthenia 300.89
compulsive 300.3
mixed compulsive states 300.3
obsession 300.3
Psychiatric disorder or problem NEC 300.9
Psychogenic — *see also* condition
factors associated with physical conditions 316
Psychoneurosis, psychoneurotic — *see also* Neurosis 300.9
anxiety (state) 300.00
climacteric 627.2
compensation 300.16
compulsion 300.3
conversion hysteria 300.11
depersonalization 300.6
depressive type 300.4
dissociative hysteria 300.15
hypochondriacal 300.7
hysteria 300.10
conversion type 300.11
dissociative type 300.15
mixed NEC 300.89
neurasthenic 300.5
obsessional 300.3
obsessive-compulsive 300.3
occupational 300.89
personality NEC 301.89
phobia 300.20
senile NEC 300.89
Psychopathic — *see also* condition
constitution, posttraumatic 310.2
with psychosis 293.9
personality 301.9
amoral trends 301.7
antisocial trends 301.7
asocial trends 301.7
mixed types 301.7
state 301.9
Psychopathy, sexual — *see also* Deviation, sexual 302.9
Psychophysiologic, psychophysiological condition — *see* Reaction, psychophysiologic
Psychose passionelle 297.8
Psychosexual identity disorder 302.6
adult-life 302.85
childhood 302.6
Psychosis 298.9
acute hysterical 298.1
affecting management of pregnancy, childbirth, or puerperium 648.4 ☑

Psychosis — *continued*
  affective (*see also* Disorder, mood) 296.90

> *Note — Use the following fifth-digit subclassification with categories 296.0–296.6:*
> 0 *unspecified*
> 1 *mild*
> 2 *moderate*
> 3 *severe, without mention of psychotic behavior*
> 4 *severe, specified as with psychotic behavior*
> 5 *in partial or unspecified remission*
> 6 *in full remission*

    drug-induced 292.84
    due to or associated with physical condition 293.83
    involutional 293.83
      recurrent episode 296.3 ☑
      single episode 296.2 ☑
    manic-depressive 296.80
      circular (alternating) 296.7
        currently depressed 296.5 ☑
        currently manic 296.4 ☑
      depressed type 296.2 ☑
        atypical 296.82
        recurrent episode 296.3 ☑
        single episode 296.2 ☑
      manic 296.0 ☑
        atypical 296.81
        recurrent episode 296.1 ☑
        single episode 296.0 ☑
      mixed type NEC 296.89
      specified type NEC 296.89
    senile 290.21
    specified type NEC 296.99
  alcoholic 291.9
    with
      anxiety 291.89
      delirium tremens 291.0
      delusions 291.5
      dementia 291.2
      hallucinosis 291.3
      jealousy 291.5
      mood disturbance 291.89
      paranoia 291.5
      persisting amnesia 291.1
      sexual dysfunction 291.89
      sleep disturbance 291.89
    amnestic confabulatory 291.1
    delirium tremens 291.0
    hallucinosis 291.3
    Korsakoff's, Korsakov's, Korsakow's 291.1
    paranoid type 291.5
    pathological intoxication 291.4
    polyneuritic 291.1
    specified type NEC 291.89
  alternating (*see also* Psychosis, manic-depressive, circular) 296.7
  anergastic (*see also* Psychosis, organic) 294.9
  arteriosclerotic 290.40
    with
      acute confusional state 290.41
      delirium 290.41
      delusions 290.42
      depressed mood 290.43
    depressed type 290.43
    paranoid type 290.42
    simple type 290.40
    uncomplicated 290.40
  atypical 298.9
    depressive 296.82
    manic 296.81
  borderline (schizophrenia) (*see also* Schizophrenia) 295.5 ☑
    of childhood (*see also* Psychosis, childhood) 299.8 ☑
    prepubertal 299.8 ☑
  brief reactive 298.8
  childhood, with origin specific to 299.9 ☑

> *Note — Use the following fifth-digit subclassification with category 299:*
> 0 *current or active state*
> 1 *residual state*

    atypical 299.8 ☑
    specified type NEC 299.8 ☑
  circular (*see also* Psychosis, manic-depressive, circular) 296.7
  climacteric (*see also* Psychosis, involutional) 298.8
  confusional 298.9
    acute 293.0
    reactive 298.2
    subacute 293.1
  depressive (*see also* Psychosis, affective) 296.2 ☑
    atypical 296.82
    involutional 296.2 ☑
      with hypomania (bipolar II) 296.89
      recurrent episode 296.3 ☑
      single episode 296.2 ☑
    psychogenic 298.0
    reactive (emotional stress) (psychological trauma) 298.0
    recurrent episode 296.3 ☑
      with hypomania (bipolar II) 296.89
    single episode 296.2 ☑
  disintegrative, childhood (*see also* Psychosis, childhood) 299.1 ☑
  drug 292.9
    with
      affective syndrome 292.84
      amnestic syndrome 292.83
      anxiety 292.89
      delirium 292.81
        withdrawal 292.0
      delusions 292.11
      dementia 292.82
      depressive state 292.84
      hallucinations 292.12
      hallucinosis 292.12
      mood disorder 292.84
      mood disturbance 292.84
      organic personality syndrome NEC 292.89
      sexual dysfunction 292.89
      sleep disturbance 292.89
      withdrawal syndrome (and delirium) 292.0
    affective syndrome 292.84
    delusions 292.11
    hallucinatory state 292.12
    hallucinosis 292.12
    paranoid state 292.11
    specified type NEC 292.89
    withdrawal syndrome (and delirium) 292.0
  due to or associated with physical condition (*see also* Psychosis, organic) 293.9
  epileptic NEC 294.8
  excitation (psychogenic) (reactive) 298.1
  exhaustive (*see also* Reaction, stress, acute) 308.9
  hypomanic (*see also* Psychosis, affective) 296.0 ☑
    recurrent episode 296.1 ☑
    single episode 296.0 ☑
  hysterical 298.8
    acute 298.1
  in
    conditions classified elsewhere
      with
        delusions 293.81
        hallucinations 293.82
    pregnancy, childbirth, or puerperium 648.4 ☑
  incipient 298.8
    schizophrenic (*see also* Schizophrenia) 295.5 ☑
  induced 297.3
  infantile (*see also* Psychosis, childhood) 299.0 ☑
  infective 293.9
    acute 293.0
    subacute 293.1
  interactional (childhood) (*see also* Psychosis, childhood) 299.1 ☑
  involutional 298.8
    depressive (*see also* Psychosis, affective) 296.2 ☑
      recurrent episode 296.3 ☑
      single episode 296.2 ☑
    melancholic 296.2 ☑
      recurrent episode 296.3 ☑
      single episode 296.2 ☑
    paranoid state 297.2
    paraphrenia 297.2
  Korsakoff's, Korakov's, Korsakow's (nonalcoholic) 294.0
    alcoholic 291.1
  mania (phase) (*see also* Psychosis, affective) 296.0 ☑
    recurrent episode 296.1 ☑
    single episode 296.0 ☑
  manic (*see also* Psychosis, affective) 296.0 ☑
    atypical 296.81
    recurrent episode 296.1 ☑
    single episode 296.0 ☑
  manic-depressive 296.80
    circular 296.7
      currently
        depressed 296.5 ☑
        manic 296.4 ☑
      mixed 296.6 ☑
    depressive 296.2 ☑
      recurrent episode 296.3 ☑
        with hypomania (bipolar II) 296.89
      single episode 296.2 ☑
    hypomanic 296.0 ☑
      recurrent episode 296.1 ☑
      single episode 296.0 ☑
    manic 296.0 ☑
      atypical 296.81
      recurrent episode 296.1 ☑
      single episode 296.0 ☑
    mixed NEC 296.89
    perplexed 296.89
    stuporous 296.89
  menopausal (*see also* Psychosis, involutional) 298.8
  mixed schizophrenic and affective (*see also* Schizophrenia) 295.7 ☑
  multi-infarct (cerebrovascular) (*see also* Psychosis, arteriosclerotic) 290.40
  organic NEC 294.9
    due to or associated with
      addiction
        alcohol (*see also* Psychosis, alcoholic) 291.9
        drug (*see also* Psychosis, drug) 292.9
      alcohol intoxication, acute (*see also* Psychosis, alcoholic) 291.9
      alcoholism (*see also* Psychosis, alcoholic) 291.9
      arteriosclerosis (cerebral) (*see also* Psychosis, arteriosclerotic) 290.40
      cerebrovascular disease
        acute (psychosis) 293.0
        arteriosclerotic (*see also* Psychosis, arteriosclerotic) 290.40
      childbirth — *see* Psychosis, puerperal
      dependence
        alcohol (*see also* Psychosis, alcoholic) 291.9
        drug 292.9
      disease
        alcoholic liver (*see also* Psychosis, alcoholic) 291.9
        brain
          arteriosclerotic (*see also* Psychosis, arteriosclerotic) 290.40
        cerebrovascular
          acute (psychosis) 293.0
          arteriosclerotic (*see also* Psychosis, arteriosclerotic) 290.40
        endocrine or metabolic 293.9
          acute (psychosis) 293.0
          subacute (psychosis) 293.1
        Jakob-Creutzfeldt 046.19
          with behavioral disturbance 046.19 *[294.11]*
          without behavioral disturbance 046.19 *[294.10]*
          familial 046.19
          iatrogenic 046.19
          specified NEC 046.19
          sporadic 046.19
          variant 046.11
            with dementia
              with behavioral disturbance 046.11 *[294.11]*
              without behavioral disturbance 046.11 *[294.10]*
        liver, alcoholic (*see also* Psychosis, alcoholic) 291.9
      disorder
        cerebrovascular
          acute (psychosis) 293.0
        endocrine or metabolic 293.9
          acute (psychosis) 293.0
          subacute (psychosis) 293.1
      epilepsy
        with behavioral disturbance 345.9 ☑ *[294.11]*
        without behavioral disturbance 345.9 ☑ *[294.10]*
        transient (acute) 293.0
      Huntington's chorea
        with behavioral disturbance 333.4 *[294.11]*
        without behavioral disturbance 333.4 *[294.10]*
      infection
        brain 293.9
          acute (psychosis) 293.0
          chronic 294.8
          subacute (psychosis) 293.1
        intracranial NEC 293.9
          acute (psychosis) 293.0
          chronic 294.8
          subacute (psychosis) 293.1
      intoxication
        alcoholic (acute) (*see also* Psychosis, alcoholic) 291.9
          pathological 291.4
        drug (*see also* Psychosis, drug) 292.2
      ischemia
        cerebrovascular (generalized) (*see also* Psychosis, arteriosclerotic) 290.40

Puerperal — *continued*
- endophlebitis — *see* Puerperal, phlebitis
- endotrachelitis 646.6 ☑
- engorgement, breasts 676.2 ☑
- erysipelas 670.0 ☑
- failure
  - lactation 676.4 ☑
  - renal, acute 669.3 ☑
- fever 670.0 ☑
  - meaning pyrexia (of unknown origin) 672.0 ☑
  - meaning sepsis 670.0 ☑
- fissure, nipple 676.1 ☑
- fistula
  - breast 675.1 ☑
  - mammary gland 675.1 ☑
  - nipple 675.0 ☑
- galactophoritis 675.2 ☑
- galactorrhea 676.6 ☑
- gangrene
  - gas 670.0 ☑
  - uterus 670.0 ☑
- gonorrhea (conditions classifiable to 098) 647.1 ☑
- hematoma, subdural 674.0 ☑
- hematosalpinx, infectional 670.0 ☑
- hemiplegia, cerebral 674.0 ☑
- hemorrhage 666.1 ☑
  - brain 674.0 ☑
  - bulbar 674.0 ☑
  - cerebellar 674.0 ☑
  - cerebral 674.0 ☑
  - cortical 674.0 ☑
  - delayed (after 24 hours) (uterine) 666.2 ☑
  - extradural 674.0 ☑
  - internal capsule 674.0 ☑
  - intracranial 674.0 ☑
  - intrapontine 674.0 ☑
  - meningeal 674.0 ☑
  - pontine 674.0 ☑
  - subarachnoid 674.0 ☑
  - subcortical 674.0 ☑
  - subdural 674.0 ☑
  - uterine, delayed 666.2 ☑
  - ventricular 674.0 ☑
- hemorrhoids 671.8 ☑
- hepatorenal syndrome 674.8 ☑
- hypertrophy
  - breast 676.3 ☑
  - mammary gland 676.3 ☑
- induration breast (fibrous) 676.3 ☑
- infarction
  - lung — *see* Puerperal, embolism
  - pulmonary — *see* Puerperal, embolism
- infection
  - Bartholin's gland 646.6 ☑
  - breast 675.2 ☑
    - with nipple 675.9 ☑
      - specified type NEC 675.8 ☑
  - cervix 646.6 ☑
  - endocervix 646.6 ☑
  - fallopian tube 670.0 ☑
  - generalized 670.0 ☑
  - genital tract (major) 670.0 ☑
    - minor or localized 646.6 ☑
  - kidney (bacillus coli) 646.6 ☑
  - mammary gland 675.2 ☑
    - with nipple 675.9 ☑
      - specified type NEC 675.8 ☑
  - nipple 675.0 ☑
    - with breast 675.9 ☑
      - specified type NEC 675.8 ☑
  - ovary 670.0 ☑
  - pelvic 670.0 ☑
  - peritoneum 670.0 ☑
  - renal 646.6 ☑
  - tubo-ovarian 670.0 ☑
  - urinary (tract) NEC 646.6 ☑
    - asymptomatic 646.5 ☑
  - uterus, uterine 670.0 ☑
  - vagina 646.6 ☑

Puerperal — *continued*
- inflammation (*see also* Puerperal, infection)
  - areola 675.1 ☑
  - Bartholin's gland 646.6 ☑
  - breast 675.2 ☑
  - broad ligament 670.0 ☑
  - cervix (uteri) 646.6 ☑
  - fallopian tube 670.0 ☑
  - genital organs 670.0 ☑
    - localized 646.6 ☑
  - mammary gland 675.2 ☑
  - nipple 675.0 ☑
  - ovary 670.0 ☑
  - oviduct 670.0 ☑
  - pelvis 670.0 ☑
  - periuterine 670.0 ☑
  - tubal 670.0 ☑
  - vagina 646.6 ☑
  - vein — *see* Puerperal, phlebitis
- inversion, nipple 676.3 ☑
- ischemia, cerebral 674.0 ☑
- lymphangitis 670.0 ☑
  - breast 675.2 ☑
- malaria (conditions classifiable to 084) 647.4 ☑
- malnutrition 648.9 ☑
- mammillitis 675.0 ☑
- mammitis 675.2 ☑
- mania 296.0 ☑
  - recurrent episode 296.1 ☑
  - single episode 296.0 ☑
- mastitis 675.2 ☑
  - purulent 675.1 ☑
  - retromammary 675.1 ☑
  - submammary 675.1 ☑
- melancholia 296.2 ☑
  - recurrent episode 296.3 ☑
  - single episode 296.2 ☑
- mental disorder (conditions classifiable to 290–303, 305.0, 305.2–305.9, 306–316, 317–319) 648.4 ☑
- metritis (septic) (suppurative) 670.0 ☑
- metroperitonitis 670.0 ☑
- metrorrhagia 666.2 ☑
- metrosalpingitis 670.0 ☑
- metrovaginitis 670.0 ☑
- milk leg 671.4 ☑
- monoplegia, cerebral 674.0 ☑
- necrosis
  - kidney, tubular 669.3 ☑
  - liver (acute) (subacute) (conditions classifiable to 570) 674.8 ☑
  - ovary 670.0 ☑
  - renal cortex 669.3 ☑
- nephritis or nephrosis (conditions classifiable to 580–589) 646.2 ☑
  - with hypertension 642.1 ☑
- nutritional deficiency (conditions classifiable to 260–269) 648.9 ☑
- occlusion, precerebral artery 674.0 ☑
- oliguria 669.3 ☑
- oophoritis 670.0 ☑
- ovaritis 670.0 ☑
- paralysis
  - bladder (sphincter) 665.5 ☑
  - cerebral 674.0 ☑
- paralytic stroke 674.0 ☑
- parametritis 670.0 ☑
- paravaginitis 646.6 ☑
- pelviperitonitis 670.0 ☑
- perimetritis 670.0 ☑
- perimetrosalpingitis 670.0 ☑
- perinephritis 646.6 ☑
- perioophoritis 670.0 ☑
- periphlebitis — *see* Puerperal, phlebitis
- perisalpingitis 670.0 ☑
- peritoneal infection 670.0 ☑
- peritonitis (pelvic) 670.0 ☑
- perivaginitis 646.6 ☑
- phlebitis 671.9 ☑
  - deep 671.4 ☑

Puerperal — *continued*
- phlebitis — *continued*
  - intracranial sinus (venous) 671.5 ☑
  - pelvic 671.4 ☑
  - specified site NEC 671.5 ☑
  - superficial 671.2 ☑
- phlegmasia alba dolens 671.4 ☑
- placental polyp 674.4 ☑
- pneumonia, embolic — *see* Puerperal, embolism
- prediabetes 648.8 ☑
- pre-eclampsia (mild) 642.4 ☑
  - with pre-existing hypertension 642.7 ☑
  - severe 642.5 ☑
- psychosis, unspecified (*see also* Psychosis, puerperal) 293.89
- pyelitis 646.6 ☑
- pyelocystitis 646.6 ☑
- pyelohydronephrosis 646.6 ☑
- pyelonephritis 646.6 ☑
- pyelonephrosis 646.6 ☑
- pyemia 670.0 ☑
- pyocystitis 646.6 ☑
- pyohemia 670.0 ☑
- pyometra 670.0 ☑
- pyonephritis 646.6 ☑
- pyonephrosis 646.6 ☑
- pyo-oophoritis 670.0 ☑
- pyosalpingitis 670.0 ☑
- pyosalpinx 670.0 ☑
- pyrexia (of unknown origin) 672.0 ☑
- renal
  - disease NEC 646.2 ☑
  - failure, acute 669.3 ☑
- retention
  - decidua (fragments) (with delayed hemorrhage) 666.2 ☑
    - without hemorrhage 667.1 ☑
  - placenta (fragments) (with delayed hemorrhage) 666.2 ☑
    - without hemorrhage 667.1 ☑
  - secundines (fragments) (with delayed hemorrhage) 666.2 ☑
    - without hemorrhage 667.1 ☑
- retracted nipple 676.0 ☑
- rubella (conditions classifiable to 056) 647.5 ☑
- salpingitis 670.0 ☑
- salpingo-oophoritis 670.0 ☑
- salpingo-ovaritis 670.0 ☑
- salpingoperitonitis 670.0 ☑
- sapremia 670.0 ☑
- secondary perineal tear 674.2 ☑
- sepsis (pelvic) 670.0 ☑
- septicemia 670.0 ☑
- subinvolution (uterus) 674.8 ☑
- sudden death (cause unknown) 674.9 ☑
- suppuration — *see* Puerperal, abscess
- syphilis (conditions classifiable to 090–097) 647.0 ☑
- tetanus 670.0 ☑
- thelitis 675.0 ☑
- thrombocytopenia 666.3 ☑
- thrombophlebitis (superficial) 671.2 ☑
  - deep 671.4 ☑
  - pelvic 671.4 ☑
  - specified site NEC 671.5 ☑
- thrombosis (venous) — *see* Thrombosis, puerperal
- thyroid dysfunction (conditions classifiable to 240–246) 648.1 ☑
- toxemia (*see also* Toxemia, of pregnancy) 642.4 ☑
  - eclamptic 642.6 ☑
    - with pre-existing hypertension 642.7 ☑
  - pre-eclamptic (mild) 642.4 ☑
    - with
      - convulsions 642.6 ☑
      - pre-existing hypertension 642.7 ☑

Puerperal — *continued*
- toxemia (*see also* Toxemia, of pregnancy) — *continued*
  - pre-eclamptic — *continued*
    - severe 642.5 ☑
- tuberculosis (conditions classifiable to 010–018) 647.3 ☑
- uremia 669.3 ☑
- vaginitis (conditions classifiable to 616.1) 646.6 ☑
- varicose veins (legs) 671.0 ☑
  - vulva or perineum 671.1 ☑
- vulvitis (conditions classifiable to 616.1) 646.6 ☑
- vulvovaginitis (conditions classifiable to 616.1) 646.6 ☑
- white leg 671.4 ☑

Pulled muscle — *see* Sprain, by site

Pulmolithiasis 518.89

Pulmonary — *see* condition

Pulmonitis (unknown etiology) 486

Pulpitis (acute) (anachoretic) (chronic) (hyperplastic) (putrescent) (suppurative) (ulcerative) 522.0

Pulpless tooth 522.9

Pulse
- alternating 427.89
  - psychogenic 306.2
- bigeminal 427.89
- fast 785.0
- feeble, rapid, due to shock following injury 958.4
- rapid 785.0
- slow 427.89
- strong 785.9
- trigeminal 427.89
- water-hammer (*see also* Insufficiency, aortic) 424.1
- weak 785.9

Pulseless disease 446.7

Pulsus
- alternans or trigeminy 427.89
  - psychogenic 306.2

Punch drunk 310.2

Puncta lacrimalia occlusion 375.52

Punctiform hymen 752.49

Puncture (traumatic) — *see also* Wound, open, by site
- accidental, complicating surgery 998.2
- bladder, nontraumatic 596.6
- by
  - device, implant, or graft — *see* Complications, mechanical
  - foreign body
    - internal organs (*see also* Injury, internal, by site)
      - by ingested object — *see* Foreign body
    - left accidentally in operation wound 998.4
  - instrument (any) during a procedure, accidental 998.2
- internal organs, abdomen, chest, or pelvis — *see* Injury, internal, by site
- kidney, nontraumatic 593.89

Pupil — *see* condition

Pupillary membrane 364.74
- persistent 743.46

Pupillotonia 379.46
- pseudotabetic 379.46

Purpura 287.2
- abdominal 287.0
- allergic 287.0
- anaphylactoid 287.0
- annularis telangiectodes 709.1
- arthritic 287.0
- autoerythrocyte sensitization 287.2
- autoimmune 287.0
- bacterial 287.0
- Bateman's (senile) 287.2
- capillary fragility (hereditary) (idiopathic) 287.8
- cryoglobulinemic 273.2
- devil's pinches 287.2

Purpura — *continued*
- fibrinolytic (*see also* Fibrinolysis) 286.6
- fulminans, fulminous 286.6
- gangrenous 287.0
- hemorrhagic (*see also* Purpura, thrombocytopenic) 287.39
  - nodular 272.7
  - nonthrombocytopenic 287.0
  - thrombocytopenic 287.39
- Henoch's (purpura nervosa) 287.0
- Henoch-Schönlein (allergic) 287.0
- hypergammaglobulinemic (benign primary) (Waldenström's) 273.0
- idiopathic 287.31
  - nonthrombocytopenic 287.0
  - thrombocytopenic 287.31
- immune thrombocytopenic 287.31
- infectious 287.0
- malignant 287.0
- neonatorum 772.6
- nervosa 287.0
- newborn NEC 772.6
- nonthrombocytopenic 287.2
  - hemorrhagic 287.0
  - idiopathic 287.0
- nonthrombopenic 287.2
- peliosis rheumatica 287.0
- pigmentaria, progressiva 709.09
- posttransfusion 287.4
- primary 287.0
- primitive 287.0
- red cell membrane sensitivity 287.2
- rheumatica 287.0
- Schönlein (-Henoch) (allergic) 287.0
- scorbutic 267
- senile 287.2
- simplex 287.2
- symptomatica 287.0
- telangiectasia annularis 709.1
- thrombocytopenic (*see also* Thrombocytopenia) 287.30
  - congenital 287.33
  - essential 287.30
  - hereditary 287.31
  - idiopathic 287.31
  - immune 287.31
  - neonatal, transitory (*see also* Thrombocytopenia, neonatal transitory) 776.1
  - primary 287.30
  - puerperal, postpartum 666.3 ☑
  - thrombotic 446.6
- thrombohemolytic (*see also* Fibrinolysis) 286.6
- thrombopenic (*see also* Thrombocytopenia) 287.30
  - congenital 287.33
  - essential 287.30
  - thrombotic 446.6
    - thrombocytic 446.6
    - thrombocytopenic 446.6
- toxic 287.0
- variolosa 050.0
- vascular 287.0
- visceral symptoms 287.0
- Werlhof's (*see also* Purpura, thrombocytopenic) 287.39

Purpuric spots 782.7

Purulent — *see* condition

Pus
- absorption, general — *see* Septicemia
- in
  - stool 792.1
  - urine 791.9
- tube (rupture) (*see also* Salpingo-oophoritis) 614.2

Pustular rash 782.1

Pustule 686.9
- malignant 022.0
- nonmalignant 686.9

Putnam-Dana syndrome (subacute combined sclerosis with pernicious anemia) 281.0 *[336.2]*

Putnam's disease (subacute combined sclerosis with pernicious anemia) 281.0 *[336.2]*

Putrefaction, intestinal 569.89

Putrescent pulp (dental) 522.1

Pyarthritis — *see* Pyarthrosis

Pyarthrosis — *see also* Arthritis, pyogenic 711.0 ☑
- tuberculous — *see* Tuberculosis, joint

Pycnoepilepsy, pycnolepsy (idiopathic) — *see also* Epilepsy 345.0 ☑

Pyelectasia 593.89

Pyelectasis 593.89

Pyelitis (congenital) (uremic) 590.80
- with
  - abortion — *see* Abortion, by type, with specified complication NEC
  - contracted kidney 590.00
  - ectopic pregnancy (*see also* categories 633.0–633.9) 639.8
  - molar pregnancy (*see also* categories 630–632) 639.8
- acute 590.10
  - with renal medullary necrosis 590.11
- chronic 590.00
  - with
    - renal medullary necrosis 590.01
- complicating pregnancy, childbirth, or puerperium 646.6 ☑
  - affecting fetus or newborn 760.1
- cystica 590.3
  - following
    - abortion 639.8
    - ectopic or molar pregnancy 639.8
- gonococcal 098.19
  - chronic or duration of 2 months or over 098.39
- tuberculous (*see also* Tuberculosis) 016.0 ☑ *[590.81]*

Pyelocaliectasis 593.89

Pyelocystitis — *see also* Pyelitis 590.80

Pyelohydronephrosis 591

Pyelonephritis — *see also* Pyelitis 590.80
- acute 590.10
  - with renal medullary necrosis 590.11
- chronic 590.00
- syphilitic (late) 095.4
- tuberculous (*see also* Tuberculosis) 016.0 ☑ *[590.81]*

Pyelonephrosis — *see also* Pyelitis 590.80
- chronic 590.00

Pyelophlebitis 451.89

Pyelo-ureteritis cystica 590.3

Pyemia, pyemic (purulent) — *see also* Septicemia 038.9
- abscess — *see* Abscess
- arthritis (*see also* Arthritis, pyogenic) 711.0 ☑
- Bacillus coli 038.42
- embolism (*see also* Septicemia) 415.12
- fever 038.9
- infection 038.9
- joint (*see also* Arthritis, pyogenic) 711.0 ☑
- liver 572.1
- meningococcal 036.2
- newborn 771.81
- phlebitis — *see* Phlebitis
- pneumococcal 038.2
- portal 572.1
- postvaccinal 999.39
- specified organism NEC 038.8
- staphylococcal 038.10
  - aureus 038.11
    - methicillin
      - resistant 038.12
      - susceptible 038.11
  - specified organism NEC 038.19
- streptococcal 038.0

Pyemia, pyemic — *see also* Septicemia — *continued*
- tuberculous — *see* Tuberculosis, miliary

Pygopagus 759.4

Pykno-epilepsy, pyknolepsy (idiopathic) — *see also* Epilepsy 345.0 ☑

Pyle (-Cohn) disease (craniometaphyseal dysplasia) 756.89

Pylephlebitis (suppurative) 572.1

Pylethrombophlebitis 572.1

Pylethrombosis 572.1

Pyloritis — *see also* Gastritis 535.5 ☑

Pylorospasm (reflex) 537.81
- congenital or infantile 750.5
- neurotic 306.4
- newborn 750.5
- psychogenic 306.4

Pylorus, pyloric — *see* condition

Pyoarthrosis — *see* Pyarthrosis

Pyocele
- mastoid 383.00
- sinus (accessory) (nasal) (*see also* Sinusitis) 473.9
- turbinate (bone) 473.9
- urethra (*see also* Urethritis) 597.0

Pyococcal dermatitis 686.00

Pyococcide, skin 686.00

Pyocolpos — *see also* Vaginitis 616.10

Pyocyaneus dermatitis 686.09

Pyocystitis — *see also* Cystitis 595.9

Pyoderma, pyodermia 686.00
- gangrenosum 686.01
- specified type NEC 686.09
- vegetans 686.8

Pyodermatitis 686.00
- vegetans 686.8

Pyogenic — *see* condition

Pyohemia — *see* Septicemia

Pyohydronephrosis — *see also* Pyelitis 590.80

Pyometra 615.9

Pyometritis — *see also* Endometritis 615.9

Pyometrium — *see also* Endometritis 615.9

Pyomyositis 728.0
- ossificans 728.19
- tropical (bungpagga) 040.81

Pyonephritis — *see also* Pyelitis 590.80
- chronic 590.00

Pyonephrosis (congenital) — *see also* Pyelitis 590.80
- acute 590.10

Pyo-oophoritis — *see also* Salpingo-oophoritis 614.2

Pyo-ovarium — *see also* Salpingo-oophoritis 614.2

Pyopericarditis 420.99

Pyopericardium 420.99

Pyophlebitis — *see* Phlebitis

Pyopneumopericardium 420.99

Pyopneumothorax (infectional) 510.9
- with fistula 510.0
- subdiaphragmatic (*see also* Peritonitis) 567.29
- subphrenic (*see also* Peritonitis) 567.29
- tuberculous (*see also* Tuberculosis, pleura) 012.0 ☑

Pyorrhea (alveolar) (alveolaris) 523.40
- degenerative 523.5

Pyosalpingitis — *see also* Salpingo-oophoritis 614.2

Pyosalpinx — *see also* Salpingo-oophoritis 614.2

Pyosepticemia — *see* Septicemia

Pyosis
- Corlett's (impetigo) 684
- Manson's (pemphigus contagiosus) 684

Pyothorax 510.9
- with fistula 510.0
- tuberculous (*see also* Tuberculosis, pleura) 012.0 ☑

Pyoureter 593.89

Pyoureter — *continued*
- tuberculous (*see also* Tuberculosis) 016.2 ☑

Pyramidopallidonigral syndrome 332.0

Pyrexia (of unknown origin) (P.U.O.) 780.60
- atmospheric 992.0
- during labor 659.2 ☑
- environmentally-induced newborn 778.4
- heat 992.0
- newborn, environmentally-induced 778.4
- puerperal 672.0 ☑

Pyroglobulinemia 273.8

Pyromania 312.33

Pyrosis 787.1

Pyrroloporphyria 277.1

Pyuria (bacterial) 791.9

Q

Q fever 083.0
- with pneumonia 083.0 *[484.8]*

Quadricuspid aortic valve 746.89

Quadrilateral fever 083.0

Quadriparesis — *see* Quadriplegia
- meaning muscle weakness 728.87

Quadriplegia 344.00
- with fracture, vertebra (process) — *see* Fracture, vertebra, cervical, with spinal cord injury
- brain (current episode) 437.8
- C1-C4
  - complete 344.01
  - incomplete 344.02
- C5-C7
  - complete 344.03
  - incomplete 344.04
- cerebral (current episode) 437.8
- congenital or infantile (cerebral) (spastic) (spinal) 343.2
- cortical 437.8
- embolic (current episode) (*see also* Embolism, brain) 434.1 ☑
- functional 780.72
- infantile (cerebral) (spastic) (spinal) 343.2
- newborn NEC 767.0
- specified NEC 344.09
- thrombotic (current episode) (*see also* Thrombosis, brain) 434.0 ☑
- traumatic — *see* Injury, spinal, cervical

Quadruplet
- affected by maternal complications of pregnancy 761.5
- healthy liveborn — *see* Newborn, multiple
- pregnancy (complicating delivery) NEC 651.8 ☑
  - with fetal loss and retention of one or more fetus(es) 651.5 ☑
  - following (elective) fetal reduction 651.7 ☑

Quarrelsomeness 301.3

Quartan
- fever 084.2
- malaria (fever) 084.2

Queensland fever 083.0
- coastal 083.0
- seven-day 100.89

Quervain's disease 727.04
- thyroid (subacute granulomatous thyroiditis) 245.1

Queyrat's erythroplasia (M8080/2)
- specified site — *see* Neoplasm, skin, in situ
- unspecified site 233.5

Quincke's disease or edema — *see* Edema, angioneurotic

Quinquaud's disease (acne decalvans) 704.09

Quinsy (gangrenous) 475

Quintan fever 083.1

Quintuplet
affected by maternal complications of pregnancy 761.5
healthy liveborn — *see* Newborn, multiple
pregnancy (complicating delivery) NEC 651.2 ☑
with fetal loss and retention of one or more fetus(es) 651.6 ☑
following (elective) fetal reduction 651.7 ☑
Quotidian
fever 084.0
malaria (fever) 084.0

R

Rabbia 071
Rabbit fever — *see also* Tularemia 021.9
Rabies 071
contact V01.5
exposure to V01.5
inoculation V04.5
reaction — *see* Complications, vaccination
vaccination, prophylactic (against) V04.5
Rachischisis — *see also* Spina bifida 741.9 ☑
Rachitic — *see also* condition
deformities of spine 268.1
pelvis 268.1
with disproportion (fetopelvic) 653.2 ☑
affecting fetus or newborn 763.1
causing obstructed labor 660.1 ☑
affecting fetus or newborn 763.1
Rachitis, rachitism — *see* also Rickets
acute 268.0
fetalis 756.4
renalis 588.0
tarda 268.0
Racket nail 757.5
Radial nerve — *see* condition
Radiation effects or sickness — *see also* Effect, adverse, radiation
cataract 366.46
dermatitis 692.82
sunburn (*see also* Sunburn) 692.71
Radiculitis (pressure) (vertebrogenic) 729.2
accessory nerve 723.4
anterior crural 724.4
arm 723.4
brachial 723.4
cervical NEC 723.4
due to displacement of intervertebral disc — *see* Neuritis, due to, displacement intervertebral disc
leg 724.4
lumbar NEC 724.4
lumbosacral 724.4
rheumatic 729.2
syphilitic 094.89
thoracic (with visceral pain) 724.4
Radiculomyelitis 357.0
toxic, due to
Clostridium tetani 037
Corynebacterium diphtheriae 032.89
Radiculopathy — *see also* Radiculitis 729.2
Radioactive substances, adverse effect — *see* Effect, adverse, radioactive substance
Radiodermal burns (acute) (chronic) (occupational) — *see* Burn, by site
Radiodermatitis 692.82
Radionecrosis — *see* Effect, adverse, radiation
Radiotherapy session V58.0
Radium, adverse effect — *see* Effect, adverse, radioactive substance
Raeder-Harbitz syndrome (pulseless disease) 446.7
Rage — *see also* Disturbance, conduct 312.0 ☑
meaning rabies 071
Rag sorters' disease 022.1
Raillietiniasis 123.8
Railroad neurosis 300.16
Railway spine 300.16
Raised — *see* Elevation
Raiva 071
Rake teeth, tooth 524.39
Rales 786.7
Ramifying renal pelvis 753.3
Ramsay Hunt syndrome (herpetic geniculate ganglionitis) 053.11
meaning dyssynergia cerebellaris myoclonica 334.2
Ranke's primary infiltration — *see also* Tuberculosis 010.0 ☑
Ranula 527.6
congenital 750.26
Rape
adult 995.83
alleged, observation or examination V71.5
child 995.53
Rapid
feeble pulse, due to shock, following injury 958.4
heart (beat) 785.0
psychogenic 306.2
respiration 786.06
psychogenic 306.1
second stage (delivery) 661.3 ☑
affecting fetus or newborn 763.6
time-zone change syndrome 327.35
Rarefaction, bone 733.99
Rash 782.1
canker 034.1
diaper 691.0
drug (internal use) 693.0
contact 692.3
ECHO 9 virus 078.89
enema 692.89
food (*see also* Allergy, food) 693.1
heat 705.1
napkin 691.0
nettle 708.8
pustular 782.1
rose 782.1
epidemic 056.9
of infants 057.8
scarlet 034.1
serum (prophylactic) (therapeutic) 999.5
toxic 782.1
wandering tongue 529.1
Rasmussen's aneurysm — *see also* Tuberculosis 011.2 ☑
Rat-bite fever 026.9
due to Streptobacillus moniliformis 026.1
spirochetal (morsus muris) 026.0
Rathke's pouch tumor (M9350/1) 237.0
Raymond (-Céstan) syndrome 433.8 ☑
Raynaud's
disease or syndrome (paroxysmal digital cyanosis) 443.0
gangrene (symmetric) 443.0 *[785.4]*
phenomenon (paroxysmal digital cyanosis) (secondary) 443.0
RDS 769
Reaction
acute situational maladjustment (*see also* Reaction, adjustment) 309.9
adaptation (*see also* Reaction, adjustment) 309.9
adjustment 309.9
with
anxious mood 309.24
with depressed mood 309.28
conduct disturbance 309.3
combined with disturbance of emotions 309.4
Reaction — *continued*
adjustment — *continued*
with — *continued*
depressed mood 309.0
brief 309.0
with anxious mood 309.28
prolonged 309.1
elective mutism 309.83
mixed emotions and conduct 309.4
mutism, elective 309.83
physical symptoms 309.82
predominant disturbance (of)
conduct 309.3
emotions NEC 309.29
mixed 309.28
mixed, emotions and conduct 309.4
specified type NEC 309.89
specific academic or work inhibition 309.23
withdrawal 309.83
depressive 309.0
with conduct disturbance 309.4
brief 309.0
prolonged 309.1
specified type NEC 309.89
adverse food NEC 995.7
affective (*see also* Psychosis, affective) 296.90
specified type NEC 296.99
aggressive 301.3
unsocialized (*see also* Disturbance, conduct) 312.0 ☑
allergic (*see also* Allergy) 995.3
drug, medicinal substance, and biological — *see* Allergy, drug
food — *see* Allergy, food
serum 999.5
anaphylactic — *see* Shock, anaphylactic
anesthesia — *see* Anesthesia, complication
anger 312.0 ☑
antisocial 301.7
antitoxin (prophylactic) (therapeutic) — *see* Complications, vaccination
anxiety 300.00
Arthus 995.21
asthenic 300.5
compulsive 300.3
conversion (anesthetic) (autonomic) (hyperkinetic) (mixed paralytic) (paresthetic) 300.11
deoxyribonuclease (DNA) (DNase) hypersensitivity NEC 287.2
depressive 300.4
acute 309.0
affective (*see also* Psychosis, affective) 296.2 ☑
recurrent episode 296.3 ☑
single episode 296.2 ☑
brief 309.0
manic (*see also* Psychosis, affective) 296.80
neurotic 300.4
psychoneurotic 300.4
psychotic 298.0
dissociative 300.15
drug NEC (*see also* Table of Drugs and Chemicals) 995.20
allergic (*see also* Allergy, drug) 995.27
correct substance properly administered 995.20
obstetric anesthetic or analgesic NEC 668.9 ☑
affecting fetus or newborn 763.5
specified drug — *see* Table of Drugs and Chemicals
overdose or poisoning 977.9
specified drug — *see* Table of Drugs and Chemicals
specific to newborn 779.4
Reaction — *continued*
drug (*see also* Table of Drugs and Chemicals) — *continued*
transmitted via placenta or breast milk — *see* Absorption, drug, through placenta
withdrawal NEC 292.0
infant of dependent mother 779.5
wrong substance given or taken in error 977.9
specified drug — *see* Table of Drugs and Chemicals
dyssocial 301.7
dystonic, acute, due to drugs 333.72
erysipeloid 027.1
fear 300.20
child 313.0
fluid loss, cerebrospinal 349.0
food (*see also* Allergy, food)
adverse NEC 995.7
anaphylactic shock — *see* Anaphylactic shock, due to, food
foreign
body NEC 728.82
in operative wound (inadvertently left) 998.4
due to surgical material intentionally left — *see* Complications, due to (presence of) any device, implant, or graft classified to 996.0–996.5 NEC
substance accidentally left during a procedure (chemical) (powder) (talc) 998.7
body or object (instrument) (sponge) (swab) 998.4
graft-versus-host (GVH) 279.50
grief (acute) (brief) 309.0
prolonged 309.1
gross stress (*see also* Reaction, stress, acute) 308.9
group delinquent (*see also* Disturbance, conduct) 312.2 ☑
Herxheimer's 995.0
hyperkinetic (*see also* Hyperkinesia) 314.9
hypochondriacal 300.7
hypoglycemic, due to insulin 251.0
therapeutic misadventure 962.3
hypomanic (*see also* Psychosis, affective) 296.0 ☑
recurrent episode 296.1 ☑
single episode 296.0 ☑
hysterical 300.10
conversion type 300.11
dissociative 300.15
id (bacterial cause) 692.89
immaturity NEC 301.89
aggressive 301.3
emotional instability 301.59
immunization — *see* Complications, vaccination
incompatibility
blood group (ABO) (infusion) (transfusion) 999.6
Rh (factor) (infusion) (transfusion) 999.7
inflammatory — *see* Infection
infusion — *see* Complications, infusion
inoculation (immune serum) — *see* Complications, vaccination
insulin 995.23
involutional
paranoid 297.2
psychotic (*see also* Psychosis, affective, depressive) 296.2 ☑
leukemoid (basophilic) (lymphocytic) (monocytic) (myelocytic) (neutrophilic) 288.62
LSD (*see also* Abuse, drugs, nondependent) 305.3 ☑
lumbar puncture 349.0

Rejection — *continued*
- transplant — *continued*
  - skin — *continued*
    - decellularized allodermis 996.55

Relapsing fever 087.9
- Carter's (Asiatic) 087.0
- Dutton's (West African) 087.1
- Koch's 087.9
- louse-borne (epidemic) 087.0
- Novy's (American) 087.1
- Obermeyer's (European) 087.0
- Spirillum 087.9
- tick-borne (endemic) 087.1

Relaxation
- anus (sphincter) 569.49
  - due to hysteria 300.11
- arch (foot) 734
  - congenital 754.61
- back ligaments 728.4
- bladder (sphincter) 596.59
- cardio-esophageal 530.89
- cervix (*see also* Incompetency, cervix) 622.5
- diaphragm 519.4
- inguinal rings — *see* Hernia, inguinal
- joint (capsule) (ligament) (paralytic) (*see also* Derangement, joint) 718.90
  - congenital 755.8
- lumbosacral joint 724.6
- pelvic floor 618.89
- pelvis 618.89
- perineum 618.89
- posture 729.90
- rectum (sphincter) 569.49
- sacroiliac (joint) 724.6
- scrotum 608.89
- urethra (sphincter) 599.84
- uterus (outlet) 618.89
- vagina (outlet) 618.89
- vesical 596.59

Remains
- canal of Cloquet 743.51
- capsule (opaque) 743.51

Remittent fever (malarial) 084.6

Remnant
- canal of Cloquet 743.51
- capsule (opaque) 743.51
- cervix, cervical stump (acquired) (postoperative) 622.8
- cystic duct, postcholecystectomy 576.0
- fingernail 703.8
  - congenital 757.5
- meniscus, knee 717.5
- thyroglossal duct 759.2
- tonsil 474.8
  - infected 474.00
- urachus 753.7

Remote effect of cancer — *see* condition

Removal (of)
- catheter (urinary) (indwelling) V53.6
  - from artificial opening — *see* Attention to, artificial, opening
  - non-vascular V58.82
  - vascular V58.81
- cerebral ventricle (communicating) shunt V53.01
- device (*see also* Fitting (of))
  - contraceptive V25.42
  - fixation
    - external V54.89
    - internal V54.01
  - traction V54.89
- drains V58.49
- dressing
  - wound V58.30
    - nonsurgical V58.30
    - surgical V58.31
- ileostomy V55.2
- Kirschner wire V54.89
- nonvascular catheter V58.82
- pin V54.01
- plaster cast V54.89
- plate (fracture) V54.01

Removal — *continued*
- rod V54.01
- screw V54.01
- splint, external V54.89
- staples V58.32
- subdermal implantable contraceptive V25.43
- sutures V58.32
- traction device, external V54.89
- vascular catheter V58.81
- wound packing V58.30
  - nonsurgical V58.30
  - surgical V58.31

Ren
- arcuatus 753.3
- mobile, mobilis (*see also* Disease, renal) 593.0
  - congenital 753.3
- unguliformis 753.3

Renal — *see also* condition
- glomerulohyalinosis-diabetic syndrome 250.4 ☑ *[581.81]*
  - due to secondary diabetes 249.4 ☑ *[581.81]*

Rendu-Osler-Weber disease or syndrome (familial hemorrhagic telangiectasia) 448.0

Reninoma (M8361/1) 236.91

Rénon-Delille syndrome 253.8

Repair
- pelvic floor, previous, in pregnancy or childbirth 654.4 ☑
  - affecting fetus or newborn 763.89
- scarred tissue V51.8

Replacement by artificial or mechanical device or prosthesis of — *see also* Fitting (of
- artificial skin V43.83
- bladder V43.5
- blood vessel V43.4
- breast V43.82
- eye globe V43.0
- heart
  - with
    - assist device V43.21
    - fully implantable artificial heart V43.22
  - valve V43.3
- intestine V43.89
- joint V43.60
  - ankle V43.66
  - elbow V43.62
  - finger V43.69
  - hip (partial) (total) V43.64
  - knee V43.65
  - shoulder V43.61
  - specified NEC V43.69
  - wrist V43.63
- kidney V43.89
- larynx V43.81
- lens V43.1
- limb(s) V43.7
- liver V43.89
- lung V43.89
- organ NEC V43.89
- pancreas V43.89
- skin (artificial) V43.83
- tissue NEC V43.89

Reprogramming
- cardiac pacemaker V53.31

Request for expert evidence V68.2

Reserve, decreased or low
- cardiac — *see* Disease, heart
  - kidney (*see also* Disease, renal) 593.9

Residual — *see also* condition
- bladder 596.8
- foreign body — *see* Retention, foreign body
- state, schizophrenic (*see also* Schizophrenia) 295.6 ☑
- urine 788.69

Resistance, resistant (to)
- activated protein C 289.81

> *Note — use the following subclassification for categories V09.5, V09.7, V09.8, V09.9:*
>
> 0 *without mention of resistance to multiple drugs*
>
> 1 *with resistance to multiple drugs*
>
> *V09.5 quinolones and fluoroquinolones*
>
> *V09.7 antimycobacterial agents*
>
> *V09.8 specified drugs NEC*
>
> *V09.9 unspecified drugs*

- drugs by microorganisms V09.9 ☑
  - Amikacin V09.4
  - aminoglycosides V09.4
  - Amodiaquine V09.5 ☑
  - Amoxicillin V09.0
  - Ampicillin V09.0
  - antimycobacterial agents V09.7 ☑
  - Azithromycin V09.2
  - Azlocillin V09.0
  - Aztreonam V09.1
  - Bacampicillin V09.0
  - Bacitracin V09.8 ☑
  - Benznidazole V09.8 ☑
  - B-lactam antibiotics V09.1
  - Capreomycin V09.7 ☑
  - Carbenicillin V09.0
  - Cefaclor V09.1
  - Cefadroxil V09.1
  - Cefamandole V09.1
  - Cefatetan V09.1
  - Cefazolin V09.1
  - Cefixime V09.1
  - Cefonicid V09.1
  - Cefoperazone V09.1
  - Ceforanide V09.1
  - Cefotaxime V09.1
  - Cefoxitin V09.1
  - Ceftazidime V09.1
  - Ceftizoxime V09.1
  - Ceftriaxone V09.1
  - Cefuroxime V09.1
  - Cephalexin V09.1
  - Cephaloglycin V09.1
  - Cephaloridine V09.1
  - Cephalosporins V09.1
  - Cephalothin V09.1
  - Cephapirin V09.1
  - Cephradine V09.1
  - Chloramphenicol V09.8 ☑
  - Chloraquine V09.5 ☑
  - Chlorguanide V09.8 ☑
  - Chlorproguanil V09.8 ☑
  - Chlortetracyline V09.3
  - Cinoxacin V09.5 ☑
  - Ciprofloxacin V09.5 ☑
  - Clarithromycin V09.2
  - Clindamycin V09.8 ☑
  - Clioquinol V09.5 ☑
  - Clofazimine V09.7 ☑
  - Cloxacillin V09.0
  - Cyclacillin V09.0
  - Cycloserine V09.7 ☑
  - Dapsone [DZ] V09.7 ☑
  - Demeclocycline V09.3
  - Dicloxacillin V09.0
  - Doxycycline V09.3
  - Enoxacin V09.5 ☑
  - Erythromycin V09.2
  - Ethambutol [EMB] V09.7 ☑
  - Ethionamide [ETA] V09.7 ☑
  - fluoroquinolones V09.5 ☑
  - Gentamicin V09.4
  - Halofantrine V09.8 ☑
  - Imipenem V09.1
  - Iodoquinol V09.5 ☑
  - Isoniazid [INH] V09.7 ☑
  - Kanamycin V09.4
  - macrolides V09.2
  - Mafenide V09.6

Resistance, resistant — *continued*
- drugs by microorganisms — *continued*
  - MDRO (multiple drug resistant organisms) NOS V09.91
  - Mefloquine V09.8 ☑
  - Melasoprol V09.8 ☑
  - Methacycline V09.3
  - Methenamine V09.8 ☑
  - Methicillin — *see* Infection, Methicillin V09.0
  - Metronidazole V09.8 ☑
  - Mezlocillin V09.0
  - Minocycline V09.3
  - multiple drug resistant organisms NOS V09.91
  - Nafcillin V09.0
  - Nalidixic acid V09.5 ☑
  - Natamycin V09.2
  - Neomycin V09.4
  - Netilmicin V09.4
  - Nimorazole V09.8 ☑
  - Nitrofurantoin V09.8 ☑
  - Nitrofurtimox V09.8 ☑
  - Norfloxacin V09.5 ☑
  - Nystatin V09.2
  - Ofloxacin V09.5 ☑
  - Oleandomycin V09.2
  - Oxacillin V09.0
  - Oxytetracycline V09.3
  - Para-amino salicylic acid [PAS] V09.7 ☑
  - Paromomycin V09.4
  - Penicillin (G) (V) (VK) V09.0
  - penicillins V09.0
  - Pentamidine V09.8 ☑
  - Piperacillin V09.0
  - Primaquine V09.5 ☑
  - Proguanil V09.8 ☑
  - Pyrazinamide [PZA] V09.7 ☑
  - Pyrimethamine/Sulfalene V09.8 ☑
  - Pyrimethamine/Sulfodoxine V09.8 ☑
  - Quinacrine V09.5 ☑
  - Quinidine V09.8 ☑
  - Quinine V09.8 ☑
  - quinolones V09.5 ☑
  - Rifabutin V09.7 ☑
  - Rifampin [RIF] V09.7 ☑
  - Rifamycin V09.7 ☑
  - Rolitetracycline V09.3
  - specified drugs NEC V09.8 ☑
  - Spectinomycin V09.8 ☑
  - Spiramycin V09.2
  - Streptomycin [SM] V09.4
  - Sulfacetamide V09.6
  - Sulfacytine V09.6
  - Sulfadiazine V09.6
  - Sulfadoxine V09.6
  - Sulfamethoxazole V09.6
  - Sulfapyridine V09.6
  - Sulfasalizine V09.6
  - Sulfasoxazole V09.6
  - sulfonamides V09.6
  - Sulfoxone V09.7 ☑
  - tetracycline V09.3
  - tetracyclines V09.3
  - Thiamphenicol V09.8 ☑
  - Ticarcillin V09.0
  - Tinidazole V09.8 ☑
  - Tobramycin V09.4
  - Triamphenicol V09.8 ☑
  - Trimethoprim V09.8 ☑
  - Vancomycin V09.8 ☑
- insulin 277.7
- thyroid hormone 246.8

Resorption
- biliary 576.8
  - purulent or putrid (*see also* Cholecystitis) 576.8
- dental (roots) 521.40
  - alveoli 525.8
  - pathological
    - external 521.42
    - internal 521.41

- **Resorption** — *continued*
  - dental — *continued*
    - pathological — *continued*
      - specified NEC 521.49
  - septic — *see* Septicemia
  - teeth (roots) 521.40
    - pathological
      - external 521.42
      - internal 521.41
      - specified NEC 521.49
- **Respiration**
  - asymmetrical 786.09
  - bronchial 786.09
  - Cheyne-Stokes (periodic respiration) 786.04
  - decreased, due to shock following injury 958.4
  - disorder of 786.00
    - psychogenic 306.1
    - specified NEC 786.09
  - failure 518.81
    - acute 518.81
    - acute and chronic 518.84
    - chronic 518.83
    - newborn 770.84
  - insufficiency 786.09
    - acute 518.82
    - newborn NEC 770.89
  - Kussmaul (air hunger) 786.09
  - painful 786.52
  - periodic 786.09
    - high altitude 327.22
  - poor 786.09
    - newborn NEC 770.89
  - sighing 786.7
    - psychogenic 306.1
  - wheezing 786.07
- **Respiratory** — *see also* condition
  - distress 786.09
    - acute 518.82
    - fetus or newborn NEC 770.89
    - syndrome (newborn) 769
      - adult (following shock, surgery, or trauma) 518.5
        - specified NEC 518.82
  - failure 518.81
    - acute 518.81
    - acute and chronic 518.84
    - chronic 518.83
- **Respiratory syncytial virus (RSV)** 079.6
  - bronchiolitis 466.11
  - pneumonia 480.1
  - vaccination, prophylactic (against) V04.82
- **Response**
  - photoallergic 692.72
  - phototoxic 692.72
- **Restless legs syndrome (RLS)** 333.94
- **Restlessness** 799.2
- **Restoration of organ continuity from previous sterilization** (tuboplasty) (vasoplasty) V26.0
- **Rest, rests**
  - mesonephric duct 752.89
    - fallopian tube 752.11
  - ovarian, in fallopian tubes 752.19
  - wolffian duct 752.89
- **Restriction of housing space** V60.1
- **Restzustand, schizophrenic** — *see also* Schizophrenia 295.6 ☑
- **Retained** — *see* Retention
- **Retardation**
  - development, developmental, specific (*see also* Disorder, development, specific) 315.9
    - learning, specific 315.2
      - arithmetical 315.1
      - language (skills) 315.31
        - expressive 315.31
        - mixed receptive-expressive 315.32
      - mathematics 315.1
      - reading 315.00
        - phonological 315.39
      - written expression 315.2
    - motor 315.4

- **Retardation** — *continued*
  - endochondral bone growth 733.91
  - growth (physical) in childhood 783.43
    - due to malnutrition 263.2
    - fetal (intrauterine) 764.9 ☑
      - affecting management of pregnancy 656.5 ☑
  - intrauterine growth 764.9 ☑
    - affecting management of pregnancy 656.5 ☑
  - mental 319
    - borderline V62.89
    - mild, IQ 50-70 317
    - moderate, IQ 35-49 318.0
    - profound, IQ under 20 318.2
    - severe, IQ 20-34 318.1
  - motor, specific 315.4
  - physical 783.43
    - child 783.43
    - due to malnutrition 263.2
    - fetus (intrauterine) 764.9 ☑
      - affecting management of pregnancy 656.5 ☑
  - psychomotor NEC 307.9
  - reading 315.00
- **Retching** — *see* Vomiting
- **Retention, retained**
  - bladder (*see also* Retention, urine) 788.20
    - psychogenic 306.53
  - carbon dioxide 276.2
  - cholelithiasis 997.4
  - cyst — *see* Cyst
  - dead
    - fetus (after 22 completed weeks gestation) 656.4 ☑
      - early fetal death (before 22 completed weeks gestation) 632
    - ovum 631
  - decidua (following delivery) (fragments) (with hemorrhage) 666.2 ☑
    - without hemorrhage 667.1 ☑
  - deciduous tooth 520.6
  - dental root 525.3
  - fecal (*see also* Constipation) 564.00
  - fluid 276.6
  - foreign body (*see also* Foreign body, retained)
    - bone 733.99
    - current trauma — *see* Foreign body, by site or type
    - middle ear 385.83
    - muscle 729.6
    - soft tissue NEC 729.6
  - gallstones 997.4
  - gastric 536.8
  - membranes (following delivery) (with hemorrhage) 666.2 ☑
    - with abortion — *see* Abortion, by type
    - without hemorrhage 667.1 ☑
  - menses 626.8
  - milk (puerperal) 676.2 ☑
  - nitrogen, extrarenal 788.99
  - placenta (total) (with hemorrhage) 666.0 ☑
    - with abortion — *see* Abortion, by type
    - without hemorrhage 667.0 ☑
    - portions or fragments 666.2 ☑
      - without hemorrhage 667.1 ☑
  - products of conception
    - early pregnancy (fetal death before 22 completed weeks gestation) 632
    - following
      - abortion — *see* Abortion, by type
      - delivery 666.2 ☑
        - with hemorrhage 666.2 ☑
        - without hemorrhage 667.1 ☑
  - secundines (following delivery) (with hemorrhage) 666.2 ☑
    - with abortion — *see* Abortion, by type

- **Retention, retained** — *continued*
  - secundines — *continued*
    - without hemorrhage 667.1 ☑
    - complicating puerperium (delayed hemorrhage) 666.2 ☑
  - smegma, clitoris 624.8
  - urine NEC 788.20
    - bladder, incomplete emptying 788.21
      - due to
        - benign prostatic hypertrophy (BPH) — see category 600
    - due to
      - benign prostatic hypertrophy (BPH) — see category 600
    - psychogenic 306.53
    - specified NEC 788.29
  - water (in tissue) (*see also* Edema) 782.3
- **Reticulation, dust** (occupational) 504
- **Reticulocytosis** NEC 790.99
- **Reticuloendotheliosis**
  - acute infantile (M9722/3) 202.5 ☑
  - leukemic (M9940/3) 202.4 ☑
  - malignant (M9720/3) 202.3 ☑
  - nonlipid (M9722/3) 202.5 ☑
- **Reticulohistiocytoma** (giant cell) 277.89
- **Reticulohistiocytosis, multicentric** 272.8
- **Reticulolymphosarcoma** (diffuse) (M9613/3) 200.8 ☑
  - follicular (M9691/3) 202.0 ☑
  - nodular (M9691/3) 202.0 ☑
- **Reticulosarcoma** (M9640/3) 200.0 ☑
  - nodular (M9642/3) 200.0 ☑
  - pleomorphic cell type (M9641/3) 200.0 ☑
- **Reticulosis** (skin)
  - acute of infancy (M9722/3) 202.5 ☑
  - familial hemophagocytic 288.4
  - histiocytic medullary (M9721/3) 202.3 ☑
  - lipomelanotic 695.89
  - malignant (M9720/3) 202.3 ☑
  - Sézary's (M9701/3) 202.2 ☑
- **Retina, retinal** — *see* condition
- **Retinitis** — *see also* Chorioretinitis 363.20
  - albuminurica 585.9 *[363.10]*
  - arteriosclerotic 440.8 *[362.13]*
  - central angiospastic 362.41
  - Coat's 362.12
  - diabetic 250.5 ☑ *[362.01]*
    - due to secondary diabetes 249.5 ☑ *[362.01]*
  - disciformis 362.52
  - disseminated 363.10
    - metastatic 363.14
    - neurosyphilitic 094.83
    - pigment epitheliopathy 363.15
  - exudative 362.12
  - focal 363.00
    - in histoplasmosis 115.92
      - capsulatum 115.02
      - duboisii 115.12
    - juxtapapillary 363.05
    - macular 363.06
    - paramacular 363.06
    - peripheral 363.08
    - posterior pole NEC 363.07
  - gravidarum 646.8 ☑
  - hemorrhagica externa 362.12
  - juxtapapillary (Jensen's) 363.05
  - luetic — *see* Retinitis, syphilitic
  - metastatic 363.14
  - pigmentosa 362.74
  - proliferans 362.29
  - proliferating 362.29
  - punctata albescens 362.76
  - renal 585.9 *[363.13]*
  - syphilitic (secondary) 091.51
    - congenital 090.0 *[363.13]*
    - early 091.51
    - late 095.8 *[363.13]*

- **Retinitis** — *see also* Chorioretinitis — *continued*
  - syphilitica, central, recurrent 095.8 *[363.13]*
  - tuberculous (*see also* Tuberculous) 017.3 ☑ *[363.13]*
- **Retinoblastoma** (M9510/3) 190.5
  - differentiated type (M9511/3) 190.5
  - undifferentiated type (M9512/3) 190.5
- **Retinochoroiditis** — *see also* Chorioretinitis 363.20
  - central angiospastic 362.41
  - disseminated 363.10
    - metastatic 363.14
    - neurosyphilitic 094.83
    - pigment epitheliopathy 363.15
    - syphilitic 094.83
  - due to toxoplasmosis (acquired) (focal) 130.2
  - focal 363.00
    - in histoplasmosis 115.92
      - capsulatum 115.02
      - duboisii 115.12
    - juxtapapillary (Jensen's) 363.05
    - macular 363.06
    - paramacular 363.06
    - peripheral 363.08
    - posterior pole NEC 363.07
  - juxtapapillaris 363.05
  - syphilitic (disseminated) 094.83
- **Retinopathy** (background) 362.10
  - arteriosclerotic 440.8 *[362.13]*
  - atherosclerotic 440.8 *[362.13]*
  - central serous 362.41
  - circinate 362.10
  - Coat's 362.12
  - diabetic 250.5 ☑ *[362.01]*
    - due to secondary diabetes 249.5 ☑ *[362.01]*
    - nonproliferative 250.5 ☑ *[362.03]*
      - due to secondary diabetes 249.5 ☑ *[362.03]*
      - mild 250.5 ☑ *[362.04]*
        - due to secondary diabetes 249.5 ☑ *[362.04]*
      - moderate 250.5 ☑ *[362.05]*
        - due to secondary diabetes 249.5 ☑ *[362.05]*
      - severe 250.5 ☑ *[362.06]*
        - due to secondary diabetes 249.5 ☑ *[362.06]*
    - proliferative 250.5 ☑ *[362.02]*
      - due to secondary diabetes 249.5 ☑ *[362.02]*
  - exudative 362.12
  - hypertensive 362.11
  - nonproliferative
    - diabetic 250.5 ☑ *[362.03]*
      - due to secondary diabetes 249.5 ☑ *[362.03]*
      - mild 250.5 ☑ *[362.04]*
        - due to secondary diabetes 249.5 ☑ *[362.04]*
      - moderate 250.5 ☑ *[362.05]*
        - due to secondary diabetes 249.5 ☑ *[362.05]*
      - severe 250.5 ☑ *[362.06]*
        - due to secondary diabetes 249.5 ☑ *[362.06]*
  - of prematurity 362.20
    - cicatricial 362.21
    - stage
      - 0 362.22
      - 1 362.23
      - 2 362.24
      - 3 362.25
      - 4 362.26
      - 5 362.27
  - pigmentary, congenital 362.74
  - proliferative 362.29
    - diabetic 250.5 ☑ *[362.02]*
      - due to secondary diabetes 249.5 ☑ *[362.02]*
    - sickle-cell 282.60 *[362.29]*
  - solar 363.31
- **Retinoschisis** 361.10

- **Rupture, ruptured** — *continued*
  - sigmoid — *continued*
    - traumatic — *see* Injury, internal, colon, sigmoid
  - sinus of Valsalva 747.29
  - spinal cord (*see also* Injury, spinal, by site)
    - due to injury at birth 767.4
    - fetus or newborn 767.4
    - syphilitic 094.89
    - traumatic (*see also* Injury, spinal, by site)
      - with fracture — *see* Fracture, vertebra, by site, with spinal cord injury
  - spleen 289.59
    - congenital 767.8
    - due to injury at birth 767.8
    - malarial 084.9
    - nontraumatic 289.59
    - spontaneous 289.59
    - traumatic 865.04
      - with open wound into cavity 865.14
  - splenic vein 459.0
  - stomach 537.89
    - due to injury at birth 767.8
    - traumatic — *see* Injury, internal, stomach
    - ulcer — *see* Ulcer, stomach, with perforation
  - synovium 727.50
    - specified site NEC 727.59
  - tendon (traumatic) (*see also* Sprain, by site)
    - with open wound — *see* Wound, open, by site
    - Achilles 845.09
      - nontraumatic 727.67
    - ankle 845.09
      - nontraumatic 727.68
    - biceps (long bead) 840.8
      - nontraumatic 727.62
    - foot 845.10
      - interphalangeal (joint) 845.13
      - metatarsophalangeal (joint) 845.12
      - nontraumatic 727.68
      - specified site NEC 845.19
      - tarsometatarsal (joint) 845.11

- **Rupture, ruptured** — *continued*
  - tendon (*see also* Sprain, by site) — *continued*
    - hand 842.10
      - carpometacarpal (joint) 842.11
      - interphalangeal (joint) 842.13
      - metacarpophalangeal (joint) 842.12
      - nontraumatic 727.63
        - extensors 727.63
        - flexors 727.64
      - specified site NEC 842.19
    - nontraumatic 727.60
      - specified site NEC 727.69
    - patellar 844.8
      - nontraumatic 727.66
    - quadriceps 844.8
      - nontraumatic 727.65
    - rotator cuff (capsule) 840.4
      - nontraumatic, complete 727.61
    - wrist 842.00
      - carpal (joint) 842.01
      - nontraumatic 727.63
        - extensors 727.63
        - flexors 727.64
      - radiocarpal (joint) (ligament) 842.02
      - radioulnar (joint), distal 842.09
      - specified site NEC 842.09
  - testis (traumatic) 878.2
    - complicated 878.3
    - due to syphilis 095.8
  - thoracic duct 457.8
  - tonsil 474.8
  - traumatic
    - with open wound — *see* Wound, open, by site
    - aorta — *see* Rupture, aorta, traumatic
    - ear drum — *see* Wound, open, ear, drum
    - external site — *see* Wound, open, by site
    - eye 871.2
    - globe (eye) — *see* Wound, open, eyeball
    - internal organ (abdomen, chest, or pelvis) (*see also* Injury, internal, by site)

- **Rupture, ruptured** — *continued*
  - traumatic — *continued*
    - internal organ (*see also* Injury, internal, by site) — *continued*
      - heart — *see* Rupture, myocardium, traumatic
      - kidney — *see* Rupture, kidney
      - liver — *see* Rupture, liver
      - spleen — *see* Rupture, spleen, traumatic
    - ligament, muscle, or tendon (*see also* Sprain, by site)
      - with open wound — *see* Wound, open, by site
    - meaning hernia — *see* Hernia
  - tricuspid (heart) (valve) — *see* Endocarditis, tricuspid
  - tube, tubal 620.8
    - abscess (*see also* Salpingo-oophoritis) 614.2
    - due to pregnancy — *see* Pregnancy, tubal
  - tympanum, tympanic (membrane) (*see also* Perforation, tympanum) 384.20
    - with otitis media — *see* Otitis media
    - traumatic — *see* Wound, open, ear, drum
  - umbilical cord 663.8 ☑
    - fetus or newborn 772.0
  - ureter (traumatic) (*see also* Injury, internal, ureter) 867.2
    - nontraumatic 593.89
  - urethra 599.84
    - with
      - abortion — *see* Abortion, by type, with damage to pelvic organs
      - ectopic pregnancy (*see also* categories 633.0–633.9) 639.2
      - molar pregnancy (*see also* categories 630–632) 639.2
    - following
      - abortion 639.2
      - ectopic or molar pregnancy 639.2
    - obstetrical trauma 665.5 ☑

- **Rupture, ruptured** — *continued*
  - urethra — *continued*
    - traumatic — *see* Injury, internal urethra
  - uterosacral ligament 620.8
  - uterus (traumatic) (*see also* Injury, internal uterus)
    - affecting fetus or newborn 763.89
    - during labor 665.1 ☑
    - nonpuerperal, nontraumatic 621.8
    - nontraumatic 621.8
    - pregnant (during labor) 665.1 ☑
      - before labor 665.0 ☑
  - vagina 878.6
    - complicated 878.7
    - complicating delivery — *see* Laceration, vagina, complicating delivery
  - valve, valvular (heart) — *see* Endocarditis
  - varicose vein — *see* Varicose, vein
  - varix — *see* Varix
  - vena cava 459.0
  - ventricle (free wall) (left) (*see also* Infarct, myocardium) 410.9 ☑
  - vesical (urinary) 596.6
    - traumatic — *see* Injury, internal, bladder
  - vessel (blood) 459.0
    - pulmonary 417.8
  - viscus 799.89
  - vulva 878.4
    - complicated 878.5
    - complicating delivery 664.0 ☑
- **Russell's dwarf** (uterine dwarfism and craniofacial dysostosis) 759.89
- **Russell's dysentery** 004.8
- **Russell (-Silver) syndrome** (congenital hemihypertrophy and short stature) 759.89
- **Russian spring-summer type encephalitis** 063.0
- **Rust's disease** (tuberculous spondylitis) 015.0 ☑ *[720.81]*
- **Rustitskii's disease** (multiple myeloma) (M9730/3) 203.0 ☑
- **Ruysch's disease** (Hirschsprung's disease) 751.3
- **Rytand-Lipsitch syndrome** (complete atrioventricular block) 426.0

S

Saber
  shin 090.5
  tibia 090.5
Saccharomyces infection — *see also* Candidiasis 112.9
Saccharopinuria 270.7
Saccular — *see* condition
Sacculation
  aorta (nonsyphilitic) (*see also* Aneurysm, aorta) 441.9
    ruptured 441.5
    syphilitic 093.0
  bladder 596.3
  colon 569.89
  intralaryngeal (congenital) (ventricular) 748.3
  larynx (congenital) (ventricular) 748.3
  organ or site, congenital — *see* Distortion
  pregnant uterus, complicating delivery 654.4 ☑
    affecting fetus or newborn 763.1
    causing obstructed labor 660.2 ☑
      affecting fetus or newborn 763.1
  rectosigmoid 569.89
  sigmoid 569.89
  ureter 593.89
  urethra 599.2
  vesical 596.3
Sachs (-Tay) disease (amaurotic familial idiocy) 330.1
Sacks-Libman disease 710.0 *[424.91]*
Sac, lacrimal — *see* condition
Sacralgia 724.6
Sacralization
  fifth lumbar vertebra 756.15
  incomplete (vertebra) 756.15
Sacrodynia 724.6
Sacroiliac joint — *see* condition
Sacroiliitis NEC 720.2
Sacrum — *see* condition
Saddle
  back 737.8
  embolus, aorta 444.0
  nose 738.0
    congenital 754.0
    due to syphilis 090.5
Sadism (sexual) 302.84
Saemisch's ulcer 370.04
Saenger's syndrome 379.46
Sago spleen 277.39
Sailors' skin 692.74
Saint
  Anthony's fire (*see also* Erysipelas) 035
  Guy's dance — *see* Chorea
  Louis-type encephalitis 062.3
  triad (*see also* Hernia, diaphragm) 553.3
  Vitus' dance — *see* Chorea
Salicylism
  correct substance properly administered 535.4 ☑
  overdose or wrong substance given or taken 965.1
Salivary duct or gland — *see also* condition
  virus disease 078.5
Salivation (excessive) — *see also* Ptyalism 527.7
Salmonella (aertrycke) (choleraesuis) (enteritidis) (gallinarum) (suipestifer) (typhimurium) — *see also* Infection, Salmonella 003.9
  arthritis 003.23
  carrier (suspected) of V02.3
  meningitis 003.21
  osteomyelitis 003.24
  pneumonia 003.22
  septicemia 003.1
  typhosa 002.0
    carrier (suspected) of V02.1
Salmonellosis 003.0
Salmonellosis — *continued*
  with pneumonia 003.22
Salpingitis (catarrhal) (fallopian tube) (nodular) (pseudofollicular) (purulent) (septic) — *see also* Salpingo-oophoritis 614.2
  ear 381.50
    acute 381.51
    chronic 381.52
  Eustachian (tube) 381.50
    acute 381.51
    chronic 381.52
  follicularis 614.1
  gonococcal (chronic) 098.37
    acute 098.17
  interstitial, chronic 614.1
  isthmica nodosa 614.1
  old — *see* Salpingo-oophoritis, chronic
  puerperal, postpartum, childbirth 670.0 ☑
  specific (chronic) 098.37
    acute 098.17
  tuberculous (acute) (chronic) (*see also* Tuberculosis) 016.6 ☑
  venereal (chronic) 098.37
    acute 098.17
Salpingocele 620.4
Salpingo-oophoritis (catarrhal) (purulent) (ruptured) (septic) (suppurative) 614.2
  acute 614.0
    with
      abortion — *see* Abortion, by type, with sepsis
      ectopic pregnancy (*see also* categories 633.0–633.9) 639.0
      molar pregnancy (*see also* categories 630–632) 639.0
    following
      abortion 639.0
      ectopic or molar pregnancy 639.0
    gonococcal 098.17
    puerperal, postpartum, childbirth 670.0 ☑
    tuberculous (*see also* Tuberculosis) 016.6 ☑
  chronic 614.1
    gonococcal 098.37
    tuberculous (see also Tuberculosis) 016.6 ☑
  complicating pregnancy 646.6 ☑
    affecting fetus or newborn 760.8
  gonococcal (chronic) 098.37
    acute 098.17
  old — *see* Salpingo-oophoritis, chronic
  puerperal 670.0 ☑
  specific — *see* Salpingo-oophoritis, gonococcal
  subacute (*see also* Salpingo-oophoritis, acute) 614.0
  tuberculous (acute) (chronic) (*see also* Tuberculosis) 016.6 ☑
  venereal — *see* Salpingo-oophoritis, gonococcal
Salpingo-ovaritis — *see also* Salpingo-oophoritis 614.2
Salpingoperitonitis — *see also* Salpingo-oophoritis 614.2
Salt-losing
  nephritis (*see also* Disease, renal) 593.9
  syndrome (*see also* Disease, renal) 593.9
Salt-rheum — *see also* Eczema 692.9
Salzmann's nodular dystrophy 371.46
Sampling
  chorionic villus V28.89
Sampson's cyst or tumor 617.1
Sandblasters'
  asthma 502
  lung 502
Sander's disease (paranoia) 297.1
Sandfly fever 066.0
Sandhoff's disease 330.1
Sanfilippo's syndrome (mucopolysaccharidosis III) 277.5
Sanger-Brown's ataxia 334.2
San Joaquin Valley fever 114.0
Sao Paulo fever or typhus 082.0
Saponification, mesenteric 567.89
Sapremia — *see* Septicemia
Sarcocele (benign)
  syphilitic 095.8
    congenital 090.5
Sarcoepiplocele — *see also* Hernia 553.9
Sarcoepiplomphalocele — *see also* Hernia, umbilicus 553.1
Sarcoid (any site) 135
  with lung involvement 135 *[517.8]*
  Boeck's 135
  Darier-Roussy 135
  Spiegler-Fendt 686.8
Sarcoidosis 135
  cardiac 135 *[425.8]*
  lung 135 *[517.8]*
Sarcoma (M8800/3) — *see also* Neoplasm, connective tissue, malignant
  alveolar soft part (M9581/3) — *see* Neoplasm, connective tissue, malignant
  ameloblastic (M9330/3) 170.1
    upper jaw (bone) 170.0
  botryoid (M8910/3) — *see* Neoplasm, connective tissue, malignant
  botryoides (M8910/3) — *see* Neoplasm, connective tissue, malignant
  cerebellar (M9480/3) 191.6
    circumscribed (arachnoidal) (M9471/3) 191.6
  circumscribed (arachnoidal) cerebellar (M9471/3) 191.6
  clear cell, of tendons and aponeuroses (M9044/3) — *see* Neoplasm, connective tissue, malignant
  embryonal (M8991/3) — *see* Neoplasm, connective tissue, malignant
  endometrial (stromal) (M8930/3) 182.0
    isthmus 182.1
  endothelial (M9130/3) (*see also* Neoplasm, connective tissue, malignant)
    bone (M9260/3) — *see* Neoplasm, bone, malignant
  epithelioid cell (M8804/3) — *see* Neoplasm, connective tissue, malignant
  Ewing's (M9260/3) — *see* Neoplasm, bone, malignant
  follicular dendritic cell 202.9 ☑
  germinoblastic (diffuse) (M9632/3) 202.8 ☑
    follicular (M9697/3) 202.0 ☑
  giant cell (M8802/3) (*see also* Neoplasm, connective tissue, malignant)
    bone (M9250/3) — *see* Neoplasm, bone, malignant
  glomoid (M8710/3) — *see* Neoplasm, connective tissue, malignant
  granulocytic (M9930/3) 205.3 ☑
  hemangioendothelial (M9130/3) — *see* Neoplasm, connective tissue, malignant
  hemorrhagic, multiple (M9140/3) — *see* Kaposi's, sarcoma
  Hodgkin's (M9662/3) 201.2 ☑
  immunoblastic (M9612/3) 200.8 ☑
  interdigitating dendritic cell 202.9 ☑
  Kaposi's (M9140/3) — *see* Kaposi's, sarcoma
  Kupffer cell (M9124/3) 155.0
  Langerhans cell 202.9 ☑
  leptomeningeal (M9530/3) — *see* Neoplasm, meninges, malignant
Sarcoma — *see also* Neoplasm, connective tissue, malignant — *continued*
  lymphangioendothelial (M9170/3) — *see* Neoplasm, connective tissue, malignant
  lymphoblastic (M9630/3) 200.1 ☑
  lymphocytic (M9620/3) 200.1 ☑
  mast cell (M9740/3) 202.6 ☑
  melanotic (M8720/3) — *see* Melanoma
  meningeal (M9530/3) — *see* Neoplasm, meninges, malignant
  meningothelial (M9530/3) — *see* Neoplasm, meninges, malignant
  mesenchymal (M8800/3) (*see also* Neoplasm, connective tissue, malignant)
    mixed (M8990/3) — *see* Neoplasm, connective tissue, malignant
  mesothelial (M9050/3) — *see* Neoplasm, by site, malignant
  monstrocellular (M9481/3)
    specified site — *see* Neoplasm, by site, malignant
    unspecified site 191.9
  myeloid (M9930/3) 205.3 ☑
  neurogenic (M9540/3) — *see* Neoplasm, connective tissue, malignant
  odontogenic (M9270/3) 170.1
    upper jaw (bone) 170.0
  osteoblastic (M9180/3) — *see* Neoplasm, bone, malignant
  osteogenic (M9180/3) (*see also* Neoplasm, bone, malignant)
    juxtacortical (M9190/3) — *see* Neoplasm, bone, malignant
    periosteal (M9190/3) — *see* Neoplasm, bone, malignant
  periosteal (M8812/3) (*see also* Neoplasm, bone, malignant)
    osteogenic (M9190/3) — *see* Neoplasm, bone, malignant
  plasma cell (M9731/3) 203.8 ☑
  pleomorphic cell (M8802/3) — *see* Neoplasm, connective tissue, malignant
  reticuloendothelial (M9720/3) 202.3 ☑
  reticulum cell (M9640/3) 200.0 ☑
    nodular (M9642/3) 200.0 ☑
    pleomorphic cell type (M9641/3) 200.0 ☑
  round cell (M8803/3) — *see* Neoplasm, connective tissue, malignant
  small cell (M8803/3) — *see* Neoplasm, connective tissue, malignant
  spindle cell (M8801/3) — *see* Neoplasm, connective tissue, malignant
  stromal (endometrial) (M8930/3) 182.0
    isthmus 182.1
  synovial (M9040/3) (*see also* Neoplasm, connective tissue, malignant)
    biphasic type (M9043/3) — *see* Neoplasm, connective tissue, malignant
    epithelioid cell type (M9042/3) — *see* Neoplasm, connective tissue, malignant
    spindle cell type (M9041/3) — *see* Neoplasm, connective tissue, malignant
Sarcomatosis
  meningeal (M9539/3) — *see* Neoplasm, meninges, malignant
  specified site NEC (M8800/3) — *see* Neoplasm, connective tissue, malignant
  unspecified site (M8800/6) 171.9
Sarcosinemia 270.8
Sarcosporidiosis 136.5
Satiety, early 780.94

Satisfactory smear but lacking transformation zone
- anal 796.77
- cervical 795.07

Saturnine — *see* condition
Saturnism 984.9
- specified type of lead — *see* Table of Drugs and Chemicals

Satyriasis 302.89
Sauriasis — *see* Ichthyosis
Sauriderma 757.39
Sauriosis — *see* Ichthyosis
Savill's disease (epidemic exfoliative dermatitis) 695.89
SBE (subacute bacterial endocarditis) 421.0
Scabies (any site) 133.0
Scabs 782.8
Scaglietti-Dagnini syndrome (acromegalic macrospondylitis) 253.0
Scald, scalded — *see also* Burn, by site
- skin syndrome 695.81

Scalenus anticus (anterior) syndrome 353.0
Scales 782.8
Scalp — *see* condition
Scaphocephaly 756.0
Scaphoiditis, tarsal 732.5
Scapulalgia 733.90
Scapulohumeral myopathy 359.1
Scarabiasis 134.1
Scarlatina 034.1
- anginosa 034.1
- maligna 034.1
- myocarditis, acute 034.1 *[422.0]*
  - old (*see also* Myocarditis) 429.0
- otitis media 034.1 *[382.02]*
- ulcerosa 034.1

Scarlatinella 057.8
Scarlet fever (albuminuria) (angina) (convulsions) (lesions of lid) (rash) 034.1
Scar, scarring — *see also* Cicatrix 709.2
- adherent 709.2
- atrophic 709.2
- cervix
  - in pregnancy or childbirth 654.6 ☑
    - affecting fetus or newborn 763.89
    - causing obstructed labor 660.2 ☑
      - affecting fetus or newborn 763.1
- cheloid 701.4
- chorioretinal 363.30
  - disseminated 363.35
  - macular 363.32
  - peripheral 363.34
  - posterior pole NEC 363.33
- choroid (*see also* Scar, chorioretinal) 363.30
- compression, pericardial 423.9
- congenital 757.39
- conjunctiva 372.64
- cornea 371.00
  - xerophthalmic 264.6
- due to previous cesarean delivery, complicating pregnancy or childbirth 654.2 ☑
  - affecting fetus or newborn 763.89
- duodenal (bulb) (cap) 537.3
- hypertrophic 701.4
- keloid 701.4
- labia 624.4
- lung (base) 518.89
- macula 363.32
  - disseminated 363.35
  - peripheral 363.34
- muscle 728.89
- myocardium, myocardial 412
- painful 709.2
- papillary muscle 429.81
- posterior pole NEC 363.33
  - macular — *see* Scar, macula
- postnecrotic (hepatic) (liver) 571.9
- psychic V15.49

Scar, scarring — *see also* Cicatrix — *continued*
- retina (*see also* Scar, chorioretinal) 363.30
- trachea 478.9
- uterus 621.8
  - in pregnancy or childbirth NEC 654.9 ☑
    - affecting fetus or newborn 763.89
    - due to previous cesarean delivery 654.2 ☑
- vulva 624.4

Schamberg's disease, dermatitis, or dermatosis (progressive pigmentary dermatosis) 709.09
Schatzki's ring (esophagus) (lower) (congenital) 750.3
- acquired 530.3

Schaufenster krankheit 413.9
Schaumann's
- benign lymphogranulomatosis 135
- disease (sarcoidosis) 135
- syndrome (sarcoidosis) 135

Scheie's syndrome (mucopolysaccharidosis IS) 277.5
Schenck's disease (sporotrichosis) 117.1
Scheuermann's disease or osteochondrosis 732.0
Scheuthauer-Marie-Sainton syndrome (cleidocranialis dysostosis) 755.59
Schilder (-Flatau) disease 341.1
Schilling-type monocytic leukemia (M9890/3) 206.9 ☑
Schimmelbusch's disease, cystic mastitis, or hyperplasia 610.1
Schirmer's syndrome (encephalocutaneous angiomatosis) 759.6
Schistocelia 756.79
Schistoglossia 750.13
Schistosoma infestation — *see* Infestation, Schistosoma
Schistosomiasis 120.9
- Asiatic 120.2
- bladder 120.0
- chestermani 120.8
- colon 120.1
- cutaneous 120.3
- due to
  - S. hematobium 120.0
  - S. japonicum 120.2
  - S. mansoni 120.1
  - S. mattheii 120.8
- eastern 120.2
- genitourinary tract 120.0
- intestinal 120.1
- lung 120.2
- Manson's (intestinal) 120.1
- Oriental 120.2
- pulmonary 120.2
- specified type NEC 120.8
- vesical 120.0

Schizencephaly 742.4
Schizo-affective psychosis — *see also* Schizophrenia 295.7 ☑
Schizodontia 520.2
Schizoid personality 301.20
- introverted 301.21
- schizotypal 301.22

Schizophrenia, schizophrenic (reaction) 295.9 ☑

> *Note — Use the following fifth-digit subclassification with category 295:*
>
> *0 unspecified*
>
> *1 subchronic*
>
> *2 chronic*
>
> *3 subchronic with acute exacerbation*
>
> *4 chronic with acute exacerbation*
>
> *5 in remission*

- acute (attack) NEC 295.8 ☑
  - episode 295.4 ☑
- atypical form 295.8 ☑

Schizophrenia, schizophrenic — *continued*
- borderline 295.5 ☑
- catalepsy 295.2 ☑
- catatonic (type) (acute) (excited) (withdrawn) 295.2 ☑
- childhood (type) (*see also* Psychosis, childhood) 299.9 ☑
- chronic NEC 295.6 ☑
- coenesthesiopathic 295.8 ☑
- cyclic (type) 295.7 ☑
- disorganized (type) 295.1 ☑
- flexibilitas cerea 295.2 ☑
- hebephrenic (type) (acute) 295.1 ☑
- incipient 295.5 ☑
- latent 295.5 ☑
- paranoid (type) (acute) 295.3 ☑
- paraphrenic (acute) 295.3 ☑
- prepsychotic 295.5 ☑
- primary (acute) 295.0 ☑
- prodromal 295.5 ☑
- pseudoneurotic 295.5 ☑
- pseudopsychopathic 295.5 ☑
- reaction 295.9 ☑
- residual type (state) 295.6 ☑
- restzustand 295.6 ☑
- schizo-affective (type) (depressed) (excited) 295.7 ☑
- schizophreniform type 295.4 ☑
- simple (type) (acute) 295.0 ☑
- simplex (acute) 295.0 ☑
- specified type NEC 295.8 ☑
- syndrome of childhood NEC (*see also* Psychosis, childhood) 299.9 ☑
- undifferentiated type 295.9 ☑
  - acute 295.8 ☑
  - chronic 295.6 ☑

Schizothymia 301.20
- introverted 301.21
- schizotypal 301.22

Schlafkrankheit 086.5
Schlatter-Osgood disease (osteochondrosis, tibial tubercle) 732.4
Schlatter's tibia (osteochondrosis) 732.4
Schloffer's tumor — *see also* Peritonitis 567.29
Schmidt's syndrome
- sphallo-pharyngo-laryngeal hemiplegia 352.6
- thyroid-adrenocortical insufficiency 258.1
- vagoaccessory 352.6

Schmincke
- carcinoma (M8082/3) — *see* Neoplasm, nasopharynx, malignant
- tumor (M8082/3) — *see* Neoplasm, nasopharynx, malignant

Schmitz (-Stutzer) dysentery 004.0
Schmorl's disease or nodes 722.30
- lumbar, lumbosacral 722.32
- specified region NEC 722.39
- thoracic, thoracolumbar 722.31

Schneiderian
- carcinoma (M8121/3)
  - specified site — *see* Neoplasm, by site, malignant
  - unspecified site 160.0
- papilloma (M8121/0)
  - specified site — *see* Neoplasm, by site, benign
  - unspecified site 212.0

Schneider's syndrome 047.9
Schnitzler syndrome 273.1
Schoffer's tumor — *see also* Peritonitis 567.29
Scholte's syndrome (malignant carcinoid) 259.2
Scholz's disease 330.0
Scholz (-Bielschowsky-Henneberg) syndrome 330.0
Schönlein (-Henoch) disease (primary) (purpura) (rheumatic) 287.0
School examination V70.3
Schottmüller's disease — *see also* Fever, paratyphoid 002.9
Schroeder's syndrome (endocrine-hypertensive) 255.3
Schüller-Christian disease or syndrome (chronic histiocytosis X) 277.89
Schultz's disease or syndrome (agranulocytosis) 288.09
Schultze's acroparesthesia, simple 443.89
Schwalbe-Ziehen-Oppenheimer disease 333.6
Schwannoma (M9560/0) — *see also* Neoplasm, connective tissue, benign
- malignant (M9560/3) — *see* Neoplasm, connective tissue, malignant

Schwartz-Bartter syndrome (inappropriate secretion of antidiuretic hormone) 253.6
Schwartz (-Jampel) syndrome 359.23
Schweninger-Buzzi disease (macular atrophy) 701.3
Sciatic — *see* condition
Sciatica (infectional) 724.3
- due to
  - displacement of intervertebral disc 722.10
  - herniation, nucleus pulposus 722.10
- wallet 724.3

Scimitar syndrome (anomalous venous drainage, right lung to inferior vena cava) 747.49
Sclera — *see* condition
Sclerectasia 379.11
Scleredema
- adultorum 710.1
- Buschke's 710.1
- newborn 778.1

Sclerema
- adiposum (newborn) 778.1
- adultorum 710.1
- edematosum (newborn) 778.1
- neonatorum 778.1
- newborn 778.1

Scleriasis — *see* Scleroderma
Scleritis 379.00
- with corneal involvement 379.05
- anterior (annular) (localized) 379.03
- brawny 379.06
- granulomatous 379.09
- posterior 379.07
- specified NEC 379.09
- suppurative 379.09
- syphilitic 095.0
- tuberculous (nodular) (*see also* Tuberculosis) 017.3 ☑ *[379.09]*

Sclerochoroiditis — *see also* Scleritis 379.00
Scleroconjunctivitis — *see also* Scleritis 379.00
Sclerocystic ovary (syndrome) 256.4
Sclerodactylia 701.0
Scleroderma, sclerodermia (acrosclerotic) (diffuse) (generalized) (progressive) (pulmonary) 710.1
- circumscribed 701.0
- linear 701.0
- localized (linear) 701.0
- newborn 778.1

Sclerokeratitis 379.05
- meaning sclerosing keratitis 370.54
- tuberculous (*see also* Tuberculosis) 017.3 ☑ *[379.09]*

Scleromalacia
- multiple 731.0
- perforans 379.04

Scleroma, trachea 040.1
Scleromyxedema 701.8
Scleroperikeratitis 379.05
Sclerose en plaques 340
Sclerosis, sclerotic
- adrenal (gland) 255.8
- Alzheimer's 331.0
  - with dementia — *see* Alzheimer's, dementia

- **Spasm, spastic, spasticity** — *see also* condition — *continued*
  - pharynx — *continued*
    - psychogenic — *continued*
      - specified as conversion reaction 300.11
  - pregnant uterus, complicating delivery 661.4 ☑
  - psychogenic 306.0
  - pylorus 537.81
    - adult hypertrophic 537.0
    - congenital or infantile 750.5
    - psychogenic 306.4
  - rectum (sphincter) 564.6
    - psychogenic 306.4
  - retinal artery NEC (*see also* Occlusion, retina, artery) 362.30
  - sacroiliac 724.6
  - salaam (infantile) (*see also* Epilepsy) 345.6 ☑
  - saltatory 781.0
  - sigmoid 564.9
    - psychogenic 306.4
  - sphincter of Oddi (*see also* Disease, gallbladder) 576.5
  - stomach 536.8
    - neurotic 306.4
  - throat 478.29
    - hysterical 300.11
    - psychogenic 306.1
      - specified as conversion reaction 300.11
  - tic 307.20
    - chronic 307.22
    - transient (of childhood) 307.21
  - tongue 529.8
  - torsion 333.6
  - trigeminal nerve 350.1
    - postherpetic 053.12
  - ureter 593.89
  - urethra (sphincter) 599.84
  - uterus 625.8
    - complicating labor 661.4 ☑
      - affecting fetus or newborn 763.7
  - vagina 625.1
    - psychogenic 306.51
  - vascular NEC 443.9
  - vasomotor NEC 443.9
  - vein NEC 459.89
  - vesical (sphincter, external or internal) 596.8
  - viscera 789.0 ☑
- **Spasmus nutans** 307.3
- **Spastic** — *see also* Spasm
  - child 343.9
- **Spasticity** — *see also* Spasm
  - cerebral, child 343.9
- **Speakers' throat** 784.49
- **Specific, specified** — *see* condition
- **Speech**
  - defect, disorder, disturbance, impediment NEC 784.5
    - psychogenic 307.9
  - therapy V57.3
- **Spells** 780.39
  - breath-holding 786.9
- **Spencer's disease** (epidemic vomiting) 078.82
- **Spens' syndrome** (syncope with heart block) 426.9
- **Spermatic cord** — *see* condition
- **Spermatocele** 608.1
  - congenital 752.89
- **Spermatocystitis** 608.4
- **Spermatocytoma** (M9063/3)
  - specified site — *see* Neoplasm, by site, malignant
  - unspecified site 186.9
- **Spermatorrhea** 608.89
- **Sperm counts**
  - fertility testing V26.21
  - following sterilization reversal V26.22
  - postvasectomy V25.8
- **Sphacelus** — *see also* Gangrene 785.4
- **Sphenoidal** — *see* condition
- **Sphenoiditis** (chronic) — *see also* Sinusitis, sphenoidal 473.3
- **Sphenopalatine ganglion neuralgia** 337.09
- **Sphericity, increased, lens** 743.36
- **Spherocytosis** (congenital) (familial) (hereditary) 282.0
  - hemoglobin disease 282.7
  - sickle-cell (disease) 282.60
- **Spherophakia** 743.36
- **Sphincter** — *see* condition
- **Sphincteritis, sphincter of Oddi** — *see also* Cholecystitis 576.8
- **Sphingolipidosis** 272.7
- **Sphingolipodystrophy** 272.7
- **Sphingomyelinosis** 272.7
- **Spicule tooth** 520.2
- **Spider**
  - finger 755.59
  - nevus 448.1
  - vascular 448.1
- **Spiegler-Fendt sarcoid** 686.8
- **Spielmeyer-Stock disease** 330.1
- **Spielmeyer-Vogt disease** 330.1
- **Spina bifida** (aperta) 741.9 ☑

> *Note — Use the following fifth-digit subclassification with category 741:*
>
> *0 unspecified region*
>
> *1 cervical region*
>
> *2 dorsal [thoracic] region*
>
> *3 lumbar region*

  - with hydrocephalus 741.0 ☑
    - fetal (suspected), affecting management of pregnancy 655.0 ☑
  - occulta 756.17
- **Spindle, Krukenberg's** 371.13
- **Spine, spinal** — *see* condition
- **Spiradenoma** (eccrine) (M8403/0) — *see* Neoplasm, skin, benign
- **Spirillosis** NEC — *see also* Fever, relapsing 087.9
- **Spirillum minus** 026.0
- **Spirillum obermeieri infection** 087.0
- **Spirochetal** — *see* condition
- **Spirochetosis** 104.9
  - arthritic, arthritica 104.9 *[711.8]* ☑
  - bronchopulmonary 104.8
  - icterohemorrhagica 100.0
  - lung 104.8
- **Spitting blood** — *see also* Hemoptysis 786.3
- **Splanchnomegaly** 569.89
- **Splanchnoptosis** 569.89
- **Spleen, splenic** — *see also* condition
  - agenesis 759.0
  - flexure syndrome 569.89
  - neutropenia syndrome 289.53
  - sequestration syndrome 289.52
- **Splenectasis** — *see also* Splenomegaly 789.2
- **Splenitis** (interstitial) (malignant) (nonspecific) 289.59
  - malarial (*see also* Malaria) 084.6
  - tuberculous (*see also* Tuberculosis) 017.7 ☑
- **Splenocele** 289.59
- **Splenomegalia** — *see* Splenomegaly
- **Splenomegalic** — *see* condition
- **Splenomegaly** 789.2
  - Bengal 789.2
  - cirrhotic 289.51
  - congenital 759.0
  - congestive, chronic 289.51
  - cryptogenic 789.2
  - Egyptian 120.1
  - Gaucher's (cerebroside lipidosis) 272.7
  - idiopathic 789.2
  - malarial (*see also* Malaria) 084.6
  - neutropenic 289.53
  - Niemann-Pick (lipid histiocytosis) 272.7
  - siderotic 289.51
  - syphilitic 095.8
    - congenital 090.0
- **Splenomegaly** — *continued*
  - tropical (Bengal) (idiopathic) 789.2
- **Splenopathy** 289.50
- **Splenopneumonia** — *see* Pneumonia
- **Splenoptosis** 289.59
- **Splinter** — *see* Injury, superficial, by site
- **Split, splitting**
  - heart sounds 427.89
  - lip, congenital (*see also* Cleft, lip) 749.10
  - nails 703.8
  - urinary stream 788.61
- **Spoiled child reaction** — *see also* Disturbance, conduct 312.1 ☑
- **Spondylarthritis** — *see also* Spondylosis 721.90
- **Spondylarthrosis** — *see also* Spondylosis 721.90
- **Spondylitis** 720.9
  - ankylopoietica 720.0
  - ankylosing (chronic) 720.0
  - atrophic 720.9
    - ligamentous 720.9
  - chronic (traumatic) (*see also* Spondylosis) 721.90
  - deformans (chronic) (*see also* Spondylosis) 721.90
  - gonococcal 098.53
  - gouty 274.0
  - hypertrophic (*see also* Spondylosis) 721.90
  - infectious NEC 720.9
  - juvenile (adolescent) 720.0
  - Kümmell's 721.7
  - Marie-Strümpell (ankylosing) 720.0
  - muscularis 720.9
  - ossificans ligamentosa 721.6
  - osteoarthritica (*see also* Spondylosis) 721.90
  - posttraumatic 721.7
  - proliferative 720.0
  - rheumatoid 720.0
  - rhizomelica 720.0
  - sacroiliac NEC 720.2
  - senescent (*see also* Spondylosis) 721.90
  - senile (*see also* Spondylosis) 721.90
  - static (*see also* Spondylosis) 721.90
  - traumatic (chronic) (*see also* Spondylosis) 721.90
  - tuberculous (*see also* Tuberculosis) 015.0 ☑ *[720.81]*
  - typhosa 002.0 *[720.81]*
- **Spondyloarthrosis** — *see also* Spondylosis 721.90
- **Spondylolisthesis** (congenital) (lumbosacral) 756.12
  - with disproportion (fetopelvic) 653.3 ☑
    - affecting fetus or newborn 763.1
    - causing obstructed labor 660.1 ☑
      - affecting fetus or newborn 763.1
  - acquired 738.4
  - degenerative 738.4
  - traumatic 738.4
    - acute (lumbar) — *see* Fracture, vertebra, lumbar
      - site other than lumbosacral — *see* Fracture, vertebra, by site
- **Spondylolysis** (congenital) 756.11
  - acquired 738.4
  - cervical 756.19
  - lumbosacral region 756.11
    - with disproportion (fetopelvic) 653.3 ☑
      - affecting fetus or newborn 763.1
      - causing obstructed labor 660.1 ☑
        - affecting fetus or newborn 763.1
- **Spondylopathy**
  - inflammatory 720.9
    - specified type NEC 720.89
  - traumatic 721.7
- **Spondylose rhizomelique** 720.0
- **Spondylosis** 721.90
- **Spondylosis** — *continued*
  - with
    - disproportion 653.3 ☑
      - affecting fetus or newborn 763.1
      - causing obstructed labor 660.1 ☑
        - affecting fetus or newborn 763.1
    - myelopathy NEC 721.91
  - cervical, cervicodorsal 721.0
    - with myelopathy 721.1
  - inflammatory 720.9
  - lumbar, lumbosacral 721.3
    - with myelopathy 721.42
  - sacral 721.3
    - with myelopathy 721.42
  - thoracic 721.2
    - with myelopathy 721.41
  - traumatic 721.7
- **Sponge**
  - divers' disease 989.5
  - inadvertently left in operation wound 998.4
  - kidney (medullary) 753.17
- **Spongioblastoma** (M9422/3)
  - multiforme (M9440/3)
    - specified site — *see* Neoplasm, by site, malignant
    - unspecified site 191.9
  - polare (M9423/3)
    - specified site — *see* Neoplasm, by site, malignant
    - unspecified site 191.9
  - primitive polar (M9443/3)
    - specified site — *see* Neoplasm, by site, malignant
    - unspecified site 191.9
  - specified site — *see* Neoplasm, by site, malignant
  - unspecified site 191.9
- **Spongiocytoma** (M9400/3)
  - specified site — *see* Neoplasm, by site, malignant
  - unspecified site 191.9
- **Spongioneuroblastoma** (M9504/3) — *see* Neoplasm, by site, malignant
- **Spontaneous** — *see also* condition
  - fracture — *see* Fracture, pathologic
- **Spoon nail** 703.8
  - congenital 757.5
- **Sporadic** — *see* condition
- **Sporotrichosis** (bones) (cutaneous) (disseminated) (epidermal) (lymphatic) (lymphocutaneous) (mucous membranes) (pulmonary) (skeletal) (visceral) 117.1
- **Sporotrichum schenckii infection** 117.1
- **Spots, spotting**
  - atrophic (skin) 701.3
  - Bitôt's (in the young child) 264.1
  - café au lait 709.09
  - cayenne pepper 448.1
  - complicating pregnancy 649.5 ☑
  - cotton wool (retina) 362.83
  - de Morgan's (senile angiomas) 448.1
  - Fúchs' black (myopic) 360.21
  - intermenstrual
    - irregular 626.6
    - regular 626.5
  - interpalpebral 372.53
  - Koplik's 055.9
  - liver 709.09
  - Mongolian (pigmented) 757.33
  - of pregnancy 649.5 ☑
  - purpuric 782.7
  - ruby 448.1
- **Spotted fever** — *see* Fever, spotted
- **Sprain, strain** (joint) (ligament) (muscle) (tendon) 848.9
  - abdominal wall (muscle) 848.8
  - Achilles tendon 845.09
  - acromioclavicular 840.0
  - ankle 845.00
    - and foot 845.00
  - anterior longitudinal, cervical 847.0

Sprain, strain — *continued*
- arm 840.9
  - upper 840.9
    - and shoulder 840.9
- astragalus 845.00
- atlanto-axial 847.0
- atlanto-occipital 847.0
- atlas 847.0
- axis 847.0
- back (*see also* Sprain, spine) 847.9
- breast bone 848.40
- broad ligament — *see* Injury, internal, broad ligament
- calcaneofibular 845.02
- carpal 842.01
- carpometacarpal 842.11
- cartilage
  - costal, without mention of injury to sternum 848.3
    - involving sternum 848.42
  - ear 848.8
  - knee 844.9
    - with current tear (*see also* Tear, meniscus) 836.2
  - semilunar (knee) 844.8
    - with current tear (*see also* Tear, meniscus) 836.2
  - septal, nose 848.0
  - thyroid region 848.2
  - xiphoid 848.49
- cervical, cervicodorsal, cervicothoracic 847.0
- chondrocostal, without mention of injury to sternum 848.3
  - involving sternum 848.42
- chondrosternal 848.42
- chronic (joint) — *see* Derangement, joint
- clavicle 840.9
- coccyx 847.4
- collar bone 840.9
- collateral, knee (medial) (tibial) 844.1
  - lateral (fibular) 844.0
  - recurrent or old 717.89
    - lateral 717.81
    - medial 717.82
- coracoacromial 840.8
- coracoclavicular 840.1
- coracohumeral 840.2
- coracoid (process) 840.9
- coronary, knee 844.8
- costal cartilage, without mention of injury to sternum 848.3
  - involving sternum 848.42
- cricoarytenoid articulation 848.2
- cricothyroid articulation 848.2
- cruciate
  - knee 844.2
  - old 717.89
    - anterior 717.83
    - posterior 717.84
- deltoid
  - ankle 845.01
  - shoulder 840.8
- dorsal (spine) 847.1
- ear cartilage 848.8
- elbow 841.9
  - and forearm 841.9
  - specified site NEC 841.8
- femur (proximal end) 843.9
  - distal end 844.9
- fibula (proximal end) 844.9
  - distal end 845.00
- fibulocalcaneal 845.02
- finger(s) 842.10
- foot 845.10
  - and ankle 845.00
- forearm 841.9
  - and elbow 841.9
  - specified site NEC 841.8
- glenoid (shoulder) (*see also* SLAP lesion) 840.8
- hand 842.10
- hip 843.9
  - and thigh 843.9
- humerus (proximal end) 840.9

Sprain, strain — *continued*
- humerus — *continued*
  - distal end 841.9
- iliofemoral 843.0
- infraspinatus 840.3
- innominate
  - acetabulum 843.9
  - pubic junction 848.5
  - sacral junction 846.1
- internal
  - collateral, ankle 845.01
  - semilunar cartilage 844.8
    - with current tear (*see also* Tear, meniscus) 836.2
    - old 717.5
- interphalangeal
  - finger 842.13
  - toe 845.13
- ischiocapsular 843.1
- jaw (cartilage) (meniscus) 848.1
  - old 524.69
- knee 844.9
  - and leg 844.9
  - old 717.5
    - collateral
      - lateral 717.81
      - medial 717.82
    - cruciate
      - anterior 717.83
      - posterior 717.84
- late effect — *see* Late, effects (of), sprain
- lateral collateral, knee 844.0
  - old 717.81
- leg 844.9
  - and knee 844.9
- ligamentum teres femoris 843.8
- low back 846.9
- lumbar (spine) 847.2
- lumbosacral 846.0
  - chronic or old 724.6
- mandible 848.1
  - old 524.69
- maxilla 848.1
- medial collateral, knee 844.1
  - old 717.82
- meniscus
  - jaw 848.1
    - old 524.69
  - knee 844.8
    - with current tear (*see also* Tear, meniscus) 836.2
    - old 717.5
  - mandible 848.1
    - old 524.69
  - specified site NEC 848.8
- metacarpal 842.10
  - distal 842.12
  - proximal 842.11
- metacarpophalangeal 842.12
- metatarsal 845.10
- metatarsophalangeal 845.12
- midcarpal 842.19
- midtarsal 845.19
- multiple sites, except fingers alone or toes alone 848.8
- neck 847.0
- nose (septal cartilage) 848.0
- occiput from atlas 847.0
- old — *see* Derangement, joint
- orbicular, hip 843.8
- patella(r) 844.8
  - old 717.89
- pelvis 848.5
- phalanx
  - finger 842.10
  - toe 845.10
- radiocarpal 842.02
- radiohumeral 841.2
- radioulnar 841.9
  - distal 842.09
- radius, radial (proximal end) 841.9
  - and ulna 841.9
    - distal 842.09
  - collateral 841.0
  - distal end 842.00

Sprain, strain — *continued*
- recurrent — *see* Sprain, by site
- rib (cage), without mention of injury to sternum 848.3
  - involving sternum 848.42
- rotator cuff (capsule) 840.4
- round ligament (*see also* Injury, internal, round ligament)
  - femur 843.8
- sacral (spine) 847.3
- sacrococcygeal 847.3
- sacroiliac (region) 846.9
  - chronic or old 724.6
  - ligament 846.1
  - specified site NEC 846.8
- sacrospinatus 846.2
- sacrospinous 846.2
- sacrotuberous 846.3
- scaphoid bone, ankle 845.00
- scapula(r) 840.9
- semilunar cartilage (knee) 844.8
  - with current tear (*see also* Tear, meniscus) 836.2
  - old 717.5
- septal cartilage (nose) 848.0
- shoulder 840.9
  - and arm, upper 840.9
  - blade 840.9
- specified site NEC 848.8
- spine 847.9
  - cervical 847.0
  - coccyx 847.4
  - dorsal 847.1
  - lumbar 847.2
  - lumbosacral 846.0
    - chronic or old 724.6
  - sacral 847.3
  - sacroiliac (*see also* Sprain, sacroiliac) 846.9
    - chronic or old 724.6
  - thoracic 847.1
- sternoclavicular 848.41
- sternum 848.40
- subglenoid (*see also* SLAP lesion) 840.8
- subscapularis 840.5
- supraspinatus 840.6
- symphysis
  - jaw 848.1
    - old 524.69
  - mandibular 848.1
    - old 524.69
  - pubis 848.5
- talofibular 845.09
- tarsal 845.10
- tarsometatarsal 845.11
- temporomandibular 848.1
  - old 524.69
- teres
  - ligamentum femoris 843.8
  - major or minor 840.8
- thigh (proximal end) 843.9
  - and hip 843.9
  - distal end 844.9
- thoracic (spine) 847.1
- thorax 848.8
- thumb 842.10
- thyroid cartilage or region 848.2
- tibia (proximal end) 844.9
  - distal end 845.00
- tibiofibular
  - distal 845.03
  - superior 844.3
- toe(s) 845.10
- trachea 848.8
- trapezoid 840.8
- ulna, ulnar (proximal end) 841.9
  - collateral 841.1
  - distal end 842.00
- ulnohumeral 841.3
- vertebrae (*see also* Sprain, spine) 847.9
  - cervical, cervicodorsal, cervicothoracic 847.0
- wrist (cuneiform) (scaphoid) (semilunar) 842.00

Sprain, strain — *continued*
- xiphoid cartilage 848.49

Sprengel's deformity (congenital) 755.52

Spring fever 309.23

Sprue 579.1
- celiac 579.0
- idiopathic 579.0
- meaning thrush 112.0
- nontropical 579.0
- tropical 579.1

Spur — *see also* Exostosis
- bone 726.91
  - calcaneal 726.73
- calcaneal 726.73
- iliac crest 726.5
- nose (septum) 478.19
  - bone 726.91
- septal 478.19

Spuria placenta — *see* Placenta, abnormal

Spurway's syndrome (brittle bones and blue sclera) 756.51

Sputum, abnormal (amount) (color) (excessive) (odor) (purulent) 786.4
- bloody 786.3

Squamous — *see also* condition
- cell metaplasia
  - bladder 596.8
  - cervix — *see* condition
- epithelium in
  - cervical canal (congenital) 752.49
  - uterine mucosa (congenital) 752.3
- metaplasia
  - bladder 596.8
  - cervix — *see* condition

Squashed nose 738.0
- congenital 754.0

Squeeze, divers' 993.3

Squint — *see also* Strabismus 378.9
- accommodative (*see also* Esotropia) 378.00
- concomitant (*see also* Heterotropia) 378.30

Stab — *see also* Wound, open, by site
- internal organs — *see* Injury, internal, by site, with open wound

Staggering gait 781.2
- hysterical 300.11

Staghorn calculus 592.0

Stain, staining
- meconium 779.84
- port wine 757.32
- tooth, teeth (hard tissues) 521.7
  - due to
    - accretions 523.6
    - deposits (betel) (black) (green) (materia alba) (orange) (tobacco) 523.6
    - metals (copper) (silver) 521.7
    - nicotine 523.6
    - pulpal bleeding 521.7
    - tobacco 523.6

Stälh's
- ear 744.29
- pigment line (cornea) 371.11

Stälhi's pigment lines (cornea) 371.11

Stammering 307.0

Standstill
- atrial 426.6
- auricular 426.6
- cardiac (*see also* Arrest, cardiac) 427.5
- sinoatrial 426.6
- sinus 426.6
- ventricular (*see also* Arrest, cardiac) 427.5

Stannosis 503

Stanton's disease (melioidosis) 025

Staphylitis (acute) (catarrhal) (chronic) (gangrenous) (membranous) (suppurative) (ulcerative) 528.3

Staphylococcemia 038.10
- aureus 038.11
- specified organism NEC 038.19

Staphylococcus, staphylococcal — *see* condition

Staphyloderma (skin) 686.00

- **Staphyloma** 379.11
  - anterior, localized 379.14
  - ciliary 379.11
  - cornea 371.73
  - equatorial 379.13
  - posterior 379.12
  - posticum 379.12
  - ring 379.15
  - sclera NEC 379.11
- **Starch eating** 307.52
- **Stargardt's disease** 362.75
- **Starvation** (inanition) (due to lack of food) 994.2
  - edema 262
  - voluntary NEC 307.1
- **Stasis**
  - bile (duct) (*see also* Disease, biliary) 576.8
  - bronchus (*see also* Bronchitis) 490
  - cardiac (*see also* Failure, heart) 428.0
  - cecum 564.89
  - colon 564.89
  - dermatitis (*see also* Varix, with stasis dermatitis) 454.1
  - duodenal 536.8
  - eczema (*see also* Varix, with stasis dermatitis) 454.1
  - edema (*see also* Hypertension, venous) 459.30
  - foot 991.4
  - gastric 536.3
  - ileocecal coil 564.89
  - ileum 564.89
  - intestinal 564.89
  - jejunum 564.89
  - kidney 586
  - liver 571.9
    - cirrhotic — *see* Cirrhosis, liver
  - lymphatic 457.8
  - pneumonia 514
  - portal 571.9
  - pulmonary 514
  - rectal 564.89
  - renal 586
    - tubular 584.5
  - stomach 536.3
  - ulcer
    - with varicose veins 454.0
    - without varicose veins 459.81
  - urine NEC (*see also* Retention, urine) 788.20
  - venous 459.81
- **State**
  - affective and paranoid, mixed, organic psychotic 294.8
  - agitated 307.9
    - acute reaction to stress 308.2
  - anxiety (neurotic) (*see also* Anxiety) 300.00
    - specified type NEC 300.09
  - apprehension (*see also* Anxiety) 300.00
    - specified type NEC 300.09
  - climacteric, female 627.2
    - following induced menopause 627.4
  - clouded
    - epileptic (*see also* Epilepsy) 345.9 ☑
    - paroxysmal (idiopathic) (*see also* Epilepsy) 345.9 ☑
  - compulsive (mixed) (with obsession) 300.3
  - confusional 298.9
    - acute 293.0
      - with
        - arteriosclerotic dementia 290.41
        - presenile brain disease 290.11
        - senility 290.3
      - alcoholic 291.0
      - drug-induced 292.81
    - epileptic 293.0
    - postoperative 293.9

State — *continued*
  - confusional — *continued*
    - reactive (emotional stress) (psychological trauma) 298.2
    - subacute 293.1
  - constitutional psychopathic 301.9
  - convulsive (*see also* Convulsions) 780.39
  - depressive NEC 311
    - induced by drug 292.84
    - neurotic 300.4
  - dissociative 300.15
  - hallucinatory 780.1
    - induced by drug 292.12
  - hypercoagulable (primary) 289.81
    - secondary 289.82
  - hyperdynamic beta-adrenergic circulatory 429.82
  - locked-in 344.81
  - menopausal 627.2
    - artificial 627.4
    - following induced menopause 627.4
  - neurotic NEC 300.9
    - with depersonalization episode 300.6
  - obsessional 300.3
  - oneiroid (*see also* Schizophrenia) 295.4 ☑
  - panic 300.01
  - paranoid 297.9
    - alcohol-induced 291.5
    - arteriosclerotic 290.42
    - climacteric 297.2
    - drug-induced 292.11
    - in
      - presenile brain disease 290.12
      - senile brain disease 290.20
    - involutional 297.2
    - menopausal 297.2
    - senile 290.20
    - simple 297.0
  - postleukotomy 310.0
  - pregnant (*see also* Pregnancy) V22.2
  - psychogenic, twilight 298.2
  - psychotic, organic (*see also* Psychosis, organic) 294.9
    - mixed paranoid and affective 294.8
    - senile or presenile NEC 290.9
    - transient NEC 293.9
      - with
        - anxiety 293.84
        - delusions 293.81
        - depression 293.83
        - hallucinations 293.82
  - residual schizophrenic (*see also* Schizophrenia) 295.6 ☑
  - tension (*see also* Anxiety) 300.9
  - transient organic psychotic 293.9
    - anxiety type 293.84
    - depressive type 293.83
    - hallucinatory type 293.83
    - paranoid type 293.81
    - specified type NEC 293.89
  - twilight
    - epileptic 293.0
    - psychogenic 298.2
  - vegetative (persistent) 780.03
- **Status** (post)
  - absence
    - epileptic (*see also* Epilepsy) 345.2
    - of organ, acquired (postsurgical) — *see* Absence, by site, acquired
  - administration of tPA(rtPA) in a different institution within the last 24 hours prior to admission to facility V45.88
  - anastomosis of intestine (for bypass) V45.3
  - anginosus 413.9
  - angioplasty, percutaneous transluminal coronary V45.82
  - ankle prosthesis V43.66
  - aortocoronary bypass or shunt V45.81
  - arthrodesis V45.4

Status — *continued*
  - artificially induced condition NEC V45.89
  - artificial opening (of) V44.9
    - gastrointestinal tract NEC V44.4
    - specified site NEC V44.8
    - urinary tract NEC V44.6
    - vagina V44.7
  - aspirator V46.0
  - asthmaticus (*see also* Asthma) 493.9 ☑
  - awaiting organ transplant V49.83
  - bariatric surgery V45.86
    - complicating pregnancy, childbirth, or the puerperium 649.2 ☑
  - bed confinement V49.84
  - breast
    - correction V43.82
    - implant removal V45.83
    - reconstruction V43.82
  - cardiac
    - device (in situ) V45.00
      - carotid sinus V45.09
        - fitting or adjustment V53.39
      - defibrillator, automatic implantable V45.02
      - pacemaker V45.01
        - fitting or adjustment V53.31
  - carotid sinus stimulator V45.09
  - cataract extraction V45.61
  - chemotherapy V66.2
    - current V58.69
  - circumcision, female 629.20
  - clitorectomy (female genital mutilation type I) 629.21
    - with excision of labia minora (female genital mutilation type II) 629.22
  - colonization — *see* Carrier (suspected) of
  - colostomy V44.3
  - contraceptive device V45.59
    - intrauterine V45.51
    - subdermal V45.52
  - convulsivus idiopathicus (*see also* Epilepsy) 345.3
  - coronary artery bypass or shunt V45.81
  - current military deployment status V62.22
  - cutting
    - female genital 629.20
      - specified NEC 629.29
      - type I 629.21
      - type II 629.22
      - type III 629.23
      - type IV 629.29
  - cystostomy V44.50
    - appendico-vesicostomy V44.52
    - cutaneous-vesicostomy V44.51
    - specified type NEC V44.59
  - defibrillator, automatic implantable cardiac V45.02
  - dental crowns V45.84
  - dental fillings V45.84
  - dental restoration V45.84
  - dental sealant V49.82
  - dialysis (hemo) (peritoneal) V45.11
  - donor V59.9
  - drug therapy or regimen V67.59
    - high-risk medication NEC V67.51
  - elbow prosthesis V43.62
  - enterostomy V44.4
  - epileptic, epilepticus (absence) (grand mal) (*see also* Epilepsy) 345.3
    - focal motor 345.7 ☑
    - partial 345.7 ☑
    - petit mal 345.2
    - psychomotor 345.7 ☑
    - temporal lobe 345.7 ☑
  - estrogen receptor
    - negative [ER-] V86.1
    - positive [ER+] V86.0
  - eye (adnexa) surgery V45.69
  - female genital
    - cutting 629.20

Status — *continued*
  - female genital — *continued*
    - cutting — *continued*
      - specified NEC 629.29
      - type I 629.21
      - type II 629.22
      - type III 629.23
      - type IV 629.29
    - mutilation 629.20
      - type I 629.21
      - type II 629.22
      - type III 629.23
      - type IV 629.29
  - filtering bleb (eye) (postglaucoma) V45.69
    - with rupture or complication 997.99
    - postcataract extraction (complication) 997.99
  - finger joint prosthesis V43.69
  - gastric
    - banding V45.86
      - complicating pregnancy, childbirth, or the puerperium 649.2 ☑
    - bypass for obesity V45.86
      - complicating pregnancy, childbirth, or the puerperium 649.2 ☑
  - gastrostomy V44.1
  - grand mal 345.3
  - heart valve prosthesis V43.3
  - hemodialysis V45.11
  - hip prosthesis (joint) (partial) (total) V43.64
  - hysterectomy V88.01
    - partial with remaining cervical stump V88.02
    - total V88.01
  - ileostomy V44.2
  - infibulation (female genital mutilation type III) 629.23
  - insulin pump V45.85
  - intestinal bypass V45.3
  - intrauterine contraceptive device V45.51
  - jejunostomy V44.4
  - knee joint prosthesis V43.65
  - lacunaris 437.8
  - lacunosis 437.8
  - low birth weight V21.30
    - less than 500 grams V21.31
    - 1000–1499 grams V21.33
    - 1500–1999 grams V21.34
    - 2000–2500 grams V21.35
    - 500–999 grams V21.32
  - lymphaticus 254.8
  - malignant neoplasm, ablated or excised — *see* History, malignant neoplasm
  - marmoratus 333.79
  - mutilation, female 629.20
    - type I 629.21
    - type II 629.22
    - type III 629.23
    - type IV 629.29
  - nephrostomy V44.6
  - neuropacemaker NEC V45.89
    - brain V45.89
    - carotid sinus V45.09
    - neurologic NEC V45.89
  - obesity surgery V45.86
    - compliating pregnancy, childbirth, or the puerperium 649.2 ☑
  - organ replacement
    - by artificial or mechanical device or prosthesis of
      - artery V43.4
      - artificial skin V43.83
      - bladder V43.5
      - blood vessel V43.4
      - breast V43.82
      - eye globe V43.0
      - heart
        - assist device V43.21

Status — *continued*
organ replacement — *continued*
by artificial or mechanical device or prosthesis of — *continued*
heart — *continued*
fully implantable artificial heart V43.22
valve V43.3
intestine V43.89
joint V43.60
ankle V43.66
elbow V43.62
finger V43.69
hip (partial) (total) V43.64
knee V43.65
shoulder V43.61
specified NEC V43.69
wrist V43.63
kidney V43.89
larynx V43.81
lens V43.1
limb(s) V43.7
liver V43.89
lung V43.89
organ NEC V43.89
pancreas V43.89
skin (artificial) V43.83
tissue NEC V43.89
vein V43.4
by organ transplant (heterologous) (homologous) — *see* Status, transplant
pacemaker
brain V45.89
cardiac V45.01
carotid sinus V45.09
neurologic NEC V45.89
specified site NEC V45.89
percutaneous transluminal coronary angioplasty V45.82
peritoneal dialysis V45.11
petit mal 345.2
postcommotio cerebri 310.2
postmenopausal (age related) (natural) V49.81
postoperative NEC V45.89
postpartum NEC V24.2
care immediately following delivery V24.0
routine follow-up V24.2
postsurgical NEC V45.89
renal dialysis V45.11
noncompliance V45.12
respirator [ventilator] V46.11
encounter
during
mechanical failure V46.14
power failure V46.12
for weaning V46.13
reversed jejunal transposition (for bypass) V45.3
sex reassignment surgery (*see also* Trans-sexualism) 302.50
shoulder prosthesis V43.61
shunt
aortocoronary bypass V45.81
arteriovenous (for dialysis) V45.11
cerebrospinal fluid V45.2
vascular NEC V45.89
aortocoronary (bypass) V45.81
ventricular (communicating) (for drainage) V45.2
sterilization
tubal ligation V26.51
vasectomy V26.52
subdermal contraceptive device V45.52
thymicolymphaticus 254.8
thymicus 254.8
thymolymphaticus 254.8
tooth extraction 525.10
tracheostomy V44.0
transplant
blood vessel V42.89
bone V42.4

Status — *continued*
transplant — *continued*
bone — *continued*
marrow V42.81
cornea V42.5
heart V42.1
valve V42.2
intestine V42.84
kidney V42.0
liver V42.7
lung V42.6
organ V42.9
removal (due to complication, failure, rejection or infection) V45.87
specified site NEC V42.89
pancreas V42.83
peripheral stem cells V42.82
skin V42.3
stem cells, peripheral V42.82
tissue V42.9
specified type NEC V42.89
vessel, blood V42.89
tubal ligation V26.51
ureterostomy V44.6
urethrostomy V44.6
vagina, artificial V44.7
vascular shunt NEC V45.89
aortocoronary (bypass) V45.81
vasectomy V26.52
ventilator [respirator] V46.11
encounter
during
mechanical failure V46.14
power failure V46.12
for weaning V46.13
wheelchair confinement V46.3
wrist prosthesis V43.63

Stave fracture — *see* Fracture, metacarpus, metacarpal bone(s)

Steal
subclavian artery 435.2
vertebral artery 435.1

Stealing, solitary, child problem — *see also* Disturbance, conduct 312.1 ☑

Steam burn — *see* Burn, by site

Steatocystoma multiplex 706.2

Steatoma (infected) 706.2
eyelid (cystic) 374.84
infected 373.13

Steatorrhea (chronic) 579.8
with lacteal obstruction 579.2
idiopathic 579.0
adult 579.0
infantile 579.0
pancreatic 579.4
primary 579.0
secondary 579.8
specified cause NEC 579.8
tropical 579.1

Steatosis 272.8
heart (*see also* Degeneration, myocardial) 429.1
kidney 593.89
liver 571.8

Steele-Richardson (-Olszewski) Syndrome 333.0

Steinbrocker's syndrome — *see also* Neuropathy, peripheral, autonomic 337.9

Steinert's disease 359.21

Stein-Leventhal syndrome (polycystic ovary) 256.4

Stein's syndrome (polycystic ovary) 256.4

STEMI (ST elevation myocardial infarction — *see also* — Infarct, myocardium, ST elevation 410.9 ☑

Stenocardia — *see also* Angina 413.9

Stenocephaly 756.0

Stenosis (cicatricial) — *see also* Stricture
ampulla of Vater 576.2
with calculus, cholelithiasis, or stones — *see* Choledocholithiasis
anus, anal (canal) (sphincter) 569.2

Stenosis — *see also* Stricture — *continued*
anus, anal — *continued*
congenital 751.2
aorta (ascending) 747.22
arch 747.10
arteriosclerotic 440.0
calcified 440.0
aortic (valve) 424.1
with
mitral (valve)
insufficiency or incompetence 396.2
stenosis or obstruction 396.0
atypical 396.0
congenital 746.3
rheumatic 395.0
with
insufficiency, incompetency or regurgitation 395.2
with mitral (valve) disease 396.8
mitral (valve)
disease (stenosis) 396.0
insufficiency or incompetence 396.2
stenosis or obstruction 396.0
specified cause, except rheumatic 424.1
syphilitic 093.22
aqueduct of Sylvius (congenital) 742.3
with spina bifida (*see also* Spina bifida) 741.0 ☑
acquired 331.4
artery NEC (*see also* Arteriosclerosis) 447.1
basilar — *see* Narrowing, artery, basilar
carotid (common) (internal) — *see* Narrowing, artery, carotid
celiac 447.4
cerebral 437.0
due to
embolism (*see also* Embolism, brain) 434.1 ☑
thrombus (*see also* Thrombosis, brain) 434.0 ☑
extremities 440.20
precerebral — *see* Narrowing, artery, precerebral
pulmonary (congenital) 747.3
acquired 417.8
renal 440.1
vertebral — *see* Narrowing, artery, vertebral
bile duct or biliary passage (*see also* Obstruction, biliary) 576.2
congenital 751.61
bladder neck (acquired) 596.0
congenital 753.6
brain 348.8
bronchus 519.19
syphilitic 095.8
cardia (stomach) 537.89
congenital 750.7
cardiovascular (*see also* Disease, cardiovascular) 429.2
carotid artery — *see* Narrowing, artery, carotid
cervix, cervical (canal) 622.4
congenital 752.49
in pregnancy or childbirth 654.6 ☑
affecting fetus or newborn 763.89
causing obstructed labor 660.2 ☑
affecting fetus or newborn 763.1
colon (*see also* Obstruction, intestine) 560.9
congenital 751.2
colostomy 569.62
common bile duct (*see also* Obstruction, biliary) 576.2
congenital 751.61

Stenosis — *see also* Stricture — *continued*
coronary (artery) — *see* Arteriosclerosis, coronary
cystic duct (*see also* Obstruction, gallbladder) 575.2
congenital 751.61
due to (presence of) any device, implant, or graft classifiable to 996.0–996.5 — *see* Complications, due to (presence of) any device, implant, or graft classified to 996.0–996.5 NEC
duodenum 537.3
congenital 751.1
ejaculatory duct NEC 608.89
endocervical os — *see* Stenosis, cervix
enterostomy 569.62
esophagostomy 530.87
esophagus 530.3
congenital 750.3
syphilitic 095.8
congenital 090.5
external ear canal 380.50
secondary to
inflammation 380.53
surgery 380.52
trauma 380.51
gallbladder (*see also* Obstruction, gallbladder) 575.2
glottis 478.74
heart valve (acquired) (*see also* Endocarditis)
congenital NEC 746.89
aortic 746.3
mitral 746.5
pulmonary 746.02
tricuspid 746.1
hepatic duct (*see also* Obstruction, biliary) 576.2
hymen 623.3
hypertrophic subaortic (idiopathic) 425.1
infundibulum cardiac 746.83
intestine (*see also* Obstruction, intestine) 560.9
congenital (small) 751.1
large 751.2
lacrimal
canaliculi 375.53
duct 375.56
congenital 743.65
punctum 375.52
congenital 743.65
sac 375.54
congenital 743.65
lacrimonasal duct 375.56
congenital 743.65
neonatal 375.55
larynx 478.74
congenital 748.3
syphilitic 095.8
congenital 090.5
mitral (valve) (chronic) (inactive) 394.0
with
aortic (valve)
disease (insufficiency) 396.1
insufficiency or incompetence 396.1
stenosis or obstruction 396.0
incompetency, insufficiency or regurgitation 394.2
with aortic valve disease 396.8
active or acute 391.1
with chorea (acute) (rheumatic) (Sydenham's) 392.0
congenital 746.5
specified cause, except rheumatic 424.0
syphilitic 093.21
myocardium, myocardial (*see also* Degeneration, myocardial) 429.1
hypertrophic subaortic (idiopathic) 425.1
nares (anterior) (posterior) 478.19

Stenosis — *see also* Stricture — *continued*
nares — *continued*
congenital 748.0
nasal duct 375.56
congenital 743.65
nasolacrimal duct 375.56
congenital 743.65
neonatal 375.55
organ or site, congenital NEC — *see* Atresia
papilla of Vater 576.2
with calculus, cholelithiasis, or stones — *see* Choledocholithiasis
pulmonary (artery) (congenital) 747.3
with ventricular septal defect, dextraposition of aorta and hypertrophy of right ventricle 745.2
acquired 417.8
infundibular 746.83
in tetralogy of Fallot 745.2
subvalvular 746.83
valve (*see also* Endocarditis, pulmonary) 424.3
congenital 746.02
vein 747.49
acquired 417.8
vessel NEC 417.8
pulmonic (congenital) 746.02
infundibular 746.83
subvalvular 746.83
pylorus (hypertrophic) 537.0
adult 537.0
congenital 750.5
infantile 750.5
rectum (sphincter) (*see also* Stricture, rectum) 569.2
renal artery 440.1
salivary duct (any) 527.8
sphincter of Oddi (*see also* Obstruction, biliary) 576.2
spinal 724.00
cervical 723.0
lumbar, lumbosacral 724.02
nerve (root) NEC 724.9
specified region NEC 724.09
thoracic, thoracolumbar 724.01
stomach, hourglass 537.6
subaortic 746.81
hypertrophic (idiopathic) 425.1
supra (valvular)-aortic 747.22
trachea 519.19
congenital 748.3
syphilitic 095.8
tuberculous (*see also* Tuberculosis) 012.8 ☑
tracheostomy 519.02
tricuspid (valve) (*see also* Endocarditis, tricuspid) 397.0
congenital 746.1
nonrheumatic 424.2
tubal 628.2
ureter (*see also* Stricture, ureter) 593.3
congenital 753.29
urethra (*see also* Stricture, urethra) 598.9
vagina 623.2
congenital 752.49
in pregnancy or childbirth 654.7 ☑
affecting fetus or newborn 763.89
causing obstructed labor 660.2 ☑
affecting fetus or newborn 763.1
valve (cardiac) (heart) (*see also* Endocarditis) 424.90
congenital NEC 746.89
aortic 746.3
mitral 746.5
pulmonary 746.02
tricuspid 746.1
urethra 753.6

Stenosis — *see also* Stricture — *continued*
valvular (*see also* Endocarditis) 424.90
congenital NEC 746.89
urethra 753.6
vascular graft or shunt 996.1
atherosclerosis — *see* Arteriosclerosis, extremities
embolism 996.74
occlusion NEC 996.74
thrombus 996.74
vena cava (inferior) (superior) 459.2
congenital 747.49
ventricular shunt 996.2
vulva 624.8
Stercolith — *see also* Fecalith 560.39
appendix 543.9
Stercoraceous, stercoral ulcer 569.82
anus or rectum 569.41
Stereopsis, defective
with fusion 368.33
without fusion 368.32
Stereotypes NEC 307.3
Sterility
female — *see* Infertility, female
male (*see also* Infertility, male) 606.9
Sterilization, admission for V25.2
status
tubal ligation V26.51
vasectomy V26.52
Sternalgia — *see also* Angina 413.9
Sternopagus 759.4
Sternum bifidum 756.3
Sternutation 784.99
Steroid
effects (adverse) (iatrogenic)
cushingoid
correct substance properly administered 255.0
overdose or wrong substance given or taken 962.0
diabetes — *see* Diabetes, secondary
correct substance properly administered 251.8
overdose or wrong substance given or taken 962.0
due to
correct substance properly administered 255.8
overdose or wrong substance given or taken 962.0
fever
correct substance properly administered 780.60
overdose or wrong substance given or taken 962.0
withdrawal
correct substance properly administered 255.41
overdose or wrong substance given or taken 962.0
responder 365.03
Stevens-Johnson disease or syndrome (erythema multiforme exudativum) 695.13
toxic epidermal necrolysis overlap (SJS-TEN overlap syndrome) 695.14
Stewart-Morel syndrome (hyperostosis frontalis interna) 733.3
Sticker's disease (erythema infectiosum) 057.0
Stickler syndrome 759.89
Sticky eye 372.03
Stieda's disease (calcification, knee joint) 726.62
Stiff
back 724.8
neck (*see also* Torticollis) 723.5
Stiff-baby 759.89
Stiff-man syndrome 333.91
Stiffness, joint NEC 719.50
ankle 719.57
back 724.8
elbow 719.52

Stiffness, joint — *continued*
finger 719.54
hip 719.55
knee 719.56
multiple sites 719.59
sacroiliac 724.6
shoulder 719.51
specified site NEC 719.58
spine 724.9
surgical fusion V45.4
wrist 719.53
Stigmata, congenital syphilis 090.5
Stillbirth, stillborn NEC 779.9
Still's disease or syndrome 714.30
adult onset 714.2
Stiller's disease (asthenia) 780.79
Still-Felty syndrome (rheumatoid arthritis with splenomegaly and leukopenia) 714.1
Stilling-Türk-Duane syndrome (ocular retraction syndrome) 378.71
Stimulation, ovary 256.1
Sting (animal) (bee) (fish) (insect) (jellyfish) (Portuguese man-o-war) (wasp) (venomous) 989.5
anaphylactic shock or reaction 989.5
plant 692.6
Stippled epiphyses 756.59
Stitch
abscess 998.59
burst (in external operation wound) (*see also* Dehiscence) 998.32
internal 998.31
in back 724.5
Stojano's (subcostal) **syndrome** 098.86
Stokes-Adams syndrome (syncope with heart block) 426.9
Stokes' disease (exophthalmic goiter) 242.0 ☑
Stokvis' (-Talma) disease (enterogenous cyanosis) 289.7
Stomach — *see* condition
Stoma malfunction
colostomy 569.62
cystostomy 997.5
enterostomy 569.62
esophagostomy 530.87
gastrostomy 536.42
ileostomy 569.62
nephrostomy 997.5
tracheostomy 519.02
ureterostomy 997.5
Stomatitis 528.00
angular 528.5
due to dietary or vitamin deficiency 266.0
aphthous 528.2
bovine 059.11
candidal 112.0
catarrhal 528.00
denture 528.9
diphtheritic (membranous) 032.0
due to
dietary deficiency 266.0
thrush 112.0
vitamin deficiency 266.0
epidemic 078.4
epizootic 078.4
follicular 528.00
gangrenous 528.1
herpetic 054.2
herpetiformis 528.2
malignant 528.00
membranous acute 528.00
monilial 112.0
mycotic 112.0
necrotic 528.1
ulcerative 101
necrotizing ulcerative 101
parasitic 112.0
septic 528.00
specified NEC 528.09
spirochetal 101
suppurative (acute) 528.00
ulcerative 528.00
necrotizing 101

Stomatitis — *continued*
ulceromembranous 101
vesicular 528.00
with exanthem 074.3
Vincent's 101
Stomatocytosis 282.8
Stomatomycosis 112.0
Stomatorrhagia 528.9
Stone(s) — *see also* Calculus
bladder 594.1
diverticulum 594.0
cystine 270.0
heart syndrome (*see also* Failure, ventricular, left) 428.1
kidney 592.0
prostate 602.0
pulp (dental) 522.2
renal 592.0
salivary duct or gland (any) 527.5
ureter 592.1
urethra (impacted) 594.2
urinary (duct) (impacted) (passage) 592.9
bladder 594.1
diverticulum 594.0
lower tract NEC 594.9
specified site 594.8
xanthine 277.2
Stonecutters' lung 502
tuberculous (*see also* Tuberculosis) 011.4 ☑
Stonemasons'
asthma, disease, or lung 502
tuberculous (*see also* Tuberculosis) 011.4 ☑
phthisis (*see also* Tuberculosis) 011.4 ☑
Stoppage
bowel (*see also* Obstruction, intestine) 560.9
heart (*see also* Arrest, cardiac) 427.5
intestine (*see also* Obstruction, intestine) 560.9
urine NEC (*see also* Retention, urine) 788.20
Storm, thyroid (apathetic) — *see also* Thyrotoxicosis 242.9 ☑
Strabismus (alternating) (congenital) (nonparalytic) 378.9
concomitant (*see also* Heterotropia) 378.30
convergent (*see also* Esotropia) 378.00
divergent (*see also* Exotropia) 378.10
convergent (*see also* Esotropia) 378.00
divergent (*see also* Exotropia) 378.10
due to adhesions, scars — *see* Strabismus, mechanical
in neuromuscular disorder NEC 378.73
intermittent 378.20
vertical 378.31
latent 378.40
convergent (esophoria) 378.41
divergent (exophoria) 378.42
vertical 378.43
mechanical 378.60
due to
Brown's tendon sheath syndrome 378.61
specified musculofascial disorder NEC 378.62
paralytic 378.50
third or oculomotor nerve (partial) 378.51
total 378.52
fourth or trochlear nerve 378.53
sixth or abducens nerve 378.54
specified type NEC 378.73
vertical (hypertropia) 378.31
Strain — *see also* Sprain, by site
eye NEC 368.13
heart — *see* Disease, heart
meaning gonorrhea — *see* Gonorrhea
on urination 788.65

- **Stricture** — *see also* Stenosis — *continued*
  - spermatic cord 608.85
  - stoma (following) (of)
    - colostomy 569.62
    - cystostomy 997.5
    - enterostomy 569.62
    - esophagostomy 530.87
    - gastrostomy 536.42
    - ileostomy 569.62
    - nephrostomy 997.5
    - tracheostomy 519.02
    - ureterostomy 997.5
  - stomach 537.89
    - congenital 750.7
    - hourglass 537.6
  - subaortic 746.81
    - hypertrophic (acquired) (idiopathic) 425.1
  - subglottic 478.74
  - syphilitic NEC 095.8
  - tendon (sheath) 727.81
  - trachea 519.19
    - congenital 748.3
    - syphilitic 095.8
    - tuberculous (*see also* Tuberculosis) 012.8 ☑
  - tracheostomy 519.02
  - tricuspid (valve) (*see also* Endocarditis, tricuspid) 397.0
    - congenital 746.1
    - nonrheumatic 424.2
  - tunica vaginalis 608.85
  - ureter (postoperative) 593.3
    - congenital 753.29
    - tuberculous (*see also* Tuberculosis) 016.2 ☑
  - ureteropelvic junction 593.3
    - congenital 753.21
  - ureterovesical orifice 593.3
    - congenital 753.22
  - urethra (anterior) (meatal) (organic) (posterior) (spasmodic) 598.9
    - associated with schistosomiasis (*see also* Schistosomiasis) 120.9 *[598.01]*
    - congenital (valvular) 753.6
    - due to
      - infection 598.00
        - syphilis 095.8 *[598.01]*
      - trauma 598.1
    - gonococcal 098.2 *[598.01]*
    - gonorrheal 098.2 *[598.01]*
    - infective 598.00
    - late effect of injury 598.1
    - postcatheterization 598.2
    - postobstetric 598.1
    - postoperative 598.2
    - specified cause NEC 598.8
    - syphilitic 095.8 *[598.01]*
    - traumatic 598.1
    - valvular, congenital 753.6
  - urinary meatus (*see also* Stricture, urethra) 598.9
    - congenital 753.6
  - uterus, uterine 621.5
    - os (external) (internal) — *see* Stricture, cervix
  - vagina (outlet) 623.2
    - congenital 752.49
  - valve (cardiac) (heart) (*see also* Endocarditis) 424.90
    - congenital (cardiac) (heart) NEC 746.89
      - aortic 746.3
      - mitral 746.5
      - pulmonary 746.02
      - tricuspid 746.1
      - urethra 753.6
  - valvular (*see also* Endocarditis) 424.90
  - vascular graft or shunt 996.1
    - atherosclerosis — see Arteriosclerosis, extremities
    - embolism 996.74
    - occlusion NEC 996.74

- **Stricture** — *see also* Stenosis — *continued*
  - vascular graft or shunt — *continued*
    - thrombus 996.74
  - vas deferens 608.85
    - congenital 752.89
  - vein 459.2
  - vena cava (inferior) (superior) NEC 459.2
    - congenital 747.49
  - ventricular shunt 996.2
  - vesicourethral orifice 596.0
    - congenital 753.6
  - vulva (acquired) 624.8
- **Stridor** 786.1
  - congenital (larynx) 748.3
- **Stridulous** — *see* condition
- **Strippling of nails** 703.8
- **Stroke** 434.91
  - apoplectic (*see also* Disease, cerebrovascular, acute) 436
  - brain — *see* Infarct, brain
  - embolic 434.11
  - epileptic — *see* Epilepsy
  - healed or old V12.54
  - heart — *see* Disease, heart
  - heat 992.0
  - hemorrhagic — see Hemorrhage, brain
  - iatrogenic 997.02
  - in evolution 434.91
  - ischemic 434.91
  - late effect — *see* Late effect(s) (of) cerebrovascular disease
  - lightning 994.0
  - paralytic — *see* Infarct, brain
  - postoperative 997.02
  - progressive 435.9
  - thrombotic 434.01
- **Stromatosis, endometrial** (M8931/1) 236.0
- **Strong pulse** 785.9
- **Strongyloides stercoralis infestation** 127.2
- **Strongyloidiasis** 127.2
- **Strongyloidosis** 127.2
- **Strongylus** (gibsoni) infestation 127.7
- **Strophulus** (newborn) 779.89
  - pruriginosus 698.2
- **Struck by lightning** 994.0
- **Struma** — *see also* Goiter 240.9
  - fibrosa 245.3
  - Hashimoto (struma lymphomatosa) 245.2
  - lymphomatosa 245.2
  - nodosa (simplex) 241.9
    - endemic 241.9
    - multinodular 241.1
    - sporadic 241.9
    - toxic or with hyperthyroidism 242.3 ☑
      - multinodular 242.2 ☑
      - uninodular 242.1 ☑
    - toxicosa 242.3 ☑
      - multinodular 242.2 ☑
      - uninodular 242.1 ☑
    - uninodular 241.0
  - ovarii (M9090/0) 220
    - and carcinoid (M9091/1) 236.2
    - malignant (M9090/3) 183.0
  - Riedel's (ligneous thyroiditis) 245.3
  - scrofulous (*see also* Tuberculosis) 017.2 ☑
  - tuberculous (*see also* Tuberculosis) 017.2 ☑
    - abscess 017.2 ☑
    - adenitis 017.2 ☑
    - lymphangitis 017.2 ☑
    - ulcer 017.2 ☑
- **Strumipriva cachexia** — *see also* Hypothyroidism 244.9
- **Strümpell-Marie disease or spine** (ankylosing spondylitis) 720.0
- **Strümpell-Westphal pseudosclerosis** (hepatolenticular degeneration) 275.1

- **Stuart's disease** (congenital factor X deficiency) — *see also* Defect, coagulation 286.3
- **Stuart-Prower factor deficiency** (congenital factor X deficiency) — *see also* Defect, coagulation 286.3
- **Students' elbow** 727.2
- **Stuffy nose** 478.19
- **Stump** — *see also* Amputation
  - cervix, cervical (healed) 622.8
- **Stupor** 780.09
  - catatonic (*see also* Schizophrenia) 295.2 ☑
  - circular (*see also* Psychosis, manic-depressive, circular) 296.7
  - manic 296.89
  - manic-depressive (*see also* Psychosis, affective) 296.89
  - mental (anergic) (delusional) 298.9
  - psychogenic 298.8
  - reaction to exceptional stress (transient) 308.2
  - traumatic NEC (*see also* Injury, intracranial)
    - with spinal (cord)
      - lesion — *see* Injury, spinal, by site
      - shock — *see* Injury, spinal, by site
- **Sturge (-Weber) (-Dimitri) disease or syndrome** (encephalocutaneous angiomatosis) 759.6
- **Sturge-Kalischer-Weber syndrome** (encephalocutaneous angiomatosis) 759.6
- **Stuttering** 307.0
- **Sty, stye** 373.11
  - external 373.11
  - internal 373.12
  - meibomian 373.12
- **Subacidity, gastric** 536.8
  - psychogenic 306.4
- **Subacute** — *see* condition
- **Subarachnoid** — *see* condition
- **Subclavian steal syndrome** 435.2
- **Subcortical** — *see* condition
- **Subcostal syndrome** 098.86
  - nerve compression 354.8
- **Subcutaneous, subcuticular** — *see* condition
- **Subdelirium** 293.1
- **Subdural** — *see* condition
- **Subendocardium** — *see* condition
- **Subependymoma** (M9383/1) 237.5
- **Suberosis** 495.3
- **Subglossitis** — *see* Glossitis
- **Subhemophilia** 286.0
- **Subinvolution** (uterus) 621.1
  - breast (postlactational) (postpartum) 611.89
  - chronic 621.1
  - puerperal, postpartum 674.8 ☑
- **Sublingual** — *see* condition
- **Sublinguitis** 527.2
- **Subluxation** — *see also* Dislocation, by site
  - congenital NEC (*see also* Malposition, congenital)
    - hip (unilateral) 754.32
      - with dislocation of other hip 754.35
      - bilateral 754.33
    - joint
      - lower limb 755.69
      - shoulder 755.59
      - upper limb 755.59
    - lower limb (joint) 755.69
    - shoulder (joint) 755.59
    - upper limb (joint) 755.59
  - lens 379.32
    - anterior 379.33
    - posterior 379.34
  - rotary, cervical region of spine — *see* Fracture, vertebra, cervical
- **Submaxillary** — *see* condition
- **Submersion** (fatal) (nonfatal) 994.1

- **Submissiveness** (undue), in child 313.0
- **Submucous** — *see* condition
- **Subnormal, subnormality**
  - accommodation (*see also* Disorder, accommodation) 367.9
  - mental (*see also* Retardation, mental) 319
    - mild 317
    - moderate 318.0
    - profound 318.2
    - severe 318.1
  - temperature (accidental) 991.6
    - not associated with low environmental temperature 780.99
- **Subphrenic** — *see* condition
- **Subscapular nerve** — *see* condition
- **Subseptus uterus** 752.3
- **Subsiding appendicitis** 542
- **Substernal thyroid** — *see also* Goiter 240.9
  - congenital 759.2
- **Substitution disorder** 300.11
- **Subtentorial** — *see* condition
- **Subtertian**
  - fever 084.0
  - malaria (fever) 084.0
- **Subthyroidism** (acquired) — *see also* Hypothyroidism 244.9
  - congenital 243
- **Succenturiata placenta** — *see* Placenta, abnormal
- **Succussion sounds, chest** 786.7
- **Sucking thumb, child** 307.9
- **Sudamen** 705.1
- **Sudamina** 705.1
- **Sudanese kala-azar** 085.0
- **Sudden**
  - death, cause unknown (less than 24 hours) 798.1
    - cardiac (SCD)
      - family history of V17.41
      - personal history of, successfully resuscitated V12.53
    - during childbirth 669.9 ☑
    - infant 798.0
    - puerperal, postpartum 674.9 ☑
  - hearing loss NEC 388.2
  - heart failure (*see also* Failure, heart) 428.9
  - infant death syndrome 798.0
- **Sudeck's atrophy, disease, or syndrome** 733.7
- **SUDS** (sudden unexplained death) 798.2
- **Suffocation** — *see also* Asphyxia 799.01
  - by
    - bed clothes 994.7
    - bunny bag 994.7
    - cave-in 994.7
    - constriction 994.7
    - drowning 994.1
    - inhalation
      - food or foreign body (*see also* Asphyxia, food or foreign body) 933.1
      - oil or gasoline (*see also* Asphyxia, food or foreign body) 933.1
    - overlying 994.7
    - plastic bag 994.7
    - pressure 994.7
    - strangulation 994.7
  - during birth 768.1
  - mechanical 994.7
- **Sugar**
  - blood
    - high 790.29
    - low 251.2
  - in urine 791.5
- **Suicide, suicidal** (attempted)
  - by poisoning — *see* Table of Drugs and Chemicals
  - ideation V62.84
  - risk 300.9
  - tendencies 300.9
  - trauma NEC (*see also* nature and site of injury) 959.9

- **Suipestifer infection** — *see also* Infection, Salmonella 003.9
- **Sulfatidosis** 330.0
- **Sulfhemoglobinemia, sulphemoglobinemia** (acquired) (congenital) 289.7
- **Sumatran mite fever** 081.2
- **Summer** — *see* condition
- **Sunburn** 692.71
  - first degree 692.71
  - second degree 692.76
  - third degree 692.77
  - dermatitis 692.71
  - due to
    - other ultraviolet radiation 692.82
    - tanning bed 692.82
- **SUNCT** (short lasting unilateral neuralgiform headache with conjunctival injection and tearing) 339.05
- **Sunken**
  - acetabulum 718.85
  - fontanels 756.0
- **Sunstroke** 992.0
- **Superfecundation** 651.9 ☑
  - with fetal loss and retention of one or more fetus(es) 651.6 ☑
  - following (elective) fetal reduction 651.7 ☑
- **Superfetation** 651.9 ☑
  - with fetal loss and retention of one or more fetus(es) 651.6 ☑
  - following (elective) fetal reduction 651.7 ☑
- **Superinvolution uterus** 621.8
- **Supernumerary** (congenital)
  - aortic cusps 746.89
  - auditory ossicles 744.04
  - bone 756.9
  - breast 757.6
  - carpal bones 755.56
  - cusps, heart valve NEC 746.89
    - mitral 746.5
    - pulmonary 746.09
  - digit(s) 755.00
    - finger 755.01
    - toe 755.02
  - ear (lobule) 744.1
  - fallopian tube 752.19
  - finger 755.01
  - hymen 752.49
  - kidney 753.3
  - lacrimal glands 743.64
  - lacrimonasal duct 743.65
  - lobule (ear) 744.1
  - mitral cusps 746.5
  - muscle 756.82
  - nipples 757.6
  - organ or site NEC — *see* Accessory ossicles, auditory 744.04
  - ovary 752.0
  - oviduct 752.19
  - pulmonic cusps 746.09
  - rib 756.3
    - cervical or first 756.2
      - syndrome 756.2
  - roots (of teeth) 520.2
  - spinal vertebra 756.19
  - spleen 759.0
  - tarsal bones 755.67
  - teeth 520.1
    - causing crowding 524.31
  - testis 752.89
  - thumb 755.01
  - toe 755.02
  - uterus 752.2
  - vagina 752.49
  - vertebra 756.19
- **Supervision** (of)
  - contraceptive method previously prescribed V25.40
    - intrauterine device V25.42
    - oral contraceptive (pill) V25.41
    - specified type NEC V25.49
    - subdermal implantable contraceptive V25.43
  - dietary (for) V65.3
    - allergy (food) V65.3
    - colitis V65.3
    - diabetes mellitus V65.3
    - food allergy intolerance V65.3
    - gastritis V65.3
    - hypercholesterolemia V65.3
    - hypoglycemia V65.3
    - intolerance (food) V65.3
    - obesity V65.3
    - specified NEC V65.3
  - lactation V24.1
  - pregnancy — *see* Pregnancy, supervision of
- **Supplemental teeth** 520.1
  - causing crowding 524.31
- **Suppression**
  - binocular vision 368.31
  - lactation 676.5 ☑
  - menstruation 626.8
  - ovarian secretion 256.39
  - renal 586
  - urinary secretion 788.5
  - urine 788.5
- **Suppuration, suppurative** — *see also* condition
  - accessory sinus (chronic) (*see also* Sinusitis) 473.9
  - adrenal gland 255.8
  - antrum (chronic) (*see also* Sinusitis, maxillary) 473.0
  - bladder (*see also* Cystitis) 595.89
  - bowel 569.89
  - brain 324.0
    - late effect 326
  - breast 611.0
    - puerperal, postpartum 675.1 ☑
  - dental periosteum 526.5
  - diffuse (skin) 686.00
  - ear (middle) (*see also* Otitis media) 382.4
    - external (*see also* Otitis, externa) 380.10
    - internal 386.33
  - ethmoidal (sinus) (chronic) (*see also* Sinusitis, ethmoidal) 473.2
  - fallopian tube (*see also* Salpingo-oophoritis) 614.2
  - frontal (sinus) (chronic) (*see also* Sinusitis, frontal) 473.1
  - gallbladder (*see also* Cholecystitis, acute) 575.0
  - gum 523.30
  - hernial sac — *see* Hernia, by site
  - intestine 569.89
  - joint (*see also* Arthritis, suppurative) 711.0 ☑
  - labyrinthine 386.33
  - lung 513.0
  - mammary gland 611.0
    - puerperal, postpartum 675.1 ☑
  - maxilla, maxillary 526.4
    - sinus (chronic) (*see also* Sinusitis, maxillary) 473.0
  - muscle 728.0
  - nasal sinus (chronic) (*see also* Sinusitis) 473.9
  - pancreas 577.0
  - parotid gland 527.2
  - pelvis, pelvic
    - female (*see also* Disease, pelvis, inflammatory) 614.4
      - acute 614.3
    - male (*see also* Peritonitis) 567.21
  - pericranial (*see also* Osteomyelitis) 730.2 ☑
  - salivary duct or gland (any) 527.2
  - sinus (nasal) (*see also* Sinusitis) 473.9
  - sphenoidal (sinus) (chronic) (*see also* Sinusitis, sphenoidal) 473.3
  - thymus (gland) 254.1
  - thyroid (gland) 245.0
  - tonsil 474.8
  - uterus (*see also* Endometritis) 615.9
  - vagina 616.10
  - wound (*see also* Wound, open, by site, complicated)
    - dislocation — *see* Dislocation, by site, compound
    - fracture — *see* Fracture, by site, open
    - scratch or other superficial injury — *see* Injury, superficial, by site
- **Supraeruption, teeth** 524.34
- **Supraglottitis** 464.50
  - with obstruction 464.51
- **Suprapubic drainage** 596.8
- **Suprarenal** (gland) — *see* condition
- **Suprascapular nerve** — *see* condition
- **Suprasellar** — *see* condition
- **Supraspinatus syndrome** 726.10
- **Surfer knots** 919.8
  - infected 919.9
- **Surgery**
  - cosmetic NEC V50.1
    - breast reconstruction following mastectomy V51.0
    - following healed injury or operation V51.8
    - hair transplant V50.0
  - elective V50.9
    - breast
      - augmentation or reduction V50.1
      - reconstruction following mastectomy V51.0
    - circumcision, ritual or routine (in absence of medical indication) V50.2
    - cosmetic NEC V50.1
    - ear piercing V50.3
    - face-lift V50.1
    - following healed injury or operation V51.8
    - hair transplant V50.0
  - not done because of
    - contraindication V64.1
    - patient's decision V64.2
    - specified reason NEC V64.3
  - plastic
    - breast
      - augmentation or reduction V50.1
      - reconstruction following mastectomy V51.0
    - cosmetic V50.1
    - face-lift V50.1
    - following healed injury or operation V51.8
    - repair of scarred tissue (following healed injury or operation) V51.8
    - specified type NEC V50.8
  - previous, in pregnancy or childbirth
    - cervix 654.6 ☑
      - affecting fetus or newborn (*see also* Newborn, affected by) 760.63
      - causing obstructed labor 660.2 ☑
        - affecting fetus or newborn 763.1
    - pelvic soft tissues NEC 654.9 ☑
      - affecting fetus or newborn (*see also* Newborn, affected by) 760.63
      - causing obstructed labor 660.2 ☑
        - affecting fetus or newborn 763.1
    - perineum or vulva 654.8 ☑
    - uterus NEC 654.9 ☑
      - affecting fetus or newborn (*see also* Newborn, affected by) 760.63
      - causing obstructed labor 660.2 ☑
        - affecting fetus or newborn 763.1
      - due to previous cesarean delivery 654.2 ☑
    - vagina 654.7 ☑
- **Surgical**
  - abortion — *see* Abortion, legal
  - emphysema 998.81
  - kidney (*see also* Pyelitis) 590.80
  - operation NEC 799.9
  - procedures, complication or misadventure — *see* Complications, surgical procedure
  - shock 998.0
- **Survey**
  - fetal anatomic V28.81
- **Susceptibility**
  - genetic
    - to
      - MEN (multiple endocrine neoplasia) V84.81
      - neoplasia
        - multiple endocrine [MEN] V84.81
      - neoplasm
        - malignant, of
          - breast V84.01
          - endometrium V84.04
          - other V84.09
          - ovary V84.02
          - prostate V84.03
      - specified disease V84.89
- **Suspected condition, ruled out** — *see also* Observation, suspected V71.9
  - specified condition NEC V71.89
- **Suspended uterus, in pregnancy or childbirth** 654.4 ☑
  - affecting fetus or newborn 763.89
  - causing obstructed labor 660.2 ☑
    - affecting fetus or newborn 763.1
- **Sutton and Gull's disease** (arteriolar nephrosclerosis) — *see also* Hypertension, kidney 403.90
- **Sutton's disease** 709.09
- **Suture**
  - burst (in external operation wound) (*see also* Dehiscence) 998.32
    - internal 998.31
  - inadvertently left in operation wound 998.4
  - removal V58.32
  - Shirodkar, in pregnancy (with or without cervical incompetence) 654.5 ☑
- **Swab inadvertently left in operation wound** 998.4
- **Swallowed, swallowing**
  - difficulty (*see also* Dysphagia) 787.20
  - foreign body NEC (*see also* Foreign body) 938
- **Swamp fever** 100.89
- **Swan neck hand** (intrinsic) 736.09
- **Sweat(s), sweating**
  - disease or sickness 078.2
  - excessive (*see also* Hyperhidrosis) 780.8
  - fetid 705.89
  - fever 078.2
  - gland disease 705.9
    - specified type NEC 705.89
  - miliary 078.2
  - night 780.8
- **Sweeley-Klionsky disease** (angiokeratoma corporis diffusum) 272.7
- **Sweet's syndrome** (acute febrile neutrophilic dermatosis) 695.89
- **Swelling** 782.3
  - abdominal (not referable to specific organ) 789.3 ☑
  - adrenal gland, cloudy 255.8

Syndrome — *see also* Disease — *continued*
- Flajani (-Basedow) (exophthalmic goiter) 242.0 ☑
- flat back
  - acquired 737.29
  - postprocedural 738.5
- floppy
  - infant 781.99
  - iris 364.81
  - valve (mitral) 424.0
- flush 259.2
- Foix-Alajouanine 336.1
- Fong's (hereditary osteo-onychodysplasia) 756.89
- foramen magnum 348.4
- Forbes-Albright (nonpuerperal amenorrhea and lactation associated with pituitary tumor) 253.1
- Foster-Kennedy 377.04
- Foville's (peduncular) 344.89
- fragile X 759.83
- Franceschetti's (mandibulofacial dysostosis) 756.0
- Fraser's 759.89
- Freeman-Sheldon 759.89
- Frey's (auriculotemporal) 705.22
- Friderichsen-Waterhouse 036.3
- Friedrich-Erb-Arnold (acropachyderma) 757.39
- Fröhlich's (adiposogenital dystrophy) 253.8
- Froin's 336.8
- Frommel-Chiari 676.6 ☑
- frontal lobe 310.0
- Fukuhara 277.87
- Fuller Albright's (osteitis fibrosa disseminata) 756.59
- functional
  - bowel 564.9
  - prepubertal castrate 752.89
- Gaisböck's (polycythemia hypertonica) 289.0
- ganglion (basal, brain) 333.90
  - geniculi 351.1
- Ganser's, hysterical 300.16
- Gardner-Diamond (autoerythrocyte sensitization) 287.2
- gastroesophageal junction 530.0
- gastroesophageal laceration-hemorrhage 530.7
- gastrojejunal loop obstruction 537.89
- Gayet-Wernicke's (superior hemorrhagic polioencephalitis) 265.1
- Gee-Herter-Heubner (nontropical sprue) 579.0
- Gélineau's (*see also* Narcolepsy) 347.00
- genito-anorectal 099.1
- Gerhardt's (vocal cord paralysis) 478.30
- Gerstmann's (finger agnosia) 784.69
- Gerstmann-Sträussler-Scheinker (GSS) 046.71
- Gianotti Crosti 057.8
  - due to known virus — *see* Infection, virus
  - due to unknown virus 057.8
- Gilbert's 277.4
- Gilford (-Hutchinson) (progeria) 259.8
- Gilles de la Tourette's 307.23
- Gillespie's (dysplasia oculodentodigitalis) 759.89
- Glénard's (enteroptosis) 569.89
- Glinski-Simmonds (pituitary cachexia) 253.2
- glucuronyl transferase 277.4
- glue ear 381.20
- Goldberg (-Maxwell) (-Morris) (testicular feminization) 259.51
- Goldenhar's (oculoauriculovertebral dysplasia) 756.0
- Goldflam-Erb 358.00
- Goltz-Gorlin (dermal hypoplasia) 757.39
- Good's 279.06

Syndrome — *see also* Disease — *continued*
- Goodpasture's (pneumorenal) 446.21
- Gopalan's (burning feet) 266.2
- Gorlin-Chaudhry-Moss 759.89
- Gougerot-Blum (pigmented purpuric lichenoid dermatitis) 709.1
- Gougerot-Carteaud (confluent reticulate papillomatosis) 701.8
- Gougerot (-Houwer)-Sjögren (keratoconjunctivitis sicca) 710.2
- Gouley's (constrictive pericarditis) 423.2
- Gowers' (vasovagal attack) 780.2
- Gowers-Paton-Kennedy 377.04
- Gradenigo's 383.02
- gray or grey (chloramphenicol) (newborn) 779.4
- Greig's (hypertelorism) 756.0
- GSS (Gerstmann-Sträussler-Scheinker) 046.71
- Gubler-Millard 344.89
- Guérin-Stern (arthrogryposis multiplex congenita) 754.89
- Guillain-Barré (-Strohl) 357.0
- Gunn's (jaw-winking syndrome) 742.8
- Günther's (congenital erythropoietic porphyria) 277.1
- gustatory sweating 350.8
- H_3O 759.81
- Hadfield-Clarke (pancreatic infantilism) 577.8
- Haglund-Läwen-Fründ 717.89
- hairless women 257.8
- hair tourniquet (*see also* Injury, superficial, by site)
  - finger 915.8
    - infected 915.9
  - penis 911.8
    - infected 911.9
  - toe 917.8
    - infected 917.9
- Hallermann-Streiff 756.0
- Hallervorden-Spatz 333.0
- Hamman's (spontaneous mediastinal emphysema) 518.1
- Hamman-Rich (diffuse interstitial pulmonary fibrosis) 516.3
- hand-foot 693.0
- Hand-Schüller-Christian (chronic histiocytosis X) 277.89
- Hanot-Chauffard (-Troisier) (bronze diabetes) 275.0
- Harada's 363.22
- Hare's (M8010/3) (carcinoma, pulmonary apex) 162.3
- Harkavy's 446.0
- harlequin color change 779.89
- Harris' (organic hyperinsulinism) 251.1
- Hart's (pellagra-cerebellar ataxia-renal aminoaciduria) 270.0
- Hayem-Faber (achlorhydric anemia) 280.9
- Hayem-Widal (acquired hemolytic jaundice) 283.9
- headache — *see* Headache, syndrome
- Heberden's (angina pectoris) 413.9
- Hedinger's (malignant carcinoid) 259.2
- Hegglin's 288.2
- Heller's (infantile psychosis) (*see also* Psychosis, childhood) 299.1 ☑
- H.E.L.L.P 642.5 ☑
- hemolytic-uremic (adult) (child) 283.11
- hemophagocytic 288.4
  - infection-associated 288.4
- Hench-Rosenberg (palindromic arthritis) (*see also* Rheumatism, palindromic) 719.3 ☑
- Henoch-Schönlein (allergic purpura) 287.0
- hepatic flexure 569.89
- hepatorenal 572.4
  - due to a procedure 997.4
  - following delivery 674.8 ☑

Syndrome — *see also* Disease — *continued*
- hepatourologic 572.4
- Herrick's (hemoglobin S disease) 282.61
- Herter (-Gee) (nontropical sprue) 579.0
- Heubner-Herter (nontropical sprue) 579.0
- Heyd's (hepatorenal) 572.4
- HHHO 759.81
- high grade myelodysplastic 238.73
  - with 5q deletion 238.73
- Hilger's 337.09
- histocytic 288.4
- Hoffa (-Kastert) (liposynovitis prepatellaris) 272.8
- Hoffmann's 244.9 *[359.5]*
- Hoffmann-Bouveret (paroxysmal tachycardia) 427.2
- Hoffmann-Werdnig 335.0
- Holländer-Simons (progressive lipodystrophy) 272.6
- Holmes' (visual disorientation) 368.16
- Holmes-Adie 379.46
- Hoppe-Goldflam 358.00
- Horner's (*see also* Neuropathy, peripheral, autonomic) 337.9
  - traumatic — *see* Injury, nerve, cervical sympathetic
- hospital addiction 301.51
- hungry bone 275.5
- Hunt's (herpetic geniculate ganglionitis) 053.11
  - dyssynergia cerebellaris myoclonica 334.2
- Hunter (-Hurler) (mucopolysaccharidosis II) 277.5
- hunterian glossitis 529.4
- Hurler (-Hunter) (mucopolysaccharidosis II) 277.5
- Hutchinson-Boeck (sarcoidosis) 135
- Hutchinson-Gilford (progeria) 259.8
- Hutchinson's incisors or teeth 090.5
- hydralazine
  - correct substance properly administered 695.4
  - overdose or wrong substance given or taken 972.6
- hydraulic concussion (abdomen) (*see also* Injury, internal, abdomen) 868.00
- hyperabduction 447.8
- hyperactive bowel 564.9
- hyperaldosteronism with hypokalemic alkalosis (Bartter's) 255.13
- hypercalcemic 275.42
- hypercoagulation NEC 289.89
- hypereosinophilic (idiopathic) 288.3
- hyperkalemic 276.7
- hyperkinetic (*see also* Hyperkinesia)
  - heart 429.82
- hyperlipemia-hemolytic anemia-icterus 571.1
- hypermobility 728.5
- hypernatremia 276.0
- hyperosmolarity 276.0
- hyperperfusion 997.01
- hypersomnia-bulimia 349.89
- hypersplenic 289.4
- hypersympathetic (*see also* Neuropathy, peripheral, autonomic) 337.9
- hypertransfusion, newborn 776.4
- hyperventilation, psychogenic 306.1
- hyperviscosity (of serum) NEC 273.3
  - polycythemic 289.0
  - sclerothymic 282.8
- hypoglycemic (familial) (neonatal) 251.2
  - functional 251.1
- hypokalemic 276.8
- hypophyseal 253.8
- hypophyseothalamic 253.8
- hypopituitarism 253.2
- hypoplastic left heart 746.7
- hypopotassemia 276.8

Syndrome — *see also* Disease — *continued*
- hyposmolality 276.1
- hypotension, maternal 669.2 ☑
- hypothenar hammer 443.89
- hypotonia-hypomentia-hypogonadism-obesity 759.81
- ICF (intravascular coagulation-fibrinolysis) (*see also* Fibrinolysis) 286.6
- idiopathic cardiorespiratory distress, newborn 769
- idiopathic nephrotic (infantile) 581.9
- iliotibial band 728.89
- Imerslund (-Gräsbeck) (anemia due to familial selective vitamin B_{12} malabsorption) 281.1
- immobility (paraplegic) 728.3
- immunity deficiency, combined 279.2
- impending coronary 411.1
- impingement
  - shoulder 726.2
  - vertebral bodies 724.4
- inappropriate secretion of antidiuretic hormone (ADH) 253.6
- incomplete
  - mandibulofacial 756.0
- infant
  - death, sudden (SIDS) 798.0
  - Hercules 255.2
  - of diabetic mother 775.0
  - shaken 995.55
- infantilism 253.3
- inferior vena cava 459.2
- influenza-like 487.1
- inspissated bile, newborn 774.4
- insufficient sleep 307.44
- intermediate coronary (artery) 411.1
- internal carotid artery (*see also* Occlusion, artery, carotid) 433.1 ☑
- interspinous ligament 724.8
- intestinal
  - carcinoid 259.2
  - gas 787.3
  - knot 560.2
- intraoperative floppy iris (IFIS) 364.81
- intravascular
  - coagulation-fibrinolysis (ICF) (*see also* Fibrinolysis) 286.6
  - coagulopathy (*see also* Fibrinolysis) 286.6
- inverted Marfan's 759.89
- IRDS (idiopathic respiratory distress, newborn) 769
- irritable
  - bowel 564.1
  - heart 306.2
  - weakness 300.5
- ischemic bowel (transient) 557.9
  - chronic 557.1
  - due to mesenteric artery insufficiency 557.1
- Itsenko-Cushing (pituitary basophilism) 255.0
- IVC (intravascular coagulopathy) (*see also* Fibrinolysis) 286.6
- Ivemark's (asplenia with congenital heart disease) 759.0
- Jaccoud's 714.4
- Jackson's 344.89
- Jadassohn-Lewandowski (pachyonchia congenita) 757.5
- Jaffe-Lichtenstein (-Uehlinger) 252.01
- Jahnke's (encephalocutaneous angiomatosis) 759.6
- Jakob-Creutzfeldt 046.19
  - with dementia
    - with behavioral disturbance 046.19 *[294.11]*
    - without behavioral disturbance 046.19 *[294.10]*
  - variant 046.11
    - with dementia
      - with behavioral disturbance 046.11 *[294.11]*

Synoviosarcoma (M9040/3) — *see* Neoplasm, connective tissue, malignant
Synovitis (*see also* Tenosynovitis) 727.00
  chronic crepitant, wrist 727.2
  due to crystals — *see* Arthritis, due to crystals
  gonococcal 098.51
  gouty 274.0
  specified NEC 727.09
  syphilitic 095.7
    congenital 090.0
  traumatic, current — *see* Sprain, by site
  tuberculous — *see* Tuberculosis, synovitis
  villonodular 719.20
    ankle 719.27
    elbow 719.22
    foot 719.27
    hand 719.24
    hip 719.25
    knee 719.26
    multiple sites 719.29
    pelvic region 719.25
    shoulder (region) 719.21
    specified site NEC 719.28
    wrist 719.23
Syphilide 091.3
  congenital 090.0
  newborn 090.0
  tubercular 095.8
    congenital 090.0
Syphilis, syphilitic (acquired) 097.9
  with lung involvement 095.1
  abdomen (late) 095.2
  acoustic nerve 094.86
  adenopathy (secondary) 091.4
  adrenal (gland) 095.8
    with cortical hypofunction 095.8
  age under 2 years NEC (*see also* Syphilis, congenital) 090.9
    acquired 097.9
  alopecia (secondary) 091.82
  anemia 095.8
  aneurysm (artery) (ruptured) 093.89
    aorta 093.0
    central nervous system 094.89
    congenital 090.5
  anus 095.8
    primary 091.1
    secondary 091.3
  aorta, aortic (arch) (abdominal) (insufficiency) (pulmonary) (regurgitation) (stenosis) (thoracic) 093.89
    aneurysm 093.0
  arachnoid (adhesive) 094.2
  artery 093.89
    cerebral 094.89
    spinal 094.89
  arthropathy (neurogenic) (tabetic) 094.0 *[713.5]*
  asymptomatic — *see* Syphilis, latent
  ataxia, locomotor (progressive) 094.0
  atrophoderma maculatum 091.3
  auricular fibrillation 093.89
  Bell's palsy 094.89
  bladder 095.8
  bone 095.5
    secondary 091.61
  brain 094.89
  breast 095.8
  bronchus 095.8
  bubo 091.0
  bulbar palsy 094.89
  bursa (late) 095.7
  cardiac decompensation 093.89
  cardiovascular (early) (late) (primary) (secondary) (tertiary) 093.9
    specified type and site NEC 093.89
  causing death under 2 years of age (*see also* Syphilis, congenital) 090.9
    stated to be acquired NEC 097.9

Syphilis, syphilitic — *continued*
  central nervous system (any site) (early) (late) (latent) (primary) (recurrent) (relapse) (secondary) (tertiary) 094.9
    with
      ataxia 094.0
      paralysis, general 094.1
        juvenile 090.40
      paresis (general) 094.1
        juvenile 090.40
      tabes (dorsalis) 094.0
        juvenile 090.40
      taboparesis 094.1
        juvenile 090.40
    aneurysm (ruptured) 094.87
    congenital 090.40
    juvenile 090.40
    remission in (sustained) 094.9
    serology doubtful, negative, or positive 094.9
    specified nature or site NEC 094.89
    vascular 094.89
  cerebral 094.89
    meningovascular 094.2
    nerves 094.89
    sclerosis 094.89
    thrombosis 094.89
  cerebrospinal 094.89
    tabetic 094.0
  cerebrovascular 094.89
  cervix 095.8
  chancre (multiple) 091.0
    extragenital 091.2
    Rollet's 091.2
  Charcôt's joint 094.0 *[713.5]*
  choked disc 094.89 *[377.00]*
  chorioretinitis 091.51
    congenital 090.0 *[363.13]*
    late 094.83
  choroiditis 091.51
    congenital 090.0 *[363.13]*
    late 094.83
    prenatal 090.0 *[363.13]*
  choroidoretinitis (secondary) 091.51
    congenital 090.0 *[363.13]*
    late 094.83
  ciliary body (secondary) 091.52
    late 095.8 *[364.11]*
  colon (late) 095.8
  combined sclerosis 094.89
  complicating pregnancy, childbirth or puerperium 647.0 ☑
    affecting fetus or newborn 760.2
  condyloma (latum) 091.3
  congenital 090.9
    with
      encephalitis 090.41
      paresis (general) 090.40
      tabes (dorsalis) 090.40
      taboparesis 090.40
    chorioretinitis, choroiditis 090.0 *[363.13]*
    early or less than 2 years after birth NEC 090.2
      with manifestations 090.0
      latent (without manifestations) 090.1
        negative spinal fluid test 090.1
        serology, positive 090.1
      symptomatic 090.0
    interstitial keratitis 090.3
    juvenile neurosyphilis 090.40
    late or 2 years or more after birth NEC 090.7
      chorioretinitis, choroiditis 090.5 *[363.13]*
      interstitial keratitis 090.3
      juvenile neurosyphilis NEC 090.40
      latent (without manifestations) 090.6
        negative spinal fluid test 090.6
        serology, positive 090.6

Syphilis, syphilitic — *continued*
  congenital — *continued*
    late or 2 years or more after birth — *continued*
      symptomatic or with manifestations NEC 090.5
        interstitial keratitis 090.3
  conjugal 097.9
    tabes 094.0
  conjunctiva 095.8 *[372.10]*
  contact V01.6
  cord, bladder 094.0
  cornea, late 095.8 *[370.59]*
  coronary (artery) 093.89
    sclerosis 093.89
  coryza 095.8
    congenital 090.0
  cranial nerve 094.89
  cutaneous — *see* Syphilis, skin
  dacryocystitis 095.8
  degeneration, spinal cord 094.89
  d'emblée 095.8
  dementia 094.1
    paralytica 094.1
      juvenilis 090.40
  destruction of bone 095.5
  dilatation, aorta 093.0
  due to blood transfusion 097.9
  dura mater 094.89
  ear 095.8
    inner 095.8
      nerve (eighth) 094.86
      neurorecurrence 094.86
  early NEC 091.0
    cardiovascular 093.9
    central nervous system 094.9
      paresis 094.1
      tabes 094.0
    latent (without manifestations) (less than 2 years after infection) 092.9
      negative spinal fluid test 092.9
      serological relapse following treatment 092.0
      serology positive 092.9
    paresis 094.1
    relapse (treated, untreated) 091.7
    skin 091.3
    symptomatic NEC 091.89
      extragenital chancre 091.2
      primary, except extragenital chancre 091.0
      secondary (*see also* Syphilis, secondary) 091.3
        relapse (treated, untreated) 091.7
    tabes 094.0
    ulcer 091.3
  eighth nerve 094.86
  endemic, nonvenereal 104.0
  endocarditis 093.20
    aortic 093.22
    mitral 093.21
    pulmonary 093.24
    tricuspid 093.23
  epididymis (late) 095.8
  epiglottis 095.8
  epiphysitis (congenital) 090.0
  esophagus 095.8
  Eustachian tube 095.8
  exposure to V01.6
  eye 095.8 *[363.13]*
    neuromuscular mechanism 094.85
  eyelid 095.8 *[373.5]*
    with gumma 095.8 *[373.5]*
    ptosis 094.89
  fallopian tube 095.8
  fracture 095.5
  gallbladder (late) 095.8
  gastric 095.8
    crisis 094.0
    polyposis 095.8
  general 097.9
    paralysis 094.1
      juvenile 090.40
  genital (primary) 091.0

Syphilis, syphilitic — *continued*
  glaucoma 095.8
  gumma (late) NEC 095.9
    cardiovascular system 093.9
    central nervous system 094.9
    congenital 090.5
    heart or artery 093.89
  heart 093.89
    block 093.89
    decompensation 093.89
    disease 093.89
    failure 093.89
    valve (*see also* Syphilis, endocarditis) 093.20
  hemianesthesia 094.89
  hemianopsia 095.8
  hemiparesis 094.89
  hemiplegia 094.89
  hepatic artery 093.89
  hepatitis 095.3
  hepatomegaly 095.3
    congenital 090.0
  hereditaria tarda (*see also* Syphilis, congenital, late) 090.7
  hereditary (*see also* Syphilis, congenital) 090.9
    interstitial keratitis 090.3
  Hutchinson's teeth 090.5
  hyalitis 095.8
  inactive — *see* Syphilis, latent
  infantum NEC (*see also* Syphilis, congenital) 090.9
  inherited — *see* Syphilis, congenital
  internal ear 095.8
  intestine (late) 095.8
  iris, iritis (secondary) 091.52
    late 095.8 *[364.11]*
  joint (late) 095.8
  keratitis (congenital) (early) (interstitial) (late) (parenchymatous) (punctata profunda) 090.3
  kidney 095.4
  lacrimal apparatus 095.8
  laryngeal paralysis 095.8
  larynx 095.8
  late 097.0
    cardiovascular 093.9
    central nervous system 094.9
    latent or 2 years or more after infection (without manifestations) 096
      negative spinal fluid test 096
      serology positive 096
    paresis 094.1
    specified site NEC 095.8
    symptomatic or with symptoms 095.9
    tabes 094.0
  latent 097.1
    central nervous system 094.9
    date of infection unspecified 097.1
    early or less than 2 years after infection 092.9
    late or 2 years or more after infection 096
    serology
      doubtful
        follow-up of latent syphilis 097.1
          central nervous system 094.9
          date of infection unspecified 097.1
          early or less than 2 years after infection 092.9
          late or 2 years or more after infection 096
      positive, only finding 097.1
        date of infection unspecified 097.1
        early or less than 2 years after infection 097.1
        late or 2 years or more after infection 097.1
  lens 095.8
  leukoderma 091.3

Syphilis, syphilitic — *continued*
leukoderma — *continued*
late 095.8
lienis 095.8
lip 091.3
chancre 091.2
late 095.8
primary 091.2
Lissauer's paralysis 094.1
liver 095.3
secondary 091.62
locomotor ataxia 094.0
lung 095.1
lymphadenitis (secondary) 091.4
lymph gland (early) (secondary) 091.4
late 095.8
macular atrophy of skin 091.3
striated 095.8
maternal, affecting fetus or newborn 760.2
manifest syphilis in newborn — *see* Syphilis, congenital
mediastinum (late) 095.8
meninges (adhesive) (basilar) (brain) (spinal cord) 094.2
meningitis 094.2
acute 091.81
congenital 090.42
meningoencephalitis 094.2
meningovascular 094.2
congenital 090.49
mesarteritis 093.89
brain 094.89
spine 094.89
middle ear 095.8
mitral stenosis 093.21
monoplegia 094.89
mouth (secondary) 091.3
late 095.8
mucocutaneous 091.3
late 095.8
mucous
membrane 091.3
late 095.8
patches 091.3
congenital 090.0
mulberry molars 090.5
muscle 095.6
myocardium 093.82
myositis 095.6
nasal sinus 095.8
neonatorum NEC (*see also* Syphilis, congenital) 090.9
nerve palsy (any cranial nerve) 094.89
nervous system, central 094.9
neuritis 095.8
acoustic nerve 094.86
neurorecidive of retina 094.83
neuroretinitis 094.85
newborn (*see also* Syphilis, congenital) 090.9
nodular superficial 095.8
nonvenereal, endemic 104.0
nose 095.8
saddle back deformity 090.5
septum 095.8
perforated 095.8
occlusive arterial disease 093.89
ophthalmic 095.8 *[363.13]*
ophthalmoplegia 094.89
optic nerve (atrophy) (neuritis) (papilla) 094.84
orbit (late) 095.8
orchitis 095.8
organic 097.9
osseous (late) 095.5
osteochondritis (congenital) 090.0
osteoporosis 095.5
ovary 095.8
oviduct 095.8
palate 095.8
gumma 095.8
perforated 090.5
pancreas (late) 095.8
pancreatitis 095.8
paralysis 094.89

Syphilis, syphilitic — *continued*
paralysis — *continued*
general 094.1
juvenile 090.40
paraplegia 094.89
paresis (general) 094.1
juvenile 090.40
paresthesia 094.89
Parkinson's disease or syndrome 094.82
paroxysmal tachycardia 093.89
pemphigus (congenital) 090.0
penis 091.0
chancre 091.0
late 095.8
pericardium 093.81
perichondritis, larynx 095.8
periosteum 095.5
congenital 090.0
early 091.61
secondary 091.61
peripheral nerve 095.8
petrous bone (late) 095.5
pharynx 095.8
secondary 091.3
pituitary (gland) 095.8
placenta 095.8
pleura (late) 095.8
pneumonia, white 090.0
pontine (lesion) 094.89
portal vein 093.89
primary NEC 091.2
anal 091.1
and secondary (*see also* Syphilis, secondary) 091.9
cardiovascular 093.9
central nervous system 094.9
extragenital chancre NEC 091.2
fingers 091.2
genital 091.0
lip 091.2
specified site NEC 091.2
tonsils 091.2
prostate 095.8
psychosis (intracranial gumma) 094.89
ptosis (eyelid) 094.89
pulmonary (late) 095.1
artery 093.89
pulmonum 095.1
pyelonephritis 095.4
recently acquired, symptomatic NEC 091.89
rectum 095.8
respiratory tract 095.8
retina
late 094.83
neurorecidive 094.83
retrobulbar neuritis 094.85
salpingitis 095.8
sclera (late) 095.0
sclerosis
cerebral 094.89
coronary 093.89
multiple 094.89
subacute 094.89
scotoma (central) 095.8
scrotum 095.8
secondary (and primary) 091.9
adenopathy 091.4
anus 091.3
bone 091.61
cardiovascular 093.9
central nervous system 094.9
chorioretinitis, choroiditis 091.51
hepatitis 091.62
liver 091.62
lymphadenitis 091.4
meningitis, acute 091.81
mouth 091.3
mucous membranes 091.3
periosteum 091.61
periostitis 091.61
pharynx 091.3
relapse (treated) (untreated) 091.7
skin 091.3

Syphilis, syphilitic — *continued*
secondary — *continued*
specified form NEC 091.89
tonsil 091.3
ulcer 091.3
viscera 091.69
vulva 091.3
seminal vesicle (late) 095.8
seronegative
with signs or symptoms — *see* Syphilis, by site or stage
seropositive
with signs or symptoms — *see* Syphilis, by site and stage
follow-up of latent syphilis — *see* Syphilis, latent
only finding — *see* Syphilis, latent
seventh nerve (paralysis) 094.89
sinus 095.8
sinusitis 095.8
skeletal system 095.5
skin (early) (secondary) (with ulceration) 091.3
late or tertiary 095.8
small intestine 095.8
spastic spinal paralysis 094.0
spermatic cord (late) 095.8
spinal (cord) 094.89
with
paresis 094.1
tabes 094.0
spleen 095.8
splenomegaly 095.8
spondylitis 095.5
staphyloma 095.8
stigmata (congenital) 090.5
stomach 095.8
synovium (late) 095.7
tabes dorsalis (early) (late) 094.0
juvenile 090.40
tabetic type 094.0
juvenile 090.40
taboparesis 094.1
juvenile 090.40
tachycardia 093.89
tendon (late) 095.7
tertiary 097.0
with symptoms 095.8
cardiovascular 093.9
central nervous system 094.9
multiple NEC 095.8
specified site NEC 095.8
testis 095.8
thorax 095.8
throat 095.8
thymus (gland) 095.8
thyroid (late) 095.8
tongue 095.8
tonsil (lingual) 095.8
primary 091.2
secondary 091.3
trachea 095.8
tricuspid valve 093.23
tumor, brain 094.89
tunica vaginalis (late) 095.8
ulcer (any site) (early) (secondary) 091.3
late 095.9
perforating 095.9
foot 094.0
urethra (stricture) 095.8
urogenital 095.8
uterus 095.8
uveal tract (secondary) 091.50
late 095.8 *[363.13]*
uveitis (secondary) 091.50
late 095.8 *[363.13]*
uvula (late) 095.8
perforated 095.8
vagina 091.0
late 095.8
valvulitis NEC 093.20
vascular 093.89
brain or cerebral 094.89
vein 093.89
cerebral 094.89

Syphilis, syphilitic — *continued*
ventriculi 095.8
vesicae urinariae 095.8
viscera (abdominal) 095.2
secondary 091.69
vitreous (hemorrhage) (opacities) 095.8
vulva 091.0
late 095.8
secondary 091.3
Syphiloma 095.9
cardiovascular system 093.9
central nervous system 094.9
circulatory system 093.9
congenital 090.5
Syphilophobia 300.29
Syringadenoma (M8400/0) — *see also* Neoplasm, skin, benign
papillary (M8406/0) — *see* Neoplasm, skin, benign
Syringobulbia 336.0
Syringocarcinoma (M8400/3) — *see* Neoplasm, skin, malignant
Syringocystadenoma (M8400/0) — *see also* Neoplasm, skin, benign
papillary (M8406/0) — *see* Neoplasm, skin, benign
Syringocystoma (M8407/0) — *see* Neoplasm, skin, benign
Syringoma (M8407/0) — *see also* Neoplasm, skin, benign
chondroid (M8940/0) — *see* Neoplasm, by site, benign
Syringomyelia 336.0
Syringomyelitis 323.9
late effect — *see* category 326
Syringomyelocele — *see also* Spina bifida 741.9 ☑
Syringopontia 336.0
disease, combined — *see* Degeneration, combined
fibrosclerosing syndrome 710.8
inflammatory response syndrome (SIRS) 995.90
due to
infectious process 995.91
with organ dysfunction 995.92
non-infectious process 995.93
with organ dysfunction 995.94
lupus erythematosus 710.0
inhibitor 286.5
System, systemic — *see also* condition
disease, combined — *see* Degeneration, combined
fibrosclerosing syndrome 710.8
inflammatory response syndrome (SIRS) 995.90
due to
infectious process 995.91
with acute organ dysfunction 995.92
non-infectious process 995.93
with acute organ dysfunction 995.94
lupus erythematosus 710.0
inhibitor 286.5

T

Tab — *see* Tag
Tabacism 989.84
Tabacosis 989.84
Tabardillo 080
flea-borne 081.0
louse-borne 080
Tabes, tabetic
with
central nervous system syphilis 094.0
Charcôt's joint 094.0 *[713.5]*
cord bladder 094.0
crisis, viscera (any) 094.0
paralysis, general 094.1
paresis (general) 094.1
perforating ulcer 094.0

- **Thrombosis, thrombotic** — *continued*
  - retina, retinal — *continued*
    - vein — *continued*
      - tributary (branch) 362.36
  - scrotum 608.83
  - seminal vesicle 608.83
  - sigmoid (venous) sinus — *see* Thrombosis, intracranial venous sinus 325
  - silent NEC 453.9
  - sinus, intracranial (venous) (any) (*see also* Thrombosis, intracranial venous sinus) 325
  - softening, brain (*see also* Thrombosis, brain) 434.0 ☑
  - specified site NEC 453.8
  - spermatic cord 608.83
  - spinal cord 336.1
    - due to syphilis 094.89
    - in pregnancy or puerperium 671.5 ☑
    - pyogenic origin 324.1
      - late effect — *see* category 326
  - spleen, splenic 289.59
    - artery 444.89
  - testis 608.83
  - traumatic (complication) (early) (*see also* Injury, blood vessel, by site) 904.9
  - tricuspid — *see* Endocarditis, tricuspid
  - tumor — see Neoplasm, by site
  - tunica vaginalis 608.83
  - umbilical cord (vessels) 663.6 ☑
    - affecting fetus or newborn 762.6
  - vas deferens 608.83
  - vein
    - deep 453.40
    - lower extremity — see Thrombosis, lower extremity
  - vena cava (inferior) (superior) 453.2
- **Thrombus** — *see* Thrombosis
- **Thrush** 112.0
  - newborn 771.7
- **Thumb** — *see also* condition
  - gamekeeper's 842.12
  - sucking (child problem) 307.9
- **Thygeson's superficial punctate keratitis** 370.21
- **Thymergasia** — *see also* Psychosis, affective 296.80
- **Thymitis** 254.8
- **Thymoma** (benign) (M8580/0) 212.6
  - malignant (M8580/3) 164.0
- **Thymus, thymic** (gland) — *see* condition
- **Thyrocele** — *see also* Goiter 240.9
- **Thyroglossal** — *see also* condition
  - cyst 759.2
  - duct, persistent 759.2
- **Thyroid** (body) (gland) — *see also* condition
  - hormone resistance 246.8
  - lingual 759.2
- **Thyroiditis** 245.9
  - acute (pyogenic) (suppurative) 245.0
    - nonsuppurative 245.0
  - autoimmune 245.2
  - chronic (nonspecific) (sclerosing) 245.8
    - fibrous 245.3
    - lymphadenoid 245.2
    - lymphocytic 245.2
    - lymphoid 245.2
  - complicating pregnancy, childbirth, or puerperium 648.1 ☑
  - de Quervain's (subacute granulomatous) 245.1
  - fibrous (chronic) 245.3
  - giant (cell) (follicular) 245.1
  - granulomatous (de Quervain's) (subacute) 245.1
  - Hashimoto's (struma lymphomatosa) 245.2
  - iatrogenic 245.4
  - invasive (fibrous) 245.3
  - ligneous 245.3
- **Thyroiditis** — *continued*
  - lymphocytic (chronic) 245.2
  - lymphoid 245.2
  - lymphomatous 245.2
  - pseudotuberculous 245.1
  - pyogenic 245.0
  - radiation 245.4
  - Riedel's (ligneous) 245.3
  - subacute 245.1
  - suppurative 245.0
  - tuberculous (*see also* Tuberculosis) 017.5 ☑
  - viral 245.1
  - woody 245.3
- **Thyrolingual duct, persistent** 759.2
- **Thyromegaly** 240.9
- **Thyrotoxic**
  - crisis or storm (*see also* Thyrotoxicosis) 242.9 ☑
  - heart failure (*see also* Thyrotoxicosis) 242.9 ☑ *[425.7]*
- **Thyrotoxicosis** 242.9 ☑

Note — Use the following fifth-digit subclassification with category 242:

0 without mention of thyrotoxic crisis or storm

1 with mention of thyrotoxic crisis or storm

  - with
    - goiter (diffuse) 242.0 ☑
      - adenomatous 242.3 ☑
        - multinodular 242.2 ☑
        - uninodular 242.1 ☑
      - nodular 242.3 ☑
        - multinodular 242.2 ☑
        - uninodular 242.1 ☑
    - infiltrative
      - dermopathy 242.0 ☑
      - ophthalmopathy 242.0 ☑
    - thyroid acropachy 242.0 ☑
  - complicating pregnancy, childbirth, or puerperium 648.1 ☑
  - due to
    - ectopic thyroid nodule 242.4 ☑
    - ingestion of (excessive) thyroid material 242.8 ☑
    - specified cause NEC 242.8 ☑
  - factitia 242.8 ☑
  - heart 242.9 ☑ *[425.7]*
  - neonatal (transient) 775.3
- **TIA** (transient ischemic attack) 435.9
  - with transient neurologic deficit 435.9
  - late effect — *see* Late effect(s) (of) cerebrovascular disease
- **Tibia vara** 732.4
- **Tic** 307.20
  - breathing 307.20
  - child problem 307.21
  - compulsive 307.22
  - convulsive 307.20
  - degenerative (generalized) (localized) 333.3
    - facial 351.8
  - douloureux (*see also* Neuralgia, trigeminal) 350.1
    - atypical 350.2
  - habit 307.20
    - chronic (motor or vocal) 307.22
    - transient (of childhood) 307.21
  - lid 307.20
    - transient (of childhood) 307.21
  - motor-verbal 307.23
  - occupational 300.89
  - orbicularis 307.20
    - transient (of childhood) 307.21
  - organic origin 333.3
  - postchoreic — *see* Chorea
  - psychogenic 307.20
    - compulsive 307.22
  - salaam 781.0
  - spasm 307.20
    - chronic (motor or vocal) 307.22
    - transient (of childhood) 307.21
- **Tick-bite fever** NEC 066.1
- **Tick-bite fever** — *continued*
  - African 087.1
  - Colorado (virus) 066.1
  - Rocky Mountain 082.0
- **Tick (-borne) fever** NEC 066.1
  - American mountain 066.1
  - Colorado 066.1
  - hemorrhagic NEC 065.3
    - Crimean 065.0
    - Kyasanur Forest 065.2
    - Omsk 065.1
  - mountain 066.1
  - nonexanthematous 066.1
- **Tick paralysis** 989.5
- **Tics and spasms, compulsive** 307.22
- **Tietze's disease or syndrome** 733.6
- **Tight, tightness**
  - anus 564.89
  - chest 786.59
  - fascia (lata) 728.9
  - foreskin (congenital) 605
  - hymen 623.3
  - introitus (acquired) (congenital) 623.3
  - rectal sphincter 564.89
  - tendon 727.81
    - Achilles (heel) 727.81
  - urethral sphincter 598.9
- **Tilting vertebra** 737.9
- **Timidity, child** 313.21
- **Tinea** (intersecta) (tarsi) 110.9
  - amiantacea 110.0
  - asbestina 110.0
  - barbae 110.0
  - beard 110.0
  - black dot 110.0
  - blanca 111.2
  - capitis 110.0
  - corporis 110.5
  - cruris 110.3
  - decalvans 704.09
  - flava 111.0
  - foot 110.4
  - furfuracea 111.0
  - imbricata (Tokelau) 110.5
  - lepothrix 039.0
  - manuum 110.2
  - microsporic (*see also* Dermatophytosis) 110.9
  - nigra 111.1
  - nodosa 111.2
  - pedis 110.4
  - scalp 110.0
  - specified site NEC 110.8
  - sycosis 110.0
  - tonsurans 110.0
  - trichophytic (*see also* Dermatophytosis) 110.9
  - unguium 110.1
  - versicolor 111.0
- **Tingling sensation** — *see also* Disturbance, sensation 782.0
- **Tin-miners' lung** 503
- **Tinnitus** (aurium) 388.30
  - audible 388.32
  - objective 388.32
  - subjective 388.31
- **Tipped, teeth** 524.33
- **Tipping**
  - pelvis 738.6
    - with disproportion (fetopelvic) 653.0 ☑
      - affecting fetus or newborn 763.1
      - causing obstructed labor 660.1 ☑
        - affecting fetus or newborn 763.1
  - teeth 524.33
- **Tiredness** 780.79
- **Tissue** — *see* condition
- **Tobacco**
  - abuse (affecting health) NEC (*see also* Abuse, drugs, nondependent) 305.1
  - heart 989.84
- **Tobacco** — *continued*
  - use disorder complicating pregnancy, childbirth, or the puerperium 649.0 ☑
- **Tobias' syndrome** (carcinoma, pulmonary apex) (M8010/3) 162.3
- **Tocopherol deficiency** 269.1
- **Todd's**
  - cirrhosis — *see* Cirrhosis, biliary
  - paralysis (postepileptic transitory paralysis) 344.89
- **Toe** — *see* condition
- **Toilet, artificial opening** — *see also* Attention to, artificial, opening V55.9
- **Tokelau ringworm** 110.5
- **Tollwut** 071
- **Tolosa-Hunt syndrome** 378.55
- **Tommaselli's disease**
  - correct substance properly administered 599.70
  - overdose or wrong substance given or taken 961.4
- **Tongue** — *see also* condition
  - worms 134.1
- **Tongue tie** 750.0
- **Tonic pupil** 379.46
- **Toni-Fanconi syndrome** (cystinosis) 270.0
- **Tonsil** — *see* condition
- **Tonsillitis** (acute) (catarrhal) (croupous) (follicular) (gangrenous) (infective) (lacunar) (lingual) (malignant) (membranous) (phlegmonous) (pneumococcal) (pseudomembranous) (purulent) (septic) (staphylococcal) (subacute) (suppurative) (toxic) (ulcerative) (vesicular) (viral) 463
  - with influenza, flu, or grippe 487.1
  - chronic 474.00
  - diphtheritic (membranous) 032.0
  - hypertrophic 474.00
  - influenzal 487.1
  - parenchymatous 475
  - streptococcal 034.0
  - tuberculous (*see also* Tuberculosis) 012.8 ☑
  - Vincent's 101
- **Tonsillopharyngitis** 465.8
- **Toothache** 525.9
- **Tooth, teeth** — *see* condition
- **Topagnosis** 782.0
- **Tophi** (gouty) 274.0
  - ear 274.81
  - heart 274.82
  - specified site NEC 274.82
- **TORCH infection** — *see also* Infection, congenital 760.2
- **Torn** — *see* Tear, torn
- **Tornwaldt's bursitis** (disease) (pharyngeal bursitis) 478.29
  - cyst 478.26
- **Torpid liver** 573.9
- **Torsion**
  - accessory tube 620.5
  - adnexa (female) 620.5
  - aorta (congenital) 747.29
    - acquired 447.1
  - appendix
    - epididymis 608.24
    - testis 608.23
  - bile duct 576.8
    - with calculus, choledocholithiasis or stones — *see* Choledocholithiasis
    - congenital 751.69
  - bowel, colon, or intestine 560.2
  - cervix — *see* Malposition, uterus
  - duodenum 537.3
  - dystonia — *see* Dystonia, torsion
  - epididymis 608.24
    - appendix 608.24
  - fallopian tube 620.5
  - gallbladder (*see also* Disease, gallbladder) 575.8

- **Torsion** — *continued*
  - gallbladder (*see also* Disease, gallbladder) — *continued*
    - congenital 751.69
  - gastric 537.89
  - hydatid of Morgagni (female) 620.5
  - kidney (pedicle) 593.89
  - Meckel's diverticulum (congenital) 751.0
  - mesentery 560.2
  - omentum 560.2
  - organ or site, congenital NEC — *see* Anomaly, specified type NEC
  - ovary (pedicle) 620.5
    - congenital 752.0
  - oviduct 620.5
  - penis 607.89
    - congenital 752.69
  - renal 593.89
  - spasm — *see* Dystonia, torsion
  - spermatic cord 608.22
    - extravaginal 608.21
    - intravaginal 608.22
  - spleen 289.59
  - testicle, testis 608.20
    - appendix 608.23
  - tibia 736.89
  - umbilical cord — *see* Compression, umbilical cord
  - uterus (*see also* Malposition, uterus) 621.6
- **Torticollis** (intermittent) (spastic) 723.5
  - congenital 754.1
    - sternomastoid 754.1
  - due to birth injury 767.8
  - hysterical 300.11
  - ocular 781.93
  - psychogenic 306.0
    - specified as conversion reaction 300.11
  - rheumatic 723.5
  - rheumatoid 714.0
  - spasmodic 333.83
  - traumatic, current NEC 847.0
- **Tortuous**
  - artery 447.1
  - fallopian tube 752.19
  - organ or site, congenital NEC — *see* Distortion
  - renal vessel (congenital) 747.62
  - retina vessel (congenital) 743.58
    - acquired 362.17
  - ureter 593.4
  - urethra 599.84
  - vein — *see* Varicose, vein
- **Torula, torular** (infection) 117.5
  - histolytica 117.5
  - lung 117.5
- **Torulosis** 117.5
- **Torus**
  - fracture
    - fibula 823.41
      - with tibia 823.42
    - radius 813.45
    - tibia 823.40
      - with fibula 823.42
  - mandibularis 526.81
  - palatinus 526.81
- **Touch, vitreous** 997.99
- **Touraine-Solente-Golé syndrome** (acropachyderma) 757.39
- **Touraine's syndrome** (hereditary osteo-onychodysplasia) 756.89
- **Tourette's disease** (motor-verbal tic) 307.23
- **Tower skull** 756.0
  - with exophthalmos 756.0
- **Toxemia** 799.89
  - with
    - abortion — *see* Abortion, by type, with toxemia
  - bacterial — *see* Septicemia
  - biliary (*see also* Disease, biliary) 576.8
  - burn — *see* Burn, by site
  - congenital NEC 779.89
  - eclamptic 642.6 ☑
- **Toxemia** — *continued*
  - eclamptic — *continued*
    - with pre-existing hypertension 642.7 ☑
  - erysipelatous (*see also* Erysipelas) 035
  - fatigue 799.89
  - fetus or newborn NEC 779.89
  - food (*see also* Poisoning, food) 005.9
  - gastric 537.89
  - gastrointestinal 558.2
  - intestinal 558.2
  - kidney (*see also* Disease, renal) 593.9
  - lung 518.89
  - malarial NEC (*see also* Malaria) 084.6
  - maternal (of pregnancy), affecting fetus or newborn 760.0
  - myocardial — *see* Myocarditis, toxic
  - of pregnancy (mild) (pre-eclamptic) 642.4 ☑
    - with
      - convulsions 642.6 ☑
      - pre-existing hypertension 642.7 ☑
    - affecting fetus or newborn 760.0
    - severe 642.5 ☑
  - pre-eclamptic — *see* Toxemia, of pregnancy
  - puerperal, postpartum — *see* Toxemia, of pregnancy
  - pulmonary 518.89
  - renal (*see also* Disease, renal) 593.9
  - septic (*see also* Septicemia) 038.9
  - small intestine 558.2
  - staphylococcal 038.10
    - aureus 038.11
    - due to food 005.0
    - specified organism NEC 038.19
  - stasis 799.89
  - stomach 537.89
  - uremic (*see also* Uremia) 586
  - urinary 586
- **Toxemica cerebropathia psychica** (nonalcoholic) 294.0
  - alcoholic 291.1
- **Toxic** (poisoning) — *see also* condition
  - from drug or poison — *see* Table of Drugs and Chemicals
  - oil syndrome 710.5
  - shock syndrome 040.82
  - thyroid (gland) (*see also* Thyrotoxicosis) 242.9 ☑
- **Toxicemia** — *see* Toxemia
- **Toxicity**
  - dilantin
    - asymptomatic 796.0
    - symptomatic — *see* Table of Drugs and Chemicals
  - drug
    - asymptomatic 796.0
    - symptomatic — *see* Table of Drugs and Chemicals
  - fava bean 282.2
  - from drug or poison
    - asymptomatic 796.0
    - symptomatic — *see* Table of Drugs and Chemicals
- **Toxicosis** — *see also* Toxemia 799.89
  - capillary, hemorrhagic 287.0
- **Toxinfection** 799.89
  - gastrointestinal 558.2
- **Toxocariasis** 128.0
- **Toxoplasma infection, generalized** 130.9
- **Toxoplasmosis** (acquired) 130.9
  - with pneumonia 130.4
  - congenital, active 771.2
  - disseminated (multisystemic) 130.8
  - maternal
    - with suspected damage to fetus affecting management of pregnancy 655.4 ☑
    - affecting fetus or newborn 760.2
      - manifest toxoplasmosis in fetus or newborn 771.2
  - multiple sites 130.8
  - multisystemic disseminated 130.8
- **Toxoplasmosis** — *continued*
  - specified site NEC 130.7
- **Trabeculation, bladder** 596.8
- **Trachea** — *see* condition
- **Tracheitis** (acute) (catarrhal) (infantile) (membranous) (plastic) (pneumococcal) (septic) (suppurative) (viral) 464.10
  - with
    - bronchitis 490
      - acute or subacute 466.0
      - chronic 491.8
      - tuberculosis — *see* Tuberculosis, pulmonary
    - laryngitis (acute) 464.20
      - with obstruction 464.21
      - chronic 476.1
      - tuberculous (*see also* Tuberculosis, larynx) 012.3 ☑
    - obstruction 464.11
  - chronic 491.8
    - with
      - bronchitis (chronic) 491.8
      - laryngitis (chronic) 476.1
    - due to external agent — *see* Condition, respiratory, chronic, due to
  - diphtheritic (membranous) 032.3
    - due to external agent — *see* Inflammation, respiratory, upper, due to
  - edematous 464.11
  - influenzal 487.1
  - streptococcal 034.0
  - syphilitic 095.8
  - tuberculous (*see also* Tuberculosis) 012.8 ☑
- **Trachelitis** (nonvenereal) — *see also* Cervicitis 616.0
  - trichomonal 131.09
- **Tracheobronchial** — *see* condition
- **Tracheobronchitis** — *see also* Bronchitis 490
  - acute or subacute 466.0
    - with bronchospasm or obstruction 466.0
  - chronic 491.8
  - influenzal 487.1
  - senile 491.8
- **Tracheobronchomegaly** (congenital) 748.3
  - with bronchiectasis 494.0
    - with (acute) exacerbation 494.1
  - acquired 519.19
    - with bronchiectasis 494.0
      - with (acute) exacerbation 494.1
- **Tracheobronchopneumonitis** — *see* Pneumonia, broncho
- **Tracheocele** (external) (internal) 519.19
  - congenital 748.3
- **Tracheomalacia** 519.19
  - congenital 748.3
- **Tracheopharyngitis** (acute) 465.8
  - chronic 478.9
    - due to external agent — *see* Condition, respiratory, chronic, due to
  - due to external agent — *see* Inflammation, respiratory, upper, due to
- **Tracheostenosis** 519.19
  - congenital 748.3
- **Tracheostomy**
  - attention to V55.0
  - complication 519.00
  - granuloma 519.09
  - hemorrhage 519.09
  - infection 519.01
  - malfunctioning 519.02
  - obstruction 519.09
  - sepsis 519.01
  - status V44.0
  - stenosis 519.02
- **Trachoma, trachomatous** 076.9
  - active (stage) 076.1
  - contraction of conjunctiva 076.1
  - dubium 076.0
- **Trachoma, trachomatous** — *continued*
  - healed or late effect 139.1
  - initial (stage) 076.0
  - Türck's (chronic catarrhal laryngitis) 476.0
- **Trachyphonia** 784.49
- **Training**
  - insulin pump V65.46
  - orthoptic V57.4
  - orthotic V57.81
- **Train sickness** 994.6
- **Trait**
  - hemoglobin
    - abnormal NEC 282.7
      - with thalassemia 282.49
    - C (*see also* Disease, hemoglobin, C) 282.7
      - with elliptocytosis 282.7
    - S (Hb-S) 282.5
  - Lepore 282.49
    - with other abnormal hemoglobin NEC 282.49
  - paranoid 301.0
  - sickle-cell 282.5
    - with
      - elliptocytosis 282.5
      - spherocytosis 282.5
- **Traits, paranoid** 301.0
- **Tramp** V60.0
- **Trance** 780.09
  - hysterical 300.13
- **Transaminasemia** 790.4
- **Transfusion, blood**
  - without reported diagnosis V58.2
  - donor V59.01
    - stem cells V59.02
  - fetal twin to twin 678.0 ☑
  - incompatible 999.6
  - reaction or complication — *see* Complications, transfusion
  - related acute lung injury (TRALI) 518.7
  - syndrome
    - fetomaternal 772.0
    - twin-to-twin
      - blood loss (donor twin) 772.0
      - recipient twin 776.4
  - twin to twin fetal 678.0 ☑
- **Transient** — *see also* condition
  - alteration of awareness 780.02
  - blindness 368.12
  - deafness (ischemic) 388.02
  - global amnesia 437.7
  - person (homeless) NEC V60.0
- **Transitional, lumbosacral joint of vertebra** 756.19
- **Translocation**
  - autosomes NEC 758.5
    - 13-15 758.1
    - 16-18 758.2
    - 21 or 22 758.0
    - balanced in normal individual 758.4
    - D_1 758.1
    - E_3 758.2
    - G 758.0
  - balanced autosomal in normal individual 758.4
  - chromosomes NEC 758.89
  - Down's syndrome 758.0
- **Translucency, iris** 364.53
- **Transmission of chemical substances through the placenta** (affecting fetus or newborn) 760.70
  - alcohol 760.71
  - anticonvulsants 760.77
  - antifungals 760.74
  - anti-infective agents 760.74
  - antimetabolics 760.78
  - cocaine 760.75
  - "crack" 760.75
  - diethylstilbestrol [DES] 760.76
  - hallucinogenic agents 760.73
  - medicinal agents NEC 760.79
  - narcotics 760.72

Tuberculosis, tubercular, tuberculous — *continued*
- curvature, spine 015.0 ☑ *[737.40]*
- cutis (colliquativa) (primary) 017.0 ☑
- cystitis 016.1 ☑
- cyst, ovary 016.6 ☑
- dacryocystitis 017.3 ☑ *[375.32]*
- dactylitis 015.5 ☑
- diarrhea 014.8 ☑
- diffuse (*see also* Tuberculosis, miliary) 018.9 ☑
  - lung — *see* Tuberculosis, pulmonary
  - meninges 013.0 ☑
- digestive tract 014.8 ☑
- disseminated (*see also* Tuberculosis, miliary) 018.9 ☑
  - meninges 013.0 ☑
- duodenum 014.8 ☑
- dura (mater) 013.9 ☑
  - abscess 013.8 ☑
    - cerebral 013.3 ☑
    - spinal 013.5 ☑
- dysentery 014.8 ☑
- ear (inner) (middle) 017.4 ☑
  - bone 015.6 ☑
  - external (primary) 017.0 ☑
  - skin (primary) 017.0 ☑
- elbow 015.8 ☑
- emphysema — *see* Tuberculosis, pulmonary
- empyema 012.0 ☑
- encephalitis 013.6 ☑
- endarteritis 017.9 ☑
- endocarditis (any valve) 017.9 ☑ *[424.91]*
- endocardium (any valve) 017.9 ☑ *[424.91]*
- endocrine glands NEC 017.9 ☑
- endometrium 016.7 ☑
- enteric, enterica 014.8 ☑
- enteritis 014.8 ☑
- enterocolitis 014.8 ☑
- epididymis 016.4 ☑
- epididymitis 016.4 ☑
- epidural abscess 013.8 ☑
  - brain 013.3 ☑
  - spinal cord 013.5 ☑
- epiglottis 012.3 ☑
- episcleritis 017.3 ☑ *[379.00]*
- erythema (induratum) (nodosum) (primary) 017.1 ☑
- esophagus 017.8 ☑
- Eustachian tube 017.4 ☑
- exposure to V01.1
- exudative 012.0 ☑
  - primary, progressive 010.1 ☑
- eye 017.3 ☑
- eyelid (primary) 017.0 ☑
  - lupus 017.0 ☑ *[373.4]*
- fallopian tube 016.6 ☑
- fascia 017.9 ☑
- fauces 012.8 ☑
- finger 017.9 ☑
- first infection 010.0 ☑
- fistula, perirectal 014.8 ☑
- Florida 011.6 ☑
- foot 017.9 ☑
- funnel pelvis 137.3
- gallbladder 017.9 ☑
- galloping (*see also* Tuberculosis, pulmonary) 011.9 ☑
- ganglionic 015.9 ☑
- gastritis 017.9 ☑
- gastrocolic fistula 014.8 ☑
- gastroenteritis 014.8 ☑
- gastrointestinal tract 014.8 ☑
- general, generalized 018.9 ☑
  - acute 018.0 ☑
  - chronic 018.8 ☑
- genital organs NEC 016.9 ☑
  - female 016.7 ☑
  - male 016.5 ☑
- genitourinary NEC 016.9 ☑

Tuberculosis, tubercular, tuberculous — *continued*
- genu 015.2 ☑
- glandulae suprarenalis 017.6 ☑
- glandular, general 017.2 ☑
- glottis 012.3 ☑
- grinders' 011.4 ☑
- groin 017.2 ☑
- gum 017.9 ☑
- hand 017.9 ☑
- heart 017.9 ☑ *[425.8]*
- hematogenous — *see* Tuberculosis, miliary
- hemoptysis (*see also* Tuberculosis, pulmonary) 011.9 ☑
- hemorrhage NEC (*see also* Tuberculosis, pulmonary) 011.9 ☑
- hemothorax 012.0 ☑
- hepatitis 017.9 ☑
- hilar lymph nodes 012.1 ☑
  - primary, progressive 010.8 ☑
- hip (disease) (joint) 015.1 ☑
  - bone 015.1 ☑ *[730.85]*
- hydrocephalus 013.8 ☑
- hydropneumothorax 012.0 ☑
- hydrothorax 012.0 ☑
- hypoadrenalism 017.6 ☑
- hypopharynx 012.8 ☑
- ileocecal (hyperplastic) 014.8 ☑
- ileocolitis 014.8 ☑
- ileum 014.8 ☑
- iliac spine (superior) 015.0 ☑ *[730.88]*
- incipient NEC (*see also* Tuberculosis, pulmonary) 011.9 ☑
- indurativa (primary) 017.1 ☑
- infantile 010.0 ☑
- infection NEC 011.9 ☑
  - without clinical manifestation 010.0 ☑
- infraclavicular gland 017.2 ☑
- inguinal gland 017.2 ☑
- inguinalis 017.2 ☑
- intestine (any part) 014.8 ☑
- iris 017.3 ☑ *[364.11]*
- iritis 017.3 ☑ *[364.11]*
- ischiorectal 014.8 ☑
- jaw 015.7 ☑ *[730.88]*
- jejunum 014.8 ☑
- joint 015.9 ☑
  - hip 015.1 ☑
  - knee 015.2 ☑
  - specified site NEC 015.8 ☑
  - vertebral 015.0 ☑ *[730.88]*
- keratitis 017.3 ☑ *[370.31]*
  - interstitial 017.3 ☑ *[370.59]*
- keratoconjunctivitis 017.3 ☑ *[370.31]*
- kidney 016.0 ☑
- knee (joint) 015.2 ☑
- kyphoscoliosis 015.0 ☑ *[737.43]*
- kyphosis 015.0 ☑ *[737.41]*
- lacrimal apparatus, gland 017.3 ☑
- laryngitis 012.3 ☑
- larynx 012.3 ☑
- leptomeninges, leptomeningitis (cerebral) (spinal) 013.0 ☑
- lichenoides (primary) 017.0 ☑
- linguae 017.9 ☑
- lip 017.9 ☑
- liver 017.9 ☑
- lordosis 015.0 ☑ *[737.42]*
- lung — *see* Tuberculosis, pulmonary
- luposa 017.0 ☑
  - eyelid 017.0 ☑ *[373.4]*
- lymphadenitis — *see* Tuberculosis, lymph gland
- lymphangitis — *see* Tuberculosis, lymph gland
- lymphatic (gland) (vessel) — *see* Tuberculosis, lymph gland
- lymph gland or node (peripheral) 017.2 ☑
  - abdomen 014.8 ☑
  - bronchial 012.1 ☑
    - primary, progressive 010.8 ☑

Tuberculosis, tubercular, tuberculous — *continued*
- lymph gland or node — *continued*
  - cervical 017.2 ☑
  - hilar 012.1 ☑
    - primary, progressive 010.8 ☑
  - intrathoracic 012.1 ☑
    - primary, progressive 010.8 ☑
  - mediastinal 012.1 ☑
    - primary, progressive 010.8 ☑
  - mesenteric 014.8 ☑
  - peripheral 017.2 ☑
  - retroperitoneal 014.8 ☑
  - tracheobronchial 012.1 ☑
    - primary, progressive 010.8 ☑
- malignant NEC (*see also* Tuberculosis, pulmonary) 011.9 ☑
- mammary gland 017.9 ☑
- marasmus NEC (*see also* Tuberculosis, pulmonary) 011.9 ☑
- mastoiditis 015.6 ☑
- maternal, affecting fetus or newborn 760.2
- mediastinal (lymph) gland or node 012.1 ☑
  - primary, progressive 010.8 ☑
- mediastinitis 012.8 ☑
  - primary, progressive 010.8 ☑
- mediastinopericarditis 017.9 ☑ *[420.0]*
- mediastinum 012.8 ☑
  - primary, progressive 010.8 ☑
- medulla 013.9 ☑
  - brain 013.2 ☑
  - spinal cord 013.4 ☑
- melanosis, Addisonian 017.6 ☑
- membrane, brain 013.0 ☑
- meninges (cerebral) (spinal) 013.0 ☑
- meningitis (basilar) (brain) (cerebral) (cerebrospinal) (spinal) 013.0 ☑
- meningoencephalitis 013.0 ☑
- mesentery, mesenteric 014.8 ☑
  - lymph gland or node 014.8 ☑
- miliary (any site) 018.9 ☑
  - acute 018.0 ☑
  - chronic 018.8 ☑
  - specified type NEC 018.8 ☑
- millstone makers' 011.4 ☑
- miners' 011.4 ☑
- moulders' 011.4 ☑
- mouth 017.9 ☑
- multiple 018.9 ☑
  - acute 018.0 ☑
  - chronic 018.8 ☑
- muscle 017.9 ☑
- myelitis 013.6 ☑
- myocarditis 017.9 ☑ *[422.0]*
- myocardium 017.9 ☑ *[422.0]*
- nasal (passage) (sinus) 012.8 ☑
- nasopharynx 012.8 ☑
- neck gland 017.2 ☑
- nephritis 016.0 ☑ *[583.81]*
- nerve 017.9 ☑
- nose (septum) 012.8 ☑
- ocular 017.3 ☑
- old NEC 137.0
  - without residuals V12.01
- omentum 014.8 ☑
- oophoritis (acute) (chronic) 016.6 ☑
- optic 017.3 ☑ *[377.39]*
  - nerve trunk 017.3 ☑ *[377.39]*
  - papilla, papillae 017.3 ☑ *[377.39]*
- orbit 017.3 ☑
- orchitis 016.5 ☑ *[608.81]*
- organ, specified NEC 017.9 ☑
- orificialis (primary) 017.0 ☑
- osseous (*see also* Tuberculosis, bone) 015.9 ☑ *[730.8]* ☑
- osteitis (*see also* Tuberculosis, bone) 015.9 ☑ *[730.8]* ☑
- osteomyelitis (*see also* Tuberculosis, bone) 015.9 ☑ *[730.8]* ☑
- otitis (media) 017.4 ☑
- ovaritis (acute) (chronic) 016.6 ☑
- ovary (acute) (chronic) 016.6 ☑

Tuberculosis, tubercular, tuberculous — *continued*
- oviducts (acute) (chronic) 016.6 ☑
- pachymeningitis 013.0 ☑
- palate (soft) 017.9 ☑
- pancreas 017.9 ☑
- papulonecrotic (primary) 017.0 ☑
- parathyroid glands 017.9 ☑
- paronychia (primary) 017.0 ☑
- parotid gland or region 017.9 ☑
- pelvic organ NEC 016.9 ☑
  - female 016.7 ☑
  - male 016.5 ☑
- pelvis (bony) 015.7 ☑ *[730.85]*
- penis 016.5 ☑
- peribronchitis 011.3 ☑
- pericarditis 017.9 ☑ *[420.0]*
- pericardium 017.9 ☑ *[420.0]*
- perichondritis, larynx 012.3 ☑
- perineum 017.9 ☑
- periostitis (*see also* Tuberculosis, bone) 015.9 ☑ *[730.8]* ☑
- periphlebitis 017.9 ☑
  - eye vessel 017.3 ☑ *[362.18]*
  - retina 017.3 ☑ *[362.18]*
- perirectal fistula 014.8 ☑
- peritoneal gland 014.8 ☑
- peritoneum 014.0 ☑
- peritonitis 014.0 ☑
- pernicious NEC (*see also* Tuberculosis, pulmonary) 011.9 ☑
- pharyngitis 012.8 ☑
- pharynx 012.8 ☑
- phlyctenulosis (conjunctiva) 017.3 ☑ *[370.31]*
- phthisis NEC (*see also* Tuberculosis, pulmonary) 011.9 ☑
- pituitary gland 017.9 ☑
- placenta 016.7 ☑
- pleura, pleural, pleurisy, pleuritis (fibrinous) (obliterative) (purulent) (simple plastic) (with effusion) 012.0 ☑
  - primary, progressive 010.1 ☑
- pneumonia, pneumonic 011.6 ☑
- pneumothorax 011.7 ☑
- polyserositis 018.9 ☑
  - acute 018.0 ☑
  - chronic 018.8 ☑
- potters' 011.4 ☑
- prepuce 016.5 ☑
- primary 010.9 ☑
  - complex 010.0 ☑
  - complicated 010.8 ☑
    - with pleurisy or effusion 010.1 ☑
  - progressive 010.8 ☑
    - with pleurisy or effusion 010.1 ☑
  - skin 017.0 ☑
- proctitis 014.8 ☑
- prostate 016.5 ☑ *[601.4]*
- prostatitis 016.5 ☑ *[601.4]*
- pulmonaris (*see also* Tuberculosis, pulmonary) 011.9 ☑
- pulmonary (artery) (incipient) (malignant) (multiple round foci) (pernicious) (reinfection stage) 011.9 ☑
  - cavitated or with cavitation 011.2 ☑
    - primary, progressive 010.8 ☑
  - childhood type or first infection 010.0 ☑
  - chromogenic acid-fast bacilli 795.39
  - fibrosis or fibrotic 011.4 ☑
  - infiltrative 011.0 ☑
    - primary, progressive 010.9 ☑
  - nodular 011.1 ☑
  - specified NEC 011.8 ☑
  - sputum positive only 795.39
  - status following surgical collapse of lung NEC 011.9 ☑

Tuberculosis, tubercular, tuberculous — *continued*
pyelitis 016.0 ☑ *[590.81]*
pyelonephritis 016.0 ☑ *[590.81]*
pyemia — *see* Tuberculosis, miliary
pyonephrosis 016.0 ☑
pyopneumothorax 012.0 ☑
pyothorax 012.0 ☑
rectum (with abscess) 014.8 ☑
fistula 014.8 ☑
reinfection stage (*see also* Tuberculosis, pulmonary) 011.9 ☑
renal 016.0 ☑
renis 016.0 ☑
reproductive organ 016.7 ☑
respiratory NEC (*see also* Tuberculosis, pulmonary) 011.9 ☑
specified site NEC 012.8 ☑
retina 017.3 ☑ *[363.13]*
retroperitoneal (lymph gland or node) 014.8 ☑
gland 014.8 ☑
retropharyngeal abscess 012.8 ☑
rheumatism 015.9 ☑
rhinitis 012.8 ☑
sacroiliac (joint) 015.8 ☑
sacrum 015.0 ☑ *[730.88]*
salivary gland 017.9 ☑
salpingitis (acute) (chronic) 016.6 ☑
sandblasters' 011.4 ☑
sclera 017.3 ☑ *[379.09]*
scoliosis 015.0 ☑ *[737.43]*
scrofulous 017.2 ☑
scrotum 016.5 ☑
seminal tract or vesicle 016.5 ☑ *[608.81]*
senile NEC (*see also* Tuberculosis, pulmonary) 011.9 ☑
septic NEC (*see also* Tuberculosis, miliary) 018.9 ☑
shoulder 015.8 ☑
blade 015.7 ☑ *[730.8]* ☑
sigmoid 014.8 ☑
sinus (accessory) (nasal) 012.8 ☑
bone 015.7 ☑ *[730.88]*
epididymis 016.4 ☑
skeletal NEC (*see also* Osteomyelitis, due to tuberculosis) 015.9 ☑ *[730.8]* ☑
skin (any site) (primary) 017.0 ☑
small intestine 014.8 ☑
soft palate 017.9 ☑
spermatic cord 016.5 ☑
spinal
column 015.0 ☑ *[730.88]*
cord 013.4 ☑
disease 015.0 ☑ *[730.88]*
medulla 013.4 ☑
membrane 013.0 ☑
meninges 013.0 ☑
spine 015.0 ☑ *[730.88]*
spleen 017.7 ☑
splenitis 017.7 ☑
spondylitis 015.0 ☑ *[720.81]*
spontaneous pneumothorax — *see* Tuberculosis, pulmonary
sternoclavicular joint 015.8 ☑
stomach 017.9 ☑
stonemasons' 011.4 ☑
struma 017.2 ☑
subcutaneous tissue (cellular) (primary) 017.0 ☑
subcutis (primary) 017.0 ☑
subdeltoid bursa 017.9 ☑
submaxillary 017.9 ☑
region 017.9 ☑
supraclavicular gland 017.2 ☑
suprarenal (capsule) (gland) 017.6 ☑
swelling, joint (*see also* Tuberculosis, joint) 015.9 ☑
symphysis pubis 015.7 ☑ *[730.88]*
synovitis 015.9 ☑ *[727.01]*
hip 015.1 ☑ *[727.01]*
knee 015.2 ☑ *[727.01]*

Tuberculosis, tubercular, tuberculous — *continued*
synovitis — *continued*
specified site NEC 015.8 ☑ *[727.01]*
spine or vertebra 015.0 ☑ *[727.01]*
systemic — *see* Tuberculosis, miliary
tarsitis (eyelid) 017.0 ☑ *[373.4]*
ankle (bone) 015.5 ☑ *[730.87]*
tendon (sheath) — *see* Tuberculosis, tenosynovitis
tenosynovitis 015.9 ☑ *[727.01]*
hip 015.1 ☑ *[727.01]*
knee 015.2 ☑ *[727.01]*
specified site NEC 015.8 ☑ *[727.01]*
spine or vertebra 015.0 ☑ *[727.01]*
testis 016.5 ☑ *[608.81]*
throat 012.8 ☑
thymus gland 017.9 ☑
thyroid gland 017.5 ☑
toe 017.9 ☑
tongue 017.9 ☑
tonsil (lingual) 012.8 ☑
tonsillitis 012.8 ☑
trachea, tracheal 012.8 ☑
gland 012.1 ☑
primary, progressive 010.8 ☑
isolated 012.2 ☑
tracheobronchial 011.3 ☑
glandular 012.1 ☑
primary, progressive 010.8 ☑
isolated 012.2 ☑
lymph gland or node 012.1 ☑
primary, progressive 010.8 ☑
tubal 016.6 ☑
tunica vaginalis 016.5 ☑
typhlitis 014.8 ☑
ulcer (primary) (skin) 017.0 ☑
bowel or intestine 014.8 ☑
specified site NEC — *see* Tuberculosis, by site
unspecified site — *see* Tuberculosis, pulmonary
ureter 016.2 ☑
urethra, urethral 016.3 ☑
urinary organ or tract 016.3 ☑
kidney 016.0 ☑
uterus 016.7 ☑
uveal tract 017.3 ☑ *[363.13]*
uvula 017.9 ☑
vaccination, prophylactic (against) V03.2
vagina 016.7 ☑
vas deferens 016.5 ☑
vein 017.9 ☑
verruca (primary) 017.0 ☑
verrucosa (cutis) (primary) 017.0 ☑
vertebra (column) 015.0 ☑ *[730.88]*
vesiculitis 016.5 ☑ *[608.81]*
viscera NEC 014.8 ☑
vulva 016.7 ☑ *[616.51]*
wrist (joint) 015.8 ☑
bone 015.5 ☑ *[730.83]*

Tuberculum
auriculae 744.29
occlusal 520.2
paramolare 520.2

Tuberosity
jaw, excessive 524.07
maxillary, entire 524.07

Tuberous sclerosis (brain) 759.5

Tube, tubal, tubular — *see also* condition
ligation, admission for V25.2

Tubo-ovarian — *see* condition

Tuboplasty, after previous sterilization V26.0

Tubotympanitis 381.10

Tularemia 021.9
with
conjunctivitis 021.3
pneumonia 021.2
bronchopneumonic 021.2
conjunctivitis 021.3
cryptogenic 021.1
disseminated 021.8

Tularemia — *continued*
enteric 021.1
generalized 021.8
glandular 021.8
intestinal 021.1
oculoglandular 021.3
ophthalmic 021.3
pneumonia 021.2
pulmonary 021.2
specified NEC 021.8
typhoidal 021.1
ulceroglandular 021.0
vaccination, prophylactic (against) V03.4

Tularensis conjunctivitis 021.3

Tumefaction — *see also* Swelling
liver (*see also* Hypertrophy, liver) 789.1

Tumor (M8000/1) — *see also* Neoplasm, by site, unspecified nature
Abrikossov's (M9580/0) (*see also* Neoplasm, connective tissue, benign)
malignant (M9580/3) — *see* Neoplasm, connective tissue, malignant
acinar cell (M8550/1) — *see* Neoplasm, by site, uncertain behavior
acinic cell (M8550/1) — *see* Neoplasm, by site, uncertain behavior
adenomatoid (M9054/0) (*see also* Neoplasm, by site, benign)
odontogenic (M9300/0) 213.1
upper jaw (bone) 213.0
adnexal (skin) (M8390/0) — *see* Neoplasm, skin, benign
adrenal
cortical (benign) (M8370/0) 227.0
malignant (M8370/3) 194.0
rest (M8671/0) — *see* Neoplasm, by site, benign
alpha cell (M8152/0)
malignant (M8152/3)
pancreas 157.4
specified site NEC — *see* Neoplasm, by site, malignant
unspecified site 157.4
pancreas 211.7
specified site NEC — *see* Neoplasm, by site, benign
unspecified site 211.7
aneurysmal (*see also* Aneurysm) 442.9
aortic body (M8691/1) 237.3
malignant (M8691/3) 194.6
argentaffin (M8241/1) — *see* Neoplasm, by site, uncertain behavior
basal cell (M8090/1) (*see also* Neoplasm, skin, uncertain behavior)
benign (M8000/0) — *see* Neoplasm, by site, benign
beta cell (M8151/0)
malignant (M8151/3)
pancreas 157.4
specified site — *see* Neoplasm, by site, malignant
unspecified site 157.4
pancreas 211.7
specified site NEC — *see* Neoplasm, by site, benign
unspecified site 211.7
blood — *see* Hematoma
Brenner (M9000/0) 220
borderline malignancy (M9000/1) 236.2
malignant (M9000/3) 183.0
proliferating (M9000/1) 236.2
Brooke's (M8100/0) — *see* Neoplasm, skin, benign
brown fat (M8880/0) — *see* Lipoma, by site
Burkitt's (M9750/3) 200.2 ☑
calcifying epithelial odontogenic (M9340/0) 213.1

Tumor — *see also* Neoplasm, by site, unspecified nature — *continued*
calcifying epithelial odontogenic — *continued*
upper jaw (bone) 213.0
carcinoid (M8240/1) 209.60
benign 209.60
appendix 209.51
ascending colon 209.53
bronchus 209.61
cecum 209.52
colon 209.50
descending colon 209.55
duodenum 209.41
foregut 209.65
hindgut 209.67
ileum 209.43
jejunum 209.42
kidney 209.64
large intestine 209.50
lung 209.61
midgut 209.66
rectum 209.57
sigmoid colon 209.56
small intestine 209.40
specified NEC 209.69
stomach 209.63
thymus 209.62
transverse colon 209.54
malignant (of) 209.20
appendix 209.11
ascending colon 209.13
bronchus 209.21
cecum 209.12
colon 209.10
descending colon 209.15
duodenum 209.01
foregut 209.25
hindgut 209.27
ileum 209.03
jejunum 209.02
kidney 209.24
large intestine 209.10
lung 209.21
midgut 209.26
rectum 209.17
sigmoid colon 209.16
small intestine 209.00
specified NEC 209.29
stomach 209.23
thymus 209.22
transverse colon 209.14
carotid body (M8692/1) 237.3
malignant (M8692/3) 194.5
Castleman's (mediastinal lymph node hyperplasia) 785.6
cells (M8001/1) (*see also* Neoplasm, by site, unspecified nature)
benign (M8001/0) — *see* Neoplasm, by site, benign
malignant (M8001/3) — *see* Neoplasm, by site, malignant
uncertain whether benign or malignant (M8001/1) — *see* Neoplasm, by site, uncertain nature
cervix
in pregnancy or childbirth 654.6 ☑
affecting fetus or newborn 763.89
causing obstructed labor 660.2 ☑
affecting fetus or newborn 763.1
chondromatous giant cell (M9230/0) — *see* Neoplasm, bone, benign
chromaffin (M8700/0) (*see also* Neoplasm, by site, benign)
malignant (M8700/3) — *see* Neoplasm, by site, malignant
Cock's peculiar 706.2
Codman's (benign chondroblastoma) (M9230/0) — *see* Neoplasm, bone, benign
dentigerous, mixed (M9282/0) 213.1
upper jaw (bone) 213.0

Tumor — *see also* Neoplasm, by site, unspecified nature — *continued*
- uterus — *continued*
  - in pregnancy or childbirth — *continued*
    - causing obstructed labor 660.2 ☑
      - affecting fetus or newborn 763.1
- vagina
  - in pregnancy or childbirth 654.7 ☑
    - affecting fetus or newborn 763.89
    - causing obstructed labor 660.2 ☑
      - affecting fetus or newborn 763.1
- varicose (*see also* Varicose, vein) 454.9
- von Recklinghausen's (M9540/1) 237.71
- vulva
  - in pregnancy or childbirth 654.8 ☑
    - affecting fetus or newborn 763.89
    - causing obstructed labor 660.2 ☑
      - affecting fetus or newborn 763.1
- Warthin's (salivary gland) (M8561/0) 210.2
- white (*see also* Tuberculosis, arthritis)
- White-Darier 757.39
- Wilms' (nephroblastoma) (M8960/3) 189.0
- yolk sac (M9071/3)
  - specified site — *see* Neoplasm, by site, malignant
  - unspecified site
    - female 183.0
    - male 186.9

Tumorlet (M8040/1) — *see* Neoplasm, by site, uncertain behavior

Tungiasis 134.1

Tunica vasculosa lentis 743.39

Tunnel vision 368.45

Turban tumor (M8200/0) 216.4

Türck's trachoma (chronic catarrhal laryngitis) 476.0

Türk's syndrome (ocular retraction syndrome) 378.71

Turner's
- hypoplasia (tooth) 520.4
- syndrome 758.6
- tooth 520.4

Turner-Kieser syndrome (hereditary osteo-onychodysplasia) 756.89

Turner-Varny syndrome 758.6

Turricephaly 756.0

Tussis convulsiva — *see also* Whooping cough 033.9

Twiddler's syndrome (due to)
- automatic implantable defibrillator 996.04
- pacemaker 996.01

Twin
- affected by maternal complications of pregnancy 761.5
- conjoined 759.4
  - fetal 678.1 ☑
- healthy liveborn — *see* Newborn, twin
- pregnancy (complicating delivery) NEC 651.0 ☑
  - with fetal loss and retention of one fetus 651.3 ☑
  - conjoined 678.1 ☑
  - following (elective) fetal reduction

Twinning, teeth 520.2

Twist, twisted
- bowel, colon, or intestine 560.2
- hair (congenital) 757.4
- mesentery 560.2
- omentum 560.2
- organ or site, congenital NEC — *see* Anomaly, specified type NEC
- ovarian pedicle 620.5
  - congenital 752.0

Twist, twisted — *continued*
- umbilical cord — *see* Compression, umbilical cord

Twitch 781.0

Tylosis 700
- buccalis 528.6
- gingiva 523.8
- linguae 528.6
- palmaris et plantaris 757.39

Tympanism 787.3

Tympanites (abdominal) (intestine) 787.3

Tympanitis — *see* Myringitis

Tympanosclerosis 385.00
- involving
  - combined sites NEC 385.09
    - with tympanic membrane 385.03
  - tympanic membrane 385.01
    - with ossicles 385.02
      - and middle ear 385.03

Tympanum — *see* condition

Tympany
- abdomen 787.3
- chest 786.7

Typhlitis — *see also* Appendicitis 541

Typhoenteritis 002.0

Typhogastric fever 002.0

Typhoid (abortive) (ambulant) (any site) (fever) (hemorrhagic) (infection) (intermittent) (malignant) (rheumatic) 002.0
- with pneumonia 002.0 *[484.8]*
- abdominal 002.0
- carrier (suspected) of V02.1
- cholecystitis (current) 002.0
- clinical (Widal and blood test negative) 002.0
- endocarditis 002.0 *[421.1]*
- inoculation reaction — *see* Complications, vaccination
- meningitis 002.0 *[320.7]*
- mesenteric lymph nodes 002.0
- myocarditis 002.0 *[422.0]*
- osteomyelitis (*see also* Osteomyelitis, due to, typhoid) 002.0 *[730.8]* ☑
- perichondritis, larynx 002.0 *[478.71]*
- pneumonia 002.0 *[484.8]*
- spine 002.0 *[720.81]*
- ulcer (perforating) 002.0
- vaccination, prophylactic (against) V03.1
- Widal negative 002.0

Typhomalaria (fever) — *see also* Malaria 084.6

Typhomania 002.0

Typhoperitonitis 002.0

Typhus (fever) 081.9
- abdominal, abdominalis 002.0
- African tick 082.1
- amarillic (*see also* Fever, Yellow) 060.9
- brain 081.9
- cerebral 081.9
- classical 080
- endemic (flea-borne) 081.0
- epidemic (louse-borne) 080
- exanthematic NEC 080
- exanthematicus SAI 080
  - brillii SAI 081.1
  - Mexicanus SAI 081.0
  - pediculo vestimenti causa 080
  - typhus murinus 081.0
- flea-borne 081.0
- Indian tick 082.1
- Kenya tick 082.1
- louse-borne 080
- Mexican 081.0
  - flea-borne 081.0
  - louse-borne 080
  - tabardillo 080
- mite-borne 081.2
- murine 081.0
- North Asian tick-borne 082.2
- petechial 081.9
- Queensland tick 082.3
- rat 081.0
- recrudescent 081.1

Typhus — *continued*
- recurrent (*see also* Fever, relapsing) 087.9
- São Paulo 082.0
- scrub (China) (India) (Malaya) (New Guinea) 081.2
- shop (of Malaya) 081.0
- Siberian tick 082.2
- tick-borne NEC 082.9
- tropical 081.2
- vaccination, prophylactic (against) V05.8

Tyrosinemia 270.2
- neonatal 775.89

Tyrosinosis (Medes) (Sakai) 270.2

Tyrosinuria 270.2

Tyrosyluria 270.2

U

Uehlinger's syndrome (acropachyderma) 757.39

Uhl's anomaly or disease (hypoplasia of myocardium, right ventricle) 746.84

Ulcerosa scarlatina 034.1

Ulcer, ulcerated, ulcerating, ulceration, ulcerative 707.9
- with gangrene 707.9 *[785.4]*
- abdomen (wall) (*see also* Ulcer, skin) 707.8
- ala, nose 478.19
- alveolar process 526.5
- amebic (intestine) 006.9
  - skin 006.6
- anastomotic — *see* Ulcer, gastrojejunal
- anorectal 569.41
- antral — *see* Ulcer, stomach
- anus (sphincter) (solitary) 569.41
  - varicose — *see* Varicose, ulcer, anus
- aorta — *see* Aneuysm
- aphthous (oral) (recurrent) 528.2
  - genital organ(s)
    - female 616.50
    - male 608.89
  - mouth 528.2
- arm (*see also* Ulcer, skin) 707.8
- arteriosclerotic plaque — *see* Arteriosclerosis, by site
- artery NEC 447.2
  - without rupture 447.8
- atrophic NEC — *see* Ulcer, skin
- Barrett's (chronic peptic ulcer of esophagus) 530.85
- bile duct 576.8
- bladder (solitary) (sphincter) 596.8
  - bilharzial (*see also* Schistosomiasis) 120.9 *[595.4]*
  - submucosal (*see also* Cystitis) 595.1
  - tuberculous (*see also* Tuberculosis) 016.1 ☑
- bleeding NEC — *see* Ulcer, peptic, with hemorrhage
- bone 730.9 ☑
- bowel (*see also* Ulcer, intestine) 569.82
- breast 611.0
- bronchitis 491.8
- bronchus 519.19
- buccal (cavity) (traumatic) 528.9
- burn (acute) — *see* Ulcer, duodenum
- Buruli 031.1
- buttock (*see also* Ulcer, skin) 707.8
  - decubitus (*see also* Ulcer, pressure) 707.00
- cancerous (M8000/3) — *see* Neoplasm, by site, malignant
- cardia — *see* Ulcer, stomach
- cardio-esophageal (peptic) 530.20
  - with bleeding 530.21
- cecum (*see also* Ulcer, intestine) 569.82
- cervix (uteri) (trophic) 622.0
  - with mention of cervicitis 616.0

Ulcer, ulcerated, ulcerating, ulceration, ulcerative — *continued*
- chancroidal 099.0
- chest (wall) (*see also* Ulcer, skin) 707.8
- Chiclero 085.4
- chin (pyogenic) (*see also* Ulcer, skin) 707.8
- chronic (cause unknown) (*see also* Ulcer, skin)
  - penis 607.89
- Cochin-China 085.1
- colitis — *see* Colitis, ulcerative
- colon (*see also* Ulcer, intestine) 569.82
- conjunctiva (acute) (postinfectional) 372.00
- cornea (infectional) 370.00
  - with perforation 370.06
  - annular 370.02
  - catarrhal 370.01
  - central 370.03
  - dendritic 054.42
  - marginal 370.01
  - mycotic 370.05
  - phlyctenular, tuberculous (*see also* Tuberculosis) 017.3 ☑ *[370.31]*
  - ring 370.02
  - rodent 370.07
  - serpent, serpiginous 370.04
  - superficial marginal 370.01
  - tuberculous (*see also* Tuberculosis) 017.3 ☑ *[370.31]*
- corpus cavernosum (chronic) 607.89
- crural — *see* Ulcer, lower extremity
- Curling's — *see* Ulcer, duodenum
- Cushing's — *see* Ulcer, peptic
- cystitis (interstitial) 595.1
- decubitus (unspecified site) (*see also* Ulcer, pressure) 707.00
  - with gangrene 707.00 *[785.4]*
  - ankle 707.06
  - back
    - lower 707.03
    - upper 707.02
  - buttock 707.05
  - elbow 707.01
  - head 707.09
  - heel 707.07
  - hip 707.04
  - other site 707.09
  - sacrum 707.03
  - shoulder blades 707.02
- dendritic 054.42
- diabetes, diabetic (mellitus) 250.8 ☑ *[707.9]*
  - due to secondary diabetes 249.8 ☑ *[707.9]*
  - lower limb 250.8 ☑ *[707.10]*
    - ankle 250.8 ☑ *[707.13]*
      - due to secondary diabetes 249.8 ☑ *[707.13]*
    - calf 250.8 ☑ *[707.12]*
      - due to secondary diabetes 249.8 ☑ *[707.12]*
    - due to secondary diabetes 249.8 ☑ *[707.10]*
    - foot 250.8 ☑ *[707.15]*
      - due to secondary diabetes 249.8 ☑ *[707.15]*
    - heel 250.8 ☑ *[707.14]*
      - due to secondary diabetes 249.8 ☑ *[707.14]*
    - knee 250.8 ☑ *[707.19]*
      - due to secondary diabetes 249.8 ☑ *[707.19]*
    - specified site NEC 250.8 ☑ *[707.19]*
      - due to secondary diabetes 249.8 ☑ *[707.19]*
    - thigh 250.8 ☑ *[707.11]*
      - due to secondary diabetes 249.8 ☑ *[707.11]*
    - toes 250.8 ☑ *[707.15]*
      - due to secondary diabetes 249.8 ☑ *[707.15]*

Ulcer, ulcerated, ulcerating, ulceration, ulcerative — *continued*
proctitis — *continued*
with ulcerative sigmoiditis 556.3
prostate 601.8
pseudopeptic — *see* Ulcer, peptic
pyloric — *see* Ulcer, stomach
rectosigmoid 569.82
with perforation 569.83
rectum (sphincter) (solitary) 569.41
stercoraceous, stercoral 569.41
varicose — *see* Varicose, ulcer, anus
retina (*see also* Chorioretinitis) 363.20
rodent (M8090/3) (*see also* Neoplasm, skin, malignant)
cornea 370.07
round — *see* Ulcer, stomach
sacrum (region) (*see also* Ulcer, skin) 707.8
Saemisch's 370.04
scalp (*see also* Ulcer, skin) 707.8
sclera 379.09
scrofulous (*see also* Tuberculosis) 017.2 ☑
scrotum 608.89
tuberculous (*see also* Tuberculosis) 016.5 ☑
varicose 456.4
seminal vesicle 608.89
sigmoid 569.82
with perforation 569.83
skin (atrophic) (chronic) (neurogenic) (non-healing) (perforating) (pyogenic) (trophic) 707.9
with gangrene 707.9 *[785.4]*
amebic 006.6
decubitus (*see also* Ulcer, pressure) 707.00
with gangrene 707.00 *[785.4]*
in granulocytopenia 288.09
lower extremity (*see also* Ulcer, lower extremity) 707.10
with gangrene 707.10 *[785.4]*
arteriosclerotic 440.24
ankle 707.13
arteriosclerotic 440.23
with gangrene 440.24
calf 707.12
foot 707.15
heel 707.14
knee 707.19
specified site NEC 707.19
thigh 707.11
toes 707.15
mycobacterial 031.1
syphilitic (early) (secondary) 091.3
tuberculous (primary) (*see also* Tuberculosis) 017.0 ☑
varicose — *see* Ulcer, varicose
sloughing NEC — *see* Ulcer, skin
soft palate 528.9
solitary, anus or rectum (sphincter) 569.41
sore throat 462
streptococcal 034.0
spermatic cord 608.89
spine (tuberculous) 015.0 ☑ *[730.88]*
stasis (leg) (venous) 454.0
with varicose veins 454.0
without varicose veins 459.81
inflamed or infected 454.2
stercoral, stercoraceous 569.82
with perforation 569.83
anus or rectum 569.41
stomach (eroded) (peptic) (round) 531.9 ☑

Note — Use the following fifth-digit subclassification with categories 531–534:
0 without mention of obstruction
1 with obstruction

with
hemorrhage 531.4 ☑

Ulcer, ulcerated, ulcerating, ulceration, ulcerative — *continued*
stomach — *continued*
with — *continued*
hemorrhage — *continued*
and perforation 531.6 ☑
perforation (chronic) 531.5 ☑
and hemorrhage 531.6 ☑
acute 531.3 ☑
with
hemorrhage 531.0 ☑
and perforation 531.2 ☑
perforation 531.1 ☑
and hemorrhage 531.2 ☑
bleeding (recurrent) — *see* Ulcer, stomach, with hemorrhage
chronic 531.7 ☑
with
hemorrhage 531.4 ☑
and perforation 531.6 ☑
perforation 531.5 ☑
and hemorrhage 531.6 ☑
penetrating — *see* Ulcer, stomach, with perforation
perforating — *see* Ulcer, stomach, with perforation
stoma, stomal — *see* Ulcer, gastrojejunal
stomatitis 528.00
stress — *see* Ulcer, peptic
strumous (tuberculous) (*see also* Tuberculosis) 017.2 ☑
submental (*see also* Ulcer, skin) 707.8
submucosal, bladder 595.1
syphilitic (any site) (early) (secondary) 091.3
late 095.9
perforating 095.9
foot 094.0
testis 608.89
thigh — *see* Ulcer, lower extremity
throat 478.29
diphtheritic 032.0
toe — *see* Ulcer, lower extremity
tongue (traumatic) 529.0
tonsil 474.8
diphtheritic 032.0
trachea 519.19
trophic — *see* Ulcer, skin
tropical NEC (*see also* Ulcer, skin) 707.9
tuberculous — *see* Tuberculosis, ulcer
tunica vaginalis 608.89
turbinate 730.9 ☑
typhoid (fever) 002.0
perforating 002.0
umbilicus (newborn) 771.4
unspecified site NEC — *see* Ulcer, skin
urethra (meatus) (*see also* Urethritis) 597.89
uterus 621.8
cervix 622.0
with mention of cervicitis 616.0
neck 622.0
with mention of cervicitis 616.0
vagina 616.89
valve, heart 421.0
varicose (lower extremity, any part) 454.0
anus — *see* Varicose, ulcer, anus
broad ligament 456.5
esophagus (*see also* Varix, esophagus) 456.1
bleeding (*see also* Varix, esophagus, bleeding) 456.0
inflamed or infected 454.2
nasal septum 456.8
perineum 456.6
rectum — *see* Varicose, ulcer, anus
scrotum 456.4
specified site NEC 456.8
sublingual 456.3
vulva 456.6
vas deferens 608.89
vesical (*see also* Ulcer, bladder) 596.8

Ulcer, ulcerated, ulcerating, ulceration, ulcerative — *continued*
vulva (acute) (infectional) 616.50
Behçet's syndrome 136.1 *[616.51]*
herpetic 054.12
tuberculous 016.7 ☑ *[616.51]*
vulvobuccal, recurring 616.50
x-ray — *see* Ulcer, by site
yaws 102.4
Ulcus — *see also* Ulcer
cutis tuberculosum (*see also* Tuberculosis) 017.0 ☑
duodeni — *see* Ulcer, duodenum
durum 091.0
extragenital 091.2
gastrojejunale — *see* Ulcer, gastrojejunal
hypostaticum — *see* Ulcer, varicose
molle (cutis) (skin) 099.0
serpens corneae (pneumococcal) 370.04
ventriculi — *see* Ulcer, stomach
Ulegyria 742.4
Ulerythema
acneiforma 701.8
centrifugum 695.4
ophryogenes 757.4
Ullrich-Feichtiger syndrome 759.89
Ullrich (-Bonnevie) (-Turner) syndrome 758.6
Ulnar — *see* condition
Ulorrhagia 523.8
Ulorrhea 523.8
Umbilicus, umbilical — *see also* condition
cord necrosis, affecting fetus or newborn 762.6
Unacceptable
existing dental restoration
contours 525.65
morphology 525.65
Unavailability of medical facilities (at) V63.9
due to
investigation by social service agency V63.8
lack of services at home V63.1
remoteness from facility V63.0
waiting list V63.2
home V63.1
outpatient clinic V63.0
specified reason NEC V63.8
Uncinaria americana infestation 126.1
Uncinariasis — *see also* Ancylostomiasis 126.9
Unconscious, unconsciousness 780.09
Underdevelopment — *see also* Undeveloped
sexual 259.0
Underfill, endodontic 526.63
Undernourishment 269.9
Undernutrition 269.9
Under observation — *see* Observation
Underweight 783.22
for gestational age — *see* Light-for-dates
Underwood's disease (sclerema neonatorum) 778.1
Undescended — *see also* Malposition, congenital
cecum 751.4
colon 751.4
testis 752.51
Undetermined diagnosis or cause 799.9
Undeveloped, undevelopment — *see also* Hypoplasia
brain (congenital) 742.1
cerebral (congenital) 742.1
fetus or newborn 764.9 ☑
heart 746.89
lung 748.5
testis 257.2
uterus 259.0
Undiagnosed (disease) 799.9
Undulant fever — *see also* Brucellosis 023.9

Unemployment, anxiety concerning V62.0
Unequal leg (acquired) (length) 736.81
congenital 755.30
Unerupted teeth, tooth 520.6
Unextracted dental root 525.3
Unguis incarnatus 703.0
Unicornis uterus 752.3
Unicorporeus uterus 752.3
Uniformis uterus 752.3
Unilateral — *see also* condition
development, breast 611.89
organ or site, congenital NEC — *see* Agenesis
vagina 752.49
Unilateralis uterus 752.3
Unilocular heart 745.8
Uninhibited bladder 596.54
with cauda equina syndrome 344.61
neurogenic — *see also* Neurogenic, bladder 596.54
Union, abnormal — *see also* Fusion
divided tendon 727.89
larynx and trachea 748.3
Universal
joint, cervix 620.6
mesentery 751.4
Unknown
cause of death 799.9
diagnosis 799.9
Unna's disease (seborrheic dermatitis) 690.10
Unresponsiveness, adrenocorticotropin (ACTH) 255.41
Unsatisfactory
cytology smear
anal 796.78
cervical 795.08
vaginal 795.18
restoration, tooth (existing) 525.60
specified NEC 525.69
Unsoundness of mind — *see also* Psychosis 298.9
Unspecified cause of death 799.9
Unstable
back NEC 724.9
colon 569.89
joint — *see* Instability, joint
lie 652.0 ☑
affecting fetus or newborn (before labor) 761.7
causing obstructed labor 660.0 ☑
affecting fetus or newborn 763.1
lumbosacral joint (congenital) 756.19
acquired 724.6
sacroiliac 724.6
spine NEC 724.9
Untruthfulness, child problem — *see also* Disturbance, conduct 312.0 ☑
Unverricht (-Lundborg) disease, syndrome, or epilepsy 333.2
Unverricht-Wagner syndrome (dermatomyositis) 710.3
Upper respiratory — *see* condition
Upset
gastric 536.8
psychogenic 306.4
gastrointestinal 536.8
psychogenic 306.4
virus (*see also* Enteritis, viral) 008.8
intestinal (large) (small) 564.9
psychogenic 306.4
menstruation 626.9
mental 300.9
stomach 536.8
psychogenic 306.4
Urachus — *see also* condition
patent 753.7
persistent 753.7
Uratic arthritis 274.0
Urbach's lipoid proteinosis 272.8
Urbach-Oppenheim disease or syndrome (necrobiosis lipoidica diabeticorum) 250.8 ☑ *[709.3]*

Urbach-Oppenheim disease or syndrome — *continued*
due to secondary diabetes 249.8 ☑ *[709.3]*
Urbach-Wiethe disease or syndrome (lipoid proteinosis) 272.8
Urban yellow fever 060.1
Urea, blood, high — *see* Uremia
Uremia, uremic (absorption) (amaurosis) (amblyopia) (aphasia) (apoplexy) (coma) (delirium) (dementia) (dropsy) (dyspnea) (fever) (intoxication) (mania) (paralysis) (poisoning) (toxemia) (vomiting) 586
with
abortion — *see* Abortion, by type, with renal failure
ectopic pregnancy (*see also* categories 633.0–633.9) 639.3
hypertension (*see also* Hypertension, kidney) 403.91
molar pregnancy (*see also* categories 630–632) 639.3
chronic 585.9
complicating
abortion 639.3
ectopic or molar pregnancy 639.3
hypertension (*see also* Hypertension, kidney) 403.91
labor and delivery 669.3 ☑
congenital 779.89
extrarenal 788.99
hypertensive (chronic) (*see also* Hypertension, kidney) 403.91
maternal NEC, affecting fetus or newborn 760.1
neuropathy 585.9 *[357.4]*
pericarditis 585.9 *[420.0]*
prerenal 788.99
pyelitic (*see also* Pyelitis) 590.80
Ureteralgia 788.0
Ureterectasis 593.89
Ureteritis 593.89
cystica 590.3
due to calculus 592.1
gonococcal (acute) 098.19
chronic or duration of 2 months or over 098.39
nonspecific 593.89
Ureterocele (acquired) 593.89
congenital 753.23
Ureterolith 592.1
Ureterolithiasis 592.1
Ureterostomy status V44.6
with complication 997.5
Ureter, ureteral — *see* condition
Urethralgia 788.99
Urethra, urethral — *see* condition
Urethritis (abacterial) (acute) (allergic) (anterior) (chronic) (nonvenereal) (posterior) (recurrent) (simple) (subacute) (ulcerative) (undifferentiated) 597.80
diplococcal (acute) 098.0
chronic or duration of 2 months or over 098.2
due to Trichomonas (vaginalis) 131.02
gonococcal (acute) 098.0

Urethritis — *continued*
gonococcal — *continued*
chronic or duration of 2 months or over 098.2
nongonococcal (sexually transmitted) 099.40
Chlamydia trachomatis 099.41
Reiter's 099.3
specified organism NEC 099.49
nonspecific (sexually transmitted) (*see also* Urethritis, nongonococcal) 099.40
not sexually transmitted 597.80
Reiter's 099.3
trichomonal or due to Trichomonas (vaginalis) 131.02
tuberculous (*see also* Tuberculosis) 016.3 ☑
venereal NEC (*see also* Urethritis, nongonococcal) 099.40
Urethrocele
female 618.03
with uterine prolapse 618.4
complete 618.3
incomplete 618.2
male 599.5
Urethrolithiasis 594.2
Urethro-oculoarticular syndrome 099.3
Urethro-oculosynovial syndrome 099.3
Urethrorectal — *see* condition
Urethrorrhagia 599.84
Urethrorrhea 788.7
Urethrostomy status V44.6
with complication 997.5
Urethrotrigonitis 595.3
Urethrovaginal — *see* condition
Urhidrosis, uridrosis 705.89
Uric acid
diathesis 274.9
in blood 790.6
Uricacidemia 790.6
Uricemia 790.6
Uricosuria 791.9
Urination
frequent 788.41
painful 788.1
urgency 788.63
Urinemia — *see* Uremia
Urine, urinary — *see also* condition
abnormality NEC 788.69
blood in (*see also* Hematuria) 599.70
discharge, excessive 788.42
enuresis 788.30
nonorganic origin 307.6
extravasation 788.8
frequency 788.41
hesitancy 788.64
incontinence 788.30
active 788.30
female 788.30
stress 625.6
and urge 788.33
male 788.30
stress 788.32
and urge 788.33
mixed (stress and urge) 788.33
neurogenic 788.39
nonorganic origin 307.6

Urine, urinary — *see also* condition — *continued*
incontinence — *continued*
overflow 788.38
stress (female) 625.6
male NEC 788.32
intermittent stream 788.61
pus in 791.9
retention or stasis NEC 788.20
bladder, incomplete emptying 788.21
psychogenic 306.53
specified NEC 788.29
secretion
deficient 788.5
excessive 788.42
frequency 788.41
strain 788.65
stream
intermittent 788.61
slowing 788.62
splitting 788.61
weak 788.62
urgency 788.63
Urinoma NEC 599.9
bladder 596.8
kidney 593.89
renal 593.89
ureter 593.89
urethra 599.84
Uroarthritis, infectious 099.3
Urodialysis 788.5
Urolithiasis 592.9
Uronephrosis 593.89
Uropathy 599.9
obstructive 599.60
Urosepsis 599.0
meaning sepsis 995.91
meaning urinary tract infection 599.0
Urticaria 708.9
with angioneurotic edema 995.1
hereditary 277.6
allergic 708.0
cholinergic 708.5
chronic 708.8
cold, familial 708.2
dermatographic 708.3
due to
cold or heat 708.2
drugs 708.0
food 708.0
inhalants 708.0
plants 708.8
serum 999.5
factitial 708.3
giant 995.1
hereditary 277.6
gigantea 995.1
hereditary 277.6
idiopathic 708.1
larynx 995.1
hereditary 277.6
neonatorum 778.8
nonallergic 708.1
papulosa (Hebra) 698.2
perstans hemorrhagica 757.39
pigmentosa 757.33
recurrent periodic 708.8

Urticaria — *continued*
serum 999.5
solare 692.72
specified type NEC 708.8
thermal (cold) (heat) 708.2
vibratory 708.4
Urticarioides acarodermatitis 133.9
Use of
methadone 304.00
nonprescribed drugs (*see also* Abuse, drugs, nondependent) 305.9 ☑
patent medicines (*see also* Abuse, drugs, nondependent) 305.9 ☑
Usher-Senear disease (pemphigus erythematosus) 694.4
Uta 085.5
Uterine size-date discrepancy 649.6 ☑
Uteromegaly 621.2
Uterovaginal — *see* condition
Uterovesical — *see* condition
Uterus — *see* condition
Utriculitis (utriculus prostaticus) 597.89
Uveal — *see* condition
Uveitis (anterior) — *see also* Iridocyclitis 364.3
acute or subacute 364.00
due to or associated with
gonococcal infection 098.41
herpes (simplex) 054.44
zoster 053.22
primary 364.01
recurrent 364.02
secondary (noninfectious) 364.04
infectious 364.03
allergic 360.11
chronic 364.10
due to or associated with
sarcoidosis 135 *[364.11]*
tuberculosis (*see also* Tuberculosis) 017.3 ☑ *[364.11]*
due to
operation 360.11
toxoplasmosis (acquired) 130.2
congenital (active) 771.2
granulomatous 364.10
heterochromic 364.21
lens-induced 364.23
nongranulomatous 364.00
posterior 363.20
disseminated — *see* Chorioretinitis, disseminated
focal — *see* Chorioretinitis, focal
recurrent 364.02
sympathetic 360.11
syphilitic (secondary) 091.50
congenital 090.0 *[363.13]*
late 095.8 *[363.13]*
tuberculous (*see also* Tuberculosis) 017.3 ☑ *[364.11]*
Uveoencephalitis 363.22
Uveokeratitis — *see also* Iridocyclitis 364.3
Uveoparotid fever 135
Uveoparotitis 135
Uvula — *see* condition
Uvulitis (acute) (catarrhal) (chronic) (gangrenous) (membranous) (suppurative) (ulcerative) 528.3

V

Vaccination
complication or reaction — *see* Complications, vaccination
delayed V64.00
not carried out V64.00
because of
acute illness V64.01
allergy to vaccine or component V64.04
caregiver refusal V64.05
chronic illness V64.02
guardian refusal V64.05
immune compromised state V64.03
parent refusal V64.05
patient had disease being vaccinated against V64.08
patient refusal V64.06
reason NEC V64.09
religious reasons V64.07
prophylactic (against) V05.9
arthropod-borne viral
disease NEC V05.1
encephalitis V05.0
chickenpox V05.4
cholera (alone) V03.0
with typhoid-paratyphoid (cholera + TAB) V06.0
common cold V04.7
diphtheria (alone) V03.5
with
poliomyelitis (DTP+ polio) V06.3
tetanus V06.5
pertussis combined (DTP) (DTaP) V06.1
typhoid-paratyphoid (DTP + TAB) V06.2
disease (single) NEC V05.9
bacterial NEC V03.9
specified type NEC V03.89
combination NEC V06.9
specified type NEC V06.8
specified type NEC V05.8
encephalitis, viral, arthropod-borne V05.0
Hemophilus influenzae, type B [Hib] V03.81
hepatitis, viral V05.3
influenza V04.81
with
Streptococcus pneumoniae [pneumococcus] V06.6
leishmaniasis V05.2
measles (alone) V04.2
with mumps-rubella (MMR) V06.4
mumps (alone) V04.6
with measles and rubella (MMR) V06.4
pertussis alone V03.6
plague V03.3
poliomyelitis V04.0
with diphtheria-tetanus-pertussis (DTP + polio) V06.3
rabies V04.5
respiratory syncytial virus (RSV) V04.82
rubella (alone) V04.3
with measles and mumps (MMR) V06.4
smallpox V04.1
Streptococcus pneumoniae [pneumococcus] V03.82
with
influenza V06.6
tetanus toxoid (alone) V03.7
with diphtheria [Td] [DT] V06.5
with
pertussis (DTP) (DTaP) V06.1
with poliomyelitis (DTP+polio) V06.3
tuberculosis (BCG) V03.2
Vaccination — *continued*
prophylactic — *continued*
tularemia V03.4
typhoid-paratyphoid (TAB) (alone) V03.1
with diphtheria-tetanus-pertussis (TAB + DTP) V06.2
varicella V05.4
viral
disease NEC V04.89
encephalitis, arthropod-borne V05.0
hepatitis V05.3
yellow fever V04.4
Vaccinia (generalized) 999.0
without vaccination 051.02
congenital 771.2
conjunctiva 999.39
eyelids 999.0 *[373.5]*
localized 999.39
nose 999.39
not from vaccination 051.02
eyelid 051.02 *[373.5]*
sine vaccinatione 051.02
Vacuum
extraction of fetus or newborn 763.3
in sinus (accessory) (nasal) (*see also* Sinusitis) 473.9
Vagabond V60.0
Vagabondage V60.0
Vagabonds' disease 132.1
Vaginalitis (tunica) 608.4
Vagina, vaginal — *see also* condition
high risk human papillomavirus (HPV) DNA test positive 795.15
low risk human papillomavirus (HPV) DNA test positive 795.19
Vaginismus (reflex) 625.1
functional 306.51
hysterical 300.11
psychogenic 306.51
Vaginitis (acute) (chronic) (circumscribed) (diffuse) (emphysematous) (Hemophilus vaginalis) (nonspecific) (nonvenereal) (ulcerative) 616.10
with
abortion — *see* Abortion, by type, with sepsis
ectopic pregnancy (*see also* categories 633.0–633.9) 639.0
molar pregnancy (*see also* categories 630–632) 639.0
adhesive, congenital 752.49
atrophic, postmenopausal 627.3
bacterial 616.10
blennorrhagic (acute) 098.0
chronic or duration of 2 months or over 098.2
candidal 112.1
chlamydial 099.53
complicating pregnancy or puerperium 646.6 ☑
affecting fetus or newborn 760.8
congenital (adhesive) 752.49
due to
C. albicans 112.1
Trichomonas (vaginalis) 131.01
following
abortion 639.0
ectopic or molar pregnancy 639.0
gonococcal (acute) 098.0
chronic or duration of 2 months or over 098.2
granuloma 099.2
Monilia 112.1
mycotic 112.1
pinworm 127.4 *[616.11]*
postirradiation 616.10
postmenopausal atrophic 627.3
senile (atrophic) 627.3
syphilitic (early) 091.0
late 095.8
trichomonal 131.01
tuberculous (*see also* Tuberculosis) 016.7 ☑
venereal NEC 099.8
Vaginosis — *see* Vaginitis
Vagotonia 352.3
Vagrancy V60.0
VAIN I (vaginal intraepithelial neoplasia I) 623.0
VAIN II (vaginal intraepithelial neoplasia II) 623.0
VAIN III (vaginal intraepithelial neoplasia III) 233.31
Vallecula — *see* condition
Valley fever 114.0
Valsuani's disease (progressive pernicious anemia, puerperal) 648.2 ☑
Valve, valvular (formation) — *see also* condition
cerebral ventricle (communicating) in situ V45.2
cervix, internal os 752.49
colon 751.5
congenital NEC — *see* Atresia
formation, congenital NEC — *see* Atresia
heart defect — *see* Anomaly, heart, valve
ureter 753.29
pelvic junction 753.21
vesical orifice 753.22
urethra 753.6
Valvulitis (chronic) — *see also* Endocarditis 424.90
rheumatic (chronic) (inactive) (with chorea) 397.9
active or acute (aortic) (mitral) (pulmonary) (tricuspid) 391.1
syphilitic NEC 093.20
aortic 093.22
mitral 093.21
pulmonary 093.24
tricuspid 093.23
Valvulopathy — *see* Endocarditis
van Bogaert-Nijssen (-Peiffer) disease 330.0
van Bogaert's leukoencephalitis (sclerosing) (subacute) 046.2
van Buchem's syndrome (hyperostosis corticalis) 733.3
Vancomycin (glycopeptide)
intermediate staphylococcus aureus (VISA/GISA) V09.8 ☑
resistant
enterococcus (VRE) V09.8 ☑
staphylococcus aureus (VRSA/GRSA) V09.8 ☑
van Creveld-von Gierke disease (glycogenosis I) 271.0
van den Bergh's disease (enterogenous cyanosis) 289.7
van der Hoeve-Halbertsma-Waardenburg syndrome (ptosis-epicanthus) 270.2
van der Hoeve-Waardenburg-Gualdi syndrome (ptosis epicanthus) 270.2
van der Hoeve's syndrome (brittle bones and blue sclera, deafness) 756.51
Vanillism 692.89
Vanishing lung 492.0
Vanishing twin 651.33
van Neck (-Odelberg) disease or syndrome (juvenile osteochondrosis) 732.1
Vapor asphyxia or suffocation NEC 987.9
specified agent — *see* Table of Drugs and Chemicals
Vaquez's disease (M9950/1) 238.4
Vaquez-Osler disease (polycythemia vera) (M9950/1) 238.4
Variance, lethal ball, prosthetic heart valve 996.02
Variants, thalassemic 282.49
Variations in hair color 704.3
Varicella 052.9
with
complication 052.8
specified NEC 052.7
Varicella — *continued*
with — *continued*
pneumonia 052.1
vaccination and inoculation (prophylactic) V05.4
exposure to V01.71
vaccination and inoculation (against) (prophylactic) V05.4
Varices — *see* Varix
Varicocele (scrotum) (thrombosed) 456.4
ovary 456.5
perineum 456.6
spermatic cord (ulcerated) 456.4
Varicose
aneurysm (ruptured) (*see also* Aneurysm) 442.9
dermatitis (lower extremity) — *see* Varicose, vein, inflamed or infected
eczema — *see* Varicose, vein
phlebitis — *see* Varicose, vein, inflamed or infected
placental vessel — *see* Placenta, abnormal
tumor — *see* Varicose, vein
ulcer (lower extremity, any part) 454.0
anus 455.8
external 455.5
internal 455.2
esophagus (*see also* Varix, esophagus) 456.1
bleeding (*see also* Varix, esophagus, bleeding) 456.0
inflamed or infected 454.2
nasal septum 456.8
perineum 456.6
rectum — *see* Varicose, ulcer, anus
scrotum 456.4
specified site NEC 456.8
vein (lower extremity) (ruptured) (*see also* Varix) 454.9
with
complications NEC 454.8
edema 454.8
inflammation or infection 454.1
ulcerated 454.2
pain 454.8
stasis dermatitis 454.1
with ulcer 454.2
swelling 454.8
ulcer 454.0
inflamed or infected 454.2
anus — *see* Hemorrhoids
broad ligament 456.5
congenital (peripheral) 747.60
gastrointestinal 747.61
lower limb 747.64
renal 747.62
specified NEC 747.69
upper limb 747.63
esophagus (ulcerated) (*see also* Varix, esophagus) 456.1
bleeding (*see also* Varix, esophagus, bleeding) 456.0
inflamed or infected 454.1
with ulcer 454.2
in pregnancy or puerperium 671.0 ☑
vulva or perineum 671.1 ☑
nasal septum (with ulcer) 456.8
pelvis 456.5
perineum 456.6
in pregnancy, childbirth, or puerperium 671.1 ☑
rectum — *see* Hemorrhoids
scrotum (ulcerated) 456.4
specified site NEC 456.8
sublingual 456.3
ulcerated 454.0
inflamed or infected 454.2
umbilical cord, affecting fetus or newborn 762.6
urethra 456.8
vulva 456.6
in pregnancy, childbirth, or puerperium 671.1 ☑

W

Water — *continued*
in joint (*see also* Effusion, joint) 719.0 ☑
intoxication 276.6
itch 120.3
lack of 994.3
loading 276.6
on
brain — *see* Hydrocephalus
chest 511.89
poisoning 276.6
Waterbrash 787.1
Water-hammer pulse — *see also* Insufficiency, aortic 424.1
Waterhouse (-Friderichsen) disease or syndrome 036.3
Water-losing nephritis 588.89
Wax in ear 380.4
Waxy
degeneration, any site 277.39
disease 277.39
kidney 277.39 *[583.81]*
liver (large) 277.39
spleen 277.39
Weak, weakness (generalized) 780.79
arches (acquired) 734
congenital 754.61
bladder sphincter 596.59
congenital 779.89
eye muscle — *see* Strabismus
facial 781.94
foot (double) — *see* Weak, arches
heart, cardiac (*see also* Failure, heart) 428.9
congenital 746.9
mind 317
muscle (generalized) 728.87
myocardium (*see also* Failure, heart) 428.9
newborn 779.89
pelvic fundus
pubocervical tissue 618.81
rectovaginal tissue 618.82
pulse 785.9
senile 797
urinary stream 788.62
valvular — *see* Endocarditis
Wear, worn, tooth, teeth (approximal) (hard tissues) (interproximal) (occlusal) — *see also* Attrition, teeth 521.10
Weather, weathered
effects of
cold NEC 991.9
specified effect NEC 991.8
hot (*see also* Heat) 992.9
skin 692.74
Weber-Christian disease or syndrome (nodular nonsuppurative panniculitis) 729.30
Weber-Cockayne syndrome (epidermolysis bullosa) 757.39
Weber-Dimitri syndrome 759.6
Weber-Gubler syndrome 344.89
Weber-Leyden syndrome 344.89
Weber-Osler syndrome (familial hemorrhagic telangiectasia) 448.0
Weber's paralysis or syndrome 344.89
Web, webbed (congenital) — *see also* Anomaly, specified type NEC
canthus 743.63
digits (*see also* Syndactylism) 755.10
duodenal 751.5
esophagus 750.3
fingers (*see also* Syndactylism, fingers) 755.11
larynx (glottic) (subglottic) 748.2
neck (pterygium colli) 744.5
Paterson-Kelly (sideropenic dysphagia) 280.8
popliteal syndrome 756.89
toes (*see also* Syndactylism, toes) 755.13
Wedge-shaped or wedging vertebra — *see also* Osteoporosis 733.00
Wegener's granulomatosis or syndrome 446.4
Wegner's disease (syphilitic osteochondritis) 090.0
Weight
gain (abnormal) (excessive) 783.1
during pregnancy 646.1 ☑
insufficient 646.8 ☑
less than 1000 grams at birth 765.0 ☑
loss (cause unknown) 783.21
Weightlessness 994.9
Weil's disease (leptospiral jaundice) 100.0
Weill-Marchesani syndrome (brachymorphism and ectopia lentis) 759.89
Weingarten's syndrome (tropical eosinophilia) 518.3
Weir Mitchell's disease (erythromelalgia) 443.82
Weiss-Baker syndrome (carotid sinus syncope) 337.01
Weissenbach-Thibierge syndrome (cutaneous systemic sclerosis) 710.1
Wen — *see also* Cyst, sebaceous 706.2
Wenckebach's phenomenon, heart block (second degree) 426.13
Werdnig-Hoffmann syndrome (muscular atrophy) 335.0
Werlhof-Wichmann syndrome — *see also* Purpura, thrombocytopenic 287.39
Werlhof's disease — *see also* Purpura, thrombocytopenic 287.39
Wermer's syndrome or disease (polyendocrine adenomatosis) 258.01
Werner's disease or syndrome (progeria adultorum) 259.8
Werner-His disease (trench fever) 083.1
Werner-Schultz disease (agranulocytosis) 288.09
Wernicke's encephalopathy, disease, or syndrome (superior hemorrhagic polioencephalitis) 265.1
Wernicke-Korsakoff syndrome or psychosis (nonalcoholic) 294.0
alcoholic 291.1
Wernicke-Posadas disease — *see also* Coccidioidomycosis 114.9
Wesselsbron fever 066.3
West African fever 084.8
West Nile
encephalitis 066.41
encephalomyelitis 066.41
fever 066.40
with
cranial nerve disorders 066.42
encephalitis 066.41
optic neuritis 066.42
other complications 066.49
other neurologic manifestations 066.42
polyradiculitis 066.42
virus 066.40
Westphal-Strümpell syndrome (hepatolenticular degeneration) 275.1
Wet
brain (alcoholic) (*see also* Alcoholism) 303.9 ☑
feet, tropical (syndrome) (maceration) 991.4
lung (syndrome)
adult 518.5
newborn 770.6
Wharton's duct — *see* condition
Wheal 709.8
Wheelchair confinement status V46.3
Wheezing 786.07
Whiplash injury or syndrome 847.0
Whipple's disease or syndrome (intestinal lipodystrophy) 040.2
Whipworm 127.3
"Whistling face" syndrome (craniocarpotarsal dystrophy) 759.89
White — *see also* condition
White — *see also* condition — *continued*
kidney
large — *see* Nephrosis
small 582.9
leg, puerperal, postpartum, childbirth 671.4 ☑
nonpuerperal 451.19
mouth 112.0
patches of mouth 528.6
sponge nevus of oral mucosa 750.26
spot lesions, teeth 521.01
White's disease (congenital) (keratosis follicularis) 757.39
Whitehead 706.2
Whitlow (with lymphangitis) 681.01
herpetic 054.6
Whitmore's disease or fever (melioidosis) 025
Whooping cough 033.9
with pneumonia 033.9 *[484.3]*
due to
Bordetella
bronchoseptica 033.8
with pneumonia 033.8 *[484.3]*
parapertussis 033.1
with pneumonia 033.1 *[484.3]*
pertussis 033.0
with pneumonia 033.0 *[484.3]*
specified organism NEC 033.8
with pneumonia 033.8 *[484.3]*
vaccination, prophylactic (against) V03.6
Wichmann's asthma (laryngismus stridulus) 478.75
Widal (-Abrami) syndrome (acquired hemolytic jaundice) 283.9
Widening aorta — *see also* Aneurysm, aorta 441.9
ruptured 441.5
Wilkie's disease or syndrome 557.1
Wilkinson-Sneddon disease or syndrome (subcorneal pustular dermatosis) 694.1
Willan's lepra 696.1
Willan-Plumbe syndrome (psoriasis) 696.1
Willebrand (-Jürgens) syndrome or thrombopathy (angiohemophilia) 286.4
Willi-Prader syndrome (hypogenital dystrophy with diabetic tendency) 759.81
Willis' disease (diabetes mellitus) — *see also* Diabetes 250.0 ☑
due to secondary diabetes 249.0 ☑
Wilms' tumor or neoplasm (nephroblastoma) (M8960/3) 189.0
Wilson's
disease or syndrome (hepatolenticular degeneration) 275.1
hepatolenticular degeneration 275.1
lichen ruber 697.0
Wilson-Brocq disease (dermatitis exfoliativa) 695.89
Wilson-Mikity syndrome 770.7
Window — *see also* Imperfect, closure
aorticopulmonary 745.0
Winged scapula 736.89
Winter — *see also* condition
vomiting disease 078.82
Wise's disease 696.2
Wiskott-Aldrich syndrome (eczema-thrombocytopenia) 279.12
Withdrawal symptoms, syndrome
alcohol 291.81
delirium (acute) 291.0
chronic 291.1
newborn 760.71
drug or narcotic 292.0
newborn, infant of dependent mother 779.5
Withdrawal symptoms, syndrome — *continued*
steroid NEC
correct substance properly administered 255.41
overdose or wrong substance given or taken 962.0
Withdrawing reaction, child or adolescent 313.22
Witts' anemia (achlorhydric anemia) 280.9
Witzelsucht 301.9
Woakes' syndrome (ethmoiditis) 471.1
Wohlfart-Kugelberg-Welander disease 335.11
Woillez's disease (acute idiopathic pulmonary congestion) 518.5
Wolff-Parkinson-White syndrome (anomalous atrioventricular excitation) 426.7
Wolhynian fever 083.1
Wolman's disease (primary familial xanthomatosis) 272.7
Wood asthma 495.8
Woolly, wooly hair (congenital) (nevus) 757.4
Wool-sorters' disease 022.1
Word
blindness (congenital) (developmental) 315.01
secondary to organic lesion 784.61
deafness (secondary to organic lesion) 784.69
developmental 315.31
Worm(s) (colic) (fever) (infection) (infestation) (ulcer) — *see also* Infestation 128.9
guinea 125.7
in intestine NEC 127.9
Worm-eaten soles 102.3
Worn out — *see also* Exhaustion 780.79
joint prosthesis (*see also* Complications, mechanical, device NEC, prosthetic NEC, joint) 996.46
"Worried well" V65.5
Wound, open (by cutting or piercing instrument) (by firearms) (cut) (dissection) (incised) (laceration) (penetration) (perforating) (puncture) (with initial hemorrhage, not internal) 879.8

Note — For fracture with open wound, see Fracture.

For laceration, traumatic rupture, tear or penetrating wound of internal organs, such as heart, lung, liver, kidney, pelvic organs, etc., whether or not accompanied by open wound or fracture in the same region, see Injury, internal.

For contused wound, see Contusion. For crush injury, see Crush. For abrasion, insect bite (nonvenomous), blister, or scratch, see Injury, superficial.

Complicated includes wounds with:

delayed healing

delayed treatment

foreign body

primary infection

For late effect of open wound, see Late, effect, wound, open, by site.

abdomen, abdominal (external) (muscle) 879.2
complicated 879.3
wall (anterior) 879.2
complicated 879.3
lateral 879.4
complicated 879.5
alveolar (process) 873.62
complicated 873.72
ankle 891.0
with tendon involvement 891.2
complicated 891.1

Yaws — *continued*
nodular, late (ulcerated) 102.4
osteitis 102.6
papilloma, papillomata (palmar) (plantar) 102.1
periostitis (hypertrophic) 102.6
ulcers 102.4
wet crab 102.1
Yeast infection — *see also* Candidiasis 112.9
Yellow
atrophy (liver) 570
chronic 571.8
Yellow — *continued*
atrophy — *continued*
resulting from administration of blood, plasma, serum, or other biological substance (within 8 months of administration) — *see* Hepatitis, viral
fever — *see* Fever, yellow
jack (*see also* Fever, yellow) 060.9
jaundice (*see also* Jaundice) 782.4
vernix syndrome 762.2
Yersinia septica 027.8

Z

Zagari's disease (xerostomia) 527.7
Zahorsky's disease (exanthema subitum) (*see also* Exanthem subitum) 058.10
syndrome (herpangina) 074.0
Zellweger syndrome 277.86
Zenker's diverticulum (esophagus) 530.6
Ziehen-Oppenheim disease 333.6
Zieve's syndrome (jaundice, hyperlipemia, and hemolytic anemia) 571.1
Zika fever 066.3
Zollinger-Ellison syndrome (gastric hypersecretion with pancreatic islet cell tumor) 251.5
Zona — *see also* Herpes, zoster 053.9
Zoophilia (erotica) 302.1
Zoophobia 300.29
Zoster (herpes) — *see also* Herpes, zoster 053.9
Zuelzer (-Ogden) anemia or syndrome (nutritional megaloblastic anemia) 281.2
Zygodactyly — *see also* Syndactylism 755.10
Zygomycosis 117.7
Zymotic — *see* condition

SECTION 2

Alphabetic Index to Poisoning and External Causes of Adverse Effects of Drugs and Other Chemical Substances

TABLE OF DRUGS AND CHEMICALS

This table contains a classification of drugs and other chemical substances to identify poisoning states and external causes of adverse effects.

Each of the listed substances in the table is assigned a code according to the poisoning classification (960-989). These codes are used when there is a statement of poisoning, overdose, wrong substance given or taken, or intoxication.

The table also contains a listing of external causes of adverse effects. An adverse effect is a pathologic manifestation due to ingestion or exposure to drugs or other chemical substances (e.g., dermatitis, hypersensitivity reaction, aspirin gastritis). The adverse effect is to be identified by the appropriate code found in Section 1, Index to Diseases and Injuries. An external cause code can then be used to identify the circumstances involved. The table headings pertaining to external causes are defined below:

Accidental poisoning (E850-E869) — accidental overdose of drug, wrong substance given or taken, drug taken inadvertently, accidents in the usage of drugs and biologicals in medical and surgical procedures, and to show external causes of poisonings classifiable to 980-989.

Therapeutic use (E930-E949) — a correct substance properly administered in therapeutic or prophylactic dosage as the external cause of adverse effects.

Suicide attempt (E950-E952) — instances in which self-inflicted injuries or poisonings are involved.

Assault (E961-E962) — injury or poisoning inflicted by another person with the intent to injure or kill.

Undetermined (E980-E982) — to be used when the intent of the poisoning or injury cannot be determined whether it was intentional or accidental.

The American Hospital Formulary Service list numbers are included in the table to help classify new drugs not identified in the table by name. The AHFS list numbers are keyed to the continually revised American Hospital Formulary Service (AHFS).* These listings are found in the table under the main term **Drug**.

Excluded from the table are radium and other radioactive substances. The classification of adverse effects and complications pertaining to these substances will be found in Section 1, Index to Diseases and Injuries, and Section 3, Index to External Causes of Injuries.

Although certain substances are indexed with one or more subentries, the majority are listed according to one use or state. It is recognized that many substances may be used in various ways, in medicine and in industry, and may cause adverse effects whatever the state of the agent (solid, liquid, or fumes arising from a liquid). In cases in which the reported data indicates a use or state not in the table, or which is clearly different from the one listed, an attempt should be made to classify the substance in the form which most nearly expresses the reported facts.

*American Hospital Formulary Service, 2 vol. (Washington, D.C.: American Society of Hospital Pharmacists, 1959-)

Substance	Poisoning	External Cause (E-Code) Accident	Therapeutic Use	Suicide Attempt	Assault	Undetermined
1-propanol	980.3	E860.4	—	E950.9	E962.1	E980.9
2-propanol	980.2	E860.3	—	E950.9	E962.1	E980.9
2, 4-D (dichlorophenoxyacetic acid)	989.4	E863.5	—	E950.6	E962.1	E980.7
2, 4-toluene diisocyanate	983.0	E864.0	—	E950.7	E962.1	E980.6
2, 4, 5-T (trichlorophenoxyacetic acid)	989.2	E863.5	—	E950.6	E962.1	E980.7
14-hydroxydihydromorphinone	965.09	E850.2	E935.2	E950.0	E962.0	E980.0
ABOB	961.7	E857	E931.7	E950.4	E962.0	E980.4
Abrus (seed)	988.2	E865.3	—	E950.9	E962.1	E980.9
Absinthe	980.0	E860.1	—	E950.9	E962.1	E980.9
beverage	980.0	E860.0	—	E950.9	E962.1	E980.9
Acenocoumarin, acenocoumarol	964.2	E858.2	E934.2	E950.4	E962.0	E980.4
Acepromazine	969.1	E853.0	E939.1	E950.3	E962.0	E980.3
Acetal	982.8	E862.4	—	E950.9	E962.1	E980.9
Acetaldehyde (vapor)	987.8	E869.8	—	E952.8	E962.2	E982.8
liquid	989.89	E866.8	—	E950.9	E962.1	E980.9
Acetaminophen	965.4	E850.4	E935.4	E950.0	E962.0	E980.0
Acetaminosalol	965.1	E850.3	E935.3	E950.0	E962.0	E980.0
Acetanilid(e)	965.4	E850.4	E935.4	E950.0	E962.0	E980.0
Acetarsol, acetarsone	961.1	E857	E931.1	E950.4	E962.0	E980.4
Acetazolamide	974.2	E858.5	E944.2	E950.4	E962.0	E980.4
Acetic						
acid	983.1	E864.1	—	E950.7	E962.1	E980.6
with sodium acetate (ointment)	976.3	E858.7	E946.3	E950.4	E962.0	E980.4
irrigating solution	974.5	E858.5	E944.5	E950.4	E962.0	E980.4
lotion	976.2	E858.7	E946.2	E950.4	E962.0	E980.4
anhydride	983.1	E864.1	—	E950.7	E962.1	E980.6
ether (vapor)	982.8	E862.4	—	E950.9	E962.1	E980.9
Acetohexamide	962.3	E858.0	E932.3	E950.4	E962.0	E980.4
Acetomenaphthone	964.3	E858.2	E934.3	E950.4	E962.0	E980.4
Acetomorphine	965.01	E850.0	E935.0	E950.0	E962.0	E980.0
Acetone (oils) (vapor)	982.8	E862.4	—	E950.9	E962.1	E980.9
Acetophenazine (maleate)	969.1	E853.0	E939.1	E950.3	E962.0	E980.3
Acetophenetidin	965.4	E850.4	E935.4	E950.0	E962.0	E980.0
Acetophenone	982.0	E862.4	—	E950.9	E962.1	E980.9
Acetorphine	965.09	E850.2	E935.2	E950.0	E962.0	E980.0
Acetosulfone (sodium)	961.8	E857	E931.8	E950.4	E962.0	E980.4
Acetrizoate (sodium)	977.8	E858.8	E947.8	E950.4	E962.0	E980.4
Acetylcarbromal	967.3	E852.2	E937.3	E950.2	E962.0	E980.2
Acetylcholine (chloride)	971.0	E855.3	E941.0	E950.4	E962.0	E980.4
Acetylcysteine	975.5	E858.6	E945.5	E950.4	E962.0	E980.4
Acetyldigitoxin	972.1	E858.3	E942.1	E950.4	E962.0	E980.4
Acetyldihydrocodeine	965.09	E850.2	E935.2	E950.0	E962.0	E980.0
Acetyldihydrocodeinone	965.09	E850.2	E935.2	E950.0	E962.0	E980.0
Acetylene (gas) (industrial)	987.1	E868.1	—	E951.8	E962.2	E981.8
incomplete combustion of — see Carbon monoxide, fuel, utility						
tetrachloride (vapor)	982.3	E862.4	—	E950.9	E962.1	E980.9
Acetyliodosalicylic acid	965.1	E850.3	E935.3	E950.0	E962.0	E980.0
Acetylphenylhydrazine	965.8	E850.8	E935.8	E950.0	E962.0	E980.0
Acetylsalicylic acid	965.1	E850.3	E935.3	E950.0	E962.0	E980.0
Achromycin	960.4	E856	E930.4	E950.4	E962.0	E980.4
ophthalmic preparation	976.5	E858.7	E946.5	E950.4	E962.0	E980.4
topical NEC	976.0	E858.7	E946.0	E950.4	E962.0	E980.4
Acidifying agents	963.2	E858.1	E933.2	E950.4	E962.0	E980.4
Acids (corrosive) NEC	983.1	E864.1	—	E950.7	E962.1	E980.6
Aconite (wild)	988.2	E865.4	—	E950.9	E962.1	E980.9
Aconitine (liniment)	976.8	E858.7	E946.8	E950.4	E962.0	E980.4
Aconitum ferox	988.2	E865.4	—	E950.9	E962.1	E980.9
Acridine	983.0	E864.0	—	E950.7	E962.1	E980.6
vapor	987.8	E869.8	—	E952.8	E962.2	E982.8
Acriflavine	961.9	E857	E931.9	E950.4	E962.0	E980.4
Acrisorcin	976.0	E858.7	E946.0	E950.4	E962.0	E980.4
Acrolein (gas)	987.8	E869.8	—	E952.8	E962.2	E982.8
liquid	989.89	E866.8	—	E950.9	E962.1	E980.9
Actaea spicata	988.2	E865.4	—	E950.9	E962.1	E980.9
Acterol	961.5	E857	E931.5	E950.4	E962.0	E980.4
ACTH	962.4	E858.0	E932.4	E950.4	E962.0	E980.4
Acthar	962.4	E858.0	E932.4	E950.4	E962.0	E980.4
Actinomycin (C) (D)	960.7	E856	E930.7	E950.4	E962.0	E980.4
Adalin (acetyl)	967.3	E852.2	E937.3	E950.2	E962.0	E980.2
Adenosine (phosphate)	977.8	E858.8	E947.8	E950.4	E962.0	E980.4
ADH	962.5	E858.0	E932.5	E950.4	E962.0	E980.4
Adhesives	989.89	E866.6	—	E950.9	E962.1	E980.9
Adicillin	960.0	E856	E930.0	E950.4	E962.0	E980.4
Adiphenine	975.1	E855.6	E945.1	E950.4	E962.0	E980.4
Adjunct, pharmaceutical	977.4	E858.8	E947.4	E950.4	E962.0	E980.4
Adrenal (extract, cortex or medulla) (glucocorticoids) (hormones) (mineralocorticoids)	962.0	E858.0	E932.0	E950.4	E962.0	E980.4
ENT agent	976.6	E858.7	E946.6	E950.4	E962.0	E980.4
ophthalmic preparation	976.5	E858.7	E946.5	E950.4	E962.0	E980.4
topical NEC	976.0	E858.7	E946.0	E950.4	E962.0	E980.4
Adrenalin	971.2	E855.5	E941.2	E950.4	E962.0	E980.4
Adrenergic blocking agents	971.3	E855.6	E941.3	E950.4	E962.0	E980.4
Adrenergics	971.2	E855.5	E941.2	E950.4	E962.0	E980.4
Adrenochrome (derivatives)	972.8	E858.3	E942.8	E950.4	E962.0	E980.4
Adrenocorticotropic hormone	962.4	E858.0	E932.4	E950.4	E962.0	E980.4
Adrenocorticotropin	962.4	E858.0	E932.4	E950.4	E962.0	E980.4
Adriamycin	960.7	E856	E930.7	E950.4	E962.0	E980.4
Aerosol spray — see Sprays						
Aerosporin	960.8	E856	E930.8	E950.4	E962.0	E980.4
ENT agent	976.6	E858.7	E946.6	E950.4	E962.0	E980.4
ophthalmic preparation	976.5	E858.7	E946.5	E950.4	E962.0	E980.4
topical NEC	976.0	E858.7	E946.0	E950.4	E962.0	E980.4
Aethusa cynapium	988.2	E865.4	—	E950.9	E962.1	E980.9
Afghanistan black	969.6	E854.1	E939.6	E950.3	E962.0	E980.3
Aflatoxin	989.7	E865.9	—	E950.9	E962.1	E980.9
African boxwood	988.2	E865.4	—	E950.9	E962.1	E980.9
Agar (-agar)	973.3	E858.4	E943.3	E950.4	E962.0	E980.4
Agricultural agent NEC	989.89	E863.9	—	E950.6	E962.1	E980.7
Agrypnal	967.0	E851	E937.0	E950.1	E962.0	—
Air contaminant(s), source or type not specified	987.9	E869.9	—	E952.9	E962.2	E982.9
specified type — see specific substance						
Akee	988.2	E865.4	—	E950.9	E962.1	E980.9
Akrinol	976.0	E858.7	E946.0	E950.4	E962.0	E980.4
Alantolactone	961.6	E857	E931.6	E950.4	E962.0	E980.4
Albamycin	960.8	E856	E930.8	E950.4	E962.0	E980.4
Albumin (normal human serum)	964.7	E858.2	E934.7	E950.4	E962.0	E980.4
Albuterol	975.7	E858.6	E945.7	E950.4	E962.0	E980.4
Alcohol	980.9	E860.9	—	E950.9	E962.1	E980.9
absolute	980.0	E860.1	—	E950.9	E962.1	E980.9
beverage	980.0	E860.0	E947.8	E950.9	E962.1	E980.9
amyl	980.3	E860.4	—	E950.9	E962.1	E980.9
antifreeze	980.1	E860.2	—	E950.9	E962.1	E980.9
butyl	980.3	E860.4	—	E950.9	E962.1	E980.9
dehydrated	980.0	E860.1	—	E950.9	E862.1	E980.9
beverage	980.0	E860.0	E947.8	E950.9	E962.1	E980.9
denatured	980.0	E860.1	—	E950.9	E962.1	E980.9
deterrents	977.3	E858.8	E947.3	E950.4	E962.0	E980.4
diagnostic (gastric function)	977.8	E858.8	E947.8	E950.4	E962.0	E980.4
ethyl	980.0	E860.1	—	E950.9	E962.1	E980.9
beverage	980.0	E860.0	E947.8	E950.9	E962.1	E980.9
grain	980.0	E860.1	—	E950.9	E962.1	E980.9
beverage	980.0	E860.0	E947.8	E950.9	E962.1	E980.9
industrial	980.9	E860.9	—	E950.9	E962.1	E980.9
isopropyl	980.2	E860.3	—	E950.9	E962.1	E980.9
methyl	980.1	E860.2	—	E950.9	E962.1	E980.9
preparation for consumption	980.0	E860.0	E947.8	E950.9	E962.1	E980.9
propyl	980.3	E860.4	—	E950.9	E962.1	E980.9
secondary	980.2	E860.3	—	E950.9	E962.1	E980.9
radiator	980.1	E860.2	—	E950.9	E962.1	E980.9
rubbing	980.2	E860.3	—	E950.9	E962.1	E980.9
specified type NEC	980.8	E860.8	—	E950.9	E962.1	E980.9
surgical	980.9	E860.9	—	E950.9	E962.1	E980.9
vapor (from any type of alcohol)	987.8	E869.8	—	E952.8	E962.2	E982.8
wood	980.1	E860.2	—	E950.9	E962.1	E980.9
Alcuronium chloride	975.2	E858.6	E945.2	E950.4	E962.0	E980.4
Aldactone	974.4	E858.5	E944.4	E950.4	E962.0	E980.4
Aldicarb	989.3	E863.2	—	E950.6	E962.1	E980.7
Aldomet	972.6	E858.3	E942.6	E950.4	E962.0	E980.4
Aldosterone	962.0	E858.0	E932.0	E950.4	E962.0	E980.4
Aldrin (dust)	989.2	E863.0	—	E950.6	E962.1	E980.7
Algeldrate	973.0	E858.4	E943.0	E950.4	E962.0	E980.4
Alidase	963.4	E858.1	E933.4	E950.4	E962.0	E980.4
Aliphatic thiocyanates	989.0	E866.8	—	E950.9	E962.1	E980.9
Alkaline antiseptic solution (aromatic)	976.6	E858.7	E946.6	E950.4	E962.0	E980.4

		External Cause (E-Code)				
	Poisoning	Accident	Therapeutic Use	Suicide Attempt	Assault	Undetermined
Alkalinizing agents (medicinal)	963.3	E858.1	E933.3	E950.4	E962.0	E980.4
Alkalis, caustic	983.2	E864.2	—	E950.7	E962.1	E980.6
Alkalizing agents (medicinal)	963.3	E858.1	E933.3	E950.4	E962.0	E980.4
Alka-seltzer	965.1	E850.3	E935.3	E950.0	E962.0	E980.0
Alkavervir	972.6	E858.3	E942.6	E950.4	E962.0	E980.4
Allegron	969.0	E854.0	E939.0	E950.3	E962.0	E980.3
Alleve — Naproxen						
Allobarbital, allobarbitone	967.0	E851	E937.0	E950.1	E962.0	E980.1
Allopurinol	974.7	E858.5	E944.7	E950.4	E962.0	E980.4
Allylestrenol	962.2	E858.0	E932.2	E950.4	E962.0	E980.4
Allylisopropylacetylurea	967.8	E852.8	E937.8	E950.2	E962.0	E980.2
Allylisopropylmalonylurea	967.0	E851	E937.0	E950.1	E962.0	E980.1
Allyltribromide	967.3	E852.2	E937.3	E950.2	E962.0	E980.2
Aloe, aloes, aloin	973.1	E858.4	E943.1	E950.4	E962.0	E980.4
Alosetron	973.8	E858.4	E943.8	E950.4	E962.0	E980.4
Aloxidone	966.0	E855.0	E936.0	E950.4	E962.0	E980.4
Aloxiprin	965.1	E850.3	E935.3	E950.0	E962.0	E980.0
Alpha-1 blockers	971.3	E855.6	E941.3	E950.4	E962.0	E980.4
Alpha amylase	963.4	E858.1	E933.4	E950.4	E962.0	E980.4
Alphaprodine (hydrochloride)	965.09	E850.2	E935.2	E950.0	E962.0	E980.0
Alpha tocopherol	963.5	E858.1	E933.5	E950.4	E962.0	E980.4
Alseroxylon	972.6	E858.3	E942.6	E950.4	E962.0	E980.4
Alum (ammonium) (potassium)	983.2	E864.2	—	E950.7	E962.1	E980.6
medicinal (astringent) NEC	976.2	E858.7	E946.2	E950.4	E962.0	E980.4
Aluminium, aluminum (gel) (hydroxide)	973.0	E858.4	E943.0	E950.4	E962.0	E980.4
acetate solution	976.2	E858.7	E946.2	E950.4	E962.0	E980.4
aspirin	965.1	E850.3	E935.3	E950.0	E962.0	E980.0
carbonate	973.0	E858.4	E943.0	E950.4	E962.0	E980.4
glycinate	973.0	E858.4	E943.0	E950.4	E962.0	E980.4
nicotinate	972.2	E858.3	E942.2	E950.4	E962.0	E980.4
ointment (surgical) (topical)	976.3	E858.7	E946.3	E950.4	E962.0	E980.4
phosphate	973.0	E858.4	E943.0	E950.4	E962.0	E980.4
subacetate	976.2	E858.7	E946.2	E950.4	E962.0	E980.4
topical NEC	976.3	E858.7	E946.3	E950.4	E962.0	E980.4
Alurate	967.0	E851	E937.0	E950.1	E962.0	E980.1
Alverine (citrate)	975.1	E858.6	E945.1	E950.4	E962.0	E980.4
Alvodine	965.09	E850.2	E935.2	E950.0	E962.0	E980.0
Amanita phalloides	988.1	E865.5	—	E950.9	E962.1	E980.9
Amantadine (hydrochloride)	966.4	E855.0	E936.4	E950.4	E962.0	E980.4
Ambazone	961.9	E857	E931.9	E950.4	E962.0	E980.4
Ambenonium	971.0	E855.3	E941.0	E950.4	E962.0	E980.4
Ambutonium bromide	971.1	E855.4	E941.1	E950.4	E962.0	E980.4
Ametazole	977.8	E858.8	E947.8	E950.4	E962.0	E980.4
Amethocaine (infiltration) (topical)	968.5	E855.2	E938.5	E950.4	E962.0	E980.4
nerve block (peripheral) (plexus)	968.6	E855.2	E938.6	E950.4	E962.0	E980.4
spinal	968.7	E855.2	E938.7	E950.4	E962.0	E980.4
Amethopterin	963.1	E858.1	E933.1	E950.4	E962.0	E980.4
Amfepramone	977.0	E858.8	E947.0	E950.4	E962.0	E980.4
Amidon	965.02	E850.1	E935.1	E950.0	E962.0	E980.0
Amidopyrine	965.5	E850.5	E935.5	E950.0	E962.0	E980.0
Aminacrine	976.0	E858.7	E946.0	E950.4	E962.0	E980.4
Aminitrozole	961.5	E857	E931.5	E950.4	E962.0	E980.4
Aminoacetic acid	974.5	E858.5	E944.5	E950.4	E962.0	E980.4
Amino acids	974.5	E858.5	E944.5	E950.4	E962.0	E980.4
Aminocaproic acid	964.4	E858.2	E934.4	E950.4	E962.0	E980.4
Aminoethylisothiourium	963.8	E858.1	E933.8	E950.4	E962.0	E980.4
Aminoglutethimide	966.3	E855.0	E936.3	E950.4	E962.0	E980.4
Aminometradine	974.3	E858.5	E944.3	E950.4	E962.0	E980.4
Aminopentamide	971.1	E855.4	E941.1	E950.4	E962.0	E980.4
Aminophenazone	965.5	E850.5	E935.5	E950.0	E962.0	E980.0
Aminophenol	983.0	E864.0	—	E950.7	E962.1	E980.6
Aminophenylpyridone	969.5	E853.8	E939.5	E950.3	E962.0	E980.3
Aminophyllin	975.7	E858.6	E945.7	E950.4	E962.0	E980.4
Aminopterin	963.1	E858.1	E933.1	E950.4	E962.0	E980.4
Aminopyrine	965.5	E850.5	E935.5	E950.0	E962.0	E980.0
Aminosalicylic acid	961.8	E857	E931.8	E950.4	E962.0	E980.4
Amiphenazole	970.1	E854.3	E940.1	E950.4	E962.0	E980.4
Amiquinsin	972.6	E858.3	E942.6	E950.4	E962.0	E980.4
Amisometradine	974.3	E858.5	E944.3	E950.4	E962.0	E980.4
Amitriptyline	969.0	E854.0	E939.0	E950.3	E962.0	E980.3
Ammonia (fumes) (gas) (vapor)	987.8	E869.8	—	E952.8	E962.2	E982.8
liquid (household) NEC	983.2	E861.4	—	E950.7	E962.1	E980.6
Ammonia — *continued*						
spirit, aromatic	970.8	E854.3	E940.8	E950.4	E962.0	E980.4
Ammoniated mercury	976.0	E858.7	E946.0	E950.4	E962.0	E980.4
Ammonium						
carbonate	983.2	E864.2	—	E950.7	E962.1	E980.6
chloride (acidifying agent)	963.2	E858.1	E933.2	E950.4	E962.0	E980.4
expectorant	975.5	E858.6	E945.5	E950.4	E962.0	E980.4
compounds (household) NEC	983.2	E861.4	—	E950.7	E962.1	E980.6
fumes (any usage)	987.8	E869.8	—	E952.8	E962.2	E982.8
industrial	983.2	E864.2	—	E950.7	E962.1	E980.6
ichthyosulfonate	976.4	E858.7	E946.4	E950.4	E962.0	E980.4
mandelate	961.9	E857	E931.9	E950.4	E962.0	E980.4
Amobarbital	967.0	E851	E937.0	E950.1	E962.0	E980.1
Amodiaquin(e)	961.4	E857	E931.4	E950.4	E962.0	E980.4
Amopyroquin(e)	961.4	E857	E931.4	E950.4	E962.0	E980.4
Amphenidone	969.5	E853.8	E939.5	E950.3	E962.0	E980.3
Amphetamine	969.7	E854.2	E939.7	E950.3	E962.0	E980.3
Amphomycin	960.8	E856	E930.8	E950.4	E962.0	E980.4
Amphotericin B	960.1	E856	E930.1	E950.4	E962.0	E980.4
topical	976.0	E858.7	E946.0	E950.4	E962.0	E980.4
Ampicillin	960.0	E856	E930.0	E950.4	E962.0	E980.4
Amprotropine	971.1	E855.4	E941.1	E950.4	E962.0	E980.4
Amygdalin	977.8	E858.8	E947.8	E950.4	E962.0	E980.4
Amyl						
acetate (vapor)	982.8	E862.4	—	E950.9	E962.1	E980.9
alcohol	980.3	E860.4	—	E950.9	E962.1	E980.9
nitrite (medicinal)	972.4	E858.3	E942.4	E950.4	E962.0	E980.4
Amylase (alpha)	963.4	E858.1	E933.4	E950.4	E962.0	E980.4
Amylene hydrate	980.8	E860.8	—	E950.9	E962.1	E980.9
Amylobarbitone	967.0	E851	E937.0	E950.1	E962.0	E980.1
Amylocaine	968.9	E855.2	E938.9	E950.4	E962.0	E980.4
infiltration (subcutaneous)	968.5	E855.2	E938.5	E950.4	E962.0	E980.4
nerve block (peripheral) (plexus)	968.6	E855.2	E938.6	E950.4	E962.0	E980.4
spinal	968.7	E855.2	E938.7	E950.4	E962.0	E980.4
topical (surface)	968.5	E855.2	E938.5	E950.4	E962.0	E980.4
Amytal (sodium)	967.0	E851	E937.0	E950.1	E962.0	E980.1
Analeptics	970.0	E854.3	E940.0	E950.4	E962.0	E980.4
Analgesics	965.9	E850.9	E935.9	E950.0	E962.0	E980.0
aromatic NEC	965.4	E850.4	E935.4	E950.0	E962.0	E980.0
non-narcotic NEC	965.7	E850.7	E935.7	E950.0	E962.0	E980.0
specified NEC	965.8	E850.8	E935.8	E950.0	E962.0	E980.0
Anamirta cocculus	988.2	E865.3	—	E950.9	E962.1	E980.9
Ancillin	960.0	E856	E930.0	E950.4	E962.0	E980.4
Androgens (anabolic congeners)	962.1	E858.0	E932.1	E950.4	E962.0	E980.4
Androstalone	962.1	E858.0	E932.1	E950.4	E962.0	E980.4
Androsterone	962.1	E858.0	E932.1	E950.4	E962.0	E980.4
Anemone pulsatilla	988.2	E865.4	—	E950.9	E962.1	E980.9
Anesthesia, anesthetic (general) NEC	968.4	E855.1	E938.4	E950.4	E962.0	E980.4
block (nerve) (plexus)	968.6	E855.2	E938.6	E950.4	E962.0	E980.4
gaseous NEC	968.2	E855.1	E938.2	E950.4	E962.0	E980.4
halogenated hydrocarbon derivatives NEC	968.2	E855.1	E938.2	E950.4	E962.0	E980.4
infiltration (intradermal) (subcutaneous) (submucosal)	968.5	E855.2	E938.5	E950.4	E962.0	E980.4
intravenous	968.3	E855.1	E938.3	E950.4	E962.0	E980.4
local NEC	968.9	E855.2	E938.9	E950.4	E962.0	E980.4
nerve blocking (peripheral) (plexus)	968.6	E855.2	E938.6	E950.4	E962.0	E980.4
rectal NEC	968.3	E855.1	E938.3	E950.4	E962.0	E980.4
spinal	968.7	E855.2	E938.7	E950.4	E962.0	E980.4
surface	968.5	E855.2	E938.5	E950.4	E962.0	E980.4
topical	968.5	E855.2	E938.5	E950.4	E962.0	E980.4
Aneurine	963.5	E858.1	E933.5	E950.4	E962.0	E980.4
Anginine — *see* Glyceryl trinitrate						
Angio-Conray	977.8	E858.8	E947.8	E950.4	E962.0	E980.4
Angiotensin	971.2	E855.5	E941.2	E950.4	E962.0	E980.4
Anhydrohydroxyprogesterone	962.2	E858.0	E932.2	E950.4	E962.0	E980.4
Anhydron	974.3	E858.5	E944.3	E950.4	E962.0	E980.4
Anileridine	965.09	E850.2	E935.2	E950.0	E962.0	E980.0
Aniline (dye) (liquid)	983.0	E864.0	—	E950.7	E962.1	E980.6
analgesic	965.4	E850.4	E935.4	E950.0	E962.0	E980.0
derivatives, therapeutic NEC	965.4	E850.4	E935.4	E950.0	E962.0	E980.0
vapor	987.8	E869.8	—	E952.8	E962.2	E982.8
Aniscoropine	971.1	E855.4	E941.1	E950.4	E962.0	E980.4

Substance	Poisoning	External Cause (E-Code): Accident	Therapeutic Use	Suicide Attempt	Assault	Undetermined
Anisindione	964.2	E858.2	E934.2	E950.4	E962.0	E980.4
Anorexic agents	977.0	E858.8	E947.0	E950.4	E962.0	E980.4
Ant (bite) (sting)	—	E905.5	—	E950.9	E962.1	E980.9
Antabuse	977.3	E858.8	E947.3	E950.4	E962.0	E980.4
Antacids	973.0	E858.4	E943.0	E950.4	E962.0	E980.4
Antazoline	963.0	E858.1	E933.0	E950.4	E962.0	E980.4
Anthralin	976.4	E858.7	E946.4	E950.4	E962.0	E980.4
Anthramycin	960.7	E856	E930.7	E950.4	E962.0	E980.4
Antiadrenergics	971.3	E855.6	E941.3	E950.4	E962.0	E980.4
Antiallergic agents	963.0	E858.1	E933.0	E950.4	E962.0	E980.4
Antianemic agents NEC	964.1	E858.2	E934.1	E950.4	E962.0	E980.4
Antiaris toxicaria	988.2	E865.4	—	E950.9	E962.1	E980.9
Antiarteriosclerotic agents	972.2	E858.3	E942.2	E950.4	E962.0	E980.4
Antiasthmatics	975.7	E858.6	E945.7	E950.4	E962.0	E980.4
Antibiotics	960.9	E856	E930.9	E950.4	E962.0	E980.4
— antifungal	960.1	E856	E930.1	E950.4	E962.0	E980.4
— antimycobacterial	960.6	E856	E930.6	E950.4	E962.0	E980.4
— antineoplastic	960.7	E856	E930.7	E950.4	E962.0	E980.4
— cephalosporin (group)	960.5	E856	E930.5	E950.4	E962.0	E980.4
— chloramphenicol (group)	960.2	E856	E930.2	E950.4	E962.0	E980.4
— macrolides	960.3	E856	E930.3	E950.4	E962.0	E980.4
— specified NEC	960.8	E856	E930.8	E950.4	E962.0	E980.4
— tetracycline (group)	960.4	E856	E930.4	E950.4	E962.0	E980.4
Anticancer agents NEC	963.1	E858.1	E933.1	E950.4	E962.0	E980.4
— antibiotics	960.7	E856	E930.7	E950.4	E962.0	E980.4
Anticholinergics	971.1	E855.4	E941.1	E950.4	E962.0	E980.4
Anticholinesterase (organophosphorus) (reversible)	971.0	E855.3	E941.0	E950.4	E962.0	E980.4
Anticoagulants	964.2	E858.2	E934.2	E950.4	E962.0	E980.4
— antagonists	964.5	E858.2	E934.5	E950.4	E962.0	E980.4
Anti-common cold agents NEC	975.6	E858.6	E945.6	E950.4	E962.0	E980.4
Anticonvulsants NEC	966.3	E855.0	E936.3	E950.4	E962.0	E980.4
Antidepressants	969.0	E854.0	E939.0	E950.3	E962.0	E980.3
Antidiabetic agents	962.3	E858.0	E932.3	E950.4	E962.0	E980.4
Antidiarrheal agents	973.5	E858.4	E943.5	E950.4	E962.0	E980.4
Antidiuretic hormone	962.5	E858.0	E932.5	E950.4	E962.0	E980.4
Antidotes NEC	977.2	E858.8	E947.2	E950.4	E962.0	E980.4
Antiemetic agents	963.0	E858.1	E933.0	E950.4	E962.0	E980.4
Antiepilepsy agent NEC	966.3	E855.0	E936.3	E950.4	E962.0	E980.4
Antifertility pills	962.2	E858.0	E932.2	E950.4	E962.0	E980.4
Antiflatulents	973.8	E858.4	E943.8	E950.4	E962.0	E980.4
Antifreeze	989.89	E866.8	—	E950.9	E962.1	E980.9
— alcohol	980.1	E860.2	—	E950.9	E962.1	E980.9
— ethylene glycol	982.8	E862.4	—	E950.9	E962.1	E980.9
Antifungals (nonmedicinal) (sprays)	989.4	E863.6	—	E950.6	E962.1	E980.7
— medicinal NEC	961.9	E857	E931.9	E950.4	E962.0	E980.4
— — antibiotic	960.1	E856	E930.1	E950.4	E962.0	E980.4
— — topical	976.0	E858.7	E946.0	E950.4	E962.0	E980.4
Antigastric secretion agents	973.0	E858.4	E943.0	E950.4	E962.0	E980.4
Antihelmintics	961.6	E857	E931.6	E950.4	E962.0	E980.4
Antihemophilic factor (human)	964.7	E858.2	E934.7	E950.4	E962.0	E980.4
Antihistamine	963.0	E858.1	E933.0	E950.4	E962.0	E980.4
Antihypertensive agents NEC	972.6	E858.3	E942.6	E950.4	E962.0	E980.4
Anti-infectives NEC	961.9	E857	E931.9	E950.4	E962.0	E980.4
— antibiotics	960.9	E856	E930.9	E950.4	E962.0	E980.4
— — specified NEC	960.8	E856	E930.8	E950.4	E962.0	E980.4
— antihelmintic	961.6	E857	E931.6	E950.4	E962.0	E980.4
— antimalarial	961.4	E857	E931.4	E950.4	E962.0	E980.4
— antimycobacterial NEC	961.8	E857	E931.8	E950.4	E962.0	E980.4
— — antibiotics	960.6	E856	E930.6	E950.4	E962.0	E980.4
— antiprotozoal NEC	961.5	E857	E931.5	E950.4	E962.0	—
— — blood	961.4	E857	E931.4	E950.4	E962.0	E980.4
— antiviral	961.7	E857	E931.7	E950.4	E962.0	E980.4
— arsenical	961.1	E857	E931.1	E950.4	E962.0	E980.4
— ENT agents	976.6	E858.7	E946.6	E950.4	E962.0	E980.4
— heavy metals NEC	961.2	E857	E931.2	E950.4	E962.0	E980.4
— local	976.0	E858.7	E946.0	E950.4	E962.0	E980.4
— ophthalmic preparation	976.5	E858.7	E946.5	E950.4	E962.0	E980.4
— topical NEC	976.0	E858.7	E946.0	E950.4	E962.0	E980.4
Anti-inflammatory agents (topical)	976.0	E858.7	E946.0	E950.4	E962.0	E980.4
Antiknock (tetraethyl lead)	984.1	E862.1	—	E950.9	—	E980.9
Antilipemics	972.2	E858.3	E942.2	E950.4	E962.0	E980.4
Antimalarials	961.4	E857	E931.4	E950.4	E962.0	E980.4
Antimony (compounds) (vapor) NEC	985.4	E866.2	—	E950.9	E962.1	E980.9
— anti-infectives	961.2	E857	E931.2	E950.4	E962.0	E980.4
— pesticides (vapor)	985.4	E863.4	—	E950.6	E962.2	E980.7
— potassium tartrate	961.2	E857	E931.2	E950.4	E962.0	E980.4
— tartrated	961.2	E857	E931.2	E950.4	E962.0	E980.4
Antimuscarinic agents	971.1	E855.4	E941.1	E950.4	E962.0	E980.4
Antimycobacterials NEC	961.8	E857	E931.8	E950.4	E962.0	E980.4
— antibiotics	960.6	E856	E930.6	E950.4	E962.0	E980.4
Antineoplastic agents	963.1	E858.1	E933.1	E950.4	E962.0	E980.4
— antibiotics	960.7	E856	E930.7	E950.4	E962.0	E980.4
Anti-Parkinsonism agents	966.4	E855.0	E936.4	E950.4	E962.0	E980.4
Antiphlogistics	965.69	E850.6	E935.6	E950.0	E962.0	E980.0
Antiprotozoals NEC	961.5	E857	E931.5	E950.4	E962.0	E980.4
— blood	961.4	E857	E931.4	E950.4	E962.0	E980.4
Antipruritics (local)	976.1	E858.7	E946.1	E950.4	E962.0	E980.4
Antipsychotic agents NEC	969.3	E853.8	E939.3	E950.3	E962.0	E980.3
Antipyretics	965.9	E850.9	E935.9	E950.0	E962.0	E980.0
— specified NEC	965.8	E850.8	E935.8	E950.0	E962.0	E980.0
Antipyrine	965.5	E850.5	E935.5	E950.0	E962.0	E980.0
Antirabies serum (equine)	979.9	E858.8	E949.9	E950.4	E962.0	E980.4
Antirheumatics	965.69	E850.6	E935.6	E950.0	E962.0	E980.0
Antiseborrheics	976.4	E858.7	E946.4	E950.4	E962.0	E980.4
Antiseptics (external) (medicinal)	976.0	E858.7	E946.0	E950.4	E962.0	E980.4
Antistine	963.0	E858.1	E933.0	E950.4	E962.0	E980.4
Antithyroid agents	962.8	E858.0	E932.8	E950.4	E962.0	E980.4
Antitoxin, any	979.9	E858.8	E949.9	E950.4	E962.0	E980.4
Antituberculars	961.8	E857	E931.8	E950.4	E962.0	E980.4
— antibiotics	960.6	E856	E930.6	E950.4	E962.0	E980.4
Antitussives	975.4	E858.6	E945.4	E950.4	E962.0	E980.4
Antivaricose agents (sclerosing)	972.7	E858.3	E942.7	E950.4	E962.0	E980.4
Antivenin (crotaline) (spider-bite)	979.9	E858.8	E949.9	E950.4	E962.0	E980.4
Antivert	963.0	E858.1	E933.0	E950.4	E962.0	E980.4
Antivirals NEC	961.7	E857	E931.7	E950.4	E962.0	E980.4
Ant poisons — *see* Pesticides						
Antrol	989.4	E863.4	—	E950.6	E962.1	E980.7
— fungicide	989.4	E863.6	—	E950.6	E962.1	E980.7
Apomorphine hydrochloride (emetic)	973.6	E858.4	E943.6	E950.4	E962.0	E980.4
Appetite depressants, central	977.0	E858.8	E947.0	E950.4	E962.0	E980.4
Apresoline	972.6	E858.3	E942.6	E950.4	E962.0	E980.4
Aprobarbital, aprobarbitone	967.0	E851	E937.0	E950.1	E962.0	E980.1
Apronalide	967.8	E852.8	E937.8	E950.2	E962.0	E980.2
Aqua fortis	983.1	E864.1	—	E950.7	E962.1	E980.6
Arachis oil (topical)	976.3	E858.7	E946.3	E950.4	E962.0	E980.4
— cathartic	973.2	E858.4	E943.2	E950.4	E962.0	E980.4
Aralen	961.4	E857	E931.4	E950.4	E962.0	E980.4
Arginine salts	974.5	E858.5	E944.5	E950.4	E962.0	E980.4
Argyrol	976.0	E858.7	E946.0	E950.4	E962.0	E980.4
— ENT agent	976.6	E858.7	E946.6	E950.4	E962.0	E980.4
— ophthalmic preparation	976.5	E858.7	E946.5	E950.4	E962.0	E980.4
Aristocort	962.0	E858.0	E932.0	E950.4	E962.0	E980.4
— ENT agent	976.6	E858.7	E946.6	E950.4	E962.0	E980.4
— ophthalmic preparation	976.5	E858.7	E946.5	E950.4	E962.0	E980.4
— topical NEC	976.0	E858.7	E946.0	E950.4	E962.0	E980.4
Aromatics, corrosive	983.0	E864.0	—	E950.7	E962.1	E980.6
— disinfectants	983.0	E861.4	—	E950.7	E962.1	E980.6
Arsenate of lead (insecticide)	985.1	E863.4	—	E950.8	E962.1	E980.8
— herbicide	985.1	E863.5	—	E950.8	E962.1	E980.8
Arsenic, arsenicals (compounds) (dust) (fumes) (vapor) NEC	985.1	E866.3	—	E950.8	E962.1	E980.8
— anti-infectives	961.1	E857	E931.1	E950.4	E962.0	E980.4
— pesticide (dust) (fumes)	985.1	E863.4	—	E950.8	E962.1	E980.8
Arsine (gas)	985.1	E866.3	—	E950.8	E962.1	E980.8
Arsphenamine (silver)	961.1	E857	E931.1	E950.4	E962.0	E980.4
Arsthinol	961.1	E857	E931.1	E950.4	E962.0	E980.4
Artane	971.1	E855.4	E941.1	E950.4	E962.0	E980.4
Arthropod (venomous) NEC	989.5	E905.5	—	E950.9	E962.1	E980.9
Asbestos	989.81	E866.8	—	E950.9	E962.1	E980.9
Ascaridole	961.6	E857	E931.6	E950.4	E962.0	E980.4
Ascorbic acid	963.5	E858.1	E933.5	E950.4	E962.0	E980.4
Asiaticoside	976.0	E858.7	E946.0	E950.4	E962.0	E980.4
Aspidium (oleoresin)	961.6	E857	E931.6	E950.4	E962.0	E980.4

		External Cause (E-Code)				
	Poisoning	Accident	Therapeutic Use	Suicide Attempt	Assault	Undetermined
Aspirin	965.1	E850.3	E935.3	E950.0	E962.0	E980.0
Astringents (local)	976.2	E858.7	E946.2	E950.4	E962.0	E980.4
Atabrine	961.3	E857	E931.3	E950.4	E962.0	E980.4
Ataractics	969.5	E853.8	E939.5	E950.3	E962.0	E980.3
Atonia drug, intestinal	973.3	E858.4	E943.3	E950.4	E962.0	E980.4
Atophan	974.7	E858.5	E944.7	E950.4	E962.0	E980.4
Atropine	971.1	E855.4	E941.1	E950.4	E962.0	E980.4
Attapulgite	973.5	E858.4	E943.5	E950.4	E962.0	E980.4
Attenuvax	979.4	E858.8	E949.4	E950.4	E962.0	E980.4
Aureomycin	960.4	E856	E930.4	E950.4	E962.0	E980.4
ophthalmic preparation	976.5	E858.7	E946.5	E950.4	E962.0	E980.4
topical NEC	976.0	E858.7	E946.0	E950.4	E962.0	E980.4
Aurothioglucose	965.69	E850.6	E935.6	E950.0	E962.0	E980.0
Aurothioglycanide	965.69	E850.6	E935.6	E950.0	E962.0	E980.0
Aurothiomalate	965.69	E850.6	E935.6	E950.0	E962.0	E980.0
Automobile fuel	981	E862.1	—	E950.9	E962.1	E980.9
Autonomic nervous system agents NEC	971.9	E855.9	E941.9	E950.4	E962.0	E980.4
Avlosulfon	961.8	E857	E931.8	E950.4	E962.0	E980.4
Avomine	967.8	E852.8	E937.8	E950.2	E962.0	E980.2
Azacyclonol	969.5	E853.8	E939.5	E950.3	E962.0	E980.3
Azapetine	971.3	E855.6	E941.3	E950.4	E962.0	E980.4
Azaribine	963.1	E858.1	E933.1	E950.4	E962.0	E980.4
Azaserine	960.7	E856	E930.7	E950.4	E962.0	E980.4
Azathioprine	963.1	E858.1	E933.1	E950.4	E962.0	E980.4
Azosulfamide	961.0	E857	E931.0	E950.4	E962.0	E980.4
Azulfidine	961.0	E857	E931.0	E950.4	E962.0	E980.4
Azuresin	977.8	E858.8	E947.8	E950.4	E962.0	E980.4
Bacimycin	976.0	E858.7	E946.0	E950.4	E962.0	E980.4
ophthalmic preparation	976.5	E858.7	E946.5	E950.4	E962.0	E980.4
Bacitracin	960.8	E856	E930.8	E950.4	E962.0	E980.4
ENT agent	976.6	E858.7	E946.6	E950.4	E962.0	E980.4
ophthalmic preparation	976.5	E858.7	E946.5	E950.4	E962.0	E980.4
topical NEC	976.0	E858.7	E946.0	E950.4	E962.0	E980.4
Baking soda	963.3	E858.1	E933.3	E950.4	E962.0	E980.4
BAL	963.8	E858.1	E933.8	E950.4	E962.0	E980.4
Bamethan (sulfate)	972.5	E858.3	E942.5	E950.4	E962.0	E980.4
Bamipine	963.0	E858.1	E933.0	E950.4	E962.0	E980.4
Baneberry	988.2	E865.4	—	E950.9	E962.1	E980.9
Banewort	988.2	E865.4	—	E950.9	E962.1	E980.9
Barbenyl	967.0	E851	E937.0	E950.1	E962.0	E980.1
Barbital, barbitone	967.0	E851	E937.0	E950.1	E962.0	E980.1
Barbiturates, barbituric acid	967.0	E851	E937.0	E950.1	E962.0	E980.1
anesthetic (intravenous)	968.3	E855.1	E938.3	E950.4	E962.0	E980.4
Barium (carbonate) (chloride) (sulfate)	985.8	E866.4	—	E950.9	E962.1	E980.9
diagnostic agent	977.8	E858.8	E947.8	E950.4	E962.0	E980.4
pesticide	985.8	E863.4	—	E950.6	E962.1	E980.7
rodenticide	985.8	E863.7	—	E950.6	E962.1	E980.7
Barrier cream	976.3	E858.7	E946.3	E950.4	E962.0	E980.4
Battery acid or fluid	983.1	E864.1	—	E950.7	E962.1	E980.6
Bay rum	980.8	E860.8	—	E950.9	E962.1	E980.9
BCG vaccine	978.0	E858.8	E948.0	E950.4	E962.0	E980.4
Bearsfoot	988.2	E865.4	—	E950.9	E962.1	E980.9
Beclamide	966.3	E855.0	E936.3	E950.4	E962.0	E980.4
Bee (sting) (venom)	989.5	E905.3	—	E950.9	E962.1	E980.9
Belladonna (alkaloids)	971.1	E855.4	E941.1	E950.4	E962.0	E980.4
Bemegride	970.0	E854.3	E940.0	E950.4	E962.0	E980.4
Benactyzine	969.8	E855.8	E939.8	E950.3	E962.0	E980.3
Benadryl	963.0	E858.1	E933.0	E950.4	E962.0	E980.4
Bendrofluazide	974.3	E858.5	E944.3	E950.4	E962.0	E980.4
Bendroflumethiazide	974.3	E858.5	E944.3	E950.4	E962.0	E980.4
Benemid	974.7	E858.5	E944.7	E950.4	E962.0	E980.4
Benethamine penicillin G	960.0	E856	E930.0	E950.4	E962.0	E980.4
Benisone	976.0	E858.7	E946.0	E950.4	E962.0	E980.4
Benoquin	976.8	E858.7	E946.8	E950.4	E962.0	E980.4
Benoxinate	968.5	E855.2	E938.5	E950.4	E962.0	E980.4
Bentonite	976.3	E858.7	E946.3	E950.4	E962.0	E980.4
Benzalkonium (chloride)	976.0	E858.7	E946.0	E950.4	E962.0	E980.4
ophthalmic preparation	976.5	E858.7	E946.5	E950.4	E962.0	E980.4
Benzamidosalicylate (calcium)	961.8	E857	E931.8	E950.4	E962.0	E980.4
Benzathine penicillin	960.0	E856	E930.0	E950.4	E962.0	E980.4
Benzcarbimine	963.1	E858.1	E933.1	E950.4	E962.0	E980.4
Benzedrex	971.2	E855.5	E941.2	E950.4	E962.0	E980.4
Benzedrine (amphetamine)	969.7	E854.2	E939.7	E950.3	E962.0	E980.3
Benzene (acetyl) (dimethyl) (methyl) (solvent) (vapor)	982.0	E862.4	—	E950.9	E962.1	E980.9
hexachloride (gamma) (insecticide) (vapor)	989.2	E863.0	—	E950.6	E962.1	E980.7

		External Cause (E-Code)				
	Poisoning	Accident	Therapeutic Use	Suicide Attempt	Assault	Undetermined
Benzethonium	976.0	E858.7	E946.0	E950.4	E962.0	E980.4
Benzhexol (chloride)	966.4	E855.0	E936.4	E950.4	E962.0	E980.4
Benzilonium	971.1	E855.4	E941.1	E950.4	E962.0	E980.4
Benzin(e) — *see* Ligroin						
Benziodarone	972.4	E858.3	E942.4	E950.4	E962.0	E980.4
Benzocaine	968.5	E855.2	E938.5	E950.4	E962.0	E980.4
Benzodiapin	969.4	E853.2	E939.4	E950.3	E962.0	E980.3
Benzodiazepines (tranquilizers) NEC	969.4	E853.2	E939.4	E950.3	E962.0	E980.3
Benzoic acid (with salicylic acid) (anti-infective)	976.0	E858.7	E946.0	E950.4	E962.0	E980.4
Benzoin	976.3	E858.7	E946.3	E950.4	E962.0	E980.4
Benzol (vapor)	982.0	E862.4	—	E950.9	E962.1	E980.9
Benzomorphan	965.09	E850.2	E935.2	E950.0	E962.0	E980.0
Benzonatate	975.4	E858.6	E945.4	E950.4	E962.0	E980.4
Benzothiadiazides	974.3	E858.5	E944.3	E950.4	E962.0	E980.4
Benzoylpas	961.8	E857	E931.8	E950.4	E962.0	E980.4
Benzperidol	969.5	E853.8	E939.5	E950.3	E962.0	E980.3
Benzphetamine	977.0	E858.8	E947.0	E950.4	E962.0	E980.4
Benzpyrinium	971.0	E855.3	E941.0	E950.4	E962.0	E980.4
Benzquinamide	963.0	E858.1	E933.0	E950.4	E962.0	E980.4
Benzthiazide	974.3	E858.5	E944.3	E950.4	E962.0	E980.4
Benztropine	971.1	E855.4	E941.1	E950.4	E962.0	E980.4
Benzyl						
acetate	982.8	E862.4	—	E950.9	E962.1	E980.9
benzoate (anti-infective)	976.0	E858.7	E946.0	E950.4	E962.0	E980.4
morphine	965.09	E850.2	E935.2	E950.0	E962.0	E980.0
penicillin	960.0	E856	E930.0	E950.4	E962.0	E980.4
Bephenium hydroxynapthoate	961.6	E857	E931.6	E950.4	E962.0	E980.4
Bergamot oil	989.89	E866.8	—	E950.9	E962.1	E980.9
Berries, poisonous	988.2	E865.3	—	E950.9	E962.1	E980.9
Beryllium (compounds) (fumes)	985.3	E866.4	—	E950.9	E962.1	E980.9
Beta-carotene	976.3	E858.7	E946.3	E950.4	E962.0	E980.4
Beta-Chlor	967.1	E852.0	E937.1	E950.2	E962.0	E980.2
Betamethasone	962.0	E858.0	E932.0	E950.4	E962.0	E980.4
topical	976.0	E858.7	E946.0	E950.4	E962.0	E980.4
Betazole	977.8	E858.8	E947.8	E950.4	E962.0	E980.4
Bethanechol	971.0	E855.3	E941.0	E950.4	E962.0	E980.4
Bethanidine	972.6	E858.3	E942.6	E950.4	E962.0	E980.4
Betula oil	976.3	E858.7	E946.3	E950.4	E962.0	E980.4
Bhang	969.6	E854.1	E939.6	E950.3	E962.0	E980.3
Bialamicol	961.5	E857	E931.5	E950.4	E962.0	E980.4
Bichloride of mercury — *see* Mercury, chloride						
Bichromates (calcium) (crystals) (potassium) (sodium)	983.9	E864.3	—	E950.7	E962.1	E980.6
fumes	987.8	E869.8	—	E952.8	E962.2	E982.8
Biguanide derivatives, oral	962.3	E858.0	E932.3	E950.4	E962.0	E980.4
Biligrafin	977.8	E858.8	E947.8	E950.4	E962.0	E980.4
Bilopaque	977.8	E858.8	E947.8	E950.4	E962.0	E980.4
Bioflavonoids	972.8	E858.3	E942.8	E950.4	E962.0	E980.4
Biological substance NEC	979.9	E858.8	E949.9	E950.4	E962.0	E980.4
Biperiden	966.4	E855.0	E936.4	E950.4	E962.0	E980.4
Bisacodyl	973.1	E858.4	E943.1	E950.4	E962.0	E980.4
Bishydroxycoumarin	964.2	E858.2	E934.2	E950.4	E962.0	E980.4
Bismarsen	961.1	E857	E931.1	E950.4	E962.0	E980.4
Bismuth (compounds) NEC	985.8	E866.4	—	E950.9	E962.1	E980.9
anti-infectives	961.2	E857	E931.2	E950.4	E962.0	E980.4
subcarbonate	973.5	E858.4	E943.5	E950.4	E962.0	E980.4
sulfarsphenamine	961.1	E857	E931.1	E950.4	E962.0	E980.4
Bisphosphonates						
intravenous	963.1	E858.1	E933.7	E950.4	E962.0	E980.4
oral	963.1	E858.1	E933.6	E950.4	E962.0	E980.4
Bithionol	961.6	E857	E931.6	E950.4	E962.0	E980.4
Bitter almond oil	989.0	E866.8	—	E950.9	E962.1	E980.9
Bittersweet	988.2	E865.4	—	E950.9	E962.1	E930.9
Black						
flag	989.4	E863.4	—	E950.6	E962.1	E980.7
henbane	988.2	E865.4	—	E950.9	E962.1	E980.9
leaf (40)	989.4	E863.4	—	E950.6	E962.1	E980.7
widow spider (bite)	989.5	E905.1	—	E950.9	E962.1	E980.9
antivenin	979.9	E858.8	E949.9	E950.4	E962.0	E980.4
Blast furnace gas (carbon monoxide from)	986	E868.8	—	E952.1	E962.2	E982.1
Bleach NEC	983.9	E864.3	—	E950.7	E962.1	E980.6
Bleaching solutions	983.9	E864.3	—	E950.7	E962.1	E980.6
Bleomycin (sulfate)	960.7	E856	E930.7	E950.4	E962.0	E980.4

	Poisoning	External Cause (E-Code)				
		Accident	Therapeutic Use	Suicide Attempt	Assault	Undetermined
Blockain	968.9	E855.2	E938.9	E950.4	E962.0	E980.4
infiltration (subcutaneous)	968.5	E855.2	E938.5	E950.4	E962.0	E980.4
nerve block (peripheral) (plexus)	968.6	E855.2	E938.6	E950.4	E962.0	E980.4
topical (surface)	968.5	E855.2	E938.5	E950.4	E962.0	E980.4
Blood (derivatives) (natural) (plasma) (whole)	964.7	E858.2	E934.7	E950.4	E962.0	E980.4
affecting agent	964.9	E858.2	E934.9	E950.4	E962.0	E980.4
specified NEC	964.8	E858.2	E934.8	E950.4	E962.0	E980.4
substitute (macromolecular)	964.8	E858.2	E934.8	E950.4	E962.0	E980.4
Blue velvet	965.09	E850.2	E935.2	E950.0	E962.0	E980.0
Bone meal	989.89	E866.5	—	E950.9	E962.1	E980.9
Bonine	963.0	E858.1	E933.0	E950.4	E962.0	E980.4
Boracic acid	976.0	E858.7	E946.0	E950.4	E962.0	E980.4
ENT agent	976.6	E858.7	E946.6	E950.4	E962.0	E980.4
ophthalmic preparation	976.5	E858.7	E946.5	E950.4	E962.0	E980.4
Borate (cleanser) (sodium)	989.6	E861.3	—	E950.9	E962.1	E980.9
Borax (cleanser)	989.6	E861.3	—	E950.9	E962.1	E980.9
Boric acid	976.0	E858.7	E946.0	E950.4	E962.0	E980.4
ENT agent	976.6	E858.7	E946.6	E950.4	E962.0	E980.4
ophthalmic preparation	976.5	E858.7	E946.5	E950.4	E962.0	E980.4
Boron hydride NEC	989.89	E866.8	—	E950.9	E962.1	E980.9
fumes or gas	987.8	E869.8	—	E952.8	E962.2	E982.8
Botox	975.3	E858.6	E945.3	E950.4	E962.0	E980.4
Brake fluid vapor	987.8	E869.8	—	E952.8	E962.2	E982.8
Brass (compounds) (fumes)	985.8	E866.4	—	E950.9	E962.1	E980.9
Brasso	981	E861.3	—	E950.9	E962.1	E980.9
Bretylium (tosylate)	972.6	E858.3	E942.6	E950.4	E962.0	E980.4
Brevital (sodium)	968.3	E855.1	E938.3	E950.4	E962.0	E980.4
British antilewisite	963.8	E858.1	E933.8	E950.4	E962.0	E980.4
Bromal (hydrate)	967.3	E852.2	E937.3	E950.2	E962.0	E980.2
Bromelains	963.4	E858.1	E933.4	E950.4	E962.0	E980.4
Bromides NEC	967.3	E852.2	E937.3	E950.2	E962.0	E980.2
Bromine (vapor)	987.8	E869.8	—	E952.8	E962.2	E982.8
compounds (medicinal)	967.3	E852.2	E937.3	E950.2	E962.0	E980.2
Bromisovalum	967.3	E852.2	E937.3	E950.2	E962.0	E980.2
Bromobenzyl cyanide	987.5	E869.3	—	E952.8	E962.2	E982.8
Bromodiphenhydramine	963.0	E858.1	E933.0	E950.4	E962.0	E980.4
Bromoform	967.3	E852.2	E937.3	E950.2	E962.0	E980.2
Bromophenol blue reagent	977.8	E858.8	E947.8	E950.4	E962.0	E980.4
Bromosalicylhydroxamic acid	961.8	E857	E931.8	E950.4	E962.0	E980.4
Bromo-seltzer	965.4	E850.4	E935.4	E950.0	E962.0	E980.0
Brompheniramine	963.0	E858.1	E933.0	E950.4	E962.0	E980.4
Bromural	967.3	E852.2	E937.3	E950.2	E962.0	E980.2
Brown spider (bite) (venom)	989.5	E905.1	—	E950.9	E962.1	E980.9
Brucia	988.2	E865.3	—	E950.9	E962.1	E980.9
Brucine	989.1	E863.7	—	E950.6	E962.1	E980.7
Brunswick green — *see* Copper						
Bruten — *see* Ibuprofen						
Bryonia (alba) (dioica)	988.2	E865.4	—	E950.9	E962.1	E980.9
Buclizine	969.5	E853.8	E939.5	E950.3	E962.0	E980.3
Bufferin	965.1	E850.3	E935.3	E950.0	E962.0	E980.0
Bufotenine	969.6	E854.1	E939.6	E950.3	E962.0	E980.3
Buphenine	971.2	E855.5	E941.2	E950.4	E962.0	E980.4
Bupivacaine	968.9	E855.2	E938.9	E950.4	E962.0	E980.4
infiltration (subcutaneous)	968.5	E855.2	E938.5	E950.4	E962.0	E980.4
nerve block (peripheral) (plexus)	968.6	E855.2	E938.6	E950.4	E962.0	E980.4
Busulfan	963.1	E858.1	E933.1	E950.4	E962.0	E980.4
Butabarbital (sodium)	967.0	E851	E937.0	E950.1	E962.0	E980.1
Butabarbitone	967.0	E851	E937.0	E950.1	E962.0	E980.1
Butabarpal	967.0	E851	E937.0	E950.1	E962.0	E980.1
Butacaine	968.5	E855.2	E938.5	E950.4	E962.0	E980.4
Butallylonal	967.0	E851	E937.0	E950.1	E962.0	E980.1
Butane (distributed in mobile container)	987.0	E868.0	—	E951.1	E962.2	E981.1
distributed through pipes	987.0	E867	—	E951.0	E962.2	E981.0
incomplete combustion of — *see* Carbon monoxide, butane						
Butanol	980.3	E860.4	—	E950.9	E962.1	E980.9
Butanone	982.8	E862.4	—	E950.9	E962.1	E980.9
Butaperazine	969.1	E853.0	E939.1	E950.3	E962.0	E980.3
Butazolidin	965.5	E850.5	E935.5	E950.0	E962.0	E980.0
Butethal	967.0	E851	E937.0	E950.1	E962.0	E980.1
Butethamate	971.1	E855.4	E941.1	E950.4	E962.0	E980.4
Buthalitone (sodium)	968.3	E855.1	E938.3	E950.4	E962.0	E980.4
Butisol (sodium)	967.0	E851	E937.0	E950.1	E962.0	E980.1

	Poisoning	External Cause (E-Code)				
		Accident	Therapeutic Use	Suicide Attempt	Assault	Undetermined
Butobarbital, butobarbitone	967.0	E851	E937.0	E950.1	E962.0	E980.1
Butriptyline	969.0	E854.0	E939.0	E950.3	E962.0	E980.3
Buttercups	988.2	E865.4	—	E950.9	E962.1	E980.9
Butter of antimony — *see* Antimony						
Butyl						
acetate (secondary)	982.8	E862.4	—	E950.9	E962.1	E980.9
alcohol	980.3	E860.4	—	E950.9	E962.1	E980.9
carbinol	980.8	E860.8	—	E950.9	E962.1	E980.9
carbitol	982.8	E862.4	—	E950.9	E962.1	E980.9
cellosolve	982.8	E862.4	—	E950.9	E962.1	E980.9
chloral (hydrate)	967.1	E852.0	E937.1	E950.2	E962.0	E980.2
formate	982.8	E862.4	—	E950.9	E962.1	E980.9
scopolammonium bromide	971.1	E855.4	E941.1	E950.4	E962.0	E980.4
Butyn	968.5	E855.2	E938.5	E950.4	E962.0	E980.4
Butyrophenone (-based tranquilizers)	969.2	E853.1	E939.2	E950.3	E962.0	E980.3
Cacodyl, cacodylic acid — *see* Arsenic						
Cactinomycin	960.7	E856	E930.7	E950.4	E962.0	E980.4
Cade oil	976.4	E858.7	E946.4	E950.4	E962.0	E980.4
Cadmium (chloride) (compounds) (dust) (fumes) (oxide)	985.5	E866.4	—	E950.9	E962.1	E980.9
sulfide (medicinal) NEC	976.4	E858.7	E946.4	E950.4	E962.0	E980.4
Caffeine	969.7	E854.2	E939.7	E950.3	E962.0	E980.3
Calabar bean	988.2	E865.4	—	E950.9	E962.1	E980.9
Caladium seguinium	988.2	E865.4	—	E950.9	E962.1	E980.9
Calamine (liniment) (lotion)	976.3	E858.7	E946.3	E950.4	E962.0	E980.4
Calciferol	963.5	E858.1	E933.5	E950.4	E962.0	E980.4
Calcium (salts) NEC	974.5	E858.5	E944.5	E950.4	E962.0	E980.4
acetylsalicylate	965.1	E850.3	E935.3	E950.0	E962.0	E980.0
benzamidosalicylate	961.8	E857	E931.8	E950.4	E962.0	E980.4
carbaspirin	965.1	E850.3	E935.3	E950.0	E962.0	E980.0
carbimide (citrated)	977.3	E858.8	E947.3	E950.4	E962.0	E980.4
carbonate (antacid)	973.0	E858.4	E943.0	E950.4	E962.0	E980.4
cyanide (citrated)	977.3	E858.8	E947.3	E950.4	E962.0	E980.4
dioctyl sulfosuccinate	973.2	E858.4	E943.2	E950.4	E962.0	E980.4
disodium edathamil	963.8	E858.1	E933.8	E950.4	E962.0	E980.4
disodium edetate	963.8	E858.1	E933.8	E950.4	E962.0	E980.4
EDTA	963.8	E858.1	E933.8	E950.4	E962.0	E980.4
hydrate, hydroxide	983.2	E864.2	—	E950.7	E962.1	E980.6
mandelate	961.9	E857	E931.9	E950.4	E962.0	E980.4
oxide	983.2	E864.2	—	E950.7	E962.1	E980.6
Calomel — see Mercury, chloride						
Caloric agents NEC	974.5	E858.5	E944.5	E950.4	E962.0	E980.4
Calusterone	963.1	E858.1	E933.1	E950.4	E962.0	E980.4
Camoquin	961.4	E857	E931.4	E950.4	E962.0	E980.4
Camphor (oil)	976.1	E858.7	E946.1	E950.4	E962.0	E980.4
Candeptin	976.0	E858.7	E946.0	E950.4	E962.0	E980.4
Candicidin	976.0	E858.7	E946.0	E950.4	E962.0	E980.4
Cannabinols	969.6	E854.1	E939.6	E950.3	E962.0	E980.3
Cannabis (derivatives) (indica) (sativa)	969.6	E854.1	E939.6	E950.3	E962.0	E980.3
Canned heat	980.1	E860.2	—	E950.9	E962.1	E980.9
Cantharides, cantharidin, cantharis	976.8	E858.7	E946.8	E950.4	E962.0	E980.4
Capillary agents	972.8	E858.3	E942.8	E950.4	E962.0	E980.4
Capreomycin	960.6	E856	E930.6	E950.4	E962.0	E980.4
Captodiame, captodiamine	969.5	E853.8	E939.5	E950.3	E962.0	E980.3
Caramiphen (hydrochloride)	971.1	E855.4	E941.1	E950.4	E962.0	E980.4
Carbachol	971.0	E855.3	E941.0	E950.4	E962.0	E980.4
Carbacrylamine resins	974.5	E858.5	E944.5	E950.4	E962.0	E980.4
Carbamate (sedative)	967.8	E852.8	E937.8	E950.2	E962.0	E980.2
herbicide	989.3	E863.5	—	E950.6	E962.1	E980.7
insecticide	989.3	E863.2	—	E950.6	E962.1	E980.7
Carbamazepine	966.3	E855.0	E936.3	E950.4	E962.0	E980.4
Carbamic esters	967.8	E852.8	E937.8	E950.2	E962.0	E980.2
Carbamide	974.4	E858.5	E944.4	E950.4	E962.0	E980.4
topical	976.8	E858.7	E946.8	E950.4	E962.0	E980.4
Carbamylcholine chloride	971.0	E855.3	E941.0	E950.4	E962.0	E980.4
Carbarsone	961.1	E857	E931.1	E950.4	E962.0	E980.4
Carbaryl	989.3	E863.2	—	E950.6	E962.1	E980.7
Carbaspirin	965.1	E850.3	E935.3	E950.0	E962.0	E980.0
Carbazochrome	972.8	E858.3	E942.8	E950.4	E962.0	E980.4
Carbenicillin	960.0	E856	E930.0	E950.4	E962.0	E980.4
Carbenoxolone	973.8	E858.4	E943.8	E950.4	E962.0	E980.4
Carbetapentane	975.4	E858.6	E945.4	E950.4	E962.0	E980.4
Carbimazole	962.8	E858.0	E932.8	E950.4	E962.0	E980.4
Carbinol	980.1	E860.2	—	E950.9	E962.1	E980.9

		External Cause (E-Code)				
	Poisoning	Accident	Therapeutic Use	Suicide Attempt	Assault	Undetermined
Carbinoxamine	963.0	E858.1	E933.0	E950.4	E962.0	E980.4
Carbitol	982.8	E862.4	—	E950.9	E962.1	E980.9
Carbocaine	968.9	E855.2	E938.9	E950.4	E962.0	E980.4
infiltration (subcutaneous)	968.5	E855.2	E938.5	E950.4	E962.0	E980.4
nerve block (peripheral) (plexus)	968.6	E855.2	E938.6	E950.4	E962.0	E980.4
topical (surface)	968.5	E855.2	E938.5	E950.4	E962.0	E980.4
Carbol-fuchsin solution	976.0	E858.7	E946.0	E950.4	E962.0	E980.4
Carbolic acid — *see also* Phenol)	983.0	E864.0	—	E950.7	E962.1	E980.6
Carbomycin	960.8	E856	E930.8	E950.4	E962.0	E980.4
Carbon						
bisulfide (liquid) (vapor)	982.2	E862.4	—	E950.9	E962.1	E980.9
dioxide (gas)	987.8	E869.8	—	E952.8	E962.2	E982.8
disulfide (liquid) (vapor)	982.2	E862.4	—	E950.9	E962.1	E980.9
monoxide (from incomplete combustion of) (in)						
NEC	986	E868.9	—	E952.1	E962.2	E982.1
blast furnace gas	986	E868.8	—	E952.1	E962.2	E982.1
butane (distributed in mobile container)	986	E868.0	—	E951.1	E962.2	E981.1
distributed through pipes	986	E867	—	E951.0	E962.2	E981.0
charcoal fumes	986	E868.3	—	E952.1	E962.2	E982.1
coal						
gas (piped)	986	E867	—	E951.0	E962.2	E981.0
solid (in domestic stoves, fireplaces)	986	E868.3	—	E952.1	E962.2	E982.1
coke (in domestic stoves, fireplaces)	986	E868.3	—	E952.1	E962.2	E982.1
exhaust gas (motor) not in transit	986	E868.2	—	E952.0	E962.2	E982.0
combustion engine, any not in watercraft	986	E868.2	—	E952.0	E962.2	E982.0
farm tractor, not in transit	986	E868.2	—	E952.0	E962.2	E982.0
gas engine	986	E868.2	—	E952.0	E962.2	E982.0
motor pump	986	E868.2	—	E952.0	E962.2	E982.0
motor vehicle, not in transit	986	E868.2	—	E952.0	E962.2	E982.0
fuel (in domestic use)	986	E868.3	—	E952.1	E962.2	E982.1
gas (piped)	986	E867	—	E951.0	E962.2	E981.0
in mobile container	986	E868.0	—	E951.1	E962.2	E981.1
utility	986	E868.1	—	E951.8	E962.2	E981.1
in mobile container	986	E868.0	—	E951.1	E962.2	E981.1
piped (natural)	986	E867	—	E951.0	E962.2	E981.0
illuminating gas	986	E868.1	—	E951.8	E962.2	E981.8
industrial fuels or gases, any	986	E868.8	—	E952.1	E962.2	E982.1
kerosene (in domestic stoves, fireplaces)	986	E868.3	—	E952.1	E962.2	E982.1
kiln gas or vapor	986	E868.8	—	E952.1	E962.2	E982.1
motor exhaust gas, not in transit	986	E868.2	—	E952.0	E962.2	E982.0
piped gas (manufactured) (natural)	986	E867	—	E951.0	E962.2	E981.0
producer gas	986	E868.8	—	E952.1	E962.2	E982.1
propane (distributed in mobile container)	986	E868.0	—	E951.1	E962.2	E981.1
distributed through pipes	986	E867	—	E951.0	E962.2	E981.0
specified source NEC	986	E868.8	—	E952.1	E962.2	E982.1
stove gas	986	E868.1	—	E951.8	E962.2	E981.8
piped	986	E867	—	E951.0	E962.2	E981.0
utility gas	986	E868.1	—	E951.8	E962.2	E981.8
piped	986	E867	—	E951.0	E962.2	E981.0
water gas	986	E868.1	—	E951.8	E962.2	E981.8
wood (in domestic stoves, fireplaces)	986	E868.3	—	E952.1	E962.2	E982.1
tetrachloride (vapor) NEC	987.8	E869.8	—	E952.8	E962.2	E982.8
liquid (cleansing agent) NEC	982.1	E861.3	—	E950.9	E962.1	E980.9
solvent	982.1	E862.4	—	E950.9	E962.1	E980.9
Carbonic acid (gas)	987.8	E869.8	—	E952.8	E962.2	E982.8
anhydrase inhibitors	974.2	E858.5	E944.2	E950.4	E962.0	E980.4
Carbowax	976.3	E858.7	E946.3	E950.4	E962.0	E980.4
Carbrital	967.0	E851	E937.0	E950.1	E962.0	E980.1
Carbromal (derivatives)	967.3	E852.2	E937.3	E950.2	E962.0	E980.2
Cardiac						
depressants	972.0	E858.3	E942.0	E950.4	E962.0	E980.4
rhythm regulators	972.0	E858.3	E942.0	E950.4	E962.0	E980.4
Cardiografin	977.8	E858.8	E947.8	E950.4	E962.0	E980.4
Cardio-green	977.8	E858.8	E947.8	E950.4	E962.0	E980.4
Cardiotonic glycosides	972.1	E858.3	E942.1	E950.4	E962.0	E980.4
Cardiovascular agents NEC	972.9	E858.3	E942.9	E950.4	E962.0	E980.4
Cardrase	974.2	E858.5	E944.2	E950.4	E962.0	E980.4
Carfusin	976.0	E858.7	E946.0	E950.4	E962.0	E980.4
Carisoprodol	968.0	E855.1	E938.0	E950.4	E962.0	E980.4
Carmustine	963.1	E858.1	E933.1	E950.4	E962.0	E980.4
Carotene	963.5	E858.1	E933.5	E950.4	E962.0	E980.4
Carphenazine (maleate)	969.1	E853.0	E939.1	E950.3	E962.0	E980.3
Carter's Little Pills	973.1	E858.4	E943.1	E950.4	E962.0	E980.4
Cascara (sagrada)	973.1	E858.4	E943.1	E950.4	E962.0	E980.4
Cassava	988.2	E865.4	—	E950.9	E962.1	E980.9
Castellani's paint	976.0	E858.7	E946.0	E950.4	E962.0	E980.4
Castor						
bean	988.2	E865.3	—	E950.9	E962.1	E980.9
oil	973.1	E858.4	E943.1	E950.4	E962.0	E980.4
Caterpillar (sting)	989.5	E905.5	—	E950.9	E962.1	E980.9
Catha (edulis)	970.8	E854.3	E940.8	E950.4	E962.0	E980.4
Cathartics NEC	973.3	E858.4	E943.3	E950.4	E962.0	E980.4
contact	973.1	E858.4	E943.1	E950.4	E962.0	E980.4
emollient	973.2	E858.4	E943.2	E950.4	E962.0	E980.4
intestinal irritants	973.1	E858.4	E943.1	E950.4	E962.0	E980.4
saline	973.3	E858.4	E943.3	E950.4	E962.0	E980.4
Cathomycin	960.8	E856	E930.8	E950.4	E962.0	E980.4
Caustic(s)	983.9	E864.4	—	E950.7	E962.1	E980.6
alkali	983.2	E864.2	—	E950.7	E962.1	E980.6
hydroxide	983.2	E864.2	—	E950.7	E962.1	E980.6
potash	983.2	E864.2	—	E950.7	E962.1	E980.6
soda	983.2	E864.2	—	E950.7	E962.1	E980.6
specified NEC	983.9	E864.3	—	E950.7	E962.1	E980.6
Ceepryn	976.0	E858.7	E946.0	E950.4	E962.0	E980.4
ENT agent	976.6	E858.7	E946.6	E950.4	E962.0	E980.4
lozenges	976.6	E858.7	E946.6	E950.4	E962.0	E980.4
Celestone	962.0	E858.0	E932.0	E950.4	E962.0	E980.4
topical	976.0	E858.7	E946.0	E950.4	E962.0	E980.4
Cellosolve	982.8	E862.4	—	E950.9	E962.1	E980.9
Cell stimulants and proliferants	976.8	E858.7	E946.8	E950.4	E962.0	E980.4
Cellulose derivatives, cathartic	973.3	E858.4	E943.3	E950.4	E962.0	E980.4
nitrates (topical)	976.3	E858.7	E946.3	E950.4	E962.0	E980.4
Centipede (bite)	989.5	E905.4	—	E950.9	E962.1	E980.9
Central nervous system						
depressants	968.4	E855.1	E938.4	E950.4	E962.0	E980.4
anesthetic (general) NEC	968.4	E855.1	E938.4	E950.4	E962.0	E980.4
gases NEC	968.2	E855.1	E938.2	E950.4	E962.0	E980.4
intravenous	968.3	E855.1	E938.3	E950.4	E962.0	E980.4
barbiturates	967.0	E851	E937.0	E950.1	E962.0	E980.1
bromides	967.3	E852.2	E937.3	E950.2	E962.0	E980.2
cannabis sativa	969.6	E854.1	E939.6	E950.3	E962.0	E980.3
chloral hydrate	967.1	E852.0	E937.1	E950.2	E962.0	E980.2
hallucinogenics	969.6	E854.1	E939.6	E950.3	E962.0	E980.3
hypnotics	967.9	E852.9	E937.9	E950.2	E962.0	E980.2
specified NEC	967.8	E852.8	E937.8	E950.2	E962.0	E980.2
muscle relaxants	968.0	E855.1	E938.0	E950.4	E962.0	E980.4
paraldehyde	967.2	E852.1	E937.2	E950.2	E962.0	E980.2
sedatives	967.9	E852.9	E937.9	E950.2	E962.0	E980.2
mixed NEC	967.6	E852.5	E937.6	E950.2	E962.0	E980.2
specified NEC	967.8	E852.8	E937.8	E950.2	E962.0	E980.2
muscle-tone depressants	—	—	—	—	—	E980.4
stimulants	970.9	E854.3	E940.9	E950.4	E962.0	E980.4
amphetamines	969.7	E854.2	E939.7	E950.3	E962.0	E980.3
analeptics	970.0	E854.3	E940.0	E950.4	E962.0	E980.4
antidepressants	969.0	E854.0	E939.0	E950.3	E962.0	E980.3
opiate antagonists	970.1	E854.3	E940.0	E950.4	E962.0	E980.4
specified NEC	970.8	E854.3	E940.8	E950.4	E962.0	E980.4
Cephalexin	960.5	E856	E930.5	E950.4	E962.0	E980.4
Cephaloglycin	960.5	E856	E930.5	E950.4	E962.0	E980.4
Cephaloridine	960.5	E856	E930.5	E950.4	E962.0	E980.4
Cephalosporins NEC	960.5	E856	E930.5	E950.4	E962.0	E980.4
N (adicillin)	960.0	E856	E930.0	E950.4	E962.0	E980.4
Cephalothin (sodium)	960.5	E856	E930.5	E950.4	E962.0	E980.4
Cerbera (odallam)	988.2	E865.4	—	E950.9	E962.1	E980.9
Cerberin	972.1	E858.3	E942.1	E950.4	E962.0	E980.4
Cerebral stimulants	970.9	E854.3	E940.9	E950.4	E962.0	E980.4
psychotherapeutic	969.7	E854.2	E939.7	E950.3	E962.0	E980.3
specified NEC	970.8	E854.3	E940.8	E950.4	E962.0	E980.4
Cetalkonium (chloride)	976.0	E858.7	E946.0	E950.4	E962.0	E980.4
Cetoxime	963.0	E858.1	E933.0	E950.4	E962.0	E980.4
Cetrimide	976.2	E858.7	E946.2	E950.4	E962.0	E980.4

	Poisoning	External Cause (E-Code) Accident	Therapeutic Use	Suicide Attempt	Assault	Undetermined
Cetylpyridinium	976.0	E858.7	E946.0	E950.4	E962.0	E980.4
ENT agent	976.6	E858.7	E946.6	E950.4	E962.0	E980.4
lozenges	976.6	E858.7	E946.6	E950.4	E962.0	E980.4
Cevadilla — see Sabadilla						
Cevitamic acid	963.5	E858.1	E933.5	E950.4	E962.0	E980.4
Chalk, precipitated	973.0	E858.4	E943.0	E950.4	E962.0	E980.4
Charcoal						
fumes (carbon monoxide)	986	E868.3	—	E952.1	E962.2	E982.1
industrial	986	E868.8	—	E952.1	E962.2	E982.1
medicinal (activated)	973.0	E858.4	E943.0	E950.4	E962.0	E980.4
Chelating agents NEC	977.2	E858.8	E947.2	E950.4	E962.0	E980.4
Chelidonium majus	988.2	E865.4	—	E950.9	E962.1	E980.9
Chemical substance	989.9	E866.9	—	E950.9	E962.1	E980.9
specified NEC	989.89	E866.8	—	E950.9	E962.1	E980.9
Chemotherapy, antineoplastic	963.1	E858.1	E933.1	E950.4	E962.0	E980.4
Chenopodium (oil)	961.6	E857	E931.6	E950.4	E962.0	E980.4
Cherry laurel	988.2	E865.4	—	E950.9	E962.1	E980.9
Chiniofon	961.3	E857	E931.3	E950.4	E962.0	E980.4
Chlophedianol	975.4	E858.6	E945.4	E950.4	E962.0	E980.4
Chloral (betaine) (formamide) (hydrate)	967.1	E852.0	E937.1	E950.2	E962.0	E980.2
Chloralamide	967.1	E852.0	E937.1	E950.2	E962.0	E980.2
Chlorambucil	963.1	E858.1	E933.1	E950.4	E962.0	E980.4
Chloramphenicol	960.2	E856	E930.2	E950.4	E962.0	E980.4
ENT agent	976.6	E858.7	E946.6	E950.4	E962.0	E980.4
ophthalmic preparation	976.5	E858.7	E946.5	E950.4	E962.0	E980.4
topical NEC	976.0	E858.7	E946.0	E950.4	E962.0	E980.4
Chlorate(s) (potassium) (sodium) NEC	983.9	E864.3	—	E950.7	E962.1	E980.6
herbicides	989.4	E863.5	—	E950.6	E962.1	E980.7
Chlorcylizine	963.0	E858.1	E933.0	E950.4	E962.0	E980.4
Chlordan(e) (dust)	989.2	E863.0	—	E950.6	E962.1	E980.7
Chlordantoin	976.0	E858.7	E946.0	E950.4	E962.0	E980.4
Chlordiazepoxide	969.4	E853.2	E939.4	E950.3	E962.0	E980.3
Chloresium	976.8	E858.7	E946.8	E950.4	E962.0	E980.4
Chlorethiazol	967.1	E852.0	E937.1	E950.2	E962.0	E980.2
Chlorethyl — *see* Ethyl, chloride						
Chloretone	967.1	E852.0	E937.1	E950.2	E962.0	E980.2
Chlorex	982.3	E862.4	—	E950.9	E962.1	E980.9
Chlorhexadol	967.1	E852.0	E937.1	E950.2	E962.0	E980.2
Chlorhexidine (hydrochloride)	976.0	E858.7	E946.0	E950.4	E962.0	E980.4
Chlorhydroxyquinolin	976.0	E858.7	E946.0	E950.4	E962.0	E980.4
Chloride of lime (bleach)	983.9	E864.3	—	E950.7	E962.1	E980.6
Chlorinated						
camphene	989.2	E863.0	—	E950.6	E962.1	E980.7
diphenyl	989.89	E866.8	—	E950.9	E962.1	E980.9
hydrocarbons NEC	989.2	E863.0	—	E950.6	E962.1	E980.7
solvent	982.3	E862.4	—	E950.9	E962.1	E980.9
lime (bleach)	983.9	E864.3	—	E950.7	E962.1	E980.6
naphthalene — see Naphthalene						
pesticides NEC	989.2	E863.0	—	E950.6	E962.1	E980.7
soda — see Sodium, hypochlorite						
Chlorine (fumes) (gas)	987.6	E869.8	—	E952.8	E962.2	E982.8
bleach	983.9	E864.3	—	E950.7	E962.1	E980.6
compounds NEC	983.9	E864.3	—	E950.7	E962.1	E980.6
disinfectant	983.9	E861.4	—	E950.7	E962.1	E980.6
releasing agents NEC	983.9	E864.3	—	E950.7	E962.1	E980.6
Chlorisondamine	972.3	E858.3	E942.3	E950.4	E962.0	E980.4
Chlormadinone	962.2	E858.0	E932.2	E950.4	E962.0	E980.4
Chlormerodrin	974.0	E858.5	E944.0	E950.4	E962.0	E980.4
Chlormethiazole	967.1	E852.0	E937.1	E950.2	E962.0	E980.2
Chlormethylenecycline	960.4	E856	E930.4	E950.4	E962.0	E980.4
Chlormezanone	969.5	E853.8	E939.5	E950.3	E962.0	E980.3
Chloroacetophenone	987.5	E869.3	—	E952.8	E962.2	E982.8
Chloroaniline	983.0	E864.0	—	E950.7	E962.1	E980.6
Chlorobenzene, chlorobenzol	982.0	E862.4	—	E950.9	E962.1	E980.9
Chlorobutanol	967.1	E852.0	E937.1	E950.2	E962.0	E980.2
Chlorodinitrobenzene	983.0	E864.0	—	E950.7	E962.1	E980.6
dust or vapor	987.8	E869.8	—	E952.8	E962.2	E982.8
Chloroethane — see Ethyl, chloride						
Chloroform (fumes) (vapor)	987.8	E869.8	—	E952.8	E962.2	E982.8
anesthetic (gas)	968.2	E855.1	E938.2	E950.4	E962.0	E980.4
liquid NEC	968.4	E855.1	E938.4	E950.4	E962.0	E980.4
solvent	982.3	E862.4	—	E950.9	E962.1	E980.9
Chloroguanide	961.4	E857	E931.4	E950.4	E962.0	E980.4
Chloromycetin	960.2	E856	E930.2	E950.4	E962.0	E980.4
ENT agent	976.6	E858.7	E946.6	E950.4	E962.0	E980.4
ophthalmic preparation	976.5	E858.7	E946.5	E950.4	E962.0	E980.4
otic solution	976.6	E858.7	E946.6	E950.4	E962.0	E980.4
topical NEC	976.0	E858.7	E946.0	E950.4	E962.0	E980.4
Chloronitrobenzene	983.0	E864.0	—	E950.7	E962.1	E980.6
dust or vapor	987.8	E869.8	—	E952.8	E962.2	E982.8
Chlorophenol	983.0	E864.0	—	E950.7	E962.1	E980.6
Chlorophenothane	989.2	E863.0	—	E950.6	E962.1	E980.7
Chlorophyll (derivatives)	976.8	E858.7	E946.8	E950.4	E962.0	E980.4
Chloropicrin (fumes)	987.8	E869.8	—	E952.8	E962.2	E982.8
fumigant	989.4	E863.8	—	E950.6	E962.1	E980.7
fungicide	989.4	E863.6	—	E950.6	E962.1	E980.7
pesticide (fumes)	989.4	E863.4	—	E950.6	E962.1	E980.7
Chloroprocaine	968.9	E855.2	E938.9	E950.4	E962.0	E980.4
infiltration (subcutaneous)	968.5	E855.2	E938.5	E950.4	E962.0	E980.4
nerve block (peripheral) (plexus)	968.6	E855.2	E938.6	E950.4	E962.0	E980.4
Chloroptic	976.5	E858.7	E946.5	E950.4	E962.0	E980.4
Chloropurine	963.1	E858.1	E933.1	E950.4	E962.0	E980.4
Chloroquine (hydrochloride) (phosphate)	961.4	E857	E931.4	E950.4	E962.0	E980.4
Chlorothen	963.0	E858.1	E933.0	E950.4	E962.0	E980.4
Chlorothiazide	974.3	E858.5	E944.3	E950.4	E962.0	E980.4
Chlorotrianisene	962.2	E858.0	E932.2	E950.4	E962.0	E980.4
Chlorovinyldichloroarsine	985.1	E866.3	—	E950.8	E962.1	E980.8
Chloroxylenol	976.0	E858.7	E946.0	E950.4	E962.0	E980.4
Chlorphenesin (carbamate)	968.0	E855.1	E938.0	E950.4	E962.0	E980.4
topical (antifungal)	976.0	E858.7	E946.0	E950.4	E962.0	E980.4
Chlorpheniramine	963.0	E858.1	E933.0	E950.4	E962.0	E980.4
Chlorphenoxamine	966.4	E855.0	E936.4	E950.4	E962.0	E980.4
Chlorphentermine	977.0	E858.8	E947.0	E950.4	E962.0	E980.4
Chlorproguanil	961.4	E857	E931.4	E950.4	E962.0	E980.4
Chlorpromazine	969.1	E853.0	E939.1	E950.3	E962.0	E980.3
Chlorpropamide	962.3	E858.0	E932.3	E950.4	E962.0	E980.4
Chlorprothixene	969.3	E853.8	E939.3	E950.3	E962.0	E980.3
Chlorquinaldol	976.0	E858.7	E946.0	E950.4	E962.0	E980.4
Chlortetracycline	960.4	E856	E930.4	E950.4	E962.0	E980.4
Chlorthalidone	974.4	E858.5	E944.4	E950.4	E962.0	E980.4
Chlortrianisene	962.2	E858.0	E932.2	E950.4	E962.0	E980.4
Chlor-Trimeton	963.0	E858.1	E933.0	E950.4	E962.0	E980.4
Chlorzoxazone	968.0	E855.1	E938.0	E950.4	E962.0	E980.4
Choke damp	987.8	E869.8	—	E952.8	E962.2	E982.8
Cholebrine	977.8	E858.8	E947.8	E950.4	E962.0	E980.4
Cholera vaccine	978.2	E858.8	E948.2	E950.4	E962.0	E980.4
Cholesterol-lowering agents	972.2	E858.3	E942.2	E950.4	E962.0	E980.4
Cholestyramine (resin)	972.2	E858.3	E942.2	E950.4	E962.0	E980.4
Cholic acid	973.4	E858.4	E943.4	E950.4	E962.0	E980.4
Choline						
dihydrogen citrate	977.1	E858.8	E947.1	E950.4	E962.0	E980.4
salicylate	965.1	E850.3	E935.3	E950.0	E962.0	E980.0
theophyllinate	974.1	E858.5	E944.1	E950.4	E962.0	E980.4
Cholinergics	971.0	E855.3	E941.0	E950.4	E962.0	E980.4
Cholografin	977.8	E858.8	E947.8	E950.4	E962.0	E980.4
Chorionic gonadotropin	962.4	E858.0	E932.4	E950.4	E962.0	E980.4
Chromates	983.9	E864.3	—	E950.7	E962.1	E980.6
dust or mist	987.8	E869.8	—	E952.8	E962.2	E982.8
lead	984.0	E866.0	—	E950.9	E962.1	E980.9
paint	984.0	E861.5	—	E950.9	E962.1	E980.9
Chromic acid	983.9	E864.3	—	E950.7	E962.1	E980.6
dust or mist	987.8	E869.8	—	E952.8	E962.2	E982.8
Chromium	985.6	E866.4	—	E950.9	E962.1	E980.9
compounds — see Chromates						
Chromonar	972.4	E858.3	E942.4	E950.4	E962.0	E980.4
Chromyl chloride	983.9	E864.3	—	E950.7	E962.1	E980.6
Chrysarobin (ointment)	976.4	E858.7	E946.4	E950.4	E962.0	E980.4
Chrysazin	973.1	E858.4	E943.1	E950.4	E962.0	E980.4
Chymar	963.4	E858.1	E933.4	E950.4	E962.0	E980.4
ophthalmic preparation	976.5	E858.7	E946.5	E950.4	E962.0	E980.4
Chymotrypsin	963.4	E858.1	E933.4	E950.4	E962.0	E980.4
ophthalmic preparation	976.5	E858.7	E946.5	E950.4	E962.0	E980.4
Cicuta maculata or virosa	988.2	E865.4	—	E950.9	E962.1	E980.9
Cigarette lighter fluid	981	E862.1	—	E950.9	E962.1	E980.9
Cinchocaine (spinal)	968.7	E855.2	E938.7	E950.4	E962.0	E980.4
topical (surface)	968.5	E855.2	E938.5	E950.4	E962.0	E980.4
Cinchona	961.4	E857	E931.4	E950.4	E962.0	E980.4
Cinchonine alkaloids	961.4	E857	E931.4	E950.4	E962.0	E980.4
Cinchophen	974.7	E858.5	E944.7	E950.4	E962.0	E980.4
Cinnarizine	963.0	E858.1	E933.0	E950.4	E962.0	E980.4
Citanest	968.9	E855.2	E938.9	E950.4	E962.0	E980.4

Substance	Poisoning	External Cause (E-Code) Accident	Therapeutic Use	Suicide Attempt	Assault	Undetermined
Citanest — *continued*						
infiltration (subcutaneous)	968.5	E855.2	E938.5	E950.4	E962.0	E980.4
nerve block (peripheral) (plexus)	968.6	E855.2	E938.6	E950.4	E962.0	E980.4
Citric acid	989.89	E866.8	—	E950.9	E962.1	E980.9
Citrovorum factor	964.1	E858.2	E934.1	E950.4	E962.0	E980.4
Claviceps purpurea	988.2	E865.4	—	E950.9	E962.1	E980.9
Cleaner, cleansing agent NEC	989.89	E861.3	—	E950.9	E962.1	E980.9
of paint or varnish	982.8	E862.9	—	E950.9	E962.1	E980.9
Clematis vitalba	988.2	E865.4	—	E950.9	E962.1	E980.9
Clemizole	963.0	E858.1	E933.0	E950.4	E962.0	E980.4
penicillin	960.0	E856	E930.0	E950.4	E962.0	E980.4
Clidinium	971.1	E855.4	E941.1	E950.4	E962.0	E980.4
Clindamycin	960.8	E856	E930.8	E950.4	E962.0	E980.4
Cliradon	965.09	E850.2	E935.2	E950.0	E962.0	E980.0
Clocortolone	962.0	E858.0	E932.0	E950.4	E962.0	E980.4
Clofedanol	975.4	E858.6	E945.4	E950.4	E962.0	E980.4
Clofibrate	972.2	E858.3	E942.2	E950.4	E962.0	E980.4
Clomethiazole	967.1	E852.0	E937.1	E950.2	E962.0	E980.2
Clomiphene	977.8	E858.8	E947.8	E950.4	E962.0	E980.4
Clonazepam	969.4	E853.2	E939.4	E950.3	E962.0	E980.3
Clonidine	972.6	E858.3	E942.6	E950.4	E962.0	E980.4
Clopamide	974.3	E858.5	E944.3	E950.4	E962.0	E980.4
Clorazepate	969.4	E853.2	E939.4	E950.3	E962.0	E980.3
Clorexolone	974.4	E858.5	E944.4	E950.4	E962.0	E980.4
Clorox (bleach)	983.9	E864.3	—	E950.7	E962.1	E980.6
Clortermine	977.0	E858.8	E947.0	E950.4	E962.0	E980.4
Clotrimazole	976.0	E858.7	E946.0	E950.4	E962.0	E980.4
Cloxacillin	960.0	E856	E930.0	E950.4	E962.0	E980.4
Coagulants NEC	964.5	E858.2	E934.5	E950.4	E962.0	E980.4
Coal (carbon monoxide from) — *see also* Carbon, monoxide, coal						
oil — see Kerosene						
tar NEC	983.0	E864.0	—	E950.7	E962.1	E980.6
fumes	987.8	E869.8	—	E952.8	E962.2	E982.8
medicinal (ointment)	976.4	E858.7	E946.4	E950.4	E962.0	E980.4
analgesics NEC	965.5	E850.5	E935.5	E950.0	E962.0	E980.0
naphtha (solvent)	981	E862.0	—	E950.9	E962.1	E980.9
Cobalt (fumes) (industrial)	985.8	E866.4	—	E950.9	E962.1	E980.9
Cobra (venom)	989.5	E905.0	—	E950.9	E962.1	E980.9
Coca (leaf)	970.8	E854.3	E940.8	E950.4	E962.0	E980.4
Cocaine (hydrochloride) (salt)	970.8	E854.3	E940.8	E950.4	E962.0	E980.4
topical anesthetic	968.5	E855.2	E938.5	E950.4	E962.0	E980.4
Coccidioidin	977.8	E858.8	E947.8	E950.4	E962.0	E980.4
Cocculus indicus	988.2	E865.3	—	E950.9	E962.1	E980.9
Cochineal	989.89	E866.8	—	E950.9	E962.1	E980.9
medicinal products	977.4	E858.8	E947.4	E950.4	E962.0	E980.4
Codeine	965.09	E850.2	E935.2	E950.0	E962.0	E980.0
Coffee	989.89	E866.8	—	E950.9	E962.1	E980.9
Cogentin	971.1	E855.4	E941.1	E950.4	E962.0	E980.4
Coke fumes or gas (carbon monoxide)	986	E868.3	—	E952.1	E962.2	E982.1
industrial use	986	E868.8	—	E952.1	E962.2	E982.1
Colace	973.2	E858.4	E943.2	E950.4	E962.0	E980.4
Colchicine	974.7	E858.5	E944.7	E950.4	E962.0	E980.4
Colchicum	988.2	E865.3	—	E950.9	E962.1	E980.9
Cold cream	976.3	E858.7	E946.3	E950.4	E962.0	E980.4
Colestipol	972.2	E858.3	E942.2	E950.4	E962.0	E980.4
Colistimethate	960.8	E856	E930.8	E950.4	E962.0	E980.4
Colistin	960.8	E856	E930.8	E950.4	E962.0	E980.4
Collagen	977.8	E866.8	E947.8	E950.9	E962.1	E980.9
Collagenase	976.8	E858.7	E946.8	E950.4	E962.0	E980.4
Collodion (flexible)	976.3	E858.7	E946.3	E950.4	E962.0	E980.4
Colocynth	973.1	E858.4	E943.1	E950.4	E962.0	E980.4
Coloring matter — *see* Dye(s)						
Combustion gas — see Carbon, monoxide						
Compazine	969.1	E853.0	E939.1	E950.3	E962.0	E980.3
Compound						
42 (warfarin)	989.4	E863.7	—	E950.6	E962.1	E980.7
269 (endrin)	989.2	E863.0	—	E950.6	E962.1	E980.7
497 (dieldrin)	989.2	E863.0	—	E950.6	E962.1	E980.7
1080 (sodium fluoroacetate)	989.4	E863.7	—	E950.6	E962.1	E980.7
3422 (parathion)	989.3	E863.1	—	E950.6	E962.1	E980.7
3911 (phorate)	989.3	E863.1	—	E950.6	E962.1	E980.7
3956 (toxaphene)	989.2	E863.0	—	E950.6	E962.1	E980.7
4049 (malathion)	989.3	E863.1	—	E950.6	E962.1	E980.7
Compound — *continued*						
4124 (dicapthon)	989.4	E863.4	—	E950.6	E962.1	E980.7
E (cortisone)	962.0	E858.0	E932.0	E950.4	E962.0	E980.4
F (hydrocortisone)	962.0	E858.0	E932.0	E950.4	E962.0	E980.4
Congo red	977.8	E858.8	E947.8	E950.4	E962.0	E980.4
Coniine, conine	965.7	E850.7	E935.7	E950.0	E962.0	E980.0
Conium (maculatum)	988.2	E865.4	—	E950.9	E962.1	E980.9
Conjugated estrogens (equine)	962.2	E858.0	E932.2	E950.4	E962.0	E980.4
Contac	975.6	E858.6	E945.6	E950.4	E962.0	E980.4
Contact lens solution	976.5	E858.7	E946.5	E950.4	E962.0	E980.4
Contraceptives (oral)	962.2	E858.0	E932.2	E950.4	E962.0	E980.4
vaginal	976.8	E858.7	E946.8	E950.4	E962.0	E980.4
Contrast media (roentgenographic)	977.8	E858.8	E947.8	E950.4	E962.0	E980.4
Convallaria majalis	988.2	E865.4	—	E950.9	E962.1	E980.9
Copper (dust) (fumes) (salts) NEC	985.8	E866.4	—	E950.9	E962.1	E980.9
arsenate, arsenite	985.1	E866.3	—	E950.8	E962.1	E980.8
insecticide	985.1	E863.4	—	E950.8	E962.1	E980.8
emetic	973.6	E858.4	E943.6	E950.4	E962.0	E980.4
fungicide	985.8	E863.6	—	E950.6	E962.1	E980.7
insecticide	985.8	E863.4	—	E950.6	E962.1	E980.7
oleate	976.0	E858.7	E946.0	E950.4	E962.0	E980.4
sulfate	983.9	E864.3	—	E950.7	E962.1	E980.6
cupric	973.6	E858.4	E943.6	E950.4	E962.0	E980.4
cuprous	983.9	E864.3	—	E950.7	E962.1	E980.6
fungicide	983.9	E863.6	—	E950.7	E962.1	E980.6
Copperhead snake (bite) (venom)	989.5	E905.0	—	E950.9	E962.1	E980.9
Coral (sting)	989.5	E905.6	—	E950.9	E962.1	E980.9
snake (bite) (venom)	989.5	E905.0	—	E950.9	E962.1	E980.9
Cordran	976.0	E858.7	E946.0	E950.4	E962.0	E980.4
Corn cures	976.4	E858.7	E946.4	E950.4	E962.0	E980.4
Cornhusker's lotion	976.3	E858.7	E946.3	E950.4	E962.0	E980.4
Corn starch	976.3	E858.7	E946.3	E950.4	E962.0	E980.4
Corrosive	983.9	E864.4	—	E950.7	E962.1	E980.6
acids NEC	983.1	E864.1	—	E950.7	E962.1	E980.6
aromatics	983.0	E864.0	—	E950.7	E962.1	E980.6
disinfectant	983.0	E861.4	—	E950.7	E962.1	E980.6
fumes NEC	987.9	E869.9	—	E952.9	E962.2	E982.9
specified NEC	983.9	E864.3	—	E950.7	E962.1	E980.6
sublimate — see Mercury, chloride						
Cortate	962.0	E858.0	E932.0	E950.4	E962.0	E980.4
Cort-Dome	962.0	E858.0	E932.0	E950.4	E962.0	E980.4
ENT agent	976.6	E858.7	E946.6	E950.4	E962.0	E980.4
ophthalmic preparation	976.5	E858.7	E946.5	E950.4	E962.0	E980.4
topical NEC	976.0	E858.7	E946.0	E950.4	E962.0	E980.4
Cortef	962.0	E858.0	E932.0	E950.4	E962.0	E980.4
ENT agent	976.6	E858.7	E946.6	E950.4	E962.0	E980.4
ophthalmic preparation	976.5	E858.7	E946.5	E950.4	E962.0	E980.4
topical NEC	976.0	E858.7	E946.0	E950.4	E962.0	E980.4
Corticosteroids (fluorinated)	962.0	E858.0	E932.0	E950.4	E962.0	E980.4
ENT agent	976.6	E858.7	E946.6	E950.4	E962.0	E980.4
ophthalmic preparation	976.5	E858.7	E946.5	E950.4	E962.0	E980.4
topical NEC	976.0	E858.7	E946.0	E950.4	E962.0	E980.4
Corticotropin	962.4	E858.0	E932.4	E950.4	E962.0	E980.4
Cortisol	962.0	E858.0	E932.0	E950.4	E962.0	E980.4
ENT agent	976.6	E858.7	E946.6	E950.4	E962.0	E980.4
ophthalmic preparation	976.5	E858.7	E946.5	E950.4	E962.0	E980.4
topical NEC	976.0	E858.7	E946.0	E950.4	E962.0	E980.4
Cortisone derivatives (acetate)	962.0	E858.0	E932.0	E950.4	E962.0	E980.4
ENT agent	976.6	E858.7	E946.6	E950.4	E962.0	E980.4
ophthalmic preparation	976.5	E858.7	E946.5	E950.4	E962.0	E980.4
topical NEC	976.0	E858.7	E946.0	E950.4	E962.0	E980.4
Cortogen	962.0	E858.0	E932.0	E950.4	E962.0	E980.4
ENT agent	976.6	E858.7	E946.6	E950.4	E962.0	E980.4
ophthalmic preparation	976.5	E858.7	E946.5	E950.4	E962.0	E980.4
Cortone	962.0	E858.0	E932.0	E950.4	E962.0	E980.4
ENT agent	976.6	E858.7	E946.6	E950.4	E962.0	E980.4
ophthalmic preparation	976.5	E858.7	E946.5	E950.4	E962.0	E980.4
Cortril	962.0	E858.0	E932.0	E950.4	E962.0	E980.4
ENT agent	976.6	E858.7	E946.6	E950.4	E962.0	E980.4
ophthalmic preparation	976.5	E858.7	E946.5	E950.4	E962.0	E980.4
topical NEC	976.0	E858.7	E946.0	E950.4	E962.0	E980.4
Cosmetics	989.89	E866.7	—	E950.9	E962.1	E980.9
Cosyntropin	977.8	E858.8	E947.8	E950.4	E962.0	E980.4
Cotarnine	964.5	E858.2	E934.5	E950.4	E962.0	E980.4

Substance	Poisoning	External Cause (E-Code) Accident	Therapeutic Use	Suicide Attempt	Assault	Undetermined
Cottonseed oil	976.3	E858.7	E946.3	E950.4	E962.0	E980.4
Cough mixtures (antitussives)	975.4	E858.6	E945.4	E950.4	E962.0	E980.4
containing opiates	965.09	E850.2	E935.2	E950.0	E962.0	E980.0
expectorants	975.5	E858.6	E945.5	E950.4	E962.0	E980.4
Coumadin	964.2	E858.2	E934.2	E950.4	E962.0	E980.4
rodenticide	989.4	E863.7	—	E950.6	E962.1	E980.7
Coumarin	964.2	E858.2	E934.2	E950.4	E962.0	E980.4
Coumetarol	964.2	E858.2	E934.2	E950.4	E962.0	E980.4
Cowbane	988.2	E865.4	—	E950.9	E962.1	E980.9
Cozyme	963.5	E858.1	E933.5	E950.4	E962.0	E980.4
Crack	970.8	E854.3	E940.8	E950.4	E962.0	E980.4
Creolin	983.0	E864.0	—	E950.7	E962.1	E980.6
disinfectant	983.0	E861.4	—	E950.7	E962.1	E980.6
Creosol (compound)	983.0	E864.0	—	E950.7	E962.1	E980.6
Creosote (beechwood) (coal tar)	983.0	E864.0	—	E950.7	E962.1	E980.6
medicinal (expectorant)	975.5	E858.6	E945.5	E950.4	E962.0	E980.4
syrup	975.5	E858.6	E945.5	E950.4	E962.0	E980.4
Cresol	983.0	E864.0	—	E950.7	E962.1	E980.6
disinfectant	983.0	E861.4	—	E950.7	E962.1	E980.6
Cresylic acid	983.0	E864.0	—	E950.7	E962.1	E980.6
Cropropamide	965.7	E850.7	E935.7	E950.0	E962.0	E980.0
with crotethamide	970.0	E854.3	E940.0	E950.4	E962.0	E980.4
Crotamiton	976.0	E858.7	E946.0	E950.4	E962.0	E980.4
Crotethamide	965.7	E850.7	E935.7	E950.0	E962.0	E980.0
with cropropamide	970.0	E854.3	E940.0	E950.4	E962.0	E980.4
Croton (oil)	973.1	E858.4	E943.1	E950.4	E962.0	E980.4
chloral	967.1	E852.0	E937.1	E950.2	E962.0	E980.2
Crude oil	981	E862.1	—	E950.9	E962.1	E980.9
Cryogenine	965.8	E850.8	E935.8	E950.0	E962.0	E980.0
Cryolite (pesticide)	989.4	E863.4	—	E950.6	E962.1	E980.7
Cryptenamine	972.6	E858.3	E942.6	E950.4	E962.0	E980.4
Crystal violet	976.0	E858.7	E946.0	E950.4	E962.0	E980.4
Cuckoopint	988.2	E865.4	—	E950.9	E962.1	E980.9
Cumetharol	964.2	E858.2	E934.2	E950.4	E962.0	E980.4
Cupric sulfate	973.6	E858.4	E943.6	E950.4	E962.0	E980.4
Cuprous sulfate	983.9	E864.3	—	E950.7	E962.1	E980.6
Curare, curarine	975.2	E858.6	E945.2	E950.4	E962.0	E980.4
Cyanic acid — *see* Cyanide(s)						
Cyanide(s) (compounds) (hydrogen) (potassium) (sodium) NEC	989.0	E866.8	—	E950.9	E962.1	E980.9
dust or gas (inhalation) NEC	987.7	E869.8	—	E952.8	E962.2	E982.8
fumigant	989.0	E863.8	—	E950.6	E962.1	E980.7
mercuric — see Mercury						
pesticide (dust) (fumes)	989.0	E863.4	—	E950.6	E962.1	E980.7
Cyanocobalamin	964.1	E858.2	E934.1	E950.4	E962.0	E980.4
Cyanogen (chloride) (gas) NEC	987.8	E869.8	—	E952.8	E962.2	E982.8
Cyclaine	968.5	E855.2	E938.5	E950.4	E962.0	E980.4
Cyclamen europaeum	988.2	E865.4	—	E950.9	E962.1	E980.9
Cyclandelate	972.5	E858.3	E942.5	E950.4	E962.0	E980.4
Cyclazocine	965.09	E850.2	E935.2	E950.0	E962.0	E980.0
Cyclizine	963.0	E858.1	E933.0	E950.4	E962.0	E980.4
Cyclobarbital, cyclobarbitone	967.0	E851	E937.0	E950.1	E962.0	E980.1
Cycloguanil	961.4	E857	E931.4	E950.4	E962.0	E980.4
Cyclohexane	982.0	E862.4	—	E950.9	E962.1	E980.9
Cyclohexanol	980.8	E860.8	—	E950.9	E962.1	E980.9
Cyclohexanone	982.8	E862.4	—	E950.9	E962.1	E980.9
Cyclomethycaine	968.5	E855.2	E938.5	E950.4	E962.0	E980.4
Cyclopentamine	971.2	E855.5	E941.2	E950.4	E962.0	E980.4
Cyclopenthiazide	974.3	E858.5	E944.3	E950.4	E962.0	E980.4
Cyclopentolate	971.1	E855.4	E941.1	E950.4	E962.0	E980.4
Cyclophosphamide	963.1	E858.1	E933.1	E950.4	E962.0	E980.4
Cyclopropane	968.2	E855.1	E938.2	E950.4	E962.0	E980.4
Cycloserine	960.6	E856	E930.6	E950.4	E962.0	E980.4
Cyclothiazide	974.3	E858.5	E944.3	E950.4	E962.0	E980.4
Cycrimine	966.4	E855.0	E936.4	E950.4	E962.0	E980.4
Cymarin	972.1	E858.3	E942.1	E950.4	E962.0	E980.4
Cyproheptadine	963.0	E858.1	E933.0	E950.4	E962.0	E980.4
Cyprolidol	969.0	E854.0	E939.0	E950.3	E962.0	E980.3
Cytarabine	963.1	E858.1	E933.1	E950.4	E962.0	E980.4
Cytisus						
laburnum	988.2	E865.4	—	E950.9	E962.1	E980.9
scoparius	988.2	E865.4	—	E950.9	E962.1	E980.9
Cytomel	962.7	E858.0	E932.7	E950.4	E962.0	E980.4
Cytosine (antineoplastic)	963.1	E858.1	E933.1	E950.4	E962.0	E980.4
Cytoxan	963.1	E858.1	E933.1	E950.4	E962.0	E980.4
Dacarbazine	963.1	E858.1	E933.1	E950.4	E962.0	E980.4
Dactinomycin	960.7	E856	E930.7	E950.4	E962.0	E980.4
DADPS	961.8	E857	E931.8	E950.4	E962.0	E980.4
Dakin's solution (external)	976.0	E858.7	E946.0	E950.4	E962.0	E980.4
Dalmane	969.4	E853.2	E939.4	E950.3	E962.0	E980.3
DAM	977.2	E858.8	E947.2	E950.4	E962.0	E980.4
Danilone	964.2	E858.2	E934.2	E950.4	E962.0	E980.4
Danthron	973.1	E858.4	E943.1	E950.4	E962.0	E980.4
Dantrolene	975.2	E858.6	E945.2	E950.4	E962.0	E980.4
Daphne (gnidium) (mezereum)	988.2	E865.4	—	E950.9	E962.1	E980.9
berry	988.2	E865.3	—	E950.9	E962.1	E980.9
Dapsone	961.8	E857	E931.8	E950.4	E962.0	E980.4
Daraprim	961.4	E857	E931.4	E950.4	E962.0	E980.4
Darnel	988.2	E865.3	—	E950.9	E962.1	E980.9
Darvon	965.8	E850.8	E935.8	E950.0	E962.0	E980.0
Daunorubicin	960.7	E856	E930.7	E950.4	E962.0	E980.4
DBI	962.3	E858.0	E932.3	E950.4	E962.0	E980.4
D-Con (rodenticide)	989.4	E863.7	—	E950.6	E962.1	E980.7
DDS	961.8	E857	E931.8	E950.4	E962.0	E980.4
DDT	989.2	E863.0	—	E950.6	E962.1	E980.7
Deadly nightshade	988.2	E865.4	—	E950.9	E962.1	E980.9
berry	988.2	E865.3	—	E950.9	E962.1	E980.9
Deanol	969.7	E854.2	E939.7	E950.3	E962.0	E980.3
Debrisoquine	972.6	E858.3	E942.6	E950.4	E962.0	E980.4
Decaborane	989.89	E866.8	—	E950.9	E962.1	E980.9
fumes	987.8	E869.8	—	E952.8	E962.2	E982.8
Decadron	962.0	E858.0	E932.0	E950.4	E962.0	E980.4
ENT agent	976.6	E858.7	E946.6	E950.4	E962.0	E980.4
ophthalmic preparation	976.5	E858.7	E946.5	E950.4	E962.0	E980.4
topical NEC	976.0	E858.7	E946.0	E950.4	E962.0	E980.4
Decahydronaphthalene	982.0	E862.4	—	E950.9	E962.1	E980.9
Decalin	982.0	E862.4	—	E950.9	E962.1	E980.9
Decamethonium	975.2	E858.6	E945.2	E950.4	E962.0	E980.4
Decholin	973.4	E858.4	E943.4	E950.4	E962.0	E980.4
sodium (diagnostic)	977.8	E858.8	E947.8	E950.4	E962.0	E980.4
Declomycin	960.4	E856	E930.4	E950.4	E962.0	E980.4
Deferoxamine	963.8	E858.1	E933.8	E950.4	E962.0	E980.4
Dehydrocholic acid	973.4	E858.4	E943.4	E950.4	E962.0	E980.4
DeKalin	982.0	E862.4	—	E950.9	E962.1	E980.9
Delalutin	962.2	E858.0	E932.2	E950.4	E962.0	E980.4
Delphinium	988.2	E865.3	—	E950.9	E962.1	E980.9
Deltasone	962.0	E858.0	E932.0	E950.4	E962.0	E980.4
Deltra	962.0	E858.0	E932.0	E950.4	E962.0	E980.4
Delvinal	967.0	E851	E937.0	E950.1	E962.0	E980.1
Demecarium (bromide)	971.0	E855.3	E941.0	E950.4	E962.0	E980.4
Demeclocycline	960.4	E856	E930.4	E950.4	E962.0	E980.4
Demecolcine	963.1	E858.1	E933.1	E950.4	E962.0	E980.4
Demelanizing agents	976.8	E858.7	E946.8	E950.4	E962.0	E980.4
Demerol	965.09	E850.2	E935.2	E950.0	E962.0	E980.0
Demethylchlortetracycline	960.4	E856	E930.4	E950.4	E962.0	E980.4
Demethyltetracycline	960.4	E856	E930.4	E950.4	E962.0	E980.4
Demeton	989.3	E863.1	—	E950.6	E962.1	E980.7
Demulcents	976.3	E858.7	E946.3	E950.4	E962.0	E980.4
Demulen	962.2	E858.0	E932.2	E950.4	E962.0	E980.4
Denatured alcohol	980.0	E860.1	—	E950.9	E962.1	E980.9
Dendrid	976.5	E858.7	E946.5	E950.4	E962.0	E980.4
Dental agents, topical	976.7	E858.7	E946.7	E950.4	E962.0	E980.4
Deodorant spray (feminine hygiene)	976.8	E858.7	E946.8	E950.4	E962.0	E980.4
Deoxyribonuclease	963.4	E858.1	E933.4	E950.4	E962.0	E980.4
Depressants						
appetite, central	977.0	E858.8	E947.0	E950.4	E962.0	E980.4
cardiac	972.0	E858.3	E942.0	E950.4	E962.0	E980.4
central nervous system (anesthetic)	968.4	E855.1	E938.4	E950.4	E962.0	E980.4
psychotherapeutic	969.5	E853.9	E939.5	E950.3	E962.0	E980.3
Dequalinium	976.0	E858.7	E946.0	E950.4	E962.0	E980.4
Dermolate	976.2	E858.7	E946.2	E950.4	E962.0	E980.4
DES	962.2	E858.0	E932.2	E950.4	E962.0	E980.4
Desenex	976.0	E858.7	E946.0	E950.4	E962.0	E980.4
Deserpidine	972.6	E858.3	E942.6	E950.4	E962.0	E980.4
Desipramine	969.0	E854.0	E939.0	E950.3	E962.0	E980.3
Deslanoside	972.1	E858.3	E942.1	E950.4	E962.0	E980.4
Desocodeine	965.09	E850.2	E935.2	E950.0	E962.0	E980.0
Desomorphine	965.09	E850.2	E935.2	E950.0	E962.0	E980.0
Desonide	976.0	E858.7	E946.0	E950.4	E962.0	E980.4
Desoxycorticosterone derivatives	962.0	E858.0	E932.0	E950.4	E962.0	E980.4
Desoxyephedrine	969.7	E854.2	E939.7	E950.3	E962.0	E980.3
DET	969.6	E854.1	E939.6	E950.3	E962.0	E980.3

		External Cause (E-Code)				
	Poisoning	Accident	Therapeutic Use	Suicide Attempt	Assault	Undetermined
Detergents (ingested) (synthetic)	989.6	E861.0	—	E950.9	E962.1	E980.9
ENT agent	976.6	E858.7	E946.6	E950.4	E962.0	E980.4
external medication	976.2	E858.7	E946.2	E950.4	E962.0	E980.4
ophthalmic preparation	976.5	E858.7	E946.5	E950.4	E962.0	E980.4
topical NEC	976.0	E858.7	E946.0	E950.4	E962.0	E980.4
Deterrent, alcohol	977.3	E858.8	E947.3	E950.4	E962.0	E980.4
Detrothyronine	962.7	E858.0	E932.7	E950.4	E962.0	E980.4
Dettol (external medication)	976.0	E858.7	E946.0	E950.4	E962.0	E980.4
Dexamethasone	962.0	E858.0	E932.0	E950.4	E962.0	E980.4
Dexamphetamine	969.7	E854.2	E939.7	E950.3	E962.0	E980.3
Dexedrine	969.7	E854.2	E939.7	E950.3	E962.0	E980.3
Dexpanthenol	963.5	E858.1	E933.5	E950.4	E962.0	E980.4
Dextran	964.8	E858.2	E934.8	E950.4	E962.0	E980.4
Dextriferron	964.0	E858.2	E934.0	E950.4	E962.0	E980.4
Dextroamphetamine	969.7	E854.2	E939.7	E950.3	E962.0	E980.3
Dextro calcium pantothenate	963.5	E858.1	E933.5	E950.4	E962.0	E980.4
Dextromethorphan	975.4	E858.6	E945.4	E950.4	E962.0	E980.4
Dextromoramide	965.09	E850.2	E935.2	E950.0	E962.0	E980.0
Dextro pantothenyl alcohol	963.5	E858.1	E933.5	E950.4	E962.0	E980.4
topical	976.8	E858.7	E946.8	E950.4	E962.0	E980.4
Dextropropoxyphene (hydrochloride)	965.8	E850.8	E935.8	E950.0	E962.0	E980.0
Dextrorphan	965.09	E850.2	E935.2	E950.0	E962.0	E980.0
Dextrose NEC	974.5	E858.5	E944.5	E950.4	E962.0	E980.4
Dextrothyroxin	962.7	E858.0	E932.7	E950.4	E962.0	E980.4
DFP	971.0	E855.3	E941.0	E950.4	E962.0	E980.4
DHE-45	972.9	E858.3	E942.9	E950.4	E962.0	E980.4
Diabinese	962.3	E858.0	E932.3	E950.4	E962.0	E980.4
Diacetyl monoxime	977.2	E858.8	E947.2	E950.4	E962.0	E980.4
Diacetylmorphine	965.01	E850.0	E935.0	E950.0	E962.0	E980.0
Diagnostic agents	977.8	E858.8	E947.8	E950.4	E962.0	E980.4
Dial (soap)	976.2	E858.7	E946.2	E950.4	E962.0	E980.4
sedative	967.0	E851	E937.0	E950.1	E962.0	E980.1
Diallylbarbituric acid	967.0	E851	E937.0	E950.1	E962.0	E980.1
Diaminodiphenylsulfone	961.8	E857	E931.8	E950.4	E962.0	E980.4
Diamorphine	965.01	E850.0	E935.0	E950.0	E962.0	E980.0
Diamox	974.2	E858.5	E944.2	E950.4	E962.0	E980.4
Diamthazole	976.0	E858.7	E946.0	E950.4	E962.0	E980.4
Diaphenylsulfone	961.8	E857	E931.8	E950.4	E962.0	E980.4
Diasone (sodium)	961.8	E857	E931.8	E950.4	E962.0	E980.4
Diazepam	969.4	E853.2	E939.4	E950.3	E962.0	E980.3
Diazinon	989.3	E863.1	—	E950.6	E962.1	E980.7
Diazomethane (gas)	987.8	E869.8	—	E952.8	E962.2	E982.8
Diazoxide	972.5	E858.3	E942.5	E950.4	E962.0	E980.4
Dibenamine	971.3	E855.6	E941.3	E950.4	E962.0	E980.4
Dibenzheptropine	963.0	E858.1	E933.0	E950.4	E962.0	E980.4
Dibenzyline	971.3	E855.6	E941.3	E950.4	E962.0	E980.4
Diborane (gas)	987.8	E869.8	—	E952.8	E962.2	E982.8
Dibromomannitol	963.1	E858.1	E933.1	E950.4	E962.0	E980.4
Dibucaine (spinal)	968.7	E855.2	E938.7	E950.4	E962.0	E980.4
topical (surface)	968.5	E855.2	E938.5	E950.4	E962.0	E980.4
Dibunate sodium	975.4	E858.6	E945.4	E950.4	E962.0	E980.4
Dibutoline	971.1	E855.4	E941.1	E950.4	E962.0	E980.4
Dicapthon	989.4	E863.4	—	E950.6	E962.1	E980.7
Dichloralphenazone	967.1	E852.0	E937.1	E950.2	E962.0	E980.2
Dichlorodifluoromethane	987.4	E869.2	—	E952.8	E962.2	E982.8
Dichloroethane	982.3	E862.4	—	E950.9	E962.1	E980.9
Dichloroethylene	982.3	E862.4	—	E950.9	E962.1	E980.9
Dichloroethyl sulfide	987.8	E869.8	—	E952.8	E962.2	E982.8
Dichlorohydrin	982.3	E862.4	—	E950.9	E962.1	E980.9
Dichloromethane (solvent) (vapor)	982.3	E862.4	—	E950.9	E962.1	E980.9
Dichlorophen(e)	961.6	E857	E931.6	E950.4	E962.0	E980.4
Dichlorphenamide	974.2	E858.5	E944.2	E950.4	E962.0	E980.4
Dichlorvos	989.3	E863.1	—	E950.6	E962.1	E980.7
Diclofenac sodium	965.69	E850.6	E935.6	E950.0	E962.0	E980.0
Dicoumarin, dicumarol	964.2	E858.2	E934.2	E950.4	E962.0	E980.4
Dicyanogen (gas)	987.8	E869.8	—	E952.8	E962.2	E982.8
Dicyclomine	971.1	E855.4	E941.1	E950.4	E962.0	E980.4
Dieldrin (vapor)	989.2	E863.0	—	E950.6	E962.1	E980.7
Dienestrol	962.2	E858.0	E932.2	E950.4	E962.0	E980.4
Dietetics	977.0	E858.8	E947.0	E950.4	E962.0	E980.4
Diethazine	966.4	E855.0	E936.4	E950.4	E962.0	E980.4
Diethyl						
barbituric acid	967.0	E851	E937.0	E950.1	E962.0	E980.1
carbamazine	961.6	E857	E931.6	E950.4	E962.0	E980.4
carbinol	980.8	E860.8	—	E950.9	E962.1	E980.9
carbonate	982.8	E862.4	—	E950.9	E962.1	E980.9
Diethyl — *continued*						
dioxide	982.8	E862.4	—	E950.9	E962.1	E980.9
ether (vapor) — see ther(s)						
glycol (monoacetate) (monoethyl ether)	982.8	E862.4	—	E950.9	E962.1	E980.9
propion	977.0	E858.8	E947.0	E950.4	E962.0	E980.4
stilbestrol	962.2	E858.0	E932.2	E950.4	E962.0	E980.4
Diethylene						
Diethylsulfone-diethylmethane	967.8	E852.8	E937.8	E950.2	E962.0	E980.2
Difencloxazine	965.09	E850.2	E935.2	E950.0	E962.0	E980.0
Diffusin	963.4	E858.1	E933.4	E950.4	E962.0	E980.4
Diflos	971.0	E855.3	E941.0	E950.4	E962.0	E980.4
Digestants	973.4	E858.4	E943.4	E950.4	E962.0	E980.4
Digitalin(e)	972.1	E858.3	E942.1	E950.4	E962.0	E980.4
Digitalis glycosides	972.1	E858.3	E942.1	E950.4	E962.0	E980.4
Digitoxin	972.1	E858.3	E942.1	E950.4	E962.0	E980.4
Digoxin	972.1	E858.3	E942.1	E950.4	E962.0	E980.4
Dihydrocodeine	965.09	E850.2	E935.2	E950.0	E962.0	E980.0
Dihydrocodeinone	965.09	E850.2	E935.2	E950.0	E962.0	E980.0
Dihydroergocristine	972.9	E858.3	E942.9	E950.4	E962.0	E980.4
Dihydroergotamine	972.9	E858.3	E942.9	E950.4	E962.0	E980.4
Dihydroergotoxine	972.9	E858.3	E942.9	E950.4	E962.0	E980.4
Dihydrohydroxycodeinone	965.09	E850.2	E935.2	E950.0	E962.0	E980.0
Dihydrohydroxymorphinone	965.09	E850.2	E935.2	E950.0	E962.0	E980.0
Dihydroisocodeine	965.09	E850.2	E935.2	E950.0	E962.0	E980.0
Dihydromorphine	965.09	E850.2	E935.2	E950.0	E962.0	E980.0
Dihydromorphinone	965.09	E850.2	E935.2	E950.0	E962.0	E980.0
Dihydrostreptomycin	960.6	E856	E930.6	E950.4	E962.0	E980.4
Dihydrotachysterol	962.6	E858.0	E932.6	E950.4	E962.0	E980.4
Dihydroxyanthraquinone	973.1	E858.4	E943.1	E950.4	E962.0	E980.4
Dihydroxycodeinone	965.09	E850.2	E935.2	E950.0	E962.0	E980.0
Diiodohydroxyquin	961.3	E857	E931.3	E950.4	E962.0	E980.4
topical	976.0	E858.7	E946.0	E950.4	E962.0	E980.4
Diiodohydroxyquinoline	961.3	E857	E931.3	E950.4	E962.0	E980.4
Dilantin	966.1	E855.0	E936.1	E950.4	E962.0	E980.4
Dilaudid	965.09	E850.2	E935.2	E950.0	E962.0	E980.0
Diloxanide	961.5	E857	E931.5	E950.4	E962.0	E980.4
Dimefline	970.0	E854.3	E940.0	E950.4	E962.0	E980.4
Dimenhydrinate	963.0	E858.1	E933.0	E950.4	E962.0	E980.4
Dimercaprol	963.8	E858.1	E933.8	E950.4	E962.0	E980.4
Dimercaptopropanol	963.8	E858.1	E933.8	E950.4	E962.0	E980.4
Dimetane	963.0	E858.1	E933.0	E950.4	E962.0	E980.4
Dimethicone	976.3	E858.7	E946.3	E950.4	E962.0	E980.4
Dimethindene	963.0	E858.1	E933.0	E950.4	E962.0	E980.4
Dimethisoquin	968.5	E855.2	E938.5	E950.4	E962.0	E980.4
Dimethisterone	962.2	E858.0	E932.2	E950.4	E962.0	E980.4
Dimethoxanate	975.4	E858.6	E945.4	E950.4	E962.0	E980.4
Dimethyl						
arsine, arsinic acid — see Arsenic						
carbinol	980.2	E860.3	—	E950.9	E962.1	E980.9
diguanide	962.3	E858.0	E932.3	E950.4	E962.0	E980.4
ketone	982.8	E862.4	—	E950.9	E962.1	E980.9
vapor	987.8	E869.8	—	E952.8	E962.2	E982.8
meperidine	965.09	E850.2	E935.2	E950.0	E962.0	E980.0
parathion	989.3	E863.1	—	E950.6	E962.1	E980.7
polysiloxane	973.8	E858.4	E943.8	E950.4	E962.0	E980.4
sulfate (fumes)	987.8	E869.8	—	E952.8	E962.2	E982.8
liquid	983.9	E864.3	—	E950.7	E962.1	E980.6
sulfoxide NEC	982.8	E862.4	—	E950.9	E962.1	E980.9
medicinal	976.4	E858.7	E946.4	E950.4	E962.0	E980.4
triptamine	969.6	E854.1	E939.6	E950.3	E962.0	E980.3
tubocurarine	975.2	E858.6	E945.2	E950.4	E962.0	E980.4
Dindevan	964.2	E858.2	E934.2	E950.4	E962.0	E980.4
Dinitrobenzene	983.0	E864.0	—	E950.7	E962.1	E980.6
vapor	987.8	E869.8	—	E952.8	E962.2	E982.8
Dinitro (-ortho-) cresol (herbicide) (spray)	989.4	E863.5	—	E950.6	E962.1	E980.7
insecticide	989.4	E863.4	—	E950.6	E962.1	E980.7
Dinitro-orthocresol (herbicide)	989.4	E863.5	—	E950.6	E962.1	E980.7
insecticide	989.4	E863.4	—	E950.6	E962.1	E980.7
Dinitrophenol (herbicide) (spray)	989.4	E863.5	—	E950.6	E962.1	E980.7
insecticide	989.4	E863.4	—	E950.6	E962.1	E980.7
Dinoprost	975.0	E858.6	E945.0	E950.4	E962.0	E980.4
Dioctyl sulfosuccinate (calcium) (sodium)	973.2	E858.4	E943.2	E950.4	E962.0	E980.4
Diodoquin	961.3	E857	E931.3	E950.4	E962.0	E980.4
Dione derivatives NEC	966.3	E855.0	E936.3	E950.4	E962.0	E980.4
Dionin	965.09	E850.2	E935.2	E950.0	E962.0	E980.0

	Poisoning	External Cause (E-Code) Accident	Therapeutic Use	Suicide Attempt	Assault	Undetermined
Dioxane	982.8	E862.4	—	E950.9	E962.1	E980.9
Dioxin — *see* Herbicide						
Dioxyline	972.5	E858.3	E942.5	E950.4	E962.0	E980.4
Dipentene	982.8	E862.4	—	E950.9	E962.1	E980.9
Diphemanil	971.1	E855.4	E941.1	E950.4	E962.0	E980.4
Diphenadione	964.2	E858.2	E934.2	E950.4	E962.0	E980.4
Diphenhydramine	963.0	E858.1	E933.0	E950.4	E962.0	E980.4
Diphenidol	963.0	E858.1	E933.0	E950.4	E962.0	E980.4
Diphenoxylate	973.5	E858.4	E943.5	E950.4	E962.0	E980.4
Diphenylchloroarsine	985.1	E866.3	—	E950.8	E962.1	E980.8
Diphenylhydantoin (sodium)	966.1	E855.0	E936.1	E950.4	E962.0	E980.4
Diphenylpyraline	963.0	E858.1	E933.0	E950.4	E962.0	E980.4
Diphtheria						
antitoxin	979.9	E858.8	E949.9	E950.4	E962.0	E980.4
toxoid	978.5	E858.8	E948.5	E950.4	E962.0	E980.4
with tetanus toxoid	978.9	E858.8	E948.9	E950.4	E962.0	E980.4
with pertussis component	978.6	E858.8	E948.6	E950.4	E962.0	E980.4
vaccine	978.5	E858.8	E948.5	E950.4	E962.0	E980.4
Dipipanone	965.09	E850.2	E935.2	E950.0	E962.0	E980.0
Diplovax	979.5	E858.8	E949.5	E950.4	E962.0	E980.4
Diprophylline	975.1	E858.6	E945.1	E950.4	E962.0	E980.4
Dipyridamole	972.4	E858.3	E942.4	E950.4	E962.0	E980.4
Dipyrone	965.5	E850.5	E935.5	E950.0	E962.0	E980.0
Diquat	989.4	E863.5	—	E950.6	E962.1	E980.7
Disinfectant NEC	983.9	E861.4	—	E950.7	E962.1	E980.6
alkaline	983.2	E861.4	—	E950.7	E962.1	E980.6
aromatic	983.0	E861.4	—	E950.7	E962.1	E980.6
Disipal	966.4	E855.0	E936.4	E950.4	E962.0	E980.4
Disodium edetate	963.8	E858.1	E933.8	E950.4	E962.0	E980.4
Disulfamide	974.4	E858.5	E944.4	E950.4	E962.0	E980.4
Disulfanilamide	961.0	E857	E931.0	E950.4	E962.0	E980.4
Disulfiram	977.3	E858.8	E947.3	E950.4	E962.0	E980.4
Dithiazanine	961.6	E857	E931.6	E950.4	E962.0	E980.4
Dithioglycerol	963.8	E858.1	E933.8	E950.4	E962.0	E980.4
Dithranol	976.4	E858.7	E946.4	E950.4	E962.0	E980.4
Diucardin	974.3	E858.5	E944.3	E950.4	E962.0	E980.4
Diupres	974.3	E858.5	E944.3	E950.4	E962.0	E980.4
Diuretics NEC	974.4	E858.5	E944.4	E950.4	E962.0	E980.4
carbonic acid anhydrase inhibitors	974.2	E858.5	E944.2	E950.4	E962.0	E980.4
mercurial	974.0	E858.5	E944.0	E950.4	E962.0	E980.4
osmotic	974.4	E858.5	E944.4	E950.4	E962.0	E980.4
purine derivatives	974.1	E858.5	E944.1	E950.4	E962.0	E980.4
saluretic	974.3	E858.5	E944.3	E950.4	E962.0	E980.4
Diuril	974.3	E858.5	E944.3	E950.4	E962.0	E980.4
Divinyl ether	968.2	E855.1	E938.2	E950.4	E962.0	E980.4
D-lysergic acid diethylamide	969.6	E854.1	E939.6	E950.3	E962.0	E980.3
DMCT	960.4	E856	E930.4	E950.4	E962.0	E980.4
DMSO	982.8	E862.4	—	E950.9	E962.1	E980.9
DMT	969.6	E854.1	E939.6	E950.3	E962.0	E980.3
DNOC	989.4	E863.5	—	E950.6	E962.1	E980.7
DOCA	962.0	E858.0	E932.0	E950.4	E962.0	E980.4
Dolophine	965.02	E850.1	E935.1	E950.0	E962.0	E980.0
Doloxene	965.8	E850.8	E935.8	E950.0	E962.0	E980.0
DOM	969.6	E854.1	E939.6	E950.3	E962.0	E980.3
Domestic gas — *see* Gas, utility						
Domiphen (bromide) (lozenges)	976.6	E858.7	E946.6	E950.4	E962.0	E980.4
Dopa (levo)	966.4	E855.0	E936.4	E950.4	E962.0	E980.4
Dopamine	971.2	E855.5	E941.2	E950.4	E962.0	E980.4
Doriden	967.5	E852.4	E937.5	E950.2	E962.0	E980.2
Dormiral	967.0	E851	E937.0	E950.1	E962.0	E980.1
Dormison	967.8	E852.8	E937.8	E950.2	E962.0	E980.2
Dornase	963.4	E858.1	E933.4	E950.4	E962.0	E980.4
Dorsacaine	968.5	E855.2	E938.5	E950.4	E962.0	E980.4
Dothiepin hydrochloride	969.0	E854.0	E939.0	E950.3	E962.0	E980.3
Doxapram	970.0	E854.3	E940.0	E950.4	E962.0	E980.4
Doxepin	969.0	E854.0	E939.0	E950.3	E962.0	E980.3
Doxorubicin	960.7	E856	E930.7	E950.4	E962.0	E980.4
Doxycycline	960.4	E856	E930.4	E950.4	E962.0	E980.4
Doxylamine	963.0	E858.1	E933.0	E950.4	E962.0	E980.4
Dramamine	963.0	E858.1	E933.0	E950.4	E962.0	E980.4
Drano (drain cleaner)	983.2	E864.2	—	E950.7	E962.1	E980.6
Dromoran	965.09	E850.2	E935.2	E950.0	E962.0	E980.0
Dromostanolone	962.1	E858.0	E932.1	E950.4	E962.0	E980.4
Droperidol	969.2	E853.1	E939.2	E950.3	E962.0	E980.3
Drotrecogin alfa	964.2	E858.2	E934.2	E950.4	E962.0	E980.4
Drug	977.9	E858.9	E947.9	E950.5	E962.0	E980.5

	Poisoning	External Cause (E-Code) Accident	Therapeutic Use	Suicide Attempt	Assault	Undetermined
Drug — *continued*						
AHFS List						
4:00 antihistamine drugs	963.0	E858.1	E933.0	E950.4	E962.0	E980.4
8:04 amebacides	961.5	E857	E931.5	E950.4	E962.0	E980.4
arsenical anti-infectives	961.1	E857	E931.1	E950.4	E962.0	E980.4
quinoline derivatives	961.3	E857	E931.3	E950.4	E962.0	E980.4
8:08 anthelmintics	961.6	E857	E931.6	E950.4	E962.0	E980.4
quinoline derivatives	961.3	E857	E931.3	E950.4	E962.0	E980.4
8:12.04 antifungal antibiotics	960.1	E856	E930.1	E950.4	E962.0	E980.4
8:12.06 cephalosporins	960.5	E856	E930.5	E950.4	E962.0	E980.4
8:12.08 chloramphenicol	960.2	E856	E930.2	E950.4	E962.0	E980.4
8:12.12 erythromycins	960.3	E856	E930.3	E950.4	E962.0	E980.4
8:12.16 penicillins	960.0	E856	E930.0	E950.4	E962.0	E980.4
8:12.20 streptomycins	960.6	E856	E930.6	E950.4	E962.0	E980.4
8:12.24 tetracyclines	960.4	E856	E930.4	E950.4	E962.0	E980.4
8:12.28 other antibiotics	960.8	E856	E930.8	E950.4	E962.0	E980.4
antimycobacterial	960.6	E856	E930.6	E950.4	E962.0	E980.4
macrolides	960.3	E856	E930.3	E950.4	E962.0	E980.4
8:16 antituberculars	961.8	E857	E931.8	E950.4	E962.0	E980.4
antibiotics	960.6	E856	E930.6	E950.4	E962.0	E980.4
8:18 antivirals	961.7	E857	E931.7	E950.4	E962.0	E980.4
8:20 plasmodicides (antimalarials)	961.4	E857	E931.4	E950.4	E962.0	E980.4
8:24 sulfonamides	961.0	E857	E931.0	E950.4	E962.0	E980.4
8:26 sulfones	961.8	E857	E931.8	E950.4	E962.0	E980.4
8:28 treponemicides	961.2	E857	E931.2	E950.4	E962.0	E980.4
8:32 trichomonacides	961.5	E857	E931.5	E950.4	E962.0	E980.4
nitrofuran derivatives	961.9	E857	E931.9	E950.4	E962.0	E980.4
quinoline derivatives	961.3	E857	E931.3	E950.4	E962.0	E980.4
8:36 urinary germicides	961.9	E857	E931.9	E950.4	E962.0	E980.4
quinoline derivatives	961.3	E857	E931.3	E950.4	E962.0	E980.4
8:40 other anti-infectives	961.9	E857	E931.9	E950.4	E962.0	E980.4
10:00 antineoplastic agents	963.1	E858.1	E933.1	E950.4	E962.0	E980.4
antibiotics	960.7	E856	E930.7	E950.4	E962.0	E980.4
progestogens	962.2	E858.0	E932.2	E950.4	E962.0	E980.4
12:04 parasympathomimetic (cholinergic) agents	971.0	E855.3	E941.0	E950.4	E962.0	E980.4
12:08 parasympatholytic (cholinergic-blocking) agents	971.1	E855.4	E941.1	E950.4	E962.0	E980.4
12:12 Sympathomimetic (adrenergic) agents	971.2	E855.5	E941.2	E950.4	E962.0	E980.4
12:16 sympatholytic (adrenergic-blocking) agents	971.3	E855.6	E941.3	E950.4	E962.0	E980.4
12:20 skeletal muscle relaxants						
central nervous system muscle-tone depressants	968.0	E855.1	E938.0	E950.4	E962.0	E980.4
myoneural blocking agents	975.2	E858.6	E945.2	E950.4	E962.0	E980.4
16:00 blood derivatives	964.7	E858.2	E934.7	E950.4	E962.0	E980.4
20:04.04 iron preparations	964.0	E858.2	E934.0	E950.4	E962.0	E980.4
20:04.08 liver and stomach preparations	964.1	E858.2	E934.1	E950.4	E962.0	E980.4
20:04 antianemia drugs	964.1	E858.2	E934.1	E950.4	E962.0	E980.4
20:12.04 anticoagulants	964.2	E858.2	E934.2	E950.4	E962.0	E980.4
20:12.08 antiheparin agents	964.5	E858.2	E934.5	E950.4	E962.0	E980.4
20:12.12 coagulants	964.5	E858.2	E934.5	E950.4	E962.0	E980.4
20:12.16 hemostatics NEC	964.5	E858.2	E934.5	E950.4	E962.0	E980.4
capillary active drugs	972.8	E858.3	E942.8	E950.4	E962.0	E980.4
24:04 cardiac drugs	972.9	E858.3	E942.9	E950.4	E962.0	E980.4
cardiotonic agents	972.1	E858.3	E942.1	E950.4	E962.0	E980.4
rhythm regulators	972.0	E858.3	E942.0	E950.4	E962.0	E980.4
24:06 antilipemic agents	972.2	E858.3	E942.2	E950.4	E962.0	E980.4
thyroid derivatives	962.7	E858.0	E932.7	E950.4	E962.0	E980.4
24:08 hypotensive agents	972.6	E858.3	E942.6	E950.4	E962.0	E980.4
adrenergic blocking agents	971.3	E855.6	E941.3	E950.4	E962.0	E980.4
ganglion blocking agents	972.3	E858.3	E942.3	E950.4	E962.0	E980.4
vasodilators	972.5	E858.3	E942.5	E950.4	E962.0	E980.4
24:12 vasodilating agents NEC	972.5	E858.3	E942.5	E950.4	E962.0	E980.4
coronary	972.4	E858.3	E942.4	E950.4	E962.0	E980.4
nicotinic acid derivatives	972.2	E858.3	E942.2	E950.4	E962.0	E980.4
24:16 sclerosing agents	972.7	E858.3	E942.7	E950.4	E962.0	E980.4
28:04 general anesthetics	968.4	E855.1	E938.4	E950.4	E962.0	E980.4
gaseous anesthetics	968.2	E855.1	E938.2	E950.4	E962.0	E980.4
halothane	968.1	E855.1	E938.1	E950.4	E962.0	E980.4

		External Cause (E-Code)				
	Poisoning	Accident	Therapeutic Use	Suicide Attempt	Assault	Undetermined
Drug — *continued*						
28:04 general anesthetics — *continued*						
intravenous anesthetics	968.3	E855.1	E938.3	E950.4	E962.0	E980.4
28:08 analgesics and antipyretics	965.9	E850.9	E935.9	E950.0	E962.0	E980.0
antirheumatics	965.69	E850.6	E935.6	E950.0	E962.0	E980.0
aromatic analgesics	965.4	E850.4	E935.4	E950.0	E962.0	E980.0
non-narcotic NEC	965.7	E850.7	E935.7	E950.0	E962.0	E980.0
opium alkaloids	965.00	E850.2	E935.2	E950.0	E962.0	E980.0
heroin	965.01	E850.0	E935.0	E950.0	E962.0	E980.0
methadone	965.02	E850.1	E935.1	E950.0	E962.0	E980.0
specified type NEC	965.09	E850.2	E935.2	E950.0	E962.0	E980.0
pyrazole derivatives	965.5	E850.5	E935.5	E950.0	E962.0	E980.0
salicylates	965.1	E850.3	E935.3	E950.0	E962.0	E980.0
specified NEC	965.8	E850.8	E935.8	E950.0	E962.0	E980.0
28:10 narcotic antagonists	970.1	E854.3	E940.1	E950.4	E962.0	E980.4
28:12 anticonvulsants	966.3	E855.0	E936.3	E950.4	E962.0	E980.4
barbiturates	967.0	E851	E937.0	E950.1	E962.0	E980.1
benzodiazepine-based tranquilizers	969.4	E853.2	E939.4	E950.3	E962.0	E980.3
bromides	967.3	E852.2	E937.3	E950.2	E962.0	E980.2
hydantoin derivatives	966.1	E855.0	E936.1	E950.4	E962.0	E980.4
oxazolidine (derivatives)	966.0	E855.0	E936.0	E950.4	E962.0	E980.4
succinimides	966.2	E855.0	E936.2	E950.4	E962.0	E980.4
28:16.04 antidepressants	969.0	E854.0	E939.0	E950.3	E962.0	E980.3
28:16.08 tranquilizers	969.5	E853.9	E939.5	E950.3	E962.0	E980.3
benzodiazepine-based	969.4	E853.2	E939.4	E950.3	E962.0	E980.3
butyrophenone-based	969.2	E853.1	E939.2	E950.3	E962.0	E980.3
major NEC	969.3	E853.8	E939.3	E950.3	E962.0	E980.3
phenothiazine-based	969.1	E853.0	E939.1	E950.3	E962.0	E980.3
28:16.12 other psychotherapeutic agents	969.8	E855.8	E939.8	E950.3	E962.0	E980.3
28:20 respiratory and cerebral stimulants	970.9	E854.3	E940.9	E950.4	E962.0	E980.4
analeptics	970.0	E854.3	E940.0	E950.4	E962.0	E980.4
anorexigenic agents	977.0	E858.8	E947.0	E950.4	E962.0	E980.4
psychostimulants	969.7	E854.2	E939.7	E950.3	E962.0	E980.3
specified NEC	970.8	E854.3	E940.8	E950.4	E962.0	E980.4
28:24 sedatives and hypnotics	967.9	E852.9	E937.9	E950.2	E962.0	E980.2
barbiturates	967.0	E851	E937.0	E950.1	E962.0	E980.1
benzodiazepine-based tranquilizers	969.4	E853.2	E939.4	E950.3	E962.0	E980.3
chloral hydrate (group)	967.1	E852.0	E937.1	E950.2	E962.0	E980.2
glutethamide group	967.5	E852.4	E937.5	E950.2	E962.0	E980.2
intravenous anesthetics	968.3	E855.1	E938.3	E950.4	E962.0	E980.4
methaqualone (compounds)	967.4	E852.3	E937.4	E950.2	E962.0	E980.2
paraldehyde	967.2	E852.1	E937.2	E950.2	E962.0	E980.2
phenothiazine-based tranquilizers	969.1	E853.0	E939.1	E950.3	E962.0	E980.3
specified NEC	967.8	E852.8	E937.8	E950.2	E962.0	E980.2
thiobarbiturates	968.3	E855.1	E938.3	E950.4	E962.0	E980.4
tranquilizer NEC	969.5	E853.9	E939.5	E950.3	E962.0	E980.3
36:04 to 36:88 diagnostic agents	977.8	E858.8	E947.8	E950.4	E962.0	E980.4
40:00 electrolyte, caloric, and water balance agents NEC	974.5	E858.5	E944.5	E950.4	E962.0	E980.4
40:04 acidifying agents	963.2	E858.1	E933.2	E950.4	E962.0	E980.4
40:08 alkalinizing agents	963.3	E858.1	E933.3	E950.4	E962.0	E980.4
40:10 ammonia detoxicants	974.5	E858.5	E944.5	E950.4	E962.0	E980.4
40:12 replacement solutions	974.5	E858.5	E944.5	E950.4	E962.0	E980.4
plasma expanders	964.8	E858.2	E934.8	E950.4	E962.0	E980.4
40:16 sodium-removing resins	974.5	E858.5	E944.5	E950.4	E962.0	E980.4
40:18 potassium-removing resins	974.5	E858.5	E944.5	E950.4	E962.0	E980.4
40:20 caloric agents	974.5	E858.5	E944.5	E950.4	E962.0	E980.4
40:24 salt and sugar substitutes	974.5	E858.5	E944.5	E950.4	E962.0	E980.4
40:28 diuretics NEC	974.4	E858.5	E944.4	E950.4	E962.0	E980.4
carbonic acid anhydrase inhibitors	974.2	E858.5	E944.2	E950.4	E962.0	E980.4
mercurials	974.0	E858.5	E944.0	E950.4	E962.0	E980.4
purine derivatives	974.1	E858.5	E944.1	E950.4	E962.0	E980.4
saluretics	974.3	E858.5	E944.3	E950.4	E962.0	E980.4
thiazides	974.3	E858.5	E944.3	E950.4	E962.0	E980.4
40:36 irrigating solutions	974.5	E858.5	E944.5	E950.4	E962.0	E980.4
Drug — *continued*						
40:40 uricosuric agents	974.7	E858.5	E944.7	E950.4	E962.0	E980.4
44:00 enzymes	963.4	E858.1	E933.4	E950.4	E962.0	E980.4
fibrinolysis-affecting agents	964.4	E858.2	E934.4	E950.4	E962.0	E980.4
gastric agents	973.4	E858.4	E943.4	E950.4	E962.0	E980.4
48:00 expectorants and cough preparations						
antihistamine agents	963.0	E858.1	E933.0	E950.4	E962.0	E980.4
antitussives	975.4	E858.6	E945.4	E950.4	E962.0	E980.4
codeine derivatives	965.09	E850.2	E935.2	E950.0	E962.0	E980.0
expectorants	975.5	E858.6	E945.5	E950.4	E962.0	E980.4
narcotic agents NEC	965.09	E850.2	E935.2	E950.0	E962.0	E980.0
52:04.04 antibiotics (EENT)						
ENT agent	976.6	E858.7	E946.6	E950.4	E962.0	E980.4
ophthalmic preparation	976.5	E858.7	E946.5	E950.4	E962.0	E980.4
52:04.06 antivirals (EENT)						
ENT agent	976.6	E858.7	E946.6	E950.4	E962.0	E980.4
ophthalmic preparation	976.5	E858.7	E946.5	E950.4	E962.0	E980.4
52:04.08 sulfonamides (EENT)						
ENT agent	976.6	E858.7	E946.6	E950.4	E962.0	E980.4
ophthalmic preparation	976.5	E858.7	E946.5	E950.4	E962.0	E980.4
52:04.12 miscellaneous anti-infectives (EENT)						
ENT agent	976.6	E858.7	E946.6	E950.4	E962.0	E980.4
ophthalmic preparation	976.5	E858.7	E946.5	E950.4	E962.0	E980.4
52:04 anti-infectives (EENT)						
ENT agent	976.6	E858.7	E946.6	E950.4	E962.0	E980.4
ophthalmic preparation	976.5	E858.7	E946.5	E950.4	E962.0	E980.4
52:08 anti-inflammatory agents (EENT)						
ENT agent	976.6	E858.7	E946.6	E950.4	E962.0	E980.4
ophthalmic preparation	976.5	E858.7	E946.5	E950.4	E962.0	E980.4
52:10 carbonic anhydrase inhibitors	974.2	E858.5	E944.2	E950.4	E962.0	E980.4
52:12 contact lens solutions	976.5	E858.7	E946.5	E950.4	E962.0	E980.4
52:16 local anesthetics (EENT)	968.5	E855.2	E938.5	E950.4	E962.0	E980.4
52:20 miotics	971.0	E855.3	E941.0	E950.4	E962.0	E980.4
52:24 mydriatics						
adrenergics	971.2	E855.5	E941.2	E950.4	E962.0	E980.4
anticholinergics	971.1	E855.4	E941.1	E950.4	E962.0	E980.4
antimuscarinics	971.1	E855.4	E941.1	E950.4	E962.0	E980.4
parasympatholytics	971.1	E855.4	E941.1	E950.4	E962.0	E980.4
spasmolytics	971.1	E855.4	E941.1	E950.4	E962.0	E980.4
sympathomimetics	971.2	E855.5	E941.2	E950.4	E962.0	E980.4
52:28 mouth washes and gargles	976.6	E858.7	E946.6	E950.4	E962.0	E980.4
52:32 vasoconstrictors (EENT)	971.2	E855.5	E941.2	E950.4	E962.0	E980.4
52:36 unclassified agents (EENT)						
ENT agent	976.6	E858.7	E946.6	E950.4	E962.0	E980.4
ophthalmic preparation	976.5	E858.7	E946.5	E950.4	E962.0	E980.4
56:04 antacids and adsorbents	973.0	E858.4	E943.0	E950.4	E962.0	E980.4
56:08 antidiarrhea agents	973.5	E858.4	E943.5	E950.4	E962.0	E980.4
56:10 antiflatulents	973.8	E858.4	E943.8	E950.4	E962.0	E980.4
56:12 cathartics NEC	973.3	E858.4	E943.3	E950.4	E962.0	E980.4
emollients	973.2	E858.4	E943.2	E950.4	E962.0	E980.4
irritants	973.1	E858.4	E943.1	E950.4	E962.0	E980.4
56:16 digestants	973.4	E858.4	E943.4	E950.4	E962.0	E980.4
56:20 emetics and antiemetics						
antiemetics	963.0	E858.1	E933.0	E950.4	E962.0	E980.4
emetics	973.6	E858.4	E943.6	E950.4	E962.0	E980.4
56:24 lipotropic agents	977.1	E858.8	E947.1	E950.4	E962.0	E980.4
56:40 miscellaneous G.I. drugs	973.8	E858.4	E943.8	E950.4	E962.0	E980.4
60:00 gold compounds	965.69	E850.6	E935.6	E950.0	E962.0	E980.0
64:00 heavy metal antagonists	963.8	E858.1	E933.8	E950.4	E962.0	E980.4
68:04 adrenals	962.0	E858.0	E932.0	E950.4	E962.0	E980.4
68:08 androgens	962.1	E858.0	E932.1	E950.4	E962.0	E980.4
68:12 contraceptives, oral	962.2	E858.0	E932.2	E950.4	E962.0	E980.4
68:16 estrogens	962.2	E858.0	E932.2	E950.4	E962.0	E980.4
68:18 gonadotropins	962.4	E858.0	E932.4	E950.4	E962.0	E980.4
68:20.08 insulins	962.3	E858.0	E932.3	E950.4	E962.0	E980.4
68:20 insulins and antidiabetic agents	962.3	E858.0	E932.3	E950.4	E962.0	E980.4
68:24 parathyroid	962.6	E858.0	E932.6	E950.4	E962.0	E980.4
68:28 pituitary (posterior)	962.5	E858.0	E932.5	E950.4	E962.0	E980.4
anterior	962.4	E858.0	E932.4	E950.4	E962.0	E980.4

	Poisoning	External Cause (E-Code) Accident	Therapeutic Use	Suicide Attempt	Assault	Undetermined
Drug — *continued*						
68:32 progestogens	962.2	E858.0	E932.2	E950.4	E962.0	E980.4
68:34 other corpus luteum hormones NEC	962.2	E858.0	E932.2	E950.4	E962.0	E980.4
68:36 thyroid and antithyroid						
antithyroid	962.8	E858.0	E932.8	E950.4	E962.0	E980.4
thyroid (derivatives)	962.7	E858.0	E932.7	E950.4	E962.0	E980.4
72:00 local anesthetics NEC	968.9	E855.2	E938.9	E950.4	E962.0	E980.4
infiltration (intradermal) (subcutaneous) (submucosal)	968.5	E855.2	E938.5	E950.4	E962.0	E980.4
nerve blocking (peripheral) (plexus) (regional)	968.6	E855.2	E938.6	E950.4	E962.0	E980.4
spinal	968.7	E855.2	E938.7	E950.4	E962.0	E980.4
topical (surface)	968.5	E855.2	E938.5	E950.4	E962.0	E980.4
76:00 oxytocics	975.0	E858.6	E945.0	E950.4	E962.0	E980.4
78:00 radioactive agents	990	—	—	—	—	—
80:04 serums NEC	979.9	E858.8	E949.9	E950.4	E962.0	E980.4
immune gamma globulin (human)	964.6	E858.2	E934.6	E950.4	E962.0	E980.4
80:08 toxoids NEC	978.8	E858.8	E948.8	E950.4	E962.0	E980.4
diphtheria	978.5	E858.8	E948.5	E950.4	E962.0	E980.4
and diphtheria	978.9	E858.8	E948.9	E950.4	E962.0	E980.4
with pertussis component	978.6	E858.8	E948.6	E950.4	E962.0	E980.4
and tetanus	978.9	E858.8	E948.9	E950.4	E962.0	E980.4
with pertussis component	978.6	E858.8	E948.6	E950.4	E962.0	E980.4
tetanus	978.4	E858.8	E948.4	E950.4	E962.0	E980.4
80:12 vaccines	979.9	E858.8	E949.9	E950.4	E962.0	E980.4
bacterial NEC	978.8	E858.8	E948.8	E950.4	E962.0	E980.4
with						
other bacterial components	978.9	E858.8	E948.9	E950.4	E962.0	E980.4
pertussis component	978.6	E858.8	E948.6	E950.4	E962.0	E980.4
viral and rickettsial components	979.7	E858.8	E949.7	E950.4	E962.0	E980.4
rickettsial NEC	979.6	E858.8	E949.6	E950.4	E962.0	E980.4
with						
bacterial component	979.7	E858.8	E949.7	E950.4	E962.0	E980.4
pertussis component	978.6	E858.8	E948.6	E950.4	E962.0	E980.4
viral component	979.7	E858.8	E949.7	E950.4	E962.0	E980.4
viral NEC	979.6	E858.8	E949.6	E950.4	E962.0	E980.4
with						
bacterial component	979.7	E858.8	E949.7	E950.4	E962.0	E980.4
pertussis component	978.6	E858.8	E948.6	E950.4	E962.0	E980.4
rickettsial component	979.7	E858.8	E949.7	E950.4	E962.0	E980.4
84:04.04 antibiotics (skin and mucous membrane)	976.0	E858.7	E946.0	E950.4	E962.0	E980.4
84:04.08 fungicides (skin and mucous membrane)	976.0	E858.7	E946.0	E950.4	E962.0	E980.4
84:04.12 scabicides and pediculicides (skin and mucous membrane)	976.0	E858.7	E946.0	E950.4	E962.0	E980.4
84:04.16 miscellaneous local anti-infectives (skin and mucous membrane)	976.0	E858.7	E946.0	E950.4	E962.0	E980.4
84:06 anti-inflammatory agents (skin and mucous membrane)	976.0	E858.7	E946.0	E950.4	E962.0	E980.4
84:08 antipruritics and local anesthetics						
antipruritics	976.1	E858.7	E946.1	E950.4	E962.0	E980.4
local anesthetics	968.5	E855.2	E938.5	E950.4	E962.0	E980.4
84:12 astringents	976.2	E858.7	E946.2	E950.4	E962.0	E980.4
84:16 cell stimulants and proliferants	976.8	E858.7	E946.8	E950.4	E962.0	E980.4
84:20 detergents	976.2	E858.7	E946.2	E950.4	E962.0	E980.4
84:24 emollients, demulcents, and protectants	976.3	E858.7	E946.3	E950.4	E962.0	E980.4
84:28 keratolytic agents	976.4	E858.7	E946.4	E950.4	E962.0	E980.4
84:32 keratoplastic agents	976.4	E858.7	E946.4	E950.4	E962.0	E980.4
84:36 miscellaneous agents (skin and mucous membrane)	976.8	E858.7	E946.8	E950.4	E962.0	E980.4

	Poisoning	External Cause (E-Code) Accident	Therapeutic Use	Suicide Attempt	Assault	Undetermined
Drug — *continued*						
86:00 spasmolytic agents	975.1	E858.6	E945.1	E950.4	E962.0	E980.4
antiasthmatics	975.7	E858.6	E945.7	E950.4	E962.0	E980.4
papaverine	972.5	E858.3	E942.5	E950.4	E962.0	E980.4
theophylline	974.1	E858.5	E944.1	E950.4	E962.0	E980.4
88:04 vitamin A	963.5	E858.1	E933.5	E950.4	E962.0	E980.4
88:08 vitamin B complex	963.5	E858.1	E933.5	E950.4	E962.0	E980.4
hematopoietic vitamin	964.1	E858.2	E934.1	E950.4	E962.0	E980.4
nicotinic acid derivatives	972.2	E858.3	E942.2	E950.4	E962.0	E980.4
88:12 vitamin C	963.5	E858.1	E933.5	E950.4	E962.0	E980.4
88:16 vitamin D	963.5	E858.1	E933.5	E950.4	E962.0	E980.4
88:20 vitamin E	963.5	E858.1	E933.5	E950.4	E962.0	E980.4
88:24 vitamin K activity	964.3	E858.2	E934.3	E950.4	E962.0	E980.4
88:28 multivitamin preparations	963.5	E858.1	E933.5	E950.4	E962.0	E980.4
92:00 unclassified therapeutic agents	977.8	E858.8	E947.8	E950.4	E962.0	E980.4
specified NEC	977.8	E858.8	E947.8	E950.4	E962.0	E980.4
Duboisine	971.1	E855.4	E941.1	E950.4	E962.0	E980.4
Dulcolax	973.1	E858.4	E943.1	E950.4	E962.0	E980.4
Duponol (C) (EP)	976.2	E858.7	E946.2	E950.4	E962.0	E980.4
Durabolin	962.1	E858.0	E932.1	E950.4	E962.0	E980.4
Dyclone	968.5	E855.2	E938.5	E950.4	E962.0	E980.4
Dyclonine	968.5	E855.2	E938.5	E950.4	E962.0	E980.4
Dydrogesterone	962.2	E858.0	E932.2	E950.4	E962.0	E980.4
Dyes NEC	989.89	E866.8	—	E950.9	E962.1	E980.9
diagnostic agents	977.8	E858.8	E947.8	E950.4	E962.0	E980.4
pharmaceutical NEC	977.4	E858.8	E947.4	E950.4	E962.0	E980.4
Dyfols	971.0	E855.3	E941.0	E950.4	E962.0	E980.4
Dymelor	962.3	E858.0	E932.3	E950.4	E962.0	E980.4
Dynamite	989.89	E866.8	—	E950.9	E962.1	E980.9
fumes	987.8	E869.8	—	E952.8	E962.2	E982.8
Dyphylline	975.1	E858.6	E945.1	E950.4	E962.0	E980.4
Ear preparations	976.6	E858.7	E946.6	E950.4	E962.0	E980.4
Echothiopate, ecothiopate	971.0	E855.3	E941.0	E950.4	E962.0	E980.4
Ecstasy	969.7	E854.2	E939.7	E950.3	E962.0	E980.3
Ectylurea	967.8	E852.8	E937.8	E950.2	E962.0	E980.2
Edathamil disodium	963.8	E858.1	E933.8	E950.4	E962.0	E980.4
Edecrin	974.4	E858.5	E944.4	E950.4	E962.0	E980.4
Edetate, disodium (calcium)	963.8	E858.1	E933.8	E950.4	E962.0	E980.4
Edrophonium	971.0	E855.3	E941.0	E950.4	E962.0	E980.4
Elase	976.8	E858.7	E946.8	E950.4	E962.0	E980.4
Elaterium	973.1	E858.4	E943.1	E950.4	E962.0	E980.4
Elder	988.2	E865.4	—	E950.9	E962.1	E980.9
berry (unripe)	988.2	E865.3	—	E950.9	E962.1	E980.9
Electrolytes NEC	974.5	E858.5	E944.5	E950.4	E962.0	E980.4
Electrolytic agent NEC	974.5	E858.5	E944.5	E950.4	E962.0	E980.4
Embramine	963.0	E858.1	E933.0	E950.4	E962.0	E980.4
Emetics	973.6	E858.4	E943.6	E950.4	E962.0	E980.4
Emetine (hydrochloride)	961.5	E857	E931.5	E950.4	E962.0	E980.4
Emollients	976.3	E858.7	E946.3	E950.4	E962.0	E980.4
Emylcamate	969.5	E853.8	E939.5	E950.3	E962.0	E980.3
Encyprate	969.0	E854.0	E939.0	E950.3	E962.0	E980.3
Endocaine	968.5	E855.2	E938.5	E950.4	E962.0	E980.4
Endrin	989.2	E863.0	—	E950.6	E962.1	E980.7
Enflurane	968.2	E855.1	E938.2	E950.4	E962.0	E980.4
Enovid	962.2	E858.0	E932.2	E950.4	E962.0	E980.4
ENT preparations (anti-infectives)	976.6	E858.7	E946.6	E950.4	E962.0	E980.4
Enzodase	963.4	E858.1	E933.4	E950.4	E962.0	E980.4
Enzymes NEC	963.4	E858.1	E933.4	E950.4	E962.0	E980.4
Epanutin	966.1	E855.0	E936.1	E950.4	E962.0	E980.4
Ephedra (tincture)	971.2	E855.5	E941.2	E950.4	E962.0	E980.4
Ephedrine	971.2	E855.5	E941.2	E950.4	E962.0	E980.4
Epiestriol	962.2	E858.0	E932.2	E950.4	E962.0	E980.4
Epilim — see Sodium valproate						
Epinephrine	971.2	E855.5	E941.2	E950.4	E962.0	E980.4
Epsom salt	973.3	E858.4	E943.3	E950.4	E962.0	E980.4
Equanil	969.5	E853.8	E939.5	E950.3	E962.0	E980.3
Equisetum (diuretic)	974.4	E858.5	E944.4	E950.4	E962.0	E980.4
Ergometrine	975.0	E858.6	E945.0	E950.4	E962.0	E980.4
Ergonovine	975.0	E858.6	E945.0	E950.4	E962.0	E980.4
Ergot NEC	988.2	E865.4	—	E950.9	E962.1	E980.9
medicinal (alkaloids)	975.0	E858.6	E945.0	E950.4	E962.0	E980.4
Ergotamine (tartrate) (for migraine) NEC	972.9	E858.3	E942.9	E950.4	E962.0	E980.4
Ergotrate	975.0	E858.6	E945.0	E950.4	E962.0	E980.4
Erythrityl tetranitrate	972.4	E858.3	E942.4	E950.4	E962.0	E980.4
Erythrol tetranitrate	972.4	E858.3	E942.4	E950.4	E962.0	E980.4
Erythromycin	960.3	E856	E930.3	E950.4	E962.0	E980.4
ophthalmic preparation	976.5	E858.7	E946.5	E950.4	E962.0	E980.4

		External Cause (E-Code)				
	Poisoning	Accident	Therapeutic Use	Suicide Attempt	Assault	Undetermined
Erythromycin — *continued*						
topical NEC	976.0	E858.7	E946.0	E950.4	E962.0	E980.4
Eserine	971.0	E855.3	E941.0	E950.4	E962.0	E980.4
Eskabarb	967.0	E851	E937.0	E950.1	E962.0	E980.1
Eskalith	969.8	E855.8	E939.8	E950.3	E962.0	E980.3
Estradiol (cypionate) (dipropionate) (valerate)	962.2	E858.0	E932.2	E950.4	E962.0	E980.4
Estriol	962.2	E858.0	E932.2	E950.4	E962.0	E980.4
Estrogens (with progestogens)	962.2	E858.0	E932.2	E950.4	E962.0	E980.4
Estrone	962.2	E858.0	E932.2	E950.4	E962.0	E980.4
Etafedrine	971.2	E855.5	E941.2	E950.4	E962.0	E980.4
Ethacrynate sodium	974.4	E858.5	E944.4	E950.4	E962.0	E980.4
Ethacrynic acid	974.4	E858.5	E944.4	E950.4	E962.0	E980.4
Ethambutol	961.8	E857	E931.8	E950.4	E962.0	E980.4
Ethamide	974.2	E858.5	E944.2	E950.4	E962.0	E980.4
Ethamivan	970.0	E854.3	E940.0	E950.4	E962.0	E980.4
Ethamsylate	964.5	E858.2	E934.5	E950.4	E962.0	E980.4
Ethanol	980.0	E860.1	—	E950.9	E962.1	E980.9
beverage	980.0	E860.0	—	E950.9	E962.1	E980.9
Ethchlorvynol	967.8	E852.8	E937.8	E950.2	E962.0	E980.2
Ethebenecid	974.7	E858.5	E944.7	E950.4	E962.0	E980.4
Ether(s) (diethyl) (ethyl) (vapor)	987.8	E869.8	—	E952.8	E962.2	E982.8
anesthetic	968.2	E855.1	E938.2	E950.4	E962.0	E980.4
petroleum — see Ligroin						
solvent	982.8	E862.4	—	E950.9	E962.1	E980.9
Ethidine chloride (vapor)	987.8	E869.8	—	E952.8	E962.2	E982.8
liquid (solvent)	982.3	E862.4	—	E950.9	E962.1	E980.9
Ethinamate	967.8	E852.8	E937.8	E950.2	E962.0	E980.2
Ethinylestradiol	962.2	E858.0	E932.2	E950.4	E962.0	E980.4
Ethionamide	961.8	E857	E931.8	E950.4	E962.0	E980.4
Ethisterone	962.2	E858.0	E932.2	E950.4	E962.0	E980.4
Ethobral	967.0	E851	E937.0	E950.1	E962.0	E980.1
Ethocaine (infiltration) (topical)	968.5	E855.2	E938.5	E950.4	E962.0	E980.4
nerve block (peripheral) (plexus)	968.6	E855.2	E938.6	E950.4	E962.0	E980.4
spinal	968.7	E855.2	E938.7	E950.4	E962.0	E980.4
Ethoheptazine (citrate)	965.7	E850.7	E935.7	E950.0	E962.0	E980.0
Ethopropazine	966.4	E855.0	E936.4	E950.4	E962.0	E980.4
Ethosuximide	966.2	E855.0	E936.2	E950.4	E962.0	E980.4
Ethotoin	966.1	E855.0	E936.1	E950.4	E962.0	E980.4
Ethoxazene	961.9	E857	E931.9	E950.4	E962.0	E980.4
Ethoxzolamide	974.2	E858.5	E944.2	E950.4	E962.0	E980.4
Ethyl						
acetate (vapor)	982.8	E862.4	—	E950.9	E962.1	E980.9
alcohol	980.0	E860.1	—	E950.9	E962.1	E980.9
beverage	980.0	E860.0	—	E950.9	E962.1	E980.9
aldehyde (vapor)	987.8	E869.8	—	E952.8	E962.2	E982.8
liquid	989.89	E866.8	—	E950.9	E962.1	E980.9
aminobenzoate	968.5	E855.2	E938.5	E950.4	E962.0	E980.4
biscoumacetate	964.2	E858.2	E934.2	E950.4	E962.0	E980.4
bromide (anesthetic)	968.2	E855.1	E938.2	E950.4	E962.0	E980.4
carbamate (antineoplastic)	963.1	E858.1	E933.1	E950.4	E962.0	E980.4
carbinol	980.3	E860.4	—	E950.9	E962.1	E980.9
chaulmoograte	961.8	E857	E931.8	E950.4	E962.0	E980.4
chloride (vapor)	987.8	E869.8	—	E952.8	E962.2	E982.8
anesthetic (local)	968.5	E855.2	E938.5	E950.4	E962.0	E980.4
inhaled	968.2	E855.1	E938.2	E950.4	E962.0	E980.4
solvent	982.3	E862.4	—	E950.9	E962.1	E980.9
estranol	962.1	E858.0	E932.1	E950.4	E962.0	E980.4
ether — see Ether(s)						
formate (solvent) NEC	982.8	E862.4	—	E950.9	E962.1	E980.9
iodoacetate	987.5	E869.3	—	E952.8	E962.2	E982.8
lactate (solvent) NEC	982.8	E862.4	—	E950.9	E962.1	E980.9
methylcarbinol	980.8	E860.8	—	E950.9	E962.1	E980.9
morphine	965.09	E850.2	E935.2	E950.0	E962.0	E980.0
Ethylene (gas)	987.1	E869.8	—	E952.8	E962.2	E982.8
anesthetic (general)	968.2	E855.1	E938.2	E950.4	E962.0	E980.4
chlorohydrin (vapor)	982.3	E862.4	—	E950.9	E962.1	E980.9
dichloride (vapor)	982.3	E862.4	—	E950.9	E962.1	E980.9
glycol(s) (any) (vapor)	982.8	E862.4	—	E950.9	E962.1	E980.9
Ethylidene						
chloride NEC	982.3	E862.4	—	E950.9	E962.1	E980.9
diethyl ether	982.8	E862.4	—	E950.9	E962.1	E980.9
Ethynodiol	962.2	E858.0	E932.2	E950.4	E962.0	E980.4
Etidocaine	968.9	E855.2	E938.9	E950.4	E962.0	E980.4
infiltration (subcutaneous)	968.5	E855.2	E938.5	E950.4	E962.0	E980.4
nerve (peripheral) (plexus)	968.6	E855.2	E938.6	E950.4	E962.0	E980.4
Etilfen	967.0	E851	E937.0	E950.1	E962.0	E980.1
Etomide	965.7	E850.7	E935.7	E950.0	E962.0	E980.0
Etorphine	965.09	E850.2	E935.2	E950.0	E962.0	E980.0
Etoval	967.0	E851	E937.0	E950.1	E962.0	E980.1
Etryptamine	969.0	E854.0	E939.0	E950.3	E962.0	E980.3
Eucaine	968.5	E855.2	E938.5	E950.4	E962.0	E980.4
Eucalyptus (oil) NEC	975.5	E858.6	E945.5	E950.4	E962.0	E980.4
Eucatropine	971.1	E855.4	E941.1	E950.4	E962.0	E980.4
Eucodal	965.09	E850.2	E935.2	E950.0	E962.0	E980.0
Euneryl	967.0	E851	E937.0	E950.1	E962.0	E980.1
Euphthalmine	971.1	E855.4	E941.1	E950.4	E962.0	E980.4
Eurax	976.0	E858.7	E946.0	E950.4	E962.0	E980.4
Euresol	976.4	E858.7	E946.4	E950.4	E962.0	E980.4
Euthroid	962.7	E858.0	E932.7	E950.4	E962.0	E980.4
Evans blue	977.8	E858.8	E947.8	E950.4	E962.0	E980.4
Evipal	967.0	E851	E937.0	E950.1	E962.0	E980.1
sodium	968.3	E855.1	E938.3	E950.4	E962.0	E980.4
Evipan	967.0	E851	E937.0	E950.1	E962.0	E980.1
sodium	968.3	E855.1	E938.3	E950.4	E962.0	E980.4
Exalgin	965.4	E850.4	E935.4	E950.0	E962.0	E980.0
Excipients, pharmaceutical	977.4	E858.8	E947.4	E950.4	E962.0	E980.4
Exhaust gas — *see* Carbon, monoxide						
Ex-Lax (phenolphthalein)	973.1	E858.4	E943.1	E950.4	E962.0	E980.4
Expectorants	975.5	E858.6	E945.5	E950.4	E962.0	E980.4
External medications (skin) (mucous membrane)	976.9	E858.7	E946.9	E950.4	E962.0	E980.4
dental agent	976.7	E858.7	E946.7	E950.4	E962.0	E980.4
ENT agent	976.6	E858.7	E946.6	E950.4	E962.0	E980.4
ophthalmic preparation	976.5	E858.7	E946.5	E950.4	E962.0	E980.4
specified NEC	976.8	E858.7	E946.8	E950.4	E962.0	E980.4
Eye agents (anti-infective)	976.5	E858.7	E946.5	E950.4	E962.0	E980.4
Factor IX complex (human)	964.5	E858.2	E934.5	E950.4	E962.0	E980.4
Fecal softeners	973.2	E858.4	E943.2	E950.4	E962.0	E980.4
Fenbutrazate	977.0	E858.8	E947.0	E950.4	E962.0	E980.4
Fencamfamin	970.8	E854.3	E940.8	E950.4	E962.0	E980.4
Fenfluramine	977.0	E858.8	E947.0	E950.4	E962.0	E980.4
Fenoprofen	965.61	E850.6	E935.6	E950.0	E962.0	E980.0
Fentanyl	965.09	E850.2	E935.2	E950.0	E962.0	E980.0
Fentazin	969.1	E853.0	E939.1	E950.3	E962.0	E980.3
Fenticlor, fentichlor	976.0	E858.7	E946.0	E950.4	E962.0	E980.4
Fer de lance (bite) (venom)	989.5	E905.0	—	E950.9	E962.1	E980.9
Ferric — *see* Iron						
Ferrocholinate	964.0	E858.2	E934.0	E950.4	E962.0	E980.4
Ferrous fumerate, gluconate, lactate, salt NEC, sulfate (medicinal)	964.0	E858.2	E934.0	E950.4	E962.0	E980.4
Ferrum — see Iron						
Fertilizers NEC	989.89	E866.5	—	E950.9	E962.1	E980.4
with herbicide mixture	989.4	E863.5	—	E950.6	E962.1	E980.7
Fibrinogen (human)	964.7	E858.2	E934.7	E950.4	E962.0	E980.4
Fibrinolysin	964.4	E858.2	E934.4	E950.4	E962.0	E980.4
Fibrinolysis-affecting agents	964.4	E858.2	E934.4	E950.4	E962.0	E980.4
Filix mas	961.6	E857	E931.6	E950.4	E962.0	E980.4
Fiorinal	965.1	E850.3	E935.3	E950.0	E962.0	E980.0
Fire damp	987.1	E869.8	—	E952.8	E962.2	E982.8
Fish, nonbacterial or noxious	988.0	E865.2	—	E950.9	E962.1	E980.9
shell	988.0	E865.1	—	E950.9	E962.1	E980.9
Flagyl	961.5	E857	E931.5	E950.4	E962.0	E980.4
Flavoxate	975.1	E858.6	E945.1	E950.4	E962.0	E980.4
Flaxedil	975.2	E858.6	E945.2	E950.4	E962.0	E980.4
Flaxseed (medicinal)	976.3	E858.7	E946.3	E950.4	E962.0	E980.4
Flomax	971.3	E855.6	E941.3	E950.4	E962.0	E980.4
Florantyrone	973.4	E858.4	E943.4	E950.4	E962.0	E980.4
Floraquin	961.3	E857	E931.3	E950.4	E962.0	E980.4
Florinef	962.0	E858.0	E932.0	E950.4	E962.0	E980.4
ENT agent	976.6	E858.7	E946.6	E950.4	E962.0	E980.4
ophthalmic preparation	976.5	E858.7	E946.5	E950.4	E962.0	E980.4
topical NEC	976.0	E858.7	E946.0	E950.4	E962.0	E980.4
Flowers of sulfur	976.4	E858.7	E946.4	E950.4	E962.0	E980.4
Floxuridine	963.1	E858.1	E933.1	E950.4	E962.0	E980.4
Flucytosine	961.9	E857	E931.9	E950.4	E962.0	E980.4
Fludrocortisone	962.0	E858.0	E932.0	E950.4	E962.0	E980.4
ENT agent	976.6	E858.7	E946.6	E950.4	E962.0	E980.4
ophthalmic preparation	976.5	E858.7	E946.5	E950.4	E962.0	E980.4
topical NEC	976.0	E858.7	E946.0	E950.4	E962.0	E980.4
Flumethasone	976.0	E858.7	E946.0	E950.4	E962.0	E980.4
Flumethiazide	974.3	E858.5	E944.3	E950.4	E962.0	E980.4
Flumidin	961.7	E857	E931.7	E950.4	E962.0	E980.4

		External Cause (E-Code)				
	Poisoning	Accident	Therapeutic Use	Suicide Attempt	Assault	Undetermined
Flunitrazepam	969.4	E853.2	E939.4	E950.3	E962.0	E980.3
Fluocinolone	976.0	E858.7	E946.0	E950.4	E962.0	E980.4
Fluocortolone	962.0	E858.0	E932.0	E950.4	E962.0	E980.4
Fluohydrocortisone	962.0	E858.0	E932.0	E950.4	E962.0	E980.4
ENT agent	976.6	E858.7	E946.6	E950.4	E962.0	E980.4
ophthalmic preparation	976.5	E858.7	E946.5	E950.4	E962.0	E980.4
topical NEC	976.0	E858.7	E946.0	E950.4	E962.0	E980.4
Fluonid	976.0	E858.7	E946.0	E950.4	E962.0	E980.4
Fluopromazine	969.1	E853.0	E939.1	E950.3	E962.0	E980.3
Fluoracetate	989.4	E863.7	—	E950.6	E962.1	E980.7
Fluorescein (sodium)	977.8	E858.8	E947.8	E950.4	E962.0	E980.4
Fluoride(s) (pesticides) (sodium) NEC	989.4	E863.4	—	E950.6	E962.1	E980.7
hydrogen — see Hydrofluoric acid						
medicinal	976.7	E858.7	E946.7	E950.4	E962.0	E980.4
not pesticide NEC	983.9	E864.4	—	E950.7	E962.1	E980.6
stannous	976.7	E858.7	E946.7	E950.4	E962.0	E980.4
Fluorinated corticosteroids	962.0	E858.0	E932.0	E950.4	E962.0	E980.4
Fluorine (compounds) (gas)	987.8	E869.8	—	E952.8	E962.2	E982.8
salt — see Fluoride(s)						
Fluoristan	976.7	E858.7	E946.7	E950.4	E962.0	E980.4
Fluoroacetate	989.4	E863.7	—	E950.6	E962.1	E980.7
Fluorodeoxyuridine	963.1	E858.1	E933.1	E950.4	E962.0	E980.4
Fluorometholone (topical) NEC	976.0	E858.7	E946.0	E950.4	E962.0	E980.4
ophthalmic preparation	976.5	E858.7	E946.5	E950.4	E962.0	E980.4
Fluorouracil	963.1	E858.1	E933.1	E950.4	E962.0	E980.4
Fluothane	968.1	E855.1	E938.1	E950.4	E962.0	E980.4
Fluoxetine hydrochloride	969.0	E854.0	E939.0	E950.3	E962.0	E980.3
Fluoxymesterone	962.1	E858.0	E932.1	E950.4	E962.0	E980.4
Fluphenazine	969.1	E853.0	E939.1	E950.3	E962.0	E980.3
Fluprednisolone	962.0	E858.0	E932.0	E950.4	E962.0	E980.4
Flurandrenolide	976.0	E858.7	E946.0	E950.4	E962.0	E980.4
Flurazepam (hydrochloride)	969.4	E853.2	E939.4	E950.3	E962.0	E980.3
Flurbiprofen	965.61	E850.6	E935.6	E950.0	E962.0	E980.0
Flurobate	976.0	E858.7	E946.0	E950.4	E962.0	E980.4
Flurothyl	969.8	E855.8	E939.8	E950.3	E962.0	E980.3
Fluroxene	968.2	E855.1	E938.2	E950.4	E962.0	E980.4
Folacin	964.1	E858.2	E934.1	E950.4	E962.0	E980.4
Folic acid	964.1	E858.2	E934.1	E950.4	E962.0	E980.4
Follicle stimulating hormone	962.4	E858.0	E932.4	E950.4	E962.0	E980.4
Food, foodstuffs, nonbacterial or noxious	988.9	E865.9	—	E950.9	E962.1	E980.9
berries, seeds	988.2	E865.3	—	E950.9	E962.1	E980.9
fish	988.0	E865.2	—	E950.9	E962.1	E980.9
mushrooms	988.1	E865.5	—	E950.9	E962.1	E980.9
plants	988.2	E865.9	—	E950.9	E962.1	E980.9
specified type NEC	988.2	E865.4	—	E950.9	E962.1	E980.9
shellfish	988.0	E865.1	—	E950.9	E962.1	E980.9
specified NEC	988.8	E865.8	—	E950.9	E962.1	E980.9
Fool's parsley	988.2	E865.4	—	E950.9	E962.1	E980.9
Formaldehyde (solution)	989.89	E861.4	—	E950.9	E962.1	E980.9
fungicide	989.4	E863.6	—	E950.6	E962.1	E980.7
gas or vapor	987.8	E869.8	—	E952.8	E962.2	E982.8
Formalin	989.89	E861.4	—	E950.9	E962.1	E980.9
fungicide	989.4	E863.6	—	E950.6	E962.1	E980.7
vapor	987.8	E869.8	—	E952.8	E962.2	E982.8
Formic acid	983.1	E864.1	—	E950.7	E962.1	E980.6
automobile	981	E862.1	—	E950.9	E962.1	E980.9
exhaust gas, not in transit	986	E868.2	—	E952.0	E962.2	E982.0
vapor NEC	987.1	E869.8	—	E952.8	E962.2	E982.8
gas (domestic use) (*see also* Carbon, monoxide, fuel) utility	987.1	E868.1	—	E951.8	E962.2	E981.8
incomplete combustion of — see Carbon, monoxide, fuel, utility						
in mobile container	987.0	E868.0	—	E951.1	E962.2	E981.1
piped (natural)	987.1	E867	—	E951.0	E962.2	E981.0
industrial, incomplete combustion	986	E868.3	—	E952.1	E962.2	E982.1
vapor	987.8	E869.8	—	E952.8	E962.2	E982.8
Fowler's solution	985.1	E866.3	—	E950.8	E962.1	E980.8
Foxglove	988.2	E865.4	—	E950.9	E962.1	E980.9
Fox green	977.8	E858.8	E947.8	E950.4	E962.0	E980.4
Framycetin	960.8	E856	E930.8	E950.4	E962.0	E980.4
Frangula (extract)	973.1	E858.4	E943.1	E950.4	E962.0	E980.4
Frei antigen	977.8	E858.8	E947.8	E950.4	E962.0	E980.4
Freons	987.4	E869.2	—	E952.8	E962.2	E982.8
Fructose	974.5	E858.5	E944.5	E950.4	E962.0	E980.4
Frusemide	974.4	E858.5	E944.4	E950.4	E962.0	E980.4
FSH	962.4	E858.0	E932.4	E950.4	E962.0	E980.4
Fuel						
Fugillin	960.8	E856	E930.8	E950.4	E962.0	E980.4
Fulminate of mercury	985.0	E866.1	—	E950.9	E962.1	E980.9
Fulvicin	960.1	E856	E930.1	E950.4	E962.0	E980.4
Fumadil	960.8	E856	E930.8	E950.4	E962.0	E980.4
Fumagillin	960.8	E856	E930.8	E950.4	E962.0	E980.4
Fumes (from)	987.9	E869.9	—	E952.9	E962.2	E982.9
carbon monoxide — see Carbon, monoxide						
charcoal (domestic use)	986	E868.3	—	E952.1	E962.2	E982.1
chloroform — see Chloroform						
coke (in domestic stoves, fireplaces)	986	E868.3	—	E952.1	E962.2	E982.1
corrosive NEC	987.8	E869.8	—	E952.8	E962.2	E982.8
ether — see Ether(s)						
freons	987.4	E869.2	—	E952.8	E962.2	E982.8
hydrocarbons	987.1	E869.8	—	E952.8	E962.2	E982.8
petroleum (liquefied)	987.0	E868.0	—	E951.1	E962.2	E981.1
distributed through pipes (pure or mixed with air)	987.0	E867	—	E951.0	E962.2	E981.0
lead — see Lead						
metals — see specified metal						
nitrogen dioxide	987.2	E869.0	—	E952.8	E962.2	E982.8
pesticides — see Pesticides						
petroleum (liquefied)	987.0	E868.0	—	E951.1	E962.2	E981.1
distributed through pipes (pure or mixed with air)	987.0	E867	—	E951.0	E962.2	E981.0
polyester	987.8	E869.8	—	E952.8	E962.2	E982.8
specified, source other (*see also* substance specified)	987.8	E869.8	—	E952.8	E962.2	E982.8
sulfur dioxide	987.3	E869.1	—	E952.8	E962.2	E982.8
Fumigants	989.4	E863.8	—	E950.6	E962.1	E980.7
Fungicides — *see also* Antifungals	989.4	E863.6	—	E950.6	E962.1	E980.7
Fungi, noxious, used as food	988.1	E865.5	—	E950.9	E962.1	E980.9
Fungizone	960.1	E856	E930.1	E950.4	E962.0	E980.4
topical	976.0	E858.7	E946.0	E950.4	E962.0	E980.4
Furacin	976.0	E858.7	E946.0	E950.4	E962.0	E980.4
Furadantin	961.9	E857	E931.9	E950.4	E962.0	E980.4
Furazolidone	961.9	E857	E931.9	E950.4	E962.0	E980.4
Furnace (coal burning) (domestic), gas from	986	E868.3	—	E952.1	E962.2	E982.1
industrial	986	E868.8	—	E952.1	E962.2	E982.1
Furniture polish	989.89	E861.2	—	E950.9	E962.1	E980.9
Furosemide	974.4	E858.5	E944.4	E950.4	E962.0	E980.4
Furoxone	961.9	E857	E931.9	E950.4	E962.0	E980.4
Fusel oil (amyl) (butyl) (propyl)	980.3	E860.4	—	E950.9	E962.1	E980.9
Fusidic acid	960.8	E856	E930.8	E950.4	E962.0	E980.4
Gallamine	975.2	E858.6	E945.2	E950.4	E962.0	E980.4
Gallotannic acid	976.2	E858.7	E946.2	E950.4	E962.0	E980.4
Gamboge	973.1	E858.4	E943.1	E950.4	E962.0	E980.4
Gamimune	964.6	E858.2	E934.6	E950.4	E962.0	E980.4
Gamma-benzene hexachloride (vapor)	989.2	E863.0	—	E950.6	E962.1	E980.7
Gamma globulin	964.6	E858.2	E934.6	E950.4	E962.0	E980.4
Gamma hydroxy butyrate (GHB)	968.4	E855.1	E938.4	E950.4	E962.0	E980.4
Gamulin	964.6	E858.2	E934.6	E950.4	E962.0	E980.4
Ganglionic blocking agents	972.3	E858.3	E942.3	E950.4	E962.0	E980.4
Ganja	969.6	E854.1	E939.6	E950.3	E962.0	E980.3
Garamycin	960.8	E856	E930.8	E950.4	E962.0	E980.4
ophthalmic preparation	976.5	E858.7	E946.5	E950.4	E962.0	E980.4
topical NEC	976.0	E858.7	E946.0	E950.4	E962.0	E980.4
Gardenal	967.0	E851	E937.0	E950.1	E962.0	E980.1
Gardepanyl	967.0	E851	E937.0	E950.1	E962.0	E980.1
Gas	987.9	E869.9	—	E952.9	E962.2	E982.9
acetylene	987.1	E868.1	—	E951.8	E962.2	E981.8
incomplete combustion of — see Carbon, monoxide, fuel, utility						
air contaminants, source or type not specified	987.9	E869.9	—	E952.9	E962.2	E982.9

		External Cause (E-Code)				
	Poisoning	Accident	Therapeutic Use	Suicide Attempt	Assault	Undetermined
Gas — *continued*						
anesthetic (general) NEC	968.2	E855.1	E938.2	E950.4	E962.0	E980.4
blast furnace	986	E868.8	—	E952.1	E962.2	E982.1
butane — see Butane						
carbon monoxide — see Carbon, monoxide						
chlorine	987.6	E869.8	—	E952.8	E962.2	E982.8
coal — see Carbon, monoxide, coal						
cyanide	987.7	E869.8	—	E952.8	E962.2	E982.8
dicyanogen	987.8	E869.8	—	E952.8	E962.2	E982.8
domestic — see Gas, utility						
exhaust — see Carbon, monoxide, exhaust gas						
from wood- or coal-burning stove or fireplace	986	E868.3	—	E952.1	E962.2	E982.1
fuel (domestic use) (*see also* Carbon, monoxide, fuel)						
industrial use	986	E868.8	—	E952.1	E962.2	E982.1
utility	987.1	E868.1	—	E951.8	E962.2	E981.8
incomplete combustion of — see Carbon, monoxide, fuel, utility						
in mobile container	987.0	E868.0	—	E951.1	E962.2	E981.1
piped (natural)	987.1	E867	—	E951.0	E962.2	E981.0
garage	986	E868.2	—	E952.0	E962.2	E982.0
hydrocarbon NEC	987.1	E869.8	—	E952.8	E962.2	E982.8
incomplete combustion of — see Carbon, monoxide, fuel, utility						
liquefied (mobile container)	987.0	E868.0	—	E951.1	E962.2	E981.1
piped	987.0	E867	—	E951.0	E962.2	E981.0
hydrocyanic acid	987.7	E869.8	—	E952.8	E962.2	E982.8
illuminating — see Gas, utility						
incomplete combustion, any — see Carbon, monoxide						
kiln	986	E868.8	—	E952.1	E962.2	E982.1
lacrimogenic	987.5	E869.3	—	E952.8	E962.2	E982.8
marsh	987.1	E869.8	—	E952.8	E962.2	E982.8
motor exhaust, not in transit	986	E868.8	—	E952.1	E962.2	E982.1
mustard — see Mustard, gas						
natural	987.1	E867	—	E951.0	E962.2	E981.0
nerve (war)	987.9	E869.9	—	E952.9	E962.2	E982.9
oils	981	E862.1	—	E950.9	E962.1	E980.9
petroleum (liquefied) (distributed in mobile containers)	987.0	E868.0	—	E951.1	E962.2	E981.1
piped (pure or mixed with air)	987.0	E867	—	E951.1	E962.2	E981.1
piped (manufactured) (natural) NEC	987.1	E867	—	E951.0	E962.2	E981.0
producer	986	E868.8	—	E952.1	E962.2	E982.1
propane — see Propane						
refrigerant (freon)	987.4	E869.2	—	E952.8	E962.2	E982.8
not freon	987.9	E869.9	—	E952.9	E962.2	E982.9
sewer	987.8	E869.8	—	E952.8	E962.2	E982.8
specified source NEC (see also substance specified)	987.8	E869.8	—	E952.8	E962.2	E982.8
stove — see Gas, utility						
tear	987.5	E869.3	—	E952.8	E962.2	E982.8
utility (for cooking, heating, or lighting) (piped) NEC	987.1	E868.1	—	E951.8	E962.2	E981.8
incomplete combustion of — see Carbon, monoxide, fuel, utilty						
in mobile container	987.0	E868.0	—	E951.1	E962.2	E981.1
piped (natural)	987.1	E867	—	E951.0	E962.2	E981.0
water	987.1	E868.1	—	E951.8	E962.2	E981.8
incomplete combustion of — see Carbon, monoxide, fuel, utility						
Gaseous substance — see Gas						
Gasoline, gasolene	981	E862.1	—	E950.9	E962.1	E980.9
vapor	987.1	E869.8	—	E952.8	E962.2	E982.8
Gastric enzymes	973.4	E858.4	E943.4	E950.4	E962.0	E980.4
Gastrografin	977.8	E858.8	E947.8	E950.4	E962.0	E980.4
Gastrointestinal agents	973.9	E858.4	E943.9	E950.4	E962.0	E980.4
specified NEC	973.8	E858.4	E943.8	E950.4	E962.0	E980.4
Gaultheria procumbens	988.2	E865.4	—	E950.9	E962.1	E980.9
Gelatin (intravenous)	964.8	E858.2	E934.8	E950.4	E962.0	E980.4
absorbable (sponge)	964.5	E858.2	E934.5	E950.4	E962.0	E980.4

		External Cause (E-Code)				
	Poisoning	Accident	Therapeutic Use	Suicide Attempt	Assault	Undetermined
Gelfilm	976.8	E858.7	E946.8	E950.4	E962.0	E980.4
Gelfoam	964.5	E858.2	E934.5	E950.4	E962.0	E980.4
Gelsemine	970.8	E854.3	E940.8	E950.4	E962.0	E980.4
Gelsemium (sempervirens)	988.2	E865.4	—	E950.9	E962.1	E980.9
Gemonil	967.0	E851	E937.0	E950.1	E962.0	E980.1
Gentamicin	960.8	E856	E930.8	E950.4	E962.0	E980.4
ophthalmic preparation	976.5	E858.7	E946.5	E950.4	E962.0	E980.4
topical NEC	976.0	E858.7	E946.0	E950.4	E962.0	E980.4
Gentian violet	976.0	E858.7	E946.0	E950.4	E962.0	E980.4
Gexane	976.0	E858.7	E946.0	E950.4	E962.0	E980.4
Gila monster (venom)	989.5	E905.0	—	E950.9	E962.1	E980.9
Ginger, Jamaica	989.89	E866.8	—	E950.9	E962.1	E980.9
Gitalin	972.1	E858.3	E942.1	E950.4	E962.0	E980.4
Gitoxin	972.1	E858.3	E942.1	E950.4	E962.0	E980.4
Glandular extract (medicinal) NEC	977.9	E858.9	E947.9	E950.5	E962.0	E980.5
Glaucarubin	961.5	E857	E931.5	E950.4	E962.0	E980.4
Globin zinc insulin	962.3	E858.0	E932.3	E950.4	E962.0	E980.4
Glucagon	962.3	E858.0	E932.3	E950.4	E962.0	E980.4
Glucochloral	967.1	E852.0	E937.1	E950.2	E962.0	E980.2
Glucocorticoids	962.0	E858.0	E932.0	E950.4	E962.0	E980.4
Glucose	974.5	E858.5	E944.5	E950.4	E962.0	E980.4
oxidase reagent	977.8	E858.8	E947.8	E950.4	E962.0	E980.4
Glucosulfone sodium	961.8	E857	E931.8	E950.4	E962.0	E980.4
Glue(s)	989.89	E866.6	—	E950.9	E962.1	E980.9
Glutamic acid (hydrochloride)	973.4	E858.4	E943.4	E950.4	E962.0	E980.4
Glutaraldehyde	989.89	E861.4	—	E950.9	E962.1	E980.9
Glutathione	963.8	E858.1	E933.8	E950.4	E962.0	E980.4
Glutethimide (group)	967.5	E852.4	E937.5	E950.2	E962.0	E980.2
Glycerin (lotion)	976.3	E858.7	E946.3	E950.4	E962.0	E980.4
Glycerol (topical)	976.3	E858.7	E946.3	E950.4	E962.0	E980.4
Glyceryl						
guaiacolate	975.5	E858.6	E945.5	E950.4	E962.0	E980.4
triacetate (topical)	976.0	E858.7	E946.0	E950.4	E962.0	E980.4
trinitrate	972.4	E858.3	E942.4	E950.4	E962.0	E980.4
Glycine	974.5	E858.5	E944.5	E950.4	E962.0	E980.4
Glycobiarsol	961.1	E857	E931.1	E950.4	E962.0	E980.4
Glycols (ether)	982.8	E862.4	—	E950.9	E962.1	E980.9
Glycopyrrolate	971.1	E855.4	E941.1	E950.4	E962.0	E980.4
Glymidine	962.3	E858.0	E932.3	E950.4	E962.0	E980.4
Gold (compounds) (salts)	965.69	E850.6	E935.6	E950.0	E962.0	E980.0
Golden sulfide of antimony	985.4	E866.2	—	E950.9	E962.1	E980.9
Goldylocks	988.2	E865.4	—	E950.9	E962.1	E980.9
Gonadal tissue extract	962.9	E858.0	E932.9	E950.4	E962.0	E980.4
beverage	980.0	E860.0	—	E950.9	E962.1	E980.9
female	962.2	E858.0	E932.2	E950.4	E962.0	E980.4
male	962.1	E858.0	E932.1	E950.4	E962.0	E980.4
Gonadotropin	962.4	E858.0	E932.4	E950.4	E962.0	E980.4
Grain alcohol	980.0	E860.1	—	E950.9	E962.1	E980.9
Gramicidin	960.8	E856	E930.8	E950.4	E962.0	E980.4
Gratiola officinalis	988.2	E865.4	—	E950.9	E962.1	E980.9
Grease	989.89	E866.8	—	E950.9	E962.1	E980.9
Green hellebore	988.2	E865.4	—	E950.9	E962.1	E980.9
Green soap	976.2	E858.7	E946.2	E950.4	E962.0	E980.4
Grifulvin	960.1	E856	E930.1	E950.4	E962.0	E980.4
Griseofulvin	960.1	E856	E930.1	E950.4	E962.0	E980.4
Growth hormone	962.4	E858.0	E932.4	E950.4	E962.0	E980.4
Guaiacol	975.5	E858.6	E945.5	E950.4	E962.0	E980.4
Guaiac reagent	977.8	E858.8	E947.8	E950.4	E962.0	E980.4
Guaifenesin	975.5	E858.6	E945.5	E950.4	E962.0	E980.4
Guaiphenesin	975.5	E858.6	E945.5	E950.4	E962.0	E980.4
Guanatol	961.4	E857	E931.4	E950.4	E962.0	E980.4
Guanethidine	972.6	E858.3	E942.6	E950.4	E962.0	E980.4
Guano	989.89	E866.5	—	E950.9	E962.1	E980.9
Guanochlor	972.6	E858.3	E942.6	E950.4	E962.0	E980.4
Guanoctine	972.6	E858.3	E942.6	E950.4	E962.0	E980.4
Guanoxan	972.6	E858.3	E942.6	E950.4	E962.0	E980.4
Hair treatment agent NEC	976.4	E858.7	E946.4	E950.4	E962.0	E980.4
Halcinonide	976.0	E858.7	E946.0	E950.4	E962.0	E980.4
Halethazole	976.0	E858.7	E946.0	E950.4	E962.0	E980.4
Hallucinogens	969.6	E854.1	E939.6	E950.3	E962.0	E980.3
Haloperidol	969.2	E853.1	E939.2	E950.3	E962.0	E980.3
Haloprogin	976.0	E858.7	E946.0	E950.4	E962.0	E980.4
Halotex	976.0	E858.7	E946.0	E950.4	E962.0	E980.4
Halothane	968.1	E855.1	E938.1	E950.4	E962.0	E980.4
Halquinols	976.0	E858.7	E946.0	E950.4	E962.0	E980.4
Hand sanitizer	976.0	E858.7	E946.0	E950.4	E962.0	E980.4
Harmonyl	972.6	E858.3	E942.6	E950.4	E962.0	E980.4
Hartmann's solution	974.5	E858.5	E944.5	E950.4	E962.0	E980.4

		External Cause (E-Code)				
	Poisoning	Accident	Therapeutic Use	Suicide Attempt	Assault	Undetermined
Hashish	969.6	E854.1	E939.6	E950.3	E962.0	E980.3
Hawaiian wood rose seeds	969.6	E854.1	E939.6	E950.3	E962.0	E980.3
Headache cures, drugs, powders NEC	977.9	E858.9	E947.9	E950.5	E962.0	E980.9
Heavenly Blue (morning glory)	969.6	E854.1	E939.6	E950.3	E962.0	E980.3
Heavy metal antagonists	963.8	E858.1	E933.8	E950.4	E962.0	E980.4
anti-infectives	961.2	E857	E931.2	E950.4	E962.0	E980.4
Hedaquinium	976.0	E858.7	E946.0	E950.4	E962.0	E980.4
Hedge hyssop	988.2	E865.4	—	E950.9	E962.1	E980.9
Heet	976.8	E858.7	E946.8	E950.4	E962.0	E980.4
Helenin	961.6	E857	E931.6	E950.4	E962.0	E980.4
Hellebore (black) (green) (white)	988.2	E865.4	—	E950.9	E962.1	E980.9
Hemlock	988.2	E865.4	—	E950.9	E962.1	E980.9
Hemostatics	964.5	E858.2	E934.5	E950.4	E962.0	E980.4
capillary active drugs	972.8	E858.3	E942.8	E950.4	E962.0	E980.4
Henbane	988.2	E865.4	—	E950.9	E962.1	E980.9
Heparin (sodium)	964.2	E858.2	E934.2	E950.4	E962.0	E980.4
Heptabarbital, heptabarbitone	967.0	E851	E937.0	E950.1	E962.0	E980.1
Heptachlor	989.2	E863.0	—	E950.6	E962.1	E980.7
Heptalgin	965.09	E850.2	E935.2	E950.0	E962.0	E980.0
Herbicides	989.4	E863.5	—	E950.6	E962.1	E980.7
Heroin	965.01	E850.0	E935.0	E950.0	E962.0	E980.0
Herplex	976.5	E858.7	E946.5	E950.4	E962.0	E980.4
HES	964.8	E858.2	E934.8	E950.4	E962.0	E980.4
Hetastarch	964.8	E858.2	E934.8	E950.4	E962.0	E980.4
Hexachlorocyclohexane	989.2	E863.0	—	E950.6	E962.1	E980.7
Hexachlorophene	976.2	E858.7	E946.2	E950.4	E962.0	E980.4
Hexadimethrine (bromide)	964.5	E858.2	E934.5	E950.4	E962.0	E980.4
Hexafluorenium	975.2	E858.6	E945.2	E950.4	E962.0	E980.4
Hexa-germ	976.2	E858.7	E946.2	E950.4	E962.0	E980.4
Hexahydrophenol	980.8	E860.8	—	E950.9	E962.1	E980.9
Hexalin	980.8	E860.8	—	E950.9	E962.1	E980.9
Hexamethonium	972.3	E858.3	E942.3	E950.4	E962.0	E980.4
Hexamethyleneamine	961.9	E857	E931.9	E950.4	E962.0	E980.4
Hexamine	961.9	E857	E931.9	E950.4	E962.0	E980.4
Hexanone	982.8	E862.4	—	E950.9	E962.1	E980.9
Hexapropymate	967.8	E852.8	E937.8	E950.2	E962.0	E980.2
Hexestrol	962.2	E858.0	E932.2	E950.4	E962.0	E980.4
Hexethal (sodium)	967.0	E851	E937.0	E950.1	E962.0	E980.1
Hexetidine	976.0	E858.7	E946.0	E950.4	E962.0	E980.4
Hexobarbital, hexobarbitone	967.0	E851	E937.0	E950.1	E962.0	E980.1
sodium (anesthetic)	968.3	E855.1	E938.3	E950.4	E962.0	E980.4
soluble	968.3	E855.1	E938.3	E950.4	E962.0	E980.4
Hexocyclium	971.1	E855.4	E941.1	E950.4	E962.0	E980.4
Hexoestrol	962.2	E858.0	E932.2	E950.4	E962.0	E980.4
Hexone	982.8	E862.4	—	E950.9	E962.1	E980.9
Hexylcaine	968.5	E855.2	E938.5	E950.4	E962.0	E980.4
Hexylresorcinol	961.6	E857	E931.6	E950.4	E962.0	E980.4
Hinkle's pills	973.1	E858.4	E943.1	E950.4	E962.0	E980.4
Histalog	977.8	E858.8	E947.8	E950.4	E962.0	E980.4
Histamine (phosphate)	972.5	E858.3	E942.5	E950.4	E962.0	E980.4
Histoplasmin	977.8	E858.8	E947.8	E950.4	E962.0	E980.4
Holly berries	988.2	E865.3	—	E950.9	E962.1	E980.9
Homatropine	971.1	E855.4	E941.1	E950.4	E962.0	E980.4
Homo-tet	964.6	E858.2	E934.6	E950.4	E962.0	E980.4
Hormones (synthetic substitute) NEC	962.9	E858.0	E932.9	E950.4	E962.0	E980.4
adrenal cortical steroids	962.0	E858.0	E932.0	E950.4	E962.0	E980.4
antidiabetic agents	962.3	E858.0	E932.3	E950.4	E962.0	E980.4
follicle stimulating	962.4	E858.0	E932.4	E950.4	E962.0	E980.4
gonadotropic	962.4	E858.0	E932.4	E950.4	E962.0	E980.4
growth	962.4	E858.0	E932.4	E950.4	E962.0	E980.4
ovarian (substitutes)	962.2	E858.0	E932.2	E950.4	E962.0	E980.4
parathyroid (derivatives)	962.6	E858.0	E932.6	E950.4	E962.0	E980.4
pituitary (posterior)	962.5	E858.0	E932.5	E950.4	E962.0	E980.4
anterior	962.4	E858.0	E932.4	E950.4	E962.0	E980.4
thyroid (derivative)	962.7	E858.0	E932.7	E950.4	E962.0	E980.4
Hornet (sting)	989.5	E905.3	—	E950.9	E962.1	E980.9
Horticulture agent NEC	989.4	E863.9	—	E950.6	E962.1	E980.7
Hyaluronidase	963.4	E858.1	E933.4	E950.4	E962.0	E980.4
Hyazyme	963.4	E858.1	E933.4	E950.4	E962.0	E980.4
Hycodan	965.09	E850.2	E935.2	E950.0	E962.0	E980.0
Hydantoin derivatives	966.1	E855.0	E936.1	E950.4	E962.0	E980.4
Hydeltra	962.0	E858.0	E932.0	E950.4	E962.0	E980.4
Hydergine	971.3	E855.6	E941.3	E950.4	E962.0	E980.4
Hydrabamine penicillin	960.0	E856	E930.0	E950.4	E962.0	E980.4
Hydralazine, hydrallazine	972.6	E858.3	E942.6	E950.4	E962.0	E980.4
Hydrargaphen	976.0	E858.7	E946.0	E950.4	E962.0	E980.4
Hydrazine	983.9	E864.3	—	E950.7	E962.1	E980.6
Hydriodic acid	975.5	E858.6	E945.5	E950.4	E962.0	E980.4
Hydrocarbon gas	987.1	E869.8	—	E952.8	E962.2	E982.8
incomplete combustion of — see Carbon, monoxide, fuel, utility						
liquefied (mobile container)	987.0	E868.0	—	E951.1	E962.2	E981.1
piped (natural)	987.0	E867	—	E951.0	E962.2	E981.0
Hydrochloric acid (liquid)	983.1	E864.1	—	E950.7	E962.1	E980.6
medicinal	973.4	E858.4	E943.4	E950.4	E962.0	E980.4
vapor	987.8	E869.8	—	E952.8	E962.2	E982.8
Hydrochlorothiazide	974.3	E858.5	E944.3	E950.4	E962.0	E980.4
Hydrocodone	965.09	E850.2	E935.2	E950.0	E962.0	E980.0
Hydrocortisone	962.0	E858.0	E932.0	E950.4	E962.0	E980.4
ENT agent	976.6	E858.7	E946.6	E950.4	E962.0	E980.4
ophthalmic preparation	976.5	E858.7	E946.5	E950.4	E962.0	E980.4
topical NEC	976.0	E858.7	E946.0	E950.4	E962.0	E980.4
Hydrocortone	962.0	E858.0	E932.0	E950.4	E962.0	E980.4
ENT agent	976.6	E858.7	E946.6	E950.4	E962.0	E980.4
ophthalmic preparation	976.5	E858.7	E946.5	E950.4	E962.0	E980.4
topical NEC	976.0	E858.7	E946.0	E950.4	E962.0	E980.4
Hydrocyanic acid — see Cyanide(s)						
Hydroflumethiazide	974.3	E858.5	E944.3	E950.4	E962.0	E980.4
Hydrofluoric acid (liquid)	983.1	E864.1	—	E950.7	E962.1	E980.6
vapor	987.8	E869.8	—	E952.8	E962.2	E982.8
Hydrogen	987.8	E869.8	—	E952.8	E962.2	E982.8
arsenide	985.1	E866.3	—	E950.8	E962.1	E980.8
arseniureted	985.1	E866.3	—	E950.8	E962.1	E980.8
cyanide (salts)	989.0	E866.8	—	E950.9	E962.1	E980.9
gas	987.7	E869.8	—	E952.8	E962.2	E982.8
fluoride (liquid)	983.1	E864.1	—	E950.7	E962.1	E980.6
vapor	987.8	E869.8	—	E952.8	E962.2	E982.8
peroxide (solution)	976.6	E858.7	E946.6	E950.4	E962.0	E980.4
phosphureted	987.8	E869.8	—	E952.8	E962.2	E982.8
sulfide (gas)	987.8	E869.8	—	E952.8	E962.2	E982.8
arseniureted	985.1	E866.3	—	E950.8	E962.1	E980.8
sulfureted	987.8	E869.8	—	E952.8	E962.2	E982.8
Hydromorphinol	965.09	E850.2	E935.2	E950.0	E962.0	E980.0
Hydromorphinone	965.09	E850.2	E935.2	E950.0	E962.0	E980.0
Hydromorphone	965.09	E850.2	E935.2	E950.0	E962.0	E980.0
Hydromox	974.3	E858.5	E944.3	E950.4	E962.0	E980.4
Hydrophilic lotion	976.3	E858.7	E946.3	E950.4	E962.0	E980.4
Hydroquinone	983.0	E864.0	—	E950.7	E962.1	E980.6
vapor	987.8	E869.8	—	E952.8	E962.2	E982.8
Hydrosulfuric acid (gas)	987.8	E869.8	—	E952.8	E962.2	E982.8
Hydrous wool fat (lotion)	976.3	E858.7	E946.3	E950.4	E962.0	E980.4
Hydroxide, caustic	983.2	E864.2	—	E950.7	E962.1	E980.6
Hydroxocobalamin	964.1	E858.2	E934.1	E950.4	E962.0	E980.4
Hydroxyamphetamine	971.2	E855.5	E941.2	E950.4	E962.0	E980.4
Hydroxychloroquine	961.4	E857	E931.4	E950.4	E962.0	E980.4
Hydroxydihydrocodeinone	965.09	E850.2	E935.2	E950.0	E962.0	E980.0
Hydroxyethyl starch	964.8	E858.2	E934.8	E950.4	E962.0	E980.4
Hydroxyphenamate	969.5	E853.8	E939.5	E950.3	E962.0	E980.3
Hydroxyphenylbutazone	965.5	E850.5	E935.5	E950.0	E962.0	E980.0
Hydroxyprogesterone	962.2	E858.0	E932.2	E950.4	E962.0	E980.4
Hydroxyquinoline derivatives	961.3	E857	E931.3	E950.4	E962.0	E980.4
Hydroxystilbamidine	961.5	E857	E931.5	E950.4	E962.0	E980.4
Hydroxyurea	963.1	E858.1	E933.1	E950.4	E962.0	E980.4
Hydroxyzine	969.5	E853.8	E939.5	E950.3	E962.0	E980.3
Hyoscine (hydrobromide)	971.1	E855.4	E941.1	E950.4	E962.0	E980.4
Hyoscyamine	971.1	E855.4	E941.1	E950.4	E962.0	E980.4
Hyoscyamus (albus) (niger)	988.2	E865.4	—	E950.9	E962.1	E980.9
Hypaque	977.8	E858.8	E947.8	E950.4	E962.0	E980.4
Hypertussis	964.6	E858.2	E934.6	E950.4	E962.0	E980.4
Hypnotics NEC	967.9	E852.9	E937.9	E950.2	E962.0	E980.2
Hypochlorites — *see* Sodium, hypochlorite						
Hypotensive agents NEC	972.6	E858.3	E942.6	E950.4	E962.0	E980.4
Ibufenac	965.69	E850.6	E935.6	E950.0	E962.0	E980.0
Ibuprofen	965.61	E850.6	E935.6	E950.0	E962.0	E980.0
ICG	977.8	E858.8	E947.8	E950.4	E962.0	E980.4
Ichthammol	976.4	E858.7	E946.4	E950.4	E962.0	E980.4
Ichthyol	976.4	E858.7	E946.4	E950.4	E962.0	E980.4
Idoxuridine	976.5	E858.7	E946.5	E950.4	E962.0	E980.4
IDU	976.5	E858.7	E946.5	E950.4	E962.0	E980.4
Iletin	962.3	E858.0	E932.3	E950.4	E962.0	E980.4

		External Cause (E-Code)				
	Poisoning	Accident	Therapeutic Use	Suicide Attempt	Assault	Undetermined
Ilex	988.2	E865.4	—	E950.9	E962.1	E980.9
Illuminating gas — see Gas, utility						
Ilopan	963.5	E858.1	E933.5	E950.4	E962.0	E980.4
Ilotycin	960.3	E856	E930.3	E950.4	E962.0	E980.4
ophthalmic preparation	976.5	E858.7	E946.5	E950.4	E962.0	E980.4
topical NEC	976.0	E858.7	E946.0	E950.4	E962.0	E980.4
Imipramine	969.0	E854.0	E939.0	E950.3	E962.0	E980.3
Immu-G	964.6	E858.2	E934.6	E950.4	E962.0	E980.4
Immuglobin	964.6	E858.2	E934.6	E950.4	E962.0	E980.4
Immune serum globulin	964.6	E858.2	E934.6	E950.4	E962.0	E980.4
Immunosuppressive agents	963.1	E858.1	E933.1	E950.4	E962.0	E980.4
Immu-tetanus	964.6	E858.2	E934.6	E950.4	E962.0	E980.4
Indandione (derivatives)	964.2	E858.2	E934.2	E950.4	E962.0	E980.4
Inderal	972.0	E858.3	E942.0	E950.4	E962.0	E980.4
Indian						
hemp	969.6	E854.1	E939.6	E950.3	E962.0	E980.3
tobacco	988.2	E865.4	—	E950.9	E962.1	E980.9
Indigo carmine	977.8	E858.8	E947.8	E950.4	E962.0	E980.4
Indocin	965.69	E850.6	E935.6	E950.0	E962.0	E980.0
Indocyanine green	977.8	E858.8	E947.8	E950.4	E962.0	E980.4
Indomethacin	965.69	E850.6	E935.6	E950.0	E962.0	E980.0
Industrial						
alcohol	980.9	E860.9	—	E950.9	E962.1	E980.9
fumes	987.8	E869.8	—	E952.8	E962.2	E982.8
solvents (fumes) (vapors)	982.8	E862.9	—	E950.9	E962.1	E980.9
Influenza vaccine	979.6	E858.8	E949.6	E950.4	E962.0	E982.8
Ingested substances NEC	989.9	E866.9	—	E950.9	E962.1	E980.9
INH (isoniazid)	961.8	E857	E931.8	E950.4	E962.0	E980.4
Inhalation, gas (noxious) — *see* Gas						
Ink	989.89	E866.8	—	E950.9	E962.1	E980.9
Innovar	967.6	E852.5	E937.6	E950.2	E962.0	E980.2
Inositol niacinate	972.2	E858.3	E942.2	E950.4	E962.0	E980.4
Inproquone	963.1	E858.1	E933.1	E950.4	E962.0	E980.4
Insecticides — *see also* Pesticides	989.4	E863.4	—	E950.6	E962.1	E980.7
chlorinated	989.2	E863.0	—	E950.6	E962.1	E980.7
mixtures	989.4	E863.3	—	E950.6	E962.1	E980.7
organochlorine (compounds)	989.2	E863.0	—	E950.6	E962.1	E980.7
organophosphorus (compounds)	989.3	E863.1	—	E950.6	E962.1	E980.7
Insect (sting), venomous	989.5	E905.5	—	E950.9	E962.1	E980.9
Insular tissue extract	962.3	E858.0	E932.3	E950.4	E962.0	E980.4
Insulin (amorphous) (globin) (isophane) (Lente) (NPH) (protamine) (Semilente) (Ultralente) (zinc)	962.3	E858.0	E932.3	E950.4	E962.0	E980.4
Intranarcon	968.3	E855.1	E938.3	E950.4	E962.0	E980.4
Inulin	977.8	E858.8	E947.8	E950.4	E962.0	E980.4
Invert sugar	974.5	E858.5	E944.5	E950.4	E962.0	E980.4
Inza — *see* Naproxen						
Iodide NEC — *see also* Iodine	976.0	E858.7	E946.0	E950.4	E962.0	E980.4
mercury (ointment)	976.0	E858.7	E946.0	E950.4	E962.0	E980.4
methylate	976.0	E858.7	E946.0	E950.4	E962.0	E980.4
potassium (expectorant) NEC	975.5	E858.6	E945.5	E950.4	E962.0	E980.4
Iodinated glycerol	975.5	E858.6	E945.5	E950.4	E962.0	E980.4
Iodine (antiseptic, external) (tincture) NEC	976.0	E858.7	E946.0	E950.4	E962.0	E980.4
diagnostic	977.8	E858.8	E947.8	E950.4	E962.0	E980.4
for thyroid conditions (antithyroid)	962.8	E858.0	E932.8	E950.4	E962.0	E980.4
vapor	987.8	E869.8	—	E952.8	E962.2	E982.8
Iodized oil	977.8	E858.8	E947.8	E950.4	E962.0	E980.4
Iodobismitol	961.2	E857	E931.2	E950.4	E962.0	E980.4
Iodochlorhydroxyquin	961.3	E857	E931.3	E950.4	E962.0	E980.4
topical	976.0	E858.7	E946.0	E950.4	E962.0	E980.4
Iodoform	976.0	E858.7	E946.0	E950.4	E962.0	E980.4
Iodopanoic acid	977.8	E858.8	E947.8	E950.4	E962.0	E980.4
Iodophthalein	977.8	E858.8	E947.8	E950.4	E962.0	E980.4
Ion exchange resins	974.5	E858.5	E944.5	E950.4	E962.0	E980.4
Iopanoic acid	977.8	E858.8	E947.8	E950.4	E962.0	E980.4
Iophendylate	977.8	E858.8	E947.8	E950.4	E962.0	E980.4
Iothiouracil	962.8	E858.0	E932.8	E950.4	E962.0	E980.4
Ipecac	973.6	E858.4	E943.6	E950.4	E962.0	E980.4
Ipecacuanha	973.6	E858.4	E943.6	E950.4	E962.0	E980.4
Ipodate	977.8	E858.8	E947.8	E950.4	E962.0	E980.4
Ipral	967.0	E851	E937.0	E950.1	E962.0	E980.1
Ipratropium	975.1	E858.6	E945.1	E950.4	E962.0	E980.4
Iproniazid	969.0	E854.0	E939.0	E950.3	E962.0	E980.3
Iron (compounds) (medicinal) (preparations)	964.0	E858.2	E934.0	E950.4	E962.0	E980.4
dextran	964.0	E858.2	E934.0	E950.4	E962.0	E980.4
nonmedicinal (dust) (fumes) NEC	985.8	E866.4	—	E950.9	E962.1	E980.9
Irritant drug	977.9	E858.9	E947.9	E950.5	E962.0	E980.5
Ismelin	972.6	E858.3	E942.6	E950.4	E962.0	E980.4
Isoamyl nitrite	972.4	E858.3	E942.4	E950.4	E962.0	E980.4
Isobutyl acetate	982.8	E862.4	—	E950.9	E962.1	E980.9
Isocarboxazid	969.0	E854.0	E939.0	E950.3	E962.0	E980.3
Isoephedrine	971.2	E855.5	E941.2	E950.4	E962.0	E980.4
Isoetharine	971.2	E855.5	E941.2	E950.4	E962.0	E980.4
Isofluorophate	971.0	E855.3	E941.0	E950.4	E962.0	E980.4
Isoniazid (INH)	961.8	E857	E931.8	E950.4	E962.0	E980.4
Isopentaquine	961.4	E857	E931.4	E950.4	E962.0	E980.4
Isophane insulin	962.3	E858.0	E932.3	E950.4	E962.0	E980.4
Isopregnenone	962.2	E858.0	E932.2	E950.4	E962.0	E980.4
Isoprenaline	971.2	E855.5	E941.2	E950.4	E962.0	E980.4
Isopropamide	971.1	E855.4	E941.1	E950.4	E962.0	E980.4
Isopropanol	980.2	E860.3	—	E950.9	E962.1	E980.9
topical (germicide)	976.0	E858.7	E946.0	E950.4	E962.0	E980.4
Isopropyl						
acetate	982.8	E862.4	—	E950.9	E962.1	E980.9
alcohol	980.2	E860.3	—	E950.9	E962.1	E980.9
topical (germicide)	976.0	E858.7	E946.0	E950.4	E962.0	E980.4
ether	982.8	E862.4	—	E950.9	E962.1	E980.9
Isoproterenol	971.2	E855.5	E941.2	E950.4	E962.0	E980.4
Isosorbide dinitrate	972.4	E858.3	E942.4	E950.4	E962.0	E980.4
Isothipendyl	963.0	E858.1	E933.0	E950.4	E962.0	E980.4
Isoxazolyl penicillin	960.0	E856	E930.0	E950.4	E962.0	E980.4
Isoxsuprine hydrochloride	972.5	E858.3	E942.5	E950.4	E962.0	E980.4
I-thyroxine sodium	962.7	E858.0	E932.7	E950.4	E962.0	E980.4
Jaborandi (pilocarpus) (extract)	971.0	E855.3	E941.0	E950.4	E962.0	E980.4
Jalap	973.1	E858.4	E943.1	E950.4	E962.0	E980.4
Jamaica						
dogwood (bark)	965.7	E850.7	E935.7	E950.0	E962.0	E980.0
ginger	989.89	E866.8	—	E950.9	E962.1	E980.9
Jatropha	988.2	E865.4	—	E950.9	E962.1	E980.9
curcas	988.2	E865.3	—	E950.9	E962.1	E980.9
Jectofer	964.0	E858.2	E934.0	E950.4	E962.0	E980.4
Jellyfish (sting)	989.5	E905.6	—	E950.9	E962.1	E980.9
Jequirity (bean)	988.2	E865.3	—	E950.9	E962.1	E980.9
Jimson weed	988.2	E865.4	—	E950.9	E962.1	E980.9
seeds	988.2	E865.3	—	E950.9	E962.1	E980.9
Juniper tar (oil) (ointment)	976.4	E858.7	E946.4	E950.4	E962.0	E980.4
Kallikrein	972.5	E858.3	E942.5	E950.4	E962.0	E980.4
Kanamycin	960.6	E856	E930.6	E950.4	E962.0	E980.4
Kantrex	960.6	E856	E930.6	E950.4	E962.0	E980.4
Kaolin	973.5	E858.4	E943.5	E950.4	E962.0	E980.4
Karaya (gum)	973.3	E858.4	E943.3	E950.4	E962.0	E980.4
Kemithal	968.3	E855.1	E938.3	E950.4	E962.0	E980.4
Kenacort	962.0	E858.0	E932.0	E950.4	E962.0	E980.4
Keratolytics	976.4	E858.7	E946.4	E950.4	E962.0	E980.4
Keratoplastics	976.4	E858.7	E946.4	E950.4	E962.0	E980.4
Kerosene, kerosine (fuel) (solvent) NEC	981	E862.1	—	E950.9	E962.1	E980.9
insecticide	981	E863.4	—	E950.6	E962.1	E980.7
vapor	987.1	E869.8	—	E952.8	E962.2	E982.8
Ketamine	968.3	E855.1	E938.3	E950.4	E962.0	E980.4
Ketobemidone	965.09	E850.2	E935.2	E950.0	E962.0	E980.0
Ketols	982.8	E862.4	—	E950.9	E962.1	E980.9
Ketone oils	982.8	E862.4	—	E950.9	E962.1	E980.9
Ketoprofen	965.61	E850.6	E935.6	E950.0	E962.0	E980.0
Kiln gas or vapor (carbon monoxide)	986	E868.8	—	E952.1	E962.2	E982.1
Konsyl	973.3	E858.4	E943.3	E950.4	E962.0	E980.4
Kosam seed	988.2	E865.3	—	E950.9	E962.1	E980.9
Krait (venom)	989.5	E905.0	—	E950.9	E962.1	E980.9
Kwell (insecticide)	989.2	E863.0	—	E950.6	E962.1	E980.7
anti-infective (topical)	976.0	E858.7	E946.0	E950.4	E962.0	E980.4
Laburnum (flowers) (seeds)	988.2	E865.3	—	E950.9	E962.1	E980.9
leaves	988.2	E865.4	—	E950.9	E962.1	E980.9
Lacquers	989.89	E861.6	—	E950.9	E962.1	E980.9
Lacrimogenic gas	987.5	E869.3	—	E952.8	E962.2	E982.8
Lactic acid	983.1	E864.1	—	E950.7	E962.1	E980.6
Lactobacillus acidophilus	973.5	E858.4	E943.5	E950.4	E962.0	E980.4
Lactoflavin	963.5	E858.1	E933.5	E950.4	E962.0	E980.4

		External Cause (E-Code)				
	Poisoning	Accident	Therapeutic Use	Suicide Attempt	Assault	Undetermined
Lactuca (virosa) (extract)	967.8	E852.8	E937.8	E950.2	E962.0	E980.2
Lactucarium	967.8	E852.8	E937.8	E950.2	E962.0	E980.2
Laevulose	974.5	E858.5	E944.5	E950.4	E962.0	E980.4
Lanatoside (C)	972.1	E858.3	E942.1	E950.4	E962.0	E980.4
Lanolin (lotion)	976.3	E858.7	E946.3	E950.4	E962.0	E980.4
Largactil	969.1	E853.0	E939.1	E950.3	E962.0	E980.3
Larkspur	988.2	E865.3	—	E950.9	E962.1	E980.9
Laroxyl	969.0	E854.0	E939.0	E950.3	E962.0	E980.3
Lasix	974.4	E858.5	E944.4	E950.4	E962.0	E980.4
Latex	989.82	E866.8	—	E950.9	E962.1	E980.9
Lathyrus (seed)	988.2	E865.3	—	E950.9	E962.1	E980.9
Laudanum	965.09	E850.2	E935.2	E950.0	E962.0	E980.0
Laudexium	975.2	E858.6	E945.2	E950.4	E962.0	E980.4
Laurel, black or cherry	988.2	E865.4	—	E950.9	E962.1	E980.9
Laurolinium	976.0	E858.7	E946.0	E950.4	E962.0	E980.4
Lauryl sulfoacetate	976.2	E858.7	E946.2	E950.4	E962.0	E980.4
Laxatives NEC	973.3	E858.4	E943.3	E950.4	E962.0	E980.4
emollient	973.2	E858.4	E943.2	E950.4	E962.0	E980.4
L-dopa	966.4	E855.0	E936.4	E950.4	E962.0	E980.4
Lead (dust) (fumes) (vapor) NEC	984.9	E866.0	—	E950.9	E962.1	E980.9
acetate (dust)	984.1	E866.0	—	E950.9	E962.1	E980.9
anti-infectives	961.2	E857	E931.2	E950.4	E962.0	E980.4
antiknock compound (tetraethyl)	984.1	E862.1	—	E950.9	E962.1	E980.9
arsenate, arsenite (dust) (insecticide) (vapor)	985.1	E863.4	—	E950.8	E962.1	E980.8
herbicide	985.1	E863.5	—	E950.8	E962.1	E980.8
carbonate	984.0	E866.0	—	E950.9	E962.1	E980.9
paint	984.0	E861.5	—	E950.9	E962.1	E980.9
chromate	984.0	E866.0	—	E950.9	E962.1	E980.9
paint	984.0	E861.5	—	E950.9	E962.1	E980.9
dioxide	984.0	E866.0	—	E950.9	E962.1	E980.9
inorganic (compound)	984.0	E866.0	—	E950.9	E962.1	E980.9
paint	984.0	E861.5	—	E950.9	E962.1	E980.9
iodide	984.0	E866.0	—	E950.9	E962.1	E980.9
pigment (paint)	984.0	E861.5	—	E950.9	E962.1	E980.9
monoxide (dust)	984.0	E866.0	—	E950.9	E962.1	E980.9
paint	984.0	E861.5	—	E950.9	E962.1	E980.9
organic	984.1	E866.0	—	E950.9	E962.1	E980.9
oxide	984.0	E866.0	—	E950.9	E962.1	E980.9
paint	984.0	E861.5	—	E950.9	E962.1	E980.9
paint	984.0	E861.5	—	E950.9	E962.1	E980.9
salts	984.0	E866.0	—	E950.9	E962.1	E980.9
specified compound NEC	984.8	E866.0	—	E950.9	E962.1	E980.9
tetra-ethyl	984.1	E862.1	—	E950.9	E962.1	E980.9
Lebanese red	969.6	E854.1	E939.6	E950.3	E962.0	E980.3
Lente Iletin (insulin)	962.3	E858.0	E932.3	E950.4	E962.0	E980.4
Leptazol	970.0	E854.3	E940.0	E950.4	E962.0	E980.4
Leritine	965.09	E850.2	E935.2	E950.0	E962.0	E980.0
Letter	962.7	E858.0	E932.7	E950.4	E962.0	E980.4
Lettuce opium	967.8	E852.8	E937.8	E950.2	E962.0	E980.2
Leucovorin (factor)	964.1	E858.2	E934.1	E950.4	E962.0	E980.4
Leukeran	963.1	E858.1	E933.1	E950.4	E962.0	E980.4
Levalbuterol	975.7	E858.6	E945.7	E950.4	E962.0	E980.4
Levallorphan	970.1	E854.3	E940.1	E950.4	E962.0	E980.4
Levanil	967.8	E852.8	E937.8	E950.2	E962.0	E980.2
Levarterenol	971.2	E855.5	E941.2	E950.4	E962.0	E980.4
Levodopa	966.4	E855.0	E936.4	E950.4	E962.0	E980.4
Levo-dromoran	965.09	E850.2	E935.2	E950.0	E962.0	E980.0
Levoid	962.7	E858.0	E932.7	E950.4	E962.0	E980.4
Levo-iso-methadone	965.02	E850.1	E935.1	E950.0	E962.0	E980.0
Levomepromazine	967.8	E852.8	E937.8	E950.2	E962.0	E980.2
Levoprome	967.8	E852.8	E937.8	E950.2	E962.0	E980.2
Levopropoxyphene	975.4	E858.6	E945.4	E950.4	E962.0	E980.4
Levorphan, levophanol	965.09	E850.2	E935.2	E950.0	E962.0	E980.0
Levothyroxine (sodium)	962.7	E858.0	E932.7	E950.4	E962.0	E980.4
Levsin	971.1	E855.4	E941.1	E950.4	E962.0	E980.4
Levulose	974.5	E858.5	E944.5	E950.4	E962.0	E980.4
Lewisite (gas)	985.1	E866.3	—	E950.8	E962.1	E980.8
Librium	969.4	E853.2	E939.4	E950.3	E962.0	E980.3
Lidex	976.0	E858.7	E946.0	E950.4	E962.0	E980.4
Lidocaine (infiltration) (topical)	968.5	E855.2	E938.5	E950.4	E962.0	E980.4
nerve block (peripheral) (plexus)	968.6	E855.2	E938.6	E950.4	E962.0	E980.4
spinal	968.7	E855.2	E938.7	E950.4	E962.0	E980.4
Lighter fluid	981	E862.1	—	E950.9	E962.1	E980.9
Lignocaine (infiltration) (topical)	968.5	E855.2	E938.5	E950.4	E962.0	E980.4
Lignocaine — *continued*						
nerve block (peripheral) (plexus)	968.6	E855.2	E938.6	E950.4	E962.0	E980.4
spinal	968.7	E855.2	E938.7	E950.4	E962.0	E980.4
Ligroin(e) (solvent)	981	E862.0	—	E950.9	E962.1	E980.9
vapor	987.1	E869.8	—	E952.8	E962.2	E982.8
Ligustrum vulgare	988.2	E865.3	—	E950.9	E962.1	E980.9
Lily of the valley	988.2	E865.4	—	E950.9	E962.1	E980.9
Lime (chloride)	983.2	E864.2	—	E950.7	E962.1	E980.6
solution, sulferated	976.4	E858.7	E946.4	E950.4	E962.0	E980.4
Limonene	982.8	E862.4	—	E950.9	E962.1	E980.9
Lincomycin	960.8	E856	E930.8	E950.4	E962.0	E980.4
Lindane (insecticide) (vapor)	989.2	E863.0	—	E950.6	E962.1	E980.7
anti-infective (topical)	976.0	E858.7	E946.0	E950.4	E962.0	E980.4
Liniments NEC	976.9	E858.7	E946.9	E950.4	E962.0	E980.4
Linoleic acid	972.2	E858.3	E942.2	E950.4	E962.0	E980.4
Liothyronine	962.7	E858.0	E932.7	E950.4	E962.0	E980.4
Liotrix	962.7	E858.0	E932.7	E950.4	E962.0	E980.4
Lipancreatin	973.4	E858.4	E943.4	E950.4	E962.0	E980.4
Lipo-Lutin	962.2	E858.0	E932.2	E950.4	E962.0	E980.4
Lipotropic agents	977.1	E858.8	E947.1	E950.4	E962.0	E980.4
Liquefied petroleum gases	987.0	E868.0	—	E951.1	E962.2	E981.1
piped (pure or mixed with air)	987.0	E867	—	E951.0	E962.2	E981.0
Liquid petrolatum	973.2	E858.4	E943.2	E950.4	E962.0	E980.4
substance	989.9	E866.9	—	E950.9	E962.1	E980.9
specified NEC	989.89	E866.8	—	E950.9	E962.1	E980.9
Lirugen	979.4	E858.8	E949.4	E950.4	E962.0	E980.4
Lithane	969.8	E855.8	E939.8	E950.3	E962.0	E980.3
Lithium	985.8	E866.4	—	E950.9	E962.1	E980.9
carbonate	969.8	E855.8	E939.8	E950.3	E962.0	E980.3
Lithonate	969.8	E855.8	E939.8	E950.3	E962.0	E980.3
Liver (extract) (injection) (preparations)	964.1	E858.2	E934.1	E950.4	E962.0	E980.4
Lizard (bite) (venom)	989.5	E905.0	—	E950.9	E962.1	E980.9
LMD	964.8	E858.2	E934.8	E950.4	E962.0	E980.4
Lobelia	988.2	E865.4	—	E950.9	E962.1	E980.9
Lobeline	970.0	E854.3	E940.0	E950.4	E962.0	E980.4
Locorten	976.0	E858.7	E946.0	E950.4	E962.0	E980.4
Lolium temulentum	988.2	E865.3	—	E950.9	E962.1	E980.9
Lomotil	973.5	E858.4	E943.5	E950.4	E962.0	E980.4
Lomustine	963.1	E858.1	E933.1	E950.4	E962.0	E980.4
Lophophora williamsii	969.6	E854.1	E939.6	E950.3	E962.0	E980.3
Lorazepam	969.4	E853.2	E939.4	E950.3	E962.0	E980.3
Lotions NEC	976.9	E858.7	E946.9	E950.4	E962.0	E980.4
Lotronex	973.8	E858.4	E943.8	E950.4	E962.0	E980.4
Lotusate	967.0	E851	E937.0	E950.1	E962.0	E980.1
Lowila	976.2	E858.7	E946.2	E950.4	E962.0	E980.4
Loxapine	969.3	E853.8	E939.3	E950.3	E962.0	E980.3
Lozenges (throat)	976.6	E858.7	E946.6	E950.4	E962.0	E980.4
LSD (25)	969.6	E854.1	E939.6	E950.3	E962.0	E980.3
L-Tryptophan — *see* amino acid						
Lubricating oil NEC	981	E862.2	—	E950.9	E962.1	E980.9
Lucanthone	961.6	E857	E931.6	E950.4	E962.0	E980.4
Luminal	967.0	E851	E937.0	E950.1	E962.0	E980.1
Lung irritant (gas) NEC	987.9	E869.9	—	E952.9	E962.2	E982.9
Lutocylol	962.2	E858.0	E932.2	E950.4	E962.0	E980.4
Lutromone	962.2	E858.0	E932.2	E950.4	E962.0	E980.4
Lututrin	975.0	E858.6	E945.0	E950.4	E962.0	E980.4
Lye (concentrated)	983.2	E864.2	—	E950.7	E962.1	E980.6
Lygranum (skin test)	977.8	E858.8	E947.8	E950.4	E962.0	E980.4
Lymecycline	960.4	E856	E930.4	E950.4	E962.0	E980.4
Lymphogranuloma venereum antigen	977.8	E858.8	E947.8	E950.4	E962.0	E980.4
Lynestrenol	962.2	E858.0	E932.2	E950.4	E962.0	E980.4
Lyovac Sodium Edecrin	974.4	E858.5	E944.4	E950.4	E962.0	E980.4
Lypressin	962.5	E858.0	E932.5	E950.4	E962.0	E980.4
Lysergic acid (amide) (diethylamide)	969.6	E854.1	E939.6	E950.3	E962.0	E980.3
Lysergide	969.6	E854.1	E939.6	E950.3	E962.0	E980.3
Lysine vasopressin	962.5	E858.0	E932.5	E950.4	E962.0	E980.4
Lysol	983.0	E864.0	—	E950.7	E962.1	E980.6
Lytta (vitatta)	976.8	E858.7	E946.8	E950.4	E962.0	E980.4
Mace	987.5	E869.3	—	E952.8	E962.2	E982.8
Macrolides (antibiotics)	960.3	E856	E930.3	E950.4	E962.0	E980.4
Mafenide	976.0	E858.7	E946.0	E950.4	E962.0	E980.4
Magaldrate	973.0	E858.4	E943.0	E950.4	E962.0	E980.4
Magic mushroom	969.6	E854.1	E939.6	E950.3	E962.0	E980.3
Magnamycin	960.8	E856	E930.8	E950.4	E962.0	E980.4
Magnesia magma	973.0	E858.4	E943.0	E950.4	E962.0	E980.4

Substance	Poisoning	External Cause (E-Code) Accident	Therapeutic Use	Suicide Attempt	Assault	Undetermined
Magnesium (compounds) (fumes) NEC	985.8	E866.4	—	E950.9	E962.1	E980.9
antacid	973.0	E858.4	E943.0	E950.4	E962.0	E980.4
carbonate	973.0	E858.4	E943.0	E950.4	E962.0	E980.4
cathartic	973.3	E858.4	E943.3	E950.4	E962.0	E980.4
citrate	973.3	E858.4	E943.3	E950.4	E962.0	E980.4
hydroxide	973.0	E858.4	E943.0	E950.4	E962.0	E980.4
oxide	973.0	E858.4	E943.0	E950.4	E962.0	E980.4
sulfate (oral)	973.3	E858.4	E943.3	E950.4	E962.0	E980.4
intravenous	966.3	E855.0	E936.3	E950.4	E962.0	E980.4
trisilicate	973.0	E858.4	E943.0	E950.4	E962.0	E980.4
Malathion (insecticide)	989.3	E863.1	—	E950.6	E962.1	E980.7
Male fern (oleoresin)	961.6	E857	E931.6	E950.4	E962.0	E980.4
Mandelic acid	961.9	E857	E931.9	E950.4	E962.0	E980.4
Manganese compounds (fumes) NEC	985.2	E866.4	—	E950.9	E962.1	E980.9
Mannitol (diuretic) (medicinal) NEC	974.4	E858.5	E944.4	E950.4	E962.0	E980.4
hexanitrate	972.4	E858.3	E942.4	E950.4	E962.0	E980.4
mustard	963.1	E858.1	E933.1	E950.4	E962.0	E980.4
Mannomustine	963.1	E858.1	E933.1	E950.4	E962.0	E980.4
MAO inhibitors	969.0	E854.0	E939.0	E950.3	E962.0	E980.3
Mapharsen	961.1	E857	E931.1	E950.4	E962.0	E980.4
Marcaine	968.9	E855.2	E938.9	E950.4	E962.0	E980.4
infiltration (subcutaneous)	968.5	E855.2	E938.5	E950.4	E962.0	E980.4
nerve block (peripheral) (plexus)	968.6	E855.2	E938.6	E950.4	E962.0	E980.4
Marezine	963.0	E858.1	E933.0	E950.4	E962.0	E980.4
Marihuana, marijuana (derivatives)	969.6	E854.1	E939.6	E950.3	E962.0	E980.3
Marine animals or plants (sting)	989.5	E905.6	—	E950.9	E962.1	E980.9
Marplan	969.0	E854.0	E939.0	E950.3	E962.0	E980.3
Marsh gas	987.1	E869.8	—	E952.8	E962.2	E982.8
Marsilid	969.0	E854.0	E939.0	E950.3	E962.0	E980.3
Matulane	963.1	E858.1	E933.1	E950.4	E962.0	E980.4
Mazindol	977.0	E858.8	E947.0	E950.4	E962.0	E980.4
MDMA	969.7	E854.2	E939.7	E950.3	E962.0	E980.3
Meadow saffron	988.2	E865.3	—	E950.9	E962.1	E980.9
Measles vaccine	979.4	E858.8	E949.4	E950.4	E962.0	E980.4
Meat, noxious or nonbacterial	988.8	E865.0	—	E950.9	E962.1	E980.9
Mebanazine	969.0	E854.0	E939.0	E950.3	E962.0	E980.3
Mebaral	967.0	E851	E937.0	E950.1	E962.0	E980.1
Mebendazole	961.6	E857	E931.6	E950.4	E962.0	E980.4
Mebeverine	975.1	E858.6	E945.1	E950.4	E962.0	E980.4
Mebhydroline	963.0	E858.1	E933.0	E950.4	E962.0	E980.4
Mebrophenhydramine	963.0	E858.1	E933.0	E950.4	E962.0	E980.4
Mebutamate	969.5	E853.8	E939.5	E950.3	E962.0	E980.3
Mecamylamine (chloride)	972.3	E858.3	E942.3	E950.4	E962.0	E980.4
Mechlorethamine hydrochloride	963.1	E858.1	E933.1	E950.4	E962.0	E980.4
Meclizene (hydrochloride)	963.0	E858.1	E933.0	E950.4	E962.0	E980.4
Meclofenoxate	970.0	E854.3	E940.0	E950.4	E962.0	E980.4
Meclozine (hydrochloride)	963.0	E858.1	E933.0	E950.4	E962.0	E980.4
Medazepam	969.4	E853.2	E939.4	E950.3	E962.0	E980.3
Medicine, medicinal substance	977.9	E858.9	E947.9	E950.5	E962.0	E980.5
specified NEC	977.8	E858.8	E947.8	E950.4	E962.0	E980.4
Medinal	967.0	E851	E937.0	E950.1	E962.0	E980.1
Medomin	967.0	E851	E937.0	E950.1	E962.0	E980.1
Medroxyprogesterone	962.2	E858.0	E932.2	E950.4	E962.0	E980.4
Medrysone	976.5	E858.7	E946.5	E950.4	E962.0	E980.4
Mefenamic acid	965.7	E850.7	E935.7	E950.0	E962.0	E980.0
Megahallucinogen	969.6	E854.1	E939.6	E950.3	E962.0	E980.3
Megestrol	962.2	E858.0	E932.2	E950.4	E962.0	E980.4
Meglumine	977.8	E858.8	E947.8	E950.4	E962.0	E980.4
Meladinin	976.3	E858.7	E946.3	E950.4	E962.0	E980.4
Melanizing agents	976.3	E858.7	E946.3	E950.4	E962.0	E980.4
Melarsoprol	961.1	E857	E931.1	E950.4	E962.0	E980.4
Melia azedarach	988.2	E865.3	—	E950.9	E962.1	E980.9
Mellaril	969.1	E853.0	E939.1	E950.3	E962.0	E980.3
Meloxine	976.3	E858.7	E946.3	E950.4	E962.0	E980.4
Melphalan	963.1	E858.1	E933.1	E950.4	E962.0	E980.4
Menadiol sodium diphosphate	964.3	E858.2	E934.3	E950.4	E962.0	E980.4
Menadione (sodium bisulfite)	964.3	E858.2	E934.3	E950.4	E962.0	E980.4
Menaphthone	964.3	E858.2	E934.3	E950.4	E962.0	E980.4
Meningococcal vaccine	978.8	E858.8	E948.8	E950.4	E962.0	E980.4
Menningovax-C	978.8	E858.8	E948.8	E950.4	E962.0	E980.4
Menotropins	962.4	E858.0	E932.4	E950.4	E962.0	E980.4
Menthol NEC	976.1	E858.7	E946.1	E950.4	E962.0	E980.4
Mepacrine	961.3	E857	E931.3	E950.4	E962.0	E980.4
Meparfynol	967.8	E852.8	E937.8	E950.2	E962.0	E980.2
Mepazine	969.1	E853.0	E939.1	E950.3	E962.0	E980.3
Mepenzolate	971.1	E855.4	E941.1	E950.4	E962.0	E980.4
Meperidine	965.09	E850.2	E935.2	E950.0	E962.0	E980.0
Mephenamin(e)	966.4	E855.0	E936.4	E950.4	E962.0	E980.4
Mephenesin (carbamate)	968.0	E855.1	E938.0	E950.4	E962.0	E980.4
Mephenoxalone	969.5	E853.8	E939.5	E950.3	E962.0	E980.3
Mephentermine	971.2	E855.5	E941.2	E950.4	E962.0	E980.4
Mephenytoin	966.1	E855.0	E936.1	E950.4	E962.0	E980.4
Mephobarbital	967.0	E851	E937.0	E950.1	E962.0	E980.1
Mepiperphenidol	971.1	E855.4	E941.1	E950.4	E962.0	E980.4
Mepivacaine	968.9	E855.2	E938.9	E950.4	E962.0	E980.4
infiltration (subcutaneous)	968.5	E855.2	E938.5	E950.4	E962.0	E980.4
nerve block (peripheral) (plexus)	968.6	E855.2	E938.6	E950.4	E962.0	E980.4
topical (surface)	968.5	E855.2	E938.5	E950.4	E962.0	E980.4
Meprednisone	962.0	E858.0	E932.0	E950.4	E962.0	E980.4
Meprobam	969.5	E853.8	E939.5	E950.3	E962.0	E980.3
Meprobamate	969.5	E853.8	E939.5	E950.3	E962.0	E980.3
Mepyramine (maleate)	963.0	E858.1	E933.0	E950.4	E962.0	E980.4
Meralluride	974.0	E858.5	E944.0	E950.4	E962.0	E980.4
Merbaphen	974.0	E858.5	E944.0	E950.4	E962.0	E980.4
Merbromin	976.0	E858.7	E946.0	E950.4	E962.0	E980.4
Mercaptomerin	974.0	E858.5	E944.0	E950.4	E962.0	E980.4
Mercaptopurine	963.1	E858.1	E933.1	E950.4	E962.0	E980.4
Mercumatilin	974.0	E858.5	E944.0	E950.4	E962.0	E980.4
Mercuramide	974.0	E858.5	E944.0	E950.4	E962.0	E980.4
Mercuranin	976.0	E858.7	E946.0	E950.4	E962.0	E980.4
Mercurochrome	976.0	E858.7	E946.0	E950.4	E962.0	E980.4
Mercury, mercuric, mercurous (compounds) (cyanide) (fumes) (nonmedicinal) (vapor) NEC	985.0	E866.1	—	E950.9	E962.1	E980.9
ammoniated	976.0	E858.7	E946.0	E950.4	E962.0	E980.4
anti-infective	961.2	E857	E931.2	E950.4	E962.0	E980.4
topical	976.0	E858.7	E946.0	E950.4	E962.0	E980.4
chloride (antiseptic) NEC	976.0	E858.7	E946.0	E950.4	E962.0	E980.4
fungicide	985.0	E863.6	—	E950.6	E962.1	E980.7
diuretic compounds	974.0	E858.5	E944.0	E950.4	E962.0	E980.4
fungicide	985.0	E863.6	—	E950.6	E962.1	E980.7
organic (fungicide)	985.0	E863.6	—	E950.6	E962.1	E980.7
Merethoxylline	974.0	E858.5	E944.0	E950.4	E962.0	E980.4
Mersalyl	974.0	E858.5	E944.0	E950.4	E962.0	E980.4
Merthiolate (topical)	976.0	E858.7	E946.0	E950.4	E962.0	E980.4
ophthalmic preparation	976.5	E858.7	E946.5	E950.4	E962.0	E980.4
Meruvax	979.4	E858.8	E949.4	E950.4	E962.0	E980.4
Mescal buttons	969.6	E854.1	E939.6	E950.3	E962.0	E980.3
Mescaline (salts)	969.6	E854.1	E939.6	E950.3	E962.0	E980.3
Mesoridazine besylate	969.1	E853.0	E939.1	E950.3	E962.0	E980.3
Mestanolone	962.1	E858.0	E932.1	E950.4	E962.0	E980.4
Mestranol	962.2	E858.0	E932.2	E950.4	E962.0	E980.4
Metacresylacetate	976.0	E858.7	E946.0	E950.4	E962.0	E980.4
Metaldehyde (snail killer) NEC	989.4	E863.4	—	E950.6	E962.1	E980.7
Metals (heavy) (nonmedicinal) NEC	985.9	E866.4	—	E950.9	E962.1	E980.9
dust, fumes, or vapor NEC	985.9	E866.4	—	E950.9	E962.1	E980.9
light NEC	985.9	E866.4	—	E950.9	E962.1	E980.9
dust, fumes, or vapor NEC	985.9	E866.4	—	E950.9	E962.1	E980.9
pesticides (dust) (vapor)	985.9	E863.4	—	E950.6	E962.1	E980.7
Metamucil	973.3	E858.4	E943.3	E950.4	E962.0	E980.4
Metaphen	976.0	E858.7	E946.0	E950.4	E962.0	E980.4
Metaproterenol	975.1	E858.6	E945.1	E950.4	E962.0	E980.4
Metaraminol	972.8	E858.3	E942.8	E950.4	E962.0	E980.4
Metaxalone	968.0	E855.1	E938.0	E950.4	E962.0	E980.4
Metformin	962.3	E858.0	E932.3	E950.4	E962.0	E980.4
Methacycline	960.4	E856	E930.4	E950.4	E962.0	E980.4
Methadone	965.02	E850.1	E935.1	E950.0	E962.0	E980.0
Methallenestril	962.2	E858.0	E932.2	E950.4	E962.0	E980.4
Methamphetamine	969.7	E854.2	E939.7	E950.3	E962.0	E980.3
Methandienone	962.1	E858.0	E932.1	E950.4	E962.0	E980.4
Methandriol	962.1	E858.0	E932.1	E950.4	E962.0	E980.4
Methandrostenolone	962.1	E858.0	E932.1	E950.4	E962.0	E980.4
Methane gas	987.1	E869.8	—	E952.8	E962.2	E982.8
Methanol	980.1	E860.2	—	E950.9	E962.1	E980.9
vapor	987.8	E869.8	—	E952.8	E962.2	E982.8
Methantheline	971.1	E855.4	E941.1	E950.4	E962.0	E980.4

	Poisoning	External Cause (E-Code) Accident	Therapeutic Use	Suicide Attempt	Assault	Undetermined
Methaphenilene	963.0	E858.1	E933.0	E950.4	E962.0	E980.4
Methapyrilene	963.0	E858.1	E933.0	E950.4	E962.0	E980.4
Methaqualone (compounds)	967.4	E852.3	E937.4	E950.2	E962.0	E980.2
Metharbital, metharbitone	967.0	E851	E937.0	E950.1	E962.0	E980.1
Methazolamide	974.2	E858.5	E944.2	E950.4	E962.0	E980.4
Methdilazine	963.0	E858.1	E933.0	E950.4	E962.0	E980.4
Methedrine	969.7	E854.2	E939.7	E950.3	E962.0	E980.3
Methenamine (mandelate)	961.9	E857	E931.9	E950.4	E962.0	E980.4
Methenolone	962.1	E858.0	E932.1	E950.4	E962.0	E980.4
Methergine	975.0	E858.6	E945.0	E950.4	E962.0	E980.4
Methiacil	962.8	E858.0	E932.8	E950.4	E962.0	E980.4
Methicillin (sodium)	960.0	E856	E930.0	E950.4	E962.0	E980.4
Methimazole	962.8	E858.0	E932.8	E950.4	E962.0	E980.4
Methionine	977.1	E858.8	E947.1	E950.4	E962.0	E980.4
Methisazone	961.7	E857	E931.7	E950.4	E962.0	E980.4
Methitural	967.0	E851	E937.0	E950.1	E962.0	E980.1
Methixene	971.1	E855.4	E941.1	E950.4	E962.0	E980.4
Methobarbital, methobarbitone	967.0	E851	E937.0	E950.1	E962.0	E980.1
Methocarbamol	968.0	E855.1	E938.0	E950.4	E962.0	E980.4
Methohexital, methohexitone (sodium)	968.3	E855.1	E938.3	E950.4	E962.0	E980.4
Methoin	966.1	E855.0	E936.1	E950.4	E962.0	E980.4
Methopholine	965.7	E850.7	E935.7	E950.0	E962.0	E980.0
Methorate	975.4	E858.6	E945.4	E950.4	E962.0	E980.4
Methoserpidine	972.6	E858.3	E942.6	E950.4	E962.0	E980.4
Methotrexate	963.1	E858.1	E933.1	E950.4	E962.0	E980.4
Methotrimeprazine	967.8	E852.8	E937.8	E950.2	E962.0	E980.2
Methoxa-Dome	976.3	E858.7	E946.3	E950.4	E962.0	E980.4
Methoxamine	971.2	E855.5	E941.2	E950.4	E962.0	E980.4
Methoxsalen	976.3	E858.7	E946.3	E950.4	E962.0	E980.4
Methoxybenzyl penicillin	960.0	E856	E930.0	E950.4	E962.0	E980.4
Methoxychlor	989.2	E863.0	—	E950.6	E962.1	E980.7
Methoxyflurane	968.2	E855.1	E938.2	E950.4	E962.0	E980.4
Methoxyphenamine	971.2	E855.5	E941.2	E950.4	E962.0	E980.4
Methoxypromazine	969.1	E853.0	E939.1	E950.3	E962.0	E980.3
Methoxypsoralen	976.3	E858.7	E946.3	E950.4	E962.0	E980.4
Methscopolamine (bromide)	971.1	E855.4	E941.1	E950.4	E962.0	E980.4
Methsuximide	966.2	E855.0	E936.2	E950.4	E962.0	E980.4
Methyclothiazide	974.3	E858.5	E944.3	E950.4	E962.0	E980.4
Methyl						
acetate	982.8	E862.4	—	E950.9	E962.1	E980.9
acetone	982.8	E862.4	—	E950.9	E962.1	E980.9
alcohol	980.1	E860.2	—	E950.9	E962.1	E980.9
amphetamine	969.7	E854.2	E939.7	E950.3	E962.0	E980.3
androstanolone	962.1	E858.0	E932.1	E950.4	E962.0	E980.4
atropine	971.1	E855.4	E941.1	E950.4	E962.0	E980.4
benzene	982.0	E862.4	—	E950.9	E962.1	E980.9
bromide (gas)	987.8	E869.8	—	E952.8	E962.2	E982.8
fumigant	987.8	E863.8	—	E950.6	E962.2	E980.7
butanol	980.8	E860.8	—	E950.9	E962.1	E980.9
carbinol	980.1	E860.2	—	E950.9	E962.1	E980.9
cellosolve	982.8	E862.4	—	E950.9	E962.1	E980.9
cellulose	973.3	E858.4	E943.3	E950.4	E962.0	E980.4
chloride (gas)	987.8	E869.8	—	E952.8	E962.2	E982.8
cyclohexane	982.8	E862.4	—	E950.9	E962.1	E980.9
cyclohexanone	982.8	E862.4	—	E950.9	E962.1	E980.9
dihydromorphinone	965.09	E850.2	E935.2	E950.0	E962.0	E980.0
ergometrine	975.0	E858.6	E945.0	E950.4	E962.0	E980.4
ergonovine	975.0	E858.6	E945.0	E950.4	E962.0	E980.4
ethyl ketone	982.8	E862.4	—	E950.9	E962.1	E980.9
hydrazine	983.9	E864.3	—	E950.7	E962.1	E980.6
isobutyl ketone	982.8	E862.4	—	E950.9	E962.1	E980.9
morphine NEC	965.09	E850.2	E935.2	E950.0	E962.0	E980.0
parafynol	967.8	E852.8	E937.8	E950.2	E962.0	E980.2
parathion	989.3	E863.1	—	E950.6	E962.1	E980.7
pentynol NEC	967.8	E852.8	E937.8	E950.2	E962.0	E980.2
peridol	969.2	E853.1	E939.2	E950.3	E962.0	E980.3
phenidate	969.7	E854.2	E939.7	E950.3	E962.0	E980.3
prednisolone	962.0	E858.0	E932.0	E950.4	E962.0	E980.4
ENT agent	976.6	E858.7	E946.6	E950.4	E962.0	E980.4
ophthalmic preparation	976.5	E858.7	E946.5	E950.4	E962.0	E980.4
topical NEC	976.0	E858.7	E946.0	E950.4	E962.0	E980.4
propylcarbinol	980.8	E860.8	—	E950.9	E962.1	E980.9
rosaniline NEC	976.0	E858.7	E946.0	E950.4	E962.0	E980.4
salicylate NEC	976.3	E858.7	E946.3	E950.4	E962.0	E980.4
sulfate (fumes)	987.8	E869.8	—	E952.8	E962.2	E982.8
liquid	983.9	E864.3	—	E950.7	E962.1	E980.6
sulfonal	967.8	E852.8	E937.8	E950.2	E962.0	E980.2
testosterone	962.1	E858.0	E932.1	E950.4	E962.0	E980.4
Methyl — *continued*						
thiouracil	962.8	E858.0	E932.8	E950.4	E962.0	E980.4
Methylated spirit	980.0	E860.1	—	E950.9	E962.1	E980.9
Methyldopa	972.6	E858.3	E942.6	E950.4	E962.0	E980.4
Methylene						
blue	961.9	E857	E931.9	E950.4	E962.0	E980.4
chloride or dichloride (solvent) NEC	982.3	E862.4	—	E950.9	E962.1	E980.9
Methylhexabital	967.0	E851	E937.0	E950.1	E962.0	E980.1
Methylparaben (ophthalmic)	976.5	E858.7	E946.5	E950.4	E962.0	E980.4
Methyprylon	967.5	E852.4	E937.5	E950.2	E962.0	E980.2
Methysergide	971.3	E855.6	E941.3	E950.4	E962.0	E980.4
Metoclopramide	963.0	E858.1	E933.0	E950.4	E962.0	E980.4
Metofoline	965.7	E850.7	E935.7	E950.0	E962.0	E980.0
Metopon	965.09	E850.2	E935.2	E950.0	E962.0	E980.0
Metronidazole	961.5	E857	E931.5	E950.4	E962.0	E980.4
Metycaine	968.9	E855.2	E938.9	E950.4	E962.0	E980.4
infiltration (subcutaneous)	968.5	E855.2	E938.5	E950.4	E962.0	E980.4
nerve block (peripheral) (plexus)	968.6	E855.2	E938.6	E950.4	E962.0	E980.4
topical (surface)	968.5	E855.2	E938.5	E950.4	E962.0	E980.4
Metyrapone	977.8	E858.8	E947.8	E950.4	E962.0	E980.4
Mevinphos	989.3	E863.1	—	E950.6	E962.1	E980.7
Mezereon (berries)	988.2	E865.3	—	E950.9	E962.1	E980.9
Micatin	976.0	E858.7	E946.0	E950.4	E962.0	E980.4
Miconazole	976.0	E858.7	E946.0	E950.4	E962.0	E980.4
Midol	965.1	E850.3	E935.3	E950.0	E962.0	E980.0
Mifepristone	962.9	E858.0	E932.9	E950.4	E962.0	E980.4
Milk of magnesia	973.0	E858.4	E943.0	E950.4	E962.0	E980.4
Millipede (tropical) (venomous)	989.5	E905.4	—	E950.9	E962.1	E980.9
Miltown	969.5	E853.8	E939.5	E950.3	E962.0	E980.3
Mineral						
oil (medicinal)	973.2	E858.4	E943.2	E950.4	E962.0	E980.4
nonmedicinal	981	E862.1	—	E950.9	E962.1	E980.9
topical	976.3	E858.7	E946.3	E950.4	E962.0	E980.4
salts NEC	974.6	E858.5	E944.6	E950.4	E962.0	E980.4
spirits	981	E862.0	—	E950.9	E962.1	E980.9
Minocycline	960.4	E856	E930.4	E950.4	E962.0	E980.4
Mithramycin (antineoplastic)	960.7	E856	E930.7	E950.4	E962.0	E980.4
Mitobronitol	963.1	E858.1	E933.1	E950.4	E962.0	E980.4
Mitomycin (antineoplastic)	960.7	E856	E930.7	E950.4	E962.0	E980.4
Mitotane	963.1	E858.1	E933.1	E950.4	E962.0	E980.4
Moderil	972.6	E858.3	E942.6	E950.4	E962.0	E980.4
Mogadon — *see* Nitrazepam						
Molindone	969.3	E853.8	E939.3	E950.3	E962.0	E980.3
Monistat	976.0	E858.7	E946.0	E950.4	E962.0	E980.4
Monkshood	988.2	E865.4	—	E950.9	E962.1	E980.9
Monoamine oxidase inhibitors	969.0	E854.0	E939.0	E950.3	E962.0	E980.3
Monochlorobenzene	982.0	E862.4	—	E950.9	E962.1	E980.9
Monosodium glutamate	989.89	E866.8	—	E950.9	E962.1	E980.9
Monoxide, carbon — *see* Carbon, monoxide						
Moperone	969.2	E853.1	E939.2	E950.3	E962.0	E980.3
Morning glory seeds	969.6	E854.1	E939.6	E950.3	E962.0	E980.3
Moroxydine (hydrochloride)	961.7	E857	E931.7	E950.4	E962.0	E980.4
Morphazinamide	961.8	E857	E931.8	E950.4	E962.0	E980.4
Morphinans	965.09	E850.2	E935.2	E950.0	E962.0	E980.0
Morphine NEC	965.09	E850.2	E935.2	E950.0	E962.0	E980.0
antagonists	970.1	E854.3	E940.1	E950.4	E962.0	E980.4
Morpholinylethylmorphine	965.09	E850.2	E935.2	E950.0	E962.0	E980.0
Morrhuate sodium	972.7	E858.3	E942.7	E950.4	E962.0	E980.4
Moth balls — *see also* Pesticides	989.4	E863.4	—	E950.6	E962.1	E980.7
naphthalene	983.0	E863.4	—	E950.7	E962.1	E980.6
Motor exhaust gas — see Carbon, monoxide, exhaust gas						
Mouth wash	976.6	E858.7	E946.6	E950.4	E962.0	E980.4
Mucolytic agent	975.5	E858.6	E945.5	E950.4	E962.0	E980.4
Mucomyst	975.5	E858.6	E945.5	E950.4	E962.0	E980.4
Mucous membrane agents (external)	976.9	E858.7	E946.9	E950.4	E962.0	E980.4
specified NEC	976.8	E858.7	E946.8	E950.4	E962.0	E980.4
Mumps						
immune globulin (human)	964.6	E858.2	E934.6	E950.4	E962.0	E980.4
skin test antigen	977.8	E858.8	E947.8	E950.4	E962.0	E980.4
vaccine	979.6	E858.8	E949.6	E950.4	E962.0	E980.4

		External Cause (E-Code)				
	Poisoning	Accident	Therapeutic Use	Suicide Attempt	Assault	Undetermined
Mumpsvax	979.6	E858.8	E949.6	E950.4	E962.0	E980.4
Muriatic acid — *see* Hydrochloric acid						
Muscarine	971.0	E855.3	E941.0	E950.4	E962.0	E980.4
Muscle affecting agents NEC	975.3	E858.6	E945.3	E950.4	E962.0	E980.4
oxytocic	975.0	E858.6	E945.0	E950.4	E962.0	E980.4
relaxants	975.3	E858.6	E945.3	E950.4	E962.0	E980.4
central nervous system	968.0	E855.1	E938.0	E950.4	E962.0	E980.4
skeletal	975.2	E858.6	E945.2	E950.4	E962.0	E980.4
smooth	975.1	E858.6	E945.1	E950.4	E962.0	E980.4
Mushrooms, noxious	988.1	E865.5	—	E950.9	E962.1	E980.9
Mussel, noxious	988.0	E865.1	—	E950.9	E962.1	E980.9
Mustard (emetic)	973.6	E858.4	E943.6	E950.4	E962.0	E980.4
gas	987.8	E869.8	—	E952.8	E962.2	E982.8
nitrogen	963.1	E858.1	E933.1	E950.4	E962.0	E980.4
Mustine	963.1	E858.1	E933.1	E950.4	E962.0	E980.4
M-vac	979.4	E858.8	E949.4	E950.4	E962.0	E980.4
Mycifradin	960.8	E856	E930.8	E950.4	E962.0	E980.4
topical	976.0	E858.7	E946.0	E950.4	E962.0	E980.4
Mycitracin	960.8	E856	E930.8	E950.4	E962.0	E980.4
ophthalmic preparation	976.5	E858.7	E946.5	E950.4	E962.0	E980.4
Mycostatin	960.1	E856	E930.1	E950.4	E962.0	E980.4
topical	976.0	E858.7	E946.0	E950.4	E962.0	E980.4
Mydriacyl	971.1	E855.4	E941.1	E950.4	E962.0	E980.4
Myelobromal	963.1	E858.1	E933.1	E950.4	E962.0	E980.4
Myleran	963.1	E858.1	E933.1	E950.4	E962.0	E980.4
Myochrysin(e)	965.69	E850.6	E935.6	E950.0	E962.0	E980.0
Myoneural blocking agents	975.2	E858.6	E945.2	E950.4	E962.0	E980.4
Myristica fragrans	988.2	E865.3	—	E950.9	E962.1	E980.9
Myristicin	988.2	E865.3	—	E950.9	E962.1	E980.9
Mysoline	966.3	E855.0	E936.3	E950.4	E962.0	E980.4
Nafcillin (sodium)	960.0	E856	E930.0	E950.4	E962.0	E980.4
Nail polish remover	982.8	E862.4	—	E950.9	E962.1	E908.9
Nalidixic acid	961.9	E857	E931.9	E950.4	E962.0	E980.4
Nalorphine	970.1	E854.3	E940.1	E950.4	E962.0	E980.4
Naloxone	970.1	E854.3	E940.1	E950.4	E962.0	E980.4
Nandrolone (decanoate) (phenproprioate)	962.1	E858.0	E932.1	E950.4	E962.0	E980.4
Naphazoline	971.2	E855.5	E941.2	E950.4	E962.0	E980.4
Naphtha (painter's) (petroleum)	981	E862.0	—	E950.9	E962.1	E980.9
solvent	981	E862.0	—	E950.9	E962.1	E980.9
vapor	987.1	E869.8	—	E952.8	E962.2	E982.8
Naphthalene (chlorinated)	983.0	E864.0	—	E950.7	E962.1	E980.6
insecticide or moth repellent	983.0	E863.4	—	E950.7	E962.1	E980.6
vapor	987.8	E869.8	—	E952.8	E962.2	E982.8
Naphthol	983.0	E864.0	—	E950.7	E962.1	E980.6
Naphthylamine	983.0	E864.0	—	E950.7	E962.1	E980.6
Naprosyn — see Naproxen						
Naproxen	965.61	E850.6	E935.6	E950.0	E962.0	E980.0
Narcotic (drug)	967.9	E852.9	E937.9	E950.2	E962.0	E980.2
analgesic NEC	965.8	E850.8	E935.8	E950.0	E962.0	E980.0
antagonist	970.1	E854.3	E940.1	E950.4	E962.0	E980.4
specified NEC	967.8	E852.8	E937.8	E950.2	E962.0	E980.2
Narcotine	975.4	E858.6	E945.4	E950.4	E962.0	E980.4
Nardil	969.0	E854.0	E939.0	E950.3	E962.0	E980.3
Natrium cyanide — see Cyanide(s)						
Natural						
blood (product)	964.7	E858.2	E934.7	E950.4	E962.0	E980.4
gas (piped)	987.1	E867	—	E951.0	E962.2	E981.0
incomplete combustion	986	E867	—	E951.0	E962.2	E981.0
Nealbarbital, nealbarbitone	967.0	E851	E937.0	E950.1	E962.0	E980.1
Nectadon	975.4	E858.6	E945.4	E950.4	E962.0	E980.4
Nematocyst (sting)	989.5	E905.6	—	E950.9	E962.1	E980.9
Nembutal	967.0	E851	E937.0	E950.1	E962.0	E980.1
Neoarsphenamine	961.1	E857	E931.1	E950.4	E962.0	E980.4
Neocinchophen	974.7	E858.5	E944.7	E950.4	E962.0	E980.4
Neomycin	960.8	E856	E930.8	E950.4	E962.0	E980.4
ENT agent	976.6	E858.7	E946.6	E950.4	E962.0	E980.4
ophthalmic preparation	976.5	E858.7	E946.5	E950.4	E962.0	E980.4
topical NEC	976.0	E858.7	E946.0	E950.4	E962.0	E980.4
Neonal	967.0	E851	E937.0	E950.1	E962.0	E980.1
Neoprontosil	961.0	E857	E931.0	E950.4	E962.0	E980.4
Neosalvarsan	961.1	E857	E931.1	E950.4	E962.0	E980.4
Neosilversalvarsan	961.1	E857	E931.1	E950.4	E962.0	E980.4
Neosporin	960.8	E856	E930.8	E950.4	E962.0	E980.4
Neosporin — *continued*						
ENT agent	976.6	E858.7	E946.6	E950.4	E962.0	E980.4
opthalmic preparation	976.5	E858.7	E946.5	E950.4	E962.0	E980.4
topical NEC	976.0	E858.7	E946.0	E950.4	E962.0	E980.4
Neostigmine	971.0	E855.3	E941.0	E950.4	E962.0	E980.4
Neraval	967.0	E851	E937.0	E950.1	E962.0	E980.1
Neravan	967.0	E851	E937.0	E950.1	E962.0	E980.1
Nerium oleander	988.2	E865.4	—	E950.9	E962.1	E980.9
Nerve gases (war)	987.9	E869.9	—	E952.9	E962.2	E982.9
Nesacaine	968.9	E855.2	E938.9	E950.4	E962.0	E980.4
infiltration (subcutaneous)	968.5	E855.2	E938.5	E950.4	E962.0	E980.4
nerve block (peripheral) (plexus)	968.6	E855.2	E938.6	E950.4	E962.0	E980.4
Neurobarb	967.0	E851	E937.0	E950.1	E962.0	E980.1
Neuroleptics NEC	969.3	E853.8	E939.3	E950.3	E962.0	E980.3
Neuroprotective agent	977.8	E858.8	E947.8	E950.4	E962.0	E980.4
Neutral spirits	980.0	E860.1	—	E950.9	E962.1	E980.9
beverage	980.0	E860.0	—	E950.9	E962.1	E980.9
Niacin, niacinamide	972.2	E858.3	E942.2	E950.4	E962.0	E980.4
Nialamide	969.0	E854.0	E939.0	E950.3	E962.0	E980.3
Nickle (carbonyl) (compounds) (fumes) (tetracarbonyl) (vapor)	985.8	E866.4	—	E950.9	E962.1	E980.9
Niclosamide	961.6	E857	E931.6	E950.4	E962.0	E980.4
Nicomorphine	965.09	E850.2	E935.2	E950.0	E962.0	E980.0
Nicotinamide	972.2	E858.3	E942.2	E950.4	E962.0	E980.4
Nicotine (insecticide) (spray) (sulfate) NEC	989.4	E863.4	—	E950.6	E962.1	E980.7
not insecticide	989.89	E866.8	—	E950.9	E962.1	E980.9
Nicotinic acid (derivatives)	972.2	E858.3	E942.2	E950.4	E962.0	E980.4
Nicotinyl alcohol	972.2	E858.3	E942.2	E950.4	E962.0	E980.4
Nicoumalone	964.2	E858.2	E934.2	E950.4	E962.0	E980.4
Nifenazone	965.5	E850.5	E935.5	E950.0	E962.0	E980.0
Nifuraldezone	961.9	E857	E931.9	E950.4	E962.0	E980.4
Nightshade (deadly)	988.2	E865.4	—	E950.9	E962.1	E980.9
Nikethamide	970.0	E854.3	E940.0	E950.4	E962.0	E980.4
Nilstat	960.1	E856	E930.1	E950.4	E962.0	E980.4
topical	976.0	E858.7	E946.0	E950.4	E962.0	E980.4
Nimodipine	977.8	E858.8	E947.8	E950.4	E962.0	E980.4
Niridazole	961.6	E857	E931.6	E950.4	E962.0	E980.4
Nisentil	965.09	E850.2	E935.2	E950.0	E962.0	E980.0
Nitrates	972.4	E858.3	E942.4	E950.4	E962.0	E980.4
Nitrazepam	969.4	E853.2	E939.4	E950.3	E962.0	E980.3
Nitric						
acid (liquid)	983.1	E864.1	—	E950.7	E962.1	E980.6
vapor	987.8	E869.8	—	E952.8	E962.2	E982.8
oxide (gas)	987.2	E869.0	—	E952.8	E962.2	E982.8
Nitrite, amyl (medicinal) (vapor)	972.4	E858.3	E942.4	E950.4	E962.0	E980.4
Nitroaniline	983.0	E864.0	—	E950.7	E962.1	E980.6
vapor	987.8	E869.8	—	E952.8	E962.2	E982.8
Nitrobenzene, nitrobenzol	983.0	E864.0	—	E950.7	E962.1	E980.6
vapor	987.8	E869.8	—	E952.8	E962.2	E982.8
Nitrocellulose	976.3	E858.7	E946.3	E950.4	E962.0	E980.4
Nitrofuran derivatives	961.9	E857	E931.9	E950.4	E962.0	E980.4
Nitrofurantoin	961.9	E857	E931.9	E950.4	E962.0	E980.4
Nitrofurazone	976.0	E858.7	E946.0	E950.4	E962.0	E980.4
Nitrogen (dioxide) (gas) (oxide)	987.2	E869.0	—	E952.8	E962.2	E982.8
mustard (antineoplastic)	963.1	E858.1	E933.1	E950.4	E962.0	E980.4
nonmedicinal	989.89	E866.8	—	E950.9	E962.1	E980.9
fumes	987.8	E869.8	—	E952.8	E962.2	E982.8
Nitroglycerin, nitroglycerol (medicinal)	972.4	E858.3	E942.4	E950.4	E962.0	E980.4
Nitrohydrochloric acid	983.1	E864.1	—	E950.7	E962.1	E980.6
Nitromersol	976.0	E858.7	E946.0	E950.4	E962.0	E980.4
Nitronaphthalene	983.0	E864.0	—	E950.7	E962.2	E980.6
Nitrophenol	983.0	E864.0	—	E950.7	E962.2	E980.6
Nitrothiazol	961.6	E857	E931.6	E950.4	E962.0	E980.4
Nitrotoluene, nitrotoluol	983.0	E864.0	—	E950.7	E962.1	E980.6
vapor	987.8	E869.8	—	E952.8	E962.2	E982.8
Nitrous	968.2	E855.1	E938.2	E950.4	E962.0	E980.4
acid (liquid)	983.1	E864.1	—	E950.7	E962.1	E980.6
fumes	987.2	E869.0	—	E952.8	E962.2	E982.8
oxide (anesthetic) NEC	968.2	E855.1	E938.2	E950.4	E962.0	E980.4
Nitrozone	976.0	E858.7	E946.0	E950.4	E962.0	E980.4
Noctec	967.1	E852.0	E937.1	E950.2	E962.0	E980.2
Noludar	967.5	E852.4	E937.5	E950.2	E962.0	E980.2
Noptil	967.0	E851	E937.0	E950.1	E962.0	E980.1
Noradrenalin	971.2	E855.5	E941.2	E950.4	E962.0	E980.4
Noramidopyrine	965.5	E850.5	E935.5	E950.0	E962.0	E980.0

		External Cause (E-Code)				
	Poisoning	Accident	Therapeutic Use	Suicide Attempt	Assault	Undetermined
Norepinephrine	971.2	E855.5	E941.2	E950.4	E962.0	E980.4
Norethandrolone	962.1	E858.0	E932.1	E950.4	E962.0	E980.4
Norethindrone	962.2	E858.0	E932.2	E950.4	E962.0	E980.4
Norethisterone	962.2	E858.0	E932.2	E950.4	E962.0	E980.4
Norethynodrel	962.2	E858.0	E932.2	E950.4	E962.0	E980.4
Norlestrin	962.2	E858.0	E932.2	E950.4	E962.0	E980.4
Norlutin	962.2	E858.0	E932.2	E950.4	E962.0	E980.4
Normison — see Benzodiazepines						
Normorphine	965.09	E850.2	E935.2	E950.0	E962.0	E980.0
Nortriptyline	969.0	E854.0	E939.0	E950.3	E962.0	E980.3
Noscapine	975.4	E858.6	E945.4	E950.4	E962.0	E980.4
Nose preparations	976.6	E858.7	E946.6	E950.4	E962.0	E980.4
Novobiocin	960.8	E856	E930.8	E950.4	E962.0	E980.4
Novocain (infiltration) (topical)	968.5	E855.2	E938.5	E950.4	E962.0	E980.4
nerve block (peripheral) (plexus)	968.6	E855.2	E938.6	E950.4	E962.0	E980.4
spinal	968.7	E855.2	E938.7	E950.4	E962.0	E980.4
Noxythiolin	961.9	E857	E931.9	E950.4	E962.0	E980.4
NPH Iletin (insulin)	962.3	E858.0	E932.3	E950.4	E962.0	E980.4
Numorphan	965.09	E850.2	E935.2	E950.0	E962.0	E980.0
Nunol	967.0	E851	E937.0	E950.1	E962.0	E980.1
Nupercaine (spinal anesthetic)	968.7	E855.2	E938.7	E950.4	E962.0	E980.4
topical (surface)	968.5	E855.2	E938.5	E950.4	E962.0	E980.4
Nutmeg oil (liniment)	976.3	E858.7	E946.3	E950.4	E962.0	E980.4
Nux vomica	989.1	E863.7	—	E950.6	E962.1	E980.7
Nydrazid	961.8	E857	E931.8	E950.4	E962.0	E980.4
Nylidrin	971.2	E855.5	E941.2	E950.4	E962.0	E980.4
Nystatin	960.1	E856	E930.1	E950.4	E962.0	E980.4
topical	976.0	E858.7	E946.0	E950.4	E962.0	E980.4
Nytol	963.0	E858.1	E933.0	E950.4	E962.0	E980.4
Oblivion	967.8	E852.8	E937.8	E950.2	E962.0	E980.2
Octyl nitrite	972.4	E858.3	E942.4	E950.4	E962.0	E980.4
Oestradiol (cypionate) (dipropionate) (valerate)	962.2	E858.0	E932.2	E950.4	E962.0	E980.4
Oestriol	962.2	E858.0	E932.2	E950.4	E962.0	E980.4
Oestrone	962.2	E858.0	E932.2	E950.4	E962.0	E980.4
Oil (of) NEC	989.89	E866.8	—	E950.9	E962.1	E980.9
bitter almond	989.0	E866.8	—	E950.9	E962.1	E980.9
camphor	976.1	E858.7	E946.1	E950.4	E962.0	E980.4
colors	989.89	E861.6	—	E950.9	E962.1	E980.9
fumes	987.8	E869.8	—	E952.8	E962.2	E982.8
lubricating	981	E862.2	—	E950.9	E962.1	E980.9
specified source, other — see substance specified						
vitriol (liquid)	983.1	E864.1	—	E950.7	E962.1	E980.6
fumes	987.8	E869.8	—	E952.8	E962.2	E982.8
wintergreen (bitter) NEC	976.3	E858.7	E946.3	E950.4	E962.0	E980.4
Ointments NEC	976.9	E858.7	E946.9	E950.4	E962.0	E980.4
Oleander	988.2	E865.4	—	E950.9	E962.1	E980.9
Oleandomycin	960.3	E856	E930.3	E950.4	E962.0	E980.4
Oleovitamin A	963.5	E858.1	E933.5	E950.4	E962.0	E980.4
Oleum ricini	973.1	E858.4	E943.1	E950.4	E962.0	E980.4
Olive oil (medicinal) NEC	973.2	E858.4	E943.2	E950.4	E962.0	E980.4
OMPA	989.3	E863.1	—	E950.6	E962.1	E980.7
Oncovin	963.1	E858.1	E933.1	E950.4	E962.0	E980.4
Ophthaine	968.5	E855.2	E938.5	E950.4	E962.0	E980.4
Ophthetic	968.5	E855.2	E938.5	E950.4	E962.0	E980.4
Opiates, opioids, opium NEC	965.00	E850.2	E935.2	E950.0	E962.0	E980.0
antagonists	970.1	E854.3	E940.1	E950.4	E962.0	E980.4
Oracon	962.2	E858.0	E932.2	E950.4	E962.0	E980.4
Oragrafin	977.8	E858.8	E947.8	E950.4	E962.0	E980.4
Oral contraceptives	962.2	E858.0	E932.2	E950.4	E962.0	E980.4
Orciprenaline	975.1	E858.6	E945.1	E950.4	E962.0	E980.4
Organidin	975.5	E858.6	E945.5	E950.4	E962.0	E980.4
Organophosphates	989.3	E863.1	—	E950.6	E962.1	E980.7
Orimune	979.5	E858.8	E949.5	E950.4	E962.0	E980.4
Orinase	962.3	E858.0	E932.3	E950.4	E962.0	E980.4
Orphenadrine	966.4	E855.0	E936.4	E950.4	E962.0	E980.4
Ortal (sodium)	967.0	E851	E937.0	E950.1	E962.0	E980.1
Orthoboric acid	976.0	E858.7	E946.0	E950.4	E962.0	E980.4
ENT agent	976.6	E858.7	E946.6	E950.4	E962.0	E980.4
ophthalmic preparation	976.5	E858.7	E946.5	E950.4	E962.0	E980.4
Orthocaine	968.5	E855.2	E938.5	E950.4	E962.0	E980.4
Ortho-Novum	962.2	E858.0	E932.2	E950.4	E962.0	E980.4
Orthotolidine (reagent)	977.8	E858.8	E947.8	E950.4	E962.0	E980.4
Osmic acid (liquid)	983.1	E864.1	—	E950.7	E962.1	E980.6
fumes	987.8	E869.8	—	E952.8	E962.2	E982.8
Osmotic diuretics	974.4	E858.5	E944.4	E950.4	E962.0	E980.4
Ouabain	972.1	E858.3	E942.1	E950.4	E962.0	E980.4
Ovarian hormones (synthetic substitutes)	962.2	E858.0	E932.2	E950.4	E962.0	E980.4
Ovral	962.2	E858.0	E932.2	E950.4	E962.0	E980.4
Ovulation suppressants	962.2	E858.0	E932.2	E950.4	E962.0	E980.4
Ovulen	962.2	E858.0	E932.2	E950.4	E962.0	E980.4
Oxacillin (sodium)	960.0	E856	E930.0	E950.4	E962.0	E980.4
Oxalic acid	983.1	E864.1	—	E950.7	E962.1	E980.6
Oxanamide	969.5	E853.8	E939.5	E950.3	E962.0	E980.3
Oxandrolone	962.1	E858.0	E932.1	E950.4	E962.0	E980.4
Oxaprozin	965.61	E850.6	E935.6	E950.0	E962.0	E980.0
Oxazepam	969.4	E853.2	E939.4	E950.3	E962.0	E980.3
Oxazolidine derivatives	966.0	E855.0	E936.0	E950.4	E962.0	E980.4
Ox bile extract	973.4	E858.4	E943.4	E950.4	E962.0	E980.4
Oxedrine	971.2	E855.5	E941.2	E950.4	E962.0	E980.4
Oxeladin	975.4	E858.6	E945.4	E950.4	E962.0	E980.4
Oxethazaine NEC	968.5	E855.2	E938.5	E950.4	E962.0	E980.4
Oxidizing agents NEC	983.9	E864.3	—	E950.7	E962.1	E980.6
Oxolinic acid	961.3	E857	E931.3	E950.4	E962.0	E980.4
Oxophenarsine	961.1	E857	E931.1	E950.4	E962.0	E980.4
Oxsoralen	976.3	E858.7	E946.3	E950.4	E962.0	E980.4
Oxtriphylline	975.7	E858.6	E945.7	E950.4	E962.0	E980.4
Oxybuprocaine	968.5	E855.2	E938.5	E950.4	E962.0	E980.4
Oxybutynin	975.1	E858.6	E945.1	E950.4	E962.0	E980.4
Oxycodone	965.09	E850.2	E935.2	E950.0	E962.0	E980.0
Oxygen	987.8	E869.8	—	E952.8	E962.2	E982.8
Oxylone	976.0	E858.7	E946.0	E950.4	E962.0	E980.4
ophthalmic preparation	976.5	E858.7	E946.5	E950.4	E962.0	E980.4
Oxymesterone	962.1	E858.0	E932.1	E950.4	E962.0	E980.4
Oxymetazoline	971.2	E855.5	E941.2	E950.4	E962.0	E980.4
Oxymetholone	962.1	E858.0	E932.1	E950.4	E962.0	E980.4
Oxymorphone	965.09	E850.2	E935.2	E950.0	E962.0	E980.0
Oxypertine	969.0	E854.0	E939.0	E950.3	E962.0	E980.3
Oxyphenbutazone	965.5	E850.5	E935.5	E950.0	E962.0	E980.0
Oxyphencyclimine	971.1	E855.4	E941.1	E950.4	E962.0	E980.4
Oxyphenisatin	973.1	E858.4	E943.1	E950.4	E962.0	E980.4
Oxyphenonium	971.1	E855.4	E941.1	E950.4	E962.0	E980.4
Oxyquinoline	961.3	E857	E931.3	E950.4	E962.0	E980.4
Oxytetracycline	960.4	E856	E930.4	E950.4	E962.0	E980.4
Oxytocics	975.0	E858.6	E945.0	E950.4	E962.0	E980.4
Oxytocin	975.0	E858.6	E945.0	E950.4	E962.0	E980.4
Ozone	987.8	E869.8	—	E952.8	E962.2	E982.8
PABA	976.3	E858.7	E946.3	E950.4	E962.0	E980.4
Packed red cells	964.7	E858.2	E934.7	E950.4	E962.0	E980.4
Paint NEC	989.89	E861.6	—	E950.9	E962.1	E980.9
cleaner	982.8	E862.9	—	E950.9	E962.1	E980.9
fumes NEC	987.8	E869.8	—	E952.8	E962.1	E982.8
lead (fumes)	984.0	E861.5	—	E950.9	E962.1	E980.9
solvent NEC	982.8	E862.9	—	E950.9	E962.1	E980.9
stripper	982.8	E862.9	—	E950.9	E962.1	E980.9
Palfium	965.09	E850.2	E935.2	E950.0	E962.0	E980.0
Palivizumab	979.9	E858.8	E949.6	E950.4	E962.0	E980.4
Paludrine	961.4	E857	E931.4	E950.4	E962.0	E980.4
PAM	977.2	E855.8	E947.2	E950.4	E962.0	E980.4
Pamaquine (naphthoate)	961.4	E857	E931.4	E950.4	E962.0	E980.4
Pamprin	965.1	E850.3	E935.3	E950.0	E962.0	E980.0
Panadol	965.4	E850.4	E935.4	E950.0	E962.0	E980.0
Pancreatic dornase (mucolytic)	963.4	E858.1	E933.4	E950.4	E962.0	E980.4
Pancreatin	973.4	E858.4	E943.4	E950.4	E962.0	E980.4
Pancrelipase	973.4	E858.4	E943.4	E950.4	E962.0	E980.4
Pangamic acid	963.5	E858.1	E933.5	E950.4	E962.0	E980.4
Panthenol	963.5	E858.1	E933.5	E950.4	E962.0	E980.4
topical	976.8	E858.7	E946.8	E950.4	E962.0	E980.4
Pantopaque	977.8	E858.8	E947.8	E950.4	E962.0	E980.4
Pantopon	965.00	E850.2	E935.2	E950.0	E962.0	E980.0
Pantothenic acid	963.5	E858.1	E933.5	E950.4	E962.0	E980.4
Panwarfin	964.2	E858.2	E934.2	E950.4	E962.0	E980.4
Papain	973.4	E858.4	E943.4	E950.4	E962.0	E980.4
Papaverine	972.5	E858.3	E942.5	E950.4	E962.0	E980.4
Para-aminobenzoic acid	976.3	E858.7	E946.3	E950.4	E962.0	E980.4
Para-aminophenol derivatives	965.4	E850.4	E935.4	E950.0	E962.0	E980.0
Para-aminosalicylic acid (derivatives)	961.8	E857	E931.8	E950.4	E962.0	E980.4
Paracetaldehyde (medicinal)	967.2	E852.1	E937.2	E950.2	E962.0	E980.2
Paracetamol	965.4	E850.4	E935.4	E950.0	E962.0	E980.0
Paracodin	965.09	E850.2	E935.2	E950.0	E962.0	E980.0
Paradione	966.0	E855.0	E936.0	E950.4	E962.0	E980.4

		External Cause (E-Code)				
	Poisoning	Accident	Therapeutic Use	Suicide Attempt	Assault	Undetermined
Paraffin(s) (wax)	981	E862.3	—	E950.9	E962.1	E980.9
liquid (medicinal)	973.2	E858.4	E943.2	E950.4	E962.0	E980.4
nonmedicinal (oil)	981	E962.1	—	E950.9	E962.1	E980.9
Paraldehyde (medicinal)	967.2	E852.1	E937.2	E950.2	E962.0	E980.2
Paramethadione	966.0	E855.0	E936.0	E950.4	E962.0	E980.4
Paramethasone	962.0	E858.0	E932.0	E950.4	E962.0	E980.4
Paraquat	989.4	E863.5	—	E950.6	E962.1	E980.7
Parasympatholytics	971.1	E855.4	E941.1	E950.4	E962.0	E980.4
Parasympathomimetics	971.0	E855.3	E941.0	E950.4	E962.0	E980.4
Parathion	989.3	E863.1	—	E950.6	E962.1	E980.7
Parathormone	962.6	E858.0	E932.6	E950.4	E962.0	E980.4
Parathyroid (derivatives)	962.6	E858.0	E932.6	E950.4	E962.0	E980.4
Paratyphoid vaccine	978.1	E858.8	E948.1	E950.4	E962.0	E980.4
Paredrine	971.2	E855.5	E941.2	E950.4	E962.0	E980.4
Paregoric	965.00	E850.2	E935.2	E950.0	E962.0	E980.0
Pargyline	972.3	E858.3	E942.3	E950.4	E962.0	E980.4
Paris green	985.1	E866.3	—	E950.8	E962.1	E980.8
insecticide	985.1	E863.4	—	E950.8	E962.1	E980.8
Parnate	969.0	E854.0	E939.0	E950.3	E962.0	E980.3
Paromomycin	960.8	E856	E930.8	E950.4	E962.0	E980.4
Paroxypropione	963.1	E858.1	E933.1	E950.4	E962.0	E980.4
Parzone	965.09	E850.2	E935.2	E950.0	E962.0	E980.0
PAS	961.8	E857	E931.8	E950.4	E962.0	E980.4
PCBs	981	E862.3	—	E950.9	E962.1	E980.9
PCP (pentachlorophenol)	989.4	E863.6	—	E950.6	E962.1	E980.7
herbicide	989.4	E863.5	—	E950.6	E962.1	E980.7
insecticide	989.4	E863.4	—	E950.6	E962.1	E980.7
phencyclidine	968.3	E855.1	E938.3	E950.4	E962.0	E980.4
Peach kernel oil (emulsion)	973.2	E858.4	E943.2	E950.4	E962.0	E980.4
Peanut oil (emulsion) NEC	973.2	E858.4	E943.2	E950.4	E962.0	E980.4
topical	976.3	E858.7	E946.3	E950.4	E962.0	E980.4
Pearly Gates (morning glory seeds)	969.6	E854.1	E939.6	E950.3	E962.0	E980.3
Pecazine	969.1	E853.0	E939.1	E950.3	E962.0	E980.3
Pecilocin	960.1	E856	E930.1	E950.4	E962.0	E980.4
Pectin (with kaolin) NEC	973.5	E858.4	E943.5	E950.4	E962.0	E980.4
Pelletierine tannate	961.6	E857	E931.6	E950.4	E962.0	E980.4
Pemoline	969.7	E854.2	E939.7	E950.3	E962.0	E980.3
Pempidine	972.3	E858.3	E942.3	E950.4	E962.0	E980.4
Penamecillin	960.0	E856	E930.0	E950.4	E962.0	E980.4
Penethamate hydriodide	960.0	E856	E930.0	E950.4	E962.0	E980.4
Penicillamine	963.8	E858.1	E933.8	E950.4	E962.0	E980.4
Penicillin (any type)	960.0	E856	E930.0	E950.4	E962.0	E980.4
Penicillinase	963.4	E858.1	E933.4	E950.4	E962.0	E980.4
Pentachlorophenol (fungicide)	989.4	E863.6	—	E950.6	E962.1	E980.7
herbicide	989.4	E863.5	—	E950.6	E962.1	E980.7
insecticide	989.4	E863.4	—	E950.6	E962.1	E980.7
Pentaerythritol	972.4	E858.3	E942.4	E950.4	E962.0	E980.4
chloral	967.1	E852.0	E937.1	E950.2	E962.0	E980.2
tetranitrate NEC	972.4	E858.3	E942.4	E950.4	E962.0	E980.4
Pentagastrin	977.8	E858.8	E947.8	E950.4	E962.0	E980.4
Pentalin	982.3	E862.4	—	E950.9	E962.1	E980.9
Pentamethonium (bromide)	972.3	E858.3	E942.3	E950.4	E962.0	E980.4
Pentamidine	961.5	E857	E931.5	E950.4	E962.0	E980.4
Pentanol	980.8	E860.8	—	E950.9	E962.1	E980.9
Pentaquine	961.4	E857	E931.4	E950.4	E962.0	E980.4
Pentazocine	965.8	E850.8	E935.8	E950.0	E962.0	E980.0
Penthienate	971.1	E855.4	E941.1	E950.4	E962.0	E980.4
Pentobarbital, pentobarbitone (sodium)	967.0	E851	E937.0	E950.1	E962.0	E980.1
Pentolinium (tartrate)	972.3	E858.3	E942.3	E950.4	E962.0	E980.4
Pentothal	968.3	E855.1	E938.3	E950.4	E962.0	E980.4
Pentylenetetrazol	970.0	E854.3	E940.0	E950.4	E962.0	E980.4
Pentylsalicylamide	961.8	E857	E931.8	E950.4	E962.0	E980.4
Pepsin	973.4	E858.4	E943.4	E950.4	E962.0	E980.4
Peptavlon	977.8	E858.8	E947.8	E950.4	E962.0	E980.4
Percaine (spinal)	968.7	E855.2	E938.7	E950.4	E962.0	E980.4
topical (surface)	968.5	E855.2	E938.5	E950.4	E962.0	E980.4
Perchloroethylene (vapor)	982.3	E862.4	—	E950.9	E962.1	E980.9
medicinal	961.6	E857	E931.6	E950.4	E962.0	E980.4
Percodan	965.09	E850.2	E935.2	E950.0	E962.0	E980.0
Percogesic	965.09	E850.2	E935.2	E950.0	E962.0	E980.0
Percorten	962.0	E858.0	E932.0	E950.4	E962.0	E980.4
Pergonal	962.4	E858.0	E932.4	E950.4	E962.0	E980.4
Perhexiline	972.4	E858.3	E942.4	E950.4	E962.0	E980.4
Periactin	963.0	E858.1	E933.0	E950.4	E962.0	E980.4
Periclor	967.1	E852.0	E937.1	E950.2	E962.0	E980.2
Pericyazine	969.1	E853.0	E939.1	E950.3	E962.0	E980.3
Peritrate	972.4	E858.3	E942.4	E950.4	E962.0	E980.4
Permanganates NEC	983.9	E864.3	—	E950.7	E962.1	E980.6

		External Cause (E-Code)				
	Poisoning	Accident	Therapeutic Use	Suicide Attempt	Assault	Undetermined
Permanganates — *continued*						
potassium (topical)	976.0	E858.7	E946.0	E950.4	E962.0	E980.4
Pernocton	967.0	E851	E937.0	E950.1	E962.0	E980.1
Pernoston	967.0	E851	E937.0	E950.1	E962.0	E980.1
Peronin(e)	965.09	E850.2	E935.2	E950.0	E962.0	E980.0
Perphenazine	969.1	E853.0	E939.1	E950.3	E962.0	E980.3
Pertofrane	969.0	E854.0	E939.0	E950.3	E962.0	E980.3
Pertussis						
immune serum (human)	964.6	E858.2	E934.6	E950.4	E962.0	E980.4
vaccine (with diphtheria toxoid) (with tetanus toxoid)	978.6	E858.8	E948.6	E950.4	E962.0	E980.4
Peruvian balsam	976.8	E858.7	E946.8	E950.4	E962.0	E980.4
Pesticides (dust) (fumes) (vapor)	989.4	E863.4	—	E950.6	E962.1	E980.7
arsenic	985.1	E863.4	—	E950.8	E962.1	E980.8
chlorinated	989.2	E863.0	—	E950.6	E962.1	E980.7
cyanide	989.0	E863.4	—	E950.6	E962.1	E980.7
kerosene	981	E863.4	—	E950.6	E962.1	E980.7
mixture (of compounds)	989.4	E863.3	—	E950.6	E962.1	E980.7
naphthalene	983.0	E863.4	—	E950.7	E962.1	E980.6
organochlorine (compounds)	989.2	E863.0	—	E950.6	E962.1	E980.7
petroleum (distillate) (products) NEC	981	E863.4	—	E950.6	E962.1	E980.7
specified ingredient NEC	989.4	E863.4	—	E950.6	E962.1	E980.7
strychnine	989.1	E863.4	—	E950.6	E962.1	E980.7
thallium	985.8	E863.7	—	E950.6	E962.1	E980.7
Pethidine (hydrochloride)	965.09	E850.2	E935.2	E950.0	E962.0	E980.0
Petrichloral	967.1	E852.0	E937.1	E950.2	E962.0	E980.2
Petrol	981	E862.1	—	E950.9	E962.1	E980.9
vapor	987.1	E869.8	—	E952.8	E962.2	E982.8
Petrolatum (jelly) (ointment)	976.3	E858.7	E946.3	E950.4	E962.0	E980.4
hydrophilic	976.3	E858.7	E946.3	E950.4	E962.0	E980.4
liquid	973.2	E858.4	E943.2	E950.4	E962.0	E980.4
topical	976.3	E858.7	E946.3	E950.4	E962.0	E980.4
nonmedicinal	981	E862.1	—	E950.9	E962.1	E980.9
Petroleum (cleaners) (fuels) (products) NEC	981	E862.1	—	E950.9	E962.1	E980.9
benzin(e) — see Ligroin						
ether — see Ligroin						
jelly — see Petrolatum						
naphtha — see Ligroin						
pesticide	981	E863.4	—	E950.6	E962.1	E980.7
solids	981	E862.3	—	E950.9	E962.1	E980.9
solvents	981	E862.0	—	E950.9	E962.1	E980.9
vapor	987.1	E869.8	—	E952.8	E962.2	E982.8
Peyote	969.6	E854.1	E939.6	E950.3	E962.0	E980.3
Phanodorm, phanodorn	967.0	E851	E937.0	E950.1	E962.0	E980.1
Phanquinone, phanquone	961.5	E857	E931.5	E950.4	E962.0	E980.4
Pharmaceutical excipient or adjunct	977.4	E858.8	E947.4	E950.4	E962.0	E980.4
Phenacemide	966.3	E855.0	E936.3	E950.4	E962.0	E980.4
Phenacetin	965.4	E850.4	E935.4	E950.0	E962.0	E980.0
Phenadoxone	965.09	E850.2	E935.2	E950.0	E962.0	E980.0
Phenaglycodol	969.5	E853.8	E939.5	E950.3	E962.0	E980.3
Phenantoin	966.1	E855.0	E936.1	E950.4	E962.0	E980.4
Phenaphthazine reagent	977.8	E858.8	E947.8	E950.4	E962.0	E980.4
Phenazocine	965.09	E850.2	E935.2	E950.0	E962.0	E980.0
Phenazone	965.5	E850.5	E935.5	E950.0	E962.0	E980.0
Phenazopyridine	976.1	E858.7	E946.1	E950.4	E962.0	E980.4
Phenbenicillin	960.0	E856	E930.0	E950.4	E962.0	E980.4
Phenbutrazate	977.0	E858.8	E947.0	E950.4	E962.0	E980.4
Phencyclidine	968.3	E855.1	E938.3	E950.4	E962.0	E980.4
Phendimetrazine	977.0	E858.8	E947.0	E950.4	E962.0	E980.4
Phenelzine	969.0	E854.0	E939.0	E950.3	E962.0	E980.3
Phenergan	967.8	E852.8	E937.8	E950.2	E962.0	E980.2
Phenethicillin (potassium)	960.0	E856	E930.0	E950.4	E962.0	E980.4
Phenetsal	965.1	E850.3	E935.3	E950.0	E962.0	E980.0
Pheneturide	966.3	E855.0	E936.3	E950.4	E962.0	E980.4
Phenformin	962.3	E858.0	E932.3	E950.4	E962.0	E980.4
Phenglutarimide	971.1	E855.4	E941.1	E950.4	E962.0	E980.4
Phenicarbazide	965.8	E850.8	E935.8	E950.0	E962.0	E980.0
Phenindamine (tartrate)	963.0	E858.1	E933.0	E950.4	E962.0	E980.4
Phenindione	964.2	E858.2	E934.2	E950.4	E962.0	E980.4
Pheniprazine	969.0	E854.0	E939.0	E950.3	E962.0	E980.3
Pheniramine (maleate)	963.0	E858.1	E933.0	E950.4	E962.0	E980.4
Phenmetrazine	977.0	E858.8	E947.0	E950.4	E962.0	E980.4
Phenobal	967.0	E851	E937.0	E950.1	E962.0	E980.1
Phenobarbital	967.0	E851	E937.0	E950.1	E962.0	E980.1
Phenobarbitone	967.0	E851	E937.0	E950.1	E962.0	E980.1
Phenoctide	976.0	E858.7	E946.0	E950.4	E962.0	E980.4

		External Cause (E-Code)				
	Poisoning	Accident	Therapeutic Use	Suicide Attempt	Assault	Undetermined
Phenol (derivatives) NEC	983.0	E864.0	—	E950.7	E962.1	E980.6
disinfectant	983.0	E864.0	—	E950.7	E962.1	E980.6
pesticide	989.4	E863.4	—	E950.6	E962.1	E980.7
red	977.8	E858.8	E947.8	E950.4	E962.0	E980.4
Phenolphthalein	973.1	E858.4	E943.1	E950.4	E962.0	E980.4
Phenolsulfonphthalein	977.8	E858.8	E947.8	E950.4	E962.0	E980.4
Phenomorphan	965.09	E850.2	E935.2	E950.0	E962.0	E980.0
Phenonyl	967.0	E851	E937.0	E950.1	E962.0	E980.1
Phenoperidine	965.09	E850.2	E935.2	E950.0	E962.0	E980.0
Phenoquin	974.7	E858.5	E944.7	E950.4	E962.0	E980.4
Phenothiazines (tranquilizers) NEC	969.1	E853.0	E939.1	E950.3	E962.0	E980.3
insecticide	989.3	E863.4	—	E950.6	E962.1	E980.7
Phenoxybenzamine	971.3	E855.6	E941.3	E950.4	E962.0	E980.4
Phenoxymethyl penicillin	960.0	E856	E930.0	E950.4	E962.0	E980.4
Phenprocoumon	964.2	E858.2	E934.2	E950.4	E962.0	E980.4
Phensuximide	966.2	E855.0	E936.2	E950.4	E962.0	E980.4
Phentermine	977.0	E858.8	E947.0	E950.4	E962.0	E980.4
Phentolamine	971.3	E855.6	E941.3	E950.4	E962.0	E980.4
Phenyl						
butazone	965.5	E850.5	E935.5	E950.0	E962.0	E980.0
enediamine	983.0	E864.0	—	E950.7	E962.1	E980.6
hydrazine	983.0	E864.0	—	E950.7	E962.1	E980.6
antineoplastic	963.1	E858.1	E933.1	E950.4	E962.0	E980.4
mercuric compounds — see Mercury						
salicylate	976.3	E858.7	E946.3	E950.4	E962.0	E980.4
Phenylephrin	971.2	E855.5	E941.2	E950.4	E962.0	E980.4
Phenylethylbiguanide	962.3	E858.0	E932.3	E950.4	E962.0	E980.4
Phenylpropanolamine	971.2	E855.5	E941.2	E950.4	E962.0	E980.4
Phenylsulfthion	989.3	E863.1	—	E950.6	E962.1	E980.7
Phenyramidol, phenyramidon	965.7	E850.7	E935.7	E950.0	E962.0	E980.0
Phenytoin	966.1	E855.0	E936.1	E950.4	E962.0	E980.4
pHisoHex	976.2	E858.7	E946.2	E950.4	E962.0	E980.4
Pholcodine	965.09	E850.2	E935.2	E950.0	E962.0	E980.0
Phorate	989.3	E863.1	—	E950.6	E962.1	E980.7
Phosdrin	989.3	E863.1	—	E950.6	E962.1	E980.7
Phosgene (gas)	987.8	E869.8	—	E952.8	E962.2	E982.8
Phosphate (tricresyl)	989.89	E866.8	—	E950.9	E962.1	E980.9
organic	989.3	E863.1	—	E950.6	E962.1	E980.7
solvent	982.8	E862.4	—	E950.9	E926.1	E980.9
Phosphine	987.8	E869.8	—	E952.8	E962.2	E982.8
fumigant	987.8	E863.8	—	E950.6	E962.2	E980.7
Phospholine	971.0	E855.3	E941.0	E950.4	E962.0	E980.4
Phosphoric acid	983.1	E864.1	—	E950.7	E962.1	E980.6
Phosphorus (compounds) NEC	983.9	E864.3	—	E950.7	E962.1	E980.6
rodenticide	983.9	E863.7	—	E950.7	E962.1	E980.6
Phthalimidoglutarimide	967.8	E852.8	E937.8	E950.2	E962.0	E980.2
Phthalylsulfathiazole	961.0	E857	E931.0	E950.4	E962.0	E980.4
Phylloquinone	964.3	E858.2	E934.3	E950.4	E962.0	E980.4
Physeptone	965.02	E850.1	E935.1	E950.0	E962.0	E980.0
Physostigma venenosum	988.2	E865.4	—	E950.9	E962.1	E980.9
Physostigmine	971.0	E855.3	E941.0	E950.4	E962.0	E980.4
Phytolacca decandra	988.2	E865.4	—	E950.9	E962.1	E980.9
Phytomenadione	964.3	E858.2	E934.3	E950.4	E962.0	E980.4
Phytonadione	964.3	E858.2	E934.3	E950.4	E962.0	E980.4
Picric (acid)	983.0	E864.0	—	E950.7	E962.1	E980.6
Picrotoxin	970.0	E854.3	E940.0	E950.4	E962.0	E980.4
Pilocarpine	971.0	E855.3	E941.0	E950.4	E962.0	E980.4
Pilocarpus (jaborandi) extract	971.0	E855.3	E941.0	E950.4	E962.0	E980.4
Pimaricin	960.1	E856	E930.1	E950.4	E962.0	E980.4
Piminodine	965.09	E850.2	E935.2	E950.0	E962.0	E980.0
Pine oil, pinesol (disinfectant)	983.9	E861.4	—	E950.7	E962.1	E980.6
Pinkroot	961.6	E857	E931.6	E950.4	E962.0	E980.4
Pipadone	965.09	E850.2	E935.2	E950.0	E962.0	E980.0
Pipamazine	963.0	E858.1	E933.0	E950.4	E962.0	E980.4
Pipazethate	975.4	E858.6	E945.4	E950.4	E962.0	E980.4
Pipenzolate	971.1	E855.4	E941.1	E950.4	E962.0	E980.4
Piperacetazine	969.1	E853.0	E939.1	E950.3	E962.0	E980.3
Piperazine NEC	961.6	E857	E931.6	E950.4	E962.0	E980.4
estrone sulfate	962.2	E858.0	E932.2	E950.4	E962.0	E980.4
Piper cubeba	988.2	E865.4	—	E950.9	E962.1	E980.9
Piperidione	975.4	E858.6	E945.4	E950.4	E962.0	E980.4
Piperidolate	971.1	E855.4	E941.1	E950.4	E962.0	E980.4
Piperocaine	968.9	E855.2	E938.9	E950.4	E962.0	E980.4
infiltration (subcutaneous)	968.5	E855.2	E938.5	E950.4	E962.0	E980.4
Piperocaine — *continued*						
nerve block (peripheral) (plexus)	968.6	E855.2	E938.6	E950.4	E962.0	E980.4
topical (surface)	968.5	E855.2	E938.5	E950.4	E962.0	E980.4
Pipobroman	963.1	E858.1	E933.1	E950.4	E962.0	E980.4
Pipradrol	970.8	E854.3	E940.8	E950.4	E962.0	E980.4
Piscidia (bark) (erythrina)	965.7	E850.7	E935.7	E950.0	E962.0	E980.0
Pitch	983.0	E864.0	—	E950.7	E962.1	E980.6
Pitkin's solution	968.7	E855.2	E938.7	E950.4	E962.0	E980.4
Pitocin	975.0	E858.6	E945.0	E950.4	E962.0	E980.4
Pitressin (tannate)	962.5	E858.0	E932.5	E950.4	E962.0	E980.4
Pituitary extracts (posterior)	962.5	E858.0	E932.5	E950.4	E962.0	E980.4
anterior	962.4	E858.0	E932.4	E950.4	E962.0	E980.4
Pituitrin	962.5	E858.0	E932.5	E950.4	E962.0	E980.4
Placental extract	962.9	E858.0	E932.9	E950.4	E962.0	E980.4
Placidyl	967.8	E852.8	E937.8	E950.2	E962.0	E980.2
Plague vaccine	978.3	E858.8	E948.3	E950.4	E962.0	E980.4
Plant foods or fertilizers NEC	989.89	E866.5	—	E950.9	E962.1	E980.9
mixed with herbicides	989.4	E863.5	—	E950.6	E962.1	E980.7
Plants, noxious, used as food	988.2	E865.9	—	E950.9	E962.1	E980.9
berries and seeds	988.2	E865.3	—	E950.9	E962.1	E980.9
specified type NEC	988.2	E865.4	—	E950.9	E962.1	E980.9
Plasma (blood)	964.7	E858.2	E934.7	E950.4	E962.0	E980.4
expanders	964.8	E858.2	E934.8	E950.4	E962.0	E980.4
Plasmanate	964.7	E858.2	E934.7	E950.4	E962.0	E980.4
Plegicil	969.1	E853.0	E939.1	E950.3	E962.0	E980.3
Podophyllin	976.4	E858.7	E946.4	E950.4	E962.0	E980.4
Podophyllum resin	976.4	E858.7	E946.4	E950.4	E962.0	E980.4
Poison NEC	989.9	E866.9	—	E950.9	E962.1	E980.9
Poisonous berries	988.2	E865.3	—	E950.9	E962.1	E980.9
Pokeweed (any part)	988.2	E865.4	—	E950.9	E962.1	E980.9
Poldine	971.1	E855.4	E941.1	E950.4	E962.0	E980.4
Poliomyelitis vaccine	979.5	E858.8	E949.5	E950.4	E962.0	E980.4
Poliovirus vaccine	979.5	E858.8	E949.5	E950.4	E962.0	E980.4
Polish (car) (floor) (furniture) (metal) (silver)	989.89	E861.2	—	E950.9	E962.1	E980.9
abrasive	989.89	E861.3	—	E950.9	E962.1	E980.9
porcelain	989.89	E861.3	—	E950.9	E962.1	E980.9
Poloxalkol	973.2	E858.4	E943.2	E950.4	E962.0	E980.4
Polyaminostyrene resins	974.5	E858.5	E944.5	E950.4	E962.0	E980.4
Polychlorinated biphenyl — *see* PCBs						
Polycycline	960.4	E856	E930.4	E950.4	E962.0	E980.4
Polyester resin hardener	982.8	E862.4	—	E950.9	E962.1	E980.9
fumes	987.8	E869.8	—	E952.8	E962.2	E982.8
Polyestradiol (phosphate)	962.2	E858.0	E932.2	E950.4	E962.0	E980.4
Polyethanolamine alkyl sulfate	976.2	E858.7	E946.2	E950.4	E962.0	E980.4
Polyethylene glycol	976.3	E858.7	E946.3	E950.4	E962.0	E980.4
Polyferose	964.0	E858.2	E934.0	E950.4	E962.0	E980.4
Polymyxin B	960.8	E856	E930.8	E950.4	E962.0	E980.4
ENT agent	976.6	E858.7	E946.6	E950.4	E962.0	E980.4
ophthalmic preparation	976.5	E858.7	E946.5	E950.4	E962.0	E980.4
topical NEC	976.0	E858.7	E946.0	E950.4	E962.0	E980.4
Polynoxylin(e)	976.0	E858.7	E946.0	E950.4	E962.0	E980.4
Polyoxymethyleneurea	976.0	E858.7	E946.0	E950.4	E962.0	E980.4
Polytetrafluoroethylene (inhaled)	987.8	E869.8	—	E952.8	E962.2	E982.8
Polythiazide	974.3	E858.5	E944.3	E950.4	E962.0	E980.4
Polyvinylpyrrolidone	964.8	E858.2	E934.8	E950.4	E962.0	E980.4
Pontocaine (hydrochloride) (infiltration) (topical)	968.5	E855.2	E938.5	E950.4	E962.0	E980.4
nerve block (peripheral) (plexus)	968.6	E855.2	E938.6	E950.4	E962.0	E980.4
spinal	968.7	E855.2	E938.7	E950.4	E962.0	E980.4
Pot	969.6	E854.1	E939.6	E950.3	E962.0	E980.3
Potash (caustic)	983.2	E864.2	—	E950.7	E962.1	E980.6
Potassic saline injection (lactated)	974.5	E858.5	E944.5	E950.4	E962.0	E980.4
Potassium (salts) NEC	974.5	E858.5	E944.5	E950.4	E962.0	E980.4
aminosalicylate	961.8	E857	E931.8	E950.4	E962.0	E980.4
arsenite (solution)	985.1	E866.3	—	E950.8	E962.1	E980.8
bichromate	983.9	E864.3	—	E950.7	E962.1	E980.6
bisulfate	983.9	E864.3	—	E950.7	E962.1	E980.6
bromide (medicinal) NEC	967.3	E852.2	E937.3	E950.2	E962.0	E980.2
carbonate	983.2	E864.2	—	E950.7	E962.1	E980.6
chlorate NEC	983.9	E864.3	—	E950.7	E962.1	E980.6
cyanide — see Cyanide						

		External Cause (E-Code)				
	Poisoning	Accident	Therapeutic Use	Suicide Attempt	Assault	Undetermined
Potassium (salts) — *continued*						
hydroxide	983.2	E864.2	—	E950.7	E962.1	E980.6
iodide (expectorant) NEC	975.5	E858.6	E945.5	E950.4	E962.0	E980.4
nitrate	989.89	E866.8	—	E950.9	E962.1	E980.9
oxalate	983.9	E864.3	—	E950.7	E962.1	E980.6
perchlorate NEC	977.8	E858.8	E947.8	E950.4	E962.0	E980.4
antithyroid	962.8	E858.0	E932.8	E950.4	E962.0	E980.4
permanganate	976.0	E858.7	E946.0	E950.4	E962.0	E980.4
nonmedicinal	983.9	E864.3	—	E950.7	E962.1	E980.6
Povidone-iodine (anti-infective) NEC	976.0	E858.7	E946.0	E950.4	E962.0	E980.4
Practolol	972.0	E858.3	E942.0	E950.4	E962.0	E980.4
Pralidoxime (chloride)	977.2	E858.8	E947.2	E950.4	E962.0	E980.4
Pramoxine	968.5	E855.2	E938.5	E950.4	E962.0	E980.4
Prazosin	972.6	E858.3	E942.6	E950.4	E962.0	E980.4
Prednisolone	962.0	E858.0	E932.0	E950.4	E962.0	E980.4
ENT agent	976.6	E858.7	E946.6	E950.4	E962.0	E980.4
ophthalmic preparation	976.5	E858.7	E946.5	E950.4	E962.0	E980.4
topical NEC	976.0	E858.7	E946.0	E950.4	E962.0	E980.4
Prednisone	962.0	E858.0	E932.0	E950.4	E962.0	E980.4
Pregnanediol	962.2	E858.0	E932.2	E950.4	E962.0	E980.4
Pregneninolone	962.2	E858.0	E932.2	E950.4	E962.0	E980.4
Preludin	977.0	E858.8	E947.0	E950.4	E962.0	E980.4
Premarin	962.2	E858.0	E932.2	E950.4	E962.0	E980.4
Prenylamine	972.4	E858.3	E942.4	E950.4	E962.0	E980.4
Preparation H	976.8	E858.7	E946.8	E950.4	E962.0	E980.4
Preservatives	989.89	E866.8	—	E950.9	E962.1	E980.9
Pride of China	988.2	E865.3	—	E950.9	E962.1	E980.9
Prilocaine	968.9	E855.2	E938.9	E950.4	E962.0	E980.4
infiltration (subcutaneous)	968.5	E855.2	E938.5	E950.4	E962.0	E980.4
nerve block (peripheral) (plexus)	968.6	E855.2	E938.6	E950.4	E962.0	E980.4
Primaquine	961.4	E857	E931.4	E950.4	E962.0	E980.4
Primidone	966.3	E855.0	E936.3	E950.4	E962.0	E980.4
Primula (veris)	988.2	E865.4	—	E950.9	E962.1	E980.9
Prinadol	965.09	E850.2	E935.2	E950.0	E962.0	E980.0
Priscol, Priscoline	971.3	E855.6	E941.3	E950.4	E962.0	E980.4
Privet	988.2	E865.4	—	E950.9	E962.1	E980.9
Privine	971.2	E855.5	E941.2	E950.4	E962.0	E980.4
Pro-Banthine	971.1	E855.4	E941.1	E950.4	E962.0	E980.4
Probarbital	967.0	E851	E937.0	E950.1	E962.0	E980.1
Probenecid	974.7	E858.5	E944.7	E950.4	E962.0	E980.4
Procainamide (hydrochloride)	972.0	E858.3	E942.0	E950.4	E962.0	E980.4
Procaine (hydrochloride) (infiltration) (topical)	968.5	E855.2	E938.5	E950.4	E962.0	E980.4
nerve block (peripheral) (plexus)	968.6	E855.2	E938.6	E950.4	E962.0	E980.4
penicillin G	960.0	E856	E930.0	E950.4	E962.0	E980.4
spinal	968.7	E855.2	E938.7	E950.4	E962.0	E980.4
Procalmidol	969.5	E853.8	E939.5	E950.3	E962.0	E980.3
Procarbazine	963.1	E858.1	E933.1	E950.4	E962.0	E980.4
Prochlorperazine	969.1	E853.0	E939.1	E950.3	E962.0	E980.3
Procyclidine	966.4	E855.0	E936.4	E950.4	E962.0	E980.4
Producer gas	986	E868.8	—	E952.1	E962.2	E982.1
Profenamine	966.4	E855.0	E936.4	E950.4	E962.0	E980.4
Profenil	975.1	E858.6	E945.1	E950.4	E962.0	E980.4
Progesterones	962.2	E858.0	E932.2	E950.4	E962.0	E980.4
Progestin	962.2	E858.0	E932.2	E950.4	E962.0	E980.4
Progestogens (with estrogens)	962.2	E858.0	E932.2	E950.4	E962.0	E980.4
Progestone	962.2	E858.0	E932.2	E950.4	E962.0	E980.4
Proguanil	961.4	E857	E931.4	E950.4	E962.0	E980.4
Prolactin	962.4	E858.0	E932.4	E950.4	E962.0	E980.4
Proloid	962.7	E858.0	E932.7	E950.4	E962.0	E980.4
Proluton	962.2	E858.0	E932.2	E950.4	E962.0	E980.4
Promacetin	961.8	E857	E931.8	E950.4	E962.0	E980.4
Promazine	969.1	E853.0	E939.1	E950.3	E962.0	E980.3
Promedol	965.09	E850.2	E935.2	E950.0	E962.0	E980.0
Promethazine	967.8	E852.8	E937.8	E950.2	E962.0	E980.2
Promin	961.8	E857	E931.8	E950.4	E962.0	E980.4
Pronestyl (hydrochloride)	972.0	E858.3	E942.0	E950.4	E962.0	E980.4
Pronetalol, pronethalol	972.0	E858.3	E942.0	E950.4	E962.0	E980.4
Prontosil	961.0	E857	E931.0	E950.4	E962.0	E980.4
Propamidine isethionate	961.5	E857	E931.5	E950.4	E962.0	E980.4
Propanal (medicinal)	967.8	E852.8	E937.8	E950.2	E962.0	E980.2
Propane (gas) (distributed in mobile container)	987.0	E868.0	—	E951.1	E962.2	E981.1
distributed through pipes	987.0	E867	—	E951.0	E962.2	E981.0
incomplete combustion of — see Carbon monoxide, Propane						

		External Cause (E-Code)				
	Poisoning	Accident	Therapeutic Use	Suicide Attempt	Assault	Undetermined
Propanidid	968.3	E855.1	E938.3	E950.4	E962.0	E980.4
Propanol	980.3	E860.4	—	E950.9	E962.1	E980.9
Propantheline	971.1	E855.4	E941.1	E950.4	E962.0	E980.4
Proparacaine	968.5	E855.2	E938.5	E950.4	E962.0	E980.4
Propatyl nitrate	972.4	E858.3	E942.4	E950.4	E962.0	E980.4
Propicillin	960.0	E856	E930.0	E950.4	E962.0	E980.4
Propiolactone (vapor)	987.8	E869.8	—	E952.8	E962.2	E982.8
Propiomazine	967.8	E852.8	E937.8	E950.2	E962.0	E980.2
Propionaldehyde (medicinal)	967.8	E852.8	E937.8	E950.2	E962.0	E980.2
Propionate compound	976.0	E858.7	E946.0	E950.4	E962.0	E980.4
Propion gel	976.0	E858.7	E946.0	E950.4	E962.0	E980.4
Propitocaine	968.9	E855.2	E938.9	E950.4	E962.0	E980.4
infiltration (subcutaneous)	968.5	E855.2	E938.5	E950.4	E962.0	E980.4
nerve block (peripheral) (plexus)	968.6	E855.2	E938.6	E950.4	E962.0	E980.4
Propoxur	989.3	E863.2	—	E950.6	E962.1	E980.7
Propoxycaine	968.9	E855.2	E938.9	E950.4	E962.0	E980.4
infiltration (subcutaneous)	968.5	E855.2	E938.5	E950.4	E962.0	E980.4
nerve block (peripheral) (plexus)	968.6	E855.2	E938.6	E950.4	E962.0	E980.4
topical (surface)	968.5	E855.2	E938.5	E950.4	E962.0	E980.4
Propoxyphene (hydrochloride)	965.8	E850.8	E935.8	E950.0	E962.0	E980.0
Propranolol	972.0	E858.3	E942.0	E950.4	E962.0	E980.4
Propyl						
alcohol	980.3	E860.4	—	E950.9	E962.1	E980.9
carbinol	980.3	E860.4	—	E950.9	E962.1	E980.9
hexadrine	971.2	E855.5	E941.2	E950.4	E962.0	E980.4
iodone	977.8	E858.8	E947.8	E950.4	E962.0	E980.4
thiouracil	962.8	E858.0	E932.8	E950.4	E962.0	E980.4
Propylene	987.1	E869.8	—	E952.8	E962.2	E982.8
Propylparaben (ophthalmic)	976.5	E858.7	E946.5	E950.4	E962.0	E980.4
Proscillaridin	972.1	E858.3	E942.1	E950.4	E962.0	E980.4
Prostaglandins	975.0	E858.6	E945.0	E950.4	E962.0	E980.4
Prostigmin	971.0	E855.3	E941.0	E950.4	E962.0	E980.4
Protamine (sulfate)	964.5	E858.2	E934.5	E950.4	E962.0	E980.4
zinc insulin	962.3	E858.0	E932.3	E950.4	E962.0	E980.4
Protectants (topical)	976.3	E858.7	E946.3	E950.4	E962.0	E980.4
Protein hydrolysate	974.5	E858.5	E944.5	E950.4	E962.0	E980.4
Prothiaden — *see* Dothiepin hydrochloride						
Prothionamide	961.8	E857	E931.8	E950.4	E962.0	E980.4
Prothipendyl	969.5	E853.8	E939.5	E950.3	E962.0	E980.3
Protokylol	971.2	E855.5	E941.2	E950.4	E962.0	E980.4
Protopam	977.2	E858.8	E947.2	E950.4	E962.0	E980.4
Protoveratrine(s) (A) (B)	972.6	E858.3	E942.6	E950.4	E962.0	E980.4
Protriptyline	969.0	E854.0	E939.0	E950.3	E962.0	E980.3
Provera	962.2	E858.0	E932.2	E950.4	E962.0	E980.4
Provitamin A	963.5	E858.1	E933.5	E950.4	E962.0	E980.4
Proxymetacaine	968.5	E855.2	E938.5	E950.4	E962.0	E980.4
Proxyphylline	975.1	E858.6	E945.1	E950.4	E962.0	E980.4
Prozac — *see* Fluoxetine hydrochloride						
Prunus						
laurocerasus	988.2	E865.4	—	E950.9	E962.1	E980.9
virginiana	988.2	E865.4	—	E950.9	E962.1	E980.9
Prussic acid	989.0	E866.8	—	E950.9	E962.1	E980.9
vapor	987.7	E869.8	—	E952.8	E962.2	E982.8
Pseudoephedrine	971.2	E855.5	E941.2	E950.4	E962.0	E980.4
Psilocin	969.6	E854.1	E939.6	E950.3	E962.0	E980.3
Psilocybin	969.6	E854.1	E939.6	E950.3	E962.0	E980.3
PSP	977.8	E858.8	E947.8	E950.4	E962.0	E980.4
Psychedelic agents	969.6	E854.1	E939.6	E950.3	E962.0	E980.3
Psychodysleptics	969.6	E854.1	E939.6	E950.3	E962.0	E980.3
Psychostimulants	969.7	E854.2	E939.7	E950.3	E962.0	E980.3
Psychotherapeutic agents	969.9	E855.9	E939.9	E950.3	E962.0	E980.3
antidepressants	969.0	E854.0	E939.0	E950.3	E962.0	E980.3
specified NEC	969.8	E855.8	E939.8	E950.3	E962.0	E980.3
tranquilizers NEC	969.5	E853.9	E939.5	E950.3	E962.0	E980.3
Psychotomimetic agents	969.6	E854.1	E939.6	E950.3	E962.0	E980.3
Psychotropic agents	969.9	E854.8	E939.9	E950.3	E962.0	E980.3
specified NEC	969.8	E854.8	E939.8	E950.3	E962.0	E980.3
Psyllium	973.3	E858.4	E943.3	E950.4	E962.0	E980.4
Pteroylglutamic acid	964.1	E858.2	E934.1	E950.4	E962.0	E980.4
Pteroyltriglutamate	963.1	E858.1	E933.1	E950.4	E962.0	E980.4
PTFE	987.8	E869.8	—	E952.8	E962.2	E982.8
Pulsatilla	988.2	E865.4	—	E950.9	E962.1	E980.9
Purex (bleach)	983.9	E864.3	—	E950.7	E962.1	E980.6
Purine diuretics	974.1	E858.5	E944.1	E950.4	E962.0	E980.4

		External Cause (E-Code)				
	Poisoning	Accident	Therapeutic Use	Suicide Attempt	Assault	Undetermined
Purinethol	963.1	E858.1	E933.1	E950.4	E962.0	E980.4
PVP	964.8	E858.2	E934.8	E950.4	E962.0	E980.4
Pyrabital	965.7	E850.7	E935.7	E950.0	E962.0	E980.0
Pyramidon	965.5	E850.5	E935.5	E950.0	E962.0	E980.0
Pyrantel (pamoate)	961.6	E857	E931.6	E950.4	E962.0	E980.4
Pyrathiazine	963.0	E858.1	E933.0	E950.4	E962.0	E980.4
Pyrazinamide	961.8	E857	E931.8	E950.4	E962.0	E980.4
Pyrazinoic acid (amide)	961.8	E857	E931.8	E950.4	E962.0	E980.4
Pyrazole (derivatives)	965.5	E850.5	E935.5	E950.0	E962.0	E980.0
Pyrazolone (analgesics)	965.5	E850.5	E935.5	E950.0	E962.0	E980.0
Pyrethrins, pyrethrum	989.4	E863.4	—	E950.6	E962.1	E980.7
Pyribenzamine	963.0	E858.1	E933.0	E950.4	E962.0	E980.4
Pyridine (liquid) (vapor)	982.0	E862.4	—	E950.9	E962.1	E980.9
aldoxime chloride	977.2	E858.8	E947.2	E950.4	E962.0	E980.4
Pyridium	976.1	E858.7	E946.1	E950.4	E962.0	E980.4
Pyridostigmine	971.0	E855.3	E941.0	E950.4	E962.0	E980.4
Pyridoxine	963.5	E858.1	E933.5	E950.4	E962.0	E980.4
Pyrilamine	963.0	E858.1	E933.0	E950.4	E962.0	E980.4
Pyrimethamine	961.4	E857	E931.4	E950.4	E962.0	E980.4
Pyrogallic acid	983.0	E864.0	—	E950.7	E962.1	E980.6
Pyroxylin	976.3	E858.7	E946.3	E950.4	E962.0	E980.4
Pyrrobutamine	963.0	E858.1	E933.0	E950.4	E962.0	E980.4
Pyrrocitine	968.5	E855.2	E938.5	E950.4	E962.0	E980.4
Pyrvinium (pamoate)	961.6	E857	E931.6	E950.4	E962.0	E980.4
PZI	962.3	E858.0	E932.3	E950.4	E962.0	E980.4
Quaalude	967.4	E852.3	E937.4	E950.2	E962.0	E980.2
Quaternary ammonium derivatives	971.1	E855.4	E941.1	E950.4	E962.0	E980.4
Quicklime	983.2	E864.2	—	E950.7	E962.1	E980.6
Quinacrine	961.3	E857	E931.3	E950.4	E962.0	E980.4
Quinaglute	972.0	E858.3	E942.0	E950.4	E962.0	E980.4
Quinalbarbitone	967.0	E851	E937.0	E950.1	E962.0	E980.1
Quinestradiol	962.2	E858.0	E932.2	E950.4	E962.0	E980.4
Quinethazone	974.3	E858.5	E944.3	E950.4	E962.0	E980.4
Quinidine (gluconate) (polygalacturonate) (salts) (sulfate)	972.0	E858.3	E942.0	E950.4	E962.0	E980.4
Quinine	961.4	E857	E931.4	E950.4	E962.0	E980.4
Quiniobine	961.3	E857	E931.3	E950.4	E962.0	E980.4
Quinolines	961.3	E857	E931.3	E950.4	E962.0	E980.4
Quotane	968.5	E855.2	E938.5	E950.4	E962.0	E980.4
Rabies						
immune globulin (human)	964.6	E858.2	E934.6	E950.4	E962.0	E980.4
vaccine	979.1	E858.8	E949.1	E950.4	E962.0	E980.4
Racemoramide	965.09	E850.2	E935.2	E950.0	E962.0	E980.0
Racemorphan	965.09	E850.2	E935.2	E950.0	E962.0	E980.0
Radiator alcohol	980.1	E860.2	—	E950.9	E962.1	E980.9
Radio-opaque (drugs) (materials)	977.8	E858.8	E947.8	E950.4	E962.0	E980.4
Ranunculus	988.2	E865.4	—	E950.9	E962.1	E980.9
Rat poison	989.4	E863.7	—	E950.6	E962.1	E980.7
Rattlesnake (venom)	989.5	E905.0	—	E950.9	E962.1	E980.9
Raudixin	972.6	E858.3	E942.6	E950.4	E962.0	E980.4
Rautensin	972.6	E858.3	E942.6	E950.4	E962.0	E980.4
Rautina	972.6	E858.3	E942.6	E950.4	E962.0	E980.4
Rautotal	972.6	E858.3	E942.6	E950.4	E962.0	E980.4
Rauwiloid	972.6	E858.3	E942.6	E950.4	E962.0	E980.4
Rauwoldin	972.6	E858.3	E942.6	E950.4	E962.0	E980.4
Rauwolfia (alkaloids)	972.6	E858.3	E942.6	E950.4	E962.0	E980.4
Realgar	985.1	E866.3	—	E950.8	E962.1	E980.8
Red cells, packed	964.7	E858.2	E934.7	E950.4	E962.0	E980.4
Reducing agents, industrial NEC	983.9	E864.3	—	E950.7	E962.1	E980.6
Refrigerant gas (freon)	987.4	E869.2	—	E952.8	E962.2	E982.8
central nervous system	968.0	E855.1	E938.0	E950.4	E962.0	E980.4
not freon	987.9	E869.9	—	E952.9	E962.2	E982.9
Regroton	974.4	E858.5	E944.4	E950.4	E962.0	E980.4
Rela	968.0	E855.1	E938.0	E950.4	E962.0	E980.4
Relaxants, skeletal muscle (autonomic)	975.2	E858.6	E945.2	E950.4	E962.0	E980.4
Renese	974.3	E858.5	E944.3	E950.4	E962.0	E980.4
Renografin	977.8	E858.8	E947.8	E950.4	E962.0	E980.4
Replacement solutions	974.5	E858.5	E944.5	E950.4	E962.0	E980.4
Rescinnamine	972.6	E858.3	E942.6	E950.4	E962.0	E980.4
Reserpine	972.6	E858.3	E942.6	E950.4	E962.0	E980.4
Resorcin, resorcinol	976.4	E858.7	E946.4	E950.4	E962.0	E980.4
Respaire	975.5	E858.6	E945.5	E950.4	E962.0	E980.4
Respiratory agents NEC	975.8	E858.6	E945.8	E950.4	E962.0	E980.4
Retinoic acid	976.8	E858.7	E946.8	E950.4	E962.0	E980.4
Retinol	963.5	E858.1	E933.5	E950.4	E962.0	E980.4
Rh (D) immune globulin (human)	964.6	E858.2	E934.6	E950.4	E962.0	E980.4
Rhodine	965.1	E850.3	E935.3	E950.0	E962.0	E980.0
RhoGAM	964.6	E858.2	E934.6	E950.4	E962.0	E980.4
Riboflavin	963.5	E858.1	E933.5	E950.4	E962.0	E980.4
Ricin	989.89	E866.8	—	E950.9	E962.1	E980.9
Ricinus communis	988.2	E865.3	—	E950.9	E962.1	E980.9
Rickettsial vaccine NEC	979.6	E858.8	E949.6	E950.4	E962.0	E980.4
with viral and bacterial vaccine	979.7	E858.8	E949.7	E950.4	E962.0	E980.4
Rifampin	960.6	E856	E930.6	E950.4	E962.0	E980.4
Rimifon	961.8	E857	E931.8	E950.4	E962.0	E980.4
Ringer's injection (lactated)	974.5	E858.5	E944.5	E950.4	E962.0	E980.4
Ristocetin	960.8	E856	E930.8	E950.4	E962.0	E980.4
Ritalin	969.7	E854.2	E939.7	E950.3	E962.0	E980.3
Roach killers — *see* Pesticides						
Rocky Mountain spotted fever vaccine	979.6	E858.8	E949.6	E950.4	E962.0	E980.4
Rodenticides	989.4	E863.7	—	E950.6	E962.1	E980.7
Rohypnol	969.4	E853.2	E939.4	E950.3	E962.0	E980.3
Rolaids	973.0	E858.4	E943.0	E950.4	E962.0	E980.4
Rolitetracycline	960.4	E856	E930.4	E950.4	E962.0	E980.4
Romilar	975.4	E858.6	E945.4	E950.4	E962.0	E980.4
Rose water ointment	976.3	E858.7	E946.3	E950.4	E962.0	E980.4
Rosuvastatin calcium	972.1	E858.3	E942.2	E950.4	E962.0	E980.4
Rotenone	989.4	E863.7	—	E950.6	E962.1	E980.7
Rotoxamine	963.0	E858.1	E933.0	E950.4	E962.0	E980.4
Rough-on-rats	989.4	E863.7	—	E950.6	E962.1	E980.7
RU486	962.9	E858.0	E932.9	E950.4	E962.0	E980.4
Rubbing alcohol	980.2	E860.3	—	E950.9	E962.1	E980.9
Rubella virus vaccine	979.4	E858.8	E949.4	E950.4	E962.0	E980.4
Rubelogen	979.4	E858.8	E949.4	E950.4	E962.0	E980.4
Rubeovax	979.4	E858.8	E949.4	E950.4	E962.0	E980.4
Rubidomycin	960.7	E856	E930.7	E950.4	E962.0	E980.4
Rue	988.2	E865.4	—	E950.9	E962.1	E980.9
Ruta	988.2	E865.4	—	E950.9	E962.1	E980.9
Sabadilla (medicinal)	976.0	E858.7	E946.0	E950.4	E962.0	E980.4
pesticide	989.4	E863.4	—	E950.6	E962.1	E980.7
Sabin oral vaccine	979.5	E858.8	E949.5	E950.4	E962.0	E980.4
Saccharated iron oxide	964.0	E858.2	E934.0	E950.4	E962.0	E980.4
Saccharin	974.5	E858.5	E944.5	E950.4	E962.0	E980.4
Safflower oil	972.2	E858.3	E942.2	E950.4	E962.0	E980.4
Salbutamol sulfate	975.7	E858.6	E945.7	E950.4	E962.0	E980.4
Salicylamide	965.1	E850.3	E935.3	E950.0	E962.0	E980.0
Salicylate(s)	965.1	E850.3	E935.3	E950.0	E962.0	E980.0
methyl	976.3	E858.7	E946.3	E950.4	E962.0	E980.4
theobromine calcium	974.1	E858.5	E944.1	E950.4	E962.0	E980.4
Salicylazosulfapyridine	961.0	E857	E931.0	E950.4	E962.0	E980.4
Salicylhydroxamic acid	976.0	E858.7	E946.0	E950.4	E962.0	E980.4
Salicylic acid (keratolytic) NEC	976.4	E858.7	E946.4	E950.4	E962.0	E980.4
congeners	965.1	E850.3	E935.3	E950.0	E962.0	E980.0
salts	965.1	E850.3	E935.3	E950.0	E962.0	E980.0
Saliniazid	961.8	E857	E931.8	E950.4	E962.0	E980.4
Salol	976.3	E858.7	E946.3	E950.4	E962.0	E980.4
Salt (substitute) NEC	974.5	E858.5	E944.5	E950.4	E962.0	E980.4
Saluretics	974.3	E858.5	E944.3	E950.4	E962.0	E980.4
Saluron	974.3	E858.5	E944.3	E950.4	E962.0	E980.4
Salvarsan 606 (neosilver) (silver)	961.1	E857	E931.1	E950.4	E962.0	E980.4
Sambucus canadensis	988.2	E865.4	—	E950.9	E962.1	E980.9
berry	988.2	E865.3	—	E950.9	E962.1	E980.9
Sandril	972.6	E858.3	E942.6	E950.4	E962.0	E980.4
Sanguinaria canadensis	988.2	E865.4	—	E950.9	E962.1	E980.9
Saniflush (cleaner)	983.9	E861.3	—	E950.7	E962.1	E980.6
Santonin	961.6	E857	E931.6	E950.4	E962.0	E980.4
Santyl	976.8	E858.7	E946.8	E950.4	E962.0	E980.4
Sarkomycin	960.7	E856	E930.7	E950.4	E962.0	E980.4
Saroten	969.0	E854.0	E939.0	E950.3	E962.0	E980.3
Saturnine — *see* Lead						
Savin (oil)	976.4	E858.7	E946.4	E950.4	E962.0	E980.4
Scammony	973.1	E858.4	E943.1	E950.4	E962.0	E980.4
Scarlet red	976.8	E858.7	E946.8	E950.4	E962.0	E980.4
Scheele's green	985.1	E866.3	—	E950.8	E962.1	E980.8
insecticide	985.1	E863.4	—	E950.8	E962.1	E980.8
Schradan	989.3	E863.1	—	E950.6	E962.1	E980.7
Schweinfurt(h) green	985.1	E866.3	—	E950.8	E962.1	E980.8
insecticide	985.1	E863.4	—	E950.8	E962.1	E980.8
Scilla — see Squill						
Sclerosing agents	972.7	E858.3	E942.7	E950.4	E962.0	E980.4

		External Cause (E-Code)				
	Poisoning	Accident	Therapeutic Use	Suicide Attempt	Assault	Undetermined
Scopolamine	971.1	E855.4	E941.1	E950.4	E962.0	E980.4
Scouring powder	989.89	E861.3	—	E950.9	E962.1	E980.9
Sea						
anemone (sting)	989.5	E905.6	—	E950.9	E962.1	E980.9
cucumber (sting)	989.5	E905.6	—	E950.9	E962.1	E980.9
snake (bite) (venom)	989.5	E905.0	—	E950.9	E962.1	E980.9
urchin spine (puncture)	989.5	E905.6	—	E950.9	E962.1	E980.9
Secbutabarbital	967.0	E851	E937.0	E950.1	E962.0	E980.1
Secbutabarbitone	967.0	E851	E937.0	E950.1	E962.0	E980.1
Secobarbital	967.0	E851	E937.0	E950.1	E962.0	E980.1
Seconal	967.0	E851	E937.0	E950.1	E962.0	E980.1
Secretin	977.8	E858.8	E947.8	E950.4	E962.0	E980.4
Sedatives, nonbarbiturate	967.9	E852.9	E937.9	E950.2	E962.0	E980.2
specified NEC	967.8	E852.8	E937.8	E950.2	E962.0	E980.2
Sedormid	967.8	E852.8	E937.8	E950.2	E962.0	E980.2
Seed (plant)	988.2	E865.3	—	E950.9	E962.1	E980.9
disinfectant or dressing	989.89	E866.5	—	E950.9	E962.1	E980.9
Selenium (fumes) NEC	985.8	E866.4	—	E950.9	E962.1	E980.9
disulfide or sulfide	976.4	E858.7	E946.4	E950.4	E962.0	E980.4
Selsun	976.4	E858.7	E946.4	E950.4	E962.0	E980.4
Senna	973.1	E858.4	E943.1	E950.4	E962.0	E980.4
Septisol	976.2	E858.7	E946.2	E950.4	E962.0	E980.4
Serax	969.4	E853.2	E939.4	E950.3	E962.0	E980.3
Serenesil	967.8	E852.8	E937.8	E950.2	E962.0	E980.2
Serenium (hydrochloride)	961.9	E857	E931.9	E950.4	E962.0	E980.4
Serepax — *see* Oxazepam						
Sernyl	968.3	E855.1	E938.3	E950.4	E962.0	E980.4
Serotonin	977.8	E858.8	E947.8	E950.4	E962.0	E980.4
Serpasil	972.6	E858.3	E942.6	E950.4	E962.0	E980.4
Sewer gas	987.8	E869.8	—	E952.8	E962.2	E982.8
Shampoo	989.6	E861.0	—	E950.9	E962.1	E980.9
Shellfish, nonbacterial or noxious	988.0	E865.1	—	E950.9	E962.1	E980.9
Silicones NEC	989.83	E866.8	E947.8	E950.9	E962.1	E980.9
Silvadene	976.0	E858.7	E946.0	E950.4	E962.0	E980.4
Silver (compound) (medicinal) NEC	976.0	E858.7	E946.0	E950.4	E962.0	E980.4
anti-infectives	976.0	E858.7	E946.0	E950.4	E962.0	E980.4
arsphenamine	961.1	E857	E931.1	E950.4	E962.0	E980.4
nitrate	976.0	E858.7	E946.0	E950.4	E962.0	E980.4
ophthalmic preparation	976.5	E858.7	E946.5	E950.4	E962.0	E980.4
toughened (keratolytic)	976.4	E858.7	E946.4	E950.4	E962.0	E980.4
nonmedicinal (dust)	985.8	E866.4	—	E950.9	E962.1	E980.9
protein (mild) (strong)	976.0	E858.7	E946.0	E950.4	E962.0	E980.4
salvarsan	961.1	E857	E931.1	E950.4	E962.0	E980.4
Simethicone	973.8	E858.4	E943.8	E950.4	E962.0	E980.4
Sinequan	969.0	E854.0	E939.0	E950.3	E962.0	E980.3
Singoserp	972.6	E858.3	E942.6	E950.4	E962.0	E980.4
Sintrom	964.2	E858.2	E934.2	E950.4	E962.0	E980.4
Sitosterols	972.2	E858.3	E942.2	E950.4	E962.0	E980.4
Skeletal muscle relaxants	975.2	E858.6	E945.2	E950.4	E962.0	E980.4
Skin						
agents (external)	976.9	E858.7	E946.9	E950.4	E962.0	E980.4
specified NEC	976.8	E858.7	E946.8	E950.4	E962.0	E980.4
test antigen	977.8	E858.8	E947.8	E950.4	E962.0	E980.4
Sleep-eze	963.0	E858.1	E933.0	E950.4	E962.0	E980.4
Sleeping draught (drug) (pill) (tablet)	967.9	E852.9	E937.9	E950.2	E962.0	E980.2
Smallpox vaccine	979.0	E858.8	E949.0	E950.4	E962.0	E980.4
Smelter fumes NEC	985.9	E866.4	—	E950.9	E962.1	E980.9
Smog	987.3	E869.1	—	E952.8	E962.2	E982.8
Smoke NEC	987.9	E869.9	—	E952.9	E962.2	E982.9
Smooth muscle relaxant	975.1	E858.6	E945.1	E950.4	E962.0	E980.4
Snail killer	989.4	E863.4	—	E950.6	E962.1	E980.7
Snake (bite) (venom)	989.5	E905.0	—	E950.9	E962.1	E980.9
Snuff	989.89	E866.8	—	E950.9	E962.1	E980.9
Soap (powder) (product)	989.6	E861.1	—	E950.9	E962.1	E980.9
bicarb	963.3	E858.1	E933.3	E950.4	E962.0	E980.4
chlorinated — see Sodium, hypochlorite						
medicinal, soft	976.2	E858.7	E946.2	E950.4	E962.0	E980.4
Soda (caustic)	983.2	E864.2	—	E950.7	E962.1	E980.6
Sodium						
acetosulfone	961.8	E857	E931.8	E950.4	E962.0	E980.4
acetrizoate	977.8	E858.8	E947.8	E950.4	E962.0	E980.4
amytal	967.0	E851	E937.0	E950.1	E962.0	E980.1
arsenate — see Arsenic						
bicarbonate	963.3	E858.1	E933.3	E950.4	E962.0	E980.4
bichromate	983.9	E864.3	—	E950.7	E962.1	E980.6
biphosphate	963.2	E858.1	E933.2	E950.4	E962.0	E980.4
bisulfate	983.9	E864.3	—	E950.7	E962.1	E980.6
Sodium — *continued*						
borate (cleanser)	989.6	E861.3	—	E950.9	E962.1	E980.9
bromide NEC	967.3	E852.2	E937.3	E950.2	E962.0	E980.2
cacodylate (nonmedicinal) NEC	978.8	E858.8	E948.8	E950.4	E962.0	E980.4
anti-infective	961.1	E857	E931.1	E950.4	E962.0	E980.4
herbicide	989.4	E863.5	—	E950.6	E962.1	E980.7
calcium edetate	963.8	E858.1	E933.8	E950.4	E962.0	E980.4
carbonate NEC	983.2	E864.2	—	E950.7	E962.1	E980.6
chlorate NEC	983.9	E864.3	—	E950.7	E962.1	E980.6
herbicide	983.9	E863.5	—	E950.7	E962.1	E980.6
chloride NEC	974.5	E858.5	E944.5	E950.4	E962.0	E980.4
chromate	983.9	E864.3	—	E950.7	E962.1	E980.6
citrate	963.3	E858.1	E933.3	E950.4	E962.0	E980.4
cyanide — see Cyanide(s)						
cyclamate	974.5	E858.5	E944.5	E950.4	E962.0	E980.4
diatrizoate	977.8	E858.8	E947.8	E950.4	E962.0	E980.4
dibunate	975.4	E858.6	E945.4	E950.4	E962.0	E980.4
dioctyl sulfosuccinate	973.2	E858.4	E943.2	E950.4	E962.0	E980.4
edetate	963.8	E858.1	E933.8	E950.4	E962.0	E980.4
ethacrynate	974.4	E858.5	E944.4	E950.4	E962.0	E980.4
fluoracetate (dust) (rodenticide)	989.4	E863.7	—	E950.6	E962.1	E980.7
fluoride — see Fluoride(s)						
free salt	974.5	E858.5	E944.5	E950.4	E962.0	E980.4
glucosulfone	961.8	E857	E931.8	E950.4	E962.0	E980.4
hydroxide	983.2	E864.2	—	E950.7	E962.1	E980.6
hypochlorite (bleach) NEC	983.9	E864.3	—	E950.7	E962.1	E980.6
disinfectant	983.9	E861.4	—	E950.7	E962.1	E980.6
medicinal (anti-infective) (external)	976.0	E858.7	E946.0	E950.4	E962.0	E980.4
vapor	987.8	E869.8	—	E952.8	E962.2	E982.8
hyposulfite	976.0	E858.7	E946.0	E950.4	E962.0	E980.4
indigotindisulfonate	977.8	E858.8	E947.8	E950.4	E962.0	E980.4
iodide	977.8	E858.8	E947.8	E950.4	E962.0	E980.4
iothalamate	977.8	E858.8	E947.8	E950.4	E962.0	E980.4
iron edetate	964.0	E858.2	E934.0	E950.4	E962.0	E980.4
lactate	963.3	E858.1	E933.3	E950.4	E962.0	E980.4
lauryl sulfate	976.2	E858.7	E946.2	E950.4	E962.0	E980.4
L-triiodothyronine	962.7	E858.0	E932.7	E950.4	E962.0	E980.4
metrizoate	977.8	E858.8	E947.8	E950.4	E962.0	E980.4
monofluoracetate (dust) (rodenticide)	989.4	E863.7	—	E950.6	E962.1	E980.7
morrhuate	972.7	E858.3	E942.7	E950.4	E962.0	E980.4
nafcillin	960.0	E856	E930.0	E950.4	E962.0	E980.4
nitrate (oxidizing agent)	983.9	E864.3	—	E950.7	E962.1	E980.6
nitrite (medicinal)	972.4	E858.3	E942.4	E950.4	E962.0	E980.4
nitroferricyanide	972.6	E858.3	E942.6	E950.4	E962.0	E980.4
nitroprusside	972.6	E858.3	E942.6	E950.4	E962.0	E980.4
para-aminohippurate	977.8	E858.8	E947.8	E950.4	E962.0	E980.4
perborate (nonmedicinal) NEC	989.89	E866.8	—	E950.9	E962.1	E980.9
medicinal	976.6	E858.7	E946.6	E950.4	E962.0	E980.4
soap	989.6	E861.1	—	E950.9	E962.1	E980.9
percarbonate — see Sodium, perborate						
phosphate	973.3	E858.4	E943.3	E950.4	E962.0	E980.4
polystyrene sulfonate	974.5	E858.5	E944.5	E950.4	E962.0	E980.4
propionate	976.0	E858.7	E946.0	E950.4	E962.0	E980.4
psylliate	972.7	E858.3	E942.7	E950.4	E962.0	E980.4
removing resins	974.5	E858.5	E944.5	E950.4	E962.0	E980.4
salicylate	965.1	E850.3	E935.3	E950.0	E962.0	E980.0
sulfate	973.3	E858.4	E943.3	E950.4	E962.0	E980.4
sulfoxone	961.8	E857	E931.8	E950.4	E962.0	E980.4
tetradecyl sulfate	972.7	E858.3	E942.7	E950.4	E962.0	E980.4
thiopental	968.3	E855.1	E938.3	E950.4	E962.0	E980.4
thiosalicylate	965.1	E850.3	E935.3	E950.0	E962.0	E980.0
thiosulfate	976.0	E858.7	E946.0	E950.4	E962.0	E980.4
tolbutamide	977.8	E858.8	E947.8	E950.4	E962.0	E980.4
tyropanoate	977.8	E858.8	E947.8	E950.4	E962.0	E980.4
valproate	966.3	E855.0	E936.3	E950.4	E962.0	E980.4
Solanine	977.8	E858.8	E947.8	E950.4	E962.0	E980.4
Solanum dulcamara	988.2	E865.4	—	E950.9	E962.1	E980.9
Solapsone	961.8	E857	E931.8	E950.4	E962.0	E980.4
Solasulfone	961.8	E857	E931.8	E950.4	E962.0	E980.4
Soldering fluid	983.1	E864.1	—	E950.7	E962.1	E980.6
Solid substance	989.9	E866.9	—	E950.9	E962.1	E980.9
specified NEC	989.9	E866.8	—	E950.9	E962.1	E980.9
Solvents, industrial	982.8	E862.9	—	E950.9	E962.1	E980.9
naphtha	981	E862.0	—	E950.9	E962.1	E980.9
petroleum	981	E862.0	—	E950.9	E962.1	E980.9
specified NEC	982.8	E862.4	—	E950.9	E962.1	E980.9

	Poisoning	External Cause (E-Code) Accident	Therapeutic Use	Suicide Attempt	Assault	Undetermined
Soma	968.0	E855.1	E938.0	E950.4	E962.0	E980.4
Somatotropin	962.4	E858.0	E932.4	E950.4	E962.0	E980.4
Sominex	963.0	E858.1	E933.0	E950.4	E962.0	E980.4
Somnos	967.1	E852.0	E937.1	E950.2	E962.0	E980.2
Somonal	967.0	E851	E937.0	E950.1	E962.0	E980.1
Soneryl	967.0	E851	E937.0	E950.1	E962.0	E980.1
Soothing syrup	977.9	E858.9	E947.9	E950.5	E962.0	E980.5
Sopor	967.4	E852.3	E937.4	E950.2	E962.0	E980.2
Soporific drug	967.9	E852.9	E937.9	E950.2	E962.0	E980.2
specified type NEC	967.8	E852.8	E937.8	E950.2	E962.0	E980.2
Sorbitol NEC	977.4	E858.8	E947.4	E950.4	E962.0	E980.4
Sotradecol	972.7	E858.3	E942.7	E950.4	E962.0	E980.4
Spacoline	975.1	E858.6	E945.1	E950.4	E962.0	E980.4
Spanish fly	976.8	E858.7	E946.8	E950.4	E962.0	E980.4
Sparine	969.1	E853.0	E939.1	E950.3	E962.0	E980.3
Sparteine	975.0	E858.6	E945.0	E950.4	E962.0	E980.4
Spasmolytics	975.1	E858.6	E945.1	E950.4	E962.0	E980.4
anticholinergics	971.1	E855.4	E941.1	E950.4	E962.0	E980.4
Spectinomycin	960.8	E856	E930.8	E950.4	E962.0	E980.4
Speed	969.7	E854.2	E939.7	E950.3	E962.0	E980.3
Spermicides	976.8	E858.7	E946.8	E950.4	E962.0	E980.4
Spider (bite) (venom)	989.5	E905.1	—	E950.9	E962.1	E980.9
antivenin	979.9	E858.8	E949.9	E950.4	E962.0	E980.4
Spigelia (root)	961.6	E857	E931.6	E950.4	E962.0	E980.4
Spiperone	969.2	E853.1	E939.2	E950.3	E962.0	E980.3
Spiramycin	960.3	E856	E930.3	E950.4	E962.0	E980.4
Spirilene	969.5	E853.8	E939.5	E950.3	E962.0	E980.3
Spirit(s) (neutral) NEC	980.0	E860.1	—	E950.9	E962.1	E980.9
beverage	980.0	E860.0	—	E950.9	E962.1	E980.9
industrial	980.9	E860.9	—	E950.9	E962.1	E980.9
mineral	981	E862.0	—	E950.9	E962.1	E980.9
of salt — see Hydrochloric acid						
surgical	980.9	E860.9	—	E950.9	E962.1	E980.9
Spironolactone	974.4	E858.5	E944.4	E950.4	E962.0	E980.4
Sponge, absorbable (gelatin)	964.5	E858.2	E934.5	E950.4	E962.0	E980.4
Sporostacin	976.0	E858.7	E946.0	E950.4	E962.0	E980.4
Sprays (aerosol)	989.89	E866.8	—	E950.9	E962.1	E980.9
cosmetic	989.89	E866.7	—	E950.9	E962.1	E980.9
medicinal NEC	977.9	E858.9	E947.9	E950.5	E962.0	E980.5
pesticides — see Pesticides						
specified content — see substance specified						
Spurge flax	988.2	E865.4	—	E950.9	E962.1	E980.9
Spurges	988.2	E865.4	—	E950.9	E962.1	E980.9
Squill (expectorant) NEC	975.5	E858.6	E945.5	E950.4	E962.0	E980.4
rat poison	989.4	E863.7	—	E950.6	E962.1	E980.7
Squirting cucumber (cathartic)	973.1	E858.4	E943.1	E950.4	E962.0	E980.4
Stains	989.89	E866.8	—	E950.9	E962.1	E980.9
Stannous — *see also* Tin						
fluoride	976.7	E858.7	E946.7	E950.4	E962.0	E980.4
Stanolone	962.1	E858.0	E932.1	E950.4	E962.0	E980.4
Stanozolol	962.1	E858.0	E932.1	E950.4	E962.0	E980.4
Staphisagria or stavesacre (pediculicide)	976.0	E858.7	E946.0	E950.4	E962.0	E980.4
Stelazine	969.1	E853.0	E939.1	E950.3	E962.0	E980.3
Stemetil	969.1	E853.0	E939.1	E950.3	E962.0	E980.3
Sterculia (cathartic) (gum)	973.3	E858.4	E943.3	E950.4	E962.0	E980.4
Sternutator gas	987.8	E869.8	—	E952.8	E962.2	E982.8
Steroids NEC	962.0	E858.0	E932.0	E950.4	E962.0	E980.4
ENT agent	976.6	E858.7	E946.6	E950.4	E962.0	E980.4
ophthalmic preparation	976.5	E858.7	E946.5	E950.4	E962.0	E980.4
topical NEC	976.0	E858.7	E946.0	E950.4	E962.0	E980.4
Stibine	985.8	E866.4	—	E950.9	E962.1	E980.9
Stibophen	961.2	E857	E931.2	E950.4	E962.0	E980.4
Stilbamide, stilbamidine	961.5	E857	E931.5	E950.4	E962.0	E980.4
Stilbestrol	962.2	E858.0	E932.2	E950.4	E962.0	E980.4
Stimulants (central nervous system)	970.9	E854.3	E940.9	E950.4	E962.0	E980.4
analeptics	970.0	E854.3	E940.0	E950.4	E962.0	E980.4
opiate antagonist	970.1	E854.3	E940.1	E950.4	E962.0	E980.4
psychotherapeutic NEC	969.0	E854.0	E939.0	E950.3	E962.0	E980.3
specified NEC	970.8	E854.3	E940.8	E950.4	E962.0	E980.4
Storage batteries (acid) (cells)	983.1	E864.1	—	E950.7	E962.1	E980.6
Stovaine	968.9	E855.2	E938.9	E950.4	E962.0	E980.4
infiltration (subcutaneous)	968.5	E855.2	E938.5	E950.4	E962.0	E980.4
nerve block (peripheral) (plexus)	968.6	E855.2	E938.6	E950.4	E962.0	E980.4
spinal	968.7	E855.2	E938.7	E950.4	E962.0	E980.4
Stovaine — *continued*						
topical (surface)	968.5	E855.2	E938.5	E950.4	E962.0	E980.4
Stovarsal	961.1	E857	E931.1	E950.4	E962.0	E980.4
Stove gas — *see* Gas, utility						
Stoxil	976.5	E858.7	E946.5	E950.4	E962.0	E980.4
STP	969.6	E854.1	E939.6	E950.3	E962.0	E980.3
Stramonium (medicinal) NEC	971.1	E855.4	E941.1	E950.4	E962.0	E980.4
natural state	988.2	E865.4	—	E950.9	E962.1	E980.9
Streptodornase	964.4	E858.2	E934.4	E950.4	E962.0	E980.4
Streptoduocin	960.6	E856	E930.6	E950.4	E962.0	E980.4
Streptokinase	964.4	E858.2	E934.4	E950.4	E962.0	E980.4
Streptomycin	960.6	E856	E930.6	E950.4	E962.0	E980.4
Streptozocin	960.7	E856	E930.7	E950.4	E962.0	E980.4
Stripper (paint) (solvent)	982.8	E862.9	—	E950.9	E962.1	E980.9
Strobane	989.2	E863.0	—	E950.6	E962.1	E980.7
Strophanthin	972.1	E858.3	E942.1	E950.4	E962.0	E980.4
Strophanthus hispidus or kombe	988.2	E865.4	—	E950.9	E962.1	E980.9
Strychnine (rodenticide) (salts)	989.1	E863.7	—	E950.6	E962.1	E980.7
medicinal NEC	970.8	E854.3	E940.8	E950.4	E962.0	E980.4
Strychnos (ignatii) — see Strychnine						
Styramate	968.0	E855.1	E938.0	E950.4	E962.0	E980.4
Styrene	983.0	E864.0	—	E950.7	E962.1	E980.6
Succinimide (anticonvulsant)	966.2	E855.0	E936.2	E950.4	E962.0	E980.4
mercuric — see Mercury						
Succinylcholine	975.2	E858.6	E945.2	E950.4	E962.0	E980.4
Succinylsulfathiazole	961.0	E857	E931.0	E950.4	E962.0	E980.4
Sucrose	974.5	E858.5	E944.5	E950.4	E962.0	E980.4
Sulfacetamide	961.0	E857	E931.0	E950.4	E962.0	E980.4
ophthalmic preparation	976.5	E858.7	E946.5	E950.4	E962.0	E980.4
Sulfachlorpyridazine	961.0	E857	E931.0	E950.4	E962.0	E980.4
Sulfacytine	961.0	E857	E931.0	E950.4	E962.0	E980.4
Sulfadiazine	961.0	E857	E931.0	E950.4	E962.0	E980.4
silver (topical)	976.0	E858.7	E946.0	E950.4	E962.0	E980.4
Sulfadimethoxine	961.0	E857	E931.0	E950.4	E962.0	E980.4
Sulfadimidine	961.0	E857	E931.0	E950.4	E962.0	E980.4
Sulfaethidole	961.0	E857	E931.0	E950.4	E962.0	E980.4
Sulfafurazole	961.0	E857	E931.0	E950.4	E962.0	E980.4
Sulfaguanidine	961.0	E857	E931.0	E950.4	E962.0	E980.4
Sulfamerazine	961.0	E857	E931.0	E950.4	E962.0	E980.4
Sulfameter	961.0	E857	E931.0	E950.4	E962.0	E980.4
Sulfamethizole	961.0	E857	E931.0	E950.4	E962.0	E980.4
Sulfamethoxazole	961.0	E857	E931.0	E950.4	E962.0	E980.4
Sulfamethoxydiazine	961.0	E857	E931.0	E950.4	E962.0	E980.4
Sulfamethoxypyridazine	961.0	E857	E931.0	E950.4	E962.0	E980.4
Sulfamethylthiazole	961.0	E857	E931.0	E950.4	E962.0	E980.4
Sulfamylon	976.0	E858.7	E946.0	E950.4	E962.0	E980.4
Sulfan blue (diagnostic dye)	977.8	E858.8	E947.8	E950.4	E962.0	E980.4
Sulfanilamide	961.0	E857	E931.0	E950.4	E962.0	E980.4
Sulfanilylguanidine	961.0	E857	E931.0	E950.4	E962.0	E980.4
Sulfaphenazole	961.0	E857	E931.0	E950.4	E962.0	E980.4
Sulfaphenylthiazole	961.0	E857	E931.0	E950.4	E962.0	E980.4
Sulfaproxyline	961.0	E857	E931.0	E950.4	E962.0	E980.4
Sulfapyridine	961.0	E857	E931.0	E950.4	E962.0	E980.4
Sulfapyrimidine	961.0	E857	E931.0	E950.4	E962.0	E980.4
Sulfarsphenamine	961.1	E857	E931.1	E950.4	E962.0	E980.4
Sulfasalazine	961.0	E857	E931.0	E950.4	E962.0	E980.4
Sulfasomizole	961.0	E857	E931.0	E950.4	E962.0	E980.4
Sulfasuxidine	961.0	E857	E931.0	E950.4	E962.0	E980.4
Sulfinpyrazone	974.7	E858.5	E944.7	E950.4	E962.0	E980.4
Sulfisoxazole	961.0	E857	E931.0	E950.4	E962.0	E980.4
ophthalmic preparation	976.5	E858.7	E946.5	E950.4	E962.0	E980.4
Sulfomyxin	960.8	E856	E930.8	E950.4	E962.0	E980.4
Sulfonal	967.8	E852.8	E937.8	E950.2	E962.0	E980.2
Sulfonamides (mixtures)	961.0	E857	E931.0	E950.4	E962.0	E980.4
Sulfones	961.8	E857	E931.8	E950.4	E962.0	E980.4
Sulfonethylmethane	967.8	E852.8	E937.8	E950.2	E962.0	E980.2
Sulfonmethane	967.8	E852.8	E937.8	E950.2	E962.0	E980.2
Sulfonphthal, sulfonphthol	977.8	E858.8	E947.8	E950.4	E962.0	E980.4
Sulfonylurea derivatives, oral	962.3	E858.0	E932.3	E950.4	E962.0	E980.4
Sulfoxone	961.8	E857	E931.8	E950.4	E962.0	E980.4
Sulfur, sulfureted, sulfuric, sulfurous, sulfuryl (compounds) NEC	989.89	E866.8	—	E950.9	E962.1	E980.9
acid	983.1	E864.1	—	E950.7	E962.1	E980.6
dioxide	987.3	E869.1	—	E952.8	E962.2	E982.8

	Poisoning	External Cause (E-Code) Accident	Therapeutic Use	Suicide Attempt	Assault	Undetermined
Sulfur, sulfureted, sulfuric, sulfurous, sulfuryl (compounds) — *continued*						
ether — see Ether(s)						
hydrogen	987.8	E869.8	—	E952.8	E962.2	E982.8
medicinal (keratolytic) (ointment) NEC	976.4	E858.7	E946.4	E950.4	E962.0	E980.4
pesticide (vapor)	989.4	E863.4	—	E950.6	E962.1	E980.7
vapor NEC	987.8	E869.8	—	E952.8	E962.2	E982.8
Sulkowitch's reagent	977.8	E858.8	E947.8	E950.4	E962.0	E980.4
Sulphadione	961.8	E857	E931.8	E950.4	E962.0	E980.4
Sulph — *see also* Sulf-						
Sulthiame, sultiame	966.3	E855.0	E936.3	E950.4	E962.0	E980.4
Superinone	975.5	E858.6	E945.5	E950.4	E962.0	E980.4
Suramin	961.5	E857	E931.5	E950.4	E962.0	E980.4
Surfacaine	968.5	E855.2	E938.5	E950.4	E962.0	E980.4
Surital	968.3	E855.1	E938.3	E950.4	E962.0	E980.4
Sutilains	976.8	E858.7	E946.8	E950.4	E962.0	E980.4
Suxamethonium (bromide) (chloride) (iodide)	975.2	E858.6	E945.2	E950.4	E962.0	E980.4
Suxethonium (bromide)	975.2	E858.6	E945.2	E950.4	E962.0	E980.4
Sweet oil (birch)	976.3	E858.7	E946.3	E950.4	E962.0	E980.4
Sym-dichloroethyl ether	982.3	E862.4	—	E950.9	E962.1	E980.9
Sympatholytics	971.3	E855.6	E941.3	E950.4	E962.0	E980.4
Sympathomimetics	971.2	E855.5	E941.2	E950.4	E962.0	E980.4
Synagis	979.6	E858.8	E949.6	E950.4	E962.0	E980.4
Synalar	976.0	E858.7	E946.0	E950.4	E962.0	E980.4
Synthroid	962.7	E858.0	E932.7	E950.4	E962.0	E980.4
Syntocinon	975.0	E858.6	E945.0	E950.4	E962.0	E980.4
Syrosingopine	972.6	E858.3	E942.6	E950.4	E962.0	E980.4
Systemic agents (primarily)	963.9	E858.1	E933.9	E950.4	E962.0	E980.4
specified NEC	963.8	E858.1	E933.8	E950.4	E962.0	E980.4
Tablets — *see also* specified substance	977.9	E858.9	E947.9	E950.5	E962.0	E980.5
Tace	962.2	E858.0	E932.2	E950.4	E962.0	E980.4
Tacrine	971.0	E855.3	E941.0	E950.4	E962.0	E980.4
Talbutal	967.0	E851	E937.0	E950.1	E962.0	E980.1
Talc	976.3	E858.7	E946.3	E950.4	E962.0	E980.4
Talcum	976.3	E858.7	E946.3	E950.4	E962.0	E980.4
Tamsulosin	971.3	E855.6	E941.3	E950.4	E962.0	E980.4
Tandearil, tanderil	965.5	E850.5	E935.5	E950.0	E962.0	E980.0
Tannic acid	983.1	E864.1	—	E950.7	E962.1	E980.6
medicinal (astringent)	976.2	E858.7	E946.2	E950.4	E962.0	E980.4
Tannin — see Tannic acid						
Tansy	988.2	E865.4	—	E950.9	E962.1	E980.9
TAO	960.3	E856	E930.3	E950.4	E962.0	E980.4
Tapazole	962.8	E858.0	E932.8	E950.4	E962.0	E980.4
Tar NEC	983.0	E864.0	—	E950.7	E962.1	E980.6
camphor — see Naphthalene						
fumes	987.8	E869.8	—	E952.8	E962.2	E982.8
Taractan	969.3	E853.8	E939.3	E950.3	E962.0	E980.3
Tarantula (venomous)	989.5	E905.1	—	E950.9	E962.1	E980.9
Tartar emetic (anti-infective)	961.2	E857	E931.2	E950.4	E962.0	E980.4
Tartaric acid	983.1	E864.1	—	E950.7	E962.1	E980.6
Tartrated antimony (anti-infective)	961.2	E857	E931.2	E950.4	E962.0	E980.4
TCA — *see* Trichloroacetic acid						
TDI	983.0	E864.0	—	E950.7	E962.1	E980.6
vapor	987.8	E869.8	—	E952.8	E962.2	E982.8
Tear gas	987.5	E869.3	—	E952.8	E962.2	E982.8
Teclothiazide	974.3	E858.5	E944.3	E950.4	E962.0	E980.4
Tegretol	966.3	E855.0	E936.3	E950.4	E962.0	E980.4
Telepaque	977.8	E858.8	E947.8	E950.4	E962.0	E980.4
Tellurium	985.8	E866.4	—	E950.9	E962.1	E980.9
fumes	985.8	E866.4	—	E950.9	E962.1	E980.9
TEM	963.1	E858.1	E933.1	E950.4	E962.0	E980.4
Temazepan — see Benzodiazepines						
TEPA	963.1	E858.1	E933.1	E950.4	E962.0	E980.4
TEPP	989.3	E863.1	—	E950.6	E962.1	E980.7
Terbutaline	971.2	E855.5	E941.2	E950.4	E962.0	E980.4
Teroxalene	961.6	E857	E931.6	E950.4	E962.0	E980.4
Terpin hydrate	975.5	E858.6	E945.5	E950.4	E962.0	E980.4
Terramycin	960.4	E856	E930.4	E950.4	E962.0	E980.4
Tessalon	975.4	E858.6	E945.4	E950.4	E962.0	E980.4
Testosterone	962.1	E858.0	E932.1	E950.4	E962.0	E980.4
Tetanus (vaccine)	978.4	E858.8	E948.4	E950.4	E962.0	E980.4
antitoxin	979.9	E858.8	E949.9	E950.4	E962.0	E980.4
immune globulin (human)	964.6	E858.2	E934.6	E950.4	E962.0	E980.4
toxoid	978.4	E858.8	E948.4	E950.4	E962.0	E980.4

	Poisoning	External Cause (E-Code) Accident	Therapeutic Use	Suicide Attempt	Assault	Undetermined
Tetanus — *continued*						
toxoid — *continued*						
with diphtheria toxoid	978.9	E858.8	E948.9	E950.4	E962.0	E980.4
with pertussis	978.6	E858.8	E948.6	E950.4	E962.0	E980.4
Tetrabenazine	969.5	E853.8	E939.5	E950.3	E962.0	E980.3
Tetracaine (infiltration) (topical)	968.5	E855.2	E938.5	E950.4	E962.0	E980.4
nerve block (peripheral) (plexus)	968.6	E855.2	E938.6	E950.4	E962.0	E980.4
spinal	968.7	E855.2	E938.7	E950.4	E962.0	E980.4
Tetrachlorethylene — see Tetrachloroethylene						
Tetrachlormethiazide	974.3	E858.5	E944.3	E950.4	E962.0	E980.4
Tetrachloroethane (liquid) (vapor)	982.3	E862.4	—	E950.9	E962.1	E980.9
paint or varnish	982.3	E861.6	—	E950.9	E962.1	E980.9
Tetrachloroethylene (liquid) (vapor)	982.3	E862.4	—	E950.9	E962.1	E980.9
medicinal	961.6	E857	E931.6	E950.4	E962.0	E980.4
Tetrachloromethane — see Carbon, tetrachloride						
Tetracycline	960.4	E856	E930.4	E950.4	E962.0	E980.4
ophthalmic preparation	976.5	E858.7	E946.5	E950.4	E962.0	E980.4
topical NEC	976.0	E858.7	E946.0	E950.4	E962.0	E980.4
Tetraethylammonium chloride	972.3	E858.3	E942.3	E950.4	E962.0	E980.4
Tetraethyl lead (antiknock compound)	984.1	E862.1	—	E950.9	E962.1	E980.9
Tetraethyl pyrophosphate	989.3	E863.1	—	E950.6	E962.1	E980.7
Tetraethylthiuram disulfide	977.3	E858.8	E947.3	E950.4	E962.0	E980.4
Tetrahydroaminoacridine	971.0	E855.3	E941.0	E950.4	E962.0	E980.4
Tetrahydrocannabinol	969.6	E854.1	E939.6	E950.3	E962.0	E980.3
Tetrahydronaphthalene	982.0	E862.4	—	E950.9	E962.1	E980.9
Tetrahydrozoline	971.2	E855.5	E941.2	E950.4	E962.0	E980.4
Tetralin	982.0	E862.4	—	E950.9	E962.1	E980.9
Tetramethylthiuram (disulfide) NEC	989.4	E863.6	—	E950.6	E962.1	E980.7
medicinal	976.2	E858.7	E946.2	E950.4	E962.0	E980.4
Tetronal	967.8	E852.8	E937.8	E950.2	E962.0	E980.2
Tetryl	983.0	E864.0	—	E950.7	E962.1	E980.6
Thalidomide	967.8	E852.8	E937.8	E950.2	E962.0	E980.2
Thallium (compounds) (dust) NEC	985.8	E866.4	—	E950.9	E962.1	E980.9
pesticide (rodenticide)	985.8	E863.7	—	E950.6	E962.1	E980.7
THC	969.6	E854.1	E939.6	E950.3	E962.0	E980.3
Thebacon	965.09	E850.2	E935.2	E950.0	E962.0	E980.0
Thebaine	965.09	E850.2	E935.2	E950.0	E962.0	E980.0
Theobromine (calcium salicylate)	974.1	E858.5	E944.1	E950.4	E962.0	E980.4
Theophylline (diuretic)	974.1	E858.5	E944.1	E950.4	E962.0	E980.4
ethylenediamine	975.7	E858.6	E945.7	E950.4	E962.0	E980.4
Thiabendazole	961.6	E857	E931.6	E950.4	E962.0	E980.4
Thialbarbital, thialbarbitone	968.3	E855.1	E938.3	E950.4	E962.0	E980.4
Thiamine	963.5	E858.1	E933.5	E950.4	E962.0	E980.4
Thiamylal (sodium)	968.3	E855.1	E938.3	E950.4	E962.0	E980.4
Thiazesim	969.0	E854.0	E939.0	E950.3	E962.0	E980.3
Thiazides (diuretics)	974.3	E858.5	E944.3	E950.4	E962.0	E980.4
Thiethylperazine	963.0	E858.1	E933.0	E950.4	E962.0	E980.4
Thimerosal (topical)	976.0	E858.7	E946.0	E950.4	E962.0	E980.4
ophthalmic preparation	976.5	E858.7	E946.5	E950.4	E962.0	E980.4
Thioacetazone	961.8	E857	E931.8	E950.4	E962.0	E980.4
Thiobarbiturates	968.3	E855.1	E938.3	E950.4	E962.0	E980.4
Thiobismol	961.2	E857	E931.2	E950.4	E962.0	E980.4
Thiocarbamide	962.8	E858.0	E932.8	E950.4	E962.0	E980.4
Thiocarbarsone	961.1	E857	E931.1	E950.4	E962.0	E980.4
Thiocarlide	961.8	E857	E931.8	E950.4	E962.0	E980.4
Thioguanine	963.1	E858.1	E933.1	E950.4	E962.0	E980.4
Thiomercaptomerin	974.0	E858.5	E944.0	E950.4	E962.0	E980.4
Thiomerin	974.0	E858.5	E944.0	E950.4	E962.0	E980.4
Thiopental, thiopentone (sodium)	968.3	E855.1	E938.3	E950.4	E962.0	E980.4
Thiopropazate	969.1	E853.0	E939.1	E950.3	E962.0	E980.3
Thioproperazine	969.1	E853.0	E939.1	E950.3	E962.0	E980.3
Thioridazine	969.1	E853.0	E939.1	E950.3	E962.0	E980.3
Thio-TEPA, thiotepa	963.1	E858.1	E933.1	E950.4	E962.0	E980.4
Thiothixene	969.3	E853.8	E939.3	E950.3	E962.0	E980.3
Thiouracil	962.8	E858.0	E932.8	E950.4	E962.0	E980.4
Thiourea	962.8	E858.0	E932.8	E950.4	E962.0	E980.4
Thiphenamil	971.1	E855.4	E941.1	E950.4	E962.0	E980.4

		External Cause (E-Code)				
	Poisoning	Accident	Therapeutic Use	Suicide Attempt	Assault	Undetermined
Thiram NEC	989.4	E863.6	—	E950.6	E962.1	E980.7
medicinal	976.2	E858.7	E946.2	E950.4	E962.0	E980.4
Thonzylamine	963.0	E858.1	E933.0	E950.4	E962.0	E980.4
Thorazine	969.1	E853.0	E939.1	E950.3	E962.0	E980.3
Thornapple	988.2	E865.4	—	E950.9	E962.1	E980.9
Throat preparation (lozenges) NEC	976.6	E858.7	E946.6	E950.4	E962.0	E980.4
Thrombin	964.5	E858.2	E934.5	E950.4	E962.0	E980.4
Thrombolysin	964.4	E858.2	E934.4	E950.4	E962.0	E980.4
Thymol	983.0	E864.0	—	E950.7	E962.1	E980.6
Thymus extract	962.9	E858.0	E932.9	E950.4	E962.0	E980.4
Thyroglobulin	962.7	E858.0	E932.7	E950.4	E962.0	E980.4
Thyroid (derivatives) (extract)	962.7	E858.0	E932.7	E950.4	E962.0	E980.4
Thyrolar	962.7	E858.0	E932.7	E950.4	E962.0	E980.4
Thyrothrophin, thyrotropin	977.8	E858.8	E947.8	E950.4	E962.0	E980.4
Thyroxin(e)	962.7	E858.0	E932.7	E950.4	E962.0	E980.4
Tigan	963.0	E858.1	E933.0	E950.4	E962.0	E980.4
Tigloidine	968.0	E855.1	E938.0	E950.4	E962.0	E980.4
Tin (chloride) (dust) (oxide) NEC	985.8	E866.4	—	E950.9	E962.1	E980.9
anti-infectives	961.2	E857	E931.2	E950.4	E962.0	E980.4
Tinactin	976.0	E858.7	E946.0	E950.4	E962.0	E980.4
Tincture, iodine — *see* Iodine						
Tindal	969.1	E853.0	E939.1	E950.3	E962.0	E980.3
Titanium (compounds) (vapor)	985.8	E866.4	—	E950.9	E962.1	E980.9
ointment	976.3	E858.7	E946.3	E950.4	E962.0	E980.4
Titroid	962.7	E858.0	E932.7	E950.4	E962.0	E980.4
TMTD — *see* Tetramethylthiuram disulfide						
TNT	989.89	E866.8	—	E950.9	E962.1	E980.9
fumes	987.8	E869.8	—	E952.8	E962.2	E982.8
Toadstool	988.1	E865.5	—	E950.9	E962.1	E980.9
Tobacco NEC	989.84	E866.8	—	E950.9	E962.1	E980.9
Indian	988.2	E865.4	—	E950.9	E962.1	E980.9
smoke, second-hand	987.8	E869.4	—	—	—	—
Tocopherol	963.5	E858.1	E933.5	E950.4	E962.0	E980.4
Tocosamine	975.0	E858.6	E945.0	E950.4	E962.0	E980.4
Tofranil	969.0	E854.0	E939.0	E950.3	E962.0	E980.3
Toilet deodorizer	989.89	E866.8	—	E950.9	E962.1	E980.9
Tolazamide	962.3	E858.0	E932.3	E950.4	E962.0	E980.4
Tolazoline	971.3	E855.6	E941.3	E950.4	E962.0	E980.4
Tolbutamide	962.3	E858.0	E932.3	E950.4	E962.0	E980.4
sodium	977.8	E858.8	E947.8	E950.4	E962.0	E980.4
Tolmetin	965.69	E850.6	E935.6	E950.0	E962.0	E980.0
Tolnaftate	976.0	E858.7	E946.0	E950.4	E962.0	E980.4
Tolpropamine	976.1	E858.7	E946.1	E950.4	E962.0	E980.4
Tolserol	968.0	E855.1	E938.0	E950.4	E962.0	E980.4
Toluene (liquid) (vapor)	982.0	E862.4	—	E950.9	E962.1	E980.9
diisocyanate	983.0	E864.0	—	E950.7	E962.1	E980.6
Toluidine	983.0	E864.0	—	E950.7	E962.1	E980.6
vapor	987.8	E869.8	—	E952.8	E962.2	E982.8
Toluol (liquid) (vapor)	982.0	E862.4	—	E950.9	E962.1	E980.9
Tolylene-2, 4-diisocyanate	983.0	E864.0	—	E950.7	E962.1	E980.6
Tonics, cardiac	972.1	E858.3	E942.1	E950.4	E962.0	E980.4
Toxaphene (dust) (spray)	989.2	E863.0	—	E950.6	E962.1	E980.7
Toxoids NEC	978.8	E858.8	E948.8	E950.4	E962.0	E980.4
Tractor fuel NEC	981	E862.1	—	E950.9	E962.1	E980.9
Tragacanth	973.3	E858.4	E943.3	E950.4	E962.0	E980.4
Tramazoline	971.2	E855.5	E941.2	E950.4	E962.0	E980.4
Tranquilizers	969.5	E853.9	E939.5	E950.3	E962.0	E980.3
benzodiazepine-based	969.4	E853.2	E939.4	E950.3	E962.0	E980.3
butyrophenone-based	969.2	E853.1	E939.2	E950.3	E962.0	E980.3
major NEC	969.3	E853.8	E939.3	E950.3	E962.0	E980.3
phenothiazine-based	969.1	E853.0	E939.1	E950.3	E962.0	E980.3
specified NEC	969.5	E853.8	E939.5	E950.3	E962.0	E980.3
Trantoin	961.9	E857	E931.9	E950.4	E962.0	E980.4
Tranxene	969.4	E853.2	E939.4	E950.3	E962.0	E980.3
Tranylcypromine (sulfate)	969.0	E854.0	E939.0	E950.3	E962.0	E980.3
Trasentine	975.1	E858.6	E945.1	E950.4	E962.0	E980.4
Travert	974.5	E858.5	E944.5	E950.4	E962.0	E980.4
Trecator	961.8	E857	E931.8	E950.4	E962.0	E980.4
Tretinoin	976.8	E858.7	E946.8	E950.4	E962.0	E980.4
Triacetin	976.0	E858.7	E946.0	E950.4	E962.0	E980.4
Triacetyloleandomycin	960.3	E856	E930.3	E950.4	E962.0	E980.4
Triamcinolone	962.0	E858.0	E932.0	E950.4	E962.0	E980.4
ENT agent	976.6	E858.7	E946.6	E950.4	E962.0	E980.4
medicinal (keratolytic)	976.4	E858.7	E946.4	E950.4	E962.0	E980.4
ophthalmic preparation	976.5	E858.7	E946.5	E950.4	E962.0	E980.4

		External Cause (E-Code)				
	Poisoning	Accident	Therapeutic Use	Suicide Attempt	Assault	Undetermined
Triamcinolone — *continued*						
topical NEC	976.0	E858.7	E946.0	E950.4	E962.0	E980.4
Triamterene	974.4	E858.5	E944.4	E950.4	E962.0	E980.4
Triaziquone	963.1	E858.1	E933.1	E950.4	E962.0	E980.4
Tribromacetaldehyde	967.3	E852.2	E937.3	E950.2	E962.0	E980.2
Tribromoethanol	968.2	E855.1	E938.2	E950.4	E962.0	E980.4
Tribromomethane	967.3	E852.2	E937.3	E950.2	E962.0	E980.2
Trichlorethane	982.3	E862.4	—	E950.9	E962.1	E980.9
Trichlormethiazide	974.3	E858.5	E944.3	E950.4	E962.0	E980.4
Trichloroacetic acid	983.1	E864.1	—	E950.7	E962.1	E980.6
Trichloroethanol	967.1	E852.0	E937.1	E950.2	E962.0	E980.2
Trichloroethylene (liquid) (vapor)	982.3	E862.4	—	E950.9	E962.1	E980.9
anesthetic (gas)	968.2	E855.1	E938.2	E950.4	E962.0	E980.4
Trichloroethyl phosphate	967.1	E852.0	E937.1	E950.2	E962.0	E980.2
Trichlorofluoromethane NEC	987.4	E869.2	—	E952.8	E962.2	E982.8
Trichlorotriethylamine	963.1	E858.1	E933.1	E950.4	E962.0	E980.4
Trichomonacides NEC	961.5	E857	E931.5	E950.4	E962.0	E980.4
Trichomycin	960.1	E856	E930.1	E950.4	E962.0	E980.4
Triclofos	967.1	E852.0	E937.1	E950.2	E962.0	E980.2
Tricresyl phosphate	989.89	E866.8	—	E950.9	E962.1	E980.9
solvent	982.8	E862.4	—	E950.9	E962.1	E980.9
Tricyclamol	966.4	E855.0	E936.4	E950.4	E962.0	E980.4
Tridesilon	976.0	E858.7	E946.0	E950.4	E962.0	E980.4
Tridihexethyl	971.1	E855.4	E941.1	E950.4	E962.0	E980.4
Tridione	966.0	E855.0	E936.0	E950.4	E962.0	E980.4
Triethanolamine NEC	983.2	E864.2	—	E950.7	E962.1	E980.6
detergent	983.2	E861.0	—	E950.7	E962.1	E980.6
trinitrate	972.4	E858.3	E942.4	E950.4	E962.0	E980.4
Triethanomelamine	963.1	E858.1	E933.1	E950.4	E962.0	E980.4
Triethylene melamine	963.1	E858.1	E933.1	E950.4	E962.0	E980.4
Triethylenephosphoramide	963.1	E858.1	E933.1	E950.4	E962.0	E980.4
Triethylenethiophosphoramide	963.1	E858.1	E933.1	E950.4	E962.0	E980.4
Trifluoperazine	969.1	E853.0	E939.1	E950.3	E962.0	E980.3
Trifluperidol	969.2	E853.1	E939.2	E950.3	E962.0	E980.3
Triflupromazine	969.1	E853.0	E939.1	E950.3	E962.0	E980.3
Trihexyphenidyl	971.1	E855.4	E941.1	E950.4	E962.0	E980.4
Triiodothyronine	962.7	E858.0	E932.7	E950.4	E962.0	E980.4
Trilene	968.2	E855.1	E938.2	E950.4	E962.0	E980.4
Trimeprazine	963.0	E858.1	E933.0	E950.4	E962.0	E980.4
Trimetazidine	972.4	E858.3	E942.4	E950.4	E962.0	E980.4
Trimethadione	966.0	E855.0	E936.0	E950.4	E962.0	E980.4
Trimethaphan	972.3	E858.3	E942.3	E950.4	E962.0	E980.4
Trimethidinium	972.3	E858.3	E942.3	E950.4	E962.0	E980.4
Trimethobenzamide	963.0	E858.1	E933.0	E950.4	E962.0	E980.4
Trimethylcarbinol	980.8	E860.8	—	E950.9	E962.1	E980.9
Trimethylpsoralen	976.3	E858.7	E946.3	E950.4	E962.0	E980.4
Trimeton	963.0	E858.1	E933.0	E950.4	E962.0	E980.4
Trimipramine	969.0	E854.0	E939.0	E950.3	E962.0	E980.3
Trimustine	963.1	E858.1	E933.1	E950.4	E962.0	E980.4
Trinitrin	972.4	E858.3	E942.4	E950.4	E962.0	E980.4
Trinitrophenol	983.0	E864.0	—	E950.7	E962.1	E980.6
Trinitrotoluene	989.89	E866.8	—	E950.9	E962.1	E980.9
fumes	987.8	E869.8	—	E952.8	E962.2	E982.8
Trional	967.8	E852.8	E937.8	E950.2	E962.0	E980.2
Trioxide of arsenic — *see* Arsenic						
Trioxsalen	976.3	E858.7	E946.3	E950.4	E962.0	E980.4
Tripelennamine	963.0	E858.1	E933.0	E950.4	E962.0	E980.4
Triperidol	969.2	E853.1	E939.2	E950.3	E962.0	E980.3
Triprolidine	963.0	E858.1	E933.0	E950.4	E962.0	E980.4
Trisoralen	976.3	E858.7	E946.3	E950.4	E962.0	E980.4
Troleandomycin	960.3	E856	E930.3	E950.4	E962.0	E980.4
Trolnitrate (phosphate)	972.4	E858.3	E942.4	E950.4	E962.0	E980.4
Trometamol	963.3	E858.1	E933.3	E950.4	E962.0	E980.4
Tromethamine	963.3	E858.1	E933.3	E950.4	E962.0	E980.4
Tronothane	968.5	E855.2	E938.5	E950.4	E962.0	E980.4
Tropicamide	971.1	E855.4	E941.1	E950.4	E962.0	E980.4
Troxidone	966.0	E855.0	E936.0	E950.4	E962.0	E980.4
Tryparsamide	961.1	E857	E931.1	E950.4	E962.0	E980.4
Trypsin	963.4	E858.1	E933.4	E950.4	E962.0	E980.4
Tryptizol	969.0	E854.0	E939.0	E950.3	E962.0	E980.3
Tuaminoheptane	971.2	E855.5	E941.2	E950.4	E962.0	E980.4
Tuberculin (old)	977.8	E858.8	E947.8	E950.4	E962.0	E980.4
Tubocurare	975.2	E858.6	E945.2	E950.4	E962.0	E980.4
Tubocurarine	975.2	E858.6	E945.2	E950.4	E962.0	E980.4
Turkish green	969.6	E854.1	E939.6	E950.3	E962.0	E980.3
Turpentine (spirits of) (liquid) (vapor)	982.8	E862.4	—	E950.9	E962.1	E980.9
Tybamate	969.5	E853.8	E939.5	E950.3	E962.0	E980.3

		External Cause (E-Code)				
	Poisoning	Accident	Therapeutic Use	Suicide Attempt	Assault	Undetermined
Tyloxapol	975.5	E858.6	E945.5	E950.4	E962.0	E980.4
Tymazoline	971.2	E855.5	E941.2	E950.4	E962.0	E980.4
Typhoid vaccine	978.1	E858.8	E948.1	E950.4	E962.0	E980.4
Typhus vaccine	979.2	E858.8	E949.2	E950.4	E962.0	E980.4
Tyrothricin	976.0	E858.7	E946.0	E950.4	E962.0	E980.4
ENT agent	976.6	E858.7	E946.6	E950.4	E962.0	E980.4
ophthalmic preparation	976.5	E858.7	E946.5	E950.4	E962.0	E980.4
Undecenoic acid	976.0	E858.7	E946.0	E950.4	E962.0	E980.4
Undecylenic acid	976.0	E858.7	E946.0	E950.4	E962.0	E980.4
Unna's boot	976.3	E858.7	E946.3	E950.4	E962.0	E980.4
Uracil mustard	963.1	E858.1	E933.1	E950.4	E962.0	E980.4
Uramustine	963.1	E858.1	E933.1	E950.4	E962.0	E980.4
Urari	975.2	E858.6	E945.2	E950.4	E962.0	E980.4
Urea	974.4	E858.5	E944.4	E950.4	E962.0	E980.4
topical	976.8	E858.7	E946.8	E950.4	E962.0	E980.4
Urethan(e) (antineoplastic)	963.1	E858.1	E933.1	E950.4	E962.0	E980.4
Urginea (maritima) (scilla) — *see* Squill						
Uric acid metabolism agents NEC	974.7	E858.5	E944.7	E950.4	E962.0	E980.4
Urokinase	964.4	E858.2	E934.4	E950.4	E962.0	E980.4
Urokon	977.8	E858.8	E947.8	E950.4	E962.0	E980.4
Urotropin	961.9	E857	E931.9	E950.4	E962.0	E980.4
Urtica	988.2	E865.4	—	E950.9	E962.1	E980.9
Utility gas — *see* Gas, utility						
Vaccine NEC	979.9	E858.8	E949.9	E950.4	E962.0	E980.4
bacterial NEC	978.8	E858.8	E948.8	E950.4	E962.0	E980.4
with						
other bacterial component	978.9	E858.8	E948.9	E950.4	E962.0	E980.4
pertussis component	978.6	E858.8	E948.6	E950.4	E962.0	E980.4
viral-rickettsial component	979.7	E858.8	E949.7	E950.4	E962.0	E980.4
mixed NEC	978.9	E858.8	E948.9	E950.4	E962.0	E980.4
BCG	978.0	E858.8	E948.0	E950.4	E962.0	E980.4
cholera	978.2	E858.8	E948.2	E950.4	E962.0	E980.4
diphtheria	978.5	E858.8	E948.5	E950.4	E962.0	E980.4
influenza	979.6	E858.8	E949.6	E950.4	E962.0	E980.4
measles	979.4	E858.8	E949.4	E950.4	E962.0	E980.4
meningococcal	978.8	E858.8	E948.8	E950.4	E962.0	E980.4
mumps	979.6	E858.8	E949.6	E950.4	E962.0	E980.4
paratyphoid	978.1	E858.8	E948.1	E950.4	E962.0	E980.4
pertussis (with diphtheria toxoid) (with tetanus toxoid)	978.6	E858.8	E948.6	E950.4	E962.0	E980.4
plague	978.3	E858.8	E948.3	E950.4	E962.0	E980.4
poliomyelitis	979.5	E858.8	E949.5	E950.4	E962.0	E980.4
poliovirus	979.5	E858.8	E949.5	E950.4	E962.0	E980.4
rabies	979.1	E858.8	E949.1	E950.4	E962.0	E980.4
respiratory syncytial virus	979.6	E858.8	E949.6	E950.4	E962.0	E980.4
rickettsial NEC	979.6	E858.8	E949.6	E950.4	E962.0	E980.4
with						
bacterial component	979.7	E858.8	E949.7	E950.4	E962.0	E980.4
pertussis component	978.6	E858.8	E948.6	E950.4	E962.0	E980.4
viral component	979.7	E858.8	E949.7	E950.4	E962.0	E980.4
Rocky mountain spotted fever	979.6	E858.8	E949.6	E950.4	E962.0	E980.4
rotavirus	979.6	E858.8	E949.6	E950.4	E962.0	E980.4
rubella virus	979.4	E858.8	E949.4	E950.4	E962.0	E980.4
sabin oral	979.5	E858.8	E949.5	E950.4	E962.0	E980.4
smallpox	979.0	E858.8	E949.0	E950.4	E962.0	E980.4
tetanus	978.4	E858.8	E948.4	E950.4	E962.0	E980.4
typhoid	978.1	E858.8	E948.1	E950.4	E962.0	E980.4
typhus	979.2	E858.8	E949.2	E950.4	E962.0	E980.4
viral NEC	979.6	E858.8	E949.6	E950.4	E962.0	E980.4
with						
bacterial component	979.7	E858.8	E949.7	E950.4	E962.0	E980.4
pertussis component	978.6	E858.8	E948.6	E950.4	E962.0	E980.4
rickettsial component	979.7	E858.8	E949.7	E950.4	E962.0	E980.4
yellow fever	979.3	E858.8	E949.3	E950.4	E962.0	E980.4
Vaccinia immune globulin (human)	964.6	E858.2	E934.6	E950.4	E962.0	E980.4
Vaginal contraceptives	976.8	E858.7	E946.8	E950.4	E962.0	E980.4
Valethamate	971.1	E855.4	E941.1	E950.4	E962.0	E980.4
Valisone	976.0	E858.7	E946.0	E950.4	E962.0	E980.4
Valium	969.4	E853.2	E939.4	E950.3	E962.0	E980.3
Valmid	967.8	E852.8	E937.8	E950.2	E962.0	E980.2
Vanadium	985.8	E866.4	—	E950.9	E962.1	E980.9
Vancomycin	960.8	E856	E930.8	E950.4	E962.0	E980.4
Vapor — *see also* Gas	987.9	E869.9	—	E952.9	E962.2	E982.9
kiln (carbon monoxide)	986	E868.8	—	E952.1	E962.2	E982.1
lead — see Lead						

		External Cause (E-Code)				
	Poisoning	Accident	Therapeutic Use	Suicide Attempt	Assault	Undetermined
Vapor — *see also* Gas — *continued*						
specified source NEC (see also specific substance)	987.8	E869.8	—	E952.8	E962.2	E982.8
Varidase	964.4	E858.2	E934.4	E950.4	E962.0	E980.4
Varnish	989.89	E861.6	—	E950.9	E962.1	E980.9
cleaner	982.8	E862.9	—	E950.9	E962.1	E980.9
Vaseline	976.3	E858.7	E946.3	E950.4	E962.0	E980.4
Vasodilan	972.5	E858.3	E942.5	E950.4	E962.0	E980.4
Vasodilators NEC	972.5	E858.3	E942.5	E950.4	E962.0	E980.4
coronary	972.4	E858.3	E942.4	E950.4	E962.0	E980.4
Vasopressin	962.5	E858.0	E932.5	E950.4	E962.0	E980.4
Vasopressor drugs	962.5	E858.0	E932.5	E950.4	E962.0	E980.4
Venom, venomous (bite) (sting)	989.5	E905.9	—	E950.9	E962.1	E980.9
arthropod NEC	989.5	E905.5	—	E950.9	E962.1	E980.9
bee	989.5	E905.3	—	E950.9	E962.1	E980.9
centipede	989.5	E905.4	—	E950.9	E962.1	E980.9
hornet	989.5	E905.3	—	E950.9	E962.1	E980.9
lizard	989.5	E905.0	—	E950.9	E962.1	E980.9
marine animals or plants	989.5	E905.6	—	E950.9	E962.1	E980.9
millipede (tropical)	989.5	E905.4	—	E950.9	E962.1	E980.9
plant NEC	989.5	E905.7	—	E950.9	E962.1	E980.9
marine	989.5	E905.6	—	E950.9	E962.1	E980.9
scorpion	989.5	E905.2	—	E950.9	E962.1	E980.9
snake	989.5	E905.0	—	E950.9	E962.1	E980.9
specified NEC	989.5	E905.8	—	E950.9	E962.1	E980.9
spider	989.5	E905.1	—	E950.9	E962.1	E980.9
wasp	989.5	E905.3	—	E950.9	E962.1	E980.9
Ventolin — *see* Salbutamol sulfate						
Veramon	967.0	E851	E937.0	E950.1	E962.0	E980.1
Veratrum						
album	988.2	E865.4	—	E950.9	E962.1	E980.9
alkaloids	972.6	E858.3	E942.6	E950.4	E962.0	E980.4
viride	988.2	E865.4	—	E950.9	E962.1	E980.9
Verdigris — *see also* Copper	985.8	E866.4	—	E950.9	E962.1	E980.9
Veronal	967.0	E851	E937.0	E950.1	E962.0	E980.1
Veroxil	961.6	E857	E931.6	E950.4	E962.0	E980.4
Versidyne	965.7	E850.7	E935.7	E950.0	E962.0	E980.0
Viagra	972.5	E858.3	E942.5	E950.4	E962.0	E980.4
Vienna						
green	985.1	E866.3	—	E950.8	E962.1	E980.8
insecticide	985.1	E863.4	—	E950.6	E962.1	E980.7
red	989.89	E866.8	—	E950.9	E962.1	E980.9
pharmaceutical dye	977.4	E858.8	E947.4	E950.4	E962.0	E980.4
Vinbarbital, vinbarbitone	967.0	E851	E937.0	E950.1	E962.0	E980.1
Vinblastine	963.1	E858.1	E933.1	E950.4	E962.0	E980.4
Vincristine	963.1	E858.1	E933.1	E950.4	E962.0	E980.4
Vinesthene, vinethene	968.2	E855.1	E938.2	E950.4	E962.0	E980.4
Vinyl						
bital	967.0	E851	E937.0	E950.1	E962.0	E980.1
ether	968.2	E855.1	E938.2	E950.4	E962.0	E980.4
Vioform	961.3	E857	E931.3	E950.4	E962.0	E980.4
topical	976.0	E858.7	E946.0	E930.4	E962.0	E980.4
Viomycin	960.6	E856	E930.6	E950.4	E962.0	E980.4
Viosterol	963.5	E858.1	E933.5	E950.4	E962.0	E980.4
Viper (venom)	989.5	E905.0	—	E950.9	E962.1	E980.9
Viprynium (embonate)	961.6	E857	E931.6	E950.4	E962.0	E980.4
Virugon	961.7	E857	E931.7	E950.4	E962.0	E980.4
Visine	976.5	E858.7	E946.5	E950.4	E962.0	E980.4
Vitamins NEC	963.5	E858.1	E933.5	E950.4	E962.0	E980.4
B_{12}	964.1	E858.2	E934.1	E950.4	E962.0	E980.4
hematopoietic	964.1	E858.2	E934.1	E950.4	E962.0	E980.4
K	964.3	E858.2	E934.3	E950.4	E962.0	E980.4
Vleminckx's solution	976.4	E858.7	E946.4	E950.4	E962.0	E980.4
Voltaren — *see* Diclofenac sodium						
Warfarin (potassium) (sodium)	964.2	E858.2	E934.2	E950.4	E962.0	E980.4
rodenticide	989.4	E863.7	—	E950.6	E962.1	E980.7
Wasp (sting)	989.5	E905.3	—	E950.9	E962.1	E980.9
Water						
balance agents NEC	974.5	E858.5	E944.5	E950.4	E962.0	E980.4
gas	987.1	E868.1	—	E951.8	E962.2	E981.8
incomplete combustion of — see Carbon, monoxide, fuel, utility						
hemlock	988.2	E865.4	—	E950.9	E962.1	E980.9
moccasin (venom)	989.5	E905.0	—	E950.9	E962.1	E980.9

	Poisoning	External Cause (E-Code)				
		Accident	Therapeutic Use	Suicide Attempt	Assault	Undetermined
Wax (paraffin) (petroleum)	981	E862.3	—	E950.9	E962.1	E980.9
automobile	989.89	E861.2	—	E950.9	E962.1	E980.9
floor	981	E862.0	—	E950.9	E962.1	E980.9
Weed killers NEC	989.4	E863.5	—	E950.6	E962.1	E980.7
Welldorm	967.1	E852.0	E937.1	E950.2	E962.0	E980.2
White						
arsenic — see Arsenic						
hellebore	988.2	E865.4	—	E950.9	E962.1	E980.9
lotion (keratolytic)	976.4	E858.7	E946.4	E950.4	E962.0	E980.4
spirit	981	E862.0	—	E950.9	E962.1	E980.9
Whitewashes	989.89	E861.6	—	E950.9	E962.1	E980.9
Whole blood	964.7	E858.2	E934.7	E950.4	E962.0	E980.4
Wild						
black cherry	988.2	E865.4	—	E950.9	E962.1	E980.9
poisonous plants NEC	988.2	E865.4	—	E950.9	E962.1	E980.9
Window cleaning fluid	989.89	E861.3	—	E950.9	E962.1	E980.9
Wintergreen (oil)	976.3	E858.7	E946.3	E950.4	E962.0	E980.4
Witch hazel	976.2	E858.7	E946.2	E950.4	E962.0	E980.4
Wood						
alcohol	980.1	E860.2	—	E950.9	E962.1	E980.9
spirit	980.1	E860.2	—	E950.9	E962.1	E980.9
Woorali	975.2	E858.6	E945.2	E950.4	E962.0	E980.4
Wormseed, American	961.6	E857	E931.6	E950.4	E962.0	E980.4
Xanthine diuretics	974.1	E858.5	E944.1	E950.4	E962.0	E980.4
Xanthocillin	960.0	E856	E930.0	E950.4	E962.0	E980.4
Xanthotoxin	976.3	E858.7	E946.3	E950.4	E962.0	E980.4
Xigris	964.2	E858.2	E934.2	E950.4	E962.0	E980.4
Xylene (liquid) (vapor)	982.0	E862.4	—	E950.9	E962.1	E980.9
Xylocaine (infiltration) (topical)	968.5	E855.2	E938.5	E950.4	E962.0	E980.4
nerve block (peripheral) (plexus)	968.6	E855.2	E938.6	E950.4	E962.0	E980.4
spinal	968.7	E855.2	E938.7	E950.4	E962.0	E980.4
Xylol (liquid) (vapor)	982.0	E862.4	—	E950.9	E962.1	E980.9
Xylometazoline	971.2	E855.5	E941.2	E950.4	E962.0	E980.4
Yellow						
fever vaccine	979.3	E858.8	E949.3	E950.4	E962.0	E980.4
jasmine	988.2	E865.4	—	E950.9	E962.1	E980.9
Yew	988.2	E865.4	—	E950.9	E962.1	E980.9
Zactane	965.7	E850.7	E935.7	E950.0	E962.0	E980.0
Zaroxolyn	974.3	E858.5	E944.3	E950.4	E962.0	E980.4
Zephiran (topical)	976.0	E858.7	E946.0	E950.4	E962.0	E980.4
ophthalmic preparation	976.5	E858.7	E946.5	E950.4	E962.0	E980.4
Zerone	980.1	E860.2	—	E950.9	E962.1	E980.9
Zinc (compounds) (fumes) (salts) (vapor) NEC	985.8	E866.4	—	E950.9	E962.1	E980.9
anti-infectives	976.0	E858.7	E946.0	E950.4	E962.0	E980.4
antivaricose	972.7	E858.3	E942.7	E950.4	E962.0	E980.4
bacitracin	976.0	E858.7	E946.0	E950.4	E962.0	E980.4
chloride	976.2	E858.7	E946.2	E950.4	E962.0	E980.4
gelatin	976.3	E858.7	E946.3	E950.4	E962.0	E980.4
oxide	976.3	E858.7	E946.3	E950.4	E962.0	E980.4
peroxide	976.0	E858.7	E946.0	E950.4	E962.0	E980.4
pesticides	985.8	E863.4	—	E950.6	E962.1	E980.7
phosphide (rodenticide)	985.8	E863.7	—	E950.6	E962.1	E980.7
stearate	976.3	E858.7	E946.3	E950.4	E962.0	E980.4
sulfate (antivaricose)	972.7	E858.3	E942.7	E950.4	E962.0	E980.4
ENT agent	976.6	E858.7	E946.6	E950.4	E962.0	E980.4
ophthalmic solution	976.5	E858.7	E946.5	E950.4	E962.0	E980.4
topical NEC	976.0	E858.7	E946.0	E950.4	E962.0	E980.4
undecylenate	976.0	E858.7	E946.0	E950.4	E962.0	E980.4
Zovant	964.2	E858.2	E934.2	E950.4	E962.0	E980.4
Zoxazolamine	968.0	E855.1	E938.0	E950.4	E962.0	E980.4
Zygadenus (venenosus)	988.2	E865.4	—	E950.9	E962.1	E980.9

SECTION 3

Alphabetic Index to External Causes of Injury and Poisoning (E Code)

This section contains the index to the codes which classify environmental events, circumstances, and other conditions as the cause of injury and other adverse effects. Where a code from the section Supplementary Classification of External Causes of Injury and Poisoning (E800-E999) is applicable, it is intended that the E code shall be used in addition to a code from the main body of the classification, Chapters 1 to 17.

The alphabetic index to the E codes is organized by main terms which describe the accident, circumstance, event, or specific agent which caused the injury or other adverse effect.

Note — Transport accidents (E800-E848) include accidents involving:

aircraft and spacecraft (E840-E845)

watercraft (E830-E838)

motor vehicle (E810-E825)

railway (E800-E807)

other road vehicles (E826-E829)

For definitions and examples related to transport accidents — see Volume 1 code categories E800-E848.

The fourth-digit subdivisions for use with categories E800-E848 to identify the injured person are found at the end of this section.

For identifying the place in which an accident or poisoning occurred (circumstances classifiable to categories E850-E869 and E880-E928) — see the listing in this section under "Accident, occurring."

See the Table of Drugs and Chemicals (Section 2 of this volume) for identifying the specific agent involved in drug overdose or a wrong substance given or taken in error, and for intoxication or poisoning by a drug or other chemical substance.

The specific adverse effect, reaction, or localized toxic effect to a correct drug or substance properly administered in therapeutic or prophylactic dosage should be classified according to the nature of the adverse effect (e.g., allergy, dermatitis, tachycardia) listed in Section 1 of this volume.

A

- **Abandonment**
  - causing exposure to weather conditions — *see* Exposure
  - child, with intent to injure or kill E968.4
  - helpless person, infant, newborn E904.0
    - with intent to injure or kill E968.4
- **Abortion, criminal, injury to child** E968.8
- **Abuse** (alleged) (suspected)
  - adult
    - by
      - child E967.4
      - ex-partner E967.3
      - ex-spouse E967.3
      - father E967.0
      - grandchild E967.7
      - grandparent E967.6
      - mother E967.2
      - non-related caregiver E967.8
      - other relative E967.7
      - other specified person E967.1
      - partner E967.3
      - sibling E967.5
      - spouse E967.3
      - stepfather E967.0
      - stepmother E967.2
      - unspecified person E967.9
  - child
    - by
      - boyfriend of parent or guardian E967.0
      - child E967.4
      - father E967.0
      - female partner of parent or guardian E967.2
      - girlfriend of parent or guardian E967.2
      - grandchild E967.7
      - grandparent E967.6
      - male partner of parent or guardian E967.0
      - mother E967.2
      - non-related caregiver E967.8
      - other relative E967.7
      - other specified person(s) E967.1
      - sibling E967.5
      - stepfather E967.0
      - stepmother E967.2
      - unspecified person E967.9
- **Accident (to)** E928.9
  - aircraft (in transit) (powered) E841 ☑
    - at landing, take-off E840 ☑
    - due to, caused by cataclysm — *see* categories E908 ☑, E909 ☑
    - late effect of E929.1
    - unpowered (*see also* Collision, aircraft, unpowered) E842 ☑
    - while alighting, boarding E843 ☑
  - amphibious vehicle
    - on
      - land — *see* Accident, motor vehicle
      - water — *see* Accident, watercraft
  - animal-drawn vehicle NEC E827 ☑
  - animal, ridden NEC E828 ☑
  - balloon (*see also* Collision, aircraft, unpowered) E842 ☑
  - caused by, due to
    - abrasive wheel (metalworking) E919.3
    - animal NEC E906.9
      - being ridden (in sport or transport) E828 ☑
    - avalanche NEC E909.2
    - band saw E919.4
    - bench saw E919.4
    - bore, earth-drilling or mining (land) (seabed) E919.1
    - bulldozer E919.7

Accident (to) — *continued*

- caused by, due to — *continued*
  - cataclysmic
    - earth surface movement or eruption E909.9
    - storm E908.9
  - chain
    - hoist E919.2
      - agricultural operations E919.0
      - mining operations E919.1
    - saw E920.1
  - circular saw E919.4
  - cold (excessive) (*see also* Cold, exposure to) E901.9
  - combine E919.0
  - conflagration — *see* Conflagration
  - corrosive liquid, substance NEC E924.1
  - cotton gin E919.8
  - crane E919.2
    - agricultural operations E919.0
    - mining operations E919.1
  - cutting or piercing instrument (*see also* Cut) E920.9
  - dairy equipment E919.8
  - derrick E919.2
    - agricultural operations E919.0
    - mining operations E919.1
  - drill E920.1
    - earth (land) (seabed) E919.1
    - hand (powered) E920.1
      - not powered E920.4
    - metalworking E919.3
    - woodworking E919.4
  - earth(-)
    - drilling machine E919.1
    - moving machine E919.7
    - scraping machine E919.7
  - electric
    - current (*see also* Electric shock) E925.9
    - motor (*see also* Accident, machine, by type of machine)
      - current (of) — *see* Electric shock
  - elevator (building) (grain) E919.2
    - agricultural operations E919.0
    - mining operations E919.1
  - environmental factors NEC E928.9
  - excavating machine E919.7
  - explosive material (*see also* Explosion) E923.9
  - farm machine E919.0
  - firearm missile — *see* Shooting
  - fire, flames (*see also* Fire)
    - conflagration — *see* Conflagration
  - forging (metalworking) machine E919.3
  - forklift (truck) E919.2
    - agricultural operations E919.0
    - mining operations E919.1
  - gas turbine E919.5
  - harvester E919.0
  - hay derrick, mower, or rake E919.0
  - heat (excessive) (*see also* Heat) E900.9
  - hoist (*see also* Accident, caused by, due to, lift) E919.2
    - chain — *see* Accident, caused by, due to, chain
    - shaft E919.1
  - hot
    - liquid E924.0
      - caustic or corrosive E924.1
    - object (not producing fire or flames) E924.8
    - substance E924.9
      - caustic or corrosive E924.1
      - liquid (metal) NEC E924.0
      - specified type NEC E924.8
  - human bite E928.3
  - ignition — *see* Ignition
  - internal combustion engine E919.5
  - landslide NEC E909.2

Accident (to) — *continued*

- caused by, due to — *continued*
  - lathe (metalworking) E919.3
    - turnings E920.8
    - woodworking E919.4
  - lift, lifting (appliances) E919.2
    - agricultural operations E919.0
    - mining operations E919.1
    - shaft E919.1
  - lightning NEC E907
  - machine, machinery (*see also* Accident, machine)
    - drilling, metal E919.3
    - manufacturing, for manufacture of
      - beverages E919.8
      - clothing E919.8
      - foodstuffs E919.8
      - paper E919.8
      - textiles E919.8
    - milling, metal E919.3
    - moulding E919.4
    - power press, metal E919.3
    - printing E919.8
    - rolling mill, metal E919.3
    - sawing, metal E919.3
    - specified type NEC E919.8
    - spinning E919.8
    - weaving E919.8
  - natural factor NEC E928.9
  - overhead plane E919.4
  - plane E920.4
    - overhead E919.4
  - powered
    - hand tool NEC E920.1
    - saw E919.4
      - hand E920.1
  - printing machine E919.8
  - pulley (block) E919.2
    - agricultural operations E919.0
    - mining operations E919.1
    - transmission E919.6
  - radial saw E919.4
  - radiation — *see* Radiation
  - reaper E919.0
  - road scraper E919.7
    - when in transport under its own power — *see* categories E810-E825 ☑
  - roller coaster E919.8
  - sander E919.4
  - saw E920.4
    - band E919.4
    - bench E919.4
    - chain E920.1
    - circular E919.4
    - hand E920.4
      - powered E920.1
    - powered, except hand E919.4
    - radial E919.4
  - sawing machine, metal E919.3
  - shaft
    - hoist E919.1
    - lift E919.1
    - transmission E919.6
  - shears E920.4
    - hand E920.4
      - powered E920.1
    - mechanical E919.3
  - shovel E920.4
    - steam E919.7
  - spinning machine E919.8
  - steam (*see also* Burning, steam)
    - engine E919.5
    - shovel E919.7
  - thresher E919.0
  - thunderbolt NEC E907
  - tractor E919.0
    - when in transport under its own power — *see* categories E810-E825 ☑
  - transmission belt, cable, chain, gear, pinion, pulley, shaft E919.6
  - turbine (gas) (water driven) E919.5
  - under-cutter E919.1

Accident (to) — *continued*

- caused by, due to — *continued*
  - weaving machine E919.8
  - winch E919.2
    - agricultural operations E919.0
    - mining operations E919.1
- diving E883.0
  - with insufficient air supply E913.2
- glider (hang) (*see also* Collision, aircraft, unpowered) E842 ☑
- hovercraft
  - on
    - land — *see* Accident, motor vehicle
    - water — *see* Accident, watercraft
- ice yacht (*see also* Accident, vehicle NEC) E848
- in
  - medical, surgical procedure
    - as, or due to misadventure — *see* Misadventure
    - causing an abnormal reaction or later complication without mention of misadventure — *see* Reaction, abnormal
- kite carrying a person (*see also* Collision, involving aircraft, unpowered) E842 ☑
- land yacht (*see also* Accident, vehicle NEC) E848
- late effect of — *see* Late effect
- launching pad E845 ☑
- machine, machinery (*see also* Accident, caused by, due to, by specific type of machine) E919.9
  - agricultural including animal-powered E919.0
  - earth-drilling E919.1
  - earth moving or scraping E919.7
  - excavating E919.7
  - involving transport under own power on highway or transport vehicle — *see* categories E810-E825 ☑, E840-E845 ☑
  - lifting (appliances) E919.2
  - metalworking E919.3
  - mining E919.1
  - prime movers, except electric motors E919.5
    - electric motors — *see* Accident, machine, by specific type of machine
  - recreational E919.8
  - specified type NEC E919.8
  - transmission E919.6
  - watercraft (deck) (engine room) (galley) (laundry) (loading) E836 ☑
  - woodworking or forming E919.4
- motor vehicle (on public highway) (traffic) E819 ☑
  - due to cataclysm — *see* categories E908 ☑, E909 ☑
  - involving
    - collision (*see also* Collision, motor vehicle) E812 ☑
  - nontraffic, not on public highway — *see* categories E820-E825 ☑
  - not involving collision — *see* categories E816-E819 ☑
- nonmotor vehicle NEC E829 ☑
  - nonroad — *see* Accident, vehicle NEC
  - road, except pedal cycle, animal-drawn vehicle, or animal being ridden E829 ☑
- nonroad vehicle NEC — *see* Accident, vehicle NEC
- not elsewhere classifiable involving
  - cable car (not on rails) E847
    - on rails E829 ☑
  - coal car in mine E846

Accident (to) — *continued*
  not elsewhere classifiable involving — *continued*
    hand truck — *see* Accident, vehicle NEC
    logging car E846
    sled(ge), meaning snow or ice vehicle E848
    tram, mine or quarry E846
    truck
      mine or quarry E846
      self-propelled, industrial E846
      station baggage E846
    tub, mine or quarry E846
    vehicle NEC E848
      snow and ice E848
      used only on industrial premises E846
    wheelbarrow E848
  occurring (at) (in)
    apartment E849.0
    baseball field, diamond E849.4
    construction site, any E849.3
    dock E849.8
      yard E849.3
    dormitory E849.7
    factory (building) (premises) E849.3
    farm E849.1
      buildings E849.1
      house E849.0
    football field E849.4
    forest E849.8
    garage (place of work) E849.3
      private (home) E849.0
    gravel pit E849.2
    gymnasium E849.4
    highway E849.5
    home (private) (residential) E849.0
      institutional E849.7
    hospital E849.7
    hotel E849.6
    house (private) (residential) E849.0
      movie E849.6
      public E849.6
    institution, residential E849.7
    jail E849.7
    mine E849.2
    motel E849.6
    movie house E849.6
    office (building) E849.6
    orphanage E849.7
    park (public) E849.4
      mobile home E849.8
      trailer E849.8
    parking lot or place E849.8
    place
      industrial NEC E849.3
      parking E849.8
      public E849.8
        specified place NEC E849.5
      recreational NEC E849.4
      sport NEC E849.4
    playground (park) (school) E849.4
    prison E849.6
    public building NEC E849.6
    quarry E849.2
    railway
      line NEC E849.8
      yard E849.3
    residence
      home (private) E849.0
    resort (beach) (lake) (mountain) (seashore) (vacation) E849.4
    restaurant E849.6
    sand pit E849.2
    school (building) (private) (public) (state) E849.6
      reform E849.7
      riding E849.4
    seashore E849.8
      resort E849.4
    shop (place of work) E849.3
      commercial E849.6
    skating rink E849.4
    sports palace E849.4
    stadium E849.4

Accident (to) — *continued*
  occurring — *continued*
    store E849.6
    street E849.5
    swimming pool (public) E849.4
      private home or garden E849.0
    tennis court, public E849.4
    theatre, theater E849.6
    trailer court E849.8
    tunnel E849.8
      under construction E849.2
    warehouse E849.3
    yard
      dock E849.3
      industrial E849.3
      private (home) E849.0
      railway E849.3
  off-road type motor vehicle (not on public highway) NEC E821 ☑
    on public highway — *see* categories E810-E819 ☑
  pedal cycle E826 ☑
  railway E807 ☑
    due to cataclysm — *see* categories E908 ☑, E909 ☑
    involving
      avalanche E909.2
      burning by engine, locomotive, train (*see also* Explosion, railway engine) E803 ☑
      collision (*see also* Collision, railway) E800 ☑
      derailment (*see also* Derailment, railway) E802 ☑
      explosion (*see also* Explosion, railway engine) E803 ☑
      fall (*see also* Fall, from, railway rolling stock) E804 ☑
      fire (*see also* Explosion, railway engine) E803 ☑
      hitting by, being struck by
        object falling in, on, from, rolling stock, train, vehicle E806 ☑
        rolling stock, train, vehicle E805 ☑
      overturning, railway rolling stock, train, vehicle (*see also* Derailment, railway) E802 ☑
      running off rails, railway (*see also* Derailment, railway) E802 ☑
      specified circumstances NEC E806 ☑
      train or vehicle hit by
        avalanche E909.2
        falling object (earth, rock, tree) E806 ☑
          due to cataclysm — *see* categories E908 ☑, E909 ☑
        landslide E909.2
  roller skate E885.1
  scooter (nonmotorized) E885.0
  skateboard E885.2
  ski(ing) E885.3
    jump E884.9
    lift or tow (with chair or gondola) E847
  snowboard E885.4
  snow vehicle, motor driven (not on public highway) E820 ☑
    on public highway — *see* categories E810-E819 ☑
  spacecraft E845 ☑
  specified cause NEC E928.8
  street car E829 ☑
  traffic NEC E819 ☑
  vehicle NEC (with pedestrian) E848
    battery powered
      airport passenger vehicle E846
      truck (baggage) (mail) E846

Accident (to) — *continued*
  vehicle — *continued*
    powered commercial or industrial (with other vehicle or object within commercial or industrial premises) E846
  watercraft E838 ☑
    with
      drowning or submersion resulting from
        accident other than to watercraft E832 ☑
        accident to watercraft E830 ☑
      injury, except drowning or submersion, resulting from
        accident other than to watercraft — *see* categories E833-E838 ☑
        accident to watercraft E831 ☑
    due to, caused by cataclysm — *see* categories E908 ☑, E909 ☑
    machinery E836 ☑
Acid throwing E961
Acosta syndrome E902.0
Aeroneurosis E902.1
Aero-otitis media — *see* Effects of, air pressure
Aerosinusitis — *see* Effects of, air pressure
After-effect, late — *see* Late effect
Air
  blast
    in
      terrorism E979.2
      war operations E993
  embolism (traumatic) NEC E928.9
    in
      infusion or transfusion E874.1
      perfusion E874.2
  sickness E903
Alpine sickness E902.0
Altitude sickness — *see* Effects of, air pressure
Anaphylactic shock, anaphylaxis — *see also* Table of Drugs and Chemicals E947.9
  due to bite or sting (venomous) — *see* Bite, venomous
Andes disease E902.0
Apoplexy
  heat — *see* Heat
Arachnidism E905.1
Arson E968.0
Asphyxia, asphyxiation
  by
    chemical
      in
        terrorism E979.7
        war operations E997.2
    explosion — *see* Explosion
    food (bone) (regurgitated food) (seed) E911
    foreign object, except food E912
    fumes
      in
        terrorism (chemical weapons) E979.7
        war operations E997.2
    gas (*see also* Table of Drugs and Chemicals)
      in
        terrorism E979.7
        war operations E997.2
      legal
        execution E978
        intervention (tear) E972
      tear E972
    mechanical means (*see also* Suffocation) E913.9
  from
    conflagration — *see* Conflagration
    fire (*see also* Fire) E899
      in
        terrorism E979.3

Asphyxia, asphyxiation — *continued*
  from — *continued*
    fire (*see also* Fire) — *continued*
      in — *continued*
        war operations E990.9
    ignition — *see* Ignition
Aspiration
  foreign body — *see* Foreign body, aspiration
  mucus, not of newborn (with asphyxia, obstruction respiratory passage, suffocation) E912
  phlegm (with asphyxia, obstruction respiratory passage, suffocation) E912
  vomitus (with asphyxia, obstruction respiratory passage, suffocation) (*see also* Foreign body, aspiration, food) E911
Assassination (attempt) — *see also* Assault E968.9
Assault (homicidal) (by) (in) E968.9
  acid E961
    swallowed E962.1
  air gun E968.6
  BB gun E968.6
  bite NEC E968.8
    of human being E968.7
  bomb ((placed in) car or house) E965.8
    antipersonnel E965.5
    letter E965.7
    petrol E965.6
  brawl (hand) (fists) (foot) E960.0
  burning, burns (by fire) E968.0
    acid E961
      swallowed E962.1
    caustic, corrosive substance E961
      swallowed E962.1
    chemical from swallowing caustic, corrosive substance NEC E962.1
    hot liquid E968.3
    scalding E968.3
    vitriol E961
      swallowed E962.1
  caustic, corrosive substance E961
    swallowed E962.1
  cut, any part of body E966
  dagger E966
  drowning E964
  explosive(s) E965.9
    bomb (*see also* Assault, bomb) E965.8
    dynamite E965.8
  fight (hand) (fists) (foot) E960.0
    with weapon E968.9
      blunt or thrown E968.2
      cutting or piercing E966
      firearm — *see* Shooting, homicide
  fire E968.0
  firearm(s) — *see* Shooting, homicide
  garrotting E963
  gunshot (wound) — *see* Shooting, homicide
  hanging E963
  injury NEC E968.9
  knife E966
  late effect of E969
  ligature E963
  poisoning E962.9
    drugs or medicinals E962.0
    gas(es) or vapors, except drugs and medicinals E962.2
    solid or liquid substances, except drugs and medicinals E962.1
  puncture, any part of body E966
  pushing
    before moving object, train, vehicle E968.5
    from high place E968.1
  rape E960.1
  scalding E968.3
  shooting — *see* Shooting, homicide
  sodomy E960.1
  stab, any part of body E966

- **Assault** — *continued*
  - strangulation E963
  - submersion E964
  - suffocation E963
  - transport vehicle E968.5
  - violence NEC E968.9
  - vitriol E961
    - swallowed E962.1
  - weapon E968.9
    - blunt or thrown E968.2
    - cutting or piercing E966
    - firearm — *see* Shooting, homicide
  - wound E968.9
    - cutting E966
    - gunshot — *see* Shooting, homicide
    - knife E966
    - piercing E966
    - puncture E966
    - stab E966
- **Attack by animal** NEC E906.9
- **Avalanche** E909.2
  - falling on or hitting
    - motor vehicle (in motion) (on public highway) E909.2
    - railway train E909.2
- **Aviators' disease** E902.1

B

- **Barotitis, barodontalgia, barosinusitis, barotrauma** (otitic) (sinus) — *see* Effects of, air pressure
- **Battered**
  - baby or child (syndrome) — *see* Abuse, child; category E967 ☑
  - person other than baby or child — *see* Assault
- **Bayonet wound** — *see also* Cut, by bayonet E920.3
  - in
    - legal intervention E974
    - terrorism E979.8
    - war operations E995
- **Bean in nose** E912
- **Bed set on fire NEC** E898.0
- **Beheading** (by guillotine)
  - homicide E966
  - legal execution E978
- **Bending, injury in** E927.8
- **Bends** E902.0
- **Bite**
  - animal NEC E906.5
    - other specified (except arthropod) E906.3
    - venomous NEC E905.9
  - arthropod (nonvenomous) NEC E906.4
    - venomous — *see* Sting
  - black widow spider E905.1
  - cat E906.3
  - centipede E905.4
  - cobra E905.0
  - copperhead snake E905.0
  - coral snake E905.0
  - dog E906.0
  - fer de lance E905.0
  - gila monster E905.0
  - human being
    - accidental E928.3
    - assault E968.7
  - insect (nonvenomous) E906.4
    - venomous — *see* Sting
  - krait E905.0
  - late effect of — *see* Late effect
  - lizard E906.2
    - venomous E905.0
  - mamba E905.0
  - marine animal
    - nonvenomous E906.3
      - snake E906.2
    - venomous E905.6
      - snake E905.0
  - millipede E906.4
    - venomous E905.4
  - moray eel E906.3
  - rat E906.1
  - rattlesnake E905.0
  - rodent, except rat E906.3
- **Bite** — *continued*
  - serpent — *see* Bite, snake
  - shark E906.3
  - snake (venomous) E905.0
    - nonvenomous E906.2
    - sea E905.0
  - spider E905.1
    - nonvenomous E906.4
  - tarantula (venomous) E905.1
  - venomous NEC E905.9
    - by specific animal — *see category* E905 ☑
  - viper E905.0
  - water moccasin E905.0
- **Blast** (air)
  - from nuclear explosion E996
  - in
    - terrorism E979.2
      - from nuclear explosion E979.5
      - underwater E979.0
    - war operations E993
      - from nuclear explosion E996
      - underwater E992
- **Blizzard** E908.3
- **Blow** E928.9
  - by law-enforcing agent, police (on duty) E975
    - with blunt object (baton) (nightstick) (stave) (truncheon) E973
- **Blowing up** — *see also* Explosion E923.9
- **Brawl** (hand) (fists) (foot) E960.0
- **Breakage** (accidental)
  - cable of cable car not on rails E847
  - ladder (causing fall) E881.0
  - part (any) of
    - animal-drawn vehicle E827 ☑
    - ladder (causing fall) E881.0
    - motor vehicle
      - in motion (on public highway) E818 ☑
      - not on public highway E825 ☑
    - nonmotor road vehicle, except animal-drawn vehicle or pedal cycle E829 ☑
    - off-road type motor vehicle (not on public highway) NEC E821 ☑
      - on public highway E818 ☑
    - pedal cycle E826 ☑
    - scaffolding (causing fall) E881.1
    - snow vehicle, motor-driven (not on public highway) E820 ☑
      - on public highway E818 ☑
    - vehicle NEC — *see* Accident, vehicle
- **Broken**
  - glass
    - fall on E888.0
    - injury by E920.8
  - power line (causing electric shock) E925.1
- **Bumping against, into** (accidentally)
  - object (moving) E917.9
    - caused by crowd E917.1
      - with subsequent fall E917.6
    - furniture E917.3
      - with subsequent fall E917.7
    - in
      - running water E917.2
      - sports E917.0
        - with subsequent fall E917.5
    - stationary E917.4
      - with subsequent fall E917.8
  - person(s) E917.9
    - with fall E886.9
      - in sports E886.0
    - as, or caused by, a crowd E917.1
      - with subsequent fall E917.6
    - in sports E917.0
      - with fall E886.0
- **Burning, burns** (accidental) (by) (from) (on) E899
  - acid (any kind) E924.1
    - swallowed — *see* Table of Drugs and Chemicals
- **Burning, burns** — *continued*
  - bedclothes (*see also* Fire, specified NEC) E898.0
  - blowlamp (*see also* Fire, specified NEC) E898.1
  - blowtorch (*see also* Fire, specified NEC) E898.1
  - boat, ship, watercraft — *see* categories E830 ☑, E831 ☑, E837 ☑
  - bonfire (controlled) E897
    - uncontrolled E892
  - candle (*see also* Fire, specified NEC) E898.1
  - caustic liquid, substance E924.1
    - swallowed — *see* Table of Drugs and Chemicals
  - chemical E924.1
    - from swallowing caustic, corrosive substance — *see* Table of Drugs and Chemicals
    - in
      - terrorism E979.7
      - war operations E997.2
  - cigar(s) or cigarette(s) (*see also* Fire, specified NEC) E898.1
  - clothes, clothing, nightdress — *see* Ignition, clothes
    - with conflagration — *see* Conflagration
  - conflagration — *see* Conflagration
  - corrosive liquid, substance E924.1
    - swallowed — *see* Table of Drugs and Chemicals
  - electric current (*see also* Electric shock) E925.9
  - fire, flames (*see also* Fire) E899
  - flare, Verey pistol E922.8
  - heat
    - from appliance (electrical) E924.8
    - in local application, or packing during medical or surgical procedure E873.5
  - homicide (attempt) (*see also* Assault, burning) E968.0
  - hot
    - liquid E924.0
      - caustic or corrosive E924.1
    - object (not producing fire or flames) E924.8
    - substance E924.9
      - caustic or corrosive E924.1
      - liquid (metal) NEC E924.0
      - specified type NEC E924.8
    - tap water E924.2
  - ignition (*see also* Ignition)
    - clothes, clothing, nightdress (*see also* Ignition, clothes)
      - with conflagration — *see* Conflagration
    - highly inflammable material (benzine) (fat) (gasoline) (kerosene) (paraffin) (petrol) E894
  - in
    - terrorism E979.3
      - from nuclear explosion E979.5
      - petrol bomb E979.3
    - war operations (from fire-producing device or conventional weapon) E990.9
      - from nuclear explosion E996
      - petrol bomb E990.0
  - inflicted by other person
    - stated as
      - homicidal, intentional (*see also* Assault, burning) E968.0
      - undetermined whether accidental or intentional (*see also* Burn, stated as undetermined whether accidental or intentional) E988.1
  - internal, from swallowed caustic, corrosive liquid, substance — *see* Table of Drugs and Chemicals
  - lamp (*see also* Fire, specified NEC) E898.1
- **Burning, burns** — *continued*
  - late effect of NEC E929.4
  - lighter (cigar) (cigarette) (*see also* Fire, specified NEC) E898.1
  - lightning E907
  - liquid (boiling) (hot) (molten) E924.0
    - caustic, corrosive (external) E924.1
      - swallowed — *see* Table of Drugs and Chemicals
  - local application of externally applied substance in medical or surgical care E873.5
  - machinery — *see* Accident, machine
  - matches (*see also* Fire, specified NEC) E898.1
  - medicament, externally applied E873.5
  - metal, molten E924.0
  - object (hot) E924.8
    - producing fire or flames — *see* Fire
  - oven (electric) (gas) E924.8
  - pipe (smoking) (*see also* Fire, specified NEC) E898.1
  - radiation — *see* Radiation
  - railway engine, locomotive, train (*see also* Explosion, railway engine) E803 ☑
  - self-inflicted (unspecified whether accidental or intentional) E988.1
    - caustic or corrosive substance NEC E988.7
    - stated as intentional, purposeful E958.1
      - caustic or corrosive substance NEC E958.7
  - stated as undetermined whether accidental or intentional E988.1
    - caustic or corrosive substance NEC E988.7
  - steam E924.0
    - pipe E924.8
  - substance (hot) E924.9
    - boiling or molten E924.0
    - caustic, corrosive (external) E924.1
      - swallowed — *see* Table of Drugs and Chemicals
  - suicidal (attempt) NEC E958.1
    - caustic substance E958.7
    - late effect of E959
  - tanning bed E926.2
  - therapeutic misadventure
    - overdose of radiation E873.2
  - torch, welding (*see also* Fire, specified NEC) E898.1
  - trash fire (*see also* Burning, bonfire) E897
  - vapor E924.0
  - vitriol E924.1
  - x-rays E926.3
    - in medical, surgical procedure — *see* Misadventure, failure, in dosage, radiation
- **Butted by animal** E906.8

C

- **Cachexia, lead or saturnine** E866.0
  - from pesticide NEC (*see also* Table of Drugs and Chemicals) E863.4
- **Caisson disease** E902.2
- **Capital punishment** (any means) E978
- **Car sickness** E903
- **Casualty** (not due to war) NEC E928.9
  - terrorism E979.8
  - war (*see also* War operations) E995
- **Cat**
  - bite E906.3
  - scratch E906.8
- **Cataclysmic** (any injury)
  - earth surface movement or eruption E909.9
    - specified type NEC E909.8
  - storm or flood resulting from storm E908.9
    - specified type NEC E909.8
- **Catching fire** — *see* Ignition

- **Caught**
  - between
    - objects (moving) (stationary and moving) E918
      - and machinery — *see* Accident, machine
  - by cable car, not on rails E847
  - in
    - machinery (moving parts of) — *see*, Accident, machine
    - object E918
- **Cave-in** (causing asphyxia, suffocation (by pressure)) — *see also* Suffocation, due to, cave-in E913.3
  - with injury other than asphyxia or suffocation E916
    - with asphyxia or suffocation (*see also* Suffocation, due to, cave-in) E913.3
  - struck or crushed by E916
    - with asphyxia or suffocation (*see also* Suffocation, due to, cave-in) E913.3
- **Change(s) in air pressure** — *see also* Effects of, air pressure
  - sudden, in aircraft (ascent) (descent) (causing aeroneurosis or aviators' disease) E902.1
- **Chilblains** E901.0
  - due to manmade conditions E901.1
- **Choking** (on) (any object except food or vomitus) E912
  - apple E911
  - bone E911
  - food, any type (regurgitated) E911
  - mucus or phlegm E912
  - seed E911
- **Civil insurrection** — *see* War operations
- **Cloudburst** E908.8
- **Cold, exposure to** (accidental) (excessive) (extreme) (place) E901.9
  - causing chilblains or immersion foot E901.0
  - due to
    - manmade conditions E901.1
    - specified cause NEC E901.8
    - weather (conditions) E901.0
  - late effect of NEC E929.5
  - self-inflicted (undetermined whether accidental or intentional) E988.3
    - suicidal E958.3
  - suicide E958.3
- **Colic, lead, painter's, or saturnine** — *see* category E866 ☑
- **Collapse**
  - building E916
    - burning (uncontrolled fire) E891.8
      - in terrorism E979.3
    - private E890.8
  - dam E909.3
  - due to heat — *see* Heat
  - machinery — *see* Accident, machine or vehicle
  - man-made structure E909.3
  - postoperative NEC E878.9
  - structure
    - burning (uncontrolled fire) NEC E891.8
      - in terrorism E979.3
- **Collision** (accidental)

Note — In the case of collisions between different types of vehicles, persons and objects, priority in classification is in the following order:

Aircraft
Watercraft
Motor vehicle
Railway vehicle
Pedal cycle
Animal-drawn vehicle
Animal being ridden
Streetcar or other nonmotor road vehicle
Other vehicle
Pedestrian or person using pedestrian conveyance
Object (except where falling from or set in motion by vehicle etc. listed above)

In the listing below, the combinations are listed only under the vehicle etc. having priority. For definitions, see Supplementary Classification of External Causes of Injury and Poisoning (E800-E999).

  - aircraft (with object or vehicle) (fixed) (movable) (moving) E841 ☑
    - with
      - person (while landing, taking off) (without accident to aircraft) E844 ☑
    - powered (in transit) (with unpowered aircraft) E841 ☑
      - while landing, taking off E840 ☑
    - unpowered E842 ☑
    - while landing, taking off E840 ☑
  - animal being ridden (in sport or transport) E828 ☑
    - and
      - animal (being ridden) (herded) (unattended) E828 ☑
      - nonmotor road vehicle, except pedal cycle or animal-drawn vehicle E828 ☑
      - object (fallen) (fixed) (movable) (moving) not falling from or set in motion by vehicle of higher priority E828 ☑
      - pedestrian (conveyance or vehicle) E828 ☑
  - animal-drawn vehicle E827 ☑
    - and
      - animal (being ridden) (herded) (unattended) E827 ☑
      - nonmotor road vehicle, except pedal cycle E827 ☑
      - object (fallen) (fixed) (movable) (moving) not falling from or set in motion by vehicle of higher priority E827 ☑
      - pedestrian (conveyance or vehicle) E827 ☑
      - streetcar E827 ☑
  - motor vehicle (on public highway) (traffic accident) E812 ☑
    - after leaving, running off, public highway (without antecedent collision) (without re-entry) E816 ☑
      - with antecedent collision on public highway — *see* categories E810-E815 ☑
      - with re-entrance collision with another motor vehicle E811 ☑
    - and
      - abutment (bridge) (overpass) E815 ☑

Collision — *continued*
  - motor vehicle — *continued*
    - and — *continued*
      - animal (herded) (unattended) E815 ☑
        - carrying person, property E813 ☑
      - animal-drawn vehicle E813 ☑
      - another motor vehicle (abandoned) (disabled) (parked) (stalled) (stopped) E812 ☑
        - with, involving re-entrance (on same roadway) (across median strip) E811 ☑
      - any object, person, or vehicle off the public highway resulting from a noncollision motor vehicle nontraffic accident E816 ☑
      - avalanche, fallen or not moving E815 ☑
        - falling E909.2
      - boundary fence E815 ☑
      - culvert E815 ☑
      - fallen
        - stone E815 ☑
        - tree E815 ☑
      - guard post or guard rail E815 ☑
      - inter-highway divider E815 ☑
      - landslide, fallen or not moving E815 ☑
        - moving E909 ☑
      - machinery (road) E815 ☑
      - nonmotor road vehicle NEC E813 ☑
      - object (any object, person, or vehicle off the public highway resulting from a noncollision motor vehicle nontraffic accident) E815 ☑
        - off, normally not on, public highway resulting from a noncollision motor vehicle traffic accident E816 ☑
      - pedal cycle E813 ☑
      - pedestrian (conveyance) E814 ☑
      - person (using pedestrian conveyance) E814 ☑
      - post or pole (lamp) (light) (signal) (telephone) (utility) E815 ☑
      - railway rolling stock, train, vehicle E810 ☑
      - safety island E815 ☑
      - street car E813 ☑
      - traffic signal, sign, or marker (temporary) E815 ☑
      - tree E815 ☑
      - tricycle E813 ☑
      - wall of cut made for road E815 ☑
    - due to cataclysm — *see* categories E908 ☑, E909 ☑
    - not on public highway, nontraffic accident E822 ☑
      - and
        - animal (carrying person, property) (herded) (unattended) E822 ☑
        - animal-drawn vehicle E822 ☑
        - another motor vehicle (moving), except off-road motor vehicle E822 ☑
          - stationary E823 ☑
        - avalanche, fallen, not moving E823 ☑
          - moving E909.2
        - landslide, fallen, not moving E823 ☑
          - moving E909.2

Collision — *continued*
  - motor vehicle — *continued*
    - not on public highway, nontraffic accident — *continued*
      - and — *continued*
        - nonmotor vehicle (moving) E822 ☑
          - stationary E823 ☑
        - object (fallen) (normally) (fixed) (movable but not in motion) (stationary) E823 ☑
          - moving, except when falling from, set in motion by, aircraft or cataclysm E822 ☑
        - pedal cycle (moving) E822 ☑
          - stationary E823 ☑
        - pedestrian (conveyance) E822 ☑
        - person (using pedestrian conveyance) E822 ☑
        - railway rolling stock, train, vehicle (moving) E822 ☑
          - stationary E823 ☑
        - road vehicle (any) (moving) E822 ☑
          - stationary E823 ☑
        - tricycle (moving) E822 ☑
          - stationary E823 ☑
  - off-road type motor vehicle (not on public highway) E821 ☑
    - and
      - animal (being ridden) (-drawn vehicle) E821 ☑
      - another off-road motor vehicle, except snow vehicle E821 ☑
      - other motor vehicle, not on public highway E821 ☑
      - other object or vehicle NEC, fixed or movable, not set in motion by aircraft, motor vehicle on highway, or snow vehicle, motor driven E821 ☑
      - pedal cycle E821 ☑
      - pedestrian (conveyance) E821 ☑
      - railway train E821 ☑
    - on public highway — *see* Collision, motor vehicle
  - pedal cycle E826 ☑
    - and
      - animal (carrying person, property) (herded) (unherded) E826 ☑
      - animal-drawn vehicle E826 ☑
      - another pedal cycle E826 ☑
      - nonmotor road vehicle E826 ☑
      - object (fallen) (fixed) (movable) (moving) not falling from or set in motion by aircraft, motor vehicle, or railway train NEC E826 ☑
      - pedestrian (conveyance) E826 ☑
      - person (using pedestrian conveyance) E826 ☑
      - street car E826 ☑
  - pedestrian(s) (conveyance) E917.9
    - with fall E886.9
      - in sports E886.0
    - and
      - crowd, human stampede E917.1
        - with subsequent fall E917.6
      - furniture E917.3
        - with subsequent fall E917.7
      - machinery — *see* Accident, machine
      - object (fallen) (moving) not falling from NEC, fixed or set in motion by any vehicle classifiable to E800-E848 ☑, E917.9

Cut, cutting — *continued*
- by — *continued*
  - ice pick E920.4
  - knife E920.3
    - electric E920.2
  - lathe turnings E920.8
  - lawn mower E920.4
    - powered E920.0
    - riding E919.8
  - machine — *see* Accident, machine
  - meat
    - grinder E919.8
    - slicer E919.8
  - nails E920.8
  - needle E920.4
    - hypodermic E920.5
  - object, edged, pointed, sharp — *see* category E920 ☑
    - following fall E888.0
  - paper cutter E920.4
  - piercing instrument (*see also* category) E920 ☑
    - late effect of E929.8
  - pitchfork E920.4
  - powered
    - can opener E920.2
    - garden cultivator E920.1
      - riding E919.8
    - hand saw E920.1
    - hand tool NEC E920.1
    - hedge clipper E920.1
    - household appliance or implement E920.2
    - lawn mower (hand) E920.0
      - riding E919.8
    - rivet gun E920.1
    - staple gun E920.1
  - rake E920.4
  - saw
    - circular E919.4
    - hand E920.4
  - scissors E920.4
  - screwdriver E920.4
  - sewing machine (electric) (powered) E920.2
    - not powered E920.4
  - shears E920.4
  - shovel E920.4
  - spade E920.4
  - splinters E920.8
  - sword E920.3
  - tin can lid E920.8
  - wood slivers E920.8
- homicide (attempt) E966
- inflicted by other person
  - stated as
    - intentional, homicidal E966
    - undetermined whether accidental or intentional E986
- late effect of NEC E929.8
- legal
  - execution E978
  - intervention E974
- self-inflicted (unspecified whether accidental or intentional) E986
  - stated as intentional, purposeful E956
- stated as undetermined whether accidental or intentional E986
- suicidal (attempt) E956
- terrorism E979.8
- war operations E995

Cyclone E908.1

D

Death due to injury occurring one year or more previous — *see* Late effect

Decapitation (accidental circumstances) NEC E928.9
- homicidal E966
- legal execution (by guillotine) E978

Deprivation — *see also* Privation
- homicidal intent E968.4

Derailment (accidental)
- railway (rolling stock) (train) (vehicle) (with subsequent collision) E802 ☑
  - with
    - collision (antecedent) (*see also* Collision, railway) E800 ☑
    - explosion (subsequent) (without antecedent collision) E802 ☑
      - antecedent collision E803 ☑
    - fall (without collision (antecedent)) E802 ☑
    - fire (without collision (antecedent)) E802 ☑
- street car E829 ☑

Descent
- parachute (voluntary) (without accident to aircraft) E844 ☑
  - due to accident to aircraft — *see* categories E840-E842 ☑

Desertion
- child, with intent to injure or kill E968.4
- helpless person, infant, newborn E904.0
  - with intent to injure or kill E968.4

Destitution — *see* Privation

Disability, late effect or sequela of injury — *see* Late effect

Disease
- Andes E902.0
- aviators' E902.1
- caisson E902.2
- range E902.0

Divers' disease, palsy, paralysis, squeeze E902.0

Dog bite E906.0

Dragged by
- cable car (not on rails) E847
  - on rails E829 ☑
- motor vehicle (on highway) E814 ☑
  - not on highway, nontraffic accident E825 ☑
- street car E829 ☑

Drinking poison (accidental) — *see* Table of Drugs and Chemicals

Drowning — *see* Submersion

Dust in eye E914

E

Earth falling (on) (with asphyxia or suffocation (by pressure)) — *see also* Suffocation, due to, cave-in E913.3
- as, or due to, a cataclysm (involving any transport vehicle) — *see* categories E908 ☑, E909 ☑
- not due to cataclysmic action E913.3
  - motor vehicle (in motion) (on public highway) E813 ☑
    - not on public highway E825 ☑
  - nonmotor road vehicle NEC E829 ☑
  - pedal cycle E826 ☑
  - railway rolling stock, train, vehicle E806 ☑
  - street car E829 ☑
  - struck or crushed by E916
    - with asphyxiation or suffocation E913.3
    - with injury other than asphyxia, suffocation E916

Earthquake (any injury) E909.0

Effect(s) (adverse) of
- air pressure E902.9
  - at high altitude E902.9
    - in aircraft E902.1
    - residence or prolonged visit (causing conditions classifiable to E902.0) E902.0
  - due to
    - diving E902.2
    - specified cause NEC E902.8
  - in aircraft E902.1

Effect(s) (adverse) of — *continued*
- cold, excessive (exposure to) (*see also* Cold, exposure to) E901.9
- heat (excessive) (*see also* Heat) E900.9
- hot
  - place — *see* Heat
  - weather E900.0
- insulation — *see* Heat
- late — *see* Late effect of
- motion E903
- nuclear explosion or weapon
  - in
    - terrorism E979.5
    - war operations (blast) (fireball) (heat) (radiation) (direct) (secondary) E996
- radiation — *see* Radiation
- terrorism, secondary E979.9
- travel E903

Electric shock, electrocution (accidental) (from exposed wire, faulty appliance, high voltage cable, live rail, open socket) (by) (in) E925.9
- appliance or wiring
  - domestic E925.0
  - factory E925.2
  - farm (building) E925.8
    - house E925.0
  - home E925.0
  - industrial (conductor) (control apparatus) (transformer) E925.2
  - outdoors E925.8
  - public building E925.8
  - residential institution E925.8
  - school E925.8
  - specified place NEC E925.8
- caused by other person
  - stated as
    - intentional, homicidal E968.8
    - undetermined whether accidental or intentional E988.4
- electric power generating plant, distribution station E925.1
- electroshock gun (taser) (stun gun) E925.8
  - caused by other person E968.8
    - legal intervention E975
    - stated as accidental E925.8
    - stated as intentional E968.8
  - due to legal intervention E975
  - stated as intentional self-harm (suicidal attempt) E958.4
  - stated as undetermined whether accidental or intentional E988.4
  - suicide (attempt) E958.4
- homicidal (attempt) E968.8
- legal execution E978
- lightning E907
- machinery E925.9
  - domestic E925.0
  - factory E925.2
  - farm E925.8
  - home E925.0
- misadventure in medical or surgical procedure
  - in electroshock therapy E873.4
- self-inflicted (undetermined whether accidental or intentional) E988.4
- stated as intentional E958.4
- stated as undetermined whether accidental or intentional E988.4
- suicidal (attempt) E958.4
- transmission line E925.1

Electrocution — *see* Electric shock

Embolism
- air (traumatic) NEC — *see* Air, embolism

Encephalitis
- lead or saturnine E866.0
  - from pesticide NEC E863.4

Entanglement
- in
  - bedclothes, causing suffocation E913.0
  - wheel of pedal cycle E826 ☑

Entry of foreign body, material, any — *see* Foreign body

Execution, legal (any method) E978

Exertion, excessive physical, from prolonged activity E927.2

Exhaustion
- cold — *see* Cold, exposure to
- due to excessive exertion E927.8
- heat — *see* Heat

Explosion (accidental) (in) (of) (on) E923.9
- acetylene E923.2
- aerosol can E921.8
- aircraft (in transit) (powered) E841 ☑
  - at landing, take-off E840 ☑
  - in
    - terrorism E979.1
    - war operations E994
  - unpowered E842 ☑
- air tank (compressed) (in machinery) E921.1
- anesthetic gas in operating theatre E923.2
- automobile tire NEC E921.8
  - causing transport accident — *see* categories E810-E825 ☑
- blasting (cap) (materials) E923.1
- boiler (machinery), not on transport vehicle E921.0
  - steamship — *see* Explosion, watercraft
- bomb E923.8
  - in
    - terrorism E979.2
    - war operations E993
      - after cessation of hostilities E998
      - atom, hydrogen or nuclear E996
      - injury by fragments from E991.9
        - antipersonnel bomb E991.3
- butane E923.2
- caused by
  - other person
    - stated as
      - intentional, homicidal — *see* Assault, explosive
      - undetermined whether accidental or homicidal E985.5
- coal gas E923.2
- detonator E923.1
- dynamite E923.1
- explosive (material) NEC E923.9
  - gas(es) E923.2
  - missile E923.8
    - in
      - terrorism E979.2
      - war operations E993
        - injury by fragments from E991.9
          - antipersonnel bomb E991.3
  - used in blasting operations E923.1
- fire-damp E923.2
- fireworks E923.0
- gas E923.2
  - cylinder (in machinery) E921.1
  - pressure tank (in machinery) E921.1
- gasoline (fumes) (tank) not in moving motor vehicle E923.2
- grain store (military) (munitions) E923.8
- grenade E923.8
  - in
    - terrorism E979.2
    - war operations E993

F

Foreign body, object or material — *continued*
- inhalation — *see* Foreign body, aspiration
- intestine (causing injury or obstruction) E915
- iris E914
- lacrimal apparatus E914
- larynx — *see* Foreign body, air passage
- late effect of NEC E929.8
- lung — *see* Foreign body, air passage
- mouth — *see* Foreign body, alimentary canal, mouth
- nasal passage — *see* Foreign body, air passage, nose
- nose — *see* Foreign body, air passage, nose
- ocular muscle E914
- operation wound (left in) — *see* Misadventure, foreign object
- orbit E914
- pharynx — *see* Foreign body, alimentary canal, pharynx
- rectum (causing injury or obstruction) E915
- stomach (hairball) (causing injury or obstruction) E915
- tear ducts or glands E914
- trachea — *see* Foreign body, air passage
- urethra (causing injury or obstruction) E915
- vagina (causing injury or obstruction) E915

Found dead, injured
- from exposure (to) — *see* Exposure
- on
  - public highway E819 ☑
  - railway right of way E807 ☑

Fracture (circumstances unknown or unspecified) E887
- due to specified external means — *see* manner of accident
- late effect of NEC E929.3
- occurring in water transport NEC E835 ☑

Freezing — *see* Cold, exposure to

Frostbite E901.0
- due to manmade conditions E901.1

Frozen — *see* Cold, exposure to

G

Garrotting, homicidal (attempted) E963

Gored E906.8

Gunshot wound — *see also* Shooting E922.9

H

Hailstones, injury by E904.3

Hairball (stomach) (with obstruction) E915

Hanged himself — *see also* Hanging, self-inflicted E983.0

Hang gliding E842 ☑

Hanging (accidental) E913.8
- caused by other person
  - in accidental circumstances E913.8
  - stated as
    - intentional, homicidal E963
    - undetermined whether accidental or intentional E983.0
- homicide (attempt) E963
- in bed or cradle E913.0
- legal execution E978
- self-inflicted (unspecified whether accidental or intentional) E983.0
  - in accidental circumstances E913.8
  - stated as intentional, purposeful E953.0
- stated as undetermined whether accidental or intentional E983.0
- suicidal (attempt) E953.0

Heat (apoplexy) (collapse) (cramps) (effects of) (excessive) (exhaustion) (fever) (prostration) (stroke) E900.9
- due to
  - manmade conditions (as listed in E900.1, except boat, ship, watercraft) E900.1
  - weather (conditions) E900.0
- from
  - electric heating appartus causing burning E924.8
  - nuclear explosion
    - in
      - terrorism E979.5
      - war operations E996
- generated in, boiler, engine, evaporator, fire room of boat, ship, watercraft E838 ☑
- inappropriate in local application or packing in medical or surgical procedure E873.5
- late effect of NEC E989

Hemorrhage
- delayed following medical or surgical treatment without mention of misadventure — *see* Reaction, abnormal
- during medical or surgical treatment as misadventure — *see* Misadventure, cut

High
- altitude, effects E902.9
- level of radioactivity, effects — *see* Radiation
- pressure effects (*see also* Effects of, air pressure)
  - from rapid descent in water (causing caisson or divers' disease, palsy, or paralysis) E902.2
- temperature, effects — *see* Heat

Hit, hitting (accidental) by
- aircraft (propeller) (without accident to aircraft) E844 ☑
  - unpowered E842 ☑
- avalanche E909.2
- being thrown against object in or part of
  - motor vehicle (in motion) (on public highway) E818 ☑
    - not on public highway E825 ☑
  - nonmotor road vehicle NEC E829 ☑
  - street car E829 ☑
- boat, ship, watercraft
  - after fall from watercraft E838 ☑
    - damaged, involved in accident E831 ☑
  - while swimming, water skiing E838 ☑
- bullet (*see also* Shooting) E922.9
  - from air gun E922.4
  - in
    - terrorism E979.4
    - war operations E991.2
      - rubber E991.0
- flare, Verey pistol (*see also* Shooting) E922.8
- hailstones E904.3
- landslide E909.2
- law-enforcing agent (on duty) E975
  - with blunt object (baton) (night stick) (stave) (truncheon) E973
- machine — *see* Accident, machine
- missile
  - firearm (*see also* Shooting) E922.9
  - in
    - terrorism — *see* Terrorism, missile
    - war operations — *see* War operations, missile
- motor vehicle (on public highway) (traffic accident) E814 ☑
  - not on public highway, nontraffic accident E822 ☑
- nonmotor road vehicle NEC E829 ☑

Hit, hitting by — *continued*
- object
  - falling E916
    - from, in, on
      - aircraft E844 ☑
        - due to accident to aircraft — *see* categories E840-E842 ☑
        - unpowered E842 ☑
      - boat, ship, watercraft E838 ☑
        - due to accident to watercraft E831 ☑
      - building E916
        - burning (uncontrolled fire) E891.8
          - in terrorism E979.3
          - private E890.8
      - cataclysmic
        - earth surface movement or eruption E909.9
        - storm E908.9
      - cave-in E916
        - with asphyxiation or suffocation (*see also* Suffocation, due to, cave-in) E913.3
      - earthquake E909.0
      - motor vehicle (in motion) (on public highway) E818 ☑
        - not on public highway E825 ☑
        - stationary E916
      - nonmotor road vehicle NEC E829 ☑
      - pedal cycle E826 ☑
      - railway rolling stock, train, vehicle E806 ☑
      - street car E829 ☑
      - structure, burning NEC E891.8
      - vehicle, stationary E916
  - moving NEC — *see* Striking against, object
  - projected NEC — *see* Striking against, object
  - set in motion by
    - compressed air or gas, spring, striking, throwing — *see* Striking against, object
    - explosion — *see* Explosion
  - thrown into, on, or towards
    - motor vehicle (in motion) (on public highway) E818 ☑
      - not on public highway E825 ☑
    - nonmotor road vehicle NEC E829 ☑
    - pedal cycle E826 ☑
    - street car E829 ☑
- off-road type motor vehicle (not on public highway) E821 ☑
  - on public highway E814 ☑
- other person(s) E917.9
  - with blunt or thrown object E917.9
    - in sports E917.0
      - with subsequent fall E917.5
    - intentionally, homicidal E968.2
  - as, or caused by, a crowd E917.1
    - with subsequent fall E917.6
  - in sports E917.0
- pedal cycle E826 ☑
- police (on duty) E975
  - with blunt object (baton) (nightstick) (stave) (truncheon) E973
- railway, rolling stock, train, vehicle (part of) E805 ☑
- shot — *see* Shooting
- snow vehicle, motor-driven (not on public highway) E820 ☑
  - on public highway E814 ☑
- street car E829 ☑
- vehicle NEC — *see* Accident, vehicle NEC

Homicide, homicidal (attempt) (justifiable) — *see also* Assault E968.9

Hot
- liquid, object, substance, accident caused by (*see also* Accident, caused by, hot, by type of substance)
  - late effect of E929.8
- place, effects — *see* Heat
- weather, effects E900.0

Humidity, causing problem E904.3

Hunger E904.1
- resulting from
  - abandonment or neglect E904.0
  - transport accident — *see* categories E800-E848 ☑

Hurricane (any injury) E908.0

Hypobarism, hypobaropathy — *see* Effects of, air pressure

Hypothermia — *see* Cold, exposure to

I

Ictus
- caloris — *see* Heat
- solaris E900.0

Ignition (accidental)
- anesthetic gas in operating theatre E923.2
- bedclothes
  - with
    - conflagration — *see* Conflagration
    - ignition (of)
      - clothing — *see* Ignition, clothes
      - highly inflammable material (benzine) (fat) (gasoline) (kerosene) (paraffin) (petrol) E894
- benzine E894
- clothes, clothing (from controlled fire) (in building) E893.9
  - with conflagration — *see* Conflagration
  - from
    - bonfire E893.2
    - highly inflammable material E894
    - sources or material as listed in E893.8
    - trash fire E893.2
    - uncontrolled fire — *see* Conflagration
  - in
    - private dwelling E893.0
    - specified building or structure, except private dwelling E893.1
  - not in building or structure E893.2
- explosive material — *see* Explosion
- fat E894
- gasoline E894
- kerosene E894
- material
  - explosive — *see* Explosion
  - highly inflammable E894
    - with conflagration — *see* Conflagration
    - with explosion E923.2
- nightdress — *see* Ignition, clothes
- paraffin E894
- petrol E894

Immersion — *see* Submersion

Implantation of quills of porcupine E906.8

Inanition (from) E904.9
- hunger — *see* Lack of, food
- resulting from homicidal intent E968.4
- thirst — *see* Lack of, water

Inattention after, at birth E904.0
- homicidal, infanticidal intent E968.4

Infanticide — *see also* Assault

Ingestion
- foreign body (causing injury) (with obstruction) — *see* Foreign body, alimentary canal
- poisonous substance NEC — *see* Table of Drugs and Chemicals

Inhalation
- excessively cold substance, manmade E901.1
- foreign body — *see* Foreign body, aspiration
- liquid air, hydrogen, nitrogen E901.1
- mucus, not of newborn (with asphyxia, obstruction respiratory passage, suffocation) E912
- phlegm (with asphyxia, obstruction respiratory passage, suffocation) E912
- poisonous gas — *see* Table of Drugs and Chemicals
- smoke from, due to
  - fire — *see* Fire
  - tobacco, second-hand E869.4
- vomitus (with asphyxia, obstruction respiratory passage, suffocation) E911

Injury, injured (accidental(ly)) NEC E928.9
- by, caused by, from
  - air rifle (BB gun) E922.4
  - animal (not being ridden) NEC E906.9
    - being ridden (in sport or transport) E828 ☑
  - assault (*see also* Assault) E968.9
  - avalanche E909.2
  - bayonet (*see also* Bayonet wound) E920.3
  - being thrown against some part of, or object in
    - motor vehicle (in motion) (on public highway) E818 ☑
      - not on public highway E825 ☑
    - nonmotor road vehicle NEC E829 ☑
    - off-road motor vehicle NEC E821 ☑
    - railway train E806 ☑
    - snow vehicle, motor-driven E820 ☑
    - street car E829 ☑
  - bending E927.8
  - bite, human E928.3
  - broken glass E920.8
  - bullet — *see* Shooting
  - cave-in (*see also* Suffocation, due to, cave-in) E913.3
    - without asphyxiation or suffocation E916
    - earth surface movement or eruption E909.9
    - storm E908.9
  - cloudburst E908.8
  - cutting or piercing instrument (*see also* Cut) E920.9
  - cyclone E908.1
  - earthquake E909.0
  - earth surface movement or eruption E909.9
  - electric current (*see also* Electric shock) E925.9
  - explosion (*see also* Explosion) E923.9
  - fire — *see* Fire
  - flare, Verey pistol E922.8
  - flood E908.2
  - foreign body — *see* Foreign body
  - hailstones E904.3
  - hurricane E908.0
  - landslide E909.2
  - law-enforcing agent, police, in course of legal intervention — *see* Legal intervention
  - lightning E907

Injury, injured — *continued*
- by, caused by, from — *continued*
  - live rail or live wire — *see* Electric shock
  - machinery (*see also* Accident, machine)
    - aircraft, without accident to aircraft E844 ☑
    - boat, ship, watercraft (deck) (engine room) (galley) (laundry) (loading) E836 ☑
  - missile
    - explosive E923.8
    - firearm — *see* Shooting
    - in
      - terrorism — see Terrorism, missile
      - war operations — *see* War operations, missile
  - moving part of motor vehicle (in motion) (on public highway) E818 ☑
    - not on public highway, nontraffic accident E825 ☑
    - while alighting, boarding, entering, leaving — *see* Fall, from, motor vehicle, while alighting, boarding
  - nail E920.8
  - needle (sewing) E920.4
    - hypodermic E920.5
  - noise E928.1
  - object
    - fallen on
      - motor vehicle (in motion) (on public highway) E818 ☑
        - not on public highway E825 ☑
    - falling — *see* Hit by, object, falling
  - paintball gun E922.5
  - radiation — *see* Radiation
  - railway rolling stock, train, vehicle (part of) E805 ☑
    - door or window E806 ☑
  - rotating propeller, aircraft E844 ☑
  - rough landing of off-road type motor vehicle (after leaving ground or rough terrain) E821 ☑
    - snow vehicle E820 ☑
  - saber (*see also* Wound, saber) E920.3
  - shot — *see* Shooting
  - sound waves E928.1
  - splinter or sliver, wood E920.8
  - straining E927.8
  - street car (door) E829 ☑
  - suicide (attempt) E958.9
  - sword E920.3
  - terrorism — *see* Terrorism
  - third rail — *see* Electric shock
  - thunderbolt E907
  - tidal wave E909.4
    - caused by storm E908.0
  - tornado E908.1
  - torrential rain E908.2
  - twisting E927.8
  - vehicle NEC — *see* Accident, vehicle NEC
  - vibration E928.2
  - volcanic eruption E909.1
  - weapon burst, in war operations E993
  - weightlessness (in spacecraft, real or simulated) E928.0
  - wood splinter or sliver E920.8
- due to
  - civil insurrection — *see* War operations
    - occurring after cessation of hostilities E998
  - terrorism — see Terrorism

Injury, injured — *continued*
- due to — *continued*
  - war operations — *see* War operations
    - occurring after cessation of hostilities E998
- homicidal (*see also* Assault) E968.9
- inflicted (by)
  - in course of arrest (attempted), suppression of disturbance, maintenance of order, by law enforcing agents — *see* Legal intervention
  - law-enforcing agent (on duty) — *see* Legal intervention
  - other person
    - stated as
      - accidental E928.9
      - homicidal, intentional — *see* Assault
      - undetermined whether accidental or intentional — *see* Injury, stated as undetermined
  - police (on duty) — *see* Legal intervention
- in, on
  - civil insurrection — *see* War operations
  - fight E960.0
  - parachute descent (voluntary) (without accident to aircraft) E844 ☑
    - with accident to aircraft — *see* categories E840-E842 ☑
  - public highway E819 ☑
  - railway right of way E807 ☑
  - terrorism — *see* Terrorism
  - war operations — *see* War operations
- late effect of E929.9
- purposely (inflicted) by other person(s) — *see* Assault
- self-inflicted (unspecified whether accidental or intentional) E988.9
  - stated as
    - accidental E928.9
    - intentionally, purposely E958.9
- specified cause NEC E928.8
- stated as
  - hanging E983.0
  - knife E986
  - late effect of E989
  - puncture (any part of body) E986
  - shooting — *see* Shooting, stated as undetermined whether accidental or intentional
  - specified means NEC E988.8
  - stab (any part of body) E986
  - strangulation — *see* Suffocation, stated as undetermined whether accidental or intentional
  - submersion E984
  - suffocation — *see* Suffocation, stated as undetermined whether accidental or intentional
  - undetermined whether accidentally or purposely inflicted (by) E988.9
    - cut (any part of body) E986
    - cutting or piercing instrument (classifiable to E920) E986
    - drowning E984
    - explosive(s) (missile) E985.5
    - falling from high place E987.9
      - manmade structure, except residential E987.1
    - natural site E987.2
    - residential premises E987.0
- to child due to criminal abortion E968.8

Insufficient nourishment — *see also* Lack of, food

Insufficient nourishment — *see also* Lack of, food — *continued*
- homicidal intent E968.4

Insulation, effects — *see* Heat

Interruption of respiration by
- food lodged in esophagus E911
- foreign body, except food, in esophagus E912

Intervention, legal — *see* Legal intervention

Intoxication, drug or poison — *see* Table of Drugs and Chemicals

Irradiation — *see* Radiation

J

Jammed (accidentally)
- between objects (moving) (stationary and moving) E918
- in object E918

Jumped or fell from high place, so stated — *see* Jumping, from, high place, stated as
- in undetermined circumstances

Jumping
- before train, vehicle or other moving object (unspecified whether accidental or intentional) E988.0
  - stated as
    - intentional, purposeful E958.0
    - suicidal (attempt) E958.0
- from
  - aircraft
    - by parachute (voluntarily) (without accident to aircraft) E844 ☑
    - due to accident to aircraft — *see* categories E840-E842 ☑
  - boat, ship, watercraft (into water)
    - after accident to, fire on, watercraft E830 ☑
      - and subsequently struck by (part of) boat E831 ☑
    - burning, crushed, sinking E830 ☑
      - and subsequently struck by (part of) boat E831 ☑
    - voluntarily, without accident (to boat) with injury other than drowning or submersion E883.0
  - building (*see also* Jumping, from, high place)
    - burning (uncontrolled fire) E891.8
      - in terrorism E979.3
      - private E890.8
  - cable car (not on rails) E847
    - on rails E829 ☑
  - high place
    - in accidental circumstances or in sport — *see* categories E880-E884 ☑
    - stated as
      - with intent to injure self E957.9
        - man-made structures NEC E957.1
        - natural sites E957.2
        - residential premises E957.0
      - in undetermined circumstances E987.9
        - man-made structures NEC E987.1
        - natural sites E987.2
        - residential premises E987.0
      - suicidal (attempt) E957.9
        - man-made structures NEC E957.1
        - natural sites E957.1
        - residential premises E957.0
  - motor vehicle (in motion) (on public highway) — *see* Fall, from, motor vehicle

T

V

W

War operations — *continued*
shell — *continued*
sea-based E992
shooting E991.2
after cessation of hostilities E998
bullet(s) E991.2
rubber E991.0
pellet(s) (rifle) E991.1
shrapnel E991.9
submersion E995
torpedo E992

War operations — *continued*
unconventional warfare, except by nuclear weapon E997.9
biological (warfare) E997.1
gas, fumes, chemicals E997.2
laser(s) E997.0
specified type NEC E997.8
underwater blast E992
vesicant (chemical) (fumes) (gas) E997.2
weapon burst E993

Washed
away by flood — *see* Flood
away by tidal wave — *see* Tidal wave
off road by storm (transport vehicle) E908.9
overboard E832 ☑

Weather exposure — *see also* Exposure
cold E901.0
hot E900.0

Weightlessness (causing injury) (effects of) (in spacecraft, real or simulated) E928.0

Wound (accidental) NEC — *see also* Injury E928.9
battle (*see also* War operations) E995
bayonet E920.3
in
legal intervention E974
war operations E995
gunshot — *see* Shooting
incised — *see* Cut
saber, sabre E920.3
in war operations E995

Railway Accidents (E800-E807)

The following fourth-digit subdivisions are for use with categories E800-E807 to identify the injured person:

.0 Railway employee
Any person who by virtue of his employment in connection with a railway, whether by the railway company or not, is at increased risk of involvement in a railway accident, such as:
catering staff on train
postal staff on train
driver
railway fireman
guard
shunter
porter
sleeping car attendant

.1 Passenger on railway
Any authorized person traveling on a train, except a railway employee
EXCLUDES intending passenger waiting at station (.8)
unauthorized rider on railway vehicle (.8)

.2 Pedestrian See definition (r), E-Codes-2

.3 Pedal cyclist See definition (p), E-Codes-2

.8 Other specified person Intending passenger waiting at station
Unauthorized rider on railway vehicle

.9 Unspecified person

Motor Vehicle Traffic and Nontraffic Accidents (E810-E825)

The following fourth-digit subdivisions are for use with categories E810-E819 and E820-E825 to identify the injured person:

.0 Driver of motor vehicle other than motorcycle See definition (1), E-Codes-2

.1 Passenger in motor vehicle other than motorcycle See definition (1), E-Codes-2

.2 Motorcyclist See definition (1), E-Codes-2

.3 Passenger on motorcycle See definition (1), E-Codes-2

.4 Occupant of streetcar

.5 Rider of animal; occupant of animal-drawn vehicle

.6 Pedal cyclist See definition (p), E-Codes-2

.7 Pedestrian See definition (r), E-Codes-2

.8 Other specified person
Occupant of vehicle other than above
Person in railway train involved in accident
Unauthorized rider of motor vehicle

.9 Unspecified person

Other Road Vehicle Accidents (E826-E829)

(animal-drawn vehicle, streetcar, pedal cycle, and other nonmotor road vehicle accidents)

The following fourth-digit subdivisions are for use with categories E826-E829 to identify the injured person:

.0 Pedestrian See definition (r), E-Codes-2

.1 Pedal cyclist (does not apply to codes E827, E828, E829) See definition (p), E-Codes-2

.2 Rider of animal (does not apply to code E829)

.3 Occupant of animal-drawn vehicle (does not apply to codes E828, E829)

.4 Occupant of streetcar

.8 Other specified person

.9 Unspecified person

Water Transport Accidents (E830-E838)

The following fourth-digit subdivisions are for use with categories E830-E838 to identify the injured person:

.0 Occupant of small boat, unpowered

.1 Occupant of small boat, powered See definition (t), E-Codes-2
EXCLUDES water skier (.4)

.2 Occupant of other watercraft — crew
Persons:
engaged in operation of watercraft
providing passenger services [cabin attendants, ship's physician, catering personnel]
working on ship during voyage in other capacity [musician in band, operators of shops and beauty parlors]

.3 Occupant of other watercraft — other than crew
Passenger
Occupant of lifeboat, other than crew, after abandoning ship

.4 Water skier

.5 Swimmer

.6 Dockers, stevedores
Longshoreman employed on the dock in loading and unloading ships

.8 Other specified person
Immigration and custom officials on board ship
Persons:
accompanying passenger or member of crew visiting boat
Pilot (guiding ship into port)

.9 Unspecified person

Air and Space Transport Accidents (E840-E845)

The following fourth-digit subdivisions are for use with categories E840-E845 to identify the injured person:

.0 Occupant of spacecraft
Crew
Passenger (civilian)
(military)
Troops
} in military aircraft [air force] [army] [national guard] [navy]

.1 Occupant of military aircraft, any
EXCLUDES occupants of aircraft operated under jurisdiction of police departments (.5) parachutist (.7)

.2 Crew of commercial aircraft (powered) in surface to surface transport

.3 Other occupant of commercial aircraft (powered) in surface to surface transport
Flight personnel:
not part of crew
on familiarization flight Passenger on aircraft

.4 Occupant of commercial aircraft (powered) in surface to air transport
Occupant [crew] [passenger] of aircraft (powered) engaged in activities, such as:
air drops of emergency supplies
air drops of parachutists, except from military craft
crop dusting
lowering of construction material [bridge or telephone pole]
sky writing

.5 Occupant of other powered aircraft
Occupant [crew] [passenger] of aircraft (powered) engaged in activities, such as:
aerial spraying (crops)(fire retardants)
aerobatic flying
aircraft racing
rescue operation
storm surveillance
traffic suveillance
Occupant of private plane NOS

.6 Occupant of unpowered aircraft, except parachutist
Occupant of aircraft classifiable to E842

.7 Parachutist (military)(other)
Person making voluntary descent
person making descent after accident to aircraft (.1-.6)

.8 Ground crew, airline employee
Persons employed at airfields (civil)(military) or launching pads, not occupants of aircraft

.9 Other person

Chapter 1: Infections and Parasitic Diseases (001–139)

Communicable diseases as well as diseases of unknown origin but possibly due to infectious organisms are found in this chapter. Infections confined to a specific body system are classified to chapters covering the specific body site. Congenitally acquired infections, postoperative infections, and infections complicating pregnancy and delivery are classified elsewhere. An additional code from the "Infectious and Parasitic Disease" chapter may be used in combination with the codes from other chapters to further describe the nature of the infection.

Infective organisms classified to categories 001–139 include arthropods, bacteria, chlamydia, fungi, helminths, mycoplasms, protozoans, rickettsias, and viruses. This chapter classifies infectious and parasitic diseases by anatomic site, by type of infectious organism or parasite, as well as by a combination of site and type of organism.

Steps to coding infection:

1. Locate the main term "Infection" in the alphabetic index.
2. Locate the subterm for the causal organism.
3. The subterm for the organism takes precedence over the more general subterms such as acute or chronic.
4. When the index directs the user to another chapter to code the infection, an additional code from the "Infectious and Parasitic Disease" chapter is generally required to further describe the nature of the infection.
5. The coder may also search the alphabetic index under the main term for the condition.
6. Locate the code in the tabular list and read all "includes" and "excludes" notes for the category to verify code assignments.

Intestinal Infectious Diseases (001–009)

This subchapter includes diseases specific to the intestines caused by infectious organisms and parasites (except for helminthiases, which are classified to subcategories 120.0–129). Some of the main categories in this subchapter include cholera, typhoid, salmonella, shigellosis, food poisoning, amebiasis, Escherichia coli (E. coli), septicemia and enteritis.

Important notes for coding this subsection:

- Determine whether the infection is acute or chronic.
- Determine from documentation in the medical record positive identification of the organism.
- Note the site of infection, whether localized or generalized.
- Note extraintestinal complications due to the infection.

Tuberculosis (010–018)

Infectious diseases caused primarily by the acid fast bacilli Mycobacterium tuberculosis, but also M. bovis, M. africanum, M. leprae and other variants are included in this subchapter. Infection occurs almost exclusively through the respiratory system by inhalation of the tubercule bacilli released by an infected host. The disease spreads from the primary lesion in the lung to other parts of the body. Tuberculosis is first coded according to site or type.

Other Bacterial Diseases (030–041)

Leprosy, diphtheria, whooping cough, scarlet fever, streptococcal sore throat, meningitis, tetanus, septicemia, actinomycotic infections, and gas gangrene are grouped as other bacterial diseases in this subchapter.

Methicillin-resistant *Staphylococcus aureus* (MRSA) is a variant form of the bacterium that is resistant to traditional beta lactam class of antibiotics such as penicillin, methicillin, and cephalosporins. Sometimes referred to as a "superbug," MRSA is a major cause of hospital-acquired infections as well as community-acquired infections. Community-acquired MRSA infections (CA-MRSA) are generally not life-threatening skin, and soft tissue infections are spread through direct contact. The term methicillin-susceptible *Staphylococcus aureus* (MSSA) identifies certain strains of *Staphylococcus aureus* that are penicillin-resistant yet susceptible or treatable with methicillin.

Note that category 041 is provided to identify the bacterial agent in diseases classified elsewhere, or of an unspecified nature or site. For example an E. coli infection of an unspecified site of the urinary tract is coded first to urinary tract infection 599.0. The instructional note under this subcategory directs the use of an additional code to identify the organism, in this case E. coli. The complete code assignment is 599.0 and 041.4.

Septicemia (038)

Septicemia is a systemic infection associated with the presence and persistence of microorganisms and their toxins in the blood. Since it is a systemic disease, site-specific or organ-specific sepsis is not coded as septicemia.

Certain forms of septicemia are more appropriately classified elsewhere. Search the alphabetic index under the main term "Septicemia" for subterms that identify particular forms of septicemia. Septicemia, not otherwise specified, is reported with code 038.9. When reporting the diagnosis of sepsis, however, the instructional note at subcategory 995.9 directs the coder to sequence the underlying cause of the infection first. The default code assigned for the underlying infection is 038.9 Unspecified septicemia. If the physician documents only the diagnosis of "sepsis," two codes are required to report the condition: 038.9 (septicemia) and 995.9 (sepsis). Systemic inflammatory response syndrome (SIRS) generally is a systemic response to infection, trauma/burns, or other insult (such as cancer). The term 'sepsis' generally refers to SIRS due to infection. Severe sepsis is sepsis with associated acute organ dysfunction.

Coding of SIRS, sepsis and severe sepsis requires a minimum of 2 codes: a code for the underlying cause (such as infection or trauma) and a code from subcategory 995.9 Systemic inflammatory response syndrome (SIRS). The code for the underlying cause must be sequenced before the code from subcategory 995.9 Systemic inflammatory response syndrome (SIRS). For sepsis, if the causal organism is not documented, assign code 038.9, Unspecified septicemia. Severe sepsis requires additional code(s) for the associated acute organ dysfunction(s).

If sepsis or severe sepsis is present on admission, and meets the definition of principal diagnosis, the systemic infection code (e.g., 038.xx, 112.5, etc) should be assigned as the principal diagnosis, followed by code 995.91, Sepsis, or 995.92, Severe sepsis, as required by the sequencing rules. When sepsis or severe sepsis develops during the encounter (not present on admission), the systemic infection code and code 995.91 or 995.92 should be assigned as secondary diagnoses.

Septic shock is a form of organ dysfunction, and circulatory failure, associated with systemic inflammatory response syndrome (SIRS) due to infectious process which cannot occur in the absence of severe sepsis. Septic shock can be stated as severe sepsis with shock. Note: severe sepsis with shock involves persistent hypotension with systolic blood pressure < 90 mmHg, or a 40 mmHg drop in previous blood pressure, with no response to adequate fluid resuscitation. As a result, reduced myocardial performance occurs, or heart failure is an inherent characteristic of severe sepsis. Therefore, heart failure is inclusive in the code 785.52 and should not be listed separately.

For all cases of septic shock, the code for the systemic infection should be sequenced first, followed by codes 995.92 and 785.52. Any additional codes for other acute organ dysfunctions should also be assigned. Septic shock cannot be assigned as a principal diagnosis.

Other Specified Botulism (040.4)

Botulism, an uncommon but serious neuromuscular poisoning caused by the toxin Clostridium botulinum, occurs in three forms. Food-borne botulism is a result of ingesting foods containing the botulism toxin and is reported with code 005.1. Wound botulism (040.42), caused by a toxin produced from a wound infected with Clostridium botulinum, is frequently the result of a traumatic injury or a deep puncture wound. Often caused by abscess formation due to self-injected illegal drugs, its manifestations include neurological symptoms with onset typically two weeks following the initial wound or trauma. To report wound botulism or botulism classifiable to code 040.42, use an additional code to identify the complicated wound, by site.

Infant botulism (040.41) is a result of consuming the spores of the botulinum bacteria and occurs most often in infants less than six months of age. The spores colonize in the large intestine, frequently resulting in constipation and progressing to neuromuscular paralysis. All forms of botulism can be fatal, with life-threatening impairment of respiratory function being one of the greatest complications.

Human Immunodeficiency Virus Infection (042)

Human immunodeficiency virus (HIV) disease is coded to category 042. Manifestations of AIDS and HIV infection are often numerous and all should be coded.

Category 042 is assigned only when the physician states a positive diagnosis. Code 042 is sequenced first when a patient is seen for an HIV infection or complication due to the presence of the HIV infection. Additional codes identify associated complications.

Code 042 is not sequenced first if the patient is seen for a condition unrelated to HIV infection. Rather, 042 is assigned as a secondary diagnosis. For example, a patient is seen for a fractured wrist, the fracture is sequenced first and the code for HIV is sequenced second.

An asymptomatic patient with a positive HIV test result is assigned V08 Asymptomatic human immunodeficiency virus [HIV] infection status. As an asymptomatic patient develops HIV related symptoms assign code 042 for subsequent visits.

Patients with nonspecific serologic evidence of HIV infection but with inconclusive HIV test results are assigned code 795.71 Nonspecific serologic evidence of human immunodeficiency virus [HIV].

A patient concerned about HIV status is reported by code V73.89 Screening for other specified viral disease.

Slow Virus Infections and Prion Diseases of Central Nervous System (046)

Prion diseases or transmissible spongiform encephalopathies (TSE) are a family of rare progressive neurodegenerative disorders that affect both humans and animals. They are distinguished by long incubation periods, characteristic spongiform changes associated with neuronal loss, and a failure to induce inflammatory response. The causative agent of TSEs is believed to be a prion, an abnormal, transmissible agent that is able to induce abnormal folding of normal cellular prion proteins in the brain, leading to brain damage and the characteristic signs and symptoms of the disease.

Other Human Herpesviruses (058)

Human herpesviruses type 6 (HHV-6) and HHV-7 infect the majority of individuals primarily during childhood and are associated with various clinical manifestations such as fever, rash, and seizures. Immunocompromised hosts, such as transplant recipients or those with AIDS, are at increased risk for symptomatic primary disease or reactivation disease.

Code category 058 reports specific herpesviruses not specifically classifiable elsewhere to type. Herpesvirus infections that are classifiable elsewhere in chapter 1 include cytomegalovirus/HHV-5 (078.5), Epstein-Barr/HHV-4 (075), and other forms of human herpesviruses (categories 052–054).

Other Poxvirus Infections (059)

Global travel and imported animals have increased the concern for exposure to poxvirus infections. Humans may be intentionally (e.g., smallpox vaccination) or unintentionally (e.g., secondary spread from a vaccine or infection from a dairy-associated wild type strain) infected with vaccinia virus. Code category 059 Other poxvirus infections, excludes cowpox (051.01) and other vaccinia and paravaccinia infections classified elsewhere. Generalized vaccinia (cutaneous and sometimes systemic reactions associated with vaccination) is reported with code 999.0, whereas vaccinia not from vaccine is reported with code 051.02. Infection due to vaccinia virus spread as an inadvertent inoculation of site other than the vaccination site is reported with code 051.02. For example, vaccinia of the eyelid requires two codes: 051.02 and 373.5 (Other infective dermatitis of eyelid).

Arthropod-borne Viral Diseases (060–066)

This section includes the viral diseases transmitted by arthropods, that phylum of exoskeletal organisms having paired and jointed legs.

Notable among these diseases is West Nile virus. Report code 066.41 if diagnosed with encephalitis, code 066.42 for other neurologic manifestations, code 066.49 for other complications, and code 066.40 if the West Nile virus is unspecified.

Other Diseases Due to Viruses and Chlamydiae (070–079)

Viral hepatitis, rabies, mumps, infectious mononucleosis, trachoma, viral warts, cat-scratch fever, cytomegaloviral disease (CMV), respiratory syncitial virus (RSV), and coxsackie viral infections are included in this section.

Viral hepatitis is classified according to virus type A, B, C, or E. Secondly, viral hepatitis is classified according to hepatic coma. For example, viral hepatitis B with hepatic coma is assigned 070.20 and viral hepatitis B without mention of hepatic coma is coded 070.30

A fifth-digit assignment for viral hepatitis B identifies the presence of hepatitis D (hepatitis delta) as well as whether the condition is acute or chronic. Hepatitis D occurs simultaneously or after an infection of hepatitis B and may increase the severity of the disease.

Verrucae (warts) are classified according to site and type. Code 078.10 is assigned for verruca vulgaris, or the common wart of the hands and fingers. This is also the default code assignment for verruca NOS. Warts specified as "condyloma" or "genital" are coded to 078.11 Condyloma acuminatum. Verruca plantaris, verruca of the sole of the feet, is assigned code 078.12. Verruca plana, flat wart of the face, neck, hands, wrists, and back is assigned code 078.19.

Parvovirus B19 (079.83), the only parvovirus that causes disease in humans, may be referred to as human parvovirus. Parvovirus B19 infection may manifest with anemia or neurological symptoms. When polyneuropathy is associated with parvovirus B19, reporting the condition requires mandatory manifestation/etiology dual coding, whereby codes 079.83 Parvovirus B19 and 711.5x Arthropathy associated with other viral diseases are reported.

Syphilis and Other Venereal Diseases (090–099)

Syphilis is classified by type, early or late, and whether symptomatic, latent, or unspecified. Syphilis affecting the cardiovascular or nervous system is classified separately.

Venereal disease is classified by type, whether acute or chronic, and by site of complication. For example, acute gonococcal infection of the bladder is coded 098.11. Chronic gonococcal infection of the seminal vesicles is codes 098.34.

Mycoses (110–118)

Diseases caused by a fungus are found in this section of the classification system, excluding Actinomycotic infections, which are coded to category 039. Additional coding is necessary to identify manifestations of the disease. For example, systemic cryptococcosis with meningitis is coded 117.5 and 321.0

Helminthiases (120–129)

Helminths are parasitic worms that cause a number of diseases including schistomsomiasis (120.x), hydatid disease (122.x), tapeworm infection (123.x), trichinosis (124.x), roundworm infection (127.0), and pinworm infection (127.4).

Late Effects of Infectious and Parasitic Diseases (137–139)

Late effects of tuberculosis (137), acute poliomyelitis (138), and other infectious and parasitic diseases (139) are classified to this section. Since the infection is no longer present, a code from one of these three categories is assigned in conjunction with the residual condition code. For example, nephropathy from past episode of tuberculosis of the kidney is coded 583.81 and 137.2.

1. INFECTIOUS AND PARASITIC DISEASES (001-139)

Note: Categories for "late effects" of infectious and parasitic diseases are to be found at 137-139.

INCLUDES diseases generally recognized as communicable or transmissible as well as a few diseases of unknown but possibly infectious origin

EXCLUDES *acute respiratory infections (460-466)*
carrier or suspected carrier of infectious organism (V02.0-V02.9)
certain localized infections
influenza (487.0-487.8, 488)

INTESTINAL INFECTIOUS DISEASES (001-009)

EXCLUDES *helminthiases (120.0-129)*

✓4th **001 Cholera**

DEF: An acute infectious enteritis caused by a potent enterotoxin elaborated by *Vibrio cholerae*; the vibrio produces a toxin in the intestinal tract that changes the permeability of the mucosa leading to diarrhea and dehydration.

001.0 Due to Vibrio cholerae

001.1 Due to Vibrio cholerae el tor

001.9 Cholera, unspecified

✓4th **002 Typhoid and paratyphoid fevers**

DEF: Typhoid fever: an acute generalized illness caused by *Salmonella typhi;* notable clinical features are fever, headache, abdominal pain, cough, toxemia, leukopenia, abnormal pulse, rose spots on the skin, bacteremia, hyperplasia of intestinal lymph nodes, mesenteric lymphadenopathy, and Peyer's patches in the intestines.

DEF: Paratyphoid fever: a prolonged febrile illness, much like typhoid but usually less severe; caused by salmonella serotypes other than *S. typhi*, especially *S. enteritidis* serotypes paratyphi A and B and *S. choleraesuis.*

002.0 Typhoid fever
Typhoid (fever) (infection) [any site]

002.1 Paratyphoid fever A

002.2 Paratyphoid fever B

002.3 Paratyphoid fever C

002.9 Paratyphoid fever, unspecified

✓4th **003 Other salmonella infections**

INCLUDES infection or food poisoning by Salmonella [any serotype]

DEF: Infections caused by a genus of gram-negative, anaerobic bacteria of the family *Enterobacteriaceae;* affecting warm-blooded animals, like humans; major symptoms are enteric fevers, acute gastroenteritis and septicemia.

003.0 Salmonella gastroenteritis
Salmonellosis

003.1 Salmonella septicemia

✓5th **003.2 Localized salmonella infections**

003.20 Localized salmonella infection, unspecified

003.21 Salmonella meningitis

003.22 Salmonella pneumonia

003.23 Salmonella arthritis

003.24 Salmonella osteomyelitis

003.29 Other

003.8 Other specified salmonella infections

003.9 Salmonella infection, unspecified

✓4th **004 Shigellosis**

INCLUDES bacillary dysentery

DEF: Acute infectious dysentery caused by the genus *Shigella*, of the family *Enterobacteriaceae;* affecting the colon causing the release of blood-stained stools with accompanying tenesmus, abdominal cramps and fever.

004.0 Shigella dysenteriae
Infection by group A Shigella (Schmitz) (Shiga)

004.1 Shigella flexneri
Infection by group B Shigella

004.2 Shigella boydii
Infection by group C Shigella

004.3 Shigella sonnei
Infection by group D Shigella

004.8 Other specified Shigella infections

004.9 Shigellosis, unspecified

✓4th **005 Other food poisoning (bacterial)**

EXCLUDES *salmonella infections (003.0-003.9)*
toxic effect of:
food contaminants (989.7)
noxious foodstuffs (988.0-988.9)

DEF: Enteritis caused by ingesting contaminated foods and characterized by diarrhea, abdominal pain, vomiting; symptoms may be mild or life threatening.

005.0 Staphylococcal food poisoning
Staphylococcal toxemia specified as due to food

005.1 Botulism food poisoning
Botulism NOS
Food poisoning due to Clostridium botulinum

EXCLUDES *infant botulism (040.41)*
wound botulism (040.42)

005.2 Food poisoning due to Clostridium perfringens [C. welchii]
Enteritis necroticans

005.3 Food poisoning due to other Clostridia

005.4 Food poisoning due to Vibrio parahaemolyticus

✓5th **005.8 Other bacterial food poisoning**

EXCLUDES *salmonella food poisoning (003.0-003.9)*

005.81 Food poisoning due to Vibrio vulnificus

005.89 Other bacterial food poisoning
Food poisoning due to Bacillus cereus

005.9 Food poisoning, unspecified

✓4th **006 Amebiasis**

INCLUDES infection due to Entamoeba histolytica

EXCLUDES *amebiasis due to organisms other than Entamoeba histolytica (007.8)*

DEF: Infection of the large intestine caused by *Entamoeba histolytica;* usually asymptomatic but symptoms may range from mild diarrhea to profound life-threatening dysentery. Extraintestinal complications include hepatic abscess, which may rupture into the lung, pericardium or abdomen, causing life-threatening infections.

006.0 Acute amebic dysentery without mention of abscess
Acute amebiasis

DEF: Sudden, severe *Entamoeba histolytica* infection causing bloody stools.

006.1 Chronic intestinal amebiasis without mention of abscess
Chronic:
amebiasis
amebic dysentery

006.2 Amebic nondysenteric colitis

DEF: *Entamoeba histolytica* infection with inflamed colon but no dysentery.

006.3 Amebic liver abscess
Hepatic amebiasis

006.4 Amebic lung abscess
Amebic abscess of lung (and liver)

006.5 Amebic brain abscess
Amebic abscess of brain (and liver) (and lung)

006.6 Amebic skin ulceration
Cutaneous amebiasis

006.8 Amebic infection of other sites
Amebic:
appendicitis
balanitis
Ameboma

EXCLUDES *specific infections by free-living amebae (136.21-136.29)*

006.9 Amebiasis, unspecified
Amebiasis NOS

✓4th **007 Other protozoal intestinal diseases**

INCLUDES protozoal:
colitis
diarrhea
dysentery

007.0 Balantidiasis
Infection by Balantidium coli

007.1 Giardiasis
Infection by Giardia lamblia
Lambliasis

007.2 Coccidiosis
Infection by Isospora belli and Isospora hominis
Isosporiasis

007.3 Intestinal trichomoniasis
DEF: Colitis, diarrhea, or dysentery caused by the protozoa *Trichomonas.*

007.4 Cryptosporidiosis
DEF: An intestinal infection by protozoan parasites causing intractable diarrhea in patients with AIDS and other immunosuppressed individuals.

007.5 Cyclosporiasis
DEF: An infection of the small intestine by the protozoal organism, *Cyclospora caytenanesis,* spread to humans though ingestion of contaminated water or food. Symptoms include watery diarrhea with frequent explosive bowel movements, loss of appetite, loss of weight, bloating, increased gas, stomach cramps, nausea, vomiting, muscle aches, low grade fever, and fatigue.

007.8 Other specified protozoal intestinal diseases
Amebiasis due to organisms other than Entamoeba histolytica

007.9 Unspecified protozoal intestinal disease
Flagellate diarrhea
Protozoal dysentery NOS

✓4th **008 Intestinal infections due to other organisms**
INCLUDES any condition classifiable to 009.0-009.3 with mention of the responsible organisms
EXCLUDES *food poisoning by these organisms (005.0-005.9)*

✓5th **008.0 Escherichia coli [E. coli]**

008.00 E. coli, unspecified
E. coli enteritis NOS

008.01 Enteropathogenic E. coli
DEF: *E. coli* causing inflammation of intestines.

008.02 Enterotoxigenic E. coli
DEF: A toxic reaction to *E. coli* of the intestinal mucosa, causing voluminous watery secretions.

008.03 Enteroinvasive E. coli
DEF: *E. coli* infection penetrating intestinal mucosa.

008.04 Enterohemorrhagic E. coli
DEF: *E. coli* infection penetrating the intestinal mucosa, producing microscopic ulceration and bleeding.

008.09 Other intestinal E. coli infections

008.1 Arizona group of paracolon bacilli

008.2 Aerobacter aerogenes
Enterobacter aeogenes

008.3 Proteus (mirabilis) (morganii)

✓5th **008.4 Other specified bacteria**

008.41 Staphylococcus
Staphylococcal enterocolitis

008.42 Pseudomonas

008.43 Campylobacter

008.44 Yersinia enterocolitica

008.45 Clostridium difficile
Pseudomembranous colitis
DEF: An overgrowth of a species of bacterium that is a part of the normal colon flora in human infants and sometimes in adults; produces a toxin that causes pseudomembranous enterocolitis.; typically is seen in patients undergoing antibiotic therapy.

008.46 Other anaerobes
Anaerobic enteritis NOS
Bacteroides (fragilis)
Gram-negative anaerobes

008.47 Other gram-negative bacteria
Gram-negative enteritis NOS
EXCLUDES *gram-negative anaerobes (008.46)*

008.49 Other

008.5 Bacterial enteritis, unspecified

✓5th **008.6 Enteritis due to specified virus**

008.61 Rotavirus

008.62 Adenovirus

008.63 Norwalk virus
Norwalk-like agent

008.64 Other small round viruses [SRVs]
Small round virus NOS

008.65 Calicivirus
DEF: Enteritis due to a subgroup of *Picornaviruses.*

008.66 Astrovirus

008.67 Enterovirus NEC
Coxsackie virus
Echovirus
EXCLUDES *poliovirus (045.0-045.9)*

008.69 Other viral enteritis
Torovirus

008.8 Other organism, not elsewhere classified
Viral:
enteritis NOS
gastroenteritis
EXCLUDES *influenza with involvement of gastrointestinal tract (487.8)*

✓4th **009 Ill-defined intestinal infections**
EXCLUDES *diarrheal disease or intestinal infection due to specified organism (001.0-008.8)*
diarrhea following gastrointestinal surgery (564.4)
intestinal malabsorption (579.0-579.9)
ischemic enteritis (557.0-557.9)
other noninfectious gastroenteritis and colitis (558.1-558.9)
regional enteritis (555.0-555.9)
ulcerative colitis (556)

009.0 Infectious colitis, enteritis, and gastroenteritis
Colitis, Enteritis, Gastroenteritis } septic
Dysentery:
NOS
catarrhal
hemorrhagic
DEF: Colitis: An inflammation of mucous membranes of the colon.
DEF: Enteritis: An inflammation of mucous membranes of the small intestine.
DEF: Gastroenteritis: An inflammation of mucous membranes of stomach and intestines.

009.1 Colitis, enteritis, and gastroenteritis of presumed infectious origin
EXCLUDES *colitis NOS (558.9)*
enteritis NOS (558.9)
gastroenteritis NOS (558.9)

009.2 Infectious diarrhea
Diarrhea:
dysenteric
epidemic
Infectious diarrheal disease NOS

009.3 Diarrhea of presumed infectious origin
EXCLUDES *diarrhea NOS (787.91)*

TUBERCULOSIS (010-018)

INCLUDES infection by Mycobacterium tuberculosis (human) (bovine)

EXCLUDES *congenital tuberculosis (771.2)*
late effects of tuberculosis (137.0-137.4)

The following fifth digit subclassification is for use with categories 010-018:

0 unspecified
1 bacteriological or histological examination not done
2 bacteriological or histological examination unknown (at present)
3 tubercle bacilli found (in sputum) by microscopy
4 tubercle bacilli not found (in sputum) by microscopy, but found by bacterial culture
5 tubercle bacilli not found by bacteriological examination, but tuberculosis confirmed histologically
6 tubercle bacilli not found by bacteriological or histological examination but tuberculosis confirmed by other methods [inoculation of animals]

DEF: An infection by *Mycobacterium tuberculosis* causing the formation of small, rounded nodules, called tubercles, that can disseminate throughout the body via lymph and blood vessels. Localized tuberculosis is most often seen in the lungs.

✓4th **010 Primary tuberculous infection**

DEF: Tuberculosis of the lungs occurring when the patient is first infected.

✓5th **010.0 Primary tuberculous infection**
[0-6]
EXCLUDES *nonspecific reaction to tuberculin skin test without active tuberculosis (795.5)*
positive PPD (795.5)
positive tuberculin skin test without active tuberculosis (795.5)

DEF: Hilar or paratracheal lymph node enlargement in pulmonary tuberculosis.

✓5th **010.1 Tuberculous pleurisy in primary progressive tuberculosis**
[0-6]

DEF: Inflammation and exudation in the lining of the tubercular lung.

✓5th **010.8 Other primary progressive tuberculosis**
[0-6]
EXCLUDES *tuberculous erythema nodosum (017.1)*

✓5th **010.9 Primary tuberculous infection, unspecified**
[0-6]

✓4th **011 Pulmonary tuberculosis**

Use additional code to identify any associated silicosis (502)

✓5th **011.0 Tuberculosis of lung, infiltrative**
[0-6]

✓5th **011.1 Tuberculosis of lung, nodular**
[0-6]

✓5th **011.2 Tuberculosis of lung with cavitation**
[0-6]

✓5th **011.3 Tuberculosis of bronchus**
[0-6]
EXCLUDES *isolated bronchial tuberculosis (012.2)*

✓5th **011.4 Tuberculous fibrosis of lung**
[0-6]

✓5th **011.5 Tuberculous bronchiectasis**
[0-6]

✓5th **011.6 Tuberculous pneumonia [any form]**
[0-6]
DEF: Inflammatory pulmonary reaction to tuberculous cells.

✓5th **011.7 Tuberculous pneumothorax**
[0-6]
DEF: Spontaneous rupture of damaged tuberculous pulmonary tissue.

✓5th **011.8 Other specified pulmonary tuberculosis**
[0-6]

✓5th **011.9 Pulmonary tuberculosis, unspecified**
[0-6]
Respiratory tuberculosis NOS
Tuberculosis of lung NOS

✓4th **012 Other respiratory tuberculosis**

EXCLUDES *respiratory tuberculosis, unspecified (011.9)*

✓5th **012.0 Tuberculous pleurisy**
[0-6]
Tuberculosis of pleura
Tuberculous empyema
Tuberculous hydrothorax
EXCLUDES *pleurisy with effusion without mention of cause (511.9)*
tuberculous pleurisy in primary progressive tuberculosis (010.1)

DEF: Inflammation and exudation in the lining of the tubercular lung.

✓5th **012.1 Tuberculosis of intrathoracic lymph nodes**
[0-6]
Tuberculosis of lymph nodes:
- hilar
- mediastinal
- tracheobronchial

Tuberculous tracheobronchial adenopathy
EXCLUDES *that specified as primary (010.0-010.9)*

✓5th **012.2 Isolated tracheal or bronchial tuberculosis**
[0-6]

✓5th **012.3 Tuberculous laryngitis**
[0-6]
Tuberculosis of glottis

✓5th **012.8 Other specified respiratory tuberculosis**
[0-6]
Tuberculosis of:
- mediastinum
- nasopharynx
- nose (septum)
- sinus [any nasal]

✓4th **013 Tuberculosis of meninges and central nervous system**

✓5th **013.0 Tuberculous meningitis**
[0-6]
Tuberculosis of meninges (cerebral) (spinal)
Tuberculous:
- leptomeningitis
- meningoencephalitis

EXCLUDES *tuberculoma of meninges (013.1)*

✓5th **013.1 Tuberculoma of meninges**
[0-6]

✓5th **013.2 Tuberculoma of brain**
[0-6]
Tuberculosis of brain (current disease)

✓5th **013.3 Tuberculous abscess of brain**
[0-6]

✓5th **013.4 Tuberculoma of spinal cord**
[0-6]

✓5th **013.5 Tuberculous abscess of spinal cord**
[0-6]

✓5th **013.6 Tuberculous encephalitis or myelitis**
[0-6]

✓5th **013.8 Other specified tuberculosis of central nervous system**
[0-6]

✓5th **013.9 Unspecified tuberculosis of central nervous system**
[0-6]
Tuberculosis of central nervous system NOS

✓4th **014 Tuberculosis of intestines, peritoneum, and mesenteric glands**

✓5th **014.0 Tuberculous peritonitis**
[0-6]
Tuberculous ascites

DEF: Tuberculous inflammation of the membrane lining the abdomen.

✓5th **014.8 Other**
[0-6]
Tuberculosis (of):
- anus
- intestine (large) (small)
- mesenteric glands
- rectum
- retroperitoneal (lymph nodes)

Tuberculous enteritis

✓4th 015 Tuberculosis of bones and joints

Use additional code to identify manifestation, as:
tuberculous:
arthropathy (711.4)
necrosis of bone (730.8)
osteitis (730.8)
osteomyelitis (730.8)
synovitis (727.01)
tenosynovitis (727.01)

✓5th 015.0 Vertebral column
[0-6]
Pott's disease
Use additional code to identify manifestation, as:
curvature of spine [Pott's] (737.4)
kyphosis (737.4)
spondylitis (720.81)

✓5th 015.1 Hip
[0-6]

✓5th 015.2 Knee
[0-6]

✓5th 015.5 Limb bones
[0-6]
Tuberculous dactylitis

✓5th 015.6 Mastoid
[0-6]
Tuberculous mastoiditis

✓5th 015.7 Other specified bone
[0-6]

✓5th 015.8 Other specified joint
[0-6]

✓5th 015.9 Tuberculosis of unspecified bones and joints
[0-6]

✓4th 016 Tuberculosis of genitourinary system

✓5th 016.0 Kidney
[0-6]
Renal tuberculosis
Use additional code to identify manifestation, as:
tuberculous:
nephropathy (583.81)
pyelitis (590.81)
pyelonephritis (590.81)

✓5th 016.1 Bladder
[0-6]

✓5th 016.2 Ureter
[0-6]

✓5th 016.3 Other urinary organs
[0-6]

✓5th 016.4 Epididymis
[0-6]

✓5th 016.5 Other male genital organs
[0-6]
Use additional code to identify manifestation, as:
tuberculosis of:
prostate (601.4)
seminal vesicle (608.81)
testis (608.81)

✓5th 016.6 Tuberculous oophoritis and salpingitis
[0-6]

✓5th 016.7 Other female genital organs
[0-6]
Tuberculous:
cervicitis
endometritis

✓5th 016.9 Genitourinary tuberculosis, unspecified
[0-6]

✓4th 017 Tuberculosis of other organs

✓5th 017.0 Skin and subcutaneous cellular tissue
[0-6]
Lupus:
exedens
vulgaris
Scrofuloderma
Tuberculosis:
colliquativa
cutis
lichenoides
papulonecrotica
verrucosa cutis

EXCLUDES *lupus erythematosus (695.4)*
disseminated (710.0)
lupus NOS (710.0)
nonspecific reaction to tuberculin skin test without active tuberculosis (795.5)
positive PPD (795.5)
positive tuberculin skin test without active tuberculosis (795.5)

✓5th 017.1 Erythema nodosum with hypersensitivity reaction in tuberculosis
[0-6]
Bazin's disease
Erythema:
induratum
nodosum, tuberculous
Tuberculosis indurativa

EXCLUDES *erythema nodosum NOS (695.2)*

DEF: Tender, inflammatory, bilateral nodules appearing on the shins and thought to be an allergic reaction to tuberculotoxin.

✓5th 017.2 Peripheral lymph nodes
[0-6]
Scrofula
Scrofulous abscess
Tuberculous adenitis

EXCLUDES *tuberculosis of lymph nodes:*
bronchial and mediastinal (012.1)
mesenteric and retroperitoneal (014.8)
tuberculous tracheobronchial adenopathy (012.1)

DEF: Scrofula: Old name for tuberculous cervical lymphadenitis.

✓5th 017.3 Eye
[0-6]
Use additional code to identify manifestation, as:
tuberculous:
chorioretinitis, disseminated (363.13)
episcleritis (379.09)
interstitial keratitis (370.59)
iridocyclitis, chronic (364.11)
keratoconjunctivitis (phlyctenular) (370.31)

✓5th 017.4 Ear
[0-6]
Tuberculosis of ear
Tuberculous otitis media

EXCLUDES *tuberculous mastoiditis (015.6)*

✓5th 017.5 Thyroid gland
[0-6]

✓5th 017.6 Adrenal glands
[0-6]
Addison's disease, tuberculous

✓5th 017.7 Spleen
[0-6]

✓5th 017.8 Esophagus
[0-6]

✓5th 017.9 Other specified organs
[0-6]
Use additional code to identify manifestation, as:
tuberculosis of:
endocardium [any valve] (424.91)
myocardium (422.0)
pericardium (420.0)

✓4th 018 Miliary tuberculosis

INCLUDES tuberculosis:
disseminated
generalized
miliary, whether of a single specified site, multiple sites, or unspecified site
polyserositis

DEF: A form of tuberculosis caused by caseous material carried through the bloodstream planting seedlike tubercles in various body organs.

✓5th 018.0 Acute miliary tuberculosis
[0-6]

✓5th 018.8 Other specified miliary tuberculosis
[0-6]

✓5th **018.9 Miliary tuberculosis, unspecified**
[0-6]

ZOONOTIC BACTERIAL DISEASES (020-027)

✓4th **020 Plague**
INCLUDES infection by Yersinia [Pasteurella] pestis

020.0 Bubonic
DEF: Most common acute and severe form of plague characterized by lymphadenopathy (buboes), chills, fever and headache.

020.1 Cellulocutaneous
DEF: Plague characterized by inflammation and necrosis of skin.

020.2 Septicemic
DEF: Plague characterized by massive infection in the bloodstream.

020.3 Primary pneumonic
DEF: Plague characterized by massive pulmonary infection.

020.4 Secondary pneumonic
DEF: Lung infection as a secondary complication of plague.

020.5 Pneumonic, unspecified

020.8 Other specified types of plague
Abortive plague
Ambulatory plague
Pestis minor

020.9 Plague, unspecified

✓4th **021 Tularemia**
INCLUDES deerfly fever
infection by Francisella [Pasteurella] tularensis
rabbit fever

DEF: A febrile disease transmitted by the bites of deer flies, fleas and ticks, by inhalations of aerosolized *F. tularensis* or by ingestion of contaminated food or water; patients quickly develop fever, chills, weakness, headache, backache and malaise.

021.0 Ulceroglandular tularemia
DEF: Lesions occur at the site *Francisella tularensis* organism enters body, usually the fingers or hands.

021.1 Enteric tularemia
Tularemia:
cryptogenic
intestinal
typhoidal

021.2 Pulmonary tularemia
Bronchopneumonic tularemia

021.3 Oculoglandular tularemia
DEF: Painful conjunctival infection by *Francisella tularensis* organism with possible corneal, preauricular lymph, or lacrimal involvement.

021.8 Other specified tularemia
Tularemia:
generalized or disseminated
glandular

021.9 Unspecified tularemia

✓4th **022 Anthrax**
DEF: An infectious bacterial disease usually transmitted by contact with infected animals or their discharges or products; it is classified by primary routes of inoculation as cutaneous, gastrointestinal and by inhalation.

022.0 Cutaneous anthrax
Malignant pustule

022.1 Pulmonary anthrax
Respiratory anthrax
Wool-sorters' disease

022.2 Gastrointestinal anthrax

022.3 Anthrax septicemia

022.8 Other specified manifestations of anthrax

022.9 Anthrax, unspecified

✓4th **023 Brucellosis**
INCLUDES fever:
Malta
Mediterranean
undulant

DEF: An infectious disease caused by gram-negative, aerobic coccobacilli organisms; it is transmitted to humans through contact with infected tissue or dairy products; fever, sweating, weakness and aching are symptoms.

023.0 Brucella melitensis
DEF: Infection from direct or indirect contact with infected sheep or goats.

023.1 Brucella abortus
DEF: Infection from direct or indirect contact with infected cattle.

023.2 Brucella suis
DEF: Infection from direct or indirect contact with infected swine.

023.3 Brucella canis
DEF: Infection from direct or indirect contact with infected dogs.

023.8 Other brucellosis
Infection by more than one organism

023.9 Brucellosis, unspecified

024 Glanders
Infection by:
Actinobacillus mallei
Farcy
Malleomyces mallei
Malleus
Pseudomonas mallei

DEF: Equine infection causing mucosal inflammation and skin ulcers in humans.

025 Melioidosis
Infection by:
Malleomyces pseudomallei
Pseudoglanders
Pseudomonas pseudomallei
Whitmore's bacillus

DEF: Rare infection caused by *Pseudomonas pseudomallei;* clinical symptoms range from localized infection to fatal septicemia.

✓4th **026 Rat-bite fever**

026.0 Spirillary fever
Rat-bite fever due to Spirillum minor [S. minus]
Sodoku

026.1 Streptobacillary fever
Epidemic arthritic erythema
Haverhill fever
Rat-bite fever due to Streptobacillus moniliformis

026.9 Unspecified rat-bite fever

✓4th **027 Other zoonotic bacterial diseases**

027.0 Listeriosis
Infection } by Listeria monocytogenes
Septicemia }

Use additional code to identify manifestation, as meningitis (320.7)

EXCLUDES *congenital listeriosis (771.2)*

027.1 Erysipelothrix infection
Erysipeloid (of Rosenbach)
Infection } by Erysipelothrix insidiosa [E. rhusiopathiae]
Septicemia }

DEF: Usually associated with handling of fish, meat, or poultry; symptoms range from localized inflammation to septicemia.

027.2 Pasteurellosis
Pasteurella pseudotuberculosis infection
Mesenteric adenitis } by Pasteurella multocida [P. septica]
Septic infection (cat bite) (dog bite) }

EXCLUDES *infection by:*
Francisella [Pasteurella] tularensis (021.0-021.9)
Yersinia [Pasteurella] pestis (020.0-020.9)

DEF: Swelling, abscesses, or septicemia from *Pasteurella multocida,* commonly transmitted to humans by a dog or cat scratch.

027.8 Other specified zoonotic bacterial diseases

027.9 Unspecified zoonotic bacterial disease

OTHER BACTERIAL DISEASES (030-041)

EXCLUDES *bacterial venereal diseases (098.0-099.9)*
bartonellosis (088.0)

✓4th **030 Leprosy**

INCLUDES Hansen's disease
infection by Mycobacterium leprae

030.0 Lepromatous [type L]
Lepromatous leprosy (macular) (diffuse) (infiltrated) (nodular) (neuritic)
DEF: Infectious, disseminated leprosy bacilli with lesions and deformities.

030.1 Tuberculoid [type T]
Tuberculoid leprosy (macular) (maculoanesthetic) (major) (minor) (neuritic)
DEF: Relatively benign, self-limiting leprosy with neuralgia and scales.

030.2 Indeterminate [group I]
Indeterminate [uncharacteristic] leprosy (macular) (neuritic)
DEF: Uncharacteristic leprosy, frequently an early manifestation.

030.3 Borderline [group B]
Borderline or dimorphous leprosy (infiltrated) (neuritic)
DEF: Transitional form of leprosy, neither lepromatous nor tuberculoid.

030.8 Other specified leprosy

030.9 Leprosy, unspecified

✓4th **031 Diseases due to other mycobacteria**

031.0 Pulmonary
Battey disease
Infection by Mycobacterium:
avium
intracellulare [Battey bacillus]
kansasii

031.1 Cutaneous
Buruli ulcer
Infection by Mycobacterium:
marinum [M. balnei]
ulcerans

031.2 Disseminated
Disseminated mycobacterium avium-intracellulare complex (DMAC)
Mycobacterium avium-intracellulare complex (MAC) bacteremia
DEF: Disseminated mycobacterium avium-intracellulare complex (DMAC): A serious systemic form of MAC commonly observed in patients in the late course of AIDS.
DEF: Mycobacterium avium-intracellulare complex (MAC) bacterium: Human pulmonary disease, lymphadenitis in children and systemic disease in immunocompromised individuals caused by a slow growing, gram-positive, aerobic organism.

031.8 Other specified mycobacterial diseases

031.9 Unspecified diseases due to mycobacteria
Atypical mycobacterium infection NOS

✓4th **032 Diphtheria**

INCLUDES infection by Corynebacterium diphtheriae

032.0 Faucial diphtheria
Membranous angina, diphtheritic
DEF: Diphtheria of the throat.

032.1 Nasopharyngeal diphtheria

032.2 Anterior nasal diphtheria

032.3 Laryngeal diphtheria
Laryngotracheitis, diphtheritic

✓5th **032.8 Other specified diphtheria**

032.81 Conjunctival diphtheria
Pseudomembranous diphtheritic conjunctivitis

032.82 Diphtheritic myocarditis

032.83 Diphtheritic peritonitis

032.84 Diphtheritic cystitis

032.85 Cutaneous diphtheria

032.89 Other

032.9 Diphtheria, unspecified

✓4th **033 Whooping cough**

INCLUDES pertussis

Use additional code to identify any associated pneumonia (484.3)

DEF: An acute, highly contagious respiratory tract infection caused by *Bordetella pertussis* and *B. bronchiseptica;* characteristic paroxysmal cough.

033.0 Bordetella pertussis [B. pertussis]

033.1 Bordetella parapertussis [B. parapertussis]

033.8 Whooping cough due to other specified organism
Bordetella bronchiseptica [B. bronchiseptica]

033.9 Whooping cough, unspecified organism

✓4th **034 Streptococcal sore throat and scarlet fever**

034.0 Streptococcal sore throat
Septic:
angina
sore throat
Streptococcal:
angina
aryngitis
pharyngitis
tonsillitis

034.1 Scarlet fever
Scarlatina
EXCLUDES *parascarlatina (057.8)*
DEF: Streptococcal infection and fever with red rash spreading from trunk.

035 Erysipelas

EXCLUDES *postpartum or puerperal erysipelas (670)*

DEF: An acute superficial cellulitis involving the dermal lymphatics; it is often caused by group A streptococci.

✓4th **036 Meningococcal infection**

036.0 Meningococcal meningitis
Cerebrospinal fever (meningococcal)
Meningitis:
cerebrospinal
epidemic

036.1 Meningococcal encephalitis

036.2 Meningococcemia
Meningococcal septicemia

036.3 Waterhouse-Friderichsen syndrome, meningococcal
Meningococcal hemorrhagic adrenalitis
Meningococcic adrenal syndrome
Waterhouse-Friderichsen syndrome NOS

✓5th **036.4 Meningococcal carditis**

036.40 Meningococcal carditis, unspecified

036.41 Meningococcal pericarditis
DEF: Meningococcal infection of the outer membrane of the heart.

036.42 Meningococcal endocarditis
DEF: Meningococcal infection of the membranes lining the cavities of the heart.

036.43 Meningococcal myocarditis
DEF: Meningococcal infection of the muscle of the heart.

✓5th **036.8 Other specified meningococcal infections**

036.81 Meningococcal optic neuritis

036.82 Meningococcal arthropathy

036.89 Other

036.9 Meningococcal infection, unspecified
Meningococcal infection NOS

037 Tetanus

EXCLUDES *tetanus:*
complicating:
abortion (634-638 with .0, 639.0)
ectopic or molar pregnancy (639.0)
neonatorum (771.3)
puerperal (670)

DEF: An acute, often fatal, infectious disease caused by the anaerobic, spore-forming bacillus *Clostridium tetani;* the bacillus most often enters the body through a contaminated wound, burns, surgical wounds, or cutaneous ulcers. Symptoms include lockjaw, spasms, seizures, and paralysis.

✓4th **038 Septicemia**

Use additional code for systemic inflammatory response syndrome (SIRS) (995.91-995.92)

EXCLUDES *bacteremia (790.7)*
during labor (659.3)
following ectopic or molar pregnancy (639.0)
following infusion, injection, transfusion, or vaccination (999.3)
postpartum, puerperal (670)
septicemia (sepsis) of newborn (771.81)
that complicating abortion (634-638 with .0, 639.0)

DEF: A systemic disease associated with the presence and persistence of pathogenic microorganisms or their toxins in the blood.

038.0 Streptococcal septicemia

✓5th **038.1 Staphylococcal septicemia**

038.10 Staphylococcal septicemia, unspecified

038.11 Methicillin susceptible Staphylococcus aureus septicemia
MSSA septicemia
Staphylococcus aureus septicemia NOS

038.12 Methicillin resistant Staphylococcus aureus septicemia

038.2 Pneumococcal septicemia [Streptococcus pneumoniae septicemia]

038.3 Septicemia due to anaerobes
Septicemia due to bacteroides

EXCLUDES *gas gangrene (040.0)*
that due to anaerobic streptococci (038.0)

✓5th **038.4 Septicemia due to other gram-negative organisms**

DEF: Infection of blood by microorganisms categorized as gram-negative by Gram's method of staining for identification of bacteria.

038.40 Gram-negative organism, unspecified
Gram-negative septicemia NOS

038.41 Hemophilus influenzae [H. influenzae]

038.42 Escherichia coli [E. coli]

038.43 Pseudomonas

038.44 Serratia

038.49 Other

038.8 Other specified septicemias

EXCLUDES *septicemia (due to):*
anthrax (022.3)
gonococcal (098.89)
herpetic (054.5)
meningococcal (036.2)
septicemic plague (020.2)

038.9 Unspecified septicemia
Septicemia NOS

EXCLUDES *bacteremia NOS (790.7)*

✓4th **039 Actinomycotic infections**

INCLUDES actinomycotic mycetoma
infection by Actinomycetales, such as species of Actinomyces, Actinomadura, Nocardia, Streptomyces
maduromycosis (actinomycotic)
schizomycetoma (actinomycotic)

DEF: Inflammatory lesions and abscesses at site of infection by *Actinomyces israelii.*

039.0 Cutaneous
Erythrasma
Trichomycosis axillaris

039.1 Pulmonary
Thoracic actinomycosis

039.2 Abdominal

039.3 Cervicofacial

039.4 Madura foot

EXCLUDES *madura foot due to mycotic infection (117.4)*

039.8 Of other specified sites

039.9 Of unspecified site
Actinomycosis NOS
Maduromycosis NOS
Nocardiosis NOS

✓4th **040 Other bacterial diseases**

EXCLUDES *bacteremia NOS (790.7)*
bacterial infection NOS (041.9)

040.0 Gas gangrene
Gas bacillus infection or gangrene
Infection by Clostridium:
histolyticum
oedematiens
perfringens [welchii]
septicum
sordellii
Malignant edema
Myonecrosis, clostridial
Myositis, clostridial

040.1 Rhinoscleroma

DEF: Growths on the nose and nasopharynx caused by *Klebsiella rhinoscleromatis.*

040.2 Whipple's disease
Intestinal lipodystrophy

040.3 Necrobacillosis

DEF: Infection with *Fusobacterium necrophorum* causing abscess or necrosis.

✓5th **040.4 Other specified botulism**
Non-foodborne intoxication due to toxins of Clostridium botulinum [C. botulinum]

EXCLUDES *botulism NOS (005.1)*
food poisoning due to toxins of Clostridium botulinum (005.1)

040.41 Infant botulism

DEF: Colonization of Clostridium botulinum spores in the large intestine; poisoning due to release of neurotoxins results in constipation; may progress to neuromuscular paralysis; affects infants of less than six months of age.

040.42 Wound botulism
Non-foodborne botulism NOS
Use additional code to identify complicated open wound

✓5th **040.8 Other specified bacterial diseases**

040.81 Tropical pyomyositis

040.82 Toxic shock syndrome
Use additional code to identify the organism

DEF: Syndrome caused by staphylococcal exotoxin that may rapidly progress to severe and intractable shock; symptoms include characteristic sunburn-like rash with peeling of skin on palms and soles, sudden onset high fever, vomiting, diarrhea, myalgia, and hypotension.

040.89 Other

✓4th **041 Bacterial infection in conditions classified elsewhere and of unspecified site**

Note: This category is provided to be used as an additional code to identify the bacterial agent in diseases classified elsewhere. This category will also be used to classify bacterial infections of unspecified nature or site.

EXCLUDES *septicemia (038.0-038.9)*

✓5th **041.0 Streptococcus**

041.00 Streptococcus, unspecified

041.01 Group A

041.02 Group B

041.03 **Group C**

041.04 **Group D [Enterococcus]**

041.05 **Group G**

041.09 **Other Streptococcus**

✓5th 041.1 **Staphylococcus**

041.10 **Staphylococcus, unspecified**

041.11 **Methicillin susceptible Staphylococcus aureus**
MSSA
Staphylococcus aureus NOS

041.12 **Methicillin resistant Staphylococcus aureus**
Methicillin-resistant staphylococcus aureus (MRSA)

041.19 **Other Staphylococcus**

041.2 **Pneumococcus**

041.3 **Friedländer's bacillus**
Infection by Klebsiella pneumoniae

041.4 **Escherichia coli [E. coli]**

041.5 **Hemophilus influenzae [H. influenzae]**

041.6 **Proteus (mirabilis) (morganii)**

041.7 **Pseudomonas**

✓5th 041.8 **Other specified bacterial infections**

041.81 **Mycoplasma**
Eaton's agent
Pleuropneumonia-like organisms [PPLO]

041.82 **Bacteroides fragilis**
DEF: Anaerobic gram-negative bacilli of the gastrointestinal tract; frequently implicated in intra-abdominal infection; commonly resistant to antibiotics.

041.83 **Clostridium perfringens**

041.84 **Other anaerobes**
Gram-negative anaerobes
EXCLUDES *Helicobacter pylori (041.86)*

041.85 **Other gram-negative organisms**
Aerobacter aerogenes
Gram-negative bacteria NOS
Mima polymorpha
Serratia
EXCLUDES *gram-negative anaerobes (041.84)*

041.86 **Helicobacter pylori [H. pylori]**

041.89 **Other specified bacteria**

041.9 **Bacterial infection, unspecified**

HUMAN IMMUNODEFICIENCY VIRUS (HIV) INFECTION (042)

042 **Human immunodeficiency virus [HIV] disease**
Acquired immune deficiency syndrome
Acquired immunodeficiency syndrome
AIDS
AIDS-like syndrome
AIDS-related complex
ARC
HIV infection, symptomatic

Use additional code(s) to identify all manifestations of HIV

Use additional code to identify HIV-2 infection (079.53)

EXCLUDES *asymptomatic HIV infection status (V08)*
exposure to HIV virus (V01.79)
nonspecific serologic evidence of HIV (795.71)

POLIOMYELITIS AND OTHER NON-ARTHROPOD-BORNE VIRAL DISEASES AND PRION DISEASES OF CENTRAL NERVOUS SYSTEM (045-049)

✓4th 045 **Acute poliomyelitis**

EXCLUDES *late effects of acute poliomyelitis (138)*

The following fifth-digit subclassification is for use with category 045:
0 poliovirus, unspecified type
1 poliovirus type I
2 poliovirus type II
3 poliovirus type III

✓5th 045.0 **Acute paralytic poliomyelitis specified as bulbar**
[0-3]
Infantile paralysis (acute) } specified as bulbar
Poliomyelitis (acute) (anterior) } specified as bulbar
Polioencephalitis (acute) (bulbar)
Polioencephalomyelitis (acute) (anterior) (bulbar)
DEF: Acute paralytic infection occurring where the brain merges with the spinal cord; affecting breathing, swallowing, and heart rate.

✓5th 045.1 **Acute poliomyelitis with other paralysis**
[0-3]
Paralysis:
acute atrophic, spinal
infantile, paralytic
Poliomyelitis (acute) anterior epidemic } with paralysis except bulbar
DEF: Paralytic infection affecting peripheral or spinal nerves.

✓5th 045.2 **Acute nonparalytic poliomyelitis**
[0-3]
Poliomyelitis (acute) anterior epidemic } specified as nonparalytic
DEF: Nonparalytic infection causing pain, stiffness, and paresthesias.

✓5th 045.9 **Acute poliomyelitis, unspecified**
[0-3]
infantile paralysis
Poliomyelitis (acute) anterior epidemic } unspecified whether paralytic or nonparalytic

✓4th 046 **Slow virus infections and prion diseases of central nervous system**

046.0 **Kuru**
DEF: A chronic, progressive, fatal nervous system disorder; clinical symptoms include cerebellar ataxia, trembling, spasticity and progressive dementia.

✓5th 046.1 **Jakob-Creutzfeldt disease**

046.11 **Variant Creutzfeldt-Jakob disease**
vCJD

046.19 **Other and unspecified Creutzfeldt-Jakob disease**
CJD
Familial Creutzfeldt-Jakob disease
Iatrogenic Creutzfeldt-Jakob disease
Jakob-Creutzfeldt disease, unspecified
Sporadic Creutzfeldt-Jakob disease
Subacute spongiform encephalopathy
EXCLUDES *variant Creutzfeldt-Jakob disease (vCJD) (046.11)*
DEF: Communicable, progressive spongiform encephalopathy thought to be caused by an infectious particle known as a "prion" (proteinaceous infection particle). This is a progressive, fatal disease manifested principally by mental deterioration.

046.2 **Subacute sclerosing panencephalitis**
Dawson's inclusion body encephalitis
Van Bogaert's sclerosing leukoencephalitis
DEF: Progressive viral infection causing cerebral dysfunction, blindness, dementia, and death (SSPE).

046.3 **Progressive multifocal leukoencephalopathy**
Multifocal leukoencephalopathy NOS
DEF: Infection affecting cerebral cortex in patients with weakened immune systems.

✓5th **046.7 Other specified prion diseases of central nervous system**

EXCLUDES *Creutzfeldt-Jakob disease (046.11-046.19)*
Jakob-Creutzfeldt disease (046.11-046.19)
kuru (046.0)
variant Creutzfeldt-Jakob disease (vCJD) (046.11)

046.71 Gerstmann-Sträussler-Scheinker syndrome
GSS syndrome

046.72 Fatal familial insomnia
FFI

046.79 Other and unspecified prion disease of central nervous system

046.8 Other specified slow virus infection of central nervous system

046.9 Unspecified slow virus infection of central nervous system

✓4th **047 Meningitis due to enterovirus**

INCLUDES meningitis:
abacterial
aseptic
viral

EXCLUDES *meningitis due to:*
adenovirus (049.1)
arthropod-borne virus (060.0-066.9)
leptospira (100.81)
virus of:
herpes simplex (054.72)
herpes zoster (053.0)
lymphocytic choriomeningitis (049.0)
mumps (072.1)
poliomyelitis (045.0-045.9)
any other infection specifically classified elsewhere

047.0 Coxsackie virus

047.1 ECHO virus
Meningo-eruptive syndrome

047.8 Other specified viral meningitis

047.9 Unspecified viral meningitis
Viral meningitis NOS

048 Other enterovirus diseases of central nervous system
Boston exanthem

✓4th **049 Other non-arthropod-borne viral diseases of central nervous system**

EXCLUDES *late effects of viral encephalitis (139.0)*

049.0 Lymphocytic choriomeningitis
Lymphocytic:
meningitis (serous) (benign)
meningoencephalitis (serous) (benign)

049.1 Meningitis due to adenovirus
DEF: Inflammation of lining of brain caused by Arenaviruses and usually occurring in adults in fall and winter months.

049.8 Other specified non-arthropod-borne viral diseases of central nervous system
Encephalitis:
acute:
inclusion body
necrotizing
epidemic
lethargica
Rio Bravo
von Economo's disease

EXCLUDES *human herpesvirus 6 encephalitis (058.21)*
other human herpesvirus encephalitis (058.29)

049.9 Unspecified non-arthropod-borne viral diseases of central nervous system
Viral encephalitis NOS

VIRAL DISEASES ACCOMPANIED BY EXANTHEM (050-059)

EXCLUDES *arthropod-borne viral diseases (060.0-066.9)*
Boston exanthem (048)

✓4th **050 Smallpox**

050.0 Variola major
Hemorrhagic (pustular) smallpox
Malignant smallpox
Purpura variolosa
DEF: Form of smallpox known for its high mortality; exists only in laboratories.

050.1 Alastrim
Variola minor
DEF: Mild form of smallpox known for its low mortality rate.

050.2 Modified smallpox
Varioloid
DEF: Mild form occurring in patients with history of infection or vaccination.

050.9 Smallpox, unspecified

✓4th **051 Cowpox and paravaccinia**

✓5th **051.0 Cowpox and vaccinia not from vaccination**

051.01 Cowpox
DEF: A disease contracted by milking infected cows; vesicles usually appear on the fingers, may spread to hands and adjacent areas and usually disappear without scarring; other associated features of the disease may include local edema, lymphangitis and regional lymphadenitis with or without fever.

051.02 Vaccinia not from vaccination

EXCLUDES *vaccinia (generalized) (from vaccination) (999.0)*

051.1 Pseudocowpox
Milkers' node
DEF: Hand lesions and mild fever in dairy workers caused by exposure to paravaccinia.

051.2 Contagious pustular dermatitis
Ecthyma contagiosum
Orf
DEF: Skin eruptions caused by exposure to poxvirus-infected sheep or goats.

051.9 Paravaccinia, unspecified

✓4th **052 Chickenpox**
DEF: Contagious infection by *Varicella-zoster* virus causing rash with pustules and fever.

052.0 Postvaricella encephalitis
Postchickenpox encephalitis

052.1 Varicella (hemorrhagic) pneumonitis

052.2 Postvaricella myelitis
Postchickenpox myelitis

052.7 With other specified complications

052.8 With unspecified complication

052.9 Varicella without mention of complication
Chickenpox NOS
Varicella NOS

✓4th **053 Herpes zoster**

INCLUDES shingles
zona

DEF: Self-limiting infection by *varicella-zoster* virus causing unilateral eruptions and neuralgia along affected nerves.

053.0 With meningitis
DEF: *Varicella-zoster* virus infection causing inflammation of the lining of the brain and/or spinal cord.

✓5th **053.1 With other nervous system complications**

053.10 With unspecified nervous system complication

053.11 Geniculate herpes zoster
Herpetic geniculate ganglionitis
DEF: Unilateral eruptions and neuralgia along the facial nerve geniculum affecting face and outer and middle ear.

053.12 Postherpetic trigeminal neuralgia
DEF: Severe oral or nasal pain following a herpes zoster infection.

053.13 Postherpetic polyneuropathy
DEF: Multiple areas of pain following a herpes zoster infection.

053.14 Herpes zoster myelitis

053.19 Other

✓5th **053.2 With ophthalmic complications**

053.20 Herpes zoster dermatitis of eyelid
Herpes zoster ophthalmicus

053.21 Herpes zoster keratoconjunctivitis

053.22 Herpes zoster iridocyclitis

053.29 Other

✓5th **053.7 With other specified complications**

053.71 Otitis externa due to herpes zoster

053.79 Other

053.8 With unspecified complication

053.9 Herpes zoster without mention of complication
Herpes zoster NOS

✓4th **054 Herpes simplex**

EXCLUDES *congenital herpes simplex (771.2)*

054.0 Eczema herpeticum
Kaposi's varicelliform eruption
DEF: Herpes simplex virus invading site of preexisting skin inflammation.

✓5th **054.1 Genital herpes**

054.10 Genital herpes, unspecified
Herpes progenitalis

054.11 Herpetic vulvovaginitis

054.12 Herpetic ulceration of vulva

054.13 Herpetic infection of penis

054.19 Other

054.2 Herpetic gingivostomatitis

054.3 Herpetic meningoencephalitis
Herpes encephalitis
Simian B disease
EXCLUDES *human herpesvirus 6 encephalitis (058.21)*
other human herpesvirus encephalitis (058.29)
DEF: Inflammation of the brain and its lining, caused by infection of herpes simplex 1 in adults and simplex 2 in newborns.

✓5th **054.4 With ophthalmic complications**

054.40 With unspecified ophthalmic complication

054.41 Herpes simplex dermatitis of eyelid

054.42 Dendritic keratitis

054.43 Herpes simplex disciform keratitis

054.44 Herpes simplex iridocyclitis

054.49 Other

054.5 Herpetic septicemia

054.6 Herpetic whitlo
Herpetic felon
DEF: A primary infection of the terminal segment of a finger by herpes simplex; intense itching and pain start the disease, vesicles form, and tissue ultimately is destroyed.

✓5th **054.7 With other specified complications**

054.71 Visceral herpes simplex

054.72 Herpes simplex meningitis

054.73 Herpes simplex otitis externa

054.74 Herpes simplex myelitis

054.79 Other

054.8 With unspecified complication

054.9 Herpes simplex without mention of complication

✓4th **055 Measles**

INCLUDES morbilli
rubeola

055.0 Postmeasles encephalitis

055.1 Postmeasles pneumonia

055.2 Postmeasles otitis media

✓5th **055.7 With other specified complications**

055.71 Measles keratoconjunctivitis
Measles keratitis

055.79 Other

055.8 With unspecified complication

055.9 Measles without mention of complication

✓4th **056 Rubella**

INCLUDES German measles
EXCLUDES *congenital rubella (771.0)*
DEF: Acute but usually benign togavirus infection causing fever, sore throat, and rash; associated with complications to fetus as a result of maternal infection.

✓5th **056.0 With neurological complications**

056.00 With unspecified neurological complication

056.01 Encephalomyelitis due to rubella
Encephalitis } due to rubella
Meningoencephalitis } due to rubella

056.09 Other

✓5th **056.7 With other specified complications**

056.71 Arthritis due to rubella

056.79 Other

056.8 With unspecified complications

056.9 Rubella without mention of complication

✓4th **057 Other viral exanthemata**
DEF: Skin eruptions or rashes and fever caused by viruses, including poxviruses.

057.0 Erythema infectiosum [fifth disease]
DEF: A moderately contagious, benign, epidemic disease, usually seen in children, and of probable viral etiology; a red macular rash appears on the face and may spread to the limbs and trunk.

057.8 Other specified viral exanthemata
Dukes (-Filatow) disease
Fourth disease
Parascarlatina
Pseudoscarlatina
EXCLUDES *exanthema subitum [sixth disease] (058.10-058.12)*
roseola infantum (058.10-058.12)

057.9 Viral exanthem, unspecified

✓4th **058 Other human herpesvirus**

EXCLUDES *congenital herpes (771.2)*
cytomegalovirus (078.5)
Epstein-Barr virus (075)
herpes NOS (054.0-054.9)
herpes simplex (054.0-054.9)
herpes zoster (053.0-053.9)
human herpesvirus NOS (054.0-054.9)
human herpesvirus 1 (054.0-054.9)
human herpesvirus 2 (054.0-054.9)
human herpesvirus 3 (052.0-053.9)
human herpesvirus 4 (075)
human herpesvirus 5 (078.5)
varicella (052.0-052.9)
varicella-zoster virus (052.0-053.9)

✓5th **058.1 Roseola infantum**
Exanthema subitum [sixth disease]

058.10 Roseola infantum, unspecified
Exanthema subitum [sixth disease], unspecified

058.11 **Roseola infantum due to human herpesvirus 6**
Exanthema subitum [sixth disease] due to human herpesvirus 6

058.12 **Roseola infantum due to human herpesvirus 7**
Exanthema subitum [sixth disease] due to human herpesvirus 7

✓5th 058.2 **Other human herpesvirus encephalitis**
EXCLUDES *herpes encephalitis NOS (054.3)*
herpes simplex encephalitis (054.3)
human herpesvirus encephalitis NOS (054.3)
simian B herpesvirus encephalitis (054.3)

058.21 **Human herpesvirus 6 encephalitis**

058.29 **Other human herpesvirus encephalitis**
Human herpesvirus 7 encephalitis

✓5th 058.8 **Other human herpesvirus infections**

058.81 **Human herpesvirus 6 infection**

058.82 **Human herpesvirus 7 infection**

058.89 **Other human herpesvirus infection**
Human herpesvirus 8 infection
Kaposi's sarcoma-associated herpesvirus infection

✓4th 059 **Other poxvirus infections**
EXCLUDES *contagious pustular dermatitis (051.2)*
cowpox (051.01)
ecthyma contagiosum (051.2)
milker's nodule (051.1)
orf (051.2)
paravaccinia NOS (051.9)
pseudocowpox (051.1)
smallpox (050.0-050.9)
vaccinia (generalized) (from vaccination) (999.0)
vaccinia not from vaccination (051.02)

✓5th 059.0 **Other orthopoxvirus infections**

059.00 **Orthopoxvirus infection, unspecified**

059.01 **Monkeypox**

059.09 **Other orthopoxvirus infection**

✓5th 059.1 **Other parapoxvirus infections**

059.10 **Parapoxvirus infection, unspecified**

059.11 **Bovine stomatitis**

059.12 **Sealpox**

059.19 **Other parapoxvirus infections**

✓5th 059.2 **Yatapoxvirus infections**

059.20 **Yatapoxvirus infection, unspecified**

059.21 **Tanapox**

059.22 **Yaba monkey tumor virus**

059.8 **Other poxvirus infections**

059.9 **Poxvirus infections, unspecified**

ARTHROPOD-BORNE VIRAL DISEASES (060-066)

Use additional code to identify any associated meningitis (321.2)
EXCLUDES *late effects of viral encephalitis (139.0)*

✓4th 060 **Yellow fever**
DEF: Fever and jaundice from infection by mosquito-borne virus of genus *Flavivirus*.

060.0 **Sylvatic**
Yellow fever:
jungle
sylvan
DEF: Yellow fever transmitted from animal to man, via mosquito.

060.1 **Urban**
DEF: Yellow fever transmitted from man to man, via mosquito.

060.9 **Yellow fever, unspecified**

061 **Dengue**
Breakbone fever
EXCLUDES *hemorrhagic fever caused by dengue virus (065.4)*
DEF: Acute, self-limiting infection by mosquito-borne virus characterized by fever and generalized aches.

✓4th 062 **Mosquito-borne viral encephalitis**

062.0 **Japanese encephalitis**
Japanese B encephalitis
DEF: Flavivirus causing inflammation of the brain, with a wide range of clinical manifestations.

062.1 **Western equine encephalitis**
DEF: Alphavirus WEE infection causing inflammation of the brain, found in areas west of the Mississippi; transmitted horse to mosquito to man.

062.2 **Eastern equine encephalitis**
EXCLUDES *Venezuelan equine encephalitis (066.2)*
DEF: Alphavirus EEE causing inflammation of the brain and spinal cord, found as far north as Canada and south into South America and Mexico; transmitted horse to mosquito to man.

062.3 **St. Louis encephalitis**
DEF: Epidemic form caused by Flavivirus and transmitted by mosquito, and characterized by fever, difficulty in speech, and headache.

062.4 **Australian encephalitis**
Australian arboencephalitis
Australian X disease
Murray Valley encephalitis
DEF: Flavivirus causing inflammation of the brain, occurring in Australia and New Guinea.

062.5 **California virus encephalitis**
Encephalitis:
California
La Crosse
Tahyna fever
DEF: Bunyamwere virus causing inflammation of the brain.

062.8 **Other specified mosquito-borne viral encephalitis**
Encephalitis by Ilheus virus
EXCLUDES *West Nile virus (066.40-066.49)*

062.9 **Mosquito-borne viral encephalitis, unspecified**

✓4th 063 **Tick-borne viral encephalitis**
INCLUDES diphasic meningoencephalitis

063.0 **Russian spring-summer [taiga] encephalitis**

063.1 **Louping ill**
DEF: Inflammation of brain caused by virus transmitted sheep to tick to man; incidence usually limited to British Isles.

063.2 **Central European encephalitis**
DEF: Inflammation of brain caused by virus transmitted by tick; limited to central Europe and presenting with two distinct phases.

063.8 **Other specified tick-borne viral encephalitis**
Langat encephalitis
Powassan encephalitis

063.9 **Tick-borne viral encephalitis, unspecified**

064 **Viral encephalitis transmitted by other and unspecified arthropods**
Arthropod-borne viral encephalitis, vector unknown
Negishi virus encephalitis
EXCLUDES *viral encephalitis NOS (049.9)*

✓4th 065 **Arthropod-borne hemorrhagic fever**

065.0 **Crimean hemorrhagic fever [CHF Congo virus]**
Central Asian hemorrhagic fever

065.1 **Omsk hemorrhagic fever**

065.2 **Kyasanur Forest disease**

065.3 **Other tick-borne hemorrhagic fever**

065.4 **Mosquito-borne hemorrhagic fever**
Chikungunya hemorrhagic fever
Dengue hemorrhagic fever
EXCLUDES *Chikungunya fever (066.3)*
dengue (061)
yellow fever (060.0-060.9)

065.8 Other specified arthropod-borne hemorrhagic fever
Mite-borne hemorrhagic fever

065.9 Arthropod-borne hemorrhagic fever, unspecified
Arbovirus hemorrhagic fever NOS

✓4th **066 Other arthropod-borne viral diseases**

066.0 Phlebotomus fever
Changuinola fever
Sandfly fever
DEF: Sandfly-borne viral infection occurring in Asia, Mideast and South America.

066.1 Tick-borne fever
Nairobi sheep disease
Tick fever:
American mountain
Colorado
Kemerovo
Quaranfil

066.2 Venezuelan equine fever
Venezuelan equine encephalitis
DEF: Alphavirus VEE infection causing inflammation of the brain, usually limited to South America, Mexico, and Florida; transmitted horse to mosquito to man.

066.3 Other mosquito-borne fever
Fever (viral):
Bunyamwera
Bwamba
Chikungunya
Guama
Mayaro
Mucambo
O'Nyong-Nyong
Fever (viral):
Oropouche
Pixuna
Rift valley
Ross river
Wesselsbron
Zika
EXCLUDES *dengue (061)*
yellow fever (060.0-060.9)

✓5th **066.4 West Nile fever**
DEF: Mosquito-borne fever causing fatal inflammation of the brain, the lining of the brain, or of the lining of the brain and spinal cord.

066.40 West Nile fever, unspecified
West Nile fever NOS
West Nile fever without complications
West Nile virus NOS

066.41 West Nile fever with encephalitis
West Nile encephalitis
West Nile encephalomyelitis

066.42 West Nile fever with other neurologic manifestation
Use additional code to specify the neurologic manifestation

066.49 West Nile fever with other complications
Use additional code to specify the other conditions

066.8 Other specified arthropod-borne viral diseases
Chandipura fever
Piry fever

066.9 Arthropod-borne viral disease, unspecified
Arbovirus infection NOS

OTHER DISEASES DUE TO VIRUSES AND CHLAMYDIAE (070-079)

✓4th **070 Viral hepatitis**
INCLUDES viral hepatitis (acute) (chronic)
EXCLUDES *cytomegalic inclusion virus hepatitis (078.5)*

The following fifth-digit subclassification is for use with categories 070.2 and 070.3:
0 acute or unspecified, without mention of hepatitis delta
1 acute or unspecified, with hepatitis delta
2 chronic, without mention of hepatitis delta
3 chronic, with hepatitis delta

DEF: Hepatitis A: HAV infection is self-limiting with flulike symptoms; transmission, fecal-oral.
DEF: Hepatitis B: HBV infection can be chronic and systemic; transmission, bodily fluids.
DEF: Hepatitis C: HCV infection can be chronic and systemic; transmission, blood transfusion and unidentified agents.
DEF: Hepatitis D (delta): HDV occurs only in the presence of hepatitis B virus.
DEF: Hepatitis E: HEV is epidemic form; transmission and nature under investigation.

070.0 Viral hepatitis A with hepatic coma

070.1 Viral hepatitis A without mention of hepatic coma
Infectious hepatitis

✓5th **070.2 Viral hepatitis B with hepatic coma**
[0-3]

✓5th **070.3 Viral hepatitis B without mention of hepatic coma**
[0-3]
Serum hepatitis

✓5th **070.4 Other specified viral hepatitis with hepatic coma**

070.41 Acute hepatitis C with hepatic coma

070.42 Hepatitis delta without mention of active hepatitis B disease with hepatic coma
Hepatitis delta with hepatitis B carrier state

070.43 Hepatitis E with hepatic coma

070.44 Chronic hepatitis C with hepatic coma

070.49 Other specified viral hepatitis with hepatic coma

✓5th **070.5 Other specified viral hepatitis without mention of hepatic coma**

070.51 Acute hepatitis C without mention of hepatic coma

070.52 Hepatitis delta without mention of active hepatitis B disease or hepatic coma

070.53 Hepatitis E without mention of hepatic coma

070.54 Chronic hepatitis C without mention of hepatic coma

070.59 Other specified viral hepatitis without mention of hepatic coma

070.6 Unspecified viral hepatitis with hepatic coma
EXCLUDES *unspecified viral hepatitis C with hepatic coma (070.71)*

✓5th **070.7 Unspecified viral hepatitis C**

070.70 Unspecified viral hepatitis C without hepatic coma
Unspecified viral hepatitis C NOS

070.71 Unspecified viral hepatitis C with hepatic coma

070.9 Unspecified viral hepatitis without mention of hepatic coma
Viral hepatitis NOS
EXCLUDES *unspecified viral hepatitis C without hepatic coma (070.70)*

071 Rabies

Hydrophobia
Lyssa

DEF: Acute infectious disease of the CNS caused by a rhabdovirus; usually spread by virus-laden saliva from bites by infected animals; it progresses from fever, restlessness, and extreme excitability, to hydrophobia, seizures, confusion and death.

✓4th **072 Mumps**

DEF: Acute infectious disease caused by paramyxovirus; usually seen in children less than 15 years of age; salivary glands are typically enlarged, and other organs, such as testes, pancreas and meninges, are often involved.

072.0 Mumps orchitis

072.1 Mumps meningitis

072.2 Mumps encephalitis

Mumps meningoencephalitis

072.3 Mumps pancreatitis

✓5th **072.7 Mumps with other specified complications**

072.71 Mumps hepatitis

072.72 Mumps polyneuropathy

072.79 Other

072.8 Mumps with unspecified complication

072.9 Mumps without mention of complication

Epidemic parotitis
Infectious parotitis

✓4th **073 Ornithosis**

INCLUDES parrot fever
psittacosis

DEF: *Chlamydia psittaci* infection often transmitted from birds to humans.

073.0 With pneumonia

Lobular pneumonitis due to ornithosis

073.7 With other specified complications

073.8 With unspecified complication

073.9 Ornithosis, unspecified

✓4th **074 Specific diseases due to Coxsackie virus**

EXCLUDES *Coxsackie virus:*
infection NOS (079.2)
meningitis (047.0)

074.0 Herpangina

Vesicular pharyngitis

DEF: Acute infectious coxsackie virus infection causing throat lesions, fever, and vomiting; generally affects children in summer.

074.1 Epidemic pleurodynia

Bornholm disease
Devil's grip
Epidemic:
myalgia
myositis

DEF: Paroxysmal pain in chest, accompanied by fever and usually limited to children and young adults; caused by coxsackie virus.

✓5th **074.2 Coxsackie carditis**

074.20 Coxsackie carditis, unspecified

074.21 Coxsackie pericarditis

DEF: Coxsackie infection of the outer lining of the heart.

074.22 Coxsackie endocarditis

DEF: Coxsackie infection within the heart's cavities.

074.23 Coxsackie myocarditis

Aseptic myocarditis of newborn

DEF: Coxsackie infection of the muscle of the heart.

074.3 Hand, foot, and mouth disease

Vesicular stomatitis and exanthem

DEF: Mild coxsackie infection causing lesions on hands, feet and oral mucosa, most commonly seen in preschool children.

074.8 Other specified diseases due to Coxsackie virus

Acute lymphonodular pharyngitis

075 Infectious mononucleosis

Glandular fever
Monocytic angina
Pfeiffer's disease

DEF: Acute infection by Epstein-Barr virus causing fever, sore throat, enlarged lymph glands and spleen, and fatigue; usually seen in teens and young adults.

✓4th **076 Trachoma**

EXCLUDES *late effect of trachoma (139.1)*

DEF: A chronic infectious disease of the cornea and conjunctiva caused by a strain of the bacteria *Chlamydia trachomatis;* the infection can cause photophobia, pain, excessive tearing and sometimes blindness.

076.0 Initial stage

Trachoma dubium

076.1 Active stage

Granular conjunctivitis (trachomatous)
Trachomatous:
follicular conjunctivitis
pannus

076.9 Trachoma, unspecified

Trachoma NOS

✓4th **077 Other diseases of conjunctiva due to viruses and Chlamydiae**

EXCLUDES *ophthalmic complications of viral diseases classified elsewhere*

077.0 Inclusion conjunctivitis

Paratrachoma
Swimming pool conjunctivitis

EXCLUDES *inclusion blennorrhea (neonatal) (771.6)*

DEF: Pus in conjunctiva caused by *Chlamydiae trachomatis.*

077.1 Epidemic keratoconjunctivitis

Shipyard eye

DEF: Highly contagious corneal or conjunctival infection caused by adenovirus type 8; symptoms include inflammation and corneal infiltrates.

077.2 Pharyngoconjunctival fever

Viral pharyngoconjunctivitis

077.3 Other adenoviral conjunctivitis

Acute adenoviral follicular conjunctivitis

077.4 Epidemic hemorrhagic conjunctivitis

Apollo:
conjunctivitis
disease
Conjunctivitis due to enterovirus type 70
Hemorrhagic conjunctivitis (acute) (epidemic)

077.8 Other viral conjunctivitis

Newcastle conjunctivitis

✓5th **077.9 Unspecified diseases of conjunctiva due to viruses and Chlamydiae**

077.98 Due to Chlamydiae

077.99 Due to viruses

Viral conjunctivitis NOS

✓4th **078 Other diseases due to viruses and Chlamydiae**

EXCLUDES *viral infection NOS (079.0-079.9)*
viremia NOS (790.8)

078.0 Molluscum contagiosum

DEF: Benign poxvirus infection causing small bumps on the skin or conjunctiva; transmitted by close contact.

✓5th **078.1 Viral warts**

Viral warts due to human papilloma virus

DEF: A keratotic papilloma of the epidermis caused by the human papilloma virus; the superficial vegetative lesions last for varying durations and eventually regress spontaneously.

078.10 Viral warts, unspecified

Verruca:
Vulgaris
Warts (infectious)

078.11 Condyloma acuminatum

Condyloma NOS
Genital warts NOS

DEF: Clusters of mucosa or epidermal lesions on external genitalia; viral infection is sexually transmitted.

078.12 Plantar wart

Verruca plantaris

078.19 Other specified viral warts

Common wart
Flat wart
Verruca plana

078.2 Sweating fever
Miliary fever
Sweating disease
DEF: A viral infection characterized by profuse sweating; various papular, vesicular and other eruptions cause the blockage of sweat glands.

078.3 Cat-scratch disease
Benign lymphoreticulosis (of inoculation)
Cat-scratch fever

078.4 Foot and mouth disease
Aphthous fever
Epizootic:
aphthae
stomatitis
DEF: Ulcers on oral mucosa, legs, and feet after exposure to infected animal.

078.5 Cytomegaloviral disease
Cytomegalic inclusion disease
Salivary gland virus disease
Use additional code to identify manifestation, as:
cytomegalic inclusion virus:
hepatitis (573.1)
pneumonia (484.1)
EXCLUDES *congenital cytomegalovirus infection (771.1)*
DEF: A herpesvirus inclusion associated with serious disease morbidity including fever, leukopenia, pneumonia, retinitis, hepatitis and organ transplant; often leads to syndromes such as hepatomegaly, splenomegaly and thrombocytopenia; a common post-transplant complication for organ transplant recipients.

078.6 Hemorrhagic nephrosonephritis
Hemorrhagic fever:
epidemic
Korean
Russian
with renal syndrome
DEF: Viral infection causing kidney dysfunction and bleeding disorders.

078.7 Arenaviral hemorrhagic fever
Hemorrhagic fever:
Argentine
Bolivian
Junin virus
Machupo virus

✓5th **078.8 Other specified diseases due to viruses and Chlamydiae**
EXCLUDES *epidemic diarrhea (009.2)*
lymphogranuloma venereum (099.1)

078.81 Epidemic vertigo

078.82 Epidemic vomiting syndrome
Winter vomiting disease

078.88 Other specified diseases due to Chlamydiae

078.89 Other specified diseases due to viruses
Epidemic cervical myalgia
Marburg disease
Tanapox

✓4th **079 Viral and chlamydial infection in conditions classified elsewhere and of unspecified site**
Note: This category is provided to be used as an additional code to identify the viral agent in diseases classifiable elsewhere. This category will also be used to classify virus infection of unspecified nature or site.

079.0 Adenovirus

079.1 ECHO virus
DEF: An "orphan" enteric RNA virus, certain serotypes of which are associated with human disease, especially aseptic meningitis.

079.2 Coxsackie virus
DEF: A heterogenous group of viruses associated with aseptic meningitis, myocarditis, pericarditis, and acute onset juvenile diabetes.

079.3 Rhinovirus
DEF: Rhinoviruses affect primarily the upper respiratory tract. Over 100 distinct types infect humans.

079.4 Human papillomavirus
DEF: Viral infection caused by the genus *Papillomavirus* causing cutaneous and genital warts, including verruca vulgaris and condyloma acuminatum; certain types are associated with cervical dysplasia, cancer and other genital malignancies.

✓5th **079.5 Retrovirus**
EXCLUDES *human immunodeficiency virus, type 1 [HIV-1] (042)*
human T-cell lymphotrophic virus, type III [HTLV-III] (042)
lymphadenopathy-associated virus [LAV] (042)
DEF: A large group of RNA viruses that carry reverse transcriptase and include the leukoviruses and lentiviruses.

079.50 Retrovirus, unspecified

079.51 Human T-cell lymphotrophic virus, type I [HTLV-I]

079.52 Human T-cell lymphotrophic virus, type II [HTLV-II]

079.53 Human immunodeficiency virus, type 2 [HIV-2]

079.59 Other specified retrovirus

079.6 Respiratory syncytial virus [RSV]
DEF: The major respiratory pathogen of young children, causing severe bronchitis and bronchopneumonia, and minor infection in adults.

✓5th **079.8 Other specified viral and chlamydial infections**

079.81 Hantavirus
DEF: An infection caused by the Muerto Canyon virus whose primary rodent reservoir is the deer mouse Peromyscus maniculatus; commonly characterized by fever, myalgias, headache, cough and rapid decline.

079.82 SARS-associated coronavirus
DEF: A life-threatening respiratory disease described as severe acute respiratory syndrome (SARS); etiology coronavirus; most common presenting symptoms may range from mild to more severe forms of flu-like conditions; fever, chills, cough, headache, myalgia; diagnosis of SARS is based upon clinical, laboratory, and epidemiological criteria.

079.83 Parvovirus B19
Human parvovirus
Parvovirus NOS
EXCLUDES *erythema infectiosum [fifth disease] (057.0)*
DEF: The only known parvovirus to cause disease in humans; most common manifestation is erythema infectiosum; also associated with polyarthropathy, chronic anemia, red cell aplasia, and fetal hydrops.

079.88 Other specified chlamydial infection

079.89 Other specified viral infection

✓5th **079.9 Unspecified viral and chlamydial infections**
EXCLUDES *viremia NOS (790.8)*

079.98 Unspecified chlamydial infection
Chlamydial infections NOS

079.99 Unspecified viral infection
Viral infections NOS

RICKETTSIOSES AND OTHER ARTHROPOD-BORNE DISEASES (080-088)

EXCLUDES *arthropod-borne viral diseases (060.0-066.9)*

080 Louse-borne [epidemic] typhus
Typhus (fever):
classical
epidemic
exanthematic NOS
louse-borne
DEF: *Rickettsia prowazekii;* causes severe headache, rash, high fever.

✓4th 081 Other typhus

081.0 Murine [endemic] typhus
Typhus (fever):
endemic
flea-borne
DEF: Milder typhus caused by *Rickettsia typhi (mooseri)*; transmitted by rat flea.

081.1 Brill's disease
Brill-Zinsser disease
Recrudescent typhus (fever)

081.2 Scrub typhus
Japanese river fever
Kedani fever
Mite-borne typhus
Tsutsugamushi

081.9 Typhus, unspecified
Typhus (fever) NOS

✓4th 082 Tick-borne rickettsioses

082.0 Spotted fevers
Rocky mountain spotted fever
Sao Paulo fever

082.1 Boutonneuse fever
African tick typhus
India tick typhus
Kenya tick typhus
Marseilles fever
Mediterranean tick fever

082.2 North Asian tick fever
Siberian tick typhus

082.3 Queensland tick typhus

✓5th 082.4 Ehrlichiosis

082.40 Ehrlichiosis, unspecified

082.41 Ehrlichiosis chaffeensis [E. chaffeensis]
DEF: A febrile illness caused by bacterial infection, also called human monocytic ehrlichiosis (HME). Causal organism is *Ehrlichia chaffeensis*, transmitted by the Lone Star tick, *Amblyomma americanum*. Symptoms include fever, chills, myalgia, nausea, vomiting, diarrhea, confusion, and severe headache occurring one week after a tick bite. Clinical findings are lymphadenopathy, rash, thrombocytopenia, leukopenia, and abnormal liver function tests.

082.49 Other ehrlichiosis

082.8 Other specified tick-borne rickettsioses
Lone star fever

082.9 Tick-borne rickettsiosis, unspecified
Tick-borne typhus NOS

✓4th 083 Other rickettsioses

083.0 Q fever
DEF: Infection of *Coxiella burnettii* usually acquired through airborne organisms.

083.1 Trench fever
Quintan fever
Wolhynian fever

083.2 Rickettsialpox
Vesicular rickettsiosis
DEF: Infection of *Rickettsia akari* usually acquired through a mite bite.

083.8 Other specified rickettsioses

083.9 Rickettsiosis, unspecified

✓4th 084 Malaria

Note: Subcategories 084.0-084.6 exclude the listed conditions with mention of pernicious complications (084.8-084.9).

EXCLUDES *congenital malaria (771.2)*

DEF: Mosquito-borne disease causing high fever and prostration and cataloged by species of *Plasmodium: P. falciparum, P. malariae, P. ovale, and P. vivax.*

084.0 Falciparum malaria [malignant tertian]
Malaria (fever):
by Plasmodium falciparum
subtertian

084.1 Vivax malaria [benign tertian]
Malaria (fever) by Plasmodium vivax

084.2 Quartan malaria
Malaria (fever) by Plasmodium malariae
Malariae malaria

084.3 Ovale malaria
Malaria (fever) by Plasmodium ovale

084.4 Other malaria
Monkey malaria

084.5 Mixed malaria
Malaria (fever) by more than one parasite

084.6 Malaria, unspecified
Malaria (fever) NOS

084.7 Induced malaria
Therapeutically induced malaria
EXCLUDES *accidental infection from syringe, blood transfusion, etc. (084.0-084.6, above, according to parasite species)*
transmission from mother to child during delivery (771.2)

084.8 Blackwater fever
Hemoglobinuric:
fever (bilious)
malaria
Malarial hemoglobinuria
DEF: Severe hemic and renal complication of *Plasmodium falciparum* infection.

084.9 Other pernicious complications of malaria
Algid malaria
Cerebral malaria
Use additional code to identify complication, as:
malarial:
hepatitis (573.2)
nephrosis (581.81)

✓4th 085 Leishmaniasis

085.0 Visceral [kala-azar]
Dumdum fever
Infection by Leishmania:
donovani
infantum
Leishmaniasis:
dermal, post-kala-azar
Mediterranean
visceral (Indian)

085.1 Cutaneous, urban
Aleppo boi
Baghdad boil
Delhi boil
Infection by Leishmania tropica (minor)
Leishmaniasis, cutaneous:
dry form
late
recurrent
ulcerating
Oriental sore

085.2 Cutaneous, Asian desert
Infection by Leishmania tropica major
Leishmaniasis, cutaneous:
acute necrotizing
rural
wet form
zoonotic form

085.3 Cutaneous, Ethiopian
Infection by Leishmania ethiopica
Leishmaniasis, cutaneous:
diffuse
lepromatous

085.4 Cutaneous, American
Chiclero ulcer
Infection by Leishmania mexicana
Leishmaniasis tegumentaria diffusa

085.5 Mucocutaneous (American)
Espundia
Infection by Leishmania braziliensis
Uta

085.9 Leishmaniasis, unspecified

✓4th **086 Trypanosomiasis**

Use additional code to identify manifestations, as:
trypanosomiasis:
encephalitis (323.2)
meningitis (321.3)

086.0 Chagas' disease with heart involvement

American trypanosomiasis } with heart involvement
Infection by Trypanosoma cruzi } with heart involvement

Any condition classifiable to 086.2 with heart involvement

086.1 Chagas' disease with other organ involvement

American trypanosomiasis } with involvement of organ other than heart
Infection by Trypanosoma cruzi } with involvement of organ other than heart

Any condition classifiable to 086.2 with involvement of organ other than heart

086.2 Chagas' disease without mention of organ involvement

American trypanosomiasis
Infection by Trypanosoma cruzi

086.3 Gambian trypanosomiasis

Gambian sleeping sickness
Infection by Trypanosoma gambiense

086.4 Rhodesian trypanosomiasis

Infection by Trypanosoma rhodesiense
Rhodesian sleeping sickness

086.5 African trypanosomiasis, unspecified

Sleeping sickness NOS

086.9 Trypanosomiasis, unspecified

✓4th **087 Relapsing fever**

INCLUDES recurrent fever

DEF: Infection of *Borrelia;* symptoms are episodic and include fever and arthralgia.

087.0 Louse-borne

087.1 Tick-borne

087.9 Relapsing fever, unspecified

✓4th **088 Other arthropod-borne diseases**

088.0 Bartonellosis

Carrión's disease
Oroya fever
Verruga peruana

✓5th **088.8 Other specified arthropod-borne diseases**

088.81 Lyme disease

Erythema chronicum migrans

DEF: A recurrent multisystem disorder caused by the spirochete *Borrelia burgdorferi* with the carrier being the tick *Ixodes dammini;* the disease begins with lesions of erythema chronicum migrans; it is followed by arthritis of the large joints, myalgia, malaise, and neurological and cardiac manifestations.

088.82 Babesiosis

Babesiasis

DEF: A tick-borne disease caused by infection of *Babesia,* characterized by fever, malaise, listlessness, severe anemia and hemoglobinuria.

088.89 Other

088.9 Arthropod-borne disease, unspecified

SYPHILIS AND OTHER VENEREAL DISEASES (090-099)

EXCLUDES *nonvenereal endemic syphilis (104.0)*
urogenital trichomoniasis (131.0)

✓4th **090 Congenital syphilis**

DEF: Infection by spirochete *Treponema pallidum* acquired in utero from the infected mother.

090.0 Early congenital syphilis, symptomatic

Congenital syphilitic:
choroiditis
coryza (chronic)
hepatomegaly
mucous patches
periostitis

Congenital syphilitic:
splenomegaly

Syphilitic (congenital):
epiphysitis
osteochondritis
pemphigus

Any congenital syphilitic condition specified as early or manifest less than two years after birth

090.1 Early congenital syphilis, latent

Congenital syphilis without clinical manifestations, with positive serological reaction and negative spinal fluid test, less than two years after birth

090.2 Early congenital syphilis, unspecified

Congenital syphilis NOS, less than two years after birth

090.3 Syphilitic interstitial keratitis

Syphilitic keratitis:
parenchymatous
punctata profunda

EXCLUDES *interstitial keratitis NOS (370.50)*

✓5th **090.4 Juvenile neurosyphilis**

Use additional code to identify any associated mental disorder

DEF: *Treponema pallidum* infection involving the nervous system.

090.40 Juvenile neurosyphilis, unspecified

Congenital neurosyphilis
Dementia paralytica juvenilis
Juvenile:
general paresis
tabes
taboparesis

090.41 Congenital syphilitic encephalitis

DEF: Congenital *Treponema pallidum* infection involving the brain.

090.42 Congenital syphilitic meningitis

DEF: Congenital *Treponema pallidum* infection involving the lining of the brain and/or spinal cord.

090.49 Other

090.5 Other late congenital syphilis, symptomatic

Gumma due to congenital syphilis
Hutchinson's teeth
Syphilitic saddle nose

Any congenital syphilitic condition specified as late or manifest two years or more after birth

090.6 Late congenital syphilis, latent

Congenital syphilis without clinical manifestations, with positive serological reaction and negative spinal fluid test, two years or more after birth

090.7 Late congenital syphilis, unspecified

Congenital syphilis NOS, two years or more after birth

090.9 Congenital syphilis, unspecified

✓4th **091 Early syphilis, symptomatic**

EXCLUDES *early cardiovascular syphilis (093.0-093.9)*
early neurosyphilis (094.0-094.9)

091.0 Genital syphilis (primary)

Genital chancre

DEF: Genital lesion at the site of initial infection by *Treponema pallidum.*

091.1 Primary anal syphilis

DEF: Anal lesion at the site of initial infection by *Treponema pallidum.*

091.2 Other primary syphilis

Primary syphilis of:
breast
fingers
lip
tonsils

DEF: Lesion at the site of initial infection by *Treponema pallidum.*

091.3 Secondary syphilis of skin or mucous membranes
Condyloma latum
Secondary syphilis of:
anus
mouth
pharynx
skin
tonsils
vulva
DEF: Transitory or chronic lesions following initial syphilis infection.

091.4 Adenopathy due to secondary syphilis
Syphilitic adenopathy (secondary)
Syphilitic lymphadenitis (secondary)

✓5th **091.5 Uveitis due to secondary syphilis**

091.50 Syphilitic uveitis, unspecified

091.51 Syphilitic chorioretinitis (secondary)
DEF: Inflammation of choroid and retina as a secondary infection.

091.52 Syphilitic iridocyclitis (secondary)
DEF: Inflammation of iris and ciliary body as a secondary infection.

✓5th **091.6 Secondary syphilis of viscera and bone**

091.61 Secondary syphilitic periostitis
DEF: Inflammation of outer layers of bone as a secondary infection.

091.62 Secondary syphilitic hepatitis
Secondary syphilis of liver

091.69 Other viscera

091.7 Secondary syphilis, relapse
Secondary syphilis, relapse (treated) (untreated)
DEF: Return of symptoms of syphilis following asymptomatic period.

✓5th **091.8 Other forms of secondary syphilis**

091.81 Acute syphilitic meningitis (secondary)
DEF: Sudden, severe inflammation of the lining of the brain and/or spinal cord as a secondary infection.

091.82 Syphilitic alopecia
DEF: Hair loss following initial syphillis infection.

091.89 Other

091.9 Unspecified secondary syphilis

✓4th **092 Early syphilis, latent**
INCLUDES syphilis (acquired) without clinical manifestations, with positive serological reaction and negative spinal fluid test, less than two years after infection

092.0 Early syphilis, latent, serological relapse after treatment

092.9 Early syphilis, latent, unspecified

✓4th **093 Cardiovascular syphilis**

093.0 Aneurysm of aorta, specified as syphilitic
Dilatation of aorta, specified as syphilitic

093.1 Syphilitic aortitis
DEF: Inflammation of the aorta – the main artery leading from the heart.

✓5th **093.2 Syphilitic endocarditis**
DEF: Inflammation of the tissues lining the cavities of the heart.

093.20 Valve, unspecified
Syphilitic ostial coronary disease

093.21 Mitral valve

093.22 Aortic valve
Syphilitic aortic incompetence or stenosis

093.23 Tricuspid valve

093.24 Pulmonary valve

✓5th **093.8 Other specified cardiovascular syphilis**

093.81 Syphilitic pericarditis
DEF: Inflammation of the outer lining of the heart.

093.82 Syphilitic myocarditis
DEF: Inflammation of the muscle of the heart.

093.89 Other

093.9 Cardiovascular syphilis, unspecified

✓4th **094 Neurosyphilis**
Use additional code to identify any associated mental disorder

094.0 Tabes dorsalis
Locomotor ataxia (progressive)
Posterior spinal sclerosis (syphilitic)
Tabetic neurosyphilis
Use additional code to identify manifestation, as:
neurogenic arthropathy [Charcot's joint disease] (713.5)
DEF: Progressive degeneration of nerves associated with long-term syphilis; causing pain, wasting away, incontinence, and ataxia.

094.1 General paresis
Dementia paralytica
General paralysis (of the insane) (progressive)
Paretic neurosyphilis
Taboparesis
DEF: Degeneration of brain associated with long-term syphilis, causing loss of brain function, progressive dementia, and paralysis.

094.2 Syphilitic meningitis
Meningovascular syphilis
EXCLUDES *acute syphilitic meningitis (secondary) (091.81)*
DEF: Inflammation of the lining of the brain and/or spinal cord.

094.3 Asymptomatic neurosyphilis

✓5th **094.8 Other specified neurosyphilis**

094.81 Syphilitic encephalitis

094.82 Syphilitic Parkinsonism
DEF: Decreased motor function, tremors, and muscular rigidity.

094.83 Syphilitic disseminated retinochoroiditis
DEF: Inflammation of retina and choroid due to neurosyphilis.

094.84 Syphilitic optic atrophy
DEF: Degeneration of the eye and its nerves due to neurosyphilis.

094.85 Syphilitic retrobulbar neuritis
DEF: Inflammation of the posterior optic nerve to neurosyphilis.

094.86 Syphilitic acoustic neuritis
DEF: Inflammation of acoustic nerve due to neurosyphilis.

094.87 Syphilitic ruptured cerebral aneurysm

094.89 Other

094.9 Neurosyphilis, unspecified
Gumma (syphilitic) } of central nervous system NOS
Syphilis (early) (late) } of central nervous system NOS
Syphiloma } of central nervous system NOS

095 Other forms of late syphilis, with symptoms
INCLUDES gumma (syphilitic)
syphilis, late, tertiary, or unspecified stage

095.0 Syphilitic episcleritis

095.1 Syphilis of lung

095.2 Syphilitic peritonitis

095.3 Syphilis of liver

095.4 Syphilis of kidney

095.5 Syphilis of bone

095.6 Syphilis of muscle
Syphilitic myositis

095.7 Syphilis of synovium, tendon, and bursa
Syphilitic:
bursitis
synovitis

095.8 Other specified forms of late symptomatic syphilis

EXCLUDES *cardiovascular syphilis (093.0-093.9)*
neurosyphilis (094.0-094.9)

095.9 Late symptomatic syphilis, unspecified

096 Late syphilis, latent

Syphilis (acquired) without clinical manifestations, with positive serological reaction and negative spinal fluid test, two years or more after infection

4th **097 Other and unspecified syphilis**

097.0 Late syphilis, unspecified

097.1 Latent syphilis, unspecified

Positive serological reaction for syphilis

097.9 Syphilis, unspecified

Syphilis (acquired) NOS

EXCLUDES *syphilis NOS causing death under two years of age (090.9)*

4th **098 Gonococcal infections**

DEF: *Neisseria gonorrhoeae* infection generally acquired in utero or in sexual congress.

098.0 Acute, of lower genitourinary tract

Gonococcal:
- Bartholinitis (acute)
- urethritis (acute)
- vulvovaginitis (acute)

Gonorrhea (acute):
- NOS
- genitourinary (tract) NOS

5th **098.1 Acute, of upper genitourinary tract**

098.10 Gonococcal infection (acute) of upper genitourinary tract, site unspecified

098.11 Gonococcal cystitis (acute) upper Gonorrhea (acute) of bladder

098.12 Gonococcal prostatitis (acute)

098.13 Gonococcal epididymo-orchitis (acute)

Gonococcal orchitis (acute)

DEF: Acute inflammation of the testes.

098.14 Gonococcal seminal vesiculitis (acute)

Gonorrhea (acute) of seminal vesicle

098.15 Gonococcal cervicitis (acute)

Gonorrhea (acute) of cervix

098.16 Gonococcal endometritis (acute)

Gonorrhea (acute) of uterus

098.17 Gonococcal salpingitis, specified as acute

DEF: Acute inflammation of the fallopian tubes.

098.19 Other

098.2 Chronic, of lower genitourinary tract

Gonococcal:
- Bartholinitis
- urethritis
- vulvovaginitis

Gonorrhea:
- NOS
- genitourinary (tract)

} specified as chronic or with duration of two months or more

Any condition classifiable to 098.0 specified as chronic or with duration of two months or more

5th **098.3 Chronic, of upper genitourinary tract**

INCLUDES any condition classifiable to 098.1 stated as chronic or with a duration of two months or more

098.30 Chronic gonococcal infection of upper genitourinary tract, site unspecified

098.31 Gonococcal cystitis, chronic

Gonorrhea of bladder, chronic

Any condition classifiable to 098.11, specified as chronic

098.32 Gonococcal prostatitis, chronic

Any condition classifiable to 098.12, specified as chronic

098.33 Gonococcal epididymo-orchitis, chronic

Chronic gonococcal orchitis

Any condition classifiable to 098.13, specified as chronic

DEF: Chronic inflammation of the testes.

098.34 Gonococcal seminal vesiculitis, chronic

Gonorrhea of seminal vesicle, chronic

Any condition classifiable to 098.14, specified as chronic

098.35 Gonococcal cervicitis, chronic

Gonorrhea of cervix, chronic

Any condition classifiable to 098.15, specified as chronic

098.36 Gonococcal endometritis, chronic

Any condition classifiable to 098.16, specified as chronic

DEF: Chronic inflammation of the uterus.

098.37 Gonococcal salpingitis (chronic)

DEF: Chronic inflammation of the fallopian tubes.

098.39 Other

5th **098.4 Gonococcal infection of eye**

098.40 Gonococcal conjunctivitis (neonatorum)

Gonococcal ophthalmia (neonatorum)

DEF: Infection of conjunctiva present at birth.

098.41 Gonococcal iridocyclitis

DEF: Inflammation and infection of iris and ciliary body.

098.42 Gonococcal endophthalmia

DEF: Inflammation and infection of contents of eyeball.

098.43 Gonococcal keratitis

DEF: Inflammation and infection of the cornea.

098.49 Other

5th **098.5 Gonococcal infection of joint**

098.50 Gonococcal arthritis

Gonococcal infection of joint NOS

098.51 Gonococcal synovitis and tenosynovitis

098.52 Gonococcal bursitis

DEF: Inflammation of the sac-like cavities in a joint.

098.53 Gonococcal spondylitis

098.59 Other

Gonococcal rheumatism

098.6 Gonococcal infection of pharynx

098.7 Gonococcal infection of anus and rectum

Gonococcal proctitis

5th **098.8 Gonococcal infection of other specified sites**

098.81 Gonococcal keratosis (blennorrhagica)

DEF: Pustular skin lesions caused by *Neisseria gonorrhoeae.*

098.82 Gonococcal meningitis

DEF: Inflammation of lining of brain and/or spinal cord.

098.83 Gonococcal pericarditis

DEF: Inflammation of the outer lining of the heart.

098.84 Gonococcal endocarditis

DEF: Inflammation of tissues lining the cavities of heart.

098.85 Other gonococcal heart disease

098.86 Gonococcal peritonitis

DEF: Inflammation of the membrane lining the abdomen.

098.89 Other

Gonococcemia

✓4th **099 Other venereal diseases**

099.0 Chancroid
Bubo (inguinal):
chancroidal
due to Hemophilus ducreyi
Chancre:
Ducrey's
simple
soft
Ulcus molle (cutis)(skin)
DEF: A sexually transmitted disease caused by *Haemophilus ducreyi;* it is identified by a painful primary ulcer at the site of inoculation (usually external genitalia) with related lymphadenitis.

099.1 Lymphogranuloma venereum
Climatic or tropical bubo
(Durand-) Nicolas-Favre disease
Esthiomene
Lymphogranuloma inguinale
DEF: Sexually transmitted infection of *Chlamydia trachomatis* causing skin lesions.

099.2 Granuloma inguinale
Donovanosis
Granuloma pudendi (ulcerating)
Granuloma venereum
Pudendal ulcer
DEF: Chronic, sexually transmitted infection of *Calymmatobac-terium granulomatis* causing progressive, anogenital skin ulcers.

099.3 Reiter's disease
Reiter's syndrome
Use additional code for associated:
arthropathy (711.1)
conjunctivitis (372.33)
DEF: A symptom complex of unknown etiology consisting of urethritis, conjunctivitis, arthritis and myocutaneous lesions. It occurs most commonly in young men and patients with HIV and may precede or follow AIDS. Also a form of reactive arthritis.

✓5th **099.4 Other nongonococcal urethritis [NGU]**

099.40 Unspecified
Nonspecific urethritis

099.41 Chlamydia trachomatis

099.49 Other specified organism

✓5th **099.5 Other venereal diseases due to Chlamydia trachomatis**
EXCLUDES *Chlamydia trachomatis infection of conjunctiva (076.0-076.9, 077.0, 077.9)*
Lymphogranuloma venereum (099.1)
DEF: Venereal diseases caused by *Chlamydia trachomatis* at other sites besides the urethra (e.g., pharynx, anus and rectum, conjunctiva and peritoneum).

099.50 Unspecified site

099.51 Pharynx

099.52 Anus and rectum

099.53 Lower genitourinary sites
Use additional code to specify site of infection, such as:
bladder (595.4)
cervix (616.0)
vagina and vulva (616.11)
EXCLUDES *urethra (099.41)*

099.54 Other genitourinary sites
Use additional code to specify site of infection, such as:
pelvic inflammatory disease NOS (614.9)
testis and epididymis (604.91)

099.55 Unspecified genitourinary site

099.56 Peritoneum
Perihepatitis

099.59 Other specified site

099.8 Other specified venereal diseases

099.9 Venereal disease, unspecified

OTHER SPIROCHETAL DISEASES (100-104)

✓4th **100 Leptospirosis**
DEF: An infection of any spirochete of the genus Leptospire in blood. This zoonosis is transmitted to humans most often by exposure with contaminated animal tissues or water and less often by contact with urine. Patients present with flulike symptoms, the most common being muscle aches involving the thighs and low back. Treatment is with hydration and antibiotics.

100.0 Leptospirosis icterohemorrhagica
Leptospiral or spirochetal jaundice (hemorrhagic)
Weil's disease

✓5th **100.8 Other specified leptospiral infections**

100.81 Leptospiral meningitis (aseptic)

100.89 Other
Fever:
Fort Bragg
pretibial
swamp
Infection by Leptospira:
australis
bataviae
pyrogenes

100.9 Leptospirosis, unspecified

101 Vincent's angina
Acute necrotizing ulcerative:
gingivitis
stomatitis
Fusospirochetal pharyngitis
Spirochetal stomatitis
Trench mouth
Vincent's:
gingivitis
infection [any site]
DEF: Painful ulceration with edema and hypermic patches of the oropharyngeal and throat membranes; it is caused by spreading of acute ulcerative gingivitis.

✓4th **102 Yaws**
INCLUDES frambesia
pian
DEF: An infectious, endemic, tropical disease caused by *Treponema pertenue;* it usually affects persons 15 years old or younger; a primary cutaneous lesion develops, then a granulomatous skin eruption, and occasionally lesions that destroy skin and bone.

102.0 Initial lesions
Chancre of yaws
Frambesia, initial or primary
Initial frambesial ulcer
Mother yaw

102.1 Multiple papillomata and wet crab yaws
Butter yaws
Frambesioma
Pianoma
Plantar or palmar papilloma of yaws

102.2 Other early skin lesions
Cutaneous yaws, less than five years after infection
Early yaws (cutaneous) (macular) (papular) (maculopapular) (micropapular)
Frambeside of early yaws

102.3 Hyperkeratosis
Ghoul hand
Hyperkeratosis, palmar or plantar (early) (late) due to yaws
Worm-eaten soles
DEF: Overgrowth of skin of palm of bottoms of feet, due to yaws.

102.4 Gummata and ulcers
Gummatous frambeside
Nodular late yaws (ulcerated)
DEF: Rubbery lesions and areas of dead skin caused by yaws.

102.5 Gangosa
Rhinopharyngitis mutilans
DEF: Massive, mutilating lesions of the nose and oral cavity caused by yaws.

102.6 Bone and joint lesions

Goundou
Gumma, bone
Gummatous osteitis or periostitis } of yaws (late)

Hydrarthrosis
Osteitis
Periostitis (hypertrophic) } of yaws (early) (late)

102.7 Other manifestations

Juxta-articular nodules of yaws
Mucosal yaws

102.8 Latent yaws

Yaws without clinical manifestations, with positive serology

102.9 Yaws, unspecified

✓4th **103 Pinta**

DEF: A chronic form of treponematosis, endemic in areas of tropical America; it is identified by the presence of red, violet, blue, coffee-colored or white spots on the skin.

103.0 Primary lesions

Chancre (primary)
Papule (primary)
Pintid } of pinta [carate]

103.1 Intermediate lesions

Erythematous plaques
Hyperchronic lesions
Hyperkeratosis } of pinta [carate]

103.2 Late lesions

Cardiovascular lesions
Skin lesions:
achromic
cicatricial
dyschromic
Vitiligo } of pinta [carate]

103.3 Mixed lesions

Achromic and hyperchromic skin lesions of pinta [carate]

103.9 Pinta, unspecified

✓4th **104 Other spirochetal infection**

104.0 Nonvenereal endemic syphilis

Bejel
Njovera

DEF: *Treponema pallidum, T. pertenue, or T. caroteum* infection transmitted non-sexually, causing lesions on mucosa and skin.

104.8 Other specified spirochetal infections

EXCLUDES *relapsing fever (087.0-087.9)*
syphilis (090.0-097.9)

104.9 Spirochetal infection, unspecified

MYCOSES (110-118)

Use additional code to identify manifestation as:
arthropathy (711.6)
meningitis (321.0-321.1)
otitis externa (380.15)

EXCLUDES *infection by Actinomycetales, such as species of Actinomyces, Actinomadura, Nocardia, Streptomyces (039.0-039.9)*

✓4th **110 Dermatophytosis**

INCLUDES infection by species of Epidermophyton, Microsporum, and Trichophyton
tinea, any type except those in 111

DEF: Superficial infection of the skin caused by a parasitic fungus.

110.0 Of scalp and beard

Kerion
Sycosis, mycotic
Trichophytic tinea [black dot tinea], scalp

110.1 Of nail

Dermatophytic onychia
Onychomycosis
Tinea unguium

110.2 Of hand

Tinea manuum

110.3 Of groin and perianal area

Dhobie itch
Eczema marginatum
Tinea cruris

110.4 Of foot

Athlete's foot
Tinea pedis

110.5 Of the body

Herpes circinatus
Tinea imbricata [Tokelau]

110.6 Deep seated dermatophytosis

Granuloma trichophyticum
Majocchi's granuloma

110.8 Of other specified sites

110.9 Of unspecified site

Favus NOS
Microsporic tinea NOS
Ringworm NOS

✓4th **111 Dermatomycosis, other and unspecified**

111.0 Pityriasis versicolor

Infection by Malassezia [Pityrosporum] furfur
Tinea flava
Tinea versicolor

111.1 Tinea nigra

Infection by Cladosporium species
Keratomycosis nigricans
Microsporosis nigra
Pityriasis nigra
Tinea palmaris nigra

111.2 Tinea blanca

Infection by Trichosporon (beigelii) cutaneum
White piedra

111.3 Black piedra

Infection by Piedraia hortai

111.8 Other specified dermatomycoses

111.9 Dermatomycosis, unspecified

✓4th **112 Candidiasis**

INCLUDES infection by Candida species
moniliasis

EXCLUDES *neonatal monilial infection (771.7)*

DEF: Fungal infection caused by Candida; usually seen in mucous membranes or skin.

112.0 Of mouth

Thrush (oral)

112.1 Of vulva and vagina

Candidal vulvovaginitis
Monilial vulvovaginitis

112.2 Of other urogenital sites

Candidal balanitis

112.3 Of skin and nails

Candidal intertrigo
Candidal onychia
Candidal perionyxis [paronychia]

112.4 Of lung

Candidal pneumonia

112.5 Disseminated

Systemic candidiasis

✓5th **112.8 Of other specified sites**

112.81 Candidal endocarditis

112.82 Candidal otitis externa

Otomycosis in moniliasis

112.83 Candidal meningitis

112.84 Candidal esophagitis

112.85 Candidal enteritis

112.89 Other

112.9 Of unspecified site

4th 114 Coccidioidomycosis

INCLUDES infection by Coccidioides (immitis)
Posada-Wernicke disease

DEF: A fungal disease caused by inhalation of dust particles containing arthrospores of *Coccidiodes immitis;* a self-limited respiratory infection; the primary form is known as San Joaquin fever, desert fever or valley fever.

114.0 Primary coccidioidomycosis (pulmonary)
Acute pulmonary coccidioidomycosis
Coccidioidomycotic pneumonitis
Desert rheumatism
Pulmonary coccidioidomycosis
San Joaquin Valley fever

DEF: Acute, self-limiting *Coccidioides immitis* infection of the lung.

114.1 Primary extrapulmonary coccidioidomycosis
Chancriform syndrome
Primary cutaneous coccidioidomycosis

DEF: Acute, self-limiting *Coccidioides immitis* infection in nonpulmonary site.

114.2 Coccidioidal meningitis

DEF: *Coccidioides immitis* infection of the lining of the brain and/or spinal cord.

114.3 Other forms of progressive coccidioidomycosis
Coccidioidal granuloma
Disseminated coccidioidomycosis

114.4 Chronic pulmonary coccidioidomycosis

114.5 Pulmonary coccidioidomycosis, unspecified

114.9 Coccidioidomycosis, unspecified

4th 115 Histoplasmosis

The following fifth-digit subclassification is for use with category 115:
0 without mention of manifestation
1 meningitis
2 retinitis
3 pericarditis
4 endocarditis
5 pneumonia
9 other

5th 115.0 Infection by Histoplasma capsulatum
[0-5, 9] American histoplasmosis
Darling's disease
Reticuloendothelial cytomycosis
Small form histoplasmosis

5th 115.1 Infection by Histoplasma duboisii
[0-5, 9] African histoplasmosis
Large form histoplasmosis

5th 115.9 Histoplasmosis, unspecified
[0-5, 9] Histoplasmosis NOS

4th 116 Blastomycotic infection

116.0 Blastomycosis
Blastomycotic dermatitis
Chicago disease
Cutaneous blastomycosis
Disseminated blastomycosis
Gilchrist's disease
Infection by Blastomyces [Ajellomyces] dermatitidis
North American blastomycosis
Primary pulmonary blastomycosis

116.1 Paracoccidioidomycosis
Brazilian blastomycosis
Infection by Paracoccidioides [Blastomyces] brasiliensis
Lutz-Splendore-Almeida disease
Mucocutaneous-lymphangitic paracoccidioidomycosis
Pulmonary paracoccidioidomycosis
South American blastomycosis
Visceral paracoccidioidomycosis

116.2 Lobomycosis
Infections by Loboa [Blastomyces] loboi
Keloidal blastomycosis
Lobo's disease

4th 117 Other mycoses

117.0 Rhinosporidiosis
Infection by Rhinosporidium seeberi

117.1 Sporotrichosis
Cutaneous sporotrichosis
Disseminated sporotrichosis
Infection by Sporothrix [Sporotrichum] schenckii
Lymphocutaneous sporotrichosis
Pulmonary sporotrichosis
Sporotrichosis of the bones

117.2 Chromoblastomycosis
Chromomycosis
Infection by Cladosporidium carrionii, Fonsecaea compactum, Fonsecaea pedrosoi, Phialophora verrucosa

117.3 Aspergillosis
Infection by Aspergillus species, mainly A. fumigatus, A. flavus group, A. terreus group

117.4 Mycotic mycetomas
Infection by various genera and species of Ascomycetes and Deuteromycetes, such as Acremonium [Cephalosporium] falciforme, Neotestudina rosatii, Madurella grisea, Madurella mycetomii, Pyrenochaeta romeroi, Zopfia [Leptosphaeria] senegalensis
Madura foot, mycotic
Maduromycosis, mycotic

EXCLUDES *actinomycotic mycetomas (039.0-039.9)*

117.5 Cryptococcosis
Busse-Buschke's disease
European cryptococcosis
Infection by Cryptococcus neoformans
Pulmonary cryptococcosis
Systemic cryptococcosis
Torula

117.6 Allescheriosis [Petriellidosis]
Infections by Allescheria [Petriellidium] boydii [Monosporium apiospermum]

EXCLUDES *mycotic mycetoma (117.4)*

117.7 Zygomycosis [Phycomycosis or Mucormycosis]
Infection by species of Absidia, Basidiobolus, Conidiobolus, Cunninghamella, Entomophthora, Mucor, Rhizopus, Saksenaea

117.8 Infection by dematiacious fungi, [Phaehyphomycosis]
Infection by dematiacious fungi, such as Cladosporium trichoides [bantianum], Dreschlera hawaiiensis, Phialophora gougerotii, Phialophora jeanselmi

117.9 Other and unspecified mycoses

118 Opportunistic mycoses
Infection of skin, subcutaneous tissues, and/or organs by a wide variety of fungi generally considered to be pathogenic to compromised hosts only (e.g., infection by species of Alternaria, Dreschlera, Fusarium)

Use additional code to identify manifestation, such as:
keratitis (370.8)

HELMINTHIASES (120-129)

4th 120 Schistosomiasis [bilharziasis]

DEF: Infection caused by *Schistosoma,* a genus of flukes or trematode parasites.

120.0 Schistosoma haematobium
Vesical schistosomiasis NOS

120.1 Schistosoma mansoni
Intestinal schistosomiasis NOS

120.2 Schistosoma japonicum
Asiatic schistosomiasis NOS
Katayama disease or fever

120.3 Cutaneous
Cercarial dermatitis
Infection by cercariae of Schistosoma
Schistosome dermatitis
Swimmers' itch

120.8 Other specified schistosomiasis
Infection by Schistosoma:
bovis
intercalatum
mattheii
spindale
Schistosomiasis chestermani

120.9 Schistosomiasis, unspecified
Blood flukes NOS
Hemic distomiasis

4th 121 Other trematode infections

121.0 Opisthorchiasis
Infection by:
cat liver fluke
Opisthorchis (felineus) (tenuicollis) (viverrini)

121.1 Clonorchiasis
Biliary cirrhosis due to clonorchiasis
Chinese liver fluke disease
Hepatic distomiasis due to Clonorchis sinensis
Oriental liver fluke disease

121.2 Paragonimiasis
Infection by Paragonimus
Lung fluke disease (oriental)
Pulmonary distomiasis

121.3 Fascioliasis
Infection by Fasciola:
gigantica
hepatica
Liver flukes NOS
Sheep liver fluke infection

121.4 Fasciolopsiasis
Infection by Fasciolopsis (buski)
Intestinal distomiasis

121.5 Metagonimiasis
Infection by Metagonimus yokogawai

121.6 Heterophyiasis
Infection by:
Heterophyes heterophyes
Stellantchasmus falcatus

121.8 Other specified trematode infections
Infection by:
Dicrocoelium dendriticum
Echinostoma ilocanum
Gastrodiscoides hominis

121.9 Trematode infection, unspecified
Distomiasis NOS
Fluke disease NOS

4th 122 Echinococcosis

INCLUDES echinococciasis
hydatid disease
hydatidosis

DEF: Infection caused by larval forms of tapeworms of the genus *Echinococcus.*

122.0 Echinococcus granulosus infection of liver

122.1 Echinococcus granulosus infection of lung

122.2 Echinococcus granulosus infection of thyroid

122.3 Echinococcus granulosus infection, other

122.4 Echinococcus granulosus infection, unspecified

122.5 Echinococcus multilocularis infection of liver

122.6 Echinococcus multilocularis infection, other

122.7 Echinococcus multilocularis infection, unspecified

122.8 Echinococcosis, unspecified, of liver

122.9 Echinococcosis, other and unspecified

4th 123 Other cestode infection

123.0 Taenia solium infection, intestinal form
Pork tapeworm (adult) (infection)

123.1 Cysticercosis
Cysticerciasis
Infection by Cysticercus cellulosae [larval form of Taenia solium]

123.2 Taenia saginata infection
Beef tapeworm (infection)
Infection by Taeniarhynchus saginatus

123.3 Taeniasis, unspecified

123.4 Diphyllobothriasis, intestinal
Diphyllobothrium (adult) (latum) (pacificum) infection
Fish tapeworm (infection)

123.5 Sparganosis [larval diphyllobothriasis]
Infection by:
Diphyllobothrium larvae
Sparganum (mansoni) (proliferum)
Spirometra larvae

123.6 Hymenolepiasis
Dwarf tapeworm (infection)
Hymenolepis (diminuta) (nana) infection
Rat tapeworm (infection)

123.8 Other specified cestode infection
Diplogonoporus (grandis) } infection
Dipylidium (caninum) } infection
Dog tapeworm (infection)

123.9 Cestode infection, unspecified
Tapeworm (infection) NOS

124 Trichinosis
Trichinella spiralis infection
Trichinellosis
Trichiniasis

DEF: Infection by *Trichinella spiralis,* the smallest of the parasitic nematodes.

4th 125 Filarial infection and dracontiasis

125.0 Bancroftian filariasis
Chyluria } due to Wuchereria bancrofti
Elephantiasis } due to Wuchereria bancrofti
Infection } due to Wuchereria bancrofti
Lymphadenitis } due to Wuchereria bancrofti
Lymphangitis } due to Wuchereria bancrofti
Wuchereriasis

125.1 Malayan filariasis
Brugia filariasis } due to Wuchereria bancrofti
Chyluria } due to Wuchereria bancrofti
Elephantiasis } due to Wuchereria bancrofti
Infection } due to Wuchereria bancrofti
Lymphadenitis } due to Wuchereria bancrofti
Lymphangitis } due to Wuchereria bancrofti

125.2 Loiasis
Eyeworm disease of Africa
Loa loa infection

125.3 Onchocerciasis
Onchocerca volvulus infection
Onchocercosis

125.4 Dipetalonemiasis
Infection by:
Acanthocheilonema perstans
Dipetalonema perstans

125.5 Mansonella ozzardi infection
Filariasis ozzardi

125.6 Other specified filariasis
Dirofilaria infection
Infection by:
Acanthocheilonema streptocerca
Dipetalonema streptocerca

125.7 Dracontiasis
Guinea-worm infection
Infection by Dracunculus medinensis

125.9 Unspecified filariasis

4th 126 Ancylostomiasis and necatoriasis

INCLUDES cutaneous larva migrans due to Ancylostoma
hookworm (disease) (infection)
uncinariasis

126.0 Ancylostoma duodenale

126.1 Necator americanus

126.2 Ancylostoma braziliense

126.3 Ancylostoma ceylanicum

126.8 Other specified Ancylostoma

126.9 Ancylostomiasis and necatoriasis, unspecified
Creeping eruption NOS
Cutaneous larva migrans NOS

✓4th 127 Other intestinal helminthiases

127.0 Ascariasis
Ascaridiasis
Infection by Ascaris lumbricoides
Roundworm infection

127.1 Anisakiasis
Infection by Anisakis larva

127.2 Strongyloidiasis
Infection by Strongyloides stercoralis
EXCLUDES *trichostrongyliasis (127.6)*

127.3 Trichuriasis
Infection by Trichuris trichiuria
Trichocephaliasis
Whipworm (disease) (infection)

127.4 Enterobiasis
Infection by Enterobius vermicularis
Oxyuriasis
Oxyuris vermicularis infection
Pinworm (disease) (infection)
Threadworm infection

127.5 Capillariasis
Infection by Capillaria philippinensis
EXCLUDES *infection by Capillaria hepatica (128.8)*

127.6 Trichostrongyliasis
Infection by Trichostrongylus species

127.7 Other specified intestinal helminthiasis
Infection by:
- Oesophagostomum apiostomum and related species
- Ternidens diminutus
- other specified intestinal helminth

Physalopteriasis

127.8 Mixed intestinal helminthiasis
Infection by intestinal helminths classified to more than one of the categories 120.0-127.7
Mixed helminthiasis NOS

127.9 Intestinal helminthiasis, unspecified

✓4th 128 Other and unspecified helminthiases

128.0 Toxocariasis
Larva migrans visceralis
Toxocara (canis) (cati) infection
Visceral larva migrans syndrome

128.1 Gnathostomiasis
Infection by Gnathostoma spinigerum and related species

128.8 Other specified helminthiasis
Infection by:
- Angiostrongylus cantonensis
- Capillaria hepatica
- other specified helminth

128.9 Helminth infection, unspecified
Helminthiasis NOS
Worms NOS

129 Intestinal parasitism, unspecified

OTHER INFECTIOUS AND PARASITIC DISEASES (130–136)

✓4th 130 Toxoplasmosis

INCLUDES infection by toxoplasma gondii
toxoplasmosis (acquired)
EXCLUDES *congenital toxoplasmosis (771.2)*

130.0 Meningoencephalitis due to toxoplasmosis
Encephalitis due to acquired toxoplasmosis

130.1 Conjunctivitis due to toxoplasmosis

130.2 Chorioretinitis due to toxoplasmosis
Focal retinochoroiditis due to acquired toxoplasmosis

130.3 Myocarditis due to toxoplasmosis

130.4 Pneumonitis due to toxoplasmosis

130.5 Hepatitis due to toxoplasmosis

130.7 Toxoplasmosis of other specified sites

130.8 Multisystemic disseminated toxoplasmosis
Toxoplasmosis of multiple sites

130.9 Toxoplasmosis, unspecified

131 Trichomoniasis

INCLUDES infection due to Trichomonas (vaginalis)

✓5th 131.0 Urogenital trichomoniasis

131.00 Urogenital trichomoniasis, unspecified
Fluor (vaginalis) } trichomonal or due to Trichomonas (vaginalis)
Leukorrhea (vaginalis) } trichomonal or due to Trichomonas (vaginalis)

DEF: ***Trichomonas vaginalis*** **infection of reproductive and urinary organs, transmitted through coitus.**

131.01 Trichomonal vulvovaginitis
Vaginitis, trichomonal or due to Trichomonas (vaginalis)

DEF: ***Trichomonas vaginalis*** **infection of vulva and vagina; often asymptomatic, transmitted through coitus.**

131.02 Trichomonal urethritis

DEF: ***Trichomonas vaginalis*** **infection of the urethra.**

131.03 Trichomonal prostatitis

DEF: ***Trichomonas vaginalis*** **infection of the prostate.**

131.09 Other

131.8 Other specified sites
EXCLUDES *intestinal (007.3)*

131.9 Trichomoniasis, unspecified

✓4th 132 Pediculosis and phthirus infestation

132.0 Pediculus capitis [head louse]

132.1 Pediculus corporis [body louse]

132.2 Phthirus pubis [pubic louse]
Pediculus pubis

132.3 Mixed infestation
Infestation classifiable to more than one of the categories 132.0-132.2

132.9 Pediculosis, unspecified

✓4th 133 Acariasis

133.0 Scabies
Infestation by Sarcoptes scabiei
Norwegian scabies
Sarcoptic itch

133.8 Other acariasis
Chiggers
Infestation by:
- Demodex folliculorum
- Trombicula

133.9 Acariasis, unspecified
Infestation by mites NOS

✓4th 134 Other infestation

134.0 Myiasis
Infestation by:
- Dermatobia (hominis)
- fly larvae
- Gasterophilus (intestinalis)
- maggots
- Oestrus ovis

134.1 Other arthropod infestation
Infestation by:
- chigoe
- sand flea
- Tunga penetrans

Jigger disease
Scarabiasis
Tungiasis

134.2 Hirudiniasis
Hirudiniasis (external) (internal)
Leeches (aquatic) (land)

134.8 Other specified infestations

134.9 Infestation, unspecified
Infestation (skin) NOS
Skin parasites NOS

135 Sarcoidosis
Besnier-Boeck-Schaumann disease
Lupoid (miliary) of Boeck
Lupus pernio (Besnier)
Lymphogranulomatosis, benign (Schaumann's)
Sarcoid (any site):
NOS
Boeck
Darier-Roussy
Uveoparotid fever

DEF: A chronic, granulomatous reticulosis (abnormal increase in cells), affecting any organ or tissue; acute form has high rate of remission; chronic form is progressive.

✓4th **136 Other and unspecified infectious and parasitic diseases**

136.0 Ainhum
Dactylolysis spontanea
DEF: A disease affecting the toes, especially the fifth digit, and sometimes the fingers, especially seen in black adult males; it is characterized by a linear constriction around the affected digit leading to spontaneous amputation of the distal part of the digit.

136.1 Behçet's syndrome
DEF: A chronic inflammatory disorder of unknown etiology involving the small blood vessels; it is characterized by recurrent aphthous ulceration of the oral and pharyngeal mucous membranes and the genitalia, skin lesions, severe uvetis, retinal vascularitis and optic atrophy.

✓5th **136.2 Specific infections by free-living amebae**

136.21 Specific infection due to acanthamoeba
Use additional code to identify manifestation, such as:
keratitis (370.8)

136.29 Other specific infections by free-living amebae
Meningoencephalitis due to Naegleria

136.3 Pneumocystosis
Pneumonia due to Pneumocystis carinii
Pneumonia due to Pneumocystis jiroveci
DEF: *Pneumocystis carinii* fungus causing pneumonia in immunocompromised patients; a leading cause of death among AIDS patients.

136.4 Psorospermiasis

136.5 Sarcosporidiosis
Infection by Sarcocystis lindemanni
DEF: *Sarcocystis* infection causing muscle cysts of intestinal inflammation.

136.8 Other specified infectious and parasitic diseases
Candiru infestation

136.9 Unspecified infectious and parasitic diseases
Infectious disease NOS
Parasitic disease NOS

LATE EFFECTS OF INFECTIOUS AND PARASITIC DISEASES (137-139)

✓4th **137 Late effects of tuberculosis**

Note: This category is to be used to indicate conditions classifiable to 010-018 as the cause of late effects, which are themselves classified elsewhere. The "late effects" include those specified as such, as sequelae, or as due to old or inactive tuberculosis, without evidence of active disease.

137.0 Late effects of respiratory or unspecified tuberculosis

137.1 Late effects of central nervous system tuberculosis

137.2 Late effects of genitourinary tuberculosis

137.3 Late effects of tuberculosis of bones and joints

137.4 Late effects of tuberculosis of other specified organs

138 Late effects of acute poliomyelitis

Note: This category is to be used to indicate conditions classifiable to 045 as the cause of late effects, which are themselves classified elsewhere. The "late effects" include conditions specified as such, or as sequelae, or as due to old or inactive poliomyelitis, without evidence of active disease.

✓4th **139 Late effects of other infectious and parasitic diseases**

Note: This category is to be used to indicate conditions classifiable to categories 001-009, 020-041, 046-136 as the cause of late effects, which are themselves classified elsewhere. The "late effects" include conditions specified as such; they also include sequela of diseases classifiable to the above categories if there is evidence that the disease itself is no longer present.

139.0 Late effects of viral encephalitis
Late effects of conditions classifiable to 049.8-049.9, 062-064

139.1 Late effects of trachoma
Late effects of conditions classifiable to 076

139.8 Late effects of other and unspecified infectious and parasitic diseases

Chapter 2: Neoplasms (140–239)

Code neoplasms by behavior and site. According to the most widely accepted definition, a neoplasm is an abnormal mass of tissue, the growth of which exceeds and is uncoordinated with that of the normal tissues and persists in the same excessive manner after cessation of the stimulus that evoked the change.

For ICD-9-CM classification purposes, neoplasms are described in the following four ways:

- Behavior - malignant, benign, uncertain, and unspecified
- Malignant neoplasms are further differentiated into three types. Primary neoplasm identifies the originating site of the tumor. Secondary neoplasm identifies the site to which a primary tumor has metastasized. And carcinoma in situ identifies tumors that are confined to their point of origin and have not invaded surrounding tissue.
- Site - anatomic location of the neoplasm and is used as a subdivision for each of the four types of behaviors
- Functional activity - effects certain neoplasms have on tissues that are functionally active
- Morphology - classification of neoplasms according to tissue type or cell origin

The morphology of a neoplasm is reported using M codes, which are provided as a separate code listing in ICD-9-CM, appendix A. Morphology codes are usually reported only by the hospital health information management (HIM) department to the national cancer registry. Physician offices do not report the morphology of neoplasms to the payers or registry.

Metastatic (secondary) neoplasms are classified to categories 196–198.

Benign neoplasms, classified to categories 210–229, are tumors in which the dividing cells adhere to each other, with the resulting neoplastic mass remaining as a circumscribed lesion.

Uncertain behavior is the term used to describe neoplasms whose behavior cannot be determined at the time of discovery and continued study is necessary to accurately classify the neoplasm by behavior.

Unspecified behavior is assigned when the medical documentation does not specify the behavior of the neoplasm.

The major groups of malignant neoplasms are carcinomas, sarcomas, and mixed tissue tumors. Examples of the mixed tissue tumors are tumors of the kidney, ovary, and testes.

Steps in coding neoplasms using the alphabetic index and neoplasm table:

- Locate the main term for the morphologic type in the alphabetic index.
- Review the subterm entries.
- Look for cross-references and site.
- If the site is not listed as a subterm refer to the neoplasm table according to the cross-reference.
- Locate the anatomical site in the table that lists sites alphabetically.
- Select the appropriate behavior type for the neoplasm.
- Select the appropriate code and verify the code in the tabular list.

Example:

> Primary hepatic cell carcinoma.
>
> Using the alphabetic index: Under the main term "Carcinoma" in the alphabetic index locate the subterm hepatic cell. The index directs the coder to the code 155.0. The tabular verifies that code 155.0 includes hepatocellular carcinoma specified as primary. Note that the morphology code indicates this is a primary site malignancy.
>
> Carcinoma (M8010/3)—see also Neoplasm, by site, malignant
> hepatic cell (M8170/3) 155.0
> hepatocellular (M8170/3) 155.0 and bile duct, mixed (M8180/3) 155.0

Using the Neoplasm Table

To locate the code for primary hepatic cell carcinoma using the table, search the table for the main entry of anatomic site. In this case hepatic cell carcinoma is neoplasm of the liver. Locate the main term "liver" in the table. The entry contains the subterm "primary." Since the diagnostic statement and the behavior code for primary hepatic cell (liver) carcinoma indicate that this neoplasm is of a primary malignant nature, the coder uses the code listed under the table heading "Malignant." Again the code choice is 155.0.

Coding Metastatic Neoplasms

For neoplasms that have multiple metastatic sites, code all as secondary and code the primary site if indicated.

Example:

> Metastatic neoplasm of the lung and brain from the oropharynx. The oropharynx is the primary site (146.8) and the lung (197.0) and brain (198.3) are secondary sites.

When either the primary or the secondary site is not indicated or documented, code 199.1 Malignant neoplasm without specification of site, is assigned. For neoplasms that have multiple metastatic sites and no primary site indicated, code all as secondary and code the primary site to 199.1.

In those cases where the neoplasm is a single metastatic site and the morphologic type is indicated, the coder first locates the morphologic term in the alphabetic index either as a separate entry or under the main term "Carcinoma."

For example, metastatic hepatic cell carcinoma of the stomach is coded 155.0 and 197.8. The user is directed by the index under the main term "Carcinoma" to code hepatic cell carcinoma 155.0 Malignant neoplasm, liver, primary. The secondary site is the stomach and is coded as 197.8. Do not assign the unspecified code 199.1 when the morphologic type indicates a primary site.

If the morphology does not indicate a primary site and the neoplasm is identified as a single metastatic site, assign code 199.1, indicating the unspecified primary site. In addition, assign a code identifying the single specified metastatic site.

For patients who are in remission or are no longer considered to have a malignant neoplasm, personal history of malignant neoplasm codes V10.00–V10.9, should be updated.

Malignant Neoplasms of Solid Tumor Type (140–199)

Solid tumors have the capacity to spread to adjacent (direct extension metastasis) or distant sites in the body (embolic metastasis). The method of spreading is not reflected in the code assignment, only the fact that there has been metastasis. When there has been direct extension and the site of origin cannot be determined (i.e., the neoplasm exists over two adjacent [contiguous] sites), ICD-9-CM classifies that neoplasm as other specified site, fourth digit of 8.

Code 199.2 reports malignant neoplasm associated with a transplanted organ. Organ recipients are routinely placed on immunosuppressive drugs to prevent rejection of the transplanted organ, but this immunosuppression also renders them vulnerable to infection and disease, including malignancy. Additionally, a transplanted organ may contain malignant cells that were undetected prior to transplant. Multiple transplant operations may be a result of transplanted organ failure, rejection, or other complications such as neoplasm. Instructional notes are included with code 199.2 Malignant neoplasm associated with transplanted organ to "code first complication of transplanted organ (996.80–996.89)" and "use additional code for specific malignancy site." Multiple codes are required and are reported in a specific sequence.

Malignant Neoplasms of Lymphatic and Hematopoietic Tissue (200–208)

Malignant neoplasms of the lymphatic and hematopoetic tissues are considered primary neoplasms and are not considered to spread to secondary sites. The malignant cells circulate to other areas but these are not considered secondary sites.

Some of the types of neoplasms included in this section are lymphosarcomas, Hodgkin's disease, lymphomas, malignant histocytosis, multiple myeloma, myeloid leukemia, acute leukemia and chronic leukemia.

Fifth-digit subclassification used with categories 200–202 specifies the lymph node involvement with the disease. It is acceptable to assign two different fourth-digit codes from the same three-digit category. For example, a patient diagnosed with T-cell lymphoma and Sezary syndrome is assigned both 202.2x Sezary syndrome, and 202.1x Mycosis fungoides.

Relapse, or recurrence, of leukemia occurs when the disease returns either during therapy or after being successfully treated (remission). Relapse during or soon after the completion of treatment is generally considered less favorable than relapse after remission has been achieved. Interventions and treatments may vary from induction (primary) therapy, and may be more aggressive in nature. Due to the increased risks associated with treating leukemia that relapsed prior to achieving remission, the fifth-digit definitions to the hematopoietic neoplasm code categories 203–208 facilitate tracking disease progression of relapse with or without having achieved remission.

Sequencing guidelines governing code assignment for cases involving neoplasms depends on focus of the treatment. If treatment is directed to the primary site, code the primary malignancy first. If treatment is directed toward the secondary site only, code the secondary neoplasm as principal diagnosis. When a patient is admitted only for chemotherapy or radiotherapy, assign code V58.0 or V58.1 [V58.11], respectively, with the malignancy coded as a secondary diagnosis. For treatment directed toward a complication of therapy, code the complication as primary and the malignancy as a secondary code.

Neuroendocrine tumors (209)

Carcinoid tumors are a specific type of slow-growing malignant neoplasms originating in the cells of the neuroendocrine system. Although the terms "carcinoid" and "neuroendocrine" may be used interchangeably in the clinical environment to describe specific types of neoplasm, carcinoid tumor is one type of neuroendocrine neoplasm. Neuroendocrine cells produce and secrete regulatory hormones. Tumors comprised of these cells are consequently capable of producing hormonal syndromes (e.g., carcinoid syndrome), in which the normal hormonal balance required to support body system functions is adversely affected. Symptoms caused by neuroendocrine tumors arise from the abnormal secretion of hormones due to the presence of neoplastic growth and its affected tissues. As a result, many of these tumors are associated with a diverse range of characteristic hormonal syndromes such as multiple endocrine neoplasia syndromes, classifiable to subcategory 258.0 and carcinoid syndrome (259.2). Carcinoid syndrome (259.2) is the most common systemic syndrome associated with carcinoid tumors. Carcinoid syndrome causes patients to have flushing, diarrhea, and heart disease. It is caused by an abnormally high concentration of serotonin secretion. Carcinoid tumors occur most commonly in the respiratory and gastrointestinal tract, and usually originate in hormone-producing cells in the linings of these organs. They can also occur in the pancreas, testes, ovaries, or lungs. Gastrointestinal carcinoid tumors are classified according to the presumed embryonic site of origin: the foregut (bronchi and stomach), the midgut (small intestine and appendix), and the hindgut (colon and rectum). Carcinoid tumors have different expected outcomes than more common neoplasms, and require different treatments. For example, an adenocarcinoma may be treated with cytotoxic chemotherapy, while a neuroendocrine tumor is likely to be more responsive to hormonal therapies due to the nature of the neoplasm.

Benign Neoplasms (210–229)

Benign neoplasms, classified to categories 210–229, are tumors in which the dividing cells adhere to each other, with the resulting neoplastic mass remaining as a circumscribed lesion. These tumor cells, which are not cancerous, do not metastasize or invade adjacent structures.

Carcinoma In Situ (230–234)

Carcinoma in situ are neoplasms that have the potential for spreading to surrounding tissue but remain limited and have not extended beyond the basement membrane of the epithelial tissue. Other common terms used to describe carcinoma in situ are noninfiltrating, noninvasive, intraepithelial, or preinvasive carcinoma. Neoplasms classified to this section of ICD-9-CM include carcinoma of the digestive tract, respiratory system, skin, breast, and genitourinary system.

For example, in situ carcinoma of the breast, lower outer quadrant is coded 233.0. Coders may use either the neoplasm table or the Index to locate this code. In the Index under the main term "Carcinoma" locate the subterm "in situ (M8010/2)—see also Neoplasm, by site, in situ." This indicates that the coder should refer to the neoplasm table under "Breast, in situ."

Certain severe dysplasias are classified as carcinoma in situ. Dysplastic tissue may be described as an alteration of cellular organization, size, and shape. These alterations may progress to cancerous conditions. Dysplasia and carcinoma in situ are definitive diagnoses based upon histological examination of biopsied tissue.

For example, vaginal intraepithelial neoplasia (VAIN III) is reported with code 233.31 Carcinoma in situ of other and unspecified female genital organs, vagina, while vulvar intraepithelial neoplasia (VIN III) is reported with code 233.32 Carcinoma in situ of other and unspecified female genital organs, vulva.

Neoplasms of Uncertain Behavior (235–238)

Neoplasms of uncertain behavior consist of cells in an intermediate stage that require further testing to determine subsequent behavior. These neoplasms are classified to category codes 235–238. Codes from this column should only be used when "uncertain behavior" appears on the pathology report. Note: Uncertain behavior is a histomorphological determination, as distinguished from "unspecified," which indicates lack of documentation to support a more specific code assignment. Do not confuse "uncertain behavior" with "unspecified." The two terms are not interchangeable.

Post-transplant lymphoproliferative disorder (PTLD) (238.77) is a disease of uncontrolled proliferation or production of B cell lymphocytes, often following infection with the Epstein-Barr virus for post-transplant patients. The clinical presentation of PTLD varies. The patient may present asymptomatically or with localized or systemic symptoms such as one or more nodal or extranodal tumors. Systemic presentations may range from an unexplained infectious syndrome or mononucleosis-like illness with or without lymphadenopathy to a disseminated sepsis syndrome. Symptoms of PTLD are related to the site of tumor growth. For example, gastrointestinal tumors can cause abdominal pain with hemorrhage and perforation, resulting in peritonitis. Diagnosis may be confirmed with histopathological changes on biopsy. After cessation of immunosuppressive drug therapy, PTLD may regress spontaneously.

Code 238.77 includes an instructional note to "code first complications of transplant (996.80–996.89)." Therefore, PTLD is reported as a secondary diagnosis, with the appropriate subcategory 996.8 as the first-listed diagnosis.

Neoplasms of Unspecified Nature (239)

Category 239 classifies by site neoplasms of unspecified morphology or behavior. This means the medical record contains no further information to more accurately code the condition. Neoplasm of unspecified nature indicates a lack of specific information in the documentation while neoplasm of uncertain behavior refers to incomplete assessment of the neoplasm. Other terms often documented in records with no further information include neoplasm, new growth, tumor, or growth.

2. NEOPLASMS (140-239)

Notes:

1. Content

This chapter contains the following broad groups:

140-195	Malignant neoplasms, stated or presumed to be primary, of specified sites, except of lymphatic and hematopoietic tissue
196-198	Malignant neoplasms, stated or presumed to be secondary, of specified sites
199	Malignant neoplasms, without specification of site
200-208	Malignant neoplasms, stated or presumed to be primary, of lymphatic and hematopoietic tissue
209	Neuroendocrine tumors
210-229	Benign neoplasms
230-234	Carcinoma in situ
235-238	Neoplasms of uncertain behavior [see Note, above category 235]
239	Neoplasms of unspecified nature

2. Functional activity

All neoplasms are classified in this chapter, whether or not functionally active. An additional code from Chapter 3 may be used to identify such functional activity associated with any neoplasm, e.g.:

catecholamine-producing malignant pheochromocytoma of adrenal:
code 194.0, additional code 255.6

basophil adenoma of pituitary with Cushing's syndrome:
code 227.3, additional code 255.0

3. Morphology [Histology]

For those wishing to identify the histological type of neoplasms, a comprehensive coded nomenclature, which comprises the morphology rubrics of the ICD-Oncology, is given in Appendix A.

4. Malignant neoplasms overlapping site boundaries

Categories 140-195 are for the classification of primary malignant neoplasms according to their point of origin. A malignant neoplasm that overlaps two or more subcategories within a three-digit rubric and whose point of origin cannot be determined should be classified to the subcategory .8 "Other."

For example, "carcinoma involving tip and ventral surface of tongue" should be assigned to 141.8. On the other hand, "carcinoma of tip of tongue, extending to involve the ventral surface" should be coded to 141.2, as the point of origin, the tip, is known. Three subcategories (149.8, 159.8, 165.8) have been provided for malignant neoplasms that overlap the boundaries of three-digit rubrics within certain systems.

Overlapping malignant neoplasms that cannot be classified as indicated above should be assigned to the appropriate subdivision of category 195 (Malignant neoplasm of other and ill-defined sites).

DEF: An abnormal growth, such as a tumor. Morphology determines behavior, i.e., whether it will remain intact (benign) or spread to adjacent tissue (malignant). The term mass is not synonymous with neoplasm, as it is often used to describe cysts and thickenings such as those occurring with hematoma or infection.

MALIGNANT NEOPLASM OF LIP, ORAL CAVITY, AND PHARYNX (140-149)

EXCLUDES *carcinoma in situ (230.0)*

✓4th 140 Malignant neoplasm of lip

EXCLUDES *skin of lip (173.0)*

140.0 Upper lip, vermilion border
Upper lip:
NOS
external
lipstick area

Lip

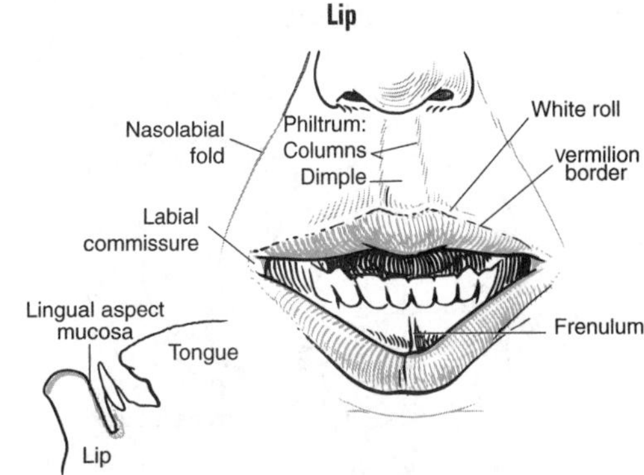

140.1 Lower lip, vermilion border
Lower lip:
NOS
external
lipstick area

140.3 Upper lip, inner aspect
Upper lip:
buccal aspect
frenulum
mucosa
oral aspect

140.4 Lower lip, inner aspect
Lower lip:
buccal aspect
frenulum
mucosa
oral aspect

140.5 Lip, unspecified, inner aspect
Lip, not specified whether upper or lower:
buccal aspect
frenulum
mucosa
oral aspect

140.6 Commissure of lip
Labial commissure

140.8 Other sites of lip
Malignant neoplasm of contiguous or overlapping sites of lip whose point of origin cannot be determined

140.9 Lip, unspecified, vermilion border
Lip, not specified as upper or lower:
NOS
external
lipstick area

✓4th 141 Malignant neoplasm of tongue

141.0 Base of tongue
Dorsal surface of base of tongue
Fixed part of tongue NOS

141.1 Dorsal surface of tongue
Anterior two-thirds of tongue, dorsal surface
Dorsal tongue NOS
Midline of tongue
EXCLUDES *dorsal surface of base of tongue (141.0)*

Tongue

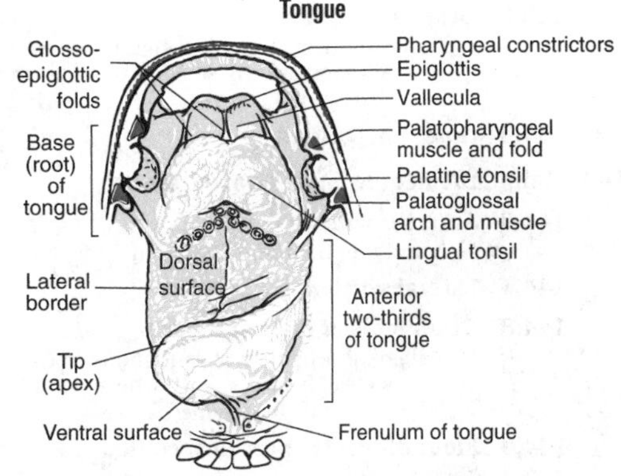

Main Salivary Glands

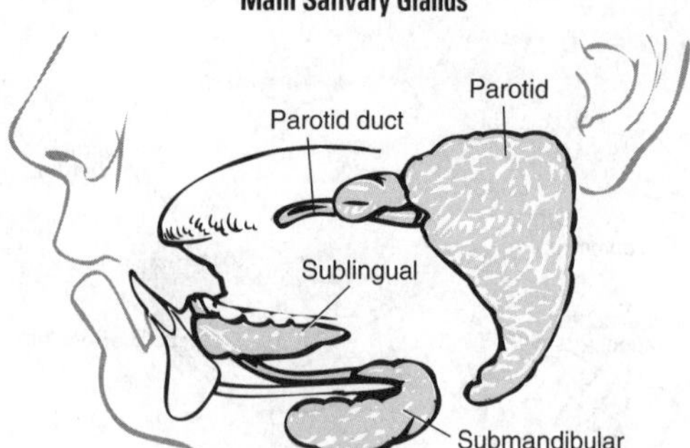

141.2 Tip and lateral border of tongue

141.3 Ventral surface of tongue
Anterior two-thirds of tongue, ventral surface
Frenulum linguae

141.4 Anterior two-thirds of tongue, part unspecified
Mobile part of tongue NOS

141.5 Junctional zone
Border of tongue at junction of fixed and mobile parts at insertion of anterior tonsillar pillar

141.6 Lingual tonsil

141.8 Other sites of tongue
Malignant neoplasm of contiguous or overlapping sites of tongue whose point of origin cannot be determined

141.9 Tongue, unspecified
Tongue NOS

4th 142 Malignant neoplasm of major salivary glands
INCLUDES salivary ducts
EXCLUDES *malignant neoplasm of minor salivary glands:*
NOS (145.9)
buccal mucosa (145.0)
soft palate (145.3)
tongue (141.0-141.9)
tonsil, palatine (146.0)

142.0 Parotid gland

142.1 Submandibular gland
Submaxillary gland

142.2 Sublingual gland

142.8 Other major salivary glands
Malignant neoplasm of contiguous or overlapping sites of salivary glands and ducts whose point of origin cannot be determined

142.9 Salivary gland, unspecified
Salivary gland (major) NOS

4th 143 Malignant neoplasm of gum
INCLUDES alveolar (ridge) mucosa
gingiva (alveolar) (marginal)
interdental papillae
EXCLUDES *malignant odontogenic neoplasms (170.0-170.1)*

143.0 Upper gum

143.1 Lower gum

143.8 Other sites of gum
Malignant neoplasm of contiguous or overlapping sites of gum whose point of origin cannot be determined

143.9 Gum, unspecified

4th 144 Malignant neoplasm of floor of mouth

144.0 Anterior portion
Anterior to the premolar-canine junction

144.1 Lateral portion

144.8 Other sites of floor of mouth
Malignant neoplasm of contiguous or overlapping sites of floor of mouth whose point of origin cannot be determined

144.9 Floor of mouth, part unspecified

Mouth

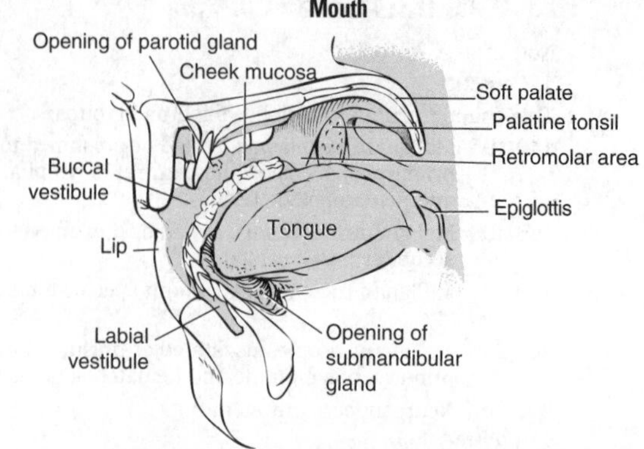

4th 145 Malignant neoplasm of other and unspecified parts of mouth
EXCLUDES *mucosa of lips (140.0-140.9)*

145.0 Cheek mucosa
Buccal mucosa
Cheek, inner aspect

145.1 Vestibule of mouth
Buccal sulcus (upper) (lower)
Labial sulcus (upper) (lower)

145.2 Hard palate

145.3 Soft palate
EXCLUDES *nasopharyngeal [posterior] [superior] surface of soft palate (147.3)*

145.4 Uvula

145.5 Palate, unspecified
Junction of hard and soft palate
Roof of mouth

145.6 Retromolar area

145.8 Other specified parts of mouth
Malignant neoplasm of contiguous or overlapping sites of mouth whose point of origin cannot be determined

145.9 Mouth, unspecified
Buccal cavity NOS
Minor salivary gland, unspecified site
Oral cavity NOS

4th 146 Malignant neoplasm of oropharynx

146.0 Tonsil
Tonsil:
NOS
faucial
palatine
EXCLUDES *lingual tonsil (141.6)*
pharyngeal tonsil (147.1)

146.1 Tonsillar fossa

146.2 Tonsillar pillars (anterior) (posterior)
Faucial pillar
Glossopalatine fold
Palatoglossal arch
Palatopharyngeal arch

Oropharynx

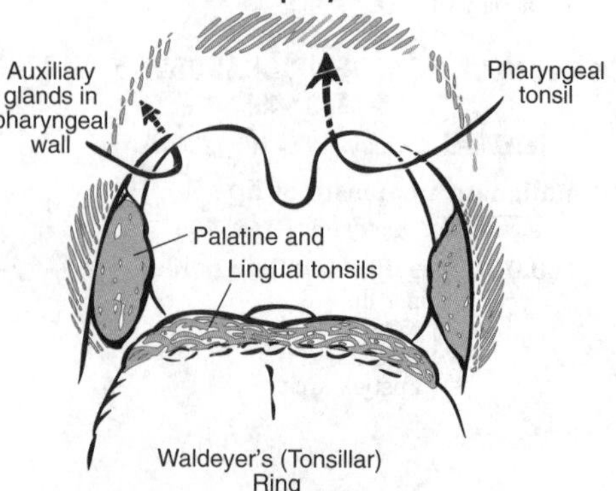

146.3 Vallecula
Anterior and medial surface of the pharyngoepiglottic fold

146.4 Anterior aspect of epiglottis
Epiglottis, free border [margin]
Glossoepiglottic fold(s)
EXCLUDES *epiglottis:*
NOS (161.1)
suprahyoid portion (161.1)

146.5 Junctional region
Junction of the free margin of the epiglottis, the aryepiglottic fold, and the pharyngoepiglottic fold

146.6 Lateral wall of oropharynx

146.7 Posterior wall of oropharynx

146.8 Other specified sites of oropharynx
Branchial cleft
Malignant neoplasm of contiguous or overlapping sites of oropharynx whose point of origin cannot be determined

146.9 Oropharynx, unspecified

✓4th **147 Malignant neoplasm of nasopharynx**

147.0 Superior wall
Roof of nasopharynx

147.1 Posterior wall
Adenoid
Pharyngeal tonsil

147.2 Lateral wall
Fossa of Rosenmüller
Opening of auditory tube
Pharyngeal recess

147.3 Anterior wall
Floor of nasopharynx
Nasopharyngeal [posterior] [superior] surface of soft palate
Posterior margin of nasal septum and choanae

147.8 Other specified sites of nasopharynx
Malignant neoplasm of contiguous or overlapping sites of nasopharynx whose point of origin cannot be determined

Nasopharynx

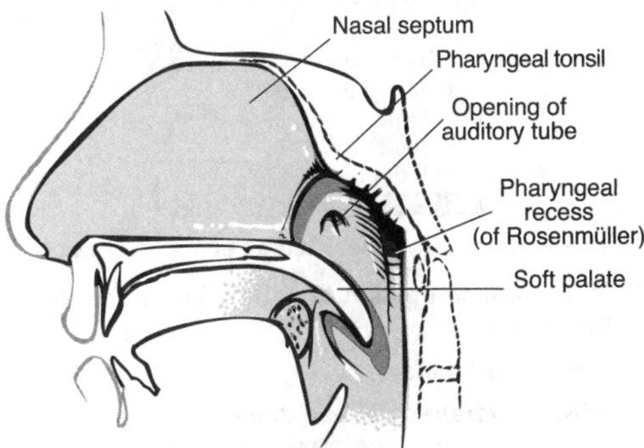

Hypopharynx

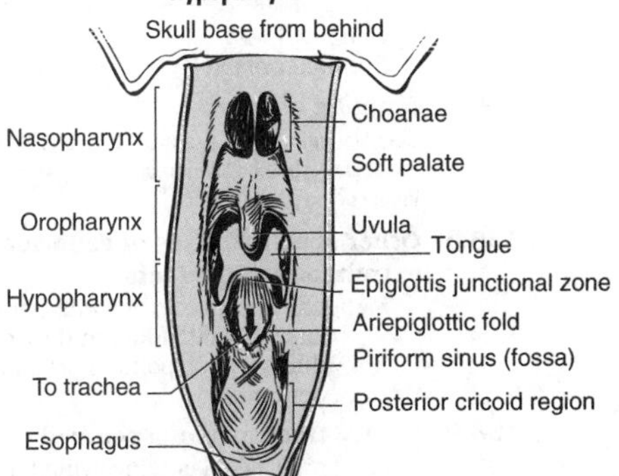

147.9 Nasopharynx, unspecified
Nasopharyngeal wall NOS

✓4th **148 Malignant neoplasm of hypopharynx**

148.0 Postcricoid region

148.1 Pyriform sinus
Pyriform fossa

148.2 Aryepiglottic fold, hypopharyngeal aspect
Aryepiglottic fold or interarytenoid fold:
NOS
marginal zone
EXCLUDES *aryepiglottic fold or interarytenoid fold, laryngeal aspect (161.1)*

148.3 Posterior hypopharyngeal wall

148.8 Other specified sites of hypopharynx
Malignant neoplasm of contiguous or overlapping sites of hypopharynx whose point of origin cannot be determined

148.9 Hypopharynx, unspecified
Hypopharyngeal wall NOS
Hypopharynx NOS

✓4th **149 Malignant neoplasm of other and ill-defined sites within the lip, oral cavity, and pharynx**

149.0 Pharynx, unspecified

149.1 Waldeyer's ring

149.8 Other
Malignant neoplasms of lip, oral cavity, and pharynx whose point of origin cannot be assigned to any one of the categories 140-148
EXCLUDES *"book leaf" neoplasm [ventral surface of tongue and floor of mouth] (145.8)*

149.9 Ill-defined

MALIGNANT NEOPLASM OF DIGESTIVE ORGANS AND PERITONEUM (150-159)

EXCLUDES *carcinoma in situ (230.1-230.9)*

✓4th **150 Malignant neoplasm of esophagus**

150.0 Cervical esophagus

150.1 Thoracic esophagus

150.2 Abdominal esophagus
EXCLUDES *adenocarcinoma (151.0)*
cardio-esophageal junction (151.0)

150.3 Upper third of esophagus
Proximal third of esophagus

150.4 Middle third of esophagus

150.5 Lower third of esophagus
Distal third of esophagus
EXCLUDES *adenocarcinoma (151.0)*
cardio-esophageal junction (151.0)

150.8 Other specified part
Malignant neoplasm of contiguous or overlapping sites of esophagus whose point of origin cannot be determined

150.9 Esophagus, unspecified

✓4th **151 Malignant neoplasm of stomach**
EXCLUDES *benign carcinoid tumor of stomach (209.63)*
malignant carcinoid tumor of stomach (209.23)

151.0 Cardia
Cardiac orifice
Cardio-esophageal junction
EXCLUDES *squamous cell carcinoma (150.2, 150.5)*

151.1 Pylorus
Prepylorus
Pyloric canal

151.2 Pyloric antrum
Antrum of stomach NOS

151.3 Fundus of stomach

151.4 Body of stomach

151.5 Lesser curvature, unspecified
Lesser curvature, not classifiable to 151.1-151.4

151.6 Greater curvature, unspecified
Greater curvature, not classifiable to 151.0-151.4

151.8 Other specified sites of stomach
Anterior wall, not classifiable to 151.0-151.4
Posterior wall, not classifiable to 151.0-151.4
Malignant neoplasm of contiguous or overlapping sites of stomach whose point of origin cannot be determined

151.9 Stomach, unspecified
Carcinoma ventriculi
Gastric cancer

✓4th **152 Malignant neoplasm of small intestine, including duodenum**
EXCLUDES *benign carcinoid tumor of small intestine and duodenum (209.40-209.43)*
malignant carcinoid tumor of small intestine and duodenum (209.00-209.03)

152.0 Duodenum

152.1 Jejunum

152.2 Ileum
EXCLUDES *ileocecal valve (153.4)*

152.3 Meckel's diverticulum

152.8 Other specified sites of small intestine
Duodenojejunal junction
Malignant neoplasm of contiguous or overlapping sites of small intestine whose point of origin cannot be determined

152.9 Small intestine, unspecified

✓4th **153 Malignant neoplasm of colon**
EXCLUDES *benign carcinoid tumor of colon (209.50-209.56)*
malignant carcinoid tumor of colon (209.10-209.16)

153.0 Hepatic flexure

153.1 Transverse colon

153.2 Descending colon
Left colon

153.3 Sigmoid colon
Sigmoid (flexure)
EXCLUDES *rectosigmoid junction (154.0)*

153.4 Cecum
Ileocecal valve

153.5 Appendix

153.6 Ascending colon
Right colon

153.7 Splenic flexure

153.8 Other specified sites of large intestine
Malignant neoplasm of contiguous or overlapping sites of colon whose point of origin cannot be determined
EXCLUDES *ileocecal valve (153.4)*
rectosigmoid junction (154.0)

153.9 Colon, unspecified
Large intestine NOS

✓4th **154 Malignant neoplasm of rectum, rectosigmoid junction, and anus**
EXCLUDES *benign carcinoid tumor of rectum (209.57)*
malignant carcinoid tumor of rectum (209.17)

154.0 Rectosigmoid junction
Colon with rectum
Rectosigmoid (colon)

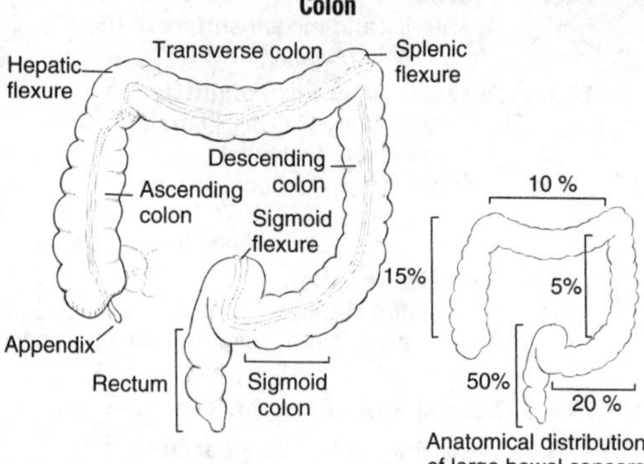

154.1 Rectum
Rectal ampulla

154.2 Anal canal
Anal sphincter
EXCLUDES *skin of anus (172.5, 173.5)*

154.3 Anus, unspecified
EXCLUDES *anus:*
margin (172.5, 173.5)
skin (172.5, 173.5)
perianal skin (172.5, 173.5)

154.8 Other
Anorectum
Cloacogenic zone
Malignant neoplasm of contiguous or overlapping sites of rectum, rectosigmoid junction, and anus whose point of origin cannot be determined

✓4th **155 Malignant neoplasm of liver and intrahepatic bile ducts**

155.0 Liver, primary
Carcinoma:
liver, specified as primary
hepatocellular
liver cell
Hepatoblastoma

155.1 Intrahepatic bile ducts
Canaliculi biliferi
Interlobular:
bile ducts
biliary canals
biliary passages
Intrahepatic:
canaliculi
gall duct
EXCLUDES *hepatic duct (156.1)*

155.2 Liver, not specified as primary or secondary

✓4th **156 Malignant neoplasm of gallbladder and extrahepatic bile ducts**

156.0 Gallbladder

156.1 Extrahepatic bile ducts
Biliary duct or passage NOS
Common bile duct
Cystic duct
Hepatic duct
Sphincter of Oddi

156.2 Ampulla of Vater
DEF: Malignant neoplasm in the area of dilation at the juncture of the common bile and pancreatic ducts near the opening into the lumen of the duodenum.

156.8 Other specified sites of gallbladder and extrahepatic bile ducts
Malignant neoplasm of contiguous or overlapping sites of gallbladder and extrahepatic bile ducts whose point of origin cannot be determined

156.9 Biliary tract, part unspecified
Malignant neoplasm involving both intrahepatic and extrahepatic bile ducts

Retroperitoneum and Peritoneum

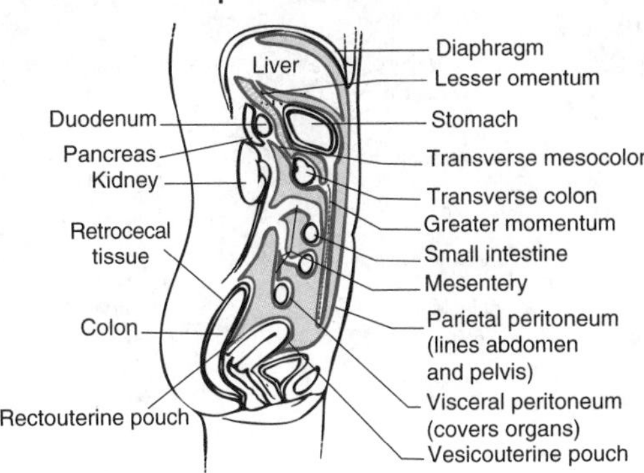

✓4th **157 Malignant neoplasm of pancreas**

157.0 Head of pancreas

157.1 Body of pancreas

157.2 Tail of pancreas

157.3 Pancreatic duct

Duct of:
- Santorini
- Wirsung

157.4 Islets of Langerhans

Islets of Langerhans, any part of pancreas

Use additional code to identify any functional activity

DEF: Malignant neoplasm within the structures of the pancreas that produce insulin, somatostatin and glucagon.

157.8 Other specified sites of pancreas

Ectopic pancreatic tissue

Malignant neoplasm of contiguous or overlapping sites of pancreas whose point of origin cannot be determined

157.9 Pancreas, part unspecified

✓4th **158 Malignant neoplasm of retroperitoneum and peritoneum**

158.0 Retroperitoneum

Periadrenal tissue
Perinephric tissue
Perirenal tissue
Retrocecal tissue

158.8 Specified parts of peritoneum

Cul-de-sac (of Douglas)

Malignant neoplasm of contiguous or overlapping sites of retroperitoneum and peritoneum whose point of origin cannot be determined

Mesentery
Mesocolon
Omentum
Peritoneum:
- parietal
- pelvic

Rectouterine pouch

158.9 Peritoneum, unspecified

✓4th **159 Malignant neoplasm of other and ill-defined sites within the digestive organs and peritoneum**

159.0 Intestinal tract, part unspecified

Intestine NOS

159.1 Spleen, not elsewhere classified

Angiosarcoma } of spleen
Fibrosarcoma }

EXCLUDES *Hodgkin's disease (201.0-201.9)*
lymphosarcoma (200.1)
reticulosarcoma (200.0)

159.8 Other sites of digestive system and intra-abdominal organs

Malignant neoplasm of digestive organs and peritoneum whose point of origin cannot be assigned to any one of the categories 150-158

EXCLUDES *anus and rectum (154.8)*
cardio-esophageal junction (151.0)
colon and rectum (154.0)

159.9 Ill-defined

Alimentary canal or tract NOS
Gastrointestinal tract NOS

EXCLUDES *abdominal NOS (195.2)*
intra-abdominal NOS (195.2)

NEOPLASM OF RESPIRATORY AND INTRATHORACIC ORGANS (160-165)

EXCLUDES *carcinoma in situ (231.0-231.9)*

✓4th **160 Malignant neoplasm of nasal cavities, middle ear, and accessory sinuses**

160.0 Nasal cavities

Cartilage of nose
Conchae, nasal
Internal nose
Septum of nose
Vestibule of nose

EXCLUDES *nasal bone (170.0)*
nose NOS (195.0)
olfactory bulb (192.0)
posterior margin of septum and choanae (147.3)
skin of nose (172.3, 173.3)
turbinates (170.0)

160.1 Auditory tube, middle ear, and mastoid air cells

Antrum tympanicum
Eustachian tube
Tympanic cavity

EXCLUDES *auditory canal (external) (172.2, 173.2)*
bone of ear (meatus) (170.0)
cartilage of ear (171.0)
ear (external) (skin) (172.2, 173.2)

160.2 Maxillary sinus

Antrum (Highmore) (maxillary)

160.3 Ethmoidal sinus

160.4 Frontal sinus

160.5 Sphenoidal sinus

160.8 Other

Malignant neoplasm of contiguous or overlapping sites of nasal cavities, middle ear, and accessory sinuses whose point of origin cannot be determined

160.9 Accessory sinus, unspecified

✓4th **161 Malignant neoplasm of larynx**

161.0 Glottis

Intrinsic larynx
Laryngeal commissure (anterior) (posterior)
True vocal cord
Vocal cord NOS

161.1 Supraglottis

Aryepiglottic fold or interarytenoid fold, laryngeal aspect
Epiglottis (suprahyoid portion) NOS
Extrinsic larynx
False vocal cords
Posterior (laryngeal) surface of epiglottis
Ventricular bands

EXCLUDES *anterior aspect of epiglottis (146.4)*
aryepiglottic fold or interarytenoid fold:
- *NOS (148.2)*
- *hypopharyngeal aspect (148.2)*
- *marginal zone (148.2)*

161.2 Subglottis

161.3 Laryngeal cartilages

Cartilage:
- arytenoid
- cricoid
- cuneiform
- thyroid

161.8 Other specified sites of larynx

Malignant neoplasm of contiguous or overlapping sites of larynx whose point of origin cannot be determined

161.9 Larynx, unspecified

✓4th **162 Malignant neoplasm of trachea, bronchus, and lung**

EXCLUDES *benign carcinoid tumor of bronchus (209.61)*
malignant carcinoid tumor of bronchus (209.21)

162.0 Trachea

Cartilage } of trachea
Mucosa } of trachea

162.2 Main bronchus

Carina
Hilus of lung

162.3 Upper lobe, bronchus or lung

162.4 Middle lobe, bronchus or lung

162.5 Lower lobe, bronchus or lung

162.8 Other parts of bronchus or lung

Malignant neoplasm of contiguous or overlapping sites of bronchus or lung whose point of origin cannot be determined

162.9 Bronchus and lung, unspecified

✓4th **163 Malignant neoplasm of pleura**

163.0 Parietal pleura

163.1 Visceral pleura

163.8 Other specified sites of pleura

Malignant neoplasm of contiguous or overlapping sites of pleura whose point of origin cannot be determined

163.9 Pleura, unspecified

✓4th **164 Malignant neoplasm of thymus, heart, and mediastinum**

164.0 Thymus

EXCLUDES *benign carcinoid tumor of the thymus (209.62)*
malignant carcinoid tumor of the thymus (209.22)

164.1 Heart

Endocardium
Epicardium
Myocardium
Pericardium

EXCLUDES *great vessels (171.4)*

164.2 Anterior mediastinum

164.3 Posterior mediastinum

164.8 Other

Malignant neoplasm of contiguous or overlapping sites of thymus, heart, and mediastinum whose point of origin cannot be determined

164.9 Mediastinum, part unspecified

✓4th **165 Malignant neoplasm of other and ill-defined sites within the respiratory system and intrathoracic organs**

165.0 Upper respiratory tract, part unspecified

165.8 Other

Malignant neoplasm of respiratory and intrathoracic organs whose point of origin cannot be assigned to any one of the categories 160-164

165.9 Ill-defined sites within the respiratory system

Respiratory tract NOS

EXCLUDES *intrathoracic NOS (195.1)*
thoracic NOS (195.1)

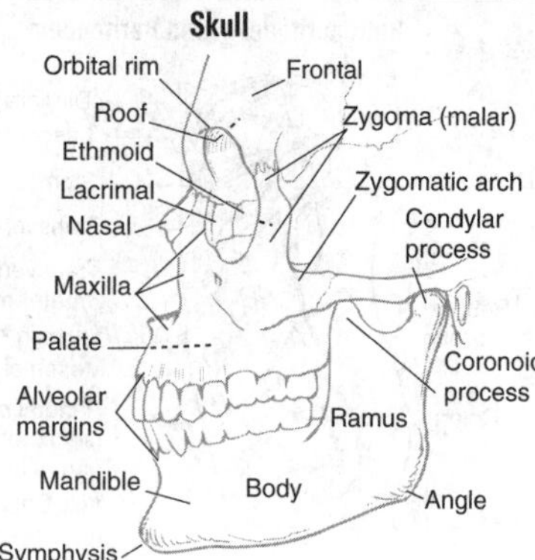

MALIGNANT NEOPLASM OF BONE, CONNECTIVE TISSUE, SKIN, AND BREAST (170-176)

EXCLUDES *carcinoma in situ:*
breast (233.0)
skin (232.0-232.9)

✓4th **170 Malignant neoplasm of bone and articular cartilage**

INCLUDES cartilage (articular) (joint)
periosteum

EXCLUDES *bone marrow NOS (202.9)*
cartilage:
ear (171.0)
eyelid (171.0)
larynx (161.3)
nose (160.0)
synovia (171.0-171.9)

170.0 Bones of skull and face, except mandible

Bone:	Bone:
ethmoid	sphenoid
frontal	temporal
malar	zygomatic
nasal	Maxilla (superior)
occipital	Turbinate
orbital	Upper jaw bone
parietal	Vomer

EXCLUDES *carcinoma, any type except intraosseous or odontogenic:*
maxilla, maxillary (sinus) (160.2)
upper jaw bone (143.0)
jaw bone (lower) (170.1)

170.1 Mandible

Inferior maxilla
Jaw bone NOS
Lower jaw bone

EXCLUDES *carcinoma, any type except intraosseous or odontogenic:*
jaw bone NOS (143.9)
lower (143.1)
upper jaw bone (170.0)

170.2 Vertebral column, excluding sacrum and coccyx

Spinal column
Spine
Vertebra

EXCLUDES *sacrum and coccyx (170.6)*

170.3 Ribs, sternum, and clavicle

Costal cartilage
Costovertebral joint
Xiphoid process

170.4 Scapula and long bones of upper limb

Acromion
Bones NOS of upper limb
Humerus
Radius
Ulna

170.5 Short bones of upper limb

Carpal	Scaphoid (of hand)
Cuneiform, wrist	Semilunar or lunate
Metacarpal	Trapezium
Navicular, of hand	Trapezoid
Phalanges of hand	Unciform
Pisiform	

170.6 Pelvic bones, sacrum, and coccyx
Coccygeal vertebra
Ilium
Ischium
Pubic bone
Sacral vertebra

170.7 Long bones of lower limb
Bones NOS of lower limb
Femur
Fibula
Tibia

170.8 Short bones of lower limb
Astragalus [talus]
Calcaneus
Cuboid
Cuneiform, ankle
Metatarsal
Navicular (of ankle)
Patella
Phalanges of foot
Tarsal

170.9 Bone and articular cartilage, site unspecified

✓4th **171 Malignant neoplasm of connective and other soft tissue**
INCLUDES blood vessel
bursa
fascia
fat
ligament, except uterine
muscle
peripheral, sympathetic, and parasympathetic nerves and ganglia
synovia
tendon (sheath)
EXCLUDES *cartilage (of):*
articular (170.0-170.9)
larynx (161.3)
nose (160.0)
connective tissue:
breast (174.0-175.9)
internal organs–code to malignant neoplasm of the site [e.g., leiomyosarcoma of stomach, 151.9]
heart (164.1)
uterine ligament (183.4)

171.0 Head, face, and neck
Cartilage of:
ear
eyelid

171.2 Upper limb, including shoulder
Arm
Finger
Forearm
Hand

171.3 Lower limb, including hip
Foot
Leg
Popliteal space
Thigh
Toe

171.4 Thorax
Axilla
Diaphragm
Great vessels
EXCLUDES *heart (164.1)*
mediastinum (164.2-164.9)
thymus (164.0)

171.5 Abdomen
Abdominal wall
Hypochondrium
EXCLUDES *peritoneum (158.8)*
retroperitoneum (158.0)

171.6 Pelvis
Buttock
Groin
Inguinal region
Perineum
EXCLUDES *pelvic peritoneum (158.8)*
retroperitoneum (158.0)
uterine ligament, any (183.3-183.5)

171.7 Trunk, unspecified
Back NOS
Flank NOS

171.8 Other specified sites of connective and other soft tissue
Malignant neoplasm of contiguous or overlapping sites of connective tissue whose point of origin cannot be determined

171.9 Connective and other soft tissue, site unspecified

✓4th **172 Malignant melanoma of skin**
INCLUDES melanocarcinoma
melanoma (skin) NOS
melanoma in situ of skin
EXCLUDES *skin of genital organs (184.0-184.9, 187.1-187.9)*
sites other than skin—code to malignant neoplasm of the site

DEF: Malignant neoplasm of melanocytes; most common in skin, may involve oral cavity, esophagus, anal canal, vagina, leptomeninges, or conjunctiva.

172.0 Lip
EXCLUDES *vermilion border of lip (140.0-140.1, 140.9)*

172.1 Eyelid, including canthus

172.2 Ear and external auditory canal
Auricle (ear)
Auricular canal, external
External [acoustic] meatus
Pinna

172.3 Other and unspecified parts of face
Cheek (external)
Chin
Eyebrow
Forehead
Nose, external
Temple

172.4 Scalp and neck

172.5 Trunk, except scrotum
Axilla
Breast
Buttock
Groin
Perianal skin
Perineum
Umbilicus
EXCLUDES *anal canal (154.2)*
anus NOS (154.3)
scrotum (187.7)

172.6 Upper limb, including shoulder
Arm
Finger
Forearm
Hand

172.7 Lower limb, including hip
Ankle
Foot
Heel
Knee
Leg
Popliteal area
Thigh
Toe

172.8 Other specified sites of skin
Malignant melanoma of contiguous or overlapping sites of skin whose point of origin cannot be determined

172.9 Melanoma of skin, site unspecified

✓4th **173 Other malignant neoplasm of skin**
INCLUDES malignant neoplasm of:
sebaceous glands
sudoriferous, sudoriparous glands
sweat glands
EXCLUDES *Kaposi's sarcoma (176.0-176.9)*
malignant melanoma of skin (172.0-172.9)
skin of genital organs (184.0-184.9, 187.1-187.9)

173.0 Skin of lip
EXCLUDES *vermilion border of lip (140.0-140.1, 140.9)*

173.1 Eyelid, including canthus
EXCLUDES *cartilage of eyelid (171.0)*

173.2 Skin of ear and external auditory canal
Auricle (ear)
Auricular canal, external
External meatus
Pinna
EXCLUDES *cartilage of ear (171.0)*

173.3 Skin of other and unspecified parts of face
Cheek, external
Chin
Eyebrow
Forehead
Nose, external
Temple

173.4 Scalp and skin of neck

173.5 Skin of trunk, except scrotum
Axillary fold
Perianal skin
Skin of:
abdominal wall
anus
back
breast
buttock
chest wall
groin
perineum
Umbilicus
EXCLUDES *anal canal (154.2)*
anus NOS (154.3)
skin of scrotum (187.7)

173.6 Skin of upper limb, including shoulder
Arm
Finger
Forearm
Hand

173.7 Skin of lower limb, including hip
Ankle
Foot
Heel
Knee
Leg
Popliteal area
Thigh
Toe

173.8 Other specified sites of skin
Malignant neoplasm of contiguous or overlapping sites of skin whose point of origin cannot be determined

173.9 Skin, site unspecified

✓4th **174 Malignant neoplasm of female breast**
Use additional code to identify estrogen receptor status (V86.0, V86.1)
INCLUDES breast (female)
connective tissue
soft parts
Paget's disease of:
breast
nipple
EXCLUDES *skin of breast (172.5, 173.5)*

174.0 Nipple and areola

174.1 Central portion

174.2 Upper-inner quadrant

174.3 Lower-inner quadrant

174.4 Upper-outer quadrant

174.5 Lower-outer quadrant

174.6 Axillary tail

174.8 Other specified sites of female breast
Ectopic sites
Inner breast
Lower breast
Midline of breast
Outer breast
Upper breast
Malignant neoplasm of contiguous or overlapping sites of breast whose point of origin cannot be determined

174.9 Breast (female), unspecified

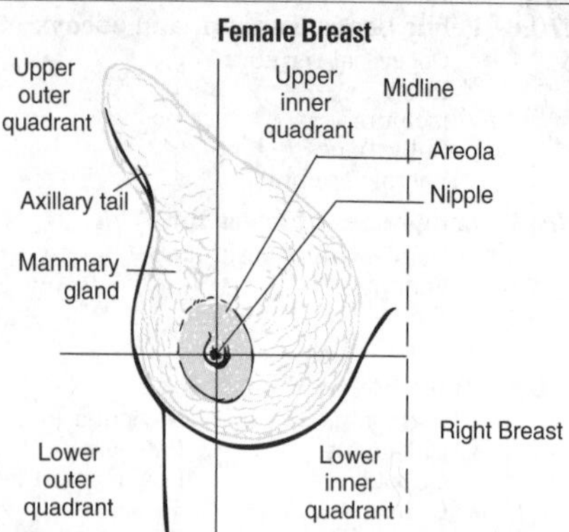

✓4th **175 Malignant neoplasm of male breast**
Use additional code to identify estrogen receptor status (V86.0, V86.1)
EXCLUDES *skin of breast (172.5, 173.5)*

175.0 Nipple and areola

175.9 Other and unspecified sites of male breast
Ectopic breast tissue, male

✓4th **176 Kaposi's sarcoma**

176.0 Skin

176.1 Soft tissue
Blood vessel
Connective tissue
Fascia
Ligament
Lymphatic(s) NEC
Muscle
EXCLUDES *lymph glands and nodes (176.5)*

176.2 Palate

176.3 Gastrointestinal sites

176.4 Lung

176.5 Lymph nodes

176.8 Other specified sites
Oral cavity NEC

176.9 Unspecified
Viscera NOS

MALIGNANT NEOPLASM OF GENITOURINARY ORGANS (179-189)

EXCLUDES *carcinoma in situ (233.1-233.9)*

179 Malignant neoplasm of uterus, part unspecified

✓4th **180 Malignant neoplasm of cervix uteri**
INCLUDES invasive malignancy [carcinoma]
EXCLUDES *carcinoma in situ (233.1)*

180.0 Endocervix
Cervical canal NOS
Endocervical canal
Endocervical gland

180.1 Exocervix

180.8 Other specified sites of cervix
Cervical stump
Squamocolumnar junction of cervix
Malignant neoplasm of contiguous or overlapping sites of cervix uteri whose point of origin cannot be determined

180.9 Cervix uteri, unspecified

181 Malignant neoplasm of placenta
Choriocarcinoma NOS
Chorioepithelioma NOS
EXCLUDES *chorioadenoma (destruens) (236.1)*
hydatidiform mole (630)
malignant (236.1)
invasive mole (236.1)
male choriocarcinoma NOS (186.0-186.9)

✓4th **182 Malignant neoplasm of body of uterus**
EXCLUDES *carcinoma in situ (233.2)*

182.0 Corpus uteri, except isthmus
Cornu
Endometrium
Fundus
Myometrium

182.1 Isthmus
Lower uterine segment

182.8 Other specified sites of body of uterus
Malignant neoplasm of contiguous or overlapping sites of body of uterus whose point of origin cannot be determined
EXCLUDES *uterus NOS (179)*

✓4th **183 Malignant neoplasm of ovary and other uterine adnexa**
EXCLUDES *Douglas' cul-de-sac (158.8)*

183.0 Ovary
Use additional code to identify any functional activity

183.2 Fallopian tube
Oviduct
Uterine tube

183.3 Broad ligament
Mesovarium
Parovarian region

183.4 Parametrium
Uterine ligament NOS
Uterosacral ligament

183.5 Round ligament

183.8 Other specified sites of uterine adnexa
Tubo-ovarian
Utero-ovarian
Malignant neoplasm of contiguous or overlapping sites of ovary and other uterine adnexa whose point of origin cannot be determined

183.9 Uterine adnexa, unspecified

✓4th **184 Malignant neoplasm of other and unspecified female genital organs**
EXCLUDES *carcinoma in situ (233.30-233.39)*

184.0 Vagina
Gartner's duct
Vaginal vault

184.1 Labia majora
Greater vestibular [Bartholin's] gland

184.2 Labia minora

184.3 Clitoris

184.4 Vulva, unspecified
External female genitalia NOS
Pudendum

184.8 Other specified sites of female genital organs
Malignant neoplasm of contiguous or overlapping sites of female genital organs whose point of origin cannot be determined

184.9 Female genital organ, site unspecified
Female genitourinary tract NOS

185 Malignant neoplasm of prostate
EXCLUDES *seminal vesicles (187.8)*

✓4th **186 Malignant neoplasm of testis**
Use additional code to identify any functional activity

186.0 Undescended testis
Ectopic testis
Retained testis

186.9 Other and unspecified testis
Testis:
NOS
descended
scrotal

✓4th **187 Malignant neoplasm of penis and other male genital organs**

187.1 Prepuce
Foreskin

187.2 Glans penis

187.3 Body of penis
Corpus cavernosum

187.4 Penis, part unspecified
Skin of penis NOS

187.5 Epididymis

187.6 Spermatic cord
Vas deferens

187.7 Scrotum
Skin of scrotum

187.8 Other specified sites of male genital organs
Seminal vesicle
Tunica vaginalis
Malignant neoplasm of contiguous or overlapping sites of penis and other male genital organs whose point of origin cannot be determined

187.9 Male genital organ, site unspecified
Male genital organ or tract NOS

✓4th **188 Malignant neoplasm of bladder**
EXCLUDES *carcinoma in situ (233.7)*

188.0 Trigone of urinary bladder

188.1 Dome of urinary bladder

188.2 Lateral wall of urinary bladder

188.3 Anterior wall of urinary bladder

188.4 Posterior wall of urinary bladder

188.5 Bladder neck
Internal urethral orifice

188.6 Ureteric orifice

188.7 Urachus

188.8 Other specified sites of bladder
Malignant neoplasm of contiguous or overlapping sites of bladder whose point of origin cannot be determined

188.9 Bladder, part unspecified
Bladder wall NOS

✓4th **189 Malignant neoplasm of kidney and other and unspecified urinary organs**
EXCLUDES *benign carcinoid tumor of kidney (209.64)*
malignant carcinoid tumor of kidney (209.24)

189.0 Kidney, except pelvis
Kidney NOS
Kidney parenchyma

189.1 Renal pelvis
Renal calyces
Ureteropelvic junction

189.2 Ureter
EXCLUDES *ureteric orifice of bladder (188.6)*

189.3 Urethra
EXCLUDES *urethral orifice of bladder (188.5)*

189.4 Paraurethral glands

189.8 Other specified sites of urinary organs
Malignant neoplasm of contiguous or overlapping sites of kidney and other urinary organs whose point of origin cannot be determined

189.9 Urinary organ, site unspecified
Urinary system NOS

MALIGNANT NEOPLASM OF OTHER AND UNSPECIFIED SITES (190-199)

EXCLUDES *carcinoma in situ (234.0-234.9)*

✓4th **190 Malignant neoplasm of eye**
EXCLUDES *carcinoma in situ (234.0)*
eyelid (skin) (172.1, 173.1)
cartilage (171.0)
optic nerve (192.0)
orbital bone (170.0)

Brain and Meninges

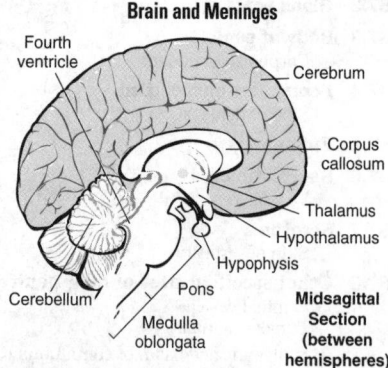

Fourth ventricle
Cerebrum
Corpus callosum
Thalamus
Hypothalamus
Hypophysis
Pons
Cerebellum
Medulla oblongata
Midsagittal Section (between hemispheres)

190.0 Eyeball, except conjunctiva, cornea, retina, and choroid
Ciliary body
Crystalline lens
Iris
Sclera
Uveal tract

190.1 Orbit
Connective tissue of orbit
Extraocular muscle
Retrobulbar
EXCLUDES *bone of orbit (170.0)*

190.2 Lacrimal gland

190.3 Conjunctiva

190.4 Cornea

190.5 Retina

190.6 Choroid

190.7 Lacrimal duct
Lacrimal sac
Nasolacrimal duct

190.8 Other specified sites of eye
Malignant neoplasm of contiguous or overlapping sites of eye whose point of origin cannot be determined

190.9 Eye, part unspecified

✓4th **191 Malignant neoplasm of brain**
EXCLUDES *cranial nerves (192.0)*
retrobulbar area (190.1)

191.0 Cerebrum, except lobes and ventricles
Basal ganglia
Cerebral cortex
Corpus striatum
Globus pallidus
Hypothalamus
Thalamus

191.1 Frontal lobe

191.2 Temporal lobe
Hippocampus
Uncus

191.3 Parietal lobe

191.4 Occipital lobe

191.5 Ventricles
Choroid plexus
Floor of ventricle

191.6 Cerebellum NOS
Cerebellopontine angle

191.7 Brain stem
Cerebral peduncle
Medulla oblongata
Midbrain
Pons

191.8 Other parts of brain
Corpus callosum
Tapetum
Malignant neoplasm of contiguous or overlapping sites of brain whose point of origin cannot be determined

191.9 Brain, unspecified
Cranial fossa NOS

✓4th **192 Malignant neoplasm of other and unspecified parts of nervous system**
EXCLUDES *peripheral, sympathetic, and parasympathetic nerves and ganglia (171.0-171.9)*

192.0 Cranial nerves
Olfactory bulb

192.1 Cerebral meninges
Dura (mater)
Falx (cerebelli) (cerebri)
Meninges NOS
Tentorium

192.2 Spinal cord
Cauda equina

192.3 Spinal meninges

192.8 Other specified sites of nervous system
Malignant neoplasm of contiguous or overlapping sites of other parts of nervous system whose point of origin cannot be determined

192.9 Nervous system, part unspecified
Nervous system (central) NOS
EXCLUDES *meninges NOS (192.1)*

193 Malignant neoplasm of thyroid gland
Thyroglossal duct
Use additional code to identify any functional activity

✓4th **194 Malignant neoplasm of other endocrine glands and related structures**
EXCLUDES *islets of Langerhans (157.4)*
neuroendocrine tumors (209.00-209.69)
ovary (183.0)
testis (186.0-186.9)
thymus (164.0)

194.0 Adrenal gland
Adrenal cortex
Adrenal medulla
Suprarenal gland

194.1 Parathyroid gland

194.3 Pituitary gland and craniopharyngeal duct
Craniobuccal pouch
Hypophysis
Rathke's pouch
Sella turcica

194.4 Pineal gland

194.5 Carotid body

194.6 Aortic body and other paraganglia
Coccygeal body
Glomus jugulare
Para-aortic body

194.8 Other
Pluriglandular involvement NOS
Note: If the sites of multiple involvements are known, they should be coded separately.

194.9 Endocrine gland, site unspecified

✓4th **195 Malignant neoplasm of other and ill-defined sites**
INCLUDES malignant neoplasms of contiguous sites, not elsewhere classified, whose point of origin cannot be determined
EXCLUDES *malignant neoplasm:*
lymphatic and hematopoietic tissue (200.0-208.9)
secondary sites (196.0-198.8)
unspecified site (199.0-199.1)

195.0 Head, face, and neck
Cheek NOS
Jaw NOS
Nose NOS
Supraclavicular region NOS

195.1 Thorax
Axilla
Chest (wall) NOS
Intrathoracic NOS

195.2 Abdomen
Intra-abdominal NOS

Lymph Nodes

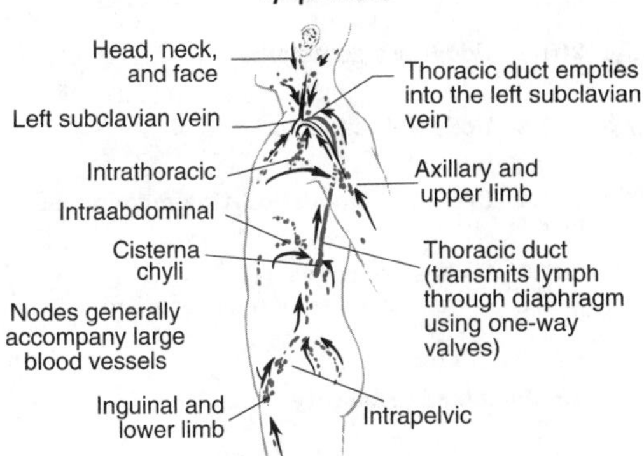

195.3 Pelvis
Groin
Inguinal region NOS
Presacral region
Sacrococcygeal region
Sites overlapping systems within pelvis, as:
rectovaginal (septum)
rectovesical (septum)

195.4 Upper limb

195.5 Lower limb

195.8 Other specified sites
Back NOS
Flank NOS
Trunk NOS

✓4th **196 Secondary and unspecified malignant neoplasm of lymph nodes**

EXCLUDES *any malignant neoplasm of lymph nodes, specified as primary (200.0-202.9)*
Hodgkin's disease (201.0-201.9)
lymphosarcoma (200.1)
other forms of lymphoma (202.0-202.9)
reticulosarcoma (200.0)

196.0 Lymph nodes of head, face, and neck
Cervical
Cervicofacial
Scalene
Supraclavicular

196.1 Intrathoracic lymph nodes
Bronchopulmonary
Intercostal
Mediastinal
Tracheobronchial

196.2 Intra-abdominal lymph nodes
Intestinal
Mesenteric
Retroperitoneal

196.3 Lymph nodes of axilla and upper limb
Brachial
Epitrochlear
Infraclavicular
Pectoral

196.5 Lymph nodes of inguinal region and lower limb
Femoral
Groin
Popliteal
Tibial

196.6 Intrapelvic lymph nodes
Hypogastric
Iliac
Obturator
Parametrial

196.8 Lymph nodes of multiple sites

196.9 Site unspecified
Lymph nodes NOS

✓4th **197 Secondary malignant neoplasm of respiratory and digestive systems**

EXCLUDES *lymph node metastasis (196.0-196.9)*

197.0 Lung
Bronchus

197.1 Mediastinum

197.2 Pleura

197.3 Other respiratory organs
Trachea

197.4 Small intestine, including duodenum

197.5 Large intestine and rectum

197.6 Retroperitoneum and peritoneum

197.7 Liver, specified as secondary

197.8 Other digestive organs and spleen

✓4th **198 Secondary malignant neoplasm of other specified sites**

EXCLUDES *lymph node metastasis (196.0-196.9)*

198.0 Kidney

198.1 Other urinary organs

198.2 Skin
Skin of breast

198.3 Brain and spinal cord

198.4 Other parts of nervous system
Meninges (cerebral) (spinal)

198.5 Bone and bone marrow

198.6 Ovary

198.7 Adrenal gland
Suprarenal gland

✓5th **198.8 Other specified sites**

198.81 Breast
EXCLUDES *skin of breast (198.2)*

198.82 Genital organs

198.89 Other
EXCLUDES *retroperitoneal lymph nodes (196.2)*

✓4th **199 Malignant neoplasm without specification of site**

EXCLUDES *malignant carcinoid tumor of unknown primary site (209.20)*
malignant neuroendocrine tumor, any site (209.30)
neuroendocrine carcinoma, any site (209.30)

199.0 Disseminated
Carcinomatosis
Generalized:
cancer
malignancy
Multiple cancer
} unspecified site (primary) (secondary)

199.1 Other
Cancer
Carcinoma
Malignancy
} unspecified site (primary) (secondary)

199.2 Malignant neoplasm associated with transplanted organ
Code first complication of transplanted organ (996.80-996.89)
Use additional code for specific malignancy site

MALIGNANT NEOPLASM OF LYMPHATIC AND HEMATOPOIETIC TISSUE (200-208)

EXCLUDES *secondary neoplasm of:*
bone marrow (198.5)
spleen (197.8)
secondary and unspecified neoplasm of lymph nodes (196.0-196.9)

The following fifth-digit subclassification is for use with categories 200-202:
0 unspecified site, extranodal and solid organ sites
1 lymph nodes of head, face, and neck
2 intrathoracic lymph nodes
3 intra-abdominal lymph nodes
4 lymph nodes of axilla and upper limb
5 lymph nodes of inguinal region and lower limb
6 intrapelvic lymph nodes
7 spleen
8 lymph nodes of multiple sites

✓4th 200 Lymphosarcoma and reticulosarcoma and other specified malignant tumors of lymphatic tissue

✓5th **200.0 Reticulosarcoma**
[0-8]
Lymphoma (malignant):
histiocytic (diffuse):
nodular
pleomorphic cell type
reticulum cell type
Reticulum cell sarcoma:
NOS
pleomorphic cell type
DEF: Malignant lymphoma of primarily histolytic cells; commonly originates in reticuloendothelium of lymph nodes.

✓5th **200.1 Lymphosarcoma**
[0-8]
Lymphoblastoma (diffuse)
Lymphoma (malignant):
lymphoblastic (diffuse)
lymphocytic (cell type) (diffuse)
lymphosarcoma type
Lymphosarcoma:
NOS
diffuse NOS
lymphoblastic (diffuse)
lymphobcytic (diffuse)
prolymphocytic
EXCLUDES *lymphosarcoma:*
follicular or nodular (202.0)
mixed cell type (200.8)
lymphosarcoma cell leukemia (207.8)
DEF: Malignant lymphoma created from anaplastic lymphoid cells resembling lymphocytes or lymphoblasts.

✓5th **200.2 Burkitt's tumor or lymphoma**
[0-8]
Malignant lymphoma, Burkitt's type
DEF: Large osteolytic lesion most common in jaw or as abdominal mass; usually found in central Africa but reported elsewhere.

✓5th **200.3 Marginal zone lymphoma**
[0-8]
Extranodal marginal zone B-cell lymphoma
Mucosa associated lymphoid tissue [MALT]
Nodal marginal zone B-cell lymphoma
Splenic marginal zone B-cell lymphoma

✓5th **200.4 Mantle cell lymphoma**
[0-8]

✓5th **200.5 Primary central nervous system lymphoma**
[0-8]

✓5th **200.6 Anaplastic large cell lymphoma**
[0-8]

✓5th **200.7 Large cell lymphoma**
[0-8]

✓5th **200.8 Other named variants**
[0-8]
Lymphoma (malignant):
lymphoplasmacytoid type
mixed lymphocytic-histiocytic (diffuse)
Lymphosarcoma, mixed cell type (diffuse)
Reticulolymphosarcoma (diffuse)

✓4th 201 Hodgkin's disease

DEF: Painless, progressive enlargement of lymph nodes, spleen and general lymph tissue; symptoms include anorexia, lassitude, weight loss, fever, pruritis, night sweats, anemia.

✓5th **201.0 Hodgkin's paragranuloma**
[0-8]

✓5th **201.1 Hodgkin's granuloma**
[0-8]

✓5th **201.2 Hodgkin's sarcoma**
[0-8]

✓5th **201.4 Lymphocytic-histiocytic predominance**
[0-8]

✓5th **201.5 Nodular sclerosis**
[0-8]
Hodgkin's disease, nodular sclerosis:
NOS
cellular phase

✓5th **201.6 Mixed cellularity**
[0-8]

✓5th **201.7 Lymphocytic depletion**
[0-8]
Hodgkin's disease, lymphocytic depletion:
NOS
diffuse fibrosis
reticular type

✓5th **201.9 Hodgkin's disease, unspecified**
[0-8]
Hodgkin's:
disease NOS
lymphoma NOS
Malignant:
lymphogranuloma
lymphogranulomatosis

✓4th 202 Other malignant neoplasms of lymphoid and histiocytic tissue

✓5th **202.0 Nodular lymphoma**
[0-8]
Brill-Symmers disease
Lymphoma:
follicular (giant)
lymphocytic, nodular
Lymphosarcoma:
follicular (giant)
nodular
DEF: Lymphomatous cells clustered into nodules within the lymph node; usually occurs in older adults and may involve all nodes and possibly extranodal sites.

✓5th **202.1 Mycosis fungoides**
[0-8]
DEF: Type of cutaneous T-cell lymphoma; may evolve into generalized lymphoma; formerly thought to be of fungoid origin.

✓5th **202.2 Sézary's disease**
[0-8]
DEF: Type of cutaneous T-cell lymphoma with erythroderma, intense pruritus, peripheral lymphadenopathy, abnormal hyperchromatic mononuclear cells in skin, lymph nodes and peripheral blood.

✓5th **202.3 Malignant histiocytosis**
[0-8]
Histiocytic medullary reticulosis
Malignant:
reticuloendotheliosis
reticulosis

✓5th **202.4 Leukemic reticuloendotheliosis**
[0-8]
Hairy-cell leukemia
DEF: Chronic leukemia with large, mononuclear cells with "hairy" appearance in marrow, spleen, liver, blood.

✓5th **202.5 Letterer-Siwe disease**
[0-8]
Acute:
differentiated progressive histiocytosis
histiocytosis X (progressive)
infantile reticuloendotheliosis
reticulosis of infancy
EXCLUDES *Hand-Schüller-Christian disease (277.89)*
histiocytosis (acute) (chronic) (277.89)
histiocytosis X (chronic) (277.89)
DEF: A recessive reticuloendotheliosis of early childhood, with a hemorrhagic tendency, eczema-like skin eruption, hepatosplenomegaly, including lymph node enlargement, and progressive anemia; it is often a fatal disease with no established cause.

✓5th **202.6 Malignant mast cell tumors**
[0-8]
Malignant:
mastocytoma
mastocytosis
Mast cell sarcoma
Systemic tissue mast cell disease
EXCLUDES *mast cell leukemia (207.8)*

✓5th **202.7 Peripheral T-cell lymphoma**
[0-8]

✓5th **202.8 Other lymphomas**
[0-8] Lymphoma (malignant):
NOS
diffuse
EXCLUDES *benign lymphoma (229.0)*

✓5th **202.9 Other and unspecified malignant neoplasms of lymphoid and histiocytic tissue**
[0-8] Follicular dendritic cell sarcoma
Interdigitating dendritic cell sarcoma
Langerhans cell sarcoma
Malignant neoplasm of bone marrow NOS

✓4th **203 Multiple myeloma and immunoproliferative neoplasms**

The following fifth-digit subclassification is for use with category 203:
0 without mention of having achieved remission
Failed remission
1 in remission
2 in relapse

✓5th **203.0 Multiple myeloma**
[0-2] Kahler's disease
Myelomatosis
EXCLUDES *solitary myeloma (238.6)*

✓5th **203.1 Plasma cell leukemia**
[0-2] Plasmacytic leukemia

✓5th **203.8 Other immunoproliferative neoplasms**
[0-2]

✓4th **204 Lymphoid leukemia**
INCLUDES leukemia:
lymphatic
lymphoblastic
lymphocytic
lymphogenous

The following fifth-digit subclassification is for use with category 204:
0 without mention of having achieved remission
Failed remission
1 in remission
2 in relapse

✓5th **204.0 Acute**
[0-2] EXCLUDES *acute exacerbation of chronic lymphoid leukemia (204.1)*

✓5th **204.1 Chronic**
[0-2]

✓5th **204.2 Subacute**
[0-2]

✓5th **204.8 Other lymphoid leukemia**
[0-2] Aleukemic leukemia:
lymphatic
lymphocytic
lymphoid

✓5th **204.9 Unspecified lymphoid leukemia**
[0-2]

✓4th **205 Myeloid leukemia**
INCLUDES leukemia:
granulocytic
myeloblastic
myelocytic
myelogenous
myelomonocytic
myelosclerotic
myelosis

The following fifth-digit subclassification is for use with category 205:
0 without mention of having achieved remission
Failed remission
1 in remission
2 in relapse

✓5th **205.0 Acute**
[0-2] Acute promyelocytic leukemia
EXCLUDES *acute exacerbation of chronic myeloid leukemia (205.1)*

✓5th **205.1 Chronic**
[0-2] Eosinophilic leukemia
Neutrophilic leukemia

✓5th **205.2 Subacute**
[0-2]

✓5th **205.3 Myeloid sarcoma**
[0-2] Chloroma
Granulocytic sarcoma

✓5th **205.8 Other myeloid leukemia**
[0-2] Aleukemic leukemia:
granulocytic
myelogenous
myeloid
Aleukemic myelosis

✓5th **205.9 Unspecified myeloid leukemia**
[0-2]

✓4th **206 Monocytic leukemia**
INCLUDES leukemia:
histiocytic
monoblastic
monocytoid

The following fifth-digit subclassification is for use with category 206:
0 without mention of having achieved remission
Failed remission
1 in remission
2 in relapse

✓5th **206.0 Acute**
[0-2] EXCLUDES *acute exacerbation of chronic monocytic leukemia (206.1)*

✓5th **206.1 Chronic**
[0-2]

✓5th **206.2 Subacute**
[0-2]

✓5th **206.8 Other monocytic leukemia**
[0-2] Aleukemic:
monocytic leukemia
monocytoid leukemia

✓5th **206.9 Unspecified monocytic leukemia**
[0-2]

✓4th **207 Other specified leukemia**
EXCLUDES *leukemic reticuloendotheliosis (202.4)*
plasma cell leukemia (203.1)

The following fifth-digit subclassification is for use with category 207:
0 without mention of having achieved remission
Failed remission
1 in remission
2 in relapse

✓5th **207.0 Acute erythremia and erythroleukemia**
[0-2] Acute erythremic myelosis
Di Guglielmo's disease
Erythremic myelosis
DEF: Erythremia: polycythemia vera.
DEF: Erythroleukemia: a malignant blood dyscrasia a myeloproliferative disorder).

✓5th **207.1 Chronic erythremia**
[0-2] Heilmeyer-Schöner disease

✓5th **207.2 Megakaryocytic leukemia**
[0-2] Megakaryocytic myelosis
Thrombocytic leukemia

✓5th **207.8 Other specified leukemia**
[0-2] Lymphosarcoma cell leukemia

✓4th **208 Leukemia of unspecified cell type**

The following fifth-digit subclassification is for use with category 208:
0 without mention of having achieved remission
Failed remission
1 in remission
2 in relapse

✓5th **208.0 Acute**
[0-2]
Acute leukemia NOS
Blast cell leukemia
Stem cell leukemia
EXCLUDES *acute exacerbation of chronic unspecified leukemia (208.1)*

✓5th **208.1 Chronic**
[0-2]
Chronic leukemia NOS

✓5th **208.2 Subacute**
[0-2]
Subacute leukemia NOS

✓5th **208.8 Other leukemia of unspecified cell type**
[0-2]

✓5th **208.9 Unspecified leukemia**
[0-2]
Leukemia NOS

NEUROENDOCRINE TUMORS (209)

✓4th **209 Neuroendocrine tumors**

Code first any associated multiple endocrine neoplasia syndrome (258.01-258.03)

Use additional code to identify associated endocrine syndrome, such as:
carcinoid syndrome (259.2)

EXCLUDES *pancreatic islet cell tumors (157.4)*

✓5th **209.0 Malignant carcinoid tumors of the small intestine**

209.00 Malignant carcinoid tumor of the small intestine, unspecified portion

209.01 Malignant carcinoid tumor of the duodenum

209.02 Malignant carcinoid tumor of the jejunum

209.03 Malignant carcinoid tumor of the ileum

✓5th **209.1 Malignant carcinoid tumors of the appendix, large intestine, and rectum**

209.10 Malignant carcinoid tumor of the large intestine, unspecified portion
Malignant carcinoid tumor of the colon NOS

209.11 Malignant carcinoid tumor of the appendix

209.12 Malignant carcinoid tumor of the cecum

209.13 Malignant carcinoid tumor of the ascending colon

209.14 Malignant carcinoid tumor of the transverse colon

209.15 Malignant carcinoid tumor of the descending colon

209.16 Malignant carcinoid tumor of the sigmoid colon

209.17 Malignant carcinoid tumor of the rectum

✓5th **209.2 Malignant carcinoid tumors of other and unspecified sites**

209.20 Malignant carcinoid tumor of unknown primary site

209.21 Malignant carcinoid tumor of the bronchus and lung

209.22 Malignant carcinoid tumor of the thymus

209.23 Malignant carcinoid tumor of the stomach

209.24 Malignant carcinoid tumor of the kidney

209.25 Malignant carcinoid tumor of the foregut NOS

209.26 Malignant carcinoid tumor of the midgut NOS

209.27 Malignant carcinoid tumor of the hindgut NOS

209.29 Malignant carcinoid tumors of other sites

✓5th **209.3 Malignant poorly differentiated neuroendocrine tumors**

209.30 Malignant poorly differentiated neuroendocrine carcinoma, any site
High grade neuroendocrine carcinoma, any site
Malignant poorly differentiated neuroendocrine tumor NOS

✓5th **209.4 Benign carcinoid tumors of the small intestine**

209.40 Benign carcinoid tumor of the small intestine, unspecified portion

209.41 Benign carcinoid tumor of the duodenum

209.42 Benign carcinoid tumor of the jejunum

209.43 Benign carcinoid tumor of the ileum

✓5th **209.5 Benign carcinoid tumors of the appendix, large intestine, and rectum**

209.50 Benign carcinoid tumor of the large intestine, unspecified portion
Benign carcinoid tumor of the colon NOS

209.51 Benign carcinoid tumor of the appendix

209.52 Benign carcinoid tumor of the cecum

209.53 Benign carcinoid tumor of the ascending colon

209.54 Benign carcinoid tumor of the transverse colon

209.55 Benign carcinoid tumor of the descending colon

209.56 Benign carcinoid tumor of the sigmoid colon

209.57 Benign carcinoid tumor of the rectum

✓5th **209.6 Benign carcinoid tumors of other and unspecified sites**

209.60 Benign carcinoid tumor of unknown primary site
Carcinoid tumor NOS
Neuroendocrine tumor NOS

209.61 Benign carcinoid tumor of the bronchus and lung

209.62 Benign carcinoid tumor of the thymus

209.63 Benign carcinoid tumor of the stomach

209.64 Benign carcinoid tumor of the kidney

209.65 Benign carcinoid tumor of the foregut NOS

209.66 Benign carcinoid tumor of the midgut NOS

209.67 Benign carcinoid tumor of the hindgut NOS

209.69 Benign carcinoid tumors of other sites

BENIGN NEOPLASMS (210-229)

✓4th 210 Benign neoplasm of lip, oral cavity, and pharynx

EXCLUDES *cyst (of):*
jaw (526.0-526.2, 526.89)
oral soft tissue (528.4)
radicular (522.8)

210.0 Lip
Frenulum labii
Lip (inner aspect) (mucosa) (vermilion border)
EXCLUDES *labial commissure (210.4)*
skin of lip (216.0)

210.1 Tongue
Lingual tonsil

210.2 Major salivary glands
Gland:
parotid
sublingual
submandibular
EXCLUDES *benign neoplasms of minor salivary glands:*
NOS (210.4)
buccal mucosa (210.4)
lips (210.0)
palate (hard) (soft) (210.4)
tongue (210.1)
tonsil, palatine (210.5)

210.3 Floor of mouth

210.4 Other and unspecified parts of mouth
Gingiva
Gum (upper) (lower)
Labial commissure
Oral cavity NOS
Oral mucosa
Palate (hard) (soft)
Uvula
EXCLUDES *benign odontogenic neoplasms of bone (213.0-213.1)*
developmental odontogenic cysts (526.0)
mucosa of lips (210.0)
nasopharyngeal [posterior] [superior] surface of soft palate (210.7)

210.5 Tonsil
Tonsil (faucial) (palatine)
EXCLUDES *lingual tonsil (210.1)*
pharyngeal tonsil (210.7)
tonsillar:
fossa (210.6)
pillars (210.6)

210.6 Other parts of oropharynx
Branchial cleft or vestiges
Epiglottis, anterior aspect
Fauces NOS
Mesopharynx NOS
Tonsillar:
fossa
pillars
Vallecula
EXCLUDES *epiglottis:*
NOS (212.1)
suprahyoid portion (212.1)

210.7 Nasopharynx
Adenoid tissue
Lymphadenoid tissue
Pharyngeal tonsil
Posterior nasal septum

210.8 Hypopharynx
Arytenoid fold
Laryngopharynx
Postcricoidregion
Pyriform fossa

210.9 Pharynx, unspecified
Throat NOS

✓4th 211 Benign neoplasm of other parts of digestive system

EXCLUDES *benign stromal tumors of digestive system (215.5)*

211.0 Esophagus

211.1 Stomach
Body, Cardia, Fundus } of stomach
Cardiac orifice
Pylorus
EXCLUDES *benign carcinoid tumors of the stomach (209.63)*

211.2 Duodenum, jejunum, and ileum
Small intestine NOS
EXCLUDES *ampulla of Vater (211.5)*
benign carcinoid tumors of the small intestine (209.40-209.43)
ileocecal valve (211.3)

211.3 Colon
Appendix
Cecum
Ileocecal valve
Large intestine NOS
EXCLUDES *benign carcinoid tumors of the large intestine (209.50-209.56)*
rectosigmoid junction (211.4)

211.4 Rectum and anal canal
Anal canal or sphincter
Anus NOS
Rectosigmoid junction
EXCLUDES *anus:*
margin (216.5)
skin (216.5)
benign carcinoid tumors of the rectum (209.57)
perianal skin (216.5)

211.5 Liver and biliary passages
Ampulla of Vater
Common bile duct
Cystic duct
Gallbladder
Hepatic duct
Sphincter of Oddi

211.6 Pancreas, except islets of Langerhans

211.7 Islets of Langerhans
Islet cell tumor
Use additional code to identify any functional activity

211.8 Retroperitoneum and peritoneum
Mesentery
Mesocolon
Omentum
Retroperitoneal tissue

211.9 Other and unspecified site
Alimentary tract NOS
Digestive system NOS
Gastrointestinal tract NOS
Intestinal tract NOS
Intestine NOS
Spleen, not elsewhere classified

✓4th 212 Benign neoplasm of respiratory and intrathoracic organs

212.0 Nasal cavities, middle ear, and accessory sinuses
Cartilage of nose
Eustachian tube
Nares
Septum of nose
Sinus:
ethmoidal
frontal
maxillary
sphenoidal
EXCLUDES *auditory canal (external) (216.2)*
bone of:
ear (213.0)
nose [turbinates] (213.0)
cartilage of ear (215.0)
ear (external) (skin) (216.2)
nose NOS (229.8)
skin (216.3)
olfactory bulb (225.1)
polyp of:
accessory sinus (471.8)
ear (385.30-385.35)
nasal cavity (471.0)
posterior margin of septum and choanae (210.7)

212.1 Larynx
Cartilage:
arytenoid
cricoid
cuneiform
thyroid
Epiglottis (suprahyoid portion) NOS
Glottis
Vocal cords (false)(true)
EXCLUDES *epiglottis, anterior aspect (210.6)*
polyp of vocal cord or larynx (478.4)

212.2 Trachea

212.3 Bronchus and lung
Carina
Hilus of lung
EXCLUDES *benign carcinoid tumors of bronchus and lung (209.61)*

212.4 Pleura

212.5 Mediastinum

212.6 Thymus
EXCLUDES *benign carcinoid tumors of thymus (209.62)*

212.7 Heart
EXCLUDES *great vessels (215.4)*

212.8 Other specified sites

212.9 Site unspecified
Respiratory organ NOS
Upper respiratory tract NOS
EXCLUDES *intrathoracic NOS (229.8)*
thoracic NOS (229.8)

✓4th 213 Benign neoplasm of bone and articular cartilage
INCLUDES cartilage (articular) (joint)
periosteum
EXCLUDES *cartilage of:*
ear (215.0)
eyelid (215.0))
larynx (212.1)
nose (212.0)
exostosis NOS (726.91
synovia (215.0-215.9)

213.0 Bones of skull and face
EXCLUDES *lower jaw bone (213.1)*

213.1 Lower jaw bone

213.2 Vertebral column, excluding sacrum and coccyx

213.3 Ribs, sternum, and clavicle

213.4 Scapula and long bones of upper limb

213.5 Short bones of upper limb

213.6 Pelvic bones, sacrum, and coccyx

213.7 Long bones of lower limb

213.8 Short bones of lower limb

213.9 Bone and articular cartilage, site unspecified

✓4th 214 Lipoma
INCLUDES angiolipoma
fibrolipoma
hibernoma
lipoma (fetal) (infiltrating) (intramuscular)
myelolipoma
myxolipoma

DEF: Benign tumor frequently composed of mature fat cells; may occasionally be composed of fetal fat cells.

214.0 Skin and subcutaneous tissue of face

214.1 Other skin and subcutaneous tissue

214.2 Intrathoracic organs

214.3 Intra-abdominal organs

214.4 Spermatic cord

214.8 Other specified sites

214.9 Lipoma, unspecified site

✓4th 215 Other benign neoplasm of connective and other soft tissue
INCLUDES blood vessel
bursa
fascia
ligament
muscle
peripheral, sympathetic, and parasympathetic nerves and ganglia
synovia
tendon (sheath)
EXCLUDES *cartilage:*
articular (213.0-213.9)
larynx (212.1)
nose (212.0)
connective tissue of:
breast (217)
internal organ, except lipoma and hemangioma–code to benign neoplasm of the site
lipoma (214.0-214.9)

215.0 Head, face, and neck

215.2 Upper limb, including shoulder

215.3 Lower limb, including hip

215.4 Thorax
EXCLUDES *heart (212.7)*
mediastinum (212.5)
thymus (212.6)

215.5 Abdomen
Abdominal wall
Benign stromal tumors of abdomen
Hypochondrium

215.6 Pelvis
Buttock
Groin
Inguinal region
Perineum
EXCLUDES *uterine:*
leiomyoma (218.0-218.9)
ligament, any (221.0)

215.7 Trunk, unspecified
Back NOS
Flank NOS

215.8 Other specified sites

215.9 Site unspecified

✓4th 216 Benign neoplasm of skin

INCLUDES blue nevus
dermatofibroma
hydrocystoma
pigmented nevus
syringoadenoma
syringoma

EXCLUDES *skin of genital organs (221.0-222.9)*

216.0 Skin of lip

EXCLUDES *vermilion border of lip (210.0)*

216.1 Eyelid, including canthus

EXCLUDES *cartilage of eyelid (215.0)*

216.2 Ear and external auditory canal

Auricle (ear)
Auricular canal, external
External meatus
Pinna

EXCLUDES *cartilage of ear (215.0)*

216.3 Skin of other and unspecified parts of face

Cheek, external
Eyebrow
Nose, external
Temple

216.4 Scalp and skin of neck

216.5 Skin of trunk, except scrotum

Axillary fold
Perianal skin
Skin of:
abdominal wall
anus
back
breast
Skin of:
buttock
chest wall
groin
perineum
Umbilicus

EXCLUDES *anal canal (211.4)*
anus NOS (211.4)
skin of scrotum (222.4)

216.6 Skin of upper limb, including shoulder

216.7 Skin of lower limb, including hip

216.8 Other specified sites of skin

216.9 Skin, site unspecified

217 Benign neoplasm of breast

Breast (male) (female):
connective tissue
glandular tissue
soft parts

EXCLUDES *adenofibrosis (610.2)*
benign cyst of breast (610.0)
fibrocystic disease (610.1)
skin of breast (216.5)

✓4th 218 Uterine leiomyoma

INCLUDES fibroid (bleeding) (uterine)
uterine:
fibromyoma
myoma

DEF: Benign tumor primarily derived from uterine smooth muscle tissue; may contain fibrous, fatty, or epithelial tissue; also called uterine fibroid or myoma.

218.0 Submucous leiomyoma of uterus

218.1 Intramural leiomyoma of uterus

Interstitial leiomyoma of uterus

218.2 Subserous leiomyoma of uterus

218.9 Leiomyoma of uterus, unspecified

✓4th 219 Other benign neoplasm of uterus

219.0 Cervix uteri

219.1 Corpus uteri

Endometrium
Fundus
Myometrium

219.8 Other specified parts of uterus

219.9 Uterus, part unspecified

Types of Uterine Fibroids

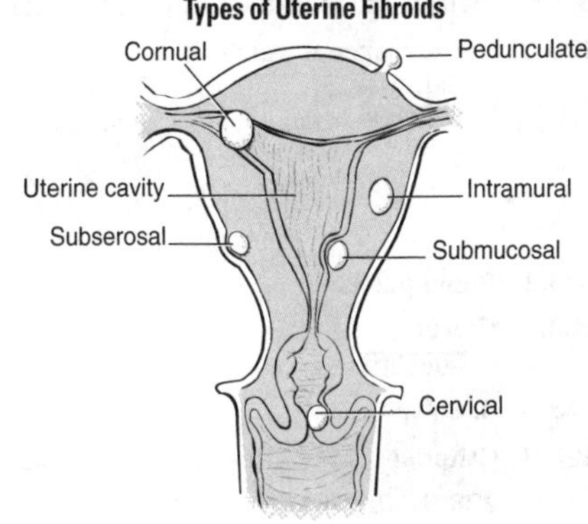

220 Benign neoplasm of ovary

Use additional code to identify any functional activity (256.0-256.1)

EXCLUDES *cyst:*
corpus albicans (620.2)
corpus luteum (620.1)
endometrial (617.1)
follicular (atretic) (620.0)
graafian follicle (620.0)
ovarian NOS (620.2)
retention (620.2)

✓4th 221 Benign neoplasm of other female genital organs

INCLUDES adenomatous polyp
benign teratoma

EXCLUDES *cyst:*
epoophoron (752.11)
fimbrial (752.11)
Gartner's duct (752.11)
parovarian (752.11)

221.0 Fallopian tube and uterine ligaments

Oviduct
Parametruim
Uterine ligament (broad) (round) (uterosacral)
Uterine tube

221.1 Vagina

221.2 Vulva

Clitoris
External female genitalia NOS
Greater vestibular [Bartholin's] gland
Labia (majora) (minora)
Pudendum

EXCLUDES *Bartholin's (duct) (gland) cyst (616.2)*

221.8 Other specified sites of female genital organs

221.9 Female genital organ, site unspecified

Female genitourinary tract NOS

✓4th 222 Benign neoplasm of male genital organs

222.0 Testis

Use additional code to identify any functional activity

222.1 Penis

Corpus cavernosum
Glans penis
Prepuce

222.2 Prostate

EXCLUDES *adenomatous hyperplasia of prostate (600.20-600.21)*
prostatic:
adenoma (600.20-600.21)
enlargement (600.00-600.01)
hypertrophy (600.00-600.01)

222.3 Epididymis

222.4 Scrotum

Skin of scrotum

222.8 Other specified sites of male genital organs

Seminal vesicle
Spermatic cord

222.9 Male genital organ, site unspecified

Male genitourinary tract NOS

✓4th **223 Benign neoplasm of kidney and other urinary organs**

223.0 Kidney, except pelvis
Kidney NOS
EXCLUDES *benign carcinoid tumors of kidney (209.64)*
renal:
calyces (223.1)
pelvis (223.1)

223.1 Renal pelvis

223.2 Ureter
EXCLUDES *ureteric orifice of bladder (223.3)*

223.3 Bladder

✓5th **223.8 Other specified sites of urinary organs**

223.81 Urethra
EXCLUDES *urethral orifice of bladder (223.3)*

223.89 Other
Paraurethral glands

223.9 Urinary organ, site unspecified
Urinary system NOS

✓4th **224 Benign neoplasm of eye**
EXCLUDES *cartilage of eyelid (215.0)*
eyelid (skin) (216.1)
optic nerve (225.1)
orbital bone (213.0)

224.0 Eyeball, except conjunctiva, cornea, retina, and choroid
Ciliary body
Iris
Sclera
Uveal tract

224.1 Orbit
EXCLUDES *bone of orbit (213.0)*

224.2 Lacrimal gland

224.3 Conjunctiva

224.4 Cornea

224.5 Retina
EXCLUDES *hemangioma of retina (228.03)*

224.6 Choroid

224.7 Lacrimal duct
Lacrimal sac
Nasolacrimal duct

224.8 Other specified parts of eye

224.9 Eye, part unspecified

✓4th **225 Benign neoplasm of brain and other parts of nervous system**
EXCLUDES *hemangioma (228.02)*
neurofibromatosis (237.7)
peripheral, sympathetic, and parasympathetic nerves and ganglia (215.0-215.9)
retrobulbar (224.1)

225.0 Brain

225.1 Cranial nerves
Acoustic neuroma

225.2 Cerebral meninges
Meninges NOS
Meningioma (cerebral)

225.3 Spinal cord
Cauda equina

225.4 Spinal meninges
Spinal meningioma

225.8 Other specified sites of nervous system

Eyeball

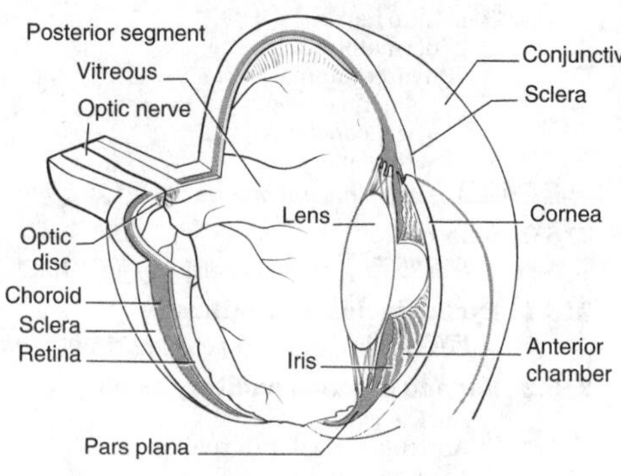

225.9 Nervous system, part unspecified
Nervous system (central) NOS
EXCLUDES *meninges NOS (225.2)*

226 Benign neoplasm of thyroid glands
Use additional code to identify any functional activity

✓4th **227 Benign neoplasm of other endocrine glands and related structures**
Use additional code to identify any functional activity
EXCLUDES *ovary (220)*
pancreas (211.6)
testis (222.0)

227.0 Adrenal gland
Suprarenal gland

227.1 Parathyroid gland

227.3 Pituitary gland and craniopharyngeal duct (pouch)
Craniobuccal pouch
Hypophysis
Rathke's pouch
Sella turcica

227.4 Pineal gland
Pineal body

227.5 Carotid body

227.6 Aortic body and other paraganglia
Coccygeal body
Glomus jugulare
Para-aortic body

227.8 Other

227.9 Endocrine gland, site unspecified

✓4th **228 Hemangioma and lymphangioma, any site**
INCLUDES angioma (benign) (cavernous) (congenital) NOS
cavernous nevus
glomus tumor
hemangioma (benign) (congenital)
EXCLUDES *benign neoplasm of spleen, except hemangioma and lymphangioma (211.9)*
glomus jugulare (227.6)
nevus:
NOS (216.0-216.9)
blue or pigmented (216.0-216.9)
vascular (757.32)

✓5th **228.0 Hemangioma, any site**
DEF: A common benign tumor usually occurring in infancy; composed of newly formed blood vessels due to malformation of angioblastic tissue.

228.00 Of unspecified site

228.01 Of skin and subcutaneous tissue

228.02 Of intracranial structures

228.03 Of retina

228.04 Of intra-abdominal structures
Peritoneum
Retroperitoneal tissue

228.09 Of other sites
Systemic angiomatosis

228.1 Lymphangioma, any site
Congenital lymphangioma
Lymphatic nevus

✓4th 229 Benign neoplasm of other and unspecified sites

229.0 Lymph nodes
EXCLUDES *lymphangioma (228.1)*

229.8 Other specified sites
Intrathoracic NOS
Thoracic NOS

229.9 Site unspecified

CARCINOMA IN SITU (230-234)

INCLUDES Bowen's disease
erythroplasia
Queyrat's erythroplasia

EXCLUDES *leukoplakia–see Alphabetic Index*

DEF: A neoplastic type; with tumor cells confined to epithelium of origin; without further invasion.

✓4th 230 Carcinoma in situ of digestive organs

230.0 Lip, oral cavity, and pharynx
Gingiva
Hypopharynx
Mouth [any part]
Nasopharynx
Oropharynx
Salivary gland or duct
Tongue
EXCLUDES *aryepiglottic fold or interarytenoid fold, laryngeal aspect (231.0)*
epiglottis:
NOS (231.0)
suprahyoid portion (231.0)
skin of lip (232.0)

230.1 Esophagus

230.2 Stomach
Body } of stomach
Cardia } of stomach
Fundus } of stomach
Cardiac orifice
Pylorus

230.3 Colon
Appendix
Cecum
Ileocecal valve
Large intestine NOS
EXCLUDES *rectosigmoid junction (230.4)*

230.4 Rectum
Rectosigmoid junction

230.5 Anal canal
Anal sphincter

230.6 Anus, unspecified
EXCLUDES *anus:*
margin (232.5)
skin (232.5)
perianal skin (232.5)

230.7 Other and unspecified parts of intestine
Duodenum
Ileum
Jejunum
Small intestine NOS
EXCLUDES *ampulla of Vater (230.8)*

230.8 Liver and biliary system
Ampulla of Vater
Common bile duct
Cystic duct
Gallbladder
Hepatic duct
Sphincter of Oddi

230.9 Other and unspecified digestive organs
Digestive organ NOS
Gastrointestinal tract NOS
Pancreas
Spleen

✓4th 231 Carcinoma in situ of respiratory system

231.0 Larynx
Cartilage:
arytenoid
cricoid
cuneiform
thyroid
Epiglottis:
NOS
posterior surface
suprahyoid portion
Vocal cords (false)(true)
EXCLUDES *aryepiglottic fold or interarytenoid fold:*
NOS (230.0)
hypopharyngeal aspect (230.0)
marginal zone (230.0)

231.1 Trachea

231.2 Bronchus and lung
Carina
Hilus of lung

231.8 Other specified parts of respiratory system
Accessory sinuses
Middle ear
Nasal cavities
Pleura
EXCLUDES *ear (external) (skin) (232.2)*
nose NOS (234.8)
skin (232.3)

231.9 Respiratory system, part unspecified
Respiratory organ NOS

✓4th 232 Carcinoma in situ of skin
INCLUDES pigment cells
EXCLUDES *melanoma in situ of skin (172.0-172.9)*

232.0 Skin of lip
EXCLUDES *vermilion border of lip (230.0)*

232.1 Eyelid, including canthus

232.2 Ear and external auditory canal

232.3 Skin of other and unspecified parts of face

232.4 Scalp and skin of neck

232.5 Skin of trunk, except scrotum
Anus, margin
Axillary fold
Perianal skin
Skin of:
abdominal wall
anus
back
Skin of:
breast
buttock
chest wall
groin
perineum
Umbilicus
EXCLUDES *anal canal (230.5)*
anus NOS (230.6)
skin of genital organs (233.30-233.39, 233.5-233.6)

232.6 Skin of upper limb, including shoulder

232.7 Skin of lower limb, including hip

232.8 Other specified sites of skin

232.9 Skin, site unspecified

✓4th 233 Carcinoma in situ of breast and genitourinary system

233.0 Breast
EXCLUDES *Paget's disease (174.0-174.9)*
skin of breast (232.5)

233.1 Cervix uteri
Adenocarcinoma in situ of cervix
Cervical intraepithelial glandular neoplasia, grade III
Cervical intraepithelial neoplasia III [CIN III]
Severe dysplasia of cervix
EXCLUDES *cervical intraepithelial neoplasia II [CIN II] (622.12)*
cytologic evidence of malignancy without histologic confirmation (795.06)
high grade squamous intraepithelial lesion (HGSIL) (795.04)
moderate dysplasia of cervix (622.12)

233.2 Other and unspecified parts of uterus

✓5th **233.3 Other and unspecified female genital organs**

233.30 Unspecified female genital organ

233.31 Vagina

Severe dysplasia of vagina
Vaginal intraepithelial neoplasia III [VAIN III]

233.32 Vulva

Severe dysplasia of vulva
Vulvar intraepithelial neoplasia III [VIN III]

233.39 Other female genital organ

233.4 Prostate

233.5 Penis

233.6 Other and unspecified male genital organs

233.7 Bladder

233.9 Other and unspecified urinary organs

✓4th **234 Carcinoma in situ of other and unspecified sites**

234.0 Eye

EXCLUDES *cartilage of eyelid (234.8)*
eyelid (skin) (232.1)
optic nerve (234.8)
orbital bone (234.8)

234.8 Other specified sites

Endocrine gland [any]

234.9 Site unspecified

Carcinoma in situ NOS

NEOPLASMS OF UNCERTAIN BEHAVIOR (235-238)

Note: Categories 235–238 classify by site certain histomorphologically well-defined neoplasms, the subsequent behavior of which cannot be predicted from the present appearance.

✓4th **235 Neoplasm of uncertain behavior of digestive and respiratory systems**

EXCLUDES *stromal tumors of uncertain behavior of digestive system (238.1)*

235.0 Major salivary glands

Gland:
parotid
sublingual
submandibular

EXCLUDES *minor salivary glands (235.1)*

235.1 Lip, oral cavity, and pharynx

Gingiva
Hypopharynx
Minor salivary glands
Mouth
Nasopharynx
Oropharynx
Tongue

EXCLUDES *aryepiglottic fold or interarytenoid fold, laryngeal aspect (235.6)*
epiglottis:
NOS (235.6)
suprahyoid portion (235.6)
skin of lip (238.2)

235.2 Stomach, intestines, and rectum

235.3 Liver and biliary passages

Ampulla of Vater
Bile ducts [any]
Gallbladder
Liver

235.4 Retroperitoneum and peritoneum

235.5 Other and unspecified digestive organs

Anal:
canal
sphincter
Anus NOS
Esophagus
Pancreas
Spleen

EXCLUDES *anus:*
margin (238.2)
skin (238.2)
perianal skin (238.2)

235.6 Larynx

EXCLUDES *aryepiglottic fold or interarytenoid fold:*
NOS (235.1)
hypopharyngeal aspect (235.1)
marginal zone (235.1)

235.7 Trachea, bronchus, and lung

235.8 Pleura, thymus, and mediastinum

235.9 Other and unspecified respiratory organs

Accessory sinuses
Middle ear
Nasal cavities
Respiratory organ NOS

EXCLUDES *ear (external) (skin) (238.2)*
nose (238.8)
skin (238.2)

✓4th **236 Neoplasm of uncertain behavior of genitourinary organs**

236.0 Uterus

236.1 Placenta

Chorioadenoma (destruens)
Invasive mole
Malignant hydatid(iform) mole

236.2 Ovary

Use additional code to identify any functional activity

236.3 Other and unspecified female genital organs

236.4 Testis

Use additional code to identify any functional activity

236.5 Prostate

236.6 Other and unspecified male genital organs

236.7 Bladder

✓5th **236.9 Other and unspecified urinary organs**

236.90 Urinary organ, unspecified

236.91 Kidney and ureter

236.99 Other

✓4th **237 Neoplasm of uncertain behavior of endocrine glands and nervous system**

237.0 Pituitary gland and craniopharyngeal duct

Use additional code to identify any functional activity

237.1 Pineal gland

237.2 Adrenal gland

Suprarenal gland

Use additional code to identify any functional activity

237.3 Paraganglia

Aortic body
Carotid body
Coccygeal body
Glomus jugulare

237.4 Other and unspecified endocrine glands

Parathyroid gland
Thyroid gland

237.5 Brain and spinal cord

237.6 Meninges

Meninges:
NOS
cerebral
spinal

✓5th **237.7 Neurofibromatosis**

von Recklinghausen's disease

DEF: An inherited condition with developmental changes in the nervous system, muscles, bones and skin; multiple soft tumors (neurofibromas) distributed over the entire body.

237.70 Neurofibromatosis, unspecified

237.71 Neurofibromatosis, type 1 [von Recklinghausen's disease]

237.72 Neurofibromatosis, type 2 [acoustic neurofibromatosis]

DEF: Inherited condition with cutaneous lesions, benign tumors of peripheral nerves and bilateral 8th nerve masses.

237.9 Other and unspecified parts of nervous system

Cranial nerves

EXCLUDES *peripheral, sympathetic, and parasympathetic nerves and ganglia (238.1)*

✓4th **238 Neoplasm of uncertain behavior of other and unspecified sites and tissues**

238.0 Bone and articular cartilage

EXCLUDES *cartilage:*
ear (238.1)
eyelid (238.1)
larynx (235.6)
nose (235.9)
synovia (238.1)

238.1 Connective and other soft tissue

Peripheral, sympathetic, and parasympathetic nerves and ganglia
Stromal tumors of digestive system

EXCLUDES *cartilage (of):*
articular (238.0)
larynx (235.6)
nose (235.9)
connective tissue of breast (238.3)

238.2 Skin

EXCLUDES *anus NOS (235.5)*
skin of genital organs (236.3, 236.6)
vermilion border of lip (235.1)

238.3 Breast

EXCLUDES *skin of breast (238.2)*

238.4 Polycythemia vera

DEF: Abnormal proliferation of all bone marrow elements, increased red cell mass and total blood volume; unknown etiology, frequently associated with splenomegaly, leukocytosis, and thrombocythemia.

238.5 Histiocytic and mast cells

Mast cell tumor NOS
Mastocytoma NOS

238.6 Plasma cells

Plasmacytoma NOS
Solitary myeloma

✓5th **238.7 Other lymphatic and hematopoietic tissues**

EXCLUDES *acute myelogenous leukemia (205.0)*
chronic myelomonocytic leukemia (205.1)
myelosclerosis NOS (289.89)
myelosis:
NOS (205.9)
megakaryocytic (207.2)

238.71 Essential thrombocythemia

Essential hemorrhagic thrombocythemia
Essential thrombocytosis
Idiopathic (hemorrhagic) thrombocythemia
Primary thrombocytosis

238.72 Low grade myelodysplastic syndrome lesions

Refractory anemia (RA)
Refractory anemia with ringed sideroblasts (RARS)
Refractory cytopenia with multilineage dysplasia (RCMD)
Refractory cytopenia with multilineage dysplasia and ringed sideroblasts (RCMD-RS)

DEF: Refractory anemia (RA): Form of bone marrow disorder (myelodysplastic syndrome) that interferes with red blood cell production in the bone marrow; malignancy unresponsive to hematinics; characteristic normal or hypercellular marrow with abnormal erythrocyte development and reticulocytopenia.

238.73 High grade myelodysplastic syndrome lesions

Refractory anemia with excess blasts-1 (RAEB-1)
Refractory anemia with excess blasts-2 (RAEB-2)

238.74 Myelodysplastic syndrome with 5q deletion

5q minus syndrome NOS

EXCLUDES *constitutional 5q deletion (758.39)*
high grade myelodysplastic syndrome with 5q deletion (238.73)

238.75 Myelodysplastic syndrome, unspecified

238.76 Myelofibrosis with myeloid metaplasia

Agnogenic myeloid metaplasia
Idiopathic myelofibrosis (chronic)
Myelosclerosis with myeloid metaplasia
Primary myelofibrosis

EXCLUDES *myelofibrosis NOS (289.83)*
myelophthisic anemia (284.2)
myelophthisis (284.2)
secondary myelofibrosis (289.83)

238.77 Post-transplant lymphoproliferative disorder [PTLD]

Code first complications of transplant (996.80-996.89)

238.79 Other lymphatic and hematopoietic tissues

Lymphoproliferative disease (chronic) NOS
Megakaryocytic myelosclerosis
Myeloproliferative disease (chronic) NOS
Panmyelosis (acute)

238.8 Other specified sites

Eye
Heart

EXCLUDES *eyelid (skin) (238.2)*
cartilage (238.1)

238.9 Site unspecified

NEOPLASMS OF UNSPECIFIED NATURE (239)

✓4th **239 Neoplasms of unspecified nature**

Note: Category 239 classifies by site neoplasms of unspecified morphology and behavior. The term "mass,"unless otherwise stated, is not to be regarded as a neoplastic growth.

INCLUDES "growth" NOS
neoplasm NOS
new growth NOS
tumor NOS

239.0 Digestive system

EXCLUDES *anus:*
margin (239.2)
skin (239.2)
perianal skin (239.2)

239.1 Respiratory system

239.2 Bone, soft tissue, and skin

EXCLUDES *anal canal (239.0)*
anus NOS (239.0)
bone marrow (202.9)
cartilage:
larynx (239.1)
nose (239.1)
connective tissue of breast (239.3)
skin of genital organs (239.5)
vermilion border of lip (239.0)

239.3 Breast

EXCLUDES *skin of breast (239.2)*

239.4 Bladder

239.5 Other genitourinary organs

239.6 Brain

EXCLUDES *cerebral meninges (239.7)*
cranial nerves (239.7)

239.7 Endocrine glands and other parts of nervous system

EXCLUDES *peripheral, sympathetic, and parasympathetic nerves and ganglia (239.2)*

239.8 Other specified sites

EXCLUDES *eyelid (skin) (239.2)*
cartilage (239.2)
great vessels (239.2)
optic nerve (239.7)

239.9 Site unspecified

Chapter 3: Endocrine, Nutritional and Metabolic Diseases, and Immunity Disorders (240–279)

Disorders of the endocrine system include a variety of specific glandular disorders that can affect any body system. Diseases of the endocrine system include hormonal disturbances that affect some of the body's most important physiological functions, including reproduction, growth and development, and energy balance. Nutritional deficiencies include dietary and nutritional disorders such as protein-calorie malnutrition, vitamin deficiencies, and mineral deficiencies. Nutritional deficiencies due to problems relating to intestinal malabsorption normally are classified to category 579 in the digestive system chapter.

Metabolic disorders include disturbances in any of the chemical processes that take place in the human body. Metabolism is divided into two phases: anabolism, the constructive phase in which smaller molecules such as amino acids are converted into larger molecules such as proteins, and catabolism, the destructive phase in which the process is reversed. The result is growth and regeneration of tissue, elimination of waste products, energy production, and energy conservation (stored reserves).

Disorders of the Thyroid Gland (240–246)

Disorders of the thyroid gland include goiter, thyrotoxicosis, hypothyroidism, thyroiditis, congenital goiter, cysts of the thyroid, hemorrhage, and infarction of the thyroid.

Congenital Hypothyroidism (243)

Congenital hypothyroidism is classified to chapter 3 rather than to chapter 14, "Congenital Anomalies," because congenital hypothyroid is not a structural anomaly but rather a functional anomaly. Severe congenital hypothyroidism in infants leads to cretinism, which is marked by arrested physical and mental development, dystrophy of the bones and lowered basal metabolism.

When coding congenital hypothyroidism use additional codes to describe any associated mental retardation. For example, a patient with mild retardation due to congenital hypothyroidism is coded 243 Congenital hypothyroidism, and 317 Mild mental retardation.

Acquired Hypothyroidism (244)

Acquired hypothyroidism (244) is a thyroid hormone deficiency also known as myxedema. The most common cause of hypothyroidism is secondary hypothyroidism due to pituitary failure (code 244.8). Acquired hypothyroidism also may be caused by surgical resection, external beam irradiation, radioactive iodine ablation, and antithyroid medications. For example, acquired hypothyroidism due to surgical resection of the thyroid to remove primary cancer is coded 244.0, Postsurgical hypothyroidism, and V10.87 History of malignant neoplasm of the thyroid.

Thyroiditis (245)

This is the inflammation of the thyroid gland. Acute thyroiditis is caused by staphylococcal, streptococcal, or other infection. Other thyroiditis results from an autoimmune response or as a result of treatment (iatrogenic), or of unknown etiology. Use an additional code to identify infectious organism. For example, acute thyroiditis due to staphylococcal infection is coded 245.0 and 041.10.

Diseases of Other Endocrine Glands (249–259)

This section covers diabetes mellitus, disorders of the pancreas, parathyroid gland, pituitary gland, thymus gland, adrenal glands, ovarian dysfunction, testicular dysfunction, polyglandular dysfunction, and other endocrine disorders.

The most complex coding issue concerning this section is coding diabetes mellitus. Each subcategory of diabetes is discussed separately since coding issues need to be addressed specifically.

Secondary Diabetes Mellitus (249)

Secondary diabetes develops due to damage or destruction of insulin-producing cells in the pancreas by the presence of chronic disease, drugs, trauma, hormonal disturbances, genetic disorders, and other conditions. Secondary diabetes mellitus presents with the same symptoms as diabetes mellitus and carries the same risks as primary diabetes, including complications such as heart conditions, stroke, diabetic retinopathy, diabetic nephropathy, diabetic neuropathy, and sexual dysfunction. Treatment of secondary diabetes involves treating the underlying cause. When the underlying cause cannot be resolved or remains unidentified, the diabetes is treated similarly to primary diabetes, with consideration given to pre-existing comorbidities. In general, this treatment focuses on controlling the level of glucose (blood sugar) with a combination of diet and exercise, and may involve insulin therapy and antidiabetic agents. Code category 249 Secondary diabetes mellitus includes 20 codes that parallel category 250. Similarly, all of the manifestation coding that applies to category 250 also applies to 249. In the same manner, instructional notes at subcategories 249.4–249.8 direct the coder to "Use additional code to identify manifestation." Sequencing of category 249 codes depends on the documentation in the medical record and forthcoming official coding guidelines.

Diabetes Mellitus (250)

Diabetes mellitus results in a chronic and progressive course of serious systemic complications. Type I patients have a complete absence of insulin secretion from the beta cells within the islets of Langerhans and have virtually no endogenous circulating insulin. This type is commonly referred to as juvenile diabetes and can be very difficult to regulate. These patients are dependent on exogenous insulin. Type II patients have some ability to secrete insulin and produce enough endogenous circulating insulin to prevent ketosis. Onset of type II diabetes is generally later in life and is commonly referred to as adult-onset diabetes. These patients may not produce sufficient amounts or may be unable to effectively utilize the insulin produced.

The fact that a patient is receiving insulin is not the determining factor to assign a fifth digit indicating type I, insulin-dependent diabetes. In some cases Type II supplemental insulin is required.

The first axis of coding for category 250 is the identification of complications present due to the diabetes. Patients with diabetes mellitus can have a variety of complications, which may or may not be due to the diabetic condition. When the condition is caused by the diabetes, ICD-9-CM provides codes to designate a causal relationship between the condition and the disease. For example, 250.4X Diabetes with renal manifestations. The source document must support the causal relationship to assign these codes. When a casual relationship is established, the diabetic code from category 250 is sequenced first followed by the code describing the complication or manifestation.

The second axis of coding is the fifth-digit assignment for the category 250, which indicates both type of diabetes and status of control of the disease. The physician MUST document the type of diabetes in order to assign a fifth-digit. The status of uncontrolled must also be stated by the physician in order to assign a fifth-digit indicating uncontrolled status. When the physician specifically states that the patient has uncontrolled diabetes, then and only then is a fifth-digit assignment of 2 or 3 made.

Both type I and type II diabetes may exist without complications.

Diabetes with Ketoacidosis (250.1)

Ketoacidosis is a form of metabolic acidosis characterized by raised levels of circulating ketone (acetone) bodies. Ketone bodies accumulate due to metabolization of fatty acids in place of carbohydrates. The carbohydrates are not being utilized due to a lack of insulin to metabolize them.

Diabetes with Hyperosmolarity (250.2)

Coma due to very high glucose concentrations in the blood and an increased concentration of osmotically active particles (e.g., sodium and potassium). For example, hyperosmolar coma in type II diabetic patient, stated as out of control, is coded 250.22.

Diabetes with Renal Manifestations (250.4)

Diabetes with renal manifestation presents as severe thickening of the capillary basement membrane of the kidney which eventually impairs renal function. There are two basic types of diabetic nephropathy, diffuse and nodular, which may coexist. In the diffuse type, the entire suspensitory structure of the renal glomerulus thickens, causing glomerulosclerosis. With nodular diabetic nephropathy (also known as Kimmelstiel-Wilson syndrome and intercapillary glomerulosclerosis), fibrin caps, capsular drops, and adhesions form in one or several areas of the glomerulus, causing glomerulosclerosis. Clinical manifestations as a result of glomerulosclerosis are known as nephrotic syndrome.

Nephritis is the first stage of kidney disease that may progress to nephrosis leading to chronic kidney disease (CKD). Code only to the most severe stage exhibited by the patient's condition. For example, type I diabetes stated as uncontrolled with diabetic nephritis and nephrosis is coded 250.43 and 583.81.

Diabetes with Ophthalmic Manifestations (250.5)

Ophthalmic disorders such as retinopathy and cataracts can result as complications of diabetes. Diabetic retinopathy is the most common ophthalmic complication and a leading cause of blindness in the United States. There are two basic types of diabetic retinopathy: background (nonproliferative or simple) and proliferative. For example, type I diabetes stated as uncontrolled with proliferative diabetic retinopathy is coded 250.53 and 362.02.

Cataracts or retinopathies are classified to this subcategory only when the physician specifies a cause and effect relationship with diabetes mellitus. Do not code cataracts as diabetic cataracts in the presence of diabetes mellitus unless the record supports a relationship between the disease and the manifestation. Diabetics may develop senile cataracts that have no causal relationship to the diabetes.

Diabetes with Neurological Manifestations (250.6)

Common long-term complications of diabetes encompass several distinct syndromes that differ with respect to anatomical distribution, neurological deficits, and clinical course. Diabetic neuropathy can affect the peripheral nerves alone or in combination with the autonomic nerves. Involvement of just a single nerve trunk is called mononeuropathy. Mononeuropathies usually are acute, self-limiting disorders most often affecting the extraocular muscles, but they can affect any single nerve trunk.

Involvement of the nerves of the peripheral nervous system is called polyneuropathy or peripheral polyneuropathy. Diabetic neuropathy affecting the part of the nervous system that regulates involuntary vital functions, particularly in the gastrointestinal system, urogenital system, and cardiovascular system, are called autonomic neuropathies. Since the autonomic nervous system includes the peripheral nerves involved in regulating cardiovascular, respiratory, endocrine, and other autonomic body functions, the term "peripheral autonomic neuropathy" (polyneuropathy) often is used.

Diabetes with Peripheral Circulatory Disorders (250.7)

Complications of diabetes that affect the blood vessels outside the heart and the lymphatic vessels are coded to this subcategory. Peripheral circulatory disorders usually are attributed to atherosclerosis and can generally be divided into two groups: macroangiopathy and microangiopathy. Macroangiopathy is disease that affects the major arterial systems; microangiopathy is disease that affects the capillary basement membranes and is a characteristic lesion of diabetes. Diabetics are more likely than nondiabetics to develop atherosclerosis and arteriosclerosis, and they tend to develop the diseases earlier.

Androgen Insensitivity Syndromes (259.5)

Androgen insensitivity syndrome (AIS) is a more accurate term for the condition formerly known as testicular feminization, Goldberg- Maxwell Syndrome, or pseudohermaphroditism. The male fetus has one X chromosome, which contains a gene that enables the body to recognize and react to androgens. However, people with AIS have a functioning Y chromosome and an abnormality on the X chromosome that prohibits the body, either completely or in part, from recognizing the androgens produced. As a result, two types of AIS develop: complete (CAIS) or partial (PAIS). In CAIS (259.51), the external genitalia development appears characteristically female. Internally, the patient may have a short vagina but no internal female organs and testicles that may require surgical removal due to possible cancer risk. Diagnosis may be delayed until amenorrhea is recognized during the teen years, in which the absence of a uterus and other reproductive organs is discovered. In PAIS (259.52), the external genitalia may be characteristically male or female, or a degree of both. People with this condition may identify as male, female, or intergendered.

Nutritional Deficiencies (260–269)

Nutritionally related diseases are reported with code 260–269. Categories 262 and 263 describe protein-caloric malnutrition. Note that categories 264–269 report the lack of specific nutrients and may identify their manifestation or associated disease process.

Gout (274)

Gout is a chronic disorder of uric metabolism manifested by hyperuricemia and recurrent characteristic inflammatory arthritis. Monosodium urate or monohydrate crystals may be deposited in and around joints. Pseudogout (chondrocalcinosis), classified to code 275.49, is a disorder of calcium metabolism. Joint disease due to deposits of dicalcium phosphate or pyrophosphate crystals is a manifestation of pseudogout. Dual coding is required to indicate joint involvement. For example, pseudogout of the ankle and foot due to dicalcium phosphate crystal deposits is coded 275.49 and 712.17.

Hungry Bone Syndrome (275.5)

Hungry bone syndrome (HBS) describes a state of severe or long-standing hypocalcemia, most commonly due to primary or secondary (including post-surgical) hypoparathyroidism. Elevated levels of parathyroid hormone and bone demineralization cause the bone to sequester calcium. This results in increased bone formation (density) and decreased bone resorption, characterized by a rapid fall in plasma calcium, phosphorus, and magnesium levels. The resultant metabolic imbalance may precede osteoporosis and associated pathological fracture, tetany, or seizures. Other causal conditions for HBS include neoplasm or associated therapies, systemic metabolic acidosis, or other chronic disease *(e.g., chronic renal disease). Code any causal conditions such as* neoplasm, chronic disease, or certain postsurgical states (e.g., parathyroidectomy) documented in the medical record. Code also any other specified manifestations, as appropriate.

Volume Depletion (276.5)

Disorders of fluid, electrolyte, and acid-base balance dehydration involve (276.51), volume depletion (276.50), or hypovolemia (276.52) are imbalances of homeostasis brought on by depletion of water in the body. The manifestations of dehydration (276.51) include lethargy, weakness, and reduced alertness. Since dehydration is usually a result of another condition (i.e., gastroenteritis, renal failure, burns, urinary tract infection, and so forth), code sequencing can be confusing. Many of the conditions that precipitate dehydration are not usually severe enough to warrant admission, yet the dehydration may be. Physician documentation is the deciding factor in sequencing the condition, since the physician must make the determination of the condition that necessitates reason for the visit.

Graft-versus-host disease (279.5)

Graft-versus-host disease (GVHD) was previously classified exclusively to code 996.85 Complications of transplanted organ, Bone marrow. GVHD does occur most often as a complication of bone marrow transplant. However, GVHD can also occur following blood transfusion or any organ transplant when white blood cells are present in the organ that is transplanted. GVHD may be either acute or chronic in nature. Acute on chronic GVHD describes an acute exacerbation of a chronic GVHD status. Acute GVHD may affect the skin (ranging from maculopapular rash to desquamation), gastrointestinal tract (with diarrhea), and liver (with elevated bilirubin), and cause increased susceptibility to infection (which may be in part a direct effect and in part due to treatment of GVHD). Chronic GVHD with onset more than three months after transplant may exhibit manifestations similar to acute GVHD. The chronic nature of the disease increases the severity of the symptoms. Treatment of GVHD involves corticosteroids and other immune suppressants. Since GVHD is a manifestation of an underlying condition, mandatory dual coding is required. Also, multiple codes may be required to describe associated manifestations.

3. ENDOCRINE, NUTRITIONAL AND METABOLIC DISEASES, AND IMMUNITY DISORDERS (240-279)

EXCLUDES *endocrine and metabolic disturbances specific to the fetus and newborn (775.0-775.9)*

Note: All neoplasms, whether functionally active or not, are classified in Chapter 2. Codes in Chapter 3 (i.e., 242.8, 246.0, 251-253, 255-259) may be used to identify such functional activity associated with any neoplasm, or by ectopic endocrine tissue.

DISORDERS OF THYROID GLAND (240-246)

✓4th **240 Simple and unspecified goiter**

DEF: An enlarged thyroid gland often caused by an inadequate dietary intake of iodine.

240.0 Goiter, specified as simple

Any condition classifiable to 240.9, specified as simple

240.9 Goiter, unspecified

Enlargement of thyroid
Goiter or struma:
- NOS
- diffuse colloid
- endemic
- hyperplastic
- nontoxic (diffuse)
- parenchymatous
- sporadic

EXCLUDES *congenital (dyshormonogenic) goiter (246.1)*

✓4th **241 Nontoxic nodular goiter**

EXCLUDES *adenoma of thyroid (226)*
cystadenoma of thyroid (226)

241.0 Nontoxic uninodular goiter

Thyroid nodule
Uninodular goiter (nontoxic)

DEF: Enlarged thyroid, commonly due to decreased thyroid production, with single nodule; no clinical hypothyroidism.

241.1 Nontoxic multinodular goiter

Multinodular goiter (nontoxic)

DEF: Enlarged thyroid, commonly due to decreased thyroid production with multiple nodules; no clinical hypothyroidism.

241.9 Unspecified nontoxic nodular goiter

Adenomatous goiter
Nodular goiter (nontoxic) NOS
Struma nodosa (simplex)

✓4th **242 Thyrotoxicosis with or without goiter**

EXCLUDES *neonatal thyrotoxicosis (775.3)*

DEF: A condition caused by excess quantities of thyroid hormones being introduced into the tissues

The following fifth-digit subclassification is for use with categories 242:
0 without mention of thyrotoxic crisis or storm
1 with mention of thyrotoxic crisis or storm

✓5th **242.0 Toxic diffuse goiter**
[0-1]

Basedow's disease
Exophthalmic or toxic goiter NOS
Graves' disease
Primary thyroid hyperplasia

DEF: Diffuse thyroid enlargement accompanied by hyperthyroidism, bulging eyes, and dermopathy.

✓5th **242.1 Toxic uninodular goiter**
[0-1]

Thyroid nodule } toxic or with
Uninodular goiter } hyperthyroidism

DEF: Symptomatic hyperthyroidism with a single nodule on the enlarged thyroid gland. Abrupt onset of symptoms; including extreme nervousness, insomnia, weight loss, tremors, and psychosis or coma.

The Endocrine System

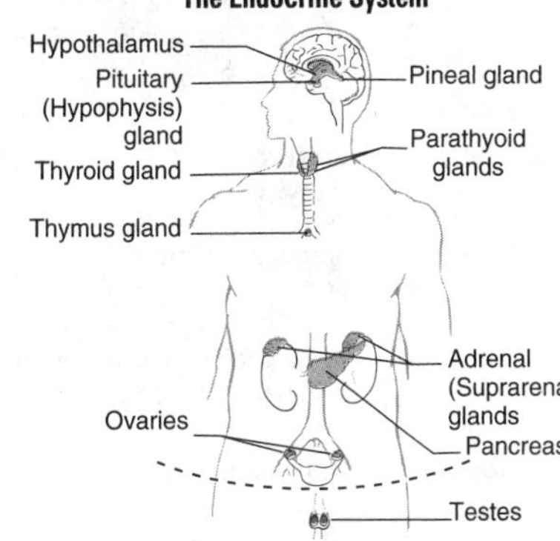

✓5th **242.2 Toxic multinodular goiter**
[0-1]

Secondary thyroid hyperplasia

DEF: Symptomatic hyperthyroidism with multiple nodules on the enlarged thyroid gland. Abrupt onset of symptoms; including extreme nervousness, insomnia, weight loss, tremors, and psychosis or comaThe Endocrine System

✓5th **242.3 Toxic nodular goiter, unspecified**
[0-1]

Adenomatous goiter } toxic or with
Nodular goiter } hyperthyroidism
Struma nodosa }

Any condition classifiable to 241.9 specified as toxic or with hyperthyroidism

✓5th **242.4 Thyrotoxicosis from ectopic thyroid nodule**
[0-1]

✓5th **242.8 Thyrotoxicosis of other specified origin**
[0-1]

Overproduction of thyroid-stimulating hormone [TSH]
Thyrotoxicosis:
- factitia from ingestion of excessive thyroid material

Use additional E code to identify cause, if drug-induced

✓5th **242.9 Thyrotoxicosis without mention of goiter or other cause**
[0-1]

Hyperthyroidism NOS
Thyrotoxicosis NOS

243 Congenital hypothyroidism

Congenital thyroid insufficiency
Cretinism (athyrotic) (endemic)

Use additional code to identify associated mental retardation

EXCLUDES *congenital (dyshormonogenic) goiter (246.1)*

DEF: Underproduction of thyroid hormone present from birth.

✓4th **244 Acquired hypothyroidism**

INCLUDES athyroidism (acquired)
hypothyroidism (acquired)
myxedema (adult) (juvenile)
thyroid (gland) insufficiency (acquired)

244.0 Postsurgical hypothyroidism

DEF: Underproduction of thyroid hormone due to surgical removal of all or part of the thyroid gland.

244.1 Other postablative hypothyroidism

Hypothyroidism following therapy, such as irradiation

244.2 Iodine hypothyroidism

Hypothyroidism resulting from administration or ingestion of iodide

Use additional E code to identify drug

244.3 Other iatrogenic hypothyroidism

Hypothyroidism resulting from:
- P-aminosalicylic acid [PAS]
- Phenylbutazone
- Resorcinol

Iatrogenic hypothyroidism NOS

Use additional E code to identify drug

244.8 Other specified acquired hypothyroidism

Secondary hypothyroidism NEC

244.9 Unspecified hypothyroidism
Hypothyroidism } primary or NOS
Myxedema }

✓4th 245 Thyroiditis

245.0 Acute thyroiditis
Abscess of thyroid
Thyroiditis:
nonsuppurative, acute
pyogenic
suppurative
Use additional code to identify organism
DEF: Inflamed thyroid caused by infection, with abscess and liquid puris.

245.1 Subacute thyroiditis
Thyroiditis:
de Quervain's
giant cell
granulomatous
viral
DEF: Inflammation of the thyroid, characterized by fever and painful enlargement of the thyroid gland, with granulomas in the gland.

245.2 Chronic lymphocytic thyroiditis
Hashimoto's disease
Struma lymphomatosa
Thyroiditis:
autoimmune
lymphocytic (chronic)
DEF: Autoimmune disease of thyroid; lymphocytes infiltrate the gland and thyroid antibodies are produced; women more often affected.

245.3 Chronic fibrous thyroiditis
Struma fibrosa
Thyroiditis:
invasive (fibrous)
ligneous
Riedel's
DEF: Persistent fibrosing inflammation of thyroid with adhesions to nearby structures; rare condition

245.4 Iatrogenic thyroiditis
Use additional code to identify cause
DEF: Thyroiditis resulting from treatment or intervention by physician or in a patient intervention setting.

245.8 Other and unspecified chronic thyroiditis
Chronic thyroiditis:
NOS
nonspecific

245.9 Thyroiditis, unspecified
Thyroiditis NOS

✓4th 246 Other disorders of thyroid

246.0 Disorders of thyrocalcitonin secretion
Hypersecretion of calcitonin or thyrocalcitonin

246.1 Dyshormonogenic goiter
Congenital (dyshormonogenic) goiter
Goiter due to enzyme defect in synthesis of thyroid hormone
Goitrous cretinism (sporadic)

246.2 Cyst of thyroid
EXCLUDES *cystadenoma of thyroid (226)*

246.3 Hemorrhage and infarction of thyroid

246.8 Other specified disorders of thyroid
Abnormality of thyroid-binding globulin
Atrophy of thyroid
Hyper-TBG-nemia
Hypo-TBG-nemia

246.9 Unspecified disorder of thyroid

DISEASES OF OTHER ENDOCRINE GLANDS (249-259)

✓4th 249 Secondary diabetes mellitus
INCLUDES diabetes mellitus (due to) (in) (secondary) (with):
drug-induced or chemical induced
infection
Use additional code to identify any associated insulin use (V58.67)
EXCLUDES *gestational diabetes (648.8)*
hyperglycemia NOS (790.29)
neonatal diabetes mellitus (775.1)
nonclinical diabetes (790.29)
Type I diabetes – see category 250
Type II diabetes – see category 250

The following fifth-digit subclassification is for use with category 249:
0 not stated as uncontrolled, or unspecified
1 uncontrolled

✓5th 249.0 Secondary diabetes mellitus without mention of complication
[0-1]
Secondary diabetes mellitus without mention of complication or manifestation classifiable to 249.1-249.9
Secondary diabetes mellitus NOS

✓5th 249.1 Secondary diabetes mellitus with ketoacidosis
[0-1]
Secondary diabetes mellitus with diabetic acidosis without mention of coma
Secondary diabetes mellitus with diabetic ketosis without mention of coma

✓5th 249.2 Secondary diabetes mellitus with hyperosmolarity
[0-1]
Secondary diabetes mellitus with hyperosmolar (nonketotic) coma

✓5th 249.3 Secondary diabetes mellitus with other coma
[0-1]
Secondary diabetes mellitus with diabetic coma (with ketoacidosis)
Secondary diabetes mellitus with diabetic hypoglycemic coma
Secondary diabetes mellitus with insulin coma NOS
EXCLUDES *secondary diabetes mellitus with hyperosmolar coma (249.2)*

✓5th 249.4 Secondary diabetes mellitus with renal manifestations
[0-1]
Use additional code to identify manifestation, as:
chronic kidney disease (585.1-585.9)
diabetic nephropathy NOS (583.81)
diabetic nephrosis (581.81)
intercapillary glomerulosclerosis (581.81)
Kimmelstiel-Wilson syndrome (581.81)

✓5th 249.5 Secondary diabetes mellitus with ophthalmic manifestations
[0-1]
Use additional code to identify manifestation, as:
diabetic blindness (369.00-369.9)
diabetic cataract (366.41)
diabetic glaucoma (365.44)
diabetic macular edema (362.07)
diabetic retinal edema (362.07)
diabetic retinopathy (362.01-362.07)

✓5th 249.6 Secondary diabetes mellitus with neurological manifestations
[0-1]
Use additional code to identify manifestation, as:
diabetic amyotrophy (353.5)
diabetic gastroparalysis (536.3)
diabetic gastroparesis (536.3)
diabetic mononeuropathy (354.0-355.9)
diabetic neurogenic arthropathy (713.5)
diabetic peripheral autonomic neuropathy (337.1)
diabetic polyneuropathy (357.2)

✓5th 249.7 Secondary diabetes mellitus with peripheral circulatory disorders
[0-1]
Use additional code to identify manifestation, as:
diabetic gangrene (785.4)
diabetic peripheral angiopathy (443.81)

✓5th **249.8 Secondary diabetes mellitus with other specified manifestations**
[0-1]
Secondary diabetic hypoglycemia in diabetes mellitus
Secondary hypoglycemic shock in diabetes mellitus
Use additional code to identify manifestation, as:
any associated ulceration (707.10-707.9)
diabetic bone changes (731.8)

✓5th **249.9 Secondary diabetes mellitus with unspecified complication**
[0-1]

✓4th **250 Diabetes mellitus**

EXCLUDES *gestational diabetes (648.8)*
hyperglycemia NOS (790.29)
neonatal diabetes mellitus (775.1)
nonclinical diabetes (790.29)
secondary diabetes (249.0-249.9)

The following fifth-digit subclassification is for use with category 250:
0 type II or unspecified type, not state as uncontrolled
Fifth-digit 0 is for use for type II patients, even if the patient requires insulin
Use additional code, if applicable, for associated long-term (current) insulin use V58.67
1 type I [juvenile type], not stated as uncontrolled
2 type II or unspecified type, uncontrolled
Fifth-digit 2 is for use for type II patients, even if the patient requires insulin
Use additional code, if applicable, for associated long-term (current) insulin use V58.67
3 type I [juvenile type], uncontrolled

DEF: Diabetes mellitus: Inability to metabolize carbohydrates, proteins, and fats with insufficient secretion of insulin. Symptoms may be unremarkable, with long-term complications, involving kidneys, nerves, blood vessels, and eyes.

DEF: Uncontrolled diabetes: A nonspecific term indicating that the current treatment regimen does not keep the blood sugar level of a patient within acceptable levels.

✓5th **250.0 Diabetes mellitus without mention of complication**
[0-3]
Diabetes mellitus without mention of complication or manifestation classifiable to 250.1-250.9
Diabetes (mellitus) NOS

✓5th **250.1 Diabetes with ketoacidosis**
[0-3]
Diabetic:
acidosis } without mention of coma
ketosis }
DEF: Diabetic hyperglycemic crisis causing ketone presence in body fluids.

✓5th **250.2 Diabetes with hyperosmolarity**
[0-3]
Hyperosmolar (nonketotic) coma

✓5th **250.3 Diabetes with other coma**
[0-3]
Diabetic coma (with ketoacidosis)
Diabetic hypoglycemic coma
Insulin coma NOS
EXCLUDES *diabetes with hyperosmolar coma (250.2)*
DEF: Coma (not hyperosmolar) caused by hyperglycemia or hypoglycemia as complication of diabetes.

✓5th **250.4 Diabetes with renal manifestations**
[0-3]
Use additional code to identify manifestation, as:
chronic kidney disease (585.1-585.9)
diabetic:
nephropathy NOS (583.81)
nephrosis (581.81)
intercapillary glomerulosclerosis (581.81)
Kimmelstiel-Wilson syndrome (581.81)

✓5th **250.5 Diabetes with ophthalmic manifestations**
[0-3]
Use additional code to identify manifestation, as:
diabetic:
blindness (369.00-369.9)
cataract (366.41)
glaucoma (365.44)
macular edema (362.07)
retinal edema (362.07)
retinopathy (362.01-362.07)

✓5th **250.6 Diabetes with neurological manifestations**
[0-3]
Use additional code to identify manifestation, as:
diabetic:
amyotrophy (353.5)
gastroparalysis (536.3)
gastroparesis (536.3)
mononeuropathy (354.0-355.9)
neurogenic arthropathy (713.5)
peripheral autonomic neuropathy (337.1)
polyneuropathy (357.2)

✓5th **250.7 Diabetes with peripheral circulatory disorders**
[0-3]
Use additional code to identify manifestation, as:
diabetic:
gangrene (785.4)
peripheral angiopathy (443.81)
DEF: Blood vessel damage or disease, usually in the feet, legs, or hands, as a complication of diabetes.

✓5th **250.8 Diabetes with other specified manifestations**
[0-3]
Diabetic hypoglycemia NOS
Hypoglycemic shock NOS
Use additional code to identify manifestation, as:
any associated ulceration (707.10-707.9)
diabetic bone changes (731.8)

✓5th **250.9 Diabetes with unspecified complication**
[0-3]

✓4th **251 Other disorders of pancreatic internal secretion**

251.0 Hypoglycemic coma
Iatrogenic hyperinsulinism
Non-diabetic insulin coma
Use additional E code to identify cause, if drug-induced
EXCLUDES *hypoglycemic coma in diabetes mellitus (249.3, 250.3)*
DEF: Coma induced by low blood sugar in non-diabetic patient.

251.1 Other specified hypoglycemia
Hyperinsulinism:
NOS
ectopic
functional
Hyperplasia of pancreatic islet beta cells NOS
EXCLUDES *hypoglycemia:*
in diabetes mellitus (249.8, 250.8)
in infant of diabetic mother (775.0)
hypoglycemic coma (251.0)
neonatal hypoglycemia (775.6)
Use additional E code to identify cause, if drug-induced.
DEF: Excessive production of insulin by the pancreas; associated with obesity and insulin-producing tumors.

251.2 Hypoglycemia, unspecified
Hypoglycemia:
NOS
reactive
spontaneous
EXCLUDES *hypoglycemia:*
with coma (251.0)
in diabetes mellitus (249.8, 250.8)
leucine-induced (270.3)

251.3 Postsurgical hypoinsulinemia
Hypoinsulinemia following complete or partial pancreatectomy
Postpancreatectomy hyperglycemia

251.4 Abnormality of secretion of glucagon
Hyperplasia of pancreatic islet alpha cells with glucagon excess
DEF: Production malfunction of a pancreatic hormone secreted by cells of the islets of Langerhans.

251.5 Abnormality of secretion of gastrin
Hyperplasia of pancreatic alpha cells with gastrin excess
Zollinger-Ellison syndrome

251.8 Other specified disorders of pancreatic internal secretion

251.9 Unspecified disorder of pancreatic internal secretion
Islet cell hyperplasia NOS

Dorsal View of Parathyroid Glands

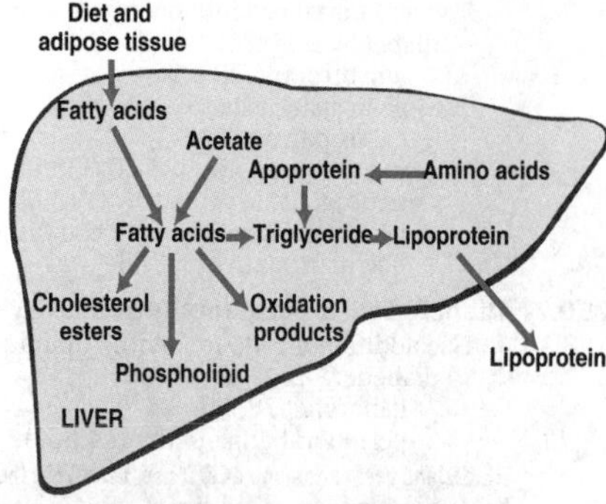

✓4th 252 Disorders of parathyroid gland

EXCLUDES *hungry bone syndrome (275.5)*

✓5th 252.0 Hyperparathyroidism

EXCLUDES *ectopic hyperparathyroidism (259.3)*

DEF: Abnormally high secretion of parathyroid hormones causing bone deterioration, reduced renal function, kidney stones.

252.00 Hyperparathyroidism, unspecified

252.01 Primary hyperparathyroidism

Hyperplasia of parathyroid

DEF: Parathyroid dysfunction commonly caused by hyperplasia of two or more glands; characteristic hyper-calcemia and increased parathyroid hormone levels.

252.02 Secondary hyperparathyroidism, non-renal

EXCLUDES *secondary hyperparathyroidism (of renal origin) (588.81)*

DEF: Underlying disease of nonrenal origin decreases blood levels of calcium causing the parathyroid to release increased levels of parathyroid hormone; para-thyroid hormone levels return to normal once underlying condition is treated and blood calcium levels are normal.

252.08 Other hyperparathyroidism

Tertiary hyperparathyroidism

DEF: Tertiary hyperparathyroidism: chronic secondary hyperparathyroidism leads to adenomatous parathyroid causing irreversible abnormal production of parathyroid hormone (PTH); PTH remains high after the serum calcium levels are brought under control.

252.1 Hypoparathyroidism

Parathyroiditis (autoimmune)
Tetany:
 parathyroid
 parathyroprival

EXCLUDES *pseudohypoparathyroidism (275.4)*
pseudopseudohypoparathyroidism (275.4)
tetany NOS (781.7)
transitory neonatal hypoparathyroidism (775.4)

DEF: Abnormally low secretion of parathyroid hormones which causes decreased calcium and increased phosphorus in the blood. Resulting in muscle cramps, tetany, urinary frequency and cataracts.

252.8 Other specified disorders of parathyroid gland

Cyst } of parathyroid
Hemorrhage } of parathyroid

252.9 Unspecified disorder of parathyroid gland

✓4th 253 Disorders of the pituitary gland and its hypothalamic control

INCLUDES the listed conditions whether the disorder is in the pituitary or the hypothalamus

EXCLUDES *Cushing's syndrome (255.0)*

253.0 Acromegaly and gigantism

Overproduction of growth hormone

DEF: Acromegaly: chronic, beginning in middle age; caused by hypersecretion of the pituitary growth hormone; produces enlarged parts of skeleton, especially the nose, ears, jaws, fingers and toes.

DEF: Gigantism: pituitary gigantism caused by excess growth of short flat bones; men may grow 78 to 80 inches tall.

253.1 Other and unspecified anterior pituitary hyperfunction

Forbes-Albright syndrome

EXCLUDES *overproduction of:*
 ACTH (255.3)
 thyroid-stimulating hormone [TSH] (242.8)

DEF: Spontaneous galactorrhea-amenorrhea syndrome unrelated to pregnancy; usually related to presence of pituitary tumor.

253.2 Panhypopituitarism

Cachexia, pituitary
Necrosis of pituitary (postpartum)
Pituitary insufficiency NOS
Sheehan's syndrome
Simmonds' disease

EXCLUDES *iatrogenic hypopituitarism (253.7)*

DEF: Damage to or absence of pituitary gland leading to impaired sexual function, weight loss, fatigue, bradycardia, hypotension, pallor, depression, and impaired growth in children; called Simmonds' disease if cachexia is prominent.

253.3 Pituitary dwarfism

Isolated deficiency of (human) growth hormone [HGH]
Lorain-Levi dwarfism

DEF: Dwarfism with infantile physical characteristics due to abnormally low secretion of growth hormone and gonadotropin deficiency.

253.4 Other anterior pituitary disorders

Isolated or partial deficiency of an anterior pituitary hormone, other than growth hormone
Prolactin deficiency

253.5 Diabetes insipidus

Vasopressin deficiency

EXCLUDES *nephrogenic diabetes insipidus (588.1)*

DEF: Metabolic disorder causing insufficient antidiuretic hormone release; symptoms include frequent urination, thirst, ravenous hunger, loss of weight, fatigue.

253.6 Other disorders of neurohypophysis

Syndrome of inappropriate secretion of antidiuretic hormone [ADH]

EXCLUDES *ectopic antidiuretic hormone secretion (259.3)*

253.7 Iatrogenic pituitary disorders

Hypopituitarism:
 hormone-induced
 hypophysectomy-induced
 postablative
 radiotherapy-induced

Use additional E code to identify cause

DEF: Pituitary dysfunction that results from drug therapy, radiation therapy, or surgery, causing mild to severe symptoms.

253.8 Other disorders of the pituitary and other syndromes of diencephalohypophyseal origin

Abscess of pituitary
Adiposogenital dystrophy
Cyst of Rathke's pouch
Fröhlich's syndrome

EXCLUDES *craniopharyngioma (237.0)*

253.9 Unspecified

Dyspituitarism

✓4th 254 Diseases of thymus gland

EXCLUDES *aplasia or dysplasia with immunodeficiency (279.2)*
hypoplasia with immunodeficiency (279.2)
myasthenia gravis (358.00-358.01)

254.0 Persistent hyperplasia of thymus
Hypertrophy of thymus
DEF: Continued abnormal growth of the twin lymphoid lobes that produce T lymphocytes.

254.1 Abscess of thymus

254.8 Other specified diseases of thymus gland
Astrophy } of thymus
Cyst } of thymus
EXCLUDES *thymoma (212.6)*

254.9 Unspecified disease of thymus gland

✓4th **255 Disorders of adrenal glands**
INCLUDES the listed conditions whether the basic disorder is in the adrenals or is pituitary-induced

255.0 Cushing's syndrome
Adrenal hyperplasia due to excess ACTH
Cushing's syndrome:
NOS
iatrogenic
idiopathic
pituitary-dependent
Ectopic ACTH syndrome
Iatrogenic syndrome of excess cortisol
Overproduction of cortisol
Use additional E code to identify cause, if drug-induced
EXCLUDES *congenital adrenal hyperplasia (255.2)*
DEF: Due to adrenal cortisol oversecretion or glucocorticoid medications; may cause fatty tissue of the face, neck and body; osteoporosis and curvature of spine, hypertension, diabetes mellitus, female genitourinary problems, male impotence, degeneration of muscle tissues, weakness.

✓5th **255.1 Hyperaldosteronism**
DEF: Oversecretion of aldosterone causing fluid retention, hypertension.

255.10 Hyperaldosteronism, unspecified
Aldosteronism NOS
Primary aldosteronism, unspecified
EXCLUDES *Conn's syndrome (255.12)*

255.11 Glucocorticoid-remediable aldosteronism
Familial aldosteronism type I
EXCLUDES *Conn's syndrome (255.12)*
DEF: A rare autosomal dominant familial form of primary aldosteronism in which the secretion of aldosterone is under the influence of adrenocortiotrophic hormone (ACTH) rather than the renin-angiotensin mechanism; characterized by moderate hypersecretion of aldosterone and suppressed plasma renin activity rapidly reversed by administration of glucosteroids; symptoms include hypertension and mild hypokalemia.

255.12 Conn's syndrome
DEF: A type of primary aldosteronism caused by an adenoma of the glomerulosa cells in the adrenal cortex; presence of hypertension.

255.13 Bartter's syndrome
DEF: A cluster of symptoms caused by a defect in the ability of the kidney to reabsorb potassium; signs include alkalosis (hypokalemic alkalosis), increased aldosterone, increased plasma renin, and normal blood pressure; symptoms include muscle cramping, weakness, constipation, frequency of urination, and failure to grow; also known as urinary potassium wasting or juxtaglomerular cell hyperplasia.

255.14 Other secondary aldosteronism

255.2 Adrenogenital disorders
Achard-Thiers syndrome
Adrenogenital syndromes, virilizing or feminizing, whether acquired or associated with congenital adrenal hyperplasia consequent on inborn enzyme defects in hormone synthesis
Congenital adrenal hyperplasia
Female adrenal pseudohermaphroditism
Male:
macrogenitosomia praecox
sexual precocity with adrenal hyperplasia
Virilization (female) (suprarenal)
EXCLUDES *adrenal hyperplasia due to excess ACTH (255.0)*
isosexual virilization (256.4)

255.3 Other corticoadrenal overactivity
Acquired benign adrenal androgenic overactivity
Overproduction of ACTH

✓5th **255.4 Corticoadrenal insufficiency**
EXCLUDES *tuberculous Addison's disease (017.6)*
DEF: Underproduction of adrenal hormones causing low blood pressure.

255.41 Glucocorticoid deficiency
Addisonian crisis
Addison's disease NOS
Adrenal atrophy (autoimmune)
Adrenal calcification
Adrenal crisis
Adrenal hemorrhage
Adrenal infarction
Adrenal insufficiency NOS
Combined glucocorticoid and mineralocorticoid deficiency
Corticoadrenal insufficiency NOS
DEF: Decreased function of the adrenal cortex resulting in insufficient production of glucocorticoid, the hormone regulating carbohydrate, fat, and protein metabolism; manifestations include hyponatremia, hyperpigmentation, orthostatic hypotension, anemia, loss of appetite, and malaise.

255.42 Mineralocorticoid deficiency
Hypoaldosteronism
EXCLUDES *combined glucocorticoid and mineralocorticoid deficiency (255.41)*
DEF: Decreased function of the adrenal cortex resulting in insufficient production of mineralocorticoid, the hormone regulating electrolyte and water balance; manifestations include hyponatremia, hyperkalemia, and mild acidosis.

255.5 Other adrenal hypofunction
Adrenal medullary insufficiency
EXCLUDES *Waterhouse-Friderichsen syndrome (meningococcal) (036.3)*

255.6 Medulloadrenal hyperfunction
Catecholamine secretion by pheochromocytoma

255.8 Other specified disorders of adrenal glands
Abnormality of cortisol-binding globulin

255.9 Unspecified disorder of adrenal glands

✓4th **256 Ovarian dysfunction**

256.0 Hyperestrogenism
DEF: Excess secretion of estrogen by the ovaries; characterized by ovaries containing multiple follicular cysts filled with serous fluid.

256.1 Other ovarian hyperfunction
Hypersecretion of ovarian androgens

256.2 Postablative ovarian failure
Ovarian failure:
iatrogenic
postirradiation
postsurgical
Use additional code for states associated with artificial menopause (627.4)
EXCLUDES *acquired absence of ovary (V45.77)*
asymptomatic age-related (natural) postmenopausal status (V49.81)
DEF: Failed ovarian function after medical or surgical intervention.

✓5th **256.3 Other ovarian failure**

Use additional code for states associated with natural menopause (627.2)

EXCLUDES *asymptomatic age-related (natural) postmenopausal status (V49.81)*

256.31 Premature menopause

DEF: Permanent cessation of ovarian function before the age of 40 occuring naturally of unknown cause.

256.39 Other ovarian failure

Delayed menarche
Ovarian hypofunction
Primary ovarian failure NOS

256.4 Polycystic ovaries

Isosexual virilization
Stein-Leventhal syndrome

DEF: Multiple serous filled cysts of ovary; symptoms of infertility, hirsutism, oligomenorrhea or amenorrhea.

256.8 Other ovarian dysfunction

256.9 Unspecified ovarian dysfunction

✓4th **257 Testicular dysfunction**

257.0 Testicular hyperfunction

Hypersecretion of testicular hormones

257.1 Postablative testicular hypofunction

Testicular hypofunction:
- iatrogenic
- postirradiation
- postsurgical

257.2 Other testicular hypofunction

Defective biosynthesis of testicular androgen
Eunuchoidism:
- NOS
- hypogonadotropic

Failure:
- Leydig's cell, adult
- seminiferous tubule, adult

Testicular hypogonadism

EXCLUDES *azoospermia (606.0)*

257.8 Other testicular dysfunction

EXCLUDES *androgen insensitivity syndromes (259.50-259.52)*

257.9 Unspecified testicular dysfunction

✓4th **258 Polyglandular dysfunction and related disorders**

✓5th **258.0 Polyglandular activity in multiple endocrine adenomatosis**

Multiple endocrine neoplasia [MEN] syndromes

Use additional codes to identify any malignancies and other conditions associated with the syndromes

258.01 Multiple endocrine neoplasia [MEN] type I

Wermer's syndrome

DEF: Wermer's syndrome: A rare hereditary condition characterized by the presence of adenomas or hyperplasia in more than one endocrine gland causing premature aging.

258.02 Multiple endocrine neoplasia [MEN] type IIA

Sipple's syndrome

DEF: Sipple's syndrome: A hereditary disorder caused by a defect in the RET gene that causes overactivity of the thyroid, adrenal, and parathyroid glands, resulting in neoplasm; commonly adrenal pheochromocytoma and thyroid medullary carcinoma.

258.03 Multiple endocrine neoplasia [MEN] type IIB

258.1 Other combinations of endocrine dysfunction

Lloyd's syndrome
Schmidt's syndrome

258.8 Other specified polyglandular dysfunction

258.9 Polyglandular dysfunction, unspecified

✓4th **259 Other endocrine disorders**

259.0 Delay in sexual development and puberty, not elsewhere classified

Delayed puberty

259.1 Precocious sexual development and puberty, not elsewhere classified

Sexual precocity:
- NOS
- constitutional
- cryptogenic
- idiopathic

259.2 Carcinoid syndrome

Hormone secretion by carcinoid tumors

DEF: Presence of carcinoid tumors that spread to liver; characterized by cyanotic flushing of skin, diarrhea, bronchospasm, acquired tricuspid and pulmonary stenosis, sudden drops in blood pressure, edema, ascites.

259.3 Ectopic hormone secretion, not elsewhere classified

Ectopic:
- antidiuretic hormone secretion [ADH]
- hyperparathyroidism

EXCLUDES *ectopic ACTH syndrome (255.0)*

259.4 Dwarfism, not elsewhere classified

Dwarfism:
- NOS
- constitutional

EXCLUDES *dwarfism:*
- *achondroplastic (756.4)*
- *intrauterine (759.7)*
- *nutritional (263.2)*
- *pituitary (253.3)*
- *renal (588.0)*

progeria (259.8)

✓5th **259.5 Androgen insensitivity syndrome**

DEF: chromosome abnormality that prohibits the body from recognizing androgen; XY genotype with ambiguous genitalia.

259.50 Androgen insensitivity, unspecified

259.51 Androgen insensitivity syndrome

Complete androgen insensitivity
de Quervain's syndrome
Goldberg-Maxwell Syndrome

259.52 Partial androgen insensitivity

Partial androgen insensitivity syndrome
Reifenstein syndrome

259.8 Other specified endocrine disorders

Pineal gland dysfunction
Progeria
Werner's syndrome

259.9 Unspecified endocrine disorder

Disturbance:
- endocrine NOS
- hormone NOS

Infantilism NOS

NUTRITIONAL DEFICIENCIES (260-269)

EXCLUDES *deficiency anemias (280.0-281.9)*

260 Kwashiorkor

Nutritional edema with dyspigmentation of skin and hair

DEF: Syndrome, particularly of children; excessive carbohydrate with inadequate protein intake, inhibited growth potential, anomalies in skin and hair pigmentation, edema and liver disease.

261 Nutritional marasmus

Nutritional atrophy
Severe calorie deficiency
Severe malnutrition NOS

DEF: Protein-calorie malabsorption or malnutrition of children; characterized by tissue wasting, dehydration, and subcutaneous fat depletion; may occur with infectious disease; also called infantile atrophy.

262 Other severe, protein-calorie malnutrition

Nutritional edema without mention of dyspigmentation of skin and hair

✓4th 263 Other and unspecified protein-calorie malnutrition

263.0 Malnutrition of moderate degree
DEF: Malnutrition characterized by biochemical changes in electrolytes, lipids, blood plasma.

263.1 Malnutrition of mild degree

263.2 Arrested development following protein-calorie malnutrition
Nutritional dwarfism
Physical retardation due to malnutrition

263.8 Other protein-calorie malnutrition

263.9 Unspecified protein-calorie malnutrition
Dystrophy due to malnutrition
Malnutrition (calorie) NOS
EXCLUDES *nutritional deficiency NOS (269.9)*

✓4th 264 Vitamin A deficiency

264.0 With conjunctival xerosis
DEF: Vitamin A deficiency with conjunctival dryness.

264.1 With conjunctival xerosis and Bitot's spot
Bitot's spot in the young child
DEF: Vitamin A deficiency with conjunctival dryness, superficial spots of keratinized epithelium.

264.2 With corneal xerosis
DEF: Vitamin A deficiency with corneal dryness.

264.3 With corneal ulceration and xerosis
DEF: Vitamin A deficiency with corneal dryness, epithelial ulceration.

264.4 With keratomalacia
DEF: Vitamin A deficiency creating corneal dryness; progresses to corneal insensitivity, softness, necrosis; usually bilateral.

264.5 With night blindness
DEF: Vitamin A deficiency causing vision failure in dim light.

264.6 With xerophthalmic scars of cornea
DEF: Vitamin A deficiency with corneal scars from dryness.

264.7 Other ocular manifestations of vitamin A deficiency
Xerophthalmia due to vitamin A deficiency

264.8 Other manifestations of vitamin A deficiency
Follicular keratosis } due to vitamin A deficiency
Xeroderma }

264.9 Unspecified vitamin A deficiency
Hypovitaminosis A NOS

✓4th 265 Thiamine and niacin deficiency states

265.0 Beriberi
DEF: Inadequate vitamin B_1 (thiamine) intake, affects heart and peripheral nerves; individual may become edematous and develop cardiac disease due to the excess fluid; alcoholics and people with a diet of excessive polished rice prone to the disease.

265.1 Other and unspecified manifestations of thiamine deficiency
Other vitamin B_1 deficiency states

265.2 Pellagra
Deficiency:
niacin (-tryptophan)
nicotinamide
nicotinic acid
vitamin PP
Pellagra (alcoholic)
DEF: Niacin deficiency causing dermatitis, inflammation of mucous membranes, diarrhea, and psychic disturbances.

✓4th 266 Deficiency of B-complex components

266.0 Ariboflavinosis
Riboflavin [vitamin B_2] deficiency
DEF: Vitamin B_2 (riboflavin) deficiency marked by swollen lips and tongue fissures, corneal vascularization, scaling lesions, and anemia.

266.1 Vitamin B_6 deficiency
Deficiency:
pyridoxal
pyridoxamine
pyridoxine
Vitamin B_6 deficiency syndrome
EXCLUDES *vitamin B_6-responsive sideroblastic anemia (285.0)*
DEF: Vitamin B_6 deficiency causing skin, lip, and tongue disturbances, peripheral neuropathy; and convulsions in infants.

266.2 Other B-complex deficiencies
Deficiency:
cyanocobalamin
folic acid
vitamin B_{12}
EXCLUDES *combined system disease with anemia (281.0-281.1)*
deficiency anemias (281.0-281.9)
subacute degeneration of spinal cord with anemia (281.0-281.1)

266.9 Unspecified vitamin B deficiency

267 Ascorbic acid deficiency
Deficiency of vitamin C
Scurvy
EXCLUDES *scorbutic anemia (281.8)*
DEF: Vitamin C deficiency causing swollen gums, myalgia, weight loss, and weakness.

✓4th 268 Vitamin D deficiency
EXCLUDES *vitamin D-resistant:*
osteomalacia (275.3)
rickets (275.3)

268.0 Rickets, active
EXCLUDES *celiac rickets (579.0)*
renal rickets (588.0)
DEF: Inadequate vitamin D intake, usually in pediatrics, that affects bones most involved with muscular action; may cause nodules on ends and sides of bones; delayed closure of fontanels in infants; symptoms may include muscle soreness, and profuse sweating.

268.1 Rickets, late effect
Any condition specified as due to rickets and stated to be a late effect or sequela of rickets
Code first the nature of late effect
DEF: Distorted or demineralized bones as a result of vitamin D deficiency.

268.2 Osteomalacia, unspecified
DEF: Softening of bones due to decrease in calcium; marked by pain, tenderness, muscular weakness, anorexia, and weight loss.

268.9 Unspecified vitamin D deficiency
Avitaminosis D

✓4th 269 Other nutritional deficiencies

269.0 Deficiency of vitamin K
EXCLUDES *deficiency of coagulation factor due to vitamin K deficiency (286.7)*
vitamin K deficiency of newborn (776.0)

269.1 Deficiency of other vitamins
Deficiency:
vitamin E
vitamin P

269.2 Unspecified vitamin deficiency
Multiple vitamin deficiency NOS

269.3 Mineral deficiency, not elsewhere classified
Deficiency:
calcium, dietary
iodine
EXCLUDES *deficiency:*
calcium NOS (275.4)
potassium (276.8)
sodium (276.1)

269.8 Other nutritional deficiency
EXCLUDES *adult failure to thrive (783.7)*
failure to thrive in childhood (783.41)
feeding problems (783.3)
newborn (779.3)

269.9 Unspecified nutritional deficiency

OTHER METABOLIC AND IMMUNITY DISORDERS (270-279)

Use additional code to identify any associated mental retardation

✓4th 270 Disorders of amino-acid transport and metabolism

EXCLUDES *abnormal findings without manifest disease (790.0-796.9)*
disorders of purine and pyrimidine metabolism (277.1-277.2)
gout (274.0-274.9)

270.0 Disturbances of amino-acid transport
Cystinosis
Cystinuria
Fanconi (-de Toni) (-Debré) syndrome
Glycinuria (renal)
Hartnup disease

270.1 Phenylketonuria [PKU]
Hyperphenylalaninemia

DEF: Inherited metabolic condition causing excess phenylpyruvic and other acids in urine; results in mental retardation, neurological manifestations, including spasticity and tremors, light pigmentation, eczema, and mousy odor.

270.2 Other disturbances of aromatic amino-acid metabolism
Albinism
Alkaptonuria
Alkaptonuric ochronosis
Disturbances of metabolismof tyrosine and tryptophan
Homogentisic acid defects
Hydroxykynureninuria
Hypertyrosinemia
Indicanuria
Kynureninase defects
Oasthouse urine disease
Ochronosis
Tyrosinosis
Tyrosinuria
Waardenburg syndrome

EXCLUDES *vitamin B_6-deficiency syndrome (266.1)*

270.3 Disturbances of branched-chain amino-acid metabolism
Disturbances of metabolism of leucine, isoleucine, and valine
Hypervalinemia
Intermittent branched-chain ketonuria
Leucine-induced hypoglycemia
Leucinosis
Maple syrup urine disease

270.4 Disturbances of sulphur-bearing amino-acid metabolism
Cystathioninemia
Cystathioninuria
Disturbances of metabolism of methionine, homocystine, and cystathionine
Homocystinuria
Hypermethioninemia
Methioninemia

270.5 Disturbances of histidine metabolism
Carnosinemia
Histidinemia
Hyperhistidinemia
Imidazole aminoaciduria

270.6 Disorders of urea cycle metabolism
Argininosuccinic aciduria
Citrullinemia
Disorders of metabolism of ornithine, citrulline, argininosuccinic acid, arginine, and ammonia
Hyperammonemia
Hyperornithinemia

270.7 Other disturbances of straight-chainamino-acid metabolism
Glucoglycinuria
Glycinemia (with methyl-malonic acidemia)
Hyperglycinemia
Hyperlysinemia
Other disturbances of metabolism of glycine, threonine, serine, glutamine, and lysine
Pipecolic acidemia
Saccharopinuria

270.8 Other specified disorders of amino-acid metabolism
Alaninemia
Ethanolaminuria
Glycoprolinuria
Hydroxyprolinemia
Hyperprolinemia
Iminoacidopathy
Prolinemia
Prolinuria
Sarcosinemia

270.9 Unspecified disorder of amino-acid metabolism

✓4th 271 Disorders of carbohydrate transport and metabolism

EXCLUDES *abnormality of secretion of glucagon (251.4)*
diabetes mellitus (249.0-249.9, 250.0-250.9)
hypoglycemia NOS (251.2)
mucopolysaccharidosis (277.5)

271.0 Glycogenosis
Amylopectinosis
Glucose-6-phosphatase deficiency
Glycogen storage disease
McArdle's disease
Pompe's disease
von Gierke's disease

271.1 Galactosemia
Galactose-1-phosphate uridyl transferase deficiency
Galactosuria

DEF: Any of three genetic disorders due to defective galactose metabolism; symptoms include failure to thrive in infancy, jaundice, liver and spleen damage, cataracts, and mental retardation.

271.2 Hereditary fructose intolerance
Essential benign fructosuria
Fructosemia

DEF: Chromosome recessive disorder of carbohydrate metabolism; in infants, occurs after dietary sugar introduced; characterized by enlarged spleen, yellowish cast to skin, and progressive inability to thrive.

271.3 Intestinal disaccharidase deficiencies and disaccharide malabsorption
Intolerance or malabsorption (congenital) (of):
glucose-galactose
lactose
sucrose-isomaltose

271.4 Renal glycosuria
Renal diabetes

DEF: Persistent abnormal levels of glucose in urine, with normal blood glucose levels; caused by failure of the renal tubules to reabsorb glucose.

271.8 Other specified disorders of carbohydrate transport and metabolism
Essential benign pentosuria
Fucosidosis
Glycolic aciduria
Hyperoxaluria (primary)
Mannosidosis
Oxalosis
Xylosuria
Xylulosuria

271.9 Unspecified disorder of carbohydrate transport and metabolism

✓4th 272 Disorders of lipoid metabolism

EXCLUDES *localized cerebral lipidoses (330.1)*

272.0 Pure hypercholesterolemia
Familial hypercholesterolemia
Fredrickson Type IIa hyperlipoproteinemia
Hyperbetalipoproteinemia
Hyperlipidemia, Group A
Low-density-lipoid-type [LDL] hyperlipoproteinemia

272.1 Pure hyperglyceridemia
Endogenous hyperglyceridemia
Fredrickson Type IV hyperlipoproteinemia
Hyperlipidemia, Group B
Hyperprebetalipoproteinemia
Hypertriglyceridemia, essential
Very-low-density-lipoid-type [VLDL] hyperlipoproteinemia

Lipid Metabolism

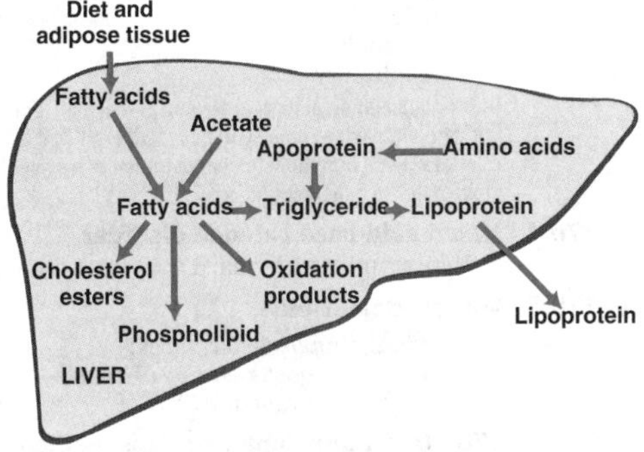

272.2 Mixed hyperlipidemia
Broad- or floating-betalipoproteinemia
Fredrickson Type IIb or III hyperlipoproteinemia
Hypercholesterolemia with endogenous hyperglyceridemia
Hyperbetalipoproteinemia with prebetalipoproteinemia
Tubo-eruptive xanthoma
Xanthoma tuberosum
DEF: Elevated levels of lipoprotein, a complex of fats and proteins, in blood due to inherited metabolic disorder.

272.3 Hyperchylomicronemia
Bürger-Grütz syndrome
Fredrickson type I or V hyperlipoproteinemia
Hyperlipidemia, Group D
Mixed hyperglyceridemia

272.4 Other and unspecified hyperlipidemia
Alpha-lipoproteinemia
Combined hyperlipidemia
Hyperlipidemia NOS
Hyperlipoproteinemia NOS
DEF: Hyperlipoproteinemia: elevated levels of transient chylomicrons in the blood which are a form of lipoproteins which transport dietary cholesterol and triglycerides from the small intestine to the blood.

272.5 Lipoprotein deficiencies
Abetalipoproteinemia
Bassen-Kornzweig syndrome
High-density lipoid deficiency
Hypoalphalipoproteinemia
Hypobetalipoproteinemia (familial)
DEF: Abnormally low levels of lipoprotein, a complex of fats and protein, in the blood.

272.6 Lipodystrophy
Barraquer-Simons disease
Progressive lipodystrophy
Use additional E code to identify cause, if iatrogenic
EXCLUDES *intestinal lipodystrophy (040.2)*
DEF: Disturbance of fat metabolism resulting in loss of fatty tissue in some areas of the body.

272.7 Lipidoses
Chemically-induced lipidosis
Disease:
Anderson's
Fabry's
Gaucher's
I cell [mucolipidosis I]
lipoid storage NOS
Niemann-Pick
pseudo-Hurler's or mucolipdosis III
triglyceride storage, Type I or II
Wolman's or triglyceride storage, Type III
Mucolipidosis II
Primary familial xanthomatosis
EXCLUDES *cerebral lipidoses (330.1)*
Tay-Sachs disease (330.1)
DEF: Lysosomal storage diseases marked by an abnormal amount of lipids in reticuloendothelial cells.

272.8 Other disorders of lipoid metabolism
Hoffa's disease or liposynovitis prepatellaris
Launois-Bensaude's lipomatosis
Lipoid dermatoarthritis

272.9 Unspecified disorder of lipoid metabolism

✓4th **273 Disorders of plasma protein metabolism**
EXCLUDES *agammaglobulinemia and hypogammaglobulinemia (279.0-279.2)*
coagulation defects (286.0-286.9)
hereditary hemolytic anemias (282.0-282.9)

273.0 Polyclonal hypergammaglobulinemia
Hypergammaglobulinemic purpura:
benign primary
Waldenström's
DEF: Elevated blood levels of gamma globulins, frequently found in patients with chronic infectious diseases.

273.1 Monoclonal paraproteinemia
Benign monoclonal hypergammaglobulinemia [BMH]
Monoclonal gammopathy:
NOS
associated with lymphoplasmacytic dyscrasias
benign
Paraproteinemia:
benign (familial)
secondary to malignant or inflammatory disease

273.2 Other paraproteinemias
Cryoglobulinemic:
purpura
vasculitis
Mixed cryoglobulinemia

273.3 Macroglobulinemia
Macroglobulinemia (idiopathic) (primary)
Waldenström's macroglobulinemia
DEF: Elevated blood levels of macroglobulins (plasma globulins of high weight); characterized by malignant neoplasms of bone marrow, spleen, liver, or lymph nodes; symptoms include weakness, fatigue, bleeding disorders, and vision problems.

273.4 Alpha-1-antitrypsin deficiency
AAT deficiency
DEF: Disorder of plasma protein metabolism that results in a deficiency of Alpha-1-antitrypsin, an acute-phase reactive protein, released into the blood in response to infection or injury to protect tissue against the harmful effect of enzymes.

273.8 Other disorders of plasma protein metabolism
Abnormality of transport protein
Bisalbuminemia

273.9 Unspecified disorder of plasma protein metabolism

✓4th **274 Gout**
EXCLUDES *lead gout (984.0-984.9)*
DEF: Purine and pyrimidine metabolic disorders; manifested by hyperuricemia and recurrent acute inflammatory arthritis; monosodium urate or monohydrate crystals may be deposited in and around the joints, leading to joint destruction, and severe crippling.

274.0 Gouty arthropathy

✓5th **274.1 Gouty nephropathy**

274.10 Gouty nephropathy, unspecified

274.11 Uric acid nephrolithiasis
DEF: Sodium urate stones in the kidney.

274.19 Other

✓5th **274.8 Gout with other specified manifestations**

274.81 Gouty tophi of ear
DEF: Chalky sodium urate deposit in the ear due to gout; produces chronic inflammation of external ear.

274.82 Gouty tophi of other sites
Gouty tophi of heart

274.89 Other
Use additional code to identify manifestations, as:
gouty:
iritis (364.11)
neuritis (357.4)

274.9 Gout, unspecified

✓4th **275 Disorders of mineral metabolism**

EXCLUDES *abnormal findings without manifest disease (790.0-796.9)*

275.0 Disorders of iron metabolism
Bronzed diabetes
Hemochromatosis
Pigmentary cirrhosis (of liver)
EXCLUDES *anemia:*
iron deficiency (280.0-280.9)
sideroblastic (285.0)

275.1 Disorders of copper metabolism
Hepatolenticular degeneration
Wilson's disease

275.2 Disorders of magnesium metabolism
Hypermagnesemia
Hypomagnesemia

275.3 Disorders of phosphorus metabolism
Familial hypophosphatemia
Hypophosphatasia
Vitamin D-resistant:
osteomalacia
rickets

✓5th **275.4 Disorders of calcium metabolism**
EXCLUDES *hungry bone syndrome (275.5)*
parathyroid disorders (252.00-252.9)
vitamin D deficiency (268.0-268.9)

275.40 Unspecified disorder of calcium metabolism

275.41 Hypocalcemia
DEF: Abnormally decreased blood calcium level; symptoms include hyperactive deep tendon reflexes, muscle, abdominal cramps, and carpopedal spasm.

275.42 Hypercalcemia
DEF: Abnormally increased blood calcium level; symptoms include muscle weakness, fatigue, nausea, depression, and constipation.

275.49 Other disorders of calcium metabolism
Nephrocalcinosis
Pseudohypoparathyroidism
Pseudopseudohypoparathyroidism
DEF: Nephrocalcinosis: calcium phosphate deposits in the tubules of the kidney with resultant renal insufficiency.
DEF: Pseudohypoparathyroidism: inherited disorder with signs and symptoms of hypoparathyroidism; caused by inadequate response to parathyroid hormone, not hormonal deficiency. Symptoms include muscle cramps, tetany, urinary frequency, blurred vision due to cataracts, and dry scaly skin.
DEF: Pseudopseudohypoparathyroidism: clinical manifestations of hypoparathyroidism without affecting blood calcium levels.

275.5 Hungry bone syndrome

275.8 Other specified disorders of mineral metabolism

275.9 Unspecified disorder of mineral metabolism

✓4th **276 Disorders of fluid, electrolyte, and acid-base balance**

EXCLUDES *diabetes insipidus (253.5)*
familial periodic paralysis (359.3)

276.0 Hyperosmolality and/or hypernatremia Sodium [Na] excess
Sodium [Na] overload

276.1 Hyposmolality and/or hyponatremia
Sodium [Na] deficiency

276.2 Acidosis
Acidosis:
NOS
lactic
metabolic
respiratory
EXCLUDES *diabetic acidosis (249.1, 250.1)*
DEF: Disorder involves decrease of pH (hydrogen ion) concentration in blood and cellular tissues; caused by increase in acid and decrease in bicarbonate.

276.3 Alkalosis
Alkalosis:
NOS
metabolic
respiratory
DEF: Accumulation of base (non-acid part of salt), or loss of acid without relative loss of base in body fluids; caused by increased arterial plasma bicarbonate concentration or loss of carbon dioxide due to hyperventilation.

276.4 Mixed acid-base balance disorder
Hypercapnia with mixed acid-base disorder

✓5th **276.5 Volume depletion**
EXCLUDES *hypovolemic shock:*
postoperative (998.0)
traumatic (958.4)

276.50 Volume depletion, unspecified
DEF: Depletion of total body water (dehydration) and/or contraction of total intravascular plasma (hypovolemia).

276.51 Dehydration
DEF: Depletion of total body water; blood volume may be normal while fluid is pulled from other tissues.

276.52 Hypovolemia
Depletion of volume of plasma
DEF: Depletion of volume plasma; depletion of total blood volume.

276.6 Fluid overload
Fluid retention
EXCLUDES *ascites (789.51-789.59)*
localized edema (782.3)

276.7 Hyperpotassemia
Hyperkalemia
Potassium [K]:
excess
intoxication
overload
DEF: Elevated blood levels of potassium; symptoms include abnormal EKG readings, weakness; related to defective renal excretion.

276.8 Hypopotassemia
Hypokalemia
Potassium [K] deficiency
DEF: Decreased blood levels of potassium; symptoms include neuromuscular disorders.

276.9 Electrolyte and fluid disorders not elsewhere classified
Electrolyte imbalance
Hyperchloremia
Hypochloremia
EXCLUDES *electrolyte imbalance:*
associated with hyperemesis gravidarum (643.1)
complicating labor and delivery (669.0)
following abortion and ectopic or molar pregnancy (634-638 with .4, 639.4)

✓4th **277 Other and unspecified disorders of metabolism**

✓5th **277.0 Cystic fibrosis**
Fibrocystic disease of the pancreas
Mucoviscidosis
DEF: Generalized, genetic disorder of infants, children, and young adults marked by exocrine gland dysfunction; characterized by chronic pulmonary disease with excess mucus production, pancreatic deficiency, high levels of electrolytes in the sweat.

277.00 Without mention of meconiumileus
Cystic fibrosis NOS

277.01 With meconium ileus
Meconium:
ileus (of newborn)
obstruction of intestine in mucoviscidosis

277.1 Disorders of porphyrin metabolism
Hematoporphyria
Hematoporphyrinuria
Hereditary coproporphyria
Porphyria
Porphyrinuria
Protocoproporphyria
Protoporphyria
Pyrroloporphyria

277.2 Other disorders of purine and pyrimidine metabolism
Hypoxanthine-guanine-phosphoribosyltransferase deficiency [HG-PRT deficiency]
Lesch-Nyhan syndrome
Xanthinuria
EXCLUDES *gout (274.0-274.9)*
orotic aciduric anemia (281.4)

✓5th **277.3 Amyloidosis**
DEF: Conditions of diverse etiologies characterized by the accumulation of insoluble fibrillar proteins (amyloid) in various organs and tissues of the body, compromising vital functions.

277.30 Amyloidosis, unspecified
Amyloidosis NOS

277.31 Familial Mediterranean fever
Benign paroxysmal peritonitis
Hereditary amyloid nephropathy
Periodic familial polyserositis
Recurrent polyserositis
DEF: Childhood or early-life onset of recurrent attacks characterized by high fevers with pain and inflammation of chest and abdominal cavities, skin and joints, also rash or vasculitis. Underlying cause is unknown, or possibly genetic, but may be precipitated by stress, trauma or exertion.

277.39 Other amyloidosis
Hereditary cardiac amyloidosis
Inherited systemic amyloidosis
Neuropathic (Portuguese) (Swiss) amyloidosis
Secondary amyloidosis

277.4 Disorders of bilirubin excretion
Hyperbilirubinemia:
congenital
constitutional
Syndrome:
Crigler-Najjar
Dubin-Johnson
Gilbert's
Rotor's
EXCLUDES *hyperbilirubinemias specific to the perinatal period (774.0-774.7)*

277.5 Mucopolysaccharidosis
Gargoylism
Hunter's syndrome
Hurler's syndrome
Lipochondrodystrophy
Maroteaux-Lamy syndrome
Morquio-Brailsford disease
Osteochondrodystrophy
Sanfilippo's syndrome
Scheie's syndrome
DEF: Metabolism disorders evidenced by excretion of various mucopolysaccharides in urine and infiltration of these substances into connective tissue, with resulting various defects of bone, cartilage and connective tissue.

277.6 Other deficiencies of circulating enzymes
Hereditary angioedema

277.7 Dysmetabolic syndrome X
Use additional code for associated manifestation, such as:
cardiovascular disease (414.00-414.07)
obesity (278.00-278.01)
DEF: A specific group of metabolic disorders that are related to the state of insulin resistance (decreased cellular response to insulin) without elevated blood sugars; often related to elevated cholesterol and triglycerides, obesity, cardiovascular disease, and high blood pressure.

✓5th **277.8 Other specified disorders of metabolism**

277.81 Primary carnitine deficiency

277.82 Carnitine deficiency due to inborn errors of metabolism

277.83 Iatrogenic carnitine deficiency
Carnitine deficiency due to:
hemodialysis
valproic acid therapy

277.84 Other secondary carnitine deficiency

277.85 Disorders of fatty acid oxidation
Carnitine palmitoyltransferase deficiencies (CPT1, CPT2)
Glutaric aciduria type II (type IIA, IIB, IIC)
Long chain 3-hydroxyacyl CoA dehydrogenase deficiency (LCHAD)
Long chain/very long chain acyl CoA dehydrogenase deficiency (LCAD, VLCAD)
Medium chain acyl CoA dehydrogenase deficiency (MCAD)
Short chain acyl CoA dehydrogenase deficiency (SCAD)
EXCLUDES *primary carnitine deficiency (277.81)*

277.86 Peroxisomal disorders
Adrenomyeloneuropathy
Neonatal adrenoleukodystrophy
Rhizomelic chrondrodysplasia punctata
X-linked adrenoleukodystrophy
Zellweger syndrome
EXCLUDES *infantile Refsum disease (356.3)*

277.87 Disorders of mitochondrial metabolism
Kearns-Sayre syndrome
Mitochondrial Encephalopathy, Lactic Acidosis and Stroke-like episodes (MELAS syndrome)
Mitochondrial Neurogastrointestinal Encephalopathy syndrome (MNGIE)
Myoclonus with Epilepsy and with Ragged Red Fibers (MERRF syndrome)
Neuropathy, Ataxia and Retinitis Pigmentosa (NARP syndrome)
Use additional code for associated conditions
EXCLUDES *disorders of pyruvate metabolism (271.8)*
Leber's optic atrophy (377.16)
Leigh's subacute necrotizing encephalopathy (330.8)
Reye's syndrome (331.81)

277.89 Other specified disorders of metabolism
Hand-Schüller-Christian disease
Histiocytosis (acute) (chronic)
Histiocytosis X (chronic)
EXCLUDES *histiocytosis:*
acute differentiated progressive (202.5)
X, acute (progressive) (202.5)

277.9 Unspecified disorder of metabolism
Enzymopathy NOS

✓4th **278 Overweight, obesity and other hyperalimentation**
EXCLUDES *hyperalimentation NOS (783.6)*
poisoning by vitamins NOS (963.5)
polyphagia (783.6)

✓5th **278.0 Overweight and obesity**
Use additional code to identify Body Mass Index (BMI), if known (V85.0-V85.54)
EXCLUDES *adiposogenital dystrophy (253.8)*
obesity of endocrine origin NOS (259.9)

278.00 Obesity, unspecified
Obesity NOS
DEF: BMI (body mass index) between 30.0 and 38.9.

278.01 Morbid obesity
Severe obesity
DEF: Increased weight beyond limits of skeletal and physical requirements (125 percent or more over ideal body weight), as a result of excess fat in subcutaneous connective tissues.
DEF: BMI (body mass index) greater than 39.

278.02 Overweight
DEF: BMI (body mass index) between 25 and 29.9.

278.1 Localized adiposity
Fat pad

278.2 Hypervitaminosis A

278.3 Hypercarotinemia
DEF: Elevated blood carotene level due to ingesting excess carotenoids or the inability to convert carotenoids to vitamin A.

278.4 Hypervitaminosis D
DEF: Weakness, fatigue, loss of weight, and other symptoms resulting from ingesting excessive amounts of vitamin D.

278.8 Other hyperalimentation

✓4th **279 Disorders involving the immune mechanism**

✓5th **279.0 Deficiency of humoral immunity**
DEF: Inadequate immune response to bacterial infections with potential reinfection by viruses due to lack of circulating immunoglobulins (acquired antibodies).

279.00 Hypogammaglobulinemia, unspecified
Agammaglobulinemia NOS

279.01 Selective IgA immunodeficiency

279.02 Selective IgM immunodeficiency

279.03 Other selective immunoglobulin deficiencies
Selective deficiency of IgG

279.04 Congenital hypogammaglobulinemia
Agammaglobulinemia:
- Bruton's type
- X-linked

279.05 Immunodeficiency with increased IgM
Immunodeficiency with hyper-IgM:
- autosomal recessive
- X-linked

279.06 Common variable immunodeficiency
Dysgammaglobulinemia (acquired) (congenital) (primary)
Hypogammaglobulinemia:
- acquired primary
- congenital non-sex-linked
- sporadic

279.09 Other
Transient hypogammaglobulinemia of infancy

✓5th **279.1 Deficiency of cell-mediated immunity**

279.10 Immunodeficiency with predominant T-cell defect, unspecified

279.11 DiGeorge's syndrome
Pharyngeal pouch syndrome
Thymic hypoplasia
DEF: Congenital disorder due to defective development of the third and fourth pharyngeal pouches; results in hypoplasia or aplasia of the thymus, parathyroid glands; related to congenital heart defects, anomalies of the great vessels, esophageal atresia, and abnormalities of facial structures.

279.12 Wiskott-Aldrich syndrome
DEF: A disease characterized by chronic conditions, such as eczema, suppurative otitis media and anemia; it results from an X-linked recessive gene and is classified as an immune deficiency syndrome.

279.13 Nezelof's syndrome
Cellular immunodeficiency with abnormal immunoglobulin deficiency
DEF: Immune system disorder characterized by a patholo-gical deficiency in cellular immunity and humoral anti-bodies resulting in inability to fight infectious diseases.

279.19 Other
EXCLUDES *ataxia-telangiectasia (334.8)*

279.2 Combined immunity deficiency
Agammaglobulinemia:
- autosomal recessive
- Swiss-type
- x-linked recessive

Severe combined immunodeficiency [SCID]
Thymic:
- alymophoplasia
- aplasia or dysplasia with immunodeficiency

EXCLUDES *thymic hypoplasia (279.11)*
DEF: Agammaglobulinemia: No immunoglobulins in the blood.
DEF: Thymic alymphoplasia: Severe combined immunodeficiency; result of failed lymphoid tissue development.

279.3 Unspecified immunity deficiency

279.4 Autoimmune disease, not elsewhere classified
Autoimmune disease NOS
EXCLUDES *transplant failure or rejection (996.80-996.89)*

✓5th **279.5 Graft-versus-host disease**
Code first underlying cause, such as:
- complication of transplanted organ (bone marrow) (996.80-996.89)
- complication of blood transfusion (998.89)

Use additional code to identify associated manifestations, such as:
- desquamative dermatitis (695.89)
- diarrhea (787.91)
- elevated bilirubin (782.4)
- hair loss (704.09)

279.50 Graft-versus-host disease, unspecified

279.51 Acute graft-versus-host disease

279.52 Chronic graft-versus-host disease

279.53 Acute on chronic graft-versus-host disease

279.8 Other specified disorders involving the immune mechanism
Single complement [C_1-C_9] deficiency or dysfunction

279.9 Unspecified disorder of immune mechanism

Chapter 4: Diseases of the Blood and Blood-Forming Organs (280–289)

This ICD-9-CM chapter classifies diseases and disorders of blood and blood-forming (hemopoietic) organs, including the following:

- Anemias
- Coagulation defects
- Purpura and other hemorrhagic conditions
- Diseases of white blood cells
- Other diseases of blood and blood-forming organs

The term "anemia" refers to a lower than normal erythrocyte count or level of hemoglobin in the circulating blood. A clinical sign rather than a diagnostic entity, anemia can be classified by three morphological variations of the erythrocyte: size (volume), hemoglobin content, and shape. These variations give clinicians clues to the specific type of anemia.

In laboratory blood tests, erythrocyte size is gauged by estimating the volume of red cells in the circulating blood. Red cell volume, or mean corpuscular volume, is estimated by dividing the patient's hematocrit (percentage of red blood cells in whole blood) by the red blood cell count. Normal values are normocytic; abnormally low values are microcytic; and abnormally high values are macrocytic.

Hemoglobin content refers to the average amount of hemoglobin in each red blood cell. This value, called the mean cell hemoglobin, is calculated by dividing the patient's hemoglobin by the number of red blood cells. Normal values are normochromic, less than normal values are hypochromic, and greater than normal values are hyperchromic.

Shape is determined by microscopy. Normally, red blood cells have a smooth concave shape. Erythrocytes with irregular shapes are called poikilocytes, a general term meaning abnormally shaped. Terms referring to specific abnormal cell shapes include acanthocytes, leptocytes, nucleated erythrocytes, macro-ovalocytes, schistocytes, helmet cells, teardrop cells, sickle cells, and target cells.

Once the cell morphology is determined, the anemia can be classified further based on certain physiological and pathological criteria. For example, constitutional aplastic anemia (subcategory 284.0) is classified physiologically as an anemia of hypoproliferation and pathologically as an inborn error of heredity.

The "coagulation defects" refers to deficiencies or disorders of hemostasis. A complicated process involving substances in the injured tissues, formed elements of blood (platelets, monocytes) and the coagulation proteins, coagulation requires the production of thrombin, a substance that stabilizes the platelet plug and forms the fibrin clot. Together they mechanically block the extravasation of blood from ruptured vessels.

The coagulation process can be interrupted by a genetic or disease-caused protein deficiency, interrupted by an increase in the catabolism of coagulation proteins or inhibited by antibodies directed against the coagulation proteins. There are many proteins involved in coagulation, many of which are identified by the term "factor" followed by a roman numeral. The activated form of a coagulation factor is indicated by the appropriate roman numeral followed by the suffix "a." For example, the protein factor II (prothrombin) is activated by the enzyme thrombin; when this occurs, it is designated factor IIa.

The term "purpura" refers to a condition characterized by hemorrhage, or extravasation of blood, into the tissues, producing bruises and small red patches on the skin. Purpura may be associated with thrombocytopenia or can occur in a nonthrombocytopenic form. Thrombocytopenia is a decrease of the number of platelets in the circulating blood and may be primary (hereditary or idiopathic) or secondary to a known cause.

Category, 288 Diseases of white blood cells classifies increases or decreases in levels and genetic or idiopathic anomalies of white blood cells not associated with malignant disease, such as leukemias which are classified to categories 200–208.

Iron Deficiency Anemias (280) and Other Deficiency Anemias (281)

Iron deficiency anemia is a chronic hypochromic, microcytic anemia characterized by small, pale erythrocytes and a depletion of iron stores. In adults, iron deficiency anemia is almost always due to blood loss; loss of as little as 2 to 4 ml of blood per day may deplete iron stores. This condition is also known as hypoferric anemia, hypochromic or microcytic anemia, and chlorosis.

Iron deficiency anemias secondary to inadequate dietary iron intake (280.1) is due to excretion of iron that exceeds normal dietary intake. Iron is recycled metabolically so that less than 1 mg is lost through excretion per day. A normal diet consists of 12–15 mg of iron, of which 0.6–1.5 mg are absorbed. Neonates and young children may develop iron deficiency anemia due to new blood formation and increased iron utilization that exceeds dietary intake.

Other specified iron deficiency anemias (280.8) are iron deficiency anemias of other specified types and causes, such as gastrectomy, excessive blood donation, and upper small-bowel malabsorption syndromes.

Iron deficiency anemia, unspecified (280.9) is a hypochromic anemia or iron deficiency anemia due to an unspecified or unknown cause. Included are microcytic or hypochromic anemias not otherwise specified and iron deficiency anemia due to impaired iron absorption not otherwise specified.

Pernicious anemia (281.0) is a progressive anemia of vitamin B-12 deficiency due to an absorption defect. Also known as Addison's or Biermer's anemia, it rarely occurs before the fourth decade of life. The condition may be due to an inherited genetic defect characterized by a deficiency of intrinsic factor, a substance essential for B-12 absorption.

Folate deficiency anemia (281.2) is macrocytic anemia caused by a deficiency of the anionic form of folic acid. If drug induced, use an additional E code to identify the drug.

Hereditary Hemolytic Anemias (282)

Hereditary hemolytic anemias include thalassemia, sickle cell trait, sickle cell anemia, and other hemoglobinopathies.

Thalassemia (282.4x) is a microcytic, hypochromic hemolytic anemia that results from a hereditary defect causing deficient hemoglobin synthesis. The severity, treatment, and prognosis of thalassemia depends on the globin gene arrangement and deletion type. Thalassemia major, the most severe form, is evident soon after birth and requires life-long blood transfusions.

Sickle-cell trait (282.5) is a heterozygous carrier of both the hemoglobin S and hemoglobin A genes. The condition rarely is associated with a clinical disorder.

Sickle-cell disease (282.6x) is a severe, chronic, and incurable form of anemia occurring in patients who inherit hemoglobin S genes from both parents. Less severe variations of the disease occur when the patient inherits a hemoglobin S gene from one parent and a hemoglobin C, D, or E gene from the other.

Acquired Hemolytic Anemias (283)

Acquired hemolytic anemia is characterized by the premature destruction of erythrocytes, exclusive of an inherited erythrocyte disorder. Hemolytic anemias may be acquired through infection, drugs, blood transfusions (autoimmune), or other intrinsic or extrinsic causes. Hemolytic uremic syndrome (hemolytic anemia and thrombocytopenia occurring with acute renal failure) is a common nonautoimmune hemolytic anemia. For example, hemolytic-uremic syndrome with acute renal failure is coded 283.11 Hemolytic-uremic syndrome, and 584.9 Acute renal failure, unspecified.

Aplastic Anemia and Other Bone Marrow Failure Syndromes (284)

Aplastic anemia is the failure of bone marrow to generate blood cells, resulting in a deficiency of all of the formed elements of the blood (erythrocytes, platelets, and leukocytes).

Aplastic anemia may be a direct result of chemotherapy for a malignant tumor. If treatment is directed toward the anemia, code as 284.8 and E933.1. This should not be confused with anemia due to the neoplastic process (e.g., 285.22).

Pure red cell aplasia (PRCA) describes a condition in which RBC precursors in bone marrow are nearly absent, while megakaryocytes and WBC precursors are usually present at normal levels. This condition is recognized as being a different entity from aplastic anemia. Although separate classifications exist for congenital red cell aplasia, the default code for the disease is the acquired form, code 284.81 Red cell aplasia. Code 284.89 Other specified aplastic anemias classifies other aplastic anemia due to chronic systemic disease or other external factors. Use an additional code to identify cause, such as drugs and radiation.

Other and Unspecified Anemias (285)

Secondary anemia caused by chronic illness (infections and neoplastic disease) or treatment for disease is assigned code 285.2x Anemia in chronic disease, only when no further information concerning the specific anemia is available. When the type of anemia is specified, the more specific anemia code should be assigned. In addition, assign codes to describe the specific chronic condition or specific malignancy (unless it's ESRD, which is contained in the code description) and an appropriate E code, if due to treatment.

Purpura and Other Hemorrhagic Conditions (287)

Purpura is hemorrhages of the skin. Initially red, the lesions darken to purple, fade to brownish-yellow and typically disappear in two to three weeks. Causes include allergic reactions, blood disorders, vascular abnormalities, and trauma.

Thrombocytopenia is a disorder distinguished by an abnormal decrease in the number of blood platelets and the presence of purpural skin hemorrhages. Secondary thrombocytopenia (287.4) may be caused by underlying conditions such as lupus erythematosus, Gaucher's disease, tuberculosis, or may be a result of massive blood transfusion, extracorporeal circulation of the blood, drugs, and platelet alloimmunization.

Diseases of White Blood Cells (288)

Neutropenia, also known as granulocytopenia or agranulocytosis, is a condition in which the neutrophil or granulocyte count in the blood is diminished, resulting in an increased susceptibility to bacterial and fungal infections. Elevated and decreased white blood cell counts are often clinically findings that lead to further patient assessment. Separate codes classify the various forms of neutropenia. Instructional notes direct the coder to use an additional E code to identify the drug in drug-induced neutropenia, or an additional code to report fever associated (but not inherent to) neutropenia.

Bandemia is a CBC laboratory finding in which there is an increase in early neutrophil cells, or band cells. The nucleus is not segmented but forms a continuous band. Code 288.66 Bandemia, is intended for reporting when a definitive diagnosis such as infection has not yet been established. If documentation states that bandemia is associated with a confirmed cause such as infection, code only the infection.

Other Diseases of Blood and Blood-Forming Organs (289)

Polycythemia, secondary (289.0) is the increase in the normal number of red blood cells. Secondary polycythemia also is known as secondary erythrocytosis, spurious polycythemia and reactive polycythemia. Spurious polycythemia, which is characterized by increased hematocrit and normal or increased erythrocyte total mass, results from a decrease in plasma volume and hemoconcentration. Reactive polycythemia is a condition characterized by excessive production of circulating erythrocytes due to an identifiable secondary condition such as hypoxia or an underlying disease such as a neoplasm.

Chronic lymphadenitis (289.1) is an inflammation of the lymph nodes. Any pathogen can cause lymphadenitis. Lymphadenitis may be generalized or restricted to regional lymph nodes and may occur with systemic infections.

Nonspecific mesenteric lymphadenitis (289.2) is a lymphadenitis occurring in the double layer of peritoneum attached to the abdominal wall, which encloses a portion or all of one of the abdominal viscera.

Hypersplenism (289.4) is a clinical syndrome characterized by splenic hyperactivity and splenomegaly. The condition results in a peripheral blood cell deficiency because the spleen traps and destroys the circulating peripheral blood cells.

Code 289.84 distinguishes heparin-induced thrombocytopenia (HIT) from other forms of secondary thrombocytopenia (287.4).Heparin is one of the most frequently prescribed medications, and its usage can lead to a particularly challenging adverse thrombocytopenic reaction (HIT). It is one of the three most common causes of iatrogenic thrombocytopenia, along with sepsis (with or without DIC) and the adverse effects of other drugs. Fifty percent or more of those with HIT will have thrombotic complications. These thromboembolic events may be arterial or venous and can lead to limb amputation, pulmonary emboli, strokes, and myocardial infarction. Although treatment should be initiated immediately if HIT is clinically suspected, the diagnosis can be confirmed by serologic tests for the pathogenic antibody. The serologic tests include commercially available ELISAs that detect the pathogenic antibodies to modified PF4, or functional assays demonstrating the activation of platelets in the presence of patient serum and heparin. Treatment includes the initiation of an alternative anticoagulant with thrombin inhibitors. Prolonged anticoagulation after recovery is essential to prevent thromboembolic events. Assign 287.4 for secondary thrombocytopenia due to drugs other than heparin or due to other treatment such as extracorporeal circulation of blood or massive blood transfusion. While clinically the same, heparin-induced thrombocytopenia has been given its own code due to the prevalence of heparin treatment and increased rate of subsequent adverse reactions.

4. DISEASES OF THE BLOOD AND BLOOD-FORMING ORGANS (280-289)

EXCLUDES *anemia complicating pregnancy or the puerperium (648.2)*

✓4th 280 Iron deficiency anemias

INCLUDES anemia:
- asiderotic
- hypochromic-microcytic
- sideropenic

EXCLUDES *familial microcytic anemia (282.49)*

280.0 Secondary to blood loss (chronic)
Normocytic anemia due to blood loss
EXCLUDES *acute posthemorrhagic anemia (285.1)*

280.1 Secondary to inadequate dietary iron intake

280.8 Other specified iron deficiency anemias
Paterson-Kelly syndrome
Plummer-Vinson syndrome
Sideropenic dysphagia

280.9 Iron deficiency anemia, unspecified
Anemia:
- achlorhydric
- chlorotic
- idiopathic hypochromic
- iron [Fe] deficiency NOS

✓4th 281 Other deficiency anemias

281.0 Pernicious anemia
Anemia:
- Addison's
- Biermer's
- congenital pernicious

Congenital intrinsic factor [Castle's] deficiency
EXCLUDES *combined system disease without mention of anemia (266.2)*
subacute degeneration of spinal cord without mention of anemia (266.2)

DEF: Chronic progressive anemia due to Vitamin B12 malabsorption; caused by lack of a secretion known as intrinsic factor, which is produced by the gastric mucosa of the stomach.

281.1 Other vitamin B_{12} deficiency anemia
Anemia:
- vegan's
- vitamin B_{12} deficiency (dietary)
- due to selective vitamin B_{12} malabsorption with proteinuria

Syndrome:
- Imerslund's
- Imerslund-Gräsbeck

EXCLUDES *combined system disease without mention of anemia (266.2)*
subacute degeneration of spinal cord without mention of anemia (266.2)

281.2 Folate-deficiency anemia
Congenital folate malabsorption
Folate or folic acid deficiency anemia:
- NOS
- dietary
- drug-induced

Goat's milk anemia
Nutritional megaloblastic anemia (of infancy)
Use additional E code to identify drug

DEF: Macrocytic anemia resembles pernicious anemia but without absence of hydrochloric acid secretions; responsive to folic acid therapy.

281.3 Other specified megaloblastic anemias not elsewhere classified
Combined B_{12} and folate-deficiency anemia
Refractory megaloblastic anemia

DEF: Megaloblasts predominant in bone marrow with few normoblasts; rare familial type associated with proteinuria and genitourinary tract anomalies.

281.4 Protein-deficiency anemia
Amino-acid-deficiency anemia

281.8 Anemia associated with other specified nutritional deficiency
Scorbutic anemia

281.9 Unspecified deficiency anemia
Anemia:
- dimorphic
- macrocytic
- megaloblastic NOS
- nutritional NOS
- simple chronic

✓4th 282 Hereditary hemolytic anemias

DEF: Escalated rate of erythrocyte destruction; similar to all anemias, occurs when imbalance exists between blood loss and blood production.

282.0 Hereditary spherocytosis
Acholuric (familial) jaundice
Congenital hemolytic anemia (spherocytic)
Congenital spherocytosis
Minkowski-Chauffard syndrome
Spherocytosis (familial)
EXCLUDES *hemolytic anemia of newborn (773.0-773.5)*

DEF: Hereditary, chronic illness marked by abnormal red blood cell membrane; symptoms include enlarged spleen, jaundice; and anemia in severe cases.

282.1 Hereditary elliptocytosis
Elliptocytosis (congenital)
Ovalocytosis (congenital) (hereditary)

DEF: Genetic hemolytic anemia characterized by malformed, elliptical erythrocytes; there is increased destruction of red cells with resulting anemia.

282.2 Anemias due to disorders of glutathione metabolism
Anemia:
- 6-phosphogluconic dehydrogenase deficiency
- enzyme deficiency, drug-induced
- erythrocytic glutathione deficiency
- glucose-6-phosphate dehydrogenase [G-6-PD] deficiency
- glutathione-reductase deficiency
- hemolytic nonspherocytic (hereditary), type I

Disorder of pentose phosphate pathway
Favism

282.3 Other hemolytic anemias due to enzyme deficiency
Anemia:
- hemolytic nonspherocytic (hereditary), type II
- hexokinase deficiency
- pyruvate kinase [PK] deficiency
- triosephosphate isomerase deficiency

✓5th 282.4 Thalassemias
EXCLUDES *sickle-cell:*
disease (282.60-282.69)
trait (282.5)

DEF: A group of inherited hemolytic disorders characterized by decreased production of at least one of the four polypeptide globin chains which results in defective hemoglobin synthesis; symptoms include severe anemia, expanded marrow spaces, transfusional and absorptive iron overload, impaired growth rate, thickened cranial bones, and pathologic fractures.

282.41 Sickle-cell thalassemia without crisis
Sickle-cell thalassemia NOS
Thalassemia Hb-S disease without crisis

282.42 Sickle-cell thalassemia with crisis
Sickle-cell thalassemia with vaso-occlusive pain
Thalassemia Hb-S disease with crisis
Use additional code for type of crisis, such as:
- acute chest syndrome (517.3)
- splenic sequestration (289.52)

282.49 Other thalassemia
Cooley's anemia
Hb-Bart's disease
Hereditary leptocytosis
Mediterranean anemia (with other hemoglobinopathy)
Microdrepanocytosis
Thalassemia (alpha) (beta) (intermedia) (major) (minima) (minor) (mixed) (trait) (with other hemoglobinopathy)
Thalassemia NOS

282.5 Sickle-cell trait
Hb-AS genotype
Hemoglobin S [Hb-S] trait
Heterozygous:
hemoglobin S
Hb-S
EXCLUDES *that with other hemoglobinopathy (282.60-282.69)*
that with thalassemia (282.49)
DEF: Heterozygous genetic makeup characterized by one gene for normal hemoglobin and one for sickle-cell hemoglobin; clinical disease rarely present.

✓5th **282.6 Sickle-cell disease**
Sickle-cell anemia
EXCLUDES *sickle-cell thalassemia (282.41-282.42)*
sickle-cell trait (282.5)
DEF: Inherited blood disorder; sickle-shaped red blood cells are hard and pointed, clogging blood flow; anemia characterized by, periodic episodes of pain, acute abdominal discomfort, skin ulcerations of the legs, increased infections; occurs primarily in persons of African descent.

282.60 Sickle-cell disease, unspecified
Sickle-cell anemia NOS

282.61 Hb-SS disease without crisis

282.62 Hb-SS disease with crisis
Hb-SS disease with vaso-occlusive pain
Sickle-cell crisis NOS
Use additional code for type of crisis, such as:
acute chest syndrome (517.3)
splenic sequestration (289.52)

282.63 Sickle-cell/Hb-C disease without crisis
Hb-S/Hb-C disease without crisis

282.64 Sickle-cell/Hb-C disease with crisis
Hb-S/Hb-C disease with crisis
Sickle-cell/Hb-C disease with vaso-occlusive pain
Use additional code for type of crisis, such as:
acute chest syndrome (517.3)
splenic sequestration (289.52)

282.68 Other sickle-cell disease without crisis
Hb-S/Hb-D } diseases without crisis
Hb-S/Hb-E
Sickle-cell/Hb-D
Sickle-cell/Hb-E

282.69 Other sickle-cell disease with crisis
Hb-S/Hb-D } diseases with crisis
Hb-S/Hb-E
Sickle-cell/Hb-D
Sickle-cell/Hb-E
Other sickle-cell disease with vaso-occlusive pain
Use additional code for type of crisis, such as:
acute chest syndrome (517.3)
splenic sequestration (289.52)

282.7 Other hemoglobinopathies
Abnormal hemoglobin NOS
Congenital Heinz-body anemia
Disease:
hemoglobin C [Hb-C]
hemoglobin D [Hb-D]
hemoglobin E [Hb-E]
hemoglobin Zurich [Hb-Zurich]
Hemoglobinopathy NOS
Hereditary persistence of fetal hemoglobin [HPFH]
Unstable hemoglobin hemolytic disease
EXCLUDES *familial polycythemia (289.6)*
hemoglobin M [Hb-M] disease (289.7)
high-oxygen-affinity hemoglobin (289.0)
DEF: Any disorder of hemoglobin due to alteration of molecular structure; may include overt anemia.

282.8 Other specified hereditary hemolytic anemias
Stomatocytosis

282.9 Hereditary hemolytic anemia, unspecified
Hereditary hemolytic anemia NOS

✓4th **283 Acquired hemolytic anemias**
DEF: Non-heriditary anemia characterized by premature destruction of red blood cells; caused by infectious organisms, poisons, and physical agents

283.0 Autoimmune hemolytic anemias
Autoimmune hemolytic disease (cold type) (warm type)
Chronic cold hemagglutinin disease
Cold agglutinin disease or hemoglobinuria
Hemolytic anemia:
cold type (secondary) (symptomatic)
drug-induced
warm type (secondary) (symptomatic)
Use additional E code to identify cause, if drug-induced
EXCLUDES *Evans' syndrome (287.32)*
hemolytic disease of newborn (773.0-773.5)

✓5th **283.1 Non-autoimmune hemolytic anemias**
Use additional E code to identify cause
DEF: Hemolytic anemia and thrombocytopenia with acute renal failure; relatively rare condition; 50 percent of patients require renal dialysis.

283.10 Non-autoimmune hemolytic anemia, unspecified

283.11 Hemolytic-uremic syndrome

283.19 Other non-autoimmune hemolytic anemias
Hemolytic anemia:
mechanical
microangiopathic
toxic

283.2 Hemoglobinuria due to hemolysis from external causes
Acute intravascular hemolysis
Hemoglobinuria:
from exertion
march
paroxysmal (cold) (nocturnal)
due to other hemolysis
Marchiafava-Micheli syndrome
Use additional E code to identify cause

283.9 Acquired hemolytic anemia, unspecified
Acquired hemolytic anemia NOS
Chronic idiopathic hemolytic anemia

✓4th **284 Aplastic anemia and other bone marrow failure syndromes**
DEF: Bone marrow failure to produce the normal amount of blood components; generally non-responsive to usual therapy.

✓5th **284.0 Constitutional aplastic anemia**

284.01 Constitutional red blood cell aplasia
Aplasia, (pure) red cell:
congenital
of infants
primary
Blackfan-Diamond syndrome
Familial hypoplastic anemia

284.09 Other constitutional aplastic anemia
Fanconi's anemia
Pancytopenia with malformations

284.1 Pancytopenia
EXCLUDES *pancytopenia (due to) (with):*
aplastic anemia NOS (284.9)
bone marrow infiltration (284.2)
constitutional red blood cell aplasia (284.01)
drug induced (284.89)
hairy cell leukemia (202.4)
human immunodeficiency virus disease (042)
leukoerythroblastic anemia (284.2)
malformations (284.09)
myelodysplastic syndromes (238.72-238.75)
myeloproliferative disease (238.79)
other constitutional aplastic anemia (284.09)

284.2 *Myelophthisis*
Leukoerythroblastic anemia
Myelophthisic anemia
Code first the underlying disorder, such as:
malignant neoplasm of breast (174.0-174.9, 175.0-175.9)
tuberculosis (015.0-015.9)
EXCLUDES *idiopathic myelofibrosis (238.76)*
myelofibrosis NOS (289.83)
myelofibrosis with myeloid metaplasia (238.76)
primary myelofibrosis (238.76)
secondary myelofibrosis (289.83)
DEF: A secondary disease process involving replacement of normal hematopoeitic tissue in the bone marrow with abnormal tissue, such as fibrous tissue or tumors. Occurs with advanced-stage neoplasms, granulomatous diseases such as miliary tuberculosis, and other inflammatory or infectious diseases or in countries where access to medical care is not readily available.

✓5th **284.8 Other specified aplastic anemias**

284.81 Red cell aplasia (acquired) (adult) (with thymoma)
Red cell aplasia NOS

284.89 Other specified aplastic anemias
Aplastic anemia (due to):
chronic systemic disease
drugs
infection
radiation
toxic (paralytic)
Use additional E code to identify cause

284.9 Aplastic anemia, unspecified
Anemia:
aplastic (idiopathic) NOS
aregenerative
hypoplastic NOS
nonregenerative
Medullary hypoplasia
EXCLUDES *refractory anemia (238.72)*

✓4th **285 Other and unspecified anemias**

285.0 Sideroblastic anemia
Anemia:
hypochromic with iron loading
sideroachrestic
sideroblastic:
acquired
congenital
hereditary
primary
secondary (drug-induced) (due to disease)
sex-linked hypochromic
vitamin B6-responsive
Pyridoxine-responsive (hypochromic) anemia
Use additional E code to identify cause, if drug induced
EXCLUDES *refractory sideroblastic anemia (238.72)*
DEF: Characterized by a disruption of final heme synthesis; results in iron overload of reticuloendothelial tissues.

285.1 Acute posthemorrhagic anemia
Anemia due to acute blood loss
EXCLUDES *anemia due to chronic blood loss (280.0)*
blood loss anemia NOS (280.0)

✓5th **285.2 Anemia of chronic disease**
Anemia in chronic illness

285.21 Anemia in chronic kidney disease
Anemia in end stage renal disease
Erythropoietin-resistant anemia (EPO resistant anemia)

285.22 Anemia in neoplastic disease

285.29 Anemia of other chronic disease
Anemia in other chronic illness

285.8 Other specified anemias
Anemia:
dyserythropoietic (congenital)
dyshematopoietic (congenital)
von Jaksch's
Infantile pseudoleukemia

285.9 Anemia, unspecified
Anemia:
NOS
essential
normocytic, not due to blood loss
profound
progressive
secondary
Oligocythemia
EXCLUDES *anemia (due to):*
blood loss:
acute (285.1)
chronic or unspecified (280.0)
iron deficiency (280.0-280.9)

✓4th **286 Coagulation defects**

286.0 Congenital factor VIII disorder
Antihemophilic globulin [AHG] deficiency
Factor VIII (functional)deficiency
Hemophilia:
NOS
A
classical
familial
hereditary
Subhemophilia
EXCLUDES *factor VIII deficiency with vascular defect (286.4)*
DEF: Hereditary, sex-linked, results in missing antihemophilic globulin (AHG) (factor VIII); causes abnormal coagulation characterized by increased tendency to bleeding, large bruises of skin, soft tissue; may also be bleeding in mouth, nose, gastrointestinal tract; after childhood, hemorrhages in joints, resulting in swelling and impaired function.

286.1 Congenital factor IX disorder
Christmas disease
Deficiency:
factor IX (functional)
plasma thromboplastin component [PTC]
Hemophilia B
DEF: Deficiency of plasma thromboplastin component (PTC) (factor IX) and plasma thromboplastin antecedent (PTA); PTC deficiency clinically indistinguishable from classical hemophilia; PTA deficiency found in both sexes.

286.2 Congenital factor XI deficiency
Hemophilia C
Plasma thromboplastin antecedent [PTA] deficiency
Rosenthal's disease

286.3 Congenital deficiency of other clotting factors
Congenital afibrinogenemia
Deficiency:
AC globulin factor:
I [fibrinogen]
II [prothrombin]
V [labile]
VII [stable]
X [Stuart-Prower]
XII [Hageman]
XIII [fibrin stabilizing]
Laki-Lorand factor
proaccelerin
Disease
Owren's
Stuart-Prower
Dysfibrinogenemia (congenital)
Dysprothrombinemia (constitutional)
Hypoproconvertinemia
Hypoprothrombinemia (hereditary)
Parahemophilia

286.4 von Willebrand's disease
Angiohemophilia (A) (B)
Constitutional thrombopathy
Factor VIII deficiency with vascular defect
Pseudohemophilia type B
Vascular hemophilia
von Willebrand's (-Jürgens') disease
EXCLUDES *factor VIII deficiency:*
NOS (286.0)
with functional defect (286.0)
hereditary capillary fragility (287.8)

DEF: Abnormal blood coagulation caused by deficient blood Factor VII; congenital; symptoms include excess or prolonged bleeding, such as hemorrhage during menstruation, following birthing, or after surgical procedure.

286.5 Hemorrhagic disorder due to intrinsic circulating anticoagulants
Antithrombinemia
Antithromboplastinemia
Antithromboplastino-genemia
Hyperheparinemia
Increase in:
anti-VIIIa
anti-IXa
anti-Xa
anti-XIa
antithrombin
Secondary hemophilia
Systemic lupus erythematosus [SLE] inhibitor

286.6 Defibrination syndrome
Afibrinogenemia, acquired
Consumption coagulopathy
Diffuse or disseminated intravascular coagulation [DIC syndrome]
Fibrinolytic hemorrhage, acquired
Hemorrhagic fibrinogenolysis
Pathologic fibrinolysis
Purpura:
fibrinolytic
fulminans
EXCLUDES *that complicating:*
abortion (634-638 with .1, 639.1)
pregnancy or the puerperium (641.3, 666.3)
disseminated intravascular coagulation in newborn (776.2)

DEF: Characterized by destruction of circulating fibrinogen; often precipitated by other conditions, such as injury, causing release of thromboplastic particles in blood stream.

286.7 Acquired coagulation factor deficiency
Deficiency of coagulation factor due to:
liver disease
vitamin K deficiency
Hypoprothrombinemia, acquired
Use additional E code to identify cause, if drug induced
EXCLUDES *vitamin K deficiency of newborn (776.0)*

286.9 Other and unspecified coagulation defects
Defective coagulation NOS
Deficiency, coagulation factor NOS
Delay, coagulation
Disorder:
coagulation
hemostasis
EXCLUDES *abnormal coagulation profile (790.92)*
hemorrhagic disease of newborn (776.0)
that complicating:
abortion (634-638 with .1, 639.1)
pregnancy or the puerperium (641.3, 666.3)

✓4th **287 Purpura and other hemorrhagic conditions**
EXCLUDES *hemorrhagic thrombocythemia (238.79)*
purpura fulminans (286.6)

287.0 Allergic purpura
Peliosis rheumatica
Purpura:
anaphylactoid
autoimmune
Henoch's
nonthrombocytopenic:
hemorrhagic
idiopathic
rheumatica
Schönlein-Henoch
vascular
Vasculitis, allergic
EXCLUDES *hemorrhagic purpura (287.39)*
purpura annularis telangiectodes (709.1)

DEF: Any hemorrhagic condition, thrombocytic or nonthrombocytopenic in origin, caused by a presumed allergic reaction.

287.1 Qualitative platelet defects
Thrombasthenia (hemorrhagic) (hereditary)
Thrombocytasthenia
Thrombocytopathy (dystrophic)
Thrombopathy (Bernard-Soulier)
EXCLUDES *von Willebrand's disease (286.4)*

287.2 Other nonthrombocytopenic purpuras
Purpura:
NOS
senile
simplex

✓5th **287.3 Primary thrombocytopenia**
EXCLUDES *thrombotic thrombocytopenic purpura (446.6)*
transient thrombocytopenia of newborn (776.1)

DEF: Decrease in number of blood platelets in circulating blood and purpural skin hemorrhages.

287.30 Primary thrombocytopenia, unspecified
Megakaryocytic hypoplasia

287.31 Immune thrombocytopenic purpura
Idiopathic thrombocytopenic purpura
Tidal platelet dysgenesis

DEF: Tidal platelet dysgenesis: Platelet counts fluctuate from normal to very low within periods of 20 to 40 days and may involve autoimmune platelet destruction.

287.32 Evans' syndrome

DEF: Combination of immunohemolytic anemia and autoimmune hemolytic anemia, sometimes with neutropenia.

287.33 Congenital and hereditary thrombocytopenic purpura
Congenital and hereditary thrombocytopenia
Thrombocytopenia with absent radii (TAR) syndrome
EXCLUDES *Wiskott-Aldrich syndrome (279.12)*

DEF: Thrombocytopenia with absent radii (TAR) syndrome: autosomal recessive syndrome characterized by thrombocytopenia and bilateral radial aplasia; manifestations include skeletal, gastrointestinal, hematologic, and cardiac system abnormalities.

287.39 Other primary thrombocytopenia

287.4 Secondary thrombocytopenia
Posttransfusion purpura
Thrombocytopenia (due to):
dilutional
drugs
extracorporeal circulation of blood
massive blood transfusion
platelet alloimmunization
Use additional E code to identify cause
EXCLUDES *heparin-induced thrombocytopenia (HIT) (289.84)*
transient thrombocytopenia of newborn (776.1)

DEF: Reduced number of platelets in circulating blood as consequence of an underlying disease or condition.

287.5 Thrombocytopenia, unspecified

287.8 Other specified hemorrhagic conditions
Capillary fragility (hereditary)
Vascular pseudohemophilia

287.9 Unspecified hemorrhagic conditions
Hemorrhagic diathesis (familial)

✓4th **288 Diseases of white blood cells**
EXCLUDES *leukemia (204.0-208.9)*

✓5th **288.0 Neutropenia**
Decreased absolute neutrophil count [ANC]
Use additional code for any associated:
fever (780.61)
mucositis (478.11, 528.00-528.09, 538, 616.81)
EXCLUDES *neutropenic splenomegaly (289.53)*
transitory neonatal neutropenia (776.7)
DEF: Sudden, severe condition characterized by reduced number of white blood cells; results in sores in the throat, stomach or skin; symptoms include chills, fever; some drugs can bring on condition.

288.00 Neutropenia, unspecified

288.01 Congenital neutropenia
Congenital agranulocytosis
Infantile genetic agranulocytosis
Kostmann's syndrome

288.02 Cyclic neutropenia
Cyclic hematopoiesis
Periodic neutropenia

288.03 Drug induced neutropenia
Use additional E code to identify drug

288.04 Neutropenia due to infection

288.09 Other neutropenia
Agranulocytosis
Neutropenia:
immune
toxic

288.1 Functional disorders of polymorphonuclear neutrophils
Chronic (childhood) granulomatous disease
Congenital dysphagocytosis
Job's syndrome
Lipochrome histiocytosis (familial)
Progressive septic granulomatosis

288.2 Genetic anomalies of leukocytes
Anomaly (granulation) (gran ulocyte) or syndrome:
Alder's (-Reilly)
Chédiak-Steinbrinck (-Higashi)
Jordan's
May-Hegglin
Pelger-Huet
Hereditary:
hypersegmentation
hyposegmentation
leukomelanopathy

288.3 Eosinophilia
Eosinophilia:
allergic
hereditary
idiopathic
secondary
Eosinophilic leukocytosis
EXCLUDES *Löffler's syndrome (518.3)*
pulmonary eosinophilia (518.3)
DEF: Elevated number of eosinophils in the blood; characteristic of allergic states and various parasitic infections.

288.4 Hemophagocytic syndromes
Familial hemophagocytic lymphohistiocytosis
Familial hemophagocytic reticulosis
Hemophagocytic syndrome, infection-associated
Histiocytic syndromes
Macrophage activation syndrome

✓5th **288.5 Decreased white blood cell count**
EXCLUDES *neutropenia (288.01-288.09)*

288.50 Leukocytopenia, unspecified
Decreased leukocytes, unspecified
Decreased white blood cell count, unspecified
Leukopenia NOS

288.51 Lymphocytopenia
Decreased lymphocytes

288.59 Other decreased white blood cell count
Basophilic leukopenia
Eosinophilic leukopenia
Monocytopenia
Plasmacytopenia

✓5th **288.6 Elevated white blood cell count**
EXCLUDES *eosinophilia (288.3)*

288.60 Leukocytosis, unspecified
Elevated leukocytes, unspecified
Elevated white blood cell count, unspecified

288.61 Lymphocytosis (symptomatic)
Elevated lymphocytes

288.62 Leukemoid reaction
Basophilic leukemoid reaction
Lymphocytic leukemoid reaction
Monocytic leukemoid reaction
Myelocytic leukemoid reaction
Neutrophilic leukemoid reaction

288.63 Monocytosis (symptomatic)
EXCLUDES *infectious mononucleosis (075)*

288.64 Plasmacytosis

288.65 Basophilia

288.66 Bandemia
Bandemia without diagnosis of specific infection
EXCLUDES *confirmed infection–code to infection*
leukemia (204.00-208.9)
DEF: Increase in early neutrophil cells, called band cells; may indicate infection.

288.69 Other elevated white blood cell count

288.8 Other specified disease of white blood cells
EXCLUDES *decreased white blood cell counts (288.50-288.59)*
elevated white blood cell counts (288.60-288.69)
immunity disorders (279.0-279.9)

288.9 Unspecified disease of white blood cells

✓4th **289 Other diseases of blood and blood-forming organs**

289.0 Polycythemia, secondary
High-oxygen-affinity hemoglobin
Polycythemia:
acquired
benign
due to:
fall in plasma volume
high altitude
emotional
erythropoietin
hypoxemic
nephrogenous
relative
spurious
stress
EXCLUDES *polycythemia:*
neonatal (776.4)
primary (238.4)
vera (238.4)
DEF: Elevated number of red blood cells in circulating blood as result of reduced oxygen supply to the tissues.

289.1 Chronic lymphadenitis
Chronic:
adenitis } any lymph node, except mesenteric
lymphadenitis }
EXCLUDES *acute lymphadenitis (683)*
mesenteric (289.2)
enlarged glands NOS (785.6)
DEF: Persistent inflammation of lymph node tissue; origin of infection is usually elsewhere.

289.2 Nonspecific mesenteric lymphadenitis
Mesenteric lymphadenitis (acute) (chronic)
DEF: Inflammation of the lymph nodes in peritoneal fold that encases abdominal organs; disease resembles acute appendicitis; unknown etiology.

289.3 Lymphadenitis, unspecified, except mesenteric

289.4 Hypersplenism
"Big spleen" syndrome
Dyssplenism
Hypersplenia
EXCLUDES *primary splenic neutropenia (289.53)*
DEF: An overactive spleen; it causes a deficiency of the peripheral blood components, an increase in bone marrow cells and sometimes a notable increase in the size of the spleen.

✓5th **289.5 Other diseases of spleen**

289.50 Disease of spleen, unspecified

289.51 Chronic congestive splenomegaly

289.52 *Splenic sequestration*
Code first sickle-cell disease in crisis (282.42, 282.62, 282.64, 282.69)
DEF: Blood is entrapped in the spleen due to vessel occlusion; most often associated with sickle-cell disease; spleen becomes enlarged and there is a sharp drop in hemoglobin.

289.53 Neutropenic splenomegaly

289.59 Other
Lien migrans
Perisplenitis
Splenic:
- abscess
- atrophy
- cyst
- fibrosis
- infarction
- rupture, nontraumatic

Splenitis
Wandering spleen
EXCLUDES *bilharzial splenic fibrosis (120.0-120.9)*
hepatolienal fibrosis (571.5)
splenomegaly NOS (789.2)

289.6 Familial polycythemia
Familial:
- benign polycythemia
- erythrocytosis

DEF: Elevated number of red blood cells.

289.7 Methemoglobinemia
Congenital NADH [DPNH]-methemoglobin-reductase deficiency
Hemoglobin M [Hb-M] disease
Methemoglobinemia:
- NOS
- acquired (with sulfhemoglobinemia)
- hereditary
- toxic

Stokvis' disease
Sulfhemoglobinemia
Use additional E code to identify cause
DEF: Presence in the blood of methemoglobin, a chemically altered form of hemoglobin; causes cyanosis, headache, dizziness, ataxia dyspnea, tachycardia, nausea, stupor, coma, and, rarely, death.

✓5th **289.8 Other specified diseases of blood and blood-forming organs**
DEF: Hypercoagulable states: a group of inherited or acquired abnormalities of specific proteins and anticoagulant factors; also called thromboembolic states or thrombotic disorders, these disorders result in the abnormal development of blood clots.

289.81 Primary hypercoagulable state
Activated protein C resistance
Antithrombin III deficiency
Factor V Leiden mutation
Lupus anticoagulant
Protein C deficiency
Protein S deficiency
Prothrombin gene mutation
DEF: Activated protein C resistance: decreased effectiveness of protein C to degrade factor V, necessary to inhibit clotting cascade; also called Factor V Leiden mutation.
DEF: Antithrombin III deficiency: deficiency in plasma antithrombin III one of six naturally occurring antithrombins that limit coagulation.
DEF: Factor V Leiden mutation: also called activated protein C resistance.
DEF: Lupus anticoagulant: deficiency in a circulating anticoagulant that inhibits the conversion of prothrombin into thrombin; autoimmune antibodies induce procoagulant surfaces in platelets; also called anti-phospholipid syndrome.
DEF: Protein C deficiency: deficiency of activated protein C which functions to bring the blood-clotting process into balance; same outcome as factor V Leiden mutation.
DEF: Protein S deficiency: similar to protein C deficiency; protein S is a vitamin K dependent cofactor in the activation of protein C.
DEF: Prothrombin gene mutation: increased levels of prothrombin, or factor II, a plasma protein that is converted to thrombin, which acts upon fibrinogen to form the fibrin.

289.82 Secondary hypercoagulable state
EXCLUDES *heparin-induced thrombocytopenia (HIT) (289.84)*

289.83 Myelofibrosis
Myelofibrosis NOS
Secondary myelofibrosis
Code first the underlying disorder, such as:
malignant neoplasm of breast (174.0-174.9, 175.0-175.9)
Use additional code for associated therapy-related myelodysplastic syndrome, if applicable (238.72, 238.73)
Use additional external cause code if due to anti-neoplastic chemotherapy (E933.1)
EXCLUDES *idiopathic myelofibrosis (238.76)*
leukoerythroblastic anemia (284.2)
myelofibrosis with myeloid metaplasia (238.76)
myelophthisic anemia (284.2)
myelophthisis (284.2)
primary myelofibrosis (238.76)
DEF: A progressive bone marrow disease characterized by the replacement of bone marrow with the overgrowth of neoplastic stem cells and fibrotic tissue, also progressive anemia and enlarged spleen.

289.84 Heparin-induced thrombocytopenia [HIT]

289.89 Other specified diseases of blood and blood-forming organs
Hypergammaglobulinemia
Pseudocholinesterase deficiency

289.9 Unspecified diseases of blood and blood-forming organs
Blood dyscrasia NOS
Erythroid hyperplasia

Chapter 5: Mental Disorders (290–319)

The fifth chapter of ICD-9-CM is "Mental Disorders," including:

- Psychoses
- Neuroses
- Transient stress disorders
- Personality disorders
- Sexual deviation and dysfunction
- Psychophysiological disorders

A suggested hierarchy for coding psychiatric disorders is provided by the World Health Organization as follows: All organically based psychiatric illnesses are given precedence over functional ones, and within the functional group the order then may be psychoses, neuroses, personality disorders, and others.

The American Psychiatric Association has developed a classification system to record diagnostic and statistical data on psychiatric patients. The Diagnostic and Statistical Manual (DSM-IV-TR) is based on a multiaxial system which evaluates each patient on five axes. Psychiatric hospitals and treatment centers frequently use both DSM-IV-TR and ICD-9-CM to record diagnosis and statistical data on their patients. Physician offices, however, should use the ICD-9-CM coding system to code for reimbursement. The clinical definitions of the diagnostic codes between ICD-9-CM and DSM-IV-TR are nearly identical. Differences occur in the other axes, such as axis IV for psychosocial and environmental factors and axis V for global assessment of functioning (GAF).

When coding mental disorders associated with physical conditions, assign as many codes as necessary to fully describe the condition.

The following sections are included in chapter 5, "Mental Disorders."

- Psychoses (290–299)
  - organic psychotic conditions (290–294)
  - other psychoses (295–299)
- Neurotic disorders, personality disorders, and other nonpsychotic mental disorders (300–316)

Organic Psychotic Conditions (290–294)

Organic psychotic conditions are defined as impairments of mental function to a degree that interferes with the activities of daily living and the ability to maintain contact with reality. Note that this section classifies conditions that are referred to as psychotic, a gross impairment of reality. Nonpsychotic organic brain syndromes are classified to categories 310–316. Conditions classified to this section include senile and presenile dementia, arteriosclerotic dementia, alcoholic dementia and withdrawal hallucinosis, drug psychosis and withdrawal syndromes, and organic brain syndromes.

Senile and presenile organic psychotic conditions (290) are characterized by severely impaired mental and social function. Signs and symptoms include memory loss, impaired comprehension, impaired orientation, poor judgment, and changes in personality or mood.

Excluded from category 290 are psychoses occurring in old age without dementia or delirium (295.0x–298.8); (310.1); and transient organic psychotic conditions (293.0–293.9).

If mental or behavioral problems are unspecified, code V40.9 may be used. However, this is not an acceptable principal diagnosis for Medicare patients.

Vascular dementia (290.4x) results from multiple infarcts and is attributable to degenerative arterial disease of the brain. Use an additional code to identify cerebral atherosclerosis. For example, vascular dementia with delirium due to cerebral arteriosclerosis is coded 290.41 Arteriosclerotic dementia with delirium, and 437.0, Cerebral arteriosclerosis.

Alcohol-Induced Mental Disorders (291)

Alcohol-induced psychoses result from excessive alcohol consumption, usually in association with nutritional deficits. This category excludes alcoholism without psychosis, which is classified to category 303. However, when alcohol dependence or abuse results in a psychotic condition, code both the psychotic condition and the dependence (303) or abuse (305.0x). For example, alcoholic withdrawal due to chronic alcoholism is coded 291.81 and 303.90.

Alcohol withdrawal delirium (291.0) is delirium resulting from the abrupt cessation of the use of alcohol by an individual who habitually consumes alcohol.

Alcohol-induced persisting amnestic syndrome (291.1) is the prominent and lasting reduction of memory span, including loss of recent memory, disordered time appreciation and confabulation, occurring in alcoholics, usually as a sequel to alcoholic psychosis.

Other alcohol-induced persisting dementia (291.2) is a nonhallucinatory dementia associated with alcoholism but without features of delirium tremens or Korsakov's psychosis.

Alcohol-induced psychotic disorder with hallucinations (291.3) is a psychosis usually lasting less than six months with slight or no clouding of consciousness in which auditory hallucinations predominate.

Idiosyncratic alcohol intoxication (291.4) is a unique behavioral pattern including belligerence, after the intake of relatively small amounts of alcohol. This behavior is not due to excessive consumption and is without conspicuous neurological signs of intoxication.

Drug-Induced Mental Disorders (292)

Drug psychoses include drug-induced mental disorders and organic brain disorders associated with drug abuse, dependence, or use. Additional E codes identify the drug. Assign additional codes to indicate associated drug dependence (304.0x–304.9x). The coding guidelines to assign drug-induced mental disorders is very similar to the guidelines to code alcohol induced psychoses.

The subcategories include drug withdrawal (292.0), paranoid and/or hallucinatory states induced by drugs (292.1x), pathological drug intoxication (292.2), and other (292.8x) and unspecified (292.9x) drug-induced mental disorders.

Other Organic Mental Disorders due to Conditions Classified Elsewhere (Persistent) (294)

This category includes dementia in conditions classified elsewhere, amnestic syndrome, and other chronic organic brain syndromes not classified elsewhere.

The term behavioral disturbances in subcategory 294.1 Dementia in conditions classified elsewhere with and without behavioral disturbances, is defined as aggressive, combative, violent, or wandering-off behavior as distinguished from more organic psychotic conditions such as hallucinations, delirium, and delusions. The more specific organic psychotic conditions (hallucinations, delirium, and delusions) are included in the code descriptions for the conditions that produce them. For example, arteriosclerotic dementia, presenile and senile dementia, alcohol and drug psychoses have code options specific to the manifestation of an organic psychotic conditions.

Behavioral disturbances are patterns of activity that interfere with normal functioning and increase resource utilization in cases of long term care. The existence of behavioral conditions in dementia in conditions classified elsewhere is a mandatory multiple coding situation. Code first the underlying condition followed by the dementia code.

Schizophrenic Disorders (295)

These are mental disorders characterized by disturbances in thinking, feeling and behavior. Informally, schizophrenia is referred to as "split personality." Signs and symptoms include: hypersensitivity, shyness, unsociability, lack of affect, paranoia, auditory hallucinations, difficulties in personal relationships, thought disorders such as unclear thinking, perplexity, affective emotional changes such as blunting, mood disturbances, and inappropriateness.

To support a diagnosis of schizophrenia, a characteristic disturbance of at least two of these areas is seen: thought, perception, mood, conduct, and personality.

The first axis of coding schizophrenia is to identify the type (i.e., simple, disordered, paranoid, latent, residual, etc.). Identify the course of illness with a fifth digit.

Episodic mood Disorder (296)

Bipolar I disorder is a recurrent, severe disturbances of mood accompanied by one or more of the following: delusions, perplexity, disturbed attitude to self, disorder of perception and behavior. Patients with bipolar I disorder have a strong characteristic toward suicide. This category includes mild disorders of mood if the symptoms closely match the descriptions.

Subcategories identify the type (i.e., manic or major depressive, bipolar, etc.) and episodic nature (i.e., single, recurrent, etc.). A fifth-digit assignment identifies severity of the episode.

Neurotic Disorders, Personality Disorders and Other Nonpsychotic Mental Disorders (300–316)

Neurotic disorders (300) are mental disorders without any obvious evidence of an organic etiology. In neurotic disorders, fantasies are not confused with reality, nor is personality disorganized. These include panic disorder, neurotic depression, hysteria, conversion disorder, psychogenic fugue, phobic disorders, obsessive-compulsive disorders, hypochondriasis and others.

Personality disorders (301) include paranoid, affective, chronic hypomanic, schizoid, explosive, compulsive, histrionic, dependent, antisocial, narcissistic, avoidant, borderline, and passive-aggressive types.

Sexual deviations and disorders (302) include ego-dystonic homosexuality, zoophilia, pedophilia, transvestism, exhibitionism, transexualism, psychosexual identity disorder, fetishism, voyeurism, sadism, and others.

Alcohol Dependence Syndrome (303)

Alcohol dependence syndrome is a psychotic and often physical state caused by alcohol. It is characterized by behavioral and other responses that always include the need to consume alcohol on a continuous or periodic basis. Fifth-digit assignment indicates pattern of use.

Use additional codes to identify any associated condition such as alcoholic psychoses (291.0–291.9), drug dependence (304.0x–304.9x), or physical complications such as cerebral degeneration (331.7), cirrhosis of the liver (571.2), epilepsy and recurrent seizures (345.0x–345.9x), hepatitis (571.1), and liver damage (571.3).

Dependence (304)

The first axis of classification in this category is the class of drug to which the patient is addicted (e.g. opioids, hallucinogens). Fifth-digit assignment indicates pattern of use.

Nondependent Drug Abuse (305)

Nondependent abuse is the maladaptive, but nondependent, effect of a drug taken by a patient on his or her own to the detriment of health and/or social functioning. The subcategories reflect the type of drug, and the fifth-digit subclassification identifies the documented pattern of use.

Tobacco dependence (305.1) is included in this category. Tobacco dependence is included here rather than under category 304, because tobacco differs from other drugs of dependence in its psychotoxic effects.

Post-concussion Syndrome (310.2)

Post-concussion syndrome is a nonpsychotic disorder due to brain trauma that causes symptoms unrelated to any disease process. Symptoms include amnesia, serial headaches, rapid heartbeat, fatigue, disrupted sleep patterns, and inability to concentrate. Use an additional code to identify associated post-traumatic headache, if applicable (339.20–339.22). Subcategory 339.2 Post-traumatic headache includes three codes that classify post-traumatic headache by severity as acute, chronic, or unspecified. Headache is a common symptom of post-concussion syndrome. According to the instructional note, it is appropriate to report an additional code for post-traumatic headache when associated with postconcussion syndrome.

Specific Delays in Development (315)

Code category 315 classifies certain specific developmental delay disorders. These disorders are separate from delays of an intellectual, educational, or neurological nature, and instead are often the result of other biological or nonbiological factors.

Children born with hearing loss or deafness, whether permanent or intermittent, are at significantly greater risk for not acquiring normal, age-appropriate language and speech abilities. Code 315.34 Speech and language developmental delay due to hearing loss should be reported for cases specific to congenital hearing loss that results in developmental delays.

Mental Retardation (317–319)

Mental retardation is the condition of arrested or incomplete development of the mind characterized by subnormal intelligence.

Assign a code based on the individual's current level of function without regard to the nature or cause of retardation. However, when mental retardation involves psychiatric disturbances or develops as a result of some physical disease or injury, use an additional code or codes to identify the associated condition.

5. MENTAL DISORDERS (290-319)

PSYCHOSES (290-299)

EXCLUDES *mental retardation (317-319)*

ORGANIC PSYCHOTIC CONDITIONS (290-294)

INCLUDES psychotic organic brain syndrome

EXCLUDES *nonpsychotic syndromes of organic etiology (310.0-310.9)*
psychoses classifiable to 295-298 and without impairment of orientation, comprehension, calculation, learning capacity, and judgment, but associated with physical disease, injury, or condition affecting the brain [eg., following childbirth] (295.0-298.8)

✓4th **290 Dementias**

Code first the associated neurological condition

EXCLUDES *dementia due to alcohol (291.0-291.2)*
dementia due to drugs (292.82)
dementia not classified as senile, presenile, or arteriosclerotic (294.10-294.11)
psychoses classifiable to 295-298 occurring in the senium without dementia or delirium (295.0-298.8)
senility with mental changes of nonpsychotic severity (310.1)
transient organic psychotic conditions (293.0-293.9)

290.0 Senile dementia, uncomplicated
Senile dementia:
NOS
simple type
EXCLUDES *mild memory disturbances, not amounting to dementia, associated with senile brain disease (310.1)*
senile dementia with:
delirium or confusion (290.3)
delusional [paranoid] features (290.20)
depressive features (290.21)

✓5th **290.1 Presenile dementia**
Brain syndrome with presenile brain disease
EXCLUDES *arteriosclerotic dementia (290.40-290.43)*
dementia associated with other cerebral conditions (294.10-294.11)

290.10 Presenile dementia, uncomplicated
Presenile dementia:
NOS
simple type

290.11 Presenile dementia with delirium
Presenile dementia with acute confusional state

290.12 Presenile dementia with delusional features
Presenile dementia, paranoid type

290.13 Presenile dementia with depressive features
Presenile dementia, depressed type

✓5th **290.2 Senile dementia with delusional or depressive features**
EXCLUDES *senile dementia:*
NOS (290.0)
with delirium and/or confusion (290.3)

290.20 Senile dementia with delusional features
Senile dementia, paranoid type
Senile psychosis NOS

290.21 Senile dementia with depressive features

290.3 Senile dementia with delirium
Senile dementia with acute confusional state
EXCLUDES *senile:*
dementia NOS (290.0)
psychosis NOS (290.20)

✓5th **290.4 Vascular dementia**
Multi-infarct dementia or psychosis
Use additional code to identify cerebral atherosclerosis (437.0)
EXCLUDES *suspected cases with no clear evidence of arteriosclerosis (290.9)*

290.40 Vascular dementia, uncomplicated
Arteriosclerotic dementia:
NOS
simple type

290.41 Vascular dementia with delirium
Arteriosclerotic dementia with acute confusional state

290.42 Vascular dementia with delusions
Arteriosclerotic dementia, paranoid type

290.43 Vascular dementia with depressed mood
Arteriosclerotic dementia, depressed type

290.8 Other specified senile psychotic conditions
Presbyophrenic psychosis

290.9 Unspecified senile psychotic condition

✓4th **291 Alcohol induced mental disorders**

EXCLUDES *alcoholism without psychosis (303.0-303.9)*

291.0 Alcohol withdrawal delirium
Alcoholic delirium
Delirium tremens
EXCLUDES *alcohol withdrawal (291.81)*

291.1 Alcohol induced persisting amnestic disorder
Alcoholic polyneuritic psychosis
Korsakoff's psychosis, alcoholic
Wernicke-Korsakoff syndrome (alcoholic)
DEF: Prominent and lasting reduced memory span, disordered time appreciation and confabulation, occurring in alcoholics, as sequel to acute alcoholic psychosis.

291.2 Alcohol induced persisting dementia
Alcoholic dementia NOS
Alcoholism associated with dementia NOS
Chronic alcoholic brain syndrome

291.3 Alcohol induced psychotic disorder with hallucinations
Alcoholic:
hallucinosis (acute)
psychosis with hallucinosis
EXCLUDES *alcohol withdrawal with delirium (291.0)*
schizophrenia (295.0-295.9) and paranoid states (297.0-297.9) taking the form of chronic hallucinosis with clear consciousness in an alcoholic
DEF: Psychosis lasting less than six months with slight or no clouding of consciousness in which auditory hallucinations predominate.

291.4 Idiosyncratic alcohol intoxication
Pathologic:
alcohol intoxication
drunkenness
EXCLUDES *acute alcohol intoxication (305.0)*
in alcoholism (303.0)
simple drunkenness (305.0)
DEF: Unique behavioral patterns, like belligerence, after intake of relatively small amounts of alcohol; behavior not due to excess consumption.

291.5 Alcohol induced psychotic disorder with delusions
Alcoholic:
paranoia
psychosis, paranoid type
EXCLUDES *nonalcoholic paranoid states (297.0-297.9)*
schizophrenia, paranoid type (295.3)

✓5th **291.8 Other specified alcohol induced mental disorders**

291.81 Alcohol withdrawal

Alcohol:
abstinence syndrome or symptoms
withdrawal syndrome or symptoms

EXCLUDES *alcohol withdrawal:*
delirium (291.0)
hallucinosis (291.3)
delirium tremens (291.0)

291.82 Alcohol induced sleep disorders

Alcohol induced circadian rhythm sleep disorders
Alcohol induced hypersomnia
Alcohol induced insomnia
Alcohol induced parasomnia

291.89 Other

Alcohol induced anxiety disorder
Alcohol induced mood disorder
Alcohol induced sexual dysfunction

291.9 Unspecified alcohol induced mental disorders

Alcoholic:
mania NOS
psychosis NOS
Alcoholism (chronic) with psychosis
Alcohol related disorder NOS

✓4th **292 Drug induced mental disorders**

INCLUDES organic brain syndrome associated with consumption of drugs

Use additional code for any associated drug dependence (304.0-304.9)

Use additional E code to identify drug

292.0 Drug withdrawal

Drug:
abstinence syndrome or symptoms
withdrawal syndrome or symptoms

✓5th **292.1 Drug induced psychotic disorders**

292.11 Drug induced psychotic disorder with delusions

Paranoid state induced by drugs

292.12 Drug induced psychotic disorder with hallucinations

Hallucinatory state induced by drugs

EXCLUDES *states following LSD or other hallucinogens, lasting only a few days or less ["bad trips"] (305.3)*

292.2 Pathological drug intoxication

Drug reaction:
NOS } resulting in brief psychotic states
idiosyncratic }
pathologic }

EXCLUDES *expected brief psychotic reactions to hallucinogens ["bad trips"] (305.3)*
physiological side-effects of drugs (e.g., dystonias)

✓5th **292.8 Other specified drug induced mental disorders**

292.81 Drug induced delirium

292.82 Drug induced persisting dementia

292.83 Drug induced persisting amnestic disorder

292.84 Drug induced mood disorder

Depressive state induced by drugs

292.85 Drug induced sleep disorders

Drug induced circadian rhythm sleep disorder
Drug induced hypersomnia
Drug induced insomnia
Drug induced parasomnia

292.89 Other

Drug induced anxiety disorder
Drug induced organic personality syndrome
Drug induced sexual dysfunction
Drug intoxication

292.9 Unspecified drug induced mental disorder

Drug related disorder NOS
Organic psychosis NOS due to or associated with drugs

✓4th **293 Transient mental disorders due to conditions classified elsewhere**

INCLUDES transient organic mental disorders not associated with alcohol or drugs

Code first the associated physical or neurological condition

EXCLUDES *confusional state or delirium superimposed on senile dementia (290.3)*
dementia due to:
alcohol (291.0-291.9)
arteriosclerosis (290.40-290.43)
drugs (292.82)
senility (290.0)

293.0 Delirium due to conditions classified elsewhere

Acute:
confusional state
infective psychosis
organic reaction
posttraumatic organic psychosis
psycho-organic syndrome
Acute psychosis associated with endocrine, metabolic, or cerebrovascular disorder
Epileptic:
confusional state
twilight state

293.1 Subacute delirium

Subacute:
confusional state
infective psychosis
organic reaction
posttraumatic organic psychosis
psycho-organic syndrome
psychosis associated with endocrine or metabolic disorder

✓5th **293.8 Other specified transient mental disorders due to conditions classified elsewhere**

293.81 Psychotic disorder with delusions in conditions classified elsewhere

Transient organic psychotic condition, paranoid type

293.82 Psychotic disorder with hallucinations in conditions classified elsewhere

Transient organic psychotic condition, hallucinatory type

293.83 Mood disorder in conditions classified elsewhere

Transient organic psychotic condition, depressive type

293.84 Anxiety disorder in conditions classified elsewhere

293.89 Other

Catatonic disorder in conditions classified elsewhere

293.9 Unspecified transient mental disorder in conditions classified elsewhere

Organic psychosis:
infective NOS
posttraumatic NOS
transient NOS
Psycho-organic syndrome

✓4th **294 Persistent mental disorders due to conditions classified elsewhere**

INCLUDES organic psychotic brain syndromes (chronic), not elsewhere classified

294.0 Amnestic disorder in conditions classified elsewhere

Korsakoff's psychosis or syndrome (nonalcoholic)

Code first underlying condition

EXCLUDES *alcoholic:*
amnestic syndrome (291.1)
Korsakoff's psychosis (291.1)

✓5th **294.1 Dementia in conditions classified elsewhere**
Dementia of the Alzheimer's type
Code first any underlying physical condition, as:
dementia in:
Alzheimer's disease (331.0)
cerebral lipidoses (330.1)
dementia with Lewy bodies (331.82)
dementia with Parkinsonism (331.82)
epilepsy (345.0-345.9)
frontal dementia (331.19)
frontotemporal dementia (331.19)
general paresis [syphilis] (094.1)
hepatolenticular degeneration (275.1)
Huntington's chorea (333.4)
Jakob-Creutzfeldt disease (046.19)
multiple sclerosis (340)
Pick's disease of the brain (331.11)
polyarteritis nodosa (446.0)
syphilis (094.1)
EXCLUDES *dementia:*
arteriosclerotic (290.40-290.43)
presenile (290.10-290.13)
senile (290.0)
epileptic psychosis NOS (294.8)

294.10 Dementia in conditions classified elsewhere without behavioral disturbance
Dementia in conditions classified elsewhere NOS

294.11 Dementia in conditions classified elsewhere with behavioral disturbance
Aggressive behavior
Combative behavior
Violent behavior
Wandering off

294.8 Other persistent mental disorders due to conditions classified elsewhere
Amnestic disorder NOS
Dementia NOS
Epileptic psychosis NOS
Mixed paranoid and affective organic psychotic states
Use additional code for associated epilepsy (345.0-345.9)
EXCLUDES *mild memory disturbances, not amounting to dementia (310.1)*

294.9 Unspecified persistent mental disorders due to conditions classified elsewhere
Cognitive disorder NOS
Organic psychosis (chronic)

OTHER PSYCHOSES (295-299)

Use additional code to identify any associated physical disease, injury, or condition affecting the brain with psychoses classifiable to 295-298

✓4th **295 Schizophrenic disorders**
INCLUDES schizophrenia of the types described in 295.0-295.9 occurring in children
EXCLUDES *childhood type schizophrenia (299.9)*
infantile autism (299.0)

The following fifth-digit subclassification is for use with category 295:
0 unspecified
1 subchronic
2 chronic
3 subchronic with acute exacerbation
4 chronic with acute exacerbation
5 in remission

DEF: Group of disorders with disturbances in thought (delusions, hallucinations), mood (blunted, flattened, inappropriate affect), sense of self, relationship to world; also bizarre, purposeless behavior, repetitious activity, or inactivity.

✓5th **295.0 Simple type**
[0-5]
Schizophrenia simplex
EXCLUDES *latent schizophrenia (295.5)*

✓5th **295.1 Disorganized type**
[0-5]
Hebephrenia
Hebephrenic type schizophrenia
DEF: Inappropriate behavior; results in extreme incoherence and disorganization of time, place and sense of social appropriateness; withdrawal from routine social interaction may occur.

✓5th **295.2 Catatonic type**
[0-5]
Catatonic (schizophrenia):
agitation
excitation
excited type
stupor
withdrawn type
Schizophrenic:
catalepsy
catatonia
flexibilitas cerea
DEF: Extreme changes in motor activity; one extreme is decreased response or reaction to the environment and the other is spontaneous activity.

✓5th **295.3 Paranoid type**
[0-5]
Paraphrenic schizophrenia
EXCLUDES *involutional paranoid state (297.2)*
paranoia (297.1)
paraphrenia (297.2)
DEF: Preoccupied with delusional suspicions and auditory hallucinations related to single theme; usually hostile, grandiose, overly religious, occasionally hypochondriacal.

✓5th **295.4 Schizophreniform disorder**
[0-5]
Oneirophrenia
Schizophreniform:
attack
psychosis, confusional type
EXCLUDES *acute forms of schizophrenia of:*
catatonic type (295.2)
hebephrenic type (295.1)
paranoid type (295.3)
simple type (295.0)
undifferentiated type (295.8)

✓5th **295.5 Latent schizophrenia**
[0-5]
Latent schizophrenic reaction
Schizophrenia:
borderline
incipient
prepsychotic
prodromal
pseudoneurotic
pseudopsychopathic
EXCLUDES *schizoid personality (301.20-301.22)*

✓5th **295.6 Residual type**
[0-5]
Chronic undifferentiated schizophrenia
Restzustand (schizophrenic)
Schizophrenic residual state

✓5th **295.7 Schizoaffective disorder**
[0-5]
Cyclic schizophrenia
Mixed schizophrenic and affective psychosis
Schizo-affective psychosis
Schizophreniform psychosis, affective type

✓5th **295.8 Other specified types of schizophrenia**
[0-5]
Acute (undifferentiated) schizophrenia
Atypical schizophrenia
Cenesthopathic schizophrenia
EXCLUDES *infantile autism (299.0)*

✓5th **295.9 Unspecified schizophrenia**
[0-5]
Schizophrenia:
NOS
mixed NOS
undifferentiated NOS
undifferentiated type
Schizophrenic reaction NOS
Schizophreniform psychosis NOS

✓4th 296 Episodic mood disorders

INCLUDES episodic affective disorders

EXCLUDES *neurotic depression (300.4)*
reactive depressive psychosis (298.0)
reactive excitation (298.1)

The following fifth-digit subclassification is for use with categories 296.0-296.6:
0 unspecified
1 mild
2 moderate
3 severe, without mention of psychotic behavior
4 severe, specified as with psychotic behavior
5 in partial or unspecified remission
6 in full remission

✓5th 296.0 Bipolar I disorder, single manic episode
[0-6]
Hypomania (mild) NOS
Hypomanic psychosis
Mania (momopolar) NOS
Manic-depressive psychosis or reaction:
hypomanic
manic
} single episode or unspecified

EXCLUDES *circular type, if there was a previous attack of depression (296.4)*

DEF: Mood disorder identified by hyperactivity; may show extreme agitation or exaggerated excitability; speech and thought processes may be accelerated.

✓5th 296.1 Manic disorder, recurrent episode
[0-6]
Any condition classifiable to 296.0, stated to be recurrent

EXCLUDES *circular type, if there was a previous attack of depression (296.4)*

✓5th 296.2 Major depressive disorder, single episode
[0-6]
Depressive psychosis
Endogenous depression
Involutional melancholia
Manic-depressive psychosis or reaction, depressed type
Monopolar depression
Psychotic depression
} single episode or unspecified

EXCLUDES *circular type, if previous attack was of manic type (296.5)*
depression NOS (311)
reactive depression (neurotic) (300.4)
psychotic (298.0)

DEF: Mood disorder that produces depression; may exhibit as sadness, low self-esteem, or guilt feelings; other manifestations may be withdrawal from friends and family; interrupted sleep.

✓5th 296.3 Major depressive disorder, recurrent episode
[0-6]
Any condition classifiable to 296.2, stated to be recurrent

EXCLUDES *circular type, if previous attack was of manic type (296.5)*
depression NOS (311)
reactive depression (neurotic) (300.4)
psychotic (298.0)

✓5th 296.4 Bipolar I disorder, most recent episode (or current) manic
[0-6]
Bipolar disorder, now manic
Manic-depressive psychosis, circular type but currently manic

EXCLUDES *brief compensatory or rebound mood swings (296.99)*

✓5th 296.5 Bipolar I disorder, most recent episode (or current) depressed
[0-6]
Bipolar disorder, now depressed
Manic-depressive psychosis, circular type but currently depressed

EXCLUDES *brief compensatory or rebound mood swings (296.99)*

✓5th 296.6 Bipolar I disorder, most recent episode (or current) mixed
[0-6]
Manic-depressive psychosis, circular type, mixed

296.7 Bipolar I disorder, most recent episode (or current) unspecified
Atypical bipolar affective disorder NOS
Manic-depressive psychosis, circular type, current condition not specified as either manic or depressive

DEF: Manic-depressive disorder referred to as bipolar because of the mood range from manic to depressive.

✓5th 296.8 Other and unspecified bipolar disorders

296.80 Bipolar disorder, unspecified
Bipolar disorder NOS
Manic-depressive:
reaction NOS
syndrome NOS

296.81 Atypical manic disorder

296.82 Atypical depressive disorder

296.89 Other
Bipolar II disorder
Manic-depressive psychosis, mixed type

✓5th 296.9 Other and unspecified episodic mood disorder

EXCLUDES *psychogenic affective psychoses (298.0-298.8)*

296.90 Unspecified episodic mood disorder
Affective psychosis NOS
Melancholia NOS
Mood disorder NOS

296.99 Other specified episodic mood disorder
Mood swings:
brief compensatory
rebound

✓4th 297 Delusional disorders

INCLUDES paranoid disorders

EXCLUDES *acute paranoid reaction (298.3)*
alcoholic jealousy or paranoid state (291.5)
paranoid schizophrenia (295.3)

297.0 Paranoid state, simple

297.1 Delusional disorder
Chronic paranoid psychosis
Sander's disease
Systematized delusions

EXCLUDES *paranoid personality disorder (301.0)*

297.2 Paraphrenia
Involutional paranoid state
Late paraphrenia
Paraphrenia (involutional)

DEF: Paranoid schizophrenic disorder that persists over a prolonged period but does not distort personality despite persistent delusions.

297.3 Shared psychotic disorder
Folie à deux
Induced psychosis or paranoid disorder

DEF: Mental disorder two people share; first person with the delusional disorder convinces second person because of a close relationship and shared experiences to accept the delusions.

297.8 Other specified paranoid states
Paranoia querulans
Sensitiver Beziehungswahn

EXCLUDES *acute paranoid reaction or state (298.3)*
senile paranoid state (290.20)

297.9 Unspecified paranoid state
Paranoid:
disorder NOS
psychosis NOS
reaction NOS
state NOS

✓4th 298 Other nonorganic psychoses

INCLUDES psychotic conditions due to or provoked by:
emotional stress
environmental factors as major part of etiology

298.0 Depressive type psychosis
Psychogenic depressive psychosis
Psychotic reactive depression
Reactive depressive psychosis
EXCLUDES *manic-depressive psychosis, depressed type (296.2-296.3)*
neurotic depression (300.4)
reactive depression NOS (300.4)

298.1 Excitative type psychosis
Acute hysterical psychosis
Psychogenic excitation
Reactive excitation
EXCLUDES *manic-depressive psychosis, manic type (296.0-296.1)*
DEF: Affective disorder similar to manic-depressive psychosis, in the manic phase, seemingly brought on by stress.

298.2 Reactive confusion
Psychogenic confusion
Psychogenic twilight state
EXCLUDES *acute confusional state (293.0)*
DEF: Confusion, disorientation, cloudiness in consciousness; brought on by severe emotional upheaval.

298.3 Acute paranoid reaction
Acute psychogenic paranoid psychosis
Bouffée délirante
EXCLUDES *paranoid states (297.0-297.9)*

298.4 Psychogenic paranoid psychosis
Protracted reactive paranoid psychosis

298.8 Other and unspecified reactive psychosis
Brief psychotic disorder
Brief reactive psychosis NOS
Hysterical psychosis
Psychogenic psychosis NOS
Psychogenic stupor
EXCLUDES *acute hysterical psychosis (298.1)*

298.9 Unspecified psychosis
Atypical psychosis
Psychosis NOS
Psychotic disorder NOS

✓4th 299 Pervasive developmental disorders

EXCLUDES *adult type psychoses occurring in childhood, as:*
affective disorders (296.0-296.9)
manic-depressive disorders (296.0-296.9)
schizophrenia (295.0-295.9)

The following fifth-digit subclassification is for use with category 299:
0 current or active state
1 residual state

✓5th 299.0 Autistic disorder
[0-1]
Childhood autism
Infantile psychosis
Kanner's syndrome
EXCLUDES *disintegrative psychosis (299.1)*
Heller's syndrome (299.1)
schizophrenic syndrome of childhood (299.9)
DEF: Severe mental disorder of children, results in impaired social behavior; abnormal development of communicative skills, appears to be unaware of the need for emotional support and offers little emotional response to family members.

✓5th 299.1 Childhood disintegrative disorder
[0-1]
Heller's syndrome
Use additional code to identify any associated neurological disorder
EXCLUDES *infantile autism (299.0)*
schizophrenic syndrome of childhood (299.9)
DEF: Mental disease of children identified by impaired development of reciprocal social skills, verbal and nonverbal communication skills, imaginative play.

✓5th 299.8 Other specified pervasive developmental disorders
[0-1]
Asperger's disorder
Atypical childhood psychosis
Borderline psychosis of childhood
EXCLUDES *simple stereotypes without psychotic disturbance (307.3)*

✓5th 299.9 Unspecified pervasive developmental disorder
[0-1]
Child psychosis NOS
Pervasive developmental disorder NOS
Schizophrenia, childhood type NOS
Schizophrenic syndrome of childhood NOS
EXCLUDES *schizophrenia of adult type occurring in childhood (295.0-295.9)*

NEUROTIC DISORDERS, PERSONALITY DISORDERS, AND OTHER NONPSYCHOTIC MENTAL DISORDERS (300-316)

✓4th 300 Anxiety, dissociative and somatoform disorders

✓5th 300.0 Anxiety states
EXCLUDES *anxiety in:*
acute stress reaction (308.0)
transient adjustment reaction (309.24)
neurasthenia (300.5)
psychophysiological disorders (306.0-306.9)
separation anxiety (309.21)
DEF: Mental disorder characterized by anxiety and avoidance be-havior not particularly related to any specific situation or stimulus; symptoms include emotional instability, apprehension, fatigue.

300.00 Anxiety state, unspecified
Anxiety:
neurosis
reaction
state (neurotic)
Atypical anxiety disorder

300.01 Panic disorder without agoraphobia
Panic:
attack
state
EXCLUDES *panic disorder with agoraphobia (300.21)*
DEF: Neurotic disorder characterized by recurrent panic or anxiety, apprehension, fear or terror; symptoms include shortness of breath, palpitations, dizziness, faintness or shakiness; fear of dying may persist or fear of other morbid consequences.

300.02 Generalized anxiety disorder

300.09 Other

✓5th 300.1 Dissociative, conversion and factitious disorders
EXCLUDES *adjustment reaction (309.0-309.9)*
anorexia nervosa (307.1)
gross stress reaction (308.0-308.9)
hysterical personality (301.50-301.59)
psychophysiologic disorders (306.0-306.9)

300.10 Hysteria, unspecified

300.11 Conversion disorder
Astasia-abasia, hysterical
Conversion hysteria or reaction
Hysterical:
blindness
deafness
paralysis
DEF: Mental disorder that impairs physical functions with no physiological basis; sensory motor symptoms include seizures, paralysis, temporary blindness; increase in stress or avoidance of unpleasant responsibilities may precipitate.

300.12 Dissociative amnesia
Hysterical amnesia

300.13 Dissociative fugue
Hysterical fugue
DEF: Dissociative hysteria; identified by loss of memory, flight from familiar surroundings; conscious activity is not associated with perception of surroundings, no later memory of episode.

300.14 Dissociative identity disorder

300.15 Dissociative disorder or reaction, unspecified
DEF: Hysterical neurotic episode; sudden but temporary changes in perceived identity, memory, consciousness, segregated memory patterns exist separate from dominant personality.

300.16 Factitious disorder with predominantly psychological signs and symptoms
Compensation neurosis
Ganser's syndrome, hysterical
DEF: A disorder characterized by the purposeful assumption of mental illness symptoms; the symptoms are not real, possibly representing what the patient imagines mental illness to be like, and are acted out more often when another person is present.

300.19 Other and unspecified factitious illness
Factitious disorder (with combined psychological and physical signs and symptoms) (with predominantly physical signs and symptoms) NOS
EXCLUDES *multiple operations or hospital addiction syndrome (301.51)*

✓5th **300.2 Phobic disorders**
EXCLUDES *anxiety state not associated with a specific situation or object (300.00-300.09)*
obsessional phobias (300.3)

300.20 Phobia, unspecified
Anxiety-hysteria NOS
Phobia NOS

300.21 Agoraphobia with panic disorder
Fear of:
open spaces, streets, travel } with panic attacks
Panic disorder with agoraphobia
EXCLUDES *agoraphobia without panic disorder (300.22)*
panic disorder without agoraphobia (300.01)

300.22 Agoraphobia without mention of panic attacks
Any condition classifiable to 300.21 without mention of panic attacks

300.23 Social phobia
Fear of:
eating in public
public speaking
washing in public

300.29 Other isolated or specific phobias
Acrophobia
Animal phobias
Claustrophobia
Fear of crowds

300.3 Obsessive-compulsive disorders
Anancastic neurosis
Compulsive neurosis
Obsessional phobia [any]
EXCLUDES *obsessive-compulsive symptoms occurring in:*
endogenous depression (296.2-296.3)
organic states (eg., encephalitis)
schizophrenia (295.0-295.9)

300.4 Dysthymic disorder
Anxiety depression
Depression with anxiety
Depressive reaction
Neurotic depressive state
Reactive depression
EXCLUDES *adjustment reaction with depressive symptoms (309.0-309.1)*
depression NOS (311)
manic-depressive psychosis, depressed type (296.2-296.3)
reactive depressive psychosis (298.0)
DEF: Depression without psychosis; less severe depression related to personal change or unexpected circumstances; also referred to as "reactional depression."

300.5 Neurasthenia
Fatigue neurosis
Nervous debility
Psychogenic:
asthenia
general fatigue
Use additional code to identify any associated physical disorder
EXCLUDES *anxiety state (300.00-300.09)*
neurotic depression (300.4)
psychophysiological disorders (306.0-306.9)
specific nonpsychotic mental disorders following organic brain damage (310.0-310.9)
DEF: Physical and mental symptoms caused primarily by what is known as mental exhaustion; symptoms include chronic weakness, fatigue.

300.6 Depersonalization disorder
Derealization (neurotic)
Neurotic state with depersonalization episode
EXCLUDES *depersonalization associated with:*
anxiety (300.00-300.09)
depression (300.4)
manic-depressive disorder or psychosis (296.0-296.9)
schizophrenia (295.0-295.9)
DEF: Dissociative disorder characterized by feelings of strangeness about self or body image; symptoms include dizziness, anxiety, fear of insanity, loss of reality of surroundings.

300.7 Hypochondriasis
Body dysmorphic disorder
EXCLUDES *hypochondriasis in:*
hysteria (300.10-300.19)
manic-depressive psychosis, depressed type (296.2-296.3)
neurasthenia (300.5)
obsessional disorder (300.3)
schizophrenia (295.0-295.9)

✓5th **300.8 Somatoform disorders**

300.81 Somatization disorder
Briquet's disorder
Severe somatoform disorder

300.82 Undifferentiated somatoform disorder
Atypical somatoform disorder
Somatoform disorder NOS
DEF: Disorders in which patients have symptoms that suggest an organic disease but no evidence of physical disorder after repeated testing.

300.89 Other somatoform disorders
Occupational neurosis, including writers' cramp
Psychasthenia
Psychasthenic neurosis

300.9 Unspecified nonpsychotic mental disorder
Psychoneurosis NOS

✓4th **301 Personality disorders**

INCLUDES character neurosis

Use additional code to identify any associated neurosis or psychosis, or physical condition

EXCLUDES *nonpsychotic personality disorder associated with organic brain syndromes (310.0-310.9)*

301.0 Paranoid personality disorder

Fanatic personality
Paranoid personality (disorder)
Paranoid traits

EXCLUDES *acute paranoid reaction (298.3)*
alcoholic paranoia (291.5)
paranoid schizophrenia (295.3)
paranoid states (297.0-297.9)

✓5th **301.1 Affective personality disorder**

EXCLUDES *affective psychotic disorders (296.0-296.9)*
neurasthenia (300.5)
neurotic depression (300.4)

301.10 Affective personality disorder, unspecified

301.11 Chronic hypomanic personality disorder

Chronic hypomanic disorder
Hypomanic personality

301.12 Chronic depressive personality disorder

Chronic depressive disorder
Depressive character or personality

301.13 Cyclothymic disorder

Cycloid personality
Cyclothymia
Cyclothymic personality

✓5th **301.2 Schizoid personality disorder**

EXCLUDES *schizophrenia (295.0-295.9)*

301.20 Schizoid personality disorder, unspecified

301.21 Introverted personality

301.22 Schizotypal personality disorder

301.3 Explosive personality disorder

Aggressive:
personality
reaction
Aggressiveness
Emotional instability (excessive)
Pathological emotionality
Quarrelsomeness

EXCLUDES *dyssocial personality (301.7)*
hysterical neurosis (300.10-300.19)

301.4 Obsessive-compulsive personality disorder

Anancastic personality
Obsessional personality

EXCLUDES *obsessive-compulsive disorder (300.3)*
phobic state (300.20-300.29)

✓5th **301.5 Histrionic personality disorder**

EXCLUDES *hysterical neurosis (300.10-300.19)*

DEF: Extreme emotional behavior, often theatrical; often concerned about own appeal; may demand attention, exhibit seductive behavior.

301.50 Histrionic personality disorder, unspecified

Hysterical personality NOS

301.51 Chronic factitious illness with physical symptoms

Hospital addiction syndrome
Multiple operations syndrome
Munchausen syndrome

301.59 Other histrionic personality disorder

Personality:
emotionally unstable
labile
psychoinfantile

301.6 Dependent personality disorder

Asthenic personality
Inadequate personality
Passive personality

EXCLUDES *neurasthenia (300.5)*
passive-aggressive personality (301.84)

DEF: Overwhelming feeling of helplessness; fears of abandonment may persist; difficulty in making personal decisions without confirmation by others; low self-esteem due to irrational sensitivity to criticism.

301.7 Antisocial personality disorder

Amoral personality
Asocial personality
Dyssocial personality
Personality disorder with predominantly sociopathic or asocial manifestation

EXCLUDES *disturbance of conduct without specifiable personality disorder (312.0-312.9)*
explosive personality (301.3)

DEF: Continuous antisocial behavior that violates rights of others; social traits include extreme aggression, total disregard for traditional social rules.

✓5th **301.8 Other personality disorders**

301.81 Narcissistic personality disorder

DEF: Grandiose fantasy or behavior, lack of social empathy, hypersensitive to the lack of others' judgment, exploits others; also sense of entitlement to have expectations met, need for continual admiration.

301.82 Avoidant personality disorder

DEF: Personality disorder marked by feelings of social inferiority; sensitivity to criticism, emotionally restrained due to fear of rejection.

301.83 Borderline personality disorder

DEF: Personality disorder characterized by unstable moods, self-image, and interpersonal relationships; uncontrolled anger, impulsive and self-destructive acts, fears of abandonment, feelings of emptiness and boredom, recurrent suicide threats or self-mutilation.

301.84 Passive-aggressive personality

DEF: Pattern of procrastination and refusal to meet standards; introduce own obstacles to success and exploit failure.

301.89 Other

Personality:
eccentric
"haltlose" type
immature
masochistic
psychoneurotic

EXCLUDES *psychoinfantile personality (301.59)*

301.9 Unspecified personality disorder

Pathological personality NOS
Personality disorder NOS
Psychopathic:
constitutional state
personality (disorder)

✓4th **302 Sexual and gender identity disorders**

EXCLUDES *sexual disorder manifest in:*
organic brain syndrome (290.0-294.9, 310.0-310.9)
psychosis (295.0-298.9)

302.0 Ego-dystonic sexual orientation

Ego-dystonic lesbianism
Sexual orientation conflict disorder

EXCLUDES *homosexual pedophilia (302.2)*

302.1 Zoophilia

Bestiality

DEF: A sociodeviant disorder marked by engaging in sexual intercourse with animals.

302.2 Pedophilia

DEF: A sociodeviant condition of adults characterized by sexual activity with children.

302.3 Transvestic fetishism

EXCLUDES *trans-sexualism (302.5)*

DEF: The desire to dress in clothing of opposite sex.

302.4 Exhibitionism

DEF: Sexual deviant behavior; exposure of genitals to strangers; behavior prompted by intense sexual urges and fantasies.

✓5th **302.5 Trans-sexualism**

Sex reassignment surgery status

EXCLUDES *transvestism (302.3)*

DEF: Gender identity disturbance; overwhelming desire to change anatomic sex, due to belief that individual is a member of the opposite sex.

302.50 With unspecified sexual history

302.51 With asexual history

302.52 With homosexual history

302.53 With heterosexual history

302.6 Gender identity disorder in children

Feminism in boys
Gender identity disorder NOS

EXCLUDES *gender identity disorder in adult (302.85)*
trans-sexualism (302.50-302.53)
transvestism (302.3)

✓5th **302.7 Psychosexual dysfunction**

EXCLUDES *impotence of organic origin (607.84)*
normal transient symptoms from ruptured hymen
transient or occasional failures of erection due to fatigue, anxiety, alcohol, or drugs

302.70 Psychosexual dysfunction, unspecified

Sexual dysfunction NOS

302.71 Hypoactive sexual desire disorder

EXCLUDES *decreased sexual desire NOS (799.81)*

302.72 With inhibited sexual excitement

Female sexual arousal disorder
Frigidity
Impotence
Male erectile disorder

302.73 Female orgasmic disorder

302.74 Male orgasmic disorder

302.75 Premature ejaculation

302.76 Dyspareunia, psychogenic

DEF: Difficult or painful sex due to psychosomatic state.

302.79 With other specified psychosexual dysfunctions

Sexual aversion disorder

✓5th **302.8 Other specified psychosexual disorders**

302.81 Fetishism

DEF: Psychosexual disorder noted for intense sexual urges and arousal precipitated by fantasies; use of inanimate objects, such as clothing, to stimulate sexual arousal, orgasm.

302.82 Voyeurism

DEF: Psychosexual disorder characterized by uncontrollable impulse to observe others, without their knowledge, who are nude or engaged in sexual activity.

302.83 Sexual masochism

DEF: Psychosexual disorder noted for need to achieve sexual gratification through humiliating or hurtful acts inflicted on self.

302.84 Sexual sadism

DEF: Psychosexual disorder noted for need to achieve sexual gratification through humiliating or hurtful acts inflicted on someone else.

302.85 Gender identity disorder in adolescents or adults

Use additional code to identify sex reassignment surgery status (302.5)

EXCLUDES *gender identity disorder NOS (302.6)*
gender identity disorder in children (302.6)

302.89 Other

Frotteurism
Nymphomania
Satyriasis

302.9 Unspecified psychosexual disorder

Paraphilia NOS
Pathologic sexuality NOS
Sexual deviation NOS
Sexual disorder NOS

✓4th **303 Alcohol dependence syndrome**

Use additional code to identify any associated condition, as:
alcoholic psychoses (291.0-291.9)
drug dependence (304.0-304.9)
physical complications of alcohol, such as:
cerebral degeneration (331.7)
cirrhosis of liver (571.2)
epilepsy (345.0-345.9)
gastritis (535.3)
hepatitis (571.1)
liver damage NOS (571.3)

EXCLUDES *drunkenness NOS (305.0)*

The following fifth-digit subclassification is for use with category 303:
0 unspecified
1 continuous
2 episodic
3 in remission

✓5th **303.0 Acute alcoholic intoxication**

[0-3] Acute drunkenness in alcoholism

✓5th **303.9 Other and unspecified alcohol dependence**

[0-3] Chronic alcoholism
Dipsomania

✓4th **304 Drug dependence**

EXCLUDES *nondependent abuse of drugs (305.1-305.9)*

The following fifth-digit subclassification is for use with category 304:
0 unspecified
1 continuous
2 episodic
3 in remission

✓5th **304.0 Opioid type dependence**

[0-3] Heroin
Meperidine
Methadone
Morphine
Opium
Opium alkaloids and their derivatives
Synthetics with morphine-like effects

✓5th **304.1 Sedative, hypnotic or anxiolytic dependence**

[0-3] Barbiturates
Nonbarbiturate sedatives and tranquilizers with a similar effect:
chlordiazepoxide
diazepam
glutethimide
meprobamate
methaqualone

✓5th **304.2 Cocaine dependence**

[0-3] Coca leaves and derivatives

✓5th **304.3 Cannabis dependence**

[0-3] Hashish
Hemp
Marihuana

✓5th **304.4 Amphetamine and other psychostimulant dependence**

[0-3] Methylphenidate
Phenmetrazine

✓5th **304.5 Hallucinogen dependence**

[0-3] Dimethyltryptamine [DMT]
Lysergic acid diethylamide [LSD] and derivatives
Mescaline
Psilocybin

✓5th **304.6 Other specified drug dependence**
[0-3]
Absinthe addiction
Glue sniffing
Inhalant dependence
Phencyclidine dependence
EXCLUDES *tobacco dependence (305.1)*

✓5th **304.7 Combinations of opioid type drug with any other**
[0-3]

✓5th **304.8 Combinations of drug dependence excluding opioid type drug**
[0-3]

✓5th **304.9 Unspecified drug dependence**
[0-3]
Drug addiction NOS
Drug dependence NOS

✓4th **305 Nondependent abuse of drugs**

Note: Includes cases where a person, for whom no other diagnosis is possible, has come under medical care because of the maladaptive effect of a drug on which he is not dependent and that he has taken on his own initiative to the detriment of his health or social functioning.

EXCLUDES *alcohol dependence syndrome (303.0-303.9)*
drug dependence (304.0-304.9)
drug withdrawal syndrome (292.0)
poisoning by drugs or medicinal substances (960.0-979.9)

The following fifth-digit subclassification is for use with codes 305.0, 305.2-305.9:
0 unspecified
1 continuous
2 episodic
3 in remission

✓5th **305.0 Alcohol abuse**
[0-3]
Drunkenness NOS
Excessive drinking of alcohol NOS
"Hangover" (alcohol)
Inebriety NOS
EXCLUDES *acute alcohol intoxication in alcoholism (303.0)*
alcoholic psychoses (291.0-291.9)

305.1 Tobacco use disorder
Tobacco dependence
EXCLUDES *history of tobacco use (V15.82)*
smoking complicating pregnancy (649.0)
tobacco use disorder complicating pregnancy (649.0)

✓5th **305.2 Cannabis abuse**
[0-3]

✓5th **305.3 Hallucinogen abuse**
[0-3]
Acute intoxication from hallucinogens ["bad trips"]
LSD reaction

✓5th **305.4 Sedative, hypnotic or anxiolytic abuse**
[0-3]

✓5th **305.5 Opioid abuse**
[0-3]

✓5th **305.6 Cocaine abuse**
[0-3]

✓5th **305.7 Amphetamine or related acting sympathomimetic abuse**
[0-3]

✓5th **305.8 Antidepressant type abuse**
[0-3]

✓5th **305.9 Other, mixed, or unspecified drug abuse**
[0-3]
Caffeine intoxication
Inhalant abuse
"Laxative habit"
Misuse of drugs NOS
Nonprescribed use of drugs or patent medicinals
Phencyclidine abuse

✓4th **306 Physiological malfunction arising from mental factors**

INCLUDES psychogenic:
physical symptoms } not involving tissue damage
physiological manifestations } not involving tissue damage

EXCLUDES *hysteria (300.11-300.19)*
physical symptoms secondary to a psychiatric disorder classified elsewhere
psychic factors associated with physical conditions involving tissue damage classified elsewhere (316)
specific nonpsychotic mental disorders following organic brain damage (310.0-310.9)

DEF: Functional disturbances or interruptions due to mental or psychological causes; no tissue damage sustained in these conditions.

306.0 Musculoskeletal
Psychogenic paralysis
Psychogenic torticollis
EXCLUDES *Gilles de la Tourette's syndrome (307.23)*
paralysis as hysterical or conversion reaction (300.11)
tics (307.20-307.22)

306.1 Respiratory
Psychogenic:
air hunger
cough
hiccough
hyperventilation
yawning
EXCLUDES *psychogenic asthma (316 and 493.9)*

306.2 Cardiovascular
Cardiac neurosis
Cardiovascular neurosis
Neurocirculatory asthenia
Psychogenic cardiovascular disorder
EXCLUDES *psychogenic paroxysmal tachycardia (316 and 427.2)*

DEF: Neurocirculatory asthenia: functional nervous and circulatory irregularities with palpitations, dyspnea, fatigue, rapid pulse, precordial pain, fear of effort, discomfort during exercise, anxiety; also called DaCosta's syndrome, Effort syndrome, Irritable or Soldier's Heart.

306.3 Skin
Psychogenic pruritus
EXCLUDES *psychogenic:*
alopecia (316 and 704.00)
dermatitis (316 and 692.9)
eczema (316 and 691.8 or 692.9)
urticaria (316 and 708.0-708.9)

306.4 Gastrointestinal
Aerophagy
Cyclical vomiting, psychogenic
Diarrhea, psychogenic
Nervous gastritis
Psychogenic dyspepsia
EXCLUDES *cyclical vomiting NOS (536.2)*
associated with migraine (346.2)
globus hystericus (300.11)
mucous colitis (316 and 564.9)
psychogenic:
cardiospasm (316 and 530.0)
duodenal ulcer (316 and 532.0-532.9)
gastric ulcer (316 and 531.0-531.9)
peptic ulcer NOS (316 and 533.0-533.9)
vomiting NOS (307.54)

DEF: Aerophagy: excess swallowing of air, usually unconscious; related to anxiety; results in distended abdomen or belching, often interpreted by the patient as a physical disorder.

✓5th **306.5 Genitourinary**
EXCLUDES *enuresis, psychogenic (307.6)*
frigidity (302.72)
impotence (302.72)
psychogenic dyspareunia (302.76)

306.50 Psychogenic genitourinary malfunction, unspecified

306.51 Psychogenic vaginismus
Functional vaginismus
DEF: Psychogenic response resulting in painful contractions of vaginal canal muscles; can be severe enough to prevent sexual intercourse.

306.52 Psychogenic dysmenorrhea

306.53 Psychogenic dysuria

306.59 Other

306.6 Endocrine

306.7 Organs of special sense
EXCLUDES *hysterical blindness or deafness (300.11)*
psychophysical visual disturbances (368.16)

306.8 Other specified psychophysiological malfunction
Bruxism
Teeth grinding

306.9 Unspecified psychophysiological malfunction
Psychophysiologic disorder NOS
Psychosomatic disorder NOS

✓4th **307 Special symptoms or syndromes, not elsewhere classified**
Note: This category is intended for use if the psychopathology is manifested by a single specific symptom or group of symptoms which is not part of an organic illness or other mental disorder classifiable elsewhere.
EXCLUDES *those due to mental disorders classified elsewhere*
those of organic origin

307.0 Stuttering
EXCLUDES *dysphasia (784.5)*
lisping or lalling (307.9)
retarded development of speech (315.31-315.39)

307.1 Anorexia nervosa
EXCLUDES *eating disturbance NOS (307.50)*
feeding problem (783.3)
of nonorganic origin (307.59)
loss of appetite (783.0)
of nonorganic origin (307.59)

✓5th **307.2 Tics**
EXCLUDES *nail-biting or thumb-sucking (307.9)*
stereotypes occurring in isolation (307.3)
tics of organic origin (333.3)
DEF: Involuntary muscle response usually confined to the face, shoulders.

307.20 Tic disorder, unspecified
Tic disorder NOS

307.21 Transient tic disorder

307.22 Chronic motor or vocal tic disorder

307.23 Tourette's disorder
Motor-verbal tic disorder
DEF: Syndrome of facial and vocal tics in childhood; progresses to spontaneous or involuntary jerking, obscene utterances, other uncontrollable actions considered inappropriate.

307.3 Stereotypic movement disorder
Body-rocking
Head banging
Spasmus nutans
Stereotypes NOS
EXCLUDES *tics (307.20-307.23)*
of organic origin (333.3)

✓5th **307.4 Specific disorders of sleep of nonorganic origin**
EXCLUDES *narcolepsy (347.00-347.11)*
organic hypersomnia (327.10-327.19)
organic insomnia (327.00-327.09)
those of unspecified cause (780.50-780.59)

307.40 Nonorganic sleep disorder, unspecified

307.41 Transient disorder of initiating or maintaining sleep
Adjustment insomnia
Hyposomnia / Insomnia / Sleeplessness } associated with intermittent emotional reactions or conflicts

307.42 Persistent disorder of initiating or maintaining sleep
Hyposomnia, insomnia, or sleeplessness associated with:
anxiety
conditioned arousal
depression (major) (minor)
psychosis
Idiopathic insomnia
Paradoxical insomnia
Primary insomnia
Psychophysiological insomnia

307.43 Transient disorder of initiating or maintaining wakefulness
Hypersomnia associated with acute or intermittent emotional reactions or conflicts

307.44 Persistent disorder of initiating or maintaining wakefulness
Hypersomnia associated with depression (major) (minor)
Insufficient sleep syndrome
Primary hypersomnia
EXCLUDES *sleep deprivation (V69.4)*

307.45 Circadian rhythm sleep disorder of nonorganic origin

307.46 Sleep arousal disorder
Night terror disorder
Night terrors
Sleep terror disorder
Sleepwalking
Somnambulism
DEF: Sleepwalking marked by extreme terror, panic, screaming, confusion; no recall of event upon arousal; term may refer to simply the act of sleepwalking.

307.47 Other dysfunctions of sleep stages or arousal from sleep
Nightmare disorder
Nightmares:
NOS
REM-sleep type
Sleep drunkenness

307.48 Repetitive intrusions of sleep
Repetitive intrusion of sleep with:
atypical polysomnographic features
environmental disturbances
repeated REM-sleep interruptions

307.49 Other
"Short-sleeper"
Subjective insomnia complaint

✓5th **307.5 Other and unspecified disorders of eating**
EXCLUDES *anorexia:*
nervosa (307.1)
of unspecified cause (783.0)
overeating, of unspecified cause (783.6)
vomiting:
NOS (787.03)
cyclical (536.2)
associated with migraine (346.2)
psychogenic (306.4)

307.50 Eating disorder, unspecified
Eating disorder NOS

307.51 Bulimia nervosa
Overeating of nonorganic origin
DEF: Mental disorder commonly characterized by binge eating followed by self-induced vomiting; perceptions of being fat; and fear the inability to stop eating voluntarily.

307.52 Pica
Perverted appetite of nonorganic origin
DEF: Compulsive eating disorder characterized by craving for substances, other than food; such as paint chips or dirt.

307.53 Rumination disorder
Regurgitation, of nonorganic origin, of food with reswallowing
EXCLUDES *obsessional rumination (300.3)*

307.54 Psychogenic vomiting

307.59 Other
Feeding disorder of infancy or early childhood of nonorganic origin
Infantile feeding disturbances } of nonorganic origin
Loss of appetite } of nonorganic origin

307.6 Enuresis
Enuresis (primary) (secondary) of nonorganic origin
EXCLUDES *enuresis of unspecified cause (788.3)*
DEF: Involuntary urination past age of normal control; also called bedwetting; no trace to biological problem; focus on psychological issues.

307.7 Encopresis
Encopresis (continuous) (discontinuous) of nonorganic origin
EXCLUDES *encopresis of unspecified cause (787.6)*
DEF: Inability to control bowel movements; cause traced to psychological, not biological, problems.

✓5th **307.8 Pain disorders related to psychological factors**

307.80 Psychogenic pain, site unspecified

307.81 Tension headache
EXCLUDES *headache:*
NOS (784.0)
migraine (346.0-346.9)
syndromes (339.00-339.89)
tension type (339.10-339.12)

307.89 Other
Code first to type or site of pain
EXCLUDES *pain disorder exclusively attributed to psychological factors (307.80)*
psychogenic pain (307.80)

307.9 Other and unspecified special symptoms or syndromes, not elsewhere classified
Communication disorder NOS
Hair plucking
Lalling
Lisping
Masturbation
Nail-biting
Thumb-sucking

✓4th **308 Acute reaction to stress**
INCLUDES catastrophic stress
combat fatigue
gross stress reaction (acute)
transient disorders in response to exceptional physical or mental stress which usually subside within hours or days
EXCLUDES *adjustment reaction or disorder (309.0-309.9)*
chronic stress reaction (309.1-309.9)

308.0 Predominant disturbance of emotions
Anxiety } as acute reaction to exceptional [gross] stress
Emotional crisis } as acute reaction to exceptional [gross] stress
Panic state } as acute reaction to exceptional [gross] stress

308.1 Predominant disturbance of consciousness
Fugues as acute reaction to exceptional [gross] stress

308.2 Predominant psychomotor disturbance
Agitation states } as acute reaction to exceptional [gross] stress
Stupor } as acute reaction to exceptional [gross] stress

308.3 Other acute reactions to stress
Acute situational disturbance
Acute stress disorder
EXCLUDES *prolonged posttraumatic emotional disturbance (309.81)*

308.4 Mixed disorders as reaction to stress

308.9 Unspecified acute reaction to stress

✓4th **309 Adjustment reaction**
INCLUDES adjustment disorders
reaction (adjustment) to chronic stress
EXCLUDES *acute reaction to major stress (308.0-308.9)*
neurotic disorders (300.0-300.9)

309.0 Adjustment disorder with depressed mood
Grief reaction
EXCLUDES *affective psychoses (296.0-296.9)*
neurotic depression (300.4)
prolonged depressive reaction (309.1)
psychogenic depressive psychosis (298.0)

309.1 Prolonged depressive reaction
EXCLUDES *affective psychoses (296.0-296.9)*
brief depressive reaction (309.0)
neurotic depression (300.4)
psychogenic depressive psychosis (298.0)

✓5th **309.2 With predominant disturbance of other emotions**

309.21 Separation anxiety disorder
DEF: Abnormal apprehension by a child when physically separated from support environment; byproduct of abnormal symbiotic child-parent relationship.

309.22 Emancipation disorder of adolescence and early adult life
DEF: Adjustment reaction of late adolescence; conflict over independence from parental supervision; symptoms include difficulty in making decisions, increased reliance on parental advice, deliberate adoption of values in opposition of parents.

309.23 Specific academic or work inhibition

309.24 Adjustment disorder with anxiety

309.28 Adjustment disorder with mixed anxiety and depressed mood
Adjustment reaction with anxiety and depression

309.29 Other
Culture shock

309.3 Adjustment disorder with disturbance of conduct
Conduct disturbance } as adjustment reaction
Destructiveness } as adjustment reaction
EXCLUDES *destructiveness in child (312.9)*
disturbance of conduct NOS (312.9)
dyssocial behavior without manifest psychiatric disorder (V71.01-V71.02)
personality disorder with predominantly sociopathic or asocial manifestations (301.7)

309.4 Adjustment disorder with mixed disturbance of emotions and conduct

✓5th **309.8 Other specified adjustment reactions**

309.81 Posttraumatic stress disorder
Chronic posttraumatic stress disorder
Concentration camp syndrome
Posttraumatic stress disorder NOS
Post-traumatic stress disorder (PTSD)
EXCLUDES *acute stress disorder (308.3)*
posttraumatic brain syndrome:
nonpsychotic (310.2)
psychotic (293.0-293.9)
DEF: Preoccupation with traumatic events beyond normal experience; i.e., rape, personal assault, combat, natural disasters, accidents, torture precip- itate disorder; also recurring flashbacks of trauma; symptoms include difficulty remembering, sleeping, or concentrating, and guilt feelings for surviving.

309.82 Adjustment reaction with physical symptoms

309.83 Adjustment reaction with withdrawal
Elective mutism as adjustment reaction
Hospitalism (in children) NOS

309.89 Other

309.9 Unspecified adjustment reaction
Adaptation reaction NOS
Adjustment reaction NOS

✓4th 310 Specific nonpsychotic mental disorders due to brain damage

EXCLUDES *neuroses, personality disorders, or other nonpsychotic conditions occurring in a form similar to that seen with functional disorders but in association with a physical condition (300.0-300.9, 301.0-301.9)*

310.0 Frontal lobe syndrome
Lobotomy syndrome
Postleucotomy syndrome [state]
EXCLUDES *postcontusion syndrome (310.2)*

310.1 Personality change due to conditions classified elsewhere
Cognitive or personality change of other type, of nonpsychotic severity
Organic psychosyndrome of nonpsychotic severity
Presbyophrenia NOS
Senility with mental changes of nonpsychotic severity
EXCLUDES *memory loss of unknown cause (780.93)*
DEF: Personality disorder caused by organic factors, such as brain lesions, head trauma, or cerebrovascular accident (CVA).

310.2 Postconcussion syndrome
Postcontusion syndrome or encephalopathy
Posttraumatic brain syndrome, nonpsychotic
Status postcommotio cerebri
Use additional code to identify associated post-traumatic headache, if applicable (339.20-339.22)
EXCLUDES *frontal lobe syndrome (310.0)*
postencephalitic syndrome (310.8)
any organic psychotic conditions following head injury (293.0-294.0)
DEF: Nonpsychotic disorder due to brain trauma, causes symptoms unrelated to any disease process; symptoms include amnesia, serial headaches, rapid heartbeat, fatigue, disrupted sleep patterns, inability to concentrate.

310.8 Other specified nonpsychotic mental disorders following organic brain damage
Mild memory disturbance
Postencephalitic syndrome
Other focal (partial) organic psychosyndromes

310.9 Unspecified nonpsychotic mental disorder following organic brain damage

311 Depressive disorder, not elsewhere classified
Depressive disorder NOS
Depressive state NOS
Depression NOS
EXCLUDES *acute reaction to major stress with depressive symptoms (308.0)*
affective personality disorder (301.10-301.13)
affective psychoses (296.0-296.9)
brief depressive reaction (309.0)
depressive states associated with stressful events (309.0-309.1)
disturbance of emotions specific to childhood and adolescence, with misery and unhappiness (313.1)
mixed adjustment reaction with depressive symptoms (309.4)
neurotic depression (300.4)
prolonged depressive adjustment reaction (309.1)
psychogenic depressive psychosis (298.0)

✓4th 312 Disturbance of conduct, not elsewhere classified

EXCLUDES *adjustment reaction with disturbance of conduct (309.3)*
drug dependence (304.0-304.9)
dyssocial behavior without manifest psychiatric disorder (V71.01-V71.02)
personality disorder with predominantly sociopathic or asocial manifestations (301.7)
sexual deviations (302.0-302.9)

The following fifth-digit subclassification is for use with categories 312.0-312.2
0 unspecified
1 mild
2 moderate
3 severe

✓5th 312.0 Undersocialized conduct disorder, aggressive type
[0-3]
Aggressive outburst
Anger reaction
Unsocialized aggressive disorder
DEF: Mental condition identified by behaviors disrespectful of others' rights and of age-appropriate social norms or rules; symptoms include bullying, vandalism, verbal and physical abusiveness, lying, stealing, defiance.

✓5th 312.1 Undersocialized conduct disorder, unaggressive type
[0-3]
Childhood truancy, unsocialized
Solitary stealing
Tantrums

✓5th 312.2 Socialized conduct disorder
[0-3]
Childhood truancy, socialized
Group delinquency
EXCLUDES *gang activity without manifest psychiatric disorder (V71.01)*

✓5th 312.3 Disorders of impulse control, not elsewhere classified

312.30 Impulse control disorder, unspecified

312.31 Pathological gambling

312.32 Kleptomania

312.33 Pyromania

312.34 Intermittent explosive disorder

312.35 Isolated explosive disorder

312.39 Other
Trichotillomania

312.4 Mixed disturbance of conduct and emotions
Neurotic delinquency
EXCLUDES *compulsive conduct disorder (312.3)*

✓5th 312.8 Other specified disturbances of conduct, not elsewhere classified

312.81 Conduct disorder, childhood onset type

312.82 Conduct disorder, adolescent onset type

312.89 Other conduct disorder
Conduct disorder of unspecified onset

312.9 Unspecified disturbance of conduct
Delinquency (juvenile)
Disruptive behavior disorder NOS

✓4th 313 Disturbance of emotions specific to childhood and adolescence

EXCLUDES *adjustment reaction (309.0-309.9)*
emotional disorder of neurotic type (300.0-300.9)
masturbation, nail-biting, thumbsucking, and other isolated symptoms (307.0-307.9)

313.0 Overanxious disorder
Anxiety and fearfulness } of childhood and adolescence
Overanxious disorder }
EXCLUDES *abnormal separation anxiety (309.21)*
anxiety states (300.00-300.09)
hospitalism in children (309.83)
phobic state (300.20-300.29)

313.1 Misery and unhappiness disorder
EXCLUDES *depressive neurosis (300.4)*

✓5th **313.2 Sensitivity, shyness, and social withdrawal disorder**
EXCLUDES *infantile autism (299.0)*
schizoid personality (301.20-301.22)
schizophrenia (295.0-295.9)

313.21 Shyness disorder of childhood
Sensitivity reaction of childhood or adolescence

313.22 Introverted disorder of childhood
Social withdrawal } of childhood and adolescence
Withdrawal reaction } of childhood and adolescence

313.23 Selective mutism
EXCLUDES *elective mutism as adjustment reaction (309.83)*

313.3 Relationship problems
Sibling jealousy
EXCLUDES *relationship problems associated with aggression, destruction, or other forms of conduct disturbance (312.0-312.9)*

✓5th **313.8 Other or mixed emotional disturbances of childhood or adolescence**

313.81 Oppositional defiant disorder
DEF: Mental disorder of children noted for pervasive opposition, defiance of authority.

313.82 Identity disorder
Identity problem
DEF: Distress of adolescents caused by inability to form acceptable self-identity; uncertainty about career choice, sexual orientation, moral values.

313.83 Academic underachievement disorder

313.89 Other
Reactive attachment disorder of infancy or early childhood

313.9 Unspecified emotional disturbance of childhood or adolescence
Mental disorder of infancy, childhood or adolescence NOS

✓4th **314 Hyperkinetic syndrome of childhood**
EXCLUDES *hyperkinesis as symptom of underlying disorder–code the underlying disorder*

✓5th **314.0 Attention deficit disorder**
Adult
Child
DEF: A behavioral disorder usually diagnosed at an early age; characterized by the inability to focus attention for a normal period of time.

314.00 Without mention of hyperactivity
Predominantly inattentive type

314.01 With hyperactivity
Combined type
Overactivity NOS
Predominantly hyperactive/impulsive type
Simple disturbance of attention with overactivity

314.1 Hyperkinesis with developmental delay
Developmental disorder of hyperkinesis
Use additional code to identify any associated neurological disorder

314.2 Hyperkinetic conduct disorder
Hyperkinetic conduct disorder without developmental delay
EXCLUDES *hyperkinesis with significant delays in specific skills (314.1)*

314.8 Other specified manifestations of hyperkinetic syndrome

314.9 Unspecified hyperkinetic syndrome
Hyperkinetic reaction of childhood or adolescence NOS
Hyperkinetic syndrome NOS

✓4th **315 Specific delays in development**
EXCLUDES *that due to a neurological disorder (320.0-389.9)*

✓5th **315.0 Specific reading disorder**

315.00 Reading disorder, unspecified

315.01 Alexia
DEF: Lack of ability to understand written language; manifestation of aphasia.

315.02 Developmental dyslexia
DEF: Serious impairment of reading skills unexplained in relation to general intelligence and teaching processes; it can be inherited or congenital.

315.09 Other
Specific spelling difficulty

315.1 Mathematics disorder
Dyscalculia

315.2 Other specific learning difficulties
Disorder of written expression
EXCLUDES *specific arithmetical disorder (315.1)*
specific reading disorder (315.00-315.09)

✓5th **315.3 Developmental speech or language disorder**

315.31 Expressive language disorder
Developmental aphasia
Word deafness
EXCLUDES *acquired aphasia (784.3)*
elective mutism (309.83, 313.0, 313.23)

315.32 Mixed receptive-expressive language disorder
Central auditory processing disorder
EXCLUDES *acquired auditory processing disorder (388.45)*

315.34 Speech and language developmental delay due to hearing loss

315.39 Other
Developmental articulation disorder
Dyslalia
Phonological disorder
EXCLUDES *lisping and lalling (307.9)*
stammering and stuttering (307.0)

315.4 Developmental coordination disorder
Clumsiness syndrome
Dyspraxia syndrome
Specific motor development disorder

315.5 Mixed development disorder

315.8 Other specified delays in development

315.9 Unspecified delay in development
Developmental disorder NOS
Learning disorder NOS

316 Psychic factors associated with diseases classified elsewhere
Psychologic factors in physical conditions classified elsewhere
Use additional code to identify the associated physical condition, as:
psychogenic:
asthma (493.9)
dermatitis (692.9)
duodenal ulcer (532.0-532.9)
eczema (691.8, 692.9)
gastric ulcer (531.0-531.9)
mucous colitis (564.9)
paroxysmal tachycardia (427.2)
ulcerative colitis (556)
urticaria (708.0-708.9)
psychosocial dwarfism (259.4)
EXCLUDES *physical symptoms and physiological malfunctions, not involving tissue damage, of mental origin (306.0-306.9)*

MENTAL RETARDATION (317-319)

Use additional code(s) to identify any associated psychiatric or physical condition(s)

317 Mild mental retardation
High-grade defect
IQ 50-70
Mild mental subnormality

✓4th **318 Other specified mental retardation**

318.0 Moderate mental retardation
IQ 35-49
Moderate mental subnormality

318.1 Severe mental retardation
IQ 20-34
Severe mental subnormality

318.2 Profound mental retardation
IQ under 20
Profound mental subnormality

319 Unspecified mental retardation
Mental deficiency NOS
Mental subnormality NOS

Chapter 6: Nervous System and Sense Organs (320–389)

This chapter classifies diseases and disorders of the nervous system and the sense organs.

Inflammatory Diseases of the Central Nervous System (320–326)

Inflammatory diseases such as meningitis, encephalitis, cerebral abscesses, late effects of infections of the central nervous system and other types of inflammations such as meningitis due to sarcoidosis, and lead poisoning (toxic) encephalitis are grouped together in this subchapter. However, many infections of the central nervous system considered communicable or transmissable are excluded from this section and are classified to chapter 1, "Infectious and Parasitic Diseases."

Meningitis (320)

Bacterial meningitis is the inflammation of the covering of the meninges due to a bacterial organism. Bacterial meningitis can be caused by a variety of pyogenic bacterial organisms, most commonly Haemophilus influenzae (type B), Streptococcus pneumoniae, Pneumococcus, Neisseria meningitidis, Staphylococcus aureus, Klebsiella, Pseudomonas, and Escherichia coli.

Encephalitis, Myelitis, and Encephalomyelitis (323)

These are inflammations of the central nervous system that alter the function of various portions of the brain (encephalitis), spinal cord (myelitis), or both (encephalomyelitis). These diseases usually result from either a direct invasion of the central nervous system by a virus or postinfection involvement of the central nervous system after a viral disease. They also may be caused by bacteria, medications, toxic substances, and parasites. Encephalitis or myelitis infection resulting from direct invasion is most often caused by arthropod-borne viruses as seen in mosquito or tick bites classified to categories 062, 063, and 064.

Assign fourth and fifth digits to identify the causative organism. Since encephalitis classified to codes 323.0x, 323.1, 323.2, 323.4x, 323.6x, and 323.7x is a manifestation of another disease process, code the underlying disease first. If the organism is unspecified or the encephalitis has a noninfectious or toxic etiology, see codes 323.5, 323.8, and 323.9.

Late Effects of Intracranial Abscess or Pyogenic Infection (326)

This category is used to indicate late effects of meningitis, encephalitis, myelitis, encephalomyelitis, intracranial and intraspinal abscess, phlebitis or thrombophlebitis of the intracranial sinuses except when these conditions are manifestations of another disease process identified by italics in the ICD-9-CM tabular list. These late effects include conditions specified as such and may occur any time after the resolution of the causal condition. Use an additional code to identify the residual condition.

Hereditary and Degenerative Diseases of the Central Nervous System (330–337)

Alzheimer's disease (331.0) is a form of presenile dementia caused by the destruction of the subcortical white matter of the brain and characterized by increasing loss of intellectual functioning beginning with minor memory loss and eventually resulting in total loss of ability to function. Assign an additional code to identify any mental condition, such as presenile dementia (290.10), associated with the current condition.

Other Cerebral Degenerations (331)

Code category 331 classifies Alzheimer's disease (331.0), frontotemporal dementias (331.1x), acquired hydrocephalus, and senile and other degenerative cerebral disorders.

Normal pressure hydrocephalus (NPH) results from a disruption in the CSF circulation, leading to gradual enlargement of the ventricles and emergence of symptoms. This syndrome, when secondary to disease processes such as subarachnoid hemorrhage, traumatic brain injury, cerebral infarction, and meningitis, is referred to as secondary NPH, or communicating hydrocephalus. Secondary NPH is appropriately coded as communicating hydrocephalus, 331.3. Hydrocephalus in patients without known etiologies may be documented as idiopathic normal pressure hydrocephalus (INPH), which is reported with code 331.5. Congenital hydrocephalus associated with spina bifida (741.0) and congenital obstructive hydrocephalus (742.3) are classified to chapter 14, "Congenital Anomalies."

Parkinson's Disease (332)

Paralysis agitans (332.0) is an idiopathic neurological disease causing degeneration and dysfunction of the basal ganglia. This disease, also known as Parkinsonism or Parkinson's disease, is due to a toxic degeneration of the nigral neurons, a group of specialized cells in the midbrain that contain neuromelanin and manufacture the neurotransmitter substance dopamine. When 75 percent to 80 percent of the dopamine innervation is destroyed, signs and symptoms of Parkinsonism appear. Secondary Parkinsonism (332.1) is a neurologic disease with features similar to paralysis agitans affecting the central nervous system. It is caused by a number of diseases or by the adverse affect of certain drugs and chemicals.

Huntington's Chorea (333.4)

This is a fatal hereditary disease affecting the basal ganglia and cerebral cortex. The onset varies but usually begins in the fourth decade of life. Death usually follows within 15 years of onset.

Disorders of the Autonomic Nervous System (337)

This category includes disorders of the peripheral autonomic, sympathetic, and parasympathetic nervous system.

Subcategory 337 includes fifth-digit subclassification codes for unspecified (337.00) and other (337.09) idiopathic peripheral neuropathies, and a specific code to report carotid sinus syndrome (337.01). Carotid sinus syndrome (CSS) (a.k.a., carotid sinus syncope, carotid sinus hypersensitivity) is an idiopathic peripheral autonomic neuropathy that exhibits as exaggerated vagal response stimulation due to pressure on the carotid sinus. CSS is characterized by recurrent dizziness, syncope or near syncope, unexplained falls, and symptoms associated with head turning or constriction of the neck. CSS contributes to increased incidence of falls, fracture, and other injury.

110Peripheral autonomic neuropathy is a chronic and progressive disorder of the peripheral autonomic nerves most often associated with diabetes mellitus, usually insulin dependent or of long-standing duration. Other common etiologies include amyloidosis, botulism, porphyria, and multiple endocrine adenomas. Code the etiology of the peripheral autonomic neuropathy first, such as diabetes mellitus (250.6x) or amyloidosis (277.3), then code 337.1.

Pain (338)

Category 338 includes pain that cannot be more specifically classified elsewhere, such as generalized pain (780.96), pain due to psychological factors (307.8x), headache syndromes (339.00–339.89), migraines (346.0–346.9), vulvodynia (625.70–625.79), and localized pain, which should be coded to pain by site. Use an additional code (307.89) to identify pain associated with psychological factors. Category 338 codes may be used in conjunction with codes from other categories and chapters to provide detailed reporting of the acute or chronic pain and neoplasm-related pain. A code from subcategories 338.1 and 338.2 should not be assigned if the underlying (definitive) diagnosis is known and the encounter is for management of the underlying condition. However, if the reason for the encounter is pain control or management, subcategory 338 codes may be sequenced as a first-listed or principal diagnosis. An admission or encounter for a procedure aimed at treating an underlying condition (e.g., fracture) is reported with the code for the underlying condition assigned as the first-listed diagnosis. In these cases, do not report an additional code from category 338.

Other Disorders of the Central Nervous System (340–349)

Other Headache Syndromes (339)

Diagnostic differentiation between the various types of headache, such as cluster headache and migraine (346), can be difficult. To further complicate matters, patients may experience overlapping types of headache, such as a migraine and cluster headache combination. There are many clinical variations of headache pain with distinct characteristics and treatments. Treatment is reliant upon accurate diagnosis; therefore, differentiation between headache syndromes is essential.

Cluster headaches that have been formerly classified to 346.2 are now more appropriately classifiable to codes 339.00–339.02.When reporting 339.3 Drug induced headache, assign the appropriate E code to report the causal drug or medication. Category 339 specifically excludes migraine headache (346.0–346.9), headache NOS (784.0), and headache due to lumbar puncture (349.0). Also note the classification difference between tension headache (307.81) and tension **type** headache (339.10-339.12). Tension headache triggered by psychological factors is classified to pain disorders due to psychological factors (307.8). This is the default classification for tension headache NOS. Tension type headache is due to physiological factors rather than psychological.

Hemiplegia and Hemiparesis (342)

Hemiplegia and hemiparesis codes are used when hemiplegia (complete) (incomplete) is reported without further specification, or is stated to be old or long standing but of unspecified cause. The category is used also in multiple coding to identify these types of hemiplegia resulting from any cause. Hemiplegia and hemiparesis resulting from cerebrovascular disease is classified to category 438.

Epilepsy and Recurrent Seizures (345)

Epilepsy is a disorder characterized by recurrent transient disturbances of the cerebral function. An abnormal paroxysmal neuronal discharge in the brain usually results in convulsive seizures, but may result in loss of consciousness, abnormal behavior, sensory disturbances, or any combination. Epilepsy may be secondary to prior trauma, hemorrhage, intoxication (toxins), chemical imbalances, anoxia, infections, neoplasms, or congenital defects.

A series of seizures at intervals too brief to allow consciousness between attacks is known as status epilepticus and can result in death. Status epilepticus, not otherwise specified, is classified to code 345.3 Grand mal status. However, status epilepticus can occur in other specified forms of epilepsy.

Migraine (346)

Migraine is a vascular-type headache usually located in the temporal lobe and unilateral in nature. These headaches are commonly associated with irritability, nausea, vomiting, and often photophobia. Preceding the attacks, the cranial arteries constrict resulting in warning sensory symptoms. In addition to classic and common, migraine headache can take several other forms. The terms "classic" and "common" have been replaced by "with aura" and "without aura" in the titles of codes 346.0 and 346.1. Fifth-digit subclassifications describe migraines with or without associated complications. Status migrainosus describes a severe, debilitating migraine lasting more than 72 hours. This is a relatively rare, but life-threatening, migraine complication that could result in a potentially fatal ischemic stroke. Except for its prolonged duration, the headache characteristics are the same as for typical migraine. Intractable migraine describes frequently occurring, continuous, unremitting, or other migraine recalcitrant to conventional medical therapy that often requires acute care to resolve.

Dural Tear (349)

Dural tears include unintended, accidental, and incidental laceration or puncture to the dura mater. They are relatively commonplace during spine surgery or other invasive extradural procedures. Most dural tears are repaired intraoperatively with suturing, fat grafts, and/or fibrin glue. The most common risk associated with dural tear is cerebrospinal fluid leakage. Multiple surgical factors increase the risk for dural tear (e.g., surgical site, type of surgery performed, and number of spine levels involved). An exclusion note was added to 998.2 Accidental puncture or laceration during a procedure to differentiate dural tear that is an unavoidable event due to anatomy or predictable surgical factors from puncture that is a complication of the procedure.

Disorders of the Peripheral Nervous System (350–359)

This subchapter classifies disorders of the peripheral nervous system based upon the specific nerve or nerve complex, involvement, or condition.

Categories 356–359 are hereditary and idiopathic peripheral neuropathies, inflammatory neuropathies, myoneural and myotonic disorders, and muscular dystrophies. Many of the conditions included in this subchapter are manifestations of other diseases and are used in addition to the code for the underlying condition. For example, polyneuropathy in diabetes, code 357.2, is used in addition to the code for the underlying condition, diabetes, 250.6x.

Acute infective polyneuritis (357.0) is a polyneuropathy due to an infective organism, most commonly herpes zoster. Guillain-Barre syndrome (357.0), usually preceded by a herpes infection, is the most common diagnosis classified here.

Disorders of the Eye and Adnexa (360–379)

Retinopathy of prematurity (ROP) is a progressive vasoproliferative disorder in premature infants and is a leading cause of blindness in children. ROP (formerly called retrolental fibroplasia) is caused by injury to the retina from O_2 therapy for the treatment of hypoxia associated with delayed lung maturation. Severe forms may progress to vision loss due to the retinal scarring and damage. Stage 5 is the end stage of the disease with a completely detached retina and severe vision loss. The term "retrolental fibroplasia" applies only to scarred retina (cicatrical disease) and has been differentiated from the more appropriate term "retinopathy of prematurity" (362.20–362.27) for this vasoproliferative condition. Retrolental fibroplasia is coded to 362. 21.

Plateau iris (364.82) is a common secondary angle-closure glaucoma characterized by closing of the anterior chamber angle due to to a large or anteriorly positioned ciliary body that mechanically alters the position of the peripheral iris in relation to the trabecular meshwork. If the angle remains capable of closure after iridotomy, the condition is then termed plateau iris syndrome, a postoperative condition that increases the risk of glaucoma.

Glaucoma (365) as defined as an increase in intraocular pressure due to an abnormality in the outflow of aqueous humor from the anterior chamber or, rarely, from an above normal rate of aqueous humor production by the ciliary body. Open-angle glaucoma (365.1x). Increase in intraocular pressure despite free access of the aqueous humor to the trabecular network, the drainage apparatus in the angle of the anterior chamber.

Primary angle-closure glaucoma (365.2x) as in increase in intraocular pressure due to the iris occluding the anterior chamber structures and preventing the aqueous humor from reaching its usual outflow channel in the tralecular meshwork.

Cataract (366): Partial or total opacity of the crystalline lens or lens capsule. Cataracts form gradually and usually occur bilaterally in patients over 70 years of age, with the exception of traumatic and congenital cataracts. Cataracts are classified by the zones of the lens involved in the opacity: anterior and posterior cortical, equatorial cortical, supranuclear, and nuclear. They are further subdivided into congenital, degenerative, traumatic, secondary, or complicated (due to ocular or systemic disease, radiation, or other external influences), toxic, and after-cataracts (meaning one remaining in the lens or capsule following cataract extraction). They may be classified according to the degree of opacity present (e.g., mature, immature) or on the basis of the appearance of the cataract, such as lamellar.

Pingueculitis (372.34) occurs when a pinguecula becomes acutely inflamed and vascularized, causing redness and irritation. A pingueculum is a yellowish, slightly raised, lipid-like deposit in the nasal and temporal limbal conjunctiva, probably produced by sunlight damage. Normally pingueculae are asymptomatic and an incidental finding. However, pingueculae can lead to the formation of pterygia, an abnormal fold of the membrane in the interpalpebral fissure. Both pingueculae and pterygia can become vascularized and inflamed, and may be associated with corneal punctuate epitheliopathy and corneal dellen (corneal thinning secondary to dryness).

Diseases of the Ear and Mastoid Process (380–389)

Hearing loss is reported with codes beginning with 389. The types of loss include conductive (389.0x) from external or middle ear problems, sensory (389.11) from disorders of the inner ear, neural disorder (389.12) of the auditory nerve, sensorineural (389.10, 389.15–389.18) and central disorder (389.14) originating in the brain. Occasionally, a conductive hearing loss occurs in combination with a sensorineural hearing loss in that damage occurs in the outer or middle ear as well as in the inner ear (cochlea) or auditory nerve. This type of hearing loss is referred to as a mixed hearing loss (389.2x).

6. DISEASES OF THE NERVOUS SYSTEM AND SENSE ORGANS (320-389)

INFLAMMATORY DISEASES OF THE CENTRAL NERVOUS SYSTEM (320-326)

✓4th **320 Bacterial meningitis**

INCLUDES arachnoiditis, leptomeningitis, meningitis, meningoencephalitis, meningomyelitis, pachymeningitis } bacterial

DEF: Bacterial infection causing inflammation of the lining of the brain and/or spinal cord.

320.0 Hemophilus meningitis
Meningitis due to Hemophilus influenzae [H. influenzae]

320.1 Pneumococcal meningitis

320.2 Streptococcal meningitis

320.3 Staphylococcal meningitis

320.7 Meningitis in other bacterial diseases classified elsewhere
Code first underlying disease, as:
actinomycosis (039.8)
listeriosis (027.0)
typhoid fever (002.0)
whooping cough (033.0-033.9)
EXCLUDES *meningitis (in):*
epidemic (036.0)
gonococcal (098.82)
meningococcal (036.0)
salmonellosis (003.21)
syphilis:
NOS (094.2)
congenital (090.42)
meningovascular (094.2)
secondary (091.81)
tuberculous (013.0)

✓5th **320.8 Meningitis due to other specified bacteria**

320.81 Anaerobic meningitis
Bacteroides (fragilis)
Gram-negative anaerobes

320.82 Meningitis due to gram-negative bacteria, not elsewhere classified
Aerobacter aerogenes pneumoniae
Escherichia coli [E. coli]
Friedländer bacillus
Klebsiella
Proteus morganii
Pseudomonas
EXCLUDES *gram-negative anaerobes (320.81)*

320.89 Meningitis due to other specified bacteria
Bacillus pyocyaneus

320.9 Meningitis due to unspecified bacterium
Meningitis:
bacterial NOS
purulent NOS
pyogenic NOS
suppurative NOS

✓4th **321 Meningitis due to other organisms**

INCLUDES arachnoiditis, leptomeningitis, meningitis, pachymeningitis } due to organisms other than bacterial

DEF: Infection causing inflammation of the lining of the brain and/or spinal cord, due to organisms other than bacteria.

321.0 Cryptococcal meningitis
Code first underlying disease (117.5)

321.1 Meningitis in other fungal diseases
Code first underlying disease (110.0-118)
EXCLUDES *meningitis in:*
candidiasis (112.83)
coccidioidomycosis (114.2)
histoplasmosis (115.01, 115.11, 115.91)

321.2 Meningitis due to viruses not elsewhere classified
Code first underlying disease, as:
meningitis due to arbovirus (060.0-066.9)
EXCLUDES *meningitis (due to):*
abacterial (047.0-047.9)
adenovirus (049.1)
aseptic NOS (047.9)
Coxsackie (virus)(047.0)
ECHO virus (047.1)
enterovirus (047.0-047.9)
herpes simplex virus (054.72)
herpes zoster virus (053.0)
lymphocytic choriomeningitis virus (049.0)
mumps (072.1)
viral NOS (047.9)
meningo-eruptive syndrome (047.1)

321.3 Meningitis due to trypanosomiasis
Code first underlying disease (086.0-086.9)

321.4 Meningitis in sarcoidosis
Code first underlying disease (135)

321.8 Meningitis due to other nonbacterial organisms classified elsewhere
Code first underlying disease
EXCLUDES *leptospiral meningitis (100.81)*

✓4th **322 Meningitis of unspecified cause**

INCLUDES arachnoiditis, leptomeningitis, meningitis, pachymeningitis } with no organism specified as cause

DEF: Infection causing inflammation of the lining of the brain and/or spinal cord, due to unspecified cause.

322.0 Nonpyogenic meningitis
Meningitis with clear cerebrospinal fluid

322.1 Eosinophilic meningitis

322.2 Chronic meningitis

322.9 Meningitis, unspecified

✓4th **323 Encephalitis, myelitis, and encephalomyelitis**

INCLUDES acute disseminated encephalomyelitis
meningoencephalitis, except bacterial
meningomyelitis, except bacterial
myelitis:
ascending
transverse

EXCLUDES *acute transverse myelitis NOS (341.20)*
acute transverse myelitis in conditions classified elsewhere (341.21)
bacterial:
meningoencephalitis (320.0-320.9)
meningomyelitis (320.0-320.9)
idiopathic transverse myelitis (341.22)

DEF: Encephalitis: inflammation of brain tissues.

DEF: Myelitis: inflammation of the spinal cord.

DEF: Encephalomyelitis: inflammation of brain and spinal cord.

✓5th **323.0 Encephalitis, myelitis, and encephalomyelitis in viral diseases classified elsewhere**
Code first underlying disease, as:
cat-scratch disease (078.3)
infectious mononucleosis (075)
ornithosis (073.7)

323.01 *Encephalitis and encephalomyelitis in viral diseases classified elsewhere*

EXCLUDES *encephalitis (in):*
arthropod-borne viral (062.0-064)
herpes simplex (054.3)
mumps (072.2)
other viral diseases of central nervous system (049.8-049.9)
poliomyelitis (045.0-045.9)
rubella (056.01)
slow virus infections of central nervous system (046.0-046.9)
viral NOS (049.9)
West Nile (066.41)

323.02 *Myelitis in viral diseases classified elsewhere*

EXCLUDES *myelitis (in):*
herpes simplex (054.74)
herpes zoster (053.14)
poliomyelitis (045.0-045.9)
rubella (056.01)
other viral diseases of central nervous system (049.8-049.9)

323.1 *Encephalitis, myelitis, and encephalomyelitis in rickettsial diseases classified elsewhere*

Code first underlying disease (080-083.9)

DEF: Inflammation of the brain caused by rickettsial disease carried by louse, tick, or mite.

323.2 *Encephalitis, myelitis, and encephalomyelitis in protozoal diseases classified elsewhere*

Code first underlying disease, as:
malaria (084.0-084.9)
trypanosomiasis (086.0-086.9)

DEF: Inflammation of the brain caused by protozoal disease carried by mosquitoes and flies.

✓5th **323.4 Other encephalitis, myelitis, and encephalomyelitis due to infection classified elsewhere**

Code first underlying disease

323.41 *Other encephalitis and encephalomyelitis due to infection classified elsewhere*

EXCLUDES *encephalitis (in):*
meningococcal (036.1)
syphilis:
NOS (094.81)
congenital (090.41)
toxoplasmosis (130.0)
tuberculosis (013.6)
meningoencephalitis due to free-living ameba [Naegleria] (136.29)

323.42 *Other myelitis due to infection classified elsewhere*

EXCLUDES *myelitis (in):*
syphilis (094.89)
tuberculosis (013.6)

✓5th **323.5 Encephalitis, myelitis, and encephalomyelitis following immunization procedures**

Use additional E code to identify vaccine

323.51 Encephalitis and encephalomyelitis following immunization procedures

Encephalitis postimmunization or postvaccinal
Encephalomyelitis postimmunization or postvaccinal

323.52 Myelitis following immunization procedures

Myelitis postimmunization or postvaccinal

✓5th **323.6 Postinfectious encephalitis, myelitis, and encephalomyelitis**

Code first underlying disease

DEF: Infection, inflammation of brain several weeks following the outbreak of a systemic infection.

323.61 *Infectious acute disseminated encephalomyelitis [ADEM]*

Acute necrotizing hemorrhagic encephalopathy

EXCLUDES *noninfectious acute disseminated encephalomyelitis (ADEM) (323.81)*

323.62 *Other postinfectious encephalitis and encephalomyelitis*

EXCLUDES *encephalitis:*
postchickenpox (052.0)
postmeasles (055.0)

323.63 *Postinfectious myelitis*

EXCLUDES *postchickenpox myelitis (052.2)*
herpes simplex myelitis (054.74)
herpes zoster myelitis (053.14)

✓5th **323.7 Toxic encephalitis, myelitis, and encephalomyelitis**

Code first underlying cause, as:
carbon tetrachloride (982.1)
hydroxyquinoline derivatives (961.3)
lead (984.0-984.9)
mercury (985.0)
thallium (985.8)

323.71 *Toxic encephalitis and encephalomyelitis*

323.72 *Toxic myelitis*

✓5th **323.8 Other causes of encephalitis, myelitis, and encephalomyelitis**

323.81 Other causes of encephalitis and encephalomyelitis

Noninfectious acute disseminated encephalomyelitis (ADEM)

323.82 Other causes of myelitis

Transverse myelitis NOS

323.9 Unspecified cause of encephalitis, myelitis, and encephalomyelitis

✓4th **324 Intracranial and intraspinal abscess**

324.0 Intracranial abscess

Abscess (embolic):
cerebellar
cerebral
Abscess (embolic) of brain [any part]:
epidural
extradural
otogenic
subdural

EXCLUDES *tuberculous (013.3)*

324.1 Intraspinal abscess

Abscess (embolic) of spinal cord [any part]:
epidural
extradural
subdural

EXCLUDES *tuberculous (013.5)*

324.9 Of unspecified site

Extradural or subdural abscess NOS

325 Phlebitis and thrombophlebitis of intracranial venous sinuses

Embolism, Endophlebitis, Phlebitis, septic or suppurative, Thrombophlebitis, Thrombosis — of cavernous, lateral or other intracranial or unspecified intracranial venous sinus

EXCLUDES *that specified as:*
complicating pregnancy, childbirth, or the puerperium (671.5)
of nonpyogenic origin (437.6)

DEF: Inflammation and formation of blood clot in a vein within the brain or its lining.

326 Late effects of intracranial abscess or pyogenic infection

Note: This category is to be used to indicate conditions whose primary classification is to 320-325 [excluding 320.7, 321.0-321.8, 323.01-323.42, 323.6-323.7] as the cause of late effects, themselves classifiable elsewhere. The "late effects" include conditions specified as such, or as sequelae, which may occur at any time after the resolution of the causal condition.

Use additional code to identify condition, as:
hydrocephalus (331.4)
paralysis (342.0-342.9, 344.0-344.9)

ORGANIC SLEEP DISORDERS (327)

✓4th **327 Organic sleep disorders**

✓5th **327.0 Organic disorders of initiating and maintaining sleep [Organic insomnia]**

EXCLUDES *insomnia NOS (780.52)*
insomnia not due to a substance or known physiological condition (307.41-307.42)
insomnia with sleep apnea NOS (780.51)

327.00 Organic insomnia, unspecified

327.01 Insomnia due to medical condition classified elsewhere

Code first underlying condition
EXCLUDES *insomnia due to mental disorder (327.02)*

327.02 Insomnia due to mental disorder

Code first mental disorder
EXCLUDES *alcohol induced insomnia (291.82)*
drug induced insomnia (292.85)

327.09 Other organic insomnia

✓5th **327.1 Organic disorder of excessive somnolence [Organic hypersomnia]**

EXCLUDES *hypersomnia NOS (780.54)*
hypersomnia not due to a substance or known physiological condition (307.43-307.44)
hypersomnia with sleep apnea NOS (780.53)

327.10 Organic hypersomnia, unspecified

327.11 Idiopathic hypersomnia with long sleep time

327.12 Idiopathic hypersomnia without long sleep time

327.13 Recurrent hypersomnia
Kleine-Levin syndrome
Menstrual related hypersomnia

327.14 Hypersomnia due to medical condition classified elsewhere

Code first underlying condition
EXCLUDES *hypersomnia due to mental disorder (327.15)*

327.15 Hypersomnia due to mental disorder

Code first mental disorder
EXCLUDES *alcohol induced hypersomnia (291.82)*
drug induced hypersomnia (292.85)

327.19 Other organic hypersomnia

✓5th **327.2 Organic sleep apnea**

EXCLUDES *Cheyne-Stokes breathing (786.04)*
hypersomnia with sleep apnea NOS (780.53)
insomnia with sleep apnea NOS (780.51)
sleep apnea in newborn (770.81-770.82)
sleep apnea NOS (780.57)

327.20 Organic sleep apnea, unspecified

327.21 Primary central sleep apnea

327.22 High altitude periodic breathing

327.23 Obstructive sleep apnea (adult) (pediatric)

327.24 Idiopathic sleep related nonobstructive alveolar hypoventilation
Sleep related hypoxia

327.25 Congenital central alveolar hypoventilation syndrome

327.26 Sleep related hypoventilation/ hypoxemia in conditions classifiable elsewhere

Code first underlying condition

327.27 Central sleep apnea in conditions classified elsewhere

Code first underlying condition

327.29 Other organic sleep apnea

✓5th **327.3 Circadian rhythm sleep disorder**

Organic disorder of sleep wake cycle
Organic disorder of sleep wake schedule

EXCLUDES *alcohol induced circadian rhythm sleep disorder (291.82)*
circadian rhythm sleep disorder of nonorganic origin (307.45)
disruption of 24 hour sleep wake cycle NOS (780.55)
drug induced circadian rhythm sleep disorder (292.85)

327.30 Circadian rhythm sleep disorder, unspecified

327.31 Circadian rhythm sleep disorder, delayed sleep phase type

327.32 Circadian rhythm sleep disorder, advanced sleep phase type

327.33 Circadian rhythm sleep disorder, irregular sleep-wake type

327.34 Circadian rhythm sleep disorder, free-running type

327.35 Circadian rhythm sleep disorder, jet lag type

327.36 Circadian rhythm sleep disorder, shift work type

327.37 Circadian rhythm sleep disorder in conditions classified elsewhere

Code first underlying condition

327.39 Other circadian rhythm sleep disorder

✓5th **327.4 Organic parasomnia**

EXCLUDES *alcohol induced parasomnia (291.82)*
drug induced parasomnia (292.85)
parasomnia not due to a known physiological condition (307.47)

327.40 Organic parasomnia, unspecified

327.41 Confusional arousals

327.42 REM sleep behavior disorder

327.43 Recurrent isolated sleep paralysis

327.44 Parasomnia in conditions classified elsewhere

Code first underlying condition

327.49 Other organic parasomnia

✓5th **327.5 Organic sleep related movement disorders**

EXCLUDES *restless legs syndrome (333.94)*
sleep related movement disorder NOS (780.58)

327.51 Periodic limb movement disorder

Periodic limb movement sleep disorder

327.52 Sleep related leg cramps

327.53 Sleep related bruxism

327.59 Other organic sleep related movement disorders

327.8 Other organic sleep disorders

HEREDITARY AND DEGENERATIVE DISEASES OF THE CENTRAL NERVOUS SYSTEM (330-337)

EXCLUDES *hepatolenticular degeneration (275.1)*
multiple sclerosis (340)
other demyelinating diseases of central nervous system (341.0-341.9)

✓4th **330 Cerebral degenerations usually manifest in childhood**

Use additional code to identify associated mental retardation

330.0 Leukodystrophy

Krabbe's disease
Leukodystrophy:
NOS
globoid cell
metachromatic
sudanophilic
Pelizaeus-Merzbacher disease
Sulfatide lipidosis

DEF: Hereditary disease of arylsulfatase or cerebroside sulfatase; characterized by a diffuse loss of myelin in CNS; infantile form causes blindness, motor disturbances, rigidity, mental deterioration and, occasionally, convulsions.

330.1 Cerebral lipidoses

Amaurotic (familial) idiocy
Disease:
Batten
Jansky-Bielschowsky
Kufs'
Spielmeyer-Vogt
Tay-Sachs
Gangliosidosis

DEF: Genetic disorder causing abnormal lipid accumulation in the reticuloendothelial cells of the brain.

330.2 Cerebral degeneration in generalized lipidoses

Code first underlying disease, as:
Fabry's disease (272.7)
Gaucher's disease (272.7)
Niemann-Pick disease (272.7)
sphingolipidosis (272.7)

330.3 Cerebral degeneration of childhood in other diseases classified elsewhere

Code first underlying disease, as:
Hunter's disease (277.5)
mucopolysaccharidosis (277.5)

330.8 Other specified cerebral degenerations in childhood

Alpers' disease or gray-matter degeneration
Infantile necrotizing encephalomyelopathy
Leigh's disease
Subacute necrotizing encephalopathy or encephalomyelopathy

330.9 Unspecified cerebral degeneration in childhood

✓4th **331 Other cerebral degenerations**

Use additional code, where applicable, to identify dementia:
with behavioral disturbance (294.11)
without behavioral disturbance (294.10)

331.0 Alzheimer's disease

DEF: Diffuse atrophy of cerebral cortex; causing a progressive decline in intellectual and physical functions, including memory loss, personality changes and profound dementia.

✓5th **331.1 Frontotemporal dementia**

DEF: Rare, progressive degenerative brain disease, similar to Alzheimer's; cortical atrophy affects the frontal and temporal lobes.

331.11 Pick's disease

DEF: A less common form of progressive frontotemporal dementia with asymmetrical atrophy of the frontal and temporal regions of the cerebral cortex including abnormal rounded brain cells called Pick cells together with the presence of abnormal staining of protein (called tau) within the cells, called Pick bodies; symptoms include prominent apathy, deterioration of social skills, behavioral changes such as disinhibition and restlessness, echolalia, impairment of language, memory, and intellect, increased carelessness, poor personal hygiene, and decreased attention span.

331.19 Other frontotemporal dementia

Frontal dementia

331.2 Senile degeneration of brain

EXCLUDES *senility NOS (797)*

331.3 Communicating hydrocephalus

Secondary normal pressure hydrocephalus

EXCLUDES *congenital hydrocephalus (742.3)*
idiopathic normal pressure hydrocephalus (331.5)
normal pressure hydrocephalus (331.5)
spina bifida with hydrocephalus (741.0)

DEF: Subarachnoid hemorrhage and meningitis causing excess buildup of cerebrospinal fluid in cavities due to nonabsorption of fluid back through fluid pathways.

331.4 Obstructive hydrocephalus

Acquired hydrocephalus NOS

EXCLUDES *congenital hydrocephalus (742.3)*
idiopathic normal pressure hydrocephalus (331.5)
normal pressure hydrocephalus (331.5)
spina bifida with hydrocephalus (741.0)

DEF: Obstruction of cerebrospinal fluid passage from brain into spinal canal.

331.5 Idiopathic normal pressure hydrocephalus [INPH]

Normal pressure hydrocephalus NOS

EXCLUDES *congenital hydrocephalus (742.3)*
secondary normal pressure hydrocephalus (331.3)
spina bifida with hydrocephalus (741.0)

DEF: Abnormal increase of cerebrospinal fluid in the brain's ventricles; results in dementia, progressive mental impairment, gait disturbance, and impaired bladder control.

331.7 Cerebral degeneration in diseases classified elsewhere

Code first underlying disease, as:
alcoholism (303.0-303.9)
beriberi (265.0)
cerebrovascular disease (430-438)
congenital hydrocephalus (741.0, 742.3)
myxedema (244.0-244.9)
neoplastic disease (140.0-239.9)
vitamin B_{12} deficiency (266.2)

EXCLUDES *cerebral degeneration in:*
Jakob-Creutzfeldt disease (046.19)
progressive multifocal leukoencephalopathy (046.3)
subacute spongiform encephalopathy (046.1)

✓5th **331.8 Other cerebral degeneration**

331.81 Reye's syndrome

DEF: Rare childhood illness, often developed after a viral upper respiratory infection; characterized by vomiting, elevated serum transaminase, changes in liver and other viscera; symptoms may be followed by an encephalopathic phase with brain swelling, disturbances of consciousness and seizures; can be fatal.

331.82 Dementia with Lewy bodies

Dementia with Parkinsonism
Lewy body dementia
Lewy body disease

DEF: A cerebral dementia with neurophysiologic changes including increased hippocampal volume, hypoperfusion in the occipital lobes, and beta amyloid deposits with neurofibrillarity tangles, atrophy of cortex and brainstem, hallmark neuropsychologic characteristics are fluctuating cognition with pronounced variation in attention and alertness; recurrent hallucinations; and parkinsonism.

331.83 Mild cognitive impairment, so stated

EXCLUDES *altered mental status (780.97)*
cerebral degeneration (331.0-331.9)
change in mental status (780.97)
cognitive deficits following (late effects of) cerebral hemorrhage or infarction (438.0)
cognitive impairment due to intracranial or head injury (850-854, 959.01)
cognitive impairment due to late effect of intracranial injury (907.0)
dementia (290.0-290.43, 294.8)
mild memory disturbance (310.8)
neurologic neglect syndrome (781.8)
personality change, nonpsychotic (310.1)

331.89 Other

Cerebral ataxia

331.9 Cerebral degeneration, unspecified

✓4th **332 Parkinson's disease**

EXCLUDES *dementia with Parkinsonism (331.82)*

332.0 Paralysis agitans

Parkinsonism or Parkinson's disease:
NOS
idiopathic
primary

DEF: Form of progressive parkinsonism characterized by mask-like facial expressions, inability to stand or walk smoothly, muscle weakness, and involuntary trembling movement.

332.1 Secondary Parkinsonism Neuroleptic-induced Parkinsonism

Parkinsonism due to drugs

Use additional E code to identify drug, if drug-induced

EXCLUDES *Parkinsonism (in):*
Huntington's disease (333.4)
progressive supranuclear palsy (333.0)
Shy-Drager syndrome (333.0)
syphilitic (094.82)

✓4th **333 Other extrapyramidal disease and abnormal movement disorders**

INCLUDES other forms of extrapyramidal, basal ganglia, or striatopallidal disease

EXCLUDES *abnormal movements of head NOS (781.0)*
sleep related movement disorders (327.51-327.59)

333.0 Other degenerative diseases of the basal ganglia

Atrophy or degeneration:
olivopontocerebellar [Déjérine-Thomas syndrome]
pigmentary pallidal [Hallervorden-Spatz disease]
striatonigral
Parkinsonian syndrome associated with:
idiopathic orthostatic hypotension
symptomatic orthostatic hypotension
Progressive supranuclear ophthalmoplegia
Shy-Drager syndrome

333.1 Essential and other specified forms of tremor

Benign essential tremor
Familial tremor
Medication-induced postural tremor

Use additional E code to identify drug, if drug-induced

EXCLUDES *tremor NOS (781.0)*

333.2 Myoclonus

Familial essential myoclonus
Progressive myoclonic epilepsy
Unverricht-Lundborg disease

Use additional E code to identify drug, if drug-induced

DEF: Spontaneous movements or contractions of muscles.

333.3 Tics of organic origin

Use additional E code to identify drug, if drug-induced

EXCLUDES *Gilles de la Tourette's syndrome (307.23)*
habit spasm (307.22)
tic NOS (307.20)

333.4 Huntington's chorea

DEF: Genetic disease characterized by chronic progressive men tal deterioration; dementia and death within 15 years of onset.

333.5 Other choreas

Hemiballism(us)
Paroxysmal choreo-athetosis

Use additional E code to identify drug, if drug-induced

EXCLUDES *Sydenham's or rheumatic chorea (392.0-392.9)*

333.6 Genetic torsion dystonia

Dystonia:
deformans progressiva
musculorum deformans
(Schwalbe-) Ziehen-Oppenheim disease

DEF: Sustained muscular contractions, causing twisting and repetitive movements that result in abnormal postures of trunk and limbs; etiology unknown.

✓5th **333.7 Acquired torsion dystonia**

333.71 Athetoid cerebral palsy

Double athetosis (syndrome)
Vogt's disease

EXCLUDES *infantile cerebral palsy (343.0-343.9)*

333.72 Acute dystonia due to drugs

Acute dystonic reaction due to drugs
Neuroleptic induced acute dystonia

Use additional E code to identify drug

EXCLUDES *blepharospasm due to drugs (333.85)*
orofacial dyskinesia due to drugs (333.85)
secondary Parkinsonism (332.1)
subacute dyskinesia due to drugs (333.85)
tardive dyskinesia (333.85)

333.79 Other acquired torsion dystonia

✓5th **333.8 Fragments of torsion dystonia**

Use additional E code to identify drug, if drug-induced

333.81 Blepharospasm

EXCLUDES *blepharospasm due to drugs (333.85)*

DEF: Uncontrolled winking or blinking due to orbicularis oculi muscle spasm.

333.82 Orofacial dyskinesia
EXCLUDES *orofacial dyskinesia due to drugs (333.85)*
DEF: Uncontrolled movement of mouth or facial muscles.

333.83 Spasmodic torticollis
EXCLUDES *torticollis:*
NOS (723.5)
hysterical (300.11)
psychogenic (306.0)
DEF: Uncontrolled movement of head due to spasms of neck muscle.

333.84 Organic writers' cramp
EXCLUDES *pychogenic (300.89)*

333.85 Subacute dyskinesia due to drugs
Blepharospasm due to drugs
Orofacial dyskinesia due to drugs
Tardive dyskinesia
Use additional E code to identify drug
EXCLUDES *acute dystonia due to drugs (333.72)*
acute dystonic reaction due to drugs (333.72)
secondary Parkinsonism (332.1)

333.89 Other

5th **333.9 Other and unspecified extrapyramidal diseases and abnormal movement disorders**

333.90 Unspecified extrapyramidal disease and abnormal movement disorder
Medication-induced movement disorders NOS
Use additional E code to identify drug, if drug-induced

333.91 Stiff-man syndrome

333.92 Neuroleptic malignant syndrome
Use additional E code to identify drug
EXCLUDES *neuroleptic induced Parkinsonism (332.1)*

333.93 Benign shuddering attacks

333.94 Restless legs syndrome [RLS]
DEF: Neurological disorder of unknown etiology with an irresistible urge to move the legs, which may temporarily relieve the symptoms, is accompanied by motor restlessness and sensations of pain, burning, prickling, or tingling.

333.99 Other
Neuroleptic-induced acute akathisia
Use additional E code to identify drug, if drug-induced

4th **334 Spinocerebellar disease**
EXCLUDES *olivopontocerebellar degeneration (333.0)*
peroneal muscular atrophy (356.1)

334.0 Friedreich's ataxia
DEF: Genetic recessive disease of children; sclerosis of dorsal, lateral spinal cord columns; characterized by ataxia, speech impairment, swaying and irregular movements, with muscle paralysis, especially of lower limbs.

334.1 Hereditary spastic paraplegia

334.2 Primary cerebellar degeneration
Cerebellar ataxia:
Marie's
Sanger-Brown
Dyssynergia cerebellaris myoclonica
Primary cerebellar degeneration:
NOS
hereditary
sporadic

334.3 Other cerebellar ataxia
Cerebellar ataxia NOS
Use additional E code to identify drug, if drug-induced

334.4 Cerebellar ataxia in diseases classified elsewhere
Code first underlying disease, as:
alcoholism (303.0-303.9)
myxedema (244.0-244.9)
neoplastic disease (140.0-239.9)

334.8 Other spinocerebellar diseases
Ataxia-telangiectasia [Louis-Bar syndrome]
Corticostriatal-spinal degeneration

334.9 Spinocerebellar disease, unspecified

4th **335 Anterior horn cell disease**

335.0 Werdnig-Hoffmann disease
Infantile spinal muscular atrophy
Progressive muscular atrophy of infancy
DEF: Spinal muscle atrophy manifested in prenatal period or shortly after birth; symptoms include hypotonia, atrophy of skeletal muscle; death occurs in infancy.

5th **335.1 Spinal muscular atrophy**

335.10 Spinal muscular atrophy, unspecified335.11

Kugelberg-Welander disease
Spinal muscular atrophy:
familial
juvenile
DEF: Hereditary; juvenile muscle atrophy; appears during first two decades of life; due to lesions of anterior horns of spinal cord; includes wasting, diminution of lower body muscles and twitching.

335.19 Other
Adult spinal muscular atrophy

5th **335.2 Motor neuron disease**

335.20 Amyotrophic lateral sclerosis
Motor neuron disease (bulbar) (mixed type)

335.21 Progressive muscular atrophy
Duchenne-Aran muscular atrophy
Progressive muscular atrophy (pure)

335.22 Progressive bulbar palsy

335.23 Pseudobulbar palsy

335.24 Primary lateral sclerosis

335.29 Other

335.8 Other anterior horn cell diseases

335.9 Anterior horn cell disease, unspecified

4th **336 Other diseases of spinal cord**

336.0 Syringomyelia and syringobulbia

336.1 Vascular myelopathies
Acute infarction of spinal cord (embolic) (nonembolic)
Arterial thrombosis of spinal cord
Edema of spinal cord
Hematomyelia
Subacute necrotic myelopathy

336.2 Subacute combined degeneration of spinal cord in diseases classified elsewhere
Code first underlying disease, as:
pernicious anemia (281.0)
other vitamin B_{12} deficiency anemia (281.1)
vitamin B_{12} deficiency (266.2)

336.3 Myelopathy in other diseases classified elsewhere
Code first underlying disease, as:
myelopathy in neoplastic disease (140.0-239.9)
EXCLUDES *myelopathy in:*
intervertebral disc disorder (722.70-722.73)
spondylosis (721.1, 721.41-721.42, 721.91)

336.8 Other myelopathy
Myelopathy:
drug-induced
radiation-induced
Use additonal E code to identify cause

336.9 Unspecified disease of spinal cord
Cord compression NOS
Myelopathy NOS
EXCLUDES *myelitis (323.02, 323.1, 323.2, 323.42, 323.52, 323.63, 323.72, 323.82, 323.9)*
spinal (canal) stenosis (723.0, 724.00-724.09)

✓4th **337 Disorders of the autonomic nervous system**
INCLUDES disorders of peripheral autonomic, sympathetic, parasympathetic, or vegetative system
EXCLUDES *familial dysautonomia [Riley-Day syndrome] (742.8)*

✓5th **337.0 Idiopathic peripheral autonomic neuropathy**

337.00 Idiopathic peripheral autonomic neuropathy, unspecified

337.01 Carotid sinus syndrome
Carotid sinus syncope

337.09 Other idiopathic peripheral autonomic neuropathy
Cervical sympathetic dystrophy or paralysis

337.1 Peripheral autonomic neuropathy in disorders classified elsewhere
Code first underlying disease, as:
amyloidosis (277.30-277.39)
diabetes (249.6, 250.6)

✓5th **337.2 Reflex sympathetic dystrophy**
DEF: Disturbance of the sympathetic nervous system evidenced by sweating, pain, pallor and edema following injury to nerves or blood vessels.

337.20 Reflex sympathetic dystrophy, unspecified
Complex regional pain syndrome type I, unspecified

337.21 Reflex sympathetic dystrophy of the upper limb
Complex regional pain syndrome type I of the upper limb

337.22 Reflex sympathetic dystrophy of the lower limb
Complex regional pain syndrome type I of the lower limb

337.29 Reflex sympathetic dystrophy of other specified site
Complex regional pain syndrome type I of other specified site

337.3 Autonomic dysreflexia
Use additional code to identify the cause, such as:
pressure ulcer (707.00-707.09)
fecal impaction (560.39)
urinary tract infection (599.0)
DEF: Noxious stimuli evokes paroxysmal hypertension, bradycardia, excess sweating, headache, pilomotor responses, facial flushing, and nasal congestion due to uncontrolled parasympathetic nerve response; usually occurs in patients with spinal cord injury above major sympathetic outflow tract (T_6).

337.9 Unspecified disorder of autonomic nervous system

PAIN (338)

✓4th **338 Pain, not elsewhere classified**
Use additional code to identify:
pain associated with psychological factors (307.89)
EXCLUDES *generalized pain (780.96)*
headache syndromes (339.00-339.89)
localized pain, unspecified type–code to pain by site
migraines (346.0-346.9)
pain disorder exclusively attributed to psychological factors (307.80)
vulvar vestibulitis (625.71)
vulvodynia (625.70-625.79)

338.0 Central pain syndrome
Déjérine-Roussy syndrome
Myelopathic pain syndrome
Thalamic pain syndrome (hyperesthetic)

✓5th **338.1 Acute pain**

338.11 Acute pain due to trauma

338.12 Acute post-thoracotomy pain
Post-thoracotomy pain NOS

338.18 Other acute postoperative pain
Postoperative pain NOS

338.19 Other acute pain
EXCLUDES *neoplasm related acute pain (338.3)*

✓5th **338.2 Chronic pain**
EXCLUDES *causalgia (355.9)*
lower limb (355.71)
upper limb (354.4)
chronic pain syndrome (338.4)
myofascial pain syndrome (729.1)
neoplasm related chronic pain (338.3)
reflex sympathetic dystrophy (337.20-337.29)

338.21 Chronic pain due to trauma

338.22 Chronic post-thoracotomy pain

338.28 Other chronic postoperative pain

338.29 Other chronic pain

338.3 Neoplasm related pain (acute) (chronic)
Cancer associated pain
Pain due to malignancy (primary) (secondary)
Tumor associated pain

338.4 Chronic pain syndrome
Chronic pain associated with significant psychosocial dysfunction

OTHER HEADACHE SYNDROMES (339)

✓4th **339 Other headache syndromes**
EXCLUDES *headache:*
NOS (784.0)
due to lumbar puncture (349.0)
migraine (346.0-346.9)

✓5th **339.0 Cluster headaches and other trigeminal autonomic cephalgias**
TACS

339.00 Cluster headache syndrome, unspecified
Ciliary neuralgia
Cluster headache NOS
Histamine cephalgia
Lower half migraine
Migrainous neuralgia

339.01 Episodic cluster headache

339.02 Chronic cluster headache

339.03 Episodic paroxysmal hemicrania
Paroxysmal hemicrania NOS

339.04 Chronic paroxysmal hemicrania

339.05 Short lasting unilateral neuralgiform headache with conjunctival injection and tearing
SUNCT

339.09 Other trigeminal autonomic cephalgias

✓5th **339.1 Tension type headache**
EXCLUDES *tension headache NOS (307.81)*
tension headache related to psychological factors (307.81)

339.10 Tension type headache, unspecified

339.11 Episodic tension type headache

339.12 Chronic tension type headache

✓5th **339.2 Post-traumatic headache**

339.20 Post-traumatic headache, unspecified

339.21 Acute post-traumatic headache

339.22 Chronic post-traumatic headache

339.3 Drug induced headache, not elsewhere classified
Medication overuse headache
Rebound headache

✓5th **339.4 Complicated headache syndromes**

339.41 Hemicrania continua

339.42 New daily persistent headache
NDPH

339.43 Primary thunderclap headache

339.44 Other complicated headache syndrome

✓5th **339.8 Other specified headache syndromes**

339.81 Hypnic headache

339.82 Headache associated with sexual activity
Orgasmic headache
Preorgasmic headache

339.83 Primary cough headache

339.84 Primary exertional headache

339.85 Primary stabbing headache

339.89 Other specified headache syndromes

OTHER DISORDERS OF THE CENTRAL NERVOUS SYSTEM (340-349)

340 Multiple sclerosis
Disseminated or multiple sclerosis:
NOS
brain stem
cord
generalized

✓4th **341 Other demyelinating diseases of central nervous system**

341.0 Neuromyelitis optica

341.1 Schilder's disease
Baló's concentric sclerosis
Encephalitis periaxialis:
concentrica [Baló's]
diffusa [Schilder's]
DEF: Chronic leukoencephalopathy of children and adolescents; symptoms include blindness, deafness, bilateral spasticity and progressive mental deterioration.

✓5th **341.2 Acute (transverse) myelitis**
EXCLUDES *acute (transverse) myelitis (in) (due to):*
following immunization procedures (323.52)
infection classified elsewhere (323.42)
postinfectious (323.63)
protozoal diseases classified elsewhere (323.2)
rickettsial diseases classified elsewhere (323.1)
toxic (323.72)
viral diseases classified elsewhere (323.02)
transverse myelitis NOS (323.82)

341.20 Acute (transverse) myelitis NOS

341.21 Acute (transverse) myelitis in conditions classified elsewhere
Code first underlying condition

341.22 Idiopathic transverse myelitis

341.8 Other demyelinating diseases of central nervous system
Central demyelination of corpus callosum
Central pontine myelinosis
Marchiafava (-Bignami) disease

341.9 Demyelinating disease of central nervous system, unspecified

✓4th **342 Hemiplegia and hemiparesis**
Note: This category is to be used when hemiplegia (complete) (incomplete) is reported without further specification, or is stated to be old or long-standing but of unspecified cause. The category is also for use in multiple coding to identify these types of hemiplegia resulting from any cause.
EXCLUDES *congenital (343.1)*
hemiplegia due to late effect of cerebrovascular accident (438.20-438.22)
infantile NOS (343.4)

The following fifth-diits are for use with codes 342.0-342.9:
0 affecting unspecified side
1 affecting dominant side
2 affecting nondominant side

✓5th **342.0 Flaccid hemiplegia**
[0-2]

342.1 Spastic hemiplegia
[0-2]

✓5th **342.8 Other specified hemiplegia**
[0-2]

✓5th **342.9 Hemiplegia, unspecified**
[0-2]

✓4th **343 Infantile cerebral palsy**
INCLUDES cerebral:
palsy NOS
spastic infantile paralysis
congenital spastic paralysis (cerebral)
Little's disease
paralysis (spastic) due to birth injury:
intracranial
spinal
EXCLUDES *athetoid cerebral palsy (333.71)*
hereditary cerebral paralysis, such as:
hereditary spastic paraplegia (334.1)
Vogt's disease (333.71)
spastic paralysis specified as noncongenital or noninfantile (344.0-344.9)

343.0 Diplegic
Congenital diplegia
Congenital paraplegia
DEF: Paralysis affecting both sides of the body simultaneously.

343.1 Hemiplegic
Congenital hemiplegia
EXCLUDES *infantile hemiplegia NOS (343.4)*

343.2 Quadriplegic
Tetraplegic

343.3 Monoplegic

343.4 Infantile hemiplegia
Infantile hemiplegia (postnatal) NOS

343.8 Other specified infantile cerebral palsy

343.9 Infantile cerebral palsy, unspecified
Cerebral palsy NOS

✓4th **344 Other paralytic syndromes**
Note: This category is to be used when the listed conditions are reported without further specification or are stated to be old or long-standing but of unspecified cause. The category is also for use in multiple coding to identify these conditions resulting from any cause.
INCLUDES paralysis (complete) (incomplete), except as classifiable to 342 and 343
EXCLUDES *congenital or infantile cerebral palsy (343.0-343.9)*
hemiplegia (342.0-342.9)
congenital or infantile (343.1, 343.4)

✓5th **344.0 Quadriplegia and quadriparesis**

344.00 Quadriplegia unspecified

344.01 C_1-C_4 complete

344.02 C_1-C_4 incomplete

344.03 C_5-C_7 complete

344.04 C_5-C_7 incomplete

344.09 Other

344.1 Paraplegia
Paralysis of both lower limbs
Paraplegia (lower)

344.2 Diplegia of upper limbs
Diplegia (upper)
Paralysis of both upper limbs

✓5th **344.3 Monoplegia of lower limb**
Paralysis of lower limb
EXCLUDES *monoplegia of lower limb due to late effect of cerebrovascular accident (438.40-438.42)*

344.30 Affecting unspecified side

344.31 Affecting dominant side

344.32 Affecting nondominant side

✓5th **344.4 Monoplegia of upper limb**
Paralysis of upper limb
EXCLUDES *monoplegia of upper limb due to late effect of cerebrovascular accident (438.30-438.32)*

344.40 Affecting unspecified side

344.41 Affecting dominant side

344.42 Affecting nondominant side

344.5 Unspecified monoplegia

✓5th **344.6 Cauda equina syndrome**
DEF: Dull pain and paresthesias in sacrum, perineum and bladder due to compression of spinal nerve roots; pain radiates down buttocks, back of thigh, calf of leg and into foot with prickling, burning sensations.

344.60 Without mention of neurogenic

344.61 With neurogenic bladder
Acontractile bladder
Autonomic hyperreflexia of bladder
Cord bladder
Detrusor hyperreflexia

✓5th **344.8 Other specified paralytic syndromes**

344.81 Locked-in state
DEF: State of consciousness where patients are paralyzed and unable to respond to environmental stimuli; patients have eye movements, and stimuli can enter the brain but patients cannot respond to stimuli.

344.89 Other specified paralytic syndrome

344.9 Paralysis, unspecified

✓4th **345 Epilepsy and recurrent seizures**

The following fifth-digit subclassification is for use with categories 345.0, .1, .4-.9:
0 without mention of intractable eilepsy
1 with intractable epilepsy

EXCLUDES *progressive myoclonic epilepsy (333.2)*
DEF: Brain disorder characterized by electrical-like disturbances; may include occasional impairment or loss of consciousness, abnormal motor phenomena and psychic or sensory disturbances.

✓5th **345.0 Generalized nonconvulsive epilepsy**
[0-1]
Absences:
atonic
typical
Minor epilepsy
Petit mal
Pykno-epilepsy
Seizures:
akinetic
atonic

✓5th **345.1 Generalized convulsive epilepsy**
[0-1]
Epileptic seizures:
clonic
myoclonic
tonic
tonic-clonic
Grand mal
Major epilepsy
EXCLUDES *convulsions:*
NOS (780.39)
infantile (780.39)
newborn (779.0)
infantile spasms (345.6)
DEF: Convulsive seizures with tension of limbs (tonic) or rhythmic contractions (clonic).

345.2 Petit mal status
Epileptic absence status
DEF: Minor myoclonic spasms and sudden momentary loss of consciousness in epilepsy.

345.3 Grand mal status
Status epilepticus NOS
EXCLUDES *epilepsia partialis continua (345.7)*
status:
psychomotor (345.7)
temporal lobe (345.7)
DEF: Sudden loss of consciousness followed by generalized convulsions in epilepsy.

✓5th **345.4 Localization-related (focal) (partial) epilepsy and epileptic syndromes with complex partial seizures**
[0-1]
Epilepsy:
limbic system
partial:
secondarily generalized
with impairment of consciousness
with memory and ideational disturbances
psychomotor
psychosensory
temporal lobe
Epileptic automatism

✓5th **345.5 Localization-related (focal) (partial) epilepsy and epileptic syndromes with simple partial seizures**
[0-1]
Epilepsy:
Bravais-Jacksonian NOS
focal (motor) NOS
Jacksonian NOS
motor partial
partial NOS:
without impairment of consciousness
sensory-induced
somatomotor
somatosensory
visceral
visual

✓5th **345.6 Infantile spasms**
[0-1]
Hypsarrhythmia
Lightning spasms
Salaam attacks
EXCLUDES *salaam tic (781.0)*

✓5th **345.7 Epilepsia partialis continua**
[0-1]
Kojevnikov's epilepsy
DEF: Continuous muscle contractions and relaxation; result of abnormal neural discharge.

✓5th **345.8 Other forms of epilepsy and recurrent seizures**
[0-1]
Epilepsy:
cursive [running]
gelastic

✓5th **345.9 Epilepsy, unspecified**
[0-1]
Epileptic convulsions, fits, or seizures NOS
Recurrent seizures NOS
Seizure disorder NOS
EXCLUDES *convulsion (convulsive) disorder (780.39)*
convulsive seizure or fit NOS (780.39)
recurrent convulsions (780.39)

4th 346 Migraine

EXCLUDES *headache:*
NOS (784.0)
syndromes (339.00-339.89)

The following fifth-digit subclassification is for use with category 346:

0 without mention of intractable migraine without mention of status migrainosus
1 with intractable migraine, so stated without mention of status migrainosus
2 without mention of intractable migraine with status migrainosus
3 with intractable migraine, so stated, with status migrainosus

DEF: Benign vascular headache of extreme pain; commonly associated with irritability, nausea, vomiting and often photophobia; premonitory visual hallucination of a crescent in the visual field (scotoma).

5th 346.0 Migraine with aura
[0-3]
Basilar migraine
Classic migraine
Migraine preceded or accompanied by transient focal neurological phenomena
Migraine triggered seizures
Migraine with acute-onset aura
Migraine with aura without headache (migraine equivalents)
Migraine with prolonged aura
Migraine with typical aura
Retinal migraine
EXCLUDES *persistent migraine aura (346.5, 346.6)*

5th 346.1 Migraine without aura
[0-3]
Common migraine

5th 346.2 Variants of migraine, not elsewhere classified
[0-3]
Abdominal migraine
Cyclical vomiting associated with migraine
Ophthalmoplegic migraine
Periodic headache syndromes in child or adolescent
EXCLUDES *cyclical vomiting NOS (536.2)*
psychogenic cyclical vomiting (306.4)

5th 346.3 Hemiplegic migraine
[0-3]
Familial migraine
Sporadic migraine

5th 346.4 Menstrual migraine
[0-3]
Menstrual headache
Menstrually related migraine
Premenstrual headache
Premenstrual migraine
Pure menstrual migraine

5th 346.5 Persistent migraine aura without cerebral infarction
[0-3]
Persistent migraine aura NOS

5th 346.6 Persistent migraine aura with cerebral infarction
[0-3]

5th 346.7 Chronic migraine without aura
[0-3]
Transformed migraine without aura

5th 346.8 Other forms of migraine
[0-3]

5th 346.9 Migraine, unspecified
[0-3]

4th 347 Cataplexy and narcolepsy

DEF: Cataplexy: Sudden onset of muscle weakness with loss of tone and strength; caused by aggressive or spontaneous emotions.

DEF: Narcolepsy: Brief, recurrent, uncontrollable episodes of sound sleep.

5th 347.0 Narcolepsy

347.00 Without cataplexy
Narcolepsy NOS

347.01 With cataplexy

5th 347.1 Narcolepsy in conditions classified elsewhere
Code first underlying condition

347.10 Without cataplexy

347.11 With cataplexy

4th 348 Other conditions of brain

348.0 Cerebral cysts
Arachnoid cyst
Porencephalic cyst
Porencephaly, acquired
Pseudoporencephaly
EXCLUDES *porencephaly (congenital) (742.4)*

348.1 Anoxic brain damage
EXCLUDES *that occurring in:*
abortion (634-638 with .7, 639.8)
ectopic or molar pregnancy (639.8)
labor or delivery (668.2, 669.4)
that of newborn (767.0, 768.0-768.9, 772.1-772.2)

Use additional E code to identify cause

DEF: Brain injury due to lack of oxygen, other than birth trauma.

348.2 Benign intracranial hypertension
Pseudotumor cerebri
EXCLUDES *hypertensive encephalopathy (437.2)*

DEF: Elevated pressure in brain due to fluid retention in brain cavities.

5th 348.3 Encephalopathy, not elsewhere classified

348.30 Encephalopathy, unspecified

348.31 Metabolic encephalopathy
Septic encephalopathy
EXCLUDES *toxic metabolic encephalopathy (349.82)*

348.39 Other encephalopathy
EXCLUDES *encephalopathy:*
alcoholic (291.2)
hepatic (572.2)
hypertensive (437.2)
toxic (349.82)

348.4 Compression of brain
Compression } brain (stem)
Herniation }
Posterior fossa compression syndrome

DEF: Elevated pressure in brain due to blood clot, tumor, fracture, abscess, other condition.

348.5 Cerebral edema

DEF: Elevated pressure in the brain due to fluid retention in brain tissues.

348.8 Other conditions of brain
Cerebral:
calcification
fungus

348.9 Unspecified condition of brain

4th 349 Other and unspecified disorders of the nervous system

349.0 Reaction to spinal or lumbar puncture
Headache following lumbar puncture

349.1 Nervous system complications from surgically implanted device
EXCLUDES *immediate postoperative complications (997.00-997.09)*
mechanical complications of nervous system device (996.2)

349.2 Disorders of meninges, not elsewhere classified
Adhesions, meningeal (cerebral) (spinal)
Cyst, spinal meninges
Meningocele, acquired
Pseudomeningocele, acquired

5th 349.3 Dural tear

349.31 Accidental puncture or laceration of dura during a procedure
Incidental (inadvertent) durotomy

349.39 Other dural tear

5th 349.8 Other specified disorders of nervous system

349.81 Cerebrospinal fluid rhinorrhea
EXCLUDES *cerebrospinal fluid otorrhea (388.61)*
DEF: Cerebrospinal fluid discharging from the nose; caused by fracture of frontal bone with tearing of dura mater and arachnoid.

349.82 Toxic encephalopathy
Toxic metabolic encephalopathy
Use additional E code to identify cause
DEF: Brain tissue degeneration due to toxic substance.

349.89 Other

349.9 Unspecified disorders of nervous system
Disorder of nervous system (central) NOS

DISORDERS OF THE PERIPHERAL NERVOUS SYSTEM (350-359)

EXCLUDES *diseases of:*
acoustic [8th] nerve (388.5)
oculomotor [3rd, 4th, 6th] nerves (378.0-378.9)
optic [2nd] nerve (377.0-377.9)
peripheral autonomic nerves (337.0-337.9)
neuralgia, neuritis, radiculitis — NOS or "rheumatic" (729.2)
peripheral neuritis in pregnancy (646.4)

✓4th **350 Trigeminal nerve disorders**
INCLUDES disorders of 5th cranial nerve

350.1 Trigeminal neuralgia
Tic douloureux
Trifacial neuralgia
Trigeminal neuralgia NOS
EXCLUDES *postherpetic (053.12)*

350.2 Atypical face pain

350.8 Other specified trigeminal nerve disorders

350.9 Trigeminal nerve disorder, unspecified

✓4th **351 Facial nerve disorders**
INCLUDES disorders of 7th cranial nerve
EXCLUDES *that in newborn (767.5)*

351.0 Bell's palsy
Facial palsy
DEF: Unilateral paralysis of face due to lesion on facial nerve; produces facial distortion.

Trigeminal and Facial Nerve Branches

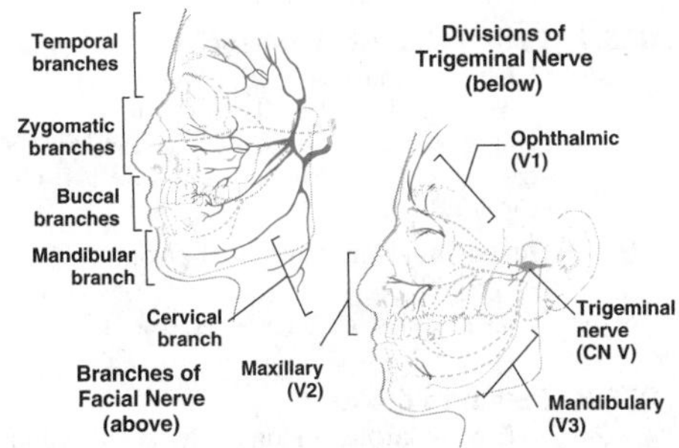

Cranial Nerves

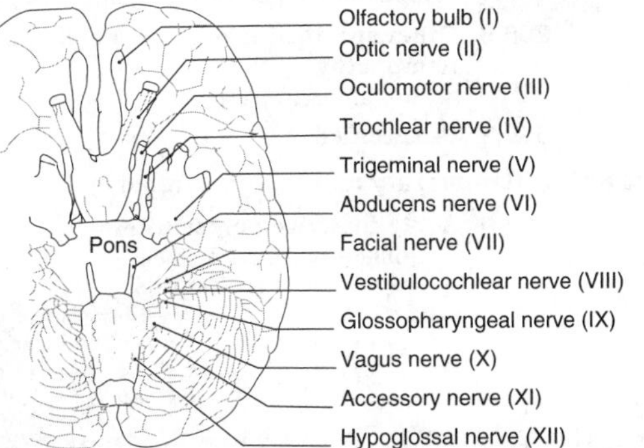

351.1 Geniculate ganglionitis
Geniculate ganglionitis NOS
EXCLUDES *herpetic (053.11)*
DEF: Inflammation of tissue at bend in facial nerve.

351.8 Other facial nerve disorders
Facial myokymia
Melkersson's syndrome

351.9 Facial nerve disorder, unspecified

✓4th **352 Disorders of other cranial nerves**

352.0 Disorders of olfactory [lst] nerve

352.1 Glossopharyngeal neuralgia
DEF: Pain between throat and ear along petrosal and jugular ganglia.

352.2 Other disorders of glossopharyngeal [9th] nerve

352.3 Disorders of pneumogastric [10th] nerve
Disorders of vagal nerve
EXCLUDES *paralysis of vocal cords or larynx (478.30-478.34)*
DEF: Nerve disorder affecting ear, tongue, pharynx, larynx, esophagus, viscera and thorax.

352.4 Disorders of accessory [11th] nerve
DEF: Nerve disorder affecting palate, pharynx, larynx, thoracic viscera, sternocleidomastoid and trapezius muscles.

352.5 Disorders of hypoglossal [12th] nerve
DEF: Nerve disorder affecting tongue muscles.

352.6 Multiple cranial nerve palsies
Collet-Sicard syndrome
Polyneuritis cranialis

352.9 Unspecified disorder of cranial nerves

✓4th **353 Nerve root and plexus disorders**
EXCLUDES *conditions due to:*
intervertebral disc disorders (722.0-722.9)
spondylosis (720.0-721.9)
vertebrogenic disorders (723.0-724.9)

353.0 Brachial plexus lesions
Cervical rib syndrome
Costoclavicular syndrome
Scalenus anticus syndrome
Thoracic outlet syndrome
EXCLUDES *brachial neuritis or radiculitis NOS (723.4)*
that in newborn (767.6)
DEF: Acquired disorder in tissue along nerves in shoulder; causes corresponding motor and sensory dysfunction.

353.1 Lumbosacral plexus lesions
DEF: Acquired disorder in tissue along nerves in lower back; causes corresponding motor and sensory dysfunction.

353.2 Cervical root lesions, not elsewhere classified

353.3 Thoracic root lesions, not elsewhere classified

353.4 Lumbosacral root lesions, not elsewhere classified

353.5 Neuralgic amyotrophy
Parsonage-Aldren-Turner syndrome
Code first any associated underlying disease, such as:
diabetes mellitus (249.6, 250.6)

353.6 Phantom limb (syndrome)
DEF: Abnormal tingling or a burning sensation, transient aches, and intermittent or continuous pain perceived as originating in the absent limb.

353.8 Other nerve root and plexus disorders

353.9 Unspecified nerve root and plexus disorder

Peripheral Nervous System

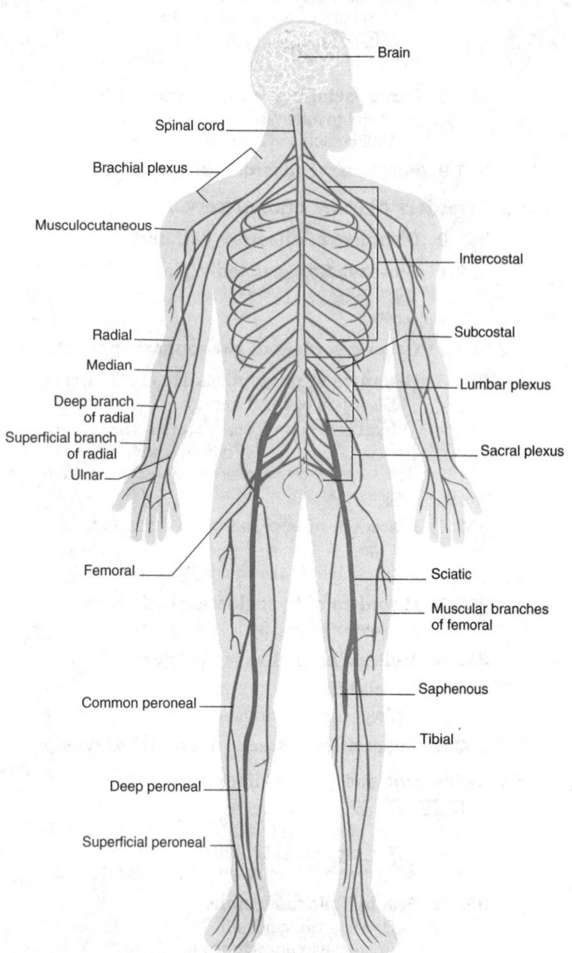

✓4th 354 Mononeuritis of upper limb and mononeuritis multiplex

DEF: Inflammation of a single nerve; known as mononeuritis multiplex when several nerves in unrelated body areas are affected.

354.0 Carpal tunnel syndrome
Median nerve entrapment
Partial thenar atrophy
DEF: Compression of median nerve by tendons; causes pain, tingling, numbness and burning sensation in hand.

354.1 Other lesion of median nerve
Median nerve neuritis

354.2 Lesion of ulnar nerve
Cubital tunnel syndrome
Tardy ulnar nerve palsy

354.3 Lesion of radial nerve
Acute radial nerve palsy

354.4 Causalgia of upper limb
Complex regional pain syndrome type II of the upper limb
EXCLUDES *causalgia:*
NOS (355.9)
lower limb (355.71)
complex regional pain syndrome type II of the lower limb (355.71)
DEF: Peripheral nerve damage, upper limb; usually due to injury; causes burning sensation and trophic skin changes.

354.5 Mononeuritis multiplex
Combinations of single conditions classifiable to 354 or 355

354.8 Other mononeuritis of upper limb

354.9 Mononeuritis of upper limb, unspecified

✓4th 355 Mononeuritis of lower limb

355.0 Lesion of sciatic nerve
EXCLUDES *sciatica NOS (724.3)*
DEF: Acquired disorder of sciatic nerve; causes motor and sensory dysfunction in back, buttock and leg.

355.1 Meralgia paresthetica
Lateral cutaneous femoral nerve of thigh compression or syndrome
DEF: Inguinal ligament entraps lateral femoral cutaneous nerve; causes tingling, pain and numbness along outer thigh.

355.2 Other lesion of femoral nerve

355.3 Lesion of lateral popliteal nerve
Lesion of common peroneal nerve

355.4 Lesion of medial popliteal nerve

355.5 Tarsal tunnel syndrome
DEF: Compressed, entrapped posterior tibial nerve; causes tingling, pain and numbness in sole of foot.

355.6 Lesion of plantar nerve
Morton's metatarsalgia, neuralgia, or neuroma

✓5th 355.7 Other mononeuritis of lower limb

355.71 Causalgia of lower limb
EXCLUDES *causalgia:*
NOS (355.9)
upper limb (354.4)
complex regional pain syndrome type II of upper limb (354.4)
DEF: Dysfunction of lower limb peripheral nerve, usually due to injury; causes burning pain and trophic skin changes.

355.79 Other mononeuritis of lower limb

355.8 Mononeuritis of lower limb, unspecified

355.9 Mononeuritis of unspecified site
Causalgia NOS
Complex regional pain syndrome NOS
EXCLUDES *causalgia:*
lower limb (355.71)
upper limb (354.4)
complex regional pain syndrome:
lower limb (355.71)
upper limb (354.4)

✓4th 356 Hereditary and idiopathic peripheral neuropathy

356.0 Hereditary peripheral neuropathy
Déjérine-Sottas disease

356.1 Peroneal muscular atrophy
Charcôt-Marie-Tooth disease
Neuropathic muscular atrophy
DEF: Genetic disorder, in muscles innervated by peroneal nerves; symptoms include muscle wasting in lower limbs and locomotor difficulties.

356.2 Hereditary sensory neuropathy
DEF: Inherited disorder in dorsal root ganglia, optic nerve, and cerebellum, causing sensory losses, shooting pains, and foot ulcers.

356.3 Refsum's disease
Heredopathia atactica polyneuritiformis
DEF: Genetic disorder of lipid metabolism; causes persistent, painful inflammation of nerves and retinitis pigmentosa.

356.4 Idiopathic progressive polyneuropathy

356.8 Other specified idiopathic peripheral neuropathy
Supranuclear paralysis

356.9 Unspecified

✓4th 357 Inflammatory and toxic neuropathy

357.0 Acute infective polyneuritis
Guillain-Barré syndrome
Postinfectious polyneuritis
DEF: Guillain-Barré syndrome: acute demyelinatry polyneuropathy preceded by viral illness (i.e., herpes, cytomegalovirus [CMV], Epstein-Barr virus [EBV]) or a bacterial illness; areflexic motor paralysis with mild sensory disturbance and acellular rise in spinal fluid protein.

357.1 ***Polyneuropathy in collagen vascular disease***

Code first underlying disease, as:
disseminated lupus erythematosus (710.0)
polyarteritis nodosa (446.0)
rheumatoid arthritis (714.0)

357.2 ***Polyneuropathy in diabetes***

Code first underlying disease (249.6, 250.6)

357.3 ***Polyneuropathy in malignant disease***

Code first underlying disease (140.0-208.9)

357.4 ***Polyneuropathy in other diseases classified elsewhere***

Code first underlying disease, as:
amyloidosis (277.30-277.39)
beriberi (265.0)
chronic uremia (585.9)
deficiency of B vitamins (266.0-266.9)
diphtheria (032.0-032.9)
hypoglycemia (251.2)
pellagra (265.2)
porphyria (277.1)
sarcoidosis (135)
uremia NOS (586)

EXCLUDES *polyneuropathy in:*
herpes zoster (053.13)
mumps (072.72)

357.5 Alcoholic polyneuropathy

357.6 Polyneuropathy due to drugs

Use additional E code to identify drug

357.7 Polyneuropathy due to other toxic agents

Use additional E code to identify toxic agent

✓5th **357.8 Other**

357.81 Chronic inflammatory demyelinating polyneuritis

DEF: Inflammation of peripheral nerves resulting in destruction of myelin sheath; associated with diabetes mellitus, dys-proteinemias, renal failure and malnutrition; symptoms in-clude tingling, numbness, burning pain, diminished tendon reflexes, weakness, and atrophy in lower extremities.

357.82 Critical illness polyneuropathy

Acute motor neuropathy

DEF: An acute axonal neuropathy, both sensory and motor, that is associated with Systemic Inflammatory Response Syndrome (SIRS).

357.89 Other inflammatory and toxic neuropathy

357.9 Unspecified

✓4th **358 Myoneural disorders**

✓5th **358.0 Myasthenia gravis**

DEF: Autoimmune disorder of acetylcholine at neuromuscular junction; causing fatigue of voluntary muscles.

358.00 Myasthenia gravis without (acute) exacerbation

Myasthenia gravis NOS

358.01 Myasthenia gravis with (acute) exacerbation

Myasthenia gravis in crisis

358.1 ***Myasthenic syndromes in diseases classified elsewhere***

Eaton-Lambert syndrome from stated cause classified elsewhere

Code first underlying disease, as:
botulism (005.1, 040.41-040.42)
hypothyroidism (244.0-244.9)
malignant neoplasm (140.0-208.9)
pernicious anemia (281.0)
thyrotoxicosis (242.0-242.9)

358.2 Toxic myoneural disorders

Use additional E code to identify toxic agent

358.8 Other specified myoneural disorders

358.9 Myoneural disorders, unspecified

✓4th **359 Muscular dystrophies and other myopathies**

EXCLUDES *idiopathic polymyositis (710.4)*

359.0 Congenital hereditary muscular dystrophy

Benign congenital myopathy
Central core disease
Centronuclear myopathy
Myotubular myopathy
Nemaline body disease

EXCLUDES *arthrogryposis multiplex congenita (754.89)*

DEF: Genetic disorder; causing progressive or nonprogressive muscle weakness.

359.1 Hereditary progressive muscular dystrophy

Muscular dystrophy:
NOS
distal
Duchenne
Erb's
fascioscapulohumeral
Gower's
Landouzy-Déjérine
limb-girdle
ocular
oculopharyngeal

DEF: Genetic degenerative, muscle disease; causes progressive weakness, wasting of muscle with no nerve involvement.

✓5th **359.2 Myotonic disorders**

EXCLUDES *periodic paralysis (359.3)*

DEF: Impaired movement due to spasmatic, rigid muscles.

359.21 Myotonic muscular dystrophy

Dystrophia myotonica
Myotonia atrophica
Myotonic dystrophy
Proximal myotonic myopathy [PROMM]
Steinert's disease

359.22 Myotonia congenita

Acetazolamide responsive myotonia congenita
Dominant form [Thomsen's disease]
Recessive form [Becker's disease]

359.23 Myotonic chondrodystrophy

Congenital myotonic chondrodystrophy
Schwartz-Jampel disease

359.24 Drug induced myotonia

Use additional E code to identify drug

359.29 Other specified myotonic disorder

Myotonia fluctuans
Myotonia levior
Myotonia permanens
Paramyotonia congenita (of von Eulenburg)

359.3 Periodic paralysis

Familial periodic paralysis
Hypokalemic familial periodic paralysis
Hyperkalemic periodic paralysis
Hypokalemic periodic paralysis
Potassium sensitive periodic paralysis

EXCLUDES *paramyotonia congenita (of von Eulenburg) (359.29)*

DEF: Genetic disorder; characterized by rapidly progressive flaccid paralysis; attacks often occur after exercise or exposure to cold or dietary changes.

359.4 Toxic myopathy

Use additional E code to identify toxic agent

DEF: Muscle disorder caused by toxic agent.

359.5 ***Myopathy in endocrine diseases classified elsewhere***

Code first underlying disease, as:
Addison's disease (255.41)
Cushing's syndrome (255.0)
hypopituitarism (253.2)
myxedema (244.0-244.9)
thyrotoxicosis (242.0-242.9)

DEF: Muscle disorder secondary to dysfunction in hormone secretion.

359.6 *Symptomatic inflammatory myopathy in diseases classified elsewhere*

Code first underlying disease, as:
amyloidosis (277.30-277.39)
disseminated lupus erythematosus (710.0)
malignant neoplasm (140.0-208.9)
polyarteritis nodosa (446.0)
rheumatoid arthritis (714.0)
sarcoidosis (135)
scleroderma (710.1)
Sjögren's disease (710.2)

✓5th **359.8 Other myopathies**

359.81 Critical illness myopathy
Acute necrotizing myopathy
Acute quadriplegic myopathy
Intensive care (ICU) myopathy
Myopathy of critical illness

359.89 Other myopathies

359.9 Myopathy, unspecified

DISORDERS OF THE EYE AND ADNEXA (360-379)

Use additional external cause code, if applicable, to identify the cause of the eye condition

✓4th **360 Disorders of the globe**

INCLUDES disorders affecting multiple structures of eye

✓5th **360.0 Purulent endophthalmitis**

EXCLUDES *bleb associated endophthalmitis (379.63)*

360.00 Purulent endophthalmitis,unspecifiecd

360.01 Acute endophthalmitis

360.02 Panophthalmitis

360.03 Chronic endophthalmitis

360.04 Vitreous abscess

✓5th **360.1 Other endophthalmitis**

EXCLUDES *bleb associated endophthalmitis (379.63)*

360.11 Sympathetic uveitis

DEF: Inflammation of vascular layer of uninjured eye; follows injury to other eye.

360.12 Panuveitis

DEF: Inflammation of entire vascular layer of eye, including choroid, iris and ciliary body.

360.13 Parasitic endophthalmitis NOS

DEF: Parasitic infection causing inflammation of the entire eye.

360.14 Ophthalmia nodosa

DEF: Conjunctival inflammation caused by embedded hairs.

360.19 Other
Phacoanaphylactic endophthalmitis

✓5th **360.2 Degenerative disorders of globe**

360.20 Degenerative disorder of globe, unspecified

360.21 Progressive high (degenerative) myopia
Malignant myopia

DEF: Severe, progressive nearsightedness in adults, complicated by serious disease of the choroid; leads to retinal detachment and blindness.

360.23 Siderosis

DEF: Iron pigment deposits within tissue of eyeball; caused by high iron content of blood.

360.24 Other metallosis
Chalcosis

DEF: Metal deposits, other than iron, within eyeball tissues.

360.29 Other

EXCLUDES *xerophthalmia (264.7)*

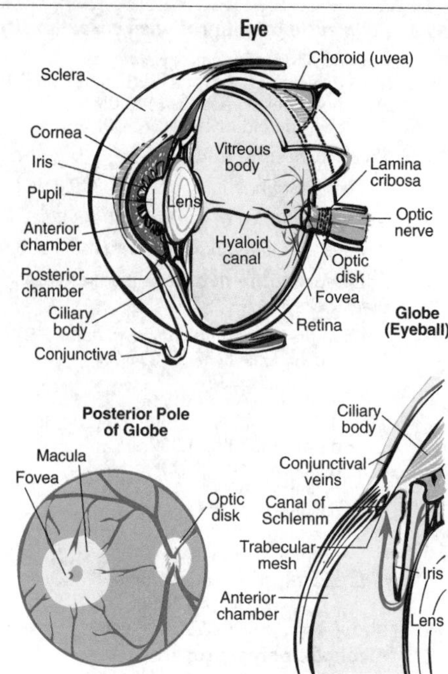

✓5th **360.3 Hypotony of eye**

360.30 Hypotony, unspecified

DEF: Low osmotic pressure causing lack of tone, tension and strength.

360.31 Primary hypotony

360.32 Ocular fistula causing hypotony

DEF: Low intraocular pressure due to leak through abnormal passage.

360.33 Hypotony associated with other ocular disorders

360.34 Flat anterior chamber

DEF: Low pressure behind cornea, causing compression.

✓5th **360.4 Degenerated conditions of globe**

360.40 Degenerated globe or eye, unspecified

360.41 Blind hypotensive eye
Atrophy of globe
Phthisis bulbi

DEF: Vision loss due to extremely low intraocular pressure.

360.42 Blind hypertensive eye
Absolute glaucoma

DEF: Vision loss due to painful, high intraocular pressure.

360.43 Hemophthalmos, except current injury

EXCLUDES *traumatic (871.0-871.9, 921.0-921.9)*

DEF: Pool of blood within eyeball, not from current injury.

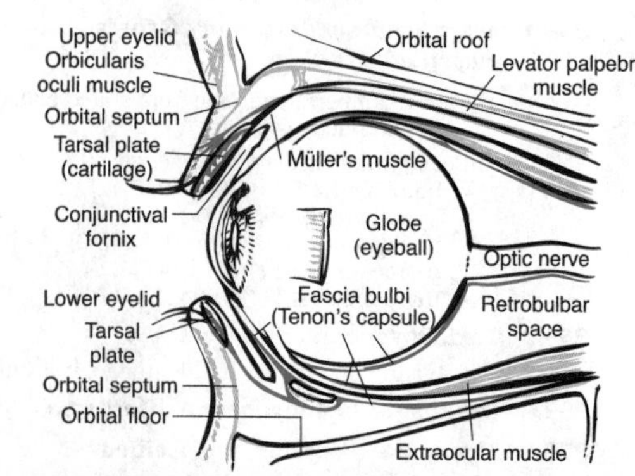

360.44 Leucocoria
DEF: Whitish mass or reflex in the pupil behind lens; also called cat's eye reflex; often indicative of retinoblastoma.

✓5th **360.5 Retained (old) intraocular foreign body, magnetic**
EXCLUDES *current penetrating injury with magnetic foreign body (871.5)*
retained (old) foreign body of orbit (376.6)

360.50 Foreign body, magnetic, intraocular, unspecified

360.51 Foreign body, magnetic, in anterior chamber

360.52 Foreign body, magnetic, in iris or ciliary body

360.53 Foreign body, magnetic, in lens

360.54 Foreign body, magnetic, in vitreous

360.55 Foreign body, magnetic, in posterior wall

360.59 Foreign body, magnetic, in other or multiple sites

✓5th **360.6 Retained (old) intraocular foreign body, nonmagnetic**
Retained (old) foreign body:
NOS
nonmagnetic
EXCLUDES *current penetrating injury with (nonmagnetic) foreign body (871.6)*
retained (old) foreign body in orbit (376.6)

360.60 Foreign body, intraocular, unspecified

360.61 Foreign body in anterior chamber

360.62 Foreign body in iris or ciliary body

360.63 Foreign body in lens

360.64 Foreign body in vitreous

360.65 Foreign body in posterior wall

360.69 Foreign body in other or multiple sites

✓5th **360.8 Other disorders of globe**

360.81 Luxation of globe
DEF: Displacement of eyeball.

360.89 Other

360.9 Unspecified disorder of globe

✓4th **361 Retinal detachments and defects**
DEF: Light-sensitive layer at back of eye, separates from blood supply; disrupting vision.

✓5th **361.0 Retinal detachment with retinal defect**
Rhegmatogenous retinal detachment
EXCLUDES *detachment of retinal pigment epithelium (362.42-362.43)*
retinal detachment (serous) (without defect) (361.2)

361.00 Retinal detachment with retinal defect, unspecified

361.01 Recent detachment, partial, with single defect

361.02 Recent detachment, partial, with multiple defects

361.03 Recent detachment, partial, with giant tear

361.04 Recent detachment, partial, with retinal dialysis
Dialysis (juvenile) of retina (with detachment)

361.05 Recent detachment, total or subtotal

361.06 Old detachment, partial
Delimited old retinal detachment

361.07 Old detachment, total or subtotal

✓5th **361.1 Retinoschisis and retinal cysts**
EXCLUDES *juvenile retinoschisis (362.73)*
microcystoid degeneration of retina (362.62)
parasitic cyst of retina (360.13)

361.10 Retinoschisis, unspecified
DEF: Separation of retina due to degenerative process of aging; should not be confused with acute retinal detachment.

361.11 Flat retinoschisis
DEF: Slow, progressive split of retinal sensory layers

361.12 Bullous retinoschisis
DEF: Fluid retention between split retinal sensory layers.

361.13 Primary retinal cysts

361.14 Secondary retinal cysts

361.19 Other
Pseudocyst of retina

361.2 Serous retinal detachment
Retinal detachment without retinal defect
EXCLUDES *central serous retinopathy (362.41)*
retinal pigment epithelium detachment (362.42-362.43)

✓5th **361.3 Retinal defects without detachment**
EXCLUDES *chorioretinal scars after surgery for detachment (363.30-363.35)*
peripheral retinal degeneration without defect (362.60-362.66)

361.30 Retinal defect, unspecified
Retinal break(s) NOS

361.31 Round hole of retina without detachment

361.32 Horseshoe tear of retina without detachment
Operculum of retina without mention of detachment

361.33 Multiple defects of retina without detachment

✓5th **361.8 Other forms of retinal detachment**

361.81 Traction detachment of retina
Traction detachment with vitreoretinal organization

361.89 Other

361.9 Unspecified retinal detachment

✓4th **362 Other retinal disorders**
EXCLUDES *chorioretinal scars (363.30-363.35)*
chorioretinitis (363.0-363.2)

✓5th **362.0 Diabetic retinopathy**
Code first diabetes (249.5, 250.5)
DEF: Retinal changes in diabetes of long duration; causes hemorrhages, microaneurysms, waxy deposits and proliferative noninflammatory degenerative disease of retina.

362.01 Background diabetic retinopathy
Diabetic retinal microaneurysms
Diabetic retinopathy NOS

362.02 Proliferative diabetic retinopathy
DEF: Occurrence of the ischemic effects of vessel blockages result in neovascularization; new blood vessels begin to form to compensate for restricted blood flow; multiple areas of the retina and inner vitreous may be affected.

362.03 Nonproliferative diabetic retinopathy NOS

362.04 Mild nonproliferative diabetic retinopathy
DEF: Early stages of degenerative condition of the retina due to diabetes; microaneurysm formation; small balloon-like swelling of the retinal vessels.

362.05 ***Moderate nonproliferative diabetic retinopathy***
DEF: Stage of degenerative condition of the retina due to diabetes with pronounced microaneurysms; vessel blockages can occur.

362.06 ***Severe nonproliferative diabetic retinopathy***
DEF: Stage of degenerative condition of the retina due to diabetes in which vascular breakdown in the retina results in multiple vascular blockages, or "beadings," intraretinal hemorrhages can be numerous.

362.07 ***Diabetic macular edema***
Note: Code 362.07 must be used with a code for diabetic retinopathy (362.01-362.06)
Diabetic retinal edema
DEF: Leakage from retinal blood vessels causes swelling of the macula and impaired vision; exudates or plaques may develop in the posterior pole of the retina due to the breakdown of retinal vasculature.

✓5th **362.1 Other background retinopathy and retinal vascular changes**

362.10 Background retinopathy, unspecified

362.11 Hypertensive retinopathy
DEF: Retinal irregularities caused by systemic hypertension.

362.12 Exudative retinopathy
Coats' syndrome

362.13 Changes in vascular appearance
Vascular sheathing of retina
Use additional code for any associated atherosclerosis (440.8)

362.14 Retinal microaneurysms NOS
DEF: Microscopic dilation of retinal vessels in nondiabetic.

362.15 Retinal telangiectasia
DEF:Dilation of blood vessels of the retina.

362.16 Retinal neovascularization NOS
Neovascularization:
- choroidal
- subretinal

DEF: New and abnormal vascular growth in the retina.

362.17 Other intraretinal microvascular abnormalities
Retinal sclerosis
Retinal varices

362.18 Retinal vasculitis
Eales' disease
Retinal:
- arteritis
- endarteritis
- perivasculitis
- phlebitis

DEF: Inflammation of retinal blood vessels.

✓5th **362.2 Other proliferative retinopathy**

362.20 Retinopathy of prematurity, unspecified
Retinopathy of prematurity NOS

362.21 Retrolental fibroplasia
Cicatricial retinopathy of prematurity
DEF: Fibrous tissue in vitreous, from retina to lens, causing blindness; associated with premature infants requiring high amounts of oxygen.

362.22 Retinopathy of prematurity, stage 0

362.23 Retinopathy of prematurity, stage 1

362.24 Retinopathy of prematurity, stage 2

362.25 Retinopathy of prematurity, stage 3

362.26 Retinopathy of prematurity, stage 4

362.27 Retinopathy of prematurity, stage 5

362.29 Other nondiabetic proliferative retinopathy

✓5th **362.3 Retinal vascular occlusion**
DEF: Obstructed blood flow to and from retina.

362.30 Retinal vascular occlusion, unspecified

362.31 Central retinal artery occlusion

362.32 Arterial branch occlusion

362.33 Partial arterial occlusion
Hollenhorst plaque
Retinal microembolism

362.34 Transient arterial occlusion
Amaurosis fugax

362.35 Central retinal vein occlusion

362.36 Venous tributary (branch) occlusion

362.37 Venous engorgement
Occlusion:
- incipient } of retinal vein
- partial } of retinal vein

✓5th **362.4 Separation of retinal layers**
EXCLUDES *retinal detachment (serous) (361.2)*
rhegmatogenous (361.00-361.07)

362.40 Retinal layer separation, unspecified

362.41 Central serous retinopathy
DEF: Serous-filled blister causing detachment of retina from pigment epithelium.

362.42 Serous detachment of retinal pigment epithelium
Exudative detachment of retinal pigment epithelium
DEF: Blister of fatty fluid causing detachment of retina from pigment epithelium.

362.43 Hemorrhagic detachment of retinal pigment epithelium
DEF: Blood-filled blister causing detachment of retina from pigment epithelium.

✓5th **362.5 Degeneration of macula and posterior pole**
EXCLUDES *degeneration of optic disc (377.21-377.24)*
hereditary retinal degeneration [dystrophy] (362.70-362.77)

362.50 Macular degeneration (senile), unspecified

362.51 Nonexudative senile macular degeneration
Senile macular degeneration:
- atrophic
- dry

362.52 Exudative senile macular degeneration
Kuhnt-Junius degeneration
Senile macular degeneration:
- disciform
- wet

DEF: Leakage in macular blood vessels with loss of visual acuity.

362.53 Cystoid macular degeneration
Cystoid macular edema
DEF: Retinal swelling and cyst formation in macula.

362.54 Macular cyst, hole, or pseudohole

362.55 Toxic maculopathy
Use additional E code to identify drug, if drug induced

362.56 Macular puckering
Preretinal fibrosis

362.57 Drusen (degenerative)
DEF: White, hyaline deposits on Bruch's membrane (lamina basalis choroideae).

✓5th **362.6 Peripheral retinal degenerations**
EXCLUDES *hereditary retinal degeneration [dystrophy] (362.70-362.77)*
retinal degeneration with retinal defect (361.00-361.07)

362.60 Peripheral retinal degeneration, unspecified

362.61 Paving stone degeneration
DEF: Degeneration of peripheral retina; causes thinning through which choroid is visible.

362.62 Microcystoid degeneration
Blessig's cysts
Iwanoff's cysts

362.63 Lattice degeneration
Palisade degeneration of retina
DEF: Degeneration of retina; often bilateral, usually benign; characterized by lines intersecting at irregular intervals in peripheral retina; retinal thinning and retinal holes may occur.

362.64 Senile reticular degeneration
DEF: Net-like appearance of retina; sign of degeneration.

362.65 Secondary pigmentary degeneration
Pseudoretinitis pigmentosa

362.66 Secondary vitreoretinal degenerations

✓5th **362.7 Hereditary retinal dystrophies**
DEF: Genetically induced progressive changes in retina.

362.70 Hereditary retinal dystrophy, unspecified

362.71 Retinal dystrophy in systemic or cerebroretinal lipidoses
Code first underlying disease, as:
cerebroretinal lipidoses (330.1)
systemic lipidoses (272.7)

362.72 Retinal dystrophy in other systemic disorders and syndromes
Code first underlying disease, as:
Bassen-Kornzweig syndrome (272.5)
Refsum's disease (356.3)

362.73 Vitreoretinal dystrophies
Juvenile retinoschisis

362.74 Pigmentary retinal dystrophy
Retinal dystrophy, albipunctate
Retinitis pigmentosa

362.75 Other dystrophies primarily involving the sensory retina
Progressive cone(-rod) dystrophy
Stargardt's disease

362.76 Dystrophies primarily involving the retinal pigment epithelium
Fundus flavimaculatus
Vitelliform dystrophy

362.77 Dystrophies primarily involving Bruch's membrane
Dystrophy:
hyaline
pseudoinflammatory foveal
Hereditary drusen

✓5th **362.8 Other retinal disorders**
EXCLUDES *chorioretinal inflammations (363.0-363.2)*
chorioretinal scars (363.30-363.35)

362.81 Retinal hemorrhage
Hemorrhage:
preretinal
retinal (deep) (superficial)
subretinal

362.82 Retinal exudates and deposits

362.83 Retinal edema
Retinal:
cotton wool spots
edema (localized) (macular) (peripheral)
DEF: Retinal swelling due to fluid accumulation.

362.84 Retinal ischemia
DEF: Reduced retinal blood supply.

362.85 Retinal nerve fiber bundle defects

362.89 Other retinal disorders

362.9 Unspecified retinal disorder

✓4th **363 Chorioretinal inflammations, scars, and other disorders of choroid**

✓5th **363.0 Focal chorioretinitis and focal retinochoroiditis**
EXCLUDES *focal chorioretinitis or retinochoroiditis in:*
histoplasmosis (115.02, 115.12, 115.92)
toxoplasmosis (130.2)
congenital infection (771.2)

363.00 Focal chorioretinitis, unspecified
Focal:
choroiditis or chorioretinitis NOS
retinitis or retinochoroiditis NOS

363.01 Focal choroiditis and chorioretinitis, juxtapapillary

363.03 Focal choroiditis and chorioretinitis of other posterior pole

363.04 Focal choroiditis and chorioretinitis, peripheral

363.05 Focal retinitis and retinochoroiditis, juxtapapillary
Neuroretinitis

363.06 Focal retinitis and retinochoroiditis, macular or paramacular

363.07 Focal retinitis and retinochoroiditis of other posterior pole

363.08 Focal retinitis and retinochoroiditis, peripheral

✓5th **363.1 Disseminated chorioretinitis and disseminated retinochoroiditis**
EXCLUDES *disseminated choroiditis or chorioretinitis in secondary syphilis (091.51)*
neurosyphilitic disseminated retinitis or retinochoroiditis (094.83)
retinal (peri)vasculitis (362.18)

363.10 Disseminated chorioretinitis, unspecified
Disseminated:
choroiditis or chorioretinitis NOS
retinitis or retinochoroiditis NOS

363.11 Disseminated choroiditis and chorioretinitis, posterior pole

363.12 Disseminated choroiditis and chorioretinitis, peripheral

363.13 Disseminated choroiditis and chorioretinitis, generalized
Code first any underlying disease, as:
tuberculosis (017.3)

363.14 Disseminated retinitis and retinochoroiditis, metastatic

363.15 Disseminated retinitis and retinochoroiditis, pigment epitheliopathy
Acute posterior multifocal placoid pigment epitheliopathy
DEF: Widespread inflammation of retina and choroid; characterized by pigmented epithelium involvement.

✓5th **363.2 Other and unspecified forms of chorioretinitis and retinochoroiditis**
EXCLUDES *panophthalmitis (360.02)*
sympathetic uveitis (360.11)
uveitis NOS (364.3)

363.20 Chorioretinitis, unspecified
Choroiditis NOS
Retinitis NOS
Uveitis, posterior NOS

363.21 Pars planitis
Posterior cyclitis
DEF: Inflammation of peripheral retina and ciliary body; characterized by bands of white cells.

363.22 Harada's disease
DEF: Retinal detachment and bilateral widespread exudative choroiditis; symptoms include headache, vomiting, increased lymphocytes in cerebrospinal fluid; and temporary or permanent deafness may occur.

✓5th **363.3 Chorioretinal scars**
Scar (postinflammatory) (postsurgical) (posttraumatic):
choroid
retina

363.30 Chorioretinal scar, unspecified

363.31 Solar retinopathy
DEF: Retinal scarring caused by solar radiation.

363.32 Other macular scars

363.33 Other scars of posterior pole

363.34 Peripheral scars

363.35 Disseminated scars

✓5th **363.4 Choroidal degenerations**

363.40 Choroidal degeneration, unspecified
Choroidal sclerosis NOS

363.41 Senile atrophy of choroid
DEF: Wasting away of choroid; due to aging.

363.42 Diffuse secondary atrophy of choroid
DEF: Wasting away of choroid in systemic disease.

363.43 Angioid streaks of choroid
DEF: Degeneration of choroid; characterized by dark brown steaks radiating from optic disk; occurs with pseudoxanthoma, elasticum or Paget's disease.

✓5th **363.5 Hereditary choroidal dystrophies**
Hereditary choroidal atrophy:
partial [choriocapillaris]
total [all vessels]

363.50 Hereditary choroidal dystrophy or atrophy, unspecified

363.51 Circumpapillary dystrophy of choroid, partial

363.52 Circumpapillary dystrophy of choroid, total
Helicoid dystrophy of choroid

363.53 Central dystrophy of choroid, partial
Dystrophy, choroidal:
central areolar
circinate

363.54 Central choroidal atrophy, total
Dystrophy, choroidal:
central gyrate
serpiginous

363.55 Choroideremia
DEF: Hereditary choroid degeneration, occurs in first decade; characterized by constricted visual field and ultimately blindness in males; less debilitating in females.

363.56 Other diffuse or generalized dystrophy, partial
Diffuse choroidal sclerosis

363.57 Other diffuse or generalized dystrophy, total
Generalized gyrate atrophy, choroid

✓5th **363.6 Choroidal hemorrhage and rupture**

363.61 Choroidal hemorrhage, unspecified

363.62 Expulsive choroidal hemorrhage

363.63 Choroidal rupture

✓5th **363.7 Choroidal detachment**

363.70 Choroidal detachment, unspecified

363.71 Serous choroidal detachment
DEF: Detachment of choroid from sclera; due to blister of serous fluid.

363.72 Hemorrhagic choroidal detachment
DEF: Detachment of choroid from sclera; due to blood-filled blister.

363.8 Other disorders of choroid

363.9 Unspecified disorder of choroid

✓4th **364 Disorders of iris and ciliary body**

✓5th **364.0 Acute and subacute iridocyclitis**
Anterior uveitis, Cylitis, Iridocyclitis, Iritis } acute, subacute

EXCLUDES *gonococcal (098.41)*
herpes simplex (054.44)
herpes zoster (053.22)

364.00 Acute and subacute iridocyclitis, unspecified

364.01 Primary iridocyclitis

364.02 Recurrent iridocyclitis

364.03 Secondary iridocyclitis, infectious

364.04 Secondary iridocyclitis, noninfectious
Aqueous:
cells
fibrin
flare

364.05 Hypopyon
DEF: Accumulation of white blood cells between cornea and lens.

✓5th **364.1 Chronic iridocyclitis**
EXCLUDES *posterior cyclitis (363.21)*

364.10 Chronic iridocyclitis, unspecified

364.11 Chronic iridocyclitis in diseases classified elsewhere
Code first underlying disease, as:
sarcoidosis (135)
tuberculosis (017.3)
EXCLUDES *syphilitic iridocyclitis (091.52)*
DEF: Persistent inflammation of iris and ciliary body; due to underlying disease or condition.

✓5th **364.2 Certain types of iridocyclitis**
EXCLUDES *posterior cyclitis (363.21)*
sympathetic uveitis (360.11)

364.21 Fuchs' heterochromic cyclitis
DEF: Chronic cyclitis characterized by differences in the color of the two irises; the lighter iris appears in the inflamed eye.

364.22 Glaucomatocyclitic crises
DEF: One-sided form of secondary open angle glaucoma; recurrent, uncommon and of short duration; causes high intraocular pressure, rarely damage.

364.23 Lens-induced iridocyclitis
DEF: Inflammation of iris; due to immune reaction to proteins in lens following trauma or other lens abnormality.

364.24 Vogt-Koyanagi syndrome
DEF: Uveomeningitis with exudative iridocyclitis and choroiditis; causes depigmentation of hair and skin, detached retina; tinnitus and loss of hearing may occur.

364.3 Unspecified iridocyclitis
Uveitis NOS

✓5th **364.4 Vascular disorders of iris and ciliary body**

364.41 Hyphema
Hemorrhage of iris or ciliary body
DEF: Hemorrhage in anterior chamber; also called hyphemia or "blood shot" eyes.

364.42 Rubeosis iridis
Neovascularization of iris or ciliary body
DEF: Blood vessel and connective tissue formation on surface of iris; symptomatic of diabetic retinopathy, central retinal vein occlusion and retinal detachment.

✓5th **364.5 Degenerations of iris and ciliary body**

364.51 Essential or progressive iris atrophy

364.52 Iridoschisis

DEF: Splitting of the iris into two layers.

364.53 Pigmentary iris degeneration

Acquired heterochromia } of iris
Pigment dispersion syndrome } of iris
Translucency } of iris

364.54 Degeneration of pupillary margin

Atrophy of sphincter } of iris
Ectropion of pigment epithelium } of iris

364.55 Miotic cysts of pupillary margin

DEF: Serous-filled sacs in pupillary margin of iris.

364.56 Degenerative changes of chamber angle

364.57 Degenerative changes of ciliary body

364.59 Other iris atrophy

Iris atrophy (generalized) (sector shaped)

✓5th **364.6 Cysts of iris, ciliary body, and anterior chamber**

EXCLUDES *miotic pupillary cyst (364.55)*
parasitic cyst (360.13)

364.60 Idiopathic cysts

DEF: Fluid-filled sacs in iris or ciliary body; unknown etiology.

364.61 Implantation cysts

Epithelial down-growth, anterior chamber
Implantation cysts (surgical) (traumatic)

364.62 Exudative cysts of iris or anterior chamber

364.63 Primary cyst of pars plana

DEF: Fluid-filled sacs of outermost ciliary ring.

364.64 Exudative cyst of pars plana

DEF: Protein, fatty-filled sacs of outermost ciliary ring; due to fluid lead from blood vessels.

✓5th **364.7 Adhesions and disruptions of iris and ciliary body**

EXCLUDES *flat anterior chamber (360.34)*

364.70 Adhesions of iris, unspecified

Synechiae (iris) NOS

364.71 Posterior synechiae

DEF: Adhesion binding iris to lens.

364.72 Anterior synechiae

DEF: Adhesion binding the iris to cornea.

364.73 Goniosynechiae

Peripheral anterior synechiae

DEF: Adhesion binding the iris to cornea at the angle of the anterior chamber.

364.74 Pupillary membranes

Iris bombé
Pupillary:
occlusion
Pupillary:
seclusion

DEF: Membrane traversing the pupil and blocking vision.

364.75 Pupillary abnormalities

Deformed pupil
Ectopic pupil
Rupture of sphincter, pupil

364.76 Iridodialysis

DEF: Separation of the iris from the ciliary body base; due to trauma or surgical accident.

364.77 Recession of chamber angle

DEF: Receding of anterior chamber angle of the eye; restricts vision.

✓5th **364.8 Other disorders of iris and ciliary body**

364.81 Floppy iris syndrome

Intraoperative floppy iris syndrome [IFIS]

Use additional E code to identify cause, such as:
sympatholytics [antiadrenergics] causing adverse effect in therapeutic use (E941.3)

DEF: Condition complicating cataract surgery for patients who have received alpha blocker treatment for urinary retention problems; iris dilator muscle fails to dilate, and the iris may billow or flap.

364.82 Plateau iris syndrome

364.89 Other disorders of iris and ciliary body

Prolapse of iris NOS

EXCLUDES *prolapse of iris in recent wound (871.1)*

364.9 Unspecified disorder of iris and ciliary body

✓4th **365 Glaucoma**

EXCLUDES *blind hypertensive eye [absolute glaucoma] (360.42)*
congenital glaucoma (743.20-743.22)

DEF: Rise in intraocular pressure restricting blood flow; multiple causes.

✓5th **365.0 Borderline glaucoma [glaucoma suspect]**

365.00 Preglaucoma, unspecified

365.01 Open angle with borderline findings

Open angle with:
borderline intraocular pressure
cupping of optic discs

DEF: Minor block of aqueous outflow from eye.

365.02 Anatomical narrow angle

365.03 Steroid responders

365.04 Ocular hypertension

DEF: High fluid pressure within eye; no apparent cause.

✓5th **365.1 Open-angle glaucoma**

365.10 Open-angle glaucoma, unspecified

Wide-angle glaucoma NOS

365.11 Primary open angle glaucoma

Chronic simple glaucoma

DEF: High intraocular pressure, despite free flow of aqueous.

365.12 Low tension glaucoma

365.13 Pigmentary glaucoma

DEF: High intraocular pressure; due to iris pigment granules blocking aqueous flow.

365.14 Glaucoma of childhood

Infantile or juvenile glaucoma

365.15 Residual stage of open angle glaucoma

✓5th **365.2 Primary angle-closure glaucoma**

365.20 Primary angle-closure glaucoma, unspecified

365.21 Intermittent angle-closure glaucoma

Angle-closure glaucoma:
interval
subacute

DEF: Recurring attacks of high intraocular pressure; due to blocked aqueous flow.

365.22 Acute angle-closure glaucoma

DEF: Sudden, severe rise in intraocular pressure due to blockage in aqueous drainage.

365.23 Chronic angle-closure glaucoma

365.24 Residual stage of angle-closure glaucoma

✓5th **365.3 Corticosteroid-induced glaucoma**

DEF: Elevated intraocular pressure; due to long-term corticosteroid therapy.

365.31 Glaucomatous stage

365.32 Residual stage

✓5th **365.4 Glaucoma associated with congenital anomalies, dystrophies, and systemic syndromes**

365.41 Glaucoma associated with chamber angle anomalies

365.42 Glaucoma associated with anomalies of iris

365.43 Glaucoma associated with other anterior segment anomalies

365.44 Glaucoma associated with systemic syndromes

Code first associated disease, as
neurofibromatosis (237.7)
Sturge-Weber (-Dimitri) syndrome (759.6)

✓5th **365.5 Glaucoma associated with disorders of the lens**

365.51 Phacolytic glaucoma

DEF: Elevated intraocular pressure; due to lens protein blocking aqueous flow.

365.52 Pseudoexfoliation glaucoma

DEF: Glaucoma characterized by small grayish particles deposited on the lens.

365.59 Glaucoma associated with other lens disorders

✓5th **365.6 Glaucoma associated with other ocular disorders**

365.60 Glaucoma associated with unspecified ocular disorder

365.61 Glaucoma associated with pupillary block

DEF: Acute, open-angle glaucoma caused by mature cataract; aqueous flow is blocked by lens material and macrophages.

365.62 Glaucoma associated with ocular inflammations

365.63 Glaucoma associated with vascular disorders

365.64 Glaucoma associated with tumors or cysts

365.65 Glaucoma associated with ocular trauma

✓5th **365.8 Other specified forms of glaucoma**

365.81 Hypersecretion glaucoma

365.82 Glaucoma with increased episcleral venous pressure

365.83 Aqueous misdirection

Malignant glaucoma

DEF: A form of glaucoma that occurs when aqueous humor flows into the posterior chamber of the eye (vitreous) rather than through the normal recycling channels into the anterior chamber.

365.89 Other specified glaucoma

365.9 Unspecified glaucoma

Aqueus Misdirection Syndrome

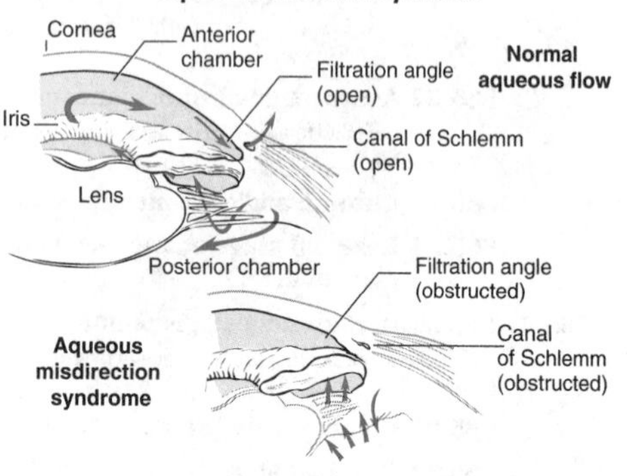

✓4th **366 Cataract**

EXCLUDES *congenital cataract (743.30-743.34)*

DEF: A variety of conditions that create a cloudy, or calcified lens that obstructs vision.

✓5th **366.0 Infantile, juvenile, and presenile cataract**

366.00 Nonsenile cataract, unspecified

366.01 Anterior subcapsular polar cataract

DEF: Defect within the front, center lens surface.

366.02 Posterior subcapsular polar cataract

DEF: Defect within the rear, center lens surface.

366.03 Cortical, lamellar, or zonular cataract

DEF: Opacities radiating from center to edge of lens; appear as thin, concentric layers of lens.

366.04 Nuclear cataract

366.09 Other and combined forms of nonsenile cataract

✓5th **366.1 Senile cataract**

366.10 Senile cataract, unspecified

366.11 Pseudoexfoliation of lens capsule

366.12 Incipient cataract

Cataract:
- coronary
- immature NOS
- punctate

Water clefts

DEF: Minor disorders of lens not affecting vision; due to aging.

366.13 Anterior subcapsular polar senile cataract

366.14 Posterior subcapsular polar senile cataract

366.15 Cortical senile cataract

366.16 Nuclear sclerosis

Cataracta brunescens
Nuclear cataract

366.17 Total or mature cataract

366.18 Hypermature cataract

Morgagni cataract

366.19 Other and combined forms of senile cataract

✓5th **366.2 Traumatic cataract**

366.20 Traumatic cataract, unspecified

366.21 Localized traumatic opacities

Vossius' ring

366.22 Total traumatic cataract

366.23 Partially resolved traumatic cataract

✓5th **366.3 Cataract secondary to ocular disorders**

366.30 Cataracta complicata, unspecified

366.31 Glaucomatous flecks (subcapsular)

Code first underlying glaucoma (365.0-365.9)

Cataract

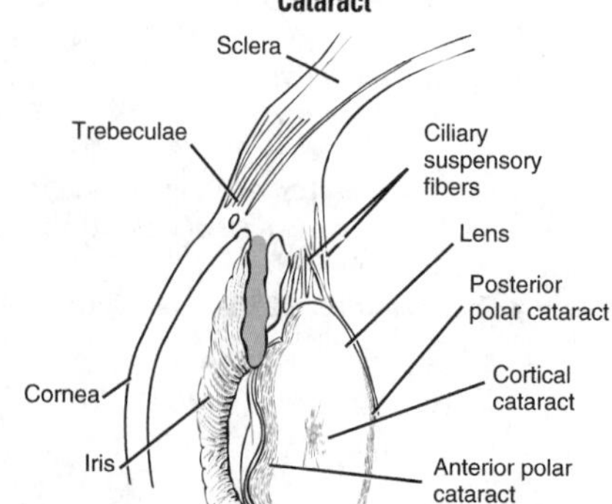

366.32 Cataract in inflammatory disorders
Code first underlying condition, as:
chronic choroiditis (363.0-363.2)

366.33 Cataract with neovascularization
Code first underlying condition, as:
chronic iridocyclitis (364.10)

366.34 Cataract in degenerative disorders
Sunflower cataract
Code first underlying condition, as:
chalcosis (360.24)
degenerative myopia (360.21)
pigmentary retinal dystrophy (362.74)

✓5th **366.4 Cataract associated with other disorders**

366.41 Diabetic cataract
Code first diabetes (249.5, 250.5)

366.42 Tetanic cataract
Code first underlying disease, as:
calcinosis (275.4)
hypoparathyroidism (252.1)

366.43 Myotonic cataract
Code first underlying disorder (359.21, 359.23)

366.44 Cataract associated with other syndromes
Code first underlying condition, as:
craniofacial dysostosis (756.0)
galactosemia (271.1)

366.45 Toxic cataract
Drug-induced cataract
Use additional E code to identify drug or other toxic substance

366.46 Cataract associated with radiation and other physical influences
Use additional E code to identify cause

✓5th **366.5 After-cataract**

366.50 After-cataract, unspecified
Secondary cataract NOS

366.51 Soemmering's ring
DEF: A donut-shaped lens remnant and a capsule behind the pupil as a result of cataract surgery or trauma.

366.52 Other after-cataract, not obscuring vision

366.53 After-cataract, obscuring vision

366.8 Other cataract
Calcification of lens

366.9 Unspecified cataract

✓4th **367 Disorders of refraction and accommodation**

367.0 Hypermetropia
Far-sightedness
Hyperopia
DEF: Refraction error, called also hyperopia, focal point is posterior to retina; abnormally short anteroposterior diameter or subnormal refractive power; causes farsightedness.

367.1 Myopia
Near-sightedness
DEF: Refraction error, focal point is anterior to retina; causes near-sightedness.

✓5th **367.2 Astigmatism**

367.20 Astigmatism, unspecified

367.21 Regular astigmatism

367.22 Irregular astigmatism

✓5th **367.3 Anisometropia and aniseikonia**

367.31 Anisometropia
DEF: Eyes with refractive powers that differ by at least one diopter.

367.32 Aniseikonia
DEF: Eyes with unequal retinal imaging; usually due to refractive error.

367.4 Presbyopia
DEF: Loss of crystalline lens elasticity; causes errors of accommodation; due to aging.

✓5th **367.5 Disorders of accommodation**

367.51 Paresis of accommodation
Cycloplegia
DEF: Partial paralysis of ciliary muscle; causing focus problems.

367.52 Total or complete internal ophthalmoplegia
DEF: Total paralysis of ciliary muscle; large pupil incapable of focus.

367.53 Spasm of accommodation
DEF: Abnormal contraction of ciliary muscle; causes focus problems.

✓5th **367.8 Other disorders of refraction and accommodation**

367.81 Transient refractive change

367.89 Other
Drug-induced } disorders of refraction and accommodation
Toxic }

367.9 Unspecified disorder of refraction and accommodation

✓4th **368 Visual disturbances**
EXCLUDES *electrophysiological disturbances (794.11-794.14)*

✓5th **368.0 Amblyopia ex anopsia**
DEF: Vision impaired due to disuse; esotropia often cause.

368.00 Amblyopia, unspecified

368.01 Strabismic amblyopia
Suppression amblyopia

368.02 Deprivation amblyopia
DEF: Decreased vision associated with suppressed retinal image of one eye.

368.03 Refractive amblyopia

✓5th **368.1 Subjective visual disturbances**

368.10 Subjective visual disturbance, unspecified

368.11 Sudden visual loss

368.12 Transient visual loss
Concentric fading
Scintillating scotoma

368.13 Visual discomfort
Asthenopia
Eye strain
Photophobia

368.14 Visual distortions of shape and size
Macropsia
Metamorphopsia
Micropsia

368.15 Other visual distortions and entoptic phenomena
Photopsia
Refractive:
diplopia
polyopia
Visual halos

368.16 Psychophysical visual disturbances
Prosopagnosia
Visual:
agnosia
disorientation syndrome
hallucinations
object agnosia

368.2 Diplopia
Double vision

✓5th **368.3 Other disorders of binocular vision**

368.30 Binocular vision disorder, unspecified

368.31 Suppression of binocular vision

368.32 Simultaneous visual perception without fusion

368.33 Fusion with defective stereopsis
DEF: Faulty depth perception though normal ability to focus.

368.34 Abnormal retinal correspondence

✓5th **368.4 Visual field defects**

368.40 Visual field defect, unspecified

368.41 Scotoma involving central area
Scotoma:
central
centrocecal
paracentral
DEF: Vision loss (blind spot) in central five degrees of visual field.

368.42 Scotoma of blind spot area
Enlarged:
angioscotoma
blind spot
Paracecal scotoma

368.43 Sector or arcuate defects
Scotoma:
arcuate
Bjerrum
Seidel
DEF: Arc-shaped blind spot caused by retinal nerve damage.

368.44 Other localized visual field defect
Scotoma:
NOS
ring
Visual field defect:
nasal step
peripheral

368.45 Generalized contraction or constriction

368.46 Homonymous bilateral field defects
Hemianopsia (altitudinal) (homonymous)
Quadrant anopia
DEF: Disorders found in the corresponding vertical halves of the visual fields of both eyes.

368.47 Heteronymous bilateral field defects
Hemianopsia:
binasal
bitemporal
DEF: Disorders in the opposite halves of the visual fields of both eyes.

✓5th **368.5 Color vision deficiencies**
Color blindness

368.51 Protan defect
Protanomaly
Protanopia
DEF: Mild difficulty distinguishing green and red hues with shortened spectrum; sex-linked affecting one percent of males.

368.52 Deutan defect
Deuteranomaly
Deuteranopia
DEF: Male-only disorder; difficulty in distinguishing green and red, no shortened spectrum.

368.53 Tritan defect
Tritanomaly
Tritanopia
DEF: Difficulty in distinguishing blue and yellow; occurs often due to drugs, retinal detachment and central nervous system diseases.

368.54 Achromatopsia
Monochromatism (cone) (rod)
DEF: Complete color blindness; caused by disease, injury to retina, optic nerve or pathway.

368.55 Acquired color vision deficiencies

368.59 Other color vision deficiencies

✓5th **368.6 Night blindness**
Nyctalopia
DEF: Nyctalopia: disorder of vision in dim light or night blindness.

368.60 Night blindness, unspecified

368.61 Congenital night blindness
Hereditary night blindness
Oguchi's disease

368.62 Acquired night blindness
EXCLUDES *that due to vitamin A deficiency (264.5)*

368.63 Abnormal dark adaptation curve
Abnormal threshold } of cones or rods
Delayed adaptation } of cones or rods

368.69 Other night blindness

368.8 Other specified visual disturbances
Blurred vision NOS

368.9 Unspecified visual disturbance

✓4th **369 Blindness and low vision**

Note: Visual impairment refers to a functional limitation of the eye (e.g., limited visual acuity or visual field). It should be distinguished from visual disability, indicating a limitation of the abilities of the individual (e.g., limited reading skills, vocational skills), and from visual handicap, indicating a limitation of personal and socioeconomic indepen- dence (e.g., limited mobility, limited employability).

The levels of impairment defined in the table on the next page are based on the recommendations of the WHO Study Group on Prevention of Blindness (Geneva, November 6-10, 1972; WHO Technical Report Series 518), and of the International Council of Ophthalmology (1976).

Note that definitions of blindness vary in different settings.

For international reporting WHO defines blindness as profound impairment. This definition can be applied to blindness of one eye (369.1, 369.6) and to blindness of the individual (369.0).

For determination of benefits in the U.S.A., the definition of legal blindness as severe impairment is often used. This definition applies to blindness of the individual only.

EXCLUDES *correctable impaired vision due to refractive errors (367.0-367.9)*

✓5th **369.0 Profound impairment, both eyes**

369.00 Impairment level not further specified
Blindness:
NOS according to WHO definition
both eyes

369.01 Better eye: total impairment; lesser eye: total impairment

369.02 Better eye: near-total impairment; lesser eye: not further specified

369.03 Better eye: near-total impairment; lesser eye: total impairment

369.04 Better eye: near-total impairment; lesser eye: near-total impairment

369.05 Better eye: profound impairment; lesser eye: not further specified

369.06 Better eye: profound impairment; lesser eye: total impairment

369.07 Better eye: profound impairment; lesser eye: near-total impairment

369.08 Better eye: profound impairment; lesser eye: profound impairment

✓4th **369.1 Moderate or severe impairment, better eye, profound impairment lesser eye**

369.10 Impairment level not further specified
Blindness, one eye, low vision other eye

369.11 Better eye: severe impairment; lesser eye: blind, not further specified

369.12 Better eye: severe impairment; lesser eye: total impairment

369.13 Better eye: severe impairment; lesser eye: near-total impairment

369.14 Better eye: severe impairment; lesser eye: profound impairment

369.15 Better eye: moderate impairment; lesser eye: blind, not further specified

369.16 Better eye: moderate impairment; lesser eye: total impairment

369.17 Better eye: moderate impairment; lesser eye: near-total impairment

369.18 Better eye: moderate impairment; lesser eye: profound impairment

✓5th **369.2 Moderate or severe impairment, both eyes**

369.20 Impairment level not further specified
Low vision, both eyes NOS

369.21 Better eye: severe impairment; lesser eye: not further specified

369.22 Better eye: severe impairment; lesser eye: severe impairment

369.23 Better eye: moderate impairment; lesser eye: not further specified

369.24 Better eye: moderate impairment; lesser eye: severe impairment

369.25 Better eye: moderate impairment; lesser eye: moderate impairment

369.3 Unqualified visual loss, both eyes
EXCLUDES *blindness NOS:*
legal [U.S.A. definition] (369.4)
WHO definition (369.00)

369.4 Legal blindness, as defined in U.S.A.
Blindness NOS according to U.S.A. definition
EXCLUDES *legal blindness with specification of impairment level (369.01-369.08, 369.11-369.14, 369.21-369.22)*

✓5th **369.6 Profound impairment, one eye**

369.60 Impairment level not further specified
Blindness, one eye

369.61 One eye: total impairment; other eye: not specified

369.62 One eye: total impairment; other eye: near normal vision

369.63 One eye: total impairment; other eye: normal vision

369.64 One eye: near-total impairment; other eye: not specified

369.65 One eye: near-total impairment; other eye: near-normal vision

369.66 One eye: near-total impairment; other eye: normal vision

369.67 One eye: profound impairment; other eye: not specified

369.68 One eye: profound impairment; other eye: near-normal vision

369.69 One eye: profound impairment; other eye: normal vision

✓5th **369.7 Moderate or severe impairment, one eye**

369.70 Impairment level not further specified
Low vision, one eye

369.71 One eye: severe impairment; other eye: not specified

369.72 One eye: severe impairment; other eye: near-normal vision

369.73 One eye: severe impairment; other eye: normal vision

369.74 One eye: moderate impairment; other eye: not specified

369.75 One eye: moderate impairment; other eye: near-normal vision

369.76 One eye: moderate impairment; other eye: normal vision

369.8 Unqualified visual loss, one eye

369.9 Unspecified visual loss

✓4th **370 Keratitis**

✓5th **370.0 Corneal ulcer**
EXCLUDES *that due to vitamin A deficiency (264.3)*

370.00 Corneal ulcer, unspecified

370.01 Marginal corneal ulcer

370.02 Ring corneal ulcer

370.03 Central corneal ulcer

370.04 Hypopyon ulcer
Serpiginous ulcer
DEF: Corneal ulcer with an accumulation of pus in the eye's anterior chamber.

370.05 Mycotic corneal ulcer
DEF: Fungal infection causing corneal tissue loss.

370.06 Perforated corneal ulcer
DEF: Tissue loss through all layers of cornea.

370.07 Mooren's ulcer
DEF: Tissue loss, with chronic inflammation, at junction of cornea and sclera; seen in elderly.

✓5th **370.2 Superficial keratitis without conjunctivitis**
EXCLUDES *dendritic [herpes simplex] keratitis (054.42)*

370.20 Superficial keratitis, unspecified

370.21 Punctate keratitis
Thygeson's superficial punctate keratitis
DEF: Formation of cellular and fibrinous deposits (keratic precipitates) on posterior surface; deposits develop after injury or iridocyclitis.

Classification: "legal"	Classification: WHO	LEVELS OF VISUAL IMPAIRMENT — Visual acuity and/or visual field limitation (whichever is worse)	Additional descriptors which may be encountered
	(NEAR-) NORMAL VISION	RANGE OF NORMAL VISION 20/10 20/13 20/16 20/20 20/25 2.0 1.6 1.25 1.0 0.8	
		NEAR-NORMAL VISION 20/30 20/40 20/50 20/60 0.7 0.6 0.5 0.4 0.3	
	LOW VISION	MODERATE VISUAL IMPAIRMENT 20/70 20/80 20/100 20/125 20/160 0.25 0.20 0.16 0.12	Moderate low vision
LEGAL BLINDNESS (U.S.A.) both eyes		SEVERE VISUAL IMPAIRMENT 20/200 20/250 20/320 20/400 0.10 0.08 0.06 0.05 Visual field: 20 degrees or less	Severe low vision, "Legal" blindness
	BLINDNESS (WHO) one or both eyes	PROFOUND VISUAL IMPAIRMENT 20/500 20/630 20/800 20/1000 0.04 0.03 0.025 0.02 Count fingers at: less than 3m (10 ft.) Visual field: 10 degrees or less	Profound low vision, Moderate blindness
		NEAR-TOTAL VISUAL IMPAIRMENT Visual acuity: less than 0.02 (20/1000) Count fingers at: 1m (3 ft.) or less Hand movements: 5m (15 ft.) or less Light projection, light perception Visual field: 5 degrees or less	Severe blindness; Near-total blindness
		TOTAL VISUAL IMPAIRMENT No light perception (NLP)	Total blindness

Visual acuity refers to best achievable acuity with correction.
Non-listed Snellen fractions may be classified by converting to the nearest decimal equivalent, e.g. 10/200 = 0.05, 6/30 = 0.20.
CF (count fingers) without designation of distance, may be classified to profound impairment.
HM (hand motion) without designation of distance, may be classified to near-total impairment.
Visual field measurements refer to the largest field diameter for a 1/100 white test object.

370.22 Macular keratitis
Keratitis: areolar, nummular
Keratitis: stellate, striate

370.23 Filamentary keratitis
DEF: Keratitis characterized by twisted filaments of mucoid material on the cornea's surface.

370.24 Photokeratitis
Snow blindness
Welders' keratitis
DEF: Painful, inflamed cornea; due to extended exposure to ultraviolet light.

✓5th **370.3 Certain types of keratoconjunctivitis**

370.31 Phlyctenular keratoconjunctivitis
Phlyctenulosis
Use additional code for any associated tuberculosis (017.3)
DEF: Miniature blister on conjunctiva or cornea; associated with tuberculosis and malnutrition disorders.

370.32 Limbar and corneal involvement in vernal conjunctivitis
Use additional code for vernal conjunctivitis (372.13)
DEF: Corneal itching and inflammation in conjunctivitis; often limited to lining of eyelids.

370.33 Keratoconjunctivitis sicca, not specified as Sjögren's
EXCLUDES *Sjögren's syndrome (710.2)*
DEF: Inflammation of conjunctiva and cornea; characterized by "horny" looking tissue and excess blood in these areas; decreased flow of lacrimal (tear) is a contributing factor.

370.34 Exposure keratoconjunctivitis
DEF: Incomplete closure of eyelid causing dry, inflamed eye.

370.35 Neurotrophic keratoconjunctivitis

✓5th **370.4 Other and unspecified keratoconjunctivitis**

370.40 Keratoconjunctivitis, unspecified
Superficial keratitis with conjunctivitis NOS

370.44 Keratitis or keratoconjunctivitis in exanthema
Code first underlying condition (050.0-052.9)
EXCLUDES *herpes simplex (054.43)*
herpes zoster (053.21)
measles (055.71)

370.49 Other
EXCLUDES *epidemic keratoconjunctivitis (077.1)*

✓5th **370.5 Interstitial and deep keratitis**

370.50 Interstitial keratitis, unspecified

370.52 Diffuse interstitial keratitis
Cogan's syndrome
DEF: Inflammation of cornea; with deposits in middle corneal layers; may obscure vision.

370.54 Sclerosing keratitis
DEF: Chronic corneal inflammation leading to opaque scarring.

370.55 Corneal abscess
DEF: Pocket of pus and inflammation on the cornea.

370.59 Other
EXCLUDES *disciform herpes simplex keratitis (054.43)*
syphilitic keratitis (090.3)

✓5th **370.6 Corneal neovascularization**

370.60 Corneal neovascularization, unspecified

370.61 Localized vascularization of cornea
DEF: Limited infiltration of cornea by new blood vessels.

370.62 Pannus (corneal)
DEF: Buildup of superficial vascularization and granulated tissue under epithelium of cornea.

370.63 Deep vascularization of cornea
DEF: Deep infiltration of cornea by new blood vessels.

370.64 Ghost vessels (corneal)

370.8 Other forms of keratitis
Code first underlying condition, such as:
Acanthamoeba (136.21)
Fusarium (118)

370.9 Unspecified keratitis

✓4th **371 Corneal opacity and other disorders of cornea**

✓5th **371.0 Corneal scars and opacities**
EXCLUDES *that due to vitamin A deficiency (264.6)*

371.00 Corneal opacity, unspecified
Corneal scar NOS

371.01 Minor opacity of cornea
Corneal nebula

371.02 Peripheral opacity of cornea
Corneal macula not interfering with central vision

371.03 Central opacity of cornea
Corneal:
leucoma, macula } interfering with central vision

371.04 Adherent leucoma
DEF: Dense, opaque corneal growth adhering to the iris; also spelled as leukoma.

371.05 Phthisical cornea
Code first underlying tuberculosis (017.3)

✓5th **371.1 Corneal pigmentations and deposits**

371.10 Corneal deposit, unspecified

371.11 Anterior pigmentations
Stähli's lines

371.12 Stromal pigmentations
Hematocornea

371.13 Posterior pigmentations
Krukenberg spindle

371.14 Kayser-Fleischer ring
DEF: Copper deposits forming ring at outer edge of cornea; seen in Wilson's disease and other liver disorders.

371.15 Other deposits associated with metabolic disorders

371.16 Argentous deposits
DEF: Silver deposits in cornea.

✓5th **371.2 Corneal edema**

371.20 Corneal edema, unspecified

371.21 Idiopathic corneal edema
DEF: Corneal swelling and fluid retention of unknown cause.

371.22 Secondary corneal edema
DEF: Corneal swelling and fluid retention caused by an underlying disease, injury, or condition.

371.23 Bullous keratopathy
DEF: Corneal degeneration; characterized by recurring, rupturing epithelial "blisters;" ruptured blebs expose corneal nerves, cause great pain; occurs in glaucoma, iridocyclitis and Fuchs' epithelial dystrophy.

371.24 Corneal edema due to wearing of contact lenses

✓5th **371.3 Changes of corneal membranes**

371.30 Corneal membrane change, unspecified

371.31 Folds and rupture of Bowman's membrane

371.32 Folds in Descemet's membrane

371.33 Rupture in Descemet's membrane

✓5th **371.4 Corneal degenerations**

371.40 Corneal degeneration, unspecified

371.41 Senile corneal changes
Arcus senilis
Hassall-Henle bodies

371.42 Recurrent erosion of cornea
EXCLUDES *Mooren's ulcer (370.07)*

371.43 Band-shaped keratopathy
DEF: Horizontal bands of superficial corneal calcium deposits.

371.44 Other calcerous degenerations of cornea

371.45 Keratomalacia NOS
EXCLUDES *that due to vitamin A deficiency (264.4)*
DEF: Destruction of the cornea by keratinization of the epithelium with ulceration and perforation of the cornea; seen in cases of vitamin A deficiency.

371.46 Nodular degeneration of cornea
Salzmann's nodular dystrophy

371.48 Peripheral degenerations of cornea
Marginal degeneration of cornea [Terrien's]

371.49 Other
Discrete colliquative keratopathy

✓5th **371.5 Hereditary corneal dystrophies**
DEF: Genetic disorder; leads to opacities, edema or lesions of cornea.

371.50 Corneal dystrophy, unspecified

371.51 Juvenile epithelial corneal dystrophy

371.52 Other anterior corneal dystrophies
Corneal dystrophy:
microscopic cystic
ring-like

371.53 Granular corneal dystrophy

371.54 Lattice corneal dystrophy

371.55 Macular corneal dystrophy

371.56 Other stromal corneal dystrophies
Crystalline corneal dystrophy

371.57 Endothelial corneal dystrophy
Combined corneal dystrophy
Cornea guttata
Fuchs' endothelial dystrophy

371.58 Other posterior corneal dystrophies
Polymorphous corneal dystrophy

✓5th **371.6 Keratoconus**
DEF: Bilateral bulging protrusion of anterior cornea; often due to noninflammatory thinning.

371.60 Keratoconus, unspecified

371.61 Keratoconus, stable condition

371.62 Keratoconus, acute hydrops

✓5th **371.7 Other corneal deformities**

371.70 Corneal deformity, unspecified

371.71 Corneal ectasia
DEF: Bulging protrusion of thinned, scarred cornea.

371.72 Descemetocele
DEF: Protrusion of Descemet's membrane into cornea.

371.73 Corneal staphyloma
DEF: Protrusion of cornea into adjacent tissue.

✓5th **371.8 Other corneal disorders**

371.81 Corneal anesthesia and hypoesthesia
DEF: Decreased or absent sensitivity of cornea.

371.82 Corneal disorder due to contact lens
EXCLUDES *corneal edema due to contact lens (371.24)*
DEF: Contact lens wear causing cornea disorder, excluding swelling.

371.89 Other

371.9 Unspecified corneal disorder

✓4th **372 Disorders of conjunctiva**
EXCLUDES *keratoconjunctivitis (370.3-370.4)*

✓5th **372.0 Acute conjunctivitis**

372.00 Acute conjunctivitis, unspecified

372.01 Serous conjunctivitis, except viral
EXCLUDES *viral conjunctivitis NOS (077.9)*

372.02 Acute follicular conjunctivitis
Conjunctival folliculosis NOS
EXCLUDES *conjunctivitis:*
adenoviral (acute follicular) (077.3)
epidemic hemorrhagic (077.4)
inclusion (077.0)
Newcastle (077.8)
epidemic keratoconjunctivitis (077.1)
pharyngoconjunctival fever (077.2)
DEF: Severe conjunctival inflammation with dense infiltrations of lymphoid tissues of inner eyelids; may be traced to a viral or chlamydial etiology.

372.03 Other mucopurulent conjunctivitis
Catarrhal conjunctivitis
EXCLUDES *blennorrhea neonatorum (gonococcal) (098.40)*
neonatal conjunctivitis(771.6)
ophthalmia neonatorum NOS (771.6)

372.04 Pseudomembranous conjunctivitis
Membranous conjunctivitis
EXCLUDES *diphtheritic conjunctivitis (032.81)*
DEF: Severe inflammation of conjunctiva; false membrane develops on inner surface of eyelid; membrane can be removed without harming epithelium, due to bacterial infections, toxic and allergic factors, and viral infections.

372.05 Acute atopic conjunctivitis
DEF: Sudden, severe conjunctivitis due to allergens.

✓5th **372.1 Chronic conjunctivitis**

372.10 Chronic conjunctivitis, unspecified

372.11 Simple chronic conjunctivitis

372.12 Chronic follicular conjunctivitis
DEF: Persistent conjunctival inflammation with dense, localized infiltrations of lymphoid tissues of inner eyelids.

372.13 Vernal conjunctivitis

372.14 Other chronic allergic conjunctivitis

372.15 Parasitic conjunctivitis
Code first underlying disease, as:
filariasis (125.0-125.9)
mucocutaneous leishmaniasis (085.5)

✓5th **372.2 Blepharoconjunctivitis**

372.20 Blepharoconjunctivitis, unspecified

372.21 Angular blepharoconjunctivitis
DEF: Inflammation at junction of upper and lower eyelids; may block lacrimal secretions.

372.22 Contact blepharoconjunctivitis

✓5th **372.3 Other and unspecified conjunctivitis**

372.30 Conjunctivitis, unspecified

372.31 Rosacea conjunctivitis
Code first underlying rosacea dermatitis (695.3)

372.33 Conjunctivitis in mucocutaneous disease
Code first underlying disease, as:
erythema multiforme (695.10-695.19)
Reiter's disease (099.3)
EXCLUDES *ocular pemphigoid (694.61)*

372.34 Pingueculitis

372.39 Other

✓5th **372.4 Pterygium**

EXCLUDES *pseudopterygium (372.52)*

DEF: Wedge-shaped, conjunctival thickening that advances from the inner corner of the eye toward the cornea.

372.40 Pterygium, unspecified

372.41 Peripheral pterygium, stationary

372.42 Peripheral pterygium, progressive

372.43 Central pterygium

372.44 Double pterygium

372.45 Recurrent pterygium

✓5th **372.5 Conjunctival degenerations and deposits**

372.50 Conjunctival degeneration, unspecified

372.51 Pinguecula

DEF: Proliferative spot on the bulbar conjunctiva located near the sclerocorneal junction, usually on the nasal side; it is seen in elderly people.

372.52 Pseudopterygium

DEF: Conjunctival scar joined to the cornea; it looks like a pterygium but is not attached to the tissue.

372.53 Conjunctival xerosis

EXCLUDES *conjunctival xerosis due to vitamin A deficiency (264.0, 264.1, 264.7)*

DEF: Dry conjunctiva due to vitamin A deficiency; related to Bitot's spots; may develop into xerophthalmia and keratomalacia.

372.54 Conjunctival concretions

DEF: Calculus or deposit on conjunctiva.

372.55 Conjunctival pigmentations

Conjunctival argyrosis

DEF: Color deposits in conjunctiva.

372.56 Conjunctival deposits

✓5th **372.6 Conjunctival scars**

372.61 Granuloma of conjunctiva

372.62 Localized adhesions and strands of conjunctiva

DEF: Abnormal fibrous connections in conjunctiva.

372.63 Symblepharon

Extensive adhesions of conjunctiva

DEF: Adhesion of the eyelids to the eyeball.

372.64 Scarring of conjunctiva

Contraction of eye socket (after enucleation)

✓5th **372.7 Conjunctival vascular disorders and cysts**

372.71 Hyperemia of conjunctiva

DEF: Conjunctival blood vessel congestion causing eye redness.

372.72 Conjunctival hemorrhage

Hyposphagma
Subconjunctival hemorrhage

372.73 Conjunctival edema

Chemosis of conjunctiva
Subconjunctival edema

DEF: Fluid retention and swelling in conjunctival tissue.

372.74 Vascular abnormalities of conjunctiva

Aneurysm(ata) of conjunctiva

372.75 Conjunctival cysts

DEF: Abnormal sacs of fluid in conjunctiva.

✓5th **372.8 Other disorders of conjunctiva**

372.81 Conjunctivochalasis

DEF: Bilateral condition of redundant conjunctival tissue between globe and lower eyelid margin; may cover lower punctum, interferring with normal tearing.

372.89 Other disorders of conjunctiva

372.9 Unspecified disorder of conjunctiva

✓4th **373 Inflammation of eyelids**

✓5th **373.0 Blepharitis**

EXCLUDES *blepharoconjunctivitis (372.20-372.22)*

373.00 Blepharitis, unspecified

373.01 Ulcerative blepharitis

373.02 Squamous blepharitis

✓5th **373.1 Hordeolum and other deep inflammation of eyelid**

DEF: Purulent, localized, staphylococcal infection in sebaceous glands of eyelids.

373.11 Hordeolum externum

Hordeolum NOSStye

DEF: Infection of the oil glands in the eyelash follicles.

373.12 Hordeolum internum

Infection of meibomian gland

DEF: Infection of the oil gland of the eyelid margin.

373.13 Abscess of eyelid

Furuncle of eyelid

DEF: Inflamed pocket of pus on the eyelid.

373.2 Chalazion

Meibomian (gland) cyst

EXCLUDES *infected meibomian gland (373.12)*

DEF: Chronic inflammation of the meibomian gland, causing an eyelid mass.

✓5th **373.3 Noninfectious dermatoses of eyelid**

373.31 Eczematous dermatitis of eyelid

373.32 Contact and allergic dermatitis of eyelid

373.33 Xeroderma of eyelid

373.34 Discoid lupus erythematosus of eyelid

373.4 *Infective dermatitis of eyelid of types resulting in deformity*

Code first underlying disease, as:
leprosy (030.0-030.9)
lupus vulgaris (tuberculous) (017.0)
yaws (102.0-102.9)

373.5 *Other infective dermatitis of eyelid*

Code first underlying disease, as:
actinomycosis (039.3)
impetigo (684)
mycotic dermatitis (110.0-111.9)
vaccinia (051.0)
postvaccination (999.0)

EXCLUDES *herpes:*
simplex (054.41)
zoster (053.20)

373.6 *Parasitic infestation of eyelid*

Code first underlying disease, as:
leishmaniasis (085.0-085.9)
loiasis (125.2)
onchocerciasis (125.3)
pediculosis (132.0)

373.8 Other inflammations of eyelids

373.9 Unspecified inflammation of eyelid

✓4th **374 Other disorders of eyelids**

✓5th **374.0 Entropion and trichiasis of eyelid**

DEF: Entropion: turning inward of eyelid edge toward eyeball.

DEF: Trichiasis: ingrowing eyelashes marked by irritation with possible distortion of sight.

374.00 Entropion, unspecified

374.01 Senile entropion

374.02 Mechanical entropion

374.03 Spastic entropion

374.04 Cicatricial entropion

374.05 Trichiasis without entropion

✓5th **374.1 Ectropion**

DEF: Turning outward (eversion) of eyelid edge; exposes palpebral conjunctiva; dryness irritation result.

374.10 Ectropion, unspecified

374.11 Senile ectropion

374.12 Mechanical ectropion

374.13 Spastic ectropion

374.14 Cicatricial ectropion

✓5th **374.2 Lagophthalmos**

DEF: Incomplete closure of eyes; causes dry eye and other complications.

374.20 Lagophthalmos, unspecified

374.21 Paralytic lagophthalmos

374.22 Mechanical lagophthalmos

374.23 Cicatricial lagophthalmos

✓5th **374.3 Ptosis of eyelid**

374.30 Ptosis of eyelid, unspecified

374.31 Paralytic ptosis

DEF: Drooping of upper eyelid due to nerve disorder.

374.32 Myogenic ptosis

DEF: Drooping of upper eyelid due to muscle disorder.

374.33 Mechanical ptosis

DEF: Outside force causes drooping of upper eyelid.

374.34 Blepharochalasis

Pseudoptosis

DEF: Loss of elasticity, thickened or indurated skin of eyelids associated with recurrent episodes of idiopathic edema causing intracellular tissue atrophy.

✓5th **374.4 Other disorders affecting eyelid function**

EXCLUDES *blepharoclonus (333.81)*
blepharospasm (333.81)
facial nerve palsy (351.0)
third nerve palsy or paralysis (378.51-378.52)
tic (psychogenic) (307.20-307.23)
organic (333.3)

374.41 Lid retraction or lag

374.43 Abnormal innervation syndrome

Jaw-blinking
Paradoxical facial movements

374.44 Sensory disorders

374.45 Other sensorimotor disorders

Deficient blink reflex

374.46 Blepharophimosis

Ankyloblepharon

DEF: Narrowing of palpebral fissure horizontally; caused by laterally displaced inner canthi; either acquired or congenital.

✓5th **374.5 Degenerative disorders of eyelid and periocular area**

374.50 Degenerative disorder of eyelid, unspecified

374.51 Xanthelasma

Xanthoma (planum) (tuberosum) of eyelid

Code first underlying condition (272.0-272.9)

DEF: Fatty tumors of the eyelid linked to high fat content of blood.

374.52 Hyperpigmentation of eyelid

Chloasma
Dyspigmentation

DEF: Excess pigment of eyelid.

Entropion and Ectropion

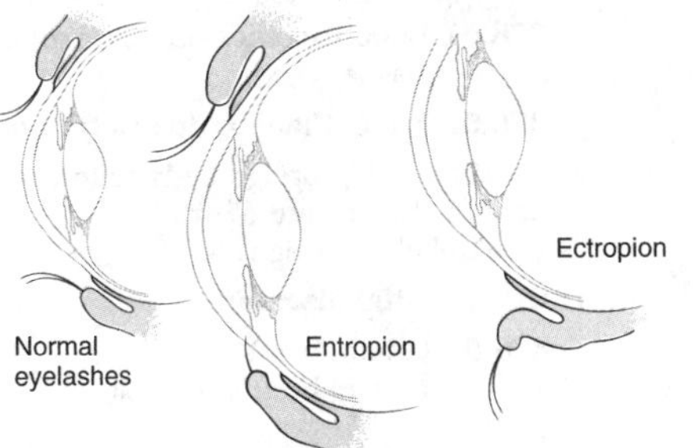

374.53 Hypopigmentation of eyelid

Vitiligo of eyelid

DEF: Lack of color pigment of the eyelid.

374.54 Hypertrichosis of eyelid

DEF: Excessive eyelash growth.

374.55 Hypotrichosis of eyelid

Madarosis of eyelid

DEF: Less than normal, or absent, eyelashes.

374.56 Other degenerative disorders of skin affecting eyelid

✓5th **374.8 Other disorders of eyelid**

374.81 Hemorrhage of eyelid

EXCLUDES *black eye (921.0)*

374.82 Edema of eyelid

Hyperemia of eyelid

DEF: Swelling and fluid retention in eyelid.

374.83 Elephantiasis of eyelid

DEF: Filarial disease causing dermatitis and enlargement of eyelid.

374.84 Cysts of eyelids

Sebaceous cyst of eyelid

374.85 Vascular anomalies of eyelid

374.86 Retained foreign body of eyelid

374.87 Dermatochalasis

DEF: Acquired form of connective tissue disorder associated with decreased elastic tissue and abnormal elastin formation resulting in loss of elasticity of the skin of the eyelid, generally associated with aging.

374.89 Other disorders of eyelid

374.9 Unspecified disorder of eyelid

✓4th **375 Disorders of lacrimal system**

✓5th **375.0 Dacryoadenitis**

375.00 Dacryoadenitis, unspecified

375.01 Acute dacryoadenitis

DEF: Severe, sudden inflammation of the lacrimal gland.

375.02 Chronic dacryoadenitis

DEF: Persistent inflammation of the lacrimal gland.

375.03 Chronic enlargement of lacrimal gland

✓5th **375.1 Other disorders of lacrimal gland**

375.11 Dacryops

DEF: Overproduction and constant flow of tears; may cause distended lacrimal duct.

375.12 Other lacrimal cysts and cystic degeneration

375.13 Primary lacrimal atrophy

375.14 Secondary lacrimal atrophy

DEF: Wasting away of the lacrimal gland due to another disease.

375.15 Tear film insufficiency, unspecified

Dry eye syndrome

DEF: Eye dryness and irritation from insufficient tear production.

375.16 Dislocation of lacrimal gland

Lacrimal System

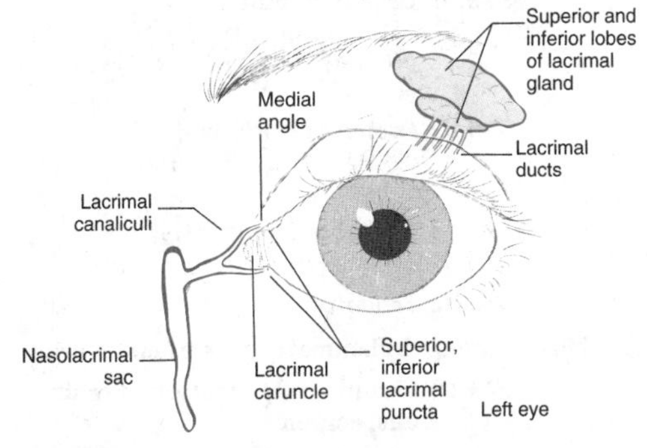

✓5th **375.2 Epiphora**
DEF: Abnormal development of tears due to stricture of lacrimal passages.

375.20 Epiphora, unspecified as to cause

375.21 Epiphora due to excess lacrimation
DEF: Tear overflow due to overproduction.

375.22 Epiphora due to insufficient drainage
DEF: Tear overflow due to blocked drainage.

✓5th **375.3 Acute and unspecified inflammation of lacrimal passages**
EXCLUDES *neonatal dacryocystitis (771.6)*

375.30 Dacryocystitis, unspecified

375.31 Acute canaliculitis, lacrimal

375.32 Acute dacryocystitis
Acute peridacryocystitis

375.33 Phlegmonous dacryocystitis
DEF: Infection of the tear sac with pockets of pus.

✓5th **375.4 Chronic inflammation of lacrimal passages**

375.41 Chronic canaliculitis

375.42 Chronic dacryocystitis

375.43 Lacrimal mucocele

✓5th **375.5 Stenosis and insufficiency of lacrimal passages**

375.51 Eversion of lacrimal punctum
DEF: Abnormal turning outward of the tear duct.

375.52 Stenosis of lacrimal punctum
DEF: Abnormal narrowing of the tear duct.

375.53 Stenosis of lacrimal canaliculi

375.54 Stenosis of lacrimal sac
DEF: Abnormal narrowing of the tear sac.

375.55 Obstruction of nasolacrimal duct, neonatal
EXCLUDES *congenital anomaly of nasolacrimal duct (743.65)*
DEF: Acquired, abnormal obstruction of tear drainage system from the eye to the nose; in an infant.

375.56 Stenosis of nasolacrimal duct, acquired

375.57 Dacryolith
DEF: Concretion or stone anywhere in lacrimal system.

✓5th **375.6 Other changes of lacrimal passages**

375.61 Lacrimal fistula
DEF: Abnormal communication from the lacrimal system.

375.69 Other

✓5th **375.8 Other disorders of lacrimal system**

375.81 Granuloma of lacrimal passages
DEF: Abnormal nodules within lacrimal system.

375.89 Other

375.9 Unspecified disorder of lacrimal system

✓4th **376 Disorders of the orbit**

✓5th **376.0 Acute inflammation of orbit**

376.00 Acute inflammation of orbit, unspecified

376.01 Orbital cellulitis
Abscess of orbit
DEF: Infection of tissue between the orbital bone and eyeball.

376.02 Orbital periostitis
DEF: Inflammation of connective tissue covering the orbital bone.

376.03 Orbital osteomyelitis
DEF: Inflammation of the orbital bone.

376.04 Tenonitis

✓5th **376.1 Chronic inflammatory disorders of orbit**

376.10 Chronic inflammation of orbit, unspecified

376.11 Orbital granuloma
Pseudotumor (inflammatory) of orbit
DEF: Abnormal nodule between orbital bone and eyeball.

376.12 Orbital myositis
DEF: Painful inflammation of the muscles of the eye.

376.13 Parasitic infestation of orbit
Code first underlying disease, as:
hydatid infestation of orbit (122.3, 122.6, 122.9)
myiasis of orbit (134.0)

✓5th **376.2 Endocrine exophthalmos**
Code first underlying thyroid disorder (242.0-242.9)

376.21 Thyrotoxic exophthalmos
DEF: Painful inflammation of eye muscles.

376.22 Exophthalmic ophthalmoplegia
DEF: Inability to rotate eye as a result of bulging eyes.

✓5th **376.3 Other exophthalmic conditions**

376.30 Exophthalmos, unspecified
DEF: Abnormal protrusion of eyeball.

376.31 Constant exophthalmos
DEF: Continuous, abnormal protrusion or bulging of eyeball.

376.32 Orbital hemorrhage
DEF: Bleeding behind the eyeball, causing it to bulge forward.

376.33 Orbital edema or congestion
DEF: Fluid retention behind eyeball, causing forward bulge.

376.34 Intermittent exophthalmos

376.35 Pulsating exophthalmos
DEF: Bulge or protrusion; associated with a carotid-cavernous fistula.

376.36 Lateral displacement of globe
DEF: Abnormal displacement of the eyeball away from nose, toward temple.

✓5th **376.4 Deformity of orbit**

376.40 Deformity of orbit, unspecified

376.41 Hypertelorism of orbit
DEF: Abnormal increase in interorbital distance; associated with congenital facial deformities; may be accompanied by mental deficiency.

376.42 Exostosis of orbit
DEF: Abnormal bony growth of orbit.

376.43 Local deformities due to bone disease
DEF: Acquired abnormalities of orbit; due to bone disease.

376.44 Orbital deformities associated with craniofacial deformities

376.45 Atrophy of orbit
DEF: Wasting away of bone tissue of orbit.

376.46 Enlargement of orbit

376.47 Deformity due to trauma or surgery

✓5th **376.5 Enophthalmos**
DEF: Recession of eyeball deep into eye socket.

376.50 Enophthalmos, unspecified as to cause

376.51 Enophthalmos due to atrophy of orbital tissue

376.52 Enophthalmos due to trauma or surgery

376.6 Retained (old) foreign body following penetrating wound of orbit
Retrobulbar foreign body

✓5th **376.8 Other orbital disorders**

376.81 Orbital cysts
Encephalocele of orbit

376.82 Myopathy of extraocular muscles
DEF: Disease in the muscles that control eyeball movement.

376.89 Other

376.9 Unspecified disorder of orbit

✓4th **377 Disorders of optic nerve and visual pathways**

✓5th **377.0 Papilledema**

377.00 Papilledema, unspecified

377.01 Papilledema associated with increased intracranial pressure

377.02 Papilledema associated with decreased ocular pressure

377.03 Papilledema associated with retinal disorder

377.04 Foster-Kennedy syndrome
DEF: Retrobulbar optic neuritis, central scotoma and optic atrophy; caused by tumors in frontal lobe of brain that press downward.

✓5th **377.1 Optic atrophy**

377.10 Optic atrophy, unspecified

377.11 Primary optic atrophy
EXCLUDES *neurosyphilitic optic atrophy (094.84)*

377.12 Postinflammatory optic atrophy
DEF: Adverse effect of inflammation causing wasting away of eye.

377.13 Optic atrophy associated with retinal dystrophies
DEF: Progressive changes in retinal tissue due to metabolic disorder causing wasting away of eye.

377.14 Glaucomatous atrophy [cupping] of optic disc

377.15 Partial optic atrophy
Temporal pallor of optic disc

377.16 Hereditary optic atrophy
Optic atrophy:
dominant hereditary
Leber's

✓5th **377.2 Other disorders of optic disc**

377.21 Drusen of optic disc

377.22 Crater-like holes of optic disc

377.23 Coloboma of optic disc
DEF: Ocular malformation caused by the failure of fetal fissure of optic stalk to close.

377.24 Pseudopapilledema

✓5th **377.3 Optic neuritis**
EXCLUDES *meningococcal optic neuritis (036.81)*

377.30 Optic neuritis, unspecified

377.31 Optic papillitis
DEF: Swelling and inflammation of the optic disc.

377.32 Retrobulbar neuritis (acute)
EXCLUDES *syphilitic retrobulbar neuritis (094.85)*
DEF: Inflammation of optic nerve immediately behind the eyeball.

377.33 Nutritional optic neuropathy
DEF: Malnutrition causing optic nerve disorder.

377.34 Toxic optic neuropathy
Toxic amblyopia
DEF: Toxic substance causing optic nerve disorder.

377.39 Other
EXCLUDES *ischemic optic neuropathy (377.41)*

✓5th **377.4 Other disorders of optic nerve**

377.41 Ischemic optic neuropathy
DEF: Decreased blood flow affecting optic nerve.

377.42 Hemorrhage in optic nerve sheaths
DEF: Bleeding in meningeal lining of optic nerve.

377.43 Optic nerve hypoplasia

377.49 Other
Compression of optic nerve

✓5th **377.5 Disorders of optic chiasm**

377.51 Associated with pituitary neoplasms and disorders
DEF: Abnormal pituitary growth causing disruption in nerve chain from retina to brain.

377.52 Associated with other neoplasms
DEF: Abnormal growth, other than pituitary, causing disruption in nerve chain from retina to brain.

377.53 Associated with vascular disorders
DEF: Vascular disorder causing disruption in nerve chain from retina to brain.

377.54 Associated with inflammatory
DEF: Inflammatory disease causing disruption in nerve chain from retina to brain.

✓5th **377.6 Disorders of other visual pathways**

377.61 Associated with neoplasms

377.62 Associated with vascular disorders

377.63 Associated with inflammatory

✓5th **377.7 Disorders of visual cortex**
EXCLUDES *visual:*
agnosia (368.16)
hallucinations (368.16)
halos (368.15)

377.71 Associated with neoplasms

377.72 Associated with vascular disorders

377.73 Associated with inflammatory

377.75 Cortical blindness
DEF: Blindness due to brain disorder, rather than eye disorder.

377.9 Unspecified disorder of optic nerve and visual pathways

✓4th **378 Strabismus and other disorders of binocular eye movements**
EXCLUDES *nystagmus and other irregular eye movements (379.50-379.59)*
DEF: Misalignment of the eyes due to imbalance in extraocular muscles.

✓5th **378.0 Esotropia**
Convergent concomitant strabismus
EXCLUDES *intermittent esotropia (378.20-378.22)*
DEF: Visual axis deviation created by one eye fixing upon an image and the other eye deviating inward.

378.00 Esotropia, unspecified

378.01 Monocular esotropia

378.02 Monocular esotropia with A pattern

378.03 Monocular esotropia with V pattern

378.04 Monocular esotropia with other noncomitancies
Monocular esotropia with X or Y pattern

Eye Musculature

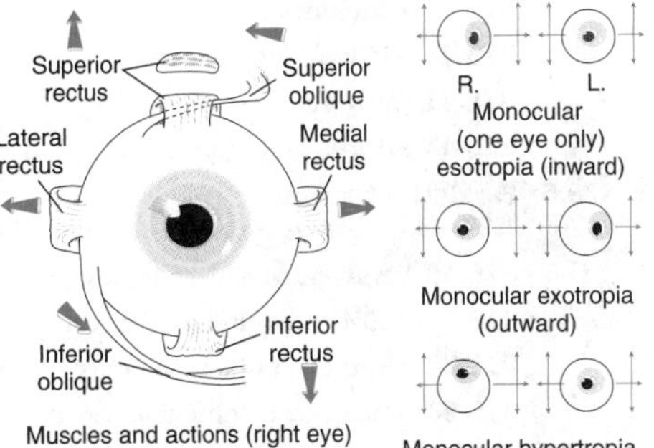

378.05 Alternating esotropia

378.06 Alternating esotropia with A pattern

378.07 Alternating esotropia with V pattern

378.08 Alternating esotropia with other noncomitancies
Alternating esotropia with X or Y pattern

✓5th **378.1 Exotropia**
Divergent concomitant strabismus
EXCLUDES *intermittent exotropia (378.20, 378.23-378.24)*
DEF: Visual axis deviation created by one eye fixing upon an image and the other eye deviating outward.

378.10 Exotropia, unspecified

378.11 Monocular exotropia

378.12 Monocular exotropia with A pattern

378.13 Monocular exotropia with V pattern

378.14 Monocular exotropia with other noncomitancies
Monocular exotropia with X or Y pattern

378.15 Alternating exotropia

378.16 Alternating exotropia with A pattern

378.17 Alternating exotropia with V pattern

378.18 Alternating exotropia with other noncomitancies
Alternating exotropia with X or Y pattern

✓5th **378.2 Intermittent heterotropia**
EXCLUDES *vertical heterotropia (intermittent) (378.31)*
DEF: Deviation of eyes seen only at intervals; it is also called strabismus.

378.20 Intermittent heterotropia, unspecified
Intermittent:
esotropia NOS
exotropia NOS

378.21 Intermittent esotropia, monocular

378.22 Intermittent esotropia, alternating

378.23 Intermittent exotropia, monocular

378.24 Intermittent exotropia, alternating

✓5th **378.3 Other and unspecified heterotropia**

378.30 Heterotropia, unspecified

378.31 Hypertropia
Vertical heterotropia (constant) (intermittent)

378.32 Hypotropia

378.33 Cyclotropia

378.34 Monofixation syndrome
Microtropia

378.35 Accommodative component in esotropia

✓5th **378.4 Heterophoria**
DEF: Deviation occurring only when the other eye is covered.

378.40 Heterophoria, unspecified

378.41 Esophoria

378.42 Exophoria

378.43 Vertical heterophoria

378.44 Cyclophoria

378.45 Alternating hyperphoria

✓5th **378.5 Paralytic strabismus**
DEF: Deviation of the eye due to nerve paralysis affecting muscle.

378.50 Paralytic strabismus, unspecified

378.51 Third or oculomotor nerve palsy, partial

378.52 Third or oculomotor nerve palsy, total

378.53 Fourth or trochlear nerve palsy

378.54 Sixth or abducens nerve palsy

378.55 External ophthalmoplegia

378.56 Total ophthalmoplegia

✓5th **378.6 Mechanical strabismus**
DEF: Deviation of the eye due to an outside force upon the extraocular muscles.

378.60 Mechanical strabismus, unspecified

378.61 Brown's (tendon) sheath syndrome
DEF: Congenital or acquired shortening of the anterior sheath of the superior oblique muscle; the eye is unable to move upward and inward; it is usually unilateral.

378.62 Mechanical strabismus from other musculofascial disorders

378.63 Limited duction associated with other conditions

✓5th **378.7 Other specified strabismus**

378.71 Duane's syndrome
DEF: Congenital, affects one eye; due to abnormal fibrous bands attached to rectus muscle; inability to abduct affected eye with retraction of globe.

378.72 Progressive external ophthalmoplegia
DEF: Paralysis progressing from one eye muscle to another.

378.73 Strabismus in other neuromuscular disorders

✓5th **378.8 Other disorders of binocular eye movements**
EXCLUDES *nystagmus (379.50-379.56)*

378.81 Palsy of conjugate gaze
DEF: Paralysis progressing from one eye muscle to another.

378.82 Spasm of conjugate gaze
DEF: Muscle contractions impairing parallel movement of eye.

378.83 Convergence insufficiency or palsy

378.84 Convergence excess or spasm

378.85 Anomalies of divergence

378.86 Internuclear ophthalmoplegia
DEF: Eye movement anomaly due to brainstem lesion.

378.87 Other dissociated deviation of eye movements
Skew deviation

378.9 Unspecified disorder of eye movements
Ophthalmoplegia NOS
Strabismus NOS

✓4th **379 Other disorders of eye**

✓5th **379.0 Scleritis and episcleritis**
EXCLUDES *syphilitic episcleritis (095.0)*

379.00 Scleritis, unspecified
Episcleritis NOS

379.01 Episcleritis periodica fugax
DEF: Hyperemia (engorgement) of the sclera and overlying conjunctiva characterized by a sudden onset and short duration.

379.02 Nodular episcleritis
DEF: Inflammation of the outermost layer of the sclera, with formation of nodules.

379.03 Anterior scleritis

379.04 Scleromalacia perforans
DEF: Scleral thinning, softening and degeneration; seen with rheumatoid arthritis.

379.05 Scleritis with corneal involvement
Scleroperikeratitis

379.06 Brawny scleritis
DEF: Severe scleral inflammation with thickening corneal margins.

379.07 Posterior scleritis
Sclerotenonitis

379.09 Other
Scleral abscess

✓5th **379.1 Other disorders of sclera**
EXCLUDES *blue sclera (743.47)*

379.11 Scleral ectasia
Scleral staphyloma NOS
DEF: Protrusion of the contents of the eyeball where the sclera has thinned.

379.12 Staphyloma posticum
DEF: Ring-shaped protrusion or bulging of sclera and uveal tissue at posterior pole of eye.

379.13 Equatorial staphyloma
DEF: Ring-shaped protrusion or bulging of sclera and uveal tissue midway between front and back of eye.

379.14 Anterior staphyloma, localized

379.15 Ring staphyloma

379.16 Other degenerative disorders of sclera

379.19 Other

✓5th **379.2 Disorders of vitreous body**
DEF: Disorder of clear gel that fills space between retina and lens.

379.21 Vitreous degeneration
Vitreous:
cavitation
detachment
liquefaction

379.22 Crystalline deposits in vitreous
Asteroid hyalitis
Synchysis scintillans

379.23 Vitreous hemorrhage

379.24 Other vitreous opacities
Vitreous floaters

379.25 Vitreous membranes and strands

379.26 Vitreous prolapse
DEF: Slipping of vitreous from normal position.

379.29 Other disorders of vitreous
EXCLUDES *vitreous abscess (360.04)*

✓5th **379.3 Aphakia and other disorders of lens**
EXCLUDES *after-cataract (366.50-366.53)*

379.31 Aphakia
EXCLUDES *cataract extraction status (V45.61)*
DEF: Absence of eye's crystalline lens.

379.32 Subluxation of lens

379.33 Anterior dislocation of lens
DEF: Lens displaced toward iris.

379.34 Posterior dislocation of lens
DEF: Lens displaced backward toward vitreous.

379.39 Other disorders of lens

✓5th **379.4 Anomalies of pupillary function**

379.40 Abnormal pupillary function, unspecified

379.41 Anisocoria
DEF: Unequal pupil diameter.

379.42 Miosis (persistent), not due to miotics
DEF: Abnormal contraction of pupil less than 2 mil.

379.43 Mydriasis (persistent), not due to mydriatics
DEF: Morbid dilation of pupil.

379.45 Argyll Robertson pupil, atypical
Argyll Robertson phenomenon or pupil, nonsyphilitic
EXCLUDES *Argyll Robertson pupil (syphilitic) (094.89)*
DEF: Failure of pupil to respond to light; affects both eyes; may be caused by diseases such as syphilis of the central nervous system or miosis.

379.46 Tonic pupillary reaction
Adie's pupil or syndrome

379.49 Other
Hippus
Pupillary paralysis

✓5th **379.5 Nystagmus and other irregular eye movements**

379.50 Nystagmus, unspecified
DEF: Involuntary, rapid, rhythmic movement of eyeball; vertical, horizontal, rotatory or mixed; cause may be congenital, acquired, physiological, neurological, myopathic, or due to ocular diseases.

379.51 Congenital nystagmus

379.52 Latent nystagmus

379.53 Visual deprivation nystagmus

379.54 Nystagmus associated with disorders of the vestibular system

379.55 Dissociated nystagmus

379.56 Other forms of nystagmus

379.57 Deficiencies of saccadic eye movements
Abnormal optokinetic response
DEF: Saccadic eye movements; small, rapid, involuntary movements by both eyes simultaneously, due to changing point of fixation on visualized object.

379.58 Deficiencies of smooth pursuit movements

379.59 Other irregularities of eye movements
Opsoclonus

✓5th **379.6 Inflammation (infection) of postprocedural bleb**
Postprocedural blebitis

379.60 Inflammation (infection) of postprocedural bleb, unspecified

379.61 Inflammation (infection) of postprocedural bleb, stage 1

379.62 Inflammation (infection) of postprocedural bleb, stage 2

379.63 Inflammation (infection) of postprocedural bleb, stage 3
Bleb associated endophthalmitis

379.8 Other specified disorders of eye and adnexa

✓5th **379.9 Unspecified disorder of eye and adnexa**

379.90 Disorder of eye, unspecified

379.91 Pain in or around eye

379.92 Swelling or mass of eye

379.93 Redness or discharge of eye

379.99 Other ill-defined disorders of eye
EXCLUDES *blurred vision NOS (368.8)*

DISEASES OF THE EAR AND MASTOID PROCESS (380-389)

Use additional external cause code, if applicable, to identify the cause of the ear condition

✓4th **380 Disorders of external ear**

✓5th **380.0 Perichondritis and chondritis of pinna**
Chondritis of auricle
Perichondritis of auricle

380.00 Perichondritis of pinna, unspecified

380.01 Acute perichondritis of pinna

380.02 Chronic perichondritis of pinna

380.03 Chondritis of pinna
DEF: Infection that has progressed into the cartilage; presents as indurated and edematous skin over the pinna; vascular compromise occurs with tissue necrosis and deformity.

✓5th **380.1 Infective otitis externa**

380.10 Infective otitis externa, unspecified
Otitis externa (acute):
NOS
circumscribed
diffuse
hemorrhagica
infective NOS

380.11 Acute infection of pinna
EXCLUDES *furuncular otitis externa (680.0)*

380.12 Acute swimmers' ear
Beach ear
Tank ear
DEF: Otitis externa due to swimming.

380.13 Other acute infections of external ear
Code first underlying disease, as:
erysipelas (035)
impetigo (684)
seborrheic dermatitis (690.10-690.18)
EXCLUDES *herpes simplex (054.73)*
herpes zoster (053.71)

380.14 Malignant otitis externa
DEF: Severe necrotic otitis externa; due to bacteria.

380.15 Chronic mycotic otitis externa
Code first underlying disease, as:
aspergillosis (117.3)
otomycosis NOS (111.9)
EXCLUDES *candidal otitis externa (112.82)*

380.16 Other chronic infective otitis externa
Chronic infective otitis externa NOS

✓5th **380.2 Other otitis externa**

380.21 Cholesteatoma of external ear
Keratosis obturans of external ear (canal)
EXCLUDES *cholesteatoma NOS (385.30-385.35)*
postmastoidectomy (383.32)
DEF: Cystlike mass filled with debris, including cholesterol; rare, congenital condition.

380.22 Other acute otitis externa
Acute otitis externa:
actinic
chemical
contact
eczematoid
reactive

380.23 Other chronic otitis externa
Chronic otitis externa NOS

✓5th **380.3 Noninfectious disorders of pinna**

380.30 Disorder of pinna, unspecified

380.31 Hematoma of auricle or pinna

380.32 Acquired deformities of auricle or pinna
EXCLUDES *cauliflower ear (738.7)*

380.39 Other
EXCLUDES *gouty tophi of ear (274.81)*

380.4 Impacted cerumen
Wax in ear

✓5th **380.5 Acquired stenosis of external ear canal**
Collapse of external ear canal

380.50 Acquired stenosis of external ear canal, unspecified as to cause

380.51 Secondary to trauma
DEF: Narrowing of the external ear canal; due to trauma.

380.52 Secondary to surgery
DEF: Postsurgical narrowing of the external ear canal.

Ear and Mastoid Process

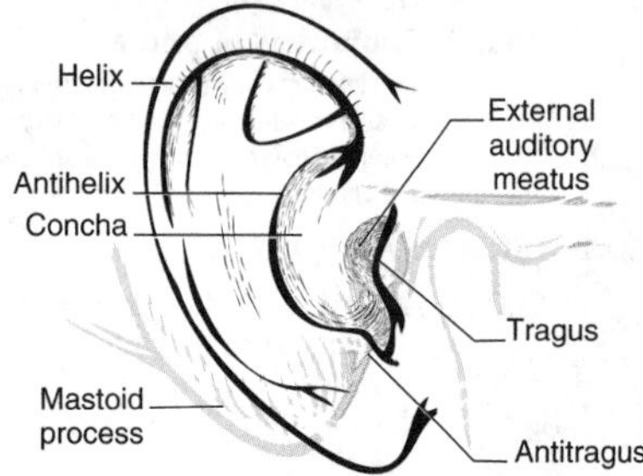

380.53 Secondary to inflammation
DEF: Narrowing of the external ear canal; due to chronic inflammation.

✓5th **380.8 Other disorders of external ear**

380.81 Exostosis of external ear canal

380.89 Other

380.9 Unspecified disorder of external ear

✓4th **381 Nonsuppurative otitis media and Eustachian tube disorders**

✓5th **381.0 Acute nonsuppurative otitis media**
Acute tubotympanic catarrh
Otitis media, acute or subacute:
catarrhal
exudative
transudative
with effusion
EXCLUDES *otitic barotrauma (993.0)*

381.00 Acute nonsuppurative otitis media, unspecified

381.01 Acute serous otitis media
Acute or subacute secretory otitis media
DEF: Sudden, severe infection of the middle ear.

381.02 Acute mucoid otitis media
Acute or subacute seromucinous otitis media
Blue drum syndrome
DEF: Sudden, severe infection of the middle ear, with mucous.

381.03 Acute sanguinous otitis media
DEF: Sudden, severe infection of the middle ear, with blood.

381.04 Acute allergic serous otitis media

381.05 Acute allergic mucoid otitis media

381.06 Acute allergic sanguinous otitis media

✓5th **381.1 Chronic serous otitis media**
Chronic tubotympanic catarrh

381.10 Chronic serous otitis media, simple or unspecified
DEF: Persistent infection of the middle ear, without pus.

381.19 Other
Serosanguinous chronic otitis media

✓5th **381.2 Chronic mucoid otitis media**
Glue ear
EXCLUDES *adhesive middle ear disease (385.10-385.19)*
DEF: Chronic condition; characterized by viscous fluid in middle ear; due to obstructed Eustachian tube.

381.20 Chronic mucoid otitis media, simple or unspecified

381.29 Other
Mucosanguinous chronic otitis media

381.3 Other and unspecified chronic nonsuppurative otitis media
Otitis media, chronic:
allergic
exudative
secretory
Otitis media, chronic:
seromucinous
transudative
with effusion

381.4 Nonsuppurative otitis media, not specified as acute or chronic
Otitis media:
allergic
catarrhal
exudative
mucoid
Otitis media:
secretory
seromucinous
serous
transudative
with effusion

✓5th **381.5 Eustachian salpingitis**

381.50 Eustachian salpingitis, unspecified

381.51 Acute Eustachian salpingitis
DEF: Sudden, severe inflammation of the Eustachian tube.

381.52 **Chronic Eustachian salpingitis**
DEF: Persistent inflammation of the Eustachian tube.

✓5th 381.6 **Obstruction of Eustachian tube**
Stenosis } of Eustachian tube
Stricture } of Eustachian tube

381.60 **Obstruction of Eustachian tube, unspecified**

381.61 **Osseous obstruction of Eustachian tube**
Obstruction of Eustachian tube from cholesteatoma, polyp, or other osseous lesion

381.62 **Intrinsic cartilaginous obstruction of Eustachian tube**
DEF: Blockage of Eustachian tube; due to cartilage overgrowth.

381.63 **Extrinsic cartilaginous obstruction of Eustachian tube**
Compression of Eustachian tube

381.7 **Patulous Eustachian tube**
DEF: Distended, oversized Eustachian tube.

✓5th 381.8 **Other disorders of Eustachian tube**

381.81 **Dysfunction of Eustachian tube**

381.89 **Other**

381.9 **Unspecified Eustachian tube disorder**

✓4th 382 **Suppurative and unspecified otitis media**

✓5th 382.0 **Acute suppurative otitis media**
Otitis media, acute:
necrotizing NOS
purulent

382.00 **Acute suppurative otitis media without spontaneous rupture of ear drum**
DEF: Sudden, severe inflammation of middle ear, with pus.

382.01 **Acute suppurative otitis media with spontaneous rupture of ear drum**
DEF: Sudden, severe inflammation of middle ear, with pressure tearing ear drum tissue.

*382.02 **Acute suppurative otitis media in diseases classified elsewhere***
Code first underlying disease, as:
influenza (487.8)
scarlet fever (034.1)
EXCLUDES *postmeasles otitis (055.2)*

382.1 **Chronic tubotympanic suppurative otitis media**
Benign chronic suppurative otitis media } (with anterior perforation of ear drum)
Chronic tubotympanic disease } (with anterior perforation of ear drum)
DEF: Inflammation of tympanic cavity and auditory tube; with pus formation.

382.2 **Chronic atticoantral suppurative otitis media**
Chronic atticoantral disease } (with posterior or superior maginal perforation of ear drum)
Persistent mucosal disease } (with posterior or superior maginal perforation of ear drum)
DEF: Inflammation of upper tympanic membrane and mastoid antrum with pus formation.

382.3 **Unspecified chronic suppurative otitis media**
Chronic purulent otitis media
EXCLUDES *tuberculous otitis media (017.4)*

382.4 **Unspecified suppurative otitis media**
Purulent otitis media NOS

382.9 **Unspecified otitis media**
Otitis media:
NOS
acute NOS
chronic NOS

✓4th 383 **Mastoiditis and related conditions**

✓5th 383.0 **Acute mastoiditis**
Abscess of mastoid
Empyema of mastoid

383.00 **Acute mastoiditis without complications**
DEF: Sudden, severe inflammation of mastoid air cells.

383.01 **Subperiosteal abscess of mastoid**
DEF: Pocket of pus within the mastoid bone.

383.02 **Acute mastoiditis with other complications**
Gradenigo's syndrome

383.1 **Chronic mastoiditis**
Caries of mastoid
Fistula of mastoid
EXCLUDES *tuberculous mastoiditis (015.6)*
DEF: Persistent inflammation of the mastoid air cells.

✓5th 383.2 **Petrositis**
Coalescing osteitis } of pertrous bone
Inflammation } of pertrous bone
Osteomyelitis } of pertrous bone

383.20 **Petrositis, unspecified**

383.21 **Acute petrositis**
DEF: Sudden, severe inflammation of dense bone behind the ear.

383.22 **Chronic petrositis**
DEF: Persistent inflammation of dense bone behind the ear.

✓5th 383.3 **Complications following mastoidectomy**

383.30 **Postmastoidectomy complication, unspecified**

383.31 **Mucosal cyst of postmastoidectomy cavity**
DEF: Mucous-lined cyst cavity following removal of mastoid bone.

383.32 **Recurrent cholesteatoma of postmastoidectomy cavity**
DEF: Cystlike mass of cell debris in cavity following removal of mastoid bone.

383.33 **Granulations of postmastoidectomy cavity**
Chronic inflammation of postmastoidectomy cavity
DEF: Granular tissue in cavity following removal of mastoid bone.

✓5th 383.8 **Other disorders of mastoid**

383.81 **Postauricular fistula**
DEF: Abnormal passage behind mastoid cavity.

383.89 **Other**

383.9 **Unspecified mastoiditis**

✓4th 384 **Other disorders of tympanic membrane**

✓5th 384.0 **Acute myringitis without mention of otitis media**

384.00 **Acute myringitis, unspecified**
Acute tympanitis NOS
DEF: Sudden, severe inflammation of ear drum.

384.01 **Bullous myringitis**
Myringitis bullosa hemorrhagica
DEF: Type of viral otitis media characterized by the appearance of serous or hemorrhagic blebs on the tympanic membrane.

384.09 **Other**

384.1 **Chronic myringitis without mention of otitis media**
Chronic tympanitis
DEF: Persistent inflammation of ear drum; with no evidence of middle ear infection.

5th **384.2 Perforation of tympanic membrane**
Perforation of ear drum:
NOS
persistent posttraumatic
postinflammatory
EXCLUDES *otitis media with perforation of tympanic membrane (382.00-382.9)*
traumatic perforation [current injury] (872.61)

384.20 Perforation of tympanic membrane, unspecified

384.21 Central perforation of tympanic membrane

384.22 Attic perforation of tympanic membrane
Pars flaccida

384.23 Other marginal perforation of tympanic membrane

384.24 Multiple perforations of tympanic membrane

384.25 Total perforation of tympanic membrane

5th **384.8 Other specified disorders of tympanic membrane**

384.81 Atrophic flaccid tympanic membrane
Healed perforation of ear drum

384.82 Atrophic nonflaccid tympanic membrane

384.9 Unspecified disorder of tympanic membrane

4th **385 Other disorders of middle ear and mastoid**
EXCLUDES *mastoiditis (383.0-383.9)*

5th **385.0 Tympanosclerosis**

385.00 Tympanosclerosis, unspecified as to involvement

385.01 Tympanosclerosis involving tympanic membrane only
DEF: Tough, fibrous tissue impeding functions of ear drum.

385.02 Tympanosclerosis involving tympanic membrane and ear ossicles
DEF: Tough, fibrous tissue impeding functions of middle ear bones (stapes, malleus, incus).

385.03 Tympanosclerosis involving tympanic membrane, ear ossicles, and middle ear
DEF: Tough, fibrous tissue impeding functions of ear drum, middle ear bones and middle ear canal.

385.09 Tympanosclerosis involving other combination of structures

5th **385.1 Adhesive middle ear disease**
Adhesive otitis
Otitis media:
chronic adhesive
fibrotic
EXCLUDES *glue ear (381.20-381.29)*
DEF: Adhesions of middle ear structures.

385.10 Adhesive middle ear disease, unspecified as to involvement

Middle and Inner Ear

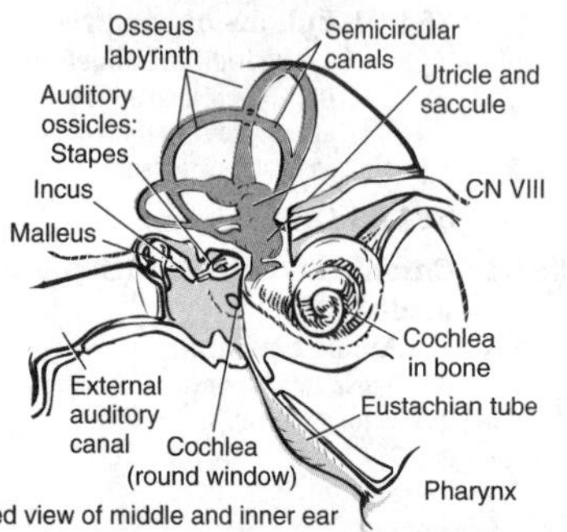

Exposed view of middle and inner ear

Cholesteatoma

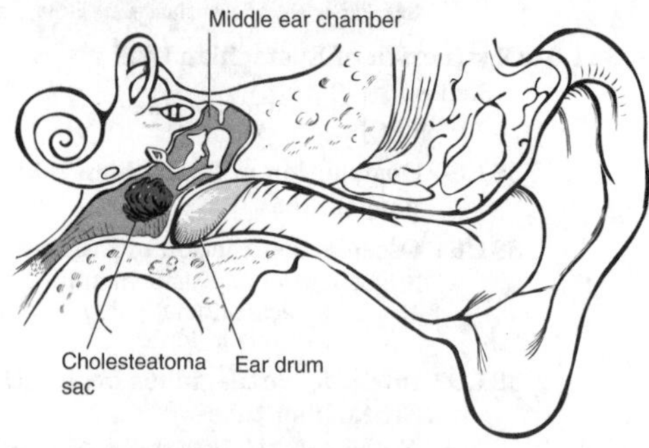

385.11 Adhesions of drum head to incus

385.12 Adhesions of drum head to stapes

385.13 Adhesions of drum head to promontorium

385.19 Other adhesions and combinations

5th **385.2 Other acquired abnormality of ear ossicles**

385.21 Impaired mobility of malleus
Ankylosis of malleus

385.22 Impaired mobility of other ear ossicles
Ankylosis of ear ossicles, except malleus

385.23 Discontinuity or dislocation of ear ossicles
DEF: Disruption in auditory chain; created by malleus, incus and stapes.

385.24 Partial loss or necrosis of ear ossicles
DEF: Tissue loss in malleus, incus and stapes.

5th **385.3 Cholesteatoma of middle ear and mastoid**
Cholesterosis, Epidermosis, Keratosis, Polyp } of (middle) ear
EXCLUDES *cholesteatoma:*
external ear canal (380.21)
recurrent of postmastoidectomy cavity (383.32)
DEF: Cystlike mass of middle ear and mastoid antrum filled with debris, including cholesterol.

385.30 Cholesteatoma, unspecified

385.31 Cholesteatoma of attic

385.32 Cholesteatoma of middle ear

385.33 Cholesteatoma of middle ear and mastoid
DEF: Cystlike mass of cell debris in middle ear and mastoid air cells behind ear.

385.35 Diffuse cholesteatosis

5th **385.8 Other disorders of middle ear and mastoid**

385.82 Cholesterin granuloma
DEF: Granuloma formed of fibrotic tissue; contains cholesterol crystals surrounded by foreign-body cells; found in the middle ear and mastoid area.

385.83 Retained foreign body of middle ear

385.89 Other

385.9 Unspecified disorder of middle ear and mastoid

4th **386 Vertiginous syndromes and other disorders of vestibular system**
EXCLUDES *vertigo NOS (780.4)*

5th **386.0 Ménière's disease**
Endolymphatic hydrops
Lermoyez's syndrome
Ménière's syndrome or vertigo
DEF: Distended membranous labyrinth of middle ear from endolymphatic hydrops; causes ischemia, failure of nerve function; hearing and balance dysfunction; symptoms include fluctuating deafness, ringing in ears and dizziness.

386.00 Ménière's disease, unspecified
Ménière's disease (active)

386.01 Active Ménière's disease, cochleovestibular

386.02 Active Ménière's disease, cochlear

386.03 Active Ménière's disease, vestibular

386.04 Inactive Ménière's disease
Ménière's disease in remission

✓5th **386.1 Other and unspecified peripheral vertigo**
EXCLUDES *epidemic vertigo (078.81)*

386.10 Peripheral vertigo, unspecified

386.11 Benign paroxysmal positional vertigo
Benign paroxysmal positional nystagmus

386.12 Vestibular neuronitis
Acute (and recurrent) peripheral vestibulopathy
DEF: Transient benign vertigo, unknown cause; characterized by response to caloric stimulation on one side, nystagmus with rhythmic movement of eyes; normal auditory function present; occurs in young adults.

386.19 Other
Aural vertigo
Otogenic vertigo

386.2 Vertigo of central origin
Central positional nystagmus
Malignant positional vertigo

✓5th **386.3 Labyrinthitis**

386.30 Labyrinthitis, unspecified

386.31 Serous labyrinthitis
Diffuse labyrinthitis
DEF: Inflammation of labyrinth; with fluid buildup.

386.32 Circumscribed labyrinthitis
Focal labyrinthitis

386.33 Suppurative labyrinthitis
Purulent labyrinthitis
DEF: Inflammation of labyrinth; with pus.

386.34 Toxic labyrinthitis
DEF: Inflammation of labyrinth; due to toxic reaction.

386.35 Viral labyrinthitis

✓5th **386.4 Labyrinthine fistula**

386.40 Labyrinthine fistula, unspecified

386.41 Round window fistula

386.42 Oval window fistula

386.43 Semicircular canal fistula

386.48 Labyrinthine fistula of combined sites

✓5th **386.5 Labyrinthine dysfunction**

386.50 Labyrinthine dysfunction, unspecified

386.51 Hyperactive labyrinth, unilateral
DEF: Abnormal increased sensitivity of labyrinth to stimuli such as sound, pressure or gravitational change, affecting one ear.

386.52 Hyperactive labyrinth, bilateral
DEF: Abnormal increased sensitivity of labyrinth to stimuli such as sound, pressure or gravitational change, affecting both ears.

386.53 Hypoactive labyrinth, unilateral
DEF: Abnormal decreased sensitivity of labyrinth to stimuli such as sound, pressure or gravitational change, affecting one ear.

386.54 Hypoactive labyrinth, bilateral
DEF: Abnormal decreased sensitivity of labyrinth to stimuli such as sound, pressure or gravitational change, affecting both ears.

386.55 Loss of labyrinthine reactivity, unilateral
DEF: Decreased function of the labyrinth sensors, affecting one ear

386.56 Loss of labyrinthine reactivity, bilateral
DEF: Decreased function of the labyrinth sensors, affecting both ears

386.58 Other forms and combinations

386.8 Other disorders of labyrinth

386.9 Unspecified vertiginous syndromes and labyrinthine disorders

✓4th **387 Otosclerosis**
INCLUDES otospongiosis
DEF: Synonym for otospongiosis, spongy bone formation in the labyrinth bones of the ear; it causes progressive hearing impairment.

387.0 Otosclerosis involving oval window, nonobliterative
DEF: Tough, fibrous tissue impeding functions of oval window.

387.1 Otosclerosis involving oval window, obliterative
DEF: Tough, fibrous tissue blocking oval window.

387.2 Cochlear otosclerosis
Otosclerosis involving:
otic capsule
round window
DEF: Tough, fibrous tissue impeding functions of cochlea.

387.8 Other otosclerosis

387.9 Otosclerosis, unspecified

✓4th **388 Other disorders of ear**

✓5th **388.0 Degenerative and vascular disorders of ear**

388.00 Degenerative and vascular disorders, unspecified

388.01 Presbyacusis
DEF: Progressive, bilateral perceptive hearing loss caused by advancing age; it is also known as presbycusis.

388.02 Transient ischemic deafness
DEF: Restricted blood flow to auditory organs causing temporary hearing loss.

✓5th **388.1 Noise effects on inner ear**

388.10 Noise effects on inner ear, unspecified

388.11 Acoustic trauma (explosive) to ear
Otitic blast injury

388.12 Noise-induced hearing loss

388.2 Sudden hearing loss, unspecified

✓5th **388.3 Tinnitus**
DEF: Abnormal noises in ear; may be heard by others beside the affected individual; noises include ringing, clicking, roaring and buzzing.

388.30 Tinnitus, unspecified

388.31 Subjective tinnitus

388.32 Objective tinnitus

✓5th **388.4 Other abnormal auditory perception**

388.40 Abnormal auditory perception, unspecified

388.41 Diplacusis
DEF: Perception of a single auditory sound as two sounds at two different levels of intensity.

388.42 Hyperacusis
DEF: Exceptionally acute sense of hearing caused by such conditions as Bell's palsy; this term may also refer to painful sensitivity to sounds.

388.43 Impairment of auditory discrimination
DEF: Impaired ability to distinguish tone of sound.

388.44 Recruitment
DEF: Perception of abnormally increased loudness caused by a slight increase in sound intensity; it is a term used in audiology.

388.45 Acquired auditory processing disorder
Auditory processing disorder NOS
EXCLUDES *central auditory processing disorder (315.32)*
DEF: Difficulty in recognizing and interpreting sounds; a failure of the brain to process auditory information; due to neurological problems due to injury, infection, and degenerative conditions.

388.5 Disorders of acoustic nerve
Acoustic neuritis
Degeneration } of acoustic or eighth nerve
Disorder } of acoustic or eighth nerve
EXCLUDES *acoustic neuroma (225.1)*
syphilitic acoustic neuritis (094.86)

✓5th **388.6 Otorrhea**

388.60 Otorrhea, unspecified
Discharging ear NOS

388.61 Cerebrospinal fluid otorrhea
EXCLUDES *cerebrospinal fluid rhinorrhea (349.81)*
DEF: Spinal fluid leakage from ear.

388.69 Other
Otorrhagia

✓5th **388.7 Otalgia**

388.70 Otalgia, unspecified
Earache NOS

388.71 Otogenic pain

388.72 Referred pain

388.8 Other disorders of ear

388.9 Unspecified disorder of ear

✓4th **389 Hearing loss**

✓5th **389.0 Conductive hearing loss**
Conductive deafness
EXCLUDES *mixed conductive and sensorineural hearing loss (389.20-389.22)*
DEF: Dysfunction in sound-conducting structures of external or middle ear causing hearing loss.

389.00 Conductive hearing loss, unspecified

389.01 Conductive hearing loss, external ear

389.02 Conductive hearing loss, tympanic membrane

389.03 Conductive hearing loss, middle ear

389.04 Conductive hearing loss, inner ear

389.05 Conductive hearing loss, unilateral

389.06 Conductive hearing loss, bilateral

389.08 Conductive hearing loss of combined types

✓5th **389.1 Sensorineural hearing loss**
Perceptive hearing loss or deafness
EXCLUDES *abnormal auditory perception (388.40-388.44)*
mixed conductive and sensorineural hearing loss (389.20-389.22)
psychogenic deafness (306.7)
DEF: Nerve conduction causing hearing loss.

389.10 Sensorineural hearing loss, unspecified

389.11 Sensory hearing loss, bilateral

389.12 Neural hearing loss, bilateral

389.13 Neural hearing loss, unilateral

389.14 Central hearing loss

389.15 Sensorineural hearing loss, unilateral

389.16 Sensorineural hearing loss, asymmetrical

389.17 Sensory hearing loss, unilateral

389.18 Sensorineural hearing loss, bilateral

✓5th **389.2 Mixed conductive and sensorineural hearing loss**
Deafness or hearing loss of type classifiable to 389.00-389.08 with type classifiable to 389.10-389.18

389.20 Mixed hearing loss, unspecified

389.21 Mixed hearing loss, unilateral

389.22 Mixed hearing loss, bilateral

389.7 Deaf, non-speaking, not elsewhere classifiable

389.8 Other specified forms of hearing loss

389.9 Unspecified hearing loss
Deafness NOS

Chapter 7: Circulatory System (390–459)

Very specific guidelines and instructions affect assignment of codes within this category. Pay careful attention to instruction notes in both the alphabetic index and the tabular list. Many of the conditions within this chapter are complex and interrelated. Physicians may use a variety of terms and phrases to describe a diagnosis.

Acute Rheumatic Fever (390–392)

Rheumatic fever is a febrile disease occurring mainly in children or young adults following throat infection by Group A Streptococci. Symptoms include sudden occurrence of fever and joint pain; followed by lesions of the heart, blood vessels, and joint connective tissue, abdominal pain, skin changes, and chorea.

The instructional notes below each of the subcategories further define and clarify the subcategory. These instructional notes assist the user to assign codes accurately even though a variety of terms and phrases may be used to describe diagnosis. For example, the Includes" notes below category 390 indicate that the conditions rheumatic arthritis (acute or subacute), rheumatic fever (active or acute), and articular rheumatism (acute or subacute) are included in this category. "Excludes" notes under category 392 indicate that if the medical documentation states the condition to be chorea, NOS, or Huntington's chorea, a code from category 392 is not an appropriate assignment.

Chronic Rheumatic Heart Disease (393–398)

Heart disease as a consequence of acute rheumatic fever commonly involves damage to the heart valves during the acute phase of the streptococcal infection. ICD-9-CM makes the presumption that certain conditions of the mitral valve such as stenosis, stenosis with insufficiency, and failure of unknown etiology are of rheumatic fever origin. None of the disorders of the aortic valve are presumed to be of rheumatic origin, however, and must be specified by documentation as "rheumatic" to be classified to these categories. However, when disorders to both mitral and aortic valves are described with the terms stenosis, stenosis with insufficiency, and failure, then ICD-9-CM presumes rheumatic origin.

Hypertensive Disease (401–405)

Hypertension is the condition of abnormally elevated arterial blood pressure. The blood pressure range considered to be hypertensive varies, but most commonly a 140/ 90 mm. Hg. is considered hypertensive.

Hypertension is classified using three axes: First, by type (i.e., primary or secondary); second is by nature of hypertension (i.e., benign, malignant, or unspecified); and third indicates associated heart disease, renal disease, or both heart and renal disease. Refer to instructional notes in coding hypertension. There are many diagnostic terms used to describe the types of hypertension.

The hypertension table, a complete list of diagnoses associated with or due to hypertension, is located in the alphabetic index under the main term "Hypertension."

Three terms "malignant," "benign," and "unspecified," serve as headings in the table to assist the user to select the most specific code to describe the diagnosis. They are defined as follows:

Malignant: This type of hypertension is considered the most severe and difficult to treat. A malignant diagnosis is made when the patient's diastolic blood pressure is consistently greater than 140 and if other clinical features are present, such as cardiac and renal involvement, and neuroretinopathy.

Benign: This type of hypertension is considered relatively mild and usually is chronic or occurs over a prolonged period of time.

Unspecified: This term is selected when the physician does not specify the type of hypertension as benign or malignant. If the physician has not specified the type, request clarification of the diagnosis.

Essential hypertension (401) is also referred to as primary, idiopathic, or systolic hypertension, and is defined as hypertension without apparent cause. The physician must document in the medical record whether the hypertension is malignant or benign to assign a fourth digit of 0 or 1 respectively. When no entry in the medical record supports either designation, assign a fifth digit of 9, unspecified.

Hypertensive heart disease is assigned to category 402. Chronic elevated blood pressure often produces changes in the heart myocardium as a result of the increased workload against the elevated blood pressure in the vessels. Hypertensive heart disease includes cardiomegaly, cardiopathy, cardiovascular disease, and heart failure. The first axis of coding is the kind of hypertension (i.e., malignant, benign, or unspecified). The second axis indicates hypertension, with or without heart failure.

In order to assign a code from the 402 category, the diagnostic statement must indicate a causal relationship between the hypertension and the heart disease. Phrases such as "due to hypertension" and "hypertensive" indicate a causal relationship. For example, hypertensive heart disease without heart failure, unspecified, is coded 402.90.

A diagnostic statement "with hypertension" does not indicate a casual relationship between the heart disease and the hypertension and the combination code 402 is inappropriate. In this case, code the heart disease and the hypertension separately. For example, congestive heart failure with hypertension, unspecified, is coded 428.0, 401.9.

Heart disease in combination with an associated hypertensive heart condition classifiable to 428, 429.0–429.3, 429.8, 429.9 is presumed by ICD-9-CM to be hypertensive. For example, congestive heart failure with unspecified hypertensive cardiovascular disease is coded 402.91.

A causal relationship between hypertension and kidney disease is assumed when the diagnostic statement indicates both conditions, even though the statement does not specify hypertensive kidney disease. Hypertensive chronic kidney disease is assigned to the category 403. Fourth-digit assignment, as with other hypertension subcategories, indicates malignant (0), benign (1), or unspecified (9). Fifth-digit assignment indicates without mention of chronic kidney disease (0) or with chronic kidney disease (1). To report chronic renal insufficiency (CRI) with hypertension, assign 403.90 Hypertensive chronic kidney disease stage I through stage IV, or unspecified and code 585.9 Chronic kidney disease, unspecified.

Category 404 includes conditions of hypertensive heart and kidney disease. This category is reviewed when the diagnostic statement indicates both hypertensive heart disease (402) and hypertensive kidney disease (403). Fifth-digit assignment in this category indicates the presence of congestive heart failure, chronic kidney disease, both conditions, or neither. Assign codes from combination category 404 Hypertensive heart and kidney disease, when both hypertensive kidney disease and hypertensive heart disease are stated in the diagnosis. Assume a relationship between the hypertension and the kidney disease, whether or not the condition is so designated.

A patient may have an elevated blood pressure reading during an outpatient visit without having a known diagnosis of hypertension. In this situation, code 796.2, which describes an elevated blood pressure reading that may be the result of emotional problems or stress. This diagnosis code can be found in the alphabetic index under the main term "Elevation" and subterms "blood pressure," "reading," and "no diagnosis of hypertension."

Secondary hypertension is coded to category 405 and is defined as high blood pressure due to or with a variety of primary diseases, such as renal disorders, disorders of the central nervous system, endocrine diseases, and vascular diseases.

The fourth- digit assignment identifies whether the condition is malignant (.0), benign (.1), or unspecified (.9). The fifth-digit assignment of 1 indicates that the underlying condition is renovascular in origin and assignment of "9" is used to designate all others.

Ischemic Heart Disease (410–414)

Myocardial Infarction (410)

An acute myocardial infarction (AMI) results from an interruption of the blood supply to an area of the myocardium. Physicians associate the condition as part of acute ischemic heart disease, which is classified to category 410. Category 410 has subcategories that identify the site of the myocardial infarction and fifth digits to indicate the episode of care involved with the myocardial infarction. ICD-9-CM classifies myocardial infarctions according to the site involved as identified by EKG, such as anterolateral wall.

The fifth digits indicate new acute myocardial infarctions and patients who are admitted within eight weeks of an acute myocardial infarction. The fifth digit of "1" (initial episode of care) covers all care during the acute phase of treatment, and is used principally in acutefacility care.

The fifth digit of "2" (subsequent episode of care) covers further observation, evaluation, or treatment rendered after the initial treatment (discharge), but within an eight week period since the myocardial infarction. For example, AMI of anterolateral wall, occurring two weeks ago is coded 410.02. Acute myocardial infarctions within eight weeks or that are unspecified require the use of a fifth digit of "2" or "0 (unspecified)." A myocardial infarction of greater than eight weeks duration with persistent symptoms is coded to 414.8.

Ischemic Heart Disease (411)

Intermediate coronary syndrome (411.1) is a condition representing an intermediate stage between angina of effort and acute myocardial infarction. It is often documented by the physician as "unstable angina." Other terms for this condition are impending infarction, preinfarction angina, and preinfarction syndrome.

Old myocardial infarction, code 412, is assigned for diagnosis of an old or healed myocardial infarction diagnosed by EKG but currently presenting no symptoms.

Other Forms of Chronic Ischemic Heart Disease (414)

Fifth-digit subclassifications are required when reporting coronary atherosclerosis. The fifth digit specifies the type of vessel affected by atherosclerotic disease; whether a native vessel, previously grafted vessel, or vessel of a transplanted heart.

A complete blockage of a coronary artery that has been present for an extended duration is known as a chronic total occlusion of the coronary artery (414.2). Collateral flow may avoid myocardial infarction, despite the chronic total occlusion of the coronary artery. However, this flow could not likely increase much during exercise and so would be likely to greatly limit activity.

Chronic total occlusion of a coronary artery may be treated with angioplasty or stent placement, usually with a drug-eluting stent. When reporting chronic total occlusion of coronary artery (414.2), code first the appropriate code for coronary atherosclerosis classifiable to codes 414.00–414.07.

Lipid-rich atherosclerotic plaques (414.3) are particularly unstable and vulnerable to rupture, increasing the risk of acute coronary events such as thrombosis, arrhythmia, and myocardial infarction. Atherosclerotic plaques containing lipid-rich cores have been identified as a cause of arterial filling defects during angiography procedures. In atherogenesis, plaque stability depends on multiple factors, including plaque composition, size and location of the core, arterial wall stress, and relationship of plaque to blood flow. Since lipid-rich plaque is present in some coronary atherosclerotic diseased vessels (but perhaps not all vessels), the presence of this code is an indicator of disease severity. Lipid-rich plaque of coronary vessels cannot be present without coronary atherosclerosis. Therefore, the appropriate coronary atherosclerosis code from subcategory 414.0 should be sequenced first, followed by code 414.3, when documented as such.

Congestive Heart Failure (428)

Congestive heart failure (CHF) is a syndrome of impaired contraction, or power failure (in pumping of the heart), pressure volume overload, and impaired filling of the heart, in which the heart may be functioning normally otherwise.

Congestive heart failure affects either the left or right ventricles of the heart. Left heart failure is the inability of the heart to meet the metabolic demands of the body. It occurs when the left ventricle has an overload of fluid due to the inability of the ventricle to contract, or pump, blood from the lungs.

Right heart failure occurs secondary to left heart failure when the left ventricle has failed completely to contract and move blood into systemic circulation. Once the left ventricle fails, patients evolving into heart failure have a grave prognosis, since the pumping mechanism of the heart is so severely damaged.

some instances the heart muscle may "compensate" during heart failure by increasing the force of the contraction, raising the arterial pressure, or increasing ventricular dilation. The heart may perform at near normal functional levels. When these compensating factors no longer are effective, decompensation is said to occur. The heart can no longer work at increased levels. Heart failure may be stated as compensated or decompensated, but ICD-9-CM code selection is still 428.0.

Cerebrovascular Disease (430–438)

Occlusion and Stenosis of Precerebral and Cerebral Arteries (433–434)

Determine the artery where the site of the stenosis or occlusion occurs before coding from this section. The code category 433 includes occlusion and stenosis of the precerebral arteries. The second step is to determine the presence of cerebral infarction. A fifth-digit assignment of "0" indicates "without mention of infarction" and the fifth-digit assignment of "1" indicates "with cerebral infarction." CVA and stroke NOS are assigned code 434.9x since the vast majority of strokes and CVA are attributed to cerebral artery occlusion. The same general guidelines apply to occlusion and stenosis of the cerebral arteries, although the first axis of classification differentiates between thrombosis and embolism instead of identification of the cerebral artery.

Report V45.88 for the administration of tPA (rtPA) to patients transferred from a different facility within the last 24 hours. Code V45.88 is reported in addition to the code for the acute condition requiring tPA administration, such as acute cerebral infarction classifiable to categories 433 and 434.

Late Effects of Cerebrovascular Disease (438)

The lead instructional note to this category explains the use of these codes.This category is used to indicate conditions in categories 430–437 as the cause of the late effect, which is classifiable elsewhere. The "late effect" includes conditions specified as such, or as sequalae, which may occur any time after the onset of the causal condition. Assignment of a code from the 438 category is inappropriate in cases of past history of cerebrovascular disease which resulted in no neurological deficits. The appropriate code assignment is V12.54 Personal history of other diseases of the circulatory system.

Category 438 is used to indicate conditions classifiable to categories 430–437 as the causes of late effects (neurologic deficits), themselves classified elsewhere. These "late effects" include neurologic deficits that persist after initial onset of conditions classifiable to 430–437. The neurologic deficits caused by cerebrovascular disease may be present from the onset or may arise at any time after the onset of the condition classifiable to 430–437. A code from category 438 may be assigned on a medical record with codes from 430–437, if the patient has a current CVA and deficits from an old CVA.

Diseases of Arteries, Arterioles, and Capillaries (440-449)

This section includes conditions affecting the arterial vasculature, which include atherosclerosis, thrombus, and embolism (clots) and other forms of peripheral vascular disease.

Atherosclerosis (440)

Atherosclerosis may be loosely defined as "hardening" of the arteries, whereby plaque formations adhere to the arterial walls, impairing their elasticity, patency, and functionality. Arteriosclerosis (occlusive) of the extremities is reported with code 440.2x. However, chronic total occlusion of an artery in the extremities (440.4) generally develops over a long time period, with partial occlusion present initially. This can cause symptoms such as intermittent claudication (leg pain with exercise) when arteries to the lower extremities are involved.

When reporting chronic occlusive disease (440.4), code first the underlying disease, atherosclerosis of arteries of extremities (440.20–440.29, 440.30–440.32). Code 440.4 excludes acute occlusion of artery of extremity (444.21–444.22).

7. DISEASES OF THE CIRCULATORY SYSTEM (390-459)

ACUTE RHEUMATIC FEVER (390-392)

DEF: Febrile disease occurs mainly in children or young adults following throat infection by group A streptococci; symptoms include fever, joint pain, lesions of heart, blood vessels and joint connective tissue, abdominal pain, skin changes, and chorea.

390 Rheumatic fever without mention of heart involvement

Arthritis, rheumatic, acute or subacute
Rheumatic fever (active) (acute)
Rheumatism, articular, acute or subacute

EXCLUDES *that with heart involvement (391.0-391.9)*

✓4th **391 Rheumatic fever with heart involvement**

EXCLUDES *chronic heart diseases of rheumatic origin (393-398.99) unless rheumatic fever is also present or there is evidence of recrudescence or activity of the rheumatic process*

391.0 Acute rheumatic pericarditis

Rheumatic:
- fever (active) (acute) with pericarditis
- pericarditis (acute)

Any condition classifiable to 390 with pericarditis

EXCLUDES *that not specified as rheumatic (420.0-420.9)*

DEF: Sudden, severe inflammation of heart lining due to rheumatic fever.

391.1 Acute rheumatic endocarditis

Rheumatic:
- endocarditis, acute
- fever (active) (acute) with endocarditis or valvulitis
- valvulitis acute

Any condition classifiable to 390 with endocarditis or valvulitis

DEF: Sudden, severe inflammation of heart cavities due to rheumatic fever.

391.2 Acute rheumatic myocarditis

Rheumatic fever (active) (acute) with myocarditis

Any condition classifiable to 390 with myocarditis

DEF: Sudden, severe inflammation of heart muscles due to rheumatic fever.

391.8 Other acute rheumatic heart disease

Rheumatic:
- fever (active) (acute) with other or multiple types of heart involvement
- pancarditis, acute

Any condition classifiable to 390 with other or multiple types of heart involvement

391.9 Acute rheumatic heart disease, unspecified

Rheumatic:
- carditis, acute
- fever (active) (acute) with unspecified type of heart involvement
- heart disease, active or acute

Any condition classifiable to 390 with unspecified type of heart involvement

✓4th **392 Rheumatic chorea**

INCLUDES Sydenham's chorea

EXCLUDES *chorea:*
- *NOS (333.5)*
- *Huntington's (333.4)*

DEF: Childhood disease linked with rheumatic fever and streptococcal infections; symptoms include spasmodic, involuntary movements of limbs or facial muscles, psychic symptoms, and irritability.

392.0 With heart involvement

Rheumatic chorea with heart involvement of any type classifiable to 391

392.9 Without mention of heart involvement

CHRONIC RHEUMATIC HEART DISEASE (393-398)

393 Chronic rheumatic pericarditis

Adherent pericardium, rheumatic
Chronic rheumatic:
- mediastinopericarditis
- myopericarditis

EXCLUDES *pericarditis NOS or not specified as rheumatic (423.0-423.9)*

DEF: Persistent inflammation of heart lining due to rheumatic heart disease.

✓4th **394 Diseases of mitral valve**

EXCLUDES *that with aortic valve involvement (396.0-396.9)*

394.0 Mitral stenosis

Mitral (valve):
- obstruction (rheumatic)
- stenosis NOS

DEF: Narrowing, of mitral valve between left atrium and left ventricle; due to rheumatic heart disease.

394.1 Rheumatic mitral insufficiency

Rheumatic mitral:
- incompetence
- regurgitation

EXCLUDES *that not specified as rheumatic (424.0)*

DEF: Malfunction of mitral valve between left atrium and left ventricle; due to rheumatic heart disease.

394.2 Mitral stenosis with insufficiency

Mitral stenosis with incompetence or regurgitation

DEF: A narrowing or stricture of the mitral valve situated between the left atrium and left ventricle. The stenosis interferes with blood flow from the atrium into the ventricle. If the valve does not completely close, it becomes insufficient (inadequate) and cannot prevent regurgitation (abnormal backward flow) into the atrium when the left ventricle contracts. This abnormal function is also called incompetence.

394.9 Other and unspecified mitral valve diseases

Mitral (valve):
- disease (chronic)
- failure

✓4th **395 Diseases of aortic valve**

EXCLUDES *that not specified as rheumatic (424.1)*
that with mitral valve involvement (396.0-396.9)

395.0 Rheumatic aortic stenosis

Rheumatic aortic (valve) obstruction

DEF: Narrowing of the aortic valve; results in backflow into ventricle; due to rheumatic heart disease.

395.1 Rheumatic aortic insufficiency

Rheumatic aortic:
- incompetence
- regurgitation

DEF: Malfunction of the aortic valve; results in backflow into left ventricle; due to rheumatic heart disease.

395.2 Rheumatic aortic stenosis with insufficiency

Rheumatic aortic stenosis with incompetence or regurgitation

DEF: Malfunction and narrowing, of the aortic valve; results in backflow into left ventricle; due to rheumatic heart disease.

395.9 Other and unspecified rheumatic aortic diseases

Rheumatic aortic (valve) disease

✓4th **396 Diseases of mitral and aortic valves**

INCLUDES involvement of both mitral and aortic valves, whether specified as rheumatic or not

396.0 Mitral valve stenosis and aortic valve stenosis

Atypical aortic (valve) stenosis
Mitral and aortic (valve) obstruction (rheumatic)

396.1 Mitral valve stenosis and aortic valve insufficiency

396.2 Mitral valve insufficiency and aortic valve stenosis

396.3 Mitral valve insufficiency and aortic valve insufficiency

Mitral and aortic (valve):
- incompetence
- regurgitation

396.8 Multiple involvement of mitral and aortic valves
Stenosis and insufficiency of mitral or aortic valve with stenosis or insufficiency, or both, of the other valve

396.9 Mitral and aortic valve diseases, unspecified

✓4th 397 Diseases of other endocardial structures

397.0 Diseases of tricuspid valve
Tricuspid (valve) (rheumatic):
disease
insufficiency
obstruction
regurgitation
stenosis

DEF: Malfunction of the valve between right atrium and right ventricle; due to rheumatic heart disease.

397.1 Rheumatic diseases of pulmonary valve
EXCLUDES *that not specified as rheumatic (424.3)*

397.9 Rheumatic diseases of endocardium, valve unspecified
Rheumatic:
endocarditis (chronic)
valvulitis (chronic)
EXCLUDES *that not specified as rheumatic (424.90-424.99)*

✓4th 398 Other rheumatic heart disease

398.0 Rheumatic myocarditis
Rheumatic degeneration of myocardium
EXCLUDES *myocarditis not specified as rheumatic (429.0)*

DEF: Chronic inflammation of heart muscle; due to rheumatic heart disease.

✓5th 398.9 Other and unspecified rheumatic heart diseases

398.90 Rheumatic heart disease, unspecified
Rheumatic:
carditis
heart disease NOS
EXCLUDES *carditis not specified as rheumatic (429.89)*
heart disease NOS not specified as rheumatic (429.9)

398.91 Rheumatic heart failure (congestive)
Rheumatic left ventricular failure

DEF: Decreased cardiac output, edema and hypertension; due to rheumatic heart disease.

398.99 Other

HYPERTENSIVE DISEASE (401-405)

EXCLUDES *that complicating pregnancy, childbirth, or the puerperium (642.0-642.9)*
that involving coronary vessels (410.00-414.9)

✓4th 401 Essential hypertension
INCLUDES high blood pressure
hyperpiesia
hyperpiesis
hypertension (arterial) (essential) (primary) (systemic)
hypertensive vascular:
degeneration
disease
EXCLUDES *elevated blood pressure without diagnosis of hypertension (796.2)*
pulmonary hypertension (416.0-416.9)
that involving vessels of:
brain (430-438)
eye (362.11)

DEF: Hypertension that occurs without apparent organic cause; idiopathic.

401.0 Malignant

DEF: Severe high arterial blood pressure; results in necrosis in kidney, retina, etc.; hemorrhages occur and death commonly due to uremia or rupture of cerebral vessel.

401.1 Benign

DEF: Mildly elevated arterial blood pressure.

401.9 Unspecified

✓4th 402 Hypertensive heart disease
INCLUDES hypertensive:
cardiomegaly
cardiopathy
cardiovascular disease
heart (disease) (failure)
any condition classifiable to 429.0-429.3, 429.8, 429.9 due to hypertension
Use additional code to specify type of heart failure (428.0-428.43), if known

✓5th 402.0 Malignant
402.00 Without heart failure
402.01 With heart failure

✓5th 402.1 Benign
402.10 Without heart failure
402.11 With heart failure

✓5th 402.9 Unspecified
402.90 Without heart failure
402.91 With heart failure

✓4th 403 Hypertensive chronic kidney disease
INCLUDES arteriolar nephritis
arteriosclerosis of:
kidney
renal arterioles
arteriosclerotic nephritis (chronic) (interstitial)
hypertensive:
nephropathy
renal failure
uremia (chronic)
nephrosclerosis
renal sclerosis with hypertension
any condition classifiable to 585 with any condition classifiable to 401
EXCLUDES *acute renal failure (584.5-584.9)*
renal disease stated as not due to hypertension
renovascular hypertension (405.0-405.9 with fifth-digit 1)

The following fifth-digit subclassification is for use with category 403:
0 with chronic kidney disease stage I through stage IV, or unspecified
Use additional code to identify the stage of chronic kidney disease (585.1-585.4, 585.9)
1 with chronic kidney disease stage V or end stage renal disease
Use additional code to identify the stage of chronic kidney disease (585.5, 585.6)

✓5th 403.0 Malignant
[0-1]

✓5th 403.1 Benign
[0-1]

✓5th 403.9 Unspecified
[0-1]

✓4th 404 Hypertensive heart and chronic kidney disease

INCLUDES disease:
cardiorenal
cardiovascular renal
any condition classifiable to 402 with any condition classifiable to 403

Use additional code to specify type of heart failure (428.0-428.43), if known

The following fifth-digit subclassification is for use with category 404:

0 without heart failure and with chronic kidney disease stage I through stage IV, or unspecified
Use additional code to identify the stage of chronic kidney disease (585.1-585.4, 585.9)

1 with heart failure and with chronic kidney disease stage I through stage IV, or unspecified
Use additional code to identify the stage of chronic kidney disease (585.1-585.4, 585.9)

2 without heart failure and with chronic kidney disease stage V or end stage renal disease
Use additional code to identify the stage of chronic kidney disease (585.5, 585.6)

3 with heart failure and chronic kidney disease stage V or end stage renal disease
Use additional code to identify the stage of chronic kidney disease (585.5, 585.6)

✓5th 404.0 Malignant
[0-3]

✓5th 404.1 Benign
[0-3]

✓5th 404.9 Unspecified
[0-3]

✓4th 405 Secondary hypertension

DEF: High arterial blood pressure due to or with a variety of primary diseases, such as renal disorders, CNS disorders, endocrine, and vascular diseases.

✓5th 405.0 Malignant

405.01 Renovascular

405.09 Other

✓5th 405.1 Benign

405.11 Renovascular

405.19 Other

✓5th 405.9 Unspecified

405.91 Renovascular

405.99 Other

Acute Myocardial Infarction

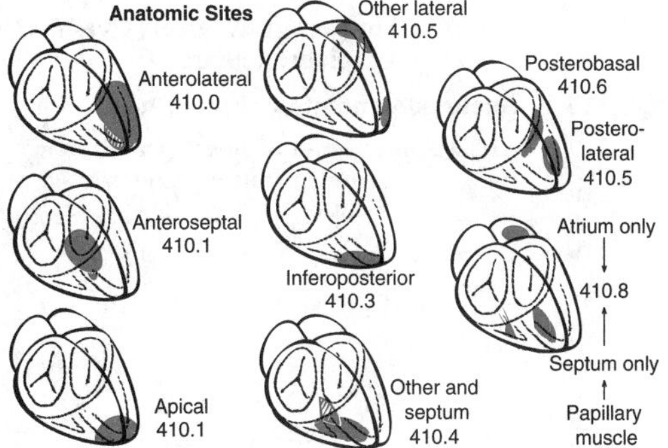

ISCHEMIC HEART DISEASE (410-414)

INCLUDES that with mention of hypertension

Use additional code to identify presence of hypertension (401.0-405.9)

✓4th 410 Acute myocardial infarction

INCLUDES cardiac infarction
coronary (artery):
embolism
occlusion
rupture
thrombosis
infarction of heart, myocardium, or ventricle
rupture of heart, myocardium, or ventricle
ST elevation (STEMI) and non-ST elevation (NSTEMI) myocardial infarction
any condition classifiable to 414.1-414.9 specified as acute or with a stated duration of 8 weeks or less

The following fifth-digit subclassification is for use with category 410:

0 episode of care unspecified
Use when the source document does not contain sufficient information for the assigment of fifth-digit 1 or 2.

1 initial episode of care
Use fifth-digit 1 to designate the first episode of care (regardless of facility site) for a newly diagnosed myocardial infarction. The fifth-digit 1 is assigned regardless of the number of times a patient may be transferred during the initial episode of care.

2 subsequent episode of care
Use fifth-digit 2 to designate an episode of care following the initial episode when the patient is admitted for further observation, evaluation or treatment for a myocardial infarction that has received initial treatment, but is still less than 8 weeks old.

DEF: A sudden insufficiency of blood supply to an area of the heart muscle; usually due to a coronary artery occlusion.

✓5th 410.0 Of anterolateral wall
[0-2] ST elevation myocardial infarction (STEMI) of anterolateral wall

✓5th 410.1 Of other anterior wall
[0-2] Infarction:
anterior (wall) NOS, anteroapical, anteroseptal } (with contiguous portion of intraventricular septum)
ST elevation myocardial infarction (STEMI) of other anterior wall

✓5th 410.2 Of inferolateral wall
[0-2] ST elevation myocardial infarction (STEMI) of inferolateral wall

✓5th 410.3 Of inferoposterior wall
[0-2] ST elevation myocardial infarction (STEMI) of inferoposterior wall

✓5th 410.4 Of other inferior wall
[0-2] Infarction:
diaphragmatic wall NOS, inferior (wall) NOS } (with contiguous portion of intraventricular septum)
ST elevation myocardial infarction (STEMI) of other inferior wall

✓5th 410.5 Of other lateral wall
[0-2] Infarction:
apical-lateral
basal-lateral
high lateral
posterolateral
ST elevation myocardial infarction (STEMI) of other lateral wall

✓5th 410.6 True posterior wall infarction
[0-2] Infarction:
posterobasal
strictly posterior
ST elevation myocardial infarction (STEMI) of true posterior wall

✓5th **410.7 Subendocardial infarction**
[0-2]
Non-ST elevation myocardial infarction (NSTEMI)
Nontransmural infarction

✓5th **410.8 Of other specified sites**
[0-2]
Infarction of:
atrium
papillary muscle
septum alone
ST elevation myocardial infarction (STEMI) of other specified sites

✓5th **410.9 Unspecified site**
[0-2]
Acute myocardial infarction NOS
Coronary occlusion NOS
Myocardial infarction NOS

✓4th **411 Other acute and subacute forms of ischemic heart disease**

411.0 Postmyocardial infarction syndrome
Dressler's syndrome
DEF: Complication developing several days/weeks after myocardial infarction; symptoms include fever, leukocytosis, chest pain, evi-dence of pericarditis, pleurisy, and pneumonitis; tendency to recur.

411.1 Intermediate coronary syndrome
Impending infarction
Preinfarction angina
Preinfarction syndrome
Unstable angina
EXCLUDES *angina (pectoris) (413.9)*
decubitus (413.0)
DEF: A condition representing an intermediate stage between angina of effort and acute myocardial infarction. It is often documented by the physician as "unstable angina."

✓5th **411.8 Other**

411.81 Acute coronary occlusion without myocardial infarction
Acute coronary (artery):
embolism, obstruction, occlusion, thrombosis } without or not resulting in myocardial infarction
EXCLUDES *obstruction without infarction due to atherosclerosis (414.00-414.07)*
occlusion without infarction due to atherosclerosis (414.00-414.07)
DEF: Interrupted blood flow to a portion of the heart; without tissue death.

411.89 Other
Coronary insufficiency (acute)
Subendocardial ischemia

412 Old myocardial infarction
Healed myocardial infarction
Past myocardial infarction diagnosed on ECG [EKG] or other special investigation, but currently presenting no symptoms

✓4th **413 Angina pectoris**
DEF: Severe constricting pain in the chest, often radiating from the precordium to the left shoulder and down the arm, due to ischemia of the heart muscle; usually caused by coronary disease; pain is often precipitated by effort or excitement.

413.0 Angina decubitus
Nocturnal angina
DEF: Angina occurring only in the recumbent position.

413.1 Prinzmetal angina
Variant angina pectoris
DEF Angina occurring when patient is recumbent; associated with ST-segment elevations.

413.9 Other and unspecified angina pectoris
Angina:
NOS
cardiac
of effort
Anginal syndrome
Status anginosus
Stenocardia
Syncope anginosa
EXCLUDES *preinfarction angina (411.1)*

✓4th **414 Other forms of chronic ischemic heart disease**
EXCLUDES *arteriosclerotic cardiovascular disease [ASCVD] (429.2)*
cardiovascular:
arteriosclerosis or sclerosis (429.2)
degeneration or disease (429.2)

✓5th **414.0 Coronary atherosclerosis**
Arteriosclerotic heart disease [ASHD]
Atherosclerotic heart disease
Coronary (artery):
arteriosclerosis
arteritis or endarteritis
atheroma
sclerosis
stricture
Use additional code, if applicable, to identify chronic total occlusion of coronary artery (414.2)
EXCLUDES *embolism of graft (996.72)*
occlusion NOS of graft (996.72)
thrombus of graft (996.72)
DEF: A chronic condition marked by thickening and loss of elasticity of the coronary artery; caused by deposits of plaque containing cholesterol, lipoid material and lipophages.

414.00 Of unspecified type of vessel, native or graft

414.01 Of native coronary artery
DEF: Plaque deposits in natural heart vessels.

414.02 Of autologous vein bypass graft
DEF: Plaque deposit in grafted vein originating within patient.

414.03 Of nonautologous biological bypass graft
DEF: Plaque deposits in grafted vessel originating outside patient.

414.04 Of artery bypass graft
Internal mammary artery
DEF: Plaque deposits in grafted artery originating within patient.

414.05 Of unspecified type of bypass graft
Bypass graft NOS

414.06 Of native coronary artery of transplanted heart

414.07 Of bypass graft (artery) (vein) of transplanted heart

✓5th **414.1 Aneurysm and dissection of heart**

414.10 Aneurysm of heart (wall)
Aneurysm (arteriovenous):
mural
ventricular

Arteries of the Heart

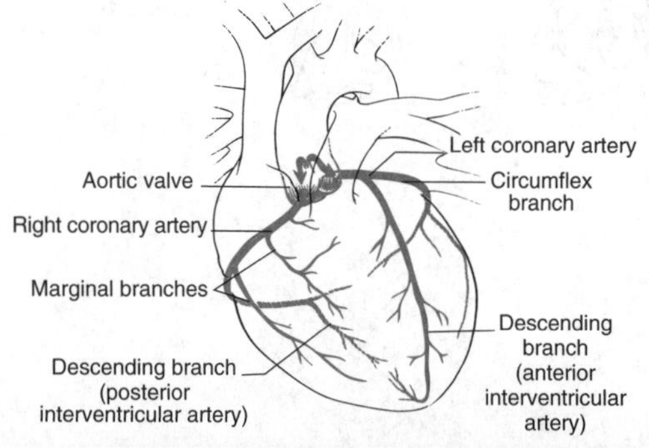

414.11 Aneurysm of coronary vessels
Aneurysm (arteriovenous) of coronary vessels
DEF: Dilatation of all three-vessel wall layers forming a sac filled with blood.

414.12 Dissection of coronary artery
DEF: A tear in the intimal arterial wall of a coronary artery resulting in the sudden intrusion of blood within the layers of the wall.

414.19 Other aneurysm of heart
Arteriovenous fistula, acquired, of heart

414.2 Chronic total occlusion of coronary artery
Complete occlusion of coronary artery
Total occlusion of coronary artery
Code first coronary atherosclerosis (414.00-414.07)
EXCLUDES *acute coronary occlusion with myocardial infarction (410.00-410.92)*
acute coronary occlusion without myocardial infarction (411.81)
DEF: Complete blockage of coronary artery due to plaque accumulation over an extended period of time; results in substantial reduction of blood flow.

414.3 Coronary atherosclerosis due to lipid rich plaque
Code first coronary atherosclerosis (414.00-414.07)

414.8 Other specified forms of chronic ischemic heart disease
Chronic coronary insufficiency
Ischemia, myocardial (chronic)
Any condition classifiable to 410 specified as chronic, or presenting with symptoms after 8 weeks from date of infarction
EXCLUDES *coronary insufficiency (acute) (411.89)*

414.9 Chronic ischemic heart disease, unspecified
Ischemic heart disease NOS

DISEASES OF PULMONARY CIRCULATION (415-417)

✓4th **415 Acute pulmonary heart disease**

415.0 Acute cor pulmonale
EXCLUDES *cor pulmonale NOS (416.9)*
DEF: A heart-lung disease marked by dilation and failure of the right side of heart; due to pulmonary embolism; ventilatory function is impaired and pulmonary hypertension results within hours.

✓5th **415.1 Pulmonary embolism and infarction**
Pulmonary (artery) (vein):
- apoplexy
- embolism
- infarction (hemorrhagic)
- thrombosis

EXCLUDES *that complicating:*
abortion (634-638 with .6, 639.6)
ectopic or molar pregnancy (639.6)
pregnancy, childbirth, or the puerperium (673.0-673.8)
DEF: Embolism: Closure of the pulmonary artery or branch; due to thrombosis (blood clot).
DEF: Infarction: Necrosis of lung tissue; due to obstructed arterial blood supply, most often by pulmonary embolism.

415.11 Iatrogenic pulmonary embolism and infarction
Use additional code for associated septic pulmonary embolism, if applicable, 415.12

415.12 Septic pulmonary embolism
Septic embolism NOS
Code first underlying infection, such as: septicemia (038.0-038.9)
EXCLUDES *septic arterial embolism (449)*

415.19 Other

✓4th **416 Chronic pulmonary heart disease**

416.0 Primary pulmonary hypertension
Idiopathic pulmonary arteriosclerosis
Pulmonary hypertension (essential) (idiopathic) (primary)
DEF: A rare increase in pulmonary circulation, often resulting in right ventricular failure or fatal syncope.

416.1 Kyphoscoliotic heart disease
DEF: High blood pressure within the lungs as a result of curvature of the spine.

416.8 Other chronic pulmonary heart diseases
Pulmonary hypertension, secondary

416.9 Chronic pulmonary heart disease, unspecified
Chronic cardiopulmonary disease
Cor pulmonale (chronic) NOS

✓4th **417 Other diseases of pulmonary circulation**

417.0 Arteriovenous fistula of pulmonary vessels
EXCLUDES *congenital arteriovenous fistula (747.3)*
DEF: Abnormal communication between blood vessels within lung.

417.1 Aneurysm of pulmonary artery
EXCLUDES *congenital aneurysm (747.3)*

417.8 Other specified diseases of pulmonary circulation
Pulmonary:
- arteritis
- endarteritis

Rupture } of pulmonary vessel
Stricture }

417.9 Unspecified disease of pulmonary circulation

OTHER FORMS OF HEART DISEASE (420-429)

✓4th **420 Acute pericarditis**
INCLUDES acute:
- mediastinopericarditis
- myopericarditis
- pericardial effusion
- pleuropericarditis
- pneumopericarditis

EXCLUDES *acute rheumatic pericarditis (391.0)*
postmyocardial infarction syndrome [Dressler's] (411.0)
DEF: Inflammation of the pericardium (heart sac); pericardial friction rub results from this inflammation and is heard as a scratchy or leathery sound.

420.0 Acute pericarditis in diseases classified elsewhere
Code first underlying disease, as:
- actinomycosis (039.8)
- amebiasis (006.8)
- chronic uremia (585.9)
- nocardiosis (039.8)
- tuberculosis (017.9)
- uremia NOS (586)

EXCLUDES *pericarditis (acute) (in):*
Coxsackie (virus) (074.21)
gonococcal (098.83)
histoplasmosis (115.0-115.9 with fifth-digit 3)
meningococcal infection (036.41)
syphilitic (093.81)

✓5th **420.9 Other and unspecified acute pericarditis**

420.90 Acute pericarditis, unspecified
Pericarditis (acute):
- NOS
- infective NOS
- sicca

420.91 Acute idiopathic pericarditis
Pericarditis, acute:
- benign
- nonspecific
- viral

Anatomy

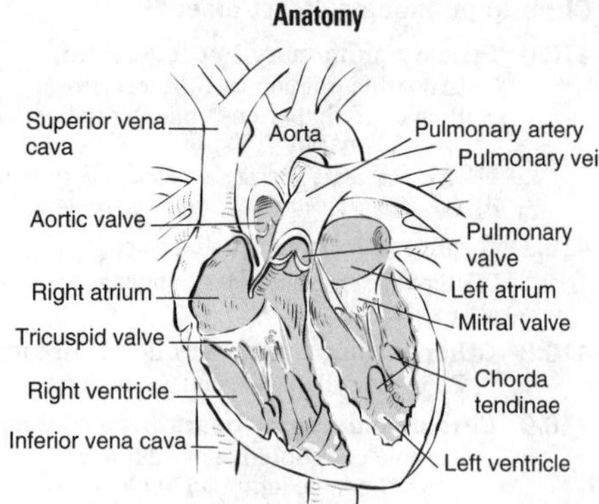

420.99 Other

Pericarditis (acute):
- pneumococcal
- purulent
- staphylococcal
- streptococcal
- suppurative

Pneumopyopericardium
Pyopericardium

EXCLUDES *pericarditis in diseases classified elsewhere (420.0)*

✓4th 421 Acute and subacute endocarditis

DEF: Bacterial inflammation of the endocardium (intracardiac area); major symptoms include fever, fatigue, heart murmurs, splenomegaly, embolic episodes and areas of infarction.

421.0 Acute and subacute bacterial endocarditis

Endocarditis (acute)(chronic) (subacute):
- bacterial
- infective NOS
- lenta
- malignant
- purulent
- septic
- ulcerative
- vegetative

Infective aneurysm
Subacute bacterial endocarditis [SBE]

Use additional code to identify infectious organism [e.g., Streptococcus 041.0, Staphylococcus 041.1]

421.1 Acute and subacute infective endocarditis in diseases classified elsewhere

Code first underlying disease, as:
- blastomycosis (116.0)
- Q fever (083.0)
- typhoid (fever) (002.0)

EXCLUDES *endocarditis (in):*
- *Coxsackie (virus) (074.22)*
- *gonococcal (098.84)*
- *histoplasmosis (115.0-115.9 with fifth-digit 4)*
- *meningococcal infection (036.42)*
- *monilial (112.81)*

421.9 Acute endocarditis, unspecified

Endocarditis, Myoendocarditis, Periendocarditis } acute or subacute

EXCLUDES *acute rheumatic endocarditis (391.1)*

✓4th 422 Acute myocarditis

EXCLUDES *acute rheumatic myocarditis (391.2)*

DEF: Acute inflammation of the muscular walls of the heart (myocardium).

422.0 Acute myocarditis in diseases classified elsewhere

Code first underlying disease, as:
- myocarditis (acute):
  - influenzal (487.8)
  - tuberculous (017.9)

EXCLUDES *myocarditis (acute) (due to):*
- *aseptic, of newborn (074.23)*
- *Coxsackie (virus) (074.23)*
- *diphtheritic (032.82)*
- *meningococcal infection (036.43)*
- *syphilitic (093.82)*
- *toxoplasmosis (130.3)*

✓5th 422.9 Other and unspecified acute myocarditis

422.90 Acute myocarditis, unspecified

Acute or subacute (interstitial) myocarditis

422.91 Idiopathic myocarditis

Myocarditis (acute or subacute):
- Fiedler's
- giant cell
- isolated (diffuse) (granulomatous)
- nonspecific granulomatous

422.92 Septic myocarditis

Myocarditis, acute or subacute:
- pneumococcal
- staphylococcal

Use additional code to identify infectious organism [e.g., Staphylococcus 041.1]

EXCLUDES *myocarditis, acute or subacute:*
- *in bacterial diseases classified elsewhere (422.0)*
- *streptococcal (391.2)*

422.93 Toxic myocarditis

DEF: Inflammation of the heart muscle due to an adverse reaction to certain drugs or chemicals reaching the heart through the bloodstream.

422.99 Other

✓4th 423 Other diseases of pericardium

EXCLUDES *that specified as rheumatic (393)*

423.0 Hemopericardium

DEF: Blood in the pericardial sac (pericardium).

423.1 Adhesive pericarditis

Adherent pericardium
Fibrosis of pericardium
Milk spots
Pericarditis:
- adhesive
- obliterative

Soldiers' patches

DEF: Two layers of serous pericardium adhere to each other by fibrous adhesions.

423.2 Constrictive pericarditis

Concato's disease
Pick's disease of heart (and liver)

DEF: Inflammation identified by a rigid, thickened and sometimes calcified pericardium; ventricles of the heart cannot be adequately filled and congestive heart failure may result.

423.3 Cardiac tamponade

Code first the underlying cause

DEF: Life-threatening condition in which fluid or blood accumulates between the muscle of the heart (myocardium) and the outer sac (pericardium), resulting in compression of the heart, which decreases cardiac output.

423.8 Other specified diseases of pericardium

Calcification, Fistula } of pericardium

Cardiac Tamponade

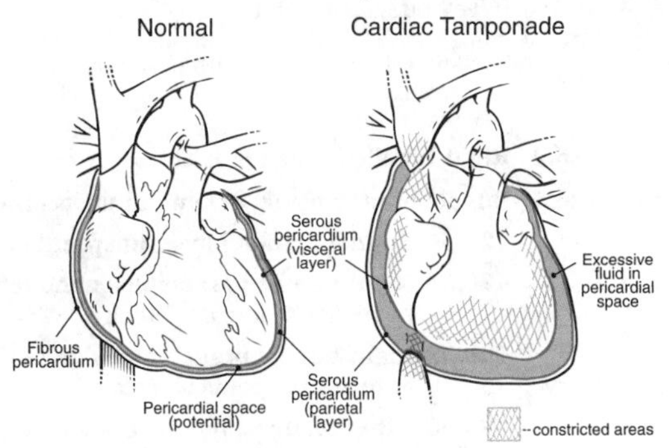

423.9 Unspecified disease of pericardium

✓4th 424 Other diseases of endocardium

EXCLUDES *bacterial endocarditis (421.0-421.9)*
rheumatic endocarditis (391.1, 394.0-397.9)
syphilitic endocarditis (093.20-093.24)

424.0 Mitral valve disorders

Mitral (valve):
- incompetence } NOS of specified cause, except rheumatic
- insufficiency
- regurgitation

EXCLUDES *mitral (valve):*
- *disease (394.9)*
- *failure (394.9)*
- *stenosis (394.0)*

the listed conditions:
- *specified as rheumatic (394.1)*
- *unspecified as to cause but with mention of:*
  - *diseases of aortic valve (396.0-396.9)*
  - *mitral stenosis or obstruction (394.2)*

424.1 Aortic valve disorders

Aortic (valve):
- incompetence } NOS of specified cause, except rheumatic
- insufficiency
- regurgitation
- stenosis

EXCLUDES *hypertrophic subaortic stenosis (425.1)*
that specified as rheumatic (395.0-395.9)
that of unspecified cause but with mention of diseases of mitral valve (396.0-396.9)

424.2 Tricuspid valve disorders, specified as nonrheumatic

Tricuspid valve:
- incompetence } of specified cause, except rheumatic
- insufficiency
- regurgitation
- stenosis

EXCLUDES *rheumatic or of unspecified cause (397.0)*

424.3 Pulmonary valve disorders

Pulmonic:
- incompetence NOS
- insufficiency NOS
- regurgitation NOS
- stenosis NOS

EXCLUDES *that specified as rheumatic (397.1)*

✓5th 424.9 Endocarditis, valve unspecified

424.90 Endocarditis, valve unspecified, unspecified cause

Endocarditis (chronic):
- NOS
- nonbacterial thrombotic

Valvular:
- incompetence } of unspecified valve, unspecified cause
- insufficiency
- regurgitation
- stenosis

Valvulitis (chronic)

Heart Valve Disorders

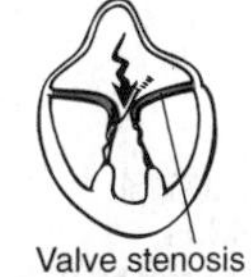

Normal Heart Valve Function

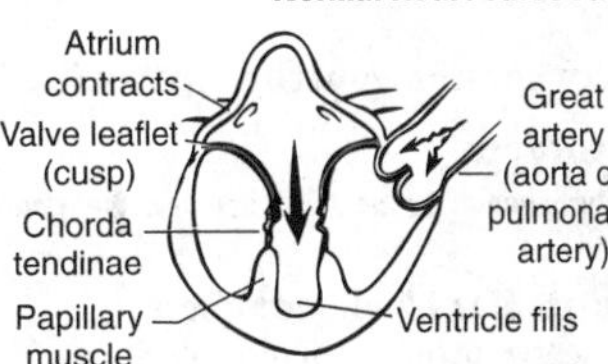

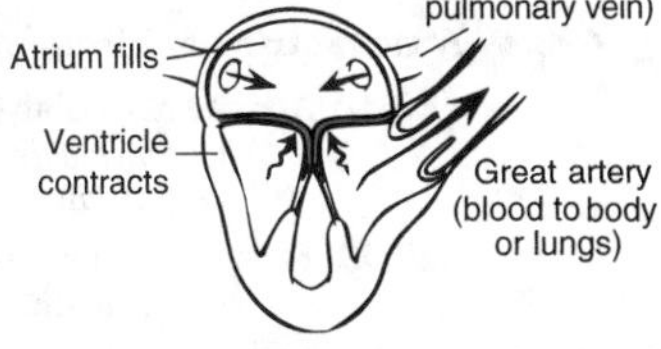

424.91 Endocarditis in diseases classified elsewhere

Code first underlying disease as:
- atypical verrucous endocarditis [Libman-Sacks] (710.0)
- disseminated lupus erythematosus (710.0)
- tuberculosis (017.9)

EXCLUDES *syphilitic (093.20-093.24)*

424.99 Other

Any condition classifiable to 424.90 with specified cause, except rheumatic

EXCLUDES *endocardial fibroelastosis (425.3)*
that specified as rheumatic (397.9)

✓4th 425 Cardiomyopathy

INCLUDES myocardiopathy

425.0 Endomyocardial fibrosis

425.1 Hypertrophic obstructive cardiomyopathy

Hypertrophic subaortic stenosis (idiopathic)

DEF: Cardiomyopathy marked by left ventricle hypertrophy, enlarged septum; results in obstructed blood flow.

425.2 Obscure cardiomyopathy of Africa

Becker's disease
Idiopathic mural endomyocardial disease

425.3 Endocardial fibroelastosis

Elastomyofibrosis

DEF: A condition marked by left ventricle hypertrophy and conversion of the endocardium into a thick fibroelastic coat; capacity of the ventricle may be reduced, but is often increased.

425.4 Other primary cardiomyopathies

Cardiomyopathy:
- NOS
- congestive
- constrictive
- familial
- hypertrophic

Cardiomyopathy:
- idiopathic
- nonobstructive
- obstructive
- restrictive

Cardiovascular collagenosis

425.5 Alcoholic cardiomyopathy

DEF: Heart disease as result of excess alcohol consumption.

425.7 *Nutritional and metabolic cardiomyopathy*

Code first underlying disease, as:
amyloidosis (277.30-277.39)
beriberi (265.0)
cardiac glycogenosis (271.0)
mucopolysaccharidosis (277.5)
thyrotoxicosis (242.0-242.9)

EXCLUDES *gouty tophi of heart (274.82)*

425.8 *Cardiomyopathy in other diseases classified elsewhere*

Code first underlying disease, as:
Friedreich's ataxia (334.0)
myotonia atrophica (359.21)
progressive muscular dystrophy (359.1)
sarcoidosis (135)

EXCLUDES *cardiomyopathy in Chagas' disease (086.0)*

425.9 Secondary cardiomyopathy, unspecified

✓4th **426 Conduction disorders**

DEF: Disruption or disturbance in the electrical impulses that regulate heartbeats.

426.0 Atrioventricular block, complete

Third degree atrioventricular block

✓5th **426.1 Atrioventricular block, other and unspecified**

426.10 Atrioventricular block, unspecified

Atrioventricular [AV] block (incomplete) (partial)

426.11 First degree atrioventricular block

Incomplete atrioventricular block, first degree
Prolonged P-R interval NOS

426.12 Mobitz (type) II atrioventricular block

Incomplete atrioventricular block:
Mobitz (type) II
second degree, Mobitz (type) II

DEF: Impaired conduction of excitatory impulse from cardiac atrium to ventricle through AV node.

426.13 Other second degree atrioventricular block

Incomplete atrioventricular block:
Mobitz (type) I [Wenckebach's]
second degree:
NOS
Mobitz (type) I
with 2:1 atrioventricular response [block]
Wenckebach's phenomenon

DEF: Wenckebach's phenomenon: impulses generated at constant rate to sinus node, P-R interval lengthens; results in cycle of ventricular inadequacy and shortened P-R interval; second-degree A-V block commonly called "Mobitz type 1."

426.2 Left bundle branch hemiblock

Block:
left anterior fascicular
left posterior fascicular

426.3 Other left bundle branch block

Left bundle branch block:
NOS
anterior fascicular with posterior fascicular
complete
main stem

426.4 Right bundle branch block

✓5th **426.5 Bundle branch block, other and unspecified**

426.50 Bundle branch block, unspecified

426.51 Right bundle branch block and left posterior fascicular block

426.52 Right bundle branch block and left anterior fascicular block

426.53 Other bilateral bundle branch block

Bifascicular block NOS
Bilateral bundle branch block NOS
Right bundle branch with left bundle branch block (incomplete) (main stem)

426.54 Trifascicular block

426.6 Other heart block

Intraventricular block:
NOS
diffuse
myofibrillar
Sinoatrial block
Sinoauricular block

426.7 Anomalous atrioventricular excitation

Atrioventricular conduction:
accelerated
accessory
pre-excitation
Ventricular pre-excitation
Wolff-Parkinson-White syndrome

DEF: Wolff-Parkinson-White: normal conduction pathway is bypassed; results in short P-R interval on EKG; tendency to supraventricular tachycardia.

✓5th **426.8 Other specified conduction disorders**

426.81 Lown-Ganong-Levine syndrome

Syndrome of short P-R interval, normal QRS complexes, and supraventricular tachycardias

426.82 Long QT syndrome

DEF: Condition characterized by recurrent syncope, malignant arrhythmias, and sudden death; characteristic prolonged Q-T interval on electrocardiogram.

426.89 Other

Dissociation:
atrioventricular [AV]
interference
isorhythmic
Nonparoxysmal AV nodal tachycardia

426.9 Conduction disorder, unspecified

Heart block NOS
Stokes-Adams syndrome

Nerve Conduction of the Heart

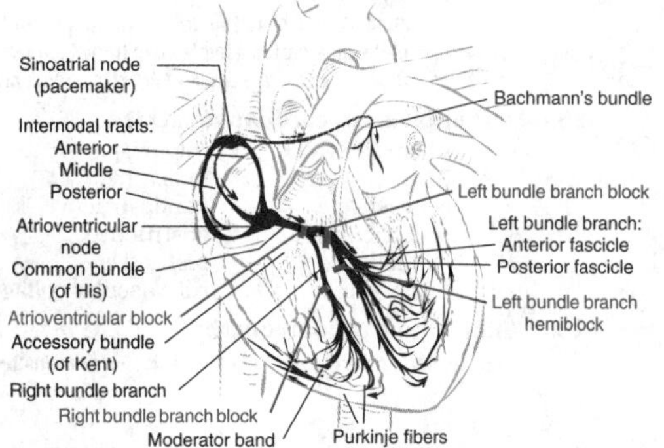

Normal and Long QT Electrocardiogram

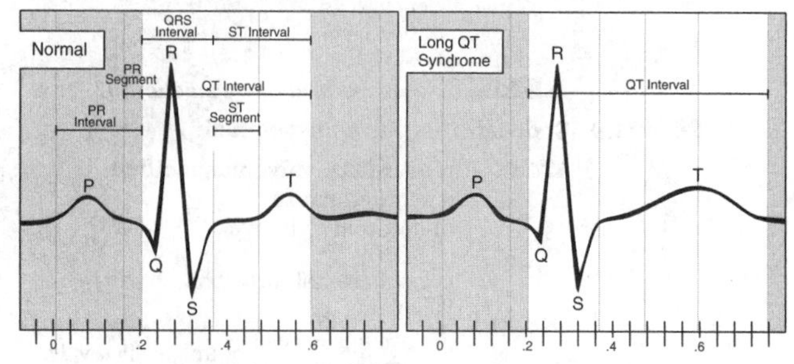

✓4th **427 Cardiac dysrhythmias**

EXCLUDES *that complicating:*
abortion (634-638 with .7, 639.8)
ectopic or molar pregnancy (639.8)
labor or delivery (668.1, 669.4)

DEF: Disruption or disturbance in the rhythm of heartbeats.

427.0 Paroxysmal supraventricular tachycardia
Paroxysmal tachycardia:
atrial [PAT]
atrioventricular [AV]
junctional
nodal

DEF: Rapid atrial rhythm.

427.1 Paroxysmal ventricular tachycardia
Ventricular tachycardia (paroxysmal)

DEF: Rapid ventricular rhythm.

427.2 Paroxysmal tachycardia, unspecified
Bouveret-Hoffmann syndrome
Paroxysmal tachycardia:
essential
NOS

✓5th **427.3 Atrial fibrillation and flutter**

427.31 Atrial fibrillation

DEF: Irregular, rapid atrial contractions.

427.32 Atrial flutter

DEF: Regular, rapid atrial contractions.

✓5th **427.4 Ventricular fibrillation and flutter**

427.41 Ventricular fibrillation

DEF: Irregular, rapid ventricular contractions.

427.42 Ventricular flutter

DEF: Regular, rapid, ventricular contractions.

427.5 Cardiac arrest
Cardiorespiratory arrest

✓5th **427.6 Premature beats**

427.60 Premature beats, unspecified
Ectopic beats
Extrasystoles
Extrasystolic arrhythmia
Premature contractions or systoles NOS

427.61 Supraventricular premature beats
Atrial premature beats, contractions, or systoles

427.69 Other
Ventricular premature beats, contractions, or systoles

✓5th **427.8 Other specified cardiac dysrhythmias**

427.81 Sinoatrial node dysfunction
Sinus bradycardia:
persistent
severe
Syndrome:
sick sinus
tachycardia-bradycardia

EXCLUDES *sinus bradycardia NOS (427.89)*

DEF: Complex cardiac arrhythmia; appears as severe sinus bradycardia, sinus bradycardia with tachycardia, or sinus bradycardia with atrioventricular block.

427.89 Other
Rhythm disorder:
coronary sinus
ectopic
nodal
Wandering (atrial) pacemaker

EXCLUDES *carotid sinus syncope (337.0)*
neonatal bradycardia (779.81)
neonatal tachycardia (779.82)
reflex bradycardia (337.0)
tachycardia NOS (785.0)

427.9 Cardiac dysrhythmia, unspecified
Arrhythmia (cardiac) NOS

Echocardiography of Heart Failure

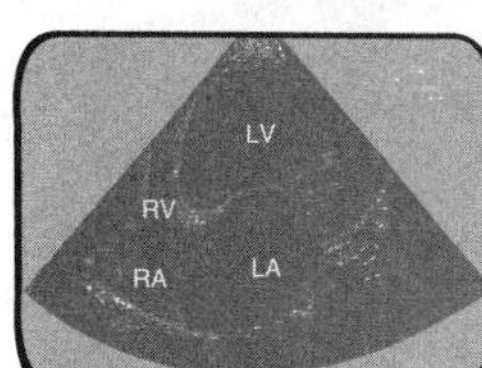

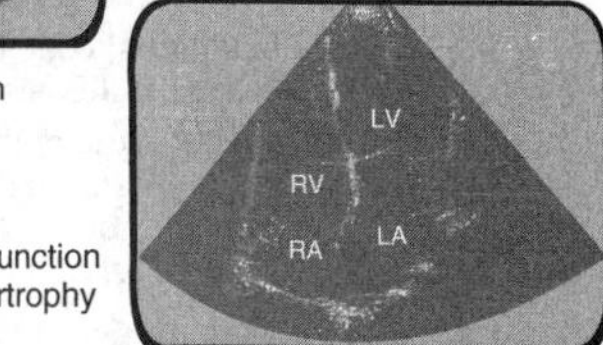

Four-chamber echocardiograms, two-dimensional views.
LV: Left ventricle
RV: Right ventricle
RA: Right atrium
LA: Left atrium

Systolic dysfunction with dilated LV

Diastolic dysfunction with LV hypertrophy

✓4th **428 Heart failure**

Code, if applicable, heart failure due to hypertension first (402.0-402.9, with fifth-digit 1 or 404.0-404.9 with fifth-digit 1 or 3)

EXCLUDES *following cardiac surgery (429.4)*
rheumatic (398.91)
that complicating:
abortion (634-638 with .7, 639.8)
ectopic or molar pregnancy (639.8)
labor or delivery (668.1, 669.4)

428.0 Congestive heart failure, unspecified
Congestive heart disease
Right heart failure (secondary to left heart failure)

EXCLUDES *fluid overload NOS (276.6)*

DEF: Mechanical inadequacy; caused by inability of heart to pump and circulate blood; results in fluid collection in lungs, hypertension, congestion and edema of tissue.

428.1 Left heart failure
Acute edema of lung } with heart disease NOS or heart failure
Acute pulmonary edema } with heart disease NOS or heart failure
Cardiac asthma
Left ventricular failure

DEF: Mechanical inadequacy of left ventricle; causing fluid in lungs.

✓5th **428.2 Systolic heart failure**

EXCLUDES *combined systolic and diastolic heart failure (428.40-428.43)*

DEF: Heart failure due to a defect in expulsion of blood caused by an abnormality in systolic function, or ventricular contractile dysfunction.

428.20 Unspecified

428.21 Acute

428.22 Chronic

428.23 Acute on chronic

✓5th **428.3 Diastolic heart failure**

EXCLUDES *combined systolic and diastolic heart failure (428.40-428.43)*

DEF: Heart failure due to resistance to ventricular filling caused by an abnormality in the diastolic function.

428.30 Unspecified

428.31 Acute

428.32 Chronic

428.33 Acute on chronic

✓5th **428.4 Combined systolic and diastolic heart failure**

428.40 Unspecified

428.41 Acute

428.42 Chronic

428.43 Acute on chronic

428.9 Heart failure, unspecified
Cardiac failure NOS
Heart failure NOS
Myocardial failure NOS
Weak heart

4th 429 Ill-defined descriptions and complications of heart disease

429.0 Myocarditis, unspecified

Myocarditis:
NOS
chronic (interstitial
fibroid
senile
} (with mention of arteriosclerosis)

Use additional code to identify presence of arteriosclerosis

EXCLUDES *acute or subacute (422.0-422.9)*
rheumatic (398.0)
acute (391.2)
that due to hypertension (402.0-402.9)

429.1 Myocardial degeneration

Degeneration of heart or myocardium:
fatty
mural
muscular
Myocardial:
degeneration
disease
} (with mention of arteriosclerosis)

Use additional code to identify presence of arteriosclerosis

EXCLUDES *that due to hypertension (402.0-402.9)*

429.2 Cardiovascular disease, unspecified

Arteriosclerotic cardiovascular disease [ASCVD]
Cardiovascular arteriosclerosis
Cardiovascular:
degeneration
disease
sclerosis
} (with mention of arteriosclerosis)

Use additional code to identify presence of arteriosclerosis

EXCLUDES *that due to hypertension (402.0-402.9)*

429.3 Cardiomegaly

Cardiac:
dilatation
hypertrophy
Ventricular dilatation

EXCLUDES *that due to hypertension (402.0-402.9)*

429.4 Functional disturbances following cardiac surgery

Cardiac insufficiency
Heart failure
} following cardiac surgery or due to presthesis

Postcardiotomy syndrome
Postvalvulotomy syndrome

EXCLUDES *cardiac failure in the immediate postoperative period (997.1)*

429.5 Rupture of chordae tendineae

DEF: Torn tissue, between heart valves and papillary muscles.

429.6 Rupture of papillary muscle

DEF: Torn muscle, between chordae tendineae and heart wall.

5th 429.7 Certain sequelae of myocardial infarction, not elsewhere classified

Use additional code to identify the associated myocardial infarction:
with onset of 8 weeks or less (410.00-410.92)
with onset of more than 8 weeks (414.8)

EXCLUDES *congenital defects of heart (745, 746)*
coronary aneurysm (414.11)
disorders of papillary muscle (429.6, 429.81)
postmyocardial infarction syndrome (411.0)
rupture of chordae tendineae (429.5)

429.71 Acquired cardiac septal defect

EXCLUDES *acute septal infarction (410.00-410.92)*

DEF: Abnormal communication, between opposite heart chambers; due to defect of septum; not present at birth.

429.79 Other

Mural thrombus (atrial) (ventricular), acquired, following myocardial infarction

5th 429.8 Other ill-defined heart diseases

429.81 Other disorders of papillary muscle

Papillary muscle:
atrophy
degeneration
dysfunction
incompetence
incoordination
scarring

429.82 Hyperkinetic heart disease

DEF: Condition of unknown origin in young adults; marked by increased cardiac output at rest, increased rate of ventricular ejection; may lead to heart failure.

429.83 Takotsubo syndrome

Broken heart syndrome
Reversible left ventricular dysfunction following sudden emotional stress
Stress induced cardiomyopathy
Transient left ventricular apical ballooning syndrome

429.89 Other

Carditis

EXCLUDES *that due to hypertension (402.0-402.9)*

429.9 Heart disease, unspecified

Heart disease (organic) NOS
Morbus cordis NOS

EXCLUDES *that due to hypertension (402.0-402.9)*

CEREBROVASCULAR DISEASE (430-438)

INCLUDES with mention of hypertension (conditions classifiable to 401-405)

Use additional code to identify presence of hypertension

EXCLUDES *any condition classifiable to 430-434, 436, 437 occurring during pregnancy, childbirth, or the puerperium, or specified as puerperal (674.0)*
iatrogenic cerebrovascular infarction or hemorrhage (997.02)

430 Subarachnoid hemorrhage

Meningeal hemorrhage
Ruptured:
berry aneurysm
(congenital) cerebral aneurysm NOS

EXCLUDES *syphilitic ruptured cerebral aneurysm (094.87)*

DEF: Bleeding in space between brain and lining.

431 Intracerebral hemorrhage

Hemorrhage (of):
basilar
bulbar
cerebellar
cerebral
cerebromeningeal
cortical

Hemorrhage (of):
internal capsule
intrapontine
pontine
subcortical
ventricular

Rupture of blood vessel in brain

DEF: Bleeding within the brain.

4th 432 Other and unspecified intracranial hemorrhage

432.0 Nontraumatic extradural hemorrhage

Nontraumatic epidural hemorrhage

DEF: Bleeding, nontraumatic, between skull and brain lining.

Berry Aneurysms

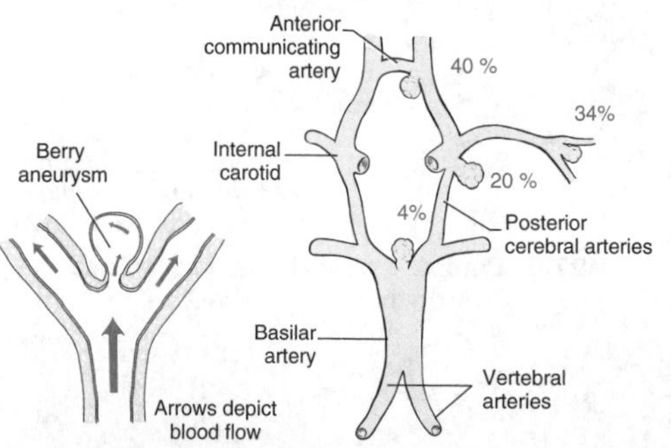

Cerebrovascular Arteries

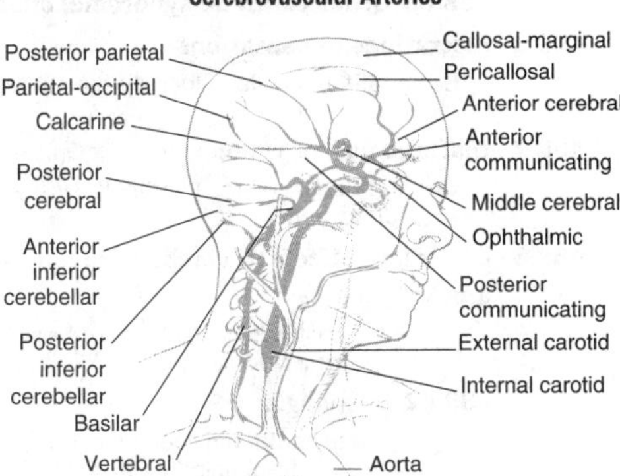

432.1 Subdural hemorrhage
Subdural hematoma, nontraumatic
DEF: Bleeding, between outermost and other layers of brain lining.

432.9 Unspecified intracranial hemorrhage
Intracranial hemorrhage NOS

✓4th **433 Occlusion and stenosis of precerebral arteries**

INCLUDES embolism, narrowing, obstruction, thrombosis of basilar, carotid, and vertebral arteries

Use additional code, if applicable, to identify status post administration of tPA (rtPA) in a different facility within the last 24 hours prior to admission to current facility (V45.88)

EXCLUDES *insufficiency NOS of precerebral arteries (435.0-435.9)*

The following fifth-digit subclassification is for use with category 433:
0 without mention of cerebral infarction
1 with cerebral infarction

DEF: Blockage, stricture, arteries branching into brain.

✓5th **433.0 Basilar artery**
[0-1]

✓5th **433.1 Carotid artery**
[0-1]

✓5th **433.2 Vertebral artery**
[0-1]

✓5th **433.3 Multiple and bilateral**
[0-1]

✓5th **433.8 Other specified precerebral artery**
[0-1]

✓5th **433.9 Unspecified precerebral artery**
[0-1] Precerebral artery NOS

✓4th **434 Occlusion of cerebral arteries**
Use additional code, if applicable, to identify status post administration of tPA (rtPA) in a different facility within the last 24 hours prior to admission to current facility (V45.88)

The following fifth-digit subclassification is for use with category 434:
0 without mention of cerebral infarction
1 with cerebral infarction

✓5th **434.0 Cerebral thrombosis**
[0-1] Thrombosis of cerebral arteries

✓5th **434.1 Cerebral embolism**
[0-1]

✓5th **434.9 Cerebral artery occlusion, unspecified**
[0-1]

✓4th **435 Transient cerebral ischemia**

INCLUDES cerebrovascular insufficiency (acute) with transient focal neurological signs and symptoms
insufficiency of basilar, carotid, and vertebral arteries
spasm of cerebral arteries

EXCLUDES *acute cerebrovascular insufficiency NOS (437.1)*
that due to any condition classifiable to 433 (433.0-433.9)

435.0 Basilar artery syndrome

435.1 Vertebral artery syndrome

435.2 Subclavian steal syndrome
DEF: Cerebrovascular insufficiency, due to occluded subclavian artery; symptoms include pain in mastoid and posterior head regions, flaccid paralysis of arm and diminished or absent radial pulse on affected side.

435.3 Vertebrobasilar artery syndrome
DEF: Transient ischemic attack; due to brainstem dysfunction; symptoms include confusion, vertigo, binocular blindness, diplopia, unilateral or bilateral weakness and paresthesis of extremities.

435.8 Other specified transient cerebral ischemias

435.9 Unspecified transient cerebral ischemia
Impending cerebrovascular accident
Intermittent cerebral ischemia
Transient ischemic attack [TIA]

436 Acute, but ill-defined, cerebrovascular disease
Apoplexy, apoplectic:
NOS
attack
cerebral
seizure
Cerebral seizure

EXCLUDES *any condition classifiable to categories 430-435*
cerebrovascular accident (434.91)
CVA (ischemic) (434.91)
embolic (434.11)
hemorrhagic (430, 431, 432.0-432.9)
thrombotic (434.01)
postoperative cerebrovascular accident (997.02)
stroke (ischemic) (434.91)
embolic (434.11)
hemorrhagic (430, 431, 432.0-432.9)
thrombotic (434.01)

✓4th **437 Other and ill-defined cerebrovascular disease**

437.0 Cerebral atherosclerosis
Atheroma of cerebral arteries
Cerebral arteriosclerosis

437.1 Other generalized ischemic cerebrovascular disease
Acute cerebrovascular insufficiency NOS
Cerebral ischemia (chronic)

437.2 Hypertensive encephalopathy
DEF: Cerebral manifestations (such as visual disturbances and headache) due to high blood pressure.

437.3 Cerebral aneurysm, nonruptured
Internal carotid artery, intracranial portion
Internal carotid artery NOS

EXCLUDES *congenital cerebral aneurysm, nonruptured (747.81)*
internal carotid artery, extracranial portion (442.81)

437.4 Cerebral arteritis
DEF: Inflammation of a cerebral artery or arteries.

437.5 Moyamoya disease
DEF: Cerebrovascular ischemia; vessels occlude and rupture causing tiny hemorrhages at base of brain; predominantly affects Japanese.

437.6 Nonpyogenic thrombosis of intracranial venous sinus

EXCLUDES *pyogenic (325)*

437.7 Transient global amnesia
DEF: Episode of short-term memory loss, not often recurrent; pathogenesis unknown; with no signs or symptoms of neurological disorder.

437.8 Other

437.9 Unspecified

Cerebrovascular disease or lesion NOS

✓4th **438 Late effects of cerebrovascular disease**

Note: This category is to be used to indicate conditions in 430-437 as the cause of late effects. The "late effects" include conditions specified as such, as sequelae, which may occur at any time after the onset of the causal condition.

EXCLUDES *personal history of:*
cerebral infarction without residual deficits (V12.54)
PRIND [Prolonged reversible ischemic neurologic deficit] (V12.54)
RIND [Reversible ischemic neurological deficit] (V12.54)
transient ischemic attack [TIA] (V12.54)

438.0 Cognitive deficits

✓5th **438.1 Speech and language deficits**

438.10 Speech and language deficit, unspecified

438.11 Aphasia

DEF: Impairment or absence of the ability to communicate by speech, writing or signs or to comprehend the spoken or written language due to disease or injury to the brain. Total aphasia is the loss of function of both sensory and motor areas of the brain.

438.12 Dysphasia

DEF: Impaired speech; marked by inability to sequence language.

438.19 Other speech and language deficits

✓5th **438.2 Hemiplegia/hemiparesis**

DEF: Paralysis of one side of the body.

438.20 Hemiplegia affecting unspecified side

438.21 Hemiplegia affecting dominant side

438.22 Hemiplegia affecting nondominant side

✓5th **438.3 Monoplegia of upper limb**

DEF: Paralysis of one limb or one muscle group.

438.30 Monoplegia of upper limb affecting unspecified side

438.31 Monoplegia of upper limb affecting dominant side

438.32 Monoplegia of upper limb affecting nondominant side

✓5th **438.4 Monoplegia of lower limb**

438.40 Monoplegia of lower limb affecting unspecified side

438.41 Monoplegia of lower limb affecting dominant side

438.42 Monoplegia of lower limb affecting nondominant side

✓5th **438.5 Other paralytic syndrome**

Use additional code to identify type of paralytic syndrome, such as:
locked-in state (344.81)
quadriplegia (344.00-344.09)

EXCLUDES *late effects of cerebrovascular accident with:*
hemiplegia/hemiparesis (438.20-438.22)
monoplegia of lower limb (438.40-438.42)
monoplegia of upper limb (438.30-438.32)

438.50 Other paralytic syndrome affecting unspecified side

438.51 Other paralytic syndrome affecting dominant side

438.52 Other paralytic syndrome affecting nondominant side

438.53 Other paralytic syndrome, bilateral

438.6 Alterations of sensations

Use additional code to identify the altered sensation

438.7 Disturbances of vision

Use additional code to identify the visual disturbance

✓5th **438.8 Other late effects of cerebrovascular disease**

438.81 Apraxia

DEF: Inability to activate learned movements; no known sensory or motor impairment.

438.82 Dysphagia

Use additional code to identify the type of dysphagia, if known (787.20-787.29)

DEF: Inability or difficulty in swallowing.

438.83 Facial weakness

Facial droop

438.84 Ataxia

438.85 Vertigo

438.89 Other late effects of cerebrovascular disease

Use additional code to identify the late effect

438.9 Unspecified late effects of cerebrovascular disease

DISEASES OF ARTERIES, ARTERIOLES, AND CAPILLARIES (440-449)

✓4th **440 Atherosclerosis**

INCLUDES arteriolosclerosis
arteriosclerosis (obliterans) (senile)
arteriosclerotic vascular disease
atheroma
degeneration:
arterial
arteriovascular
vascular
endarteritis deformans or obliterans
senile:
arteritis
endarteritis

EXCLUDES *atheroembolism (445.01-445.89)*
atherosclerosis of bypass graft of the extremities (440.30-440.32)

DEF: Stricture and reduced elasticity of an artery; due to plaque deposits.

440.0 Of aorta

440.1 Of renal artery

EXCLUDES *atherosclerosis of renal arterioles (403.00-403.91)*

✓5th **440.2 Of native arteries of the extremities**

Use additional code, if applicable, to identify chronic total occlusion of artery of the extremities (440.4)

EXCLUDES *atherosclerosis of bypass graft of the extremities (440.30-440.32)*

440.20 Atherosclerosis of the extremities, unspecified

440.21 Atherosclerosis of the extremities with intermittent claudication

DEF: Atherosclerosis; marked by pain, tension and weakness after walking; no symptoms while at rest.

440.22 Atherosclerosis of the extremities with rest pain

INCLUDES any condition classifiable to 440.21

DEF: Atherosclerosis, marked by pain, tension and weakness while at rest.

Map of Major Arteries

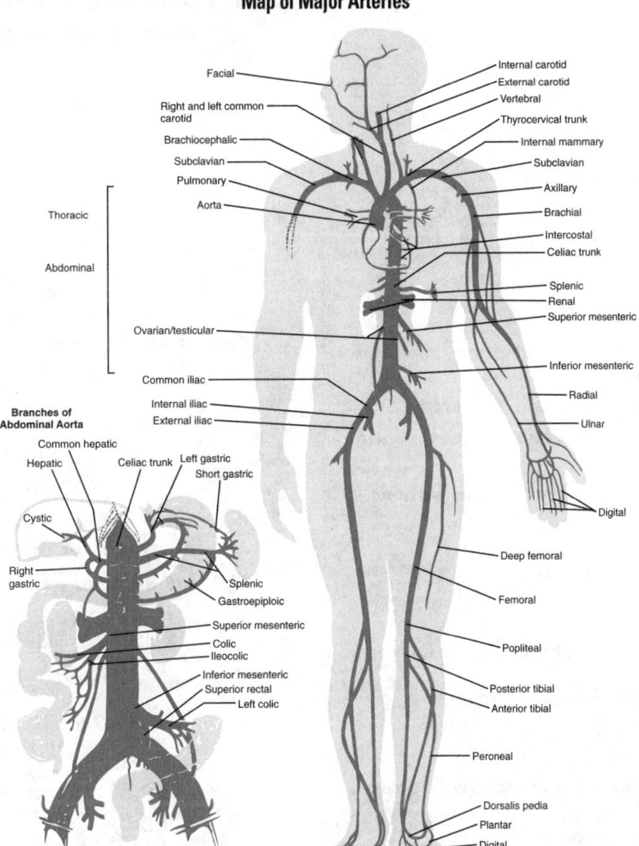

440.23 Atherosclerosis of the extremities with ulceration

INCLUDES any condition classifiable to 440.21 and 440.22

Use additional code for any associated ulceration (707.10-707.9)

440.24 Atherosclerosis of the extremities with gangrene

INCLUDES any condition classifiable to 440.21, 440.22, and 440.23 with ischemic gangrene 785.4

Use additional code for any associated ulceration (707.10-707.9)

EXCLUDES *gas gangrene (040.0)*

440.29 Other

✓5th **440.3 Of bypass graft of extremities**

EXCLUDES *atherosclerosis of native arteries of the extremities (440.21-440.24)*
embolism [occlusion NOS] [thrombus] of graft (996.74)

440.30 Of unspecified graft

440.31 Of autologous vein bypass graft

440.32 Of nonautologous biological bypass graft

440.4 Chronic total occlusion of artery of the extremities

Complete occlusion of artery of the extremities
Total occlusion of artery of the extremities

Code first atherosclerosis of arteries of the extremities (440.20-440.29, 440.30-440.32)

EXCLUDES *acute occlusion of artery of extremity (444.21-444.22)*

440.8 Of other specified arteries

EXCLUDES *basilar (433.0)*
carotid (433.1)
cerebral (437.0)
coronary (414.00-414.07)
mesenteric (557.1)
precerebral (433.0-433.9)
pulmonary (416.0)
vertebral (433.2)

440.9 Generalized and unspecified atherosclerosis

Arteriosclerotic vascular disease NOS

EXCLUDES *arteriosclerotic cardiovascular disease [ASCVD] (429.2)*

✓4th **441 Aortic aneurysm and dissection**

EXCLUDES *syphilitic aortic aneurysm (093.0)*
traumatic aortic aneurysm (901.0, 902.0)

✓5th **441.0 Dissection of aorta**

DEF: Dissection or splitting of wall of the aorta; due to blood entering through intimal tear or interstitial hemorrhage.

441.00 Unspecified site

441.01 Thoracic

441.02 Abdominal

441.03 Thoracoabdominal

441.1 Thoracic aneurysm, ruptured

441.2 Thoracic aneurysm without mention of rupture

441.3 Abdominal aneurysm, ruptured

441.4 Abdominal aneurysm without mention of rupture

Thoracic and Abdominal Aortic Aneurysm

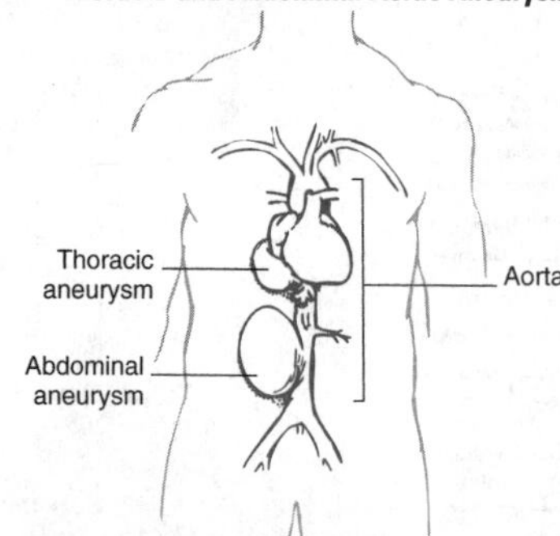

441.5 Aortic aneurysm of unspecified site, ruptured
Rupture of aorta NOS

441.6 Thoracoabdominal aneurysm, ruptured

441.7 Thoracoabdominal aneurysm, without mention of rupture

441.9 Aortic aneurysm of unspecified site without mention of rupture
Aneurysm
Dilatation
Hyaline necrosis } of aorta

✓4th **442 Other aneurysm**
INCLUDES aneurysm (ruptured) (cirsoid) (false) (varicose)
aneurysmal varix
EXCLUDES *arteriovenous aneurysm or fistula:*
acquired (447.0)
congenital (747.60-747.69)
traumatic (900.0-904.9)
DEF: Dissection or splitting of arterial wall; due to blood entering through intimal tear or interstitial hemorrhage.

442.0 Of artery of upper extremity

442.1 Of renal artery

442.2 Of iliac artery

442.3 Of artery of lower extremity
Aneurysm:
femoral artery
popliteal artery

✓5th **442.8 Of other specified artery**

442.81 Artery of neck
Aneurysm of carotid artery (common) (external) (internal, extracranial portion)
EXCLUDES *internal carotid artery, intracranial portion (437.3)*

442.82 Subclavian artery

442.83 Splenic artery

442.84 Other visceral artery
Aneurysm:
celiac
gastroduodenal
gastroepiploic
hepatic
pancreaticoduodenal
superior mesenteric } artery

442.89 Other
Aneurysm:
mediastinal artery
spinal artery
EXCLUDES *cerebral (nonruptured) (437.3)*
congenital (747.81)
ruptured (430)
coronary (414.11)
heart (414.10)
pulmonary (417.1)

442.9 Of unspecified site

✓4th **443 Other peripheral vascular disease**

443.0 Raynaud's syndrome
Raynaud's:
disease
phenomenon (secondary)
Use additional code to identify gangrene (785.4)
DEF: Constriction of the arteries, due to cold or stress; bilateral ischemic attacks of fingers, toes, nose or ears; symptoms include pallor, paresthesia and pain; more common in females.

443.1 Thromboangiitis obliterans [Buerger's disease]
Presenile gangrene
DEF: Inflammatory disease of extremity blood vessels, mainly the lower; occurs primarily in young men and leads to tissue ischemia and gangrene.

✓5th **443.2 Other arterial dissection**
EXCLUDES *dissection of aorta (441.00-441.03)*
dissection of coronary arteries (414.12)

443.21 Dissection of carotid artery

443.22 Dissection of iliac artery

443.23 Dissection of renal artery

443.24 Dissection of vertebral artery

443.29 Dissection of other artery

✓5th **443.8 Other specified peripheral vascular diseases**

443.81 Peripheral angiopathy in diseases classified elsewhere
Code first underlying disease, as:
diabetes mellitus (249.7, 250.7)

443.82 Erythromelalgia
DEF: Rare syndrome of paroxysmal vasodilation; maldistribution of blood flow causes redness, pain, increased skin temperature, and burning sensations in various parts of the body.

443.89 Other
Acrocyanosis
Acroparesthesia:
simple [Schultze's type]
vasomotor [Nothnagel's type]
Erythrocyanosis
EXCLUDES *chilblains (991.5)*
frostbite (991.0-991.3)
immersion foot (991.4)

443.9 Peripheral vascular disease, unspecified
Intermittent claudication NOS
Peripheral:
angiopathy NOS
vascular disease NOS
Spasm of artery
EXCLUDES *atherosclerosis of the arteries of the extremities (440.20-440.22)*
spasm of cerebral artery (435.0-435.9)

✓4th **444 Arterial embolism and thrombosis**
INCLUDES infarction:
embolic
thrombotic
occlusion
EXCLUDES *atheroembolism (445.01-445.89)*
that complicating:
abortion (634-638 with .6, 639.6)
ectopic or molar pregnancy (639.6)
pregnancy, childbirth, or the pueperium (673.0-673.8)
septic arterial embolism (449)

444.0 Of abdominal aorta
Aortic bifurcation syndrome
Aortoiliac obstruction
Leriche's syndrome
Saddle embolus

444.1 Of thoracic aorta
Embolism or thrombosis of aorta (thoracic)

✓5th **444.2 Of arteries of the extremities**

444.21 Upper extremity

Arterial Diseases and Disorders

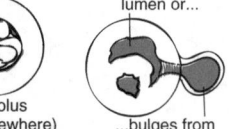

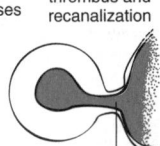

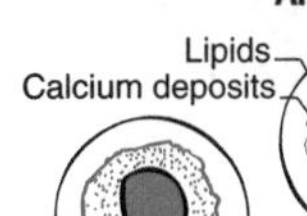
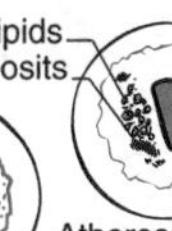
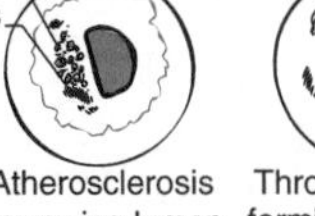
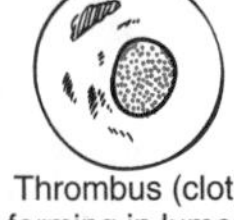

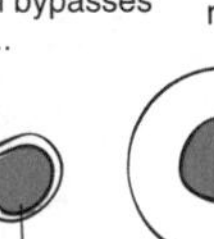

444.22 Lower extremity
Arterial embolism or thrombosis:
femoral
peripheral NOS
popliteal
EXCLUDES *iliofemoral (444.81)*

✓5th **444.8 Of other specified artery**

444.81 Iliac artery

444.89 Other
EXCLUDES *basilar (433.0)*
carotid (433.1)
cerebral (434.0-434.9)
coronary (410.00-410.92)
mesenteric (557.0)
ophthalmic (362.30-362.34)
precerebral (433.0-433.9)
pulmonary (415.19)
renal (593.81)
retinal (362.30-362.34)
vertebral (433.2)

444.9 Of unspecified artery

445 Atheroembolism
INCLUDES atherothrombotic microembolism
cholesterol embolism

✓5th **445.0 Of extremities**

445.01 Upper extremity

445.02 Lower extremity

✓5th **445.8 Of other sites**

445.81 Kidney
Use additional code for any associated acute renal failure or chronic kidney disease (584, 585)

445.89 Other site

✓4th **446 Polyarteritis nodosa and allied conditions**

446.0 Polyarteritis nodosa
Disseminated necrotizing periarteritis
Necrotizing angiitis
Panarteritis (nodosa)
Periarteritis (nodosa)
DEF: Inflammation of small and mid-size arteries; symptoms related to involved arteries in kidneys, muscles, gastrointestinal tract and heart; results in tissue death.

446.1 Acute febrile mucocutaneous lymph node syndrome [MCLS]
Kawasaki disease
DEF: Acute febrile disease of children; marked by erythema of conjunctiva and mucous membranes of upper respiratory tract, skin eruptions and edema.

✓5th **446.2 Hypersensitivity angiitis**
EXCLUDES *antiglomerular basement membrane disease without pulmonary hemorrhage (583.89)*

446.20 Hypersensitivity angiitis, unspecified

446.21 Goodpasture's syndrome
Antiglomerular basement membrane antibody-mediated nephritis with pulmonary hemorrhage
Use additional code to identify renal disease (583.81)
DEF: Glomerulonephritis associated with hematuria, progresses rapidly; results in death from renal failure.

446.29 Other specified hypersensitivity angiitis

446.3 Lethal midline granuloma
Malignant granuloma of face
DEF: Granulomatous lesion; in nose or paranasal sinuses; often fatal; occurs chiefly in males.

446.4 Wegener's granulomatosis
Necrotizing respiratory granulomatosis
Wegener's syndrome
DEF: A disease occurring mainly in men; marked by necrotizing granulomas and ulceration of the upper respiratory tract; underlying condition is a vasculitis affecting small vessels and is possibly due to an immune disorder.

446.5 Giant cell arteritis
Bagratuni's syndrome
Cranial arteritis
Horton's disease
Temporal arteritis
DEF: Inflammation of arteries; due to giant cells affecting carotid artery branches, resulting in occlusion; symptoms include fever, headache and neurological problems; occurs in elderly.

446.6 Thrombotic microangiopathy
Moschcowitz's syndrome
Thrombotic thrombocytopenic purpura
DEF: Blockage of small blood vessels; due to hyaline deposits; symptoms include purpura, CNS disorders; results in protracted disease or rapid death.

446.7 Takayasu's disease
Aortic arch arteritis
Pulseless disease
DEF: Progressive obliterative arteritis of brachiocephalic trunk, left subclavian, and left common carotid arteries above aortic arch; results in ischemia in brain, heart and arm; pulses impalpable in head, neck and arms; more common in young adult females.

✓4th **447 Other disorders of arteries and arterioles**

447.0 Arteriovenous fistula, acquired
Arteriovenous aneurysm, acquired
EXCLUDES *cerebrovascular (437.3)*
coronary (414.19)
pulmonary (417.0)
surgically created arteriovenous shunt or fistula:
complication (996.1, 996.61-996.62)
status or presence (V45.11)
traumatic (900.0-904.9)
DEF: Communication between an artery and vein caused by error in healing.

447.1 Stricture of artery

447.2 Rupture of artery
Erosion
Fistula, except arteriovenous } of artery
Ulcer
EXCLUDES *traumatic rupture of artery (900.0-904.9)*

447.3 Hyperplasia of renal artery
Fibromuscular hyperplasia of renal artery
DEF: Overgrowth of cells in muscular lining of renal artery.

447.4 Celiac artery compression syndrome
Celiac axis syndrome
Marable's syndrome

447.5 Necrosis of artery

Map of Major Veins

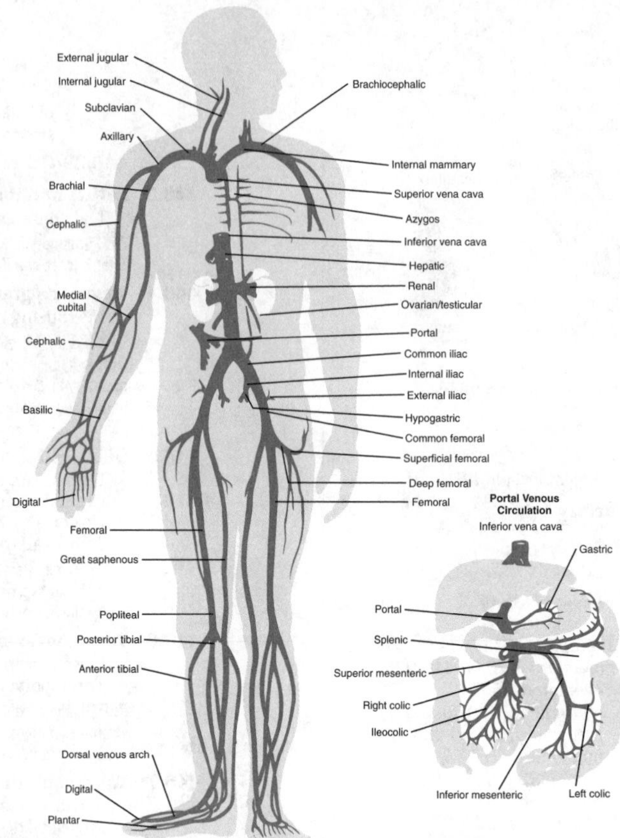

447.6 Arteritis, unspecified
Aortitis NOS
Endarteritis NOS
EXCLUDES *arteritis, endarteritis:*
aortic arch (446.7)
cerebral (437.4)
coronary (414.00-414.07)
deformans (440.0-440.9)
obliterans (440.0-440.9)
pulmonary (417.8)
senile (440.0-440.9)
polyarteritis NOS (446.0)
syphilitic aortitis (093.1)

447.8 Other specified disorders of arteries and arterioles
Fibromuscular hyperplasia of arteries, except renal

447.9 Unspecified disorders of arteries and arterioles

✓4th **448 Disease of capillaries**

448.0 Hereditary hemorrhagic telangiectasia
Rendu-Osler-Weber disease
DEF: Genetic disease with onset after puberty; results in multiple telangiectases, dilated venules on skin and mucous membranes; recurrent bleeding may occur.

448.1 Nevus, non-neoplastic
Nevus:
araneus
senile
spider
stellar
EXCLUDES *neoplastic (216.0-216.9)*
port wine (757.32)
strawberry (757.32)
DEF: Enlarged or malformed blood vessels of skin; results in reddish swelling, skin patch, or birthmark.

448.9 Other and unspecified capillary diseases
Capillary:
hemorrhage
hyperpermeability
thrombosis
EXCLUDES *capillary fragility (hereditary) (287.8)*

449 Septic arterial embolism
Code first underlying infection, such as:
infective endocarditis (421.0)
lung abscess (513.0)
Use additional code to identify the site of the embolism (433.0-433.9, 444.0-444.9)
EXCLUDES *septic pulmonary embolism (415.12)*

DISEASES OF VEINS AND LYMPHATICS, AND OTHER DISEASES OF CIRCULATORY SYSTEM (451-459)

✓4th **451 Phlebitis and thrombophlebitis**
INCLUDES endophlebitis
inflammation, vein
periphlebitis
suppurative phlebitis
Use additional E code to identify drug, if drug-induced
EXCLUDES *that complicating:*
abortion (634-638 with .7, 639.8)
ectopic or molar pregnancy (639.8)
pregnancy, childbirth, or the puerperium (671.0-671.9)
that due to or following:
implant or catheter device (996.61-996.62)
infusion, perfusion, or transfusion (999.2)
DEF: Inflammation of a vein (phlebitis) with formation of a thrombus (thrombophlebitis).

451.0 Of superficial vessels of lower extremities
Saphenous vein (greater) (lesser)

✓5th **451.1 Of deep vessels of lower extremities**

451.11 Femoral vein (deep) (superficial)

451.19 Other
Femoropopliteal vein
Popliteal vein
Tibial vein

451.2 Of lower extremities, unspecified

✓5th **451.8 Of other sites**

EXCLUDES *intracranial venous sinus (325)*
nonpyogenic (437.6)
portal (vein) (572.1)

451.81 Iliac vein

451.82 Of superficial veins of upper extremities
Antecubital vein
Basilic vein
Cephalic vein

451.83 Of deep veins of upper extremities
Brachial vein
Radial vein
Ulnar vein

451.84 Of upper extremities, unspecified

451.89 Other
Axillary vein
Jugular vein
Subclavian vein
Thrombophlebitis of breast (Mondor's disease)

451.9 Of unspecified site

452 Portal vein thrombosis
Portal (vein) obstruction

EXCLUDES *hepatic vein thrombosis (453.0)*
phlebitis of portal vein (572.1)

DEF: Formation of a blood clot in main vein of liver.

✓4th **453 Other venous embolism and thrombosis**

EXCLUDES *that complicating:*
abortion (634-638 with .7, 639.8)
ectopic or molar pregnancy (639.8)
pregnancy, childbirth, or the puerperium (671.0-671.9)
that with inflammation, phlebitis, and thrombophlebitis (451.0-451.9)

453.0 Budd-Chiari syndrome
Hepatic vein thrombosis

DEF: Thrombosis or other obstruction of hepatic vein; symptoms include enlarged liver, extensive collateral vessels, intractable ascites and severe portal hypertension.

453.1 Thrombophlebitis migrans

DEF: Slow, advancing thrombophlebitis; appearing first in one vein then another.

453.2 Of vena cava

453.3 Of renal vein

✓5th **453.4 Venous embolism and thrombosis of deep vessels of lower extremity**

453.40 Venous embolism and thrombosis of unspecified deep vessels of lower extremity
Deep vein thrombosis NOS
DVT NOS

453.41 Venous embolism and thrombosis of deep vessels of proximal lower extremity
Femoral
Iliac
Popliteal
Thigh
Upper leg NOS

453.42 Venous embolism and thrombosis of deep vessels of distal lower extremity
Calf
Lower leg NOS
Peroneal
Tibial

453.8 Of other specified veins

EXCLUDES *cerebral (434.0-434.9)*
coronary (410.00-410.92)
intracranial venous sinus (325)
nonpyogenic (437.6)
mesenteric (557.0)
portal (452)
precerebral (433.0-433.9)
pulmonary (415.19)

453.9 Of unspecified site
Embolism of vein
Thrombosis (vein)

✓4th **454 Varicose veins of lower extremities**

EXCLUDES *that complicating pregnancy, childbirth, or the puerperium (671.0)*

DEF: Dilated leg veins; due to incompetent vein valves that allow reversed blood flow and cause tissue erosion or weakness of wall; may be painful.

454.0 With ulcer
Varicose ulcer (lower extremity, any part)
Varicose veins with ulcer of lower extremity [any part] or of unspecified site
Any condition classifiable to 454.9 with ulcer or specified as ulcerated

454.1 With inflammation
Stasis dermatitis
Varicose veins with inflammation of lower extremity [any part] or of unspecified site
Any condition classifiable to 454.9 with inflammation or specified as inflamed

454.2 With ulcer and inflammation
Varicose veins with ulcer and inflammation of lower extremity [any part] or of unspecified site
Any condition classifiable to 454.9 with ulcer and inflammation

454.8 With other complications
Edema
Pain
Swelling

454.9 Asymptomatic varicose veins
Phlebectasia, Varicose veins, Varix } of lower extremity [any part] or of unspecified site
Varicose veins NOS

✓4th **455 Hemorrhoids**

INCLUDES hemorrhoids (anus) (rectum)
piles
varicose veins, anus or rectum

EXCLUDES *that complicating pregnancy, childbirth, or the puerperium (671.8)*

DEF: Varicose condition of external hemorrhoidal veins causing painful swellings at the anus.

455.0 Internal hemorrhoids without mention of complication

455.1 Internal thrombosed hemorrhoids

455.2 Internal hemorrhoids with other complication
Internal hemorrhoids:
bleeding
prolapsed
strangulated
ulcerated

455.3 External hemorrhoids without mention of complication

455.4 External thrombosed hemorrhoids

455.5 External hemorrhoids with other complication
External hemorrhoids:
bleeding
prolapsed
strangulated
ulcerated

455.6 Unspecified hemorrhoids without mention of complication
Hemorrhoids NOS

455.7 Unspecified thrombosed hemorrhoids
Thrombosed hemorrhoids, unspecified whether internal or external

455.8 Unspecified hemorrhoids with other complication
Hemorrhoids, unspecified whether internal or external:
bleeding
prolapsed
strangulated
ulcerated

455.9 Residual hemorrhoidal skin tags
Skin tags, anus or rectum

4th 456 Varicose veins of other sites

456.0 Esophageal varices with bleeding
DEF: Distended, tortuous, veins of lower esophagus, usually due to portal hypertension.

456.1 Esophageal varices without mention of bleeding

5th 456.2 Esophageal varices in diseases classified elsewhere
Code first underlying cause, as:
cirrhosis of liver (571.0-571.9)
portal hypertension (572.3)

456.20 With bleeding

456.21 Without mention of bleeding

456.3 Sublingual varices
DEF: Distended, tortuous veins beneath tongue.

456.4 Scrotal varices
Varicocele

456.5 Pelvic varices
Varices of broad ligament

456.6 Vulval varices
Varices of perineum
EXCLUDES *that complicating pregnancy, childbirth, or the puerperium (671.1)*

456.8 Varices of other sites
Varicose veins of nasal septum (with ulcer)
EXCLUDES *placental varices (656.7)*
retinal varices (362.17)
varicose ulcer of unspecified site (454.0)
varicose veins of unspecified site (454.9)

4th 457 Noninfectious disorders of lymphatic channels

457.0 Postmastectomy lymphedema syndrome
Elephantiasis } due to mastectomy
Obliteration of lymphatic vessel } due to mastectomy
DEF: Reduced lymphatic circulation following mastectomy; symptoms include swelling of the arm on the operative side.

457.1 Other lymphedema
Elephantiasis (nonfilarial) NOS
Lymphangiectasis
Lymphedema:
acquired (chronic)
praecox
secondary
Obliteration, lymphatic vessel
EXCLUDES *elephantiasis (nonfilarial):*
congenital (757.0)
eyelid (374.83)
vulva (624.8)
DEF: Fluid retention due to reduced lymphatic circulation; due to other than mastectomy.

457.2 Lymphangitis
Lymphangitis:
NOS
chronic
subacute
EXCLUDES *acute lymphangitis (682.0-682.9)*

457.8 Other noninfectious disorders of lymphatic channels
Chylocele (nonfilarial)
Chylous:
ascites
cyst
Lymph node or vessel:
fistula
infarction
rupture
EXCLUDES *chylocele:*
filarial (125.0-125.9)
tunica vaginalis (nonfilarial) (608.84)

457.9 Unspecified noninfectious disorder of lymphatic channels

4th 458 Hypotension
INCLUDES hypopiesis
EXCLUDES *cardiovascular collapse (785.50)*
maternal hypotension syndrome (669.2)
shock (785.50-785.59)
Shy-Drager syndrome (333.0)

458.0 Orthostatic hypotension
Hypotension:
orthostatic (chronic)
postural
DEF: Low blood pressure; occurs when standing.

458.1 Chronic hypotension
Permanent idiopathic hypotension
DEF: Persistent low blood pressure.

5th 458.2 Iatrogenic hypotension
DEF: Abnormally low blood pressure; due to medical treatment.

458.21 Hypotension of hemodialysis
Intra-dialytic hypotension

458.29 Other iatrogenic hypotension
Postoperative hypotension

458.8 Other specified hypotension

458.9 Hypotension, unspecified
Hypotension (arterial) NOS

4th 459 Other disorders of circulatory system

459.0 Hemorrhage, unspecified
Rupture of blood vessel NOS
Spontaneous hemorrhage NEC
EXCLUDES *hemorrhage:*
gastrointestinal NOS (578.9)
in newborn NOS (772.9)
secondary or recurrent following trauma (958.2)
traumatic rupture of blood vessel (900.0-904.9)
nontraumatic hematoma of soft tissue (729.92)

5th 459.1 Postphlebitic syndrome
Chronic venous hypertension due to deep vein thrombosis
EXCLUDES *chronic venous hypertension without deep vein thrombosis (459.30-459.39)*
DEF: Various conditions following deep vein thrombosis; including edema, pain, stasis dermatitis, cellulitis, varicose veins and ulceration of the lower leg.

459.10 Postphlebitic syndrome without complications
Asymptomatic postphlebitic syndrome
Postphlebitic syndrome NOS

459.11 Postphlebitic syndrome with ulcer

459.12 Postphlebitic syndrome with inflammation

459.13 Postphlebitic syndrome with ulcer and inflammation

459.19 Postphlebitic syndrome with other complication

459.2 Compression of vein
Stricture of vein
Vena cava syndrome (inferior) (superior)

5th 459.3 Chronic venous hypertension (idiopathic)
Stasis edema
EXCLUDES *chronic venous hypertension due to deep vein thrombosis (459.10-459.9)*
varicose veins (454.0-454.9)

459.30 Chronic venous hypertension without complications
Asymptomatic chronic venous hypertension
Chronic venous hypertension NOS

459.31 Chronic venous hypertension with ulcer

459.32 Chronic venous hypertension with inflammation

459.33 Chronic venous hypertension with ulcer and inflammation

459.39 Chronic venous hypertension with other complication

✓5th **459.8 Other specified disorders of circulatory system**

459.81 Venous (peripheral) insufficiency, unspecified

Chronic venous insufficiency NOS

Use additional code for any associated ulceration (707.10-707.9)

DEF: Insufficient drainage, venous blood, any part of body, results in edema or dermatosis.

459.89 Other

Collateral circulation (venous), any site
Phlebosclerosis
Venofibrosis

459.9 Unspecified circulatory system disorder

Chapter 8: Respiratory System (460–519)

Conditions related to the respiratory system may be difficult to code because some conditions are classified in chapter 1, "Infectious and Parasitic Diseases." All other conditions are classified to this chapter, Diseases of the Respiratory System, with use of an additional code from category 041 or 079 if an infectious organism is known.

This complex of organs includes pulmonary ventilation and the exchange of oxygen and carbon dioxide between the lungs and the ambient air. The organs of the respiratory system also perform nonrespiratory functions such as warming and moisturizing air passing into the lungs, air flow for the larynx and vocal cords for speech and thermoregulation, and homeostasis through release of excess body heat. The lung also performs important metabolic and embolic filtering functions.

Acute Respiratory Infections (460–466)

This subchapter includes infections of the respiratory tract, excluding pneumonia and influenza, and is organized by site.

Common Cold (460)

Acute infective nasopharyngitis, or the common cold, is classified to category 460. This category excludes allergic and chronic rhinitis, acute and chronic pharyngitis and sore throat.

Sore Throat (462)

Acute pharyngitis is a prolonged inflammatory disorder of the throat, which may be caused by a virus or bacteria.

Acute Tonsillitis (463)

Acute tonsillitis is classified to code 463. This includes follicular, gangrenous, infective, pneumococcal, septic, staphylococcal, suppurative, ulcerative, and viral tonsillitis. Chronic tonsillitis is classified to category 474. The alphabetic index directs the coder to code acute adenoiditis to 463 as well.

Acute Upper Respiratory Infection of Multiple or Unspecified Sites (URI) (465)

Category 465 classifies those upper respiratory infections of multiple or unspecified sites such as acute larygopharyngitis, multiple upper respiratory infection (URI) and acute URI, NOS.

Other Diseases of the Upper Respiratory Tract (470–478)

This section includes the noninfective disorders and chronic conditions of the upper respiratory tract.

Chronic Tonsillitis and Adenoiditis (474)

This category classifies chronic tonsillitis, chronic adenoiditis or a combination of the two conditions. Acute conditions are classified to 463.

Pneumonia and Influenza (480–488)

Pneumonia and influenza are inflammations in the alveolar parenchyma of the lung caused by microbial infection, irradiation or physicochemical agents. Microbial agents include viral, bacterial, fungal, protozoa mycobacterial, mycoplasmal or rickettsial pathogens. Physicochemical agents may be inhaled or reach the lung via the bloodstream. Inhaled agents include toxic gases, irritant particles, or irritant fluids such as gastric juice.

Pneumonia (480–486)

Pneumonia is classified by infective organism such as:

- Viral (480)
- Streptococcal (481)
- Other bacterial (482)
- Other specified organisms (483)

or classified as:

- Pneumonia in infectious disease classified elsewhere (484)
- Bronchopneumonia (485)
- Pneumonia unspecified (486)

Many forms of pneumonia are classified to other chapters of ICD-9-CM because of their etiology. Always refer to the Index under the main terms "Pneumonia" and "Pneumonitis" as a first step in coding pneumonia.

Methicillin-resistant *Staphylococcus aureus* (MRSA) is a variant form of the bacterium *Staphylococcus aureus (S. aureus)* that is resistant to traditional beta-lactam antibiotic therapies for *S. aureus* infections, which include penicillin, methicillin, and cephalosporins. The term methicillin-susceptible *Staphylococcus aureus* (MSSA) identifies certain strains of *Staphylococcus aureus* that are penicillin-resistant, yet susceptible or treatable with methicillin. Due to the clinical challenges MRSA poses, it is sometimes referred to as a "superbug." Previously limited to nosocomial infections, community-acquired pneumonia (CAP) caused by the *Staphylococcus aureus (S. aureus)* bacterium is occurring with increasing frequency, including that caused by antibiotic-resistant and antibiotic-susceptible (MRSA and MSSA) strains. Although rare, MRSA pneumonia can be particularly severe and rapidly fatal, affecting otherwise healthy young people. Some MRSA strains contain toxins (e.g., Panton-Valentine leukocidin) that have been identified as responsible for the severity of illness.

Certain genetic elements for methicillin resistance have been identified in specific, highly virulent MSSA strains, posing significant public health concern. The presence of a toxin may contribute to the changing epidemiology and clinical presentation of staphylococcal pneumonia whether it is due to MSSA or MRSA. Community-acquired MRSA strains have an increased genetic predisposition for such concomitant toxins, although not all currently known MRSA strains are toxin-producing. Increased risk is associated with certain strains of influenza, or patients with a history of MRSA skin infections, or those who have had exposure to persons with MRSA infection. Diagnosis relies upon early recognition, empiric treatment, and microbiological confirmation to ensure appropriate infection control precautions. Treatment includes vancomycin or linezolid therapies when MRSA community-acquired pneumonia is suspected. Assign code 482.42 for methicillin resistant pneumonia due to *Staphylococcus aureus* (MRSA). Code 482.41 reports pneumonia due to methicillin susceptible *Staphylococcus aureus* (MSSA). Pneumonia due to *Staphylococcus aureus* NOS is classified as methicillin susceptible, not methicillin resistant. V codes have been created to report MRSA (V02.53) and MSSA (V02.54) colonization status and personal history of MRSA infection (V12.04).

Influenza (487)

Influenza is an acute viral respiratory infection characterized by the abrupt onset of tracheobronchitis. The severity of the disease varies from a mild upper respiratory infection to an extensive pneumonia. Influenza virus type A is the most common and can cause epidemics of varying severity. Influenza virus type B is associated with more limited epidemics and has been linked to Reye's syndrome. Influenza virus type C is an uncommon strain that causes very mild upper respiratory symptoms.

Four-digit subclassification identifies associated manifestations such as influenzal laryngitis, pharyngitis, or URI (487.1).

Influenza type A affects a number of different animal species, with the largest variety found among birds. Waterfowl are considered a natural reservoir for influenza type A viruses. Only three subtypes of influenza type A are currently known to be circulating in humans: H1N1, H1N2, and H3N2. Human influenza due to H5N1 has generally been associated with close contact with birds. There has not been any wide human-to-human transmission, although it is not clear whether isolated instances may have occurred. The diagnosis of avian influenza should be definitive before assigning code 488 Influenza due to identified avian influenza virus. Code 488 is a valid three-digit code that is not further subdivided.

Chronic Obstructive Pulmonary Disease and Allied Conditions (490–496)

Chronic obstructive pulmonary disease (COPD) is a term that causes confusion for many coders. COPD describes many disorders that cause persistent obstruction of the bronchial air flow. This general term, COPD, may refer to the following conditions:

Code	Conditions
491.20	Emphysematous chronic bronchitis, obstructive chronic bronchitis, bronchitis with airway obstruction, bronchitis with emphysema
491.21	COPD with acute exacerbation.
491.22	Chronic obstructive bronchitis with acute bronchitis, acute bronchitis with COPD
491.8	Chronic tracheitis, chronic tracheobronchitis
493.2x	Chronic obstructive asthma, asthma with chronic obstructive pulmonary disease (COPD), chronic asthmatic bronchitis
495.9	Chronic obstructive lung disease with allergic alveolitis
496	Chronic airway obstruction NOS, nonspecific chronic lung disease, obstructive lung disease, COPD NOS, diffuse chronic obstructive lung disease with fibrosis

Obstructive Chronic Bronchitis (491.2x)

Chronic bronchitis combined with obstructive lung disease is defined as a persistent cough with sputum production occurring on most days for at least three months of the year and for at least two years. Obstructive lung disease is defined as a chronic or recurrent reduction in expiratory airflow within the lung. Obstructive chronic bronchitis is characterized by an increased mass of mucous glands in the lung, resulting in an increase in the thickness of the bronchial mucosa. Its most common etiology is cigarette smoking, but it also may be caused by environmental pollution or inhalation of irritant chemicals.

Emphysema (492)

The term "emphysema" refers to any condition in which air is present in a small area of an organ or tissue, for example, subcutaneous emphysema, characterized by air in the subcutaneous tissue. Emphysema classified to category 492 refers to pulmonary emphysema only.

Asthma (493)

Asthma is a narrowing of the airways due to increased responsiveness of the trachea and bronchi to various stimuli. Asthma is reversible, changing in severity either spontaneously or as a result of treatment. Asthma is associated with bronchospasm and pathologic features such as increased mucous secretion, mucosal edema and hyperemia, hypertrophy of bronchial smooth muscle, and acute inflammation. The most serious condition is "status asthmaticus," in which attacks are severe and prolonged.

Asthma has traditionally been classified as extrinsic, intrinsic, or unspecified. This differentiation is considered archaic by many clinicians because manifestations of both extrinsic and intrinsic disease commonly occur in the same patient.

The following fifth-digit assignment is used with category 493:

0	without mention of status asthmaticus or acute exacerbation or unspecified
1	with status asthmaticus
2	with acute exacerbation

Status asthmaticus is severe and does not respond to normal therapeutic measures.

Pneumoconioses (500–505)

Pneumoconioses are diseases marked by permanent deposits of particulate matter within the lungs. The sources of the matter are usually environmental or occupational.

Other Diseases of Respiratory System (510–519)

Empyema (510)

Empyema is the accumulation of pus within the pleural space. Use an additional code to identify the infectious organism from category 041.

Pleurisy (511)

Pleurisy is the inflammation of the serous membrane of the lungs and lining of the thoracic cavity. Exudation develops in the cavity or on the surface of the membrane. This category excludes pleurisy mentioned with tuberculosis (012.0). Use an additional code to identify any causal organism. Malignant pleural effusion is an abnormal accumulation of fluid in the pleura. The pleural space lies between the outside of the lung and the wall of the chest cavity. Malignant pleural effusion commonly occurs as a result of a cancerous neoplastic process in the lung, breast, lymph glands, and vessels or within the chest cavity. Malignant pleural effusions may be attributed to the presence of a metastatic secondary neoplasm of the pleura from primary tumors elsewhere in the body, or they may arise as a primary neoplasm of the pleura, as a thoracic lymphoma, or as an integral part of progressive primary lung cancer. As the malignant fluid accumulates in the pleural space, the lung collapses, resulting in chest pain, cough, hypoxia, and shortness of breath.

Prior to October 1, 2008, malignant pleural effusion defaulted to code 197.2 as a secondary malignant neoplasm of the pleura. Clinically, this was not a valid default code. Therefore, a unique classification has been created to report malignant pleural effusion (511.81). Additionally, malignant pleural effusion is a sign used in the staging of lung cancer. An instructional note has been listed at code 511.81 to "code first malignant neoplasm, if known."

Pneumothorax (512)

Pneumothorax is an accumulation of gas or air in the pleural space. The degree of lung collapse is determined by the amount of air or gas trapped in the intrapleural space. Postoperative pneumothorax is coded as 512.1. Traumatic pneumothorax is classified to 860.0–860.1 and 860.4–860.5.

Acute Respiratory Failure (518.81)

Acute respiratory failure is the failure of oxygenation and/or ventilation severe enough to impair or threaten the function of vital organs.

Associated conditions include:

- Chronic obstructive lung disease such as chronic obstructive bronchitis, emphysema, cystic fibrosis
- Acute obstructive lung disease such as asthma, pneumonia, acute bronchitis
- Disorder of respiratory control such as drug overdose, cerebrovascular accident
- Neuromuscular abnormalities such as poliomyelitis, myasthenia gravis, Guillain-Barre syndrome
- Chest wall trauma such as flail chest

If both acute respiratory failure and pneumonia are present on admission and both conditions are treated equally, either condition may be sequenced as the principal diagnosis. According to *The Official Guidelines for Coding and Reporting* (section II.C. Selection of Principal Diagnosis), "In the unusual instance when two or more diagnoses equally meet the criteria for principal diagnosis as determined by the circumstances of admission, diagnostic workup, and/or therapy provided, and the Alphabetic Index, Tabular List, or another coding guideline does not provide sequencing direction, any one of the diagnoses may be sequenced first."

Acute Bronchospasm (519.11)

By definition, bronchospasm is an abnormal contraction of the smooth muscle of the bronchi, resulting in an acute narrowing and obstruction of the respiratory airway. This is chiefly characterized by a cough with generalized wheezing and a sensation of tightness in the chest. Bronchospasm is a component of asthma and bronchitis, and thought to be a precursor to diagnosis. However, many other conditions exhibit manifestation of bronchospasm, including abscess of bronchus, atrophy of trachea, bronchostenosis and calcification of bronchus. Code 519.11 Acute bronchospasm, is used to report and monitor incidences and recurrences of bronchospasm in patients that have not yet been diagnosed with asthma, and/or do not meet bronchitis criteria.

8. DISEASES OF THE RESPIRATORY SYSTEM (460-519)

Use additional code to identify infectious organism

ACUTE RESPIRATORY INFECTIONS (460-466)

EXCLUDES *pneumonia and influenza (480.0-488)*

460 Acute nasopharyngitis [common cold]

Coryza (acute)
Nasal catarrh, acute
Nasopharyngitis:
  NOS
  acute
  infective NOS
Rhinitis:
  acute
  infective

EXCLUDES *nasopharyngitis, chronic (472.2)*
pharyngitis:
  acute or unspecified (462)
  chronic (472.1)
rhinitis:
  allergic (477.0-477.9)
  chronic or unspecified (472.0)
sore throat:
  acute or unspecified (462)
  chronic (472.1)

DEF: Acute inflammation of mucous membranes; extends from nares to pharynx.

✓4th **461 Acute sinusitis**

INCLUDES abscess, empyema, infection, inflammation, suppuration } acute, of sinus (accessory) (nasal)

EXCLUDES *chronic or unspecified sinusitis (473.0-473.9)*

461.0 Maxillary
Acute antritis

461.1 Frontal

461.2 Ethmoidal

461.3 Sphenoidal

461.8 Other acute sinusitis
Acute pansinusitis

461.9 Acute sinusitis, unspecified
Acute sinusitis NOS

462 Acute pharyngitis

Acute sore throat NOS
Pharyngitis (acute):
  NOS
  gangrenous
  infective
  phlegmonous
  pneumococcal
  staphylococca
  suppurative
  ulcerative
Sore throat (viral) NOS
Viral pharyngitis

EXCLUDES *abscess:*
  peritonsillar [quinsy] (475)
  pharyngeal NOS (478.29)
  retropharyngeal (478.24)
chronic pharyngitis (472.1)
infectious mononucleosis (075)
that specified as (due to):
  Coxsackie (virus) (074.0)
  gonococcus (098.6)
  herpes simplex (054.79)
  influenza (487.1)
  septic (034.0)
  streptococcal (034.0)

Respiratory System

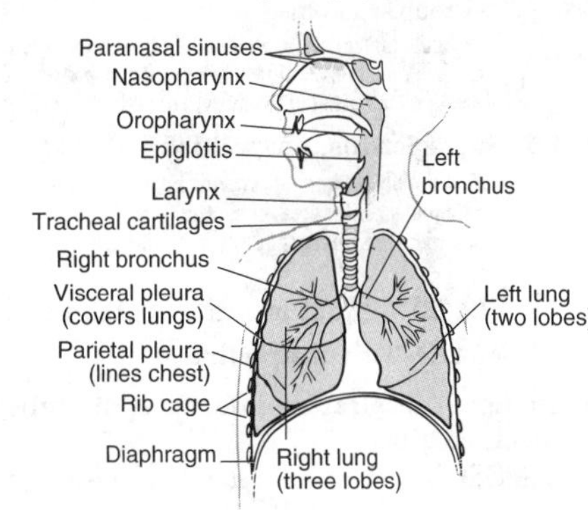

463 Acute tonsillitis

Tonsillitis (acute):
  NOS
  follicular
  gangrenous
  infective
  pneumococcal
  septic
  staphylococcal
  suppurative
  ulcerative
  viral

EXCLUDES *chronic tonsillitis (474.0)*
hypertrophy of tonsils (474.1)
peritonsillar abscess [quinsy] (475)
sore throat:
  acute or NOS (462)
  septic (034.0)
streptococcal tonsillitis (034.0)

✓4th **464 Acute laryngitis and tracheitis**

EXCLUDES *that associated with influenza (487.1)*
that due to Streptococcus (034.0)

✓5th **464.0 Acute laryngitis**
Laryngitis (acute):
  NOS
  edematous
  Hemophilus influenzae [H. influenzae]
  pneumococcal
  septic
  suppurative
  ulcerative

EXCLUDES *chronic laryngitis (476.0-476.1)*
influenzal laryngitis (487.1)

464.00 Without mention of obstruction

464.01 With obstruction

✓5th **464.1 Acute tracheitis**
Tracheitis (acute):
  NOS
  catarrhal
  viral

EXCLUDES *chronic tracheitis (491.8)*

464.10 Without mention of obstruction

464.11 With obstruction

✓5th **464.2 Acute laryngotracheitis**
Laryngotracheitis (acute)
Tracheitis (acute) with laryngitis (acute)

EXCLUDES *chronic laryngotracheitis (476.1)*

464.20 Without mention of obstruction

464.21 With obstruction

✓5th **464.3 Acute epiglottitis**
Viral epiglottitis

EXCLUDES *epiglottitis, chronic (476.1)*

464.30 Without mention of obstruction

464.31 With obstruction

464.4 Croup
Croup syndrome
DEF: Acute laryngeal obstruction due to allergy, foreign body or infection; symptoms include barking cough, hoarseness and harsh, persistent high-pitched respiratory sound.

✓5th **464.5 Supraglottitis, unspecified**
DEF: A rapidly advancing generalized upper respiratory infection of the lingual tonsillar area, epiglottic folds, false vocal cords, and the epiglottis; seen most commonly in children, but can affect people of any age.

464.50 Without mention of obstruction

464.51 With obstruction

✓4th **465 Acute upper respiratory infections of multiple or unspecified sites**
EXCLUDES *upper respiratory infection due to:*
influenza (487.1)
Streptococcus (034.0)

465.0 Acute laryngopharyngitis
DEF: Acute infection of the vocal cords and pharynx.

465.8 Other multiple sites
Multiple URI

465.9 Unspecified site
Acute URI NOS
Upper respiratory infection (acute)

✓4th **466 Acute bronchitis and bronchiolitis**
INCLUDES that with:
bronchospasm
obstruction

466.0 Acute bronchitis
Bronchitis, acute or subacute:
fibrinous
membranous
pneumococcal
purulent
septic
viral
with tracheitis
Croupous bronchitis
Tracheobronchitis, acute
EXCLUDES *acute bronchitis with chronic obstructive pulmonary disease (491.22)*
DEF: Acute inflammation of main branches of bronchial tree due to infectious or irritant agents; symptoms include cough with a varied production of sputum, fever, substernal soreness, and lung rales.

✓5th **466.1 Acute bronchiolitis**
Bronchiolitis (acute)
Capillary pneumonia
DEF: Acute inflammation of finer subdivisions of bronchial tree due to infectious or irritant agents; symptoms include cough with a varied production of sputum, fever, substernal soreness, and lung rales.

466.11 Acute bronchiolitis due to respiratory syncytial virus (RSV)

466.19 Acute bronchiolitis due to other infectious organisms
Use additional code to identify organism

OTHER DISEASES OF THE UPPER RESPIRATORY TRACT (470-478)

470 Deviated nasal septum
Deflected septum (nasal) (acquired)
EXCLUDES *congenital (754.0)*

✓4th **471 Nasal polyps**
EXCLUDES *adenomatous polyps (212.0)*

471.0 Polyp of nasal cavity
Polyp:
choanal
nasopharyngeal

471.1 Polypoid sinus degeneration
Woakes' syndrome or ethmoiditis

Upper Respiratory System

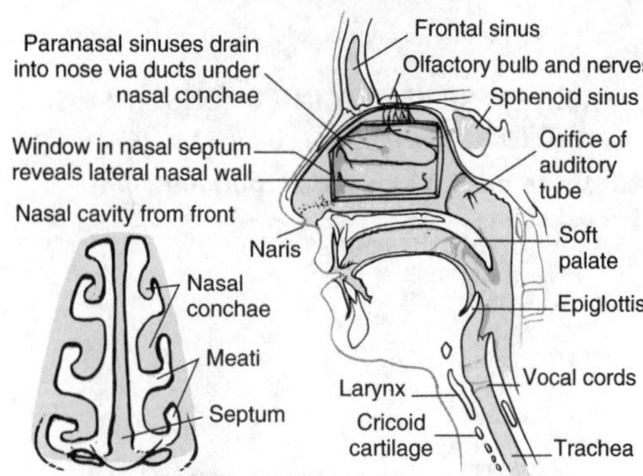

471.8 Other polyp of sinus
Polyp of sinus:
accessory
ethmoidal
maxillary
sphenoidal

471.9 Unspecified nasal polyp
Nasal polyp NOS

✓4th **472 Chronic pharyngitis and nasopharyngitis**

472.0 Chronic rhinitis
Ozena
Rhinitis:
NOS
atrophic
granulomatous
hypertrophic
obstructive
purulent
ulcerative
EXCLUDES *allergic rhinitis (477.0-477.9)*
DEF: Persistent inflammation of mucous membranes of nose.

472.1 Chronic pharyngitis
Chronic sore throat
Pharyngitis:
atrophic
granular (chronic)
hypertrophic

472.2 Chronic nasopharyngitis
EXCLUDES *acute or unspecified nasopharyngitis (460)*
DEF: Persistent inflammation of mucous membranes extending from nares to pharynx.

✓4th **473 Chronic sinusitis**
INCLUDES abscess, empyema, infection, suppuration } (chronic) of sinus (accessory) (nasal)
EXCLUDES *acute sinusitis (461.0-461.9)*

473.0 Maxillary
Antritis (chronic)

473.1 Frontal

Paranasal Sinuses

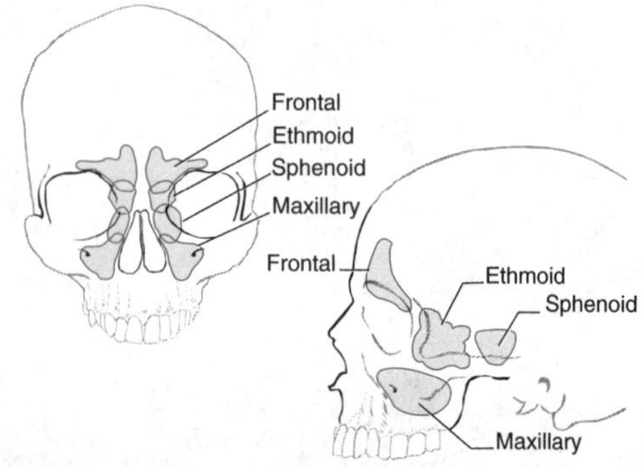

473.2 Ethmoidal

EXCLUDES *Woakes' ethmoiditis (471.1)*

473.3 Sphenoidal

473.8 Other chronic sinusitis

Pansinusitis (chronic)

473.9 Unspecified sinusitis (chronic)

Sinusitis (chronic) NOS

✓4th 474 Chronic disease of tonsils and adenoids

✓5th 474.0 Chronic tonsillitis and adenoiditis

EXCLUDES *acute or unspecified tonsillitis (463)*

474.00 Chronic tonsillitis

474.01 Chronic adenoiditis

474.02 Chronic tonsillitis and adenoiditis

✓5th 474.1 Hypertrophy of tonsils and adenoids

Enlargement / Hyperplasia / Hypertrophy } of tonsils or adenoids

EXCLUDES *that with:*
adenoiditis (474.01)
adenoiditis and tonsillitis (474.02)
tonsillitis (474.00)

474.10 Tonsils with adenoids

474.11 Tonsils alone

474.12 Adenoids alone

474.2 Adenoid vegetations

DEF: Fungus-like growth of lymph tissue between the nares and pharynx.

474.8 Other chronic disease of tonsils and adenoids

Amygdalolith
Calculus, tonsil
Cicatrix of tonsil (and adenoid)
Tonsillar tag
Ulcer, tonsil

474.9 Unspecified chronic disease of tonsils and adenoids

Disease (chronic) of tonsils (and adenoids)

475 Peritonsillar abscess

Abscess of tonsil
Peritonsillar cellulitis
Quinsy

EXCLUDES *tonsillitis:*
acute or NOS (463)
chronic (474.0)

✓4th 476 Chronic laryngitis and laryngotracheitis

476.0 Chronic laryngitis

Laryngitis:
catarrhal
hypertrophic
sicca

476.1 Chronic laryngotracheitis

Laryngitis, chronic, with tracheitis (chronic)
Tracheitis, chronic, with laryngitis

EXCLUDES *chronic tracheitis (491.8)*
laryngitis and tracheitis, acute or unspecified (464.00-464.51)

✓4th 477 Allergic rhinitis

INCLUDES allergic rhinitis (nonseasonal) (seasonal)
hay fever
spasmodic rhinorrhea

EXCLUDES *allergic rhinitis with asthma (bronchial) (493.0)*

DEF: True immunoglobulin E (IgE)-mediated allergic reaction of nasal mucosa; seasonal (typical hay fever) or perennial (year-round allergens: dust, food, dander).

477.0 Due to pollen

Pollinosis

477.1 Due to food

477.2 Due to animal (cat) (dog) hair and dander

477.8 Due to other allergen

477.9 Cause unspecified

✓4th 478 Other diseases of upper respiratory tract

478.0 Hypertrophy of nasal turbinates

DEF: Overgrowth, enlargement of shell-shaped bones, in nasal cavity.

✓5th 478.1 Other diseases of nasal cavity and sinuses

EXCLUDES *varicose ulcer of nasal septum (456.8)*

478.11 Nasal mucositis (ulcerative)

Use additional E code to identify adverse effects of therapy, such as:
antineoplastic and immunosuppressive drugs (E930.7, E933.1)
radiation therapy (E879.2)

478.19 Other diseases of nasal cavity and sinuses

Abscess / Necrosis / Ulcer } of nose (septum)

Cyst or mucocele of sinus (nasal)
Rhinolith

✓5th 478.2 Other diseases of pharynx, not elsewhere classified

478.20 Unspecified disease of pharynx

478.21 Cellulitis of pharynx or nasopharynx

478.22 Parapharyngeal abscess

478.24 Retropharyngeal abscess

DEF: Purulent infection, behind pharynx and front of precerebral fascia.

478.25 Edema of pharynx or nasopharynx

478.26 Cyst of pharynx or nasopharynx

478.29 Other

Abscess of pharynx or nasopharynx

EXCLUDES *ulcerative pharyngitis (462)*

✓5th 478.3 Paralysis of vocal cords or larynx

DEF: Loss of motor ability of vocal cords or larynx; due to nerve or muscle damage.

478.30 Paralysis, unspecified

Laryngoplegia
Paralysis of glottis

478.31 Unilateral, partial

478.32 Unilateral, complete

478.33 Bilateral, partial

478.34 Bilateral, complete

478.4 Polyp of vocal cord or larynx

EXCLUDES *adenomatous polyps (212.1)*

478.5 Other diseases of vocal cords

Abscess / Cellulitis / Granuloma / Leukoplakia } of vocal cords

Chorditis (fibrinous) (nodosa) (tuberosa)
Singers' nodes

478.6 Edema of larynx

Edema (of):
glottis
subglottic
supraglottic

✓5th 478.7 Other diseases of larynx, not elsewhere classified

478.70 Unspecified disease of larynx

478.71 Cellulitis and perichondritis of larynx

DEF: Inflammation of deep soft tissues or lining of bone of the larynx.

478.74 Stenosis of larynx

478.75 Laryngeal spasm

Laryngismus (stridulus)

DEF: Involuntary muscle contraction of the larynx.

478.79 Other

Abscess, Necrosis, Obstruction, Pachyderma, Ulcer } of larynx

EXCLUDES *ulcerative laryngitis (464.00-464.01)*

478.8 Upper respiratory tract hypersensitivity reaction, site unspecified

EXCLUDES *hypersensitivity reaction of lower respiratory tract, as:*
extrinsic allergic alveolitis (495.0-495.9)
pneumoconiosis (500-505)

478.9 Other and unspecified diseases of upper respiratory tract

Abscess, Cicatrix } of trachea

PNEUMONIA AND INFLUENZA (480-488)

EXCLUDES *pneumonia:*
allergic or eosinophilic (518.3)
aspiration:
NOS (507.0)
newborn (770.18)
solids and liquids (507.0-507.8)
congenital (770.0)
lipoid (507.1)
passive (514)
rheumatic (390)
ventilator-associated (997.31)

✓4th **480 Viral pneumonia**

480.0 Pneumonia due to adenovirus

480.1 Pneumonia due to respiratory syncytial virus

480.2 Pneumonia due to parainfluenza virus

480.3 Pneumonia due to SARS-associated coronavirus

DEF: A severe adult respiratory syndrome caused by the coronavirus, specified as inflammation of the lungs with consolidation.

480.8 Pneumonia due to other virus not elsewhere classified

EXCLUDES *congenital rubella pneumonitis (771.0)*
influenza with pneumonia, any form (487.0)
pneumonia complicating viral diseases classified elsewhere (484.1-484.8)

480.9 Viral pneumonia, unspecified

481 Pneumococcal pneumonia [Streptococcus pneumoniae pneumonia]

Lobar pneumonia, organism unspecified

✓4th **482 Other bacterial pneumonia**

482.0 Pneumonia due to Klebsiella pneumoniae

482.1 Pneumonia due to Pseudomonas

482.2 Pneumonia due to Hemophilus influenzae [H. influenzae]

✓5th **482.3 Pneumonia due to Streptococcus**

EXCLUDES *Streptococcus pneumoniae (481)*

482.30 Streptococcus, unspecified

482.31 Group A

482.32 Group B

482.39 Other Streptococcus

✓5th **482.4 Pneumonia due to Staphylococcus**

482.40 Pneumonia due to Staphylococcus, unspecified

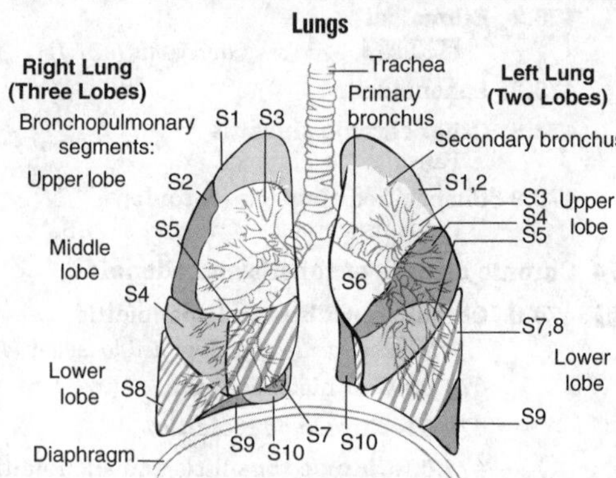

482.41 Methicillin susceptible pneumonia due to Staphylococcus aureus

Staphylococcus aureus
MSSA pneumonia
Pneumonia due to Staphylococcus aureus NOS

482.42 Methicillin resistant pneumonia due to Staphylococcus aureus

482.49 Other Staphylococcus pneumonia

✓5th **482.8 Pneumonia due to other specified bacteria**

EXCLUDES *pneumonia, complicating infectious disease classified elsewhere (484.1-484.8)*

482.81 Anaerobes

Bacteroides (melaninogenicus)
Gram-negative anaerobes

482.82 Escherichia coli [E. coli]

482.83 Other gram-negative bacteria

Gram-negative pneumonia NOS
Proteus
Serratia marcescens

EXCLUDES *gram-negative anaerobes (482.81)*
Legionnaires' disease (482.84)

482.84 Legionnaires' disease

DEF: Severe and often fatal infection by Legionella pneumophilia; symptoms include high fever, gastrointestinal pain, headache, myalgia, dry cough, and pneumonia; transmitted airborne via air conditioning systems, humidifiers, water faucets, shower heads; not person-to-person contact.

482.89 Other specified bacteria

482.9 Bacterial pneumonia unspecified

✓4th **483 Pneumonia due to other specified organism**

483.0 Mycoplasma pneumoniae

Eaton's agent
Pleuropneumonia-like organism [PPLO]

483.1 Chlamydia

483.8 Other specified organism

✓4th **484 Pneumonia in infectious diseases classified elsewhere**

EXCLUDES *influenza with pneumonia, any form (487.0)*

484.1 Pneumonia in cytomegalic inclusion disease

Code first underlying disease (078.5)

484.3 Pneumonia in whooping cough

Code first underlying disease (033.0-033.9)

484.5 Pneumonia in anthrax

Code first underlying disease (022.1)

484.6 Pneumonia in aspergillosis

Code first underlying disease (117.3)

484.7 *Pneumonia in other systemic mycoses*

Code first underlying disease

EXCLUDES *pneumonia in:*
candidiasis (112.4)
coccidioidomycosis (114.0)
histoplasmosis (115.0-115.9 with fifth-digit 5)

484.8 *Pneumonia in other infectious diseases classified elsewhere*

Code first underlying disease, as:
Q fever (083.0)
typhoid fever (002.0)

EXCLUDES *pneumonia in:*
actinomycosis (039.1)
measles (055.1)
nocardiosis (039.1)
ornithosis (073.0)
Pneumocystis carinii (136.3)
salmonellosis (003.22)
toxoplasmosis (130.4)
tuberculosis (011.6)
tularemia (021.2)
varicella (052.1)

485 Bronchopneumonia, organism unspecified

Bronchopneumonia:
hemorrhagic
terminal
Pleurobronchopneumonia
Pneumonia:
lobular
segmental

EXCLUDES *bronchiolitis (acute) (466.11-466.19)*
chronic (491.8)
lipoid pneumonia (507.1)

486 Pneumonia, organism unspecified

EXCLUDES *hypostatic or passive pneumonia (514)*
influenza with pneumonia, any form (487.0)
inhalation or aspiration pneumonia due to foreign materials (507.0-507.8)
pneumonitis due to fumes and vapors (506.0)

✓4th **487 Influenza**

EXCLUDES *Hemophilus influenzae [H. influenzae]:*
infection NOS (041.5)
influenza due to identified avian influenza virus (488)
laryngitis (464.00-464.01)
meningitis (320.0)

487.0 With pneumonia

Influenza with pneumonia, any form
Influenzal:
bronchopneumonia
pneumonia

Use additional code to identify the type of pneumonia (480.0-480.9, 481, 482.0-482.9, 483.0-483.8, 485)

487.1 With other respiratory manifestations

Influenza NOS
Influenzal:
laryngitis
pharyngitis
respiratory infection (upper) (acute)

487.8 With other manifestations

Encephalopathy due to influenza
Influenza with involvement of gastrointestinal tract

EXCLUDES *"intestinal flu" [viral gastroenteritis] (008.8)*

Bronchioli and Alveoli

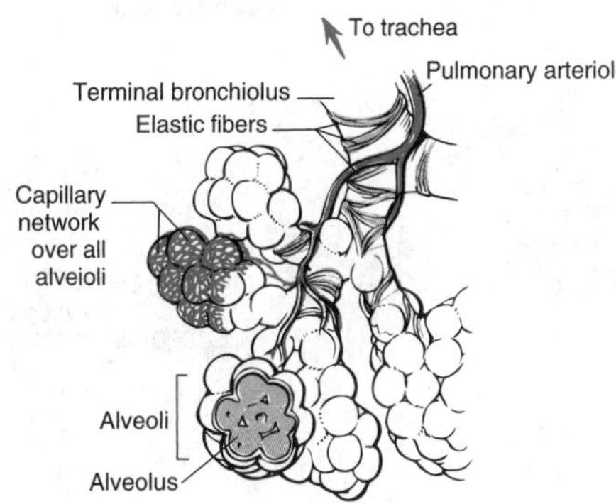

488 Influenza due to identified avian influenza virus

Note: Influenza caused by influenza viruses that normally infect only birds and, less commonly, other animals

EXCLUDES *influenza caused by other influenza viruses (487)*

DEF: Infection caused by contact with bird influenza viruses; results in flu-like symptoms that may progress to other severe and life-threatening complications.

CHRONIC OBSTRUCTIVE PULMONARY DISEASE AND ALLIED CONDITIONS (490-496)

490 Bronchitis, not specified as acute or chronic

Bronchitis NOS:
catarrhal
with tracheitis NOS
Tracheobronchitis NOS

EXCLUDES *bronchitis:*
allergic NOS (493.9)
asthmatic NOS (493.9)
due to fumes and vapors (506.0)

✓4th **491 Chronic bronchitis**

EXCLUDES *chronic obstructive asthma (493.2)*

491.0 Simple chronic bronchitis

Catarrhal bronchitis, chronic
Smokers' cough

491.1 Mucopurulent chronic bronchitis

Bronchitis (chronic) (recurrent):
fetid
mucopurulent
purulent

DEF: Chronic bronchial infection characterized by both mucus and pus secretions in the bronchial tree; recurs after asymptomatic periods; signs are coughing, expectoration and secondary changes in the lung.

✓5th **491.2 Obstructive chronic bronchitis**

Bronchitis:
emphysematous
obstructive (chronic) (diffuse)
Bronchitis with:
chronic airway obstruction
emphysema

EXCLUDES *asthmatic bronchitis (acute) NOS (493.9)*
chronic obstructive asthma (493.2)

491.20 Without exacerbation

Emphysema with chronic bronchitis

491.21 With (acute) exacerbation

Acute exacerbation of chronic obstructive pulmonary disease [COPD]
Decompensated chronic obstructive pulmonary disease [COPD]
Decompensated chronic obstructive pulmonary disease [COPD] with exacerbation

EXCLUDES *chronic obstructive asthma with acute exacerbation (493.22)*

491.22 With acute bronchitis

Interrelationship Between Chronic Airway Obstruction, Chronic Bronchitis, and Emphysema

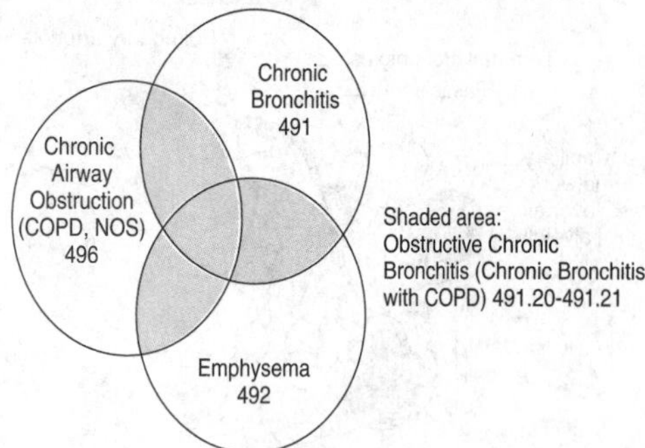

491.8 Other chronic bronchitis
Chronic:
tracheitis
tracheobronchitis

491.9 Unspecified chronic bronchitis

✓4th 492 Emphysema

492.0 Emphysematous bleb
Giant bullous emphysema
Ruptured emphysematous bleb
Tension pneumatocele
Vanishing lung
DEF: Formation of vesicle or bulla in emphysematous lung, more than one millimeter; contains serum or blood.

492.8 Other emphysema
Emphysema (lung or pulmonary):
NOS
centriacinar
centrilobular
obstructive
panacinar
panlobular
unilateral
vesicular
MacLeod's syndrome
Swyer-James syndrome
Unilateral hyperlucent lung
EXCLUDES *emphysema:*
with chronic bronchitis (491.20-491.22)
compensatory (518.2)
due to fumes and vapors (506.4)
interstitial (518.1)
newborn (770.2)
mediastinal (518.1)
surgical (subcutaneous) (998.81)
traumatic (958.7)

✓4th 493 Asthma

EXCLUDES *wheezing NOS (786.07)*

The following fifth-digit subclassification is for use with codes 493.0-493.2, 493.9:
0 unspecified
1 with status asthmaticus
2 with (acute) exacerbation

DEF: Status asthmaticus: severe, intractable episode of asthma unresponsive to normal therapeutic measures.

✓5th **493.0 Extrinsic asthma**
[0-2]
Asthma:
allergic with stated cause
atopic
childhood
hay
platinum
Hay fever with asthma
EXCLUDES *asthma:*
allergic NOS (493.9)
detergent (507.8)
miners' (500)
wood (495.8)
DEF: Transient stricture of airway diameters of bronchi; due to environmental factor; also called allergic (bronchial) asthma.

✓5th **493.1 Intrinsic asthma**
[0-2]
Late-onset asthma
DEF: Transient stricture, of airway diameters of bronchi; due to pathophysiological disturbances.

✓5th **493.2 Chronic obstructive asthma**
[0-2]
Asthma with chronic obstructive pulmonary disease [COPD]
Chronic asthmatic bronchitis
EXCLUDES *acute bronchitis (466.0)*
chronic obstructive bronchitis (491.20-491.22)
DEF: Persistent narrowing of airway diameters in the bronchial tree, restricting airflow and causing constant labored breathing.

✓5th **493.8 Other forms of asthma**

493.81 Exercise induced bronchospasm

493.82 Cough variant asthma

✓5th **493.9 Asthma, unspecified**
[0-2]
Asthma (bronchial) (allergic NOS)
Bronchitis:
allergic
asthmatic

✓4th 494 Bronchiectasis

Bronchiectasis (fusiform) (postinfectious) (recurrent)
Bronchiolectasis
EXCLUDES *congenital (748.61)*
tuberculous bronchiectasis (current disease) (011.5)
DEF: Dilation of bronchi; due to infection or chronic conditions; causes decreased lung capacity and recurrent infections of lungs.

494.0 Bronchiectasis without acute exacerbation

494.1 Bronchiectasis with acute exacerbation

✓4th 495 Extrinsic allergic alveolitis

INCLUDES allergic alveolitis and pneumonitis due to inhaled organic dust particles of fungal, thermophilic actinomycete, or other origin
DEF: Pneumonitis due to particles inhaled into lung, often at workplace; symptoms include cough, chills, fever, increased heart and respiratory rates; develops within hours of exposure.

495.0 Farmers' lung

495.1 Bagassosis

495.2 Bird-fanciers' lung
Budgerigar-fanciers' disease or lung
Pigeon-fanciers' disease or lung

495.3 Suberosis
Cork-handlers' disease or lung

495.4 Malt workers' lung
Alveolitis due to Aspergillus clavatus

495.5 Mushroom workers' lung

495.6 Maple bark-strippers' lung
Alveolitis due to Cryptostroma corticale

495.7 "Ventilation" pneumonitis
Allergic alveolitis due to fungal, thermophilic actinomycete, and other organisms growing in ventilation [air conditioning] systems

495.8 Other specified allergic alveolitis and pneumonitis
Cheese-washers' lung
Coffee workers' lung
Fish-meal workers' lung
Furriers' lung
Grain-handlers' disease or lung
Pituitary snuff-takers' disease
Sequoiosis or red-cedar asthma
Wood asthma

495.9 Unspecified allergic alveolitis and pneumonitis
Alveolitis, allergic (extrinsic)
Hypersensitivity pneumonitis

496 Chronic airway obstruction, not elsewhere classified

Note: This code is not to be used with any code from categories 491-493

Chronic:
- nonspecific lung disease
- obstructive lung disease
- obstructive pulmonary disease [COPD] NOS

EXCLUDES *chronic obstructive lung disease [COPD] specified (as) (with):*
- *allergic alveolitis (495.0-495.9)*
- *asthma (493.20-493.22)*
- *bronchiectasis (494.0-494.1)*
- *bronchitis (491.20-491.22)*
  - *with emphysema (491.20-491.22)*
- *decompensated (491.21)*
- *emphysema (492.0-492.8)*

PNEUMOCONIOSES AND OTHER LUNG DISEASES DUE TO EXTERNAL AGENTS (500-508)

DEF: Permanent deposits of particulate matter, within lungs; due to occupational or environmental exposure; results in chronic induration and fibrosis. (See specific listings in 500-508 code range)

500 Coal workers' pneumoconiosis

Anthracosilicosis
Anthracosis
Black lung disease
Coal workers' lung
Miner's asthma

501 Asbestosis

502 Pneumoconiosis due to other silica or silicates

Pneumoconiosis due to talc
Silicotic fibrosis (massive) of lung
Silicosis (simple) (complicated)

503 Pneumoconiosis due to other inorganic dust

Aluminosis (of lung)
Baritosis
Bauxite fibrosis (of lung)
Berylliosis
Graphite fibrosis (of lung)
Siderosis
Stannosis

504 Pneumonopathy due to inhalation of other dust

Byssinosis
Cannabinosis
Flax-dressers' disease

EXCLUDES *allergic alveolitis (495.0-495.9)*
asbestosis (501)
bagassosis (495.1)
farmers' lung (495.0)

505 Pneumoconiosis, unspecified

✓4th **506 Respiratory conditions due to chemical fumes and vapors**

Use additional E code to identify cause

506.0 Bronchitis and pneumonitis due to fumes and vapors

Chemical bronchitis (acute)

506.1 Acute pulmonary edema due to fumes and vapors

Chemical pulmonary edema (acute)

EXCLUDES *acute pulmonary edema NOS (518.4)*
chronic or unspecified pulmonary edema (514)

506.2 Upper respiratory inflammation due to fumes and vapors

506.3 Other acute and subacute respiratory conditions due to fumes and vapors

506.4 Chronic respiratory conditions due to fumes and vapors

Emphysema (diffuse) (chronic)
Obliterative bronchiolitis (chronic) (subacute)
Pulmonary fibrosis (chronic)
} due to inhalation of chemical fumes and vapors

506.9 Unspecified respiratory conditions due to fumes and vapors

Silo-fillers' disease

✓4th **507 Pneumonitis due to solids and liquids**

EXCLUDES *fetal aspiration pneumonitis (770.18)*

507.0 Due to inhalation of food or vomitus

Aspiration pneumonia (due to):
- NOS
- food (regurgitated)
- gastric secretions
- milk
- saliva
- vomitus

507.1 Due to inhalation of oils and essences

Lipoid pneumonia (exogenous)

EXCLUDES *endogenous lipoid pneumonia (516.8)*

507.8 Due to other solids and liquids

Detergent asthma

✓4th **508 Respiratory conditions due to other and unspecified external agents**

Use additional E code to identify cause

508.0 Acute pulmonary manifestations due to radiation

Radiation pneumonitis

508.1 Chronic and other pulmonary manifestations due to radiation

Fibrosis of lung following radiation

508.8 Respiratory conditions due to other specified external agents

508.9 Respiratory conditions due to unspecified external agent

OTHER DISEASES OF RESPIRATORY SYSTEM (510-519)

✓4th **510 Empyema**

Use additional code to identify infectious organism (041.0-041.9)

EXCLUDES *abscess of lung (513.0)*

DEF: Purulent infection; within pleural space.

510.0 With fistula

Fistula:
- bronchocutaneous
- bronchopleural
- hepatopleural
- mediastinal
- pleural
- thoracic

Any condition classifiable to 510.9 with fistula

DEF: Purulent infection of respiratory cavity; with communication from cavity to another structure.

510.9 Without mention of fistula

Abscess:
- pleura
- thorax

Empyema (chest) (lung) (pleura)
Fibrinopurulent pleurisy
Pleurisy:
- purulent
- septic
- seropurulent
- suppurative

Pyopneumothorax
Pyothorax

✓4th **511 Pleurisy**

EXCLUDES *pleurisy with mention of tuberculosis, current disease (012.0)*

DEF: Inflammation of serous membrane of lungs and lining of thoracic cavity; causes exudation in cavity or membrane surface.

511.0 Without mention of effusion or current tuberculosis

Adhesion, lung or pleura
Calcification of pleura
Pleurisy (acute) (sterile):
diaphragmatic
fibrinous
interlobar
Pleurisy:
NOS
pneumococcal
staphylococcal
streptococcal
Thickening of pleura

511.1 With effusion, with mention of a bacterial cause other than tuberculosis

Pleurisy with effusion (exudative) (serous):
pneumococcal
staphylococcal
streptococcal
other specified nontuberculous bacterial cause

✓5th **511.8 Other specified forms of effusion, except tuberculous**

EXCLUDES *traumatic (860.2-860.5, 862.29, 862.39)*

511.81 Malignant pleural effusion

Code first malignant neoplasm, if known

511.89 Other specified forms of effusion, except tuberculous

Encysted pleurisy
Hemopneumothorax
Hemothorax
Hydropneumothorax
Hydrothorax

511.9 Unspecified pleural effusion

Pleural effusion NOS
Pleurisy:
exudative
serofibrinous
serous
with effusion NOS

✓4th **512 Pneumothorax**

DEF: Collapsed lung; due to gas or air in pleural space.

512.0 Spontaneous tension pneumothorax

DEF: Leaking air from lung into lining causing collapse.

512.1 Iatrogenic pneumothorax

Postoperative pneumothorax

DEF: Air trapped in the lining of the lung following surgery.

512.8 Other spontaneous pneumothorax

Pneumothorax:
NOS
acute
chronic

EXCLUDES *pneumothorax:*
congenital (770.2)
traumatic (860.0-860.1, 860.4-860.5)
tuberculous, current disease (011.7)

✓4th **513 Abscess of lung and mediastinum**

513.0 Abscess of lung

Abscess (multiple) of lung
Gangrenous or necrotic pneumonia
Pulmonary gangrene or necrosis

513.1 Abscess of mediastinum

514 Pulmonary congestion and hypostasis

Hypostatic:
bronchopneumonia
pneumonia
Passive pneumonia
Pulmonary congestion (chronic) (passive)
Pulmonary edema:
NOS
chronic

EXCLUDES *acute pulmonary edema:*
NOS (518.4)
with mention of heart disease or failure (428.1)
hypostatic pneumonia due to or specified as a specific type of pneumonia–code to the type of pneumonia (480.0-480.9, 481, 482.0-482.49, 483.0-483.8, 485, 486, 487.0)

DEF: Excessive retention of interstitial fluid in the lungs and pulmonary vessels; due to poor circulation.

515 Postinflammatory pulmonary fibrosis

Cirrhosis of lung
Fibrosis of lung (atrophic)
(confluent) (massive)
(perialveolar)
(peribronchial)
Induration of lung
} chronic or unspecified

DEF: Fibrosis and scarring of the lungs due to inflammatory reaction.

✓4th **516 Other alveolar and parietoalveolar pneumonopathy**

516.0 Pulmonary alveolar proteinosis

DEF: Reduced ventilation; due to proteinaceous deposits on alveoli; symptoms include dyspnea, cough, chest pain, weakness, weight loss, and hemoptysis.

516.1 Idiopathic pulmonary hemosiderosis

Code first underlying disease (275.0)
Essential brown induration of lung

DEF: Fibrosis of alveolar walls; marked by abnormal amounts hemosiderin in lungs; primarily affects children; symptoms include anemia, fluid in lungs, and blood in sputum; etiology unknown.

516.2 Pulmonary alveolar microlithiasis

DEF: Small calculi in pulmonary alveoli resembling sand-like particles on x-ray.

516.3 Idiopathic fibrosing alveolitis

Alveolar capillary block
Diffuse (idiopathic) (interstitial) pulmonary fibrosis
Hamman-Rich syndrome

516.8 Other specified alveolar and parietoalveolar pneumonopathies

Endogenous lipoid pneumonia
Interstitial pneumonia (desquamative) (lymphoid)

EXCLUDES *lipoid pneumonia, exogenous or unspecified (507.1)*

516.9 Unspecified alveolar and parietoalveolar pneumonopathy

✓4th **517 Lung involvement in conditions classified elsewhere**

EXCLUDES *rheumatoid lung (714.81)*

517.1 Rheumatic pneumonia

Code first underlying disease (390)

517.2 Lung involvement in systemic sclerosis

Code first underlying disease (710.1)

517.3 Acute chest syndrome

Code first sickle-cell disease in crisis (282.42, 282.62, 282.64, 282.69)

517.8 Lung involvement in other diseases classified elsewhere

Code first underlying disease, as:
amyloidosis (277.30-277.39)
polymyositis (710.4)
sarcoidosis (135)
Sjögren's disease (710.2)
systemic lupus erythematosus (710.0)

EXCLUDES *syphilis (095.1)*

✓4th 518 Other diseases of lung

518.0 Pulmonary collapse
Atelectasis
Collapse of lung
Middle lobe syndrome
EXCLUDES *atelectasis:*
congenital (partial) (770.5)
primary (770.4)
tuberculous, current disease (011.8)

518.1 Interstitial emphysema
Mediastinal emphysema
EXCLUDES *surgical (subcutaneous) emphysema (998.81)*
that in fetus or newborn (770.2)
traumatic emphysema (958.7)

DEF: Escaped air from the alveoli trapped in the interstices of the lung; trauma or cough may cause the disease.

518.2 Compensatory emphysema
DEF: Distention of all or part of the lung caused by disease processes or surgical intervention that decreased volume in another part of the lung; overcompensation reaction to the loss of capacity in another part of the lung.

518.3 Pulmonary eosinophilia
Eosinophilic asthma
Löffler's syndrome
Pneumonia:
allergic
eosinophilic
Tropical eosinophilia

DEF: Infiltration, into pulmonary parenchyma of eosinophilia; results in cough, fever, and dyspnea.

518.4 Acute edema of lung, unspecified
Acute pulmonary edema NOS
Pulmonary edema, postoperative
EXCLUDES *pulmonary edema:*
acute, with mention of heart disease or failure (428.1)
chronic or unspecified (514)
due to external agents (506.0-508.9)

DEF: Severe, sudden fluid retention within lung tissues.

518.5 Pulmonary insufficiency following trauma and surgery
Adult respiratory distress syndrome
Pulmonary insufficiency following:
shock
surgery
trauma
Shock lung
EXCLUDES *adult respiratory distress syndrome associated with other conditions (518.82)*
pneumonia:
aspiration (507.0)
hypostatic (514)
respiratory failure in other conditions (518.81, 518.83-518.84)

518.6 Allergic bronchopulmonary aspergillosis
DEF: Noninvasive hypersensitive reaction; due to allergic reaction to *Aspergillus fumigatus* (mold).

518.7 Transfusion related acute lung injury [TRALI]
DEF: A relatively rare, but serious pulmonary complication of blood transfusion, with acute respiratory distress, noncardiogenic pulmonary edema, cyanosis, hypoxemia, hypotension, fever and chills.

✓5th 518.8 Other diseases of lung

518.81 Acute respiratory failure
Respiratory failure NOS
EXCLUDES *acute and chronic respiratory failure (518.84)*
acute respiratory distress (518.82)
chronic respiratory failure (518.83)
respiratory arrest (799.1)
respiratory failure, newborn (770.84)

518.82 Other pulmonary insufficiency, not elsewhere classified
Acute respiratory distress
Acute respiratory insufficiency
Adult respiratory distress syndrome NEC
EXCLUDES *adult respiratory distress syndrome associated with trauma and surgery (518.5)*
pulmonary insufficiency following trauma and surgery (518.5)
respiratory distress:
NOS (786.09)
newborn (770.89)
syndrome, newborn (769)
shock lung (518.5)

518.83 Chronic respiratory failure

518.84 Acute and chronic respiratory failure
Acute on chronic respiratory failure

518.89 Other diseases of lung, not elsewhere classified
Broncholithiasis
Calcification of lung
Lung disease NOS
Pulmolithiasis

DEF: Broncholithiasis: calculi in lumen of transbronchial tree.

DEF: Pulmolithiasis: calculi in lung.

✓4th 519 Other diseases of respiratory system

✓5th 519.0 Tracheostomy complications

519.00 Tracheostomy complication, unspecified

519.01 Infection of tracheostomy
Use additional code to identify type of infection, such as:
abscess or cellulitis of neck (682.1)
septicemia (038.0-038.9)
Use additional code to identify organism (041.00-041.9)

519.02 Mechanical complication of tracheostomy
Tracheal stenosis due to tracheostomy

519.09 Other tracheostomy complications
Hemorrhage due to tracheostomy
Tracheoesophageal fistula due to tracheostomy

✓5th 519.1 Other diseases of trachea and bronchus, not elsewhere classified

519.11 Acute bronchospasm
Bronchospasm NOS
EXCLUDES *acute bronchitis with bronchospasm (466.0)*
asthma (493.00-493.92)
exercise induced bronchospasm (493.81)

519.19 Other diseases of trachea and bronchus
Calcification, Stenosis, Ulcer } of bronchus or trachea

519.2 Mediastinitis
DEF: Inflammation of tissue between organs behind sternum.

519.3 Other diseases of mediastinum, not elsewhere classified
Fibrosis, Hernia, Retraction } of mediastinum

519.4 Disorders of diaphragm
Diaphragmitis
Paralysis of diaphragm
Relaxation of diaphragm
EXCLUDES *congenital defect of diaphragm (756.6)*
diaphragmatic hernia (551-553 with .3)
congenital (756.6)

519.8 Other diseases of respiratory system, not elsewhere classified

519.9 Unspecified disease of respiratory system

Respiratory disease (chronic) NOS

Chapter 9: Digestive System (520–579)

This chapter classifies diseases and disorders of all of the organs along the alimentary (digestive) tract - the long, muscular tube beginning at the oral cavity and ending at the anus. The major digestive organs include the pharynx, esophagus, stomach, and intestines. Accessory, or secondary, organs include the salivary and parotid glands, jaw, teeth and the supporting structures of teeth, liver, gallbladder and biliary tract, pancreas, and peritoneum.

The primary function of the digestive system is to mechanically break down and chemically dissolve food in order to provide the body with essential vitamins, proteins, minerals, and water. Diseases and disorders that interfere with this function are classified here, along with diseases and disorders that affect the organs of the digestive tract, even though they may have no direct affect on digestion. For example, dental caries have a direct effect on digestion because they interfere with mastication, the mechanical breakdown of food by chewing. Portal hypertension does not directly affect digestion, but is included here because it represents a disease of a digestive system organ.

The main subchapters of chapter 9, "Diseases of the Digestive System," are as follows:

- Diseases of oral cavity, salivary glands, and jaws (520–529)
- Diseases of esophagus, stomach, and duodenum (530–538)
- Appendicitis (540–543)
- Hernia of abdominal cavity (550–553)
- Noninfectious enteritis and colitis (555–558)
- Other diseases of intestines and peritoneum (560–569)
- Other diseases of digestive system (570–579)

Diseases of Oral Cavity, Salivary Glands, and Jaws (520–529)

This category includes diseases and disorders of the jaw, salivary and parotid glands, teeth, gingiva and periodontium, lips, oral mucosa, and tongue.

Disorders of Tooth Development and Eruption (520)

Disorders of tooth development and eruption in all patients regardless of age are included in this category. This is one of the few categories in ICD-9-CM that classifies congenital anomalies and hereditary disturbances outside of chapter 14, "Congenital Anomalies."

Dentofacial Anomalies, Including Malocclusion (524)

Anomalies in the alignment of the jaw to the cranium can cause problems with the ability to chew food, may obstruct swallowing, and obstruct opening or closure of the mouth and cause physical distortion to the appearance of the face. Also included in this category are disorders of the temporomandibular joint.

Diseases of the Salivary Glands (527)

Diseases of the salivary glands include atrophy, hypertrophy, sialoadenitis, abscess, fistula, sialolithiasis, and disturbances of salivary secretion.

Diseases of the Oral Soft Tissues (528)

Excluded from this category are lesions specific to the gingiva and tongue, which are included in category 529. Included are cellulitis of the mouth, cysts, diseases of the lips, leukoplakia, and others.

DISEASES OF ESOPHAGUS, STOMACH, AND DUODENUM (530–538)

This category includes diseases and disorders of the esophagus, the muscular, tubular structure that serves as a conduit for the passage of food and water from the pharynx to the stomach. The esophagus functions by transporting food and fluids from the mouth to the stomach (and sometimes in the reverse direction). The esophagus is equipped with two sphincters. The first is the pharyngoesophageal sphincter located at the level of the cricoid cartilage; the second is the gastroesophageal sphincter (also known as the lower esophageal sphincter) located at the level of the esophageal hiatus of the diaphragm.

Esophagitis (530.1)

Esophagitis is the inflammation of the esophagus due to reflux, chemicals and infection. Reflux esophagitis, is the most common form and is caused by acid and pepsin from the stomach rising past the gastroesophageal sphincter into the esophagus. Underlying causes include: hiatal hernia, pregnancy, certain drugs (e.g., calcium channel blockers, beta-adrenergic agonists), scleroderma, obesity, and surgeries.

Gastric Ulcer (531)

Gastric ulcer is a condition formed by tissue destruction within the lumen of the stomach. The destruction is due to the action of hydrochloric (gastric) acid and pepsin on areas of gastric mucosa having a decreased resistance to ulceration. Also known as pyloric ulcer, stomach ulcer or prepyloric ulcer. Note peptic ulcer NOS is classified to category 533 when the site is unspecified. Fifth-digit assignment for category 531 indicates whether there is mention of obstruction.

Peptic Ulcer, Site Unspecified (533)

A peptic ulcer is an acute or chronic benign ulcer occurring in a portion of the digestive tract accessible to gastric secretions. Peptic ulcers result from the corrosive action of acid gastric juice on vulnerable epithelium. This category (533) includes only peptic ulcers for which no site has been specified. Peptic ulcers may occur in the esophagus (530.2), stomach (531), duodenum (532), jejunum and gastrojejunum (534), and ileum (569.82). Fifth-digit assignment for category 533 indicates whether there is mention of obstruction. When ulcers are drug induced, an additional E code is assigned.

Gastritis and Duodenitis (535)

Gastritis and duodenitis are self-limiting illnesses characterized by nausea, vomiting, anorexia, epigastric pain, and some systemic symptoms. Fifth-digit assignment identifies the complication of hemorrhage.

Eosinophilic gastrointestinal disorders (EGIDs) selectively affect the lining of the gastrointestinal tract through the accumulation of eosinophil cells in the intestinal tissue, causing inflammation. In this disease, eosinophil accumulation occurs in the absence of known causes for eosinophilia (e.g., drug reactions, parasitic infection, connective tissue disease, or malignancy). EGIDs are characterized by inflammation of the esophagus, stomach, or intestine. Symptoms and features of EGIDs mimic those of food allergy and immune dysregulation but do not clearly fit those disease categories. While these conditions may be difficult to diagnose, they are being identified with increasing frequency. Inflammation may not always be present visually during an endoscopic exam, but it may be seen under the microscope. Abnormally high numbers of eosinophils within the digestive tract may not provide a conclusive diagnosis of an EGID. Fifth-digit assignment for subcategory 535.7 identifies the complication of hemorrhage.

Appendicitis (540–543)

Appendicitis is an inflammation of the vermiform appendix and is usually initiated by obstruction. The obstruction is then followed by infection, edema, and frequently infarction of the appendiceal wall.

Subcategory levels of 540 indicate whether there is peritonitis or peritoneal abscess.

Hernia of Abdominal Cavity (550–553)

Hernias included in this section are acquired and congenital except diaphragmatic or hiatal.

Steps for coding hernias are as follows:

1. Determine the site.
2. Determine if gangrene is a complication.
3. Determine if there is obstruction.

4. For some categories, fifth-digit assignment identifies the nature (recurrent or not) and laterality (unilateral or bilateral).

Noninfectious Enteritis and Colitis (555–558)

Regional enteritis is a form of inflammatory bowel disease and is also known as Crohn's disease. Regional enteritis most often affects the large intestines but may occur anywhere along the gastrointestinal tract. Often, enteritis, gastroenteritis and diarrhea, when specified as due to an underlying condition, should be classified to a category other than 555. Infectious disease is the most frequent cause of gastritis and gastroenteritis and is classified to chapter 1, "Infectious and Parasitic Diseases."

Commonly caused by infection, diarrhea may also be caused by numerous disorders such as chronic bowel disease, malabsorption, food poisoning, adverse reactions to medications, dietary factors such as malnutrition and food allergy, pancreatic disease, metabolic disease, neurological disease, psychogenic disorders, heavy metal poisoning, laxative abuse, and immunodeficiency disease.

OTHER DISEASES OF INTESTINES AND PERITONEUM (560–579)

Intussusception and Volvulus (560.X)

Intussusception is the prolapse of one part of the intestine into another part below. It occurs primarily in children and its chief symptoms are paroxysmal pain, vomiting, and passage of blood and mucus via the rectum.

Volvulus is a looped or entangled bowel causing intestinal obstruction, particularly in the sigmoid flexure. Circulation of the bowel may be severely compromised in severe cases.

Diverticula of Colon (562.1X)

Diverticula is the formation of a pouch or sac in the colon. Acquired diverticula are herniations of the mucosa through the muscle. Congenital diverticula are herniations of the entire thickness of the intestinal wall. This tends to occur in higher pressure areas such as the sigmoid colon. Diverticulosis is the presence of diverticula in the absence of inflammation. Diverticulitis is the inflammation of the diverticula.

Peritonitis and Retroperitoneal Infections (567)

Peritonitis is the acute or chronic inflammation of the peritoneum. Inflammation and infection may be in response to agents such as bacteria, viruses, bile, hydrochloric acid, chemicals, parasites, fungi, and foreign bodies such as barium sulfate used in diagnostic imaging studies. Ruptured viscus and surgical procedures are two common underlying factors in secondary peritonitis and retroperitoneal abscess. Chronic peritonitis can lead to dense, widespread abdominal adhesions.

Other Disorders of Intestine (569)

This section includes other intestinal disorders not classifiable elsewhere, including anorectal disorders, intestinal abscesses, fistula and angiodysplasias, and colostomy complications.

Anal Sphincter Tear (Healed) (Old) (Nontraumatic) (569.43)

Anal sphincter tears often result in fecal incontinence. Fecal incontinence may be the first symptom that leads to a diagnosis of an old, nonhealed anal sphincter tear. Anal sphincter tears can occur during delivery independent of third-degree lacerations, and such tears may not be identified until they complicate a subsequent delivery. Report code 569.43 Anal sphincter tear (healed) (old), for nongravid patients presenting for treatment of complications of an old tear. Report code 664.6x Anal sphincter tear complicating delivery, when not associated with third-degree perineal laceration. When reporting code 569.43, use an additional code for any associated fecal incontinence (787.6).

Chronic Liver Disease and Cirrhosis (571)

Cirrhosis of the liver is a chronic, progressive disease characterized by damage to the hepatic parenchymal cells and nodular regeneration, fibrosis formation, and disturbance of the normal architecture. Two different types of cirrhosis have been described based on the amount of regenerative activity in the liver: chronic sclerosing cirrhosis, in which the liver is small and hard, and nodular cirrhosis in which the liver may be quite enlarged initially.

Chronic hepatitis is defined as an inflammation and necrosis of the liver. Chronic hepatitis due to viral infection (070) is classified with the infectious and parasitic diseases of chapter 1. There are several forms of nonviral chronic hepatitis, based upon localization and extent of liver injury: active, aggressive, recurrent, and persistent. Code assignment is based upon the form of chronic hepatitis or upon the etiology of the liver disease.

Example:

> Chronic liver disease due to chronic persistent hepatitis is coded as 571.41.
>
> Acute alcoholic hepatitis is coded as 571.1.
>
> Acute viral hepatitis C without hepatic coma is coded as 070.51.
>
> Nonalocholic cirrhosis of the liver is coded as 571.5.
>
> Autoimmune hepatitis is coded to 571.42.

Acute Cholecystitis (575.0)

Acute cholecystitis without mention of cholelithiasis (calculi or "gallstones" of the gallbladder or bile ducts) is classified to 575.0. This condition may be caused by obstruction of the cystic duct by another process (such as a malignant tumor), bile stasis ("sludge" formation), or infection due to organisms such as Escherichia coli, Clostridia, or Salmonella typhi.

Most cases (95 percent) of acute cholecystitis are due to obstruction of the cystic duct by an impacted gallstone and are classified to category 574.

Gastrointestinal Hemorrhage (578)

Gastrointestinal hemorrhage is bleeding of the stomach, ileum, jejunum, duodenum, and/or colon. The condition may be described as acute or chronic and involve a grossly bloody (visible) appearance or be detected by laboratory examination only (occult bleeding). GI bleeding is classified as either hematemesis (vomiting of blood) or blood in stool, which includes melena (partially digested blood showing as dark tarry stools) and hematochezia (passage of red blood in stools not specified as hematemesis or blood in stool).

This category excludes bleeding of the anus and rectum for classification purposes.

The terms "upper" and "lower" have no value as modifiers for classification of GI bleeding; the codes are distinguished by the presentation of the GI bleeding, not the site. Unspecified GI bleeding must be assigned to code 578.9 Hemorrhage of gastrointestinal tract, unspecified, when not stated as hematemesis or blood in stool (melena).

Hematemesis (578.0)

Hematemesis is the vomiting of frank red or partially digested blood and is usually indicative of bleeding of the upper gastrointestinal tract. Occult bleeding can be detected by analysis of vomitus or nasogastric tube aspiration.

Blood in Stool (578.1)

Blood in stool is the passage of frank red or partially digested blood in the stools, which may be due to a lower GI bleed. Blood in the stool without further documentation of GI bleeding is classified to code 792.1 Nonspecific abnormal findings in stool contents.

9. DISEASES OF THE DIGESTIVE SYSTEM (520-579)

DISEASES OF ORAL CAVITY, SALIVARY GLANDS, AND JAWS (520-529)

✓4th 520 Disorders of tooth development and eruption

520.0 Anodontia
Absence of teeth (complete) (congenital) (partial)
Hypodontia
Oligodontia
EXCLUDES *acquired absence of teeth (525.10-525.19)*

520.1 Supernumerary teeth
Distomolar
Fourth molar
Mesiodens
Paramolar
Supplemental teeth
EXCLUDES *supernumerary roots (520.2)*

520.2 Abnormalities of size and form
Concrescence } of teeth
Fusion } of teeth
Gemination } of teeth
Dens evaginatus
Dens in dente
Dens invaginatus
Enamel pearls
Macrodontia
Microdontia
Peg-shaped [conical] teeth
Supernumerary roots
Taurodontism
Tuberculum paramolare
EXCLUDES *that due to congenital syphilis (090.5)*
tuberculum Carabelli, which is regarded as a normal variation

520.3 Mottled teeth
Mottling of enamel
Dental fluorosis
Nonfluoride enamel opacities

Digestive System

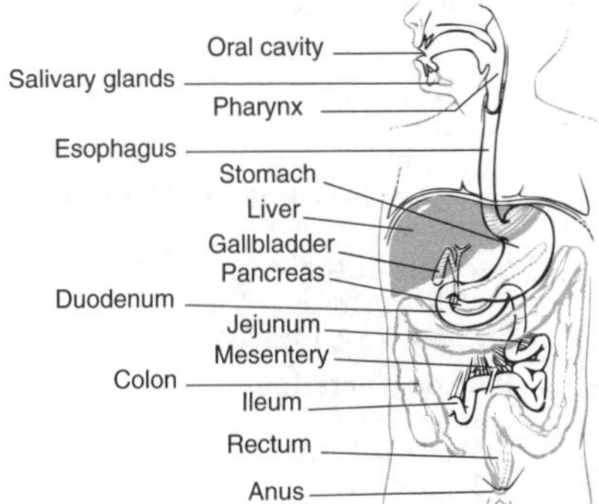

The Oral Cavity

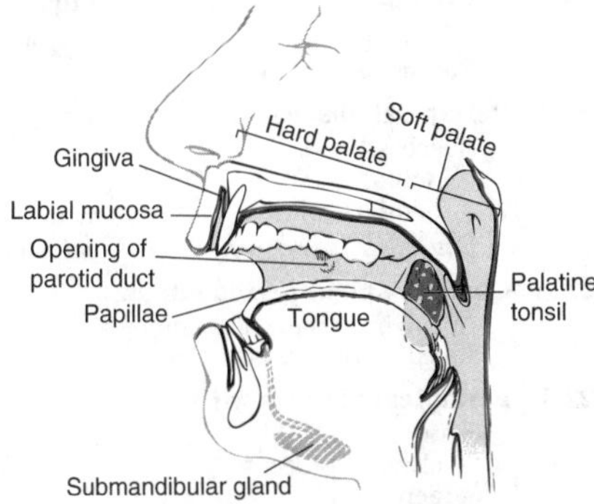

Teeth

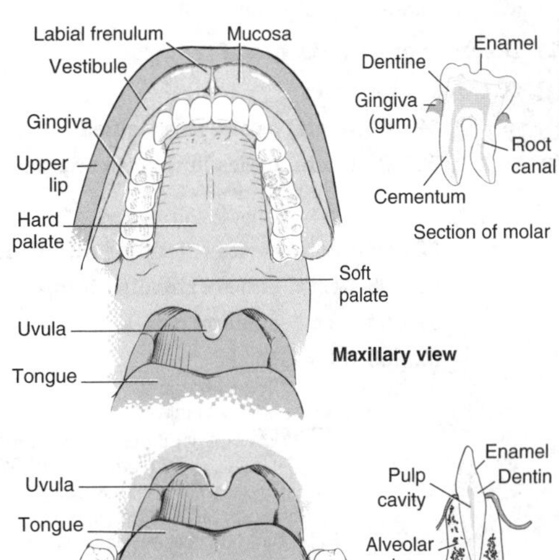

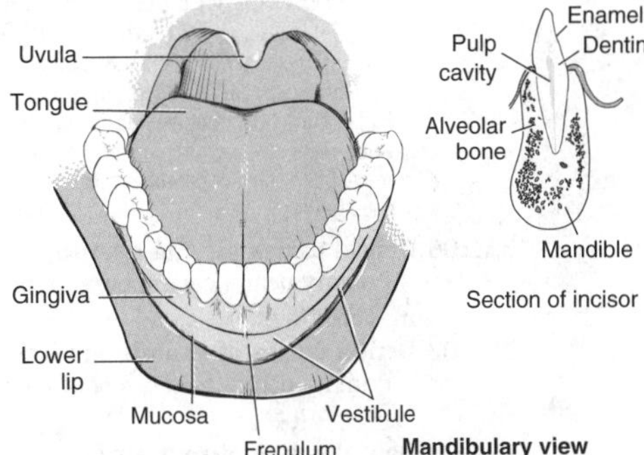

520.4 Disturbances of tooth formation
Aplasia and hypoplasia of cementum
Dilaceration of tooth
Enamel hypoplasia (neonatal) (postnatal) (prenatal)
Horner's teeth
Hypocalcification of teeth
Regional odontodysplasia
Turner's tooth
EXCLUDES *Hutchinson's teeth and mulberry molars in congenital syphilis (090.5)*
mottled teeth (520.3)

520.5 Hereditary disturbances in tooth structure, not elsewhere classified
Amelogensis } imperfecta
Dentinogenesis } imperfecta
Odontogenesis } imperfecta
Dentinal dysplasia
Shell teeth

520.6 Disturbances in tooth eruption
Teeth:
- embedded
- impacted
- natal
- neonatal
- prenatal
- primary [deciduous]:
  - persistent
  - shedding, premature

Tooth eruption:
- late
- obstructed
- premature

EXCLUDES *exfoliation of teeth (attributable to disease of surrounding tissues) (525.0-525.19)*

520.7 Teething syndrome

520.8 Other specified disorders of tooth development and eruption
Color changes during tooth formation
Pre-eruptive color changes
EXCLUDES *posteruptive color changes (521.7)*

520.9 Unspecified disorder of tooth development and eruption

✓4th **521 Diseases of hard tissues of teeth**

✓5th **521.0 Dental caries**

521.00 Dental caries, unspecified

521.01 Dental caries limited to enamel

Initial caries
White spot lesion

521.02 Dental caries extending into dentine

521.03 Dental caries extending into pulp

521.04 Arrested dental caries

521.05 Odontoclasia

Infantile melanodontia
Melanodontoclasia

EXCLUDES *internal and external resorption of teeth (521.40-521.49)*

DEF: A pathological dental condition described as stained areas, loss of tooth substance, and hypoplasia linked to nutritional deficiencies during tooth develop-ment and to cariogenic oral conditions; synonyms are melanodontoclasia and infantile melanodontia.

521.06 Dental caries pit and fissure

Primary dental caries, pit and fissure origin

521.07 Dental caries of smooth surface

Primary dental caries, smooth surface origin

521.08 Dental caries of root surface

Primary dental caries, root surface

521.09 Other dental caries

✓5th **521.1 Excessive attrition (approximal wear) (occlusal wear)**

521.10 Excessive attrition, unspecified

521.11 Excessive attrition, limited to enamel

521.12 Excessive attrition, extending into dentine

521.13 Excessive attrition, extending into pulp

521.14 Excessive attrition, localized

521.15 Excessive attrition, generalized

✓5th **521.2 Abrasion**

Abrasion:
- dentifrice
- habitual
- occupational
- ritual
- traditional

} of teeth

Wedge defect NOS } of teeth

521.20 Abrasion, unspecified

521.21 Abrasion, limited to enamel

521.22 Abrasion, extending into dentine

521.23 Abrasion, extending into pulp

521.24 Abrasion, localized

521.25 Abrasion, generalized

✓5th **521.3 Erosion**

Erosion of teeth:
- NOS
- due to:
  - medicine
  - persistent vomiting
- idiopathic
- occupational

521.30 Erosion, unspecified

521.31 Erosion, limited to enamel

521.32 Erosion, extending into dentine

521.33 Erosion, extending into pulp

521.34 Erosion, localized

521.35 Erosion, generalized

✓5th **521.4 Pathological resorption**

DEF: Loss of dentin and cementum due to disease process.

521.40 Pathological resorption, unspecified

521.41 Pathological resorption, internal

521.42 Pathological resorption, external

521.49 Other pathological resorption

Internal granuloma of pulp

521.5 Hypercementosis

Cementation hyperplasia

DEF: Excess deposits of cementum, on tooth root. Primary dental caries, root surface

521.6 Ankylosis of teeth

DEF: Adhesion of tooth to surrounding bone.

521.7 Intrinsic posteruptive color changes

Staining [discoloration] of teeth:
- NOS
- due to:
  - drugs
  - metals
  - pulpal bleeding

EXCLUDES *accretions [deposits] on teeth (523.6)*
extrinsic color changes (523.6)
pre-eruptive color changes (520.8)

✓5th **521.8 Other specified diseases of hard tissues of teeth**

521.81 Cracked tooth

EXCLUDES *asymptomatic craze lines in enamel — omit code*
broken tooth due to trauma (873.63, 873.73)
fractured tooth due to trauma (873.63, 873.73)

521.89 Other specified diseases of hard tissues of teeth

Irradiated enamel
Sensitive dentin

521.9 Unspecified disease of hard tissues of teeth

✓4th **522 Diseases of pulp and periapical tissues**

522.0 Pulpitis

Pulpal:
- abscess
- polyp

Pulpitis:
- acute
- chronic (hyperplastic) (ulcerative)
- suppurative

522.1 Necrosis of the pulp

Pulp gangrene

DEF: Death of pulp tissue.

522.2 Pulp degeneration

Denticles
Pulp calcifications
Pulp stones

522.3 Abnormal hard tissue formation in pulp

Secondary or irregular dentin

522.4 Acute apical periodontitis of pulpal origin

DEF: Severe inflammation of periodontal ligament due to pulpal inflammation or necrosis.

522.5 Periapical abscess without sinus

Abscess:
- dental
- dentoalveolar

EXCLUDES *periapical abscess with sinus (522.7)*

522.6 Chronic apical periodontitis

Apical or periapical granuloma
Apical periodontitis NOS

522.7 Periapical abscess with sinus

Fistula:
- alveolar process
- dental

522.8 Radicular cyst
Cyst:
apical (periodontal)
periapical
radiculodental
residual radicular
EXCLUDES *lateral developmental or lateral periodontal cyst (526.0)*
DEF: Cyst in tissue around tooth apex due to chronic infection of granuloma around root.

522.9 Other and unspecified diseases of pulp and periapical tissues

✓4th **523 Gingival and periodontal diseases**

✓5th **523.0 Acute gingivitis**
EXCLUDES *acute necrotizing ulcerative gingivitis (101)*
herpetic gingivostomatitis (054.2)

523.00 Acute gingivitis, plaque induced
Acute gingivitis NOS

523.01 Acute gingivitis, non-plaque induced

✓5th **523.1 Chronic gingivitis**
Gingivitis (chronic):
desquamative
hyperplastic
simple marginal
ulcerative
EXCLUDES *herpetic gingivostomatitis (054.2)*

523.10 Chronic gingivitis, plaque induced
Chronic gingivitis NOS
Gingivitis NOS

523.11 Chronic gingivitis, non-plaque induced

✓5th **523.2 Gingival recession**
Gingival recession (postinfective) (postoperative)

523.20 Gingival recession, unspecified

523.21 Gingival recession, minimal

523.22 Gingival recession, moderate

523.23 Gingival recession, severe

523.24 Gingival recession, localized

523.25 Gingival recession, generalized

✓5th **523.3 Aggressive and acute periodontitis**
Acute:
pericementitis
pericoronitis
EXCLUDES *acute apical periodontitis (522.4)*
periapical abscess (522.5, 522.7)
DEF: Severe inflammation, of tissues supporting teeth.

523.30 Aggressive periodontitis, unspecified

523.31 Aggressive periodontitis, localized
Periodontal abscess

523.32 Aggressive periodontitis, generalized

523.33 Acute periodontitis

✓5th **523.4 Chronic periodontitis**
Chronic pericoronitis
Pericementitis (chronic)
Periodontitis:
complex
simplex
NOS
EXCLUDES *chronic apical periodontitis (522.6)*

523.40 Chronic periodontitis, unspecified

523.41 Chronic periodontitis, localized

523.42 Chronic periodontitis, generalized

523.5 Periodontosis

523.6 Accretions on teeth
Dental calculus:
subgingival
supragingival
Deposits on teeth:
betel
materia alba
soft
tartar
tobacco
Extrinsic discoloration of teeth
EXCLUDES *intrinsic discoloration of teeth (521.7)*
DEF: Foreign material on tooth surface, usually plaque or calculus.

523.8 Other specified periodontal diseases
Giant cell:
epulis
peripheral granuloma
Gingival:
cysts
enlargement NOS
fibromatosis
Gingival polyp
Periodontal lesions due to traumatic occlusion
Peripheral giant cell granuloma
EXCLUDES *leukoplakia of gingiva (528.6)*

523.9 Unspecified gingival and periodontal disease

✓4th **524 Dentofacial anomalies, including malocclusion**

✓5th **524.0 Major anomalies of jaw size**
EXCLUDES *hemifacial atrophy or hypertrophy (754.0)*
unilateral condylar hyperplasia or hypoplasia of mandible (526.89)

524.00 Unspecified anomaly
DEF: Unspecified deformity of jaw size.

524.01 Maxillary hyperplasia
DEF: Overgrowth or over development of upper jaw bone.

524.02 Mandibular hyperplasia
DEF: Overgrowth or over development of lower jaw bone.

524.03 Maxillary hypoplasia
DEF: Incomplete or underdeveloped, upper jaw bone.

524.04 Mandibular hypoplasia
DEF: Incomplete or underdeveloped, lower jaw bone.

524.05 Macrogenia
DEF: Enlarged, jaw, especially chin; affects bone, soft tissue, or both.

524.06 Microgenia
DEF: Underdeveloped mandible, characterized by an extremely small chin.

524.07 Excessive tuberosity of jaw
Entire maxillary tuberosity

524.09 Other specified anomaly

✓5th **524.1 Anomalies of relationship of jaw to cranial base**

524.10 Unspecified anomaly
Prognathism
Retrognathism
DEF: Prognathism: protrusion of lower jaw.
DEF: Retrognathism: jaw is located posteriorly to a normally positioned jaw; backward position of mandible.

524.11 Maxillary asymmetry
DEF: Absence of symmetry of maxilla.

524.12 Other jaw asymmetry

524.19 Other specified anomaly

Angle's Classification of Malocclusion

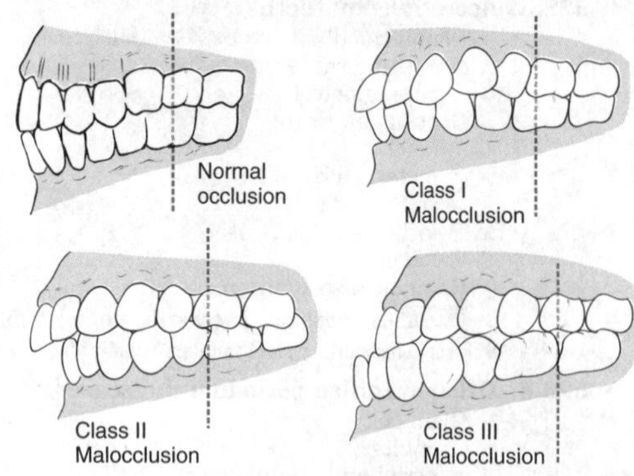

✓5th **524.2 Anomalies of dental arch relationship**
Anomaly of dental arch
EXCLUDES *hemifacial atrophy or hypertrophy (754.0)*
soft tissue impingement (524.81-524.82)
unilateral condylar hyperplasia or hypoplasia of mandible (526.89)

524.20 Unspecified anomaly of dental arch relationship

524.21 Malocclusion, Angle's class I
Neutro-occlusion

524.22 Malocclusion, Angle's class II
Disto-occlusion Division I
Disto-occlusion Division II

524.23 Malocclusion, Angle's class III
Mesio-occlusion

524.24 Open anterior occlusal relationship
Anterior open bite

524.25 Open posterior occlusal relationship
Posterior open bite

524.26 Excessive horizontal overlap
Excessive horizontal overjet

524.27 Reverse articulation
Anterior articulation
Crossbite
Posterior articulation

524.28 Anomalies of interarch distance
Excessive interarch distance
Inadequate interarch distance

524.29 Other anomalies of dental arch relationship
Other anomalies of dental arch

✓5th **524.3 Anomalies of tooth position of fully erupted teeth**
EXCLUDES *impacted or embedded teeth with abnormal position of such teeth or adjacent teeth (520.6)*

524.30 Unspecified anomaly of tooth position
Diastema of teeth NOS
Displacement of teeth NOS
Transposition of teeth NOS

524.31 Crowding of teeth

524.32 Excessive spacing of teeth

524.33 Horizontal displacement of teeth
Tipped teeth
Tipping of teeth

524.34 Vertical displacement of teeth
Extruded tooth
Infraeruption of teeth
Intruded tooth
Supraeruption of teeth

524.35 Rotation of tooth/teeth

524.36 Insufficient interocclusal distance of teeth (ridge)
Lack of adequate intermaxillary vertical dimension

524.37 Excessive interocclusal distance of teeth
Excessive intermaxillary vertical dimension
Loss of occlusal vertical dimension

524.39 Other anomalies of tooth position

524.4 Malocclusion, unspecified
DEF: Malposition of top and bottom teeth; interferes with chewing.

✓5th **524.5 Dentofacial functional abnormalities**

524.50 Dentofacial functional abnormality, unspecified

524.51 Abnormal jaw closure

524.52 Limited mandibular range of motion

524.53 Deviation in opening and closing of the mandible

524.54 Insufficient anterior guidance
Insufficient anterior occlusal guidance

524.55 Centric occlusion maximum intercuspation discrepancy
Centric occlusion of teeth discrepancy

524.56 Non-working side interference
Balancing side interference

524.57 Lack of posterior occlusal support

524.59 Other dentofacial functional abnormalities
Abnormal swallowing
Mouth breathing
Sleep postures
Tongue, lip, or finger habits

✓5th **524.6 Temporomandibular joint disorders**
EXCLUDES *current temporomandibular joint:*
dislocation (830.0-830.1)
strain (848.1)

524.60 Temporomandibular joint disorders, unspecified
Temporomandibular joint-pain-dysfunction syndrome [TMJ]

524.61 Adhesions and ankylosis (bony or fibrous)
DEF: Stiffening or union of temporomandibular joint due to bony or fibrous union across joint.

524.62 Arthralgia of temporomandibular joint
DEF: Pain in temporomandibular joint; not inflammatory in nature.

524.63 Articular disc disorder (reducing or non-reducing)

524.64 Temporomandibular joint sounds on opening and/or closing the jaw

524.69 Other specified temporomandibular joint disorders

✓5th **524.7 Dental alveolar anomalies**

524.70 Unspecified alveolar anomaly

524.71 Alveolar maxillary hyperplasia
DEF: Excessive tissue formation in the dental alveoli of upper jaw.

524.72 Alveolar mandibular hyperplasia
DEF: Excessive tissue formation in the dental alveoli of lower jaw.

524.73 Alveolar maxillary hypoplasia
DEF: Incomplete or underdeveloped, alveolar tissue of upper jaw.

524.74 Alveolar mandibular hypoplasia
DEF: Incomplete or underdeveloped, alveolar tissue of lower jaw.

524.75 Vertical displacement of alveolus and teeth
Extrusion of alveolus and teeth

524.76 Occlusal plane deviation

524.79 Other specified alveolar anomaly

✓5th **524.8 Other specified dentofacial anomalies**

524.81 Anterior soft tissue impingement

524.82 Posterior soft tissue impingement

524.89 Other specified dentofacial anomalies

524.9 Unspecified dentofacial anomalies

✓4th **525 Other diseases and conditions of the teeth and supporting structures**

525.0 Exfoliation of teeth due to systemic causes

DEF: Deterioration of teeth and surrounding structures due to systemic disease.

✓5th **525.1 Loss of teeth due to trauma, extraction, or periodontal disease**

Code first class of edentulism (525.40-525.44, 525.50-525.54)

525.10 Acquired absence of teeth, unspecified

Tooth extraction status, NOS

525.11 Loss of teeth due to trauma

525.12 Loss of teeth due to periodontal disease

525.13 Loss of teeth due to caries

525.19 Other loss of teeth

✓5th **525.2 Atrophy of edentulous alveolar ridge**

525.20 Unspecified atrophy of edentulous alveolar ridge

Atrophy of the mandible NOS
Atrophy of the maxilla NOS

525.21 Minimal atrophy of the mandible

525.22 Moderate atrophy of the mandible

525.23 Severe atrophy of the mandible

525.24 Minimal atrophy of the maxilla

525.25 Moderate atrophy of the maxilla

525.26 Severe atrophy of the maxilla

525.3 Retained dental root

✓5th **525.4 Complete edentulism**

Use additional code to identify cause of edentulism (525.10-525.19)

525.40 Complete edentulism, unspecified

Edentulism NOS

525.41 Complete edentulism, class I

525.42 Complete edentulism, class II

525.43 Complete edentulism, class III

525.44 Complete edentulism, class IV

✓5th **525.5 Partial edentulism**

Use additional code to identify cause of edentulism (525.10-525.19)

525.50 Partial edentulism, unspecified

525.51 Partial edentulism, class I

525.52 Partial edentulism, class II

525.53 Partial edentulism, class III

525.54 Partial edentulism, class IV

✓5th **525.6 Unsatisfactory restoration of tooth**

Defective bridge, crown, fillings
Defective dental restoration

EXCLUDES *dental restoration status (V45.84)*
unsatisfactory endodontic treatment (526.61-526.69)

525.60 Unspecified unsatisfactory restoration of tooth

Unspecified defective dental restoration

525.61 Open restoration margins

Dental restoration failure of marginal integrity
Open margin on tooth restoration

525.62 Unrepairable overhanging of dental restorative materials

Overhanging of tooth restoration

525.63 Fractured dental restorative material without loss of material

EXCLUDES *cracked tooth (521.81)*
fractured tooth (873.63, 873.73)

525.64 Fractured dental restorative material with loss of material

EXCLUDES *cracked tooth (521.81)*
fractured tooth (873.63, 873.73)

525.65 Contour of existing restoration of tooth biologically incompatible with oral health

Dental restoration failure of periodontal anatomical integrity
Unacceptable contours of existing restoration
Unacceptable morphology of existing restoration

525.66 Allergy to existing dental restorative material

Use additional code to identify the specific type of allergy

525.67 Poor aesthetics of existing restoration

Dental restoration aesthetically inadequate or displeasing

525.69 Other unsatisfactory restoration of existing tooth

✓5th **525.7 Endosseous dental implant failure**

525.71 Osseointegration failure of dental implant

Failure of dental implant due to infection
Failure of dental implant due to unintentional loading
Failure of dental implant osseointegration due to premature loading
Failure of dental implant to osseointegrate prior to intentional prosthetic loading
Hemorrhagic complications of dental implant placement
Iatrogenic osseointegration failure of dental implant
Osseointegration failure of dental implant due to complications of systemic disease
Osseointegration failure of dental implant due to poor bone quality
Pre-integration failure of dental implant NOS
Pre-osseointegration failure of dental implant

525.72 Post-osseointegration biological failure of dental implant

Failure of dental implant due to lack of attached gingiva
Failure of dental implant due to occlusal trauma (caused by poor prosthetic design)
Failure of dental implant due to parafunctional habits
Failure of dental implant due to periodontal infection (peri-implantitis)
Failure of dental implant due to poor oral hygiene
Failure of dental implant to osseointegrate following intentional prosthetic loading
Iatrogenic post-osseointegration failure of dental implant
Post-osseointegration failure of dental implant due to complications of systemic disease

525.73 Post-osseointegration mechanic failure of dental implant
Failure of dental prosthesis causing loss of dental implant
Fracture of dental implant
Mechanical failure of dental implant NOS
EXCLUDES *cracked tooth (521.81)*
fractured dental restorative material with loss of material (525.64)
fractured dental restorative material without loss of material (525.63)
fractured tooth (873.63, 873.73)

525.79 Other endosseous dental implant failure
Dental implant failure NOS

525.8 Other specified disorders of the teeth and supporting structures
Enlargement of alveolar ridge NOS
Irregular alveolar process

525.9 Unspecified disorder of the teeth and supporting structures

✓4th **526 Diseases of the jaws**

526.0 Developmental odontogenic cysts
Cyst:
dentigerous
eruption
follicular
lateral developmental
lateral periodontal
primordial
Keratocyst
EXCLUDES *radicular cyst (522.8)*

526.1 Fissural cysts of jaw
Cyst:
globulomaxillary
incisor canal
median anterior maxillary
median palatal
nasopalatine
palatine of papilla
EXCLUDES *cysts of oral soft tissues (528.4)*

526.2 Other cysts of jaws
Cyst of jaw
NOS
aneurysmal
hemorrhagic
traumatic

526.3 Central giant cell (reparative) granuloma
EXCLUDES *peripheral giant cell granuloma (523.8)*

526.4 Inflammatory conditions
Abscess, Osteitis, Osteomyelitis (neonatal), Periostitis } of jaw (acute) (chronic) (suppurative)
Sequestrum of jaw bone
EXCLUDES *alveolar osteitis (526.5)*
osteonecrosis of jaw (733.45)

526.5 Alveolitis of jaw
Alveolar osteitis
Dry socket
DEF: Inflammation, of alveoli or tooth socket.

✓5th **526.6 Periradicular pathology associated with previous endodontic treatment**

526.61 Perforation of root canal space

526.62 Endodontic overfill

526.63 Endodontic underfill

526.69 Other periradicular pathology associated with previous endodontic treatment

✓5th **526.8 Other specified diseases of the jaws**

526.81 Exostosis of jaw
Torus mandibularis
Torus palatinus
DEF: Spur or bony outgrowth on the jaw.

526.89 Other
Cherubism, Fibrous dysplasia, Latent bone cyst, Osteoradionecrosis } of jaw(s)
Unilateral condylar hyperplasia or hypoplasia of mandible

526.9 Unspecified disease of the jaws

✓4th **527 Diseases of the salivary glands**

527.0 Atrophy
DEF: Wasting away, necrosis of salivary gland tissue.

527.1 Hypertrophy
DEF: Overgrowth or overdeveloped salivary gland tissue.

527.2 Sialoadenitis
Parotitis:
NOS
allergic
toxic
Sialoangitis
Sialodochitis
EXCLUDES *epidemic or infectious parotitis (072.0-072.9)*
uveoparotid fever (135)
DEF: Inflammation of salivary gland.

527.3 Abscess

527.4 Fistula
EXCLUDES *congenital fistula of salivary gland (750.24)*

527.5 Sialolithiasis
Calculus, Stone } of salivary gland or duct
Sialodocholithiasis

527.6 Mucocele
Mucous:
extravasation cyst of salivary gland
retention cyst of salivary gland
Ranula
DEF: Dilated salivary gland cavity filled with mucous.

527.7 Disturbance of salivary secretion
Hyposecretion
Ptyalism
Sialorrhea
Xerostomia

527.8 Other specified diseases of the salivary glands
Benign lymphoepithelial lesion of salivary gland
Sialectasia
Sialosis
Stenosis, Stricture } of salivary duct

527.9 Unspecified disease of the salivary glands

✓4th **528 Diseases of the oral soft tissues, excluding lesions specific for gingiva and tongue**

✓5th **528.0 Stomatitis and mucositis (ulcerative)**
EXCLUDES *cellulitis and abscess of mouth (528.3)*
diphtheritic stomatitis (032.0)
epizootic stomatitis (078.4)
gingivitis (523.0-523.1)
oral thrush (112.0)
Stevens-Johnson syndrome (695.13)
stomatitis:
acute necrotizing ulcerative (101)
aphthous (528.2)
gangrenous (528.1)
herpetic (054.2)
Vincent's (101)
DEF: Stomatitis: Inflammation of oral mucosa; labial and buccal mucosa, tongue, palate, floor of the mouth, and gingivae.

528.00 Stomatitis and mucositis, unspecified
Mucositis NOS
Ulcerative mucositis NOS
Ulcerative stomatitis NOS
Vesicular stomatitis NOS

528.01 Mucositis (ulcerative) due to antineoplastic therapy
Use additional E code to identify adverse effects of therapy, such as:
antineoplastic and immunosuppressive drugs (E930.7, E933.1)
radiation therapy (E879.2)

528.02 Mucositis (ulcerative) due to other drugs
Use additional E code to identify drug

528.09 Other stomatitis and mucositis (ulcerative)

528.1 Cancrum oris
Gangrenous stomatitis
Noma
DEF: A severely gangrenous lesion of mouth due to fusospirochetal infection; destroys buccal, labial and facial tissues; can be fatal; found primarily in debilitated and malnourished children.

528.2 Oral aphthae
Aphthous stomatitis
Canker sore
Periadenitis mucosa necrotica recurrens
Recurrent aphthous ulcer
Stomatitis herpetiformis
EXCLUDES *herpetic stomatitis (054.2)*
DEF: Small oval or round ulcers of the mouth marked by a grayish exudate and a red halo effect.

528.3 Cellulitis and abscess
Cellulitis of mouth (floor)
Ludwig's angina
Oral fistula
EXCLUDES *abscess of tongue (529.0)*
cellulitis or abscess of lip (528.5)
fistula (of):
dental (522.7)
lip (528.5)
gingivitis (523.00-523.11)

528.4 Cysts
Dermoid cyst } or mouth
Epidermoid cyst } or mouth
Epstein's pearl } or mouth
Lymphoepithelial cyst } or mouth
Nasoalveolar cyst } or mouth
Nasolabial cyst } or mouth
EXCLUDES *cyst:*
gingiva (523.8)
tongue (529.8)

528.5 Diseases of lips
Abscess } of lips
Cellulitis } of lips
Fistula } of lips
Hypertrophy } of lips
Cheilitis:
NOS
angular
Cheilodynia
Cheilosis
EXCLUDES *actinic cheilitis (692.79)*
congenital fistula of lip (750.25)
leukoplakia of lips (528.6)

528.6 Leukoplakia of oral mucosa, including tongue
Leukokeratosis of oral mucosa
Leukoplakia of:
gingiva
lips
tongue
EXCLUDES *carcinoma in situ (230.0, 232.0)*
leukokeratosis nicotina palati (528.79)
DEF: Thickened white patches of epithelium on mucous membranes of mouth.

✓5th **528.7 Other disturbances of oral epithelium, including tongue**
EXCLUDES *carcinoma in situ (230.0, 232.0)*
leukokeratosis NOS (702.8)

528.71 Minimal keratinized residual ridge mucosa
Minimal keratinization of alveolar ridge mucosa

528.72 Excessive keratinized residual ridge mucosa
Excessive keratinization of alveolar ridge mucosa

528.79 Other disturbances of oral epithelium, including tongue
Erythroplakia of mouth or tongue
Focal epithelial hyperplasia of mouth or tongue
Leukoedema of mouth or tongue
Leukokeratosis nicotina palate
Other oral epithelium disturbances

528.8 Oral submucosal fibrosis, including of tongue

528.9 Other and unspecified diseases of the oral soft tissues
Cheek and lip biting
Denture sore mouth
Denture stomatitis
Melanoplakia
Papillary hyperplasia of palate
Eosinophilic granuloma } of oral mucosa
Irritative hyperplasisa } of oral mucosa
Pyogenic granuloma } of oral mucosa
Ulcer (traumatic) } of oral mucosa

✓4th **529 Diseases and other conditions of the tongue**

529.0 Glossitis
Abscess } of tongue
Ulceration (traumatic) } of tongue
EXCLUDES *glossitis:*
benign migratory (529.1)
Hunter's (529.4)
median rhomboid (529.2)
Moeller's (529.4)

529.1 Geographic tongue
Benign migratory glossitis
Glossitis areata exfoliativa
DEF: Chronic glossitis; marked by filiform papillae atrophy and inflammation; no known etiology.

529.2 Median rhomboid glossitis
DEF: A noninflammatory, congenital disease characterized by rhomboid-like lesions at the middle third of the tongue's dorsal surface.

529.3 Hypertrophy of tongue papillae
Black hairy tongue
Coated tongue
Hypertrophy of foliate papillae
Lingua villosa nigra

529.4 Atrophy of tongue papillae
Bald tongue
Glazed tongue
Glossitis:
Hunter's
Moeller's
Glossodynia exfoliativa
Smooth atrophic tongue

529.5 Plicated tongue
Fissured } tongue
Furrowed } tongue
Scrotal } tongue
EXCLUDES *fissure of tongue, congenital (750.13)*
DEF: Cracks, fissures or furrows, on dorsal surface of tongue.

529.6 Glossodynia
Glossopyrosis
Painful tongue
EXCLUDES *glossodynia exfoliativa (529.4)*

529.8 Other specified conditions of the tongue

Atrophy
Crenated
Enlargement
Hypertrophy
} (of) tongue

Glossocele
Glossoptosis

EXCLUDES *erythroplasia of tongue (528.79)*
leukoplakia of tongue (528.6)
macroglossia (congenital) (750.15)
microglossia (congenital) (750.16)
oral submucosal fibrosis (528.8)

529.9 Unspecified condition of the tongue

DISEASES OF ESOPHAGUS, STOMACH, AND DUODENUM (530-538)

✓4th **530 Diseases of esophagus**

EXCLUDES *esophageal varices (456.0-456.2)*

530.0 Achalasia and cardiospasm

Achalasia (of cardia)
Aperistalsis of esophagus
Megaesophagus

EXCLUDES *congenital cardiospasm (750.7)*

DEF: Failure of smooth muscle fibers to relax, at gastrointestinal junctures; such as esophagogastric sphincter when swallowing.

✓5th **530.1 Esophagitis**

Esophagitis:
chemical
peptic
postoperative
regurgitant

Use additional E code to identify cause, if induced by chemical

EXCLUDES *tuberculous esophagitis (017.8)*

530.10 Esophagitis, unspecified

Esophagitis NOS

530.11 Reflux esophagitis

DEF: Inflammation of lower esophagus; due to regurgitated gastric acid.

530.12 Acute esophagitis

DEF: An acute inflammation of the mucous lining or submucosal coat of the esophagus.

530.13 Eosinophilic esophagitis

530.19 Other esophagitis

Abscess of esophagus

✓5th **530.2 Ulcer of esophagus**

Ulcer of esophagus:
fungal
peptic

Ulcer of esophagus due to ingestion of:
aspirin
chemicals
medicines

Use additional E code to identify cause, if induced by chemical or drug

530.20 Ulcer of esophagus without bleeding

Ulcer of esophagus NOS

530.21 Ulcer of esophagus with bleeding

EXCLUDES *bleeding esophageal varices (456.0, 456.20)*

530.3 Stricture and stenosis of esophagus

Compression of esophagus
Obstruction of esophagus

EXCLUDES *congenital stricture of esophagus (750.3)*

530.4 Perforation of esophagus

Rupture of esophagus

EXCLUDES *traumatic perforation of esophagus (862.22, 862.32, 874.4-874.5)*

530.5 Dyskinesia of esophagus

Corkscrew esophagus
Curling esophagus
Esophagospasm
Spasm of esophagus

EXCLUDES *cardiospasm (530.0)*

DEF: Difficulty performing voluntary esophageal movements.

Esophagus

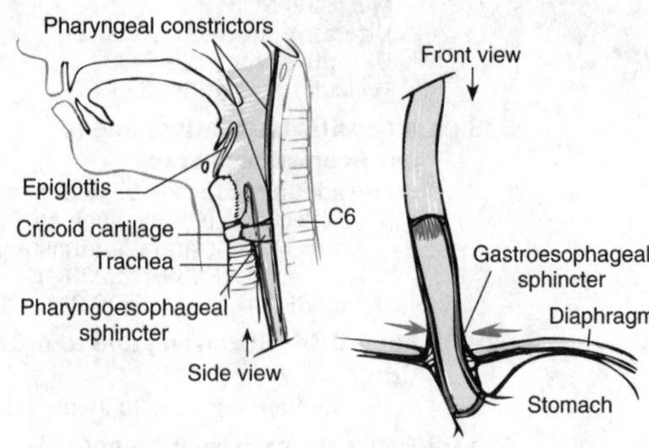

530.6 Diverticulum of esophagus, acquired

Diverticulum, acquired:
epiphrenic
pharyngoesophageal
pulsion
subdiaphragmatic
traction
Zenker's (hypopharyngeal)

Esophageal pouch, acquired
Esophagocele, acquired

EXCLUDES *congenital diverticulum of esophagus (750.4)*

530.7 Gastroesophageal laceration-hemorrhage syndrome

Mallory-Weiss syndrome

DEF: Laceration of distal esophagus and proximal stomach due to vomiting, hiccups or other sustained activity.

✓5th **530.8 Other specified disorders of esophagus**

530.81 Esophageal reflux

Gastroesophageal reflux

EXCLUDES *reflux esophagitis (530.11)*

DEF: Regurgitation of the gastric contents into esophagus and possibly pharynx; where aspiration may occur between the vocal cords and down into the trachea.

530.82 Esophageal hemorrhage

EXCLUDES *hemorrhage due to esophageal varices (456.0-456.2)*

530.83 Esophageal leukoplakia

530.84 Tracheoesophageal fistula

EXCLUDES *congenital tracheoesophageal fistula (750.3)*

530.85 Barrett's esophagus

DEF: A metaplastic disorder in which specialized colum-nar epithelial cells replace the normal squamous epith-elial cells; an acquired condition secondary to chronic gastroesophageal reflux damage to the mucosa; assoc-iated with increased risk of developing adenocarcinoma.

530.86 Infection of esophagostomy

Use additional code to specify infection

530.87 Mechanical complication of esophagostomy

Malfunction of esophagostomy

530.89 Other

EXCLUDES *Paterson-Kelly syndrome (280.8)*

Stomach

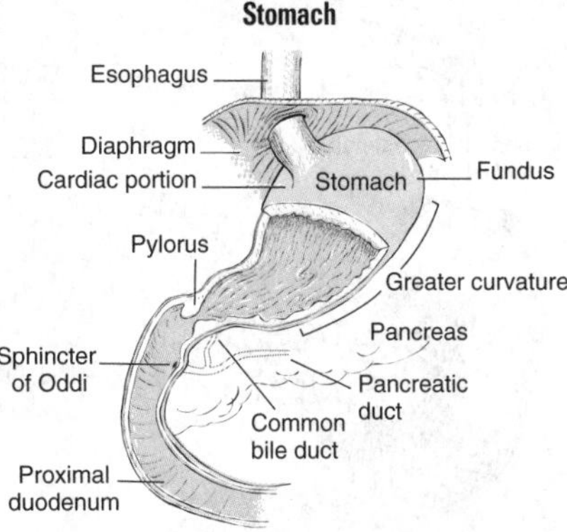

530.9 Unspecified disorder of esophagus

✓4th 531 Gastric ulcer

INCLUDES ulcer (peptic):
prepyloric
pylorus
stomach

Use additional E code to identify drug, if drug-induced

EXCLUDES *peptic ulcer NOS (533.0-533.9)*

The following fifth-digit subclassification is for use with category 531:
0 without mention of obstruction
1 with obstruction

DEF: Destruction of tissue in lumen of stomach due to action of gastric acid and pepsin on gastric mucosa decreasing resistance to ulcers.

✓5th **531.0 Acute with hemorrhage**
[0-1]

✓5th **531.1 Acute with perforation**
[0-1]

✓5th **531.2 Acute with hemorrhage and perforation**
[0-1]

✓5th **531.3 Acute without mention of hemorrhage or perforation**
[0-1]

✓5th **531.4 Chronic or unspecified with hemorrhage**
[0-1]

✓5th **531.5 Chronic or unspecified with perforation**
[0-1]

✓5th **531.6 Chronic or unspecified with hemorrhage and perforation**
[0-1]

✓5th **531.7 Chronic without mention of hemorrhage or perforation**
[0-1]

✓5th **531.9 Unspecified as acute or chronic, without mention of hemorrhage or perforation**
[0-1]

✓4th 532 Duodenal ulcer

INCLUDES erosion (acute) of duodenum
ulcer (peptic):
duodenum
postpyloric

Use additional E code to identify drug, if drug-induced

EXCLUDES *peptic ulcer NOS (533.0-533.9)*

The following fifth-digit subclassification is for use with category 532:
0 without mention of obstruction
1 with obstruction

DEF: Ulcers in duodenum due to action of gastric acid and pepsin on mucosa decreasing resistance to ulcers.

✓5th **532.0 Acute with hemorrhage**
[0-1]

✓5th **532.1 Acute with perforation**
[0-1]

✓5th **532.2 Acute with hemorrhage and perforation**
[0-1]

✓5th **532.3 Acute without mention of hemorrhage or perforation**
[0-1]

✓5th **532.4 Chronic or unspecified with hemorrhage**
[0-1]

✓5th **532.5 Chronic or unspecified with perforation**
[0-1]

✓5th **532.6 Chronic or unspecified with hemorrhage and perforation**
[0-1]

✓5th **532.7 Chronic without mention of hemorrhage or perforation**
[0-1]

✓5th **532.9 Unspecified as acute or chronic, without mention of hemorrhage or perforation**
[0-1]

✓4th 533 Peptic ulcer, site unspecified

INCLUDES gastroduodenal ulcer NOS
peptic ulcer NOS
stress ulcer NOS

Use additional E code to identify drug, if drug-induced

EXCLUDES *peptic ulcer:*
duodenal (532.0-532.9)
gastric (531.0-531.9)

The following fifth-digit subclassification is for use with category 533:
0 without mention of obstruction
1 with obstruction

DEF: Ulcer of mucous membrane of esophagus, stomach or duodenum due to gastric acid secretion.

✓5th **533.0 Acute with hemorrhage**
[0-1]

✓5th **533.1 Acute with perforation**
[0-1]

✓5th **533.2 Acute with hemorrhage and perforation**
[0-1]

✓5th **533.3 Acute without mention of hemorrhage and perforation**
[0-1]

✓5th **533.4 Chronic or unspecified with hemorrhage**
[0-1]

✓5th **533.5 Chronic or unspecified with perforation**
[0-1]

✓5th **533.6 Chronic or unspecified with hemorrhage and perforation**
[0-1]

✓5th **533.7 Chronic without mention of hemorrhage or perforation**
[0-1]

✓5th **533.9 Unspecified as acute or chronic, without mention of hemorrhage or perforation**
[0-1]

✓4th 534 Gastrojejunal ulcer

INCLUDES ulcer (peptic) or erosion:
anastomotic
gastrocolic
gastrointestinal
gastrojejunal
jejunal
marginal
stomal

EXCLUDES *primary ulcer of small intestine (569.82)*

The following fifth-digit subclassification is for use with category 534:
0 without mention of obstruction
1 with obstruction

✓5th **534.0 Acute with hemorrhage**
[0-1]

✓5th **534.1 Acute with perforation**
[0-1]

✓5th **534.2 Acute with hemorrhage and perforation**
[0-1]

✓5th **534.3 Acute without mention of hemorrhage or perforation**
[0-1]

✓5th **534.4 Chronic or unspecified with hemorrhage**
[0-1]

✓5th **534.5 Chronic or unspecified with perforation**
[0-1]

✓5th **534.6 Chronic or unspecified with hemorrhage and perforation**
[0-1]

✓5th **534.7 Chronic without mention of hemorrhage or perforation**
[0-1]

✓5th **534.9 Unspecified as acute or chronic, without mention of hemorrhage or perforation**
[0-1]

✓4th **535 Gastritis and duodenitis**

The following fifth-digit subclassification is for use with category 535:
0 without mention of hemorrhage
1 with hemorrhage

✓5th **535.0 Acute gastritis**
[0-1]

✓5th **535.1 Atrophic gastritis**
[0-1]
Gastritis:
atrophic-hyperplastic
chronic (atrophic)

DEF: Inflammation of stomach, with mucous membrane atrophy and peptic gland destruction.

✓5th **535.2 Gastric mucosal hypertrophy**
[0-1]
Hypertrophic gastritis

✓5th **535.3 Alcoholic gastritis**
[0-1]

✓5th **535.4 Other specified gastritis**
[0-1]
Gastritis:
allergic
bile induced
irritant
superficial
toxic

EXCLUDES *eosinophilic gastritis (535.7)*

✓5th **535.5 Unspecified gastritis and gastroduodenitis**
[0-1]

✓5th **535.6 Duodenitis**
[0-1]
DEF: Inflammation of intestine, between pylorus and jejunum.

✓5th **535.7 Eosinophilic gastritis**
[0-1]

✓4th **536 Disorders of function of stomach**

EXCLUDES *functional disorders of stomach specified as psychogenic (306.4)*

536.0 Achlorhydria

DEF: Absence of gastric acid due to gastric mucosa atrophy; unresponsive to histamines; also known as gastric anacidity.

536.1 Acute dilatation of stomachAcute distention of stomach

536.2 Persistent vomiting
Cyclical vomiting
Habit vomiting
Persistent vomiting [not of pregnancy]
Uncontrollable vomiting

EXCLUDES *excessive vomiting in pregnancy (643.0-643.9)*
vomiting NOS (787.03)
cyclical, associated with migraine (346.2)

536.3 Gastroparesis
Gastroparalysis
Code first underlying disease, such as: diabetes mellitus (249.6, 250.6)

DEF: Slight degree of paralysis within muscular coat of stomach.

✓5th **536.4 Gastrostomy complications**

536.40 Gastrostomy complication, unspecified

Duodenum

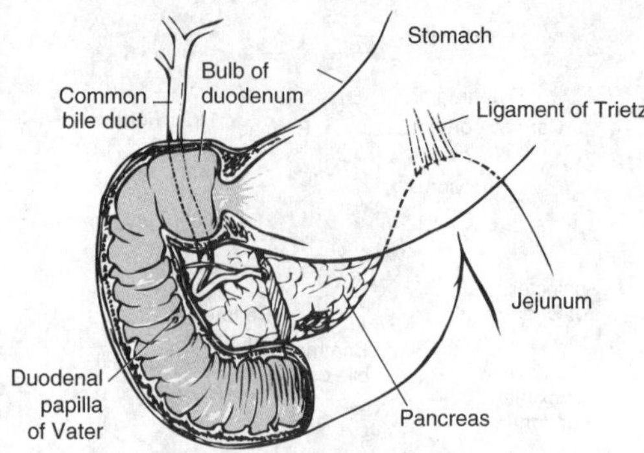

536.41 Infection of gastrostomy
Use additional code to specify type of infection, such as:
abscess or cellulitis of abdomen (682.2)
septicemia (038.0-038.9)
Use additional code to identify organism (041.00-041.9)

536.42 Mechanical complication of gastrostomy

536.49 Other gastrostomy complications

536.8 Dyspepsia and other specified disorders of function of stomach
Achylia gastrica
Hourglass contraction of stomach
Hyperacidity
Hyperchlorhydria
Hypochlorhydria
Indigestion
Tachygastria

EXCLUDES *achlorhydria (536.0)*
heartburn (787.1)

536.9 Unspecified functional disorder of stomach
Functional gastrointestinal:
disorder
disturbance
irritation

✓4th **537 Other disorders of stomach and duodenum**

537.0 Acquired hypertrophic pyloric stenosis
Constriction, Obstruction, Stricture } of pylorus, acquired or adult

EXCLUDES *congenital or infantile pyloric stenosis (750.5)*

537 .1 Gastric diverticulum

EXCLUDES *congenital diverticulum of stomach (750.7)*

DEF: Herniated sac or pouch, within stomach or duodenum.

537.2 Chronic duodenal ileus

DEF: Persistent obstruction between pylorus and jejunum.

537.3 Other obstruction of duodenum
Cicatrix, Stenosis, Stricture, Volvulus } of duodenum

EXCLUDES *congenital obstruction of duodenum (751.1)*

537.4 Fistula of stomach or duodenum
Gastrocolic fistula
Gastrojejunocolic fistula

537.5 Gastroptosis

DEF: Downward displacement of stomach.

537.6 Hourglass stricture or stenosis of stomach
Cascade stomach

EXCLUDES *congenital hourglass stomach (750.7)*
hourglass contraction of stomach (536.8)

✓5th 537.8 Other specified disorders of stomach and duodenum

537.81 Pylorospasm

EXCLUDES *congenital pylorospasm (750.5)*

DEF: Spasm of the pyloric sphincter.

537.82 Angiodysplasia of stomach and duodenum (without mention of hemorrhage)

537.83 Angiodysplasia of stomach and duodenum with hemorrhage

DEF: Bleeding of stomach and duodenum due to vascular abnormalities.

537.84 Dieulafoy lesion (hemorrhagic) of stomach and duodenum

DEF: An abnormally large and convoluted submucosal artery protruding through a defect in the mucosa in the stomach or intestines that can erode the epithelium causing hemorrhaging; also called Dieulafoy's vascular malformation.

537.89 Other

Gastric or duodenal:
- prolapse
- rupture

Intestinal metaplasia of gastric mucosa
Passive congestion of stomach

EXCLUDES *diverticula of duodenum (562.00-562.01)*
gastrointestinal hemorrhage (578.0-578.9)

537.9 Unspecified disorder of stomach and duodenum

538 Gastrointestinal mucositis (ulcerative)

Use additional E code to identify adverse effects of therapy, such as:
antineoplastic and immunosuppressive drugs (E930.7, E933.1)
radiation therapy (E879.2)

EXCLUDES *mucositis (ulcerative) of mouth and oral soft tissue (528.00- 528.09)*

APPENDICITIS (540-543)

✓4th 540 Acute appendicitis

DEF: Inflammation of vermiform appendix due to fecal obstruction, neoplasm or foreign body of appendiceal lumen; causes infection, edema and infarction of appendiceal wall; may result in mural necrosis, and perforation.

540.0 With generalized peritonitis

Appendicitis (acute) with: { perforation, peritonitis (generalized), rupture } { fulminating, gangrenous, obstructive }

Cecitis (acute) with perforation, peritonitis (generalized), rupture
Rupture of appendix

EXCLUDES *acute appendicitis with peritoneal abscess (540.1)*

540.1 With peritoneal abscess

Abscess of appendix
With generalized peritonitis

540.9 Without mention of peritonitis

Acute appendicitis without mention of perforation, peritonitis, or rupture:
- fulminating
- gangrenous
- inflamed
- obstructive

Acute cecitis without mention of perforation, peritonitis, or rupture

541 Appendicitis, unqualified

542 Other appendicitis

Appendicitis:
- chronic
- recurrent

Appendicitis:
- relapsing
- subacute

EXCLUDES *hyperplasia (lymphoid) of appendix (543.0)*

Appendix

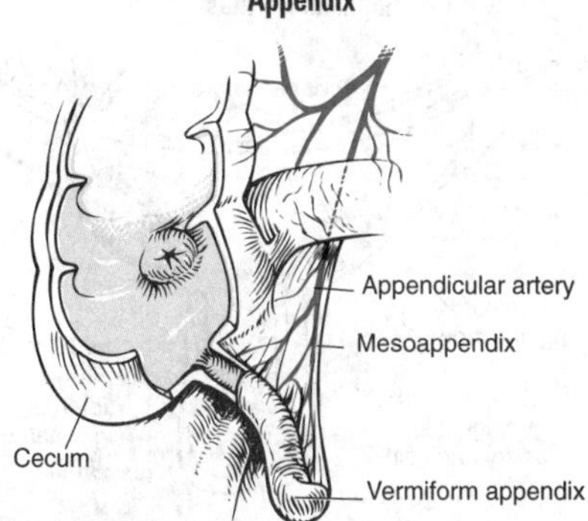

✓4th 543 Other diseases of appendix

543.0 Hyperplasia of appendix (lymphoid)

DEF: Proliferation of cells in appendix tissue.

543.9 Other and unspecified diseases of appendix

Appendicular or appendiceal:
- colic
- concretion
- fistula

Diverticulum, Fecalith, Intussusception, Mucocele, Stercolith } of appendix

HERNIA OF ABDOMINAL CAVITY (550-553)

INCLUDES hernia:
- acquired
- congenital, except diaphragmatic or hiatal

✓4th 550 Inguinal hernia

INCLUDES bubonocele
inguinal hernia (direct) (double) (indirect) (oblique) (sliding)
scrotal hernia

The following fifth-digit subclassification is for use with category 550:
- **0 unilateral or unspecified (not specified as recurrent)**
  Unilateral NOS
- **1 unilateral or unspecified, recurrent**
- **2 bilateral (not specified as recurrent)**
  Bilateral NOS
- **3 bilateral, recurrent**

DEF: Hernia protrusion of an abdominal organ or tissue through inguinal canal.

DEF: Indirect inguinal hernia: (external or oblique) leaves abdomen through deep inguinal ring, passes through inguinal canal lateral to the inferior epigastric artery.

DEF: Direct inguinal hernia: (internal) emerges between inferior epigastric artery and rectus muscle edge.

✓5th 550.0 Inguinal hernia, with gangrene
[0-3] Inguinal hernia with gangrene (and obstruction)

✓5th 550.1 Inguinal hernia, with obstruction, without mention of gangrene
[0-3] Inguinal hernia with mention of incarceration, irreducibility, or strangulation

✓5th 550.9 Inguinal hernia, without mention of obstruction or gangrene
[0-3] Inguinal hernia NOS

✓4th 551 Other hernia of abdominal cavity, with gangrene

INCLUDES *that with gangrene (and obstruction)*

✓5th 551.0 Femoral hernia with gangrene

551.00 Unilateral or unspecified (not specified as recurrent)

Femoral hernia NOS with gangrene

551.01 Unilateral or unspecified, recurrent

551.02 Bilateral (not specified as recurrent)

551.03 Bilateral, recurrent

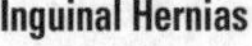

Inguinal Hernias

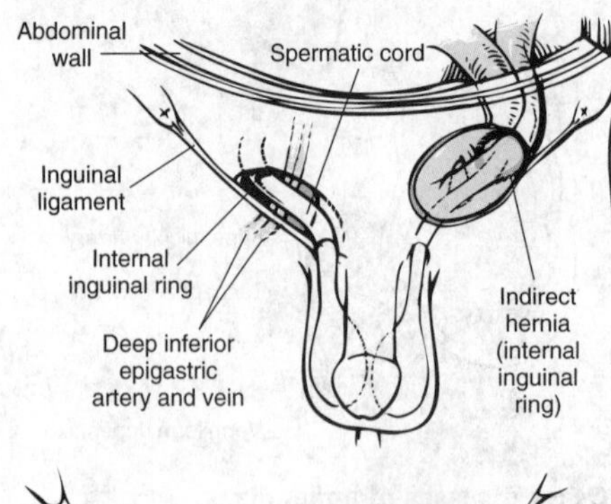

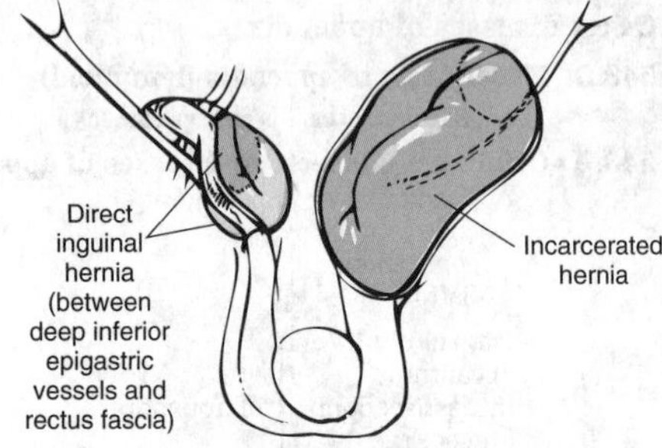

551.1 Umbilical hernia with gangrene
Parumbilical hernia specified as gangrenous

✓5th **551.2 Ventral hernia with gangrene**

551.20 Ventral, unspecified, with gangrene

551.21 Incisional, with gangrene
Hernia:
postoperative } specified as gangrenous
recurrent, ventral } specified as gangrenous

551.29 Other
Epigastric hernia specified as gangrenous

551.3 Diaphragmatic hernia with gangrene
Hernia:
hiatal (esophageal) (sliding) } specified as gangrenous
paraesophageal } specified as gangrenous
Thoracic stomach } specified as gangrenous

EXCLUDES *congenital diaphragmatic hernia (756.6)*

551.8 Hernia of other specified sites, with gangrene
Any condition classifiable to 553.8 if specified as gangrenous

551.9 Hernia of unspecified site, with gangrene
Any condition classifiable to 553.9 if specified as gangrenous

✓4th **552 Other hernia of abdominal cavity, with obstruction, but without mention of gangrene**

EXCLUDES *that with mention of gangrene (551.0-551.9)*

✓5th **552.0 Femoral hernia with obstruction**
Femoral hernia specified as incarcerated, irreducible, strangulated, or causing obstruction

552.00 Unilateral or unspecified (not specified as recurrent)

552.01 Unilateral or unspecified, recurrent

552.02 Bilateral (not specified as recurrent)

552.03 Bilateral, recurrent

552.1 Umbilical hernia with obstruction
Parumbilical hernia specified as incarcerated, irreducible, strangulated, or causing obstruction

✓5th **552.2 Ventral hernia with obstruction**
Ventral hernia specified as incarcerated, irreducible, strangulated, or causing obstruction

552.20 Ventral, unspecified, with obstruction

552.21 Incisional, with obstruction
Hernia:
postoperative } specified as incarcerated, irreducible, strangulated, or causing obstruction
recurrent, } specified as incarcerated, irreducible, strangulated, or causing obstruction
ventral } specified as incarcerated, irreducible, strangulated, or causing obstruction

552.29 Other
Epigastric hernia specified as incarcerated, irreducible, strangulated, or causing obstruction

552.3 Diaphragmatic hernia with obstruction
Hernia:
hiatal (esophageal) (sliding) } specified as caracerated, irreducible, strangulated, or causing obstruction
paraesophageal } specified as caracerated, irreducible, strangulated, or causing obstruction
Thoracic stomach } specified as caracerated, irreducible, strangulated, or causing obstruction

EXCLUDES *congenital diaphragmatic hernia (756.6)*

552.8 Hernia of other specified sites, with obstruction
Any condition classifiable to 553.8 if specified as incarcerated, irreducible, strangulated, or causing obstruction

EXCLUDES *hernia due to adhesion with obstruction (560.81)*

552.9 Hernia of unspecified site, with obstruction
Any condition classifiable to 553.9 if specified as incarcerated, irreducible, strangulated, or causing obstruction

✓4th **553 Other hernia of abdominal cavity without mention of obstruction or gangrene**

EXCLUDES *the listed conditions with mention of:*
gangrene (and obstruction) (551.0-551.9)
obstruction (552.0-552.9)

✓5th **553.0 Femoral hernia**

553.00 Unilateral or unspecified (not specified as recurrent)
Femoral hernia NOS

553.01 Unilateral or unspecified, recurrent

553.02 Bilateral (not specified as recurrent)

553.03 Bilateral, recurrent

553.1 Umbilical hernia
Parumbilical hernia

Hernias of Abdominal Cavity

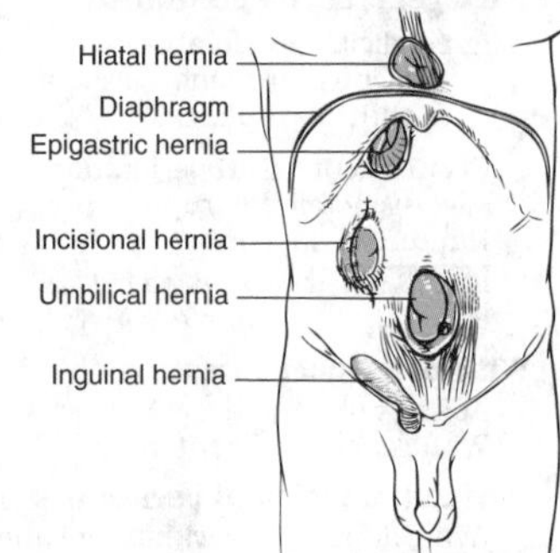

Femoral Hernia

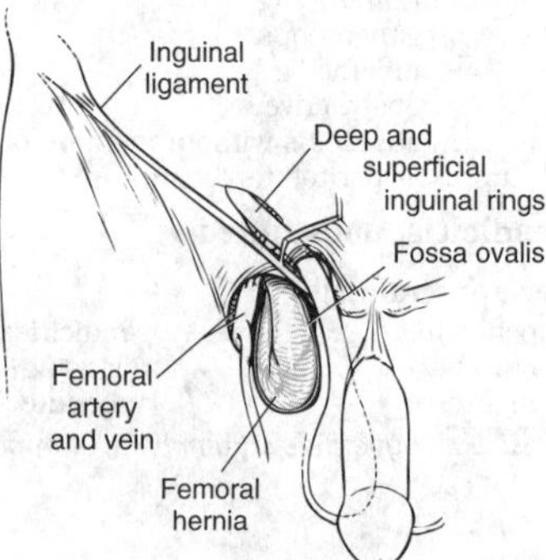

✓5th **553.2 Ventral hernia**

553.20 Ventral, unspecified

553.21 Incisional

Hernia:
- postoperative
- recurrent, ventral

553.29 Other

Hernia:
- epigastric
- spigelian

553.3 Diaphragmatic hernia

Hernia:
- hiatal (esophageal) (sliding)
- paraesophageal

Thoracic stomach

EXCLUDES *congenital:*
diaphragmatic hernia (756.6)
hiatal hernia (750.6)
esophagocele (530.6)

553.8 Hernia of other specified sites

Hernia:
- ischiatic
- ischiorectal
- lumbar
- obturator
- pudendal
- retroperitoneal
- sciatic

Other abdominal hernia of specified site

EXCLUDES *vaginal enterocele (618.6)*

553.9 Hernia of unspecified site

Enterocele
Epiplocele
Rupture (nontraumatic)
Sarcoepiplocele

Hernia:
- NOS
- interstitial
- intestinal
- intra-abdominal

Diaphragmatic Hernias

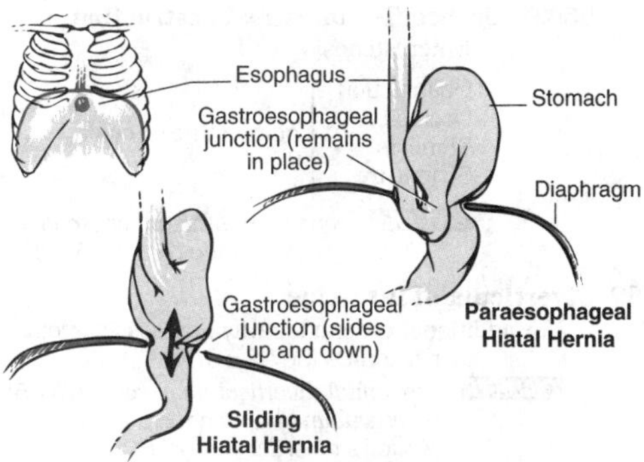

Large Intestine

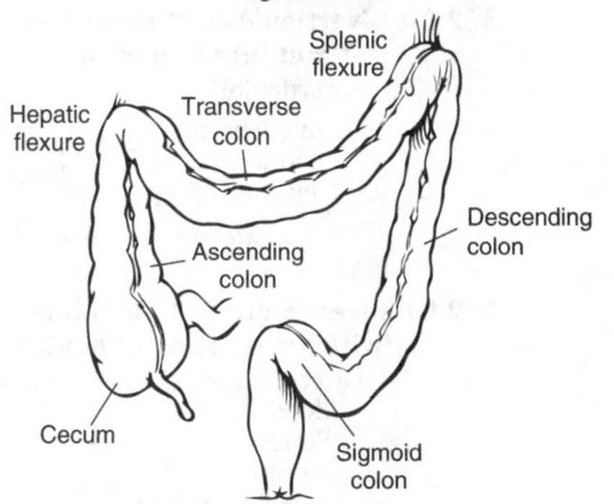

NONINFECTIOUS ENTERITIS AND COLITIS (555-558)

✓4th **555 Regional enteritis**

INCLUDES Crohn's disease
Granulomatous enteritis

EXCLUDES *ulcerative colitis (556)*

DEF: Inflammation of intestine; classified to site.

555.0 Small intestine

Ileitis:
- regional
- segmental
- terminal

Regional enteritis or Crohn's disease of:
- duodenum
- ileum
- jejunum

555.1 Large intestine

Colitis:
- granulmatous
- regional
- transmural

Regional enteritis or Crohn's disease of:
- colon
- large bowel
- rectum

555.2 Small intestine with large intestine

Regional ileocolitis

555.9 Unspecified site

Crohn's disease NOS
Regional enteritis NOS

✓4th **556 Ulcerative colitis**

DEF: Chronic inflammation of mucosal lining of intestinal tract; may be single area or entire colon.

556.0 Ulcerative (chronic) enterocolitis

556.1 Ulcerative (chronic) ileocolitis

556.2 Ulcerative (chronic) proctitis

556.3 Ulcerative (chronic) proctosigmoiditis

556.4 Pseudopolyposis of colon

556.5 Left-sided ulcerative (chronic) colitis

556.6 Universal ulcerative (chronic) colitis

Pancolitis

556.8 Other ulcerative colitis

556.9 Ulcerative colitis, unspecified

Ulcerative enteritis NOS

✓4th **557 Vascular insufficiency of intestine**

EXCLUDES *necrotizing enterocolitis of the newborn (777.50–777.53)*

DEF: Inadequacy of intestinal vessels.

557.0 Acute vascular insufficiency of intestine

Acute:
- hemorrhagic enterocolitis
- ischemic colitis, enteritis, or enterocolitis
- massive necrosis of intestine

Bowel infarction
Embolism of mesenteric artery
Fulminant enterocolitis
Hemorrhagic necrosis of intestine
Infarction of appendices epiploicae
Intestinal gangrene
Intestinal infarction (acute) (agnogenic) (hemorrhagic) (nonocclusive)
Mesenteric infarction (embolic) (thrombotic)
Necrosis of intestine
Terminal hemorrhagic enteropathy
Thrombosis of mesenteric artery

557.1 Chronic vascular insufficiency of intestine
Angina, abdominal

Chronic ischemic colitis, enteritis, or enterocolitis
Ischemic stricture of intestine

Mesenteric:
- angina
- artery syndrome (superior)
- vascular insufficiency

557.9 Unspecified vascular insufficiency of intestine
Alimentary pain due to vascular insufficiency
Ischemic colitis, enteritis, or enterocolitis NOS

✓4th **558 Other and unspecified noninfectious gastroenteritis and colitis**
EXCLUDES *infectious:*
colitis, enteritis, or gastroenteritis (009.0-009.1)
diarrhea (009.2-009.3)

558.1 Gastroenteritis and colitis due to radiation
Radiation enterocolitis

558.2 Toxic gastroenteritis and colitis
Use additional E code to identify cause

558.3 Allergic gastroenteritis and colitis
Use additional code to identify type of food allergy (V15.01-V15.05)
DEF: True immunoglobulin E (IgE)-mediated allergic reaction of the lining of the stomach, intestines, or colon to food proteins; causes nausea, vomiting, diarrhea, and abdominal cramping.

✓5th **558.4 Eosinophilic gastroenteritis and colitis**

558.41 Eosinophilic gastroenteritis
Eosinophilic enteritis

558.42 Eosinophilic colitis

558.9 Other and unspecified noninfectious gastroenteritis and colitis

Colitis, Enteritis, Gastroenteritis, Ileitis, Jejunitis, Sigmoiditis } NOS, dietetic, or noninfectious

OTHER DISEASES OF INTESTINES AND PERITONEUM (560-569)

✓4th **560 Intestinal obstruction without mention of hernia**
EXCLUDES *duodenum (537.2-537.3)*
inguinal hernia with obstruction (550.1)
intestinal obstruction complicating hernia (552.0-552.9)
mesenteric:
embolism (557.0)
infarction (557.0)
thrombosis (557.0)
neonatal intestinal obstruction (277.01, 777.1-777.2, 777.4)

560.0 Intussusception
Intussusception (colon) (intestine) (rectum)
Invagination of intestine or colon
EXCLUDES *intussusception of appendix (543.9)*
DEF: Prolapse of a bowel section into adjacent section; occurs primarily in children; symptoms include paroxysmal pain, vomiting, presence of lower abdominal tumor and blood, and mucous passage from rectum.

560.1 Paralytic ileus
Adynamic ileus
Ileus (of intestine) (of bowel) (of colon)
Paralysis of intestine or colon
EXCLUDES *gallstone ileus (560.31)*
DEF: Obstruction of ileus due to inhibited bowel motility.

560.2 Volvulus

Knotting, Strangulation, Torsion, Twist } if intestine, bowel, or colon

DEF: Entanglement of bowel; causes obstruction; may compromise bowel circulation.

Volvulus and Diverticulitis

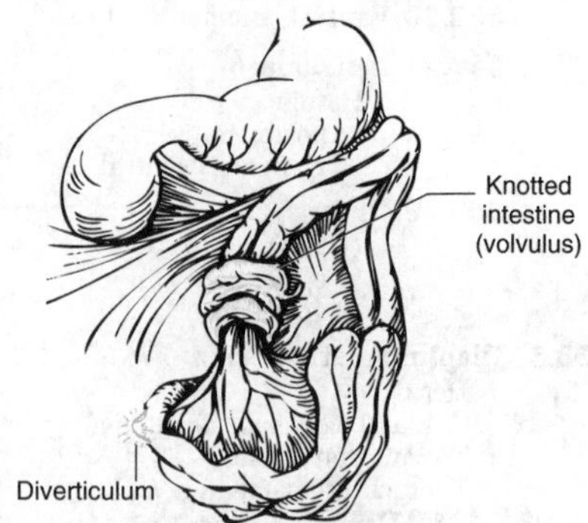

✓5th **560.3 Impaction of intestine**

560.30 Impaction of intestine, unspecified
Impaction of colon

560.31 Gallstone ileus
Obstruction of intestine by gallstone

560.39 Other
Concretion of intestine
Enterolith
Fecal impaction

✓5th **560.8 Other specified intestinal obstruction**

560.81 Intestinal or peritoneal adhesions with obstruction (postoperative) (postinfection)
EXCLUDES *adhesions without obstruction (568.0)*
DEF: Obstruction of peritoneum or intestine due to abnormal union of tissues.

560.89 Other
Acute pseudo-obstruction of intestine
Mural thickening causing obstruction
EXCLUDES *ischemic stricture of intestine (557.1)*

560.9 Unspecified intestinal obstruction
Enterostenosis

Obstruction, Occlusion, Stenosis, Stricture } of intestine or colon

EXCLUDES *congenital stricture or stenosis of intestine (751.1-751.2)*

✓4th **562 Diverticula of intestine**
Use additional code to identify any associated:
peritonitis (567.0-567.9)
EXCLUDES *congenital diverticulum of colon (751.5)*
diverticulum of appendix (543.9)
Meckel's diverticulum (751.0)

✓5th **562.0 Small intestine**

562.00 Diverticulosis of small intestine (without mention of hemorrhage)
Diverticulosis:
duodenum, ileum, jejunum } without mention of diverticulitis
DEF: Saclike herniations of mucous lining of small intestine.

562.01 Diverticulitis of small intestine (without mention of hemorrhage)
Diverticulitis (with diverticulosis):
duodenum
ileum
jejunum
small intestine
DEF: Inflamed saclike herniations of mucous lining of small intestine

562.02 Diverticulosis of small intestine with hemorrhage

562.03 Diverticulitis of small intestine with hemorrhage

✓5th **562.1 Colon**

562.10 Diverticulosis of colon (without mention of hemorrhage)
Diverticulosis:
NOS } without mention of diverticulitis
intestine (large) }
Diverticular disease (colon) without mention of diverticulitis
DEF: Saclike herniations of mucous lining of large intestine.

562.11 Diverticulitis of colon (without mention of hemorrhage)
Diverticulitis (with diverticulosis):
NOS
colon
intestine (large)
DEF: Inflamed saclike herniations of mucosal lining of large intestine.

562.12 Diverticulosis of colon with hemorrhage

562.13 Diverticulitis of colon with hemorrhage

✓4th **564 Functional digestive disorders, not elsewhere classified**

EXCLUDES *functional disorders of stomach (536.0-536.9)*
those specified as psychogenic (306.4)

✓5th **564.0 Constipation**

564.00 Constipation, unspecified

564.01 Slow transit constipation
DEF: Delay in the transit of fecal material through the colon secondary to smooth muscle dysfunction or decreased peristaltic contractions along the colon: also called colonic inertia or delayed transit.

564.02 Outlet dysfunction constipation
DEF: Failure to relax the paradoxical contractions of the striated pelvic floor muscles during the attempted defecation.

564.09 Other constipation

564.1 Irritable bowel syndrome
Irritable colon
Spastic colon
DEF: Functional gastrointestinal disorder (FGID); symptoms following meals include diarrhea, constipation, abdominal pain; other symptoms include bloating, gas, distended abdomen, nausea, vomiting, appetite loss, emotional distress, and depression.

564.2 Postgastric surgery syndromes
Dumping syndrome
Jejunal syndrome
Postgastrectomy syndrome
Postvagotomy syndrome
EXCLUDES *malnutrition following gastrointestinal surgery (579.3)*
postgastrojejunostomy ulcer (534.0-534.9)

564.3 Vomiting following gastrointestinal surgery
Vomiting (bilious) following gastrointestinal surgery

564.4 Other postoperative functional disorders
Diarrhea following gastrointestinal surgery
EXCLUDES *colostomy and enterostomy complications (569.60-569.69)*

564.5 Functional diarrhea
EXCLUDES *diarrhea:*
NOS (787.91)
psychogenic (306.4)
DEF: Diarrhea with no detectable organic cause.

564.6 Anal spasm
Proctalgia fugax

Anal Fistula and Abscess

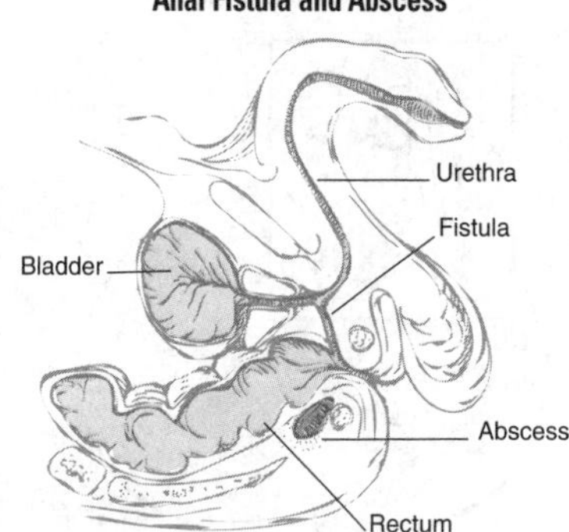

564.7 Megacolon, other than Hirschsprung's
Dilatation of colon
EXCLUDES *megacolon:*
congenital [Hirschsprung's] (751.3)
toxic (556)
DEF: Enlarged colon; congenital or acquired; can occur acutely or become chronic.

✓5th **564.8 Other specified functional disorders of intestine**
EXCLUDES *malabsorption (579.0-579.9)*

564.81 Neurogenic bowel
DEF: Disorder of bowel due to spinal cord lesion above conus medullaris; symptoms include precipitous micturition, nocturia, catheter intolerance, headache, sweating, nasal obstruction and spastic contractions.

564.89 Other functional disorders of intestine
Atony of colon

564.9 Unspecified functional disorder of intestine

✓4th **565 Anal fissure and fistula**

565.0 Anal fissure
EXCLUDES *anal sphincter tear (healed) (non-traumatic) (old) (569.43)*
traumatic (863.89, 863.99)
DEF: Ulceration of cleft at anal mucosa; causes pain, itching, bleeding, infection, and sphincter spasm; may occur with hemorrhoids.

565.1 Anal fistula
Fistula:
anorectal
rectal
rectum to skin
EXCLUDES *fistula of rectum to internal organs–see Alphabetic Index*
ischiorectal fistula (566)
rectovaginal fistula (619.1)
DEF: Abnormal opening on cutaneous surface near anus; may lack connection with rectum.

566 Abscess of anal and rectal regions
Abscess:
ischiorectal
perianal
perirectal
Cellulitis:
anal
perirectal
rectal
Ischiorectal fistula

✓4th **567 Peritonitis and retroperitoneal infections**
EXCLUDES *peritonitis:*
benign paroxysmal (277.31)
pelvic, female (614.5, 614.7)
periodic familial (277.31)
puerperal (670)
with or following:
abortion (634-638 with .0, 639.0)
appendicitis (540.0-540.1)
ectopic or molar pregnancy (639.0)
DEF: Inflammation of the peritoneal cavity.

Psoas Muscle Abscess

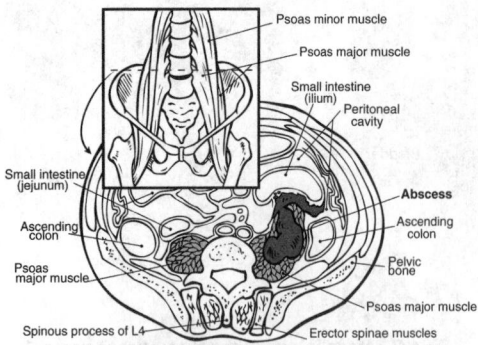

567.0 *Peritonitis in infectious diseases classified elsewhere*

Code first underlying disease

EXCLUDES *peritonitis:*
gonococcal (098.86)
syphilitic (095.2)
tuberculous (014.0)

567.1 Pneumococcal peritonitis

✓5th **567.2 Other suppurative peritonitis**

567.21 Peritonitis (acute) generalized

Pelvic peritonitis, male

567.22 Peritoneal abscess

Abscess (of):
abdominopelvic
mesenteric
omentum
peritoneum
retrocecal
subdiaphragmatic
subhepatic
subphrenic

567.23 Spontaneous bacterial peritonitis

EXCLUDES *bacterial peritonitis NOS (567.29)*

567.29 Other suppurative peritonitis

Subphrenic peritonitis

✓5th **567.3 Retroperitoneal infections**

567.31 Psoas muscle abscess

DEF: Infection that extends into or around the psoas muscle that connects the lumbar vertebrae to the femur.

567.38 Other retroperitoneal abscess

567.39 Other retroperitoneal infections

✓5th **567.8 Other specified peritonitis**

567.81 Choleperitonitis

Peritonitis due to bile

DEF: Inflammation or infection due to presence of bile in the peritoneum resulting from rupture of the bile passages or gallbladder.

567.82 Sclerosing mesenteritis

Fat necrosis of peritoneum
(Idiopathic) sclerosing mesenteric fibrosis
Mesenteric lipodystrophy
Mesenteric panniculitis
Retractile mesenteritis

DEF: Inflammatory processes involving the mesenteric fat; progresses to fibrosis and necrosis of tissue.

567.89 Other specified peritonitis

Chronic proliferative peritonitis
Mesenteric saponification
Peritonitis due to urine

567.9 Unspecified peritonitis

Peritonitis NOS
Peritonitis of unspecified cause

✓4th **568 Other disorders of peritoneum**

568.0 Peritoneal adhesions (postoperative) (postinfection)

Adhesions (of):
abdominal (wall)
diaphragm
intestine
male pelvis
mesenteric
omentum
stomach
Adhesive bands

EXCLUDES *adhesions:*
pelvic, female (614.6)
with obstruction:
duodenum (537.3)
intestine (560.81)

DEF: Abnormal union of tissues in peritoneum.

✓5th **568.8 Other specified disorders of peritoneum**

568.81 Hemoperitoneum (nontraumatic)

568.82 Peritoneal effusion (chronic)

EXCLUDES *ascites NOS (789.51-789.59)*

DEF: Persistent leakage of fluid within peritoneal cavity.

568.89 Other

Peritoneal:
cyst
granuloma

568.9 Unspecified disorder of peritoneum

✓4th **569 Other disorders of intestine**

569.0 Anal and rectal polyp

Anal and rectal polyp NOS

EXCLUDES *adenomatous anal and rectal polyp (211.4)*

569.1 Rectal prolapse

Procidentia:
anus (sphincter)
rectum (sphincter)
Proctoptosis
Prolapse:
anal canal
rectal mucosa

EXCLUDES *prolapsed hemorrhoids (455.2, 455.5)*

569.2 Stenosis of rectum and anus

Stricture of anus (sphincter)

569.3 Hemorrhage of rectum and anus

EXCLUDES *gastrointestinal bleeding NOS (578.9)*
melena (578.1)

✓5th **569.4 Other specified disorders of rectum and anus**

569.41 Ulcer of anus and rectum

Solitary ulcer } of anus (sphincter) or rectum (sphincter)
Stercoral ulcer }

569.42 Anal or rectal pain

Rectum and Anus

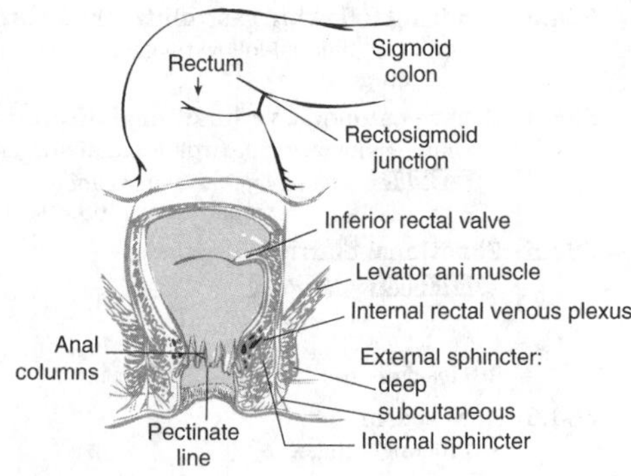

569.43 Anal sphincter tear (healed) (old)
Tear of anus, nontraumatic
Use additional code for any associated fecal incontinence (787.6)
EXCLUDES *anal fissure (565.0)*
anal sphincter tear (healed) (old) complicating delivery (654.8)

569.44 Dysplasia of anus
Anal intraepithelial neoplasia I and II (AIN I and II) (histologically confirmed)
Dysplasia of anus NOS
Mild and moderate dysplasia of anus (histologically confirmed)
EXCLUDES *abnormal results from anal cytologic examination without histologic confirmation (796.70-796.79)*
anal intraepithelial neoplasia III (230.5, 230.6)
carcinoma in situ of anus (230.5, 230.6)
HGSIL of anus (796.74)
severe dysplasia of anus (230.5, 230.6)

569.49 Other
Granuloma } of rectum (sphincter)
Rupture } of rectum (sphincter)
Hypertrophy of anal papillae
Proctitis NOS
EXCLUDES *fistula of rectum to:*
internal organs–see Alphabetic Index
skin (565.1)
hemorrhoids (455.0-455.9)
incontinence of sphincter ani (787.6)

569.5 Abscess of intestine
EXCLUDES *appendiceal abscess (540.1)*

✓5th **569.6 Colostomy and enterostomy complications**
DEF: Complication in a surgically created opening, from intestine to surface skin.

569.60 Colostomy and enterostomy complication, unspecified

569.61 Infection of colostomy or enterostomy
Use additional code to identify organism (041.00-041.9)
Use additional code to specify type of infection, such as:
abscess or cellulitis of abdomen (682.2)
septicemia (038.0-038.9)

569.62 Mechanical complication of colostomy and enterostomy
Malfunction of colostomy and enterostomy

569.69 Other complication
Fistula
Hernia
Prolapse

✓5th **569.8 Other specified disorders of intestine**

569.81 Fistula of intestine, excluding rectum and anus
Fistula:
abdominal wall
enterocolic
enteroenteric
ileorectal
EXCLUDES *fistula of intestine to internal organs–see Alphabetic Index*
persistent postoperative fistula (998.6)

569.82 Ulceration of intestine
Primary ulcer of intestine
Ulceration of colon
EXCLUDES *that with perforation (569.83)*

569.83 Perforation of intestine

569.84 Angiodysplasia of intestine (without mention of hemorrhage)
DEF: Small vascular abnormalities of the intestinal tract without bleeding problems.

569.85 Angiodysplasia of intestine with hemorrhage
DEF: Small vascular abnormalities of the intestinal tract with bleeding problems.

569.86 Dieulafoy lesion (hemorrhagic) of intestine

569.89 Other
Enteroptosis
Granuloma } of intestine
Prolapse } of intestine
Pericolitis
Perisigmoiditis
Visceroptosis
EXCLUDES *gangrene of intestine, mesentery, or omentum (557.0)*
hemorrhage of intestine NOS (578.9)
obstruction of intestine (560.0-560.9)

569.9 Unspecified disorder of intestine

OTHER DISEASES OF DIGESTIVE SYSTEM (570-579)

570 Acute and subacute necrosis of liver
Acute hepatic failure
Acute or subacute hepatitis, not specified as infective
Necrosis of liver (acute) (diffuse) (massive) (subacute)
Parenchymatous degeneration of liver
Yellow atrophy (liver) (acute) (subacute)
EXCLUDES *icterus gravis of newborn (773.0-773.2)*
serum hepatitis (070.2-070.3)
that with:
abortion (634-638 with .7, 639.8)
ectopic or molar pregnancy (639.8)
pregnancy, childbirth, or the puerperium (646.7)
viral hepatitis (070.0-070.9)

✓4th **571 Chronic liver disease and cirrhosis**

571.0 Alcoholic fatty liver

571.1 Acute alcoholic hepatitis
Acute alcoholic liver disease

571.2 Alcoholic cirrhosis of liver
Florid cirrhosis
Laennec's cirrhosis (alcoholic)
DEF: Fibrosis and dysfunction, of liver; due to alcoholic liver disease.

571.3 Alcoholic liver damage, unspecified

✓5th **571.4 Chronic hepatitis**
EXCLUDES *viral hepatitis (acute) (chronic) (070.0-070.9)*

571.40 Chronic hepatitis, unspecified

571.41 Chronic persistent hepatitis

571.42 Autoimmune hepatitis

571.49 Other
Chronic hepatitis:
active
aggressive
Recurrent hepatitis

Liver

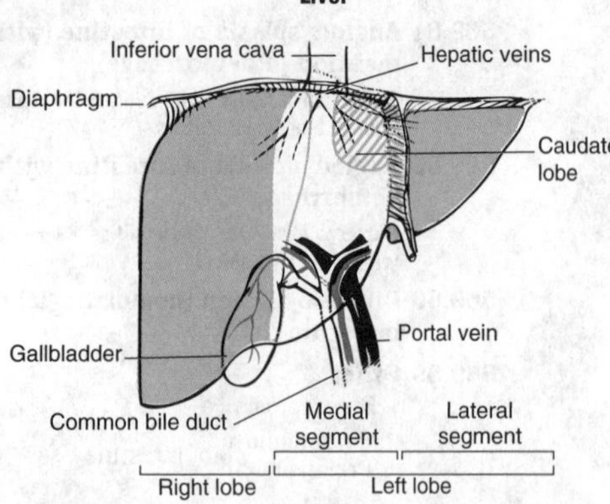

571.5 Cirrhosis of liver without mention of alcohol
Cirrhosis of liver:
NOS
cryptogenic
macronodular
micronodular
posthepatitic
postnecrotic
Healed yellow atrophy (liver)
Portal cirrhosis
Code first, if applicable, viral hepatitis (acute) (chronic) (070.0-070.9)
DEF: Fibrosis and dysfunction of liver; not alcohol related.

571.6 Biliary cirrhosis
Chronic nonsuppurative destructive cholangitis
Cirrhosis:
cholangitic
cholestatic

571.8 Other chronic nonalcoholic liver disease
Chronic yellow atrophy (liver)
Fatty liver, without mention of alcohol

571.9 Unspecified chronic liver disease without mention of alcohol

✓4th **572 Liver abscess and sequelae of chronic liver disease**

572.0 Abscess of liver
EXCLUDES *amebic liver abscess (006.3)*

572.1 Portal pyemia
Phlebitis of portal vein
Portal thrombophlebitis
Pylephlebitis
Pylethrombophlebitis
DEF: Inflammation of portal vein or branches; may be due to intestinal disease; symptoms include fever, chills, jaundice, sweating, and abscess in various body parts.

572.2 Hepatic coma
Hepatic encephalopathy
Hepatocerebral intoxication
Portal-systemic encephalopathy
EXCLUDES *hepatic coma associated with viral hepatitis–see category 070*

572.3 Portal hypertension
DEF: Abnormally high blood pressure in the portal vein.

572.4 Hepatorenal syndrome
EXCLUDES *that following delivery (674.8)*
DEF: Hepatic and renal failure characterized by cirrhosis with ascites or obstructive jaundice, oliguria, and low sodium concentration.

572.8 Other sequelae of chronic liver disease

✓4th **573 Other disorders of liver**
EXCLUDES *amyloid or lardaceous degeneration of liver (277.39)*
congenital cystic disease of liver (751.62)
glycogen infiltration of liver (271.0)
hepatomegaly NOS (789.1)
portal vein obstruction (452)

573.0 Chronic passive congestion of liver
DEF: Blood accumulation in liver tissue.

573.1 Hepatitis in viral diseases classified elsewhere
Code first underlying disease as:
Coxsackie virus disease (074.8)
cytomegalic inclusion virus disease (078.5)
infectious mononucleosis (075)
EXCLUDES *hepatitis (in):*
mumps (072.71)
viral (070.0-070.9)
yellow fever (060.0-060.9)

573.2 Hepatitis in other infectious diseases classified elsewhere
Code first underlying disease, as:
malaria (084.9)
EXCLUDES *hepatitis in:*
late syphilis (095.3)
secondary syphilis (091.62)
toxoplasmosis (130.5)

573.3 Hepatitis, unspecified
Toxic (noninfectious) hepatitis
Use additional E code to identify cause

573.4 Hepatic infarction

573.8 Other specified disorders of liver
Hepatoptosis

573.9 Unspecified disorder of liver

✓4th **574 Cholelithiasis**

The following fifth-digit subclassification is for use with category 574:
0 without mention of obstruction
1 with obstruction

✓5th **574.0 Calculus of gallbladder with acute cholecystitis**
[0-1]
Billary calculus
Calculus of cystic duct
Cholelithiasis
} with acute cholecystitis

Any condition classifiable to 574.2 with acute cholecystitis

✓5th **574.1 Calculus of gallbladder with other cholecystitis**
[0-1]
Billary calculus
Calculus of cystic duct
Cholelithiasis
} with cholecystitis

Cholecystitis with cholelithiasis NOS
Any condition classifiable to 574.2 with cholecystitis (chronic)

✓5th **574.2 Calculus of gallbladder without mention of cholecystitis**
[0-1]
Biliary:
calculus NOS
colic NOS
Calculus of cystic duct
Cholelithiasis NOS
Colic (recurrent) of gallbladder
Gallstone (impacted)

✓5th **574.3 Calculus of bile duct with acute cholecystitis**
[0-1]
Calculus of bile duct (any)
Choledocholithiasis
} with acute cholecystitis

Any condition classifiable to 574.5 with acute cholecystitis

✓5th **574.4 Calculus of bile duct with other cholecystitis**
[0-1]
Calculus of bile duct (any)
Choledocholithiasis
} with cholecystitis (chronic)

Any condition classifiable to 574.5 with cholecystitis (chronic)

✓5th **574.5 Calculus of bile duct without mention of cholecystitis**
[0-1]
Calculus of:
bile duct [any]
common duct
hepatic duct
Choledocholithiasis
Hepatic:
colic (recurrent)
lithiasis

Gallbladder and Bile Ducts

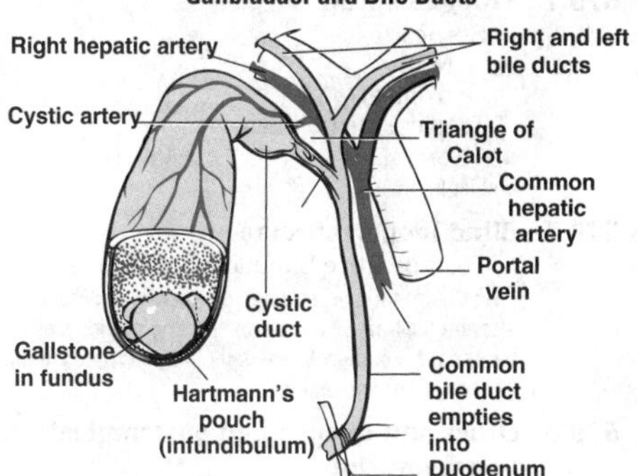

✓5th **574.6 Calculus of gallbladder and bile duct with acute cholecystitis**
[0-1]
Any condition classifiable to 574.0 and 574.3

✓5th **574.7 Calculus of gallbladder and bile duct with other cholecystitis**
[0-1]
Any condition classifiable to 574.1 and 574.4

✓5th **574.8 Calculus of gallbladder and bile duct with acute and chronic cholecystitis**
[0-1]
Any condition classifiable to 574.6 and 574.7

✓5th **574.9 Calculus of gallbladder and bile duct without cholecystitis**
[0-1]
Any condition classifiable to 574.2 and 574.5

✓4th **575 Other disorders of gallbladder**

575.0 Acute cholecystitis

Abscess of gallbladder
Angiocholecystitis
Cholecystitis:
  emphysematous (acute)
  gangrenous
  suppurative
Empyema of gallbladder
Gangrene of gallbladder
} without mention of calculus

EXCLUDES *that with:*
acute and chronic cholecystitis (575.12)
choledocholithiasis (574.3)
choledocholithiasis and cholelithiasis (574.6)
cholelithiasis (574.0)

✓5th **575.1 Other cholecystitis**

Cholecystitis:
  NOS
  chronic
} without mention of calculus

EXCLUDES *that with:*
choledocholithiasis (574.4)
choledocholithiasis and cholelithiasis (574.8)
cholelithiasis (574.1)

575.10 Cholecystitis, unspecified
Cholecystitis NOS

575.11 Chronic cholecystitis

575.12 Acute and chronic cholecystitis

575.2 Obstruction of gallbladder

Occlusion
Stenosis
Stricture
} of cystic duct or gallbladder without mention of calculus

EXCLUDES *that with calculus (574.0-574.2 with fifth-digit 1)*

575.3 Hydrops of gallbladder
Mucocele of gallbladder
DEF: Serous fluid accumulation in bladder.

575.4 Perforation of gallbladder
Rupture of cystic duct or gallbladder

575.5 Fistula of gallbladder
Fistula:
  cholecystoduodenal
  cholecystoenteric

575.6 Cholesterolosis of gallbladder
Strawberry gallbladder
DEF: Cholesterol deposits in gallbladder tissue.

575.8 Other specified disorders of gallbladder

Adhesions
Atrophy
Cyst
Hypertrophy
Nonfunctioning
Ulcer
} of cystic duct or gallbladder

Biliary dyskinesia

EXCLUDES *Hartmann's pouch of intestine (V44.3)*
nonvisualization of gallbladder (793.3)

575.9 Unspecified dmisorder of gallbladder

✓4th **576 Other disorders of biliary tract**

EXCLUDES *that involving the:*
cystic duct (575.0-575.9)
gallbladder (575.0-575.9)

576.0 Postcholecystectomy syndrome
DEF: Jaundice or abdominal pain following cholecystectomy.

576.1 Cholangitis
Cholangitis:
  NOS
  acute
  ascending
  chronic
  primary
  recurrent
  sclerosing
  secondary
  stenosing
  suppurative

576.2 Obstruction of bile duct

Occlusion
Stenosis
Stricture
} of bile duct, except cystic duct, without mention of calculus

EXCLUDES *congenital (751.61)*
that with calculus (574.3-574.5 with fifth-digit 1)

576.3 Perforation of bile duct
Rupture of bile duct, except cystic duct

576.4 Fistula of bile duct
Choledochoduodenal fistula

576.5 Spasm of sphincter of Oddi

576.8 Other specified disorders of biliary tract

Adehesions
Atrophy
Cyst
Hypertrophy
Nonfunctioning
Ulcer
} of bile duct (any)

EXCLUDES *congenital choledochal cyst (751.69)*

576.9 Unspecified disorder of biliary tract

✓4th **577 Diseases of pancreas**

577.0 Acute pancreatitis
Abscess of pancreas
Necrosis of pancreas:
  acute
  infective
Pancreatitis:
  NOS
  acute (recurrent)
  apoplectic
  hemorrhagic
  subacute
  suppurative

EXCLUDES *mumps pancreatitis (072.3)*

577.1 Chronic pancreatitis

Chronic pancreatitis:	Pancreatitis:
NOS	painless
infectious	recurrent
interstitial	relapsing

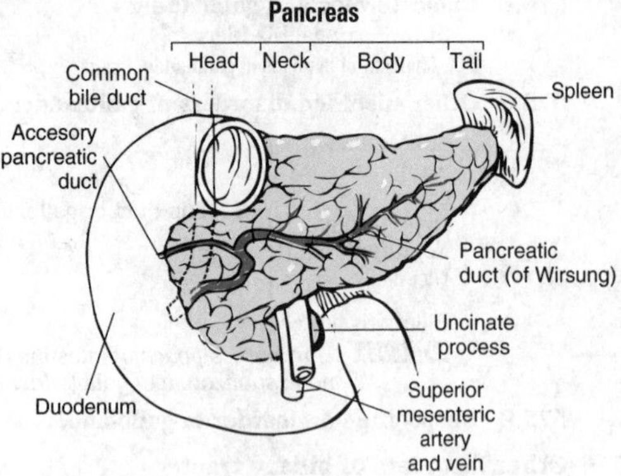

577.2 Cyst and pseudocyst of pancreas

577.8 Other specified diseases of pancreas

Atrophy, Calculus, Cirrhosis, Fibrosis } of pancreas

Pancreatic:
- infantilism
- necrosis:
  - NOS
  - aseptic
  - fat

Pancreatolithiasis

EXCLUDES *fibrocystic disease of pancreas (277.00-277.09)*
islet cell tumor of pancreas (211.7)
pancreatic steatorrhea (579.4)

577.9 Unspecified disease of pancreas

✓4th 578 Gastrointestinal hemorrhage

EXCLUDES *that with mention of:*
- *angiodysplasia of stomach and duodenum (537.83)*
- *angiodysplasia of intestine (569.85)*
- *diverticulitis, intestine:*
  - *large (562.13)*
  - *small (562.03)*
- *diverticulosis, intestine:*
  - *large (562.12)*
  - *small (562.02)*
- *gastritis and duodenitis (535.0-535.6)*
- *ulcer:*
  - *duodenal, gastric, gastrojejunal or peptic (531.00-534.91)*

578.0 Hematemesis

Vomiting of blood

578.1 Blood in stool

Melena

EXCLUDES *melena of the newborn (772.4, 777.3)*
occult blood (792.1)

578.9 Hemorrhage of gastrointestinal tract, unspecified

Gastric hemorrhage
Intestinal hemorrhage

✓4th 579 Intestinal malabsorption

579.0 Celiac disease

Celiac:
- crisis
- infantilism
- rickets

Gee (-Herter) disease
Gluten enteropathy
Idiopathic steatorrhea
Nontropical sprue

DEF: Malabsorption syndrome due to gluten consumption; symptoms include fetid, bulky, frothy, oily stools; distended abdomen, gas, weight loss, asthenia, electrolyte depletion and vitamin B, D and K deficiency.

579.1 Tropical sprue

Sprue:
- NOS
- tropical

Tropical steatorrhea

DEF: Diarrhea, occurs in tropics; may be due to enteric infection and malnutrition.

579.2 Blind loop syndrome

Postoperative blind loop syndrome

DEF: Obstruction or impaired passage in small intestine due to alterations, from strictures or surgery; causes stasis, abnormal bacterial flora, diarrhea, weight loss, multiple vitamin deficiency, and megaloblastic anemia.

579.3 Other and unspecified postsurgical nonabsorption

Hypoglycemia, Malnutrition } following gastrointestinal surgery

579.4 Pancreatic steatorrhea

DEF: Excess fat in feces due to absence of pancreatic juice in intestine.

579.8 Other specified intestinal malabsorption

Enteropathy:
- exudative
- protein-losing

Steatorrhea (chronic)

579.9 Unspecified intestinal malabsorption

Malabsorption syndrome NOS

Chapter 10: Genitourinary System (580–629)

Diseases of the genitourinary system are classified to chapter 10 of ICD-9-CM and include the following subchapters:

- Nephritis, nephrotic syndrome and nephrosis (580–589)
- Other diseases of urinary system (590–599)
- Diseases of male genital organs (600–608)
- Disorders of breast (610–612)
- Inflammatory disease of female pelvic organs (614–616)
- Other disorders of female genital tract (617–629)

Conditions relating to the female genitourinary system complicating pregnancy, childbirth, and the puerperium are classified to chapter 11, "Complications of Pregnancy, Childbirth and the Puerperium." Some infectious diseases affecting the genitourinary system are also classified to chapter 1, "Infectious and Parasitic Diseases." The nephritis, nephrotic syndrome and nephrosis (580–589) section classifies those conditions affecting the kidney, excluding those conditions associated with hypertensive renal disease (403.00–403.91).

Acute Glomerulonephritis (580)

Acute glomerulonephritis is a prolonged inflammation in the glomeruli of the kidney and may also be known as acute hemorrhagic glomerulonephritis or acute nephritis.

Acute glomerulonephritis with lesion or rapidly progressive glomerulonephritis (580.4) is characterized by rapid deterioration of kidney function.

Nephrotic Syndrome (581)

Usually due to some form of glomerulonephritis, nephrotic syndrome may result in chronic renal failure. The nephrotic syndrome is the end point of the glomerulonephritis and should not be coded in addition to the syndrome.

Example:

> Nephrotic syndrome with lesions of proliferative glomerulonephritis is coded as 581.0.
>
> Do not assign an additional code for the proliferative glomerulnephritis (580.0, acute or 582.0, chronic).

Nephrotic syndrome may or may not be present with chronic renal failure, code only when nephrotic syndrome is stated by the physician.

Chronic Glomerulonephritis (582)

Chronic glomerulonephritis is a slowly progressing disease characterized by inflammation of the glomeruli, which results in sclerosis, scarring, and eventual chronic renal failure. Etiologies for chronic glomerulonephritis include primary renal disorders (classified to categories 580 and 581) and systemic diseases, such as lupus erythematosus, amyloidosis, and hemolytic-uremic syndrome.

Acute Renal Failure (584)

Acute renal failure is the sudden interruption of renal function following any one of a variety or conditions affecting the normal kidney. Although usually reversible with treatment, acute renal failure may progress to chronic renal insufficiency, chronic renal failure or death.

The causes of acute renal failure are classified as prerenal, intrinsic (renal), or postrenal. Prerenal failure is due to diminished blood flow to the kidneys and may be caused by conditions such as dehydration, shock, or other emergent conditions. Intrinsic failure results from diseases and disorders of the kidneys themselves, such as acute tubular necrosis. Postrenal failure is caused by bilateral obstruction of urinary outflow, as caused by stones, clots, neoplasms, strictures, or benign prostatic hypertrophy.category excludes renal failure due to trauma, which is classified to 958.5.

Chronic Kidney Disease (585)

Chronic kidney disease (CKD) can be defined as structural or functional abnormalities of the kidneys over a period of three months or greater and is indicated by pathologic or laboratory abnormalities. The condition is divided into five stages of increasing severity based on the GFR. At the final stage, there is total or near-total loss of kidney function, necessitating dialysis or transplantation.

The GFR is a standard measure of how well the kidneys filter waste products from the blood, and is an overall expression of kidney function. The GFR falls from its normal values of approximately 100–140 mL/min. in men, and 85–115 mL/min in women as CKD progresses. These values are estimated using calculations that include factoring in the serum creatinine, blood urea nitrogen, serum albumin, and a patient's age, race, and sex. ESRD is a term defined by the federal government that indicates a patient is undergoing chronic treatment by dialysis or transplantation for stage 5 chronic kidney disease.

Urinary Tract Infection (599.0)

Urinary tract infection, site not specified, covers a wide variety of clinical conditions characterized by a significant number of micro-organisms in an unspecified part of the urinary tract. Predisposing factors include calculi or other urinary tract obstructions or foreign bodies, pregnancy, and diabetes mellitus among many others. Many urinary tract infections recur due to bacterial persistence or reinfection from new organisms outside the urinary tract.

When the bacterial organism is identified, an additional code should be used (E.coli, 041.4).

Urinalysis and urine culture are the most important indicators for urinary tract infection.

Hematuria (599.7)

Hematuria is a common presenting symptom of multiple genitourinary diseases, including bladder cancer. Hematuria may be visible to the naked eye (gross) or visible only under a microscope (microscopic). It is usually painless, but patients presenting with hematuria are at high risk for bladder cancer and may have other distinct risk factors for bladder cancer. A number of these risk factors include smoking, voiding dysfunction, exposure to toxic metals and chemicals, and personal history of urinary disorder or disease. Several conditions can cause hematuria, many of which are not serious. Hematuria may also occur in the absence of any other related health problems. Treatment for hematuria depends on establishing the underlying cause by further diagnostic examination. Code 599.7 Hematuria has includes fifth-digit subclassifications to provide unique codes for gross (599.71), microscopic (599.72), and unspecified (599.70) hematuria. Review of personal history may indicate factors associated with an increased risk of bladder cancer. A V code should be assigned to indicate factors influencing health.

Diseases of Male Genital Organs (600–608)

Conditions classified to this section include prostate disease, disorders of the penis, disorders of the testes, and other structural and functional disorders of the male genital system.

Hyperplasia of Prostate (600)

Hyperplasia of prostate describes several conditions believed to arise as fibrostromal proliferation in the periurethral glands. The etiology is unknown, but a relationship between aging and prostate enlargement is well documented.

Other terms used to describe hyperplasia of the prostate include: hypertrophy (benign) of the prostate (BPH) (600.0); nodular prostate (600.1); adenoma (benign) of the prostate (600.2); cyst of prostate (600.3); and prostatic obstruction (600.9).

The term with or without LUTS (lower urinary tract symptoms) has been added to hypertrophy and hyperplasia codes in order to specify that whether or not urinary obstruction is present, lower urinary tract symptoms are present. An instructional note directs the coder to assign a code for each in addition to the code for the underlying condition (BPH).

DISORDERS OF BREAST (610-612)

Other Specified Disorders of Breast (611.8)

Historically, ICD-9-CM codes have not clearly identified the various stages for which a breast reconstruction encounter may occur, or distinguished between the disorders of reconstructed breasts and native breasts. This subcategory includes codes which provide unique classifications for the following conditions:

Breast ptosis (611.81): Drooping breasts. In general, it is a naturally occurring process of aging coinciding with loosening of the skin and suspensory ligaments. Early ptosis can occur from reduction in the volume of breast tissue, such as after pregnancy or significant weight loss.

Breast hypoplasia (611.82): May refer to postpubertal underdevelopment of breast tissue, although many surgeons use this diagnosis in reference to small breasts for patients who wish to undergo elective augmentation procedures. Clinically, there is no objective definition of hypoplasia, as normal breast development is relatively unrelated to breast size. True hypoplasia refers to the congenital underdevelopment of the pectoral muscle.

Capsular contracture of breast implant (611.83): An abnormal response of the immune system to an artificial breast implant. Collagen fibers form around the implant as a normal immune response to a foreign body. Contracture occurs when the collagen fibers form too tightly around the implant, causing a painful compression of the implant capsule, with possible associated distortion and asymmetry. Risk factors include rupture, leakage, and hematoma formation. Surgery is normally required to correct capsular contractures.

Deformity and Disproportion of Reconstructed Breast (612)

Breast reconstruction procedures are often performed to correct defects as a result of prior surgery or trauma to the breast. Depending on the nature of the defect and type of procedure indicated, breast reconstructive procedures may be performed in a single operative episode or separately, in staged procedures over the course of months or years. When a patient undergoes mastectomy, breast tissue is removed according to the size, location, and nature of the tumor. The patient may also have a biopsy scar to consider in the reconstructive surgery plan. When significant breast tissue is excised, tissue expanders are routinely inserted over time into the chest wall to create a soft pocket for a permanent implant. Attaining symmetry and aesthetic balance with the natural breast can pose a challenge for the surgeon. Post-mastectomy, circulation and healing of breast tissue may be compromised, delaying the insertion of a permanent implant or resulting in an unfavorable anatomic appearance. Examples of breast reconstructive procedures include insertion of tissue expanders or implants, revisions involving matching or balancing procedures to mimic the appearance of the native breast and areolar and nipple grafting, or tattooing. When these procedures result in a deformity or disproportion when compared with the native breast, surgical revision is usually required to restore desired anatomic appearance.

Category 612 contains two fourth-digit subclassification codes for deformities (612.0) and disproportions (612.1) of a reconstructed breast. Coding options for acquired breast deformity not related to reconstruction are found under category 611.

Inflammatory Disease of Female Pelvic Organs (614–616)

Use additional codes to identify the infectious organism such as Staphylococcus (041.1x) or Streptococcus (041.0x). This section excludes conditions complicating pregnancy, childbirth and the puerperium. Also excluded from this section are endometriosis (617) and gonococcal (098) and tuberculous (016) infections.

Other disorders of Female genital tract (612-629)

Endometriosis (617)

Endometriosis is the presence of tissues that ordinarily line only the uterine cavity occurring outside of the uterine vault. The etiology is unknown, but previous uterine surgery or heredity may be predisposing factors. Endometriosis is classified by site, such as the rectovaginal septum (617.4) and intestine (617.5).

Genital Prolapse (618)

Genital prolapse includes vaginal wall, uterine, uterovaginal, and vaginal enterocele. Prolapse may cause urinary incontinence, which should be identified by using an additional code from 625.6, 788.31, or 788.33–788.39.

Dystrophy of Vulva (624.0x)

Vulvar intraepithelial neoplasia (VIN), a precancerous condition of the vulva, is a pathological process within the vulva's epithelial cells that results in the formation and growth of a tumor. VIN is relatively rare but appears to have a high risk of becoming cancerous if left untreated. HPV-16, a prevalent causative agent of cervical cancer, can cause vulvar intraepithelial neoplasia. Subcategory 624.0 classifies vulvar intraepithelial neoplasia type I, II and other dystrophies of vulva not classifiable elsewhere. This subcategory excludes vulvar carcinoma in situ, severe dysplasia, and VIN III, all of which are appropriately reported with code 233.32.

Vulvodynia (625.7)

Vulvodynia may be defined as persistent vulvar pain without an identifiable cause. The most commonly reported symptoms include severe and persistent burning, stinging and/or rawness, itching, and dyspareunia. Symptoms include constant or intermittent pain lasting for months or even years, which can vanish as mysteriously as it started. As a result, the patient's quality of life is affected by sexual, physical, and psychological limitations. Although the underlying cause is unknown, contributing factors have been identified such as previous injury to pelvic nerves, history of infection, allergies or localized hypersensitivity, muscle spasm, or hormonal changes associated with menopause. Vulvar vestibulitis (625.71) is a specific type of vulvodynia often associated with premenopausal hormone changes that is characterized by localized tenderness within the vulvar vestibulum, and focal or diffuse vestibular erythema. History of certain procedures such as carbon dioxide laser therapy, cryotherapy, or allergic drug reactions, including recent use of chemical irritants, have also been identified as possible precipitating factors. Other vulvodynia is indexed to code 625.79.

10. DISEASES OF THE GENITOURINARY SYSTEM (580-629)

NEPHRITIS, NEPHROTIC SYNDROME, AND NEPHROSIS (580-589)

EXCLUDES *hypertensive chronic kidney disease (403.00-403.91, 404.00-404.93)*

✓4th 580 Acute glomerulonephritis

INCLUDES acute nephritis

DEF: Acute, severe inflammation in tuft of capillaries that filter the kidneys.

580.0 With lesion of proliferative glomerulonephritis
Acute (diffuse) proliferative glomerulonephritis
Acute poststreptococcal glomerulonephritis

580.4 With lesion of rapidly progressive glomerulonephritis
Acute nephritis with lesion of necrotizing glomerulitis

DEF: Acute glomerulonephritis; progresses to ESRD with diffuse epithelial proliferation.

✓5th 580.8 With other specified pathological lesion in kidney

580.81 Acute glomerulonephritis in diseases classified elsewhere

Code first underlying disease, as:
infectious hepatitis (070.0-070.9)
mumps (072.79)
subacute bacterial endocarditis (421.0)
typhoid fever (002.0)

580.89 Other
Glomerulonephritis, acute, with lesion of:
exudative nephritis
interstitial (diffuse) (focal) nephritis

580.9 Acute glomerulonephritis with unspecified pathological lesion in kidney

Glomerulonephritis NOS, hemorrhagic; Nephritis; Nephropathy — specified as acute

✓4th 581 Nephrotic syndrome

DEF: Disease process marked by symptoms such as; extensive edema, notable proteinuria, hypoalbuminemia, and susceptibility to intercurrent infections.

581.0 With lesion of proliferative glomerulonephritis

581.1 With lesion of membranous glomerulonephritis
Epimembranous nephritis
Idiopathic membranous glomerular disease
Nephrotic syndrome with lesion of:
focal glomerulosclerosis
sclerosing membranous glomerulonephritis
segmental hyalinosis

581.2 With lesion of membranoproliferative glomerulonephritis
Nephrotic syndrome with lesion (of):

endothelial; hypocomplementemic persistent; lobular; mesangiocapillary; mixed membranous and proliferative — glomerulonephritis

DEF: Glomerulonephritis combined with clinical features of nephrotic syndrome; characterized by uneven thickening of glomerular capillary walls and mesangial cell increase; slowly progresses to ESRD.

581.3 With lesion of minimal change glomerulonephritis
Foot process disease
Lipoid nephrosis
Minimal change:
glomerular disease
glomerulitis
nephrotic syndrome

Kidney

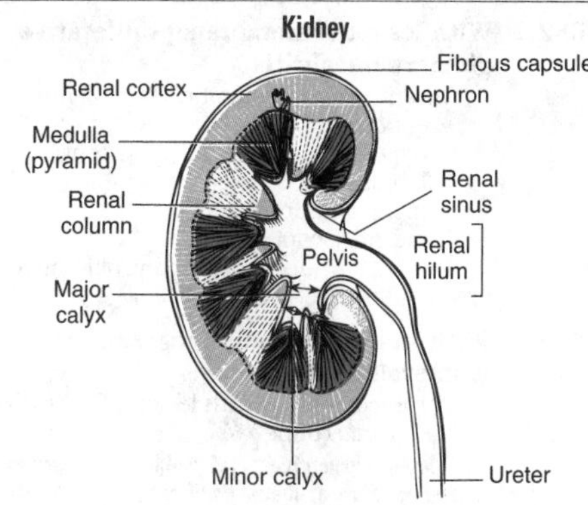

Nephron

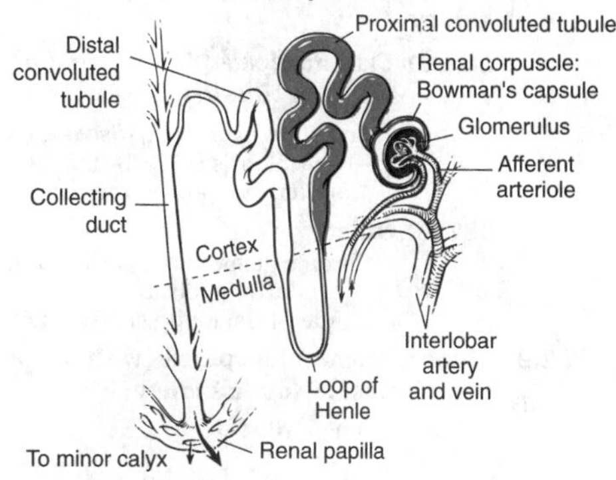

✓5th 581.8 With other specified pathological lesion in kidney

581.81 Nephrotic syndrome in diseases classified elsewhere

Code first underlying disease, as:
amyloidosis (277.30-277.39)
diabetes mellitus (249.4, 250.4)
malaria (084.9)
polyarteritis (446.0)
systemic lupus erythematosus (710.0)

EXCLUDES *nephrosis in epidemic hemorrhagic fever (078.6)*

581.89 Other
Glomerulonephritis with edema and lesion of:
exudative nephritis
interstitial (diffuse) (focal) nephritis

581.9 Nephrotic syndrome with unspecified pathological lesion in kidney
Glomerulonephritis with edema NOS
Nephritis:
nephrotic NOS
with edema NOS
Nephrosis NOS
Renal disease with edema NOS

✓4th 582 Chronic glomerulonephritis

INCLUDES chronic nephritis

DEF: Slow progressive type of nephritis characterized by inflammation of the capillary loops in the glomeruli of the kidney, which leads to renal failure.

582.0 With lesion of proliferative glomerulonephritis
Chronic (diffuse) proliferative glomerulonephritis

582.1 With lesion of membranous glomerulonephritis
Chronic glomerulonephritis:
membranous
sclerosing
Focal glomerulosclerosis
Segmental hyalinosis

582.2 With lesion of membranoproliferative glomerulonephritis

Chronic glomerulonephritis:
- endothelial
- hypocomplementemic persistent
- lobular
- membranoproliferative
- mesangiocapillary
- mixed membranous and proliferative

DEF: Chronic glomerulonephritis with mesangial cell proliferation.

582.4 With lesion of rapidly progressive glomerulonephritis

Chronic nephritis with lesion of necrotizing glomerulitis

DEF: Chronic glomerulonephritisrapidly progresses to ESRD; marked by diffuse epithelial proliferation.

✓5th **582.8 With other specified pathological lesion in kidney**

582.81 Chronic glomerulonephritis in diseases classified elsewhere

Code first underlying disease, as:
- amyloidosis (277.30-277.39)
- systemic lupus erythematosus (710.0)

582.89 Other

Chronic glomerulonephritis with lesion of:
- exudative nephritis
- interstitial (diffuse) (focal) nephritis

582.9 Chronic glomerulonephritis with unspecified pathological lesion in kidney

Glomerulonephritis:
- NOS
- hemorrhagic

Nephritis
Nephropathy
} specified as chronic

✓4th **583 Nephritis and nephropathy, not specified as acute or chronic**

INCLUDES "renal disease" so stated, not specified as acute or chronic but with stated pathology or cause

583.0 With lesion of proliferative glomerulonephritis

Proliferative:
- glomerulonephritis (diffuse) NOS
- nephritis NOS
- nephropathy NOS

583.1 With lesion of membranous glomerulonephritis

Membranous:
- glomerulonephritis NOS
- nephritis NOS

Membranous nephropathy NOS

DEF: Kidney inflammation or dysfunction with deposits on glomerular capillary basement membranes.

583.2 With lesion of membranoproliferative glomerulonephritis

Membranoproliferative:
- glomerulonephritis NOS
- nephritis NOS
- nephropathy NOS

Nephritis NOS, with lesion of:
- hypocomplementemic persistant
- lobular
- mesangiocapillary
- mixed membranous and proliferative

} glomerulonephritis

DEF: Kidney inflammation or dysfunction with mesangial cell proliferation.

583.4 With lesion of rapidly progressive glomerulonephritis

Necrotizing or rapidly progressive:
- glomerulitis NOS
- glomerulonephritis NOS
- nephritis NOS
- nephropathy NOS

Nephritis, unspecified, with lesion of necrotizing glomerulitis

DEF: Kidney inflammation or dysfunction; rapidly progresses to ESRD marked by diffuse epithelial proliferation.

583.6 With lesion of renal cortical necrosis

Nephritis, NOS
Nephropathy NS
} with (renal) cortical necrosis

Renal cortical necrosis NOS

583.7 With lesion of renal medullary necrosis

Nephritis, NOS
Nephropathy NOS
} with (renal) medullary [papillary] necrosis

583.8 With other specified pathological lesion in kidney

583.81 Nephritis and nephropathy, not specified as acute or chronic, in diseases classified elsewhere

Code first underlying disease, as:
- amyloidosis (277.30-277.39)
- diabetes mellitus (249.4, 250.4)
- gonococcal infection (098.19)
- Goodpasture's syndrome (446.21)
- systemic lupus erythematosus (710.0)
- tuberculosis (016.0)

EXCLUDES *gouty nephropathy (274.10)*
syphilitic nephritis (095.4)

583.89 Other

Glomerulitis
Glomerulonephritis
Nephritis
Nephropathy
Renal disease
} with lesions of: exudative nephritis, interstitial nephritis

583.9 With unspecified pathological lesion in kidney

Glomerulitis
Glomerulonephritis
Nephritis
Nephropathy
} NOS

EXCLUDES *nephropathy complicating pregnancy, labor, or the puerperium (642.0-642.9, 646.2)*
renal disease NOS with no stated cause (593.9)

✓4th **584 Acute renal failure**

EXCLUDES *following labor and delivery (669.3)*
posttraumatic (958.5)
that complicating:
abortion (634-638 with .3, 639.3)
ectopic or molar pregnancy (639.3)

DEF: State resulting from increasing urea and related substances from the blood (azotemia), often with urine output of less than 500 ml per day.

584.5 With lesion of tubular necrosis

Lower nephron nephrosis
Renal failure with (acute) tubular necrosis
Tubular necrosis:
- NOS
- acute

DEF: Acute decline in kidney efficiency with destruction of tubules.

584.6 With lesion of renal cortical necrosis

DEF: Acute decline in kidney efficiency with destruction of renal tissues that filter blood.

584.7 With lesion of renal medullary [papillary] necrosis

Necrotizing renal papillitis

DEF: Acute decline in kidney efficiency with destruction of renal tissues that collect urine.

584.8 With other specified pathological lesion in kidney

584.9 Acute renal failure, unspecified

Acute kidney injury (nontraumatic)

EXCLUDES *traumatic kidney injury (866.00-866.13)*

✓4th **585 Chronic kidney disease [CKD]**
Chronic uremia
Code first hypertensive chronic kidney disease, if applicable, (403.00-403.91, 404.00-404.93)
Use additional code to identify kidney transplant status, if applicable (V42.0)
Use additional code to identify manifestation as:
uremic:
neuropathy (357.4)
pericarditis (420.0)

585.1 Chronic kidney disease, Stage I
DEF: Some kidney damage; normal or slightly increased GFR (> 90).

585.2 Chronic kidney disease, Stage II (mild)
DEF: Kidney damage with mild decrease in GFR (60–89).

585.3 Chronic kidney disease, Stage III (moderate)
DEF: Kidney damage with moderate decrease in GFR (30–59).

585.4 Chronic kidney disease, Stage IV (severe)
DEF: Kidney damage with severe decrease in GFR (15–29).

585.5 Chronic kidney disease, Stage V
EXCLUDES *chronic kidney disease, stage V requiring chronic dialysis (585.6)*
DEF: Kidney failure with GFR value of less than 15.

585.6 End stage renal disease
Chronic kidney disease requiring chronic dialysis
DEF: Federal government indicator of a stage V CKD patient undergoing treatment by dialysis or transplantation.

585.9 Chronic kidney disease, unspecified
Chronic renal disease
Chronic renal failure NOS
Chronic renal insufficiency

586 Renal failure, unspecified
Uremia NOS
EXCLUDES *following labor and delivery (669.3)*
posttraumatic renal failure (958.5)
that complicating:
abortion (634-638 with .3, 639.3)
ectopic or molar pregnancy (639.3)
uremia:
extrarenal (788.9)
prerenal (788.9)
DEF: Renal failure: kidney functions cease; malfunction may be due to inability to excrete metabolized substances or retain level of electrolytes.
DEF: Uremia: excess urea, creatinine and other nitrogenous products of protein and amino acid metabolism in blood due to reduced excretory function in bilateral kidney disease; also called azotemia.

587 Renal sclerosis, unspecified
Atrophy of kidney
Contracted kidney
Renal:
cirrhosis
fibrosis

✓4th **588 Disorders resulting from impaired renal function**

588.0 Renal osteodystrophy
Azotemic osteodystrophy
Phosphate-losing tubular disorders
Renal:
dwarfism
infantilism
rickets
DEF: Bone disorder that results in various bone diseases such as osteomalacia, osteoporosis or osteosclerosis; caused by impaired renal function, an abnormal level of phosphorus in the blood and impaired stimulation of the parathyroid.

588.1 Nephrogenic diabetes insipidus
EXCLUDES *diabetes insipidus NOS (253.5)*
DEF: Type of diabetes due to renal tubules inability to reabsorb water; not responsive to vasopressin; may develop into chronic renal insufficiency.

✓5th **588.8 Other specified disorders resulting from impaired renal function**
EXCLUDES *secondary hypertension (405.0-405.9)*

588.81 Secondary hyperparathyroidism (of renal origin)
Secondary hyperparathyroidism NOS
DEF: Parathyroid dysfunction caused by chronic renal failure; phosphate clearance is impaired, phosphate is released from bone, vitamin D is not produced, intestinal calcium absorption is low, and blood levels of calcium are lowered causing excessive production of parathyroid hormone.

588.89 Other specified disorders resulting from impaired renal function
Hypokalemic nephropathy

588.9 Unspecified disorder resulting from impaired renal function

✓4th **589 Small kidney of unknown cause**

589.0 Unilateral small kidney

589.1 Bilateral small kidneys

589.9 Small kidney, unspecified

OTHER DISEASES OF URINARY SYSTEM (590-599)

✓4th **590 Infections of kidney**
Use additional code to identify organism, such as Escherichia coli [E. coli] (041.4)

✓5th **590.0 Chronic pyelonephritis**
Chronic pyelitis
Chronic pyonephrosis
Code if applicable, any casual condition first

590.00 Without lesion of renal medullary necrosis

590.01 With lesion of renal medullary necrosis

✓5th **590.1 Acute pyelonephritis**
Acute pyelitis
Acute pyonephrosis

590.10 Without lesion of renal medullary necrosis

590.11 With lesion of renal medullary necrosis

590.2 Renal and perinephric abscess
Abscess:
kidney
nephritic
perirenal
Carbuncle of kidney

590.3 Pyeloureteritis cystica
Infection of renal pelvis and ureter
Ureteritis cystica
DEF: Inflammation and formation of submucosal cysts in the kidney, pelvis, and ureter.

✓5th **590.8 Other pyelonephritis or pyonephrosis, not specified as acute or chronic**

590.80 Pyelonephritis, unspecified
Pyelitis NOS
Pyelonephritis NOS

Genitourinary System

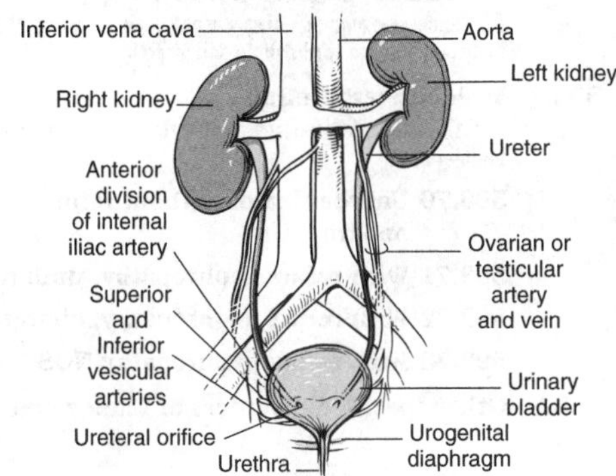

590.81 *Pyelitis or pyelonephritis in diseases classified elsewhere*

Code first underlying disease, as:
tuberculosis (016.0)

590.9 Infection of kidney, unspecified

EXCLUDES *urinary tract infection NOS (599.0)*

591 Hydronephrosis

Hydrocalycosis
Hydronephrosis
Hydroureteronephrosis

EXCLUDES *congenital hydronephrosis (753.29)*
hydroureter (593.5)

DEF: Distention of kidney and pelvis, with urine build-up due to ureteral obstruction; pyonephrosis may result.

✓4th **592 Calculus of kidney and ureter**

EXCLUDES *nephrocalcinosis (275.4)*

592.0 Calculus of kidney

Nephrolithiasis NOS
Renal calculus or stone
Staghorn calculus
Stone in kidney

EXCLUDES *uric acid nephrolithiasis (274.11)*

592.1 Calculus of ureter

Ureteric stone
Ureterolithiasis

592.9 Urinary calculus, unspecified

✓4th **593 Other disorders of kidney and ureter**

593.0 Nephroptosis

Floating kidney
Mobile kidney

593.1 Hypertrophy of kidney

593.2 Cyst of kidney, acquired

Cyst (multiple) (solitary) of kidney, not congenital
Peripelvic (lymphatic) cyst

EXCLUDES *calyceal or pyelogenic cyst of kidney (591)*
congenital cyst of kidney (753.1)
polycystic (disease of) kidney (753.1)

DEF: Abnormal, fluid-filled sac in the kidney, not present at birth.

593.3 Stricture or kinking of ureter

Angulation } of ureter (post-operative)
Constriction } of ureter (post-operative)
Stricture of pelviureteric junction

DEF: Stricture or knot in tube connecting kidney to bladder.

593.4 Other ureteric obstruction

Idiopathic retroperitoneal fibrosis
Occlusion NOS of ureter

EXCLUDES *that due to calculus (592.1)*

593.5 Hydroureter

EXCLUDES *congenital hydroureter (753.22)*
hydroureteronephrosis (591)

593.6 Postural proteinuria

Benign postural proteinuria
Orthostatic proteinuria

EXCLUDES *proteinuria NOS (791.0)*

DEF: Excessive amounts of serum protein in the urine caused by the body position, e.g., orthostatic and lordotic.

✓5th **593.7 Vesicoureteral reflux**

DEF: Backflow of urine, from bladder into ureter due to obstructed bladder neck.

593.70 Unspecified or without reflux nephropathy

593.71 With reflux nephropathy, unilateral

593.72 With reflux nephropathy, bilateral

593.73 With reflux nephropathy NOS

✓5th **593.8 Other specified disorders of kidney and ureter**

593.81 Vascular disorders of kidney

Renal (artery):
embolism
hemorrhage
thrombosis
Renal infarction

593.82 Ureteral fistula

Intestinoureteral fistula

EXCLUDES *fistula between ureter and female genital tract (619.0)*

DEF: Abnormal communication, between tube connecting kidney to bladder and another structure.

593.89 Other

Adhesions, kidney or ureter
Periureteritis
Polyp of ureter
Pyelectasia
Ureterocele

EXCLUDES *tuberculosis of ureter (016.2)*
ureteritis cystica (590.3)

593.9 Unspecified disorder of kidney and ureter

Acute renal disease
Acute renal insufficiency
Renal disease NOS
Salt-losing nephritis or syndrome

EXCLUDES *chronic renal insufficiency (585.9)*
cystic kidney disease (753.1)
nephropathy, so stated (583.0-583.9)
renal disease:
arising in pregnancy or the puerperium (642.1-642.2, 642.4-642.7, 646.2)
not specified as acute or chronic, but with stated pathology or cause (583.0-583.9)

✓4th **594 Calculus of lower urinary tract**

594.0 Calculus in diverticulum of bladder

DEF: Stone or mineral deposit in abnormal sac on the bladder wall.

594.1 Other calculus in bladder

Urinary bladder stone

EXCLUDES *staghorn calculus (592.0)*

DEF: Stone or mineral deposit in bladder.

594.2 Calculus in urethra

DEF: Stone or mineral deposit in tube that empties urine from bladder.

594.8 Other lower urinary tract calculus

594.9 Calculus of lower urinary tract, unspecified

EXCLUDES *calculus of urinary tract NOS (592.9)*

✓4th **595 Cystitis**

EXCLUDES *prostatocystitis (601.3)*

Use additional code to identify organism, such as Escherichia coli [E. coli] (041.4)

595.0 Acute cystitis

EXCLUDES *trigonitis (595.3)*

DEF: Acute inflammation of bladder.

595.1 Chronic interstitial cystitis

Hunner's ulcer
Panmural fibrosis of bladder
Submucous cystitis

DEF: Inflamed lesion affecting bladder wall; symptoms include urinary frequency, pain on bladder filling, nocturia, and distended bladder.

595.2 Other chronic cystitis

Chronic cystitis NOS
Subacute cystitis

EXCLUDES *trigonitis (595.3)*

DEF: Persistent inflammation of bladder.

595.3 Trigonitis

Follicular cystitis
Trigonitis (acute) (chronic)
Urethrotrigonitis

DEF: Inflammation of the triangular area of the bladder called the trigonum vesicae.

Bladder

Anterior View
Fundus
Left ureter
Right ureter
Lateral wall
Ureteral orifice
Trigone
Uvula of bladder
Urethra

Lateral View

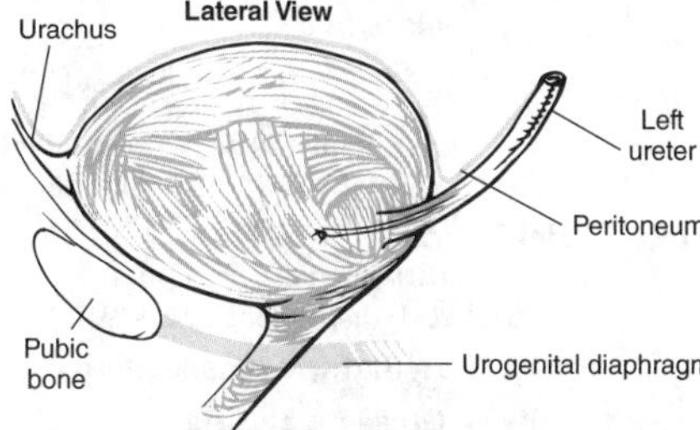

595.4 ***Cystitis in diseases classified elsewhere***

Code first underlying disease, as:
actinomycosis (039.8)
amebiasis (006.8)
bilharziasis (120.0-120.9)
Echinococcus infestation (122.3, 122.6)

EXCLUDES *cystitis:*
diphtheritic (032.84)
gonococcal (098.11, 098.31)
monilial (112.2)
trichomonal (131.09)
tuberculous (016.1)

✓5th **595.8 Other specified types of cystitis**

595.81 Cystitis cystica

DEF: Inflammation of the bladder characterized by formation of multiple cysts.

595.82 Irradiation cystitis

Use additional E code to identify cause

DEF: Inflammation of the bladder due to effects of radiation.

595.89 Other

Abscess of bladder:
Cystitis:
bullous
emphysematous
glandularis

595.9 Cystitis, unspecified

✓4th **596 Other disorders of bladder**

Use additional code to identify urinary incontinence (625.6, 788.30-788.39)

596.0 Bladder neck obstruction

Contracture (acquired) / Obstruction (acquired) / Stenosis (acquired) } of bladder neck or vesicourethral orifice

EXCLUDES *congenital (753.6)*

DEF: Bladder outlet and vesicourethral obstruction; occurs more often in males as a consequence of benign prostatic hypertrophy or prostatic cancer; may also occur in either sex due to strictures, following radiation, cystoscopy, catheterization, injury, infection, blood clots, bladder cancer, impaction or disease compressing bladder neck.

596.1 Intestinovesical fistula

Fistula:
enterovesical
vesicocolic
vesicoenteric
vesicorectal

DEF: Abnormal communication, between intestine and bladder.

596.2 Vesical fistula, not elsewhere classified

Fistula:
bladder NOS
urethrovesical
vesicocutaneous
vesicoperineal

EXCLUDES *fistula between bladder and female genital tract (619.0)*

DEF: Abnormal communication between bladder and another structure.

596.3 Diverticulum of bladder

Diverticulitis / Diverticulum (acquired) (false) } of bladder

EXCLUDES *that with calculus in diverticulum of bladder (594.0)*

DEF: Abnormal pouch in bladder wall.

596.4 Atony of bladder

High compliance bladder
Hypotonicity / Inertia } of bladder

EXCLUDES *neurogenic bladder (596.54)*

DEF: Distended, bladder with loss of expulsive force; linked to CNS disease.

✓5th **596.5 Other functional disorders of bladder**

EXCLUDES *cauda equina syndrome with neurogenic bladder (344.61)*

596.51 Hypertonicity of bladder

Hyperactivity
Overactive bladder

DEF: Abnormal tension of muscular wall of bladder; may appear after surgery of voluntary nerve.

596.52 Low bladder compliance

DEF: Low bladder capacity; causes increased pressure and frequent urination.

596.53 Paralysis of bladder

DEF: Impaired bladder motor function due to nerve or muscle damage.

596.54 Neurogenic bladder NOS

DEF: Unspecified dysfunctional bladder due to lesion of central, peripheral nervous system; may result in incontinence, residual urine retention, urinary infection, stones and renal failure.

596.55 Detrusor sphincter dyssynergia

DEF: Instability of the urinary bladder sphincter muscle associated with urinary incontinence.

596.59 Other functional disorder of bladder

Detrusor instability

DEF: Detrusor instability: instability of bladder; marked by uninhibited contractions often leading to incontinence.

596.6 Rupture of bladder, nontraumatic

596.7 Hemorrhage into bladder wall

Hyperemia of bladder

EXCLUDES *acute hemorrhagic cystitis (595.0)*

596.8 Other specified disorders of bladder

Bladder:
calcified
contracted
hemorrhage
hypertrophy

EXCLUDES *cystocele, female (618.01-618.02, 618.09, 618.2-618.4)*
hernia or prolapse of bladder, female (618.01-618.02, 618.09, 618.2-618.4)

596.9 Unspecified disorder of bladder

✓4th **597 Urethritis, not sexually transmitted, and urethral syndrome**

EXCLUDES *nonspecific urethritis, so stated (099.4)*

597.0 Urethral abscess

Abscess:
- periurethral
- urethral (gland)

Abscess of:
- bulbourethral gland
- Cowper's gland
- Littré's gland

Periurethral cellulitis

EXCLUDES *urethral caruncle (599.3)*

DEF: Pocket of pus in tube that empties urine from the bladder.

✓5th **597.8 Other urethritis**

597.80 Urethritis, unspecified

597.81 Urethral syndrome NOS

597.89 Other

Adenitis, Skene's glands
Cowperitis
Meatitis, urethral
Ulcer, urethra (meatus)
Verumontanitis

EXCLUDES *trichomonal (131.02)*

✓4th **598 Urethral stricture**

Use additional code to identify urinary incontinence (625.6, 788.30-788.39)

INCLUDES pinhole meatus
stricture of urinary meatus

EXCLUDES *congenital stricture of urethra and urinary meatus (753.6)*

DEF: Narrowing of tube that empties urine from bladder.

✓5th **598.0 Urethral stricture due to infection**

598.00 Due to unspecified infection

598.01 Due to infective diseases classified elsewhere

Code first underlying disease, as:
- gonococcal infection (098.2)
- schistosomiasis (120.0-120.9)
- syphilis (095.8)

598.1 Traumatic urethral stricture

Stricture of urethra:
- late effect of injury
- postobstetric

EXCLUDES *postoperative following surgery on genitourinary tract (598.2)*

598.2 Postoperative urethral stricture

Postcatheterization stricture of urethra

598.8 Other specified causes of urethral stricture

598.9 Urethral stricture, unspecified

✓4th **599 Other disorders of urethra and urinary tract**

599.0 Urinary tract infection, site not specified

EXCLUDES *candidiasis of urinary tract (112.2)*
urinary tract infection of newborn (771.82)

Use additional code to identify organism, such as Escherichia coli [E. coli] (041.4)

599.1 Urethral fistula

Fistula:
- urethroperineal
- urethrorectal

Urinary fistula NOS

EXCLUDES *fistula:*
- *urethroscrotal (608.89)*
- *urethrovaginal (619.0)*
- *urethrovesicovaginal (619.0)*

599.2 Urethral diverticulum

DEF: Abnormal pouch in urethral wall.

599.3 Urethral caruncle

Polyp of urethra

599.4 Urethral false passage

DEF: Abnormal opening in urethra due to surgery; trauma or disease.

599.5 Prolapsed urethral mucosa

Prolapse of urethra
Urethrocele

EXCLUDES *urethrocele, female (618.03, 618.09, 618.2-618.4)*

✓5th **599.6 Urinary obstruction**

Use additional code to identify urinary incontinence (625.6, 788.30-788.39)

EXCLUDES *obstructive nephropathy NOS (593.89)*

599.60 Urinary obstruction, unspecified

Obstructive uropathy NOS
Urinary (tract) obstruction NOS

599.69 Urinary obstruction, not elsewhere classified

Code, if applicable, any causal condition first, such as:
hyperplasia of prostate (600.0-600.9 with fifth-digit 1)

✓5th **599.7 Hematuria**

Hematuria (benign) (essential)

EXCLUDES *hemoglobinuria (791.2)*

599.70 Hematuria, unspecified

599.71 Gross hematuria

599.72 Microscopic hematuria

✓5th **599.8 Other specified disorders of urethra and urinary tract**

Use additional code to identify urinary incontinence (625.6, 788.30-788.39), if present

EXCLUDES *symptoms and other conditions classifiable to 788.0-788.2, 788.4-788.9, 791.0-791.9*

599.81 Urethral hypermobility

DEF: Hyperactive urethra.

599.82 Intrinsic (urethral) sphincter deficiency [ISD]

DEF: Malfunctioning urethral sphincter.

599.83 Urethral instability

DEF: Inconsistent functioning of urethra.

599.84 Other specified disorders of urethra

Rupture of urethra (nontraumatic)
Urethral:
- cyst
- granuloma

DEF: Rupture of urethra due to herniation or breaking down of tissue; not due to trauma.

DEF: Urethral cyst: abnormal sac in urethra; usually fluid filled.

DEF: Granuloma: inflammatory cells forming small nodules in urethra.

599.89 Other specified disorders of urinary tract

599.9 Unspecified disorder of urethra and urinary tract

DISEASES OF MALE GENITAL ORGANS (600-608)

✓4th **600 Hyperplasia of prostate**

INCLUDES enlarged prostate

DEF: Fibrostromal proliferation in periurethral glands, causes blood in urine; etiology unknown.

✓5th **600.0 Hypertrophy (benign) of prostate**

Benign prostatic hypertrophy
Enlargement of prostate
Smooth enlarged prostate
Soft enlarged prostate

600.00 Hypertrophy (benign) of prostate without urinary obstruction and other lower urinary tract symptoms [LUTS]

Hypertrophy (benign) of prostate NOS

Male Pelvic Organs

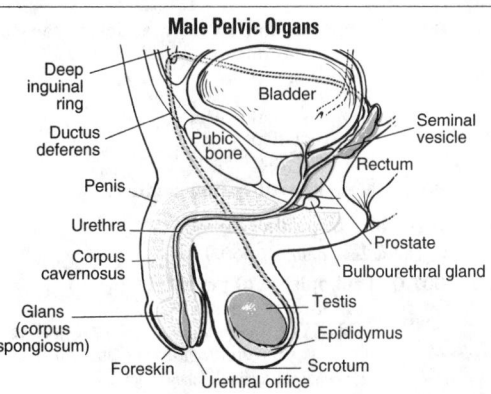

600.01 Hypertrophy (benign) of prostate with urinary obstruction and other lower urinary tract symptoms [LUTS]
Hypertrophy (benign) of prostate with urinary retention
Use additional code to identify symptoms:
incomplete bladder emptying (788.21)
nocturia (788.43)
straining on urination (788.65)
urinary frequency (788.41)
urinary hesitancy (788.64)
urinary incontinence (788.30-788.39)
urinary obstruction (599.69)
urinary retention (788.20)
urinary urgency (788.63)
weak urinary stream (788.62)

✓5th **600.1 Nodular prostate**
Hard, firm prostate
Multinodular prostate
EXCLUDES *malignant neoplasm of prostate (185)*
DEF: Hard, firm nodule in prostate.

600.10 Nodular prostate without urinary obstruction
Nodular prostate NOS

600.11 Nodular prostate with urinary obstruction
Nodular prostate with urinary retention

✓5th **600.2 Benign localized hyperplasia of prostate**
Adenofibromatous hypertrophy of prostate
Adenoma of prostate
Fibroadenoma of prostate
Fibroma of prostate
Myoma of prostate
Polyp of prostate
EXCLUDES *benign neoplasms of prostate (222.2)*
hypertrophy of prostate (600.00-600.01)
malignant neoplasm of prostate (185)
DEF: Benign localized hyperplasia is a clearly defined epithelial tumor. Other terms used for this condition are adenofibromatous hypertrophy of prostate, adenoma of prostate, fibroadenoma of prostate, fibroma of prostate, myoma of prostate, and polyp of prostate.

600.20 Benign localized hyperplasia of prostate without urinary obstruction and other lower urinary tract symptoms [LUTS]
Benign localized hyperplasia of prostate NOS

600.21 Benign localized hyperplasia of prostate with urinary obstruction and other lower urinary tract symptoms [LUTS]
Benign localized hyperplasia of prostate with urinary retention
Use additional code to identify symptoms:
incomplete bladder emptying (788.21)
nocturia (788.43)
straining on urination (788.65)
urinary frequency (788.41)
urinary hesitancy (788.64)
urinary incontinence (788.30-788.39)
urinary obstruction (599.69)
urinary retention (788.20)
urinary urgency (788.63)
weak urinary stream (788.62)

600.3 Cyst of prostate
DEF: Sacs of fluid, which differentiate this from either nodular or adenomatous tumors.

✓5th **600.9 Hyperplasia of prostate, unspecified**
Median bar
Prostatic obstruction NOS

600.90 Hyperplasia of prostate, unspecified, without urinary obstruction and other lower urinary tract symptoms [LUTS]
Hyperplasia of prostate NOS

600.91 Hyperplasia of prostate, unspecified with urinary obstruction and other lower urinary tract symptoms [LUTS]
Hyperplasia of prostate, unspecified, with urinary retention
Use additional code to identify symptoms:
incomplete bladder emptying (788.21)
nocturia (788.43)
straining on urination (788.65)
urinary frequency (788.41)
urinary hesitancy (788.64)
urinary incontinence (788.30-788.39)
urinary obstruction (599.69)
urinary retention (788.20)
urinary urgency (788.63)
weak urinary stream (788.62)

✓4th **601 Inflammatory diseases of prostate**
Use additional code to identify organism, such as Staphylococcus (041.1), or Streptococcus (041.0)

601.0 Acute prostatitis

601.1 Chronic prostatitis

601.2 Abscess of prostate

601.3 Prostatocystitis

601.4 Prostatitis in diseases classified elsewhere
Code first underlying disease, as:
actinomycosis (039.8)
blastomycosis (116.0)
syphilis (095.8)
tuberculosis (016.5)
EXCLUDES *prostatitis:*
gonococcal (098.12, 098.32)
monilial (112.2)
trichomonal (131.03)

601.8 Other specified inflammatory diseases of prostate
Prostatitis:
cavitary
diverticular
granulomatous

601.9 Prostatitis, unspecified
Prostatitis NOS

✓4th **602 Other disorders of prostate**

602.0 Calculus of prostate
Prostatic stone
DEF: Stone or mineral deposit in prostate.

602.1 Congestion or hemorrhage of prostate
DEF: Bleeding or fluid collection in prostate.

602.2 Atrophy of prostate

602.3 Dysplasia of prostate
Prostatic intraepithelial neoplasia I (PIN I)
Prostatic intraepithelial neoplasia II (PIN II)
EXCLUDES *prostatic intraepithelial neoplasia III (PIN III) (233.4)*
DEF: Abnormality of shape and size of the intraepithelial tissues of the prostate; pre-malignant condition characterized by stalks and absence of a basilar cell layer; synonyms are intraductal dysplasia, large acinar atypical hyperplasia, atypical primary hyperplasia, hyperplasia with malignant changes, marked atypia, or duct-acinar dysplasia.

602.8 Other specified disorders of prostate
Fistula } of prostate
Infarction } of prostate
Stricture } of prostate
Periprostatic adhesions

602.9 Unspecified disorder of prostate

Common Inguinal Canal Anomalies

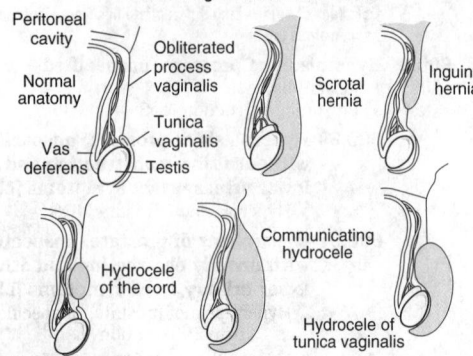

✓4th 603 Hydrocele

INCLUDES hydrocele of spermatic cord, testis or tunica vaginalis

EXCLUDES *congenital (778.6)*

DEF: Circumscribed collection of fluid in tunica vaginalis, spermatic cord or testis.

603.0 Encysted hydrocele

603.1 Infected hydrocele

Use additional code to identify organism

603.8 Other specified types of hydrocele

603.9 Hydrocele, unspecified

✓4th 604 Orchitis and epididymitis

Use additional code to identify organism, such as Escherichia coli [E. coli] (041.4), Staphylococcus (041.1), or Streptococcus (041.0)

604.0 Orchitis, epididymitis, and epididymo-orchitis, with abscess

Abscess of epididymis or testis

✓5th 604.9 Other orchitis, epididymitis, and epididymo-orchitis, without mention of abscess

604.90 Orchitis and epididymitis, unspecified

604.91 Orchitis and epididymitis in diseases classified elsewhere

Code first underlying disease, as:
diphtheria (032.89)
filariasis (125.0-125.9)
syphilis (095.8)

EXCLUDES *orchitis:*
gonococcal (098.13, 098.33)
mumps (072.0)
tuberculous (016.5)
tuberculous epididymitis (016.4)

604.99 Other

605 Redundant prepuce and phimosis

Adherent prepuce
Paraphimosis
Phimosis (congenital)
Tight foreskin

DEF: Constriction of preputial orifice causing inability of the prepuce to be drawn back over the glans; it may be congenital or caused by infection.

✓4th 606 Infertility, male

606.0 Azoospermia

Absolute infertility
Infertility due to:
germinal (cell) aplasia
spermatogenic arrest (complete)

DEF: Absence of spermatozoa in the semen or inability to produce spermatozoa.

606.1 Oligospermia

Infertility due to:
germinal cell desquamation
hypospermatogenesis
incomplete spermatogenic arrest

DEF: Insufficient number of sperm in semen.

606.8 Infertility due to extratesticular causes

Infertility due to:
drug therapy
infection
obstruction of efferent ducts
radiation
systemic disease

606.9 Male infertility, unspecified

✓4th 607 Disorders of penis

EXCLUDES *phimosis (605)*

607.0 Leukoplakia of penis

Kraurosis of penis

EXCLUDES *carcinoma in situ of penis (233.5)*
erythroplasia of Queyrat (233.5)

DEF: White, thickened patches on glans penis.

607.1 Balanoposthitis

Balanitis

Use additional code to identify organism

DEF: Inflammation of glans penis and prepuce.

607.2 Other inflammatory disorders of penis

Abscess, Boil, Carbuncle, Cellulitis } of corpus cavernosum or penis

Cavernitis (penis)

Use additional code to identify organism

EXCLUDES *herpetic infection (054.13)*

607.3 Priapism

Painful erection

DEF: Prolonged penile erection without sexual stimulation.

✓5th 607.8 Other specified disorders of penis

607.81 Balanitis xerotica obliterans

Induratio penis plastica

DEF: Inflammation of the glans penis, caused by stricture of the opening of the prepuce.

607.82 Vascular disorders of penis

Embolisim, Hematoma (nontraumatic), Hemorrhage, Thrombosis } of corpus cavernosum or penis

607.83 Edema of penis

DEF: Fluid retention within penile tissues.

607.84 Impotence of organic origin

EXCLUDES *nonorganic (302.72)*

DEF: Physiological cause interfering with erection.

607.85 Peyronie's disease

DEF: A severe curvature of the erect penis due to fibrosis of the cavernous sheaths.

607.89 Other

Atrophy, Fibrosis, Hypertrophy, Ulcer (chronic) } of corpus cavernosum or penis

607.9 Unspecified disorder of penis

✓4th 608 Other disorders of male genital organs

608.0 Seminal vesiculitis

Abscess, Cellulitis } of seminal vesicle

Vesiculitis (seminal)

Use additional code to identify organism

EXCLUDES *gonococcal infection (098.14, 098.34)*

DEF: Inflammation of seminal vesicle.

608.1 Spermatocele

DEF: Cystic enlargement of the epididymis or the testis; the cysts contain spermatozoa.

Torsion of the Testis

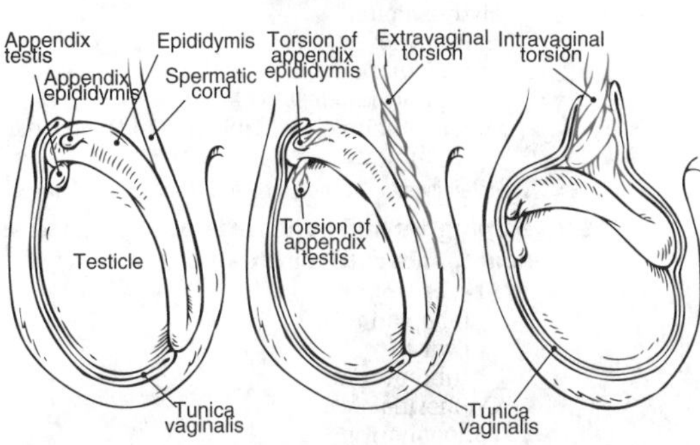

✓5th **608.2 Torsion of testis**

DEF: Twisted or rotated testis; may compromise blood flow.

608.20 Torsion of testis, unspecified

608.21 Extravaginal torsion of spermatic cord

DEF: Torsion of the spermatic cord just below the tunica vaginalis attachments. Often manifests in the neonatal period after having developed in utero. This type of torsion accounts for approximately 5% of all torsions. It is usually associated with high birth weight.

608.22 Intravaginal torsion of spermatic cord

Torsion of spermatic cord NOS

DEF: Torsion within the tunica vaginalis also called the "bell-clapper" anomaly. It usually occurs in older children, with peak incidence occurring at approximately 13 years of age. This type of torsion accounts for roughly 16% emergency room torsion encounters. Of note, the left testis is most frequently affected, with only 2% cases presenting as bilateral torsions.

608.23 Torsion of appendix testis

DEF: Torsion of small solid projection of tissue on the upper outer surface of the testis (hydatid of Morgagni); a remnant of the embryologic mullerian duct.

608.24 Torsion of appendix epididymis

DEF: Torsion of small stalked appendage of the head of the epididymis (pedunculated hydatid); a detached embryologic efferent duct.

608.3 Atrophy of testis

608.4 Other inflammatory disorders of male genital organs

Abscess / Boil / Carbuncle / Cellulitis } of scrotum, spermatic cord, testis [except abscess], tunica vaginalis, or vas deferens

Vasitis

Use additional code to identify organism

EXCLUDES *abscess of testis (604.0)*

✓5th **608.8 Other specified disorders of male genital organs**

608.81 Disorders of male genital organs in diseases classified elsewhere

Code first underlying disease, as:
filariasis (125.0-125.9)
tuberculosis (016.5)

608.82 Hematospermia

DEF: Presence of blood in the ejaculate; relatively common, affecting men of any age after puberty; cause is often difficult to determine since the semen originates in several organs, often the result of a viral or bacterial infection and inflammation.

608.83 Vascular disorders

Hematoma (non-traumatic) / Hemorrhage / Thrombosis } of seminal vessel, spermatic cord, testis, scrotum, tunica vaginalis, or vas deferens

Hematocele NOS, male

608.84 Chylocele of tunica vaginalis

DEF: Chylous effusion into tunica vaginalis; due to infusion of lymphatic fluids.

608.85 Stricture

Stricture of:
spermatic cord
tunica vaginalis
vas deferens

608.86 Edema

608.87 Retrograde ejaculation

DEF: Condition where the semen travels to the bladder rather than out through the urethra due to damaged nerves causing the bladder neck to remain open during ejaculation.

608.89 Other

Atrophy / Fibrosis / Hypertrophy / Ulcer } of seminal vessel, spermatic cord, testis, scrotum, tunica vaginalis, or vas deferens

EXCLUDES *atrophy of testis (608.3)*

608.9 Unspecified disorder of male genital organs

DISORDERS OF BREAST (610-612)

✓4th **610 Benign mammary dysplasias**

610.0 Solitary cyst of breast

Cyst (solitary) of breast

610.1 Diffuse cystic mastopathy

Chronic cystic mastitis
Cystic breast
Fibrocystic disease of breast

DEF: Extensive formation of nodular cysts in breast tissue; symptoms include tenderness, change in size and hyperplasia of ductal epithelium.

610.2 Fibroadenosis of breast

Fibroadenosis of breast:
NOS
chronic
cystic
diffuse
periodic
segmental

DEF: Non-neoplastic nodular condition of breast.

610.3 Fibrosclerosis of breast

DEF: Fibrous tissue in breast.

610.4 Mammary duct ectasia

Comedomastitis
Duct ectasia
Mastitis:
periductal
plasma cell

DEF: Atrophy of duct epithelium; causes distended collecting ducts of mammary gland; drying up of breast secretion, intraductal inflammation and periductal and interstitial chronic inflammatory reaction.

610.8 Other specified benign mammary dysplasias

Mazoplasia
Sebaceous cyst of breast

610.9 Benign mammary dysplasia, unspecified

✓4th **611 Other disorders of breast**

EXCLUDES *that associated with lactation or the puerperium (675.0-676.9)*

611.0 Inflammatory disease of breast

Abscess (acute) (chronic) (nonpuerperal) of:
areola
breast
Mammillary fistula
Mastitis (acute) (subacute) (nonpuerperal):
NOS
infective
retromammary
submammary

EXCLUDES *carbuncle of breast (680.2)*
chronic cystic mastitis (610.1)
neonatal infective mastitis (771.5)
thrombophlebitis of breast [Mondor's disease] (451.89)

611.1 Hypertrophy of breast
Gynecomastia
Hypertrophy of breast:
NOS
massive pubertal
EXCLUDES *breast engorgement in newborn (778.7)*
disproportion of reconstructed breast (612.1)

611.2 Fissure of nipple

611.3 Fat necrosis of breast
Fat necrosis (segmental) of breast
Code first breast necrosis due to breast graft (996.79)
DEF: Splitting of neutral fats in adipose tissue cells as a result of trauma; a firm circumscribed mass is then formed in the breast.

611.4 Atrophy of breast

611.5 Galactocele

611.6 Galactorrhea not associated with childbirth

✓5th **611.7 Signs and symptoms in breast**

611.71 Mastodynia
Pain in breast

611.72 Lump or mass in breast

611.79 Other
Induration of breast
Inversion of nipple
Nipple discharge
Retraction of nipple

✓5th **611.8 Other specified disorders of breast**

611.81 Ptosis of breast
EXCLUDES *ptosis of native breast in relation to reconstructed breast (612.1)*

611.82 Hypoplasia of breast
Micromastia
EXCLUDES *hypoplasia of native breast in relation to reconstructed breast (612.1)*

611.83 Capsular contracture of breast implant

611.89 Other specified disorders of breast
Hematoma (nontraumatic) of breast
Infarction of breast
Occlusion of breast duct
Subinvolution of breast (postlactational) (postpartum)

611.9 Unspecified breast disorder

✓4th **612 Deformity and disproportion of reconstructed breast**

612.0 Deformity of reconstructed breast
Contour irregularity in reconstructed breast
Excess tissue in reconstructed breast
Misshapen reconstructed breast

612.1 Disproportion of reconstructed breast
Breast asymmetry between native breast and reconstructed breast
Disproportion between native breast and reconstructed breast

INFLAMMATORY DISEASE OF FEMALE PELVIC ORGANS (614-616)

Use additional code to identify organism, such as Staphylococcus (041.1), or Streptococcus (041.0)
EXCLUDES *that associated with pregnancy, abortion, childbirth, or the puerperium (630-676.9)*

✓4th **614 Inflammatory disease of ovary, fallopian tube, pelvic cellular tissue, and peritoneum**
EXCLUDES *endometritis (615.0-615.9)*
major infection following delivery (670)
that complicating:
abortion (634-638 with .0, 639.0)
ectopic or molar pregnancy (639.0)
pregnancy or labor (646.6)

614.0 Acute salpingitis and oophoritis
Any condition classifiable to 614.2, specified as acute or subacute
DEF: Acute inflammation, of ovary and fallopian tube.

614.1 Chronic salpingitis and oophoritis
Hydrosalpinx
Salpingitis:
follicularis
isthmica nodosa
Any condition classifiable to 614.2, specified as chronic
DEF: Persistent inflammation of ovary and fallopian tube.

614.2 Salpingitis and oophoritis not specified as acute, subacute, or chronic
Abscess (of):
fallopian tube
ovary
tubo-ovarian
Oophoritis
Perioophoritis
Perisalpingitis
Pyosalpinx
Salpingitis
Salpingo-oophoritis
Tubo-ovarian inflammatory disease
EXCLUDES *gonococcal infection (chronic) (098.37)*
acute (098.17)
tuberculous (016.6)

614.3 Acute parametritis and pelvic cellulitis
Acute inflammatory pelvic disease
Any condition classifiable to 614.4, specified as acute
DEF: Parametritis: inflammation of the parametrium; pelvic cellulitis is a synonym for parametritis.

614.4 Chronic or unspecified parametritis and pelvic cellulitis
Abscess (of):
broad ligament } chronic or NOS
parametrium } chronic or NOS
pelvis, femal } chronic or NOS
pouch of Douglas } chronic or NOS
Chronic inflammatory pelvic disease
Pelvic cellulitis, female
EXCLUDES *tuberculous (016.7)*

614.5 Acute or unspecified pelvic peritonitis, female

614.6 Pelvic peritoneal adhesions, female (postoperative) (postinfection)
Adhesions:
peritubal
tubo-ovarian
Use additional code to identify any associated infertility (628.2)
DEF: Fibrous scarring abnormally joining structures within abdomen.

614.7 Other chronic pelvic peritonitis, female
EXCLUDES *tuberculous (016.7)*

614.8 Other specified inflammatory disease of female pelvic organs and tissues

614.9 Unspecified inflammatory disease of female pelvic organs and tissues
Pelvic infection or inflammation, female NOS
Pelvic inflammatory disease [PID]

✓4th **615 Inflammatory diseases of uterus, except cervix**
EXCLUDES *following delivery (670)*
hyperplastic endometritis (621.30-621.33)
that complicating:
abortion (634-638 with .0, 639.0)
ectopic or molar pregnancy (639.0)
pregnancy or labor (646.6)

615.0 Acute
Any condition classifiable to 615.9, specified as acute or subacute

615.1 Chronic
Any condition classifiable to 615.9, specified as chronic

615.9 Unspecified inflammatory disease of uterus
Endometritis
Endomyometritis
Intrauterine infection
Metritis
Myometritis
Perimetritis
Pyometra
Uterine abscess

✓4th **616 Inflammatory disease of cervix, vagina, and vulva**
EXCLUDES *that complicating:*
abortion (634-638 with .0, 639.0)
ectopic or molar pregnancy (639.0)
pregnancy, childbirth, or the puerperium (646.6)

616.0 Cervicitis and endocervicitis
Cervicitis } with or without mention of erosion or ectropion
Endocervicitis }
Nabothian (gland) cyst or follicle
EXCLUDES *erosion or ectropion without mention of cervicitis (622.0)*

✓5th **616.1 Vaginitis and vulvovaginitis**
EXCLUDES *vulvar vestibulitis (625.71)*
DEF: Inflammation or infection of vagina or external female genitalia.

616.10 Vaginitis and vulvovaginitis, unspecified
Vaginitis:
NOS
postirradiation
Vulvitis NOS
Vulvovaginitis NOS
Use additional code to identify organism, such as Escherichia coli [E. coli] (041.4), Staphylococcus (041.1), or Streptococcus (041.0)
EXCLUDES *noninfective leukorrhea (623.5)*
postmenopausal or senile vaginitis (627.3)

616.11 Vaginitis and vulvovaginitis in diseases classified elsewhere
Code first underlying disease, as:
pinworm vaginitis (127.4)
EXCLUDES *herpetic vulvovaginitis (054.11)*
monilial vulvovaginitis (112.1)
trichomonal vaginitis or vulvovaginitis (131.01)

616.2 Cyst of Bartholin's gland
Bartholin's duct cyst
DEF: Fluid-filled sac within gland of vaginal orifice.

616.3 Abscess of Bartholin's gland
Vulvovaginal gland abscess

616.4 Other abscess of vulva
Abscess }
Carbuncle } of vulva
Furuncle }

✓5th **616.5 Ulceration of vulva**

616.50 Ulceration of vulva, unspecified
Ulcer NOS of vulva

616.51 Ulceration of vulva in diseases classified elsewhere
Code first underlying disease, as:
Behçet's syndrome (136.1)
tuberculosis (016.7)
EXCLUDES *vulvar ulcer (in):*
gonococcal (098.0)
herpes simplex (054.12)
syphilitic (091.0)

✓5th **616.8 Other specified inflammatory diseases of cervix,vagina, and vulva**
EXCLUDES *noninflammatory disorders of:*
cervix (622.0-622.9)
vagina (623.0-623.9)
vulva (624.0-624.9)

616.81 Mucositis (ulcerative) of cervix, vagina, and vulva
Use additional E code to identify adverse effects of therapy, such as:
antineoplastic and immunosuppressive drugs (E930.7, E933.1)
radiation therapy (E879.2)

616.89 Other inflammatory disease of cervix, vagina and vulva
Caruncle, vagina or labium
Ulcer, vagina

616.9 Unspecified inflammatory disease of cervix, vagina, and vulva

OTHER DISORDERS OF FEMALE GENITAL TRACT (617-629)

✓4th **617 Endometriosis**

617.0 Endometriosis of uterus
Adenomyosis
Endometriosis:
cervix
internal
myometrium
EXCLUDES *stromal endometriosis (236.0)*
DEF: Aberrant uterine mucosal tissue; creating products of menses and inflamed uterine tissues.

617.1 Endometriosis of ovary
Chocolate cyst of ovary
Endometrial cystoma of ovary
DEF: Aberrant uterine tissue; creating products of menses and inflamed ovarian tissues.

617.2 Endometriosis of fallopian tube
DEF: Aberrant uterine tissue; creating products of menses and inflamed tissues of fallopian tubes.

617.3 Endometriosis of pelvic peritoneum
Endometriosis:
broad ligament
cul-de-sac (Douglas')
parametrium
round ligament
DEF: Aberrant uterine tissue; creating products of menses and inflamed peritoneum tissues.

Female Genitourinary System

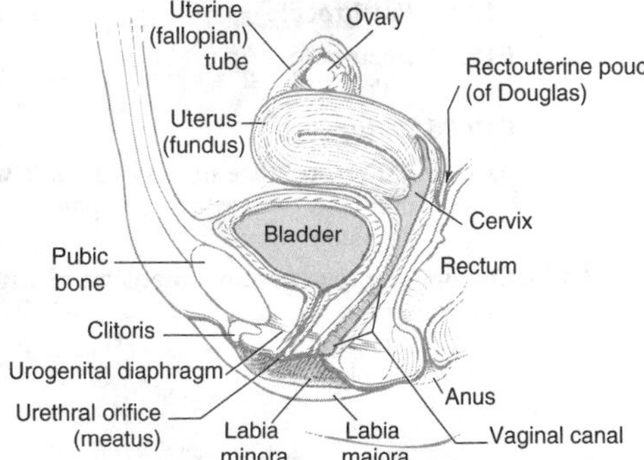

Common Sites of Endometriosis

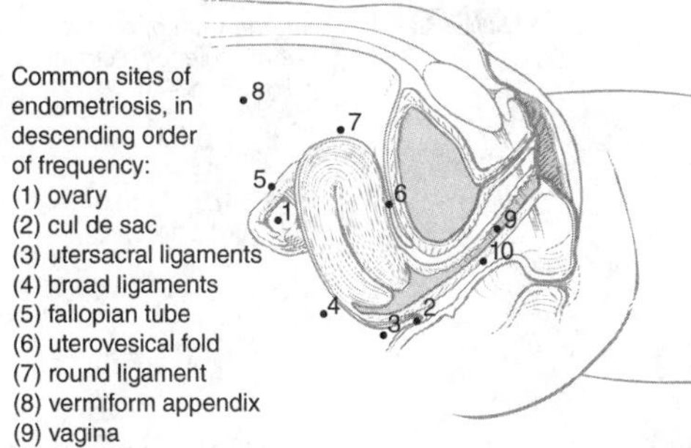

617.4 Endometriosis of rectovaginal septum and vagina

DEF: Aberrant uterine tissue; creating products of menses and inflamed tissues in and behind vagina.

617.5 Endometriosis of intestine

Endometriosis:
- appendix
- colon

Endometriosis:
- rectum

DEF: Aberrant uterine tissue; creating products of menses and inflamed intestinal tissues.

617.6 Endometriosis in scar of skin

617.8 Endometriosis of other specified sites

Endometriosis:
- bladder
- lung
- umbilicus
- vulva

617.9 Endometriosis, site unspecified

✓4th **618 Genital prolapse**

Use additional code to identify urinary incontinence (625.6, 788.31, 788.33-788.39)

EXCLUDES *that complicating pregnancy, labor, or delivery (654.4)*

✓5th **618.0 Prolapse of vaginal walls without mention of uterine prolapse**

EXCLUDES *that with uterine prolapse (618.2-618.4)*
enterocele (618.6)
vaginal vault prolapse following hysterectomy (618.5)

618.00 Unspecified prolapse of vaginal walls

Vaginal prolapse NOS

618.01 Cystocele, midline

Cystocele NOS

DEF: Defect in the pubocervical fascia, the supportive layer of the bladder, causing bladder drop and herniated into the vagina along the midline.

618.02 Cystocele, lateral

Paravaginal

DEF: Loss of support of the lateral attachment of the vagina at the arcus tendinous results in bladder drop; bladder herniates into the vagina laterally; also called paravaginal defect.

618.03 Urethrocele

618.04 Rectocele

Proctocele

618.05 Perineocele

618.09 Other prolapse of vaginal walls without mention of uterine prolapse

Cystourethrocele

618.1 Uterine prolapse without mention of vaginal wall prolapse

Descensus uteri

Uterine prolapse:
- NOS
- complete
- first degree
- second degree
- third degree

EXCLUDES *that with mention of cystocele, urethrocele, or rectocele (618.2-618.4)*

Vaginal Midline Cystocele

Uterus
Pubocervical fascia
Bladder
Midline cystocele
Rectum
Urethra
Rectovaginal fascia
Uterus
Vaginal epithelium
Normal vaginal support
Bladder
Urethra
Defect of pubocervical fascia

Vaginal Lateral Cystocele

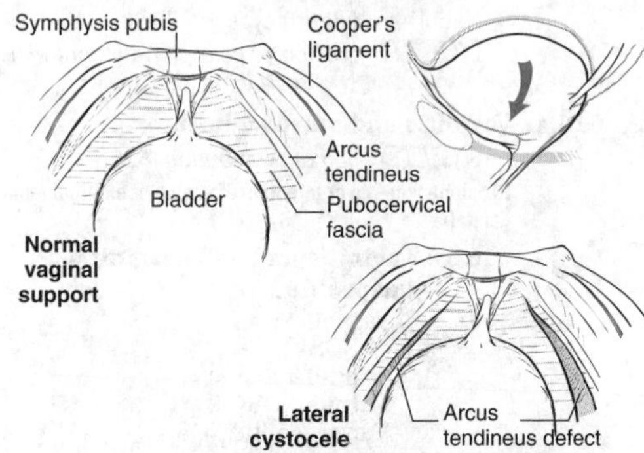

618.2 Uterovaginal prolapse, incomplete

DEF: Downward displacement of uterus downward into vagina.

618.3 Uterovaginal prolapse, complete

DEF: Downward displacement of uterus exposed within external genitalia.

618.4 Uterovaginal prolapse, unspecified

618.5 Prolapse of vaginal vault after hysterectomy

618.6 Vaginal enterocele, congenital or acquired

Pelvic enterocele, congenital or acquired

DEF: Vaginal vault hernia formed by the loop of the small intestine protruding into the rectal vaginal pouch; can also accompany uterine prolapse or follow hysterectomy.

618.7 Old laceration of muscles of pelvic floor

✓5th **618.8 Other specified genital prolapse**

618.81 Incompetence or weakening of pubocervical tissue

618.82 Incompetence or weakening of rectovaginal tissue

618.83 Pelvic muscle wasting

Disuse atrophy of pelvic muscles and anal sphincter

618.84 Cervical stump prolapse

Types of Vaginal Hernias

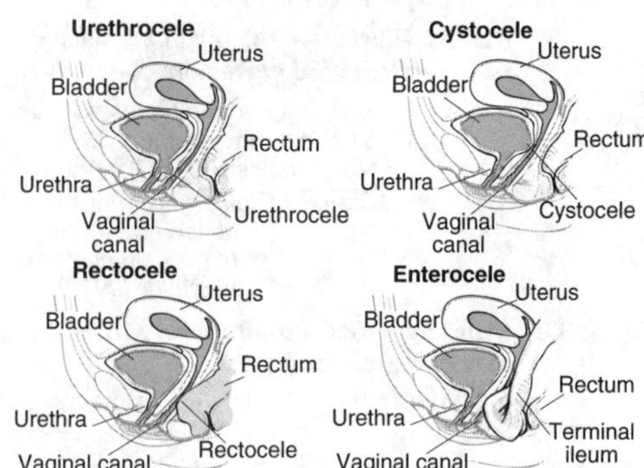

618.89 Other specified genital prolapse

618.9 Unspecified genital prolapse

✓4th **619 Fistula involving female genital tract**

EXCLUDES *vesicorectal and intestinovesical fistula (596.1)*

619.0 Urinary-genital tract fistula, female

Fistula:
- cervicovesical
- ureterovaginal
- urethrovaginal
- urethrovesicovaginal
- uteroureteric
- uterovesical
- vesicocervicovaginal
- vesicovaginal

619.1 Digestive-genital tract fistula, female

Fistula:
- intestinouterine
- intestinovaginal
- rectovaginal
- rectovulval
- sigmoidovaginal
- uterorectal

619.2 Genital tract-skin fistula, female

Fistula:
- uterus to abdominal wall
- vaginoperineal

619.8 Other specified fistulas involving female genital tract

Fistula:
- cervix
- cul-de-sac (Douglas')
- uterus
- vagina

619.9 Unspecified fistula involving female genital tract

✓4th **620 Noninflammatory disorders of ovary, fallopian tube, and broad ligament**

EXCLUDES *hydrosalpinx (614.1)*

620.0 Follicular cyst of ovary

Cyst of graafian follicle

DEF: Fluid-filled, encapsulated cyst due to occluded follicle duct that secretes hormones into ovaries.

620.1 Corpus luteum cyst or hematoma

Corpus luteum hemorrhage or rupture
Lutein cyst

DEF: Fluid-filled cyst due to serous developing from corpus luteum or clotted blood.

620.2 Other and unspecified ovarian cyst

Cyst:
- NOS } of ovary
- corpus albicans } of ovary
- retention NOS } of ovary
- serous } of ovary
- theca-lutein } of ovary

Simple cystoma of ovary

EXCLUDES *cystadenoma (benign) (serous) (220)*
developmental cysts (752.0)
neoplastic cysts (220)
polycystic ovaries (256.4)
Stein-Leventhal syndrome (256.4)

Uterus and Ovaries

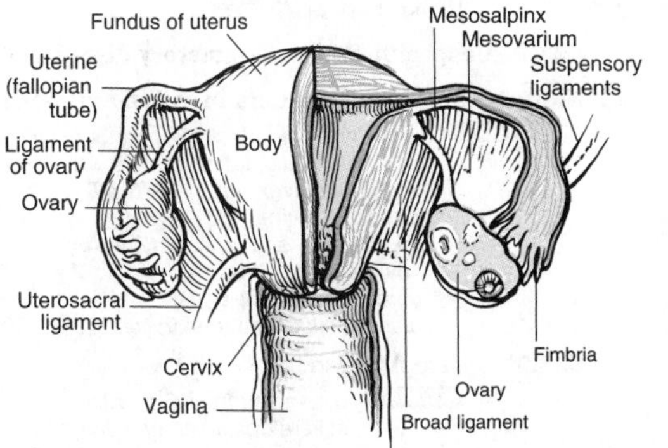

620.3 Acquired atrophy of ovary and fallopian tube

Senile involution of ovary

620.4 Prolapse or hernia of ovary and fallopian tube

Displacement of ovary and fallopian tube
Salpingocele

620.5 Torsion of ovary, ovarian pedicle, or fallopian tube

Torsion:
- accessory tube
- hydatid of Morgagni

620.6 Broad ligament laceration syndrome

Masters-Allen syndrome

620.7 Hematoma of broad ligament

Hematocele, broad ligament

DEF: Blood within peritoneal fold that supports uterus.

620.8 Other noninflammatory disorders of ovary, fallopian tube, and broad ligament

Cyst } of broad ligament or fallopian tube
Polyp } of broad ligament or fallopian tube

Infarction } of ovary or fallopian tube
Rupture } of ovary or fallopian tube

Hematosalpinx

EXCLUDES *hematosalpinx in ectopic pregnancy (639.2)*
peritubal adhesions (614.6)
torsion of ovary, ovarian pedicle, or fallopian tube (620.5)

620.9 Unspecified noninflammatory disorder of ovary, fallopian tube, and broad ligament

✓4th **621 Disorders of uterus, not elsewhere classified**

621.0 Polyp of corpus uteri

Polyp:
- endometrium
- uterus NOS

EXCLUDES *cervical polyp NOS (622.7)*

621.1 Chronic subinvolution of uterus

EXCLUDES *puerperal (674.8)*

DEF: Abnormal size of uterus after delivery; the uterus does not return to its normal size after the birth of a child.

621.2 Hypertrophy of uterus

Bulky or enlarged uterus

EXCLUDES *puerperal (674.8)*

✓5th **621.3 Endometrial hyperplasia**

Hyperplasia (adenomatous) (cystic) (glandular) of endometrium

DEF: Abnormal cystic overgrowth of endometrial tissue.

621.30 Endometrial hyperplasia, unspecified

Endometrial hyperplasia NOS

621.31 Simple endometrial hyperplasia without atypia

621.32 Complex endometrial hyperplasia without atypia

621.33 Endometrial hyperplasia with atypia

621.4 Hematometra

Hemometra

EXCLUDES *that in congenital anomaly (752.2-752.3)*

DEF: Accumulated blood in uterus.

621.5 Intrauterine synechiae

Adhesions of uterus
Band(s) of uterus

621.6 Malposition of uterus

Anteversion } of uterus
Retroflexion } of uterus
Retroversion } of uterus

EXCLUDES *malposition complicating pregnancy, labor, or delivery (654.3-654.4)*

621.7 Chronic inversion of uterus

EXCLUDES *current obstetrical trauma (665.2)*
prolapse of uterus (618.1-618.4)

621.8 Other specified disorders of uterus, not elsewhere classified

Atrophy, acquired | Cyst | Fibrosis NOS | Old laceration (postpartum) | Ulcer — of uterus

EXCLUDES *bilharzial fibrosis (120.0-120.9)*
endometriosis (617.0)
fistulas (619.0-619.8)
inflammatory diseases (615.0-615.9)

621.9 Unspecified disorder of uterus

✓4th **622 Noninflammatory disorders of cervix**

EXCLUDES *abnormality of cervix complicating pregnancy, labor, or delivery (654.5-654.6)*
fistula (619.0-619.8)

622.0 Erosion and ectropion of cervix

Eversion | Ulcer — of cervix

EXCLUDES *that in chronic cervicitis (616.0)*

DEF: Ulceration or turning outward of uterine cervix.

✓5th **622.1 Dysplasia of cervix (uteri)**

EXCLUDES *abnormal results from cervical cytologic examination without histologic confirmation (795.00-795.09)*
carcinoma in situ of cervix (233.1)
cervical intraepithelial neoplasia III [CIN III] (233.1)
HGSIL of cervix (795.04)

DEF: Abnormal cell structures in portal between uterus and vagina.

622.10 Dysplasia of cervix, unspecified

Anaplasia of cervix
Cervical atypism
Cervical dysplasia NOS

622.11 Mild dysplasia of cervix

Cervical intraepithelial neoplasia I [CIN I]

622.12 Moderate dysplasia of cervix

Cervical intraepithelial neoplasia II [CIN II]

EXCLUDES *carcinoma in situ of cervix (233.1)*
cervical intraepithelial neo-plasia III [CIN III] (233.1)
severe dysplasia (233.1)

622.2 Leukoplakia of cervix (uteri)

EXCLUDES *carcinoma in situ of cervix (233.1)*

DEF: Thickened, white patches on portal between uterus and vagina.

622.3 Old laceration of cervix

Adhesions | Band(s) | Cicatrix (postpartum) — of cervix

EXCLUDES *current obstetrical trauma (665.3)*

DEF: Scarring or other evidence of old wound on cervix.

622.4 Stricture and stenosis of cervix

Atresia (acquired) | Contracture | Occlusion — of cervix

Pinpoint os uteri

EXCLUDES *congenital (752.49)*
that complicating labor (654.6)

622.5 Incompetence of cervix

EXCLUDES *complicating pregnancy (654.5)*
that affecting fetus or newborn (761.0)

DEF: Inadequate functioning of cervix; marked by abnormal widening during pregnancy; causing miscarriage.

622.6 Hypertrophic elongation of cervix

DEF: Overgrowth of cervix tissues extending down into vagina.

622.7 Mucous polyp of cervix

Polyp NOS of cervix

EXCLUDES *adenomatous polyp of cervix (219.0)*

622.8 Other specified noninflammatory disorders of cervix

Atrophy (senile) | Cyst | Fibrosis | Hemorrhage — of cervix

EXCLUDES *endometriosis (617.0)*
fistula (619.0-619.8)
inflammatory diseases (616.0)

622.9 Unspecified noninflammatory disorder of cervix

✓4th **623 Noninflammatory disorders of vagina**

EXCLUDES *abnormality of vagina complicating pregnancy, labor, or delivery (654.7)*
congenital absence of vagina (752.49)
congenital diaphragm or bands (752.49)
fistulas involving vagina (619.0-619.8)

623.0 Dysplasia of vagina

Mild and moderate dysplasia of vagina
Vaginal intraepithelial neoplasia I and II [VAIN I and II]

EXCLUDES *abnormal results from vaginal cytological examination without histologic confirmation (795.10-795.19)*
carcinoma in situ of vagina (233.31)
HGSIL of vagina (795.14)
severe dysplasia of vagina (233.31)
vaginal intraepithelial neoplasia III [VAIN III] (233.31)

623.1 Leukoplakia of vagina

DEF: Thickened white patches on vaginal canal.

623.2 Stricture or atresia of vagina

Adhesions (postoperative) (postradiation) of vagina
Occlusion of vagina
Stenosis, vagina

Use additional E code to identify any external cause

EXCLUDES *congenital atresia or stricture (752.49)*

623.3 Tight hymenal ring

Rigid hymen | Tight hymenal ring | Tight introitus — acquired or congenital

EXCLUDES *imperforate hymen (752.42)*

623.4 Old vaginal laceration

EXCLUDES *old laceration involving muscles of pelvic floor (618.7)*

DEF: Scarring or other evidence of old wound on vagina.

623.5 Leukorrhea, not specified as infective

Leukorrhea NOS of vagina
Vaginal discharge NOS

EXCLUDES *trichomonal (131.00)*

DEF: Viscid whitish discharge, from vagina.

623.6 Vaginal hematoma

EXCLUDES *current obstetrical trauma (665.7)*

623.7 Polyp of vagina

623.8 Other specified noninflammatory disorders of vagina

Cyst | Hemorrhage — of vagina

623.9 Unspecified noninflammatory disorder of vagina

✓4th **624 Noninflammatory disorders of vulva and perineum**

EXCLUDES *abnormality of vulva and perineum complicating pregnancy, labor, or delivery (654.8)*
condyloma acuminatum (078.10)
fistulas involving:
perineum – see Alphabetic Index
vulva (619.0-619.8)
vulval varices (456.6)
vulvar involvement in skin conditions (690-709.9)

✓5th **624.0 Dystrophy of vulva**

EXCLUDES *carcinoma in situ of vulva (233.32)*
severe dysplasia of vulva (233.32)
vulvar intraepithelial neoplasia III [VIN III] (233.32)

624.01 Vulvar intraepithelial neoplasia I [VIN I]
Mild dysplasia of vulva

624.02 Vulvar intraepithelial neoplasia II [VIN II]
Moderate dysplasia of vulva

624.09 Other dystrophy of vulva
Kraurosis of vulva
Leukoplakia of vulva

624.1 Atrophy of vulva

624.2 Hypertrophy of clitoris
EXCLUDES *that in endocrine disorders (255.2, 256.1)*

624.3 Hypertrophy of labia
Hypertrophy of vulva NOS
DEF: Overgrowth of fleshy folds on either side of vagina.

624.4 Old laceration or scarring of vulva
DEF: Scarring or other evidence of old wound on external female genitalia.

624.5 Hematoma of vulva
EXCLUDES *that complicating delivery (664.5)*
DEF: Blood in tissue of external genitalia.

624.6 Polyp of labia and vulva

624.8 Other specified noninflammatory disorders of vulva and perineum
Cyst, Edema, Stricture } of vulva

624.9 Unspecified noninflammatory disorder of vulva and perineum

✓4th 625 Pain and other symptoms associated with female genital organs

625.0 Dyspareunia
EXCLUDES *psychogenic dyspareunia (302.76)*
DEF: Difficult or painful sexual intercourse.

625.1 Vaginismus
Colpospasm
Vulvismus
EXCLUDES *psychogenic vaginismus (306.51)*
DEF: Vaginal spasms; due to involuntary contraction of musculature; prevents intercourse.

625.2 Mittelschmerz
Intermenstrual pain
Ovulation pain
DEF: Pain occurring between menstrual periods.

625.3 Dysmenorrhea
Painful menstruation
EXCLUDES *psychogenic dysmenorrhea (306.52)*

625.4 Premenstrual tension syndromes
Menstrual molimen
Premenstrual dysphoric disorder
Premenstrual syndrome
Premenstrual tension NOS
EXCLUDES *menstrual migraine (346.4)*

625.5 Pelvic congestion syndrome
Congestion-fibrosis syndrome
Taylor's syndrome
DEF: Excessive accumulation of blood in vessels of pelvis; may occur after orgasm; causes abnormal menstruation, lower back pain and vaginal discharge.

625.6 Stress incontinence, female
EXCLUDES *mixed incontinence (788.33)*
stress incontinence, male (788.32)
DEF: Involuntary leakage of urine due to insufficient sphincter control; occurs upon sneezing, laughing, coughing, sudden movement or lifting.

✓5th **625.7 Vulvodynia**

625.70 Vulvodynia, unspecified
Vulvodynia NOS

625.71 Vulvar vestibulitis

625.79 Other vulvodynia

625.8 Other specified symptoms associated with female genital organs

625.9 Unspecified symptom associated with female genital organs

✓4th 626 Disorders of menstruation and other abnormal bleeding from female genital tract

EXCLUDES *menopausal and premenopausal bleeding (627.0)*
pain and other symptoms associated with menstrual cycle (625.2-625.4)
postmenopausal bleeding (627.1)

626.0 Absence of menstruation
Amenorrhea (primary) (secondary)

626.1 Scanty or infrequent menstruation
Hypomenorrhea
Oligomenorrhea

626.2 Excessive or frequent menstruation
Heavy periods
Menometrorrhagia
Menorrhagia
Plymenorrhea
EXCLUDES *premenopausal (627.0)*
that in puberty (626.3)

626.3 Puberty bleeding
Excessive bleeding associated with onset of menstrual periods
Pubertal menorrhagia

626.4 Irregular menstrual cycle
Irregular:
- bleeding NOS
- menstruation
- periods

626.5 Ovulation bleeding
Regular intermenstrual bleeding

626.6 Metrorrhagia
Bleeding unrelated to menstrual cycle
Irregular intermenstrual bleeding

626.7 Postcoital bleeding
DEF: Bleeding from vagina after sexual intercourse.

626.8 Other
Dysfunctional or functional uterine hemorrhage NOS
Menstruation:
- retained
- suppression of

626.9 Unspecified

✓4th 627 Menopausal and postmenopausal disorders

EXCLUDES *asymptomatic age-related (natural) postmenopausal status (V49.81)*

627.0 Premenopausal menorrhagia
Excessive bleeding associated with onset of menopause
Menorrhagia:
- climacteric
- menopausal
- preclimacteric

627.1 Postmenopausal bleeding

627.2 Symptomatic menopausal or female climacteric states
Symptoms, such as flushing, sleeplessness, headache, lack of concentration, associated with the menopause

627.3 Postmenopausal atrophic vaginitis
Senile (atrophic) vaginitis

627.4 Symptomatic states associated with artificial menopause
Postartificial menopause syndromes
Any condition classifiable to 627.1, 627.2, or 627.3 which follows induced menopause
DEF: Conditions arising after hysterectomy.

627.8 Other specified menopausal and postmenopausal disorders
EXCLUDES *premature menopause NOS (256.31)*

627.9 Unspecified menopausal and postmenopausal disorder

✓4th **628 Infertility, female**

INCLUDES primary and secondary sterility

DEF: Infertility: inability to conceive for at least one year with regular intercourse.

DEF: Primary infertility: occurring in patients who have never conceived.

DEF: Secondary infertility: occurring in patients who have previously conceived.

628.0 Associated with anovulation
Anovulatory cycle
Use additional code for any associated Stein-Leventhal syndrome (256.4)

628.1 Of pituitary-hypothalamic origin
Code first underlying cause, as:
adiposogenital dystrophy (253.8)
anterior pituitary disorder (253.0-253.4)

628.2 Of tubal origin
Infertility associated with congenital anomaly of tube
Tubal:
block
occlusion
stenosis
Use additional code for any associated peritubal adhesions (614.6)

628.3 Of uterine origin
Infertility associated with congenital anomaly of uterus
Nonimplantation
Use additional code for any associated tuberculous endometritis (016.7)

628.4 Of cervical or vaginal origin
Infertility associated with:
anomaly of cervical mucus
congenital structural anomaly
dysmucorrhea

628.8 Of other specified origin

628.9 Of unspecified origin

✓4th **629 Other disorders of female genital organs**

629.0 Hematocele, female, not elsewhere classified
EXCLUDES *hematocele or hematoma:*
broad ligament (620.7)
fallopian tube (620.8)
that associated with ectopic pregnancy (633.00-633.91)
uterus (621.4)
vagina (623.6)
vulva (624.5)

629.1 Hydrocele, canal of Nuck
Cyst of canal of Nuck (acquired)
EXCLUDES *congenital (752.41)*

✓5th **629.2 Female genital mutilation status**
Female circumcision status
Female genital cutting

629.20 Female genital mutilation status, unspecified
Female genital cutting status, unspecified
Female genital mutilation status NOS

629.21 Female genital mutilation Type I status
Clitorectomy status
Female genital cutting Type I status
DEF: Female genital mutilation involving clitorectomy, with part or all of the clitoris removed.

629.22 Female genital mutilation Type II status
Clitorectomy with excision of labia minora status
Female genital cutting Type II status
DEF: Female genital mutilation involving clitoris and the labia minora amputation.

629.23 Female genital mutilation Type III status
Female genital cutting Type III status
Infibulation status
DEF: Female genital mutilation involving removal, most or all of the labia minora excised, labia majora incised which is then made into a hood of skin over the urethral and vaginal opening.

629.29 Other female genital mutilation status
Female genital cutting Type IV status
Female genital mutilation Type IV status
Other female genital cutting status

✓5th **629.8 Other specified disorders of female genital organs**

629.81 Habitual aborter without current pregnancy
EXCLUDES *habitual aborter with current pregnancy (646.3)*

629.89 Other specified disorders of female genital organs

629.9 Unspecified disorder of female genital organs

Chapter 11: Complications of Pregnancy, Childbirth, and the Puerperium (630–679)

Chapter 11 of the tabular list provides codes for normal delivery as well as for obstetrical complications. Obstetrical terms can be found in the alphabetic index under the main terms "Pregnancy," Delivery," "Labor," and "Puerperal." The coder must decide whether the condition specified in the diagnostic statement is a complication of the pregnancy, labor or delivery, or whether it occurred after delivery.

The categories in chapter 11 are:

- Ectopic and molar pregnancy (630–633)
- Other pregnancy with abortive outcome (634–639)
- Complications mainly related to pregnancy (640–649)
- Normal delivery, and other indications for care in pregnancy, labor and delivery (650–659)
- Complications occurring mainly in the course of labor and delivery (660–669)
- Complications of the puerperium (670–677)
- Other maternal and fetal complications contains two categories: 678 Other fetal conditions and 679 Complications of in utero procedures.

Ectopic and Molar Pregnancy (630–633)

An hydatidiform mole (630) is an abnormal product of conception that results in a mass of cells that resembles a bunch of grapes. This condition also is called cystic or vesicular mole.

Missed abortion (632) is the retention of a fetus before completion of 22 weeks of gestation for at least four weeks after fetal demise. (This period of time varies according to state law. It may be as few as 19 weeks.) This excludes retained products of conception following spontaneous (634) or induced abortion (637), delivery, or missed delivery (656.4X)

Ectopic pregnancy (633) is the implantation of fertilized ovum in an anatomic location other than the uterus. The most common site of ectopic pregnancy is the fallopian tube, but it may occur in other locations of the body such as the abdomen, ovary, or cervix.

Legally Induced Abortion (635)

Legally induced abortion is the termination of a pregnancy with removal of some but not all of the products of conception, with or without an identifiable fetus weighing less than 500 grams or before completion of 22 weeks of gestation for therapeutic or elective reasons.

Terms that apply to this category are:

- Termination of pregnancy
- Elective abortion
- Legal abortion
- Therapeutic abortion

Fourth-digit subcategories specify complications that arise during the current episode of care.

Fifth-digit assignment indicates the stage of the abortion as, unspecified, incomplete, or complete. Generally, induced abortions are complete at the time of initial episode of care and a fifth digit of "2" is assigned.

Use an additional code from categories 640–648 and 651–657 to identify the complication or reason for the induced abortion. When assigning these additional codes use the fifth digit of "3," antepartum condition or complication.abortion, complete, complicated by an electrolyte imbalance during the episode of care. For example the reason for the termination of pregnancy is maternal primary genital syphilis. Code as follows:

Example:

635.42 Legally induced abortion complicated by metabolic disorder, complete

647.03 Pregnancy complicated by infection in the mother, syphilis, fifth-digit assignment of antepartum condition or complication

091.0 Genital syphilis, primary

Complications Following Abortion and Ectopic and Molar Pregnancy (639)

Complications under the 639 category include:

- Genital tract and pelvic infection (639.0)
- Delayed or excessive hemorrhage (639.1)
- Damage to the pelvic organs or tissues (639.2)
- Renal failure (639.3)
- Metabolic disorders (electrolyte imbalance) (639.4)
- Shock (639.5)
- Embolism (639.6)
- Other specified complication (cardiac arrest, UTI, cerebral anoxia, etc.) (639.8)
- Unspecified complication (639.9)

Complications Mainly Related to Pregnancy (640–649)

These codes describe conditions that affect the management of labor, pregnancy or delivery, and the puerperium, even if the condition was present before pregnancy. Multiple coding may be necessary to fully describe complications relating to the pregnancy. Sequencing of the codes depends upon the main focus of and the reason for the episode of care.

Categories include:

- Hemorrhage in early pregnancy (640)
- Antepartum hemorrhage, abruptio placentae and placenta previa (641)
- Hypertension complicating pregnancy, childbirth, and the puerperium (642)
- Excessive vomiting in pregnancy (643)
- Early or threatened labor (644)
- Late pregnancy (645)
- Other complications, not elsewhere classified (646)
- Infectious and parasitic conditions in the mother classifiable elsewhere but complicating pregnancy, childbirth, or the puerperium (647)
- Other current conditions in the mother classifiable elsewhere but complicating pregnancy, childbirth or the puerperium (648)
- Other conditions or status of the mother complicating pregnancy, childbirth or puerperium (649) are general guidelines to follow when coding complications of pregnancy, childbirth or the puerperium classifiable to categories 640–649.

First, the fourth-digit subcategories generally add specificity to the described complication.

The fifth-digit subclassification denotes the current episode of care or the stage of pregnancy, childbirth or puerperium at which the complication occurred.

0 Unspecified as to episode of care or not applicable

1 Delivered, with or without mention of antepartum condition

2 Delivered, with mention of postpartum complication

3 Antepartum condition or complication (delivery does not occur during this episode of care)

4 Postpartum condition or complication (following previous episode of care resulting in delivery)

Multiple coding is used to fully describe the complications affecting the pregnancy, childbirth, and the puerperium. Appropriate fifth-digit assignment is needed to specify the episode of care and the stage during which the complication arose.

A postpartum complication is any complication occurring within the six-week period following delivery. Codes from this section may also be used to describe pregnancy- related complications after the six-week period should the physician document that a condition is pregnancy related. Postpartum complications that occur during the same admission as the delivery are identified with a fifth digit of "2." Subsequent admissions for postpartum complications should identified with a fifth digit of "4."

Complications Occurring Mainly in the Course of Labor and Delivery (660-669)

Anal Sphincter Tear Complicating Delivery, Not Associated with Third-Degree Perineal Laceration (664.6x)

Anal sphincter tears can occur during delivery independent of third-degree lacerations, and such tears may not be identified until they complicate a subsequent delivery. Conversely, a third-degree tear may occur independently of an anal sphincter tear. Report code 664.6x Anal sphincter tear complicating delivery, when the anal sphincter tear complicates delivery but is not associated with a third-degree perineal laceration. When reporting code 664.6, assign the appropriate fifth digit to indicate episode of care.

OTHER MATERNAL AND FETAL COMPLICATIONS (678–679)

Other Fetal Conditions (678)

Section "Other Maternal and Fetal Complications" includes categories 678 and 679. Valid fifth-digit subclassifications 0–4 are listed at the beginning of the section and are required to denote the episode of care. Category 679 contains two subcategories: one representing maternal complications and one representing fetal complications from in utero procedures.

Category 678 includes two subcategories that classify both fetal hematological conditions (678.0) and fetal conjoined twins (678.1). Fetal hemorrhagic conditions classified under this subcategory include only conditions affecting the fetus during pregnancy or affecting the management of the mother during delivery. These codes are reported on the mother's medical record. This subcategory excludes isoimmunization incompatability and fetal-maternal hemorrhage. Fetal hematological disorders include fetal anemia, whereby red blood cells are inadequately produced or are destroyed faster than they can be produced. Causal conditions include maternal-fetal incompatibility, viral infection, or other infectious process. If anemia is diagnosed or suspected, the pregnancy will require close observation, as it can be fatal for the fetus. Treatment of severe fetal anemia may include intrauterine blood transfusion.

Fetal thrombocytopenia is a potentially fatal condition whereby the fetus's platelet (blood clotting) cell count is abnormally low or deficient, possibly due to maternal-fetal immune incompatibility. Risks include fetal hemorrhage which, if it occurs in the central nervous system, can result in a fetal stroke. Early detection and treatment of fetal hematological disorders (678.0X) is essential to optimal outcomes. However, the procedures used to manage these diagnoses carry some risk to the pregnancy and fetus. Anemic infants may have short-term complications from their anemia or low platelet counts after birth, requiring transfusions or other specialized treatments.

A pregnancy complicated by twin-to-twin transfusion syndrome (TTTS) carries significant risk of severe disabilities or death of one or both twins. TTTS occurs when monozygotic (identical) twins share the same placenta and blood vessels and results from an intrauterine blood transfusion from one twin to the other. If TTTS develops after 26 weeks, the babies can usually be delivered and have a greater chance of survival without disability. There are a number of different therapies used to treat TTTS, with varying rates of success, including serial amniocentesis from recipient twin, or fetoscopic laser ablation of communicating blood vessels.

Conjoined twins (678.1X) are identical twins that fail to completely separate into two individuals. They are most often joined at the head, chest, or pelvis and may share one or more internal organs. The success of separation surgery often depends on the anatomic site or sites of connection and which or how many organs are shared. Conjoined twins pose significant risks during pregnancy. Identification can be made by ultrasound imaging as early as the 12th week of pregnancy, with specific anatomic details apparent by the 20th week. Approximately half of conjoined twins develop excessive amniotic fluid (polyhydramnios), which increases the risk of premature rupture of the membranes, problems with the umbilical cord, and stillbirth. About 40 percent of conjoined twins are stillborn. Vaginal delivery is rarely possible. If the parents choose to continue the pregnancy, cesarean section delivery is usually required.

Complications from In Utero Procedures (679)

Fetal surgery is a relatively new surgical specialty that enables treatment of certain fetal conditions and anomalies previously considered untreatable. Diagnostic imaging technologies help in early detection of fetal anomalies and associated gestational risks. Conditions treatable by in utero surgery include:

- Twin-to-twin transfusion syndrome (TTTS) by laser photocoagulation
- Vasa previa by YAG laser photocoagulation of placental blood vessels
- Bladder outlet obstruction by cystoscopy-guided laser incision or vesicoamniotic shunting
- Myelomeningocele by open neurosurgical repair by hysterotomy
- Congenital cystic pulmonary adenoma by resection or thoracoamniotic shunt
- Sacrococcygeal teratoma by open surgical repair via hysterotomy
- Congenital diaphragmatic hernia repair by fetal tracheal occlusion

In utero interventional procedures provide opportunities to improve outcomes for pregnancies complicated by fetal conditions previously not amenable to treatment. However, these procedures are not without risk for both the fetus and the mother, depending on the nature of the diagnosis and type of intervention. The greatest risk is loss of fetal life by preterm labor, hemorrhage, or other surgical complication. For the mother, damage can occur to the uterus, precluding or complicating future pregnancies.

11. COMPLICATIONS OF PREGNANCY, CHILDBIRTH, AND THE PUERPERIUM (630-679)

ECTOPIC AND MOLAR PREGNANCY (630-633)

Use additional code from category 639 to identify any complications

630 Hydatidiform mole

Trophoblastic disease NOS
Vesicular mole

EXCLUDES *chorioadenoma (destruens) (236.1)*
chorionepithelioma (181)
malignant hydatidiform mole (236.1)

DEF: Abnormal product of pregnancy; marked by mass of cysts resembling bunch of grapes due to chorionic villi proliferation, and dissolution; must be surgically removed.

631 Other abnormal product of conception

Blighted ovum
Mole:
NOS
carneous
fleshy
stone

632 Missed abortion

Early fetal death before completion of 22 weeks' gestation with retention of dead fetus
Retained products of conception, not following spontaneous or induced abortion or delivery

EXCLUDES *failed induced abortion (638.0-638.9)*
fetal death (intrauterine) (late) (656.4)
missed delivery (656.4)
that with abnormal product of conception (630, 631)

✓4th **633 Ectopic pregnancy**

INCLUDES ruptured ectopic pregnancy

DEF: Fertilized egg develops outside uterus.

✓5th **633.0 Abdominal pregnancy**

Intraperitoneal pregnancy

633.00 Abdominal pregnancy without intrauterine pregnancy

633.01 Abdominal pregnancy with intrauterine pregnancy

✓5th **633.1 Tubal pregnancy**

Fallopian pregnancy
Rupture of (fallopian) tube due to pregnancy
Tubal abortion

633.10 Tubal pregnancy without intrauterine pregnancy

633.11 Tubal pregnancy with intrauterine pregnancy

✓5th **633.2 Ovarian pregnancy**

633.20 Ovarian pregnancy without intrauterine pregnancy

633.21 Ovarian pregnancy with intrauterine pregnancy

✓5th **633.8 Other ectopic pregnancy**

Pregnancy:
cervical
combined
cornual
intraligamentous
mesometric
mural

633.80 Other ectopic pregnancy without intrauterine pregnancy

633.81 Other ectopic pregnancy with intrauterine pregnancy

✓5th **633.9 Unspecified ectopic pregnancy**

633.90 Unspecified ectopic pregnancy without intrauterine pregnancy

633.91 Unspecified ectopic pregnancy with intrauterine pregnancy

Ectopic Pregnancy Sites

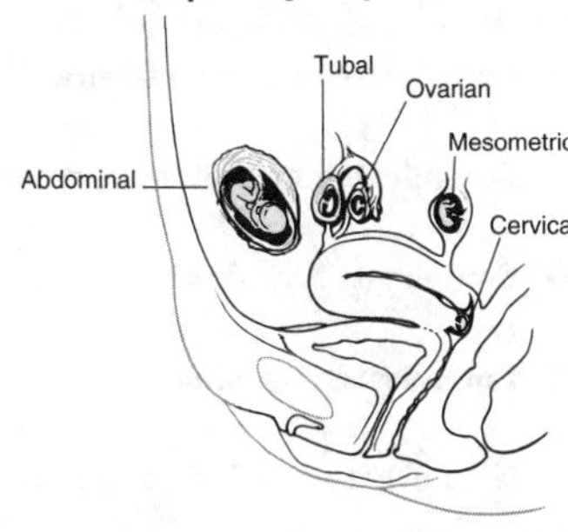

OTHER PREGNANCY WITH ABORTIVE OUTCOME (634-639)

The following fourth-digit subdivisions are for use with categories 634-638:

.0 Complicated by genital tract and pelvic infection

Endometritis
Salpingo-oophoritis
Sepsis NOS
Septicemia NOS
Any condition classifiable to 639.0 with condition classifiable to 634-638

EXCLUDES *urinary tract infection (634-638 with .7)*

.1 Complicated by delayed or excessive hemorrhage

Afibrinogenemia
Defibrination syndrome
Intravascular hemolysis
Any condition classifiable to 639.1 with condition classifiable to 634-638

.2 Complicated by damage to pelvic organs and tissues

Laceration, perforation, or tear of:
bladder
uterus
Any condition classifiable to 639.2 with condition classifiable to 634-638

.3 Complicated by renal failure

Oliguria
Uremia
Any condition classifiable to 639.3, with condition classifiable to 634-638

.4 Complicated by metabolic disorder

Electrolyte imbalance with conditions classfiable to 634-638

.5 Complicated by shock

Circulatory collapse
Shock (postoperative) (septic)
Any condition classifiable to 639.5 with condition classifiable to 634-638

.6 Complicated by embolism

Embolism:
NOS
amniotic fluid
pulmonary
Any condition classifiable to 639.6, with condition classifiable to 634-638

.7 With other specified complications

Cardiac arrest or failure
Urinary tract infection
Any condition classiable to 639.8 with condition classifiable to 634-638

.8 With unspecified complication

.9 Without mention of complication

✓4th **634 Spontaneous abortion**

Requires fifth-digit to identify stage:
0 unspecified
1 incomplete
2 complete

INCLUDES miscarriage
spontaneous abortion

DEF: Spontaneous premature expulsion of the products of conception from the uterus.

✓5th **634.0 Complicated by genital tract and pelvic infection**
[0-2]

✓5th **634.1 Complicated by delayed or excessive hemorrhage**
[0-2]

✓5th **634.2 Complicated by damage to pelvic organs or tissues**
[0-2]

✓5th **634.3 Complicated by renal failure**
[0-2]

✓5th **634.4 Complicated by metabolic disorder**
[0-2]

✓5th **634.5 Complicated by shock**
[0-2]

✓5th **634.6 Complicated by embolism**
[0-2]

✓5th **634.7 With other specified complications**
[0-2]

✓5th **634.8 With unspecified complication**
[0-2]

✓5th **634.9 Without mention of complication**
[0-2]

✓4th **635 Legally induced abortion**

Requires fifth-digit to identify stage:
0 unspecified
1 incomplete
2 complete

INCLUDES abortion or termination of pregnancy:
elective
legal
therapeutic

EXCLUDES *menstrual extraction or regulation (V25.3)*

DEF: Intentional expulsion of products of conception from uterus performed by medical professionals inside boundaries of law.

✓5th **635.0 Complicated by genital tract and pelvic infection**
[0-2]

✓5th **635.1 Complicated by delayed or excessive hemorrhage**
[0-2]

✓5th **635.2 Complicated by damage to pelvic organs or tissues**
[0-2]

✓5th **635.3 Complicated by renal failure**
[0-2]

✓5th **635.4 Complicated by metabolic disorder**
[0-2]

✓5th **635.5 Complicated by shock**
[0-2]

✓5th **635.6 Complicated by embolism**
[0-2]

✓5th **635.7 With other specified complications**
[0-2]

✓5th **635.8 With unspecified complication**
[0-2]

✓5th **635.9 Without mention of complication**
[0-2]

✓4th **636 Illegally induced abortion**

Requires fifth-digit to identify stage:
0 unspecified
1 incomplete
2 complete

INCLUDES abortion:
criminal
illegal
self-induced

DEF: Intentional expulsion of products of conception from uterus; outside boundaries of law.

✓5th **636.0 Complicated by genital tract and pelvic infection**
[0-2]

✓5th **636.1 Complicated by delayed or excessive hemorrhage**
[0-2]

✓5th **636.2 Complicated by damage to pelvic organs or tissues**
[0-2]

✓5th **636.3 Complicated by renal failure**
[0-2]

✓5th **636.4 Complicated by metabolic disorder**
[0-2]

✓5th **636.5 Complicated by shock**
[0-2]

✓5th **636.6 Complicated by embolism**
[0-2]

✓5th **636.7 With other specified complications**
[0-2]

✓5th **636.8 With unspecified complication**
[0-2]

✓5th **636.9 Without mention of complication**
[0-2]

✓4th **637 Unspecified abortion**

Requires fifth-digit to identify stage:
0 unspecified
1 incomplete
2 complete

INCLUDES abortion NOS
retained products of conception following abortion, not classifiable elsewhere

✓5th **637.0 Complicated by genital tract and pelvic infection**
[0-2]

✓5th **637.1 Complicated by delayed or excessive hemorrhage**
[0-2]

✓5th **637.2 Complicated by damage to pelvic organs or tissues**
[0-2]

✓5th **637.3 Complicated by renal failure**
[0-2]

✓5th **637.4 Complicated by metabolic disorder**
[0-2]

✓5th **637.5 Complicated by shock**
[0-2]

✓5th **637.6 Complicated by embolism**
[0-2]

✓5th **637.7 With other specified complications**
[0-2]

✓5th **637.8 With unspecified complication**
[0-2]

✓5th **637.9 Without mention of complication**
[0-2]

✓4th **638 Failed attempted abortion**

INCLUDES failure of attempted induction of (legal) abortion

EXCLUDES *incomplete abortion (634.0-637.9)*

DEF: Continued pregnancy despite an attempted legal abortion.

638.0 Complicated by genital tract and pelvic infection

638.1 Complicated by delayed or excessive hemorrhage

638.2 Complicated by damage to pelvic organs or tissues

638.3 Complicated by renal failure

638.4 Complicated by metabolic disorder

638.5 Complicated by shock

638.6 Complicated by embolism

638.7 With other specified complications

638.8 With unspecified complication

638.9 Without mention of complication

✓4th 639 Complications following abortion and ectopic and molar pregnancies

Note: This category is provided for use when it is required to classify separately the complications classifiable to the fourth-digit level in categories 634-638; for example:

a) when the complication itself was responsible for an episode of medical care, the abortion, ectopic or molar pregnancy itself having been dealt with at a previous episode

b) when these conditions are immediate complications of ectopic or molar pregnancies classifiable to 630-633 where they cannot be identified at fourth-digit level.

639.0 Genital tract and pelvic infection

Endometritis
Parametritis
Pelvic peritonitis
Salpingitis
Salpingo-oophoritis
Sepsis NOS
Septicemia NOS
} following conditions classifiable to 630-638

EXCLUDES *urinary tract infection (639.8)*

639.1 Delayed or excessive hemorrhage

Afibrinogenemia
Defibrination syndrome
Intravascular
} following conditions classfiable to 630-638

639.2 Damage to pelvic organs and tissues

Laceration, perforation, or tear of:
bladder
bowel
broad ligament
cervix
periurethral tissue
uterus
vagina
} following conditions classifiable to 630-638

639.3 Renal failure

Oliguria
Renal:
failure (acute)
shutdown
tubular necrosis
Uremia
} following conditions classifiable to 630-638

639.4 Metabolic disorders

Electrolyte imbalance following conditions classifiable to 630-638

639.5 Shock

Circulatory collapse
Shock (postoperative) (septic)
} following conditions classifiable to 630-638

639.6 Embolism

Embolism:
NOS
air
amniotic fluid
blood-clot
fat
pulmonary
pyemic
septic
soap
} following conditions classifiable to 630-638

639.8 Other specified complications following abortion or ectopic and molar pregnancy

Acute yellow atrophy or necrosis of liver
Cardiac arrest or failure
Cerebral anoxia
Urinary tract infection
} following conditons classifiable to 630-638

639.9 Unspecified complication following abortion or ectopic and molar pregnancy

Complication(s) not further specified following conditions classifiable to 630-638

Placenta Previa

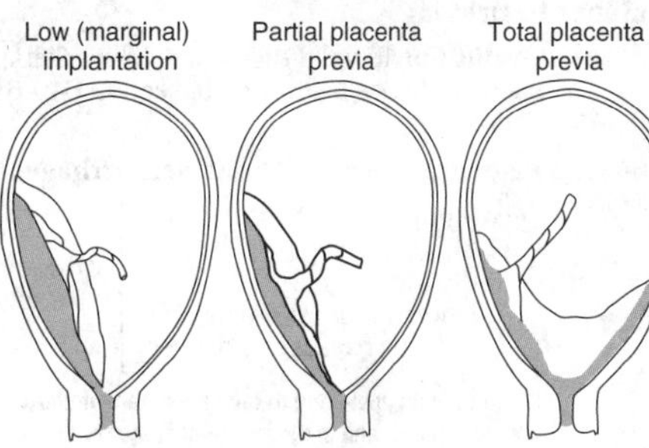

Abruptio Placentae

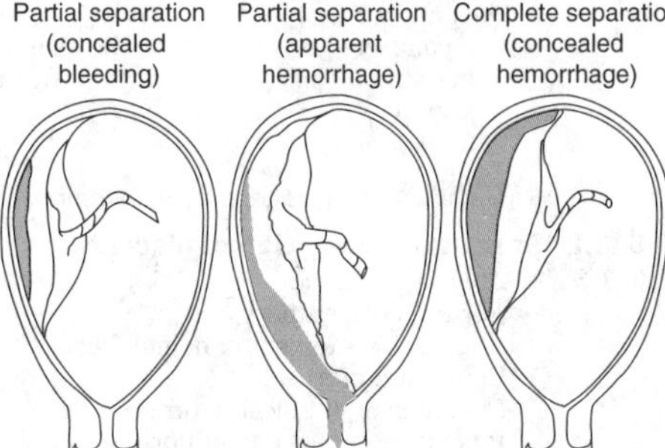

COMPLICATIONS MAINLY RELATED TO PREGNANCY (640-649)

INCLUDES the listed conditions even if they arose or were present during labor, delivery, or the puerperium

The following fifth-digit subclassification is for use with categories 640-649 to denote the current episode of care. Valid fifth-digits are in [brackets] under each code.

0 unspecified as to episode of care or not applicable

1 delivered, with or without mention of antepartum condition

Antepartum condition with delivery
Delivery NOS (with mention of antepartum complication during current episode of care)
Intrapartum obstetric condition (with mention of antepartum complication during current episode of care)
Pregnancy, delivered (with mention of antepartum complication during current episode of care)

2 delivered, with mention of postpartum complication

Delivery with mention of puerperal complication during current episode of care

3 antepartum condition or complication

Antepartum obstetric condtion, not delivered during the current episode of care

4 postpartum condition of complication

Postpartum or puerperal obstetric condition or complication following delivery that occurred:
during previous episode of care
outside hospital, with subsequent admission for observation or care

✓4th 640 Hemorrhage in early pregnancy

Requires fifth-digit; valid digits are in [brackets] under each code. See beginning of section 640-649 for definitions.

INCLUDES hemorrhage before completion of 22 weeks' gestation

✓5th **640.0 Threatened abortion**
[0,1,3] **DEF: Bloody discharge during pregnancy; cervix may be dilated and pregnancy is threatened, but the pregnancy is not terminated.**

✓5th **640.8 Other specified hemorrhage in early**
[0,1,3] **pregnancy**

✓5th **640.9 Unspecified hemorrhage in early**
[0,1,3] **pregnancy**

✓4th 641 Antepartum hemorrhage, abruptio placentae, and placenta previa

Requires fifth-digit; valid digits are in [brackets] under each code. See beginning of section 640-649 for definitions.

✓5th 641.0 Placenta previa without hemorrhage
[0,1,3]

Low implantation of placenta
Placenta previa noted:
during pregnancy
before labor (and delivered by caesarean delivery
} without hemorrhage

DEF: Placenta implanted in lower segment of uterus; commonly causes hemorrhage in the last trimester of pregnancy.

✓5th 641.1 Hemorrhage from placenta previa
[0,1,3]

Low-lying placenta
Placenta previa
incomplete
marginal
partial
total
} NOS or with hemorrhage (intrapartum)

EXCLUDES *hemorrhage from vasa previa (663.5)*

✓5th 641.2 Premature separation of placenta
[0,1,3]

Ablatio placentae
Abruptio placentae
Accidental antepartum hemorrhage
Couvelaire uterus
Detachment of placenta (premature)
Premature separation of normally implanted placenta

DEF: Abruptio placentae: premature detachment of the placenta, characterized by shock, oliguria and decreased fibrinogen.

✓5th 641.3 Antepartum hemorrhage associated with coagulation defects
[0,1,3]

Antepartum or intrapartum hemorrhage associated with:
afibrinogenemia
hyperfibrinolysis
hypofibrinogenemia

EXCLUDES *coagulation defects not associated with antepartum hemorrhage (649.3)*

DEF: Uterine hemorrhage prior to delivery.

✓5th 641.8 Other antepartum hemorrhage
[0,1,3]

Antepartum or intrapartum hemorrhage associated with:
trauma
uterine leiomyoma

✓5th 641.9 Unspecified antepartum hemorrhage
[0,1,3]

Hemorrhage:
antepartum NOS
intrapartum NOS

Hemorrhage:
of pregnancy NOS

✓4th 642 Hypertension complicating pregnancy, childbirth, and the puerperium

Requires fifth-digit; valid digits are in [brackets] under each code. See beginning of section 640-649 for definitions.

✓5th 642.0 Benign essential hypertension complicating pregnancy, childbirth, and the puerperium
[0-4]

Hypertension
benign essential
chronic NOS
essential
pre-existing NOS
} specified as complicating, or as reason for obstetric care during pregnancy, childbirth, or the puerperium

✓5th 642.1 Hypertension secondary to renal disease, complicating pregnancy, childbirth, and the puerperium
[0-4]

Hypertension secondary to renal disease, specified as complicating, or as a reason for obstetric care during pregnancy, childbirth, or the puerperium

✓5th 642.2 Other pre-existing hypertension complicating pregnancy, childbirth, and the puerperium
[0-4]

Hypertensive
chronic kidney disease
heart and chronic kidney disease
heart disease
Malignant hypertension
} specified as complicating, or as a reason for obstetric care during pregnancy, childbirth, or the puerperium

✓5th 642.3 Transient hypertension of pregnancy
[0-4]

Gestational hypertension
Transient hypertension, so described, in pregnancy, childbirth, or the puerperium

✓5th 642.4 Mild or unspecified pre-eclampsia
[0-4]

Hypertension in pregnancy, childbirth, or the puerperium, not specified as pre-existing, with either albuminuria or edema, or both; mild or unspecified
Pre-eclampsia:
NOS
mild
Toxemia (pre-eclamptic):
NOS
mild

EXCLUDES *albuminuria in pregnancy, without mention of hypertension (646.2)*
edema in pregnancy, without mention of hypertension (646.1)

✓5th 642.5 Severe pre-eclampsia
[0-4]

Hypertension in pregnancy, childbirth, or the puerperium, not specified as pre-existing, with either albuminuria or edema, or both; specified as severe
Pre-eclampsia, severe
Toxemia (pre-eclamptic), severe

✓5th 642.6 Eclampsia
[0-4]

Toxemia:
eclamptic
with convulsions

✓5th 642.7 Pre-eclampsia or eclampsia superimposed on pre-existing hypertension
[0-4]

Conditions classifiable to 642.4-642.6, with conditions classifiable to 642.0-642.2

✓5th 642.9 Unspecified hypertension complicating pregnancy, childbirth, or the puerperium
[0-4]

Hypertension NOS, without mention of albuminuria or edema, complicating pregnancy, childbirth, or the puerperium

✓4th 643 Excessive vomiting in pregnancy

Requires fifth-digit; valid digits are in [brackets] under each code. See beginning of section 640-649 for definitions.

INCLUDES
hyperemesis
vomiting:
persistent
vicious
} arising during pregnancy
hyperemesis gravidarum

✓5th 643.0 Mild hyperemesis gravidarum
[0,1,3]

Hyperemesis gravidarum, mild or unspecified, starting before the end of the 22nd week of gestation

DEF: Detrimental vomiting and nausea.

✓5th 643.1 Hyperemesis gravidarum with metabolic disturbance
[0,1,3]

Hyperemesis gravidarum, starting before the end of the 22nd week of gestation, with metabolic disturbance, such as:
carbohydrate depletion
dehydration
electrolyte imbalance

✓5th 643.2 Late vomiting of pregnancy
[0,1,3]

Excessive vomiting starting after 22 completed weeks of gestation

√5th **643.8 Other vomiting complicating pregnancy**
[0,1,3] Vomiting due to organic disease or other cause, specified as complicating pregnancy, or as a reason for obstetric care during pregnancy
Use additional code to specify cause

√5th **643.9 Unspecified vomiting of pregnancy**
[0,1,3] Vomiting as a reason for care during pregnancy, length of gestation unspecified

√4th **644 Early or threatened labor**
Requires fifth-digit; valid digits are in [brackets] under each code. See beginning of section 640-649 for definitions.

√5th **644.0 Threatened premature labor**
[0,3] Premature labor after 22 weeks, but before 37 completed weeks of gestation without delivery
EXCLUDES *that occurring before 22 completed weeks of gestation (640.0)*

√5th **644.1 Other threatened labor**
[0,3] False labor:
NOS } without delivery
after 37 completed weeks of gestation } without delivery
Threatened labor NOS } without delivery

√5th **644.2 Early onset of delivery**
[0,1] Onset (spontaneous) of delivery } before 37 completed weeks of gestation
Premature labor with onset of delivery } before 37 completed weeks of gestation

√4th **645 Late pregnancy**
Requires fifth-digit; valid digits are in [brackets] under each code. See beginning of section 640-649 for definitions.

√5th **645.1 Post term pregnancy**
[0,1,3] Pregnancy over 40 completed weeks to 42 completed weeks gestation

√5th **645.2 Prolonged pregnancy**
[0,1,3] Pregnancy which has advanced beyond 42 completed weeks gestation

√4th **646 Other complications of pregnancy, not elsewhere classified**
Requires fifth-digit; valid digits are in [brackets] under each code. See beginning of section 640-649 for definitions.
Use additional code(s) to further specify complication

√5th **646.0 Papyraceous fetus**
[0,1,3] **DEF: Fetus that dies in the second trimester of pregnancy and is retained in the uterus, with subsequent atrophy and mummification; commonly occurs in twin pregnancy, nonviable fetus becomes compressed by growth of living twin and exhibits parchment-like skin.**

√5th **646.1 Edema or excessive weight gain in pregnancy, without mention of hypertension**
[0-4] Gestational edema
Maternal obesity syndrome
EXCLUDES *that with mention of hypertension (642.0-642.9)*

√5th **646.2 Unspecified renal disease in pregnancy, without mention of hypertension**
[0-4]
Albuminuria } in pregnancy or the puerperium, without mention of hypertension
Nephropathy NOS } in pregnancy or the puerperium, without mention of hypertension
Renal disease NOS } in pregnancy or the puerperium, without mention of hypertension
Uremia } in pregnancy or the puerperium, without mention of hypertension
Gestational proteinuria
EXCLUDES *that with mention of hypertension (642.0-642.9)*

√5th **646.3 Habitual aborter**
[0,1,3] EXCLUDES *with current abortion (634.0-634.9)*
without current pregnancy (629.81)
DEF: Three or more consecutive spontaneous abortions.

√5th **646.4 Peripheral neuritis in pregnancy**
[0-4]

√5th **646.5 Asymptomatic bacteriuria in pregnancy**
[0-4]

√5th **646.6 Infections of genitourinary tract in pregnancy**
[0-4] Conditions classifiable to 590, 595, 597, 599.0, 616 complicating pregnancy, childbirth, or the puerperium
Conditions classifiable to 614.0-614.5, 614.7-614.9, 615 complicating pregnancy or labor
EXCLUDES *major puerperal infection (670)*

√5th **646.7 Liver disorders in pregnancy**
[0,1,3]
Acute yellow atrophy of liver (obstetric) (true) } of pregnancy
Icterus gravis } of pregnancy
Necrosis of liver } of pregnancy
EXCLUDES *hepatorenal syndrome following delivery (674.8)*
viral hepatitis (647.6)

√5th **646.8 Other specified complications of pregnancy**
[0-4] Fatigue during pregnancy
Herpes gestationis
Insufficient weight gain of pregnancy

√5th **646.9 Unspecified complication of pregnancy**
[0,1,3]

√4th **647 Infectious and parasitic conditions in the mother classifiable elsewhere, but complicating pregnancy, childbirth, or the puerperium**
Requires fifth-digit; valid digits are in [brackets] under each code. See beginning of section 640-649 for definitions.
INCLUDES the listed conditions when complicating the pregnant state, aggravated by the pregnancy, or when a main reason for obstetric care
EXCLUDES *those conditions in the mother known or suspected to have affected the fetus (655.0-655.9)*
Use additional code(s) to further specify complication

√5th **647.0 Syphilis**
[0-4] Conditions classifiable to 090-097

√5th **647.1 Gonorrhea**
[0-4] Conditions classifiable to 098

√5th **647.2 Other venereal diseases**
[0-4] Conditions classifiable to 099

√5th **647.3 Tuberculosis**
[0-4] Conditions classifiable to 010-018

√5th **647.4 Malaria**
[0-4] Conditions classifiable to 084

√5th **647.5 Rubella**
[0-4] Conditions classifiable to 056

√5th **647.6 Other viral diseases**
[0-4] Conditions classifiable to 042, 050-055, 057-079, 795.05, 795.15, 796.75

√5th **647.8 Other specified infectious and parasitic diseases**
[0-4]

√5th **647.9 Unspecified infection or infestation**
[0-4]

√4th **648 Other current conditions in the mother classifiable elsewhere, but complicating pregnancy, childbirth, or the puerperium**
Requires fifth-digit; valid digits are in [brackets] under each code. See beginning of section 640-649 for definitions.
INCLUDES the listed conditions when complicating the pregnant state, aggravated by the pregnancy, or when a main reason for obstetric care
EXCLUDES *those conditions in the mother known or suspected to have affected the fetus (655.0-655.9)*
Use additional code(s) to identify the condition

✓5th **648.0 Diabetes mellitus**
[0-4] Conditions classifiable to 249, 250
EXCLUDES *gestational diabetes (648.8)*

✓5th **648.1 Thyroid dysfunction**
[0-4] Conditions classifiable to 240-246

✓5th **648.2 Anemia**
[0-4] Conditions classifiable to 280-285

✓5th **648.3 Drug dependence**
[0-4] Conditions classifiable to 304

✓5th **648.4 Mental disorders**
[0-4] Conditions classifiable to 290-303, 305.0, 305.2-305.9, 306-316, 317-319

✓5th **648.5 Congenital cardiovascular disorders**
[0-4] Conditions classifiable to 745-747

✓5th **648.6 Other cardiovascular diseases**
[0-4] Conditions classifiable to 390-398, 410-429
EXCLUDES *cerebrovascular disorders in the puerperium (674.0)*
peripartum cardiomyopathy (674.5)
venous complications (671.0-671.9)

✓5th **648.7 Bone and joint disorders of back, pelvis, and lower limbs**
[0-4] Conditions classifiable to 720-724, and those classifiable to 711-719 or 725-738, specified as affecting the lower limbs

✓5th **648.8 Abnormal glucose tolerance**
[0-4] Conditions classifiable to 790.21-790.29
Gestational diabetes
Use additional code, if applicable, for associated long-term (current) insulin use (V58.67)
DEF: Glucose intolerance arising in pregnancy, resolving at end of pregnancy.

✓5th **648.9 Other current conditions classifiable elsewhere**
[0-4] Conditions classifiable to 440-459, 795.01-795.04, 795.06, 795.10-795.14, 795.16, 796.70-796.74, 796.76

✓4th **649 Other conditions or status of the mother complicating pregnancy, childbirth, or the puerperium**

Requires fifth-digit; valid digits are in [brackets] under each code. See beginning of section 640-649 for definitions.

✓5th **649.0 Tobacco use disorder complicating pregnancy, childbirth, or the puerperium**
[0-4] Smoking complicating pregnancy, childbirth, or the puerperium

✓5th **649.1 Obesity complicating pregnancy, childbirth, or the puerperium**
[0-4] Use additional code to identify the obesity (278.00, 278.01)

✓5th **649.2 Bariatric surgery status complicating pregnancy, childbirth, or the puerperium**
[0-4] Gastric banding status complicating pregnancy, childbirth, or the puerperium
Gastric bypass status for obesity complicating pregnancy, childbirth, or the puerperium
Obesity surgery status complicating pregnancy, childbirth, or the puerperium

✓5th **649.3 Coagulation defects complicating pregnancy, childbirth, or the puerperium**
[0-4] Conditions classifiable to 286, 287, 289
Use additional code to identify the specific coagulation defect (286.0-286.9, 287.0-287.9, 289.0-289.9)
EXCLUDES *coagulation defects causing antepartum hemorrhage (641.3)*
postpartum coagulation defects (666.3)

✓5th **649.4 Epilepsy complicating pregnancy, childbirth, or the puerperium**
[0-4] Conditions classifiable to 345
Use additional code to identify the specific type of epilepsy (345.00-345.91)
EXCLUDES *eclampsia (642.6)*

✓5th **649.5 Spotting complicating pregnancy**
[0,1,3] EXCLUDES *antepartum hemorrhage (641.0-641.9)*
hemorrhage in early pregnancy (640.0-640.9)

✓5th **649.6 Uterine size date discrepancy**
[0-4] EXCLUDES *suspected problem with fetal growth not found (V89.04)*

✓5th **649.7 Cervical shortening**
[0,1,3] EXCLUDES *suspected cervical shortening not found (V89.05)*

NORMAL DELIVERY, AND OTHER INDICATIONS FOR CARE IN PREGNANCY, LABOR, AND DELIVERY (650-659)

The following fifth-digit subclassification is for use with categories 651-659 to denote the current episode of care. Valid fifth-digits are in [brackets] under each code.
0 unspecified as to episode of care or not applicable
1 delivered, with or without mention of antepartum condition
2 delivered, with mention of postpartum complication
3 antepartum condition or complication
4 postpartum condition or complication

650 Normal delivery

Delivery requiring minimal or no assistance, with or without episiotomy, without fetal manipulation [e.g., rotation version] or instrumentation [forceps] of spontaneous, cephalic, vaginal, full-term, single, live-born infant. This code is for use as a single diagnosis code and is not to be used with any other code in the range 630-676.
Use additional code to indicate outcome of delivery (V27.0)
EXCLUDES *breech delivery (assisted) (spontaneous) NOS (652.2)*
delivery by vacuum extractor, forceps, cesarean section, or breech extraction, without specified complication (669.5-669.7)

✓4th **651 Multiple gestation**

Requires fifth-digit; valid digits are in [brackets] under each code. See beginning of section 650-659 for definitions.

✓5th **651.0 Twin pregnancy**
[0,1,3] EXCLUDES fetal conjoined twins (678.1)

✓5th **651.1 Triplet pregnancy**
[0,1,3]

✓5th **651.2 Quadruplet pregnancy**
[0,1,3]

✓5th **651.3 Twin pregnancy with fetal loss andr etention of one fetus**
[0,1,3] Vanishing twin syndrome (651.33)

✓5th **651.4 Triplet pregnancy with fetal loss and retention of one or more fetus(es)**
[0,1,3]

✓5th **651.5 Quadruplet pregnancy with fetal loss and retention of one or more fetus(es)**
[0,1,3]

✓5th **651.6 Other multiple pregnancy with fetal loss and retention of one or more fetus(es)**
[0,1,3]

✓5th **651.7 Multiple gestation following (elective) fetal reduction**
[0,1,3] Fetal reduction of multiple fetuses reduced to single fetus

✓5th **651.8 Other specified multiple gestation**
[0,1,3]

✓5th **651.9 Unspecified multiple gestation**
[0,1,3]

✓4th **652 Malposition and malpresentation of fetus**

Requires fifth-digit; valid digits are in [brackets] under each code. See beginning of section 650-659 for definitions.
Code first any associated obstructed labor (660.0)

✓5th **652.0 Unstable lie**
[0,1,3] **DEF: Changing fetal position.**

Malposition and Malpresentation

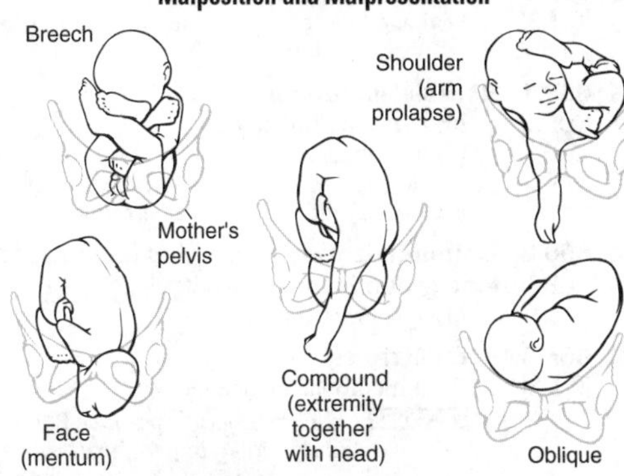

✓5th **652.1 Breech or other malpresentation successfully converted to cephalic presentation**
[0,1,3]
Cephalic version NOS
DEF: Fetal presentation of buttocks or feet at birth canal.

✓5th **652.2 Breech presentation without mention of version**
[0,1,3]
Breech delivery (assisted) (spontaneous) NOS
Buttocks presentation
Complete breech
Frank breech
EXCLUDES *footling presentation (652.8)*
incomplete breech (652.8)

✓5th **652.3 Transverse or oblique presentation**
[0,1,3]
Oblique lie Transverse lie
EXCLUDES *transverse arrest of fetal head (660.3)*

✓5th **652.4 Face or brow presentation**
[0,1,3]
Mentum presentation

✓5th **652.5 High head at term**
[0,1,3]
Failure of head to enter pelvic brim

✓5th **652.6 Multiple gestation with malpresentation of one fetus or more**
[0,1,3]

✓5th **652.7 Prolapsed arm**
[0,1,3]

✓5th **652.8 Other specified malposition or malpresentation**
[0,1,3]
Compound presentation

✓5th **652.9 Unspecified malposition or malpresentation**
[0,1,3]

✓4th **653 Disproportion**

Requires fifth-digit; valid digits are in [brackets] under each code. See beginning of section 650-659 for definitions.
Code first any associated obstructed labor (660.1)

✓5th **653.0 Major abnormality of bony pelvis, not further specified**
[0,1,3]
Pelvic deformity NOS

✓5th **653.1 Generally contracted pelvis**
[0,1,3]
Contracted pelvis NOS

✓5th **653.2 Inlet contraction of pelvis**
[0,1,3]
Inlet contraction (pelvis)

✓5th **653.3 Outlet contraction of pelvis**
[0,1,3]
Outlet contraction (pelvis)

✓5th **653.4 Fetopelvic disproportion**
[0,1,3]
Cephalopelvic disproportion NOS
Disproportion of mixed maternal and fetal origin, with normally formed fetus

✓5th **653.5 Unusually large fetus causing disproportion**
[0,1,3]
Disproportion of fetal origin with normally formed fetus
Fetal disproportion NOS
EXCLUDES *that when the reason for medical care was concern for the fetus (656.6)*

Cephalopelvic Disproportion

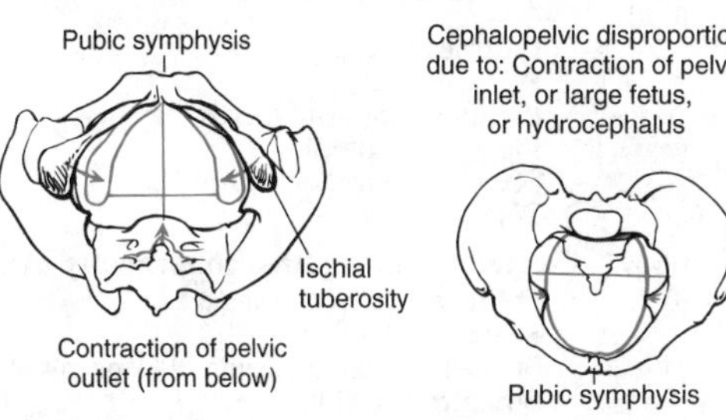

✓5th **653.6 Hydrocephalic fetus causing disproportion**
[0,1,3]
EXCLUDES *that when the reason for medical care was concern for the fetus (655.0)*

✓5th **653.7 Other fetal abnormality causing disproportion**
[0,1,3]
Fetal:
- ascites
- hydrops
- myelomeningocele
- sacral teratoma
- tumor

EXCLUDES *conjoined twins causing disproportion (678.1)*

✓5th **653.8 Disproportion of other origin**
[0,1,3]
EXCLUDES *shoulder (girdle) dystocia (660.4)*

✓5th **653.9 Unspecified disproportion**
[0,1,3]

✓4th **654 Abnormality of organs and soft tissues of pelvis**

Requires fifth-digit; valid digits are in [brackets] under each code. See beginning of section 650-659 for definitions.
INCLUDES the listed conditions during pregnancy, childbirth, or the puerperium
Code first any associated obstructed labor (660.2)
EXCLUDES *trauma to perineum and vulva complicating current delivery (664.0-664.9)*

✓5th **654.0 Congenital abnormalities of uterus**
[0-4]
Double uterus
Uterus bicornis

✓5th **654.1 Tumors of body of uterus**
[0-4]
Uterine fibroids

✓5th **654.2 Previous cesarean delivery**
[0,1,3]
Uterine scar from previous cesarean delivery

✓5th **654.3 Retroverted and incarcerated gravid uterus**
[0-4]
DEF: Retroverted: tilted back uterus; no change in angle of longitudinal axis.
DEF: Incarcerated: immobile, fixed uterus.

✓5th **654.4 Other abnormalities in shape or position of gravid uterus and of neighboring structures**
[0-4]
Cystocele
Pelvic floor repair
Pendulous abdomen
Prolapse of gravid uterus
Rectocele
Rigid pelvic floor

✓5th **654.5 Cervical incompetence**
[0-4]
Presence of Shirodkar suture with or without mention of cervical incompetence
DEF: Abnormal cervix; tendency to dilate in second trimester; causes premature fetal expulsion.
DEF: Shirodkar suture: purse-string suture used to artificially close incompetent cervix.

✓5th **654.6 Other congenital or acquired abnormality of cervix**
[0-4]
Cicatricial cervix
Polyp of cervix
Previous surgery to cervix
Rigid cervix (uteri)
Stenosis or stricture of cervix
Tumor of cervix

✓5th **654.7 Congenital or acquired abnormality of vagina**
[0-4]
Previous surgery to vagina
Septate vagina
Stenosis of vagina (acquired) (congenital)
Stricture of vagina
Tumor of vagina

✓5th **654.8 Congenital or acquired abnormality of vulva**
[0-4]
Anal sphincter tear (healed) (old) complicating delivery
Fibrosis of perineum
Persistent hymen
Previous surgery to perineum or vulva
Rigid perineum
Tumor of vulva
EXCLUDES *anal sphincter tear (healed) (old) not associated with delivery (569.43)*
varicose veins of vulva (671.1)

✓5th **654.9 Other and unspecified**
[0-4]
Uterine scar NEC

✓4th **655 Known or suspected fetal abnormality affecting management of mother**
Requires fifth-digit; valid digits are in [brackets] under each code. See beginning of section 650-659 for definitions.
INCLUDES the listed conditions in the fetus as a reason for observation or obstetrical care of the mother, or for termination of pregnancy

✓5th **655.0 Central nervous system malformation in fetus**
[0,1,3]
Fetal or suspected fetal:
anencephaly
hydrocephalus
spina bifida (with myelomeningocele)

✓5th **655.1 Chromosomal abnormality in fetus**
[0,1,3]

✓5th **655.2 Hereditary disease in family possibly affecting fetus**
[0,1,3]

✓5th **655.3 Suspected damage to fetus from viral disease in the mother**
[0,1,3]
Suspected damage to fetus from maternal rubella

✓5th **655.4 Suspected damage to fetus from other disease in the mother**
[0,1,3]
Suspected damage to fetus from maternal:
alcohol addiction
listeriosis
toxoplasmosis

✓5th **655.5 Suspected damage to fetus from drugs**
[0,1,3]

✓5th **655.6 Suspected damage to fetus from radiation**
[0,1,3]

✓5th **655.7 Decreased fetal movements**
[0,1,3]

✓5th **655.8 Other known or suspected fetal abnormality, not elsewhere classified**
[0,1,3]
Suspected damage to fetus from:
environmental toxins
intrauterine contraceptive device

✓5th **655.9 Unspecified**
[0,1,3]

✓4th **656 Other known or suspected fetal and placental problems affecting management of mother**
Requires fifth-digit; valid digits are in [brackets] under each code. See beginning of section 650-659 for definitions.
EXCLUDES *fetal hematologic conditions (678.0)*
suspected placental problems not found (V89.02)

✓5th **656.0 Fetal-maternal hemorrhage**
[0,1,3]
Leakage (microscopic) of fetal blood into maternal circulation

✓5th **656.1 Rhesus isoimmunization**
[0,1,3]
Anti-D [Rh] antibodies
Rh incompatibility
DEF: Antibodies developing against Rh factor; mother with Rh negative develops antibodies against Rh positive fetus.

✓5th **656.2 Isoimmunization from other and unspecified lood-group incompatibility**
[0,1,3]
ABO isoimmunization

✓5th **656.3 Fetal distress**
[0,1,3]
Fetal metabolic acidemia
EXCLUDES *abnormal fetal acid-base balance (656.8)*
abnormality in fetal heart rate or rhythm (659.7)
fetal bradycardia (659.7)
fetal tachycardia (659.7)
meconium in liquor (656.8)
DEF: Life-threatening disorder; fetal anoxia, hemolytic disease and other miscellaneous diseases cause fetal distress.

✓5th **656.4 Intrauterine death**
[0,1,3]
Fetal death:
NOS
after completion of 22 weeks' gestation
late
Missed delivery
EXCLUDES *missed abortion (632)*

✓5th **656.5 Poor fetal growth**
[0,1,3]
"Light-for-dates"
"Placental insufficiency"
"Small-for-dates"

✓5th **656.6 Excessive fetal growth**
[0,1,3]
"Large-for-dates"

✓5th **656.7 Other placental conditions**
[0,1,3]
Abnormal placenta
Placental infarct
EXCLUDES *placental polyp (674.4)*
placentitis (658.4)

✓5th **656.8 Other specified fetal and placental problems**
[0,1,3]
Abnormal acid-base balance
Intrauterine acidosis
Lithopedian
Meconium in liquor
Subchorionic hematoma
DEF: Lithopedion: Calcified fetus; not expelled by mother.

✓5th **656.9 Unspecified fetal and placental problem**
[0,1,3]

✓4th **657 Polyhydramnios**
[0,1,3] Requires fifth-digit; valid digits are in [brackets] under each code. See beginning of section 650-659 for definitions.
EXCLUDES *suspected polyhydramnios not found (V89.01)*

✓5th Use 0 as fourth-digit for this category
Hydramnios
DEF: Excess amniotic fluid.

✓4th **658 Other problems associated with amniotic cavity and membranes**
EXCLUDES *amniotic fluid embolism (673.1)*
suspected problems with amniotic cavity and membranes not found (V89.01)

✓5th **658.0 Oligohydramnios**
[0,1,3]
Oligohydramnios without mention of rupture of membranes
DEF: Deficient amount of amniotic fluid.

✓5th **658.1 Premature rupture of membranes**
[0,1,3]
Rupture of amniotic sac less than 24 hours prior to the onset of labor

✓5th **658.2 Delayed delivery after spontaneous or unspecified rupture of membranes**
[0,1,3]
Prolonged rupture of membranes NOS
Rupture of amniotic sac 24 hours or more prior to the onset of labor

✓5th **658.3 Delayed delivery after artificial rupture of membranes**
[0,1,3]

✓5th **658.4 Infection of amniotic cavity**
[0,1,3]
Amnionitis
Chorioamnionitis
Membranitis
Placentitis

✓5th **658.8 Other**
[0,1,3]
Amnion nodosum
Amniotic cyst

✓5th **658.9 Unspecified**
[0,1,3]

✓4th **659 Other indications for care or intervention related to labor and delivery, not elsewhere classified**

Requires fifth-digit; valid digits are in [brackets] under each code. See beginning of section 650-659 for definitions.

✓5th **659.0 Failed mechanical induction**
[0,1,3]
Failure of induction of labor by surgical or other instrumental methods

✓5th **659.1 Failed medical or unspecified induction**
[0,1,3]
Failed induction NOS
Failure of induction of labor by medical methods, such as oxytocic drugs

✓5th **659.2 Maternal pyrexia during labor, unspecified**
[0,1,3]
DEF: Fever during labor.

✓5th **659.3 Generalized infection during labor**
[0,1,3]
Septicemia during labor

✓5th **659.4 Grand multiparity**
[0,1,3]
EXCLUDES **supervision only, in pregnancy (V23.3)**
without current pregnancy (V61.5)
DEF: Having borne six or more children previously.

✓5th **659.5 Elderly primigravida**
[0,1,3]
First pregnancy in a woman who will be 35 years of age or older at expected date of delivery
EXCLUDES *supervision only, in pregnancy (V23.81)*

✓5th **659.6 Elderly multigravida**
[0,1,3]
Second or more pregnancy in a woman who will be 35 years of age or older at expected date of delivery
EXCLUDES *elderly primigravida 659.5*
supervision only, in pregnancy (V23.82)

✓5th **659.7 Abnormality in fetal heart rate or rhythm**
[0,1,3]
Depressed fetal heart tones
Fetal:
bradycardia
tachycardia
Fetal heart rate decelerations
Non-reassuring fetal heart rate or rhythm

✓5th **659.8 Other specified indications for care or intervention related to labor and delivery**
[0,1,3]
Pregnancy in a female less than 16 years old at expected date of delivery
Very young maternal age

✓5th **659.9 Unspecified indication for care or intervention related to labor and delivery**
[0,1,3]

COMPLICATIONS OCCURRING MAINLY IN THE COURSE OF LABOR AND DELIVERY (660-669)

The following fifth-digit subclassification is for use with categories 660-669 to denote the current episode of care. Valid fifth-digits are in [brackets] under each code.

0 unspecified as to episode of care or not applicable
1 delivered, with or without mention of antepartum condition
2 delivered, with mention of postpartum complication
3 antepartum condition or complication
4 postpartum condition or complication

✓4th **660 Obstructed labor**

Requires fifth-digit; valid digits are in [brackets] under each code. See beginning of section 660-669 for definitions.

✓5th **660.0 Obstruction caused by malposition of fetus at onset of labor**
[0,1,3]
Any condition classifiable to 652, causing obstruction during labor
Use additional code from 652.0-652.9 to identify condition

✓5th **660.1 Obstruction by bony pelvis**
[0,1,3]
Any condition classifiable to 653, causing obstruction during labor
Use additional code from 653.0-653.9 to identify condition

✓5th **660.2 Obstruction by abnormal pelvic soft tissues**
[0,1,3]
Prolapse of anterior lip of cervix
Any condition classifiable to 654, causing obstruction during labor
Use additional code from 654.0-654.9 to identify condition

✓5th **660.3 Deep transverse arrest and persistent occipitoposterior position**
[0,1,3]

✓5th **660.4 Shoulder (girdle) dystocia**
[0,1,3]
Impacted shoulders
DEF: Obstructed labor due to impacted fetal shoulders.

✓5th **660.5 Locked twins**
[0,1,3]

✓5th **660.6 Failed trial of labor, unspecified**
[0,1,3]
Failed trial of labor, without mention of condition or suspected condition

✓5th **660.7 Failed forceps or vacuum extractor, unspecified**
[0,1,3]
Application of ventouse or forceps, without mention of condition

✓5th **660.8 Other causes of obstructed labor**
[0,1,3]
Use additional code to identify condition

✓5th **660.9 Unspecified obstructed labor**
[0,1,3]
Dystocia:
NOS
fetal NOS
maternal NO

✓4th **661 Abnormality of forces of labor**

Requires fifth-digit; valid digits are in [brackets] under each code. See beginning of section 660-669 for definitions.

✓5th **661.0 Primary uterine inertia**
[0,1,3]
Failure of cervical dilation
Hypotonic uterine dysfunction, primary
Prolonged latent phase of labor
DEF: Lack of efficient contractions during labor causing prolonged labor.

✓5th **661.1 Secondary uterine inertia**
[0,1,3]
Arrested active phase of labor
Hypotonic uterine dysfunction, secondary

✓5th **661.2 Other and unspecified uterine inertia**
[0,1,3]
Atony of uterus without hemorrhage
Desultory labor
Irregular labor
Poor contractions
Slow slope active phase of labor
EXCLUDES *atony of uterus with hemorrhage (666.1)*
postpartum atony of uterus without hemorrhage (669.8)

✓5th **661.3 Precipitate labor**
[0,1,3]
DEF: Rapid labor and delivery.

✓5th **661.4 Hypertonic, incoordinate, or prolonged uterine contractions**
[0,1,3]
Cervical spasm
Contraction ring (dystocia)
Dyscoordinate labor
Hourglass contraction of uterus
Hypertonic uterine dysfunction
Incoordinate uterine action
Retraction ring (Bandl's) (pathological)
Tetanic contractions
Uterine dystocia NOS
Uterine spasm

✓5th **661.9 Unspecified abnormality of labor**
[0,1,3]

✓4th **662 Long labor**
Requires fifth-digit; valid digits are in [brackets] under each code. See beginning of section 660-669 for definitions.

✓5th **662.0 Prolonged first stage**
[0,1,3]

✓5th **662.1 Prolonged labor, unspecified**
[0,1,3]

✓5th **662.2 Prolonged second stage**
[0,1,3]

✓5th **662.3 Delayed delivery of second twin, triplet, etc.**
[0,1,3]

✓4th **663 Umbilical cord complications**
Requires fifth-digit; valid digits are in [brackets] under each code. See beginning of section 660-669 for definitions.

✓5th **663.0 Prolapse of cord**
[0,1,3] Presentation of cord
DEF: Abnormal presentation of fetus; marked by protruding umbilical cord during labor; can cause fetal death.

✓5th **663.1 Cord around neck, with compression**
[0,1,3] Cord tightly around neck

✓5th **663.2 Other and unspecified cord entanglement, with compression**
[0,1,3] Entanglement of cords of twins in mono-amniotic sac
Knot in cord (with compression)

✓5th **663.3 Other and unspecified cord entanglement, without mention of compression**
[0,1,3]

✓5th **663.4 Short cord**
[0,1,3]

✓5th **663.5 Vasa previa**
[0,1,3] DEF: Abnormal presentation of fetus marked by blood vessels of umbilical cord in front of fetal head.

✓5th **663.6 Vascular lesions of cord**
[0,1,3] Bruising of cord
Hematoma of cord
Thrombosis of vessels of cord

✓5th **663.8 Other umbilical cord complications**
[0,1,3] Velamentous insertion of umbilical cord

✓5th **663.9 Unspecified umbilical cord complication**
[0,1,3]

✓4th **664 Trauma to perineum and vulva during delivery**
Requires fifth-digit; valid digits are in [brackets] under each code. See beginning of section 660-669 for definitions.
INCLUDES damage from instruments
that from extension of episiotomy

✓5th **664.0 First-degree perineal laceration**
[0,1,4] Perineal laceration, rupture, or tear involving:
fourchette
hymen
labia
skin
vagina
vulva

✓5th **664.1 Second-degree perineal laceration**
[0,1,4] Perineal laceration, rupture, or tear (following episiotomy) involving:
pelvic floor
perineal muscles
vaginal muscles
EXCLUDES *that involving anal sphincter (664.2)*

Perineal Lacerations

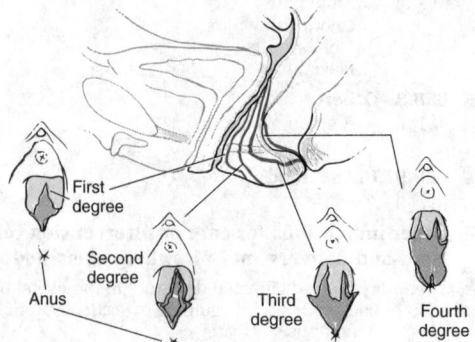

✓5th **664.2 Third-degree perineal laceration**
[0,1,4] Perineal laceration, rupture, or tear (following episiotomy) involving:
anal sphincter
rectovaginal septum
sphincter NOS
EXCLUDES *anal sphincter tear during delivery not associated with third-degree perineal laceration (664.6)*
that with anal or rectal mucosal laceration (664.3)

✓5th **664.3 Fourth-degree perineal laceration**
[0,1,4] Perineal laceration, rupture, or tear as classifiable to 664.2 and involving also:
anal mucosa
rectal mucosa

✓5th **664.4 Unspecified perineal laceration**
[0,1,4] Central laceration

✓5th **664.5 Vulval and perineal hematoma**
[0,1,4]

✓5th **664.6 Anal sphincter tear complicating delivery, not associated with third-degree perineal laceration**
[0,1,4]
EXCLUDES *third-degree perineal laceration (664.2)*

✓5th **664.8 Other specified trauma to perineum and vulva**
[0,1,4]

✓5th **664.9 Unspecified trauma to perineum and vulva**
[0,1,4]

✓4th **665 Other obstetrical trauma**
Requires fifth-digit; valid digits are in [brackets] under each code. See beginning of section 660-669 for definitions.
INCLUDES damage from instruments

✓5th **665.0 Rupture of uterus before onset of labor**
[0,1,3]

✓5th **665.1 Rupture of uterus during labor**
[0,1] Rupture of uterus NOS

✓5th **665.2 Inversion of uterus**
[0,2,4]

✓5th **665.3 Laceration of cervix**
[0,1,4]

✓5th **665.4 High vaginal laceration**
[0,1,4] Laceration of vaginal wall or sulcus without mention of perineal laceration

✓5th **665.5 Other injury to pelvic organs**
[0,1,4] Injury to:
bladder
urethra

✓5th **665.6 Damage to pelvic joints and ligaments**
[0,1,4] Avulsion of inner symphyseal cartilage
Damage to coccyx
Separation of symphysis (pubis)

✓5th **665.7 Pelvic hematoma**
[0-2, 4] Hematoma of vagina

✓5th **665.8 Other specified obstetrical trauma**
[0-4]

5th **665.9 Unspecified obstetrical trauma**
[0-4]

4th **666 Postpartum hemorrhage**
Requires fifth-digit; valid digits are in [brackets] under each code. See beginning of section 660-669 for definitions.

5th **666.0 Third-stage hemorrhage**
[0,2,4] Hemorrhage associated with retained, trapped, or adherent placenta
Retained placenta NOS

5th **666.1 Other immediate postpartum hemorrhage**
[0,2,4] Atony of uterus with hemorrhage
Hemorrhage within the first 24 hours following delivery of placenta
Postpartum atony of uterus with hemorrhage
Postpartum hemorrhage (atonic) NOS
EXCLUDES *atony of uterus without hemorrhage (661.2)*
postpartum atony of uterus without hemorrhage (669.8)

5th **666.2 Delayed and secondary postpartum hemorrhage**
[0,2,4] Hemorrhage:
after the first 24 hours following delivery
associated with retained portions of placenta or membranes
Postpartum hemorrhage specified as delayed or secondary
Retained products of conception NOS, following delivery

5th **666.3 Postpartum coagulation defects**
[0,2,4] Postpartum:
afibrinogenemia
fibrinolysis

4th **667 Retained placenta or membranes, without hemorrhage**
Requires fifth-digit; valid digits are in [brackets] under each code. See beginning of section 660-669 for definitions.
DEF: Postpartum condition resulting from failure to expel placental membrane tissues due to failed contractions of uterine wall.

5th **667.0 Retained placenta without hemorrhage**
[0,2,4] Placenta accreta } without hemorrhage
Retained placenta: } without hemorrhage
NOS } without hemorrhage
total } without hemorrhage

5th **667.1 Retained portions of placenta or membranes, without hemorrhage**
[0,2,4] Retained products of conception following delivery, without hemorrhage

4th **668 Complications of the administration of anesthetic or other sedation in labor and delivery**
Requires fifth-digit; valid digits are in [brackets] under each code. See beginning of section 660-669 for definitions.
INCLUDES complications arising from the administration of a general or local anesthetic, analgesic, or other sedation in labor and delivery
EXCLUDES *reaction to spinal or lumbar puncture (349.0)*
spinal headache (349.0)
Use additional code(s) to further specify complication

5th **668.0 Pulmonary complications**
[0-4] Inhalation (aspiration) of stomach contents or secretions } following anesthesia or other sedation in labor or delivery
Mendelson's syndrome } following anesthesia or other sedation in labor or delivery
Pressure collapse of lung } following anesthesia or other sedation in labor or delivery

5th **668.1 Cardiac complications**
[0-4] Cardiac arrest or failure following anesthesia or other sedation in labor and delivery

5th **668.2 Central nervous system complications**
[0-4] Cerebral anoxia following anesthesia or other sedation in labor and delivery

5th **668.8 Other complications of anesthesia or other sedation in labor and delivery**
[0-4]

5th **668.9 Unspecified complication of anesthesia and other sedation**
[0-4]

4th **669 Other complications of labor and delivery, not elsewhere classified**
Requires fifth-digit; valid digits are in [brackets] under each code. See beginning of section 660-669 for definitions.

5th **669.0 Maternal distress**
[0-4] Metabolic disturbance in labor and delivery

5th **669.1 Shock during or following labor and delivery**
[0-4] Obstetric shock

5th **669.2 Maternal hypotension syndrome**
[0-4] **DEF: Low arterial blood pressure, in mother, during labor and delivery.**

5th **669.3 Acute renal failure following labor and delivery**
[0,2,4]

5th **669.4 Other complications of obstetrical surgery and procedures**
[0-4] Cardiac:
arrest } following cesarean or other obstetrical surgery or procedure, including delivery NOS
failure } following cesarean or other obstetrical surgery or procedure, including delivery NOS
Cerebral } following cesarean or other obstetrical surgery or procedure, including delivery NOS
anoxia } following cesarean or other obstetrical surgery or procedure, including delivery NOS
EXCLUDES *complications of obstetrical surgical wounds (674.1-674.3)*

5th **669.5 Forceps or vacuum extractor delivery without mention of indication**
[0,1] Delivery by ventouse, without mention of indication

5th **669.6 Breech extraction, without mention of indication**
[0,1]
EXCLUDES *breech delivery NOS (652.2)*

5th **669.7 Cesarean delivery, without mention of indication**
[0,1]

5th **669.8 Other complications of labor and delivery**
[0-4]

5th **669.9 Unspecified complication of labor and delivery**
[0-4]

COMPLICATIONS OF THE PUERPERIUM (670-677)

Note: Categories 671 and 673-676 include the listed conditions even if they occur during pregnancy or childbirth.

The following fifth-digit subclassification is for use with categories 670-676 to denote the current episode of care. Valid fifth-digits are in [brackets] under each code.
0 unspecified as to episode of care or not applicable
1 delivered, with or without mention of antepartum condition
2 delivered, with mention of postpartum complication
3 antepartum condition or complication
4 postpartum condition or complication

4th **670 Major puerperal infection**
[0,2,4] Requires fifth-digit; valid digits are in [brackets] under each code. See beginning of section 670-676 for definitions.

5th Use 0 as fourth-digit for this category
Puerperal:
endometritis
fever (septic)
pelvic:
cellulitis
sepsis
peritonitis
pyemia
salpingitis
septicemia
EXCLUDES *infection following abortion (639.0)*
minor genital tract infection following delivery (646.6)
puerperal pyrexia NOS (672)
puerperal fever NOS (672)
puerperal pyrexia of unknown origin (672)
urinary tract infection following delivery (646.6)
DEF: Infection and inflammation, following childbirth.

✓4th **671 Venous complications in pregnancy and the puerperium**

Requires fifth-digit; valid digits are in [brackets] under each code. See beginning of section 670-676 for definitions.

✓5th **671.0 Varicose veins of legs**
[0-4] Varicose veins NOS
DEF: Distended, tortuous veins on legs associated with pregnancy.

✓5th **671.1 Varicose veins of vulva and perineum**
[0-4]
DEF: Distended, tortuous veins on external female genitalia associated with pregnancy.

✓5th **671.2 Superficial thrombophlebitis**
[0-4] Thrombophlebitis (superficial)

✓5th **671.3 Deep phlebothrombosis, antepartum**
[0,1,3] Deep vein thrombosis antepartum

✓5th **671.4 Deep phlebothrombosis, postpartum**
[0,2,4] Deep-vein thrombosis, postpartum
Pelvic thrombophlebitis, postpartum
Phlegmasia alba dolens (puerperal)

✓5th **671.5 Other phlebitis and thrombosis**
[0-4] Cerebral venous thrombosis
Thrombosis of intracranial venous sinus

✓5th **671.8 Other venous complications**
[0-4] Hemorrhoids

✓5th **671.9 Unspecified venous complication**
[0-4] Phlebitis NOS
Thrombosis NOS

✓4th **672 Pyrexia of unknown origin during the puerperium**
[0,2,4]

Requires fifth-digit; valid digits are in [brackets] under each code. See beginning of section 670-676 for definitions.

✓5th Use 0 as fourth-digit for this category
Postpartum fever NOS
Puerperal fever NOS
Puerperal pyrexia NOS
DEF: Fever of unknown origin experienced by the mother after childbirth.

✓4th **673 Obstetrical pulmonary embolism**

INCLUDES pulmonary emboli in pregnancy, childbirth, or the puerperium, or specified as puerperal

EXCLUDES *embolism following abortion (639.6)*

✓5th **673.0 Obstetrical air embolism**
[0-4] DEF: Sudden blocking of pulmonary artery with air or nitrogen bubbles during puerperium.

✓5th **673.1 Amniotic fluid embolism**
[0-4] DEF: Sudden onset of pulmonary artery blockage from amniotic fluid entering the mother's circulation near the end of pregnancy due to strong uterine contractions.

✓5th **673.2 Obstetrical blood-clot embolism**
[0-4] Puerperal pulmonary embolism NOS
DEF: Blood clot blocking artery in the lung; associated with pregnancy.

✓5th **673.3 Obstetrical pyemic and septic embolism**
[0-4]

✓5th **673.8 Other pulmonary embolism**
[0-4] Fat embolism

✓4th **674 Other and unspecified complications of the puerperium, not elsewhere classified**

Requires fifth-digit; valid digits are in [brackets] under each code. See beginning of section 670-676 for definitions.

✓5th **674.0 Cerebrovascular disorders in the puerperium**
[0-4] Any condition classifiable to 430-434, 436-437 occurring during pregnancy, childbirth, or the puerperium, or specified as puerperal

EXCLUDES *intracranial venous sinus thrombosis (671.5)*

✓5th **674.1 Disruption of cesarean wound**
[0,2,4] Dehiscence or disruption of uterine wound

EXCLUDES *uterine rupture before onset of labor (665.0)*
uterine rupture during labor (665.1)

✓5th **674.2 Disruption of perineal wound**
[0,2,4] Breakdown of perineum
Disruption of wound of:
episiotomy
perineal laceration
Secondary perineal tear

✓5th **674.3 Other complications of obstetrical surgical wounds**
[0,2,4]
Hematoma, Hemorrhage, Infection } of cesarean section or perineal wound

EXCLUDES *damage from instruments in delivery (664.0-665.9)*

✓5th **674.4 Placental polyp**
[0,2,4]

✓5th **674.5 Peripartum cardiomyopathy**
[0-4] Postpartum cardiomyopathy
DEF: Any structural or functional abnormality of the ventricular myocardium, non-inflammatory disease of obscure or unknown etiology with onset during the postpartum period.

✓5th **674.8 Other**
[0,2,4] Hepatorenal syndrome, following delivery
Postpartum:
subinvolution of uterus
uterine hypertrophy

✓5th **674.9 Unspecified**
[0,2,4] Sudden death of unknown cause during the puerperium

✓4th **675 Infections of the breast and nipple associated with childbirth**

Requires fifth-digit; valid digits are in [brackets] under each code. See beginning of section 670-676 for definitions.

INCLUDES the listed conditions during pregnancy, childbirth, or the puerperium

✓5th **675.0 Infections of nipple**
[0-4] Abscess of nipple

✓5th **675.1 Abscess of breast**
[0-4] Abscess:
mammary
subareolar
submammary
purulent
retromammary
submammary

✓5th **675.2 Nonpurulent mastitis**
[0-4] Lymphangitis of breast
Mastitis:
NOS
interstitial
parenchymatous

Lactation Process: Ejection Reflex Arc

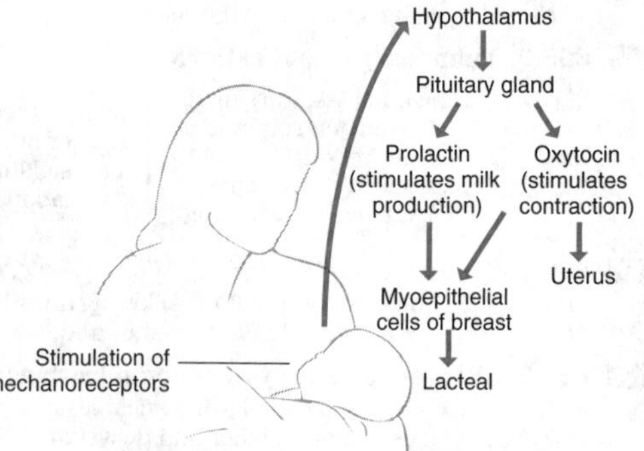

✓5th **675.8 Other specified infections of the breast and nipple**
[0-4]

✓5th **675.9 Unspecified infection of the breast and nipple**
[0-4]

✓4th **676 Other disorders of the breast associated with childbirth and disorders of lactation**

Requires fifth-digit; valid digits are in [brackets] under each code. See beginning of section 670-676 for definitions.

INCLUDES the listed conditions during pregnancy, the puerperium, or lactation

✓5th **676.0 Retracted nipple**
[0-4]

✓5th **676.1 Cracked nipple**
[0-4] Fissure of nipple

✓5th **676.2 Engorgement of breasts**
[0-4]
DEF: Abnormal accumulation of milk in ducts of breast.

✓5th **676.3 Other and unspecified disorder of breast**
[0-4]

✓5th **676.4 Failure of lactation**
[0-4] Agalactia
DEF: Abrupt ceasing of milk secretion by breast.

✓5th **676.5 Suppressed lactation**
[0-4]

✓5th **676.6 Galactorrhea**
[0-4] EXCLUDES *galactorrhea not associated with childbirth (611.6)*
DEF: Excessive or persistent milk secretion by breast; may be in absence of nursing.

✓5th **676.8 Other disorders of lactation**
[0-4] Galactocele
DEF: Galactocele: Obstructed mammary gland, creating retention cyst, results in milk-filled cysts enlarging mammary gland.

✓5th **676.9 Unspecified disorder of lactation**
[0-4]

677 Late effect of complication of pregnancy, childbirth, and the puerperium

Note: This category is to be used to indicate conditions in 632-648.9 and 651-676.9 as the cause of the late effect, themselves classifiable elsewhere. The "late effects" include conditions specified as such, or as sequelae, which may occur at any time after puerperium.

Code first any sequelae

OTHER MATERNAL AND FETAL COMPLICATIONS (678-679)

The following fifth-digit subclassification is for use with categories 678-679 to denote the current episode of care. Valid fifth-digits are in [brackets] under each code.

0 unspecified as to episode of care or not applicable
1 delivered, with or without mention of antepartum condition
2 delivered, with mention of postpartum complication
3 antepartum condition or complication
4 postpartum condition or complication

✓4th **678 Other fetal conditions**

✓5th **678.0 Fetal hematologic conditions**
[0,1,3] Fetal anemia
Fetal thrombocytopenia
Fetal twin to twin transfusion
EXCLUDES *fetal and neonatal hemorrhage (772.0-772.9)*
fetal hematologic disorders affecting newborn (776.0-776.9)
fetal-maternal hemorrhage (656.00-656.03)
isoimmunization incompatibility (656.10-656.13, 656.20-656.23)

✓5th **678.1 Fetal conjoined twins**
[0,1,3]

✓4th **679 Complications of in utero procedures**

✓5th **679.0 Maternal complications from in utero procedure**
[0-4]
EXCLUDES *maternal history of in utero procedure during previous pregnancy (V23.86)*

✓5th **679.1 Fetal complications from in utero procedure**
[0-4] Fetal complications from amniocentesis
EXCLUDES *newborn affected by in utero procedure (760.61-760.64)*

Chapter 12: Skin and Subcutaneous Tissue (680–709)

This chapter classifies diseases and disorders of the epidermis, dermis, subcutaneous tissue, nails, scar tissue, sebaceous glands, sweat glands, hair, and hair follicles. The sections of this chapter are as follows:

- Infections of skin and subcutaneous tissue (680–686)
- Other inflammatory conditions of skin and subcutaneous tissue (690–698)
- Other diseases of skin and subcutaneous tissue (700–709)

Infections of the Skin and Subcutaneous Tissue (680–686)

Certain infections and parasitic diseases of the skin and subcutaneous tissue such as herpes simplex and herpes zoster, viral warts, and molluscum contagiosum are classified to chapter 1. Refer to the alphabetic index for instruction concerning the correct classification of infectious conditions of the skin and subcutaneous tissue.

This subchapter classifies diseases and disorders such as boils, carbuncles, furuncles, cellulitis, abscess, lymphadenitis, local infections, and pilonidal cysts.

When assigning a code from categories 680–686, also assign a code (as a secondary code) to identify the infective organism, such as Staphylococcus (subcategory 041.1).

Carbuncle and Furuncle (680)

Carbuncle and furuncle are infections caused by either aerobic or anaerobic bacterial organisms. A carbuncle is a collection of pus contained in a cavity or sac. A furuncle is a painful nodule formed by circumscribed inflammation of the skin and subcutaneous tissue, which encloses a central core.

Use an additional code to identify the infective organism, typically Streptococcus or Staphylococcus. Use the appropriate fourth digit to indicate the anatomic location of the furuncle or carbuncle.

Cellulitis and Abscess (681–682)

Cellulitis is a diffuse infection of the dermis and subcutaneous tissues often caused by group A Strep or Staphylococcus aureus, but sometimes caused by other organisms. Cellulitis may be associated with an abscess, which is a collection of pus resulting from an acute or chronic localized infection with tissue destruction. Category 681 includes lymphangitis and abscess and is often associated with cellulitis of the skin affecting fingers and toes.

Use an additional code to identify the infective organism, typically Streptococcus or Staphylococcus.

Abscess and lymphangitis are included in category 681. Do not code in addition to the cellulitis.

When cellulitis occurs with chronic skin ulcer (category 707), code both conditions.

Example:

> Chronic pressure ulcer of the heel with cellulitis, unspecified organism, is coded 707.07 Pressure ulcer, heel and 682. 7. Sequencing is dependent upon circumstances of the episode of care.

When cellulitis occurs secondary to a superficial injury (e.g., frostbite or burn) two codes are required sequenced according to the circumstances of the episode of care. Example:

Patient seen for care of staphylococcal cellulitis of a second-degree burn on the hand is coded:

682.4	Cellulitis of the hand, except fingers and thumb
944.20	Burn, second degree of hand, unspecified site
041.10	Staphylococcus, unspecified

There are sites other than skin and subcutaneous tissue where cellulitis may occur. These sites include the cervix, larynx, nose, penis and tonsils. Coders should follow the instructions in the alphabetic index to code these sites.

Other Inflammatory Conditions of Skin and Subcutaneous Tissue (690–698)

Other inflammatory conditions that affect the skin such as dermatitis, eczema, sunburn, rosacea, lupus erythematosus, psoriasis, and lichen are classified to this section.

Contact Dermatitis and Other Eczema (692)

Contact dermatitis is classified by agent. The fourth digit specifies the agent such as detergents, solvents, medicines and drugs, food in contact with skin, solar radiation, and metals.

Palmar Plantar Erythrodysesthesia (693.0)

Palmar plantar erythrodysesthesia (PPE), also called hand and foot syndrome, may be described as an adverse effect of certain cancer therapies that occurs as a result of small amounts of antineoplastic or biologic drugs leaking from the capillaries into the tissues. Tissue damage occurs in the palms of the hands and soles of the feet due to the friction and heat generated during the course of normal daily activities. Symptoms include tenderness, redness, and peeling skin resembling a sunburn. Palmar plantar erythrodysesthesia is reported as drug dermatitis, with code 693.0 Dermatitis due to substances taken internally. Assign the appropriate E code for the adverse effect of drug. In addition, report the malignancy.

Erythematous Conditions (695.1)

Clinical classifications for erythema multiforme are based on the pattern and distribution of cutaneous lesions. Different causes, characteristics, and risk factors exist between erythema multiforme, Stevens-Johnson syndrome, and toxic epidermal necrolysis. The term "erythema multiforme" (EM) refers to the "multiple forms" in which these conditions, characterized by redness of the skin, are manifest. The characteristic redness (erythema) is produced by congestion of the capillaries. The "multiforme" portion of the diagnosis refers to the wide range of clinical presentation in which it appears, from the nature of symptoms and associated conditions to the variance in degrees of severity.

Erythema multiforme (695.10–695.12) is a hypersensitivity (allergic) reaction that can occur at any age but primarily affects children or young adults. It may occur in response to medications, infections, or illness. The causal agent induces damage to dermal blood vessels and tissues. Clinical presentation may range from a mild, self-limited rash (minor) to a more severe, life-threatening form involving mucous membranes. These erythematous conditions are characterized by the sudden onset of multiple, symmetrical pruritic (itching) skin lesions of the limbs and face that may spread and form blisters. Other associated symptoms include fever, malaise, and joint pain. Facial lesions are often associated with painful conjunctivitis, vision abnormalities, and buccal lesions. Erythema multiforme minor accounts for approximately 80 percent of EM cases.

In Stevens-Johnson syndrome (695.13–695.14), the lesions are more extensive than those characteristic of erythema multiforme major, and the systemic symptoms are more severe. Multiple body areas are usually involved, especially the mucous membranes. An overlap condition with an intermediate percent of body surface area affected (10 to 30 percent) is identified as SJS-TEN overlap syndrome (695.14). TEN (toxic epidermal necrolysis) (695.15) (also called Lyell's syndrome) involves multiple large blisters with exfoliation of all or most of the skin and mucous membranes, generally involving over 30 percent of the body surface area—similar to the skin loss with a severe burn, necessitating treatment in a burn unit.

SJS is part of the same spectrum of disease as TEN, although it generally involves body surface area of less than 10 percent. Erythema multiforme major has been strongly associated with herpes virus infection, while Stevens-Johnson syndrome and TEN have been associated with severe adverse drug reactions to certain medications that cause an extreme immunologically mediated abnormal metabolic reaction in sensitive people.

Three instructional notes at subcategory 695.1 Erythema multiforme provide important coding and sequencing information. Multiple codes may be necessary to report any associated manifestations, causal drug E codes, and the percentage of skin exfoliation.

Lupus Erythematosus (695.4)

Lupus erythematosus is a chronic disease that causes inflammation of the connective tissue of the skin only. This disease affects nine times as many women as men, usually those of childbearing age.

Note that this subcategory includes discoid lupus erythematosus, but excludes systemic lupus erythematosus.

Exfoliation Due to Erythematous Conditions According to Extent of Body Surface Involved (695.5)

Erythematous conditions are skin disorders characterized by diffuse redness (erythema). Exfoliation describes scaling and flaking off of the epidermal layers of the skin. Many of the conditions classified to code subcategory 695.1 result in scaling and flaking of the skin. The percentage of body surface involved correlates to the severity of presentation and represents the level of clinical care required. Specific codes indicate the severity of erythematous conditions. To help indicate severity, the percentage of skin exfoliation due to these conditions is reported with an additional code from subcategory 695.5. An instructional note is included with this subcategory to "Code first the erythematous condition causing exfoliation." These additional codes report the percentage of body surface involved, ranging from less than 10 percent to 90 percent or more of body surface.

Psoriasis (696)

Psoriasis is a common skin disease characterized by patches of inflamed, red skin, covered by silvery scales and sometimes accompanied by painful swelling and stiffness of joints (arthritis). The skin stratum becomes thickened, particularly over the elbows, knees, scalp, and trunk.

Other Diseases of Skin and Subcutaneous Tissue (700–709)

These codes describe conditions of the skin and subcutaneous tissues. The conditions in this section are benign but may require treatment.

Categories include:

- Corns and callosities (700)
- Other hypertrophic and atrophic conditions of skin (701)

Chronic Ulcer of Skin (707) and Pressure [Decubitus] Ulcer Staging (707.2)

Subclassification 707.0 reports conditions also known as bedsores or pressure sores. These lesions initially affect superficial tissues and, depending on the state of patient's health and other circumstances, may progress to affect muscle and bone. Patients at risk for developing pressure ulcers include the bedridden, those who are unconscious or immobile such as stroke patients, or those with paralysis and limited motion. Intrinsic loss of pain and pressure sensations, disuse atrophy, malnutrition, anemia, and infection contribute to the formation and progression of pressure ulcers. In the early stages, the condition is reversible, but left untended, the pressure ulcer can become extensively infected, necrotic and, ultimately, irreversible.

Code assignment reflects the National Pressure Ulcer Advisory Panel (NPUAP) definition and staging of pressure ulcers. A pressure ulcer is defined as a "localized injury to the skin and/or underlying tissue, usually over a bony prominence, as a result of pressure, or pressure in combination with shear and/or friction." Clinicians ordinarily characterize pressure ulcers by location, shape, depth, and healing status. The depth of the lesion or stage of ulcer is the most important element in clinical measurement:

- Unstageable (702.25): Lesion inaccessible for evaluation due to nonremovable dressings, eschar, sterile blister, or suspected deep injury in evolution are unstageable. Deep tissue injury may be difficult to detect in individuals with dark skin tones, and as such evolution of the wound may progress rapidly. Suspected deep tissue injury may be characterized by purple or maroon discoloration of the skin with or without blistering. Affected tissue may be painful and variant in temperature and texture from surrounding normal tissue.
- Stage I (707.21): Nonblanching erythema (a reddened area on the skin)
- Stage II (707.22): Abrasion, blister, shallow open crater, or other partial-thickness skin loss
- Stage III (707.23): Full-thickness skin loss involving damage or necrosis into subcutaneous soft tissues
- Stage IV (707.24): Full-thickness skin loss with necrosis of soft tissues through to the muscle, tendons, or tissues around underlying bone

Previous ICD-9-CM coding did not differentiate stages, with unique codes only for pressure ulcers for the more common anatomic sites (707.05 for buttock, for example). This method of classification precluded the use of coded records to accurately reflect severity data for quality improvement initiatives. Assign the appropriate code for the site of ulcer from subcategory 707.0 with an additional code from subcategory 707.2 to specify the stage of the ulcer.

12. DISEASES OF THE SKIN AND SUBCUTANEOUS TISSUE (680-709)

INFECTIONS OF SKIN AND SUBCUTANEOUS TISSUE (680-686)

EXCLUDES *certain infections of skin classified under "Infectious and Parasitic Diseases," such as:*
erysipelas (035)
erysipeloid of Rosenbach (027.1)
herpes:
simplex (054.0-054.9)
zoster (053.0-053.9)
molluscum contagiosum (078.0)
viral warts (078.10)

✓4th 680 Carbuncle and furuncle

INCLUDES boil
furunculosis

DEF: Carbuncle: necrotic boils in skin and subcutaneous tissue of neck or back mainly due to staphylococcal infection.

DEF: Furuncle: circumscribed inflammation of corium and subcutaneous tissue due to staphylococcal infection.

680.0 Face
Ear [any part]
Face [any part, except eye]
Nose (septum)
Temple (region)
EXCLUDES *eyelid (373.13)*
lacrimal apparatus (375.31)
orbit (376.01)

680.1 Neck

680.2 Trunk
Abdominal wall
Back [any part, except buttocks]
Breast
Chest wall
Flank
Groin
Pectoral region
Perineum
Umbilicus
EXCLUDES *buttocks (680.5)*
external genital organs:
female (616.4)
male (607.2, 608.4)

680.3 Upper arm and forearm
Arm [any part, except hand]
Axilla
Shoulder

680.4 Hand
Finger [any]
Thumb
Wrist

680.5 Buttock
Anus
Gluteal region

680.6 Leg, except foot
Ankle
Hip
Knee
Thigh

680.7 Foot
Heel
Toe

680.8 Other specified sites
Head [any part, except face]
Scalp
EXCLUDES *external genital organs:*
female (616.4)
male (607.2, 608.4)

680.9 Unspecified site
Boil NOS
Carbuncle NOS
Furuncle NOS

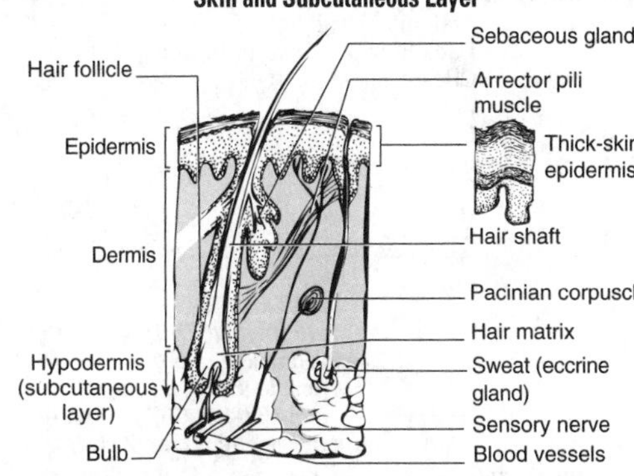

✓4th 681 Cellulitis and abscess of finger and toe

INCLUDES that with lymphangitis

Use additional code to identify organism, such as Staphylococcus (041.1)

DEF: Acute suppurative inflammation and edema in subcutaneous tissue or muscle of finger or toe.

✓5th 681.0 Finger

681.00 Cellulitis and abscess, unspecified

681.01 Felon
Pulp abscess
Whitlow
EXCLUDES *herpetic whitlow (054.6)*
DEF: Painful abscess of fingertips caused by infection in the closed space of terminal phalanx.

681.02 Onychia and paronychia of finger
Panaritium } of finger
Perionychia }
DEF: Onychia: inflammation of nail matrix; causes nail loss.
DEF: Paronychia: inflammation of tissue folds around nail.

✓5th 681.1 Toe

681.10 Cellulitis and abscess, unspecified

681.11 Onychia and paronychia of toe
Panaritium } of toe
Perionychia }

681.9 Cellulitis and abscess of unspecified digit
Infection of nail NOS

✓4th 682 Other cellulitis and abscess

INCLUDES abscess (acute) } (with lymphangitis) except of finger or toe
cellulitis (diffuse) }
lymphangitis, acute }

Use additional code to identify organism, such as Staphylococcus (041.1)

EXCLUDES *lymphangitis (chronic) (subacute) (457.2)*

DEF: Cellulitis: Acute suppurative inflammation of deep subcutaneous tissue and sometimes muscle due to infection of wound, burn or other lesion.

682.0 Face
Cheek, external
Chin
Forehead
Nose, external
Submandibular
Temple (region)
EXCLUDES *ear [any part] (380.10-380.16)*
eyelid (373.13)
lacrimal apparatus (375.31)
lip (528.5)
mouth (528.3)
nose (internal) (478.1)
orbit (376.01)

682.1 Neck

682.2 Trunk
Abdominal wall
Back [any part, except buttock]
Chest wall
Flank
Groin
Pectoral region
Perineum
Umbilicus, except newborn
EXCLUDES *anal and rectal regions (566)*
breast:
NOS (611.0)
puerperal (675.1)
external genital organs:
female (616.3-616.4)
male (604.0, 607.2, 608.4)
umbilicus, newborn (771.4)

682.3 Upper arm and forearm
Arm [any part, except hand]
Axilla
Shoulder
EXCLUDES *hand (682.4)*

682.4 Hand, except fingers and thumb
Wrist
EXCLUDES *finger and thumb (681.00-681.02)*

682.5 Buttock
Gluteal region
EXCLUDES *anal and rectal regions (566)*

682.6 Leg, except foot
Ankle
Hip
Knee
Thigh

682.7 Foot, except toes
Heel
EXCLUDES *toe (681.10-681.11)*

682.8 Other specified sites
Head [except face]
Scalp
EXCLUDES *face (682.0)*

682.9 Unspecified site
Abscess NOS
Cellulitis NOS
Lymphangitis, acute NOS
EXCLUDES *lymphangitis NOS (457.2)*

683 Acute lymphadenitis
Abscess (acute) / Adenitis, acute / Lymphadenitis, acute } lymph gland or node, except mesenteric
Use additional code to identify organism, such as Staphylococcus (041.1)
EXCLUDES *enlarged glands NOS (785.6)*
lymphadenitis:
chronic or subacute, except mesenteric (289.1)
mesenteric (acute) (chronic) (subacute) (289.2)
unspecified (289.3)

DEF: Acute inflammation of lymph nodes due to primary infection located elsewhere in the body.

Lymphatic System of Head and Neck

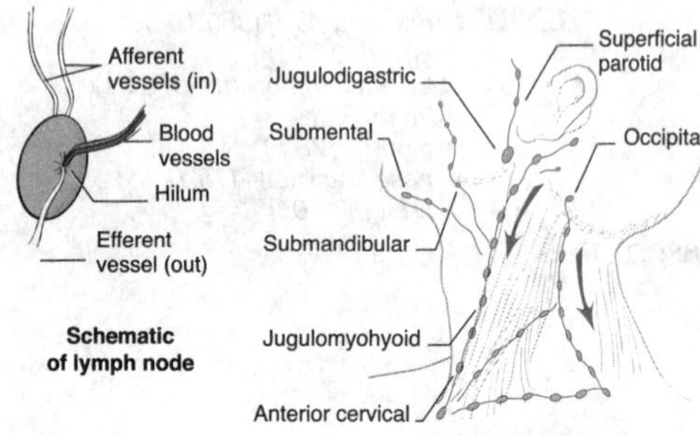

Stages of Pilonidal Disease

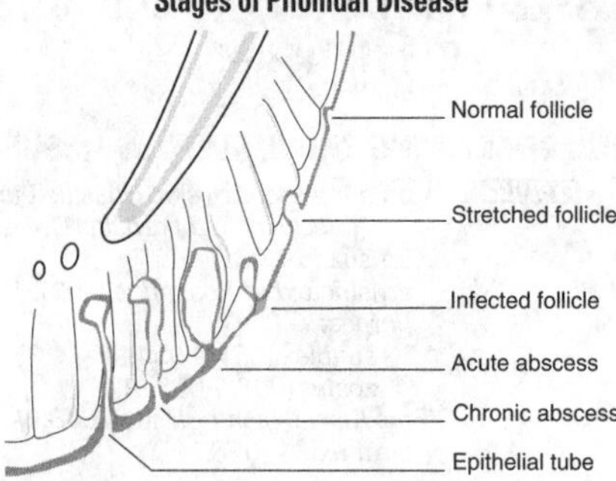

684 Impetigo
Impetiginization of other dermatoses
Impetigo (contagiosa) [any site] [any organism]:
bullous
circinate
neonatorum
simplex
Pemphigus neonatorum
EXCLUDES *impetigo herpetiformis (694.3)*

DEF: Infectious skin disease commonly occurring in children; caused by group A streptococci or *Staphylococcus aureus;* skin lesions usually appear on the face and consist of subcorneal vesicles and bullae that burst and form yellow crusts.

✓4th **685 Pilonidal cyst**
INCLUDES fistula / sinus } coccygeal or pilonidal

DEF: Hair-containing cyst or sinus in the tissues of the sacrococcygeal area; often drains through opening at the postanal dimple.

685.0 With abscess

685.1 Without mention of abscess

✓4th **686 Other local infections of skin and subcutaneous tissue**
Use additional code to identify any infectious organism (041.0-041.8)

✓5th **686.0 Pyoderma**
Dermatitis:
purulent
septic
Dermatitis:
suppurative

DEF: Nonspecific purulent skin disease related most to furuncles, pustules, or possibly carbuncles.

686.00 Pyoderma, unspecified

686.01 Pyoderma gangrenosum
DEF: Persistent debilitating skin disease, characterized by irregular, boggy, blue-red ulcerations, with central healing and undermined edges.

686.09 Other pyoderma

686.1 Pyogenic granuloma
Granuloma:
septic
suppurative
telangiectaticum
EXCLUDES *pyogenic granuloma of oral mucosa (528.9)*

DEF: Solitary polypoid capillary hemangioma often asociated with local irritation, trauma, and superimposed inflammation; located on the skin and gingival or oral mucosa.

686.8 Other specified local infections of skin and subcutaneous tissue
Bacterid (pustular)
Dermatitis vegetans
Ecthyma
Perlèche
EXCLUDES *dermatitis infectiosa eczematoides (690.8)*
panniculitis (729.30-729.39)

686.9 Unspecified local infection of skin and subcutaneous tissue
Fistula of skin NOS
Skin infection NOS
EXCLUDES *fistula to skin from internal organs – see Alphabetic Index*

OTHER INFLAMMATORY CONDITIONS OF SKIN AND SUBCUTANEOUS TISSUE (690-698)

EXCLUDES *panniculitis (729.30-729.39)*

✓4th **690 Erythematosquamous dermatosis**

EXCLUDES *eczematous dermatitis of eyelid (373.31)*
parakeratosis variegata (696.2)
psoriasis (696.0-696.1)
seborrheic keratosis (702.11-702.19)

✓5th **690.1 Seborrheic dermatitis**

690.10 Seborrheic dermatitis, unspecified
Seborrheic dermatitis NOS

690.11 Seborrhea capitis
Cradle cap

690.12 Seborrheic infantile dermatitis

690.18 Other seborrheic dermatitis

690.8 Other erythematosquamous dermatosis

✓4th **691 Atopic dermatitis and related conditions**

DEF: Atopic dermatitis: chronic, pruritic, inflammatory skin disorder found on the face and antecubital and popliteal fossae; noted in persons with a hereditary predisposition to pruritus, and often accompanied by allergic rhinitis, hay fever, asthma, and extreme itching; also called allergic dermatitis, allergic or atopic eczema, or disseminated neurodermatitis.

691.0 Diaper or napkin rash
Ammonia dermatitis
Diaper or napkin:
dermatitis
erythema
rash
Psoriasiform napkin eruption

691.8 Other atopic dermatitis and related conditions
Atopic dermatitis
Besnier's prurigo
Eczema:
atopic
flexural
intrinsic (allergic)
Neurodermatitis:
atopic
diffuse (of Brocq)

✓4th **692 Contact dermatitis and other eczema**

INCLUDES dermatitis:
NOS
contact
occupational
venenata
eczema (acute) (chronic):
NOS
allergic
erythematous
occupational

EXCLUDES *allergy NOS (995.3)*
contact dermatitis of eyelids (373.32)
dermatitis due to substances taken internally (693.0-693.9)
eczema of external ear (380.22)
perioral dermatitis (695.3)
urticarial reactions (708.0-708.9, 995.1)

DEF: Contact dermatitis: acute or chronic dermatitis caused by initial irritant effect of a substance, or by prior sensitization to a substance coming once again in contact with skin.

692.0 Due to detergents

692.1 Due to oils and greases

692.2 Due to solvents
Dermatitis due to solvents of:
chlorocompound, cyclohexane, ester, glycol, hydrocarbon, ketone } group

692.3 Due to drugs and medicines in contact with skin
Dermatitis (allergic) (contact) due to:
arnica
fungicides
iodine
keratolytics
mercurials
neomycin
pediculocides
phenols
scabicides
any drug applied to skin
Dermatitis medicamentosa due to drug applied to skin
Use additional E code to identify drug

EXCLUDES *allergy NOS due to drugs (995.27)*
dermatitis due to ingested drugs (693.0)
dermatitis medicamentosa NOS (693.0)

692.4 Due to other chemical products
Dermatitis due to:
acids
adhesive plaster
alkalis
caustics
dichromate
insecticide
nylon
plastic
rubber

692.5 Due to food in contact with skin
Dermatitis, contact, due to:
cereals
fish
flour
fruit
meat
milk

EXCLUDES *dermatitis due to:*
dyes (692.89)
ingested foods (693.1)
preservatives (692.89)

692.6 Due to plants [except food]
Dermatitis due to:
lacquer tree [Rhus verniciflua]
poison:
ivy [Rhus toxicodendron]
oak [Rhus diversiloba]
sumac [Rhus venenata]
vine [Rhus radicans]
primrose [Primula]
ragweed [Senecio jacobae]
other plants in contact with the skin

EXCLUDES *allergy NOS due to pollen (477.0)*
nettle rash (708.8)

✓5th **692.7 Due to solar radiation**

EXCLUDES *sunburn due to other ultraviolet radiation exposure (692.82)*

692.70 Unspecified dermatitis due to sun

692.71 Sunburn
First degree sunburn
Sunburn NOS

692.72 Acute dermatitis due to solar radiation
Acute solar skin damage NOS
Berlogue dermatitis
Photoallergic response
Phototoxic response
Polymorphus light eruption
Use additional E code to identify drug, if drug induced
EXCLUDES *sunburn (692.71, 692.76-692.77)*
DEF: Berloque dermatitis: Phytophotodermatitis due to sun exposure after use of a product containing bergamot oil; causes red patches, which may turn brown.
DEF: Photoallergic response: Dermatitis due to hypersensitivity to the sun; causes papulovesicular, eczematous or exudative eruptions.
DEF: Phototoxic response: Chemically induced sensitivity to sun causes burn-like reaction, occasionally vesiculation and subsequent hyperpigmentation.
DEF: Polymorphous light eruption: Inflammatory skin eruptions due to sunlight exposure; eruptions differ in size and shape.
DEF: Acute solar skin damage (NOS): Rapid, unspecified injury to skin from sun.

692.73 Actinic reticuloid and actinic granuloma
DEF: Actinic reticuloid: Dermatosis aggravated by light, causes chronic eczema-like eruption on exposed skin which extends to other unexposed surfaces; occurs in the eldery.
DEF: Actinic granuloma: Inflammatory response of skin to sun causing small nodule of microphages.

692.74 Other chronic dermatitis due to solar radiation
Chronic solar skin damage NOS
Solar elastosis
EXCLUDES *actinic [solar] keratosis (702.0)*
DEF: Solar elastosis: Premature aging of skin of light-skinned people; causes inelasticity, thinning or thickening, wrinkling, dryness, scaling and hyperpigmentation.
DEF: Chronic solar skin damage (NOS): Chronic skin impairment due to exposure to the sun, not otherwise specified.

692.75 Disseminated superficial actinic porokeratosis [DSAP]
DEF: Autosomal dominant skin condition occurring in skin that has been overexposed to the sun. Primarily affects women over the age of 16; characterized by numerous superficial annular, keratotic, brownish-red spots or thickenings with depressed centers and sharp, ridged borders. High risk that condition will evolve into squamous cell carcinoma.

692.76 Sunburn of second degree

692.77 Sunburn of third degree

692.79 Other dermatitis due to solar radiation
Hydroa aestivale
Photodermatitis } (due to sun)
Photosensitiveness } (due to sun)
Solar skin damage NOS

✓5th **692.8 Due to other specified agents**

692.81 Dermatitis due to cosmetics

692.82 Dermatitis due to other radiation
Infrared rays
Light, except from sun
Radiation NOS
Tanning bed
Ultraviolet rays, except from sun
X-rays
EXCLUDES *solar radiation (692.70-692.79)*

692.83 Dermatitis due to metals
Jewelry

692.84 Due to animal (cat) (dog) dander
Due to animal (cat) (dog) hair

692.89 Other
Dermatitis due to:
cold weather
dyes
hot weather
preservatives
EXCLUDES *allergy (NOS) (rhinitis) due to animal hair or dander (477.2)*
allergy to dust (477.8)
sunburn (692.71, 692.76-692.77)

692.9 Unspecified cause
Dermatitis:
NOS
contact NOS
venenata NOS
Eczema NOS

✓4th **693 Dermatitis due to substances taken internally**
EXCLUDES *adverse effect NOS of drugs and medicines (995.20)*
allergy NOS (995.3)
contact dermatitis (692.0-692.9)
urticarial reactions (708.0-708.9, 995.1)
DEF: Inflammation of skin due to ingested substance.

693.0 Due to drugs and medicines
Dermatitis medicamentosa NOS
Use additional E code to identify drug
EXCLUDES *that due to drugs in contact with skin (692.3)*

693.1 Due to food

693.8 Due to other specified substances taken internally

693.9 Due to unspecified substance taken internally
EXCLUDES *dermatitis NOS (692.9)*

✓4th **694 Bullous dermatoses**

694.0 Dermatitis herpetiformis
Dermatosis herpetiformis
Duhring's disease
Hydroa herpetiformis
EXCLUDES *herpes gestationis (646.8)*
dermatitis herpetiformis:
juvenile (694.2)
senile (694.5)
DEF: Chronic, relapsing multisystem disease manifested most in the cutaneous system; seen as an extremely pruritic eruption of various combinations of lesions that frequently heal leaving hyperpigmentation or hypopigmentation and occasionally scarring; usually associated with an asymptomatic gluten-sensitive enteropathy, and immunogenic factors are believed to play a role in its origin.

694.1 Subcorneal pustular dermatosis
Sneddon-Wilkinson disease or syndrome
DEF: Chronic relapses of sterile pustular blebs beneath the horny skin layer of the trunk and skin folds; resembles dermatitis herpetiformis.

694.2 Juvenile dermatitis herpetiformis
Juvenile pemphigoid

694.3 Impetigo herpetiformis
DEF: Rare dermatosis associated with pregnancy; marked by itching pustules in third trimester, hypocalcemia, tetany, fever and lethargy; may result in maternal or fetal death.

694.4 Pemphigus
Pemphigus:
NOS
erythematosus
foliaceus
malignant
vegetans
vulgaris
EXCLUDES *pemphigus neonatorum (684)*
DEF: Chronic, relapsing, sometimes fatal skin diseases; causes vesicles, bullae; autoantibodies against intracellular connections cause acantholysis.

694.5 Pemphigoid
Benign pemphigus NOS
Bullous pemphigoid
Herpes circinatus bullosus
Senile dermatitis herpetiformis

✓5th **694.6 Benign mucous membrane pemphigoid**
Cicatricial pemphigoid
Mucosynechial atrophic bullous dermatitis

694.60 Without mention of ocular involvement

694.61 With ocular involvement
Ocular pemphigus
DEF: Mild self-limiting, subepidermal blistering of mucosa including the conjunctiva, seen predominantly in the elderly. It produces adhesions and scarring.

694.8 Other specified bullous dermatoses
EXCLUDES *herpes gestationis (646.8)*

694.9 Unspecified bullous dermatoses

✓4th **695 Erythematous conditions**

695.0 Toxic erythema
Erythema venenatum

✓5th **695.1 Erythema multiforme**
Use additional code to identify associated manifestations, such as:
arthropathy associated with dermatological disorders (713.3)
conjunctival edema (372.73)
conjunctivitis (372.04, 372.33)
corneal scars and opacities (371.00-371.05)
corneal ulcer (370.00-370.07)
edema of eyelid (374.82)
inflammation of eyelid (373.8)
keratoconjunctivitis sicca (370.33)
mechanical lagophthalmos (374.22)
mucositis (478.11, 528.00, 538, 616.81)
stomatitis (528.00)
symblepharon (372.63)
Use additional E-code to identify drug, if drug-induced
Use additional code to identify percentage of skin exfoliation (695.50-695.59)
EXCLUDES *(Staphylococcal) scalded skin syndrome (695.81)*
DEF: Symptom complex with a varied skin eruption pattern of macular, bullous, papular, nodose, or vesicular lesions on the neck, face, and legs; gastritis and rheumatic pains are also noticeable, first-seen symptoms; complex is secondary to a number of factors, including infections, ingestants, physical agents, malignancy and pregnancy.

695.10 Erythema multiforme, unspecified
Erythema iris
Herpes iris

695.11 Erythema multiforme minor

695.12 Erythema multiforme major

695.13 Stevens-Johnson syndrome

695.14 Stevens-Johnson syndrome-toxic epidermal necrolysis overlap syndrome
SJS-TEN overlap syndrome

695.15 Toxic epidermal necrolysis
Lyell's syndrome

695.19 Other erythema multiforme

695.2 Erythema nodosum
EXCLUDES *tuberculous erythema nodosum (017.1)*
DEF: Panniculitis (an inflammatory reaction of the subcutaneous fat) of women, usually seen as a hypersensitivity reaction to various infections, drugs, sarcoidosis, and specific enteropathies; the acute stage is often associated with other symptoms, including fever, malaise, and arthralgia; the lesions are pink to blue in color, appear in crops as tender nodules and are found on the front of the legs below the knees.

695.3 Rosacea
Acne:
erythematosa
rosacea
Perioral dermatitis
Rhinophyma
DEF: Chronic skin disease, usually of the face, characterized by persistent erythema and sometimes by telangiectasis with acute episodes of edema, engorgement papules, and pustules.

695.4 Lupus erythematosus
Lupus:
erythematodes (discoid)
erythematosus (discoid), not disseminated
EXCLUDES *lupus (vulgaris) NOS (017.0)*
systemic [disseminated] lupus erythematosus (710.0)
DEF: Group of connective tissue disorders occurring as various cutaneous diseases of unknown origin; it primarily affects women between the ages of 20 and 40.

✓5th **695.5 Exfoliation due to erythematous conditions according to extent of body surface involved**
Code first erythematous condition causing exfoliation, such as:
Ritter's disease (695.81)
(Staphylococcal) scalded skin syndrome (695.81)
Stevens-Johnson syndrome (695.13)
Stevens-Johnson syndrome-toxic epidermal necrolysis overlap syndrome (695.14)
toxic epidermal necrolysis (695.15)

695.50 Exfoliation due to erythematous condition involving less than 10 percent of body surface
Exfoliation due to erythematous condition NOS

695.51 Exfoliation due to erythematous condition involving 10-19 percent of body surface

695.52 Exfoliation due to erythematous condition involving 20-29 percent of body surface

695.53 Exfoliation due to erythematous condition involving 30-39 percent of body surface

695.54 Exfoliation due to erythematous condition involving 40-49 percent of body surface

695.55 Exfoliation due to erythematous condition involving 50-59 percent of body surface

695.56 Exfoliation due to erythematous condition involving 60-69 percent of body surface

695.57 Exfoliation due to erythematous condition involving 70-79 percent of body surface

695.58 Exfoliation due to erythematous condition involving 80-89 percent of body surface

695.59 Exfoliation due to erythematous condition involving 90 percent or more of body surface

✓5th **695.8 Other specified erythematous conditions**

695.81 Ritter's disease
Dermatitis exfoliativa neonatorum
(Staphylococcal) Scalded skin syndrome
Use additional code to identify percentage of skin exfoliation (695.50-695.59)
DEF: Infectious skin disease of infants and young children marked by eruptions ranging from a localized bullous type to widespread development of easily ruptured fine vesicles and bullae; results in exfoliation of large planes of skin and leaves raw areas.

695.89 Other
Erythema intertrigo
Intertrigo
Pityriasis rubra (Hebra)
EXCLUDES *mycotic intertrigo (111.0-111.9)*

695.9 Unspecified erythematous condition
Erythema NOS
Erythroderma (secondary)

✓4th **696 Psoriasis and similar disorders**

696.0 Psoriatic arthropathy
DEF: Psoriasis associated with inflammatory arthritis; often involves interphalangeal joints.

696.1 Other psoriasis
Acrodermatitis continua
Dermatitis repens
Psoriasis:
NOS
any type, except arthropathic
EXCLUDES *psoriatic arthropathy (696.0)*

696.2 Parapsoriasis
Parakeratosis variegata
Parapsoriasis lichenoides chronica
Pityriasis lichenoides et varioliformis
DEF: Erythrodermas similar to lichen, planus and psoriasis; symptoms include redness and itching; resistant to treatment.

696.3 Pityriasis rosea
Pityriasis circinata (et maculata)
DEF: Common, self-limited rash of unknown etiology marked by a solitary erythematous, salmon or fawn-colored herald plaque on the trunk, arms or thighs; followed by development of papular or macular lesions that tend to peel and form a scaly collarette.

696.4 Pityriasis rubra pilaris
Devergie's disease
Lichen ruber acuminatus
EXCLUDES *pityriasis rubra (Hebra) (695.89)*
DEF: Inflammatory disease of hair follicles; marked by firm, red lesions topped by horny plugs; may form patches; occurs on fingers elbows, knees.

696.5 Other and unspecified pityriasis
Pityriasis:
NOS
alba
streptogenes
EXCLUDES *pityriasis:*
simplex (690.18)
versicolor (111.0)

696.8 Other

✓4th **697 Lichen**
EXCLUDES *lichen:*
obtusus corneus (698.3)
pilaris (congenital) (757.39)
ruber acuminatus (696.4)
sclerosus et atrophicus (701.0)
scrofulosus (017.0)
simplex chronicus (698.3)
spinulosus (congenital) (757.39)
urticatus (698.2)

697.0 Lichen planus
Lichen:
planopilaris
ruber planus
DEF: Inflammatory, pruritic skin disease; marked by angular, flat-top, violet-colored papules; may be acute and widespread or chronic and localized.

697.1 Lichen nitidus
Pinkus' disease
DEF: Chronic, inflammatory, usually asymptomatic skin disorder, characterized by numerous glistening, flat-topped, discrete, smooth, skin-colored micropapules most often on penis, lower abdomen, inner thighs, wrists, forearms, breasts and buttocks.

697.8 Other lichen, not elsewhere classified
Lichen:
ruber moniliforme
striata

697.9 Lichen, unspecified

✓4th **698 Pruritus and related conditions**
EXCLUDES *pruritus specified as psychogenic (306.3)*
DEF: Pruritus: Intense, persistent itching due to irritation of sensory nerve endings from organic or psychogenic causes.

698.0 Pruritus ani
Perianal itch

698.1 Pruritus of genital organs

698.2 Prurigo
Lichen urticatus
Prurigo:
NOS
Hebra's
mitis
simplex
Urticaria papulosa (Hebra)
EXCLUDES *prurigo nodularis (698.3)*

698.3 Lichenification and lichen simplex chronicus
Hyde's disease
Neurodermatitis (circumscripta) (local)
Prurigo nodularis
EXCLUDES *neurodermatitis, diffuse (of Brocq) (691.8)*
DEF: Lichenification: thickening of skin due to prolonged rubbing or scratching.
DEF: Lichen simplex chronicus: eczematous dermatitis, of face, neck, extremities, scrotum, vulva, and perianal region due to repeated itching, rubbing and scratching; spontaneous or evolves with other dermatoses.

698.4 Dermatitis factitia [artefacta]
Dermatitis ficta
Neurotic excoriation
Use additional code to identify any associated mental disorder
DEF: Various types of self-inflicted skin lesions characterized in appearance as an erythema to a gangrene.

698.8 Other specified pruritic conditions
Pruritus:
hiemalis
senilis
Winter itch

698.9 Unspecified pruritic disorder
Itch NOS
Pruritus NOS

OTHER DISEASES OF SKIN AND SUBCUTANEOUS TISSUE (700-709)

EXCLUDES *conditions confined to eyelids (373.0-374.9)*
congenital conditions of skin, hair, and nails (757.0-757.9)

700 Corns and callosities
Callus
Clavus
DEF: Corns: Conical or horny thickening of skin on toes, due to friction, pressure from shoes and hosiery; pain and inflammation may develop.
DEF: Callosities: Localized overgrowth (hyperplasia) of the horny epidermal layer due to pressure or friction.

✓4th **701 Other hypertrophic and atrophic conditions of skin**
EXCLUDES *dermatomyositis (710.3)*
hereditary edema of legs (757.0)
scleroderma (generalized) (710.1)

701.0 Circumscribed scleroderma
Addison's keloid
Dermatosclerosis, localized
Lichen sclerosus et atrophicus
Morphea
Scleroderma, circumscribed or localized
DEF: Thickened, hardened, skin and subcutaneous tissue; may involve musculoskeletal system.

701.1 Keratoderma, acquired
Acquired:
ichthyosis
keratoderma palmaris et plantaris
Elastosis perforans serpiginosa
Hyperkeratosis:
NOS
follicularis in cutem penetrans
palmoplantaris climacterica
Keratoderma:
climactericum
tylodes, progressive
Keratosis (blennorrhagica)
EXCLUDES *Darier's disease [keratosis follicularis] (congenital) (757.39)*
keratosis:
arsenical (692.4)
gonococcal (098.81)

701.2 Acquired acanthosis nigricans
Keratosis nigricans
DEF: Diffuse velvety hyperplasia of the spinous skin layer of the axilla and other body folds marked by gray, brown, or black pigmentation; in adult form it is often associated with an internal carcinoma (malignant acanthosis nigricans) in a benign, nevoid form it is relatively generalized; benign juvenile form with obesity is sometimes caused by an endocrine disturbance.

701.3 Striae atrophicae
Atrophic spots of skin
Atrophoderma maculatum
Atrophy blanche (of Milian)
Degenerative colloid atrophy
Senile degenerative atrophy
Striae distensae
DEF: Bands of atrophic, depressed, wrinkled skin associated with stretching of skin from pregnancy, obesity, or rapid growth during puberty.

701.4 Keloid scar
Cheloid
Hypertrophic scar
Keloid
DEF: Overgrowth of scar tissue due to excess amounts of collagen during connective tissue repair; occurs mainly on upper trunk, face.

701.5 Other abnormal granulation tissue
Excessive granulation

701.8 Other specified hypertrophic and atrophic conditions of skin
Acrodermatitis atrophicans chronica
Atrophia cutis senilis
Atrophoderma neuriticum
Confluent and reticulate papillomatosis
Cutis laxa senilis
Elastosis senilis
Folliculitis ulerythematosa reticulata
Gougerot-Carteaud syndrome or disease

701.9 Unspecified hypertrophic and atrophic conditions of skin
Atrophoderma
Skin tag

✓4th **702 Other dermatoses**
EXCLUDES *carcinoma in situ (232.0-232.9)*

702.0 Actinic keratosis
DEF: Wart-like growth, red or skin-colored; may form a cutaneous horn.

✓5th **702.1 Seborrheic keratosis**
DEF: Common, benign, lightly pigmented, warty growth composed of basaloid cells.

702.11 Inflamed seborrheic keratosis

702.19 Other seborrheic keratosis
Seborrheic keratosis NOS

702.8 Other specified dermatoses

✓4th **703 Diseases of nail**
EXCLUDES *congenital anomalies (757.5)*
onychia and paronychia (681.02, 681.11)

703.0 Ingrowing nail
Ingrowing nail with infection
Unguis incarnatus
EXCLUDES *infection, nail NOS (681.9)*

703.8 Other specified diseases of nail
Dystrophia unguium
Hypertrophy of nail
Koilonychia
Leukonychia (punctata) (striata)
Onychauxis
Onychogryposis
Onycholysis

703.9 Unspecified disease of nail

✓4th **704 Diseases of hair and hair follicles**
EXCLUDES *congenital anomalies (757.4)*

✓5th **704.0 Alopecia**
EXCLUDES *madarosis (374.55)*
syphilitic alopecia (091.82)
DEF: Lack of hair, especially on scalp; often called baldness; may be partial or total; occurs at any age.

704.00 Alopecia, unspecified
Baldness
Loss of hair

704.01 Alopecia areata
Ophiasis
DEF: Alopecia areata: usually reversible, inflammatory, patchy hair loss found in beard or scalp.
DEF: Ophiasis: alopecia areata of children; marked by band around temporal and occipital scalp margins.

704.02 Telogen effluvium
DEF: Shedding of hair from premature telogen development in follicles due to stress, including shock, childbirth, surgery, drugs or weight loss.

704.09 Other
Folliculitis decalvans
Hypotrichosis:
NOS
postinfectional NOS
Pseudopelade

704.1 Hirsutism
Hypertrichosis:
NOS
lanuginosa, acquired
Polytrichia
EXCLUDES *hypertrichosis of eyelid (374.54)*
DEF: Excess hair growth; often in unexpected places and amounts.

704.2 Abnormalities of the hair
Atrophic hair
Clastothrix
Fragilitas crinium
Trichiasis:
NOS
cicatrical
Trichorrhexis (nodosa)
EXCLUDES *trichiasis of eyelid (374.05)*

704.3 Variations in hair color
Canities (premature)
Grayness, hair (premature)
Heterochromia of hair
Poliosis:
NOS
circumscripta, acquired

704.8 Other specified diseases of hair and hair follicles
Folliculitis:
NOS
abscedens et suffodiens
pustular
Perifolliculitis:
NOS
capitis abscedens et suffodiens
scalp
Sycosis:
NOS
barbae [not parasitic]
lupoid
vulgaris

704.9 Unspecified disease of hair and hair follicles

✓4th 705 Disorders of sweat glands

705.0 Anhidrosis
Hypohidrosis
Oligohidrosis
DEF: Lack or deficiency of ability to sweat.

705.1 Prickly heat
Heat rash
Miliaria rubra (tropicalis)
Sudamina

✓5th **705.2 Focal hyperhidrosis**
EXCLUDES *generalized (secondary) hyperhidrosis (780.8)*

705.21 Primary focal hyperhidrosis
Focal hyperhidrosis NOS
Hyperhidrosis NOS
Hyperhidrosis of:
- axilla
- face
- palms
- soles

DEF: A rare condition that is a disorder of the sweat glands resulting in excessive production of sweat; occurs in the absence of any underlying or causative condition and is almost always focal, confined to one or more specific areas of the body.

705.22 Secondary focal hyperhidrosis
Frey's syndrome
DEF: Secondary focal hyperhidrosis: a symptom of an underlying disease process resulting in excessive sweating beyond what the body requires to maintain thermal control, confined to one or more specific areas of the body.
DEF: Frey's syndrome: an auriculotemporal syndrome due to lesion on the parotid gland; characteristic redness and excessive sweating on the cheek in connection with eating.

✓5th **705.8 Other specified disorders of sweat glands**

705.81 Dyshidrosis
Cheiropompholyx
Pompholyx
DEF: Vesicular eruption, on hands, feet causing itching and burning.

705.82 Fox-Fordyce disease
DEF: Chronic, usually pruritic disease chiefly of women evidenced by small follicular papular eruptions, especially in the axillary and pubic areas; develops from the closure and rupture of the affected apocrine glands' intraepidermal portion of the ducts.

705.83 Hidradenitis
Hidradenitis suppurativa
DEF: Inflamed sweat glands.

705.89 Other
Bromhidrosis
Chromhidrosis
Granulosis rubra nasi
Urhidrosis
EXCLUDES *generalized hyperhidrosis (780.8)*
hidrocystoma (216.0-216.9)
DEF: Bromhidrosis: foul-smelling axillary sweat due to decomposed bacteria.
DEF: Chromhidrosis: secretion of colored sweat.
DEF: Granulosis rubra nasi: ideopathic condition of children; causes redness, sweating around nose, face and chin; tends to end by puberty.
DEF: Urhidrosis: urinous substance, such as uric acid, in sweat; occurs in uremia.

705.9 Unspecified disorder of sweat glands
Disorder of sweat glands NOS

✓4th 706 Diseases of sebaceous glands

706.0 Acne varioliformis
Acne:
- frontalis
- necrotica

DEF: Rare form of acne characterized by persistent brown papulo-pustules usually on the brow and temporoparietal part of the scalp.

706.1 Other acne
Acne:
- NOS
- conglobata
- cystic
- pustular
- vulgaris

Blackhead
Comedo
EXCLUDES *acne rosacea (695.3)*

706.2 Sebaceous cyst
Atheroma, skin
Keratin cyst
Wen
DEF: Benign epidermal cyst, contains sebum and keratin; presents as firm, circumscribed nodule.

706.3 Seborrhea
EXCLUDES *seborrhea:*
capitis (690.11)
sicca (690.18)
seborrheic
dermatitis (690.10)
keratosis (702.11-702.19)
DEF: Seborrheic dermatitis marked by excessive secretion of sebum; the sebum forms an oily coating, crusts, or scales on the skin; it is also called hypersteatosis.

706.8 Other specified diseases of sebaceous glands
Asteatosis (cutis)
Xerosis cutis

706.9 Unspecified disease of sebaceous glands

✓4th 707 Chronic ulcer of skin

INCLUDES non-infected sinus of skin
non-healing ulcer

✓5th **707.0 Pressure ulcer**
Bed sore
Decubitus ulcer
Plaster ulcer
Use additional code to identify pressure ulcer stage (707.20-707.25)

707.00 Unspecified

707.01 Elbow

707.02 Upper back
Shoulder blades

707.03 Lower back
Sacrum

707.04 Hip

707.05 Buttock

Cutaneous Lesions

Surface Lesions
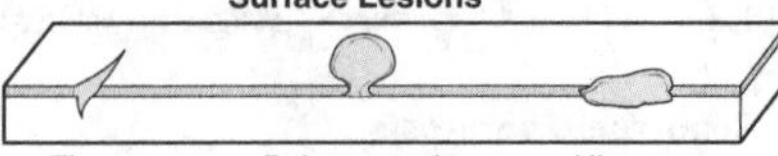

Solid Lesions

Sac Lesions

Four Stages of Decubitus Ulcers

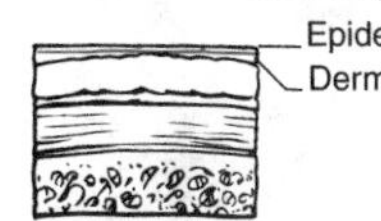

First Stage
Persistent focal erythema

Second Stage
Partial thickness skin loss involving epidermis, dermis, or both

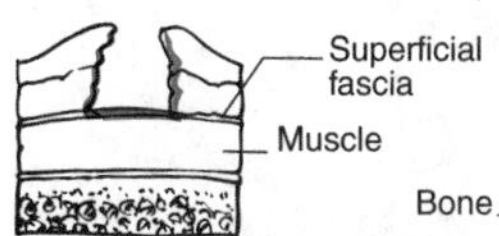

Third Stage
Full thickness skin loss extending through subcutaneous tissue

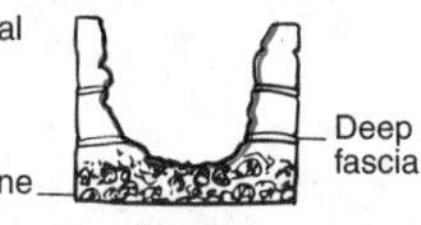

Fourth Stage
Necrosis of soft tissue extending to muscle and bone

707.06 Ankle

707.07 Heel

707.09 Other site
Head

✓5th **707.1 Ulcer of lower limbs, except pressure ulcer**
Ulcer, chronic:
neurogenic } of lower limb
trophic }
Code, if applicable, any causal condition first:
atherosclerosis of the extremities with ulceration (440.23)
chronic venous hypertension with ulcer (459.31)
chronic venous hypertension with ulcer and inflammation (459.33)
diabetes mellitus (249.80-249.81, 250.80-250.83)
postphlebitic syndrome with ulcer (459.11)
postphlebitic syndrome with ulcer and inflammation (459.13)

707.10 Ulcer of lower limb, unspecified

707.11 Ulcer of thigh

707.12 Ulcer of calf

707.13 Ulcer of ankle

707.14 Ulcer of heel and midfoot
Plantar surface of midfoot

707.15 Ulcer of other part of foot
Toes

707.19 Ulcer of other part of lower limb

✓5th **707.2 Pressure ulcer stages**
Code first site of pressure ulcer (707.00-707.09)

707.20 Pressure ulcer, unspecified stage
Healing pressure ulcer NOS
Healing pressure ulcer, unspecified stage

707.21 Pressure ulcer stage I
Healing pressure ulcer, stage I
Pressure pre-ulcer skin changes limited to persistent focal erythema

707.22 Pressure ulcer stage II
Healing pressure ulcer, stage II
Pressure ulcer with abrasion, blister, partial thickness skin loss involving epidermis and/or dermis

707.23 Pressure ulcer stage III
Healing pressure ulcer, stage III
Pressure ulcer with full thickness skin loss involving damage or necrosis of subcutaneous tissue

707.24 Pressure ulcer stage IV
Healing pressure ulcer, stage IV
Pressure ulcer with necrosis of soft tissues through to underlying muscle, tendon, or bone

707.25 Pressure ulcer, unstageable

707.8 Chronic ulcer of other specified sites
Ulcer, chronic:
neurogenic } of other specified sites
trophic }

707.9 Chronic ulcer of unspecified site
Chronic ulcer NOS
Trophic ulcer NOS
Tropical ulcer NOS
Ulcer of skin NOS

✓4th **708 Urticaria**

EXCLUDES *edema:*
angioneurotic (995.1)
Quincke's (995.1)
hereditary angioedema (277.6)
urticaria:
giant (995.1)
papulosa (Hebra) (698.2)
pigmentosa (juvenile) (congenital) (757.33)

DEF: Skin disorder marked by raised edematous patches of skin or mucous membrane with intense itching; also called hives.

708.0 Allergic urticaria

708.1 Idiopathic urticaria

708.2 Urticaria due to cold and heat
Thermal urticaria

708.3 Dermatographic urticaria
Dermatographia
Factitial urticaria

708.4 Vibratory urticaria

708.5 Cholinergic urticaria

708.8 Other specified urticaria
Nettle rash
Urticaria:
chronic
recurrent periodic

708.9 Urticaria, unspecified
Hives NOS

✓4th **709 Other disorders of skin and subcutaneous tissue**

✓5th **709.0 Dyschromia**

EXCLUDES *albinism (270.2)*
pigmented nevus (216.0-216.9)
that of eyelid (374.52-374.53)

DEF: Pigment disorder of skin or hair.

709.00 Dyschromia, unspecified

709.01 Vitiligo

DEF: Persistent, progressive development of nonpigmented white patches on otherwise normal skin.

709.09 Other

709.1 Vascular disorders of skin
Angioma serpiginosum
Purpura (primary)annularis telangiectodes

709.2 Scar conditions and fibrosis of skin
Adherent scar (skin)
Cicatrix
Disfigurement (due to scar)
Fibrosis, skin NOS
Scar NOS

EXCLUDES *keloid scar (701.4)*

709.3 Degenerative skin disorders
Calcinosis:
circumscripta
cutis
Colloid milium
Degeneration, skin
Deposits, skin
Senile dermatosis NOS
Subcutaneous calcification

709.4 Foreign body granuloma of skin and subcutaneous tissue

EXCLUDES *residual foreign body without granuloma of skin and subcutaneous tissue (729.6)*
that of muscle (728.82)

709.8 Other specified disorders of skin

Epithelial hyperplasia
Menstrual dermatosis
Vesicular eruption

DEF: Epithelial hyperplasia: increased number of epitheleal cells.

DEF: Vesicular eruption: liquid-filled structures appearing through skin.

709.9 Unspecified disorder of skin and subcutaneous tissue

Dermatosis NOS

Chapter 13: Musculoskeletal System and Connective Tissue (710–739)

Diseases and disorders of the bones, muscles, cartilage, fascia, ligaments, synovia, tendons, and bursa are classified to this chapter. The major sections of this chapter are as follows:

- Arthropathies and related disorder (710–719)
- Dorsopathies (720–724)
- Rheumatism, excluding the back (725–729)
- Osteopathies, chondropathies, and acquired musculoskeletal deformities (730–739)

Connective tissue disorders classified to chapter 13 are those primarily affecting the musculoskeletal system. Injuries and certain congenital disorders of the musculoskeletal system are classified elsewhere.

Many codes for the manifestation of musculoskeletal diseases due to specified infections and other diseases and disorders classified elsewhere are included in this chapter. Also included are many codes describing the residuals of previous diseases, disorders, and injuries classified as late effects. These codes often can be identified by the term "acquired" in the description.

Arthropathies and Related Disorders (710–719)

Arthropathy is defined as any joint disease, including arthritis (inflammatory) and arthrosis (noninflammatory). This section excludes myelopathy, disorders of the spinal cord, and dorsopathy, disorders of the spine.

Diffuse Diseases of Connective Tissue (710)

This is a group of diseases in which the primary lesion appears to be damage to collagen, a protein that is the major component of connective tissue. Collagen diseases, attributed largely to disorders of the immune complex mechanisms include dermatomyositis, systemic sclerosis, Sicca syndrome, polymyositis, collagen disease NOS, multifocal fibrosclerosis, and systemic lupus erythematosus. Many of these conditions, such as polyarteritis nodosa (a connective tissue disease that is a form of vasculitis) are classified to other chapters.

Rheumatoid Arthritis (714.0)

Rheumatoid arthritis is a chronic, systemic inflammatory disease of unknown etiology, characterized by a variable but prolonged course with exacerbations and remissions of joint pains and swelling. In early stages, the disease attacks the joints of the hands and feet. As the disease progresses, more joints become involved. Also known as primary progressive arthritis and proliferative arthritis, the disease often leads to progressive deformities, which may develop rapidly, and produce permanent disability.

Osteoarthrosis and Allied Disorders (715)

Osteoarthrosis is a degenerative, rather than inflammatory, disease of one joint or more than one joint. Also known as osteoarthritis and degenerative joint disease, osteoarthrosis is most conspicuous in the large joints and is initiated by local deterioration of the articular cartilage. It progressively destroys the cartilage, remodels the subchondral bone and causes a secondary inflammation of the synovial membrane.

Assignment of the fourth-digit to codes in this category is based on whether the disease is generalized or localized and whether it is primary or secondary. In these subcategories localized includes bilateral involvement of the same site.

Example:

> Primary localized osteoarthritis of the hand is coded 715.14, whether unilateral or bilateral and is not considered generalized osteoarthritis because of the bilateral nature of the condition.

Generalized disease is defined as osteoarthrosis involving many joints without any known pre-existing abnormality. There are three code choices for generalized arthritis or osteoarthrosis for unspecified site (715.00), the hand (715.04) or for multiple sites (715.09).

Localized osteoarthrosis is a disease confined to a limited number of sites. The distinction between generalized and localized can be difficult for the clinician because the disease may be generalized, but detectable in only one or two of the larger weight- bearing joints such as the hip or knee. The physician must document localized or generalized, or the coder should assign the unspecified code.

Dorsopathies (720–724)

Dorsopathies classified to this section exclude curvature of the spine (737) and osteochondrosis of the spine (732.0 Juvenile, and 732.8 Adult).

Included in this section are:

- Ankylosing spondylitis (720)
- Spondylosis (721)
- Intervertebral disc disorders (722)
- Other disorders of the cervical region (723)
- Other and unspecified disorders of the back (724)

Other Disorders of the Synovium, Tendon and Bursa (727)

Synovitis is the inflammation of a synovial membrane, especially the synovium that lines articular joints. In a normal joint, the smooth and reciprocally shaped cartilaginous opposing surfaces permit a fluid, frictionless and painless articulation. Irregularities, disease, and damage to the articular surfaces lead to progressive degenerative changes resulting in pain and limitation of movement. The joint capsule is particularly sensitive to stretching and increased fluid pressure.

Tenosynovitis is the inflammation of a tendon and its synovial sheath. It is also known as tendosynovitis, tendovaginitis, tenontothecitis, and vaginal or tendinous synovitis. At sites of friction, the tendon is enveloped by a sheath consisting of a visceral and parietal layer of synovial membrane and is lubricated by a synovial-like fluid. The synovial sheath is in turn covered by a dense, fibrous tissue sheath. Irregularities, disease, and damage to the tendon's attachment to the articular joints may lead to progressive degenerative changes with resultant limitation of movement and pain. The synovial membranes of tendon sheaths and bursae are capable of the same inflammatory reactions to abnormal conditions as the synovial membranes of joints.

Ganglions and cysts of synovium, tendon, and bursa (727.4x) are thin-walled cystic lesions of unknown etiology containing thick, clear, mucinous fluid, possibly due to mucoid degeneration. Ganglions are limited to the hands and feet and are most common in the dorsum of the wrist.

Synovial cyst of popliteal space (727.51), such as a Baker's cysts, is sometimes called popliteal cysts. In children, Baker's cysts are common but usually are asymptomatic and regress spontaneously. In adults, Baker's cysts, in conjunction with synovial effusion due to rheumatoid arthritis or degenerative joint disease, may produce significant impairment. Baker's cysts are classified to subcategory 727.5.

Post-traumatic Seroma, Nontraumatic Hematoma of Soft Tissue (729.9)

A nontraumatic hematoma is a localized collection of blood in a tissue or space due to the breakage in the wall of a blood vessel that does not occur as a result of any obvious injury to the affected area. When nontraumatic hematoma occurs in the muscle, it is often characterized by a localized lump or swollen area that may be painful or associated with a decreased range of motion of the affected area. Depending on the depth of hematoma into the muscle and soft tissues, associated skin discoloration may vary. A seroma is a localized accumulation of serum (fluid) within a tissue or space resulting in swelling. As fluid accumulates, a hematoma may subsequently develop with a seroma in the soft tissue of the affected area. Nontraumatic hematoma may be caused by circulatory disorders, vascular anomalies, or the effects of other disease processes. Post-traumatic seroma occurs as a result of injury in which the lymph vessels or lymph nodes sustain damage. In either case, the accumulation of blood (hematoma) and clear fluid (seroma) in the soft tissue may require incision and drainage.

Osteopathies, Chondropathies and Acquired Musculoskeletal Deformities (730–739)

This category includes a broad spectrum of bone infections. Osteomyelitis is an inflammation of bone and/or bone marrow. The condition is virtually always due to a pathogen such as bacteria, virus, protozoa, or fungus. Periostitis is an inflammation of the periosteum, the thick fibrous membrane covering all the surfaces of bones except at the articular cartilage.

Other Disorders of Bone and Cartilage (733)

Osteoporosis (733.0) is a generalized bone disease characterized by decreased formation of matrix combined with increased resorption of bone, resulting in a marked decrease in bone mass. Osteoporosis often presents with osteopenia, which is a decrease in bone mineralization. Clinically, osteoporosis is classified into two major groups: primary and secondary. Primary osteoporosis implies that the condition is a fundamental disease entity itself. Secondary osteoporosis attributes the condition to an underlying clinical disease, medical condition, or medication.

When the osteoporosis is due to drug use, assign the appropriate drug code and E code in addition to the code for osteoporosis.

Pathologic Fractures (733.1)

Pathological fractures occur at a site weakened by pre-existing disease. They are often differentiated from traumatic fractures by clinically assessing the magnitude of the trauma or stress causing the fracture. A relatively minor trauma or stress can cause a pathological fracture in bones diseased by osteoporosis and other metabolic bone disease, disseminated bone disorders, inflammatory bone diseases, or any other condition that can compromise bone strength and integrity. Other terms used to describe pathologic fractures are spontaneous and secondary fractures.

Code the underlying disease in addition to the appropriate code from subcategory 733.1. Sequencing of the codes depends on whether only the fracture or the fracture and the underlying disease were treated. Code the fracture first if the treatment is toward the fracture only. If treatment of the underlying disease is addressed then code the underlying disease first.

Necrosis of Bone; Jaw (733.45)

A possible relationship between osteonecrosis of the jaw (ONJ) and the use of bisphosphonates and other medications is being studied in the oral and maxillofacial surgery (OMS) patient population. Without a specific reporting mechanism, the incidence of this occurrence is not being captured. The American Association of Oral and Maxillofacial Surgeons' (AAOMS) case definition of osteonecrosis is "any patient who has not received radiation therapy to the oral cavity or neck and who has exposed bone in the maxillofacial area that occurred spontaneously or following dental surgery and has no evidence of healing for more than 3–6 weeks after appropriate care." As noted in the definition, osteonecrosis differs from osteoradionecrosis, which is caused by radiation therapy.

Use an additional E code to identify the drug, if drug-induced. Codes E933.6 Oral bisphosphonates and E933.7 Intravenous bisphosphonates, report the adverse effects of these prescribed bisphosphonates. Bisphosphonate drugs include Boniva, Fosamax, and Zometa. Do not assign 733.45 Aseptic necrosis of bone, jaw for osteoradionecrosis of jaw (526.89).

Stress Fracture (733.9)

Stress fractures are classified separately from pathological fractures (733.1X). Stress fractures may occur as a result of overexertion, strenuous, repetitive motion, static positioning, and load-bearing injuries, and sudden traumatic and cumulative trauma injuries. Subcategory 733.9 includes an instructional note to "Use additional external cause code(s) to identify the cause of the stress fracture" with codes 733.93–733.98.

Curvature of the Spine (737)

Kyphosis (737.0–737.1x) is the abnormal increase in the thoracic convexity of the spine as viewed from the side.

Lordosis (737.2x) is the anterior convexity of the cervical and lumbar spine as viewed from the side.

Scoliosis (737.3x) is the lateral curvature of the spine described as structural or nonstructural depending on whether the condition is reversible.

Kyphoscoliosis (737.3x) the lateral curvature of the spine with extensive flexion.

Acquired deformities of the spine associated with disease classified elsewhere are coded to subcategory 737.4. Code first the underlying condition. The fifth digit identifies the type of deformity.

13. DISEASES OF THE MUSCULOSKELETAL SYSTEM AND CONNECTIVE TISSUE (710-739)

Use additional external cause code, if applicable, to identify the cause of the musculoskeletal condition

The following fifth-digit subclassification is for use with categories 711-712, 715-716, 718-719, and 730:

0 site unspecified

1 shoulder region
- Acromioclavicular joint(s)
- Clavicle
- Glenohumeral joint(s)
- Scapula
- Sternoclavicular joint(s)

2 upper arm
- Elbow joint
- Humerus

3 forearm
- Radius
- Ulna
- Wrist joint

4 hand
- Carpus
- Metacarpus
- Phalanges [fingers]

5 pelvic region and thigh
- Buttock
- Femur
- Hip (joint)

6 lower leg
- Fibula
- Knee joint
- Patella
- Tibia

7 ankle and foot
- Ankle joint
- Digits [toes]
- Metatarsus
- Phalanges, foot
- Tarsus
- Other joints in foot

8 other specified sites
- Head
- Neck
- Ribs
- Skull
- Trunk
- Vertebral column

9 multiple sites

ARTHROPATHIES AND RELATED DISORDERS (710-719)

EXCLUDES *disorders of spine (720.0-724.9)*

4th 710 Diffuse diseases of connective tissue

INCLUDES all collagen diseases whose effects are not mainly confined to a single system

EXCLUDES *those affecting mainly the cardiovascular system, i.e., polyarteritis nodosa and allied conditions (446.0-446.7)*

710.0 Systemic lupus erythematosus

Disseminated lupus erythematosus
Libman-Sacks disease

Use additional code to identify manifestation, as:
endocarditis (424.91)
nephritis (583.81)
chronic (582.81)
nephrotic syndrome (581.81)

EXCLUDES *lupus erythematosus (discoid) NOS (695.4)*

DEF: A chronic multisystemic inflammatory disease affecting connective tissue; marked by anemia, leukopenia, muscle and joint pains, fever, rash of a butterfly pattern around cheeks and forehead area; of unknown etiology.

710.1 Systemic sclerosis

Acrosclerosis
CRST syndrome
Progressive systemic sclerosis
Scleroderma

Use additional code to identify manifestation, as:
lung involvement (517.2)
myopathy (359.6)

EXCLUDES *circumscribed scleroderma (701.0)*

DEF: Systemic disease, involving excess fibrotic collagen build-up; symptoms include thickened skin; fibrotic degenerative changes in various organs; and vascular abnomalities; condition occurs more often in females.

Joint Structures

Muscle
Periosteum (covers bone)
Cortical bone
Medullary bone
Fascia over Muscle
Sesamoid bone
Bursa (with synovial fluid)
Tendon (muscle to bone)
Muscle insertion into bone (crosses one or more joints)
Retinaculum
Tendon sheath around
Tendon
Synovium lines
Joint capsule around
Synovial cavity (with fluid)
Articular cartilage
Ligament (bone to bone)
Bursa
Bone covered with periosteum

710.2 Sicca syndrome

Keratoconjunctivitis sicca
Sjögren's disease

DEF: Autoimmune disease; associated with keratoconjunctivitis, laryngopharyngitis, rhinitis, dry mouth, enlarged parotid gland, and chronic polyarthritis.

710.3 Dermatomyositis

Poikilodermatomyositis
Polymyositis with skin involvement

DEF: Polymyositis associated with flat-top purple papules on knuckles; marked by upper eyelid rash, edema of eyelids and orbit area, red rash on forehead, neck, shoulders, trunk and arms; symptoms include fever, weight loss aching muscles; visceral cancer (in individuals older than 40).

710.4 Polymyositis

DEF: Chronic, progressive, inflammatory skeletal muscle disease; causes weakness of limb girdles, neck, pharynx; may precede or follow scleroderma, Sjogren's disease, systemic lupus erythematosus, arthritis, or malignancy.

710.5 Eosinophilia myalgia syndrome

Toxic oil syndrome

Use additional E code to identify drug, if drug induced

DEF: Eosinophilia myalgia syndrome (EMS): inflammatory, multisystem fibrosis; associated with ingesting elementary L-tryptophan; symptoms include myalgia, weak limbs and bulbar muscles, distal sensory loss, areflexia, arthralgia, cough, fever, fatigue, skin rashes, myopathy, and eosinophil counts greater than 1000/microliter.

DEF: Toxic oil syndrome: syndrome similar to EMS due to ingesting contaminated cooking oil.

710.8 Other specified diffuse diseases of connective tissue

Multifocal fibrosclerosis (idiopathic) NEC
Systemic fibrosclerosing syndrome

710.9 Unspecified diffuse connective tissue disease

Collagen disease NOS

4th 711 Arthropathy associated with infections

INCLUDES arthritis, arthropathy, polyarthritis, polyarthropathy } associated with conditions classifiable below

EXCLUDES *rheumatic fever (390)*

The following fifth-digit subclassification is for use with category 711; valid digits are in [brackets] under each code. See list at beginning of chapter for definitions.

0 site unspecified
1 shoulder region
2 upper arm
3 forearm
4 hand
5 pelvic region and thigh
6 lower leg
7 ankle and foot
8 other specified sites
9 multiple sites

✓5th **711.0 Pyogenic arthritis**
[0-9]
Arthritis or polyarthritis (due to):
- coliform [Escherichia coli]
- Hemophilus influenzae [H. influenzae]
- pneumococcal
- Pseudomonas
- staphylococcal
- streptococcal

Pyarthrosis

Use additional code to identify infectious organism (041.0-041.8)

DEF: Infectious arthritis caused by various bacteria; marked by inflamed synovial membranes, and purulent effusion in joints.

✓5th ***711.1 Arthropathy associated with Reiter's disease and nonspecific urethritis***
[0-9]
Code first underlying disease as:
- nonspecific urethritis (099.4)
- Reiter's disease (099.3)

DEF: Reiter's disease: joint disease marked by diarrhea, urethritis, conjunctivitis, keratosis and arthritis; of unknown etiology; affects young males.

DEF: Urethritis: inflamed urethra.

✓5th ***711.2 Arthropathy in Behçet's syndrome***
[0-9]
Code first underlying disease (136.1)

DEF: Behçet's syndrome: Chronic inflammatory disorder, of unknown etiology; affects small blood vessels; causes ulcers of oral and pharyngeal mucous membranes and genitalia, skin lesions, retinal vasculitis, optic atrophy and severe uveitis.

✓5th ***711.3 Postdysenteric arthropathy***
[0-9]
Code first underlying disease as:
- dysentery (009.0)
- enteritis, infectious (008.0-009.3)
- paratyphoid fever (002.1-002.9)
- typhoid fever (002.0)

EXCLUDES *salmonella arthritis (003.23)*

✓5th ***711.4 Arthropathy associated with other bacterial diseases***
[0-9]
Code first underlying disease as:
- diseases classifiable to 010-040, 090-099, except as in 711.1, 711.3, and 713.5
- leprosy (030.0-030.9)
- tuberculosis (015.0-015.9)

EXCLUDES *gonococcal arthritis (098.50)*
meningococcal arthritis (036.82)

✓5th ***711.5 Arthropathy associated with other viral diseases***
[0-9]
Code first underlying disease as:
- diseases classifiable to 045-049, 050-079, 480, 487
- O'nyong nyong (066.3)

EXCLUDES *that due to rubella (056.71)*

✓5th ***711.6 Arthropathy associated with mycoses***
[0-9]
Code first underlying disease (110.0-118)

✓5th ***711.7 Arthropathy associated with helminthiasis***
[0-9]
Code first underlying disease as:
- filariasis (125.0-125.9)

✓5th ***711.8 Arthropathy associated with other infectious and parasitic diseases***
[0-9]
Code first underlying disease as:
- diseases classifiable to 080-088, 100-104, 130-136

EXCLUDES *arthropathy associated with sarcoidosis (713.7)*

✓5th **711.9 Unspecified infective arthritis**
[0-9]
Infective arthritis or polyarthritis (acute) (chronic) (subacute) NOS

✓4th **712 Crystal arthropathies**

INCLUDES crystal-induced arthritis and synovitis

EXCLUDES *gouty arthropathy (274.0)*

DEF: Joint disease due to urate crystal deposit in joints or synovial membranes.

The following fifth-digit subclassification is for use with category 712; valid digits are in [brackets] under each code. See list at beginning of chapter for definitions.

- **0 site unspecified**
- **1 shoulder region**
- **2 upper arm**
- **3 forearm**
- **4 hand**
- **5 pelvic region and thigh**
- **6 lower leg**
- **7 ankle and foot**
- **8 other specified sites**
- **9 multiple sites**

✓5th ***712.1 Chondrocalcinosis due to dicalcium phosphate crystals***
[0-9]
Chondrocalcinosis due to dicalcium phosphate crystals (with other crystals)

Code first underlying disease (275.4)

✓5th ***712.2 Chondrocalcinosis due to pyrophosphate crystals***
[0-9]
Code first underlying disease (275.4)

✓5th ***712.3 Chondrocalcinosis, unspecified***
[0-9]
Code first underlying disease (275.4)

✓5th **712.8 Other specified crystal arthropathies**
[0-9]

✓5th **712.9 Unspecified crystal arthropathy**
[0-9]

✓4th **713 Arthropathy associated with other disorders classified elsewhere**

INCLUDES arthritis, arthropathy, polyarthritis, polyarthropathy } associated with conditions classifiable below

713.0 Arthropathy associated with other endocrine and metabolic disorders

Code first underlying disease as:
- acromegaly (253.0)
- hemochromatosis (275.0)
- hyperparathyroidism (252.00-252.08)
- hypogammaglobulinemia (279.00-279.09)
- hypothyroidism (243-244.9)
- lipoid metabolism disorder (272.0-272.9)
- ochronosis (270.2)

EXCLUDES *arthropathy associated with:*
- *amyloidosis (713.7)*
- *crystal deposition disorders, except gout (712.1-712.9)*
- *diabetic neuropathy (713.5)*
- *gouty arthropathy (274.0)*

713.1 Arthropathy associated with gastrointestinal conditions other than infections

Code first underlying disease as:
- regional enteritis (555.0-555.9)
- ulcerative colitis (556)

713.2 Arthropathy associated with hematological disorders

Code first underlying disease as:
- hemoglobinopathy (282.4-282.7)
- hemophilia (286.0-286.2)
- leukemia (204.0-208.9)
- malignant reticulosis (202.3)
- multiple myelomatosis (203.0)

EXCLUDES *arthropathy associated with Henoch-Schönlein purpura (713.6)*

713.3 *Arthropathy associated with dermatological disorders*

Code first underlying disease as:
erythema multiforme (695.10-695.19)
erythema nodosum (695.2)

EXCLUDES *psoriatic arthropathy (696.0)*

713.4 *Arthropathy associated with respiratory disorders*

Code first underlying disease as:
diseases classifiable to 490-519

EXCLUDES *arthropathy associated with respiratory infections (711.0, 711.4-711.8)*

713.5 *Arthropathy associated with neurological disorders*

Charcôt's arthropathy } associated with diseases
Neuropathic arthritis } classifiable elsewhere

Code first underlying disease as:
neuropathic joint disease [Charcôt's joints]:
NOS (094.0)
diabetic (249.6, 250.6)
syringomyelic (336.0)
tabetic [syphilitic] (094.0)

713.6 *Arthropathy associated with hypersensitivity reaction*

Code first underlying disease as:
Henoch (-Schönlein) purpura (287.0)
serum sickness (999.5)

EXCLUDES *allergic arthritis NOS (716.2)*

713.7 *Other general diseases with articular involvement*

Code first underlying disease as:
amyloidosis (277.30-277.39)
familial Mediterranean fever (277.31)
sarcoidosis (135)

713.8 *Arthropathy associated with other condition classifiable elsewhere*

Code first underlying disease as:
conditions classifiable elsewhere except as in 711.1-711.8, 712, and 713.0-713.7

✓4th **714 Rheumatoid arthritis and other inflammatory polyarthropathies**

EXCLUDES *rheumatic fever (390)*
rheumatoid arthritis of spine NOS (720.0)

714.0 Rheumatoid arthritis

Arthritis or polyarthritis:
atrophic
rheumatic (chronic)

Use additional code to identify manifestation, as:
myopathy (359.6)
polyneuropathy (357.1)

EXCLUDES *juvenile rheumatoid arthritis NOS (714.30)*

DEF: Chronic systemic disease principally of joints, manifested by inflammatory changes in articular structures and synovial membranes, atrophy, and loss in bone density.

714.1 Felty's syndrome

Rheumatoid arthritis with splenoadenomegaly and leukopenia

DEF: Syndrome marked by rheumatoid arthritis, splenomegaly, leukopenia, pigmented spots on lower extremity skin, anemia, and thrombocytopenia.

714.2 Other rheumatoid arthritis with visceral or systemic involvement

Rheumatoid carditis

✓5th **714.3 Juvenile chronic polyarthritis**

DEF: Rheumatoid arthritis of more than one joint; lasts longer than six weeks in age 17 or younger; symptoms include fever, erythematous rash, weight loss, lymphadenopathy, hepatosplenomegaly and pericarditis.

714.30 Polyarticular juvenile rheumatoid arthritis, chronic or unspecified

Juvenile rheumatoid arthritis NOS
Still's disease

714.31 Polyarticular juvenile rheumatoid arthritis, acute

714.32 Pauciarticular juvenile rheumatoid arthritis

714.33 Monoarticular juvenile rheumatoid arthritis

714.4 Chronic postrheumatic arthropathy

Chronic rheumatoid nodular fibrositis
Jaccoud's syndrome

DEF: Persistent joint disorder; follows previous rheumatic infection.

✓5th **714.8 Other specified inflammatory polyarthropathies**

714.81 Rheumatoid lung

Caplan's syndrome
Diffuse interstitial rheumatoid disease of lung
Fibrosing alveolitis, rheumatoid

DEF: Lung disorders associated with rheumatoid arthritis.

714.89 Other

714.9 Unspecified inflammatory polyarthropathy

Inflammatory polyarthropathy or polyarthritis NOS

EXCLUDES *polyarthropathy NOS (716.5)*

✓4th **715 Osteoarthrosis and allied disorders**

Note: Localized, in the subcategories below, includes bilateral involvement of the same site.

INCLUDES arthritis or polyarthritis:
degenerative
hypertrophic
degenerative joint disease
osteoarthritis

EXCLUDES *Marie-Strümpell spondylitis (720.0)*
osteoarthrosis [osteoarthritis] of spine (721.0-721.9)

The following fifth-digit subclassification is for use with category 715; valid digits are in [brackets] under each code. See list at beginning of chapter for definitions.

0 site unspecified
1 shoulder region
2 upper arm
3 forearm
4 hand
5 pelvic region and thigh
6 lower leg
7 ankle and foot
8 other specified sites
9 multiple sites

✓5th **715.0 Osteoarthrosis, generalized**
[0,4,9]

Degenerative joint disease, involving multiple joints
Primary generalized hypertrophic osteoarthrosis

DEF: Chronic noninflammatory arthritis; marked by degenerated articular cartilage and enlarged bone; symptoms include pain and stiffness with activity; occurs among elderly.

✓5th **715.1 Osteoarthrosis, localized, primary**
[0-8]

Localized osteoarthropathy, idiopathic

✓5th **715.2 Osteoarthrosis, localized, secondary**
[0-8]

Coxae malum senilis

✓5th **715.3 Osteoarthrosis, localized, not specified whether primary or secondary**
[0-8]

Otto's pelvis

✓5th **715.8 Osteoarthrosis involving, or with mention of more than one site, but not specified as generalized**
[0,9]

✓5th **715.9 Osteoarthrosis, unspecified whether generalized or localized**
[0-8]

4th 716 Other and unspecified arthropathies

EXCLUDES *cricoarytenoid arthropathy (478.79)*

The following fifth-digit subclassification is for use with category 716; valid digits are in [brackets] under each code. See list at beginning of chapter for definitions.

0 site unspecified
1 shoulder region
2 upper arm
3 forearm
4 hand
5 pelvic region and thigh
6 lower leg
7 ankle and foot
8 other specified sites
9 multiple sites

5th 716.0 Kaschin-Beck disease
[0-9] Endemic polyarthritis

DEF: Chronic degenerative disease of spine and peripheral joints; occurs in eastern Siberian, northern Chinese, and Korean youth; may be a mycotoxicosis caused by eating cereals infected with fungus.

5th 716.1 Traumatic arthropathy
[0-9]

5th 716.2 Allergic arthritis
[0-9] EXCLUDES *arthritis associated with Henoch-Schönlein purpura or serum sickness (713.6)*

5th 716.3 Climacteric arthritis
[0-9] Menopausal arthritis

DEF: Ovarian hormone deficiency; causes pain in small joints, shoulders, elbows or knees; affects females at menopause; also called arthropathia ovaripriva.

5th 716.4 Transient arthropathy
[0-9] EXCLUDES *palindromic rheumatism (719.3)*

5th 716.5 Unspecified polyarthropathy or polyarthritis
[0-9]

5th 716.6 Unspecified monoarthritis
[0-8] Coxitis

5th 716.8 Other specified arthropathy
[0-9]

5th 716.9 Arthropathy, unspecified
[0-9]
Arthritis } (acute) (chronic) (subacute)
Arthropathy } (acute) (chronic) (subacute)
Articular rheumatism (chronic)
Inflammation of joint NOS

4th 717 Internal derangement of knee

INCLUDES degeneration, rupture, old, tear, old } of articular cartilage or meniscus of knee

EXCLUDES *acute derangement of knee (836.0-836.6)*
ankylosis (718.5)
contracture (718.4)
current injury (836.0-836.6)
deformity (736.4-736.6)
recurrent dislocation (718.3)

717.0 Old bucket handle tear of medial meniscus
Old bucket handle tear of unspecified cartilage

717.1 Derangement of anterior horn of medial meniscus

717.2 Derangement of posterior horn of medial meniscus

717.3 Other and unspecified derangement of medial meniscus
Degeneration of internal semilunar cartilage

5th 717.4 Derangement of lateral meniscus

717.40 Derangement of lateral meniscus, unspecified

717.41 Bucket handle tear of lateral meniscus

717.42 Derangement of anterior horn of lateral meniscus

Disruption and Tears of Meniscus

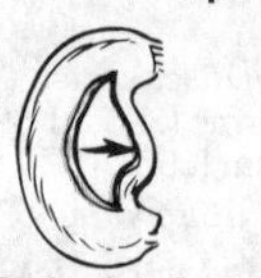

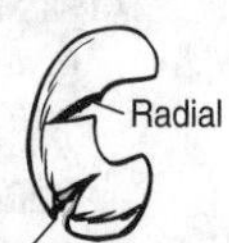

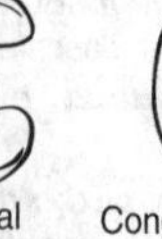

Internal Derangements of Knee

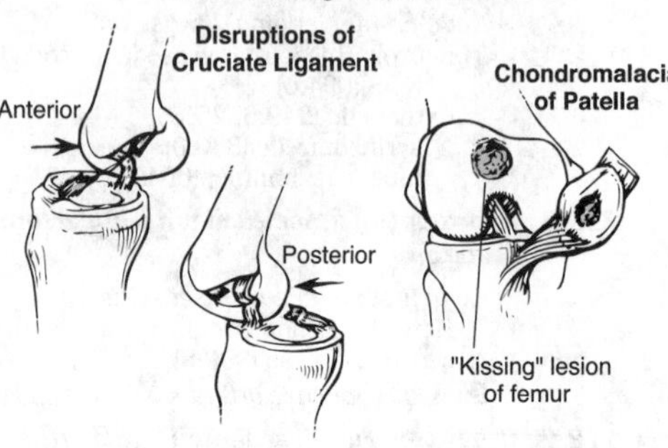

717.43 Derangement of posterior horn of lateral meniscus

717.49 Other

717.5 Derangement of meniscus, not elsewhere classified
Congenital discoid meniscus
Cyst of semilunar cartilage
Derangement of semilunar cartilage NOS

717.6 Loose body in knee
Joint mice, knee
Rice bodies, knee (joint)

DEF: The presence in the joint synovial area of a small, frequently calcified, loose body created from synovial membrane, organized fibrin fragments of articular cartilage or arthritis osteophytes.

717.7 Chondromalacia of patella
Chondromalacia patellae
Degeneration [softening] of articular cartilage of patella

DEF: Softened patella cartilage.

5th 717.8 Other internal derangement of knee

717.81 Old disruption of lateral collateral ligament

717.82 Old disruption of medial collateral ligament

717.83 Old disruption of anterior cruciate ligament

717.84 Old disruption of posterior cruciate ligament

717.85 Old disruption of other ligaments of knee
Capsular ligament of knee

717.89 Other
Old disruption of ligaments NOS

717.9 Unspecified internal derangement of knee
Derangement NOS of knee

✓4th 718 Other derangement of joint

EXCLUDES *current injury (830.0-848.9)*
jaw (524.60-524.69)

The following fifth-digit subclassification is for use with category 718; valid digits are in [brackets] under each code. See list at beginning of chapter for definitions.

0 site unspecified
1 shoulder region
2 upper arm
3 forearm
4 hand
5 pelvic region and thigh
6 lower leg
7 ankle and foot
8 other specified sites
9 multiple sites

✓5th 718.0 Articular cartilage disorder
[0-5,7-9]
Meniscus:
disorder
rupture, old
Meniscus:
tear, old
Old rupture of ligament(s) of joint NOS

EXCLUDES *articular cartilage disorder:*
in ochronosis (270.2)
knee (717.0-717.9)
chondrocalcinosis (275.4)
metastatic calcification (275.4)

✓5th 718.1 Loose body in joint
[0-5,7-9] Joint mice

EXCLUDES *knee (717.6)*

DEF: Calcified loose bodies in synovial fluid; due to arthritic osteophytes.

✓5th 718.2 Pathological dislocation
[0-9] Dislocation or displacement of joint, not recurrent and not current injury
Spontaneous dislocation (joint)

✓5th 718.3 Recurrent dislocation of joint
[0-9]

✓5th 718.4 Contracture of joint
[0-9]

✓5th 718.5 Ankylosis of joint
[0-9] Ankylosis of joint (fibrous) (osseous)

EXCLUDES *spine (724.9)*
stiffness of joint without mention of ankylosis (719.5)

DEF: Immobility and solidification, of joint; due to disease, injury or surgical procedure.

✓5th 718.6 Unspecified intrapelvic protrusion of acetabulum
[0,5] Protrusio acetabuli, unspecified

DEF: Sinking of the floor of acetabulum; causing femoral head to protrude, limits hip movement; of unknown etiology.

✓5th 718.7 Developmental dislocation of joint
[0-9]

EXCLUDES *congenital dislocation of joint (754.0-755.8)*
traumatic dislocation of joint (830-839)

✓5th 718.8 Other joint derangement, not elsewhere classified
[0-9] Flail joint (paralytic) Instability of joint

EXCLUDES *deformities classifiable to 736 (736.0-736.9)*

✓5th 718.9 Unspecified derangement of joint
[0-5,7-9] EXCLUDES *knee (717.9)*

Joint Derangements and Disorders

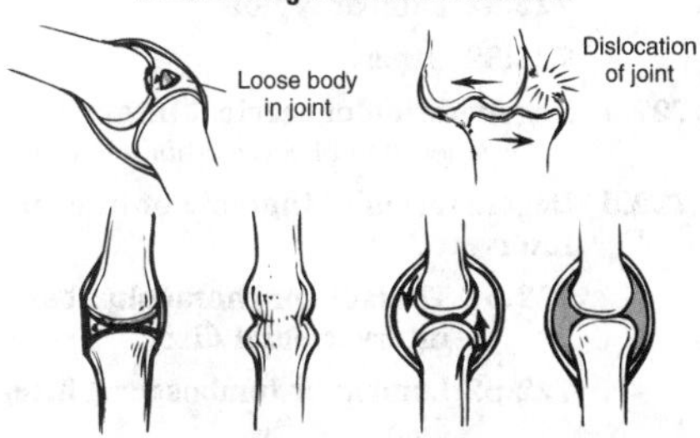

✓4th 719 Other and unspecified disorders of joint

EXCLUDES *jaw (524.60-524.69)*

The following fifth-digit subclassification is for use with codes 719.0-719.6, 719.8-719.9; valid digits are in [brackets] under each code. See list at beginning of chapter for definitions.

0 site unspecified
1 shoulder region
2 upper arm
3 forearm
4 hand
5 pelvic region and thigh
6 lower leg
7 ankle and foot
8 other specified sites
9 multiple sites

✓5th 719.0 Effusion of joint
[0-9] Hydrarthrosis
Swelling of joint, with or without pain

EXCLUDES *intermittent hydrarthrosis (719.3)*

✓5th 719.1 Hemarthrosis
[0-9] EXCLUDES **current injury (840.0-848.9)**

✓5th 719.2 Villonodular synovitis
[0-9]

DEF: Overgrowth of synovial tissue, especially at knee joint; due to macrophage infiltration of giant cells in synovial villi and fibrous nodules.

✓5th 719.3 Palindromic rheumatism
[0-9] Hench-Rosenberg syndrome
Intermittent hydrarthrosis

DEF: Recurrent episodes of afebrile arthritis and periarthritis marked by their complete disappearance after a few days or hours; causes swelling, redness, and disability usually affecting only one joint; no known cause; affects adults of either sex.

✓5th 719.4 Pain in joint
[0-9] Arthralgia

✓5th 719.5 Stiffness of joint, not elsewhere classified
[0-9]

✓5th 719.6 Other symptoms referable to joint
[0-9] Joint crepitus
Snapping hip

719.7 Difficulty in walking

EXCLUDES *abnormality of gait (781.2)*

✓5th 719.8 Other specified disorders of joint
[0-9] Calcification of joint
Fistula of joint

EXCLUDES *temporomandibular joint-pain-dysfunction syndrome [Costen's syndrome] (524.60)*

✓5th 719.9 Unspecified disorder of joint
[0-9]

DORSOPATHIES (720-724)

EXCLUDES *curvature of spine (737.0-737.9)*
osteochondrosis of spine (juvenile) (732.0)
adult (732.8)

✓4th 720 Ankylosing spondylitis and other inflammatory spondylopathies

720.0 Ankylosing spondylitis
Rheumatoid arthritis of spine NOS
Spondylitis:
Marie-Strümpell
rheumatoid

DEF: Rheumatoid arthritis of spine and sacroiliac joints; fusion and deformity in spine follows; affects mainly males; cause unknown.

720.1 Spinal enthesopathy
Disorder of peripheral ligamentous or muscular attachments of spine
Romanus lesion

DEF: Tendinous or muscular vertebral bone attachment abnormality.

720.2 Sacroiliitis, not elsewhere classified
Inflammation of sacroiliac joint NOS

DEF: Pain due to inflammation in joint, at juncture of sacrum and hip.

✓5th **720.8 Other inflammatory spondylopathies**

720.81 Inflammatory spondylopathies in diseases classified elsewhere

Code first underlying disease as:
tuberculosis (015.0)

720.89 Other

720.9 Unspecified inflammatory spondylopathy
Spondylitis NOS

✓4th **721 Spondylosis and allied disorders**
DEF: Degenerative changes in spinal joint.

721.0 Cervical spondylosis without myelopathy
Cervical or cervicodorsal:
arthritis
osteoarthritis
spondylarthritis

721.1 Cervical spondylosis with myelopathy Anterior spinal artery compression syndrome
Spondylogenic compression of cervical spinal cord
Vertebral artery compression syndrome

721.2 Thoracic spondylosis without myelopathy
Thoracic:
arthritis
osteoarthritis
spondylarthritis

721.3 Lumbosacral spondylosis without myelopathy
Lumbar or lumbosacral:
arthritis
osteoarthritis
spondylarthritis

✓5th **721.4 Thoracic or lumbar spondylosis with myelopathy**

721.41 Thoracic region
Spondylogenic compression of thoracic spinal cord

721.42 Lumbar region
Spondylogenic compression of lumbar spinal cord

721.5 Kissing spine
Baastrup's syndrome
DEF: Compression of spinous processes of adjacent vertebrae; due to mutual contact.

721.6 Ankylosing vertebral hyperostosis

721.7 Traumatic spondylopathy
Kümmell's disease or spondylitis

721.8 Other allied disorders of spine

✓5th **721.9 Spondylosis of unspecified site**

721.90 Without mention of myelopathy
Spinal:
arthritis (deformans) (degenerative) (hypertrophic)
osteoarthritis NOS
Spondylarthrosis NOS

721.91 With myelopathy
Spondylogenic compression of spinal cord NOS

✓4th **722 Intervertebral disc disorders**

722.0 Displacement of cervical intervertebral disc without myelopathy
Neuritis (brachial) or radiculitis due to displacement or rupture of cervical intervertebral disc
Any condition classifiable to 722.2 of the cervical or cervicothoracic intervertebral disc

✓5th **722.1 Displacement of thoracic or lumbar intervertebral disc without myelopathy**

Anatomy of Vertebral Disc

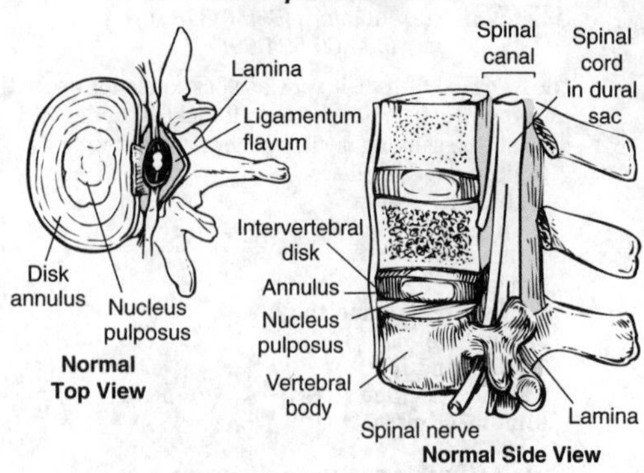

Derangement of Vertebral Disc

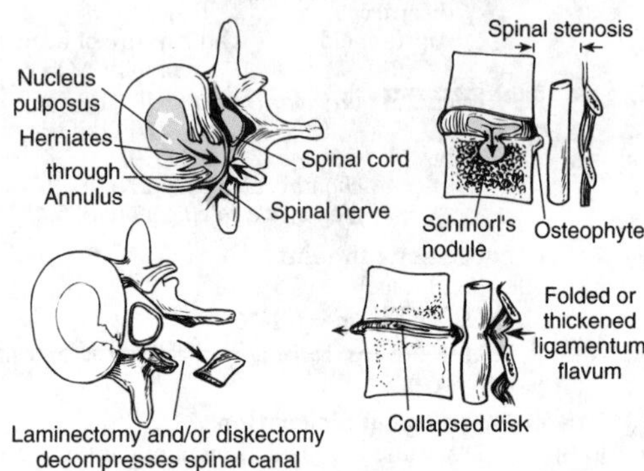

722.10 Lumbar intervertebral disc without myelopathy
Lumbago or sciatica due to displacement of intervertebral disc
Neuritis or radiculitis due to displacement or rupture of lumbar intervertebral disc
Any condition classifiable to 722.2 of the lumbar or lumbosacral intervertebral disc

722.11 Thoracic intervertebral disc without myelopathy
Any condition classifiable to 722.2 of thoracic intervertebral disc

722.2 Displacement of intervertebral disc, site unspecified, without myelopathy
Discogenic syndrome NOS
Herniation of nucleus pulposus NOS
Intervertebral disc NOS:
extrusion
prolapse
protrusion
rupture
Neuritis or radiculitis due to displacement or rupture of intervertebral disc

✓5th **722.3 Schmorl's nodes**
DEF: Irregular bone defect in the margin of the vertebral body; causes herniation into end plate of vertebral body.

722.30 Unspecified region

722.31 Thoracic region

722.32 Lumbar region

722.39 Other

722.4 Degeneration of cervical intervertebral disc
Degeneration of cervicothoracic intervertebral disc

✓5th **722.5 Degeneration of thoracic or lumbar intervertebral disc**

722.51 Thoracic or thoracolumbar intervertebral disc

722.52 Lumbar or lumbosacral intervertebral disc

Stenosis in Cervical Region

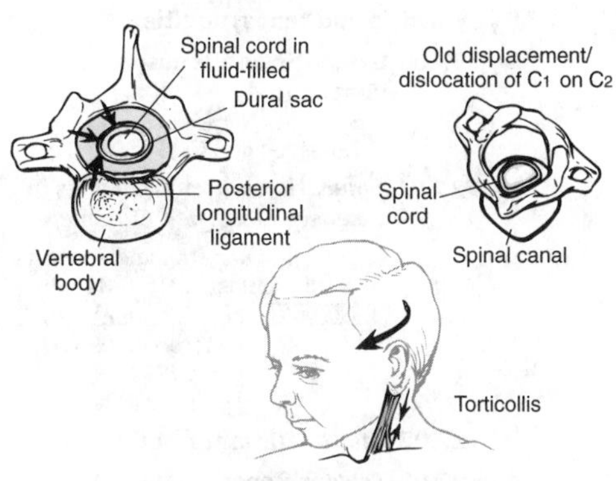

722.6 Degeneration of intervertebral disc, site unspecified
Degenerative disc disease NOS
Narrowing of intervertebral disc or space NOS

✓5th **722.7 Intervertebral disc disorder with myelopathy**
722.70 Unspecified region
722.71 Cervical region
722.72 Thoracic region
722.73 Lumbar region

✓5th **722.8 Postlaminectomy syndrome**
DEF: Spinal disorder due to spinal laminectomy surgery.
722.80 Unspecified region
722.81 Cervical region
722.82 Thoracic region
722.83 Lumbar region

✓5th **722.9 Other and unspecified disc disorder**
Calcification of intervertebral cartilage or disc
Discitis
722.90 Unspecified region
722.91 Cervical region
722.92 Thoracic region
722.93 Lumbar region

✓4th **723 Other disorders of cervical region**
EXCLUDES *conditions due to:*
intervertebral disc disorders (722.0-722.9)
spondylosis (721.0-721.9)

723.0 Spinal stenosis in cervical region

723.1 Cervicalgia
Pain in neck
DEF: Pain in cervical spine or neck region.

723.2 Cervicocranial syndrome
Barré-Liéou syndrome
Posterior cervical sympathetic syndrome
DEF: Neurologic disorder of upper cervical spine and nerve roots.

723.3 Cervicobrachial syndrome (diffuse)
DEF: Complex of symptoms due to scalenus anterior muscle compressing the brachial plexus; pain radiates from shoulder to arm or back of neck.

723.4 Brachial neuritis or radiculitis NOS
Cervical radiculitis
Radicular syndrome of upper limbs

723.5 Torticollis, unspecified
Contracture of neck
EXCLUDES *congenital (754.1)*
due to birth injury (767.8)
hysterical (300.11)
ocular torticollis (781.93)
psychogenic (306.0)
spasmodic (333.83)
traumatic, current (847.0)
DEF: Abnormally positioned neck relative to head; due to cervical muscle or fascia contractions; also called wryneck.

723.6 Panniculitis specified as affecting neck
DEF: Inflammation of the panniculus adiposus (subcutaneous fat) in the neck.

723.7 Ossification of posterior longitudinal ligament in cervical region

723.8 Other syndromes affecting cervical region
Cervical syndrome NEC
Klippel's disease
Occipital neuralgia

723.9 Unspecified musculoskeletal disorders and symptoms referable to neck
Cervical (region) disorder NOS

✓4th **724 Other and unspecified disorders of back**
EXCLUDES *collapsed vertebra (code to cause, e.g., osteoporosis, 733.00-733.09)*
conditions due to:
intervertebral disc disorders (722.0-722.9)
spondylosis (721.0-721.9)

✓5th **724.0 Spinal stenosis, other than cervical**
724.00 Spinal stenosis, unspecified region
724.01 Thoracic region
724.02 Lumbar region
724.09 Other

724.1 Pain in thoracic spine

724.2 Lumbago
Low back pain
Low back syndrome
Lumbalgia

724.3 Sciatica
Neuralgia or neuritis of sciatic nerve
EXCLUDES *specified lesion of sciatic nerve (355.0)*

724.4 Thoracic or lumbosacral neuritis or radiculitis, unspecified
Radicular syndrome of lower limbs

724.5 Backache, unspecified
Vertebrogenic (pain) syndrome NOS

724.6 Disorders of sacrum
Ankylosis } lumbosacral or sacroiliac (joint)
Instability }

✓5th **724.7 Disorders of coccyx**
724.70 Unspecified disorder of coccyx
724.71 Hypermobility of coccyx
724.79 Other
Coccygodynia

724.8 Other symptoms referable to back
Ossification of posterior longitudinal ligament NOS
Panniculitis specified as sacral or affecting back

724.9 Other unspecified back disorders
Ankylosis of spine NOS
Compression of spinal nerve root NEC
Spinal disorder NOS
EXCLUDES *sacroiliitis (720.2)*

RHEUMATISM, EXCLUDING THE BACK (725-729)

INCLUDES disorders of muscles and tendons and their attachments, and of other soft tissues

725 Polymyalgia rheumatica
DEF: Joint and muscle pain, pelvis, and shoulder girdle stiffness, high sedimentation rate and temporal arteritis; occurs in elderly.

✓4th **726 Peripheral enthesopathies and allied syndromes**
Note: Enthesopathies are disorders of peripheral ligamentous or muscular attachments.
EXCLUDES *spinal enthesopathy (720.1)*

726.0 Adhesive capsulitis of shoulder

✓5th **726.1 Rotator cuff syndrome of shoulder and allied disorders**

726.10 Disorders of bursae and tendons in shoulder region, unspecified
Rotator cuff syndrome NOS
Supraspinatus syndrome NOS

726.11 Calcifying tendinitis of shoulder

726.12 Bicipital tenosynovitis

726.19 Other specified disorders
EXCLUDES *complete rupture of rotator cuff, nontraumatic (727.61)*

726.2 Other affections of shoulder region, not elsewhere classified
Periarthritis of shoulder
Scapulohumeral fibrositis

✓5th **726.3 Enthesopathy of elbow region**

726.30 Enthesopathy of elbow, unspecified

726.31 Medial epicondylitis

726.32 Lateral epicondylitis
Epicondylitis NOS
Golfers' elbow
Tennis elbow

726.33 Olecranon bursitis
Bursitis of elbow

726.39 Other

726.4 Enthesopathy of wrist and carpus
Bursitis of hand or wrist
Periarthritis of wrist

726.5 Enthesopathy of hip region
Bursitis of hip
Gluteal tendinitis
Iliac crest spur
Psoas tendinitis
Trochanteric tendinitis

✓5th **726.6 Enthesopathy of knee**

726.60 Enthesopathy of knee, unspecified
Bursitis of knee NOS

726.61 Pes anserinus tendinitis or bursitis
DEF: Inflamed tendons of sartorius, gracilis and semitendinosus muscles of medial aspect of knee.

726.62 Tibial collateral ligament bursitis
Pellegrini-Stieda syndrome

726.63 Fibular collateral ligament bursitis

726.64 Patellar tendinitis

726.65 Prepatellar bursitis

726.69 Other
Bursitis:
  infrapatellar
  subpatellar

✓5th **726.7 Enthesopathy of ankle and tarsus**

726.70 Enthesopathy of ankle and tarsus, unspecified
Metatarsalgia NOS
EXCLUDES *Morton's metatarsalgia (355.6)*

726.71 Achilles bursitis or tendinitis

726.72 Tibialis tendinitis
Tibialis (anterior) (posterior) tendinitis

726.73 Calcaneal spur
DEF: Overgrowth of calcaneous bone; causes pain on walking; due to chronic avulsion injury of plantar fascia from calcaneus.

726.79 Other
Peroneal tendinitis

726.8 Other peripheral enthesopathies

✓5th **726.9 Unspecified enthesopathy**

726.90 Enthesopathy of unspecified site
Capsulitis NOS
Periarthritis NOS
Tendinitis NOS

726.91 Exostosis of unspecified site
Bone spur NOS

✓4th **727 Other disorders of synovium, tendon, and bursa**

✓5th **727.0 Synovitis and tenosynovitis**

727.00 Synovitis and tenosynovitis, unspecified
Synovitis NOS
Tenosynovitis NOS

727.01 Synovitis and tenosynovitis in diseases classified elsewhere
Code first underlying disease as:
tuberculosis (015.0-015.9)
EXCLUDES *crystal-induced (275.4)*
gonococcal (098.51)
gouty (274.0)
syphilitic (095.7)

727.02 Giant cell tumor of tendon sheath

727.03 Trigger finger (acquired)
DEF: Stenosing tenosynovitis or nodule in flexor tendon; cessation of flexion or extension movement in finger, followed by snapping into place.

727.04 Radial styloid tenosynovitis
de Quervain's disease

727.05 Other tenosynovitis of hand and wrist

727.06 Tenosynovitis of foot and ankle

727.09 Other

727.1 Bunion
DEF: Enlarged first metatarsal head due to inflamed bursa; results in laterally displaced great toe.

727.2 Specific bursitides often of occupational origin
Beat:
  elbow
  hand
  knee
Chronic crepitant synovitis of wrist
Miners':
  elbow
  knee

727.3 Other bursitis
Bursitis NOS
EXCLUDES *bursitis:*
  gonococcal (098.52)
  subacromial (726.19)
  subcoracoid (726.19)
  subdeltoid (726.19)
  syphilitic (095.7)
  "frozen shoulder" (726.0)

✓5th **727.4 Ganglion and cyst of synovium, tendon, and bursa**

727.40 Synovial cyst, unspecified
EXCLUDES *that of popliteal space (727.51)*

727.41 Ganglion of joint

727.42 Ganglion of tendon sheath

727.43 Ganglion, unspecified

727.49 Other
Cyst of bursa

Bunion

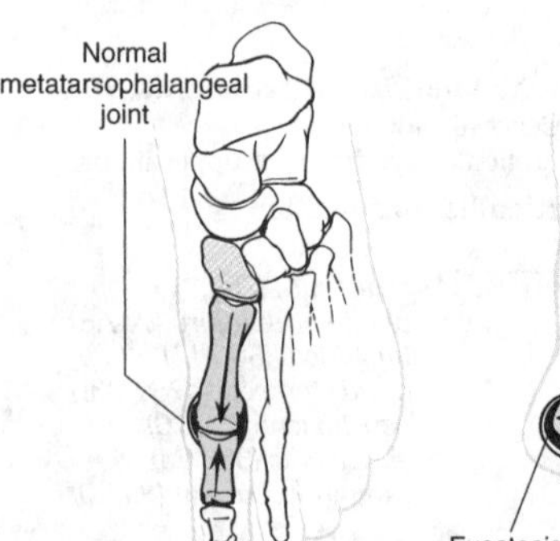

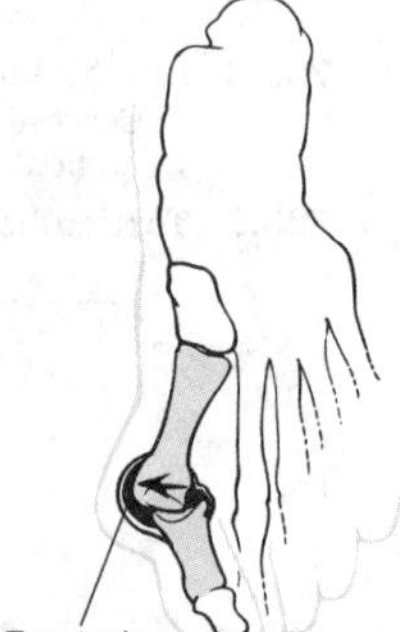

Ganglia

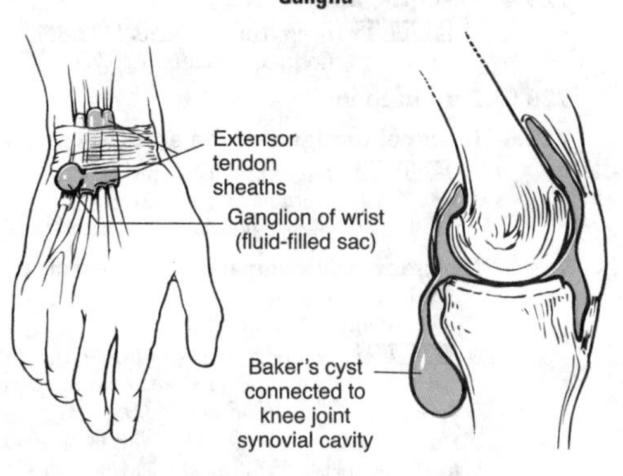

✓5th **727.5 Rupture of synovium**

727.50 Rupture of synovium, unspecified

727.51 Synovial cyst of popliteal space
Baker's cyst (knee)

727.59 Other

✓5th **727.6 Rupture of tendon, nontraumatic**

727.60 Nontraumatic rupture of unspecified tendon

727.61 Complete rupture of rotator cuff

727.62 Tendons of biceps (long head)

727.63 Extensor tendons of hand and wrist

727.64 Flexor tendons of hand and wrist

727.65 Quadriceps tendon

727.66 Patellar tendon

727.67 Achilles tendon

727.68 Other tendons of foot and ankle

727.69 Other

✓5th **727.8 Other disorders of synovium, tendon, and bursa**

727.81 Contracture of tendon (sheath)
Short Achilles tendon (acquired)

727.82 Calcium deposits in tendon and bursa
Calcification of tendon NOS
Calcific tendinitis NOS
EXCLUDES *peripheral ligamentous or muscular attachments (726.0-726.9)*

727.83 Plica syndrome
Plica knee
DEF: A fold in the synovial tissue that begins to form before birth, creating a septum between two pockets of synovial tissue; two most common plicae are the medial patellar plica and the suprapatellar plica. Plica syndrome, or plica knee, refers to symptomatic plica. Experienced by females more commonly than males.

727.89 Other
Abscess of bursa or tendon
EXCLUDES *xanthomatosis localized to tendons (272.7)*

727.9 Unspecified disorder of synovium, tendon, and bursa

✓4th **728 Disorders of muscle, ligament, and fascia**
EXCLUDES *enthesopathies (726.0-726.9)*
muscular dystrophies (359.0-359.1)
myoneural disorders (358.00-358.9)
myopathies (359.2-359.9)
nontraumatic hematoma of muscle (729.92)
old disruption of ligaments of knee (717.81-717.89)

728.0 Infective myositis
Myositis:
purulent
suppurative
EXCLUDES *myositis:*
epidemic (074.1)
interstitial (728.81)
syphilitic (095.6)
tropical (040.81)
DEF: Inflamed connective septal tissue of muscle.

✓5th **728.1 Muscular calcification and ossification**

728.10 Calcification and ossification, unspecified
Massive calcification (paraplegic)

728.11 Progressive myositis ossificans
DEF: Progressive myositic disease; marked by bony tissue formed by voluntary muscle; occurs among very young.

728.12 Traumatic myositis ossificans
Myositis ossificans (circumscripta)

728.13 Postoperative heterotopic calcification
DEF: Abnormal formation of calcium deposits in muscular tissue after surgery, marked by a corresponding loss of muscle tone and tension.

728.19 Other
Polymyositis ossificans

728.2 Muscular wasting and disuse atrophy, not elsewhere classified
Amyotrophia NOS
Myofibrosis
EXCLUDES *neuralgic amyotrophy (353.5)*
pelvic muscle wasting and disuse atrophy (618.83)
progressive muscular atrophy (335.0-335.9)

728.3 Other specific muscle disorders
Arthrogryposis
Immobility syndrome (paraplegic)
EXCLUDES *arthrogryposis multiplex congenita (754.89)*
stiff-man syndrome (333.91)

728.4 Laxity of ligament

728.5 Hypermobility syndrome

728.6 Contracture of palmar fascia
Dupuytren's contracture
DEF: Dupuytren's contracture: flexion deformity of finger, due to shortened, thickened fibrosing of palmar fascia; cause unknown; associated with long-standing epilepsy; occurs more often in males.

✓5th **728.7 Other fibromatoses**

728.71 Plantar fascial fibromatosis
Contracture of plantar fascia
Plantar fasciitis (traumatic)
DEF: Plantar fascia fibromatosis; causes nodular swelling and pain; not associated with contractures.

728.79 Other
Garrod's or knuckle pads
Nodular fasciitis
Pseudosarcomatous fibromatosis (proliferative) (subcutaneous)
DEF: Knuckle pads: Pea-size nodules on dorsal surface of interphalangeal joints; new growth of fibrous tissue with thickened dermis and epidermis.

✓5th **728.8 Other disorders of muscle, ligament, and fascia**

728.81 Interstitial myositis
DEF: Inflammation of septal connective parts of muscle tissue.

728.82 Foreign body granuloma of muscle
Talc granuloma of muscle

728.83 Rupture of muscle, nontraumatic

728.84 Diastasis of muscle
Diastasis recti (abdomen)
EXCLUDES *diastasis recti complicating pregnancy, labor, and delivery (665.8)*
DEF: Muscle separation, such as recti abdominis after repeated pregnancies.

728.85 Spasm of muscle

728.86 Necrotizing fasciitis
Use additional code to identify:
infectious organism (041.00-041.89)
gangrene (785.4), if applicable
DEF: Fulminating infection begins with extensive cellulitis, spreads to superficial and deep fascia; causes thrombosis of subcutaneous vessels, and gangrene of underlying tissue.

728.87 Muscle weakness (generalized)
EXCLUDES *generalized weakness (780.79)*

728.88 Rhabdomyolysis
DEF: A disintegration or destruction of muscle; an acute disease characterized by the excretion of myoglobin into the urine.

728.89 Other
Eosinophilic fasciitis
Use additional E code to identify drug, if drug induced
DEF: Eosinophilic fasciitis: inflammation of fascia of extremities associated with eosinophilia, edema, and swelling; occurs alone or as part of myalgia syndrome.

728.9 Unspecified disorder of muscle, ligament, and fascia

✓4th **729 Other disorders of soft tissues**
EXCLUDES *acroparesthesia (443.89)*
carpal tunnel syndrome (354.0)
disorders of the back (720.0-724.9)
entrapment syndromes (354.0-355.9)
palindromic rheumatism (719.3)
periarthritis (726.0-726.9)
psychogenic rheumatism (306.0)

729.0 Rheumatism, unspecified and fibrositis
DEF: General term describes diseases of muscle, tendon, nerve, joint, or bone; symptoms include pain and stiffness.

729.1 Myalgia and myositis, unspecified
Fibromyositis NOS
DEF: Myalgia: muscle pain.
DEF: Myositis: inflamed voluntary muscle.
DEF: Fibromyositis: inflamed fibromuscular tissue.

729.2 Neuralgia, neuritis, and radiculitis, unspecified
EXCLUDES *brachial radiculitis (723.4)*
cervical radiculitis (723.4)
lumbosacral radiculitis (724.4)
mononeuritis (354.0-355.9)
radiculitis due to intervertebral disc involvement (722.0-722.2, 722.7)
sciatica (724.3)
DEF: Neuralgia: paroxysmal pain along nerve; symptoms include brief pain and tenderness at point nerve exits.
DEF: Neuritis: inflamed nerve, symptoms include paresthesia, paralysis and loss of reflexes at nerve site.
DEF: Radiculitis: inflamed nerve root.

✓5th **729.3 Panniculitis, unspecified**
DEF: Inflammatory reaction of subcutaneous fat; causes nodules; often develops in abdominal region.

729.30 Panniculitis, unspecified site
Weber-Christian disease
DEF: Febrile, nodular, nonsuppurative, relapsing inflammation of subcutaneous fat.

729.31 Hypertrophy of fat pad, knee
Hypertrophy of infrapatellar fat pad

729.39 Other site
EXCLUDES *panniculitis specified as (affecting):*
back (724.8)
neck (723.6)
sacral (724.8)

729.4 Fasciitis, unspecified
EXCLUDES *necrotizing fasciitis (728.86)*
nodular fasciitis (728.79)

729.5 Pain in limb

729.6 Residual foreign body in soft tissue
EXCLUDES *foreign body granuloma:*
muscle (728.82)
skin and subcutaneous tissue (709.4)

✓5th **729.7 Nontraumatic compartment syndrome**
Code first, if applicable, postprocedural complication (998.89)
EXCLUDES *compartment syndrome NOS (958.90)*
traumatic compartment syndrome (958.90-958.99)
DEF: Compression of nerves and blood vessels within an enclosed space, leading to impaired blood flow and muscle and nerve damage.

729.71 Nontraumatic compartment syndrome of upper extremity
Nontraumatic compartment syndrome of shoulder, arm, forearm, wrist, hand, and fingers

729.72 Nontraumatic compartment syndrome of lower extremity
Nontraumatic compartment syndrome of hip, buttock, thigh, leg, foot, and toes

729.73 Nontraumatic compartment syndrome of abdomen

729.79 Nontraumatic compartment syndrome of other sites

✓5th **729.8 Other musculoskeletal symptoms referable to limbs**

729.81 Swelling of limb

729.82 Cramp

729.89 Other
EXCLUDES *abnormality of gait (781.2)*
tetany (781.7)
transient paralysis of limb (781.4)

✓5th **729.9 Other and unspecified disorders of soft tissue**

729.90 Disorders of soft tissue, unspecified

729.91 Post-traumatic seroma
EXCLUDES *seroma complicating a procedure (998.13)*

729.92 Nontraumatic hematoma of soft tissue
Nontraumatic hematoma of muscle

729.99 Other disorders of soft tissue
Polyalgia

OSTEOPATHIES, CHONDROPATHIES, AND ACQUIRED MUSCULOSKELETAL DEFORMITIES (730-739)

✓4th 730 Osteomyelitis, periostitis, and other infections involving bone

EXCLUDES *jaw (526.4-526.5)*
petrous bone (383.2)

Use additional code to identify organism, such as Staphylococcus (041.1)

The following fifth-digit subclassification is for use with category 730; valid digits are in [brackets] under each code. See list at beginning of chapter for definitions.

0 site unspecified
1 shoulder region
2 upper arm
3 forearm
4 hand
5 pelvic region and thigh
6 lower leg
7 ankle and foot
8 other specified sites
9 multiple sites

DEF: Osteomyelitis: bacterial inflammation of bone tissue and marrow.

DEF: Periostitis: inflammation of specialized connective tissue; causes swelling of bone and aching pain.

✓5th 730.0 Acute osteomyelitis
[0-9]
Abscess of any bone except accessory sinus, jaw, or mastoid
Acute or subacute osteomyelitis, with or without mention of periostitis
Use additional code to identify major osseous defect, if applicable (731.3)

✓5th 730.1 Chronic osteomyelitis
[0-9]
Brodie's abscess
Chronic or old osteomyelitis, with or without mention of periostitis
Sequestrum of bone
Sclerosing osteomyelitis of Garré
Use additional code to identify major osseous defect, if applicable (731.3)
EXCLUDES *aseptic necrosis of bone (733.40-733.49)*

✓5th 730.2 Unspecified osteomyelitis
[0-9]
Osteitis or osteomyelitis NOS, with or without mention of periostitis
Use additional code to identify major osseous defect, if applicable (731.3)

✓5th 730.3 Periostitis without mention of osteomyelitis
[0-9]
Abscess of periosteum } without mention of osteomyelitis
Periostosis }
EXCLUDES *that in secondary syphilis (091.61)*

✓5th 730.7 *Osteopathy resulting from poliomyelitis*
[0-9]
Code first underlying disease (045.0-045.9)

✓5th 730.8 *Other infections involving bone in diseases classified elsewhere*
[0-9]
Code first underlying disease as:
tuberculosis (015.0-015.9)
typhoid fever (002.0)
EXCLUDES *syphilis of bone NOS (095.5)*

✓5th 730.9 Unspecified infection of bone
[0-9]

✓4th 731 Osteitis deformans and osteopathies associated with other disorders classified elsewhere

DEF: Osteitis deformans: Bone disease marked by episodes of increased bone loss, excessive repair attempts follow; causes weakened, deformed bones with increased mass, bowed long bones, deformed flat bones, pain and pathological fractures; may be fatal if associated with congestive heart failure, giant cell tumors or bone sarcoma; also called Paget's disease.

731.0 Osteitis deformans without mention of bone tumor
Paget's disease of bone

731.1 Osteitis deformans in diseases classified elsewhere
Code first underlying disease as:
malignant neoplasm of bone (170.0-170.9)

731.2 Hypertrophic pulmonary osteoarthropathy
Bamberger-Marie disease
DEF: Clubbing, of fingers and toes; related to enlarged ends of long bones; due to chronic lung and heart disease.

731.3 Major osseous defects
Code first underlying disease, if known, such as:
aseptic necrosis (733.40-733.49)
malignant neoplasm of bone (170.0-170.9)
osteomyelitis (730.00-730.29)
osteoporosis (733.00-733.09)
peri-prosthetic osteolysis (996.45)

731.8 Other bone involvement in diseases classified elsewhere
Code first underlying disease as:
diabetes mellitus (249.8, 250.8)
Use additional code to specify bone condition, such as:
acute osteomyelitis (730.00-730.09)

✓4th 732 Osteochondropathies

DEF: Conditions related to both bone and cartilage, or conditions in which cartilage is converted to bone (enchondral ossification).

732.0 Juvenile osteochondrosis of spine
Juvenile osteochondrosis (of):
marginal or vertebral epiphysis (of Scheuermann)
spine NOS
Vertebral epiphysitis
EXCLUDES *adolescent postural kyphosis (737.0)*

732.1 Juvenile osteochondrosis of hip and pelvis
Coxa plana
Ischiopubic synchondrosis (of van Neck)
Osteochondrosis (juvenile) of:
acetabulum
head of femur (of Legg-Calvé-Perthes)
iliac crest (of Buchanan)
symphysis pubis (of Pierson)
Pseudocoxalgia

732.2 Nontraumatic slipped upper femoral epiphysis
Slipped upper femoral epiphysis NOS

732.3 Juvenile osteochondrosis of upper extremity
Osteochondrosis (juvenile) of:
capitulum of humerus (of Panner)
carpal lunate (of Kienbock)
hand NOS
head of humerus (of Haas)
heads of metacarpals (of Mauclaire)
lower ulna (of Burns)
radial head (of Brailsford)
upper extremity NOS

732.4 Juvenile osteochondrosis of lower extremity, excluding foot
Osteochondrosis (juvenile) of:
lower extremity NOS
primary patellar center (of Köhler)
proximal tibia (of Blount)
secondary patellar center (of Sinding-Larsen)
tibial tubercle (of Osgood-Schlatter)
Tibia vara

732.5 Juvenile osteochondrosis of foot
Calcaneal apophysitis
Epiphysitis, os calcis
Osteochondrosis (juvenile) of:
astragalus (of Diaz)
calcaneum (of Sever)
foot NOS
metatarsal
second (of Freiberg)
fifth (of Iselin)
os tibiale externum (of Haglund)
tarsal navicular (of Köhler)

Slipped Femoral Epiphysis

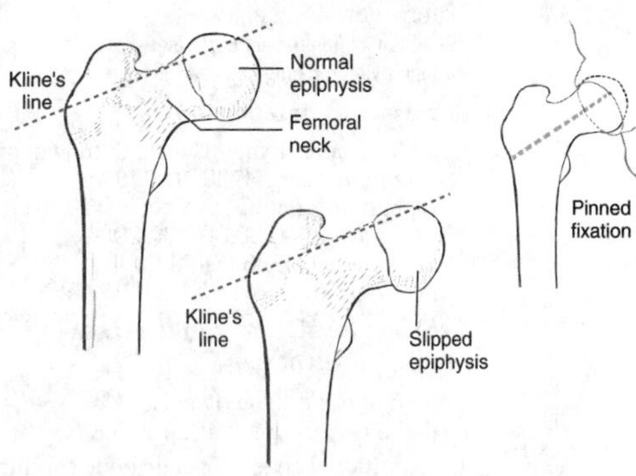

732.6 Other juvenile osteochondrosis

Apophysitis, Epiphysitis, Osteochondritis, Osteochondrosis — specified as juvenile, of other site, or site NOS

732.7 Osteochondritis dissecans

732.8 Other specified forms of osteochondropathy

Adult osteochondrosis of spine

732.9 Unspecified osteochondropathy

Apophysitis, Epiphysitis, Osteochondritis, Osteochondrosis — NOS; not specified as adult or juvenile, of unspecified site

✓4th **733 Other disorders of bone and cartilage**

EXCLUDES *bone spur (726.91)*
cartilage of, or loose body in, joint (717.0-717.9, 718.0-718.9)
giant cell granuloma of jaw (526.3)
osteitis fibrosa cystica generalisata (252.01)
osteomalacia (268.2)
polyostotic fibrous dysplasia of bone (756.54)
prognathism, retrognathism (524.1)
xanthomatosis localized to bone (272.7)

✓5th **733.0 Osteoporosis**

Use additional code to identify major osseous defect, if applicable (731.3)

Use additional code to identify personal history of pathologic (healed) fracture (V13.51)

DEF: Bone mass reduction that ultimately results in fractures after minimal trauma; dorsal kyphosis or loss of height often occur.

733.00 Osteoporosis, unspecified

Wedging of vertebra NOS

733.01 Senile osteoporosis

Postmenopausal osteoporosis

733.02 Idiopathic osteoporosis

733.03 Disuse osteoporosis

733.09 Other

Drug-induced osteoporosis

Use additional E code to identify drug

✓5th **733.1 Pathologic fracture**

Spontaneous fracture

EXCLUDES *stress fracture (733.93-733.95)*
traumatic fracture (800-829)

DEF: Fracture due to bone structure weakening by pathological processes (e.g., osteoporosis, neoplasms and osteomalacia).

733.10 Pathologic fracture, unspecified site

733.11 Pathologic fracture of humerus

733.12 Pathologic fracture of distal radius and ulna

Wrist NOS

733.13 Pathologic fracture of vertebrae

Collapse of vertebra NOS

733.14 Pathologic fracture of neck of femur

Femur NOS
Hip NOS

733.15 Pathologic fracture of other specified part of femur

733.16 Pathologic fracture of tibia or fibula

Ankle NOS

733.19 Pathologic fracture of other specified site

✓5th **733.2 Cyst of bone**

733.20 Cyst of bone (localized), unspecified

733.21 Solitary bone cyst

Unicameral bone cyst

733.22 Aneurysmal bone cyst

DEF: Solitary bone lesion, bulges into periosteum; marked by calcified rim.

733.29 Other

Fibrous dysplasia (monostotic)

EXCLUDES *cyst of jaw (526.0-526.2, 526.89)*
osteitis fibrosa cystica (252.01)
polyostotic fibrousdyplasia of bone (756.54)

733.3 Hyperostosis of skull

Hyperostosis interna frontalis
Leontiasis ossium

DEF: Abnormal bone growth on inner aspect of cranial bones.

✓5th **733.4 Aseptic necrosis of bone**

Use additional code to identify major osseous defect, if applicable (731.3)

EXCLUDES *osteochondropathies (732.0-732.9)*

DEF: Infarction of bone tissue due to a nonfectious etiology, such as a fracture, ischemic disorder or administration of immunosuppressive drugs; leads to degenerative joint disease or nonunion of fractures.

733.40 Aseptic necrosis of bone, site unspecified

733.41 Head of humerus

733.42 Head and neck of femur

Femur NOS

EXCLUDES *Legg-Calvé-Perthes disease (732.1)*

733.43 Medial femoral condyle

733.44 Talus

733.45 Jaw

Use additional E code to identify drug, if drug-induced

EXCLUDES *osteoradionecrosis of jaw (526.89)*

733.49 Other

733.5 Osteitis condensans

Piriform sclerosis of ilium

DEF: Idiopathic condition marked by low back pain; associated with oval or triangular sclerotic, opaque bone next to sacroiliac joints in the ileum.

733.6 Tietze's disease

Costochondral junction syndrome
Costochondritis

DEF: Painful, idiopathic, nonsuppurative, swollen costal cartilage sometimes confused with cardiac symptoms because the anterior chest pain resembles that of coronary artery disease.

733.7 Algoneurodystrophy

Disuse atrophy of bone
Sudeck's atrophy

✓5th **733.8 Malunion and nonunion of fracture**

733.81 Malunion of fracture

733.82 Nonunion of fracture

Pseudoarthrosis (bone)

✓5th **733.9 Other unspecified disorders of bone and cartilage**

733.90 Disorder of bone and cartilage

733.91 Arrest of bone development or growth

Epiphyseal arrest

733.92 Chondromalacia

Chondromalacia:
NOS
localized, except patella
systemic
tibial plateau

EXCLUDES *chondromalacia of patella (717.7)*

DEF: Articular cartilage softening.

733.93 Stress fracture of tibia or fibula

Stress reaction of tibia or fibula

Use additional external cause code(s) to identify the cause of the stress fracture

733.94 Stress fracture of the metatarsals

Stress reaction of metatarsals

Use additional external cause code(s) to identify the cause of the stress fracture

733.95 Stress fracture of other bone

Stress reaction of other bone

Use additional external cause code(s) to identify the cause of the stress fracture

EXCLUDES *stress fracture of:*
femoral neck (733.96)
fibula (733.93)
metatarsals (733.94)
pelvis (733.98)
shaft of femur (733.97)
tibia (733.93)

733.96 Stress fracture of femoral neck

Stress reaction of femoral neck

Use additional external cause code(s) to identify the cause of the stress fracture

733.97 Stress fracture of shaft of femur

Stress reaction of shaft of femur

Use additional external cause code(s) to identify the cause of the stress fracture

733.98 Stress fracture of pelvis

Stress reaction of pelvis

Use additional external cause code(s) to identify the cause of the stress fracture

733.99 Other

Diaphysitis
Hypertrophy of bone
Relapsing polychondritis

734 Flat foot

Pes planus (acquired)
Talipes planus (acquired)

EXCLUDES *congenital (754.61)*
rigid flat foot (754.61)
spastic (everted) flat foot (754.61)

✓4th **735 Acquired deformities of toe**

EXCLUDES *congenital (754.60-754.69, 755.65-755.66)*

735.0 Hallux valgus (acquired)

DEF: Angled displacement of the great toe, causing it to ride over or under other toes.

735.1 Hallux varus (acquired)

DEF: Angled displacement of the great toe toward the body midline, away from the other toes.

735.2 Hallux rigidus

DEF: Limited flexion movement at metatarsophalangeal joint of great toe; due to degenerative joint disease.

735.3 Hallux malleus

DEF: Extended proximal phalanx, flexed distal phalanges, of great toe; foot resembles claw or hammer.

735.4 Other hammer toe (acquired)

735.5 Claw toe (acquired)

DEF: Hyperextended proximal phalanges, flexed middle and distal phalanges.

735.8 Other acquired deformities of toe

Acquired Deformities of Toe

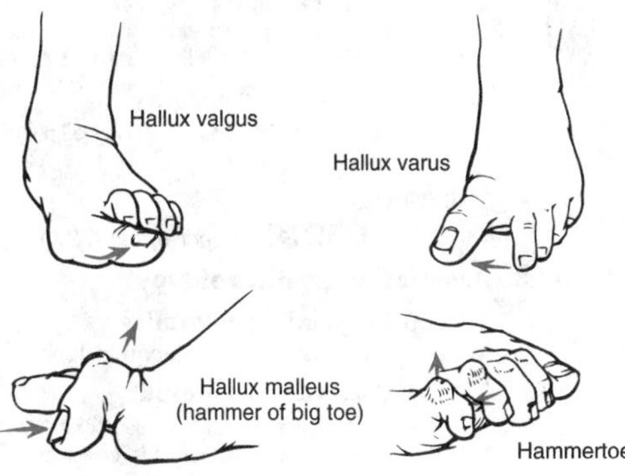

735.9 Unspecified acquired deformity of toe

✓4th **736 Other acquired deformities of limbs**

EXCLUDES *congenital (754.3-755.9)*

✓5th **736.0 Acquired deformities of forearm, excluding fingers**

736.00 Unspecified deformity

Deformity of elbow, forearm, hand, or wrist (acquired) NOS

736.01 Cubitus valgus (acquired)

DEF: Deviation of the elbow away from the body midline upon extension; it occurs when the palm is turning outward.

736.02 Cubitus varus (acquired)

DEF: Elbow joint displacement angled laterally; when the forearm is extended, it is deviated toward the midline of the body; also called "gun stock" deformity.

736.03 Valgus deformity of wrist (acquired)

DEF: Abnormal angulation away from the body midline.

736.04 Varus deformity of wrist (acquired)

DEF: Abnormal angulation toward the body midline.

736.05 Wrist drop (acquired)

DEF: Inability to extend the hand at the wrist due to extensor muscle paralysis

736.06 Claw hand (acquired)

DEF: Flexion and atrophy of the hand and fingers; found in ulnar nerve lesions, syringomyelia, and leprosy.

736.07 Club hand, acquired

DEF: Twisting of the hand out of shape or position; caused by the congenital absence of the ulna or radius.

736.09 Other

736.1 Mallet finger

DEF: Permanently flexed distal phalanx.

✓5th **736.2 Other acquired deformities of finger**

736.20 Unspecified deformity

Deformity of finger (acquired) NOS

Acquired Deformities of Forearm

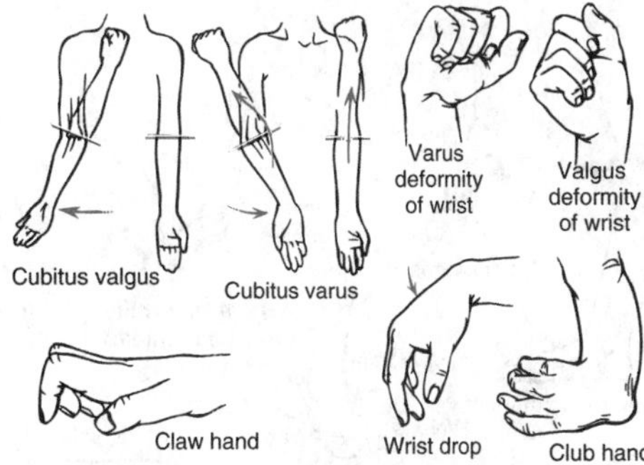

Musculoskeletal System and Connective Tissue

733.92–736.20

736.21 Boutonniere deformity

DEF: A deformity of the finger caused by flexion of the proximal interphalangeal joint and hyperextension of the distal joint; also called buttonhole deformity.

736.22 Swan-neck deformity

DEF: Flexed distal and hyperextended proximal interphalangeal joint.

736.29 Other

EXCLUDES *trigger finger (727.03)*

✓5th **736.3 Acquired deformities of hip**

736.30 Unspecified deformity

Deformity of hip (acquired) NOS

736.31 Coxa valga (acquired)

DEF: Increase of at least 140 degrees in the angle formed by the axis of the head and the neck of the femur, and the axis of its shaft.

736.32 Coxa vara (acquired)

DEF: The bending downward of the neck of the femur: causing difficulty in movement; a right angle or less may be formed by the axis of the head and neck of the femur, and the axis of its shaft.

736.39 Other

✓5th **736.4 Genu valgum or varum (acquired)**

736.41 Genu valgum (acquired)

DEF: Abnormally close together and an abnormally large space between the ankles; also called "knock-knees."

736.42 Genu varum (acquired)

DEF: Abnormally separated knees and the inward bowing of the legs; it is also called "bowlegs."

736.5 Genu recurvatum (acquired)

DEF: Hyperextended knees; also called "backknee."

736.6 Other acquired deformities of knee

Deformity of knee (acquired) NOS

✓5th **736.7 Other acquired deformities of ankle and foot**

EXCLUDES *deformities of toe (acquired) (735.0-735.9)*
pes planus (acquired) (734)

736.70 Unspecified deformity of ankle and foot, acquired

Acquired Deformities of Hip

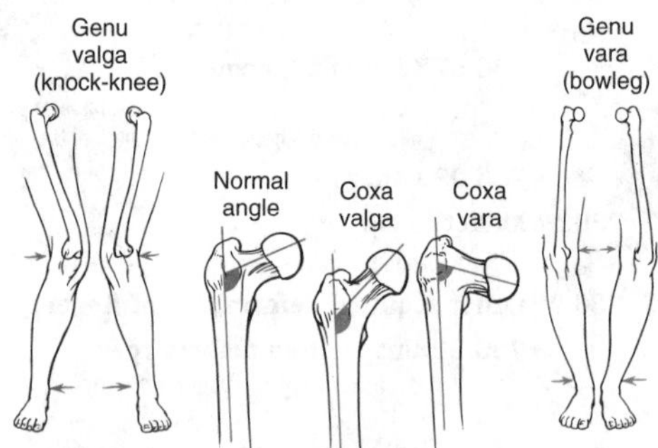

Deformities of Lower Limb

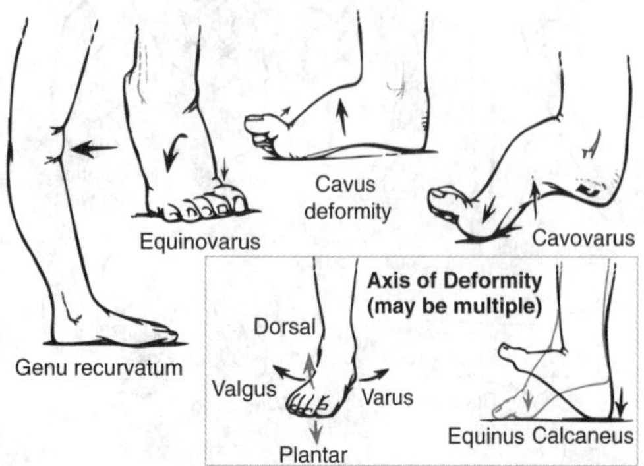

736.71 Acquired equinovarus deformity

Clubfoot, acquired

EXCLUDES *clubfoot not specified as acquired (754.5-754.7)*

736.72 Equinus deformity of foot, acquired

DEF: A plantar flexion deformity that forces people to walk on their toes.

736.73 Cavus deformity of foot

EXCLUDES *that with claw foot (736.74)*

DEF: Abnormally high longitudinal arch of the foot.

736.74 Claw foot, acquired

DEF: High foot arch with hyperextended toes at metatarsophalangeal joint and flexed toes at distal joints; also called "main en griffe."

736.75 Cavovarus deformity of foot, acquired

DEF: Inward turning of the heel from the midline of the leg and an abnormally high longitudinal arch.

736.76 Other calcaneus deformity

736.79 Other

Acquired:
- pes } not elsewhere classified
- talipes } not elsewhere classified

✓5th **736.8 Acquired deformities of other parts of limbs**

736.81 Unequal leg length (acquired)

736.89 Other

Deformity (acquired):
- arm or leg, not elsewhere classified
- shoulder

736.9 Acquired deformity of limb, site unspecified

✓4th **737 Curvature of spine**

EXCLUDES *congenital (754.2)*

737.0 Adolescent postural kyphosis

EXCLUDES *osteochondrosis of spine (juvenile) (732.0)*
adult (732.8)

✓5th **737.1 Kyphosis (acquired)**

737.10 Kyphosis (acquired) (postural)

737.11 Kyphosis due to radiation

737.12 Kyphosis, postlaminectomy

737.19 Other

EXCLUDES *that associated with conditions classifiable elsewhere (737.41)*

✓5th **737.2 Lordosis (acquired)**

DEF: Swayback appearance created by an abnormally increased spinal curvature; it is also referred to as "hollow back" or "saddle back."

737.20 Lordosis (acquired) (postural)

737.21 Lordosis, postlaminectomy

737.22 Other postsurgical lordosis

737.29 Other

EXCLUDES *that associated with conditions classifiable elsewhere (737.42)*

✓5th **737.3 Kyphoscoliosis and scoliosis**

DEF: Kyphoscoliosis: backward and lateral curvature of the spinal column; it is found in vertebral osteochondrosis.

DEF: Scoliosis: an abnormal deviation of the spine to the left or right of the midline

737.30 Scoliosis [and kyphoscoliosis], idiopathic

737.31 Resolving infantile idiopathic scoliosis

737.32 Progressive infantile idiopathic scoliosis

737.33 Scoliosis due to radiation

Kyphosis and Lordosis

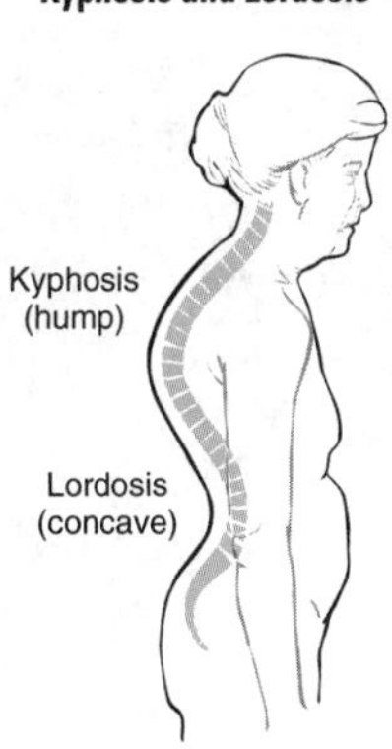

737.34 Thoracogenic scoliosis

737.39 Other

EXCLUDES *that associated with conditions classifiable elsewhere (737.43)*
that in kyphoscoliotic heart disease (416.1)

✓5th **737.4 Curvature of spine associated with other conditions**

Code first associated condition as:
Charcôt-Marie-Tooth disease (356.1)
mucopolysaccharidosis (277.5)
neurofibromatosis (237.7)
osteitis deformans (731.0)
osteitis fibrosa cystica (252.01)
osteoporosis (733.00-733.09)
poliomyelitis (138)
tuberculosis [Pott's curvature] (015.0)

737.40 *Curvature of spine, unspecified*

737.41 *Kyphosis*

737.42 *Lordosis*

737.43 *Scoliosis*

737.8 Other curvatures of spine

737.9 Unspecified curvature of spine

Curvature of spine (acquired) (idiopathic) NOS
Hunchback, acquired

EXCLUDES *deformity of spine NOS (738.5)*

✓4th **738 Other acquired deformity**

EXCLUDES *congenital (754.0-756.9, 758.0-759.9)*
dentofacial anomalies (524.0-524.9)

738.0 Acquired deformity of nose

Deformity of nose (acquired)
Overdevelopment of nasal bones

EXCLUDES *deflected or deviated nasal septum (470)*

✓5th **738.1 Other acquired deformity of head**

738.10 Unspecified deformity

Scoliosis and Kyphoscoliosis

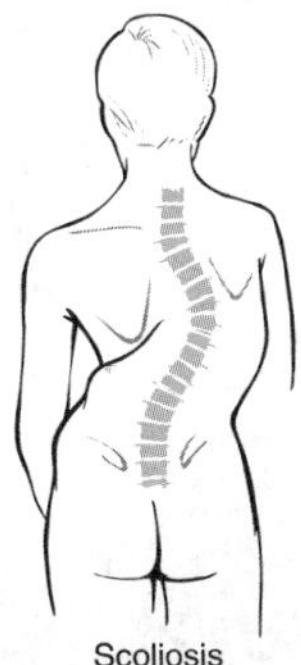

Scoliosis

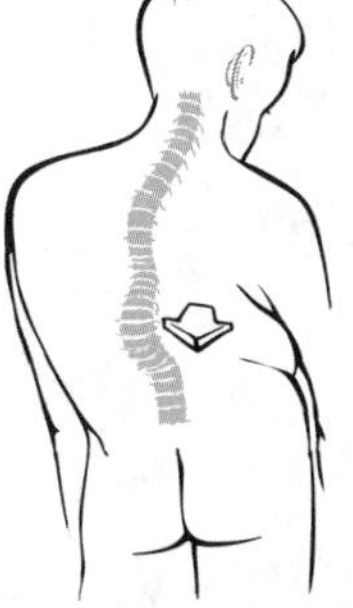

Kyphoscoliosis

738.11 Zygomatic hyperplasia

DEF: Abnormal enlargement of the zygoma (processus zygomaticus temporalis).

738.12 Zygomatic hypoplasia

DEF: Underdevelopment of the zygoma (processus zygomaticus temporalis).

738.19 Other specified deformity

738.2 Acquired deformity of neck

738.3 Acquired deformity of chest and rib

Deformity:
chest (acquired)
rib (acquired)
Pectus:
carinatum, acquired
excavatum, acquired

738.4 Acquired spondylolisthesis

Degenerative spondylolisthesis
Spondylolysis, acquired

EXCLUDES *congenital (756.12)*

DEF: Vertebra displaced forward over another; due to bilateral defect in vertebral arch, eroded articular surface of posterior facts and elongated pedicle between fifth lumbar vertebra and sacrum.

738.5 Other acquired deformity of back or spine

Deformity of spine NOS

EXCLUDES *curvature of spine (737.0-737.9)*

738.6 Acquired deformity of pelvis

Pelvic obliquity

EXCLUDES *intrapelvic protrusion of acetabulum (718.6)*
that in relation to labor and delivery (653.0-653.4, 653.8-653.9)

DEF: Pelvic obliquity: slanting or inclination of the pelvis at an angle between 55 and 60 degrees between the plane of the pelvis and the horizontal plane.

738.7 Cauliflower ear

DEF: Abnormal external ear; due to injury, subsequent perichondritis.

738.8 Acquired deformity of other specified site

Deformity of clavicle

738.9 Acquired deformity of unspecified site

✓4th **739 Nonallopathic lesions, not elsewhere classified**

INCLUDES segmental dysfunction
somatic dysfunction

DEF: Disability, loss of function or abnormality of a body part that is neither classifiable to a particular system nor brought about therapeutically to counteract another disease.

739.0 Head region

Occipitocervical region

739.1 Cervical region

Cervicothoracic region

739.2 Thoracic region

Thoracolumbar region

739.3 Lumbar region

Lumbosacral region

739.4 Sacral region

Sacrococcygeal region
Sacroiliac region

739.5 Pelvic region

Hip region
Pubic region

739.6 Lower extremities

739.7 Upper extremities

Acromioclavicular region
Sternoclavicular region

739.8 Rib cage

Costochondral region
Costovertebral region
Sternochondral region

739.9 Abdomen and other

Chapter 14: Congenital Anomalies (740–759)

Congenital anomalies may be the result of genetic factors (chromosomes), teratogens (agents causing physical defects in the embryo), or both. The anomalies may be apparent at birth or hidden and identified sometime after birth. Whatever the cause, congenital anomalies can be attributed to nearly 50 percent of deaths to full-term newborn infants.

Codes in Chapter 14 are classified according to a principal or defining defect rather than to the cause (chromosome abnormalities are the exception). Regardless of the origin, dysmorphology (clinical structural abnormality) is generally the primary indication of a congenital anomaly, and in many cases, a syndrome may be classified according to a single anatomic anomaly rather than a complex of symptoms.

ICD-9-CM does not differentiate between abnormalities that are intrinsic — related to the fetus — or extrinsic — as a result of intrauterine problems, although a note in ICD-9-CM prior to rubric 754 Certain congenital musculoskeletal deformities identifies codes as specific to extrinsic factors.

However ICD-9-CM does make a distinction in the classification of an anomaly as compared to a deformity. An anomaly is a malformation caused by abnormal fetal development, as in transposition of great vessels or spina bifida. A deformity is an alteration in structure caused by an extrinsic force, as in uterine compression.

Many congenital anomalies are patterns of multiple malformations that are considered pathogenetically related, meaning the cellular events and mechanical reactions occurring during the development of the disease are linked. These symptom complexes are called syndromes. When syndromes are not specifically indexed in ICD-9-CM, a code is assigned to each presenting manifestation of the syndrome that occurs as a set of symptoms or as multiple malformations.

This chapter classifies conditions present at birth including neurological problems, anomalies of the senses, heart anomalies, respiratory anomalies and digestive system anomalies. The chapter is organized by organ system or anatomical site affected by the congenital anomaly.

The coding guidelines for congenital anomalies follow the general guidelines for ICD-9-CM. Coders should pay close attention to the instructional notes and be aware of the various structural anomalies associated with certain syndromes, so as to not assign unnecessary additional codes. Alternately, instructional notes may also prompt the coder to report additional or separate codes, where necessary, to fully describe the condition.

Some of the more common congenital anomalies classified to this chapter are briefly outlined below.

Anomalies that arise due to the birth process are considered injuries due to the birth process, not congenital anomalies, and are classified to category 767, "Conditions in the Perinatal Period."

Obstructive Anomalies of Heart, NEC (746.84)

Multiple codes may be required to report certain obstructive cardiac anomalies. For example, an instructional note at code 746.84 directs the coder to "Use additional code for associated anomalies, such as:"

- Coarctation of aorta (747.10)
- Congenital mitral stenosis (746.5)
- Subaortic stenosis (746.81)

This instructional note alerts the coder that an additional code is necessary to describe specific anomalies associated with cardiac obstruction classifiable to code 746.84. Code first the obstruction (746.84) followed by an additional code for the specific anomaly. For example, Shone's syndrome with subaortic stenosis is reported with code 746.84, followed by code 746.81.

Patent Ductus Arteriosus (747.0)

Patent ductus arteriosus is the failure of the ductus arteriosus to close. A vessel that allows blood to bypass the nonfunctioning lungs of the fetus, the ductus arteriosus normally constricts rapidly within minutes of birth and closes completely within one to two months after birth. When the ductus arteriosus fails to close, blood from the aorta is allowed to flow into the pulmonary artery where it is recirculated to the lungs and reoxygenated, resulting in an increased workload on the left side of the heart and increased pulmonary vascular congestion.

Cleft Palate (749)

Cleft palate is the fissure or abnormal elongated opening of the palate. Cleft palate can occur either unilaterally or bilaterally and can be partial or involve the entire palate. The most common types of cleft palate are the complete left unilateral and partial midline cleft of the secondary palate. Fifth-digit assignment indicates laterality.

Meckel's Diverticulum (751.0)

Meckel's diverticulum is a diverticulum protruding from the wall of the ileum, arising from any point as close as 3 cm and as far as 100 cm from the cecum. Usually asymptomatic, Meckel's diverticulum is an incidental finding in most people.

Down's Syndrome (758.0)

Down's syndrome is a syndrome of congenital anomalies due to chromosomal abnormality, specifically an extra chromosome, usually at 21 or 22. The condition also is known as trisomy 21 or 22.

Marfan Syndrome (759.82)

Marfan syndrome is a hereditary autosomal trait disorder of connective tissue with many manifestations. It is characterized by elongation of the bones, often with associated abnormalities of the eyes and the cardiovascular system.

Finnish-type Congenital Nephrosis (759.89)

This congenital kidney disease is caused by a rare genetic recessive mutation of chromosome 19, which affects one out of 8,000 births in Finland, usually in premature and low-birth-weight babies. It occurs during the first week of life and develops to end-stage renal disease between 3 and 8 years of age. Treatment may include immune therapy, metabolic support, tube feedings, dialysis, and renal transplant.

Two codes are required to report Finnish-type congenital nephrosis: 759.89 Other specified anomalies and 581.3 Nephrotic syndrome with lesion of minimal change glomerulonephritis.

Borjeson-Forssman-Lehmann Syndrome (759.89)

Borjeson-Forssman-Lehmann syndrome is a rare X-linked recessive disorder described as a mental deficiency, epilepsy-endocrine disorder. Characteristics of this syndrome include severe mental retardation, epilepsy, obesity, hypogonadism, hypometabolism, swelling of facial subcutaneous tissue, visual problems, and large ears. Developmental delays and learning disabilities are common. Borjeson-Forssman-Lehmann syndrome is not classifiable to a single, unique code. Report code 759.89 Other specified anomalies, along with separate codes for each separate manifestation of the syndrome (e.g., mental retardation, obesity, hypogonadism, anatomical deformities).

14. CONGENITAL ANOMALIES (740-759)

✓4th 740 Anencephalus and similar anomalies

740.0 Anencephalus

Acrania
Amyelencephalus
Hemicephaly
Hemianencephaly

DEF: Fetus without cerebrum, cerebellum and flat bones of skull.

740.1 Craniorachischisis

DEF: Congenital slit in cranium and vertebral column

740.2 Iniencephaly

DEF: Spinal cord passes through enlarged occipital bone (foramen magnum); absent vertebral bone layer and spinal processes; resulting in both reduction in number and proper fusion of the vertebrae.

✓4th 741 Spina bifida

EXCLUDES *spina bifida occulta (756.17)*

The following fifth-digit subclassification is for use with category 741:

0 unspecified region
1 cervical region
2 dorsal [thoracic] region
3 lumbar region

DEF: Lack of closure of spinal cord's bony encasement; marked by cord protrusion into lumbosacral area; evident by elevated alpha-fetoprotein of amniotic fluid

✓5th **741.0 With hydrocephalus**
[0-3]

Arnold-Chiari syndrome, type II
Chiari malformation, type II
Any condition classifiable to 741.9 with any condition classifiable to 742.3

✓5th **741.9 Without mention of hydrocephalus**
[0-3]

Hydromeningocele (spinal)
Hydromyelocele
Meningocele (spinal)
Meningomyelocele
Myelocele
Myelocystocele
Rachischisis
Spina bifida (aperta)
Syringomyelocele

✓4th 742 Other congenital anomalies of nervous system

EXCLUDES *congenital central alveolar hypoventilation syndrome (327.25)*

742.0 Encephalocele

Encephalocystocele
Encephalomyelocele
Hydroencephalocele
Hydromeningocele, cranial
Meningocele, cerebral
Meningoencephalocele

DEF: Brain tissue protrudes through skull defect.

742.1 Microcephalus

Hydromicrocephaly
Micrencephaly

DEF: Extremely small head or brain.

Spina Bifida

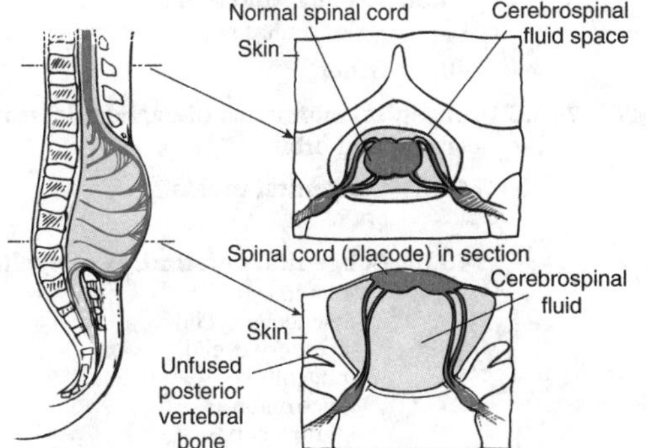

Normal Ventricles and Hydrocephalus

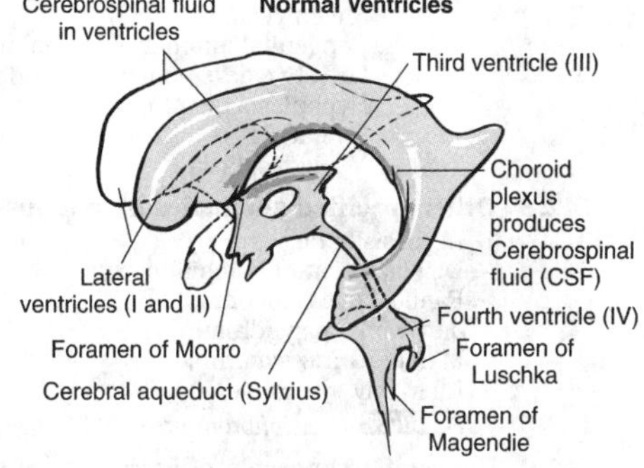

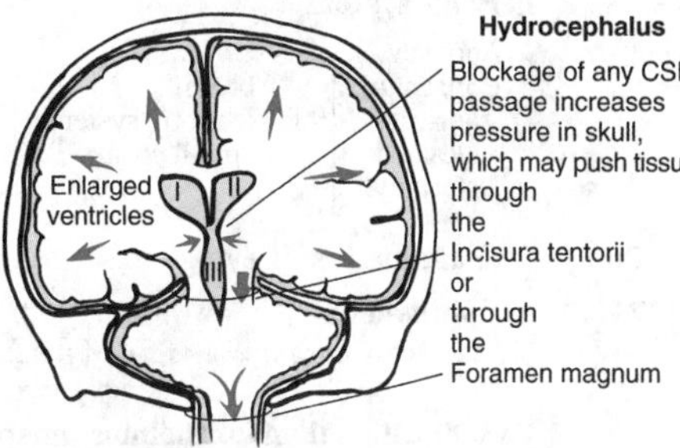

742.2 Reduction deformities of brain

Absence, Agenesis, Aplasia, Hypoplasia } of part of brain
Agyria
Arhinencephaly
Holoprosencephaly
Microgyria

742.3 Congenital hydrocephalus

Aqueduct of Sylvius:
  anomaly
  obstruction, congenital
  stenosis
Atresia of foramina of Magendie and Luschka
Hydrocephalus in newborn

EXCLUDES *hydrocephalus:*
acquired (331.3-331.4)
due to congenital toxoplasmosis (771.2)
with any condition classifiable to 741.9 (741.0)

DEF: Fluid accumulation within the skull; involves subarachnoid (external) or ventricular (internal) brain spaces.

742.4 Other specified anomalies of brain

Congenital cerebral cyst
Macroencephaly
Macrogyria
Megalencephaly
Multiple anomalies of brain NOS
Porencephaly
Ulegyria

✓5th **742.5 Other specified anomalies of spinal cord**

742.51 Diastematomyelia

DEF: Congenital anomaly often associated with spina bifida; the spinal cord is separated into halves by a bony tissue resembling a "spike" (a spicule), each half surrounded by a dural sac.

742.53 Hydromyelia

Hydrorhachis

DEF: Dilated central spinal cord canal; characterized by increased fluid accumulation.

742.59 Other
Amyelia
Atelomyelia
Congenital anomaly of spinal meninges
Defective development of cauda equina
Hypoplasia of spinal cord
Myelatelia
Myelodysplasia

742.8 Other specified anomalies of nervous system
Agenesis of nerve
Displacement of brachial plexus
Familial dysautonomia
Jaw-winking syndrome
Marcus-Gunn syndrome
Riley-Day syndrome
EXCLUDES *neurofibromatosis (237.7)*

742.9 Unspecified anomaly of brain, spinal cord, and nervous system
Anomaly } of: brain, nervous system, spinal cord
Congenital:
disease
lesion
Deformity

✓4th **743 Congenital anomalies of eye**

✓5th **743.0 Anophthalmos**
DEF: Complete absence of the eyes or the presence of vestigial eyes.

743.00 Clinical anophthalmos, unspecified
Agenesis } of eye
Cogenital absence } of eye
Anophthalmos NOS

743.03 Cystic eyeball, congenital

743.06 Cryptophthalmos
DEF: Skin is continuous over eyeball, results in apparent absence of eyelids.

✓5th **743.1 Microphthalmos**
Dysplasia } of eye
Hypoplasia } of eye
Rudimentary eye
DEF: Abnormally small eyeballs, may be opacities of cornea and lens, scarring of choroid and retina.

743.10 Microphthalmos, unspecified

743.11 Simple microphthalmos

743.12 Microphthalmos associated with other anomalies of eye and adnexa

✓5th **743.2 Buphthalmos**
Glaucoma:
congenital
newborn
Hydrophthalmos
EXCLUDES *glaucoma of childhood (365.14)*
traumatic glaucoma due to birth injury (767.8)
DEF: Distended, enlarged fibrous coats of eye; due to intraocular pressure of congenital glaucoma.

743.20 Buphthalmos, unspecified

743.21 Simple buphthalmos

743.22 Buphthalmos associated with other ocular anomalies
Keratoglobus, congenital } associated with buphthalmos
Megalocornea } associated with buphthalmos

✓5th **743.3 Congenital cataract and lens anomalies**
EXCLUDES *infantile cataract (366.00-366.09)*
DEF: Opaque eye lens.

743.30 Congenital cataract, unspecified

743.31 Capsular and subcapsular cataract

743.32 Cortical and zonular cataract

743.33 Nuclear cataract

743.34 Total and subtotal cataract, congenital

743.35 Congenital aphakia
Congenital absence of lens

743.36 Anomalies of lens shape
Microphakia
Spherophakia

743.37 Congenital ectopic lens

743.39 Other

✓5th **743.4 Coloboma and other anomalies of anterior segment**
DEF: Coloboma: ocular tissue defect associated with defect of ocular fetal intraocular fissure; may cause small pit on optic disk, major defects of iris, ciliary body, choroid, and retina.

743.41 Anomalies of corneal size and shape
Microcornea
EXCLUDES *that associated with buphthalmos (743.22)*

743.42 Corneal opacities, interfering with vision, congenital

743.43 Other corneal opacities, congenital

743.44 Specified anomalies of anterior chamber, chamber angle, and related structures
Anomaly:
Axenfeld's
Peters'
Rieger's

743.45 Aniridia
DEF: Incompletely formed or absent iris; affects both eyes; dominant trait; also called congenital hyperplasia of iris.

743.46 Other specified anomalies of iris and ciliary body
Anisocoria, congenital
Atresia of pupil
Coloboma of iris
Corectopia

743.47 Specified anomalies of sclera

743.48 Multiple and combined anomalies of anterior segment

743.49 Other

✓5th **743.5 Congenital anomalies of posterior segment**

743.51 Vitreous anomalies
Congenital vitreous opacity

743.52 Fundus coloboma
DEF: Absent retinal and choroidal tissue; occurs in lower fundus; a bright white ectatic zone of exposed sclera extends into and changes the optic disk.

743.53 Chorioretinal degeneration, congenital

743.54 Congenital folds and cysts of posterior segment

743.55 Congenital macular changes

743.56 Other retinal changes, congenital

743.57 Specified anomalies of optic disc
Coloboma of optic disc (congenital)

743.58 Vascular anomalies
Congenital retinal aneurysm

743.59 Other

✓5th **743.6 Congenital anomalies of eyelids, lacrimal system, and orbit**

743.61 Congenital ptosis
DEF: Drooping of eyelid.

743.62 Congenital deformities of eyelids
Ablepharon
Absence of eyelid
Accessory eyelid
Congenital:
ectropion
entropion

743.63 Other specified congenital anomalies of eyelid
Absence, agenesis, of cilia

743.64 Specified congenital anomalies of lacrimal gland

743.65 Specified congenital anomalies of lacrimal passages
Absence, agenesis of:
lacrimal apparatus
punctum lacrimale
Accessory lacrimal canal

743.66 Specified congenital anomalies of orbit

743.69 Other
Accessory eye muscles

743.8 Other specified anomalies of eye
EXCLUDES *congenital nystagmus (379.51)*
ocular albinism (270.2)
optic nerve hypoplasia (377.43)
retinitis pigmentosa (362.74)

743.9 Unspecified anomaly of eye
Congenital:
anomaly NOS } of eye (any part)
deformity NOS }

✓4th **744 Congenital anomalies of ear, face, and neck**
EXCLUDES *anomaly of:*
cervical spine (754.2, 756.10-756.19)
larynx (748.2-748.3)
nose (748.0-748.1)
parathyroid gland (759.2)
thyroid gland (759.2)
cleft lip (749.10-749.25)

✓5th **744.0 Anomalies of ear causing impairment of hearing**
EXCLUDES *congenital deafness without mention of cause (389.0-389.9)*

744.00 Unspecified anomaly of ear with impairment of hearing

744.01 Absence of external ear
Absence of:
auditory canal (external)
auricle (ear) (with stenosis or atresia of auditory canal)

744.02 Other anomalies of external ear with impairment of hearing
Atresia or stricture of auditory canal (external)

744.03 Anomaly of middle ear, except ossicles
Atresia or stricture of osseous meatus (ear)

744.04 Anomalies of ear ossicles
Fusion of ear ossicles

744.05 Anomalies of inner ear
Congenital anomaly of:
membranous labyrinth
organ of Corti

744.09 Other
Absence of ear, congenital

744.1 Accessory auricle
Accessory tragus
Polyotia
Preauricular appendage
Supernumerary:
ear
lobule
DEF: Redundant tissue or structures of ear.

✓5th **744.2 Other specified anomalies of ear**
EXCLUDES *that with impairment of hearing (744.00-744.09)*

744.21 Absence of ear lobe, congenital

744.22 Macrotia
DEF: Abnormally large pinna of ear.

744.23 Microtia
DEF: Hypoplasia of pinna; associated with absent or closed auditory canal.

744.24 Specified anomalies of Eustachian tube
Absence of Eustachian tube

744.29 Other
Bat ear
Darwin's tubercle
Pointed ear
Prominence of auricle
Ridge ear
EXCLUDES *preauricular sinus (744.46)*

744.3 Unspecified anomaly of ear
Congenital:
anomaly NOS } of ear, not elsewhere classified
deformity NOS }

✓5th **744.4 Branchial cleft cyst or fistula; preauricular sinus**

744.41 Branchial cleft sinus or fistula
Branchial:
sinus (external) (internal)
vestige
DEF: Cyst due to failed closure of embryonic branchial cleft.

744.42 Branchial cleft cyst

744.43 Cervical auricle

744.46 Preauricular sinus or fistula

744.47 Preauricular cyst

744.49 Other
Fistula (of):
auricle, congenital
cervicoaural

744.5 Webbing of neck
Pterygium colli
DEF: Thick, triangular skinfold, stretches from lateral side of neck across shoulder; associated with Turner's and Noonan's syndromes.

✓5th **744.8 Other specified anomalies of face and neck**

744.81 Macrocheilia
Hypertrophy of lip, congenital
DEF: Abnormally large lips.

744.82 Microcheilia
DEF: Abnormally small lips.

744.83 Macrostomia
DEF: Bilateral or unilateral anomaly, of mouth due to malformed maxillary and mandibular processes; results in mouth extending toward ear.

744.84 Microstomia
DEF: Abnormally small mouth.

744.89 Other
EXCLUDES *congenital fistula of lip (750.25)*
musculoskeletal anomalies (754.0-754.1, 756.0)

744.9 Unspecified anomalies of face and neck
Congenital:
anomaly NOS } of face [any part] or neck [any part]
deformity NOS }

✓4th **745 Bulbus cordis anomalies and anomalies of cardiac septal closure**

745.0 Common truncus
Absent septum } between aorta and pulmonary artery
Communication (abnormal) }
Aortic septal defect
Common aortopulmonary trunk
Persistent truncus arteriosus

✓5th **745.1 Transposition of great vessels**

745.10 Complete transposition of great vessels
Transposition of great vessels:
NOS
classical

Heart Defects

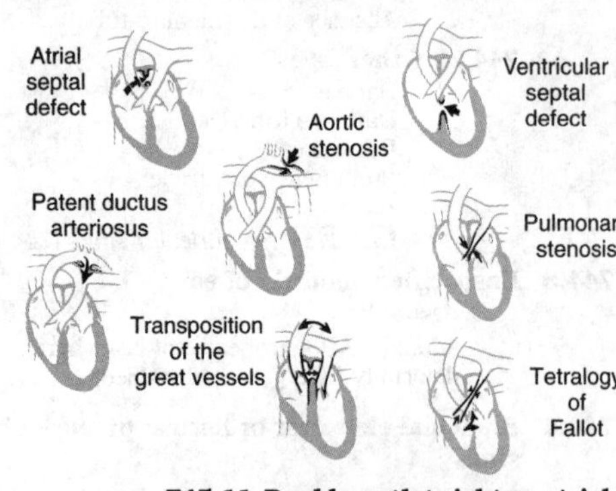

745.11 Double outlet right ventricle
Dextratransposition of aorta
Incomplete transposition of great vessels
Origin of both great vessels from right ventricle
Taussig-Bing syndrome or defect

745.12 Corrected transposition of great vessels

745.19 Other

745.2 Tetralogy of Fallot
Fallot's pentalogy
Ventricular septal defect with pulmonary stenosis or atresia, dextraposition of aorta, and hypertrophy of right ventricle
EXCLUDES *Fallot's triad (746.09)*
DEF: Obstructed cardiac outflow causes pulmonary stenosis, interventricular septal defect and right ventricular hypertrophy.

745.3 Common ventricle
Cor triloculare biatriatum
Single ventricle

745.4 Ventricular septal defect
Eisenmenger's defect or complex
Gerbo dedefect
Interventricular septal defect
Left ventricular-right atrial communication
Roger's disease
EXCLUDES *common atrioventricular canal type (745.69)*
single ventricle (745.3)

745.5 Ostium secundum type atrial septal defect
Defect:
atrium secundum
fossa ovalis
Lutembacher's syndrome
Patent or persistent:
foramen ovale
ostium secundum
DEF: Opening in atrial septum due to failure of the septum secondum and the endocardial cushions to fuse; there is a rim of septum surrounding the defect.

✓5th **745.6 Endocardial cushion defects**
DEF: Atrial and/or ventricular septal defects causing abnormal fusion of cushions in atrioventricular canal.

745.60 Endocardial cushion defect, unspecified type
DEF: Septal defect due to imperfect fusion of endocardial cushions.

745.61 Ostium primum defect
Persistent ostium primum
DEF: Opening in low, posterior septum primum; causes cleft in basal portion of atrial septum; associated with cleft mitral valve.

745.69 Other
Absence of atrial septum
Atrioventricular canal type ventricular septal defect
Common atrioventricular canal
Common atrium

745.7 Cor biloculare
Absence of atrial and ventricular septa
DEF: Atrial and ventricular septal defect; marked by heart with two cardiac chambers (one atrium, one ventricle), and one atrioventricular valve.

745.8 Other

745.9 Unspecified defect of septal closure
Septal defect NOS

✓4th **746 Other congenital anomalies of heart**
EXCLUDES *endocardial fibroelastosis (425.3)*

✓5th **746.0 Anomalies of pulmonary valve**
EXCLUDES *infundibular or subvalvular pulmonic stenosis (746.83)*
tetralogy of Fallot (745.2)

746.00 Pulmonary valve anomaly, unspecified

746.01 Atresia, congenital
Congenital absence of pulmonary valve

746.02 Stenosis, congenital
DEF: Stenosis of opening between pulmonary artery and right ventricle; causes obstructed blood outflow from right ventricle.

746.09 Other
Congenital insufficiency of pulmonary valve
Fallot's triad or trilogy

746.1 Tricuspid atresia and stenosis, congenital
Absence of tricuspid valve

746.2 Ebstein's anomaly
DEF: Malformation of the tricuspid valve characterized by septal and posterior leaflets attaching to the wall of the right ventricle; causing the right ventricle to fuse with the atrium producing a large right atrium and a small ventricle; causes a malfunction of the right ventricle with accompanying complications such as heart failure and abnormal cardiac rhythm.

746.3 Congenital stenosis of aortic valve
Congenital aortic stenosis
EXCLUDES *congenital:*
subaortic stenosis (746.81)
supravalvular aortic stenosis (747.22)
DEF: Stenosis of orifice of aortic valve; obstructs blood outflow from left ventricle.

746.4 Congenital insufficiency of aortic valveBicuspid aortic valve
Congenital aortic insufficiency
DEF: Impaired functioning of aortic valve due to incomplete closure; causes backflow (regurgitation) of blood from aorta to left ventricle.

746.5 Congenital mitral stenosis
Fused commissure } of mitral valve
Parachute deformity } of mitral valve
Supernumerary cusps } of mitral valve
DEF: Stenosis of left atrioventricular orifice.

746.6 Congenital mitral insufficiency
DEF: Impaired functioning of mitral valve due to incomplete closure; causes backflow of blood from left ventricle to left atrium.

746.7 Hypoplastic left heart syndrome
Atresia, or marked hypoplasia, of aortic orifice or valve, with hypoplasia of ascending aorta and defective development of left ventricle (with mitral valve atresia)

✓5th **746.8 Other specified anomalies of heart**

746.81 Subaortic stenosis
DEF: Stenosis, of left ventricular outflow tract due to fibrous tissue ring or septal hypertrophy below aortic valve.

746.82 Cor triatriatum
DEF: Transverse septum divides left atrium due to failed resorption of embryonic common pulmonary vein; results in three atrial chambers.

746.83 Infundibular pulmonic stenosis
Subvalvular pulmonic stenosis
DEF: Stenosis of right ventricle outflow tract within infundibulum due to fibrous diaphragm below valve or long, narrow fibromuscular channel.

746.84 Obstructive anomalies of heart, not elsewhere classified
Shone's syndrome
Uhl's disease
Use additional code for associated anomalies, such as:
coarctation of aorta (747.10)
congenital mitral stenosis (746.5)
subaortic stenosis (746.81)

746.85 Coronary artery anomaly
Anomalous origin or communication of coronary artery
Arteriovenous malformation of coronary artery
Coronary artery:
absence
arising from aorta or pulmonary trunk
single

746.86 Congenital heart block
Complete or incomplete atrioventricular [AV] block
DEF: Impaired conduction of electrical impulses; due to maldeveloped junctional tissue.

746.87 Malposition of heart and cardiac apex
Abdominal heart
Dextrocardia
Ectopia cordis
Levocardia (isolated)
Mesocardia
EXCLUDES *dextrocardia with complete transposition of viscera (759.3)*

746.89 Other
Atresia } of cardiac vein
Hypoplasia } of cardiac vein
Congenital:
cardiomegaly
diverticulum, left ventricle
pericardial defect

746.9 Unspecified anomaly of heart
Congenital:
anomaly of heart NOS
heart disease NOS

✓4th **747 Other congenital anomalies of circulatory system**

747.0 Patent ductus arteriosus
Patent ductus Botalli
Persistent ductus arteriosus
DEF: Open lumen in ductus arteriosus causes arterial blood recirculation in lungs; inhibits blood supply to aorta; symptoms such as shortness of breath more noticeable upon activity.

✓5th **747.1 Coarctation of aorta**
DEF: Localized deformity of aortic media seen as a severe constriction of the vessel lumen; major symptom is high blood pressure in the arms and low pressure in the legs; a CVA, rupture of the aorta, bacterial endocarditis or congestive heart failure can follow if left untreated.

747.10 Coarctation of aorta (preductal) (postductal)
Hypoplasia of aortic arch

747.11 Interruption of aortic arch

✓5th **747.2 Other anomalies of aorta**

747.20 Anomaly of aorta, unspecified

747.21 Anomalies of aortic arch
Anomalous origin, right subclavian artery
Dextraposition of aorta
Double aortic arch
Kommerell's diverticulum
Overriding aorta
Persistent:
convolutions, aortic arch
right aortic arch
Vascular ring
EXCLUDES *hypoplasia of aortic arch (747.10)*

747.22 Atresia and stenosis of aorta
Absence } of aorta
Aplasia } of aorta
Hypoplasia } of aorta
Stricture } of aorta
Supra (valvular)-aortic stenosis
EXCLUDES *congenital aortic (valvular) stenosis or stricture, so stated (746.3)*
hypoplasia of aorta in hypoplastic left heart syndrome (746.7)

747.29 Other
Aneurysm of sinus of Valsalva
Congenital:
aneurysm } of aorta
dilation } of aorta

747.3 Anomalies of pulmonary artery
Agenesis } of pulmonary artery
Anomaly } of pulmonary artery
Atresia } of pulmonary artery
Coarctation } of pulmonary artery
Hypoplasia } of pulmonary artery
Stenosis } of pulmonary artery
Pulmonary arteriovenous aneurysm

✓5th **747.4 Anomalies of great veins**

747.40 Anomaly of great veins, unspecified
Anomaly NOS of:
pulmonary veins
vena cava

747.41 Total anomalous pulmonary venous connection
Total anomalous pulmonary venous return [TAPVR]:
subdiaphragmatic
supradiaphragmatic

747.42 Partial anomalous pulmonary venous connection
Partial anomalous pulmonary venous return

747.49 Other anomalies of great veins
Absence } of vena cava (inferior) (superior)
Congenital stenosis } of vena cava (inferior) (superior)
Persistent:
left posterior cardinal vein
left superior vena cava
Scimitar syndrome
Transposition of pulmonary veins NOS

747.5 Absence or hypoplasia of umbilical artery
Single umbilical artery

✓5th **747.6 Other anomalies of peripheral vascular system**

Absence } of artery or vein, NEC
Anomaly
Atresia

Arteriovenous aneurysm (peripheral)
Arteriovenous malformation of the peripheral vascular system
Congenital:
- aneurysm (peripheral)
- phlebectasia
- stricture, artery
- varix

Multiple renal arteries

EXCLUDES *anomalies of:*
cerebral vessels (747.81)
pulmonary artery (747.3)
congenital retinal aneurysm (743.58)
hemangioma (228.00-228.09)
lymphangioma (228.1)

747.60 Anomaly of the peripheral vascular system, unspecified site

747.61 Gastrointestinal vessel anomaly

747.62 Renal vessel anomaly

747.63 Upper limb vessel anomaly

747.64 Lower limb vessel anomaly

747.69 Anomalies of other specified sites of peripheral vascular system

✓5th **747.8 Other specified anomalies of circulatory system**

747.81 Anomalies of cerebrovascular system

Arteriovenous malformation of brain
Cerebral arteriovenous aneurysm, congenital
Congenital anomalies of cerebral vessels

EXCLUDES *ruptured cerebral (arteriovenous) aneurysm (430)*

747.82 Spinal vessel anomaly

Arteriovenous malformation of spinal vessel

747.83 Persistent fetal circulation

Persistent pulmonary hypertension
Primary pulmonary hypertension of newborn

DEF: A return to fetal-type circulation due to constriction of pulmonary arterioles and opening of the ductus arteriosus and foramen ovale, right-to-left shunting occurs, oxygenation of the blood does not occur, and the lungs remain constricted after birth; PFC is seen in term or post-term infants causes include asphyxiation, meconium aspiration syndrome, acidosis, sepsis, and developmental immaturity.

747.89 Other

Aneurysm, congenital, specified site not elsewhere classified

EXCLUDES *congenital aneurysm:*
coronary (746.85)
peripheral (747.6)
pulmonary (747.3)
retinal (743.58)

747.9 Unspecified anomaly of circulatory system

748 Congenital anomalies of respiratory system

EXCLUDES *congenital central alveolar hypoventilation syndrome (327.25)*
congenital defect of diaphragm (756.6)

748.0 Choanal atresia

Atresia } of nares (anterior)
Congenital stenosis } (posterior)

DEF: Occluded posterior nares (choana), bony or membranous due to failure of embryonic bucconasal membrane to rupture.

Persistent Fetal Circulation

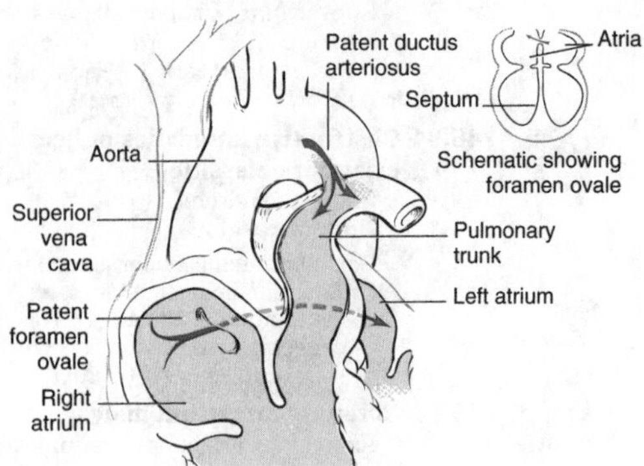

748.1 Other anomalies of nose

Absent nose
Accessory nose
Cleft nose
Congenital:
- deformity of nose
- notching of tip of nose
- perforation of wall of nasal sinus

Deformity of wall of nasal sinus

EXCLUDES *congenital deviation of nasal septum (754.0)*

748.2 Web of larynx

Web of larynx:
- NOS
- glottic
- subglottic

DEF: Malformed larynx; marked by thin, translucent, or thick, fibrotic spread between vocal folds; affects speech.

748.3 Other anomalies of larynx, trachea, and bronchus

Absence or agenesis of:
- bronchus
- larynx
- trachea

Anomaly (of):
- cricoid cartilage
- epiglottis
- thyroid cartilage
- tracheal cartilage

Atresia (of):
- epiglottis
- glottis
- larynx
- trachea

Cleft thyroid, cartilage, congenital
Congenital:
- dilation, trachea
- stenosis:
  - larynx
  - trachea
- tracheocele

Diverticulum:
- bronchus
- trachea

Fissure of epiglottis
Laryngocele
Posterior cleft of cricoid cartilage (congenital)
Rudimentary tracheal bronchus
Stridor, laryngeal, congenital

748.4 Congenital cystic lung

Disease, lung:
- cystic, congenital
- polycystic, congenital

Honeycomb lung, congenital

EXCLUDES *acquired or unspecified cystic lung (518.89)*

DEF: Enlarged air spaces of lung parenchyma.

748.5 Agenesis, hypoplasia, and dysplasia of lung

Absence of lung (fissures) (lobe) (lobe)
Aplasia of lung
Hypoplasia of lung
Sequestration of lung

✓5th **748.6 Other anomalies of lung**

748.60 Anomaly of lung, unspecified

748.61 Congenital bronchiectasis

748.69 Other

Accessory lung (lobe)
Azygos lobe (fissure), lung

748.8 Other specified anomalies of respiratory system

Abnormal communication between pericardial and pleural sacs
Anomaly, pleural folds
Atresia of nasopharynx
Congenital cyst of mediastinum

748.9 Unspecified anomaly of respiratory system

Anomaly of respiratory system NOS

✓4th **749 Cleft palate and cleft lip**

✓5th **749.0 Cleft palate**

749.00 Cleft palate, unspecified

749.01 Unilateral, complete

749.02 Unilateral, incomplete

Cleft uvula

749.03 Bilateral, complete

749.04 Bilateral, incomplete

✓5th **749.1 Cleft lip**

Cheiloschisis
Congenital fissure of lip
Harelip
Labium leporinum

749.10 Cleft lip, unspecified

749.11 Unilateral, complete

749.12 Unilateral, incomplete

749.13 Bilateral, complete

749.14 Bilateral, incomplete

✓5th **749.2 Cleft palate with cleft lip**

Cheilopalatoschisis

749.20 Cleft palate with cleft lip, unspecified

749.21 Unilateral, complete

749.22 Unilateral, incomplete

749.23 Bilateral, complete

749.24 Bilateral, incomplete

749.25 Other combinations

Cleft Lip and Palate

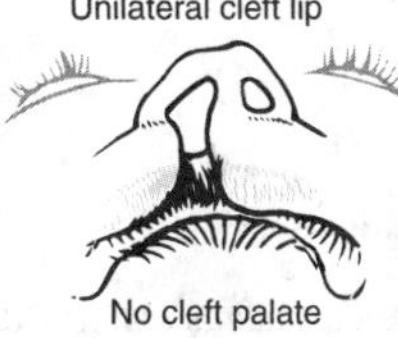

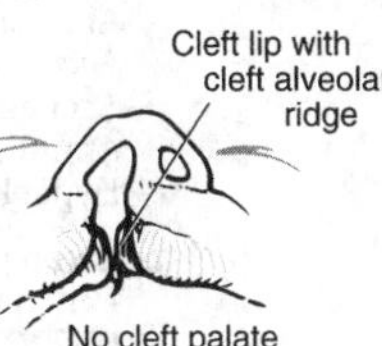

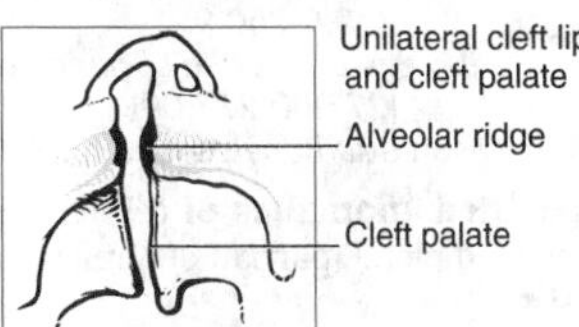

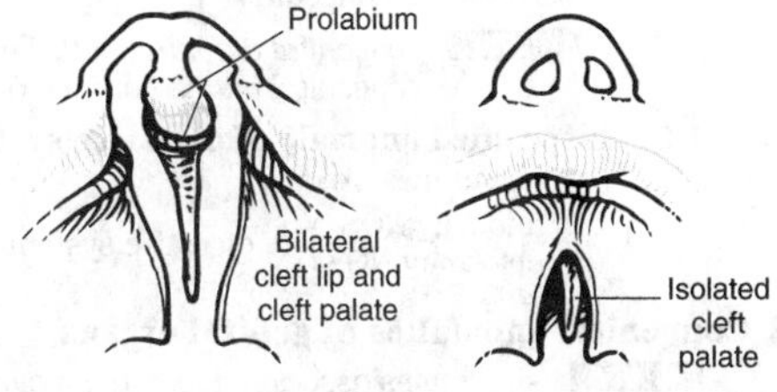

✓4th **750 Other congenital anomalies of upper alimentary tract**

EXCLUDES *dentofacial anomalies (524.0-524.9)*

750.0 Tongue tie

Ankyloglossia

DEF: Restricted tongue movement due to lingual frenum extending toward tip of tongue. Tongue may be fused to mouth floor affecting speech.

✓5th **750.1 Other anomalies of tongue**

750.10 Anomaly of tongue, unspecified

750.11 Aglossia

DEF: Absence of tongue.

750.12 Congenital adhesions of tongue

750.13 Fissure of tongue

Bifid tongue
Double tongue

750.15 Macroglossia

Congenital hypertrophy of tongue

750.16 Microglossia

Hypoplasia of tongue

750.19 Other

✓5th **750.2 Other specified anomalies of mouth and pharynx**

750.21 Absence of salivary gland

750.22 Accessory salivary gland

750.23 Atresia, salivary duct

Imperforate salivary duct

750.24 Congenital fistula of salivary gland

750.25 Congenital fistula of lip

Congenital (mucus) lip pits

750.26 Other specified anomalies of mouth

Absence of uvula

750.27 Diverticulum of pharynx

Pharyngeal pouch

750.29 Other specified anomalies of pharynx

Imperforate pharynx

750.3 Tracheoesophageal fistula, esophageal atresia and stenosis

Absent esophagus
Atresia of esophagus
Congenital:
  esophageal ring
  stenosis of esophagus
  stricture of esophagus
Congenital fistula:
  esophagobronchial
  esophagotracheal
Imperforate esophagus
Webbed esophagus

750.4 Other specified anomalies of esophagus

Dilatation, congenital; Displacement, congenital; Diverticulum; Duplication; Giant } (of) esophagus

Esophageal pouch

EXCLUDES *congenital hiatus hernia (750.6)*

750.5 Congenital hypertrophic pyloric stenosis

Congenital or infantile:
  constriction; hypertrophy; spasm; stenosis; stricture } of pylorus

DEF: Obstructed pylorus due to overgrowth of pyloric muscle.

750.6 Congenital hiatus hernia

Displacement of cardia through esophageal hiatus

EXCLUDES *congenital diaphragmatic hernia (756.6)*

750.7 Other specified anomalies of stomach

Congenital:
- cardiospasm
- hourglass stomach

Displacement of stomach
Diverticulum of stomach, congenital
Duplication of stomach
Megalogastria
Microgastria
Transposition of stomach

750.8 Other specified anomalies of upper alimentary tract

750.9 Unspecified anomaly of upper alimentary tract

Congenital:
- anomaly NOS } of upper alimentary tract [any part, except tongue]
- deformity NOS }

✓4th 751 Other congenital anomalies of digestive system

751.0 Meckel's diverticulum

Meckel's diverticulum (displaced) (hypertrophic)
Persistent:
- omphalomesenteric duct
- vitelline duct

DEF: Malformed sacs or appendages of ileum of small intestine; can cause strangulation, volvulus and intussusception.

751.1 Atresia and stenosis of small intestine

Atresia of:
- duodenum
- ileum
- intestine NOS

Congenital:
- absence } of small intestine or intestine NOS
- obstruction }
- stenosis }
- stricture }

Imperforate jejunum

751.2 Atresia and stenosis of large intestine rectum, and anal canal

Absence:
- anus (congenital)
- appendix, congenital
- large intestine, congenital
- rectum

Atresia of:
- anus
- colon
- rectum

Congenital or infantile:
- obstruction of large intestine
- occlusion of anus
- stricture of anus

Imperforate:
- anus
- rectum

Stricture of rectum, congenital

751.3 Hirschsprung's disease and other congenital functional disorders of colon

Aganglionosis
Congenital dilation of colon
Congenital megacolon
Macrocolon

DEF: Hirschsprung's disease: enlarged or dilated colon (megacolon), with absence of ganglion cells in the narrowed wall distally; causes inability to defecate.

751.4 Anomalies of intestinal fixation

Congenital adhesions:
- omental, anomalous
- peritoneal

Jackson's membrane
Malrotation of colon
Rotation of cecum or colon:
- failure of
- incomplete
- insufficient

Universal mesentery

751.5 Other anomalies of intestine

Congenital diverticulum, colon
Dolichocolon
Duplication of:
- anus
- appendix
- cecum
- intestine

Ectopic anus
Megaloappendix
Megaloduodenum
Microcolon
Persistent cloaca
Transposition of:
- appendix
- colon
- intestine

✓5th 751.6 Anomalies of gallbladder, bile ducts, and liver

751.60 Unspecified anomaly of gallbladder, bile ducts, and liver

751.61 Biliary atresia

Congenital:
- absence } of bile duct (common) of passage
- hypoplasia }
- obstruction }
- stricture }

751.62 Congenital cystic disease of liver

Congenital polycystic disease of liver
Fibrocystic disease of liver

751.69 Other anomalies of gallbladder, bile ducts, and liver

Absence of:
- gallbladder, congenital
- liver (lobe)

Accessory:
- hepatic ducts
- liver

Congenital:
- choledochal cyst
- hepatomegaly

Duplication of:
- biliary duct
- cystic duct
- gallbladder
- liver

Floating:
- gallbladder
- liver

Intrahepatic gallbladder

751.7 Anomalies of pancreas

- Absence } (of) pancreas
- Accessory }
- Agenesis }
- Annular }
- Hypoplasia }

Ectopic pancreatic tissue
Pancreatic heterotopia

EXCLUDES *diabetes mellitus (249.0-249.9, 250.0-250.9)*
fibrocystic disease of pancreas (277.00-277.09)
neonatal diabetes mellitus (775.1)

751.8 Other specified anomalies of digestive system

Absence (complete) (partial) of alimentary tract NOS
- Duplication } of digestive organs NOS
- Malposition, congenital }

EXCLUDES *congenital diaphragmatic hernia (756.6)*
congenital hiatus hernia (750.6)

751.9 Unspecified anomaly of digestive system

Congenital:
- anomaly NOS } of digestive system NOS
- deformity NOS }

✓4th 752 Congenital anomalies of genital organs

EXCLUDES *syndromes associated with anomalies in the number and form of chromosomes (758.0-758.9)*

752.0 Anomalies of ovaries

Absence, congenital } (of) ovary
Accessory
Ectopic
Streak

✓5th **752.1 Anomalies of fallopian tubes and broad ligaments**

752.10 Unspecified anomaly of fallopian tubes and broad ligaments

752.11 Embryonic cyst of fallopian tubes and broad ligaments

Cyst:
- epoophoron
- fimbrial
- parovarian

752.19 Other

Absence } (of) fallopian tube or broad ligament
Accessory
Atresia

752.2 Doubling of uterus

Didelphic uterus
Doubling of uterus [any degree] (associated with doubling of cervix and vagina)

752.3 Other anomalies of uterus

Absence, congenital } (of) uterus
Agenesis
Aplasia
Bicornuate

Uterus unicornis
Uterus with only one functioning horn

✓5th **752.4 Anomalies of cervix, vagina, and external female genitalia**

752.40 Unspecified anomaly of cervix,vagina, and external female genitalia

752.41 Embryonic cyst of cervix, vagina, and external female genitalia

Cyst of:
- canal of Nuck, congenital
- Gartner's duct
- vagina, embryonal
- vulva, congenital

DEF: Embryonic fluid-filled cysts, of cervix, vagina or external female genitalia.

752.42 Imperforate hymen

DEF: Complete closure of membranous fold around external opening of vagina.

752.49 Other anomalies of cervix, vagina, and external female genitalia

Absence } of cervix, clitoris, vagina, or vulva
Agenesis

Congenital stenosis or stricture of:
- cervical canal
- vagina

EXCLUDES *double vagina associated with total duplication (752.2)*

✓5th **752.5 Undescended and retractile testicle**

752.51 Undescended testis

Cryptorchism
Ectopic testis

752.52 Retractile testis

✓5th **752.6 Hypospadias and epispadias and other penile anomalies**

752.61 Hypospadias

DEF: Abnormal opening of urethra on the ventral surface of the penis or perineum; also a rare defect of vagina.

752.62 Epispadias

Anaspadias

DEF: Urethra opening on dorsal surface of penis; in females appears as a slit in the upper wall of urethra.

752.63 Congenital chordee

DEF: Ventral bowing of penis due to fibrous band along corpus spongiosum; occurs with hypospadias.

Hypospadias and Epispadias

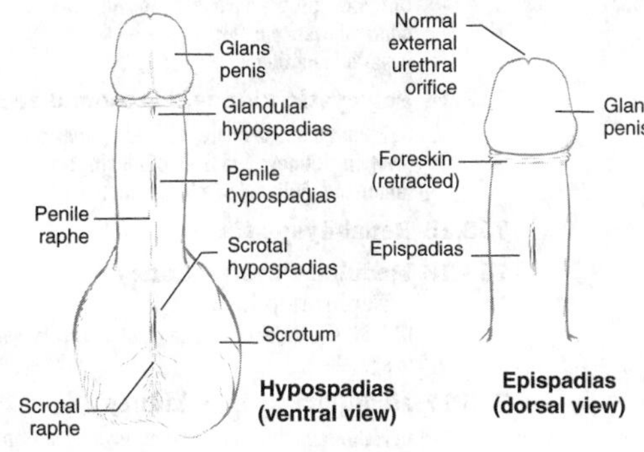

752.64 Micropenis

752.65 Hidden penis

752.69 Other penile anomalies

752.7 Indeterminate sex and pseudohermaphroditism

Gynandrism
Hermaphroditism
Ovotestis
Pseudohermaphroditism (male) (female)
Pure gonadal dysgenesis

EXCLUDES *androgen insensitivity (259.50-259.52)*
pseudohermaphroditism:
female, with adrenocortical disorder (255.2)
male, with gonadal disorder (257.8)
with specified chromosomal anomaly (758.0-758.9)
testicular feminization syndrome (259.50-259.52)

DEF: Pseudohermaphroditism: presence of gonads of one sex and external genitalia of other sex.

✓5th **752.8 Other specified anomalies of genital organs**

EXCLUDES *congenital hydrocele (778.6)*
penile anomalies (752.61-752.69)
phimosis or paraphimosis (605)

752.81 Scrotal transposition

752.89 Other specified anomalies of genital organs

Absence of:
- prostate
- spermatic cord
- vas deferens

Anorchism
Aplasia (congenital) of:
- prostate
- round ligament
- testicle

Atresia of:
- ejaculatory duct
- vas deferens

Fusion of testes
Hypoplasia of testis
Monorchism
Polyorchism

752.9 Unspecified anomaly of genital organs

Congenital:
anomaly NOS } of genital organ, not elsewhere classified
deformity NOS

✓4th **753 Congenital anomalies of urinary system**

753.0 Renal agenesis and dysgenesis

Atrophy of kidney:
- congenital
- infantile

Congenital absence of kidney(s)
Hypoplasia of kidney(s)

✓5th **753.1 Cystic kidney disease**

EXCLUDES *acquired cyst of kidney (593.2)*

753.10 Cystic kidney disease, unspecified

753.11 Congenital single renal cyst

753.12 Polycystic kidney, unspecified type

753.13 Polycystic kidney, autosomal dominant
DEF: Slow progressive disease characterized by bilateral cysts causing increased kidney size and impaired function.

753.14 Polycystic kidney, autosomal recessive
DEF: Rare disease characterized by multiple cysts involving kidneys and liver, producing renal and hepatic failure in childhood or adolescence.

753.15 Renal dysplasia

753.16 Medullary cystic kidney
Nephronopthisis
DEF: Diffuse kidney disease results in uremia onset prior to age 20.

753.17 Medullary sponge kidney
DEF: Dilated collecting tubules; usually asymptomatic but calcinosis in tubules may cause renal insufficiency.

753.19 Other specified cystic kidney disease
Multicystic kidney

✓5th **753.2 Obstructive defects of renal pelvis and ureter**

753.20 Unspecified obstructive defect of renal pelvis and ureter

753.21 Congenital obstruction of ureteropelvic junction
DEF: Stricture at junction of ureter and renal pelvis.

753.22 Congenital obstruction of ureterovesical junction
Adynamic ureter
Congenital hydroureter
DEF: Stricture at junction of ureter and bladder.

753.23 Congenital ureterocele

753.29 Other

753.3 Other specified anomalies of kidney
Accessory kidney
Congenital:
- calculus of kidney
- displaced kidney

Discoid kidney
Double kidney with double pelvis
Ectopic kidney
Fusion of kidneys
Giant kidney
Horseshoe kidney
Hyperplasia of kidney
Lobulation of kidney
Malrotation of kidney
Trifid kidney (pelvis)

753.4 Other specified anomalies of ureter
Absent ureter
Accessory ureter
Deviation of ureter
Displaced ureteric orifice
Double ureter
Ectopic ureter
Implantation, anomalous of ureter

753.5 Exstrophy of urinary bladder
Ectopia vesicae
Extroversion of bladder
DEF: Absence of lower abdominal and anterior bladder walls with posterior bladder wall protrusion.

753.6 Atresia and stenosis of urethra and bladder neck
Congenital obstruction:
- bladder neck
- urethra

Congenital stricture of:
- urethra (valvular)
- urinary meatus
- vesicourethral orifice

Imperforate urinary meatus
Impervious urethra
Urethral valve formation

753.7 Anomalies of urachus
Cyst, Fistula, Patent } (of) urachussinus
Persistent umbilical sinus

753.8 Other specified anomalies of bladder and urethra
Absence, congenital of:
- bladder
- urethra

Accessory:
- bladder
- urethra

Congenital:
- diverticulum of bladder
- hernia of bladder
- urethrorectal fistula
- prolapse of:
  - bladder (mucosa)
  - urethra

Double:
- urethra
- urinary meatus

753.9 Unspecified anomaly of urinary system
Congenital:
anomaly NOS, deformity NOS } of urinary system [any part, except urachus]

✓4th **754 Certain congenital musculoskeletal deformities**
INCLUDES nonteratogenic deformities which are considered to be due to intrauterine malposition and pressure

754.0 Of skull, face, and jaw
Asymmetry of face
Compression facies
Depressions in skull
Deviation of nasal septum, congenital
Dolichocephaly
Plagiocephaly
Potter's facies
Squashed or bent nose, congenital
EXCLUDES *dentofacial anomalies (524.0-524.9)*
syphilitic saddle nose (090.5)

754.1 Of sternocleidomastoid muscle
Congenital sternomastoid torticollis
Congenital wryneck
Contracture of sternocleidomastoid (muscle)
Sternomastoid tumor

754.2 Of spine
Congenital postural:
- lordosis
- scoliosis

✓5th **754.3 Congenital dislocation of hip**

754.30 Congenital dislocation of hip, unilateral
Congenital dislocation of hip NOS

754.31 Congenital dislocation of hip, bilateral

754.32 Congenital subluxation of hip, unilateral
Congenital flexion deformity, hip or thigh
Predislocation status of hip at birth
Preluxation of hip, congenital

754.33 Congenital subluxation of hip, bilateral

754.35 Congenital dislocation of one hip with subluxation of other hip

✓5th **754.4 Congenital genu recurvatum and bowing of long bones of leg**

754.40 Genu recurvatum
DEF: Backward curving of knee joint.

754.41 Congenital dislocation of knee (with genu recurvatum)

754.42 Congenital bowing of femur

754.43 Congenital bowing of tibia and fibula

754.44 Congenital bowing of unspecified long bones of leg

✓5th **754.5 Varus deformities of feet**
EXCLUDES *acquired (736.71, 736.75, 736.79)*

754.50 Talipes varus
Congenital varus deformity of foot, unspecified
Pes varus
DEF: Inverted foot marked by outer sole resting on ground.

754.51 Talipes equinovarus
Equinovarus (congenital)
DEF: Elevated, outward rotation of heel; also called clubfoot.

754.52 Metatarsus primus varus
DEF: Malformed first metatarsal bone, with bone angled toward body.

754.53 Metatarsus varus

754.59 Other
Talipes calcaneovarus

✓5th **754.6 Valgus deformities of feet**
EXCLUDES *valgus deformity of foot (acquired) (736.79)*

754.60 Talipes valgus
Congenital valgus deformity of foot, unspecified

754.61 Congenital pes planus
Congenital rocker bottom flat foot
Flat foot, congenital
EXCLUDES *pes planus (acquired) (734)*

754.62 Talipes calcaneovalgus

754.69 Other
Talipes:
equinovalgus
planovalgus

✓5th **754.7 Other deformities of feet**
EXCLUDES *acquired (736.70-736.79)*

754.70 Talipes, unspecified
Congenital deformity of foot NOS

754.71 Talipes cavus
Cavus foot (congenital)

754.79 Other
Asymmetric talipes
Talipes:
calcaneus
equinus

✓5th **754.8 Other specified nonteratogenic anomalies**

754.81 Pectus excavatum
Congenital funnel chest

754.82 Pectus carinatum
Congenital pigeon chest [breast]

754.89 Other
Club hand (congenital)
Congenital:
deformity of chest wall
dislocation of elbow
Generalized flexion contractures of lower limb joints, congenital
Spade-like hand (congenital)

✓4th **755 Other congenital anomalies of limbs**
EXCLUDES *those deformities classifiable to 754.0-754.8*

✓5th **755.0 Polydactyly**

755.00 Polydactyly, unspecified digits
Supernumerary digits

755.01 Of fingers
Accessory fingers

755.02 Of toes
Accessory toes

✓5th **755.1 Syndactyly**
Symphalangy
Webbing of digits

755.10 Of multiple and unspecified sites

755.11 Of fingers without fusion of bone

755.12 Of fingers with fusion of bone

755.13 Of toes without fusion of bone

755.14 Of toes with fusion of bone

✓5th **755.2 Reduction deformities of upper limb**

755.20 Unspecified reduction deformity of upper limb
Ectromelia NOS } of upper limb
Hemimelia NOS } of upper limb
Shortening of arm, congenital

755.21 Transverse deficiency of upper limb
Amelia of upper limb
Congenital absence of:
fingers, all (complete or partial)
forearm, including hand and fingers
upper limb, complete
Congenital amputation of upper limb
Transverse hemimelia of upper limb

755.22 Longitudinal deficiency of upper limb, not elsewhere classified
Phocomelia NOS of upper limb
Rudimentary arm

755.23 Longitudinal deficiency, combined, involving humerus, radius, and ulna (complete or incomplete)
Congenital absence of arm and forearm (complete or incomplete) with or without metacarpal deficiency and/or phalangeal deficiency, incomplete
Phocomelia, complete, of upper limb

755.24 Longitudinal deficiency, humeral, complete or partial (with or without distal deficiencies, incomplete)
Congenital absence of humerus (with or without absence of some [but not all] distal elements)
Proximal phocomelia of upper limb

755.25 Longitudinal deficiency, radioulnar, complete or partial (with or without distal deficiencies, incomplete)
Congenital absence of radius and ulna (with or without absence of some [but not all] distal elements)
Distal phocomelia of upper limb

755.26 Longitudinal deficiency, radial, complete or partial (with or without distal deficiencies, incomplete)
Agenesis of radius
Congenital absence of radius (with or without absence of some [but not all] distal elements)

755.27 Longitudinal deficiency, ulnar, complete or partial (with or without distal deficiencies, incomplete)
Agenesis of ulna
Congenital absence of ulna (with or without absence of some [but not all] distal elements)

755.28 Longitudinal deficiency, carpals or metacarpals, complete or partial (with or without incomplete phalangeal deficiency)

755.29 Longitudinal deficiency, phalanges, complete or partial
Absence of finger, congenital
Aphalangia of upper limb, terminal, complete or partial
EXCLUDES *terminal deficiency of all five digits (755.21)*
transverse deficiency of phalanges (755.21)

5th 755.3 Reduction deformities of lower limb

755.30 Unspecified reduction deformity of lower limb

Ectromelia NOS } of lower limb
Hemimelia NOS }
Shortening of leg, congenital

755.31 Transverse deficiency of lower limb

Amelia of lower limb
Congenital absence of:
foot
leg, including foot and toes
lower limb, complete
toes, all, complete
Transverse hemimelia of lower limb

755.32 Longitudinal deficiency of lower limb, not elsewhere classified

Phocomelia NOS of lower limb

755.33 Longitudinal deficiency, combined, involving femur, tibia, and fibula (complete or incomplete)

Congenital absence of thigh and (lower) leg (complete or incomplete) with or without metacarpal deficiency and/or phalangeal deficiency, incomplete
Phocomelia, complete, of lower limb

755.34 Longitudinal deficiency, femoral, complete or partial (with or without distal deficiencies, incomplete)

Congenital absence of femur (with or without absence of some [but not all] distal elements)
Proximal phocomelia of lower limb

755.35 Longitudinal deficiency, tibiofibular, complete or partial (with or without distal deficiencies, incomplete)

Congenital absence of tibia and fibula (with or without absence of some [but not all] distal elements)
Distal phocomelia of lower limb

755.36 Longitudinal deficiency, tibia, complete or partial (with or without distal deficiencies, incomplete)

Agenesis of tibia
Congenital absence of tibia (with or without absence of some [but not all] distal elements)

755.37 Longitudinal deficiency, fibular, complete or partial (with or without distal deficiencies, incomplete)

Agenesis of fibula
Congenital absence of fibula (with or without absence of some [but not all] distal elements)

755.38 Longitudinal deficiency, tarsals or metatarsals, complete or partial (with or without incomplete phalangeal deficiency)

755.39 Longitudinal deficiency, phalanges, complete or partial

Absence of toe, congenital
Aphalangia of lower limb, terminal, complete or partial

EXCLUDES *terminal deficiency of all five digits (755.31)*
transverse deficiency of phalanges (755.31)

755.4 Reduction deformities, unspecified limb

Absence, congenital (complete or partial) of limb NOS

Amelia }
Ectromelia } of unspecified limb
Hemimelia }
Phocomelia }

5th 755.5 Other anomalies of upper limb, including shoulder girdle

755.50 Unspecified anomaly of upper limb

755.51 Congenital deformity of clavicle

755.52 Congenital elevation of scapula

Sprengel's deformity

755.53 Radioulnar synostosis

DEF: Osseous adhesion of radius and ulna.

755.54 Madelung's deformity

DEF: Distal ulnar overgrowth or radial shortening; also called carpus curvus.

755.55 Acrocephalosyndactyly

Apert's syndrome

DEF: Premature cranial suture fusion (craniostenosis); marked by cone-shaped or pointed (acrocephaly) head and webbing of the fingers (syndactyly); similar to craniofacial dysostosis.

755.56 Accessory carpal bones

755.57 Macrodactylia (fingers)

DEF: Abnormally large fingers, toes.

755.58 Cleft hand, congenital

Lobster-claw hand

DEF: Extended separation between fingers into metacarpus; also may refer to large fingers and absent middle fingers of hand.

755.59 Other

Cleidocranial dysostosis
Cubitus:
valgus, congenital
varus, congenital

EXCLUDES *club hand (congenital) (754.89)*
congenital dislocation of elbow (754.89)

5th 755.6 Other anomalies of lower limb, including pelvic girdle

755.60 Unspecified anomaly of lower limb

755.61 Coxa valga, congenital

DEF: Abnormally wide angle between the neck and shaft of the femur.

755.62 Coxa vara, congenital

DEF: Diminished angle between neck and shaft of femur.

755.63 Other congenital deformity of hip (joint)

Congenital anteversion of femur (neck)

EXCLUDES *congenital dislocation of hip (754.30-754.35)*

755.64 Congenital deformity of knee (joint)

Congenital:
absence of patella
genu valgum [knock-knee]
genu varum [bowleg]
Rudimentary patella

755.65 Macrodactylia of toes

DEF: Abnormally large toes.

755.66 Other anomalies of toes

Congenital:
hallux valgus
hallux varus
hammer toe

755.67 Anomalies of foot, not elsewhere classified

Astragaloscaphoid synostosis
Calcaneonavicular bar
Coalition of calcaneus
Talonavicular synostosis
Tarsal coalitions

755.69 Other

Congenital:
angulation of tibia
deformity (of):
ankle (joint)
sacroiliac (joint)
fusion of sacroiliac joint

755.8 Other specified anomalies of unspecified limb

755.9 Unspecified anomaly of unspecified limb

Congenital:
- anomaly NOS } of unspecified limb
- deformity NOS } of unspecified limb

EXCLUDES *reduction deformity of unspecified limb (755.4)*

✓4th **756 Other congenital musculoskeletal anomalies**

EXCLUDES *congenital myotonic chondrodystrophy (359.23)*
those deformities classifiable to 754.0-754.8

756.0 Anomalies of skull and face bones

Absence of skull bones
Acrocephaly
Congenital deformity of forehead
Craniosynostosis
Crouzon's disease
Hypertelorism
Imperfect fusion of skull
Oxycephaly
Platybasia
Premature closure of cranial sutures
Tower skull
Trigonocephaly

EXCLUDES *acrocephalosyndactyly [Apert's syndrome] (755.55)*
dentofacial anomalies (524.0-524.9)
skull defects associated with brain anomalies, such as:
anencephalus (740.0)
encephalocele (742.0)
hydrocephalus (742.3)
microcephalus (742.1)

✓5th **756.1 Anomalies of spine**

756.10 Anomaly of spine, unspecified

756.11 Spondylolysis, lumbosacral region

Prespondylolisthesis (lumbosacral)

DEF: Bilateral or unilateral defect through the pars interarticularis of a vertebra causes spondylolisthesis.

756.12 Spondylolisthesis

DEF: Downward slipping of lumbar vertebra over next vertebra; usually related to pelvic deformity.

756.13 Absence of vertebra, congenital

756.14 Hemivertebra

DEF: Incomplete development of one side of a vertebra.

756.15 Fusion of spine [vertebra], congenital

756.16 Klippel-Feil syndrome

DEF: Short, wide neck; limits range of motion due to ab-normal number of cervical vertebra or fused hemivertebrae.

756.17 Spina bifida occulta

EXCLUDES *spina bifida (aperta) (741.0-741.9)*

DEF: Spina bifida marked by a bony spinal canal defect without a protrusion of the cord or meninges; it is diagnosed by radiography and has no symptoms.

756.19 Other

Platyspondylia
Supernumerary vertebra

756.2 Cervical rib

Supernumerary rib in the cervical region

DEF: Costa cervicalis: extra rib attached to cervical vertebra.

756.3 Other anomalies of ribs and sternum

Congenital absence of:
- rib
- sternum

Congenital:
- fissure of sternum
- fusion of ribs

Sternum bifidum

EXCLUDES *nonteratogenic deformity of chest wall (754.81-754.89)*

756.4 Chondrodystrophy

Achondroplasia
Chondrodystrophia (fetalis)
Dyschondroplasia
Enchondromatosis
Ollier's disease

EXCLUDES *congenital myotonic chondrodystrophy (359.23)*
lipochondrodystrophy [Hurler's syndrome] (277.5)
Morquio's disease (277.5)

DEF: Abnormal development of cartilage.

✓5th **756.5 Osteodystrophies**

756.50 Osteodystrophy, unspecified

756.51 Osteogenesis imperfecta

Fragilitas ossium
Osteopsathyrosis

DEF: A collagen disorder commonly characterized by brittle, osteoporotic, easily fractured bones, hypermobility of joints, blue sclerae, and a tendency to hemorrhage.

756.52 Osteopetrosis

DEF: Abnormally dense bone, optic atrophy, hepatosplenomegaly, deafness; sclerosing depletes bone marrow and nerve foramina of skull; often fatal.

756.53 Osteopoikilosis

DEF: Multiple sclerotic foci on ends of long bones, stippling in round, flat bones; identified by x-ray.

756.54 Polyostotic fibrous dysplasia of bone

DEF: Fibrous tissue displaces bone results in segmented ragged-edge café-au-lait spots; occurs in girls of early puberty.

756.55 Chondroectodermal dysplasia

Ellis-van Creveld syndrome

DEF: Inadequate enchondral bone formation; impaired development of hair and teeth, polydactyly, and cardiac septum defects.

756.56 Multiple epiphyseal dysplasia

756.59 Other

Albright (-McCune)-Sternberg syndrome

756.6 Anomalies of diaphragm

Absence of diaphragm
Congenital hernia:
- diaphragmatic
- foramen of Morgagni

Eventration of diaphragm

EXCLUDES *congenital hiatus hernia (750.6)*

✓5th **756.7 Anomalies of abdominal wall**

756.70 Anomaly of abdominal wall, unspecified

756.71 Prune belly syndrome

Eagle-Barrett syndrome
Prolapse of bladder mucosa

DEF: Prune belly syndrome: absence of lower rectus abdominis muscle and lower and medial oblique muscles; results in dilated bladder and ureters, dysplastic kidneys and hydronephrosis; more common in male infants with undescended testicles.

756.79 Other congenital anomalies of abdominal wall

Exomphalos
Gastroschisis
Omphalocele

EXCLUDES *umbilical hernia (551-553 with .1)*

DEF: Exomphalos: umbilical hernia prominent navel.

DEF: Gastroschisis: fissure of abdominal wall, results in protruding small or large intestine.

DEF: Omphalocele: hernia of umbilicus due to impaired abdominal wall; results in membrane-covered intestine protruding through peritoneum and amnion.

✓5th **756.8 Other specified anomalies of muscle, tendon, fascia, and connective tissue**

756.81 Absence of muscle and tendon

Absence of muscle (pectoral)

756.82 Accessory muscle

756.83 Ehlers-Danlos syndrome

DEF: Danlos syndrome: connective tissue disorder causes hyperextended skin and joints; results in fragile blood vessels with bleeding, poor wound healing and subcutaneous pseudotumors.

756.89 Other

Amyotrophia congenita
Congenital shortening of tendon

756.9 Other and unspecified anomalies of musculoskeletal system

Congenital:
anomaly NOS } of musculoskeletal system, not
deformity NOS } elsewhere classified

✓4th 757 Congenital anomalies of the integument

INCLUDES anomalies of skin, subcutaneous tissue, hair, nails, and breast

EXCLUDES *hemangioma (228.00-228.09)*
pigmented nevus (216.0-216.9)

757.0 Hereditary edema of legs

Congenital lymphedema
Hereditary trophedema
Milroy's disease

757.1 Ichthyosis congenita

Congenital ichthyosis
Harlequin fetus
Ichthyosiform erythroderma

DEF: Overproduction of skin cells causes scaling of skin; may result in stillborn fetus or death soon after birth.

757.2 Dermatoglyphic anomalies

Abnormal palmar creases

DEF: Abnormal skin-line patterns of fingers, palms, toes and soles; initial finding of possible chromosomal abnormalities.

✓5th **757.3 Other specified anomalies of skin**

757.31 Congenital ectodermal dysplasia

DEF: Tissues and structures originate in embryonic ectoderm; includes anhidrotic and hidrotic ectodermal dysplasia and EEC syndrome.

757.32 Vascular hamartomas

Birthmarks
Port-wine stain
Strawberry nevus

DEF: Benign tumor of blood vessels; due to malformed angioblastic tissues.

757.33 Congenital pigmentary anomalies of skin

Congenital poikiloderma
Urticaria pigmentosa
Xeroderma pigmentosum

EXCLUDES *albinism (270.2)*

757.39 Other

Accessory skin tags, congenital
Congenital scar
Epidermolysis bullosa
Keratoderma (congenital)

EXCLUDES *pilonidal cyst (685.0-685.1)*

757.4 Specified anomalies of hair

Congenital:
alopecia
atrichosis
beaded hair
hypertrichosis
monilethrix
Persistent lanugo

757.5 Specified anomalies of nails

Anonychia
Congenital:
clubnail
koilonychia
leukonychia
onychauxis
pachyonychia

757.6 Specified anomalies of breast

Absent }
Accessory } breast or nipple
Supernumerary }

EXCLUDES *absence of pectoral muscle (756.81)*
hypoplasia of breast (611.82)

757.8 Other specified anomalies of the integument

757.9 Unspecified anomaly of the integument

Congenital:
anomaly NOS } of integument
deformity NOS }

✓4th 758 Chromosomal anomalies

INCLUDES syndromes associated with anomalies in the number and form of chromosomes

Use additional codes for conditions associated with the chromosomal anomalies

758.0 Down's syndrome

Mongolism
Translocation Down's syndrome
Trisomy:
21 or 22
G

758.1 Patau's syndrome

Trisomy:
13
D_1

DEF: Trisomy of 13th chromosome; characteristic failure to thrive, severe mental impairment, seizures, abnormal eyes, low-set ears and sloped forehead.

758.2 Edwards' syndrome

Trisomy:
18
E_3

DEF: Trisomy of 18th chromosome; characteristic mental and physical impairments; mainly affects females.

✓5th **758.3 Autosomal deletion syndromes**

758.31 Cri-du-chat syndrome

Deletion 5p

DEF: Hereditary congenital syndrome caused by a microdeletion of short arm of chromosome 5; characterized by catlike cry in newborn, microenceph-aly, severe mental deficiency, and hypertelorism.

758.32 Velo-cardio-facial syndrome

Deletion 22q11.2

DEF: Microdeletion syndrome affecting multiple organs; characteristic cleft palate, heart defects, elongated face with almond-shaped eyes, wide nose, small ears, weak immune systems, weak musculature, hypothyroidism, short stature, and scoliosis; deletion at q11.2 on the long arm of the chromosome 22.

758.33 Other microdeletions

Miller-Dieker syndrome
Smith-Magenis syndrome

DEF: Miller-Dieker syndrome: deletion from the short arm of chromosome 17; characteristic mental retardation, speech and motor development delays, neurological complications, and multiple abnormalities affecting the kidneys, heart, gastrointestinal tract, and other organ; death in infancy or early childhood.

DEF: Smith-Magenis syndrome: deletion in a certain area of chromosome 17 that results in craniofacial changes, speech delay, hoarse voice, hearing loss in many, and behavioral problems, such as self-destructive head banging, wrist biting, and tearing at nails.

758.39 Other autosomal deletions

758.4 Balanced autosomal translocation in normal individual

758.5 Other conditions due to autosomal anomalies

Accessory autosomes NEC

758.6 Gonadal dysgenesis

Ovarian dysgenesis XO syndrome
Turner's syndrome

EXCLUDES *pure gonadal dysgenesis (752.7)*

758.7 Klinefelter's syndrome
XXY syndrome
DEF: Impaired embryonic development of seminiferous tubes; results in small testes, azoospermia, infertility and enlarged mammary glands.

✓5th **758.8 Other conditions due to chromosome anomalies**

758.81 Other conditions due to sex chromosome anomalies

758.89 Other

758.9 Conditions due to anomaly of unspecified chromosome

✓4th **759 Other and unspecified congenital anomalies**

759.0 Anomalies of spleen
Aberrant / Absent / Accessory } spleen
Congenital splenomegaly
Ectopic spleen
Lobulation of spleen

759.1 Anomalies of adrenal gland
Aberrant / Absent / Accessory } adrenal gland
EXCLUDES *adrenogenital disorders (255.2)*
congenital disorders of steroid metabolism (255.2)

759.2 Anomalies of other endocrine glands
Absent parathyroid gland
Accessory thyroid gland
Persistent thyroglossal or thyrolingual duct
Thyroglossal (duct) cyst
EXCLUDES *congenital:*
goiter (246.1)
hypothyroidism (243)

759.3 Situs inversus
Situs inversus or transversus:
abdominalis
thoracis
Transposition of viscera:
abdominal
thoracic
EXCLUDES *dextrocardia without mention of complete transposition (746.87)*
DEF: Laterally transposed thoracic and abdominal viscera.

759.4 Conjoined twins
Craniopagus
Dicephalus
Pygopagus
Thoracopagus
Xiphopagus

759.5 Tuberous sclerosis
Bourneville's disease
Epiloia
DEF: Hamartomas of brain, retina and viscera, impaired mental ability, seizures and adenoma sebaceum.

759.6 Other hamartoses, not elsewhere classified
Syndrome:
Peutz-Jeghers
Sturge-Weber (-Dimitri)
von Hippel-Lindau
EXCLUDES *neurofibromatosis (237.7)*
DEF: Peutz-Jeghers: hereditary syndrome characterized by hamartomas of small intestine.
DEF: Sturge-Weber: congenital syndrome characterized by unilateral port-wine stain over trigeminal nerve, underlying meninges and cerebral cortex.
DEF: von Hipple-Lindau: hereditary syndrome of congenital angiomatosis of the retina and cerebellum.

759.7 Multiple congenital anomalies, so described
Congenital:
anomaly, multiple NOS
deformity, multiple NOS

✓5th **759.8 Other specified anomalies**

759.81 Prader-Willi syndrome

759.82 Marfan syndrome

759.83 Fragile X syndrome

759.89 Other
Congenital malformation syndromes affect-ing multiple systems, not elsewhere classified
Laurence-Moon-Biedl syndrome

759.9 Congenital anomaly, unspecified

Chapter 15: Conditions in the Perinatal Period (760–779)

This chapter classifies conditions that begin during the perinatal period even if death or morbidity occurs later. The perinatal period is defined as the period of time occurring before, during, through the first 28 days following birth. These codes are used to classify causes or morbidity, and mortality in the fetus or newborn and should not be used on the mother's coded profile.

ICD-9-CM divides this chapter into the following sections:

- Maternal causes of perinatal morbidity and mortality (760–763)
- Other conditions originating in the perinatal period (764–779)

Maternal Causes of Perinatal Morbidity and Mortality (760–763)

Fetal or newborn conditions caused by systemic, metabolic, or infectious diseases of the mother are classified to this section. Maternal diseases that can affect the health or life of the fetus or newborn include hypertension, renal disease, urinary or respiratory tract infections, and chronic respiratory or circulatory diseases (e.g., pulmonary embolism, thrombophlebitis). Categories 760–763 also include fetal or newborn conditions caused by maternal nutritional disorders; maternal injury, surgery or death, maternal ingestion of drugs, chemicals, or alcohol; and maternal complications of labor, delivery, or both.

Assign an additional code to identify the condition that was a result of the maternal condition described by codes in this section, unless the resultant condition code already specifies the maternal condition.

Example:

> Syndrome of "infant of diabetic mother" need only be assigned code 775.0 rather than a code from the 760–763 range.

These codes may be used regardless of the patient's age. For example, it is not uncommon for the daughters of women who ingested DES during pregnancy to develop ovarian cancer from exposure through the placenta while in utero. Code 760.76 is assigned to women affected by DES exposure. E-code assignment is made only for first generation users of DES.

Surgical Operation on Mother and Fetus (760.6)

Subcategory 760.6 describes conditions in which a liveborn infant has been affected in some manner by interventional procedures or surgeries performed during the pregnancy, to diagnose or treat either a fetal condition or a maternal complication of the pregnancy. Fetal surgery is a relatively new surgical specialty that enables treatment of certain conditions that were previously considered untreatable. Diagnostic imaging technologies help in early detection of fetal anomalies and associated gestational risks. In utero interventional procedures provide alternatives to improve outcomes for pregnancies complicated by fetal conditions not previously amenable to treatment. However, these procedures are not without risk for both the fetus and the mother, depending on the nature of the diagnosis and type of intervention. The primary risk for the newborn is premature birth or injury as a result of a procedural intervention during the pregnancy. Premature infants face an increased risk of potentially serious complications and typically require neonatal intensive care unit (NICU) care. Some studies have suggested that amniocentesis and other interventional procedures increase the risk for clubfoot, hip dislocation, and respiratory problems in the infant. Infection of the amniotic fluid is possible, although extremely rare, less than one occurring in 1,000 procedures. Chronic infections such as HIV, cytomegalovirus, hepatitis C, and toxoplasmosis are suspected to be transmittable during in utero interventions.

Slow Fetal Growth and Fetal Malnutrition (764)

Slow fetal growth and fetal malnutrition is a condition in which a fetus is considerably below the normal weight expected for a fetus of the same gestational age. Malnutrition in a fetus may be due to defective assimilation or utilization of nutrients or to a maternal diet that is unbalanced or insufficient, as well as other factors.

This condition may be described with such terms as "small for gestational age," "intrauterine growth retardation" or "IUGR."

Conditions Originating in the Perinatal Period (764-779)

Monochorionic Gestation Complicated by Inter-twin Vascular Communication

Twin-twin transfusion syndrome (TTTS) is a complication of fetal cardiovascular development that results in a hostile intrauterine fluid volume environment. Due to the abnormal development of anastomotic blood vessels, one twin is polyhydramniotic and the other is oligohydramniotic, creating a donor-recipient situation with associated complicating conditions for each fetus. Amnioreduction can be performed to treat the polyhydramniotic twin, reducing the fluid volume and pressure. However, the definitive surgery is fetoscopic laser photocoagulation, which is performed to ablate and correct the underlying chorionic vascular anomalies that cause TTTS, and prevent further fluid loss for the oligohydramniotic twin.

Separate diagnoses are required to report a pregnancy complicated by inter-twin vascular communication and the resultant manifestations of oligohydramnios and polyhydramnios.

Code assignment for mother's record:

651.03 Twin pregnancy, antepartum complication

655.83 Other known or suspected fetal abnormality NEC, antepartum complication

657.03 Polyhydramnios, antepartum condition

658.03 Oligohydramnios, antepartum condition.

If one fetus is terminated as a result of TTTS, report code 651.73 Multiple gestation following elective reduction, antepartum condition, for the reduction diagnosis, with a secondary diagnosis of 655.83 Other known or suspected fetal abnormality.

Code assignment for newborn record:

762.3 Placental transfusion syndromes

Use an additional code to indicate any resultant condition in the fetus or newborn, such as fetal blood loss (772.0) or polycythemia neonatorum (776.4)

Post-term and Prolonged Gestation Infant (766.2x)

Post-term infant is defined as an infant with a gestation period of more than 40 to 42 completed weeks. Prolonged gestation is defined as an infant with a gestation period of more than 42 completed weeks. The definitions relate to length of gestation and not to associated conditions that may arise due to the length of gestation.

Codes 766.21 Post-term infant and 766.22 Prolonged gestation of infant may be assigned based only on the gestational age of the newborn. A specific condition or disorder does not have to be associated with the longer gestational period to assign these codes.

Necrotizing Enterocolitis (777.5)

Necrotizing enterocolitis (NEC) is a serious and life-threatening condition in premature infants. It is a gastrointestinal illness associated with some very low birth-weight (VLBW) infants. In NEC, the lining of the intestinal wall dies and the tissue sloughs off. The cause for this disorder is unknown, but it is thought that a decrease in blood flow to the bowel keeps the bowel from producing mucus that protects the gastrointestinal tract. Bacteria in the intestine may also be a contributing factor. NEC without pneumatosis (defined as gas in the bowel wall) or perforation is a vague disorder and may resolve with medical treatment. NEC with pneumatosis places the patient at higher risk for mortality and progression to serious complications, such as portal vein gas or perforation.

Stages of NEC may be classified as follows:

- Stage 1 (suspected) (777.51): Nonspecific systemic signs, including lethargy, abdominal distention, blood in stool. Radiology studies may be normal or positive for bowel dilation.
- Stage 2 (proven) (777.52): Absent bowel sounds. Radiology studies positive for intestinal dilation, ileus, pneumatosis, and possibly ascites.
- Stage 3 (advanced) (777.53): Critical illness with hypotension or shock, bradycardia, apnea, peritonitis, or bowel perforation. Appropriate use of treatments such as antenatal steroids, standardized enteric feeding regimens with human milk, and probiotics, along with careful monitoring, could substantially reduce the incidence of this serious disease. When perforation or necrotic bowel occurs, emergent surgery is necessary.

Due to the fragility of premature infants, those who suffer intestinal perforation often have high mortality rates. Assign the appropriate code for the clinical stage of disease only as documented in the medical record.

15. CERTAIN CONDITIONS ORIGINATING IN THE PERINATAL PERIOD (760-779)

INCLUDES conditions which have their origin in the perinatal period, before birth through the first 28 days after birth, even though death or morbidity occurs later

Use additional code(s) to further specify condition

MATERNAL CAUSES OF PERINATAL MORBIDITY AND MORTALITY (760-763)

✓4th **760 Fetus or newborn affected by maternal conditions which may be unrelated to present pregnancy**

INCLUDES the listed maternal conditions only when specified as a cause of mortality or morbidity of the fetus or newborn

EXCLUDES *maternal endocrine and metabolic disorders affecting fetus or newborn (775.0-775.9)*

760.0 Maternal hypertensive disorders

Fetus or newborn affected by maternal conditions classifiable to 642

760.1 Maternal renal and urinary tract diseases

Fetus or newborn affected by maternal conditions classifiable to 580-599

760.2 Maternal infections

Fetus or newborn affected by maternal infectious disease classifiable to 001-136 and 487, but fetus or newborn not manifesting that disease

EXCLUDES *congenital infectious diseases (771.0-771.8)*
maternal genital tract and other localized infections (760.8)

760.3 Other chronic maternal circulatory and respiratory diseases

Fetus or newborn affected by chronic maternal conditions classifiable to 390-459, 490-519, 745-748

760.4 Maternal nutritional disorders

Fetus or newborn affected by:
maternal disorders classifiable to 260-269
maternal malnutrition NOS

EXCLUDES *fetal malnutrition (764.10-764.29)*

760.5 Maternal injury

Fetus or newborn affected by maternal conditions classifiable to 800-995

✓5th **760.6 Surgical operation on mother and fetus**

EXCLUDES *cesarean section for present delivery (763.4)*
damage to placenta from amniocentesis, cesarean section, or surgical induction (762.1)

760.61 Newborn affected by amniocentesis

EXCLUDES *fetal complications from amniocentesis (679.1)*

760.62 Newborn affected by other in utero procedure

EXCLUDES *fetal complications of in utero procedure (679.1)*

760.63 Newborn affected by other surgical operations on mother during pregnancy

EXCLUDES *newborn affected by previous surgical procedure on mother not associated with pregnancy (760.64)*

760.64 Newborn affected by previous surgical procedure on mother not associated with pregnancy

✓5th **760.7 Noxious influences affecting fetus or newborn via placenta or breast milk**

Fetus or newborn affected by noxious substance transmitted via placenta or breast milk

EXCLUDES *anesthetic and analgesic drugs administered during labor and delivery (763.5)*
drug withdrawal syndrome in newborn (779.5)

760.70 Unspecified noxious substance

Fetus or newborn affected by:
Drug NEC

760.71 Alcohol

Fetal alcohol syndrome

760.72 Narcotics

760.73 Hallucinogenic agents

760.74 Anti-infectives

Antibiotics
Antifungals

760.75 Cocaine

760.76 Diethylstilbestrol [DES]

760.77 Anticonvulsants

Carbamazepine
Phenobarbital
Phenytoin
Valproic acid

760.78 Antimetabolic agents

Methotrexate
Retinoic acid
Statins

760.79 Other

Fetus or newborn affected by:
immune sera } transmitted via placenta or breast
medicinal agents NEC } transmitted via placenta or breast
toxic substance NEC } transmitted via placenta or breast

760.8 Other specified maternal conditions affecting fetus or newborn

Maternal genital tract and other localized infection affecting fetus or newborn, but fetus or newborn not manifesting that disease

EXCLUDES *maternal urinary tract infection affecting fetus or newborn (760.1)*

760.9 Unspecified maternal condition affecting fetus or newborn

✓4th **761 Fetus or newborn affected by maternal complications of pregnancy**

INCLUDES the listed maternal conditions only when specified as a cause of mortality or morbidity of the fetus or newborn

761.0 Incompetent cervix

DEF: Inadequate functioning of uterine cervix.

761.1 Premature rupture of membranes

761.2 Oligohydramnios

EXCLUDES *that due to premature rupture of membranes (761.1)*

DEF: Deficient amniotic fluid.

761.3 Polyhydramnios

Hydramnios (acute) (chronic)

DEF: Excess amniotic fluid.

761.4 Ectopic pregnancy

Pregnancy:
abdominal
intraperitoneal
tubal

761.5 Multiple pregnancy

Triplet (pregnancy)
Twin (pregnancy)

761.6 Maternal death

761.7 Malpresentation before labor

Breech presentation, External version, Oblique lie, Transverse lie, Unstable lie } before labor

761.8 Other specified maternal complications of pregnancy affecting fetus or newborn

Spontaneous abortion, fetus

761.9 Unspecified maternal complication of pregnancy affecting fetus or newborn

✓4th **762 Fetus or newborn affected by complications of placenta, cord, and membranes**

INCLUDES the listed maternal conditions only when specified as a cause of mortality or morbidity in the fetus or newborn

762.0 Placenta previa

DEF: Placenta developed in lower segment of uterus; causes hemorrhaging in last trimester.

762.1 Other forms of placental separation and hemorrhage

Abruptio placentae
Antepartum hemorrhage
Damage to placenta from amniocentesis, cesarean section, or surgical induction
Maternal blood loss
Premature separation of placenta
Rupture of marginal sinus

762.2 Other and unspecified morphological and functional abnormalities of placenta

Placental:
- dysfunction
- infarction
- insufficiency

762.3 Placental transfusion syndromes

Placental and cord abnormality resulting in twin-to-twin or other transplacental transfusion

Use additional code to indicate resultant condition in fetus or newborn:
- fetal blood loss (772.0)
- polycythemia neonatorum (776.4)

762.4 Prolapsed cord

Cord presentation

762.5 Other compression of umbilical cord

Cord around neck
Entanglement of cord
Knot in cord
Torsion of cord

762.6 Other and unspecified conditions of umbilical cord

Short cord

Thrombosis, Varices, Velamentous insertion, Vasa previa } of umbilical cord

EXCLUDES *infection of umbilical cord (771.4)*
single umbilical artery (747.5)

762.7 Chorioamnionitis

Amnionitis
Membranitis
Placentitis

DEF: Inflamed fetal membrane.

762.8 Other specified abnormalities of chorion and amnion

762.9 Unspecified abnormality of chorion and amnion

✓4th **763 Fetus or newborn affected by other complications of labor and delivery**

INCLUDES the listed conditions only when specified as a cause of mortality or morbidity in the fetus or newborn

EXCLUDES *newborn affected by surgical procedures on mother (760.61-760.64)*

763.0 Breech delivery and extraction

763.1 Other malpresentation, malposition, and disproportion during labor and delivery

Fetus or newborn affected by:
- abnormality of bony pelvis
- contracted pelvis
- persistent occipitoposterior position
- shoulder presentation
- transverse lie

Fetus or newborn affected by conditions classifiable to 652, 653, and 660

763.2 Forceps delivery

Fetus or newborn affected by forceps extraction

763.3 Delivery by vacuum extractor

763.4 Cesarean delivery

EXCLUDES *placental separation or hemorrhage from cesarean section (762.1)*

763.5 Maternal anesthesia and analgesia

Reactions and intoxications from maternal opiates and tranquilizers during labor and delivery

EXCLUDES *drug withdrawal syndrome in newborn (779.5)*

763.6 Precipitate delivery

Rapid second stage

763.7 Abnormal uterine contractions

Fetus or newborn affected by:
- contraction ring
- hypertonic labor
- hypotonic uterine dysfunction
- uterine inertia or dysfunction

Fetus or newborn affected by conditions classifiable to 661, except 661.3

✓5th **763.8 Other specified complications of labor and delivery affecting fetus or newborn**

763.81 Abnormality in fetal heart rate or rhythm before the onset of labor

763.82 Abnormality in fetal heart rate or rhythm during labor

763.83 Abnormality in fetal heart rate or rhythm, unspecified as to time of onset

763.84 Meconium passage during delivery

EXCLUDES *meconium aspiration (770.11, 770.12)*
meconium staining (779.84)

DEF: Fetal intestinal activity that increases in response to a distressed state during delivery; anal sphincter relaxes, and meconium is passed into the amniotic fluid.

763.89 Other specified complications of labor and delivery affecting fetus or newborn

Fetus or newborn affected by:
- abnormality of maternal soft tissues
- destructive operation on live fetus to facilitate delivery
- induction of labor (medical)
- other procedures used in labor and delivery

Fetus or newborn affected by other conditions classifiable to 650-699

763.9 Unspecified complication of labor and delivery affecting fetus or newborn

OTHER CONDITIONS ORIGINATING IN THE PERINATAL PERIOD (764-779)

The following fifth-digit subclassification is for use with category 764 and codes 765.0-765.1 to denote birthweight:

- **0 unspecified [weight]**
- **1 less than 500 grams**
- **2 500-749 grams**
- **3 750-999 grams**
- **4 1,000-1,249 grams**
- **5 1,250-1,499 grams**
- **6 1,500-1,749 grams**
- **7 1,750-1,999 grams**
- **8 2,000-2,499 grams**
- **9 2,500 grams and over**

✓4th **764 Slow fetal growth and fetal malnutrition**

✓5th **764.0 "Light-for-dates" without mention of fetal malnutrition**
[0-9]
Infants underweight for gestational age
"Small-for-dates"

✓5th **764.1 "Light-for-dates" with signs of fetal malnutrition**
[0-9]
Infants "light-for-dates" classifiable to 764.0, who in addition show signs of fetal malnutrition, such as dry peeling skin and loss of subcutaneous tissue

✓5th **764.2 Fetal malnutrition without mention of "light-for-dates"**
[0-9]
Infants, not underweight for gestational age, showing signs of fetal malnutrition, such as dry peeling skin and loss of subcutaneous tissue
Intrauterine malnutrition

✓5th **764.9 Fetal growth retardation, unspecified**
[0-9]
Intrauterine growth retardation

✓4th **765 Disorders relating to short gestation and low birthweight**

INCLUDES the listed conditions, without further specification, as causes of mortality, morbidity, or additional care, in fetus or newborn

✓5th **765.0 Extreme immaturity**
[0-9]
Note: Usually implies a birthweight of less than 1000 grams.
Use additional code for weeks of gestation (765.20-765.29)

✓5th **765.1 Other preterm infants**
[0-9]
Note: Usually implies a birthweight of 1000-2499 grams.
Prematurity NOS
Prematurity or small size, not classifiable to 765.0 or as "light-for-dates" in 764
Use additional code for weeks of gestation (765.20-765.29)

✓5th **765.2 Weeks of gestation**

765.20 Unspecified weeks of gestation

765.21 Less than 24 completed weeks ofgestation

765.22 24 completed weeks of gestation

765.23 25-26 completed weeks of gestation

765.24 27-28 completed weeks of gestation

765.25 29-30 completed weeks of gestation

765.26 31-32 completed weeks of gestation

765.27 33-34 completed weeks of gestation

765.28 35-36 completed weeks of gestation

765.29 37 or more completed weeks of gestation

✓4th **766 Disorders relating to long gestation and high birthweight**

INCLUDES the listed conditions, without further specification, as causes of mortality, morbidity, or additional care, in fetus or newborn

766.0 Exceptionally large baby
Note: Usually implies a birthweight of 4500 grams or more.

766.1 Other "heavy-for-dates" infants
Other fetus or infant "heavy-" or "large-for-dates" regardless of period of gestation

✓5th **766.2 Late infant, not "heavy-for-dates"**

766.21 Post-term infant
Infant with gestation period over 40 completed weeks to 42 completed weeks

766.22 Prolonged gestation of infant
Infant with gestation period over 42 completed weeks
Postmaturity NOS

✓4th **767 Birth trauma**

767.0 Subdural and cerebral hemorrhage
Subdural and cerebral hemorrhage, whether described as due to birth trauma or to intrapartum anoxia or hypoxia
Subdural hematoma (localized)
Tentorial tear
Use additional code to identify cause

EXCLUDES *intraventricular hemorrhage (772.10-772.14)*
subarachnoid hemorrhage (772.2)

✓5th **767.1 Injuries to scalp**

767.11 Epicranial subaponeurotic hemorrhage (massive)
Subgaleal hemorrhage

DEF: A hemorrhage that occurs within the space between the galea aponeurotica, or epicranial aponeurosis, a thin tendinous structure that is attached to the skull laterally and provides an insertion site for the occipitalis posteriorly and the frontalis muscle anteriorly, and the periosteum of the skull.

767.19 Other injuries to scalp
Caput succedaneum
Cephalhematoma
Chignon (from vacuum extraction)

767.2 Fracture of clavicle

767.3 Other injuries to skeleton
Fracture of:
long bones
skull

EXCLUDES *congenital dislocation of hip (754.30-754.35)*
fracture of spine, congenital (767.4)

Epicranial Aponeurosis

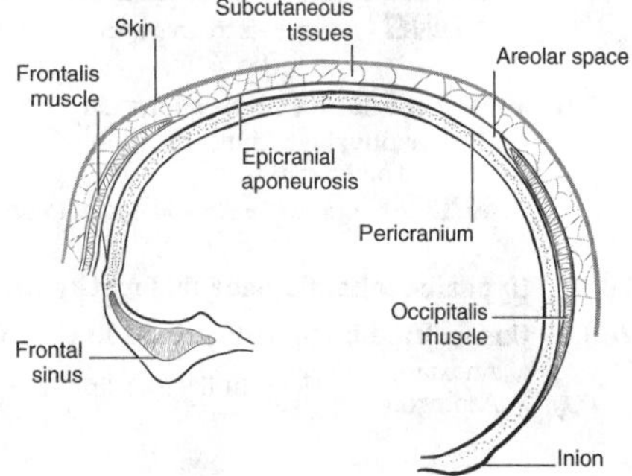

767.4 Injury to spine and spinal cord

Dislocation, Fracture, Laceration, Rupture } of spine or spinal cord due to birth trauma

767.5 Facial nerve injury

Facial palsy

767.6 Injury to brachial plexus

Palsy or paralysis:
- brachial
- Erb (-Duchenne)
- Klumpke (-Déjérine)

767.7 Other cranial and peripheral nerve injuries

Phrenic nerve paralysis

767.8 Other specified birth trauma

Eye damage

Hematoma of:
- liver (subcapsular)
- testes
- vulva

Rupture of:
- liver
- spleen

Scalpel wound

Traumatic glaucoma

EXCLUDES *hemorrhage classifiable to 772.0-772.9*

767.9 Birth trauma, unspecified

Birth injury NOS

✓4th 768 Intrauterine hypoxia and birth asphyxia

Use only when associated with newborn morbidity classifiable elsewhere

EXCLUDES *acidemia NOS of newborn (775.81)*
acidosis NOS of newborn (775.81)
cerebral ischemia NOS (779.2)
hypoxia NOS of newborn (770.88)
mixed metabolic and respiratory acidosis of newborn (775.81)
respiratory arrest of newborn (770.87)

DEF: Oxygen intake insufficiency due to interrupted placental circulation or premature separation of placenta.

768.0 Fetal death from asphyxia or anoxia before onset of labor or at unspecified time

768.1 Fetal death from asphyxia or anoxia during labor

768.2 Fetal distress before onset of labor, in liveborn infant

Fetal metabolic acidemia before onset of labor, in liveborn infant

768.3 Fetal distress first noted during labor and delivery, in liveborn infant

Fetal metabolic acidemia first noted during labor and delivery, in liveborn infant

768.4 Fetal distress, unspecified as to time of onset, in liveborn infant

Fetal metabolic acidemia unspecified as to time of onset, in liveborn infant

768.5 Severe birth asphyxia

Birth asphyxia with neurologic involvement

EXCLUDES *hypoxic-ischemic encephalopathy [HIE] (768.7)*

768.6 Mild or moderate birth asphyxia

Birth asphyxia (without mention of neurologic involvement)

EXCLUDES *hypoxic-ischemic encephalopathy [HIE] (768.7)*

768.7 Hypoxic-ischemic encephalopathy [HIE]

768.9 Unspecified birth asphyxia in liveborn infant

Anoxia, Asphyxia } NOS, in liveborn infant

769 Respiratory distress syndrome

Cardiorespiratory distress syndrome of newborn
Hyaline membrane disease (pulmonary)
Idiopathic respiratory distress syndrome [IRDS or RDS] of newborn
Pulmonary hypoperfusion syndrome

EXCLUDES *transient tachypnea of newborn (770.6)*

DEF: Severe chest contractions upon air intake and expiratory grunting; infant appears blue due to oxygen deficiency and has rapid respiratory rate; formerly called hyaline membrane disease.

✓4th 770 Other respiratory conditions of fetus and newborn

770.0 Congenital pneumonia

Infective pneumonia acquired prenatally

EXCLUDES *pneumonia from infection acquired after birth (480.0-486)*

✓5th 770.1 Fetal and newborn aspiration

EXCLUDES *aspiration of postnatal stomach contents (770.85, 770.86)*
meconium passage during delivery (763.84)
meconium staining (779.84)

770.10 Fetal and newborn aspiration, unspecified

770.11 Meconium aspiration without respiratory symptoms

Meconium aspiration NOS

770.12 Meconium aspiration with respiratory symptoms

Meconium aspiration pneumonia
Meconium aspiration pneumonitis
Meconium aspiration syndrome NOS

Use additional code to identify any secondary pulmonary hypertension (416.8), if applicable

DEF: Meconium aspiration syndrome: aspiration of fetal intestinal material during or prior to delivery, usually a complication of placental insufficiency, causing pneumonitis and bronchial obstruction (inflammatory reaction of lungs).

770.13 Aspiration of clear amniotic fluid without respiratory symptoms

Aspiration of clear amniotic fluid NOS

770.14 Aspiration of clear amniotic fluid with respiratory symptoms

Aspiration of clear amniotic fluid with pneumonia
Aspiration of clear amniotic fluid with pneumonitis

Use additional code to identify any secondary pulmonary hypertension (416.8), if applicable

770.15 Aspiration of blood without respiratory symptoms

Aspiration of blood NOS

770.16 Aspiration of blood with respiratory symptoms

Aspiration of blood with pneumonia
Aspiration of blood with pneumonitis

Use additional code to identify any secondary pulmonary hypertension (416.8), if applicable

770.17 Other fetal and newborn aspiration without respiratory symptoms

770.18 Other fetal and newborn aspiration with respiratory symptoms

Other aspiration pneumonia
Other aspiration pneumonitis

Use additional code to identify any secondary pulmonary hypertension (416.8), if applicable

770.2 Interstitial emphysema and related conditions

Pneumomediastinum, Pneumopericardium, Pneumothorax } originating in the perinatal period

770.3 Pulmonary hemorrhage
Hemorrhage:
alveolar (lung) } originating in the perinatal period
intra-alveolar (lung)
massive pulmonary

770.4 Primary atelectasis
Pulmonary immaturity NOS
DEF: Alveoli fail to expand causing insufficient air intake by newborn.

770.5 Other and unspecified atelectasis
Atelectasis: } originating in the perinatal period
NOS
partial
secondary
Pulmonary collapse

770.6 Transitory tachypnea of newborn
Idiopathic tachypnea of newborn
Wet lung syndrome
EXCLUDES *respiratory distress syndrome (769)*
DEF: Quick, shallow breathing of newborn; short-term problem.

770.7 Chronic respiratory disease arising in the perinatal period
Bronchopulmonary dysplasia
Interstitial pulmonary fibrosis of prematurity
Wilson-Mikity syndrome

✓5th **770.8 Other respiratory problems after birth**
EXCLUDES *mixed metabolic and respiratory acidosis of newborn (775.81)*

770.81 Primary apnea of newborn
Apneic spells of newborn NOS
Essential apnea of newborn
Sleep apnea of newborn
DEF: Cessation of breathing when a neonate makes no respiratory effort for 15 seconds, resulting in cyanosis and bradycardia.

770.82 Other apnea of newborn
Obstructive apnea of newborn

770.83 Cyanotic attacks of newborn

770.84 Respiratory failure of newborn
EXCLUDES *respiratory distress syndrome (769)*

770.85 Aspiration of postnatal stomach contents without respiratory symptoms
Aspiration of postnatal stomach contents NOS

770.86 Aspiration of postnatal stomach contents with respiratory symptoms
Aspiration of postnatal stomach contents with pneumonia
Aspiration of postnatal stomach contents with pneumonitis
Use additional code to identify any secondary pulmonary hypertension (416.8), if applicable

770.87 Respiratory arrest of newborn

770.88 Hypoxemia of newborn
Hypoxia NOS of newborn

770.89 Other respiratory problems after birth

770.9 Unspecified respiratory condition of fetus and newborn

✓4th **771 Infections specific to the perinatal period**
INCLUDES infections acquired before or during birth or via the umbilicus or during the first 28 days after birth
EXCLUDES *congenital pneumonia (770.0)*
congenital syphilis (090.0-090.9)
infant botulism (040.41)
maternal infectious disease as a cause of mortality or morbidity in fetus or newborn, but fetus or newborn not manifesting the disease (760.2)
ophthalmia neonatorum due to gonococcus (098.40)
other infections not specifically classified to this category

771.0 Congenital rubel
Congenital rubella pneumonitis

771.1 Congenital cytomegalovirus infection
Congenital cytomegalic inclusion disease

771.2 Other congenital infections
Congenital:
herpes simplex
listeriosis
malaria
Congenital:
toxoplasmosis
tuberculosis

771.3 Tetanus neonatorum
Tetanus omphalitis
EXCLUDES *hypocalcemic tetany (775.4)*
DEF: Severe infection of central nervous system; due to exotoxin of tetanus bacillus from navel infection prompted by nonsterile technique during umbilical ligation.

771.4 Omphalitis of the newborn
Infection:
navel cord
umbilical stump
EXCLUDES *tetanus omphalitis (771.3)*
DEF: Inflamed umbilicus.

771.5 Neonatal infective mastitis
EXCLUDES *noninfective neonatal mastitis (778.7)*

771.6 Neonatal conjunctivitis and dacryocystitis
Ophthalmia neonatorum NOS
EXCLUDES *ophthalmia neonatorum due to gonococcus (098.40)*

771.7 Neonatal Candida infection
Neonatal moniliasis
Thrush in newborn

✓5th **771.8 Other infection specific to the perinatal period**
Use additional code to identify organism (041.00-041.9)

771.81 Septicemia [sepsis] of newborn
Use additional codes to identify severe sepsis (995.92) and any associated acute organ dysfunction, if applicable

771.82 Urinary tract infection of newborn

771.83 Bacteremia of newborn

771.89 Other infections specific to the perinatal period
Intra-amniotic infection of fetus NOS
Infection of newborn NOS

✓4th **772 Fetal and neonatal hemorrhage**
EXCLUDES *hematological disorders of fetus and newborn (776.0-776.9)*

772.0 Fetal blood loss
Fetal blood loss from:
cut end of co-twin's cord
placenta
ruptured cord
vasa previa
Fetal exsanguination
Fetal hemorrhage into:
co-twin
mother's circulation

5th 772.1 Intraventricular hemorrhage
Intraventricular hemorrhage from any perinatal cause

772.10 Unspecified grade

772.11 Grade I
Bleeding into germinal matrix

772.12 Grade II
Bleeding into ventricle

772.13 Grade III
Bleeding with enlargement of ventricle

772.14 Grade IV
Bleeding into cerebral cortex

772.2 Subarachnoid hemorrhage
Subarachnoid hemorrhage from any perinatal cause
EXCLUDES *subdural and cerebral hemorrhage (767.0)*

772.3 Umbilical hemorrhage after birth
Slipped umbilical ligature

772.4 Gastrointestinal hemorrhage
EXCLUDES *swallowed maternal blood (777.3)*

772.5 Adrenal hemorrhage

772.6 Cutaneous hemorrhage
Bruising, Ecchymoses, Petechiae, Superficial hematoma } in fetus or newborn

772.8 Other specified hemorrhage of fetus or newborn
EXCLUDES *hemorrhagic disease of newborn (776.0)*
pulmonary hemorrhage (770.3)

772.9 Unspecified hemorrhage of newborn

4th 773 Hemolytic disease of fetus or newborn, due to isoimmunization
DEF: Hemolytic anemia of fetus or newborn due to maternal antibody formation against fetal erythrocytes; infant blood contains nonmaternal antigen.

773.0 Hemolytic disease due to Rh isoimmunization
Anemia, Erythroblastosis (fetalis), Hemolytic disease (fetus) (newborn), Jaundice } due to RH: antibodies, isoimmunization, maternal/fetal incompatibility
Rh hemolytic disease
Rh isoimmunization

773.1 Hemolytic disease due to ABO isoimmumization
ABO hemolytic disease
ABO isoimmunization
Anemia, Erythroblastosis (fetalis), Hemolytic disease (fetus) (newborn), Jaundice } due to ABO: antibodies, isoimmunization, maternal/fetal incompatibility
DEF: Incompatible Rh fetal-maternal blood grouping; prematurely destroys red blood cells; detected by Coombs test.

773.2 Hemolytic disease due to other and unspecified isoimmunization
Eythroblastosis (fetalis) (neonatorum) NOS
Hemolytic disease (fetus) (newborn) NOS
Jaundice or anemia due to other and unspecified blood-group incompatibility

773.3 Hydrops fetalis due to isoimmunization
Use additional code to identify type of isoimmunization (773.0-773.2)
DEF: Massive edema of entire body and severe anemia; may result in fetal death or stillbirth.

773.4 Kernicterus due to isoimmunization
Use additional code to identify type of isoimmunization (773.0-773.2)
DEF: Complication of erythroblastosis fetalis associated with severe neural symptoms, high blood bilirubin levels and nerve cell destruction; results in bilirubin-pigmented gray matter of central nervous system.

773.5 Late anemia due to isoimmunization

4th 774 Other perinatal jaundice

774.0 Perinatal jaundice from hereditary hemolytic anemias
Code first underlying disease (282.0-282.9)

774.1 Perinatal jaundice from other excessive hemolysis
Fetal or neonatal jaundice from:
- bruising
- drugs or toxins transmitted from mother
- infection
- polycythemia
- swallowed maternal blood

Use additional code to identify cause
EXCLUDES *jaundice due to isoimmunization (773.0-773.2)*

774.2 Neonatal jaundice associated with preterm delivery
Hyperbilirubinemia of prematurity
Jaundice due to delayed conjugation associated with preterm delivery

5th 774.3 Neonatal jaundice due to delayed conjugation from other causes

774.30 Neonatal jaundice due to delayed conjugation, cause unspecified
DEF: Jaundice of newborn with abnormal bilirubin metabolism; causes excess accumulated unconjugated bilirubin in blood.

774.31 Neonatal jaundice due to delayed conjugation in diseases classified elsewhere
Code first underlying diseases as:
- congenital hypothyroidism (243)
- Crigler-Najjar syndrome (277.4)
- Gilbert's syndrome (277.4)

774.39 Other
Jaundice due to delayed conjugation from causes, such as:
- breast milk inhibitors
- delayed development of conjugating system

774.4 Perinatal jaundice due to hepatocellular damage
Fetal or neonatal hepatitis
Giant cell hepatitis
Inspissated bile syndrome

774.5 Perinatal jaundice from other causes
Code first underlying cause as:
- congenital obstruction of bile duct (751.61)
- galactosemia (271.1)
- mucoviscidosis (277.00-277.09)

774.6 Unspecified fetal and neonatal jaundice
Icterus neonatorum
Neonatal hyperbilirubinemia (transient)
Physiologic jaundice NOS in newborn
EXCLUDES *that in preterm infants (774.2)*

774.7 Kernicterus not due to isoimmunization
Bilirubin encephalopathy
Kernicterus of newborn NOS
EXCLUDES *kernicterus due to isoimmunization (773.4)*

4th 775 Endocrine and metabolic disturbances specific to the fetus and newborn
INCLUDES transitory endocrine and metabolic disturb-ances caused by the infant's response to maternal endocrine and metabolic factors, its removal from them, or its adjustment to extrauterine existence

775.0 Syndrome of "infant of a diabetic mother"
Maternal diabetes mellitus affecting fetus or newborn (with hypoglycemia)

775.1 Neonatal diabetes mellitus
Diabetes mellitus syndrome in newborn infant

775.2 Neonatal myasthenia gravis

775.3 Neonatal thyrotoxicosis
Neonatal hyperthydroidism (transient)

775.4 Hypocalcemia and hypomagnesemia of newborn
Cow's milk hypocalcemia
Hypocalcemic tetany, neonatal
Neonatal hypoparathyroidism
Phosphate-loading hypocalcemia

775.5 Other transitory neonatal electrolyte disturbances
Dehydration, neonatal

775.6 Neonatal hypoglycemia
EXCLUDES *infant of mother with diabetes mellitus (775.0)*

775.7 Late metabolic acidosis of newborn

775.8 Other neonatal endocrine and metabolic disturbances

775.81 Other acidosis of newborn
Acidemia NOS of newborn
Acidosis of newborn NOS
Mixed metabolic and respiratory acidosis of newborn

775.89 Other neonatal endocrine and metabolic disturbances
Amino-acid metabolic disorders described as transitory

775.9 Unspecified endocrine and metabolic disturbances specific to the fetus and newborn

✓4th **776 Hematological disorders of newborn**
INCLUDES disorders specific to the newborn though possibly originating in utero
EXCLUDES *fetal hematologic conditions (678.0)*

776.0 Hemorrhagic disease of newborn
Hemorrhagic diathesis of newborn
Vitamin K deficiency of newborn
EXCLUDES *fetal or neonatal hemorrhage (772.0-772.9)*

776.1 Transient neonatal thrombocytopenia
Neonatal thrombocytopenia due to:
exchange transfusion
idiopathic maternal thrombocytopenia
isoimmunization
DEF: Temporary decrease in blood platelets of newborn.

776.2 Disseminated intravascular coagulation in newborn
DEF: Disseminated intravascular coagulation of newborn: clotting disorder due to excess thromboplastic agents in blood as a result of disease or trauma; causes blood clotting within vessels and reduces available elements necessary for blood coagulation.

776.3 Other transient neonatal disorders of coagulation
Transient coagulation defect, newborn

776.4 Polycythemia neonatorum
Plethora of newborn
Polycythemia due to:
donor twin transfusion
maternal-fetal transfusion
DEF: Abnormal increase of total red blood cells of newborn.

776.5 Congenital anemia
Anemia following fetal blood loss
EXCLUDES *anemia due to isoimmunization (773.0-773.2, 773.5)*
hereditary hemolytic anemias (282.0-282.9)

776.6 Anemia of prematurity

776.7 Transient neonatal neutropenia
Isoimmune neutropenia
Maternal transfer neutropenia
EXCLUDES *congenital neutropenia (nontransient) (288.01)*
DEF: Decreased neutrophilic leukocytes in blood of newborn.

776.8 Other specified transient hematological disorders

776.9 Unspecified hematological disorder specific to fetus or newborn

✓4th **777 Perinatal disorders of digestive system**
INCLUDES disorders specific to the fetus and newborn
EXCLUDES *intestinal obstruction classifiable to 560.0-560.9*

777.1 Meconium obstruction
Congenital fecaliths
Delayed passage of meconium
Meconium ileus NOS
Meconium plug syndrome
EXCLUDES *meconium ileus in cystic fibrosis (277.01)*
DEF: Meconium blocked digestive tract of newborn.

777.2 Intestinal obstruction due to inspissated milk

777.3 Hematemesis and melena due to swallowed maternal blood
Swallowed blood syndrome in newborn
EXCLUDES *that not due to swallowed maternal blood (772.4)*

777.4 Transitory ileus of newborn
EXCLUDES *Hirschsprung's disease (751.3)*

✓5th **777.5 Necrotizing enterocolitis in newborn**
Pseudomembranous enterocolitis in newborn
DEF: Acute inflammation of small intestine due to pseudomembranous plaque over ulceration; may be due to aggressive antibiotic therapy.

777.50 Necrotizing enterocolitis in newborn, unspecified
Necrotizing enterocolitis in newborn, NOS

777.51 Stage I necrotizing enterocolitis in newborn

777.52 Stage II necrotizing enterocolitis in newborn
Necrotizing enterocolitis with pneumatosis, without perforation

777.53 Stage III necrotizing enterocolitis in newborn
Necrotizing enterocolitis with perforation
Necrotizing enterocolitis with pneumatosis and perforation

777.6 Perinatal intestinal perforation
Meconium peritonitis

777.8 Other specified perinatal disorders of digestive system

777.9 Unspecified perinatal disorder of digestive system

✓4th **778 Conditions involving the integument and temperature regulation of fetus and newborn**

778.0 Hydrops fetalis not due to isoimmunization
Idiopathic hydrops
EXCLUDES *hydrops fetalis due to isoimmunization (773.3)*
DEF: Edema of entire body, unrelated to immune response.

778.1 Sclerema neonatorum
Subcutaneous fat necrosis
DEF: Diffuse, rapidly progressing white, waxy, nonpitting hardening of tissue, usually of legs and feet, life-threatening; found in preterm or debilitated infants; unknown etiology.

778.2 Cold injury syndrome of newborn

778.3 Other hypothermia of newborn

778.4 Other disturbances of temperature regulation of newborn
Dehydration fever in newborn
Environmentally-induced pyrexia
Hyperthermia in newborn
Transitory fever of newborn

778.5 Other and unspecified edema of newborn
Edema neonatorum

778.6 Congenital hydrocele
Congenital hydrocele of tunica vaginalis

778.7 Breast engorgement in newborn
Noninfective mastitis of newborn
EXCLUDES *infective mastitis of newborn (771.5)*

778.8 Other specified conditions involving the integument of fetus and newborn

Urticaria neonatorum

EXCLUDES *impetigo neonatorum (684)*
pemphigus neonatorum (684)

778.9 Unspecified condition involving the integument and temperature regulation of fetus and newborn

✓4th 779 Other and ill-defined conditions originating in the perinatal period

779.0 Convulsions in newborn

Fits } in newborn
Seizures

779.1 Other and unspecified cerebral irritability in newborn

779.2 Cerebral depression, coma, and other abnormal cerebral signs

Cerebral ischemia NOS of newborn
CNS dysfunction in newborn NOS

EXCLUDES *cerebral ischemia due to birth trauma (767.0)*
intrauterine cerebral ischemia (768.2-768.9)
intraventricular hemorrhage (772.10-772.14)

779.3 Feeding problems in newborn

Regurgitation of food }
Slow feeding } in newborn
Vomiting }

779.4 Drug reactions and intoxications specific to newborn

Gray syndrome from chloramphenicol administration in newborn

EXCLUDES *fetal alcohol syndrome (760.71)*
reactions and intoxications from maternal opiates and tranquilizers (763.5)

779.5 Drug withdrawal syndrome in newborn

Drug withdrawal syndrome in infant of dependent mother

EXCLUDES *fetal alcohol syndrome (760.71)*

779.6 Termination of pregnancy (fetus)

Fetal death due to:
induced abortion
termination of pregnancy

EXCLUDES *spontaneous abortion (fetus) (761.8)*

779.7 Periventricular leukomalacia

DEF: Necrosis of white matter adjacent to lateral ventricles with the formation of cysts; cause of PVL has not been firmly established, but thought to be related to inadequate blood flow in certain areas of the brain.

✓5th 779.8 Other specified conditions originating in the perinatal period

779.81 Neonatal bradycardia

EXCLUDES *abnormality in fetal heart rate or rhythm complicating labor and delivery (763.81-763.83)*
bradycardia due to birth asphyxia (768.5-768.9)

779.82 Neonatal tachycardia

EXCLUDES *abnormality in fetal heart rate or rhythm complicating labor and delivery (763.81-763.83)*

779.83 Delayed separation of umbilical cord

779.84 Meconium staining

EXCLUDES *meconium aspiration (770.11, 770.12)*
meconium passage during delivery (763.84)

779.85 Cardiac arrest of newborn

779.89 Other specified conditions originating in the perinatal period

Use additional code to specify condition

779.9 Unspecified condition originating in the perinatal period

Congenital debility NOS
Stillbirth NEC

Chapter 16: Symptoms, Signs, and Ill-defined Conditions (780–799)

This chapter includes symptoms, signs, and abnormal results of laboratory or other investigative procedures, as well as ill-defined conditions for which there are no other, more specific diagnoses classifiable elsewhere.

Symptoms are subjective observations reported to the physician by the patient. These observations depart from the structure, function or sensation that the patient normally experiences.

In general, codes from this chapter are used to report symptoms, signs, and ill-defined conditions that point with equal suspicion to two or more diagnoses or represent important problems in medical care that may affect management of the patient.

In addition, this chapter provides codes to classify abnormal findings that are reported without a corresponding definitive diagnosis. Codes for such findings can be located in the alphabetic index under such terms as "Abnormal, abnormality, abnormalities," "Decrease, decreased," "Elevation" and "Findings, abnormal, without diagnosis."

Codes from this chapter also are used to report:

- Symptoms and signs that existed on initial encounter but proved to be transient and whose causes could not be determined
- Provisional diagnoses for patients who fail to return for further investigation
- Cases referred elsewhere for further investigation before being diagnosed
- Cases in which a more definitive diagnosis was not available for other reasons

Do not assign a code from categories 780–799 when the symptoms, signs, and abnormal findings pertain to and are integral to a definitive diagnosis.

Example:

A patient with acute appendicitis would not need additional codes for abdominal pain (789.00) and abdominal rigidity (789.40). These signs and symptoms are integral to acute appendicitis and add no value to the patient's coding profile when assigned as secondary codes.

However, you may use a code from this chapter to report symptoms, signs, and abnormal findings that pertain to a particular clinical diagnosis if they represent important problems in medical care. Such problems may be useful to record because they may affect treatment plans. In this case, list the definitive condition as the principal diagnosis and the symptoms as secondary.

List as a secondary diagnosis any symptoms, signs, and abnormal findings that are not integral to the principal diagnosis but coexist at the time of current episode of care and affect treatment, clinical evaluation, or increased monitoring or care. For example, a patient with benign prostatic hypertrophy NOS (600.00) seen for urinary retention may have acute urinary retention listed as a secondary diagnosis (788.20). Acute urinary retention is not integral to the disease process for benign prostatic hypertrophy, but it is an indication for an aggressive treatment plan. Acute urinary retention can be viewed as an "important medical problem" when the medical record documentation indicates the need for diagnostic procedures, therapeutic treatment, or monitoring to determine the cause.

List as the principal diagnosis any symptoms, signs, and abnormal findings that, after study, cannot be attributed to a definitive diagnosis classifiable to another chapter. The official coding guideline for coding symptoms, signs, and ill-defined conditions for outpatient services states that codes describing symptoms and signs, as opposed to diagnoses, are acceptable for reporting purposes when an established diagnosis has not been confirmed by the physician.

Symptoms that are integral to the disease process should not be assigned additional codes. However, those symptoms that are not routinely exhibited by patients with the disease may be coded in addition. For example, patients with Crohn's disease do not routinely exhibit intestinal obstruction. In some cases the intestinal obstruction occurs with Crohn's disease and both conditions should be coded.

The alphabetic index should be consulted to determine which symptoms and signs are to be classified here and which should be classified to more specific sections of ICD-9-CM. The residual subcategories designated as .9 subcategories are provided for other relevant symptoms that are not elsewhere classified.

Symptoms (780-789)

Fever and other Physiologic Disturbances of Temperature Regulation (780.6)

While inherent in a number of conditions, fever is considered a significant complication when associated with many chronic conditions, such as leukemia and sickle cell disease. In these chronic conditions, the presence of a fever may be a warning sign that the disease is being exacerbated or that a complicating infectious or inflammatory process is occurring in the body. Fever in chronic disease may also indicate an adverse drug or transfusion reaction, or the cause may not be known. However, the presence of a fever often affects the resources and intensity of required treatment. Code first the underlying condition when reporting code 780.61.

Functional Quadriplegia (780.72)

Functional quadriplegia is the inability to move due to another condition (e.g., dementia, severe contractures, arthritis, etc.) excluding neurological conditions. Functionally, the patient is the same as a paralyzed person. The inability to move and perform routine daily tasks for themselves renders patients immobile. This state poses certain associated health risks such as pressure ulcer, contractures, and pneumonia. The amount and type of care required to attend to these patients is greater than that of a patient with similar state of health but who is more mobile or has a greater degree of physical function.

Dysphagia (787.2x)

Dysphagia is a dynamic disorder, whereby the symptoms vary significantly depending on the affected phase of swallow. Oral-phase disorders typically result from impaired tongue control. Patients may experience trouble chewing solid food and initiating swallows. When drinking, there may be difficulty in containing the liquid in the oral cavity before swallowing, resulting in aspiration. In pharyngeal-phase dysphagia, the patient may be unable to ingest sufficiently life-sustaining amounts of food when pharyngeal clearance is severely limited. Impairment of esophageal function may cause food and liquid to be retained in the esophagus after swallowing. This can result from mechanical obstruction, motility disorder, or impaired opening of the lower esophageal sphincter.

Unique subclassification codes are available to facilitate reporting of dysphagia by the affected phase(s) of swallow as well as options for unspecified (787.20) and other (787.29) dysphagia. Dysphagia due to late effect of cerebrovascular accident (438.82) is sequenced first, if applicable.

Functional Urinary Incontinence (788.9)

Functional urinary incontinence (FUI) is defined as leakage of urine related to impairment in cognitive function or other physical disability that makes the patient unable to control bladder function. FUI may be a temporary or permanent condition, depending on the underlying cause and contributing factors. This type of urinary incontinence is common among the elderly population, particularly those who suffer from dementia or mobility issues. Precipitating causes include stroke, neurological deficits (Parkinson's, Alzheimer's), severe depression, effects of medication, or musculoskeletal deconditioning due to aging.

Ascites (789.5x)

Malignant ascites (789.51) is most often seen in patients with ovarian, endometrial, breast, colon, gastric, and pancreatic cancer. Management of malignant ascites can include systemic chemotherapy, instillation of radioisotopes or chemotherapeutic drugs into the peritoneal fluid, and peritoneal venous shunting procedures.

Code 197.6 is no longer the default code for reporting malignant ascites, as this code assumes that a secondary malignancy (metastasis) of the peritoneum or retroperitoneum exists. This default coding practice presents problems when malignant ascites is not the result of metastatic spread of a malignancy to the peritoneum. For example, malignant ascites can occur as a result of a primary ovarian malignancy, without tumor extension into the retroperitoneum or peritoneal tissues. Therefore, the default code for malignant ascites has been removed from 197.6 to 789.51. Code first the associated causal malignancy (e.g., 183.0, 197.6) when reporting malignant ascites.

Nonspecific Abnormal Findings (790–796)

Included in this section are nonspecific findings on examination of:

- Blood (790)
- Urine (791)
- Other body substances (792)
- Radiological and other examinations of body structure (793)
- Function studies (794)
- Immunological studies (795)
- Other (796)

Abnormal findings (laboratory, x-ray, pathologic, and other diagnostic results) are not assigned and reported unless the physician indicates a clinical significance or if a definitive diagnosis cannot be made. If the findings are outside the normal range and the physician has ordered other tests to evaluate the condition or prescribed treatment, it is appropriate to ask the physician whether the diagnosis should be added.

Abnormal Cytologies (795, 796)

Cytology samples may be obtained from the vagina, cervix, vulva, or anorectal canal to screen for human papillomavirus (HPV), abnormal growth such as dysplasia, anal intraepithelial neoplasia (AIN), and perianal intraepithelial neoplasia (PAIN). The correlation between abnormal cytologic smears and the risk of dysplasia and carcinoma is the same for the anus as it is for the cervix. Many pathophysiological parallels exist between cervical-vaginal and anal-rectal screening. For example, there is a transformation zone in the anus (similar to that of the cervix), which is the area between the keratinized and nonkeratinized epithelia. It is important to obtain a cytological sample from these tissues. Transformational zone tissue samples contain either squamous metaplastic and/or rectal columnar cells. Cellular analysis of transformation zone cells help diagnose and classify dysplastic changes. The histological and immunological cell changes reported with the Bethesda system are determined by cytology studies of the cell samples of the anus, cervix, vagina, and vulva as obtained by smear tests. The Bethesda system classifies cell changes by type and severity, from normal tissue to the identification of malignant cells. A pathologist interprets the findings and places the samples into the following categories:

- No pathologic change (normal) or inflammation (e.g., infection): Cells indicate the presence of inflammation that may be due to infection
- Atypical squamous cells of undetermined significance (ASCUS): Minor changes of the thin, flat surface cells due to unknown causes; may be followed up with DNA testing to identify the presence of a human papillomavirus (HPV)
- Atypical glandular cells (AGC): Abnormal mucus-producing cells due to unknown cause; favorable conditions for neoplastic growth
- Low-grade squamous intraepithelial lesion (LGSIL): Minor cellular changes unlikely to progress to cancer. Includes HPV infection, mild dysplasia, and intraepithelial neoplasia (CIN 1); may be followed up with DNA testing to identify the presence of a high-risk HPV infection
- High-grade squamous intraepithelial lesion (HGSIL): Cellular changes with a likelihood of progressing to cancer. Includes moderate to severe dysplasia, carcinoma in situ (CIS), CIN 2 and CIN 3, or changes suspicious for invasive cancer
- Malignant cells identified

The transformation zone refers to the area between the keratinized and nonkeratinized epithelia. It is important to obtain a cytological sample from these specific tissues. Transformational zone tissue samples contain squamous metaplastic and/or rectal columnar cells. Cellular analysis of transformation zone cells provides valuable information in diagnosis and classification of the specific nature of the dysplastic changes. Definitive diagnoses of carcinoma, intraepithelial neoplasia, and dysplasia are excluded from subcategory 795.0. Assign the appropriate chapter 2 neoplasm code or chapter 10 genitourinary disease code. When reporting abnormal vaginal smears, use an additional code from new category V88 to identify the acquired absence of the uterus or cervix, if applicable. Use an additional code to report associated HPV when reporting 795.19 or 796.79, when appropriate.

16. SYMPTOMS, SIGNS, AND ILL-DEFINED CONDITIONS (780-799)

This section includes symptoms, signs, abnormal results of laboratory or other investigative procedures, and ill-defined conditions regarding which no diagnosis classifiable elsewhere is recorded.

Signs and symptoms that point rather definitely to a given diagnosis are assigned to some category in the preceding part of the classification. In general, categories 780-796 include the more ill-defined conditions and symptoms that point with perhaps equal suspicion to two or more diseases or to two or more systems of the body, and without the necessary study of the case to make a final diagnosis. Practically all categories in this group could be designated as "not otherwise specified," or as "unknown etiology," or as "transient." The Alphabetic Index should be consulted to determine which symptoms and signs are to be allocated here and which to more specific sections of the classification; the residual subcategories numbered .9 are provided for other relevant symptoms which cannot be allocated elsewhere in the classification.

The conditions and signs or symptoms included in categories 780-796 consist of: (a) cases for which no more specific diagnosis can be made even after all facts bearing on the case have been investigated; (b) signs or symptoms existing at the time of initial encounter that proved to be transient and whose causes could not be determined; (c) provisional diagnoses in a patient who failed to return for further investigation or care; (d) cases referred elsewhere for investigation or treatment before the diagnosis was made; (e) cases in which a more precise diagnosis was not available for any other reason; (f) certain symptoms which represent important problems in medical care and which it might be desired to classify in addition to a known cause.

SYMPTOMS (780-789)

✓4th **780 General symptoms**

✓5th **780.0 Alteration of consciousness**

EXCLUDES *coma:*
diabetic (249.2-249.3, 250.2-250.3)
hepatic (572.2)
originating in the perinatal period (779.2)

780.01 Coma

DEF: State of unconsciousness from which the patient cannot be awakened.

780.02 Transient alteration of awareness

DEF: Temporary, recurring spells of reduced consciousness.

780.03 Persistent vegetative state

DEF: Persistent wakefulness without consciousness due to nonfunctioning cerebral cortex.

780.09 Other

Drowsiness
Semicoma
Somnolence
Stupor
Unconsciousness

780.1 Hallucinations

Hallucinations:
NOS
auditory
gustatory
olfactory
tactile

EXCLUDES *those associated with mental disorders, as functional psychoses (295.0-298.9)*
organic brain syndromes (290.0-294.9, 310.0-310.9)
visual hallucinations (368.16)

DEF: Perception of external stimulus in absence of stimulus; inability to distinguish between real and imagined.

780.2 Syncope and collapse

Blackout
Fainting
(Near) (Pre) syncope
Vasovagal attack

EXCLUDES *carotid sinus syncope (337.0)*
heat syncope (992.1)
neurocirculatory asthenia (306.2)
orthostatic hypotension (458.0)
shock NOS (785.50)

DEF: Sudden unconsciousness due to reduced blood flow to brain.

✓5th **780.3 Convulsions**

EXCLUDES *convulsions:*
epileptic (345.10-345.91)
in newborn (779.0)

DEF: Sudden, involuntary contractions of the muscles.

780.31 Febrile convulsions (simple), unspecified

Febrile seizure NOS

780.32 Complex febrile convulsions

Febrile seizure:
atypical
complex
complicated

EXCLUDES *status epilepticus (345.3)*

780.39 Other convulsions

Convulsive disorder NOS
Fit NOS
Recurrent convulsions NOS
Seizure NOS

780.4 Dizziness and giddiness

Light-headedness
Vertigo NOS

EXCLUDES *Ménière's disease and other specified vertiginous syndromes (386.0-386.9)*

DEF: Whirling sensations in head with feeling of falling.

✓5th **780.5 Sleep disturbances**

EXCLUDES *circadian rhythm sleep disorders (327.30-327.39)*
organic hypersomnia (327.10-327.19)
organic insomnia (327.00-327.09)
organic sleep apnea (327.20-327.29)
organic sleep related movement disorders (327.51-327.59)
parasomnias (327.40-327.49)
that of nonorganic origin (307.40-307.49)

780.50 Sleep disturbance, unspecified

780.51 Insomnia with sleep apnea, unspecified

DEF: Transient cessation of breathing disturbing sleep.

780.52 Insomnia, unspecified

DEF: Inability to maintain adequate sleep cycle.

780.53 Hypersomnia with sleep apnea, unspecified

DEF: Autonomic response inhibited during sleep; causes insufficient oxygen intake, acidosis and pulmonary hypertension.

780.54 Hypersomnia, unspecified

DEF: Prolonged sleep cycle.

780.55 Disruptions of 24 hour sleep wake cycle, unspecified

780.56 Dysfunctions associated with sleep stages or arousal from sleep

780.57 Unspecified sleep apnea

780.58 Sleep related movement disorder, unspecified

EXCLUDES *restless legs syndrome (333.94)*

780.59 Other

✓5th **780.6 Fever and other physiologic disturbances of temperature regulation**

EXCLUDES *effects of reduced environmental temperature (991.0-991.9)*
effects of heat and light (992.0-992.9)
fever, chills or hypothermia associated with confirmed infection – code to infection

DEF: Elevated body temperature; no known cause.

780.60 Fever, unspecified

Chills with fever
Fever NOS
Fever of unknown origin (FUO)
Hyperpyrexia NOS
Pyrexia NOS
Pyrexia of unknown origin

EXCLUDES *chills without fever (780.64)*
neonatal fever (778.4)
pyrexia of unknown origin (during):
in newborn (778.4)
labor (659.2)
the puerperium (672)

780.61 Fever presenting with conditions classifi elsewhere

Code first underlying condition when associated fever is present, such as with:
leukemia (conditions classifiable to 204-208)
neutropenia (288.00-288.09)
sickle-cell disease (282.60-282.69)

780.62 Postprocedural fever

EXCLUDES *postvaccination fever (780.63)*

780.63 Postvaccination fever

Postimmunization fever

780.64 Chills (without fever)

Chills NOS

EXCLUDES *chills with fever (780.60)*

780.65 Hypothermia not associated with low environmental temperature

EXCLUDES *hypothermia:*
associated with low environmental temperature (991.6)
due to anesthesia (995.89)
of newborn (778.2, 778.3)

✓5th **780.7 Malaise and fatigue**

EXCLUDES *debility, unspecified (799.3)*
fatigue (during):
combat (308.0-308.9)
heat (992.6)
pregnancy (646.8)
neurasthenia (300.5)
senile asthenia (797)

780.71 Chronic fatigue syndrome

DEF: Persistent fatigue, symptoms include weak muscles, sore throat, lymphadenitis, headache, depression and mild fever; no known cause; also called chronic mononucleosis, benign myalgic encephalomyelitis, Iceland disease and neurosthenia.

780.72 Functional quadriplegia

Complete immobility due to severe physical disability or frailty

EXCLUDES *hysterical paralysis (300.11)*
immobility syndrome (728.3)
neurologic quadriplegia (344.00-344.09)
quadriplegia NOS (344.00)

780.79 Other malaise and fatigue

Asthenia NOS
Lethargy
Postviral (asthenic) syndrome
Tiredness

DEF: Asthenia: Any weakness, lack of strength or loss of energy, especially neuromuscular.

DEF: Lethargy: Listlessness, drowsiness, stupor and apathy.

DEF: Malaise: Vague feeling of debility or lack of good health.

DEF: Postviral (asthenic) syndrome: Listlessness, drowsiness, stupor and apathy; follows acute viral infection.

DEF: Tiredness: General exhaustion or fatigue.

780.8 Generalized hyperhidrosis

Diaphoresis
Excessive sweating
Secondary hyperhidrosis

EXCLUDES *focal (localized) (primary) (secondary) hyperhidrosis (705.21-705.22)*
Frey's syndrome (705.22)

DEF: Excessive sweating, appears as droplets on skin; general or localized.

✓5th **780.9 Other general symptoms**

EXCLUDES *hypothermia:*
NOS (accidental) (991.6)
due to anesthesia (995.89)
of newborn (778.2-778.3)
memory disturbance as part of a pattern of mental disorder

780.91 Fussy infant (baby)

780.92 Excessive crying of infant (baby)

EXCLUDES *excessive crying of child, adolescent or adult (780.95)*

780.93 Memory loss

Amnesia (retrograde)
Memory loss NOS

EXCLUDES *mild memory disturbance due to organic brain damage (310.1)*
transient global amnesia (437.7)

780.94 Early satiety

DEF: The premature feeling of being full; mechanism of satiety is mutlifactorial.

780.95 Excessive crying of child, adolescent, or adult

EXCLUDES *excessive crying of infant (baby) (780.92)*

780.96 Generalized pain

Pain NOS

780.97 Altered mental status

Change in mental status

EXCLUDES *altered level of consciousness (780.01-780.09)*
altered mental status due to known condition–code to condition
delirium NOS (780.09)

780.99 Other general symptoms

✓4th **781 Symptoms involving nervous and musculoskeletal systems**

EXCLUDES *depression NOS (311)*
disorders specifically relating to:
back (724.0-724.9)
hearing (388.0-389.9)
joint (718.0-719.9)
limb (729.0-729.9)
neck (723.0-723.9)
vision (368.0-369.9)
pain in limb (729.5)

781.0 Abnormal involuntary movements
Abnormal head movements
Fasciculation
Spasms NOS
Tremor NOS
EXCLUDES *abnormal reflex (796.1)*
chorea NOS (333.5)
infantile spasms (345.60-345.61)
spastic paralysis (342.1, 343.0-344.9)
specified movement disorders classifiable to 333 (333.0-333.9)
that of nonorganic origin (307.2-307.3)

781.1 Disturbances of sensation of smell and taste
Anosmia
Parageusia
Parosmia
DEF: Anosmia: loss of sense of smell due to organic factors, including loss of olfactory nerve conductivity, cerebral disease, nasal fossae formation and peripheral olfactory nerve diseases; can also be psychological disorder.
DEF: Parageusia: distorted sense of taste, or bad taste in mouth.
DEF: Parosmia: distorted sense of smell.

781.2 Abnormality of gait
Gait:
ataxic
paralytic
spastic
staggering
EXCLUDES *ataxia:*
NOS (781.3)
locomotor (progressive) (094.0)
difficulty in walking (719.7)
DEF: Abnormal, asymmetric gait.

781.3 Lack of coordination
Ataxia NOS
Muscular incoordination
EXCLUDES *ataxic gait (781.2)*
cerebellar ataxia (334.0-334.9)
difficulty in walking (719.7)
vertigo NOS (780.4)

781.4 Transient paralysis of limb
Monoplegia, transient NOS
EXCLUDES *paralysis (342.0-344.9)*

781.5 Clubbing of fingers
DEF: Enlarged soft tissue of distal fingers.

781.6 Meningismus
Dupré's syndrome
Meningism
DEF: Condition with signs and symptoms that resemble meningeal irritation; it is associated with febrile illness and dehydration with no evidence of infection.

781.7 Tetany
Carpopedal spasm
EXCLUDES *tetanus neonatorum (771.3)*
tetany:
hysterical (300.11)
newborn (hypocalcemic) (775.4)
parathyroid (252.1)
psychogenic (306.0)
DEF: Nerve and muscle hyperexcitability; symptoms include muscle spasms, twitching, cramps, laryngospasm with inspiratory stridor, hyperreflexia and choreiform movements.

781.8 Neurologic neglect syndrome
Asomatognosia
Hemi-akinesia
Hemi-inattention
Hemispatial neglect
Left-sided neglect
Sensory extinction
Sensory neglect
Visuospatial neglect

✓5th **781.9 Other symptoms involving nervous and musculoskeletal systems**

781.91 Loss of height
EXCLUDES *osteoporosis (733.00-733.09)*

781.92 Abnormal posture

781.93 Ocular torticollis
DEF: Abnormal head posture as a result of a contracted state of cervical muscles to correct a visual disturbance; either double vision or a visual field defect.

781.94 Facial weakness
Facial droop
EXCLUDES *facial weakness due to late effect of cerebrovascular accident (438.83)*

781.99 Other symptoms involving nervous and musculoskeletal systems

✓4th **782 Symptoms involving skin and other integumentary tissue**
EXCLUDES *symptoms relating to breast (611.71-611.79)*

782.0 Disturbance of skin sensation
Anesthesia of skin
Burning or prickling sensation
Hyperesthesia
Hypoesthesia
Numbness
Paresthesia
Tingling

782.1 Rash and other nonspecific skin eruption
Exanthem
EXCLUDES *vesicular eruption (709.8)*

782.2 Localized superficial swelling, mass, or lump
Subcutaneous nodules
EXCLUDES *localized adiposity (278.1)*

782.3 Edema
Anasarca
Dropsy
Localized edema NOS
EXCLUDES *ascites (789.51-789.59)*
edema of:
newborn NOS (778.5)
pregnancy (642.0-642.9, 646.1)
fluid retention (276.6)
hydrops fetalis (773.3, 778.0)
hydrothorax (511.81-511.89)
nutritional edema (260, 262)
DEF: Edema: excess fluid in intercellular body tissue.
DEF: Anasarca: massive edema in all body tissues.
DEF: Dropsy: serous fluid accumulated in body cavity or cellular tissue.
DEF: Localized edema: edema in specific body areas.

782.4 Jaundice, unspecified, not of newborn
Cholemia NOS
Icterus NOS
EXCLUDES *jaundice in newborn (774.0-774.7)*
due to isoimmunization (773.0-773.2, 773.4)
DEF: Bilirubin deposits of skin, causing yellow cast.

782.5 Cyanosis
EXCLUDES *newborn (770.83)*
DEF: Deficient oxygen of blood; causes blue cast to skin.

✓5th **782.6 Pallor and flushing**

782.61 Pallor

782.62 Flushing
Excessive blushing

782.7 Spontaneous ecchymoses
Petechiae
EXCLUDES *ecchymosis in fetus or newborn (772.6)*
purpura (287.0-287.9)
DEF: Hemorrhagic spots of skin; resemble freckles.

782.8 Changes in skin texture
Induration } of skin
Thickening }

782.9 Other symptoms involving skin and integumentary tissues

4th **783 Symptoms concerning nutrition, metabolism, and development**

783.0 Anorexia
Loss of appetite
EXCLUDES *anorexia nervosa (307.1)*
loss of appetite of nonorganic origin (307.59)

783.1 Abnormal weight gain
EXCLUDES *excessive weight gain in pregnancy (646.1)*
obesity (278.00)
morbid (278.01)

5th **783.2 Abnormal loss of weight and underweight**
Use additional code to identify Body Mass Index (BMI), if known (V85.0-V85.54)

783.21 Loss of weight

783.22 Underweight

783.3 Feeding difficulties and mismanagement
Feeding problem (elderly) (infant)
EXCLUDES *feeding disturbance or problems:*
in newborn (779.3)
of nonorganic origin (307.50-307.59

5th **783.4 Lack of expected normal physiological development in childhood**
EXCLUDES *delay in sexual development and puberty (259.0)*
gonadal dysgenesis (758.6)
pituitary dwarfism (253.3)
slow fetal growth and fetal malnutrition (764.00-764.99)
specific delays in mental development (315.0-315.9)

783.40 Lack of normal physiological development, unspecified
Inadequate development
Lack of development

783.41 Failure to thrive
Failure to gain weight
DEF: Organic failure to thrive: acute or chronic illness that interferes with nutritional intake, absorption, metabolism excretion and energy requirements. Nonorganic FTT is symptom of neglect or abuse.

783.42 Delayed milestones
Late talker
Late walker

783.43 Short stature
Growth failure
Growth retardation
Lack of growth
Physical retardation
DEF: Constitutional short stature: stature inconsistent with chronological age. Genetic short stature is when skeletal maturation matches chronological age.

783.5 Polydipsia
Excessive thirst

783.6 Polyphagia
Excessive eating
Hyperalimentation NOS
EXCLUDES *disorders of eating of nonorganic origin (307.50-307.59)*

783.7 Adult failure to thrive

783.9 Other symptoms concerning nutrition, metabolism, and development
Hypometabolism
EXCLUDES *abnormal basal metabolic rate (794.7)*
dehydration (276.51)
other disorders of fluid, electrolyte, and acid-base balance (276.0-276.9)

4th **784 Symptoms involving head and neck**
EXCLUDES *encephalopathy NOS (348.30)*
specific symptoms involving neck classifiable to 723 (723.0-723.9)

784.0 Headache
Facial pain
Pain in head NOS
EXCLUDES *atypical face pain (350.2)*
migraine (346.0-346.9)
tension headache (307.81)

784.1 Throat pain
EXCLUDES *dysphagia (787.20-787.29)*
neck pain (723.1)
sore throat (462)
chronic (472.1)

784.2 Swelling, mass, or lump in head and neck
Space-occupying lesion, intracranial NOS

784.3 Aphasia
EXCLUDES *aphasia due to late effects of cerebrovascular disease (438.11)*
developmental aphasia (315.31)
DEF: Inability to communicate through speech, written word, or sign language.

5th **784.4 Voice disturbance**

784.40 Voice disturbance, unspecified

784.41 Aphonia
Loss of voice

784.49 Other
Change in voice
Dysphonia
Hoarseness
Hypernasality
Hyponasality

784.5 Other speech disturbance
Dysarthria
Dysphasia
Slurred speech
EXCLUDES *stammering and stuttering (307.0)*
that of nonorganic origin (307.0, 307.9)

5th **784.6 Other symbolic dysfunction**
EXCLUDES *developmental learning delays (315.0-315.9)*

784.60 Symbolic dysfunction, unspecified

784.61 Alexia and dyslexia
Alexia (with agraphia)
DEF: Alexia: Inability to understand written word due to central brain lesion.
DEF: Dyslexia: Ability to recognize letters but inability to read, spell, and write words; genetic.

784.69 Other
Acalculia
Agnosia
Agraphia NOS
Apraxia

784.7 Epistaxis
Hemorrhage from nose
Nosebleed

784.8 Hemorrhage from throat
EXCLUDES *hemoptysis (786.3)*

5th **784.9 Other symptoms involving head and neck**

784.91 Postnasal drip

784.99 Other symptoms involving head and neck
Choking sensation
Feeling of foreign body in throat
Halitosis
Mouth breathing
Sneezing
EXCLUDES *foreign body in throat (933.0)*

4th **785 Symptoms involving cardiovascular system**
EXCLUDES *heart failure NOS (428.9)*

785.0 Tachycardia, unspecified
Rapid heart beat
EXCLUDES *neonatal tachycardia (779.82)*
paroxysmal tachycardia (427.0-427.2)
DEF: Excessively rapid heart rate.

785.1 Palpitations
Awareness of heart beat
EXCLUDES *specified dysrhythmias (427.0-427.9)*

785.2 Undiagnosed cardiac murmurs
Heart murmurs NOS

785.3 Other abnormal heart sounds
Cardiac dullness, increased or decreased
Friction fremitus, cardiac
Precordial friction

785.4 Gangrene
Gangrene:
NOS
spreading cutaneous
Gangrenous cellulitis
Phagedena
Code first any associated underlying condition
EXCLUDES *gangrene of certain sites – see Alphabetic Index*
gangrene with atherosclerosis of the extremities (440.24)
gas gangrene (040.0
DEF: Gangrene: necrosis of skin tissue due to bacterial infection, diabetes, embolus and vascular supply loss.
DEF: Gangrenous cellulitis: group A streptococcal infection; begins with severe cellulitis, spreads to superficial and deep fascia; produces gangrene of underlying tissues.

✓5th **785.5 Shock without mention of trauma**

785.50 Shock, unspecifiedFailure of peripheral circulation
DEF: Peripheral circulatory failure due to heart insufficiencies.

785.51 Cardiogenic shock
DEF: Shock syndrome: associated with myocardial infarction, cardiac tamponade and massive pulmonary embolism; symptoms include mental confusion, reduced blood pressure, tachycardia, pallor and cold, clammy skin.

785.52 Septic shock
Shock:
endotoxic
gram-negative
Code first:
systemic inflammatory response syndrome due to infectious process with organ dysfunction (995.92)

785.59 Other
Shock:
hypovolemic
EXCLUDES *shock (due to):*
anesthetic (995.4)
anaphylactic (995.0)
due to serum (999.4)
electric (994.8)
following abortion (639.5)
lightning (994.0)
obstetrical (669.1)
postoperative (998.0)
traumatic (958.4)

785.6 Enlargement of lymph nodes
Lymphadenopathy
"Swollen glands"
EXCLUDES *lymphadenitis (chronic) (289.1-289.3)*
acute (683)

785.9 Other symptoms involving cardiovascular system
Bruit (arterial)
Weak pulse

✓4th **786 Symptoms involving respiratory system and other chest symptoms**

✓5th **786.0 Dyspnea and respiratory abnormalities**

786.00 Respiratory abnormality, unspecified

786.01 Hyperventilation
EXCLUDES *hyperventilation, psychogenic (306.1)*
DEF: Rapid breathing causes carbon dioxide loss from blood.

786.02 Orthopnea
DEF: Difficulty breathing except in upright position.

786.03 Apnea
EXCLUDES *apnea of newborn (770.81, 770.82)*
sleep apnea (780.51, 780.53, 780.57)
DEF: Cessation of breathing.

786.04 Cheyne-Stokes respiration
DEF: Rhythmic increase of depth and frequency of breathing with apnea; occurs in frontal lobe and diencephalic dysfunction.

786.05 Shortness of breath
DEF: Inability to take in sufficient oxygen.

786.06 Tachypnea
EXCLUDES *transitory tachypnea of newborn (770.6)*
DEF: Abnormal rapid respiratory rate; called hyperventilation.

786.07 Wheezing
EXCLUDES *asthma (493.00-493.92)*
DEF: Stenosis of respiratory passageway; causes whistling sound; due to asthma, coryza, croup, emphysema, hay fever, edema, and pleural effusion.

786.09 Other
Respiratory:
distress
insufficiency
EXCLUDES *respiratory distress:*
following trauma and surgery (518.5)
newborn (770.89)
syndrome (newborn) (769)
adult (518.5)
respiratory failure (518.81, 518.83-518.84)
newborn (770.84)

786.1 Stridor
EXCLUDES *congenital laryngeal stridor (748.3)*
DEF: Obstructed airway causes harsh sound.

786.2 Cough
EXCLUDES *cough:*
psychogenic (306.1)
smokers' (491.0)
with hemorrhage (786.3)

786.3 Hemoptysis
Cough with hemorrhage
Pulmonary hemorrhage NOS
EXCLUDES *pulmonary hemorrhage of newborn (770.3)*
DEF: Coughing up blood or blood-stained sputum.

786.4 Abnormal sputum
Abnormal:
amount, color, odor } sputum
Excessive septum

✓5th **786.5 Chest pain**

786.50 Chest pain, unspecified

786.51 Precordial pain
DEF: Chest pain over heart and lower thorax.

786.52 Painful respiration
Pain:
anterior chest wall
pleuritic
Pleurodynia
EXCLUDES *epidemic pleurodynia (074.1)*

786.59 Other

Discomfort, Pressure, Tightness } in chest

EXCLUDES *pain in breast (611.71)*

786.6 Swelling, mass, or lump in chest

EXCLUDES *lump in breast (611.72)*

786.7 Abnormal chest sounds

Abnormal percussion, chest
Friction sounds, chest
Rales
Tympany, chest

EXCLUDES *wheezing (786.07)*

786.8 Hiccough

EXCLUDES *psychogenic hiccough (306.1)*

786.9 Other symptoms involving respiratory system and chest

Breath-holding spell

✓4th **787 Symptoms involving digestive system**

EXCLUDES *constipation (564.00-564.09)*
pylorospasm (537.81)
congenital (750.5)

✓5th **787.0 Nausea and vomiting**

Emesis

EXCLUDES *hematemesis NOS (578.0)*
vomiting:
bilious, following gastrointestinal surgery (564.3)
cyclical (536.2)
associated with migraine (346.2)
psychogenic (306.4)
excessive, in pregnancy (643.0-643.9)
habit (536.2)
of newborn (779.3)
psychogenic NOS (307.54)

787.01 Nausea with vomiting

787.02 Nausea alone

787.03 Vomiting alone

787.1 Heartburn

Pyrosis
Waterbrash

EXCLUDES *dyspepsia or indigestion (536.8)*

✓5th **787.2 Dysphagia**

Code first, if applicable, dysphagia due to late effect of cerebrovascular accident (438.82)

787.20 Dysphagia, unspecified

Difficulty in swallowing NOS

787.21 Dysphagia, oral phase

787.22 Dysphagia, oropharyngeal phase

787.23 Dysphagia, pharyngeal phase

787.24 Dysphagia, pharyngoesophageal phase

787.29 Other dysphagia

Cervical dysphagia
Neurogenic dysphagia

Phases of Swallowing

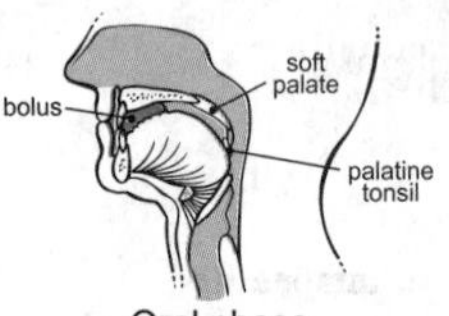

Oral phase

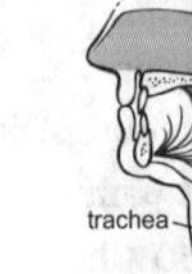

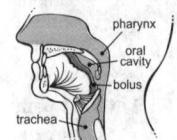

Oropharyngeal phase

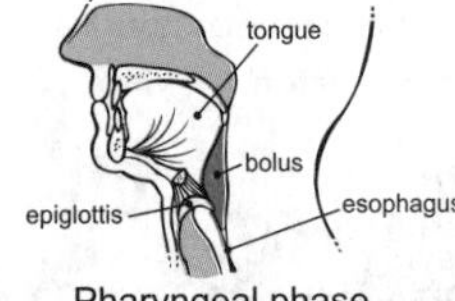

Pharyngeal phase

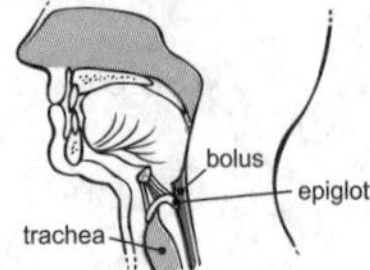

Pharyngeoesophageal phase

787.3 Flatulence, eructation, and gas pain

Abdominal distention (gaseous)
Bloating
Tympanites (abdominal) (intestinal)

EXCLUDES *aerophagy (306.4)*

DEF: Flatulence: excess air or gas in intestine or stomach.

DEF: Eructation: belching, expelling gas through mouth.

DEF: Gas pain: gaseous pressure affecting gastrointestinal system.

787.4 Visible peristalsis

Hyperperistalsis

DEF: Increase in involuntary movements of intestines.

787.5 Abnormal bowel sounds

Absent bowel sounds
Hyperactive bowel sounds

787.6 Incontinence of feces

Encopresis NOS
Incontinence of sphincter ani

EXCLUDES *that of nonorganic origin (307.7)*

787.7 Abnormal feces

Bulky stools

EXCLUDES *abnormal stool content (792.1)*
melena:
NOS (578.1)
newborn (772.4, 777.3)

✓5th **787.9 Other symptoms involving digestive system**

EXCLUDES *gastrointestinal hemorrhage (578.0-578.9)*
intestinal obstruction (560.0-560.9)
specific functional digestive disorders:
esophagus (530.0-530.9)
stomach and duodenum (536.0-536.9)
those not elsewhere classified (564.00-564.9)

787.91 Diarrhea

Diarrhea NOS

787.99 Other

Change in bowel habits
Tenesmus (rectal)

DEF: Tenesmus: Painful, ineffective straining at the rectum with limited passage of fecal matter.

✓4th **788 Symptoms involving urinary system**

EXCLUDES *hematuria (599.70-599.72)*
nonspecific findings on examination of the urine (791.0-791.9)
small kidney of unknown cause (589.0-589.9)
uremia NOS (586)
urinary obstruction (599.60, 599.69)

788.0 Renal colic

Colic (recurrent) of:
kidney
ureter

DEF: Kidney pain.

788.1 Dysuria

Painful urination
Strangury

✓5th **788.2 Retention of urine**

Code, if applicable, any causal condition first, such as:
hyperplasia of prostate (600.0-600.9 with fifth-digit 1)

DEF: Accumulation of urine in the bladder due to inability to void

788.20 Retention of urine, unspecified

788.21 Incomplete bladder emptying

788.29 Other specified retention of urine

✓5th **788.3 Urinary incontinence**

Code, if applicable, any causal condition first, such as:
congenital ureterocele (753.23)
genital prolapse (618.00-618.9)
hyperplasia of prostate (600.0-600.9 with fifth-digit 1)

EXCLUDES *functional urinary incontinence (788.91)*
that of nonorganic origin (307.6)
urinary incontinence associated with cognitive impairment (788.91)

788.30 Urinary incontinence, unspecified
Enuresis NOS

788.31 Urge incontinence
DEF: Inability to control urination, upon urge to urinate.

788.32 Stress incontinence, male
EXCLUDES *stress incontinence, female (625.6)*
DEF: Inability to control urination associated with weak sphincter in males.

788.33 Mixed incontinence, (male) (female)
Urge and stress
DEF: Urge, stress incontinence: involuntary discharge of urine due to anatomic displacement.

788.34 Incontinence without sensory awareness
DEF: Involuntary discharge of urine without sensory warning.

788.35 Post-void dribbling
DEF: Involuntary discharge of residual urine after voiding.

788.36 Nocturnal enuresis
DEF: Involuntary discharge of urine during the night.

788.37 Continuous leakage
DEF: Continuous, involuntary urine seepage.

788.38 Overflow incontinence
DEF: Leakage caused by pressure of retained urine in the bladder after the bladder has fully contracted due to weakened bladder muscles or an obstruction of the urethra.

788.39 Other urinary incontinence

✓5th **788.4 Frequency of urination and polyuria**

Code, if applicable, any causal condition first, such as:
hyperplasia of prostate (600.0-600.9 with fifth-digit 1)

788.41 Urinary frequency
Frequency of micturition

788.42 Polyuria
DEF: Excessive urination.

788.43 Nocturia
DEF: Urination affecting sleep patterns.

788.5 Oliguria and anuria
Deficient secretion of urine
Suppression of urinary secretion
EXCLUDES *that complicating:*
abortion (634-638 with .3, 639.3)
ectopic or molar pregnancy (639.3)
pregnancy, childbirth, or the puerperium (642.0-642.9, 646.2)
DEF: Oliguria: diminished urinary secretion related to fluid intake.
DEF: Anuria: lack of urinary secretion due to renal failure or obstructed urinary tract.

✓5th **788.6 Other abnormality of urination**

Code, if applicable, any causal condition first, such as:
hyperplasia of prostate (600.0-600.9 with fifth-digit 1)

788.61 Splitting of urinary stream
Intermittent urinary stream

788.62 Slowing of urinary stream
Weak stream

788.63 Urgency of urination
EXCLUDES *urge incontinence (788.31, 788.33)*
DEF: Feeling of intense need to urinate; abrupt sensation of imminent urination.

788.64 Urinary hesitancy

788.65 Straining on urination

788.69 Other

788.7 Urethral discharge
Penile discharge
Urethrorrhea

788.8 Extravasation of urine
DEF: Leaking or infiltration of urine into tissues.

✓5th **788.9 Other symptoms involving urinary system**

788.91 Functional urinary incontinence
Urinary incontinence due to cognitive impairment, or severe physical disability or immobility
EXCLUDES *urinary incontinence due to physiologic condition (788.30-788.39)*

788.99 Other symptoms involving urinary system
Extrarenal uremia
Vesical:
pain
tenesmus

✓4th **789 Other symptoms involving abdomen and pelvis**

EXCLUDES *symptoms referable to genital organs:*
female (625.0-625.9)
male (607.0-608.9)
psychogenic (302.70-302.79))

The following fifth-digit subclassification is to be used for codes 789.0. 789.3, 789.4, 789.6:
0 unspecified site
1 right upper quadrant
2 left upper quadrant
3 right lower quadrant
4 left lower quadrant
5 periumbilic
6 epigastric
7 generalized
9 other specified site
Multiple sites

✓5th **789.0 Abdominal pain**
[0-7, 9] Colic:
NOS
infantile
Cramps, abdominal
EXCLUDES *renal colic (788.0)*

789.1 Hepatomegaly
Enlargement of liver

789.2 Splenomegaly
Enlargement of spleen

✓5th **789.3 Abdominal or pelvic swelling, mass, or lump**
[0-7, 9] Diffuse or generalized swelling or mass:
abdominal NOS
umbilical
EXCLUDES *abdominal distention (gaseous) (787.3)*
ascites (789.51-789.59)

✓5th **789.4 Abdominal rigidity**
[0-7, 9]

✓5th **789.5 Ascites**
Fluid in peritoneal cavity
DEF: Serous fluid effusion and accumulation in abdominal cavity.

789.51 Malignant ascites
Code first malignancy, such as:
malignant neoplasm of ovary (183.0)
secondary malignant neoplasm of retroperitoneum and peritoneum (197.6)

789.59 Other ascites

✓5th **789.6 Abdominal tenderness**
[0-7, 9] Rebound tenderness

789.9 Other symptoms involving abdomen and pelvis
Umbilical:
bleeding
discharge

NONSPECIFIC ABNORMAL FINDINGS (790-796)

✓4th **790 Nonspecific findings on examination of blood**
EXCLUDES *abnormality of:*
platelets (287.0-287.9)
thrombocytes (287.0-287.9)
white blood cells (288.00-288.9)

✓5th **790.0 Abnormality of red blood cells**
EXCLUDES *anemia:*
congenital (776.5)
newborn, due to isoimmunization (773.0-773.2, 773.5)
of premature infant (776.6)
other specified types (280.0-285.9)
hemoglobin disorders (282.5-282.7)
polycythemia:
familial (289.6)
neonatorum (776.4)
secondary (289.0)
vera (238.4)

790.01 Precipitous drop in hematocrit Drop in hematocrit

790.09 Other abnormality of red blood cells
Abnormal red cell morphology NOS
Abnormal red cell volume NOS
Anisocytosis
Poikilocytosis

790.1 Elevated sedimentation rate

✓5th **790.2 Abnormal glucose**
EXCLUDES *diabetes mellitus (249.00-249.91, 250.00-250.93)*
dysmetabolic syndrome X (277.7)
gestational diabetes (648.8)
glycosuria (791.5)
hypoglycemia (251.2)
that complicating pregnancy, childbirth, or puerperium (648.8)

790.21 Impaired fasting glucose
Elevated fasting glucose

790.22 Impaired glucose tolerance test (oral)
Elevated glucose tolerance test

790.29 Other abnormal glucose
Abnormal glucose NOS
Abnormal non-fasting glucose
Hyperglycemia NOS
Pre-diabetes NOS

790.3 Excessive blood level of alcohol
Elevated blood-alcohol

790.4 Nonspecific elevation of levels of transaminase or lactic acid dehydrogenase [LDH]

790.5 Other nonspecific abnormal serum enzyme levels
Abnormal serum level of:
acid phosphatase
alkaline phosphatase
amylase
lipase
EXCLUDES *deficiency of circulating enzymes (277.6)*

790.6 Other abnormal blood chemistry
Abnormal blood level of:
cobalt
copper
iron
lead
lithium
magnesium
mineral
zinc
EXCLUDES *abnormality of electrolyte or acid-base balance (276.0-276.9)*
hypoglycemia NOS (251.2)
lead poisoning (984.0-984.9)
specific finding indicating abnormality of:
amino-acid transport and metabolism (270.0-270.9)
carbohydrate transport and metabolism (271.0-271.9)
lipid metabolism (272.0-272.9)
uremia NOS (586)

790.7 Bacteremia
EXCLUDES *bacteremia of newborn (771.83)*
septicemia (038)
Use additional code to identify organism (041)
DEF: Laboratory finding of bacteria in the blood in the absence of two or more signs of sepsis; transient in nature, progresses to septicemia with severe infectious process.

790.8 Viremia, unspecified
DEF: Presence of a virus in the blood stream.

✓5th **790.9 Other nonspecific findings on examination of blood**

790.91 Abnormal arterial blood gases

790.92 Abnormal coagulation profile
Abnormal or prolonged:
bleeding time
coagulation time
partial thromboplastin time [PTT]
prothrombin time [PT]
EXCLUDES *coagulation (hemorrhagic) disorders (286.0-286.9)*

790.93 Elevated prostate specific antigen, [PSA]

790.94 Euthyroid sick syndrome
DEF: Transient alteration of thyroid hormone metabolism due to nonthyroid illness or stress.

790.95 Elevated C-reactive protein [CRP]
DEF: Inflammation in an arterial wall results in elevated C-reactive protein (CRP) in the blood; CRP is a recognized risk factor in cardiovascular disease.

790.99 Other

✓4th **791 Nonspecific findings on examination of urine**
EXCLUDES *hematuria NOS (599.70-599.72)*
specific findings indicating abnormality of:
amino-acid transport and metabolism (270.0-270.9)
carbohydrate transport and metabolism (271.0-271.9)

791.0 Proteinuria
Albuminuria
Bence-Jones proteinuria
EXCLUDES *postural proteinuria (593.6)*
that arising during pregnancy or the puerperium (642.0-642.9, 646.2)
DEF: Excess protein in urine.

791.1 Chyluria
EXCLUDES *filarial (125.0-125.9)*
DEF: Excess chyle in urine.

791.2 Hemoglobinuria
DEF: Free hemoglobin in blood due to rapid hemolysis of red blood cells.

791.3 Myoglobinuria
DEF: Myoglobin (oxygen-transporting pigment) in urine.

791.4 Biliuria
DEF: Bile pigments in urine.

791.5 Glycosuria
EXCLUDES *renal glycosuria (271.4)*
DEF: Sugar in urine.

791.6 Acetonuria
Ketonuria
DEF: Excess acetone in urine.

791.7 Other cells and casts in urine

791.9 Other nonspecific findings on examination of urine
Crystalluria
Elevated urine levels of:
17-ketosteroids
catecholamines
indolacetic acid
vanillylmandelic acid [VMA]
Melanuria

✓4th **792 Nonspecific abnormal findings in other body substances**
EXCLUDES *that in chromosomal analysis (795.2)*

792.0 Cerebrospinal fluid

792.1 Stool contents
Abnormal stool color
Fat in stool
Mucus in stool
Occult stool
Pus in stool
EXCLUDES *blood in stool [melena] (578.1)*
newborn (772.4, 777.3)

792.2 Semen
Abnormal spermatozoa
EXCLUDES *azoospermia (606.0)*
oligospermia (606.1)

792.3 Amniotic fluid
DEF: Nonspecific abnormal findings in amniotic fluid.

792.4 Saliva
EXCLUDES *that in chromosomal analysis (795.2)*

792.5 Cloudy (hemodialysis) (peritoneal) dialysis effluent

792.9 Other nonspecific abnormal findings in body substances
Peritoneal fluid
Pleural fluid
Synovial fluid
Vaginal fluids

✓4th **793 Nonspecific abnormal findings on radiological and other examination of body structure**
INCLUDES nonspecific abnormal findings of:
thermography
ultrasound examination [echogram]
x-ray examination
EXCLUDES *abnormal results of function studies and radioisotope scans (794.0-794.9)*

793.0 Skull and head
EXCLUDES *nonspecific abnormal echoencephalogram (794.01)*

793.1 Lung field
Coin lesion } (of) lung
Shadow } (of) lung
DEF: Coin lesion of lung: coin-shaped, solitary pulmonary nodule.

793.2 Other intrathoracic organ
Abnormal:
echocardiogram
heart shadow
ultrasound cardiogram
Mediastinal shift

793.3 Biliary tract
Nonvisualization of gallbladder

793.4 Gastrointestinal tract

793.5 Genitourinary organs
Filling defect:
bladder
kidney
ureter

793.6 Abdominal area, including retroperitoneum

793.7 Musculoskeletal system

✓5th **793.8 Breast**

793.80 Abnormal mammogram, unspecified

793.81 Mammographic microcalcification
EXCLUDES *mammographic calcification (793.89)*
mammographic calculus (793.89)
DEF: Calcium and cellular debris deposits in the breast that cannot be felt but can be detected on a mammogram; can be a sign of cancer, benign conditions, or changes in the breast tissue as a result of inflammation, injury, or obstructed duct.

793.89 Other abnormal findings on radiological examination of breast
Mammographic calcification
Mammographic calculus

✓5th **793.9 Other**
EXCLUDES *abnormal finding by radioisotope localization of placenta (794.9)*

793.91 Image test inconclusive due to excess body fat
Use additional code to identify Body Mass Index (BMI), if known (V85.0-V85.54)

793.99 Other nonspecific abnormal findings on radiological and other examinations of body structure
Abnormal:
placental finding by x-ray or ultrasound method
radiological findings in skin and subcutaneous tissue

✓4th **794 Nonspecific abnormal results of function studies**
INCLUDES radioisotope:
scans
uptake studies
scintiphotography

✓5th **794.0 Brain and central nervous system**

794.00 Abnormal function study, unspecified

794.01 Abnormal echoencephalogram

794.02 Abnormal electroencephalogram [EEG]

794.09 Other
Abnormal brain scan

✓5th **794.1 Peripheral nervous system and special senses**

794.10 Abnormal response to nerve stimulation, unspecified

794.11 Abnormal retinal function studies
Abnormal electroretinogram [ERG]

794.12 Abnormal electro-oculogram [EOG]

794.13 Abnormal visually evoked potential

794.14 Abnormal oculomotor studies

794.15 Abnormal auditory function studies

794.16 Abnormal vestibular function studies

794.17 Abnormal electromyogram [EMG]
EXCLUDES that of eye (794.14)

794.19 Other

794.2 Pulmonary
Abnormal lung scan
Reduced:
ventilatory capacity
vital capacity

✓5th **794.3 Cardiovascular**

794.30 Abnormal function study, unspecified

794.31 Abnormal electrocardiogram [ECG] [EKG]
EXCLUDES *long QT syndrome (426.82)*

794.39 Other
Abnormal:
ballistocardiogram
phonocardiogram
vectorcardiogram

794.4 Kidney
Abnormal renal function test

794.5 Thyroid
Abnormal thyroid:
scan
uptake

794.6 Other endocrine function study

794.7 Basal metabolism
Abnormal basal metabolic rate [BMR]

794.8 Liver
Abnormal liver scan

794.9 Other
Bladder
Pancreas
Placenta
Spleen

✓4th **795 Other and nonspecific abnormal cytological, histological, immunological and DNA test findings**

EXCLUDES *abnormal cytologic smear of anus and anal HPV (796.70-796.79)*
nonspecific abnormalities of red blood cells (790.01-790.09)

✓5th **795.0 Abnormal Papanicolaou smear of cervix and cervical HPV**
Abnormal thin preparation smear of cervix
Abnormal cervical cytology

EXCLUDES *abnormal cytologic smear of vagina and vaginal HPV (795.10-795.19)*
carcinoma in situ of cervix (233.1)
cervical intraepithelial neoplasia I (CIN I) (622.11)
cervical intraepithelial neoplasia II (CIN II) (622.12)
cervical intraepithelial neoplasia III (CIN III) (233.1)
dysplasia (histologically confirmed) of cervix (uteri) NOS (622.10)
mild cervical dysplasia (histologically confirmed) (622.11)
moderate cervical dysplasia (histologically confirmed) (622.12)
severe cervical dysplasia (histologically confirmed) (233.1)

795.00 Abnormal glandular Papanicolaou smear of cervix
Atypical endocervical cells NOS
Atypical endometrial cells NOS
Atypical cervical glandular cells NOS

795.01 Papanicolaou smear of cervix with atypical squamous cells of undetermined significance [ASC-US]

795.02 Papanicolaou smear of cervix with atypical squamous cells cannot exclude high grade squamous intraepithelial lesion [ASC-H]

795.03 Papanicolaou smear of cervix with low grade squamous intraepithelial lesion [LGSIL]

795.04 Papanicolaou smear of cervix with highgrade squamous intraepithelial lesion [HGSIL]

795.05 Cervical high risk human papillomavirus [HPV] DNA test positive

795.06 Papanicolaou smear of cervix with cytologic evidence of malignancy

795.07 Satisfactory cervical smear but lacking transformation zone

795.08 Unsatisfactory cervical cytology smear
Inadequate cervical cytology sample

795.09 Other abnormal Papanicolaou smear of cervix and cervical HPV
Cervical low risk human papillomavirus (HPV) DNA test positive
Use additional code for associated human papillomavirus (079.4)

EXCLUDES *encounter for Papanicolaou cervical smear to confirm findings of recent normal smear following initial abnormal smear (V72.32)*

✓5th **795.1 Abnormal Papanicolaou smear of vagina and vaginal HPV**
Abnormal thin preparation smear of vagina NOS
Abnormal vaginal cytology NOS
Use additional code to identify acquired absence of uterus and cervix, if applicable (V88.01-V88.03)

EXCLUDES *abnormal cytologic smear of cervix and cervical HPV (795.00-795.09)*
carcinoma in situ of vagina (233.31)
carcinoma in situ of vulva (233.32)
dysplasia (histologically confirmed) of vagina NOS (623.0, 233.31)
dysplasia (histologically confirmed) of vulva NOS (624.01, 624.02, 233.32)
mild vaginal dysplasia (histologically confirmed) (623.0)
mild vulvar dysplasia (histologically confirmed) (624.01)
moderate vaginal dysplasia (histologically confirmed) (623.0)
moderate vulvar dysplasia (histologically confirmed) (624.02)
severe vaginal dysplasia (histologically confirmed) (233.31)
severe vulvar dysplasia (histologically confirmed) (233.32)
vaginal intraepithelial neoplasia I (VAIN I) (623.0)
vaginal intraepithelial neoplasia II (VAIN II) (623.0)
vaginal intraepithelial neoplasia III (VAIN III) (233.31)
vulvar intraepithelial neoplasia I (VIN I) (624.01)
vulvar intraepithelial neoplasia II (VIN II) (624.02)
vulvar intraepithelial neoplasia III (VIN III) (233.32)

795.10 Abnormal glandular Papanicolaou smear of vagina
Atypical vaginal glandular cells NOS

795.11 Papanicolaou smear of vagina with atypical squamous cells of undetermined significance [ASC-US]

795.12 Papanicolaou smear of vagina with atypical squamous cells cannot exclude high grade squamous intraepithelial lesion [ASC-H]

795.13 Papanicolaou smear of vagina with low grade squamous intraepithelial lesion [LGSIL]

795.14 Papanicolaou smear of vagina with high grade squamous intraepithelial lesion [HGSIL]

795.15 Vaginal high risk human papillomavirus [HPV] DNA test positive

EXCLUDES *condyloma acuminatum (078.11)*
genital warts (078.11)

795.16 Papanicolaou smear of vagina with cytologic evidence of malignancy

795.18 Unsatisfactory vaginal cytology smear
Inadequate vaginal cytology sample

795.19 Other abnormal Papanicolaou smear of vagina and vaginal HPV
Vaginal low risk human papillomavirus (HPV) DNA test positive
Use additional code for associated human papillomavirus (079.4)

795.2 Nonspecific abnormal findings on chromosomal analysis
Abnormal karyotype

✓5th **795.3 Nonspecific positive culture findings**
Positive culture findings in:
nose
throat
sputum
wound
EXCLUDES *that of:*
blood (790.7-790.8)
urine (791.9)

795.31 Nonspecific positive findings for anthrax
Positive findings by nasal swab

795.39 Other nonspecific positive culture findings

795.4 Other nonspecific abnormal histological findings

795.5 Nonspecific reaction to tuberculin skin test without active tuberculosis
Abnormal result of Mantoux test
PPD positive
Tuberculin (skin test):
positive
reactor

795.6 False positive serological test for syphilis
False positive Wassermann reaction

✓5th **795.7 Other nonspecific immunological findings**
EXCLUDES *abnormal tumor markers (795.81-795.89)*
elevated prostate specific antigen [PSA] (790.93)
elevated tumor associated antigens (795.81-795.89)
isoimmunization, in pregnancy (656.1-656.2)
affecting fetus or newborn (773.0-773.2)

795.71 Nonspecific serologic evidence of human immunodeficiency virus [HIV]
Inclusive human immunodeficiency [HIV] test (adult) (infant)
Note: This code is **only** to be used when a test finding is reported as nonspecific. Asymptomatic positive findings are coded to V08. If any HIV infection symptom or condition is present, see code 042. Negative findings are not coded.
EXCLUDES *acquired immunodeficiency syndrome [AIDS] (042)*
asymptomatic human immunodeficiency virus, [HIV] infection status (V08)
HIV infection, symptomatic (042)
human immunodeficiency virus [HIV] disease (042)
positive (status) NOS (V08)

795.79 Other and unspecified nonspecific immunological findings
Raised antibody titer
Raised level of immunoglobulins

✓5th **795.8 Abnormal tumor markers**
Elevated tumor associated antigens [TAA]
Elevated tumor specific antigens [TSA]
EXCLUDES *elevated prostate specific antigen [PSA] (790.93)*

795.81 Elevated carcinoembryonic antigen [CEA]

795.82 Elevated cancer antigen 125 [CA 125]

795.89 Other abnormal tumor markers

✓4th **796 Other nonspecific abnormal findings**

796.0 Nonspecific abnormal toxicological findings
Abnormal levels of heavy metals or drugs in blood, urine, or other tissue
EXCLUDES *excessive blood level of alcohol (790.3)*

796.1 Abnormal reflex

796.2 Elevated blood pressure reading without diagnosis of hypertension
Note: This category is to be used to record an episode of elevated blood pressure in a patient in whom no formal diagnosis of hypertension has been made, or as an incidental finding.

796.3 Nonspecific low blood pressure reading

796.4 Other abnormal clinical findings

796.5 Abnormal finding on antenatal screening

796.6 Abnormal findings on neonatal screening
EXCLUDES *nonspecific serologic evidence of human immunodeficiency virus [HIV] (795.71)*

✓5th **796.7 Abnormal cytologic smear of anus and anal HPV**
EXCLUDES *abnormal cytologic smear of cervix and cervical HPV (795.00-795.09)*
abnormal cytologic smear of vagina and vaginal HPV (795.10-795.19)
anal intraepithelial neoplasia I (AIN I) (569.44)
anal intraepithelial neoplasia II (AIN II) (569.44)
anal intraepithelial neoplasia III (AIN III) (230.5, 230.6)
carcinoma in situ of anus (230.5, 230.6)
dysplasia (histologically confirmed) of anus NOS (569.44)
mild anal dysplasia (histologically confirmed) (569.44)
moderate anal dysplasia (histologically confirmed) (569.44)
severe anal dysplasia (histologically confirmed) (230.5, 230.6)

796.70 Abnormal glandular Papanicolaou smear of anus
Atypical anal glandular cells NOS

796.71 Papanicolaou smear of anus with atypical squamous cells of undetermined significance [ASC-US]

796.72 Papanicolaou smear of anus with atypical squamous cells cannot exclude high grade squamous intraepithelial lesion [ASC-H]

796.73 Papanicolaou smear of anus with low grade squamous intraepithelial lesion [LGSIL]

796.74 Papanicolaou smear of anus with high grade squamous intraepithelial lesion [HGSIL]

796.75 Anal high risk human papillomavirus [HPV] DNA test positive

796.76 Papanicolaou smear of anus with cytologic evidence of malignancy

796.77 Satisfactory anal smear but lacking transformation zone

796.78 Unsatisfactory anal cytology smear

Inadequate anal cytology sample

796.79 Other abnormal Papanicolaou smear of anus and anal HPV

Anal low risk human papillomavirus (HPV) DNA test positive

Use additional code for associated human papillomavirus (079.4)

796.9 Other

ILL-DEFINED AND UNKNOWN CAUSES OF MORBIDITY AND MORTALITY (797-799)

797 Senility without mention of psychosis

Frailty
Senescence
Senile asthenia
Senile:
  debility
  exhaustion

EXCLUDES *senile psychoses (290.0-290.9)*

✓4th **798 Sudden death, cause unknown**

798.0 Sudden infant death syndrome

Cot death
Crib death
Sudden death of nonspecific cause in infancy

DEF: Death of infant under age one due to nonspecific cause.

798.1 Instantaneous death

798.2 Death occurring in less than 24 hours from onset of symptoms, not otherwise explained

Death known not to be violent or instantaneous, for which no cause could be discovered
Died without sign of disease

798.9 Unattended death

Death in circumstances where the body of the deceased was found and no cause could be discovered
Found dead

✓4th **799 Other ill-defined and unknown causes of morbidity and mortality**

✓5th **799.0 Asphyxia and hypoxemia**

EXCLUDES *asphyxia and hypoxemia (due to):*
carbon monoxide (986)
hypercapnia (786.09)
inhalation of food or foreign body (932-934.9)
newborn (768.0-768.9)
traumatic (994.7)

799.01 Asphyxia

DEF: Lack of oxygen in inspired air, causing a deficiency of oxygen in tissues (hypoxia) and elevated levels of arterial carbon dioxide (hypercapnia).

799.02 Hypoxemia

DEF: Deficient oxygenation of the blood.

799.1 Respiratory arrest

Cardiorespiratory failure

EXCLUDES *cardiac arrest (427.5)*
failure of peripheral circulation (785.50)
respiratory distress:
  NOS (786.09)
  acute (518.82)
  following trauma and surgery (518.5)
  newborn (770.89)
  syndrome (newborn) (769)
    adult (following trauma and surgery) (518.5)
  other (518.82)
respiratory failure (518.81, 518.83-518.84)
  newborn (770.84)
respiratory insufficiency (786.09)
  acute (518.82)

799.2 Nervousness

"Nerves"

799.3 Debility, unspecified

EXCLUDES *asthenia (780.79)*
nervous debility (300.5)
neurasthenia (300.5)
senile asthenia (797)

799.4 Cachexia

Wasting disease
Code first underlying condition, if known

DEF: General ill health and poor nutrition.

✓5th **799.8 Other ill-defined conditions**

799.81 Decreased libido

Decreased sexual desire

EXCLUDES *psychosexual dysfunction with inhibited sexual desire (302.71)*

799.89 Other ill-defined conditions

799.9 Other unknown and unspecified cause

Undiagnosed disease, not specified as to site or system involved
Unknown cause of morbidity or mortality

Chapter 17: Injury and Poisoning (800–999)

This chapter classifies:

- Fractures, dislocations, sprains, and strains
- Intracranial, internal, superficial, blood vessel, nerve and spinal cord, crush, and foreign body injuries
- Contusions, open wounds, and burns
- Late effects of injuries, poisonings, toxic effects, and other external causes
- Certain traumatic complications and unspecified injuries
- Poisonings and toxic effects of nonmedicinal substances
- Other and unspecified effects of external causes
- Complications of surgical and medical care, not elsewhere classified

Injuries, burns, poisoning and adverse effects, and complications of surgery and medical care are all covered in this one chapter of ICD-9-CM. Each of these areas is governed by specific coding guidelines and are discussed separately.

Injuries (800–959)

Multiple coding is encouraged in ICD-9-CM to provide specific detail regarding the nature and extent of injuries. Combination categories for multiple injuries are provided for use when there is insufficient detail available to record a code for each component. When the component sites of injury are specified, the term "with" indicates involvement of both sites, and the term "and" indicates involvement of either or both sites. For example, in category 823, fracture of tibia and fibula, the term "and" between tibia and fibula indicates fractures of the tibia alone, fibula alone, or fibula with tibia. The fifth-digit assignment for this category emphasizes this point. A fifth-digit assignment of "0" indicates tibia involvement alone, "1" indicates fibula involvement alone, and "2" indicates that both fubula and tibia are involved.

Code fractures and other injuries as current conditions during the healing phase as long as they continue to require monitoring and treatment.

The sequencing of codes for fractures and other injuries depends on the circumstances of the admission.

Example:

A patient is seen for treatment of a pressure ulcer of the elbow (code 707.01) but also has a plaster cast on his left arm for a fracture of the humerus suffered six weeks prior to the visit. Only if the patient requires additional care because of the cast would code V54.11, Aftercare for healing traumatic fracture of upper arm, be listed as a secondary diag- nosis since the condition had a bearing on the episode of care.

Example:

A patient is seen for treatment of a new displacement of humeral fracture initially suffered six weeks prior. At the time of the visit, the patient also is noted to have pressure ulcers requiring application of a dressing. In this case, the humeral fracture would be listed as the principal diagnosis, followed by a secondary code for pressure ulcer.

Fracture (800–829)

A fracture is a structural break in the continuity of a bone that occurs as the result

of physical forces exerted on the rigid bone tissue beyond its ability to accommodate by resistance, elasticity, or bending. ICD-9-CM classifies fractures by anatomic site: skull (800–804), neck and trunk (805–809), upper limb (810–819), and lower limb (820–829).

Fractures may occur as a result of direct injury, such as a forceful blow to the bone by a heavy object, or indirect injury, such as indirect transmission of force through one or more joints (e.g., a stress fracture of the distal tibia caused by jogging).

Fractures may be defined as closed or open. A closed fracture is one in which the skin is intact at the site of the fracture. An open fracture is one in which there is a wound communicating from the skin surface to the fracture site. Open fractures may occur when an external object penetrates the skin to fracture the bone or when a bone or bone fragment penetrates the skin from within.

Clinically, the term "fracture" may be used more broadly to include injuries classified elsewhere in the chapter. "Fracture of cartilage of knee" (836.2) is a tear of the cartilage or "fractured liver" (864) is an injury to the liver. Fractures with dislocation of the joint are classified to the fracture category only.

Fractures designated as pathological fractures are classified to subcategory 733.1 and are defined as fractures due to bone structure weakening by pathological processes (e.g., osteoporosis).

Terms normally used to describe open and closed fractures are listed in the notes to this subchapter. However, these terms are not restricted. Coders should read the documentation to determine whether the fracture should be classified as open or closed.

Example:

A "depressed skull fracture with exposed skull fragments" is coded as an open fracture of the skull, even though the term "depressed" is grouped with the terms describing closed fractures.

Note that an open wound associated with a fracture does not necessarily indicate an open fracture.

Example:

A patient with a fractured femur secondary to a motorcycle accident may also have an open wound or skin avulsion over or near the fracture site. If the wound or avulsion is superficial and does not reach and expose the fracture site, the fracture is coded as closed.

Skull Fracture (800–804)

Skull fracture (800–804) is a fracture of any of the bones of the cranial vault and facial bones. Closed skull fractures most often result from blunt trauma to the head; open skull fractures usually result from extreme trauma or missile injuries such as gunshot wounds.

A concussion is a clinical syndrome caused by a blow or whiplash injury to the head, causing the brain to strike against the skull, but not hard enough to cause a cerebral contusion. Most concussion patients recover uneventfully within 48 hours. Code category 850 is used for concussion uncomplicated by cerebral hemorrhage, laceration, or contusion.

Sprains and Strains of Joint and Adjacent Muscles (840–848)

A sprain is a complete or an incomplete tear in any one or more of the ligaments that surround and support a joint. A strain is an ill-defined injury caused by overuse or overextension of the muscles or tendons of a joint. A "charleyhorse" is an idiom for a strain of a muscle, usually one of the major muscles such as the quadriceps femoris or gastrocnemius. A "slap" lesion refers to the detachment of the superior glenoid labrum (shoulder region), and is considered an injury. These categories also include muscle, tendon, ligament, or joint capsule ruptures.

Strains and sprains are classified according to site (e.g., wrist, foot, knee, leg, etc.) at the category level. Subcategory and subclassification further specify site or structure (e.g., joint or ligament).

Open Wounds (870–897)

Open wounds are bites, avulsions, lacerations, punture wounds, and traumatic amputations. Excluded injuries are burns, crushing injuries, puncture of internal organs, superficial injuries, and those incidental to dislocation, fracture, and intracranial injury.

Complicated, when described in the fourth digit subcategory, is used to distinguish wounds documented as having delayed healing, delayed treatment, foreign body, or infection. Any wound complicated by infection requires an additional code to indentify the infection.

Many types and sites of open wounds are excluded from this code range. Review the ICD-9-CM index under "Wound, open" for "see" and "see category" instructions, as well as the excludes note at the beginning of the code range in the tabular list for proper code assignment.

Injury to Blood Vessels (900–904)

Injuries to any artery or vein due to or associated with traumatic injury are classified to this section. Penetrating trauma with injury of the blood vessel usually involves disruption of the blood vessel with extravasation of blood. Contusions and crush injuries may produce blood vessel injuries such as intimal damage or intramural hematomas with no extravasation of blood.

Late Effects of Injury, Poisoning, Toxic Effects and Other External Causes (905–909)

This category is to be used to indicate conditions classifiable to 800–999 (chapter 17, "Injury and Poisoning") as the cause of the late effects, which themselves are classified elsewhere. The "late effects" include those specified as such, or as sequelae, which may occur at any time after the acute injury.

Each section of chapter 17 has correlating "late effects" categories. For example, injuries classifiable to skull fracture (800–804) have "late effect" codes in the subcategory 905.0 Late effect of fracture of the skull and face bones. Instructional notes within each subcategory alert the coder as to the nature of the acute injury that resulted in the residual condition classifiable to that subcategory.

Burns (940–949)

Burns are injury or destruction of tissue due to the effects of thermal energy, chemicals, electricity or radiation. This section includes current unhealed burns from electricity, flame, hot object, lightening, radiation, chemicals, and scalds. Excluded are friction burns and sunburns, which are classified elsewhere.

First-degree burn, or erythema, is injury limited to tissue damage to the outer layer of the epidermis. Second-degree burn is injury extending beyond the epidermis to partial thickness of the dermis. Third-degree burn is a full thickness skin loss. Third-degree burn with presence of necrotic tissue is termed deep necrosis and is further specified as with or without loss of body parts.

Categories 940–947 classify burns by degree and site. This section is subdivided by general anatomical site at the category level. Subcategory subdivision is according to either more specific site designation (scalp, shoulder, foot), causal agent (chemical) or degree of burn (first, second, third). "Excludes" notes direct coders to the appropriate site category for such areas as mouth (947, internal organs), and scapula (943, upper arm).

Category 948 classifies burns according to the extent of body surface involved. This category is to be used when the site of the burn is unspecified or with categories 940– 947 when the site is specified.

The percentage of body surface is calculated using the "Rule of Nines." The Rule of Nines is a method of estimating the percent of body surface as illustrated. Fourth-digit subdivision indicates the total percent of body surface involved in the burn injury regardless of degree.

Poisoning by Drugs, Medicinal and Biological Substances (960–979)

These categories include situations in which a patient suffers an adverse reaction, or poisoning, from a drug, medicine, or biological substance taken in error or a correct substance improperly administered.

These codes are used primarily in inpatient and emergency settings. However, office coders should be aware of the general guidelines for these categories. E codes from the table of drugs and chemicals are used to identify the circumstances under which the poisoning occurred: accidental, suicide (attempt), assault, or undetermined. Codes identifying suicide or assault should never be assigned without specific physician documentation. Note that an E code from the therapeutic use column is never paired with a poisoning code.

Chronic conditions occurring as a result of substance abuse or dependence are not classified as poisonings. Use codes from 303–305 to classify chronic abuse or dependence.

Late effects of poisoning due to drugs, medicinal, or biological substances are coded to subcategory 909.0. Code the residual first, then the late effect code, followed by the E code for poisoning.

Adverse Effects of Drugs, Medicinal, and Biological Substances

Adverse effects of incorrectly administered drugs are not classified to this section. Note: The interaction of a prescribed drug and an over the counter drug is coded as an adverse effect if both were used correctly and both prescribed by a physician. Adverse effects are described by the following terms:

- Allergic reaction
- Toxicity (cumulative effect of a drug)
- Hypersensitivity
- Idiosyncratic reaction
- Paradoxical reaction
- Synergistic reaction

To code adverse effects, code the condition and assign an E code from the therapeutic use column in the drug table. Do not assign a code from the 960–979 categories. If the adverse effect is unspecified, use code from subcategory 995.2x Unspecified effect of drug, medicinal, and biological substance to identify that an adverse effect occurred.

If the drug is specified but not elsewhere classified, refer to the drug table under the main term "Drug" and choose the appropriate E code from the therapeutic use column. To locate drugs not listed as a main entry in the table refer to the AHFS listing in appendix C of the disease tabular section. Locate the appropriate AHFS number under the main entry "Drug."

Late Effects of Poisoning or Adverse Reactions

Late effects of either poisoning or adverse reactions to drugs, medicinal, and biological substances are classified elsewhere under the appropriate late effect categories. Refer to the alphabetic index for code assignment under main term "Late, effect(s) (of)" and subterm "adverse effect of drug, medicinal or biological substance; or poisoning due to drug, medicinal or biological substance." Code the residual condition first, then the late effect code, followed by the E code to identify the drug.

Examples:

> Urticaria due to allergic reaction to penicillin taken as prescribed is coded 708.0 Urticaria, and E930.0 External cause due to therapeutic use of penicillin.
>
> Scarring due to extreme urticaria as a late effect result of an adverse reaction to penicillin is coded 709.2, 909.5, and E930.0.

Complications of Surgical and Medical Care, Not Elsewhere Classified (996-999)

This section classifies complications of medical and surgical care not classified elsewhere. Code assignment should be based on the provider's documentation of the relationship between the condition and the procedure. Not all conditions that occur following a procedure or treatment are considered complications. Complications include those conditions that exceed routine postoperative or post-interventional expectations and those conditions in which a cause-and-effect relationship is documented by the provider. The term "complication" does not imply that the condition is a result of a mishap or other occurrence on the part of the provider. There is no time limit associated with the development of a complication. Depending on the nature of the complication, it may occur immediately, following the procedure or other care provided, or years later. Sequencing is determined by the circumstances of the admission/encounter. Complications occurring during the current episode of care, following treatment, the complication should be reported as an additional code. When the complication is the reason for the admission/encounter, the complication may be designated as the first-listed diagnosis. Instructional notes are provided throughout this section to help the coder appropriately report complication codes.

17. INJURY AND POISONING (800-999)

Use E code(s) to identify the cause and intent of the injury or poisoning (E800-E999)

Note:

1. The principle of multiple coding of injuries should be followed wherever possible. Combination categories for multiple injuries are provided for use when there is insufficient detail as to the nature of the individual conditions, or for primary tabulation purposes when it is more convenient to record a single code; otherwise, the component injuries should be coded separately.

   Where multiple sites of injury are specified in the titles, the word "with" indicates involvement of both sites, and the word "and" indicates involvement of either or both sites. The word "finger" includes thumb.

2. Categories for "late effect" of injuries are to be found at 905-909.

FRACTURES (800-829)

EXCLUDES *malunion (733.81)*
nonunion (733.82)
pathological or spontaneous fracture (733.10-733.19)
stress fractures (733.93-733.95)

The terms "condyle," "coronoid process," "ramus," and "symphysis" indicate the portion of the bone fractured, not the name of the bone involved.

The descriptions "closed" and "open" used in the fourth-digit subdivisions include the following terms:

closed (with or without delayed healing):

comminuted	impacted
depressed	linear
elevated	simple
fissured	slipped epiphysis
fracture NOS	spiral
greenstick	

open (with or without delayed healing):

compound	puncture
infected	with foreign body
missile	

Note: A fracture not indicated as closed or open should be classified as closed.

FRACTURE OF SKULL (800-804)

The following fifth-digit subclassification is for use with the appropriate codes in category 800, 801, 803, and 804:

0 unspecified state of consciousness
1 with no loss of consciousness
2 with brief [less than one hour] loss of consciousness
3 with moderate [1-24 hours] loss of consciousness
4 with prolonged [more than 24 hours] loss of consciousness and return to pre-existing conscious level
5 with prolonged [more than 24 hours] loss of consciousness, without return to pre-existing conscious level
Use fifth-digit 5 to designate a patient is unconscious and dies before regaining consciousness, regardless of the duration of the loss of consciousness
6 with loss of consciousness of unspecified duration
9 with concussion, unspecified

✓4th **800 Fracture of vault of skull**

INCLUDES frontal bone
parietal bone

DEF: Fracture of bone that forms skull dome and protects brain.

✓5th **800.0 Closed without mention of intracranial injury**
[0-6, 9]

✓5th **800.1 Closed with cerebral laceration and contusion**
[0-6, 9]

✓5th **800.2 Closed with subarachnoid, subdural, and**
[0-6, 9] **extradural hemorrhage**

✓5th **800.3 Closed with other and unspecified intracranial**
[0-6, 9] **hemorrhage**

✓5th **800.4 Closed with intracranial injury of other and**
[0-6, 9] **unspecified nature**

Fractures

Fracture-dislocation
Impacted
Avulsion
Linear (fissured)
Greenstick
Open (skin broken)
Oblique
Closed spiral
Epiphyseal
Depressed
March
Comminuted

✓5th **800.5 Open without mention of intracranial injury**
[0-6, 9]

✓5th **800.6 Open with cerebral laceration and contusion**
[0-6, 9]

✓5th **800.7 Open with subarachnoid, subdural, and**
[0-6, 9] **extradural hemorrhage**

✓5th **800.8 Open with other and unspecified intracranial**
[0-6, 9] **hemorrhage**

✓5th **800.9 Open with intracranial injury of other and**
[0-6, 9] **unspecified nature**

✓4th **801 Fracture of base of skull**

INCLUDES fossa:
anterior
middle
posterior
occiput bone
orbital roof
sinus:
ethmoid
frontal
sphenoid bone
temporal bone

DEF: Fracture of bone that forms skull floor.

✓5th **801.0 Closed without mention of intracranial injury**
[0-6, 9]

✓5th **801.1 Closed with cerebral laceration and contusion**
[0-6, 9]

✓5th **801.2 Closed with subarachnoid, subdural, and**
[0-6, 9] **extradural hemorrhage**

✓5th **801.3 Closed with other and unspecified intracranial**
[0-6, 9] **hemorrhage**

✓5th **801.4 Closed with intracranial injury of other and**
[0-6, 9] **unspecified nature**

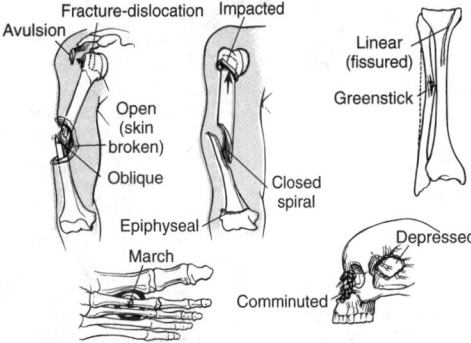

✓5th **801.5 Open without mention of intracranial injury**
[0-6, 9]

✓5th **801.6 Open with cerebral laceration and contusion**
[0-6, 9]

✓5th **801.7 Open with subarachnoid, subdural, and**
[0-6, 9] **extradural hemorrhage**

Skull

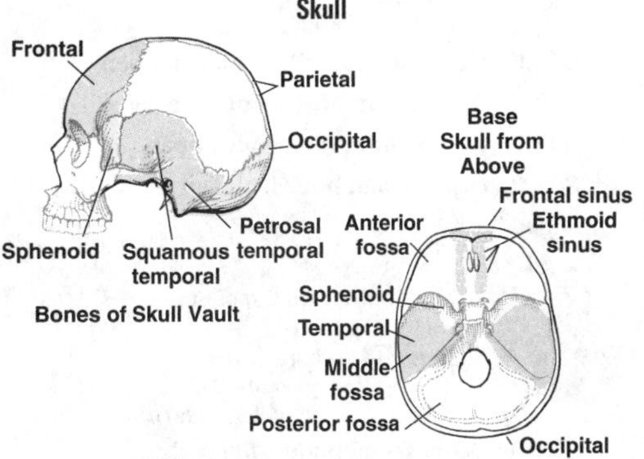

Facial Fracture

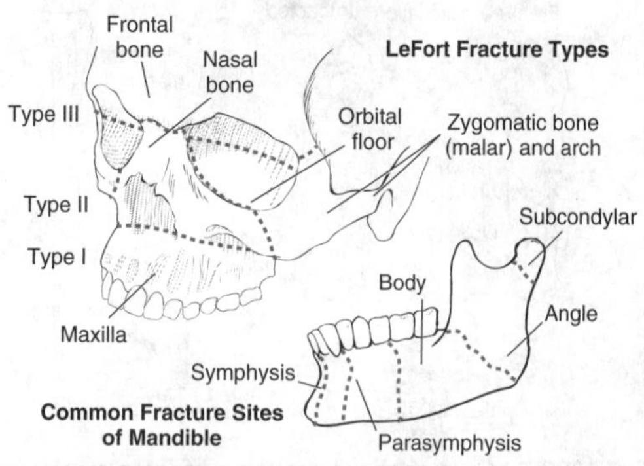

✓5th **801.8 Open with other and unspecified intracranial hemorrhage**
[0-6, 9]

✓5th **801.9 Open with intracranial injury of other and unspecified nature**
[0-6, 9]

✓4th **802 Fracture of face bones**

802.0 Nasal bones, closed

802.1 Nasal bones, open

✓5th **802.2 Mandible, closed**
Inferior maxilla
Lower jaw (bone)

802.20 Unspecified site

802.21 Condylar process

802.22 Subcondylar

802.23 Coronoid process

802.24 Ramus, unspecified

802.25 Angle of jaw

802.26 Symphysis of body

802.27 Alveolar border of body

802.28 Body, other and unspecified

802.29 Multiple sites

✓5th **802.3 Mandible, open**

802.30 Unspecified site

802.31 Condylar process

802.32 Subcondylar

802.33 Coronoid process

802.34 Ramus, unspecified

802.35 Angle of jaw

802.36 Symphysis of body

802.37 Alveolar border of body

802.38 Body, other and unspecified

802.39 Multiple sites

802.4 Malar and maxillary bones, closed
Superior maxilla
Upper jaw (bone)
Zygoma
Zygomatic arch

802.5 Malar and maxillary bones, open

802.6 Orbital floor (blow-out), closed

802.7 Orbital floor (blow-out), open

802.8 Other facial bones, closed
Alveolus
Orbit:
NOS
part other than roof or floor
Palate
EXCLUDES *orbital:*
floor (802.6)
roof (801.0-801.9)

802.9 Other facial bones, open

803 Other and unqualified skull fractures
INCLUDES skull NOS
skull multiple NOS

✓5th **803.0 Closed without mention of intracranial injury**
[0-6, 9]

✓5th **803.1 Closed with cerebral laceration and contusion**
[0-6, 9]

✓5th **803.2 Closed with subarachnoid, subdural, and extradural hemorrhage**
[0-6, 9]

✓5th **803.3 Closed with other and unspecified intracranial hemorrhage**
[0-6, 9]

✓5th **803.4 Closed with intracranial injury of other and unspecified nature**
[0-6, 9]

✓5th **803.5 Open without mention of intracranial injury**
[0-6, 9]

✓5th **803.6 Open with cerebral laceration and contusion**
[0-6, 9]

✓5th **803.7 Open with subarachnoid, subdural, and extradural hemorrhage**
[0-6, 9]

✓5th **803.8 Open with other and unspecified intracranial hemorrhage**
[0-6, 9]

✓5th **803.9 Open with intracranial injury of other and unspecified nature**
[0-6, 9]

✓4th **804 Multiple fractures involving skull or face with other bones**

✓5th **804.0 Closed without mention of intracranial injury**
[0-6, 9]

✓5th **804.1 Closed with cerebral laceration and contusion**
[0-6, 9]

✓5th **804.2 Closed with subarachnoid, subdural, and extradural hemorrhage**
[0-6, 9]

✓5th **804.3 Closed with other and unspecified intracranial hemorrhage**
[0-6, 9]

✓5th **804.4 Closed with intracranial injury of other and unspecified nature**
[0-6, 9]

✓5th **804.5 Open without mention of intracranial injury**
[0-6, 9]

✓5th **804.6 Open with cerebral laceration and contusion**
[0-6, 9]

✓5th **804.7 Open with subarachnoid, subdural, and extradural hemorrage**
[0-6, 9]

✓5th **804.8 Open with other and unspecified intracranial hemorrhage**
[0-6, 9]

✓5th **804.9 Open with intracranial injury of other and unspecified nature**
[0-6, 9]

FRACTURE OF NECK AND TRUNK (805-809)

✓4th **805 Fracture of vertebral column without mention of spinal cord injury**
INCLUDES neural arch
spine
spinous process
transverse process
vertebra

The following fifth-digit subclassification is for use with codes 805.0-805.1:
0 cervical vertebra, unspecified level
1 first cervical vertebra
2 second cervical vertebra
3 third cervical vertebra
4 fourth cervical vertebra
5 fifth cervical vertebra
6 sixth cervical vertebra
7 seventh cervical vertebra
8 multiple cervical vertebrae

✓5th **805.0 Cervical, closed**
[0-8] Atlas
Axis

Vertebral Column

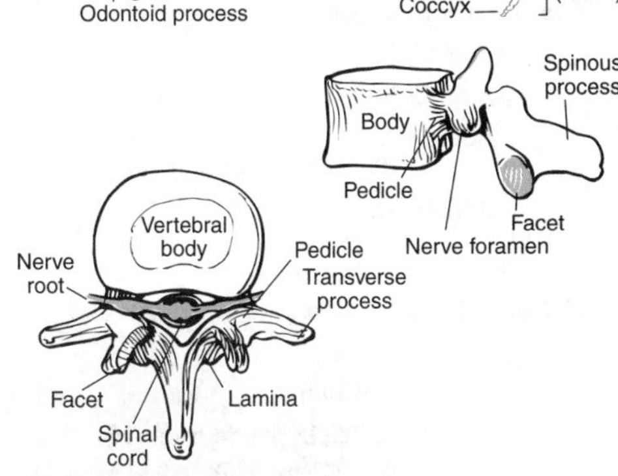

✓5th **805.1 Cervical, open**
[0-8]

805.2 Dorsal [thoracic], closed

805.3 Dorsal [thoracic], open

805.4 Lumbar, closed

805.5 Lumbar, open

805.6 Sacrum and coccyx, closed

805.7 Sacrum and coccyx, open

805.8 Unspecified, closed

805.9 Unspecified, open

✓4th **806 Fracture of vertebral column with spinal cord injury**

INCLUDES any condition classifiable to 805 with:
- complete or incomplete transverse lesion (of cord)
- hematomyelia
- injury to:
  - cauda equina
  - nerve
- paralysis
- paraplegia
- quadriplegia
- spinal concussion

✓5th **806.0 Cervical, closed**

806.00 C_1-C_4 level with unspecified spinal cord injury
Cervical region NOS with spinal cord injury NOS

806.01 C_1-C_4 level with complete lesion of cord

806.02 C_1-C_4 level with anterior cord syndrome

806.03 C_1-C_4 level with central cord Syndrome

806.04 C_1-C_4 level with other specified spinal cord injury
C_1-C_4 level with:
- incomplete spinal cord lesion NOS
- posterior cord syndrome

806.05 C_5-C_7 level with unspecified spinal cord injury

806.06 C_5-C_7 level with complete lesion of cord

806.07 C_5-C_7 level with anterior cord syndrome

806.08 C_5-C_7 level with central cord syndrome

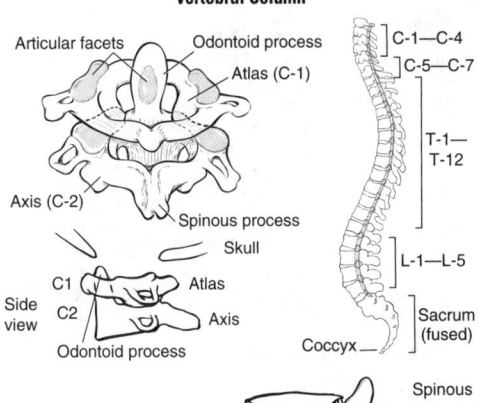

806.09 C_5-C_7 level with other specified spinal cord injury
C_5-C_7 level with:
- incomplete spinal cord lesion NOS
- posterior cord syndrome

✓5th **806.1 Cervical, open**

806.10 C_1-C_4 level with unspecified spinal cord injury

806.11 C_1-C_4 level with complete lesion of cord

806.12 C_1-C_4 level with anterior cord syndrome

806.13 C_1-C_4 level with central cord syndrome

806.14 C_1-C_4 level with other specified spinal cord injury
C_1-C_4 level with:
- incomplete spinal cord lesion NOS
- posterior cord syndrome

806.15 C_5-C_7 level with unspecified spinal cord injury

806.16 C_5-C_7 level with complete lesion of cord

806.17 C_5-C_7 level with anterior cord syndrome

806.18 C_5-C_7 level with central cord syndrome

806.19 C_5-C_7 level with other specified spinal cord injury
C_5-C_7 level with:
- incomplete spinal cord lesion NOS
- posterior cord syndrome

✓5th **806.2 Dorsal [thoracic], closed**

806.20 T_1-T_6 level with unspecified spinal cord injury
Thoracic region NOS with spinal cord injury NOS

806.21 T_1-T_6 level with complete lesion of cord

806.22 T_1-T_6 level with anterior cord syndrome

806.23 T_1-T_6 level with central cord syndrome

806.24 T_1-T_6 level with other specified spinal cord injury
T_1-T_6 level with:
- incomplete spinal cord lesion NOS
- posterior cord syndrome

806.25 T_7-T_{12} level with unspecified spinal cord injury

806.26 T_7-T_{12} level with complete lesion of cord

806.27 T_7-T_{12} level with anterior cord syndrome

806.28 T_7-T_{12} level with central cord syndrome

806.29 T_7-T_{12} level with other specified spinal cord injury
T_7-T_{12} level with:
- incomplete spinal cord lesion NOS
- posterior cord syndrome

✓5th **806.3 Dorsal [thoracic], open**

806.30 T_1-T_6 level with unspecified spinal cord injury

806.31 T_1-T_6 level with complete lesion of cord

806.32 T_1-T_6 level with anterior cord syndrome

806.33 T_1-T_6 level with central cord syndrome

806.34 T_1-T_6 level with other specified spinal cord injury
T_1-T_6 level with:
- incomplete spinal cord lesion NOS
- posterior cord syndrome

806.35 T_7-T_{12} level with unspecified spinal cord injury

806.36 T_7-T_{12} level with complete lesion of cord

806.37 T_7-T_{12} level with anterior cord syndrome

Ribs, Sternum, Larynx, and Trachea

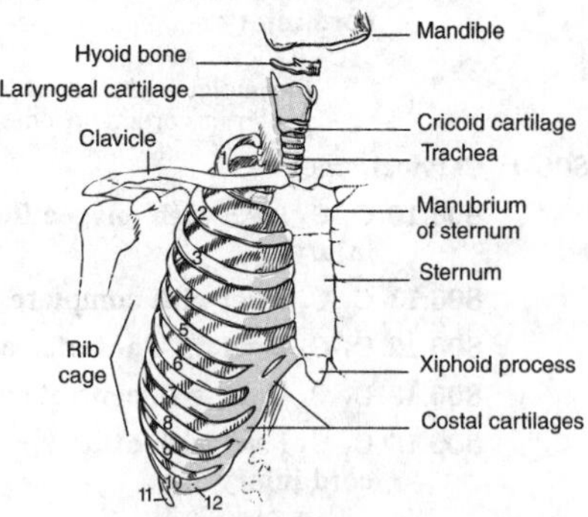

806.38 T_7-T_{12} level with central cord syndrome

806.39 T_7-T_{12} level with other specified spinal cord injury

T_7-T_{12} level with:
incomplete spinal cord lesion NOS
posterior cord syndrome

806.4 Lumbar, closed

806.5 Lumbar, open

✓5th **806.6 Sacrum and coccyx, closed**

806.60 With unspecified spinal cord injury

806.61 With complete cauda equina lesion

806.62 With other cauda equina injury

806.69 With other spinal cord injury

✓5th **806.7 Sacrum and coccyx, open**

806.70 With unspecified spinal cord injury

806.71 With complete cauda equina lesion

806.72 With other cauda equina injury

806.79 With other spinal cord injury

806.8 Unspecified, closed

806.9 Unspecified, open

✓4th **807 Fracture of rib(s), sternum, larynx, and trachea**

The following fifth-digit subclassification is for use with codes 807.0-807.1:
- **0 rib(s) unspecifed**
- **1 one rib**
- **2 two ribs**
- **3 three ribs**
- **4 four ribs**
- **5 five ribs**
- **6 six ribs**
- **7 seven ribs**
- **8 eight or more ribs**
- **9 multiple ribs, unspecified**

✓5th **807.0 Rib(s), closed**
[0-9]

✓5th **807.1 Rib(s), open**
[0-9]

807.2 Sternum, closed
DEF: Break in flat bone (breast bone) in anterior thorax.

807.3 Sternum, open
DEF: Break, with open wound, in flat bone in mid anterior thorax.

807.4 Flail chest

807.5 Larynx and trachea, closed
Hyoid bone
Thyroid cartilage
Trachea

807.6 Larynx and trachea, open

✓4th **808 Fracture of pelvis**

808.0 Acetabulum, closed

808.1 Acetabulum, open

808.2 Pubis, closed

808.3 Pubis, open

Pelvis and Pelvic Fractures

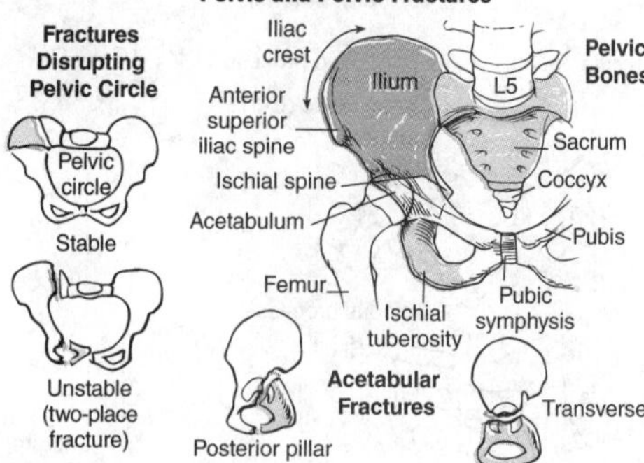

✓5th **808.4 Other specified part, closed**

808.41 Ilium

808.42 Ischium

808.43 Multiple pelvic fractures with disruption of pelvic circle

808.49 Other
Innominate bone
Pelvic rim

✓5th **808.5 Other specified part, open**

808.51 Ilium

808.52 Ischium

808.53 Multiple pelvic fractures with disruption of pelvic circle

808.59 Other

808.8 Unspecified, closed

808.9 Unspecified, open

✓4th **809 Ill-defined fractures of bones of trunk**

INCLUDES bones of trunk with other bones except those of skull and face
multiple bones of trunk

EXCLUDES *multiple fractures of:*
pelvic bones alone (808.0-808.9)
ribs alone (807.0-807.1, 807.4)
ribs or sternum with limb bones (819.0-819.1, 828.0-828.1)
skull or face with other bones (804.0-804.9)

809.0 Fracture of bones of trunk, closed

809.1 Fracture of bones of trunk, open

FRACTURE OF UPPER LIMB (810-819)

✓4th **810 Fracture of clavicle**

INCLUDES collar bone
interligamentous part of clavicle

The following fifth-digit subclassification is for use with category 810:
- **0 unspecified part**
  Clavicle NOS
- **1 sternal end of clavicle**
- **2 shaft of clavicle**
- **3 acromial end of clavicle**

✓5th **810.0 Closed**
[0-3]

✓5th **810.1 Open**
[0-3]

✓4th **811 Fracture of scapula**

INCLUDES shoulder blade

The following fifth-digit subclassification is for use with category 811:
- **0 unspecified part**
- **1 acromial process**
  Acromion (process)
- **2 coracoid process**
- **3 glenoid cavity and neck of scapula**
- **9 other**

Right Clavicle and Scapula, Anterior View

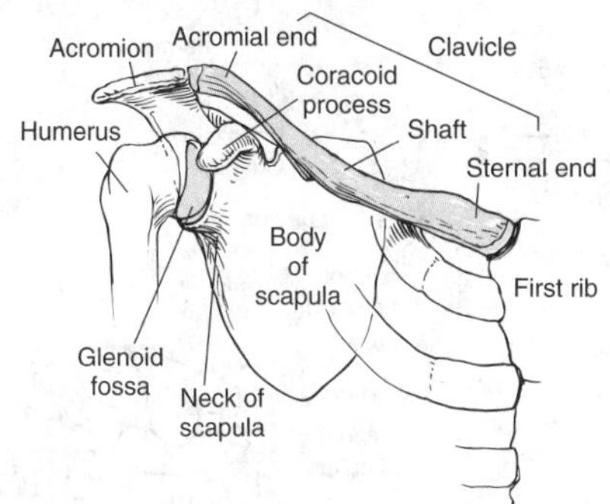

Right Humerus, Anterior View

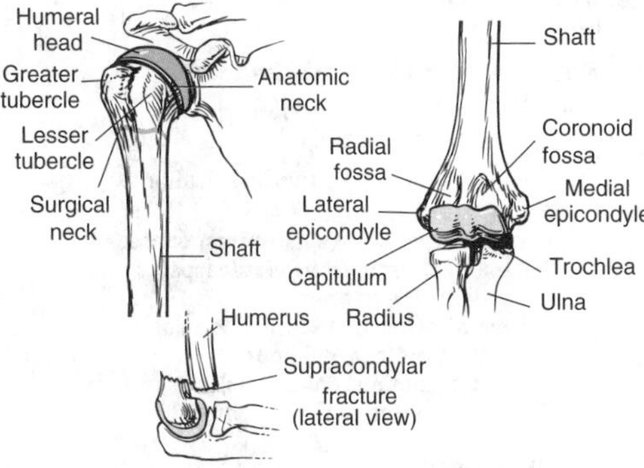

✓5th **811.0 Closed**
[0-3, 9]

✓5th **811.1 Open**
[0-3, 9]

✓4th **812 Fracture of humerus**

✓5th **812.0 Upper end, closed**

812.00 Upper end, unspecified part
Proximal end
Shoulder

812.01 Surgical neck
Neck of humerus NOS

812.02 Anatomical neck

812.03 Greater tuberosity

812.09 Other
Head
Lesser tuberosity
Upper epiphysis

✓5th **812.1 Upper end, open**

812.10 Upper end, unspecified part

812.11 Surgical neck

812.12 Anatomical neck

812.13 Greater tuberosity

812.19 Other

✓5th **812.2 Shaft or unspecified part, closed**

812.20 Unspecified part of humerus
Humerus NOS
Lesser tuberosity
Upper arm NOS

812.21 Shaft of humerus

✓5th **812.3 Shaft or unspecified part, open**

812.30 Unspecified part of humerus

812.31 Shaft of humerus

✓5th **812.4 Lower end, closed**
Distal end of humerus
Elbow

812.40 Lower end, unspecified part

812.41 Supracondylar fracture of humerus

812.42 Lateral condyle
External condyle

812.43 Medial condyle
Internal epicondyle

812.44 Condyle(s), unspecified
Articular process NOS
Lower epiphysis NOS

812.49 Other
Multiple fractures of lower end
Trochlea

✓5th **812.5 Lower end, open**

812.50 Lower end, unspecified part

812.51 Supracondylar fracture of humerus

812.52 Lateral condyle

812.53 Medial condyle

812.54 Condyle(s), unspecified

812.59 Other

✓4th **813 Fracture of radius and ulna**

✓5th **813.0 Upper end, closed**
Proximal end

813.00 Upper end of forearm, unspecified

813.01 Olecranon process of ulna

813.02 Coronoid process of ulna

813.03 Monteggia's fracture
DEF: Fracture near the head of the ulnar shaft, causing dislocation of the radial head.

813.04 Other and unspecified fractures of proximal end of ulna (alone)
Multiple fractures of ulna, upper end

813.05 Head of radius

813.06 Neck of radius

813.07 Other and unspecified fractures of proximal end of radius (alone)
Multiple fractures of radius, upper end

813.08 Radius with ulna, upper end [any part]

✓5th **813.1 Upper end, open**

813.10 Upper end of forearm, unspecified

813.11 Olecranon process of ulna

813.12 Coronoid process of ulna

813.13 Monteggia's fracture

813.14 Other and unspecified fractures of proximal end of ulna (alone)

813.15 Head of radius

813.16 Neck of radius

813.17 Other and unspecified fractures of proximal end of radius (alone)

813.18 Radius with ulna, upper end [any part]

Right Radius and Ulna, Anterior View

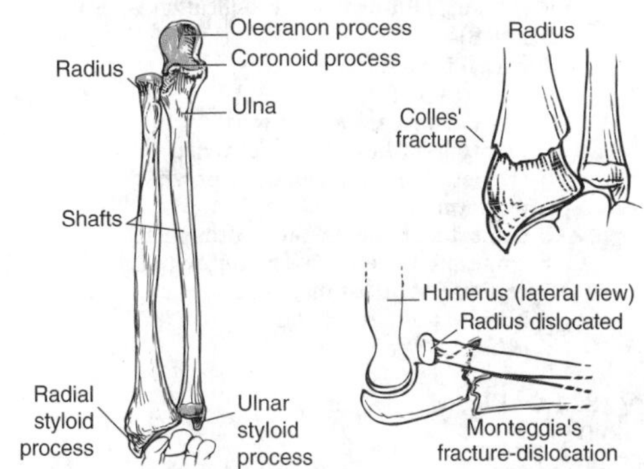

✓5th **813.2 Shaft, closed**
- **813.20 Shaft, unspecified**
- **813.21 Radius (alone)**
- **813.22 Ulna (alone)**
- **813.23 Radius with ulna**

✓5th **813.3 Shaft, open**
- **813.30 Shaft, unspecified**
- **813.31 Radius (alone)**
- **813.32 Ulna (alone)**
- **813.33 Radius with ulna**

✓5th **813.4 Lower end, closed**
Distal end
- **813.40 Lower end of forearm, unspecified**
- **813.41 Colles' fracture**
  Smith's fracture
  DEF: Break of lower end of radius; associated with backward movement of the radius lower section.
- **813.42 Other fractures of distal end of radius (alone)**
  Dupuytren's fracture, radius
  Radius, lower end
  DEF: Dupuytren's fracture: fracture and dislocation of the forearm; the fracture is of the radius above the wrist, and the dislocation is of the ulna at the lower end.
- **813.43 Distal end of ulna (alone)**
  Ulna:
  head
  lower end
  lower epiphysis
  styloid process
- **813.44 Radius with ulna, lower end**
- **813.45 Torus fracture of radius**

✓5th **813.5 Lower end, open**
- **813.50 Lower end of forearm, unspecified**
- **813.51 Colles' fracture**
- **813.52 Other fractures of distal end of radius (alone)**
- **813.53 Distal end of ulna (alone)**
- **813.54 Radius with ulna, lower end**

✓5th **813.8 Unspecified part, closed**
- **813.80 Forearm, unspecified**
- **813.81 Radius (alone)**
- **813.82 Ulna (alone)**
- **813.83 Radius with ulna**

✓5th **813.9 Unspecified part, open**
- **813.90 Forearm, unspecified**
- **813.91 Radius (alone)**
- **813.92 Ulna (alone)**
- **813.93 Radius with ulna**

✓4th **814 Fracture of carpal bone(s)**

The following fifth-digit subclassification is for use with category 814:
- **0 carpal bone, unspecified**
  Wrist NOS
- **1 navicular [scaphoid] of wrist**
- **2 lunate [semilunar] bone of wrist**
- **3 triquetral [cuneiform] bone of wrist**
- **4 pisiform**
- **5 trapezium bone [larger multangular]**
- **6 trapezoid bone [smaller multangular]**
- **7 capitate bone [os magnum]**
- **8 hamate [unciform] bone**
- **9 other**

✓5th **814.0 Closed**
[0-9]

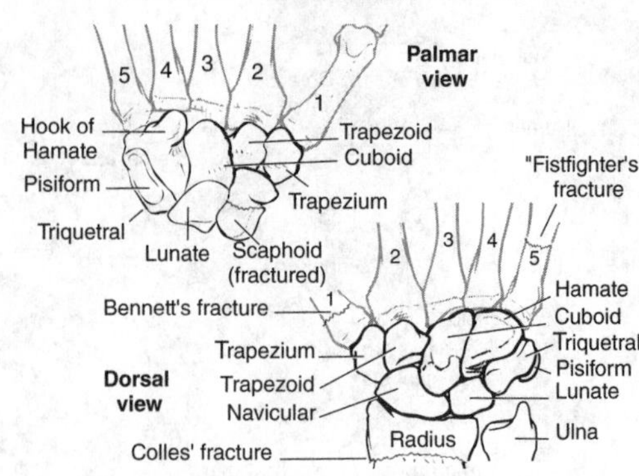

✓5th **814.1 Open**
[0-9]

✓4th **815 Fracture of metacarpal bone(s)**
INCLUDES hand [except finger]
metacarpus

The following fifth-digit subclassification is for use with category 815:
- **0 metacarpal bone(s), site unspecified**
- **1 base of thumb [first] metacarpal**
  Bennett's fracture
- **2 base of other metacarpal bone(s)**
- **3 shaft of metacarpal bone(s)**
- **4 neck of metacarpal bone(s)**
- **9 multiple sites of metacarpus**

✓5th **815.0 Closed**
[0-4, 9]

✓5th **815.1 Open**
[0-4, 9]

✓4th **816 Fracture of one or more phalanges of hand**
INCLUDES finger(s)
thumb

The following fifth-digit subclassification is for use with category 816:
- **0 phalanx or phalanges, unspecified**
- **1 middle or proximal phalanx or phalanges**
- **2 distal phalanx or phalanges**
- **3 multiple sites**

✓5th **816.0 Closed**
[0-3]

✓5th **816.1 Open**
[0-3]

✓4th **817 Multiple fractures of hand bones**
INCLUDES metacarpal bone(s) with phalanx or phalanges of same hand
- **817.0 Closed**
- **817.1 Open**

✓4th **818 Ill-defined fractures of upper limb**
INCLUDES arm NOS
multiple bones of same upper limb

EXCLUDES *multiple fractures of:*
metacarpal bone(s) with phalanx or phalanges (817.0-817.1)
phalanges of hand alone (816.0-816.1)
radius with ulna (813.0-813.9)
- **818.0 Closed**
- **818.1 Open**

✓4th **819 Multiple fractures involving both upper limbs, and upper limb with rib(s) and sternum**
INCLUDES arm(s) with rib(s) or sternum
both arms [any bones]
- **819.0 Closed**
- **819.1 Open**

FRACTURE OF LOWER LIMB (820-829)

✓4th **820 Fracture of neck of femur**

✓5th **820.0 Transcervical fracture, closed**

820.00 Intracapsular section, unspecified

820.01 Epiphysis (separation) (upper)
Transepiphyseal

820.02 Midcervical section
Transcervical NOS

820.03 Base of neck
Cervicotrochanteric section

820.09 Other
Head of femur
Subcapital

✓5th **820.1 Transcervical fracture, open**

820.10 Intracapsular section, unspecified

820.11 Epiphysis (separation) (upper)

820.12 Midcervical section

820.13 Base of neck

820.19 Other

✓5th **820.2 Pertrochanteric fracture, closed**

820.20 Trochanteric section, unspecified
Trochanter:
NOS
greater
lesser

820.21 Intertrochanteric section

820.22 Subtrochanteric section

✓5th **820.3 Pertrochanteric fracture, open**

820.30 Trochanteric section, unspecified

820.31 Intertrochanteric section

820.32 Subtrochanteric section

820.8 Unspecified part of neck of femur, closed
Hip NOS
Neck of femur NOS

820.9 Unspecified part of neck of femur, open

✓4th **821 Fracture of other and unspecified parts of femur**

✓5th **821.0 Shaft or unspecified part, closed**

821.00 Unspecified part of femur
Thigh
Upper leg
EXCLUDES *hip NOS (820.8)*

821.01 Shaft

✓5th **821.1 Shaft or unspecified part, open**

821.10 Unspecified part of femur

821.11 Shaft

✓5th **821.2 Lower end, closed**
Distal end

821.20 Lower end, unspecified part

821.21 Condyle, femoral

821.22 Epiphysis, lower (separation)

Right Femur, Anterior View

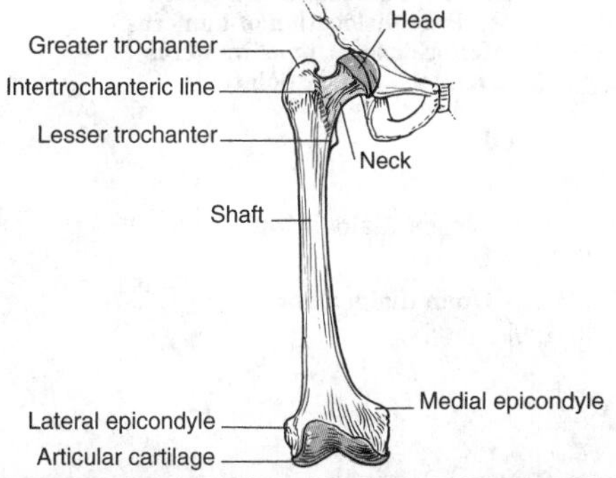

Right Tibia and Fibula, Anterior View

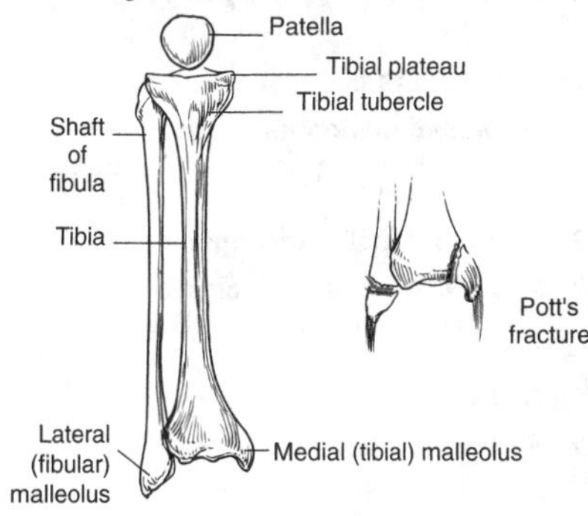

Torus Fracture

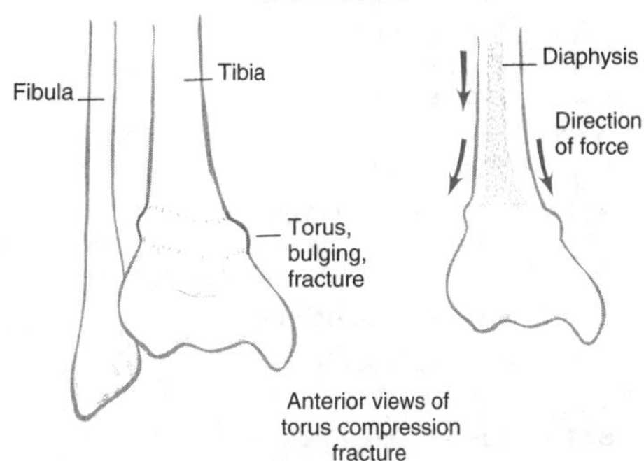

821.23 Supracondylar fracture of femur

821.29 Other
Multiple fractures of lower end

✓5th **821.3 Lower end, open**

821.30 Lower end, unspecified part

821.31 Condyle, femoral

821.32 Epiphysis, lower (separation)

821.33 Supracondylar fracture of femur

821.39 Other

✓4th **822 Fracture of patella**

822.0 Closed

822.1 Open

✓4th **823 Fracture of tibia and fibula**

EXCLUDES *Dupuytren's fracture (824.4-824.5)*
ankle (824.4-824.5)
radius (813.42, 813.52)
Pott's fracture (824.4-824.5)
that involving ankle (824.0-824.9)

The following fifth-digit subclassification is for use with category 823:
0 tibia alone
1 fibula alone
2 fibula with tibia

✓5th **823.0 Upper end, closed**
[0-2] Head
Proximal end
Tibia:
condyles
tuberosity

✓5th **823.1 Upper end, open**
[0-2]

✓5th **823.2 Shaft, closed**
[0-2]

✓5th **823.3 Shaft, open**
[0-2]

✓5th **823.4 Torus fracture**
[0-2] **DEF: A bone deformity in children, occurring commonly in the tibia and fibula, in which the bone bends and buckles but does not fracture.**

✓5th **823.8 Unspecified part, closed**
[0-2] Lower leg NOS

✓5th **823.9 Unspecified part, open**
[0-2]

✓4th 824 Fracture of ankle

824.0 Medial malleolus, closed
Tibia involving: ankle
Tibia involving: malleolus

824.1 Medial malleolus, open

824.2 Lateral malleolus, closed
Fibula involving: ankle
Fibula involving: malleolus

824.3 Lateral malleolus, open

824.4 Bimalleolar, closed
Dupuytren's fracture, fibula
Pott's fracture

DEF: Bimalleolar, closed: Breaking of both nodules (malleoli) on either side of ankle joint, without an open wound.

DEF: Dupuytren's fracture (Pott's fracture): The breaking of the farthest end of the lower leg bone (fibula), with injury to the farthest end joint of the other lower leg bone (tibia).

824.5 Bimalleolar, open

824.6 Trimalleolar, closed
Lateral and medial malleolus with anterior or posterior lip of tibia

824.7 Trimalleolar, open

824.8 Unspecified, closed
Ankle NOS

824.9 Unspecified, open

✓4th 825 Fracture of one or more tarsal and metatarsal bones

825.0 Fracture of calcaneus, closed
Heel bone
Os calcis

825.1 Fracture of calcaneus, open

✓5th **825.2 Fracture of other tarsal and metatarsal bones, closed**

825.20 Unspecified bone(s) of foot [except toes]
Instep

825.21 Astragalus
Talus

825.22 Navicular [scaphoid], foot

825.23 Cuboid

825.24 Cuneiform, foot

825.25 Metatarsal bone(s)

825.29 Other
Tarsal with metatarsal bone(s) only
EXCLUDES *calcaneus (825.0)*

✓5th **825.3 Fracture of other tarsal and metatarsal bones, open**

825.30 Unspecified bone(s) of foot [except toes]

825.31 Astragalus

825.32 Navicular [scaphoid], foot

825.33 Cuboid

825.34 Cuneiform, foot

825.35 Metatarsal bone(s)

825.39 Other

Right Foot, Dorsal

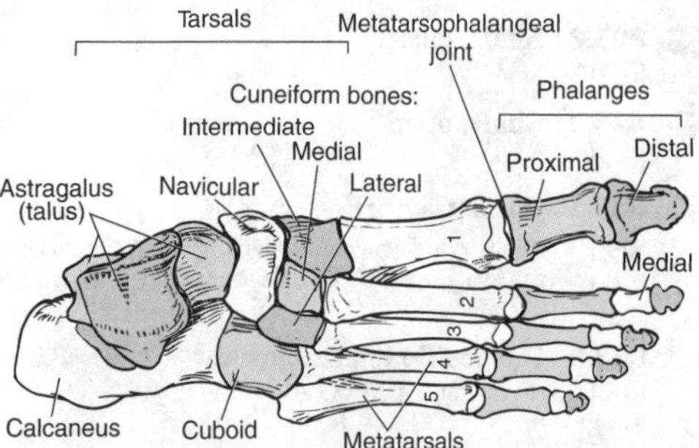

✓4th 826 Fracture of one or more phalanges of foot

INCLUDES toe(s)

826.0 Closed

826.1 Open

✓4th 827 Other, multiple, and ill-defined fractures of lower limb

INCLUDES leg NOS
multiple bones of same lower limb

EXCLUDES *multiple fractures of:*
ankle bones alone (824.4-824.9)
phalanges of foot alone (826.0-826.1)
tarsal with metatarsal bones (825.29, 825.39)
tibia with fibula (823.0-823.9 with fifth-digit 2)

827.0 Closed

827.1 Open

✓4th 828 Multiple fractures involving both lower limbs, lower with upper limb, and lower limb(s) with rib(s) and sternum

INCLUDES arm(s) with leg(s) [any bones]
both legs [any bones]
leg(s) with rib(s) or sternum

828.0 Closed

828.1 Open

✓4th 829 Fracture of unspecified bones

829.0 Unspecified bone, closed

829.1 Unspecified bone, open

DISLOCATION (830-839)

INCLUDES displacement
subluxation

EXCLUDES *congenital dislocation (754.0-755.8)*
pathological dislocation (718.2)
recurrent dislocation (718.3)

The descriptions "closed" and "open," used in the fourth-digit subdivisions, include the following terms:

closed:	open:
complete	compound
dislocation NOS	infected
partial	with foreign body
simple	
uncomplicated	

A dislocation not indicated as closed or open should be classified as closed.

✓4th 830 Dislocation of jaw

INCLUDES jaw (cartilage) (meniscus)
mandible
maxilla (inferior)
temporomandibular (joint)

830.0 Closed dislocation

830.1 Open dislocation

✓4th 831 Dislocation of shoulder

EXCLUDES *sternoclavicular joint (839.61, 839.71)*
sternum (839.61, 839.71)

The following fifth-digit subclassification is for use with category 831:

0 shoulder, unspecified
Humerus NOS
1 anterior dislocation of humerus
2 posterior dislocation of humerus
3 inferior dislocation of humerus
4 acromioclavicular (joint)
Clavicle
9 other
Scapula

✓5th **831.0 Closed dislocation**
[0-4, 9]

✓5th **831.1 Open dislocation**
[0-4, 9]

✓4th 832 Dislocation of elbow

The following fifth-digit subclassification is for use with category 832:
- **0 elbow, unspecified**
- **1 anterior dislocation of elbow**
- **2 posterior dislocation of elbow**
- **3 medial dislocation of elbow**
- **4 lateral dislocation of elbow**
- **9 other**

✓5th 832.0 Closed dislocation
[0-4, 9]

✓5th 832.1 Open dislocation
[0-4, 9]

✓4th 833 Dislocation of wrist

The following fifth-digit subclassification is for use with category 833:
- **0 wrist unspecified part**
  Carpal (bone)
  Radius, distal end
- **1 radioulnar (joint), distal**
- **2 radiocarpal (joint)**
- **3 midcarpal (joint)**
- **4 carpometacarpal (joint)**
- **5 metacarpal (bone), proximal end**
- **9 other**
  Ulna, distal end

✓5th 833.0 Closed dislocation
[0-5, 9]

✓5th 833.1 Open dislocation
[0-5, 9]

✓4th 834 Dislocation of finger

INCLUDES finger(s)
phalanx of hand
thumb

The following fifth-digit subclassification is for use with category 834:
- **0 finger unspecified part**
- **1 metacarpophalangeal (joint)**
  Metacarpal (bone), distal end
- **2 interphalangeal (joint), hand**

✓5th 834.0 Closed dislocation
[0-2]

✓5th 834.1 Open dislocation
[0-2]

✓4th 835 Dislocation of hip

The following fifth-digit subclassification is for use with category 835:
- **0 dislocation of hip, unspecified**
- **1 posterior dislocation**
- **2 obturator dislocation**
- **3 other anterior dislocation**

✓5th 835.0 Closed dislocation
[0-3]

✓5th 835.1 Open dislocation
[0-3]

✓4th 836 Dislocation of knee

EXCLUDES *dislocation of knee:*
old or pathological (718.2)
recurrent (718.3)
internal derangement of knee joint (717.0-717.5, 717.8-717.9)
old tear of cartilage or meniscus of knee (717.0-717.5, 717.8-717.9)

836.0 Tear of medial cartilage or meniscus of knee, current
Bucket handle tear:
NOS } current injury
medial meniscus } current injury

836.1 Tear of lateral cartilage or meniscus of knee, current

836.2 Other tear of cartilage or meniscus of knee, current
Tear of:
cartilage (semilunar) } current injury, not specified as medial or lateral
meniscus } current injury, not specified as medial or lateral

836.3 Dislocation of patella, closed

836.4 Dislocation of patella, open

✓5th 836.5 Other dislocation of knee, closed

836.50 Dislocation of knee, unspecified

836.51 Anterior dislocation of tibia, proximal end
Posterior dislocation of femur, distal end

836.52 Posterior dislocation of tibia, proximal end
Anterior dislocation of femur, distal end

836.53 Medial dislocation of tibia, proximal end

836.54 Lateral dislocation of tibia, proximal end

836.59 Other

✓5th 836.6 Other dislocation of knee, open

836.60 Dislocation of knee, unspecified

836.61 Anterior dislocation of tibia, proximal end

836.62 Posterior dislocation of tibia, proximal end

836.63 Medial dislocation of tibia,proximal end

836.64 Lateral dislocation of tibia, proximal end

836.69 Other

✓4th 837 Dislocation of ankle

INCLUDES astragalus
fibula, distal end
navicular, foot
scaphoid, foot
tibia, distal end

837.0 Closed dislocation

837.1 Open dislocation

✓4th 838 Dislocation of foot

The following fifth-digit subclassification is for use with category 838:
- **0 foot unspecified**
- **1 tarsal (bone), joint unspecified**
- **2 midtarsal (joint)**
- **3 tarsometatarsal (joint)**
- **4 metatarsal (bone), joint unspecified**
- **5 metatarsophalangeal (joint)**
- **6 interphalangeal (joint), foot**
- **9 other**
  Phalanx of foot
  Toe(s)

✓5th 838.0 Closed dislocation
[0-6, 9]

✓5th 838.1 Open dislocation
[0-6, 9]

✓4th 839 Other, multiple, and ill-defined dislocations

✓5th 839.0 Cervical vertebra, closed
Cervical spine Neck

839.00 Cervical vertebra, unspecified

839.01 First cervical vertebra

839.02 Second cervical vertebra

839.03 Third cervical vertebra

839.04 Fourth cervical vertebra

839.05 Fifth cervical vertebra

839.06 Sixth cervical vertebra

839.07 Seventh cervical vertebra

839.08 Multiple cervical vertebrae

✓5th **839.1 Cervical vertebra, open**

839.10 Cervical vertebra, unspecified

839.11 First cervical vertebra

839.12 Second cervical vertebra

839.13 Third cervical vertebra

839.14 Fourth cervical vertebra

839.15 Fifth cervical vertebra

839.16 Sixth cervical vertebra

839.17 Seventh cervical vertebra

839.18 Multiple cervical vertebrae

✓5th **839.2 Thoracic and lumbar vertebra, closed**

839.20 Lumbar vertebra

839.21 Thoracic vertebra

Dorsal [thoracic] vertebra

✓5th **839.3 Thoracic and lumbar vertebra, open**

839.30 Lumbar vertebra

839.31 Thoracic vertebra

✓5th **839.4 Other vertebra, closed**

839.40 Vertebra, unspecified site

Spine NOS

839.41 Coccyx

839.42 Sacrum

Sacroiliac (joint)

839.49 Other

✓5th **839.5 Other vertebra, open**

839.50 Vertebra, unspecified site

839.51 Coccyx

839.52 Sacrum

839.59 Other

✓5th **839.6 Other location, closed**

839.61 Sternum

Sternoclavicular joint

839.69 Other

Pelvis

✓5th **839.7 Other location, open**

839.71 Sternum

839.79 Other

839.8 Multiple and ill-defined, closed

Arm
Back
Hand
Multiple locations, except fingers or toes alone
Other ill-defined locations
Unspecified location

839.9 Multiple and ill-defined, open

SPRAINS AND STRAINS OF JOINTS AND ADJACENT MUSCLES (840-848)

INCLUDES avulsion, hemarthrosis, laceration, rupture, sprain, strain, tear of: joint capsule, ligament, muscle, tendon

EXCLUDES *laceration of tendon in open wounds (880-884 and 890-894 with .2)*

✓4th **840 Sprains and strains of shoulder and upper arm**

840.0 Acromioclavicular (joint) (ligament)

840.1 Coracoclavicular (ligament)

840.2 Coracohumeral (ligament)

840.3 Infraspinatus (muscle) (tendon)

840.4 Rotator cuff (capsule)

EXCLUDES *complete rupture of rotator cuff, nontraumatic (727.61)*

840.5 Subscapularis (muscle)

840.6 Supraspinatus (muscle) (tendon)

840.7 Superior glenoid labrum lesion

SLAP lesion

DEF: Detachment injury of the superior aspect of the glenoid labrum which is the ring of fibrocartilage attached to the rim of the glenoid cavity of the scapula.

840.8 Other specified sites of shoulder and upper arm

840.9 Unspecified site of shoulder and upper arm

Arm NOS   Shoulder NOS

✓4th **841 Sprains and strains of elbow and forearm**

841.0 Radial collateral ligament

841.1 Ulnar collateral ligament

841.2 Radiohumeral (joint)

841.3 Ulnohumeral (joint)

841.8 Other specified sites of elbow and forearm

841.9 Unspecified site of elbow and forearm

Elbow NOS

✓4th **842 Sprains and strains of wrist and hand**

✓5th **842.0 Wrist**

842.00 Unspecified site

842.01 Carpal (joint)

842.02 Radiocarpal (joint) (ligament)

842.09 Other

Radioulnar joint, distal

✓5th **842.1 Hand**

842.10 Unspecified site

842.11 Carpometacarpal (joint)

842.12 Metacarpophalangeal (joint)

842.13 Interphalangeal (joint)

842.19 Other

Midcarpal (joint)

✓4th **843 Sprains and strains of hip and thigh**

843.0 Iliofemoral (ligament)

843.1 Ischiocapsular (ligament)

843.8 Other specified sites of hip and thigh

843.9 Unspecified site of hip and thigh

Hip NOS   Thigh NOS

✓4th **844 Sprains and strains of knee and leg**

844.0 Lateral collateral ligament of knee

844.1 Medial collateral ligament of knee

844.2 Cruciate ligament of knee

844.3 Tibiofibular (joint) (ligament), superior

844.8 Other specified sites of knee and leg

844.9 Unspecified site of knee and leg

Knee NOS   Leg NOS

✓4th **845 Sprains and strains of ankle and foot**

✓5th **845.0 Ankle**

845.00 Unspecified site

845.01 Deltoid (ligament), ankle

Internal collateral (ligament), ankle

845.02 Calcaneofibular (ligament)

845.03 Tibiofibular (ligament), distal

845.09 Other

Achilles tendon

✓5th **845.1 Foot**

845.10 Unspecified site

845.11 Tarsometatarsal (joint) (ligament)

845.12 Metatarsophalangeal (joint)

845.13 Interphalangeal (joint), toe

845.19 Other

✓4th **846 Sprains and strains of sacroiliac region**

846.0 Lumbosacral (joint) (ligament)

846.1 Sacroiliac ligament

846.2 Sacrospinatus (ligament)

846.3 Sacrotuberous (ligament)

846.8 Other specified sites of sacroiliac region

846.9 Unspecified site of sacroiliac region

✓4th **847 Sprains and strains of other and unspecified parts of back**

EXCLUDES *lumbosacral (846.0)*

847.0 Neck

Anterior longitudinal (ligament), cervical
Atlanto-axial (joints)
Atlanto-occipital (joints)
Whiplash injury

EXCLUDES *neck injury NOS (959.0)*
thyroid region (848.2)

847.1 Thoracic

847.2 Lumbar

847.3 Sacrum

Sacrococcygeal (ligament)

847.4 Coccyx

847.9 Unspecified site of back

Back NOS

✓4th **848 Other and ill-defined sprains and strains**

848.0 Septal cartilage of nose

848.1 Jaw

Temporomandibular (joint) (ligament)

848.2 Thyroid region

Cricoarytenoid (joint) (ligament)
Cricothyroid (joint) (ligament)
Thyroid cartilage

848.3 Ribs

Chondrocostal (joint) } without mention of
Costal cartilage } injury to sternum

✓5th **848.4 Sternum**

848.40 Unspecified site

848.41 Sternoclavicular (joint) (ligament)

848.42 Chondrosternal (joint)

848.49 Other

Xiphoid cartilage

848.5 Pelvis

Symphysis pubis

EXCLUDES *that in childbirth (665.6)*

848.8 Other specified sites of sprains and strains

848.9 Unspecified site of sprain and strain

INTRACRANIAL INJURY, EXCLUDING THOSE WITH SKULL FRACTURE (850-854)

EXCLUDES *intracranial injury with skull fracture (800-801 and 803-804, except .0 and .5)*
open wound of head without intracranial injury (870.0-873.9)
skull fracture alone (800-801 and 803-804 with .0, .5)

Note: The description "with open intracranial wound," used in the fourth-digit subdivisions, includes those specified as open or with mention of infection or foreign body.

The following fifth-digit subclassification is for use with categories 851-854:

0 unspecified state of consciousness
1 with no loss of consciousness
2 with brief [less than one hour] loss of consciousness
3 with moderate [1-24 hours] loss of consciousness
4 with prolonged [more than 24 hours] loss of consciousness and returen to pre-existing conscious level
5 with prolonged [more than 24 hours] loss of consciousness without return to pre-existing conscious level
Use fifth-digit 5 to designate when a patient is unconscious and dies before regaining consciousness, regardless of the duration of the loss of consciousness
6 with loss of consciousness of unspecified duration
9 with concussion, unspecified

850 Concussion

INCLUDES commotio cerebri

EXCLUDES *concussion with:*
cerebral laceration or contusion (851.0-851.9)
cerebral hemorrhage (852-853)
head injury NOS (959.01)

850.0 With no loss of consciousness

Concussion with mental confusion or disorientation, without loss of consciousness

✓5th **850.1 With brief loss of consciousness**

Loss of consciousness for less than one hour

850.11 With loss of consciousness of 30 minutes or less

850.12 With loss of consciousness from 31 to 59 minutes

850.2 With moderate loss of consciousness

Loss of consciousness for 1-24 hours

850.3 With prolonged loss of consciousness and return to pre-existing conscious level

Loss of consciousness for more than 24 hours with complete recovery

850.4 With prolonged loss of consciousness, without return to pre-existing conscious level

850.5 With loss of consciousness of unspecified duration

850.9 Concussion, unspecified

✓4th **851 Cerebral laceration and contusion**

✓5th **851.0 Cortex (cerebral) contusion without mention of** [0-6, 9] **open intracranial wound**

✓5th **851.1 Cortex (cerebral) contusion with open** [0-6, 9] **intracranial wound**

✓5th **851.2 Cortex (cerebral) laceration without mention of** [0-6, 9] **open intracranial wound**

✓5th **851.3 Cortex (cerebral) laceration with open** [0-6, 9] **intracranial wound**

✓5th **851.4 Cerebellar or brain stem contusion without** [0-6, 9] **mention of open intracranial wound**

✓5th **851.5 Cerebellar or brain stem contusion with open** [0-6, 9] **intracranial wound**

✓5th **851.6 Cerebellar or brain stem contusion with open** [0-6, 9] **intracranial wound**

✓5th **851.7 Cerebellar or brain stem laceration with open** [0-6, 9] **intracranial wound**

Brain

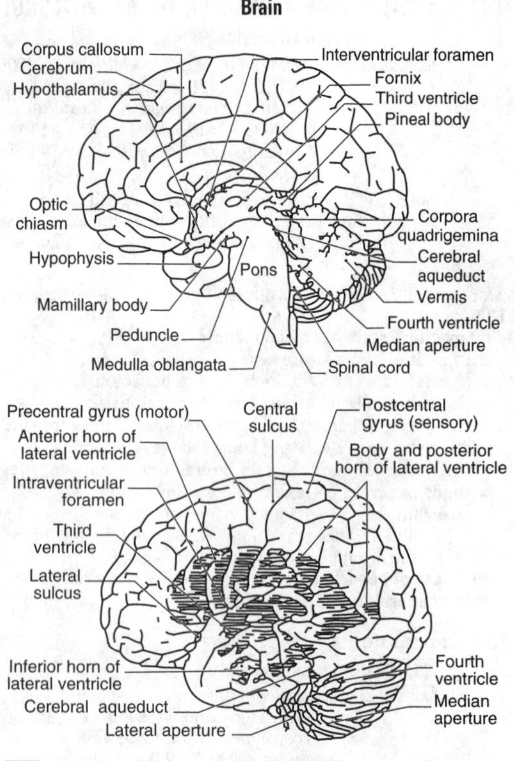

✓5th **851.8 Other and unspecified cerebral laceration and contusion, without mention of open intracranial wound**
[0-6, 9]
Brain (membrane) NOS

✓5th **851.9 Other and unspecified cerebral laceration and contusion, with open intracranial wound**
[0-6, 9]

✓4th **852 Subarachnoid, subdural, and extradural hemorrhage, following injury**

EXCLUDES *Cerebral contusion or laceration (with hemorrhage) (851.0-851.9)*

DEF: Bleeding from lining of brain; due to injury.

✓5th **852.0 Subarachnoid hemorrhage following injury without mention of open intracranial wound**
[0-6, 9]
Middle meningeal hemorrhage following injury

✓5th **852.1 Subarachnoid hemorrhage following injury with open intracranial wound**
[0-6, 9]

✓5th **852.2 Subdural hemorrhage following injury without mention of open intracranial wound**
[0-6, 9]

✓5th **852.3 Subdural hemorrhage following injury with open intracranial wound**
[0-6, 9]

✓5th **852.4 Extradural hemorrhage following injury without mention of open intracranial wound**
[0-6, 9]
Epidural hematoma following injury

✓5th **852.5 Extradural hemorrhage following injury with open intracranial wound**
[0-6, 9]

✓4th **853 Other and unspecified intracranial hemorrhage following injury**

✓5th **853.0 Without mention of open intracranial wound**
[0-6, 9]
Cerebral compression due to injury
Intracranial hematoma following injury
Traumatic cerebral hemorrhage

✓5th **853.1 With open intracranial wound**
[0-6, 9]

✓4th **854 Intracranial injury of other and unspecified nature**

INCLUDES brain injury NOS
cavernous sinus
intracranial injury

EXCLUDES *any condition classifiable to 850-853*
head injury NOS (959.01)

✓5th **854.0 Without mention of open intracranial wound**
[0-6, 9]

✓5th **854.1 With open intracranial wound**
[0-6, 9]

INTERNAL INJURY OF THORAX, ABDOMEN, AND PELVIS (860-869)

INCLUDES blast injuries, blunt trauma, bruise, concussion injuries (except cerebral), crushing, hematoma, laceration, puncture, tear, traumatic rupture } of internal organs

EXCLUDES *concussion NOS (850.0-850.9)*
flail chest (807.4)
foreign body entering through orifice (930.0-939.9)
injury to blood vessels (901.0-902.9)

Note: The description "with open wound," used in the fourth-digit subdivisions, includes those with mention of infection or foreign body.

✓4th **860 Traumatic pneumothorax and hemothorax**

DEF: Traumatic pneumothorax: air or gas leaking into pleural space of lung due to trauma.

DEF: Traumatic hemothorax: blood buildup in pleural space of lung due to trauma.

860.0 Pneumothorax without mention of open wound into thorax

860.1 Pneumothorax with open wound into thorax

860.2 Hemothorax without mention of open wound into thorax

860.3 Hemothorax with open wound into thorax

860.4 Pneumohemothorax without mention of open wound into thorax

860.5 Pneumohemothorax with open wound into thorax

✓4th **861 Injury to heart and lung**

EXCLUDES *injury to blood vessels of thorax (901.0-901.9)*

✓5th **861.0 Heart, without mention of open wound into thorax**

861.00 Unspecified injury

861.01 Contusion
Cardiac contusion
Myocardial contusion

DEF: Bruising within the pericardium with no mention of open wound.

861.02 Laceration without penetration of heart chambers

DEF: Tearing injury of heart tissue, without penetration of chambers; no open wound.

861.03 Laceration with penetration of heart chambers

✓5th **861.1 Heart, with open wound into thorax**

861.10 Unspecified injury

861.11 Contusion

861.12 Laceration without penetration of heart chambers

861.13 Laceration with penetration of heart chambers

✓5th **861.2 Lung, without mention of open wound into thorax**

861.20 Unspecified injury

861.21 ContusionDEF: Bruising of lung without mention of open wound.

861.22 Laceration

✓5th **861.3 Lung, with open wound into thorax**

861.30 Unspecified injury

861.31 Contusion

861.32 Laceration

✓4th **862 Injury to other and unspecified intrathoracic organs**

EXCLUDES *injury to blood vessels of thorax (901.0-901.9)*

862.0 Diaphragm, without mention of open wound into cavity

862.1 Diaphragm, with open wound into cavity

✓5th **862.2 Other specified intrathoracic organs, without mention of open wound into cavity**

862.21 Bronchus

862.22 Esophagus

862.29 Other

Pleura
Thymus gland

✓5th **862.3 Other specified intrathoracic organs, with open wound into cavity**

862.31 Bronchus

862.32 Esophagus

862.39 Other

862.8 Multiple and unspecified intrathoracic organs, without mention of open wound into cavity

Crushed chest
Multiple intrathoracic organs

862.9 Multiple and unspecified intrathoracic organs, with open wound into cavity

✓4th **863 Injury to gastrointestinal tract**

EXCLUDES *anal sphincter laceration during delivery (664.2)*
bile duct (868.0-868.1 with fifth-digit 2)
gallbladder (868.0-868.1 with fifth-digit 2)

863.0 Stomach, without mention of open wound into cavity

863.1 Stomach, with open wound into cavity

✓5th **863.2 Small intestine, without mention of open wound into cavity**

863.20 Small intestine, unspecified site

863.21 Duodenum

863.29 Other

✓5th **863.3 Small intestine, with open wound into cavity**

863.30 Small intestine, unspecified site

863.31 Duodenum

863.39 Other

✓5th **863.4 Colon or rectum, without mention of open wound into cavity**

863.40 Colon, unspecified site

863.41 Ascending [right] colon

863.42 Transverse colon

863.43 Descending [left] colon

863.44 Sigmoid colon

863.45 Rectum

863.46 Multiple sites in colon and rectum

863.49 Other

✓5th **863.5 Colon or rectum, with open wound into cavity**

863.50 Colon, unspecified site

863.51 Ascending [right] colon

863.52 Transverse colon

863.53 Descending [left] colon

863.54 Sigmoid colon

863.55 Rectum

863.56 Multiple sites in colon and rectum

863.59 Other

✓5th **863.8 Other and unspecified gastrointestinal sites, without mention of open wound into cavity**

863.80 Gastrointestinal tract, unspecified site

863.81 Pancreas, head

863.82 Pancreas, body

863.83 Pancreas, tail

863.84 Pancreas, multiple and unspecified sites

863.85 Appendix

863.89 Other

Intestine NOS

✓5th **863.9 Other and unspecified gastrointestinal sites, with open wound into cavity**

863.90 Gastrointestinal tract, unspecified site

863.91 Pancreas, head

863.92 Pancreas, body

863.93 Pancreas, tail

863.94 Pancreas, multiple and unspecified sites

863.95 Appendix

863.99 Other

✓4th **864 Injury to liver**

The following fifth-digit subclassification is for use with category 864:

0 unspecified injury
1 hematoma and contusion
2 laceration, minor
Laceration involving capsule only, or without significant involvement of hepatic parenchyma [i.e., less than 1 cm deep]
3 laceration, moderate
Laceration involving parenchyma but without major disruption of parenchyma [i.e., less than 10 cm long and less than 3 cm deep]
4 laceration, major
Laceration with significant disruption of hepatic parenchyma [i.e., 10 cm long and 3 cm deep]
Multiple moderate lacerations, with or without hematoma
Stellate lacerations of liver
5 laceration, unspecified
9 other

✓5th **864.0 Without mention of open wound into cavity**
[0-5, 9]

✓5th **864.1 With open wound into cavity**
[0-5, 9]

✓4th **865 Injury to spleen**

The following fifth-digit subclassification is for use with category 865:

0 unspecified injury
1 hematoma without rupture of capsule
2 capsular tears, without major disruption of parenchyma
3 laceration extending into parenchyma
4 massive parenchymal disruption
9 other

✓5th **865.0 Without mention of wound into cavity**
[0-4, 9]

✓5th **865.1 With open wound into cavity**
[0-4, 9]

✓4th **866 Injury to kidney**

EXCLUDES *acute kidney injury (nontraumatic) (584.9)*

The following fifth-digit subclassification is for use with category 866:

0 unspecified injury
1 hematoma without rupture of capsule
2 laceration
3 complete disruption of kidney parenchyma

✓5th **866.0 Without mention of open wound into cavity**
[0-3]

✓5th **866.1 With open wound into cavity**
[0-3]

✓4th **867 Injury to pelvic organs**

EXCLUDES *injury during delivery (664.0-665.9)*

867.0 Bladder and urethra, without mention of open wound into cavity

867.1 Bladder and urethra, with open wound into cavity

867.2 Ureter, without mention of open wound into cavity

867.3 Ureter, with open wound into cavity

867.4 Uterus, without mention of open wound into cavity

867.5 Uterus, with open wound into cavity

867.6 Other specified pelvic organs, without mention of open wound into cavity
Fallopian tube
Ovary
Prostate
Seminal vesicle
Vas deferens

867.7 Other specified pelvic organs, with open wound into cavity

867.8 Unspecified pelvic organ, without mention of open wound into cavity

867.9 Unspecified pelvic organ, with open wound into cavity

✓4th **868 Injury to other intra-abdominal organs**

The following fifth-digit subclassification is for use with category 868:
0 unspecified intra-abdominal organ
1 adrenal gland
2 bile duct and gallbladder
3 peritoneum
4 retroperitoneum
9 other and multiple intra-abdominal organs

✓5th **868.0 Without mention of open wound into cavity**
[0-4,9]

✓5th **868.1 With open wound into cavity**
[0-4,9]

✓4th **869 Internal injury to unspecified or ill-defined organs**

INCLUDES internal injury NOS
multiple internal injury NOS

869.0 Without mention of open wound into cavity

869.1 With open wound into cavity

OPEN WOUND (870-897)

INCLUDES animal bite
avulsion
cut
laceration
puncture wound
traumatic amputation

Use additional code to identify infection

EXCLUDES *burn (940.0-949.5)*
crushing (925-929.9)
puncture of internal organs (860.0-869.1)
superficial injury (910.0-919.9)
that incidental to:
dislocation (830.0-839.9)
fracture (800.0-829.1)
internal injury (860.0-869.1)
intracranial injury (851.0-854.1)

Note: The description "complicated" used in the fourth-digit subdivisions includes those with mention of delayed healing, delayed treatment, foreign body, or infection.

OPEN WOUND OF HEAD, NECK, AND TRUNK (870-879)

✓4th **870 Open wound of ocular adnexa**

870.0 Laceration of skin of eyelid and periocular area

870.1 Laceration of eyelid, full-thickness, not involving lacrimal passages

870.2 Laceration of eyelid involving lacrimal passages

870.3 Penetrating wound of orbit, without mention of foreign body

870.4 Penetrating wound of orbit with foreign body

EXCLUDES *retained (old) foreign body in orbit (376.6)*

870.8 Other specified open wounds of ocular adnexa

870.9 Unspecified open wound of ocular adnexa

✓4th **871 Open wound of eyeball**

EXCLUDES *2nd cranial nerve [optic] injury (950.0-950.9)*
3rd cranial nerve [oculomotor] injury (951.0)

871.0 Ocular laceration without prolapse of intraocular tissue
DEF: Tear in ocular tissue without displacing structures.

871.1 Ocular laceration with prolapse or exposure of intraocular tissue

871.2 Rupture of eye with partial loss of intraocular tissue
DEF: Forcible tearing of eyeball, with tissue loss.

871.3 Avulsion of eye
Traumatic enucleation
DEF: Traumatic extraction of eyeball from socket.

871.4 Unspecified laceration of eye

871.5 Penetration of eyeball with magnetic foreign body

EXCLUDES *retained (old) magnetic foreign body in globe (360.50-360.59)*

871.6 Penetration of eyeball with (nonmagnetic) foreign body

EXCLUDES *retained (old) (nonmagnetic) foreign body in globe (360.60-360.69)*

871.7 Unspecified ocular penetration

871.9 Unspecified open wound of eyeball

✓4th **872 Open wound of ear**

✓5th **872.0 External ear, without mention of complication**

872.00 External ear, unspecified site

872.01 Auricle, ear
Pinna
DEF: Open wound of fleshy, outer ear.

872.02 Auditory canal
DEF: Open wound of passage from external ear to eardrum.

✓5th **872.1 External ear, complicated**

872.10 External ear, unspecified site

872.11 Auricle, ear

872.12 Auditory canal

✓5th **872.6 Other specified parts of ear, without mention of complication**

872.61 Ear drum
Drumhead
Tympanic membrane

872.62 Ossicles

872.63 Eustachian tube
DEF: Open wound of channel between nasopharynx and tympanic cavity.

872.64 Cochlea
DEF: Open wound of snail shell shaped tube of inner ear.

872.69 Other and multiple sites

✓5th **872.7 Other specified parts of ear, complicated**

872.71 Ear drum

872.72 Ossicles

872.73 Eustachian tube

872.74 **Cochlea**

872.79 **Other and multiple sites**

872.8 **Ear, part unspecified, without mention of complication**
Ear NOS

872.9 **Ear, part unspecified, complicated**

✓4th **873 Other open wound of head**

873.0 **Scalp, without mention of complication**

873.1 **Scalp, complicated**

✓5th 873.2 **Nose, without mention of complication**

873.20 **Nose, unspecified site**

873.21 **Nasal septum**
DEF: Open wound between nasal passages.

873.22 **Nasal cavity**
DEF: Open wound of nostrils.

873.23 **Nasal sinus**
DEF: Open wound of mucous-lined respiratory cavities.

873.29 **Multiple sites**

✓5th 873.3 **Nose, complicated**

873.30 **Nose, unspecified site**

873.31 **Nasal septum**

873.32 **Nasal cavity**

873.33 **Nasal sinus**

873.39 **Multiple sites**

✓5th 873.4 **Face, without mention of complication**

873.40 **Face, unspecified site**

873.41 **Cheek**

873.42 **Forehead**
Eyebrow

873.43 **Lip**

873.44 **Jaw**

873.49 **Other and multiple sites**

✓5th 873.5 **Face, complicated**

873.50 **Face, unspecified site**

873.51 **Cheek**

873.52 **Forehead**

873.53 **Lip**

873.54 **Jaw**

873.59 **Other and multiple sites**

✓5th 873.6 **Internal structures of mouth, without mention of complication**

873.60 **Mouth, unspecified site**

873.61 **Buccal mucosa**
DEF: Open wound of inside of cheek.

873.62 **Gum (alveolar process)**

873.63 **Tooth (broken) (fractured) (due to trauma)**
EXCLUDES *cracked tooth (521.81)*

873.64 **Tongue and floor of mouth**

873.65 **Palate**
DEF: Open wound of roof of mouth.

873.69 **Other and multiple sites**

✓5th 873.7 **Internal structures of mouth, complicated**

873.70 **Mouth, unspecified site**

873.71 **Buccal mucosa**

873.72 **Gum (alveolar process)**

873.73 **Tooth (broken) (fractured) (due to trauma)**
EXCLUDES *cracked tooth (521.81)*

873.74 **Tongue and floor of mouth**

873.75 **Palate**

873.79 **Other and multiple sites**

873.8 **Other and unspecified open wound of head without mention of complication**
Head NOS

873.9 **Other and unspecified open wound of head, complicated**

✓4th **874 Open wound of neck**

✓5th 874.0 **Larynx and trachea, without mention of complication**

874.00 **Larynx with trachea**

874.01 **Larynx**

874.02 **Trachea**

✓5th 874.1 **Larynx and trachea, complicated**

874.10 **Larynx with trachea**

874.11 **Larynx**

874.12 **Trachea**

874.2 **Thyroid gland, without mention of complication**

874.3 **Thyroid gland, complicated**

874.4 **Pharynx, without mention of complication**
Cervical esophagus

874.5 **Pharynx, complicated**

874.8 **Other and unspecified parts, without mention of complication**
Nape of neck
Supraclavicular region
Throat NOS

874.9 **Other and unspecified parts, complicated**

✓4th **875 Open wound of chest (wall)**
EXCLUDES *open wound into thoracic cavity (860.0-862.9)*
traumatic pneumothorax and hemothorax (860.1, 860.3, 860.5)

875.0 **Without mention of complication**

875.1 **Complicated**

✓4th **876 Open wound of back**
INCLUDES loin
lumbar region
EXCLUDES *open wound into thoracic cavity (860.0-862.9)*
traumatic pneumothorax and hemothorax (860.1, 860.3, 860.5)

876.0 **Without mention of complication**

876.1 **Complicated**

✓4th **877 Open wound of buttock**
INCLUDES sacroiliac region

877.0 **Without mention of complication**

877.1 **Complicated**

✓4th **878 Open wound of genital organs (external), including traumatic amputation**
EXCLUDES *injury during delivery (664.0-665.9)*
internal genital organs (867.0-867.9)

878.0 **Penis, without mention of complication**

878.1 **Penis, complicated**

878.2 **Scrotum and testes, without mention of complication**

878.3 **Scrotum and testes, complicated**

878.4 **Vulva, without mention of complication**
Labium (majus) (minus)

878.5 **Vulva, complicated**

878.6 **Vagina, without mention of complication**

878.7 **Vagina, complicated**

878.8 **Other and unspecified parts, without mention of complication**

878.9 Other and unspecified parts, complicated

✓4th **879 Open wound of other and unspecified sites, except limbs**

879.0 Breast, without mention of complication

879.1 Breast, complicated

879.2 Abdominal wall, anterior, without mention of complication
Abdominal wall NOS
Epigastric region
Hypogastric region
Pubic region
Umbilical region

879.3 Abdominal wall, anterior, complicated

879.4 Abdominal wall, lateral, without mention of complication
Flank
Groin
Hypochondrium
Iliac (region)
Inguinal region

879.5 Abdominal wall, lateral, complicated

879.6 Other and unspecified parts of trunk, without mention of complication
Pelvic region
Perineum
Trunk NOS

879.7 Other and unspecified parts of trunk, complicated

879.8 Open wound(s) (multiple) of unspecified site(s) without mention of complication
Multiple open wounds NOS
Open wound NOS

879.9 Open wound(s) (multiple) of unspecified site(s), complicated

OPEN WOUND OF UPPER LIMB (880-887)

✓4th **880 Open wound of shoulder and upper arm**

The following fifth-digit subclassification is for use with category 880:
0 shoulder region
1 scapular region
2 axillary region
3 upper arm
9 multiple sites

✓5th **880.0 Without mention of complication**
[0-3,9]

✓5th **880.1 Complicated**
[0-3,9]

✓5th **880.2 With tendon involvement**
[0-3,9]

881 Open wound of elbow, forearm, and wrist

The following fifth-digit subclassification is for use with category 881:
0 forearm
1 elbow
2 wrist

✓5th **881.0 Without mention of complication**
[0-2]

✓5th **881.1 Complicated**
[0-2]

✓5th **881.2 With tendon involvement**
[0-2]

✓4th **882 Open wound of hand except finger(s) alone**

882.0 Without mention of complication

882.1 Complicated

882.2 With tendon involvement

✓4th **883 Open wound of finger(s)**
INCLUDES fingernail
thumb (nail)

883.0 Without mention of complication

883.1 Complicated

883.2 With tendon involvement

884 Multiple and unspecified open wound of upper limb
INCLUDES arm NOS
multiple sites of one upper limb
upper limb NOS

884.0 Without mention of complication

884.1 Complicated

884.2 With tendon involvement

✓4th **885 Traumatic amputation of thumb (complete) (partial)**
INCLUDES thumb(s) (with finger(s) of either hand)

885.0 Without mention of complication

885.1 Complicated

✓4th **886 Traumatic amputation of other finger(s) (complete) (partial)**
INCLUDES finger(s) of one or both hands, without mention of thumb(s)

886.0 Without mention of complication

886.1 Complicated

✓4th **887 Traumatic amputation of arm and hand (complete) (partial)**

887.0 Unilateral, below elbow, without mention of complication

887.1 Unilateral, below elbow, complicated

887.2 Unilateral, at or above elbow, without mention of complication

887.3 Unilateral, at or above elbow, complicated

887.4 Unilateral, level not specified, without mention of complication

887.5 Unilateral, level not specified, complicated

887.6 Bilateral [any level], without mention of complication
One hand and other arm

887.7 Bilateral [any level], complicated

OPEN WOUND OF LOWER LIMB (890-897)

✓4th **890 Open wound of hip and thigh**

890.0 Without mention of complication

890.1 Complicated

890.2 With tendon involvement

✓4th **891 Open wound of knee, leg [except thigh], and ankle**
INCLUDES leg NOS
multiple sites of leg, except thigh
EXCLUDES *that of thigh (890.0-890.2)*
with multiple sites of lower limb (894.0-894.2)

891.0 Without mention of complication

891.1 Complicated

891.2 With tendon involvement

✓4th **892 Open wound of foot except toe(s) alone**
INCLUDES heel

892.0 Without mention of complication

892.1 Complicated

892.2 With tendon involvement

✓4th **893 Open wound of toe(s)**
INCLUDES toenail

893.0 Without mention of complication

893.1 Complicated

893.2 With tendon involvement

✓4th 894 Multiple and unspecified open wound of lower limb

INCLUDES lower limb NOS
multiple sites of one lower limb, with thigh

894.0 Without mention of complication

894.1 Complicated

894.2 With tendon involvement

✓4th 894 Multiple and unspecified open wound of lower limb

INCLUDES lower limb NOS
multiple sites of one lower limb, with thigh

894.0 Without mention of complication

894.1 Complicated

894.2 With tendon involvement

✓4th 895 Traumatic amputation of toe(s) (complete) (partial)

INCLUDES toe(s) of one or both feet

895.0 Without mention of complication

895.1 Complicated

✓4th 896 Traumatic amputation of foot (complete) (partial)

896.0 Unilateral, without mention of complication

896.1 Unilateral, complicated

896.2 Bilateral, without mention of complication

EXCLUDES *one foot and other leg (897.6-897.7)*

896.3 Bilateral, complicated

✓4th 897 Traumatic amputation of leg(s) (complete) (partial)

897.0 Unilateral, below knee, without mention of complication

897.1 Unilateral, below knee, complicated

897.2 Unilateral, at or above knee, withoutmention of complication

897.3 Unilateral, at or above knee, complicated

897.4 Unilateral, level not specified, without mention of complication

897.5 Unilateral, level not specified, complicated

897.6 Bilateral [any level], without mention of complication

One foot and other leg

897.7 Bilateral [any level], complicated

INJURY TO BLOOD VESSELS (900-904)

INCLUDES arterial hematoma, avulsion, cut, laceration, rupture, traumatic aneurysm or fistula (arteriovenous) } of blood vessel secondary to other injuries, e.g.; fracture or open wound

EXCLUDES *accidental puncture or laceration during medical procedure (998.2)*
intracranial hemorrhage following injury (851.0-854.1)

✓4th 900 Injury to blood vessels of head and neck

✓5th 900.0 Carotid artery

900.00 Carotid artery, unspecified

900.01 Common carotid artery

900.02 External carotid artery

900.03 Internal carotid artery

900.1 Internal jugular vein

✓5th 900.8 Other specified blood vessels of head and neck

900.81 External jugular vein

Jugular vein NOS

900.82 Multiple blood vessels of head and neck

900.89 Other

900.9 Unspecified blood vessel of head and neck

✓4th 901 Injury to blood vessels of thorax

EXCLUDES *traumatic hemothorax (860.2-860.5)*

901.0 Thoracic aorta

901.1 Innominate and subclavian arteries

901.2 Superior vena cava

901.3 Innominate and subclavian veins

✓5th 901.4 Pulmonary blood vessels

901.40 Pulmonary vessel(s), unspecified

901.41 Pulmonary artery

901.42 Pulmonary vein

✓5th 901.8 Other specified blood vessels of thorax

901.81 Intercostal artery or vein

901.82 Internal mammary artery or vein

901.83 Multiple blood vessels of thorax

901.89 Other

Azygos vein
Hemiazygos vein

901.9 Unspecified blood vessel of thorax

✓4th 902 Injury to blood vessels of abdomen and pelvis

902.0 Abdominal aorta

✓5th 902.1 Inferior vena cava

902.10 Inferior vena cava, unspecified

902.11 Hepatic veins

902.19 Other

✓5th 902.2 Celiac and mesenteric arteries

902.20 Celiac and mesenteric arteries, unspecified

902.21 Gastric artery

902.22 Hepatic artery

902.23 Splenic artery

902.24 Other specified branches of celiac axis

902.25 Superior mesenteric artery (trunk)

902.26 Primary branches of superior mesenteric artery

Ileocolic artery

902.27 Inferior mesenteric artery

902.29 Other

✓5th 902.3 Portal and splenic veins

902.31 Superior mesenteric vein and primary subdivisions

Ileocolic vein

902.32 Inferior mesenteric vein

902.33 Portal vein

902.34 Splenic vein

902.39 Other

Cystic vein
Gastric vein

✓5th 902.4 Renal blood vessels

902.40 Renal vessel(s), unspecified

902.41 Renal artery

902.42 Renal vein

902.49 Other

Suprarenal arteries

✓5th 902.5 Iliac blood vessels

902.50 Iliac vessel(s), unspecified

902.51 Hypogastric artery

902.52 Hypogastric vein

902.53 Iliac artery

902.54 Iliac vein

902.55 Uterine artery

902.56 **Uterine vein**

902.59 **Other**

✓5th 902.8 **Other specified blood vessels of abdomen and pelvis**

902.81 **Ovarian artery**

902.82 **Ovarian vein**

902.87 **Multiple blood vessels of abdomen and pelvis**

902.89 **Other**

902.9 **Unspecified blood vessel of abdomen and pelvis**

✓4th **903 Injury to blood vessels of upper extremity**

✓5th 903.0 **Axillary blood vessels**

903.00 **Axillary vessel(s), unspecified**

903.01 **Axillary artery**

903.02 **Axillary vein**

903.1 **Brachial blood vessels**

903.2 **Radial blood vessels**

903.3 **Ulnar blood vessels**

903.4 **Palmar artery**

903.5 **Digital blood vessels**

903.8 **Other specified blood vessels of upper extremity**
Multiple blood vessels of upper extremity

903.9 **Unspecified blood vessel of upper extremity**

✓4th **904 Injury to blood vessels of lower extremity and unspecified sites**

904.0 **Common femoral artery**
Femoral artery above profunda origin

904.1 **Superficial femoral artery**

904.2 **Femoral veins**

904.3 **Saphenous veins**
Saphenous vein (greater) (lesser)

✓5th 904.4 **Popliteal blood vessels**

904.40 **Popliteal vessel(s), unspecified**

904.41 **Popliteal artery**

904.42 **Popliteal vein**

✓5th 904.5 **Tibial blood vessels**

904.50 **Tibial vessel(s), unspecified**

904.51 **Anterior tibial artery**

904.52 **Anterior tibial vein**

904.53 **Posterior tibial artery**

904.54 **Posterior tibial vein**

904.6 **Deep plantar blood vessels**

904.7 **Other specified blood vessels of lower extremity**
Multiple blood vessels of lower extremity

904.8 **Unspecified blood vessel of lower extremity**

904.9 **Unspecified site**
Injury to blood vessel NOS

LATE EFFECTS OF INJURIES, POISONINGS, TOXIC EFFECTS, AND OTHER EXTERNAL CAUSES (905-909)

Note: These categories are to be used to indicate conditions classifiable to 800-999 as the cause of late effects, which are themselves classified elsewhere. The "late effects" include those specified as such, or as sequelae, which may occur at any time after the acute injury.

✓4th **905 Late effects of musculoskeletal and connective tissue injuries**

905.0 **Late effect of fracture of skull and face bones**
Late effect of injury classifiable to 800-804

905.1 **Late effect of fracture of spine and trunk without mention of spinal cord lesion**
Late effect of injury classifiable to 805, 807-809

905.2 **Late effect of fracture of upper extremities**
Late effect of injury classifiable to 810-819

905.3 **Late effect of fracture of neck of femur**
Late effect of injury classifiable to 820

905.4 **Late effect of fracture of lower extremities**
Late effect of injury classifiable to 821-827

905.5 **Late effect of fracture of multiple and unspecified bones**
Late effect of injury classifiable to 828-829

905.6 **Late effect of dislocation**
Late effect of injury classifiable to 830-839

905.7 **Late effect of sprain and strain without mention of tendon injury**
Late effect of injury classifiable to 840-848, except tendon injury

905.8 **Late effect of tendon injury**
Late effect of tendon injury due to:
open wound [injury classifiable to 880-884 with .2, 890-894 with .2]
sprain and strain [injury classifiable to 840-848]

905.9 **Late effect of traumatic amputation**
Late effect of injury classifiable to 885-887, 895-897

EXCLUDES *late amputation stump complication (997.60-997.69)*

✓4th **906 Late effects of injuries to skin and subcutaneous tissues**

906.0 **Late effect of open wound of head, neck, and trunk**
Late effect of injury classifiable to 870-879

906.1 **Late effect of open wound of extremities without mention of tendon injury**
Late effect of injury classifiable to 880-884, 890-894 except .2

906.2 **Late effect of superficial injury**
Late effect of injury classifiable to 910-919

906.3 **Late effect of contusion**
Late effect of injury classifiable to 920-924

906.4 **Late effect of crushing**
Late effect of injury classifiable to 925-929

906.5 **Late effect of burn of eye, face, head, and neck**
Late effect of injury classifiable to 940-941

906.6 **Late effect of burn of wrist and hand**
Late effect of injury classifiable to 944

906.7 **Late effect of burn of other extremities**
Late effect of injury classifiable to 943 or 945

906.8 **Late effect of burns of other specified sites**
Late effect of injury classifiable to 942, 946-947

906.9 **Late effect of burn of unspecified site**
Late effect of injury classifiable to 948-949

✓4th **907 Late effects of injuries to the nervous system**

907.0 **Late effect of intracranial injury without mention of skull fracture**
Late effect of injury classifiable to 850-854

907.1 **Late effect of injury to cranial nerve**
Late effect of injury classifiable to 950-951

907.2 **Late effect of spinal cord injury**
Late effect of injury classifiable to 806, 952

907.3 **Late effect of injury to nerve root(s), spinal plexus(es), and other nerves of trunk**
Late effect of injury classifiable to 953-954

907.4 **Late effect of injury to peripheral nerve of shoulder girdle and upper limb**
Late effect of injury classifiable to 955

907.5 **Late effect of injury to peripheral nerve of pelvic girdle and lower limb**
Late effect of injury classifiable to 956

907.9 Late effect of injury to other and unspecified nerve
Late effect of injury classifiable to 957

✓4th 908 Late effects of other and unspecified injuries

908.0 Late effect of internal injury to chest
Late effect of injury classifiable to 860-862

908.1 Late effect of internal injury to intra-abdominal organs
Late effect of injury classifiable to 863-866, 868

908.2 Late effect of internal injury to other internal organs
Late effect of injury classifiable to 867 or 869

908.3 Late effect of injury to blood vessel of head, neck, and extremities
Late effect of injury classifiable to 900, 903-904

908.4 Late effect of injury to blood vessel of thorax, abdomen, and pelvis
Late effect of injury classifiable to 901-902

908.5 Late effect of foreign body in orifice
Late effect of injury classifiable to 930-939

908.6 Late effect of certain complications of trauma
Late effect of complications classifiable to 958

908.9 Late effect of unspecified injury
Late effect of injury classifiable to 959

✓4th 909 Late effects of other and unspecified external causes

909.0 Late effect of poisoning due to drug, medicinal or biological substance
Late effect of conditions classifiable to 960-979
EXCLUDES *late effect of adverse effect of drug, medicinal or biological substance (909.5)*

909.1 Late effect of toxic effects of nonmedical substances
Late effect of conditions classifiable to 980-989

909.2 Late effect of radiation
Late effect of conditions classifiable to 990

909.3 Late effect of complications of surgical and medical care
Late effect of conditions classifiable to 996-999

909.4 Late effect of certain other external causes
Late effect of conditions classifiable to 991-994

909.5 Late effect of adverse effect of drug, medical or biological substance
EXCLUDES *late effect of poisoning due to drug, medicinal or biological substance (909.0)*

909.9 Late effect of other and unspecified external causes

SUPERFICIAL INJURY (910-919)

EXCLUDES *burn (blisters) (940.0-949.5)*
contusion (920-924.9)
foreign body:
granuloma (728.82)
inadvertently left in operative wound (998.4)
residual in soft tissue (729.6)
insect bite, venomous (989.5)
open wound with incidental foreign body (870.0-897.7)

✓4th 910 Superficial injury of face, neck, and scalp except eye
INCLUDES cheek
ear
gum
lip
nose
throat
EXCLUDES *eye and adnexa (918.0-918.9)*

910.0 Abrasion or friction burn without mention of infection

910.1 Abrasion or friction burn, infected

910.2 Blister without mention of infection

910.3 Blister, infected

910.4 Insect bite, nonvenomous, without mention of infection

910.5 Insect bite, nonvenomous, infected

910.6 Superficial foreign body (splinter) without major open wound and without mention of infection

910.7 Superficial foreign body (splinter) without major open wound, infected

910.8 Other and unspecified superficial injury of face, neck, and scalp without mention of infection

910.9 Other and unspecified superficial injury of face, neck, and scalp, infected

✓4th 911 Superficial injury of trunk
INCLUDES abdominal wall
anus
back
breast
buttock
chest wall
flank
groin
interscapular region
labium (majus) (minus)
penis
perineum
scrotum
testis
vagina
vulva
EXCLUDES *hip (916.0-916.9)*
scapular region (912.0-912.9)

911.0 Abrasion or friction burn without mention of infection

911.1 Abrasion or friction burn, infected

911.2 Blister without mention of infection

911.3 Blister, infected

911.4 Insect bite, nonvenomous, without mention of infection

911.5 Insect bite, nonvenomous, infected

911.6 Superficial foreign body (splinter) without major open wound and without mention of infection

911.7 Superficial foreign body (splinter) without major open wound, infected

911.8 Other and unspecified superficial injury of trunk without mention of infection

911.9 Other and unspecified superficial injury of trunk, infected

✓4th 912 Superficial injury of shoulder and upper arm
INCLUDES axilla
scapular region

912.0 Abrasion or friction burn without mention of infection

912.1 Abrasion or friction burn, infected

912.2 Blister without mention of infection

912.3 Blister, infected

912.4 Insect bite, nonvenomous, without mention of infection

912.5 Insect bite, nonvenomous, infected

912.6 Superficial foreign body (splinter) without major open wound and without mention of infection

912.7 Superficial foreign body (splinter) without major open wound, infected

912.8 Other and unspecified superficial injury of shoulder and upper arm without mention of infection

912.9 Other and unspecified superficial injury of shoulder and upper arm, infected

✓4th 913 Superficial injury of elbow, forearm, and wrist

913.0 Abrasion or friction burn without mention of infection

913.1 Abrasion or friction burn, infected

913.2 Blister without mention of infection

913.3 Blister, infected

913.4 Insect bite, nonvenomous, without mention of infection

913.5 Insect bite, nonvenomous, infected

913.6 Superficial foreign body (splinter) without major open wound and without mention of infection

913.7 Superficial foreign body (splinter) without major open wound, infected

913.8 Other and unspecified superficial injury of elbow, forearm, and wrist without mention of infection

913.9 Other and unspecified superficial injury of elbow, forearm, and wrist, infected

✓4th 914 Superficial injury of hand(s) except finger(s) alone

914.0 Abrasion or friction burn without mention of infection

914.1 Abrasion or friction burn, infected

914.2 Blister without mention of infection

914.3 Blister, infected

914.4 Insect bite, nonvenomous, without mention of infection

914.5 Insect bite, nonvenomous, infected

914.6 Superficial foreign body (splinter) without major open wound and without mention of infection

914.7 Superficial foreign body (splinter) without major open wound, infected

914.8 Other and unspecified superficial injury of hand without mention of infection

914.9 Other and unspecified superficial injury of hand, infected

✓4th 915 Superficial injury of finger(s)

INCLUDES fingernail
thumb (nail)

915.0 Abrasion or friction burn without mention of infection

915.1 Abrasion or friction burn, infected

915.2 Blister without mention of infection

915.3 Blister, infected

915.4 Insect bite, nonvenomous, without mention of infection

915.5 Insect bite, nonvenomous, infected

915.6 Superficial foreign body (splinter) without major open wound and without mention of infection

915.7 Superficial foreign body (splinter) without major open wound, infected

915.8 Other and unspecified superficial injury of fingers without mention of infection

915.9 Other and unspecified superficial injury of fingers, infected

✓4th 916 Superficial injury of hip, thigh, leg, and ankle

916.0 Abrasion or friction burn without mention of infection

916.1 Abrasion or friction burn, infected

916.2 Blister without mention of infection

916.3 Blister, infected

916.4 Insect bite, nonvenomous, without mention of infection

916.5 Insect bite, nonvenomous, infected

916.6 Superficial foreign body (splinter) without major open wound and without mention of infection

916.7 Superficial foreign body (splinter) without major open wound, infected

916.8 Other and unspecified superficial injury of hip, thigh, leg, and ankle without mention of infection

916.9 Other and unspecified superficial injury of hip, thigh, leg, and ankle, infected

✓4th 917 Superficial injury of foot and toe(s)

INCLUDES heel
toenail

917.0 Abrasion or friction burn without mention of infection

917.1 Abrasion or friction burn, infected

917.2 Blister without mention of infection

917.3 Blister, infected

917.4 Insect bite, nonvenomous, without mention of infection

917.5 Insect bite, nonvenomous, infected

917.6 Superficial foreign body (splinter) without major open wound and without mention of infection

917.7 Superficial foreign body (splinter) without major open wound, infected

917.8 Other and unspecified superficial injury of foot and toes without mention of infection

917.9 Other and unspecified superficial injury of foot and toes, infected

✓4th 918 Superficial injury of eye and adnexa

EXCLUDES *burn (940.0-940.9)*
foreign body on external eye (930.0-930.9)

918.0 Eyelids and periocular area

Abrasion
Insect bite
Superficial foreign body (splinter)

918.1 Cornea

Corneal abrasion
Superficial laceration

EXCLUDES *corneal injury due to contact lens (371.82)*

918.2 Conjunctiva

918.9 Other and unspecified superficial injuries of eye

Eye (ball) NOS

✓4th 919 Superficial injury of other, multiple, and unspecified sites

EXCLUDES *multiple sites classifiable to the same three-digit category (910.0-918.9)*

919.0 Abrasion or friction burn without mention of infection

919.1 Abrasion or friction burn, infected

919.2 Blister without mention of infection

919.3 Blister, infected

919.4 Insect bite, nonvenomous, without mention of infection

919.5 Insect bite, nonvenomous, infected

919.6 Superficial foreign body (splinter) without major open wound and without mention of infection

919.7 Superficial foreign body (splinter) without major open wound, infected

919.8 Other and unspecified superficial injury without mention of infection

919.9 Other and unspecified superficial injury, infected

CONTUSION WITH INTACT SKIN SURFACE (920-924)

INCLUDES bruise } without fracture or open wound
hematoma

EXCLUDES *concussion (850.0-850.9)*
hemarthrosis (840.0-848.9)
internal organs (860.0-869.1)
that incidental to:
crushing injury (925-929.9)
dislocation (830.0-839.9)
fracture (800.0-829.1)
internal injury (860.0-869.1)
intracranial injury (850.0-854.1)
nerve injury (950.0-957.9)
open wound (870.0-897.7)

920 Contusion of face, scalp, and neck except eye(s)
Cheek
Ear (auricle)
Gum
Lip
Mandibular joint area
Nose
Throat

✓4th **921 Contusion of eye and adnexa**

921.0 Black eye, not otherwise specified

921.1 Contusion of eyelids and periocular area

921.2 Contusion of orbital tissues

921.3 Contusion of eyeball

921.9 Unspecified contusion of eye
Injury of eye NOS

✓4th **922 Contusion of trunk**

922.0 Breast

922.1 Chest wall

922.2 Abdominal wall
Flank
Groin

✓5th **922.3 Back**

922.31 Back
EXCLUDES *interscapular region (922.33)*

922.32 Buttock

922.33 Interscapular region

922.4 Genital organs
Labium (majus) (minus)
Penis
Perineum
Scrotum
Vagina
Vulva

922.8 Multiple sites of trunk

922.9 Unspecified part
Trunk NOS

✓4th **923 Contusion of upper limb**

✓5th **923.0 Shoulder and upper arm**

923.00 Shoulder region

923.01 Scapular region

923.02 Axillary region

923.03 Upper arm

923.09 Multiple sites

✓5th **923.1 Elbow and forearm**

923.10 Forearm

923.11 Elbow

✓5th **923.2 Wrist and hand(s), except finger(s) alone**

923.20 Hand(s)

923.21 Wrist

923.3 Finger
Fingernail
Thumb (nail)

923.8 Multiple sites of upper limb

923.9 Unspecified part of upper limb
Arm NOS

✓4th **924 Contusion of lower limb and of other and unspecified sites**

✓5th **924.0 Hip and thigh**

924.00 Thigh

924.01 Hip

✓5th **924.1 Knee and lower leg**

924.10 Lower leg

924.11 Knee

✓5th **924.2 Ankle and foot, excluding toe(s)**

924.20 Foot
Heel

924.21 Ankle

924.3 Toe
Toenail

924.4 Multiple sites of lower limb

924.5 Unspecified part of lower limb
Leg NOS

924.8 Multiple sites, not elsewhere classified

924.9 Unspecified site

CRUSHING INJURY (925-929)

Use additional code to identify any associated injuries, such as:
fractures (800-829)
internal injuries (860.0-869.1)
intracranial injuries (850.0-854.1)

✓4th **925 Crushing injury of face, scalp, and neck**
Cheek
Ear
Larynx
Pharynx
Throat

925.1 Crushing injury of face and scalp
Cheek
Ear

925.2 Crushing injury of neck
Larynx
Pharynx
Throat

✓4th **926 Crushing injury of trunk**

926.0 External genitalia
Labium (majus) (minus)
Penis
Scrotum
Testis
Vulva

✓5th **926.1 Other specified sites**

926.11 Back

926.12 Buttock

926.19 Other
Breast

926.8 Multiple sites of trunk

926.9 Unspecified site
Trunk NOS

✓4th **927 Crushing injury of upper limb**

✓5th **927.0 Shoulder and upper arm**

927.00 Shoulder region

927.01 Scapular region

927.02 Axillary region

927.03 Upper arm

927.09 Multiple sites

✓5th **927.1 Elbow and forearm**

927.10 Forearm

927.11 Elbow

✓5th **927.2 Wrist and hand(s), except finger(s) alone**

927.20 Hand(s)

927.21 Wrist

927.3 Finger(s)

927.8 Multiple sites of upper limb

927.9 Unspecified site
Arm NOS

✓4th **928 Crushing injury of lower limb**

✓5th **928.0 Hip and thigh**

928.00 Thigh

928.01 Hip

✓5th **928.1 Knee and lower leg**

928.10 Lower leg

928.11 Knee

✓5th **928.2 Ankle and foot, excluding toe(s) alone**

928.20 Foot

Heel

928.21 Ankle

928.3 Toe(s)

928.8 Multiple sites of lower limb

928.9 Unspecified site

Leg NOS

✓4th **929 Crushing injury of multiple and unspecified sites**

929.0 Multiple sites, not elsewhere classified

929.9 Unspecified site

EFFECTS OF FOREIGN BODY ENTERING THROUGH ORIFICE (930-939)

EXCLUDES *foreign body:*
granuloma (728.82)
inadvertently left in operative wound (998.4, 998.7)
in open wound (800-839, 851-897)
residual in soft tissues (729.6)
superficial without major open wound (910-919 with .6 or .7)

✓4th **930 Foreign body on external eye**

EXCLUDES *foreign body in penetrating wound of:*
eyeball (871.5-871.6)
retained (old) (360.5-360.6)
ocular adnexa (870.4)
retained (old) (376.6)

930.0 Corneal foreign body

930.1 Foreign body in conjunctival sac

930.2 Foreign body in lacrimal punctum

930.8 Other and combined sites

930.9 Unspecified site

External eye NOS

931 Foreign body in ear

Auditory canal
Auricle

932 Foreign body in nose

Nasal sinus
Nostril

✓4th **933 Foreign body in pharynx and larynx**

933.0 Pharynx

Nasopharynx
Throat NOS

933.1 Larynx

Asphyxia due to foreign body
Choking due to:
food (regurgitated)
phlegm

✓4th **934 Foreign body in trachea, bronchus, and lung**

934.0 Trachea

934.1 Main bronchus

934.8 Other specified parts

Bronchioles
Lung

934.9 Respiratory tree, unspecified

Inhalation of liquid or vomitus, lower respiratory tract NOS

✓4th **935 Foreign body in mouth, esophagus, and stomach**

935.0 Mouth

935.1 Esophagus

935.2 Stomach

936 Foreign body in intestine and colon

937 Foreign body in anus and rectum

Rectosigmoid (junction)

938 Foreign body in digestive system, unspecified

Alimentary tract NOS
Swallowed foreign body

✓4th **939 Foreign body in genitourinary tract**

939.0 Bladder and urethra

939.1 Uterus, any part

EXCLUDES *intrauterine contraceptive device:*
complications from (996.32, 996.65)
presence of (V45.51)

939.2 Vulva and vagina

939.3 Penis

939.9 Unspecified site

BURNS (940-949)

INCLUDES burns from:
electrical heating appliance
electricity
flame
hot object
lightning
radiation
chemical burns (external) (internal)
scalds

EXCLUDES *friction burns (910-919 with .0, .1)*
sunburn (692.71, 692.76-692.77)

✓4th **940 Burn confined to eye and adnexa**

940.0 Chemical burn of eyelids and periocular area

940.1 Other burns of eyelids and periocular area

940.2 Alkaline chemical burn of cornea and conjunctival sac

940.3 Acid chemical burn of cornea and conjunctival sac

940.4 Other burn of cornea and conjunctival sac

940.5 Burn with resulting rupture and destruction of eyeball

940.9 Unspecified burn of eye and adnexa

✓4th **941 Burn of face, head, and neck**

EXCLUDES *mouth (947.0)*

The following fifth-digit subclassification is for use with category 941:
0 face and head, unspecified site
1 ear [any part]
2 eye (with other parts of face, head, and neck)
3 lip(s)
4 chin
5 nose (septum)
6 scalp [any part]
Temple (region)
7 forehead and cheek
8 neck
9 multiple sites [except with eye] of face, head, and neck

✓5th **941.0 Unspecified degree**
[0-9]

✓5th **941.1 Erythema [first degree]**
[0-9]

✓5th **941.2 Blisters, epidermal loss [second degree]**
[0-9]

✓5th **941.3 Full-thickness skin loss [third degree NOS]**
[0-9]

✓5th **941.4 Deep necrosis of underlying tissues [deep third degree] without mention of loss of a body part**
[0-9]

✓5th **941.5 Deep necrosis of underlying tissues [deep third degree] with loss of a body part**
[0-9]

✓4th **942 Burn of trunk**

EXCLUDES *scapular region (943.0-943.5 with fifth-digit 6)*

The following fifth-digit subclassificaiton is for use with category 942:

0 trunk, unspecified
1 breast
2 chest wall, excluding breast and nipple
3 abdominal wall
Flank
Groin
4 back [any part]
Buttock
Interscapular region
5 genitalia
Labium (majus) (minus
Penis
Perineum
Scrotum
Testis
Vulva
9 other and multiple sites of trunk

✓5th **942.0 Unspecified degree**
[0-5, 9]

✓5th **942.1 Erythema [first degree]**
[0-5, 9]

✓5th **942.2 Blisters, epidermal loss [second degree]**
[0-5, 9]

✓5th **942.3 Full-thickness skin loss [third degree NOS]**
[0-5, 9]

✓5th **942.4 Deep necrosis of underlying tissues [deep third degree] without mention of loss of a body part**
[0-5, 9]

✓5th **942.5 Deep necrosis of underlying tissues [deep third degree] with loss of a body part**
[0-5, 9]

✓4th **943 Burn of upper limb, except wrist and hand**

The following fifth-digit subclassificaiton is for use with category 943:

0 upper limb, unspecified site
1 forearm
2 elbow
3 upper arm
4 axilla
5 shoulder
6 scapular region
9 multiple sites of upper limb, except wrist and hand

✓5th **943.0 Unspecified degree**
[0-6, 9]

✓5th **943.1 Erythema [first degree]**
[0-6, 9]

✓5th **943.2 Blisters, epidermal loss [second degree]**
[0-6, 9]

✓5th **943.3 Full-thickness skin loss [third degree NOS]**
[0-6, 9]

✓5th **943.4 Deep necrosis of underlying tissues [deep third degree] without mention of loss of a body part**
[0-6, 9]

✓5th **943.5 Deep necrosis of underlying tissues [deep third degree] with loss of a body part**
[0-6, 9]

✓4th **944 Burn of wrist(s) and hand(s)**

The following fifth-digit subclassification is for use with category 944:

0 hand, unspecified site
1 single digit [finger (nail)] other than thumb
2 thumb (nail)
3 two or more digits, not including thumb
4 two or more digits including thumb
5 palm
6 back of hand
7 wrist
8 multiple sites of wrist(s) and hand(s)

✓5th **944.0 Unspecified degree**
[0-8]

✓5th **944.1 Erythema [first degree]**
[0-8]

✓5th **944.2 Blisters, epidermal loss [second degree]**
[0-8]

✓5th **944.3 Full-thickness skin loss [third degree NOS]**
[0-8]

✓5th **944.4 Deep necrosis of underlying tissues [deep third degree] without mention of loss of a body part**
[0-8]

✓5th **944.5 Deep necrosis of underlying tissues [deep third degree] with loss of a body part**
[0-8]

✓4th **945 Burn of lower limb(s)**

The following fifth-digit subclassification is for use with category 945:

0 lower limb [leg], unspecified site
1 toe(s) (nail)
2 foot
3 ankle
4 lower leg
5 knee
6 thigh [any part]
9 multiple sites of lower limb(s)

✓5th **945.0 Unspecified degree**
[0-8]

✓5th **945.1 Erythema [first degree]**
[0-8]

✓5th **945.2 Blisters, epidermal loss [second degree]**
[0-8]

✓5th **945.3 Full-thickness skin loss [third degree NOS]**
[0-8]

✓5th **945.4 Deep necrosis of underlying tissues [deep third degree] without mention of loss of a body part**
[0-8]

✓5th **945.5 Deep necrosis of underlying tissues [deep third degree] with loss of a body part**
[0-8]

✓4th **946 Burns of multiple specified sites**

INCLUDES burns of sites classifiable to more than one three-digit category in 940-945

EXCLUDES *multiple burns NOS (949.0-949.5)*

946.0 Unspecified degree

946.1 Erythema [first degree]

946.2 Blisters, epidermal loss [second degree]

946.3 Full-thickness skin loss [third degree NOS]

946.4 Deep necrosis of underlying tissues [deep third degree] without mention of loss of a body part

946.5 Deep necrosis of underlying tissues [deep third degree] with loss of a body part

✓4th **947 Burn of internal organs**

INCLUDES burns from chemical agents (ingested)

947.0 Mouth and pharynx
Gum Tongue

947.1 Larynx, trachea, and lung

947.2 Esophagus

947.3 Gastrointestinal tract
Colon Small intestine
Rectum Stomach

947.4 Vagina and uterus

947.8 Other specified sites

947.9 Unspecified site

✓4th **948 Burns classified according to extent of body surface involved**

Note: This category is to be used when the site of the burn is unspecified, or with categories 940-947 when the site is specified.

EXCLUDES *sunburn (692.71, 692.76-692.77)*

The following fifth-digit subclassification is for use with category 948 to indicate the percent of body surface with third degree burn; valid digits are in [brackets] under each code:

0 less than 10 percent or unspecified
1 10-19%
2 20-29%
3 30-39%
4 40-49%
5 50-59%
6 60-69%
7 70-79%
8 80-89%
9 90% or more of body surface

✓5th **948.0 Burn [any degree] involving less than 10 percent of body surface**
[0]

✓5th **948.1 10-19 percent of body surface**
[0-1]

✓5th **948.2 20-29 percent of body surface**
[0-2]

✓5th **948.3 30-39 percent of body surface**
[0-3]

✓5th **948.4 40-49 percent of body surface**
[0-4]

✓5th **948.5 50-59 percent of body surface**
[0-5]

✓5th **948.6 60-69 percent of body surface**
[0-6]

✓5th **948.7 70-79 percent of body surface**
[0-7]

✓5th **948.8 80-89 percent of body surface**
[0-8]

✓5th **948.9 90 percent or more of body surface**
[0-9]

✓4th **949 Burn, unspecified**

INCLUDES burn NOS
multiple burns NOS

EXCLUDES *burn of unspecified site but with statement of the extent of body surface involved (948.0-948.9)*

949.0 Unspecified degree

949.1 Erythema [first degree]

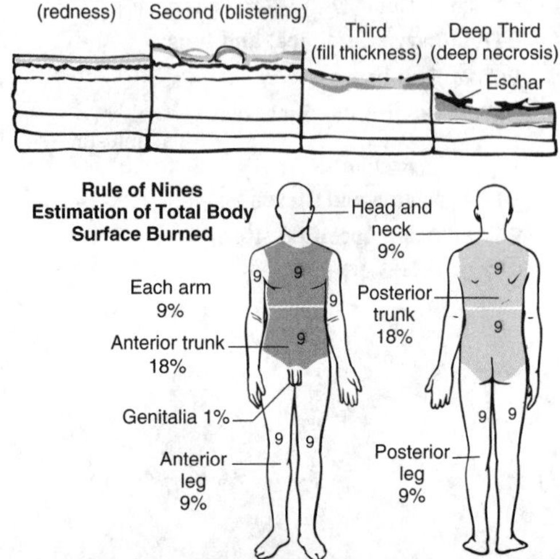

949.2 Blisters, epidermal loss [second degree]

949.3 Full-thickness skin loss [third degree NOS]

949.4 Deep necrosis of underlying tissues [deep third degree] without mention of loss of a body part

949.5 Deep necrosis of underlying tissues [deep third degree] with loss of a body part

INJURY TO NERVES AND SPINAL CORD (950-957)

INCLUDES division of nerve
lesion in continuity
traumatic neuroma
traumatic transient paralysis
} (with open wound)

EXCLUDES *accidental puncture or laceration during medical procedure (998.2)*

✓4th **950 Injury to optic nerve and pathways**

950.0 Optic nerve injury
Second cranial nerve

950.1 Injury to optic chiasm

950.2 Injury to optic pathways

950.3 Injury to visual cortex

950.9 Unspecified
Traumatic blindness NOS

✓4th **951 Injury to other cranial nerve(s)**

951.0 Injury to oculomotor nerve
Third cranial nerve

951.1 Injury to trochlear nerve
Fourth cranial nerve

951.2 Injury to trigeminal nerve
Fifth cranial nerve

951.3 Injury to abducens nerve
Sixth cranial nerve

951.4 Injury to facial nerve
Seventh cranial nerve

951.5 Injury to acoustic nerve
Auditory nerve
Eighth cranial nerve
Traumatic deafness NOS

951.6 Injury to accessory nerve
Eleventh cranial nerve

951.7 Injury to hypoglossal nerve
Twelfth cranial nerve

951.8 Injury to other specified cranial nerves
Glossopharyngeal [9th cranial] nerve
Olfactory [1st cranial] nerve
Pneumogastric [10th cranial] nerve
Traumatic anosmia NOS
Vagus [10th cranial] nerve

951.9 Injury to unspecified cranial nerve

✓4th **952 Spinal cord injury without evidence of spinal bone injury**

✓5th **952.0 Cervical**

952.00 C_1-C_4 level with unspecified spinal cord injury
Spinal cord injury, cervical region NOS

952.01 C_1-C_4 level with complete lesion of spinal cord

952.02 C_1-C_4 level with anterior cord syndrome

952.03 C_1-C_4 level with central cord syndrome

952.04 C_1-C_4 level with other specified spinal cord injury
Incomplete spinal cord lesion at C_1-C_4 level:
NOS
with posterior cord syndrome

952.05 C_5-C_7 level with unspecified spinal cord injury

952.06 C_5-C_7 level with complete lesion of spinal cord

Spinal Nerve Roots

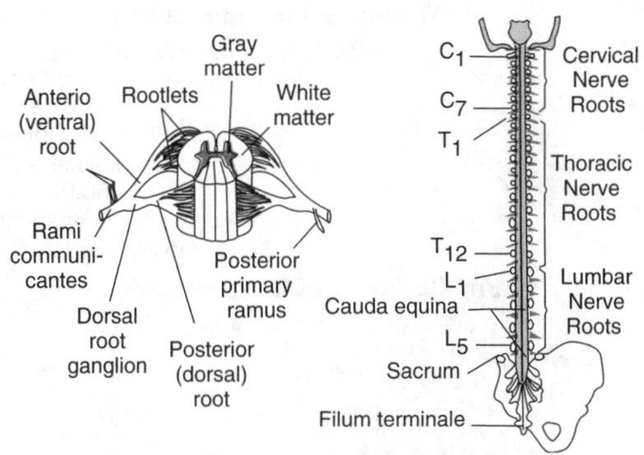

952.07 C_5-C_7 level with anterior cord syndrome

952.08 C_5-C_7 level with central cord syndrome

952.09 C_5-C_7 level with other specified spinal cord injury
Incomplete spinal cord lesion at C_5-C_7 level:
NOS
with posterior cord syndrome

✓5th **952.1 Dorsal [thoracic]**

952.10 T_1-T_6 level with unspecified spinal cord injury
Spinal cord injury, thoracic region NOS

952.11 T_1-T_6 level with complete lesion of spinal cord

952.12 T_1-T_6 level with anterior cord syndrome

952.13 T_1-T_6 level with central cord syndrome

952.14 T_1-T_6 level with other specified spinal cord injury
Incomplete spinal cord lesion at T_1-T_6 level:
NOS
with posterior cord syndrome

952.15 T_7-T_{12} level with unspecified spinal cord injury

952.16 T_7-T_{12} level with complete lesion of spinal cord

952.17 T_7-T_{12} level with anterior cord syndrome

952.18 T_7-T_{12} level with central cord syndrome

952.19 T_7-T_{12} level with other specified spinal cord injury
Incomplete spinal cord lesion at T_7-T_{12} level:
NOS
with posterior cord syndrome

952.2 Lumbar

952.3 Sacral

952.4 Cauda equina

952.8 Multiple sites of spinal cord

952.9 Unspecified site of spinal cord

✓4th **953 Injury to nerve roots and spinal plexus**

953.0 Cervical root

953.1 Dorsal root

953.2 Lumbar root

953.3 Sacral root

953.4 Brachial plexus

953.5 Lumbosacral plexus

953.8 Multiple sites

953.9 Unspecified site

✓4th **954 Injury to other nerve(s) of trunk, excluding shoulder and pelvic girdles**

954.0 Cervical sympathetic

954.1 Other sympathetic
Celiac ganglion or plexus
Inferior mesenteric plexus
Splanchnic nerve(s)
Stellate ganglion

954.8 Other specified nerve(s) of trunk

954.9 Unspecified nerve of trunk

✓4th **955 Injury to peripheral nerve(s) of shoulder girdle and upper limb**

955.0 Axillary nerve

955.1 Median nerve

955.2 Ulnar nerve

955.3 Radial nerve

955.4 Musculocutaneous nerve

955.5 Cutaneous sensory nerve, upper limb

955.6 Digital nerve

955.7 Other specified nerve(s) of shoulder girdle and upper limb

955.8 Multiple nerves of shoulder girdle and upper limb

955.9 Unspecified nerve of shoulder girdle and upper limb

✓4th **956 Injury to peripheral nerve(s) of pelvic girdle and lower limb**

956.0 Sciatic nerve

956.1 Femoral nerve

956.2 Posterior tibial nerve

956.3 Peroneal nerve

956.4 Cutaneous sensory nerve, lower limb

956.5 Other specified nerve(s) of pelvic girdle and lower limb

956.8 Multiple nerves of pelvic girdle and lower limb

956.9 Unspecified nerve of pelvic girdle and lower limb

✓4th **957 Injury to other and unspecified nerves**

957.0 Superficial nerves of head and neck

957.1 Other specified nerve(s)

957.8 Multiple nerves in several parts
Multiple nerve injury NOS

957.9 Unspecified site
Nerve injury NOS

CERTAIN TRAUMATIC COMPLICATIONS AND UNSPECIFIED INJURIES (958-959)

✓4th **958 Certain early complications of trauma**

EXCLUDES *adult respiratory distress syndrome (518.5)*
flail chest (807.4)
post-traumatic seroma (729.91)
shock lung (518.5)
that occurring during or following medical procedures (996.0-999.9)

958.0 Air embolism
Pneumathemia
EXCLUDES *that complicating:*
abortion (634-638 with .6, 639.6)
ectopic or molar pregnancy (639.6)
pregnancy, childbirth, or the puerperium (673.0)

DEF: Arterial obstruction due to introduction of air bubbles into the veins following surgery or trauma.

958.1 Fat embolism

EXCLUDES *that complicating:*
abortion (634-638 with .6, 639.6)
pregnancy, childbirth, or the puerperium (673.8)

DEF: Arterial blockage due to the entrance of fat in circulatory system, after fracture of large bones or administration of corticosteroids.

958.2 Secondary and recurrent hemorrhage

958.3 Posttraumatic wound infection, not elsewhere classified

EXCLUDES *infected open wounds-code to complicated open wound of site*

958.4 Traumatic shock

Shock (immediate) (delayed) following injury

EXCLUDES *shock:*
anaphylactic (995.0)
due to serum (999.4)
anesthetic (995.4)
electric (994.8)
following abortion (639.5)
lightning (994.0)
nontraumatic NOS (785.50)
obstetric (669.1)
postoperative (998.0)

DEF: Shock, immediate or delayed following injury.

958.5 Traumatic anuria

Crush syndrome
Renal failure following crushing

EXCLUDES *that due to a medical procedure (997.5)*

DEF: Complete suppression of urinary secretion by kidneys due to trauma.

958.6 Volkmann's ischemic contracture

Posttraumatic muscle contracture

DEF: Muscle deterioration due to loss of blood supply from injury or tourniquet; causes muscle contraction and results in inability to extend the muscles fully.

958.7 Traumatic subcutaneous emphysema

EXCLUDES *subcutaneous emphysema resulting from a procedure (998.81)*

958.8 Other early complications of trauma

✓5th **958.9 Traumatic compartment syndrome**

EXCLUDES *nontraumatic compartment syndrome (729.71-729.79)*

DEF: Compression of nerves and blood vessels within an enclosed space due to previous trauma, which leads to impaired blood flow and muscle and nerve damage.

958.90 Compartment syndrome, unspecified

958.91 Traumatic compartment syndrome of upper extremity

Traumatic compartment syndrome of shoulder, arm, forearm, wrist, hand, and fingers

958.92 Traumatic compartment syndrome of lower extremity

Traumatic compartment syndrome of hip, buttock, thigh, leg, foot, and toes

958.93 Traumatic compartment syndrome of abdomen

958.99 Traumatic compartment syndrome of other sites

✓4th **959 Injury, other and unspecified**

INCLUDES injury NOS

EXCLUDES *injury NOS of:*
blood vessels (900.0-904.9)
eye (921.0-921.9)
internal organs (860.0-869.1)
intracranial sites (854.0-854.1)
nerves (950.0-951.9, 953.0-957.9)
spinal cord (952.0-952.9)

✓5th **959.0 Head, face and neck**

959.01 Head injury, unspecified

EXCLUDES *concussion (850.1-850.9)*
with head injury NOS (850.1-850.9)
head injury NOS with loss of consciousness (850.1-850.5)
specified intracranial injuries (850.0-854.1)

959.09 Injury of face and neck

Cheek
Ear
Eyebrow
Lip
Mouth
Nose
Throat

✓5th **959.1 Trunk**

EXCLUDES *scapular region (959.2)*

959.11 Other injury of chest wall

959.12 Other injury of abdomen

959.13 Fracture of corpus cavernosum penis

959.14 Other injury of external genitals

959.19 Other injury of other sites of trunk

Injury of trunk NOS

959.2 Shoulder and upper arm

Axilla
Scapular region

959.3 Elbow, forearm, and wrist

959.4 Hand, except finger

959.5 Finger

Fingernail
Thumb (nail)

959.6 Hip and thigh

Upper leg

959.7 Knee, leg, ankle, and foot

959.8 Other specified sites, including multiple

EXCLUDES *multiple sites classifiable to the same four-digit category (959.0-959.7)*

959.9 Unspecified site

POISONING BY DRUGS, MEDICINAL AND BIOLOGICAL SUBSTANCES (960-979)

INCLUDES overdose of these substances
wrong substance given or taken in error

Use additional code to specify the effects of the poisoning

EXCLUDES *adverse effects ["hypersensitivity," "reaction," etc.] of correct substance properly administered. Such cases are to be classified according to the nature of the adverse effect, such as:*
adverse effect NOS (995.20)
allergic lymphadenitis (289.3)
aspirin gastritis (535.4)
blood disorders (280.0-289.9)
dermatitis:
contact (692.0-692.9)
due to ingestion (693.0-693.9)
nephropathy (583.9)
[The drug giving rise to the adverse effect may be identified by use of categories E930-E949.]
drug dependence (304.0-304.9)
drug reaction and poisoning affecting the newborn (760.0-779.9)
nondependent abuse of drugs (305.0-305.9)
pathological drug intoxication (292.2)

✓4th **960 Poisoning by antibiotics**

EXCLUDES *antibiotics:*
ear, nose, and throat (976.6)
eye (976.5)
local (976.0)

960.0 Penicillins
Ampicillin
Carbenicillin
Cloxacillin
Penicillin G

960.1 Antifungal antibiotics
Amphotericin B
Griseofulvin
Nystatin
Trichomycin
EXCLUDES *preparations intended for topical use (976.0-976.9)*

960.2 Chloramphenicol group
Chloramphenicol
Thiamphenicol

960.3 Erythromycin and other macrolides
Oleandomycin
Spiramycin

960.4 Tetracycline group
Doxycycline
Minocycline
Oxytetracycline

960.5 Cephalosporin group
Cephalexin
Cephaloglycin
Cephaloridine
Cephalothin

960.6 Antimycobacterial antibiotics
Cycloserine
Kanamycin
Rifampin
Streptomycin

960.7 Antineoplastic antibiotics
Actinomycin such as:
Bleomycin
Cactinomycin
Dactinomycin
Daunorubicin
Mitomycin

960.8 Other specified antibiotics

960.9 Unspecified antibiotic

✓4th **961 Poisoning by other anti-infectives**
EXCLUDES *anti-infectives:*
ear, nose, and throat (976.6)
eye (976.5)
local (976.0)

961.0 Sulfonamides
Sulfadiazine
Sulfafurazole
Sulfamethoxazole

961.1 Arsenical anti-infectives

961.2 Heavy metal anti-infectives
Compounds of:
antimony
bismuth
lead
mercury
EXCLUDES *mercurial diuretics (974.0)*

961.3 Quinoline and hydroxyquinoline derivatives
Chiniofon
Diiodohydroxyquin
EXCLUDES *antimalarial drugs (961.4)*

961.4 Antimalarials and drugs acting on other blood protozoa
Chloroquine
Cycloguanil
Primaquine
Proguanil [chloroguanide]
Pyrimethamine
Quinine

961.5 Other antiprotozoal drugs
Emetine

961.6 Anthelmintics
Hexylresorcinol
Piperazine
Thiabendazole

961.7 Antiviral drugs
Methisazone
EXCLUDES *amantadine (966.4)*
cytarabine (963.1)
idoxuridine (976.5)

961.8 Other antimycobacterial drugs
Ethambutol
Ethionamide
Isoniazid
Para-aminosalicylic acid derivatives
Sulfones

961.9 Other and unspecified anti-infectives
Flucytosine
Nitrofuran derivatives

✓4th **962 Poisoning by hormones and synthetic substitutes**
EXCLUDES *oxytocic hormones (975.0)*

962.0 Adrenal cortical steroids
Cortisone derivatives
Desoxycorticosterone derivatives
Fluorinated corticosteroids

962.1 Androgens and anabolic congeners
Methandriol
Nandrolone
Oxymetholone
Testosterone

962.2 Ovarian hormones and synthetic substitutes
Contraceptives, oral
Estrogens
Estrogens and progestogens, combined
Progestogens

962.3 Insulins and antidiabetic agents
Acetohexamide
Biguanide derivatives, oral
Chlorpropamide
Glucagon
Insulin
Phenformin
Sulfonylurea derivatives, oral
Tolbutamide

962.4 Anterior pituitary hormones
Corticotropin
Gonadotropin
Somatotropin [growth hormone]

962.5 Posterior pituitary hormones
Vasopressin
EXCLUDES *oxytocic hormones (975.0)*

962.6 Parathyroid and parathyroid derivatives

962.7 Thyroid and thyroid derivatives
Dextrothyroxin
Levothyroxine sodium
Liothyronine
Thyroglobulin

962.8 Antithyroid agents
Iodides
Thiouracil
Thiourea

962.9 Other and unspecified hormones and synthetic substitutes

✓4th **963 Poisoning by primarily systemic agents**

963.0 Antiallergic and antiemetic drugs
Antihistamines
Chlorpheniramine
Diphenhydramine
Diphenylpyraline
Thonzylamine
Tripelennamine
EXCLUDES *phenothiazine-based tranquilizers (969.1)*

963.1 Antineoplastic and immunosuppressive drugs
Azathioprine
Busulfan
Chlorambucil
Cyclophosphamide
Cytarabine
Fluorouracil
Mercaptopurine
thio-TEPA
EXCLUDES *antineoplastic antibiotics (960.7)*

963.2 Acidifying agents

963.3 Alkalizing agents

963.4 Enzymes, not elsewhere classified
Penicillinase

963.5 Vitamins, not elsewhere classified
Vitamin A
Vitamin D
EXCLUDES *nicotinic acid (972.2)*
vitamin K (964.3)

963.8 Other specified systemic agents
Heavy metal antagonists

963.9 Unspecified systemic agent

✓4th **964 Poisoning by agents primarily affecting blood constituents**

964.0 Iron and its compounds
Ferric salts
Ferrous sulfate and other ferrous salts

964.1 Liver preparations and other antianemic agents
Folic acid

964.2 Anticoagulants
Coumarin
Heparin
Phenindione
Warfarin sodium

964.3 Vitamin K [phytonadione]

964.4 Fibrinolysis-affecting drugs
Aminocaproic acid
Streptodornase
Streptokinase
Urokinase

964.5 Anticoagulant antagonists and other coagulants
Hexadimethrine
Protamine sulfate

964.6 Gamma globulin

964.7 Natural blood and blood products
Blood plasma
Human fibrinogen
Packed red cells
Whole blood
EXCLUDES *transfusion reactions (999.4-999.8)*

964.8 Other specified agents affecting blood constituents
Macromolecular blood substitutes
Plasma expanders

964.9 Unspecified agent affecting blood constituents

✓4th **965 Poisoning by analgesics, antipyretics, and antirheumatics**
EXCLUDES *drug dependence (304.0-304.9)*
nondependent abuse (305.0-305.9)

✓5th **965.0 Opiates and related narcotics**

965.00 Opium (alkaloids), unspecified

965.01 Heroin
Diacetylmorphine

965.02 Methadone

965.09 Other
Codeine [methylmorphine]
Meperidine [pethidine]
Morphine

965.1 Salicylates
Acetylsalicylic acid [aspirin]
Salicylic acid salts

965.4 Aromatic analgesics, not elsewhere classified
Acetanilid
Paracetamol [acetaminophen]
Phenacetin [acetophenetidin]

965.5 Pyrazole derivatives
Aminophenazone [aminopyrine]
Phenylbutazone

✓5th **965.6 Antirheumatics [antiphlogistics]**
EXCLUDES *salicylates (965.1)*
steroids (962.0-962.9)

965.61 Propionic acid derivatives
Fenoprofen
Flurbiprofen
Ibuprofen
Ketoprofen
Naproxen
Oxaprozin

965.69 Other antirheumatics
Gold salts
Indomethacin

965.7 Other non-narcotic analgesics
Pyrabital

965.8 Other specified analgesics and antipyretics
Pentazocine

965.9 Unspecified analgesic and antipyretic

✓4th **966 Poisoning by anticonvulsants and anti-Parkinsonism drugs**

966.0 Oxazolidine derivatives
Paramethadione
Trimethadione

966.1 Hydantoin derivatives
Phenytoin

966.2 Succinimides
Ethosuximide
Phensuximide

966.3 Other and unspecified anticonvulsants
Primidone
EXCLUDES *barbiturates (967.0)*
sulfonamides (961.0)

966.4 Anti-Parkinsonism drugs
Amantadine
Ethopropazine [profenamine]
Levodopa [L-dopa]

✓4th **967 Poisoning by sedatives and hypnotics**
EXCLUDES *drug dependence (304.0-304.9)*
nondependent abuse (305.0-305.9)

967.0 Barbiturates
Amobarbital [amylobarbitone]
Barbital [barbitone]
Butabarbital [butabarbitone]
Pentobarbital [pentobarbitone]
Phenobarbital [phenobarbitone]
Secobarbital [quinalbarbitone]
EXCLUDES *thiobarbiturate anesthetics (968.3)*

967.1 Chloral hydrate group

967.2 Paraldehyde

967.3 Bromine compounds
Bromide
Carbromal (derivatives)

967.4 Methaqualone compounds

967.5 Glutethimide group

967.6 Mixed sedatives, not elsewhere classified

967.8 Other sedatives and hypnotics

967.9 Unspecified sedative or hypnotic
Sleeping:
drug } NOS
pill } NOS
tablet } NOS

✓4th 968 Poisoning by other central nervous system depressants and anesthetics

EXCLUDES *drug dependence (304.0-304.9)*
nondependent abuse (305.0-305.9)

968.0 Central nervous system muscle-tone depressants
Chlorphenesin (carbamate)
Mephenesin
Methocarbamol

968.1 Halothane

968.2 Other gaseous anesthetics
Ether
Halogenated hydrocarbon derivatives, except halothane
Nitrous oxide

968.3 Intravenous anesthetics
Ketamine
Methohexital [methohexitone]
Thiobarbiturates, such as thiopental sodium

968.4 Other and unspecified general anesthetics

968.5 Surface [topical] and infiltration anesthetics
Cocaine
Lidocaine [lignocaine]
Procaine
Tetracaine

968.6 Peripheral nerve- and plexus-blocking anesthetics

968.7 Spinal anesthetics

968.9 Other and unspecified local anesthetics

✓4th 969 Poisoning by psychotropic agents

EXCLUDES *drug dependence (304.0-304.9)*
nondependent abuse (305.0-305.9)

969.0 Antidepressants
Amitriptyline
Imipramine
Monoamine oxidase [MAO] inhibitors

969.1 Phenothiazine-based tranquilizers
Chlorpromazine
Fluphenazine
Prochlorperazine
Promazine

969.2 Butyrophenone-based tranquilizers
Haloperidol
Spiperone
Trifluperidol

969.3 Other antipsychotics, neuroleptics, and major tranquilizers

969.4 Benzodiazepine-based tranquilizers
Chlordiazepoxide
Diazepam
Flurazepam
Lorazepam
Medazepam
Nitrazepam

969.5 Other tranquilizers
Hydroxyzine
Meprobamate

969.6 Psychodysleptics [hallucinogens]
Cannabis (derivatives)
Lysergide [LSD]
Marihuana (derivatives)
Mescaline
Psilocin
Psilocybin

969.7 Psychostimulants
Amphetamine
Caffeine
EXCLUDES *central appetite depressants (977.0)*

969.8 Other specified psychotropic agents

969.9 Unspecified psychotropic agent

✓4th 970 Poisoning by central nervous system stimulants

970.0 Analeptics
Lobeline
Nikethamide

970.1 Opiate antagonists
Levallorphan
Nalorphine
Naloxone

970.8 Other specified central nervous system stimulants

970.9 Unspecified central nervous system stimulant

✓4th 971 Poisoning by drugs primarily affecting the autonomic nervous system

971.0 Parasympathomimetics [cholinergics]
Acetylcholine
Anticholinesterase:
organophosphorus
reversible
Pilocarpine

971.1 Parasympatholytics [anticholinergics and antimuscarinics] and spasmolytics
Atropine
Homatropine
Hyoscine [scopolamine]
Quaternary ammonium derivatives
EXCLUDES *papaverine (972.5)*

971.2 Sympathomimetics [adrenergics]
Epinephrine [adrenalin]
Levarterenol [noradrenalin]

971.3 Sympatholytics [antiadrenergics]
Phenoxybenzamine
Tolazolinehydrochloride

971.9 Unspecified drug primarily affecting autonomic nervous system

✓4th 972 Poisoning by agents primarily affecting the cardiovascular system

972.0 Cardiac rhythm regulators
Practolol
Procainamide
Propranolol
Quinidine
EXCLUDES *lidocaine (968.5)*

972.1 Cardiotonic glycosides and drugs of similar action
Digitalis glycosides
Digoxin
Strophanthins

972.2 Antilipemic and antiarteriosclerotic drugs
Clofibrate
Nicotinic acid derivatives

972.3 Ganglion-blocking agents
Pentamethonium bromide

972.4 Coronary vasodilators
Dipyridamole
Nitrates [nitroglycerin]
Nitrites

972.5 Other vasodilators
Cyclandelate
Diazoxide
Papaverine
EXCLUDES *nicotinic acid (972.2)*

972.6 Other antihypertensive agents
Clonidine
Guanethidine
Rauwolfia alkaloids
Reserpine

972.7 Antivaricose drugs, including sclerosing agents
Sodium morrhuate
Zinc salts

972.8 Capillary-active drugs
Adrenochrome derivatives
Metaraminol

972.9 Other and unspecified agents primarily affecting the cardiovascular system

973 Poisoning by agents primarily affecting the gastrointestinal system

973.0 Antacids and antigastric secretion drugs
Aluminum hydroxide
Magnesium trisilicate

973.1 Irritant cathartics
Bisacodyl
Castor oil
Phenolphthalein

973.2 Emollient cathartics
Dioctyl sulfosuccinates

973.3 Other cathartics, including intestinal atonia drugs
Magnesium sulfate

973.4 Digestants
Pancreatin
Papain
Pepsin

973.5 Antidiarrheal drugs
Kaolin
Pectin
EXCLUDES *anti-infectives (960.0-961.9)*

973.6 Emetics

973.8 Other specified agents primarily affecting the gastrointestinal system

973.9 Unspecified agent primarily affecting the gastrointestinal system

974 Poisoning by water, mineral, and uric acid metabolism drugs

974.0 Mercurial diuretics
Chlormerodrin
Mercaptomerin
Mersalyl

974.1 Purine derivative diuretics
Theobromine
Theophylline
EXCLUDES *aminophylline [theophylline ethylenediamine] (975.7)*
caffeine (969.7)

974.2 Carbonic acid anhydrase inhibitors
Acetazolamide

974.3 Saluretics
Benzothiadiazides
Chlorothiazide group

974.4 Other diuretics
Ethacrynic acid
Furosemide

974.5 Electrolytic, caloric, and water-balance agents

974.6 Other mineral salts, not elsewhere classified

974.7 Uric acid metabolism drugs
Allopurinol
Colchicine
Probenecid

975 Poisoning by agents primarily acting on the smooth and skeletal muscles and respiratory system

975.0 Oxytocic agents
Ergot alkaloids
Oxytocin
Prostaglandins

975.1 Smooth muscle relaxants
Adiphenine
Metaproterenol [orciprenaline]
EXCLUDES *papaverine (972.5)*

975.2 Skeletal muscle relaxants

975.3 Other and unspecified drugs acting on muscles

975.4 Antitussives
Dextromethorphan
Pipazethate

975.5 Expectorants
Acetylcysteine
Guaifenesin
Terpin hydrate

975.6 Anti-common cold drugs

975.7 Antiasthmatics
Aminophylline [theophylline ethylenediamine]

975.8 Other and unspecified respiratory drugs

976 Poisoning by agents primarily affecting skin and mucous membrane, ophthalmological, otorhinolaryngological, and dental drugs

976.0 Local anti-infectives and anti-inflammatory drugs

976.1 Antipruritics

976.2 Local astringents and local detergents

976.3 Emollients, demulcents, and protectants

976.4 Keratolytics, keratoplastics, other hair treatment drugs and preparations

976.5 Eye anti-infectives and other eye drugs
Idoxuridine

976.6 Anti-infectives and other drugs and preparations for ear, nose, and throat

976.7 Dental drugs topically applied
EXCLUDES *anti-infectives (976.0)*
local anesthetics (968.5)

976.8 Other agents primarily affecting skin and mucous membrane
Spermicides [vaginal contraceptives]

976.9 Unspecified agent primarily affecting skin and mucous membrane

977 Poisoning by other and unspecified drugs and medicinal substances

977.0 Dietetics
Central appetite depressants

977.1 Lipotropic drugs

977.2 Antidotes and chelating agents, not elsewhere classified

977.3 Alcohol deterrents

977.4 Pharmaceutical excipients
Pharmaceutical adjuncts

977.8 Other specified drugs and medicinal substances
Contrast media used for diagnostic x-ray procedures
Diagnostic agents and kits

977.9 Unspecified drug or medicinal substance

978 Poisoning by bacterial vaccines

978.0 BCG

978.1 Typhoid and paratyphoid

978.2 Cholera

978.3 Plague

978.4 Tetanus

978.5 Diphtheria

978.6 Pertussis vaccine, including combinations with a pertussis component

978.8 Other and unspecified bacterial vaccines

978.9 Mixed bacterial vaccines, except combinations with a pertussis component

979 Poisoning by other vaccines and biological substances
EXCLUDES *gamma globulin (964.6)*

979.0 Smallpox vaccine

979.1 Rabies vaccine

979.2 Typhus vaccine

979.3 Yellow fever vaccine

979.4 Measles vaccine

979.5 Poliomyelitis vaccine

979.6 Other and unspecified viral and rickettsial vaccines
Mumps vaccine

979.7 Mixed viral-rickettsial and bacterial vaccines, except combinations with a pertussis component
EXCLUDES *combinations with a pertussis component (978.6)*

979.9 Other and unspecified vaccines and biological substances

TOXIC EFFECTS OF SUBSTANCES CHIEFLY NONMEDICINAL AS TO SOURCE (980-989)

Use additional code to specify the nature of the toxic effect

EXCLUDES *burns from chemical agents (ingested) (947.0-947.9)*
localized toxic effects indexed elsewhere (001.0-799.9)
respiratory conditions due to external agents (506.0-508.9)

✓4th **980 Toxic effect of alcohol**

980.0 Ethyl alcohol
Denatured alcohol Grain alcohol
Ethanol

Use additional code to identify any associated:
acute alcohol intoxication (305.0)
in alcoholism (303.0)
drunkenness (simple) (305.0)
pathological (291.4)

980.1 Methyl alcohol
Methanol
Wood alcohol

980.2 Isopropyl alcohol
Dimethyl carbinol
Isopropanol
Rubbing alcohol

980.3 Fusel oil
Alcohol:
amyl
butyl
propyl

980.8 Other specified alcohols

980.9 Unspecified alcohol

981 Toxic effect of petroleum products
Benzine
Gasoline
Kerosene
Paraffin wax
Petroleum:
ether
naphtha
spirit

✓4th **982 Toxic effect of solvents other than petroleum-based**

982.0 Benzene and homologues

982.1 Carbon tetrachloride

982.2 Carbon disulfide
Carbon bisulfide

982.3 Other chlorinated hydrocarbon solvents
Tetrachloroethylene
Trichloroethylene
EXCLUDES *chlorinated hydrocarbon preparations other than solvents (989.2)*

982.4 Nitroglycol

982.8 Other nonpetroleum-based solvents
Acetone

✓4th **983 Toxic effect of corrosive aromatics, acids, and caustic alkalis**

983.0 Corrosive aromatics
Carbolic acid or phenol
Cresol

983.1 Acids
Acid:
hydrochloric
nitric
sulfuric

983.2 Caustic alkalis
Lye
Potassium hydroxide
Sodium hydroxide

983.9 Caustic, unspecified

✓4th **984 Toxic effect of lead and its compounds (including fumes)**
INCLUDES that from all sources except medicinal substances

984.0 Inorganic lead compounds
Lead dioxide
Lead salts

984.1 Organic lead compounds
Lead acetate
Tetraethyl lead

984.8 Other lead compounds

984.9 Unspecified lead compound

✓4th **985 Toxic effect of other metals**
INCLUDES that from all sources except medicinal substances

985.0 Mercury and its compounds
Minamata disease

985.1 Arsenic and its compounds

985.2 Manganese and its compounds

985.3 Beryllium and its compounds

985.4 Antimony and its compounds

985.5 Cadmium and its compounds

985.6 Chromium

985.8 Other specified metals
Brass fumes
Copper salts
Iron compounds
Nickel compounds

985.9 Unspecified metal

986 Toxic effect of carbon monoxide
Carbon monoxide from any source

✓4th **987 Toxic effect of other gases, fumes, or vapors**

987.0 Liquefied petroleum gases
Butane
Propane

987.1 Other hydrocarbon gas

987.2 Nitrogen oxides
Nitrogen dioxide
Nitrous fumes

987.3 Sulfur dioxide

987.4 Freon
Dichloromonofluoromethane

987.5 Lacrimogenic gas
Bromobenzyl cyanide
Chloroacetophenone
Ethyliodoacetate

987.6 Chlorine gas

987.7 Hydrocyanic acid gas

987.8 Other specified gases, fumes, or vapors
Phosgene
Polyester fumes

987.9 Unspecified gas, fume, or vapor

✓4th **988 Toxic effect of noxious substances eaten as food**

EXCLUDES *allergic reaction to food, such as:*
gastroenteritis (558.3)
rash (692.5, 693.1)
food poisoning (bacterial) (005.0-005.9)
toxic effects of food contaminants, such as:
aflatoxin and other mycotoxin (989.7)
mercury (985.0)

988.0 Fish and shellfish

988.1 Mushrooms

988.2 Berries and other plants

988.8 Other specified noxious substances eaten as food

988.9 Unspecified noxious substance eaten as food

✓4th **989 Toxic effect of other substances, chiefly nonmedicinal as to source**

989.0 Hydrocyanic acid and cyanides
Potassium cyanide
Sodium cyanide
EXCLUDES *gas and fumes (987.7)*

989.1 Strychnine and salts

989.2 Chlorinated hydrocarbons
Aldrin
Chlordane
DDT
Dieldrin
EXCLUDES *chlorinated hydrocarbon solvents (982.0-982.3)*

989.3 Organophosphate and carbamate
Carbaryl
Dichlorvos
Malathion
Parathion
Phorate
Phosdrin

989.4 Other pesticides, not elsewhere classified
Mixtures of insecticides

989.5 Venom
Bites of venomous snakes, lizards, and spiders
Tick paralysis

989.6 Soaps and detergents

989.7 Aflatoxin and other mycotoxin [food contaminants]

✓5th **989.8 Other substances, chiefly nonmedicinal as to source**

989.81 Asbestos
EXCLUDES *asbestosis (501)*
exposure to asbestos (V15.84)

989.82 Latex

989.83 Silicone
EXCLUDES *silicone used in medical devices, implants and grafts (996.00-996.79)*

989.84 Tobacco

989.89 Other

989.9 Unspecified substance, chiefly nonmedicinal as to source

OTHER AND UNSPECIFIED EFFECTS OF EXTERNAL CAUSES (990-995)

990 Effects of radiation, unspecified
Complication of:
phototherapy
radiation therapy
Radiation sickness
EXCLUDES *specified adverse effects of radiation. Such conditions are to be classified according to the nature of the adverse effect, as:*
burns (940.0-949.5)
dermatitis (692.7-692.8)
leukemia (204.0-208.9)
pneumonia (508.0)
sunburn (692.71, 692.76-692.77)
[The type of radiation giving rise to the adverse effect may be identified by use of the E codes.]

✓4th **991 Effects of reduced temperature**

991.0 Frostbite of face

991.1 Frostbite of hand

991.2 Frostbite of foot

991.3 Frostbite of other and unspecified sites

991.4 Immersion foot
Trench foot
DEF: Paresthesia, edema, blotchy cyanosis of foot, the skin is soft (macerated), pale and wrinkled, and the sole is swollen with surface ridging and following sustained immersion in water.

991.5 Chilblains
Erythema pernio
Perniosis
DEF: Red, swollen, itchy skin; follows damp cold exposure; also associated with pruritus and a burning feeling, in hands, feet, ears, and face in children, legs and toes in women, and hands and fingers in men.

991.6 Hypothermia
Hypothermia (accidental)
EXCLUDES *hypothermia following anesthesia (995.89)*
hypothermia not associated with low environmental temperature (780.65)
DEF: Reduced body temperature due to low environmental temperatures.

991.8 Other specified effects of reduced temperature

991.9 Unspecified effect of reduced temperature
Effects of freezing or excessive cold NOS

✓4th **992 Effects of heat and light**
EXCLUDES *burns (940.0-949.5)*
diseases of sweat glands due to heat (705.0-705.9)
malignant hyperpyrexia following anesthesia (995.86)
sunburn (692.71, 692.76-692.77)

992.0 Heat stroke and sunstroke
Heat apoplexy
Heat pyrexia
Ictus solaris
Siriasis
Thermoplegia
DEF: Headache, vertigo, cramps and elevated body temperature due to high environmental temperatures.

992.1 Heat syncope
Heat collapse

992.2 Heat cramps

992.3 Heat exhaustion, anhydrotic
Heat prostration due to water depletion
EXCLUDES *that associated with salt depletion (992.4)*

992.4 Heat exhaustion due to salt depletion
Heat prostration due to salt (and water) depletion

992.5 Heat exhaustion, unspecified
Heat prostration NOS

992.6 Heat fatigue, transient

992.7 Heat edema
DEF: Fluid retention due to high environmental temperatures.

992.8 Other specified heat effects

992.9 Unspecified

✓4th **993 Effects of air pressure**

993.0 Barotrauma, otitic
Aero-otitis media
Effects of high altitude on ears
DEF: Ringing ears, deafness, pain and vertigo due to air pressure changes.

993.1 Barotrauma, sinus
Aerosinusitis
Effects of high altitude on sinuses

993.2 Other and unspecified effects of high altitude
Alpine sickness
Andes disease
Anoxia due to high altitude
Hypobaropathy
Mountain sickness

993.3 Caisson disease
Bends
Compressed-air disease
Decompression sickness
Divers' palsy or paralysis
DEF: Rapid reduction in air pressure while breathing compressed air; symptoms include skin lesions, joint pains, respiratory and neurological problems.

993.4 Effects of air pressure caused by explosion

993.8 Other specified effects of air pressure

993.9 Unspecified effect of air pressure

✓4th **994 Effects of other external causes**
EXCLUDES *certain adverse effects not elsewhere classified (995.0-995.8)*

994.0 Effects of lightning
Shock from lightning
Struck by lightning NOS
EXCLUDES *burns (940.0-949.5)*

994.1 Drowning and nonfatal submersion
Bathing cramp
Immersion

994.2 Effects of hunger
Deprivation of food
Starvation

994.3 Effects of thirst
Deprivation of water

994.4 Exhaustion due to exposure

994.5 Exhaustion due to excessive exertion
Exhaustion due to overexertion

994.6 Motion sickness
Air sickness
Seasickness
Travel sickness

994.7 Asphyxiation and strangulation
Suffocation (by):
bedclothes
cave-in
constriction
mechanical
plastic bag
pressure
strangulation
EXCLUDES *asphyxia from:*
carbon monoxide (986)
inhalation of food or foreign body (932-934.9)
other gases, fumes, and vapors (987.0-987.9)

994.8 Electrocution and nonfatal effects of electric current
Shock from electric current
Shock from electroshock gun (taser)
EXCLUDES *electric burns (940.0-949.5)*

994.9 Other effects of external causes
Effects of:
abnormal gravitational [G] forces or states
weightlessness

✓4th **995 Certain adverse effects not elsewhere classified**
EXCLUDES *complications of surgical and medical care (996.0-999.9)*

995.0 Other anaphylactic shock
Allergic shock, Anaphylactic reaction, Anaphylaxis — NOS or due to adverse effect of correct medicinal substance properly administered

Use additional E code to identify external cause, such as:
adverse effects of correct medicinal substance properly administered [E930-E949]
EXCLUDES *anaphylactic reaction to serum (999.4)*
anaphylactic shock due to adverse food reaction (995.60-995.69)
DEF: Immediate sensitivity response after exposure to specific antigen; results in life-threatening respiratory distress; usually followed by vascular collapse, shock, urticaria, angioedema and pruritus.

995.1 Angioneurotic edema
Giant urticaria
EXCLUDES *urticaria:*
due to serum (999.5)
other specified (698.2, 708.0-708.9, 757.33)
DEF: Circulatory response of deep dermis, subcutaneous or submucosal tissues; causes localized edema and wheals.

✓5th **995.2 Other and unspecified adverse effect of drug, medicinal and biological substance**
Adverse effect, Allergic reaction, Hypersensitivity, Idiosyncrasy — (due) to correct medicinal substance properly administered

Drug:
hypersensitivity NOS
reaction NOS
EXCLUDES *pathological drug intoxication (292.2)*

995.20 Unspecified adverse effect of unspecified drug, medicinal and biological substance

995.21 Arthus phenomenon
Arthus reaction

995.22 Unspecified adverse effect of anesthesia

995.23 Unspecified adverse effect of insulin

995.27 Other drug allergy
Drug allergy NOS
Drug hypersensitivity NOS

995.29 Unspecified adverse effect of other drug,medicinal and biological substance

995.3 Allergy, unspecified
Allergic reaction NOS
Hypersensitivity NOS
Idiosyncrasy NOS
EXCLUDES *allergic reaction NOS to correct medicinal substance properly administered (995.27)*
allergy to existing dental restorative materials (525.66)
specific types of allergic reaction, such as:
allergic diarrhea (558.3)
dermatitis (691.0-693.9)
hayfever (477.0-477.9)

995.4 Shock due to anesthesia
Shock due to anesthesia in which the correct substance was properly administered
EXCLUDES *complications of anesthesia in labor or delivery (668.0-668.9)*
overdose or wrong substance given (968.0-969.9)
postoperative shock NOS (998.0)
specified adverse effects of anesthesia classified elsewhere, such as:
anoxic brain damage (348.1)
hepatitis (070.0-070.9), etc.
unspecified adverse effect of anesthesia (995.22)

Continuum of Illness Due to Infection

Bacteremia → Septicemia → Sepsis → Severe Sepsis → Severe Sepsis with Septic Shock → MODS (Multiple Organ Dysfunction Syndrome) → Death

995.5 Child maltreatment syndrome

Use additional code(s), if applicable, to identify any associated injuries

Use additional E code to identify:
- nature of abuse (E960-E968)
- perpetrator (E967.0-E967.9)

995.50 Child abuse, unspecified

995.51 Child emotional/psychological abuse

995.52 Child neglect (nutritional)

995.53 Child sexual abuse

995.54 Child physical abuse

Battered baby or child syndrome

EXCLUDES *shaken infant syndrome (995.55)*

995.55 Shaken infant syndrome

Use additional code(s) to identify any associated injuries

995.59 Other child abuse and neglect

Multiple forms of abuse

995.6 Anaphylactic shock due to adverse food reaction

Anaphylactic reaction due to food
Anaphylactic shock due to nonpoisonous foods

995.60 Due to unspecified food

995.61 Due to peanuts

995.62 Due to crustaceans

995.63 Due to fruits and vegetables

995.64 Due to tree nuts and seeds

995.65 Due to fish

995.66 Due to food additives

995.67 Due to milk products

995.68 Due to eggs

995.69 Due to other specified food

995.7 Other adverse food reactions, not elsewhere classified

Use additional code to identify the type of reaction, such as:
- hives (708.0)
- wheezing (786.07)

EXCLUDES *anaphylactic shock due to adverse food reaction (995.60-995.69)*
asthma (493.0, 493.9)
dermatitis due to food (693.1)
in contact with skin (692.5)
gastroenteritis and colitis due to food (558.3)
rhinitis due to food (477.1)

995.8 Other specified adverse effects, not elsewhere classified

995.80 Adult maltreatment, unspecified

Abused person NOS

Use additional code to identify:
- any associated injury
- perpetrator (E967.0-E967.9)

995.81 Adult physical abuse

Battered:
- person syndrome NEC
- man
- spouse
- woman

Use additional code to identify:
- any association injury
- nature of abuse (E960-E968)
- perpetrator (E967.0-E967.9)

995.82 Adult emotional/psychological abuse

Use additional E code to identify perpetrator (E967.0-E967.9)

995.83 Adult sexual abuse

Use additional code(s) to identify:
- any associated injury
- perpetrator (E967.0-E967.9)

995.84 Adult neglect (nutritional)

Use additional code(s) to identify:
- intent of neglect (E904.0, E968.4)
- perpetrator (E967.0-E967.9)

995.85 Other adult abuse and neglect

Multiple forms of abuse and neglect

Use additional code(s) to identify
- any associated injury
- intent of neglect (E904.0, E968.4)
- nature of abuse (E960-E968)
- perpetrator (E967.0-E967.9)

995.86 Malignant hyperthermia

Malignant hyperpyrexia due to anesthesia

995.89 Other

Hypothermia due to anesthesia

995.9 Systemic inflammatory response syndrome (SIRS)

DEF: Clinical response to infection or trauma that can trigger an acute inflammatory reaction and progresses to coagulation, impaired fibrinolysis, and organ failure; manifested by two or more of the following symptoms: fever, tachycardia, tachypnea, leukocytosis or leukopenia.

995.90 Systemic inflammatory response syndrome, unspecified

SIRS NOS

995.91 Sepsis

Systemic inflammatory response syndrome due to infectious process without acute organ dysfunction

Code first underlying infection

EXCLUDES *sepsis with acute organ dysfunction (995.92)*
sepsis with multiple organ dysfunction (995.92)
severe sepsis (995.92)

995.92 Severe sepsis

Sepsis with acute organ dysfunction
Sepsis with multiple organ dysfunction (MOD)
Systemic inflammatory response syndrome due to infectious process with acute organ dysfunction

Code first underlying infection

Use additional code to specify acute organ dysfunction, such as:
- acute renal failure (584.5-584.9)
- acute respiratory failure (518.81)
- critical illness myopathy (359.81)
- critical illness polyneuropathy (357.82)
- disseminated intravascular coagulopathy [DIC] (286.6)
- encephalopathy (348.31)
- hepatic failure (570)
- septic shock (785.52)

995.93 Systemic inflammatory response syndrome due to noninfectious process without acute organ dysfunction

Code first underlying conditions, such as:
acute pancreatitis (577.0)
trauma

EXCLUDES *systemic inflammatory response syndrome due to noninfectious process with acute organ dysfunction (995.94)*

995.94 Systemic inflammatory response syndrome due to noninfectious process with acute organ dysfunction

Code first underlying conditions, such as:
acute pancreatitis (577.0)
trauma

Use additional code to specify acute organ dysfunction, such as:
acute renal failure (584.5-584.9)
acute respiratory failure (518.81)
critical illness myopathy (359.81)
critical illness polyneuropathy (357.82)
disseminated intravascular coagulopathy [DIC] syndrome (286.6)
encephalopathy (348.31)
hepatic failure (570)

EXCLUDES *severe sepsis (995.92)*

COMPLICATIONS OF SURGICAL AND MEDICAL CARE, NOT ELSEWHERE CLASSIFIED (996-999)

EXCLUDES *adverse effects of medicinal agents (001.0-799.9, 995.0-995.8)*
burns from local applications and irradiation (940.0-949.5)
complications of:
conditions for which the procedure was performed
surgical procedures during abortion, labor, and delivery (630-676.9)
poisoning and toxic effects of drugs and chemicals (960.0-989.9)
postoperative conditions in which no complications are present, such as:
artificial opening status (V44.0-V44.9)
closure of external stoma (V55.0-V55.9)
fitting of prosthetic device (V52.0-V52.9)
specified complications classified elsewhere
anesthetic shock (995.4)
electrolyte imbalance (276.0-276.9)
postlaminectomy syndrome (722.80-722.83)
postmastectomy lymphedema syndrome (457.0)
postoperative psychosis (293.0-293.9)
any other condition classified elsewhere in the Alphabetic Index when described as due to a procedure

✓4th **996 Complications peculiar to certain specified procedures**

INCLUDES complications, not elsewhere classified, in the use of artificial substitutes [e.g., Dacron, metal, Silastic, Teflon] or natural sources [e.g., bone] involving:
anastomosis (internal)
graft (bypass) (patch)
implant
internal device:
catheter
electronic
fixation
prosthetic
reimplant
transplant

EXCLUDES *accidental puncture or laceration during procedure (998.2)*
capsular contracture of breast implant (611.83)
complications of internal anastomosis of:
gastrointestinal tract (997.4)
urinary tract (997.5)
endosseous dental implant failures (525.71-525.79)
intraoperative floppy iris syndrome [IFIS] (364.81)
mechanical complication of respirator (V46.14)
other specified complications classified elsewhere, such as:
hemolytic anemia (283.1)
functional cardiac disturbances (429.4)
serum hepatitis (070.2-070.3)

✓5th **996.0 Mechanical complication of cardiac device, implant, and graft**

Breakdown (mechanical)
Displacement
Leakage
Obstruction, mechanical
Perforation
Protrusion

996.00 Unspecified device, implant, and graft

996.01 Due to cardiac pacemaker (electrode)

996.02 Due to heart valve prosthesis

996.03 Due to coronary bypass graft

EXCLUDES *atherosclerosis of graft (414.02, 414.03)*
embolism [occlusion NOS] [thrombus] of graft (996.72)

996.04 Due to automatic implantable cardiac defibrillator

996.09 Other

996.1 Mechanical complication of other vascular device, implant, and graft

Mechanical complications involving:
aortic (bifurcation) graft (replacement)
arteriovenous:
dialysis catheter, fistula, shunt — surgically created
balloon (counterpulsation) device, intra-aortic
carotid artery bypass graft
femoral-popliteal bypass graft
umbrella device, vena cava

EXCLUDES *atherosclerosis of biological graft (440.30-440.32)*
embolism [occlusion NOS] [thrombus] of (biological) (synthetic) graft (996.74)
peritoneal dialysis catheter (996.56)

996.2 Mechanical complication of nervous system device, implant, and graft

Mechanical complications involving:
dorsal column stimulator
electrodes implanted in brain [brain "pacemaker"]
peripheral nerve graft
ventricular (communicating) shunt

✓5th **996.3 Mechanical complication of genitourinary device, implant, and graft**

996.30 Unspecified device, implant, and graft

996.31 Due to urethral [indwelling] catheter

996.32 Due to intrauterine contraceptive device

996.39 Other

Cystostomy catheter
Prosthetic reconstruction of vas deferens
Repair (graft) of ureter without mention of resection

EXCLUDES *complications due to:*
external stoma of urinary tract (997.5)
internal anastomosis of urinary tract (997.5)

✓5th **996.4 Mechanical complication of internal orthopedic device, implant, and graft**

Mechanical complications involving:
external (fixation) device utilizing internal screw(s), pin(s) or other methods of fixation
grafts of bone, cartilage, muscle, or tendon
internal (fixation) device such as nail, plate, rod, etc.

Use additional code to identify prosthetic joint with mechanical complication (V43.60-V43.69)

EXCLUDES *complications of external orthopedic device, such as:*
pressure ulcer due to cast (707.00-707.09)

996.40 Unspecified mechanical complication of internal orthopedic device, implant, and graft

996.41 Mechanical loosening of prosthetic joint

Aseptic loosening

996.42 Dislocation of prosthetic joint

Instability of prosthetic joint
Subluxation of prosthetic joint

996.43 Prosthetic joint implant failure

Breakage (fracture) of prosthetic joint

996.44 Peri-prosthetic fracture around prosthetic joint

996.45 Peri-prosthetic osteolysis

Use additional code to identify major osseous defect, if applicable (731.3)

996.46 Articular bearing surface wear of prosthetic joint

996.47 Other mechanical complication of prosthetic joint implant

Mechanical complication of prosthetic joint NOS

996.49 Other mechanical complication of other internal orthopedic device, implant, and graft

Breakage of internal fixation device in bone
Dislocation of internal fixation device in bone

EXCLUDES *mechanical complication of prosthetic joint implant (996.41-996.47)*

✓5th **996.5 Mechanical complication of other specified prosthetic device, implant, and graft**

Mechanical complications involving:
prosthetic implant in:
bile duct
breast
chin
orbit of eye
nonabsorbable surgical material NOS
other graft, implant, and internal device, not elsewhere classified

996.51 Due to corneal graft

996.52 Due to graft of other tissue, not elsewhere classified

Skin graft failure or rejection

EXCLUDES *failure of artificial skin graft (996.55)*
failure of decellularized allodermis (996.55)
sloughing of temporary skin allografts or xenografts (pigskin) — omit code

996.53 Due to ocular lens prosthesis

EXCLUDES *contact lenses — code to condition*

996.54 Due to breast prosthesis

Breast capsule (prosthesis)
Mammary implant

996.55 Due to artificial skin graft and decellularized allodermis

Dislodgement
Displacement
Failure
Non-adherence
Poor incorporation
Shearing

996.56 Due to peritoneal dialysis catheter

EXCLUDES *mechanical complication of arteriovenous dialysis catheter*

996.57 Due to insulin pump

996.59 Due to other implant and internal device, not elsewhere classified

Nonabsorbable surgical material NOS
Prosthetic implant in:
bile duct
chin
orbit of eye

✓5th **996.6 Infection and inflammatory reaction due to internal prosthetic device, implant, and graft**

Infection (causing obstruction), Inflammation } due to (presence of) any device, implant, and graft classifiable to 996.0-996.5

Use additional code to identify specified infections

996.60 Due to unspecified device, implant, and graft

996.61 Due to cardiac device, implant, and graft

Cardiac pacemaker or defibrillator:
electrode(s), lead(s)
pulse generator
subcutaneous pocket
Coronary artery bypass graft
Heart valve prosthesis

996.62 Due to other vascular device, implant, and graft

Arterial graft
Arteriovenous fistula or shunt
Infusion pump
Vascular catheter (arterial) (dialysis) (peripheral venous)

EXCLUDES *infection due to:*
central venous catheter (999.31)
Hickman catheter (999.31)
peripherally inserted central catheter [PICC] (999.31)
portacath (port-a-cath) (999.31)
triple lumen catheter (999.31)
umbilical venous catheter (999.31)

996.63 Due to nervous system device, implant, and graft

Electrodes implanted in brain
Peripheral nerve graft
Spinal canal catheter
Ventricular (communicating) shunt (catheter)

996.64 Due to indwelling urinary catheter
Use additional code to identify specified infections, such as:
Cystitis (595.0-595.9)
Sepsis (038.0-038.9)

996.65 Due to other genitourinary device, implant, and graft
Intrauterine contraceptive device

996.66 Due to internal joint prosthesis
Use additional code to identify infected prosthetic joint (V43.60-V43.69)

996.67 Due to other internal orthopedic device, implant, and graft
Bone growth stimulator (electrode)
Internal fixation device (pin) (rod) (screw)

996.68 Due to peritoneal dialysis catheter
Exit-site infection or inflammation

996.69 Due to other internal prostheticdevice, implant, and graft
Breast prosthesis
Ocular lens prosthesis
Prosthetic orbital implant

✓5th **996.7 Other complications of internal (biological) (synthetic) prosthetic device, implant, and graft**

Complication NOS, Occlusion NOS, Embolism, Fibrosis, Hemorrhage, Pain, Stenosis, Thrombus — due to (presence of) any device, implant, and graft classifiable to 996.0-996.5

Use additional code to identify complication, such as:
pain due to presence of device, implant or graft (338.18-338.19, 338.28-338.29)

EXCLUDES *disruption (dehiscence) of internal suture material (998.31)*
transplant rejection (996.8)

996.70 Due to unspecified device, implant, and graft

996.71 Due to heart valve prosthesis

996.72 Due to other cardiac device, implant, and graft
Cardiac pacemaker or defibrillator:
electrode(s), lead(s)
subcutaneous pocket
Coronary artery bypass (graft)
EXCLUDES *occlusion due to atherosclerosis (414.02-414.06)*

996.73 Due to renal dialysis device, implant, and graft

996.74 Due to other vascular device, implant, and graft
EXCLUDES *occlusion of biological graft due to atherosclerosis (440.30-440.32)*

996.75 Due to nervous system device, implant, and graft

996.76 Due to genitourinary device, implant, and graft

996.77 Due to internal joint prosthesis
Use additional code to identify prosthetic joint (V43.60-V43.69)

996.78 Due to other internal orthopedic device, implant, and graft

996.79 Due to other internal prosthetic device, implant, and graft

✓5th **996.8 Complications of transplanted organ**
Transplant failure or rejection
Use additional code to identify nature of complication, such as:
cytomegalovirus (CMV) infection (078.5)
graft-versus-host disease (279.50-279.53)
malignancy associated with organ transplant (199.2)
post-transplant lymphoproliferative disorder (PTLD) (238.77)

996.80 Transplanted organ, unspecified

996.81 Kidney

996.82 Liver

996.83 Heart

996.84 Lung

996.85 Bone marrow

996.86 Pancreas

996.87 Intestine

996.89 Other specified transplanted organ

✓5th **996.9 Complications of reattached extremity or body part**

996.90 Unspecified extremity

996.91 Forearm

996.92 Hand

996.93 Finger(s)

996.94 Upper extremity, other and unspecified

996.95 Foot and toe(s)

996.96 Lower extremity, other and unspecified

996.99 Other specified body part

✓4th **997 Complications affecting specified body systems, not elsewhere classified**
Use additional code to identify complications
EXCLUDES *the listed conditions when specified as:*
causing shock (998.0)
complications of:
anesthesia:
adverse effect (001.0-799.9, 995.0-995.8)
in labor or delivery (668.0-668.9)
poisoning (968.0-969.9)
implanted device or graft (996.0-996.9)
obstetrical procedures (669.0-669.4)
reattached extremity (996.90-996.96)
transplanted organ (996.80-996.89)

✓5th **997.0 Nervous system complications**

997.00 Nervous system complication, unspecified

997.01 Central nervous system complication
Anoxic brain damage
Cerebral hypoxia
EXCLUDES *cerebrovascular hemorrhage or infarction (997.02)*

997.02 Iatrogenic cerebrovascular infarction or hemorrhage
Postoperative stroke

997.09 Other nervous system complications

997.1 Cardiac complications

Cardiac: arrest, insufficiency; Cardiorespiratory failure; Heart failure — during or resulting from a procedure

EXCLUDES *the listed conditions as long-term effects of cardiac surgery or due to the presence of cardiac prosthetic device (429.4)*

997.2 Peripheral vascular complications

Phlebitis or thrombophlebitis during or resulting from a procedure

EXCLUDES *the listed conditions due to:*
implant or catheter device (996.62)
infusion, perfusion, or transfusion (999.2)
complications affecting blood vessels (997.71-997.79)

✓5th **997.3 Respiratory complications**

EXCLUDES *iatrogenic [postoperative] pneumothorax (512.1)*
iatrogenic pulmonary embolism (415.11)
Mendelson's syndrome in labor and delivery (668.0)
specified complications classified elsewhere, such as:
adult respiratory distress syndrome (518.5)
pulmonary edema, postoperative (518.4)
respiratory insufficiency, acute, postoperative (518.5)
shock lung (518.5)
tracheostomy complications (519.00-519.09)
transfusion related acute lung injury [TRALI] (518.7)

997.31 Ventilator associated pneumonia

Use additional code to identify organism

997.39 Other respiratory complications

Mendelson's syndrome resulting from a procedure
Pneumonia (aspiration) resulting from a procedure

DEF: Mendelson's syndrome: acid pneumonitis due to aspiration of gastric acids, may occur after anesthesia or sedation.

997.4 Digestive system complications

Complications of:
intestinal (internal) anastomosis and bypass, not elsewhere classified, except that involving urinary tract

Hepatic failure
Hepatorenal syndrome
Intestinal obstruction NOS
} specified as due to a procedure

EXCLUDES *gastrostomy complications (536.40-536.49)*
specified gastrointestinal complications classified elsewhere, such as:
blind loop syndrome (579.2)
colostomy and enterostomy complications (569.60-569.69)
gastrojejunal ulcer (534.0-534.9)
infection of esophagostomy (530.86)
infection of external stoma (569.61)
mechanical complication of esophagostomy (530.87)
pelvic peritoneal adhesions, female (614.6)
peritoneal adhesions (568.0)
peritoneal adhesions with obstruction (560.81)
postcholecystectomy syndrome (576.0)
postgastric surgery syndromes (564.2)
vomiting following gastrointestinal surgery (564.3)

997.5 Urinary complications

Complications of:
external stoma of urinary tract
internal anastomosis and bypass of urinary tract, including that involving intestinal tract

Oliguria or anuria
Renal:
failure (acute)
insufficiency (acute)
Tubular necrosis (acute)
} specified as due to procedure

EXCLUDES *specified complications classified elsewhere, such as:*
postoperative stricture of:
ureter (593.3)
urethra (598.2)

✓5th **997.6 Amputation stump complication**

EXCLUDES *admission for treatment for a current traumatic amputation – code to complicated traumatic amputation*
phantom limb (syndrome) (353.6)

997.60 Unspecified complication

997.61 Neuroma of amputation stump

DEF: Hyperplasia generated nerve cell mass following amputation.

997.62 Infection (chronic)

Use additional code to identify the organism

997.69 Other

✓5th **997.7 Vascular complications of other vessels**

EXCLUDES *peripheral vascular complications (997.2)*

997.71 Vascular complications of mesenteric artery

997.72 Vascular complications of renal artery

997.79 Vascular complications of other vessels

✓5th **997.9 Complications affecting other specified body systems, not elsewhere classified**

EXCLUDES *specified complications classified elsewhere, such as:*
broad ligament laceration syndrome (620.6)
postartificial menopause syndrome (627.4)
postoperative stricture of vagina (623.2)

997.91 Hypertension

EXCLUDES *essential hypertension (401.0-401.9)*

997.99 Other

Vitreous touch syndrome

DEF: Vitreous touch syndrome: vitreous protruding through pupil and attaches to corneal epithelium; causes aqueous fluid in vitreous body; marked by corneal edema, loss of lucidity; complication of cataract surgery.

✓4th **998 Other complications of procedures, not elsewhere classified**

998.0 Postoperative shock

Collapse NOS
Shock (endotoxic)
(hypovolemic septic)
} during or resulting from a surgical procedure

EXCLUDES *shock:*
anaphylactic due to serum (999.4)
anesthetic (995.4)
electric (994.8)
following abortion (639.5)
obstetric (669.1)
traumatic (958.4)

✓5th **998.1 Hemorrhage or hematoma or seroma complicating a procedure**

EXCLUDES *hemorrhage, hematoma, or seroma:*
complicating cesarean section or puerperal perineal wound (674.3)
due to implanted device or graft (996.70-996.79)

998.11 Hemorrhage complicating a procedure

998.12 Hematoma complicating a procedure

998.13 Seroma complicating a procedure

998.2 Accidental puncture or laceration during a procedure

Accidental perforation by catheter or other instrument during a procedure on:
blood vessel
nerve
organ

EXCLUDES *iatrogenic [postoperative] pneumothorax (512.1)*
puncture or laceration caused by implanted device intentionally left in operation wound (996.0-996.5)
specified complications classified elsewhere, such as:
broad ligament laceration syndrome (620.6)
dural tear (349.31)
incidental durotomy (349.31)
trauma from instruments during delivery (664.0-665.9)

✓5th **998.3 Disruption of wound**

Dehiscence } of operation wound
Rupture }

Disruption of any suture materials or other closure method

EXCLUDES *disruption of:*
cesarean wound (674.1)
perineal wound, puerperal (674.2)

998.30 Disruption of wound, unspecified

Disruption of wound NOS

998.31 Disruption of internal operation (surgical) wound

Disruption or dehiscence of closure of:
fascia, superficial or muscular
internal organ
muscle or muscle flap
ribs or rib cage
skull or craniotomy
sternum or sternotomy
tendon or ligament

Deep disruption or dehiscence of operation wound NOS

EXCLUDES *complications of internal anastomosis of:*
gastrointestinal tract (997.4)
urinary tract (997.5)

998.32 Disruption of external operation (surgical) wound

Disruption of operation wound NOS
Disruption or dehiscence of closure of:
cornea
mucosa
skin
subcutaneous tissue
Full-thickness skin disruption or dehiscence
Superficial disruption or dehiscence of operation wound

998.33 Disruption of traumatic injury wound repair

Disruption or dehiscence of closure of traumatic laceration (external) (internal)

998.4 Foreign body accidentally left during a procedure

Adhesions } due to foreign body accidentally left in operative wound or body cavity during a procedure
Obstruction }
Perforation }

EXCLUDES *obstruction or perforation caused by implanted device intentionally left in body (996.0-996.5)*

✓5th **998.5 Postoperative infection**

EXCLUDES *bleb associated endophthalmitis (379.63)*
infection due to:
implanted device (996.60-996.69)
infusion, perfusion, or transfusion (999.31-999.39)
postoperative obstetrical wound infection (674.3)

998.51 Infected postoperative seroma

Use additional code to identify organism

998.59 Other postoperative infection

Abscess: } postoperative
intra-abdominal
stitch
subphrenic
wound
Septicemia

Use additional code to identify infection

998.6 Persistent postoperative fistula

998.7 Acute reaction to foreign substance accidentally left during a procedure

Peritonitis:
aseptic
chemical

✓5th **998.8 Other specified complications of procedures, not elsewhere classified**

998.81 Emphysema (subcutaneous) (surgical) resulting from a procedure

998.82 Cataract fragments in eye following cataract surgery

998.83 Non-healing surgical wound

998.89 Other specified complications

998.9 Unspecified complication of procedure, not elsewhere classified

Postoperative complication NOS

EXCLUDES *complication NOS of obstetrical, surgery or procedure (669.4)*

999 Complications of medical care, not elsewhere classified

INCLUDES complications, not elsewhere classified, of:
dialysis (hemodialysis) (peritoneal) (renal)
extracorporeal circulation
hyperalimentation therapy
immunization
infusion
inhalation therapy
injection
inoculation
perfusion
transfusion
vaccination
ventilation therapy

Use additional code, where applicable, to identify specific complication

EXCLUDES *specified complications classified elsewhere such as:*
complications of implanted device (996.0-996.9)
contact dermatitis due to drugs (692.3)
dementia dialysis (294.8)
transient (293.9)
dialysis disequilibrium syndrome (276.0-276.9)
poisoning and toxic effects of drugs and chemicals (960.0-989.9)
postvaccinal encephalitis (323.51)
water and electrolyte imbalance (276.0-276.9)

999.0 Generalized vaccinia

EXCLUDES *vaccinia not from vaccine (051.02)*

DEF: Skin eruption, self-limiting; follows vaccination; due to transient viremia with virus localized in skin.

999.1 Air embolism

Air embolism to any site following infusion, perfusion, or transfusion

EXCLUDES *embolism specified as:*
complicating:
abortion (634-638 with .6, 639.6)
ectopic or molar pregnancy (639.6)
pregnancy, childbirth, or the puerperium (673.0)
due to implanted device (996.7)
traumatic (958.0)

999.2 Other vascular complications

Phlebitis, Thromboembolism, Thrombophlebitis } following infusion, perfusion, or transfusion

EXCLUDES *extravasation of vesicant drugs (999.81, 999.82)*
the listed conditions when specified as:
due to implanted device (996.61-996.62. 996.72-996.74)
postoperative NOS (997.2, 997.71-997.79)

999.3 Other infection

Infection, Sepsis, Septicemia } following infusion, injection, transfusion, or vaccination

Use additional code to identify the specified infection, such as:
septicemia (038.0-038.9)

EXCLUDES *the listed conditions when specified as:*
due to implanted device (996.60-996.69)
postoperative NOS (998.51-998.59)

998.30 Disruption of wound, unspecified

Disruption of wound NOS

999.31 Infection due to central venouscatheter

Catheter-related bloodstream infection (CRBSI]) NOS
Infection due to:
Hickman catheter
peripherally inserted central catheter (PICC])
portacath (port-a-cath)
triple lumen catheter
umbilical venous catheter

EXCLUDES *infection due to:*
arterial catheter (996.62)
catheter NOS (996.69)
peripheral venous catheter (996.62)
urinary catheter (996.64)

999.39 Infection following other infusion, injection, transfusion, or vaccination

999.4 Anaphylactic shock due to serum

Anaphylactic reaction due to serum

EXCLUDES *shock:*
allergic NOS (995.0)
anaphylactic:
NOS (995.0)
due to drugs and chemicals (995.0)

DEF: Life-threatening hypersensitivity to foreign serum; causes respiratory distress, vascular collapse, and shock.

999.5 Other serum reaction

Intoxication by serum
Protein sickness
Serum rash
Serum sickness
Urticaria due to serum

EXCLUDES *serum hepatitis (070.2-070.3)*

DEF: Serum sickness: Hypersensitivity to foreign serum; causes fever, hives, swelling, and lymphadenopathy.

999.6 ABO incompatibility reaction

Incompatible blood transfusion
Reaction to blood group incompatibility in infusion or transfusion

999.7 Rh incompatibility reaction

Elevation of Rh titer
Reactions due to Rh factor in infusion or transfusion

999.8 Other infusion and transfusion reaction

EXCLUDES *postoperative shock (998.0)*
transfusion related acute lung injury [TRALI] (518.7)

999.81 Extravasation of vesicant chemotherapy

Infiltration of vesicant chemotherapy

999.82 Extravasation of other vesicant agent

Infiltration of other vesicant agent

999.88 Other infusion reaction

999.89 Other transfusion reaction

Transfusion reaction NOS

Use additional code to identify graft-versus-host reaction (279.5)

999.9 Other and unspecified complications of medical care, not elsewhere classified

Complications, not elsewhere classified, of:
electroshock, inhalation, ultrasound, ventilation } therapy

Unspecified misadventure of medical care

EXCLUDES *unspecified complication of:*
phototherapy (990)
radiation therapy (999)
ventilator associated pneumonia (997.31)

V Codes: Supplementary Classification of Factors Influencing Health Status and Contact with Health Service (V01–V89)

This chapter classifies the following situations that are not classifiable to categories 001–999, specifically:

- Encounters for health services
- Problems influencing a person's health status
- Facts needed for statistical tabulations

The encounter V codes are used to record a visit or classify a patient who is not acutely ill but needs a health service for a specific purpose, such as prophylactic immunization, routine examination, or counseling. These V codes are not procedures codes. If a procedure is performed as a result of the encounter, then an appropriate procedure code must be assigned.

Example:

> Patient encounter for the purpose of receiving prophylactic tetanus immunization is coded as V03.7 Need for prophylactic vaccination and inoculation, tetanus toxoid alone.

The problem V codes describe circumstances that influence the person's health status but are not a current illness or injury, such as a colostomy status or a past history of mental illness. Except in rare cases, the problem V codes are not reported as a principal diagnosis, nor do they stand alone. They do not describe the reason for the encounter, but rather provide an item of information about the state of the patient. These V codes are used only when the circumstance influences the patient's current condition or treatment.

Example:

> Patient has a history of stomach cancer and the purpose of the encounter is screening; findings are negative. Assign codes V76.49 Special screening for malignant neoplasm and V10.04 Personal history of malignant neoplasm of the stomach.

Other V codes may provide supplementary information that is important to record but is not representative of a problem or service.

V codes are used in both inpatient and outpatient settings. V codes for encounters are more appropriate for outpatient and physician office visits.

PERSONS WITH POTENTIAL HEALTH HAZARDS RELATED TO COMMUNICABLE DISEASES (V01–V06)

This subchapter contains service and problem V codes and is especially applicable for ambulatory care settings, including the emergency department. Encounters for vaccination, isolation, and prophylactic surgery are classified here.

Encounters for contact or exposure to communicable diseases (V01) are to be used for patients who do not exhibit any signs or symptoms of the disease.

Carriers or suspected carriers of infectious disease are classified to V02. This V code provides supplementary information about the patient that may affect the course of or outcome of treatment.

Categories V03–V06 classify encounters for the reason of inoculation or vaccination as a prophylactic measure.

PERSONS WITH NEED FOR ISOLATION, OTHER POTENTIAL HEALTH HAZARDS AND PROPHYLACTIC MEASURES (V07-V09)

Encounters for the reasons of isolation and other prophylactic measures are classified to V07. This category includes isolation, desentitization to allergens, postmenopausal hormone replacement therapy, and prophylactic fluoride treatments.

Code V08, asymptomatic human immunodeficiency virus (HIV) infection status, is used for patients who have the HIV virus (i.e., have tested positive) but have not ever manifested signs or symptoms of the disease.

Infection with drug-resistant micro-organism, V09, is used to indicate that a patient has a form of infection resistant to drugs.

PERSONS WITH POTENTIAL HEALTH HAZARDS RELATED TO PERSONAL AND FAMILY HISTORY (V10–V19)

Categories V10–V19 contain personal and family history codes. Personal history codes include a history of neoplasms, mental disorders, diseases, and allergies. Family history codes include a history of neoplasms and diseases. Personal history codes are often reported to indicate the need for adjunctive surgery and treatment; family history codes are often used to indicate the need for prophylactic surgery and treatment. Family history codes are frequently used with screening codes to justify a test or procedure. This range of codes should be used as secondary codes if the historical condition or family history has an impact on current care or influences treatment.

PERSONS ENCOUNTERING HEALTH SERVICES IN CIRCUMSTANCES RELATED TO REPRODUCTION AND DEVELOPMENT (V20–V29)

This subchapter contains codes to indicate supervision of uncomplicated pregnancy and perceived problems which, after evaluation, are determined to be normal states in development (e.g., onset of menses, teething). Codes to report outcome of delivery on the mother's record (used in addition to codes from the obstetric section of ICD-9-CM) also are included here.

Category V40–V49 codes are used to describe circumstances other than a disease or an injury that influences a patient's health status. These codes describe the residual of a past disease or a condition that in some way affects the way the patient's treatment is carried out. The status codes are different from the history codes in that a history code indicates that the patient no longer has the disease. These codes should be used when the condition is documented as a diagnosis or problem.

Supervision of high-risk pregnancy (V23) is used for pregnancy with a history of conditions classifiable to 634–638. Habitual aborter is coded 646.3x.

Code V28 Antenatal screening, should be used only if no specific condition is found to exist during the screening process. Code the condition, not the screening, if one is discovered.

Code V29 Observation and evaluation of newborns for suspected condition not found, should be sequenced second after V30 Live born infant.

LIVEBORN INFANTS ACCORDING TO TYPE OF BIRTH (V30–V39)

This section contains codes for the principal diagnosis for an infant and describes the type of birth, single or multiple. These codes are used in the inpatient setting for most patients (fourth digit 0) but may be used for those born before admission (fourth digit 1) or not admitted to the hospital (fourth digit 2). The fifth digit identifies whether the delivery was vaginal (0) or cesarean (1).

PERSONS WITH A CONDITION INFLUENCING THEIR HEALTH STATUS (V40–V49)

Category V40–V49 codes are used to describe circumstances other than a disease or an injury that influences a patient's health status. These codes describe the residual of a past disease or a condition that in some way affects the way the patient's treatment is carried out. The status codes are different from the history codes in that a history code indicates that the patient no longer has the disease. These codes should be used when the condition is documented as a diagnosis or problem.

PERSONS ENCOUNTERING HEALTH SERVICES FOR SPECIFIC PROCEDURES AND AFTERCARE (V50–V59)

This subchapter contains codes to indicate reasons for care in patients who have already been treated for some disease or injury, but may need aftercare or adjunctive treatment to consolidate the treatment, deal with residual states, or prevent recurrence.

Encounters for plastic surgery are classified in two ways: procedures used for cosmetic surgery for conditions that are normal variations rather than the result of pathological states and procedures for the residual conditions of a healed injury or operation.

Also classified here are encounters for services such as chemotherapy, radiotherapy, rehabilitation and physical therapy, fittings and adjustments of devices, orthopedic aftercare, and dialysis.

The subdivision of this section includes the following categories:

PERSONS ENCOUNTERING HEALTH SERVICES IN OTHER CIRCUMSTANCES (V60–V69)

Category V60–V68 codes contain additional information that must be included in the medical record regarding family, household, administrative, follow-up, and psychosocial circumstances. Included in this section is category V64 *Persons encountering health services for specific procedures, not carried out.* Code sequencing depends on the reason the procedure was not performed.

EXAMINATION AND INVESTIGATION OF INDIVIDUALS AND POPULATIONS (V70–V82)

This subchapter contains codes to represent encounters with health services for general physical and mental examinations, routine tests on specific body systems and screenings. The special screening codes are used only when screening procedures are done on defined population groups.

These V codes are especially applicable for ambulatory care settings as well as emergency departments and are largely beyond the scope of office settings.

GENETICS (V83–V84)

Category V83 codes are used to report genetic carrier status. The codes are mainly used for women who are pregnant or are considering pregnancy and are known carriers of a disease. The codes listed are for asymptomatic carriers except for V83.02, which is for carriers of hemophilia A, who have trouble with blood coagulation. Category V84 reports genetic susceptibility to disease. Having a genetic susceptibility to a disease, in particular a malignancy, is not the same as being a carrier of a disease that may be passed on to offspring. Those people who are genetically susceptibility is a red flag a person is at higher risk and has a greater chance of getting a disease or malignant growth because of their inborn predisposition. These patients sometimes request to have the particular organ at risk removed prophylactically in the hope that taking such a step will prevent the disease from occurring. Most of these requests are for prophylactic breast or ovary removal. A V code for genetic susceptibility to a disease (V84) is assigned only after positive confirmation through genetic testing.

BODY MASS INDEX (V85)

BMI is measured in kilograms per meters squared. The calculation is based on height and weight determined by dividing a person's weight in kilograms by height in meters squared. The index score can also be calculated by multiplying a patient's weight in kilograms by 704.5, and dividing the result by the patient's height in inches twice. BMI measurements are a guideline for categorizing weight in a more specific manner than relying solely on "overweight" or "obese" terminology. By definition, an adult is generally considered overweight if he or she has a BMI between 25 and 29.9 kg/m2. Obesity is defined as a BMI of 30 or higher. Individual variances such as the presence or absence of muscle mass and the distribution of body fat also need to be taken into consideration. BMI pediatric codes are to be used for persons aged 2 to 20 years only. The percentiles specified above are based on growth charts published by the Centers for Disease Control and Prevention (CDC).

ESTROGEN RECEPTOR STATUS (V86)

In breast cancer, the hormone receptor status of the cells is a useful tool for determining treatment and prognosis. Cancers in which the cells express estrogen receptor (ER) in their nuclei generally have a better prognosis, since these cells are better differentiated and can respond to hormonal manipulation. According to the National Cancer Institute, seven out of 10 breast cancer patients have ER-positive tumors.

OTHER SPECIFIED PERSONAL EXPOSURES AND HISTORY PRESENTING HAZARDS TO HEALTH (V87)

Patients may be initially asymptomatic following exposures to drugs, chemicals, and other substances, but develop subsequent health concerns as a result. For example, individuals such as firefighters, hair stylists, truck drivers, and textile workers may have more exposure to certain chemicals and dyes, such as benzenes or aromatic amines, and are therefore at higher risk of developing adverse effects of these exposures for which they may seek medical care. These adverse effects may include medical problems that persist for months or years after treatment ends. Some therapeutic drug therapies for the treatment of cancer may result in infertility, growth problems in children, or cancer treatment-related fatigue.

ACQUIRED ABSENCE OF OTHER ORGANS AND TISSUE (V88)

Category V88 codes classify the acquired absence of cervix or uterus. Women who have had a full hysterectomy no longer need cervical Pap smears, but they do require vaginal smears to test for vaginal malignancies. Women with a cervical stump following a hysterectomy still require cervical Pap smears. These codes assist in supporting medical necessity of Pap smears for this population of patients.

OTHER SUSPECTED CONDITIONS NOT FOUND (V89)

Pregnant patients may be referred to maternal-fetal specialists for further detailed diagnostic tests when an initial prenatal screening test indicates a possible abnormality. However, in many cases the detailed exam shows no abnormality and the suspected condition is ruled out. Category V89 codes help support the medical necessity of tests and encounters for the purpose of ruling out suspected conditions that would require a higher level of care.

SEQUENCING OF V CODES

The first list is that of V codes that are only acceptable as first listed. The second list is that of V codes that may only be used as additional codes. All other V codes are sequenced according to the circumstances of the health care encounter.

These V code designations apply to outpatient coding only. Many of the primary and secondary use designations are in conflict with inpatient coding edits.

V codes in the following categories/subcategories/subclassifications are accepted only as first-listed codes:

V20	Health supervision of infant or child
V22.0	Supervision of normal first pregnancy
V22.1	Supervision of other normal pregnancy
V24	Postpartum care and examination
V26.81	Encounter for assisted reproductive fertility procedure cycle.
V30–V39	Liveborn infants according to type of birth
V46.12	Encounter for respirator dependence during power failure
V46.13	Encounter for weaning from respirator [ventilator]
V51.0	Encounter for breast reconstruction following mastectomy
V56.0	Extracorporeal dialysis
V57	Care involving use of rehabilitation procedures
V58.0	Radiotherapy
V58.11	Encounter for antineoplastic chemotherapy
	V58.0 and V58.11 may be used together on a record with either one being sequenced first, when the patient receives both chemotherapy and radiation therapy during the same session.
V58.12	Encounter for antineoplastic immunotherapy
V59	Donors
V66	Convalescence and palliative care
	EXCEPT V66.7 Palliative care
V68	Encounters for administrative purposes
V70	General medical examination
	EXCEPT V70.7 Examination of participant in clinical trial
V71	Observation and evaluation for suspected conditions not found

V codes in the following categories/subcategories/subclassifications are accepted only as additional codes, not first-listed or principal diagnosis codes:

V07.4	Hormone replacement therapy (postmenopausal)
V07.5	Prophylactic use of agents affecting estrogen receptors and estrogen levels
V09	Infection with drug resistant organism
V13.61	Personal history of hypospadias
V14	Personal history of allergy to medicinal agent
V15	Other personal history resenting health hazard,
	EXCEPT V15.7 Contraception and V15.88 History of fall
V21	Constitutional sates in development
V22.2	Pregnancy state, incidental
V26.5	Sterilization status
V27	Outcome of delivery
V42	Organ or tissue replaced by transplant
V43	Organ or tissue replaced by other means
	EXCEPT V43.22 Fully implantable artificial heart status
V44	Artificial opening status
V45	Other postsurgical states
	EXCEPT subcategory V45.7 Acquired absence of organ
V46.0	Other dependence on machines, aspirator
V46.11	Dependence on respirator, status
V46.2	Other dependence on machines, supplemental oxygen
V46.3	Wheelchair dependence
V46.8	Other dependence on machines
V49.82	Dental sealant status
V49.83	Awaiting organ transplant status
V49.85	Dual sensory impairment
V58.6	Long term (current) drug use
V60	Housing, household, and economic circumstances
V62	Other psychosocial circumstances
V64	Persons encountering health services for specified procedure, not carried out
V66.7	Palliative care
V84	Genetic susceptibility to disease
V85	Body mass index
V86	Estrogen receptor status
V87.4	Personal history of drug therapy
V88.0	Acquired absence of cervix and uterus

SUPPLEMENTARY CLASSIFICATION OF FACTORS INFLUENCING HEALTH STATUS AND CONTACT WITH HEALTH SERVICES (V01-V89)

This classification is provided to deal with occasions when circumstances other than a disease or injury classifiable to categories 001-999 (the main part of ICD) are recorded as "diagnoses" or "problems." This can arise mainly in three ways:

a) When a person who is not currently sick encounters the health services for some specific purpose, such as to act as a donor of an organ or tissue, to receive prophylactic vaccination, or to discuss a problem which is in itself not a disease or injury. This will be a fairly rare occurrence among hospital inpatients, but will be relatively more common among hospital outpatients and patients of family practitioners, health clinics, etc.

b) When a person with a known disease or injury, whether it is current or resolving, encounters the health care system for a specific treatment of that disease or injury (e.g., dialysis for renal disease; chemotherapy for malignancy; cast change).

c) When some circumstance or problem is present which influences the person's health status but is not in itself a current illness or injury. Such factors may be elicited during population surveys, when the person may or may not be currently sick, or be recorded as an additional factor to be borne in mind when the person is receiving care for some current illness or injury classifiable to categories 001-999.

In the latter circumstances the V code should be used only as a supplementary code and should not be the one selected for use in primary, single cause tabulations. Examples of these circumstances are a personal history of certain diseases, or a person with an artificial heart valve in situ.

PERSONS WITH POTENTIAL HEALTH HAZARDS RELATED TO COMMUNICABLE DISEASES (V01-V06)

EXCLUDES *family history of infectious and parasitic diseases (V18.8)*
personal history of infectious and parasitic diseases (V12.0)

✓4th **V01 Contact with or exposure to communicable diseases**

V01.0 Cholera
Conditions classifiable to 001

V01.1 Tuberculosis
Conditions classifiable to 010-018

V01.2 Poliomyelitis
Conditions classifiable to 045

V01.3 Smallpox
Conditions classifiable to 050

V01.4 Rubella
Conditions classifiable to 056

V01.5 Rabies
Conditions classifiable to 071

V01.6 Venereal diseases
Conditions classifiable to 090-099

✓5th **V01.7 Other viral diseases**
Conditions classifiable to 042-078 and V08, except as above

V01.71 Varicella

V01.79 Other viral diseases

✓5th **V01.8 Other communicable diseases**
Conditions classifiable to 001-136, except as above

V01.81 Anthrax

V01.82 Exposure to SARS-associated coronavirus

V01.83 Escherichia coli (E. coli)

V01.84 Meningococcus

V01.89 Other communicable diseases

V01.9 Unspecified communicable diseases

✓4th **V02 Carrier or suspected carrier of infectious diseases**

INCLUDES colonization status

V02.0 Cholera

V02.1 Typhoid

V02.2 Amebiasis

V02.3 Other gastrointestinal pathogens

V02.4 Diphtheria

✓5th **V02.5 Other specified bacterial diseases**

V02.51 Group B streptococcus

V02.52 Other streptococcus

V02.53 Methicillin susceptible Staphylococcus aureus
MSSA colonization

V02.54 Methicillin resistant Staphylococcus aureus
MRSA colonization

V02.59 Other specified bacterial diseases
Meningococcal
Staphylococcal

✓5th **V02.6 Viral hepatitis**
Hepatitis Australian-antigen [HAA] [SH] carrier
Serum hepatitis carrier

V02.60 Viral hepatitis carrier, unspecfied

V02.61 Hepatitis B carrier

V02.62 Hepatitis C carrier

V02.69 Other viral hepatitis carrier

V02.7 Gonorrhea

V02.8 Other venereal diseases

V02.9 Other specified infectious organism

✓4th **V03 Need for prophylactic vaccination and inoculation against bacterial diseases**

EXCLUDES *vaccination not carried out (V64.00-V64.09)*
vaccines against combinations of diseases (V06.0-V06.9)

V03.0 Cholera alone

V03.1 Typhoid-paratyphoid alone [TAB]

V03.2 Tuberculosis [BCG]

V03.3 Plague

V03.4 Tularemia

V03.5 Diphtheria alone

V03.6 Pertussis alone

V03.7 Tetanus toxoid alone

✓5th **V03.8 Other specified vaccinations against single bacterial diseases**

V03.81 Hemophilus influenza, type B [Hib]

V03.82 Streptococcus pneumoniae [pneumococcus]

V03.89 Other specified vaccination

V03.9 Unspecified single bacterial disease

✓4th **V04 Need for prophylactic vaccination and inoculation against certain viral diseases**

EXCLUDES *vaccines against combinations of diseases (V06.0-V06.9)*

V04.0 Poliomyelitis

V04.1 Smallpox

V04.2 Measles alone

V04.3 Rubella alone

V04.4 Yellow fever

V04.5 Rabies

V04.6 Mumps alone

V04.7 Common cold

✓5th **V04.8 Other viral diseases**

V04.81 Influenza

V04.82 Respiratory syncytial virus (RSV)

V04.89 Other viral diseases

V05 Need for other prophylactic vaccination and inoculation against single diseases

EXCLUDES *vaccines against combinations of diseases (V06.0-V06.9)*

V05.0 Athropod-borne viral encephalitis

V05.1 Other arthropod-borne viral diseases

V05.2 Leshmaniasis

V05.3 Viral hepatitis

V05.4 Varicella

Chickenpox

V05.8 Other specified disease

V05.9 Unspecified single disease

V06 Need for prophylactic vaccination and inoculation against combinations of diseases

Note: Use additional single vaccination codes from categories V03-V05 to identify any vaccinations not included in a combination code.

V06.0 Cholera with typhoid-paratyphoid [cholera+TAB]

V06.1 Diphtheia-tetanus-pertussis, combined [DTP] [DTaP]

V06.2 Diphtheria-tetanus-pertussis with typhoid-paratyphoid [DTP+TAB]

V06.3 Diphtheria-tetanus-pertussis with poliomyelitis [DTP+polio]

V06.4 Measles-mumps-rubella [MMR]

V06.5 Tetanus-diphtheria [Td] [DT]

V06.6 Streptococcus pneumoniae [pneumococcus] and influenza

V06.8 Other combinations

EXCLUDES *multiple single vaccination codes (V03.0-V05.9)*

V06.9 Unspecified combined vaccine

PERSONS WITH NEED FOR ISOLATION, OTHER POTENTIAL HEALTH HAZARDS AND PROPHYLACTIC MEASURES (V07-V09)

V07 Need for isolation and other prophylactic measures

EXCLUDES *prophylactic organ removal (V50.41-V50.49)*

V07.0 Isolation

Admission to protect the individual from his surroundings or for isolation of individual after contact with infectious diseases

V07.1 Desensitization to allergens

V07.2 Prophylactic immunotherapy

Administration of:
- antivenin
- immune sera [gamma globulin]
- RhoGAM
- tetanus antitoxin

V07.3 Other prophylactic chemotherapy

V07.31 Prophylactic fluoride administration

V07.39 Other prophylactic chemotherapy

EXCLUDES *maintenance chemotherapy following disease (V58.11)*

V07.4 Hormone replacement therapy (postmenopausal)

V07.5 Prophylactic use of agents affecting estrogen receptors and estrogen levels

Code first, if applicable:
- malignant neoplasm of breast (174.0-174.9, 175.0-175.9)
- malignant neoplasm of prostate (185)

Use additional code, if applicable, to identify:
- estrogen receptor positive status (V86.0)
- family history of breast cancer (V16.3)
- genetic susceptibility to cancer (V84.01-V84.09)
- personal history of breast cancer (V10.3)
- personal history of prostate cancer (V10.46)
- postmenopausal status (V49.81)

EXCLUDES *hormone replacement therapy (postmenopausal) (V07.4)*

V07.51 Prophylactic use of selective estrogen receptor modulators [SERMs]

Prophylactic use of:
- raloxifene (Evista)
- tamoxifen (Nolvadex)
- toremifene (Fareston)

V07.52 Prophylactic use of aromatase inhibitors

Prophylactic use of:
- anastrozole (Arimidex)
- exemestane (Aromasin)
- letrozole (Femara)

V07.59 Prophylactic use of other agents affecting estrogen receptors and estrogen levels

Prophylactic use of:
- estrogen receptor downregulators
- fulvestrant (Faslodex)
- gonadotropin-releasing hormone (GnRH) agonist
- goserelin acetate (Zoladex)
- leuprolide acetate (leuprorelin) (Lupron)
- megestrol acetate (Megace)

V07.8 Other specified prophylactic measure

V07.9 Unspecified prophylactic measure

V08 Asymptomatic human immunodeficiency virus [HIV] infection status

HIV positive NOS

Note: This code is only to be used when no HIV infection symptoms or conditions are present. If any HIV infec-tion symptoms or conditions are present, see code 042.

EXCLUDES *AIDS (042)*
human immunodeficiency virus [HIV] disease (042)
exposure to HIV (V01.79)
nonspecific serologic evidence of HIV (795.71)
symptomatic human immunodeficiency virus [HIV] infection (042)

V09 Infection with drug-resistant microorganisms

Note: This category is intended for use as an additional code for infectious conditions classified elsewhere to indicate the presence of drug-resistance of the infectious organism.

V09.0 Infection with microorganisms resistant to penicillins

V09.1 Infection with microorganisms resistant to cephalosporins and other B-lactam antibiotics

V09.2 Infection with microorganisms resistant to macrolides

V09.3 Infection with microorganisms resistant to tetracyclines

V09.4 Infection with microorganisms resistant to aminoglycosides

V09.5 Infection with microorganisms resistant to quinolones and fluoroquinolones

V09.50 Without mention of resistance to multiple quinolones and fluoroquinoles

V09.51 With resistance to multiple quinolones and fluoroquinoles

V09.6 Infection with microorganisms resistant to sulfonamides

✓5th **V09.7 Infection with microorganisms resistant to other specified antimycobacterial agents**

EXCLUDES *Amikacin (V09.4)*
Kanamycin (V09.4)
Streptomycin [SM] (V09.4)

V09.70 Without mention of resistance to multiple antimycobacterial agents

V09.71 With resistance to multiple antimycobacterial agents

✓5th **V09.8 Infection with microorganisms resistant to other specified drugs**

Vancomycin (glycopeptide) intermediate staphylococcus aureus (VISA/GISA)
Vancomycin (glycopeptide) resistant enterococcus (VRE)
Vancomycin (glycopeptide) resistant staphylococcus aureus (VRSA/GRSA)

V09.80 Without mention of resistance to multiple drugs

V09.81 With resistance to multiple drugs

✓5th **V09.9 Infection with drug-resistant microorganisms, unspecified**

Drug resistance, NOS

V09.90 Without mention of multiple drug resistance

V09.91 With multiple drug resistance

Multiple drug resistance NOS

PERSONS WITH POTENTIAL HEALTH HAZARDS RELATED TO PERSONAL AND FAMILY HISTORY (V10-V19)

EXCLUDES *obstetric patients where the possibility that the fetus might be affected is the reason for observation or management during pregnancy (655.0-655.9)*

✓4th **V10 Personal history of malignant neoplasm**

Code first any continuing functional activity, such as: carcinoid syndrome (259.2)

✓5th **V10.0 Gastrointestinal tract**

History of conditions classifiable to 140-159

V10.00 Gastrointestinal tract, unspecified

V10.01 Tongue

V10.02 Other and unspecified oral cavity and pharynx

V10.03 Esophagus

V10.04 Stomach

V10.05 Large Intestine

V10.06 Rectum, rectosigmoid junction, and anus

V10.07 Liver

V10.09 Other

✓5th **V10.1 Trachea, bronchus, and lung**

History of conditions classifiable to 162

V10.11 Bronchus and lung

V10.12 Trachea

✓5th **V10.2 Other respiratory and intrathoracic organs**

History of conditions classifiable to 160, 161, 163-165

V10.20 Respiratory organ, unspecified

V10.21 Larynx

V10.22 Nasal cavities, middle ear, and accessory sinuses

V10.29 Other

V10.3 Breast

History of conditions classifiable to 174 and 175

✓5th **V10.4 Genital organs**

History of conditions classifiable to 179-187

V10.40 Female genital organ, unspecfied

V10.41 Cervix uteri

V10.42 Other parts of uterus

V10.43 Ovary

V10.44 Other female genital organs

V10.45 Male genital organ, unspecfied

V10.46 Prostate

V10.47 Testis

V10.48 Epididymis

V10.49 Other male genital organs

✓5th **V10.5 Urinary organs**

History of conditions classifiable to 188 and 189

V10.50 Urinary organ, unspecified

V10.51 Bladder

V10.52 Kidney

EXCLUDES *renal pelvis (V10.53)*

V10.53 Renal pelvis

V10.59 Other

✓5th **V10.6 Leukemia**

Conditions classifiable to 204-208

EXCLUDES *leukemia in remission (204-208)*

V10.60 Leukemia, unspecified

V10.61 Lymphoid leukemia

V10.62 Myeloid leukemia

V10.63 Monocytic leukemia

V10.69 Other

✓5th **V10.7 Other lymphatic and hematopoietic neoplasms**

Conditions classifiable to 200-203

EXCLUDES *listed conditions in 200-203 in remission*

V10.71 Lymphosarcoma and reticulosarcoma

V10.72 Hodgkin's disease

V10.79 Other

✓5th **V10.8 Personal history of malignant neoplasm of other sites**

History of conditions classifiable to 170-173, 190-195

V10.81 Bone

V10.82 Malignant melanoma of skin

V10.83 Other malignant neoplasm of skin

V10.84 Eye

V10.85 Brain

V10.86 Other parts of the nervous system

EXCLUDES *peripheral sympathetic, and parasympathetic nerves (V10.89)*

V10.87 Thyroid

V10.88 Other endocrine glands and related structures

V10.89 Other

V10.9 Unspecified personal history of malignant neoplasm

✓4th **V11 Personal history of mental disorder**

V11.0 Schizophrenia

EXCLUDES *that in remission (295.0-295.9 with fifth-digit 5)*

V11.1 Affective disorders

Personal history of manic-depressive psychosis

EXCLUDES *that in remission (296.0-296.6 with fifth-digit 5, 6)*

V11.2 Neurosis

V11.3 Alcoholism

V11.8 **Other mental disorders**

V11.9 **Unspecified mental disorder**

✓4th **V12 Personal history of certain other diseases**

✓5th **V12.0 Infectious and parasitic diseases**

EXCLUDES *personal history of infectious diseases specific to a body system*

V12.00 Unspecified infectious and parasitic disease

V12.01 Tuberculosis

V12.02 Poliomyelitis

V12.03 Malaria

V12.04 Methicillin resistant Staphylococcus aureus

MRSA

V12.09 Other

V12.1 Nutritional deficiency

V12.2 Endocrine, metabolic, and immunity disorders

EXCLUDES *history of allergy (V14.0-V14.9, V15.01-V15.09)*

V12.3 Diseases of blood and blood-forming organs

✓5th **V12.4 Disorders of nervous system and sense organs**

V12.40 Unspecified disorder of nervous system and sense organs

V12.41 Benign neoplasm of the brain

V12.42 Infections of the central nervous system

Encephalitis Meningitis

V12.49 Other disorders of nervous system and sense organs

✓5th **V12.5 Diseases of circulatory system**

EXCLUDES *old myocardial infarction (412)*
postmyocardial infarction syndrome (411.0)

V12.50 Unspecified circulatory disease

V12.51 Venous thrombosis and embolism

Pulmonary embolism

V12.52 Thrombophlebitis

V12.53 Sudden cardiac arrest

Sudden cardiac death successfully resuscitated

V12.54 Transient ischemic attack [TIA], and cerebral infarction without residual deficits

Prolonged reversible ischemic neurological deficit [PRIND]
Reversible ischemic neurologic deficit [RIND]
Stroke NOS without residual deficits

EXCLUDES *late effects of cerebrovascular disease (438.0-438.9)*

V12.59 Other

✓5th **V12.6 Diseases of respiratory system**

EXCLUDES *tuberculosis (V12.01)*

V12.60 Unspecified disease of respiratory system

V12.61 Pneumonia (recurrent)

V12.69 Other diseases of respiratory system

✓5th **V12.7 Diseases of digestive system**

V12.70 Unspecified digestive disease

V12.71 Peptic ulcer disease

V12.72 Colonic polyps

V12.79 Other

✓4th **V13 Personal history of other diseases**

✓5th **V13.0 Disorders of urinary system**

V13.00 Unspecified urinary disorder

V13.01 Urinary calculi

V13.02 Urinary (tract) infection

V13.03 Nephrotic syndrome

V13.09 Other

V13.1 Trophoblastic disease

EXCLUDES *supervision during a current pregnancy (V23.1)*

✓5th **V13.2 Other genital system and obstetric disorders**

EXCLUDES *habitual aborter (646.3)*
without current pregnancy (629.81)
supervision during a current pregnancy of a woman with poor obstetric history (V23.0-V23.9)

V13.21 Personal history of pre-term labor

EXCLUDES *current pregnancy with history of pre-term labor (V23.41)*

V13.22 Personal history of cervical dysplasia

Personal history of conditions classifiable to 622.10-622.12

EXCLUDES *personal history of malignant neoplasm of cervix uteri (V10.41)*

V13.29 Other genital system and obstetric disorders

V13.3 Diseases of skin and subcutaneous tissue

V13.4 Arthritis

✓5th **V13.5 Other musculoskeletal disorders**

V13.51 Pathologic fracture

Healed pathologic fracture

EXCLUDES *personal history of traumatic fracture (V15.51)*

V13.52 Stress fracture

Healed stress fracture

EXCLUDES *personal history of traumatic fracture (V15.51)*

V13.59 Other musculoskeletal disorders

✓5th **V13.6 Congenital malformations**

V13.61 Hypospadias

V13.69 Other congenital malformations

V13.7 Perinatal problems

EXCLUDES *low birth weight status (V21.30-V21.35)*

V13.8 Other specified diseases

V13.9 Unspecified disease

✓4th **V14 Personal history of allergy to medicinal agents**

V14.0 Penicillin

V14.1 Other antibiotic agent

V14.2 Sulfonamides

V14.3 Other anti-infective agent

V14.4 Anesthetic age

V14.5 Narcotic agent

V14.6 Analgesic agent

V14.7 Serum or vaccine

V14.8 Other specified medicinal agents

V14.9 Unspecified medicinal agent

✓4th **V15 Other personal history presenting hazards to health**

EXCLUDES *personal history of drug therapy (V87.41-V87.49)*

✓5th **V15.0 Allergy, other than to medicinal agents**

EXCLUDES *allergy to food substance used as base for medicinal agent (V14.0-V14.9)*

V15.01 Allergy to peanuts

V15.02 Allergy to milk products

EXCLUDES *lactose intolerance (271.3)*

V15.03 Allergy to eggs

V15.04 Allergy to seafood
Seafood (octopus) (squid) ink
Shellfish

V15.05 Allergy to other foods
Food additives
Nuts other than peanuts

V15.06 Allergy to insects
Bugs
Insect bites and stings
Spiders

V15.07 Allergy to latex
Latex sensitivity

V15.08 Allergy to radiographic dye
Contrast media used for diagnostic x-ray procedures

V15.09 Other allergy, other than to medicinal agents

V15.1 Surgery to heart and great vessels
EXCLUDES *replacement by transplant or other means (V42.1-V42.2, V43.2-V43.4)*

✓5th **V15.2 Surgery to other organs**
EXCLUDES *replacement by transplant or other means (V42.0-V43.8)*

V15.21 Personal history of undergoing in utero procedure during pregnancy

V15.22 Personal history of undergoing in utero procedure while a fetus

V15.29 Surgery to other organs

V15.3 Irradiation
Previous exposure to therapeutic or other ionizing radiation

✓5th **V15.4 Psychological trauma**
EXCLUDES *history of condition classifiable to 290-316 (V11.0-V11.9)*

V15.41 History of physical abuse
Rape

V15.42 History of emotional abuse
Neglect

V15.49 Other

✓5th **V15.5 Injury**

V15.51 Traumatic fracture
Healed traumatic fracture
EXCLUDES *personal history of pathologic and stress fracture (V13.51, V13.52)*

V15.59 Other injury

V15.6 Poisoning

V15.7 Contraception
EXCLUDES *current contraceptive management (V25.0-V25.4)*
presence of intrauterine contraceptive device as incidental finding (V45.5)

✓5th **V15.8 Other specified personal history presenting hazards to health**
EXCLUDES *contact with and (suspected) exposure to:*
aromatic compounds and dyes (V87.11-V87.19)
arsenic and other metals (V87.01-V87.09)
molds (V87.31)

V15.81 Noncompliance with medical treatment
EXCLUDES *noncompliance with renal dialysis (V45.12)*

V15.82 History of tobacco use
EXCLUDES *tobacco dependence (305.1)*

V15.84 Exposure to asbestos

V15.85 Exposure to potentially hazardous body fluids

V15.86 Exposure to lead

V15.87 History of extracorporeal membrane oxygenation [ECMO]

V15.88 History of fall
At risk for falling

V15.89 Other
EXCLUDES *contact with and (suspected) exposure to other potentially hazardous:*
chemicals (V87.2)
substances (V87.39)

V15.9 Unspecified personal history presenting hazards to health

✓4th **V16 Family history of malignant neoplasm**

V16.0 Gastrointestinal tract
Family history of condition classifiable to 140-159

V16.1 Trachea, bronchus, and lung
Family history of condition classifiable to 162

V16.2 Other respiratory and intrathoracic organs
Family history of condition classifiable to 160-161, 163-165

V16.3 Breast
Family history of condition classifiable to 174

✓5th **V16.4 Genital organs**
Family history of condition classifiable to 179-187

V16.40 Genital organ, unspecified

V16.41 Ovary

V16.42 Prostate

V16.43 Testis

V16.49 Other

✓5th **V16.5 Urinary organs**
Family history of condition classifiable to 188-189

V16.51 Kidney

V16.52 Bladder

V16.59 Other

V16.6 Leukemia
Family history of condition classifiable to 204-208

V16.7 Other lymphatic and hematopoietic neoplasms
Family history of condition classifiable to 200-203

V16.8 Other specified malignant neoplasm
Family history of other condition classifiable to 140-199

V16.9 Unspecified malignant neoplasm

✓4th **V17 Family history of certain chronic disabling diseases**

V17.0 Psychiatric condition
EXCLUDES *family history of mental retardation (V18.4)*

V17.1 Stroke (cerebrovascular)

V17.2 Other neurological diseases
Epilepsy
Huntington's chorea

V17.3 Ischemic heart disease

✓5th **V17.4 Other cardiovascular diseases**

V17.41 Family history of sudden cardiac death [SCD]
EXCLUDES *family history of ischemic heart disease (V17.3)*
family history of myocardial infarction (V17.3)

V17.49 Family history of other cardiovascular diseases
Family history of cardiovascular disease NOS

V17.5 Asthma

V17.6 Other chronic respiratory conditions

V17.7 Arthritis

✓5th **V17.8 Other musculoskeletal diseases**

V17.81 Osteoporosis

V17.89 Other musculoskeletal diseases

V18 Family history of certain other specific conditions

V18.0 Diabetes mellitus

V18.1 Other endocrine and metabolic diseases

V18.11 Multiple endocrine neoplasia [MEN] syndrome

V18.19 Other endocrine and metabolic diseases

V18.2 Anemia

V18.3 Other blood disorders

V18.4 Mental retardation

V18.5 Digestive disorders

V18.51 Colonic polyps

EXCLUDES *family history of malignant neoplasm of gastrointestinal tract (V16.0)*

V18.59 Other digestive disorders

V18.6 Kidney diseases

V18.61 Polycystic kidney

V18.69 Other kidney diseases

V18.7 Other genitourinary diseases

V18.8 Infectious and parasitic diseases

V18.9 Genetic disease carrier

V19 Family history of other conditions

V19.0 Blindness or visual loss

V19.1 Other eye disorders

V19.2 Deafness or hearing loss

V19.3 Other ear disorders

V19.4 Skin conditions

V19.5 Congenital anomalies

V19.6 Allergic disorders

V19.7 Consanguinity

V19.8 Other condition

PERSONS ENCOUNTERING HEALTH SERVICES IN CIRCUMSTANCES RELATED TO REPRODUCTION AND DEVELOPMENT (V20-V29)

V20 Health supervision of infant or child

V20.0 Foundling

V20.1 Other healthy infant or child receiving care

Medical or nursing care supervision of healthy infant in cases of:
- maternal illness, physical or psychiatric
- socioeconomic adverse condition at home
- too many children at home preventing or interfering with normal care

V20.2 Routine infant or child health check

Developmental testing of infant or child
Immunizations appropriate for age
Initial and subsequent routine newborn check
Routine vision and hearing testing
Use additional code(s) to identify:
- special screening examination(s) performed (V73.0-V82.9)

EXCLUDES *special screening for developmental handicaps (V79.3)*

V21 Constitutional states in development

V21.0 Period of rapid growth in childhood

V21.1 Puberty

V21.2 Other adolecsence

V21.3 Low birth weight status

EXCLUDES *history of perinatal problems*

V21.30 Low birth weight status, unspecified

V21.31 Low birth weight status, less than 500 grams

V21.32 Low birth weight status, 500-999 grams

V21.33 Low birth weight status, 1000-1499 grams

V21.34 Low birth weight status, 1500-1999 grams

V21.35 Low birth weight status, 2000-2500 grams

V21.8 Other specified constitutional states in development

V21.9 Unspecified constitutional state in development

V22 Normal pregnancy

EXCLUDES *pregnancy examination or test, pregnancy unconfirmed (V72.40)*

V22.0 Supervision of normal first pregnancy

V22.1 Supervision of other normal pregnancy

V22.2 Pregnant state, incidental

Pregnant state NOS

V23 Supervision of high-risk pregnancy

V23.0 Pregnancy with history of infertility

V23.1 Pregnancy with history of trophoblastic disease

Pregnancy with history of:
- hydatidiform mole
- vesicular mole

EXCLUDES *that without current pregnancy (V13.1)*

V23.2 Pregnancy with history of abortion

Pregnancy with history of conditions classifiable to 634-638

EXCLUDES *habitual aborter:*
- *care during pregnancy (646.3)*
- *that without current pregnancy (629.81)*

V23.3 Grand multiparity

EXCLUDES *care in relation to labor and delivery (659.4)*
that without current pregnancy (V61.5)

V23.4 Pregnancy with other poor obstetric history

Pregnancy with history of other conditions classifiable to 630-676

V23.41 Pregnancy with history of pre-term labor

V23.49 Pregnancy with other poor obstetric history

V23.5 Pregnancy with other poor reproductive history

Pregnancy with history of stillbirth or neonatal death

V23.7 Insufficient prenatal care

History of little or no prenatal care

V23.8 Other high-risk pregnancy

V23.81 Elderly primigravida

First pregnancy in a woman who will be 35 years of age or older at expected date of delivery

EXCLUDES *elderly primigravida complicating pregnancy (659.5)*

V23.82 Elderly multigravida

Second or more pregnancy in a woman who will be 35 years of age or older at expected date of delivery

EXCLUDES *elderly multigravida complicating pregnancy (659.6)*

V23.83 Young primigravida

First pregnancy in a female less than 16 years old at expected date of delivery

EXCLUDES *young primigravida complicating pregnancy (659.8)*

V23.84 Young multigravida
Second or more pregnancy in a female less than 16 years old at expected date of delivery
EXCLUDES *young multigravida complicating pregnancy (659.8)*

V23.85 Pregnancy resulting from assisted reproductive technology
Pregnancy resulting from in vitro fertilization

V23.86 Pregnancy with history of in utero procedure during previous pregnancy
EXCLUDES *management of pregnancy affected by in utero procedure during current pregnancy (679.0-679.1)*

V23.89 Other high-risk pregnancy

V23.9 Unspecified high-risk pregnancy

✓4th **V24 Postpartum care and examination**

V24.0 Immediately after delivery
Care and observation in uncomplicated cases

V24.1 Lactating mother
Supervision of lactation

V24.2 Routine postpartum follow-up

✓4th **V25 Encounter for contraceptive management**

✓5th **V25.0 General counseling and advice**

V25.01 Prescription of oral contraceptives

V25.02 Initiation of other contraceptive measures
Fitting of diaphragm
Prescription of foams, creams, or other agents

V25.03 Encounter for emergency contraceptive counseling and prescription
Encounter for postcoital contraceptive counseling and prescription

V25.04 Counseling and instruction in natural family planning to avoid pregnancy

V25.09 Other
Family planning advice

V25.1 Insertion of intrauterine contraceptive device

V25.2 Sterilization
Admission for interruption of fallopian tubes or vas deferens

V25.3 Menstrual extraction
Menstrual regulation

✓5th **V25.4 Surveillance of previously prescribed contraceptive methods**
Checking, reinsertion, or removal of contraceptive device
Repeat prescription for contraceptive method
Routine examination in connection with contraceptive maintenance
EXCLUDES *presence of intrauterine contraceptive device as incidental finding (V45.5)*

V25.40 Contraceptive surveillance, unspecified

V25.41 Contraceptive pill

V25.42 Intrauterine contraceptive device
Checking, reinsertion, or removal of intrauterine device

V25.43 Implantable subdermal contraceptive

V25.49 Other contraceptive method

V25.5 Insertion of implantable subdermal contraceptive

V25.8 Other specified contraceptive management
Postvasectomy sperm count
EXCLUDES *sperm count following sterilization reversal (V26.22)*
sperm count for fertility testing (V26.21)

V25.9 Unspecified contraceptive management

✓4th **V26 Procreative management**

V26.0 Tuboplasty or vasoplasty after previous sterilization

V26.1 Artificial insemination

✓5th **V26.2 Investigation and testing**
EXCLUDES *postvasectomy sperm count (V25.8)*

V26.21 Fertility testing
Fallopian insufflation
Sperm count for fertility testing
EXCLUDES *genetic counseling and testing (V26.31-V26.39)*

V26.22 Aftercare following sterilization reversal
Fallopian insufflation following sterilization reversal
Sperm count following sterilization reversal

V26.29 Other investigation and testing

✓5th **V26.3 Genetic counseling and testing**
EXCLUDES *fertility testing (V26.21)*
nonprocreative genetic screening (V82.71, V82.79)

V26.31 Testing of female for genetic disease carrier status

V26.32 Other genetic testing of female
Use additional code to identify habitual aborter (629.81, 646.3)

V26.33 Genetic counseling

V26.34 Testing of male for genetic disease carrier status

V26.35 Encounter for testing of male partner of habitual aborter

V26.39 Other genetic testing of male

✓5th **V26.4 General counseling and advice**

V26.41 Procreative counseling and advice using natural family planning

V26.49 Other procreative management, counseling and advice

✓5th **V26.5 Sterilization status**

V26.51 Tubal ligation status
EXCLUDES *infertility not due to previous tu-bal ligation (628.0-628.9)*

V26.52 Vasectomy status

✓5th **V26.8 Other specified procreative management**

V26.81 Encounter for assisted reproductive fertility procedure cycle
Patient undergoing in vitro fertilization cycle
Use additional code to identify the type of infertility
EXCLUDES *pre-cycle diagnosis and testing—code to reason for encounter*

V26.89 Other specified procreative management

V26.9 Unspecified procreative management

✓4th **V27 Outcome of delivery**

Note: This category is intended for the coding of the outcome of delivery on the mother's record.

V27.0 Single liveborn

V27.1 Single stillborn

V27.2 Twins, both liveborn

V27.3 Twins, one liveborn and one stillborn

V27.4 Twins, both stillborn

V27.5 Other multiple birth, all liveborn

V27.6 Other multiple birth, some liveborn

V27.7 Other multiple birth, all stillborn

V27.9 Unspecified outcome of delivery

Single birth / Multiple birth } outcome to infant unspecified

✓4th **V28 Encounter for antenatal screening of mother**

EXCLUDES *abnormal findings on screening — code to findings*
routine prenatal care (V22.0-V23.9)
suspected fetal conditions affecting management of pregnancy (655.00-655.93, 656.00-656.93, 657.00-657.03, 658.00-658.93)
suspected fetal conditions not found (V89.01-V89.09)

V28.0 Screening for chromosomal anomalies by amniocentesis

V28.1 Screening for raised alpha-fetoprotein levels in amniotic fluid

V28.2 Other screening based on amniocentesis

V28.3 Encounter for routine screening for malformation using ultrasonics

Encounter for routine fetal ultrasound NOS

EXCLUDES *encounter for fetal anatomic survey (V28.81)*
genetic counseling and testing (V26.31-V26.39)

V28.4 Screening for fetal growth retardation using ultrasonics

V28.5 Screening for isoimmunization

V28.6 Screening for Streptococcus B

✓5th **V28.8 Other specified antenatal screening**

V28.81 Encounter for fetal anatomic survey

V28.82 Encounter for screening for risk of pre-term labor

V28.89 Other specified antenatal screening

Chorionic villus sampling
Genomic screening
Nuchal translucency testing
Proteomic screening

V28.9 Unspecified antenatal screening

✓4th **V29 Observation and evaluation of newborns and infants for suspected condition not found**

Note: This category is to be used for newborns, within the neonatal period, (the first 28 days of life) who are suspected of having an abnormal condition resulting from exposure from the mother or the birth process, but without signs or symptoms, and, which after examination and observation, is found not to exist.

EXCLUDES *suspected fetal conditions not found (V89.01-V89.09)*

V29.0 Observation for suspected infectious condition

V29.1 Observation for suspected neurological condition

V29.2 Observation for suspected respiratory condition

V29.3 Observation for suspected genetic or metabolic condition

V29.8 Observation for other specified suspected condition

V29.9 Observation for unspecified suspected condition

LIVEBORN INFANTS ACCORDING TO TYPE OF BIRTH (V30-V39)

Note: These categories are intended for the coding of liveborn infants who are consuming health care [e.g., crib or bassinet occupancy].

The following fouth-digit subdivisions are for use with categories V30-V39

✓5th **0 Born in hospital**
1 Born before admission to hospital
2 Born outside hospital and not hospitalized

The following two fifth-digits are for use with the fourth-digit .0, Born in hospital:

0 delivered without mention of cesarean delivery
1 delivered by cesarean delivery

✓4th **V30 Single liveborn**

✓4th **V31 Twin, mate liveborn**

✓4th **V32 Twin, mate stillborn**

✓4th **V33 Twin, unspecified**

✓4th **V34 Other multiple, mates all liveborn**

✓4th **V35 Other multiple, mates all stillborn**

✓4th **V36 Other multiple, mates live and stillborn**

✓4th **V37 Other multiple, unspecified**

✓4th **V39 Unspecified**

PERSONS WITH A CONDITION INFLUENCING THEIR HEALTH STATUS (V40-V49)

Note: These categories are intended for use when these conditions are recorded as "diagnoses" or "problems."

✓4th **V40 Mental and behavioral problems**

V40.0 Problems with learning

V40.1 Problems with communication [including speech]

V40.2 Other mental problems

V40.3 Other behavioral problems

V40.9 Unspecified mental or behavioral problem

✓4th **V41 Problems with special senses and other special functions**

V41.0 Problems with sight

V41.1 Other eye problems

V41.2 Problems with hearing

V41.3 Other ear problems

V41.4 Problems with voice production

V41.5 Problems with smell and taste

V41.6 Problems with swallowing and mastication

V41.7 Problems with sexual function

EXCLUDES *marital problems (V61.10)*
psychosexual disorders (302.0-302.9)

V41.8 Other problems with special functions

V41.9 Unspecified problem with special functions

✓4th **V42 Organ or tissue replaced by transplant**

INCLUDES *homologous or heterologous (animal) (human) transplant organ status*

V42.0 Kidney

V42.1 Heart

V42.2 Heart valve

V42.3 Skin

V42.4 Bone

V42.5 Cornea

V42.6 Lung

V42.7 Liver

✓5th **V42.8 Other specified organ or tissue**

V42.81 Bone marrow

V42.82 **Peripheral stem cells**

V42.83 **Pancreas**

V42.84 **Intestines**

V42.89 **Other**

V42.9 **Unspecified organ or tissue**

✓4th **V43 Organ or tissue replaced by other means**

INCLUDES organ or tissue assisted by other means
replacement of organ by:
artificial device
mechanical device
prosthesis

EXCLUDES *cardiac pacemaker in situ (V45.01)*
fitting and adjustment of prosthetic device (V52.0-V52.9)
renal dialysis status (V45.11)

V43.0 **Eye globe**

V43.1 **Lens**
Pseudophakos

✓5th V43.2 **Heart**

V43.21 **Heart assist device**

V43.22 **Fully implantable artificial heart**

V43.3 **Heart valve**

V43.4 **Blood vessel**

V43.5 **Bladder**

✓5th V43.6 **Joint**

V43.60 **Unspecified joint**

V43.61 **Shoulder**

V43.62 **Elbow**

V43.63 **Wrist**

V43.64 **Hip**

V43.65 **Knee**

V43.66 **Ankle**

V43.69 **Other**

V43.7 **Limb**

✓5th V43.8 **Other organ or tissue**

V43.81 **Larynx**

V43.82 **Breast**

V43.83 **Artificial skin**

V43.89 **Other**

✓4th **V44 Artificial opening status**

EXCLUDES *artificial openings requiring attention or management (V55.0-V55.9)*

V44.0 **Tracheostomy**

V44.1 **Gastrostomy**

V44.2 **Ileostomy**

V44.3 **Colostomy**

V44.4 **Other artificial opening of gastrointestinal tract**

✓5th V44.5 **Cystostomy**

V44.50 **Cystostomy, unspecified**

V44.51 **Cutaneous-vesicostomy**

V44.52 **Appendico-vesicostomy**

V44.59 **Other cystostomy**

V44.6 **Other artificial opening of urinary tract**
Nephrostomy
Ureterostomy
Urethrostomy

V44.7 **Artificial vagina**

V44.8 **Other artificial opening status**

V44.9 **Unspecified artificial opening status**

✓4th **V45 Other postprocedural states**

EXCLUDES *aftercare management (V51-V58.9)*
malfunction or other complication — code to condition

✓5th V45.0 **Cardiac device in situ**

EXCLUDES *artificial heart (V43.22)*
heart assist device (V43.21)

V45.00 **Unspecified cardiac device**

V45.01 **Cardiac pacemaker**

V45.02 **Automatic implantable cardiac defibrillator**

V45.09 **Other specified cardiac device**
Carotid sinus pacemaker in situ

✓5th V45.1 **Renal dialysis status**

EXCLUDES *admission for dialysis treatment or session (V56.0)*

V45.11 **Renal dialysis status**
Hemodialysis status
Patient requiring intermittent renal dialysis
Peritoneal dialysis status
Presence of arterial-venous shunt (for dialysis)

V45.12 **Noncompliance with renal dialysis**

V45.2 **Presence of cerebrospinal fluid drainage device**
Cerebral ventricle (communicating) shunt, valve, or device in situ

EXCLUDES *malfunction (996.2)*

V45.3 **Intestinal bypass or anastomosis status**

EXCLUDES *bariatric surgery status (V45.86)*
gastric bypass status (V45.86)
obesity surgery status (V45.86)

V45.4 **Arthrodesis status**

✓5th V45.5 **Presence of contraceptive device**

EXCLUDES *checking, reinsertion, or removal of device (V25.42)*
complication from device (996.32)
insertion of device (V25.1)

V45.51 **Intrauterine contraceptive device**

V45.52 **Subdermal contraceptive implant**

V45.59 **Other**

✓5th V45.6 **States following surgery of eye and adnexa**

Cataract extraction
Filtering bleb
Surgical eyelid adhesion
} state following eye surgery

EXCLUDES *aphakia (379.31)*
artificial eye globe (V43.0)

V45.61 **Cataract extraction status**
Use additional code for associated artificial lens status (V43.1)

V45.69 **Other states following surgery of eye and adnexa**

✓5th V45.7 **Acquired absence of organ**

V45.71 **Acquired absence of breast and nipple**

V45.72 **Acquired absence of intestine (large)(small)**

V45.73 **Acquired absence of kidney**

V45.74 **Other parts of urinary tract**
Bladder

V45.75 **Stomach**

V45.76 **Lung**

V45.77 **Genital organs**

EXCLUDES *acquired absence of cervix and uterus (V88.01-V88.03)*
female genital mutilation status (629.20-629.29)

V45.78 **Eye**

V45.79 **Other acquired absence of organ**

✓5th **V45.8 Other postprocedural status**

V45.81 Aortocoronary bypass status

V45.82 Percutaneous transluminal coronary angioplasty status

V45.83 Breast implant removal status

V45.84 Dental restoration status

Dental crowns status
Dental fillings status

V45.85 Insulin pump status

V45.86 Bariatric surgery status

Gastric banding status
Gastric bypass status for obesity
Obesity surgery status

EXCLUDES *bariatric surgery status complicating pregnancy, childbirth or the puerperium (649.2)*
intestinal bypass or anastomosis status (V45.3)

V45.87 Transplanted organ removal status

Transplanted organ previously removed due to complication, failure, rejection or infection

EXCLUDES *encounter for removal of transplanted organ — code to complication of transplanted organ (996.80-996.89)*

V45.88 Status post administration of tPA (rtPA) in a different facility within the last 24 hours prior to admission to current facility

Code first condition requiring tPA administration, such as:
acute cerebral infarction (433.0-433.9 with fifth-digit 1, 434.0-434.9 with fifth digit 1)
acute myocardial infarction (410.00-410.92)

V45.89 Other

Presence of neuropacemaker or other electronic device

EXCLUDES *artificial heart valve in situ (V43.3)*
vascular prosthesis in situ (V43.4)

✓4th **V46 Other dependence on machines and devices**

V46.0 Aspirator

✓5th **V46.1 Respirator [Ventilator]**

Iron lung

V46.11 Dependence on respirator, status

V46.12 Encounter for respirator dependence during power failure

V46.13 Encounter for weaning from respirator [ventilator]

V46.14 Mechanical complication of respirator [ventilator]

Mechanical failure of respirator [ventilator]

V46.2 Supplemental oxygen

Long-term oxygen therapy

V46.3 Wheelchair dependence

Wheelchair confinement status

Code first cause of dependence, such as:
muscular dystrophy (359.1)
obesity (278.00, 278.01)

V46.8 Other enabling machines

Hyperbaric chamber
Possum [Patient-Operated-Selector-Mechanism]

EXCLUDES *cardiac pacemaker (V45.0)*
kidney dialysis machine (V45.11)

V46.9 Unspecified machine dependence

✓4th **V47 Other problems with internal organs**

V47.0 Deficiencies of internal organs

V47.1 Mechanical and motor problems with internal organs

V47.2 Other cardiorespiratory problems

Cardiovascular exercise intolerance with pain (with):
at rest
less than ordinary activity
ordinary activity

V47.3 Other digestive problems

V47.4 Other urinary problems

V47.5 Other genital problems

V47.9 Unspecified

✓4th **V48 Problems with head, neck, and trunk**

V48.0 Deficiencies of head

EXCLUDES *deficiencies of ears, eyelids, and nose (V48.8)*

V48.1 Deficiencies of neck and trunk

V48.2 Mechanical and motor problems with head

V48.3 Mechanical and motor problems with neck and trunk

V48.4 Sensory problem with head

V48.5 Sensory problem with neck and trunk

V48.6 Disfigurements of head

V48.7 Disfigurements of neck and trunk

V48.8 Other problems with head, neck, and trunk

V48.9 Unspecified problem with head, neck, or trunk

✓4th **V49 Other conditions influencing health status**

V49.0 Deficiencies of limbs

V49.1 Mechanical problems with limbs

V49.2 Motor problems with limbs

V49.3 Sensory problems with limbs

V49.4 Disfigurements of limbs

V49.5 Other problems of limbs

✓5th **V49.6 Upper limb amputation status**

V49.60 Unspecified level

V49.61 Thumb

V49.62 Other finger(s)

V49.63 Hand

V49.64 Wrist

Disarticulation of wrist

V49.65 Below elbow

V49.66 Above elbow

Disarticulation of elbow

V49.67 Shoulder

Disarticulation of shoulder

✓5th **V49.7 Lower limb amputation status**

V49.70 Unspecified level

V49.71 Great toe

V49.72 Other toe(s)

V49.73 Foot

V49.74 Ankle

Disarticulation of ankle

V49.75 Below knee

V49.76 Above knee

Disarticulation of knee

V49.77 Hip

Disarticulation of hip

✓5th **V49.8 Other specified conditions influencing health status**

V49.81 Asymptomatic postmenopausal status (age-related) (natural)

EXCLUDES *menopausal and premenopausal disorder (627.0-627.9)*
postsurgical menopause (256.2)
premature menopause (256.31)
symptomatic menopause (627.0-627.9)

V49.82 Dental sealant status

V49.83 Awaiting organ transplant status

V49.84 Bed confinement status

V49.85 Dual sensory impairment

Blindness with deafness
Combined visual hearing impairment
Code first:
hearing impairment (389.00-389.9)
visual impairment (369.00-369.9)

V49.89 Other specified conditions influencing health status

V49.9 Unspecified

PERSONS ENCOUNTERING HEALTH SERVICES FOR SPECIFIC PROCEDURES AND AFTERCARE (V50-V59)

Note: Categories V51-V59 are intended for use to indicate a reason for care in patients who may have already been treated for some disease or injury not now present, or who are receiving care to consolidate the treatment, to deal with residual states, or to prevent recurrence.

EXCLUDES *follow-up examination for medical surveillance following treatment (V67.0-V67.9)*

✓4th **V50 Elective surgery for purposes other than remedying health states**

V50.0 Hair transplant

V50.1 Other plastic surgery for unacceptable cosmetic appearance

Breast augmentation or reduction
Face-lift

EXCLUDES *encounter for breast reduction (611.1)*
plastic surgery following healed injury or operation (V51.0-V51.8)

V50.2 Routine or ritual circumcision

Circumcision in the absence of significant medical indication

V50.3 Ear piercing

✓5th **V50.4 Prophylactic organ removal**

EXCLUDES *organ donations (V59.0-V59.9)*
therapeutic organ removal — code to condition

V50.41 Breast

V50.42 Ovary

V50.49 Other

V50.8 Other

V50.9 Unspecified

✓4th **V51 Aftercare involving the use of plastic surgery**

Plastic surgery following healed injury or operation

EXCLUDES *cosmetic plastic surgery (V50.1)*
plastic surgery as treatment for current condtion or injury — code to condition or injury
repair of scarred tissue — code to scar

V51.0 Encounter for breast reconstruction following mastectomy

EXCLUDES *deformity and disproportion of reconstructed breast (612.0-612.1)*

V51.8 Other aftercare involving the use of plastic surgery

✓4th **V52 Fitting and adjustment of prosthetic device and implant**

INCLUDES removal of device

EXCLUDES *malfunction or complication of prosthetic device (996.0-996.7)*
status only, without need for care (V43.0-V43.8)

V52.0 Artificial arm (complete) (partial)

V52.1 Artificial leg (complete) (partial)

V52.2 Artificial eye

V52.3 Dental prosthetic device

V52.4 Breast prosthesis and implant

Elective implant exchange (different material) (different size)
Removal of tissue expander without synchronous insertion of permanent implant

EXCLUDES *admission for initial breast implant insertion for breast augmentation (V50.1)*
complications of breast implant (996.54, 996.69, 996.79)
encounter for breast reconstruction following mastectomy (V51.0)

V52.8 Other specified prosthetic device

V52.9 Unspecified prosthetic device

✓4th **V53 Fitting and adjustment of other device**

INCLUDES removal of device
replacement of device

EXCLUDES *status only, without need for care (V45.0-V45.8)*

✓5th **V53.0 Devices related to nervous system and special senses**

V53.01 Fitting and adjustment of cerebral ventricular (communicating) shunt

V53.02 Neuropacemaker (brain) (peripheral nerve) (spinal cord)

V53.09 Fitting and adjustment of other devices related to nervous system and special senses

Auditory substitution device
Visual substitution device

V53.1 Spectacles and contact lenses

V53.2 Hearing aid

✓5th **V53.3 Cardiac device**

Reprogramming

V53.31 Cardiac pacemaker

EXCLUDES *mechanical complication of cardiac pacemaker (996.01)*

V53.32 Automatic implantable cardiac defibrillator

V53.39 Other cardiac device

V53.4 Orthodontic devices

V53.5 Other intestinal appliance

EXCLUDES *colostomy (V55.3)*
ileostomy (V55.2)
other artificial opening of digestive tract (V55.4)

V53.6 Urinary devices

Urinary catheter

EXCLUDES *cystostomy (V55.5)*
nephrostomy (V55.6)
ureterostomy (V55.6)
urethrostomy (V55.6)

V53.7 Orthopedic devices

Orthopedic:
brace
cast
corset
shoes

EXCLUDES *other orthopedic aftercare (V54)*

V53.8 Wheelchair

✓5th **V53.9 Other and unspecified device**

V53.90 Unspecified device

V53.91 Fitting and adjustment of insulin pump
Insulin pump titration

V53.99 Other device

✓4th **V54 Other orthopedic aftercare**

EXCLUDES *fitting and adjustment of orthopedic devices (V53.7)*
malfunction of internal orthopedic device (996.40-996.49)
other complication of nonmechanical nature (996.60-996.79)

✓5th **V54.0 Aftercare involving internal fixation device**

EXCLUDES *malfunction of internal orthopedic device (996.40-996.49)*
other complication of nonmechanical nature (996.60-996.79)
removal of external fixation device (V54.89)

V54.01 Encounter for removal of internal fixation device

V54.02 Encounter for lengthening/adjustment of growth rod

V54.09 Other aftercare involving internal fixation device

✓5th **V54.1 Aftercare for healing traumatic fracture**

EXCLUDES *aftercare for amputation stump (V54.89)*

V54.10 Aftercare for healing traumatic fracture of arm, unspecified

V54.11 Aftercare for healing traumatic fracture of upper arm

V54.12 Aftercare for healing traumatic fracture of lower arm

V54.13 Aftercare for healing traumatic fracture of hip

V54.14 Aftercare for healing traumatic fracture of leg, unspecified

V54.15 Aftercare for healing traumatic fracture of upper leg

EXCLUDES *aftercare for healing traumatic fracture of hip (V54.13)*

V54.16 Aftercare for healing traumatic fracture of lower leg

V54.17 Aftercare for healing traumatic fracture of vertebrae

V54.19 Aftercare for healing traumatic fracture of other bone

✓5th **V54.2 Aftercare for healing pathologic fracture**

V54.20 Aftercare for healing pathologic fracture of arm, unspecified

V54.21 Aftercare for healing pathologic fracture of upper arm

V54.22 Aftercare for healing pathologic fracture of lower arm

V54.23 Aftercare for healing pathologic fracture of hip

V54.24 Aftercare for healing pathologic fracture of leg, unspecified

V54.25 Aftercare for healing pathologic fracture of upper leg

EXCLUDES *aftercare for healing pathologic fracture of hip (V54.23)*

V54.26 Aftercare for healing pathologic fracture of lower leg

V54.27 Aftercare for healing pathologic fracture of vertebrae

V54.29 Aftercare for healing pathologic fracture of other bone

✓5th **V54.8 Other orthopedic aftercare**

V54.81 Aftercare following joint replacement
Use additional code to identify joint replacement site (V43.60-V43.69)

V54.89 Other orthopedic aftercare
Aftercare for healing fracture NOS

V54.9 Unspecified orthopedic aftercare

✓4th **V55 Attention to artificial openings**

INCLUDES adjustment or repositioning of catheter
closure
passage of sounds or bougies
reforming
removal or replacement of catheter
toilet or cleansing

EXCLUDES *complications of external stoma (519.00-519.09, 569.60-569.69, 997.4, 997.5)*
status only, without need for care (V44.0-V44.9)

V55.0 Tracheostomy

V55.1 Gastrostomy

V55.2 Ileostomy

V55.3 Colostomy

V55.4 Other artificial opening of digestive tract

V55.5 Cystostomy

V55.6 Other artificial opening of urinary tract
Nephrostomy
Urethrostomy
Ureterostomy

V55.7 Artificial vagina

V55.8 Other specified artificial opening

V55.9 Unspecified artificial opening

✓4th **V56 Encounter for dialysis and dialysis catheter care**
Use additional code to identify the associated condition

EXCLUDES *dialysis preparation — code to condition*

V56.0 Extracorporeal dialysis
Dialysis (renal) NOS

EXCLUDES *dialysis status (V45.11)*

V56.1 Fitting and adjustment of extracorporeal dialysis catheter
Removal or replacement of catheter
Toilet or cleansing
Use additional code for any concurrent extracorporeal dialysis (V56.0)

V56.2 Fitting and adjustment of peritoneal dialysis catheter
Use additional code for any concurrent peritoneal dialysis (V56.8)

✓5th **V56.3 Encounter for adequacy testing for dialysis**

V56.31 Encounter for adequacy testing for hemodialysis

V56.32 Encounter for adequacy testing for peritoneal dialysis
Peritoneal equilibration test

V56.8 Other dialysis
Peritoneal dialysis

✓4th **V57 Care involving use of rehabilitation procedures**
Use additional code to identify underlying condition

V57.0 Breathing exercises

V57.1 Other physical therapy
Therapeutic and remedial exercises, except breathing

✓5th **V57.2 Occupational therapy and vocational rehabilitation**

V57.21 Encounter for occupational therapy

V57.22 Encounter for vocational therapy

V57.3 Speech therapy

V57.4 Orthoptic training

✓5th **V57.8 Other specified rehabilitation procedure**

V57.81 Orthotic training
Gait training in the use of artificial limbs

V57.89 Other
Multiple training or therapy

V57.9 Unspecified rehabilitation procedure

✓4th **V58 Encounter for other and unspecified procedures and aftercare**
EXCLUDES *convalescence and palliative care (V66)*

V58.0 Radiotherapy
Encounter or admission for radiotherapy
EXCLUDES *encounter for radioactive implant — code to condition*
radioactive iodine therapy — code to condition

✓5th **V58.1 Encounter for antineoplastic chemotherapy and immunotherapy**
Encounter or admission for chemotherapy
EXCLUDES *chemotherapy and immunotherapy for nonneoplastic conditions — code to condition*

V58.11 Encounter for antineoplastic chemotherapy

V58.12 Encounter for antineoplastic immunotherapy

V58.2 Blood transfusion, without reported diagnosis

✓5th **V58.3 Attention to dressings and sutures**
Change or removal of wound packing
EXCLUDES *attention to drains (V58.49)*
planned postoperative wound closure (V58.41)

V58.30 Encounter for change or removal of nonsurgical wound dressing
Encounter for change or removal of wound dressing NOS

V58.31 Encounter for change or removal of surgical wound dressing

V58.32 Encounter for removal of sutures
Encounter for removal of staples

✓5th **V58.4 Other aftercare following surgery**
Note: Codes from this subcategory should be used in conjunction with other aftercare codes to fully identify the reason for the aftercare encounter
EXCLUDES *aftercare following sterilization reversal surgery (V26.22)*
attention to artificial openings (V55.0-V55.9)
orthopedic aftercare (V54.0-V54.9)

V58.41 Encounter for planned postoperative wound closure
EXCLUDES *disruption of operative wound (998.31-998.32)*
encounter for dressings and suture aftercare (V58.30-V58.32)

V58.42 Aftercare following surgery for neoplasm
Conditions classifiable to 140-239

V58.43 Aftercare following surgery for injury and trauma
Conditions classifiable to 800-999
EXCLUDES *aftercare for healing traumatic fracture (V54.10-V54.19)*

V58.44 Aftercare following organ transplant
Use additional code to identify the organ transplanted (V42.0-V42.9)

V58.49 Other specified aftercare following surgery
Change or removal of drains

V58.5 Orthodontics
EXCLUDES *fitting and adjustment of orthodontic device (V53.4)*

✓5th **V58.6 Long-term (current) drug use**
EXCLUDES *drug abuse and dependence complicating pregnancy (648.3-648.4)*
drug abuse (305.00-305.93)
drug dependence (304.00-304.93)
hormone replacement therapy (postmenopausal) (V07.4)
prophylactic use of agents affecting estrogen receptors and estrogen levels (V07.51-V07.59)

V58.61 Long-term (current) use of anticoagulants
EXCLUDES *long-term (current) use of aspirin (V58.66)*

V58.62 Long-term (current) use of antibiotics

V58.63 Long-term (current) use of antiplatelets/antithrombotics
EXCLUDES *long-term (current) use of aspirin (V58.66)*

V58.64 Long-term (current) use of non-steroidal anti-inflammatories (NSAID)
EXCLUDES *long-term (current) use of aspirin (V58.66)*

V58.65 Long-term (current) use of steroids

V58.66 Long-term (current) use of aspirin

V58.67 Long-term (current) use of insulin

V58.69 Long-term (current) use of other medications
Other high-risk medications
Long term current use of methadone
Long term current use of opiate analgesic

✓5th **V58.7 Aftercare following surgery to specified body systems, not elsewhere classified**
Note: Codes from this subcategory should be used in conjunction with other aftercare codes to fully identify the reason for the aftercare encounter
EXCLUDES *aftercare following organ transplant (V58.44)*
aftercare following surgery for neoplasm (V58.42)

V58.71 Aftercare following surgery of the sense organs, NEC
Conditions classifiable to 360-379, 380-389

V58.72 Aftercare following surgery of the nervous system, NEC
Conditions classifiable to 320-359
EXCLUDES *aftercare following surgery of the sense organs, NEC (V58.71)*

V58.73 Aftercare following surgery of the circulatory system, NEC
Conditions classifiable to 390-459

V58.74 Aftercare following surgery of the respiratory system, NEC
Conditions classifiable to 460-519

V58.75 Aftercare following surgery of the teeth, oral cavity and digestive system, NEC
Conditions classifiable to 520-579

V58.76 Aftercare following surgery of the genitourinary system, NEC
Conditions classifiable to 580-629
EXCLUDES *aftercare following sterilization reversal (V26.22)*

V58.77 Aftercare following surgery of the skin and subcutaneous tissue, NEC
Conditions classifiable to 680-709

V58.78 Aftercare following surgery of the musculoskeletal system, NEC
Conditions classifiable to 710-739
EXCLUDES *orthopedic aftercare (V54.01-V54.9)*

✓5th **V58.8 Other specified procedures and aftercare**

V58.81 Fitting and adjustment of vascular catheter
Removal or replacement of catheter
Toilet or cleansing
EXCLUDES *complication of renal dialysis (996.73)*
complication of vascular catheter (996.74)
dialysis preparation — code to condition
encounter for dialysis (V56.0-V56.8)
fitting and adjustment of dialysis catheter (V56.1)

V58.82 Fitting and adjustment of nonvascular catheter, NEC
Removal or replacement of catheter
Toilet or cleansing
EXCLUDES *fitting and adjustment of peritoneal dialysis catheter (V56.2)*
fitting and adjustment of urinary catheter (V53.6)

V58.83 Encounter for therapeutic drug monitoring
Use additional code for any associated long- term (current) drug use (V58.61-V58.69)
EXCLUDES *blood-drug testing for medicolegal reasons (V70.4)*
DEF: Drug monitoring: Measurement of the level of a specific drug in the body or measurement of a specific function to assess effectiveness of a drug.

V58.89 Other specified aftercare

V58.9 Unspecified aftercare

✓4th **V59 Donors**
EXCLUDES *examination of potential donor (V70.8)*
self-donation of organ or tissue — code to condition

✓5th **V59.0 Blood**

V59.01 Whole blood

V59.02 Stem cells

V59.09 Other

V59.1 Skin

V59.2 Bone

V59.3 Bone marrow

V59.4 Kidney

V59.5 Cornea

V59.6 Liver

✓5th **V59.7 Egg (oocyte) (ovum)**

V59.70 Egg (oocyte) (ovum) donor, unspecified

V59.71 Egg (oocyte) (ovum) donor, under age 35, anonymous recipient
Egg donor, under age 35 NOS

V59.72 Egg (oocyte) (ovum) donor, under age 35, designated recipient

V59.73 Egg (oocyte) (ovum) donor, age 35 and over, anonymous recipient
Egg donor, age 35 and over NOS

V59.74 Egg (oocyte) (ovum) donor, age 35 and over, designated recipient

V59.8 Other specified organ or tissue

V59.9 Unspecified organ or tissue

PERSONS ENCOUNTERING HEALTH SERVICES IN OTHER CIRCUMSTANCES (V60-V69)

✓4th **V60 Housing, household, and economic circumstances**

V60.0 Lack of housing
Hobos
Social migrants
Tramps
Transients
Vagabonds

V60.1 Inadequate housing
Lack of heating
Restriction of space
Technical defects in home preventing adequate care

V60.2 Inadequate material resources
Economic problem
Poverty NOS

V60.3 Person living alone

V60.4 No other household member able to render care
Person requiring care (has) (is):
family member too handicapped, ill, or otherwise unsuited to render care
partner temporarily away from home
temporarily away from usual place of abode
EXCLUDES *holiday relief care (V60.5)*

V60.5 Holiday relief care
Provision of health care facilities to a person normally cared for at home, to enable relatives to take a vacation

V60.6 Person living in residential institution
Boarding school resident

V60.8 Other specified housing or economic circumstances

V60.9 Unspecified housing or economic circumstance

✓4th **V61 Other family circumstances**
INCLUDES when these circumstances or fear of them, affecting the person directly involved or others, are mentioned as the reason, justified or not, for seeking or receiving medical advice or care

✓5th **V61.0 Family disruption**

V61.01 Family disruption due to family member on military deployment
Individual or family affected by other family member being on deployment

V61.02 Family disruption due to return of family member from military deployment
Individual or family affected by other family member having returned from deployment (current or past conflict)

V61.03 Family disruption due to divorce or legal separation

V61.04 Family disruption due to parent-child estrangement
EXCLUDES *other family estrangement (V61.09)*

V61.05 Family disruption due to child in welfare custody

V61.06 Family disruption due to child in foster care or in care of non-parental family member

V61.09 Other family disruption
Family estrangement NOS

✓5th **V61.1 Counseling for marital and partner problems**
EXCLUDES *problems related to:*
psychosexual disorders (302.0-302.9)
sexual function (V41.7)

V61.10 Counseling for marital and partner problems, unspecified
Marital conflict
Marital relationship problem
Partner conflict
Partner relationship problem

V61.11 Counseling for victim of spousal and partner abuse
EXCLUDES *encounter for treatment of current injuries due to abuse (995.80-995.85)*

V61.12 Counseling for perpetrator of spousal and partner abuse

✓5th **V61.2 Parent-child problems**

V61.20 Counseling for parent-child problem, unspecified
Concern about behavior of child
Parent-child conflict
Parent-child relationship problem

V61.21 Counseling for victim of child abuse
Child battering
Child neglect
EXCLUDES *current injuries due to abuse (995.50-995.59)*

V61.22 Counseling for perpetrator of parental child abuse
EXCLUDES *counseling for non-parental abuser (V62.83)*

V61.29 Other
Problem concerning adopted or foster child

V61.3 Problems with aged parents or in-laws

✓5th **V61.4 Health problems within family**

V61.41 Alcoholism in family

V61.49 Other
Care of } sick or handicapped person in family or household
Presence of }

V61.5 Multiparity

V61.6 Illegitimacy or illegitimate pregnancy

V61.7 Other unwanted pregnancy

V61.8 Other specified family circumstances
Problems with family members NEC
Sibling relationship problem

V61.9 Unspecified family circumstance

✓4th **V62 Other psychosocial circumstances**
INCLUDES those circumstances or fear of them, affecting the person directly involved or others, mentioned as the reason, justified or not, for seeking or receiving medical advice or care
EXCLUDES *previous psychological trauma (V15.41-V15.49)*

V62.0 Unemployment
EXCLUDES *circumstances when main problem is economic inadequacy or poverty (V60.2)*

V62.1 Adverse effects of work environment

✓5th **V62.2 Other occupational circumstances or maladjustment**

V62.21 Personal current military deployment status
Individual (civilian or military) currently deployed in theater or in support of military war, peacekeeping and humanitarian operations

V62.22 Personal history of return from military deployment
Individual (civilian or military) with past history of military war, peacekeeping and humanitarian deployment (current or past conflict)

V62.29 Other occupational circumstances or maladjustment
Career choice problem
Dissatisfaction with employment
Occupational problem

V62.3 Educational circumstances
Academic problem
Dissatisfaction with school environment
Educational handicap

V62.4 Social maladjustment
Acculturation problem
Cultural deprivation
Political, religious, or sex discrimination
Social:
isolation
persecution

V62.5 Legal circumstances
Imprisonment
Legal investigation
Litigation
Prosecution

V62.6 Refusal of treatment for reasons of religion or conscience

✓5th **V62.8 Other psychological or physical stress, not elsewhere classified**

V62.81 Interpersonal problems, not elsewhere classified
Relational problem NOS

V62.82 Bereavement, uncomplicated
EXCLUDES *bereavement as adjustment reaction (309.0)*

V62.83 Counseling for perpetrator of physical/sexual abuse
EXCLUDES *counseling for perpetrator of parental child abuse (V61.22)*
counseling for perpetrator of spousal and partner abuse (V61.12)

V62.84 Suicidal ideation
EXCLUDES *suicidal tendencies (300.9)*
DEF: Thoughts of committing suicide; no actual attempt of suicide has been made.

V62.89 Other
Borderline intellectual functioning
Life circumstance problems
Phase of life problems
Religious or spiritual problem

V62.9 Unspecified psychosocial circumstance

✓4th **V63 Unavailability of other medical facilities for care**

V63.0 Residence remote from hospital or other health care facility

V63.1 Medical services in home not available
EXCLUDES *no other household member able to render care (V60.4)*

V63.2 Person awaiting admission to adequate facility elsewhere

V63.8 Other specified reasons for unavailability of medical facilities
Person on waiting list undergoing social agency investigation

V63.9 Unspecified reason for unavailability of medical facilities

✓4th **V64 Persons encountering health services for specific procedures, not carried out**

✓5th **V64.0 Vaccination not carried out**

V64.00 Vaccination not carried out, unspecified reason

V64.01 Vaccination not carried out because of acute illness

V64.02 Vaccination not carried out because of chronic illness or condition

V64.03 Vaccination not carried out because of immune compromised state

V64.04 Vaccination not carried out because of allergy to vaccine or component

V64.05 Vaccination not carried out because of caregiver refusal

Guardian refusal
Parent refusal

EXCLUDES *vaccination not carried out because of caregiver refusal for religious reasons (V64.07)*

V64.06 Vaccination not carried out because of patient refusal

V64.07 Vaccination not carried out for religious reasons

V64.08 Vaccination not carried out because patient had disease being vaccinated against

V64.09 Vaccination not carried out for other reason

V64.1 Surgical or other procedure not carried out because of contraindication

V64.2 Surgical or other procedure not carried out because of patient's decision

V64.3 Procedure not carried out for other reasons

✓5th **V64.4 Closed surgical procedure converted to open procedure**

V64.41 Laparoscopic surgical procedure converted to open procedure

V64.42 Thoracoscopic surgical procedure converted to open procedure

V64.43 Arthroscopic surgical procedure converted to open procedure

✓4th **V65 Other persons seeking consultation**

V65.0 Healthy person accompanying sick person

Boarder

✓5th **V65.1 Person consulting on behalf of another person**

Advice or treatment for nonattending third party

EXCLUDES *concern (normal) about sick person in family (V61.41-V61.49)*

V65.11 Pediatric pre-birth visit for expectant mother

V65.19 Other person consulting on behalf of another person

V65.2 Person feigning illness

Malingerer
Peregrinating patient

V65.3 Dietary surveillance and counseling

Dietary surveillance and counseling (in):
- NOS
- colitis
- diabetes mellitus
- food allergies or intolerance
- gastritis
- hypercholesterolemia
- hypoglycemia
- obesity

Use additional code to identify Body Mass Index (BMI), if known (V85.0-V85.54)

✓5th **V65.4 Other counseling, not elsewhere classified**

Health:
- advice
- education
- instruction

EXCLUDES *counseling (for):*
- *contraception (V25.40-V25.49)*
- *genetic (V26.31-V26.39)*
- *on behalf of third party (V65.11-V65.19)*
- *procreative management (V26.41-V26.49)*

V65.40 Counseling NOS

V65.41 Exercise counseling

V65.42 Counseling on substance use and abuse

V65.43 Counseling on injury prevention

V65.44 Human immunodeficiency virus [HIV] counseling

V65.45 Counseling on other sexually transmitted diseases

V65.46 Encounter for insulin pump training

V65.49 Other specified counseling

V65.5 Person with feared complaint in whom no diagnosis was made

Feared condition not demonstrated
Problem was normal state
"Worried well"

V65.8 Other reasons for seeking consultation

EXCLUDES *specified symptoms*

V65.9 Unspecified reason for consultation

✓4th **V66 Convalescence and palliative care**

V66.0 Following surgery

V66.1 Following radiotherapy

V66.2 Following chemotherapy

V66.3 Following psychotherapy and other treatment for mental disorder

V66.4 Following treatment of fracture

V66.5 Following other treatment

V66.6 Following combined treatment

V66.7 Encounter for palliative care

End of life care
Hospice care
Terminal care

Code first underlying disease

V66.9 Unspecified convalescence

✓4th **V67 Follow-up examination**

INCLUDES surveillance only following completed treatment

EXCLUDES *surveillance of contraception (V25.40-V25.49)*

✓5th **V67.0 Following surgery**

V67.00 Following surgery, unspecified

V67.01 Follow-up vaginal pap smear

Vaginal pap-smear, status-post hysterectomy for malignant condition

Use additional code to identify:
- acquired absence of uterus (V88.01-V88.03)
- personal history of malignant neoplasm (V10.40-V10.44)

EXCLUDES *vaginal pap smear status-post hysterectomy for non-malignant condition (V76.47)*

V67.09 Following other surgery

EXCLUDES *sperm count following sterilization reversal (V26.22)*
sperm count for fertility testing (V26.21)

V67.1 Following radiotherapy

V67.2 Following chemotherapy

Cancer chemotherapy follow-up

V67.3 Following psychotherapy and other treatment for mental disorder

V67.4 Following treatment of healed fracture

EXCLUDES *current (healing) fracture aftercare (V54.0-V54.9)*

5th V67.5 **Following other treatment**

V67.51 **Following completed treatment with high-risk medications, not elsewhere classified**

EXCLUDES *long-term (current) drug use (V58.61-V58.69)*

V67.59 **Other**

V67.6 **Following combined treatment**

V67.9 **Unspecified follow-up examination**

4th **V68 Encounters for administrative purposes**

5th V68.0 **Issue of medical certificates**

EXCLUDES *encounter for general medical examination (V70.0-V70.9)*

V68.01 **Disability examination**

Use additional code(s) to identify specific examination(s), screening and testing performed (V72.0-V82.9)

V68.09 **Other issue of medical certificates**

V68.1 **Issue of repeat prescriptions**

Issue of repeat prescription for:
- appliance
- glasses
- medications

EXCLUDES *repeat prescription for contraceptives (V25.41-V25.49)*

V68.2 **Request for expert evidence**

5th V68.8 **Other specified administrative purpose**

V68.81 **Referral of patient without examination or treatment**

V68.89 **Other**

V68.9 **Unspecified administrative purpose**

4th **V69 Problems related to lifestyle**

V69.0 **Lack of physical exercise**

V69.1 **Inappropriate diet and eating habits**

EXCLUDES *anorexia nervosa (307.1)*
bulimia (783.6)
malnutrition and other nutritional deficiencies (260-269.9)
other and unspecified eating disorders (307.50-307.59)

V69.2 **High-risk sexual behavior**

V69.3 **Gambling and betting**

EXCLUDES *pathological gambling (312.31)*

V69.4 **Lack of adequate sleep**

Sleep deprivation

EXCLUDES *insomnia (780.52)*

V69.5 **Behavioral insomnia of childhood**

DEF: Behaviors on the part of the child or caregivers that cause negative compliance with a child's sleep schedule; results in lack of adequate sleep.

V69.8 **Other problems related to lifestyle**

Self-damaging behavior

V69.9 **Problem related to lifestyle, unspecified**

PERSONS WITHOUT REPORTED DIAGNOSIS ENCOUNTERED DURING EXAMINATION AND INVESTIGATION OF INDIVIDUALS AND POPULATIONS (V70-V82)

Note: Nonspecific abnormal findings disclosed at the time of these examinations are classifiable to categories 790-796.

4th **V70 General medical examination**

Use additional code(s) to identify any special screening examination(s) performed (V73.0-V82.9)

V70.0 **Routine general medical examination at a health care facility**

Health checkup

EXCLUDES *health checkup of infant or child (V20.2)*
pre-procedural general physical examination (V72.83)

V70.1 **General psychiatric examination, requested by the authority**

V70.2 **General psychiatric examination, other and unspecified**

V70.3 **Other medical examination for administrative purposes**

General medical examination for:
- admission to old age home
- adoption
- camp
- driving license
- immigration and naturalization
- insurance certification
- marriage
- prison
- school admission
- sports competition

EXCLUDES *attendance for issue of medical certificates (V68.0)*
pre-employment screening (V70.5)

V70.4 **Examination for medicolegal reasons**

Blood-alcohol tests Paternity testing
Blood-drug tests

EXCLUDES *examination and observation following:*
accidents (V71.3, V71.4)
assault (V71.6)
rape (V71.5)

V70.5 **Health examination of defined subpopulations**

- Armed forces personnel
- Inhabitants of institutions
- Occupational healthexaminations
- Pre-employment screening
- Preschool children
- Prisoners
- Prostitutes
- Refugees
- School children
- Students

V70.6 **Health examination in population surveys**

EXCLUDES *special screening (V73.0-V82.9)*

V70.7 **Examination of participant in clinical trial**

Examination of participant or control in clinical research

V70.8 **Other specified general medical examinations**

Examination of potential donor of organ or tissue

V70.9 **Unspecified general medical examination**

4th **V71 Observation and evaluation for suspected conditions not found**

INCLUDES This category is to be used when persons without a diagnosis are suspected of having an abnormal condition, without signs or symptoms, which requires study, but after examination and observation, is found not to exist. This category is also for use for administrative and legal observation status.

EXCLUDES *suspected maternal and fetal conditions not found (V89.01-V89.09)*

5th V71.0 **Observation for suspected mental condition**

V71.01 **Adult antisocial behavior**

Dyssocial behavior or gang activity in adult without manifest psychiatric disorder

V71.02 **Childhood or adolescent antisocial behavior**

Dyssocial behavior or gang activity in child or adolescent without manifest psychiatric disorder

V71.09 **Other suspected mental condition**

V71.1 **Observation for suspected malignant neoplasm**

V71.2 **Observation for suspected tuberculosis**

V71.3 **Observation following accident at work**

V71.4 **Observation following other accident**

Examination of individual involved in motor vehicle traffic accident

V71.5 Observation following alleged rape or seduction
Examination of victim or culprit

V71.6 Observation following other inflicted injury
Examination of victim or culprit

V71.7 Observation for suspected cardiovascular disease

✓5th **V71.8 Observation and evaluation for other specified suspected conditions**
EXCLUDES *contact with and (suspected) exposure to (potentially) hazardous substances (V15.84-V15.86, V87.0-V87.31)*

V71.81 Abuse and neglect
EXCLUDES *adult abuse and neglect (995.80-995.85)*
child abuse and neglect (995.50-995.59)

V71.82 Observation and evaluation for suspected exposure to anthrax

V71.83 Observation and evaluation for suspected exposure to other biological agent

V71.89 Other specified suspected conditions

V71.9 Observation for unspecified suspected condition

✓4th **V72 Special investigations and examinations**
INCLUDES routine examination of specific system
Use additional code(s) to identify any special screening examination(s) performed (V73.0-V82.9)
EXCLUDES *general medical examination (V70.0-V70.4)*
general screening examination of defined population groups (V70.5, V70.6, V70.7)
routine examination of infant or child (V20.2)

V72.0 Examination of eyes and vision

✓5th **V72.1 Examination of ears and hearing**

V72.11 Encounter for hearing examination following failed hearing screening

V72.12 Encounter for hearing conservation and treatment

V72.19 Other examination of ears and hearing

V72.2 Dental examination

✓5th **V72.3 Gynecological examination**
EXCLUDES *cervical Papanicolaou smear without general gynecological examination (V76.2)*
routine examination in contraceptive management (V25.40-V25.49)

V72.31 Routine gynecological examination
General gynecological examination with or without Papanicolaou cervical smear
Pelvic examination (annual) (periodic)
Use additional code to identify:
human papillomavirus (HPV) screening (V73.81)
routine vaginal Papanicolaou smear (V76.47)

V72.32 Encounter for Papanicolaou cervical smear to confirm findings of recent normal smear following initial abnormal smear

✓5th **V72.4 Pregnancy examination or test**

V72.40 Pregnancy examination or test, pregnancy unconfirmed
Possible pregnancy, not (yet) confirmed

V72.41 Pregnancy examination or test, negative result

V72.42 Pregnancy examination or test, positive result

V72.5 Radiological examination, not elsewhere classified
Routine chest x-ray
EXCLUDES *examination for suspected tuberculosis (V71.2)*

V72.6 Laboratory examination
EXCLUDES *that for suspected disorder (V71.0-V71.9)*

V72.7 Diagnostic skin and sensitization tests
Allergy tests
Skin tests for hypersensitivity
EXCLUDES *diagnostic skin tests for bacterial diseases (V74.0-V74.9)*

✓5th **V72.8 Other specified examinations**

V72.81 Pre-operative cardiovascular examination
Pre-procedural cardiovascular examination

V72.82 Pre-operative respiratory examination
Pre-procedural respiratory examination

V72.83 Other specified pre-operative examination
Other pre-procedural examination
Pre-procedural general physical examination
EXCLUDES *routine general medical examination (V70.0)*

V72.84 Pre-operative examination, unspecified
Pre-procedural examination, unspecified

V72.85 Other specified examination

V72.86 Encounter for blood typing

V72.9 Unspecified examination

✓4th **V73 Special screening examination for viral and chlamydial diseases**

V73.0 Poliomyelitis

V73.1 Smallpox

V73.2 Measles

V73.3 Rubella

V73.4 Yellow fever

V73.5 Other arthropod-borne viral diseases
Dengue fever
Hemorrhagic fever
Viral encephalitis:
mosquito-borne
tick-borne

V73.6 Trachoma

✓5th **V73.8 Other specified viral and chlamydial diseases**

V73.81 Human papillomavirus [HPV]

V73.88 Other specified chlamydial diseases

V73.89 Other specified viral diseases

✓5th **V73.9 Unspecified viral and chlamydial disease**

V73.98 Unspecified chlamydial disease

V73.99 Unspecified viral disease

✓4th **V74 Special screening examination for bacterial and spirochetal diseases**
INCLUDES diagnostic skin tests for these diseases

V74.0 Cholera

V74.1 Pulmonary tuberculosis

V74.2 Leprosy [Hansen's disease]

V74.3 Diphtheria

V74.4 Bacterial conjunctivitis

V74.5 Venereal disease
Screening for bacterial and spirochetal sexually transmitted diseases
Screening for sexually transmitted diseases NOS
EXCLUDES *special screening for nonbacterial sexually transmitted diseases (V73.81-V73.89, V75.4, V75.8)*

V74.6 Yaws

V74.8 Other specified bacterial and spirochetal diseases
Brucellosis
Leptospirosis
Plague
Tetanus
Whooping cough

V74.9 Unspecified bacterial and spirochetal disease

✓4th **V75 Special screening examination for other infectious diseases**

V75.0 Rickettsial diseases

V75.1 Malaria

V75.2 Leishmaniasis

V75.3 Trypanosomiasis
Chagas' disease
Sleeping sickness

V75.4 Mycotic infections

V75.5 Schistosomiasis

V75.6 Filariasis

V75.7 Intestinal helminthiasis

V75.8 Other specified parasitic infections

V75.9 Unspecified infectious disease

✓4th **V76 Special screening for malignant neoplasms**

V76.0 Respiratory organs

✓5th **V76.1 Breast**

V76.10 Breast screening, unspecified

V76.11 Screening mammogram for high-risk patient

V76.12 Other screening mammogram

V76.19 Other screening breast examination

V76.2 Cervix
Routine cervical Papanicolaou smear
EXCLUDES *special screening for human papillomavirus (V73.81)*
that as part of a general gynecological examination (V72.31)

V76.3 Bladder

✓5th **V76.4 Other sites**

V76.41 Rectum

V76.42 Oral cavity

V76.43 Skin

V76.44 Prostate

V76.45 Testis

V76.46 Ovary

V76.47 Vagina
Vaginal pap smear status-post hysterectomy for non-malignant condition
Use additional code to identify acquired absence of uterus (V88.01-V88.03)
EXCLUDES *vaginal pap smear status-post hysterectomy for malignant condition (V67.01)*

V76.49 Other sites

✓5th **V76.5 Intestine**

V76.50 Intestine, unspecified

V76.51 Colon
EXCLUDES *rectum (V76.41)*

V76.52 Small intestine

✓5th **V76.8 Other neoplasm**

V76.81 Nervous system

V76.89 Other neoplasm

V76.9 Unspecified

✓4th **V77 Special screening for endocrine, nutritional, metabolic, and immunity disorders**

V77.0 Thyroid disorders

V77.1 Diabetes mellitus

V77.2 Malnutrition

V77.3 Phenylketonuria [PKU]

V77.4 Galactosemia

V77.5 Gout

V77.6 Cystic fibrosis
Screening for mucoviscidosis

V77.7 Other inborn errors of metabolism

V77.8 Obesity

✓5th **V77.9 Other and unspecified endocrine, nutritional, metabolic, and immunity disorders**

V77.91 Screening for lipoid disorders
Screening for cholesterol level
Screening for hypercholesterolemia
Screening for hyperlipidemia

V77.99 Other and unspecified endocrine, nutritional, metabolic, and immunity disorders

✓4th **V78 Special screening for disorders of blood and blood-forming organs**

V78.0 Iron deficiency anemia

V78.1 Other and unspecified deficiency anemia

V78.2 Sickle cell disease or trait

V78.3 Other hemoglobinopathies

V78.8 Other disorders of blood and blood-forming organs

V78.9 Unspecified disorder of blood and blood-forming organs

✓4th **V79 Special screening for mental disorders and developmental handicaps**

V79.0 Depression

V79.1 Alcoholism

V79.2 Mental retardation

V79.3 Developmental handicaps in early childhood

V79.8 Other specified mental disorders and developmental handicaps

V79.9 Unspecified mental disorder and developmental handicap

✓4th **V80 Special screening for neurological, eye, and ear diseases**

V80.0 Neurological conditions

V80.1 Glaucoma

V80.2 Other eye conditions
Screening for:
cataract
congenital anomaly of eye
senile macular lesions
EXCLUDES *general vision examination (V72.0)*

V80.3 Ear diseases
EXCLUDES *general hearing examination (V72.11-V72.19)*

✓4th V81 Special screening for cardiovascular, respiratory, and genitourinary diseases

V81.0 Ischemic heart disease

V81.1 Hypertension

V81.2 Other and unspecified cardiovascular conditions

V81.3 Chronic bronchitis and emphysema

V81.4 Other and unspecified respiratory conditions

EXCLUDES *screening for:*
lung neoplasm (V76.0)
pulmonary tuberculosis (V74.1)

V81.5 Nephropathy

Screening for asymptomatic bacteriuria

V81.6 Other and unspecified genitourinary conditions

✓4th V82 Special screening for other conditions

V82.0 Skin conditions

V82.1 Rheumatoid arthritis

V82.2 Other rheumatic disorders

V82.3 Congenital dislocation of hip

V82.4 Maternal postnatal screening for chromosomal anomalies

EXCLUDES *antenatal screening by amniocentesis (V28.0)*

V82.5 Chemical poisoning and other contamination

Screening for:
heavy metal poisoning
ingestion of radioactive substance
poisoning from contaminated water supply
radiation exposure

V82.6 Multiphasic screening

✓5th V82.7 Genetic screening

EXCLUDES *genetic testing for procreative management (V26.31-V26.39)*

V82.71 Screening for genetic disease carrier status

V82.79 Other genetic screening

✓5th V82.8 Other specified conditions

V82.81 Osteoporosis

Use additional code to identify:
hormone replacement therapy (postmenopausal) status (V07.4)
postmenopausal (age-related) (natural) status (V49.81)

V82.89 Other specified conditions

V82.9 Unspecified condition

GENETICS (V83-V84)

✓4th V83 Genetic carrier status

✓5th V83.0 Hemophilia A carrier

V83.01 Asymptomatic hemophilia A carrier

V83.02 Symptomatic hemophilia A carrier

✓5th V83.8 Other genetic carrier status

V83.81 Cystic fibrosis gene carrier

V83.89 Other genetic carrier status

✓4th V84 Genetic susceptibility to disease

INCLUDES confirmed abnormal gene

Use additional code, if applicable, for any associated family history of the disease (V16-V19)

✓5th V84.0 Genetic susceptibility to malignant neoplasm

Code first, if applicable, any current malignant neoplasms (140.0-195.8, 200.0-208.9, 230.0-234.9)

Use additional code, if applicable, for any personal history of malignant neoplasm (V10.0-V10.9)

V84.01 Genetic susceptibility to malignant neoplasm of breast

V84.02 Genetic susceptibility to malignant neoplasm of ovary

V84.03 Genetic susceptibility to malignant neoplasm of prostate

V84.04 Genetic susceptibility to malignant neoplasm of endometrium

V84.09 Genetic susceptibility to other malignant neoplasm

✓5th V84.8 Genetic susceptibility to other disease

V84.81 Genetic susceptibility to multiple endocrine neoplasia [MEN]

V84.89 Genetic susceptibility to other disease

BODY MASS INDEX (V85)

✓4th V85 Body Mass Index [BMI]

Kilograms per meters squared

Note: BMI adult codes are for use for persons over 20 years old

V85.0 Body Mass Index less than 19, adult

V85.1 Body Mass Index between 19-24, adult

✓5th V85.2 Body Mass Index between 25-29, adult

V85.21 Body Mass Index 25.0-25.9, adult

V85.22 Body Mass Index 26.0-26.9, adult

V85.23 Body Mass Index 27.0-27.9, adult

V85.24 Body Mass Index 28.0-28.9, adult

V85.25 Body Mass Index 29.0-29.9, adult

✓5th V85.3 Body Mass Index between 30-39, adult

V85.30 Body Mass Index 30.0-30.9, adult

V85.31 Body Mass Index 31.0-31.9, adult

V85.32 Body Mass Index 32.0-32.9, adult

V85.33 Body Mass Index 33.0-33.9, adult

V85.34 Body Mass Index 34.0-34.9, adult

V85.35 Body Mass Index 35.0-35.9, adult

V85.36 Body Mass Index 36.0-36.9, adult

V85.37 Body Mass Index 37.0-37.9, adult

V85.38 Body Mass Index 38.0-38.9, adult

V85.39 Body Mass Index 39.0-39.9, adult

V85.4 Body Mass Index 40 and over, adult

✓5th V85.5 Body Mass Index, pediatric

Note: BMI pediatric codes are for use for persons age 2-20 years old. These percentiles are based on the growth charts published by the Centers for Disease Control and Prevention (CDC)

V85.51 Body Mass Index, pediatric, less than 5th percentile for age

V85.52 Body Mass Index, pediatric, 5th percentile to less than 85th percentile for age

V85.53 Body Mass Index, pediatric, 85th percentile to less than 95th percentile for age

V85.54 Body Mass Index, pediatric, greater than or equal to 95th percentile for age

ESTROGEN RECEPTOR STATUS (V86)

✓4th V86 Estrogen receptor status

Code first malignant neoplasm of breast (174.0-174.9, 175.0-175.9)

V86.0 Estrogen receptor positive status [ER+]

V86.1 Estrogen receptor negative status [ER-]

OTHER SPECIFIED PERSONAL EXPOSURES AND HISTORY PRESENTING HAZARDS TO HEALTH (V87)

✓4th **V87 Other specified personal exposures and history presenting hazards to health**

✓5th **V87.0 Contact with and (suspected) exposure to hazardous metals**

EXCLUDES *exposure to lead (V15.86)*
toxic effect of metals (984.0-985.9)

V87.01 Arsenic

V87.09 Other hazardous metals
Chromium compounds
Nickel dust

✓5th **V87.1 Contact with and (suspected) exposure to hazardous aromatic compounds**

EXCLUDES *toxic effects of aromatic compounds (982.0, 983.0)*

V87.11 Aromatic amines

V87.12 Benzene

V87.19 Other hazardous aromatic compounds
Aromatic dyes NOS
Polycyclic aromatic hydrocarbons

V87.2 Contact with and (suspected) exposure to other potentially hazardous chemicals
Dyes NOS

EXCLUDES *exposure to asbestos (V15.84)*
toxic effect of chemicals (980-989)

✓5th **V87.3 Contact with and (suspected) exposure to other potentially hazardous substances**

EXCLUDES *contact with and (suspected) exposure to potentially hazardous body fluids (V15.85)*
toxic effect of substances (980-989)

V87.31 Exposure to mold

V87.39 Contact with and (suspected) exposure to other potentially hazardous substances

✓5th **V87.4 Personal history of drug therapy**

EXCLUDES *long-term (current) drug use (V58.61-V58.69)*

V87.41 Personal history of antineoplastic chemotherapy

V87.42 Personal history of monoclonal drug therapy

V87.49 Personal history of other drug therapy

ACQUIRED ABSENCE OF OTHER ORGANS AND TISSUE (V88)

✓4th **V88 Acquired absence of other organs and tissue**

✓5th **V88.0 Acquired absence of cervix and uterus**

V88.01 Acquired absence of both cervix and uterus
Acquired absence of uterus NOS
Status post total hysterectomy

V88.02 Acquired absence of uterus with remaining cervical stump
Status post partial hysterectomy with remaining cervical stump

V88.03 Acquired absence of cervix with remaining uterus

OTHER SUSPECTED CONDITIONS NOT FOUND (V89)

✓4th **V89 Other suspected conditions not found**

✓5th **V89.0 Suspected maternal and fetal conditions not found**

EXCLUDES *known or suspected fetal anomalies affecting management of mother, not ruled out (655.00, 655.93, 656.00-656.93, 657.00-657.03, 658.00-658.93)*
newborn and perinatal conditions — code to condition

V89.01 Suspected problem with amniotic cavity and membrane not found
Suspected oligohydramnios not found
Suspected polyhydramnios not found

V89.02 Suspected placental problem not found

V89.03 Suspected fetal anomaly not found

V89.04 Suspected problem with fetal growth not found

V89.05 Suspected cervical shortening not found

V89.09 Other suspected maternal and fetal condition not found

E Codes Supplementary Classification of External Causes of Injury and Poisoning (E800-E999.1)

The section titled "Supplementary Classification of External Causes of Injury and Poisoning" is commonly referred to as "E codes." E codes provide a classification of external causes that relate to the condition or injury being coded. E codes may indicate how an accident occurred; what caused an injury; whether a drug overdose was accidental; an adverse drug reaction; or, the location of occurrence of the injury.

Some major categories of E codes include the following:

- Transport accidents
- Poisoning and adverse effects of drugs, medicinal substances, and biologicals
- Accidental falls
- Accidents caused by fire and flames
- Accidents due to natural and environmental factors
- Late effects of accidents, assaults, or self-injury
- Assaults or purposely inflicted injury
- Suicide or self-inflicted injury

Coding Principles for E Codes

The E codes are assigned primarily by inpatient and other specialty facilities. However, office coders should be aware of the principles of E code assignment. The following principles are used to assign E codes: Look for the causes (fire, accident, fall, shooting) in section 3 of the alphabetic index. For adverse reactions to medical or surgical care, look under the main term "Reaction" in the alphabetic index. When listing an E code on a claim, be sure to use the letter "E" with the code number.

E codes are never used alone.

An E code is never used as a primary, principal or first-listed diagnosis.

An E code may be used with any code in the range of 001.0–V89.09, which indicates an injury, poisoning or adverse effect due to an external cause.

Use the full range of E codes to completely describe the cause, the intent and the place of occurrence, if applicable, for all injuries, poisonings, and adverse effects of drugs. Assign as many E codes as necessary to fully explain each cause. If only one E code can be recorded, assign the E code most related to the principal diagnosis.

Use an additional code from category E849 to identify the place of occurrence, if stated.

Late effect E codes exist for injuries and poisonings but not for adverse effects of drugs, misadventures, and surgical complications. A late effect E code (E929, E959, E969, E977, E989 or E999) should be assigned to report a late effect or sequela resulting from a previous injury or poisoning (905–909) and never to be used with an injury code.

There are several guidelines to follow when assigning multiple E codes. The hierarchy of reporting E codes is as follows:

- E codes for child and adult abuse take priority over all other E codes.
- E codes for cataclysmic events take priority over all other E codes except child and adult abuse.
- E codes for transport accidents take priority over all other E codes except cataclysmic events and child and adult abuse.

E codes provide information concerning intent (unintentional, or accidental or intentional, such as suicide or assault). If the intent (accident, self-harm, assault) of the cause of an injury or poisoning is unknown, questionable, probable or suspected or unspecified, code the intent as undetermined E980–E989.

TRANSPORT ACCIDENTS (E800–E848)

Transport accidents (E800–E848) involve a vehicle that is used primarily to transport people or products. Agriculture and construction vehicle accidents are considered transport accidents if the machinery is under its own power on a highway. Report the code for the injury sustained in the accident before the E code.

According to ICD-9-CM guidelines, a motor vehicle accident (E810–E819) is a transport accident involving a vehicle that is motorized. A motor vehicle accident is an accident that occurs on the highway and is assumed to have occurred on the highway unless otherwise specified. An accident that involves an off-road vehicle, such as an ATV or a snowmobile, is considered a nontraffic accident (E820–E825) unless otherwise specified. All codes require fourth digits.

ACCIDENTAL POISONING BY DRUGS, MEDICINAL SUBSTANCES AND BIOLOGICALS (E850–E858)

Poisoning by drugs, medicinal, and biological substances is the major cause of childhood accidents in the home and can occur by many routes, including oral ingestion, inhalation, dermal absorption, and ocular instillation.

Accidental poisoning codes identify accidental overdose of a drug, a wrong substance given or taken, a drug taken inadvertently, and accidents in the use of drugs and biologicals in medical and surgical procedures. The alphabetical index of ICD-9-CM can give a more complete list of specific drugs classified under a fourth-digit category; however, codes should not be assigned directly from the table of drugs and chemicals. Always consult the tabular section of ICD-9-CM before assigning the accidental poisoning codes. Many of the common medications can be found in the pharmacological listings found in the back of ICD-9-CM. When coding accidental poisoning use as many codes as necessary to completely describe the drug, medicinal, or biological poisoning. Sequence poisoning first, manifestation second, and the E code third. Assign an additional code for drug dependency, if applicable.

MISADVENTURES TO PATIENTS DURING SURGICAL AND MEDICAL CARE (E870–E876)

Many people are incapacitated as a result of medical errors. These errors increase health care costs significantly. The following kinds of errors unfortunately are often made: prescribing the wrong medication, administering an anesthetic improperly, operating a mechanical device incorrectly, causing an infection by improper wound treatment, contaminating blood or other pathological tests, completing a surgical procedure incorrectly. The physician should document clearly that a misadventure occurred and the nature of the complication.

ACCIDENTAL FALLS (E880–E888)

Codes for accidental fall codes are one of the most frequently assigned series of E codes. A fall is the most common cause of fatal injury in the elderly and a common cause of injury in children. Accidental falls are broken down into specific types depending on whether the fall was from a bed, a chair, a ladder, the toilet, or the sidewalk curb. Also included in this category is a fall that results in the person striking against an object. Excluded from this section is a fall in or from a burning building; into a fire; into water with submerging and drowning; in or from operating machinery; on an edged, painted, or sharp object; and in or from a transport or other vehicle.

Accidents (E916–E928)

Environmental Exposure to Harmful Algae and Toxins (E928.6)

Red tide is the reddish-brown color of sea water caused by an overconcentration of microscopic algae. Red tides are not always red but can vary in color or even look normal during a "bloom." Blooms are caused by a multitude of factors, including temperature shifts, rainfall accumulations, and changes in wind currents. A red tide begins offshore and moves shoreward, which accounts for beaches littered with dead marine mammals and fish. Red tides are natural phenomena, apparently unrelated to, though possibly exacerbated by, man-made pollution.

Irritation of the eyes, nose, throat, and tingling lips and tongue are common symptoms that occur in humans from airborne toxins during a red tide. Waves, wind, and boat propellers disperse toxin particles into the air, creating irritants for people along the shore. People suffering from severe or chronic respiratory conditions should avoid red tide areas, as the airborne irritants can exacerbate these conditions. Swimming in a red tide is unadvisable and may cause skin and mucous membrane irritation. Red tide can also be responsible for illnesses caused by consuming contaminated shellfish.

Code E928.6 Environmental exposure to harmful algae and toxins is assigned as a secondary diagnosis to describe the external cause of environmental exposure to harmful algae and toxins. Code first the manifestation (e.g., 462 Acute pharyngitis and E928.6 Environmental exposure to harmful algae and toxins).

Overexertion and Strenuous Movements (E927)

Overexertion and strenuous movements may cause small tears in the muscle, which are referred to as muscle strain. This occurs when the muscle is suddenly stretched beyond its limit. Muscle strains are graded according to their severity. Muscle strains can heal rapidly in the cases of mild strain or take months to heal for more severe strains. Standard treatment for muscle strains is rest, ice, compression, and elevation. Properly warming up, using correct body mechanics, strengthening muscles, and regular exercise can prevent muscle strains.

Drugs, Medicinal and Biological Substances Causing Adverse Effects in Therapeutic Use (E930–E949)

Codes E930–E949 report adverse medication reactions related to therapeutic use. This section is not used to report overdoses but rather allergic reaction or hypersensitivity. Symptoms can range from hives or skin rash to anaphylactic shock. Anaphylaxis is a severe allergic reaction and, in some cases, can produce life-threatening bronchospasm and laryngeal edema.

Adverse Effects of Oral (E933.6) and Intravenous (E933.7) Bisphosphonates

Codes E933.6 and E933.7 enable tracking of adverse effects of bisphosphonates drugs (e.g., Boniva, Fosamax, and Zometa) in therapeutic use. A causal relationship between osteonecrosis of the jaw and bisphosphonate medications is currently under investigation. The route of administration of these external causes is distinguished as either oral (E933.6) or intravenous (E933.7).

SUICIDE AND SELF-INFLICTED INJURY (E950–E959)

Codes E950–E959 report suicide and self-inflicted injury, which includes injury and suicide by self-inflicted poisoning, hanging, strangulating, suffocating, shooting, submerging, and drowning, and cutting or piercing. Near drowning is now more commonly referred to as a submersion accident. If the intent is not specified, is unknown, or documented as questionable, probable, or suspected, assign the E code for cause undetermined.

HOMICIDE AND INJURY PURPOSELY INFLICTED BY OTHER PERSONS (E960–E969)

This section includes fights, rape, assault by corrosive substance, assault by poisoning, and assault by firearm. Also included in this section are codes to describe the perpetrator of child and adult abuse. E codes for child and adult abuse take priority over all other E codes. An E code for the type of abuse should be listed first, followed by the code for perpetrator. Report an accidental neglect code first if the intent is an accidental abandonment of an adult or a child. If the intent is not specified, unknown, or documented as questionable, probable, or suspected, assign the E code for cause undetermined.

INJURY RESULTING FROM OPERATIONS OF WAR (E990–E999)

Section E990–E999 reports injury resulting from operations of war. Operations of war are injuries to military personnel and civilians caused by war and civil revolt and occurring during the time of war. Excluded from this section are accidents during training of military personnel, manufacture of war material, and transport, unless attributable to enemy action.

SUPPLEMENTARY CLASSIFICATION OF EXTERNAL CAUSES OF INJURY AND POISONING (E800-E999)

This section is provided to permit the classification of environmental events, circumstances, and conditions as the cause of injury, poisoning, and other adverse effects. Where a code from this section is applicable, it is intended that it shall be used in addition to a code from one of the main chapters of ICD-9-CM, indicating the nature of the condition. Certain other conditions which may be stated to be due to external causes are classified in Chapters 1 to 16 of ICD-9-CM. For these, the "E" code classification should be used as an additional code for more detailed analysis.

Machinery accidents [other than those connected with transport] are classifiable to category E919, in which the fourth-digit allows a broad classification of the type of machinery involved. If a more detailed classification of type of machinery is required, it is suggested that the "Classification of Industrial Accidents according to Agency," prepared by the International Labor Office, be used in addition. This is reproduced in Appendix D for optional use.

Categories for "late effects" of accidents and other external causes are to be found at E929, E959, E969, E977, E989, and E999.

DEFINITIONS AND EXAMPLES RELATED TO TRANSPORT ACCIDENTS

(a) A **transport accident** (E800-E848) is any accident involving a device designed primarily for, or being used at the time primarily for, conveying persons or goods from one place to another.

INCLUDES accidents involving:
- aircraft and spacecraft (E840-E845)
- watercraft (E830-E838)
- motor vehicle (E810-E825)
- railway (E800-E807)
- other road vehicles (E826-E829)

In classifying accidents which involve more than one kind of transport, the above order of precedence of transport accidents should be used.

Accidents involving agricultural and construction machines, such as tractors, cranes, and bulldozers, are regarded as transport accidents only when these vehicles are under their own power on a highway [otherwise the vehicles are regarded as machinery]. Vehicles which can travel on land or water, such as hovercraft and other amphibious vehicles, are regarded as watercraft when on the water, as motor vehicles when on the highway, and as off-road motor vehicles when on land, but off the highway.

EXCLUDES *accidents:*
- *in sports which involve the use of transport but where the transport vehicle itself was not involved in the accident*
- *involving vehicles which are part of industrial equipment used entirely on industrial premises*
- *occurring during transportation but unrelated to the hazards associated with the means of transportation [e.g., injuries received in a fight on board ship; transport vehicle involved in a cataclysm such as an earthquake]*
- *to persons engaged in the maintenance or repair of transport equipment or vehicle not in motion, unlesss injured by another vehicle in motion*

(b) A **railway accident** is a transport accident involving a railway train or other railway vehicle operated on rails, whether in motion or not.

EXCLUDES *accidents:*
- *in repair shops*
- *in roundhouse or on turntable*
- *on railway premises but not involving a train or other railway vehicle*

(c) A **railway train** or **railway vehicle** is any device with or without cars coupled to it, desiged for traffic on a railway.

INCLUDES interurban:
- electric car, street car (operated chiefly on its own right-of-way, not open to other traffic)
- railway train, any power [diesel] [electric] [steam]
  - funicular
  - monorail or two-rail
  - subterranean or elevated
- other vehicle designed to run on a railway track

EXCLUDES *interurban electric cars [streetcars] specified to be operating on a right-of-way that forms part of the public street or highway [definition (h)]*

(d) A **railway** or **railroad** is a right-of-way designed for traffic on rails, which is used by carriages or wagons transporting passengers or freight, and by other rolling stock, and which is not open to other public vehicular traffic.

(e) A **motor vehicle accident** is a transport accident involving a motor vehicle. It is defined as a motor vehicle traffic accident or as a motor vehicle nontraffic accident according to whether the accident occurs on a public highway or elsewhere.

EXCLUDES *injury or damage due to cataclysm*
injury or damage while a motor vehicle, not under its own power, is being loaded on, or unloaded from, another conveyance

(f) A **motor vehicle traffic accident** is any motor vehicle accident occurring on a public highway [i.e., originating, terminating, or involving a vehicle partially on the highway]. A motor vehicle accident is assumed to have occurred on the highway unless another place is specified, except in the case of accidents involving only off-road motor vehicles which are classified as nontraffic accidents unless the contrary is stated.

(g) A **motor vehicle nontraffic accident** is any motor vehicle accident which occurs entirely in any place other than a public highway.

(h) A **public highway [trafficway]** or **street** is the entire width between property lines [or other boundary lines] of every way or place, of which any part is open to the use of the public for purposes of vehicular traffic as a matter of right or custom. A **roadway** is that part of the public highway designed, improved, and ordinarily used, for vehicular travel.

INCLUDES approaches (public) to:
- docks
- public building
- station

EXCLUDES *driveway (private)*
parking lot
ramp
roads in:
- *airfield*
- *farm*
- *industrial premises*
- *mine*
- *private grounds*
- *quarry*

(i) A **motor vehicle** is any mechanically or electrically powered device, not operated on rails, upon which any person or property may be transported or drawn upon a highway. Any object such as a trailer, coaster, sled, or wagon being towed by a motor vehicle is considered a part of the motor vehicle.

INCLUDES automobile [any type]
bus
construction machinery, farm and industrial machinery, steam roller, tractor, army tank, highway grader, or similar vehicle on wheels or treads, while in transport under own power
fire engine (motorized)
motorcycle
motorized bicycle [moped] or scooter
trolley bus not operating on rails
truck
van

EXCLUDES *devices used solely to move persons or materials within the confines of a building and its premises, such as:*
building elevator
coal car in mine
electric baggage or mail truck used solely within a railroad station
electric truck used solely within an industrial plant
moving overhead crane

(j) A **motorcycle** is a two-wheeled motor vehicle having one or two riding saddles and sometimes having a third wheel for the support of a sidecar. The sidecar is considered part of the motorcycle.

INCLUDES motorized:
bicycle [moped]
scooter
tricycle

(k) An **off-road motor vehicle** is a motor vehicle of special design, to enable it to negotiate rough or soft terrain or snow. Examples of special design are high construction, special wheels and tires, driven by treads, or support on a cushion of air.

INCLUDES all terrain vehicle [ATV]
army tank
hovercraft, on land or swamp
snowmobile

(l) A **driver** of a motor vehicle is the occupant of the motor vehicle operating it or intending to operate it. A **motorcyclist** is the driver of a motorcycle. Other authorized occupants of a motor vehicle are **passengers**.

(m) An **other road vehicle** is any device, except a motor vehicle, in, on, or by which any person or property may be transported on a highway.

INCLUDES animal carrying a person or goods
animal-drawn vehicles
animal harnessed to conveyance
bicycle [pedal cycle]
streetcar
tricycle (pedal)

EXCLUDES *pedestrian conveyance [definition (q)]*

(n) A **streetcar** is a device designed and used primarily for transporting persons within a municipality, running on rails, usually subject to normal traffic control signals, and operated principally on a right-of-way that forms part of the traffic way. A trailer being towed by a streetcar is considered a part of the streetcar.

INCLUDES interurban or intraurban electric or streetcar, when specified to be operating on a street or public highway
tram (car)
trolley (car)

(o) A **pedal cycle** is any road transport vehicle operated solely by pedals.

INCLUDES bicycle
pedal cycle
tricycle

EXCLUDES *motorized bicycle [definition (j)]*

(p) A **pedal cyclist** is any person riding on a pedal cycle or in a sidecar attached to such a vehicle.

(q) A **pedestrian conveyance** is any human powered device by which a pedestrian may move other than by walking or by which a walking person may move another pedestrian.

INCLUDES baby carriage
coaster wagon
heelies, wheelies
ice skates
perambulator
pushcart
pushchair
roller skates
scooter
skateboard
skis
sled
wheelchair

(r) A **pedestrian** is any person involved in an accident who was not at the time of the accident riding in or on a motor vehicle, railroad train, streetcar, animal-drawn or other vehicle, or on a bicycle or animal.

INCLUDES person:
changing tire of vehicle
in or operating a pedestrian conveyance
making adjustment to motor of vehicle
on foot

(s) A **watercraft** is any device for transporting passengers or goods on the water.

(t) A **small boat** is any watercraft propelled by paddle, oars, or small motor, with a passenger capacity of less than ten.

INCLUDES boat NOS
canoe
coble
dinghy
punt
raft
rowboat
rowing shell
scull
skiff
small motorboat

EXCLUDES *barge*
lifeboat (used after abandoning ship)
raft (anchored) being used as a diving platform
yacht

(u) An **aircraft** is any device for transporting passengers or goods in the air.

INCLUDES airplane [any type]
balloon
bomber
dirigible
glider (hang)
military aircraft
parachute

(v) A **commercial transport aircraft** is any device for collective passenger or freight transportation by air, whether run on commercial lines for profit or by government authorities, with the exception of military craft.

RAILWAY ACCIDENTS (E800-E807)

Note: For definitions of railway accident and related terms see definitions (a) to (d).

EXCLUDES *accidents involving railway train and:*
aircraft (E840.0-E845.9)
motor vehicle (E810.0-E825.9)
watercraft (E830.0-E838.9)

The following fourth-digit subdivisions are for use with categories E800-E807 to identify the injured person:

.0 Railway employee
Any person who by virtue of his employment in connection with a railway, whether by the railway company or not, is at increased risk of involvement in a railway accident, such as:
catering staff of train
driver
guard
porter
postal staff on train
railway fireman
shunter
sleeping car attendant

.1 Passenger on railway
Any authorized person traveling on a train, except a railway employee.
EXCLUDES *intending passenger waiting at station (.8)*
unauthorized rider on railway vehicle (.8)

.2 Pedestrian
See definition (r)

.3 Pedal cyclist
See definition (p)

.8 Other specified person
Intending passenger or bystander waiting at station
Unauthorized rider on railway vehicle

.9 Unspecified person

✓4th E800 Railway accident involving collision with rolling stock
INCLUDES collision between railway trains or railway vehicles, any kind
collision NOS on railway
derailment with antecedent collision with rolling stock or NOS

✓4th E801 Railway accident involving collision with other object
INCLUDES collision of railway train with:
buffers
fallen tree on railway
gates
platform
rock on railway
streetcar
other nonmotor vehicle
other object

EXCLUDES *collision with:*
aircraft (E840.0-E842.9)
motor vehicle (E810.0-E810.9, E820.0-E822.9)

✓4th E802 Railway accident involving derailment without antecedent collision

✓4th E803 Railway accident involving explosion, fire, or burning
EXCLUDES *explosion or fire, with antecedent derailment (E802.0-E802.9)*
explosion or fire, with mention of antecedent collision (E800.0-E801.9)

✓4th E804 Fall in, on, or from railway train
INCLUDES fall while alighting from or boarding railway train
EXCLUDES *fall related to collision, derailment, or explosion of railway train (E800.0-E803.9)*

✓4th E805 Hit by rolling stock
INCLUDES crushed, injured, killed, knocked down, run over } by railway train or part
EXCLUDES *pedestrian hit by object set in motion by railway train (E806.0-E806.9)*

✓4th E806 Other specified railway accident
INCLUDES hit by object falling in railway train
injured by door or window on railway train
nonmotor road vehicle or pedestrian hit by object set in motion by railway train
railway train hit by falling:
earth NOS
rock
tree
other object
EXCLUDES *railway accident due to cataclysm (E908-E909)*

✓4th E807 Railway accident of unspecified nature
INCLUDES found dead, injured } on railway right-of-way NOS
railway accident NOS

MOTOR VEHICLE TRAFFIC ACCIDENTS (E810-E819)

Note: For definitions of motor vehicle traffic accident, and related terms, see definitions (e) to (k).

EXCLUDES *accidents involving motor vehicle and aircraft (E840.0-E845.9)*

The following fourth-digit subdivisions are for use with categories E810-E819 to identify the injured person:

.0 Driver of motor vehicle other than motorcycle
See definition (l)

.1 Passenger in motor vehicle other than motorcycle
See definition (l)

.2 Motorcyclist
See definition (l)

.3 Passenger on motorcycle
See definition (l)

.4 Occupant of streetcar

.5 Rider of animal; occupant of animal-drawn vehicle

.6 Pedal cyclist
See definition (p)

.7 Pedestrian
See definition (r)

.8 Other specified person
Occupant of vehicle other than above
Person in railway train involved in accident
Unauthorized rider of motor vehicle

.9 Unspecified person

✓4th E810 Motor vehicle traffic accident involving collision with train
EXCLUDES *motor vehicle collision with object set in motion by railway train (E815.0-E815.9)*
railway train hit by object set in motion by motor vehicle (E818.0-E818.9)

✓4th E811 Motor vehicle traffic accident involving re-entrant collision with another motor vehicle
INCLUDES collision between motor vehicle which accidentally leaves the roadway then re-enters the same roadway, or the opposite roadway on a divided highway, and another motor vehicle
EXCLUDES *collision on the same roadway when none of the motor vehicles involved have left and re-entered the highway (E812.0-E812.9)*

✓4th E812 Other motor vehicle traffic accident involving collision with motor vehicle

INCLUDES collision with another motor vehicle parked, stopped, stalled, disabled, or abandoned on the highway
motor vehicle collision NOS

EXCLUDES *collision with object set in motion by another motor vehicle (E815.0-E815.9)*
re-entrant collision with another motor vehicle (E811.0-E811.9)

✓4th E813 Motor vehicle traffic accident involving collision with other vehicle

INCLUDES collision between motor vehicle, any kind, and:
other road (nonmotor transport) vehicle, such as:
animal carrying a person
animal-drawn vehicle
pedal cycle
streetcar

EXCLUDES *collision with:*
object set in motion by nonmotor road vehicle (E815.0-E815.9)
pedestrian (E814.0-E814.9)
nonmotor road vehicle hit by object set in motion by motor vehicle (E818.0-E818.9)

✓4th E814 Motor vehicle traffic accident involving collision with pedestrian

INCLUDES collision between motor vehicle, any kind, and pedestrian
pedestrian dragged, hit, or run over by motor vehicle, any kind

EXCLUDES *pedestrian hit by object set in motion by motor vehicle (E818.0-E818.9)*

✓4th E815 Other motor vehicle traffic accident involving collision on the highway

INCLUDES collision (due to loss of control) (on highway) between motor vehicle, any kind, and:
abutment (bridge) (overpass)
animal (herded) (unattended)
fallen stone, traffic sign, tree, utility pole
guard rail or boundary fence
interhighway divider
landslide (not moving)
object set in motion by railway train or road vehicle (motor) (nonmotor)
object thrown in front of motor vehicle
other object, fixed, movable, or moving
safety island
temporary traffic sign or marker
wall of cut made for road

EXCLUDES *collision with:*
any object off the highway (resulting from loss of control) (E816.0-E816.9)
any object which normally would have been off the highway and is not stated to have been on it (E816.0-E816.9)
motor vehicle parked, stopped, stalled, disabled, or abandoned on highway (E812.0-E812.9)
moving landslide (E909)
motor vehicle hit by object:
set in motion by railway train or road vehicle (motor) (nonmotor) (E818.0-E818.9)
thrown into or on vehicle (E818.0-E818.9)

✓4th E816 Motor vehicle traffic accident due to loss of control, without collision on the highway

INCLUDES motor vehicle:

failing to make curve going out of control (due to): blowout burst tire driver falling asleep drive inattention excessive speed failure of mechanical part	and: coliding with object off the highway overturning stopping abruptly off the highway

EXCLUDES *collision on highway following loss of control (E810.0-E815.9)*
loss of control of motor vehicle following collision on the highway (E810.0-E815.9)

✓4th E817 Noncollision motor vehicle traffic accident while boarding or alighting

INCLUDES

fall down stairs of motor bus fall from car in street injured by moving part of the vehicle trapped by door of motor bus	while boarding or alighting

✓4th E818 Other noncollision motor vehicle traffic accident

INCLUDES

accidental poisoning from exhaust gas generated by breakage of any part of explosion of any part of fall, jump, or being accidentally pushed from fire starting in hit by object thrown into or on injured by being thrown against some part of, or object in injury from moving part of object falling in or on object thrown on	motor vehicle while in motion

collision of railway train or road vehicle except motor vehicle, with object set in motion by motor vehicle
motor vehicle hit by object set in motion by railway train or road vehicle (motor) (nonmotor)
pedestrian, railway train, or road vehicle (motor) (nonmotor) hit by object set in motion by motor vehicle

EXCLUDES *collision between motor vehicle and:*
object set in motion by railway train or road vehicle (motor) (nonmotor) (E815.0-E815.9)
object thrown towards the motor vehicle (E815.0-E815.9)
person overcome by carbon monoxide generated by stationary motor vehicle off the roadway with motor running (E868.2)

✓4th E819 Motor vehicle traffic accident of unspecified nature

INCLUDES motor vehicle traffic accident NOS
traffic accident NOS

MOTOR VEHICLE NONTRAFFIC ACCIDENTS (E820-E825)

Note: For definitions of motor vehicle nontraffic accident and related terms see definition (a) to (k).

INCLUDES accidents involving motor vehicles being used in recreational or sporting activities off the highway
collision and noncollision motor vehicle accidents occurring entirely off the highway

EXCLUDES *accidents involving motor vehicle and:*
aircraft (E840.0-E845.9)
watercraft (E830.0-E838.9)
accidents, not on the public highway, involving agricultural and construction machinery but not involving another motor vehicle (E919.0, E919.2, E919.7)

The following fourth-digit subdivisions are for use with categories E820-E825 to identify the injured person:

.0 Driver of motor vehicle other than motorcycle
See definition (l)
.1 Passenger in motor vehicle other than motorcycle
See definition (l)
.2 Motorcyclist
See definition (l)
.3 Passenger on motorcycle
See definition (l)
.4 Occupant of streetcar
.5 Rider of animal; occupant of animal-drawn vehicle
.6 Pedal cyclist
See definition (p)
.7 Pedestrian
See definition (r)
.8 Other specified person
Occupant of vehicle other than above
Person in railway train involved in accident
Unauthorized rider of motor vehicle
.9 Unspecified person

✓4th E820 Nontraffic accident involving motor-driven snow vehicle

INCLUDES breakage of part of / fall from / hit by / overturning of / run over or dragged by } motor-driven snow vehicle (not on public highway)
collision of motor-driven snow vehicle with:
animal (being ridden) (-drawn vehicle)
another off-road motor vehicle
other motor vehicle, not on public highway
railway train
other object, fixed or movable
injury caused by rough landing of motor-driven snow vehicle (after leaving ground on rough terrain)

EXCLUDES *accident on the public highway involving motor driven snow vehicle (E810.0-E819.9)*

✓4th E821 Nontraffic accident involving other off-road motor vehicle

INCLUDES breakage of part of / fall from / hit by / overturning of / run over or dragged by / thrown against some part of or object in } off-road motorvehicle except snow vehicle (not on public highway
collision with:
animal (being ridden) (-drawn vehicle)
another off-road motor vehicle, except snow vehicle
other motor vehicle, not on public highway
other object, fixed or movable

EXCLUDES *accident on public highway involving off-road motor vehicle (E810.0-E819.9)*
collision between motor driven snow vehicle and other off-road motor vehicle (E820.0-E820.9)
hovercraft accident on water (E830.0-E838.9)

✓4th E822 Other motor vehicle nontraffic accident involving collision with moving object

INCLUDES collision, not on public highway, between motor vehicle, except off-road motor vehicle and:
animal
nonmotor vehicle
other motor vehicle, except off-road motor vehicle
pedestrian
railway train
other moving object

EXCLUDES *collision with:*
motor-driven snow vehicle (E820.0-E820.9)
other off-road motor vehicle (E821.0-E821.9)

✓4th E823 Other motor vehicle nontraffic accident involving collision with stationary object

INCLUDES collision, not on public highway, between motor vehicle, except off-road motor vehicle, and any object, fixed or movable, but not in motion

✓4th E824 Other motor vehicle nontraffic accident while boarding and alighting

INCLUDES fall / injury from oving part of motor vehicle / trapped by door of motor vehhicle } while boarding or alighting from motor vehicle, except off-road motor vehicle, not on public highway

✓4th E825 Other motor vehicle nontraffic accident of other and unspecified nature

INCLUDES accidental poisoning from carbon monoxide generated by / breakage of any part of / explosion of any part of / fall, jump, or being accidentally pushed from / fire starting in / hit by object thrown into, towards, or on / injured by being thrown against some part of, or object in / injury from moving part of / object falling in or on } motor vehicle while in motion, not on public highway
motor vehicle nontraffic accident NOS

EXCLUDES *fall from or in stationary motor vehicle (E884.9, E885.9)*
overcome by carbon monoxide or exhaust gas generated by stationary motor vehicle off the roadway with motor running (E868.2)
struck by falling object from or in stationary motor vehicle (E916)

OTHER ROAD VEHICLE ACCIDENTS (E826-E829)

Note: Other road vehicle accidents are transport accidents involving road vehicles other than motor vehicles. For definitions of other road vehicle and related terms see definitions (m) to (o).

INCLUDES accidents involving other road vehicles being used in recreational or sporting activities

EXCLUDES *collision of other road vehicle [any] with:*
aircraft (E840.0-E845.9)
motor vehicle (E813.0-E813.9, E820.0-E822.9)
railway train (E801.0-E801.9))

The following fourth-digit subdivisions are for use with categories E826-E829 to identify the injured person:

.0 Pedestrian
See definition (r)
.1 Pedal cyclist
See definition (p)
.2 Rider of animal
.3 Occupant of animal-drawn vehicle
.4 Occupant of streetcar
.8 Other specified person
.9 Unspecified person

4th E826 Pedal cycle accident

[0-9] INCLUDES breakage of any part of pedal cycle
collision between pedal cycle and:
animal (being ridden) (herded) (unattended)
another pedal cycle
any pedestrian
nonmotor road vehicle
other object, fixed, movable, or moving, not set in motion by motor vehicle, railway train, or aircraft
entanglement in wheel of pedal cycle
fall from pedal cycle
hit by object falling or thrown on the pedal cycle
pedal cycle accident NOS
pedal cycle overturned

4th E827 Animal-drawn vehicle accident

[0,2,4,8,9] INCLUDES breakage of any part of vehicle
collision between animal-drawn vehicle and:
animal (being ridden) (herded) (unattended)
nonmotor road vehicle, except pedal cycle
pedestrian, pedestrian conveyance, or pedestrian vehicle
other object, fixed, movable, or moving, not set in motion by motor vehicle, railway train, or aircraft
fall from, knocked down by, overturning of, running over by, thrown from } animal drawn vehicle

EXCLUDES *collision of animal-drawn vehicle with pedal cycle (E826.0-E826.9)*

4th E828 Accident involving animal being ridden

[0,2,4,8,9] INCLUDES collision between animal being ridden and:
another animal
nonmotor road vehicle, except pedal cycle, and animal-drawn vehicle
pedestrian, pedestrian conveyance, or pedestrian vehicle
other object, fixed, movable, or moving, not set in motion by motor vehicle, railway train, or aircraft
fall from, knocked down by, thrown from, trampled by } animal being ridden
ridden animal stumbled and fell

EXCLUDES *collision of animal being ridden with:*
animal-drawn vehicle (E827.0-E827.9)
pedal cycle (E826.0-E826.9)

4th E829 Other road vehicle accidents

[0,4,8,9] INCLUDES accident while boarding or alighting from, blow from object in, breakage of any part of, caught in door of, derailment of, fall in, on, or from, fire in } streetcar nonmotor road vehicle not classifiable to E826-E828
collision between streetcar or nonmotor road vehicle, except as in E826-E828, and:
animal (not being ridden)
another nonmotor road vehicle not classifiable to E826-E828
pedestrian
other object, fixed, movable, or moving, not set in motion by motor vehicle, railway train, or aircraft
nonmotor road vehicle accident NOS
streetcar accident NOS

EXCLUDES *collision with:*
animal being ridden (E828.0-E828.9)
animal-drawn vehicle (E827.0-E827.9)
pedal cycle (E826.0-E826.9)

WATER TRANSPORT ACCIDENTS (E830-E838)

Note: For definitions of water transport accident and related terms see definitions (a), (s), and (t).

INCLUDES watercraft accidents in the course of recreational activities

EXCLUDES *accidents involving both aircraft, including objects set in motion by aircraft, and watercraft (E840.0-E845.9)*

The following fourth-digit subdivisions are for use with categories E830-E838 to identify the injured person:

.0 Occupant of small boat, unpowered
.1 Occupant of small boat, powered
See definition (t)
EXCLUDES *water skier (.4)*
.2 Occupant of other watercraft – crew
Persons:
engaged in operation of watercraft
providing passenger services [cabin attendants, ship's physician, catering personnel]
working on ship during voyage in other capacity [musician in band, operators of shops and beauty parlors
.3 Occupant of other watercraft – other than crew
Passenger
Occupant of lifeboat, other than crew, after abandoning ship
.4 Water skier
.5 Swimmer
.6 Dockers, stevedores
Longshoreman employed on the dock in loading and unloading ships
.8 Other specified person
Immigration and custom officials on board ship
Person:
accompanying passenger or member of crew visiting boat
Pilot (guiding ship into port)
.9 Unspecified person

4th E830 Accident to watercraft causing submersion

INCLUDES submersion and drowning due to:
boat overturning
boat submerging
falling or jumping from burning ship
falling or jumping from crushed watercraft
ship sinking
other accident to watercraft

✓4th E831 Accident to watercraft causing other injury

INCLUDES any injury, except submersion and drowning, as a result of an accident to watercraft
burned while ship on fire
crushed between ships in collision
crushed by lifeboat after abandoning ship
fall due to collision or other accident to watercraft
hit by falling object due to accident to watercraft
injured in watercraft accident involving collision
struck by boat or part thereof after fall or jump from damaged boat

EXCLUDES *burns from localized fire or explosion on board ship (E837.0-E837.9)*

✓4th E832 Other accidental submersion or drowning in water transport accident

INCLUDES submersion or drowning as a result of an accident other than accident to the watercraft, such as:
fall:
from gangplank
from ship
overboard
thrown overboard by motion of ship
washed overboard

EXCLUDES *submersion or drowning of swimmer or diver who voluntarily jumps from boat not involved in an accident (E910.0-E910.9)*

✓4th E833 Fall on stairs or ladders in water transport

EXCLUDES *fall due to accident to watercraft (E831.0-E831.9)*

✓4th E834 Other fall from one level to another in water transport

EXCLUDES *fall due to accident to watercraft (E831.0-E831.9)*

✓4th E835 Other and unspecified fall in water transport

EXCLUDES *fall due to accident to watercraft (E831.0-E831.9)*

✓4th E836 Machinery accident in water transport

INCLUDES injuries in water transport caused by:
deck, engine room, galley, laundry, loading } machinery

✓4th E837 Explosion, fire, or burning in watercraft

INCLUDES explosion of boiler on steamship
localized fire on ship

EXCLUDES *burning ship (due to collision or explosion) resulting in:*
submersion or drowning (E830.0-E830.9)
other injury (E831.0-E831.9)

✓4th E838 Other and unspecified water transport accident

INCLUDES accidental poisoning by gases or fumes on ship
atomic power plant malfunction in watercraft
crushed between ship and stationary object [wharf]
crushed between ships without accident to watercraft
crushed by falling object on ship or while loading or unloading
hit by boat while water skiing
struck by boat or part thereof (after fall from boat)
watercraft accident NOS

AIR AND SPACE TRANSPORT ACCIDENTS (E840-E845)

Note:For definition of aircraft and related terms see definitions (u) and (v).

The following fourth-digit subdivisions are for use with categories E840-E845 to identify the injured person. Valid fourth digits are in [brackets] under codes E842-E845:

.0 Occupant of spacecraft

.1 Occupant of military aircraft, any
Crew in military aircraft [air force] [army] [national guard] [navy]
Passenger (civilian) (military) in military aircraft [air force] [army] [national guard] [navy]
Troops in military aircraft [air force] [army] [national guard] [navy]

EXCLUDES *occupants of aircraft operated under jurisdiction of police departments (.5)*
parachutist (.7)

.2 Crew of commercial aircraft (powered) in surface to surface transport

.3 Other occupant of commercial aircraft (powered) in surface to surface transport
Flight personnel:
not part of crew
on familiarization flight
Passenger on aircraft (powered) NOS

.4 Occupant of commercial aircraft (powered) in surface to air transport
Occupant [crew] [passenger] of aircraft (powered) engaged in activities, such as:
aerial spraying (crops) (fire retardants)
air drops of emergency supplies
air drops of parachutists, except from military craft
crop dusting
lowering of construction material [bridge or telephone pole]
sky writing

.5 Occupant of other powered aircraft
Occupant [crew] [passenger] of aircraft (powered) engaged in activities, such as:
aerobatic flying
aircraft racing
rescue operation
storm surveillance
traffic surveillance
Occupant of private plane NOS

.6 Occupant of unpowered aircraft, except parachutist
Occupant of aircraft classifiable to E842

.7 Parachutist (military) (other)
Person making voluntary descent

EXCLUDES *person making descent after accident to aircraft (.1-.6)*

.8 Ground crew, airline employee
Persons employed at airfields (civil) (military) or launching pads, not occupants of aircraft

.9 Other person

✓4th E840 Accident to powered aircraft at takeoff or landing

INCLUDES collision of aircraft with any object, fixed, movable, or moving; crash; explosion on aircraft; fire on aircraft; forced landing } while taking off or landing

✓4th E841 Accident to powered aircraft, other and unspecified

INCLUDES aircraft accident NOS
aircraft crash or wreck NOS
any accident to powered aircraft while in transit or when not specified whether in transit, taking off, or landing
collision of aircraft with another aircraft, bird, or any object, while in transit
explosion on aircraft while in transit
fire on aircraft while in transit

✓4th E842 Accident to unpowered aircraft
[6-9] INCLUDES any accident, except collision with powered aircraft, to:
balloon
glider
hang glider
kite carrying a person
hit by object falling from unpowered aircraft

✓4th E843 Fall in, on, or from aircraft
[0-9] INCLUDES accident in boarding or alighting from aircraft, any kind
fall in, on, or from aircraft [any kind], while in transit, taking off, or landing, except when as a result of an accident to aircraft

✓4th E844 Other specified air transport accidents
[0-9] INCLUDES hit by:
aircraft
object falling from aircraft
injury by or from:
machinery of aircraft
rotating propellar
voluntary parachute descent
poisoning by carbon monoxide from aircraft while in transit
sucked into jet
} without accident to aircraft
any accident involving other transport vehicle (motor) (nonmotor) due to being hit by object set in motion by aircraft (powered)
EXCLUDES *air sickness (E903)*
effects of:
high altitude (E902.0-E902.1)
pressure change (E902.0-E902.1)
injury in parachute descent due to accident to aircraft (E840.0-E842-9)

§ **✓4th E845 Accident involving spacecraft**
[0,8,9] INCLUDES launching pad accident
EXCLUDES *effects of weightlessness in spacecraft (E928.0)*

VEHICLE ACCIDENTS NOT ELSEWHERE CLASSIFIABLE (E846-E848)

E846 Accidents involving powered vehicles used solely within the buildings and premises of industrial or commercial establishment
Accident to, on, or involving:
battery powered airport passenger vehicle
battery powered trucks (baggage) (mail)
coal car in mine
logging car
self propelled truck, industrial
station baggage truck (powered)
tram, truck, or tub (powered) in mine or quarry
Collision with:
pedestrian
other vehicle or object within premises
Explosion of
Fall from
Overturning of
Struck by
} powered vehicle, industrial or commercial
EXCLUDES *accidental poisoning by exhaust gas from vehicle not elsewhere classifiable (E868.2)*
injury by crane, lift (fork), or elevator (E919.2)

E847 Accidents involving cable cars not running on rails
Accident to, on, or involving:
cable car, not on rails
ski chair-lift
ski-lift with gondola
téléférique
Breakage of cable
Caught or dragged by
Fall or jump from
Object thrown from or in
} cable car, not on rails

E848 Accidents involving other vehicles, not elsewhere classifiable
Accident to, on, or involving:
ice yacht
land yacht
nonmotor, nonroad vehicle NOS

✓4th E849 Place of occurrence
The following category is for use to denote the place where the injury or poisoning occurred.

E849.0 Home
Apartment
Boarding house
Farm house
Home premises
House (residential)
Noninstitutional place of residence
Private:
driveway
garage
garden
home
walk
Swimming pool in private house or garden
Yard of home
EXCLUDES *home under construction but not yet occupied (E849.3)*
institutional place of residence (E849.7)

E849.1 Farm
Farm:
buildings
land under cultivation
EXCLUDES *farm house and home premises of farm (E849.0)*

E849.2 Mine and quarry
Gravel pit
Sand pit
Tunnel under construction

E849.3 Industrial place and premises
Building under construction
Dockyard
Dry dock
Factory
building
premises
Garage (place of work)
Industrial yard
Loading platform (factory) (store)
Plant, industrial
Railway yard
Shop (place of work)
Warehouse
Workhouse

E849.4 Place for recreation and sport

Amusement park
Baseball field
Basketball court
Beach resort
Cricket ground
Fives court
Football field
Golf course
Gymnasium
Hockey field
Holiday camp
Ice palace
Lake resort
Mountain resort
Playground, including school playground
Public park
Racecourse
Resort NOS
Riding school
Rifle range
Seashore resort
Skating rink
Sports palace
Stadium
Swimming pool, public
Tennis court
Vacation resort

EXCLUDES *that in private house or garden (E849.0)*

E849.5 Street and highway

E849.6 Public building

Building (including adjacent grounds) used by the general public or by a particular group of the public, such as:
airport
bank
café
casino
church
cinema
clubhouse
courthouse
dance hall
garage building (for car storage)
hotel
market (grocery or other commodity)
movie house
music hall
nightclub
office
office building
opera house
post office
public hall
radio broadcasting station
restaurant
school (state) (public) (private)
shop, commercial
station (bus) (railway)
store
theater

EXCLUDES *home garage (E849.0)*
industrial building or workplace (E849.3)

E849.7 Residential institution

Children's home
Dormitory
Hospital
Jail
Old people's home
Orphanage
Prison
Reform school

E849.8 Other specified places

Beach NOS
Canal
Caravan site NOS
Derelict house
Desert
Dock
Forest
Harbor
Hill
Lake NOS
Mountain
Parking lot
Parking place
Pond or pool (natural)
Prairie
Public place NOS
Railway line
Reservoir
River
Sea
Seashore NOS
Stream
Swamp
Trailer court
Woods

E849.9 Unspecified place

ACCIDENTAL POISONING BY DRUGS, MEDICINAL SUBSTANCES, AND BIOLOGICALS (E850-E858)

INCLUDES accidental overdose of drug, wrong drug given or taken in error, and drug taken inadvertently
accidents in the use of drugs and biologicals in medical and surgical procedures

EXCLUDES *administration with suicidal or homicidal intent or intent to harm, or in circumstances classifiable to E980-E989 (E950.0-E950.5, E962.0, E980.0-E980.5)*
correct drug properly administered in therapeutic or prophylactic dosage, as the cause of adverse effect (E930.0-E949.9)

See Alphabetic Index for more complete list of specific drugs to be classified under the fourth-digit subdivisions. The American Hospital Formulary numbers can be used to classify new drugs listed by the American Hospital Formulary Service (AHFS). See Appendix C.

✓4th E850 Accidental poisoning by analgesics, antipyretics, and antirheumatics

E850.0 Heroin

Diacetylmorphine

E850.1 Methadone

E850.2 Other opiates and related narcotics

Codeine [methylmorphine]
Meperidine [pethidine]
Morphine
Opium (alkaloids)

E850.3 Salicylates

Acetylsalicylic acid [aspirin]
Amino derivatives of salicylic acid
Salicylic acid salts

E850.4 Aromatic analgesics, not elsewhere classified

Acetanilid
Paracetamol [acetaminophen]
Phenacetin [acetophenetidin]

E850.5 Pyrazole derivatives

Aminophenazone [amidopyrine]
Phenylbutazone

E850.6 Antirheumatics [antiphlogistics]

Gold salts
Indomethacin

EXCLUDES *salicylates (E850.3)*
steroids (E858.0)

E850.7 Other non-narcotic analgesics

Pyrabital

E850.8 Other specified analgesics and antipyretics

Pentazocine

E850.9 Unspecified analgesic or antipyretic

E851 Accidental poisoning by barbiturates
Amobarbital [amylobarbitone]
Barbital [barbitone]
Butabarbital [butabarbitone]
Pentobarbital [pentobarbitone]
Phenobarbital [phenobarbitone]
Secobarbital [quinalbarbitone]

EXCLUDES *thiobarbiturates (E855.1)*

✓4th **E852 Accidental poisoning by other sedatives and hypnotics**

E852.0 Chloral hydrate group

E852.1 Paraldehyde

E852.2 Bromine compounds
Bromides
Carbromal (derivatives)

E852.3 Methaqualone compounds

E852.4 Glutethimide group

E852.5 Mixed sedatives, not elsewhere classified

E852.8 Other specified sedatives and hypnotics

E852.9 Unspecified sedative or hypnotic
Sleeping:
drug } NOS
pill } NOS
tablet } NOS

✓4th **E853 Accidental poisoning by tranquilizers**

E853.0 Phenothiazine-based tranquilizers
Chlorpromazine
Fluphenazine
Prochlorperazine
Promazine

E853.1 Butyrophenone-based tranquilizers
Haloperidol
Spiperone
Trifluperidol

E853.2 Benzodiazepine-based tranquilizers
Chlordiazepoxide
Diazepam
Flurazepam
Lorazepam
Medazepam
Nitrazepam

E853.8 Other specified tranquilizers
Hydroxyzine
Meprobamate

E853.9 Unspecified tranquilizer

✓4th **E854 Accidental poisoning by other psychotropic agents**

E854.0 Antidepressants
Amitriptyline
Imipramine
Monoamine oxidase [MAO] inhibitors

E854.1 Psychodysleptics [hallucinogens]
Cannabis derivatives
Lysergide [LSD]
Marihuana (derivatives)
Mescaline
Psilocin
Psilocybin

E854.2 Psychostimulants
Amphetamine
Caffeine

EXCLUDES *central appetite depressants (E858.8)*

E854.3 Central nervous system stimulants
Analeptics
Opiate antagonists

E854.8 Other psychotropic agents

✓4th **E855 Accidental poisoning by other drugs acting on central and autonomic nervous system**

E855.0 Anticonvulsant and anti-Parkinsonism drugs
Amantadine
Hydantoin derivatives
Levodopa [L-dopa]
Oxazolidine derivatives [paramethadione] [trimethadione]
Succinimides

E855.1 Other central nervous system depressants
Ether
Gaseous anesthetics
Halogenated hydrocarbon derivatives
Intravenous anesthetics
Thiobarbiturates, such as thiopental sodium

E855.2 Local anesthetics
Cocaine
Lidocaine [lignocaine]
Procaine
Tetracaine

E855.3 Parasympathomimetics [cholinergics]
Acetylcholine
Anticholinesterase:
organophosphorus
reversible
Pilocarpine

E855.4 Parasympatholytics [anticholinergics and antimuscarinics] and spasmolytics
Atropine
Homatropine
Hyoscine [scopolamine]
Quaternary ammonium derivatives

E855.5 Sympathomimetics [adrenergics]
Epinephrine [adrenalin]
Levarterenol [noradrenalin]

E855.6 Sympatholytics [antiadrenergics]
Phenoxybenzamine
Tolazoline hydrochloride

E855.8 Other specified drugs acting on central and autonomic nervous systems

E855.9 Unspecified drug acting on central and autonomic nervous systems

E856 Accidental poisoning by antibiotics

E857 Accidental poisoning by other anti-infectives

✓4th **E858 Accidental poisoning by other drugs**

E858.0 Hormones and synthetic substitutes

E858.1 Primarily systemic agents

E858.2 Agents primarily affecting blood constituents

E858.3 Agents primarily affecting cardiovascular system

E858.4 Agents primarily affecting gastrointestinal system

E858.5 Water, mineral, and uric acid metabolism drugs

E858.6 Agents primarily acting on the smooth and skeletal muscles and respiratory system

E858.7 Agents primarily affecting skin and mucous membrane, ophthalmological, otorhinolaryngological, and dental drugs

E858.8 Other specified drugs
Central appetite depressants

E858.9 Unspecified drug

ACCIDENTAL POISONING BY OTHER SOLID AND LIQUID SUBSTANCES, GASES, AND VAPORS (E860-E869)

Note: Categories in this section are intended primarily to indicate the external cause of poisoning states classifiable to 980-989. They may also be used to indicate external causes of localized effects classifiable to 001-799.

✓4th E860 Accidental poisoning by alcohol, not elsewhere classified

E860.0 Alcoholic beverages
Alcohol in preparations intended for consumption

E860.1 Other and unspecified ethyl alcohol and its products
Denatured alcohol
Ethanol NOS
Grain alcohol NOS
Methylated spirit

E860.2 Methyl alcohol
Methanol
Wood alcohol

E860.3 Isopropyl alcohol
Dimethyl carbinol
Isopropanol
Rubbing alcohol subsitute
Secondary propyl alcohol

E860.4 Fusel oil
Alcohol:
amyl
butyl
propyl

E860.8 Other specified alcohols

E860.9 Unspecified alcohol

✓4th E861 Accidental poisoning by cleansing and polishing agents, disinfectants, paints, and varnishes

E861.0 Synthetic detergents and shampoos

E861.1 Soap products

E861.2 Polishes

E861.3 Other cleansing and polishing agents
Scouring powders

E861.4 Disinfectants
Household and other disinfectants not ordinarily used on the person
EXCLUDES *carbolic acid or phenol (E864.0)*

E861.5 Lead paints

E861.6 Other paints and varnishes
Lacquers
Oil colors
Paints, other than lead
White washes

E861.9 Unspecified

✓4th E862 Accidental poisoning by petroleum products, other solvents and their vapors, not elsewhere classified

E862.0 Petroleum solvents
Petroleum:
ether
benzine
naphtha

E862.1 Petroleum fuels and cleaners
Antiknock additives to petroleum fuels
Gas oils
Gasoline or petrol
Kerosene
EXCLUDES *kerosene insecticides (E863.4)*

E862.2 Lubricating oils

E862.3 Petroleum solids
Paraffin wax

E862.4 Other specified solvents
Benzene

E862.9 Unspecified solvent

✓4th E863 Accidental poisoning by agricultural and horticultural chemical and pharmaceutical preparations other than plant foods and fertilizers
EXCLUDES *plant foods and fertilizers (E866.5)*

E863.0 Insecticides of organochlorine compounds
Benzene hexachloride
Chlordane
DDT
Dieldrin
Endrine
Toxaphene

E863.1 Insecticides of organophosphorus compounds
Demeton
Diazinon
Dichlorvos
Malathion
Methyl parathion
Parathion
Phenylsulphthion
Phorate
Phosdrin

E863.2 Carbamates
Aldicarb
Carbaryl
Propoxur

E863.3 Mixtures of insecticides

E863.4 Other and unspecified insecticides
Kerosene insecticides

E863.5 Herbicides
2, 4-Dichlorophenoxyacetic acid [2, 4-D]
2, 4, 5-Trichlorophenoxyacetic acid [2, 4, 5-T]
Chlorates
Diquat
Mixtures of plant foods and fertilizers with herbicides
Paraquat

E863.6 Fungicides
Organic mercurials (used in seed dressing)
Pentachlorophenols

E863.7 Rodenticides
Fluoroacetates
Squill and derivatives
Thallium
Warfarin
Zinc phosphide

E863.8 Fumigants
Cyanides
Methyl bromide
Phosphine

E863.9 Other and unspecified

✓4th E864 Accidental poisoning by corrosives and caustics, not elsewhere classified
EXCLUDES *those as components of disinfectants (E861.4)*

E864.0 Corrosive aromatics
Carbolic acid or phenol

E864.1 Acids
Acid:
hydrochloric
nitric
sulfuric

E864.2 Caustic alkalis
Lye

E864.3 Other specified corrosives and caustics

E864.4 Unspecified corrosives and caustics

✓4th E865 Accidental poisoning from poisonous foodstuffs and poisonous plants

INCLUDES any meat, fish, or shellfish
plants, berries, and fungi eaten as, or in mistake for, food, or by a child

EXCLUDES *anaphylactic shock due to adverse food reaction (995.60-995.69)*
food poisoning (bacterial) (005.0-005.9)
poisoning and toxic reactions to venomous plants (E905.6-E905.7)

E865.0 Meat

E865.1 Shellfish

E865.2 Other fish

E865.3 Berries and seeds

E865.4 Other specified plants

E865.5 Mushrooms and other fungi

E865.8 Other specified foods

E865.9 Unspecified foodstuff or poisonous plant

✓4th E866 Accidental poisoning by other and unspecified solid and liquid substances

EXCLUDES *these substances as a component of:*
medicines (E850.0-E858.9)
paints (E861.5-E861.6)
pesticides (E863.0-E863.9)
petroleum fuels (E862.1)

E866.0 Lead and its compounds and fumes

E866.1 Mercury and its compounds and fumes

E866.2 Antimony and its compounds and fumes

E866.3 Arsenic and its compounds and fumes

E866.4 Other metals and their compounds and fumes
Beryllium (compounds)
Brass fumes
Cadmium (compounds)
Copper salts
Iron (compounds)
Manganese (compounds)
Nickel (compounds)
Thallium (compounds)

E866.5 Plant foods and fertilizers

EXCLUDES *mixtures with herbicides (E863.5)*

E866.6 Glues and adhesives

E866.7 Cosmetics

E866.8 Other specified solid or liquid substances

E866.9 Unspecified solid or liquid substance

E867 Accidental poisoning by gas distributed by pipeline
Carbon monoxide from incomplete combustion of piped gas
Coal gas NOS
Liquefied petroleum gas distributed through pipes (pure or mixed with air)
Piped gas (natural) (manufactured)

✓4th E868 Accidental poisoning by other utility gas and other carbon monoxide

E868.0 Liquefied petroleum gas distributed in mobile containers
Butane
Liquefied hydrocarbon gas NOS
Propane
} or carbon monoxide from incomplete conbustion of these gases

E868.1 Other and unspecified utility gas
Acetylene
Gas NOS used for lighting, heating, or cooking
Water gas
} or carbon monoxide from incomplete conbustion of these gases

E868.2 Motor vehicle exhaust gas
Exhaust gas from:
farm tractor, not in transit
gas engine
motor pump
motor vehicle, not in transit
any type of combustion engine not in watercraft

EXCLUDES *poisoning by carbon monoxide from:*
aircraft while in transit (E844.0-E844.9)
motor vehicle while in transit (E818.0-E818.9)
watercraft whether or not in transit (E838.0-E838.9)

E868.3 Carbon monoxide from incomplete combustion of other domestic fuels
Carbon monoxide from incomplete combustion of:
coal
coke
kerosene
wood
} in domestic stove or fireplace

EXCLUDES *carbon monoxide from smoke and fumes due to conflagration (E890.0-E893.9)*

E868.8 Carbon monoxide from other sources
Carbon monoxide from:
blast furnace gas
incomplete combustion of fuels in industrial use
kiln vapor

E868.9 Unspecified carbon monoxide

✓4th E869 Accidental poisoning by other gases and vapors

EXCLUDES *effects of gases used as anesthetics (E855.1, E938.2)*
fumes from heavy metals (E866.0-E866.4)
smoke and fumes due to conflagration or explosion (E890.0-E899)

E869.0 Nitrogen oxides

E869.1 Sulfur dioxide

E869.2 Freon

E869.3 Lacrimogenic gas [tear gas]
Bromobenzyl cyanide
Chloroacetophenone
Ethyliodoacetate

E869.4 Second-hand tobacco smoke

E869.8 Other specified gases and vapors
Chlorine
Hydrocyanic acid gas

E869.9 Unspecified gases and vapors

MISADVENTURES TO PATIENTS DURING SURGICAL AND MEDICAL CARE (E870-E876)

EXCLUDES *accidental overdose of drug and wrong drug given in error (E850.0-E858.9)*
surgical and medical procedures as the cause of abnormal reaction by the patient, without mention of misadventure at the time of procedure (E878.0-E879.9)

✓4th E870 Accidental cut, puncture, perforation, or hemorrhage during medical care

E870.0 Surgical operation

E870.1 Infusion or transfusion

E870.2 Kidney dialysis or other perfusion

E870.3 Injection or vaccination

E870.4 Endoscopic examination

E870.5 Aspiration of fluid or tissue, puncture, and catheterization
Abdominal paracentesis
Aspirating needle biopsy
Blood sampling
Lumbar puncture
Thoracentesis
EXCLUDES *heart catheterization (E870.6)*

E870.6 Heart catheterization

E870.7 Administration of enema

E870.8 Other specified medical care

E870.9 Unspecified medical care

✓4th **E871 Foreign object left in body during procedure**

E871.0 Surgical operation

E871.1 Infusion or transfusion

E871.2 Kidney dialysis or other perfusion

E871.3 Injection or vaccination

E871.4 Endoscopic examination

E871.5 Aspiration of fluid or tissue, puncture, and catheterization
Abdominal paracentesis
Aspiration needle biopsy
Blood sampling
Lumbar puncture
Thoracentesis
EXCLUDES *heart catheterization (E871.6)*

E871.6 Heart catheterization

E871.7 Removal of catheter or packing

E871.8 Other specified procedures

E871.9 Unspecified procedure

✓4th **E872 Failure of sterile precautions during procedure**

E872.0 Surgical operation

E872.1 Infusion or transfusion

E872.2 Kidney dialysis and other perfusion

E872.3 Injection or vaccination

E872.4 Endoscopic examination

E872.5 Aspiration of fluid or tissue, puncture, and catheterization
Abdominal paracentesis
Aspiration needle biopsy
Blood sampling
Lumbar puncture
Thoracentesis
EXCLUDES *heart catheterization (E872.6)*

E872.6 Heart catheterization

E872.8 Other specified procedures

E872.9 Unspecified procedure

✓4th **E873 Failure in dosage**
EXCLUDES *accidental overdose of drug, medicinal or biological substance (E850.0-E858.9)*

E873.0 Excessive amount of blood or other fluid during transfusion or infusion

E873.1 Incorrect dilution of fluid during infusion

E873.2 Overdose of radiation in therapy

E873.3 Inadvertent exposure of patient to radiation during medical care

E873.4 Failure in dosage in electroshock or insulin-shock therapy

E873.5 Inappropriate [too hot or too cold] temperature in local application and packing

E873.6 Nonadministration of necessary drug or medicinal substance

E873.8 Other specified failure in dosage

E873.9 Unspecified failure in dosage

✓4th **E874 Mechanical failure of instrument or apparatus during procedure**

E874.0 Surgical operation

E874.1 Infusion and transfusion
Air in system

E874.2 Kidney dialysis and other perfusion

E874.3 Endoscopic examination

E874.4 Aspiration of fluid or tissue, puncture, and catheterization
Abdominal paracentesis
Aspiration needle biopsy
Blood sampling
Lumbar puncture
Thoracentesis
EXCLUDES *heart catheterization (E874.5)*

E874.5 Heart catheterization

E874.8 Other specified procedures

E874.9 Unspecified procedure

✓4th **E875 Contaminated or infected blood, other fluid, drug, or biological substance**
INCLUDES presence of:
bacterial pyrogens
endotoxin-producing bacteria
serum hepatitis-producing agent

E875.0 Contaminated substance transfused or infused

E875.1 Contaminated substance injected or used for vaccination

E875.2 Contaminated drug or biological substance administered by other means

E875.8 Other

E875.9 Unspecified

✓4th **E876 Other and unspecified misadventures during medical care**

E876.0 Mismatched blood in transfusion

E876.1 Wrong fluid in infusion

E876.2 Failure in suture and ligature during surgical operation

E876.3 Endotracheal tube wrongly placed during anesthetic procedure

E876.4 Failure to introduce or to remove other tube or instrument
EXCLUDES *foreign object left in body during procedure (E871.0-E871.9)*

E876.5 Performance of inappropriate operation

E876.8 Other specified misadventures during medical care
Performance of inappropriate treatment NEC

E876.9 Unspecified misadventure during medical care

SURGICAL AND MEDICAL PROCEDURES AS THE CAUSE OF ABNORMAL REACTION OF PATIENT OR LATER COMPLICATION, WITHOUT MENTION OF MISADVENTURE AT THE TIME OF PROCEDURE (E878-E879)

INCLUDES procedures as the cause of abnormal reaction, such as:
- displacement or malfunction of prosthetic device
- hepatorenal failure, postoperative
- malfunction of external stoma
- postoperative intestinal obstruction
- rejection of transplanted organ

EXCLUDES *anesthetic management properly carried out as the cause of adverse effect (E937.0-E938.9)*
infusion and transfusion, without mention of misadventure in the technique of procedure (E930.0-E949.9)

✓4th **E878 Surgical operation and other surgical procedures as the cause of abnormal reaction of patient, or of later complication, without mention of misadventure at the time of operation**

E878.0 Surgical operation with transplant of whole organ
Transplantation of:
- heart
- kidney
- liver

E878.1 Surgical operation with implant of artificial internal device
Cardiac pacemaker
Electrodes implanted in brain
Heart valve prosthesis
Internal orthopedic device

E878.2 Surgical operation with anastomosis, bypass, or graft, with natural or artificial tissues used as implant
Anastomosis:
- arteriovenous
- gastrojejunal

Graft of blood vessel, tendon, or skin

EXCLUDES *external stoma (E878.3)*

E878.3 Surgical operation with formation of external stoma
Colostomy
Cystostomy
Duodenostomy
Gastrostomy
Ureterostomy

E878.4 Other restorative surgery

E878.5 Amputation of limb(s)

E878.6 Removal of other organ (partial) (total)

E878.8 Other specified surgical operations and procedures

E878.9 Unspecified surgical operations and procedures

✓4th **E879 Other procedures, without mention of misadventure at the time of procedure, as the cause of abnormal reaction of patient, or of later complication**

E879.0 Cardiac catheterization

E879.1 Kidney dialysis

E879.2 Radiological procedure and radiotherapy

EXCLUDES *radio-opaque dyes for diagnostic x-ray procedures (E947.8)*

E879.3 Shock therapy
Electroshock therapy
Insulin-shock therapy

E879.4 Aspiration of fluid
Lumbar puncture
Thoracentesis

E879.5 Insertion of gastric or duodenal sound

E879.6 Urinary catheterization

E879.7 Blood sampling

E879.8 Other specified procedures
Blood transfusion

E879.9 Unspecified procedure

ACCIDENTAL FALLS (E880-E888)

EXCLUDES *falls (in or from):*
- *burning building (E890.8, E891.8)*
- *into fire (E890.0-E899)*
- *into water (with submersion or drowning) (E910.0-E910.9)*
- *machinery (in operation) (E919.0-E919.9)*
- *on edged, pointed, or sharp object (E920.0-E920.9)*
- *transport vehicle (E800.0-E845.9)*
- *vehicle not elsewhere classifiable (E846-E848)*

✓4th **E880 Fall on or from stairs or steps**

E880.0 Escalator

E880.1 Fall on or from sidewalk curb

EXCLUDES *fall from moving sidewalk (E885.9)*

E880.9 Other stairs or steps

✓4th **E881 Fall on or from ladders or scaffolding**

E881.0 Fall from ladder

E881.1 Fall from scaffolding

E882 Fall from or out of building or other structure
Fall from:
- balcony
- bridge
- building
- flagpole
- tower
- turret
- viaduct
- wall
- window

Fall through roof

EXCLUDES *collapse of a building or structure (E916)*
fall or jump from burning building (E890.8, E891.8)

✓4th **E883 Fall into hole or other opening in surface**

INCLUDES fall into:
- cavity
- dock
- hole
- pit
- quarry
- shaft
- swimming pool
- tank
- well

EXCLUDES *fall into water NOS (E910.9)*
that resulting in drowning or submersion without mention of injury (E910.0-E910.9)

E883.0 Accident from diving or jumping into water [swimming pool]
Strike or hit:
- against bottom when jumping or diving into water
- wall or board of swimming pool
- water surface

EXCLUDES *diving with insufficient air supply (E913.2)*
effects of air pressure from diving (E902.2)

E883.1 Accidental fall into well

E883.2 Accidental fall into storm drain or manhole

E883.9 Fall into other hole or other opening in surface

✓4th E884 Other fall from one level to another

E884.0 Fall from playground equipment

EXCLUDES *recreational machinery (E919.8)*

E884.1 Fall from cliff

E884.2 Fall from chair

E884.3 Fall from wheelchair

E884.4 Fall from bed

E884.5 Fall from other furniture

E884.6 Fall from commode

Toilet

E884.9 Other fall from one level to another

Fall from:
embankment
haystack
stationary vehicle
tree

✓4th E885 Fall on same level from slipping, tripping, or stumbling

E885.0 Fall from (nonmotorized) scooter

E885.1 Fall from roller skates

Heelies
In-line skates
Wheelies

E885.2 Fall from skateboard

E885.3 Fall from skis

E885.4 Fall from snowboard

E885.9 Fall from other slipping, tripping, or stumbling

Fall on moving sidewalk

✓4th E886 Fall on same level from collision, pushing, or shoving, by or with other person

EXCLUDES *crushed or pushed by a crowd or human stampede (E917.1, E917.6)*

E886.0 In sports

Tackles in sports

EXCLUDES *kicked, stepped on, struck by object, in sports (E917.0, E917.5)*

E886.9 Other and unspecified

Fall from collision of pedestrian (conveyance) with another pedestrian (conveyance)

E887 Fracture, cause unspecified

✓4th E888 Other and unspecified fall

Accidental fall NOS
Fall on same level NOS

E888.0 Fall resulting in striking against sharp object

Use additional external cause code to identify object (E920)

E888.1 Fall resulting in striking against other object

E888.8 Other fall

E888.9 Unspecified fall

Fall NOS

ACCIDENTS CAUSED BY FIRE AND FLAMES (E890-E899)

INCLUDES asphyxia or poisoning due to conflagration or ignition
burning by fire
secondary fires resulting from explosion

EXCLUDES *arson (E968.0)*
fire in or on:
machinery (in operation) (E919.0-E919.9)
transport vehicle other than stationary vehicle (E800.0-E845.9)
vehicle not elsewhere classifiable (E846-E848)

✓4th E890 Conflagration in private dwelling

INCLUDES conflagration in:
apartment
boarding house
camping place
caravan
farmhouse
house
lodging house
mobile home
private garage
rooming house
tenement
conflagration originating from sources classifiable to E893-E898 in the above buildings

E890.0 Explosion caused by conflagration

E890.1 Fumes from combustion of polyvinylchloride [PVC] and similar material in conflagration

E890.2 Other smoke and fumes from conflagration

Carbon monoxide / Fumes NOS / Smoke NOS } from conflagration in private building

E890.3 Burning caused by conflagration

E890.8 Other accident resulting from conflagration

Collapse of / Fall from / Hit by object falling from / Jump from } burning private building

E890.9 Unspecified accident resulting from conflagration in private dwelling

✓4th E891 Conflagration in other and unspecified building or structure

Conflagration in:
barn
church
convalescent and other residential home
dormitory of educational institution
factory
farm outbuildings
hospital
hotel
school
store
theater
Conflagration originating from sources classifiable to E893-E898, in the above buildings

E891.0 Explosion caused by conflagration

E891.1 Fumes from combustion of polyvinylchloride [PVC] and similar material in conflagration

E891.2 Other smoke and fumes from conflagration

Carbon monoxide / Fumes NOS / Smoke NOS } from conflagration in private building or structure

E891.3 Burning caused by conflagration

E891.8 Other accident resulting from conflagration

Collapse of / Fall from / Hit by object falling from / Jump from } burning private building or structure

E891.9 Unspecified accident resulting from conflagration of other and unspecified building or structure

E892 Conflagration not in building or structure

Fire (uncontrolled) (in) (of):
- forest
- grass
- hay
- lumber
- mine
- prairie
- transport vehicle [any], except while in transit
- tunnel

✓4th E893 Accident caused by ignition of clothing

EXCLUDES *ignition of clothing:*
from highly inflammable material (E894)
with conflagration (E890.0-E892)

E893.0 From controlled fire in private dwelling

Ignition of clothing from:
normal fire (charcoal) (coal) (electric) (gas) (wood) in: brazier, fireplace, furnace, stove } in private dwelling (as listed in E890)

E893.1 From controlled fire in other building or structure

Ignition of clothing from:
normal fire (charcoal) (coal) (electric) (gas) (wood) in: brazier, fireplace, furnace, stove } in other building or structure (as listed in E891)

E893.2 From controlled fire not in building or structure

Ignition of clothing from:
- bonfire (controlled)
- brazier fire (controlled), not in building or structure
- trash fire (controlled)

EXCLUDES *conflagration not in building (E892)*
trash fire out of control (E892)

E893.8 From other specified sources

Ignition of clothing from:
- blowlamp
- blowtorch
- burning bedspread
- candle
- cigar
- cigarette
- lighter
- matches
- pipe
- welding torch

E893.9 Unspecified source

Ignition of clothing (from controlled fire NOS) (in building NOS) NOS

E894 Ignition of highly inflammable material

Ignition of:
benzine, gasoline, fat, kerosene, paraffin, petrol } (with ignition of clothing)

EXCLUDES *ignition of highly inflammable material with:*
conflagration (E890.0-E892)
explosion (E923.0-E923.9)

E895 Accident caused by controlled fire in private dwelling

Burning by (flame of) normal fire (charcoal) (coal) (electric) (gas) (wood) in:
brazier, fireplace, furnace, stove } in private dwelling (as listed in E890)

EXCLUDES *burning by hot objects not producing fire or flames (E924.0-E924.9)*
ignition of clothing from these sources (E893.0)
poisoning by carbon monoxide from incomplete combustion of fuel (E867-E868.9)
that with conflagration (E890.0-E890.9)

E896 Accident caused by controlled fire in other and unspecified building or structure

Burning by (flame of) normal fire (charcoal) (coal)(electric)(gas)(wood) in:
brazier, fireplace, furnace, stove } in other building or structure (as listed in E891)

EXCLUDES *burning by hot objects not producing fire or flames (E924.0-E924.9)*
ignition of clothing from these sources (E893.1)
poisoning by carbon monoxide from incomplete combustion of fuel (E867-E868.9)
that with conflagration (E891.0-E891.9)

E897 Accident caused by controlled fire not in building or structure

Burns from flame of:
bonfire, brazier fire, not in building or structure, trash fire } controlled

EXCLUDES *ignition of clothing from these sources (E893.2)*
trash fire out of control (E892)
that with conflagration (E892)

✓4th E898 Accident caused by other specified fire and flames

EXCLUDES *conflagration (E890.0-E892)*
that with ignition of:
clothing (E893.0-E893.9)
highly inflammable material (E894)

E898.0 Burning bedclothes

Bed set on fire NOS

E898.1 Other

Burning by:
- blowlamp
- blowtorch
- candle
- cigar
- cigarette
- fire in room NOS
- lamp
- lighter
- matches
- pipe
- welding torch

E899 Accident caused by unspecified fire

Burning NOS

ACCIDENTS DUE TO NATURAL AND ENVIRONMENTAL FACTORS (E900-E909)

✓4th E900 Excessive heat

E900.0 Due to weather conditions

Excessive heat as the external cause of:
- ictus solaris
- siriasis
- sunstroke

E900.1 Of man-made origin
Heat (in):
boiler room
drying room
factory
furnace room
generated in transport vehicle
kitchen

E900.9 Of unspecified origin

✓4th E901 Excessive cold

E901.0 Due to weather conditions
Excessive cold as the cause of:
chilblains NOS
immersion foot

E901.1 Of man-made origin
Contact with or inhalation of:
dry ice
liquid air
liquid hydrogen
liquid nitrogen
Prolonged exposure in:
deep freeze unit
refrigerator

E901.8 Other specified origin

E901.9 Of unspecified origin

✓4th E902 High and low air pressure and changes in air pressure

E902.0 Residence or prolonged visit at high altitude
Residence or prolonged visit at high altitude as the cause of:
Acosta syndrome
Alpine sickness
altitude sickness
Andes disease
anoxia, hypoxia
barotitis, barodontalgia, barosinusitis, otitic barotrauma
hypobarism, hypobaropathy
mountain sickness
range disease

E902.1 In aircraft
Sudden change in air pressure in aircraft during ascent or descent as the cause of:
aeroneurosis
aviators' disease

E902.2 Due to diving
High air pressure from rapid descent in water / Reduction in atmospheric pressure while surfacing from deep water diving } as the cause of:
caisson disease
divers' disease
divers' palsy or paralysis

E902.8 Due to other specified causes
Reduction in atmospheric pressure whilesurfacing from underground

E902.9 Unspecified cause

E903 Travel and motion

✓4th E904 Hunger, thirst, exposure, and neglect
EXCLUDES *any condition resulting from homicidal intent (E968.0-E968.9)*
hunger, thirst, and exposure resulting from accidents connected with transport (E800.0-E848)

E904.0 Abandonment or neglect of infants and helpless persons
Exposure to weather conditions / Hunger or thirst } resulting from abandonment or neglect
Desertion of newborn
Inattention at or after birth
Lack of care (helpless person) (infant)
EXCLUDES *criminal [purposeful] neglect (E968.4)*

E904.1 Lack of food
Lack of food as the cause of:
inanition
insufficient nourishment
starvation
EXCLUDES *hunger resulting from abandonment or neglect (E904.0)*

E904.2 Lack of water
Lack of water as the cause of:
dehydration
inanition
EXCLUDES *dehydration due to acute fluid loss (276.51)*

E904.3 Exposure (to weather conditions), not elsewhere classifiable
Exposure NOS
Humidity
Struck by hailstones
EXCLUDES *struck by lightning (E907)*

E904.9 Privation, unqualified
Destitution

✓4th E905 Venomous animals and plants as the cause of poisoning and toxic reactions
INCLUDES chemical released by animal
insects
release of venom through fangs, hairs, spines, tentacles, and other venom apparatus
EXCLUDES *eating of poisonous animals or plants (E865.0-E865.9)*

E905.0 Venomous snakes and lizards
Cobra
Copperhead snake
Coral snake
Fer de lance
Gila monster
Krait
Mamba
Rattlesnake
Sea snake
Snake (venomous)
Viper
Water moccasin
EXCLUDES *bites of snakes and lizards known to be nonvenomous (E906.2)*

E905.1 Venomous spiders
Black widow spider
Brown spider
Tarantula (venomous)

E905.2 Scorpion

E905.3 Hornets, wasps, and bees
Yellow jacket

E905.4 Centipede and venomous millipede (tropical)

E905.5 Other venomous arthropods
Sting of:
ant
caterpillar

E905.6 Venomous marine animals and plants
Puncture by sea urchin spine
Sting of:
coral
jelly fish
nematocysts
sea anemone
sea cucumber
other marine animal or plant
EXCLUDES *bites and other injuries caused by nonvenomous marine animal (E906.2-E906.8)*
bite of sea snake (venomous) (E905.0)

E905.7 Poisoning and toxic reactions caused by other plants
Injection of poisons or toxins into or through skin by plant thorns, spines, or other mechanisms
EXCLUDES *puncture wound NOS by plant thorns or spines (E920.8)*

E905.8 Other specified

E905.9 Unspecified
Sting NOS
Venomous bite NOS

✓4th E906 Other injury caused by animals
EXCLUDES *poisoning and toxic reactions caused by venomous animals and insects (E905.0-E905.9)*
road vehicle accident involving animals (E827.0-E828.9)
tripping or falling over an animal (E885.9)

E906.0 Dog bite

E906.1 Rat bite

E906.2 Bite of nonvenomous snakes and lizards

E906.3 Bite of other animal except arthropod
Cats
Moray eel
Rodents, except rats
Shark

E906.4 Bite of nonvenomous arthropod
Insect bite NOS

E906.5 Bite by unspecified animal
Animal bite NOS

E906.8 Other specified injury caused by animal
Butted by animal
Fallen on by horse or other animal, not being ridden
Gored by animal
Implantation of quills of porcupine
Pecked by bird
Run over by animal, not being ridden
Stepped on by animal, not being ridden
EXCLUDES *injury by animal being ridden (E828.0-E828.9)*

E906.9 Unspecified injury caused by animal

E907 Lightning
EXCLUDES *injury from:*
fall of tree or other object caused by lightning (E916)
fire caused by lightning (E890.0-E892)

✓4th E908 Cataclysmic storms, and floods resulting from storms
EXCLUDES *collapse of dam or man-made structure causing flood (E909.3)*

E908.0 Hurricane
Storm surge
"Tidal wave" caused by storm action
Typhoon

E908.1 Tornado
Cyclone
Twisters

E908.2 Floods
Torrential rainfall
Flash flood
EXCLUDES *collapse of dam or man-made structure causing flood (E909.3)*

E908.3 Blizzard (snow)(ice)

E908.4 Dust storm

E908.8 Other cataclysmic storms
Cloudburst

E908.9 Unspecified cataclysmic storms, and floods resulting from storms
Storm NOS

✓4th E909 Cataclysmic earth surface movements and eruptions

E909.0 Earthquakes

E909.1 Volcanic eruptions
Burns from lava
Ash inhalation

E909.2 Avalanche, landslide, or mudslide

E909.3 Collapse of dam or man-made structure

E909.4 Tidalwave caused by earthquake
Tidalwave NOS
Tsunami
EXCLUDES *tidalwave caused by tropical storm (E908.0)*

E909.8 Other cataclysmic earth surface movements and eruptions

E909.9 Unspecified cataclysmic earth surface movements and eruptions

ACCIDENTS CAUSED BY SUBMERSION, SUFFOCATION, AND FOREIGN BODIES (E910-E915)

✓4th E910 Accidental drowning and submersion
INCLUDES immersion
swimmers' cramp
EXCLUDES *diving accident (NOS) (resulting in injury except drowning) (E883.0)*
diving with insufficient air supply (E913.2)
drowning and submersion due to:
cataclysm (E908-E909)
machinery accident (E919.0-E919.9)
transport accident (E800.0-E845.9)
effect of high and low air pressure (E902.2)
injury from striking against objects while in running water (E917.2)

E910.0 While water-skiing
Fall from water skis with submersion or drowning
EXCLUDES *accident to water-skier involving a watercraft and resulting in submersion or other injury (E830.4, E831.4)*

E910.1 While engaged in other sport or recreational activity with diving equipment
Scuba diving NOS
Skin diving NOS
Underwater spear fishing NOS

E910.2 While engaged in other sport or recreational activity without diving equipment
Fishing or hunting, except from boat or with diving equipment
Ice skating
Playing in water
Surfboarding
Swimming NOS
Voluntarily jumping from boat, not involved in accident, for swim NOS
Wading in water
EXCLUDES *jumping into water to rescue another person (E910.3)*

E910.3 While swimming or diving for purposes other than recreation or sport
Marine salvage
Pearl diving
Placement of fishing nets
Rescue (attempt) of another person
Underwater construction or repairs
} (with diving equipment)

E910.4 In bathtub

E910.8 Other accidental drowning or submersion
Drowning in:
quenching tank
swimming pool

E910.9 Unspecified accidental drowning or submersion
Accidental fall into water NOS
Drowning NOS

E911 Inhalation and ingestion of food causing obstruction of respiratory tract or suffocation
Aspiration and inhalation of food [any] (into respiratory tract) NOS
Asphyxia by / Choked on / Suffocation by } food [including bone, seed in food, regurgitated food]
Compression of trachea / Interruption of respiration / Obstruction of respiration } by food lodged in esophagus
Obstruction of pharynx by food (bolus)
EXCLUDES *injury, except asphyxia and obstruction of respiratory passage, caused by food (E915)*
obstruction of esophagus by food without mention of asphyxia or obstruction of respiratory passage (E915)

E912 Inhalation and ingestion of other object causing obstruction of respiratory tract or suffocation
Aspiration and inhalation of foreign body except food (into respiratory tract) NOS
Foreign object [bean] [marble] in nose
Obstruction of pharynx by foreign body
Compression / Interruption of respiration / Obstruction of respiration } by foreign body in esophagus
EXCLUDES *injury, except asphyxia and obstruction of respiratory passage, caused by foreign body (E915)*
obstruction of esophagus by foreign body without mention of asphyxia or obstruction in respiratory passage (E915)

✓4th **E913 Accidental mechanical suffocation**
EXCLUDES *mechanical suffocation from or by:*
accidental inhalation or ingestion of:
food (E911)
foreign object (E912)
cataclysm (E908-E909)
explosion (E921.0-E921.9, E923.0-E923.9)
machinery accident (E919.0-E919.9)

E913.0 In bed or cradle
EXCLUDES *suffocation by plastic bag (E913.1)*

E913.1 By plastic bag

E913.2 Due to lack of air (in closed place)
Accidentally closed up in refrigerator or other airtight enclosed space
Diving with insufficient air supply
EXCLUDES *suffocation by plastic bag (E913.1)*

E913.3 By falling earth or other substance
Cave-in NOS
EXCLUDES *cave-in caused by cataclysmic earth surface movements and eruptions (E909)*
struck by cave-in without asphyxiation or suffocation (E916)

E913.8 Other specified means
Accidental hanging, except in bed or cradle

E913.9 Unspecified means
Asphyxia, mechanical NOS
Strangulation NOS
Suffocation NOS

E914 Foreign body accidentally entering eye and adnexa
EXCLUDES *corrosive liquid (E924.1)*

E915 Foreign body accidentally entering other orifice
EXCLUDES *aspiration and inhalation of foreign body, any, (into respiratory tract) NOS (E911-E912)*

OTHER ACCIDENTS (E916-E928)

E916 Struck accidentally by falling object
Collapse of building, except on fire
Falling:
rock
snowslide NOS
stone
tree
Object falling from:
machine, not in operation
stationary vehicle
Code first:
collapse of building on fire (E890.0-E891.9)
falling object in:
cataclysm (E908-E909)
machinery accidents (E919.0-E919.9)
transport accidents (E800.0-E845.9)
vehicle accidents not elsewhere classifiable (E846-E848)
object set in motion by:
explosion (E921.0-E921.9, E923.0-E923.9)
firearm (E922.0-E922.9)
projected object (E917.0-E917.9)

✓4th **E917 Striking against or struck accidentally by objects or persons**
INCLUDES bumping into or against / colliding with / kicking against / stepping on / struck by } object (moving) (projected) (stationary) / pedestrian conveyance / person
EXCLUDES *fall from:*
collision with another person, except when caused by a crowd (E886.0-E886.9)
stumbling over object (E885.9)
fall resulting in striking against object (E888.0, E888.1)
injury caused by:
assault (E960.0-E960.1, E967.0-E967.9)
cutting or piercing instrument (E920.0-E920.9)
explosion (E921.0-E921.9, E923.0-E923.9)
firearm (E922.0-E922.9)
machinery (E919.0-E919.9)
transport vehicle (E800.0-E845.9)
vehicle not elsewhere classifiable (E846-E848)

E917.0 In sports without subsequent fall
Kicked or stepped on during game (football) (rugby)
Struck by hit or thrown ball
Struck by hockey stick or puck

E917.1 Caused by a crowd, by collective fear or panic without subsequent fall
Crushed / Pushed / Stepped on } by crowd or human stampede

E917.2 In running water without subsequent fall
EXCLUDES *drowning or submersion (E910.0-E910.9)*
that in sports (E917.0, E917.5)

E917.3 Furniture without subsequent fall
EXCLUDES *fall from furniture (E884.2, E884.4-E884.5)*

E917.4 Other stationary object without subsequent fall
Bath tub
Fence
Lamp-post

E917.5 Object in sports with subsequent fall
Knocked down while boxing

E917.6 Caused by a crowd, by collective fear or panic with subsequent fall

E Codes

E917.7 Furniture with subsequent fall

EXCLUDES *fall from furniture (E884.2, E884.4-E884.5)*

E917.8 Other stationary object with subsequent fall

Bath tub
Fence
Lamp-post

E917.9 Other striking against with or without subsequent fall

E918 Caught accidentally in or between objects

Caught, crushed, jammed, or pinched in or between moving or stationary objects, such as:
- escalator
- folding object
- hand tools, appliances, or implements
- sliding door and door frame
- under packing crate
- washing machine wringer

EXCLUDES *injury caused by:*
- *cutting or piercing instrument (E920.0-E920.9)*
- *machinery (E919.0-E919.9)*
- *transport vehicle (E800.0-E845.9)*
- *vehicle not elsewhere classifiable (E846-E848)*

struck accidentally by:
- *falling object (E916)*
- *object (moving) (projected) (E917.0-E917.9)*

✓4th **E919 Accidents caused by machinery**

INCLUDES burned by } machinery (accident)
caught in (moving parts of) } machinery (accident)
collapse of } machinery (accident)
crushed by } machinery (accident)
cut or pierced by } machinery (accident)
drowning or submersion caused by } machinery (accident)
expolosion of, on, in } machinery (accident)
fall from or into moving part of } machinery (accident)
fire starting in or on } machinery (accident)
mechanical suffocation caused by } machinery (accident)
object falling from, on, in motion by } machinery (accident)
overturning of } machinery (accident)
pinned under } machinery (accident)
run over by } machinery (accident)
struck by } machinery (accident)
thrown from } machinery (accident)
caught between machinery and other object
machinery accident NOS

EXCLUDES *accidents involving machinery, not in operation (E884.9, E916-E918)*

injury caused by:
- *electric current in connection with machinery (E925.0-E925.9)*
- *escalator (E880.0, E918)*
- *explosion of pressure vessel in connection with machinery (E921.0-E921.9)*
- *moving sidewalk (E885.9)*
- *powered hand tools, appliances, and implements (E916-E918, E920.0-E921.9, E923.0-E926.9)*
- *transport vehicle accidents involving machinery (E800.0-E848)*
- *poisoning by carbon monoxide generated by machine (E868.8)*

E919.0 Agricultural machines

Animal-powered agricultural machine
Combine
Derrick, hay
Farm machinery NOS
Farm tractor
Harvester
Hay mower or rake
Reaper
Thresher

EXCLUDES *that in transport under own power on the highway (E810.0-E819.9)*
that being towed by another vehicle on the highway (E810.0-E819.9, E827.0-E827.9, E829.0-E829.9)
that involved in accident classifiable to E820-E829 (E820.0-E829.9)

E919.1 Mining and earth-drilling machinery

Bore or drill (land) (seabed)
Shaft hoist
Shaft lift
Under-cutter

EXCLUDES *coal car, tram, truck, and tub in mine (E846)*

E919.2 Lifting machines and appliances

Chain hoist } except in agricultural or mining operations
Crane } except in agricultural or mining operations
Derrick } except in agricultural or mining operations
Elevator (building) (grain) } except in agricultural or mining operations
Forklift truck } except in agricultural or mining operations
Lift } except in agricultural or mining operations
Pulley block } except in agricultural or mining operations
Winch } except in agricultural or mining operations

EXCLUDES *that being towed by another vehicle on the highway (E810.0-E819.9, E827.0-E827.9, E829.0-829.9)*
that in transport under own power on the highway (E810.0-E819.9)
that involved in accident classifiable to E820-E829 (E820.0-E829.9)

E919.3 Metalworking machines

Abrasive wheel
Forging machine
Lathe
Mechanical shears
Metal:
- drilling machine
- milling machine
- power press
- rolling-mill
- sawing machine

E919.4 Woodworking and forming machines

Band saw
Bench saw
Circular saw
Molding machine
Overhead plane
Powered saw
Radial saw
Sander

EXCLUDES *hand saw (E920.1)*

E919.5 Prime movers, except electrical motors

Gas turbine
Internal combustion engine
Steam engine
Water driven turbine

EXCLUDES *that being towed by other vehicle on the highway (E810.0-E819.9, E827.0-E827.9, E829.0-E829.9)*
that in transport under own power on the highway (E810.0-E819.9)

E919.6 Transmission machinery
Transmission:
belt
cable
chain
gear
pinion
pulley
shaft

E919.7 Earth moving, scraping, and other excavating machines
Bulldozer
Road scraper
Steam shovel

EXCLUDES *that being towed by other vehicle on the highway (E810.0-E819.9, E827.0-E827.9, E829.0-E829.9)*
that in transport under own power on the highway (E810.0-E819.9)

E919.8 Other specified machinery
Machines for manufacture of:
clothing
foodstuffs and beverages
paper
Printing machine
Recreational machinery
Spinning, weaving, and textile machines

E919.9 Unspecified machinery

✓4th **E920 Accidents caused by cutting and piercing instruments or objects**

INCLUDES accidental injury (by) object } edged, pointed, sharp

E920.0 Powered lawn mower

E920.1 Other powered hand tools
Any powered hand tool [compressed air] [electric] [explosive cartridge] [hydraulic power], such as:
drill
hand saw
hedge clipper
rivet gun
snow blower
staple gun

EXCLUDES *band saw (E919.4)*
bench saw (E919.4)

E920.2 Powered household appliances and implements
Blender
Electric:
beater or mixer
can opener
fan
knife
sewing machine
Garbage disposal appliance

E920.3 Knives, swords, and daggers

E920.4 Other hand tools and implements
Axe
Can opener NOS
Chisel
Fork
Hand saw
Hoe
Ice pick
Needle (sewing)
Paper cutter
Pitchfork
Rake
Scissors
Screwdriver
Sewing machine, not powered
Shovel

E920.5 Hypodermic needle
Contaminated needle
Needle stick

E920.8 Other specified cutting and piercing instruments or objects
Arrow
Broken glass
Dart
Edge of stiff paper
Lathe turnings
Nail
Plant thorn
Splinter
Tin can lid

EXCLUDES *animal spines or quills (E906.8)*
flying glass due to explosion (E921.0-E923.9)

E920.9 Unspecified cutting and piercing instrument or object

✓4th **E921 Accident caused by explosion of pressure vessel**

INCLUDES accidental explosion of pressure vessels, whether or not part of machinery

EXCLUDES *explosion of pressure vessel on transport vehicle (E800.0-E845.9)*

E921.0 Boilers

E921.1 Gas cylinders
Air tank
Pressure gas tank

E921.8 Other specified pressure vessels
Aerosol can
Automobile tire
Pressure cooker

E921.9 Unspecified pressure vessel

✓4th **E922 Accident caused by firearm, and air gun missile**

E922.0 Handgun
Pistol
Revolver

EXCLUDES *Verey pistol (E922.8)*

E922.1 Shotgun (automatic)

E922.2 Hunting rifle

E922.3 Military firearms
Army rifle
Machine gun

E922.4 Air gun
BB gun
Pellet gun

E922.5 Paintball gun

E922.8 Other specified firearm missile
Verey pistol [flare]

E922.9 Unspecified firearm missile
Gunshot wound NOS
Shot NOS

✓4th **E923 Accident caused by explosive material**

INCLUDES flash burns and other injuries resulting from explosion of explosive material
ignition of highly explosive material with explosion

EXCLUDES *explosion:*
in or on machinery (E919.0-E919.9)
on any transport vehicle, except stationary motor vehicle (E800.0-E848)
with conflagration (E890.0, E891.0,E892)
secondary fires resulting from explosion (E890.0-E899)

E923.0 Fireworks

E923.1 Blasting materials
Blasting cap
Detonator
Dynamite
Explosive [any] used in blasting operations

E923.2 Explosive gases
Acetylene
Butane
Coal gas
Explosion in mine NOS
Fire damp
Gasoline fumes
Methane
Propane

E923.8 Other explosive materials
Bomb
Explosive missile
Grenade
Mine
Shell
Torpedo
Explosion in munitions:
dump
factory

E923.9 Unspecified explosive material
Explosion NOS

✓4th E924 Accident caused by hot substance or object, caustic or corrosive material, and steam

EXCLUDES *burning NOS (E899)*
chemical burn resulting from swallowing a corrosive substance (E860.0-E864.4)
fire caused by these substances and objects (E890.0-E894)
radiation burns (E926.0-E926.9)
therapeutic misadventures (E870.0-E876.9)

E924.0 Hot liquids and vapors, including steam
Burning or scalding by:
boiling water
hot or boiling liquids not primarily caustic or corrosive
liquid metal
steam
other hot vapor

EXCLUDES *hot (boiling) tap water (E924.2)*

E924.1 Caustic and corrosive substances
Burning by:
acid [any kind]
ammonia
caustic oven cleaner or other substance
corrosive substance
lye
vitriol

E924.2 Hot (boiling) tap water

E924.8 Other
Burning by:
heat from electric heating appliance
hot object NOS
light bulb
steam pipe

E924.9 Unspecified

✓4th E925 Accident caused by electric current

INCLUDES electric current from exposed wire, faulty appliance, high voltage cable, live rail, or open electric socket as the cause of:
burn
cardiac fibrillation
convulsion
electric shock
electrocution
puncture wound
respiratory paralysis

EXCLUDES *burn by heat from electrical appliance (E924.8)*
lightning (E907)

E925.0 Domestic wiring and appliances

E925.1 Electric power generating plants, distribution stations, transmission lines
Broken power line

E925.2 Industrial wiring, appliances, and electrical machinery
Conductors
Control apparatus
Electrical equipment and machinery
Transformers

E925.8 Other electric current
Wiring and appliances in or on:
farm [not farmhouse]
outdoors
public building
residential institutions
schools

E925.9 Unspecified electric current
Burns or other injury from electric current NOS
Electric shock NOS
Electrocution NOS

✓4th E926 Exposure to radiation

EXCLUDES *abnormal reaction to or complication of treatment without mention of misadventure (E879.2)*
atomic power plant malfunction in water transport (E838.0-E838.9)
misadventure to patient in surgical and medical procedures (E873.2-E873.3)
use of radiation in war operations (E996-E997.9)

E926.0 Radiofrequency radiation

Overexposure to:	from:
microwave radiation radar radiation radiofrequency radiofrequency radiation [any]	high-powered radio and television transmitters industrial radiofrequency induction heaters radar installations

E926.1 Infrared heaters and lamps
Exposure to infrared radiation from heaters and lamps as the cause of:
blistering
burning
charring
inflammatory change

EXCLUDES *physical contact with heater or lamp (E924.8)*

E926.2 Visible and ultraviolet light sources
Arc lamps
Black light sources
Electrical welding arc
Oxygas welding torch
Sun rays
Tanning bed

EXCLUDES *excessive heat from these sources (E900.1-E900.9)*

E926.3 X-rays and other electromagnetic ionizing radiation
Gamma rays
X-rays (hard) (soft)

E926.4 Lasers

E926.5 Radioactive isotopes
Radiobiologicals
Radiopharmaceuticals

E926.8 Other specified radiation
Artificially accelerated beams of ionized particles generated by:
betatrons
synchrotrons

E926.9 Unspecified radiation
Radiation NOS

✓4th E927 Overexertion and strenuous and repetitive movements or loads

E927.0 Overexertion from sudden strenuous movement
Sudden trauma from strenuous movement

E927.1 Overexertion from prolonged static position
Overexertion from maintaining prolonged positions, such as:
holding
sitting
standing

E927.2 Excessive physical exertion from prolonged activity

E927.3 Cumulative trauma from repetitive motion
Cumulative trauma from repetitive movements

E927.4 Cumulative trauma from repetitive impact

E927.8 Other overexertion and strenuous and repetitive movements or loads

E927.9 Unspecified overexertion and strenuous and repetitive movements or loads

✓4th E928 Other and unspecified environmental and accidental causes

E928.0 Prolonged stay in weightless environment
Weightlessness in spacecraft (simulator)

E928.1 Exposure to noise
Noise (pollution)
Sound waves
Supersonic waves

E928.2 Vibration

E928.3 Human bite

E928.4 External constriction caused by hair

E928.5 External constriction caused by other object

E928.6 Environmental exposure to harmful algae and toxins
Algae bloom NOS
Blue-green algae bloom
Brown tide
Cyanobacteria bloom
Florida red tide
Harmful algae bloom
Pfiesteria piscicida
Red tide

E928.8 Other

E928.9 Unspecified accident

Accident NOS Blow NOS Casualty (not due to war) Decapitation	stated as accidentally inflicted
Knocked down Killed Injury [any part of body, or unspecified] Mangled Wound	stated as accidentally inflicted, but not otherwise specified

EXCLUDES *fracture, cause unspecified (E887)*
injuries undetermined whether accidentally or purposely inflicted (E980.0-E989)

LATE EFFECTS OF ACCIDENTAL INJURY (E929)

Note: This category is to be used to indicate accidental injury as the cause of death or disability from late effects, which are themselves classifiable elsewhere. The "late effects" include conditions reported as such, or as sequelae which may occur at any time after the attempted suicide or self-inflicted injury.

✓4th E929 Late effects of accidental injury

EXCLUDES *late effects of:*
surgical and medical procedures (E870.0-E879.9)
therapeutic use of drugs and medicines (E930.0-E949.9)

E929.0 Late effects of motor vehicle accident
Late effects of accidents classifiable to E810-E825

E929.1 Late effects of other transport accident
Late effects of accidents classifiable to E800-E807, E826-E838, E840-E848

E929.2 Late effects of accidental poisoning
Late effects of accidents classifiable to E850-E858, E860-E869

E929.3 Late effects of accidental fall
Late effects of accidents classifiable to E880-E888

E929.4 Late effects of accident caused by fire
Late effects of accidents classifiable to E890-E899

E929.5 Late effects of accident due to natural and environmental factors
Late effects of accidents classifiable to E900-E909

E929.8 Late effects of other accidents
Late effects of accidents classifiable to E910-E928.8

E929.9 Late effects of unspecified accident
Late effects of accidents classifiable to E928.9

DRUGS, MEDICINAL AND BIOLOGICAL SUBSTANCES CAUSING ADVERSE EFFECTS IN THERAPEUTIC USE (E930-E949)

INCLUDES correct drug properly administered in therapeutic or prophylactic dosage, as the cause of any adverse effect including allergic or hypersensitivity reactions

EXCLUDES *accidental overdose of drug and wrong drug given or taken in error (E850.0-E858.9)*
accidents in the technique of administration of drug or biological substance, such as accidental puncture during injection, or contamination of drug (E870.0-E876.9)
administration with suicidal or homicidal intent or intent to harm, or in circumstances classifiable to E980-E989 (E950.0-E950.5, E962.0, E980.0-E980.5)

See Alphabetic Index for more complete list of specific drugs to be classified under the fourth-digit subdivisions. The American Hospital Formulary numbers can be used to classify new drugs listed by the American Hospital Formulary Service (AHFS). See Appendix C.

✓4th E930 Antibiotics

EXCLUDES *that used as eye, ear, nose, and throat [ENT], and local anti-infectives (E946.0-E946.9)*

E930.0 Penicillins
Natural
Synthetic
Semisynthetic, such as:
ampicillin
cloxacillin
nafcillin
oxacillin

E930.1 Antifungal antibiotics
Amphotericin B
Griseofulvin
Hachimycin [trichomycin]
Nystatin

E930.2 Chloramphenicol group
Chloramphenicol
Thiamphenicol

E930.3 Erythromycin and other macrolides
Oleandomycin
Spiramycin

E930.4 Tetracycline group
Doxycycline
Minocycline
Oxytetracycline

E930.5 Cephalosporin group
Cephalexin
Cephaloglycin
Cephaloridine
Cephalothin

E930.6 Antimycobacterial antibiotics
Cycloserine
Kanamycin
Rifampin
Streptomycin

E930.7 Antineoplastic antibiotics
Actinomycins, such as:
Bleomycin
Cactinomycin
Dactinomycin
Daunorubicin
Mitomycin

EXCLUDES *other antineoplastic drugs (E933.1)*

E930.8 Other specified antibiotics

E930.9 Unspecified antibiotic

✓4th **E931 Other anti-infectives**

EXCLUDES *ENT, and local anti-infectives (E946.0-E946.9)*

E931.0 Sulfonamides
Sulfadiazine
Sulfafurazole
Sulfamethoxazole

E931.1 Arsenical anti-infectives

E931.2 Heavy metal anti-infectives
Compounds of:
antimony
bismuth
lead
mercury

EXCLUDES *mercurial diuretics (E944.0)*

E931.3 Quinoline and hydroxyquinoline derivatives
Chiniofon
Diiodohydroxyquin

EXCLUDES *antimalarial drugs (E931.4)*

E931.4 Antimalarials and drugs acting on other blood protozoa
Chloroquine phosphate
Cycloguanil
Primaquine
Proguanil [chloroguanide]
Pyrimethamine
Quinine (sulphate)

E931.5 Other antiprotozoal drugs
Emetine

E931.6 Anthelmintics
Hexylresorcinol
Male fern oleoresin
Piperazine
Thiabendazole

E931.7 Antiviral drugs
Methisazone

EXCLUDES *amantadine (E936.4)*
cytarabine (E933.1)
idoxuridine (E946.5)

E931.8 Other antimycobacterial drugs
Ethambutol
Ethionamide
Isoniazid
Para-aminosalicylic acid derivatives
Sulfones

E931.9 Other and unspecified anti-infectives
Flucytosine
Nitrofuranderivatives

✓4th **E932 Hormones and synthetic substitutes**

E932.0 Adrenal cortical steroids
Cortisone derivatives
Desoxycorticosterone derivatives
Fluorinated corticosteroid

E932.1 Androgens and anabolic congeners
Nandrolone phenpropionate
Oxymetholone
Testosterone and preparations

E932.2 Ovarian hormones and synthetic substitutes
Contraceptives, oral
Estrogens
Estrogens and progestogens combined
Progestogens

E932.3 Insulins and antidiabetic agents
Acetohexamide
Biguanide derivatives, oral
Chlorpropamide
Glucagon
Insulin
Phenformin
Sulfonylurea derivatives, oral
Tolbutamide

EXCLUDES *adverse effect of insulin administered for shock therapy (E879.3)*

E932.4 Anterior pituitary hormones
Corticotropin
Gonadotropin
Somatotropin [growth hormone]

E932.5 Posterior pituitary hormones
Vasopressin

EXCLUDES *oxytocic agents (E945.0)*

E932.6 Parathyroid and parathyroid derivatives

E932.7 Thyroid and thyroid derivatives
Dextrothyroxine
Levothyroxine sodium
Liothyronine
Thyroglobulin

E932.8 Antithyroid agents
Iodides
Thiouracil
Thiourea

E932.9 Other and unspecified hormones and synthetic substitutes

✓4th **E933 Primarily systemic agents**

E933.0 Antiallergic and antiemetic drugs
Antihistamines
Chlorpheniramine
Diphenhydramine
Diphenylpyraline
Thonzylamine
Tripelennamine

EXCLUDES *phenothiazine-based tranquilizers (E939.1)*

E933.1 Antineoplastic and immunosuppressive drugs
Azathioprine
Busulfan
Chlorambucil
Cyclophosphamide
Cytarabine
Fluorouracil
Mechlorethamine hydrochloride
Mercaptopurine
Triethylenethiophosphoramide [thio-TEPA]
EXCLUDES *antineoplastic antibiotics (E930.7)*

E933.2 Acidifying agents

E933.3 Alkalizing agents

E933.4 Enzymes, not elsewhere classified
Penicillinase

E933.5 Vitamins, not elsewhere classified
Vitamin A
Vitamin D
EXCLUDES *nicotinic acid (E942.2)*
vitamin K (E934.3)

E933.6 Oral bisphosphonates

E933.7 Intravenous bisphosphonates

E933.8 Other systemic agents, not elsewhere classified
Heavy metal antagonists

E933.9 Unspecified systemic agent

✓4th **E934 Agents primarily affecting blood constituents**

E934.0 Iron and its compounds
Ferric salts
Ferrous sulphate and other ferrous salts

E934.1 Liver preparations and other antianemic agents
Folic acid

E934.2 Anticoagulants
Coumarin
Heparin
Phenindione
Prothrombin synthesis inhibitor
Warfarin sodium

E934.3 Vitamin K [phytonadione]

E934.4 Fibrinolysis-affecting drugs
Aminocaproic acid
Streptodornase
Streptokinase
Urokinase

E934.5 Anticoagulant antagonists and other coagulants
Hexadimethrine bromide
Protamine sulfate

E934.6 Gamma globulin

E934.7 Natural blood and blood products
Blood plasma
Human fibrinogen
Packed red cells
Whole blood

E934.8 Other agents affecting blood constituents
Macromolecular blood substitutes

E934.9 Unspecified agent affecting blood constituents

✓4th **E935 Analgesics, antipyretics, and antirheumatics**

E935.0 Heroin
Diacetylmorphine

E935.1 Methadone

E935.2 Other opiates and related narcotics
Codeine [methylmorphine]
Meperidine [pethidine]
Morphine
Opium (alkaloids)

E935.3 Salicylates
Acetylsalicylic acid [aspirin]
Amino derivatives of salicylic acid
Salicylic acid salts

E935.4 Aromatic analgesics, not elsewhere classified
Acetanilid
Paracetamol [acetaminophen]
Phenacetin [acetophenetidin]

E935.5 Pyrazole derivatives
Aminophenazone [aminopyrine]
Phenylbutazone

E935.6 Antirheumatics [antiphlogistics]
Gold salts
Indomethacin
EXCLUDES *salicylates (E935.3)*
steroids (E932.0)

E935.7 Other non-narcotic analgesics
Pyrabital

E935.8 Other specified analgesics and antipyretics
Pentazocine

E935.9 Unspecified analgesic and antipyretic

✓4th **E936 Anticonvulsants and anti-Parkinsonism drugs**

E936.0 Oxazolidine derivatives
Paramethadione
Trimethadione

E936.1 Hydantoin derivatives
Phenytoin

E936.2 Succinimides
Ethosuximide
Phensuximide

E936.3 Other and unspecified anticonvulsants
Beclamide
Primidone

E936.4 Anti-Parkinsonism drugs
Amantadine
Ethopropazine [profenamine]
Levodopa [L-dopa]

✓4th **E937 Sedatives and hypnotics**

E937.0 Barbiturates
Amobarbital [amylobarbitone]
Barbital [barbitone]
Butabarbital [butabarbitone]
Pentobarbital [pentobarbitone]
Phenobarbital [phenobarbitone]
Secobarbital [quinalbarbitone]
EXCLUDES *thiobarbiturates (E938.3)*

E937.1 Chloral hydrate group

E937.2 Paraldehyde

E937.3 Bromine compounds
Bromide
Carbromal (derivatives)

E937.4 Methaqualone compounds

E937.5 Glutethimide group

E937.6 Mixed sedatives, not elsewhere classified

E937.8 Other sedatives and hypnotics

E937.9 Unspecified
Sleeping:
drug } NOS
pill } NOS
tablet } NOS

✓4th **E938 Other central nervous system depressants and anesthetics**

E938.0 Central nervous system muscle-tone depressants
Chlorphenesin (carbamate)
Mephenesin
Methocarbamol

E938.1 Halothane

E938.2 Other gaseous anesthetics
Ether
Halogenated hydrocarbon derivatives, except halothane
Nitrous oxide

E938.3 Intravenous anesthetics
Ketamine
Methohexital [methohexitone]
Thiobarbiturates, such as thiopental sodium

E938.4 Other and unspecified general anesthetics

E938.5 Surface and infiltration anesthetics
Cocaine
Lidocaine [lignocaine]
Procaine
Tetracaine

E938.6 Peripheral nerve- and plexus-blocking anesthetics

E938.7 Spinal anesthetics

E938.9 Other and unspecified local anesthetics

✓4th **E939 Psychotropic agents**

E939.0 Antidepressants
Amitriptyline
Imipramine
Monoamine oxidase [MAO] inhibitors

E939.1 Phenothiazine-based tranquilizers
Chlorpromazine
Fluphenazine
Phenothiazine
Prochlorperazine
Promazine

E939.2 Butyrophenone-based tranquilizers
Haloperidol
Spiperone
Trifluperidol

E939.3 Other antipsychotics, neuroleptics, and major tranquilizers

E939.4 Benzodiazepine-based tranquilizers
Chlordiazepoxide
Diazepam
Flurazepam
Lorazepam
Medazepam
Nitrazepam

E939.5 Other tranquilizers
Hydroxyzine
Meprobamate

E939.6 Psychodysleptics [hallucinogens]
Cannabis (derivatives)
Lysergide [LSD]
Marihuana (derivatives)
Mescaline
Psilocin
Psilocybin

E939.7 Psychostimulants
Amphetamine
Caffeine

EXCLUDES *central appetite depressants (E947.0)*

E939.8 Other psychotropic agents

E939.9 Unspecified psychotropic agent

✓4th **E940 Central nervous system stimulants**

E940.0 Analeptics
Lobeline
Nikethamide

E940.1 Opiate antagonists
Levallorphan
Nalorphine
Naloxone

E940.8 Other specified central nervous system stimulants

E940.9 Unspecified central nervous system stimulant

✓4th **E941 Drugs primarily affecting the autonomic nervous system**

E941.0 Parasympathomimetics [cholinergics]
Acetylcholine
Anticholinesterase:
organophosphorus
reversible
Pilocarpine

E941.1 Parasympatholytics [anticholinergics and antimuscarinics] and spasmolytics
Atropine
Homatropine
Hyoscine [scopolamine]
Quaternary ammonium derivatives

EXCLUDES *papaverine (E942.5)*

E941.2 Sympathomimetics [adrenergics]
Epinephrine [adrenalin]
Levarterenol [noradrenalin]

E941.3 Sympatholytics [antiadrenergics]
Phenoxybenzamine
Tolazolinehydrochloride

E941.9 Unspecified drug primarily affecting the autonomic nervous system

✓4th **E942 Agents primarily affecting the cardiovascular system**

E942.0 Cardiac rhythm regulators
Practolol
Procainamide
Propranolol
Quinidine

E942.1 Cardiotonic glycosides and drugs of similar action
Digitalis glycosides
Digoxin
Strophanthins

E942.2 Antilipemic and antiarteriosclerotic drugs
Cholestyramine
Clofibrate
Nicotinic acid derivatives
Sitosterols

EXCLUDES *dextrothyroxine (E932.7)*

E942.3 Ganglion-blocking agents
Pentamethonium bromide

E942.4 Coronary vasodilators
Dipyridamole
Nitrates [nitroglycerin]
Nitrites
Prenylamine

E942.5 Other vasodilators
Cyclandelate
Diazoxide
Hydralazine
Papaverine

E942.6 Other antihypertensive agents
Clonidine
Guanethidine
Rauwolfia alkaloids
Reserpine

E942.7 Antivaricose drugs, including sclerosing agents
Monoethanolamine
Zinc salts

E942.8 Capillary-active drugs
Adrenochrome derivatives
Bioflavonoids
Metaraminol

E942.9 Other and unspecified agents primarily affecting the cardiovascular system

✓4th E943 Agents primarily affecting gastrointestinal system

E943.0 Antacids and antigastric secretion drugs
Aluminum hydroxide
Magnesium trisilicate

E943.1 Irritant cathartics
Bisacodyl
Castor oil
Phenolphthalein

E943.2 Emollient cathartics
Sodium dioctyl sulfosuccinate

E943.3 Other cathartics, including intestinal atonia drugs
Magnesium sulfate

E943.4 Digestants
Pancreatin
Papain
Pepsin

E943.5 Antidiarrheal drugs
Bismuth subcarbonate Pectin or Kaolin
EXCLUDES *anti-infectives (E930.0-E931.9)*

E943.6 Emetics

E943.8 Other specified agents primarily affecting the gastrointestinal system

E943.9 Unspecified agent primarily affecting the gastrointestinal system

✓4th E944 Water, mineral, and uric acid metabolism drugs

E944.0 Mercurial diuretics
Chlormerodrin
Mercaptomerin
Mercurophylline
Mersalyl

E944.1 Purine derivative diuretics
Theobromine
Theophylline
EXCLUDES *aminophylline [theophylline ethylenediamine] (E945.7)*

E944.2 Carbonic acid anhydrase inhibitors
Acetazolamide

E944.3 Saluretics
Benzothiadiazides
Chlorothiazide group

E944.4 Other diuretics
Ethacrynic acid
Furosemide

E944.5 Electrolytic, caloric, and water-balance agents

E944.6 Other mineral salts, not elsewhere classified

E944.7 Uric acid metabolism drugs
Cinchophen and congeners
Colchicine
Phenoquin
Probenecid

✓4th E945 Agents primarily acting on the smooth and skeletal muscles and respiratory system

E945.0 Oxytocic agents
Ergot alkaloids
Prostaglandins

E945.1 Smooth muscle relaxants
Adiphenine
Metaproterenol [orciprenaline]
EXCLUDES *papaverine (E942.5)*

E945.2 Skeletal muscle relaxants
Alcuronium chloride
Suxamethonium chloride

E945.3 Other and unspecified drugs acting on muscles

E945.4 Antitussives
Dextromethorphan
Pipazethate hydrochloride

E945.5 Expectorants
Acetylcysteine
Cocillana
Guaifenesin [glyceryl guaiacolate]
Ipecacuanha
Terpin hydrate

E945.6 Anti-common cold drugs

E945.7 Antiasthmatics
Aminophylline [theophylline ethylenediamine]

E945.8 Other and unspecified respiratory drugs

✓4th E946 Agents primarily affecting skin and mucous membrane, ophthalmological, otorhinolaryngological, and dental drugs

E946.0 Local anti-infectives and anti-inflammatory drugs

E946.1 Antipruritics

E946.2 Local astringents and local detergents

E946.3 Emollients, demulcents, and protectants

E946.4 Keratolytics, kerstoplastics, other hair treatment drugs and preparations

E946.5 Eye anti-infectives and other eye drugs
Idoxuridine

E946.6 Anti-infectives and other drugs and preparations for ear, nose, and throat

E946.7 Dental drugs topically applied

E946.8 Other agents primarily affecting skin and mucous membrane
Spermicides

E946.9 Unspecified agent primarily affecting skin and mucous membrane

✓4th E947 Other and unspecified drugs and medicinal substances

E947.0 Dietetics

E947.1 Lipotropic drugs

E947.2 Antidotes and chelating agents, not elsewhere classified

E947.3 Alcohol deterrents

E947.4 Pharmaceutical excipients

E947.8 Other drugs and medicinal substances
Contrast media used for diagnostic x-ray procedures
Diagnostic agents and kits

E947.9 Unspecified drug or medicinal substance

✓4th E948 Bacterial vaccines

E948.0 BCG vaccine

E948.1 Typhoid and paratyphoid

E948.2 Cholera

E948.3 Plague

E948.4 Tetanus

E948.5 Diphtheria

E948.6 Pertussis vaccine, including combinations with a pertussis component

E948.8 Other and unspecified bacterial vaccines

E948.9 Mixed bacterial vaccines, except combinations with a pertussis component

✓4th E949 Other vaccines and biological substances
EXCLUDES *gamma globulin (E934.6)*

E949.0 Smallpox vaccine

E949.1 Rabies vaccine

E949.2 Typhus vaccine

E949.3 Yellow fever vaccine

E949.4 Measles vaccine

E949.5 Poliomyelitis vaccine

E949.6 Other and unspecified viral and rickettsial vaccines
Mumps vaccine

E949.7 Mixed viral-rickettsial and bacterial vaccines, except combinations with a pertussis component
EXCLUDES *combinations with a pertussis component (E948.6)*

E949.9 Other and unspecified vaccines and biological substances

SUICIDE AND SELF-INFLICTED INJURY (E950-E959)

INCLUDES injuries in suicide and attempted suicide
self-inflicted injuries specified as intentional

✓4th **E950 Suicide and self-inflicted poisoning by solid or liquid substances**

E950.0 Analgesics, antipyretics, and antirheumatics

E950.1 Barbiturates

E950.2 Other sedatives and hypnotics

E950.3 Tranquilizers and other psychotropic agents

E950.4 Other specified drugs and medicinal substances

E950.5 Unspecified drug or medicinal substance

E950.6 Agricultural and horticultural chemical and pharmaceutical preparations other than plant foods and fertilizers

E950.7 Corrosive and caustic substances
Suicide and self-inflicted poisoning by substances classifiable to E864

E950.8 Arsenic and its compounds

E950.9 Other and unspecified solid and liquid substances

✓4th **E951 Suicide and self-inflicted poisoning by gases in domestic use**

E951.0 Gas distributed by pipeline

E951.1 Liquefied petroleum gas distributed in mobile containers

E951.8 Other utility gas

✓4th **E952 Suicide and self-inflicted poisoning by other gases and vapors**

E952.0 Motor vehicle exhaust gas

E952.1 Other carbon monoxide

E952.8 Other specified gases and vapors

E952.9 Unspecified gases and vapors

✓4th **E953 Suicide and self-inflicted injury by hanging, strangulation, and suffocation**

E953.0 Hanging

E953.1 Suffocation by plastic bag

E953.8 Other specified means

E953.9 Unspecified means

E954 Suicide and self-inflicted injury by submersion [drowning]

✓4th **E955 Suicide and self-inflicted injury by firearms, air guns and explosives**

E955.0 Handgun

E955.1 Shotgun

E955.2 Hunting rifle

E955.3 Military firearms

E955.4 Other and unspecified firearm
Gunshot NOS
Shot NOS

E955.5 Explosives

E955.6 Air gun
BB gun
Pellet gun

E955.7 Paintball gun

E955.9 Unspecified

E956 Suicide and self-inflicted injury by cutting and piercing instrument

✓4th **E957 Suicide and self-inflicted injuries by jumping from high place**

E957.0 Residential premises

E957.1 Other man-made structures

E957.2 Natural sites

E957.9 Unspecified

✓4th **E958 Suicide and self-inflicted injury by other and unspecified means**

E958.0 Jumping or lying before moving object

E958.1 Burns, fire

E958.2 Scald

E958.3 Extremes of cold

E958.4 Electrocution

E958.5 Crashing of motor vehicle

E958.6 Crashing of aircraft

E958.7 Caustic substances, except poisoning
EXCLUDES *poisoning by caustic substance (E950.7)*

E958.8 Other specified means

E958.9 Unspecified means

E959 Late effects of self-inflicted injury
Note: This category is to be used to indicate circumstances classifiable to E950-E958 as the cause of death or disability from late effects, which are themselves classifiable elsewhere. The "late effects" include conditions reported as such, or as sequelae which may occur at any time after the attempted suicide or self-inflicted injury.

HOMICIDE AND INJURY PURPOSELY INFLICTED BY OTHER PERSONS (E960-E969)

INCLUDES injuries inflicted by another person with intent to injure or kill, by any means

EXCLUDES *injuries due to:*
legal intervention (E970-E978)
operations of war (E990-E999)
terrorism (E979)

✓4th **E960 Fight, brawl, rape**

E960.0 Unarmed fight or brawl
Beatings NOS
Brawl or fight with hands, fists, feet
Injured or killed in fight NOS
EXCLUDES *homicidal:*
injury by weapons (E965.0-E966, E969)
strangulation (E963)
submersion (E964)

E960.1 Rape

E961 Assault by corrosive or caustic substance, except poisoning
Injury or death purposely caused by corrosive or caustic substance, such as:
acid [any]
corrosive substance
vitriol

EXCLUDES *burns from hot liquid (E968.3)*
chemical burns from swallowing a corrosive substance (E962.0-E962.9)

✓4th **E962 Assault by poisoning**

E962.0 Drugs and medicinal substances
Homicidal poisoning by any drug or medicinal substance

E962.1 Other solid and liquid substances

E962.2 Other gases and vapors

E962.9 Unspecified poisoning

E963 Assault by hanging and strangulation
Homicidal (attempt):
garrotting or ligature
hanging
strangulation
suffocation

E964 Assault by submersion [drowning]

✓4th **E965 Assault by firearms and explosives**

E965.0 Handgun
Pistol
Revolver

E965.1 Shotgun

E965.2 Hunting rifle

E965.3 Military firearms

E965.4 Other and unspecified firearm

E965.5 Antipersonnel bomb

E965.6 Gasoline bomb

E965.7 Letter bomb

E965.8 Other specified explosive
Bomb NOS (placed in):
car
house
Dynamite

E965.9 Unspecified explosive

E966 Assault by cutting and piercing instrument
Assassination (attempt), homicide (attempt) by any instrument classifiable under E920
Homicidal:
cut, puncture, stab } any part of the body
Stabbed any part of the body

✓4th **E967 Perpetrator of child and adult abuse**
Note: Selection of the correct perpetrator code is based on the relationship between the perpetrator and the victim

E967.0 By father, stepfather, or boyfriend
Male partner of child's parent or guardian

E967.1 By other specified person

E967.2 By mother, stepmother, or girlfriend
Female partner of child's parent or guardian

E967.3 By spouse or partner
Abuse of spouse or partner by ex-spouse or ex-partner

E967.4 By child

E967.5 By sibling

E967.6 By grandparent

E967.7 By other relative

E967.8 By non-related caregiver

E967.9 By unspecified person

✓4th **E968 Assault by other and unspecified means**

E968.0 Fire
Arson
Homicidal burns NOS

EXCLUDES *burns from hot liquid (E968.3)*

E968.1 Pushing from a high place

E968.2 Striking by blunt or thrown object

E968.3 Hot liquid
Homicidal burns by scalding

E968.4 Criminal neglect
Abandonment of child, infant, or other helpless person with intent to injure or kill

E968.5 Transport vehicle
Being struck by other vehicle or run down with intent to injure
Pushed in front of, thrown from, or dragged by moving vehicle with intent to injure

E968.6 Air gun
BB gun
Pellet gun

E968.7 Human bite

E968.8 Other specified means

E968.9 Unspecified means
Assassination (attempt) NOS
Homicidal (attempt):
injury NOS
wound NOS
Manslaughter (nonaccidental)
Murder (attempt) NOS
Violence, non-accidental

E969 Late effects of injury purposely inflicted by other person
Note: This category is to be used to indicate circumstances classifiable to E960-E968 as the cause of death or disability from late effects, which are themselves classifiable elsewhere. The "late effects" include conditions reported as such, or as sequelae which may occur at any time after injury purposely inflicted by another person.

LEGAL INTERVENTION (E970-E978)

INCLUDES injuries inflicted by the police or other law-enforcing agents, including military on duty, in the course of arresting or attempting to arrest lawbreakers, suppressing disturbances, maintaining order, and other legal action
legal execution

EXCLUDES *injuries caused by civil insurrections (E990.0-E999)*

E970 Injury due to legal intervention by firearms
Gunshot wound
Injury by:
machine gun
revolver
rifle pellet or rubber bullet
shot NOS

E971 Injury due to legal intervention by explosives
Injury by:
dynamite
explosive shell
grenade
mortar bomb

E972 Injury due to legal intervention by gas
Asphyxiation by gas
Injury by tear gas
Poisoning by gas

E973 Injury due to legal intervention by blunt object
Hit, struck by:
baton (nightstick)
blunt object
stave

E974 Injury due to legal intervention by cutting and piercing instrument
Cut
Incised wound
Injured by bayonet
Stab wound

E975 Injury due to legal intervention by other specified means
Blow
Manhandling

E976 Injury due to legal intervention by unspecified means

E977 Late effects of injuries due to legal intervention
Note: This category is to be used to indicate circumstances classifiable to E970-E976 as the cause of death or disability from late effects, which are themselves classifiable elsewhere. The "late effects" include conditions reported as such, or as sequelae, which may occur at any time after the injury due to legal intervention.

E978 Legal execution
All executions performed at the behest of the judiciary or ruling authority [whether permanent or temporary] as:
asphyxiation by gas
beheading, decapitation (by guillotine)
capital punishment
electrocution
hanging
poisoning
shooting
other specified means

TERRORISM (E979)

✓4th **E979 Terrorism**
Injuries resulting from the unlawful use of force or violence against persons or property to intimidate or coerce a Government, the civilian population, or any segment thereof, in furtherance of political or social objective

E979.0 Terrorism involving explosion of marine weapons
Depth-charge
Marine mine
Mine NOS, at sea or in harbour
Sea-based artillery shell
Torpedo
Underwater blast

E979.1 Terrorism involving destruction of aircraft
Aircraft used as a weapon
Aircraft:
burned
exploded
shot down
Crushed by falling aircraft

E979.2 Terrorism involving other explosions and fragments
Antipersonnel bomb (fragments)
Blast NOS
Explosion (of):
artillery shell
breech-block
cannon block
mortar bomb
munitions being used in terrorism
NOS
Fragments from:
artillery shell
bomb
grenade
guided missile
land-mine
rocket
shell
shrapnel
Mine NOS

E979.3 Terrorism involving fires, conflagration and hot substances
Burning building or structure:
collapse of
fall from
hit by falling object in
jump from
Conflagration NOS
Fire (causing):
Asphyxia
Burns
NOS
Other injury
Melting of fittings and furniture in burning
Petrol bomb
Smouldering building or structure

E979.4 Terrorism involving firearms
Bullet:
carbine
machine gun
pistol
rifle
rubber (rifle)
Pellets (shotgun)

E979.5 Terrorism involving nuclear weapons
Blast effects
Exposure to ionizing radiation from nuclear weapon
Fireball effects
Heat from nuclear weapon
Other direct and secondary effects of nuclear weapons

E979.6 Terrorism involving biological weapons
Anthrax
Cholera
Smallpox

E979.7 Terrorism involving chemical weapons
Gases, fumes, chemicals
Hydrogen cyanide
Phosgene
Sarin

E979.8 Terrorism involving other means
Drowning and submersion
Lasers
Piercing or stabbing instruments
Terrorism NOS

E979.9 Terrorism, secondary effects
Note: This code is for use to identify conditions occurring subsequent to a terrorist attack not those that are due to the initial terrorist act

EXCLUDES *late effect of terrorist attack (E999.1)*

INJURY UNDETERMINED WHETHER ACCIDENTALLY OR PURPOSELY INFLICTED (E980-E989)

Note: Categories E980-E989 are for use when it is unspecified or it cannot be determined whether the injuries are accidental (unintentional), suicide (attempted), or assault.

✓4th **E980 Poisoning by solid or liquid substances, undetermined whether accidentally or purposely inflicted**

E980.0 Analgesics, antipyretics, and antirheumatics

E980.1 Barbiturates

E980.2 Other sedatives and hypnotics

E980.3 Tranquilizers and other psychotropic agents

E980.4 Other specified drugs and medicinal substances

E980.5 Unspecified drug or medicinal substance

E980.6 Corrosive and caustic substances

Poisoning, undetermined whether accidental or purposeful, by substances classifiable to E864

E980.7 Agricultural and horticultural chemical and pharmaceutical preparations other than plant foods and fertilizers

E980.8 Arsenic and its compounds

E980.9 Other and unspecified solid and liquid substances

✓4th **E981 Poisoning by gases in domestic use, undetermined whether accidentally or purposely inflicted**

E981.0 Gas distributed by pipeline

E981.1 Liquefied petroleum gas distributed in mobile containers

E981.8 Other utility gas

✓4th **E982 Poisoning by other gases, undetermined whether accidentally or purposely inflicted**

E982.0 Motor vehicle exhaust gas

E982.1 Other carbon monoxide

E982.8 Other specified gases and vapors

E982.9 Unspecified gases and vapors

✓4th **E983 Hanging, strangulation, or suffocation, undetermined whether accidentally or purposely inflicted**

E983.0 Hanging

E983.1 Suffocation by plastic bag

E983.8 Other specified means

E983.9 Unspecified means

E984 Submersion [drowning], undetermined whether accidentally or purposely inflicted

✓4th **E985 Injury by firearms, air guns and explosives, undetermined whether accidentally or purposely inflicted**

E985.0 Handgun

E985.1 Shotgun

E985.2 Hunting rifle

E985.3 Military firearms

E985.4 Other and unspecified firearm

E985.5 Explosives

E985.6 Air gun

BB gun
Pellet gun

E985.7 Paintball gun

E986 Injury by cutting and piercing instruments, undetermined whether accidentally or purposely inflicted

✓4th **E987 Falling from high place, undetermined whether accidentally or purposely inflicted**

E987.0 Residential premises

E987.1 Other man-made structures

E987.2 Natural sites

E987.9 Unspecified site

✓4th **E988 Injury by other and unspecified means, undetermined whether accidentally or purposely inflicted**

E988.0 Jumping or lying before moving object

E988.1 Burns, fire

E988.2 Scald

E988.3 Extremes of cold

E988.4 Electrocution

E988.5 Crashing of motor vehicle

E988.6 Crashing of aircraft

E988.7 Caustic substances, except poisoning

E988.8 Other specified means

E988.9 Unspecified means

E989 Late effects of injury, undetermined whether accidentally or purposely inflicted

Note: This category is to be used to indicate circumstances classifiable to E980-E988 as the cause of death or disability from late effects, which are themselves classifiable elsewhere. The "late effects" include conditions reported as such, or as sequelae, which may occur at any time after injury, undetermined whether accidentally or purposely inflicted.

INJURY RESULTING FROM OPERATIONS OF WAR (E990-E999)

INCLUDES injuries to military personnel and civilians caused by war and civil insurrections and occurring during the time of war and insurrection

EXCLUDES *accidents during training of military personnel manufacture of war material and transport, unless attributable to enemy action*

✓4th **E990 Injury due to war operations by fires and conflagrations**

INCLUDES asphyxia, burns, or other injury originating from fire caused by a fire-producing device or indirectly by any conventional weapon

E990.0 From gasoline bomb

E990.9 From other and unspecified source

✓4th **E991 Injury due to war operations by bullets and fragments**

E991.0 Rubber bullets (rifle)

E991.1 Pellets (rifle)

E991.2 Other bullets

Bullet [any, except rubber bullets and pellets]
carbine
machine gun
pistol
rifle
shotgun

E991.3 Antipersonnel bomb (fragments)

E991.9 Other and unspecified fragments
Fragments from:
artillery shell
bombs, except anti-personnel
grenade
guided missile
land mine
rockets
shell
Shrapnel

E992 Injury due to war operations by explosion of marine weapons
Depth charge
Marine mines
Mine NOS, at sea or in harbor
Sea-based artillery shell
Torpedo
Underwater blast

E993 Injury due to war operations by other explosion
Accidental explosion of munitions being used in war
Accidental explosion of own weapons
Air blast NOS
Blast NOS
Explosion NOS
Explosion of:
artillery shell
breech block
cannon block
mortar bomb
Injury by weapon burst

E994 Injury due to war operations by destruction of aircraft
Airplane:
burned
exploded
shot down
Crushed by falling airplane

E995 Injury due to war operations by other and unspecified forms of conventional warfare
Battle wounds
Bayonet injury
Drowned in war operations

E996 Injury due to war operations by nuclear weapons
Blast effects
Exposure to ionizing radiation from nuclear weapons
Fireball effects
Heat
Other direct and secondary effects of nuclear weapons

✓4th **E997 Injury due to war operations by other forms of unconventional warfare**

E997.0 Lasers

E997.1 Biological warfare

E997.2 Gases, fumes, and chemicals

E997.8 Other specified forms of unconventional warfare

E997.9 Unspecified form of unconventional warfare

E998 Injury due to war operations but occurring after cessation of hostilities
Injuries due to operations of war but occurring after cessation of hostilities by any means classifiable under E990-E997
Injuries by explosion of bombs or mines placed in the course of operations of war, if the explosion occurred after cessation of hostilities

✓4th **E999 Late effect of injury due to war operations and terrorism**
Note: This category is to be used to indicate circumstances classifiable to E979, E990-E998 as the cause of death or disability from late effects, which are themselves classifiable elsewhere. The "late effects" include conditions reported as such, or as sequelae, which may occur at any time after the injury, resulting from operations of war or terrorism

E999.0 Late effect of injury due to war operations

E999.1 Late effect of injury due to terrorism

MORPHOLOGY OF NEOPLASMS

The World Health Organization has published an adaptation of the International Classification of Diseases for oncology (ICD-O). It contains a coded nomenclature for the morphology of neoplasms, which is reproduced here for those who wish to use it in conjunction with Chapter 2 of the International Classification of Diseases, 9th Revision, Clinical Modification.

The morphology code numbers consist of five digits; the first four identify the histological type of the neoplasm and the fifth indicates its behavior. The one-digit behavior code is as follows:

/0	Benign
/1	Uncertain whether benign or malignant Borderline malignancy
/2	Carcinoma in situ Intraepithelial Noninfiltrating Noninvasive
/3	Malignant, primary site
/6	Malignant, metastatic site Secondary site
/9	Malignant, uncertain whether primary or metastatic site

In the nomenclature below, the morphology code numbers include the behavior code appropriate to the histological type of neoplasm, but this behavior code should be changed if other reported information makes this necessary. For example, "chordoma (M9370/3)" is assumed to be malignant; the term "benign chordoma" should be coded M9370/0. Similarly, "superficial spreading adenocarcinoma (M8143/3)" described as "noninvasive" should be coded M8143/2 and "melanoma (M8720/3)" described as "secondary" should be coded M8720/6.

The following table shows the correspondence between the morphology code and the different sections of Chapter 2:

Morphology Code Histology/Behavior		ICD-9-CM Chapter 2	
Any	0	210-229	Benign neoplasms
M8000-M8004	1	239	Neoplasms of unspecified nature
M8010+	1	235-238	Neoplasms of uncertain behavior
Any	2	230-234	Carcinoma in situ
Any	3	140-195 200-208	Malignant neoplasms, stated or presumed to be primary
Any	6	196-198	Malignant neoplasms, stated or presumed to be secondary

The ICD-O behavior digit /9 is inapplicable in an ICD context, since all malignant neoplasms are presumed to be primary (/3) or secondary (/6) according to other information on the medical record.the first-listed term of the full ICD-O morphology nomenclature appears against each code number in the list below. The ICD-9-CM Alphabetical Index (Volume 2), however, includes all the ICD-O synonyms as well as a number of other morphological names still likely to be encountered on medical records but omitted from ICD-O as outdated or otherwise undesirable.

A coding difficulty sometimes arises where a morphological diagnosis contains two qualifying adjectives that have different code numbers. An example is "transitional cell epidermoid carcinoma." "Transitional cell carcinoma NOS" is M8120/3 and "epidermoid carcinoma NOS" is M8070/3. In such circumstances, the higher number (M8120/3 in this example) should be used, as it is usually more specific.

CODED NOMENCLATURE FOR MORPHOLOGY OF NEOPLASMS

M800 Neoplasms NOS

M8000/0 *Neoplasm, benign*
M8000/1 *Neoplasm, uncertain whether benign or malignant*
M8000/3 *Neoplasm, malignant*
M8000/6 *Neoplasm, metastatic*
M8000/9 *Neoplasm, malignant, uncertain whether primary or metastatic*
M8001/0 *Tumor cells, benign*
M8001/1 *Tumor cells, uncertain whether benign or malignant*
M8001/3 *Tumor cells, malignant*
M8002/3 *Malignant tumor, small cell type*
M8003/3 *Malignant tumor, giant cell type*
M8004/3 *Malignant tumor, fusiform cell type*

M801-M804 Epithelial neoplasms NOS

M8010/0 *Epithelial tumor, benign*
M8010/2 *Carcinoma in situ NOS*
M8010/3 *Carcinoma NOS*
M8010/6 *Carcinoma, metastatic NOS*
M8010/9 *Carcinomatosis*
M8011/0 *Epithelioma, benign*
M8011/3 *Epithelioma, malignant*
M8012/3 *Large cell carcinoma NOS*
M8020/3 *Carcinoma, undifferentiated type NOS*
M8021/3 *Carcinoma, anaplastic type NOS*
M8022/3 *Pleomorphic carcinoma*
M8030/3 *Giant cell and spindle cell carcinoma*
M8031/3 *Giant cell carcinoma*
M8032/3 *Spindle cell carcinoma*
M8033/3 *Pseudosarcomatous carcinoma*
M8034/3 *Polygonal cell carcinoma*
M8035/3 *Spheroidal cell carcinoma*
M8040/1 *Tumorlet*
M8041/3 *Small cell carcinoma NOS*
M8042/3 *Oat cell carcinoma*
M8043/3 *Small cell carcinoma, fusiform cell type*

M805-M808 Papillary and squamous cell neoplasms

M8050/0 *Papilloma NOS (except Papilloma of urinary bladder M8120/1)*
M8050/2 *Papillary carcinoma in situ*
M8050/3 *Papillary carcinoma NOS*
M8051/0 *Verrucous papilloma*
M8051/3 *Verrucous carcinoma NOS*
M8052/0 *Squamous cell papilloma*
M8052/3 *Papillary squamous cell carcinoma*
M8053/0 *Inverted papilloma*
M8060/0 *Papillomatosis NOS*
M8070/2 *Squamous cell carcinoma in situ NOS*
M8070/3 *Squamous cell carcinoma NOS*
M8070/6 *Squamous cell carcinoma, metastatic NOS*
M8071/3 *Squamous cell carcinoma, keratinizing type NOS*
M8072/3 *Squamous cell carcinoma, large cell, nonkeratinizing type*
M8073/3 *Squamous cell carcinoma, small cell, nonkeratinizing type*
M8074/3 *Squamous cell carcinoma, spindle cell type*
M8075/3 *Adenoid squamous cell carcinoma*
M8076/2 *Squamous cell carcinoma in situ with questionable stromal invasion*
M8076/3 *Squamous cell carcinoma, microinvasive*
M8080/2 *Queyrat's erythroplasia*
M8081/2 *Bowen's disease*
M8082/3 *Lymphoepithelial carcinoma*

M809-M811 Basal cell neoplasms

M8090/1 *Basal cell tumor*
M8090/3 *Basal cell carcinoma NOS*
M8091/3 *Multicentric basal cell carcinoma*
M8092/3 *Basal cell carcinoma, morphea type*
M8093/3 *Basal cell carcinoma, fibroepithelial type*
M8094/3 *Basosquamous carcinoma*
M8095/3 *Metatypical carcinoma*
M8096/0 *Intraepidermal epithelioma of Jadassohn*
M8100/0 *Trichoepithelioma*
M8101/0 *Trichofolliculoma*
M8102/0 *Tricholemmoma*
M8110/0 *Pilomatrixoma*

M812-M813 Transitional cell papillomas and carcinomas

M8120/0 *Transitional cell papilloma NOS*
M8120/1 *Urothelial papilloma*
M8120/2 *Transitional cell carcinoma in situ*
M8120/3 *Transitional cell carcinoma NOS*
M8121/0 *Schneiderian papilloma*
M8121/1 *Transitional cell papilloma, inverted type*
M8121/3 *Schneiderian carcinoma*
M8122/3 *Transitional cell carcinoma, spindle cell type*
M8123/3 *Basaloid carcinoma*
M8124/3 *Cloacogenic carcinoma*
M8130/3 *Papillary transitional cell carcinoma*

M814-M838 Adenomas and adenocarcinomas

M8140/0 *Adenoma NOS*
M8140/1 *Bronchial adenoma NOS*
M8140/2 *Adenocarcinoma in situ*
M8140/3 *Adenocarcinoma NOS*
M8140/6 *Adenocarcinoma, metastatic NOS*
M8141/3 *Scirrhous adenocarcinoma*
M8142/3 *Linitis plastica*
M8143/3 *Superficial spreading adenocarcinoma*
M8144/3 *Adenocarcinoma, intestinal type*
M8145/3 *Carcinoma, diffuse type*
M8146/0 *Monomorphic adenoma*
M8147/0 *Basal cell adenoma*
M8150/0 *Islet cell adenoma*
M8150/3 *Islet cell carcinoma*
M8151/0 *Insulinoma NOS*
M8151/3 *Insulinoma, malignant*
M8152/0 *Glucagonoma NOS*
M8152/3 *Glucagonoma, malignant*
M8153/1 *Gastrinoma NOS*
M8153/3 *Gastrinoma, malignant*
M8154/3 *Mixed islet cell and exocrine adenocarcinoma*
M8160/0 *Bile duct adenoma*
M8160/3 *Cholangiocarcinoma*
M8161/0 *Bile duct cystadenoma*
M8161/3 *Bile duct cystadenocarcinoma*
M8170/0 *Liver cell adenoma*
M8170/3 *Hepatocellular carcinoma NOS*

M8180/0 *Hepatocholangioma, benign*
M8180/3 *Combined hepatocellular carcinoma and cholangiocarcinoma*
M8190/0 *Trabecular adenoma*
M8190/3 *Trabecular adenocarcinoma*
M8191/0 *Embryonal adenoma*
M8200/0 *Eccrine dermal cylindroma*
M8200/3 *Adenoid cystic carcinoma*
M8201/3 *Cribriform carcinoma*
M8210/0 *Adenomatous polyp NOS*
M8210/3 *Adenocarcinoma in adenomatous polyp*
M8211/0 *Tubular adenoma NOS*
M8211/3 *Tubular adenocarcinoma*
M8220/0 *Adenomatous polyposis coli*
M8220/3 *Adenocarcinoma in adenomatous polyposis coli*
M8221/0 *Multiple adenomatous polyps*
M8230/3 *Solid carcinoma NOS*
M8231/3 *Carcinoma simplex*
M8240/1 *Carcinoid tumor NOS*
M8240/3 *Carcinoid tumor, malignant*
M8241/1 *Carcinoid tumor, argentaffin NOS*
M8241/3 *Carcinoid tumor, argentaffin, malignant*
M8242/1 *Carcinoid tumor, nonargentaffin NOS*
M8242/3 *Carcinoid tumor, nonargentaffin, malignant*
M8243/3 *Mucocarcinoid tumor, malignant*
M8244/3 *Composite carcinoid*
M8250/1 *Pulmonary adenomatosis*
M8250/3 *Bronchiolo-alveolar adenocarcinoma*
M8251/0 *Alveolar adenoma*
M8251/3 *Alveolar adenocarcinoma*
M8260/0 *Papillary adenoma NOS*
M8260/3 *Papillary adenocarcinoma NOS*
M8261/1 *Villous adenoma NOS*
M8261/3 *Adenocarcinoma in villous adenoma*
M8262/3 *Villous adenocarcinoma*
M8263/0 *Tubulovillous adenoma*
M8270/0 *Chromophobe adenoma*
M8270/3 *Chromophobe carcinoma*
M8280/0 *Acidophil adenoma*
M8280/3 *Acidophil carcinoma*
M8281/0 *Mixed acidophil-basophil adenoma*
M8281/3 *Mixed acidophil-basophil carcinoma*
M8290/0 *Oxyphilic adenoma*
M8290/3 *Oxyphilic adenocarcinoma*
M8300/0 *Basophil adenoma*
M8300/3 *Basophil carcinoma*
M8310/0 *Clear cell adenoma*
M8310/3 *Clear cell adenocarcinoma NOS*
M8311/1 *Hypernephroid tumor*
M8312/3 *Renal cell carcinoma*
M8313/0 *Clear cell adenofibroma*
M8320/3 *Granular cell carcinoma*
M8321/0 *Chief cell adenoma*
M8322/0 *Water-clear cell adenoma*
M8322/3 *Water-clear cell adenocarcinoma*
M8323/0 *Mixed cell adenoma*
M8323/3 *Mixed cell adenocarcinoma*
M8324/0 *Lipoadenoma*
M8330/0 *Follicular adenoma*
M8330/3 *Follicular adenocarcinoma NOS*
M8331/3 *Follicular adenocarcinoma, well differentiated type*
M8332/3 *Follicular adenocarcinoma, trabecular type*
M8333/0 *Microfollicular adenoma*
M8334/0 *Macrofollicular adenoma*
M8340/3 *Papillary and follicular adenocarcinoma*
M8350/3 *Nonencapsulated sclerosing carcinoma*
M8360/1 *Multiple endocrine adenomas*
M8361/1 *Juxtaglomerular tumor*
M8370/0 *Adrenal cortical adenoma NOS*
M8370/3 *Adrenal cortical carcinoma*
M8371/0 *Adrenal cortical adenoma, compact cell type*
M8372/0 *Adrenal cortical adenoma, heavily pigmented variant*
M8373/0 *Adrenal cortical adenoma, clear cell type*
M8374/0 *Adrenal cortical adenoma, glomerulosa cell type*
M8375/0 *Adrenal cortical adenoma, mixed cell type*
M8380/0 *Endometrioid adenoma NOS*
M8380/1 *Endometrioid adenoma, borderline malignancy*
M8380/3 *Endometrioid carcinoma*
M8381/0 *Endometrioid adenofibroma NOS*
M8381/1 *Endometrioid adenofibroma, borderline malignancy*
M8381/3 *Endometrioid adenofibroma, malignant*

M839-M842 Adnexal and skin appendage neoplasmsM8390/0*Skin appendage adenoma*

M8390/3 *Skin appendage carcinoma*
M8400/0 *Sweat gland adenoma*
M8400/1 *Sweat gland tumor NOS*
M8400/3 *Sweat gland adenocarcinoma*
M8401/0 *Apocrine adenoma*
M8401/3 *Apocrine adenocarcinoma*
M8402/0 *Eccrine acrospiroma*
M8403/0 *Eccrine spiradenoma*
M8404/0 *Hidrocystoma*
M8405/0 *Papillary hydradenoma*
M8406/0 *Papillary syringadenoma*
M8407/0 *Syringoma NOS*
M8410/0 *Sebaceous adenoma*
M8410/3 *Sebaceous adenocarcinoma*
M8420/0 *Ceruminous adenoma*
M8420/3 *Ceruminous adenocarcinoma*

M843 Mucoepidermoid neoplasms

M8430/1 *Mucoepidermoid tumor*
M8430/3 *Mucoepidermoid carcinoma*

M844-M849 Cystic, mucinous, and serous neoplasms

M8440/0 *Cystadenoma NOS*
M8440/3 *Cystadenocarcinoma NOS*
M8441/0 *Serous cystadenoma NOS*
M8441/1 *Serous cystadenoma, borderline malignancy*
M8441/3 *Serous cystadenocarcinoma NOS*
M8450/0 *Papillary cystadenoma NOS*
M8450/1 *Papillary cystadenoma, borderline malignancy*
M8450/3 *Papillary cystadenocarcinoma NOS*
M8460/0 *Papillary serous cystadenoma NOS*
M8460/1 *Papillary serous cystadenoma, borderline malignancy*
M8460/3 *Papillary serous cystadenocarcinoma*
M8461/0 *Serous surface papilloma NOS*
M8461/1 *Serous surface papilloma, borderline malignancy*
M8461/3 *Serous surface papillary carcinoma*
M8470/0 *Mucinous cystadenoma NOS*
M8470/1 *Mucinous cystadenoma, borderline malignancy*
M8470/3 *Mucinous cystadenocarcinoma NOS*
M8471/0 *Papillary mucinous cystadenoma NOS*
M8471/1 *Papillary mucinous cystadenoma, borderline malignancy*
M8471/3 *Papillary mucinous cystadenocarcinoma*
M8480/0 *Mucinous adenoma*
M8480/3 *Mucinous adenocarcinoma*
M8480/6 *Pseudomyxoma peritonei*
M8481/3 *Mucin-producing adenocarcinoma*
M8490/3 *Signet ring cell carcinoma*
M8490/6 *Metastatic signet ring cell carcinoma*

M850-M854 Ductal, lobular, and medullary neoplasms

M8500/2 *Intraductal carcinoma, noninfiltrating NOS*
M8500/3 *Infiltrating duct carcinoma*
M8501/2 *Comedocarcinoma, noninfiltrating*
M8501/3 *Comedocarcinoma NOS*
M8502/3 *Juvenile carcinoma of the breast*
M8503/0 *Intraductal papilloma*
M8503/2 *Noninfiltrating intraductal papillary adenocarcinoma*
M8504/0 *Intracystic papillary adenoma*
M8504/2 *Noninfiltrating intracystic carcinoma*
M8505/0 *Intraductal papillomatosis NOS*
M8506/0 *Subareolar duct papillomatosis*
M8510/3 *Medullary carcinoma NOS*
M8511/3 *Medullary carcinoma with amyloid stroma*
M8512/3 *Medullary carcinoma with lymphoid stroma*
M8520/2 *Lobular carcinoma in situ*
M8520/3 *Lobular carcinoma NOS*
M8521/3 *Infiltrating ductular carcinoma*
M8530/3 *Inflammatory carcinoma*
M8540/3 *Paget's disease, mammary*
M8541/3 *Paget's disease and infiltrating duct carcinoma of breast*
M8542/3 *Paget's disease, extramammary (except Paget's disease of bone)*

M855 Acinar cell neoplasms

M8550/0 *Acinar cell adenoma*
M8550/1 *Acinar cell tumor*
M8550/3 *Acinar cell carcinoma*

M856-M858 Complex epithelial neoplasms

M8560/3 *Adenosquamous carcinoma*
M8561/0 *Adenolymphoma*
M8570/3 *Adenocarcinoma with squamous metaplasia*
M8571/3 *Adenocarcinoma with cartilaginous and osseous metaplasia*
M8572/3 *Adenocarcinoma with spindle cell metaplasia*
M8573/3 *Adenocarcinoma with apocrine metaplasia*
M8580/0 *Thymoma, benign*
M8580/3 *Thymoma, malignant*

M859-M867 Specialized gonadal neoplasms

M8590/1 *Sex cord-stromal tumor*
M8600/0 *Thecoma NOS*
M8600/3 *Theca cell carcinoma*
M8610/0 *Luteoma NOS*
M8620/1 *Granulosa cell tumor NOS*
M8620/3 *Granulosa cell tumor, malignant*
M8621/1 *Granulosa cell-theca cell tumor*
M8630/0 *Androblastoma, benign*
M8630/1 *Androblastoma NOS*
M8630/3 *Androblastoma, malignant*
M8631/0 *Sertoli-Leydig cell tumor*
M8632/1 *Gynandroblastoma*
M8640/0 *Tubular androblastoma NOS*
M8640/3 *Sertoli cell carcinoma*
M8641/0 *Tubular androblastoma with lipid storage*
M8650/0 *Leydig cell tumor, benign*
M8650/1 *Leydig cell tumor NOS*
M8650/3 *Leydig cell tumor, malignant*
M8660/0 *Hilar cell tumor*
M8670/0 *Lipid cell tumor of ovary*

M8671/0 *Adrenal rest tumor*

M868-M871 Paragangliomas and glomus tumors

M8680/1 *Paraganglioma NOS*
M8680/3 *Paraganglioma, malignant*
M8681/1 *Sympathetic paraganglioma*
M8682/1 *Parasympathetic paraganglioma*
M8690/1 *Glomus jugulare tumor*
M8691/1 *Aortic body tumor*
M8692/1 *Carotid body tumor*
M8693/1 *Extra-adrenal paraganglioma NOS*
M8693/3 *Extra-adrenal paraganglioma, malignant*
M8700/0 *Pheochromocytoma NOS*
M8700/3 *Pheochromocytoma, malignant*
M8710/3 *Glomangiosarcoma*
M8711/0 *Glomus tumor*
M8712/0 *Glomangioma*

M872-M879 Nevi and melanomas

M8720/0 *Pigmented nevus NOS*
M8720/3 *Malignant melanoma NOS*
M8721/3 *Nodular melanoma*
M8722/0 *Balloon cell nevus*
M8722/3 *Balloon cell melanoma*
M8723/0 *Halo nevus*
M8724/0 *Fibrous papule of the nose*
M8725/0 *Neuronevus*
M8726/0 *Magnocellular nevus*
M8730/0 *Nonpigmented nevus*
M8730/3 *Amelanotic melanoma*
M8740/0 *Junctional nevus*
M8740/3 *Malignant melanoma in junctional nevus*
M8741/2 *Precancerous melanosis NOS*
M8741/3 *Malignant melanoma in precancerous melanosis*
M8742/2 *Hutchinson's melanotic freckle*
M8742/3 *Malignant melanoma in Hutchinson's melanotic freckle*
M8743/3 *Superficial spreading melanoma*
M8750/0 *Intradermal nevus*
M8760/0 *Compound nevus*
M8761/1 *Giant pigmented nevus*
M8761/3 *Malignant melanoma in giant pigmented nevus*
M8770/0 *Epithelioid and spindle cell nevus*
M8771/3 *Epithelioid cell melanoma*
M8772/3 *Spindle cell melanoma NOS*
M8773/3 *Spindle cell melanoma, type A*
M8774/3 *Spindle cell melanoma, type B*
M8775/3 *Mixed epithelioid and spindle cell melanoma*
M8780/0 *Blue nevus NOS*
M8780/3 *Blue nevus, malignant*
M8790/0 *Cellular blue nevus*

M880 Soft tissue tumors and sarcomas NOS

M8800/0 *Soft tissue tumor, benign*
M8800/3 *Sarcoma NOS*
M8800/9 *Sarcomatosis NOS*
M8801/3 *Spindle cell sarcoma*
M8802/3 *Giant cell sarcoma (except of bone M9250/3)*
M8803/3 *Small cell sarcoma*
M8804/3 *Epithelioid cell sarcoma*

M881-M883 Fibromatous neoplasms

M8810/0 *Fibroma NOS*
M8810/3 *Fibrosarcoma NOS*
M8811/0 *Fibromyxoma*
M8811/3 *Fibromyxosarcoma*
M8812/0 *Periosteal fibroma*
M8812/3 *Periosteal fibrosarcoma*
M8813/0 *Fascial fibroma*
M8813/3 *Fascial fibrosarcoma*
M8814/3 *Infantile fibrosarcoma*
M8820/0 *Elastofibroma*
M8821/1 *Aggressive fibromatosis*
M8822/1 *Abdominal fibromatosis*
M8823/1 *Desmoplastic fibroma*
M8830/0 *Fibrous histiocytoma NOS*
M8830/1 *Atypical fibrous histiocytoma*
M8830/3 *Fibrous histiocytoma, malignant*
M8831/0 *Fibroxanthoma NOS*
M8831/1 *Atypical fibroxanthoma*
M8831/3 *Fibroxanthoma, malignant*
M8832/0 *Dermatofibroma NOS*
M8832/1 *Dermatofibroma protuberans*
M8832/3 *Dermatofibrosarcoma NOS*

M884 Myxomatous neoplasms

M8840/0 *Myxoma NOS*
M8840/3 *Myxosarcoma*

M885-M888 Lipomatous neoplasms

M8850/0 *Lipoma NOS*
M8850/3 *Liposarcoma NOS*
M8851/0 *Fibrolipoma*
M8851/3 *Liposarcoma, well differentiated type*
M8852/0 *Fibromyxolipoma*
M8852/3 *Myxoid liposarcoma*
M8853/3 *Round cell liposarcoma*
M8854/3 *Pleomorphic liposarcoma*
M8855/3 *Mixed type liposarcoma*
M8856/0 *Intramuscular lipoma*
M8857/0 *Spindle cell lipoma*
M8860/0 *Angiomyolipoma*
M8860/3 *Angiomyoliposarcoma*
M8861/0 *Angiolipoma NOS*
M8861/1 *Angiolipoma, infiltrating*
M8870/0 *Myelolipoma*
M8880/0 *Hibernoma*
M8881/0 *Lipoblastomatosis*

M889-M892 Myomatous neoplasms

M8890/0 *Leiomyoma NOS*
M8890/1 *Intravascular leiomyomatosis*
M8890/3 *Leiomyosarcoma NOS*
M8891/1 *Epithelioid leiomyoma*
M8891/3 *Epithelioid leiomyosarcoma*
M8892/1 *Cellular leiomyoma*
M8893/0 *Bizarre leiomyoma*
M8894/0 *Angiomyoma*
M8894/3 *Angiomyosarcoma*
M8895/0 *Myoma*
M8895/3 *Myosarcoma*
M8900/0 *Rhabdomyoma NOS*
M8900/3 *Rhabdomyosarcoma NOS*
M8901/3 *Pleomorphic rhabdomyosarcoma*
M8902/3 *Mixed type rhabdomyosarcoma*
M8903/0 *Fetal rhabdomyoma*
M8904/0 *Adult rhabdomyoma*
M8910/3 *Embryonal rhabdomyosarcoma*
M8920/3 *Alveolar rhabdomyosarcoma*

M893-M899 Complex mixed and stromal neoplasms

M8930/3 *Endometrial stromal sarcoma*
M8931/1 *Endolymphatic stromal myosis*
M8932/0 *Adenomyoma*
M8940/0 *Pleomorphic adenoma*
M8940/3 *Mixed tumor, malignant NOS*
M8950/3 *Mullerian mixed tumor*
M8951/3 *Mesodermal mixed tumor*
M8960/1 *Mesoblastic nephroma*
M8960/3 *Nephroblastoma NOS*
M8961/3 *Epithelial nephroblastoma*
M8962/3 *Mesenchymal nephroblastoma*
M8970/3 *Hepatoblastoma*
M8980/3 *Carcinosarcoma NOS*
M8981/3 *Carcinosarcoma, embryonal type*
M8982/0 *Myoepithelioma*
M8990/0 *Mesenchymoma, benign*
M8990/1 *Mesenchymoma NOS*
M8990/3 *Mesenchymoma, malignant*
M8991/3 *Embryonal sarcoma*

M900-M903 Fibroepithelial neoplasms

M9000/0 *Brenner tumor NOS*
M9000/1 *Brenner tumor, borderline malignancy*
M9000/3 *Brenner tumor, malignant*
M9010/0 *Fibroadenoma NOS*
M9011/0 *Intracanalicular fibroadenoma NOS*
M9012/0 *Pericanalicular fibroadenoma*
M9013/0 *Adenofibroma NOS*
M9014/0 *Serous adenofibroma*
M9015/0 *Mucinous adenofibroma*
M9020/0 *Cellular intracanalicular fibroadenoma*
M9020/1 *Cystosarcoma phyllodes NOS*
M9020/3 *Cystosarcoma phyllodes, malignant*
M9030/0 *Juvenile fibroadenoma*

M904 Synovial neoplasms

M9040/0 *Synovioma, benign*
M9040/3 *Synovial sarcoma NOS*
M9041/3 *Synovial sarcoma, spindle cell type*
M9042/3 *Synovial sarcoma, epithelioid cell type*
M9043/3 *Synovial sarcoma, biphasic type*
M9044/3 *Clear cell sarcoma of tendons and aponeuroses*

M905 Mesothelial neoplasms

M9050/0 *Mesothelioma, benign*
M9050/3 *Mesothelioma, malignant*
M9051/0 *Fibrous mesothelioma, benign*
M9051/3 *Fibrous mesothelioma, malignant*
M9052/0 *Epithelioid mesothelioma, benign*
M9052/3 *Epithelioid mesothelioma, malignant*
M9053/0 *Mesothelioma, biphasic type, benign*
M9053/3 *Mesothelioma, biphasic type, malignant*
M9054/0 *Adenomatoid tumor NOS*

M906-M909 Germ cell neoplasms

M9060/3 *Dysgerminoma*
M9061/3 *Seminoma NOS*
M9062/3 *Seminoma, anaplastic type*
M9063/3 *Spermatocytic seminoma*
M9064/3 *Germinoma*
M9070/3 *Embryonal carcinoma NOS*
M9071/3 *Endodermal sinus tumor*
M9072/3 *Polyembryoma*
M9073/1 *Gonadoblastoma*
M9080/0 *Teratoma, benign*
M9080/1 *Teratoma NOS*
M9080/3 *Teratoma, malignant NOS*
M9081/3 *Teratocarcinoma*
M9082/3 *Malignant teratoma, undifferentiated type*
M9083/3 *Malignant teratoma, intermediate type*
M9084/0 *Dermoid cyst*
M9084/3 *Dermoid cyst with malignant transformation*
M9090/0 *Struma ovarii NOS*
M9090/3 *Struma ovarii, malignant*
M9091/1 *Strumal carcinoid*

M910 Trophoblastic neoplasms

M9100/0 *Hydatidiform mole NOS*
M9100/1 *Invasive hydatidiform mole*
M9100/3 *Choriocarcinoma*
M9101/3 *Choriocarcinoma combined with teratoma*
M9102/3 *Malignant teratoma, trophoblastic*

M911 Mesonephromas

M9110/0 *Mesonephroma, benign*
M9110/1 *Mesonephric tumor*
M9110/3 *Mesonephroma, malignant*
M9111/1 *Endosalpingioma*

M912-M916 Blood vessel tumors

M9120/0 *Hemangioma NOS*
M9120/3 *Hemangiosarcoma*
M9121/0 *Cavernous hemangioma*
M9122/0 *Venous hemangioma*

M9123/0 *Racemose hemangioma*
M9124/3 *Kupffer cell sarcoma*
M9130/0 *Hemangioendothelioma, benign*
M9130/1 *Hemangioendothelioma NOS*
M9130/3 *Hemangioendothelioma, malignant*
M9131/0 *Capillary hemangioma*
M9132/0 *Intramuscular hemangioma*
M9140/3 *Kaposi's sarcoma*
M9141/0 *Angiokeratoma*
M9142/0 *Verrucous keratotic hemangioma*
M9150/0 *Hemangiopericytoma, benign*
M9150/1 *Hemangiopericytoma NOS*
M9150/3 *Hemangiopericytoma, malignant*
M9160/0 *Angiofibroma NOS*
M9161/1 *Hemangioblastoma*

M917 Lymphatic vessel tumors
M9170/0 *Lymphangioma NOS*
M9170/3 *Lymphangiosarcoma*
M9171/0 *Capillary lymphangioma*
M9172/0 *Cavernous lymphangioma*
M9173/0 *Cystic lymphangioma*
M9174/0 *Lymphangiomyoma*
M9174/1 *Lymphangiomyomatosis*
M9175/0 *Hemolymphangioma*

M918-M920 Osteomas and osteosarcomas
M9180/0 *Osteoma NOS*
M9180/3 *Osteosarcoma NOS*
M9181/3 *Chondroblastic osteosarcoma*
M9182/3 *Fibroblastic osteosarcoma*
M9183/3 *Telangiectatic osteosarcoma*
M9184/3 *Osteosarcoma in Paget's disease of bone*
M9190/3 *Juxtacortical osteosarcoma*
M9191/0 *Osteoid osteoma NOS*
M9200/0 *Osteoblastoma*

M921-M924 Chondromatous neoplasms
M9210/0 *Osteochondroma*
M9210/1 *Osteochondromatosis NOS*
M9220/0 *Chondroma NOS*
M9220/1 *Chondromatosis NOS*
M9220/3 *Chondrosarcoma NOS*
M9221/0 *Juxtacortical chondroma*
M9221/3 *Juxtacortical chondrosarcoma*
M9230/0 *Chondroblastoma NOS*
M9230/3 *Chondroblastoma, malignant*
M9240/3 *Mesenchymal chondrosarcoma*
M9241/0 *Chondromyxoid fibroma*

M925 Giant cell tumors
M9250/1 *Giant cell tumor of bone NOS*
M9250/3 *Giant cell tumor of bone, malignant*
M9251/1 *Giant cell tumor of soft parts NOS*
M9251/3 *Malignant giant cell tumor of soft parts*

M926 Miscellaneous bone tumors
M9260/3 *Ewing's sarcoma*
M9261/3 *Adamantinoma of long bones*
M9262/0 *Ossifying fibroma*

M927-M934 Odontogenic tumors
M9270/0 *Odontogenic tumor, benign*
M9270/1 *Odontogenic tumor NOS*
M9270/3 *Odontogenic tumor, malignant*
M9271/0 *Dentinoma*
M9272/0 *Cementoma NOS*
M9273/0 *Cementoblastoma, benign*
M9274/0 *Cementifying fibroma*
M9275/0 *Gigantiform cementoma*
M9280/0 *Odontoma NOS*
M9281/0 *Compound odontoma*
M9282/0 *Complex odontoma*
M9290/0 *Ameloblastic fibro-odontoma*
M9290/3 *Ameloblastic odontosarcoma*
M9300/0 *Adenomatoid odontogenic tumor*
M9301/0 *Calcifying odontogenic cyst*
M9310/0 *Ameloblastoma NOS*
M9310/3 *Ameloblastoma, malignant*
M9311/0 *Odontoameloblastoma*
M9312/0 *Squamous odontogenic tumor*
M9320/0 *Odontogenic myxoma*
M9321/0 *Odontogenic fibroma NOS*
M9330/0 *Ameloblastic fibroma*
M9330/3 *Ameloblastic fibrosarcoma*
M9340/0 *Calcifying epithelial odontogenic tumor*

M935-M937 Miscellaneous tumors
M9350/1 *Craniopharyngioma*
M9360/1 *Pinealoma*
M9361/1 *Pineocytoma*
M9362/3 *Pineoblastoma*
M9363/0 *Melanotic neuroectodermal tumor*
M9370/3 *Chordoma*

M938-M948 Gliomas
M9380/3 *Glioma, malignant*
M9381/3 *Gliomatosis cerebri*
M9382/3 *Mixed glioma*
M9383/1 *Subependymal glioma*
M9384/1 *Subependymal giant cell astrocytoma*
M9390/0 *Choroid plexus papilloma NOS*
M9390/3 *Choroid plexus papilloma, malignant*
M9391/3 *Ependymoma NOS*
M9392/3 *Ependymoma, anaplastic type*
M9393/1 *Papillary ependymoma*
M9394/1 *Myxopapillary ependymoma*
M9400/3 *Astrocytoma NOS*
M9401/3 *Astrocytoma, anaplastic type*
M9410/3 *Protoplasmic astrocytoma*
M9411/3 *Gemistocytic astrocytoma*
M9420/3 *Fibrillary astrocytoma*
M9421/3 *Pilocytic astrocytoma*
M9422/3 *Spongioblastoma NOS*
M9423/3 *Spongioblastoma polare*
M9430/3 *Astroblastoma*
M9440/3 *Glioblastoma NOS*
M9441/3 *Giant cell glioblastoma*
M9442/3 *Glioblastoma with sarcomatous component*
M9443/3 *Primitive polar spongioblastoma*
M9450/3 *Oligodendroglioma NOS*
M9451/3 *Oligodendroglioma, anaplastic type*
M9460/3 *Oligodendroblastoma*
M9470/3 *Medulloblastoma NOS*
M9471/3 *Desmoplastic medulloblastoma*
M9472/3 *Medullomyoblastoma*
M9480/3 *Cerebellar sarcoma NOS*
M9481/3 *Monstrocellular sarcoma*

M949-M952 Neuroepitheliomatous neoplasms
M9490/0 *Ganglioneuroma*
M9490/3 *Ganglioneuroblastoma*
M9491/0 *Ganglioneuromatosis*
M9500/3 *Neuroblastoma NOS*
M9501/3 *Medulloepithelioma NOS*
M9502/3 *Teratoid medulloepithelioma*
M9503/3 *Neuroepithelioma NOS*
M9504/3 *Spongioneuroblastoma*
M9505/1 *Ganglioglioma*
M9506/0 *Neurocytoma*
M9507/0 *Pacinian tumor*
M9510/3 *Retinoblastoma NOS*
M9511/3 *Retinoblastoma, differentiated type*
M9512/3 *Retinoblastoma, undifferentiated type*
M9520/3 *Olfactory neurogenic tumor*
M9521/3 *Esthesioneurocytoma*
M9522/3 *Esthesioneuroblastoma*
M9523/3 *Esthesioneuroepithelioma*

M953 Meningiomas
M9530/0 *Meningioma NOS*
M9530/1 *Meningiomatosis NOS*
M9530/3 *Meningioma, malignant*
M9531/0 *Meningotheliomatous meningioma*
M9532/0 *Fibrous meningioma*
M9533/0 *Psammomatous meningioma*
M9534/0 *Angiomatous meningioma*
M9535/0 *Hemangioblastic meningioma*
M9536/0 *Hemangiopericytic meningioma*
M9537/0 *Transitional meningioma*
M9538/1 *Papillary meningioma*
M9539/3 *Meningeal sarcomatosis*

M954-M957 Nerve sheath tumor
M9540/0 *Neurofibroma NOS*
M9540/1 *Neurofibromatosis NOS*
M9540/3 *Neurofibrosarcoma*
M9541/0 *Melanotic neurofibroma*
M9550/0 *Plexiform neurofibroma*
M9560/0 *Neurilemmoma NOS*
M9560/1 *Neurinomatosis*
M9560/3 *Neurilemmoma, malignant*
M9570/0 *Neuroma NOS*

M958 Granular cell tumors and alveolar soft part sarcoma
M9580/0 *Granular cell tumor NOS*
M9580/3 *Granular cell tumor, malignant*
M9581/3 *Alveolar soft part sarcoma*

M959-M963 Lymphomas, NOS or diffuse
M9590/0 *Lymphomatous tumor, benign*
M9590/3 *Malignant lymphoma NOS*
M9591/3 *Malignant lymphoma, non Hodgkin's type*
M9600/3 *Malignant lymphoma, undifferentiated cell type NOS*
M9601/3 *Malignant lymphoma, stem cell type*
M9602/3 *Malignant lymphoma, convoluted cell type NOS*
M9610/3 *Lymphosarcoma NOS*
M9611/3 *Malignant lymphoma, lymphoplasmacytoid type*
M9612/3 *Malignant lymphoma, immunoblastic type*
M9613/3 *Malignant lymphoma, mixed lymphocytic-histiocytic NOS*
M9614/3 *Malignant lymphoma, centroblastic-centrocytic, diffuse*
M9615/3 *Malignant lymphoma, follicular center cell NOS*
M9620/3 *Malignant lymphoma, lymphocytic, well differentiated NOS*
M9621/3 *Malignant lymphoma, lymphocytic, intermediate differentiation NOS*
M9622/3 *Malignant lymphoma, centrocytic*
M9623/3 *Malignant lymphoma, follicular center cell, cleaved NOS*
M9630/3 *Malignant lymphoma, lymphocytic, poorly differentiated NOS*
M9631/3 *Prolymphocytic lymphosarcoma*
M9632/3 *Malignant lymphoma, centroblastic type NOS*
M9633/3 *Malignant lymphoma, follicular center cell, noncleaved NOS*

M964 *Reticulosarcomas*
M9640/3 *Reticulosarcoma NOS*
M9641/3 *Reticulosarcoma, pleomorphic cell type*
M9642/3 *Reticulosarcoma, nodular*

M965-M966 *Hodgkin's disease*
M9650/3 *Hodgkin's disease NOS*
M9651/3 *Hodgkin's disease, lymphocytic predominance*
M9652/3 *Hodgkin's disease, mixed cellularity*
M9653/3 *Hodgkin's disease, lymphocytic depletion NOS*
M9654/3 *Hodgkin's disease, lymphocytic depletion, diffuse fibrosis*

M9655/3 *Hodgkin's disease, lymphocytic depletion, reticular type*
M9656/3 *Hodgkin's disease, nodular sclerosis NOS*
M9657/3 *Hodgkin's disease, nodular sclerosis, cellular phase*
M9660/3 *Hodgkin's paragranuloma*
M9661/3 *Hodgkin's granuloma*
M9662/3 *Hodgkin's sarcoma*

M969 Lymphomas, nodular or follicular
M9690/3 *Malignant lymphoma, nodular NOS*
M9691/3 *Malignant lymphoma, mixed lymphocytic-histiocytic, nodular*
M9692/3 *Malignant lymphoma, centroblastic-centrocytic, follicular*
M9693/3 *Malignant lymphoma, lymphocytic, well differentiated, nodular*
M9694/3 *Malignant lymphoma, lymphocytic, intermediate differentiation, nodular*
M9695/3 *Malignant lymphoma, follicular center cell, cleaved, follicular*
M9696/3 *Malignant lymphoma, lymphocytic, poorly differentiated, nodular*
M9697/3 *Malignant lymphoma, centroblastic type, follicular*
M9698/3 *Malignant lymphoma, follicular center cell, noncleaved, follicular*

M970 Mycosis fungoides
M9700/3 *Mycosis fungoides*
M9701/3 *Sezary's disease*

M971-M972 Miscellaneous reticuloendothelial neoplasms
M9710/3 *Microglioma*
M9720/3 *Malignant histiocytosis*
M9721/3 *Histiocytic medullary reticulosis*
M9722/3 *Letterer-Siwe's disease*

M973 Plasma cell tumors
M9730/3 *Plasma cell myeloma*
M9731/0 *Plasma cell tumor, benign*
M9731/1 *Plasmacytoma NOS*
M9731/3 *Plasma cell tumor, malignant*

M974 Mast cell tumors
M9740/1 *Mastocytoma NOS*
M9740/3 *Mast cell sarcoma*
M9741/3 *Malignant mastocytosis*

M975 Burkitt's tumor
M9750/3 *Burkitt's tumor*

M980-M994 Leukemias NOS
M9800/3 Leukemias NOS
M9800/3 *Leukemia NOS*
M9801/3 *Acute leukemia NOS*
M9802/3 *Subacute leukemia NOS*
M9803/3 *Chronic leukemia NOS*
M9804/3 *Aleukemic leukemia NOS*

M981 Compound leukemias
M9810/3 *Compound leukemia*

M982 Lymphoid leukemias
M9820/3 *Lymphoid leukemia NOS*
M9821/3 *Acute lymphoid leukemia*
M9822/3 *Subacute lymphoid leukemia*
M9823/3 *Chronic lymphoid leukemia*
M9824/3 *Aleukemic lymphoid leukemia*
M9825/3 *Prolymphocytic leukemia*

M983 Plasma cell leukemias
M9830/3 *Plasma cell leukemia*

M984 Erythroleukemias
M9840/3 *Erythroleukemia*
M9841/3 *Acute erythremia*
M9842/3 *Chronic erythremia*

M985 Lymphosarcoma cell leukemias
M9850/3 *Lymphosarcoma cell leukemia*

M986 Myeloid leukemias
M9860/3 *Myeloid leukemia NOS*
M9861/3 *Acute myeloid leukemia*
M9862/3 *Subacute myeloid leukemia*
M9863/3 *Chronic myeloid leukemia*
M9864/3 *Aleukemic myeloid leukemia*
M9865/3 *Neutrophilic leukemia*
M9866/3 *Acute promyelocytic leukemia*

M987 Basophilic leukemias
M9870/3 *Basophilic leukemia*

M988 Eosinophilic leukemias
M9880/3 *Eosinophilic leukemia*

M989 Monocytic leukemias
M9890/3 *Monocytic leukemia NOS*
M9891/3 *Acute monocytic leukemia*
M9892/3 *Subacute monocytic leukemia*
M9893/3 *Chronic monocytic leukemia*
M9894/3 *Aleukemic monocytic leukemia*

M990-M994 Miscellaneous leukemias
M9900/3 *Mast cell leukemia*
M9910/3 *Megakaryocytic leukemia*
M9920/3 *Megakaryocytic myelosis*
M9930/3 *Myeloid sarcoma*
M9940/3 *Hairy cell leukemia*

M995-M997 Miscellaneous myeloproliferative and lymphoproliferative disorders
M9950/1 *Polycythemia vera*
M9951/1 *Acute panmyelosis*
M9960/1 *Chronic myeloproliferative disease*
M9961/1 *Myelosclerosis with myeloid metaplasia*
M9962/1 *Idiopathic thrombocythemia*
M9970/1 *Chronic lymphoproliferative disease*

APPENDIX B WAS OFFICIALLY DELETED OCTOBER 1, 2004

CLASSIFICATION OF DRUGS BY AMERICAN HOSPITAL FORMULARY SERVICE LIST NUMBER AND THEIR ICD-9-CM EQUIVALENTS

The coding of adverse effects of drugs is keyed to the continually revised Hospital Formulary of the American Hospital Formulary Service (AHFS) published under the direction of the American Society of Hospital Pharmacists.

The following section gives the ICD-9-CM diagnosis code for each AHFS list.

	AHFS* List	ICD-9-CM Diagnosis Code
4:00	ANTIHISTAMINE DRUGS	963.0
8:00	ANTI-INFECTIVE AGENTS	
8:04	Amebacides	961.5
	hydroxyquinoline derivatives	961.3
	arsenical anti-infectives	961.1
	quinoline derivatives	961.3
8:12.04	Antifungal Antibiotics	960.1
	nonantibiotics	961.9
8:12.06	Cephalosporins	960.5
8:12.08	Chloramphenicol	960.2
8:12.12	The Erythromycins	960.3
8:12.16	The Penicillins	960.0
8:12.20	The Streptomycins	960.6
8:12.24	The Tetracyclines	960.4
8:12.28	Other Antibiotics	960.8
	antimycobacterial antibiotics	960.6
	macrolides	960.3
8:16	Antituberculars	961.8
	antibiotics	960.6
8:18	Antivirals	961.7
8:20	Plasmodicides (antimalarials)	961.4
8:24	Sulfonamides	961.0
8:26	The Sulfones	961.8
8:28	Treponemicides	961.2
8:32	Trichomonacides	961.5
	hydroxyquinoline derivatives	961.3
	nitrofuran derivatives	961.9
8:36	Urinary Germicides	961.9
	quinoline derivatives	961.3
8:40	Other Anti-Infectives	961.9
10:00	ANTINEOPLASTIC AGENTS	963.1
	antibiotics	960.7
	progestogens	962.2
12:00	AUTONOMIC DRUGS	
12:04	Parasympathomimetic (Cholinergic) Agents	971.0
12:08	Parasympatholytic (Cholinergic Blocking) Agents	971.1
12:12	Sympathomimetic (Adrenergic) Agents	971.2
12:16	Sympatholytic (Adrenergic Blocking) Agents	971.3
12:20	Skeletal Muscle Relaxants	975.2
	central nervous system muscle-tone depressants	968.0
16:00	BLOOD DERIVATIVES	964.7
20:00	BLOOD FORMATION AND COAGULATION	
20:04	Antianemia Drugs	964.1
20:04.04	Iron Preparations	964.0
20:04.08	Liver and Stomach Preparations	964.1
20:12.04	Anticoagulants	964.2
20:12.08	Antiheparin Agents	964.5
20:12.12	Coagulants	964.5
20.12.16	Hemostatics	964.5
	capillary-active drugs	972.8
	fibrinolysis-affecting agents	964.4
	natural products	964.7
24:00	CARDIOVASCULAR DRUGS	
24:04	Cardiac Drugs	972.9
	cardiotonic agents	972.1
	rhythm regulators	972.0
24:06	Antilipemic Agents	972.2
	thyroid derivatives	962.7

	AHFS* List	ICD-9-CM Diagnosis Code
24:08	Hypotensive Agents	972.6
	adrenergic blocking agents	971.3
	ganglion-blocking agents	972.3
	vasodilators	972.5
24:12	Vasodilating Agents	972.5
	coronary	972.4
	nicotinic acid derivatives	972.2
24:16	Sclerosing Agents	972.7
28:00	CENTRAL NERVOUS SYSTEM DRUGS	
28:04	General Anesthetics	968.4
	gaseous anesthetics	968.2
	halothane	968.1
	intravenous anesthetics	968.3
28:08	Analgesics and Antipyretics	965.9
	antirheumatics	965.61-965.69
	aromatic analgesics	965.4
	non-narcotics NEC	965.7
	opium alkaloids	965.00
	heroin	965.01
	methadone	965.02
	specified type NEC	965.09
	pyrazole derivatives	965.5
	salicylates	965.1
	specified type NEC	965.8
28:10	Narcotic Antagonists	970.1
28:12	Anticonvulsants	966.3
	barbiturates	967.0
	benzodiazepine-based tranquilizers	969.4
	bromides	967.3
	hydantoin derivatives	966.1
	oxazolidine derivative	966.0
	succinimides	966.2
28:16.04	Antidepressants	969.0
28:16.08	Tranquilizers	969.5
	benzodiazepine-based	969.4
	butyrophenone-based	969.2
	major NEC	969.3
	phenothiazine-based	969.1
28:16.12	Other Psychotherapeutic Agents	969.8
28:20	Respiratory and Cerebral Stimulants	970.9
	analeptics	970.0
	anorexigenic agents	977.0
	psychostimulants	969.7
	specified type NEC	970.8
28:24	Sedatives and Hypnotics	967.9
	barbiturates	967.0
	benzodiazepine-based tranquilizers	969.4
	chloral hydrate group	967.1
	glutethamide group	967.5
	intravenous anesthetics	968.3
	methaqualone	967.4
	paraldehyde	967.2
	phenothiazine-based tranquilizers	969.1
	specified type NEC	967.8
	thiobarbiturates	968.3
	tranquilizer NEC	969.5
36:00	DIAGNOSTIC AGENTS	977.8
40:00	ELECTROLYTE, CALORIC, AND WATER BALANCE AGENTS NEC	974.5
40:04	Acidifying Agents	963.2
40:08	Alkalinizing Agents	963.3
40:10	Ammonia Detoxicants	974.5
40:12	Replacement Solutions NEC	974.5
	plasma volume expanders	964.8
40:16	Sodium-Removing Resins	974.5
40:18	Potassium-Removing Resins	974.5
40:20	Caloric Agents	974.5
40:24	Salt and Sugar Substitutes	974.5
40:28	Diuretics NEC	974.4
	carbonic acid anhydrase inhibitors	974.2
	mercurials	974.0
	purine derivatives	974.1
	saluretics	974.3
40:36	Irrigating Solutions	974.5
40:40	Uricosuric Agents	974.7

	AHFS* List	ICD-9-CM Diagnosis Code
44:00	ENZYMES NEC	963.4
	fibrinolysis-affecting agents	964.4
	gastric agents	973.4
48:00	EXPECTORANTS AND COUGH PREPARATIONS	
	antihistamine agents	963.0
	antitussives	975.4
	codeine derivatives	965.09
	expectorants	975.5
	narcotic agents NEC	965.09
52:00	EYE, EAR, NOSE, AND THROAT PREPARATIONS	
52:04	Anti-Infectives	
	ENT	976.6
	ophthalmic	976.5
52:04.04	Antibiotics	
	ENT	976.6
	ophthalmic	976.5
52:04.06	Antivirals	
	ENT	976.6
	ophthalmic	976.5
52:04.08	Sulfonamides	
	ENT	976.6
	ophthalmic	976.5
52:04.12	Miscellaneous Anti-Infectives	
	ENT	976.6
	ophthalmic	976.5
52:08	Anti-Inflammatory Agents	
	ENT	976.6
	ophthalmic	976.5
52:10	Carbonic Anhydrase Inhibitors	974.2
52:12	Contact Lens Solutions	976.5
52:16	Local Anesthetics	968.5
52:20	Miotics	971.0
52:24	Mydriatics	
	adrenergics	971.2
	anticholinergics	971.1
	antimuscarinics	971.1
	parasympatholytics	971.1
	spasmolytics	971.1
	sympathomimetics	971.2
52:28	Mouth Washes and Gargles	976.6
52:32	Vasoconstrictors	971.2
52:36	Unclassified Agents	
	ENT	976.6
	ophthalmic	976.5
56:00	GASTROINTESTINAL DRUGS	
56:04	Antacids and Absorbents	973.0
56:08	Anti-Diarrhea Agents	973.5
56:10	Antiflatulents	973.8
56:12	Cathartics NEC	973.3
	emollients	973.2
	irritants	973.1
56:16	Digestants	973.4
56:20	Emetics and Antiemetics	
	antiemetics	963.0
	emetics	973.6
56:24	Lipotropic Agents	977.1
60:00	GOLD COMPOUNDS	965.69
64:00	HEAVY METAL ANTAGONISTS	963.8
68:00	HORMONES AND SYNTHETIC SUBSTITUTES	
68:04	Adrenals	962.0
68:08	Androgens	962.1
68:12	Contraceptives	962.2
68:16	Estrogens	962.2
68:18	Gonadotropins	962.4
68:20	Insulins and Antidiabetic Agents	962.3
68:20.08	Insulins	962.3
68:24	Parathyroid	962.6
68:28	Pituitary	
	anterior	962.4
	posterior	962.5
68:32	Progestogens	962.2
68:34	Other Corpus Luteum Hormones	962.2

	AHFS* List	ICD-9-CM Diagnosis Code
68:36	Thyroid and Antithyroid	
	antithyroid	962.8
	thyroid	962.7
72:00	LOCAL ANESTHETICS NEC	968.9
	topical (surface) agents	968.5
	infiltrating agents (intradermal) (subcutaneous) (submucosal)	968.5
	nerve blocking agents (peripheral) (plexus) (regional)	968.6
	spinal	968.7
76:00	OXYTOCICS	975.0
78:00	RADIOACTIVE AGENTS	990
80:00	SERUMS, TOXOIDS, AND VACCINES	
80:04	Serums	979.9
	immune globulin (gamma) (human)	964.6
80:08	Toxoids NEC	978.8
	diphtheria	978.5
	and tetanus	978.9
	with pertussis component	978.6
	tetanus	978.4
	and diphtheria	978.9
	with pertussis component	978.6
80:12	Vaccines NEC	979.9
	bacterial NEC	978.8
	with other bacterial component	978.9
	pertussis component	978.6
	viral and rickettsial component	979.7
	rickettsial NEC	979.6
	with bacterial component	979.7
	pertussis component	978.6
	viral component	979.7
	viral NEC	979.6
	with bacterial component	979.7
	pertussis component	978.6
	rickettsial component	979.7
84:00	SKIN AND MUCOUS MEMBRANE PREPARATIONS	
84:04	Anti-Infectives	976.0
84:04.04	Antibiotics	976.0
84:04.08	Fungicides	976.0
84:04.12	Scabicides and Pediculicides	976.0
84:04.16	Miscellaneous Local Anti-Infectives	976.0
84:06	Anti-Inflammatory Agents	976.0
84:08	Antipruritics and Local Anesthetics	
	antipruritics	976.1
	local anesthetics	968.5
84:12	Astringents	976.2
84:16	Cell Stimulants and Proliferants	976.8
84:20	Detergents	976.2
84:24	Emollients, Demulcents, and Protectants	976.3
84:28	Keratolytic Agents	976.4
84:32	Keratoplastic Agents	976.4
84:36	Miscellaneous Agents	976.8
86:00	SPASMOLYTIC AGENTS	975.1
	antiasthmatics	975.7
	papaverine	972.5
	theophyllin	974.1
88:00	VITAMINS	
88:04	Vitamin A	963.5
88:08	Vitamin B Complex	963.5
	hematopoietic vitamin	964.1
	nicotinic acid derivatives	972.2
88:12	Vitamin C	963.5
88:16	Vitamin D	963.5
88:20	Vitamin E	963.5
88:24	Vitamin K Activity	964.3
88:28	Multivitamin Preparations	963.5
92:00	UNCLASSIFIED THERAPEUTIC AGENTS	977.8

* American Hospital Formulary Service

CLASSIFICATION OF INDUSTRIAL ACCIDENTS ACCORDING TO AGENCY

Annex B to the Resolution concerning Statistics of Employment Injuries adopted by the Tenth International Conference of Labor Statisticians on 12 October 1962

1 MACHINES

11 Prime-Movers, except Electrical Motors
111 *Steam engines*
112 *Internal combustion engines*
119 *Others*
12 Transmission Machinery
121 *Transmission shafts*
122 *Transmission belts, cables, pulleys, pinions, chains, gears*
129 *Others*
13 Metalworking Machines
131 *Power presses*
132 *Lathes*
133 *Milling machines*
134 *Abrasive wheels*
135 *Mechanical shears*
136 *Forging machines*
137 *Rolling-mills*
139 *Others*
14 *Wood and Assimilated Machines*
141 *Circular saws*
142 *Other saws*
143 *Molding machines*
144 *Overhand planes*
149 *Others*
15 *Agricultural Machines*
151 *Reapers (including combine reapers)*
152 *Threshers*
159 *Others*
16 *Mining Machinery*
161 *Under-cutters*
169 *Others*
19 *Other Machines Not Elsewhere Classified*
191 *Earth-moving machines, excavating and scraping machines, except means of transport*
192 *Spinning, weaving and other textile machines*
193 *Machines for the manufacture of food- stuffs and beverages*
194 *Machines for the manufacture of paper*
195 *Printing machines*
199 *Others*

2 MEANS OF TRANSPORT AND LIFTING EQUIPMENT

21 *Lifting Machines and Appliances*
211 *Cranes*
212 *Lifts and elevators*
213 *Winches*
214 *Pulley blocks*
219 *Others*
22 *Means of Rail Transport*
221 *Inter-urban railways*
222 *Rail transport in mines, tunnels, quarries, industrial establishments, docks, etc.*
229 *Others*
23 *Other Wheeled Means of Transport, Excluding Rail Transport*
231 *Tractors*
232 *Lorries*
233 *Trucks*
234 *Motor vehicles, not elsewhere classified*
235 *Animal-drawn vehicles*
236 *Hand-drawn vehicles*
239 *Others*
24 *Means of Air Transport*
25 *Means of Water Transport*
251 *Motorized means of water transport*
252 *Non-motorized means of water transport*
26 *Other Means of Transport*
261 *Cable-cars*
262 *Mechanical conveyors, except cable-cars*
269 *Others*

3 OTHER EQUIPMENT

31 *Pressure Vessels*
311 *Boilers*
312 *Pressurized containers*
313 *Pressurized piping and accessories*
314 *Gas cylinders*
315 *Caissons, diving equipment*
319 *Others*
32 *Furnaces, Ovens, Kilns*
321 *Blast furnaces*
322 *Refining furnaces*
323 *Other furnaces*
324 *Kilns*
325 *Ovens*
33 *Refrigerating Plants*
34 *Electrical Installations, Including Electric Motors, but Excluding Electric Hand Tools*
341 *Rotating machines*
342 *Conductors*
343 *Transformers*
344 *Control apparatus*
349 *Others*
35 *Electric Hand Tools*
36 *Tools, Implements, and Appliances, Except Electric Hand Tools*
361 *Power-driven hand tools, except electrichand tools*
362 *Hand tools, not power-driven*
369 *Others*
37 *Ladders, Mobile Ramps*
38 *Scaffolding*
39 *Other Equipment, Not Elsewhere Classified*

4 MATERIALS, SUBSTANCES AND RADIATIONS

41 *Explosives*
42 *Dusts, Gases, Liquids and Chemicals, Excluding Explosives*
421 *Dusts*
422 *Gases, vapors, fumes*
423 *Liquids, not elsewhere classified*
424 *Chemicals, not elsewhere classified*
43 *Flying Fragments*
44 *Radiations*
441 *Ionizing radiations*
449 *Others*
49 *Other Materials and Substances Not Elsewhere Classified*

5 WORKING ENVIRONMENT

51 *Outdoor*
511 *Weather*
512 *Traffic and working surfaces*
513 *Water*
519 *Others*
52 *Indoor*
521 *Floors*
522 *Confined quarters*
523 *Stairs*
524 *Other traffic and working surfaces*
525 *Floor openings and wall openings*
526 *Environmental factors (lighting, ventilation, temperature, noise, etc.)*

529 *Others*
53 *Underground*
531 *Roofs and faces of mine roads and tunnels, etc.*
532 *Floors of mine roads and tunnels, etc.*
533 *Working-faces of mines, tunnels, etc.*
534 *Mine shafts*
535 *Fire*
536 *Water*
539 *Others*

6 OTHER AGENCIES, NOT ELSEWHERE CLASSIFIED

61 *Animals*
611 *Live animals*
612 *Animal products*
69 *Other Agencies, Not Elsewhere Classified*

7 AGENCIES NOT CLASSIFIED FOR LACK OF SUFFICIENT DATA

LIST OF THREE-DIGIT CATEGORIES

1. INFECTIOUS AND PARASITIC DISEASES

Intestinal infectious diseases (001-009)

001 Cholera
002 Typhoid and paratyphoid fevers
003 Other salmonella infections
004 Shigellosis
005 Other food poisoning (bacterial)
006 Amebiasis
007 Other protozoal intestinal diseases
008 Intestinal infections due to other organisms
009 Ill-defined intestinal infections

Tuberculosis (010-018)

010 Primary tuberculous infection
011 Pulmonary tuberculosis
012 Other respiratory tuberculosis
013 Tuberculosis of meninges and central nervous system
014 Tuberculosis of intestines, peritoneum, and mesenteric glands
015 Tuberculosis of bones and joints
016 Tuberculosis of genitourinary system
017 Tuberculosis of other organs
018 Miliary tuberculosis

Zoonotic bacterial diseases (020-027)

020 Plague
021 Tularemia
022 Anthrax
023 Brucellosis
024 Glanders
025 Melioidosis
026 Rat-bite fever
027 Other zoonotic bacterial diseases

Other bacterial diseases (030-042)

030 Leprosy
031 Diseases due to other mycobacteria
032 Diphtheria
033 Whooping cough
034 Streptococcal sore throat and scarlatina
035 Erysipelas
036 Meningococcal infection
037 Tetanus
038 Septicemia
039 Actinomycotic infections
040 Other bacterial diseases
041 Bacterial infection in conditions classified elsewhere and of unspecified site

Human immunodeficiency virus (042)

042 Human immunodeficiency virus [HIV] disease

Poliomyelitis and other non-arthropod-borne viral diseases and prion diseases of central nervous system (045-049)

045 Acute poliomyelitis
046 Slow virus infections and prion diseases of central nervous system
047 Meningitis due to enterovirus
048 Other enterovirus diseases of central nervous system
049 Other non-arthropod-borne viral diseases of central nervous system

Viral diseases accompanied by exanthem (050-058)

050 Smallpox
051 Cowpox and paravaccinia
052 Chickenpox
053 Herpes zoster
054 Herpes simplex
055 Measles
056 Rubella
057 Other viral exanthemata
058 Other human herpesvirus
059 Other poxvirus infections

Arthropod-borne viral diseases (060-066)

060 Yellow fever
061 Dengue
062 Mosquito-borne viral encephalitis
063 Tick-borne viral encephalitis
064 Viral encephalitis transmitted by other and unspecified arthropods
065 Arthropod-borne hemorrhagic fever
066 Other arthropod-borne viral diseases

Other diseases due to viruses and Chlamydiae (070-079)

070 Viral hepatitis
071 Rabies
072 Mumps
073 Ornithosis
074 Specific diseases due to Coxsackievirus
075 Infectious mononucleosis
076 Trachoma
077 Other diseases of conjunctiva due to viruses and Chlamydiae
078 Other diseases due to viruses and Chlamydiae
079 Viral infection in conditions classified elsewhere and of unspecified site

Rickettsioses and other arthropod-borne diseases (080-088)

080 Louse-borne [epidemic] typhus
081 Other typhus
082 Tick-borne rickettsioses
083 Other rickettsioses
084 Malaria
085 Leishmaniasis
086 Trypanosomiasis
087 Relapsing fever
088 Other arthropod-borne diseases

Syphilis and other venereal diseases (090-099)

090 Congenital syphilis
091 Early syphilis, symptomatic
092 Early syphilis, latent
093 Cardiovascular syphilis
094 Neurosyphilis
095 Other forms of late syphilis, with symptoms
096 Late syphilis, latent
097 Other and unspecified syphilis
098 Gonococcal infections
099 Other venereal diseases

Other spirochetal diseases (100-104)

100 Leptospirosis
101 Vincent's angina
102 Yaws
103 Pinta
104 Other spirochetal infection

Mycoses (110-118)

110 Dermatophytosis
111 Dermatomycosis, other and unspecified
112 Candidiasis
114 Coccidioidomycosis
115 Histoplasmosis
116 Blastomycotic infection
117 Other mycoses
118 Opportunistic mycoses

Helminthiases (120-129)

120 Schistosomiasis [bilharziasis]
121 Other trematode infections
122 Echinococcosis
123 Other cestode infection
124 Trichinosis
125 Filarial infection and dracontiasis
126 Ancylostomiasis and necatoriasis
127 Other intestinal helminthiases
128 Other and unspecified helminthiases
129 Intestinal parasitism, unspecified

Other infectious and parasitic diseases (130-136)

130 Toxoplasmosis
131 Trichomoniasis
132 Pediculosis and phthirus infestation
133 Acariasis
134 Other infestation
135 Sarcoidosis
136 Other and unspecified infectious and parasitic diseases

Late effects of infectious and parasitic diseases (137-139)

137 Late effects of tuberculosis
138 Late effects of acute poliomyelitis
139 Late effects of other infectious and parasitic diseases

2. NEOPLASMS

Malignant neoplasm of lip, oral cavity, and pharynx (140-149)

140 Malignant neoplasm of lip
141 Malignant neoplasm of tongue
142 Malignant neoplasm of major salivary glands
143 Malignant neoplasm of gum
144 Malignant neoplasm of floor of mouth
145 Malignant neoplasm of other and unspecified parts of mouth
146 Malignant neoplasm of oropharynx
147 Malignant neoplasm of nasopharynx
148 Malignant neoplasm of hypopharynx
149 Malignant neoplasm of other and ill-defined sites within the lip, oral cavity, and pharynx

Malignant neoplasm of digestive organs and peritoneum (150-159)

150 Malignant neoplasm of esophagus
151 Malignant neoplasm of stomach
152 Malignant neoplasm of small intestine, including duodenum
153 Malignant neoplasm of colon
154 Malignant neoplasm of rectum, rectosigmoid junction, and anus
155 Malignant neoplasm of liver and intrahepatic bile ducts
156 Malignant neoplasm of gallbladder and extrahepatic bile ducts
157 Malignant neoplasm of pancreas
158 Malignant neoplasm of retroperitoneum and peritoneum
159 Malignant neoplasm of other and ill-defined sites within the digestive organs and peritoneum

Malignant neoplasm of respiratory and intrathoracic organs (160-165)

160 Malignant neoplasm of nasal cavities, middle ear, and accessory sinuses
161 Malignant neoplasm of larynx
162 Malignant neoplasm of trachea, bronchus, and lung
163 Malignant neoplasm of pleura
164 Malignant neoplasm of thymus, heart, and mediastinum
165 Malignant neoplasm of other and ill-defined sites within the respiratory system and intrathoracic organs

Malignant neoplasm of bone, connective tissue, skin, and breast (170-176)

170 Malignant neoplasm of bone and articular cartilage
171 Malignant neoplasm of connective and other soft tissue
172 Malignant melanoma of skin
173 Other malignant neoplasm of skin
174 Malignant neoplasm of female breast
175 Malignant neoplasm of male breast
176 Kaposi's sarcoma

Malignant neoplasm of genitourinary organs (179-189)

179 Malignant neoplasm of uterus, part unspecified
180 Malignant neoplasm of cervix uteri
181 Malignant neoplasm of placenta
182 Malignant neoplasm of body of uterus
183 Malignant neoplasm of ovary and other uterine adnexa
184 Malignant neoplasm of other and unspecified female genital organs
185 Malignant neoplasm of prostate
186 Malignant neoplasm of testis
187 Malignant neoplasm of penis and other male genital organs
188 Malignant neoplasm of bladder
189 Malignant neoplasm of kidney and other unspecified urinary organs

Malignant neoplasm of other and unspecified sites (190-199)

190 Malignant neoplasm of eye
191 Malignant neoplasm of brain
192 Malignant neoplasm of other and unspecified parts of nervous system
193 Malignant neoplasm of thyroid gland
194 Malignant neoplasm of other endocrine glands and related structures
195 Malignant neoplasm of other and ill-defined sites
196 Secondary and unspecified malignant neoplasm of lymph nodes
197 Secondary malignant neoplasm of respiratory and digestive systems
198 Secondary malignant neoplasm of other specified sites
199 Malignant neoplasm without specification of site

Malignant neoplasm of lymphatic and hematopoietic tissue (200-208)

200 Lymphosarcoma and reticulosar-coma and other specified malignant tumors of lymphatic tissue
201 Hodgkin's disease
202 Other malignant neoplasm of lymphoid and histiocytic tissue
203 Multiple myeloma and immunoproliferative neoplasms
204 Lymphoid leukemia
205 Myeloid leukemia
206 Monocytic leukemia
207 Other specified leukemia
208 Leukemia of unspecified cell type

Neuroendocrine tumors (209)

209 Neuroendocrine tumors

Benign neoplasms (210-229)

210 Benign neoplasm of lip, oral cavity, and pharynx
211 Benign neoplasm of other parts of digestive system
212 Benign neoplasm of respiratory and intrathoracic organs
213 Benign neoplasm of bone and articular cartilage
214 Lipoma
215 Other benign neoplasm of connective and other soft tissue
216 Benign neoplasm of skin
217 Benign neoplasm of breast
218 Uterine leiomyoma
219 Other benign neoplasm of uterus
220 Benign neoplasm of ovary
221 Benign neoplasm of other female genital organs
222 Benign neoplasm of male genital organs
223 Benign neoplasm of kidney and other urinary organs
224 Benign neoplasm of eye
225 Benign neoplasm of brain and other parts of nervous system
226 Benign neoplasm of thyroid gland
227 Benign neoplasm of other endocrine glands and related structures
228 Hemangioma and lymphangioma, any site
229 Benign neoplasm of other and unspecified sites

Carcinoma in situ (230-234)

230 Carcinoma in situ of digestive organs
231 Carcinoma in situ of respiratory system
232 Carcinoma in situ of skin
233 Carcinoma in situ of breast and genitourinary system
234 Carcinoma in situ of other and unspecified sites

Neoplasms of uncertain behavior (235-238)

235 Neoplasm of uncertain behavior of digestive and respiratory systems
236 Neoplasm of uncertain behavior of genitourinary organs
237 Neoplasm of uncertain behavior of endocrine glands and nervous system
238 Neoplasm of uncertain behavior of other and unspecified sites and tissues

Neoplasms of unspecified nature (239)

239 Neoplasm of unspecified nature

3. ENDOCRINE, NUTRITIONAL AND METABOLIC DISEASES, AND IMMUNITY DISORDERS

Disorders of thyroid gland (240-246)

240 Simple and unspecified goiter
241 Nontoxic nodular goiter
242 Thyrotoxicosis with or without goiter
243 Congenital hypothyroidism
244 Acquired hypothyroidism
245 Thyroiditis
246 Other disorders of thyroid

Diseases of other endocrine glands (249-259)

249 Secondary diabetes mellitus
250 Diabetes mellitus
251 Other disorders of pancreatic internal secretion
252 Disorders of parathyroid gland
253 Disorders of the pituitary gland and its hypothalamic control
254 Diseases of thymus gland
255 Disorders of adrenal glands
256 Ovarian dysfunction
257 Testicular dysfunction
258 Polyglandular dysfunction and related disorders
259 Other endocrine disorders

Nutritional deficiencies (260-269)

260 Kwashiorkor
261 Nutritional marasmus
262 Other severe protein-calorie malnutrition
263 Other and unspecified protein-calorie malnutrition
264 Vitamin A deficiency
265 Thiamine and niacin deficiency states
266 Deficiency of B-complex components
267 Ascorbic acid deficiency
268 Vitamin D deficiency
269 Other nutritional deficiencies

Other metabolic disorders and immnity disorders (270-279)

270 Disorders of amino-acid transport and metabolism
271 Disorders of carbohydrate transport and metabolism
272 Disorders of lipoid metabolism
273 Disorders of plasma protein metabolism
274 Gout
275 Disorders of mineral metabolism
276 Disorders of fluid, electrolyte, and acid-base balance
277 Other and unspecified disorders of metabolism
278 Overweight, obesity and other hyperalimentation
279 Disorders involving the immune mechanism

4. DISEASES OF BLOOD AND BLOOD-FORMING ORGANS (280-289)

280 Iron deficiency anemias
281 Other deficiency anemias
282 Hereditary hemolytic anemias
283 Acquired hemolytic anemias
284 Aplastic anemia
285 Other and unspecified anemias
286 Coagulation defects
287 Purpura and other hemorrhagic conditions
288 Diseases of white blood cells
289 Other diseases of blood and blood-forming organs

5. MENTAL DISORDERS

Organic psychotic conditions (290-294)

290 Senile and presenile organic psychotic conditions
291 Alcoholic psychoses
292 Drug psychoses
293 Transient organic psychotic conditions
294 Other organic psychotic conditions (chronic)

Other psychoses (295-299)

295 Schizophrenic psychoses
296 Affective psychoses
297 Paranoid states
298 Other nonorganic psychoses
299 Psychoses with origin specific to childhood

Neurotic disorders, personality disorders, and other nonpsychotic mental disorders (300-316)

300 Neurotic disorders
301 Personality disorders
302 Sexual and gender identity disorders
303 Alcohol dependence syndrome
304 Drug dependence
305 Nondependent abuse of drugs
306 Physiological malfunction arising from mental factors
307 Special symptoms or syndromes, not elsewhere classified
308 Acute reaction to stress
309 Adjustment reaction
310 Specific nonpsychotic mental disorders following organic brain damage
311 Depressive disorder, not elsewhereclassified
312 Disturbance of conduct, not elsewhere classified
313 Disturbance of emotions specific tochildhood and adolescence
314 Hyperkinetic syndrome of childhood
315 Specific delays in development
316 Psychic factors associated with diseases classified elsewhere

Mental retardation (317-319)

317 Mild mental retardation
318 Other specified mental retardation
319 Unspecified mental retardation

6. DISEASES OF THE NERVOUS SYSTEM AND SENSE ORGANS

Inflammatory diseases of the central nervous system (320-326)
320 Bacterial meningitis
321 Meningitis due to other organisms
322 Meningitis of unspecified cause
323 Encephalitis, myelitis, and encephalomyelitis
324 Intracranial and intraspinal abscess
325 Phlebitis and thrombophlebitis of intracranial venous sinuses
326 Late effects of intracranial abscess or pyogenic infection

Organic Sleep Disorders (327)
327 Organic sleep disorders

Hereditary and degenerative diseases of the central nervous system (330-337)
330 Cerebral degenerations usually manifest in childhood
331 Other cerebral degenerations
332 Parkinson's disease
333 Other extrapyramidal diseases and abnormal movement disorders
334 Spinocerebellar disease
335 Anterior horn cell disease
336 Other diseases of spinal cord
337 Disorders of the autonomic nervous system

Pain (338)
338 Pain, not elsewhere classified

Other headache syndromes (339)
339 Other headache syndromes

Other disorders of the central nervous system (340-349)
340 Multiple sclerosis
341 Other demyelinating diseases of central nervous system
342 Hemiplegia and hemiparesis
343 Infantile cerebral palsy
344 Other paralytic syndromes
345 Epilepsy and recurrent seizures
346 Migraine
347 Cataplexy and narcolepsy
348 Other conditions of brain
349 Other and unspecified disorders of the nervous system

Disorders of the peripheral nervous system (350-359)
350 Trigeminal nerve disorders
351 Facial nerve disorders
352 Disorders of other cranial nerves
353 Nerve root and plexus disorders
354 Mononeuritis of upper limb and mononeuritis multiplex
355 Mononeuritis of lower limb
356 Hereditary and idiopathic peripheral neuropathy
357 Inflammatory and toxic neuropathy
358 Myoneural disorders
359 Muscular dystrophies and other myopathies

Disorders of the eye and adnexa (360-379)
360 Disorders of the globe
361 Retinal detachments and defects
362 Other retinal disorders
363 Chorioretinal inflammations and scars and other disorders of choroid
364 Disorders of iris and ciliary body
365 Glaucoma
366 Cataract
367 Disorders of refraction and accommodation
368 Visual disturbances
369 Blindness and low vision
370 Keratitis
371 Corneal opacity and other disorders of cornea
372 Disorders of conjunctiva
373 Inflammation of eyelids
374 Other disorders of eyelids
375 Disorders of lacrimal system
376 Disorders of the orbit
377 Disorders of optic nerve and visual pathways
378 Strabismus and other disorders of binocular eye movements
379 Other disorders of eye

Diseases of the ear and mastoid process (380-389)
380 Disorders of external ear
381 Nonsuppurative otitis media and Eustachian tube disorders
382 Suppurative and unspecified otitis media
383 Mastoiditis and related conditions
384 Other disorders of tympanic membrane
385 Other disorders of middle ear and mastoid
386 Vertiginous syndromes and other disorders of vestibular system
387 Otosclerosis
388 Other disorders of ear
389 Hearing loss

7. DISEASES OF THE CIRCULATORY SYSTEM

Acute rheumatic fever (390-392)
390 Rheumatic fever without mention of heart involvement
391 Rheumatic fever with heart involvement
392 Rheumatic chorea

Chronic rheumatic heart disease (393-398)
393 Chronic rheumatic pericarditis
394 Diseases of mitral valve
395 Diseases of aortic valve
396 Diseases of mitral and aortic valves
397 Diseases of other endocardial structures
398 Other rheumatic heart disease

Hypertensive disease (401-405)
401 Essential hypertension
402 Hypertensive heart disease
403 Hypertensive kidney disease
404 Hypertensive heart and kidney disease
405 Secondary hypertension

Ischemic heart disease (410-414)
410 Acute myocardial infarction
411 Other acute and subacute form of ischemic heart disease
412 Old myocardial infarction
413 Angina pectoris
414 Other forms of chronic ischemic heart disease

Diseases of pulmonary circulation (415-417)
415 Acute pulmonary heart disease
416 Chronic pulmonary heart disease
417 Other diseases of pulmonary circulation

Other forms of heart disease (420-429)
420 Acute pericarditis
421 Acute and subacute endocarditis
422 Acute myocarditis
423 Other diseases of pericardium
424 Other diseases of endocardium
425 Cardiomyopathy
426 Conduction disorders
427 Cardiac dysrhythmias
428 Heart failure
429 Ill-defined descriptions and complications of heart disease

Cerebrovascular disease (430-438)
430 Subarachnoid hemorrhage
431 Intracerebral hemorrhage
432 Other and unspecified intracranial hemorrhage
433 Occlusion and stenosis of precerebral arteries
434 Occlusion of cerebral arteries
435 Transient cerebral ischemia
436 Acute but ill-defined cerebrovascular disease
437 Other and ill-defined cerebrovascular disease
438 Late effects of cerebrovascular disease

Diseases of arteries, arterioles, and capillaries (440-449)
440 Atherosclerosis
441 Aortic aneurysm and dissection
442 Other aneurysm
443 Other peripheral vascular disease
444 Arterial embolism and thrombosis
445 Atheroembolism
446 Polyarteritis nodosa and allied conditions
447 Other disorders of arteries and arterioles
448 Diseases of capillaries
449 Septic arterial embolism

Diseases of veins and lymphatics, and other diseases of circulatory system (451-459)
451 Phlebitis and thrombophlebitis
452 Portal vein thrombosis
453 Other venous embolism and thrombosis
454 Varicose veins of lower extremities
455 Hemorrhoids
456 Varicose veins of other sites
457 Noninfective disorders of lymphatic channels
458 Hypotension
459 Other disorders of circulatory system

8. DISEASES OF THE RESPIRATORY SYSTEM

Acute respiratory infections (460-466)
460 Acute nasopharyngitis [common cold]
461 Acute sinusitis
462 Acute pharyngitis
463 Acute tonsillitis
464 Acute laryngitis and tracheitis
465 Acute upper respiratory infections of multiple or unspecified sites
466 Acute bronchitis and bronchiolitis

Other diseases of upper respiratory tract (470-478)
470 Deviated nasal septum
471 Nasal polyps
472 Chronic pharyngitis and nasopharyngitis
473 Chronic sinusitis
474 Chronic disease of tonsils and adenoids
475 Peritonsillar abscess
476 Chronic laryngitis and aryngotracheitis
477 Allergic rhinitis
478 Other diseases of upper respiratory tract

Pneumonia and influenza (480-488)
480 Viral pneumonia
481 Pneumococcal pneumonia [Streptococcus pneumoniae pneumonia]
482 Other bacterial pneumonia
483 Pneumonia due to other specified organism
484 Pneumonia in infectious diseases classified elsewhere
485 Bronchopneumonia, organism unspecified
486 Pneumonia, organism unspecified
487 Influenza
488 Influenza due to identified avian influenza virus

Chronic obstructive pulmonary disease and allied conditions (490-496)

490 Bronchitis, not specified as acute or chronic
491 Chronic bronchitis
492 Emphysema
493 Asthma
494 Bronchiectasis
495 Extrinsic allergic alveolitis
496 Chronic airways obstruction, not elsewhere classified

Pneumoconioses and other lung diseases due to external agents (500-508)

500 Coal workers' pneumoconiosis
501 Asbestosis
502 Pneumoconiosis due to other silica or silicates
503 Pneumoconiosis due to other inorganic dust
504 Pneumopathy due to inhalation of other dust
505 Pneumoconiosis, unspecified
506 Respiratory conditions due to chemical fumes and vapors
507 Pneumonitis due to solids and liquids
508 Respiratory conditions due to other and unspecified external agents

Other diseases of respiratory system (510-519)

510 Empyema
511 Pleurisy
512 Pneumothorax
513 Abscess of lung and mediastinum
514 Pulmonary congestion and hypostasis
515 Postinflammatory pulmonary fibrosis
516 Other alveolar and parietoalveolar pneumopathy
517 Lung involvement in conditions classified elsewhere
518 Other diseases of lung
519 Other diseases of respiratory system

9. DISEASES OF THE DIGESTIVE SYSTEM

Diseases of oral cavity, salivary glands, and jaws (520-529)

520 Disorders of tooth development and eruption
521 Diseases of hard tissues of teeth
522 Diseases of pulp and periapical tissues
523 Gingival and periodontal diseases
524 Dentofacial anomalies, including malocclusion
525 Other diseases and conditions of the teeth and supporting structures
526 Diseases of the jaws
527 Diseases of the salivary glands
528 Diseases of the oral soft tissues, excluding lesions specific for gingiva and tongue
529 Diseases and other conditions of the tongue

Diseases of esophagus, stomach, and duodenum (530-538)

530 Diseases of esophagus
531 Gastric ulcer
532 Duodenal ulcer
533 Peptic ulcer, site unspecified
534 Gastrojejunal ulcer
535 Gastritis and duodenitis
536 Disorders of function of stomach
537 Other disorders of stomach and duodenum
538 Gastrointestinal mucositis (ulcerative)

Appendicitis (540-543)

540 Acute appendicitis
541 Appendicitis, unqualified
542 Other appendicitis
543 Other diseases of appendix

Hernia of abdominal cavity (550-553)

550 Inguinal hernia
551 Other hernia of abdominal cavity, with gangrene
552 Other hernia of abdominal cavity, with ob-struction, but without mention of gangrene
553 Other hernia of abdominal cavity without mention of obstruction or gangrene

Noninfective enteritis and colitis (555-558)

555 Regional enteritis
556 Ulcerative colitis
557 Vascular insufficiency of intestine
558 Other noninfective gastroenteritis and colitis

Other diseases of intestines and peritoneum (560-569)

560 Intestinal obstruction without mention of hernia
562 Diverticula of intestine
564 Functional digestive disorders, not elsewhere classified
565 Anal fissure and fistula
566 Abscess of anal and rectal regions
567 Peritonitis and retroperitoneal infections
568 Other disorders of peritoneum
569 Other disorders of intestine

Other diseases of digestive system (570-579)

570 Acute and subacute necrosis of liver
571 Chronic liver disease and cirrhosis
572 Liver abscess and sequelae of chronic liver disease
573 Other disorders of liver
574 Cholelithiasis
575 Other disorders of gallbladder
576 Other disorders of biliary tract
577 Diseases of pancreas
578 Gastrointestinal hemorrhage
579 Intestinal malabsorption

10. DISEASES OF THE GENITOURINARY SYSTEM

Nephritis, nephrotic syndrome, and nephrosis (580-589)

580 Acute gloerulonephritis
581 Nephrotic syndrome
582 Chronic glomerulonephritis
583 Nephritis and nephropathy, not specified as acute or chronic
584 Acute renal failure
585 Chronic kidney disease (CKD)
586 Renal failure, unspecified
587 Renal sclerosis, unspecified
588 Disorders resulting from impaired renal function
589 Small kidney of unknown cause

Other diseases of urinary system (590-599)

590 Infections of kidney
591 Hydronephrosis
592 Calculus of kidney and ureter
593 Other disorders of kidney and ureter
594 Calculus of lower urinary tract
595 Cystitis
596 Other disorders of bladder
597 Urethritis, not sexually transmitted, and urethral syndrome
598 Urethral stricture
599 Other disorders of urethra and urinary tract

Diseases of male genital organs (600-608)

600 Hyperplasia of prostate
601 Inflammatory diseases of prostate
602 Other disorders of prostate
603 Hydrocele
604 Orchitis and epididymitis
605 Redundant prepuce and phimosis
606 Infertility, male
607 Disorders of penis
608 Other disorders of male genital organs

Disorders of breast (610-612)

610 Benign mammary dysplasias
611 Other disorders of breast
612 Deformity and disproportion of reconstructed breast

Inflammatory disease of female pelvic organs (614-616)

614 Inflammatory disease of ovary, fallopian tube, pelvic cellular tissue, and peritoneum
615 Inflammatory diseases of uterus, except cervix
616 Inflammatory disease of cervix, vagina, and vulva

Other disorders of female genital tract (617-629)

617 Endometriosis
618 Genital prolapse
619 Fistula involving female genital tract
620 Noninflammatory disorders of ovary, fallopian tube, and broad ligament
621 Disorders of uterus, not elsewhere classified
622 Noninflammatory disorders of cervix
623 Noninflammatory disorders of vagina
624 Noninflammatory disorders of vulva and perineum
625 Pain and other symptoms associated with female genital organs
626 Disorders of menstruation and other abnormal bleeding from female genital tract
627 Menopausal and postmenopausal disorders
628 Infertility, female
629 Other disorders of female genital organs

11. COMPLICATIONS OF PREGNANCY, CHILDBIRTH AND THE PUERPERIUM

Ectopic and molar pregnancy and other pregnancy with abortive outcome (630-639)

630 Hydatidiform mole
631 Other abnormal product of conception
632 Missed abortion
633 Ectopic pregnancy
634 Spontaneous abortion
635 Legally induced abortion
636 Illegally induced abortion
637 Unspecified abortion
638 Failed attempted abortion
639 Complications following abortion and ectopic and molar pregnancies

Complications mainly related to pregnancy (640-649)

640 Hemorrhage in early pregnancy
641 Antepartum hemorrhage, abruptio placentae, and placenta previa
642 Hypertension complicating pregnancy, childbirth, and the puerperium
643 Excessive vomiting in pregnancy
644 Early or threatened labor
645 Prolonged pregnancy
646 Other complications of pregnancy, not elsewhere classified
647 Infective and parasitic conditions in the mother classifiable elsewhere but complicating pregnancy, childbirth, and the puerperium
648 Other current conditions in the mother classifiable elsewhere but complicating pregnancy, childbirth, and the puerperium
649 Other conditions or status of the mother complicating pregnancy, childbirth, or puerperium

Normal delivery, and other indications for care in pregnancy, labor, and delivery (650-659)

650 Normal delivery
651 Multiple gestation
652 Malposition and malpresentation of fetus
653 Disproportion
654 Abnormality of organs and soft tissues of pelvis
655 Known or suspected fetal abnormality affecting management of mother
656 Other fetal and placental problems affecting management of mother
657 Polyhydramnios
658 Other problems associated with amniotic cavity and membranes
659 Other indications for care or intervention related to labor and delivery and not elsewhere classified

Complications occurring mainly in the course of labor and delivery (660-669)

660 Obstructed labor
661 Abnormality of forces of labor
662 Long labor
663 Umbilical cord complications
664 Trauma to perineum and vulva during delivery
665 Other obstetrical trauma
666 Postpartum hemorrhage
667 Retained placenta or membranes, without hemorrhage
668 Complications of the administration of anesthetic or other sedation in labor and delivery
669 Other complications of labor and delivery, not elsewhere classified

Complications of the puerperium (670-677)

670 Major puerperal infection
671 Venous complications in pregnancy and the puerperium
672 Pyrexia of unknown origin during the puerperium
673 Obstetrical pulmonary embolism
674 Other and unspecified complications of the puerperium, not elsewhere classified
675 Infections of the breast and nipple associated with childbirth
676 Other disorders of the breast associated with childbirth, and disorders of lactation
677 Late effect of complication of pregnancy, childbirth, and the puerperium

Other maternal and fetal complications (678-679)

678 Other fetal conditions
679 Complications of in utero procedures

12. DISEASES OF THE SKIN AND SUBCUTANEOUS TISSUE

Infections of skin and subcutaneous tissue (680-686)

680 Carbuncle and furuncle
681 Cellulitis and abscess of finger and toe
682 Other cellulitis and abscess
683 Acute lymphadenitis
684 Impetigo
685 Pilonidal cyst
686 Other local infections of skin and subcutaneous tissue

Inflammatory conditions of skin and subcutaneous tissue (690-698)

690 Erythematosquamous dermatosis
691 Atopic dermatitis and related conditions
692 Contact dermatitis and other eczema
693 Dermatitis due to substances taken internally
694 Bullous dermatoses
695 Erythematous conditions
696 Psoriasis and similar disorders
697 Lichen
698 Pruritus and related conditions

Other diseases of skin and subcutaneous tissue (700-709)

700 Corns and callosities
701 Other hypertrophic and atrophic conditions of skin
702 Other dermatoses
703 Diseases of nail
704 Diseases of hair and hair follicles
705 Disorders of sweat glands
706 Diseases of sebaceous glands
707 Chronic ulcer of skin
708 Urticaria
709 Other disorders of skin and subcutaneous tissue

13. DISEASES OF THE MUSCULOSKELETAL SYSTEM AND CONNECTIVE TISSUE

Arthropathies and related disorders (710-719)

710 Diffuse diseases of connective tissue
711 Arthropathy associated with infections
712 Crystal arthropathies
713 Arthropathy associated with other disorders classified elsewhere
714 Rheumatoid arthritis and other inflammatory polyarthropathies
715 Osteoarthrosis and allied disorders
716 Other and unspecified arthropathies
717 Internal derangement of knee
718 Other derangement of joint
719 Other and unspecified disorder of joint

Dorsopathies (720-724)

720 Ankylosing spondylitis and other inflammatory spondylopathies
721 Spondylosis and allied disorders
722 Intervertebral disc disorders
723 Other disorders of cervical region
724 Other and unspecified disorders of back

Rheumatism, excluding the back (725-729)

725 Polymyalgia rheumatica
726 Peripheral enthesopathies and allied syndromes
727 Other disorders of synovium, tendon, and bursa
728 Disorders of muscle, ligament, and fascia
729 Other disorders of soft tissues

Osteopathies, chondropathies, and acquired musculoskeletal deformities (730-739)

730 Osteomyelitis, periostitis, and other infections involving bone
731 Osteitis deformans and osteopathies associated with other disorders classified elsewhere
732 Osteochondropathies
733 Other disorders of bone and cartilage
734 Flat foot
735 Acquired deformities of toe
736 Other acquired deformities of limbs
737 Curvature of spine
738 Other acquired deformity
739 Nonallopathic lesions, not elsewhere classified

14. CONGENITAL ANOMALIES

740 Anencephalus and similar anomalies
741 Spina bifida
742 Other congenital anomalies of nervous system
743 Congenital anomalies of eye
744 Congenital anomalies of ear, face, and neck
745 Bulbus cordis anomalies and anomalies of cardiac septal closure
746 Other congenital anomalies of heart
747 Other congenital anomalies of circulatory system
748 Congenital anomalies of respiratory system
749 Cleft palate and cleft lip
750 Other congenital anomalies of upper alimentary tract
751 Other congenital anomalies of digestive system
752 Congenital anomalies of genital organs
753 Congenital anomalies of urinary system
754 Certain congenital musculoskeletal deformities
755 Other congenital anomalies of limbs
756 Other congenital musculoskeletal anomalies
757 Congenital anomalies of the integument
758 Chromosomal anomalies
759 Other and unspecified congenital anomalies

15. CERTAIN CONDITIONS ORIGINATING IN THE PERINATAL PERIOD

Maternal causes of perinatal morbidity and mortality (760-763)

760 Fetus or newborn affected by maternal conditions which may be unrelated to present pregnancy
761 Fetus or newborn affected by maternal complications of pregnancy
762 Fetus or newborn affected by complications of placenta, cord, and membranes
763 Fetus or newborn affected by other complications of labor and delivery

Other conditions originating in the perinatal period (764-779)

764 Slow fetal growth and fetal malnutrition
765 Disorders relating to short gestation and unspecified low birthweight
766 Disorders relating to long gestation and high birthweight
767 Birth trauma
768 Intrauterine hypoxia and birth asphyxia
769 Respiratory distress syndrome
770 Other respiratory conditions of fetus and newborn
771 Infections specific to the perinatal period
772 Fetal and neonatal hemorrhage
773 Hemolytic disease of fetus or newborn, due to isoimmunization
774 Other perinatal jaundice
775 Endocrine and metabolic disturbances specific to the fetus and newborn
776 Hematological disorders of newborn
777 Perinatal disorders of digestive system
778 Conditions involving the integument and temperature regulation of fetus and newborn
779 Other and ill-defined conditions originating in the perinatal period

16. SYMPTOMS, SIGNS, AND ILL-DEFINED CONDITIONS

Symptoms (780-789)

780 General symptoms
781 Symptoms involving nervous and musculoskeletal systems
782 Symptoms involving skin and other integumentary tissue
783 Symptoms concerning nutrition, metabolism, and development
784 Symptoms involving head and neck

785 Symptoms involving cardiovascular system
786 Symptoms involving respiratory system and other chest symptoms
787 Symptoms involving digestive system
788 Symptoms involving urinary system
789 Other symptoms involving abdomen and pelvis

Nonspecific abnormal findings (790-796)
790 Nonspecific findings on examination of blood
791 Nonspecific findings on examination of urine
792 Nonspecific abnormal findings in other body substances
793 Nonspecific abnormal findings on radiological and other examination of body structure
794 Nonspecific abnormal results of function studies
795 Nonspecific abnormal histological and immunological findings
796 Other nonspecific abnormal findings

Ill-defined and unknown causes of morbidity and mortality (797-799)
797 Senility without mention of psychosis
798 Sudden death, cause unknown
799 Other ill-defined and unknown causes of morbidity and mortality

17. INJURY AND POISONING

Fracture of skull (800-804)
800 Fracture of vault of skull
801 Fracture of base of skull
802 Fracture of face bones
803 Other and unqualified skull fractures
804 Multiple fractures involving skull or face with other bones

Fracture of spine and trunk (805-809)
805 Fracture of vertebral column without mention of spinal cord lesion
806 Fracture of vertebral column with spinal cord lesion
807 Fracture of rib(s), sternum, larynx, and trachea
808 Fracture of pelvis
809 Ill-defined fractures of bones of trunk

Fracture of upper limb (810-819)
810 Fracture of clavicle
811 Fracture of scapula
812 Fracture of humerus
813 Fracture of radius and ulna
814 Fracture of carpal bone(s)
815 Fracture of metacarpal bone(s)
816 Fracture of one or more phalanges of hand
817 Multiple fractures of hand bones
818 Ill-defined fractures of upper limb
819 Multiple fractures involving both upper limbs, and upper limb with rib(s) and sternum

Fracture of lower limb (820-829)
820 Fracture of neck of femur
821 Fracture of other and unspecified parts of femur
822 Fracture of patella
823 Fracture of tibia and fibula
824 Fracture of ankle
825 Fracture of one or more tarsal and metatarsal bones
826 Fracture of one or more phalanges of foot
827 Other, multiple, and ill-defined fractures of lower limb
828 Multiple fractures involving both lower limbs, lower with upper limb, and lower limb(s) with rib(s) and sternum
829 Fracture of unspecified bones

Dislocation (830-839)
830 Dislocation of jaw
831 Dislocation of shoulder
832 Dislocation of elbow
833 Dislocation of wrist
834 Dislocation of finger
835 Dislocation of hip
836 Dislocation of knee
837 Dislocation of ankle
838 Dislocation of foot
839 Other, multiple, and ill-defined dislocations

Sprains and strains of joints and adjacent muscles (840-848)
840 Sprains and strains of shoulder and upper arm
841 Sprains and strains of elbow and forearm
842 Sprains and strains of wrist and hand
843 Sprains and strains of hip and thigh
844 Sprains and strains of knee and leg
845 Sprains and strains of ankle and foot
846 Sprains and strains of sacroiliac region
847 Sprains and strains of other and unspecified parts of back
848 Other and ill-defined sprains and strains

Intracranial injury, excluding those with skull fracture (850-854)
850 Concussion
851 Cerebral laceration and contusion
852 Subarachnoid, subdural, and extradural hemorrhage, following injury
853 Other and unspecified intracranial hemorrhage following injury
854 Intracranial injury of other and unspecified nature

Internal injury of chest, abdomen, and pelvis (860-869)
860 Traumatic pneumothorax and hemothorax
861 Injury to heart and lung
862 Injury to other and unspecified intrathoracic organs
863 Injury to gastrointestinal tract
864 Injury to liver
865 Injury to spleen
866 Injury to kidney
867 Injury to pelvic organs
868 Injury to other intra-abdominal organs
869 Internal injury to unspecified or ill-defined organs

Open wound of head, neck, and trunk (870-879)
870 Open wound of ocular adnexa
871 Open wound of eyeball
872 Open wound of ear
873 Other open wound of head
874 Open wound of neck
875 Open wound of chest (wall)
876 Open wound of back
877 Open wound of buttock
878 Open wound of genital organs (external), including traumatic amputation
879 Open wound of other and unspecified sites, except limbs

Open wound of upper limb (880-887)
880 Open wound of shoulder and upper arm
881 Open wound of elbow, forearm, and wrist
882 Open wound of hand except finger(s) alone
883 Open wound of finger(s)
884 Multiple and unspecified open wound of upper limb
885 Traumatic amputation of thumb (complete) (partial)
886 Traumatic amputation of other finger(s) (complete) (partial)
887 Traumatic amputation of arm and hand (complete) (partial)

Open wound of lower limb (890-897)
890 Open wound of hip and thigh
891 Open wound of knee, leg [except thigh], and ankle
892 Open wound of foot except toe(s) alone
893 Open wound of toe(s)
894 Multiple and unspecified open wound of lower limb
895 Traumatic amputation of toe(s) (complete) (partial)
896 Traumatic amputation of foot (complete) (partial)
897 Traumatic amputation of leg(s) (complete) (partial)

Injury to blood vessels (900-904)
900 Injury to blood vessels of head and neck
901 Injury to blood vessels of thorax
902 Injury to blood vessels of abdomen and pelvis
903 Injury to blood vessels of upper extremity
904 Injury to blood vessels of lower extremity and unspecified sites

Late effects of injuries, poisonings, toxic effects, and other external causes (905-909)
905 Late effects of musculoskeletal and connective tissue injuries
906 Late effects of injuries to skin and subcutaneous tissues
907 Late effects of injuries to the nervous system
908 Late effects of other and unspecified injuries
909 Late effects of other and unspecified external causes

Superficial injury (910-919)
910 Superficial injury of face, neck, and scalp except eye
911 Superficial injury of trunk
912 Superficial injury of shoulder and upper arm
913 Superficial injury of elbow, forearm, and wrist
914 Superficial injury of hand(s) except finger(s) alone
915 Superficial injury of finger(s)
916 Superficial injury of hip, thigh, leg, and ankle
917 Superficial injury of foot and toe(s)
918 Superficial injury of eye and adnexa
919 Superficial injury of other, multiple, and unspecified sites

Contusion with intact skin surface (920-924)
920 Contusion of face, scalp, and neck except eye(s)
921 Contusion of eye and adnexa
922 Contusion of trunk
923 Contusion of upper limb
924 Contusion of lower limb and of other and unspecified sites

Crushing injury (925-929)
925 Crushing injury of face, scalp, and neck
926 Crushing injury of trunk
927 Crushing injury of upper limb
928 Crushing injury of lower limb
929 Crushing injury of multiple and unspecified sites

Effects of foreign body entering through orifice (930-939)
930 Foreign body on external eye
931 Foreign body in ear
932 Foreign body in nose
933 Foreign body in pharynx and larynx

934 Foreign body in trachea, bronchus, and lung
935 Foreign body in mouth, esophagus, and stomach
936 Foreign body in intestine and colon
937 Foreign body in anus and rectum
938 Foreign body in digestive system, unspecified
939 Foreign body in genitourinary tract

Burns (940-949)
940 Burn confined to eye and adnexa
941 Burn of face, head, and neck
942 Burn of trunk
943 Burn of upper limb, except wrist and hand
944 Burn of wrist(s) and hand(s)
945 Burn of lower limb(s)
946 Burns of multiple specified sites
947 Burn of internal organs
948 Burns classified according to extent of body surface involved
949 Burn, unspecified

Injury to nerves and spinal cord (950-957)
950 Injury to optic nerve and pathways
951 Injury to other cranial nerve(s)
952 Spinal cord injury without evidence of spinal bone injury
953 Injury to nerve roots and spinal plexus
954 Injury to other nerve(s) of trunk excluding shoulder and pelvic girdles
955 Injury to peripheral nerve(s) of shoulder girdle and upper limb
956 Injury to peripheral nerve(s) of pelvic girdle and lower limb
957 Injury to other and unspecified nerves

Certain traumatic complications and unspecified injuries (958-959)
958 Certain early complications of trauma
959 Injury, other and unspecified

Poisoning by drugs, medicinals and biological substances (960-979)
960 Poisoning by antibiotics
961 Poisoning by other anti-infectives
962 Poisoning by hormones and synthetic substitutes
963 Poisoning by primarily systemic agents
964 Poisoning by agents primarily affecting blood constituents
965 Poisoning by analgesics, antipyretics, and antirheumatics
966 Poisoning by anticonvulsants and anti-Parkinsonism drugs
967 Poisoning by sedatives and hypnotics
968 Poisoning by other central nervous system depressants and anesthetics
969 Poisoning by psychotropic agents
970 Poisoning by central nervous system stimulants
971 Poisoning by drugs primarily affecting the autonomic nervous system
972 Poisoning by agents primarily affecting the cardiovascular system
973 Poisoning by agents primarily affecting the gastrointestinal system
974 Poisoning by water, mineral, and uric acid metabolism drugs
975 Poisoning by agents primarily acting on the smooth and skeletal muscles and respiratory system
976 Poisoning by agents primarily affecting skin and mucous membrane, ophthalmological, otorhinolaryngological, and dental drugs
977 Poisoning by other and unspecified drugs and medicinals
978 Poisoning by bacterial vaccines
979 Poisoning by other vaccines and biological substances

Toxic effects of substances chiefly nonmedicinal as to source (980-989)
980 Toxic effect of alcohol
981 Toxic effect of petroleum products
982 Toxic effect of solvents other than petroleum-based
983 Toxic effect of corrosive aromatics, acids, and caustic alkalis
984 Toxic effect of lead and its compounds (including fumes)
985 Toxic effect of other metals
986 Toxic effect of carbon monoxide
987 Toxic effect of other gases, fumes, or vapors
988 Effect of noxious substances eaten as food
989 Toxic effect of other substances, chiefly nonmedicinal as to source

Other and unspecified effects of external causes (990-995)
990 Effects of radiation, unspecified
991 Effects of reduced temperature
992 Effects of heat and light
993 Effects of air pressure
994 Effects of other external causes
995 Certain adverse effects, not elsewhere classified

Complications of surgical and medical care, not elsewhere classified (996-999)
996 Complications peculiar to certain specified procedures
997 Complications affecting specified body systems, not elsewhere classified
998 Other complications of procedures, not elsewhere classified
999 Complications of medical care, not elsewhere classified

SUPPLEMENTARY CLASSIFICATION OF FACTORS INFLUENCING HEALTH STATUS AND CONTACT WITH HEALTH SERVICES

Persons with potential health hazards related to communicable diseases (V01-V09)
V01 Contact with or exposure to communicable diseases
V02 Carrier or suspected carrier of infectious diseases
V03 Need for prophylactic vaccination and inoculation against bacterial diseases
V04 Need for prophylactic vaccination and inoculation against certain viral diseases
V05 Need for other prophylactic vaccination and inoculation against single diseases
V06 Need for prophylactic vaccination and inoculation against combinations of diseases
V07 Need for isolation and other prophylactic measures
V08 Asymptomatic human immunodeficiency virus [HIV] infection status
V09 Infection with drug-resistant microorganisms

Persons with potential health hazards related to personal and family history (V10-V19)
V10 Personal history of malignant neoplasm
V11 Personal history of mental disorder
V12 Personal history of certain other diseases
V13 Personal history of other diseases
V14 Personal history of allergy to medicinal agents
V15 Other personal history presenting hazards to health
V16 Family history of malignant neoplasm
V17 Family history of certain chronic disabling diseases
V18 Family history of certain other specific conditions
V19 Family history of other conditions

Persons encountering health services in circumstances related to reproduction and development (V20-V29)
V20 Health supervision of infant or child
V21 Constitutional states in development
V22 Normal pregnancy
V23 Supervision of high-risk pregnancy
V24 Postpartum care and examination
V25 Encounter for contraceptive management
V26 Procreative management
V27 Outcome of delivery
V28 Antenatal screening
V29 Observation and evaluation of newborns and infants for suspected condition not found

Liveborn infants according to type of birth (V30-V39)
V30 Single liveborn
V31 mate liveborn
V32 Twin, mate stillborn
V33 Twin, unspecified
V34 Other multiple, mates all liveborn
V35 Other multiple, mates all stillborn
V36 Other multiple, mates live- and stillborn
V37 Other multiple, unspecified
V39 Unspecified

Persons with a condition influencing their health status (V40-V49)
V40 Mental and behavioral problems
V41 Problems with special senses and other special functions
V42 Organ or tissue replaced by transplant
V43 Organ or tissue replaced by other means
V44 Artificial opening status
V45 Other postprocedural states
V46 Other dependence on machines
V47 Other problems with internal organs
V48 Problems with head, neck, and trunk
V49 Other conditions influencing health status

Persons encountering health services for specific procedures and aftercare (V50-V59)
V50 Elective surgery for purposes other than remedying health states
V51 Aftercare involving the use of plastic surgery
V52 Fitting and adjustment of prosthetic device
V53 Fitting and adjustment of other device
V54 Other orthopedic aftercare
V55 Attention to artificial openings
V56 Encounter for dialysis and dialysis catheter care
V57 Care involving use of rehabilitation procedures
V58 Encounter for other and unspecified procedures and aftercare
V59 Donors

Persons encountering health services in other circumstances (V60-V69)
V60 Housing, household, and economic circumstances
V61 Other family circumstances
V62 Other psychosocial circumstances
V63 Unavailability of other medical facilities for care
V64 Persons encountering health services for specific procedures, not carried out
V65 Other persons seeking consultation
V66 Convalescence and palliative care
V67 Follow-up examination
V68 Encounters for administrative purposes
V69 Problems related to lifestyle

Persons without reported diagnosis encountered during examination and investigation of individuals and populations (V70-V82)

V70 General medical examination
V71 Observation and evaluation for suspected conditions not found
V72 Special investigations and examinations
V73 Special screening examination for viral and chlamydial diseases
V74 Special screening examination for bacterial and spirochetal diseases
V75 Special screening examination for other infectious diseases
V76 Special screening for malignant neoplasms
V77 Special screening for endocrine, nutritional, metabolic, and immunity disorders
V78 Special screening for disorders of blood and blood-forming organs
V79 Special screening for mental disorders and developmental handicaps
V80 Special screening for neurological, eye, and ear diseases
V81 Special screening for cardiovascular, respiratory, and genitourinary diseases
V82 Special screening for other conditions

Genetics (V83-V84)

V83 Genetic carrier status
V84 Genetic susceptibility to disease

Body mass index (V85)

V85 Body Mass Index

Estrogen receptor status (V86)

V86 Estrogen receptor status

Other specified personal exposures and history presenting hazards o health (V87)

V87 Other specified personal exposures and history presenting hazards to health

Acquired absence of other organs and tissue (V88)

V88 Acquired absence of other organs and tissue

Other suspected conditions not found (V89)

V89 Other suspected conditions not found

SUPPLEMENTARY CLASSIFICATION OF EXTERNAL CAUSES OF INJURY AND POISONING

Railway accidents (E800-E807)

E800 Railway accident involving collision with rolling stock
E801 Railway accident involving collision with other object
E802 Railway accident involving derailment without antecedent collision
E803 Railway accident involving explosion, fire, or burning
E804 Fall in, on, or from railway train
E805 Hit by rolling stock
E806 Other specified railway accident
E807 Railway accident of unspecified nature

Motor vehicle traffic accidents (E810-E819)

E810 Motor vehicle traffic accident involving collision with train
E811 Motor vehicle traffic accident involving re-entrant collision with another motor vehicle
E812 Other motor vehicle traffic accident involving collision with another motor vehicle
E813 Motor vehicle traffic accident involving collision with other vehicle
E814 Motor vehicle traffic accident involving collision with pedestrian
E815 Other motor vehicle traffic accident involving collision on the highway
E816 Motor vehicle traffic accident due to loss of control, without collision on the highway
E817 Noncollision motor vehicle traffic accident while boarding or alighting
E818 Other noncollision motor vehicle traffic accident
E819 Motor vehicle traffic accident of unspecified nature

Motor vehicle nontraffic accidents (E820-E825)

E820 Nontraffic accident involving motor-driven snow vehicle
E821 Nontraffic accident involving other off-road motor vehicle
E822 Other motor vehicle nontraffic accident involving collision with moving object
E823 Other motor vehicle nontraffic accident involving collision with stationary object
E824 Other motor vehicle nontraffic accident while boarding and alighting
E825 Other motor vehicle nontraffic accident of other and unspecified nature

Other road vehicle accidents (E826-E829)

E826 Pedal cycle accident
E827 Animal-drawn vehicle accident
E828 Accident involving animal being ridden
E829 Other road vehicle accidents

Water transport accidents (E830-E838)

E830 Accident to watercraft causing submersion
E831 Accident to watercraft causing other injury
E832 Other accidental submersion or drowning in water transport accident
E833 Fall on stairs or ladders in water transport
E834 Other fall from one level to another in water transport
E835 Other and unspecified fall in water transport
E836 Machinery accident in water transport
E837 Explosion, fire, or burning in watercraft
E838 Other and unspecified water transport accident

Air and space transport accidents (E840-E845)

E840 Accident to powered aircraft at takeoff or landing
E841 Accident to powered aircraft, other and unspecified
E842 Accident to unpowered aircraft
E843 Fall in, on, or from aircraft
E844 Other specified air transport accidents
E845 Other involving spacecraft

Vehicle accidents, not elsewhere classfiable (E846-E849)

E846 Accidents involving powered vehicles used solely within the buildings and premises of an industrial or commercial establishment
E847 Accidents involving cable cars not running on rails
E848 Accidents involving other vehicles, not elsewhere classifiable
E849 Place of occurrence

Accidental poisoning by drugs, medicinal substances, and biologicals (E850-E858)

E850 Accidental poisoning by analgesics, antipyretics, and antirheumatics
E851 Accidental poisoning by barbiturates
E852 Accidental poisoning by other sedatives and hypnotics
E853 Accidental poisoning by tranquilizers
E854 Accidental poisoning by other psychotropic agents
E855 Accidental poisoning by other drugs acting on central and autonomic nervous systems
E856 Accidental poisoning by antibiotics
E857 Accidental poisoning by anti-infectives
E858 Accidental poisoning by other drugs

Accidental poisoning by other solid and liquid substances, gases, and vapors (E860-E869)

E860 Accidental poisoning by alcohol, not elsewhere classified
E861 Accidental poisoning by cleansing and polishing agents, disinfectants, paints, and varnishes
E862 Accidental poisoning by petroleum products, other solvents and their vapors, not elsewhere classified
E863 Accidental poisoning by agricultural and horticultural chemical and pharmaceutical preparations other than plant foods and fertilizers
E864 Accidental poisoning by corrosives and caustics, not elsewhere classified
E865 Accidental poisoning from poisonous foodstuffs and poisonous plants
E866 Accidental poisoning by other and unspecified solid and liquid substances
E867 Accidental poisoning by gas distributed by pipeline
E868 Accidental poisoning by other utility gas and other carbon monoxide
E869 Accidental poisoning by other gases and vapors

Misadventures to patients during surgical and medical care (E870-E876)

E870 Accidental cut, puncture, perforation, or hemorrhage during medical care
E871 Foreign object left in body during procedure
E872 Failure of sterile precautions during procedure
E873 Failure in dosage
E874 Mechanical failure of instrument or apparatus during procedure
E875 Contaminated or infected blood, other fluid, drug, or biological substance
E876 Other and unspecified misadventures during medical care

Surgical and medical procedures as the cause of abnormal reaction of patient or later complication, without mention of misadventure at the time of procedure (E878-E879)

E878 Surgical operation and other surgical procedures as the cause of abnormal reaction of patient, or of later complication, without mention of misadventure at the time of operation
E879 Other procedures, without mention of misadventure at the time of procedure, as the cause of abnormal reaction of patient, or of later complication

Accidental falls (E880-E888)

E880 Fall on or from stairs or steps
E881 Fall on or from ladders or scaffolding
E882 Fall from or out of building or other structure
E883 Fall into hole or other opening in surface
E884 Other fall from one level to another
E885 Fall on same level from slipping, tripping, or stumbling
E886 Fall on same level from collision, pushing or shoving, by or with other person
E887 Fracture, cause unspecified
E888 Other and unspecified fall

Accidents caused by fire and flames (E890-E899)

E890 Conflagration in private dwelling
E891 Conflagration in other and unspecified building or structure
E892 Conflagration not in building or structure
E893 Accident caused by ignition of clothing
E894 Ignition of highly inflammable material
E895 Accident caused by controlled fire in private dwelling
E896 Accident caused by controlled fire in other and unspecified building or structure
E897 Accident caused by controlled fire not in building or structure
E898 Accident caused by other specified fire and flames
E899 Accident caused by unspecified fire

Accidents due to natural and environmental factors (E900-E909)

E900 Excessive heat
E901 Excessive cold
E902 High and low air pressure and changes in air pressure
E903 Travel and motion
E904 Hunger, thirst, exposure, and neglect
E905 Venomous animals and plants as the cause of poisoning and toxic reactions
E906 Other injury caused by animals
E907 Lightning
E908 Cataclysmic storms, and floods resulting from storms
E909 Cataclysmic earth surface movements and eruptions

Accidents caused by submersion, suffocation, and foreign bodies (E910-E915)

E910 Accidental drowning and submersion
E911 Inhalation and ingestion of food causing obstruction of respiratory tract or suffocation
E912 Inhalation and ingestion of other object causing obstruction of respiratory tract or suffocation
E913 Accidental mechanical suffocation
E914 Foreign body accidentally entering eye and adnexa
E915 Foreign body accidentally entering other orifice

Other accidents (E916-E928)

E916 Struck accidentally by falling object
E917 Striking against or struck accidentally by objects or persons
E918 Caught accidentally in or between objects
E919 Accidents caused by machinery
E920 Accidents caused by cutting and piercing instruments or objects
E921 Accident caused by explosion of pressure vessel
E922 Accident caused by firearm missile
E923 Accident caused by explosive material
E924 Accident caused by hot substance or object, caustic or corrosive material, and steam
E925 Accident caused by electric current
E926 Exposure to radiation
E927 Overexertion and strenuous movements
E928 Other and unspecified environmental and accidental causes

Late effects of accidental injury (E929)

E929 Late effects of accidental injury

Drugs, medicinal and biological substances causing adverse effects in therapeutic use (E930-E949)

E930 Antibiotics
E931 Other anti-infectives
E932 Hormones and synthetic substitutes
E933 Primarily systemic agents
E934 Agents primarily affecting blood constituents
E935 Analgesics, antipyretics, and antirheumatics
E936 Anticonvulsants and anti-Parkinsonism drugs
E937 Sedatives and hypnotics
E938 Other central nervous system depressants and anesthetics
E939 Psychotropic agents
E940 Central nervous system stimulants
E941 Drugs primarily affecting the autonomic nervous system
E942 Agents primarily affecting the cardiovascular system
E943 Agents primarily affecting gastrointestinal system
E944 Water, mineral, and uric acid metabolism drugs
E945 Agents primarily acting on the smooth and skeletal muscles and respiratory system
E946 Agents primarily affecting skin and mucous membrane, ophthalmological, otorhinolaryngological, and dental drugs
E947 Other and unspecified drugs and medicinal substances
E948 Bacterial vaccines
E949 Other vaccines and biological substances

Suicide and self-inflicted injury (E950-E959)

E950 Suicide and self-inflicted poisoning by solid or liquid substances
E951 Suicide and self-inflicted poisoning by gases in domestic use
E952 Suicide and self-inflicted poisoning by other gases and vapors
E953 Suicide and self-inflicted injury by hanging, strangulation, and suffocation
E954 Suicide and self-inflicted injury by submersion [drowning]
E955 Suicide and self-inflicted injury by firearms and explosives
E956 Suicide and self-inflicted injury by cutting and piercing instruments
E957 Suicide and self-inflicted injuries by jumping from high place
E958 Suicide and self-inflicted injury by other and unspecified means
E959 Late effects of self-inflicted injury

Homicide and injury purposely inflicted by other persons (E960-E969)

E960 Fight, brawl, and rape
E961 Assault by corrosive or caustic substance, except poisoning
E962 Assault by poisoning
E963 Assault by hanging and strangulation
E964 Assault by submersion [drowning]
E965 Assault by firearms and explosives
E966 Assault by cutting and piercing instrument
E967 Child and adult battering and other maltreatment
E968 Assault by other and unspecified means
E969 Late effects of injury purposely inflicted by other person

Legal intervention (E970-E978)

E970 Injury due to legal intervention by firearms
E971 Injury due to legal intervention by explosives
E972 Injury due to legal intervention by gas
E973 Injury due to legal intervention by blunt object
E974 Injury due to legal intervention by cutting and piercing instruments
E975 Injury due to legal intervention by other specified means
E976 Injury due to legal intervention by unspecified means
E977 Late effects of injuries due to legal intervention
E978 Legal execution

Terrorism (E979)

E979 Terrorism

Injury undetermined whether accidentally or purposely inflicted (E980-E989)

E980 Poisoning by solid or liquid substances, undetermined whether accidentally or purposely inflicted
E981 Poisoning by gases in domestic use, undetermined whether accidentally or purposely inflicted
E982 Poisoning by other gases, undetermined whether accidentally or purposely inflicted
E983 Hanging, strangulation, or suffocation, undetermined whether accidentally or purposely inflicted
E984 Submersion [drowning], undetermined whether accidentally or purposely inflicted
E985 Injury by firearms and explosives, undetermined whether accidentally or purposely inflicted
E986 Injury by cutting and piercing instruments, undetermined whether accidentally or purposely inflicted
E987 Falling from high place, undetermined whether accidentally or purposely inflicted
E988 Injury by other and unspecified means, undetermined whether accidentally or purposely inflicted
E989 Late effects of injury, undetermined whether accidentally or purposely inflicted

Resulting from operations of war (E990-E999)

E990 Injury due to war operations by fires and conflagrations
E991 Injury due to war operations by bullets and fragments
E992 Injury due to war operations by explosion of marine weapons
E993 Injury due to war operations by other explosion
E994 Injury due to war operations by destruction of aircraft
E995 Injury due to war operations by other and unspecified forms of conventional warfare
E996 Injury due to war operations by nuclear weapons
E997 Injury due to war operations by other forms of unconventional warfare
E998 Injury due to war operations but occurring after cessation of hostilities
E999 Late effects of injury due to war operations

A

B

Biopsy — *continued*
testis NEC 62.11
closed 62.11
open 62.12
percutaneous (needle) 62.11
thymus 07.16
thyroid gland NEC 06.11
closed 06.11
open 06.12
percutaneous (aspiration) (needle) 06.11
tongue 25.01
closed (needle) 25.01
open 25.02
tonsil 28.11
trachea 31.44
brush 31.44
closed (endoscopic) 31.44
open 31.45
tunica vaginalis 61.11
umbilicus 54.22
ureter 56.33
closed (percutaneous) 56.32
endoscopic 56.33
open 56.34
transurethral 56.33
urethra 58.23
uterus, uterine (endometrial) 68.16
by
aspiration curettage 69.59
dilation and curettage 69.09
closed (endoscopic) 68.16
ligaments 68.15
closed (endoscopic) 68.15
open 68.14
open 68.13
uvula 27.22
vagina 70.24
vas deferens 63.01
vein (any site) 38.21
vulva 71.11
BiPAP 93.90
delivered by
endotracheal tube — *see* category 96.7 ☑
tracheostomy — *see* category 96.7 ☑
Bischoff operation (spinal myelotomy) 03.29
Bischoff operation (ureteroneocystostomy) 56.74
Bisection — *see also* Excision
hysterectomy 68.39
laparoscopic 68.31
ovary 65.29
laparoscopic 65.25
stapes foot plate 19.19
with incus replacement 19.11
Blalock-Hanlon operation (creation of atrial septal defect) 35.42
Blalock operation (systemic-pulmonary anastomosis) 39.0
Blalock-Taussig operation (subclavian-pulmonary anastomosis) 39.0
Blascovic operation (resection and advancement of levator palpebrae superioris) 08.33
Blepharectomy 08.20
Blepharoplasty — *see also* Reconstruction, eyelid 08.70
extensive 08.44
Blepharorrhaphy 08.52
division or severing 08.02
Blepharotomy 08.09
Blind rehabilitation therapy NEC 93.78
Block
caudal — *see* Injection, spinal
celiac ganglion or plexus 05.31
dissection
breast
bilateral 85.46
unilateral 85.45
bronchus 32.6
larynx 30.3
lymph nodes 40.50
neck 40.40
Block — *continued*
dissection — *continued*
vulva 71.5
epidural, spinal — *see* Injection, spinal
gasserian ganglion 04.81
intercostal nerves 04.81
intrathecal — *see* Injection, spinal
nerve (cranial) (peripheral) NEC 04.81
paravertebral stellate ganglion 05.31
peripheral nerve 04.81
spinal nerve root (intrathecal) — *see* Injection, spinal
stellate (ganglion) 05.31
subarachnoid, spinal — *see* Injection, spinal
sympathetic nerve 05.31
trigeminal nerve 04.81
Blood
flow study, Doppler-type (ultrasound) — *see* Ultrasonography
patch, spine (epidural) 03.95
transfusion
antihemophilic factor 99.06
autologous
collected prior to surgery 99.02
intraoperative 99.00
perioperative 99.00
postoperative 99.00
previously collected 99.02
salvage 99.00
blood expander 99.08
blood surrogate 99.09
coagulation factors 99.06
exchange 99.01
granulocytes 99.09
hemodilution 99.03
other substance 99.09
packed cells 99.04
plasma 99.07
platelets 99.05
serum, other 99.07
thrombocytes 99.05
Blount operation
femoral shortening (with blade plate) 78.25
by epiphyseal stapling 78.25
Boari operation (bladder flap) 56.74
Bobb operation (cholelithotomy) 51.04
Bone
age studies 88.33
mineral density study 88.98
Bonney operation (abdominal hysterectomy) 68.49
laparoscopic 68.41
Borthen operation (iridotasis) 12.63
Bost operation
plantar dissection 80.48
radiocarpal fusion 81.26
Bosworth operation
arthroplasty for acromioclavicular separation 81.83
fusion of posterior lumbar and lumbosacral spine 81.08
for pseudarthrosis 81.38
resection of radial head ligaments (for tennis elbow) 80.92
shelf procedure, hip 81.40
Bottle repair of hydrocele, tunica vaginalis 61.2
Boyd operation (hip disarticulation) 84.18
Brachytherapy
intravascular 92.27
Brauer operation (cardiolysis) 37.10
Breech extraction — *see* Extraction, breech
Bricker operation (ileoureterostomy) 56.51
Brisement (forcé) 93.26
Bristow operation (repair of shoulder dislocation) 81.82
Brockman operation (soft tissue release for clubfoot) 83.84
Brock operation (pulmonary valvotomy) 35.03
Bronchogram, bronchography 87.32
endotracheal 87.31
transcricoid 87.32
Bronchoplasty 33.48
Bronchorrhaphy 33.41
Bronchoscopy NEC 33.23
with biopsy 33.24
lung 33.27
brush 33.24
fiberoptic 33.22
with biopsy 33.24
lung 33.27
brush 33.24
through tracheostomy 33.21
with biopsy 33.24
lung 33.27
brush 33.24
Bronchospirometry 89.38
Bronchostomy 33.0
closure 33.42
Bronchotomy 33.0
Browne (-Denis) operation (hypospadias repair) 58.45
Brunschwig operation (temporary gastrostomy) 43.19
Buckling, scleral 14.49
with
air tamponade 14.49
implant (silicone) (vitreous) 14.41
resection of sclera 14.49
vitrectomy 14.49
vitreous implant (silicone) 14.41
Bunionectomy (radical) 77.59
with
arthrodesis 77.52
osteotomy of first metatarsal 77.51
resection of joint with prosthetic implant 77.59
soft tissue correction NEC 77.53
Bunnell operation (tendon transfer) 82.56
Burch procedure (retropubic urethral suspension for urinary stress incontinence) 59.5
Burgess operation (amputation of ankle) 84.14
Burn dressing 93.57
Burr holes 01.24
Bursectomy 83.5
hand 82.31
Bursocentesis 83.94
hand 82.92
Bursotomy 83.03
hand 82.03
Burying of fimbriae in uterine wall 66.97
Bypass
abdominal-coronary artery 36.17
aortocoronary (catheter stent) (with prosthesis) (with saphenous vein graft) (with vein graft) 36.10
one coronary vessel 36.11
two coronary vessels 36.12
three coronary vessels 36.13
four coronary vessels 36.14
arterial (graft) (mandril grown graft) (vein graft) NEC 39.29
carotid-cerebral 39.28
carotid-vertebral 39.28
extracranial-intracranial [EC-IC] 39.28
intra-abdominal NEC 39.26
intrathoracic NEC 39.23
peripheral NEC 39.29
cardiopulmonary 39.61
open 39.61
percutaneous (closed) 39.66
carotid-cerebral 39.28
carotid-vertebral 39.28
coronary (*see also* Bypass, aortocoronary) 36.10
extracranial-intracranial [EC-IC] 39.28
gastric 44.39
high 44.31
laparoscopic 44.38
Printen and Mason 44.31
Bypass — *continued*
gastroduodenostomy (Jaboulay's) 44.39
laparoscopic 44.38
percutaneous [endoscopic] 44.32
gastroenterostomy 44.39
laparoscopic 44.38
gastroepiploic-coronary artery 36.17
gastrogastrostomy 44.39
laparoscopic 44.38
graft, pressurized treatment 00.16
heart-lung (complete) (partial) 39.61
open 39.61
percutaneous (closed) 39.66
high gastric 44.31
ileo-jejunal 45.91
internal mammary-coronary artery (single) 36.15
double vessel 36.16
jejunal-ileum 45.91
pulmonary 39.61
open 39.61
percutaneous (closed) 39.66
shunt
intestine
large-to-large 45.94
small-to-large 45.93
small-to-small 45.91
stomach 44.39
high gastric 44.31
laparoscopic 44.38
terminal ileum 45.93
vascular (arterial) (graft) (mandril grown graft) (vein graft) NEC 39.29
aorta-carotid-brachial 39.22
aorta-iliac-femoral 39.25
aorta-renal 39.24
aorta-subclavian-carotid 39.22
aortic-superior mesenteric 39.26
aortocarotid 39.22
aortoceliac 39.26
aortocoronary (*see also* Bypass, aortocoronary) 36.10
aortofemoral 39.25
aortofemoral-popliteal 39.25
aortoiliac 39.25
to popliteal 39.25
aortoiliofemoral 39.25
aortomesenteric 39.26
aortopopliteal 39.25
aortorenal 39.24
aortosubclavian 39.22
axillary-brachial 39.29
axillary-femoral (superficial) 39.29
axillofemoral (superficial) 39.29
carotid-cerebral 39.28
carotid to subclavian artery 39.22
carotid-vertebral 39.28
common hepatic-common iliac-renal 39.26
coronary (*see also* Bypass, aortocoronary) 36.10
extracranial-intracranial [EC-IC] 39.28
femoral-femoral 39.29
femoroperoneal 39.29
femoropopliteal (reversed saphenous vein) (saphenous) 39.29
femorotibial (anterior) (posterior) 39.29
iliofemoral 39.25
ilioiliac 39.26
internal mammary-coronary artery (single) 36.15
double vessel 36.16
intra-abdominal (arterial) NEC 39.26
venous NEC 39.1
intrathoracic NEC 39.23
peripheral artery NEC 39.29
popliteal-tibial 39.29
renal artery 39.24
splenorenal (venous) 39.1
arterial 39.26
subclavian-axillary 39.29

Charnley operation (compression arthrodesis)
  ankle 81.11
  hip 81.21
  knee 81.22
Cheatle-Henry operation — *see* Repair, hernia, femoral
Check
  automatic implantable cardioverter/defibrillatory (AICD) (interrogation only) 89.49
  CRT-D (cardiac resynchronization defibrillator) (interrogation only) 89.49
  CRT-P (cardiac resynchronization pacemaker) (interrogation only) 89.45
  pacemaker, artificial (cardiac) (function) (interrogation only) (rate) 89.45
    amperage threshold 89.48
    artifact wave form 89.46
    electrode impedance 89.47
    voltage threshold 89.48
  vision NEC 95.09
Cheiloplasty 27.59
Cheilorrhaphy 27.51
Cheilostomatoplasty 27.59
Cheilotomy 27.0
Chemical peel, skin 86.24
Chemocauterization — *see also* Destruction, lesion, by site
  corneal epithelium 11.41
  palate 27.31
Chemodectomy 39.8
Chemoembolization 99.25
Chemolysis
  nerve (peripheral) 04.2
  spinal canal structure 03.8
Chemoneurolysis 04.2
Chemonucleolysis (nucleus pulposus) 80.52
Chemopallidectomy 01.42
Chemopeel (skin) 86.24
Chemosurgery
  esophagus 42.39
    endoscopic 42.33
  Mohs' 86.24
  skin (superficial) 86.24
  stomach 43.49
    endoscopic 43.41
Chemothalamectomy 01.41
Chemotherapy — *see also* Immunotherapy
  for cancer NEC 99.25
    brain wafer implantation 00.10
    implantation of chemotherapeutic agent 00.10
    interstitial implantation 00.10
    intracavitary implantation 00.10
    wafer chemotherapy 00.10
  Antabuse 94.25
  lithium 94.22
  methadone 94.25
  palate (bony) 27.31
Chevalier-Jackson operation (partial laryngectomy) 30.29
Child operation (radical subtotal pancreatectomy) 52.53
Cholangiocholangiostomy 51.39
Cholangiocholecystocholedochectomy 51.22
Cholangio-enterostomy 51.39
Cholangiogastrostomy 51.39
Cholangiogram 87.54
  endoscopic retrograde (ERC) 51.11
  intraoperative 87.53
  intravenous 87.52
  percutaneous hepatic 87.51
  transhepatic 87.53
Cholangiography — *see also* Cholangiogram 87.54
Cholangiojejunostomy (intrahepatic) 51.39
Cholangiopancreatography, endoscopic retrograde (ERCP) 51.10
Cholangiostomy 51.59
Cholangiotomy 51.59
Cholecystectomy
  partial 51.21
    laparoscopic 51.24
  total 51.22
    laparoscopic 51.23
Cholecystenterorrhaphy 51.91
Cholecystocecostomy 51.32
Cholecystocholangiogram 87.59
Cholecystocolostomy 51.32
Cholecystoduodenostomy 51.32
Cholecystoenterostomy (Winiwater) 51.32
Cholecystogastrostomy 51.34
Cholecystogram 87.59
Cholecystoileostomy 51.32
Cholecystojejunostomy (Roux-en-Y) (with jejunojejunostomy) 51.32
Cholecystopancreatostomy 51.33
Cholecystopexy 51.99
Cholecystorrhaphy 51.91
Cholecystostomy NEC 51.03
  by trocar 51.02
Cholecystotomy 51.04
  percutaneous 51.01
Choledochectomy 51.63
Choledochoduodenostomy 51.36
Choledochoenterostomy 51.36
Choledochojejunostomy 51.36
Choledocholithotomy 51.41
  endoscopic 51.88
Choledocholithotripsy 51.41
  endoscopic 51.88
Choledochopancreatostomy 51.39
Choledochoplasty 51.72
Choledochorrhaphy 51.71
Choledochoscopy 51.11
Choledochostomy 51.51
Choledochotomy 51.51
Cholelithotomy 51.04
Chondrectomy 80.90
  ankle 80.97
  elbow 80.92
  foot and toe 80.98
  hand and finger 80.94
  hip 80.95
  intervertebral cartilage — *see* category 80.5 ☑
  knee (semilunar cartilage) 80.6
  nasal (submucous) 21.5
  semilunar cartilage (knee) 80.6
  shoulder 80.91
  specified site NEC 80.99
  spine — *see* category 80.5 ☑
  wrist 80.93
Chondroplasty — *see* Arthroplasty
Chondrosternoplasty (for pectus excavatum repair) 34.74
Chondrotomy — *see also* Division, cartilage 80.40
  nasal 21.1
Chopart operation (midtarsal amputation) 84.12
Chordectomy, vocal 30.22
Chordotomy (spinothalmic) (anterior) (posterior) NEC 03.29
  percutaneous 03.21
  stereotactic 03.21
Ciliarotomy 12.55
Ciliectomy (ciliary body) 12.44
  eyelid margin 08.20
Cinch, cinching
  for scleral buckling (*see also* Buckling, scleral) 14.49
  ocular muscle (oblique) (rectus) 15.22
    multiple (two or more muscles) 15.4
Cineangiocardiography — *see also* Angiocardiography 88.50
Cineplasty, cineplastic prosthesis
  amputation — *see* Amputation
  arm 84.44
  biceps 84.44
  extremity 84.40
    lower 84.48
Cineplasty, cineplastic prosthesis — *continued*
  extremity — *continued*
    upper 84.44
  leg 84.48
Cineradiograph — *see* Radiography
Cingulumotomy (brain) (percutaneous radiofrequency) 01.32
Circumcision (male) 64.0
  female 71.4
CISH (classic infrafascial SEMM hysterectomy) 68.31
Clagett operation (closure of chest wall following open flap drainage) 34.72
Clamp and cautery, hemorrhoids 49.43
Clamping
  aneurysm (cerebral) 39.51
  blood vessel — *see* Ligation, blood vessel
  ventricular shunt 02.43
Clavicotomy 77.31
  fetal 73.8
Claviculectomy (partial) 77.81
  total 77.91
Clayton operation (resection of metatarsal heads and bases of phalanges) 77.88
Cleaning, wound 96.59
Clearance
  bladder (transurethral) 57.0
  pelvic
    female 68.8
    male 57.71
  prescalene fat pad 40.21
  renal pelvis (transurethral) 56.0
  ureter (transurethral) 56.0
Cleidotomy 77.31
  fetal 73.8
Clipping
  aneurysm (basilar) (carotid) (cerebellar) (cerebellopontine) (communicating artery) (vertebral) 39.51
  arteriovenous fistula 39.53
  frenulum, frenum
    labia (lips) 27.91
    lingual (tongue) 25.91
  left atrial appendage 37.36
  tip of uvula 27.72
Clitoridectomy 71.4
Clitoridotomy 71.4
Clivogram 87.02
Closure — *see also* Repair
  abdominal wall 54.63
    delayed (granulating wound) 54.62
    secondary 54.61
    tertiary 54.62
  amputation stump, secondary 84.3
  anular disc 80.54
    with graft or prosthesis 80.53
  anulus fibrosus 80.54
    with graft or prosthesis 80.53
  aorticopulmonary fenestration (fistula) 39.59
  appendicostomy 47.92
  artificial opening
    bile duct 51.79
    bladder 57.82
    bronchus 33.42
    common duct 51.72
    esophagus 42.83
    gallbladder 51.92
    hepatic duct 51.79
    intestine 46.50
      large 46.52
      small 46.51
    kidney 55.82
    larynx 31.62
    rectum 48.72
    stomach 44.62
    thorax 34.72
    trachea 31.72
    ureter 56.83
    urethra 58.42
  atrial septal defect (*see also* Repair, atrial septal defect) 35.71
Closure — *see also* Repair — *continued*
  atrial septal defect (*see also* Repair, atrial septal defect) — *continued*
    with umbrella device (King-Mills type) 35.52
    combined with repair of valvular and ventricular septal defects — *see* Repair, endocardial cushion defect
  bronchostomy 33.42
  cecostomy 46.52
  cholecystostomy 51.92
  cleft hand 82.82
  colostomy 46.52
  cystostomy 57.82
  diastema (alveolar) (dental) 24.8
  disrupted abdominal wall (postoperative) 54.61
  duodenostomy 46.51
  encephalocele 02.12
  endocardial cushion defect (*see also* Repair, endocardial cushion defect) 35.73
  enterostomy 46.50
  esophagostomy 42.83
  fenestration
    aorticopulmonary 39.59
    septal, heart (*see also* Repair, heart, septum) 35.70
  filtering bleb, corneoscleral (postglaucoma) 12.66
  fistula
    abdominothoracic 34.83
    anorectal 48.73
    anovaginal 70.73
    antrobuccal 22.71
    anus 49.73
    aorticopulmonary (fenestration) 39.59
    aortoduodenal 39.59
    appendix 47.92
    biliary tract 51.79
    bladder NEC 57.84
    branchial cleft 29.52
    bronchocutaneous 33.42
    bronchoesophageal 33.42
    bronchomediastinal 34.73
    bronchopleural 34.73
    bronchopleurocutaneous 34.73
    bronchopleuromediastinal 34.73
    bronchovisceral 33.42
    bronchus 33.42
    cecosigmoidal 46.76
    cerebrospinal fluid 02.12
    cervicoaural 18.79
    cervicosigmoidal 67.62
    cervicovesical 57.84
    cervix 67.62
    cholecystocolic 51.93
    cholecystoduodenal 51.93
    cholecystoenteric 51.93
    cholecystogastric 51.93
    cholecystojejunal 51.93
    cisterna chyli 40.63
    colon 46.76
    colovaginal 70.72
    common duct 51.72
    cornea 11.49
      with lamellar graft (homograft) 11.62
        autograft 11.61
    diaphragm 34.83
    duodenum 46.72
    ear drum 19.4
    ear, middle 19.9
    enterocolic 46.74
    enterocutaneous 46.74
    enterouterine 69.42
    enterovaginal 70.74
    enterovesical 57.83
    esophagobronchial 33.42
    esophagocutaneous 42.84
    esophagopleurocutaneous 34.73
    esophagotracheal 31.73

D

Index
Episiorrhaphy — Examination

Index
Excision — Exploration

F

Infusion — *continued*
- enzymes, thrombolytic (streptokinase) (tissue plasminogen activator) (TPA) (urokinase)
  - direct coronary artery 36.04
  - intravenous 99.10
- Eptifibatide 99.20
- gamma globulin 99.14
- GP IIb/IIIa inhibitor 99.20
- hormone substance NEC 99.24
- human B-type natriuretic peptide (hBNP) 00.13
- immunosuppressive antibody therapy 00.18
- interleukin-2
  - high-dose 00.15
  - low-dose 99.28
- nesiritide 00.13
- neuroprotective agent 99.75
- nimodipine 99.75
- nutritional substance — *see* Nutrition
- platelet inhibitor
  - direct coronary artery 36.04
  - intravenous 99.20
- Proleukin (low-dose) 99.28
  - high-dose 00.15
- prophylactic substance NEC 99.29
- radioimmunoconjugate 92.28
- radioimmunotherapy 92.28
- radioisotope (liquid brachytherapy) (liquid I-125) 92.20
- recombinant protein 00.11
- reteplase 99.10
- therapeutic substance NEC 99.29
- thrombolytic agent (enzyme) (streptokinase) 99.10
  - with percutaneous transluminal angioplasty

    Note: Also use 00.40, 00.41, 00.42, or 00.43 to show the total number of vessels treated.

    - coronary 00.66
    - non-coronary vessel(s) 39.50
    - specified site NEC 39.50
  - direct intracoronary artery 36.04
- tirofiban (HCl) 99.20
- vaccine
  - tumor 99.28
- vasopressor 00.17

Injection (into) (hypodermically) (intramuscularly) (intravenously) (acting locally or systemically)
- Actinomycin D, for cancer chemotherapy 99.25
- adhesion barrier substance 99.77
- alcohol
  - nerve — *see* Injection, nerve
  - spinal 03.8
- anterior chamber, eye (air) (liquid) (medication) 12.92
- antibiotic 99.21
  - oxazolidinone class 00.14
- anticoagulant 99.19
- anti-D (Rhesus) globulin 99.11
- antidote NEC 99.16
- anti-infective NEC 99.22
- antineoplastic agent (chemotherapeutic) NEC 99.25
  - biological response modifier [BRM] 99.28
  - cintredekin besudotox 99.28
  - high-dose interleukin-2 00.15
  - low-dose interleukin-2 99.28
- antivenin 99.16
- barrier substance, adhesion 99.77
- BCG
  - for chemotherapy 99.25
  - vaccine 99.33
- biological response modifier [BRM], antineoplastic agent 99.28
  - cintredekin besudotox 99.28
  - high-dose interleukin-2 00.15
  - low-dose interleukin-2 99.28
- bone marrow 41.92
  - transplant — *see* Transplant, bone, marrow

Injection — *continued*
- breast (therapeutic agent) 85.92
  - inert material (silicone) (bilateral) 85.52
    - unilateral 85.51
- bursa (therapeutic agent) 83.96
  - hand 82.94
- cancer chemotherapeutic agent 99.25
- caudal — *see* Injection, spinal
- cintredekin besudotox 99.28
- cortisone 99.23
- costochondral junction 81.92
- dinoprost-tromethine, intraamniotic 75.0
- ear, with alcohol 20.72
- electrolytes 99.18
- enzymes, thrombolytic (streptokinase) (tissue plasminogen activator) (TPA) (urokinase)
  - direct coronary artery 36.04
  - intravenous 99.10
- epidural, spinal — *see* Injection, spinal
- esophageal varices or blood vessel (endoscopic) (sclerosing agent) 42.33
- Eustachian tube (inert material) 20.8
- eye (orbit) (retrobulbar) 16.91
  - anterior chamber 12.92
  - subconjunctival 10.91
- fascia 83.98
  - hand 82.96
- gamma globulin 99.14
- ganglion, sympathetic 05.39
  - ciliary 12.79
  - paravertebral stellate 05.39
- gel, adhesion barrier — *see* Injection, adhesion barrier substance
- globulin
  - anti-D (Rhesus) 99.11
  - gamma 99.14
  - Rh immune 99.11
- heart 37.92
- heavy metal antagonist 99.16
- hemorrhoids (sclerosing agent) 49.42
- hormone NEC 99.24
- human B-type natriuretic peptide (hBNP) 00.13
- immune sera 99.14
- inert material — *see* Implant, inert material
- inner ear, for destruction 20.72
- insulin 99.17
- intervertebral space for herniated disc 80.52
- intra-amniotic
  - for induction of
    - abortion 75.0
    - labor 73.1
- intrathecal — *see* Injection, spinal
- joint (therapeutic agent) 81.92
  - temporomandibular 76.96
- kidney (cyst) (therapeutic substance) NEC 55.96
- larynx 31.0
- ligament (joint) (therapeutic substance) 81.92
- liver 50.94
- lung, for surgical collapse 33.32
- Methotrexate, for cancer chemotherapy 99.25
- nerve (cranial) (peripheral) 04.80
  - agent NEC 04.89
    - alcohol 04.2
    - anesthetic for analgesia 04.81
      - for operative anesthesia — *omit code*
    - neurolytic 04.2
    - phenol 04.2
  - laryngeal (external) (recurrent) (superior) 31.91
  - optic 16.91
  - sympathetic 05.39
    - alcohol 05.32
    - anesthetic for analgesia 05.31
    - neurolytic agent 05.32

Injection — *continued*
- nerve — *continued*
  - sympathetic — *continued*
    - phenol 05.32
- nesiritide 00.13
- neuroprotective agent 99.75
- nimodipine 99.75
- orbit 16.91
- pericardium 37.93
- peritoneal cavity
  - air 54.96
  - locally-acting therapeutic substance 54.97
- platelet inhibitor
  - direct coronary artery 36.04
  - intravenous 99.20
- prophylactic substance NEC 99.29
- prostate 60.92
- radioimmunoconjugate 92.28
- radioimmunotherapy 92.28
- radioisotopes (intracavitary) (intravenous) 92.28
- renal pelvis (cyst) 55.96
- retrobulbar (therapeutic substance) 16.91
  - for anesthesia — *omit code*
- Rh immune globulin 99.11
- RhoGAM 99.11
- sclerosing agent NEC 99.29
  - esophageal varices (endoscopic) 42.33
  - hemorrhoids 49.42
  - pleura 34.92
    - treatment of malignancy (cytotoxic agent) 34.92 *[99.25]*
      - with tetracycline 34.92 *[99.21]*
  - varicose vein 39.92
  - vein NEC 39.92
- semicircular canals, for destruction 20.72
- silicone — *see* Implant, inert material
- skin (sclerosing agent) (filling material) 86.02
- soft tissue 83.98
  - hand 82.96
- spinal (canal) NEC 03.92
  - alcohol 03.8
  - anesthetic agent for analgesia 03.91
    - for operative anesthesia — *omit code*
  - contrast material (for myelogram) 87.21
  - destructive agent NEC 03.8
  - neurolytic agent NEC 03.8
  - phenol 03.8
  - proteolytic enzyme (chymopapain) (chymodiactin) 80.52
  - saline (hypothermic) 03.92
  - steroid 03.92
- spinal nerve root (intrathecal) — *see* Injection, spinal
- steroid NEC 99.23
- subarachnoid, spinal — *see* Injection, spinal
- subconjunctival 10.91
- tendon 83.97
  - hand 82.95
- testis 62.92
- therapeutic agent NEC 99.29
- thoracic cavity 34.92
- thrombolytic agent (enzyme) (streptokinase) 99.10
  - with percutaneous transluminal angioplasty

    Note: Also use 00.40, 00.41, 00.42, or 00.43 to show the total number of vessels treated.

    - coronary 00.66
    - non-coronary vessel(s) 39.50
    - specified site NEC 39.50
  - direct intracoronary artery 36.04
- trachea 31.94
- tranquilizer 99.26

Injection — *continued*
- tunica vaginalis (with aspiration) 61.91
- tympanum 20.94
- urethra (inert material)
  - for repair of urinary stress incontinence
    - collagen implant 59.72
    - endoscopic injection of implant 59.72
    - fat implant 59.72
    - polytef implant 59.72
- vaccine
  - tumor 99.28
- varices, esophagus (endoscopic) (sclerosing agent) 42.33
- varicose vein (sclerosing agent) 39.92
  - esophagus (endoscopic) 42.33
- vestibule, for destruction 20.72
- vitreous substitute (silicone) 14.75
  - for reattachment of retina 14.59
- vocal cords 31.0

Inlay, tooth 23.3

Inoculation
- antitoxins — *see* Administration, antitoxins
- toxoids — *see* Administration, toxoids
- vaccine — *see* Administration, vaccine

Insemination, artificial 69.92

Insertion
- airway
  - esophageal obturator 96.03
  - nasopharynx 96.01
  - oropharynx 96.02
- Allen-Brown cannula 39.93
- arch bars (orthodontic) 24.7
  - for immobilization (fracture) 93.55
- atrial septal umbrella 35.52
- Austin-Moore prosthesis 81.52
- baffle, heart (atrial) (interatrial) (intra-atrial) 35.91
- bag, cervix (nonobstetrical) 67.0
  - after delivery or abortion 75.8
  - to assist delivery or induce labor 73.1
- Baker's (tube) (for stenting) 46.85
- balloon
  - gastric 44.93
  - heart (pulsation-type) (Kantrowitz) 37.61
  - intestine (for decompression) (for dilation) 46.85
- band (adjustable)
  - gastric, laparoscopic 44.95
  - Lap-Band™ 44.95
- Barton's tongs (skull) (with synchronous skeletal traction) 02.94
- bipolar endoprosthesis (femoral head) 81.52
- Blakemore-Sengstaken tube 96.06
- bone growth stimulator (invasive) (percutaneous) (semi-invasive) — *see* category 78.9 ☑
- bone morphogenetic protein (Infuse™) (OP-1™) (recombinant) (rhBMP) 84.52
- bone void filler 84.55
  - that with percutaneous vertebral augmentation 81.66
  - that with percutaneous vertebroplasty 81.65
- bougie, cervix, nonobstetrical 67.0
  - to assist delivery or induce labor 73.1
- breast implant (for augmentation) (bilateral) 85.54
  - unilateral 85.53
- bridge (dental) (fixed) 23.42
  - removable 23.43
- bubble (balloon), stomach 44.93
- caliper tongs (skull) (with synchronous skeletal traction) 02.94

Insertion — *continued*
- cannula
  - for extracorporeal membrane oxygenation (ECMO) — *omit code*
  - Allen-Brown 39.93
  - nasal sinus (by puncture) 22.01
    - through natural ostium 22.02
  - pancreatic duct 52.92
    - endoscopic 52.93
  - vessel to vessel 39.93
- cardiac resynchronization device
  - defibrillator (biventricular defibrillator) (BiV ICD) (BiV pacemaker with defibrillator) (BiV pacing with defibrillator) (CRT-D) (total system) (device and one or more leads) 00.51
    - left ventricular coronary venous lead only 00.52
    - pulse generator only 00.54
  - pacemaker (biventricular pacemaker) (BiV pacemaker) (CRT-P) (total system) (device and one or more leads) 00.50
    - left ventricular coronary venous lead only 00.52
    - pulse generator only 00.53
- cardiac support device (CSD) (CorCap™) 37.41
- carotid artery stent(s) (stemt graft) 00.63

Note: Also use 00.40, 00.41, 00.42, or 00.43 to show the total number of vessels treated. Use code 00.44 once to show procedure on a bifurcated vessel. In addition, use 00.45, 00.46, 00.47, or 00.48 to show the number of vascular stents inserted.

- catheter
  - abdomen of fetus, for intrauterine transfusion 75.2
  - anterior chamber (eye), for permanent drainage (glaucoma) 12.79
  - artery 38.91
  - bile duct(s) 51.59
    - common 51.51
      - endoscopic 51.87
    - endoscopic 51.87
  - bladder, indwelling 57.94
    - suprapubic 57.18
      - percutaneous (closed) 57.17
  - bronchus 96.05
    - with lavage 96.56
  - central venous NEC 38.93
    - for
      - hemodialysis 38.95
      - pressure monitoring 89.62
    - peripherally inserted central catheter (PICC) 38.93
  - chest 34.04
    - revision (with lysis of adhesions) 34.04
      - thoracoscopic 34.06
    - thoracoscopic 34.06
  - cranial cavity 01.26
    - placement via burr hole(s) 01.28
  - esophagus (nonoperative) 96.06
    - permanent tube 42.81
  - intercostal (with water seal), for drainage 34.04
    - revision (with lysis of adhesions) 34.04
      - thoracoscopic 34.06
    - thoracoscopic 34.06
  - intracerebral 01.26
    - placement via burr hole(s) 01.28
  - spinal canal space (epidural) (subarachnoid) (subdural) for infusion of therapeutic or palliative substances 03.90
  - Swan-Ganz (pulmonary) 89.64
  - transtracheal for oxygenation 31.99
  - vein NEC 38.93
    - for renal dialysis 38.95
- chest tube 34.04

Insertion — *continued*
- chest tube — *continued*
  - thoracoscopic 34.06
- choledochohepatic tube (for decompression) 51.43
  - endoscopic 51.87
- circulatory support device
  - CentriMag® 37.62
  - external heart assist device
    - biventricular 37.60
    - percutaneous 37.68
    - temporary 37.62
  - non-implantable 37.62
  - pVAD (percutaneous VAD) 37.68
  - TandemHeart® 37.68
  - temporary non-implantable circulatory assist device 37.62
- cochlear prosthetic device — *see* Implant, cochlear prosthetic device
- contraceptive device (intrauterine) 69.7
- CorCap™ 37.41
- cordis cannula 54.98
- coronary (artery)

Note: Also use 00.40, 00.41, 00.42, or 00.43 to show the total number of vessels treated. Use code 00.44 once to show procedure on a bifurcated vessel. In addition, use 00.45, 00.46, 00.47, or 00.48 to show the number of vascular stents inserted.

  - stent, drug-eluting 36.07
  - stent, non-drug-eluting 36.06
- Crosby-Cooney button 54.98
- CRT-D (biventricular defibrillator) (BiV ICD) (BiV pacemaker with defibrillator) (BiV pacing with defibrillator) (cardiac resynchronization defibrillator) (device and one or more leads) 00.51
  - left ventricular coronary venous lead only 00.52
  - pulse generator only 00.54
- CRT-P (biventricular pacemaker) (BiV pacemaker) (cardiac resynchronization pacemaker) (device and one or more leads) 00.50
  - left ventricular coronary venous lead only 00.52
  - pulse generator only 00.53
- Crutchfield tongs (skull) (with synchronous skeletal traction) 02.94
- Davidson button 54.98
- denture (total) 99.97
- device
  - adjustable gastric band and port 44.95
  - bronchial device NOS 33.79
  - bronchial substance NOS 33.79
  - bronchial valve 33.71
  - cardiac resynchronization — *see* Insertion, cardiac resynchronization device
  - cardiac support device (CSD) 37.41
  - CorCap™ 37.41
  - epicardial support device 37.41
  - Lap-Band™ 44.95
  - left atrial appendage 37.90
  - left atrial filter 37.90
  - left atrial occluder 37.90
  - prosthetic cardiac support device 37.41
  - vascular access 86.07
  - ventricular support device 37.41
- diaphragm, vagina 96.17
- drainage tube
  - kidney 55.02
    - pelvis 55.12
  - renal pelvis 55.12
- Dynesys® 84.82
- elbow prosthesis (total) 81.84
  - revision 81.97

Insertion — *continued*
- electrode(s)
  - bone growth stimulator (invasive) (percutaneous) (semi-invasive) — *see* category 78.9 ☑
  - brain 02.93
    - depth 02.93
    - foramen ovale 02.93
    - sphenoidal 02.96
  - depth 02.93
  - foramen ovale 02.93
  - gastric 04.92
  - heart (initial) (transvenous) 37.70
    - atrium (initial) 37.73
      - replacement 37.76
    - atrium and ventricle (initial) 37.72
      - replacement 37.76
    - epicardium (sternotomy or thoracotomy approach) 37.74
    - left ventricular coronary venous system 00.52
    - temporary transvenous pacemaker system 37.78
      - during and immediately following cardiac surgery 39.64
    - ventricle (initial) 37.71
      - replacement 37.76
  - intracranial 02.93
  - osteogenic (for bone growth stimulation) — *see* category 78.9 ☑
  - peripheral nerve 04.92
  - sacral nerve 04.92
  - sphenoidal 02.96
  - spine 03.93
- electroencephalographic receiver — *see* Implant, electroencephalographic receiver, by site
- electronic stimulator — *see* Implant, electronic stimulator, by site
- electrostimulator — *see* Implant, electronic stimulator, by site
- endograft(s), endovascular graft(s)
  - endovascular, abdominal aorta 39.71
  - endovascular, head and neck vessels 39.72
  - endovascular, other vessels (for aneurysm) 39.79
  - endovascular, thoracic aorta 39.73
- endoprosthesis
  - bile duct 51.87
  - femoral head (bipolar) 81.52
  - pancreatic duct 52.93
- epidural pegs 02.93
- external fixation device (bone) — *see* category 78.1 ☑
- facial bone implant (alloplastic) (synthetic) 76.92
- filling material, skin (filling of defect) 86.02
- filter
  - vena cava (inferior) (superior) (transvenous) 38.7
- fixator, mini device (bone) — *see* category 78.1 ☑
- frame (stereotactic)
  - for radiosurgery 93.59
- Gardner Wells tongs (skull) (with synchronous skeletal traction) 02.94
- gastric bubble (balloon) 44.93
- globe, into eye socket 16.69
- Greenfield filter 38.7
- halo device (skull) (with synchronous skeletal traction) 02.94
- Harrington rod (*see also* Fusion, spinal, by level)
  - with dorsal, dorsolumbar fusion 81.05
- Harris pin 79.15
- heart
  - assist system — *see* Implant, heart assist system

Insertion — *continued*
- heart — *continued*
  - cardiac support device (CSD) 37.41
  - circulatory assist system — *see* Implant, heart assist system
  - CorCap™ 37.41
  - epicardial support device 37.41
  - pacemaker — *see* Insertion, pacemaker, cardiac
  - prosthetic cardiac support device 37.41
  - pump (Kantrowitz) 37.62
  - valve — *see* Replacement, heart valve
  - ventricular support device 37.41
- hip prosthesis (partial) 81.52
  - revision NOS 81.53
    - acetabular and femoral components (total) 00.70
    - acetabular component only 00.71
    - acetabular liner and/or femoral head only 00.73
    - femoral component only 00.72
    - femoral head only and/or acetabular liner 00.73
    - partial
      - acetabular component only 00.71
      - acetabular liner and/or femoral head only 00.73
      - femoral component only 00.72
      - femoral head only and/or acetabular liner 00.73
    - total (acetabular and femoral components) 00.70
  - total 81.51
    - revision
      - acetabular and femoral components (total) 00.70
      - total (acetabular and femoral components) 00.70
- Holter valve 02.2
- Hufnagel valve — *see* Replacement, heart valve
- implant — *see* Insertion, prosthesis
- infusion pump 86.06
- interbody spinal fusion device 84.51
- intercostal catheter (with water seal), for drainage 34.04
  - revision (with lysis of adhesions) 34.04
  - thoracoscopic 34.06
- intra-arterial blood gas monitoring system 89.60
- intrauterine
  - contraceptive device 69.7
  - radium (intracavitary) 69.91
  - tamponade (nonobstetric) 69.91
- Kantrowitz
  - heart pump 37.62
  - pulsation balloon (phase-shift) 37.61
- keratoprosthesis 11.73
- King-Mills umbrella device (heart) 35.52
- Kirschner wire 93.44
  - with reduction of fracture or dislocation — *see* Reduction, fracture *and* Reduction, dislocation
- knee prosthesis (partial) (total) 81.54
  - revision NOS 81.55
    - femoral component 00.82
    - partial
      - femoral component 00.82
      - patellar component 00.83
      - tibial component 00.81
      - tibial insert 00.84
    - patellar component 00.83
    - tibial component 00.81
    - tibial insert 00.84
    - total (all components) 00.80
- laminaria, cervix 69.93

J

K

L

N

O

Q

R

Note — Also use 00.40, 00.41, 00.42, or 00.43 to show the total number of vessels treated. Use code 00.44 once to show procedure on a bifurcated vessel. In addition, use 00.45, 00.46, 00.47, or 00.48 to show the number of vascular stents inserted.

Repair — *continued*
bone (*see also* Osteoplasty — *see* category) — *continued*
for malunion, nonunion, or delayed union of fracture — *see* Repair, fracture, malunion or nonunion
accessory sinus 22.79
cranium NEC 02.06
with
flap (bone) 02.03
graft (bone) 02.04
nasal 21.89
skull NEC 02.06
with
flap (bone) 02.03
graft (bone) 02.04
bottle, hydrocele of tunica vaginalis 61.2
brain (trauma) NEC 02.92
breast (plastic) (*see also* Mammoplasty) 85.89
broad ligament 69.29
bronchus NEC 33.48
laceration (by suture) 33.41
bunionette (with osteotomy) 77.54
canaliculus, lacrimal 09.73
canthus (lateral) 08.59
cardiac pacemaker NEC 37.89
electrode(s) (lead) NEC 37.75
cardioverter/defibrillator (automatic) pocket (skin) (subcutaneous) 37.99
cerebral meninges 02.12
cervix 67.69
internal os 67.59
transabdominal 67.51
transvaginal 67.59
laceration (by suture) 67.61
obstetric (current) 75.51
old 67.69
chest wall (mesh) (silastic) NEC 34.79
chordae tendineae 35.32
choroid NEC 14.9
with retinal repair — *see* Repair, retina
cisterna chyli 40.69
claw toe 77.57
cleft
hand 82.82
laryngotracheal 31.69
lip 27.54
palate 27.62
secondary or subsequent 27.63
coarctation of aorta — *see* Excision, coarctation of aorta
cochlear prosthetic device 20.99
external components only 95.49
cockup toe 77.58
colostomy 46.43
conjunctiva NEC 10.49
with scleral repair 12.81
laceration 10.6
with repair of sclera 12.81
late effect of trachoma 10.49
cornea NEC 11.59
with
conjunctival flap 11.53
transplant — *see* Keratoplasty
postoperative dehiscence 11.52
coronary artery NEC 36.99
by angioplasty — *see* Angioplasty, coronary
by atherectomy — *see* Angioplasty, coronary
cranium NEC 02.06
with
flap (bone) 02.03
graft (bone) 02.04
cusp, valve — *see* Repair, heart, valve
cystocele 70.51
with graft or prosthesis 70.54
and rectocele 70.50
with graft or prosthesis 70.53
dental arch 24.8
diaphragm NEC 34.84

Repair — *continued*
diastasis recti 83.65
diastematomyelia 03.59
ear (external) 18.79
auditory canal or meatus 18.6
auricle NEC 18.79
cartilage NEC 18.79
laceration (by suture) 18.4
lop ear 18.79
middle NEC 19.9
prominent or protruding 18.5
ectropion 08.49
by or with
lid reconstruction 08.44
suture (technique) 08.42
thermocauterization 08.41
wedge resection 08.43
encephalocele (cerebral) 02.12
endocardial cushion defect 35.73
with
prosthesis (grafted to septa) 35.54
tissue graft 35.63
enterocele (female) 70.92
with graft or prosthesis 70.93
male 53.9
enterostomy 46.40
entropion 08.49
by or with
lid reconstruction 08.44
suture (technique) 08.42
thermocauterization 08.41
wedge resection 08.43
epicanthus (fold) 08.59
epididymis (and spermatic cord) NEC 63.59
with vas deferens 63.89
epiglottis 31.69
episiotomy
routine following delivery — *see* Episiotomy
secondary 75.69
epispadias 58.45
esophagus, esophageal NEC 42.89
fistula NEC 42.84
stricture 42.85
exstrophy of bladder 57.86
eyebrow 08.89
linear 08.81
eye, eyeball 16.89
multiple structures 16.82
rupture 16.82
socket 16.64
with graft 16.63
eyelid 08.89
full-thickness 08.85
involving lid margin 08.84
laceration 08.81
full-thickness 08.85
involving lid margin 08.84
partial-thickness 08.83
involving lid margin 08.82
linear 08.81
partial-thickness 08.83
involving lid margin 08.82
retraction 08.38
fallopian tube (with prosthesis) 66.79
by
anastomosis 66.73
reanastomosis 66.79
reimplantation into
ovary 66.72
uterus 66.74
suture 66.71
false aneurysm — *see* Repair, aneurysm
fascia 83.89
by or with
arthroplasty — *see* Arthroplasty
graft (fascial) (muscle) 83.82
hand 82.72
tendon 83.81
hand 82.79
suture (direct) 83.65
hand 82.46
hand 82.89

Repair — *continued*
fascia — *continued*
hand — *continued*
by
graft NEC 82.79
fascial 82.72
muscle 82.72
suture (direct) 82.46
joint — *see* Arthroplasty
filtering bleb (corneal) (scleral) (by excision) 12.82
by
corneal graft (*see also* Keratoplasty) 11.60
scleroplasty 12.82
suture 11.51
with conjunctival flap 11.53
fistula (*see also* Closure, fistula)
anovaginal 70.73
arteriovenous 39.53
clipping 39.53
coagulation 39.53
endovascular approach 39.79
head and neck 39.72
division 39.53
excision or resection (*see also* Aneurysmectomy, by site)
with
anastomosis — *see* Aneurysmectomy, with anasto-mosis, by site
graft replacement — *see* Aneurysmectomy, with graft replacement, by site
ligation 39.53
coronary artery 36.99
occlusion 39.53
endovascular approach 39.79
head and neck 39.72
suture 39.53
cervicovesical 57.84
cervix 67.62
choledochoduodenal 51.72
colovaginal 70.72
enterovaginal 70.74
enterovesical 57.83
esophagocutaneous 42.84
ileovesical 57.83
intestinovaginal 70.74
intestinovesical 57.83
oroantral 22.71
perirectal 48.93
pleuropericardial 37.49
rectovaginal 70.73
rectovesical 57.83
rectovesicovaginal 57.83
scrotum 61.42
sigmoidovaginal 70.74
sinus
nasal 22.71
of Valsalva 35.39
splenocolic 41.95
urethroperineovesical 57.84
urethrovesical 57.84
urethrovesicovaginal 57.84
uterovesical 57.84
vagina NEC 70.75
vaginocutaneous 70.75
vaginoenteric NEC 70.74
vaginoileal 70.74
vaginoperineal 70.75
vaginovesical 57.84
vesicocervicovaginal 57.84
vesicocolic 57.83
vesicocutaneous 57.84
vesicoenteric 57.83
vesicointestinal 57.83
vesicometrorectal 57.83
vesicoperineal 57.84
vesicorectal 57.83
vesicosigmoidal 57.83
vesicosigmoidovaginal 57.83

Repair — *continued*
fistula (*see also* Closure, fistula) — *continued*
vesicourethral 57.84
vesicourethrorectal 57.83
vesicouterine 57.84
vesicovaginal 57.84
vulva 71.72
vulvorectal 48.73
foramen ovale (patent) 35.71
with
prosthesis (open heart technique) 35.51
closed heart technique 35.52
tissue graft 35.61
fracture (*see also* Reduction, fracture)
larynx 31.64
malunion or nonunion (delayed) NEC — *see* category 78.4 ☑
with
graft — *see* Graft, bone
insertion (of)
bone growth stimulator (invasive) — *see* category 78.9 ☑
internal fixation device 78.5 ☑
manipulation for realignment — *see* Reduction, fracture, by site, closed
osteotomy
with
correction of alignment — *see* category 77.3 ☑
with internal fixation device — *see* categories 77.3 ☑ *[78.5]* ☑
with intramedullary rod — *see* categories 77.3 ☑ *[78.5]* ☑
replacement arthroplasty — *see* Arthroplasty
sequestrectomy — *see* category 77.0 ☑
Sofield type procedure — *see* categories 77.3 ☑ *[78.5]* ☑
synostosis technique — *see* Arthrodesis
vertebra 03.53
funnel chest (with implant) 34.74
gallbladder 51.91
gastroschisis 54.71
great vessels NEC 39.59
laceration (by suture) 39.30
artery 39.31
vein 39.32
hallux valgus NEC 77.59
resection of joint with prosthetic implant 77.59
hammer toe 77.56
hand 82.89
with graft or implant 82.79
fascia 82.72
muscle 82.72
tendon 82.79
heart 37.49
assist system 37.63
septum 35.70
with
prosthesis 35.50
tissue graft 35.60
atrial 35.71
with
prosthesis (open heart technique) 35.51
closed heart technique 35.52
tissue graft 35.61

Repair — *continued*
heart — *continued*
septum — *continued*
atrial — *continued*
combined with repair of valvular and ventricular septal defects — *see* Repair, endocardial cushion defect
in total repair of
tetralogy of Fallot 35.81
total anomalous pulmonary venous connection 35.82
truncus arteriosus 35.83
combined with repair of valvular defect — *see* Repair, endocardial cushion defect
ventricular 35.72
with
prosthesis (open heart technique) 35.53
closed heart technique 35.55
tissue graft 35.62
combined with repair of valvular and atrial septal defects — *see* Repair, endocardial cushion defect
in total repair of
tetralogy of Fallot 35.81
total anomalous pulmonary venous connection 35.82
truncus arteriosus 35.83
total internal biventricular replacement system 37.52
implantable battery 37.54
implantable controller 37.54
thoracic unit 37.53
transcutaneous energy transfer (TET) device 37.54
valve (cusps) (open heart technique) 35.10
with prosthesis or tissue graft 35.20
aortic (without replacement) 35.11
with
prosthesis 35.22
tissue graft 35.21
combined with repair of atrial and ventricular septal defects — *see* Repair, endocardial cushion defect
mitral (without replacement) 35.12
with
prosthesis 35.24
tissue graft 35.23
pulmonary (without replacement) 35.13
with
prosthesis 35.26
in total repair of tetralogy of Fallot 35.81
tissue graft 35.25
tricuspid (without replacement) 35.14
with
prosthesis 35.28
tissue graft 35.27
hepatic duct 51.79
hernia NEC 53.9
anterior abdominal wall NEC 53.59
with prosthesis or graft
laparoscopic 53.63
other and open 53.69
colostomy 46.42
crural 53.29
cul-de-sac (Douglas') 70.92
diaphragmatic
abdominal approach
laparoscopic 53.71

Repair — *continued*
hernia — *continued*
diaphragmatic — *continued*
abdominal approach — *continued*
other and open 53.72
unspecified 53.75
thoracic, thoracoabdominal approach 53.80
laparoscopic 53.83
other and open 53.84
epigastric 53.59
with prosthesis or graft 53.69
esophageal hiatus
abdominal approach
laparoscopic 53.71
other and open 53.72
unspecified 53.75
thoracic, thoracoabdominal approach 53.80
fascia 83.89
hand 82.89
femoral (unilateral) 53.29
with prosthesis or graft 53.21
bilateral 53.39
with prosthesis or graft 53.31
Ferguson 53.00
Halsted 53.00
Hill-Allison (hiatal hernia repair, transpleural approach) 53.80
hypogastric 53.59
with prosthesis or graft 53.69
incisional 53.51
laparoscopic with prosthesis or graft 53.62
other open with prosthesis or graft 53.61
inguinal (unilateral) 53.00
with prosthesis or graft 53.05
bilateral 53.10
with prosthesis or graft 53.17
laparoscopic 17.24
direct
laparoscopic with graft or prosthesis 17.21
other and open 53.11
with prosthesis or graft 53.14
direct and indirect
laparoscopic with graft or prosthesis 17.23
other and open 53.13
with prosthesis or graft 53.16
indirect
laparoscopic with graft or prosthesis 17.22
other and open 53.12
with prosthesis or graft 53.15
direct (unilateral)
with prosthesis or graft 53.03
and indirect (unilateral)
laparoscopic with graft or prosthesis 17.11
other and open 53.01
with prosthesis or graft 53.03
laparoscopic with graft or prosthesis 17.11
other and open 53.01
with prosthesis or graft 53.03
indirect (unilateral)
laparoscopic with graft or prosthesis 17.12
other and open 53.02
with prosthesis or graft 53.04
internal 53.9
ischiatic 53.9
ischiorectal 53.9
laparoscopic with graft or prosthesis, NOS 17.13
lumbar 53.9
manual 96.27

Repair — *continued*
hernia — *continued*
obturator 53.9
omental 53.9
paraesophageal
laparoscopic 53.71
other and open 53.72
unspecified 53.75
parahiatal
laparoscopic 53.71
other and open 53.72
unspecified 53.75
paraileostomy 46.41
parasternal 53.82
paraumbilical
laparoscopic 53.43
with graft or prosthesis 53.42
other and open with graft or prosthesis 53.41
other open 53.49
pericolostomy 46.42
perineal (enterocele) 53.9
preperitoneal 53.29
pudendal 53.9
retroperitoneal 53.9
sciatic 53.9
scrotal — *see* Repair, hernia, inguinal
spigelian 53.59
with prosthesis or graft 53.69
umbilical
laparoscopic 53.43
with graft or prosthesis 53.42
other and open with graft or prosthesis 53.41
other open 53.49
uveal 12.39
ventral 53.59
with prosthesis or graft
laparoscopic 53.63
other and open 53.69
incisional 53.51
other open with prosthesis or graft 53.61
hydrocele
round ligament 69.19
spermatic cord 63.1
tunica vaginalis 61.2
hymen 70.76
hypospadias 58.45
ileostomy 46.41
ingrown toenail 86.23
intestine, intestinal NEC 46.79
fistula — *see* Closure, fistula, intestine
laceration
large intestine 46.75
small intestine NEC 46.73
stoma — *see* Repair, stoma
inverted uterus NEC 69.29
manual
nonobstetric 69.94
obstetric 75.94
obstetrical
manual 75.94
surgical 75.93
vaginal approach 69.23
iris (rupture) NEC 12.39
jejunostomy 46.41
joint (capsule) (cartilage) NEC (*see also* Arthroplasty) 81.96
kidney NEC 55.89
knee (joint) NEC 81.47
collateral ligaments 81.46
cruciate ligaments 81.45
five-in-one 81.42
triad 81.43
labia — *see* Repair, vulva
laceration — *see* Suture, by site
lacrimal system NEC 09.99
canaliculus 09.73
punctum 09.72
for eversion 09.71
laryngostomy 31.62
laryngotracheal cleft 31.69
larynx 31.69

Repair — *continued*
larynx — *continued*
fracture 31.64
laceration 31.61
leads (cardiac) NEC 37.75
ligament (*see also* Arthroplasty) 81.96
broad 69.29
collateral, knee NEC 81.46
cruciate, knee NEC 81.45
round 69.29
uterine 69.29
lip NEC 27.59
cleft 27.54
laceration (by suture) 27.51
liver NEC 50.69
laceration 50.61
lop ear 18.79
lung NEC 33.49
lymphatic (channel) (peripheral) NEC 40.9
duct, left (thoracic) NEC 40.69
macrodactyly 82.83
mallet finger 82.84
mandibular ridge 76.64
mastoid (antrum) (cavity) 19.9
meninges (cerebral) NEC 02.12
spinal NEC 03.59
meningocele 03.51
myelomeningocele 03.52
meningocele (spinal) 03.51
cranial 02.12
mesentery 54.75
mouth NEC 27.59
laceration NEC 27.52
muscle NEC 83.87
by
graft or implant (fascia) (muscle) 83.82
hand 82.72
tendon 83.81
hand 82.79
suture (direct) 83.65
hand 82.46
transfer or transplantation (muscle) 83.77
hand 82.58
hand 82.89
by
graft or implant NEC 82.79
fascia 82.72
suture (direct) 82.46
transfer or transplantation (muscle) 82.58
musculotendinous cuff, shoulder 83.63
myelomeningocele 03.52
nasal
septum (perforation) NEC 21.88
sinus NEC 22.79
fistula 22.71
nasolabial flaps (plastic) 21.86
nasopharyngeal atresia 29.4
nerve (cranial) (peripheral) NEC 04.79
old injury 04.76
revision 04.75
sympathetic 05.81
nipple NEC 85.87
nose (external) (internal) (plastic) NEC (*see also* Rhinoplasty) 21.89
laceration (by suture) 21.81
notched lip 27.59
omentum 54.74
omphalocele
laparoscopic 53.43
with graft or prosthesis 53.42
other and open with graft or prosthesis 53.41
other open 53.49
orbit 16.89
wound 16.81
ostium
primum defect 35.73
with
prosthesis 35.54
tissue graft 35.63
secundum defect 35.71

S

Therapy — *continued*
shock — *continued*
electric 94.27
subconvulsive 94.26
insulin 94.24
speech 93.75
for correction of defect 93.74
SuperOxygenation (SSO_2) 00.49
SuperSaturated oxygen 00.49
ultrasound
heat therapy 93.35
hyperthermia for cancer treatment 99.85
physical therapy 93.35
therapeutic — *see* Ultrasound
ultraviolet light 99.82
Thermocautery — *see* Cauterization
Thermography 88.89
blood vessel 88.86
bone 88.83
breast 88.85
cerebral 88.81
eye 88.82
lymph gland 88.89
muscle 88.84
ocular 88.82
osteoarticular 88.83
specified site NEC 88.89
vein, deep 88.86
Thermokeratoplasty 11.74
Thermosclerectomy 12.62
Thermotherapy (hot packs) (paraffin bath) NEC 93.35
prostate
by
microwave 60.96
radiofrequency 60.97
transurethral microwave thermotherapy (TUMT) 60.96
transurethral needle ablation (TUNA) 60.97
TUMT (transurethral microwave thermotherapy) 60.96
TUNA (transurethral needle ablation) 60.97
Thiersch operation
anus 49.79
skin graft 86.69
hand 86.62
Thompson operation
cleft lip repair 27.54
correction of lymphedema 40.9
quadricepsplasty 83.86
thumb apposition with bone graft 82.69
Thoracectomy 34.09
for lung collapse 33.34
Thoracentesis 34.91
Thoracocentesis 34.91
Thoracolysis (for collapse of lung) 33.39
Thoracoplasty (anterior) (extrapleural) (paravertebral) (posterolateral) (complete) (partial) 33.34
Thoracoscopy, transpleural (for exploration) 34.21
Thoracostomy 34.09
for lung collapse 33.32
Thoracotomy (with drainage) 34.09
as operative approach — *omit code*
exploratory 34.02
Thoratec® implantable ventricular assist device (IVAD™) 37.66
Thoratec® ventricular assist device (VAD) system 37.66
Three-snip operation, punctum 09.51
Thrombectomy 38.00
with endarterectomy — *see* Endarterectomy
abdominal
artery 38.06
vein 38.07
aorta (arch) (ascending) (descending) 38.04
arteriovenous shunt or cannula 39.49
bovine graft 39.49
coronary artery 36.09
Thrombectomy — *continued*
head and neck vessel NEC 38.02
intracranial vessel NEC 38.01
lower limb
artery 38.08
vein 38.09
mechanical
endovascular
head and neck 39.74
pulmonary vessel 38.05
thoracic vessel NEC 38.05
upper limb (artery) (vein) 38.03
Thromboendarterectomy 38.10
abdominal 38.16
aorta (arch) (ascending) (descending) 38.14
coronary artery 36.09
open chest approach 36.03
head and neck NEC 38.12
intracranial NEC 38.11
lower limb 38.18
thoracic NEC 38.15
upper limb 38.13
Thymectomy 07.80
partial (open) (other) 07.81
thoracoscopic 07.83
total (open) (other) 07.82
thoracoscopic 07.84
transcervical 07.99
Thyrochondrotomy 31.3
Thyrocricoidectomy 30.29
Thyrocricotomy (for assistance in breathing) 31.1
Thyroidectomy NEC 06.39
by mediastinotomy (*see also* Thyroidectomy, substernal) 06.50
with laryngectomy — *see* Laryngectomy
complete or total 06.4
substernal (by mediastinotomy) (transsternal route) 06.52
transoral route (lingual) 06.6
lingual (complete) (partial) (subtotal) (total) 06.6
partial or subtotal NEC 06.39
with complete removal of remaining lobe 06.2
submental route (lingual) 06.6
substernal (by mediastinotomy) (transsternal route) 06.51
remaining tissue 06.4
submental route (lingual) 06.6
substernal (by mediastinotomy) (transsternal route) 06.50
complete or total 06.52
partial or subtotal 06.51
transoral route (lingual) 06.6
transsternal route (*see also* Thyroidectomy, substernal) 06.50
unilateral (with removal of isthmus) (with removal of portion of other lobe) 06.2
Thyroidorrhaphy 06.93
Thyroidotomy (field) (gland) NEC 06.09
postoperative 06.02
Thyrotomy 31.3
with tantalum plate 31.69
Tirofiban (HCl), infusion 99.20
Toilette
skin — *see* Debridement, skin or subcutaneous tissue
tracheostomy 96.55
Token economy (behavior therapy) 94.33
Tomkins operation (metroplasty) 69.49
Tomography — *see also* Radiography
abdomen NEC 88.02
cardiac 87.42
computerized axial NEC 88.38
abdomen 88.01
bone 88.38
quantitative 88.98
brain 87.03
cardiac 87.41
coronary 87.41
head 87.03
Tomography — *see also* Radiography — *continued*
computerized axial — *continued*
kidney 87.71
skeletal 88.38
quantitative 88.98
thorax 87.41
head NEC 87.04
kidney NEC 87.72
lung 87.42
thorax NEC 87.42
Tongue tie operation 25.91
Tonography 95.26
Tonometry 89.11
Tonsillectomy 28.2
with adenoidectomy 28.3
Tonsillotomy 28.0
Topectomy 01.32
Torek (-Bevan) operation (orchidopexy) (first stage) (second stage) 62.5
Torkildsen operation (ventriculocisternal shunt) 02.2
Torpin operation (cul-de-sac resection) 70.92
Toti operation (dacryocystorhinostomy) 09.81
Touchas operation 86.83
Touroff operation (ligation of subclavian artery) 38.85
Toxicology — *see* Examination, microscopic
TPN (total parenteral nutrition) 99.15
Trabeculectomy ab externo 12.64
Trabeculodialysis 12.59
Trabeculotomy ab externo 12.54
Trachelectomy 67.4
Trachelopexy 69.22
Tracheloplasty 67.69
Trachelorrhaphy (Emmet) (suture) 67.61
obstetrical 75.51
Trachelotomy 69.95
obstetrical 73.93
Tracheocricotomy (for assistance in breathing) 31.1
Tracheofissure 31.1
Tracheography 87.32
Tracheolaryngotomy (emergency) 31.1
permanent opening 31.29
Tracheoplasty 31.79
with artificial larynx 31.75
Tracheorrhaphy 31.71
Tracheoscopy NEC 31.42
through tracheotomy (stoma) 31.41
Tracheostomy (emergency) (temporary) (for assistance in breathing) 31.1
mediastinal 31.21
percutaneous dilatational
other permanent 31.29
temporary 31.1
permanent NEC 31.29
revision 31.74
Tracheotomy (emergency) (temporary) (for assistance in breathing) 31.1
percutaneous dilatational
other permanent 31.29
temporary 31.1
permanent 31.29
Tracing, carotid pulse with ECG lead 89.56
Traction
with reduction of fracture or dislocation — *see* Reduction, fracture *and* Reduction, dislocation
adhesive tape (skin) 93.46
boot 93.46
Bryant's (skeletal) 93.44
Buck's 93.46
caliper tongs 93.41
with synchronous insertion of device 02.94
Cortel's (spinal) 93.42
Crutchfield tongs 93.41
with synchronous insertion of device 02.94
Dunlop's (skeletal) 93.44
gallows 93.46
Traction — *continued*
Gardner Wells 93.41
with synchronous insertion of device 02.94
halo device, skull 93.41
with synchronous insertion of device 02.94
Lyman Smith (skeletal) 93.44
manual, intermittent 93.21
mechanical, intermittent 93.21
Russell's (skeletal) 93.44
skeletal NEC 93.44
intermittent 93.43
skin, limbs NEC 93.46
spinal NEC 93.42
with skull device (halo) (caliper) (Crutchfield) (Gardner Wells) (Vinke) (tongs) 93.41
with synchronous insertion of device 02.94
Thomas' splint 93.45
Vinke tongs 93.41
with synchronous insertion of device 02.94
Tractotomy
brain 01.32
medulla oblongata 01.32
mesencephalon 01.32
percutaneous 03.21
spinal cord (one-stage) (two-stage) 03.29
trigeminal (percutaneous) (radiofrequency) 04.02
Training (for) (in)
ADL (activities of daily living) 93.83
for the blind 93.78
ambulation 93.22
braille 93.77
crutch walking 93.24
dyslexia 93.71
dysphasia 93.72
esophageal speech (postlaryngectomy) 93.73
gait 93.22
joint movements 93.14
lip reading 93.75
Moon (blind reading) 93.77
orthoptic 95.35
prenatal (natural childbirth) 93.37
prosthetic or orthotic device usage 93.24
relaxation 94.33
speech NEC 93.75
for correction of defect 93.74
esophageal 93.73
use of lead dog for the blind 93.76
vocational 93.85
TRAM (transverse rectus abdominis musculocutaneous) flap of breast
free 85.73
pedicled 85.72
Transactional analysis
group 94.44
individual 94.39
Transection — *see also* Division
artery (with ligation) (*see also* Division, artery) 38.80
renal, aberrant (with reimplantation) 39.55
bone (*see also* Osteotomy) 77.30
fallopian tube (bilateral) (remaining) (solitary) 66.39
by endoscopy 66.22
unilateral 66.92
isthmus, thyroid 06.91
muscle 83.19
eye 15.13
multiple (two or more muscles) 15.3
hand 82.19
nerve (cranial) (peripheral) NEC 04.03
acoustic 04.01
root (spinal) 03.1
sympathetic 05.0
tracts in spinal cord 03.29
trigeminal 04.02

00. PROCEDURES AND INTERVENTIONS, NOT ELSEWHERE CLASSIFIED (00)

✓3rd 00 Procedures and interventions, not elsewhere classified

✓4th 00.0 Therapeutic ultrasound

EXCLUDES *diagnostic ultrasound (non-invasive) (88.71-88.79)*
intracardiac echocardiography [ICE] (heart chamber(s)) (37.28)
intravascular imaging (adjunctive) (00.21-00.29)

DEF: Interventional treatment modality using lower frequency and higher intensity levels of ultrasound energy than used in diagnostic ultrasound modality for the purpose of limiting intimal hyperplasia, or restenosis, associated with atherosclerotic vascular disease.

00.01 Therapeutic ultrasound of vessels of head and neck
Anti-restenotic ultrasound
Intravascular non-ablative ultrasound

EXCLUDES *diagnostic ultrasound of:*
eye (95.13)
head and neck (88.71)
that of inner ear (20.79)
ultrasonic:
angioplasty of non-coronary vessel (39.50)
embolectomy (38.01, 38.02)
endarterectomy (38.11, 38.12)
thrombectomy (38.01, 38.02)

00.02 Therapeutic ultrasound of heart
Anti-restenotic ultrasound
Intravascular non-ablative ultrasound

EXCLUDES *diagnostic ultrasound of heart (88.72)*
ultrasonic ablation of heart lesion (37.34)
ultrasonic angioplasty of coronary vessels (00.66, 36.09)

00.03 Therapeutic ultrasound of peripheral vascular vessels
Anti-restenotic ultrasound
Intravascular non-ablative ultrasound

EXCLUDES *diagnostic ultrasound of peripheral vascular system (88.77)*
ultrasonic angioplasty of:
non-coronary vessel (39.50)

00.09 Other therapeutic ultrasound

EXCLUDES *ultrasonic:*
fragmentation of urinary stones (59.95)
percutaneous nephrostomy with fragmentation (55.04)
physical therapy (93.35)
transurethral guided laser induced prostatectomy (TULIP) (60.21)

✓4th 00.1 Pharmaceuticals

00.10 Implantation of chemotherapeutic agent
Brain wafer chemotherapy
Interstitial/intracavitary

EXCLUDES *injection or infusion of cancer chemotherapeutic substance (99.25)*

DEF: Brain wafer chemotherapy: Placement of wafers containing antineoplastic agent against the wall of the resection cavity subsequent to the surgeon completing a tumor excision to deliver chemotherapy directly to the tumor site; used to treat glioblastoma multiforme (GBM).

00.11 Infusion of drotrecogin alfa (activated)
Infusion of recombinant protein

00.12 Administration of inhaled nitric oxide
Nitric oxide therapy

00.13 Injection or infusion of nesiritide
Human B-type natriuretic peptide (hBNP)

00.14 Injection or infusion of oxazolidinone class of antibiotics
Linezolid injection

00.15 High-dose infusion interleukin-2 [IL-2]
Infusion (IV bolus, CIV) interleukin
Injection of aldesleukin

EXCLUDES *low-dose infusion interleukin-2 (99.28)*

DEF: A high-dose anti-neoplastic therapy using a biological response modifier (BRM); the body naturally produces substances called interleukins, which are multi-function cytokines in the generation of an immune response.

00.16 Pressurized treatment of venous bypass graft [conduit] with pharmaceutical substance
Ex-vivo treatment of vessel
Hyperbaric pressurized graft [conduit]

DEF: Ex-vivo process of delivering small nucleic acid molecules that block protein transcription factors essential for the expression of genes controlling cell proliferation into graft tissue under nondistending pressure; reduces intimal hyperplasia and vein graft failure.

00.17 Infusion of vasopressor agent

00.18 Infusion of immunosuppressive antibody therapy
Monoclonal antibody therapy
Polyclonal antibody therapy

INCLUDES *during induction phase of solid organ transplantation*

00.19 Disruption of blood brain barrier via infusion [BBBD]
Infusion of substance to disrupt blood brain barrier

Code also chemotherapy (99.25)

EXCLUDES *other perfusion (39.97)*

DEF: Infusion of chemotherapy drug that temporarily allows the transport of materials into the brain through the blood brain barrier (BBB), which is the protective mechanism that limits transport of toxins while allowing necessary nutrients to pass from the blood vessels into the brain tissue; used in the treatment of brain cancers.

✓4th 00.2 Intravascular imaging of blood vessels

Note: Real-time imaging of lumen of blood vessel(s) using sound waves
Endovascular ultrasonography
Intravascular [ultrasound] imaging of blood vessels
Intravascular ultrasound (IVUS)

Code also any synchronous diagnostic or therapeutic procedures

EXCLUDES *adjunct vascular system procedures, number of vessels treated (00.40-00.43)*
diagnostic procedures on blood vessels (38.21-38.29)
diagnostic ultrasound of peripheral vascular system (88.77)
magnetic resonance imaging (MRI) (88.91-88.97)
therapeutic ultrasound (00.01-00.09)

00.21 Intravascular imaging of extracranial cerebral vessels
Common carotid vessels and branches
Intravascular ultrasound (IVUS), extracranial cerebral vessels

EXCLUDES *diagnostic ultrasound (non-invasive) of head and neck (88.71)*

00.22 Intravascular imaging of intrathoracic vessels
Aorta and aortic arch
Intravascular ultrasound (IVUS), intrathoracic vessels
Vena cava (superior) (inferior)

EXCLUDES *diagnostic ultrasound (non-invasive) of other sites of thorax (88.73)*

00.23 Intravascular imaging of peripheral vessels
Imaging of:
vessels of arm(s)
vessels of leg(s)
Intravascular ultrasound (IVUS), peripheral vessels

EXCLUDES *diagnostic ultrasound (non-invasive) of peripheral vascular system (88.77)*

00.24 Intravascular imaging of coronary vessels
Intravascular ultrasound (IVUS), coronary vessels

EXCLUDES *diagnostic ultrasound (non-invasive) of heart (88.72)*
intracardiac echocardiography [ICE] (ultrasound of heart chamber(s)) (37.28)

00.25 Intravascular imaging of renal vessels
Intravascular ultrasound (IVUS), renal vessels
Renal artery

EXCLUDES *diagnostic ultrasound (non-invasive) of urinary system (88.75)*

00.28 Intravascular imaging, other specified vessel(s)

00.29 Intravascular imaging, unspecified vessel(s)

✓4th **00.3 Computer assisted surgery [CAS]**
CT-free navigation
Image guided navigation (IGN)
Image guided surgery (IGS)
Imageless navigation
That without the use of robotic(s) technology
Code also diagnostic or therapeutic procedure

EXCLUDES *robotic assisted procedures (17.41-17.49)*
stereotactic frame application only (93.59)

00.31 Computer assisted surgery with CT/CTA

00.32 Computer assisted surgery with MR/MRA

00.33 Computer assisted surgery with fluoroscopy

00.34 Imageless computer assisted surgery

00.35 Computer assisted surgery with multiple datasets

00.39 Other computer assisted surgery
Computer assisted surgery NOS

✓4th **00.4 Adjunct vascular system procedures**
Note: These codes can apply to both coronary and peripheral vessels. These codes are to be used in conjunction with other therapeutic procedure codes to provide additional information on the number of vessels upon which a procedure was performed and/or the number of stents inserted. As appropriate, code both the number of vessels operated on (00.40-00.43), and the number of stents inserted (00.45-00.48).
Code also any:
angioplasty or atherectomy (00.61-00.62, 00.66, 39.50)
endarterectomy (38.10-38.18)
insertion of vascular stent(s) (00.55, 00.63-00.65, 36.06-36.07, 39.90)
other removal of coronary artery obstruction (36.09)

00.40 Procedure on single vessel
Number of vessels, unspecified

EXCLUDES *(aorto)coronary bypass (36.10-36.19)*
intravascular imaging of blood vessels (00.21-00.29)

00.41 Procedure on two vessels

EXCLUDES *(aorto)coronary bypass (36.10-36.19)*
intravascular imaging of blood vessels (00.21-00.29)

00.42 Procedure on three vessels

EXCLUDES *(aorto)coronary bypass (36.10-36.19)*
intravascular imaging of blood vessels (00.21-00.29)

00.43 Procedure on four or more vessels

EXCLUDES *(aorto)coronary bypass (36.10-36.19)*
intravascular imaging of blood vessels (00.21-00.29)

00.44 Procedure on vessel bifurcation
Note: This code is to be used to identify the presence of a vessel bifurcation; it does not describe a specific bifurcation stent. Use this code only once per operative episode, irrespective of the number of bifurcations in vessels.

00.45 Insertion of one vascular stent
Number of stents, unspecified

00.46 Insertion of two vascular stents

00.47 Insertion of three vascular stents

00.48 Insertion of four or more vascular stents

Stenting Techniques on Vessel Bifurcation

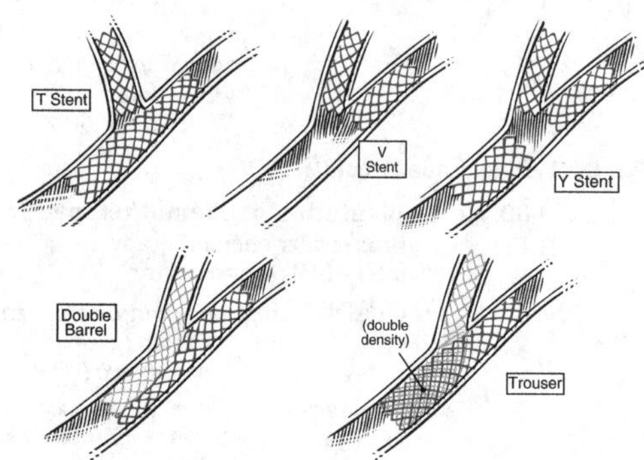

00.49 SuperSaturated oxygen therapy
Aqueous oxygen (AO) therapy
SSO_2
SuperOxygenation infusion therapy
Code also any:
injection or infusion of thrombolytic agent (99.10)
insertion of coronary artery stent(s) (36.06-36.07)
intracoronary artery thrombolytic infusion (36.04)
number of vascular stents inserted (00.45-00.48)
number of vessels treated (00.40-00.43)
open chest coronary artery angioplasty (36.03)
other removal of coronary obstruction (36.09)
percutaneous transluminal coronary angioplasty [PTCA] (00.66)
procedure on vessel bifurcation (00.44)

EXCLUDES *other oxygen enrichment (93.96)*
other perfusion (39.97)

✓4th 00.5 Other cardiovascular procedures

00.50 Implantation of cardiac resynchronization pacemaker without mention of defibrillation, total system [CRT-P]
Note: Device testing during procedure — *omit code*
Biventricular pacemaker
Biventricular pacing without internal cardiac defibrillator
BiV pacemaker
Implantation of cardiac resynchronization (biventricular) pulse generator pacing device, formation of pocket, transvenous leads including placement of lead into left ventricular coronary venous system, and intraoperative procedures for evaluation of lead signals
That with CRT-P generator and one or more leads

EXCLUDES *implantation of cardiac resynchronization defibrillator, total system [CRT-D] (00.51)*
insertion or replacement of any type pacemaker device (37.80-37.87)
replacement of cardiac resynchronization:
defibrillator, pulse generator only [CRT-D] (00.54)
pacemaker, pulse generator only [CRT-P] (00.53)

DEF: Cardiac resynchronization pacemaker: CRT-P, or bi-ventricular pacing, adds a third lead to traditional pacemaker designs that connects to the left ventricle. The device provides electrical stimulation and coordinates ventricular contractions to improve cardiac output.

00.51 Implantation of cardiac resynchronization defibrillator, total system [CRT-D]
Note: Device testing during procedure — *omit code*
BiV defibrillator
Biventricular defibrillator
Biventricular pacing with internal cardiac defibrillator
BiV ICD
BiV pacemaker with defibrillator
BiV pacing with defibrillator
Implantation of cardiac resynchronization (biventricular) pulse generator with defibrillator [AICD], formation of pocket, transvenous leads, including placement of lead into left ventricular coronary venous system, intraoperative procedures for evaluation of lead signals, and obtaining defibrillator threshold measurements
That with CRT-D generator and one or more leads

EXCLUDES *implantation of cardiac resynchronization pacemaker, total system [CRT-P] (00.50)*
implantation or replacement of automatic cardioverter/ defibrillator, total system [AICD] (37.94)
replacement of cardiac resynchronization defibrillator, pulse generator only [CRT-D] (00.54)

00.52 Implantation or replacement of transvenous lead [electrode] into left ventricular coronary venous system

EXCLUDES *implantation of cardiac resynchronization:*
defibrillator, total system [CRT-D] (00.51)
pacemaker, total system [CRT-P] (00.50)
initial insertion of transvenous lead [electrode] (37.70-37.72)
replacement of transvenous atrial and/or ventricular lead(s) [electrodes] (37.76)

00.53 Implantation or replacement of cardiac resynchronization pacemaker, pulse generator only [CRT-P]
Note: Device testing during procedure — *omit code*
Implantation of CRT-P device with removal of any existing CRT-P or other pacemaker device

EXCLUDES *implantation of cardiac resynchronization pacemaker, total system [CRT-P] (00.50)*
implantation or replacement of cardiac resynchronization defibrillator, pulse generator only [CRT-D] (00.54)
insertion or replacement of any type pacemaker device (37.80-37.87)

00.54 Implantation or replacement of cardiac resynchronization defibrillator, pulse generator device only [CRT-D]

Note: Device testing during procedure — *omit code*

Implantation of CRT-D device with removal of any existing CRT-D, CRT-P, pacemaker, or defibrillator device

EXCLUDES *implantation of automatic cardioverter/defibrillator pulse generator only (37.96)*
implantation of cardiac resynchronization defibrillator, total system [CRT-D] (00.51)
implantation or replacement of cardiac resynchronization pacemaker, pulse generator only [CRT-P] (00.53)

00.55 Insertion of drug-eluting peripheral vessel stent(s)

Endograft(s)
Endovascular graft(s)
Stent graft(s)

Code also any:
angioplasty or atherectomy of other non-coronary vessel(s) (39.50)
number of vascular stents inserted (00.45-00.48)
number of vessels treated (00.40-00.43)
procedure on vessel bifurcation (00.44)

EXCLUDES *drug-coated peripheral stents, e.g., heparin coated (39.90)*
insertion of cerebrovascular stent(s) (00.63-00.65)
insertion of drug-eluting coronary artery stent (36.07)
insertion of non-drug-eluting stent(s):
coronary artery (36.06)
peripheral vessel (39.90)
that for aneurysm repair (39.71-39.79)

00.56 Insertion or replacement of implantable pressure sensor (lead) for intracardiac hemodynamic monitoring

Code also any associated implantation or replacement of monitor (00.57)

EXCLUDES *circulatory monitoring (blood gas, arterial or venous pressure, cardiac output and coronary blood flow) (89.60-89.69)*

DEF: Insertion of an implantable device consisting of a data storage system, a single lead with a pressure sensor tip and a wireless antenna that continuously collects data on heart rate, pressures, physical activity and temperature.

00.57 Implantation or replacement of subcutaneous device for intracardiac hemodynamic monitoring

Implantation of monitoring device with formation of subcutaneous pocket and connection to intracardiac pressure sensor (lead)

Code also any associated insertion or replacement of implanted pressure sensor (lead) (00.56)

00.58 Insertion of intra-aneurysm sac pressure monitoring device (intraoperative)

Insertion of pressure sensor during endovascular repair of abdominal or thoracic aortic aneurysm(s)

00.59 Intravascular pressure measurement of coronary arteries

INCLUDES fractional flow reserve (FFR)

Code also any synchronous diagnostic or therapeutic procedures

EXCLUDES *intravascular pressure measurement of intrathoracic arteries (00.67)*

✓4th 00.6 Procedures on blood vessels

00.61 Percutaneous angioplasty or atherectomy of precerebral (extracranial) vessel(s)

Basilar
Carotid
Vertebral

Code also any:
injection or infusion of thrombolytic agent (99.10)
number of vascular stents inserted (00.45-00.48)
number of vessels treated (00.40-00.43)
percutaneous insertion of carotid artery stent(s) (00.63)
percutaneous insertion of other precerebral artery stent(s) (00.64)
procedure on vessel bifurcation (00.44)

EXCLUDES *angioplasty or atherectomy of other non-coronary vessel(s) (39.50)*
removal of cerebrovascular obstruction of vessel(s) by open approach (38.01-38.02, 38.11-38.12, 38.31-38.32, 38.41-38.42)

00.62 Percutaneous angioplasty or atherectomy intracranial vessel(s)

Code also any:
injection or infusion of thrombolytic agent (99.10)
number of vascular stents inserted (00.45-00.48)
number of vessels treated (00.40-00.43)
percutaneous insertion of intracranial stent(s) (00.65)
procedure on vessel bifurcation (00.44)

EXCLUDES *angioplasty or atherectomy of other non-coronary vessel(s) (39.50)*
removal of cerebrovascular obstruction of vessel(s) by open approach (38.01-38.02, 38.11-38.12, 38.31-38.32, 38.41-38.42)

00.63 Percutaneous insertion of carotid artery stent(s)

Includes the use of any embolic protection device, distal protection device, filter device, or stent delivery system
Non-drug-eluting stent

Code also any:
number of vascular stents inserted (00.45-00.48)
number of vessels treated (00.40-00.43)
percutaneous angioplasty or atherectomy of precerebral vessel(s) (00.61)
procedure on vessel bifurcation (00.44)

EXCLUDES *angioplasty or atherectomy of other non-coronary vessel(s) (39.50)*
insertion of drug-eluting peripheral vessel stent(s) (00.55)

00.64 Percutaneous insertion of other precerebral (extracranial) artery stent(s)

Includes the use of any embolic protection device, distal protection device, filter device, or stent delivery system

Basilar stent

Vertebral stent

Code also any:
- number of vascular stents inserted (00.45-00.48)
- number of vessels treated (00.40-00.43)
- percutaneous angioplasty or atherectomy of precerebral vessel(s) (00.61)
- procedure on vessel bifurcation (00.44)

EXCLUDES *angioplasty or atherectomy of other non-coronary vessel(s) (39.50)*
insertion of drug-eluting peripheral vessel stent(s) (00.55)

00.65 Percutaneous insertion of intracranial vascular stent(s)

Includes the use of any embolic protection device, distal protection device, filter device, or stent delivery system

Code also any:
- number of vascular stents inserted (00.45-00.48)
- number of vessels treated (00.40-00.43)
- percutaneous angioplasty or atherectomy of intracranial vessel(s) (00.62)
- procedure on vessel bifurcation (00.44)

EXCLUDES *angioplasty or atherectomy of other non-coronary vessel(s) (39.50)*
insertion of drug-eluting peripheral vessel stent(s) (00.55)

00.66 Percutaneous transluminal coronary angioplasty [PTCA] or coronary atherectomy

Balloon angioplasty of coronary artery

Coronary atherectomy

Percutaneous coronary angioplasty NOS

PTCA NOS

Code also any:
- injection or infusion of thrombolytic agent (99.10)
- insertion of coronary artery stent(s) (36.06-36.07)
- intracoronary artery thrombolytic infusion (36.04)
- number of vascular stents inserted (00.45-00.48)
- number of vessels treated (00.40-00.43)
- procedure on vessel bifurcation (00.44)
- SuperSaturated oxygen therapy (00.49)

DEF: Balloon angioplasty: Insertion of catheter with inflation of balloon to flatten plaque and widen vessels.

PTCA (Balloon Angioplasty)

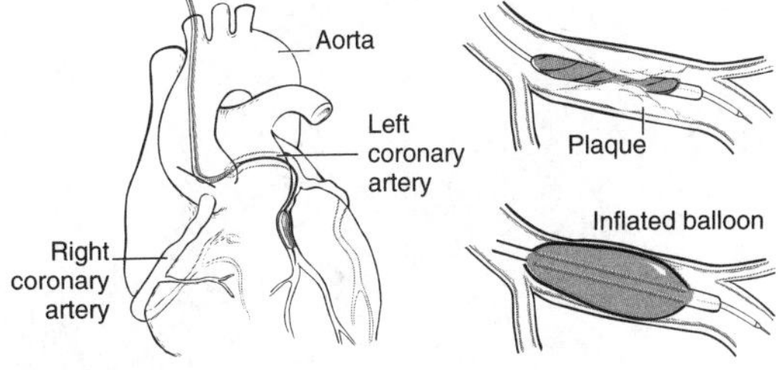

00.67 Intravascular pressure measurement of intrathoracic arteries

Assessment of:
- aorta and aortic arch
- carotid

Code also any synchronous diagnostic or therapeutic procedures

00.68 Intravascular pressure measurement of peripheral arteries

Assessment of:
- other peripheral vessels
- vessels of arm(s)
- vessels of leg(s)

Code also any synchronous diagnostic or therapeutic procedures

00.69 Intravascular pressure measurement, other specified and unspecified vessels

Assessment of:
- iliac vessels
- intra-abdominal vessels
- mesenteric vessels
- renal vessels

Code also any synchronous diagnostic or therapeutic procedures

EXCLUDES *intravascular pressure measurement of:*
coronary arteries (00.59)
intrathoracic arteries (00.67)
peripheral arteries (00.68)

✓4th 00.7 Other hip procedures

00.70 Revision of hip replacement, both acetabular and femoral components

Total hip revision

Code also any:
- removal of (cement) (joint) spacer (84.57)
- type of bearing surface, if known (00.74-00.77)

EXCLUDES *revision of hip replacement, acetabular component only (00.71)*
revision of hip replacement, femoral component only (00.72)
revision of hip replacement, not otherwise specified (81.53)
revision with replacement of acetabular liner and/or femoral head only (00.73)

00.71 Revision of hip replacement, acetabular component

Partial, acetabular component only

That with:
- exchange of acetabular cup and liner
- exchange of femoral head

Code also any type of bearing surface, if known (00.74-00.77)

EXCLUDES *revision of hip replacement, both acetabular and femoral components (00.70)*
revision of hip replacement, femoral component (00.72)
revision of hip replacement, not otherwise specified (81.53)
revision with replacement of acetabular liner and/or femoral head only (00.73)

00.72 Revision of hip replacement, femoral component
Partial, femoral component only
That with:
exchange of acetabular liner
exchange of femoral stem and head
Code also any type of bearing surface, if known (00.74-00.77)
EXCLUDES *revision of hip replacement, acetabular component (00.71)*
revision of hip replacement, both acetabular and femoral components (00.70)
revision of hip replacement, not otherwise specified (81.53)
revision with replacement of acetabular liner and/or femoral head only (00.73)

00.73 Revision of hip replacement, acetabular liner and/or femoral head only
Code also any type of bearing surface, if known (00.74-00.77)

00.74 Hip bearing surface, metal-on-polyethylene

00.75 Hip bearing surface, metal-on-metal

00.76 Hip bearing surface, ceramic-on-ceramic

00.77 Hip bearing surface, ceramic-on-polyethylene

✓4th **00.8 Other knee and hip procedures**
Note: Report up to two components using 00.81-00.83 to describe revision of knee replacements. If all three components are revised, report 00.80.

00.80 Revision of knee replacement, total (all components)
Replacement of femoral, tibial, and patellar components (all components)
Code also any removal of (cement) (joint) spacer (84.57)
EXCLUDES *revision of only one or two components (tibial, femoral or patellar component) (00.81-00.84)*

00.81 Revision of knee replacement, tibial component
Replacement of tibial baseplate and tibial insert (liner)
EXCLUDES *revision of knee replacement, total (all components) (00.80)*

00.82 Revision of knee replacement, femoral component
That with replacement of tibial insert (liner)
EXCLUDES *revision of knee replacement, total (all components) (00.80)*

00.83 Revision of knee replacement, patellar component
EXCLUDES *revision of knee replacement, total (all components) (00.80)*

00.84 Revision of total knee replacement, tibial insert (liner)
Replacement of tibial insert (liner)
EXCLUDES *that with replacement of tibial component (tibial baseplate and liner) (00.81)*

00.85 Resurfacing hip, total, acetabulum and femoral head
Hip resurfacing arthroplasty, total

00.86 Resurfacing hip, partial, femoral head
Hip resurfacing arthroplasty, NOS
Hip resurfacing arthroplasty, partial, femoral head
EXCLUDES *that with resurfacing of acetabulum (00.85)*

00.87 Resurfacing hip, partial, acetabulum
Hip resurfacing arthroplasty, partial, acetabulum
EXCLUDES *that with resurfacing of femoral head (00.85)*

✓4th **00.9 Other procedures and interventions**

00.91 Transplant from live related donor
Code also organ transplant procedure

00.92 Transplant from live non-related donor
Code also organ transplant procedure

00.93 Transplant from cadaver
Code also organ transplant procedure

00.94 Intra-operative neurophysiologic monitoring
Intra-operative neurophysiologic testing
IOM
Nerve monitoring
Neuromonitoring
INCLUDES Cranial nerve, peripheral nerve and spinal cord testing performed intra-operatively
EXCLUDES *brain temperature monitoring (01.17)*
intracranial oxygen monitoring (01.16)
intracranial pressure monitoring (01.10)
plethysmogram (89.58)

DEF: Real-time testing techniques used in brain, spinal cord, and nerve procedures to assist in lesion excision and provide ongoing neurological functioning information and/or warning of impending neural structure injury.

1. OPERATIONS ON THE NERVOUS SYSTEM (01-05)

✓3rd **01 Incision and excision of skull, brain, and cerebral meninges**

✓4th **01.0 Cranial puncture**

01.01 Cisternal puncture
Cisternal aspiration
Cisternal tap
EXCLUDES *pneumocisternogram (87.02)*
DEF: Needle insertion through subarachnoid space to withdraw cerebrospinal fluid.

01.02 Ventriculopuncture through previously implanted catheter
Puncture of ventricular shunt tubing
DEF: Piercing of artificial, fluid-diverting tubing in the brain for withdrawal of cerebrospinal fluid.

01.09 Other cranial puncture
Aspiration of:
subarachnoid space
subdural space
Cranial aspiration NOS
Puncture of anterior fontanel
Subdural tap (through fontanel)

✓4th **01.1 Diagnostic procedures on skull, brain, and cerebral meninges**

01.10 Intracranial pressure monitoring
INCLUDES insertion of catheter or probe for monitoring

01.11 Closed [percutaneous] [needle] biopsy of cerebral meninges
Burr hole approach
DEF: Needle excision of tissue sample through skin into cerebral membranes; no other procedure performed.

01.12 Open biopsy of cerebral meninges
DEF: Open surgical excision of tissue sample from cerebral membrane.

01.13 Closed [percutaneous] [needle] biopsy of brain
Burr hole approach
Stereotactic method
DEF: Removal by needle of brain tissue sample through skin.

01.14 Open biopsy of brain
DEF: Open surgical excision of brain tissue sample.

01.15 Biopsy of skull

01.16 Intracranial oxygen monitoring
Partial pressure of brain oxygen ($PbtO_2$)
INCLUDES insertion of catheter or probe for monitoring

01.17 Brain temperature monitoring
INCLUDES insertion of catheter or probe for monitoring

01.18 Other diagnostic procedures on brain and cerebral meninges
EXCLUDES *brain temperature monitoring (01.17)*
cerebral:
arteriography (88.41)
thermography (88.81)
contrast radiogram of brain (87.01-87.02)
echoencephalogram (88.71)
electroencephalogram (89.14)
intracranial oxygen monitoring (01.16)
intracranial pressure monitoring (01.10)
microscopic examination of specimen from nervous system and of spinal fluid (90.01-90.09)
neurologic examination (89.13)
phlebography of head and neck (88.61)
pneumoencephalogram (87.01)
radioisotope scan:
cerebral (92.11)
head NEC (92.12)
tomography of head:
C.A.T. scan (87.03)
other (87.04)

01.19 Other diagnostic procedures on skull
EXCLUDES *transillumination of skull (89.16)*
x-ray of skull (87.17)

✓4th **01.2 Craniotomy and craniectomy**
EXCLUDES *decompression of skull fracture (02.02)*
exploration of orbit (16.01-16.09)
that as operative approach — omit code
DEF: Craniotomy: Incision into skull.
DEF: Craniectomy: Excision of part of skull.

01.21 Incision and drainage of cranial sinus
DEF: Incision for drainage, including drainage of air cavities in skull bones.

01.22 Removal of intracranial neurostimulator lead(s)
Code also any removal of neurostimulator pulse generator (86.05)
EXCLUDES *removal with synchronous replacement (02.93)*

01.23 Reopening of craniotomy site
DEF: Reopening of skull incision.

01.24 Other craniotomy
Cranial:
decompression
exploration
trephination
Craniotomy NOS
Craniotomy with removal of:
epidural abscess
extradural hematoma
foreign body of skull
EXCLUDES *removal of foreign body with incision into brain (01.39)*

01.25 Other craniectomy
Debridement of skull NOS
Sequestrectomy of skull
EXCLUDES *debridement of compound fracture of skull (02.02)*
strip craniectomy (02.01)

01.26 Insertion of catheter(s) into cranial cavity or tissue

Code also any concomitant procedure (e.g. resection (01.59))

EXCLUDES *placement of intracerebral catheter(s) via burr hole(s) (01.28)*

01.27 Removal of catheter(s) from cranial cavity or tissue

01.28 Placement of intracerebral catheter(s) via burr hole(s)

Convection enhanced delivery
Stereotactic placement of intracerebral catheter(s)

Code also infusion of medication

EXCLUDES *insertion of catheter(s) into cranial cavity or tissue(s) (01.26)*

DEF: The strategic neurosurgical placement of catheters via burr holes into targeted brain tissue, through which therapeutic agents such as antineoplastics are microinfused.

✓4th **01.3 Incision of brain and cerebral meninges**

01.31 Incision of cerebral meninges

Drainage of:
- intracranial hygroma
- subarachnoid abscess (cerebral)
- subdural empyema

01.32 Lobotomy and tractotomy

Division of:
- brain tissue
- cerebral tracts

Percutaneous (radiofrequency) cingulotomy

DEF: Lobotomy: Incision of nerve fibers of brain lobe, usually frontal.

DEF: Tractotomy: Severing of a nerve fiber group to relieve pain.

01.39 Other incision of brain

Amygdalohippocampotomy
Drainage of intracerebral hematoma
Incision of brain NOS

EXCLUDES *division of cortical adhesions (02.91)*

✓4th **01.4 Operations on thalamus and globus pallidus**

01.41 Operations on thalamus

Chemothalamectomy
Thalamotomy

EXCLUDES *that by stereotactic radiosurgery (92.30-92.39)*

01.42 Operations on globus pallidus

Pallidoansectomy
Pallidotomy

EXCLUDES *that by stereotactic radiosurgery (92.30-92.39)*

✓4th **01.5 Other excision or destruction of brain and meninges**

01.51 Excision of lesion or tissue of cerebral meninges

Decortication
Resection
Stripping of subdural membrane
} of (cerebral) meninges

EXCLUDES *biopsy of cerebral meninges (01.11-01.12)*

01.52 Hemispherectomy

DEF: Removal of one half of the brain. Most often performed for malignant brain tumors or intractable epilepsy.

01.53 Lobectomy of brain

DEF: Excision of a brain lobe.

01.59 Other excision or destruction of lesion or tissue of brain

Curettage of brain
Debridement of brain
Marsupialization of brain cyst
Transtemporal (mastoid) excision of brain tumor

EXCLUDES *biopsy of brain (01.13-01.14)*
that by stereotactic radiosurgery (92.30-92.39)

01.6 Excision of lesion of skull

Removal of granulation tissue of cranium

EXCLUDES *biopsy of skull (01.15)*
sequestrectomy (01.25)

✓3rd **02 Other operations on skull, brain, and cerebral meninges**

✓4th **02.0 Cranioplasty**

EXCLUDES *that with synchronous repair of encephalocele (02.12)*

02.01 Opening of cranial suture

Linear craniectomy
Strip craniectomy

DEF: Opening of the lines of junction between the bones of the skull for removal of strips of skull bone.

02.02 Elevation of skull fracture fragments

Debridement of compound fracture of skull
Decompression of skull fracture
Reduction of skull fracture

Code also any synchronous debridement of brain (01.59)

EXCLUDES *debridement of skull NOS (01.25)*
removal of granulation tissue of cranium (01.6)

02.03 Formation of cranial bone flap

Repair of skull with flap

02.04 Bone graft to skull

Pericranial graft (autogenous) (heterogenous)

02.05 Insertion of skull plate

Replacement of skull plate

02.06 Other cranial osteoplasty

Repair of skull NOS
Revision of bone flap of skull

DEF: Plastic surgery repair of skull bones.

02.07 Removal of skull plate

EXCLUDES *removal with synchronous replacement (02.05)*

✓4th **02.1 Repair of cerebral meninges**

EXCLUDES *marsupialization of cerebral lesion (01.59)*

02.11 Simple suture of dura mater of brain

02.12 Other repair of cerebral meninges

Closure of fistula of cerebrospinal fluid
Dural graft
Repair of encephalocele including synchronous cranioplasty
Repair of meninges NOS
Subdural patch

02.13 Ligation of meningeal vessel

Ligation of:
- longitudinal sinus
- middle meningeal artery

02.14 Choroid plexectomy

Cauterization of choroid plexus

DEF: Excision or destruction of the ependymal cells that form the membrane lining in the third, fourth, and lateral ventricles of the brain and secrete cerebrospinal fluid.

02.2 Ventriculostomy

Anastomosis of ventricle to:
cervical subarachnoid space
cisterna magna
Insertion of Holter valve
Ventriculocisternal intubation

DEF: Surgical creation of an opening of ventricle; often performed to drain cerebrospinal fluid in treating hydrocephalus.

✓4th **02.3 Extracranial ventricular shunt**

INCLUDES that with insertion of valve

DEF: Placement of shunt or creation of artificial passage leading from skull cavities to site outside skull to relieve excess cerebrospinal fluid created in the chorioid plexuses of the third and fourth ventricles of the brain.

02.31 Ventricular shunt to structure in head and neck

Ventricle to nasopharynx shunt
Ventriculomastoid anastomosis

02.32 Ventricular shunt to circulatory system

Ventriculoatrial anastomosis
Ventriculocaval shunt

02.33 Ventricular shunt to thoracic cavity

Ventriculopleural anastomosis

02.34 Ventricular shunt to abdominal cavity and organs

Ventriculocholecystostomy
Ventriculoperitoneostomy

02.35 Ventricular shunt to urinary system

Ventricle to ureter shunt

02.39 Other operations to establish drainage of ventricle

Ventricle to bone marrow shunt
Ventricular shunt to extracranial site NEC

✓4th **02.4 Revision, removal, and irrigation of ventricular shunt**

EXCLUDES *revision of distal catheter of ventricular shunt (54.95)*

02.41 Irrigation and exploration of ventricular shunt

Exploration of ventriculoperitoneal shunt at ventricular site
Re-programming of ventriculoperitoneal shunt

02.42 Replacement of ventricular shunt

Reinsertion of Holter valve
Replacement of ventricular catheter
Revision of ventriculoperitoneal shunt at ventricular site

02.43 Removal of ventricular shunt

✓4th **02.9 Other operations on skull, brain, and cerebral meninges**

EXCLUDES *operations on:*
pineal gland (07.17, 07.51-07.59)
pituitary gland [hypophysis] (07.13-07.15, 07.61-07.79)

02.91 Lysis of cortical adhesions

DEF: Breaking up of fibrous structures in brain outer layer.

02.92 Repair of brain

02.93 Implantation or replacement of intracranial neurostimulator lead(s)

Implantation, insertion, placement, or replacement of intracranial:
brain pacemaker [neuropacemaker]
depth electrodes
epidural pegs
electroencephalographic receiver
foramen ovale electrodes
intracranial electrostimulator
subdural grids
subdural strips

Code also any insertion of neurostimulator pulse generator (86.94-86.98)

02.94 Insertion or replacement of skull tongs or halo traction device

DEF: Halo traction device: Metal or plastic band encircles the head or neck secured to the skull with four pins and attached to a metal chest plate by rods; provides support and stability for the head and neck.

DEF: Skull tongs: Device inserted into each side of the skull used to apply parallel traction to the long axis of the cervical spine.

02.95 Removal of skull tongs or halo traction device

02.96 Insertion of sphenoidal electrodes

02.99 Other

EXCLUDES *chemical shock therapy (94.24)*
electroshock therapy:
subconvulsive (94.26)
other (94.27)

✓3rd **03 Operations on spinal cord and spinal canal structures**

Code also any application or administration of an adhesion barrier substance (99.77)

✓4th **03.0 Exploration and decompression of spinal canal structures**

03.01 Removal of foreign body from spinal canal

03.02 Reopening of laminectomy site

03.09 Other exploration and decompression of spinal canal

Decompression:
laminectomy
laminotomy
Expansile laminoplasty
Exploration of spinal nerve root
Foraminotomy

Code also any synchronous insertion, replacement and revision of posterior spinal motion preservation device(s), if performed (84.80-84.85)

EXCLUDES *drainage of spinal fluid by anastomosis (03.71-03.79)*
laminectomy with excision of intervertebral disc (80.51)
spinal tap (03.31)
that as operative approach — omit code

DEF: Decompression of spinal canal: Excision of bone pieces, hematoma or other lesion to relieve spinal cord pressure.

DEF: Expansile laminoplasty: Lamina is incised at the level of the pedicle to relieve pressure; no tissue is excised.

DEF: Foraminotomy: Removal of root opening between vertebrae to relieve nerve root pressure.

Laminotomy with Decompression

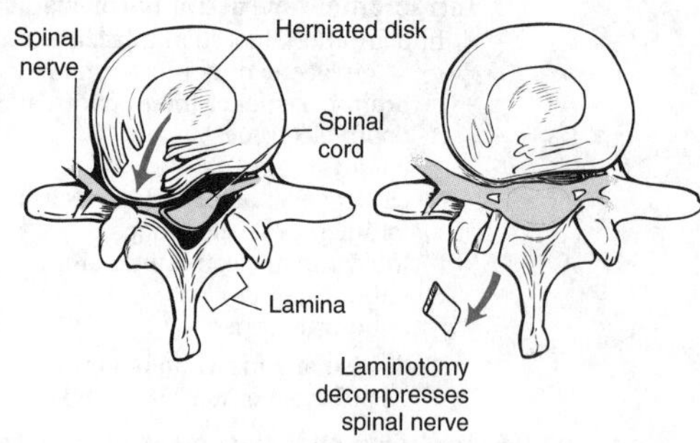

03.1 Division of intraspinal nerve root
Rhizotomy
DEF: Rhizotomy: Surgical severing of spinal nerve roots within spinal canal for pain relief.

✓4th **03.2 Chordotomy**
DEF: Chordotomy: Surgical cutting of lateral spinothalamic tract of spinal cord to relieve pain.

03.21 Percutaneous chordotomy
Stereotactic chordotomy
DEF: Percutaneous chordotomy: Insertion of hollow needle through skin to interrupt spinal nerve root.
DEF: Stereotactic chordotomy: Use of three-dimensional imaging to locate spinal nerve root for surgical interruption.

03.29 Other chordotomy
Chordotomy NOS
Tractotomy (one-stage) (two-stage) of spinal cord
Transection of spinal cord tracts
DEF: Tractotomy (one stage) (two stages) of the spinal cord: Surgical incision or severing of a nerve tract of spinal cord.
DEF: Transection of spinal cord tracts: Use of transverse incision to divide spinal nerve root.

✓4th **03.3 Diagnostic procedures on spinal cord and spinal canal structures**

03.31 Spinal tap
Lumbar puncture for removal of dye
EXCLUDES *lumbar puncture for injection of dye [myelogram] (87.21)*
DEF: Puncture into lumbar subarachnoid space to tap cerebrospinal fluid.

03.32 Biopsy of spinal cord or spinal meninges

03.39 Other diagnostic procedures on spinal cord and spinal canal structures
EXCLUDES *microscopic examination of specimen from nervous system or of spinal fluid (90.01-90.09)*
x-ray of spine (87.21-87.29)

Lumbar Spinal Puncture

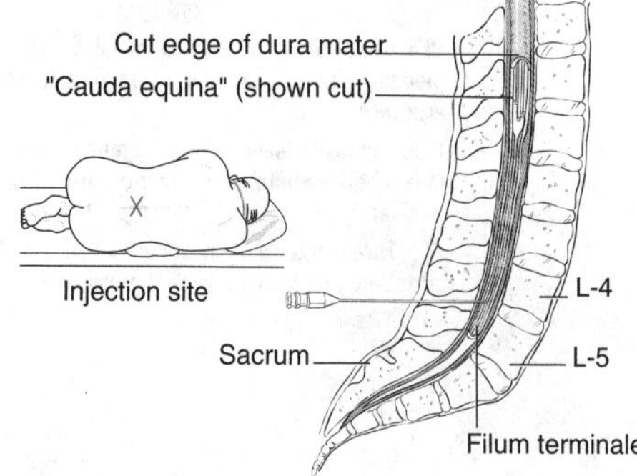

03.4 Excision or destruction of lesion of spinal cord or spinal meninges
Curettage
Debridement
Marsupialization of cyst
Resection
} of spinal cord or spinal meninges
EXCLUDES *biopsy of spinal cord or meninges (03.32)*

✓4th **03.5 Plastic operations on spinal cord structures**

03.51 Repair of spinal meningocele
Repair of meningocele NOS
DEF: Restoration of hernial protrusion of spinal meninges through defect in vertebral column.

03.52 Repair of spinal myelomeningocele
DEF: Restoration of hernial protrusion of spinal cord and meninges through defect in vertebral column.

03.53 Repair of vertebral fracture
Elevation of spinal bone fragments
Reduction of fracture of vertebrae
Removal of bony spicules from spinal canal
EXCLUDES *percutaneous vertebral augmentation (81.66)*
percutaneous vertebroplasty (81.65)

03.59 Other repair and plastic operations on spinal cord structures
Repair of:
- diastematomyelia
- spina bifida NOS
- spinal cord NOS
- spinal meninges NOS
- vertebral arch defect

03.6 Lysis of adhesions of spinal cord and nerve roots

✓4th **03.7 Shunt of spinal theca**
INCLUDES that with valve
DEF: Surgical passage created from spinal cord dura mater to another channel.

03.71 Spinal subarachnoid-peritoneal shunt

03.72 Spinal subarachnoid-ureteral shunt

03.79 Other shunt of spinal theca
Lumbar-subarachnoid shunt NOS
Pleurothecal anastomosis
Salpingothecal anastomosis

03.8 Injection of destructive agent into spinal canal

✓4th **03.9 Other operations on spinal cord and spinal canal structures**

03.90 Insertion of catheter into spinal canal for infusion of therapeutic or palliative substances
Insertion of catheter into epidural, subarachnoid, or subdural space of spine with intermittent or continuous infusion of drug (with creation of any reservoir)
Code also any implantation of infusion pump (86.06)

03.91 Injection of anesthetic into spinal canal for analgesia
EXCLUDES *that for operative anesthesia — omit code*

03.92 Injection of other agent into spinal canal
Intrathecal injection of steroid
Subarachnoid perfusion of refrigerated saline
EXCLUDES *injection of:*
contrast material for myelogram (87.21)
destructive agent into spinal canal (03.8)

03.93 Implantation or replacement of spinal neurostimulator lead(s)
Code also any insertion of neurostimulator pulse generator (86.94-86.98)

03.94 Removal of spinal neurostimulator lead(s)
Code also any removal of neurostimulator pulse generator (86.05)

03.95 Spinal blood patch
DEF: Injection of blood into epidural space to patch hole in outer spinal membrane when blood clots.

03.96 Percutaneous denervation of facet

03.97 Revision of spinal thecal shunt

03.98 Removal of spinal thecal shunt

03.99 Other

✓3rd **04 Operations on cranial and peripheral nerves**

✓4th **04.0 Incision, division, and excision of cranial and peripheral nerves**
EXCLUDES *opticociliary neurectomy (12.79)*
sympathetic ganglionectomy (05.21-05.29)

04.01 Excision of acoustic neuroma
That by craniotomy
EXCLUDES *that by stereotactic radiosurgery (92.3)*

04.02 Division of trigeminal nerve
Retrogasserian neurotomy
DEF: Transection of sensory root fibers of trigeminal nerve for relief of trigeminal neuralgia.

04.03 Division or crushing of other cranial and peripheral nerves
EXCLUDES *that of:*
glossopharyngeal nerve (29.92)
laryngeal nerve (31.91)
nerves to adrenal glands (07.42)
phrenic nerve for collapse of lung (33.31)
vagus nerve (44.00-44.03)

04.04 Other incision of cranial and peripheral nerves

04.05 Gasserian ganglionectomy

04.06 Other cranial or peripheral ganglionectomy
EXCLUDES *sympathetic ganglionectomy (05.21-05.29)*

04.07 Other excision or avulsion of cranial and peripheral nerves
Curettage, Debridement, Resection } of peripheral nerve
Excision of peripheral neuroma [Morton's]
EXCLUDES *biopsy of cranial or peripheral nerve (04.11-04.12)*

✓4th **04.1 Diagnostic procedures on peripheral nervous system**

04.11 Closed [percutaneous] [needle] biopsy of cranial or peripheral nerve or ganglion

04.12 Open biopsy of cranial or peripheral nerve or ganglion

04.19 Other diagnostic procedures on cranial and peripheral nerves and ganglia
EXCLUDES *microscopic examination of specimen from nervous system (90.01-90.09)*
neurologic examination (89.13)

Release of Carpal Tunnel

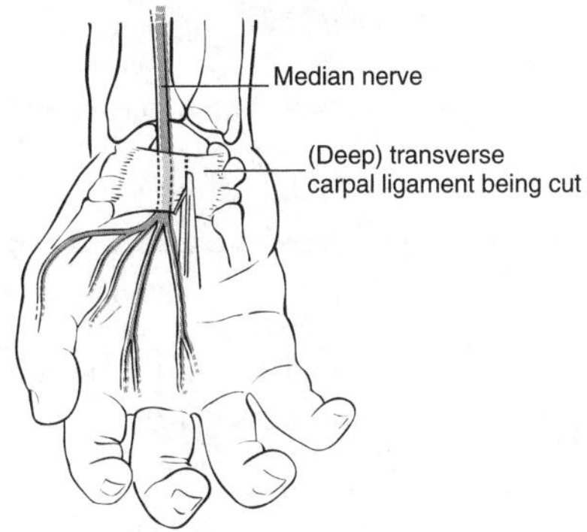

04.2 Destruction of cranial and peripheral nerves
Destruction of cranial or peripheral nerves by:
cryoanalgesia
injection of neurolytic agent
radiofrequency
Radiofrequency ablation
DEF: Radiofrequency ablation: High frequency radio waves are applied to injure the nerve resulting in interruption of the pain signal.

04.3 Suture of cranial and peripheral nerves

✓4th **04.4 Lysis of adhesions and decompression of cranial and peripheral nerves**

04.41 Decompression of trigeminal nerve root

04.42 Other cranial nerve decompression

04.43 Release of carpal tunnel

04.44 Release of tarsal tunnel

04.49 Other peripheral nerve or ganglion decompression or lysis of adhesions
Peripheral nerve neurolysis NOS

04.5 Cranial or peripheral nerve graft

04.6 Transposition of cranial and peripheral nerves
Nerve transplantation
DEF: Relocation of cranial or peripheral nerves without detaching or severing them.

✓4th **04.7 Other cranial or peripheral neuroplasty**

04.71 Hypoglossal-facial anastomosis
DEF: Surgical connection of hypoglossal nerve to facial nerve.

04.72 Accessory-facial anastomosis
DEF: Surgical connection of accessory nerve to facial nerve.

04.73 Accessory-hypoglossal anastomosis
DEF: Surgical connection of accessory nerve to hypoglossal nerve.

04.74 Other anastomosis of cranial or peripheral nerve

04.75 Revision of previous repair of cranial and peripheral nerves

04.76 Repair of old traumatic injury of cranial and peripheral nerves

04.79 Other neuroplasty

✓4th **04.8 Injection into peripheral nerve**
EXCLUDES *destruction of nerve (by injection of neurolytic agent) (04.2)*

04.80 Peripheral nerve injection, not otherwise specified

04.81 Injection of anesthetic into peripheral nerve for analgesia

EXCLUDES *that for operative anesthesia — omit code*

04.89 Injection of other agent, except neurolytic

EXCLUDES *injection of neurolytic agent (04.2)*

✓4th **04.9 Other operations on cranial and peripheral nerves**

04.91 Neurectasis

DEF: Surgical stretching of peripheral or cranial nerve.

04.92 Implantation or replacement of peripheral neurostimulator lead(s)

Code also any insertion of neurostimulator pulse generator (86.94-86.98)

DEF: Placement of or removal and replacement of neurostimulator lead(s) during the same episode.

04.93 Removal of peripheral neurostimulator lead(s)

Code also any removal of neurostimulator pulse generator (86.05)

04.99 Other

✓3rd **05 Operations on sympathetic nerves or ganglia**

EXCLUDES *paracervical uterine denervation (69.3)*

05.0 Division of sympathetic nerve or ganglion

EXCLUDES *that of nerves to adrenal glands (07.42)*

✓4th **05.1 Diagnostic procedures on sympathetic nerves or ganglia**

05.11 Biopsy of sympathetic nerve or ganglion

05.19 Other diagnostic procedures on sympathetic nerves or ganglia

✓4th **05.2 Sympathectomy**

DEF: Sympathectomy: Division of nerve pathway at a specific site of a sympathetic nerve.

05.21 Sphenopalatine ganglionectomy

05.22 Cervical sympathectomy

05.23 Lumbar sympathectomy

DEF: Excision, resection of lumber chain nerve group to relieve causalgia, Raynaud's disease, or lower extremity thromboangiitis.

05.24 Presacral sympathectomy

DEF: Excision or resection of hypogastric nerve network.

05.25 Periarterial sympathectomy

DEF: Removal of arterial sheath containing sympathetic nerve fibers.

05.29 Other sympathectomy and ganglionectomy

Excision or avulsion of sympathetic nerve NOS

Sympathetic ganglionectomy NOS

EXCLUDES *biopsy of sympathetic nerve or ganglion (05.11)*
opticociliary neurectomy (12.79)
periarterial sympathectomy (05.25)
tympanosympathectomy (20.91)

✓4th **05.3 Injection into sympathetic nerve or ganglion**

EXCLUDES *injection of ciliary sympathetic ganglion (12.79)*

05.31 Injection of anesthetic into sympathetic nerve for analgesia

05.32 Injection of neurolytic agent into sympathetic nerve

05.39 Other injection into sympathetic nerve or ganglion

✓4th **05.8 Other operations on sympathetic nerves or ganglia**

05.81 Repair of sympathetic nerve or ganglion

05.89 Other

05.9 Other operations on nervous system

2. OPERATIONS ON THE ENDOCRINE SYSTEM (06-07)

✓3rd 06 Operations on thyroid and parathyroid glands

INCLUDES incidental resection of hyoid bone

✓4th 06.0 Incision of thyroid field

EXCLUDES *division of isthmus (06.91)*

06.01 Aspiration of thyroid field

Percutaneous or needle drainage of thyroid field

EXCLUDES *aspiration biopsy of thyroid (06.11)*
drainage by incision (06.09)
postoperative aspiration of field (06.02)

06.02 Reopening of wound of thyroid field

Reopening of wound of thyroid field for:
control of (postoperative) hemorrhage
examination
exploration
removal of hematoma

06.09 Other incision of thyroid field

Drainage of hematoma
Drainage of thyroglossal tract
Exploration
neck
thyroid (field)
Removal of foreign body
Thyroidotomy NOS
} by incision

EXCLUDES *postoperative exploration (06.02)*
removal of hematoma by aspiration (06.01)

✓4th 06.1 Diagnostic procedures on thyroid and parathyroid glands

06.11 Closed [percutaneous] [needle] biopsy of thyroid gland

Aspiration biopsy of thyroid

DEF: Insertion of needle-type device for removal of thyroid tissue sample.

06.12 Open biopsy of thyroid gland

06.13 Biopsy of parathyroid gland

06.19 Other diagnostic procedures on thyroid and parathyroid glands

EXCLUDES *radioisotope scan of:*
parathyroid (92.13)
thyroid (92.01)
soft tissue x-ray of thyroid field (87.09)

06.2 Unilateral thyroid lobectomy

Complete removal of one lobe of thyroid (with removal of isthmus or portion of other lobe)
Hemithyroidectomy

EXCLUDES *partial substernal thyroidectomy (06.51)*

DEF: Excision of thyroid lobe.

Thyroidectomy

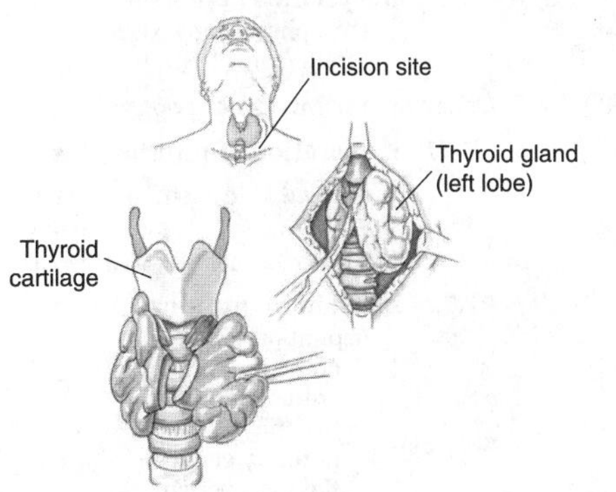

✓4th 06.3 Other partial thyroidectomy

06.31 Excision of lesion of thyroid

EXCLUDES *biopsy of thyroid (06.11-06.12)*

DEF: Removal of growth on thyroid.

06.39 Other

Isthmectomy
Partial thyroidectomy NOS

EXCLUDES *partial substernal thyroidectomy (06.51)*

06.4 Complete thyroidectomy

EXCLUDES *complete substernal thyroidectomy (06.52)*
that with laryngectomy (30.3-30.4)

✓4th 06.5 Substernal thyroidectomy

DEF: Removal of thyroid tissue below breastbone.

06.50 Substernal thyroidectomy, not otherwise specified

06.51 Partial substernal thyroidectomy

06.52 Complete substernal thyroidectomy

06.6 Excision of lingual thyroid

Excision of thyroid by:
submental route
transoral route

DEF: Excision of thyroid tissue at base of tongue.

06.7 Excision of thyroglossal duct or tract

✓4th 06.8 Parathyroidectomy

DEF: Removal of parathyroid glands.

06.81 Complete parathyroidectomy

06.89 Other parathyroidectomy

Parathyroidectomy NOS
Partial parathyroidectomy

EXCLUDES *biopsy of parathyroid (06.13)*

✓4th 06.9 Other operations on thyroid (region) and parathyroid

06.91 Division of thyroid isthmus

Transection of thyroid isthmus

DEF: Cutting or division of tissue at narrowest point of thyroid.

06.92 Ligation of thyroid vessels

06.93 Suture of thyroid gland

06.94 Thyroid tissue reimplantation

Autotransplantation of thyroid tissue

DEF: Placement of thyroid tissue graft into functional site.

DEF: Autotransplantation of thyroid tissue: Tissue graft from patient thyroid tissue to another site on thyroid.

06.95 Parathyroid tissue reimplantation

Autotransplantation of parathyroid tissue

DEF: Placement of parathyroid tissue graft into functional site.

DEF: Autotransplantation of parathyroid tissue: Use of patient parathyroid tissue for graft.

06.98 Other operations on thyroid glands

06.99 Other operations on parathyroid glands

✓3rd 07 Operations on other endocrine glands

INCLUDES operations on:
adrenal glands
pineal gland
pituitary gland
thymus

EXCLUDES *operations on:*
aortic and carotid bodies (39.8)
ovaries (65.0-65.99)
pancreas (52.01-52.99)
testes (62.0-62.99)

✓4th 07.0 Exploration of adrenal field

EXCLUDES *incision of adrenal (gland) (07.41)*

07.00 Exploration of adrenal field, not otherwise specified

07.01 Unilateral exploration of adrenal field

DEF: Investigation of one adrenal gland for diagnostic reasons.

07.02 Bilateral exploration of adrenal field

DEF: Investigation of both adrenal glands for diagnostic reasons.

4th 07.1 Diagnostic procedures on adrenal glands, pituitary gland, pineal gland, and thymus

07.11 Closed [percutaneous] [needle] biopsy of adrenal gland

07.12 Open biopsy of adrenal gland

07.13 Biopsy of pituitary gland, transfrontal approach

DEF: Excision of pituitary gland tissue for exam through frontal bone.

07.14 Biopsy of pituitary gland, transsphenoidal approach

DEF: Excision of pituitary gland tissue for exam through sphenoid bone.

07.15 Biopsy of pituitary gland, unspecified approach

07.16 Biopsy of thymus

07.17 Biopsy of pineal gland

07.19 Other diagnostic procedures on adrenal glands, pituitary gland, pineal gland, and thymus

EXCLUDES *microscopic examination of specimen from endocrine gland (90.11-90.19)*
radioisotope scan of pituitary gland (92.11)

4th 07.2 Partial adrenalectomy

07.21 Excision of lesion of adrenal gland

EXCLUDES *biopsy of adrenal gland (07.11-07.12)*

07.22 Unilateral adrenalectomy

Adrenalectomy NOS

EXCLUDES *excision of remaining adrenal gland (07.3)*

DEF: Excision of one adrenal gland.

07.29 Other partial adrenalectomy

Partial adrenalectomy NOS

07.3 Bilateral adrenalectomy

Excision of remaining adrenal gland

EXCLUDES *bilateral partial adrenalectomy (07.29)*

4th 07.4 Other operations on adrenal glands, nerves, and vessels

07.41 Incision of adrenal gland

Adrenalotomy (with drainage)

07.42 Division of nerves to adrenal glands

07.43 Ligation of adrenal vessels

07.44 Repair of adrenal gland

07.45 Reimplantation of adrenal tissue

Autotransplantation of adrenal tissue

DEF: Autotransplantation of adrenal tissue: Use of tissue graft from the patient's own body.

07.49 Other

4th 07.5 Operations on pineal gland

07.51 Exploration of pineal field

EXCLUDES *that with incision of pineal gland (07.52)*

07.52 Incision of pineal gland

07.53 Partial excision of pineal gland

EXCLUDES *biopsy of pineal gland (07.17)*

07.54 Total excision of pineal gland

Pinealectomy (complete) (total)

07.59 Other operations on pineal gland

4th 07.6 Hypophysectomy

DEF: Excision, destruction of pituitary gland.

07.61 Partial excision of pituitary gland, transfrontal approach

Cryohypophysectomy, partial
Division of hypophyseal stalk
Excision of lesion of pituitary [hypophysis]
Hypophysectomy subtotal
Infundibulectomy, hypophyseal
} transfrontal approach

EXCLUDES *biopsy of pituitary gland, transfrontal approach (07.13)*

DEF: Removal of pituitary gland, partial, through frontal bone.

07.62 Partial excision of pituitary gland, transsphenoidal approach

EXCLUDES *biopsy of pituitary gland, transsphenoidal approach (07.14)*

DEF: Removal of pituitary gland, partial, through sphenoid bone.

07.63 Partial excision of pituitary gland, unspecified approach

EXCLUDES *biopsy of pituitary gland NOS (07.15)*

07.64 Total excision of pituitary gland, transfrontal approach

Ablation of pituitary by implantation (strontiumyttrium) (y)
Cryohypophysectomy, complete
} transfrontal approach

DEF: Removal of pituitary gland, total, through frontal bone.

07.65 Total excision of pituitary gland, transsphenoidal approach

DEF: Removal of pituitary gland, total, through sphenoid bone.

07.68 Total excision of pituitary gland, other specified approach

DEF: Destroy or remove pituitary gland by a specified approach, other than those listed.

07.69 Total excision of pituitary gland, unspecified approach

Hypophysectomy NOS
Pituitectomy NOS

4th 07.7 Other operations on hypophysis

07.71 Exploration of pituitary fossa

EXCLUDES *exploration with incision of pituitary gland (07.72)*

DEF: Exploration of region of pituitary gland.

07.72 Incision of pituitary gland

Aspiration of:
- craniobuccal pouch
- craniopharyngioma
- hypophysis
- pituitary gland
- Rathke's pouch

07.79 Other
Insertion of pack into sella turcica

✓4th **07.8 Thymectomy**

07.80 Thymectomy, not otherwise specified

07.81 Other partial excision of thymus
Open partial excision of thymus
EXCLUDES *biopsy of thymus (07.16)*
thoracoscopic partial excision of thymus (07.83)

07.82 Other total excision of thymus
Open total excision of thymus
EXCLUDES *thoracoscopic total excision of thymus (07.84)*

07.83 Thoracoscopic partial excision of thymus
EXCLUDES *other partial excision of thymus (07.81)*

07.84 Thoracoscopic total excision of thymus
EXCLUDES *other total excision of thymus (07.82)*

✓4th **07.9 Other operations on thymus**

07.91 Exploration of thymus field
EXCLUDES *exploration with incision of thymus (07.92)*

07.92 Other incision of thymus
Open incision of thymus
EXCLUDES *thoracoscopic incision of thymus (07.95)*

07.93 Repair of thymus

07.94 Transplantation of thymus
DEF: Placement of thymus tissue grafts into functional area of gland.

07.95 Thoracoscopic incision of thymus
EXCLUDES *other incision of thymus (07.92)*

07.98 Other and unspecified thoracoscopic operations on thymus

07.99 Other and unspecified operations on thymus
Transcervical thymectomy
EXCLUDES *other thoracoscopic operations on thymus (07.98)*

3. OPERATIONS ON THE EYE (08-16)

√3rd **08 Operations on eyelids**

INCLUDES operations on the eyebrow

√4th **08.0 Incision of eyelid**

08.01 Incision of lid margin

DEF: Cutting into eyelid edge.

08.02 Severing of blepharorrhaphy

DEF: Freeing of eyelids previously sutured shut.

08.09 Other incision of eyelid

√4th **08.1 Diagnostic procedures on eyelid**

08.11 Biopsy of eyelid

08.19 Other diagnostic procedures on eyelid

√4th **08.2 Excision or destruction of lesion or tissue of eyelid**

Code also any synchronous reconstruction (08.61-08.74)

EXCLUDES *biopsy of eyelid (08.11)*

08.20 Removal of lesion of eyelid, not otherwise specified

Removal of meibomian gland NOS

08.21 Excision of chalazion

08.22 Excision of other minor lesion of eyelid

Excision of:
verruca
wart

08.23 Excision of major lesion of eyelid, partial-thickness

Excision involving one-fourth or more of lid margin, partial-thickness

DEF: Excision of lesion not in all eyelid layers.

08.24 Excision of major lesion of eyelid, full-thickness

Excision involving one-fourth or more of lid margin, full-thickness
Wedge resection of eyelid

DEF: Excision of growth in all eyelid layers, full thickness.

08.25 Destruction of lesion of eyelid

√4th **08.3 Repair of blepharoptosis and lid retraction**

08.31 Repair of blepharoptosis by frontalis muscle technique with suture

DEF: Correction of drooping upper eyelid with suture of frontalis muscle.

08.32 Repair of blepharoptosis by frontalis muscle technique with fascial sling

DEF: Correction of drooping upper eyelid with fascial tissue sling of frontalis muscle.

08.33 Repair of blepharoptosis by resection or advancement of levator muscle or aponeurosis

DEF: Correction of drooping upper eyelid with levator muscle, extended, cut, or by expanded tendon.

08.34 Repair of blepharoptosis by other levator muscle techniques

08.35 Repair of blepharoptosis by tarsal technique

DEF: Correction of drooping upper eyelid with tarsal muscle.

08.36 Repair of blepharoptosis by other techniques

Correction of eyelid ptosis NOS
Orbicularis oculi muscle sling for correction of blepharoptosis

08.37 Reduction of overcorrection of ptosis

DEF: Correction, release of previous plastic repair of drooping eyelid.

08.38 Correction of lid retraction

DEF: Fixing of withdrawn eyelid into normal position.

√4th **08.4 Repair of entropion or ectropion**

08.41 Repair of entropion or ectropion by thermocauterization

DEF: Restoration of eyelid margin to normal position with heat cautery.

08.42 Repair of entropion or ectropion by suture technique

DEF: Restoration of eyelid margin to normal position by suture.

08.43 Repair of entropion or ectropion with wedge resection

DEF: Restoration of eyelid margin to normal position by removing tissue.

08.44 Repair of entropion or ectropion with lid reconstruction

DEF: Reconstruction of eyelid margin.

08.49 Other repair of entropion or ectropion

√4th **08.5 Other adjustment of lid position**

08.51 Canthotomy

DEF: Incision into outer canthus of eye.

08.52 Blepharorrhaphy

Canthorrhaphy
Tarsorrhaphy

DEF: Suture together of eyelids, partial or repair; done to shorten palpebral fissure or protect cornea.

08.59 Other

Canthoplasty NOS
Repair of epicanthal fold

√4th **08.6 Reconstruction of eyelid with flaps or grafts**

EXCLUDES *that associated with repair of entropion and ectropion (08.44)*

08.61 Reconstruction of eyelid with skin flap or graft

DEF: Rebuild of eyelid by graft or flap method.

08.62 Reconstruction of eyelid with mucous membrane flap or graft

DEF: Rebuild of eyelid with mucous membrane by graft or flap method.

08.63 Reconstruction of eyelid with hair follicle graft

DEF: Rebuild of eyelid with hair follicle graft.

08.64 Reconstruction of eyelid with tarsoconjunctival flap

Transfer of tarsoconjunctival flap from opposing lid

DEF: Recreation of eyelid with tarsoconjunctival tissue.

08.69 Other reconstruction of eyelid with flaps or grafts

√4th **08.7 Other reconstruction of eyelid**

EXCLUDES *that associated with repair of entropion and ectropion (08.44)*

08.70 Reconstruction of eyelid, not otherwise specified

08.71 Reconstruction of eyelid involving lid margin, partial-thickness

DEF: Repair of eyelid margin not using all lid layers.

08.72 Other reconstruction of eyelid, partial-thickness

DEF: Reshape of eyelid not using all lid layers.

08.73 Reconstruction of eyelid involving lid margin, full-thickness

DEF: Repair of eyelid and margin using all tissue layers.

08.74 Other reconstruction of eyelid, full-thickness
DEF: Other repair of eyelid using all tissue layers.

✓4th **08.8 Other repair of eyelid**

08.81 Linear repair of laceration of eyelid or eyebrow

08.82 Repair of laceration involving lid margin, partial-thickness
DEF: Repair of laceration not involving all layers of eyelid margin.

08.83 Other repair of laceration of eyelid, partial thickness
DEF: Repair of eyelid tear not involving all eyelid layers.

08.84 Repair of laceration involving lid margin, full-thickness
DEF: Repair of eyelid margin tear involving all margin layers.

08.85 Other repair of laceration of eyelid, full-thickness
DEF: Repair of eyelid tear involving all layers.

08.86 Lower eyelid rhytidectomy
DEF: Removal of wrinkles from lower eyelid.

08.87 Upper eyelid rhytidectomy
DEF: Removal of wrinkles from upper eyelid.

08.89 Other eyelid repair

✓4th **08.9 Other operations on eyelids**

08.91 Electrosurgical epilation of eyelid
DEF: Electrical removal of eyelid hair roots.

08.92 Cryosurgical epilation of eyelid
DEF: Removal of eyelid hair roots by freezing.

08.93 Other epilation of eyelid

08.99 Other

✓3rd **09 Operations on lacrimal system**

09.0 Incision of lacrimal gland
Incision of lacrimal cyst (with drainage)

✓4th **09.1 Diagnostic procedures on lacrimal system**

09.11 Biopsy of lacrimal gland

09.12 Biopsy of lacrimal sac

09.19 Other diagnostic procedures on lacrimal system
EXCLUDES *contrast dacryocystogram (87.05)*
soft tissue x-ray of nasolacrimal duct (87.09)

✓4th **09.2 Excision of lesion or tissue of lacrimal gland**

09.20 Excision of lacrimal gland, not otherwise specified

09.21 Excision of lesion of lacrimal gland
EXCLUDES *biopsy of lacrimal gland (09.11)*

09.22 Other partial dacryoadenectomy
EXCLUDES *biopsy of lacrimal gland (09.11)*
DEF: Excision, partial, of tear gland.

09.23 Total dacryoadenectomy
DEF: Excision, total, of tear gland.

09.3 Other operations on lacrimal gland

✓4th **09.4 Manipulation of lacrimal passage**
INCLUDES removal of calculus
that with dilation
EXCLUDES *contrast dacryocystogram (87.05)*

09.41 Probing of lacrimal punctum
DEF: Exploration of tear duct entrance with flexible rod.

09.42 Probing of lacrimal canaliculi
DEF: Exploration of tear duct with flexible rod.

09.43 Probing of nasolacrimal duct
EXCLUDES *that with insertion of tube or stent (09.44)*
DEF: Exploration of passage between tear sac and nose with flexible rod.

09.44 Intubation of nasolacrimal duct
Insertion of stent into nasolacrimal duct

09.49 Other manipulation of lacrimal passage

✓4th **09.5 Incision of lacrimal sac and passages**

09.51 Incision of lacrimal punctum

09.52 Incision of lacrimal canaliculi

09.53 Incision of lacrimal sac
DEF: Cutting into lacrimal pouch of tear gland.

09.59 Other incision of lacrimal passages
Incision (and drainage) of nasolacrimal duct NOS

09.6 Excision of lacrimal sac and passage
EXCLUDES *biopsy of lacrimal sac (09.12)*
DEF: Removal of pouch and passage of tear gland.

✓4th **09.7 Repair of canaliculus and punctum**
EXCLUDES *repair of eyelid (08.81-08.89)*

09.71 Correction of everted punctum
DEF: Repair of an outwardly turned tear duct entrance.

09.72 Other repair of punctum

09.73 Repair of canaliculus

✓4th **09.8 Fistulization of lacrimal tract to nasal cavity**

09.81 Dacryocystorhinostomy [DCR]
DEF: Creation of entrance between tear gland and nasal passage for tear flow.

09.82 Conjunctivocystorhinostomy
Conjunctivodacryocystorhinostomy [CDCR]
EXCLUDES *that with insertion of tube or stent (09.83)*
DEF: Creation of tear drainage path from lacrimal sac to nasal cavity through conjunctiva.

09.83 Conjunctivorhinostomy with insertion of tube or stent
DEF: Creation of passage between eye sac membrane and nasal cavity with tube or stent.

✓4th **09.9 Other operations on lacrimal system**

09.91 Obliteration of lacrimal punctum
DEF: Destruction, total of tear gland opening in eyelid.

09.99 Other

✓3rd **10 Operations on conjunctiva**

10.0 Removal of embedded foreign body from conjunctiva by incision
EXCLUDES *removal of:*
embedded foreign body without incision (98.22)
superficial foreign body (98.21)

10.1 Other incision of conjunctiva

✓4th **10.2 Diagnostic procedures on conjunctiva**

10.21 Biopsy of conjunctiva

10.29 Other diagnostic procedures on conjunctiva

✓4th **10.3 Excision or destruction of lesion or tissue of conjunctiva**

10.31 Excision of lesion or tissue of conjunctiva
Excision of ring of conjunctiva around cornea
EXCLUDES *biopsy of conjunctiva (10.21)*
DEF: Removal of growth or tissue from eye membrane.

10.32 Destruction of lesion of conjunctiva
EXCLUDES *excision of lesion (10.31)*
thermocauterization for entropion (08.41)
DEF: Destruction of eye membrane growth; not done by excision.

10.33 Other destructive procedures on conjunctiva
Removal of trachoma follicles

✓4th **10.4 Conjunctivoplasty**
DEF: Correction of conjunctiva by plastic surgery.

10.41 Repair of symblepharon with free graft

10.42 Reconstruction of conjunctival cul-de-sac with free graft
EXCLUDES *revision of enucleation socket with graft (16.63)*
DEF: Rebuilding of eye membrane fold with graft of unattached tissue.

10.43 Other reconstruction of conjunctival cul-de-sac
EXCLUDES *revision of enucleation socket (16.64)*

10.44 Other free graft to conjunctiva

10.49 Other conjunctivoplasty
EXCLUDES *repair of cornea with conjunctival flap (11.53)*

10.5 Lysis of adhesions of conjunctiva and eyelid
Division of symblepharon (with insertion of conformer)

10.6 Repair of laceration of conjunctiva
EXCLUDES *that with repair of sclera (12.81)*

✓4th **10.9 Other operations on conjunctiva**

10.91 Subconjunctival injection

10.99 Other

✓3rd **11 Operations on cornea**

11.0 Magnetic removal of embedded foreign body from cornea
EXCLUDES *that with incision (11.1)*

11.1 Incision of cornea
Incision of cornea for removal of foreign body

✓4th **11.2 Diagnostic procedures on cornea**

11.21 Scraping of cornea for smear or culture

11.22 Biopsy of cornea

11.29 Other diagnostic procedures on cornea

✓4th **11.3 Excision of pterygium**

11.31 Transposition of pterygium
DEF: Cutting into membranous structure extending from eye membrane to cornea and suturing it in a downward position.

11.32 Excision of pterygium with corneal graft
DEF: Surgical removal and repair of membranous structure extending from eye membrane to cornea using corneal tissue transplant.

11.39 Other excision of pterygium

✓4th **11.4 Excision or destruction of tissue or other lesion of cornea**

11.41 Mechanical removal of corneal epithelium
That by chemocauterization
EXCLUDES *that for smear or culture (11.21)*
DEF: Removal of outer layer of cornea by mechanical means.

11.42 Thermocauterization of corneal lesion
DEF: Destruction of corneal lesion by electrical cautery.

11.43 Cryotherapy of corneal lesion
DEF: Destruction of corneal lesion with cold therapy.

11.49 Other removal or destruction of corneal lesion
Excision of cornea NOS
EXCLUDES *biopsy of cornea (11.22)*

✓4th **11.5 Repair of cornea**

11.51 Suture of corneal laceration

11.52 Repair of postoperative wound dehiscence of cornea
DEF: Repair of ruptured postoperative corneal wound.

11.53 Repair of corneal laceration or wound with conjunctival flap
DEF: Correction corneal wound or tear with conjunctival tissue.

11.59 Other repair of cornea

✓4th **11.6 Corneal transplant**
EXCLUDES *excision of pterygium with corneal graft (11.32)*

11.60 Corneal transplant, not otherwise specified
Note: To report donor sources – see codes 00.91-00.93
Keratoplasty NOS

11.61 Lamellar keratoplasty with autograft
DEF: Restoration of sight using patient's own corneal tissue, partial thickness.

11.62 Other lamellar keratoplasty
DEF: Restoration of sight using donor corneal tissue, partial thickness.

11.63 Penetrating keratoplasty with autograft
Perforating keratoplasty with autograft

11.64 Other penetrating keratoplasty
Perforating keratoplasty (with homograft)

11.69 Other corneal transplant

✓4th **11.7 Other reconstructive and refractive surgery on cornea**

11.71 Keratomileusis
DEF: Restoration of corneal shape by removing portion of cornea, freezing, reshaping curve and reattaching it.

11.72 Keratophakia
DEF: Correction of eye lens loss by dissecting the central zone of the cornea and replacing it with a thickened graft of the cornea.

11.73 Keratoprosthesis
DEF: Placement of corneal artificial implant.

11.74 Thermokeratoplasty
DEF: Reshaping and reforming cornea by heat application.

11.75 Radial keratotomy
DEF: Incisions around cornea radius to correct nearsightedness.

11.76 Epikeratophakia
DEF: Repair lens loss by cornea graft sutured to central corneal zone.

11.79 Other

✓4th **11.9 Other operations on cornea**

11.91 Tattooing of cornea

11.92 Removal of artificial implant from cornea

11.99 Other

✓3rd **12 Operations on iris, ciliary body, sclera, and anterior chamber**

EXCLUDES *operations on cornea (11.0-11.99)*

✓4th **12.0 Removal of intraocular foreign body from anterior segment of eye**

12.00 Removal of intraocular foreign body from anterior segment of eye, not otherwise specified

12.01 Removal of intraocular foreign body from anterior segment of eye with use of magnet

12.02 Removal of intraocular foreign body from anterior segment of eye without use of magnet

✓4th **12.1 Iridotomy and simple iridectomy**

EXCLUDES *iridectomy associated with:*
cataract extraction (13.11-13.69)
removal of lesion (12.41-12.42)
scleral fistulization (12.61-12.69)

12.11 Iridotomy with transfixion

12.12 Other iridotomy

Corectomy
Discission of iris
Iridotomy NOS

DEF: Corectomy: Incision into iris (also called iridectomy).

12.13 Excision of prolapsed iris

DEF: Removal of downwardly placed portion of iris.

12.14 Other iridectomy

Iridectomy (basal) (peripheral) (total)

DEF: Removal, partial or total of iris.

✓4th **12.2 Diagnostic procedures on iris, ciliary body, sclera, and anterior chamber**

12.21 Diagnostic aspiration of anterior chamber of eye

DEF: Suction withdrawal of fluid from anterior eye chamber for diagnostic reasons.

12.22 Biopsy of iris

12.29 Other diagnostic procedures on iris, ciliary body, sclera, and anterior chamber

✓4th **12.3 Iridoplasty and coreoplasty**

DEF: Correction or abnormal iris or pupil by plastic surgery.

12.31 Lysis of goniosynechiae

Lysis of goniosynechiae by injection of air or liquid

DEF: Freeing of fibrous structures between cornea and iris by injecting air or liquid.

Trabeculectomy Ab Externo

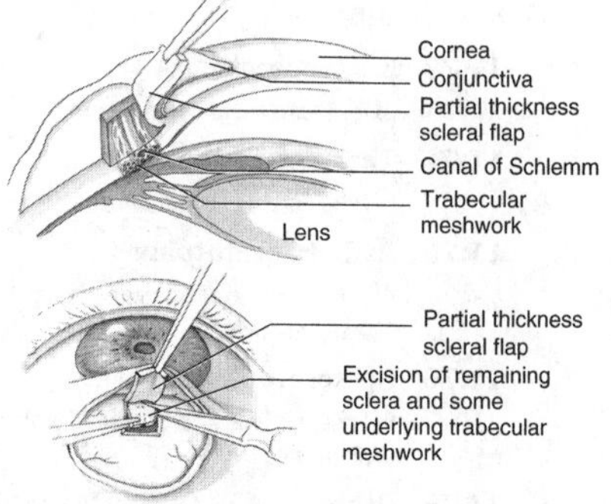

12.32 Lysis of other anterior synechiae

Lysis of anterior synechiae:
NOS
by injection of air or liquid

12.33 Lysis of posterior synechiae

Lysis of iris adhesions NOS

12.34 Lysis of corneovitreal adhesions

DEF: Release of adhesions of cornea and vitreous body.

12.35 Coreoplasty

Needling of pupillary membrane

DEF: Correction of an iris defect.

12.39 Other iridoplasty

✓4th **12.4 Excision or destruction of lesion of iris and ciliary body**

12.40 Removal of lesion of anterior segment of eye, not otherwise specified

12.41 Destruction of lesion of iris, nonexcisional

Destruction of lesion of iris by:
cauterization
cryotherapy
photocoagulation

12.42 Excision of lesion of iris

EXCLUDES *biopsy of iris (12.22)*

12.43 Destruction of lesion of ciliary body, nonexcisional

12.44 Excision of lesion of ciliary body

✓4th **12.5 Facilitation of intraocular circulation**

12.51 Goniopuncture without goniotomy

DEF: Stab incision into anterior chamber of eye to relieve optic pressure.

12.52 Goniotomy without goniopuncture

DEF: Incision into Schlemm's canal to drain aqueous and relieve pressure.

12.53 Goniotomy with goniopuncture

12.54 Trabeculotomy ab externo

DEF: Incision into supporting connective tissue strands of eye capsule, via exterior approach.

12.55 Cyclodialysis

DEF: Creation of passage between anterior chamber and suprachoroidal space.

12.59 Other facilitation of intraocular circulation

✓4th **12.6 Scleral fistulization**

EXCLUDES *exploratory sclerotomy (12.89)*

12.61 Trephination of sclera with iridectomy

DEF: Cut around sclerocornea to remove part of the iris.

12.62 Thermocauterization of sclera with iridectomy

DEF: Destruction of outer eyeball layer with partial excision of iris using heat.

12.63 Iridencleisis and iridotasis

DEF: Creation of permanent drain in iris by transposing or stretching iris tissue.

12.64 Trabeculectomy ab externo

DEF: Excision of supporting connective tissue strands of eye capsule, via exterior approach.

12.65 Other scleral fistulization with iridectomy

Holth's sclerectomy

DEF: Creation of outer eyeball layer passage with partial excision of iris.

12.66 Postoperative revision of scleral fistulization procedure
Revision of filtering bleb
EXCLUDES *repair of fistula (12.82)*

12.69 Other fistulizing procedure

✓4th **12.7 Other procedures for relief of elevated intraocular pressure**

12.71 Cyclodiathermy
DEF: Destruction of ciliary body tissue with heat.

12.72 Cyclocryotherapy
DEF: Destruction of ciliary body tissue by freezing.

12.73 Cyclophotocoagulation
DEF: Destruction of ciliary body tissue by high energy light source.

12.74 Diminution of ciliary body, not otherwise specified

12.79 Other glaucoma procedures

✓4th **12.8 Operations on sclera**
EXCLUDES *those associated with:*
retinal reattachment (14.41-14.59)
scleral fistulization (12.61-12.69)

12.81 Suture of laceration of sclera
Suture of sclera with synchronous repair of conjunctiva

12.82 Repair of scleral fistula
EXCLUDES *postoperative revision of scleral fistulization procedure (12.66)*

12.83 Revision of operative wound of anterior segment, not elsewhere classified
EXCLUDES *postoperative revision of scleral fistulization procedure (12.66)*

12.84 Excision or destruction of lesion of sclera

12.85 Repair of scleral staphyloma with graft
DEF: Repair of protruding outer eyeball layer with a graft.

12.86 Other repair of scleral staphyloma

12.87 Scleral reinforcement with graft
DEF: Restoration of outer eyeball shape with tissue graft.

12.88 Other scleral reinforcement

12.89 Other operations on sclera
Exploratory sclerotomy

✓4th **12.9 Other operations on iris, ciliary body, and anterior chamber**

12.91 Therapeutic evacuation of anterior chamber
Paracentesis of anterior chamber
EXCLUDES *diagnostic aspiration (12.21)*

12.92 Injection into anterior chamber
Injection of:
air, liquid, medication } into anterior chamber

12.93 Removal or destruction of epithelial downgrowth from anterior chamber
EXCLUDES *that with iridectomy (12.41-12.42)*
DEF: Excision or destruction of epithelial overgrowth in anterior eye chamber.

12.97 Other operations on iris

12.98 Other operations on ciliary body

12.99 Other operations on anterior chamber

✓3rd **13 Operations on lens**

✓4th **13.0 Removal of foreign body from lens**
EXCLUDES *removal of pseudophakos (13.8)*

13.00 Removal of foreign body from lens, not otherwise specified

13.01 Removal of foreign body from lens with use of magnet

13.02 Removal of foreign body from lens without use of magnet

✓4th **13.1 Intracapsular extraction of lens**
Code also any synchronous insertion of pseudophakos (13.71)

13.11 Intracapsular extraction of lens by temporal inferior route
DEF: Extraction of lens and capsule via anterior approach through outer side of eyeball.

13.19 Other intracapsular extraction of lens
Cataract extraction NOS
Cryoextraction of lens
Erysiphake extraction of cataract
Extraction of lens NOS

13.2 Extracapsular extraction of lens by linear extraction technique
DEF: Excision of lens without the posterior capsule at junction between the cornea and outer eyeball layer by means of a linear incision.

13.3 Extracapsular extraction of lens by simple aspiration (and irrigation) technique
Irrigation of traumatic cataract
DEF: Removal of lens without the posterior capsule by suctioning and flushing out the area.

✓4th **13.4 Extracapsular extraction of lens by fragmentation and aspiration technique**
DEF: Removal of lens after division into smaller pieces with posterior capsule left intact.

13.41 Phacoemulsification and aspiration of cataract

13.42 Mechanical phacofragmentation and aspiration of cataract by posterior route
Code also any synchronous vitrectomy (14.74)

13.43 Mechanical phacofragmentation and other aspiration of cataract

✓4th **13.5 Other extracapsular extraction of lens**
Code also any synchronous insertion of pseudophakos (13.71)

13.51 Extracapsular extraction of lens by temporal inferior route
DEF: Removal of lens through outer eyeball with posterior capsule left intact.

13.59 Other extracapsular extraction of lens

Extraction of Lens (with insertion of intraocular lens prosthesis)

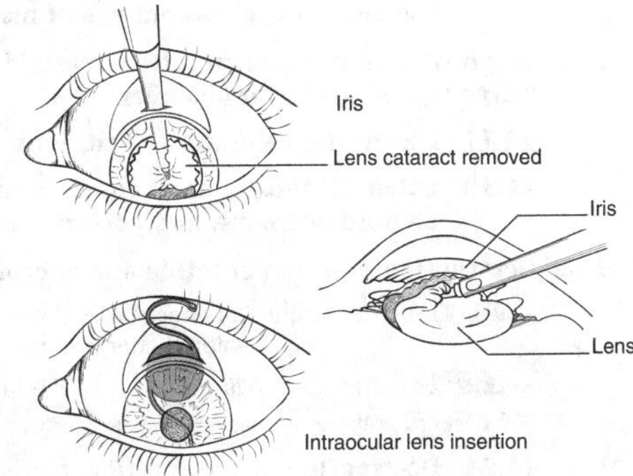

✓4th **13.6 Other cataract extraction**

Code also any synchronous insertion of pseudophakos (13.71)

13.64 Discission of secondary membrane [after cataract]

DEF: Breaking up of fibrotic lens capsule developed after previous lens extraction.

13.65 Excision of secondary membrane [after cataract]

Capsulectomy

DEF: Capsulectomy: Excision of lens capsule membrane after previous lens extraction.

13.66 Mechanical fragmentation of secondary membrane [after cataract]

DEF: Breaking up and removal of fibrotic lens capsule developed after previous lens extraction.

13.69 Other cataract extraction

✓4th **13.7 Insertion of prosthetic lens [pseudophakos]**

EXCLUDES *implantation of intraocular telescope prosthesis (13.91)*

DEF: Insertion of ocular implant, following lens extraction.

13.70 Insertion of pseudophakos, not otherwise specified

13.71 Insertion of intraocular lens prosthesis at time of cataract extraction, one-stage

Code also synchronous extraction of cataract (13.11-13.69)

13.72 Secondary insertion of intraocular lens prosthesis

13.8 Removal of implanted lens

Removal of pseudophakos

✓4th **13.9 Other operations on lens**

13.90 Operation on lens, not elsewhere classified

13.91 Implantation of intraocular telescope prosthesis

Implantable miniature telescope

INCLUDES removal of lens, any method

EXCLUDES *secondary insertion of ocular implant (16.61)*

✓3rd **14 Operations on retina, choroid, vitreous, and posterior chamber**

✓4th **14.0 Removal of foreign body from posterior segment of eye**

EXCLUDES *removal of surgically implanted material (14.6)*

14.00 Removal of foreign body from posterior segment of eye, not otherwise specified

14.01 Removal of foreign body from posterior segment of eye with use of magnet

14.02 Removal of foreign body from posterior segment of eye without use of magnet

✓4th **14.1 Diagnostic procedures on retina, choroid, vitreous, and posterior chamber**

14.11 Diagnostic aspiration of vitreous

14.19 Other diagnostic procedures on retina, choroid, vitreous, and posterior chamber

✓4th **14.2 Destruction of lesion of retina and choroid**

INCLUDES destruction of chorioretinopathy or isolated chorioretinal lesion

EXCLUDES *that for repair of retina (14.31-14.59)*

DEF: Destruction of damaged retina and choroid tissue.

14.21 Destruction of chorioretinal lesion by diathermy

Laser Surgery (YAG)

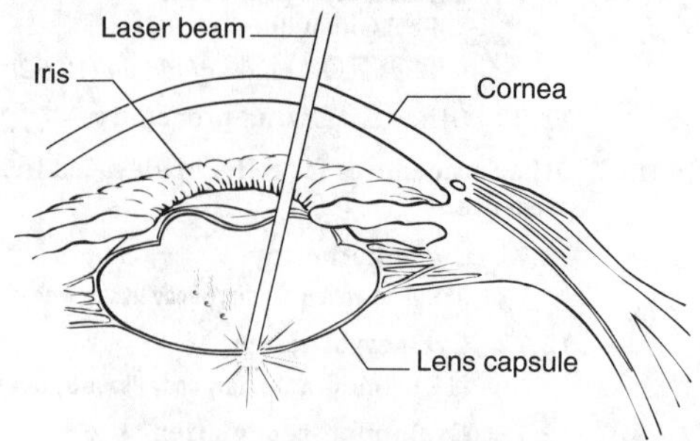

14.22 Destruction of chorioretinal lesion by cryotherapy

14.23 Destruction of chorioretinal lesion by xenon arc photocoagulation

14.24 Destruction of chorioretinal lesion by laser photocoagulation

14.25 Destruction of chorioretinal lesion by photocoagulation of unspecified type

14.26 Destruction of chorioretinal lesion by radiation therapy

14.27 Destruction of chorioretinal lesion by implantation of radiation source

14.29 Other destruction of chorioretinal lesion

Destruction of lesion of retina and choroid NOS

✓4th **14.3 Repair of retinal tear**

INCLUDES repair of retinal defect

EXCLUDES *repair of retinal detachment (14.41-14.59)*

14.31 Repair of retinal tear by diathermy

14.32 Repair of retinal tear by cryotherapy

14.33 Repair of retinal tear by xenon arc photocoagulation

14.34 Repair of retinal tear by laser photocoagulation

14.35 Repair of retinal tear by photocoagulation of unspecified type

14.39 Other repair of retinal tear

✓4th **14.4 Repair of retinal detachment with scleral buckling and implant**

DEF: Placement of material around eye to indent sclera and close a hole or tear or to reduce vitreous traction.

14.41 Scleral buckling with implant

Scleral Buckling with Implant

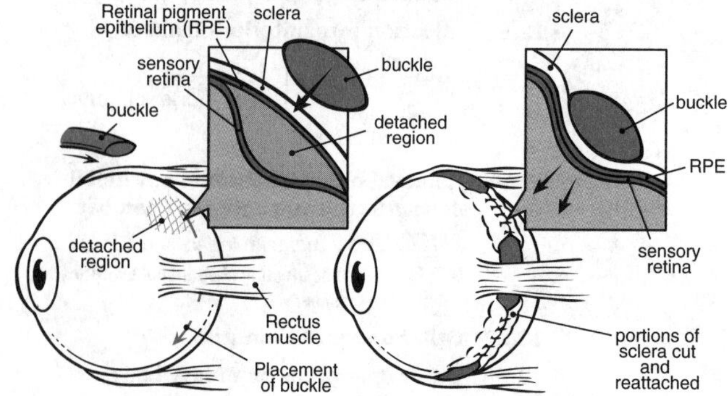

14.49 Other scleral buckling
Scleral buckling with:
air tamponade
resection of sclera
vitrectomy

✓4th **14.5 Other repair of retinal detachment**
INCLUDES that with drainage

14.51 Repair of retinal detachment with diathermy

14.52 Repair of retinal detachment with cryotherapy

14.53 Repair of retinal detachment with xenon arc photocoagulation

14.54 Repair of retinal detachment with laser photocoagulation

14.55 Repair of retinal detachment with photocoagulation of unspecified type

14.59 Other

14.6 Removal of surgically implanted material from posterior segment of eye

✓4th **14.7 Operations on vitreous**

14.71 Removal of vitreous, anterior approach
Open sky technique
Removal of vitreous, anterior approach (with replacement)
DEF: Removal of all or part of the eyeball fluid via the anterior segment of the eyeball.

14.72 Other removal of vitreous
Aspiration of vitreous by posterior sclerotomy

14.73 Mechanical vitrectomy by anterior approach
DEF: Removal of abnormal tissue in eyeball fluid to control fibrotic overgrowth in severe intraocular injury.

14.74 Other mechanical vitrectomy
Posterior approach

14.75 Injection of vitreous substitute
EXCLUDES *that associated with removal (14.71-14.72)*

14.79 Other operations on vitreous

14.9 Other operations on retina, choroid, and posterior chamber

✓3rd **15 Operations on extraocular muscles**

✓4th **15.0 Diagnostic procedures on extraocular muscles or tendons**

15.01 Biopsy of extraocular muscle or tendon

15.09 Other diagnostic procedures on extraocular muscles and tendons

✓4th **15.1 Operations on one extraocular muscle involving temporary detachment from globe**

15.11 Recession of one extraocular muscle
DEF: Detachment of exterior eye muscle with posterior reattachment to correct strabismus.

15.12 Advancement of one extraocular muscle
DEF: Detachment of exterior eye muscle with forward reattachment to correct strabismus.

15.13 Resection of one extraocular muscle

15.19 Other operations on one extraocular muscle involving temporary detachment from globe
EXCLUDES *transposition of muscle (15.5)*

Lengthening Procedure on One Extraocular Muscle

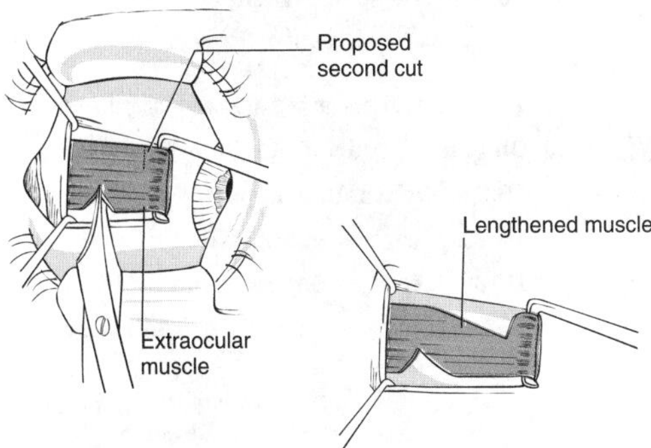

Shortening Procedure on One Extraocular Muscle

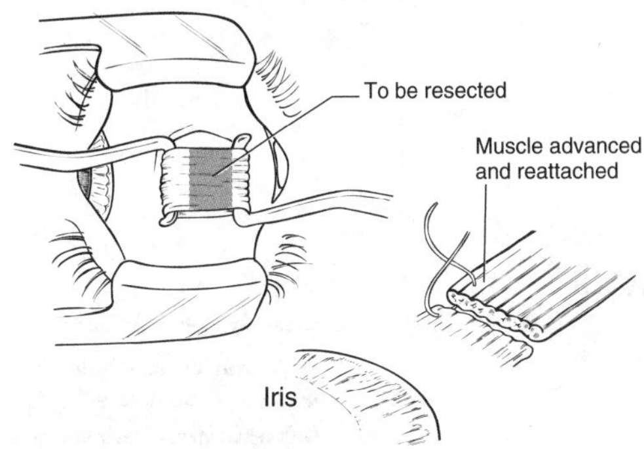

✓4th **15.2 Other operations on one extraocular muscle**

15.21 Lengthening procedure on one extraocular muscle
DEF: Extension of exterior eye muscle length.

15.22 Shortening procedure on one extraocular muscle
DEF: Shortening of exterior eye muscle.

15.29 Other

15.3 Operations on two or more extraocular muscles involving temporary detachment from globe, one or both eyes

15.4 Other operations on two or more extraocular muscles, one or both eyes

15.5 Transposition of extraocular muscles
EXCLUDES *that for correction of ptosis (08.31-08.36)*
DEF: Relocation of exterior eye muscle to a more functional site.

15.6 Revision of extraocular muscle surgery
DEF: Repair of previous exterior eye muscle surgery.

15.7 Repair of injury of extraocular muscle
Freeing of entrapped extraocular muscle
Lysis of adhesions of extraocular muscle
Repair of laceration of extraocular muscle, tendon, or Tenon's capsule

15.9 Other operations on extraocular muscles and tendons

✓3rd **16 Operations on orbit and eyeball**
EXCLUDES *reduction of fracture of orbit (76.78-76.79)*

✓4th **16.0 Orbitotomy**

16.01 Orbitotomy with bone flap
Orbitotomy with lateral approach
DEF: Incision into orbital bone with insertion of small bone piece.

16.02 Orbitotomy with insertion of orbital implant
EXCLUDES *that with bone flap (16.01)*

16.09 Other orbitotomy

16.1 Removal of penetrating foreign body from eye, not otherwise specified

EXCLUDES *removal of nonpenetrating foreign body (98.21)*

DEF: Removal of foreign body from an unspecified site in eye.

✓4th **16.2 Diagnostic procedures on orbit and eyeball**

16.21 Ophthalmoscopy

16.22 Diagnostic aspiration of orbit

16.23 Biopsy of eyeball and orbit

16.29 Other diagnostic procedures on orbit and eyeball

EXCLUDES *examination of form and structure of eye (95.11-95.16)*
general and subjective eye examination (95.01-95.09)
microscopic examination of specimen from eye (90.21-90.29)
objective functional tests of eye (95.21-95.26)
ocular thermography (88.82)
tonometry (89.11)
x-ray of orbit (87.14, 87.16)

✓4th **16.3 Evisceration of eyeball**

DEF: Removal of eyeball, leaving sclera and occasionally cornea.

16.31 Removal of ocular contents with synchronous implant into scleral shell

DEF: Removal of eyeball leaving outer eyeball layer with ocular implant into shell.

16.39 Other evisceration of eyeball

✓4th **16.4 Enucleation of eyeball**

DEF: Removal of entire eyeball after severing eye muscles and optic nerves.

16.41 Enucleation of eyeball with synchronous implant into Tenon's capsule with attachment of muscles

Integrated implant of eyeball

DEF: Removal of eyeball with insertion of ocular implant and muscle attachment.

16.42 Enucleation of eyeball with other synchronous implant

16.49 Other enucleation of eyeball

Removal of eyeball NOS

✓4th **16.5 Exenteration of orbital contents**

16.51 Exenteration of orbit with removal of adjacent structures

Radical orbitomaxillectomy

DEF: Removal of contents of bony cavity of eye as well as related tissues and structures.

DEF: Radical orbitomaxillectomy: Removal of contents of bony cavity of eye, related tissues and structures, and a portion of maxillary bone.

16.52 Exenteration of orbit with therapeutic removal of orbital bone

16.59 Other exenteration of orbit

Evisceration of orbit NOS
Exenteration of orbit with temporalis muscle transplant

✓4th **16.6 Secondary procedures after removal of eyeball**

EXCLUDES *that with synchronous:*
enucleation of eyeball (16.41-16.42)
evisceration of eyeball (16.31)

16.61 Secondary insertion of ocular implant

DEF: Insertion of ocular implant after previous eye removal.

16.62 Revision and reinsertion of ocular implant

DEF: Reimplant or correction of ocular implant.

16.63 Revision of enucleation socket with graft

DEF: Implant of tissue to correct socket after eye removal.

16.64 Other revision of enucleation socket

16.65 Secondary graft to exenteration cavity

DEF: Implant of tissue in place of eye after removal.

16.66 Other revision of exenteration cavity

16.69 Other secondary procedures after removal of eyeball

✓4th **16.7 Removal of ocular or orbital implant**

16.71 Removal of ocular implant

16.72 Removal of orbital implant

✓4th **16.8 Repair of injury of eyeball and orbit**

16.81 Repair of wound of orbit

EXCLUDES *reduction of orbital fracture (76.78-76.79)*
repair of extraocular muscles (15.7)

16.82 Repair of rupture of eyeball

Repair of multiple structures of eye

EXCLUDES *repair of laceration of:*
cornea (11.51-11.59)
sclera (12.81)

16.89 Other repair of injury of eyeball or orbit

✓4th **16.9 Other operations on orbit and eyeball**

EXCLUDES *irrigation of eye (96.51)*
prescription and fitting of low vision aids (95.31-95.33)
removal of:
eye prosthesis NEC (97.31)
nonpenetrating foreign body from eye without incision (98.21)

16.91 Retrobulbar injection of therapeutic agent

EXCLUDES *injection of radiographic contrast material (87.14)*
opticociliary injection (12.79)

16.92 Excision of lesion of orbit

EXCLUDES *biopsy of orbit (16.23)*

16.93 Excision of lesion of eye, unspecified structure

EXCLUDES *biopsy of eye NOS (16.23)*

16.98 Other operations on orbit

16.99 Other operations on eyeball

3A. OTHER MISCELLANEOUS DIAGNOSTIC AND THERAPEUTIC PROCEDURES (17)

✓3rd **17 Other miscellaneous procedures**

✓4th **17.1 Laparoscopic unilateral repair of inguinal hernia**

EXCLUDES *other and open unilateral repair of hernia (53.00-53.05)*

17.11 Laparoscopic repair of direct inguinal hernia with graft or prosthesis

Laparoscopic repair of direct and indirect inguinal hernia with graft or prosthesis

17.12 Laparoscopic repair of indirect inguinal hernia with graft or prosthesis

17.13 Laparoscopic repair of inguinal hernia with graft or prosthesis, not otherwise specified

✓4th **17.2 Laparoscopic bilateral repair of inguinal hernia**

EXCLUDES *other and open bilateral repair of hernia (53.10 – 53.17)*

17.21 Laparoscopic bilateral repair of direct inguinal hernia with graft or prosthesis

17.22 Laparoscopic bilateral repair of indirect inguinal hernia with graft or prosthesis

17.23 Laparoscopic bilateral repair of inguinal hernia, one direct and one indirect, with graft or prosthesis

17.24 Laparoscopic bilateral repair of inguinal hernia with graft or prosthesis, not otherwise specified

✓4th **17.3 Laparoscopic partial excision of large intestine**

EXCLUDES *other and open partial excision of large intestine (45.71-45.79)*

17.31 Laparoscopic multiple segmental resection of large intestine

17.32 Laparoscopic cecectomy

17.33 Laparoscopic right hemicolectomy

17.34 Laparoscopic resection of transverse colon

17.35 Laparoscopic left hemicolectomy

17.36 Laparoscopic sigmoidectomy

17.39 Other laparoscopic partial excision of large intestine

✓4th **17.4 Robotic assisted procedures**

Note: This category includes use of a computer console with (3-D) imaging, software, camera(s), visualization and instrumentation *combined* with the use of robotic arms, device(s), or system(s) at the time of the procedure.

Computer assisted robotic surgery
Computer-enhanced robotic surgery
Robotic procedure with computer assistance
Surgeon-controlled robotic surgery

Code first primary procedure

EXCLUDES *computer assisted surgery (00.31-00.35, 00.39)*

17.41 Open robotic assisted procedure

Robotic assistance in open procedure

17.42 Laparoscopic robotic assisted procedure

Robotic assistance in laparoscopic procedure

17.43 Percutaneous robotic assisted procedure

Robotic assistance in percutaneous procedure

17.44 Endoscopic robotic assisted procedure

Robotic assistance in endoscopic procedure

17.45 Thoracoscopic robotic assisted procedure

Robotic assistance in thoracoscopic procedure

17.49 Other and unspecified robotic assisted procedure

Robotic assistance in other and unspecified procedure

EXCLUDES *endoscopic robotic assisted procedure (17.44)*
laparoscopic robotic assisted procedure (17.42)
open robotic assisted procedure (17.41)
percutaneous robotic assisted procedure (17.43)
thoracoscopic robotic assisted procedure (17.45)

4. OPERATIONS ON THE EAR (18-20)

✓3rd **18 Operations on external ear**

INCLUDES operations on:
external auditory canal
skin and cartilage of:
auricle
meatus

✓4th **18.0 Incision of external ear**

EXCLUDES *removal of intraluminal foreign body (98.11)*

18.01 Piercing of ear lobe
Piercing of pinna

18.02 Incision of external auditory canal

18.09 Other incision of external ear

✓4th **18.1 Diagnostic procedures on external ear**

18.11 Otoscopy
DEF: Exam of the ear with instrument designed for visualization.

18.12 Biopsy of external ear

18.19 Other diagnostic procedures on external ear
EXCLUDES *microscopic examination of specimen from ear (90.31-90.39)*

✓4th **18.2 Excision or destruction of lesion of external ear**

18.21 Excision of preauricular sinus
Radical excision of preauricular sinus or cyst
EXCLUDES *excision of preauricular remnant [appendage] (18.29)*
DEF: Excision of preauricular sinus or cyst with adjacent tissues.

18.29 Excision or destruction of other lesion of external ear
Cauterization, Coagulation, Cryosurgery, Curettage, Electrocoagulation, Enucleation } of external ear
Excision of:
exostosis of external auditory canal
preauricular remnant [appendage]
Partial excision of ear
EXCLUDES *biopsy of external ear (18.12)*
radical excision of lesion (18.31)
removal of cerumen (96.52)

✓4th **18.3 Other excision of external ear**

EXCLUDES *biopsy of external ear (18.12)*

18.31 Radical excision of lesion of external ear
EXCLUDES *radical excision of preauricular sinus (18.21)*
DEF: Removal of damaged, diseased ear and adjacent tissue.

18.39 Other
Amputation of external ear
EXCLUDES *excision of lesion (18.21-18.29, 18.31)*

18.4 Suture of laceration of external ear

18.5 Surgical correction of prominent ear
Ear:
pinning
setback
DEF: Reformation of protruding outer ear.

18.6 Reconstruction of external auditory canal
Canaloplasty of external auditory meatus
Construction [reconstruction] of external meatus of ear:
osseous portion
skin-lined portion (with skin graft)
DEF: Repair of outer ear canal.

✓4th **18.7 Other plastic repair of external ear**

18.71 Construction of auricle of ear
Prosthetic appliance for absent ear
Reconstruction:
auricle
ear
DEF: Reformation or repair of external ear flap.

18.72 Reattachment of amputated ear

18.79 Other plastic repair of external ear
Otoplasty NOS
Postauricular skin graft
Repair of lop ear
DEF: Postauricular skin graft: Graft repair behind ear.
DEF: Repair of lop ear: Reconstruction of ear that is at right angle to head.

18.9 Other operations on external ear

EXCLUDES *irrigation of ear (96.52)*
packing of external auditory canal (96.11)
removal of:
cerumen (96.52)
foreign body (without incision) (98.11)

✓3rd **19 Reconstructive operations on middle ear**

19.0 Stapes mobilization
Division, otosclerotic:
material
process
Remobilization of stapes
Stapediolysis
Transcrural stapes mobilization
EXCLUDES *that with synchronous stapedectomy (19.11-19.19)*
DEF: Repair of innermost bone of middle ear to enable movement and response to sound.

✓4th **19.1 Stapedectomy**

EXCLUDES *revision of previous stapedectomy (19.21-19.29)*
stapes mobilization only (19.0)
DEF: Removal of innermost bone of middle ear.

19.11 Stapedectomy with incus replacement
Stapedectomy with incus:
homograft
prosthesis
DEF: Removal of innermost bone of middle ear with autograft or prosthesis replacement.

19.19 Other stapedectomy

Stapedectomy with Incus Replacement

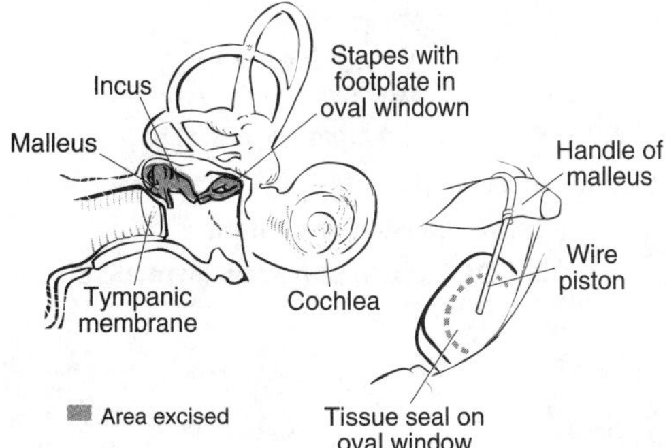

✓4th **19.2 Revision of stapedectomy**

19.21 Revision of stapedectomy with incus replacement

19.29 Other revision of stapedectomy

19.3 Other operations on ossicular chain

Incudectomy NOS
Ossiculectomy NOS
Reconstruction of ossicles, second stage

DEF: Incudectomy: Excision of middle bone of middle ear, not otherwise specified.

DEF: Ossiculectomy: Excision of middle ear bones, not otherwise specified.

DEF: Reconstruction of ossicles, second stage: Repair of middle ear bones following previous surgery.

19.4 Myringoplasty

Epitympanic, type I
Myringoplasty by:
cauterization
graft
Tympanoplasty (type I)

DEF: Epitympanic, type I: Repair over or upon eardrum.

DEF: Myringoplasty by cauterization: Plastic repair of tympanic membrane of eardrum by heat.

DEF: Graft: Plastic repair using implanted tissue.

DEF: Tympanoplasty (type I): Reconstruction of eardrum to restore hearing.

✓4th **19.5 Other tympanoplasty**

19.52 Type II tympanoplasty

Closure of perforation with graft against incus or malleus

19.53 Type III tympanoplasty

Graft placed in contact with mobile and intact stapes

19.54 Type IV tympanoplasty

Mobile footplate left exposed with air pocket between round window and graft

19.55 Type V tympanoplasty

Fenestra in horizontal semicircular canal covered by graft

19.6 Revision of tympanoplasty

DEF: Repair or correction of previous plastic surgery on eardrum.

19.9 Other repair of middle ear

Closure of mastoid fistula
Mastoid myoplasty
Obliteration of tympanomastoid cavity

DEF: Closure of mastoid fistula: Closing of abnormal channel in mastoid.

DEF: Mastoid myoplasty: Restoration or repair of mastoid muscle.

DEF: Obliteration of tympanomastoid cavity: Removal, total, of functional elements of middle ear.

✓3rd **20 Other operations on middle and inner ear**

✓4th **20.0 Myringotomy**

DEF: Myringotomy: Puncture of tympanic membrane or eardrum, also called tympanocentesis

20.01 Myringotomy with insertion of tube

Myringostomy

20.09 Other myringotomy

Aspiration of middle ear NOS

20.1 Removal of tympanostomy tube

✓4th **20.2 Incision of mastoid and middle ear**

20.21 Incision of mastoid

20.22 Incision of petrous pyramid air cells

20.23 Incision of middle ear

Atticotomy
Division of tympanum
Lysis of adhesions of middle ear

EXCLUDES *division of otosclerotic process (19.0)*
stapediolysis (19.0)
that with stapedectomy (19.11-19.19)

✓4th **20.3 Diagnostic procedures on middle and inner ear**

20.31 Electrocochleography

DEF: Measure of electric potential of eighth cranial nerve by electrode applied sound.

20.32 Biopsy of middle and inner ear

20.39 Other diagnostic procedures on middle and inner ear

EXCLUDES *auditory and vestibular function tests (89.13, 95.41-95.49)*
microscopic examination of specimen from ear (90.31-90.39)

✓4th **20.4 Mastoidectomy**

Code also any:
skin graft (18.79)
tympanoplasty (19.4-19.55)

EXCLUDES *that with implantation of cochlear prosthetic device (20.96-20.98)*

DEF: Mastoidectomy: Excision of bony protrusion behind ear.

20.41 Simple mastoidectomy

20.42 Radical mastoidectomy

20.49 Other mastoidectomy

Atticoantrostomy
Mastoidectomy:
NOS
modified radical

DEF: Atticoantrotomy: Opening of cavity of mastoid bone and middle ear.

✓4th **20.5 Other excision of middle ear**

EXCLUDES *that with synchronous mastoidectomy (20.41-20.49)*

20.51 Excision of lesion of middle ear

EXCLUDES *biopsy of middle ear (20.32)*

20.59 Other

Apicectomy of petrous pyramid
Tympanectomy

✓4th **20.6 Fenestration of inner ear**

20.61 Fenestration of inner ear (initial)

Fenestration of:
labyrinth, semicircular canals, vestibule } with graft (skin) (vein)

EXCLUDES *that with tympanoplasty, type V (19.55)*

DEF: Creation of inner ear opening.

20.62 Revision of fenestration of inner ear

✓4th **20.7 Incision, excision, and destruction of inner ear**

20.71 Endolymphatic shunt

DEF: Insertion of tube to drain fluid in inner ear cavities.

20.72 Injection into inner ear

Destruction by injection (alcohol):
inner ear
semicircular canals
vestibule

20.79 Other incision, excision, and destruction of inner ear

Decompression of labyrinth
Drainage of inner ear
Fistulization:
  endolymphatic sac
  labyrinth
Incision of endolymphatic sac
Labyrinthectomy (transtympanic)
Opening of bony labyrinth
Perilymphatic tap

EXCLUDES *biopsy of inner ear (20.32)*

DEF: Decompression of labyrinth: Controlled relief of pressure in cavities of inner ear.

DEF: Drainage of inner ear: Removal of fluid from inner ear.

DEF: Fistulization of endolymphatic sac: Creation of passage to fluid sac in inner ear cavities.

DEF: Fistulization of labyrinth: Creation of passage to inner ear cavities.

DEF: Incision of endolymphatic sac: Cutting into fluid sac in inner ear cavities.

DEF: Labyrinthectomy (transtympanic): Excision of cavities across eardrum.

DEF: Opening of bony labyrinth: Cutting into inner ear bony cavities.

DEF: Perilymphatic tap: Puncture or incision into fluid sac of inner ear cavities.

20.8 Operations on Eustachian tube

Catheterization
Inflation
Injection (Teflon paste)
Insufflation (boric acid-salicylic acid)
Intubation
Politzerization
} of Eustachian tube

DEF: Catheterization: Passing catheter into passage between pharynx and middle ear.

DEF: Inflation: Blowing air, gas or liquid into passage between pharynx and middle ear to inflate.

DEF: Injection (Teflon paste): Forcing fluid (Teflon paste) into passage between pharynx and middle ear.

DEF: Insufflation (boric acid-salicylic acid): Blowing gas or liquid into passage between pharynx and middle ear.

DEF: Intubation: Placing tube into passage between pharynx and middle ear.

DEF: Politzerization: Inflating passage between pharynx and middle ear with Politzer bag.

✓4th **20.9 Other operations on inner and middle ear**

20.91 Tympanosympathectomy

DEF: Excision or chemical suppression of impulses of middle ear nerves.

20.92 Revision of mastoidectomy

DEF: Correction of previous removal of mastoid cells from temporal or mastoid bone.

20.93 Repair of oval and round windows

Closure of fistula:
  oval window
  perilymph
  round window

DEF: Restoration of middle ear openings.

20.94 Injection of tympanum

20.95 Implantation of electromagnetic hearing device

Bone conduction hearing device

EXCLUDES *cochlear prosthetic device (20.96-20.98)*

20.96 Implantation or replacement of cochlear prosthetic device, not otherwise specified

Implantation of receiver (within skull) and insertion of electrode(s) in the cochlea

INCLUDES mastoidectomy

EXCLUDES *electromagnetic hearing device (20.95)*

20.97 Implantation or replacement of cochlear prosthetic device, single channel

Implantation of receiver (within skull) and insertion of electrode in the cochlea

INCLUDES mastoidectomy

EXCLUDES *electromagnetic hearing device (20.95)*

20.98 Implantation or replacement of cochlear prosthetic device, multiple channel

Implantation of receiver (within skull) and insertion of electrodes in the cochlea

INCLUDES mastoidectomy

EXCLUDES *electromagnetic hearing device (20.95)*

20.99 Other operations on middle and inner ear

Attachment of percutaneous abutment (screw) for prosthetic device
Repair or removal of cochlear prosthetic device (receiver) (electrode)

EXCLUDES *adjustment (external components) of cochlear prosthetic device (95.49)*
fitting of hearing aid (95.48)

5. OPERATIONS ON THE NOSE, MOUTH, AND PHARYNX (21-29)

✓3rd **21 Operations on nose**

INCLUDES operations on:
bone } of nose
skin

✓4th **21.0 Control of epistaxis**

21.00 Control of epistaxis, not otherwise specified

21.01 Control of epistaxis by anterior nasal packing

21.02 Control of epistaxis by posterior (and anterior) packing

21.03 Control of epistaxis by cauterization (and packing)

21.04 Control of epistaxis by ligation of ethmoidal arteries

21.05 Control of epistaxis by (transantral) ligation of the maxillary artery

21.06 Control of epistaxis by ligation of the external carotid artery

21.07 Control of epistaxis by excision of nasal mucosa and skin grafting of septum and lateral nasal wall

21.09 Control of epistaxis by other means

21.1 Incision of nose

Chondrotomy
Incision of skin of nose
Nasal septotomy

DEF: Chondrotomy: Incision or division of nasal cartilage.

DEF: Nasal septotomy: Incision into bone dividing nose into two chambers.

✓4th **21.2 Diagnostic procedures on nose**

21.21 Rhinoscopy

DEF: Visualization of nasal passage with nasal speculum.

21.22 Biopsy of nose

21.29 Other diagnostic procedures on nose

EXCLUDES *microscopic examination of specimen from nose (90.31-90.39)*
nasal:
function study (89.12)
x-ray (87.16)
rhinomanometry (89.12)

✓4th **21.3 Local excision or destruction of lesion of nose**

EXCLUDES *biopsy of nose (21.22)*
nasal fistulectomy (21.82)

21.30 Excision or destruction of lesion of nose, not otherwise specified

21.31 Local excision or destruction of intranasal lesion

Nasal polypectomy

21.32 Local excision or destruction of other lesion of nose

21.4 Resection of nose

Amputation of nose

21.5 Submucous resection of nasal septum

DEF: Resection, partial, of nasal septum with mucosa reimplanted after excision.

Excision of Turbinate

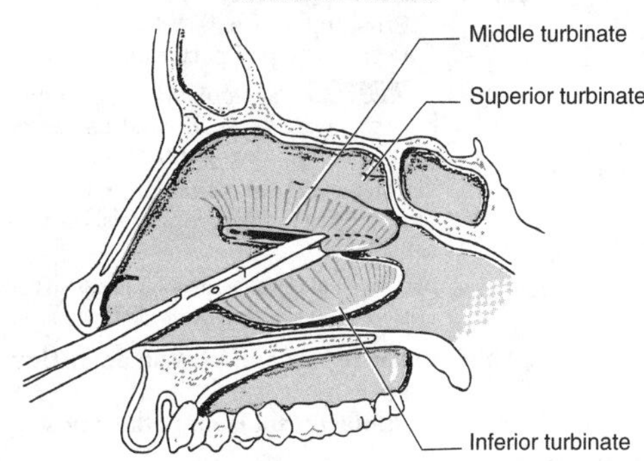

✓4th **21.6 Turbinectomy**

DEF: Removal, partial, or total of turbinate bones; inferior turbinate is most often excised.

21.61 Turbinectomy by diathermy or cryosurgery

DEF: Destruction of turbinate bone by heat or freezing.

21.62 Fracture of the turbinates

DEF: Surgical breaking of turbinate bones.

21.69 Other turbinectomy

EXCLUDES *turbinectomy associated with sinusectomy (22.31-22.39, 22.42, 22.60-22.64)*

✓4th **21.7 Reduction of nasal fracture**

21.71 Closed reduction of nasal fracture

21.72 Open reduction of nasal fracture

✓4th **21.8 Repair and plastic operations on the nose**

21.81 Suture of laceration of nose

21.82 Closure of nasal fistula

Nasolabial }
Nasopharyngeal } fistulectomy
Oronasal }

DEF: Sealing off crack or hole between nose and lip, nose and pharynx, or nose and mouth.

21.83 Total nasal reconstruction

Reconstruction of nose with:
arm flap
forehead flap

DEF: Reformation, plastic, of nasal structure with tissue flap from arm or forehead.

21.84 Revision rhinoplasty

Rhinoseptoplasty
Twisted nose rhinoplasty

DEF: Rhinoseptoplasty: Repair of nose and the bone dividing the nose into two chambers.

DEF: Twisted nose rhinoplasty: Repair of nose alignment following reconstructive surgery.

21.85 Augmentation rhinoplasty

Augmentation rhinoplasty with:
graft
synthetic implant

DEF: Implant of tissue or synthetic graft to enlarge nose.

21.86 Limited rhinoplasty

Plastic repair of nasolabial flaps
Tip rhinoplasty

DEF: Plastic repair of nasolabial flaps: Reconstruction of nasal area above lips.

DEF: Tip rhinoplasty: Reconstruction or restoration of nasal tip.

21.87 Other rhinoplasty

Rhinoplasty NOS

21.88 Other septoplasty
Crushing of nasal septum
Repair of septal perforation
EXCLUDES *septoplasty associated with submucous resection of septum (21.5)*
DEF: Crushing of nasal septum: Division and reconstruction of defects in bone dividing nasal chambers.
DEF: Repair of septal perforation: Repair of hole in bone dividing nasal chambers with adjacent tissue.

21.89 Other repair and plastic operations on nose
Reattachment of amputated nose

✓4th **21.9 Other operations on nose**

21.91 Lysis of adhesions of nose
Posterior nasal scrub
DEF: Posterior nasal scrub: Clearing out of abnormal adhesions in posterior nasal area.

21.99 Other
EXCLUDES *dilation of frontonasal duct (96.21)*
irrigation of nasal passages (96.53)
removal of:
intraluminal foreign body without incision (98.12)
nasal packing (97.32)
replacement of nasal packing (97.21)

✓3rd **22 Operations on nasal sinuses**

✓4th **22.0 Aspiration and lavage of nasal sinus**

22.00 Aspiration and lavage of nasal sinus, not otherwise specified

22.01 Puncture of nasal sinus for aspiration or lavage

22.02 Aspiration or lavage of nasal sinus through natural ostium
DEF: Withdrawal of fluid and washing of nasal cavity through natural opening.

✓4th **22.1 Diagnostic procedures on nasal sinus**

22.11 Closed [endoscopic] [needle] biopsy of nasal sinus

22.12 Open biopsy of nasal sinus

22.19 Other diagnostic procedures on nasal sinuses
Endoscopy without biopsy
EXCLUDES *transillumination of sinus (89.35)*
x-ray of sinus (87.15-87.16)

22.2 Intranasal antrotomy
EXCLUDES *antrotomy with external approach (22.31-22.39)*
DEF: Incision of intranasal sinus.

✓4th **22.3 External maxillary antrotomy**

22.31 Radical maxillary antrotomy
Removal of lining membrane of maxillary sinus using Caldwell-Luc approach
DEF: Caldwell-Luc approach: Removal of membrane lining the maxillary cavity through incision above canine teeth.

22.39 Other external maxillary antrotomy
Exploration of maxillary antrum with Caldwell-Luc approach

✓4th **22.4 Frontal sinusotomy and sinusectomy**

22.41 Frontal sinusotomy

22.42 Frontal sinusectomy
Excision of lesion of frontal sinus
Obliteration of frontal sinus (with fat)
EXCLUDES *biopsy of nasal sinus (22.11-22.12)*

✓4th **22.5 Other nasal sinusotomy**

22.50 Sinusotomy, not otherwise specified

22.51 Ethmoidotomy

22.52 Sphenoidotomy

22.53 Incision of multiple nasal sinuses

✓4th **22.6 Other nasal sinusectomy**
INCLUDES that with incidental turbinectomy
EXCLUDES *biopsy of nasal sinus (22.11-22.12)*

22.60 Sinusectomy, not otherwise specified

22.61 Excision of lesion of maxillary sinus with Caldwell-Luc approach

22.62 Excision of lesion of maxillary sinus with other approach

22.63 Ethmoidectomy
DEF: Removal of ethmoid cells and bone, partial or total includes excising mucosal lining, partial or total.

22.64 Sphenoidectomy
DEF: Removal of wedge shaped sphenoid bone at base of brain.

✓4th **22.7 Repair of nasal sinus**

22.71 Closure of nasal sinus fistula
Repair of oro-antral fistula

22.79 Other repair of nasal sinus
Reconstruction of frontonasal duct
Repair of bone of accessory sinus

22.9 Other operations on nasal sinuses
Exteriorization of maxillary sinus
Fistulization of sinus
EXCLUDES *dilation of frontonasal duct (96.21)*
DEF: Exteriorization of maxillary sinus: Creation of external maxillary cavity opening.
DEF: Fistulization of sinus: Creation of fistula canal in nasal cavity.

✓3rd **23 Removal and restoration of teeth**

✓4th **23.0 Forceps extraction of tooth**

23.01 Extraction of deciduous tooth

23.09 Extraction of other tooth
Extraction of tooth NOS

✓4th **23.1 Surgical removal of tooth**

23.11 Removal of residual root

23.19 Other surgical extraction of tooth
Odontectomy NOS
Removal of impacted tooth
Tooth extraction with elevation of mucoperiosteal flap

23.2 Restoration of tooth by filling

23.3 Restoration of tooth by inlay
DEF: Restoration of tooth by cementing in a molded filling.

✓4th **23.4 Other dental restoration**

23.41 Application of crown

23.42 Insertion of fixed bridge

23.43 Insertion of removable bridge

23.49 Other

23.5 Implantation of tooth
DEF: Insertion of a sound tooth to replace extracted tooth.

23.6 Prosthetic dental implant
Endosseous dental implant
DEF: Implant of artificial denture within bone covering tooth socket.

✓4th **23.7 Apicoectomy and root canal therapy**

23.70 Root canal, not otherwise specified

23.71 Root canal therapy with irrigation

23.72 Root canal therapy with apicoectomy
DEF: Removal of tooth root to treat damaged root canal tissue.

23.73 Apicoectomy

✓3rd **24 Other operations on teeth, gums, and alveoli**

24.0 Incision of gum or alveolar bone
Apical alveolotomy

✓4th **24.1 Diagnostic procedures on teeth, gums, and alveoli**

24.11 Biopsy of gum

24.12 Biopsy of alveolus

24.19 Other diagnostic procedures on teeth, gums, and alveoli
EXCLUDES *dental:*
examination (89.31)
x-ray:
full-mouth (87.11)
other (87.12)
microscopic examination of dental specimen (90.81-90.89)

24.2 Gingivoplasty
Gingivoplasty with bone or soft tissue graft
DEF: Repair of gum tissue.

✓4th **24.3 Other operations on gum**

24.31 Excision of lesion or tissue of gum
EXCLUDES *biopsy of gum (24.11)*
excision of odontogenic lesion (24.4)

24.32 Suture of laceration of gum

24.39 Other

24.4 Excision of dental lesion of jaw
Excision of odontogenic lesion

24.5 Alveoloplasty
Alveolectomy (interradicular) (intraseptal) (radical) (simple) (with graft or implant)
EXCLUDES *biopsy of alveolus (24.12)*
en bloc resection of alveolar process and palate (27.32)
DEF: Repair or correction of bony tooth socket.

24.6 Exposure of tooth

24.7 Application of orthodontic appliance
Application, insertion, or fitting of:
arch bars
orthodontic obturator
orthodontic wiring
periodontal splint
EXCLUDES *nonorthodontic dental wiring (93.55)*

24.8 Other orthodontic operation
Closure of diastema (alveolar) (dental)
Occlusal adjustment
Removal of arch bars
Repair of dental arch
EXCLUDES *removal of nonorthodontic wiring (97.33)*

✓4th **24.9 Other dental operations**

24.91 Extension or deepening of buccolabial or lingual sulcus

24.99 Other
EXCLUDES *dental:*
debridement (96.54)
examination (89.31)
prophylaxis (96.54)
scaling and polishing (96.54)
wiring (93.55)
fitting of dental appliance [denture] (99.97)
microscopic examination of dental specimen (90.81-90.89)
removal of dental:
packing (97.34)
prosthesis (97.35)
wiring (97.33)
replacement of dental packing (97.22)

✓3rd **25 Operations on tongue**

✓4th **25.0 Diagnostic procedures on tongue**

25.01 Closed [needle] biopsy of tongue

25.02 Open biopsy of tongue
Wedge biopsy

25.09 Other diagnostic procedures on tongue

25.1 Excision or destruction of lesion or tissue of tongue
EXCLUDES *biopsy of tongue (25.01-25.02)*
frenumectomy:
labial (27.41)
lingual (25.92)

25.2 Partial glossectomy

25.3 Complete glossectomy
Glossectomy NOS
Code also any neck dissection (40.40-40.42)

25.4 Radical glossectomy
Code also any:
neck dissection (40.40-40.42)
tracheostomy (31.1-31.29)

✓4th **25.5 Repair of tongue and glossoplasty**

25.51 Suture of laceration of tongue

25.59 Other repair and plastic operations on tongue
Fascial sling of tongue
Fusion of tongue (to lip)
Graft of mucosa or skin to tongue
EXCLUDES *lysis of adhesions of tongue (25.93)*

✓4th **25.9 Other operations on tongue**

25.91 Lingual frenotomy
EXCLUDES *labial frenotomy (27.91)*
DEF: Extension of groove between cheek and lips or cheek and tongue.

25.92 Lingual frenectomy
EXCLUDES *labial frenectomy (27.41)*
DEF: Frenectomy: Removal of vertical membrane attaching tongue to floor of mouth.

25.93 Lysis of adhesions of tongue

25.94 Other glossotomy

25.99 Other

✓3rd **26 Operations on salivary glands and ducts**
INCLUDES operations on:
lesser salivary, parotid, sublingual, submaxillry } gland and duct
Code also any neck dissection (40.40-40.42)

26.0 Incision of salivary gland or duct

Operations on the Nose, Mouth, and Pharynx 23.6–26.0

✓4th **26.1 Diagnostic procedures on salivary glands and ducts**

26.11 Closed [needle] biopsy of salivary gland or duct

26.12 Open biopsy of salivary gland or duct

26.19 Other diagnostic procedures on salivary glands and ducts

EXCLUDES *x-ray of salivary gland (87.09)*

✓4th **26.2 Excision of lesion of salivary gland**

26.21 Marsupialization of salivary gland cyst

DEF: Creation of pouch of salivary gland cyst to drain and promote healing.

26.29 Other excision of salivary gland lesion

EXCLUDES *biopsy of salivary gland (26.11-26.12)*
salivary fistulectomy (26.42)

✓4th **26.3 Sialoadenectomy**

DEF: Removal of salivary gland.

26.30 Sialoadenectomy, not otherwise specified

26.31 Partial sialoadenectomy

26.32 Complete sialoadenectomy

En bloc excision of salivary gland lesion
Radical sialoadenectomy

✓4th **26.4 Repair of salivary gland or duct**

26.41 Suture of laceration of salivary gland

26.42 Closure of salivary fistula

DEF: Closing of abnormal opening in salivary gland.

26.49 Other repair and plastic operations on salivary gland or duct

Fistulization of salivary gland
Plastic repair of salivary gland or duct NOS
Transplantation of salivary duct opening

✓4th **26.9 Other operations on salivary gland or duct**

26.91 Probing of salivary duct

26.99 Other

✓3rd **27 Other operations on mouth and face**

INCLUDES operations on:
lips
palate
soft tissue of face and mouth, except tongue and gingiva

EXCLUDES *operations on:*
gingiva (24.0-24.99)
tongue (25.01-25.99)

27.0 Drainage of face and floor of mouth

Drainage of:
facial region (abscess)
fascial compartment of face
Ludwig's angina

EXCLUDES *drainage of thyroglossal tract (06.09)*

27.1 Incision of palate

✓4th **27.2 Diagnostic procedures on oral cavity**

27.21 Biopsy of bony palate

27.22 Biopsy of uvula and soft palate

27.23 Biopsy of lip

27.24 Biopsy of mouth, unspecified structure

27.29 Other diagnostic procedures on oral cavity

EXCLUDES *soft tissue x-ray (87.09)*

✓4th **27.3 Excision of lesion or tissue of bony palate**

27.31 Local excision or destruction of lesion or tissue of bony palate

Local excision or destruction of palate by:
cautery
chemotherapy
cryotherapy

EXCLUDES *biopsy of bony palate (27.21)*

27.32 Wide excision or destruction of lesion or tissue of bony palate

En bloc resection of alveolar process and palate

✓4th **27.4 Excision of other parts of mouth**

27.41 Labial frenectomy

EXCLUDES *division of labial frenum (27.91)*

DEF: Removal of mucous membrane fold of lip.

27.42 Wide excision of lesion of lip

27.43 Other excision of lesion or tissue of lip

27.49 Other excision of mouth

EXCLUDES *biopsy of mouth NOS (27.24)*
excision of lesion of:
palate (27.31-27.32)
tongue (25.1)
uvula (27.72)
fistulectomy of mouth (27.53)
frenectomy of:
lip (27.41)
tongue (25.92)

✓4th **27.5 Plastic repair of mouth**

EXCLUDES *palatoplasty (27.61-27.69)*

27.51 Suture of laceration of lip

27.52 Suture of laceration of other part of mouth

27.53 Closure of fistula of mouth

EXCLUDES *fistulectomy:*
nasolabial (21.82)
oro-antral (22.71)
oronasal (21.82)

27.54 Repair of cleft lip

27.55 Full-thickness skin graft to lip and mouth

27.56 Other skin graft to lip and mouth

27.57 Attachment of pedicle or flap graft to lip and mouth

DEF: Repair of lip or mouth with tissue pedicle or flap still connected to original vascular base.

27.59 Other plastic repair of mouth

✓4th **27.6 Palatoplasty**

27.61 Suture of laceration of palate

27.62 Correction of cleft palate

Correction of cleft palate by push-back operation

EXCLUDES *revision of cleft palate repair (27.63)*

27.63 Revision of cleft palate repair

Secondary:
attachment of pharyngeal flap
lengthening of palate

27.64 Insertion of palatal implant

DEF: Nonabsorbable polyester implants into the soft palate at the back of the roof of the mouth; one implant placed at the soft palate midline and two are positioned on either side; to support and stiffen the palate reducing vibration (snoring).

27.69 Other plastic repair of palate

Code also any insertion of palatal implant (27.64)

EXCLUDES *fistulectomy of mouth (27.53)*

✓4th **27.7 Operations on uvula**

27.71 Incision of uvula

27.72 Excision of uvula

EXCLUDES *biopsy of uvula (27.22)*

27.73 Repair of uvula

EXCLUDES *that with synchronous cleft palate repair (27.62)*
uranostaphylorrhaphy (27.62)

27.79 Other operations on uvula

✓4th **27.9 Other operations on mouth and face**

27.91 Labial frenotomy

Division of labial frenum

EXCLUDES *lingual frenotomy (25.91)*

DEF: Division of labial frenum: Cutting and separating mucous membrane fold of lip.

27.92 Incision of mouth, unspecified structure

EXCLUDES *incision of:*
gum (24.0)
palate (27.1)
salivary gland or duct (26.0)
tongue (25.94)
uvula (27.71)

27.99 Other operations on oral cavity

Graft of buccal sulcus

EXCLUDES *removal of:*
intraluminal foreign body (98.01)
penetrating foreign body from mouth without incision (98.22)

DEF: Graft of buccal sulcus: Implant of tissue into groove of interior cheek lining.

✓3rd **28 Operations on tonsils and adenoids**

28.0 Incision and drainage of tonsil and peritonsillar structures

Drainage (oral) (transcervical) of:
parapharyngeal, peritonsillar, retropharyngeal, tonsillar } abscess

✓4th **28.1 Diagnostic procedures on tonsils and adenoids**

28.11 Biopsy of tonsils and adenoids

28.19 Other diagnostic procedures on tonsils and adenoids

EXCLUDES *soft tissue x-ray (87.09)*

28.2 Tonsillectomy without adenoidectomy

28.3 Tonsillectomy with adenoidectomy

28.4 Excision of tonsil tag

28.5 Excision of lingual tonsil

28.6 Adenoidectomy without tonsillectomy

Excision of adenoid tag

28.7 Control of hemorrhage after tonsillectomy and adenoidectomy

✓4th **28.9 Other operations on tonsils and adenoids**

28.91 Removal of foreign body from tonsil and adenoid by incision

EXCLUDES *that without incision (98.13)*

28.92 Excision of lesion of tonsil and adenoid

EXCLUDES *biopsy of tonsil and adenoid (28.11)*

28.99 Other

✓3rd **29 Operations on pharynx**

INCLUDES operations on:
hypopharynx
nasopharynx
oropharynx
pharyngeal pouch
pyriform sinus

29.0 Pharyngotomy

Drainage of pharyngeal bursa

EXCLUDES *incision and drainage of retropharyngeal abscess (28.0)*
removal of foreign body (without incision) (98.13)

✓4th **29.1 Diagnostic procedures on pharynx**

29.11 Pharyngoscopy

29.12 Pharyngeal biopsy

Biopsy of supraglottic mass

29.19 Other diagnostic procedures on pharynx

EXCLUDES *x-ray of nasopharynx:*
contrast (87.06)
other (87.09)

29.2 Excision of branchial cleft cyst or vestige

EXCLUDES *branchial cleft fistulectomy (29.52)*

✓4th **29.3 Excision or destruction of lesion or tissue of pharynx**

29.31 Cricopharyngeal myotomy

EXCLUDES *that with pharyngeal diverticulectomy (29.32)*

DEF: Removal of outward pouching of throat.

29.32 Pharyngeal diverticulectomy

29.33 Pharyngectomy (partial)

EXCLUDES *laryngopharyngectomy (30.3)*

29.39 Other excision or destruction of lesion or tissue of pharynx

29.4 Plastic operation on pharynx

Correction of nasopharyngeal atresia

EXCLUDES *pharyngoplasty associated with cleft palate repair (27.62-27.63)*

DEF: Correction of nasopharyngeal atresia: Construction of normal opening for throat stricture behind nose.

✓4th **29.5 Other repair of pharynx**

29.51 Suture of laceration of pharynx

29.52 Closure of branchial cleft fistula

DEF: Sealing off an abnormal opening of the branchial fissure in throat.

29.53 Closure of other fistula of pharynx

Pharyngoesophageal fistulectomy

29.54 Lysis of pharyngeal adhesions

29.59 Other

✓4th **29.9 Other operations on pharynx**

29.91 Dilation of pharynx

Dilation of nasopharynx

29.92 Division of glossopharyngeal nerve

29.99 Other

EXCLUDES *insertion of radium into pharynx and nasopharynx (92.27)*
removal of intraluminal foreign body (98.13)

6. OPERATIONS ON THE RESPIRATORY SYSTEM (30-34)

✓3rd 30 Excision of larynx

✓4th 30.0 Excision or destruction of lesion or tissue of larynx

30.01 Marsupialization of laryngeal cyst

DEF: Incision of cyst of larynx with the edges sutured open to create pouch.

30.09 Other excision or destruction of lesion or lesion or tissue of larynx

Stripping of vocal cords

EXCLUDES *biopsy of larynx (31.43)*
laryngeal fistulectomy (31.62)
laryngotracheal fistulectomy (31.62)

30.1 Hemilaryngectomy

DEF: Excision of one side (half) of larynx.

✓4th 30.2 Other partial laryngectomy

30.21 Epiglottidectomy

30.22 Vocal cordectomy

Excision of vocal cords

30.29 Other partial laryngectomy

Excision of laryngeal cartilage

30.3 Complete laryngectomy

Block dissection of larynx (with thyroidectomy) (with synchronous tracheostomy)
Laryngopharyngectomy

EXCLUDES *that with radical neck dissection (30.4)*

30.4 Radical laryngectomy

Complete [total] laryngectomy with radical neck dissection (with thyroidectomy) (with synchronous tracheostomy)

✓3rd 31 Other operations on larynx and trachea

31.0 Injection of larynx

Injection of inert material into larynx or vocal cords

31.1 Temporary tracheostomy

Temporary percutaneous dilatational tracheostomy [PDT]

Tracheotomy for assistance in breathing

Code also any synchronous bronchoscopy, if performed (33.21-33.24, 33.27)

✓4th 31.2 Permanent tracheostomy

31.21 Mediastinal tracheostomy

DEF: Placement of artificial breathing tube in windpipe through mediastinum, for long-term use.

31.29 Other permanent tracheostomy

Permanent percutaneous dilatational tracheostomy [PDT]

Code also any synchronous bronchoscopy, if performed (33.21-33.24, 33.27)

EXCLUDES *that with laryngectomy (30.3-30.4)*

Temporary Tracheostomy

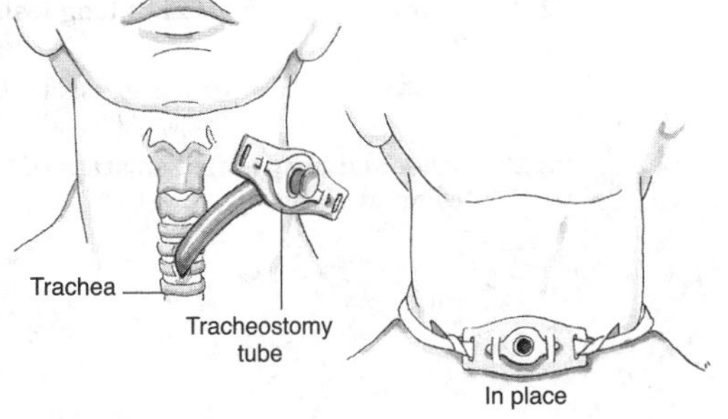

Closed Endoscopic Biopsy of Larynx

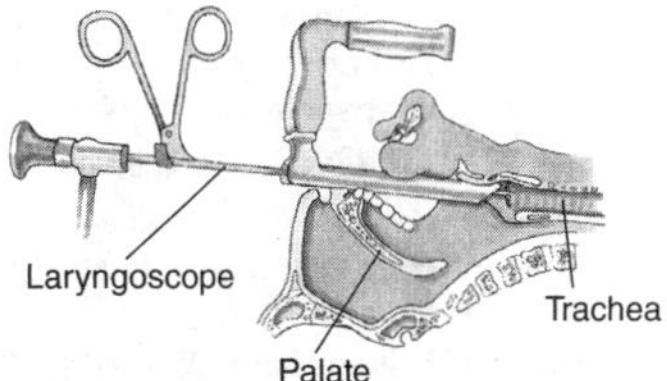

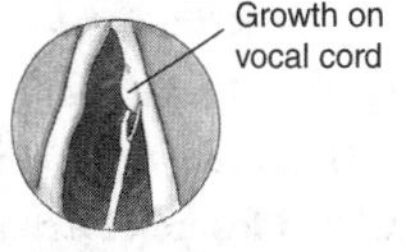

31.3 Other incision of larynx or trachea

EXCLUDES *that for assistance in breathing (31.1-31.29)*

✓4th 31.4 Diagnostic procedures on larynx and trachea

31.41 Tracheoscopy through artificial stoma

EXCLUDES *that with biopsy (31.43-31.44)*

DEF: Exam by scope of trachea through an artificial opening.

31.42 Laryngoscopy and other tracheoscopy

EXCLUDES *that with biopsy (31.43-31.44)*

31.43 Closed [endoscopic] biopsy of larynx

31.44 Closed [endoscopic] biopsy of trachea

31.45 Open biopsy of larynx or trachea

31.48 Other diagnostic procedures on larynx

EXCLUDES *contrast laryngogram (87.07)*
microscopic examination of specimen from larynx (90.31-90.39)
soft tissue x-ray of larynx NEC (87.09)

31.49 Other diagnostic procedures on trachea

EXCLUDES *microscopic examination of specimen from trachea (90.41-90.49)*
x-ray of trachea (87.49)

31.5 Local excision or destruction of lesion or tissue of trachea

EXCLUDES *biopsy of trachea (31.44-31.45)*
laryngotracheal fistulectomy (31.62)
tracheoesophageal fistulectomy (31.73)

✓4th 31.6 Repair of larynx

31.61 Suture of laceration of larynx

31.62 Closure of fistula of larynx

Laryngotracheal fistulectomy
Take-down of laryngostomy

DEF: Laryngotracheal fistulectomy: Excision and closing of passage between voice box and trachea.

DEF: Take-down of laryngostomy: Removal of laryngostomy tube and restoration of voice box.

31.63 Revision of laryngostomy

31.64 Repair of laryngeal fracture

DEF: Alignment and positioning of harder structures of larynx such as hyoid bone; following fracture.

31.69 Other repair of larynx
Arytenoidopexy
Cordopexy
Graft of larynx
Transposition of vocal cords

EXCLUDES *construction of artificial larynx (31.75)*

DEF: Arytenoidopexy: Fixation of pitcher-shaped cartilage in voice box.

DEF: Graft of larynx: Implant of graft tissue into voice box.

DEF: Transposition of the vocal cords: Placement of vocal cords into more functional positions.

✓4th **31.7 Repair and plastic operations on trachea**

31.71 Suture of laceration of trachea

31.72 Closure of external fistula of trachea
Closure of tracheotomy

31.73 Closure of other fistula of trachea
Tracheoesophageal fistulectomy

EXCLUDES *laryngotracheal fistulectomy (31.62)*

DEF: Tracheoesophageal fistulectomy: Excision and closure of abnormal opening between windpipe and esophagus.

31.74 Revision of tracheostomy

31.75 Reconstruction of trachea and construction of artificial larynx
Tracheoplasty with artificial larynx

31.79 Other repair and plastic operations on trachea

✓4th **31.9 Other operations on larynx and trachea**

31.91 Division of laryngeal nerve

31.92 Lysis of adhesions of trachea or larynx

31.93 Replacement of laryngeal or tracheal stent

DEF: Removal and substitution of tubed molding into larynx or trachea.

31.94 Injection of locally-acting therapeutic substance into trachea

31.95 Tracheoesophageal fistulization

DEF: Creation of passage between trachea and esophagus.

31.98 Other operations on larynx
Dilation } of larynx
Division of congenital web } of larynx
Removal of keel or stent } of larynx

EXCLUDES *removal of intraluminal foreign body from larynx without incision (98.14)*

DEF: Dilation: Increasing larynx size by stretching.
DEF: Division of congenital web: Cutting and separating congenital membranes around larynx.
DEF: Removal of keel or stent: Removal of prosthetic device from larynx.

31.99 Other operations on trachea

EXCLUDES *removal of:*
intraluminal foreign body from trachea without incision (98.15)
tracheostomy tube (97.37)
replacement of tracheostomy tube (97.23)
tracheostomy toilette (96.55)

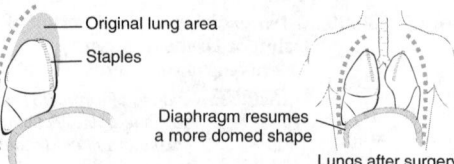

Lung Volume Reduction

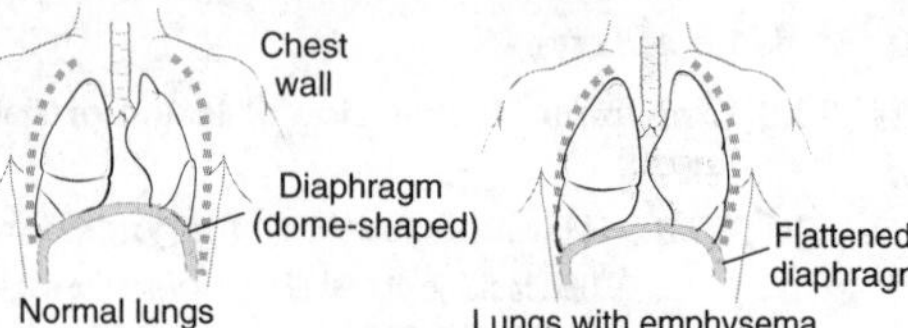

✓3rd **32 Excision of lung and bronchus**

INCLUDES rib section } as operative approach
sternotomy } as operative approach
sternum-splitting incision } as operative approach
thoracotomy } as operative approach

Code also any synchronous bronchoplasty (33.48)

DEF: Rib resection: Cutting of ribs to access operative field.
DEF: Sternotomy: Cut through breastbone as an operative approach.
DEF: Sternum-splitting incision: Breaking through breastbone to access operative field.

✓4th **32.0 Local excision or destruction of lesion or tissue of bronchus**

EXCLUDES *biopsy of bronchus (33.24-33.25)*
bronchial fistulectomy (33.42)

32.01 Endoscopic excision or destruction of lesion or tissue of bronchus

32.09 Other local excision or destruction of lesion or tissue of bronchus

EXCLUDES *that by endoscopic approach (32.01)*

32.1 Other excision of bronchus
Resection (wide sleeve) of bronchus

EXCLUDES *radical dissection [excision] of bronchus (32.6)*

DEF: Resection (wide sleeve) of bronchus: Excision and partial, lengthwise removal of a lung branch.Lung Volume Reduction

✓4th **32.2 Local excision or destruction of lesion or tissue of lung**

32.20 Thoracoscopic excision of lesion or tissue of lung
Thoracoscopic wedge resection

32.21 Plication of emphysematous bleb

DEF: Stitching of a swollen vesicle into folds or tuck.

32.22 Lung volume reduction surgery

DEF: Excision of portion of lung(s) to reduce respiratory effort in moderate to severe emphysema.

32.23 Open ablation of lung lesion or tissue

32.24 Percutaneous ablation of lung lesion or tissue

32.25 Thoracoscopic ablation of lung lesion or tissue

EXCLUDES *thoracoscopic excision of lesion or tissue of lung (32.20)*

32.26 Other and unspecified ablation of lung lesion or tissue

32.28 Endoscopic excision or destruction of lesion or tissue of lung

EXCLUDES *ablation of lung lesion or tissue:*
open (32.23)
other (32.26)
percutaneous (32.24)
thoracoscopic (32.25)
biopsy of lung (33.26-33.27)

32.29 Other local excision or destruction of lesion or tissue of lung

Resection of lung:
NOS
wedge

EXCLUDES *ablation of lung lesion or tissue:*
open (32.23)
other (32.26)
percutaneous (32.24)
thoracoscopic (32.25)
biopsy of lung (33.26-33.27)
that by endoscopic approach (32.28)
thoracoscopic excision of lesion or tissue of lung (32.20)
wide excision of lesion of lung (32.3)

✓4th **32.3 Segmental resection of lung**

Partial lobectomy

32.30 Thoracoscopic segmental resection of lung

32.39 Other and unspecified segmental resection of lung

EXCLUDES *thoracoscopic segmental resection of lung (32.30)*

✓4th **32.4 Lobectomy of lung**

Lobectomy with segmental resection of adjacent lobes of lung

EXCLUDES *that with radical dissection [excision] of thoracic structures (32.6)*

32.41 Thoracoscopic lobectomy of lung

32.49 Other lobectomy of lung

EXCLUDES *thoracoscopic lobectomy of lung (32.41)*

✓4th **32.5 Pneumonectomy**

Excision of lung NOS
Pneumonectomy (with mediastinal dissection)

32.50 Thoracoscopic pneumonectomy

32.59 Other and unspecified pneumonectomy

EXCLUDES *thoracoscopic pneumonectomy (32.50)*

32.6 Radical dissection of thoracic structures

Block [en bloc] dissection of bronchus, lobe of lung, brachial plexus, intercostal structure, ribs (transverse process), and sympathetic nerves

32.9 Other excision of lung

EXCLUDES *biopsy of lung and bronchus (33.24-33.27)*
pulmonary decortication (34.51)

Bronchoscopy with Bite Biopsy

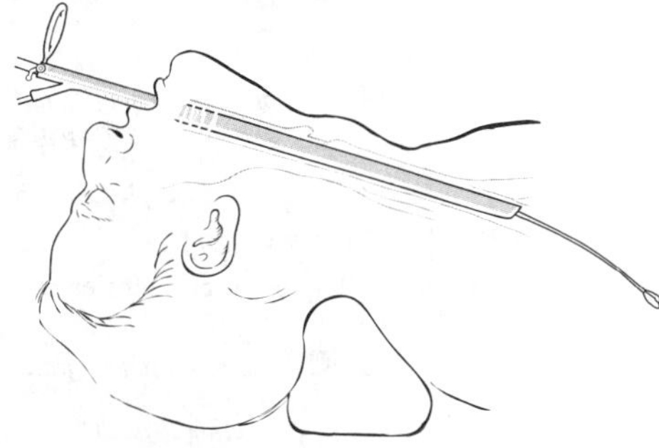

✓3rd **33 Other operations on lung and bronchus**

INCLUDES rib section, sternotomy, sternum-splitting incision, thoracotomy } as operative approach

33.0 Incision of bronchus

33.1 Incision of lung

EXCLUDES *puncture of lung (33.93)*

✓4th **33.2 Diagnostic procedures on lung and bronchus**

33.20 Thoracoscopic lung biopsy

EXCLUDES *closed endoscopic biopsy of lung (33.27)*
closed [percutaneous] [needle] biopsy of lung (33.26)
open biopsy of lung (33.28)

33.21 Bronchoscopy through artificial stoma

EXCLUDES *that with biopsy (33.24, 33.27)*

DEF: Visual exam of lung and its branches via tube through artificial opening.

33.22 Fiber-optic bronchoscopy

EXCLUDES *that with biopsy (33.24, 33.27)*

DEF: Exam of lung and bronchus via flexible optical instrument for visualization.

33.23 Other bronchoscopy

EXCLUDES *that for:*
aspiration (96.05)
biopsy (33.24, 33.27)

33.24 Closed [endoscopic] biopsy of bronchus

Bronchoscopy (fiberoptic) (rigid) with:
brush biopsy of "lung"
brushing or washing for specimen collection
excision (bite) biopsy
Diagnostic bronchoalveolar lavage (BAL)

EXCLUDES *closed biopsy of lung, other than brush biopsy of "lung" (33.26, 33.27)*
whole lung lavage (33.99)

DEF: Bronchoalveolar lavage (BAL): Saline is introduced into the subsegment of a lobe and retrieved using gentle suction; also called 'liquid biopsy'.

DEF: Brush biopsy: Obtaining cell or tissue samples via bristled instrument without incision.

33.25 Open biopsy of bronchus

EXCLUDES *open biopsy of lung (33.28)*

33.26 Closed [percutaneous] [needle] biopsy of lung

Fine needle aspiration (FNA) of lung
Transthoracic needle biopsy of lung (TTNB)

EXCLUDES *endoscopic biopsy of lung (33.27)*
thoracoscopic lung biopsy (33.20)

33.27 Closed endoscopic biopsy of lung
Fiber-optic (flexible) bronchoscopy with fluoroscopic guidance with biopsy
Transbronchial lung biopsy
EXCLUDES *brush biopsy of "lung" (33.24)*
percutaneous biopsy of lung (33.26)
thoracoscopic lung biopsy (33.20)

33.28 Open biopsy of lung

33.29 Other diagnostic procedures on lung and bronchus
EXCLUDES *contrast bronchogram:*
endotracheal (87.31)
other (87.32)
endoscopic pulmonary airway flow measurement (33.72)
lung scan (92.15)
magnetic resonance imaging (88.92)
microscopic examination of specimen from bronchus or lung (90.41-90.49)
routine chest x-ray (87.44)
ultrasonography of lung (88.73)
vital capacity determination (89.37)
x-ray of bronchus or lung NOS (87.49)

✓4th **33.3 Surgical collapse of lung**

33.31 Destruction of phrenic nerve for collapse of lung
DEF: Therapeutic deadening or destruction of diaphragmatic nerve to collapse the lung.

33.32 Artificial pneumothorax for collapse of lung
Thoracotomy for collapse of lung
DEF: Forcing air or gas into diaphragmatic space to achieve therapeutic collapse of lung.
DEF: Thoracotomy for collapse of lung: Incision into chest for therapeutic collapse of lung.

33.33 Pneumoperitoneum for collapse of lung
DEF: Forcing air or gas into abdominal serous membrane to achieve therapeutic collapse of lung.

33.34 Thoracoplasty
DEF: Removal of ribs for therapeutic collapse of lungs.

33.39 Other surgical collapse of lung
Collapse of lung NOS

✓4th **33.4 Repair and plastic operation on lung and bronchus**

33.41 Suture of laceration of bronchus

33.42 Closure of bronchial fistula
Closure of bronchostomy
Fistulectomy:
bronchocutaneous
bronchoesophageal
bronchovisceral
EXCLUDES *closure of fistula:*
bronchomediastinal (34.73)
bronchopleural (34.73)
bronchopleuromediastinal (34.73)
DEF: Closure of bronchostomy: Removal of bronchostomy tube and repair of surgical wound.
DEF: Fistulectomy: Closure of abnormal passage.
Bronchocutaneous: Between skin and lung branch.
Bronchoesophagus: Between esophagus and lung branch.
Bronchovisceral: Between an internal organ and lung branch.

33.43 Closure of laceration of lung

33.48 Other repair and plastic operations on bronchus

33.49 Other repair and plastic operations on lung
EXCLUDES *closure of pleural fistula (34.73)*

✓4th **33.5 Lung transplant**
Note: To report donor source – *see* codes 00.91-00.93
Code also cardiopulmonary bypass [extracorporeal circulation] [heart-lung machine] [39.61]
EXCLUDES *combined heart-lung transplantation (33.6)*

33.50 Lung transplantation, not otherwise specified

33.51 Unilateral lung transplantation

33.52 Bilateral lung transplantation
Double-lung transplantation
En bloc transplantation
DEF: Sequential excision and implant of both lungs.

33.6 Combined heart-lung transplantation
Note: To report donor source – *see* codes 00.91-00.93
Code also cardiopulmonary bypass [extracorporeal circulation] [heart-lung machine] (39.61)

✓4th **33.7 Other endoscopic procedures in bronchus or lung**
EXCLUDES *insertion of tracheobronchial stent (96.05)*

33.71 Endoscopic insertion or replacement of bronchial valve(s)
Endobronchial airflow redirection valve
Intrabronchial airflow redirection valve

33.72 Endoscopic pulmonary airway flow measurement
Assessment of pulmonary airway flow
Code also any diagnostic or therapeutic procedure if performed

33.78 Endoscopic removal of bronchial device(s) or substances

33.79 Endoscopic insertion of other bronchial device or substances
Biologic lung volume reduction NOS (BLVR)

✓4th **33.9 Other operations on lung and bronchus**

33.91 Bronchial dilation

33.92 Ligation of bronchus
DEF: Tying off of a lung branch.

33.93 Puncture of lung
EXCLUDES *needle biopsy (33.26)*
DEF: Piercing of lung with surgical instrument.

33.98 Other operations on bronchus
EXCLUDES *bronchial lavage (96.56)*
removal of intraluminal foreign body from bronchus without incision (98.15)

33.99 Other operations on lung
Whole lung lavage
EXCLUDES *other continuous mechanical ventilation (96.70-96.72)*
respiratory therapy (93.90-93.99)

✓3rd 34 Operations on chest wall, pleura, mediastinum, and diaphragm

EXCLUDES *operations on breast (85.0-85.99)*

✓4th 34.0 Incision of chest wall and pleura

EXCLUDES *that as operative approach — omit code*

34.01 Incision of chest wall

Extrapleural drainage

EXCLUDES *incision of pleura (34.09)*

DEF: Extrapleural drainage: Incision to drain fluid from external pleura.

34.02 Exploratory thoracotomy

34.03 Reopening of recent thoracotomy site

34.04 Insertion of intercostal catheter for drainage

Chest tube
Closed chest drainage
Revision of intercostal catheter (chest tube) (with lysis of adhesions)

EXCLUDES *thoracoscopic drainage of pleural cavity (34.06)*

DEF: Insertion of catheter between ribs for drainage.

34.05 Creation of pleuroperitoneal shunt

34.06 Thoracoscopic drainage of pleural cavity

Evacuation of empyema

34.09 Other incision of pleura

Creation of pleural window for drainage
Intercostal stab
Open chest drainage

EXCLUDES *thoracoscopy (34.21)*
thoracotomy for collapse of lung (33.32)

DEF: Creation of pleural window: Creation of circum-scribed drainage hole in serous membrane of chest.
DEF: Intercostal stab: Creation of penetrating stab wound between ribs.
DEF: Open chest drainage: Insertion of tube through ribs and serous membrane of chest for drainage.

34.1 Incision of mediastinum

EXCLUDES *mediastinoscopy (34.22)*
mediastinotomy associated with pneumonectomy (32.5)

✓4th 34.2 Diagnostic procedures on chest wall, pleura, mediastinum, and diaphragm

34.20 Thoracoscopic pleural biopsy

34.21 Transpleural thoracoscopy

DEF: Exam of chest through serous membrane using scope.

34.22 Mediastinoscopy

Code also any lymph node biopsy (40.11)

DEF: Exam of lung cavity and heart using scope.

34.23 Biopsy of chest wall

34.24 Other pleural biopsy

EXCLUDES *thoracoscopic pleural biopsy (34.20)*

34.25 Closed [percutaneous] [needle] biopsy of mediastinum

34.26 Open biopsy of mediastinum

34.27 Biopsy of diaphragm

34.28 Other diagnostic procedures on chest wall, pleura, and diaphragm

EXCLUDES *angiocardiography (88.50-88.58)*
aortography (88.42)
arteriography of:
intrathoracic vessels NEC (88.44)
pulmonary arteries (88.43)
microscopic examination of specimen from chest wall, pleura, and diaphragm (90.41-90.49)
phlebography of:
intrathoracic vessels NEC (88.63)
pulmonary veins (88.62)
radiological examinations of thorax:
C.A.T. scan (87.41)
diaphragmatic x-ray (87.49)
intrathoracic lymphangiogram (87.34)
routine chest x-ray (87.44)
sinogram of chest wall (87.38)
soft tissue x-ray of chest wall NEC (87.39)
tomogram of thorax NEC (87.42)
ultrasonography of thorax (88.73)

34.29 Other diagnostic procedures on mediastinum

EXCLUDES *mediastinal:*
pneumogram (87.33)
x-ray NEC (87.49)

34.3 Excision or destruction of lesion or tissue of mediastinum

EXCLUDES *biopsy of mediastinum (34.25-34.26)*
mediastinal fistulectomy (34.73)

34.4 Excision or destruction of lesion of chest wall

Excision of lesion of chest wall NOS (with excision of ribs)

EXCLUDES *biopsy of chest wall (34.23)*
costectomy not incidental to thoracic procedure (77.91)
excision of lesion of:
breast (85.20-85.25)
cartilage (80.89)
skin (86.2-86.3)
fistulectomy (34.73)

✓4th 34.5 Pleurectomy

34.51 Decortication of lung

EXCLUDES *thoracoscopic decortication of lung (34.52)*

DEF: Removal of thickened serous membrane for lung expansion.

34.52 Thoracoscopic decortication of lung

34.59 Other excision of pleura

Excision of pleural lesion

EXCLUDES *biopsy of pleura (34.24)*
pleural fistulectomy (34.73)

34.6 Scarification of pleura

Pleurosclerosis

EXCLUDES *injection of sclerosing agent (34.92)*

DEF: Destruction of fluid-secreting serous membrane cells of chest.

✓4th 34.7 Repair of chest wall

34.71 Suture of laceration of chest wall

EXCLUDES *suture of skin and subcutaneous tissue alone (86.59)*

34.72 Closure of thoracostomy

34.73 Closure of other fistula of thorax

Closure of:
- bronchopleural
- bronchopleurocutaneous } fistula
- bronchopleuromediastinal

34.74 Repair of pectus deformity

Repair of:
- pectus carinatum } (with implant)
- pectus excavatum

DEF: Pectus carinatum repair: Restoration of prominent chest bone defect with implant.

DEF: Pectus excavatum: Restoration of depressed chest bone defect with implant.

34.79 Other repair of chest wall

Repair of chest wall NOS

✓4th **34.8 Operations on diaphragm**

34.81 Excision of lesion or tissue of diaphragm

EXCLUDES *biopsy of diaphragm (34.27)*

34.82 Suture of laceration of diaphragm

34.83 Closure of fistula of diaphragm

- Thoracicoabdominal
- Thoracicogastric } fistulectomy
- Thoracicointestinal

DEF: Fistulectomy: Closure of abnormal passage.

34.84 Other repair of diaphragm

EXCLUDES *repair of diaphragmatic hernia (53.7-53.82)*

34.85 Implantation of diaphragmatic pacemaker

34.89 Other operations on diaphragm

✓4th **34.9 Other operations on thorax**

34.91 Thoracentesis

DEF: Puncture of pleural cavity for fluid aspiration, also called pleurocentesis.

34.92 Injection into thoracic cavity

Chemical pleurodesis
Injection of cytotoxic agent or tetracycline
Instillation into thoracic cavity
Requires additional code for any cancer chemotherapeutic substance (99.25)

EXCLUDES *that for collapse of lung (33.32)*

DEF: Chemical pleurodesis: Tetracycline hydrochloride injections to create adhesions between parietal and visceral pleura for treatment of pleural effusion.

34.93 Repair of pleura

34.99 Other

EXCLUDES *removal of:*
- *mediastinal drain (97.42)*
- *sutures (97.43)*
- *thoracotomy tube (97.41)*

DEF: Pleural tent: Extrapleural mobilization of parietal pleura that allows draping of membrane over visceral pleura to eliminate intrapleural dead space and seal visceral pleura.

7. OPERATIONS ON THE CARDIOVASCULAR SYSTEM (35-39)

✓3rd 35 Operations on valves and septa of heart

INCLUDES sternotomy (median) (tranverse), thoracotomy } as operative approach

Code also cardiopulmonary bypass [extracorporeal circulation] [heart-lung machine] (39.61)

✓4th 35.0 Closed heart valvotomy

EXCLUDES *percutaneous (balloon) valvuloplasty (35.96)*

DEF: Incision into valve to restore function.

35.00 Closed heart valvotom, unspecified valve

35.01 Closed heart valvotomy, aortic valve

35.02 Closed heart valvotomy, mitral valve

35.03 Closed heart valvotomy, pulmonary valve

35.04 Closed heart valvotomy, tricuspid valve

✓4th 35.1 Open heart valvuloplasty without replacement

INCLUDES open heart valvotomy

Code also cardiopulmonary bypass, if performed [extracorporeal circulation] [heart-lung machine] (39.61)

EXCLUDES *that associated with repair of:*
endocardial cushion defect (35.54,35.63,35.73)
percutaneous (balloon) valvuloplasty (35.96)
valvular defect associated with atrial and ventricular septal defects (35.54, 35.63, 35.73)

DEF: Incision into heart for plastic repair of valve without replacing valve.

35.10 Open heart valvuloplasty without replacement, unspecified valve

35.11 Open heart valvuloplasty of aortic valve without replacement

35.12 Open heart valvuloplasty of mitral valve without replacement

35.13 Open heart valvuloplasty of pulmonary valve without replacement

35.14 Open heart valvuloplasty of tricuspid valve without replacement

✓4th 35.2 Replacement of heart valve

INCLUDES excision of heart valve with replacement

Code also cardiopulmonary bypass [extracorporeal circulation] [heart-lung machine] (39.61)

EXCLUDES *that associated with repair of:*
endocardial cushion defect (35.54,35.63, 35.73)
valvular defect associated with atrial and ventricular septal defects (35.54, 35.63, 35.73)

DEF: Removal and replacement of valve with tissue from patient, animal, other human, or prosthetic (synthetic) valve.

35.20 Replacement of unspecified heart valve
Repair of unspecified heart valve with tissue graft or prosthetic implant

35.21 Replacement of aortic valve with tissue graft
Repair of aortic valve with tissue graft (autograft) (heterograft) (homograft)

35.22 Other replacement of aortic valve
Repair of aortic valve with replacement:
NOS
prosthetic (partial) (synthetic) (total)

35.23 Replacement of mitral valve with tissue graft
Repair of mitral valve with tissue graft (autograft) (heterograft) (homograft)

35.24 Other replacement of mitral valve
Repair of mitral valve with replacement:
NOS
prosthetic (partial) (synthetic) (total)

35.25 Replacement of pulmonary valve with tissue graft
Repair of pulmonary valve with tissue graft (autograft) (heterograft) (homograft)

35.26 Other replacement of pulmonary valve
Repair of pulmonary valve with replacement:
NOS
prosthetic (partial) (synthetic) (total)

35.27 Replacement of tricuspid valve with tissue graft
Repair of tricuspid valve with tissue graft (autograft) (heterograft) (homograft)

35.28 Other replacement of tricuspid valve
Repair of tricuspid valve with replacement:
NOS
prosthetic (partial) (synthetic) (total)

✓4th 35.3 Operations on structures adjacent to heart valves

Code also cardiopulmonary bypass [extracorporeal circulation] [heart-lung machine] (39.61)

35.31 Operations on papillary muscle
Division, Reattachment, Repair } of papillary muscle

35.32 Operations on chordae tendineae
Division, Repair } chordae tendineae

35.33 Annuloplasty
Plication of annulus

DEF: Plication of annulus: Tuck stitched in valvular ring for tightening.

35.34 Infundibulectomy
Right ventricular infundibulectomy

DEF: Infundibulectomy: Excision of funnel-shaped heart passage.

DEF: Right ventricular infundibulectomy: Excision of funnel-shaped passage in right upper heart chamber.

35.35 Operations on trabeculae carneae cordis
Division, Excision } of trabeculae carneae cordis
Excision of aortic subvalvular ring

35.39 Operations on other structures adjacent to valves of heart
Repair of sinus of Valsalva (aneurysm)

✓4th 35.4 Production of septal defect in heart

35.41 Enlargement of existing atrial septal defect
Rashkind procedure
Septostomy (atrial) (balloon)

DEF: Enlargement of partition wall defect in lower heart chamber to improve function.

DEF: Rashkind procedure: Enlargement of partition wall defect between the two lower heart chambers by balloon catheter.

35.42 Creation of septal defect in heart
Blalock-Hanlon operation

DEF: Blalock-Hanlon operation: Removal of partition wall defect in lower heart chamber.

✓4th 35.5 Repair of atrial and ventricular septa with prosthesis

INCLUDES repair of septa with synthetic implant or patch

Code also cardiopulmonary bypass [extracorporeal circulation] [heart-lung machine] (39.61)

35.50 Repair of unspecified septal defect of heart with prosthesis

EXCLUDES *that associated with repair of:*
endocardial cushion defect (35.54)
septal defect associated with valvular defect (35.54)

35.51 Repair of atrial septal defect with prosthesis, open technique

Atrioseptoplasty
Correction of atrial septal defect
Repair:
foramen ovale (patent)
ostium secundum defect
} with prosthesis

EXCLUDES *that associated with repair of:*
atrial septal defect associated with valvular and ventricular septal defects (35.54)
endocardial cushion defect (35.54)

DEF: Repair of opening or weakening in septum separating the atria; prosthesis implanted through heart incision.

35.52 Repair of atrial septal defect with prosthesis, closed technique

Insertion of atrial septal umbrella [King-Mills]

DEF: Correction of partition wall defect in lower heart chamber with artificial material; without incision into heart.

DEF: Insertion of atrial septal umbrella (King-Mills): Correction of partition wall defect in lower heart chamber with atrial septal umbrella.

35.53 Repair of ventricular septal defect with prosthesis, open technique

Correction of ventricular septal defect
Repair of supracristal defect
} with prosthesis

EXCLUDES *that associated with repair of:*
endocardial cushion defect (35.54)
ventricular defect associated with valvular and atrial septal defects (35.54)

35.54 Repair of endocardial cushion defect with prosthesis

Repair:
atrioventricular canal
ostium primum defect
valvular defect associated with atrial and ventricular septal defects
} with prosthesis (grafted to septa)

EXCLUDES *repair of isolated:*
atrial septal defect (35.51-35.52)
valvular defect (35.20, 35.22, 35.24, 35.26, 35.28)
ventricular septal defect (35.53)

35.55 Repair of ventricular septal defect with prosthesis, closed technique

✓4th 35.6 Repair of atrial and ventricular septa with tissue graft

Code also cardiopulmonary bypass [extracorporeal circulation] [heart-lung machine] (39.61)

35.60 Repair of unspecified septal defect of heart with tissue graft

EXCLUDES *that associated with repair of:*
endocardial cushion defect (35.63)
septal defect associated with valvular defect (35.63)

35.61 Repair of atrial septal defect with tissue graft

Atrioseptoplasty
Correction of atrial septal defect
Repair:
foramen ovale (patent)
ostium secundum defect
} with tissue graft

EXCLUDES *that associated with repair of:*
atrial septal defect associated with valvular and ventricular septal defects (35.63)
endocardial cushion defect (35.63)

35.62 Repair of ventricular septal defect with tissue graft

Correction of ventricular septal defect
Repair of supracristal defect
} with tissue graft

EXCLUDES *that associated with repair of:*
endocardial cushion defect (35.63)
ventricular defect associated with valvular and atrial septal defects (35.63)

35.63 Repair of endocardial cushion defect with tissue graft

Repair of:
artrioventricular canal
ostium primum defect
valvular defect associated with atrial and ventricular septal defects
} with tissue graft

EXCLUDES *repair of isolated:*
atrial septal defect (35.61)
valvular defect (35.20-35.21, 35.23, 35.25, 35.27)
ventricular septal defect (35.62)

✓4th 35.7 Other and unspecified repair of atrial and ventricular septa

Code also cardiopulmonary bypass [extracorporeal circulation] [heart-lung machine] (39.61)

35.70 Other and unspecified repair of unspecified septal defect of heart

Repair of septal defect NOS

EXCLUDES *that associated with repair of:*
endocardial cushion defect (35.73)
septal defect associated with valvular defect (35.73)

35.71 Other and unspecified repair of atrial septal defect
Repair NOS:
atrial septum
foramen ovale (patent)
ostium secundum defect

EXCLUDES *that associated with repair of:*
atrial septal defect associated with valvular and ventricular septal defects (35.73)
endocardial cushion defect (35.73)

35.72 Other and unspecified repair of ventricular septal defect
Repair NOS:
supracristal defect
ventricular septum

EXCLUDES *that associated with repair of:*
endocardial cushion defect (35.73)
ventricular septal defect associated with valvular and atrial septal defects (35.73)

35.73 Other and unspecified repair of endocardial cushion defect
Repair NOS:
atrioventricular canal
ostium primum defect
valvular defect associated with atrial and ventricular septal defects

EXCLUDES *repair of isolated:*
atrial septal defect (35.71)
valvular defect (35.20, 35.22, 35.24, 35.26, 35.28)
ventricular septal defect (35.72)

✓4th **35.8 Total repair of certain congenital cardiac anomalies**

Note: For partial repair of defect [e.g. repair of atrial septal defect in tetralogy of Fallot] – code to specific procedure

35.81 Total repair of tetralogy of Fallot
One-stage total correction of tetralogy of Fallot with or without:
commissurotomy of pulmonary valve
infundibulectomy
outflow tract prosthesis
patch graft of outflow tract
prosthetic tube for pulmonary artery
repair of ventricular septal defect (with prosthesis)
take-down of previous systemic-pulmonary artery anastomosis

35.82 Total repair of total anomalous pulmonary venous connection
One-stage total correction of total anomalous pulmonary venous connection with or without:
anastomosis between (horizontal) common pulmonary trunk and posterior wall of left atrium (side-to-side)
enlargement of foramen ovale
incision [excision] of common wall between posterior left atrium and coronary sinus and roofing of resultant defect with patch graft (synthetic)
ligation of venous connection (descending anomalous vein) (to left innominate vein) (to superior vena cava)
repair of atrial septal defect (with prosthesis)

35.83 Total repair of truncus arteriosus
One-stage total correction of truncus arteriosus with or without:
construction (with aortic homograft) (with prosthesis) of a pulmonary artery placed from right ventricle to arteries supplying the lung
ligation of connections between aorta and pulmonary artery
repair of ventricular septal defect (with prosthesis)

35.84 Total correction of transposition of great vessels, not elsewhere classified
Arterial switch operation [Jatene]
Total correction of transposition of great arteries at the arterial level by switching the great arteries, including the left or both coronary arteries, implanted in the wall of the pulmonary artery

EXCLUDES *baffle operation [Mustard] [Senning] (35.91)*
creation of shunt between right ventricle and pulmonary artery [Rastelli] (35.92)

✓4th **35.9 Other operations on valves and septa of heart**
Code also cardiopulmonary bypass, if performed [extracorporeal circulation] [heart-lung machine] (39.61)

35.91 Interatrial transposition of venous return
Baffle:
atrial
interatrial
Mustard's operation
Resection of atrial septum and insertion of patch to direct systemic venous return to tricuspid valve and pulmonary venous return to mitral valve

DEF: Atrial baffle: Correction of venous flow of abnormal or deviated lower heart chamber.

DEF: Interatrial baffle: Correction of venous flow between abnormal lower heart chambers.

DEF: Mustard's operation: Creates intra-atrial baffle using pericardial tissue to correct transposition of the great vessels.

35.92 Creation of conduit between right ventricle and pulmonary artery
Creation of shunt between right ventricle and (distal) pulmonary artery

EXCLUDES *that associated with total repair of truncus arteriosus (35.83)*

35.93 Creation of conduit between left ventricle and aorta
Creation of apicoaortic shunt
Shunt between apex of left ventricle and aorta

35.94 Creation of conduit between atrium and pulmonary artery
Fontan procedure

35.95 Revision of corrective procedure on heart
Replacement of prosthetic heart valve poppet
Resuture of prosthesis of:
septum
valve

EXCLUDES *complete revision – code to specific procedure*
replacement of prosthesis or graft of:
septum (35.50-35.63)
valve (35.20-35.28)

DEF: Replacement of prosthetic heart valve poppet: Removal and replacement of valve-supporting prosthesis.

DEF: Resuture of prosthesis of septum: Restitching of prosthesis in partition wall.

DEF: Resuture of prosthesis of valve: Restitching of prosthetic valve.

35.96 Percutaneous valvuloplasty
Percutaneous balloon valvuloplasty

DEF: Repair of valve with catheter.

DEF: Percutaneous balloon valvuloplasty: Repair of valve with inflatable catheter.

35.98 Other operations on septa of heart

35.99 Other operations on valves of heart

✓3rd 36 Operations on vessels of heart

INCLUDES sternotomy (median) (transverse), thoracotomy } as operative approach

Code also any:
injection or infusion of platelet inhibitor (99.20)
injection or infusion of thrombolytic agent (99.10)
Code also cardiopulmonary bypass, if performed [extracorporeal circulation] [heart-lung machine] (39.61)

✓4th 36.0 Removal of coronary artery obstruction and insertion of stent(s)

36.03 Open chest coronary artery angioplasty
Coronary (artery):
endarterectomy (with patch graft)
thromboendarterectomy (with patch graft)
Open surgery for direct relief of coronary artery obstruction

Code also any:
insertion of drug-eluting coronary stent(s) (36.07)
insertion of non-drug-eluting coronary stent(s) (36.06)
number of vascular stents inserted (00.45-00.48)
number of vessels treated (00.40-00.43)
procedure on vessel bifurcation (00.44)

EXCLUDES *that with coronary artery bypass graft (36.10-36.19)*

DEF: Endarterectomy (with patch graft): Excision of thickened material within coronary artery; repair with patch graft.

DEF: Thromboendarterectomy (with patch graft): Excision of blood clot and thickened material within coronary artery; repair with patch graft.

DEF: Open surgery for direct relief of coronary artery obstruction: Removal of coronary artery obstruction through opening in chest.

36.04 Intracoronary artery thrombolytic infusion
That by direct coronary artery injection, infusion, or catheterization
Enzyme infusion
Platelet inhibitor

EXCLUDES *infusion of platelet inhibitor (99.20)*
infusion of thrombolytic agent (99.10)
that associated with any procedure in 36.03

DEF: Infusion of clot breaking solution into intracoronary artery.

36.06 Insertion of non-drug-eluting coronary atery stent(s)
Bare stent(s)
Bonded stent(s)
Drug-coated stent(s), e.g., heparin coated
Endograft(s)
Endovascular graft(s)
Stent graft(s)
Code also any:
number of vascular stents inserted (00.45-00.48)
number of vessels treated (00.40-00.43)
open chest coronary artery angioplasty (36.03)
percutaneous transluminal coronary angioplasty [PTCA] or coronary atherectomy (00.66)
procedure on vessel bifurcation (00.44)

EXCLUDES *insertion of drug-eluting coronary artery stent(s) (36.07)*

DEF: Percutaneous implant via catheter of metal stent, to enlarge, maintain lumen size of coronary artery.

36.07 Insertion of drug-eluting coronary artery stent(s)
Endograft(s)
Endovascular graft(s)
Stent graft(s)
Code also any:
number of vascular stents inserted (00.45-00.48)
number of vessels treated (00.40-00.43)
open chest coronary artery angioplasty (36.03)
percutaneous transluminal coronary angioplasty [PTCA] or coronary atherectomy (00.66)
procedure on vessel bifurcation (00.44)

EXCLUDES *drug-coated stents, e.g., heparin coated (36.06)*
insertion of non-drug-eluting coronary artery stent(s) (36.06)

DEF: Drug-eluting stent technology developed to prevent the accumulation of scar tissue that can narrow reopened coronary arteries. A special polymer is used to coat the drug onto the stent, which slowly releases into the coronary artery wall tissue.

36.09 Other removal of coronary artery obstruction
Coronary angioplasty NOS
Code also any:
number of vascular stents inserted (00.45-00.48)
number of vessels treated (00.40-00.43)
procedure on vessel bifurcation (00.44)

EXCLUDES *that by open angioplasty (36.03)*
that by percutaneous transluminal coronary angioplasty [PTCA] or coronary atherectomy (00.66)

Coronary Bypass

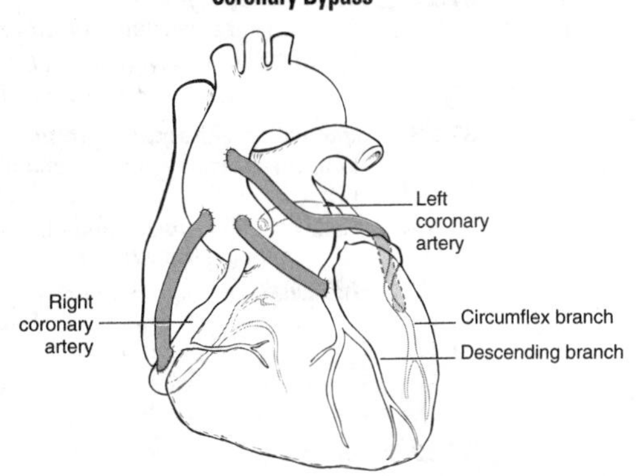

Transmyocardial Revascularization

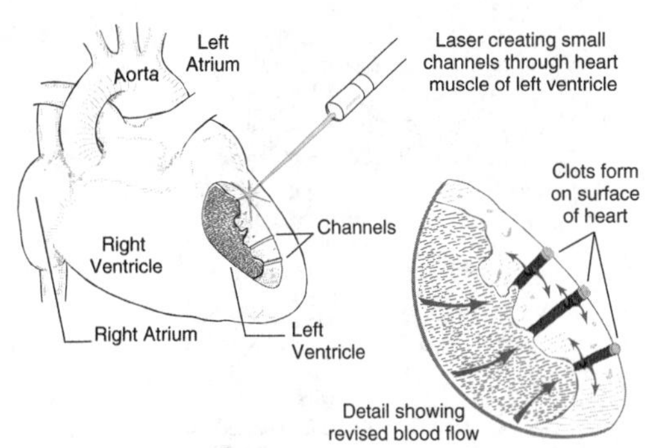

✓4th 36.1 Bypass anastomosis for heart revascularization

Note: Do not assign codes from series 00.40-00.43 with codes from series 36.10-36.19

Code also:
cardiopulmonary bypass [extracorporeal circulation] [heart-lung machine] (39.61)
pressurized treatment of venous bypass graft [conduit] with pharmaceutical substance, if performed (00.16)

DEF: Insertion of tube to bypass blocked coronary artery, correct coronary blood flow.

36.10 Aortocoronary bypass for heart revascularization, not otherwise specified

Direct revascularization:
cardiac, coronary, hear muscle, myocardial } with catheter stent, prosthesis, or vein graft

Heart revascularization NOS

36.11 (Aorto)coronary bypass of one coronary artery

36.12 (Aorto)coronary bypass of two coronary arteries

36.13 (Aorto)coronary bypass of three coronary arteries

36.14 (Aorto)coronary bypass of four or more coronary arteries

36.15 Single internal mammary-coronary artery bypass

Anastomosis (single):
mammary artery to coronary artery
thoracic artery to coronary artery

36.16 Double internal mammary-coronary artery bypass

Anastomosis, double:
mammary artery to coronary artery
thoracic artery to coronary artery

36.17 Abdominal-coronary artery bypass

Anastomosis:
gastroepiploic artery to coronary artery

36.19 Other bypass anastomosis for heart revascularization

36.2 Heart revascularization by arterial implant

Implantation of:
aortic branches [ascending aortic branches] into heart muscle
blood vessels into myocardium
internal mammary artery [internal thoracic artery] into:
heart muscle
myocardium
ventricle
ventricular wall

Indirect heart revascularization NOS

✓4th 36.3 Other heart revascularization

36.31 Open chest transmyocardial revascularization

DEF: Transmyocardial revascularization (TMR): Laser creation of channels through myocardium allows oxygenated blood flow from sinusoids to myocardial tissue.

36.32 Other transmyocardial revascularization

36.33 Endoscopic transmyocardial revascularization

Thoracoscopic transmyocardial revascularization

36.34 Percutaneous transmyocardial revascularization

Endovascular transmyocardial revascularization

36.39 Other heart revascularization

Abrasion of epicardium
Cardio-omentopexy
Intrapericardial poudrage
Myocardial graft:
mediastinal fat
omentum
pectoral muscles

DEF: Cardio-omentopexy: Suture of omentum segment to heart after drawing segment through incision in diaphragm to improve blood supply.

DEF: Intrapericardial poudrage: Application of powder to heart lining to promote fusion.

✓4th 36.9 Other operations on vessels of heart

Code also cardiopulmonary bypass [extracorporeal circulation] [heart-lung machine] (39.61)

36.91 Repair of aneurysm of coronary vessel

36.99 Other operations on vessels of heart

Exploration, Incision, Ligation } of coronary artery

Repair of arteriovenous fistula

✓3rd 37 Other operations on heart and pericardium

Code also any injection or infusion of platelet inhibitor (99.20)

37.0 Pericardiocentesis

DEF: Puncture of the heart lining to withdraw fluid.

✓4th 37.1 Cardiotomy and pericardiotomy

Code also cardiopulmonary bypass [extracorporeal circulation] [heart-lung machine] (39.61)

37.10 Incision of heart, not otherwise specified

Cardiolysis NOS

37.11 Cardiotomy

Incision of:
atrium
endocardium
myocardium
ventricle

Intracardiac Echocardiography

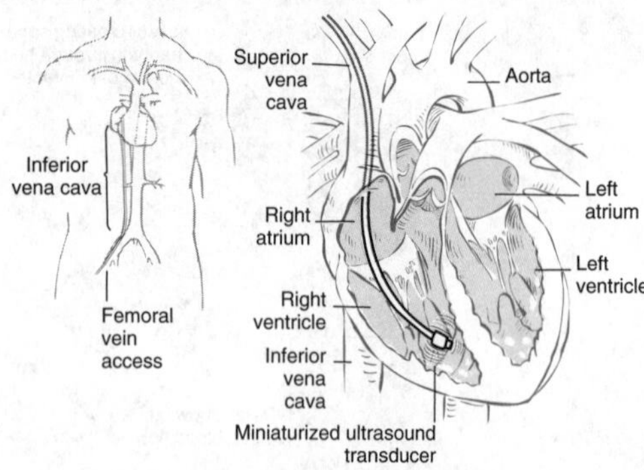

37.12 Pericardiotomy

Pericardial window operation
Pericardiolysis
Pericardiotomy

DEF: Pericardial window operation: Incision into heart lining for drainage.

DEF: Pericardiolysis: Destruction of heart tissue lining.

✓4th **37.2 Diagnostic procedures on heart and pericardium**

37.20 Non-invasive programmed electrical stimulation [NIPS]

EXCLUDES *catheter based invasive electrophysiologic testing (37.26)*
device interrogation only without arrhythmia induction (bedside check) (89.45-89.49)
that as part of intraoperative testing — omit code

DEF: Non-invasive testing of a previously implanted cardioverter-defibrillator to ensure proper lead placement and system function.

37.21 Right heart cardiac catheterization

Cardiac catheterization NOS

EXCLUDES *that with catheterization of left heart (37.23)*

37.22 Left heart cardiac catheterization

EXCLUDES *that with catheterization of right heart (37.23)*

37.23 Combined right and left heart cardiac catheterization

37.24 Biopsy of pericardium

37.25 Biopsy of heart

37.26 Catheter based invasive electrophysiologic testing

Electrophysiologic studies [EPS]

Code also any concomitant procedure

EXCLUDES *device interrogation only without arrhythmia induction (bedside check) (89.45-89.49)*
His bundle recording (37.29)
non-invasive programmed electrical stimulation (NIPS) (37.20)
that as part of intraoperative testing — omit code

DEF: Diagnostic mapping and measurement of intracardiac electrical activity; requires inserting three to six catheters into heart blood vessels and positioning catheters under fluoroscopic guidance to determine site of the tachycardia or abnormal impulse pathway; may also be used to terminate arrhythmias.

37.27 Cardiac mapping

Code also any concomitant procedure

EXCLUDES *electrocardiogram (89.52)*
His bundle recording (37.29)

37.28 Intracardiac echocardiography

Echocardiography of heart chambers
ICE

Code also any synchronous Doppler flow mapping (88.72)

EXCLUDES *intravascular imaging of coronary vessels (intravascular ultra-sound) (IVUS) (00.24)*

DEF: Creation of a two-dimensional graphic of heart using endoscopic echocardiographic equipment.

37.29 Other diagnostic procedures on heart and pericardium

EXCLUDES *angiocardiography (88.50-88.58)*
cardiac function tests (89.41-89.69)
cardiovascular radioisotopic scan and function study (92.05)
coronary arteriography (88.55-88.57)
diagnostic pericardiocentesis (37.0)
diagnostic ultrasound of heart (88.72)
x-ray of heart (87.49)

✓4th **37.3 Pericardiectomy and excision of lesion of heart**

Code also cardiopulmonary bypass [extracorporeal circulation] [heart-lung machine] (39.61)

37.31 Pericardiectomy

Excision of:
- adhesions of pericardium
- constricting scar of:
  - epicardium
  - pericardium

DEF: Excision of a portion of heart lining.

37.32 Excision of aneurysm of heart

Repair of aneurysm of heart

37.33 Excision or destruction of other lesion or tissue of heart, open approach

Ablation of heart tissue (cryoablation) (electrocurrent) (laser) (microwave) (radiofrequency) (resection), open chest approach
Cox-maze procedure
Maze procedure
Modified maze procedure, transthoracic approach

EXCLUDES *ablation, excision or destruction of lesion or tissue of heart, endovascular approach (37.34)*
excision or destruction of left atrial appendage (LAA) (37.36)

37.34 Excision or destruction of other lesion or tissue of heart, other approach

Ablation of heart tissue (cryoablation) (electrocurrent) (laser) (microwave) (radiofrequency) (resection), via peripherally inserted catheter
Modified maze procedure, endovascular approach

DEF: Destruction of heart tissue or lesion by freezing, electric current or resection.

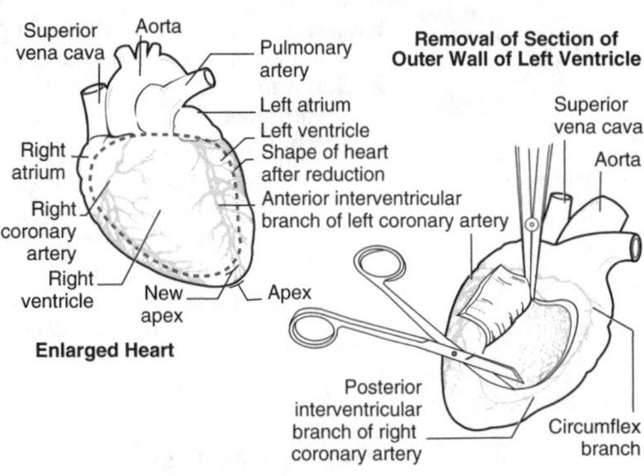

37.35 Partial ventriculectomy

Ventricular reduction surgery
Ventricular remodeling

Code also any synchronous:
mitral valve repair (35.02, 35.12)
mitral valve replacement (35.23-35.24)

DEF: Removal of elliptical slice of ventricle between anterior and posterior papillary muscle; also called Batiste operation.

37.36 Excision or destruction of left atrial appendage (LAA)

INCLUDES thoracoscopic approach, minithoracotomy approach

Clipping of left atrial appendage
Exclusion of left atrial appendage
Oversewing of left atrial appendage
Stapling of left atrial appendage

Code also any concomitant procedure performed

EXCLUDES *ablation, excision or destruction of lesion or tissue of heart, endovascular approach (37.34)*

✓4th **37.4 Repair of heart and pericardium**

37.41 Implantation of prosthetic cardiac support device around the heart

Cardiac support device (CSD)
Epicardial support device
Fabric (textile) (mesh) device
Ventricular support device on surface of heart

Code also any:
cardiopulmonary bypass [extracorporeal circulation] [heart-lung machine] if performed (39.61)
mitral valve repair (35.02, 35.12)
mitral valve replacement (35.23-35.24)
transesophageal echocardiography (88.72)

EXCLUDES *circulatory assist systems (37.61-37.68)*

DEF: Cardiac support device: any device implanted around the ventricles of the heart for cardiac support

DEF: Fabric (textile) (mesh) device: textile mesh net sutured around the heart for support.

37.49 Other repair of heart and pericardium

✓4th **37.5 Heart replacement procedures**

37.51 Heart transplantation

EXCLUDES *combined heart-lung transplantation (33.6)*

37.52 Implantation of total internal biventricular heart replacement system

Note: This procedure includes substantial removal of part or all of the biological heart. Both ventricles are resected, and the native heart is no longer intact.Ventriculectomy is included in this procedure; do not code separately.

Artificial heart

EXCLUDES *implantation of heart assist system [VAD] (37.62, 37.65, 37.66, 37.68)*

37.53 Replacement or repair of thoracic unit of (total) replacement heart system

EXCLUDES *replacement and repair of heart assist system [VAD] (37.63)*

37.54 Replacement or repair of other implantable component of (total) replacement heart system

Implantable battery
Implantable controller
Transcutaneous energy transfer [TET] device

EXCLUDES *replacement and repair of heart assist system [VAD] (37.63)*
replacement or repair of thoracic unit of (total) replacement heart system (37.53)

37.55 Removal of internal biventricular heart replacement system

Explantation of artificial heart

Code also any concomitant procedure, such as:
combined heart-lung transplantation (33.6)
heart transplantation (37.51)
implantation of internal biventricular heart replacement system (37.52)

EXCLUDES *explantation [removal] of external heart assist system (37.64)*
explantation [removal] of percutaneous external heart assist device (97.44)
nonoperative removal of heart assist system (97.44)
that with replacement or repair of heart replacement system (37.53, 37.54)

✓4th **37.6 Implantation of heart and circulatory assist system(s)**

EXCLUDES *implantation of prosthetic cardiac support system (37.41)*

DEF: Implant of device for assisting heart in circulating blood.

37.60 Implantation or insertion of biventricular external heart assist system

Note: Device (outside the body but connected to heart) with external circulation pump. Ventriculotomy is included; do not code separately.

INCLUDES open chest (sternotomy) procedure for cannulae attachments

Temporary cardiac support for both left and right ventricles, inserted in the same operative episode

EXCLUDES *implantation of internal biventricular heart replacement system (artificial heart) (37.52)*
implant of pulsation balloon (37.61)
insertion of percutaneous external heart assist device (37.68)
insertion of temporary non-implantable extracorporeal circulatory assist device (37.62)

37.61 Implant of pulsation balloon

37.62 Insertion of temporary non-implantable extracorporeal circulatory assist device

Note: Includes explantation of this device; do not code separately.

Acute circulatory support device
Insertion of heart assist system, NOS
Insertion of heart pump
Short-term circulatory support (up to six hours)

EXCLUDES *implant of external heart assist system (37.65)*
implantation of total internal biventricular heart replacement system [artificial heart] (37.52)
insertion of implantable extracorporeal heart assist system (37.66)
insertion of percutaneous external heart assist device (37.68)
removal of heart assist system (37.64)

37.63 Repair of heart assist system

Replacement of parts of an existing ventricular assist device (VAD)

EXCLUDES *replacement or repair of other implantable component of (total) replacement heart system [artificial heart] (37.54)*
replacement or repair of thoracic unit of (total) replacement heart system [artificial heart] (37.53)

37.64 Removal of external heart assist system(s) or device(s)

Explantation of external device(s) providing left and right ventricular support
Explantation of single external device and cannulae

EXCLUDES *explantation [removal] of percutaneous external heart assist device (97.44)*
nonoperative removal of heart assist system (97.44)
temporary non-implantable extracorporeal circulatory assist device (37.62)
that with replacement of implant (37.63)

37.65 Implant of single ventricular (extracorporeal) external heart assist system

Note: Device (outside the body but connected to heart) with external circulation and pump

Note: Insertion or implantation of one external VAD for left or right heart support.

INCLUDES open chest (sternotomy) procedure for cannulae attachments

EXCLUDES *implantation of total internal biventricular heart replacement system (37.52)*
implant of pulsation balloon (37.61)
insertion of implantable heart assist system (37.66)
insertion of percutaneous external heart assist device (37.68)
insertion or implantation of two external VADs for simultaneous right and left heart support (37.60)
that without sternotomy (37.62)

DEF: Insertion of short-term circulatory support device with pump outside body.

37.66 Insertion of implantable heart assist system

Note: Device directly connected to the heart and implanted in the upper left quadrant of peritoneal cavity.This device can be used for either destination therapy (DT) or bridge-to-transplant (BTT).

Axial flow heart assist system
Diagonal pump heart assist system
Left ventricular assist device (LVAD)
Pulsatile heart assist system
Right ventricular assist device (RVAD)
Rotary pump heart assist system
Transportable, implantable heart assist system
Ventricular assist device (VAD) not otherwise specified

EXCLUDES *implantation of total internal biventricular heart replacement system [artificial heart] (37.52)*
implant of pulsation balloon (37.61)
insertion of percutaneous external heart assist device (37.68)

DEF: Insertion of long-term circulatory support device with pump in body.

37.67 Implantation of cardiomyostimulation system

Note: Two-step open procedure consisting of tranfer of one end of the latissimus dorsi muscle; wrapping it around the heart; rib resection; implantation of epicardial cardiac pacing leads into the right ventricle; tunneling and pocket creation for the cardiomyostimulator.

37.68 Insertion of percutaneous external heart assist device

Circulatory assist device
Extrinsic heart assist device
pVAD
Percutaneous heart assist device

EXCLUDES *percutaneous [femoral] insertion of cannulae attachments*

✓4th **37.7 Insertion, revision, replacement, and removal of leads; insertion of temporary pacemaker system; or revision of cardiac device pocket**

Code also any insertion and replacement of pacemaker device (37.80-37.87)

EXCLUDES *implantation or replacement of transvenous lead [electrode] into left ventricular cardiac venous system (00.52)*

37.70 Initial insertion of lead [electrode], not otherwise specified

EXCLUDES *insertion of temporary transvenous pacemaker system (37.78)*
replacement of atrial and/or ventricular lead(s) (37.76)

37.71 Initial insertion of transvenous lead [electrode] into ventricle

EXCLUDES *insertion of temporary transvenous pacemaker system (37.78)*
replacement of atrial and/or ventricular lead(s) (37.76)

37.72 Initial insertion of transvenous leads [electrodes] into atrium and ventricle

EXCLUDES *insertion of temporary transvenous pacemaker system (37.78)*
replacement of atrial and/or ventricular lead(s) (37.76)

37.73 Initial insertion of transvenous lead [electrode] into atrium

EXCLUDES *insertion of temporary transvenous pacemaker system (37.78)*
replacement of atrial and/or ventricular lead(s) (37.76)

37.74 Insertion or replacement of epicardial lead [electrode] into epicardium

Insertion or replacement of epicardial lead by:
- sternotomy
- thoracotomy

EXCLUDES *replacement of atrial and/or ventricular lead(s) (37.76)*

37.75 Revision of lead [electrode]

Repair of electrode [removal with re-insertion]
Repositioning of lead(s) (AICD) (cardiac device) (CRT-D) (CRT-P) (defibrillator) (pacemaker) (pacing) (sensing) [electrode]
Revision of lead NOS

EXCLUDES *repositioning of temporary transvenous pacemaker system — omit code*

37.76 Replacement of transvenous atrial and/or ventricular lead(s) [electrode]

Removal or abandonment of existing transvenous or epicardial lead(s) with transvenous lead(s) replacement

EXCLUDES *replacement of epicardial lead [electrode] (37.74)*

37.77 Removal of lead(s) [electrode] without replacement

Removal:
- epicardial lead (transthoracic approach)
- transvenous lead(s)

EXCLUDES *removal of temporary transvenous pacemaker system — omit code*
that with replacement of:
- *atrial and/or ventricular lead(s) [electrode] (37.76)*
- *epicardial lead [electrode] (37.74)*

37.78 Insertion of temporary transvenous pacemaker system

EXCLUDES *intraoperative cardiac pacemaker (39.64)*

37.79 Revision or relocation of cardiac device pocket

Debridement and reforming pocket (skin and subcutaneous tissue)
Insertion of loop recorder
Relocation of pocket [creation of new pocket] pacemaker or CRT-P
Removal of cardiac device/pulse generator without replacement
Removal of implantable hemodynamic pressure sensor [lead] and monitor device
Removal without replacement of cardiac resynchronization defibrillator device
Repositioning of implantable hemodynamic pressure sensor [lead] and monitor device
Repositioning of pulse generator
Revision of cardioverter/defibrillator (automatic) pocket
Revision of pocket for intracardiac hemodynamic monitoring
Revision or relocation of CRT-D pocket
Revision or relocation of pacemaker, defibrillator, or other implanted cardiac device pocket

EXCLUDES *removal of loop recorder (86.05)*

Insertion of Pacemaker

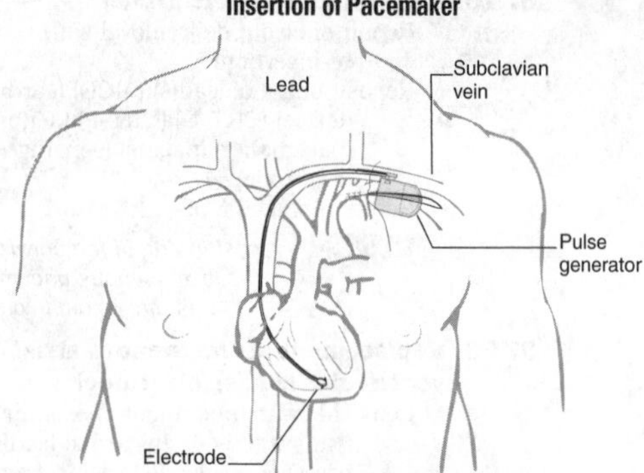

✓4th **37.8 Insertion, replacement, removal, and revision of pacemaker device**

Note: Device testing during procedure — *omit code*

Code also any lead insertion, lead replacement, lead removal and/or lead revision (37.70-37.77)

EXCLUDES *implantation of cardiac resynchronization pacemaker, total system [CRT-P] (00.50)*
implantation or replacement of cardiac resynchronization pacemaker pulse generator only [CRT-P] (00.53)

37.80 Insertion of permanent pacemaker, initial or replacement, type of device not specified

37.81 Initial insertion of single-chamber device, not specified as rate responsive

EXCLUDES *replacement of existing pacemaker device (37.85-37.87)*

37.82 Initial insertion of single-chamber device, rate responsive

Rate responsive to physiologic stimuli other than atrial rate

EXCLUDES *replacement of existing pacemaker device (37.85-37.87)*

37.83 Initial insertion of dual-chamber device

Atrial ventricular sequential device

EXCLUDES *replacement of existing pacemaker device (37.85-37.87)*

37.85 Replacement of any type pacemaker device with single-chamber device, not specified as rate responsive

37.86 Replacement of any type pacemaker device with single-chamber device, rate responsive

Rate responsive to physiologic stimuli other than atrial rate

37.87 Replacement of any type pacemaker device with dual-chamber device

Atrial ventricular sequential device

37.89 Revision or removal of pacemaker device

Removal without replacement of cardiac re-synchronization pacemaker device [CRT-P]

Repair of pacemaker device

EXCLUDES *removal of temporary transvenous pacemaker system — omit code*
replacement of existing pacemaker device (37.85-37.87)
replacement of existing pacemaker device with CRT-P pacemaker device (00.53)

Left Atrial Appendage Device Insertion

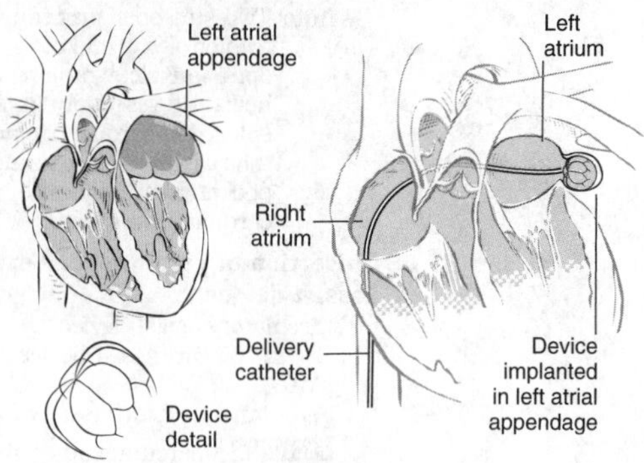

Automatic Implantable Cardioverter/Defibrillator

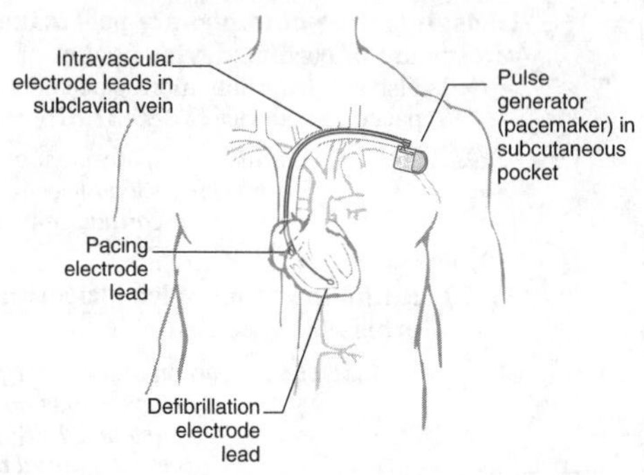

✓4th **37.9 Other operations on heart and pericardium**

37.90 Insertion of left atrial appendage device

Left atrial filter
Left atrial occluder
Transseptal catheter technique

DEF: Implantation of a filtering device within the left atrial appendage (LAA) to block emboli from exiting the LAA causing stroke or systemic thromboembolism.

37.91 Open chest cardiac massage

EXCLUDES *closed chest cardiac massage (99.63)*

DEF: Massage of heart through opening in chest wall to reinstate or maintain circulation.

37.92 Injection of therapeutic substance into heart

37.93 Injection of therapeutic substance into pericardium

37.94 Implantation or replacement of automatic cardioverter/defibrillator, total system [AICD]

Note: Device testing during procedure — *omit code*

Implantation of defibrillator with leads (epicardial patches), formation of pocket (abdominal fascia) (subcutaneous), any transvenous leads, intra-operative procedures for evaluation of lead signals, and obtaining defibrillator threshold measurements

Techniques:
- lateral thoracotomy
- medial sternotomy
- subxiphoid procedure

Code also extracorporeal circulation, if performed (39.61)

Code also any concomitant procedure [e.g., coronary bypass] (36.01-36.19)

EXCLUDES *implantation of cardiac resynchronization defibrillator, total system [CRT-D] (00.51)*

DEF: Direct insertion, of defibrillator/cardioverter system to deliver shock and restore heart rhythm.

37.95 Implantation of automatic cardioverter/defibrillator lead(s) only

37.96 Implantation of automatic cardioverter/ defibrillator pulse generator only

Note: Device testing during procedure — *omit code*

EXCLUDES *implantation or replacement of cardiac resynchronization defibrillator, pulse generator device only [CRT-D] (00.54)*

37.97 Replacement of automatic cardioverter/defibrillator lead(s) only

EXCLUDES *replacement of epicardial lead [electrode] into epicardium (37.74)*
replacement of transvenous lead [electrode] into left ventricular coronary venous system (00.52)

37.98 Replacement of automatic cardioverter defibrillator pulse generator only

Note: Device testing during procedure — *omit code*

EXCLUDES *replacement of cardiac resynchronization defibrillator, pulse generator device only [CRT-D] (00.54)*

37.99 Other

EXCLUDES *cardiac retraining (93.36)*
conversion of cardiac rhythm (99.60-99.69)
implantation of prosthetic cardiac support device (37.41)
insertion of left atrial appendage device (37.90)
maze procedure (Cox-maze), open (37.33)
maze procedure, endovascular approach (37.34)
repositioning of pulse generator (37.79)
revision of lead(s) (37.75)
revision or relocation of pacemaker, defibrillator or other implanted cardiac device pocket (37.79)

✓3rd **38 Incision, excision, and occlusion of vessels**

Code also any application or administration of an adhesion barrier substance (99.77)

Code also cardiopulmonary bypass [extracorporeal circulation] [heart-lung machine] (39.61)

EXCLUDES *that of coronary vessels (00.66, 36.03, 36.04, 36.09, 36.10-36.99)*

The following fourth-digit subclassification is for use with appropriate categories in section 38.0, 38.1, 38.3, 38.5, 38.6, and 38.8 according to site. Valid fourth-digits are in [brackets] under each code.

0 unspecified

1 intracranial vessels
- Cerebral (anterior) (middle)
- Circle of Willis
- Posterior communicating artery

2 other vessels of head and neck
- Carotid artery (common) (external) (internal)
- Jugular vein (external) (internal)

3 upper limb vessels
- Axilllary
- Brachial
- Radial
- Ulnar

4 aorta

5 other thoracic vessels
- Innominate
- Pulmonary (artery) (vein)
- Subclavian
- Vena cava, superior

6 abdominal arteries
- Celiac
- Gastric
- Hepatic
- Iliac
- Mesenteric
- Renal
- Splenic
- Umbilical

EXCLUDES *abdominal aorta (4)*

7 abdominal veins
- Iliac
- Portal
- Renal
- Splenic
- Vena cava (inferior)

8 lower limb arteries
- Femoral (common) (superficial)
- Popliteal
- Tibial

9 lower limb veins
- Femoral
- Popliteal
- Saphenous
- Tibial

✓4th **38.0 Incision of vessel**

[0-9] Embolectomy
Thrombectomy

EXCLUDES *endovascular removal of obstruction from head and neck vessel(s) (39.74)*
puncture or catheterization of any:
artery (38.91, 38.98)
vein (38.92-38.95, 38.99)

✓4th **38.1 Endarterectomy**

[0-6,8] Endarterectomy with:
- embolectomy
- patch graft
- temporary bypass during procedure
- thrombectomy

Code also any:
- number of vascular stents inserted (00.45-00.48)
- number of vessels treated (00.40-00.43)
- procedure on vessel bifurcation (00.44)

DEF: Excision of tunica intima of artery to relieve arterial walls thickened by plaque or chronic inflammation.

✓4th **38.2 Diagnostic procedures on blood vessels**

EXCLUDES *adjunct vascular system procedures (00.40-00.43)*

38.21 Biopsy of blood vessel

38.22 Percutaneous angioscopy

EXCLUDES *angioscopy of eye (95.12)*

DEF: Exam, with fiberoptic catheter inserted through peripheral artery to visualize inner lining of blood vessels.

Endarterectomy of Aortic Bifurcation

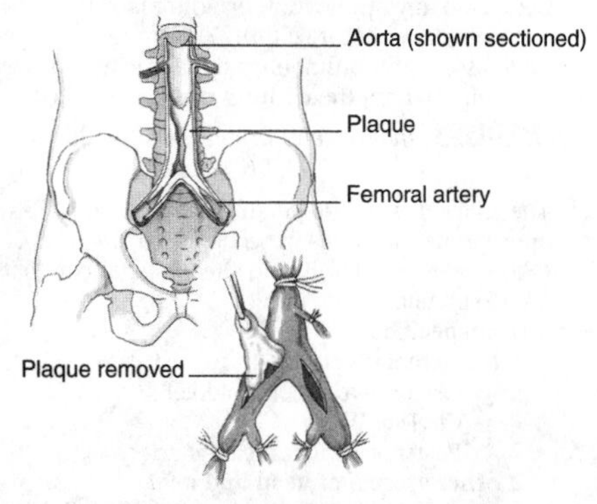

38.23 Intravascular spectroscopy

INCLUDES imaging of both coronary and peripheral vessels

Intravascular chemography

Near infrared (NIR) spectroscopy

EXCLUDES *intravascular imaging of:*
coronary vessels (00.24)
peripheral vessels (00.23)

38.29 Other diagnostic procedures on blood vessels

EXCLUDES *blood vessel thermography (88.86)*
circulatory monitoring (89.61-89.69)
contrast:
angiocardiography (88.50-88.58)
arteriography (88.40-88.49)
phlebography (88.60-88.67)
impedance phlebography (88.68)
peripheral vascular ultrasonography (88.77)
plethysmogram (89.58)

✓4th **38.3 Resection of vessel with anastomosis**

[0-9] Angiectomy

Excision of:
aneurysm (arteriovenous) } with anastomosis
blood vessel (lesion) }

DEF: Reconstruction and reconnection of vessel after partial excision.

Methods of Vessel Anastomoses

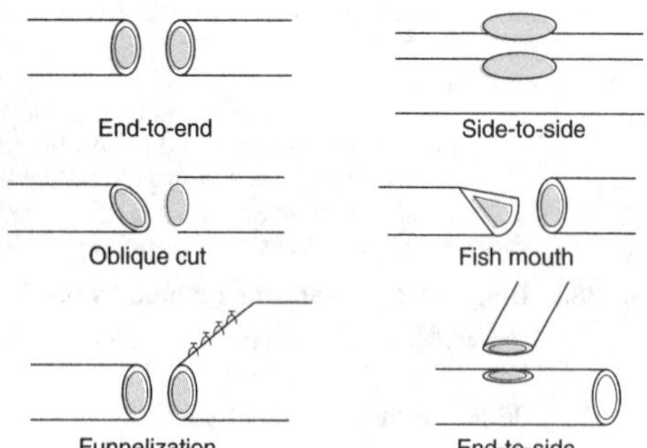

✓4th **38.4 Resection of vessel with replacement**

[0-9] Angiectomy

Excision of:
aneurysm (arteriovenous) } with replacement
or blood vessel (lesion) }

Partial resection with replacement

EXCLUDES *endovascular repair of aneurysm (39.71-39.79)*

Requires the use of one of the following fourth-digit subclassifications to identify site:

0 unspecified

1 intracranial vessels
Cerebral (anterior) (middle)
Circle of Willis
Posterior communicating artery

2 other vessels of head and neck
Carotid artery (common) (external) (internal)
Jugular vein (external) (internal)

3 upper limb vessels
Axilllary — Radial
Brachial — Ulnar

4 aorta, abdominal
Code also any thoracic vessel involvement (thoracoabdominal procedure) (38.45)

5 other thoracic vessels
Aorta (thoracic) — Subclavian
Innominate — Vena cava, superior
Pulmonary (artery) (vein)
Code also any abdominal aorta involvement (thoracoabdonminal procedure) (38.44)

6 abdominal arteries
Celiac — Mesenteric
Gastric — Renal
Hepatic — Splenic
Iliac — Umbilical
EXCLUDES *abdominal aorta (4)*

7 abdominal veins
Iliac — Splenic
Portal — Vena cava (inferior)
Renal

8 lower limb arteries
Femoral (common)(superficial)
Tibial

9 lower limb veins
Femoral — Saphenous
Popliteal — Tibial

DEF: Excision of aneurysm (arteriovenous): Excision and replacement of segment of stretched or bulging blood vessel.

DEF: Excision of blood vessel (lesion): Excision and replacement of segment of vessel containing lesion.

✓4th **38.5 Ligation and stripping of varicose veins**

[0-3,5,7,9] EXCLUDES ligation of varices:
esophageal (42.91)
gastric (44.91)

DEF: Ligation of varicose veins: Typing off vein with thread or wire to eliminate blood flow; stripping involves excising length of vein.

✓4th **38.6 Other excision of vessels**

[0-9] Excision of blood vessel (lesion) NOS

EXCLUDES *excision of vessel for aortocoronary bypass (36.10-36.14)*
excision with:
anastomosis (38.30-38.39)
graft replacement (38.40-38.49)
implant (38.40-38.49)

38.7 Interruption of the vena cava

Insertion of implant or sieve in vena cava

Ligation of vena cava (inferior) (superior)

Plication of vena cava

DEF: Interruption of the blood flow through the venous heart vessels to prevent clots from reaching the chambers of the heart by means of implanting a sieve or implant, separating off a portion or by narrowing the venous blood vessels.

✓4th 38.8 Other surgical occlusion of vessels
[0-9]

Clamping, Division, Ligation, Occlusion } of blood vessel

EXCLUDES *adrenal vessels (07.43)*
esophageal varices (42.91)
gastric or duodenal vessel for ulcer (44.40-44.49)
gastric varices (44.91)
meningeal vessel (02.13)
percutaneous transcatheter infusion embolization (99.29)
spermatic vein for varicocele (63.1)
surgical occlusion of vena cava (38.7)
that for chemoembolization (99.25)
that for control of (postoperative) hemorrhage:
anus (49.95)
bladder (57.93)
following vascular procedure (39.41)
nose (21.00-21.09)
prostate (60.94)
tonsil (28.7)
thyroid vessel (06.92)
transcatheter (infusion) 99.29

✓4th 38.9 Puncture of vessel

EXCLUDES *that for circulatory monitoring (89.60-89.69)*

38.91 Arterial catheterization

38.92 Umbilical vein catheterization

38.93 Venous catheterization, not elsewhere classified

EXCLUDES *that for cardiac catheterization (37.21-37.23)*
that for renal dialysis (38.95)

38.94 Venous cutdown

DEF: Incision of vein to place needle or catheter.

38.95 Venous catheterization for renal dialysis

EXCLUDES *insertion of totally implantable vascular access device [VAD] (86.07)*

38.98 Other puncture of artery

EXCLUDES *that for:*
arteriography (88.40-88.49)
coronary arteriography (88.55-88.57)

Typical Venous Cutdown

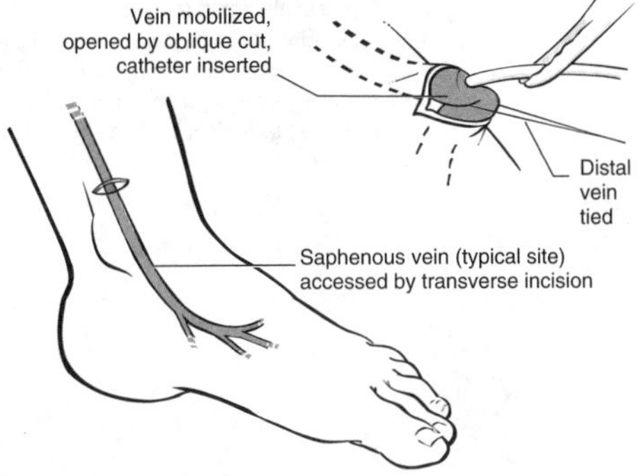

38.99 Other puncture of vein

Phlebotomy

EXCLUDES *that for:*
angiography of veins (88.60-88.68)
extracorporeal circulation (39.61, 50.92)
injection or infusion of:
sclerosing solution (39.92)
therapeutic or prophylactic substance (99.11-99.29)
perfusion (39.96, 39.97)
phlebography (88.60-88.68)
transfusion (99.01-99.09)

✓3rd 39 Other operations on vessels

EXCLUDES *those on coronary vessels (36.03-36.99)*

39.0 Systemic to pulmonary artery shunt

Descending aorta-pulmonary artery, Left to right, Subclavian-pulmonary } anastomosis (graft)

Code also cardiopulmonary bypass [extracorporeal circulation] [heart-lung machine] (39.61)

DEF: Descending aorta-pulmonary artery anastomosis (graft): Connection of descending main heart artery to pulmonary artery.

DEF: Left to right anastomosis (graft): Connection of systemic arterial blood vessel to venous pulmonary system.

DEF: Subclavian-pulmonary anastomosis (graft): Connection of subclavian artery to pulmonary artery

39.1 Intra-abdominal venous shunt

Anastomosis:
mesocaval
portacaval
portal vein to inferior vena cava
splenic and renal veins
transjugular intrahepatic portosystemic shunt [TIPS]

EXCLUDES *peritoneovenous shunt (54.94)*

DEF: Connection of two venous blood vessels within abdominal cavity.

✓4th 39.2 Other shunt or vascular bypass

Code also pressurized treatment of venous bypass graft [conduit] with pharmaceutical substance, if performed (00.16)

DEF: Creation of supplemental blood flow to area with inadequate blood supply due to disease or injury of vessels.

39.21 Caval-pulmonary artery anastomosis

Code also cardiopulmonary bypass (39.61)

39.22 Aorta-subclavian-carotid bypass

Bypass (arterial):
aorta to carotid and brachial
aorta to subclavian and carotid
carotid to subclavian

39.23 Other intrathoracic vascular shunt or bypass

Intrathoracic (arterial) bypass graft NOS

EXCLUDES *coronary artery bypass (36.10-36.19)*

39.24 Aorta-renal bypass

39.25 Aorta-iliac-femoral bypass

Bypass:
aortofemoral
aortoiliac
aortoiliac to popliteal
aortopopliteal
iliofemoral [iliac-femoral]

39.26 Other intra-abdominal vascular shunt or bypass

Bypass:
  aortoceliac
  aortic-superior mesenteric
  common hepatic-common iliac-renal
Intra-abdominal arterial bypass graft NOS

EXCLUDES *peritoneovenous shunt (54.94)*

39.27 Arteriovenostomy for renal dialysis

Anastomosis for renal dialysis
Formation of (peripheral) arteriovenous fistula for renal [kidney] dialysis

Code also any renal dialysis (39.95)

39.28 Extracranial-intracranial (EC-IC) vascular bypass

39.29 Other (peripheral) vascular shunt or bypass

Bypass (graft):
  axillary-brachial
  axillary-femoral [axillofemoral] (superficial)
  brachial
  femoral-femoral
  femoroperoneal
  femoropopliteal (arteries)
  femorotibial (anterior) (posterior)
  popliteal
  vascular NOS

EXCLUDES *peritoneovenous shunt (54.94)*

✓4th **39.3 Suture of vessel**

Repair of laceration of blood vessel

EXCLUDES *any other vascular puncture closure device — omit code*
suture of aneurysm (39.52)
that for control of hemorrhage (postoperative):
  anus (49.95)
  bladder (57.93)
  following vascular procedure (39.41)
  nose (21.00-21.09)
  prostate (60.94)
  tonsil (28.7)

39.30 Suture of unspecified blood vessel

39.31 Suture of artery

39.32 Suture of vein

✓4th **39.4 Revision of vascular procedure**

39.41 Control of hemorrhage following vascular surgery

EXCLUDES *that for control of hemorrhage (postoperative):*
  anus (49.95)
  bladder (57.93)
  nose (21.00-21.09)
  prostate (60.94)
  tonsil (28.7)

39.42 Revision of arteriovenous shunt for renal dialysis

Conversion of renal dialysis:
  end-to-end anastomosis to end-to-side
  end-to-side anastomosis to end-to-end
  vessel-to-vessel cannula to arteriovenous shunt
Removal of old arteriovenous shunt and creation of new shunt

EXCLUDES *replacement of vessel-to-vessel cannula (39.94)*

39.43 Removal of arteriovenous shunt for renal dialysis

EXCLUDES *that with replacement [revision] of shunt (39.42)*

39.49 Other revision of vascular procedure

Declotting (graft)
Revision of:
  anastomosis of blood vessel
  vascular procedure (previous)

DEF: Declotting (graft): Removal of clot from graft.

✓4th **39.5 Other repair of vessels**

39.50 Angioplasty or atherectomy of other non-coronary vessel(s)

Percutaneous transluminal angioplasty (PTA) of non-coronary vessels:
  lower extremity vessels
  mesenteric artery
  renal artery
  upper extremity vessels

Code also any:
  injection or infusion of thrombolytic agent (99.10)
  insertion of non-coronary stent(s) or stent grafts(s) (39.90)
  number of vascular stents inserted (00.45-00.48)
  number of vessels treated (00.40-00.43)
  procedure on vessel bifurcation (00.44)

EXCLUDES *percutaneous angioplasty or atherectomy of precerebral or cerebral vessel(s) (00.61-00.62)*

39.51 Clipping of aneurysm

EXCLUDES *clipping of arteriovenous fistula (39.53)*

39.52 Other repair of aneurysm

Repair of aneurysm by:
  coagulation
  electrocoagulation
  filipuncture
  methyl methacrylate
  suture
  wiring
  wrapping

EXCLUDES *endovascular repair of aneurysm (39.71-39.79)*
re-entry operation (aorta) (39.54)
that with:
  graft replacement (38.40-38.49)
  resection (38.30-38.49, 38.60-38.69)

DEF: Application of device in abnormally stretched blood vessel to prevent movement of material collected in vessel.

DEF: Repair of aneurysm by: Coagulation: Clotting or solidifying. Electrocoagulation: Electrically produced clotting. Filipuncture: Insertion of wire or thread. Methyl methacrylate: Injection or insertion of plastic material. Suture: Stitching. Wiring: Insertion of wire. Wrapping: Compression.

39.53 Repair of arteriovenous fistula

Embolization of carotid cavernous fistula
Repair of arteriovenous fistula by:
clipping
coagulation
ligation and division

EXCLUDES *repair of:*
arteriovenous shunt for renal dialysis (39.42)
head and neck vessels, endovascular approach (39.72)
that with:
graft replacement (38.40-38.49)
resection (38.30-38.49, 38.60-38.69)

DEF: Correction of arteriovenous fistula by application of clamps, causing coagulation or by tying off and dividing the connection.

39.54 Re-entry operation (aorta)

Fenestration of dissecting aneurysm of thoracic aorta

Code also cardiopulmonary bypass [extracorporeal circulation] [heart-lung machine] (39.61)

DEF: Re-entry operation: Creation of passage between stretched wall of the vessel and major arterial channel to heart.

DEF: Fenestration of dissecting aneurysm of thoracic aorta: Creation of passage between stretched arterial heart vessel and functional part of vessel.

39.55 Reimplantation of aberrant renal vessel

DEF: Reimplant of renal vessel into normal position.

39.56 Repair of blood vessel with tissue patch graft

EXCLUDES *that with resection (38.40-38.49)*

39.57 Repair of blood vessel with synthetic patch graft

EXCLUDES *that with resection (38.40-38.49)*

39.58 Repair of blood vessel with unspecified type of patch graft

EXCLUDES *that with resection (38.40-38.49)*

39.59 Other repair of vessel

Aorticopulmonary window operation
Arterioplasty NOS
Construction of venous valves (peripheral)
Plication of vein (peripheral)
Reimplantation of artery

Code also cardiopulmonary bypass [extracorporeal circulation] [heart-lung machine] (39.61)

EXCLUDES *interruption of the vena cava (38.7)*
reimplantation of renal artery (39.55)
that with:
graft (39.56-39.58)
resection (38.30-38.49, 38.60-38.69)

DEF: Aorticopulmonary window operation: Repair of abnormal opening between major heart arterial vessel above valves and pulmonary artery.

DEF: Construction of venous valves (peripheral): Reconstruction of valves within peripheral veins.

DEF: Plication of vein (peripheral): Shortening of peripheral vein.

DEF: Reimplantation of artery: Reinsertion of artery into its normal position.

✓4th **39.6 Extracorporeal circulation and procedures auxiliary to heart surgery**

39.61 Extracorporeal circulation auxiliary to open heart surgery

Artificial heart and lung
Cardiopulmonary bypass
Pump oxygenator

EXCLUDES *extracorporeal hepatic assistance (50.92)*
extracorporeal membrane oxygenation [ECMO] (39.65)
hemodialysis (39.95)
percutaneous cardiopulmonary bypass (39.66)

39.62 Hypothermia (systemic) incidental to open heart surgery

39.63 Cardioplegia

Arrest:
anoxic
circulatory

DEF: Purposely inducing electromechanical cardiac arrest.

39.64 Intraoperative cardiac pacemaker

Temporary pacemaker used during and immediately following cardiac surgery

39.65 Extracorporeal membrane oxygenation [ECMO]

EXCLUDES *extracorporeal circulation auxiliary to open heart surgery (39.61)*
percutaneous cardiopulmonary bypass (39.66)

DEF: Creation of closed-chest, heart-lung bypass or Bard cardiopulmonary assist system with tube insertion.

39.66 Percutaneous cardiopulmonary bypass

Closed chest

EXCLUDES *extracorporeal circulation auxiliary to open heart surgery (39.61)*
extracorporeal hepatic assistance (50.92)
extracorporeal membrane oxygenation [ECMO] (39.65)
hemodialysis (39.95)

DEF: Use of mechanical pump system to oxygenate and pump blood throughout the body via catheter in the femoral artery and vein.

✓4th **39.7 Endovascular repair of vessel**

Endoluminal repair

EXCLUDES *angioplasty or atherectomy of other non-coronary vessel(s) (39.50)*
insertion of non-drug-eluting peripheral vessel stent(s) (39.90)
other repair of aneurysm (39.52)
percutaneous insertion of carotid artery stent(s) (00.63)
percutaneous insertion of intracranial stent(s) (00.65)
percutaneous insertion of other precerebral artery stent(s) (00.64)
resection of abdominal aorta with replacement (38.44)
resection of lower limb arteries with replacement (38.48)
resection of thoracic aorta with replacement (38.45)
resection of upper limb vessels with replacement (38.43)

Endovascular Repair of Abdominal Aortic Aneurysm

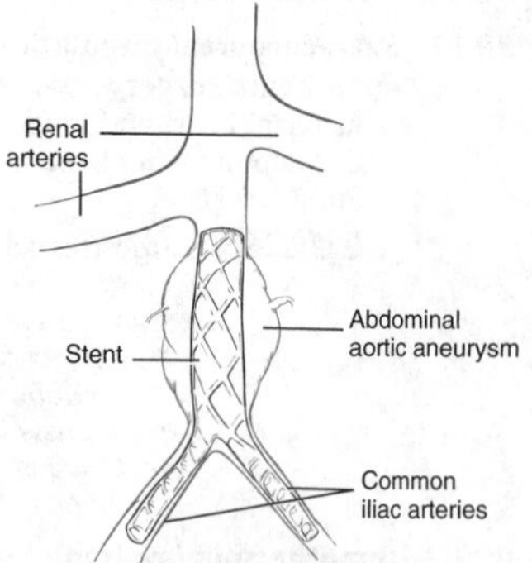

39.71 Endovascular implantation of graft in abdominal aorta

Endovascular repair of abdominal aortic aneurysm with graft
Stent graft(s)

Code also intra-aneurysm sac pressure monitoring (intraoperative) (00.58)

DEF: Replacement of a section of abdominal aorta with mesh graft; via catheters inserted through femoral arteries.

39.72 Endovascular repair or occlusion of head and neck vessels

Coil embolization or occlusion
Endograft(s)
Endovascular graft(s)
Liquid tissue adhesive (glue) embolization or occlusion
Other implant or substance for repair, embolization or occlusion
That for repair of aneurysm, arteriovenous malformation [AVM] or fistula

EXCLUDES *mechanical thrombectomy of pre-cerebral and cerebral vessels (39.74)*

DEF: Coil embolization or occlusion: Utilizing x-ray guidance a neuro-microcatheter is guided from entry in the femoral artery in the groin to the site of the aneurysm of the head and neck vessels for delivery of micro-coils that stop blood flow to the arteriovenous malfomation (AVM).

39.73 Endovascular implantation of graft in thoracic aorta

Endograft(s)
Endovascular graft(s)
Endovascular repair of defect of thoracic aorta with graft(s) or device(s)
Stent graft(s) or device(s)
That for repair of aneurysm, dissection, or injury

Code also intra-aneurysm sac pressure monitoring (intraoperative) (00.58)

EXCLUDES *fenestration of dissecting aneurysm of thoracic aorta (39.54)*

DEF: Intravascular transcatheter deployment of an expanding stent-graft for repair of thoracic aortic aneurysm, performed without opening the chest.

39.74 Endovascular removal of obstruction from head and neck vessel(s)

Endovascular embolectomy
Endovascular thrombectomy of pre-cerebral and cerebral vessels
Mechanical embolectomy or thrombectomy

Code also:
any injection or infusion of thrombolytic agent (99.10)
number of vessels treated (00.40-00.43)
procedure on vessel bifurcation (00.44)

EXCLUDES *endarterectomy of intracranial vessels and other vessels of head and neck (38.11-38.12)*
occlusive endovascular repair of head or neck vessels (39.72)
open embolectomy or thrombectomy (38.01-38.02)

39.79 Other endovascular repair (of aneurysm) of other vessels

Coil embolization or occlusion
Endograft(s)
Endovascular graft(s)
Liquid tissue adhesive (glue) embolization or occlusion
Other implant or substance for repair, embolization or occlusion

EXCLUDES *endovascular implantation of graft in thoracic aorta (39.73)*
endovascular repair or occlusion of head and neck vessels (39.72)
insertion of drug-eluting peripheral vessel stent(s) (00.55)
insertion of non-drug-eluting peripheral vessel stent(s) (for other than aneurysm repair) (39.90)
non-endovascular repair of arteriovenous fistula (39.53)
other surgical occlusion of vessels – see category 38.8
percutaneous transcatheter infusion (99.29)
transcatheter embolization for gastric or duodenal bleeding (44.44)

39.8 Operations on carotid body, carotid sinus and other vascular bodies

Chemodectomy
Denervation of:
aortic body
carotid body
Electronic stimulator
Glomectomy, carotid
Implantation or replacement of carotid sinus baroreflex activation device

EXCLUDES *excision of glomus jugulare (20.51)*
replacement of carotid sinus lead(s) only (04.92)

DEF: Chemodectomy: Removal of a chemoreceptor vascular body.

DEF: Denervation of aortic body: Destruction of nerves attending the major heart blood vessels.

DEF: Denervation of carotid body: Destruction of nerves of carotid artery.

DEF: Glomectomy, carotid: Removal of the carotid artery framework.

✓4th **39.9 Other operations on vessels**

39.90 Insertion of non-drug-eluting peripheral vessel stent(s)

Bare stent(s)
Bonded stent(s)
Drug-coated stent(s), i.e., heparin coated
Endograft(s)
Endovascular graft(s)
Endovascular recanalization techniques
Stent graft(s)

Code also any:
non-coronary angioplasty or atherectomy (39.50)
number of vascular stents inserted (00.45-00.48)
number of vessels treated (00.40-00.43)
procedure on vessel bifurcation (00.44)

EXCLUDES *insertion of drug-eluting, peripheral vessel stent(s) (00.55)*
percutaneous insertion of carotid artery stent(s) (00.63)
percutaneous insertion of intracranial stent(s) (00.65)
percutaneous insertion of other precerebral artery stent(s) (00.64)
that for aneurysm repair (39.71-39.79)

39.91 Freeing of vessel

Dissection and freeing of adherent tissue:
artery-vein-nerve bundle
vascular bundle

39.92 Injection of sclerosing agent into vein

EXCLUDES *injection:*
esophageal varices (42.33)
hemorrhoids (49.42)

39.93 Insertion of vessel-to-vessel cannula

Formation of:
arteriovenous: fistula, shunt } by external cannula

Code also any renal dialysis (39.95)

39.94 Replacement of vessel-to-vessel cannula

Revision of vessel-to-vessel cannula

39.95 Hemodialysis

Artificial kidney
Hemodiafiltration
Hemofiltration
Renal dialysis

EXCLUDES *peritoneal dialysis (54.98)*

DEF: Filtration process to treat acute and chronic renal failure by eliminating toxic end products of nitrogen metabolism from blood.

External Arteriovenous Shunt

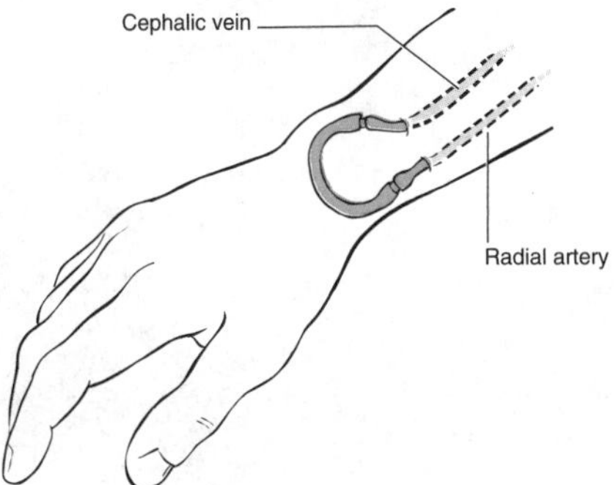

39.96 Total body perfusion

Code also substance perfused (99.21-99.29)

39.97 Other perfusion

Perfusion NOS
Perfusion, local [regional] of:
carotid artery
coronary artery
head
lower limb
neck
upper limb

Code also substance perfused (99.21-99.29)

EXCLUDES *perfusion of:*
kidney (55.95)
large intestine (46.96)
liver (50.93)
small intestine (46.95)
SuperSaturated oxygen therapy (00.49)

39.98 Control of hemorrhage, not otherwise specified

Angiotripsy
Control of postoperative hemorrhage NOS
Venotripsy

EXCLUDES *control of hemorrhage (postoperative):*
anus (49.95)
bladder (57.93)
following vascular procedure (39.41)
nose (21.00-21.09)
prostate (60.94)
tonsil (28.7)
that by:
ligation (38.80-38.89)
suture (39.30-39.32)

DEF: Angiotripsy: Clamping of tissue to stop arterial blood flow.

DEF: Venotripsy: Clamping of tissue to stop venous blood flow.

39.99 Other operations on vessels

EXCLUDES *injection or infusion of therapeutic or prophylactic substance (99.11-99.29)*
transfusion of blood and blood components (99.01-99.09)

8. OPERATIONS ON THE HEMIC AND LYMPHATIC SYSTEMS (40-41)

✓3rd **40 Operations on lymphatic system**

40.0 Incision of lymphatic structures

✓4th **40.1 Diagnostic procedures on lymphatic structures**

40.11 Biopsy of lymphatic structure

40.19 Other diagnostic procedures on lymphatic structures

EXCLUDES *lymphangiogram:*
abdominal (88.04)
cervical (87.08)
intrathoracic (87.34)
lower limb (88.36)
upper limb (88.34)
microscopic examination of specimen (90.71-90.79)
radioisotope scan (92.16)
thermography (88.89)

✓4th **40.2 Simple excision of lymphatic structure**

EXCLUDES *biopsy of lymphatic structure (40.11)*

DEF: Removal of lymphatic structure only.

40.21 Excision of deep cervical lymph node

40.22 Excision of internal mammary lymph node

40.23 Excision of axillary lymph node

40.24 Excision of inguinal lymph node

40.29 Simple excision of other lymphatic structure

Excision of:
cystic hygroma
lymphangioma
Simple lymphadenectomy

DEF: Lymphangioma: Removal of benign congenital lymphatic malformation.

DEF: Simple lymphadenectomy: Removal of lymph node.

40.3 Regional lymph node excision

Extended regional lymph node excision
Regional lymph node excision with excision of lymphatic drainage area including skin, subcutaneous tissue, and fat

DEF: Extended regional lymph node excision: Removal of lymph node group, including area around nodes.

✓4th **40.4 Radical excision of cervical lymph nodes**

Resection of cervical lymph nodes down to muscle and deep fascia

EXCLUDES *that associated with radical laryngectomy (30.4)*

40.40 Radical neck dissection, not otherwise specified

40.41 Radical neck dissection, unilateral

DEF: Dissection, total, of cervical lymph nodes on one side of neck.

40.42 Radical neck dissection, bilateral

DEF: Dissection, total, of cervical lymph nodes on both sides of neck.

✓4th **40.5 Radical excision of other lymph nodes**

EXCLUDES *that associated with radical mastectomy (85.45-85.48)*

40.50 Radical excision of lymph nodes, not otherwise specified

Radical (lymph) node dissection NOS

40.51 Radical excision of axillary lymph nodes

40.52 Radical excision of periaortic lymph nodes

40.53 Radical excision of iliac lymph nodes

40.54 Radical groin dissection

40.59 Radical excision of other lymph nodes

EXCLUDES *radical neck dissection (40.40-40.42)*

✓4th **40.6 Operations on thoracic duct**

40.61 Cannulation of thoracic duct

DEF: Placement of cannula in main lymphatic duct of chest.

40.62 Fistulization of thoracic duct

DEF: Creation of passage in main lymphatic duct of chest.

40.63 Closure of fistula of thoracic duct

DEF: Closure of fistula in main lymphatic duct of chest.

40.64 Ligation of thoracic duct

DEF: Tying off main lymphatic duct of chest.

40.69 Other operations on thoracic duct

40.9 Other operations on lymphatic structures

Anastomosis, Dilation, Ligation, Obliteration, Reconstruction, Repair, Transplantation } of peripheral lymphatics

Correction of lymphedema of limb, NOS

EXCLUDES *reduction of elephantiasis of scrotum (61.3)*

✓3rd **41 Operations on bone marrow and spleen**

✓4th **41.0 Bone marrow or hematopoietic stem cell transplant**

Note: To report donor source – see codes 00.91-00.93

EXCLUDES *aspiration of bone marrow from donor (41.91)*

41.00 Bone marrow transplant, not otherwise specified

41.01 Autologous bone marrow transplant without purging

EXCLUDES *that with purging (41.09)*

DEF: Transplant of patient's own bone marrow.

41.02 Allogeneic bone marrow transplant with purging

Allograft of bone marrow with in vitro removal (purging) of T-cells

DEF: Transplant of bone marrow from donor to patient after donor marrow purged of undesirable cells.

Partial Splenectomy

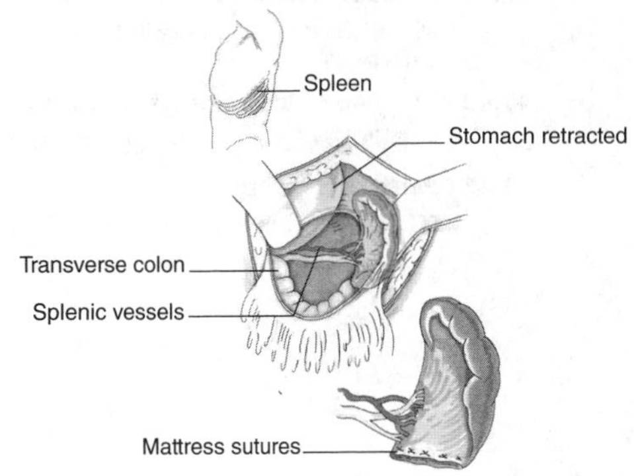

41.03 Allogeneic bone marrow transplant without purging
Allograft of bone marrow NOS

41.04 Autologous hematopoietic stem cell transplant without purging
EXCLUDES *that with purging (41.07)*

41.05 Allogeneic hematopoietic stem cell transplant without purging
EXCLUDES *that with purging (41.08)*

41.06 Cord blood stem cell transplant

41.07 Autologous hematopoietic stem cell transplant with purging
Cell depletion

41.08 Allogeneic hematopoietic stem cell transplant with purging
Cell depletion

41.09 Autologous bone marrow transplant with purging
With extracorporeal purging of malignant cells from marrow
Cell depletion

41.1 Puncture of spleen
EXCLUDES *aspiration biopsy of spleen (41.32)*

41.2 Splenotomy

✓4th **41.3 Diagnostic procedures on bone marrow and spleen**

41.31 Biopsy of bone marrow

41.32 Closed [aspiration] [percutaneous] biopsy of spleen
Needle biopsy of spleen

41.33 Open biopsy of spleen

41.38 Other diagnostic procedures on bone marrow
EXCLUDES *microscopic examination of specimen from bone marrow (90.61-90.69)*
radioisotope scan (92.05)

41.39 Other diagnostic procedures on spleen
EXCLUDES *microscopic examination of specimen from spleen (90.61-90.69)*
radioisotope scan (92.05)

✓4th **41.4 Excision or destruction of lesion or tissue of spleen**
Code also any application or administration of an adhesion barrier substance (99.77)
EXCLUDES *excision of accessory spleen (41.93)*

41.41 Marsupialization of splenic cyst
DEF: Incision of cyst of spleen with edges sutured open to create pouch.

41.42 Excision of lesion or tissue of spleen
EXCLUDES *biopsy of spleen (41.32-41.33)*

41.43 Partial splenectomy
DEF: Removal of spleen, partial.

Total Splenectomy

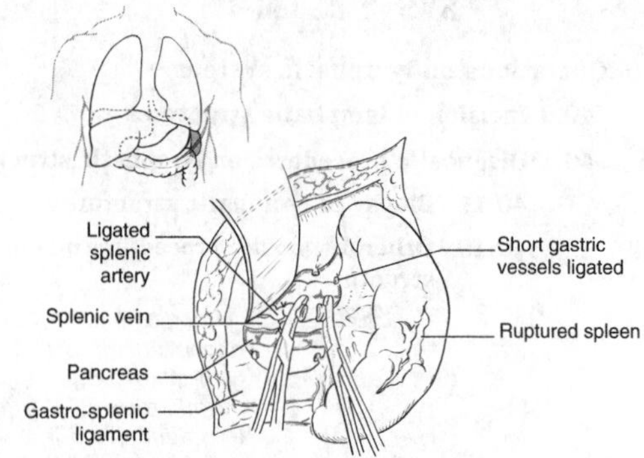

41.5 Total splenectomy
Splenectomy NOS
Code also any application or administration of an adhesion barrier substance (99.77)

✓4th **41.9 Other operations on spleen and bone marrow**
Code also any application or administration of an adhesion barrier substance (99.77)

41.91 Aspiration of bone marrow from donor for transplant
EXCLUDES *biopsy of bone marrow (41.31)*

41.92 Injection into bone marrow
EXCLUDES *bone marrow transplant (41.00-41.03)*

41.93 Excision of accessory spleen

41.94 Transplantation of spleen

41.95 Repair and plastic operations on spleen

41.98 Other operations on bone marrow

41.99 Other operations on spleen

9. OPERATIONS ON THE DIGESTIVE SYSTEM (42-54)

✓3rd **42 Operations on esophagus**

✓4th **42.0 Esophagotomy**

42.01 Incision of esophageal web

DEF: Cutting into congenital esophageal membrane.

42.09 Other incision of esophagus

Esophagotomy NOS

EXCLUDES *esophagomyotomy (42.7)*
esophagostomy (42.10-42.19)

✓4th **42.1 Esophagostomy**

42.10 Esophagostomy, not otherwise specified

42.11 Cervical esophagostomy

DEF: Creation of opening into upper region of esophagus.

42.12 Exteriorization of esophageal pouch

DEF: Transfer of section of esophageal pouch to exterior of the body.

42.19 Other external fistulization of esophagus

Thoracic esophagostomy

Code also any resection (42.40-42.42)

✓4th **42.2 Diagnostic procedures on esophagus**

42.21 Operative esophagoscopy by incision

DEF: Esophageal examination with an endoscope through incision.

42.22 Esophagoscopy through artificial stoma

EXCLUDES *that with biopsy (42.24)*

42.23 Other esophagoscopy

EXCLUDES *that with biopsy (42.24)*

42.24 Closed [endoscopic] biopsy of esophagus

Brushing or washing for specimen collection
Esophagoscopy with biopsy
Suction biopsy of the esophagus

EXCLUDES *esophagogastroduodenoscopy [EGD] with closed biopsy (45.16)*

DEF: Scope passed through mouth and throat to obtain biopsy specimen, usually by brushing and swabbing.

42.25 Open biopsy of esophagus

42.29 Other diagnostic procedures on esophagus

EXCLUDES *barium swallow (87.61)*
esophageal manometry (89.32)
microscopic examination of specimen from esophagus (90.81-90.89)

✓4th **42.3 Local excision or destruction of lesion or tissue of esophagus**

42.31 Local excision of esophageal diverticulum

44.32 Percutaneous [endoscopic] gastrojejunostomy

Bypass:
  gastroduodenostomy
PEGJJ

EXCLUDES *percutaneous (endoscopic) feeding jejunostomy (46.32)*

DEF: Percutaneous placement of a thin feeding tube through a gastrostomy tube and then pulling the tube into the proximal end of the jejunum.

42.33 Endoscopic excision or destruction of lesion or tissue of esophagus

Ablation of esophageal neoplasm
Control of esophageal bleeding
Esophageal polypectomy
Espohageal varices
Injection of esophageal varices
} by endoscopic approach

EXCLUDES *biopsy of esophagus (42.24-42.25)*
fistulectomy (42.84)
open ligation of esophageal varices (42.91)

42.39 Other destruction of lesion or tissue of esophagus

EXCLUDES *that by endoscopic approach (42.33)*

✓4th **42.4 Excision of esophagus**

EXCLUDES *esophagogastrectomy NOS 43.99)*

42.40 Esophagectomy, not otherwise specified

42.41 Partial esophagectomy

Code also any synchronous:
  anastomosis other than end-to-end (42.51-42.69)
  esophagostomy (42.10-42.19)
  gastrostomy (43.11-43.19)

DEF: Surgical removal of any part of esophagus.

42.42 Total esophagectomy

Code also any synchronous:
  gastrostomy (43.11-43.19)
  interposition or anastomosis other than end-to-end (42.51-42.69)

EXCLUDES *esophagogastrectomy (43.99)*

DEF: Surgical removal of entire esophagus.

✓4th **42.5 Intrathoracic anastomosis of esophagus**

Code also any synchronous:
  esophagectomy (42.40-42.42)
  gastrostomy (43.1)

DEF: Connection of esophagus to conduit within chest.

42.51 Intrathoracic esophagoesophagostomy

DEF: Connection of both ends of esophagus within chest cavity.

42.52 Intrathoracic esophagogastrostomy

DEF: Connection of esophagus to stomach within chest; follows esophagogastrectomy.

42.53 Intrathoracic esophageal anastomosis with interposition of small bowel

42.54 Other intrathoracic esophagoenterostomy

Anastomosis of esophagus to intestinal segment NOS

42.55 Intrathoracic esophageal anastomosis with interposition of colon

42.56 Other intrathoracic esophagocolostomy

Esophagocolostomy NOS

42.58 Intrathoracic esophageal anastomosis with other interposition

Construction of artificial esophagus
Retrosternal formation of reversed gastric tube

DEF: Construction of artificial esophagus: Creation of artificial esophagus.

DEF: Retrosternal anastomosis of reversed gastric tube: Formation of gastric tube behind breastbone.

42.59 Other intrathoracic anastomosis of esophagus

✓4th **42.6 Antesternal anastomosis of esophagus**
Code also any synchronous:
esophagectomy (42.40-42.42)
gastrostomy (43.1)

42.61 Antesternal esophagoesophagostomy

42.62 Antesternal esophagogastrostomy

42.63 Antesternal esophageal anastomosis with interposition of small bowel

42.64 Other antesternal esophagoenterostomy
Antethoracic:
esophagoenterostomy
esophagoileostomy
esophagojejunostomy

42.65 Antesternal esophageal anastomosis with interposition of colon
DEF: Connection of esophagus with colon segment.

42.66 Other antesternal esophagocolostomy
Antethoracic esophagocolostomy

42.68 Other antesternal esophageal anastomosis with interposition

42.69 Other antesternal anastomosis of esophagus

42.7 Esophagomyotomy
DEF: Division of esophageal muscle, usually distal.

✓4th **42.8 Other repair of esophagus**

42.81 Insertion of permanent tube into esophagus

42.82 Suture of laceration of esophagus

42.83 Closure of esophagostomy

42.84 Repair of esophageal fistula, not elsewhere classified
EXCLUDES *repair of fistula:*
bronchoesophageal (33.42)
esophagopleurocutaneous (34.73)
pharyngoesophageal (29.53)
tracheoesophageal (31.73)

42.85 Repair of esophageal stricture

42.86 Production of subcutaneous tunnel without esophageal anastomosis
DEF: Surgical formation of esophageal passage, without cutting, and reconnection.

42.87 Other graft of esophagus
EXCLUDES *antesternal esophageal anastomosis with interposition of:*
colon (42.65)
small bowel (42.63)
antesternal esophageal anastomosis with other interposition (42.68)
intrathoracic esophageal anastomosis with interposition of:
colon (42.55)
small bowel (42.53)
intrathoracic esophageal anastomosis with other interposition (42.58)

42.89 Other repair of esophagus

✓4th **42.9 Other operations on esophagus**

42.91 Ligation of esophageal varices
EXCLUDES *that by endoscopic approach (42.33)*
DEF: Destruction of dilated veins by suture strangulation.

42.92 Dilation of esophagus
Dilation of cardiac sphincter
EXCLUDES *intubation of esophagus (96.03, 96.06-96.08)*
DEF: Passing of balloon or hydrostatic dilators through esophagus to enlarge esophagus and relieve obstruction.

42.99 Other
EXCLUDES *insertion of Sengstaken tube (96.06)*
intubation of esophagus (96.03, 96.06-96.08)
removal of intraluminal foreign body from esophagus without incision (98.02)
tamponade of esophagus (96.06)

✓3rd **43 Incision and excision of stomach**
Code also any application or administration of an adhesion barrier substance (99.77)

43.0 Gastrotomy
EXCLUDES *gastrostomy (43.11-43.19)*
that for control of hemorrhage (44.49)

✓4th **43.1 Gastrostomy**

43.11 Percutaneous [endoscopic] gastrostomy [PEG]
Percutaneous transabdominal gastrostomy
DEF: Endoscopic positioning of tube through abdominal wall into stomach.

43.19 Other gastrostomy
EXCLUDES *percutaneous [endoscopic] gastrostomy [PEG] (43.11)*

43.3 Pyloromyotomy
DEF: Cutting into longitudinal and circular muscular membrane between stomach and small intestine.

✓4th **43.4 Local excision or destruction of lesion or tissue of stomach**

43.41 Endoscopic excision or destruction of lesion or tissue of stomach
Gastric polypectomy by endoscopic approach
Gastric varices by endoscopic approach
EXCLUDES *biopsy of stomach (44.14-44.15)*
control of hemorrhage (44.43)
open ligation of gastric varices (44.91)

43.42 Local excision of other lesion or tissue of stomach
EXCLUDES *biopsy of stomach (44.14-44.15)*
gastric fistulectomy (44.62-44.63)
partial gastrectomy (43.5-43.89)

43.49 Other destruction of lesion or tissue of stomach
EXCLUDES *that by endoscopic approach (43.41)*

43.5 Partial gastrectomy with anastomosis to esophagus
Proximal gastrectomy

Partial Gastrectomy with Anastomosis to Duodenum

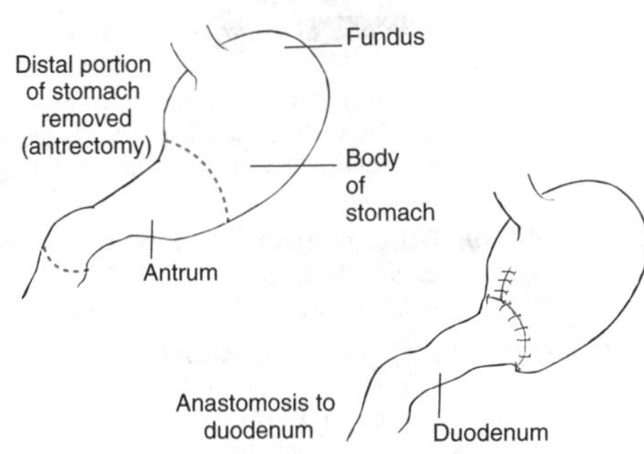

43.6 Partial gastrectomy with anastomosis to duodenum
Billroth I operation
Distal gastrectomy
Gastropylorectomy

43.7 Partial gastrectomy with anastomosis to jejunum
Billroth II operation

✓4th **43.8 Other partial gastrectomy**

43.81 Partial gastrectomy with jejunal transposition
Henley jejunal transposition operation
Code also any synchronous intestinal resection (45.51)

43.89 Other
Partial gastrectomy with bypass gastrogastrostomy
Sleeve resection of stomach

✓4th **43.9 Total gastrectomy**

43.91 Total gastrectomy with intestinal interposition

43.99 Other total gastrectomy
Complete gastroduodenectomy
Esophagoduodenostomy with complete gastrectomy
Esophagogastrectomy NOS
Esophagojejunostomy with complete gastrectomy
Radical gastrectomy

✓3rd **44 Other operations on stomach**
Code also any application or administration of an adhesion barrier substance (99.77)

✓4th **44.0 Vagotomy**

44.00 Vagotomy, not otherwise specified
Division of vagus nerve NOS
DEF: Cutting of vagus nerve to reduce acid production.

Biliopancreatic Diversion Without Duodenal Switch

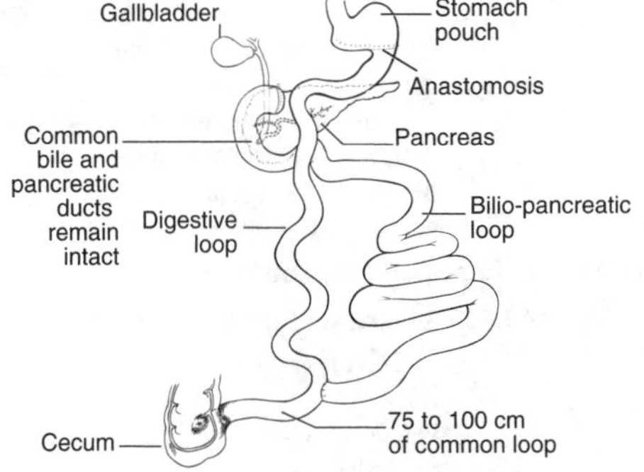

Biliopancreatic Diversion with Duodenal Switch

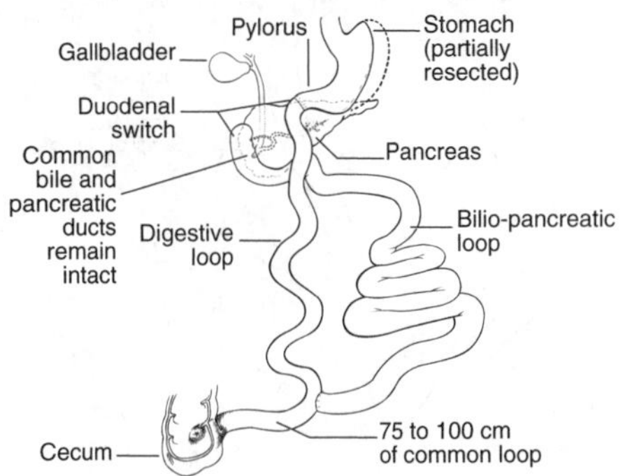

44.01 Truncal vagotomy
DEF: Surgical removal of vagus nerve segment near stomach branches.

44.02 Highly selective vagotomy
Parietal cell vagotomy
Selective proximal vagotomy
DEF: Cutting select gastric branches of vagus nerve to reduce acid production and preserve other nerve functions.

44.03 Other selective vagotomy

✓4th **44.1 Diagnostic procedures on stomach**

44.11 Transabdominal gastroscopy
Intraoperative gastroscopy
EXCLUDES *that with biopsy (44.14)*

44.12 Gastroscopy through artificial stoma
EXCLUDES *that with biopsy (44.14)*

44.13 Other gastroscopy
EXCLUDES *that with biopsy (44.14)*

44.14 Closed [endoscopic] biopsy of stomach
Brushing or washing for specimen collection
EXCLUDES *esophagogastroduodenoscopy [EGD] with closed biopsy (45.16)*

44.15 Open biopsy of stomach

44.19 Other diagnostic procedures on stomach
EXCLUDES *gastric lavage (96.33)*
microscopic examination of specimen from stomach (90.81-90.89)
upper GI series (87.62)

✓4th **44.2 Pyloroplasty**

44.21 Dilation of pylorus by incision
DEF: Cutting and suturing pylorus to relieve obstruction.

Types of Vagotomy Procedures

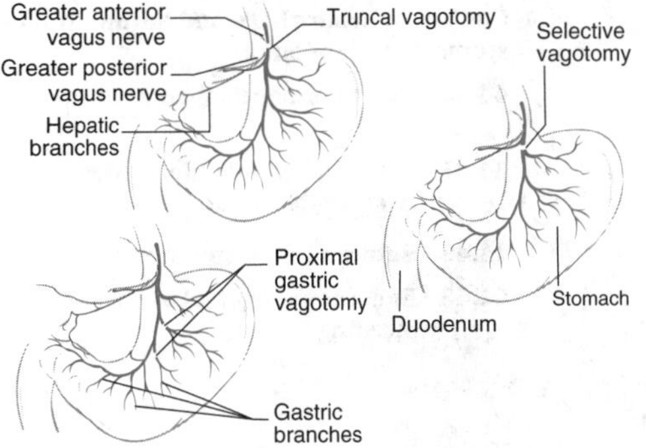

Roux-en-Y Operation (Gastrojejunostomy without gastrectomy)

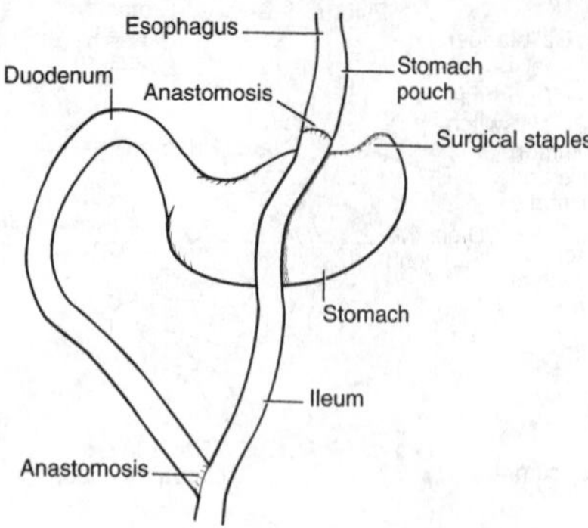

44.22 Endoscopic dilation of pylorus
Dilation with balloon endoscope
Endoscopic dilation of gastrojejunostomy site

44.29 Other pyloroplasty
Pyloroplasty NOS
Revision of pylorus

✓4th **44.3 Gastroenterostomy without gastrectomy**

44.31 High gastric bypass
Printen and Mason gastric bypass

DEF: Connection of middle part of small intestine to upper stomach to divert food passage from upper intestine.

44.32 Percutaneous [endoscopic] gastrojejunostomy
Bypass:
gastroduodenostomy
PEGJJ

EXCLUDES *percutaneous (endoscopic) feeding jejunostomy (46.32)*

DEF: Percutaneous placement of a thin feeding tube through a gastrostomy tube and then pulling the tube into the proximal end of the jejunum.

44.38 Laparoscopic gastroenterostomy
Bypass:
gastroduodenostomy
gastroenterostomy
gastrogastrostomy
Laparoscopic gastrojejunostomy without gastrectomy NEC

EXCLUDES *gastroenterostomy, open approach (44.39)*

44.39 Other gastroenterostomy
Bypass:
gastroduodenostomy
gastroenterostomy
gastrogastrostomy
Gastrojejunostomy without gastrectomy NOS

✓4th **44.4 Control of hemorrhage and suture of ulcer of stomach or duodenum**

44.40 Suture of peptic ulcer, not otherwise specified

44.41 Suture of gastric ulcer site

EXCLUDES *ligation of gastric varices (44.91)*

44.42 Suture of duodenal ulcer site

44.43 Endoscopic control of gastric or duodenal bleeding

44.44 Transcatheter embolization for gastric or duodenal bleeding

EXCLUDES *surgical occlusion of abdominal vessels (38.86-38.87)*

DEF: Therapeutic blocking of stomach or upper small intestine blood vessel to stop hemorrhaging; accomplished by introducing various substances using a catheter.

44.49 Other control of hemorrhage of stomach or duodenum
That with gastrotomy

44.5 Revision of gastric anastomosis
Closure of:
gastric anastomosis
gastroduodenostomy
gastrojejunostomy
Pantaloon operation

✓4th **44.6 Other repair of stomach**

44.61 Suture of laceration of stomach

EXCLUDES *that of ulcer site (44.41)*

44.62 Closure of gastrostomy

44.63 Closure of other gastric fistula
Closure of:
gastrocolic fistula
gastrojejunocolic fistula

44.64 Gastropexy

DEF: Suturing of stomach into position.

44.65 Esophagogastroplasty
Belsey operation
Esophagus and stomach cardioplasty

44.66 Other procedures for creation of esophagogastric sphincteric competence
Fundoplication
Gastric cardioplasty
Nissen's fundoplication
Restoration of cardio-esophageal angle

EXCLUDES *that by laparoscopy (44.67)*

44.67 Laparoscopic procedures for creation of esophagogastric sphincteric competence
Fundoplication
Gastric cardioplasty
Nissen's fundoplication
Restoration of cardio-esophageal angle

44.68 Laparoscopic gastroplasty
Banding
Silastic vertical banding
Vertical banded gastroplasty (VBG)

Code also any synchronous laparoscopic gastroenterostomy (44.38)

EXCLUDES *insertion, laparoscopic adjustable gastric band (restrictive procedure) (44.95)*
other repair of stomach, open approach (44.61-44.65, 44.69)

44.69 Other
Inversion of gastric diverticulum
Repair of stomach NOS

DEF: Inversion of gastric diverticulum: Turning stomach inward to repair outpouch of wall.

✓4th **44.9 Other operations on stomach**

44.91 Ligation of gastric varices

EXCLUDES *that by endoscopic approach (43.41)*

DEF: Destruction of dilated veins by suture or strangulation.

44.92 Intraoperative manipulation of stomach
Reduction of gastric volvulus

44.93 Insertion of gastric bubble (balloon)

44.94 Removal of gastric bubble (balloon)

44.95 Laparoscopic gastric restrictive procedure
Adjustable gastric band and port insertion

EXCLUDES *laparoscopic gastroplasty (44.68)*
other repair of stomach (44.69)

44.96 Laparoscopic revision of gastric restrictive procedure
Revision or replacement of:
adjustable gastric band
subcutaneous gastric port device

44.97 Laparoscopic removal of gastric restrictive device(s)
Removal of either or both:
adjustable gastric band
subcutaneous port device

EXCLUDES *nonoperative removal of gastric restrictive device(s) (97.86)*
open removal of gastric restrictive device(s) (44.99)

44.98 (Laparoscopic) adjustment of size of adjustable gastric restrictive device
Infusion of saline for device tightening
Withdrawal of saline for device loosening
Code also any:
abdominal ultrasound (88.76)
abdominal wall fluoroscopy (88.09)
barium swallow (87.61)

44.99 Other

EXCLUDES *change of gastrostomy tube (97.02)*
dilation of cardiac sphincter (42.92)
gastric:
cooling (96.31)
freezing (96.32)
gavage (96.35)
hypothermia (96.31)
lavage (96.33)
insertion of nasogastric tube (96.07)
irrigation of gastrostomy (96.36)
irrigation of nasogastric tube (96.34)
removal of:
gastrostomy tube (97.51)
intraluminal foreign body from stomach without incision (98.03)
replacement of:
gastrostomy tube (97.02)
(naso-)gastric tube (97.01)

✓3rd **45 Incision, excision, and anastomosis of intestine**
Code also any application or administration of an adhesion barrier substance (99.77)

✓4th **45.0 Enterotomy**

EXCLUDES *duodenocholedochotomy (51.41-51.42, 51.51)*
that for destruction of lesion (45.30-45.34)
that of exteriorized intestine (46.14, 46.24, 46.31)

45.00 Incision of intestine, not otherwise specified

45.01 Incision of duodenum

45.02 Other incision of small intestine

45.03 Incision of large intestine

EXCLUDES *proctotomy (48.0)*

✓4th **45.1 Diagnostic procedures on small intestine**
Code also any laparotomy (54.11-54.19)

45.11 Transabdominal endoscopy of small intestine
Intraoperative endoscopy of small intestine

EXCLUDES *that with biopsy (45.14)*

DEF: Endoscopic exam of small intestine through abdominal wall.

DEF: Intraoperative endoscope of small intestine: Endoscopic exam of small intestine during surgery.

45.12 Endoscopy of small intestine through artificial stoma

EXCLUDES *that with biopsy (45.14)*

45.13 Other endoscopy of small intestine
Esophagogastroduodenoscopy [EGD]

EXCLUDES *that with biopsy (45.14, 45.16)*

45.14 Closed [endoscopic] biopsy of small intestine
Brushing or washing for specimen collection

EXCLUDES *esophagogastroduodenoscopy [EGD] with closed biopsy (45.16)*

45.15 Open biopsy of small intestine

45.16 Esophagogastroduodenoscopy [EGD] with closed biopsy
Biopsy of one or more sites involving esophagus, stomach, and/or duodenum

45.19 Other diagnostic procedures on small intestine

EXCLUDES *microscopic examination of specimen from small intestine (90.91-90.99)*
radioisotope scan (92.04)
ultrasonography (88.74)
x-ray (87.61-87.69)

✓4th **45.2 Diagnostic procedures on large intestine**
Code also any laparotomy (54.11-54.19)

45.21 Transabdominal endoscopy of large intestine
Intraoperative endoscopy of large intestine

EXCLUDES *that with biopsy (45.25)*

DEF: Endoscopic exam of large intestine through abdominal wall.

DEF: Intraoperative endoscopy of large intestine: Endoscopic exam of large intestine during surgery.

45.22 Endoscopy of large intestine through artificial stoma

EXCLUDES *that with biopsy (45.25)*

DEF: Endoscopic exam of large intestine lining from rectum to cecum via colostomy stoma.

45.23 Colonoscopy
Flexible fiberoptic colonoscopy

EXCLUDES *endoscopy of large intestine through artificial stoma (45.22)*
flexible sigmoidoscopy (45.24)
rigid proctosigmoidoscopy (48.23)
transabdominal endoscopy of large intestine (45.21)

DEF: Endoscopic exam of descending colon, splenic flexure, transverse colon, hepatic flexure and cecum.

Esophagogastroduodenoscopy

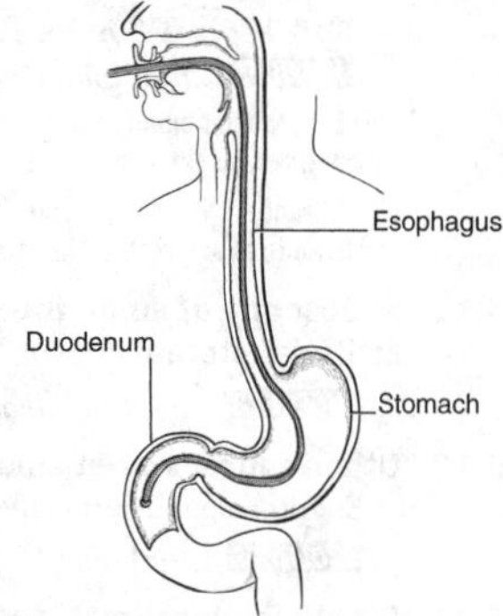

45.24 Flexible sigmoidoscopy
Endoscopy of descending colon
EXCLUDES *rigid proctosigmoidoscopy (48.23)*
DEF: Endoscopic exam of anus, rectum and sigmoid colon.

45.25 Closed [endoscopic] biopsy of large intestine
Biopsy, closed, of unspecified intestinal site
Brushing or washing for specimen collection
Colonoscopy with biopsy
EXCLUDES *proctosigmoidoscopy with biopsy (48.24)*

45.26 Open biopsy of large intestine

45.27 Intestinal biopsy, site unspecified

45.28 Other diagnostic procedures on large intestine

45.29 Other diagnostic procedures on intestine, site unspecified
EXCLUDES *microscopic examination of specimen (90.91-90.99)*
scan and radioisotope function study (92.04)
ultrasonography (88.74)
x-ray (87.61-87.69)

✓4th **45.3 Local excision or destruction of lesion or tissue of small intestine**

45.30 Endoscopic excision or destruction of lesion of duodenum
EXCLUDES *biopsy of duodenum (45.14-45.15)*
control of hemorrhage (44.43)
fistulectomy (46.72)

45.31 Other local excision of lesion of duodenum
EXCLUDES *biopsy of duodenum (45.14-45.15)*
fistulectomy (46.72)
multiple segmental resection (45.61)
that by endoscopic approach (45.30)

45.32 Other destruction of lesion of duodenum
EXCLUDES *that by endoscopic approach (45.30)*

45.33 Local excision of lesion or tissue of small intestine, except duodenum
Excision of redundant mucosa of ileostomy
EXCLUDES *biopsy of small intestine (45.14-45.15)*
fistulectomy (46.74)
multiple segmental resection (45.61)

45.34 Other destruction of lesion of small intestine, except duodenum

✓4th **45.4 Local excision or destruction of lesion or tissue of large intestine**

45.41 Excision of lesion or tissue of large intestine
Excision of redundant mucosa of colostomy
EXCLUDES *biopsy of large intestine (45.25-45.27)*
endoscopic polypectomy of large intestine (45.42)
fistulectomy (46.76)
multiple segmental resection (17.31, 45.71)
that by endoscopic approach (45.42-45.43)

45.42 Endoscopic polypectomy of large intestine
EXCLUDES *that by open approach (45.41)*
DEF: Endoscopic removal of polyp from large intestine.

45.43 Endoscopic destruction of other lesion or tissue of large intestine
Endoscopic ablation of tumor of large intestine
Endoscopic control of colonic bleeding
EXCLUDES *endoscopic polypectomy of large intestine (45.42)*

45.49 Other destruction of lesion of large intestine
EXCLUDES *that by endoscopic approach (45.43)*

✓4th **45.5 Isolation of intestinal segment**
Code also any synchronous:
anastomosis other than end-to-end (45.90-45.94)
enterostomy (46.10-46.39)

45.50 Isolation of intestinal segment, not otherwise specified
Isolation of intestinal pedicle flap
Reversal of intestinal segment
DEF: Isolation of small intestinal pedicle flap: Separation of intestinal pedicle flap.
DEF: Reversal of intestinal segment: Separation of intestinal segment.

45.51 Isolation of segment of small intestine
Isolation of ileal loop
Resection of small intestine for interposition

45.52 Isolation of segment of large intestine
Resection of colon for interposition

✓4th **45.6 Other excision of small intestine**
Code also any synchronous:
anastomosis other than end-to-end (45.90-45.93, 45.95)
colostomy (46.10-46.13)
enterostomy (46.10-46.39)
EXCLUDES *cecectomy (17.32, 45.72)*
enterocolectomy (17.39, 45.79)
gastroduodenectomy (43.6-43.99)
ileocolectomy (17.33, 45.73)
pancreatoduodenectomy (52.51-52.7)

45.61 Multiple segmental resection of small intestine
Segmental resection for multiple traumatic lesions of small intestine

Colectomy

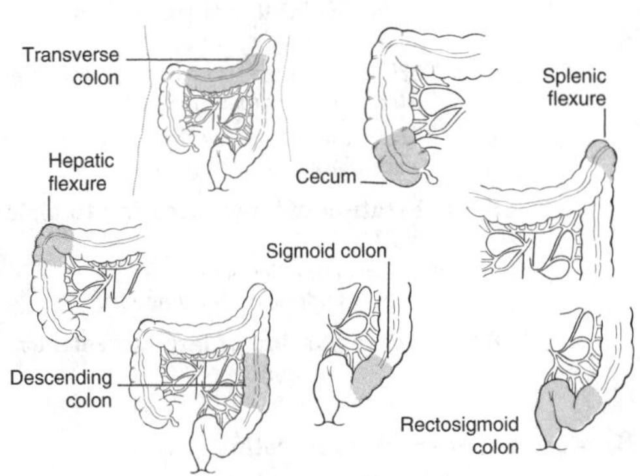

45.62 Other partial resection of small intestine
Duodenectomy
Ileectomy
Jejunectomy
EXCLUDES *duodenectomy with synchronous pancreatectomy (52.51-52.7)*
resection of cecum and terminal ileum (17.32, 45.72)

45.63 Total removal of small intestine

✓4th **45.7 Open and other partial excision of large intestine**
Code also any synchronous:
anastomosis other than end-to-end (45.92-45.94)
enterostomy (46.10-46.39)
EXCLUDES *laparoscopic partial excision of large intestine (17.31-17.39)*

45.71 Open and other multiple segmental resection of large intestine
Segmental resection for multiple traumatic lesions of large intestine

45.72 Open and other cecectomy
Resection of cecum and terminal ileum

45.73 Open and other right hemicolectomy
Ileocolectomy
Right radical colectomy

45.74 Open and other resection of transverse colon

45.75 Open and other left hemicolectomy
EXCLUDES *proctosigmoidectomy (48.41-48.69)*
second stage Mikulicz operation (46.04)
DEF: Excision of left descending large intestine.

45.76 Open and other sigmoidectomy

45.79 Other and unspecified partial excision of large intestine
Enterocolectomy NEC

✓4th **45.8 Total intra-abdominal colectomy**
Excision of cecum, colon, and sigmoid
EXCLUDES *coloproctectomy (48.41-48.69)*

45.81 Laparoscopic total intra-abdominal colectomy

45.82 Open total intra-abdominal colectomy

45.83 Other and unspecified total intra-abdominal colectomy

✓4th **45.9 Intestinal anastomosis**
Code also any synchronous resection (45.31-45.8, 48.41-48.69)
EXCLUDES *end-to-end anastomosis — omit code*

45.90 Intestinal anastomosis, not otherwise specified

45.91 Small-to-small intestinal anastomosis

Intestinal Anastomosis

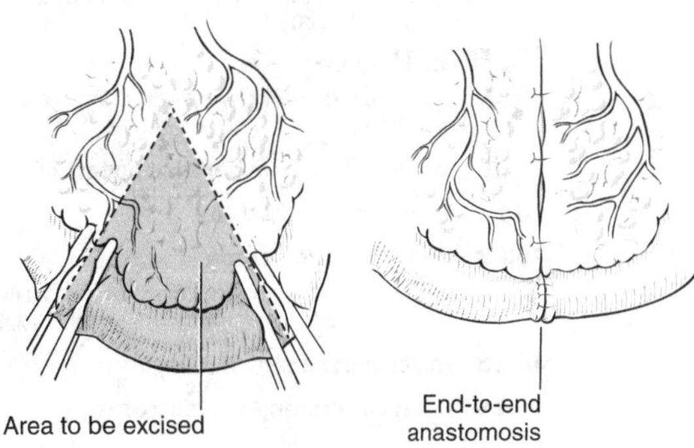

45.92 Anastomosis of small intestine to rectal stump
Hampton procedure

45.93 Other small-to-large intestinal anastomosis

45.94 Large-to-large intestinal anastomosis
EXCLUDES *rectorectostomy (48.74)*

45.95 Anastomosis to anus
Formation of endorectal ileal pouch (J-pouch) (H-pouch) (S-pouch) with anastomosis of small intestine to anus

✓3rd **46 Other operations on intestine**
Code also any application or administration of an adhesion barrier substance (99.77)

✓4th **46.0 Exteriorization of intestine**
INCLUDES loop enterostomy
multiple stage resection of intestine
DEF: Bringing intestinal segment to body surface.

46.01 Exteriorization of small intestine
Loop ileostomy

46.02 Resection of exteriorized segment of small intestine

46.03 Exteriorization of large intestine
Exteriorization of intestine NOS
First stage Mikulicz exteriorization of intestine
Loop colostomy

46.04 Resection of exteriorized segment of large intestine
Resection of exteriorized segment of intestine NOS
Second stage Mikulicz operation

✓4th **46.1 Colostomy**
Code also any synchronous resection (45.49, 45.71-45.79, 45.8)
EXCLUDES *loop colostomy (46.03)*
that with abdominoperineal resection of rectum (48.5)
that with synchronous anterior rectal resection (48.62)
DEF: Creation of opening from large intestine through abdominal wall to body surface.

46.10 Colostomy, not otherwise specified

46.11 Temporary colostomy

46.13 Permanent colostomy

46.14 Delayed opening of colostomy

4th 46.2 Ileostomy

Code also any synchronous resection (45.34, 45.61-45.63)

EXCLUDES *loop ileostomy (46.01)*

DEF: Creation of artificial anus by bringing ileum through abdominal wall to body surface.

46.20 Ileostomy, not otherwise specified

46.21 Temporary ileostomy

46.22 Continent ileostomy

DEF: Creation of opening from third part of small intestine through abdominal wall, with pouch outside abdomen.

46.23 Other permanent ileostomy

46.24 Delayed opening of ileostomy

4th 46.3 Other enterostomy

Code also any synchronous resection (45.61-45.8)

46.31 Delayed opening of other enterostomy

46.32 Percutaneous (endoscopic) jejunostomy [PEJ]

Endoscopic conversion of gastrostomy to jejunostomy
Percutaneous (endoscopic) feeding enterostomy

EXCLUDES *percutaneous [endoscopic] gastrojejunostomy (bypass) (44.32)*

DEF: Endoscopic placement of tube in midsection of small intestine through abdominal wall.

46.39 Other

Duodenostomy
Feeding enterostomy

4th 46.4 Revision of intestinal stoma

DEF: Revision of opening surgically created from intestine through abdominal wall, to skin surface.

46.40 Revision of intestinal stoma, not otherwise specified

Plastic enlargement of intestinal stoma
Reconstruction of stoma of intestine
Release of scar tissue of intestinal stoma

EXCLUDES *excision of redundant mucosa (45.41)*

46.41 Revision of stoma of small intestine

EXCLUDES *excision of redundant mucosa (45.33)*

46.42 Repair of pericolostomy hernia

46.43 Other revision of stoma of large intestine

EXCLUDES *excision of redundant mucosa (45.41)*

4th 46.5 Closure of intestinal stoma

Code also any synchronous resection (45.34, 45.49, 45.61-45.8)

46.50 Closure of intestinal stoma, not otherwise specified

46.51 Closure of stoma of small intestine

46.52 Closure of stoma of large intestine

Closure or take-down of cecostomy
Closure or take-down of colostomy
Closure or take-down of sigmoidostomy

4th 46.6 Fixation of intestine

46.60 Fixation of intestine, not otherwise specified

Fixation of intestine to abdominal wall

46.61 Fixation of small intestine to abdominal wall

Ileopexy

46.62 Other fixation of small intestine

Noble plication of small intestine
Plication of jejunum

DEF: Noble plication of small intestine: Fixing small intestine into place with tuck in small intestine.

DEF: Plication of jejunum: Fixing small intestine into place with tuck in midsection.

46.63 Fixation of large intestine to abdominal wall

Cecocoloplicopexy
Sigmoidopexy (Moschowitz)

46.64 Other fixation of large intestine

Cecofixation
Colofixation

4th 46.7 Other repair of intestine

EXCLUDES *closure of:*
ulcer of duodenum (44.42)
vesicoenteric fistula (57.83)

46.71 Suture of laceration of duodenum

46.72 Closure of fistula of duodenum

46.73 Suture of laceration of small intestine, except duodenum

46.74 Closure of fistula of small intestine, except duodenum

EXCLUDES *closure of:*
artificial stoma (46.51)
vaginal fistula (70.74)
repair of gastrojejunocolic fistula (44.63)

46.75 Suture of laceration of large intestine

46.76 Closure of fistula of large intestine

EXCLUDES *closure of:*
gastrocolic fistula (44.63)
rectal fistula (48.73)
sigmoidovesical fistula (57.83)
stoma (46.52)
vaginal fistula (70.72-70.73)
vesicocolic fistula (57.83)
vesicosigmoidovaginal fistula (57.83)

46.79 Other repair of intestine

Duodenoplasty

4th 46.8 Dilation and manipulation of intestine

46.80 Intra-abdominal manipulation of intestine, not otherwise specified

Correction of intestinal malrotation
Reduction of:
intestinal torsion
intestinal volvulus
intussusception

EXCLUDES *reduction of intussusception with:*
fluoroscopy (96.29)
ionizing radiation enema (96.29)
ultrasonography guidance (96.29)

DEF: Correction of intestinal malrotation: Repair of abnormal rotation.

DEF: Reduction of:
Intestinal torsion: Repair of twisted segment.
Intestinal volvulus: Repair of a knotted segment.
Intussusception: Repair of prolapsed segment.

46.81 Intra-abdominal manipulation of small intestine

46.82 Intra-abdominal manipulation of large intestine

46.85 Dilation of intestine
Dilation (balloon) of duodenum
Dilation (balloon) of jejunum
Endoscopic dilation (balloon) of large intestine
That through rectum or colostomy

✓4th **46.9 Other operations on intestines**

46.91 Myotomy of sigmoid colon

46.92 Myotomy of other parts of colon

46.93 Revision of anastomosis of small intestine

46.94 Revision of anastomosis of large intestine

46.95 Local perfusion of small intestine
Code also substance perfused (99.21-99.29)

46.96 Local perfusion of large intestine
Code also substance perfused (99.21-99.29)

46.97 Transplant of intestine
Note: To report donor source – see codes 00.91-00.93

46.99 Other
Ileoentectropy
EXCLUDES *diagnostic procedures on intestine (45.11-45.29)*
dilation of enterostomy stoma (96.24)
intestinal intubation (96.08)
removal of:
intraluminal foreign body from large intestine without incision (98.04)
intraluminal foreign body from small intestine without incision (98.03)
tube from large intestine (97.53)
tube from small intestine (97.52)
replacement of:
large intestine tube or enterostomy device (97.04)
small intestine tube or enterostomy device (97.03)

✓3rd **47 Operations on appendix**
INCLUDES appendiceal stump
Code also any application or administration of an adhesion barrier substance (99.77)

✓4th **47.0 Appendectomy**
EXCLUDES *incidental appendectomy, so described (47.11, 47.19)*

47.01 Laparoscopic appendectomy

47.09 Other appendectomy

✓4th **47.1 Incidental appendectomy**
DEF: Removal of appendix during abdominal surgery as prophylactic measure, without significant appendiceal pathology.

47.11 Laparoscopic incidental appendectomy

47.19 Other incidental appendectomy

47.2 Drainage of appendiceal abscess
EXCLUDES *that with appendectomy (47.0)*

✓4th **47.9 Other operations on appendix**

47.91 Appendicostomy

47.92 Closure of appendiceal fistula

47.99 Other
Anastomosis of appendix
EXCLUDES *diagnostic procedures on appendix (45.21-45.29)*

✓3rd **48 Operations on rectum, rectosigmoid, and perirectal tissue**
Code also any application or administration of an adhesion barrier substance (99.77)

48.0 Proctotomy
Decompression of imperforate anus
Panas' operation [linear proctotomy]
EXCLUDES *incision of perirectal tissue (48.81)*
DEF: Incision into rectal portion of large intestine.
DEF: Decompression of imperforate anus: opening a closed anus by means of an incision.
DEF: Panas' operation (linear proctotomy): Linear incision into rectal portion of large intestine

48.1 Proctostomy

✓4th **48.2 Diagnostic procedures on rectum, rectosigmoid, and perirectal tissue**

48.21 Transabdominal proctosigmoidoscopy
Intraoperative proctosigmoidoscopy
EXCLUDES *that with biopsy (48.24)*

48.22 Proctosigmoidoscopy through artificial stoma
EXCLUDES *that with biopsy (48.24)*

48.23 Rigid proctosigmoidoscopy
EXCLUDES *flexible sigmoidoscopy (45.24)*
DEF: Endoscopic exam of anus, rectum and lower sigmoid colon.

48.24 Closed [endoscopic] biopsy of rectum
Brushing or washing for specimen collection
Proctosigmoidoscopy with biopsy

48.25 Open biopsy of rectum

48.26 Biopsy of perirectal tissue

48.29 Other diagnostic procedures on rectum, rectosigmoid, and perirectal tissue
EXCLUDES *digital examination of rectum (89.34)*
lower GI series (87.64)
microscopic examination of specimen from rectum (90.91-90.99)

✓4th **48.3 Local excision or destruction of lesion or tissue of rectum**

48.31 Radical electrocoagulation of rectal lesion or tissue
DEF: Destruction of lesion or tissue of large intestine, rectal part.

48.32 Other electrocoagulation of rectal lesion or tissue

48.33 Destruction of rectal lesion or tissue by laser

48.34 Destruction of rectal lesion or tissue by cryosurgery

48.35 Local excision of rectal lesion or tissue
EXCLUDES *biopsy of rectum (48.24-48.25)*
[endoscopic] polypectomy of rectum (48.36)
excision of perirectal tissue (48.82)
hemorrhoidectomy (49.46)
rectal fistulectomy (48.73)

48.36 [Endoscopic] polypectomy of rectum

✓4th **48.4 Pull-through resection of rectum**
Code also any synchronous anastomosis other than end-to-end (45.90, 45.92-45.95)

48.40 Pull-through resection of rectum, not otherwise specified
Pull-through resection NOS
EXCLUDES *abdominoperineal pull-through NOS (48.50)*

48.41 Soave submucosal resection of rectum
Endorectal pull-through operation

DEF: Soave submucosal resection: Resection of submucosal rectal part of large intestine by pull-through technique.

DEF: Endorectal pull-through operation: Resection of interior large intestine by pull-through technique.

48.42 Laparoscopic pull-through resection of rectum

48.43 Open pull-through resection of rectum

48.49 Other pull-through resection of rectum
Abdominoperineal pull-through
Altemeier operation
Swenson proctectomy

EXCLUDES *Duhamel abdominoperineal pull-through (48.65)*
laparoscopic pull-through resection of rectum (48.42)
open pull-through resection of rectum (48.43)
pull-through resection of rectum, not otherwise specified (48.40)

DEF: Abdominoperineal pull-through: Resection of large intestine, latter part, by pull-through of abdomen, scrotum or vulva and anus.

DEF: Swenson proctatectomy: Excision of large intestine, rectal by pull-through and preserving muscles that close the anus.

✓4th **48.5 Abdominoperineal resection of rectum**

INCLUDES with synchronous colostomy
Combined abdominoendorectal resection
Complete proctectomy

Code also any synchronous anastomosis other than end-to-end (45.90, 45.92-45.95)

EXCLUDES *Duhamel abdominoperineal pull-through (48.65)*
that as part of pelvic exenteration (68.8)

DEF: Rectal excision through cavities formed by abdomen, anus, vulva or scrotum.

48.50 Abdominoperineal resection of the rectum, not otherwise specified

48.51 Laparoscopic abdominoperineal resection of the rectum

48.52 Open abdominoperineal resection of the rectum

48.59 Other abdominoperineal resection of the rectum

EXCLUDES *abdominoperineal resection of the rectum, NOS (48.50)*
laparoscopic abdominoperineal resection of the rectum (48.51)
open abdominoperineal resection of the rectum (48.52)

✓4th **48.6 Other resection of rectum**

Code also any synchronous anastomosis other than end-to-end (45.90, 45.92-45.95)

48.61 Transsacral rectosigmoidectomy

DEF: Excision through sacral bone area of sigmoid and last parts of large intestine.

48.62 Anterior resection of rectum with synchronous colostomy

DEF: Resection of front terminal end of large intestine and creation of colostomy.

48.63 Other anterior resection of rectum

EXCLUDES *that with synchronous colostomy (48.62)*

48.64 Posterior resection of rectum

48.65 Duhamel resection of rectum
Duhamel abdominoperineal pull-through

48.69 Other
Partial proctectomy
Rectal resection NOS

✓4th **48.7 Repair of rectum**

EXCLUDES *repair of:*
current obstetric laceration (75.62)
vaginal rectocele (70.50, 70.52, 70.53, 70.55)

48.71 Suture of laceration of rectum

48.72 Closure of proctostomy

48.73 Closure of other rectal fistula

EXCLUDES *fistulectomy:*
perirectal (48.93)
rectourethral (58.43)
rectovaginal (70.73)
rectovesical (57.83)
rectovesicovaginal (57.83)

48.74 Rectorectostomy
Rectal anastomosis NOS
Stapled transanal rectal resection (STARR)

DEF: Rectal anastomosis: Connection of two cut portions of large intestine, rectal end.

48.75 Abdominal proctopexy
Frickman procedure
Ripstein repair of rectal prolapse

DEF: Fixation of rectum to adjacent abdominal structures.

48.76 Other proctopexy
Delorme repair of prolapsed rectum
Proctosigmoidopexy
Puborectalis sling operation

EXCLUDES *manual reduction of rectal prolapse (96.26)*

DEF: Delorme repair of prolapsed rectum: Fixation of collapsed large intestine, rectal part.

DEF: Proctosigmoidopexy: Suturing of twisted large intestine, rectal part.

DEF: Puborectalis sling operation: Fixation of large intestine, rectal part by forming puborectalis muscle into sling.

48.79 Other repair of rectum
Repair of old obstetric laceration of rectum

EXCLUDES *anastomosis to:*
large intestine (45.94)
small intestine (45.92-45.93)
repair of:
current obstetrical laceration (75.62)
vaginal rectocele (70.50, 70.52)

✓4th **48.8 Incision or excision of perirectal tissue or lesion**

INCLUDES pelvirectal tissue
rectovaginal septum

48.81 Incision of perirectal tissue
Incision of rectovaginal septum

48.82 Excision of perirectal tissue

EXCLUDES *perirectal biopsy (48.26)*
perirectofistulectomy (48.93)
rectal fistulectomy (48.73)

✓4th **48.9 Other operations on rectum and perirectal tissue**

48.91 Incision of rectal stricture

48.92 Anorectal myectomy

DEF: Excision of anorectal muscle.

48.93 Repair of perirectal fistula

EXCLUDES *that opening into rectum (48.73)*

DEF: Closure of abdominal passage in tissue around large intestine, rectal part.

48.99 Other

EXCLUDES *digital examination of rectum (89.34)*
dilation of rectum (96.22)
insertion of rectal tube (96.09)
irrigation of rectum (96.38-96.39)
manual reduction of rectal prolapse (96.26)
proctoclysis (96.37)
rectal massage (99.93)
rectal packing (96.19)
removal of:
impacted feces (96.38)
intraluminal foreign body from rectum without incision (98.05)
rectal packing (97.59)
transanal enema (96.39)

✓3rd 49 Operations on anus

Code also any application or administration of an adhesion barrier substance (99.77)

✓4th 49.0 Incision or excision of perianal tissue

49.01 Incision of perianal abscess

49.02 Other incision of perianal tissue
Undercutting of perianal tissue

EXCLUDES *anal fistulotomy (49.11)*

49.03 Excision of perianal skin tags

49.04 Other excision of perianal tissue

EXCLUDES *anal fistulectomy (49.12)*
biopsy of perianal tissue (49.22)

✓4th 49.1 Incision or excision of anal fistula

EXCLUDES *closure of anal fistula (49.73)*

49.11 Anal fistulotomy

49.12 Anal fistulectomy

✓4th 49.2 Diagnostic procedures on anus and perianal tissue

49.21 Anoscopy

49.22 Biopsy of perianal tissue

49.23 Biopsy of anus

49.29 Other diagnostic procedures on anus and perianal tissue

EXCLUDES *microscopic examination of specimen from anus (90.91-90.99)*

✓4th 49.3 Local excision or destruction of other lesion or tissue of anus

Anal cryptotomy
Cauterization of lesion of anus

EXCLUDES *biopsy of anus (49.23)*
control of (postoperative) hemorrhage of anus (49.95)
hemorrhoidectomy (49.46)

49.31 Endoscopic excision or destruction of lesion or tissue of anus

49.39 Other local excision or destruction of lesion or tissue of anus

EXCLUDES *that by endoscopic approach (49.31)*

✓4th 49.4 Procedures on hemorrhoids

49.41 Reduction of hemorrhoids
DEF: Manual manipulation to reduce hemorrhoids.

49.42 Injection of hemorrhoids

49.43 Cauterization of hemorrhoids
Clamp and cautery of hemorrhoids

49.44 Destruction of hemorrhoids by cryotherapy

49.45 Ligation of hemorrhoids

49.46 Excision of hemorrhoids
Hemorrhoidectomy NOS

49.47 Evacuation of thrombosed hemorrhoids
DEF: Removal of clotted material from hemorrhoid.

49.49 Other procedures on hemorrhoids
Lord procedure

✓4th 49.5 Division of anal sphincter

49.51 Left lateral anal sphincterotomy

49.52 Posterior anal sphincterotomy

49.59 Other anal sphincterotomy
Division of sphincter NOS

49.6 Excision of anus

✓4th 49.7 Repair of anus

EXCLUDES *repair of current obstetric laceration (75.62)*

49.71 Suture of laceration of anus

49.72 Anal cerclage
DEF: Encircling anus with ring or sutures.

49.73 Closure of anal fistula

EXCLUDES *excision of anal fistula (49.12)*

49.74 Gracilis muscle transplant for anal incontinence
DEF: Moving pubic attachment of gracilis muscle to restore anal control.

49.75 Implantation or revision of artificial anal sphincter
Removal with subsequent replacement
Replacement during same or subsequent operative episode

49.76 Removal of artificial anal sphincter
Explantation or removal without replacement

EXCLUDES *revision with implantation during same operative episode (49.75)*

49.79 Other repair of anal sphincter
Repair of old obstetric laceration of anus

EXCLUDES *anoplasty with synchronous hemorrhoidectomy (49.46)*
repair of current obstetric laceration (75.62)

✓4th 49.9 Other operations on anus

EXCLUDES *dilation of anus (sphincter) (96.23)*

49.91 Incision of anal septum

49.92 Insertion of subcutaneous electrical anal stimulator

Dynamic Graciloplasty

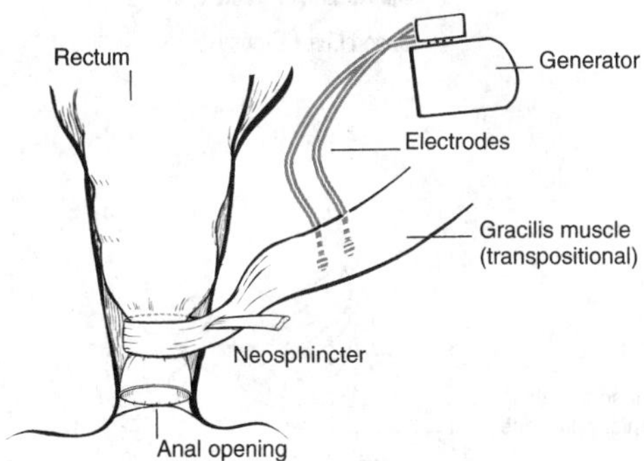

49.93 Other incision of anus
Removal of:
foreign body from anus with incision
seton from anus
EXCLUDES *anal fistulotomy (49.11)*
removal of intraluminal foreign body without incision (98.05)

49.94 Reduction of anal prolapse
EXCLUDES *manual reduction of rectal prolapse (96.26)*
DEF: Manipulation of displaced anal tissue to normal position.

49.95 Control of (postoperative) hemorrhage of anus

49.99 Other

✓3rd **50 Operations on liver**
Code also any application or administration of an adhesion barrier substance (99.77)

50.0 Hepatotomy
Incision of abscess of liver
Removal of gallstones from liver
Stromeyer-Little operation

✓4th **50.1 Diagnostic procedures on liver**

50.11 Closed (percutaneous) (needle) biopsy of liver
Diagnostic aspiration of liver

50.12 Open biopsy of liver
Wedge biopsy

50.13 Transjugular liver biopsy
Transvenous liver biopsy
EXCLUDES *closed (percutaneous) [needle] biopsy of liver (50.11)*
laparoscopic liver biopsy (50.14)

50.14 Laparoscopic liver biopsy
EXCLUDES *closed (percutaneous) [needle] biopsy of liver (50.11)*
open biopsy of liver (50.12)
transjugular liver biopsy (50.13)

50.19 Other diagnostic procedures on liver
EXCLUDES *laparoscopic liver biopsy (50.14)*
liver scan and radioisotope function study (92.02)
microscopic examination of specimen from liver (91.01-91.09)
transjugular liver biopsy (50.13)

✓4th **50.2 Local excision or destruction of liver tissue or lesion**

50.21 Marsupialization of lesion of liver
DEF: Exteriorizing lesion by incision and suturing cut edges to skin to create opening.

Closed Liver Biopsy

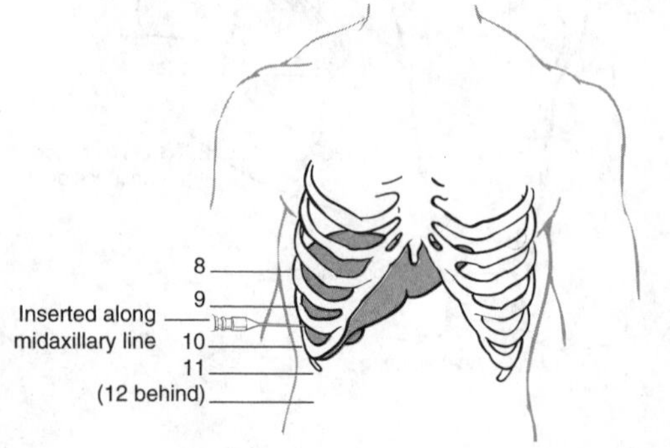

Liver Biopsy (Open, Wedge)

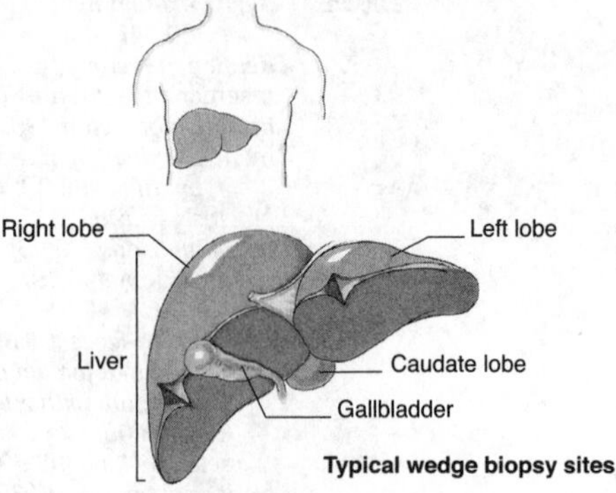

50.22 Partial hepatectomy
Wedge resection of liver
EXCLUDES *biopsy of liver (50.11-50.12)*
hepatic lobectomy (50.3)

50.23 Open ablation of liver lesion or tissue

50.24 Percutaneous ablation of liver lesion or tissue

50.25 Laparoscopic ablation of liver lesion or tissue

50.26 Other and unspecified ablation of liver lesion or tissue

50.29 Other destruction of lesion of liver
Cauterization, Enucleation, Evacuation } of hepatic lesion
EXCLUDES *ablation of liver lesion or tissue:*
laparoscopic (50.25)
open (50.23)
other (50.26)
percutaneous (50.24)
percutaneous aspiration of lesion (50.91)

50.3 Lobectomy of liver
Total hepatic lobectomy with partial excision of other lobe

50.4 Total hepatectomy

✓4th **50.5 Liver transplant**
Note: To report donor source – see codes 00.91-00.93

50.51 Auxiliary liver transplant
Auxiliary hepatic transplantation leaving patient's own liver in situ

50.59 Other transplant of liver

✓4th **50.6 Repair of liver**

50.61 Closure of laceration of liver

50.69 Other repair of liver
Hepatopexy

✓4th **50.9 Other operations on liver**
EXCLUDES *lysis of adhesions (54.5)*

50.91 Percutaneous aspiration of liver
EXCLUDES *percutaneous biopsy (50.11)*
DEF: Incision into liver through body wall to withdraw fluid.

50.92 Extracorporeal hepatic assistance
Liver dialysis
DEF: Devices used outside body to assist liver function.

50.93 Localized perfusion of liver

50.94 Other injection of therapeutic substance into liver

50.99 Other

✓3rd 51 Operations on gallbladder and biliary tract

INCLUDES operations on:
ampulla of Vater
common bile duct
cystic duct
hepatic duct
intrahepatic bile duct
sphincter of Oddi

Code also any application or administration of an adhesion barrier substance (99.77)

✓4th 51.0 Cholecystotomy and cholecystostomy

51.01 Percutaneous aspiration of gallbladder
Percutaneous cholecystotomy for drainage
That by: needle or catheter
EXCLUDES *needle biopsy (51.12)*

51.02 Trocar cholecystostomy
DEF: Creating opening in gallbladder with catheter.

51.03 Other cholecystostomy

51.04 Other cholecystotomy
Cholelithotomy NOS

✓4th 51.1 Diagnostic procedures on biliary tract

EXCLUDES *that for endoscopic procedures classifiable to 51.64, 51.84-51.88, 52.14, 52.21, 52.93 -52.94, 52.97-52.98*

51.10 Endoscopic retrograde cholangiopancreatography [ERCP]
EXCLUDES *endoscopic retrograde:*
cholangiography [ERC] (51.11)
pancreatography [ERP] (52.13)
DEF: Endoscopic and radioscopic exam of pancreatic and common bile ducts with contrast material injected in opposite direction of normal flow through catheter.

51.11 Endoscopic retrograde cholangiography [ERC]
Laparoscopic exploration of common bile duct
EXCLUDES *endoscopic retrograde:*
cholangiopancreatography [ERCP] (51.10)
pancreatography [ERP] (52.13)
DEF: Endoscopic and radioscopic exam of common bile ducts with contrast material injected in opposite direction of normal flow through catheter.

51.12 Percutaneous biopsy of gallbladder or bile ducts
Needle biopsy of gallbladder

51.13 Open biopsy of gallbladder or bile ducts

51.14 Other closed [endoscopic] biopsy of biliary duct or sphincter of Oddi
Brushing or washing for specimen collection
Closed biopsy of biliary duct or sphincter of Oddi by procedures classifiable to 51.10-51.11, 52.13
DEF: Endoscopic biopsy of muscle tissue around pancreatic and common bile ducts.

51.15 Pressure measurement of sphincter of Oddi
Pressure measurement of sphincter by procedures classifiable to 51.10-51.11, 52.13
DEF: Pressure measurement tests of muscle tissue surrounding pancreatic and common bile ducts.

Laparoscopic Cholecystectomy by Laser

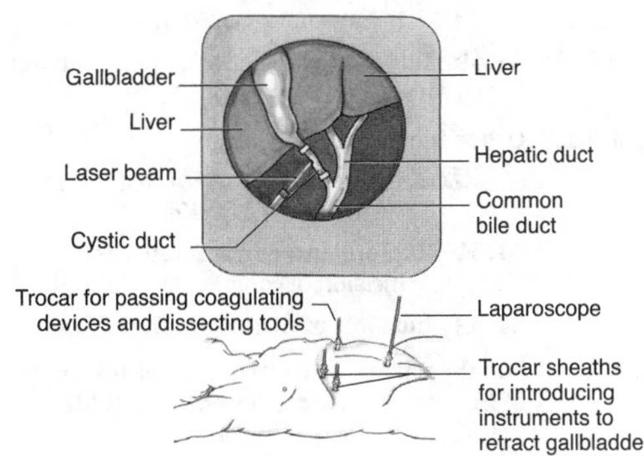

51.19 Other diagnostic procedures on biliary tract
EXCLUDES *biliary tract x-ray (87.51-87.59)*
microscopic examination of specimen from biliary tract (91.01-91.09)

✓4th 51.2 Cholecystectomy

51.21 Other partial cholecystectomy
Revision of prior cholecystectomy
EXCLUDES *that by laparoscope (51.24)*

51.22 Cholecystectomy
EXCLUDES *laparoscopic cholecystectomy (51.23)*

51.23 Laparoscopic cholecystectomy
That by laser
DEF: Endoscopic removal of gallbladder.

51.24 Laparoscopic partial cholecystectomy

✓4th 51.3 Anastomosis of gallbladder or bile duct

EXCLUDES *resection with end-to-end anastomosis (51.61-51.69)*

51.31 Anastomosis of gallbladder to hepatic ducts

51.32 Anastomosis of gallbladder to intestine

51.33 Anastomosis of gallbladder to pancreas

51.34 Anastomosis of gallbladder to stomach

51.35 Other gallbladder anastomosis
Gallbladder anastomosis NOS

51.36 Choledochoenterostomy
DEF: Connection of common bile duct to intestine.

51.37 Anastomosis of hepatic duct to gastrointestinal tract
Kasai portoenterostomy
DEF: Kaisi portoenterostomy: A duct to drain bile from the liver is formed by anastomosing the porta hepatis to a loop of bowel.

51.39 Other bile duct anastomosis
Anastomosis of bile duct NOS
Anastomosis of unspecified bile duct to:
intestine
liver
pancreas
stomach

✓4th 51.4 Incision of bile duct for relief of obstruction

51.41 Common duct exploration for removal of calculus
EXCLUDES *percutaneous extraction (51.96)*

51.42 Common duct exploration for relief of other obstruction

51.43 Insertion of choledochohepatic tube for decompression
Hepatocholedochostomy

51.49 Incision of other bile ducts for relief of obstruction

✓4th **51.5 Other incision of bile duct**
EXCLUDES *that for relief of obstruction (51.41-51.49)*

51.51 Exploration of common duct
Incision of common bile duct

51.59 Incision of other bile duct

✓4th **51.6 Local excision or destruction of lesion or tissue of biliary ducts and sphincter of Oddi**
Code also anastomosis other than end-to-end (51.31, 51.36-51.39)
EXCLUDES *biopsy of bile duct (51.12-51.13)*

51.61 Excision of cystic duct remnant

51.62 Excision of ampulla of Vater (with reimplantation of common duct)

51.63 Other excision of common duct
Choledochectomy
EXCLUDES *fistulectomy (51.72)*

51.64 Endoscopic excision or destruction of lesion of biliary ducts or sphincter of Oddi
Excision or destruction of lesion of biliary duct by procedures classifiable to 51.10-51.11, 52.13

51.69 Excision of other bile duct
Excision of lesion of bile duct NOS
EXCLUDES *fistulectomy (51.79)*

✓4th **51.7 Repair of bile ducts**

51.71 Simple suture of common bile duct

51.72 Choledochoplasty
Repair of fistula of common bile duct

51.79 Repair of other bile ducts
Closure of artificial opening of bile duct NOS
Suture of bile duct NOS
EXCLUDES *operative removal of prosthetic device (51.95)*

✓4th **51.8 Other operations on biliary ducts and sphincter of Oddi**

51.81 Dilation of sphincter of Oddi
Dilation of ampulla of Vater
EXCLUDES *that by endoscopic approach (51.84)*

DEF: Dilation of muscle around common bile and pancreatic ducts; to mitigate constriction obstructing bile flow.

51.82 Pancreatic sphincterotomy
Incision of pancreatic sphincter
Transduodenal ampullary sphincterotomy
EXCLUDES *that by endoscopic approach (51.85)*

DEF: Pancreatic sphincterotomy: Division of muscle around common bile and pancreatic ducts.

DEF: Transduodenal ampullary sphincterotomy: Incision into muscle around common bile and pancreatic ducts; closing approach through first section of small intestine.

51.83 Pancreatic sphincteroplasty

51.84 Endoscopic dilation of ampulla and biliary duct
Dilation of ampulla and biliary duct by procedures classifiable to 51.10-51.11, 52.13

51.85 Endoscopic sphincterotomy and papillotomy
Sphincterotomy and papillotomy by procedures classifiable to 51.10-51.11, 52.13

DEF: Incision of muscle around common bile and pancreatic ducts and closing the duodenal papilla.

51.86 Endoscopic insertion of nasobiliary drainage tube
Insertion of nasobiliary tube by procedures classifiable to 51.10-51.11, 52.13

51.87 Endoscopic insertion of stent (tube) into bile duct
Endoprosthesis of bile duct
Insertion of stent into bile duct by procedures classifiable to 51.10-51.11, 52.13
EXCLUDES *nasobiliary drainage tube (51.86)*
replacement of stent (tube) (97.05)

51.88 Endoscopic removal of stone(s) from biliary tract
Laparoscopic removal of stone(s) from biliary tract
Removal of biliary tract stone(s) by procedures classifiable to 51.10-51.11, 52.13
EXCLUDES *percutaneous extraction of common duct stones (51.96)*

51.89 Other operations on sphincter of Oddi

✓4th **51.9 Other operations on biliary tract**

51.91 Repair of laceration of gallbladder

51.92 Closure of cholecystostomy

51.93 Closure of other biliary fistula
Cholecystogastroenteric fistulectomy

51.94 Revision of anastomosis of biliary tract

51.95 Removal of prosthetic device from bile duct
EXCLUDES *nonoperative removal (97.55)*

51.96 Percutaneous extraction of common duct stones

51.98 Other percutaneous procedures on biliary tract
Percutaneous biliary endoscopy via existing T-tube or other tract for:
- dilation of biliary duct stricture
- removal of stone(s) except common duct stone
- exploration (postoperative)

Percutaneous transhepatic biliary drainage
EXCLUDES *percutaneous aspiration of gallbladder (51.01)*
percutaneous biopsy and/or collection of specimen by brushing or washing (51.12)
percutaneous removal of common duct stone(s) (51.96)

51.99 Other

Insertion or replacement of biliary tract prosthesis

EXCLUDES *biopsy of gallbladder (51.12-51.13)*
irrigation of cholecystostomy and other biliary tube (96.41)
lysis of peritoneal adhesions (54.5)
nonoperative removal of:
cholecystostomy tube (97.54)
tube from biliary tract or liver (97.55)

✓3rd 52 Operations on pancreas

INCLUDES operations on pancreatic duct

Code also any application or administration of an adhesion barrier substance (99.77)

✓4th 52.0 Pancreatotomy

52.01 Drainage of pancreatic cyst by catheter

52.09 Other pancreatotomy

Pancreatolithotomy

EXCLUDES *drainage by anastomosis (52.4, 52.96)*
incision of pancreatic sphincter (51.82)
marsupialization of cyst (52.3)

DEF: Pancreatolithotomy: Incision into pancreas to remove stones.

✓4th 52.1 Diagnostic procedures on pancreas

52.11 Closed [aspiration] [needle] [percutaneous] biopsy of pancreas

52.12 Open biopsy of pancreas

52.13 Endoscopic retrograde pancreatography [ERP]

EXCLUDES *endoscopic retrograde:*
cholangiography [ERC] (51.11)
cholangiopancreatography [ERCP] (51.10)
that for procedures classifiable to 51.14-51.15, 51.64, 51.84-51.88, 52.14, 52.21, 52.92-52.94, 52.97-52.98

52.14 Closed [endoscopic] biopsy of pancreatic duct

Closed biopsy of pancreatic duct by procedures classifiable to 51.10-51.11, 52.13

52.19 Other diagnostic procedures on pancreas

EXCLUDES *contrast pancreatogram (87.66)*
endoscopic retrograde pancreatography [ERP] (52.13)
microscopic examination of specimen from pancreas (91.01-91.09)

✓4th 52.2 Local excision or destruction of pancreas and pancreatic duct

EXCLUDES *biopsy of pancreas (52.11-52.12, 52.14)*
pancreatic fistulectomy (52.95)

52.21 Endoscopic excision or destruction of lesion or tissue of pancreatic duct

Excision or destruction of lesion or tissue of pancreatic duct by procedures classifiable to 51.10-51.11, 52.13

52.22 Other excision or destruction of lesion or tissue of pancreas or pancreatic duct

52.3 Marsupialization of pancreatic cyst

EXCLUDES *drainage of cyst by catheter (52.01)*

DEF: Incision into pancreas and suturing edges to form pocket; promotes drainage and healing.

52.4 Internal drainage of pancreatic cyst

Pancreaticocystoduodenostomy
Pancreaticocystogastrostomy
Pancreaticocystojejunostomy

DEF: Withdrawing fluid from pancreatic cyst by draining it through a created passage to another organ.

DEF: Pancreaticocystoduodenostomy: Creation of passage from pancreatic cyst to first portion of small intestine.

DEF: Pancreaticocystogastrostomy: Creation of passage from pancreatic cyst to stomach.

DEF: Pancreaticocystojejunostomy: Creation of passage from pancreatic cyst to midsection of small intestine.

✓4th 52.5 Partial pancreatectomy

EXCLUDES *pancreatic fistulectomy (52.95)*

52.51 Proximal pancreatectomy

Excision of head of pancreas (with part of body)
Proximal pancreatectomy with synchronous duodenectomy

52.52 Distal pancreatectomy

Excision of tail of pancreas (with part of body)

52.53 Radical subtotal pancreatectomy

52.59 Other partial pancreatectomy

52.6 Total pancreatectomy

Pancreatectomy with synchronous duodenectomy

52.7 Radical pancreaticoduodenectomy

One-stage pancreaticoduodenal resection with choledochojejunal anastomosis, pancreaticojejunal anastomosis, and gastrojejunostomy
Two-stage pancreaticoduodenal resection (first stage) (second stage)
Radical resection of the pancreas
Whipple procedure

EXCLUDES *radical subtotal pancreatectomy (52.53)*

DEF: Whipple procedure: pancreaticoduodenectomy involving the removal of the head of the pancreas and part of the small intestines; pancreaticojejunostomy, choledochojejunal anastomosis, and gastrojejunostomy included in the procedure.

✓4th 52.8 Transplant of pancreas

Note: To report donor source–see codes 00.91-00.93

52.80 Pancreatic transplant, not otherwise specified

52.81 Reimplantation of pancreatic tissue

52.82 Homotransplant of pancreas

52.83 Heterotransplant of pancreas

52.84 Autotransplantation of cells of islets of Langerhans

Homotransplantation of islet cells of pancreas

DEF: Transplantation of Islet cells from pancreas to another location of same patient.

52.85 Allotransplantation of cells of islets of Langerhans

Heterotransplantation of islet cells of pancreas

DEF: Transplantation of Islet cells from one individual to another.

52.86 Transplantation of cells of islets of Langerhans, not otherwise specified

✓4th 52.9 Other operations on pancreas

DEF: Placement of tube into pancreatic duct, without an endoscope.

52.92 Cannulation of pancreatic duct

EXCLUDES *that by endoscopic approach (52.93)*

52.93 Endoscopic insertion of stent (tube) into pancreatic duct

Insertion of cannula or stent into pancreatic duct by procedures classifiable to 51.10-51.11, 52.13

EXCLUDES *endoscopic insertion of nasopancreatic drainage tube (52.97)*
replacement of stent (tube) (97.05)

52.94 Endoscopic removal of stone(s) from pancreatic duct

Removal of stone(s) from pancreatic duct by procedures classifiable to 51.10-51.11, 52.13

52.95 Other repair of pancreas

Fistulectomy } of pancreas
Simple suture } of pancreas

52.96 Anastomosis of pancreas

Anastomosis of pancreas (duct) to:
intestine
jejunum
stomach

EXCLUDES *anastomosis to:*
bile duct (51.39)
gallbladder (51.33)

52.97 Endoscopic insertion of nasopancreatic drainage tube

Insertion of nasopancreatic drainage tube by procedures classifiable to 51.10-51.11, 52.13

EXCLUDES *drainage of pancreatic cyst by catheter (52.01)*
replacement of stent (tube) (97.05)

52.98 Endoscopic dilation of pancreatic duct

Dilation of Wirsung's duct by procedures classifiable to 51.10-51.11, 52.13

52.99 Other

Dilation of pancreatic [Wirsung's] duct } by open approach
Repair of pancreatic [Wirsung's] duct } by open approach

EXCLUDES *irrigation of pancreatic tube (96.42)*
removal of pancreatic tube (97.56)

✓3rd **53 Repair of hernia**

INCLUDES hernioplasty
herniorrhaphy

Code also any application or administration of an adhesion barrier substance (99.77)

EXCLUDES *manual reduction of hernia (96.27)*

DEF: Repair of hernia: Restoration of abnormally protruding organ or tissue.

DEF: Herniorrhaphy: Repair of hernia.

DEF: Herniotomy: Division of constricted, strangulated, irreducible hernia.

✓4th **53.0 Other unilateral repair of inguinal hernia**

EXCLUDES *laparoscopic unilateral repair of inguinal hernia (17.11-17.13)*

53.00 Unilateral repair of inguinal hernia, not otherwise specified

Inguinal herniorrhaphy NOS

53.01 Other and open repair of direct inguinal hernia

Direct and indirect inguinal hernia

53.02 Other and open repair of indirect inguinal hernia

53.03 Other and open repair of direct inguinal hernia with graft or prosthesis

53.04 Other and open repair of indirect inguinal hernia with graft or prosthesis

Indirect Repair of Hernia

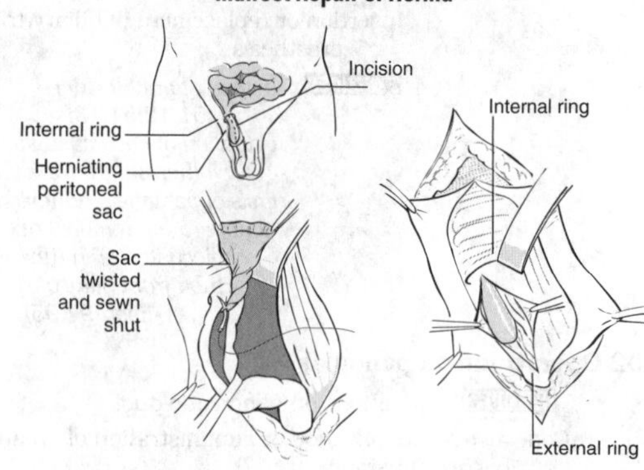

53.05 Repair of inguinal herna with graft or prosthesis, not otherwise specified

✓4th **53.1 Other bilateral repair of inguinal hernia**

EXCLUDES *laparoscopic bilateral repair of inguinal hernia (17.21-17.24)*

53.10 Bilateral repair of inguinal hernia, not otherwise specified

53.11 Other and open bilateral repair of direct inguinal hernia

53.12 Other and open bilateral repair of indirect inguinal hernia

53.13 Other and open bilateral repair of inguinal hernia, one direct and one indirect

53.14 Other and open bilateral repair of direct inguinal hernia with graft or prosthesis

53.15 Other and open bilateral repair of indirect inguinal hernia with graft or prosthesis

53.16 Other and bilateral repair of inguinal hernia, one direct and one indirect, with graft or prosthesis

53.17 Bilateral inguinal hernia repair with graft or prosthesis, not otherwise specified

✓4th **53.2 Unilateral repair of femoral hernia**

53.21 Unilateral repair of femoral hernia with graft or prosthesis

53.29 Other unilateral femoral herniorrhaphy

✓4th **53.3 Bilateral repair of femoral hernia**

53.31 Bilateral repair of femoral hernia with graft or prosthesis

53.39 Other bilateral femoral herniorrhaphy

✓4th **53.4 Repair of umbilical hernia**

EXCLUDES *repair of gastroschisis (54.71)*

53.41 Other and open repair of umbilical hernia with graft or prosthesis

53.42 Laparoscopic repair of umbilical hernia with graft or prosthesis

53.43 Other laparoscopic umbilical herniorrhaphy

53.49 Other open umbilical herniorrhaphy

EXCLUDES *other laparoscopic umbilical herniorrhaphy (53.43)*
repair of umbilical hernia with graft or prosthesis (53.41, 53.42)

✓4th **53.5 Repair of other hernia of anterior abdominal wall (without graft or prosthesis)**

53.51 Incisional hernia repair

53.59 Repair of other hernia of anterior abdominal wall

Repair of hernia:
- epigastric
- hypogastric
- spigelian
- ventral

✓4th **53.6 Repair of other hernia of anterior abdominal wall with graft or prosthesis**

53.61 Other open incisional hernia repair with graft or prosthesis

EXCLUDES *laparoscopic incisional hernia repair with graft or prosthesis (53.62)*

53.62 Laparoscopic incisional hernia repair with graft or prosthesis

53.63 Other laparoscopic repair of other hernia of anterior abdominal wall with graft or prosthesis

53.69 Other and open repair of other hernia of anterior abdominal wall with graft or prosthesis

EXCLUDES *other laparoscopic repair of other hernia of anterior abdominal wall with graft or prosthesis (53.63)*

✓4th **53.7 Repair of diaphragmatic hernia, abdominal approach**

53.71 Laparoscopic repair of diaphragmatic hernia, abdominal approach

53.72 Other and open repair of diaphragmatic hernia, abdominal approach

53.75 Repair of diaphragmatic hernia, abdominal approach, not otherwise specified

EXCLUDES *laparoscopic repair of diaphragmatic hernia (53.71)*
other and open repair of diaphragmatic hernia (53.72)

✓4th **53.8 Repair of diaphragmatic hernia, thoracic approach**

DEF: Repair of diaphragmatic hernia though abdomen and thorax.

53.80 Repair of diaphragmatic hernia with thoracic approach, not otherwise specified

Thoracoabdominal repair of diaphragmatic hernia

53.81 Plication of the diaphragm

DEF: Tuck repair of diaphragmatic hernia.

53.82 Repair of parasternal hernia

DEF: Repair of hernia protruding into breastbone area.

53.83 Laparoscopic repair of diaphragmatic hernia, with thoracic approach

53.84 Other and open repair of diaphragmatic hernia, with thoracic approach

EXCLUDES *repair of diaphragmatic hernia with thoracic approach, NOS, (53.80)*

53.9 Other hernia repair

Repair of hernia:
- ischiatic
- ischiorectal
- lumbar
- obturator
- omental
- retroperitoneal
- sciatic

EXCLUDES *relief of strangulated hernia with exteriorization of intestine (46.01, 46.03)*
repair of pericolostomy hernia (46.42)
repair of vaginal enterocele (70.92)

✓3rd **54 Other operations on abdominal region**

INCLUDES operations on:
- epigastric region
- flank
- groin region
- hypochondrium
- inguinal region
- loin region
- mesentery
- omentum
- pelvic cavity
- peritoneum
- retroperitoneal tissue space

Code also any application or administration of an adhesion barrier substance (99.77)

EXCLUDES *hernia repair (53.00-53.9)*
obliteration of cul-de-sac (70.92)
retroperitoneal tissue dissection (59.00-59.09)
skin and subcutaneous tissue of abdominal wall (86.01-86.99)

54.0 Incision of abdominal wall

Drainage of:
- abdominal wall
- extraperitoneal abscess
- retroperitoneal abscess

EXCLUDES *incision of peritoneum (54.95)*
laparotomy (54.11-54.19)

✓4th **54.1 Laparotomy**

DEF: Incision into abdomen.

54.11 Exploratory laparotomy

EXCLUDES *exploration incidental to intra-abdominal surgery — omit code*

DEF: Exam of peritoneal cavity through incision into abdomen.

54.12 Reopening of recent laparotomy site

Reopening of recent laparotomy site for:
- control of hemorrhage
- exploration
- incision of hematoma

54.19 Other laparotomy

Drainage of intraperitoneal abscess or hematoma

EXCLUDES *culdocentesis (70.0)*
drainage of appendiceal abscess (47.2)
exploration incidental to intra-abdominal surgery — omit code
Ladd operation (54.95)
percutaneous drainage of abdomen (54.91)
removal of foreign body (54.92)

✓4th **54.2 Diagnostic procedures of abdominal region**

54.21 Laparoscopy
Peritoneoscopy
EXCLUDES *laparoscopic cholecystectomy (51.23)*
that incidental to destruction of fallopian tubes (66.21-66.29)

DEF: Endoscopic exam of peritoneal cavity through abdominal incision.

54.22 Biopsy of abdominal wall or umbilicus

54.23 Biopsy of peritoneum
Biopsy of:
- mesentery
- omentum
- peritoneal implant

EXCLUDES *closed biopsy of:*
omentum (54.24)
peritoneum (54.24)

54.24 Closed [percutaneous] [needle] biopsy of intra-abdominal mass
Closed biopsy of:
- omentum
- peritoneal implant
- peritoneum

EXCLUDES *that of:*
fallopian tube (66.11)
ovary (65.11)
uterine ligaments (68.15)
uterus (68.16)

54.25 Peritoneal lavage
Diagnostic peritoneal lavage
EXCLUDES *peritoneal dialysis (54.98)*

DEF: Irrigation of peritoneal cavity with siphoning of liquid contents for analysis.

54.29 Other diagnostic procedures on abdominal region
EXCLUDES *abdominal lymphangiogram (88.04)*
abdominal x-ray NEC (88.19)
angiocardiography of venae cavae (88.51)
C.A.T. scan of abdomen (88.01)
contrast x-ray of abdominal cavity (88.11-88.15)
intra-abdominal arteriography NEC (88.47)
microscopic examination of peritoneal and retroperitoneal specimen (91.11-91.19)
phlebography of:
intra-abdominal vessels NEC (88.65)
portal venous system (88.64)
sinogram of abdominal wall (88.03)
soft tissue x-ray of abdominal wall NEC (88.09)
tomography of abdomen NEC (88.02)
ultrasonography of abdomen and retroperitoneum (88.76)

54.3 Excision or destruction of lesion or tissue of abdominal wall or umbilicus
Debridement of abdominal wall
Omphalectomy
EXCLUDES *biopsy of abdominal wall or umbilicus (54.22)*
size reduction operation (86.83)
that of skin of abdominal wall (86.22, 86.26, 86.3)

54.4 Excision or destruction of peritoneal tissue
Excision of:
- appendices epiploicae
- falciform ligament
- gastrocolic ligament
- lesion of:
  - mesentery
  - omentum
  - peritoneum
- presacral lesion NOS
- retroperitoneal lesion NOS

EXCLUDES *biopsy of peritoneum (54.23)*
endometrectomy of cul-de-sac (70.32)

✓4th **54.5 Lysis of peritoneal adhesions**
Freeing of adhesions of:
- biliary tract
- intestines
- liver
- pelvic peritoneum
- peritoneum
- spleen
- uterus

EXCLUDES *lysis of adhesions of:*
bladder (59.11)
fallopian tube and ovary (65.81, 65.89)
kidney (59.02)
ureter (59.02-59.03)

54.51 Laparoscopic lysis of peritoneal adhesions

54.59 Other lysis of peritoneal adhesions

✓4th **54.6 Suture of abdominal wall and peritoneum**

54.61 Reclosure of postoperative disruption of abdominal wall

54.62 Delayed closure of granulating abdominal wound
Tertiary subcutaneous wound closure

DEF: Closure of outer layers of abdominal wound; follows procedure to close initial layers of wound.

54.63 Other suture of abdominal wall
Suture of laceration of abdominal wall
EXCLUDES *closure of operative wound — omit code*

54.64 Suture of peritoneum
Secondary suture of peritoneum
EXCLUDES *closure of operative wound — omit code*

✓4th **54.7 Other repair of abdominal wall and peritoneum**

54.71 Repair of gastroschisis

DEF: Repair of congenital fistula of abdominal wall.

54.72 Other repair of abdominal wall

54.73 Other repair of peritoneum
Suture of gastrocolic ligament

54.74 Other repair of omentum
Epiplorrhaphy
Graft of omentum
Omentopexy
Reduction of torsion of omentum
EXCLUDES *cardio-omentopexy (36.39)*

DEF: Epiplorrhaphy: Suture of abdominal serous membrane.

DEF: Graft of omentum: Implantation of tissue into abdominal serous membrane.

DEF: Omentopexy: Anchoring of abdominal serous membrane.

DEF: Reduction of torsion of omentum: Reduction of twisted abdominal serous membrane.

54.75 Other repair of mesentery
Mesenteric plication
Mesenteropexy

DEF: Creation of folds in mesentery for shortening.

DEF: Mesenteriopexy: Fixation of torn, incised mesentery.

✓4th **54.9 Other operations of abdominal region**

EXCLUDES *removal of ectopic pregnancy (74.3)*

54.91 Percutaneous abdominal drainage
Paracentesis

EXCLUDES *creation of cutaneoperitoneal fistula (54.93)*

DEF: Puncture for removal of fluid.

54.92 Removal of foreign body from peritoneal cavity

54.93 Creation of cutaneoperitoneal fistula

DEF: Creation of opening between skin and peritoneal cavity.

54.94 Creation of peritoneovascular shunt
Peritoneovenous shunt

DEF: Peritoneal vascular shunt: Construction of shunt to connect peritoneal cavity with vascular system.

DEF: Peritoneovenous shunt: Construction of shunt to connect peritoneal cavity with vein.

54.95 Incision of peritoneum
Exploration of ventriculoperitoneal shunt at peritoneal site
Ladd operation
Revision of distal catheter of ventricular shunt
Revision of ventriculoperitoneal shunt at peritoneal site

EXCLUDES *that incidental to laparotomy (54.11-54.19)*

DEF: Ladd operation: Peritoneal attachment of incompletely rotated cecum, obstructing duodenum.

54.96 Injection of air into peritoneal cavity
Pneumoperitoneum

EXCLUDES *that for:*
collapse of lung (33.33)
radiography (88.12-88.13, 88.15)

54.97 Injection of locally-acting therapeutic substance into peritoneal cavity

EXCLUDES *peritoneal dialysis (54.98)*

54.98 Peritoneal dialysis

EXCLUDES *peritoneal lavage (diagnostic) (54.25)*

DEF: Separation of blood elements by diffusion through membrane.

54.99 Other

EXCLUDES *removal of:*
abdominal wall sutures (97.83)
peritoneal drainage device (97.82)
retroperitoneal drainage device (97.81)

10. OPERATIONS ON THE URINARY SYSTEM (55-59)

✓3rd **55 Operations on kidney**

INCLUDES operations on renal pelvis

Code also any application or administration of an adhesion barrier substance (99.77)

EXCLUDES *perirenal tissue (59.00-59.09, 59.21-59.29, 59.91-59.92)*

✓4th **55.0 Nephrotomy and nephrostomy**

EXCLUDES *drainage by:*
anastomosis (55.86)
aspiration (55.92)

55.01 Nephrotomy

Evacuation of renal cyst
Exploration of kidney
Nephrolithotomy

DEF: Nephrotomy: Incision into kidney.

DEF: Evacuation of renal cyst: Draining contents of cyst.

DEF: Exploration of kidney: Exploration through incision.

DEF: Nephrolithotomy: Removal of kidney stone through incision.

55.02 Nephrostomy

55.03 Percutaneous nephrostomy without fragmentation

Nephrostolithotomy, percutaneous (nephroscopic)
Percutaneous removal of kidney stone(s) by:
forceps extraction (nephroscopic)
basket extraction
Pyelostolithotomy, percutaneous (nephroscopic)
With placement of catheter down ureter

EXCLUDES *percutaneous removal by fragmentation (55.04)*
repeat nephroscopic removal during current episode (55.92)

DEF: Insertion of tube through abdominal wall without breaking up stones.

DEF: Nephrostolithotomy: Insertion of tube through the abdominal wall to remove stones.

DEF: Basket extraction: Removal, percutaneous of stone with grasping forceps.

DEF: Pyelostolithotomy: Removal, percutaneous of stones from funnel-shaped portion of kidney.

55.04 Percutaneous nephrostomy with fragmentation

Percutaneous nephrostomy with disruption of kidney stone by ultrasonic energy and extraction (suction) through endoscope
With placement of catheter down ureter
With fluoroscopic guidance

EXCLUDES *repeat fragmentation during current episode (59.95)*

DEF: Insertion of tube through abdominal wall into kidney to break up stones.

✓4th **55.1 Pyelotomy and pyelostomy**

EXCLUDES *drainage by anastomosis (55.86)*
percutaneous pyelostolithotomy (55.03)
removal of calculus without incision (56.0)

55.11 Pyelotomy

Exploration of renal pelvis
Pyelolithotomy

55.12 Pyelostomy

Insertion of drainage tube into renal pelvis

✓4th **55.2 Diagnostic procedures on kidney**

55.21 Nephroscopy

DEF: Endoscopic exam of renal pelvis; retrograde through ureter, percutaneous or open exposure.

55.22 Pyeloscopy

DEF: Fluoroscopic exam of kidney pelvis, calyces and ureters; follows IV or retrograde injection of contrast.

55.23 Closed [percutaneous] [needle] biopsy of kidney

Endoscopic biopsy via existing nephrostomy, nephrotomy, pyelostomy, or pyelotomy

55.24 Open biopsy of kidney

55.29 Other diagnostic procedures on kidney

EXCLUDES *microscopic examination of specimen from kidney (91.21-91.29)*
pyelogram:
intravenous (87.73)
percutaneous (87.75)
retrograde (87.74)
radioisotope scan (92.03)
renal arteriography (88.45)
tomography:
C.A.T scan (87.71)
other (87.72)

✓4th **55.3 Local excision or destruction of lesion or tissue of kidney**

55.31 Marsupialization of kidney lesion

DEF: Exteriorization of lesion by incising anterior wall and suturing cut edges to create open pouch.

55.32 Open ablation of renal lesion or tissue

55.33 Percutaneous ablation of renal lesion or tissue

55.34 Laparoscopic ablation of renal lesion or tissue

55.35 Other and unspecified ablation of renal lesion or tissue

55.39 Other local destruction or excision of renal lesion or tissue

Obliteration of calyceal diverticulum

EXCLUDES *ablation of renal lesion or tissue:*
laparoscopic (55.34)
open (55.32)
other (55.35)
percutaneous (55.33)
biopsy of kidney (55.23-55.24)
partial nephrectomy (55.4)
percutaneous aspiration of kidney (55.92)
wedge resection of kidney (55.4)

55.4 Partial nephrectomy

Calycectomy
Wedge resection of kidney

Code also any synchronous resection of ureter (56.40-56.42)

DEF: Surgical removal of a part of the kidney.

DEF: Calycectomy: Removal of indentations in kidney.

✓4th **55.5 Complete nephrectomy**

Code also any synchronous excision of:
adrenal gland (07.21-07.3)
bladder segment (57.6)
lymph nodes (40.3, 40.52-40.59)

55.51 Nephroureterectomy

Nephroureterectomy with bladder cuff
Total nephrectomy (unilateral)

EXCLUDES *removal of transplanted kidney (55.53)*

DEF: Complete removal of the kidney and all or portion of the ureter.

DEF: Nephroureterectomy with bladder cuff: Removal of kidney, ureter, and portion of bladder attached to ureter.

DEF: Total nephrectomy (unilateral): Complete excision of one kidney.

55.52 Nephrectomy of remaining kidney
Removal of solitary kidney
EXCLUDES *removal of transplanted kidney (55.53)*

55.53 Removal of transplanted or rejected kidney

55.54 Bilateral nephrectomy
EXCLUDES *complete nephrectomy NOS (55.51)*
DEF: Removal of both kidneys same operative session.

✓4th **55.6 Transplant of kidney**
Note: To report donor source – see codes 00.91-00.93

55.61 Renal autotransplantation

55.69 Other kidney transplantation

55.7 Nephropexy
Fixation or suspension of movable [floating] kidney

✓4th **55.8 Other repair of kidney**

55.81 Suture of laceration of kidney

55.82 Closure of nephrostomy and pyelostomy
DEF: Removal of tube from kidney and closure of site of tube insertion.

55.83 Closure of other fistula of kidney

55.84 Reduction of torsion of renal pedicle
DEF: Restoration of twisted renal pedicle into normal position.

55.85 Symphysiotomy for horseshoe kidney
DEF: Division of congenitally malformed kidney into two parts.

55.86 Anastomosis of kidney
Nephropyeloureterostomy
Pyeloureterovesical anastomosis
Ureterocalyceal anastomosis
EXCLUDES *nephrocystanastomosis NOS (56.73)*
DEF: Nephropyeloureterostomy: Creation of passage between kidney and ureter.
DEF: Pyeloureterovesical anastomosis: Creation of passage between kidney and bladder.
DEF: Ureterocalyceal anastomosis: Creation of passage between ureter and kidney indentations.

55.87 Correction of ureteropelvic junction

55.89 Other

✓4th **55.9 Other operations on kidney**
EXCLUDES *lysis of perirenal adhesions (59.02)*

55.91 Decapsulation of kidney
Capsulectomy } of kidney
Decortication } of kidney

Symphysiostomy for Horseshoe Kidney

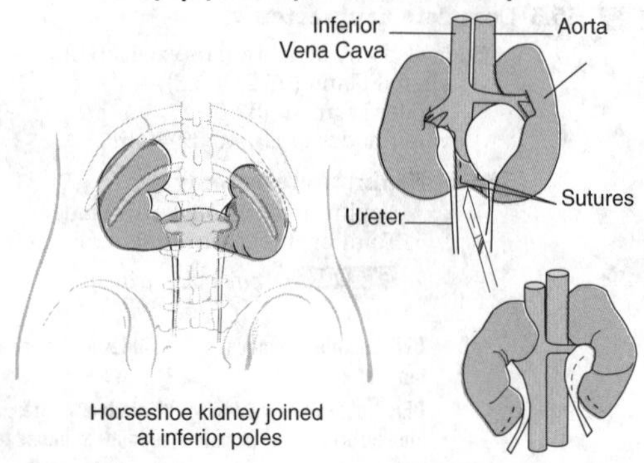

55.92 Percutaneous aspiration of kidney (pelvis)
Aspiration of renal cyst
Renipuncture
EXCLUDES *percutaneous biopsy of kidney (55.23)*
DEF: Insertion of needle into kidney to withdraw fluid.

55.93 Replacement of nephrostomy tube

55.94 Replacement of pyelostomy tube

55.95 Local perfusion of kidney
DEF: Fluid passage through kidney.

55.96 Other injection of therapeutic substance into kidney
Injection into renal cyst

55.97 Implantation or replacement of mechanical kidney

55.98 Removal of mechanical kidney

55.99 Other
EXCLUDES *removal of pyelostomy or nephrostomy tube (97.61)*

✓3rd **56 Operations on ureter**
Code also any application or administration of an adhesion barrier substance (99.77)

56.0 Transurethral removal of obstruction from ureter and renal pelvis
Removal of:
blood clot } from ureter or renal pelvis without incision
calculus } from ureter or renal pelvis without incision
foreign body } from ureter or renal pelvis without incision
EXCLUDES *manipulation without removal of obstruction (59.8)*
that by incision (55.11,56.2)
transurethral insertion of ureteral stent for passage of calculus (59.8)
DEF: Removal of obstruction by tube inserted through urethra to ureter.

56.1 Ureteral meatotomy
DEF: Incision into ureteral meatus to enlarge passage.

56.2 Ureterotomy
Incision of ureter for:
drainage
exploration
removal of calculus
EXCLUDES *cutting of ureterovesical orifice (56.1)*
removal of calculus without incision (56.0)
transurethral insertion of ureteral stent for passage of calculus (59.8)
urinary diversion (56.51-56.79)

✓4th **56.3 Diagnostic procedures on ureter**

56.31 Ureteroscopy

56.32 Closed percutaneous biopsy of ureter
EXCLUDES *endoscopic biopsy of ureter (56.33)*

56.33 Closed endoscopic biopsy of ureter
Cystourethroscopy with ureteral biopsy
Transurethral biopsy of ureter
Ureteral endoscopy with biopsy through ureterotomy
Ureteroscopy with biopsy
EXCLUDES *percutaneous biopsy of ureter (56.32)*

56.34 Open biopsy of ureter

56.35 Endoscopy (cystoscopy) (looposcopy) of ileal conduit
DEF: Endoscopic exam of created opening between ureters and one end of small intestine; other end used to form artificial opening.

56.39 Other diagnostic procedures on ureter

EXCLUDES *microscopic examination of specimen from ureter (91.21-91.29)*

√4th **56.4 Ureterectomy**

Code also anastomosis other than end-to-end (56.51-56.79)

EXCLUDES *fistulectomy (56.84)*
nephroureterectomy (55.51-55.54)

56.40 Ureterectomy, not otherwise specified

56.41 Partial ureterotomy

Excision of lesion of ureter
Shortening of ureter with reimplantation

EXCLUDES *biopsy of ureter (56.32-56.34)*

56.42 Total ureterectomy

√4th **56.5 Cutaneous uretero-ileostomy**

56.51 Formation of cutaneous uretero-ileostomy

Construction of ileal conduit
External ureteral ileostomy
Formation of open ileal bladder
Ileal loop operation
Ileoureterostomy (Bricker's) (ileal bladder)
Transplantation of ureter into ileum with external diversion

EXCLUDES *closed ileal bladder (57.87)*
replacement of ureteral defect by ileal segment (56.89)

DEF: Creation of urinary passage by connecting the terminal end of small intestine to ureter then connected to opening through abdominal wall.

DEF: Construction of ileal conduit: Formation of conduit from terminal end of small intestine.

56.52 Revision of cutaneous uretero-ileostomy

√4th **56.6 Other external urinary diversion**

56.61 Formation of other cutaneous ureterostomy

Anastomosis of ureter to skin
Ureterostomy NOS

56.62 Revision of other cutaneous ureterostomy

Revision of ureterostomy stoma

EXCLUDES *nonoperative removal of ureterostomy tube (97.62)*

√4th **56.7 Other anastomosis or bypass of ureter**

EXCLUDES *ureteropyelostomy (55.86)*

56.71 Urinary diversion to intestine

Anastomosis of ureter to intestine
Internal urinary diversion NOS

Code also any synchronous colostomy (46.10-46.13)

EXCLUDES *external ureteral ileostomy (56.51)*

56.72 Revision of ureterointestinal anastomosis

EXCLUDES *revision of external ureteral ileostomy (56.52)*

56.73 Nephrocystanastomosis, not otherwise specified

DEF: Connection of kidney to bladder.

56.74 Ureteroneocystostomy

Replacement of ureter with bladder flap
Ureterovesical anastomosis

DEF: Transfer of ureter to another site in bladder.

DEF: Ureterovesical anastomosis: Implantation of ureter into bladder.

56.75 Transureteroureterostomy

EXCLUDES *ureteroureterostomy associated with partial resection (56.41)*

DEF: Separating one ureter and joining the ends to the opposite ureter.

56.79 Other

√4th **56.8 Repair of ureter**

56.81 Lysis of intraluminal adhesions of ureter

EXCLUDES *lysis of periureteral adhesions (59.02-59.03)*
ureterolysis (59.02-59.03)

DEF: Destruction of adhesions within urethral cavity.

56.82 Suture of laceration of ureter

56.83 Closure of ureterostomy

56.84 Closure of other fistula of ureter

56.85 Ureteropexy

56.86 Removal of ligature from ureter

56.89 Other repair of ureter

Graft of ureter
Replacement of ureter with ileal segment implanted into bladder
Ureteroplication

DEF: Graft of ureter: Tissue from another site for graft replacement or repair of ureter.

DEF: Replacement of ureter with ileal segment implanted into bladder and ureter replacement with terminal end of small intestine.

DEF: Ureteroplication: Creation of tucks in ureter.

√4th **56.9 Other operations on ureter**

56.91 Dilation of ureteral meatus

56.92 Implantation of electronic ureteral stimulator

56.93 Replacement of electronic ureteral stimulator

56.94 Removal of electronic ureteral stimulator

EXCLUDES *that with synchronous replacement (56.93)*

56.95 Ligation of ureter

56.99 Other

EXCLUDES *removal of ureterostomy tube and ureteral catheter (97.62)*
ureteral catheterization (59.8)

√3rd **57 Operations on urinary bladder**

Code also any application or administration of an adhesion barrier substance (99.77)

EXCLUDES *perivesical tissue (59.11-59.29, 59.91-59.92)*
ureterovesical orifice (56.0-56.99)

57.0 Transurethral clearance of bladder

Drainage of bladder without incision
Removal of:
blood clot, calculus, foreign body } from bladder without incision

EXCLUDES *that by incision (57.19)*

DEF: Insertion of device through urethra to cleanse bladder.

√4th **57.1 Cystotomy and cystostomy**

EXCLUDES *cystotomy and cystostomy as operative approach — omit code*

DEF: Cystotomy: Incision of bladder.

DEF: Cystostomy: Creation of opening into bladder.

57.11 Percutaneous aspiration of bladder

Operations on the Urinary System

56.39–57.11

Transurethral Cystourethroscopy

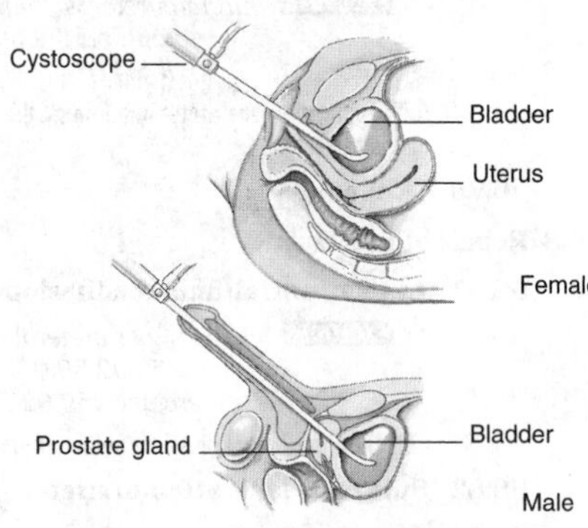

57.12 Lysis of intraluminal adhesions with incision into bladder

EXCLUDES *transurethral lysis of intraluminal adhesions (57.41)*

DEF: Incision into bladder to destroy lesions.

57.17 Percutaneous cystostomy

Closed cystostomy
Percutaneous suprapubic cystostomy

EXCLUDES *removal of cystostomy tube (97.63)*
replacement of cystostomy tube (59.94)

DEF: Incision through body wall into bladder to insert tube.

DEF: Percutaneous (closed) suprapubic cystostomy: Incision above pubic arch, through body wall, into the bladder to insert tube.

57.18 Other suprapubic cystostomy

EXCLUDES *percutaneous cystostomy (57.17)*
removal of cystostomy tube (97.63)
replacement of cystostomy tube (59.94)

57.19 Other cystotomy

Cystolithotomy

EXCLUDES *percutaneous cystostomy (57.17)*
suprapubic cystostomy (57.18)

✓4th **57.2 Vesicostomy**

EXCLUDES *percutaneous cystostomy (57.17)*
suprapubic cystostomy (57.18)

57.21 Vesicostomy

Creation of permanent opening from bladder to skin using a bladder flap

DEF: Creation of permanent opening from the bladder to the skin.

57.22 Revision or closure of vesicostomy

EXCLUDES *closure of cystostomy (57.82)*

✓4th **57.3 Diagnostic procedures on bladder**

57.31 Cystoscopy through artificial stoma

57.32 Other cystoscopy

Transurethral cystoscopy

EXCLUDES *cystourethroscopy with ureteral biopsy (56.33)*
retrograde pyelogram (87.74)
that for control of hemorrhage (postoperative):
bladder (57.93)
prostate (60.94)

57.33 Closed [transurethral] biopsy of bladder

57.34 Open biopsy of bladder

57.39 Other diagnostic procedures on bladder

EXCLUDES *cystogram NEC (87.77)*
microscopic examination of specimen from bladder (91.31-91.39)
retrograde cystourethrogram (87.76)
therapeutic distention of bladder (96.25)

✓4th **57.4 Transurethral excision or destruction of bladder tissue**

DEF: Destruction of bladder tissue with instrument inserted into urethra.

57.41 Transurethral lysis of intraluminal adhesions

57.49 Other transurethral excision or destruction of lesion or tissue of bladder

Endoscopic resection of bladder lesion

EXCLUDES *transurethral biopsy of bladder (57.33)*
transurethral fistulectomy (57.83-57.84)

✓4th **57.5 Other excision or destruction of bladder tissue**

EXCLUDES *that with transurethral approach (57.41-57.49)*

57.51 Excision of urachus

Excision of urachal sinus of bladder

EXCLUDES *excision of urachal cyst of abdominal wall (54.3)*

57.59 Open excision or destruction of other lesion or tissue of bladder

Endometrectomy of bladder
Suprapubic excision of bladder lesion

EXCLUDES *biopsy of bladder (57.33-57.34)*
fistulectomy of bladder (57.83-57.84)

DEF: Endometrectomy of bladder: Removal of inner lining.

DEF: Suprapubic excision of bladder lesion: Removal of lesion by excision above suprapubic bone arch.

57.6 Partial cystectomy

Excision of bladder dome
Trigonectomy
Wedge resection of bladder

✓4th **57.7 Total cystectomy**

INCLUDES total cystectomy with urethrectomy

57.71 Radical cystectomy

Pelvic exenteration in male
Removal of bladder, prostate, seminal vesicles and fat
Removal of bladder, urethra, and fat in a female
Code also any:
lymph node dissection (40.3, 40.5)
urinary diversion (56.51-56.79)

EXCLUDES *that as part of pelvic exenteration in female (68.8)*

DEF: Radical cystectomy: Removal of bladder and surrounding tissue.

DEF: Pelvic exenteration in male: Excision of bladder, prostate, seminal vessels and fat.

57.79 Other total cystectomy

✓4th **57.8 Other repair of urinary bladder**

EXCLUDES *repair of:*
current obstetric laceration (75.61)
cystocele (70.50-70.51)
that for stress incontinence (59.3-59.79)

57.81 Suture of laceration of bladder

57.82 Closure of cystostomy

57.83 Repair of fistula involving bladder and intestine

Rectovesicovaginal } fistulectomy
Vesicosigmoidovaginal } fistulectomy

57.84 Repair of other fistula of bladder

Cervicovesical } fistulectomy
Urethroperineovesical } fistulectomy
Uterovesical } fistulectomy
Vaginovesical } fistulectomy

EXCLUDES *vesicoureterovaginal fistulectomy (56.84)*

57.85 Cystourethroplasty and plastic repair of bladder neck

Plication of sphincter of urinary bladder
V-Y plasty of bladder neck

DEF: Cystourethroplasty: Reconstruction of narrowed portion of bladder.

DEF: Plication of sphincter or urinary bladder: Creation of tuck in bladder sphincter.

DEF: V-Y plasty of bladder neck: Surgical reconstruction of the narrowed portion of bladder by V-Y technique.

57.86 Repair of bladder exstrophy

DEF: Surgical correction of a congenital bladder wall defect.

57.87 Reconstruction of urinary bladder

Anastomosis of bladder with isolated segment of ileum
Augmentation of bladder
Replacement of bladder with ileum or sigmoid [closed ileal bladder]

Code also resection of intestine (45.50-45.52)

DEF: Anastomosis of bladder with isolated segment of ileum: Creation of connection between bladder and separated terminal end of small intestine.

57.88 Other anastomosis of bladder

Anastomosis of bladder to intestine NOS
Cystocolic anastomosis

EXCLUDES *formation of closed ileal bladder (57.87)*

57.89 Other repair of bladder

Bladder suspension, not elsewhere classified
Cystopexy NOS
Repair of old obstetric laceration of bladder

EXCLUDES *repair of current obstetric laceration (75.61)*

✓4th **57.9 Other operations on bladder**

57.91 Sphincterotomy of bladder

Division of bladder neck

57.92 Dilation of bladder neck

57.93 Control of (postoperative) hemorrhage of bladder

57.94 Insertion of indwelling urinary catheter

57.95 Replacement of indwelling urinary catheter

57.96 Implantation of electronic bladder stimulator

57.97 Replacement of electronic bladder stimulator

57.98 Removal of electronic bladder stimulator

EXCLUDES *that with synchronous replacement (57.97)*

57.99 Other

EXCLUDES *irrigation of:*
cystostomy (96.47)
other indwelling urinary catheter (96.48)
lysis of external adhesions (59.11)
removal of:
cystostomy tube (97.63)
other urinary drainage device (97.64)
therapeutic distention of bladder (96.25)

✓3rd **58 Operations on urethra**

INCLUDES operations on:
bulbourethral gland [Cowper's gland]
periurethral tissue

Code also any application or administration of an adhesion barrier substance (99.77)

58.0 Urethrotomy

Excision of urethral septum
Formation of urethrovaginal fistula
Perineal urethrostomy
Removal of calculus from urethra by incision

EXCLUDES *drainage of bulbourethral gland or periurethral tissue (58.91)*
internal urethral meatotomy (58.5)
removal of urethral calculus without incision (58.6)

58.1 Urethral meatotomy

EXCLUDES *internal urethral meatotomy (58.5)*

DEF: Incision of urethra to enlarge passage.

✓4th **58.2 Diagnostic procedures on urethra**

58.21 Perineal urethroscopy

58.22 Other urethroscopy

58.23 Biopsy of urethra

58.24 Biopsy of periurethral tissue

DEF: Removal for biopsy of tissue around urethra.

58.29 Other diagnostic procedures on urethra and periurethral tissue

EXCLUDES *microscopic examination of specimen from urethra (91.31-91.39)*
retrograde cystourethrogram (87.76)
urethral pressure profile (89.25)
urethral sphincter electromyogram (89.23)

✓4th **58.3 Excision or destruction of lesion or tissue of urethra**

EXCLUDES *biopsy of urethra (58.23)*
excision of bulbourethral gland (58.92)
fistulectomy (58.43)
urethrectomy as part of:
complete cystectomy (57.79)
pelvic evisceration (68.8)
radical cystectomy (57.71)

58.31 Endoscopic excision or destruction of lesion or tissue of urethra

Fulguration of urethral lesion

58.39 Other local excision or destruction of lesion or tissue of urethra

Excision of:
congenital valve } of urethra
lesion } of urethra
stricture } of urethra

Urethrectomy

EXCLUDES *that by endoscopic appoach (58.31)*

✓4th **58.4 Repair of urethra**

EXCLUDES *repair of current obstetric laceration (75.61)*

58.41 Suture of laceration of urethra

58.42 Closure of urethrostomy

58.43 Closure of other fistula of urethra

EXCLUDES *repair of urethroperineovesical fistula (57.84)*

58.44 Reanastomosis of urethra

Anastomosis of urethra

DEF: Repair of severed urethra.

58.45 Repair of hypospadias or epispadias

DEF: Repair of abnormal urethral opening.

58.46 Other reconstruction of urethra

Urethral construction

58.47 Urethral meatoplasty

DEF: Reconstruction of urethral opening.

58.49 Other repair of urethra

Benenenti rotation of bulbous urethra
Repair of old obstetric laceration of urethra
Urethral plication

EXCLUDES *repair of:*
current obstetric laceration (75.61)
urethrocele (70.50-70.51)

58.5 Release of urethral stricture

Cutting of urethral sphincter
Internal urethral meatotomy
Urethrolysis

58.6 Dilation of urethra

Dilation of urethrovesical junction
Passage of sounds through urethra
Removal of calculus from urethra without incision

EXCLUDES *urethral calibration (89.29)*

✓4th **58.9 Other operations on urethra and periurethral tissue**

58.91 Incision of periurethral tissue

Drainage of bulbourethral gland

DEF: Incision of tissue around urethra.

58.92 Excision of periurethral tissue

EXCLUDES *biopsy of periurethral tissue (58.24)*
lysis of periurethral adhesions (59.11-59.12)

58.93 Implantation of artificial urinary sphincter [AUS]

Placement of inflatable:
urethral sphincter
bladder sphincter
Removal with replacement of sphincter device [AUS]
With pump and/or reservoir

58.99 Other

Repair of inflatable sphincter pump and/or reservoir
Surgical correction of hydraulic pressure of inflatable sphincter device
Removal of inflatable urinary sphincter without replacement

EXCLUDES *removal of:*
intraluminal foreign body from urethra without incision (98.19)
urethral stent (97.65)

✓3rd **59 Other operations on urinary tract**

Code also any application or administration of an adhesion barrier substance (99.77)

✓4th **59.0 Dissection of retroperitoneal tissue**

59.00 Retroperitoneal dissection, not otherwise specified

59.02 Other lysis of perirenal or periureteral adhesions

EXCLUDES *that by laparoscope (59.03)*

59.03 Laparoscopic lysis of perirenal or periureteral adhesions

59.09 Other incision of perirenal or periureteral tissue

Exploration of perinephric area
Incision of perirenal abscess

DEF: Exploration of the perinephric area: Exam of tissue around the kidney by incision.

DEF: Incision of perirenal abscess: Incising abscess in tissue around kidney.

✓4th **59.1 Incision of perivesical tissue**

DEF: Incising tissue around bladder.

59.11 Other lysis of perivesical adhesions

59.12 Laparoscopic lysis of perivesical adhesions]

59.19 Other incision of perivesical tissue

Exploration of perivesical tissue
Incision of hematoma of space of Retzius
Retropubic exploration

✓4th **59.2 Diagnostic procedures on perirenal and perivesical tissue**

59.21 Biopsy of perirenal or perivesical tissue

59.29 Other diagnostic procedures on perirenal tissue, perivesical tissue, and retroperitoneum

EXCLUDES *microscopic examination of specimen from:*
perirenal tissue (91.21-91.29)
perivesical tissue (91.31-91.39)
retroperitoneum NEC (91.11-91.19)
retroperitoneal x-ray (88.14-88.16)

59.3 Plication of urethrovesical junction

Kelly-Kennedy operation on urethra
Kelly-Stoeckel urethral plication

DEF: Suturing a tuck in tissues around urethra at junction with bladder; changes angle of junction and provides support.

59.4 Suprapubic sling operation

Goebel-Frangenheim-Stoeckel urethrovesical suspension
Millin-Read urethrovesical suspension
Oxford operation for urinary incontinence
Urethrocystopexy by suprapubic suspension

DEF: Suspension of urethra from suprapubic periosteum to restore support to bladder and urethra.

59.5 Retropubic urethral suspension

Burch procedure
Marshall-Marchetti-Krantz operation
Suture of periurethral tissue to symphysis pubis
Urethral suspension NOS

DEF: Suspension of urethra from pubic bone with suture placed from symphysis pubis to paraurethral tissues; elevates urethrovesical angle, restores urinary continence.

59.6 Paraurethral suspension
Pereyra paraurethral suspension
Periurethral suspension

DEF: Suspension of bladder neck from fibrous membranes of anterior abdominal wall; upward traction applied; changes angle of urethra, improves urinary control.

✓4th **59.7 Other repair of urinary stress incontinence**

59.71 Levator muscle operation for urethrovesical suspension
Cystourethropexy with levator muscle sling
Gracilis muscle transplant for urethrovesical suspension
Pubococcygeal sling

59.72 Injection of implant into urethra and/or bladder neck
Collagen implant
Endoscopic injection of implant
Fat implant
Polytef implant

DEF: Injection of collagen into submucosal tissues to increase tissue bulk and improve urinary control.

59.79 Other
Anterior urethropexy
Repair of stress incontinence NOS
Tudor "rabbit ear" urethropexy

DEF: Pubovaginal sling for treatment of stress incontinence: A strip of fascia is harvested and the vaginal epithelium is mobilized and then sutured to the midline at the urethral level to the rectus muscle to create a sling supporting the bladder.

DEF: Vaginal wall sling with bone anchors for treatment of stress incontinence: A sling for the bladder is formed by a suture attachment of vaginal wall to the abdominal wall. In addition, a suture is run from the vagina to a bone anchor placed in the pubic bone.

DEF: Transvaginal endoscopic bladder neck suspension for treatment of stress incontinence: Endoscopic surgical suturing of the vaginal epithelium and the pubocervical fascia at the bladder neck level on both sides of the urethra. Two supporting sutures are run from the vagina to an anchor placed in the pubic bone on each side.

59.8 Ureteral catheterization
Drainage of kidney by catheter
Insertion of ureteral stent
Ureterovesical orifice dilation

Code also any ureterotomy (56.2)

EXCLUDES *that for:*
retrograde pyelogram (87.74)
transurethral removal of calculus or clot from ureter and renal pelvis (56.0)

✓4th **59.9 Other operations on urinary system**

EXCLUDES *nonoperative removal of therapeutic device (97.61-97.69)*

59.91 Excision of perirenal or perivesical tissue

EXCLUDES *biopsy of perirenal or perivesical tissue (59.21)*

59.92 Other operations on perirenal or perivesical tissue

59.93 Replacement of ureterostomy tube
Change of ureterostomy tube
Reinsertion of ureterostomy tube

EXCLUDES *nonoperative removal of ureterostomy tube (97.62)*

59.94 Replacement of cystostomy tube

EXCLUDES *nonoperative removal of cystostomy tube (97.63)*

59.95 Ultrasonic fragmentation of urinary stones
Shattered urinary stones

EXCLUDES *percutaneous nephrostomy with fragmentation (55.04)*
shockwave disintegration (98.51)

59.99 Other

EXCLUDES *instillation of medication into urinary tract (96.49)*
irrigation of urinary tract (96.45-96.48)

11. OPERATIONS ON THE MALE GENITAL ORGANS (60-64)

✓3rd **60 Operations on prostate and seminal vesicles**

INCLUDES operations on periprostatic tissue

Code also any application or administration of an adhesion barrier substance (99.77)

EXCLUDES *that associated with radical cystectomy (57.71)*

60.0 Incision of prostate

Drainage of prostatic abscess
Prostatolithotomy

EXCLUDES *drainage of periprostatic tissue only (60.81)*

✓4th **60.1 Diagnostic procedures on prostate and seminal vesicles**

60.11 Closed [percutaneous] [needle] biopsy of prostate

Approach:
transrectal
transurethral
Punch biopsy

DEF: Excision of prostate tissue by closed technique for biopsy.

60.12 Open biopsy of prostate

60.13 Closed [percutaneous] biopsy of seminal vesicles

Needle biopsy of seminal vesicles

60.14 Open biopsy of seminal vesicles

60.15 Biopsy of periprostatic tissue

60.18 Other diagnostic procedures on prostate and periprostatic tissue

EXCLUDES *microscopic examination of specimen from prostate (91.31-91.39)*
x-ray of prostate (87.92)

60.19 Other diagnostic procedures on seminal vesicles

EXCLUDES *microscopic examination of specimen from seminal vesicles (91.31-91.39)*
x-ray:
contrast seminal vesiculogram (87.91)
other (87.92)

✓4th **60.2 Transurethral prostatectomy**

EXCLUDES *local excision of lesion of prostate (60.61)*

60.21 Transurethral (ultrasound) guided laser induced prostatectomy (TULIP)

Ablation (contact) (noncontact) by laser

60.29 Other transurethral prostatectomy

Excision of median bar by transurethral approach
Transurethral electrovaporization of prostate (TEVAP)
Transurethral enucleative procedure
Transurethral prostatectomy NOS
Transurethral resection of prostate (TURP)

DEF: Excision of median bar by transurethral approach: Removal of fibrous structure of prostate.

DEF: Transurethral enucleative procedure: Transurethral prostatectomy.

Transurethral Prostatectomy

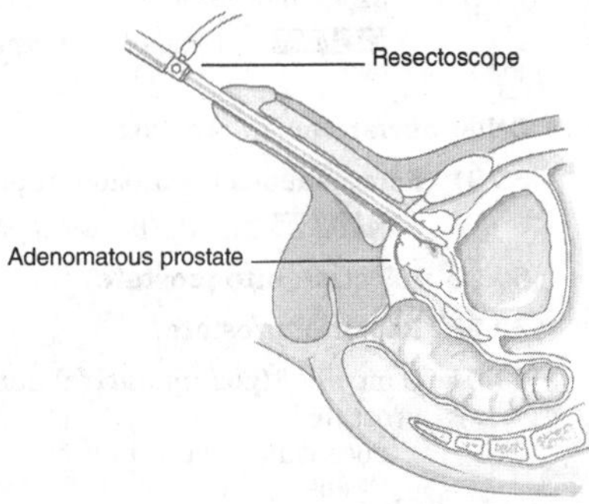

60.3 Suprapubic prostatectomy

Transvesical prostatectomy

EXCLUDES *local excision of lesion of prostate (60.61)*
radical prostatectomy (60.5)

DEF: Resection of prostate through incision in abdomen above pubic arch.

60.4 Retropubic prostatectomy

EXCLUDES *local excision of lesion of prostate (60.61)*
radical prostatectomy (60.5)

DEF: Removal of the prostate using an abdominal approach with direct cutting into prostatic capsule.

60.5 Radical prostatectomy

Prostatovesiculectomy
Radical prostatectomy by any approach

EXCLUDES *cystoprostatectomy (57.71)*

DEF: Removal of prostate, epididymis and vas ampullae.

DEF: Prostatovesiculectomy: Removal of prostate and epididymis.

✓4th **60.6 Other prostatectomy**

60.61 Local excision of lesion of prostate

Excision of prostatic lesion by any approach

EXCLUDES *biopsy of prostate (60.11-60.12)*

60.62 Perineal prostatectomy

Cryoablation of prostate
Cryoprostatectomy
Cryosurgery of prostate
Radical cryosurcial ablation of prostate (RCSA)

EXCLUDES *local excision of lesion of prostate (60.61)*

DEF: Excision of prostate tissue through incision between scrotum and anus.

60.69 Other

✓4th **60.7 Operations on seminal vesicles**

60.71 Percutaneous aspiration of seminal vesicle

EXCLUDES *needle biopsy of seminal vesicle (60.13)*

60.72 Incision of seminal vesicle

60.73 Excision of seminal vesicle

Excision of Müllerian duct cyst
Spermatocystectomy

EXCLUDES *biopsy of seminal vesicle (60.13-60.14)*
prostatovesiculectomy (60.5)

60.79 Other operations on seminal vesicles

✓4th **60.8 Incision or excision of periprostatic tissue**

60.81 Incision of periprostatic tissue

Drainage of periprostatic abscess

60.82 Excision of periprostatic tissue
Excision of lesion of periprostatic tissue
EXCLUDES *biopsy of periprostatic tissue (60.15)*

✓4th **60.9 Other operations on prostate**

60.91 Percutaneous aspiration of prostate
EXCLUDES *needle biopsy of prostate (60.11)*

60.92 Injection into prostate

60.93 Repair of prostate

60.94 Control of (postoperative) hemorrhage of prostate
Coagulation of prostatic bed
Cystoscopy for control of prostatic hemorrhage

60.95 Transurethral balloon dilation of the prostatic urethra
DEF: Insertion and inflation of balloon to stretch prostate passage.

60.96 Transurethral destruction of prostate tissue by microwave thermotherapy
Transurethral microwave thermotherapy (TUMT) of prostate
EXCLUDES *Prostatectomy:*
other (60.61-60.69)
radical (60.5)
retropubic (60.4)
suprapubic (60.3)
transurethral (60.21-60.29)

60.97 Other transurethral destruction of prostate tissue by other thermotherapy
Radiofrequency thermotherapy
Transurethral needle ablation (TUNA) of prostate
EXCLUDES *Prostatectomy:*
other (60.61-60.69)
radical (60.5)
retropubic (60.4)
suprapubic (60.3)
transurethral (60.21-60.29)

60.99 Other
EXCLUDES *prostatic massage (99.94)*

✓3rd **61 Operations on scrotum and tunica vaginalis**

61.0 Incision and drainage of scrotum and tunica vaginalis
EXCLUDES *percutaneous aspiration of hydrocele (61.91)*

✓4th **61.1 Diagnostic procedures on scrotum and tunica vaginalis**

61.11 Biopsy of scrotum or tunica vaginalis

61.19 Other diagnostic procedures on scrotum and tunica vaginalis

61.2 Excision of hydrocele (of tunica vaginalis)
Bottle repair of hydrocele of tunica vaginalis
EXCLUDES *percutaneous aspiration of hydrocele (61.91)*
DEF: Removal of fluid collected in serous membrane of testes.

Hydrocelectomy

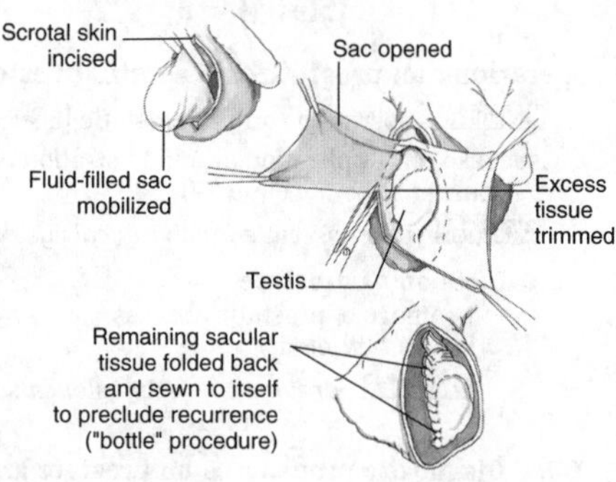

61.3 Excision or destruction of lesion or tissue of scrotum
Fulguration of lesion } of scrotum
Reduction of elephantiasis } of scrotum
Partial scrotectomy } of scrotum
EXCLUDES *biopsy of scrotum (61.11)*
scrotal fistulectomy (61.42)

✓4th **61.4 Repair of scrotum and tunica vaginalis**

61.41 Suture of laceration of scrotum and tunica vaginalis

61.42 Repair of scrotal fistula

61.49 Other repair of scrotum and tunica vaginalis
Reconstruction with rotational or pedicle flaps

✓4th **61.9 Other operations on scrotum and tunica vaginalis**

61.91 Percutaneous aspiration of tunica vaginalis
Aspiration of hydrocele of tunica vaginalis

61.92 Excision of lesion of tunica vaginalis other than hydrocele
Excision of hematocele of tunica vaginalis
DEF: Removal of blood collected in tunica vaginalis.

61.99 Other
EXCLUDES *removal of foreign body from scrotum without incision (98.24)*

✓3rd **62 Operations on testes**

62.0 Incision of testis

✓4th **62.1 Diagnostic procedures on testes**

62.11 Closed [percutaneous] [needle] biopsy of testis

62.12 Open biopsy of testis

62.19 Other diagnostic procedures on testes

62.2 Excision or destruction of testicular lesion
Excision of appendix testis
Excision of cyst of Morgagni in the male
Excision of hydatid of Morgagni in the male
EXCLUDES *biopsy of testis (62.11-62.12)*

62.3 Unilateral orchiectomy
Orchidectomy (with epididymectomy) NOS

Orchiopexy with Detorsion of Testes

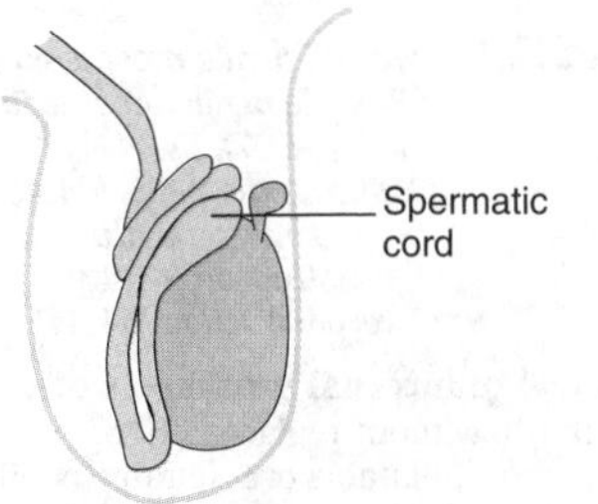

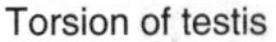

Torsion of testis

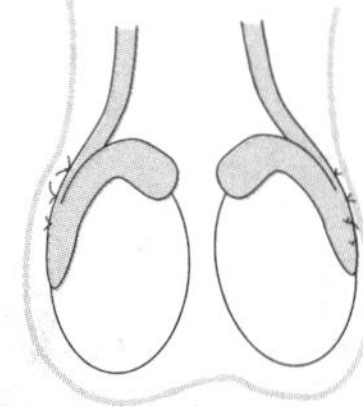

Testes after correction showing bilateral fixation

✓4th 62.4 Bilateral orchiectomy

Male castration
Radical bilateral orchiectomy (with epididymectomy)
Code also any synchronous lymph node dissection (40.3, 40.5)

DEF: Removal of both testes.

DEF: Radical bilateral orchiectomy (with epididymectomy): Excision of both testes and structures that store sperm.

62.41 Removal of both testes at same operative episode

Bilateral orchidectomy NOS

62.42 Removal of remaining testis

Removal of solitary testis

62.5 Orchiopexy

Mobilization and replacement of testis in scrotum
Orchiopexy with detorsion of testis
Torek (-Bevan) operation (orchidopexy) (first stage) (second stage)
Transplantation to and fixation of testis in scrotum

DEF: Fixation of testis in scrotum.

DEF: Orchiopexy with detorsion of testis: Fixation and placement of testis in scrotum after correcting angle.

DEF: Torek operation (first stage) (second stage): Transfer of congenitally undescended testis from inguinal canal to scrotum.

DEF: Transplantation to and fixation of testis in scrotum: Transfer of displaced testis to scrotum.

✓4th 62.6 Repair of testes

EXCLUDES *reduction of torsion (63.52)*

62.61 Suture of laceration of testis

62.69 Other repair of testis

Testicular graft

62.7 Insertion of testicular prosthesis

✓4th 62.9 Other operations on testes

62.91 Aspiration of testis

EXCLUDES *percutaneous biopsy of testis (62.11)*

62.92 Injection of therapeutic substance into testis

62.99 Other

✓3rd 63 Operations on spermatic cord, epididymis, and vas deferens

✓4th 63.0 Diagnostic procedures on spermatic cord, epididymis, and vas deferens

63.01 Biopsy of spermatic cord, epididymis, or vas deferens

Varicocelectomy

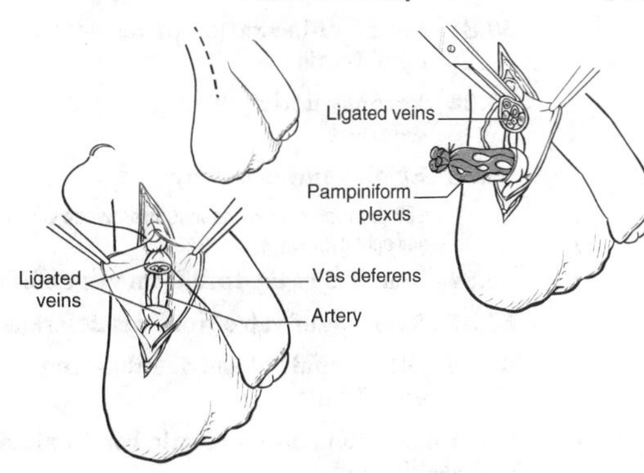

63.09 Other diagnostic procedures on spermatic cord, epididymis, and vas deferens

EXCLUDES *contrast epididymogram (87.93)*
contrast vasogram (87.94)
other x-ray of epididymis and vas deferens (87.95)

63.1 Excision of varicocele and hydrocele of spermatic cord

High ligation of spermatic vein
Hydrocelectomy of canal of Nuck

DEF: Removal of a swollen vein and collected fluid from spermatic cord.

DEF: High ligation of spermatic vein: Tying off of spermatic vein.

DEF: Hydrocelectomy of canal of Nuck: Removal of fluid collected from serous membrane of inguinal canal.

63.2 Excision of cyst of epididymis

Spermatocelectomy

63.3 Excision of other lesion or tissue of spermatic cord and epididymis

Excision of appendix epididymis

EXCLUDES *biopsy of spermatic cord or epididymis (63.01)*

63.4 Epididymectomy

EXCLUDES *that synchronous with orchiectomy (62.3-62.42)*

✓4th 63.5 Repair of spermatic cord and epididymis

63.51 Suture of laceration of spermatic cord and epididymis

63.52 Reduction of torsion of testis or spermatic cord

EXCLUDES *that associated with orchiopexy (62.5)*

DEF: Correction of twisted testicle or spermatic cord.

63.53 Transplantation of spermatic cord

63.59 Other repair of spermatic cord and epididymis

63.6 Vasotomy

Vasostomy

DEF: Vasotomy: Incision of ducts carrying sperm from testicles.

DEF: Vasostomy: Creation of an opening into duct.

✓4th 63.7 Vasectomy and ligation of vas deferens

63.70 Male sterilization procedure, not otherwise specified

63.71 Ligation of vas deferens

Crushing of vas deferens
Division of vas deferens

63.72 Ligation of spermatic cord

63.73 Vasectomy

✓4th **63.8 Repair of vas deferens and epididymis**

63.81 Suture of laceration of vas deferens and epididymis

63.82 Reconstruction of surgically divided vas deferens

63.83 Epididymovasostomy

DEF: Creation of new connection between vas deferens and epididymis.

63.84 Removal of ligature from vas deferens

63.85 Removal of valve from vas deferens

63.89 Other repair of vas deferens and epididymis

✓4th **63.9 Other operations on spermatic cord, epididymis, and vas deferens**

63.91 Aspiration of spermatocele

DEF: Puncture of cystic distention of epididymis.

63.92 Epididymotomy

DEF: Incision of epididymis.

63.93 Incision of spermatic cord

DEF: Incision into sperm storage structure.

63.94 Lysis of adhesions of spermatic cord

63.95 Insertion of valve in vas deferens

63.99 Other

64 Operations on penis

INCLUDES operations on:
corpora cavernosa
glans penis
prepuce

64.0 Circumcision

DEF: Removal of penis foreskin.

✓4th **64.1 Diagnostic procedures on the penis**

64.11 Biopsy of penis

64.19 Other diagnostic procedures on penis

64.2 Local excision or destruction of lesion of penis

EXCLUDES *biopsy of penis (64.11)*

64.3 Amputation of penis

✓4th **64.4 Repair and plastic operation on penis**

64.41 Suture of laceration of penis

64.42 Release of chordee

DEF: Correction of downward displacement of penis.

64.43 Construction of penis

64.44 Reconstruction of penis

64.45 Replantation of penis

Reattachment of amputated penis

64.49 Other repair of penis

EXCLUDES *repair of epispadias and hypospadias (58.45)*

64.5 Operations for sex transformation, not elsewhere classified

✓4th **64.9 Other operations on male genital organs**

64.91 Dorsal or lateral slit of prepuce

64.92 Incision of penis

64.93 Division of penile adhesions

64.94 Fitting of external prosthesis of penis

Penile prosthesis NOS

64.95 Insertion or replacement of non-inflatable penile prosthesis

Insertion of semi-rigid rod prosthesis into shaft of penis

EXCLUDES *external penile prosthesis (64.94)*
inflatable penile prosthesis (64.97)
plastic repair, penis (64.43-64.49)
that associated with:
construction (64.43)
reconstruction (64.44)

64.96 Removal of internal prosthesis of penis

Removal without replacement of non-inflatable or inflatable penile prosthesis

64.97 Insertion or replacement of inflatable penile prosthesis

Insertion of cylinders into shaft of penis and placement of pump and reservoir

EXCLUDES *external penile prosthesis (64.94)*
non-inflatable penile prosthesis (64.95)
plastic repair, penis (64.43-64.49)

64.98 Other operations on penis

Corpora cavernosa-corpus spongiosum shunt
Corpora-saphenous shunt
Irrigation of corpus cavernosum

EXCLUDES *removal of foreign body:*
intraluminal (98.19)
without incision (98.24)
stretching of foreskin (99.95)

DEF: Corpora cavernosa-corpus spongiosum shunt: Insertion of shunt between erectile tissues of penis.

DEF: Corpora-saphenous shunt: Insertion of shunt between erectile tissue and vein of penis.

DEF: Irrigation of corpus cavernosum: Washing of erectile tissue forming dorsum and side of penis.

64.99 Other

EXCLUDES *collection of sperm for artificial insemination (99.96)*

12. OPERATIONS ON THE FEMALE GENITAL ORGANS (65-71)

✓3rd **65 Operations on ovary**
Code also any application or administration of an adhesion barrier substance (99.77)

✓4th **65.0 Oophorotomy**
Salpingo-oophorotomy
DEF: Incision into ovary.
DEF: Salpingo-oophorotomy: Incision into ovary and the fallopian tube.

65.01 Laparoscopic oophorotomy

65.09 Other oophorotomy

✓4th **65.1 Diagnostic procedures on ovaries**

65.11 Aspiration biopsy of ovary

65.12 Other biopsy of ovary

65.13 Laparoscopic biopsy of ovary

65.14 Other laparoscopic diagnostic procedures on ovaries

65.19 Other diagnostic procedures on ovaries
EXCLUDES *microscopic examination of specimen from ovary (91.41-91.49)*

✓4th **65.2 Local excision or destruction of ovarian lesion or tissue**

65.21 Marsupialization of ovarian cyst
EXCLUDES *that by laparoscope (65.23)*
DEF: Exteriorized cyst to outside by incising anterior wall and suturing cut edges to create open pouch.

65.22 Wedge resection of ovary
EXCLUDES *that by laparoscope (65.24)*

65.23 Laparoscopic marsupialization of ovarian cyst

65.24 Laparoscopic wedge resection of ovary

65.25 Other laparoscopic local excision or destruction of ovary

65.29 Other local excision or destruction of ovary
Bisection } of ovary
Cauterization } of ovary
Parial excision } of ovary
EXCLUDES *biopsy of ovary (65.11-65.13)*
that by laparoscope (65.25)

✓4th **65.3 Unilateral oophorectomy**

65.31 Laparoscopic unilateral oophorectomy

65.39 Other unilateral oophorectomy
EXCLUDES *that by laparoscope (65.31)*

✓4th **65.4 Unilateral salpingo-oophorectomy**

65.41 Laparoscopic unilateral salpingo-oophorectomy

65.49 Other unilateral salpingo-oophorectomy

Oophorectomy

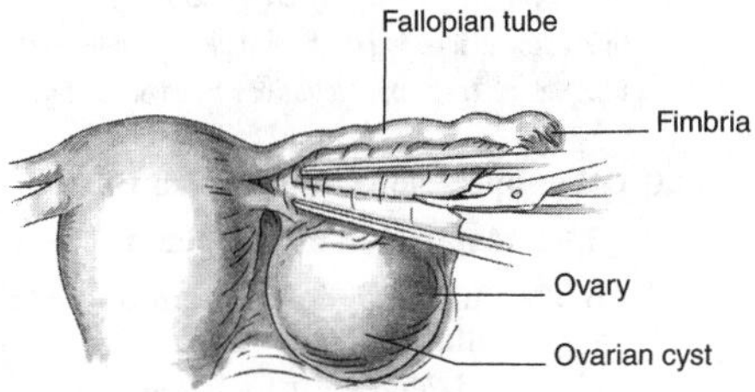

✓4th **65.5 Bilateral oophorectomy**

65.51 Other removal of both ovaries at same operative episode
Female castration
EXCLUDES *that by laparoscope (65.53)*

65.52 Other removal of remaining ovary
Removal of solitary ovary
EXCLUDES *that by laparoscope (65.54)*

65.53 Laparoscopic removal of both ovaries at same operative episode

65.54 Laparoscopic removal of remaining ovary

✓4th **65.6 Bilateral salpingo-oophorectomy**

65.61 Other removal of both ovaries and tubes at same operative episode
EXCLUDES *that by laparoscope (65.53)*

65.62 Other removal of remaining ovary and tube
Removal of solitary ovary and tube
EXCLUDES *that by laparoscope (65.54)*

65.63 Laparoscopic removal of both ovaries and tubes at the same operative episode

65.64 Laparoscopic removal of remaining ovary and tube

✓4th **65.7 Repair of ovary**
EXCLUDES *salpingo-oophorostomy (66.72)*

65.71 Other simple suture of ovary
EXCLUDES *that by laparoscope (65.74)*

65.72 Other reimplantation of ovary
EXCLUDES *that by laparoscope (65.75)*
DEF: Grafting and repositioning of ovary at same site.

65.73 Other salpingo-oophoroplasty
EXCLUDES *that by laparoscope (65.76)*

65.74 Laparoscopic simple suture of ovary

65.75 Laparoscopic reimplantation of ovary

65.76 Laparoscopic salpingo-oophoroplasty

65.79 Other repair of ovary
Oophoropexy

✓4th **65.8 Lysis of adhesions of ovary and fallopian tube**

65.81 Laparoscopic lysis of adhesions of ovary and fallopian tube

65.89 Other lysis of adhesions of ovary and fallopian tube
EXCLUDES *that by laparoscope (65.81)*

✓4th **65.9 Other operations on ovary**

65.91 Aspiration of ovary
EXCLUDES *aspiration biopsy of ovary (65.11)*

65.92 Transplantation of ovary
EXCLUDES *reimplantation of ovary (65.72, 65.75)*

65.93 Manual rupture of ovarian cyst
DEF: Breaking up an ovarian cyst using manual technique or blunt instruments.

65.94 Ovarian denervation
DEF: Destruction of nerve tracts to ovary.

65.95 Release of torsion of ovary

65.99 Other
Ovarian drilling

✓3rd **66 Operations on fallopian tubes**

Code also any application or administration of an adhesion barrier substance (99.77)

✓4th **66.0 Salpingotomy and salpingostomy**

66.01 Salpingotomy

66.02 Salpingostomy

✓4th **66.1 Diagnostic procedures on fallopian tubes**

66.11 Biopsy of fallopian tube

66.19 Other diagnostic procedures on fallopian tubes

EXCLUDES *microscopic examination of specimen from fallopian tubes (91.41-91.49)*
radiography of fallopian tubes (87.82-87.83, 87.85)
Rubin's test (66.8)

✓4th **66.2 Bilateral endoscopic destruction or occlusion of fallopian tubes**

INCLUDES bilateral endoscopic destruction or occlusion of fallopian tubes by:
culdoscopy
endoscopy
hysteroscopy
laparoscopy
peritoneoscopy
endoscopic destruction of solitary fallopian tube

DEF: Endoscopic blockage or destruction of both fallopian tubes.

DEF: Bilateral endoscopic destruction or occlusion of fallopian tubes by:

Culdoscopy: Endoscopic insertion through posterior structure of vagina.

Hysteroscopy: Endoscopic insertion through uterus.

Laparoscopy: Endoscopic insertion through abdomen.

Peritoneoscopy: Endoscopic insertion through abdominal serous membrane cavity.

Endoscopic destruction of solitary fallopian tube: Endoscopic destruction of one fallopian tube.

66.21 Bilateral endoscopic ligation and crushing of fallopian tubes

66.22 Bilateral endoscopic ligation and division of fallopian tubes

66.29 Other bilateral endoscopic destruction or occlusion of fallopian tubes

✓4th **66.3 Other bilateral destruction or occlusion of fallopian tubes**

INCLUDES destruction of solitary fallopian tube

EXCLUDES *endoscopic destruction or occlusion of fallopian tubes (66.21-66.29)*

66.31 Other bilateral ligation and crushing of fallopian tubes

Endoscopic Ligation of Fallopian Tubes

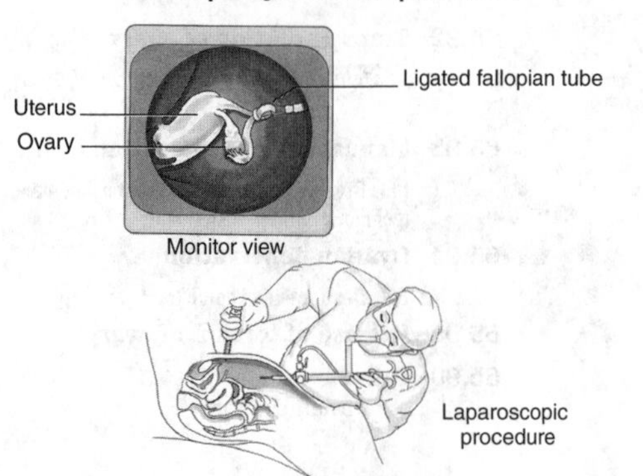

66.32 Other bilateral ligation and division of fallopian tubes

Pomeroy operation

66.39 Other bilateral destruction or occlusion of fallopian tubes

Female sterilization operation NOS

66.4 Total unilateral salpingectomy

✓4th **66.5 Total bilateral salpingectomy**

EXCLUDES *bilateral partial salpingectomy for sterilization (66.39)*
that with oophorectomy (65.61-65.64)

66.51 Removal of both fallopian tubes at same operative episode

66.52 Removal of remaining fallopian tube

Removal of solitary fallopian tube

✓4th **66.6 Other salpingectomy**

INCLUDES salpingectomy by:
cauterization
coagulation
electrocoagulation
excision

EXCLUDES *fistulectomy (66.73)*

66.61 Excision or destruction of lesion of fallopian tube

EXCLUDES *biopsy of fallopian tube (66.11)*

66.62 Salpingectomy with removal of tubal pregnancy

Code also any synchronous oophorectomy (65.31, 65.39)

66.63 Bilateral partial salpingectomy, not otherwise specified

66.69 Other partial salpingectomy

✓4th **66.7 Repair of fallopian tube**

66.71 Simple suture of fallopian tube

66.72 Salpingo-oophorostomy

66.73 Salpingo-salpingostomy

66.74 Salpingo-uterostomy

66.79 Other repair of fallopian tube

Graft of fallopian tube
Reopening of divided fallopian tube
Salpingoplasty

DEF: Graft of fallopian: Repair of fallopian tube with implanted graft.

DEF: Reopening of divided fallopian tube: Reconnection of severed fallopian tube to restore patency.

DEF: Salpingoplasty: Plastic reconstruction of fallopian tube defect.

66.8 Insufflation of fallopian tube

Insufflation of fallopian tube with:
air
dye
gas
saline
Rubin's test

EXCLUDES *insufflation of therapeutic agent (66.95)*
that for hysterosalpingography (87.82-87.83)

DEF: Forceful blowing of gas or liquid into fallopian tubes.

DEF: Rubin's test: Introduction of carbon dioxide gas into fallopian tubes.

✓4th **66.9 Other operations on fallopian tubes**

66.91 Aspiration of fallopian tube

66.92 Unilateral destruction or occlusion of fallopian tube

EXCLUDES *that of solitary tube (66.21-66.39)*

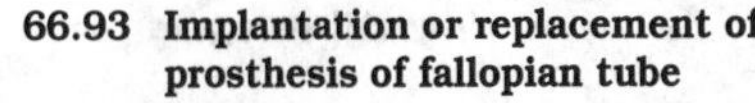

66.93 Implantation or replacement of prosthesis of fallopian tube

66.94 Removal of prosthesis of fallopian tube

66.95 Insufflation of therapeutic agent into fallopian tubes

66.96 Dilation of fallopian tube

66.97 Burying of fimbriae in uterine wall

DEF: Implantation of fallopian tube, fringed edges into uterine wall.

66.99 Other

EXCLUDES *lysis of adhesions of ovary and tube (65.81, 65.89)*

✓3rd 67 Operations on cervix

Code also any application or administration of an adhesion barrier substance (99.77)

67.0 Dilation of cervical canal

EXCLUDES *dilation and curettage (69.01-69.09)*
that for induction of labor (73.1)

✓4th 67.1 Diagnostic procedures on cervix

67.11 Endocervical biopsy

EXCLUDES *conization of cervix (67.2)*

67.12 Other cervical biopsy

Punch biopsy of cervix NOS

EXCLUDES *conization of cervix (67.2)*

67.19 Other diagnostic procedures on cervix

EXCLUDES *microscopic examination of specimen from cervix (91.41-91.49)*

67.2 Conization of cervix

EXCLUDES *that by:*
cryosurgery (67.33)
electrosurgery (67.32)

DEF: Removal of cone-shaped section from distal cervix; cervical function preserved.

✓4th 67.3 Other excision or destruction of lesion or tissue of cervix

67.31 Marsupialization of cervical cyst

DEF: Incision and then suturing open of a cyst in the neck of the uterus.

67.32 Destruction of lesion of cervix by cauterization

Electroconization of cervix
LEEP (loop electrosurgical excision procedure)
LLETZ (large loop excision of the transformation zone)

DEF: Destruction of lesion of uterine neck by applying intense heat.

DEF: Electroconization of cervix: Electrocautery excision of multilayer cone-shaped section from uterine neck.

67.33 Destruction of lesion of cervix by cryosurgery

Cryoconization of cervix

DEF: Destruction of lesion of uterine neck by freezing.

DEF: Cryoconization of cervix: Excision by freezing of multilayer cone-shaped section of abnormal tissue in uterine neck.

67.39 Other excision or destruction of lesion or tissue of cervix

EXCLUDES *biopsy of cervix (67.11-67.12)*
cervical fistulectomy (67.62)
conization of cervix (67.2)

Cerclage of Cervix

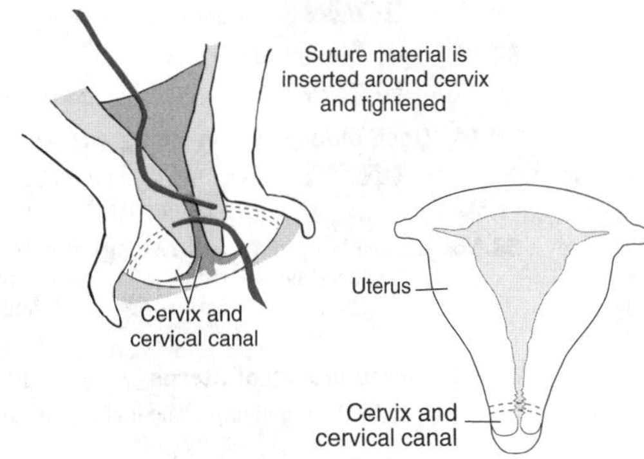

67.4 Amputation of cervix

Cervicectomy with synchronous colporrhaphy

DEF: Excision of lower uterine neck.

DEF: Cervicectomy with synchronous colporrhaphy: Excision of lower uterine neck with suture of vaginal stump.

✓4th 67.5 Repair of internal cervical os

DEF: Repair of cervical opening defect.

67.51 Transabdominal cerclage of cervix

67.59 Other repair of internal cervical os

Cerclage of isthmus uteri
McDonald operation
Shirodkar operation
Transvaginal cerclage

EXCLUDES *laparoscopically assisted supracervical hysterectomy [LASH] (68.31)*
transabdominal cerclage of cervix (67.51)

DEF: Cerclage of isthmus uteri: Placement of encircling suture between neck and body of uterus.

DEF: Shirodkar operation: Placement of purse-string suture in internal cervical opening.

✓4th 67.6 Other repair of cervix

EXCLUDES *repair of current obstetric laceration (75.51)*

67.61 Suture of laceration of cervix

67.62 Repair of fistula of cervix

Cervicosigmoidal fistulectomy

EXCLUDES *fistulectomy:*
cervicovesical (57.84)
ureterocervical (56.84)
vesicocervicovaginal (57.84)

DEF: Closure of fistula in lower uterus.

DEF: Cervicosigmoidal fistulectomy: Excision of abnormal passage between uterine neck and torsion of large intestine.

67.69 Other repair of cervix

Repair of old obstetric laceration of cervix

✓3rd 68 Other incision and excision of uterus

Code also any application or administration of an adhesion barrier substance (99.77)

68.0 Hysterotomy

Hysterotomy with removal of hydatidiform mole

EXCLUDES *hysterotomy for termination of pregnancy (74.91)*

DEF: Incision into the uterus.

✓4th 68.1 Diagnostic procedures on uterus and supporting structures

68.11 Digital examination of uterus

EXCLUDES *pelvic examination, so described (89.26)*
postpartal manual exploration of uterine cavity (75.7)

68.12 Hysteroscopy

EXCLUDES *that with biopsy (68.16)*

68.13 Open biopsy of uterus

EXCLUDES *closed biopsy of uterus (68.16)*

68.14 Open biopsy of uterine ligaments

EXCLUDES *closed biopsy of uterine ligaments (68.15)*

68.15 Closed biopsy of uterine ligaments

Endoscopic (laparoscopy) biopsy of uterine adnexa, except ovary and fallopian tube

68.16 Closed biopsy of uterus

Endoscopic (laparoscopy) (hysteroscopy) biopsy of uterus

EXCLUDES *open biopsy of uterus (68.13)*

68.19 Other diagnostic procedures on uterus and supporting structures

EXCLUDES *diagnostic:*
- *aspiration curettage (69.59)*
- *dilation and curettage (69.09)*

microscopic examination of specimen from uterus (91.41-91.49)
pelvic examination (89.26)
radioisotope scan of:
- *placenta (92.17)*
- *uterus (92.19)*

ultrasonography of uterus (88.78-88.79)
x-ray of uterus (87.81-87.89)

✓4th **68.2 Excision or destruction of lesion or tissue of uterus**

68.21 Division of endometrial synechiae

Lysis of intraluminal uterine adhesions

DEF: Separation of uterine adhesions.

DEF: Lysis of intraluminal uterine adhesion: Surgical destruction of adhesive, fibrous structures inside uterine cavity.

68.22 Incision or excision of congenital septum of uterus

68.23 Endometrial ablation

Dilation and curettage
Hysteroscopic endometrial ablation

DEF: Removal or destruction of uterine lining; usually by electrocautery or loop electrosurgical excision procedure (LEEP).

68.29 Other excision or destruction of lesion of uterus

Uterine myomectomy

EXCLUDES *biopsy of uterus (68.13)*
uterine fistulectomy (69.42)

✓4th **68.3 Subtotal abdominal hysterectomy**

68.31 Laparoscopic supracervical hysterectomy [LSH]

Classic infrafascial SEMM hysterectomy [CISH]
Laparoscopically assisted supracervical hysterectomy [LASH]

DEF: A hysterectomy that spares the cervix and maintains the integrity of the pelvic floor; SEMM version of the supracervical hysterectomy, also called the classic infrafascial Semm hysterectomy [CISH], the cardinal ligaments, or lateral cervical ligaments that merge with the pelvic diaphragm remain intact.

Vaginal Hysterectomy

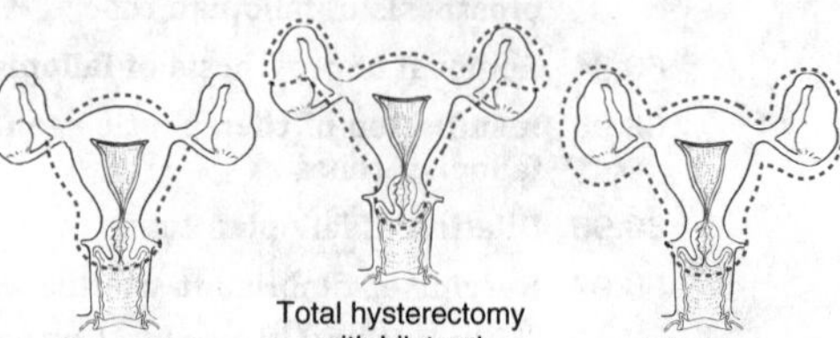

68.39 Other and unspecified subtotal abdominal hysterectomy

Supracervical hysterectomy

EXCLUDES *classic infrafascial SEMM hysterectomy [CISH] (68.31)*
laparoscopic supracervical hysterectomy [LSH] (68.31)

✓4th **68.4 Total abdominal hysterectomy**

Code also any synchronous removal of tubes and ovaries (65.31-65.64)

EXCLUDES *laparoscopic total abdominal hysterectomy (68.41)*
radical abdominal hysterectomy, any approach (68.61-68.69)

DEF: Complete excision of uterus and uterine neck through abdominal approach.

68.41 Laparoscopic total abdominal hysterectomy

Total laparoscopic hysterectomy [TLH]

68.49 Other and unspecified total abdominal hysterectomy

Hysterectomy:
- extended

✓4th **68.5 Vaginal hysterectomy**

Code also any synchronous:
- removal of tubes and ovaries (65.31-65.64)
- repair of cystocele or rectocele (70.50-70.52)
- repair of pelvic floor (70.79)

DEF: Complete excision of the uterus by a vaginal approach.

68.51 Laparoscopically assisted vaginal hysterectomy (LAVH)

68.59 Other and unspecified vaginal hysterectomy

EXCLUDES *laparoscopically assisted vaginal hysterectomy (68.51)*
radical vaginal hysterectomy (68.71-68.79)

✓4th **68.6 Radical abdominal hysterectomy**

Code also any synchronous:
- lymph gland dissection (40.3, 40.5)
- removal of tubes and ovaries (65.31-65.64)

EXCLUDES *pelvic evisceration (68.8)*

DEF: Excision of uterus, loose connective tissue and smooth muscle around uterus and vagina via abdominal approach.

68.61 Laparoscopic radical abdominal hysterectomy

Laparoscopic modified radical hysterectomy
Total laparoscopic radical hysterectomy [TLRH]

68.69 Other and unspecified radical abdominal hysterectomy
Modified radical hysterectomy
Wertheim's operation
EXCLUDES *laparoscopic radical abdominal hysterectomy (68.61)*
laparoscopic total abdominal hysterectomy (68.41)

✓4th **68.7 Radical vaginal hysterectomy**
Code also any synchronous:
lymph gland dissection (40.3, 40.5)
removal of tubes and ovaries (65.31-65.64)
EXCLUDES *abdominal hysterectomy, any approach (68.31-68.39, 68.41-68.49, 68.61-68.69, 68.9)*

DEF: Excision of uterus, loose connective tissue and smooth muscle around uterus and vagina via vaginal approach.

68.71 Laparoscopic radical vaginal hysterectomy [LRVH]

68.79 Other and unspecified radical vaginal hysterectomy
Hysterocolpectomy
Schauta operation

68.8 Pelvic evisceration
Removal of ovaries, tubes, uterus, vagina, bladder, and urethra (with removal of sigmoid colon and rectum)
Code also any synchronous:
colostomy (46.10-46.13)
lymph gland dissection (40.3, 40.5)
urinary diversion (56.51-56.79)

68.9 Other and unspecified hysterectomy
Hysterectomy NOS
EXCLUDES *abdominal hysterectomy, any approach (68.31-68.39, 68.41-68.49, 68.61-68.69)*
vaginal hysterectomy, any approach (68.51-68.59, 68.71-68.79)

✓3rd **69 Other operations on uterus and supporting structures**
Code also any application or administration of an adhesion barrier substance (99.77)

✓4th **69.0 Dilation and curettage of uterus**
EXCLUDES *aspiration curettage of uterus (69.51-69.59)*

DEF: Stretching of uterine neck to scrape tissue from walls.

69.01 Dilation and curettage for termination of pregnancy

69.02 Dilation and curettage following delivery or abortion

69.09 Other dilation and curettage
Diagnostic D and C

✓4th **69.1 Excision or destruction of lesion or tissue of uterus and supporting structures**

69.19 Other excision or destruction of uterus and supporting structures
EXCLUDES *biopsy of uterine ligament (68.14)*

Dilation and Curettage

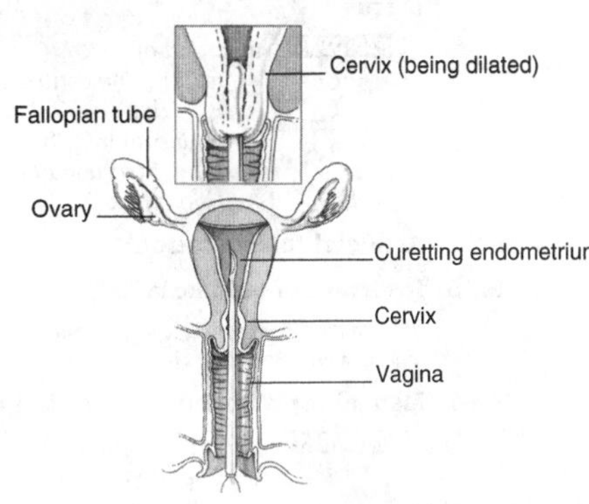

✓4th **69.2 Repair of uterine supporting structures**

69.21 Interposition operation
Watkins procedure

69.22 Other uterine suspension
Hysteropexy
Manchester operation
Plication of uterine ligament

DEF: Hysteropexy: Fixation or anchoring of uterus.

DEF: Manchester operation: Fixation or anchoring of uterus with supportive banding tissue of uterine neck and vagina.

DEF: Plication of uterine ligament: Creation of tucks in suppurative uterine banding tissue.

DEF: Repositioning or realignment of bladder and uterus.

69.23 Vaginal repair of chronic inversion of uterus

DEF: Repositioning of inverted uterus via vaginal approach.

69.29 Other repair of uterus and supporting structures

69.3 Paracervical uterine denervation

✓4th **69.4 Uterine repair**
EXCLUDES *repair of current obstetric laceration (75.50-75.52)*

69.41 Suture of laceration of uterus

69.42 Closure of fistula of uterus
EXCLUDES *uterovesical fistulectomy (57.84)*

69.49 Other repair of uterus
Repair of old obstetric laceration of uterus

✓4th **69.5 Aspiration curettage of uterus**
EXCLUDES *menstrual extraction (69.6)*

69.51 Aspiration curettage of uterus for termination of pregnancy
Therapeutic abortion NOS

69.52 Aspiration curettage following delivery or abortion

69.59 Other aspiration curettage of uterus

69.6 Menstrual extraction or regulation

DEF: Induction of menstruation by low pressure suction.

69.7 Insertion of intrauterine contraceptive device

✓4th **69.9 Other operations on uterus, cervix, and supporting structures**
EXCLUDES *obstetric dilation or incision of cervix (73.1, 73.93)*

69.91 Insertion of therapeutic device into uterus

EXCLUDES *insertion of:*
intrauterine contraceptive device (69.7)
laminaria (69.93)
obstetric insertion of bag, bougie, or pack (73.1)

69.92 Artificial insemination

69.93 Insertion of laminaria

DEF: Placement of laminaria, a sea kelp, in cervical os to induce labor; applied for six to 12 hours.

69.94 Manual replacement of inverted uterus

EXCLUDES *that in immediate postpartal period (75.94)*

69.95 Incision of cervix

EXCLUDES *that to assist delivery (73.93)*

69.96 Removal of cerclage material from cervix

DEF: Removal of ring inserted to restore uterine neck competency.

69.97 Removal of other penetrating foreign body from cervix

EXCLUDES *removal of intraluminal foreign body from cervix (98.16)*

69.98 Other operations on supporting structures of uterus

EXCLUDES *biopsy of uterine ligament (68.14)*

69.99 Other operations on cervix and uterus

EXCLUDES *removal of:*
foreign body (98.16)
intrauterine contraceptive device (97.71)
obstetric bag, bougie, or pack (97.72)
packing (97.72)

✓3rd **70 Operations on vagina and cul-de-sac**

Code also any application or administration of an adhesion barrier substance (99.77)

70.0 Culdocentesis

DEF: Insertion of needle into upper vaginal vault encircling cervix to withdraw fluid.

✓4th **70.1 Incision of vagina and cul-de-sac**

70.11 Hymenotomy

70.12 Culdotomy

DEF: Incision into pocket between terminal end of large intestine and posterior uterus.

70.13 Lysis of intraluminal adhesions of vagina

70.14 Other vaginotomy

Division of vaginal septum
Drainage of hematoma of vaginal cuff

DEF: Division of vaginal septum: Incision into partition of vaginal walls.

DEF: Drainage of hematoma of vaginal cuff: Incision into vaginal tissue to drain collected blood.

✓4th **70.2 Diagnostic procedures on vagina and cul-de-sac**

70.21 Vaginoscopy

70.22 Culdoscopy

DEF: Endoscopic exam of pelvic viscera through incision in posterior vaginal wall.

70.23 Biopsy of cul-de-sac

70.24 Vaginal biopsy

70.29 Other diagnostic procedures on vagina and cul-de-sac

✓4th **70.3 Local excision or destruction of vagina and cul-de-sac**

70.31 Hymenectomy

70.32 Excision or destruction of lesion of cul-de-sac

Endometrectomy of cul-de-sac

EXCLUDES *biopsy of cul-de-sac (70.23)*

70.33 Excision or destruction of lesion of vagina

EXCLUDES *biopsy of vagina (70.24)*
vaginal fistulectomy (70.72-70.75)

70.4 Obliteration and total excision of vagina

Vaginectomy

EXCLUDES *obliteration of vaginal vault (70.8)*

DEF: Vaginectomy: Removal of vagina.

✓4th **70.5 Repair of cystocele and rectocele**

70.50 Repair of cystocele and rectocele

EXCLUDES *repair of cystocele and rectocele with graft or prosthesis (70.53)*

DEF: Repair of anterior and posterior vaginal wall bulges.

70.51 Repair of cystocele

Anterior colporrhaphy (with urethrocele repair)

EXCLUDES *repair of cystocele and rectocele with graft or prosthesis (70.53)*
repair of cystocele with graft or prosthesis (70.54)

70.52 Repair of rectocele

Posterior colporrhaphy

EXCLUDES *repair of cystocele and rectocele with graft or prosthesis (70.53)*
repair of rectocele with graft or prosthesis (70.55)
STARR procedure (48.74)

70.53 Repair of cystocele and rectocele with graft or prosthesis

Use additional code for biological substance (70.94) or synthetic substance (70.95), if known

70.54 Repair of cystocele with graft or prosthesis

Anterior colporrhaphy (with urethrocele repair)

Use additional code for biological substance (70.94) or synthetic substance (70.95), if known

70.55 Repair of rectocele with graft or prosthesis

Posterior colporrhaphy

Use additional code for biological substance (70.94) or synthetic substance (70.95), if known

✓4th **70.6 Vaginal construction and reconstruction**

70.61 Vaginal construction

70.62 Vaginal reconstruction

70.63 Vaginal construction with graft or prosthesis

Use additional code for biological substance (70.94) or synthetic substance (70.95), if known

EXCLUDES *vaginal construction (70.61)*

70.64 Vaginal reconstruction with graft or prosthesis

Use additional code for biological substance (70.94) or synthetic substance (70.95), if known

EXCLUDES *vaginal reconstruction (70.62)*

✓4th **70.7 Other repair of vagina**

EXCLUDES *lysis of intraluminal adhesions (70.13)*
repair of current obstetric laceration (75.69)
that associated with cervical amputation (67.4)

70.71 Suture of laceration of vagina

70.72 Repair of colovaginal fistula

DEF: Correction of abnormal opening between midsection of large intestine and vagina.

70.73 Repair of rectovaginal fistula

DEF: Correction of abnormal opening between last section of large intestine and vagina.

70.74 Repair of other vaginoenteric fistula

DEF: Correction of abnormal opening between vagina and intestine; other than mid or last sections.

70.75 Repair of other fistula of vagina

EXCLUDES *repair of fistula:*
rectovesicovaginal (57.83)
ureterovaginal (56.84)
urethrovaginal (58.43)
uterovaginal (69.42)
vesicocervicovaginal (57.84)
vesicosigmoidovaginal (57.83)
vesicoureterovaginal (56.84)
vesicovaginal (57.84)

70.76 Hymenorrhaphy

DEF: Closure of vagina with suture of hymenal ring or hymenal remnant flaps.

70.77 Vaginal suspension and fixation

DEF: Repair of vaginal protrusion, sinking or laxity by suturing vagina into position.

70.78 Vaginal suspension and fixation with graft or prosthesis

Use additional code for biological substance (70.94) or synthetic substance (70.95), if known

70.79 Other repair of vagina

Colpoperineoplasty
Repair of old obstetric laceration of vagina

70.8 Obliteration of vaginal vault

LeFort operation

DEF: LeFort operation: Uniting or sewing together vaginal walls.

✓4th **70.9 Other operations on vagina and cul-de-sac**

70.91 Other operations on vagina

EXCLUDES *insertion of:*
diaphragm (96.17)
mold (96.15)
pack (96.14)
pessary (96.18)
suppository (96.49)
removal of:
diaphragm (97.73)
foreign body (98.17)
pack (97.75)
pessary (97.74)
replacement of:
diaphragm (97.24)
pack (97.26)
pessary (97.25)
vaginal dilation (96.16)
vaginal douche (96.44)

70.92 Other operations on cul-de-sac

Obliteration of cul-de-sac
Repair of vaginal enterocele

DEF: Repair of vaginal enterocele: Elimination of herniated cavity within pouch between last part of large intestine and posterior uterus.

70.93 Other operations on cul-de-sac with graft or prosthesis

Repair of vaginal enterocele with graft or prosthesis

Use additional code for biological substance (70.94) or synthetic substance (70.95), if known

70.94 Insertion of biological graft

Allogenic material or substance
Allograft
Autograft
Autologous material or substance
Heterograft
Xenogenic material or substance

Code first these procedures when done with graft or prosthesis:
Other operations on cul-de-sac (70.93)
Repair of cystocele (70.54)
Repair of cystocele and rectocele (70.53)
Repair of rectocele (70.55)
Vaginal construction (70.63)
Vaginal reconstruction (70.64)
Vaginal suspension and fixation (70.78)

70.95 Insertion of synthetic graft or prosthesis

Artificial tissue

Code first these procedures when done with graft or prosthesis:
Other operations on cul-de-sac (70.93)
Repair of cystocele (70.54)
Repair of cystocele and rectocele (70.53)
Repair of rectocele (70.55)
Vaginal construction (70.63)
Vaginal reconstruction (70.64)
Vaginal suspension and fixation (70.78)

✓3rd **71 Operations on vulva and perineum**

Code also any application or administration of an adhesion barrier substance (99.77)

✓4th **71.0 Incision of vulva and perineum**

71.01 Lysis of vulvar adhesions

71.09 Other incision of vulva and perineum

Enlargement of introitus NOS

EXCLUDES *removal of foreign body without incision (98.23)*

✓4th **71.1 Diagnostic procedures on vulva**

71.11 Biopsy of vulva

71.19 Other diagnostic procedures on vulva

✓4th **71.2 Operations on Bartholin's gland**

71.21 Percutaneous aspiration of Bartholin's gland (cyst)

71.22 Incision of Bartholin's gland (cyst)

71.23 Marsupialization of Bartholin's gland (cyst)

DEF: Incision and suturing opening of a cyst in Bartholin's gland.

71.24 Excision or other destruction of Bartholin's gland (cyst)

71.29 Other operations on Bartholin's gland

71.3 Other local excision or destruction of vulva and perineum

Division of Skene's gland

EXCLUDES *biopsy of vulva (71.11)*
vulvar fistulectomy (71.72)

Marsupialization

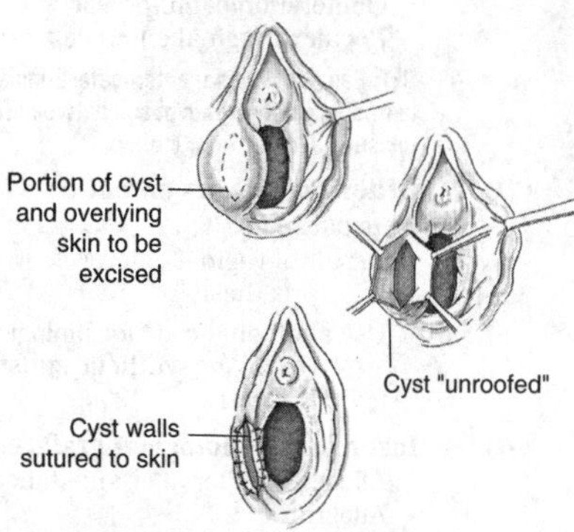

71.4 Operations on clitoris
Amputation of clitoris
Clitoridotomy
Female circumcision

DEF: Amputation of clitoris: Removal of clitoris.
DEF: Clitoridotomy: Incision into clitoris.
DEF: Female circumcision: Incision of skin fold over clitoris.

71.5 Radical vulvectomy
Code also any synchronous lymph gland dissection (40.3, 40.5)

DEF: Removal of over 80 percent of deep tissue from vulva, including tissue of abdomen, groin, labia minora, labia majora, clitoris, mons veneris, and terminal portions of urethra, vagina and other vulvar organs.

✓4th **71.6 Other vulvectomy**

71.61 Unilateral vulvectomy

71.62 Bilateral vulvectomy
Vulvectomy NOS

✓4th **71.7 Repair of vulva and perineum**

EXCLUDES *repair of current obstetric laceration (75.69)*

71.71 Suture of laceration of vulva or perineum

71.72 Repair of fistula of vulva or perineum

EXCLUDES *repair of fistula:*
urethroperineal (58.43)
urethroperineovesical (57.84)
vaginoperineal (70.75)

71.79 Other repair of vulva and perineum
Repair of old obstetric laceration of vulva or perineum

71.8 Other operations on vulva

EXCLUDES *removal of:*
foreign body without incision (98.23)
packing (97.75)
replacement of packing (97.26)

71.9 Other operations on female genital organs

13. OBSTETRICAL PROCEDURES (72-75)

✓3rd **72 Forces, vacuum, and breech delivery**

72.0 Low forceps operation
Outlet forceps operation

72.1 Low forceps operation with episiotomy
Outlet forceps operation with episiotomy

✓4th **72.2 Mid forceps operation**

72.21 Mid forceps operation with episiotomy

72.29 Other mid forceps operation

✓4th **72.3 High forceps operation**

72.31 High forceps operation with episiotomy

72.39 Other high forceps operation

72.4 Forceps rotation of fetal head
DeLee maneuver
Key-in-lock rotation
Kielland rotation
Scanzoni's maneuver
Code also any associated forceps extraction (72.0-72.39)

✓4th **72.5 Breech extraction**

72.51 Partial breech extraction with forceps to aftercoming head

72.52 Other partial breech extraction

72.53 Total breech extraction with forceps to aftercoming head

72.54 Other total breech extraction

72.6 Forceps application to aftercoming head
Piper forceps operation
EXCLUDES *partial breech extraction with forceps to aftercoming head (72.51)*
total breech extraction with forceps to aftercoming head (72.53)

✓4th **72.7 Vacuum extraction**
INCLUDES Malstöm's extraction

72.71 Vacuum extraction with episiotomy

72.79 Other vacuum extraction

72.8 Other specified instrumental delivery

72.9 Unspecified instrumental delivery

✓3rd **73 Other procedures inducing or assisting delivery**

✓4th **73.0 Artificial rupture of membranes**

73.01 Induction of labor by artificial rupture of membranes
Surgical induction NOS
EXCLUDES *artificial rupture of membranes after onset of labor (73.09)*

Breech Extraction

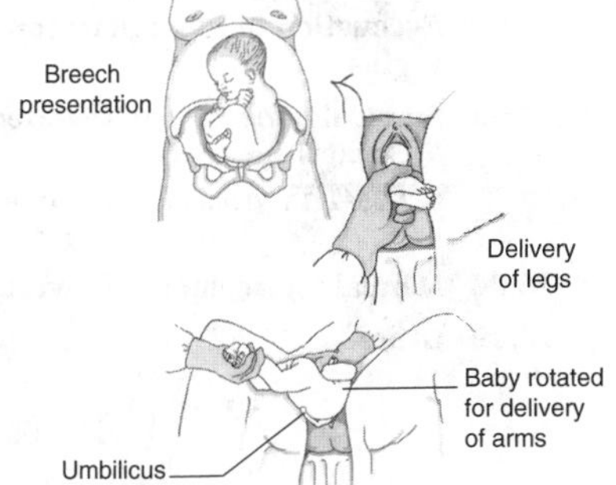

73.09 Other artificial rupture of membranes
Artificial rupture of membranes at time of delivery

73.1 Other surgical induction of labor
Induction by cervical dilation
EXCLUDES *injection for abortion (75.0)*
insertion of suppository for abortion (96.49)

✓4th **73.2 Internal and combined version and extraction**

73.21 Internal and combined version without extraction
Version NOS

73.22 Internal and combined version with extraction

73.3 Failed forceps
Application of forceps without delivery
Trial forceps

73.4 Medical induction of labor
EXCLUDES *medication to augment active labor — omit code*

✓4th **73.5 Manually assisted delivery**

73.51 Manual rotation of fetal head

73.59 Other manually assisted delivery
Assisted spontaneous delivery
Credé maneuver

73.6 Episiotomy
Episioproctotomy
Episiotomy with subsequent episiorrhaphy
EXCLUDES *that with:*
high forceps (72.31)
low forceps (72.1)
mid forceps (72.21)
outlet forceps (72.1)
vacuum extraction (72.71)

73.8 Operations on fetus to facilitate delivery
Clavicotomy on fetus
Destruction of fetus
Needling of hydrocephalic head

✓4th **73.9 Other operations assisting delivery**

73.91 External version

73.92 Replacement of prolapsed umbilical cord

73.93 Incision of cervix to assist delivery
Dührssen's incisions

73.94 Pubiotomy to assist delivery
Obstetrical symphysiotomy

73.99 Other
EXCLUDES *dilation of cervix, obstetrical, to induce labor (73.1)*
insertion of bag or bougie to induce labor (73.1)
removal of cerclage material (69.96)

✓3rd **74 Cesarean section and removal of fetus**
Code also any synchronous:
hysterectomy (68.3-68.4, 68.6, 68.8)
myomectomy (68.29)
sterilization (66.31-66.39, 66.63)

74.0 Classical cesarean section
Transperitoneal classical cesarean section

74.1 Low cervical cesarean section
Lower uterine segment cesarean section

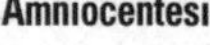
Amniocentesis

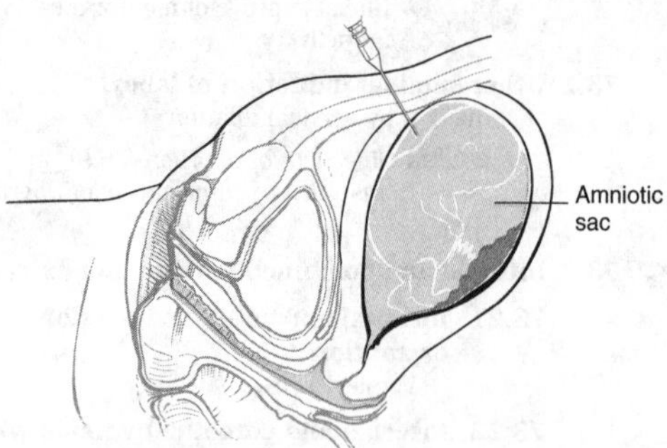

Aspiration of amniotic fluid

74.2 Extraperitoneal cesarean section
Supravesical cesarean section

74.3 Removal of extratubal ectopic pregnancy
Removal of:
ectopic abdominal pregnancy
fetus from peritoneal or extraperitoneal cavity following uterine or tubal rupture

EXCLUDES *that by salpingostomy (66.02)*
that by salpingotomy (66.01)
that with synchronous salpingectomy (66.62)

74.4 Cesarean section of other specified type
Peritoneal exclusion cesarean section
Transperitoneal cesarean section NOS
Vaginal cesarean section

✓4th **74.9 Cesarean section of unspecified type**

74.91 Hysterotomy to terminate pregnancy
Therapeutic abortion by hysterotomy

74.99 Other cesarean section of unspecified type
Cesarean section NOS
Obstetrical abdominouterotomy
Obstetrical hysterotomy

✓3rd **75 Other obstetric operations**

75.0 Intra-amniotic injection for abortion
Injection of:
prostaglandin } for induction of abortion
saline }
Termination of pregnancy by intrauterine injection

EXCLUDES *insertion of prostaglandin suppository for abortion (96.49)*

75.1 Diagnostic amniocentesis

75.2 Intrauterine transfusion
Exchange transfusion in utero
Insertion of catheter into abdomen of fetus for transfusion
Code also any hysterotomy approach (68.0)

✓4th **75.3 Other intrauterine operations on fetus and amnion**
Code also any hysterotomy approach (68.0)

75.31 Amnioscopy
Fetoscopy
Laparoamnioscopy

75.32 Fetal EKG (scalp)

75.33 Fetal blood sampling and biopsy

75.34 Other fetal monitoring
Antepartum fetal nonstress test
Fetal monitoring, not otherwise specified

EXCLUDES *fetal pulse oximetry (75.38)*

75.35 Other diagnostic procedures on fetus and amnion
Intrauterine pressure determination

EXCLUDES *amniocentesis (75.1)*
diagnostic procedures on gravid uterus and placenta (87.81, 88.46, 88.78, 92.17)

75.36 Correction of fetal defect

75.37 Amnioinfusion
Code also injection of antibiotic (99.21)

75.38 Fetal pulse oximetry
Transcervical fetal oxygen saturation monitoring
Transcervical fetal SpO_2 monitoring

DEF: Single-use sensor inserted through the birth canal and positioned to rest against the fetal cheek, forehead, or temple; infrared beam of light aimed at the fetal skin is reflected back through the sensor for analysis.

75.4 Manual removal of retained placenta

EXCLUDES *aspiration curettage (69.52)*
dilation and curettage (69.02)

✓4th **75.5 Repair of current obstetric laceration of uterus**

75.50 Repair of current obstetric laceration of uterus, not otherwise specified

75.51 Repair of current obstetric laceration of cervix

75.52 Repair of current obstetric laceration of corpus uteri

✓4th **75.6 Repair of other current obstetric laceration**
Code also episiotomy, if performed (73.6)

75.61 Repair of current obstetric laceration of bladder and urethra

75.62 Repair of current obstetric laceration of rectum and sphincter ani

75.69 Repair of other current obstetric laceration
Episioperineorrhaphy
Repair of:
pelvic floor
perineum
vagina
vulva
Secondary repair of episiotomy

75.7 Manual exploration of uterine cavity, postpartum

75.8 Obstetric tamponade of uterus or vagina

EXCLUDES *antepartum tamponade (73.1)*

✓4th **75.9 Other obstetric operations**

75.91 Evacuation of obstetrical incisional hematoma of perineum
Evacuation of hematoma of:
episiotomy
perineorrhaphy

75.92 Evacuation of other hematoma ofvulva or vagina

75.93 Surgical correction of inverted uterus
Spintelli operation

EXCLUDES *vaginal repair of chronic inversion of uterus (69.23)*

75.94 Manual replacement of inverted uterus

75.99 Other

14. OPERATIONS ON THE MUSCULOSKELETAL SYSTEM (76-84)

✓3rd **76 Operations on facial bones and joints**

EXCLUDES *accessory sinuses (22.00-22.9)*
nasal bones (21.00-21.99)
skull (01.01-02.99)

✓4th **76.0 Incision of facial bone without division**

76.01 Sequestrectomy of facial bone
Removal of necrotic bone chip from facial bone

76.09 Other incision of facial bone
Reopening of osteotomy site of facial bone

EXCLUDES *osteotomy associated with orthognathic surgery (76.61-76.69)*
removal of internal fixation device (76.97)

✓4th **76.1 Diagnostic procedures on facial bones and joints**

76.11 Biopsy of facial bone

76.19 Other diagnostic procedures on facial bones and joints

EXCLUDES *contrast arthrogram of temporomandibular joint (87.13)*
other x-ray (87.11-87.12, 87.14-87.16)

76.2 Local excision or destruction of lesion of facial bone

EXCLUDES *biopsy of facial bone (76.11)*
excision of odontogenic lesion (24.4)

✓4th **76.3 Partial ostectomy of facial bone**

76.31 Partial mandibulectomy
Hemimandibulectomy

EXCLUDES *that associated with temporomandibular arthroplasty (76.5)*

DEF: Excision, partial of lower jawbone.

DEF: Hemimandibulectomy: Excision of one-half of lower jawbone.

76.39 Partial ostectomy of other facial bone
Hemimaxillectomy (with bonegraft or prosthesis)

DEF: Excision, partial of facial bone; other than lower jawbone.

DEF: Hemimaxillectomy (with bone graft or prosthesis): Excision of one side of upper jawbone and restoration with bone graft or prosthesis.

✓4th **76.4 Excision and reconstruction of facial bones**

76.41 Total mandibulectomy with synchronous reconstruction

76.42 Other total mandibulectomy

76.43 Other reconstruction of mandible

EXCLUDES *genioplasty (76.67-76.68)*
that with synchronous total mandibulectomy (76.41)

76.44 Total ostectomy of other facial bone with synchronous reconstruction

DEF: Excision, facial bone, total with reconstruction during same operative session.

76.45 Other total ostectomy of other facial bone

76.46 Other reconstruction of other facial bone

EXCLUDES *that with synchronous total ostectomy (76.44)*

76.5 Temporomandibular arthroplasty

✓4th **76.6 Other facial bone repair and orthognathic surgery**

Code also any synchronous:
bone graft (76.91)
synthetic implant (76.92)

EXCLUDES *reconstruction of facial bones (76.41-76.46)*

76.61 Closed osteoplasty [osteotomy] of mandibular ramus
Gigli saw osteotomy

DEF: Reshaping and restoration of lower jawbone projection; closed surgical field.

DEF: Gigli saw osteotomy: Plastic repair using a flexible wire with saw teeth.

76.62 Open osteoplasty [osteotomy] of mandibular ramus

76.63 Osteoplasty [osteotomy] of body of mandible

76.64 Other orthognathic surgery on mandible
Mandibular osteoplasty NOS
Segmental or subapical osteotomy

76.65 Segmental osteoplasty [osteotomy] of maxilla
Maxillary osteoplasty NOS

76.66 Total osteoplasty [osteotomy] of maxilla

76.67 Reduction genioplasty
Reduction mentoplasty

DEF: Reduction of protruding chin or lower jawbone.

76.68 Augmentation genioplasty
Mentoplasty:
NOS
with graft or implant

DEF: Extension of the lower jawbone to a functional position by means of plastic surgery.

76.69 Other facial bone repair
Osteoplasty of facial bone NOS

✓4th **76.7 Reduction of facial fracture**

INCLUDES internal fixation

Code also any synchronous:
bone graft (76.91)
synthetic implant (76.92)

EXCLUDES *that of nasal bones (21.71-21.72)*

76.70 Reduction of facial fracture, not otherwise specified

76.71 Closed reduction of malar and zygomatic fracture

76.72 Open reduction of malar and zygomatic fracture

76.73 Closed reduction of maxillary fracture

76.74 Open reduction of maxillary fracture

76.75 Closed reduction of mandibular fracture

76.76 Open reduction of mandibular fracture

76.77 Open reduction of alveolar fracture
Reduction of alveolar fracture with stabilization of teeth

76.78 Other closed reduction of facial fracture
Closed reduction of orbital fracture

EXCLUDES *nasal bone (21.71)*

76.79 Other open reduction of facial fracture
Open reduction of orbit rim or wall

EXCLUDES *nasal bone (21.72)*

✓4th **76.9 Other operations on facial bones and joints**

76.91 Bone graft to facial bone
Autogenous, Bone bank, Heterogenous } graft to facial bone

76.92 Insertion of synthetic implant in facial bone
Alloplastic implant to facial bone

76.93 Closed reduction of temporomandibular dislocation

76.94 Open reduction of temporomandibular dislocation

76.95 Other manipulation of temporomandibular joint

76.96 Injection of therapeutic substance into temporomandibular joint

76.97 Removal of internal fixation device from facial bone

EXCLUDES *removal of:*
dental wiring (97.33)
external mandibular fixation device NEC (97.36)

76.99 Other

✓3rd 77 Incision, excision, and division of other bones

EXCLUDES *laminectomy for decompression (03.09)*
operations on:
accessory sinuses (22.00-22.9)
ear ossicles (19.0-19.55)
facial bones (76.01-76.99)
joint structures (80.00-81.99)
mastoid (19.9-20.99)
nasal bones (21.00-21.99)
skull (01.01-02.99)

The following fourth-digit subclassification is for use with appropriate categories in section 77 to identify the site. Valid fourth-digit categories are in [brackets] under each code.

0 unspecified site
1 scapula, clavicle, and thorax [ribs and sternum]
2 humerus
3 radius and ulna
4 carpals and metacarpals
5 femur
6 patella
7 tibia and fibula
8 tarsals and metatarsals
9 other
Pelvic bones
Phalanges (of foot) (of hand)
Vertebrae

✓4th 77.0 Sequestrectomy
[0-9] **DEF: Excision and removal of dead bone.**

✓4th 77.1 Other incision of bone without division
[0-9] Reopening of osteotomy site

EXCLUDES *aspiration of bone marrow, (41.31, 41.91)*
removal of internal fixation device (78.60-78.69)

DEF: Incision into bone without division of site.

✓4th 77.2 Wedge osteotomy
[0-9] EXCLUDES *that for hallux valgus (77.51)*

DEF: Removal of wedge-shaped piece of bone.

Repair of Hammer Toe

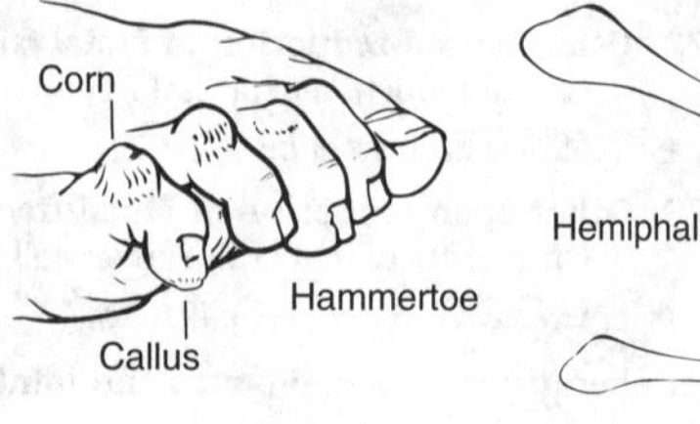

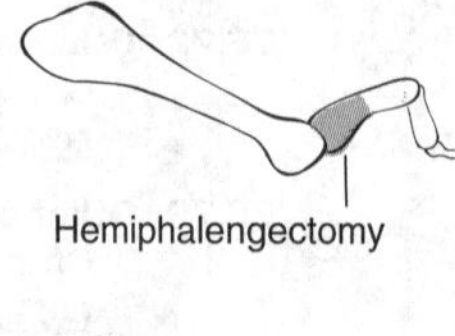

✓4th 77.3 Other division of bone
[0-9] Osteoarthrotomy

EXCLUDES *clavicotomy of fetus (73.8)*
laminotomy or incision of vertebra (03.01-03.09)
pubiotomy to assist delivery (73.94)
sternotomy incidental to thoracic operation — omit code

✓4th 77.4 Biopsy of bone
[0-9]

✓4th 77.5 Excision and repair of bunion and other toe deformities

77.51 Bunionectomy with soft tissue correction and osteotomy of the first metatarsal
DEF: Incision and removal of big toe bony prominence and reconstruction with soft tissue.

77.52 Bunionectomy with soft tissue correction and arthrodesis
DEF: Removal of big toe bony prominence and reconstruction with soft tissue and joint fixation.

77.53 Other bunionectomy with soft tissue correction

77.54 Excision or correction of bunionette
That with osteotomy
DEF: Resection of fifth metatarsal head via exposure of joint; includes imbrication of capsule.

77.56 Repair of hammer toe
Filleting } of hammer toe
Fusion } of hammer toe
Phalangectomy (partial) } of hammer toe
DEF: Repair of clawlike toe defect by joint fusion, or partial removal of toe via traction technique.

77.57 Repair of claw toe
Capsulotomy } of claw toe
Fusion } of claw toe
Phalangectomy (partial) } of claw toe
Tendon lenghening } of claw toe
DEF: Repair of clawlike toe defect by joint fusion, partial removal of toe, joint capsule incision or lengthening of fibrous muscle attachment.

77.58 Other excision, fusion, and repair of toes
Cockup toe repair
Overlapping toe repair
That with use of prosthetic materials

77.59 Other bunionectomy
Resection of hallux valgus joint with insertion of prosthesis
DEF: Resection of hallux valgus joint with insertion of prosthesis: Cutting away part of big toe with prosthesis insertion to correct bony prominence.

✓4th 77.6 Local excision of lesion or tissue of bone
[0-9] EXCLUDES *biopsy of bone (77.40-77.49)*
debridement of compound fracture (79.60-79.69)

✓4th 77.7 Excision of bone for graft
[0-9]

√4th **77.8 Other partial ostectomy**
[0-9] Condylectomy

EXCLUDES *amputation (84.00-84.19, 84.91)*
arthrectomy (80.90-80.99)
excision of bone ends associated with:
arthrodesis (81.00-81.39, 81.62-81.66)
arthroplasty (81.40-81.59, 81.71-81.85)
excision of cartilage (80.5-80.6, 80.80-80.99)
excision of head of femur with synchronous replacement (00.70-00.73, 81.51-81.53)
hemilaminectomy (03.01-03.09)
laminectomy (03.01-03.09)
ostectomy for hallux valgus (77.51-77.59)
partial amputation:
finger (84.01)
thumb (84.02)
toe (84.11)
resection of ribs incidental to thoracic operation — omit code
that incidental to other operation — omit code

√4th **77.9 Total ostectomy**
[0-9] **EXCLUDES** *amputation of limb (84.00-84.19, 84.91)*
that incidental to other operation — omit code

√3rd **78 Other operations on bones, except facial bones**

EXCLUDES *operations on:*
accessory sinuses (22.00-22.9)
facial bones (76.01-76.99)
joint structures (80.00-81.99)
nasal bones (21.00-21.99)
skull (01.01-02.99)

The following fourth-digit subclassification is for use with appropriate categories in section 78 to identify the site. Valid fourth-digit categories are in [brackets] under each code.

0 unspecified site
1 scapula, clavicle, and thorax [ribs and sternum]
2 humerus
3 radius and ulna
4 carpals and metacarpals
5 femur
6 patella
7 tibia and fibula
8 tarsals and metatarsals
9 other
Pelvic bones
Phalanges (of foot) (of hand)
Vertebrae

√4th **78.0 Bone graft**
[0-9] Bone:
bank graft
graft (autogenous) (heterogenous)
That with debridement of bone graft site (removal of sclerosed, fibrous, or necrotic bone or tissue)
Transplantation of bone

Code also any excision of bone for graft (77.70-77.79)

EXCLUDES *that for bone lengthening (78.30-78.39)*

√4th **78.1 Application of external fixator device**
[0-9] Fixator with insertion of pins/wires/screws into bone

Code also any type of fixator device, if known (84.71-84.73)

EXCLUDES *other immobilization, pressure, and attention to wound (93.51-93.59)*

√4th **78.2 Limb shortening procedures**
[0,2-5,7-9]
Epiphyseal stapling
Open epiphysiodesis
Percutaneous epiphysiodesis
Resection/osteotomy

√4th **78.3 Limb lengthening procedures**
[0,2-5,7-9]
Bone graft with or without internal fixation devices or osteotomy
Distraction technique with or without corticotomy/osteotomy

Code also any application of an external fixation device (78.10-78.19)

√4th **78.4 Other repair or plastic operations on bone**
[0-9] Other operation on bone NEC
Repair of malunion or nonunion fracture NEC

EXCLUDES *application of external fixation device (78.10-78.19)*
limb lengthening procedures (78.30-78.39)
limb shortening procedures (78.20-78.29)
osteotomy (77.3)
reconstruction of thumb (82.61-82.69)
repair of pectus deformity (34.74)
repair with bone graft (78.00-78.09)

√4th **78.5 Internal fixation of bone without fracture**
[0-9] **reduction**
Internal fixation of bone (prophylactic)
Reinsertion of internal fixation device
Revision of displaced or broken fixation device

EXCLUDES *arthroplasty and arthrodesis (81.00-81.85)*
bone graft (78.00-78.09)
limb shortening procedures (78.20-78.29)
that for fracture reduction (79.10-79.19, 79.30-79.59)

√4th **78.6 Removal of implanted devices from bone**
[0-9] External fixator device (invasive)
Internal fixation device
Removal of bone growth stimulator (invasive)
Removal of internal limb lengthening device
Removal of pedicle screw(s) used in spinal fusion

EXCLUDES *removal of cast, splint, and traction device (Kirschner wire) (Steinmann pin) (97.88)*
removal of posterior spinal motion preservation (facet replacement, pedicle-based dynamic stabilization, interspinous process) device(s) (80.09)
removal of skull tongs or halo traction device (02.95)

√4th **78.7 Osteoclasis**
[0-9] **DEF: Surgical breaking or rebreaking of bone.**

√4th **78.8 Diagnostic procedures on bone, not elsewhere**
[0-9] **classified**

EXCLUDES *biopsy of bone (77.40-77.49)*
magnetic resonance imaging (88.94)
microscopic examination of specimen from bone (91.51-91.59)
radioisotope scan (92.14)
skeletal x-ray (87.21-87.29, 87.43, 88.21-88.33)
thermography (88.83)

√4th **78.9 Insertion of bone growth stimulator**
[0-9] Insertion of:
bone stimulator (electrical) to aid bone healing
osteogenic electrodes for bone growth stimulation
totally implanted device (invasive)

EXCLUDES *non-invasive (transcutaneous) (surface) stimulator (99.86)*

3rd 79 Reduction of fracture and dislocation

INCLUDES application of cast or splint
reduction with insertion of traction device (Kirschner wire) (Steinmann pin)

Code also any:
application of external fixator device (78.10-78.19)
type of fixator device, if known (84.71-84.73)

EXCLUDES *external fixation alone for immobilization of fracture (93.51-93.56, 93.59)*
internal fixation without reduction of fracture (78.50-78.59)
operations on:
facial bones(76.70-76.79)
nasal bones (21.71-21.72)
orbit (76.78-76.79)
skull (02.02)
vertebrae (03.53)
removal of cast or splint (97.88)
replacement of cast or splint (97.11-97.14)
traction alone for reduction of fracture (93.41-93.46)

The following fourth-digit subclassification is for use with appropriate categories in section 79 to identify the site. Valid fourth-digit categories are in [brackets] under each code.
0 unspecified site
1 humerus
2 radius and ulna
Arm NOS
3 carpals and metacarpals
Hand NOS
4 phalanges of hand
5 femur
6 tibia and fibula
Leg NOS
7 tarsals and metatarsals
Foot NOS
8 phalanges of foot
9 other specified bone

4th 79.0 Closed reduction of fracture without internal fixation
[0-9]

EXCLUDES *that for separation of epiphysis (79.40-79.49)*

DEF: Manipulative realignment of fracture; without incision or internal fixation.

4th 79.1 Closed reduction of fracture with internal fixation
[0-9]

EXCLUDES *that for separation of epiphysis (79.40-79.49)*

DEF: Manipulative realignment of fracture; with internal fixation but without incision.

4th 79.2 Open reduction of fracture without internal fixation
[0-9]

EXCLUDES *that for separation of epiphysis (79.50-79.59)*

4th 79.3 Open reduction of fracture with internal fixation
[0-9]

EXCLUDES *that for separation of epiphysis (79.50-79.59)*

DEF: Realignment of fracture with incision and internal fixation.

4th 79.4 Closed reduction of separated epiphysis
[0-2,5,6,9]

Reduction with or without internal fixation

DEF: Manipulative reduction of expanded joint end of long bone to normal position without incision.

4th 79.5 Open reduction of separated epiphysis
[0-2,5,6,9]

Reduction with or without internal fixation

DEF: Reduction of expanded joint end of long bone with incision.

4th 79.6 Debridement of open fracture site
[0-9] Debridement of compound fracture

DEF: Removal of damaged tissue at fracture site.

4th 79.7 Closed reduction of dislocation

INCLUDES closed reduction (with external traction device)

EXCLUDES *closed reduction of dislocation of temporomandibular joint (76.93)*

DEF: Manipulative reduction of displaced joint without incision; with or without external traction.

79.70 Closed reduction of dislocation of unspecified site

79.71 Closed reduction of dislocation of shoulder

79.72 Closed reduction of dislocation of elbow

79.73 Closed reduction of dislocation of wrist

79.74 Closed reduction of dislocation of hand and finger

79.75 Closed reduction of dislocation of hip

79.76 Closed reduction of dislocation of knee

79.77 Closed reduction of dislocation of ankle

79.78 Closed reduction of dislocation of foot and toe

79.79 Closed reduction of dislocation of other specified sites

4th 79.8 Open reduction of dislocation

INCLUDES open reduction (with internal and external fixation devices)

EXCLUDES *open reduction of dislocation of temporomandibular joint (76.94)*

DEF: Reduction of displaced joint via incision; with or without internal and external fixation.

79.80 Open reduction of dislocation of unspecified site

79.81 Open reduction of dislocation of shoulder

79.82 Open reduction of dislocation of elbow

79.83 Open reduction of dislocation of wrist

79.84 Open reduction of dislocation of hand and finger

79.85 Open reduction of dislocation of hip

79.86 Open reduction of dislocation of knee

79.87 Open reduction of dislocation of ankle

79.88 Open reduction of dislocation of foot and toe

79.89 Open reduction of dislocation of other specified sites

4th 79.9 Unspecified operation on bone injury
[0-9]

✓3rd 80 Incision and excision of joint structures

INCLUDES operations on:
capsule of joint
cartilage
condyle
ligament
meniscus
synovial membrane

EXCLUDES *cartilage of:*
ear (18.01-18.9)
nose (21.00-21.99)
temporomandibular joint (76.01-76.99))

The following fourth-digit subclassification is for use with appropriate categories in section 80 to identify the site:
0 unspecified site
1 shoulder
2 elbow
3 wrist
4 hand and finger
5 hip
6 knee
7 ankle
8 foot and toe
9 other specified sites
Spine

✓4th 80.0 Arthrotomy for removal of prosthesis

INCLUDES removal of posterior spinal motion preservation (dynamic stabilization, facet replacement, interspinous process) device(s)

Code also any:
insertion of (cement) (joint) (methylmethacrylate) spacer (84.56)
removal of (cement) (joint) (methylmethacrylate) spacer (84.57)

EXCLUDES *removal of pedicle screws used in spinal fusion (78.69)*

DEF: Incision into joint to remove prosthesis.

✓4th 80.1 Other arthrotomy

Arthrostomy

EXCLUDES *that for:*
arthrography (88.32)
arthroscopy (80.20-80.29)
injection of drug (81.92)
operative approach — omit code

DEF: Incision into joint; other than to remove prosthesis.

DEF: Arthrostomy: Creation of opening into joint.

✓4th 80.2 Arthroscopy

✓4th 80.3 Biopsy of joint structure

Aspiration biopsy

✓4th 80.4 Division of joint capsule, ligament, or cartilage

Goldner clubfoot release
Heyman-Herndon(-Strong) correction of metatarsus varus
Release of:
adherent or constrictive joint capsule
joint
ligament

EXCLUDES *symphysiotomy to assist delivery (73.94)*
that for:
carpal tunnel syndrome (04.43)
tarsal tunnel syndrome (04.44)

DEF: Incision and separation of joint tissues, including capsule, fibrous bone attachment or cartilage.

✓4th 80.5 Excision, destruction and other repair of intervertebral disc

80.50 Excision or destruction of intervertebral disc, unspecified

Unspecified as to excision or destruction

80.51 Excision of intervertebral disc

Note: Requires additional code for any concomitant decompression of spinal nerve root at different level from excision site

Diskectomy
Level:
cervical
thoracic
lumbar (lumbosacral)
Removal of herniated nucleus pulposus
That by laminotomy or hemilaminectomy
That with decompression of spinal nerve root at same level
Code also any:
concurrent spinal fusion (81.00-81.08)
repair of the anulus fibrosus (80.53-80.54)

EXCLUDES *intervertebral chemonucleolysis (80.52)*
laminectomy for exploration of intraspinal canal (03.09)
laminotomy for decompression of spinal nerve root only (03.09)
that for insertion of (non-fusion) spinal disc replacement device (84.60-84.69)
that with corpectomy, (vertebral) (80.99)

DEF: Diskectomy: Removal of intervertebral disc.

DEF: Removal of a herniated nucleus pulposus: Removal of displaced intervertebral disc, central part.

80.52 Intervertebral chemonucleolysis

With aspiration of disc fragments
With diskography
Injection of proteolytic enzyme into intervertebral space (chymopapain)

EXCLUDES *injection of anesthetic substance (03.91)*
injection of other substances (03.92)

DEF: Destruction of intervertebral disc via injection of enzyme.

80.53 Repair of the anulus fibrosus with graft or prosthesis

INCLUDES microsurgical suture repair with fascial autograft
soft tissue re-approximation repair with tension bands
surgical mesh repair

Anular disc repair
Closure (sealing) of the anulus fibrosus defect
Code also any:
application or administration of adhesion barrier substance, if performed (99.77)
intervertebral discectomy, if performed (80.51)
locally harvested fascia for graft (83.43)

80.54 Other and unspecified repair of the anulus fibrosus

Anular disc repair
Closure (sealing) of the anulus fibrosus defect
Microsurgical suture repair without fascial autograft
Percutaneous repair of the anulus fibrosus
Code also any:
application or administration of adhesion barrier substance, if performed (99.77)
intervertebral discectomy, if performed (80.51)

80.59 Other destruction of intervertebral disc
Destruction NEC
That by laser

80.6 Excision of semilunar cartilage of knee
Excision of meniscus of knee

✓4th **80.7 Synovectomy**
Complete or partial resection of synovial membrane
EXCLUDES *excision of Baker's cyst (83.39)*
DEF: Excision of inner membrane of joint capsule.

✓4th **80.8 Other local excision or destruction of lesion of joint**

✓4th **80.9 Other excision of joint**
EXCLUDES *cheilectomy of joint (77.80-77.89)*
excision of bone ends (77.80-77.89)

✓3rd 81 Repair and palstic operations on joint structures

✓4th **81.0 Spinal fusion**
INCLUDES arthrodesis of spine with:
bone graft
internal fixation
Code also any:
insertion of interbody spinal fusion device (84.51)
insertion of recombinant bone morphogenetic protein (84.52)
synchronous excision of (locally) harvested bone for graft (77.70-77.79)
Code also the total number of vertebrae fused (81.62-81.64)
EXCLUDES *corrections of pseudarthrosis of spine (81.30-81.39)*
refusion of spine (81.30-81.39)
DEF: Spinal fusion: Immobilization of spinal column.
DEF: Anterior interbody fusion: Arthrodesis by excising disc and cartilage end plates with bone graft insertion between two vertebrae.
DEF: Lateral fusion: Arthrodesis by decorticating and bone grafting lateral surface of zygapophysial joint, pars interarticularis and transverse process.
DEF: Posterior fusion: Arthrodesis by decorticating and bone grafting of neural arches between right and left zygapophysial joints.
DEF: Posterolateral fusion: Arthrodesis by decorticating and bone grafting zygapophysial joint, pars interarticularis and transverse processes

81.00 Spinal fusion, not otherwise specified

81.01 Atlas-axis spinal fusion
Craniocervical fusion
C1–C2 fusion
Occiput C2 fusion
} by anterior transoral or posterior technique

81.02 Other cervical fusion, anterior technique
Arthrodesis of C2 level or below:
anterior (interbody) technique
anterolateral technique

81.03 Other cervical fusion, posterior technique
Arthrodesis of C2 level or below:
posterior (interbody) technique
posterolateral technique

81.04 Dorsal and dorsolumbar fusion, anterior technique
Arthrodesis of thoracic or thoracolumbar region:
anterior (interbody) technique
anterolateral technique

81.05 Dorsal and dorsolumbar fusion, posterior technique
Arthrodesis of thoracic or thoracolumbar region:
posterior (interbody) technique
posterolateral technique

Types of Grafts for Anterior Arthrodesis

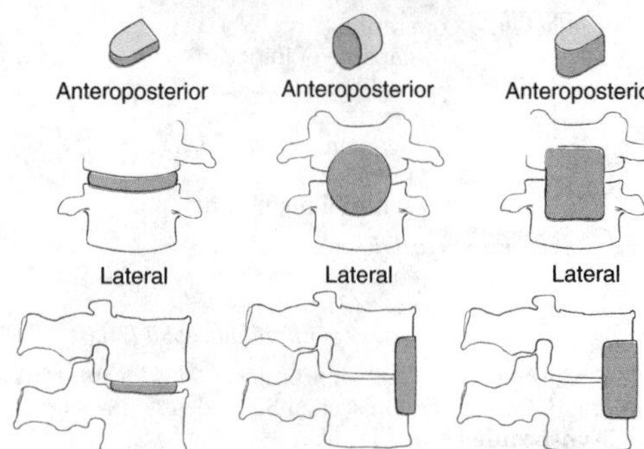

81.06 Lumbar and lumbosacral fusion, anterior technique
Anterior lumbar interbody fusion (ALIF)
Arthrodesis of lumbar or lumbosacral region:
anterior (interbody) technique
anterolateral technique

81.07 Lumbar and lumbosacral fusion, lateral transverse process technique

81.08 Lumbar and lumbosacral fusion, posterior technique
Arthrodesis of lumbar or lumbosacral region:
posterior (interbody) technique
posterolateral technique
Posterior lumbar interbody fusion (PLIF)
Transforaminal lumbar interbody fusion (TLIF)

✓4th **81.1 Arthrodesis and arthroereisis of foot and ankle**
INCLUDES arthrodesis of foot and ankle with:
bone graft
external fixation device
DEF: Fixation of foot or ankle joints.

81.11 Ankle fusion
Tibiotalar fusion

81.12 Triple arthrodesis
Talus to calcaneus and calcaneus to cuboid and navicular

81.13 Subtalar fusion
EXCLUDES *arthroereisis (81.18)*

81.14 Midtarsal fusion

81.15 Tarsometatarsal fusion

81.16 Metatarsophalangeal fusion

81.17 Other fusion of foot

81.18 Subtalar joint arthroereisis
DEF: Insertion of an endoprostheses to limit excessive valgus motion of the subtalar joint; nonfusion procedure to prevent pronation.

✓4th **81.2 Arthrodesis of other joint**
INCLUDES arthrodesis with:
bone graft
external fixation device
excision of bone ends and compression

81.20 Arthrodesis of unspecified joint

81.21 Arthrodesis of hip

81.22 Arthrodesis of knee

81.23 Arthrodesis of shoulder

81.24 Arthrodesis of elbow

81.25 Carporadial fusion

81.26 Metacarpocarpal fusion

Subtalar Joint Arthroereisis

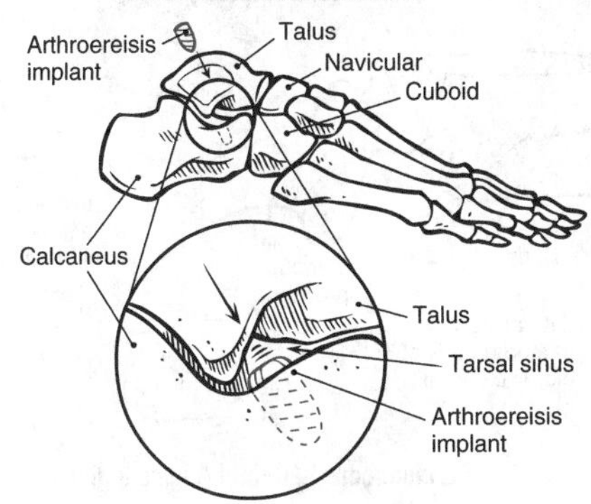

81.27 Metacarpophalangeal fusion

81.28 Interphalangeal fusion

81.29 Arthrodesis of other specified joints

✓4th **81.3 Refusion of spine**

INCLUDES arthrodesis of spine with:
bone graft
internal fixation
correction of pseudarthrosis of spine

Code also any:
insertion of interbody spinal fusion device (84.51)
insertion of recombinant bone morphogenetic protein (84.52)
synchronous excision of (locally) harvested bone for graft (77.70-77.79)

Code also the total number of vertebrae fused (81.62-81.64)

81.30 Refusion of spine, not otherwise specified

81.31 Refusion of atlas-axis spine

Craniocervical fusion, C1-C2 fusion, Occiput C2 fusion } by anterior transoral or posterior technique

81.32 Refusion of other cervical spine, anterior technique

Arthrodesis of C2 level or below:
anterior (interbody) technique
anterolateral technique

81.33 Refusion of other cervical spine, posterior technique

Arthrodesis of C2 level or below:
posterior (interbody) technique
posterolateral technique

81.34 Refusion of dorsal and dorsolumbar spine, anterior technique

Arthrodesis of thoracic or thoracolumbar region:
anterior (interbody) technique
anterolateral technique

81.35 Refusion of dorsal and dorsolumbar spine, posterior technique

Arthrodesis of thoracic or thoracolumbar region:
posterior (interbody) technique
posterolateral technique

81.36 Refusion of lumbar and lumbosacral spine, anterior technique

Anterior lumbar interbody fusion (ALIF)
Arthrodesis of lumbar or lumbosacral region:
anterior (interbody) technique
anterolateral technique

81.37 Refusion of lumbar and lumbosacral spine, lateral transverse process technique

81.38 Refusion of lumbar and lumbosacral spine, posterior technique

Arthrodesis of lumbar or lumbosacral region:
posterior (interbody) technique
posterolateral technique
Posterior lumbar interbody fusion (PLIF)
Transforaminal lumbar interbody fusion (TLIF)

81.39 Refusion of spine, not elsewhere classified

✓4th **81.4 Other repair of joint of lower extremity**

INCLUDES arthroplasty of lower extremity with:
external traction or fixation
graft of bone (chips) or cartilage
internal fixation device

81.40 Repair of hip, not elsewhere classified

81.42 Five-in-one repair of knee

Medial meniscectomy, medial collateral ligament repair, vastus medialis advancement, semitendinosus advancement, and pes anserinus transfer

81.43 Triad knee repair

Medial meniscectomy with repair of the anterior cruciate ligament and the medial collateral ligament
O'Donoghue procedure

81.44 Patellar stabilization

Roux-Goldthwait operation for recurrent dislocation of patella

DEF: Roux-Goldthwait operation: Stabilization of patella via lateral ligament transposed at insertion beneath undisturbed medial insertion; excision of capsule ellipse and medial patella retinaculum; capsule reefed for lateral patella hold.

81.45 Other repair of the cruciate ligaments

81.46 Other repair of the collateral ligaments

81.47 Other repair of knee

81.49 Other repair of ankle

✓4th **81.5 Joint replacement of lower extremity**

INCLUDES arthroplasty of lower extremity with:
external traction or fixation
graft of bone (chips) or cartilage
internal fixation device or prosthesis

81.51 Total hip replacement

Replacement of both femoral head and acetabulum by prosthesis
Total reconstruction of hip

Code also any type of bearing surface, if known (00.74-00.77)

DEF: Repair of both surfaces of hip joint with prosthesis.

81.52 Partial hip replacement

Bipolar endoprosthesis

Code also any type of bearing surface, if known (00.74-00.77)

DEF: Repair of single surface of hip joint with prosthesis.

81.53 Revision of hip replacement, not otherwise specified

Revision of hip replacement, not specified as to component(s) replaced, (acetabular, femoral or both)

Code also any:
removal of (cement) (joint) spacer (84.57)
type of bearing surface, if known (00.74-00.77)

EXCLUDES *revision of hip replacement, components specified (00.70-00.73)*

Partial Hip Replacement

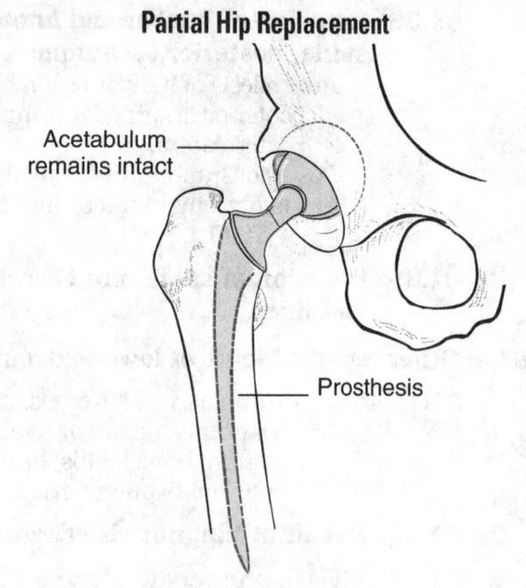

Total Hip Replacement

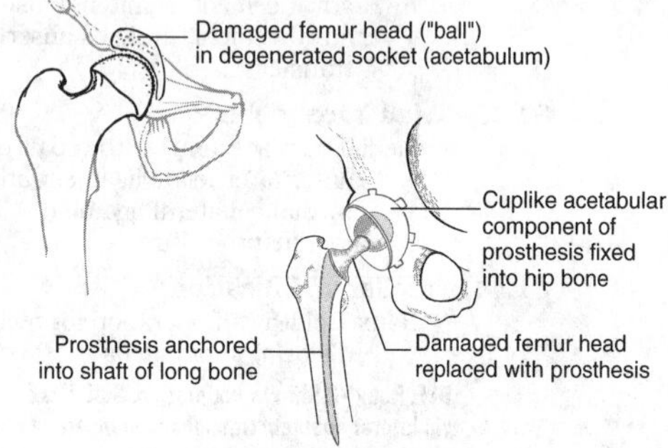

Total Knee Replacement

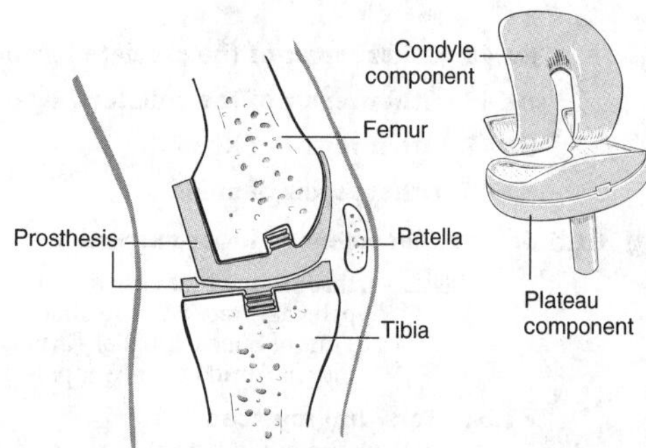

81.54 Total knee replacement
Bicompartmental
Tricompartmental
Unicompartmental (hemijoint)

DEF: Repair of a knee joint with prosthetic implant in one, two, or three compartments.

81.55 Revision of knee replacement, not otherwise specified
Code also any removal of (cement) (joint) spacer (84.57)

EXCLUDES *arthrodesis of knee (81.22)*
revision of knee replacement, components specified (00.80-00.84)

81.56 Total ankle replacement

81.57 Replacement of joint of foot and toe

81.59 Revision of joint replacement of lower extremity, not otherwise specified

Vertebroplasty

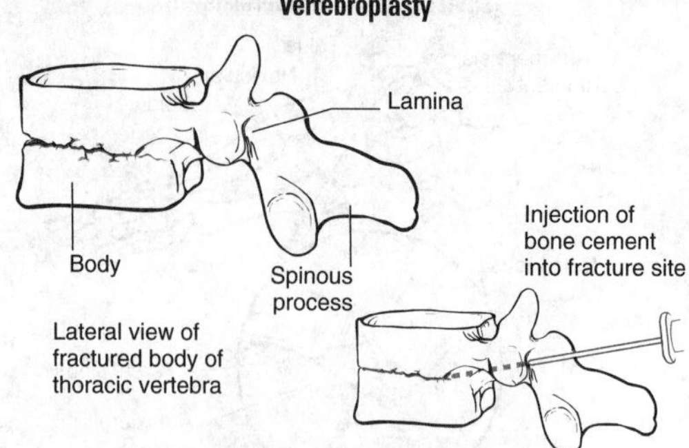

Percutaneous Vertebral Augmentation

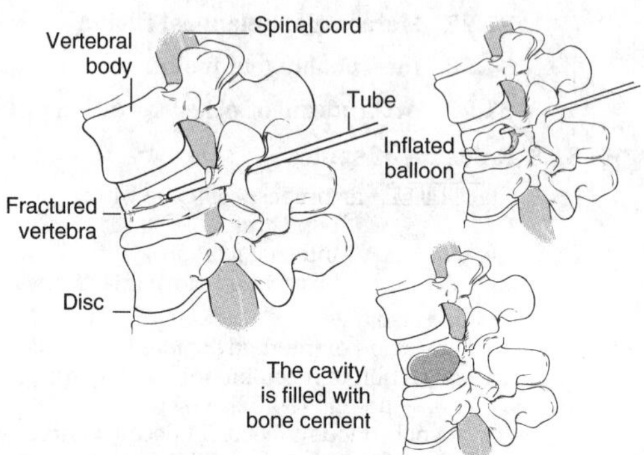

4th 81.6 Other procedures on spine

Note: Number of vertebrae

The vertebral spine consists of 25 vertebrae in the following order and number:
Cervical: C1 (atlas), C2 (axis), C3, C4, C5, C6, C7
Thoracic or Dorsal: T1, T2, T3, T4, T5, T6, T7, T8, T9, T10, T11, T12
Lumbar and Sacral: L1, L2, L3, L4, L5, S1

Coders should report only one code from the series 81.62-81.64 to show the total number of vertebrae fused on the patient.

Code also the level and approach of the fusion or refusion (81.00-81.08, 81.30-81.39)

DEF: A combined posterior and anterior fusion performed by a surgeon through one incision: lateral transverse, posterior, or anterior.

81.62 Fusion or refusion of 2-3 vertebrae

81.63 Fusion or refusion of 4-8 vertebrae

81.64 Fusion or refusion of 9 or more vertebrae

81.65 Percutaneous vertebroplasty
Injection of bone void filler (cement) (polymethylmethacrylate) (PMMA) into the diseased or fractured vertebral body

EXCLUDES *kyphoplasty (81.66)*
percutaneous vertebral augmentation (81.66)

81.66 Percutaneous vertebral augmentation
Arcuplasty
Insertion of inflatable balloon, bone tamp, or other device displacing (removing) (compacting) bone to create a space (cavity) (void) prior to the injection of bone void filler (cement) (polymethylmethacrylate) (PMMA) or other substance
Kyphoplasty
SKyphoplasty
Spineoplasty

EXCLUDES *percutaneous vertebroplasty (81.65)*

✓4th 81.7 Arthroplasty and repair of hand, fingers, and wrist

INCLUDES arthroplasty of hand and finger with:
external traction or fixation
graft of bone (chips) or cartilage
internal fixation device or prosthesis

EXCLUDES *operations on muscle, tendon, and fascia of hand (82.01-82.99)*

DEF: Plastic surgery of hand, fingers and wrist joints.

81.71 Arthroplasty of metacarpophalangeal and interphalangeal joint with implant

81.72 Arthroplasty of metacarpophalangeal and interphalangeal joint without implant

81.73 Total wrist replacement

81.74 Arthroplasty of carpocarpal or carpometacarpal joint with implant

81.75 Arthroplasty of carpocarpal or carpometacarpal joint without implant

81.79 Other repair of hand, fingers, and wrist

✓4th 81.8 Arthroplasty and repair of shoulder and elbow

INCLUDES arthroplasty of upper limb NEC with:
external traction or fixation
graft of bone (chips) or cartilage
internal fixation device or prosthesis

81.80 Total shoulder replacement

81.81 Partial shoulder replacement

81.82 Repair of recurrent dislocation of shoulder

81.83 Other repair of shoulder
Revision of arthroplasty of shoulder

81.84 Total elbow replacement

81.85 Other repair of elbow

✓4th 81.9 Other operations on joint structures

81.91 Arthrocentesis
Joint aspiration

EXCLUDES *that for:*
arthrography (88.32)
biopsy of joint structure (80.30-80.39)
injection of drug (81.92)

DEF: Insertion of needle to withdraw fluid from joint.

81.92 Injection of therapeutic substance into joint or ligament

81.93 Suture of capsule or ligament of upper extremity

EXCLUDES *that associated with arthroplasty (81.71-81.75, 81.80-81.81, 81.84)*

Arthrocentesis

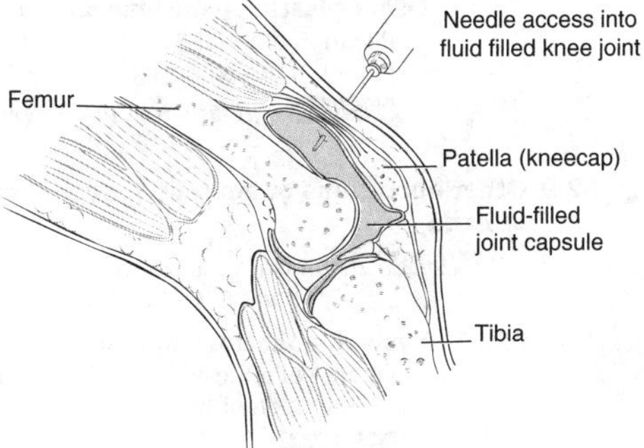

81.94 Suture of capsule or ligament of ankle and foot

EXCLUDES *that associated with arthroplasty (81.56-81.59)*

81.95 Suture of capsule or ligament of other lower extremity

EXCLUDES *that associated with arthroplasty (81.51-81.55, 81.59)*

81.96 Other repair of joint

81.97 Revision of joint replacement of upper extremity
Partial
Removal of cement spacer
Total

81.98 Other diagnostic procedures on joint structures

EXCLUDES *arthroscopy (80.20-80.29)*
biopsy of joint structure (80.30-80.39)
microscopic examination of specimen from joint (91.51-91.59)
thermography (88.83)
x-ray (87.21-87.29, 88.21-88.33)

81.99 Other

✓3rd 82 Operations on muscle, tendon, and fascia of hand

INCLUDES operations on:
aponeurosis
synovial membrane (tendon sheath)
tendon sheath

✓4th 82.0 Incision of muscle, tendon, fascia, and bursa of hand

82.01 Exploration of tendon sheath of hand
Incision of } tendon sheath of hand
Removal of rice bodies in } tendon sheath of hand

EXCLUDES *division of tendon (82.11)*

DEF: Incision into and exploring the hand's muscle and its accompanying supportive, connective tissue, bands, and sacs.

82.02 Myotomy of hand

EXCLUDES *myotomy for division (82.19)*

DEF: Incision into hand muscle.

82.03 Bursotomy of hand

82.04 Incision and drainage of palmar or thenar space

82.09 Other incision of soft tissue of hand

EXCLUDES *incision of skin and subcutaneous tissue alone (86.01-86.09)*

✓4th 82.1 Division of muscle, tendon, and fascia of hand

82.11 Tenotomy of hand
Division of tendon of hand

82.12 Fasciotomy of hand
Division of fascia of hand

82.19 Other division of soft tissue of hand
Division of muscle of hand

✓4th 82.2 Excision of lesion of muscle, tendon, and fascia of hand

82.21 Excision or lesion of tendon sheath of hand
Ganglionectomy of tendon sheath (wrist)

82.22 Excision of lesion of muscle of hand

82.29 Excision of other lesion of soft tissue of hand

EXCLUDES *excision of lesion of skin and subcutaneous tissue (86.21-86.3)*

✓4th 82.3 Other excision of soft tissue of hand

Code also any skin graft (86.61-86.62, 86.73)

EXCLUDES *excision of skin and subcutaneous tissue (86.21-86.3)*

82.31 Bursectomy of hand

82.32 Excision of tendon of hand for graft

DEF: Resection and excision of fibrous tissue connecting bone to hand muscle for grafting.

82.33 Other tenonectomy of hand

Tenosynovectomy of hand

EXCLUDES *excision of lesion of:*
tendon (82.29)
sheath (82.21)

DEF: Removal of fibrous bands connecting muscle to bone of hand.
DEF: Tenosynovectomy of hand: Excision of fibrous band connecting muscle and bone of hand and removal of coverings.

82.34 Excision of muscle or fascia of hand for graft

82.35 Other fasciectomy of hand

Release of Dupuytren's contracture

EXCLUDES *excision of lesion of fascia (82.29)*

DEF: Excision of fibrous connective tissue; other than for grafting or removing lesion.
DEF: Release of Dupuytren's contracture: Excision of fibrous connective tissue to correct flexion of fingers.

82.36 Other myectomy of hand

EXCLUDES *excision of lesion of muscle (82.22)*

82.39 Other excision of soft tissue of hand

EXCLUDES *excision of skin (86.21-86.3)*
excision of soft tissue lesion (82.29)

✓4th 82.4 Suture of muscle, tendon, and fascia of hand

82.41 Suture of tendon sheath of hand

82.42 Delayed suture of flexor tendon of hand

DEF: Suture of fibrous band between flexor muscle and bone; following initial repair.

82.43 Delayed suture of other tendon of hand

82.44 Other suture of flexor tendon of hand

EXCLUDES *delayed suture of flexor tendon of hand (82.42)*

82.45 Other suture of other tendon of hand

EXCLUDES *delayed suture of other tendon of hand (82.43)*

82.46 Suture of muscle or fascia of hand

✓4th 82.5 Transplantation of muscle and tendon of hand

82.51 Advancement of tendon of hand

DEF: Detachment of fibrous connective muscle band and bone with reattachment at advanced point of hand.

82.52 Recession of tendon of hand

DEF: Detachment of fibrous band of muscle and bone with reattachment at drawn-back point of hand.

82.53 Reattachment of tendon of hand

82.54 Reattachment of muscle of hand

82.55 Other change in hand muscle or tendon length

82.56 Other hand tendon transfer or transplantation

EXCLUDES *pollicization of thumb (82.61)*
transfer of finger, except thumb (82.81)

82.57 Other hand tendon transposition

82.58 Other hand muscle transfer or transplantation

82.59 Other hand muscle transposition

✓4th 82.6 Reconstruction of thumb

INCLUDES digital transfer to act as thumb

Code also any amputation for digital transfer (84.01, 84.11)

82.61 Pollicization operation carrying over nerves and blood supply

DEF: Creation or reconstruction of a thumb with another digit, commonly the index finger.

82.69 Other reconstruction of thumb

"Cocked-hat" procedure [skin flap and bone]
Grafts:
bone } to thumb
skin (pedicle) } to thumb

✓4th 82.7 Plastic operation on hand with graft or implant

82.71 Tendon pulley reconstruction

Reconstruction for opponensplasty

DEF: Reconstruction of fibrous band between muscle and bone of hand.

82.72 Plastic operation on hand with graft of muscle or fascia

82.79 Plastic operation on hand with other graft or implant

Tendon graft to hand

✓4th 82.8 Other plastic operations on hand

82.81 Transfer of finger, except thumb

EXCLUDES *pollicization of thumb (82.61)*

82.82 Repair of cleft hand

DEF: Correction of fissure defect of hand.

82.83 Repair of macrodactyly

DEF: Reduction in size of abnormally large fingers.

82.84 Repair of mallet finger

DEF: Repair of flexed little finger.

82.85 Other tenodesis of hand

Tendon fixation of hand NOS

DEF: Fixation of fibrous connective band between muscle and bone of hand.

82.86 Other tenoplasty of hand

Myotenoplasty of hand

DEF: Myotenoplasty of hand: Plastic repair of muscle and fibrous band connecting muscle to bone.

82.89 Other plastic operations on hand

Plication of fascia
Repair of fascial hernia

EXCLUDES *that with graft or implant (82.71-82.79)*

✓4th 82.9 Other operations on muscle, tendon, and fascia of hand

EXCLUDES *diagnostic procedures on soft tissue of hand (83.21-83.29)*

82.91 Lysis of adhesions of hand

Freeing of adhesions of fascia, muscle, and tendon of hand

EXCLUDES *decompression of carpal tunnel (04.43)*
that by stretching or manipulation only (93.26)

82.92 Aspiration of bursa of hand

82.93 Aspiration of other soft tissue of hand

EXCLUDES *skin and subcutaneous tissue (86.01)*

82.94 Injection of therapeutic substance into bursa of hand

82.95 Injection of therapeutic substance into tendon of hand

82.96 Other injection of locally-acting therapeutic substance into soft tissue of hand

EXCLUDES *subcutaneous or intramuscular injection (99.11-99.29)*

82.99 Other operations on muscle, tendon, and fascia of hand

✓3rd 83 Operations on muscle, tendon, fascia, and bursa, except hand

INCLUDES operations on:
aponeurosis
synovial membrane of bursa and tendon sheaths
tendon sheaths

EXCLUDES *diaphragm (34.81-34.89)*
hand (82.01-82.99)
muscles of eye (15.01-15.9)

✓4th 83.0 Incision of muscle, tendon, fascia, and bursa

83.01 Exploration of tendon sheath

Incision of tendon sheath
Removal of rice bodies from tendon sheath

DEF: Incision of external covering of fibrous cord for exam.

DEF: Removal of rice bodies from tendon sheath: Incision and removal of small bodies resembling grains of rice.

83.02 Myotomy

EXCLUDES *cricopharyngeal myotomy (29.31)*

83.03 Bursotomy

Removal of calcareous deposit of bursa

EXCLUDES *aspiration of bursa (percutaneous) (83.94)*

83.09 Other incision of soft tissue

Incision of fascia

EXCLUDES *incision of skin and subcutaneous tissue alone (86.01-86.09)*

✓4th 83.1 Division of muscle, tendon, and fascia

83.11 Achillotenotomy

83.12 Adductor tenotomy of hip

DEF: Incision into fibrous attachment between adductor muscle and hip bone.

83.13 Other tenotomy

Aponeurotomy
Division of tendon
Tendon release
Tendon transection
Tenotomy for thoracic outlet decompression

DEF: Aponeurotomy: Incision and separation of fibrous cords attaching a muscle to bone to aid movement.

DEF: Division of tendon: Separation of fibrous band connecting muscle to bone.

DEF: Tendon release: Surgical detachment of fibrous band from muscle and/or bone.

DEF: Tendon transection: Incision across width of fibrous bands between muscle and bone.

DEF: Tenotomy for thoracic outlet decompression: Incision of fibrous muscle with separation from bone to relieve compressed thoracic outlet.

83.14 Fasciotomy

Division of fascia
Division of iliotibial band
Fascia stripping
Release of Volkmann's contracture by fasciotomy

DEF: Division of fascia: Incision to separate fibrous connective tissue.

DEF: Division of iliotibial band: Incision to separate fibrous band connecting tibial bone to muscle in flank.

DEF: Fascia stripping: Incision and lengthwise separation of fibrous connective tissue.

DEF: Release of Volkmann's contracture by fasciotomy: Divisional incision of connective tissue to correct defect in flexion of finger(s).

83.19 Other division of soft tissue

Division of muscle
Muscle release
Myotomy for thoracic outlet decompression
Myotomy with division
Scalenotomy
Transection of muscle

✓4th 83.2 Diagnostic procedures on muscle, tendon, fascia, and bursa, including that of hand

83.21 Biopsy of soft tissue

EXCLUDES *biopsy of chest wall (34.23)*
biopsy of skin and subcutaneous tissue (86.11)

83.29 Other diagnostic procedures on muscle, tendon, fascia, and bursa, including that of hand

EXCLUDES *microscopic examination of specimen (91.51-91.-59)*
soft tissue x-ray (87.09, 87.38-87.39, 88.09, 88.35, 88.37)
thermography of muscle (88.84)

✓4th 83.3 Excision of lesion of muscle, tendon, fascia, and bursa

EXCLUDES *biopsy of soft tissue (83.21)*

83.31 Excision of lesion of tendon sheath

Excision of ganglion of tendon sheath, except of hand

83.32 Excision of lesion of muscle

Excision of:
heterotopic bone
muscle scar for release of Volkmann's contracture
myositis ossificans

DEF: Heterotopic bone: Bone lesion in muscle.

DEF: Muscle scar for release of Volkmann's contracture: Scarred muscle tissue interfering with finger flexion.

DEF: Myositis ossificans: Bony deposits in muscle.

83.39 Excision of lesion of other soft tissue

Excision of Baker's cyst

EXCLUDES *bursectomy (83.5)*
excision of lesion of skin and subcutaneous tissue (86.3)
synovectomy (80.70-80.79)

✓4th 83.4 Other excision of muscle, tendon, and fascia

83.41 Excision of tendon for graft

83.42 Other tenonectomy

Excision of:
aponeurosis
tendon sheath
Tenosynovectomy

83.43 Excision of muscle or fascia for graft

83.44 Other fasciectomy

DEF: Excision of fascia; other than for graft.

83.45 Other myectomy
Debridement of muscle NOS
Scalenectomy

DEF: Scalenectomy: Removal of thoracic scaleni muscle tissue.

83.49 Other excision of soft tissue

83.5 Bursectomy

✓4th **83.6 Suture of muscle, tendon, and fascia**

83.61 Suture of tendon sheath

83.62 Delayed suture of tendon

83.63 Rotator cuff repair

DEF: Repair of musculomembranous structure around shoulder joint capsule.

83.64 Other suture of tendon
Achillorrhaphy
Aponeurorrhaphy

EXCLUDES *delayed suture of tendon (83.62)*

DEF: Achillorrhaphy: Suture of fibrous band connecting Achilles tendon to heel bone.

DEF: Aponeurorrhaphy: Suture of fibrous cords connecting muscle to bone.

83.65 Other suture of muscle or fascia
Repair of diastasis recti

✓4th **83.7 Reconstruction of muscle and tendon**

EXCLUDES *reconstruction of muscle and tendon associated with arthroplasty*

83.71 Advancement of tendon

DEF: Detaching fibrous cord between muscle and bone with reattachment at advanced point.

83.72 Recession of tendon

DEF: Detaching fibrous cord between muscle and bone with reattachment at drawn-back point.

83.73 Reattachment of tendon

83.74 Reattachment of muscle

83.75 Tendon transfer or transplantation

83.76 Other tendon transposition

83.77 Muscle transfer or transplantation
Release of Volkmann's contracture by muscle transplantation

83.79 Other muscle transposition

✓4th **83.8 Other plastic operations on muscle, tendon, and fascia**

EXCLUDES *plastic operations on muscle, tendon, and fascia associated with arthroplasty*

83.81 Tendon graft

83.82 Graft of muscle or fascia

83.83 Tendon pulley reconstruction

DEF: Reconstruction of fibrous cord between muscle and bone; at any site other than hand.

83.84 Release of clubfoot, not elsewhere classified
Evans operation on clubfoot

83.85 Other change in muscle or tendon length
Hamstring lengthening
Heel cord shortening
Plastic achillotenotomy
Tendon plication

DEF: Plastic achillotenotomy: Increase in heel cord length.

DEF: Tendon plication: Surgical tuck of tendon.

83.86 Quadricepsplasty

DEF: Correction of quadriceps femoris muscle.

83.87 Other plastic operations on muscle
Musculoplasty
Myoplasty

83.88 Other plastic operations on tendon
Myotenoplasty
Tendon fixation
Tenodesis
Tenoplasty

83.89 Other plastic operations on fascia
Fascia lengthening
Fascioplasty
Plication of fascia

✓4th **83.9 Other operations on muscle, tendon, fascia, and bursa**

EXCLUDES *nonoperative:*
manipulation (93.25-93.29)
stretching (93.27-93.29)

83.91 Lysis of adhesions of muscle, tendon, fascia, and bursa

EXCLUDES *that for tarsal tunnel syndrome (04.44)*

DEF: Separation of created fibrous structures from muscle, connective tissues, bands and sacs.

83.92 Insertion or replacement of skeletal muscle stimulator
Implantation, insertion, placement, or replacement of skeletal muscle:
electrodes
stimulator

83.93 Removal of skeletal muscle stimulator

83.94 Aspiration of bursa

83.95 Aspiration of other soft tissue

EXCLUDES *that of skin and subcutaneous tissue (86.01)*

83.96 Injection of therapeutic substance into bursa

83.97 Injection of therapeutic substance into tendon

83.98 Injection of locally-acting therapeutic substance into other soft tissue

EXCLUDES *subcutaneous or intramuscular injection (99.11-99.29)*

83.99 Other operations on muscle, tendon, fascia, and bursa
Suture of bursa

✓3rd **84 Other procedures on musculoskeletal system**

✓4th **84.0 Amputation of upper limb**

EXCLUDES *revision of amputation stump (84.3)*

84.00 Upper limb amputation, not otherwise specified
Closed flap amputation, Kineplastic amputation, Open or guillotine amputation, Revision of current traumatic amputation — of upper limb NOS

DEF: Closed flap amputation: Sewing a created skin flap over stump end of upper limb.

DEF: Kineplastic amputation: Amputation and preparation of stump of upper limb to permit movement.

DEF: Open or guillotine amputation: Straight incision across upper limb; used when primary closure is contraindicated.

DEF: Revision of current traumatic amputation: Reconstruction of traumatic amputation of upper limb to enable closure.

84.01 Amputation and disarticulation of finger

EXCLUDES *ligation of supernumerary finger (86.26)*

84.02 Amputation and disarticulation of thumb

84.03 Amputation through hand

Amputation through carpals

84.04 Disarticulation of wrist

84.05 Amputation through forearm

Forearm amputation

84.06 Disarticulation of elbow

DEF: Amputation of forearm through elbow joint.

84.07 Amputation through humerus

Upper arm amputation

84.08 Disarticulation of shoulder

DEF: Amputation of arm through shoulder joint.

84.09 Interthoracoscapular amputation

Forequarter amputation

DEF: Removal of upper arm, shoulder bone and collarbone.

4th 84.1 Amputation of lower limb

EXCLUDES *revision of amputation stump (84.3)*

84.10 Lower limb amputation, not otherwise specified

Closed flap amputation | Kineplastic amputation | Open or guillotine amputation | Revision of current traumatic amputation } of lower limb NOS

DEF: Closed flap amputation: Sewing a created skin flap over stump of lower limb.

DEF: Kineplastic amputation: Amputation and preparation of stump of lower limb to permit movement.

DEF: Open or guillotine amputation: Straight incision across lower limb; used when primary closure is contraindicated.

DEF: Revision of current traumatic amputation: Reconstruction of traumatic amputation of lower limb to enable closure.

84.11 Amputation of toe

Amputation through metatarsophalangeal joint
Disarticulation of toe
Metatarsal head amputation
Ray amputation of foot (disarticulation of the metatarsal head of the toe extending across the forefoot, just proximal to the metatarsophalangeal crease)

EXCLUDES *ligation of supernumerary toe (86.26)*

84.12 Amputation through foot

Amputation of forefoot
Amputation through middle of foot
Chopart's amputation
Midtarsal amputation
Transmetatarsal amputation (amputation of the forefoot, including the toes)

EXCLUDES *Ray amputation of foot (84.11)*

DEF: Amputation of forefoot: Removal of foot in front of joint between toes and body of foot.

DEF: Chopart's amputation: Removal of foot with retention of heel, ankle and other associated ankle bones.

DEF: Midtarsal amputation: Amputation of foot through tarsals.

DEF: Transmetatarsal amputation: Amputation of foot through metatarsals.

84.13 Disarticulation of ankle

DEF: Removal of foot through ankle bone.

84.14 Amputation of ankle through malleoli of tibia and fibula

84.15 Other amputation below knee

Amputation of leg through tibia and fibula NOS

84.16 Disarticulation of knee

Batch, Spitler, and McFaddin amputation
Mazet amputation
S.P. Roger's amputation

DEF: Removal of lower leg through knee joint.

84.17 Amputation above knee

Amputation of leg through femur
Amputation of thigh
Conversion of below-knee amputation into above-knee amputation
Supracondylar above-knee amputation

84.18 Disarticulation of hip

DEF: Removal of leg through hip joint.

84.19 Abdominopelvic amputation

Hemipelvectomy
Hindquarter amputation

DEF: Removal of leg and portion of pelvic bone.

DEF: Hemipelvectomy: Removal of leg and lateral pelvis.

4th 84.2 Reattachment of extremity

84.21 Thumb reattachment

84.22 Finger reattachment

84.23 Forearm, wrist, or hand reattachment

84.24 Upper arm reattachment

Reattachment of arm NOS

84.25 Toe reattachment

84.26 Foot reattachment

84.27 Lower leg or ankle reattachment

Reattachment of leg NOS

84.28 Thigh reattachment

84.29 Other reattachment

84.3 Revision of amputation stump

Reamputation | Secondary closure | Trimming } of stump

EXCLUDES *revision of current traumatic amputation [revision by further amputation of current injury] (84.00-84.19, 84.91)*

4th 84.4 Implantation or fitting of prosthetic limb device

84.40 Implantation or fitting of prosthetic limb device, not otherwise specified

84.41 Fitting of prosthesis of upper arm and shoulder

84.42 Fitting of prosthesis of lower arm and hand

84.43 Fitting of prosthesis of arm, not otherwise specified

84.44 Implantation of prosthetic device of arm

84.45 Fitting of prosthesis above knee

84.46 Fitting of prosthesis below knee

84.47 Fitting of prosthesis of leg, not otherwise specified

84.48 Implantation of prosthetic device of leg

4th 84.5 Implantation of other musculoskeletal devices and substances

EXCLUDES *insertion of (non-fusion) spinal disc replacement device (84.60-84.69)*

Spinal Fusion with Metal Cage

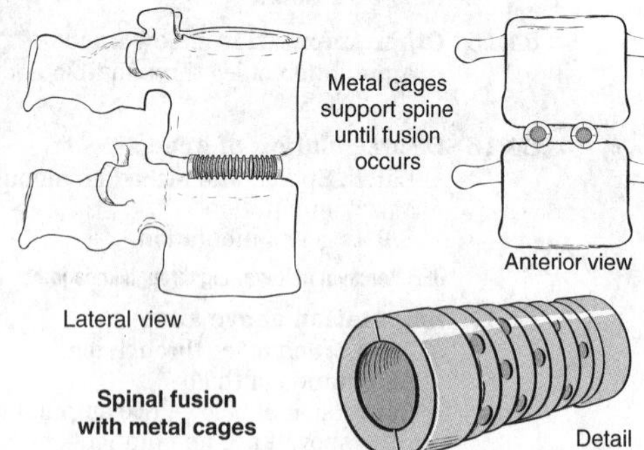

84.51 Insertion of interbody spinal fusion device
Insertion of:
cages (carbn, ceramic, metal, plastic or titanium)
interbody fusion cage
synthetic cages or spacers
threaded bone dowels
Code also refusion of spine (81.30-81.39)
Code also spinal fusion (81.00-81.08)

84.52 Insertion of recombinant bone morphogenetic protein
rhBMP
That via collagen sponge, coral, ceramic and other carriers
Code also primary procedure performed:
fracture repair (79.00-79.99)
spinal fusion (81.00-81.08)
spinal refusion (81.30-81.39)
DEF: Surgical implantation of bone morphogenetic proteins (BMP) and recombinant BMP (rhBMP) to induce new bone growth formation; clinical applications include delayed unions and nonunions, fractures, and spinal fusions.

84.53 Implantation of internal limb lengthening device with kinetic distraction
Code also limb lengthening procedure (78.30-78.39)

84.54 Implantation of other internal limb lengthening device
Implantation of internal limb lengthening device, not otherwise specified (NOS)
Code also limb lengthening procedure (78.30-78.39)

84.55 Insertion of bone void filler
Insertion of:
acrylic cement (PMMA)
bone void cement
calcium based bone void filler
polymethylmethacrylate (PMMA)
EXCLUDES *that with percutaneous vertebral augmentation (81.66)*
that with percutaneous vertebroplasty (81.65)

84.56 Insertion or replacement of (cement) spacer
Insertion or replacement of joint (methylmethacrylate) spacer
DEF: Implantation of an interspinous process decompressive (IPD) device between the spinous processes to limit extension; nonfusion, posterior approach procedure.

84.57 Removal of (cement) spacer
Removal of joint (methylmethacrylate) spacer

84.59 Insertion of other spinal devices
EXCLUDES *initial insertion of pedicle screws with spinal fusion — omit code*
insertion of facet replacement device(s) (84.84)
insertion of interspinous process device(s) (84.80)
insertion of pedicle-based dynamic stabilization device(s) (84.82)

✓4th **84.6 Replacement of spinal disc**
INCLUDES non-fusion arthroplasty of the spine with insertion of artificial disc prosthesis

84.60 Insertion of spinal disc prosthesis, not otherwise specified
Replacement of spinal disc, NOS
INCLUDES diskectomy (discectomy)

84.61 Insertion of partial spinal disc prosthesis, cervical
Nuclear replacement device, cervical
Partial artificial disc prosthesis (flexible), cervical
Replacement of nuclear disc (nucleus pulposus), cervical
INCLUDES diskectomy (discectomy)

84.62 Insertion of total spinal disc prosthesis, cervical
Replacement of cervical spinal disc, NOS
Replacement of total spinal disc, cervical
Total artificial disc prosthesis (flexible), cervical
INCLUDES diskectomy (discectomy)

84.63 Insertion of spinal disc prosthesis, thoracic
Artificial disc prosthesis (flexible), thoracic
Replacement of thoracic spinal disc, partial or total
INCLUDES diskectomy (discectomy)

84.64 Insertion of partial spinal disc prosthesis, lumbosacral
Nuclear replacement device, lumbar
Partial artificial disc prosthesis (flexible), lumbar
Replacement of nuclear disc (nucleus pulposus), lumbar
INCLUDES diskectomy (discectomy)

84.65 Insertion of total spinal disc prosthesis, lumbosacral
Replacement of lumbar spinal disc, NOS
Replacement of total spinal disc, lumbar
Total artificial disc prosthesis (flexible), lumbar
INCLUDES diskectomy (discectomy)

84.66 Revision or replacement of artificial spinal disc prosthesis, cervical
Removal of (partial) (total) spinal disc prosthesis with synchronous insertion of new (partial) (total) spinal disc prosthesis, cervical
Repair of previously inserted spinal disc prosthesis, cervical

84.67 Revision or replacement of artificial spinal disc prosthesis, thoracic
Removal of (partial) (total) spinal disc prosthesis with synchronous insertion of new (partial) (total) spinal disc prosthesis, thoracic
Repair of previously inserted spinal disc prosthesis, thoracic

84.68 Revision or replacement of artificial spinal disc prosthesis, lumbosacral
Removal of (partial) (total) spinal disc prosthesis with synchronous insertion of new (partial) (total) spinal disc prosthesis, lumbosacral
Repair of previously inserted spinal disc prosthesis, lumbosacral

84.69 Revision or replacement of artificial spinal disc prosthesis, not otherwise specified
Removal of (partial) (total) spinal disc prosthesis with synchronous insertion of new (partial) (total) spinal disc prosthesis
Repair of previously inserted spinal disc prosthesis

✓4th **84.7 Adjunct codes for external fixator devices**
Code also any primary procedure performed:
application of external fixator device (78.10, 78.12-78.13, 78.15, 78.17-78.19)
reduction of fracture and dislocation (79.00-79.89)

84.71 Application of external fixator device, monoplanar system
EXCLUDES *other hybrid device or system (84.73)*
ring device or system (84.72)

DEF: Instrumentation that provides percutaneous neutralization, compression, and /or distraction of bone in a single plane by applying force within that plane.

84.72 Application of external fixator device, ring system
Ilizarov type
Sheffield type
EXCLUDES *monoplanar device or system (84.71)*
other hybrid device or system (84.73)

DEF: Instrumentation that provides percutaneous neutralization, compression, and/or distraction of bone through 360 degrees of force application.

84.73 Application of hybrid external fixator device
Computer (assisted) (dependent) external fixator device
Hybrid system using both ring and monoplanar devices
EXCLUDES *monoplanar device or system, when used alone (84.71)*
ring device or system, when used alone (84.72)

DEF: Instrumentation that provides percutaneous neutralization, compression, and /or distraction of bone by applying multiple external forces using monoplanar and ring device combinations.

✓4th **84.8 Insertion, replacement and revision of posterior spinal motion preservation device(s)**
Dynamic spinal stabilization device(s)
INCLUDES any synchronous facetectomy (partial, total) performed at the same level
Code also any synchronous surgical decompression (foraminotomy, laminectomy, laminotomy), if performed (03.09)
EXCLUDES *fusion of spine (81.00-81.08, 81.30-81.39)*
insertion of artificial disc prosthesis (84.60-84.69)
insertion of interbody spinal fusion device (84.51)

External Fixator Devices

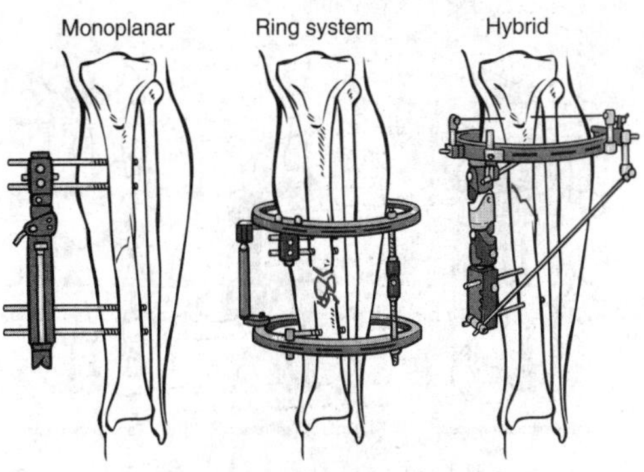

84.80 Insertion or replacement of interspinous process device(s)
Interspinous process decompression device(s)
Interspinous process distraction device(s)
EXCLUDES *insertion or replacement of facet replacement device (84.84)*
insertion or replacement of pedicle-based dynamic stabilization device (84.82)

84.81 Revision of interspinous process device(s)
Repair of previously inserted interspinous process device(s)
EXCLUDES *revision of facet replacement device(s) (84.85)*
revision of pedicle-based dynamic stabilization device (84.83)

84.82 Insertion or replacement of pedicle-based dynamic stabilization device(s)
EXCLUDES *initial insertion of pedicle screws with spinal fusion — omit code*
insertion or replacement of facet replacement device(s) (84.84)
insertion or replacement of interspinous process device(s) (84.80)
replacement of pedicle screws used in spinal fusion (78.59)

84.83 Revision of pedicle-based dynamic stabilization device(s)
Repair of previously inserted pedicle-based dynamic stabilization device(s)
EXCLUDES *removal of pedicle screws used in spinal fusion (78.69)*
replacement of pedicle screws used in spinal fusion (78.59)
revision of facet replacement device(s) (84.85)
revision of interspinous process device(s) (84.81)

Posterior Spinal Motion Preservation Devices

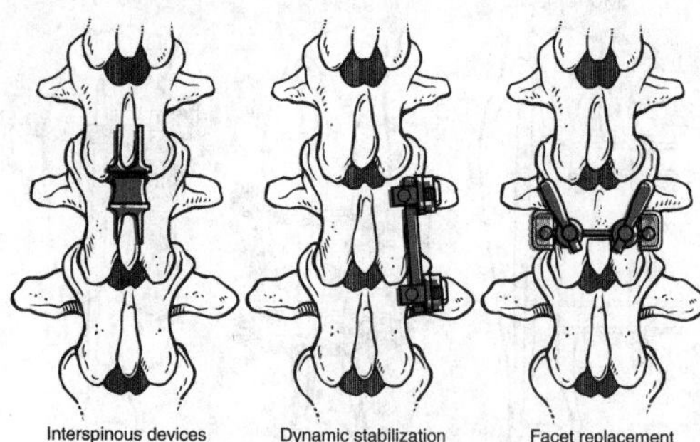

84.84 Insertion or replacement of facet replacement device(s)

Facet arthroplasty

EXCLUDES *initial insertion of pedicle screws with spinal fusion — omit code*
insertion or replacement of interspinous process device(s) (84.80)
insertion or replacement of pedicle-based dynamic stabilization device(s) (84.82)
replacement of pedicle screws used in spinal fusion (78.59)

84.85 Revision of facet replacement device(s)

Repair of previously inserted facet replacement device(s)

EXCLUDES *removal of pedicle screws used in spinal fusion (78.69)*
replacement of pedicle screws used in spinal fusion (78.59)
revision of interspinous process device(s) (84.81)
revision of pedicle-based dynamic stabilization device(s) (84.83)

✓4th **84.9 Other operations on musculoskeletal system**

EXCLUDES *nonoperative manipulation (93.25-93.29)*

84.91 Amputation, not otherwise specified

84.92 Separation of equal conjoined twins

84.93 Separation of unequal conjoined twins

Separation of conjoined twins NOS

84.99 Other

15. OPERATIONS ON THE INTEGUMENTARY SYSTEM (85-86)

✓3rd 85 Operations on the breast

INCLUDES operations on the skin and subcutaneous tissue of:
breast } female or male
previous mastectomy site } female or male
revision of previous mastectomy site

85.0 Mastotomy
Incision of breast (skin)
Mammotomy
EXCLUDES *aspiration of breast (85.91)*
removal of implant (85.94)

✓4th 85.1 Diagnostic procedures on breast

85.11 Closed [percutaneous] [needle] biopsy of breast
DEF: Mammatome biopsy: Excision of breast tissue using a needle inserted through a small incision; followed by a full cut circle of tissue surrounding the core biopsy to obtain; multiple contiguous directional sampling for definitive diagnosis and staging of cancer.

85.12 Open biopsy of breast
DEF: Excision of breast tissue for examination.

85.19 Other diagnostic procedures on breast
EXCLUDES *mammary ductogram (87.35)*
mammography NEC (87.37)
manual examination (89.36)
microscopic examination of specimen (91.61-91.69)
thermography (88.85)
ultrasonography (88.73)
xerography (87.36)

✓4th 85.2 Excision or destruction of breast tissue
EXCLUDES *mastectomy (85.41-85.48)*
reduction mammoplasty (85.31-85.32)

85.20 Excision or destruction of breast tissue, not otherwise specified

85.21 Local excision of lesion of breast
Lumpectomy
Removal of area of fibrosis from breast
EXCLUDES *biopsy of breast (85.11-85.12)*

85.22 Resection of quadrant of breast

85.23 Subtotal mastectomy
EXCLUDES *quadrant resection (85.22)*
DEF: Excision of a large portion of breast tissue.

85.24 Excision of ectopic breast tissue
Excision of accessory nipple
DEF: Excision of breast tissue outside normal breast region.

85.25 Excision of nipple
EXCLUDES *excision of accessory nipple (85.24)*

✓4th 85.3 Reduction mammoplasty and subcutaneous mammectomy

85.31 Unilateral reduction mammoplasty
Unilateral:
amputative mammoplasty
size reduction mammoplasty

85.32 Bilateral reduction mammoplasty
Amputative mammoplasty
Biesenberger operation
Reduction mammoplasty (for gynecomastia)

85.33 Unilateral subcutaneous mammectomy with synchronous implant
EXCLUDES *that without synchronous implant (85.34)*
DEF: Removal of mammary tissue, leaving skin and nipple intact with implant of prosthesis.

85.34 Other unilateral subcutaneous mammectomy
Removal of breast tissue with preservation of skin and nipple
Subcutaneous mammectomy NOS
DEF: Excision of mammary tissue, leaving skin and nipple intact.

85.35 Bilateral subcutaneous mammectomy with synchronous implant
EXCLUDES *that without synchronous implant (85.36)*
DEF: Excision of mammary tissue, both breasts, leaving skin and nipples intact; with prosthesis.

85.36 Other bilateral subcutaneous mammectomy

✓4th 85.4 Mastectomy

85.41 Unilateral simple mastectomy
Mastectomy:
NOS
complete
DEF: Removal of one breast.

85.42 Bilateral simple mastectomy
Bilateral complete mastectomy
DEF: Removal of both breasts.

85.43 Unilateral extended simple mastectomy
Extended simple mastectomy NOS
Modified radical mastectomy
Simple mastectomy with excision of regional lymph nodes
DEF: Removal of one breast and lymph nodes under arm.

85.44 Bilateral extended simple mastectomy

85.45 Unilateral radical mastectomy
Excision of breast, pectoral muscles, and regional lymph nodes [axillary, clavicular, supraclavicular]
Radical mastectomy NOS
DEF: Removal of one breast and regional lymph nodes, pectoral muscle and adjacent tissue.

85.46 Bilateral radical mastectomy

85.47 Unilateral extended radical mastectomy
Excision of breast, muscles, and lymph nodes [axillary, clavicular, supraclavicular, internal mammary, and mediastinal]
Extended radical mastectomy NOS
DEF: Removal of one breast, regional and middle chest lymph nodes, chest muscle and adjacent tissue.

Mastectomy

85.48 Bilateral extended radical mastectomy
DEF: Removal of both breasts, regional and middle chest lymph nodes, chest muscle and adjacent tissue.

✓4th **85.5 Augmentation mammoplasty**
EXCLUDES *that associated with subcutaneous mammectomy (85.33, 85.35)*
DEF: Plastic surgery to increase breast size.

85.50 Augmentation mammoplasty, not otherwise specified

85.51 Unilateral injection into breast for augmentation

85.52 Bilateral injection into breast for augmentation
Injection into breast for augmentation NOS

85.53 Unilateral breast implant

85.54 Bilateral breast implant
Breast implant NOS

85.6 Mastopexy
DEF: Anchoring of pendulous breast.

✓4th **85.7 Total reconstruction of breast**

85.70 Total reconstruction of breast, not otherwise specified
Perforator flap, free

85.71 Latissimus dorsi myocutaneous flap

85.72 Transverse rectus abdominis myocutaneous (TRAM) flap, pedicled
EXCLUDES *transverse rectus abdominis myocutaneous (TRAM) flap, free (85.73)*

85.73 Transverse rectus abdominis myocutaneous (TRAM) flap, free
EXCLUDES *transverse rectus abdominis myocutaneous (TRAM) flap, pedicled (85.72)*

85.74 Deep inferior epigastric artery perforator (DIEP) flap, free

85.75 Superficial inferior epigastric artery (SIEA) flap, free

85.76 Gluteal artery perforator (GAP) flap, free

85.79 Other total reconstruction of breast
EXCLUDES
deep inferior epigastric artery perforator (DIEP) flap, free (85.74)
gluteal artery perforator (GAP) flap, free (85.76)
latissimus dorsi myocutaneous flap (85.71)
perforator flap, free (85.70)
superficial inferior epigastric artery (SIEA) flap, free (85.75)
total reconstruction of breast, not otherwise specified (85.70)
transverse rectus abdominis myocutaneous (TRAM) flap, free (85.73)
transverse rectus abdominis myocutaneous (TRAM) flap, pedicled (85.72)

✓4th **85.8 Other repair and plastic operations on breast**
EXCLUDES *that for:*
augmentation (85.50-85.54)
reconstruction (85.70-85.76, 85.79)
reduction (85.31-85.32)

85.81 Suture of laceration of breast

85.82 Split-thickness graft to breast

85.83 Full-thickness graft to breast

85.84 Pedicle graft to breast
DEF: Implantation of transferred muscle tissue still connected to vascular source.

85.85 Muscle flap graft to breast
DEF: Relocation of nipple.

85.86 Transposition of nipple

85.87 Other repair or reconstruction of nipple

85.89 Other mammoplasty

✓4th **85.9 Other operations on the breast**

85.91 Aspiration of breast
EXCLUDES *percutaneous biopsy of breast (85.11)*

85.92 Injection of therapeutic agent into breast
EXCLUDES *that for augmentation of breast (85.51-85.52)*

85.93 Revision of implant of breast

85.94 Removal of implant of breast

85.95 Insertion of breast tissue expander
Insertion (soft tissue) of tissue expander (one or more) under muscle or platysma to develop skin flaps for donor use

85.96 Removal of breast tissue expander(s)

85.99 Other

✓3rd **86 Operations on skin and subcutaneous tissue**
INCLUDES operations on:
hair follicles
male perineum
nails
sebaceous glands
subcutaneous fat pads
sudoriferous glands
superficial fossae

EXCLUDES *those on skin of:*
anus (49.01-49.99)
breast (mastectomy site) (85.0-85.99)
ear (18.01-18.9)
eyebrow (08.01-08.99)
eyelid (08.01-08.99)
female perineum (71.01-71.9)
lips (27.0-27.99)
nose (21.00-21.99)
penis (64.0-64.99)
scrotum (61.0-61.99)
vulva (71.01-71.9)

✓4th **86.0 Incision of skin and subcutaneous tissue**

86.01 Aspiration of skin and subcutaneous tissue
Aspiration of:
abscess, hematoma, seroma } of nail, skin, or subcutaneous tissue

86.02 Injection or tattooing of skin lesion or defect
Insertion, Injection } of filling material
Pigmenting of skin
DEF: Pigmenting of skin: Adding color to skin.

86.03 Incision of pilonidal sinus or cyst
EXCLUDES *marsupialization (86.21)*

86.04 Other incision with drainage of skin and subcutaneous tissue
EXCLUDES *drainage of:*
fascial compartments of face and mouth (27.0)
palmar or thenar space (82.04)
pilonidal sinus or cyst (86.03)

86.05 Incision with removal of foreign body or device from skin and subcutaneous tissue
Removal of carotid sinus baroreflex activation device
Removal of loop recorder
Removal of neurostimulator pulse generator (single array, dual array)
Removal of tissue expander(s) from skin or soft tissue other than breast tissue
EXCLUDES *removal of foreign body without incision (98.20-98.29)*

86.06 Insertion of totally implantable infusion pump
Code also any associated catheterization
EXCLUDES *insertion of totally implantable vascular access device (86.07)*

86.07 Insertion of totally implantable vascular access device [VAD]
Totally implanted port
EXCLUDES *insertion of totally implantable infusion pump (86.06)*
DEF: Placement of vascular access infusion catheter system under skin to allow for frequent manual infusions into blood vessel.

86.09 Other incision of skin and subcutaneous tissue
Creation of thalamic stimulator pulse generator pocket, new site
Escharotomy
Exploration:
sinus tract, skin
superficial fossa
Relocation of subcutaneous device pocket NEC
Reopening subcutaneous pocket for device revision without replacement
Undercutting of hair follicle
EXCLUDES *creation of loop recorder pocket, new site and insertion/relocation of device (37.79)*
creation of pocket for implantable, patient-activated cardiac event recorder and insertion/relocation of device (37.79)
removal of catheter from cranial cavity (01.27)
that for drainage (86.04)
that of:
cardiac pacemaker pocket, new site (37.79)
fascial compartments of face and mouth (27.0)

✓4th **86.1 Diagnostic procedures on skin and subcutaneous tissue**

86.11 Biopsy of skin and subcutaneous tissue

86.19 Other diagnostic procedures on skin and subcutaneous tissue
EXCLUDES *microscopic examination of specimen from skin and subcutaneous tissue (91.61-91.79)*

✓4th **86.2 Excision or destruction of lesion or tissue of skin and subcutaneous tissue**

86.21 Excision of pilonidal cyst or sinus
Marsupialization of cyst
EXCLUDES *incision of pilonidal cyst or sinus (86.03)*
DEF: Marsupialization of cyst: Incision of cyst and suturing edges to skin to open site.

86.22 Excisional debridement of wound, infection, or burn
Removal by excision of:
devitalized tissue
necrosis
slough
EXCLUDES *debridement of:*
abdominal wall (wound) (54.3)
bone (77.60-77.69)
muscle (83.45)
of hand (82.36)
nail (bed) (fold) (86.27)
nonexcisional debridement of wound, infection, or burn (86.28)
open fracture site (79.60-79.69)
pedicle or flap graft (86.75)

86.23 Removal of nail, nail bed, or nail fold

86.24 Chemosurgery of skin
Chemical peel of skin
DEF: Chemicals applied to destroy skin tissue.
DEF: Chemical peel of skin: Chemicals used to peel skin layers.

86.25 Dermabrasion
That with laser
EXCLUDES *dermabrasion of wound to remove embedded debris (86.28)*
DEF: Removal of wrinkled or scarred skin; with fine sandpaper, wire, brushes or laser.

86.26 Ligation of dermal appendage
EXCLUDES *excision of preauricular appendage (18.29)*
DEF: Tying off extra skin.

86.27 Debridement of nail, nail bed, or nail fold
Removal of:
necrosis
slough
EXCLUDES *removal of nail, nail bed, or nail fold (86.23)*

86.28 Nonexcisional debridement of wound, infection, or burn
Debridement NOS
Maggot therapy
Removal of devitalized tissue, necrosis, and slough by such methods as:
brushing
irrigation (under pressure)
scrubbing
washing
Water scalpel (jet)
DEF: Removal of damaged skin; by methods other than excision.

86.3 Other local excision or destruction of lesion or tissue of skin and subcutaneous tissue
Destruction of skin by:
cauterization
cryosurgery
fulguration
laser beam
That with Z-plasty
EXCLUDES *adipectomy (86.83)*
biopsy of skin (86.11)
wide or radical excision of skin (86.4)
Z-plasty without excision (86.84)

86.4 Radical excision of skin lesion
Wide excision of skin lesion involving underlying or adjacent structure
Code also any lymph node dissection (40.3-40.5)

✓4th **86.5 Suture or other closure of skin and subcutaneous tissue**

86.51 Replantation of scalp

86.59 Closure of skin and subcutaneous tissue of other sites

Adhesives (surgical)(tissue)
Staples
Sutures

EXCLUDES *application of adhesive strips (butterfly) — omit code*

✓4th **86.6 Free skin graft**

INCLUDES excision of skin for autogenous graft

EXCLUDES *construction or reconstruction of:*
penis (64.43-64.44)
trachea (31.75)
vagina (70.61-70.64)

DEF: Transplantation of skin to another site.

86.60 Free skin graft, not otherwise specified

86.61 Full-thickness skin graft to hand

EXCLUDES *heterograft (86.65)*
homograft (86.66)

86.62 Other skin graft to hand

EXCLUDES *heterograft (86.65)*
homograft (86.66)

86.63 Full-thickness skin graft to other sites

EXCLUDES *heterograft (86.65)*
homograft (86.66)

86.64 Hair transplant

EXCLUDES *hair follicle transplant to eyebrow or eyelash (08.63)*

86.65 Heterograft to skin

Pigskin graft
Porcine graft

EXCLUDES *application of dressing only (93.57)*

DEF: Implantation of nonhuman tissue.

86.66 Homograft to skin

Graft to skin of:
amnionic membrane } from donor
skin } from donor

DEF: Implantation of tissue from human donor.

86.67 Dermal regenerative graft

Artificial skin, NOS
Creation of "neodermis"
Decellularized allodermis
Integumentary matrix implants
Prosthetic implant of dermal layer of skin
Regenerate dermal layer of skin

EXCLUDES *heterograft to skin (86.65)*
homograft to skin (86.66)

DEF: Replacement of dermis and epidermal layer of skin by cultured or regenerated autologous tissue; used to treat full-thickness or deep partial-thickness burns; also called cultured epidermal autograft (CEA).

86.69 Other skin graft to other sites

EXCLUDES *heterograft (86.65)*
homograft (86.66)

✓4th **86.7 Pedicle grafts or flaps**

EXCLUDES *construction or reconstruction of:*
penis (64.43-64.44)
trachea (31.75)
vagina (70.61-70.64)

DEF: Full thickness skin and subcutaneous tissue partially attached to the body by a narrow strip of tissue so that it retains its blood supply. The unattached portion is sutured to the defect.

86.70 Pedicle or flap graft, not otherwise specified

86.71 Cutting and preparation of pedicle grafts or flaps

Elevation of pedicle from its bed
Flap design and raising
Partial cutting of pedicle or tube
Pedicle delay

EXCLUDES *pollicization or digital transfer (82.61,82.81)*
revision of pedicle (86.75)

DEF: Elevation of pedicle from its bed: Separation of tissue implanted from its bed.

DEF: Flap design and raising: Planing and elevation of tissue to be implanted.

DEF: Pedicle delay: Elevation and preparation of tissue still attached to vascular bed; delayed implant.

86.72 Advancement of pedicle graft

86.73 Attachment of pedicle or flap graft to hand

EXCLUDES *pollicization or digital transfer (82.61, 82.81)*

86.74 Attachment of pedicle or flap graft to other sites

Attachment by:
advanced flap
double pedicled flap
pedicle graft
rotating flap
sliding flap
tube graft

DEF: Attachment by:

Advanced flap: Sliding tissue implant into new position.

Double pedicle flap: Implant connected to two vascular beds.

Pedicle graft: Implant connected to vascular bed.

Rotating flap: Implant rotated along curved incision.

Sliding flap: Sliding implant to site.

Tube graft: Double tissue implant to form tube with base connected to original site.

86.75 Revision of pedicle or flap graft

Debridement } of pedicle or flap graft
Defatting } of pedicle or flap graft

DEF: Connection of implant still attached to its vascular tissue.

✓4th **86.8 Other repair and reconstruction of skin and subcutaneous tissue**

DEF: Revision and tightening of excess, wrinkled facial skin.

86.81 Repair for facial weakness

86.82 Facial rhytidectomy

Face lift

EXCLUDES *rhytidectomy of eyelid (08.86-08.87)*

86.83 Size reduction plastic operation

Liposuction
Reduction of adipose tissue of:
abdominal wall (pendulous)
arms (batwing)
buttock
thighs (trochanteric lipomatosis)

EXCLUDES *breast (85.31-85.32)*

DEF: Excision and plastic repair of excess skin and underlying tissue.

86.84 Relaxation of scar or web contracture of skin

Z-plasty of skin

EXCLUDES *Z-plasty with excision of lesion (86.3)*

86.85 Correction of syndactyly

DEF: Plastic repair of webbed fingers or toes.

86.86 Onychoplasty

DEF: Plastic repair of nail or nail bed.

86.89 Other repair and reconstruction of skin and subcutaneous tissue

EXCLUDES *mentoplasty (76.67-76.68)*

✓4th **86.9 Other operations on skin and subcutaneous tissue**

86.91 Excision of skin for graft

Excision of skin with closure of donor site

EXCLUDES *that with graft at same operative episode (86.60-86.69)*

86.92 Electrolysis and other epilation of skin

EXCLUDES *epilation of eyelid (08.91-08.93)*

86.93 Insertion of tissue expander

Insertion (subcutaneous) (soft tissue) of expander (one or more) in scalp (subgaleal space), face, neck, trunk except breast, and upper and lower extremities for development of skin flaps for donor use

EXCLUDES *flap graft preparation (86.71)*
tissue expander, breast (85.95)

86.94 Insertion or replacement of single array neurostimulator pulse generator, not specified as rechargeable

Pulse generator (single array, single channel) for intracranial, spinal, and peripheral neurostimulator

Code also any associated lead implantation (02.93, 03.93, 04.92)

EXCLUDES *insertion or replacement of single array rechargeable neurostimulator pulse generator (86.97)*

86.95 Insertion or replacement of dual array neurostimulator pulse generator, not specified as rechargeable

Pulse generator (dual array, dual channel) for intracranial, spinal, and peripheral neurostimulator

Code also any associated lead implantation (02.93, 03.93, 04.92)

EXCLUDES *insertion or replacement of dual arrayrechargeable neurostimulator pulse generator (86.98)*

86.96 Insertion or replacement of other neurostimulator pulse generator

Code also any associated lead implantation (02.93, 03.93, 04.92)

EXCLUDES *insertion of dual array neurostimulator pulse generator (86.95, 86.98)*
insertion of single array neurostimulator pulse generator (86.94, 86.97)

86.97 Insertion or replacement of single array rechargeable neurostimulator pulse generator

Rechargeable pulse generator (single array, single channel) for intracranial, spinal, and peripheral neurostimulator

Code also any associated lead implantation (02.93, 03.93, 04.92)

86.98 Insertion or replacement of dual array rechargeable neurostimulator pulse generator

Rechargeable pulse generator (dual array, dual channel) for intracranial, spinal, and peripheral neurostimulator

Code also any associated lead implantation (02.93, 03.93, 04.92)

86.99 Other

EXCLUDES *removal of sutures from:*
abdomen (97.83)
head and neck (97.38)
thorax (97.43)
trunk NEC (97.84)
wound catheter:
irrigation (96.58)
replacement (97.15)

16. MISCELLANEOUS DIAGNOSTIC AND THERAPEUTIC PROCEDURES (87-99)

✓3rd **87 Diagnostic radiology**

✓4th **87.0 Soft tissue x-ray of face, head, and neck**

EXCLUDES *angiography (88.40-88.68)*

87.01 Pneumoencephalogram

DEF: Radiographic exam of cerebral ventricles and subarachnoid spaces; with injection of air or gas for contrast.

87.02 Other contrast radiogram of brain and skull

Pneumocisternogram
Pneumoventriculogram
Posterior fossa myelogram

DEF: Pneumocisternogram: radiographic exam of subarachnoid spaces after injection of gas or contrast.

DEF: Pneumoventriculography: radiographic exam of cerebral ventricles after injection of gas or contrast.

DEF: Posterior fossa myelogram: radiographic exam of posterior channel of spinal cord after injection of gas or contrast.

87.03 Computerized axial tomography of head

C.A.T. scan of head

87.04 Other tomography of head

87.05 Contrast dacryocystogram

DEF: Radiographic exam of tear sac after injection of contrast.

87.06 Contrast radiogram of nasopharynx

87.07 Contrast laryngogram

87.08 Cervical lymphangiogram

DEF: Radiographic exam of lymph vessels of neck; with or without contrast.

87.09 Other soft tissue x-ray of face, head, and neck

Noncontrast x-ray of:
- adenoid
- larynx
- nasolacrimal duct
- nasopharynx
- salivary gland
- thyroid region
- uvula

EXCLUDES *x-ray study of eye (95.14)*

✓4th **87.1 Other x-ray of face, head, and neck**

EXCLUDES *angiography (88.40-88.68)*

87.11 Full-mouth x-ray of teeth

87.12 Other dental x-ray

Orthodontic cephalogram or cephalometrics
Panorex examination of mandible
Root canal x-ray

87.13 Temporomandibular contrast arthrogram

87.14 Contrast radiogram of orbit

87.15 Contrast radiogram of sinus

87.16 Other x-ray of facial bones

X-ray of:
- frontal area
- mandible
- maxilla
- nasal sinuses
- nose
- orbit
- supraorbital area
- symphysis menti
- zygomaticomaxillary complex

87.17 Other x-ray of skull

Lateral projection } of skull
Sagittal projection } of skull
Tangential projection } of skull

DEF: Lateral projection: Side to side view of head.

DEF: Sagittal projection: View of body in plane running midline from front to back.

DEF: Tangential projection: Views from adjacent skull surfaces.

✓4th **87.2 X-ray of spine**

87.21 Contrast myelogram

DEF: Radiographic exam of space between middle and outer spinal cord coverings after injection of contrast.

87.22 Other x-ray of cervical spine

87.23 Other x-ray of thoracic spine

87.24 Other x-ray of lumbosacral spine

Sacrococcygeal x-ray

87.29 Other x-ray of spine

Spinal x-ray NOS

✓4th **87.3 Soft tissue x-ray of thorax**

EXCLUDES *angiocardiography (88.50-88.58)*
angiography (88.40-88.68)

87.31 Endotracheal bronchogram

DEF: Radiographic exam of lung, main branch, with contrast introduced through windpipe.

87.32 Other contrast bronchogram

Transcricoid bronchogram

DEF: Transcricoid bronchogram: Radiographic exam of lung, main branch, with contrast introduced through cartilage of neck.

87.33 Mediastinal pneumogram

DEF: Radiographic exam of cavity containing heart, esophagus and adjacent structures.

87.34 Intrathoracic lymphangiogram

DEF: Radiographic exam of lymphatic vessels within chest; with or without contrast.

87.35 Contrast radiogram of mammary ducts

DEF: Radiographic exam of mammary ducts; with contrast.

87.36 Xerography of breast

DEF: Radiographic exam of breast via selenium-coated plates.

87.37 Other mammography

87.38 Sinogram of chest wall

Fistulogram of chest wall

DEF: Fistulogram of chest wall: Radiographic exam of abnormal opening in chest.

87.39 Other soft tissue x-ray of chest wall

✓4th **87.4 Other x-ray of thorax**

EXCLUDES *angiocardiography (88.50-88.58)*
angiography (88.40-88.68)

87.41 Computerized axial tomography of thorax

C.A.T. scan of heart

C.A.T. scan } of thorax
Crystal linea scan of x-ray beam } of thorax
Electronic subtraction } of thorax
Photoelectric response } of thorax
Tomography with use of computer, x-rays, and camera } of thorax

87.42 Other tomography of thorax

Cardiac tomogram

EXCLUDES *C.A.T. scan of heart (87.41)*

DEF: Radiographic exam of chest plane.

87.43 X-ray of ribs, sternum, and clavicle
Examination for:
cervical rib
fracture

87.44 Routine chest x-ray, so described
X-ray of chest NOS

87.49 Other chest x-ray
X-ray of:
bronchus NOS
diaphragm NOS
heart NOS
lung NOS
mediastinum NOS
trachea NOS

✓4th **87.5 Biliary tract x-ray**

87.51 Percutaneous hepatic cholangiogram
DEF: Radiographic exam of bile tract of gallbladder; with needle injection of contrast into bile duct of liver.

87.52 Intravenous cholangiogram
DEF: Radiographic exam of bile ducts; with intravenous contrast injection.

87.53 Intraoperative cholangiogram
DEF: Radiographic exam of bile ducts; with contrast; following gallbladder removal.

87.54 Other cholangiogram

87.59 Other biliary tract x-ray
Cholecystogram

✓4th **87.6 Other x-ray of digestive system**

87.61 Barium swallow

87.62 Upper GI series

87.63 Small bowel series

87.64 Lower GI series

87.65 Other x-ray of intestine

87.66 Contrast pancreatogram

87.69 Other digestive tract x-ray

✓4th **87.7 X-ray of urinary system**
EXCLUDES *angiography of renal vessels (88.45, 88.65)*

87.71 Computerized axial tomography of kidney
C.A.T. scan of kidney

87.72 Other nephrotomogram
DEF: Radiographic exam of kidney plane.

87.73 Intravenous pyelogram
Diuretic infusion pyelogram
DEF: Radiographic exam of lower kidney, with intravenous contrast injection.
DEF: Diuretic infusion pyelogram: Radiographic exam of lower kidney with diuretic contrast.

87.74 Retrograde pyelogram

87.75 Percutaneous pyelogram

Ureteropyelography

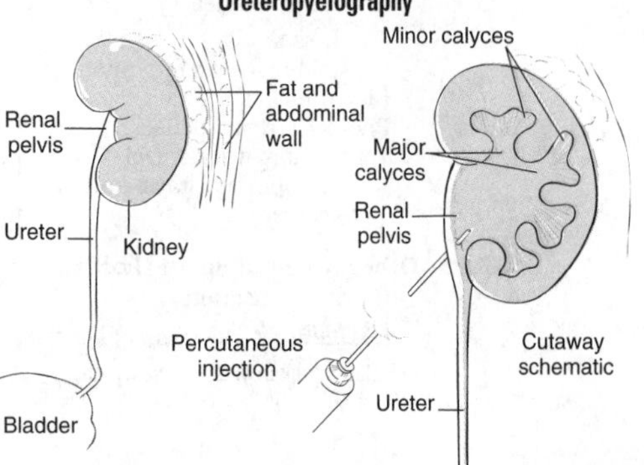

87.76 Retrograde cystourethrogram
DEF: Radiographic exam of bladder and urethra with contrast injected through catheter into bladder.

87.77 Other cystogram

87.78 Ileal conduitogram
DEF: Radiographic exam of passage created between ureter and artificial opening into abdomen.

87.79 Other x-ray of the urinary system
KUB x-ray

✓4th **87.8 X-ray of female genital organs**

87.81 X-ray of gravid uterus
Intrauterine cephalometry by x-ray

87.82 Gas contrast hysterosalpingogram
DEF: Radiographic exam of uterus and fallopian tubes; with gas contrast.

87.83 Opaque dye contrast hysterosalpingogram

87.84 Percutaneous hysterogram
DEF: Radiographic exam of uterus with contrast injected through body wall.

87.85 Other x-ray of fallopian tubes and uterus

87.89 Other x-ray of female genital organs

✓4th **87.9 X-ray of male genital organs**

87.91 Contrast seminal vesiculogram

87.92 Other x-ray of prostate and seminal vesicles

87.93 Contrast epididymogram

87.94 Contrast vasogram

87.95 Other x-ray of epididymis and vas deferens

87.99 Other x-ray of male genital organs

✓3rd **88 Other diagnostic radiology and related techniques**

✓4th **88.0 Soft tissue x-ray of abdomen**
EXCLUDES *angiography (88.40-88.68)*

88.01 Computerized axial tomography of abdomen
C.A.T. scan of abdomen
EXCLUDES *C.A.T. scan of kidney (87.71)*

88.02 Other abdomen tomography
EXCLUDES *nephrotomogram (87.72)*

88.03 Sinogram of abdominal wall
Fistulogram of abdominal wall
DEF: Radiographic exam of abnormal abdominal passage.

88.04 Abdominal lymphangiogram
DEF: Radiographic exam of abdominal lymphatic vessels; with contrast.

88.09 Other soft tissue x-ray of abdominal wall

✓4th **88.1 Other x-ray of abdomen**

88.11 Pelvic opaque dye contrast radiography

88.12 Pelvic gas contrast radiography
Pelvic pneumoperitoneum

88.13 Other peritoneal pneumogram

88.14 Retroperitoneal fistulogram

88.15 Retroperitoneal pneumogram

88.16 Other retroperitoneal x-ray

88.19 Other x-ray of abdomen
Flat plate of abdomen

✓4th **88.2 Skeletal x-ray of extremities and pelvis**

EXCLUDES *contrast radiogram of joint (88.32)*

88.21 Skeletal x-ray of shoulder and upper arm

88.22 Skeletal x-ray of elbow and forearm

88.23 Skeletal x-ray of wrist and hand

88.24 Skeletal x-ray of upper limb, not otherwise specified

88.25 Pelvimetry

DEF: Imaging of pelvic bones to measure pelvic capacity.

88.26 Other skeletal x-ray of pelvis and hip

88.27 Skeletal x-ray of thigh, knee, and lower leg

88.28 Skeletal x-ray of ankle and foot

88.29 Skeletal x-ray of lower limb, not otherwise specified

✓4th **88.3 Other x-ray**

88.31 Skeletal series

X-ray of whole skeleton

88.32 Contrast arthrogram

EXCLUDES *that of temporomandibular joint (87.13)*

88.33 Other skeletal x-ray

EXCLUDES *skeletal x-ray of:*
extremities and pelvis (88.21-88.29)
face, head, and neck (87.11-87.17)
spine (87.21-87.29)
thorax (87.43)

88.34 Lymphangiogram of upper limb

88.35 Other soft tissue x-ray of upper limb

88.36 Lymphangiogram of lower limb

88.37 Other soft tissue x-ray of lower limb

EXCLUDES *femoral angiography (88.48, 88.66)*

88.38 Other computerized axial tomography

C.A.T. scan NOS

EXCLUDES *C.A.T. scan of:*
abdomen (88.01)
head (87.03)
heart (87.41)
kidney (87.71)
thorax (87.41)

88.39 X-ray, other and unspecified

✓4th **88.4 Arteriography using contrast material**

Note: The fourth-digit subclassification identifies the site to be viewed, not the site of injection.

INCLUDES angiography of arteries
arterial puncture for injection of contrast material
radiography of arteries (by fluoroscopy)
retrograde arteriography

EXCLUDES *arteriography using:*
radioisotopes or radionuclides (92.01-92.19)
ultrasound (88.71-88.79)
fluorescein angiography of eye (95.12)

DEF: Electromagnetic wave photography of arteries; with contrast.

88.40 Arteriography using contrast material, unspecified site

88.41 Arteriography of cerebral arteries

Angiography of:
basilar artery
carotid (internal)
posterior cerebral circulation
vertebral artery

88.42 Aortography

Arteriography of aorta and aortic arch

88.43 Arteriography of pulmonary arteries

88.44 Arteriography of other intrathoracic vessels

EXCLUDES *angiocardiography (88.50-88.58)*
arteriography of coronary arteries (88.55-88.57)

88.45 Arteriography of renal arteries

88.46 Arteriography of placenta

Placentogram using contrast material

88.47 Arteriography of other intra-abdominal arteries

88.48 Arteriography of femoral and other lower extremity arteries

88.49 Arteriography of other specified sites

✓4th **88.5 Angiocardiography using contrast material**

INCLUDES arterial puncture and insertion of arterial catheter for injection of contrast material
cineangiocardiography
selective angiocardiography

Code also synchronous cardiac catheterization (37.21-37.23)

EXCLUDES *angiography of pulmonary vessels (88.43, 88.62)*

DEF: Electromagnetic wave photography of heart and great vessels; with contrast.

88.50 Angiocardiography, not otherwise specified

88.51 Angiocardiography of venae cavae

Inferior vena cavography
Phlebography of vena cava (inferior) (superior)

88.52 Angiocardiography of right heart structures

Angiocardiography of:
pulmonary valve
right atrium
right ventricle (outflow tract)

EXCLUDES *intra-operative fluorescence vascular angiography (88.59)*
that combined with left heart angiocardiography (88.54)

88.53 Angiocardiography of left heart structures

Angiocardiography of:
aortic valve
left atrium
left ventricle (outflow tract)

EXCLUDES *intra-operative fluorescence vascular angiography (88.59)*
that combined with right heart angiocardiography (88.54)

88.54 Combined right and left heart angiocardiography

EXCLUDES *intra-operative fluorescence vascular angiography (88.59)*

88.55 Coronary arteriography using a single catheter

Coronary arteriography by Sones technique
Direct selective coronary arteriography using a single catheter

EXCLUDES *intra-operative fluorescence vascular angiography (88.59)*

88.56 Coronary arteriography using two catheters
Coronary arteriography by:
Judkins technique
Ricketts and Abrams technique
Direct selective coronary arteriography using two catheters
EXCLUDES *intra-operative fluorescence vascular angiography (88.59)*

88.57 Other and unspecified coronary arteriography
Coronary arteriography NOS
EXCLUDES *intra-operative fluorescence vascular angiography (88.59)*

88.58 Negative-contrast cardiac roentgenography
Cardiac roentgenography with injection of carbon dioxide

88.59 Intra-operative fluorescence vascular angiography
Intraoperative laser arteriogram (SPY)
SPY arteriogram
SPY arteriography
DEF: Coronary artery bypass grafting (CABG) procedure imaging technology; utilizes dye with high-speed digital infrared photography. Sequence is performed for each graft; provides information on graft patency, vessel size, blood flow velocities.

✓4th **88.6 Phlebography**
Note: The fourth-digit subclassification (88.60-88.67) identifies the site to be viewed, not the site of injection.
INCLUDES angiography of veins
radiography of veins (by fluoroscopy)
retrograde phlebography
venipuncture for injection of contrast material
venography using contrast material
EXCLUDES *angiography using:*
radioisotopes or radionuclides (92.01-92.19)
ultrasound (88.71-88.79)
fluorescein angiography of eye (95.12)
DEF: Electromagnetic wave photography of veins; with contrast.

88.60 Phlebography using contrast material, unspecified site

88.61 Phlebography of veins of head and neck using contrast material

88.62 Phlebography of pulmonary veins using contrast material

88.63 Phlebography of other intrathoracic veins using contrast material

88.64 Phlebography of the portal venous system using contrast material
Splenoportogram (by splenic arteriography)

88.65 Phlebography of other intra-abdominal veins using contrast material

88.66 Phlebography of femoral and other lower extremity veins using contrast material

88.67 Phlebography of other specified sites using contrast material

88.68 Impedance phlebography

✓4th **88.7 Diagnostic ultrasound**
INCLUDES echography
non-invasive ultrasound
ultrasonic angiography
ultrasonography
EXCLUDES *intravascular imaging (adjunctive) (IVUS) (00.21-00.29)*
therapeutic ultrasound (00.01-00.09)
DEF: Graphic recording of anatomical structures via high frequency, sound-wave imaging and computer graphics.

88.71 Diagnostic ultrasound of head and neck
Determination of midline shift of brain
Echoencephalography
EXCLUDES *eye (95.13)*

88.72 Diagnostic ultrasound of heart
Echocardiography
Transesophageal echocardiography
EXCLUDES *echocardiography of heart chambers (37.28)*
intracardiac echocardiography (ICE) (37.28)
intravascular (IVUS) imaging of coronary vessels (00.24)

88.73 Diagnostic ultrasound of other sites of thorax
Aortic arch ultrasonography
Breast ultrasonography
Lung ultrasonography

88.74 Diagnostic ultrasound of digestive system

88.75 Diagnostic ultrasound of urinary system

88.76 Diagnostic ultrasound of abdomen and retroperitoneum

88.77 Diagnostic ultrasound of peripheral vascular system
Deep vein thrombosis ultrasonic scanning
EXCLUDES *adjunct vascular system procedures (00.40-00.43)*

88.78 Diagnostic ultrasound of gravid uterus
Intrauterine cephalometry:
echo
ultrasonic
Placental localization by ultrasound

88.79 Other diagnostic ultrasound
Ultrasonography of:
multiple sites
nongravid uterus
total body

✓4th **88.8 Thermography**
DEF: Infrared photography to determine various body temperatures.

88.81 Cerebral thermography

88.82 Ocular thermography

88.83 Bone thermography
Osteoarticular thermography

88.84 Muscle thermography

88.85 Breast thermography

88.86 Blood vessel thermography
Deep vein thermography

88.89 Thermographay of other sites
Lymph gland thermography
Thermography NOS

✓4th **88.9 Other diagnostic imaging**

88.90 Diagnostic imaging, not elsewhere classified

88.91 Magnetic resonance imaging of brain and brain stem

EXCLUDES *intraoperative magnetic resonance imaging (88.96)*
real-time magnetic resonance imaging (88.96)

88.92 Magnetic resonance imaging of chest and myocardium

For evaluation of hilar and mediastinal lymphadenopathy

88.93 Magnetic resonance imaging of spinal canal

Spinal cord levels:
cervical
thoracic
lumbar (lumbosacral)
Spinal cord
Spine

88.94 Magnetic resonance imaging of musculoskeletal

Bone marrow blood supply
Extremities (upper) (lower)

88.95 Magnetic resonance imaging of pelvis, prostate, and bladder

88.96 Other intraoperative magnetic resonance imaging

iMRI
Real-time magnetic resonance imaging

88.97 Magnetic resonance imaging of other and unspecified sites

Abdomen
Eye orbit
Face
Neck

88.98 Bone mineral density studies

Dual photon absorptiometry
Quantitative computed tomography (CT) studies
Radiographic densitometry
Single photon absorptiometry

DEF: Dual photon absorptiometry: Measurement of bone mineral density by comparing dissipation of emission from two separate photoelectric energy peaks.

DEF: Quantitative computed tomography (CT) studies: Computer assisted analysis of x-ray absorption through bone to determine density.

DEF: Radiographic densiometry: Measurement of bone mineral density by degree of bone radiopacity.

DEF: Single photon absorptiometry: Measurement of bone mineral density by degree of dissipation of emission from one photoelectric energy peaks emitted by gadolinium 153.

✓3rd **89 Interview, evaluation, consultation, and examination**

✓4th **89.0 Diagnostic interview, consultation, and evaluation**

EXCLUDES *psychiatric diagnostic interview (94.11-94.19)*

89.01 Interview and evaluation, described as brief

Abbreviated history and evaluation

89.02 Interview and evaluation, described as limited

Interval history and evaluation

89.03 Interview and evaluation, described as comprehensive

History and evaluation of new problem

89.04 Other interview and evaluation

89.05 Diagnostic interview and evaluation, not otherwise specified

89.06 Consultation, described as limited

Consultation on a single organ system

89.07 Consultation, described as comprehensive

89.08 Other consultation

89.09 Consulation, not otherwise specified

✓4th **89.1 Anatomic and physiologic measurements and manual examinations — nervous system and sense organs**

EXCLUDES *ear examination (95.41-95.49)*
eye examination (95.01-95.26)
the listed procedures when done as part of a general physical examination (89.7)

89.10 Intracarotid amobarbital test

Wada test

DEF: Amobarbital injections into internal carotid artery to induce hemiparalysis to determine the hemisphere that controls speech and language.

89.11 Tonometry

DEF: Pressure measurements inside eye.

89.12 Nasal function study

Rhinomanometry

DEF: Rhinomanometry: Measure of degree of nasal cavity obstruction.

89.13 Neurologic examination

89.14 Electroencephalogram

EXCLUDES *that with polysomnogram (89.17)*

DEF: Recording of electrical currents in brain via electrodes to detect epilepsy, lesions and other encephalopathies.

89.15 Other nonoperative neurologic function tests

89.16 Transillumination of newborn skull

DEF: Light passed through newborn skull for diagnostic purposes.

89.17 Polysomnogram

Sleep recording

DEF: Graphic studies of sleep patterns.

89.18 Other sleep disorder function tests

Multiple sleep latency test [MSLT]

89.19 Video and radio-telemetered electroencephalographic monitoring

Radiographic } EEG Monitoring
Video }

✓4th **89.2 Anatomic and physiologic measurements and manual examinations — genitourinary system**

EXCLUDES *the listed procedures when done as part of a general physical examination (89.7)*

89.21 Urinary manometry

Manometry through:
indwelling ureteral catheter
nephrostomy
pyelostomy
ureterostomy

DEF: Measurement of urinary pressure.

DEF: Manometry through:

Indwelling urinary catheter: Semipermanent urinary catheter.
Nephrostomy: Opening into pelvis of kidney.
Pyelostomy: Opening in lower kidney.
Ureterostomy: Opening into ureter.

89.22 Cystometrogram
DEF: Pressure recordings at various stages of bladder filling.

89.23 Urethral sphincter electromyogram

89.24 Uroflowmetry [UFR]
DEF: Continuous recording of urine flow.

89.25 Urethral pressure profile [UPP]

89.26 Gynecological examination
Pelvic examination

89.29 Other nonoperative genitourinary system measurements
Bioassay of urine
Renal clearance
Urine chemistry

✓4th **89.3 Other anatomic and physiologic measurements and manual examinations**
EXCLUDES *the listed procedures when done as part of a general physical examination (89.7)*

89.31 Dental examination
Oral mucosal survey
Periodontal survey

89.32 Esophageal manometry
DEF: Measurement of esophageal fluid and gas pressures.

89.33 Digital examination of enterostomy stoma
Digital examination of colostomy stoma

89.34 Digital examination of rectum

89.35 Transillumination of nasal sinuses

89.36 Manual examination of breast

89.37 Vital capacity determination
EXCLUDES *endoscopic pulmonary airway flow measurement (33.72)*
DEF: Measurement of expelled gas volume after full inhalation.

89.38 Other nonoperative respiratory measurements
Plethysmography for measurement of respiratory function
Thoracic impedance plethysmography
EXCLUDES *endoscopic pulmonary airway flow measurement (33.72)*
DEF: Plethysmography for measurement of respiratory function: Registering changes in respiratory function as noted in blood circulation.

89.39 Other nonoperative measurements and examinations
^{14}C-Urea breath test
Basal metabolic rate [BMR]
Gastric:
analysis
function NEC
EXCLUDES *body measurement (93.07)*
cardiac tests (89.41-89.69)
fundus photography (95.11)
limb length measurement (93.06)

✓4th **89.4 Cardiac stress tests, pacemaker and defibrillator checks**

89.41 Cardiovascular stress test using treadmill

89.42 Masters' two-step stress test

89.43 Cardiovascular stress test using bicycle ergometer
DEF: Electrocardiogram during exercise on bicycle with device capable of measuring muscular, metabolic and respiratory effects of exercise.

89.44 Other cardiovascular stress test
Thallium stress test with or without transesophageal pacing

89.45 Artificial pacemaker rate check
Artificial pacemaker function check NOS
Bedside device check of pacemaker or cardiac resynchronization pacemaker [CRT-P]
Interrogation only without arrhythmia induction
EXCLUDES *catheter based invasive electrophysiologic testing (37.26)*
non-invasive programmed electrical stimulation [NIPS] (arrhythmia induction) (37.20)

89.46 Artificial pacemaker artifact wave form check

89.47 Artificial pacemaker electrode impedance check

89.48 Artificial pacemaker voltage or amperage threshold check

89.49 Automatic implantable cardioverter/defibrillator (AICD) check
Bedside check of an AICD or cardiac resynchronization defibrillator [CRT-D]
Checking pacing thresholds of device
Interrogation only without arrhythmia induction
EXCLUDES *catheter based invasive electrophysiologic testing (37.26)*
non-invasive programmed electrical stimulation [NIPS] (arrhythmia induction) (37.20)

✓4th **89.5 Other nonoperative cardiac and vascular diagnostic procedures**
EXCLUDES *fetal EKG (75.32)*

89.50 Ambulatory cardiac monitoring
Analog devices [Holter-type]

89.51 Rhythm electrocardiogram
Rhythm EKG (with one to three leads)

89.52 Electrocardiogram
ECG NOS
EKG (with 12 or more leads)

89.53 Vectorcardiogram (with ECG)

89.54 Electrographic monitoring
Telemetry
EXCLUDES *ambulatory cardiac monitoring (89.50)*
electrographic monitoring during surgery — omit code
DEF: Evaluation of heart electrical activity by continuous screen monitoring.
DEF: Telemetry: Evaluation of heart electrical activity; with radio signals at distance from patient.

89.55 Phonocardiogram with ECG lead

89.56 Carotid pulse tracing with ECG lead
EXCLUDES *oculoplethysmography (89.58)*

89.57 Apexcardiogram (with ECG lead)

89.58 Plethysmogram
Penile plethysmography with nerve stimulation
EXCLUDES *plethysmography (for):*
measurement of respiratory function (89.38)
thoracic impedance (89.38)
DEF: Determination and recording of blood pressure variations present or passing through an organ.

Central Venous Pressure Monitoring

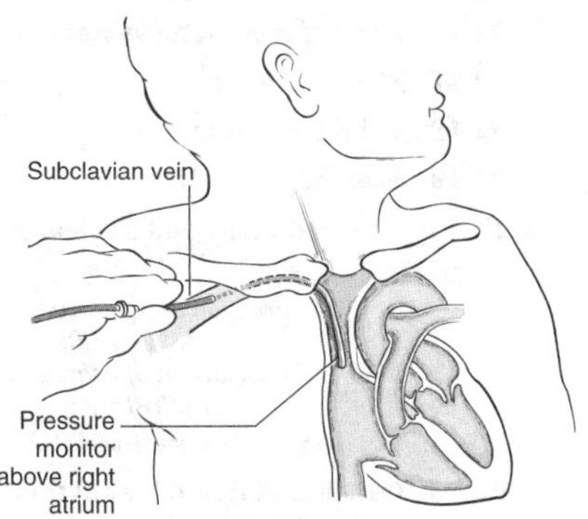

89.59 Other nonoperative cardiac and vascular measurements

✓4th **89.6 Circulatory monitoring**

EXCLUDES *electrocardiographic monitoring during surgery — omit code*
implantation or replacement of subcutaneous device for intracardiac hemodynamic monitoring (00.57)
insertion or replacement of implantable pressure sensor (lead) for intracardiac hemodynamic monitoring (00.56)

89.60 Continuous intra-arterial blood gas monitoring

Insertion of blood gas monitoring system and continuous monitoring of blood gases through an intra-arterial sensor

89.61 Systemic arterial pressure monitoring

EXCLUDES *intra-aneurysm sac pressure monitoring (intraoperative) (00.58)*
intravascular pressure measurement of intrathoracic arteries (00.67)
intravascular pressure measurement of peripheral arteries (00.68)

89.62 Central venous pressure monitoring

EXCLUDES *intravascular pressure measurement, other specified and unspecified vessels (00.69)*

89.63 Pulmonary artery pressure monitoring

EXCLUDES *pulmonary artery wedge monitoring (89.64)*

89.64 Pulmonary artery wedge monitoring

Pulmonary capillary wedge [PCW] monitoring
Swan-Ganz catheterization

DEF: Monitoring pulmonary artery pressure via catheter inserted through right lower and upper heart chambers into pulmonary artery and advancing the balloon-tip to wedge it in the distal pulmonary artery branch.

89.65 Measurement of systemic arterial blood gases

EXCLUDES *continuous intra-arterial blood gas monitoring (89.60)*

89.66 Measurement of mixed venous blood gases

89.67 Monitoring of cardiac output by oxygen consumption technique

Fick method

DEF: Fick method: Indirect measure of cardiac output through blood volume flow over pulmonary capillaries; determines oxygen absorption by measurement of arterial oxygen content versus venous oxygen content.

89.68 Monitoring of cardiac output by other technique

Cardiac output monitor by thermodilution indicator

DEF: Cardiac output monitor by thermodilution indicator: Injection of ice cold dextrose solution into right lower heart chamber; temperature sensitive catheter monitors disappearance from beat to beat to measure expelled blood volume.

89.69 Monitoring of coronary blood flow

Coronary blood flow monitoring by coincidence counting technique

EXCLUDES *intravascular pressure measurement of coronary arteries (00.59)*

89.7 General physical examination

89.8 Autopsy

✓3rd **90 Microscopic examination - I**

The following fourth-digit subclassification is for use with categories in section 90 to identify type of examination:
1 bacterial smear
2 culture
3 culture and sensitivity
4 parasitology
5 toxicology
6 cell block and Papanicolaou smear
9 other microscopic examination

✓4th **90.0 Microscopic examination of specimen from nervous system and of spinal fluid**

✓4th **90.1 Microscopic examination of specimen from endocrine gland, not elsewhere classified**

✓4th **90.2 Microscopic examination of specimen from eye**

✓4th **90.3 Microscopic examination of specimen from ear, nose, throat, and larynx**

✓4th **90.4 Microscopic examination of specimen from trachea, bronchus, pleura, lung, and other thoracic specimen, and of sputum**

✓4th **90.5 Microscopic examination of blood**

✓4th **90.6 Microscopic examination of specimen from spleen and of bone marrow**

✓4th **90.7 Microscopic examination of specimen from lymph node and of lymph**

✓4th **90.8 Microscopic examination of specimen from upper gastrointestinal tract and of vomitus**

✓4th **90.9 Microscopic examination of specimen from lower gastrointestinal tract and of stool**

✓3rd **91 Microscopic examination - II**

The following fourth-digit subclassification is for use with categories in section 91 to identify type of examination:
1 bacterial smear
2 culture
3 culture and sensitivity
4 parasitology
5 toxicology
6 cell block and Papanicolaou smear
9 other microscopic examination

✓4th **91.0 Microscopic examination of specimen from liver, biliary tract, and pancreas**

✓4th **91.1 Microscopic examination of peritoneal and retroperitoneal specimen**

✓4th **91.2 Microscopic examination of specimen from kidney, ureter, perirenal and periureteral tissue**

✓4th **91.3 Microscopic examination of specimen from bladder, urethra, prostate, seminal vesicle, perivesical tissue, and of urine and semen**

✓4th **91.4 Microscopic examination of specimen from female genital tract**
Amnionic sac
Fetus

✓4th **91.5 Microscopic examination of specimen from musculoskeletal system and of joint fluid**
Microscopic examination of:
bone
bursa
cartilage
fascia
ligament
muscle
synovial membrane
tendon

✓4th **91.6 Microscopic examination of specimen from skin and other integument**
Microscopic examination of:
hair
nails
skin
EXCLUDES *mucous membrane — code to organ site that of operative wound (91.71-91.79)*

✓4th **91.7 Microscopic examination of specimen from operative wound**

✓4th **91.8 Microscopic examination of specimen from other site**

✓4th **91.9 Microscopic examination of specimen from unspecified site**

✓3rd **92 Nuclear medicine**

✓4th **92.0 Radioisotope scan and function study**

92.01 Thyroid scan and radioisotope function studies
Iodine-131 uptake
Protein-bound iodine
Radio-iodine uptake

92.02 Liver scan and radioisotope function study

92.03 Renal scan and radioisotope function study
Renal clearance study

92.04 Gastrointestinal scan and radioisotope function study
Radio-cobalt B_{12} Schilling test
Radio-iodinated triolein study

92.05 Cardiovascular and hematopoietic scan and radioisotope function study
Bone marrow
Cardiac output
Circulation time
Radionuclide cardiac ventriculogram
Spleen
} scan or function study

92.09 Other radioisotope function studies

✓4th **92.1 Other radioisotope scan**

92.11 Cerebral scan
Pituitary

92.12 Scan of other sites of head
EXCLUDES *eye (95.16)*

92.13 Parathyroid scan

92.14 Bone scan

92.15 Pulmonary scan

92.16 Scan of lymphatic system

92.17 Placental scan

92.18 Total body scan

92.19 Scan of other sites

✓4th **92.2 Therapeutic radiology and nuclear medicine**
EXCLUDES *that for:*
ablation of pituitary gland (07.64-07.69)
destruction of chorioretinal lesion (14.26-14.27)

DEF: Radiation and nuclear isotope treatment of diseased tissue.

92.20 Infusion of liquid brachytherapy radioisotope
I-125 radioisotope
Intracavitary brachytherapy
EXCLUDES *removal of radioisotope*

92.21 Superficial radiation
Contact radiation [up to 150 KVP]

92.22 Orthovoltage radiation
Deep radiation [200-300 KVP]

92.23 Radioisotopic teleradiotherapy
Teleradiotherapy using:
cobalt-60
iodine-125
radioactive cesium

92.24 Teleradiotherapy using photons
Megavoltage NOS
Supervoltage NOS
Use of:
Betatron
linear accelerator

92.25 Teleradiotherapy using electrons
Beta particles
EXCLUDES *intra-operative electron radiation therapy (92.41)*

92.26 Teleradiotherapy of other particulate radiation
Neutrons
Protons NOS

92.27 Implantation or insertion of radioactive elements
Intravascular brachytherapy
Code also incision of site
EXCLUDES *infusion of liquid brachytherapy radioisotope (92.20)*

92.28 Injection or instillation of radioisotopes
Injection or infusion of radioimmunoconjugate
Intracavitary injection or instillation
Intravenous injection or instillation
Iodine-131 [I-131] tositumomab
Radioimmunotherapy
Ytrium-90 [Y-90] ibritumomab tiuxetan
EXCLUDES *infusion of liquid brachytherapy radioisotope (92.20)*

92.29 Other radiotherapeutic procedure

✓4th **92.3 Stereotactic radiosurgery**
Code also stereotactic head frame application (93.59)
EXCLUDES *stereotactic biopsy*

DEF: Ablation of deep intracranial lesions; single procedure; placement of head frame for 3-D analysis of lesion, followed by radiation treatment from helmet attached to frame.

92.30 Stereotactic radiosurgery, not otherwise specified

92.31 Single source photon radiosurgery
High energy x-rays
Linear accelerator (LINAC)

92.32 Multi-source photon radiosurgery
Cobalt 60 radiation
Gamma irradiation

92.33 Particulate radiosurgery
Particle beam radiation (cyclotron)
Proton accelerator

92.39 Stereotactic radiosurgery, not elsewhere classified

✓4th **92.4 Intra-operative radiation procedures**

92.41 Intra-operative electron radiation therapy
IOERT
That using a mobile linear accelerator

DEF: Use of a mobile linear accelerator unit that delivers precision electron radiation beam radiation to highly focused anatomic sites, protecting the normal surrounding tissues from exposure.

✓3rd **93 Physical therapy, respiratory therapy, rehabilitation, and related procedures**

✓4th **93.0 Diagnostic physical therapy**

93.01 Functional evaluation

93.02 Orthotic evaluation

93.03 Prosthetic evaluation

93.04 Manual testing of muscle function

93.05 Range of motion testing

93.06 Measurement of limb length

93.07 Body measurement
Girth measurement
Measurement of skull circumference

93.08 Electromyography

EXCLUDES *eye EMG (95.25)*
that with polysomnogram (89.17)
urethral sphincter EMG (89.23)

DEF: Graphic recording of electrical activity of muscle.

93.09 Other diagnostic physical therapy procedure

✓4th **93.1 Physical therapy exercises**

93.11 Assisting exercise

EXCLUDES *assisted exercise in pool (93.31)*

93.12 Other active musculoskeletal exercise

93.13 Resistive exercise

93.14 Training in joint movements

93.15 Mobilization of spine

93.16 Mobilization of other joints

EXCLUDES *manipulation of temporomandibular joint (76.95)*

93.17 Other passive musculoskeletal exercise

93.18 Breathing exercise

93.19 Exercise, not elsewhere classified

✓4th **93.2 Other physical therapy musculoskeletal manipulation**

93.21 Manual and mechanical traction

EXCLUDES *skeletal traction (93.43-93.44)*
skin traction (93.45-93.46)
spinal traction (93.41-93.42)

93.22 Ambulation and gait training

93.23 Fitting of orthotic device

93.24 Training in use of prosthetic or orthotic device
Training in crutch walking

93.25 Forced extension of limb

93.26 Manual rupture of joint adhesions

DEF: Therapeutic application of force to rupture adhesions restricting movement.

93.27 Stretching of muscle or tendon

93.28 Stretching of fascia

93.29 Other forcible correction of deformity

✓4th **93.3 Other physical therapy therapeutic procedures**

93.31 Assisted exercise in pool

93.32 Whirlpool treatment

93.33 Other hydrotherapy

93.34 Diathermy

93.35 Other heat therapy
Acupuncture with smouldering moxa
Hot packs
Hyperthermia NEC
Infrared irradiation
Moxibustion
Paraffin bath

EXCLUDES *hyperthermia for treatment of cancer (99.85)*

DEF: Moxibustion: Igniting moxa, a Chinese plant, for counterirritation of skin.

DEF: Paraffin bath: Hot wax treatment.

93.36 Cardiac retraining

DEF: Cardiac rehabilitation regimen following myocardial infarction or coronary bypass graft procedure.

93.37 Prenatal training
Training for natural childbirth

93.38 Combined physical therapy without mention of the components

93.39 Other physical therapy

✓4th **93.4 Skeletal traction and other traction**

93.41 Spinal traction using skull device
Traction using:
caliper tongs
Crutchfield tongs
halo device
Vinke tongs

EXCLUDES *insertion of tongs or halo traction device (02.94)*

DEF: Applying device to head to exert pulling force on spine.

93.42 Other spinal traction
Cotrel's traction

EXCLUDES *cervical collar (93.52)*

DEF: Pulling force exerted on spine without skull device.

93.43 Intermittent skeletal traction

93.44 Other skeletal traction
Bryant's traction
Dunlop's traction
Lyman Smith traction
Russell's traction

93.45 Thomas' splint traction

DEF: Thomas splint: Placement of ring around thigh, attached to rods running length of leg for therapeutic purposes.

93.46 Other skin traction of limbs
Adhesive tape traction
Boot traction
Buck's traction
Gallows traction

✓4th 93.5 Other immobilization, pressure, and attention to wound

EXCLUDES *external fixator device (84.71-84.73)*
wound cleansing (96.58-96.59)

93.51 Application of plaster jacket

EXCLUDES *Minerva jacket (93.52)*

93.52 Application of neck support

Application of:
- cervical collar
- Minerva jacket
- molded neck support

93.53 Application of other cast

93.54 Application of splint

Plaster splint
Tray splint

EXCLUDES *periodontal splint (24.7)*

93.55 Dental wiring

EXCLUDES *that for orthodontia (24.7)*

93.56 Application of pressure dressing

Application of:
- Gibney bandage
- Robert Jones' bandage
- Shanz dressing

93.57 Application of other wound dressing

Porcine wound dressing

93.58 Application of pressure trousers

Application of:
- anti-shock trousers
- MAST trousers
- vasopneumatic device

93.59 Other immobilization, pressure, and attention to wound

Elastic stockings
Electronic gaiter
Intermittent pressure device
Oxygenation of wound (hyperbaric)
Stereotactic head frame application
Strapping (non-traction)
Velpeau dressing

✓4th 93.6 Osteopathic manipulative treatment

93.61 Osteopathic manipulative treatment for general mobilization

General articulatory treatment

93.62 Osteopathic manipulative treatment using high-velocity, low-amplitude forces

Thrusting forces

93.63 Osteopathic manipulative treatment using low-velocity, high-amplitude forces

Springing forces

93.64 Osteopathic manipulative treatment using isotonic, isometric forces

93.65 Osteopathic manipulative treatment using indirect forces

93.66 Osteopathic manipulative treatment to move tissue fluids

Lymphatic pump

93.67 Other specified osteopathic manipulative treatment

✓4th 93.7 Speech and reading rehabilitation and rehabilitation of the blind

93.71 Dyslexia training

93.72 Dysphasia training

DEF: Speech training to coordinate and arrange words in proper sequence.

93.73 Esophageal speech training

DEF: Speech training after voice box removal; sound is produced by vibration of air column in esophagus against the cricopharangeal sphincter.

93.74 Speech defect training

93.75 Other speech training and therapy

93.76 Training in use of lead dog for the blind

93.77 Training in braille or Moon

93.78 Other rehabilitation for the blind

✓4th 93.8 Other rehabilitation therapy

93.81 Recreational therapy

Diversional therapy
Play therapy

EXCLUDES *play psychotherapy (94.36)*

93.82 Educational therapy

Education of bed-bound children
Special schooling for the handicapped

93.83 Occupational therapy

Daily living activities therapy

EXCLUDES *training in activities of daily living for the blind (93.78)*

93.84 Music therapy

93.85 Vocational rehabilitation

Sheltered employment
Vocational:
- assessment
- retraining
- training

93.89 Rehabilitation, not elsewhere classified

✓4th 93.9 Respiratory therapy

EXCLUDES *insertion of airway (96.01-96.05)*
other continuous invasive (through endotracheal tube or tracheostomy) mechanical ventilation (96.70-96.72)

93.90 Non-invasive mechanical ventilation

Note: Patients admitted on *non-invasive* mechanical ventilation that subsequently require *invasive* mechanical ventilation; code both types of mechanical ventilation

Bi-level airway pressure
BiPAP without (delivery through) endotracheal tube or tracheostomy
CPAP without (delivery through) endotracheal tube or tracheostomy
Mechanical ventilation NOS
Non-invasive positive pressure (NIPPV)
Non-invasive PPV
NPPV
That delivered by non-invasive interface:
- face mask
- nasal mask
- nasal pillow
- oral mouthpiece
- oronasal mask

EXCLUDES *invasive (through endotracheal tube or tracheostomy) continuous mechanical ventilation (96.70-96.72)*

DEF: Noninvasive ventilation support system that augments the ability to breathe spontaneously without the insertion of an endotracheal tube or tracheostomy.

93.91 Intermittent positive pressure breathing [IPPB]

93.93 Nonmechanical methods of resuscitation

Artificial respiration
Manual resuscitation
Mouth-to-mouth resuscitition

93.94 Respiratory medication administered by nebulizer
Mist therapy

93.95 Hyperbaric oxygenation
EXCLUDES *oxygenation of wound (93.59)*

93.96 Other oxygen enrichment
Catalytic oxygen therapy
Cytoreductive effect
Oxygenators
Oxygen therapy
EXCLUDES *oxygenation of wound (93.59)*
SuperSaturated oxygen therapy (00.49)

93.97 Decompression chamber

93.98 Other control of atmospheric pressure and composition
Antigen-free air conditioning
Helium therapy
EXCLUDES *inhaled nitric oxide therapy (INO) (00.12)*

93.99 Other respiratory procedures
Continuous negative pressure ventilation [CNP]
Postural drainage

✓3rd 94 Procedures related to the psyche

✓4th 94.0 Psychologic evaluation and testing

94.01 Administration of intelligence test
Administration of:
Stanford-Binet
Wechsler Adult Intelligence Scale
Wechsler Intelligence Scale for Children

94.02 Administration of psychologic test
Administration of:
Bender Visual-Motor Gestalt Test
Benton Visual Retention Test
Minnesota Multiphasic Personality Inventory
Wechsler Memory Scale

94.03 Character analysis

94.08 Other psychologic evaluation and testing

94.09 Psychologic mental status determination, not otherwise specified

✓4th 94.1 Psychiatric interviews, consultations, and evaluations

94.11 Psychiatric mental status determination
Clinical psychiatric mental status determination
Evaluation for criminal responsibility
Evaluation for testimentary capacity
Medicolegal mental status determination
Mental status determination NOS

94.12 Routine psychiatric visit, not otherwise specified

94.13 Psychiatric commitment evaluation
Pre-commitment interview

94.19 Other psychiatric interview and evaluation
Follow-up psychiatric interview NOS

✓4th 94.2 Psychiatric somatotherapy
DEF: Biological treatment of mental disorders.

94.21 Narcoanalysis
Narcosynthesis

94.22 Lithium therapy

94.23 Neuroleptic therapy

94.24 Chemical shock therapy

94.25 Other psychiatric drug therapy

94.26 Subconvulsive electroshock therapy

94.27 Other electroshock therapy
Electroconvulsive therapy (ECT)
EST

94.29 Other psychiatric somatotherapy

✓4th 94.3 Individual psychotherapy

94.31 Psychoanalysis

94.32 Hypnotherapy
Hypnodrome
Hypnosis

94.33 Behavior therapy
Aversion therapy
Behavior modification
Desensitization therapy
Extinction therapy
Relaxation training
Token economy

94.34 Individual therapy for psychosexual dysfunction
EXCLUDES *that performed in group setting (94.41)*

94.35 Crisis intervention

94.36 Play psychotherapy

94.37 Exploratory verbal psychotherapy

94.38 Supportive verbal psychotherapy

94.39 Other individual psychotherapy
Biofeedback

✓4th 94.4 Other psychotherapy and counseling

94.41 Group therapy for psychosexual dysfunction

94.42 Family therapy

94.43 Psychodrama

94.44 Other group therapy

94.45 Drug addiction counseling

94.46 Alcoholism counseling

94.49 Other counseling

✓4th 94.5 Referral for psychologic rehabilitation

94.51 Referral for psychotherapy

94.52 Referral for psychiatric aftercare
That in:
halfway house
outpatient (clinic) facility

94.53 Referral for alcoholism rehabilitation

94.54 Referral for drug addiction rehabilitation

94.55 Referral for vocational rehabilitation

94.59 Referral for other psychologic rehabilitation

✓4th 94.6 Alcohol and drug rehabilitation and detoxification

94.61 Alcohol rehabilitation
DEF: Program designed to restore social and physical functioning, free of the dependence of alcohol.

94.62 Alcohol detoxification
DEF: Treatment of physical symptoms during withdrawal from alcohol dependence.

94.63 Alcohol rehabilitation and detoxification

94.64 Drug rehabilitation
DEF: Program designed to restore social and physical functioning, free of the dependence of drugs.

94.65 Drug detoxification
DEF: Treatment of physical symptoms during withdrawal from drug dependence.

94.66 Drug rehabilitation and detoxification

94.67 Combined alcohol and drug rehabilitation

94.68 Combined alcohol and drug detoxification

94.69 Combined alcohol and drug rehabilitation and detoxification

✓3rd 95 Ophthalmologic and otologic diagnosis and treatment

✓4th 95.0 General and subjective eye examination

95.01 Limited eye examination
Eye examination with prescription of spectacles

95.02 Comprehensive eye examination
Eye examination covering all aspects of the visual system

95.03 Extended ophthalmologic work-up
Examination (for):
- glaucoma
- neuro-ophthalmology
- retinal disease

95.04 Eye examination under anesthesia
Code also type of examination

95.05 Visual field study

95.06 Color vision study

95.07 Dark adaptation study
DEF: Exam of eye's adaption to dark.

95.09 Eye examination, not otherwise specified
Vision check NOS

✓4th 95.1 Examinations of form and structure of eye

95.11 Fundus photography

95.12 Fluorescein angiography or angioscopy of eye

95.13 Ultrasound study of eye

95.14 X-ray study of eye

95.15 Ocular motility study

95.16 P_{32} and other tracer studies of eye

✓4th 95.2 Objective functional tests of eye

EXCLUDES *that with polysomnogram (89.17)*

95.21 Electroretinogram [ERG]

95.22 Electro-oculogram [EOG]

95.23 Visual evoked potential [VEP]
DEF: Measuring and recording evoked visual responses of body and senses.

95.24 Electronystagmogram [ENG]
DEF: Monitoring of brain waves to record induced and spontaneous eye movements.

95.25 Electromyogram of eye [EMG]

95.26 Tonography, provocative tests, and other glaucoma testing

✓4th 95.3 Special vision services

95.31 Fitting and dispensing of spectacles

95.32 Prescription, fitting, and dispensing of contact lens

95.33 Dispensing of other low vision aids

95.34 Ocular prosthetics

95.35 Orthoptic training

95.36 Ophthalmologic counselling and instruction
Counselling in:
- adaptation to visual loss
- use of low vision aids

✓4th 95.4 Nonoperative procedures related to hearing

95.41 Audiometry
Békésy 5-tone audiometry
Impedance audiometry
Stapedial reflex response
Subjective audiometry
Tympanogram

95.42 Clinical test of hearing
Tuning fork test
Whispered speech test

95.43 Audiological evaluation
Audiological evaluation by:
- Bárány noise machine
- blindfold test
- delayed feedback
- masking
- Weber lateralization

95.44 Clinical vestibular function tests
Thermal test of vestibular function

95.45 Rotation tests
Bárány chair
DEF: Irrigation of ear canal with warm or cold water to evaluate vestibular function.

95.46 Other auditory and vestibular function tests

95.47 Hearing examination, not otherwise specified

95.48 Fitting of hearing aid
EXCLUDES *implantation of electromagnetic hearing device (20.95)*

95.49 Other nonoperative procedures related to hearing
Adjustment (external components) of cochlear prosthetic device

✓3rd 96 Nonoperative intubation and irrigation

✓4th 96.0 Nonoperative intubation of gastrointestinal and respiratory tracts

96.01 Insertion of nasopharyngeal airway

96.02 Insertion of oropharyngeal airway

96.03 Insertion of esophageal obturator airway

96.04 Insertion of endotracheal tube

96.05 Other intubation of respiratory tract
EXCLUDES *endoscopic insertion or replacement of bronchial device or substance (33.71, 33.79)*

96.06 Insertion of Sengstaken tube
Esophageal tamponade
DEF: Insertion of Sengstaken tube: Nonsurgical emergency measure to stop esophageal bleeding using compression exerted by inflated balloons; additional tube ports to aspirate blood and clots.

Endotracheal Intubation

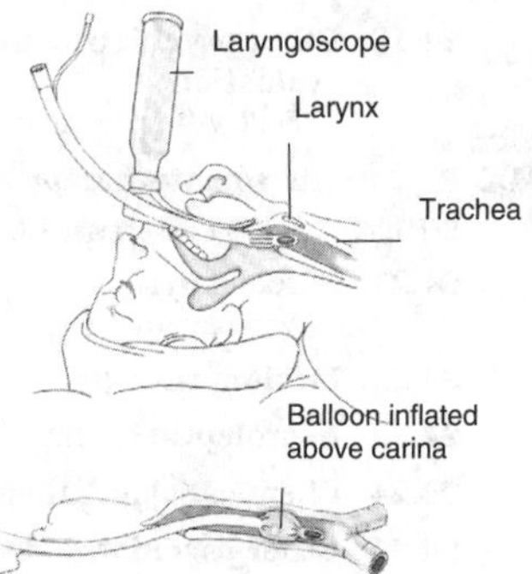

96.07 Insertion of other (naso-) gastric tube
Intubation for decompression
EXCLUDES *that for enteral infusion of nutritional substance (96.6)*

96.08 Insertion of (naso-) intestinal tube
Miller-Abbott tube (for decompression)

96.09 Insertion of rectal tube
Replacement of rectal tube

✓4th **96.1 Other nonoperative insertion**
EXCLUDES *nasolacrimal intubation (09.44)*

96.11 Packing of external auditory canal

96.14 Vaginal packing

96.15 Insertion of vaginal mold

96.16 Other vaginal dilation

96.17 Insertion of vaginal diaphragm

96.18 Insertion of other vaginal pessary

96.19 Rectal packing

✓4th **96.2 Nonoperative dilation and manipulation**

96.21 Dilation of frontonasal duct

96.22 Dilation of rectum

96.23 Dilation of anal sphincter

96.24 Dilation and manipulation of enterostomy stoma

96.25 Therapeutic distention of bladder
Intermittent distention of bladder

96.26 Manual reduction of rectal prolapse

96.27 Manual reduction of hernia

96.28 Manual reduction of enterostomy prolapse

96.29 Reduction of intussusception of alimentary tract
With:
fluoroscopy
ionizing radiation enema
ultrasonography guidance
Hydrostatic reduction
Pneumatic reduction
EXCLUDES *intra-abdominal manipulation of intestine, not otherwise specified (46.80)*

✓4th **96.3 Nonoperative alimentary tract irrigation, cleaning, and local instillation**

96.31 Gastric cooling
Gastric hypothermia
DEF: Reduction of internal stomach temperature.

96.32 Gastric freezing

96.33 Gastric lavage

96.34 Other irrigation of (naso-)gastric tube

96.35 Gastric gavage
DEF: Food forced into stomach.

96.36 Irrigation of gastrostomy or enterostomy

96.37 Proctoclysis
DEF: Slow introduction of large amounts of fluids into lower large intestine.

96.38 Removal of impacted feces
Removal of impaction:
by flushing manually

96.39 Other transanal enema
Rectal irrigation
EXCLUDES *reduction of intussusception of alimentary tract by ionizing radiation enema (96.29)*

✓4th **96.4 Nonoperative irrigation, cleaning, and local instillation of other digestive and genitourinary organs**

96.41 Irrigation of cholecystostomy and other biliary tube

96.42 Irrigation of pancreatic tube

96.43 Digestive tract instillation, except gastric gavage

96.44 Vaginal douche

96.45 Irrigation of nephrostomy and pyelostomy

96.46 Irrigation of ureterostomy and ureteral catheter

96.47 Irrigation of cystostomy

96.48 Irrigation of other indwelling urinary catheter

96.49 Other genitourinary instillation
Insertion of prostaglandin suppository

✓4th **96.5 Other nonoperative irrigation and cleaning**

96.51 Irrigation of eye
Irrigation of cornea
EXCLUDES *irrigation with removal of foreign body (98.21)*

96.52 Irrigation of ear
Irrigation with removal of cerumen

96.53 Irrigation of nasal passages

96.54 Dental scaling, polishing, and debridement
Dental prophylaxis
Plaque removal

96.55 Tracheostomy toilette

96.56 Other lavage of bronchus and trachea
EXCLUDES *diagnostic bronchoalveolar lavage (BAL) (33.24)*
whole lung lavage (33.99)

96.57 Irrigation of vascular catheter

96.58 Irrigation of wound catheter

96.59 Other irrigation of wound
Wound cleaning NOS
EXCLUDES *debridement (86.22, 86.27-86.28)*

96.6 Enteral infusion of concentrated-nutritional substances

✓4th **96.7 Other continuous invasive mechanical ventilation**

BiPAP delivered through endotracheal tube or tracheostomy (invasive interface
CPAP delivered through endotracheal tube or tracheostomy (invasive interface
Endotracheal respiratory assistance
Invasive positive pressure ventilation [IPPV]
Mechanical ventilation through invasive interface
That by tracheostomy
Weaning of an intubated (endotracheal tube) patient

Code also any associated:
endotracheal tube insertion (96.04)
tracheostomy (31.1-31.29)

EXCLUDES *continuous negative pressure ventilation [CNP] (iron lung) (cuirass) (93.99)*
intermittent positive pressure breathing [IPPB] (93.91)
non-invasive bi-level positive airway pressure [BiPAP] (93.90)
non-invasive continuous positive airway pressure [CPAP] (93.90)
non-invasive positive pressure (NIPPV) (93.90)
that by face mask (93.90-93.99)
that by nasal cannula (93.90-93.99)
that by nasal catheter (93.90-93.99)

Note: Endotracheal intubation

To calculate the number of hours (duration) of continuous mechanical ventilation during a hospitalization, begin the count from the start of the (endotracheal) intubation. The duration ends with (endotracheal) extubation.

If a patient is intubated prior to admission, begin counting the duration from the time of the admission. If a patient is transferred (discharged) while intubated, the duration would end at the time of transfer (discharge).

For patients who begin on (endotracheal) intubation and subsequently have a tracheostomy performed for mechanical ventilation, the duration begins with the (endotracheal) intubation and ends when the mechanical ventilation is turned off (after the weaning period).

Tracheostomy

To calculate the number of hours of continuous mechanical ventilation during a hospitalization, begin counting the duration when mechanical ventilation is started. The duration ends when the mechanical ventilator is turned off (after the weaning period).

If a patient has received a tracheostomy prior to admission and is on mechanical ventilation at the time of admission, begin counting the duration from the time of admission. If a patient is transferred (discharged) while still on mechanical ventilation via tracheostomy, the duration would end at the time of the transfer (discharge).

96.70 Continuous invasive mechanical ventilation of unspecified duration
Invasive mechanical ventilation NOS

96.71 Continuous invasive mechanical ventilation for less than 96 consecutive hours

96.72 Continuous invasivemechanical ventilation for 96 consecutive hours or more

✓3rd **97 Replacement and removal of therapeutic appliances**

✓4th **97.0 Nonoperative replacement of gastrointestinal appliance**

97.01 Replacement of (naso-)gastric or esophagostomy tube

97.02 Replacement of gastrostomy tube

97.03 Replacement of tube or enterostomy device of small intestine

97.04 Replacement of tube or enterostomy device of large intestine

97.05 Replacement of stent (tube) in biliary or pancreatic duct

✓4th **97.1 Nonoperative replacement of musculoskeletal and integumentary system appliance**

97.11 Replacement of cast on upper limb

97.12 Replacement of cast on lower limb

97.13 Replacement of other cast

97.14 Replacement of other device for musculoskeletal immobilization
Splinting
Strapping

97.15 Replacement of wound catheter

97.16 Replacement of wound packing or drain

EXCLUDES *repacking of:*
dental wound (97.22)
vulvar wound (97.26)

✓4th **97.2 Other nonoperative replacement**

97.21 Replacement of nasal packing

97.22 Replacement of dental packing

97.23 Replacement of tracheostomy tube

97.24 Replacement and refitting of vagina diaphragm

97.25 Replacement of other vaginal pessary

97.26 Replacement of vaginal or vulvar packing or drain

97.29 Other nonoperative replacements

✓4th **97.3 Nonoperative removal of therapeutic device from head and neck**

97.31 Removal of eye prosthesis

EXCLUDES *removal of ocular implant (16.71)*
removal of orbital implant (16.72)

97.32 Removal of nasal packing

97.33 Removal of dental wiring

97.34 Removal of dental packing

97.35 Removal of dental prosthesis

97.36 Removal of other external mandibular fixation device

97.37 Removal of tracheostomy tube

97.38 Removal of sutures from head and neck

97.39 Removal of other therapeutic device from head and neck

EXCLUDES *removal of skull tongs (02.94)*

✓4th **97.4 Nonoperative removal of therapeutic device from thorax**

97.41 Removal of thoracotomy tube or pleural cavity drain

Intraaortic Balloon Pump

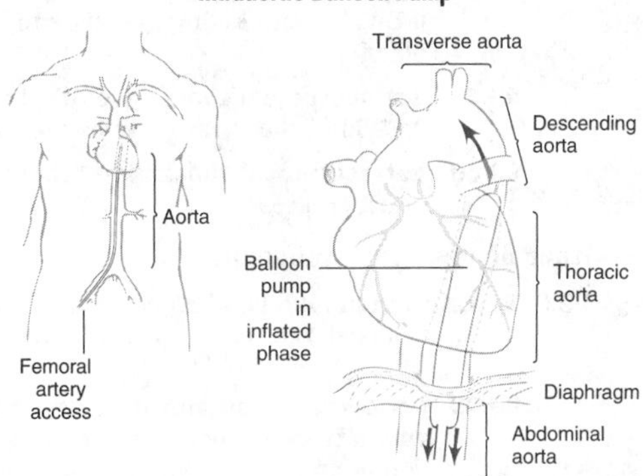

97.42 Removal of mediastinal drain

97.43 Removal of sutures from thorax

97.44 Nonoperative removal of heart assist system
Explantation [removal] of circulatory assist device
Explantation [removal] of percutaneous external heart assist device
Removal of extrinsic heart assist device
Removal of pVAD
Removal of percutaneous heart assist device

DEF: Non-invasive removal of ventricular assist systems, or intraaortic balloon pump, which is a balloon catheter placed into the descending thoracic aorta and timed to inflate and deflate with the patient's own heart rhythm to aid in blood circulation.

97.49 Removal of other device from thorax
EXCLUDES *endoscopic removal of bronchial device(s) or substances (33.78)*

✓4th **97.5 Nonoperative removal of therapeutic device from digestive system**

97.51 Removal of gastrostomy tube

97.52 Removal of tube from small intestine

97.53 Removal of tube from large intestine or appendix

97.54 Removal of cholecystostomy tube

97.55 Removal of T-tube, other bile duct tube, or liver tube
Removal of bile duct stent

97.56 Removal of pancreatic tube or drain

97.59 Removal of other device from digestive system
Removal of rectal packing

✓4th **97.6 Nonoperative removal of therapeutic device from urinary system**

97.61 Removal of pyelostomy and nephrostomy tube
DEF: Nonsurgical removal of tubes from lower part of kidney.

97.62 Removal of ureterostomy tube and ureteral catheter

97.63 Removal of cystostomy tube

97.64 Removal of other urinary drainage device
Removal of indwelling urinary catheter

97.65 Removal of urethral stent

97.69 Removal of other device from urinary system

✓4th **97.7 Nonoperative removal of therapeutic device from genital system**

97.71 Removal of intrauterine contraceptive device

97.72 Removal of intrauterine pack

97.73 Removal of vaginal diaphragm

97.74 Removal of other vaginal pessary

97.75 Removal of vaginal or vulvar packing

97.79 Removal of other device from genital tract
Removal of sutures

✓4th **97.8 Other nonoperative removal of therapeutic device**

97.81 Removal of retroperitoneal drainage device

97.82 Removal of peritoneal drainage device

97.83 Removal of abdominal wall sutures

97.84 Removal of sutures from trunk, not elsewhere classified

97.85 Removal of packing from trunk, not elsewhere classified

97.86 Removal of other device from abdomen

97.87 Removal of other device from trunk

97.88 Removal of external immobilization device
Removal of:
brace
cast
splint

97.89 Removal of other therapeutic device

✓3rd **98 Nonoperative removal of foreign body or calculus**

✓4th **98.0 Removal of intraluminal foreign body from digestive system without incision**
EXCLUDES *removal of therapeutic device (97.51-97.59)*

DEF: Retrieval of foreign body from digestive system lining without incision.

98.01 Removal of intraluminal foreign body from mouth without incision

98.02 Removal of intraluminal foreign body from esophagus without incision

98.03 Removal of intraluminal foreign body from stomach and small intestine without incision

98.04 Removal of intraluminal foreign body from large intestine without incision

98.05 Removal of intraluminal foreign body from rectum and anus without incision

✓4th **98.1 Removal of intraluminal foreign body from other sites without incision**
EXCLUDES *removal of therapeutic device (97.31-97.49, 97.61-97.89)*

98.11 Removal of intraluminal foreign body from ear without incision

98.12 Removal of intraluminal foreign body from nose without incision

98.13 Removal of intraluminal foreign body from pharynx without incision

98.14 Removal of intraluminal foreign body from larynx without incision

98.15 Removal of intraluminal foreign body from trachea and bronchus without incision

EXCLUDES *endoscopic removal of bronchial device(s) or substances (33.78)*

98.16 Removal of intraluminal foreign bodyfrom uterus without incision

EXCLUDES *removal of intrauterine contraceptive device (97.71)*

98.17 Removal of intraluminal foreign bodyfrom vagina without incision

98.18 Removal of intraluminal foreign body from artificial stoma without incision

98.19 Removal of intraluminal foreign body from urethra without incision

✓4th **98.2 Removal of other foreign body without incision**

EXCLUDES *removal of intraluminal foreign body (98.01-98.19)*

98.20 Removal of foreign body, not otherwise specified

98.21 Removal of superficial foreign body from eye without incision

98.22 Removal of other foreign body without incision from head and neck

Removal of embedded foreign body from eyelid or conjunctiva without incision

98.23 Removal of foreign body from vulva without incision

98.24 Removal of foreign body from scrotum or penis without incision

98.25 Removal of other foreign body without incision from trunk except scrotum, penis, or vulva

98.26 Removal of foreign body from hand without incision

98.27 Removal of foreign body without incision from upper limb, except hand

98.28 Removal of foreign body from foot without incision

98.29 Removal of foreign body without incision from lower limb, except foot

✓4th **98.5 Extracorporeal shockwave lithotripsy [ESWL]**

Lithotriptor tank procedure
Disintegration of stones by extracorporeal induced shockwaves
That with insertion of stent

DEF: Breaking of stones with high voltage condenser device synchronized with patient R waves.

Extracorporeal Shock Wave Lithotripsy

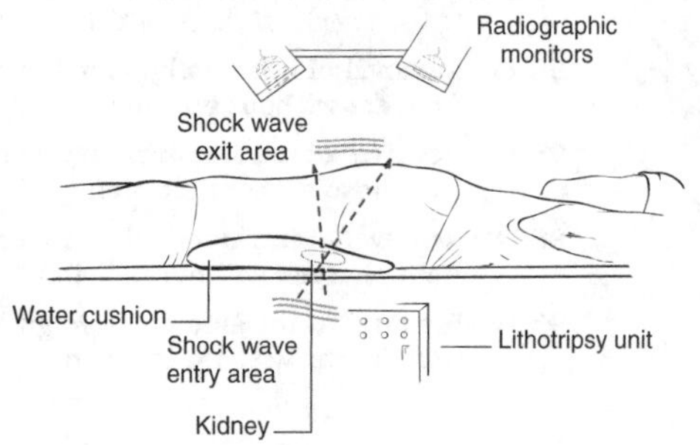

98.51 Extracorporeal shockwave lithotripsy [ESWL] of the kidney, ureter and/or bladder

98.52 Extracorporeal shockwave lithotripsy [ESWL] of the gallbladder and/or bile duct

98.59 Extracorporeal shockwave lithotripsy of other sites

✓3rd **99 Other nonoperative procedures**

✓4th **99.0 Transfusion of blood and blood components**

Use additional code for that done via catheter or cutdown (38.92-38.94)

99.00 Perioperative autologous transfusion of whole blood or blood components

Intraoperative blood collection
Postoperative blood collection
Salvage

DEF: Salvaging patient blood with reinfusion during perioperative period.

99.01 Exchange transfusion

Transfusion:
- exsanguination
- replacement

DEF: Repetitive withdrawal of blood, replaced by donor blood.

99.02 Transfusion of previously collected autologous blood

Blood component

DEF: Transfusion with patient's own previously withdrawn and stored blood.

99.03 Other transfusion of whole blood

Transfusion:
- blood NOS
- hemodilution
- NOS

99.04 Transfusion of packed cells

99.05 Transfusion of platelets

Transfusion of thrombocytes

99.06 Transfusion of coagulation factors

Transfusion of antihemophilic factor

99.07 Transfusion of other serum

Transfusion of plasma

EXCLUDES *injection [transfusion] of:*
- *antivenin (99.16)*
- *gamma globulin (99.14)*

99.08 Transfusion of blood expander

Transfusion of Dextran

99.09 Transfusion of other substance

Transfusion of:
- blood surrogate
- granulocytes

EXCLUDES *transplantation [transfusion] of bone marrow (41.0)*

✓4th **99.1 Injection or infusion of therapeutic or prophylactic substance**

INCLUDES injection or infusion given:
- hypodermically
- intramuscularly
- intravenously

} acting locally or systemically

99.10 Injection or infusion of thrombolytic agent
Alteplase
Anistreplase
Reteplase
Streptokinase
Tenecteplase
Tissue plasminogen activator (TPA)
Urokinase

EXCLUDES *aspirin — omit code*
GP IIb/IIIa platelet inhibitors (99.20)
heparin (99.19)
SuperSaturated oxygen therapy (00.49)
warfarin — omit code

99.11 Injection of Rh immune globulin
Injection of:
Anti-D (Rhesus) globulin
RhoGAM

99.12 Immunization for allergy
Desensitization

99.13 Immunization for autoimmune disease

99.14 Injection or infusion of gamma globulin
Injection of immune sera

99.15 Parenteral infusion of concentrated nutritional substances
Hyperalimentation
Total parenteral nutrition [TPN]
Peripheral parenteral nutrition [PPN]

DEF: Administration of greater than necessary amount of nutrients via other than the alimentary canal (e.g., infusion).

99.16 Injection of antidote
Injection of:
antivenin
heavy metal antagonist

99.17 Injection of insulin

99.18 Injection or infusion of electrolytes

99.19 Injection of anticoagulant

EXCLUDES *infusion of drotrecogin alfa (activated) (00.11)*

✓4th **99.2 Injection or infusion of other therapeutic or prophylactic substance**

INCLUDES injection or infusion given:
hypodermically, intramuscularly, intravenously } acting locally or systemically

Use additional code for:
injection (into):
breast (85.92)
bursa (82.94, 83.96)
intraperitoneal (cavity) (54.97)
intrathecal (03.92)
joint (76.96, 81.92)
kidney (55.96)
liver (50.94)
orbit (16.91)
other sites — see Alphabetic Index
perfusion:
NOS (39.97)
intestine (46.95, 46.96)
kidney (55.95)
liver (50.93)
total body (39.96)

EXCLUDES *SuperSaturated oxygen therapy (00.49)*

99.20 Injection or infusion of platelet inhibitor
Glycoprotein IIb/IIIa inhibitor
GP IIb-IIIa inhibitor
GP IIb/IIIa inhibitor

EXCLUDES *infusion of heparin (99.19)*
injection or infusion of thrombolytic agent (99.10)

99.21 Injection of antibiotic

EXCLUDES *injection or infusion of oxazolidinone class of antibiotics (00.14)*

99.22 Injection of other anti-infective

EXCLUDES *injection or infusion of oxazolidinone class of antibiotics (00.14)*

99.23 Injection of steroid
Injection of cortisone
Subdermal implantation of progesterone

99.24 Injection of other hormone

99.25 Injection or infusion of cancer chemotherapeutic substance
Chemoembolization
Injection or infusion of antineoplastic agent
Use additional code for disruption of blood brain barrier, if performed [BBBD] (00.19)

EXCLUDES *immunotherapy, antineoplastic (00.15, 99.28)*
implantation of chemotherapeutic agent (00.10)
injection of radioisotope (92.28)
injection or infusion of biological response modifier [BRM] as an antineoplastic agent (99.28)

99.26 Injection of tranquilizer

99.27 Iontophoresis

DEF: Iontophoresis: Introduction of soluble salts into tissues via electric current.

99.28 Injection or infusion of biological response modifier [BRM] as an antineoplastic agent
Immunotherapy, antineoplastic
Infusion of cintredekin besudotox
Interleukin therapy
Low-dose interleukin-2 [IL-2] therapy
Tumor vaccine

EXCLUDES *high-dose infusion interleukin-2 [IL-2] (00.15)*

99.29 Injection or infusion of other therapeutic or prophylactic substance

EXCLUDES *administration of neuroprotective agent (99.75)*
immunization (99.31-99.59)
infusion of blood brain barrier disruption substance (00.19)
injection of sclerosing agent into:
esophageal varices (42.33)
hemorrhoids (49.42)
veins (39.92)
injection or infusion of:
human B-type natriuretic peptide (hBNP) (00.13)
nesiritide (00.13)
platelet inhibitor (99.20)
thrombolytic agent (99.10)

✓4th **99.3 Prophylactic vaccination and inoculation against certain bacterial diseases**

DEF: Administration of a killed bacteria suspension to produce immunity.

99.31 Vaccination against cholera

99.32 Vaccination against typhoid and paratyphoid fever
Administration of TAB vaccine

99.33 Vaccination against tuberculosis
Administration of BCG vaccine

99.34 Vaccination against plague

99.35 Vaccination against tularemia

99.36 Administration of diphtheria toxoid

EXCLUDES *administration of:*
diphtheria antitoxin (99.58)
diphtheria-tetanus-pertussis, combined (99.39)

99.37 Vaccination against pertussis

EXCLUDES *administration of diphtheria-tetanus-pertussis, combined (99.39)*

99.38 Administration of tetanus toxoid

EXCLUDES *administration of:*
diphtheria-tetanus-pertussis, combined (99.39)
tetanus antitoxin (99.56)

99.39 Administration of diphtheria-tetanus-pertussis, combined

✓4th **99.4 Prophylactic vaccination and inoculation against certain viral diseases**

DEF: Administration of a killed virus suspension to produce immunity.

99.41 Administration of poliomyelitis vaccine

99.42 Vaccination against smallpox

99.43 Vaccination against yellow fever

99.44 Vaccination against rabies

99.45 Vaccination against measles

EXCLUDES *administration of measles-mumps-rubella vaccine (99.48)*

99.46 Vaccination against mumps

EXCLUDES *administration of measles-mumps-rubella vaccine (99.48)*

99.47 Vaccination against rubella

EXCLUDES *administration of measles-mumps-rubella vaccine (99.48)*

99.48 Administration of measles-mumps-rubella vaccine

✓4th **99.5 Other vaccination and inoculation**

99.51 Prophylactic vaccination against the common cold

99.52 Prophylactic vaccination against influenza

99.53 Prophylactic vaccination against arthropod-borne viral encephalitis

99.54 Prophylactic vaccination against other arthropod-borne viral diseases

99.55 Prophylactic administration of vaccine against other diseases

Vaccination against:
anthrax
brucellosis
Rocky Mountain spotted fever
Staphylococcus
Streptococcus
typhus

99.56 Administration of tetanus antitoxin

99.57 Administration of botulism antitoxin

99.58 Administration of other antitoxins

Administration of:
diphtheria antitoxin
gas gangrene antitoxin
scarlet fever antitoxin

99.59 Other vaccination and inoculation

Vaccination NOS

EXCLUDES *injection of:*
gamma globulin (99.14)
Rh immune globulin (99.11)
immunization for:
allergy (99.12)
autoimmune disease (99.13)

✓4th **99.6 Conversion of cardiac rhythm**

EXCLUDES *open chest cardiac:*
electric stimulation (37.91)
massage (37.91)

DEF: Correction of cardiac rhythm.

99.60 Cardiopulmonary resuscitation, not otherwise specified

99.61 Atrial cardioversion

DEF: Application of electric shock to upper heart chamber to restore normal heart rhythm.

99.62 Other electric countershock of heart

Cardioversion:
NOS
external
Conversion to sinus rhythm
Defibrillation
External electrode stimulation

99.63 Closed chest cardiac massage

Cardiac massage NOS
Manual external cardiac massage

DEF: Application of alternating manual pressure over breastbone to restore normal heart rhythm.

99.64 Carotid sinus stimulation

99.69 Other conversion of cardiac rhythm

✓4th **99.7 Therapeutic apheresis or other injection, administration, or infusion of other therpeutic or prophylactic substance**

99.71 Therapeutic plasmapheresis

EXCLUDES *extracorporeal immunoadsorption [ECI] (99.76)*

99.72 Therapeutic leukopheresis

Therapeutic leukocytapheresis

99.73 Therapeutic erythrocytapheresis

Therapeutic erythropheresis

99.74 Therapeutic plateletpheresis

99.75 Administration of neuroprotective agent

DEF: Direct application of neuroprotective agent (e.g., nimodipine) to miinimize ischemic injury by inhibiting toxic neurotransmitters, blocking free ions, removing free radicals, and causing vasodilation.

99.76 Extracorporeal immunoadsorption

Removal of antibodies from plasma with protein A columns

99.77 Application or administration of adhesion barrier substance

99.78 Aquapheresis

Plasma water removal
Ultrafiltration [for water removal]

EXCLUDES *hemodiafiltration (39.95)*
hemodialysis (39.95)
therapeutic plasmapheresis (99.71)

99.79 Other

Apheresis (harvest) of stem cells

✓4th **99.8 Miscellaneous physical procedures**

99.81 Hypothermia (central) (local)

EXCLUDES *gastric cooling (96.31)*
gastric freezing (96.32)
that incidental to open heart surgery (39.62)

99.82 Ultraviolet light therapy
Actinotherapy

99.83 Other phototherapy
Phototherapy of the newborn

EXCLUDES *extracorporeal photochemotherapy (99.88)*
photocoagulation of retinal lesion (14.23-14.25, 14.33-14.35, 14.53-14.55)

DEF: Treating disease with light rays of various concentrations.

99.84 Isolation
Isolation after contact with infectious disease
Protection of individual from his surroundings
Protection of surroundings from individual

99.85 Hyperthermia for treatment of cancer
Hyperthermia (adjunct therapy) induced by microwave, ultrasound, low energy radio frequency, probes (interstitial), or other means in the treatment of cancer

Code also any concurrent chemotherapy or radiation therapy

99.86 Non-invasive placement of bone growth stimulator
Transcutaneous (surface) placement of pads or patches for stimulation to aid bone healing

EXCLUDES *insertion of invasive or semi-invasive bone growth stimulators (device) (percutaneous electrodes) (78.90-78.99)*

99.88 Therapeutic photopheresis
Extracorporeal photochemotherapy
Extracorporeal photopheresis

EXCLUDES *other phototherapy (99.83)*
ultraviolet light therapy (99.82)

DEF: Extracorporeal photochemotherapy: Treating disease with drugs that react to ultraviolet radiation or sunlight.

✓4th **99.9 Other miscellaneous procedures**

99.91 Acupuncture for anesthesia

99.92 Other acupuncture

EXCLUDES *that with smouldering moxa (93.35)*

99.93 Rectal massage (for levator spasm)

99.94 Prostatic massage

99.95 Stretching of foreskin

99.96 Collection of sperm for artificial insemination

99.97 Fitting of denture

99.98 Extraction of milk from lactating breast

99.99 Other
Leech therapy

HCPCS Introduction

All experienced medical coders know and use the tools to report medical procedures and services and the diagnoses that justify the treatment. Sometimes overlooked in training, though, is another area of medical coding: nonphysician services, specific supplies, and the administration of select drugs. HCPCS Level II codes are the tools to report these types of services and supplies.

The term HCPCS (pronounced ™hick-picks½) is most accurately used as the acronym for the entire two-level Healthcare Common Procedure Coding System. The federal government refers to all procedure codes as the HCPCS system. But HCPCS is also commonly used to specifically identify HCPCS Level II national codes, the topic of this chapter. (CPT codes are Level I of the system.) The HCPCS Level II codes are maintained by the Centers for Medicare and Medicaid Services (CMS) and are updated throughout the year, with the major update effective the first of each year. Because the Level I CPT coding system does not include codes for nonphysician services many of these services are identified with a Level II code as well as specific supplies, procedures which do not have a specific CPT code and drugs.

To see how HCPCS fits within the entire CMS coding system, we offer the following overview of each of the three levels, their official names, and their popular, commonly used names.

HCPCS Level II/National Codes

More than 2,800 codes comprise the HCPCS Level II national codes. If an appropriate HCPCS Level II code exists, it usually takes precedence over a CPT code in Medicare billing. These codes are updated annually but new codes may be introduced through out the year as necessary. Codes may also be changed or deleted throughout the year.

The alphanumeric codes represent groups of services or supplies. HCPCS codes are now required to report most medical services and supplies provided in outpatient settings to Medicare and Medicaid patients. An increasing number of private insurance carriers also encourage or require the use of HCPCS codes. Most of the larger national payers, including workers' compensation, recognize HCPCS codes. HCPCS codes are available from the CMSwebsite, Medicare contractor, or from commercial publishers such as Ingenix. For Medicare, Level II codes usually supercede Level 1 codes. Many private payers prefer Level 1 codes to Level II codes when similar codes exist.

The HCPCS National Codes in Detail

HCPCS Level II-national codes may be used throughout the United States in all Medicare regions. National codes consist of one alpha character (A through V) followed by four digits (A0000±V9999). HCPCS Level II provides specific codes for supplies, services, injections and certain drugs, durable medical equipment (DME), orthotics, prosthetics, etc. HCPCS Level II codes are designed to provide more specificity than CPT codes. The HCPCS Level II coding system also contains an Index. In addition, all prescription drugs are listed in the table of drugs. In the index, under ™Drugs(s),½ the user is directed to this table.

HCPCS Codes

Each section of codes is designated by a letter code except for the last section, the table of drugs.

A codes include ambulance and transportation services, medical and surgical supplies, administrative, and miscellaneous and investigational services and supplies.

B codes include enteral and parenteral therapy.

C codes are used for facility (technical) services.

D codes include diagnostic, preventive, restorative, endodontic, periodontic, prosthodontic, prosthetic, orthodontic, and surgical dental procedures. These codes are supplied to CMS and are copyrighted by the American Dental Association.

E codes include durable medical equipment such as canes, crutches, walkers, commodes, decubitus care, bath and toilet aids, hospital beds, oxygen and related respiratory equipment, monitoring equipment, pacemakers, patient lifts, safety equipment, restraints, traction equipment, fracture frames, wheelchairs, and artificial kidney machines.

G codes include temporary procedures and professional services that are under review prior to inclusion in the CPT coding system.

H codes describe alcohol and drug abuse treatment services. These are temporary codes for state or federal agencies other than Medicare and Medicaid.

J codes include drugs that cannot ordinarily be self-administered, chemotherapy drugs, immunosuppressive drugs, inhalation solutions, and other miscellaneous drugs and solutions.

K codes are temporary codes for durable medical equipment and drugs. Once these codes are approved for permanent inclusion in HCPCS, they typically become A, E, or J codes.

L codes include orthotic and prosthetic procedures and devices, as well as scoliosis equipment, orthopedic shoes, and prosthetic implants.

M codes include office services and cardiovascular and other medical services.

P codes include certain pathology and laboratory services.

Q codes are miscellaneous temporary codes.

R codes are diagnostic radiology services codes.

S codes are not accepted by Medicare and have been developed by Blue cross/Blue Shield and other commercial payers to report drugs, services and supplies. Often these codes are replaced by a CPT code within several years of development.

T codes are for use by state Medicaid agencies and are not valid for Medicare.

V codes include vision, hearing, and speech-language pathology services.

The table of drugs lists all drugs found in HCPCS by their generic name, with amount, route of administration, and code number. Brand name drugs are also listed in the table with a reference to the appropriate generic drug.

The HCPCS Level II coding system also contains modifiers. These modifiers are two-digit suffixes that can be appended to all procedure codes (i.e., HCPCS level I or HCPCS Level II codes). HCPCS modifiers may be alpha or alphanumeric.

There are also two-character modifiers used on claims that are created by combining two single-character modifiers. These are used for ambulance services, the first digit indicating the origin and the second the destination.

Use of HCPCS

The following points summarize why practices use HCPCS:

- HCPCS codes are mandated by CMS for use on Medicare claims and are also required by most state Medicaid offices.
- HCPCS codes improve a provider's ability to communicate services or supplies correctly without resorting to narrative descriptions.
- The codes reduce resubmission of claims for correction or review.
- Up-to-date and accurate HCPCS codes on office routing slips allow office staff to assign fees quickly and efficiently to services and supplies, saving both time and money.
- Consistent submission of ™clean claims½ (claims having all correct information necessary for processing) helps avoid an audit by a carrier due to lack of specificity of claims.

- Use of HCPCS is essential for accurate and complete reimbursement from Medicare.
- Supplies billed to Medicare as "other than incidental to an office visit" (CPT code 99070) are not reimbursed unless identified with Level II/HCPCS or Level III/local codes.

The Index

The index is of tremendous help to both new and experienced HCPCS coders. All main terms are in boldface type in the Index. Main term entries include tests, services, supplies, orthotics, prostheses, medical equipment, drugs, therapies, and some medical and surgical procedures. Subterms are listed under the main term to which they apply. Where possible, entries are listed under a common main term. In some instances, the common term is a noun, while in others, the main term is a descriptor.

The steps to follow for searching the index are:

1. Analyze the provided statement or description that designates the term to be coded.
2 Identify the main term.
3. Locate the main term in the index.
4. Check for relevant subterms under the main term. Verify the meaning of any unfamiliar abbreviations.
5. Note the codes found after the selected main term or subterm.
6. Locate the code in the alphanumeric list to ensure the specificity of the code. If a code range is provided, locate the code range and review all code narratives in that code range for specificity.
7. In some cases, an entry may be listed under more than one main term. When this occurs, review all code choices suggested.
8. Never code directly from the index. Always verify the main choice in the alphanumeric list.

Tabular—Color Coding

Red — Codes that are "Not Covered" or invalid for Medicare are designated by a red color bar. Any pertinent Medicare manual references are provided. Please see the resources to review the corresponding manual citations.

Grey — Codes that have "Special Coverage Instructions" are designated by a gray color bar. Any pertinent Medicare manual references are provided. Please see the resources to review the corresponding citations.

No Color Codes not designated by a color bar are covered at "Carrier Discretion." Contact the carrier for specific instructions.

MED: — This notation precedes an instruction pertaining to this code in the Centers for Medicare and Medicaid Services [CMS] Publication 100 (Pub 100) electronic manual. These CMS sources present the rules for submitting these services to the federal goverment or its contractors. See Appendix-4 of this manual for the Pub-100 references.

AHA: — The Central Office on HCPCS issues a quarterly publication, *AHA's Coding Clinic for HCPCS* to provide consistent and accurate advice for proper application of HCPCS. References to specfic HCPCS coding issues are identified by the symbol AHA: followed by the issue, year, and page number. For example code A9600 includes AHA: 2Q, '02, 9. This means that in the second quarted publication in 2002 on page 9 there is information regarding assignment of A9600 Strontium Sr-89 chloride, therapeutic, per 50 millicuries.

HCPCS in the Physician's Office

While many of the HCPCS codes relate to supplies, such as durable medical equipment, there are a lot of codes that are used to report the provision of services and pharmaceuticals.

Providers should carefully review the codes in the G section each year. For example, many of the screening codes and services are reported from this section. As previously noted, where there is a HCPCS Level II code, it supersedes a HCPCS Level I (CPT) code for Medicare. Some of those services are listed below:

G0101	Cervical or vaginal cancer screening: pelvic and clinical breast examination
G0102	Prostate cancer screening; digital rectal examination
G0104	Colorectal cancer screening; flexible sigmoidoscopy
G0108	Diabetes outpatient self-management training services, individual per 30 minutes
G0117	Glaucoma screening for high-risk patients furnished by an optometrist or ophthalmologist
G0168	Wound closure utilizing tissue adhesive(s) only

For example, physician who performs a pelvic exam with cervical cancer screening (Pap smear) and clinical breast examination would report G0101 and not an E/M service office visit or preventive medicine examination.

Health intervention and behavioral health services for Medicare patients are reported with the codes starting with "H." Specific prenatal care codes are also included in this section as well as foster care for children and supported housing for adults. State Medicaid programs also require many of these codes. Providers should review these codes and the guidelines from their state program to correctly report services.

Perhaps the best-known set of HCPCS codes by the physician practice is the J code set for pharmaceuticals. Most of these drugs are in the injectable or intravenous format. Oral forms of the medications listed are not in this section of codes and are not covered by Medicare. The drugs are also listed in generic terms and it may be necessary to convert the drug brand name to its generic name. It is also important to verify the dosage. Some drugs are listed with multiple options for dosage. If the entire dose is not used on a single dose vial the modifier JW should be reported to indicate that the remainder was discarded and not given to another patient.

Chemotherapy drugs are also listed as J codes. Again the generic name is used and many have multiple dosing options to choose from.

Treatment of Medicare patients who received psychopharmaceutical therapy without psychotherapy is reported with M0064. Non-Medicare patients use 90862.

Many of the current HCPCS codes are considered temporary and changes are made in these sections on a yearly basis. It is important for the provider to verify these codes on a yearly basis to verify that only current codes are used. Many of these codes are assigned while the CPT process determines if a permanent CPT code will be assigned. Some of these codes replace state level codes for Medicaid that were deleted as a result of HIPAA legislation.

Modifiers

Modifiers should, or in some cases must, be used to identify circumstances that alter or enhance the description of a service or supply. As mentioned earlier, the HCPCS level II coding system also contains modifiers. These modifiers can and should be used when appropriate with either CPT or HCPCS Level II codes. In certain circumstances, modifiers must be used to report the alteration of a procedure or service.

In HCPCS Level II, modifiers are composed of two alpha- or alphanumeric characters that range from "A1" to "VP."

E0260-NU Hospital bed, semi-electric (head and foot adjustment), with any type side rails, with mattress

NU: Identifies the hospital bed as new equipment

When reporting ambulance services, separate one-character codes are used together to form a two-character modifier. The first letter indicates the origination of the patient, and the second identifies the destination.

Although both alpha and numeric modifiers are common throughout the country, some regional carriers do not recognize their use due to software limitations. It may be necessary to provide a cover letter, an invoice, or other specific documentation with the claim for clarification.

Unlisted HCPCS Codes

Unlisted HCPCS codes are unique to a section or a subsection of codes. Third-party payers designate as unlisted all HCPCS codes that include the term unlisted in the definition. In addition, payers often apply the unlisted codes to services and supplies that are described in indefinite terms, do not have a precise meaning, and/or have language open to differing interpretations. Terms and phrases commonly found in the descriptions of these unlisted HCPCS codes include the following:

- Miscellaneous
- NES (not elsewhere specified)
- NOC (not otherwise classified)
- Unclassified
- Unspecified

THE DMEPOS INDUSTRY

Wheelchairs, artificial limbs, braces, surgical dressings, and medications are all examples of durable medical equipment, prosthetics, orthotics, and supplies, known by the acronyms DME and POS, or simply DMEPOS.

The DMEPOS industry includes manufacturers, pharmaceutical companies, medical equipment and supply companies (suppliers and vendors), and providers. Entities peripheral to the DMEPOS industry–but having direct impact on its operations–include the Food and Drug Administration (FDA), which approves the use of medical devices and pharmaceuticals in the United States, and federal and state health care programs, such as Medicare and Medicaid, which provide DMEPOS coverage and/or reimbursement for millions of beneficiaries. Other third-party payers, such as Blue Cross/Blue Shield, various preferred provider organizations (PPOs), workers' compensation carriers, and managed care organizations (MCOs), also influence the DMEPOS industry.

Special Federal and Third-party Payer Definitions

For federally funded health care programs, such as Medicare and the Children's Health Insurance Program (CHIP), and for programs that are partially funded by the federal government, such as some state Medicaid programs, strict definitions of what constitutes DMEPOS are delineated. A number of commercial insurance plans and MCOs also follow this same framework–or a similar one–constructed around the prescription, dispensation, reporting, and reimbursement of DMEPOS.

Defining DME

According to CMS, the federal agency that operates the Medicare program, DME must meet specific criteria to be eligible for coverage. These criteria are shown here in the form of questions. The provider or supplier must answer yes to all of these questions for the equipment or device to be recognized as eligible for reimbursement under the Medicare program:

- Can the medical equipment withstand repeated use?
- Is the medical equipment primarily and customarily used for medical purposes?
- Is the medical equipment not of use to a person without illness or injury or in need of improvement of a malformed body part?
- Is the medical equipment appropriate for home use?

An answer of no to any of the preceding questions could render the DME ineligible for Medicare coverage.

(Special exceptions can be made by the Medicare program, some state Medicaid programs, and other third-party payers even when the DME equipment or device does not meet the accepted definition: (1) the equipment or devices are not primarily and customarily used for medical purposes, and/or (2) the equipment or devices can be used in the absence of illness, injury, or deformity. A DMEPOS item, described by one or both of these contradicting criteria, may be eligible for Medicare coverage if the therapeutic purpose is clearly distinguished, such as use of a heat lamp where the medical need for heat therapy has been established. The fact that the patient's course of treatment is under the supervision of the physician must also be in evidence.)

Defining Prostheses

Prosthetic devices, as recognized by CMS and many third-party payers, are those devices that replace all or part of an internal body organ, or replace all or part of the function of a permanently inoperative or malfunctioning internal body organ. This category of devices includes:

- Artificial limbs
- Breast and eye prostheses
- Maxillofacial devices
- Joint implants
- Devices that replace all or part of the ear or nose
- Ostomy and colostomy bags
- Irrigation and flushing equipment directly related to ostomy/colostomy care

An example of a prosthesis is a urinary collection and retention system that replaces the function of the bladder in cases of permanent urinary incontinence. Replacement of a prosthetic device may be covered, but only when the replacement is required because of a change in the beneficiary's physical condition. Adjustments to an artificial limb or other prosthetic device required by wear or by a change in the beneficiary's physical condition may likewise be covered when ordered by a physician.

Defining Orthoses

An orthosis or orthotic device is used for the correction or prevention of skeletal deformities. This includes braces for the neck, shoulder and arm, forearm, wrist and hand, hip, leg, ankle, and foot, as well as spinal or back devices. If there is a change in the beneficiary's physical condition that requires replacements and adjustments, those may also be covered. However, according to CMS, to be classified as an orthotic the brace must be a rigid or semi-rigid device used to support a weak or deformed body member, or to restrict or eliminate motion in a diseased or injured part of the body.

Defining Supplies

Within the DMEPOS industry, a supply is an item or accessory needed for the effective use of a DME, prosthetic or orthotic device, or appliance. Such supplies include those drugs and biologicals that must be placed directly into equipment to achieve the therapeutic benefit of the DME or to ensure the proper function of the equipment. An example of this is the use of heparin within a home dialysis system. To be eligible for coverage by Medicare, Medicaid, and third-party payers, supplies must be medically necessary and must be prescribed by the treating provider. Supplies eligible for reimbursement by these programs and payers are typically not those bought off-the-shelf or over-the-counter at local drug stores and grocery stores. Exceptions include recent additions to covered supplies for a patient's home use, such as supplies needed with a glucometer to monitor diabetes mellitus.

HCPC Self Test

1. A patient, involved in an auto accident, is transported by ambulance to the hospital with a possible broken leg.

   a. A0380-EH　　c. A0390-EH
   b. A0380-SH　　d. A0390-SH

2. A patient receives a 1000 ml parenteral solution of 3.5% amino acids for use at home.

   a. B4168, 2 units　　c. B4172, 2 units
   b. B4185, 2 units　　d. B4180, 2 units

3. An adult patient presents to the dentist for a cleaning.

   a. D0210　　c. D2975
   b. D1330　　d. D1110

4. A patient is seen in the office for cellulitis. The physician administers 500 mg of Rocephin.

   a. J0698　　c. J0696 X 2
   b. J0696　　d. J0692 X 2

5. A patient is seen by his psychiatrist for an adjustment of his medication.

   a. M0064　　c. G8128
   b. G0332　　d. M0300

6. The definition of HCPCS is:

   a. Health Code Practice Country System
   b. Hickpicks Common Practice Coding System
   c. Healthcare Current Procedural Coding System
   d. Healthcare Common Procedure Coding System

7. Level I HCPCS refers to:

   a. HCPCS alpha numeric codes
   b. CPT codes
   c. ICD-9 codes
   d. a and c

8. Level II HCPCS refers to:

   a. HCPCS alphanumeric codes
   b. CPT codes
   c. ICD-9 codes
   d. a and c

9. Which of the following is not a step in coding HCPCS:

   a. Locate main term from index
   b. Code from index
   c. Identify the main term
   d. Locate any subterms under the main term

10. D codes describe:

    a. Ambulance codes　　c. Temporary codes
    b. DME　　d. Dental codes

11. Assign the HCPCS codes for a disposable surgical tray:

    a. A4550　　c. A6200
    b. A4310　　d. A6206

12. A patient receives an injection of 1,200,000 units of Bicillin C-R. Assign the correct HCPCS code for the medication.

    a. J0530, units 2　　c. J0540
    b. J0550　　d. J0560

13. A patient presents to his physician's office for the administration of a flu vaccine. Assign the HCPCS code for the administration:

    a. J2405　　c. G0009
    b. G0008　　d. G0010

14. A patient presents to his orthopedic surgeons office for an injection of the shoulder joint. The patient injects the joint with 3 mg of celestone soluspan. Assign the HCPCS code for the medication:

    a. J0704　　c. J0715
    b. J0698　　d. J0702

15. A postoperative patient receives 30 mg of Toradol IV for pain relief. Assign the HCPCS code used for the medication:

    a. J1885　　c. J3301, 3 units
    b. J3280, 3 units　　d. J1885, 2 units

16. A patient presents to his dentist for a one surface amalgam filling in a permanent tooth. Assign the HCPCS code for the service:

    a. D2330　　c. D2150
    b. D2331　　d. D2140

17. HCPCS modifiers can be used with:

    a. CPT codes　　c. ICD-9 codes
    b. HCPCS codes　　d. a and b

18. A patient with a history of smoking one pack a day for the past 20 years presents to her physician's office for smoking cessation counseling, which lasts 20 minutes. Assign the HCPCS code for the service:

    a. G0375, 2 units　　c. G0376
    b. G9016　　d. D1320

19. A patient presents for fitting of a below-knee 40±50 mm Hg gradient compression stocking for the right leg. Assign the HCPCS code for this supply:

    a. A6532-RT　　c. A6532
    b. A6535-RT　　d. A6542-RT

20. A patient is directly admitted to a hospital's observation unit with a diagnosis of head injury. Assign the HCPCS code for this service:

    a. G0264　　c. G0244
    b. G0378　　d. G0379

21. A head injury patient presents for a protective helmet. The patient is given a hard prefabricated helmet with chin strap. Assign the HCPCS code for this service:

    a. A7036 and A8001　　c. A7036 and A8003
    b. A8003　　d. A8001

22. A patient receives hospice care in his home. Assign the HCPCS code for this service:

    a. Q5004　　c. Q5009
    b. Q5002　　d. Q5001

23. An epileptic patient presents for a 500 mg infusion of Keppra.

    a. J1953 X 15　　c. J1953 X 5
    b. J1953 X 50　　d. J1953 X 10

24. A Medicare patient is seen in the office for diabetes mellitus, and the physician is reporting that all quality actions for the applicable measures for this patient have been performed.

    a. G8497　　c. G8494
    b. G8499　　d. G8500

Answer Key can be found in the back of the book.

10% LMD, J7100
5% dextrose/normal saline, J7042
5% dextrose/water, J7060

A

Abarelix, J0128
Abatacept, J0129
Abbokinase, J3364, J3365
Abciximab, J0130
Abdomen/abdominal
dressing holder/binder, A4461, A4463
pad, low profle, L1270
Abduction
control, each, L2624
pillow, E1399
rotation bar, foot, L3140-L3170
Abortion, S2260-S2267
Abscess, incision and drainage, D7510-D7520
Absorption dressing, A6251-A6256
Abutments
for implants, D6056-D6057
retainers for resin bonded "Maryland bridge", D6545
Accession of brush biopsy sample, D0486
Accession of tissue, dental, D0472-D0474
Accessories
ambulation devices, E0153-E0159
artifcial kidney and machine (*see also* ESRD), E1510-E1699
beds, E0271-E0280, E0305-E0326
oxygen, E1354-E1358
wheelchairs, E0950-E1010, E1050-E1298, E2201-E2231, E2295, E2300-E2367, K0001-K0108
Access system, A4301
AccuChek
blood glucose meter, E0607
test strips, box of 50, A4253
Accurate
prosthetic sock, L8420-L8435
stump sock, L8470-L8485
Acetate concentrate for hemodialysis, A4708
Acetazolamide sodium, J1120
Acetylcysteine
inhalation solution, J7608
injection, J0132
Achromycin, J0120
Acid concentrate for hemodialysis, A4709
ACTH, J0800
Acthar, J0800
Actimmune, J9216
Action neoprene supports, L1825
Action Patriot manual wheelchair, K0004
Action Xtra, Action MVP, Action Pro-T, manual wheelchair, K0005
Active Life
convex one-piece urostomy pouch, A4421
flush away, A5051
one-piece
drainable custom pouch, A5061
pre-cut closed-end pouch, A5051
stoma cap, A5055
Activity therapy, G0176
Acyclovir, J0133
Adalimumab, J0135
Adaptor
neurostimulator, C1883
pacing lead, C1883
Addition
cushion AK, L5648
cushion BK, L5646
harness upper extremity, L6675-L6676
to lower extremity orthotic, K0672
to lower extremity prosthesis, L5970-L5990
wrist, flexion, extension, L6620
Adenocard, J0150
Adenosine, J0150-J0152
Adhesive
barrier, C1765
catheter, A4364
disc or foam pad, A5126
medical, A4364
Nu-Hope
1 oz bottle with applicator, A4364
3 oz bottle with applicator, A4364
ostomy, A4364
pads, A6203-A6205, A6212-A6214, A6219-A6221, A6237-A6239, A6245-A6247, A6254-A6256
remover, A4365, A4455
support, breast prosthesis, A4280
tape, A4450, A4452
tissue, G0168
Adjunctive services, dental, D9220-D9310
Adjustabrace 3, L2999
Adjustment, bariatric band, S2083
Administration
hepatitis B vaccine, G0010
influenza virus vaccine, G0008
medication, T1502-T1503
direct observation, H0033
pneumococcal vaccine, G0009
Adoptive immunotherapy, S2107
Adrenalin, J0170
Adrenal transplant, S2103
Adriamycin, J9000
Adrucil, J9190
AdvantaJet, A4210
AFO, E1815, E1830, L1900-L1990, L4392, L4396
Agalsidase beta, J0180
Aimsco Ultra Thin syringe, 1 cc or 1/2 cc, each, A4206
Air ambulance — *see also* Ambulance
Air bubble detector, dialysis, E1530
Aircast, L4350-L4380
Aircast air stirrup ankle brace, L1906
Air fluidized bed, E0194
Airlife Brand Misty-Neb nebulizer, E0580
Air pressure pad/mattress, E0186, E0197
AirSep, E0601
Air travel and nonemergency transportation, A0140
Airway device, E0485-E0486
Akineton, J0190
Alarm
enuresis, S8270
pressure, dialysis, E1540
Alatrofloxacin mesylate, J0200
Albumarc, P9041
Albumin, human, P9041, P9045-P9047
Albuterol, J7611, J7613
Alcohol
abuse service, G0396, G0397, H0047
pint, A4244
testing, H0048
wipes, A4245
Aldesleukin, J9015
Aldomet, J0210
Aldurazyme, J1931
Alefacept, J0215
Alemtuzumab, J9010
injection, S0088
Alferon N, J9215
Algiderm, alginate dressing, A6196-A6199
Alginate dressing, A6196-A6199
Alglucerase, J0205
Algosteril, alginate dressing, A6196-A6199
Alimta, J9305
Alkaban-AQ, J9360
Alkaline battery for blood glucose monitor, A4233-A4236
Alkeran, J8600
Allogenic cord blood harvest, S2140
Allograft
Cymetra, Q4112
GRAFTJACKET, Q4113
Allograft — *continued*
small intestine and liver, S2053
soft dental tissue, D4275
Alpha 1-proteinase inhibitor, human, J0256
Alteplase recombinant, J2997
Alternating pressure mattress/pad, E0181, E0277
pump, E0182
Alternative communication device, i.e., communication board, E1902
Alveoloplasty
with extraction(s), D7310-D7311
without extractions, D7320-D7321
Alveolus, fracture, D7770
Amalgam, restoration, dental, D2140-D2161
Amantadine hydrochloride, G9017, G9033
Ambulance, A0021-A0999
air, A0436
disposable supplies, A0382-A0398
oxygen, A0422
response, treatment, no transport, A0998
Ambulation device, E0100-E0159
Ambulation stimulator
spinal cord injured, E0762
Amcort, J3302
A-methaPred, J2920, J2930
Amevive, J0215
Amifostine, J0207
Amikacin sulfate, J0278
Aminaid, enteral nutrition, B4154
Aminolevulinic acid, topical, J7308
Aminophylline, J0280
Amiodarone hydrochloride, J0282
Amirosyn-RF, parenteral nutrition, B5000
Amitriptyline HCI, J1320
Ammonia N-13
diagnostic imaging agent, A9526
Ammonia test paper, A4774
Amobarbital, J0300
Amphocin, J0285
Amphotericin B, J0285
cholesterol sulfate, J0288
lipid complex, J0287
liposome, J0289
Ampicillin sodium, J0290
sodium/sulbactam sodium, J0295
Amputee
adapter, wheelchair, E0959
prosthesis, L5000-L7510, L7520, L7900, L8400-L8465
stump sock, L8470
wheelchair, E1170-E1190, E1200
Amygdalin, J3570
Amytal, J0300
Anabolin LA 100, J2320-J2322
Analgesia, dental, D9230, D9241, D9242
nonintravenous conscious sedation, D9248
Analysis
saliva sample, D0418
Anastrozole, S0170
Ancef, J0690
Anchor, screw, C1713
Andrest 90-4, J0900
Andro-Cyp, J1070-J1080
Andro-Estro 90-4, J0900
Androgyn L.A., J0900
Andro L.A. 200, J3130
Androlone
-D 100, J2321
Andronaq
-LA, J1070
Andronate
-100, J1070
-200, J1080
Andropository 100, J3120
Andryl 200, J3130
Anectine, J0330
Anergan (25, 50), J2550
Anesthesia
dental, D9210-D9221
dialysis, A4736-A4737
Angiography
iliac artery, G0278
magnetic resonance, C8901-C8914, C8918-C8920
reconstruction, G0288
renal artery, G0275
Angioplasty
percutaneous, G0392-G0393
Anidulafungin, J0348
Anistreplase, J0350
Ankle–foot orthotic AFO, L1900-L1990, L2106-L2116
Dorsiwedge Night Splint, L4398 or A4570 or, L2999
Specialist
Ankle Foot Orthotic, L1930
Tibial Pre-formed Fracture Brace, L2116
Surround Ankle Stirrup Braces with Floam, L1906
Antagon, S0132
Anterior-posterior orthotic
lateral orthotic, L0700, L0710
Antibiotic home infusion therapy, S9494-S9504
Antibody testing, HIV-1, S3645
Anticeptic
chlorhexidine, A4248
Anticoagulation clinic, S9401
Antiemetic drug, prescription
oral, Q0163-Q0181
Antifungal home infusion therapy, S9494-S9504
Anti-hemophilic factor (Factor VIII), J7190-J7192
Anti-hemophilic factor (Factor VIIa) recombinant, J7189
Anti-inhibitors, J7198
Anti-neoplastic drug, NOC, J9999
Antispas, J0500
Antithrombin III, J7197
Antiviral home infusion therapy, S9494-S9504
Anzemet, J1260
Apexifcation, dental, D3351-D3353
Apicoectomy, dental, D3410-D3426
A.P.L., J0725
Apligraf, Q4101
Apnea monitor, E0618-E0619
with recording feature, E0619
electrodes, A4556
lead wires, A4557
Apomorphine hydrochloride, J0364
Appliance
cleaner, A5131
orthodontic
fixed, D8220
removable, D8210
removal, D7997
pneumatic, E0655-E0673
Application
fluoride, D1203-D1206
Aprepitant, J8501
Apresoline, J0360
Aprotinin, J0365
AquaMEPHYTON, J3430
AquaPedic sectional gel flotation, E0196
Aqueous
shunt, L8612
Ara-C, J9100
Aralen, J0390
Aramine, J0380
Aranesp
ESRD, J0882
non-ESRD, J0881
Arbutamine HCl, J0395
Arch support, L3040-L3100
Aredia, J2430
Argatroban, C9121
Argyle Sentinel Seal chest drainage unit, E0460

E

Hole cutter tool, A4421
Hollister
  belt adapter, A4421
  closed pouch, A5051, A5052
  colostomy/ileostomy kit, A5061
  drainable pouches, A5061
    with flange, A5063
  medical adhesive, A4364
  pediatric ostomy belt, A4367
  remover, adhesive, A4455
  skin barrier, A4362, A5122
  skin cleanser, A4335
  skin conditioning creme, A4335
  skin gel protective dressing wipes, A5120
  stoma cap, A5055
  two-piece pediatric ostomy system, A5054, A5063, A5073
  urostomy pouch, A5071, A5072
Home health
  aide, S9122, T1030-T1031
    home health setting, G0156
  care
    certified nurse assistant, S9122, T1021
    home health aide, S9122, T1021
    management
      episodic, S0272
      hospice, S0271
      standard, S0270
    nursing care, S9122-S9124, T1030-T1031
    outside capitation arrangement, S0273-S0274
    re-certification, G0179-G0180
  gestational
    assessment, T1028
    delivery suppies, S8415
    diabetes, S9214
    hypertension, S9211
    pre-eclampsia, S9213
    preterm labor, S9208-S9209
  hydration therapy, S9373-S9379
  infusion therapy, S9325-S9379, S9494-S9497, S9537-S9810
  insertion midline venous catheter, S5523
  nursing services, S0274, S9212-S9213
  physician services, S0270-S0273
  postpartum hypertension, S9212
  services of
    clinical social worker, G0155
    occupational therapist, G0152
    physical therapist, G0151
    skilled nurse, G0154
    speech/language pathologist, G0153
  transfusion, blood products, S9538
  wound care, S9097
Home uterine monitor, S9001
Hook
  electric, L7009
  mechanical, L6706-L6707
Hospice
  care, Q5001-Q5008, S9126, T2041-T2046
  evaluation and counseling services, G0337
  referral visit, S0255
Hospital
  call
    dental, D9420
  observation
    direct admit, G0379
    per hour, G0378
Hot water bottle, E0220
Houdini security suit, E0700
House call, dental, D9410
Housing, supported, H0043-H0044
Hoyer patient lifts, E0621, E0625, E0630
H-Tron insulin pump, E0784
H-Tron Plus insulin pump, E0784
Hudson
  adult multi-vent venturi style mask, A4620
  nasal cannula, A4615
  oxygen supply tubing, A4616
  UC-BL type shoe insert, L3000
Humalog, J1815, J1817, S5550
Human insulin, J1815, J1817
Humidifer, E0550-E0560
  water chamber, A7046
Humira, J0135
Humulin insulin, J1815, J1817
Hyaluronidase
  bovine, J3470
  ovine, up to 150 units, J3471
  ovine,up to 999 units, J3472
  recombinant, J3473
Hyate, J7191
Hybolin
  decanoate, J2321
Hycamtin, J9350
Hydralazine HCl, J0360
Hydrate, J1240
Hydration therapy, S9373-S9379
Hydraulic patient lift, E0630
Hydrocollator, E0225, E0239
Hydrocolloid dressing, A6234-A6241
Hydrocortisone
  acetate, J1700
  sodium phosphate, J1710
  sodium succinate, J1720
Hydrocortone
  acetate, J1700
  phosphate, J1710
Hydrogel dressing, A6242-A6248
Hydromorphone, J1170, S0092
Hydroxyurea, S0176
Hydroxyzine HCl, J3410
  pamoate, Q0177-Q0178
Hyoscyamine sulfate, J1980
Hyperbaric oxygen chamber, topical, A4575
Hyperstat IV, J1730
Hypertonic saline solution, J7130
Hypo-Let lancet device, A4258
Hypothermia
  intragastric, M0100
HypRho-D, J2790
Hyrexin-50, J1200
Hyzine-;50, J3410

I

I-125 sodium iothalamate, A9554
I-131
  sodium iodide, A9531
    capsule, A9517, A9528
    solution, A9529-A9530
  tositumomab, A9544-A9545
I&D
  Intraoral, D7511, D7521
Ibandronate sodium injection, J1740
Ibutilide fumarate, J1742
Ice cap or collar, E0230
Idamycin, J9211
Idarubicin HCl, J9211
Ifex, J9208
Ifosfamide, J9208
IL-2, J9015
Iletin insulin, J1815, J1817, S5552
Ilfeld, hip orthotic, L1650
Images, oral/facial, D0350
Imaging, C1770
  coil, MRI, C1770
Imatinib, S0088
Imiglucerase, J1785
Imitrex, J3030
Immunoassay
  alpha microglobulin-1, S3628
Immunofluorescence
  direct, D0482
  indirect, D0483
Immunosuppressive drug, not otherwise classified, J7599
Impacted tooth, removal, D7220-D7241
Impaction
  tooth, treatment, D7283
Implant
  access system, A4301
  aqueous shunt, L8612
  auditory device
    brainstem, S2235
    middle ear, S2230
  breast, L8600
  cochlear, L8614, L8619
  collagen, urinary tract, L8603
  contraceptive, J7306
  dental
    chin, D7995
    endodontic, D3460
    endosteal/endosseous, D6010
    eposteal/subperiosteal, D6040
    facial, D7995
    maintenance, D6080
    other implant service, D6053-D6079
    supported prosthetics, D6053-D6079
      removal, D6100
      repair, D6090, D6095
    transosteal/tensosseous, D6050
  dextranomer/hyaluronic acid copolymer, urinary tract, L8604
  ganciclovir, J7310
  goserelin acetate, J9202
  hallux, L8642
  infusion pump, E0782, E0783
  injectable bulking agent, urinary tract, L8606
  interspinous process distraction device, C1821
  joint, L8630, L8641, L8658
  lacrimal duct, A4262, A4263
  levonorgestral, J7306
  maintenance procedures, D6080, D6100
  maxillofacial, D5913-D5937
  metacarpophalangeal joint, L8630
  metatarsal joint, L8641
  neurostimulator, pulse generator or receiver, E0755, L8685-L8688
  Norplant, J7306
  not otherwise specified, L8699
  ocular, L8610
  ossicular, L8613
  osteogenesis stimulator, E0749
  percutaneous access system, A4301
  prosthetic device, C9899
  removal, dental, D6100
  repair, dental, D6090
  urinary tract, L8603-L8604
  vascular access portal, A4300
  vascular graft, L8670
  yttrium 90, S2095
  Zoladex, J9202
Implantable radiation dosimeter, ea, A4650
Implantation/reimplantation, tooth, D7270
  intentional reimplantation, D3470
Impregnated gauze dressing, A6222-A6230
Imuran, J7500, J7501
Inapsine, J1790
Incontinence
  appliances and supplies, A4310, A5051-A5093, A5102-A5114, A5120-A5200
  brief or diaper, T4521-T4524, T4543
  disposable/liner, T4535
  garment, A4520
  pediatric
    brief or diaper, T4529-T4530
    pull-on protection, T4531-T4532
  reusable
    diaper or brief, T4539
    pull-on protection, T4536
  treatment system, E0740
  underpad
    disposable, T4541, T4542
Incontinence — *continued*
  underpad — *continued*
    reusable, T4537, T4540
  youth
    brief or diaper, T4533
    pull-on protection, T4534
Inderal, J1800
Indium 111
  capromab pendetide, A9507
  ibritumomab tiuxetan, A9542
  labeled
    platelets, A9571
    white blood cells, A9570
  oxyguinoline, A9547
  pentetate, A9548, A9572
  pentetreotide, A9572
  satumomab pendetide, A4642
Infant safety, CPR, training, S9447
Infergen, J9212
Infliximab injection, J1745
Infusion
  catheter, C1752
  IV, OPPS, C8957
  pump, C1772, C2626
    ambulatory, with administrative equipment, E0781
    epoprostenol, K0455
    heparin, dialysis, E1520
    implantable, E0782, E0783
    implantable, refill kit, A4220
    insulin, E0784
    mechanical, reusable, E0779, E0780
    nonprogrammable, C1891
    supplies, A4221, A4222, A4230-A4232
    Versa-Pole IV, E0776
  supplies, A4222, A4223
  therapy, home, S9347, S9351, S9497-S9504
Inhalation drugs
  acetylcysteine, J7608
  albuterol, J7609, J7610, J7611, J7613
  Alupent, J7668-J7669
  atropine, J7635-J7636
  Atrovent, J7644
  Azmacort, J7684
  beclomethasone, J7622
  betamethasone, J7624
  bitolterol mesylate, J7628-J7629
  Brcanyl, J7680-J7681
  Brethine, J7680-J7681
  budesonide, J7626-J7627, J7633-J7634
  colistimethate sodium, S0142
  cromolyn sodium, J7631
  dexamethasone, J7637-J7638
  dornase alpha, J7639
  flunisolide, J7641
  formoterol, J7606, J7640
  Gastrocrom, J7631
  glycopyrolate, J7642-J7643
  iloprost, Q4080
  Intal, J7631
  ipratropium bromide, J7644-J7645
  isoetharine HCl, J7647-J7650
  isoproterenol HCl, J7657-J7660
  levalbuterol, J7607, J7612, J7614, J7615
  metaproterenol sulfate, J7667-J7670
  methacholine chloride, J7674
  Mucomyst, J7608
  Mucosil, J7608
  Nasalcrom, J7631
  NOC, J7699
  pentamidine isethionate, J7676
  Pulmicort Respules, J7627
  terbutaline sulfate, J7680-J7681
  Tobi, J7682
  tobramycin, J7682, J7685
  Tornalate, J7628-J7629
  triamcinolone, J7683-J7684
Initial
  ECG, Medicare, G0403-G0405
  physical exam, Medicare, G0402

J

K

L

M

N

Nabilone, oral, J8650
Nafcillin sodium, S0032
Nail trim, G0127, S0390
Nalbuphine HCl, J2300
Naloxone HCl, J2310
Naltrexone depot injection, J2315
Nandrobolic L.A., J2321
Nandrolone
  decanoate, J2320-J2322
Narcan, J2310
Narrowing device, wheelchair, E0969
Nasahist B, J0945
Nasal
  application device (for CPAP device), A7032-A7034
  vaccine inhalation, J3530
Nasogastric tubing, B4081, B4082
Navelbine, J9390
ND Stat, J0945
Nebcin, J3260
Nebulizer, E0570-E0585
  aerosol compressor, E0571
  aerosol mask, A7015
  aerosols, E0580
    Airlife Brand Misty-Neb, E0580
    Power-Mist, E0580
    Up-Draft Neb-U-Mist, E0580
    Up-Mist hand-held nebulizer, E0580
  compressor, with, E0570
    Madamist II medication compressor/nebulizer, E0570
    Pulmo-Aide compressor/nebulizer, E0570
    Schuco Mist nebulizer system, E0570
  corrugated tubing
    disposable, A7010, A7018
    non-disposable, A7011
  distilled water, A7018
  filter
    disposable, A7013
    non-disposable, A7014
  heater, E1372
  large volume
    disposable, prefilled, A7008
    disposable, unfilled, A7007
  not used with oxygen
    durable glass, A7017
  pneumatic, administration set, A7003, A7005, A7006
  pneumatic, nonfiltered, A7004
  portable, E0570
  small volume, E0574
  spacer or nebulizer, S8100
    with mask, S8101
  ultrasonic, dome and mouthpiece, A7016
  ultrasonic, reservoir bottle
    nondisposable, A7009
  water, A7018
  water collection device large volume nebulizer, A7012
    distilled water, A7018
NebuPent, J2545
Needle, A4215
  with syringe, A4206-A4209
  brachytherapy, C1715
  non-coring, A4212
Negative pressure wound therapy
  dressing set, A6550
  pump, E2402
Nelarabine, J9261
Nembutal sodium solution, J2515
Neocyten, J2360
Neo-Durabolic, J2320-J2322
Neomax knee support, L1800
Neoplasms, dental, D7410-D7465
Neoquess, J0500
Neosar, J9070-J9092
Neostigmine methylsulfate, J2710
Neo-Synephrine, J2370
NephrAmine, parenteral nutrition, B5000
Nesacaine MPF, J2400
Nesiritide, J2325
Neulasta, J2505
Neumega, J2355
Neuromuscular stimulator, E0745
  ambulation of spinal cord injured, E0762
Neuro-Pulse, E0720
Neurostimulator
  functional transcutaneous, E0764
  generator, C1767, C1820
  implantable
    electrode, L8680
    pulse generator, L8685-L8688
    receiver, L8682
  lead, C1778
  patient programmer, L8681
  receiver and/or transmitter, C1816
  transmitter
    external, L8683-L8684
Neutrexin, J3305
Newington
  Legg Perthes orthotic, L1710
  mobility frame, L1500
Newport Lite hip orthotic, L1685
Nextep Contour Lower Leg Walker, L2999
Nextep Low Silhouette Lower Leg Walkers, L2999
Nicotine
  gum, S4995
  patches, S4990-S4991
Niemann-Pick disease, genetic test, S3849
Nightguard, D9940
Nipent, J9268
Nitrogen mustard, J9230
Nitrous oxide, dental analgesia, D9230
Nonchemotherapy drug, oral, J8499
Noncovered services, A9270, G0293-G0294
Nonemergency transportation, A0080-A0210
Nonimpregnated gauze dressing, A6216, A6221, A6402, A6404
Nonintravenous conscious sedation, dental, D9248
Nonprescription drug, A9150
Nonthermal pulsed high frequency radiowaves treatment device, E0761
Nordryl, J1200
Norflex, J2360
Normal saline, A4216-A4217, J7030, J7040, J7042, J7050, J7130
Norplant System contraceptive, J7306
Northwestern Suspension, socket prosthesis, L6110
Not otherwise classifed drug, J3490, J7599, J7699, J7799, J8499, J8999, J9999, Q0181
Novantrone, J9293
Novo Nordisk insulin, J1815, J1817
Novo Seven, J7189
NPH insulin, J1815, S5552
Nubain, J2300
NuHope
  adhesive, 1 oz bottle with applicator, A4364
  adhesive, 3 oz bottle with applicator, A4364
  cleaning solvent, 16 oz bottle, A4455
  cleaning solvent, 4 oz bottle, A4455
  hole cutter tool, A4421
Numorphan H.P., J2410
Nursing care, in home
  licensed practical nurse, S9124
  registered nurse, S9123
Nursing home visit, dental, D9410
Nursing services, S9211-S9212, T1000-T1004
Nutri-Source, enteral nutrition, B4155
Nutrition
  counseling
    dental, D1310, D1320
    dietary, S9452
  enteral formulae, B4150-B4162
Nutrition — *continued*
  enteral infusion pump, B9000, B9002
  medical food, S9433
  parenteral infusion pump, B9004, B9006
  parenteral solution, B4164-B5200
Nutritional counseling, dietition visit, S9470

O

O&P Express
  above knee, L5210
  ankle-foot orthotic with bilateral uprights, L1990
  anterior floor reaction orthotic, L1945
  below knee, L5105
  elbow disarticulation, L6200
  hip disarticulation, L5250
  hip-knee-ankle-foot orthotic, L2080
  interscapular thoracic, L6370
  knee-ankle-foot orthotic, L2000, L2010, L2020, L2036
  knee disarticulation, L5150, L5160
  Legg Perthes orthotic, Patten bottom type, L1755
  Legg Perthes orthotic, Scottish Rite, L1730
  partial foot, L5000, L5020
  plastic foot drop brace, L1960
  supply/accessory/service, L9900
Oasis
  burn matrix, Q4103
  wound matrix, Q4102
Observation service
  direct admission, G0379
  per hour, G0378
Obturator prosthesis
  definitive, D5932
  dental
    postsurgical, D5932
    refitting, D5933
    surgical, D5931
  interim, D5936
  surgical, D5931
Occipital/mandibular support, cervical, L0160
Occlusal
  adjustment, dental, D9951-D9952
  guard, dental, D9940
  orthotic device, D7877
Occlusion/analysis, D9950
Occupational multifocal lens, V2786
Occupational therapist
  home health setting, G0152
Occupational therapy, S9129
Octafluoropropae microspheres, Q9956
Octreotide
  intramuscular form, J2353
  subcutaneous or intravenous form, J2354
Ocular device, C1784
Ocular prosthetic implant, L8610
Oculinum, J0585
Odansetron HCl, J2405, Q0179
Odontoplasty (enameloplasty), D9971
Office service, M0064
Offobock cosmetic gloves, L6895
O-Flex, J2360
Ofloxacin, S0034
Ohio Willow
  prosthetic sheath
    above knee, L8410
    below knee, L8400
    upper limb, L8415
  prosthetic sock, L8420-L8435
  stump sock, L8470-L8485
Olanzapine, S0166
Omalizumab, J2357
Omnipen-N, J0290
Oncaspar, J9266
Oncology
  breast cancer, G9071-G9073, G9131
Oncology — *continued*
  chronic myelogenous leukemia, G9139
  colon cancer, G9083-G9089
  coordination of care, G9054
  demonstration project, G9056
  esophageal cancer, G9096-G9099
  evaluation, G9050
  expectant management, G9053
  gastric cancer, G9100-G9104
  head and neck, G9110-G9112
  management
    adheres to guidelines, G9056
    differs from guidelines, G9057-G9060, G9062
    not addressed by guidelines, G9061
  management of care, G9054
  multiple myeloma, G9128, G9130
  no directed therapy, G9053
  non-Hodgkin's lymphoma, G9123-G9125, G9134-G9138
  nonsmall cell lung cancer, G9063-G9070
  ovarian cancer, G9113-G9117, G9126
  pancreatic cancer, G9105-G9108
  prostate cancer, G9077-G9083, G9132-G9133
  rectal cancer, G9090-G9095
  staging, G9050
  supervising care, G9054
  surveillance for recurrence, G9052
  treatment decision making, G9051
  unspecified service, G9055
  work up, G9050
Oncoscint, A4642
Oncovin, J9370
Ondanestron HCl, S0181
One-Button foldaway walker, E0143
One Touch
  Basic blood glucose meter, E0607
  Basic test strips, box of 50, A4253
  Profile blood glucose meter, E0607
Onlay, dental
  fixed partial denture retainer, metallic, D6602, D6615
  metallic, D2542-D2544
  porcelain/ceramic, D2642-D2644
  resin-based composite, D2662, D2664
  titanium, D6634
Operculectomy, D7971
Oprelvekin, J2355
Oral
  airway device, E0485-E0486
  disease
    test for detection, D0431
    test for susceptibility, D0421
  examination, D0120-D0160
  hygiene instruction, D1330
  interpreter or sign language services, T1013
  pathology
    accession of tissue, D0472-D0474
    bacteriologic studies, D0415
    cytology, D0480
    other oral pathology procedures, D0502
Oral and maxillofacial surgery, D7111-D7999
Oraminic II, J0945
Organ donor procurement, S2152
Ormazine, J3230
Oropharyngeal suction catheter, A4628
Orphenadrine, J2360
Orphenate, J2360
Orthodontics, D8010-D8999
Ortho-Ease forearm crutches, E0111
Orthoflex Elastic Plaster Bandages, A4580
Orthoguard hip orthotic, L1685
Orthomedics
  ankle-foot orthotic, L1900
  pediatric hip abduction splint, L1640

Q

R

S

U

V

W

X

Y

Z

TRANSPORTATION SERVICES INCLUDING AMBULANCE A0000-A0999

This code range includes ground and air ambulance, nonemergency transportation (taxi, bus, automobile, wheelchair van), and ancillary transportation-related fees.

HCPCS Level II codes for ambulance services must be reported with modifiers that indicate pick-up origins and destinations. The modifier describing the arrangement (QM, QN) is listed first. The modifiers describing the origin and destination are listed second. Origin and destination modifiers are created by combining two alpha characters from the following list. Each alpha character, with the exception of X, represents either an origin or a destination. Each pair of alpha characters creates one modifier. The first position represents the origin and the second the destination. The modifiers most commonly used are:

D	Diagnostic or therapeutic site other than "P" or "H" when these are used as origin codes
E	Residential, domiciliary, custodial facility (other than 1819 facility)
G	Hospital-based ESRD facility
H	Hospital
I	Site of transfer (e.g., airport or helicopter pad) between modes of ambulance transport
J	Free standing ESRD facility
N	Skilled nursing facility (SNF)
P	Physician's office
R	Residence
S	Scene of accident or acute event
X	Intermediate stop at physician's office on way to hospital (destination code only)

Note: Modifier X can only be used as a destination code in the second position of a modifier.

See S0215. For Medicaid, see T codes and T modifiers.

A0021 **Ambulance service, outside state per mile, transport (Medicaid only)**

A0080 **Nonemergency transportation, per mile — vehicle provided by volunteer (individual or organization), with no vested interest**

A0090 **Nonemergency transportation, per mile — vehicle provided by individual (family member, self, neighbor) with vested interest**

A0100 **Nonemergency transportation; taxi**

A0110 **Nonemergency transportation and bus, intra- or interstate carrier**

A0120 **Nonemergency transportation: mini-bus, mountain area transports, or other transportation systems**

A0130 **Nonemergency transportation: wheelchair van**

A0140 **Nonemergency transportation and air travel (private or commercial) intra- or interstate**

A0160 **Nonemergency transportation: per mile — caseworker or social worker**

A0170 **Transportation ancillary: parking fees, tolls, other**

A0180 **Nonemergency transportation: ancillary: lodging, recipient**

A0190 **Nonemergency transportation: ancillary: meals, recipient**

A0200 **Nonemergency transportation: ancillary: lodging, escort**

A0210 **Nonemergency transportation: ancillary: meals, escort**

A0225 **Ambulance service, neonatal transport, base rate, emergency transport, one way**
MED: 100-4,1,10.1.4.1

A0380 **BLS mileage (per mile)**
See code(s): A0425
MED: 100-2,6,10; 100-4,1,10.1.4.1

A0382 **BLS routine disposable supplies**

A0384 **BLS specialized service disposable supplies; defibrillation (used by ALS ambulances and BLS ambulances in jurisdictions where defibrillation is permitted in BLS ambulances)**

A0390 **ALS mileage (per mile)**
See code(s): A0425
MED: 100-4,1,10.1.4.1

A0392 **ALS specialized service disposable supplies; defibrillation (to be used only in jurisdictions where defibrillation cannot be performed in BLS ambulances)**

A0394 **ALS specialized service disposable supplies; IV drug therapy**

A0396 **ALS specialized service disposable supplies; esophageal intubation**

A0398 **ALS routine disposable supplies**

WAITING TIME TABLE

Units	Time
1	1/2 to 1 hr.
2	1 to 1-1/2 hrs.
3	1-1/2 to 2 hrs.
4	2 to 2-1/2 hrs.
5	2-1/2 to 3 hrs.
6	3 to 3-1/2 hrs.
7	3-1/2 to 4 hrs.
8	4 to 4-1/2 hrs.
9	4-1/2 to 5 hrs.
10	5 to 5-1/2 hrs.

A0420 **Ambulance waiting time (ALS or BLS), one-half (1/2) hour increments**

A0422 **Ambulance (ALS or BLS) oxygen and oxygen supplies, life sustaining situation**

A0424 **Extra ambulance attendant, ground (ALS or BLS) or air (fixed or rotary winged); (requires medical review)**
Pertinent documentation to evaluate medical appropriateness should be included when this code is reported.

A0425 **Ground mileage, per statute mile**
MED: 100-2,6,10; 100-2,10,20; 100-4,1,10.1.4.1

A0426 **Ambulance service, advanced life support, nonemergency transport, level 1 (ALS 1)**
MED: 100-2,6,10; 100-2,10,20; 100-4,1,10.1.4.1

A0427 **Ambulance service, advanced life support, emergency transport, level 1 (ALS 1 — emergency)**
MED: 100-2,6,10; 100-2,10,20; 100-4,1,10.1.4.1

A0428 **Ambulance service, basic life support, nonemergency transport, (BLS)**
MED: 100-2,6,10; 100-2,10,20; 100-4,1,10.1.4.1

A0429 **Ambulance service, basic life support, emergency transport (BLS, emergency)**
MED: 100-2,6,10; 100-2,10,20; 100-4,1,10.1.4.1

A0430 **Ambulance service, conventional air services, transport, one way (fixed wing)**
MED: 100-2,6,10; 100-2,10,20; 100-4,1,10.1.4.1

A0431 **Ambulance service, conventional air services, transport, one way (rotary wing)**
MED: 100-2,6,10; 100-2,10,20; 100-4,1,10.1.4.1

A0432 **Paramedic intercept (PI), rural area, transport furnished by a volunteer ambulance company which is prohibited by state law from billing third-party payers**
MED: 100-2,10,20

A0433 Advanced life support, level 2 (ALS 2)

MED: 100-2,10,20

A0434 Specialty care transport (SCT)

MED: 100-2,10,20

A0435 Fixed wing air mileage, per statute mile

MED: 100-2,10,20

A0436 Rotary wing air mileage, per statute mile

MED: 100-2,10,20

A0888 Noncovered ambulance mileage, per mile (e.g., for miles traveled beyond closest appropriate facility)

MED: 100-2,10,20

A0998 Ambulance response and treatment, no transport

A0999 Unlisted ambulance service

Determine if an alternative HCPCS Level II or a CPT code better describes the service being reported. This code should be used only if a more specific code is unavailable.

MED: 100-2,10,20; 100-4,1,10.1.4.1

MEDICAL AND SURGICAL SUPPLIES A4000-A8999

This section covers a wide variety of medical, surgical, and some durable medical equipment (DME) related supplies and accessories. DME-related supplies, accessories, maintenance, and repair required to ensure the proper functioning of this equipment is generally covered by Medicare under the prosthetic devices provision.

MISCELLANEOUS SUPPLIES

These codes are to be filed with the Medicare local contractor, unless otherwise noted (if incident to a physicians' services, not separately billable) unless they represent incidental services or supplies which are referred to the DME Medicare Administrative Contractor (DME MAC).

A4206 Syringe with needle, sterile, 1 cc or less, each

A4207 Syringe with needle, sterile 2 cc, each

A4208 Syringe with needle, sterile 3 cc, each

A4209 Syringe with needle, sterile 5 cc or greater, each

A4210 Needle-free injection device, each

Sometimes covered by commercial payers with preauthorization and physician letter stating need (e.g., for insulin injection in young children).

MED: 100-3,280.1

A4211 Supplies for self-administered injections

When a drug that is usually injected by the patient (e.g., insulin or calcitonin) is injected by the physician, it is excluded from Medicare coverage unless administered in an emergency situation (e.g., diabetic coma).

MED: 100-2,15,50

A4212 Noncoring needle or stylet with or without catheter

A4213 Syringe, sterile, 20 cc or greater, each

A4215 Needle, sterile, any size, each

A4216 Sterile water, saline and/or dextrose, diluent/flush, 10 ml

MED: 100-2,15,50

A4217 Sterile water/saline, 500 ml

MED: 100-2,15,50

A4218 Sterile saline or water, metered dose dispenser, 10 ml

A4220 Refill kit for implantable infusion pump

Implantable infusion pumps are covered by Medicare for 5-FUdR therapy for unresected liver or colorectal cancer and for opioid drug therapy for intractable pain. They are not covered by Medicare for heparin therapy for thromboembolic disease. Report drugs separately.

MED: 100-3,280.14

A4221 Supplies for maintenance of drug infusion catheter, per week (list drug separately)

A4222 Infusion supplies for external drug infusion pump, per cassette or bag (list drugs separately)

A4223 Infusion supplies not used with external infusion pump, per cassette or bag (list drugs separately)

A4230 Infusion set for external insulin pump, nonneedle cannula type

Covered by some commercial payers as ongoing supply to preauthorized pump.

MED: 100-3,280.14

A4231 Infusion set for external insulin pump, needle type

Covered by some commercial payers as ongoing supply to preauthorized pump.

MED: 100-3,280.14

A4232 Syringe with needle for external insulin pump, sterile, 3 cc

Covered by some commercial payers as ongoing supply to preauthorized pump.

MED: 100-3,280.14

A4233 Replacement battery, alkaline (other than J cell), for use with medically necessary home blood glucose monitor owned by patient, each

A4234 Replacement battery, alkaline, J cell, for use with medically necessary home blood glucose monitor owned by patient, each

A4235 Replacement battery, lithium, for use with medically necessary home blood glucose monitor owned by patient, each

A4236 Replacement battery, silver oxide, for use with medically necessary home blood glucose monitor owned by patient, each

A4244 Alcohol or peroxide, per pint

A4245 Alcohol wipes, per box

A4246 Betadine or pHisoHex solution, per pint

A4247 Betadine or iodine swabs/wipes, per box

A4248 Chlorhexidine containing antiseptic, 1 ml

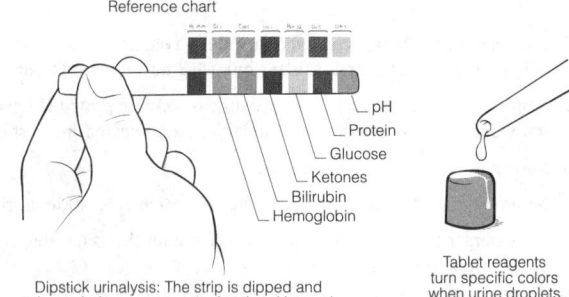

Dipstick urinalysis: The strip is dipped and color-coded squares are read at timed intervals (e.g., pH immediately; ketones at 15 sec., etc.). Results are compared against a reference chart

Tablet reagents turn specific colors when urine droplets are placed on them

A4250 Urine test or reagent strips or tablets (100 tablets or strips)

MED: 100-2,15,110

A4252 Blood ketone test or reagent strip, each

A4253 Blood glucose test or reagent strips for home blood glucose monitor, per 50 strips

Medicare covers glucose strips for diabetic patients using home glucose monitoring devices prescribed by their physicians.

MED: 100-3,40.2

A4255 Platforms for home blood glucose monitor, 50 per box

Some Medicare contractors cover monitor platforms for diabetic patients using home glucose monitoring devices prescribed by their physicians. Some commercial payers also provide this coverage to noninsulin dependent diabetics.

MED: 100-3,40.2

A4256 **Normal, low, and high calibrator solution/chips**
Some Medicare contractors cover calibration solutions or chips for diabetic patients using home glucose monitoring devices prescribed by their physicians. Some commercial payers also provide this coverage to noninsulin dependent diabetics.
MED: 100-3,40.2

A4257 **Replacement lens shield cartridge for use with laser skin piercing device, each**

A4258 **Spring-powered device for lancet, each**
Some Medicare contractors cover lancing devices for diabetic patients using home glucose monitoring devices prescribed by their physicians. Medicare jurisdiction: DME regional contractor. Some commercial payers also provide this coverage to noninsulin dependent diabetics.
MED: 100-3,40.2

A4259 **Lancets, per box of 100**
Medicare covers lancets for diabetic patients using home glucose monitoring devices prescribed by their physicians. Medicare jurisdiction: DME regional contractor. Some commercial payers also provide this coverage to noninsulin dependent diabetics.
MED: 100-3,40.2

A4261 **Cervical cap for contraceptive use**

A4262 **Temporary, absorbable lacrimal duct implant, each**
Always report concurrent to the implant procedure.

A4263 **Permanent, long-term, nondissolvable lacrimal duct implant, each**
Always report concurrent to the implant procedure.

A4265 **Paraffin, per pound**
MED: 100-3,280.1

A4266 **Diaphragm for contraceptive use**

A4267 **Contraceptive supply, condom, male, each**

A4268 **Contraceptive supply, condom, female, each**

A4269 **Contraceptive supply, spermicide (e.g., foam, gel), each**

A4270 **Disposable endoscope sheath, each**

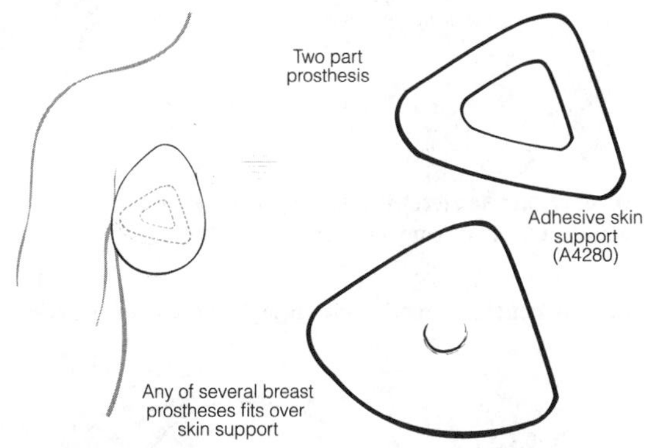

A4280 **Adhesive skin support attachment for use with external breast prosthesis, each**

A4281 **Tubing for breast pump, replacement**

A4282 **Adapter for breast pump, replacement**

A4283 **Cap for breast pump bottle, replacement**

A4284 **Breast shield and splash protector for use with breast pump, replacement**

A4285 **Polycarbonate bottle for use with breast pump, replacement**

A4286 **Locking ring for breast pump, replacement**

A4290 **Sacral nerve stimulation test lead, each**
AHA: 1Q,'02,9

VASCULAR CATHETERS

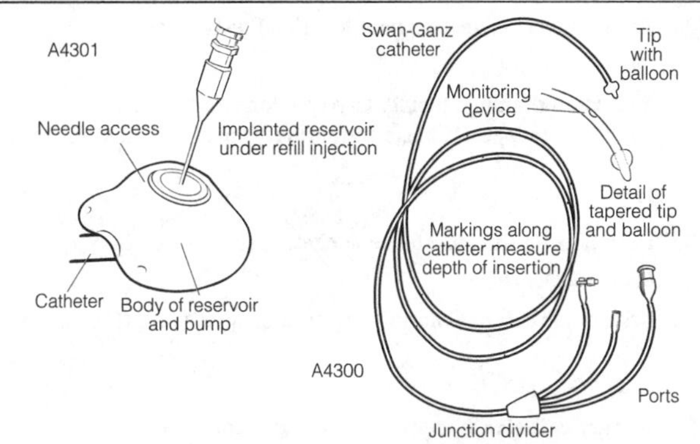

A4300 **Implantable access catheter, (e.g., venous, arterial, epidural subarachnoid, or peritoneal, etc.) external access**
MED: 100-2,15,120

A4301 **Implantable access total catheter, port/reservoir (e.g., venous, arterial, epidural, subarachnoid, peritoneal, etc.)**

A4305 **Disposable drug delivery system, flow rate of 50 ml or greater per hour**

A4306 **Disposable drug delivery system, flow rate of less than 50 ml per hour**

INCONTINENCE APPLIANCES AND CARE SUPPLIES

Covered by Medicare when the medical record indicates incontinence is permanent, or of long and indefinite duration.

A4310 **Insertion tray without drainage bag and without catheter (accessories only)**
MED: 100-2,15,120

A4311 **Insertion tray without drainage bag with indwelling catheter, Foley type, 2-way latex with coating (Teflon, silicone, silicone elastomer or hydrophilic, etc.)**
MED: 100-2,15,120

A4312 **Insertion tray without drainage bag with indwelling catheter, Foley type, 2-way, all silicone**
MED: 100-2,15,120

A4313 **Insertion tray without drainage bag with indwelling catheter, Foley type, 3-way, for continuous irrigation**
MED: 100-2,15,120

A4314 **Insertion tray with drainage bag with indwelling catheter, Foley type, 2-way latex with coating (Teflon, silicone, silicone elastomer or hydrophilic, etc.)**
MED: 100-2,15,120

A4315 **Insertion tray with drainage bag with indwelling catheter, Foley type, 2-way, all silicone**
MED: 100-2,15,120

A4316 **Insertion tray with drainage bag with indwelling catheter, Foley type, 3-way, for continuous irrigation**
MED: 100-2,15,120

A4320 **Irrigation tray with bulb or piston syringe, any purpose**
MED: 100-2,15,120

A4321 **Therapeutic agent for urinary catheter irrigation**
MED: 100-2,15,120

A4322 **Irrigation syringe, bulb or piston, each**
MED: 100-2,15,120

A4326 **Male external catheter with integral collection chamber, any type, each**
MED: 100-2,15,120

A4327 **Female external urinary collection device; meatal cup, each**
MED: 100-2,15,120

A4328 **Female external urinary collection device; pouch, each**
MED: 100-2,15,120

A4330 **Perianal fecal collection pouch with adhesive, each**
MED: 100-2,15,120

A4331 **Extension drainage tubing, any type, any length, with connector/adaptor, for use with urinary leg bag or urostomy pouch, each**
MED: 100-2,15,120

A4332 **Lubricant, individual sterile packet, each**
MED: 100-2,15,120

A4333 **Urinary catheter anchoring device, adhesive skin attachment, each**
MED: 100-2,15,120

A4334 **Urinary catheter anchoring device, leg strap, each**
MED: 100-2,15,120

A4335 **Incontinence supply; miscellaneous**
MED: 100-2,15,120

A4338 **Indwelling catheter; Foley type, 2-way latex with coating (Teflon, silicone, silicone elastomer, or hydrophilic, etc.), each**
MED: 100-2,15,120

A4340 **Indwelling catheter; specialty type, (e.g., Coude, mushroom, wing, etc.), each**
MED: 100-2,15,120

A4344 **Indwelling catheter, Foley type, 2-way, all silicone, each**
MED: 100-2,15,120

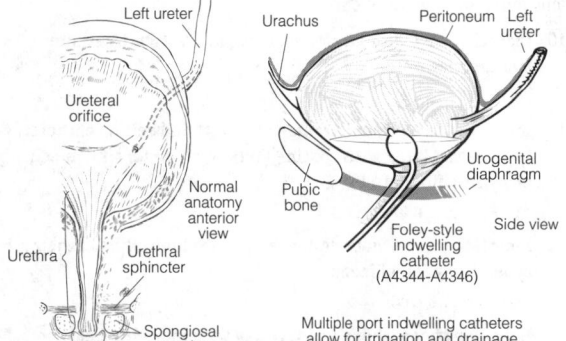

Multiple port indwelling catheters allow for irrigation and drainage

A4346 **Indwelling catheter; Foley type, 3-way for continuous irrigation, each**
MED: 100-2,15,120

A4349 **Male external catheter, with or without adhesive, disposable, each**
MED: 100-2,15,120

A4351 **Intermittent urinary catheter; straight tip, with or without coating (Teflon, silicone, silicone elastomer, or hydrophilic, etc.), each**
MED: 100-2,15,120

A4352 **Intermittent urinary catheter; Coude (curved) tip, with or without coating (Teflon, silicone, silicone elastomeric, or hydrophilic, etc.), each**
MED: 100-2,15,120

A4353 **Intermittent urinary catheter, with insertion supplies**
MED: 100-2,15,120

A4354 **Insertion tray with drainage bag but without catheter**
MED: 100-2,15,120

A4355 **Irrigation tubing set for continuous bladder irrigation through a 3-way indwelling Foley catheter, each**
MED: 100-2,15,120

EXTERNAL URINARY SUPPLIES

A4356 **External urethral clamp or compression device (not to be used for catheter clamp), each**
MED: 100-2,15,120

A4357 **Bedside drainage bag, day or night, with or without antireflux device, with or without tube, each**
MED: 100-2,15,120

A4358 **Urinary drainage bag, leg or abdomen, vinyl, with or without tube, with straps, each**
MED: 100-2,15,120

OSTOMY SUPPLIES

A4361 **Ostomy faceplate, each**
MED: 100-2,15,120

A4362 **Skin barrier; solid, 4 x 4 or equivalent; each**
See code(s) A4461 or A4463

A4363 **Ostomy clamp, any type, replacement only, each**

A4364 **Adhesive, liquid or equal, any type, per oz**
MED: 100-2,15,120

A4365 **Adhesive remover wipes, any type, per 50**
MED: 100-2,15,120

A4366 **Ostomy vent, any type, each**

A4367 **Ostomy belt, each**
MED: 100-2,15,120

A4368 **Ostomy filter, any type, each**

A4369 **Ostomy skin barrier, liquid (spray, brush, etc.), per oz**
MED: 100-2,15,120

A4371 **Ostomy skin barrier, powder, per oz**
MED: 100-2,15,120

A4372 **Ostomy skin barrier, solid 4 x 4 or equivalent, standard wear, with built-in convexity, each**
MED: 100-2,15,120

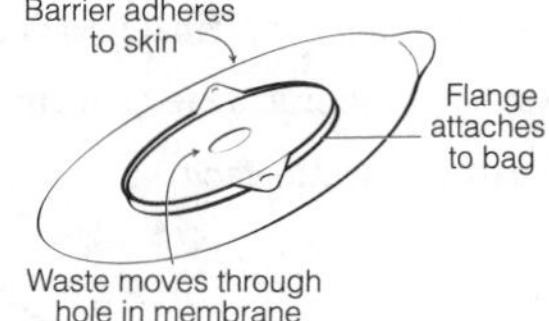

Faceplate flange and skin barrier combination (A4373)

A4373 **Ostomy skin barrier, with flange (solid, flexible or accordian), with built-in convexity, any size, each**
MED: 100-2,15,120

A4375 **Ostomy pouch, drainable, with faceplate attached, plastic, each**
MED: 100-2,15,120

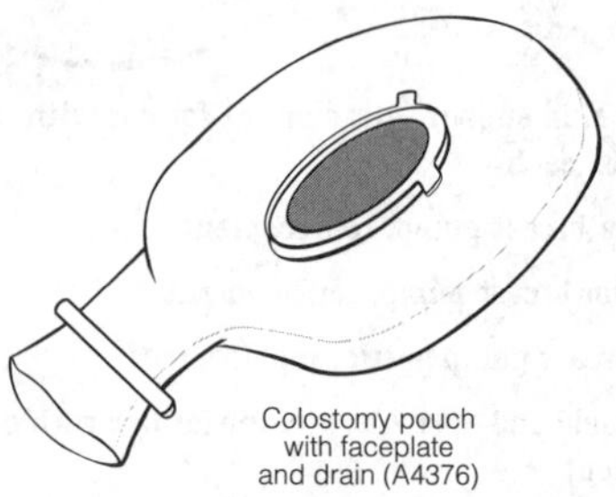

Colostomy pouch with faceplate and drain (A4376)

A4376 **Ostomy pouch, drainable, with faceplate attached, rubber, each**
MED: 100-2,15,120

A4377 **Ostomy pouch, drainable, for use on faceplate, plastic, each**
MED: 100-2,15,120

A4378 **Ostomy pouch, drainable, for use on faceplate, rubber, each**
MED: 100-2,15,120

A4379 Ostomy pouch, urinary, with faceplate attached, plastic, each
MED: 100-2,15,120

A4380 Ostomy pouch, urinary, with faceplate attached, rubber, each
MED: 100-2,15,120

A4381 Ostomy pouch, urinary, for use on faceplate, plastic, each
MED: 100-2,15,120

A4382 Ostomy pouch, urinary, for use on faceplate, heavy plastic, each
MED: 100-2,15,120

A4383 Ostomy pouch, urinary, for use on faceplate, rubber, each
MED: 100-2,15,120

A4384 Ostomy faceplate equivalent, silicone ring, each
MED: 100-2,15,120

A4385 Ostomy skin barrier, solid 4 x 4 or equivalent, extended wear, without built-in convexity, each
MED: 100-2,15,120

A4387 Ostomy pouch, closed, with barrier attached, with built-in convexity (1 piece), each
MED: 100-2,15,120

A4388 Ostomy pouch, drainable, with extended wear barrier attached, (1 piece), each
MED: 100-2,15,120

A4389 Ostomy pouch, drainable, with barrier attached, with built-in convexity (1 piece), each
MED: 100-2,15,120

A4390 Ostomy pouch, drainable, with extended wear barrier attached, with built-in convexity (1 piece), each
MED: 100-2,15,120

A4391 Ostomy pouch, urinary, with extended wear barrier attached (1 piece), each
MED: 100-2,15,120

A4392 Ostomy pouch, urinary, with standard wear barrier attached, with built-in convexity (1 piece), each
MED: 100-2,15,120

A4393 Ostomy pouch, urinary, with extended wear barrier attached, with built-in convexity (1 piece), each
MED: 100-2,15,120

A4394 Ostomy deodorant, with or without lubricant, for use in ostomy pouch, per fl oz
MED: 100-2,15,120

A4395 Ostomy deodorant for use in ostomy pouch, solid, per tablet
MED: 100-2,15,120

A4396 Ostomy belt with peristomal hernia support
MED: 100-2,15,120

A4397 Irrigation supply; sleeve, each
MED: 100-2,15,120

A4398 Ostomy irrigation supply; bag, each
MED: 100-2,15,120

A4399 Ostomy irrigation supply; cone/catheter, including brush
MED: 100-2,15,120

A4400 Ostomy irrigation set
MED: 100-2,15,120

A4402 Lubricant, per oz
MED: 100-2,15,120

A4404 Ostomy ring, each
MED: 100-2,15,120

A4405 Ostomy skin barrier, nonpectin-based, paste, per oz
MED: 100-2,15,120

A4406 Ostomy skin barrier, pectin-based, paste, per oz
MED: 100-2,15,120

A4407 Ostomy skin barrier, with flange (solid, flexible, or accordion), extended wear, with built-in convexity, 4 x 4 in or smaller, each
MED: 100-2,15,120

A4408 Ostomy skin barrier, with flange (solid, flexible or accordion), extended wear, with built-in convexity, larger than 4 x 4 in, each
MED: 100-2,15,120

A4409 Ostomy skin barrier, with flange (solid, flexible or accordion), extended wear, without built-in convexity, 4 x 4 in or smaller, each
MED: 100-2,15,120

A4410 Ostomy skin barrier, with flange (solid, flexible or accordion), extended wear, without built-in convexity, larger than 4 x 4 in, each
MED: 100-2,15,120

A4411 Ostomy skin barrier, solid 4 x 4 or equivalent, extended wear, with built-in convexity, each

A4412 Ostomy pouch, drainable, high output, for use on a barrier with flange (2 piece system), without filter, each
MED: 100-2,15,120

A4413 Ostomy pouch, drainable, high output, for use on a barrier with flange (2-piece system), with filter, each
MED: 100-2,15,120

A4414 Ostomy skin barrier, with flange (solid, flexible or accordion), without built-in convexity, 4 x 4 in or smaller, each
MED: 100-2,15,120

A4415 Ostomy skin barrier, with flange (solid, flexible or accordion), without built-in convexity, larger than 4 x 4 in, each
MED: 100-2,15,120

A4416 Ostomy pouch, closed, with barrier attached, with filter (1 piece), each

A4417 Ostomy pouch, closed, with barrier attached, with built-in convexity, with filter (1 piece), each

A4418 Ostomy pouch, closed; without barrier attached, with filter (1 piece), each

A4419 Ostomy pouch, closed; for use on barrier with nonlocking flange, with filter (2 piece), each

A4420 Ostomy pouch, closed; for use on barrier with locking flange (2 piece), each

A4421 Ostomy supply; miscellaneous
Determine if an alternative HCPCS Level II or a CPT code better describes the service being reported. This code should be used only if a more specific code is unavailable.
MED: 100-2,15,120

A4422 Ostomy absorbent material (sheet/pad/crystal packet) for use in ostomy pouch to thicken liquid stomal output, each
MED: 100-2,15,120

A4423 Ostomy pouch, closed; for use on barrier with locking flange, with filter (2 piece), each

A4424 Ostomy pouch, drainable, with barrier attached, with filter (1 piece), each

A4425 Ostomy pouch, drainable; for use on barrier with nonlocking flange, with filter (2-piece system), each

A4426 Ostomy pouch, drainable; for use on barrier with locking flange (2-piece system), each

A4427 Ostomy pouch, drainable; for use on barrier with locking flange, with filter (2-piece system), each

A4428 Ostomy pouch, urinary, with extended wear barrier attached, with faucet-type tap with valve (1 piece), each

A4429 Ostomy pouch, urinary, with barrier attached, with built-in convexity, with faucet-type tap with valve (1 piece), each

A4430 Ostomy pouch, urinary, with extended wear barrier attached, with built-in convexity, with faucet-type tap with valve (1 piece), each

A4431 Ostomy pouch, urinary; with barrier attached, with faucet-type tap with valve (1 piece), each

A4432 Ostomy pouch, urinary; for use on barrier with nonlocking flange, with faucet-type tap with valve (2 piece), each

A4433 Ostomy pouch, urinary; for use on barrier with locking flange (2 piece), each

A4434 Ostomy pouch, urinary; for use on barrier with locking flange, with faucet-type tap with valve (2 piece), each

ADDITIONAL MISCELLANEOUS SUPPLIES

A4450 Tape, nonwaterproof, per 18 sq in
See also code A4452.
MED: 100-2,15,120

A4452 Tape, waterproof, per 18 sq in
See also code A4450.
MED: 100-2,15,120

A4455 Adhesive remover or solvent (for tape, cement or other adhesive), per oz
MED: 100-2,15,120

A4458 Enema bag with tubing, reusable

A4461 Surgical dressing holder, nonreusable, each

A4463 Surgical dressing holder, reusable, each

A4465 Nonelastic binder for extremity

A4470 Gravlee jet washer
MED: 100-2,16,90; 100-3,230.5

A4480 VABRA aspirator
MED: 100-2,16,90; 100-3,230.6

A4481 Tracheostoma filter, any type, any size, each
MED: 100-2,15,120

A4483 Moisture exchanger, disposable, for use with invasive mechanical ventilation
MED: 100-2,15,120

A4490 Surgical stockings above knee length, each
MED: 100-2,15,100; 100-2,15,110; 100-3,280.1

A4495 Surgical stockings thigh length, each
MED: 100-2,15,100; 100-2,15,110; 100-3,280.1

A4500 Surgical stockings below knee length, each
MED: 100-2,15,100; 100-2,15,110; 100-3,280.1

A4510 Surgical stockings full-length, each
MED: 100-2,15,100; 100-2,15,110; 100-3,280.1

A4520 Incontinence garment, any type, (e.g., brief, diaper), each
MED: 100-3,280.1

A4550 Surgical trays

A4554 Disposable underpads, all sizes
MED: 100-2,15,120; 100-3,280.1

A4556 Electrodes (e.g., apnea monitor), per pair

A4557 Lead wires (e.g., apnea monitor), per pair

A4558 Conductive gel or paste, for use with electrical device (e.g., TENS, NMES), per oz

A4559 Coupling gel or paste, for use with ultrasound device, per oz

A4561 Pessary, rubber, any type

A4562 Pessary, nonrubber, any type
Medicare jurisdiction: DME regional contractor.

A4565 Slings
Dressings applied by a physician are included as part of the professional service. Surgical dressings obtained by the patient to perform homecare as prescribed by the physician are covered.

A4570 Splint
Dressings applied by a physician are included as part of the professional service.
MED: 100-2,6,10; 100-2,15,100; 100-4,4,240

A4575 Topical hyperbaric oxygen chamber, disposable
MED: 100-3,20.29

A4580 Cast supplies (e.g., plaster)
See Q4001-Q4048.
MED: 100-2,6,10; 100-2,15,100; 100-4,4,240

A4590 Special casting material (e.g., fiberglass)
See Q4001-Q4048.
MED: 100-2,6,10; 100-2,15,100; 100-4,4,240

A4595 Electrical stimulator supplies, 2 lead, per month, (e.g., TENS, NMES)
MED: 100-3,160.13

A4600 Sleeve for intermittent limb compression device, replacement only, each

A4601 Lithium ion battery for nonprosthetic use, replacement

A4604 Tubing with integrated heating element for use with positive airway pressure device

A4605 Tracheal suction catheter, closed system, each

A4606 Oxygen probe for use with oximeter device, replacement

A4608 Transtracheal oxygen catheter, each

SUPPLIES FOR OXYGEN AND RELATED RESPIRATORY EQUIPMENT

A4611 Battery, heavy-duty; replacement for patient-owned ventilator

A4612 Battery cables; replacement for patient-owned ventilator

A4613 Battery charger; replacement for patient-owned ventilator

A4614 Peak expiratory flow rate meter, hand held

A4615 Cannula, nasal
MED: 100-3,160.6; 100-4,20,100.2

A4616 Tubing (oxygen), per foot
MED: 100-3,160.6; 100-4,20,100.2

A4617 Mouthpiece
MED: 100-3,160.6; 100-4,20,100.2

A4618 Breathing circuits
MED: 100-3,160.6; 100-4,20,100.2

A4619 Face tent
MED: 100-3,160.6; 100-4,20,100.2

A4620 Variable concentration mask
MED: 100-3,160.6; 100-4,20,100.2

A4623 Tracheostomy, inner cannula
MED: 100-2,15,120; 100-3,20.9

A4624 Tracheal suction catheter, any type other than closed system, each

A4625 Tracheostomy care kit for new tracheostomy
MED: 100-2,15,120

A4626 Tracheostomy cleaning brush, each
MED: 100-2,15,120

A4627 Spacer, bag or reservoir, with or without mask, for use with metered dose inhaler
MED: 100-2,15,110

A4628 Oropharyngeal suction catheter, each

A4629 Tracheostomy care kit for established tracheostomy
MED: 100-2,15,120

SUPPLIES FOR OTHER DURABLE MEDICAL EQUIPMENT

A4630 Replacement batteries, medically necessary, transcutaneous electrical stimulator, owned by patient
MED: 100-3,160.7

A4633 Replacement bulb/lamp for ultraviolet light therapy system, each

A4634 Replacement bulb for therapeutic light box, tabletop model

A4635 Underarm pad, crutch, replacement, each
MED: 100-3,280.1

A4636 Replacement, handgrip, cane, crutch, or walker, each
MED: 100-3,280.1

A4637 Replacement, tip, cane, crutch, walker, each
MED: 100-3,280.1

A4638 Replacement battery for patient-owned ear pulse generator, each

A4639 Replacement pad for infrared heating pad system, each

A4640 Replacement pad for use with medically necessary alternating pressure pad owned by patient
MED: 100-3,280.1; 100-8,5,5.2.3

SUPPLIES FOR RADIOLOGIC PROCEDURES

A4641 Radiopharmaceutical, diagnostic, not otherwise classified
MED: 100-4,13,60.3.1

A4642 Indium In-111 satumomab pendetide, diagnostic, per study dose, up to 6 millicuries
Use this code for Oncoscint.

MISCELLANEOUS SUPPLIES

A4648 Tissue marker, implantable, any type, each

A4649 Surgical supply; miscellaneous
Determine if an alternative HCPCS Level II or a CPT code better describes the service being reported. This code should be used only if a more specific code is unavailable.

A4650 Implantable radiation dosimeter, each

A4651 Calibrated microcapillary tube, each

A4652 Microcapillary tube sealant

DIALYSIS SUPPLIES

A4653 Peritoneal dialysis catheter anchoring device, belt, each

A4657 Syringe, with or without needle, each

A4660 Sphygmomanometer/blood pressure apparatus with cuff and stethoscope

A4663 Blood pressure cuff only

A4670 Automatic blood pressure monitor
MED: 100-3,20.19

A4671 Disposable cycler set used with cycler dialysis machine, each

A4672 Drainage extension line, sterile, for dialysis, each

A4673 Extension line with easy lock connectors, used with dialysis

A4674 Chemicals/antiseptics solution used to clean/sterilize dialysis equipment, per 8 oz

A4680 Activated carbon filter for hemodialysis, each
MED: 100-3,230.7

A4690 Dialyzer (artificial kidneys), all types, all sizes, for hemodialysis, each

A4706 Bicarbonate concentrate, solution, for hemodialysis, per gallon

A4707 Bicarbonate concentrate, powder, for hemodialysis, per packet

A4708 Acetate concentrate solution, for hemodialysis, per gallon

A4709 Acid concentrate, solution, for hemodialysis, per gallon

A4714 Treated water (deionized, distilled, or reverse osmosis) for peritoneal dialysis, per gallon
MED: 100-3,230.7

A4719 "Y set" tubing for peritoneal dialysis

A4720 Dialysate solution, any concentration of dextrose, fluid volume greater than 249 cc, but less than or equal to 999 cc, for peritoneal dialysis

A4721 Dialysate solution, any concentration of dextrose, fluid volume greater than 999 cc but less than or equal to 1999 cc, for peritoneal dialysis

A4722 Dialysate solution, any concentration of dextrose, fluid volume greater than 1999 cc but less than or equal to 2999 cc, for peritoneal dialysis

A4723 Dialysate solution, any concentration of dextrose, fluid volume greater than 2999 cc but less than or equal to 3999 cc, for peritoneal dialysis

A4724 Dialysate solution, any concentration of dextrose, fluid volume greater than 3999 cc but less than or equal to 4999 cc, for peritoneal dialysis

A4725 Dialysate solution, any concentration of dextrose, fluid volume greater than 4999 cc but less than or equal to 5999 cc, for peritoneal dialysis

A4726 Dialysate solution, any concentration of dextrose, fluid volume greater than 5999 cc, for peritoneal dialysis

A4728 Dialysate solution, nondextrose containing, 500 ml

A4730 Fistula cannulation set for hemodialysis, each

A4736 Topical anesthetic, for dialysis, per gram

A4737 Injectable anesthetic, for dialysis, per 10 ml

A4740 Shunt accessory, for hemodialysis, any type, each

A4750 Blood tubing, arterial or venous, for hemodialysis, each

A4755 Blood tubing, arterial and venous combined, for hemodialysis, each

A4760 Dialysate solution test kit, for peritoneal dialysis, any type, each

A4765 Dialysate concentrate, powder, additive for peritoneal dialysis, per packet

A4766 Dialysate concentrate, solution, additive for peritoneal dialysis, per 10 ml

A4770 Blood collection tube, vacuum, for dialysis, per 50

A4771 Serum clotting time tube, for dialysis, per 50

A4772 Blood glucose test strips, for dialysis, per 50

A4773 Occult blood test strips, for dialysis, per 50

A4774 Ammonia test strips, for dialysis, per 50

A4802 Protamine sulfate, for hemodialysis, per 50 mg

A4860 Disposable catheter tips for peritoneal dialysis, per 10

A4870 Plumbing and/or electrical work for home hemodialysis equipment

A4890 Contracts, repair and maintenance, for hemodialysis equipment
MED: 100-2,15,110.2

A4911 Drain bag/bottle, for dialysis, each

A4913 Miscellaneous dialysis supplies, not otherwise specified
Pertinent documentation to evaluate medical appropriateness should be included when this code is reported. Determine if an alternative HCPCS Level II or a CPT code better describes the service being reported. This code should be used only if a more specific code is unavailable.

A4918 Venous pressure clamp, for hemodialysis, each

A4927 Gloves, nonsterile, per 100

A4928 Surgical mask, per 20

A4929 Tourniquet for dialysis, each

A4930 Gloves, sterile, per pair

A4931 Oral thermometer, reusable, any type, each

A4932 Rectal thermometer, reusable, any type, each

ADDITIONAL OSTOMY SUPPLIES

A5051 Ostomy pouch, closed; with barrier attached (1 piece), each
MED: 100-2,15,120

A5052 Ostomy pouch, closed; without barrier attached (1 piece), each
MED: 100-2,15,120

A5053 Ostomy pouch, closed; for use on faceplate, each
MED: 100-2,15,120

A5054 Ostomy pouch, closed; for use on barrier with flange (2 piece), each
MED: 100-2,15,120

A5055 Stoma cap
MED: 100-2,15,120

A5061 Ostomy pouch, drainable; with barrier attached, (1 piece), each

A5062 Ostomy pouch, drainable; without barrier attached (1 piece), each
MED: 100-2,15,120

A5063 Ostomy pouch, drainable; for use on barrier with flange (2-piece system), each
MED: 100-2,15,120

A5071 Ostomy pouch, urinary; with barrier attached (1 piece), each
MED: 100-2,15,120

A5072 Ostomy pouch, urinary; without barrier attached (1 piece), each
MED: 100-2,15,120

A5073 Ostomy pouch, urinary; for use on barrier with flange (2 piece), each
MED: 100-2,15,120

A5081 Continent device; plug for continent stoma
MED: 100-2,15,120

A5082 Continent device; catheter for continent stoma
MED: 100-2,15,120

A5083 Continent device, stoma absorptive cover for continent stoma

A5093 Ostomy accessory; convex insert
MED: 100-2,15,120

ADDITIONAL INCONTINENCE APPLIANCES/SUPPLIES

A5102 Bedside drainage bottle with or without tubing, rigid or expandable, each
MED: 100-2,15,120

A5105 Urinary suspensory with leg bag, with or without tube, each
MED: 100-2,15,120

A5112 Urinary leg bag; latex
MED: 100-2,15,120

A5113 Leg strap; latex, replacement only, per set
MED: 100-2,15,120

A5114 Leg strap; foam or fabric, replacement only, per set
MED: 100-2,15,120

SUPPLIES FOR EITHER INCONTINENCE OR OSTOMY APPLIANCES

For additional skin barrier codes see codes A4405-A4411.

A5120 Skin barrier, wipes or swabs, each
MED: 100-2,15,120

A5121 Skin barrier; solid, 6 x 6 or equivalent, each
MED: 100-2,15,120

A5122 Skin barrier; solid, 8 x 8 or equivalent, each
MED: 100-2,15,120

A5126 Adhesive or nonadhesive; disk or foam pad
MED: 100-2,15,120

A5131 Appliance cleaner, incontinence and ostomy appliances, per 16 oz
MED: 100-2,15,120

A5200 Percutaneous catheter/tube anchoring device, adhesive skin attachment
MED: 100-2,15,120

DIABETIC SHOES, FITTING, AND MODIFICATIONS

According to Medicare, documentation from the prescribing physician must certify the diabetic patient has one of the following conditions: peripheral neuropathy with evidence of callus formation; history of preulcerative calluses; history of ulceration; foot deformity; previous amputation; or poor circulation. The footwear must be fitted and furnished by a podiatrist, pedorthist, orthotist, or prosthetist.

A5500 For diabetics only, fitting (including follow-up), custom preparation and supply of off-the-shelf depth-inlay shoe manufactured to accommodate multidensity insert(s), per shoe
MED: 100-2,15,140

A5501 For diabetics only, fitting (including follow-up), custom preparation and supply of shoe molded from cast(s) of patient's foot (custom molded shoe), per shoe
MED: 100-2,15,140

A5503 For diabetics only, modification (including fitting) of off-the-shelf depth-inlay shoe or custom molded shoe with roller or rigid rocker bottom, per shoe
MED: 100-2,15,140

A5504 For diabetics only, modification (including fitting) of off-the-shelf depth-inlay shoe or custom molded shoe with wedge(s), per shoe
MED: 100-2,15,140

A5505 For diabetics only, modification (including fitting) of off-the-shelf depth-inlay shoe or custom molded shoe with metatarsal bar, per shoe
MED: 100-2,15,140

A5506 For diabetics only, modification (including fitting) of off-the-shelf depth-inlay shoe or custom molded shoe with off-set heel(s), per shoe
MED: 100-2,15,140

A5507 For diabetics only, not otherwise specified modification (including fitting) of off-the-shelf depth-inlay shoe or custom molded shoe, per shoe
MED: 100-2,15,140

A5508 For diabetics only, deluxe feature of off-the-shelf depth-inlay shoe or custom molded shoe, per shoe
MED: 100-2,15,140

A5510 For diabetics only, direct formed, compression molded to patient's foot without external heat source, multiple-density insert(s) prefabricated, per shoe
MED: 100-2,15,140

A5512 For diabetics only, multiple density insert, direct formed, molded to foot after external heat source of 230 degrees Fahrenheit or higher, total contact with patient's foot, including arch, base layer minimum of 1/4 inch material of shore a 35 durometer or 3/16 inch material of shore a 40 durometer (or higher), prefabricated, each

A5513 For diabetics only, multiple density insert, custom molded from model of patient's foot, total contact with patient's foot, including arch, base layer minimum of 3/16 inch material of shore a 35 durometer or higher), includes arch filler and other shaping material, custom fabricated, each

DRESSINGS

A6000 Noncontact wound-warming wound cover for use with the noncontact wound-warming device and warming card

MED: 100-2,16,20

A6010 Collagen based wound filler, dry form, sterile, per gram of collagen

MED: 100-2,15,100

A6011 Collagen based wound filler, gel/paste, sterile, per gram of collagen

MED: 100-2,15,100

A6021 Collagen dressing, sterile, pad size 16 sq in or less, each

MED: 100-2,15,100; 100-4,4,240

A6022 Collagen dressing, sterile, pad size more than 16 sq in but less than or equal to 48 sq in, each

MED: 100-2,15,100; 100-4,4,240

A6023 Collagen dressing, sterile, pad size more than 48 sq in, each

MED: 100-2,15,100; 100-4,4,240

A6024 Collagen dressing wound filler, sterile, per 6 in

MED: 100-2,15,100; 100-4,4,240

A6025 Gel sheet for dermal or epidermal application, (e.g., silicone, hydrogel, other), each

A6154 Wound pouch, each

MED: 100-2,15,100

A6196 Alginate or other fiber gelling dressing, wound cover, sterile, pad size 16 sq in or less, each dressing

MED: 100-2,15,100; 100-4,4,240

A6197 Alginate or other fiber gelling dressing, wound cover, sterile, pad size more than 16 sq in but less than or equal to 48 sq in, each dressing

MED: 100-2,15,100; 100-4,4,240

A6198 Alginate or other fiber gelling dressing, wound cover, sterile, pad size more than 48 sq in, each dressing

MED: 100-2,15,100; 100-4,4,240

A6199 Alginate or other fiber gelling dressing, wound filler, sterile, per 6 in

MED: 100-2,15,100; 100-4,4,240

A6200 Composite dressing, pad size 16 sq in or less, without adhesive border, each dressing

MED: 100-2,15,100; 100-4,4,240

A6201 Composite dressing, pad size more than 16 sq in but less than or equal to 48 sq in, without adhesive border, each dressing

MED: 100-2,15,100; 100-4,4,240

A6202 Composite dressing, pad size more than 48 sq in, without adhesive border, each dressing

MED: 100-2,15,100; 100-4,4,240

A6203 Composite dressing, sterile, pad size 16 sq in or less, with any size adhesive border, each dressing

MED: 100-2,15,100; 100-4,4,240

A6204 Composite dressing, sterile, pad size more than 16 sq in, but less than or equal to 48 sq in, with any size adhesive border, each dressing

MED: 100-2,15,100; 100-4,4,240

A6205 Composite dressing, sterile, pad size more than 48 sq in, with any size adhesive border, each dressing

MED: 100-2,15,100; 100-4,4,240

A6206 Contact layer, sterile, 16 sq in or less, each dressing

MED: 100-2,15,100; 100-4,4,240

A6207 Contact layer, sterile, more than 16 sq in but less than or equal to 48 sq in, each dressing

MED: 100-2,15,100; 100-4,4,240

A6208 Contact layer, sterile, more than 48 sq in, each dressing

MED: 100-2,15,100; 100-4,4,240

A6209 Foam dressing, wound cover, sterile, pad size 16 sq in or less, without adhesive border, each dressing

MED: 100-2,15,100; 100-4,4,240

A6210 Foam dressing, wound cover, sterile, pad size more than 16 sq in but less than or equal to 48 sq in, without adhesive border, each dressing

MED: 100-2,15,100; 100-4,4,240

A6211 Foam dressing, wound cover, sterile, pad size more than 48 sq in, without adhesive border, each dressing

MED: 100-2,15,100; 100-4,4,240

A6212 Foam dressing, wound cover, sterile, pad size 16 sq in or less, with any size adhesive border, each dressing

MED: 100-2,15,100; 100-4,4,240

A6213 Foam dressing, wound cover, sterile, pad size more than 16 sq in but less than or equal to 48 sq in, with any size adhesive border, each dressing

MED: 100-2,15,100; 100-4,4,240

A6214 Foam dressing, wound cover, sterile, pad size more than 48 sq in, with any size adhesive border, each dressing

MED: 100-2,15,100; 100-4,4,240

A6215 Foam dressing, wound filler, sterile, per gram

MED: 100-2,15,100; 100-4,4,240

A6216 Gauze, nonimpregnated, nonsterile, pad size 16 sq in or less, without adhesive border, each dressing

MED: 100-2,15,100; 100-4,4,240

A6217 Gauze, nonimpregnated, nonsterile, pad size more than 16 sq in but less than or equal to 48 sq in, without adhesive border, each dressing

MED: 100-2,15,100; 100-4,4,240

A6218 Gauze, nonimpregnated, nonsterile, pad size more than 48 sq in, without adhesive border, each dressing

MED: 100-2,15,100; 100-4,4,240

A6219 Gauze, nonimpregnated, sterile, pad size 16 sq in or less, with any size adhesive border, each dressing

MED: 100-2,15,100; 100-4,4,240

A6220 Gauze, nonimpregnated, sterile, pad size more than 16 sq in but less than or equal to 48 sq in, with any size adhesive border, each dressing

MED: 100-2,15,100; 100-4,4,240

A6221 Gauze, nonimpregnated, sterile, pad size more than 48 sq in, with any size adhesive border, each dressing

MED: 100-2,15,100; 100-4,4,240

A6222 Gauze, impregnated with other than water, normal saline, or hydrogel, sterile, pad size 16 sq in or less, without adhesive border, each dressing

MED: 100-2,15,100; 100-4,4,240

A6223 Gauze, impregnated with other than water, normal saline, or hydrogel, sterile, pad size more than 16 sq in, but less than or equal to 48 sq in, without adhesive border, each dressing

MED: 100-2,15,100; 100-4,4,240

A6224 Gauze, impregnated with other than water, normal saline, or hydrogel, sterile, pad size more than 48 sq in, without adhesive border, each dressing

MED: 100-2,15,100; 100-4,4,240

A6228 Gauze, impregnated, water or normal saline, sterile, pad size 16 sq in or less, without adhesive border, each dressing

MED: 100-2,15,100; 100-4,4,240

A6229 Gauze, impregnated, water or normal saline, sterile, pad size more than 16 sq in but less than or equal to 48 sq in, without adhesive border, each dressing

MED: 100-2,15,100; 100-4,4,240

A6230 Gauze, impregnated, water or normal saline, sterile, pad size more than 48 sq in, without adhesive border, each dressing

MED: 100-2,15,100; 100-4,4,240

A6231 Gauze, impregnated, hydrogel, for direct wound contact, sterile, pad size 16 sq in or less, each dressing

MED: 100-2,15,100; 100-4,4,240

A6232 Gauze, impregnated, hydrogel, for direct wound contact, sterile, pad size greater than 16 sq in, but less than or equal to 48 sq in, each dressing

MED: 100-2,15,100; 100-4,4,240

A6233 Gauze, impregnated, hydrogel, for direct wound contact, sterile, pad size more than 48 sq in, each dressing

MED: 100-2,15,100; 100-4,4,240

A6234 Hydrocolloid dressing, wound cover, sterile, pad size 16 sq in or less, without adhesive border, each dressing

MED: 100-2,15,100; 100-4,4,240

A6235 Hydrocolloid dressing, wound cover, sterile, pad size more than 16 sq in but less than or equal to 48 sq in, without adhesive border, each dressing

MED: 100-2,15,100; 100-4,4,240

A6236 Hydrocolloid dressing, wound cover, sterile, pad size more than 48 sq in, without adhesive border, each dressing

MED: 100-2,15,100; 100-4,4,240

A6237 Hydrocolloid dressing, wound cover, sterile, pad size 16 sq in or less, with any size adhesive border, each dressing

MED: 100-2,15,100; 100-4,4,240

A6238 Hydrocolloid dressing, wound cover, sterile, pad size more than 16 sq in but less than or equal to 48 sq in, with any size adhesive border, each dressing

MED: 100-2,15,100; 100-4,4,240

A6239 Hydrocolloid dressing, wound cover, sterile, pad size more than 48 sq in, with any size adhesive border, each dressing

MED: 100-2,15,100; 100-4,4,240

A6240 Hydrocolloid dressing, wound filler, paste, sterile, per oz

MED: 100-2,15,100; 100-4,4,240

A6241 Hydrocolloid dressing, wound filler, dry form, sterile, per gram

MED: 100-2,15,100; 100-4,4,240

A6242 Hydrogel dressing, wound cover, sterile, pad size 16 sq in or less, without adhesive border, each dressing

MED: 100-2,15,100; 100-4,4,240

A6243 Hydrogel dressing, wound cover, sterile, pad size more than 16 sq in but less than or equal to 48 sq in, without adhesive border, each dressing

MED: 100-2,15,100; 100-4,4,240

A6244 Hydrogel dressing, wound cover, sterile, pad size more than 48 sq in, without adhesive border, each dressing

MED: 100-2,15,100; 100-4,4,240

A6245 Hydrogel dressing, wound cover, sterile, pad size 16 sq in or less, with any size adhesive border, each dressing

MED: 100-2,15,100; 100-4,4,240

A6246 Hydrogel dressing, wound cover, sterile, pad size more than 16 sq in but less than or equal to 48 sq in, with any size adhesive border, each dressing

MED: 100-2,15,100; 100-4,4,240

A6247 Hydrogel dressing, wound cover, sterile, pad size more than 48 sq in, with any size adhesive border, each dressing

MED: 100-2,15,100; 100-4,4,240

A6248 Hydrogel dressing, wound filler, gel, sterile, per fl oz

MED: 100-2,15,100; 100-4,4,240

A6250 Skin sealants, protectants, moisturizers, ointments, any type, any size

Surgical dressings applied by a physician are included as part of the professional service. Surgical dressings obtained by the patient to perform homecare as prescribed by the physician are covered.

MED: 100-2,15,100; 100-4,4,240

A6251 Specialty absorptive dressing, wound cover, sterile, pad size 16 sq in or less, without adhesive border, each dressing

MED: 100-2,15,100; 100-4,4,240

A6252 Specialty absorptive dressing, wound cover, sterile, pad size more than 16 sq in but less than or equal to 48 sq in, without adhesive border, each dressing

MED: 100-2,15,100; 100-4,4,240

A6253 Specialty absorptive dressing, wound cover, sterile, pad size more than 48 sq in, without adhesive border, each dressing

MED: 100-2,15,100; 100-4,4,240

A6254 Specialty absorptive dressing, wound cover, sterile, pad size 16 sq in or less, with any size adhesive border, each dressing

MED: 100-2,15,100; 100-4,4,240

A6255 Specialty absorptive dressing, wound cover, sterile, pad size more than 16 sq in but less than or equal to 48 sq in, with any size adhesive border, each dressing

MED: 100-2,15,100; 100-4,4,240

A6256 Specialty absorptive dressing, wound cover, sterile, pad size more than 48 sq in, with any size adhesive border, each dressing

MED: 100-2,15,100; 100-4,4,240

A6257 Transparent film, sterile, 16 sq in or less, each dressing

Surgical dressings applied by a physician are included as part of the professional service. Surgical dressings obtained by the patient to perform homecare as prescribed by the physician are covered. Use this code for Polyskin, Tegaderm, and Tegaderm HP.

MED: 100-2,15,100; 100-4,4,240

A6258 Transparent film, sterile, more than 16 sq in but less than or equal to 48 sq in, each dressing

Surgical dressings applied by a physician are included as part of the professional service. Surgical dressings obtained by the patient to perform homecare as prescribed by the physician are covered.

MED: 100-2,15,100; 100-4,4,240

A6259 Transparent film, sterile, more than 48 sq in, each dressing

Surgical dressings applied by a physician are included as part of the professional service. Surgical dressings obtained by the patient to perform homecare as prescribed by the physician are covered.

MED: 100-2,15,100; 100-4,4,240

A6260 Wound cleansers, sterile, any type, any size

Surgical dressings applied by a physician are included as part of the professional service. Surgical dressings obtained by the patient to perform homecare as prescribed by the physician are covered.

MED: 100-2,15,100; 100-4,4,240

A6261 Wound filler, gel/paste, sterile, per fl oz, not otherwise specified

Surgical dressings applied by a physician are included as part of the professional service. Surgical dressings obtained by the patient to perform homecare as prescribed by the physician are covered.

MED: 100-2,15,100; 100-4,4,240

A6262 Wound filler, dry form, sterile, per gram, not otherwise specified

MED: 100-2,15,100; 100-4,4,240

A6266 Gauze, impregnated, other than water, normal saline, or zinc paste, sterile, any width, per linear yd
Surgical dressings applied by a physician are included as part of the professional service. Surgical dressings obtained by the patient to perform homecare as prescribed by the physician are covered.
MED: 100-2,15,100; 100-4,4,240

A6402 Gauze, nonimpregnated, sterile, pad size 16 sq in or less, without adhesive border, each dressing
Surgical dressings applied by a physician are included as part of the professional service. Surgical dressings obtained by the patient to perform homecare as prescribed by the physician are covered.
MED: 100-2,15,100; 100-4,4,240

A6403 Gauze, nonimpregnated, sterile, pad size more than 16 sq in, less than or equal to 48 sq in, without adhesive border, each dressing
Surgical dressings applied by a physician are included as part of the professional service. Surgical dressings obtained by the patient to perform homecare as prescribed by the physician are covered.
MED: 100-2,15,100; 100-4,4,240

A6404 Gauze, nonimpregnated, sterile, pad size more than 48 sq in, without adhesive border, each dressing
MED: 100-2,15,100; 100-4,4,240

A6407 Packing strips, nonimpregnated, sterile, up to 2 in in width, per linear yd

A6410 Eye pad, sterile, each
MED: 100-2,15,100

A6411 Eye pad, nonsterile, each
MED: 100-2,15,100

A6412 Eye patch, occlusive, each

A6413 Adhesive bandage, first aid type, any size, each

A6441 Padding bandage, nonelastic, nonwoven/nonknitted, width greater than or equal to 3 in and less than 5 in, per yd

A6442 Conforming bandage, nonelastic, knitted/woven, nonsterile, width less than 3 in, per yd

A6443 Conforming bandage, nonelastic, knitted/woven, nonsterile, width greater than or equal to 3 in and less than 5 in, per yd

A6444 Conforming bandage, nonelastic, knitted/woven, nonsterile, width greater than or equal to 5 in, per yd

A6445 Conforming bandage, nonelastic, knitted/woven, sterile, width less than 3 in, per yd

A6446 Conforming bandage, nonelastic, knitted/woven, sterile, width greater than or equal to 3 in and less than 5 in, per yd

A6447 Conforming bandage, nonelastic, knitted/woven, sterile, width greater than or equal to 5 in, per yd

A6448 Light compression bandage, elastic, knitted/woven, width less than 3 in, per yd

A6449 Light compression bandage, elastic, knitted/woven, width greater than or equal to 3 in and less than 5 in, per yd

A6450 Light compression bandage, elastic, knitted/woven, width greater than or equal to 5 in, per yd

A6451 Moderate compression bandage, elastic, knitted/woven, load resistance of 1.25 to 1.34 ft lbs at 50% maximum stretch, width greater than or equal to 3 in and less than 5 in, per yd

A6452 High compression bandage, elastic, knitted/woven, load resistance greater than or equal to 1.35 ft lbs at 50% maximum stretch, width greater than or equal to 3 in and less than 5 in, per yd

A6453 Self-adherent bandage, elastic, nonknitted/nonwoven, width less than 3 in, per yd

A6454 Self-adherent bandage, elastic, nonknitted/nonwoven, width greater than or equal to 3 in and less than 5 in, per yd

A6455 Self-adherent bandage, elastic, nonknitted/nonwoven, width greater than or equal to 5 in, per yd

A6456 Zinc paste impregnated bandage, nonelastic, knitted/woven, width greater than or equal to 3 in and less than 5 in, per yd

A6457 Tubular dressing with or without elastic, any width, per linear yard

A6501 Compression burn garment, bodysuit (head to foot), custom fabricated
MED: 100-2,15,100

A6502 Compression burn garment, chin strap, custom fabricated
MED: 100-2,15,100

A6503 Compression burn garment, facial hood, custom fabricated
MED: 100-2,15,100

A6504 Compression burn garment, glove to wrist, custom fabricated
MED: 100-2,15,100

A6505 Compression burn garment, glove to elbow, custom fabricated
MED: 100-2,15,100

A6506 Compression burn garment, glove to axilla, custom fabricated
MED: 100-2,15,100

A6507 Compression burn garment, foot to knee length, custom fabricated
MED: 100-2,15,100

A6508 Compression burn garment, foot to thigh length, custom fabricated
MED: 100-2,15,100

A6509 Compression burn garment, upper trunk to waist including arm openings (vest), custom fabricated
MED: 100-2,15,100

A6510 Compression burn garment, trunk, including arms down to leg openings (leotard), custom fabricated
MED: 100-2,15,100

A6511 Compression burn garment, lower trunk including leg openings (panty), custom fabricated
MED: 100-2,15,100

A6512 Compression burn garment, not otherwise classified
MED: 100-2,15,100

A6513 Compression burn mask, face and/or neck, plastic or equal, custom fabricated

A6530 Gradient compression stocking, below knee, 18-30 mm Hg, each

A6531 Gradient compression stocking, below knee, 30-40 mm Hg, each
MED: 100-2,15,100

A6532 Gradient compression stocking, below knee, 40-50 mm Hg, each
MED: 100-2,15,100

A6533 Gradient compression stocking, thigh length, 18-30 mm Hg, each
MED: 100-2,15,130

A6534 Gradient compression stocking, thigh length, 30-40 mm Hg, each
MED: 100-2,15,130

A6535 Gradient compression stocking, thigh length, 40-50 mm Hg, each
MED: 100-2,15,130

A6536 Gradient compression stocking, full-length/chap style, 18-30 mm Hg, each
MED: 100-2,15,130

A6537 Gradient compression stocking, full-length/chap style, 30-40 mm Hg, each
MED: 100-2,15,130

A6538 Gradient compression stocking, full-length/chap style, 40-50 mm Hg, each
MED: 100-2,15,130

A6539 Gradient compression stocking, waist length, 18-30 mm Hg, each
MED: 100-2,15,130

A6540 Gradient compression stocking, waist length, 30-40 mm Hg, each
MED: 100-2,15,130

A6541 Gradient compression stocking, waist length, 40-50 mm Hg, each
MED: 100-2,15,130

A6542 Gradient compression stocking, custom made
MED: 100-2,15,130

A6543 Gradient compression stocking, lymphedema
MED: 100-2,15,130

A6544 Gradient compression stocking, garter belt
MED: 100-2,15,130

A6545 Gradient compression wrap, nonelastic, below knee, 30-50 mm Hg, each

A6549 Gradient compression stocking, not otherwise specified
MED: 100-2,15,130

A6550 Wound care set, for negative pressure wound therapy electrical pump, includes all supplies and accessories

MISCELLANEOUS SUPPLIES

A7000 Canister, disposable, used with suction pump, each

A7001 Canister, nondisposable, used with suction pump, each

A7002 Tubing, used with suction pump, each

A7003 Administration set, with small volume nonfiltered pneumatic nebulizer, disposable

A7004 Small volume nonfiltered pneumatic nebulizer, disposable

A7005 Administration set, with small volume nonfiltered pneumatic nebulizer, nondisposable

A7006 Administration set, with small volume filtered pneumatic nebulizer

A7007 Large volume nebulizer, disposable, unfilled, used with aerosol compressor

A7008 Large volume nebulizer, disposable, prefilled, used with aerosol compressor

A7009 Reservoir bottle, nondisposable, used with large volume ultrasonic nebulizer

A7010 Corrugated tubing, disposable, used with large volume nebulizer, 100 ft

A7011 Corrugated tubing, nondisposable, used with large volume nebulizer, 10 ft

A7012 Water collection device, used with large volume nebulizer

A7013 Filter, disposable, used with aerosol compressor

A7014 Filter, nondisposable, used with aerosol compressor or ultrasonic generator

A7015 Aerosol mask, used with DME nebulizer

A7016 Dome and mouthpiece, used with small volume ultrasonic nebulizer

A7017 Nebulizer, durable, glass or autoclavable plastic, bottle type, not used with oxygen
MED: 100-3,280.1

A7018 Water, distilled, used with large volume nebulizer, 1000 ml

A7025 High frequency chest wall oscillation system vest, replacement for use with patient-owned equipment, each

A7026 High frequency chest wall oscillation system hose, replacement for use with patient-owned equipment, each

A7027 Combination oral/nasal mask, used with continuous positive airway pressure device, each

A7028 Oral cushion for combination oral/nasal mask, replacement only, each

A7029 Nasal pillows for combination oral/nasal mask, replacement only, pair

A7030 Full face mask used with positive airway pressure device, each

A7031 Face mask interface, replacement for full face mask, each

A7032 Cushion for use on nasal mask interface, replacement only, each

A7033 Pillow for use on nasal cannula type interface, replacement only, pair

A7034 Nasal interface (mask or cannula type) used with positive airway pressure device, with or without head strap

A7035 Headgear used with positive airway pressure device

A7036 Chinstrap used with positive airway pressure device

A7037 Tubing used with positive airway pressure device

A7038 Filter, disposable, used with positive airway pressure device

A7039 Filter, nondisposable, used with positive airway pressure device

A7040 One way chest drain valve

A7041 Water seal drainage container and tubing for use with implanted chest tube

A7042 Implanted pleural catheter, each

A7043 Vacuum drainage bottle and tubing for use with implanted catheter

A7044 Oral interface used with positive airway pressure device, each

A7045 Exhalation port with or without swivel used with accessories for positive airway devices, replacement only
MED: 100-3,230.17

A7046 Water chamber for humidifier, used with positive airway pressure device, replacement, each
MED: 100-3,230.17

A7501 Tracheostoma valve, including diaphragm, each
MED: 100-2,15,120

A7502 Replacement diaphragm/faceplate for tracheostoma valve, each
MED: 100-2,15,120

A7503 Filter holder or filter cap, reusable, for use in a tracheostoma heat and moisture exchange system, each
MED: 100-2,15,120

A7504 Filter for use in a tracheostoma heat and moisture exchange system, each
MED: 100-2,15,120

A7505 Housing, reusable without adhesive, for use in a heat and moisture exchange system and/or with a tracheostoma valve, each
MED: 100-2,15,120

A7506 Adhesive disc for use in a heat and moisture exchange system and/or with tracheostoma valve, any type each
MED: 100-2,15,120

A7507 Filter holder and integrated filter without adhesive, for use in a tracheostoma heat and moisture exchange system, each
MED: 100-2,15,120

A7508 Housing and integrated adhesive, for use in a tracheostoma heat and moisture exchange system and/or with a tracheostoma valve, each
MED: 100-2,15,120

A7509 Filter holder and integrated filter housing, and adhesive, for use as a tracheostoma heat and moisture exchange system, each
MED: 100-2,15,120

A7520 Tracheostomy/laryngectomy tube, noncuffed, polyvinylchloride (PVC), silicone or equal, each

A7521 Tracheostomy/laryngectomy tube, cuffed, polyvinylchloride (PVC), silicone or equal, each

A7522 Tracheostomy/laryngectomy tube, stainless steel or equal (sterilizable and reusable), each

A7523 Tracheostomy shower protector, each

A7524 Tracheostoma stent/stud/button, each

A7525 Tracheostomy mask, each

A7526 Tracheostomy tube collar/holder, each

A7527 Tracheostomy/laryngectomy tube plug/stop, each

A8000 Helmet, protective, soft, prefabricated, includes all components and accessories

A8001 Helmet, protective, hard, prefabricated, includes all components and accessories

A8002 Helmet, protective, soft, custom fabricated, includes all components and accessories

A8003 Helmet, protective, hard, custom fabricated, includes all components and accessories

A8004 Soft interface for helmet, replacement only

ADMINISTRATIVE, MISCELLANEOUS & INVESTIGATIONAL A9000-A9999

This section of codes reports items such as nonprescription drugs, noncovered items/services, exercise equipment and, most notably, radiopharmaceutical diagnostic imaging agents.

A9150 Nonprescription drugs
MED: 100-2,15,50

A9152 Single vitamin/mineral/trace element, oral, per dose, not otherwise specified

A9153 Multiple vitamins, with or without minerals and trace elements, oral, per dose, not otherwise specified

A9155 Artificial saliva, 30 ml

A9180 Pediculosis (lice infestation) treatment, topical, for administration by patient/caretaker

A9270 Noncovered item or service
MED: 100-2,16,20

A9274 External ambulatory insulin delivery system, disposable, each, includes all supplies and accessories

A9275 Home glucose disposable monitor, includes test strips

A9276 Sensor; invasive (e.g., subcutaneous), disposable, for use with interstitial continuous glucose monitoring system, 1 unit = 1 day supply

A9277 Transmitter; external, for use with interstitial continuous glucose monitoring system

A9278 Receiver (monitor); external, for use with interstitial continuous glucose monitoring system

A9279 Monitoring feature/device, stand-alone or integrated, any type, includes all accessories, components and electronics, not otherwise classified

A9280 Alert or alarm device, not otherwise classified

A9281 Reaching/grabbing device, any type, any length, each

A9282 Wig, any type, each

A9283 Foot pressure off loading/supportive device, any type, each

A9284 Spirometer, nonelectronic, includes all accessories

A9300 Exercise equipment
MED: 100-2,15,110.1; 100-3,280.1

RADIOPHARMACEUTICALS

A9500 Technetium Tc-99m sestamibi, diagnostic, per study dose, up to 40 millicuries
Use this code for Cardiolite.

A9501 Technetium Tc-99m teboroxime, diagnostic, per study dose

A9502 Technetium Tc-99m tetrofosmin, diagnostic, per study dose
Use this code for Myoview.

A9503 Technetium Tc-99m medronate, diagnostic, per study dose, up to 30 millicuries
Use this code for CIS-MDP, Draximage MDP-10, Draximage MDP-25, MDP-Bracco, Technetium Tc-99m MPI-MDP
AHA: 2Q,'02,9

A9504 Technetium Tc-99m apcitide, diagnostic, per study dose, up to 20 millicuries
Use this code for Acutect
AHA: 2Q,'02,9; 4Q,'01,5

A9505 Thallium Tl-201 thallous chloride, diagnostic, per millicurie
Use this code for MIBG, Thallous Chloride USP.
AHA: 2Q,'02,9

A9507 Indium In-111 capromab pendetide, diagnostic, per study dose, up to 10 millicuries
Use this code for Prostascint.

A9508 Iodine I-131 iobenguane sulfate, diagnostic, per 0.5 millicurie
Use this code for MIBG.
AHA: 2Q,'02,9

A9509 Iodine I-123 sodium iodide, diagnostic, per millicurie

A9510 Technetium Tc-99m disofenin, diagnostic, per study dose, up to 15 millicuries
Use this code for Hepatolite.

A9512 Technetium Tc-99m pertechnetate, diagnostic, per millicurie
Use this code for Technelite, Ultra-Technelow.

A9516 Iodine I-123 sodium iodide, diagnostic, per 100 microcuries, up to 999 microcuries

A9517 Iodine I-131 sodium iodide capsule(s), therapeutic, per millicurie

A9521 Technetium Tc-99m exametazime, diagnostic, per study dose, up to 25 millicuries
Use this code for Ceretec.

A9524 Iodine I-131 iodinated serum albumin, diagnostic, per 5 microcuries

A9526 Nitrogen N-13 ammonia, diagnostic, per study dose, up to 40 millicuries
MED: 100-3,220.6; 100-4,13,60.3.1; 100-4,13,60.3.2

A9527 Iodine I-125, sodium iodide solution, therapeutic, per millicurie

A9528 Iodine I-131 sodium iodide capsule(s), diagnostic, per millicurie

A9529 Iodine I-131 sodium iodide solution, diagnostic, per millicurie

A9530 Iodine I-131 sodium iodide solution, therapeutic, per millicurie

A9531 Iodine I-131 sodium iodide, diagnostic, per microcurie (up to 100 microcuries)

A9532 Iodine I-125 serum albumin, diagnostic, per 5 microcuries

A9535 Injection, methylene blue, 1 ml

A9536 Technetium Tc-99m depreotide, diagnostic, per study dose, up to 35 millicuries

A9537 Technetium Tc-99m mebrofenin, diagnostic, per study dose, up to 15 millicuries

A9538 Technetium Tc-99m pyrophosphate, diagnostic, per study dose, up to 25 millicuries
Use this code for CIS-PYRO, Phosphostec, Technescan Pyp Kit

A9539 Technetium Tc-99m pentetate, diagnostic, per study dose, up to 25 millicuries
Use this code for AN-DTPA, DTPA, Magnavist, MPI-DTPA Kit-Chelate, MPI Indium DTPA IN-111, Pentate Calcium Trisodium, Pentate Zinc Trisodium

A9540 Technetium Tc-99m macroaggregated albumin, diagnostic, per study dose, up to 10 millicuries

A9541 Technetium Tc-99m sulfur colloid, diagnostic, per study dose, up to 20 millicuries

A9542 Indium In-111 ibritumomab tiuxetan, diagnostic, per study dose, up to 5 millicuries
Use this code for Zevalin

A9543 Yttrium Y-90 ibritumomab tiuxetan, therapeutic, per treatment dose, up to 40 millicuries

A9544 Iodine I-131 tositumomab, diagnostic, per study dose

A9545 Iodine I-131 tositumomab, therapeutic, per treatment dose
Use this code for Bexxar.

A9546 Cobalt Co-57/58, cyanocobalamin, diagnostic, per study dose, up to 1 microcurie

A9547 Indium In-111 oxyquinoline, diagnostic, per 0.5 millicurie

A9548 Indium In-111 pentetate, diagnostic, per 0.5 millicurie

A9550 Technetium Tc-99m sodium gluceptate, diagnostic, per study dose, up to 25 millicurie

A9551 Technetium Tc-99m succimer, diagnostic, per study dose, up to 10 millicuries
Use this code for MPI-DMSA Kidney Reagent.

A9552 Fluorodeoxyglucose F-18 FDG, diagnostic, per study dose, up to 45 millicuries

A9553 Chromium Cr-51 sodium chromate, diagnostic, per study dose, up to 250 microcuries
Use this code for Chromitope Sodium.

A9554 Iodine I-125 sodium iothalamate, diagnostic, per study dose, up to 10 microcuries
Use this code for Glofil-125.

A9555 Rubidium Rb-82, diagnostic, per study dose, up to 60 millicuries
Use this code for Cardiogen 82.

A9556 Gallium Ga-67 citrate, diagnostic, per millicurie
Use this code for Ganite.

A9557 Technetium Tc-99m bicisate, diagnostic, per study dose, up to 25 millicuries
Use this code for Neurolite.

A9558 Xenon Xe-133 gas, diagnostic, per 10 millicuries

A9559 Cobalt Co-57 cyanocobalamin, oral, diagnostic, per study dose, up to 1 microcurie

A9560 Technetium Tc-99m labeled red blood cells, diagnostic, per study dose, up to 30 millicuries

A9561 Technetium Tc-99m oxidronate, diagnostic, per study dose, up to 30 millicuries
Use this code for TechneScan.

A9562 Technetium Tc-99m mertiatide, diagnostic, per study dose, up to 15 millicuries
Use this code for TechneScan MAG-3.

A9563 Sodium phosphate P-32, therapeutic, per millicurie

A9564 Chromic phosphate P-32 suspension, therapeutic, per millicurie
Use this code for Phosphocol (P32).

A9566 Technetium Tc-99m fanolesomab, diagnostic, per study dose, up to 25 millicuries

A9567 Technetium Tc-99m pentetate, diagnostic, aerosol, per study dose, up to 75 millicuries
Use this code for AN-DTPA, DTPA, MPI-DTPA Kit-Chelate, MPI Indium DTPA IN-111, Pentate Calcium Trisodium, Pentate Zinc Trisodium.

A9568 Technetium Tc-99m arcitumomab, diagnostic, per study dose, up to 45 millicuries
Use this code for CEA Scan.

A9569 Technetium Tc-99m exametazime labeled autologous white blood cells, diagnostic, per study dose
Use this code for Ceretec.

A9570 Indium In-111 labeled autologous white blood cells, diagnostic, per study dose

A9571 Indium In-111 labeled autologous platelets, diagnostic, per study dose

A9572 Indium In-111 pentetreotide, diagnostic, per study dose, up to 6 millicuries
Use this code for Ostreoscan.

A9576 Injection, gadoteridol, (ProHance multipack), per ml

A9577 Injection, gadobenate dimeglumine (MultiHance), per ml

A9578 Injection, gadobenate dimeglumine (MultiHance multipack), per ml

A9579 Injection, gadolinium-based magnetic resonance contrast agent, not otherwise specified (NOS), per ml
Use this code for Omniscan.

A9580 Sodium fluoride F-18, diagnostic, per study dose, up to 30 millicuries

A9600 Strontium Sr-89 chloride, therapeutic, per millicurie
Use this code for Metastron.
AHA: 2Q,'02,9

A9605 Samarium Sm-153 lexidronamm, therapeutic, per 50 millicuries
Use this code for Quadramet.
AHA: 2Q,'02,9

A9698 Nonradioactive contrast imaging material, not otherwise classified, per study

A9699 Radiopharmaceutical, therapeutic, not otherwise classified

A9700 Supply of injectable contrast material for use in echocardiography, per study
AHA: 4Q,'01,5

MISCELLANEOUS

A9900 Miscellaneous DME supply, accessory, and/or service component of another HCPCS code

A9901 DME delivery, set up, and/or dispensing service component of another HCPCS code

A9999 Miscellaneous DME supply or accessory, not otherwise specified

ENTERAL AND PARENTERAL THERAPY B4000-B9999

This section includes codes for supplies, formulae, nutritional solutions, and infusion pumps.

ENTERAL FORMULAE AND ENTERAL MEDICAL SUPPLIES

Certification of medical necessity is required for coverage. Submit a revision to the certification of medical necessity if the patient's daily volume changes by more than one liter; if there is a change in infusion method; or if there is a change from premix to home mix or parenteral to enteral therapy.

B4034 Enteral feeding supply kit; syringe fed, per day

MED: 100-2,15,120; 100-3,180.2; 100-4,20,100.2.2; 100-4,20,160.1

B4035 Enteral feeding supply kit; pump fed, per day

MED: 100-2,15,120; 100-3,180.2; 100-4,20,100.2.2; 100-4,20,160.1

B4036 Enteral feeding supply kit; gravity fed, per day

MED: 100-2,15,120; 100-3,180.2; 100-4,20,100.2.2; 100-4,20,160.1

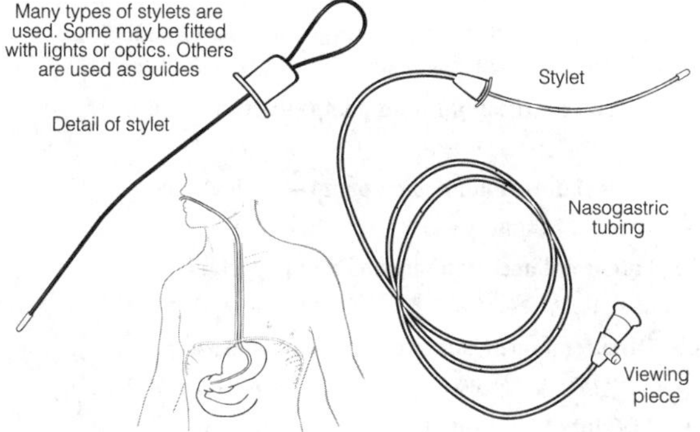
Many types of stylets are used. Some may be fitted with lights or optics. Others are used as guides
Detail of stylet
Stylet
Nasogastric tubing
Viewing piece

B4081 Nasogastric tubing with stylet

MED: 100-2,15,120; 100-3,180.2; 100-4,20,100.2.2; 100-4,20,160.1

B4082 Nasogastric tubing without stylet

MED: 100-2,15,120; 100-3,180.2; 100-4,20,100.2.2; 100-4,20,160.1

B4083 Stomach tube — Levine type

MED: 100-2,15,120; 100-3,180.2; 100-4,20,100.2.2

B4087 Gastrostomy/jejunostomy tube, standard, any material, any type, each

B4088 Gastrostomy/jejunostomy tube, low-profile, any material, any type, each

B4100 Food thickener, administered orally, per oz

B4102 Enteral formula, for adults, used to replace fluids and electrolytes (e.g., clear liquids), 500 ml = 1 unit

MED: 100-3,180.2; 100-4,20,160.1

B4103 Enteral formula, for pediatrics, used to replace fluids and electrolytes (e.g., clear liquids), 500 ml = 1 unit

MED: 100-3,180.2; 100-4,20,160.1

B4104 Additive for enteral formula (e.g., fiber)

MED: 100-3,180.2; 100-4,20,160.1

B4149 Enteral formula, manufactured blenderized natural foods with intact nutrients, includes proteins, fats, carbohydrates, vitamins and minerals, may include fiber, administered through an enteral feeding tube, 100 calories = 1 unit

MED: 100-2,15,120; 100-3,180.2; 100-4,20,100.2.2; 100-4,20,160.1

B4150 Enteral formula, nutritionally complete with intact nutrients, includes proteins, fats, carbohydrates, vitamins and minerals, may include fiber, administered through an enteral feeding tube, 100 calories = 1 unit

Use this code for Enrich, Ensure, Ensure HN, Ensure Powder, Isocal, Lonalac Powder, Meritene, Meritene Powder, Osmolite, Osmolite HN, Portagen Powder, Sustacal, Renu, Sustagen Powder, Travasorb.

MED: 100-2,15,120; 100-3,180.2; 100-4,20,100.2.2; 100-4,20,160.1

B4152 Enteral formula, nutritionally complete, calorically dense (equal to or greater than 1.5 kcal/ml) with intact nutrients, includes proteins, fats, carbohydrates, vitamins and minerals, may include fiber, administered through an enteral feeding tube, 100 calories = 1 unit

Use this code for Magnacal, Isocal HCN, Sustacal HC, Ensure Plus, Ensure Plus HN.

MED: 100-2,15,120; 100-3,180.2; 100-4,20,100.2.2; 100-4,20,160.1

B4153 Enteral formula, nutritionally complete, hydrolyzed proteins (amino acids and peptide chain), includes fats, carbohydrates, vitamins and minerals, may include fiber, administered through an enteral feeding tube, 100 calories = 1 unit

Use this code for Criticare HN, Vivonex t.e.n. (Total Enteral Nutrition), Vivonex HN, Vital (Vital HN), Travasorb HN, Isotein HN, Precision HN, Precision Isotonic.

MED: 100-2,15,120; 100-3,180.2; 100-4,20,100.2.2; 100-4,20,160.1

B4154 Enteral formula, nutritionally complete, for special metabolic needs, excludes inherited disease of metabolism, includes altered composition of proteins, fats, carbohydrates, vitamins and/or minerals, may include fiber, administered through an enteral feeding tube, 100 calories = 1 unit

Use this code for Hepatic-aid, Travasorb Hepatic, Travasorb MCT, Travasorb Renal, Traum-aid, Tramacal, Aminaid.

MED: 100-2,15,120; 100-3,180.2; 100-4,20,100.2.2; 100-4,20,160.1

B4155 Enteral formula, nutritionally incomplete/modular nutrients, includes specific nutrients, carbohydrates (e.g., glucose polymers), proteins/amino acids (e.g., glutamine, arginine), fat (e.g., medium chain triglycerides) or combination, administered through an enteral feeding tube, 100 calories = 1 unit

Use this code for Propac, Gerval Protein, Promix, Casec, Moducal, Controlyte, Polycose Liquid or Powder, Sumacal, Microlipids, MCT Oil, Nutri-source.

MED: 100-2,15,120; 100-3,180.2; 100-4,20,100.2.2; 100-4,20,160.1

B4157 Enteral formula, nutritionally complete, for special metabolic needs for inherited disease of metabolism, includes proteins, fats, carbohydrates, vitamins and minerals, may include fiber, administered through an enteral feeding tube, 100 calories = 1 unit

MED: 100-3,180.2; 100-4,20,160.1

B4158 Enteral formula, for pediatrics, nutritionally complete with intact nutrients, includes proteins, fats, carbohydrates, vitamins and minerals, may include fiber and/or iron, administered through an enteral feeding tube, 100 calories = 1 unit

MED: 100-3,180.2; 100-4,20,160.1

B4159 Enteral formula, for pediatrics, nutritionally complete soy based with intact nutrients, includes proteins, fats, carbohydrates, vitamins and minerals, may include fiber and/or iron, administered through an enteral feeding tube, 100 calories = 1 unit

MED: 100-3,180.2; 100-4,20,160.1

B4160 Enteral formula, for pediatrics, nutritionally complete calorically dense (equal to or greater than 0.7 kcal/ml) with intact nutrients, includes proteins, fats, carbohydrates, vitamins and minerals, may include fiber, administered through an enteral feeding tube, 100 calories = 1 unit

MED: 100-3,180.2; 100-4,20,160.1

B4161 Enteral formula, for pediatrics, hydrolyzed/amino acids and peptide chain proteins, includes fats, carbohydrates, vitamins and minerals, may include fiber, administered through an enteral feeding tube, 100 calories = 1 unit

MED: 100-3,180.2; 100-4,20,160.1

B4162 Enteral formula, for pediatrics, special metabolic needs for inherited disease of metabolism, includes proteins, fats, carbohydrates, vitamins and minerals, may include fiber, administered through an enteral feeding tube, 100 calories = 1 unit

MED: 100-3,180.2; 100-4,20,160.1

PARENTERAL NUTRITION SOLUTIONS AND SUPPLIES

B4164 Parenteral nutrition solution: carbohydrates (dextrose), 50% or less (500 ml = 1 unit), home mix

MED: 100-2,15,120; 100-3,180.2; 100-4,3,10.4; 100-4,20,100.2.2

B4168 Parenteral nutrition solution; amino acid, 3.5%, (500 ml = 1 unit) — home mix

MED: 100-2,15,120; 100-3,180.2; 100-4,3,10.4; 100-4,20,100.2.2

B4172 Parenteral nutrition solution; amino acid, 5.5% through 7%, (500 ml = 1 unit) — home mix

MED: 100-2,15,120; 100-3,180.2; 100-4,3,10.4; 100-4,20,100.2.2

B4176 Parenteral nutrition solution; amino acid, 7% through 8.5%, (500 ml = 1 unit) — home mix

MED: 100-2,15,120; 100-3,180.2; 100-4,3,10.4; 100-4,20,100.2.2

B4178 Parenteral nutrition solution: amino acid, greater than 8.5% (500 ml = 1 unit), home mix

MED: 100-2,15,120; 100-3,180.2; 100-4,3,10.4; 100-4,20,100.2.2

B4180 Parenteral nutrition solution: carbohydrates (dextrose), greater than 50% (500 ml = 1 unit), home mix

MED: 100-2,15,120; 100-3,180.2; 100-4,3,10.4; 100-4,20,100.2.2

B4185 Parenteral nutrition solution, per 10 grams lipids

B4189 Parenteral nutrition solution: compounded amino acid and carbohydrates with electrolytes, trace elements, and vitamins, including preparation, any strength, 10 to 51 g of protein, premix

MED: 100-2,15,120; 100-3,180.2; 100-4,3,10.4; 100-4,20,100.2.2

B4193 Parenteral nutrition solution: compounded amino acid and carbohydrates with electrolytes, trace elements, and vitamins, including preparation, any strength, 52 to 73 g of protein, premix

MED: 100-2,15,120; 100-3,180.2; 100-4,3,10.4; 100-4,20,100.2.2

B4197 Parenteral nutrition solution; compounded amino acid and carbohydrates with electrolytes, trace elements and vitamins, including preparation, any strength, 74 to 100 grams of protein — premix

MED: 100-2,15,120; 100-3,180.2; 100-4,3,10.4; 100-4,20,100.2.2

B4199 Parenteral nutrition solution; compounded amino acid and carbohydrates with electrolytes, trace elements and vitamins, including preparation, any strength, over 100 grams of protein — premix

MED: 100-2,15,120; 100-3,180.2; 100-4,3,10.4; 100-4,20,100.2.2

B4216 Parenteral nutrition; additives (vitamins, trace elements, Heparin, electrolytes), home mix, per day

MED: 100-2,15,120; 100-3,180.2; 100-4,3,10.4; 100-4,20,100.2.2

B4220 Parenteral nutrition supply kit; premix, per day

MED: 100-2,15,120; 100-3,180.2; 100-4,3,10.4; 100-4,20,100.2.2

B4222 Parenteral nutrition supply kit; home mix, per day

MED: 100-2,15,120; 100-3,180.2; 100-4,3,10.4; 100-4,20,100.2.2

B4224 Parenteral nutrition administration kit, per day

MED: 100-2,15,120; 100-3,180.2; 100-4,3,10.4; 100-4,20,100.2.2

B5000 Parenteral nutrition solution: compounded amino acid and carbohydrates with electrolytes, trace elements, and vitamins, including preparation, any strength, renal - Amirosyn RF, NephrAmine, RenAmine - premix

Use this code for Amirosyn-RF, NephrAmine, RenAmin.

MED: 100-2,15,120; 100-3,180.2; 100-4,3,10.4; 100-4,20,100.2.2

B5100 Parenteral nutrition solution: compounded amino acid and carbohydrates with electrolytes, trace elements, and vitamins, including preparation, any strength, hepatic - FreAmine HBC, HepatAmine - premix

Use this code for FreAmine HBC, HepatAmine.

MED: 100-2,15,120; 100-3,180.2; 100-4,3,10.4; 100-4,20,100.2.2

B5200 Parenteral nutrition solution: compounded amino acid and carbohydrates with electrolytes, trace elements, and vitamins, including preparation, any strength, stress - branch chain amino acids - premix

MED: 100-2,15,120; 100-3,180.2; 100-4,3,10.4; 100-4,20,100.2.2

ENTERAL AND PARENTERAL PUMPS

Submit documentation of the need for the infusion pump. Medicare will reimburse for the simplest model that meets the patient's needs.

B9000 Enteral nutrition infusion pump — without alarm

MED: 100-2,15,120; 100-3,180.2; 100-4,20,100.2.2

B9002 Enteral nutrition infusion pump — with alarm

MED: 100-2,15,120; 100-3,180.2; 100-4,20,100.2.2

B9004 Parenteral nutrition infusion pump, portable

MED: 100-2,15,120; 100-3,180.2; 100-4,3,10.4; 100-4,20,100.2.2

B9006 Parenteral nutrition infusion pump, stationary

MED: 100-2,15,120; 100-3,180.2; 100-4,3,10.4; 100-4,20,100.2.2

B9998 NOC for enteral supplies

MED: 100-2,15,120; 100-3,180.2; 100-4,3,10.4; 100-4,20,100.2.2

B9999 NOC for parenteral supplies

Determine if an alternative HCPCS Level II or a CPT code better describes the service being reported. This code should be used only if a more specific code is unavailable.

MED: 100-2,15,120; 100-3,180.2; 100-4,3,10.4; 100-4,20,100.2.2

OUTPATIENT PPS C1000-C9999

This section reports drugs, biologicals, and devices codes that must be used by OPPS hospitals. Non-OPPS hospitals, Critical Access Hospitals (CAHs), Indian Health Service Hospitals (HIS), hospitals located in American Samoa, Guam, Saipan, or the Virgin Islands, and Maryland waiver hospitals may report these codes at their discretion. The codes can only be reported for facility (technical) services.

The C series of HCPCS may include device catagories, new technology procedures, and drugs, biologicals and radiopharmaceuticals that do not have other HCPCS codes assigned. Some of these items and services are eligible for transitional pass-through payments for OPPS hospitals, have separate APC payments, or are items that are packaged. Hospitals are encouraged to report all appropriate C codes regardless of payment status.

C1300 Hyperbaric oxygen under pressure, full body chamber, per 30 minute interval

MED: 100-4,32,30.1

C1713 Anchor/screw for opposing bone-to-bone or soft tissue-to-bone (implantable)

MED: 100-4,4,61.1
AHA: 3Q,'02,5; 1Q,'01,5

C1714 Catheter, transluminal atherectomy, directional

MED: 100-4,4,61.1
AHA: 4Q,'03,8; 3Q,'02,5; 1Q,'01,5

C1715 Brachytherapy needle

MED: 100-4,4,61.1
AHA: 3Q,'02,5; 1Q,'01,5

C1716 Brachytherapy source, nonstranded, gold-198, per source

MED: 100-4,4,61.1
AHA: 3Q,'02,5; 1Q,'01,5

C1717 Brachytherapy source, nonstranded, high dose rate iridium-192, per source

MED: 100-4,4,61.1
AHA: 3Q,'02,5; 1Q,'01,5

C1719 Brachytherapy source, nonstranded, nonhigh dose rate iridium-192, per source

MED: 100-4,4,61.1
AHA: 3Q,'02,5; 1Q,'01,5

C1721 Cardioverter-defibrillator, dual chamber (implantable)

MED: 100-4,4,61.1
AHA: 3Q,'02,5; 1Q,'01,5

C1722 Cardioverter-defibrillator, single chamber (implantable)

MED: 100-4,4,61.1
AHA: 3Q,'02,5; 1Q,'01,5

C1724 Catheter, transluminal atherectomy, rotational

MED: 100-4,4,61.1
AHA: 4Q,'03,8; 3Q,'02,5; 1Q,'01,5

C1725 Catheter, transluminal angioplasty, nonlaser (may include guidance, infusion/perfusion capability)

MED: 100-4,4,61.1
AHA: 4Q,'03,8; 3Q,'02,5; 1Q,'01,5

C1726 Catheter, balloon dilatation, nonvascular

MED: 100-4,4,61.1
AHA: 3Q,'02,5; 1Q,'01,5

C1727 Catheter, balloon tissue dissector, nonvascular (insertable)

MED: 100-4,4,61.1
AHA: 3Q,'02,5; 1Q,'01,5

C1728 Catheter, brachytherapy seed administration

MED: 100-4,4,61.1
AHA: 3Q,'02,5; 1Q,'01,5

C1729 Catheter, drainage

MED: 100-4,4,61.1
AHA: 3Q,'02,5; 1Q,'01,5

C1730 Catheter, electrophysiology, diagnostic, other than 3D mapping (19 or fewer electrodes)

MED: 100-4,4,61.1
AHA: 3Q,'02,5; 1Q,'01,5

C1731 Catheter, electrophysiology, diagnostic, other than 3D mapping (20 or more electrodes)

MED: 100-4,4,61.1
AHA: 3Q,'02,5; 1Q,'01,5

C1732 Catheter, electrophysiology, diagnostic/ablation, 3D or vector mapping

MED: 100-4,4,61.1
AHA: 1Q,'01,5

C1733 Catheter, electrophysiology, diagnostic/ablation, other than 3D or vector mapping, other than cool-tip

MED: 100-4,4,61.1
AHA: 3Q,'02,5; 1Q,'01,5

C1750 Catheter, hemodialysis/peritoneal, long-term

MED: 100-4,4,61.1
AHA: 4Q,'03,8; 3Q,'02,5; 1Q,'01,5

C1751 Catheter, infusion, inserted peripherally, centrally or midline (other than hemodialysis)

MED: 100-4,4,61.1
AHA: 4Q,'03,8; 3Q,'02,5; 3Q,'01,5

C1752 Catheter, hemodialysis/peritoneal, short-term

MED: 100-4,4,61.1
AHA: 4Q,'03,8; 3Q,'02,5; 1Q,'01,5

C1753 Catheter, intravascular ultrasound

MED: 100-4,4,61.1
AHA: 4Q,'03,8; 3Q,'02,5; 1Q,'01,5

C1754 Catheter, intradiscal

MED: 100-4,4,61.1
AHA: 4Q,'03,8; 3Q,'02,5; 1Q,'01,5

C1755 Catheter, intraspinal

MED: 100-4,4,61.1
AHA: 4Q,'03,8; 3Q,'02,5; 1Q,'01,5

C1756 Catheter, pacing, transesophageal

MED: 100-4,4,61.1
AHA: 4Q,'03,8; 3Q,'02,5; 1Q,'01,5

C1757 Catheter, thrombectomy/embolectomy

MED: 100-4,4,61.1
AHA: 4Q,'03,8; 3Q,'02,5; 1Q,'01,5

C1758 Catheter, ureteral

MED: 100-4,4,61.1
AHA: 4Q,'03,8; 3Q,'02,5; 1Q,'01,6

C1759 Catheter, intracardiac echocardiography

MED: 100-4,4,61.1
AHA: 4Q,'03,8; 3Q,'02,5; 1Q,'01,5; 3Q,'01,4

C1760 Closure device, vascular (implantable/insertable)

MED: 100-4,4,61.1
AHA: 4Q,'03,8; 3Q,'02,5; 1Q,'01,6

C1762 Connective tissue, human (includes fascia lata)

MED: 100-4,4,61.1
AHA: 3Q,'03,12; 4Q,'03,8; 3Q,'02,5; 1Q,'01,6

C1763 Connective tissue, nonhuman (includes synthetic)

MED: 100-4,4,61.1
AHA: 3Q,'03,12; 4Q,'03,8; 3Q,'02,5; 1Q,'01,6

C1764 Event recorder, cardiac (implantable)

MED: 100-4,4,61.1
AHA: 4Q,'03,8; 3Q,'02,5; 1Q,'01,6

C1765 Adhesion barrier

MED: 100-4,4,61.1

C1766 Introducer/sheath, guiding, intracardiac electrophysiological, steerable, other than peel-away

MED: 100-4,4,61.1
AHA: 3Q,'02,5; 3Q,'01,5

C1767 Generator, neurostimulator (implantable), nonrechargeable
MED: 100-4,4,61.1
AHA: 4Q,'03,8; 1Q,'02,9; 3Q,'02,5

C1768 Graft, vascular
MED: 100-4,4,61.1
AHA: 4Q,'03,8; 3Q,'02,5; 1Q,'01,6

C1769 Guide wire
MED: 100-4,4,61.1
AHA: 4Q,'03,8; 3Q,'02,5; 1Q,'01,6; 3Q,'01,4

C1770 Imaging coil, magnetic resonance (insertable)
MED: 100-4,4,61.1
AHA: 4Q,'03,8; 3Q,'02,5; 1Q,'01,6

C1771 Repair device, urinary, incontinence, with sling graft
MED: 100-4,4,61.1
AHA: 4Q,'03,8; 3Q,'02,5; 1Q,'01,6

C1772 Infusion pump, programmable (implantable)
MED: 100-4,4,61.1
AHA: 3Q,'02,5; 1Q,'01,6

C1773 Retrieval device, insertable (used to retrieve fractured medical devices)
MED: 100-4,4,61.1
AHA: 4Q,'03,8; 3Q,'02,5; 1Q,'01,6

C1776 Joint device (implantable)
MED: 100-4,4,61.1
AHA: 3Q,'02,5; 1Q,'01,6; 3Q,'01,5

C1777 Lead, cardioverter-defibrillator, endocardial single coil (implantable)
MED: 100-4,4,61.1
AHA: 3Q,'02,5; 1Q,'01,6

C1778 Lead, neurostimulator (implantable)
MED: 100-4,4,61.1
AHA: 3Q,'02,5; 1Q,'02,9

C1779 Lead, pacemaker, transvenous VDD single pass
MED: 100-4,4,61.1
AHA: 3Q,'02,5; 1Q,'01,6

C1780 Lens, intraocular (new technology)
MED: 100-4,4,61.1
AHA: 3Q,'02,5; 1Q,'01,6

C1781 Mesh (implantable)
MED: 100-4,4,61.1
AHA: 3Q,'02,5; 1Q,'01,6

C1782 Morcellator
MED: 100-4,4,61.1
AHA: 3Q,'02,5; 1Q,'01,6

C1783 Ocular implant, aqueous drainage assist device
MED: 100-4,4,61.1

C1784 Ocular device, intraoperative, detached retina
MED: 100-4,4,61.1
AHA: 3Q,'02,5; 1Q,'01,6

C1785 Pacemaker, dual chamber, rate-responsive (implantable)
MED: 100-4,3,10.4; 100-4,4,61.1
AHA: 4Q,'03,8; 3Q,'02,5; 1Q,'01,6

C1786 Pacemaker, single chamber, rate-responsive (implantable)
MED: 100-4,4,61.1
AHA: 4Q,'03,8; 3Q,'02,5; 1Q,'01,6

C1787 Patient programmer, neurostimulator
MED: 100-4,4,61.1
AHA: 4Q,'03,8; 3Q,'02,5; 1Q,'01,6

C1788 Port, indwelling (implantable)
MED: 100-4,4,61.1
AHA: 4Q,'03,8; 3Q,'02,5; 1Q,'01,6; 3Q,'01,4

C1789 Prosthesis, breast (implantable)
MED: 100-4,4,61.1
AHA: 4Q,'03,8; 3Q,'02,5; 1Q,'01,6

C1813 Prosthesis, penile, inflatable
MED: 100-4,4,61.1
AHA: 4Q,'03,8; 3Q,'02,5; 1Q,'01,6

C1814 Retinal tamponade device, silicone oil
MED: 100-4,4,61.1

C1815 Prosthesis, urinary sphincter (implantable)
MED: 100-4,4,61.1
AHA: 4Q,'03,8; 3Q,'02,5; 1Q,'01,6

C1816 Receiver and/or transmitter, neurostimulator (implantable)
MED: 100-4,4,61.1
AHA: 4Q,'03,8; 3Q,'02,5; 1Q,'01,6

C1817 Septal defect implant system, intracardiac
MED: 100-4,4,61.1
AHA: 4Q,'03,8; 3Q,'02,5; 1Q,'01,6

C1818 Integrated keratoprosthesis
MED: 100-4,4,61.1
AHA: 4Q,'03,4

C1819 Surgical tissue localization and excision device (implantable)
MED: 100-4,4,61.1

C1820 Generator, neurostimulator (implantable), with rechargeable battery and charging system
MED: 100-4,4,10.12

C1821 Interspinous process distraction device (implantable)

C1874 Stent, coated/covered, with delivery system
MED: 100-4,4,61.1
AHA: 4Q,'03,8; 1Q,'01,6

C1875 Stent, coated/covered, without delivery system
MED: 100-4,4,61.1
AHA: 4Q,'03,8; 1Q,'01,6

C1876 Stent, noncoated/noncovered, with delivery system
MED: 100-4,4,61.1
AHA: 4Q,'03,8; 3Q,'02,5; 1Q,'01,6; 3Q,'01,4

C1877 Stent, noncoated/noncovered, without delivery system
MED: 100-4,4,61.1
AHA: 4Q,'03,8; 3Q,'02,5; 1Q,'01,6; 3Q,'01,4

C1878 Material for vocal cord medialization, synthetic (implantable)
MED: 100-4,4,61.1
AHA: 3Q,'02,5; 1Q,'01,6

C1879 Tissue marker (implantable)
MED: 100-4,4,61.1
AHA: 4Q,'03,8; 3Q,'02,5; 1Q,'01,6

C1880 Vena cava filter
MED: 100-4,4,61.1
AHA: 4Q,'03,8; 3Q,'02,5; 1Q,'01,6

C1881 Dialysis access system (implantable)
MED: 100-4,4,61.1
AHA: 4Q,'03,8; 3Q,'02,5; 1Q,'01,6

C1882 Cardioverter-defibrillator, other than single or dual chamber (implantable)
MED: 100-4,4,61.1
AHA: 3Q,'02,5; 1Q,'01,5

C1883 Adaptor/extension, pacing lead or neurostimulator lead (implantable)
MED: 100-4,4,61.1
AHA: 1Q,'02,9; 3Q,'02,5; 1Q,'01,5

C1884 Embolization protective system
MED: 100-4,4,61.1

C1885 Catheter, transluminal angioplasty, laser
MED: 100-4,4,61.1
AHA: 4Q,'03,8; 3Q,'02,5; 1Q,'01,5

C1887 Catheter, guiding (may include infusion/perfusion capability)
MED: 100-4,4,61.1
AHA: 3Q,'02,5; 1Q,'01,5

C1888 Catheter, ablation, noncardiac, endovascular (implantable)
MED: 100-4,4,61.1

C1891 Infusion pump, nonprogrammable, permanent (implantable)
MED: 100-4,4,61.1
AHA: 4Q,'03,8; 3Q,'02,5; 1Q,'01,6

C1892 Introducer/sheath, guiding, intracardiac electrophysiological, fixed-curve, peel-away
MED: 100-4,4,61.1
AHA: 3Q,'02,5; 1Q,'01,6

C1893 Introducer/sheath, guiding, intracardiac electrophysiological, fixed-curve, other than peel-away
MED: 100-4,4,61.1
AHA: 3Q,'02,5; 1Q,'01,6; 3Q,'01,4

C1894 Introducer/sheath, other than guiding, other than intracardiac electrophysiological, nonlaser
MED: 100-4,4,61.1
AHA: 3Q,'02,5

C1895 Lead, cardioverter-defibrillator, endocardial dual coil (implantable)
MED: 100-4,4,61.1
AHA: 3Q,'02,5; 1Q,'01,6

C1896 Lead, cardioverter-defibrillator, other than endocardial single or dual coil (implantable)
MED: 100-4,4,61.1
AHA: 3Q,'02,5; 1Q,'01,6

C1897 Lead, neurostimulator test kit (implantable)
MED: 100-4,4,61.1
AHA: 1Q,'02,9; 3Q,'02,5; 1Q,'01,6

C1898 Lead, pacemaker, other than transvenous VDD single pass
MED: 100-4,4,61.1
AHA: 1Q,'01,6; 3Q,'01,4

C1899 Lead, pacemaker/cardioverter-defibrillator combination (implantable)
MED: 100-4,4,61.1
AHA: 3Q,'02,5; 1Q,'01,6

C1900 Lead, left ventricular coronary venous system
MED: 100-4,4,61.1

C2614 Probe, percutaneous lumbar discectomy
MED: 100-4,4,61.1

C2615 Sealant, pulmonary, liquid
MED: 100-4,4,61.1
AHA: 3Q,'02,5; 1Q,'01,6

C2616 Brachytherapy source, nonstranded, yttrium-90, per source
MED: 100-4,4,61.1
AHA: 3Q,'03,11; 3Q,'02,5

C2617 Stent, noncoronary, temporary, without delivery system
MED: 100-4,4,61.1
AHA: 4Q,'03,8; 3Q,'02,5; 1Q,'01,6

C2618 Probe, cryoablation
MED: 100-4,4,61.1
AHA: 4Q,'03,8; 3Q,'02,5; 1Q,'01,6

C2619 Pacemaker, dual chamber, nonrate-responsive (implantable)
MED: 100-4,4,61.1
AHA: 3Q,'02,5; 1Q,'01,6; 3Q,'01,4

C2620 Pacemaker, single chamber, nonrate-responsive (implantable)
MED: 100-4,3,10.4; 100-4,4,61.1
AHA: 4Q,'03,8; 3Q,'02,5; 1Q,'01,6

C2621 Pacemaker, other than single or dual chamber (implantable)
MED: 100-4,3,10.4; 100-4,4,61.1
AHA: 4Q,'03,8; 1Q,'01,6

C2622 Prosthesis, penile, noninflatable
MED: 100-4,4,61.1
AHA: 4Q,'03,8; 3Q,'02,5; 1Q,'01,6

C2625 Stent, noncoronary, temporary, with delivery system
MED: 100-4,4,61.1
AHA: 4Q,'03,8; 3Q,'02,5; 1Q,'01,6

C2626 Infusion pump, nonprogrammable, temporary (implantable)
MED: 100-4,4,61.1
AHA: 3Q,'02,5; 1Q,'01,6

C2627 Catheter, suprapubic/cystoscopic
MED: 100-4,4,61.1
AHA: 4Q,'03,8; 3Q,'02,5; 1Q,'01,5

C2628 Catheter, occlusion
MED: 100-4,4,61.1
AHA: 4Q,'03,8; 3Q,'02,5; 1Q,'01,5

C2629 Introducer/sheath, other than guiding, intracardiac electrophysiological, laser
MED: 100-4,4,61.1
AHA: 3Q,'02,5; 1Q,'01,6

C2630 Catheter, electrophysiology, diagnostic/ablation, other than 3D or vector mapping, cool-tip
MED: 100-4,4,61.1
AHA: 3Q,'02,5; 1Q,'01,5

C2631 Repair device, urinary, incontinence, without sling graft
MED: 100-4,4,61.1
AHA: 4Q,'03,8; 3Q,'02,5; 1Q,'01,6

C2634 Brachytherapy source, nonstranded, high activity, iodine-125, greater than 1.01 mCi (NIST), per source
MED: 100-4,4,61.1
AHA: 2Q,'05,8

C2635 Brachytherapy source, nonstranded, high activity, palladium-103, greater than 2.2 mCi (NIST), per source
MED: 100-4,4,61.1
AHA: 2Q,'05,8

C2636 Brachytherapy linear source, nonstranded, palladium-103, per 1 mm
MED: 100-4,4,61.1

C2637 Brachytherapy source, nonstranded, ytterbium-169, per source
AHA: 3Q,'05,7

C2638 Brachytherapy source, stranded, iodine-125, per source

C2639 Brachytherapy source, nonstranded, iodine-125, per source

C2640 Brachytherapy source, stranded, palladium-103, per source

C2641 Brachytherapy source, nonstranded, palladium-103, per source

C2642 Brachytherapy source, stranded, cesium-131, per source

C2643 Brachytherapy source, nonstranded, cesium-131, per source

C2698 Brachytherapy source, stranded, not otherwise specified, per source

C2699 Brachytherapy source, nonstranded, not otherwise specified, per source

C8900 Magnetic resonance angiography with contrast, abdomen

C8901 Magnetic resonance angiography without contrast, abdomen

C8902 Magnetic resonance angiography without contrast followed by with contrast, abdomen

C8903 Magnetic resonance imaging with contrast, breast; unilateral

C8904 Magnetic resonance imaging without contrast, breast; unilateral

C8905 Magnetic resonance imaging without contrast followed by with contrast, breast; unilateral

C8906 Magnetic resonance imaging with contrast, breast; bilateral

C8907 Magnetic resonance imaging without contrast, breast; bilateral

C8908 Magnetic resonance imaging without contrast followed by with contrast, breast; bilateral

C8909 Magnetic resonance angiography with contrast, chest (excluding myocardium)

C8910 Magnetic resonance angiography without contrast, chest (excluding myocardium)

C8911 Magnetic resonance angiography without contrast followed by with contrast, chest (excluding myocardium)

C8912 Magnetic resonance angiography with contrast, lower extremity

C8913 Magnetic resonance angiography without contrast, lower extremity

C8914 Magnetic resonance angiography without contrast followed by with contrast, lower extremity

C8918 Magnetic resonance angiography with contrast, pelvis
AHA: 4Q,'03,4

C8919 Magnetic resonance angiography without contrast, pelvis
AHA: 4Q,'03,4

C8920 Magnetic resonance angiography without contrast followed by with contrast, pelvis
AHA: 4Q,'03,4

C8921 Transthoracic echocardiography with contrast, or without contrast followed by with contrast, for congenital cardiac anomalies; complete

C8922 Transthoracic echocardiography with contrast, or without contrast followed by with contrast, for congenital cardiac anomalies; follow-up or limited study

C8923 Transthoracic echocardiography with contrast, or without contrast followed by with contrast, real-time with image documentation (2D) with or without M-mode recording; complete

C8924 Transthoracic echocardiography with contrast, or without contrast followed by with contrast, real-time with image documentation (2D) with or without M-mode recording; follow-up or limited study

C8925 Transesophageal echocardiography (TEE) with contrast, or without contrast followed by with contrast, real time with image documentation (2D) (with or without M-mode recording); including probe placement, image acquisition, interpretation and report

C8926 Transesophageal echocardiography (TEE) with contrast, or without contrast followed by with contrast, for congenital cardiac anomalies; including probe placement, image acquisition, interpretation and report

C8927 Transesophageal echocardiography (TEE) with contrast, or without contrast followed by with contrast, for monitoring purposes, including probe placement, real time 2-dimensional image acquisition and interpretation leading to ongoing (continuous) assessment of (dynamically changing) cardiac pumping function and to therapeutic measures on an immediate time basis

C8928 Transthoracic echocardiography with contrast, or without contrast followed by with contrast, real-time with image documentation (2D), with or without M-mode recording, during rest and cardiovascular stress test using treadmill, bicycle exercise and/or pharmacologically induced stress, with interpretation and report

C8929 Transthoracic echocardiography with contrast, or without contrast followed by with contrast, real-time with image documentation (2D), includes M-mode recording, when performed, complete, with spectral doppler echocardiography, and with color flow doppler echocardiography

C8930 Transthoracic echocardiography, with contrast, or without contrast followed by with contrast, real-time with image documentation (2D), includes M-mode recording, when performed, during rest and cardiovascular stress test using treadmill, bicycle exercise and/or pharmacologically induced stress, with interpretation and report; including performance of continuous electrocardiographic monitoring, with physician supervision

C8957 Intravenous infusion for therapy/diagnosis; initiation of prolonged infusion (more than 8 hours), requiring use of portable or implantable pump
MED: 100-4,4,230.2.1; 100-4,4,230.2.3

C9113 Injection, pantoprazole sodium, per vial
Use this code for Protonix.

C9121 Injection, argatroban, per 5 mg

C9245 Injection, romiplostim, 10 mcg
Use this code for Nplate

C9246 Injection, gadoxetate disodium, per ml
Use this code for Eovist

C9247 Iobenguane, I-123, diagnostic, per study dose, up to 10 millicuries

C9248 Injection, clevidipine butyrate, 1 mg
Use this code for Cleviprex

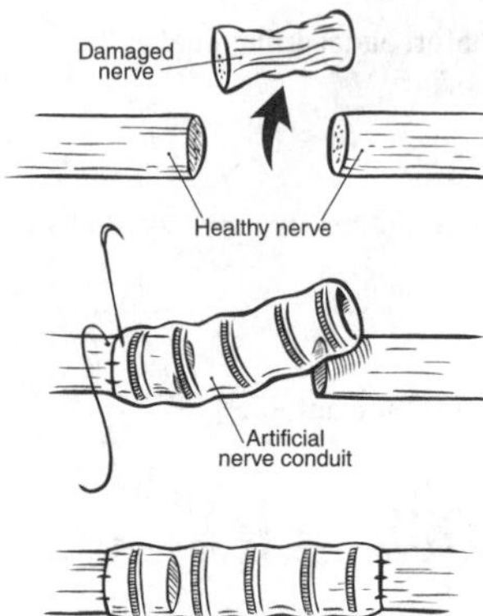

A synthetic "bridge" is affixed to each end of a severed nerve with sutures
This procedure is performed using an operating microscope

C9352 Microporous collagen implantable tube (NeuraGen Nerve Guide), per cm length

C9353 Microporous collagen implantable slit tube (NeuraWrap Nerve Protector), per cm length

C9354 Acellular pericardial tissue matrix of nonhuman origin (Veritas), per sq cm

C9355 Collagen nerve cuff (NeuroMatrix), per 0.5 cm length

C9356 Tendon, porous matrix of cross-linked collagen and glycosaminoglycan matrix (TenoGlide Tendon Protector Sheet), per sq cm

C9358 Dermal substitute, native, nondenatured collagen (SurgiMend Collagen Matrix), per 0.5 square cm

C9359 Porous purified collagen matrix bone void filler (Integra Mozaik Osteoconductive Scaffold Putty, Integra OS Osteoconductive Scaffold Putty), per 0.5 cc

C9399 Unclassified drugs or biologicals

C9716 Creations of thermal anal lesions by radiofrequency energy

C9724 Endoscopic full-thickness plication in the gastric cardia using endoscopic plication system (EPS); includes endoscopy

C9725 Placement of endorectal intracavitary applicator for high intensity brachytherapy
AHA: 3Q,'05,7

C9726 Placement and removal (if performed) of applicator into breast for radiation therapy

C9727 Insertion of implants into the soft palate; minimum of 3 implants

C9728 Placement of interstitial device(s) for radiation therapy/surgery guidance (e.g., fiducial markers, dosimeter), other than prostate (any approach), single or multiple

C9898 Radiolabeled product provided during a hospital inpatient stay

C9899 Implanted prosthetic device, payable only for inpatients who do not have inpatient coverage

DENTAL PROCEDURES D0000-D9999

The D, or dental, codes are a separate category of national codes. The Current Dental Terminology code set is copyrighted by the American Dental Association (ADA). CDT is included in HCPCS Level II. Decisions regarding the modification, deletion, or addition of CDT codes are made by the ADA and not the national panel responsible for the administration of HCPCS.

The Department of Health and Human Services has an agreement with the AMA pertaining to the use of the CPT codes for physician services; it also has an agreement with the ADA to include as a set of HCPCS Level II codes for use in billing for dental services.

Please refer to you CPT book for possible alternate code(s).

DIAGNOSTIC D0100-D0999

CLINICAL ORAL EVALUATION

D0120 **Periodic oral evaluation — established patient**
This procedure is covered if its purpose is to identify a patient's existing infections prior to kidney transplantation.

D0140 **Limited oral evaluation — problem focused**

D0145 **Oral evaluation for a patient under 3 years of age and counseling with primary caregiver**

D0150 **Comprehensive oral evaluation — new or established patient**
This procedure is covered if its purpose is to identify a patient's existing infections prior to kidney transplantation.
MED: 100-2,15,150; 100-2,16,140; 100-3,260.6

D0160 **Detailed and extensive oral evaluation — problem focused, by report**
Pertinent documentation to evaluate medical appropriateness should be included when this code is reported.

D0170 **Re-evaluation, limited, problem-focused (established patient, not postoperative visit)**

D0180 **Comprehensive periodontal evaluation — new or established patient**

RADIOGRAPHS

D0210 **Intraoral, complete series (including bitewings)**

D0220 **Intraoral, periapical, first film**

D0230 **Intraoral, periapical, each additional film**

D0240 **Intraoral — occlusal film**
MED: 100-2,15,150; 100-2,16,140

D0250 **Extraoral, first film**
MED: 100-2,15,150; 100-2,16,140

D0260 **Extraoral, each additional film**
MED: 100-2,15,150; 100-2,16,140

D0270 **Bitewing, single film**
MED: 100-2,15,150; 100-2,16,140

D0272 **Bitewings, 2 films**
MED: 100-2,15,150; 100-2,16,140

D0273 **Bitewings, 3 films**

D0274 **Bitewings, 4 films**
MED: 100-2,15,150; 100-2,16,140

D0277 **Vertical bitewings - 7 to 8 films**
MED: 100-2,15,150; 100-2,16,140

D0290 **Posterior-anterior or lateral skull and facial bone survey film**

D0310 **Sialography**

D0320 **Temporomandibular joint arthrogram, including injection**

D0321 **Other temporomandibular joint films, by report**

D0322 **Tomographic survey**
MED: 100-3,260.6

D0330 **Panoramic film**

D0340 **Cephalometric film**

D0350 **Oral/facial photographic images**
This code excludes conventional radiographs.

D0360 **Cone beam CT — craniofacial data capture**

D0362 **Cone beam, 2-dimensional image reconstruction using existing data, includes multiple images**

D0363 **Cone beam, 3-dimensional image reconstruction using existing data, includes multiple images**

TEST AND LABORATORY EXAMINATIONS

D0415 **Collection of microorganisms for culture and sensitivity**
This procedure is covered if its purpose is to identify a patient's existing infections prior to kidney transplantation.
See code(s): D0410

D0416 **Viral culture**

D0417 **Collection and preparation of saliva sample for laboratory diagnostic testing**

D0418 **Analysis of saliva sample**

D0421 **Genetic test for susceptibility to oral diseases**

D0425 **Caries susceptibility tests**
This procedure is covered by Medicare if its purpose is to identify a patient's existing infections prior to kidney transplantation.

D0431 **Adjunctive prediagnostic test that aids in detection of mucosal abnormalities including premalignant and malignant lesions, not to include cytology or biopsy procedures**

D0460 **Pulp vitality tests**
This procedure is covered by Medicare if its purpose is to identify a patient's existing infections prior to kidney transplantation.
MED: 100-2,15,150; 100-2,16,140; 100-3,260.6

D0470 **Diagnostic casts**

D0472 **Accession of tissue, gross examination, preparation, and transmission of written report**
MED: 100-2,15,150; 100-2,16,140; 100-3,260.6

D0473 **Accession of tissue, gross and microscopic examination, preparation and transmission of written report**
MED: 100-2,15,150; 100-2,16,140; 100-3,260.6

D0474 **Accession of tissue, gross and microscopic examination, including assessment of surgical margins for presence of disease, preparation and transmission of written report**
MED: 100-2,15,150; 100-2,16,140; 100-3,260.6

D0475 **Decalcification procedure**

D0476 **Special stains for microorganisms**

D0477 **Special stains, not for microorganisms**

D0478 **Immunohistochemical stains**

D0479 **Tissue in-situ hybridization, including interpretation**

D0480 **Accession of exfoliative cytologic smears, microscopic examination, preparation and transmission of written report**
MED: 100-2,15,150; 100-2,16,140; 100-3,260.6

D0481 **Electron microscopy - diagnostic**

D0482 **Direct immunofluorescence**

D0483 **Indirect immunofluorescence**

D0484 **Consultation on slides prepared elsewhere**

D0485 **Consultation, including preparation of slides from biopsy material supplied by referring source**

D0486 Laboratory accession of brush biopsy sample, microscopic examination, preparation and transmission of written report

D0502 Other oral pathology procedures, by report
Pertinent documentation to evaluate medical appropriateness should be included when this code is reported. This procedure is covered by Medicare if its purpose is to identify a patient's existing infections prior to kidney transplantation.
MED: 100-2,15,150; 100-2,16,140; 100-3,260.6

D0999 Unspecified diagnostic procedure, by report
Determine if an alternative HCPCS Level II or a CPT code better describes the service being reported. This code should be used only if a more specific code is unavailable.
MED: 100-2,15,150; 100-2,16,140; 100-3,260.6

PREVENTIVE D1000-D1999

DENTAL PROPHYLAXIS

D1110 Prophylaxis, adult

D1120 Prophylaxis, child

TOPICAL FLUORIDE TREATMENT (OFFICE PROCEDURE)

D1203 Topical application of fluoride, child

D1204 Topical application of fluoride, adult

D1206 Topical fluoride varnish; therapeutic application for moderate to high caries risk patients

OTHER PREVENTIVE SERVICES

D1310 Nutritional counseling for the control of dental disease
MED: 100-2,16,10

D1320 Tobacco counseling for the control and prevention of oral disease
MED: 100-2,16,10

D1330 Oral hygiene instruction
MED: 100-2,16,10

D1351 Sealant, per tooth

SPACE MAINTENANCE (PASSIVE APPLIANCES)

D1510 Space maintainer, fixed unilateral
MED: 100-2,16,140

D1515 Space maintainer, fixed bilateral
MED: 100-2,15,150; 100-2,16,140

D1520 Space maintainer, removable unilateral
MED: 100-2,15,150; 100-2,16,140

D1525 Space maintainer, removable bilateral
MED: 100-2,15,150; 100-2,16,140

D1550 Recementation of space maintainer
MED: 100-2,15,150; 100-2,16,140

D1555 Removal of fixed space maintainer

D2140 Amalgam—one surface, primary or permanent

D2150 Amalgam, 2 surfaces, primary or permanent

D2160 Amalgam, 3 surfaces, primary or permanent

D2161 Amalgam, 4 or more surfaces, primary or permanent

RESIN RESTORATIONS

D2330 Resin, one surface, anterior

D2331 Resin, 2 surfaces, anterior

D2332 Resin, 3 surfaces, anterior

D2335 Resin, 4 or more surfaces or involving incisal angle (anterior)

D2390 Resin-based composite crown, anterior

D2391 Resin-based composite — one surface, posterior

D2392 Resin-based composite, 2 surfaces, posterior

D2393 Resin-based composite, 3 surfaces, posterior

D2394 Resin-based composite, 4 or more surfaces, posterior

GOLD FOIL RESTORATIONS

D2410 Gold foil, one surface

D2420 Gold foil, 2 surfaces

D2430 Gold foil, 3 surfaces

INLAY/ONLAY RESTORATIONS

D2510 Inlay, metallic, one surface

D2520 Inlay, metallic, 2 surfaces

D2530 Inlay, metallic, 3 or more surfaces

D2542 Onlay, metallic, 2 surfaces

D2543 Onlay, metallic, 3 surfaces

D2544 Onlay, metallic, 4 or more surfaces

D2610 Inlay, porcelain/ceramic, one surface

D2620 Inlay, porcelain/ceramic, 2 surfaces

D2630 Inlay, porcelain/ceramic, 3 or more surfaces

D2642 Onlay, porcelain/ceramic, 2 surfaces

D2643 Onlay, porcelain/ceramic, 3 surfaces

D2644 Onlay, porcelain/ceramic, 4 or more surfaces

D2650 Inlay — resin-based composite — one surface

D2651 Inlay, resin-based composite, 2 surfaces

D2652 Inlay, resin-based composite, 3 or more surfaces

D2662 Onlay, resin-based composite, 2 surfaces

D2663 Onlay, resin-based composite, 3 surfaces

D2664 Onlay, resin-based composite, 4 or more surfaces

CROWNS - SINGLE RESTORATION ONLY

D2710 Crown — resin-based composite (indirect)

D2712 Crown — 3/4 resin-based composite (indirect)

D2720 Crown, resin with high noble metal

D2721 Crown, resin with predominantly base metal

D2722 Crown, resin with noble metal

D2740 Crown, porcelain/ceramic substrate

D2750 Crown, porcelain fused to high noble metal

D2751 Crown — porcelain fused to predominantly base metal

D2752 Crown, porcelain fused to noble metal

D2780 Crown — 3/4 cast high noble metal

D2781 Crown - 3/4 cast predominantly base metal

D2782 Crown — 3/4 cast noble metal

D2783 Crown - 3/4 porcelain/ceramic

D2790 Crown, full cast high noble metal

D2791 Crown, full cast predominantly base metal

D2792 Crown, full cast noble metal

D2794 Crown, titanium

D2799 Provisional crown
Do not use this code to report a temporary crown for routine prosthetic restoration.

OTHER RESTORATIVE SERVICES

D2910 Recement inlay, onlay or partial coverage restoration

D2915 Recement cast or prefabricated post and core

D2920 Recement crown

D2930 Prefabricated stainless steel crown, primary tooth

D2931 Prefabricated stainless steel crown, permanent tooth

D2932 Prefabricated resin crown

D2933 Prefabricated stainless steel crown with resin window

D2934 Prefabricated esthetic coated stainless steel crown - primary tooth

D2940 Sedative filling

D2950 Core buildup, including any pins

D2951 Pin retention, per tooth, in addition to restoration

D2952 Post and core in addition to crown, indirectly fabricated

D2953 Each additional indirectly fabricated post — same tooth
Report in addition to code D2952.

D2954 Prefabricated post and core in addition to crown

D2955 Post removal (not in conjunction with endodontic therapy)

D2957 Each additional prefabricated post — same tooth
Report in addition to code D2954.

D2960 Labial veneer (laminate)-chairside

D2961 Labial veneer (resin laminate), laboratory

D2962 Labial veneer (porcelain laminate), laboratory

D2970 Temporary crown (fractured tooth)

D2971 Additional procedures to construct new crown under existing partial denture framework

D2975 Coping

D2980 Crown repair, by report
Pertinent documentation to evaluate medical appropriateness should be included when this code is reported.

D2999 Unspecified restorative procedure, by report
Determine if an alternative HCPCS Level II or a CPT code better describes the service being reported. This code should be used only if a more specific code is unavailable.
MED: 100-2,15,150; 100-2,16,140

ENDODONTICS D3000-D3999

PULP CAPPING

D3110 Pulp cap, direct (excluding final restoration)

D3120 Pulp cap, indirect (excluding final restoration)

PULPOTOMY

D3220 Therapeutic pulpotomy (excluding final restoration), removal of pulp coronal to the dentinocemental junction and application of medicament
Do not use this code to report the first stage of root canal therapy.

D3221 Pulpal debridement, primary and permanent teeth

D3222 Partial pulpotomy for apexogenesis, permanent tooth with incomplete root development

PULPAL THERAPY ON PRIMARY TEETH (INCLUDES PRIMARY TEETH WITH SUCCEDANEOUS TEETH AND PLACEMENT OF RESORBABLE FILLING)

D3230 Pulpal therapy (resorbable filling), anterior, primary tooth (excluding final restoration)

D3240 Pulpal therapy (resorbable filling), posterior, primary tooth (excluding final restoration)

ROOT CANAL THERAPY (INCLUDING TREATMENT PLAN, CLINICAL PROCEDURES, AND FOLLOW-UP CARE, INCLUDES PRIMARY TEETH WITHOUT SUCCEDANEOUS TEETH AND PERMANENT TEETH)

D3310 Endodontic therapy, anterior tooth (excluding final restoration)

D3320 Endodontic therapy, bicuspid tooth (excluding final restoration)

D3330 Endodontic therapy, molar (excluding final restoration)

D3331 Treatment of root canal obstruction; nonsurgical access

D3332 Incomplete endodontic therapy; inoperable, unrestorable or fractured tooth

D3333 Internal root repair of perforation defects

D3346 Retreatment of previous root canal therapy, anterior

D3347 Retreatment of previous root canal therapy, bicuspid

D3348 Retreatment of previous root canal therapy, molar

D3351 Apexification/recalcification, initial visit (apical closure/calcific repair of perforations, root resorption, etc.)

D3352 Apexification/recalcification, interim medication replacement (apical closure/calcific repair of perforations, root resorption, etc.)

D3353 Apexification/recalcification, final visit (includes completed root canal therapy, apical closure/calcific repair of perforations, root resorption, etc.)

APICOECTOMY/PERIRADICULAR SERVICES

D3410 Apicoectomy/periradicular surgery, anterior

D3421 Apicoectomy/periradicular surgery, bicuspid (first root)

D3425 Apicoectomy/periradicular surgery, molar (first root)

D3426 Apicoectomy/periradicular surgery (each additional root)

D3430 Retrograde filling, per root

D3450 Root amputation, per root

D3460 Endodontic endosseous implant
MED: 100-2,15,150; 100-2,16,140

D3470 Intentional replantation (including necessary splinting)

OTHER ENDODONTIC PROCEDURES

D3910 Surgical procedure for isolation of tooth with rubber dam

D3920 Hemisection (including any root removal), not including root canal therapy

D3950 Canal preparation and fitting of preformed dowel or post

D3999 Unspecified endodontic procedure, by report
Determine if an alternative HCPCS Level II or a CPT code better describes the service being reported. This code should be used only if a more specific code is unavailable.
MED: 100-2,15,150; 100-2,16,140

PERIODONTICS D4000-D4999

SURGICAL SERVICES (INCLUDING USUAL POSTOPERATIVE SERVICES)

D4210 Gingivectomy or gingivoplasty, 4 or more contiguous teeth or tooth bounded spaces per quadrant

D4211 Gingivectomy or gingivoplasty, 1 to 3 contiguous teeth or tooth bounded spaces per quadrant

D4230 Anatomical crown exposure, 4 or more contiguous teeth per quadrant

D4231 Anatomical crown exposure, 1 to 3 teeth per quadrant

D4240 Gingival flap procedure, including root planing, 4 or more contiguous teeth or tooth bounded spaces per quadrant

D4241 Gingival flap procedure, including root planing, 1 to 3 contiguous teeth or tooth bounded spaces per quadrant

D4245 Apically positioned flap

D4249 Clinical crown lengthening, hard tissue

D4260 Osseous surgery (including flap entry and closure), 4 or more contiguous teeth or tooth bounded spaces per quadrant

MED: 100-2,15,150; 100-2,16,140

D4261 Osseous surgery (including flap entry and closure), 1 to 3 contiguous teeth or tooth bounded spaces per quadrant

D4263 Bone replacement graft — first site in quadrant

MED: 100-2,15,150; 100-2,16,140; 100-3,260.6

D4264 Bone replacement graft — each additional site in quadrant

MED: 100-2,15,150; 100-2,16,140; 100-3,260.6

D4265 Biologic materials to aid in soft and osseous tissue regeneration

D4266 Guided tissue regeneration — resorbable barrier, per site

D4267 Guided tissue regeneration, nonresorbable barrier, per site (includes membrane removal)

D4268 Surgical revision procedure, per tooth

MED: 100-2,15,150; 100-2,16,140

D4270 Pedicle soft tissue graft procedure

MED: 100-2,15,150; 100-2,16,140

D4271 Free soft tissue graft procedure (including donor site surgery)

MED: 100-2,15,150; 100-2,16,140

D4273 Subepithelial connective tissue graft procedures, per tooth

MED: 100-2,15,150; 100-2,16,140; 100-3,260.6

D4274 Distal or proximal wedge procedure (when not performed in conjunction with surgical procedures in the same anatomical area)

D4275 Soft tissue allograft

D4276 Combined connective tissue and double pedicle graft, per tooth

ADJUNCTIVE PERIODONTAL SERVICES

D4320 Provisional splinting, intracoronal

D4321 Provisional splinting, extracoronal

D4341 Periodontal scaling and root planing, 4 or more teeth per quadrant

D4342 Periodontal scaling and root planing, 1 to 3 teeth, per quadrant

D4355 Full mouth debridement to enable comprehensive evaluation and diagnosis

This procedure is covered by Medicare if its purpose is to identify a patient's existing infections prior to kidney transplantation.

MED: 100-2,15,150; 100-2,16,140; 100-3,260.6

D4381 Localized delivery of antimicrobial agents via a controlled release vehicle into diseased crevicular tissue, per tooth, by report

Pertinent documentation to evaluate medical appropriateness should be included when this code is reported.

MED: 100-2,15,150; 100-2,16,140; 100-3,260.6

OTHER PERIODONTAL SERVICES

D4910 Periodontal maintenance

D4920 Unscheduled dressing change (by someone other than treating dentist)

D4999 Unspecified periodontal procedure, by report

Determine if an alternative HCPCS Level II or a CPT code better describes the service being reported. This code should be used only if a more specific code is unavailable.

PROSTHODONTICS (REMOVABLE) D5000-D5899

COMPLETE DENTURES (INCLUDING ROUTINE POST DELIVERY CARE)

D5110 Complete denture — maxillary

D5120 Complete denture — mandibular

D5130 Immediate denture — maxillary

D5140 Immediate denture — mandibular

PARTIAL DENTURES (INCLUDING ROUTINE POST DELIVERY CARE)

D5211 Upper partial denture - resin base (including any conventional clasps, rests and teeth)

D5212 Lower partial denture - resin base (including any conventional clasps, rests and teeth)

D5213 Maxillary partial denture — cast metal framework with resin denture bases (including any conventional clasps, rests and teeth)

D5214 Mandibular partial denture, cast metal framework with resin denture bases (including any conventional clasps, rests, and teeth)

D5225 Maxillary partial denture - flexible base (including any clasps, rests and teeth)

D5226 Mandibular partial denture — flexible base (including any clasps, rests and teeth)

D5281 Removable unilateral partial denture, 1 piece cast metal (including clasps and teeth)

ADJUSTMENTS TO REMOVABLE PROSTHESES

D5410 Adjust complete denture — maxillary

D5411 Adjust complete denture — mandibular

D5421 Adjust partial denture — maxillary

D5422 Adjust partial denture — mandibular

REPAIRS TO COMPLETE DENTURES

D5510 Repair broken complete denture base

D5520 Replace missing or broken teeth, complete denture (each tooth)

REPAIRS TO PARTIAL DENTURES

D5610 Repair resin denture base

D5620 Repair cast framework

D5630 Repair or replace broken clasp

D5640 Replace broken teeth, per tooth

D5650 Add tooth to existing partial denture

D5660 Add clasp to existing partial denture

D5670 Replace all teeth and acrylic on cast metal framework (maxillary)

D5671 Replace all teeth and acrylic on cast metal framework (mandibular)

DENTURE REBASE PROCEDURES

D5710 Rebase complete maxillary denture

D5711 Rebase complete mandibular denture

D5720 Rebase maxillary partial denture

D5721 Rebase mandibular partial denture

DENTURE RELINE PROCEDURES

D5730 Reline complete maxillary denture (chairside)

D5731 Reline lower complete mandibular denture (chairside)

D5740 Reline maxillary partial denture (chairside)

D5741 Reline mandibular partial denture (chairside)

D5750 Reline complete maxillary denture (laboratory)

D5751 Reline complete mandibular denture (laboratory)

D5760 Reline maxillary partial denture (laboratory)

D5761 Reline mandibular partial denture (laboratory)

OTHER REMOVABLE PROSTHETIC SERVICES

D5810 Interim complete denture (maxillary)

D5811 Interim complete denture (mandibular)

D5820 Interim partial denture (maxillary)

D5821 Interim partial denture (mandibular)

D5850 Tissue conditioning, maxillary

D5851 Tissue conditioning, mandibular

D5860 Overdenture, complete, by report
Pertinent documentation to evaluate medical appropriateness should be included when this code is reported.

D5861 Overdenture, partial, by report
Pertinent documentation to evaluate medical appropriateness should be included when this code is reported.

D5862 Precision attachment, by report
Pertinent documentation to evaluate medical appropriateness should be included when this code is reported.

D5867 Replacement of replaceable part of semi-precision or precision attachment (male or female component)

D5875 Modification of removable prosthesis following implant surgery

D5899 Unspecified removable prosthodontic procedure, by report
Determine if an alternative HCPCS Level II or a CPT code better describes the service being reported. This code should be used only if a more specific code is unavailable.

MAXILLOFACIAL PROSTHETICS D5900-D5999

D5911 Facial moulage (sectional)
MED: 100-2,15,120; 100-2,15,150

D5912 Facial moulage (complete)
MED: 100-2,15,120

D5913 Nasal prosthesis

D5914 Auricular prosthesis

D5915 Orbital prosthesis
See code(s): L8611

D5916 Ocular prosthesis
See code(s): V2623, V2629

D5919 Facial prosthesis

D5922 Nasal septal prosthesis

D5923 Ocular prosthesis, interim

D5924 Cranial prosthesis

D5925 Facial augmentation implant prosthesis

D5926 Nasal prosthesis, replacement

D5927 Auricular prosthesis, replacement

D5928 Orbital prosthesis, replacement

D5929 Facial prosthesis, replacement

D5931 Obturator prosthesis, surgical

D5932 Obturator prosthesis, definitive

D5933 Obturator prosthesis, modification

D5934 Mandibular resection prosthesis with guide flange

D5935 Mandibular resection prosthesis without guide flange

D5936 Obturator/prosthesis, interim

D5937 Trismus appliance (not for TM treatment)
MED: 100-2,15,120

D5951 Feeding aid
MED: 100-2,15,120; 100-2,16,140

D5952 Speech aid prosthesis, pediatric

D5953 Speech aid prosthesis, adult

D5954 Palatal augmentation prosthesis

D5955 Palatal lift prosthesis, definitive

D5958 Palatal lift prosthesis, interim

D5959 Palatal lift prosthesis, modification

D5960 Speech aid prosthesis, modification

D5982 Surgical stent

D5983 Radiation carrier
MED: 100-2,15,150; 100-2,16,140

D5984 Radiation shield
MED: 100-2,15,150; 100-2,16,140

D5985 Radiation cone locator
MED: 100-2,15,150; 100-2,16,140

D5986 Fluoride gel carrier

D5987 Commissure splint
MED: 100-2,15,150; 100-2,16,140; 100-4,4,240

D5988 Surgical splint
MED: 100-4,4,240

D5991 Topical medicament carrier

D5999 Unspecified maxillofacial prosthesis, by report
Determine if an alternative HCPCS Level II or a CPT code better describes the service being reported. This code should be used only if a more specific code is unavailable.

IMPLANT SERVICES D6000-D6199

D6010 Surgical placement of implant body: endosteal implant

D6012 Surgical placement of interim implant body for transitional prosthesis: endosteal implant

D6040 Surgical placement: eposteal implant

D6050 Surgical placement: transosteal implant

D6053 Implant/abutment supported removable denture for completely edentulous arch
MED: 100-2,15,150

D6054 Implant/abutment supported removable denture for partially edentulous arch
MED: 100-2,15,150

D6055 Dental implant supported connecting bar
MED: 100-2,15,150

D6056 Prefabricated abutment - includes placement
MED: 100-2,15,150

D6057 Custom abutment — includes placement
MED: 100-2,15,150

D6058 Abutment supported porcelain/ceramic crown
MED: 100-2,15,150

D6059 Abutment supported porcelain fused to metal crown (high noble metal)
MED: 100-2,15,150

D6060 Abutment supported porcelain fused to metal crown (predominantly base metal)
MED: 100-2,15,150

D6061 Abutment supported porcelain fused to metal crown (noble metal)
MED: 100-2,15,150

D6062 Abutment supported cast metal crown (high noble metal)
MED: 100-2,15,150

D6063 Abutment supported cast metal crown (predominantly base metal)
MED: 100-2,15,150

D6064 Abutment supported cast metal crown (noble metal)
MED: 100-2,15,150

D6065 Implant supported porcelain/ceramic crown
MED: 100-2,15,150

D6066 Implant supported porcelain fused to metal crown (titanium, titanium alloy, high noble metal)
MED: 100-2,15,150

D6067 Implant supported metal crown (titanium, titanium alloy, high noble metal)
MED: 100-2,15,150

D6068 Abutment supported retainer for porcelain/ceramic FPD
MED: 100-2,15,150

D6069 Abutment supported retainer for porcelain fused to metal FPD (high noble metal)
MED: 100-2,15,150

D6070 Abutment supported retainer for porcelain fused to metal FPD (predominantly base metal)
MED: 100-2,15,150

D6071 Abutment supported retainer for porcelain fused to metal FPD (noble metal)
MED: 100-2,15,150

D6072 Abutment supported retainer for cast metal FPD (high noble metal)
MED: 100-2,15,150

D6073 Abutment supported retainer for cast metal FPD (predominantly base metal)
MED: 100-2,15,150

D6074 Abutment supported retainer for cast metal FPD (noble metal)
MED: 100-2,15,150

D6075 Implant supported retainer for ceramic FPD
MED: 100-2,15,150

D6076 Implant supported retainer for porcelain fused to metal FPD (titanium, titanium alloy, or high noble metal)
MED: 100-2,15,150

D6077 Implant supported retainer for cast metal FPD (titanium, titanium alloy, or high noble metal)
MED: 100-2,15,150

D6078 Implant/abutment supported fixed denture for completely edentulous arch
MED: 100-2,15,150

D6079 Implant/abutment supported fixed denture for partially edentulous arch
MED: 100-2,15,150

D6080 Implant maintenance procedures, including removal of prosthesis, cleansing of prosthesis and abutments, reinsertion of prosthesis
MED: 100-2,15,150

D6090 Repair implant-supported prosthesis, by report
Pertinent documentation to evaluate medical appropriateness should be included when this code is reported.

D6091 Replacement of semi-precision or precision attachment (male or female component) of implant/abutment supported prosthesis, per attachment

D6092 Recement implant/abutment supported crown

D6093 Recement implant/abutment supported fixed partial denture

D6094 Abutment supported crown - (titanium)

D6095 Repair implant abutment, by report
Pertinent documentation to evaluate medical appropriateness should be included when this code is reported.

D6100 Implant removal, by report
Pertinent documentation to evaluate medical appropriateness should be included when this code is reported.

D6190 Radiographic/surgical implant index, by report

D6194 Abutment supported retainer crown for FPD - (titanium)

D6199 Unspecified implant procedure, by report

D6205 Pontic — indirect resin based composite

PROSTHODONTICS (FIXED) D6200-D6999

FIXED PARTIAL DENTURE PONTICS

D6210 Pontic, cast high noble metal
Each abutment and each pontic constitute a unit in a prosthesis. An alloy of at least 60 percent gold (Au), palladium (Pd), or platinum (Pt) is considered a high noble metal.

D6211 Pontic, cast predominantly base metal
Each abutment and each pontic constitute a unit in a prosthesis. An alloy of less than 25 percent gold (Au), palladium (Pd), or platinum (Pt) is considered a high noble metal.

D6212 Pontic, cast noble metal
Each abutment and each pontic constitute a unit in a prosthesis. An alloy of at least 25 percent gold (Au), palladium (Pd), or platinum (Pt) is considered a high noble metal.

D6214 Pontic — titanium

D6240 Pontic, porcelain fused to high noble metal
Each abutment and each pontic constitute a unit in a prosthesis. An alloy of at least 60 percent gold (Au), palladium (Pd), or platinum (Pt) is considered a high noble metal.

D6241 Pontic, porcelain fused to predominantly base metal
Each abutment and each pontic constitute a unit in a prosthesis. An alloy of less than 25 percent gold (Au), palladium (Pd), or platinum (Pt) is considered a high noble metal.

D6242 Pontic, porcelain fused to noble metal
Each abutment and each pontic constitute a unit in a prosthesis. An alloy of at least 60 percent gold (Au), palladium (Pd), or platinum (Pt) is considered a high noble metal.

D6245 Pontic — porcelain/ceramic
MED: 100-2,15,150

D6250 Pontic, resin with high noble metal
Each abutment and each pontic constitute a unit in a prosthesis. An alloy of at least 60 percent gold (Au), palladium (Pd), or platinum (Pt) is considered a high noble metal.

D6251 Pontic, resin with predominantly base metal
Each abutment and each pontic constitute a unit in a prosthesis. An alloy of less than 25 percent gold (Au), palladium (Pd), or platinum (Pt) is considered a high noble metal.

D6252 Pontic, resin with noble metal
Each abutment and each pontic constitute a unit in a prosthesis. An alloy of at least 25 percent gold (Au), palladium (Pd), or platinum (Pt) is considered a high noble metal.

D6253 Provisional pontic

D6545 Retainer, cast metal for resin bonded fixed prosthesis

D6548 Retainer — porcelain/ceramic for resin bonded fixed prosthesis
MED: 100-2,15,150

D6600 Inlay, porcelain/ceramic, 2 surfaces
MED: 100-2,15,150

D6601 Inlay, porcelain/ceramic, 3 or more surfaces
MED: 100-2,15,150

D6602 Inlay, cast high noble metal, 2 surfaces
MED: 100-2,15,150

D6603 Inlay, cast high noble metal, 3 or more surfaces
MED: 100-2,15,150

D6604 Inlay, cast predominantly base metal, 2 surfaces
MED: 100-2,15,150

D6605 Inlay, cast predominantly base metal, 3 or more surfaces
MED: 100-2,15,150

D6606 Inlay, cast noble metal, 2 surfaces
MED: 100-2,15,150

D6607 Inlay, cast noble metal, 3 or more surfaces
MED: 100-2,15,150

D6608 Onlay, porcelain/ceramic, 2 surfaces
MED: 100-2,15,150

D6609 Onlay, porcelain/ceramic, 3 or more surfaces
MED: 100-2,15,150

D6610 Onlay, cast high noble metal, 2 surfaces
MED: 100-2,15,150

D6611 Onlay, cast high noble metal, 3 or more surfaces
MED: 100-2,15,150

D6612 Onlay, cast predominantly base metal, 2 surfaces
MED: 100-2,15,150

D6613 Onlay, cast predominantly base metal, 3 or more surfaces
MED: 100-2,15,150

D6614 Onlay, cast noble metal, 2 surfaces
MED: 100-2,15,150

D6615 Onlay, cast noble metal, 3 or more surfaces
MED: 100-2,15,150

D6624 Inlay — titanium

D6634 Onlay — titanium

D6710 Crown — indirect resin based composite

FIXED PARTIAL DENTURE RETAINERS - CROWNS

D6720 Crown, resin with high noble metal
An alloy of at least 60 percent gold (Au), palladium (Pd), or platinum (Pt) is considered a high noble metal.

D6721 Crown, resin with predominantly base metal
An alloy of less than 25 percent gold (Au), palladium (Pd), or platinum (Pt) is considered a base metal.

D6722 Crown, resin with noble metal
An alloy of at least 25 percent gold (Au), palladium (Pd), or platinum (Pt) is considered a noble metal.

D6740 Crown — porcelain/ceramic
MED: 100-2,15,150

D6750 Crown, porcelain fused to high noble metal
An alloy of at least 60 percent gold (Au), palladium (Pd), or platinum (Pt) is considered a high noble metal.

D6751 Crown, porcelain fused to predominantly base metal
An alloy of less than 25 percent gold (Au), palladium (Pd), or platinum (Pt) is considered a base metal.

D6752 Crown, porcelain fused to noble metal
An alloy of at least 25 percent gold (Au), palladium (Pd), or platinum (Pt) is considered a noble metal.

D6780 Crown, 3/4 cast high noble metal
An alloy of at least 60 percent gold (Au), palladium (Pd), or platinum (Pt) is considered a high noble metal.

D6781 Crown - 3/4 cast predominantly base metal
An alloy of less than 25 percent gold (Au), palladium (Pd), or platinum (Pt) is considered a base metal.
MED: 100-2,15,150

D6782 Crown — 3/4 cast noble metal
An alloy of at least 25 percent gold (Au), palladium (Pd), or platinum (Pt) is considered a noble metal.
MED: 100-2,15,150

D6783 Crown — 3/4 porcelain/ceramic
MED: 100-2,15,150

D6790 Crown, full cast high noble metal
An alloy of at least 60 percent gold (Au), palladium (Pd), or platinum (Pt) is considered a high noble metal.

D6791 Crown, full cast predominantly base metal
An alloy of less than 25 percent gold (Au), palladium (Pd), or platinum (Pt) is considered a base metal.

D6792 Crown, full cast noble metal
An alloy of at least 25 percent gold (Au), palladium (Pd), or platinum (Pt) is considered a noble metal.

D6793 Provisional retainer crown

D6794 Crown — titanium

OTHER FIXED PARTIAL DENTURE SERVICES

D6920 Connector bar
MED: 100-2,15,150; 100-2,16,140; 100-3,260.6

D6930 Recement bridge

D6940 Stress breaker

D6950 Precision attachment

D6970 Post and core in addition to fixed partial denture retainer, indirectly fabricated

D6972 Prefabricated post and core in addition to bridge retainer

D6973 Core build up for retainer, including any pins

D6975 Coping, metal

D6976 Each additional indirectly fabricated post — same tooth
Report this code in addition to codes D6970.
MED: 100-2,15,150

D6977 Each additional prefabricated post — same tooth
Report this code in addition to code D6972.
MED: 100-2,15,150

D6980 Bridge repair, by report
Pertinent documentation to evaluate medical appropriateness should be included when this code is reported.

D6985 Pediatric partial denture, fixed

D6999 Unspecified fixed prosthodontic procedure, by report
Determine if an alternative HCPCS Level II or a CPT code better describes the service being reported. This code should be used only if a more specific code is unavailable.

SURGICAL EXTRACTIONS (INCLUDES LOCAL ANESTHESIA AND ROUTINE POSTOPERATIVE CARE)

D7111 Extraction, coronal remnants — deciduous tooth
MED: 100-2,16,140

D7140 Extraction, erupted tooth or exposed root (elevation and/or forceps removal)
MED: 100-2,16,140

D7210 Surgical removal of erupted tooth requiring elevation of mucoperiosteal flap and removal of bone and/or section of tooth
MED: 100-2,15,150; 100-2,16,140

D7220 Removal of impacted tooth, soft tissue
MED: 100-2,15,150; 100-2,16,140

D7230 Removal of impacted tooth, partially bony
MED: 100-2,15,150; 100-2,16,140

D7240 Removal of impacted tooth, completely bony
MED: 100-2,15,150; 100-2,16,140

D7241 Removal of impacted tooth, completely bony, with unusual surgical complications
MED: 100-2,15,150; 100-2,16,140

D7250 Surgical removal of residual tooth roots (cutting procedure)
MED: 100-2,15,150; 100-2,16,140

OTHER SURGICAL PROCEDURES

D7260 Oral antral fistula closure
MED: 100-2,15,150; 100-2,16,140

D7261 Primary closure of a sinus perforation
See equivalent CPT code for repair of mucous membranes.
MED: 100-2,16,140

D7270 Tooth reimplantation and/or stabilization of accidentally evulsed or displaced tooth

D7272 Tooth transplantation (includes reimplantation from one site to another and splinting and/or stabilization)

D7280 Surgical access of an unerupted tooth

D7282 Mobilization of erupted or malpositioned tooth to aid eruption

D7283 Placement of device to facilitate eruption of impacted tooth

D7285 Biopsy of oral tissue — hard (bone, tooth)

D7286 Biopsy of oral tissue — soft

D7287 Exfoliative cytological sample collection

D7288 Brush biopsy — transepithelial sample collection

D7290 Surgical repositioning of teeth

D7291 Transseptal fiberotomy/supra crestal fiberotomy, by report
Pertinent documentation to evaluate medical appropriateness should be included when this code is reported.
MED: 100-2,15,150; 100-2,16,140

D7292 Surgical placement: temporary anchorage device (screw retained plate) requiring surgical flap

D7293 Surgical placement: temporary anchorage device requiring surgical flap

D7294 Surgical placement: temporary anchorage device without surgical flap

ALVEOLOPLASTY - SURGICAL PREPARATION OF RIDGE FOR DENTURES

D7310 Alveoloplasty in conjunction with extractions, 4 or more teeth or tooth spaces, per quadrant

D7311 Alveoloplasty in conjunction with extractions, 1 to 3 teeth or tooth spaces, per quadrant

D7320 Alveoloplasty not in conjunction with extractions, 4 or more teeth or tooth spaces, per quadrant

D7321 Alveoloplasty not in conjunction with extractions, 1 to 3 teeth or tooth spaces, per quadrant

VESTIBULOPLASTY

D7340 Vestibuloplasty, ridge extension (second epithelialization)

D7350 Vestibuloplasty, ridge extension (including soft tissue grafts, muscle re-attachments, revision of soft tissue attachment, and management of hypertrophied and hyperplastic tissue)

SURGICAL EXCISION OF REACTIVE INFLAMMATORY LESIONS (SCAR TISSUE OR LOCALIZED CONGENITAL LESIONS)

D7410 Excision of benign lesion up to 1.25 cm

D7411 Excision of benign lesion greater than 1.25 cm

D7412 Excision of benign lesion, complicated

D7413 Excision of malignant lesion up to 1.25 cm

D7414 Excision of malignant lesion greater than 1.25 cm

D7415 Excision of malignant lesion, complicated

D7440 Excision of malignant tumor, lesion diameter up to 1.25 cm

D7441 Excision of malignant tumor, lesion diameter greater than 1.25 cm

D7450 Removal of benign odontogenic cyst or tumor — lesion diameter up to 1.25 cm

D7451 Removal of benign odontogenic cyst or tumor, lesion diameter greater than 1.25 cm

D7460 Removal of benign nonodontogenic cyst or tumor, lesion diameter up to 1.25 cm

D7461 Removal of benign nonodontogenic cyst or tumor, lesion diameter greater than 1.25 cm

D7465 Destruction of lesion(s) by physical or chemical methods, by report
Pertinent documentation to evaluate medical appropriateness should be included when this code is reported.

D7471 Removal of lateral exostosis (maxilla or mandible)

D7472 Removal of torus palatinus

D7473 Removal of torus mandibularis

D7485 Surgical reduction of osseous tuberosity

D7490 Radical resection of maxilla or mandible

SURGICAL INCISION

D7510 Incision and drainage of abscess, intraoral soft tissue

D7511 Incision and drainage of abscess — intraoral soft tissue — complicated (includes drainage of multiple fascial spaces)

D7520 Incision and drainage of abscess, extraoral soft tissue

D7521 Incision and drainage of abscess — extraoral soft tissue — complicated (includes drainage of multiple fascial spaces)

D7530 Removal of foreign body from mucosa, skin, or subcutaneous alveolar tissue

D7540 Removal of reaction-producing foreign bodies, musculoskeletal system

D7550 Partial ostectomy/sequestrectomy for removal of nonvital bone

D7560 Maxillary sinusotomy for removal of tooth fragment or foreign body

TREATMENT OF FRACTURES - SIMPLE

D7610 Maxilla, open reduction (teeth immobilized if present)

D7620 Maxilla, closed reduction (teeth immobilized if present)

D7630 Mandible, open reduction (teeth immobilized if present)

D7640 Mandible, closed reduction (teeth immobilized if present)

D7650 Malar and/or zygomatic arch, open reduction

D7660 Malar and/or zygomatic arch, closed reduction

D7670 Alveolus - closed reduction, may include stabilization of teeth

D7671 Alveolus - open reduction, may include stabilization of teeth

D7680 Facial bones, complicated reduction with fixation and multiple surgical approaches

TREATMENT OF FRACTURES - COMPOUND

D7710 Maxilla, open reduction

D7720 Maxilla, closed reduction

D7730 Mandible, open reduction

D7740 Mandible, closed reduction

D7750 Malar and/or zygomatic arch, open reduction

D7760 Malar and/or zygomatic arch, closed reduction

D7770 Alveolus — open reduction stabilization of teeth

D7771 Alveolus, closed reduction stabilization of teeth

D7780 Facial bones, complicated reduction with fixation and multiple surgical approaches

REDUCTION OF DISLOCATION AND MANAGEMENT OF OTHER TEMPOROMANDIBULAR JOINT DYSFUNCTIONS

Procedures which are an integral part of a primary procedure should not be reported separately.

D7810 Open reduction of dislocation

D7820 Closed reduction of dislocation

D7830 Manipulation under anesthesia

D7840 Condylectomy

D7850 Surgical discectomy; with/without implant

D7852 Disc repair

D7854 Synovectomy

D7856 Myotomy

D7858 Joint reconstruction

D7860 Arthrotomy

MED: 100-2,15,150; 100-2,16,140

D7865 Arthroplasty

D7870 Arthrocentesis

D7871 Nonarthroscopic lysis and lavage

D7872 Arthroscopy, diagnosis, with or without biopsy

D7873 Arthroscopy, surgical: lavage and lysis of adhesions

D7874 Arthroscopy, surgical: disc repositioning and stabilization

D7875 Arthroscopy, surgical: synovectomy

D7876 Arthroscopy, surgical: discectomy

D7877 Arthroscopy, surgical: debridement

D7880 Occlusal orthotic appliance

D7899 Unspecified TMD therapy, by report

Determine if an alternative HCPCS Level II or a CPT code better describes the service being reported. This code should be used only if a more specific code is unavailable.

REPAIR OF TRAUMATIC WOUNDS

D7910 Suture of recent small wounds up to 5 cm

COMPLICATED SUTURING (RECONSTRUCTION REQUIRING DELICATE HANDLING OF TISSUES AND WIDE UNDERMINING FOR METICULOUS CLOSURE)

D7911 Complicated suture, up to 5 cm

D7912 Complicated suture, greater than 5 cm

OTHER REPAIR PROCEDURES

D7920 Skin graft (identify defect covered, location, and type of graft)

D7940 Osteoplasty, for orthognathic deformities

MED: 100-2,15,150; 100-2,16,140

D7941 Osteotomy — mandibular rami

D7943 Osteotomy — mandibular rami with bone graft; includes obtaining the graft

D7944 Osteotomy-segmented or subapical

D7945 Osteotomy, body of mandible

D7946 LeFort I (maxilla, total)

D7947 LeFort I (maxilla, segmented)

D7948 LeFort II or LeFort III (osteoplasty of facial bones for midface hypoplasia or retrusion), without bone graft

D7949 LeFort II or LeFort III, with bone graft

D7950 Osseous, osteoperiosteal, or cartilage graft of the mandible or maxilla, autogenous or nonautogenous, by report

Pertinent documentation to evaluate medical appropriateness should be included when this code is reported.

D7951 Sinus augmentation with bone or bone substitutes

D7953 Bone replacement graft for ridge preservation - per site

D7955 Repair of maxillofacial soft and/or hard tissue defect

D7960 Frenulectomy (frenectomy or frenotomy), separate procedure

D7963 Frenuloplasty

D7970 Excision of hyperplastic tissue, per arch

D7971 Excision of pericoronal gingiva

D7972 Surgical reduction of fibrous tuberosity

D7980 Sialolithotomy

D7981 Excision of salivary gland, by report

Pertinent documentation to evaluate medical appropriateness should be included when this code is reported.

D7982 Sialodochoplasty

D7983 Closure of salivary fistula

D7990 Emergency tracheotomy

D7991 Coronoidectomy

D7995 Synthetic graft, mandible or facial bones, by report

Pertinent documentation to evaluate medical appropriateness should be included when this code is reported.

D7996 Implant, mandible for augmentation purposes (excluding alveolar ridge), by report

Pertinent documentation to evaluate medical appropriateness should be included when this code is reported.

D7997 Appliance removal (not by dentist who placed appliance), includes removal of archbar

D7998 Intraoral placement of a fixation device not in conjunction with a fracture

D7999 Unspecified oral surgery procedure, by report

Determine if an alternative HCPCS Level II or a CPT code better describes the service being reported. This code should be used only if a more specific code is unavailable.

ORTHODONTICS D8000-D8999

D8010 Limited orthodontic treatment of the primary dentition

D8020 Limited orthodontic treatment of the transitional dentition

D8030 Limited orthodontic treatment of the adolescent dentition

D8040 Limited orthodontic treatment of the adult dentition

D8050 Interceptive orthodontic treatment of the primary dentition

D8060 Interceptive orthodontic treatment of the transitional dentition

D8070 Comprehensive orthodontic treatment of the transitional dentition

D8080 Comprehensive orthodontic treatment of the adolescent dentition

D8090 Comprehensive orthodontic treatment of the adult dentition

MINOR TREATMENT TO CONTROL HARMFUL HABITS

D8210 Removable appliance therapy

D8220 Fixed appliance therapy

OTHER ORTHODONTIC SERVICES

D8660 Orthodontic treatment (alternative billing to a contract fee)

D8670 Periodic orthodontic treatment visit (as part of contract)

D8680 Orthodontic retention (removal of appliances, construction and placement of retainer(s))

D8690 Orthodontic treatment (alternative billing to a contract fee)

D8691 Repair of orthodontic appliance

D8692 Replacement of lost or broken retainer

D8693 Rebonding or recementing; and/or repair, as required, of fixed retainers

D8999 Unspecified orthodontic procedure, by report
Determine if an alternative HCPCS Level II or a CPT code better describes the service being reported. This code should be used only if a more specific code is unavailable.

ADJUNCTIVE GENERAL SERVICES D9110-D9999

UNCLASSIFIED TREATMENT

D9110 Palliative (emergency) treatment of dental pain-minor procedures
MED: 100-2,15,150; 100-2,16,140

D9120 Fixed partial denture sectioning

ANESTHESIA

D9210 Local anesthesia not in conjunction with operative or surgical procedures

D9211 Regional block anesthesia

D9212 Trigeminal division block anesthesia

D9215 Local anesthesia

D9220 Deep sedation/general anesthesia, first 30 minutes

D9221 Deep sedation/general anesthesia, each additional 15 minutes
MED: 100-2,15,150; 100-2,16,140

D9230 Analgesia, anxiolysis, inhalation of nitrous oxide
MED: 100-2,15,150; 100-2,16,140

D9241 Intravenous conscious sedation/analgesia — first 30 minutes

D9242 Intravenous conscious sedation/analgesia — each additional 15 minutes

D9248 Nonintravenous conscious sedation

PROFESSIONAL CONSULTATION

D9310 Consultation, diagnostic service provided by dentist or physician other than requesting dentist or physician

PROFESSIONAL VISITS

D9410 House/extended care facility call

D9420 Hospital call

D9430 Office visit for observation (during regularly scheduled hours), no other services performed

D9440 Office visit, after regularly scheduled hours

D9450 Case presentation, detailed and extensive treatment planning

DRUGS

D9610 Therapeutic parenteral drug, single administration
Pertinent documentation to evaluate medical appropriateness should be included when this code is reported.

D9612 Therapeutic parenteral drugs, 2 or more administrations, different medications

D9630 Other drugs and/or medicaments, by report
Determine if an alternative HCPCS Level II or a CPT code better describes the service being reported. This code should be used only if a more specific code is unavailable.
MED: 100-2,15,150; 100-2,16,140

MISCELLANEOUS SERVICES

D9910 Application of desensitizing medicament

D9911 Application of desensitizing resin for cervical and/or root surface, per tooth

D9920 Behavior management, by report
Pertinent documentation to evaluate medical appropriateness should be included when this code is reported.

D9930 Treatment of complications (postsurgical) — unusual circumstances, by report
MED: 100-2,15,150; 100-2,16,140

D9940 Occlusal guards, by report
Pertinent documentation to evaluate medical appropriateness should be included when this code is reported.
MED: 100-2,15,150; 100-2,16,140

D9941 Fabrication of athletic mouthguard

D9942 Repair and/or reline of occlusal guard

D9950 Occlusion analysis, mounted case
MED: 100-2,15,150; 100-2,16,140

D9951 Occlusal adjustment, limited
MED: 100-2,15,150; 100-2,16,140

D9952 Occlusal adjustment, complete
MED: 100-2,15,150; 100-2,16,140

D9970 Enamel microabrasion

D9971 Odontoplasty 1-2 teeth; includes removal of enamel projections

D9972 External bleaching — per arch

D9973 External bleaching — per tooth

D9974 Internal bleaching — per tooth

D9999 Unspecified adjunctive procedure, by report
Determine if an alternative HCPCS Level II or a CPT code better describes the service being reported. This code should be used only if a more specific code is unavailable.

DURABLE MEDICAL EQUIPMENT E0100-E9999

E codes include durable medical equipment such as canes, crutches, walkers, commodes, decubitus care, bath and toilet aids, hospital beds, oxygen and related respiratory equipment, monitoring equipment, pacemakers, patient lifts, safety equipment, restraints, traction equipment, fracture frames, wheelchairs, and artificial kidney machines.

CANES

E0100 Cane, includes canes of all materials, adjustable or fixed, with tip
White canes for the blind are not covered under Medicare.
MED: 100-2,15,110.1; 100-3,280.1; 100-3,280.2

E0105 Cane, quad or 3-prong, includes canes of all materials, adjustable or fixed, with tips
MED: 100-2,15,110.1; 100-3,280.1; 100-3,280.5

CRUTCHES

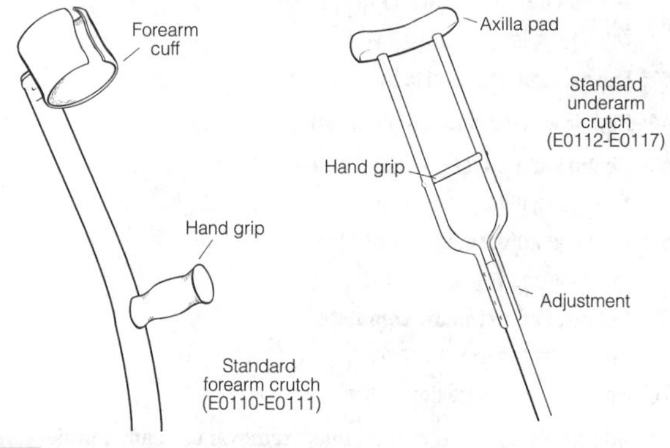

E0110 Crutches, forearm, includes crutches of various materials, adjustable or fixed, pair, complete with tips and handgrips
MED: 100-2,15,110.1; 100-3,280.1

E0111 Crutch, forearm, includes crutches of various materials, adjustable or fixed, each, with tip and handgrips
MED: 100-2,15,110.1; 100-3,280.1

E0112 Crutches, underarm, wood, adjustable or fixed, pair, with pads, tips, and handgrips
MED: 100-2,15,110.1; 100-3,280.1

E0113 Crutch, underarm, wood, adjustable or fixed, each, with pad, tip, and handgrip
MED: 100-2,15,110.1; 100-3,280.1

E0114 Crutches, underarm, other than wood, adjustable or fixed, pair, with pads, tips, and handgrips
MED: 100-2,15,110.1; 100-3,280.1

E0116 Crutch, underarm, other than wood, adjustable or fixed, with pad, tip, handgrip, with or without shock absorber, each
MED: 100-2,15,110.1; 100-3,280.1

E0117 Crutch, underarm, articulating, spring assisted, each
MED: 100-2,15,110.1

E0118 Crutch substitute, lower leg platform, with or without wheels, each
Medicare covers walkers if patient's ambulation is impaired.

ATTACHMENTS

E0153 Platform attachment, forearm crutch, each

E0154 Platform attachment, walker, each

E0155 Wheel attachment, rigid pick-up walker, per pair

E0156 Seat attachment, walker

E0157 Crutch attachment, walker, each

E0158 Leg extensions for walker, per set of 4

E0159 Brake attachment for wheeled walker, replacement, each

COMMODES

E0160 Sitz type bath or equipment, portable, used with or without commode
Medicare covers sitz baths if medical record indicates that the patient has an infection or injury of the perineal area and the sitz bath is prescribed by the physician.
MED: 100-3,280.1

E0161 Sitz type bath or equipment, portable, used with or without commode, with faucet attachment(s)
Medicare covers sitz baths if medical record indicates that the patient has an infection or injury of the perineal area and the sitz bath is prescribed by the physician.
MED: 100-3,280.1

E0162 Sitz bath chair
Medicare covers sitz baths if medical record indicates that the patient has an infection or injury of the perineal area and the sitz bath is prescribed by the physician.
MED: 100-3,280.1

E0163 Commode chair, mobile or stationary, with fixed arms
Medicare covers commodes for patients confined to their beds or rooms, for patients without indoor bathroom facilities, and to patients who cannot climb or descend the stairs necessary to reach the bathrooms in their homes.
MED: 100-2,15,110.1; 100-3,280.1

E0165 Commode chair, mobile or stationary, with detachable arms
Medicare covers commodes for patients confined to their beds or rooms, for patients without indoor bathroom facilities, and to patients who cannot climb or descend the stairs necessary to reach the bathrooms in their homes.
MED: 100-2,15,110.1; 100-3,280.1

E0167 Pail or pan for use with commode chair, replacement only
Medicare covers commodes for patients confined to their beds or rooms, for patients without indoor bathroom facilities, and to patients who cannot climb or descend the stairs necessary to reach the bathrooms in their homes.
MED: 100-3,280.1

E0168 Commode chair, extra wide and/or heavy-duty, stationary or mobile, with or without arms, any type, each

E0170 Commode chair with integrated seat lift mechanism, electric, any type

E0171 Commode chair with integrated seat lift mechanism, nonelectric, any type

E0172 Seat lift mechanism placed over or on top of toilet, any type

E0175 Footrest, for use with commode chair, each

DECUBITUS CARE EQUIPMENT

E0181 Powered pressure reducing mattress overlay/pad, alternating, with pump, includes heavy-duty
Medicare covers pads if physicians supervise their use in patients who have decubitus ulcers or susceptibility to them. Prior authorization is required by Medicare for this item.
MED: 100-3,280.1; 100-8,5,5.2.3

E0182 Pump for alternating pressure pad, for replacement only
Medicare covers pads if physicians supervise their use in patients who have decubitus ulcers or susceptibility to them. Prior authorization is required by Medicare for this item.
MED: 100-3,280.1; 100-8,5,5.2.3

E0184 Dry pressure mattress
Medicare covers pads if physicians supervise their use in patients who have decubitus ulcers or susceptibility to them. Prior authorization is required by Medicare for this item.
MED: 100-3,280.1; 100-8,5,5.2.3

E0185 Gel or gel-like pressure pad for mattress, standard mattress length and width
Medicare covers pads if physicians supervise their use in patients who have decubitus ulcers or susceptibility to them. Prior authorization is required by Medicare for this item.
MED: 100-3,280.1; 100-8,5,5.2.3

E0186 Air pressure mattress
Medicare covers pads if physicians supervise their use in patients who have decubitus ulcers or susceptibility to them.
MED: 100-3,280.1

E0187 Water pressure mattress
Medicare covers pads if physicians supervise their use in patients who have decubitus ulcers or susceptibility to them.
MED: 100-3,280.1

E0188 Synthetic sheepskin pad
Medicare covers pads if physicians supervise their use in patients who have decubitus ulcers or susceptibility to them. Prior authorization is required by Medicare for this item.
MED: 100-3,280.1; 100-8,5,5.2.3

E0189 Lambswool sheepskin pad, any size
Medicare covers pads if physicians supervise their use in patients who have decubitus ulcers or susceptibility to them. Prior authorization is required by Medicare for this item.
MED: 100-3,280.1; 100-8,5,5.2.3

E0190 Positioning cushion/pillow/wedge, any shape or size, includes all components and accessories
MED: 100-2,15,110.1

E0191 Heel or elbow protector, each

E0193 Powered air flotation bed (low air loss therapy)

E0194 Air fluidized bed
An air fluidized bed is covered by Medicare if the patient has a stage 3 or stage 4 pressure sore and, without the bed, would require institutionalization. A physician's prescription is required.
MED: 100-3,280.8

E0196 Gel pressure mattress
Medicare covers pads if physicians supervise their use in patients who have decubitus ulcers or susceptibility to them.
MED: 100-3,280.1

E0197 Air pressure pad for mattress, standard mattress length and width
Medicare covers pads if physicians supervise their use in patients who have decubitus ulcers or susceptibility to them.
MED: 100-3,280.1

E0198 Water pressure pad for mattress, standard mattress length and width
Medicare covers pads if physicians supervise their use in patients who have decubitus ulcers or susceptibility to them.
MED: 100-3,280.1

E0199 Dry pressure pad for mattress, standard mattress length and width
Medicare covers pads if physicians supervise their use in patients who have decubitus ulcers or susceptibility to them.
MED: 100-3,280.1

HEAT/COLD APPLICATION

E0200 Heat lamp, without stand (table model), includes bulb, or infrared element
MED: 100-2,15,110.1; 100-3,280.1

E0202 Phototherapy (bilirubin) light with photometer

E0203 Therapeutic lightbox, minimum 10,000 lux, table top model

E0205 Heat lamp, with stand, includes bulb, or infrared element
MED: 100-2,15,110.1; 100-3,280.1

E0210 Electric heat pad, standard
MED: 100-3,280.1

E0215 Electric heat pad, moist
MED: 100-3,280.1

E0217 Water circulating heat pad with pump
MED: 100-3,280.1

E0218 Water circulating cold pad with pump
MED: 100-3,280.1

E0220 Hot water bottle

E0221 Infrared heating pad system
MED: 100-3,270.2

E0225 Hydrocollator unit, includes pads
MED: 100-2,15,230; 100-3,280.1

E0230 Ice cap or collar

E0231 Noncontact wound-warming device (temperature control unit, AC adapter and power cord) for use with warming card and wound cover
MED: 100-2,16,20

E0232 Warming card for use with the noncontact wound-warming device and noncontact wound-warming wound cover
MED: 100-2,16,20

E0235 Paraffin bath unit, portable (see medical supply code A4265 for paraffin)
MED: 100-2,15,230; 100-3,280.1

E0236 Pump for water circulating pad
MED: 100-3,280.1

E0238 Nonelectric heat pad, moist
MED: 100-3,280.1

E0239 Hydrocollator unit, portable
MED: 100-2,15,230; 100-3,280.1

BATH AND TOILET AIDS

E0240 Bath/shower chair, with or without wheels, any size
MED: 100-3,280.1

E0241 Bathtub wall rail, each
MED: 100-2,15,110.1; 100-3,280.1

E0242 Bathtub rail, floor base
MED: 100-2,15,110.1; 100-3,280.1

E0243 Toilet rail, each
MED: 100-2,15,110.1; 100-3,280.1

E0244 Raised toilet seat
MED: 100-3,280.1

E0245 Tub stool or bench
MED: 100-3,280.1

E0246 Transfer tub rail attachment

E0247 Transfer bench for tub or toilet with or without commode opening
MED: 100-3,280.1

E0248 Transfer bench, heavy-duty, for tub or toilet with or without commode opening
MED: 100-3,280.1

E0249 Pad for water circulating heat unit
MED: 100-3,280.1

HOSPITAL BEDS AND ACCESSORIES

E0250 Hospital bed, fixed height, with any type side rails, with mattress
MED: 100-2,15,110.1; 100-3,280.7

E0251 Hospital bed, fixed height, with any type side rails, without mattress
MED: 100-2,15,110.1; 100-3,280.7

E0255 Hospital bed, variable height, hi-lo, with any type side rails, with mattress
MED: 100-2,15,110.1; 100-3,280.7

E0256 Hospital bed, variable height, hi-lo, with any type side rails, without mattress
MED: 100-2,15,110.1; 100-3,280.7

E0260 Hospital bed, semi-electric (head and foot adjustment), with any type side rails, with mattress
MED: 100-2,15,110.1; 100-3,280.7

E0261 Hospital bed, semi-electric (head and foot adjustment), with any type side rails, without mattress
MED: 100-2,15,110.1; 100-3,280.7

E0265 Hospital bed, total electric (head, foot, and height adjustments), with any type side rails, with mattress
MED: 100-2,15,110.1; 100-3,280.7

E0266 Hospital bed, total electric (head, foot, and height adjustments), with any type side rails, without mattress
MED: 100-2,15,110.1; 100-3,280.7

E0270 Hospital bed, institutional type includes: oscillating, circulating and Stryker frame, with mattress
MED: 100-3,280.1

E0271 Mattress, innerspring
MED: 100-3,280.1; 100-3,280.7

E0272 Mattress, foam rubber
MED: 100-3,280.1; 100-3,280.7

E0273 Bed board
MED: 100-3,280.1

E0274 Over-bed table
MED: 100-3,280.1

E0275 Bed pan, standard, metal or plastic
Reusable, autoclavable bedpans are covered by Medicare for bed-confined patients.
MED: 100-3,280.1

E0276 Bed pan, fracture, metal or plastic
Reusable, autoclavable bedpans are covered by Medicare for bed-confined patients.
MED: 100-3,280.1

E0277 Powered pressure-reducing air mattress
MED: 100-3,280.1

E0280 Bed cradle, any type

E0290 Hospital bed, fixed height, without side rails, with mattress
MED: 100-2,15,110.1; 100-3,280.7

E0291 Hospital bed, fixed height, without side rails, without mattress
MED: 100-2,15,110.1; 100-3,280.7

E0292 Hospital bed, variable height, hi-lo, without side rails, with mattress
MED: 100-2,15,110.1; 100-3,280.7

E0293 Hospital bed, variable height, hi-lo, without side rails, without mattress
MED: 100-2,15,110.1; 100-3,280.7

E0294 Hospital bed, semi-electric (head and foot adjustment), without side rails, with mattress
MED: 100-2,15,110.1; 100-3,280.7

E0295 Hospital bed, semi-electric (head and foot adjustment), without side rails, without mattress
MED: 100-2,15,110.1; 100-3,280.7

E0296 Hospital bed, total electric (head, foot, and height adjustments), without side rails, with mattress
MED: 100-2,15,110.1; 100-3,280.7

E0297 Hospital bed, total electric (head, foot, and height adjustments), without side rails, without mattress
MED: 100-2,15,110.1; 100-3,280.7

E0300 Pediatric crib, hospital grade, fully enclosed

E0301 Hospital bed, heavy-duty, extra wide, with weight capacity greater than 350 pounds, but less than or equal to 600 pounds, with any type side rails, without mattress
MED: 100-3,280.7

E0302 Hospital bed, extra heavy-duty, extra wide, with weight capacity greater than 600 pounds, with any type side rails, without mattress
MED: 100-3,280.7

E0303 Hospital bed, heavy-duty, extra wide, with weight capacity greater than 350 pounds, but less than or equal to 600 pounds, with any type side rails, with mattress
MED: 100-3,280.7

E0304 Hospital bed, extra heavy-duty, extra wide, with weight capacity greater than 600 pounds, with any type side rails, with mattress
MED: 100-3,280.7

E0305 Bedside rails, half-length
MED: 100-3,280.7

E0310 Bedside rails, full-length
MED: 100-3,280.7

E0315 Bed accessory: board, table, or support device, any type
MED: 100-3,280.1

E0316 Safety enclosure frame/canopy for use with hospital bed, any type

E0325 Urinal; male, jug-type, any material
MED: 100-3,280.1

E0326 Urinal; female, jug-type, any material
MED: 100-3,280.1

E0328 Hospital bed, pediatric, manual, 360 degree side enclosures, top of headboard, footboard and side rails up to 24 inches above the spring, includes mattress

E0329 Hospital bed, pediatric, electric or semi-electric, 360 degree side enclosures, top of headboard, footboard and side rails up to 24 inches above the spring, includes mattress

E0350 Control unit for electronic bowel irrigation/evacuation system

E0352 Disposable pack (water reservoir bag, speculum, valving mechanism, and collection bag/box) for use with the electronic bowel irrigation/evacuation system

E0370 Air pressure elevator for heel

E0371 Nonpowered advanced pressure reducing overlay for mattress, standard mattress length and width

E0372 Powered air overlay for mattress, standard mattress length and width

E0373 Nonpowered advanced pressure reducing mattress

OXYGEN AND RELATED RESPIRATORY EQUIPMENT

E0424 Stationary compressed gaseous oxygen system, rental; includes container, contents, regulator, flowmeter, humidifier, nebulizer, cannula or mask, and tubing

For the first claim filed for home oxygen equipment or therapy, submit a certificate of medical necessity that includes the oxygen flow rate, anticipated frequency and duration of oxygen therapy, and physician signature. Medicare accepts oxygen therapy as medically necessary in cases documenting any of the following: erythocythemia with a hematocrit greater than 56 percent; a P pulmonale on EKG; or dependent edema consistent with congestive heart failure.

MED: 100-3,240.2

E0425 Stationary compressed gas system, purchase; includes regulator, flowmeter, humidifier, nebulizer, cannula or mask, and tubing

MED: 100-3,240.2

E0430 Portable gaseous oxygen system, purchase; includes regulator, flowmeter, humidifier, cannula or mask, and tubing

MED: 100-3,240.2

E0431 Portable gaseous oxygen system, rental; includes portable container, regulator, flowmeter, humidifier, cannula or mask, and tubing

MED: 100-3,240.2

E0434 Portable liquid oxygen system, rental; includes portable container, supply reservoir, humidifier, flowmeter, refill adaptor, contents gauge, cannula or mask, and tubing

MED: 100-3,240.2

E0435 Portable liquid oxygen system, purchase; includes portable container, supply reservoir, flowmeter, humidifier, contents gauge, cannula or mask, tubing and refill adaptor

MED: 100-3,240.2

E0439 Stationary liquid oxygen system, rental; includes container, contents, regulator, flowmeter, humidifier, nebulizer, cannula or mask, & tubing

MED: 100-3,240.2

E0440 Stationary liquid oxygen system, purchase; includes use of reservoir, contents indicator, regulator, flowmeter, humidifier, nebulizer, cannula or mask, and tubing

MED: 100-3,240.2

E0441 Oxygen contents, gaseous (for use with owned gaseous stationary systems or when both a stationary and portable gaseous system are owned), 1 month's supply = 1 unit

MED: 100-3,240.2

E0442 Oxygen contents, liquid (for use with owned liquid stationary systems or when both a stationary and portable liquid system are owned), 1 month's supply = 1 unit

MED: 100-3,240.2

E0443 Portable oxygen contents, gaseous (for use only with portable gaseous systems when no stationary gas or liquid system is used), 1 month's supply = 1 unit

MED: 100-3,240.2

E0444 Portable oxygen contents, liquid (for use only with portable liquid systems when no stationary gas or liquid system is used), 1 month's supply = 1 unit

MED: 100-3,240.2

E0445 Oximeter device for measuring blood oxygen levels noninvasively

E0450 Volume control ventilator, without pressure support mode, may include pressure control mode, used with invasive interface (e.g., tracheostomy tube)

MED: 100-3,280.1

E0455 Oxygen tent, excluding croup or pediatric tents

MED: 100-3,240.2

E0457 Chest shell (cuirass)

E0459 Chest wrap

E0460 Negative pressure ventilator; portable or stationary

MED: 100-3,280.1

E0461 Volume control ventilator, without pressure support mode, may include pressure control mode, used with noninvasive interface (e.g., mask)

MED: 100-3,280.1

E0462 Rocking bed, with or without side rails

E0463 Pressure support ventilator with volume control mode, may include pressure control mode, used with invasive interface (e.g., tracheostomy tube)

E0464 Pressure support ventilator with volume control mode, may include pressure control mode, used with noninvasive interface (e.g., mask)

E0470 Respiratory assist device, bi-level pressure capability, without backup rate feature, used with noninvasive interface, e.g., nasal or facial mask (intermittent assist device with continuous positive airway pressure device)

MED: 100-3,280.1

E0471 Respiratory assist device, bi-level pressure capability, with back-up rate feature, used with noninvasive interface, e.g., nasal or facial mask (intermittent assist device with continuous positive airway pressure device)

MED: 100-3,280.1

E0472 Respiratory assist device, bi-level pressure capability, with backup rate feature, used with invasive interface, e.g., tracheostomy tube (intermittent assist device with continuous positive airway pressure device)

MED: 100-3,280.1

E0480 Percussor, electric or pneumatic, home model

MED: 100-3,280.1

E0481 Intrapulmonary percussive ventilation system and related accessories

MED: 100-3,240.5

E0482 Cough stimulating device, alternating positive and negative airway pressure

E0483 High frequency chest wall oscillation air-pulse generator system, (includes hoses and vest), each

E0484 Oscillatory positive expiratory pressure device, nonelectric, any type, each

E0485 Oral device/appliance used to reduce upper airway collapsibility, adjustable or nonadjustable, prefabricated, includes fitting and adjustment

E0486 Oral device/appliance used to reduce upper airway collapsibility, adjustable or nonadjustable, custom fabricated, includes fitting and adjustment

E0487 Spirometer, electronic, includes all accessories

IPPB MACHINES

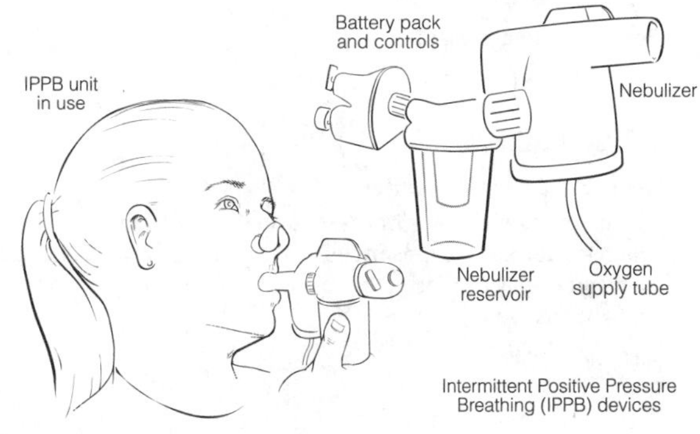

Intermittent Positive Pressure Breathing (IPPB) devices

E0500 IPPB machine, all types, with built-in nebulization; manual or automatic valves; internal or external power source

MED: 100-3,280.1

HUMIDIFIERS/COMPRESSORS/NEBULIZERS FOR USE WITH OXYGEN IPPB EQUIPMENT

E0550 Humidifier, durable for extensive supplemental humidification during IPPB treatments or oxygen delivery

MED: 100-3,280.1

E0555 Humidifier, durable, glass or autoclavable plastic bottle type, for use with regulator or flowmeter

MED: 100-3,280.1

E0560 Humidifier, durable for supplemental humidification during IPPB treatment or oxygen delivery

MED: 100-3,280.1

E0561 Humidifier, nonheated, used with positive airway pressure device

E0562 Humidifier, heated, used with positive airway pressure device

E0565 Compressor, air power source for equipment which is not self-contained or cylinder driven

E0570 Nebulizer, with compressor

MED: 100-3,280.1

E0571 Aerosol compressor, battery powered, for use with small volume nebulizer

MED: 100-3,280.1

E0572 Aerosol compressor, adjustable pressure, light duty for intermittent use

E0574 Ultrasonic/electronic aerosol generator with small volume nebulizer

E0575 Nebulizer, ultrasonic, large volume

MED: 100-3,280.1

E0580 Nebulizer, durable, glass or autoclavable plastic, bottle type, for use with regulator or flowmeter

MED: 100-3,280.1

E0585 Nebulizer, with compressor and heater

MED: 100-3,280.1

SUCTION PUMP/ROOM VAPORIZERS

E0600 Respiratory suction pump, home model, portable or stationary, electric

MED: 100-3,280.1

E0601 Continuous airway pressure (CPAP) device

MED: 100-3,240.4

E0602 Breast pump, manual, any type

E0603 Breast pump, electric (AC and/or DC), any type

E0604 Breast pump, hospital grade, electric (AC and/or DC), any type

E0605 Vaporizer, room type

MED: 100-3,280.1

E0606 Postural drainage board

MED: 100-3,280.1

MONITORING EQUIPMENT

E0607 Home blood glucose monitor

Medicare covers home blood testing devices for diabetic patients when the devices are prescribed by the patients' physicians. Many commercial payers provide this coverage to non-insulin dependent diabetics as well.

MED: 100.3,230.16

PACEMAKER MONITOR

E0610 Pacemaker monitor, self-contained, (checks battery depletion, includes audible and visible check systems)

MED: 100-3,20.8; 100-3,20.8.1; 100-3,20.8.2

E0615 Pacemaker monitor, self-contained, checks battery depletion and other pacemaker components, includes digital/visible check systems

MED: 100-3,20.8; 100-3,20.8.1; 100-3,20.8.2

E0616 Implantable cardiac event recorder with memory, activator, and programmer

E0617 External defibrillator with integrated electrocardiogram analysis

E0618 Apnea monitor, without recording feature

E0619 Apnea monitor, with recording feature

E0620 Skin piercing device for collection of capillary blood, laser, each

PATIENT LIFTS

E0621 Sling or seat, patient lift, canvas or nylon

MED: 100-3,280.1

E0625 Patient lift, bathroom or toilet, not otherwise classified

MED: 100-3,280.1

E0627 Seat lift mechanism incorporated into a combination lift-chair mechanism

MED: 100-3,280.4; 100-4,20,100; 100-4,20,130.2; 100-4,20,130.3; 100-4,20,130.4; 100-4,20,130.5

E0628 Separate seat lift mechanism for use with patient-owned furniture, electric

MED: 100-3,280.4; 100-4,20,100; 100-4,20,130.2; 100-4,20,130.3; 100-4,20,130.4; 100-4,20,130.5

E0629 Separate seat lift mechanism for use with patient-owned furniture, nonelectric

MED: 100-4,20,100; 100-4,20,130.2; 100-4,20,130.3; 100-4,20,130.4; 100-4,20,130.5

E0630 Patient lift, hydraulic or mechanical, includes any seat, sling, strap(s), or pad(s)

MED: 100-3,280.1

E0635 Patient lift, electric, with seat or sling

MED: 100-3,280.1

E0636 Multipositional patient support system, with integrated lift, patient accessible controls

E0637 Combination sit to stand system, any size including pediatric, with seatlift feature, with or without wheels

MED: 100-3,280.1

E0638 Standing frame system, one position (e.g., upright, supine, or prone stander), any size including pediatric, with or without wheels

MED: 100-3,280.1

E0639 Patient lift, moveable from room to room with disassembly and reassembly, includes all components/accessories

E0640 Patient lift, fixed system, includes all components/accessories

E0641 Standing frame system, multi-position (e.g., 3-way stander), any size including pediatric, with or without wheels

E0642 Standing frame system, mobile (dynamic stander), any size including pediatric

PNEUMATIC COMPRESSOR AND APPLIANCES

E0650 Pneumatic compressor, nonsegmental home model

MED: 100-3,280.6

E0651 Pneumatic compressor, segmental home model without calibrated gradient pressure

MED: 100-3,280.6

E0652 Pneumatic compressor, segmental home model with calibrated gradient pressure
MED: 100-3,280.6

E0655 Nonsegmental pneumatic appliance for use with pneumatic compressor, half arm
MED: 100-3,280.6

E0656 Segmental pneumatic appliance for use with pneumatic compressor, trunk

E0657 Segmental pneumatic appliance for use with pneumatic compressor, chest

E0660 Nonsegmental pneumatic appliance for use with pneumatic compressor, full leg
MED: 100-3,280.6

E0665 Nonsegmental pneumatic appliance for use with pneumatic compressor, full arm
MED: 100-3,280.6

E0666 Nonsegmental pneumatic appliance for use with pneumatic compressor, half leg
MED: 100-3,280.6

E0667 Segmental pneumatic appliance for use with pneumatic compressor, full leg
MED: 100-3,280.6

E0668 Segmental pneumatic appliance for use with pneumatic compressor, full arm
MED: 100-3,280.6

E0669 Segmental pneumatic appliance for use with pneumatic compressor, half leg
MED: 100-3,280.6

E0671 Segmental gradient pressure pneumatic appliance, full leg
MED: 100-3,280.6

E0672 Segmental gradient pressure pneumatic appliance, full arm
MED: 100-3,280.6

E0673 Segmental gradient pressure pneumatic appliance, half leg
MED: 100-3,280.6

E0675 Pneumatic compression device, high pressure, rapid inflation/deflation cycle, for arterial insufficiency (unilateral or bilateral system)

E0676 Intermittent limb compression device (includes all accessories), not otherwise specified

E0691 Ultraviolet light therapy system panel, includes bulbs/lamps, timer and eye protection, treatment area 2 sq ft or less

E0692 Ultraviolet light therapy system panel, includes bulbs/lamps, timer and eye protection, 4 ft panel

E0693 Ultraviolet light therapy system panel, includes bulbs/lamps, timer and eye protection, 6 ft panel

E0694 Ultraviolet multidirectional light therapy system in 6 ft cabinet, includes bulbs/lamps, timer, and eye protection

SAFETY EQUIPMENT

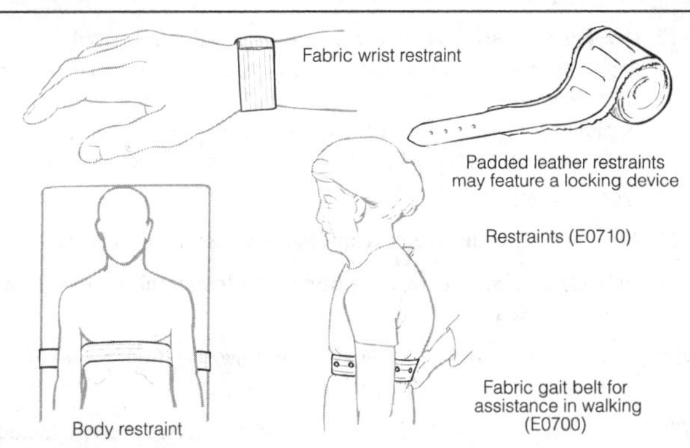

E0700 Safety equipment (e.g., belt, harness, or vest)

E0705 Transfer device, any type, each

RESTRAINTS

E0710 Restraints, any type (body, chest, wrist, or ankle)

TRANSCUTANEOUS AND/OR NEUROMUSCULAR ELECTRICAL NERVE STIMULATORS - TENS

E0720 Transcutaneous electrical nerve stimulation (TENS) device, 2 lead, localized stimulation
While TENS is covered when employed to control chronic pain, it is not covered for experimental treatment, as in motor function disorders like MS. Prior authorization is required by Medicare for this item.
MED: 100-3,40.5; 100-3,130.5; 100-3,130.6; 100-3,160.2; 100-3,160.7.1; 100-3,230.1; 100-8,5,5.2.3

E0730 Transcutaneous electrical nerve stimulation (TENS) device, 4 or more leads, for multiple nerve stimulation
While TENS is covered when employed to control chronic pain, it is not covered for experimental treatment, as in motor function disorders like MS. Prior authorization is required by Medicare for this item.
MED: 100-3,40.5; 100-3,130.5; 100-3,130.6; 100-3,160.2; 100-3,160.7.1; 100-3,230.1; 100-8,5,5.2.3

E0731 Form-fitting conductive garment for delivery of TENS or NMES (with conductive fibers separated from the patient's skin by layers of fabric)
MED: 100-3,160.13

E0740 Incontinence treatment system, pelvic floor stimulator, monitor, sensor, and/or trainer
MED: 100-3,230.8

E0744 Neuromuscular stimulator for scoliosis

E0745 Neuromuscular stimulator, electronic shock unit
MED: 100-3,160.12

E0746 Electromyography (EMG), biofeedback device
Biofeedback therapy is covered by Medicare only for re-education of specific muscles or for treatment of incapacitating muscle spasm or weakness. Medicare jurisdiction: local contractor.
MED: 100-3,30.1; 100-3,30.1.1

E0747 Osteogenesis stimulator, electrical, noninvasive, other than spinal applications
Medicare covers noninvasive osteogenic stimulation for nonunion of long bone fractures, failed fusion, or congenital pseudoarthroses.
MED: 100-3,150.2

E0748 Osteogenesis stimulator, electrical, noninvasive, spinal applications
Medicare covers noninvasive osteogenic stimulation as an adjunct to spinal fusion surgery for patients at high risk of pseudoarthroses due to previously failed spinal fusion, or for those undergoing fusion of three or more vertebrae.
MED: 100-3,150.2

E0749 Osteogenesis stimulator, electrical, surgically implanted
Medicare covers invasive osteogenic stimulation for nonunion of long bone fractures or as an adjunct to spinal fusion surgery for patients at high risk of pseudoarthroses due to previously failed spinal fusion, or for those undergoing fusion of three or more vertebrae.
MED: 100-3,150.2

E0755 Electronic salivary reflex stimulator (intraoral/noninvasive)

E0760 Osteogenesis stimulator, low intensity ultrasound, noninvasive
MED: 100-3,150.2

E0761 Nonthermal pulsed high frequency radiowaves, high peak power electromagnetic energy treatment device

E0762 Transcutaneous electrical joint stimulation device system, includes all accessories

E0764 Functional neuromuscular stimulation, transcutaneous stimulation of sequential muscle groups of ambulation with computer control, used for walking by spinal cord injured, entire system, after completion of training program

E0765 FDA approved nerve stimulator, with replaceable batteries, for treatment of nausea and vomiting

E0769 Electrical stimulation or electromagnetic wound treatment device, not otherwise classified
MED: 100-4,32,11.1

E0770 Functional electrical stimulator, transcutaneous stimulation of nerve and/or muscle groups, any type, complete system, not otherwise specified

INFUSION SUPPLIES

E0776 IV pole

E0779 Ambulatory infusion pump, mechanical, reusable, for infusion 8 hours or greater

E0780 Ambulatory infusion pump, mechanical, reusable, for infusion less than 8 hours

E0781 Ambulatory infusion pump, single or multiple channels, electric or battery operated, with administrative equipment, worn by patient
MED: 100-3,280.14

E0782 Infusion pump, implantable, nonprogrammable (includes all components, e.g., pump, catheter, connectors, etc.)
MED: 100-3,280.14

E0783 Infusion pump system, implantable, programmable (includes all components, e.g., pump, catheter, connectors, etc.)
MED: 100-3,280.14

E0784 External ambulatory infusion pump, insulin
Covered by some commercial payers with preauthorization.
MED: 100-3,280.14

E0785 Implantable intraspinal (epidural/intrathecal) catheter used with implantable infusion pump, replacement
Medicare jurisdiction: local contractor.
MED: 100-3,280.14

E0786 Implantable programmable infusion pump, replacement (excludes implantable intraspinal catheter)
Medicare jurisdiction: local contractor.
MED: 100-3,280.14

E0791 Parenteral infusion pump, stationary, single, or multichannel
MED: 100-2,15,120; 100-3,180.2; 100-4,20,100.2.2

TRACTION - ALL TYPES

E0830 Ambulatory traction device, all types, each
MED: 100-3,280.1

TRACTION - CERVICAL

E0840 Traction frame, attached to headboard, cervical traction
MED: 100-3,280.1

E0849 Traction equipment, cervical, free-standing stand/frame, pneumatic, applying traction force to other than mandible

E0850 Traction stand, freestanding, cervical traction
MED: 100-3,280.1

E0855 Cervical traction equipment not requiring additional stand or frame

E0856 Cervical traction device, cervical collar with inflatable air bladder

TRACTION - OVERDOOR

E0860 Traction equipment, overdoor, cervical
MED: 100-3,280.1

TRACTION - EXTREMITY

E0870 Traction frame, attached to footboard, extremity traction (e.g., Buck's)
MED: 100-3,280.1

E0880 Traction stand, freestanding, extremity traction (e.g., Buck's)
MED: 100-3,280.1

TRACTION - PELVIC

E0890 Traction frame, attached to footboard, pelvic traction
MED: 100-3,280.1

E0900 Traction stand, freestanding, pelvic traction (e.g., Buck's)
MED: 100-3,280.1

TRAPEZE EQUIPMENT, FRACTURE FRAME, AND OTHER ORTHOPEDIC DEVICES

E0910 Trapeze bars, also known as Patient Helper, attached to bed, with grab bar
MED: 100-3,280.1

E0911 Trapeze bar, heavy-duty, for patient weight capacity greater than 250 pounds, attached to bed, with grab bar

E0912 Trapeze bar, heavy-duty, for patient weight capacity greater than 250 pounds, freestanding, complete with grab bar

E0920 Fracture frame, attached to bed, includes weights
MED: 100-3,280.1

E0930 Fracture frame, freestanding, includes weights
MED: 100-3,280.1

E0935 Continuous passive motion exercise device for use on knee only
MED: 100-3,280.1

E0936 Continuous passive motion exercise device for use other than knee

E0940 Trapeze bar, freestanding, complete with grab bar
MED: 100-3,280.1

E0941 Gravity assisted traction device, any type
MED: 100-3,280.1

E0942 Cervical head harness/halter

E0944 Pelvic belt/harness/boot

E0945 Extremity belt/harness

E0946 Fracture frame, dual with cross bars, attached to bed (e.g., Balken, Four Poster)
MED: 100-3,280.1

E0947 Fracture frame, attachments for complex pelvic traction
MED: 100-3,280.1

E0948 Fracture frame, attachments for complex cervical traction
MED: 100-3,280.1

ROLLABOUT CHAIR

E1031 Rollabout chair, any and all types with castors 5 in or greater
MED: 100-3,280.1

E1035 Multi-positional patient transfer system, with integrated seat, operated by care giver
MED: 100-2,15,110

E1037 Transport chair, pediatric size
MED: 100-3,280.1

E1038 Transport chair, adult size, patient weight capacity up to and including 300 pounds
MED: 100-3,280.1

E1039 Transport chair, adult size, heavy-duty, patient weight capacity greater than 300 pounds

WHEELCHAIRS - FULLY RECLINING

E1050 Fully-reclining wheelchair, fixed full-length arms, swing-away detachable elevating legrests
MED: 100-3,280.1

E1060 Fully-reclining wheelchair, detachable arms, desk or full-length, swing-away detachable elevating legrests
MED: 100-3,280.1

E1070 Fully-reclining wheelchair, detachable arms (desk or full-length) swing-away detachable footrest
MED: 100-3,280.1

E1083 Hemi-wheelchair; fixed full-length arms, swing-away, detachable, elevating legrests
MED: 100-3,280.1

E1084 Hemi-wheelchair, detachable arms desk or full-length arms, swing-away detachable elevating legrests
MED: 100-3,280.1

E1085 Hemi-wheelchair, fixed full-length arms, swing-away detachable footrests
See code(s): K0002
MED: 100-3,280.1

E1086 Hemi-wheelchair, detachable arms, desk or full-length, swing-away detachable footrests
See code(s): K0002
MED: 100-3,280.1

E1087 High strength lightweight wheelchair, fixed full-length arms, swing-away detachable elevating legrests
MED: 100-3,280.1

E1088 High strength lightweight wheelchair, detachable arms desk or full-length, swing-away detachable elevating legrests
MED: 100-3,280.1

E1089 High-strength lightweight wheelchair, fixed-length arms, swing-away detachable footrest
See code(s): K0004
MED: 100-3,280.1

E1090 High-strength lightweight wheelchair, detachable arms, desk or full-length, swing-away detachable footrests
See code(s): K0004
MED: 100-3,280.1

E1092 Wide heavy-duty wheel chair, detachable arms (desk or full-length), swing-away detachable elevating legrests
MED: 100-3,280.1

E1093 Wide heavy-duty wheelchair, detachable arms, desk or full-length, swing-away detachable footrests
MED: 100-3,280.1

WHEELCHAIR - SEMI-RECLINING

E1100 Semi-reclining wheelchair, fixed full-length arms, swing-away detachable elevating legrests
MED: 100-3,280.1

E1110 Semi-reclining wheelchair, detachable arms (desk or full-length) elevating legrest
MED: 100-3,280.1

WHEELCHAIR - STANDARD

E1130 Standard wheelchair, fixed full-length arms, fixed or swing-away detachable footrests
See code(s): K0001
MED: 100-3,280.1

E1140 Wheelchair, detachable arms, desk or full-length, swing-away detachable footrests
See code(s): K0001
MED: 100-3,280.1

E1150 Wheelchair, detachable arms, desk or full-length swing-away detachable elevating legrests
MED: 100-3,280.1

E1160 Wheelchair, fixed full-length arms, swing-away detachable elevating legrests
MED: 100-3,280.1

E1161 Manual adult size wheelchair, includes tilt in space

WHEELCHAIR - AMPUTEE

E1170 Amputee wheelchair, fixed full-length arms, swing-away detachable elevating legrests
MED: 100-3,280.1

E1171 Amputee wheelchair, fixed full-length arms, without footrests or legrest
MED: 100-3,280.1

E1172 Amputee wheelchair, detachable arms (desk or full-length) without footrests or legrest
MED: 100-3,280.1

E1180 Amputee wheelchair, detachable arms (desk or full-length) swing-away detachable footrests
MED: 100-3,280.1

E1190 Amputee wheelchair, detachable arms (desk or full-length) swing-away detachable elevating legrests
MED: 100-3,280.1

E1195 Heavy-duty wheelchair, fixed full-length arms, swing-away detachable elevating legrests
MED: 100-3,280.1

E1200 Amputee wheelchair, fixed full-length arms, swing-away detachable footrest
MED: 100-3,280.1

WHEELCHAIR - SPECIAL SIZE

E1220 Wheelchair, specially sized or constructed (indicate brand name, model number, if any, and justification)
MED: 100-3,280.3

E1221 Wheelchair with fixed arm, footrests
MED: 100-3,280.3

E1222 Wheelchair with fixed arm, elevating legrests
MED: 100-3,280.3

E1223 Wheelchair with detachable arms, footrests
MED: 100-3,280.3

E1224 Wheelchair with detachable arms, elevating legrests
MED: 100-3,280.3

E1225 Wheelchair accessory, manual semi-reclining back, (recline greater than 15 degrees, but less than 80 degrees), each
MED: 100-3,280.3

E1226 Wheelchair accessory, manual fully reclining back, (recline greater than 80 degrees), each
See also K0028
MED: 100-3,280.1

E1227 Special height arms for wheelchair
MED: 100-3,280.3

E1228 Special back height for wheelchair
MED: 100-3,280.3

E1229 Wheelchair, pediatric size, not otherwise specified

E1230 Power operated vehicle (3- or 4-wheel nonhighway, specify brand name and model number
Prior authorization is required by Medicare for this item.
MED: 100-8,5,5.2.3

E1231 Wheelchair, pediatric size, tilt-in-space, rigid, adjustable, with seating system
MED: 100-3,280.1

E1232 Wheelchair, pediatric size, tilt-in-space, folding, adjustable, with seating system
MED: 100-3,280.1

E1233 Wheelchair, pediatric size, tilt-in-space, rigid, adjustable, without seating system
MED: 100-3,280.1

E1234 Wheelchair, pediatric size, tilt-in-space, folding, adjustable, without seating system
MED: 100-3,280.1

E1235 Wheelchair, pediatric size, rigid, adjustable, with seating system
MED: 100-3,280.1

E1236 Wheelchair, pediatric size, folding, adjustable, with seating system
MED: 100-3,280.1

E1237 Wheelchair, pediatric size, rigid, adjustable, without seating system
MED: 100-3,280.1

E1238 Wheelchair, pediatric size, folding, adjustable, without seating system
MED: 100-3,280.1

E1239 Power wheelchair, pediatric size, not otherwise specified

WHEELCHAIR - LIGHTWEIGHT

E1240 Lightweight wheelchair, detachable arms, (desk or full-length) swing-away detachable, elevating legrest
MED: 100-3,280.1

E1250 Lightweight wheelchair, fixed full-length arms, swing-away detachable footrest
See code(s): K0003
MED: 100-3,280.1

E1260 Lightweight wheelchair, detachable arms (desk or full-length) swing-away detachable footrest
See code(s): K0003
MED: 100-3,280.1

E1270 Lightweight wheelchair, fixed full-length arms, swing-away detachable elevating legrests
MED: 100-3,280.1

WHEELCHAIR - HEAVY-DUTY

E1280 Heavy-duty wheelchair, detachable arms (desk or full-length) elevating legrests
MED: 100-3,280.1

E1285 Heavy-duty wheelchair, fixed full-length arms, swing-away detachable footrest
See code(s): K0006
MED: 100-3,280.1

E1290 Heavy-duty wheelchair, detachable arms (desk or full-length) swing-away detachable footrest
See code(s): K0006
MED: 100-3,280.1

E1295 Heavy-duty wheelchair, fixed full-length arms, elevating legrest
MED: 100-3,280.1

E1296 Special wheelchair seat height from floor
MED: 100-3,280.3

E1297 Special wheelchair seat depth, by upholstery
MED: 100-3,280.3

E1298 Special wheelchair seat depth and/or width, by construction
MED: 100-3,280.3

WHIRLPOOL - EQUIPMENT

E1300 Whirlpool, portable (overtub type)
MED: 100-3,280.1

E1310 Whirlpool, nonportable (built-in type)
MED: 100-3,280.1

REPAIRS AND REPLACEMENT SUPPLIES

E1340 Repair or nonroutine service for durable medical equipment requiring the skill of a technician, labor component, per 15 minutes
Medicare jurisdiction: local contractor if repair or implanted DME.
MED: 100-2,15,110.2

ADDITIONAL OXYGEN RELATED EQUIPMENT

E1353 Regulator
MED: 100-3,240.2

E1354 Oxygen accessory, wheeled cart for portable cylinder or portable concentrator, any type, replacement only, each

E1355 Stand/rack
MED: 100-3,240.2

E1356 Oxygen accessory, battery pack/cartridge for portable concentrator, any type, replacement only, each

E1357 Oxygen accessory, battery charger for portable concentrator, any type, replacement only, each

E1358 Oxygen accessory, DC power adapter for portable concentrator, any type, replacement only, each

E1372 Immersion external heater for nebulizer
MED: 100-3,240.2

E1390 Oxygen concentrator, single delivery port, capable of delivering 85 percent or greater oxygen concentration at the prescribed flow rate
MED: 100-3,240.2

E1391 Oxygen concentrator, dual delivery port, capable of delivering 85 percent or greater oxygen concentration at the prescribed flow rate, each
MED: 100-3,240.2

E1392 Portable oxygen concentrator, rental

E1399 Durable medical equipment, miscellaneous
Determine if an alternative HCPCS Level II or a CPT code better describes the service being reported. This code should be used only if a more specific code is unavailable. Medicare jurisdiction: local contractor if repair or implanted DME.

E1405 Oxygen and water vapor enriching system with heated delivery
MED: 100-3,240.2; 100-4,20,20; 100-4,20,20.4

E1406 Oxygen and water vapor enriching system without heated delivery
MED: 100-3,240.2; 100-4,20,20; 100-4,20,20.4

ARTIFICIAL KIDNEY MACHINES AND ACCESSORIES

E1500 Centrifuge, for dialysis

E1510 Kidney, dialysate delivery system kidney machine, pump recirculating, air removal system, flowrate meter, power off, heater and temp control with alarm, IV poles, pressure gauge, concentrate container

E1520 Heparin infusion pump for hemodialysis

E1530 Air bubble detector for hemodialysis, each, replacement

E1540 Pressure alarm for hemodialysis, each, replacement

E1550 Bath conductivity meter for hemodialysis, each

E1560 Blood leak detector for hemodialysis, each, replacement

E1570 Adjustable chair, for ESRD patients

E1575 Transducer protectors/fluid barriers, for hemodialysis, any size, per 10

E1580 Unipuncture control system for hemodialysis

E1590 Hemodialysis machine

E1592 Automatic intermittent peritoneal dialysis system

E1594 Cycler dialysis machine for peritoneal dialysis

E1600 Delivery and/or installation charges for hemodialysis equipment

E1610 Reverse osmosis water purification system, for hemodialysis
MED: 100-3,230.7

E1615 Deionizer water purification system, for hemodialysis
MED: 100-3,230.7

E1620 Blood pump for hemodialysis, replacement

E1625 Water softening system, for hemodialysis
MED: 100-3,230.7

E1630 Reciprocating peritoneal dialysis system

E1632 Wearable artificial kidney, each

E1634 Peritoneal dialysis clamps, each

E1635 Compact (portable) travel hemodialyzer system

E1636 Sorbent cartridges, for hemodialysis, per 10

E1637 Hemostats, each

E1639 Scale, each

E1699 Dialysis equipment, not otherwise specified
Determine if an alternative HCPCS Level II or a CPT code better describes the service being reported. This code should be used only if a more specific code is unavailable. Pertinent documentation to evaluate medical appropriateness should be included when this code is reported.

JAW MOTION REHABILITATION SYSTEM AND ACCESSORIES

E1700 Jaw motion rehabilitation system
Medicare jurisdiction: local contractor.

E1701 Replacement cushions for jaw motion rehabilitation system, package of 6
Medicare jurisdiction: local contractor.

E1702 Replacement measuring scales for jaw motion rehabilitation system, package of 200
Medicare jurisdiction: local contractor.

OTHER ORTHOPEDIC DEVICES

E1800 Dynamic adjustable elbow extension/flexion device, includes soft interface material

E1801 Static progressive stretch elbow device, extension and/or flexion, with or without range of motion adjustment, includes all components and accessories

E1802 Dynamic adjustable forearm pronation/supination device, includes soft interface material

E1805 Dynamic adjustable wrist extension/flexion device, includes soft interface material

E1806 Static progressive stretch wrist device, flexion and/or extension, with or without range of motion adjustment, includes all components and accessories

E1810 Dynamic adjustable knee extension/flexion device, includes soft interface material

E1811 Static progressive stretch knee device, extension and/or flexion, with or without range of motion adjustment, includes all components and accessories

E1812 Dynamic knee, extension/flexion device with active resistance control

E1815 Dynamic adjustable ankle extension/flexion device, includes soft interface material

E1816 Static progressive stretch ankle device, flexion and/or extension, with or without range of motion adjustment, includes all components and accessories

E1818 Static progressive stretch forearm pronation/supination device, with or without range of motion adjustment, includes all components and accessories

E1820 Replacement soft interface material, dynamic adjustable extension/flexion device

E1821 Replacement soft interface material/cuffs for bi-directional static progressive stretch device

E1825 Dynamic adjustable finger extension/flexion device, includes soft interface material

E1830 Dynamic adjustable toe extension/flexion device, includes soft interface material

E1840 Dynamic adjustable shoulder flexion/abduction/rotation device, includes soft interface material

E1841 Static progressive stretch shoulder device, with or without range of motion adjustment, includes all components and accessories

E1902 Communication board, nonelectronic augmentative or alternative communication device

E2000 Gastric suction pump, home model, portable or stationary, electric

E2100 Blood glucose monitor with integrated voice synthesizer
MED: 100.3,230.16

E2101 Blood glucose monitor with integrated lancing/blood sample
MED: 100.3,230.16

E2120 Pulse generator system for tympanic treatment of inner ear endolymphatic fluid

PROCEDURES/PROFESSIONAL SERVICES (TEMPORARY) G0000-G9999

The G codes are used to identify professional health care procedures and services that would otherwise be coded in CPT but for which there are no CPT codes. Please refer to you CPT book for possible alternate code(s).

G0127 **Trimming of dystrophic nails, any number**
MED: 100-2,15,290

G0128 **Direct (face-to-face with patient) skilled nursing services of a registered nurse provided in a comprehensive outpatient rehabilitation facility, each 10 minutes beyond the first 5 minutes**
MED: 100-4,5,100.3

G0129 **Occupational therapy services requiring the skills of a qualified occupational therapist, furnished as a component of a partial hospitalization treatment program, per session (45 minutes or more)**

G0130 **Single energy x-ray absorptiometry (SEXA) bone density study, one or more sites; appendicular skeleton (peripheral) (e.g., radius, wrist, heel)**
MED: 100-2,6,10; 100-3,150.3; 100-4,4,240; 100-4,13,140

G0141 **Screening cytopathology smears, cervical or vaginal, performed by automated system, with manual rescreening, requiring interpretation by physician**
MED: 100-2,6,10

G0143 **Screening cytopathology, cervical or vaginal (any reporting system), collected in preservative fluid, automated thin layer preparation, with manual screening and rescreening by cytotechnologist under physician supervision**
MED: 100-2,6,10

G0144 **Screening cytopathology, cervical or vaginal (any reporting system), collected in preservative fluid, automated thin layer preparation, with screening by automated system, under physician supervision**
MED: 100-2,6,10

G0145 **Screening cytopathology, cervical or vaginal (any reporting system), collected in preservative fluid, automated thin layer preparation, with screening by automated system and manual rescreening under physician supervision**
MED: 100-2,6,10

G0147 **Screening cytopathology smears, cervical or vaginal, performed by automated system under physician supervision**
MED: 100-2,6,10

G0148 **Screening cytopathology smears, cervical or vaginal, performed by automated system with manual rescreening**
MED: 100-2,6,10

G0151 **Services of physical therapist in home health setting, each 15 minutes**

G0152 **Services of occupational therapist in home health setting, each 15 minutes**

G0153 **Services of speech and language pathologist in home health setting, each 15 minutes**

G0154 **Services of skilled nurse in home health setting, each 15 minutes**

G0155 **Services of clinical social worker in home health setting, each 15 minutes**

G0156 **Services of home health aide in home health setting, each 15 minutes**

G0166 **External counterpulsation, per treatment session**
MED: 100-3,20.20

G0168 **Wound closure utilizing tissue adhesive(s) only**
AHA: 3Q,'01,13; 4Q,'01,12

G0173 **Linear accelerator based stereotactic radiosurgery, complete course of therapy in one session**

G0175 **Scheduled interdisciplinary team conference (minimum of 3 exclusive of patient care nursing staff) with patient present**

G0176 **Activity therapy, such as music, dance, art or play therapies not for recreation, related to the care and treatment of patient's disabling mental health problems, per session (45 minutes or more)**

G0177 **Training and educational services related to the care and treatment of patient's disabling mental health problems per session (45 minutes or more)**

G0179 **Physician re-certification for Medicare-covered home health services under a home health plan of care (patient not present), including contacts with home health agency and review of reports of patient status required by physicians to affirm the initial implementation of the plan of care that meets patient's needs, per re-certification period**
MED: 100-4,11,40.1.3.1; 100-4,12,180; 100-4,12,180.1

G0180 **Physician certification for Medicare-covered home health services under a home health plan of care (patient not present), including contacts with home health agency and review of reports of patient status required by physicians to affirm the initial implementation of the plan of care that meets patient's needs, per certification period**
MED: 100-4,11,40.1.3.1; 100-4,12,180; 100-4,12,180.1

G0181 **Physician supervision of a patient receiving Medicare-covered services provided by a participating home health agency (patient not present) requiring complex and multidisciplinary care modalities involving regular physician development and/or revision of care plans, review of subsequent reports of patient status, review of laboratory and other studies, communication (including telephone calls) with other health care professionals involved in the patient's care, integration of new information into the medical treatment plan and/or adjustment of medical therapy, within a calendar month, 30 minutes or more**
MED: 100-4,11,40.1.3.1; 100-4,12,180; 100-4,12,180.1

G0182 **Physician supervision of a patient under a Medicare-approved hospice (patient not present) requiring complex and multidisciplinary care modalities involving regular physician development and/or revision of care plans, review of subsequent reports of patient status, review of laboratory and other studies, communication (including telephone calls) with other health care professionals involved in the patient's care, integration of new information into the medical treatment plan and/or adjustment of medical therapy, within a calendar month, 30 minutes or more**
MED: 100-4,11,40.1.3.1; 100-4,12,180; 100-4,12,180.1

G0186 **Destruction of localized lesion of choroid (for example, choroidal neovascularization); photocoagulation, feeder vessel technique (one or more sessions)**

G0202 **Screening mammography, producing direct digital image, bilateral, all views**
MED: 100-2,6,10; 100-4,4,240
AHA: 1Q,'02,3

G0204 **Diagnostic mammography, producing direct digital image, bilateral, all views**
AHA: 1Q,'03,7

G0206 **Diagnostic mammography, producing direct digital image, unilateral, all views**
AHA: 1Q,'03,7

G0219 **PET imaging whole body; melanoma for noncovered indications**
MED: 100-3,220.6
AHA: 1Q,'02,10

G0235 **PET imaging, any site, not otherwise specified**

G0237 **Therapeutic procedures to increase strength or endurance of respiratory muscles, face-to-face, one-on-one, each 15 minutes (includes monitoring)**

G0238 Therapeutic procedures to improve respiratory function, other than described by G0237, one-on-one, face-to-face, per 15 minutes (includes monitoring)

G0239 Therapeutic procedures to improve respiratory function or increase strength or endurance of respiratory muscles, 2 or more individuals (includes monitoring)

G0245 Initial physician evaluation and management of a diabetic patient with diabetic sensory neuropathy resulting in a loss of protective sensation (LOPS) which must include: (1) the diagnosis of LOPS, (2) a patient history, (3) a physical examination that consists of at least the following elements: (a) visual inspection of the forefoot, hindfoot, and toe web spaces, (b) evaluation of a protective sensation, (c) evaluation of foot structure and biomechanics, (d) evaluation of vascular status and skin integrity, and (e) evaluation and recommendation of footwear, and (4) patient education

MED: 100-3,70.2.1

AHA: 4Q,'02,9

G0246 Follow-up physician evaluation and management of a diabetic patient with diabetic sensory neuropathy resulting in a loss of protective sensation (LOPS) to include at least the following: (1) a patient history, (2) a physical examination that includes: (a) visual inspection of the forefoot, hindfoot, and toe web spaces, (b) evaluation of protective sensation, (c) evaluation of foot structure and biomechanics, (d) evaluation of vascular status and skin integrity, and (e) evaluation and recommendation of footwear, and (3) patient education

MED: 100-3,70.2.1

AHA: 4Q,'02,9

G0247 Routine foot care by a physician of a diabetic patient with diabetic sensory neuropathy resulting in a loss of protective sensation (LOPS) to include the local care of superficial wounds (i.e., superficial to muscle and fascia) and at least the following, if present: (1) local care of superficial wounds, (2) debridement of corns and calluses, and (3) trimming and debridement of nails

MED: 100-3,70.2.1

AHA: 4Q,'02,9

G0248 Demonstration, prior to initial use, of home INR monitoring for patient with either mechanical heart valve(s), chronic atrial fibrillation, or venous thromboembolism who meets Medicare coverage criteria, under the direction of a physician; includes: face-to-face demonstration of use and care of the INR monitor, obtaining at least one blood sample, provision of instructions for reporting home INR test results, and documentation of patient ability to perform testing prior to its use

MED: 100-3,210.1

AHA: 4Q,'02,9

G0249 Provision of test materials and equipment for home INR monitoring of patient with either mechanical heart valve(s), chronic atrial fibrillation, or venous thromboembolism who meets Medicare coverage criteria; includes provision of materials for use in the home and reporting of test results to physician; not occurring more frequently than once a week

MED: 100-3,210.1

AHA: 4Q,'02,9

G0250 Physician review, interpretation, and patient management of home INR testing for a patient with either mechanical heart valve(s), chronic atrial fibrillation, or venous thromboembolism who meets Medicare coverage criteria; includes face-to-face verification by the physician at least once a year (e.g., during an evaluation and management service) that the patient uses the device in the context of the management of the anticoagulation therapy following initiation of the home INR monitoring; not occurring more frequently than once a week.

MED: 100-3,210.1

AHA: 4Q,'02,9

G0251 Linear accelerator based stereotactic radiosurgery, delivery including collimator changes and custom plugging, fractionated treatment, all lesions, per session, maximum 5 sessions per course of treatment

G0252 PET imaging, full and partial-ring PET scanners only, for initial diagnosis of breast cancer and/or surgical planning for breast cancer (e.g., initial staging of axillary lymph nodes)

MED: 100-3,220.6

G0255 Current perception threshold/sensory nerve conduction test, (SNCT) per limb, any nerve

MED: 100-3,160.23

AHA: 4Q,'02,9

G0257 Unscheduled or emergency dialysis treatment for an ESRD patient in a hospital outpatient department that is not certified as an ESRD facility

AHA: 1Q,'03,9; 4Q,'02,9

G0259 Injection procedure for sacroiliac joint; arthrography

AHA: 4Q,'02,9

G0260 Injection procedure for sacroiliac joint; provision of anesthetic, steroid and/or other therapeutic agent, with or without arthrography

AHA: 4Q,'02,9

G0268 Removal of impacted cerumen (one or both ears) by physician on same date of service as audiologic function testing

AHA: 1Q,'03,12

G0269 Placement of occlusive device into either a venous or arterial access site, postsurgical or interventional procedure (e.g., angioseal plug, vascular plug)

G0270 Medical nutrition therapy; reassessment and subsequent intervention(s) following second referral in same year for change in diagnosis, medical condition or treatment regimen (including additional hours needed for renal disease), individual, face-to-face with the patient, each 15 minutes

G0271 Medical nutrition therapy, reassessment and subsequent intervention(s) following second referral in same year for change in diagnosis, medical condition, or treatment regimen (including additional hours needed for renal disease), group (2 or more individuals), each 30 minutes

G0275 Renal angiography, nonselective, one or both kidneys, performed at the same time as cardiac catheterization and/or coronary angiography, includes positioning or placement of any catheter in the abdominal aorta at or near the origins (ostia) of the renal arteries, injection of dye, flush aortogram, production of permanent images, and radiologic supervision and interpretation (List separately in addition to primary procedure)

G0278 Iliac and/or femoral artery angiography, nonselective, bilateral or ipsilateral to catheter insertion, performed at the same time as cardiac catheterization and/or coronary angiography, includes positioning or placement of the catheter in the distal aorta or ipsilateral femoral or iliac artery, injection of dye, production of permanent images, and radiologic supervision and interpretation (List separately in addition to primary procedure)

G0281 Electrical stimulation, (unattended), to one or more areas, for chronic Stage III and Stage IV pressure ulcers, arterial ulcers, diabetic ulcers, and venous stasis ulcers not demonstrating measurable signs of healing after 30 days of conventional care, as part of a therapy plan of care

MED: 100-4,32,11.1

AHA: 1Q,'03,7; 2Q,'03,7

G0282 Electrical stimulation, (unattended), to one or more areas, for wound care other than described in G0281

MED: 100-3,270.1

AHA: 1Q,'03,7; 2Q,'03,7

G0283 Electrical stimulation (unattended), to one or more areas for indication(s) other than wound care, as part of a therapy plan of care

AHA: 1Q,'03,7; 2Q,'03,7

G0288 Reconstruction, computed tomographic angiography of aorta for surgical planning for vascular surgery

G0289 Arthroscopy, knee, surgical, for removal of loose body, foreign body, debridement/shaving of articular cartilage (chondroplasty) at the time of other surgical knee arthroscopy in a different compartment of the same knee

G0290 Transcatheter placement of a drug eluting intracoronary stent(s), percutaneous, with or without other therapeutic intervention, any method; single vessel

AHA: 3Q,'03,11; 4Q,'03,7; 4Q,'02,9

G0291 Transcatheter placement of a drug eluting intracoronary stent(s), percutaneous, with or without other therapeutic intervention, any method; each additional vessel

AHA: 3Q,'03,11; 4Q,'03,7; 4Q,'02,9

G0293 Noncovered surgical procedure(s) using conscious sedation, regional, general, or spinal anesthesia in a Medicare qualifying clinical trial, per day

AHA: 4Q,'02,9

G0294 Noncovered procedure(s) using either no anesthesia or local anesthesia only, in a Medicare qualifying clinical trial, per day

AHA: 4Q,'02,9

G0295 Electromagnetic therapy, to one or more areas, for wound care other than described in G0329 or for other uses

MED: 100-3,270.1

AHA: 1Q,'03,7

G0302 Preoperative pulmonary surgery services for preparation for LVRS, complete course of services, to include a minimum of 16 days of services

G0303 Preoperative pulmonary surgery services for preparation for LVRS, 10 to 15 days of services

G0304 Preoperative pulmonary surgery services for preparation for LVRS, 1 to 9 days of services

G0305 Postdischarge pulmonary surgery services after LVRS, minimum of 6 days of services

G0306 Complete CBC, automated (HgB, HCT, RBC, WBC, without platelet count) and automated WBC differential count

G0307 Complete (CBC), automated (HgB, HCT, RBC, WBC, without platelet count)

G0328 Colorectal cancer screening; fecal occult blood test, immunoassay, 1-3 simultaneous determinations

MED: 100-4,18,60.1

G0329 Electromagnetic therapy, to one or more areas for chronic Stage III and Stage IV pressure ulcers, arterial ulcers, diabetic ulcers and venous stasis ulcers not demonstrating measurable signs of healing after 30 days of conventional care as part of a therapy plan of care

MED: 100-4,32,11.2

G0333 Pharmacy dispensing fee for inhalation drug(s); initial 30-day supply as a beneficiary

G0337 Hospice evaluation and counseling services, preelection

G0339 Image guided robotic linear accelerator-based stereotactic radiosurgery, complete course of therapy in one session, or first session of fractionated treatment

G0340 Image guided robotic linear accelerator-based stereotactic radiosurgery, delivery including collimator changes and custom plugging, fractionated treatment, all lesions, per session, second through fifth sessions, maximum 5 sessions per course of treatment

G0341 Percutaneous islet cell transplant, includes portal vein catheterization and infusion

MED: 100-3,260.3; 100-4,32,70

G0342 Laparoscopy for islet cell transplant, includes portal vein catheterization and infusion

MED: 100-3,260.3; 100-4,32,70

G0343 Laparotomy for islet cell transplant, includes portal vein catheterization and infusion

MED: 100-3,260.3; 100-4,32,70

G0364 Bone marrow aspiration performed with bone marrow biopsy through the same incision on the same date of service

G0365 Vessel mapping of vessels for hemodialysis access (services for preoperative vessel mapping prior to creation of hemodialysis access using an autogenous hemodialysis conduit, including arterial inflow and venous outflow)

G0372 Physician service required to establish and document the need for a power mobility device

G0378 Hospital observation service, per hour

MED: 100-2,6,20.6

G0379 Direct admission of patient for hospital observation care

MED: 100-2,6,20.6

G0380 Level 1 hospital emergency department visit provided in a type B emergency department; (the ED must meet at least one of the following requirements: (1) it is licensed by the state in which it is located under applicable state law as an emergency room or emergency department; (2) it is held out to the public (by name, posted signs, advertising, or other means) as a place that provides care for emergency medical conditions on an urgent basis without requiring a previously scheduled appointment; or (3) during the calendar year immediately preceding the calendar year in which a determination under 42 CFR 489.24 is being made, based on a representative sample of patient visits that occurred during that calendar year, it provides at least one-third of all of its outpatient visits for the treatment of emergency medical conditions on an urgent basis without requiring a previously scheduled appointment)

MED: 100-4,4,160

G0381 Level 2 hospital emergency department visit provided in a type B emergency department; (the ED must meet at least one of the following requirements: (1) it is licensed by the state in which it is located under applicable state law as an emergency room or emergency department; (2) it is held out to the public (by name, posted signs, advertising, or other means) as a place that provides care for emergency medical conditions on an urgent basis without requiring a previously scheduled appointment; or (3) during the calendar year immediately preceding the calendar year in which a determination under 42 CFR 489.24 is being made, based on a representative sample of patient visits that occurred during that calendar year, it provides at least one-third of all of its outpatient visits for the treatment of emergency medical conditions on an urgent basis without requiring a previously scheduled appointment)

MED: 100-4,4,160

G0382 Level 3 hospital emergency department visit provided in a type B emergency department; (the ED must meet at least one of the following requirements: (1) it is licensed by the state in which it is located under applicable state law as an emergency room or emergency department; (2) it is held out to the public (by name, posted signs, advertising, or other means) as a place that provides care for emergency medical conditions on an urgent basis without requiring a previously scheduled appointment; or (3) during the calendar year immediately preceding the calendar year in which a determination under 42 CFR 489.24 is being made, based on a representative sample of patient visits that occurred during that calendar year, it provides at least one-third of all of its outpatient visits for the treatment of emergency medical conditions on an urgent basis without requiring a previously scheduled appointment)

MED: 100-4,4,160

G0383 Level 4 hospital emergency department visit provided in a type B emergency department; (the ED must meet at least one of the following requirements: (1) it is licensed by the state in which it is located under applicable state law as an emergency room or emergency department; (2) it is held out to the public (by name, posted signs, advertising, or other means) as a place that provides care for emergency medical conditions on an urgent basis without requiring a previously scheduled appointment; or (3) during the calendar year immediately preceding the calendar year in which a determination under 42 CFR 489.24 is being made, based on a representative sample of patient visits that occurred during that calendar year, it provides at least one-third of all of its outpatient visits for the treatment of emergency medical conditions on an urgent basis without requiring a previously scheduled appointment)

MED: 100-4,4,160

G0384 Level 5 hospital emergency department visit provided in a type B emergency department; (the ED must meet at least one of the following requirements: (1) it is licensed by the state in which it is located under applicable state law as an emergency room or emergency department; (2) it is held out to the public (by name, posted signs, advertising, or other means) as a place that provides care for emergency medical conditions on an urgent basis without requiring a previously scheduled appointment; or (3) during the calendar year immediately preceding the calendar year in which a determination under 42 CFR 489.24 is being made, based on a representative sample of patient visits that occurred during that calendar year, it provides at least one-third of all of its outpatient visits for the treatment of emergency medical conditions on an urgent basis without requiring a previously scheduled appointment)

MED: 100-4,4,160

G0389 Ultrasound B-scan and/or real time with image documentation; for abdominal aortic aneurysm (AAA) screening

G0390 Trauma response team associated with hospital critical care service

G0392 Transluminal balloon angioplasty, percutaneous; for maintenance of hemodialysis access, arteriovenous fistula or graft; arterial

G0393 Transluminal balloon angioplasty, percutaneous; for maintenance of hemodialysis access, arteriovenous fistula or graft; venous

G0396 Alcohol and/or substance (other than tobacco) abuse structured assessment (e.g., AUDIT, DAST), and brief intervention 15 to 30 minutes

G0397 Alcohol and/or substance (other than tobacco) abuse structured assessment (e.g., AUDIT, DAST), and intervention, greater than 30 minutes

G0398 Home sleep study test (HST) with type II portable monitor, unattended; minimum of 7 channels: EEG, EOG, EMG, ECG/heart rate, airflow, respiratory effort and oxygen saturation

G0399 Home sleep test (HST) with type III portable monitor, unattended; minimum of 4 channels: 2 respiratory movement/airflow, 1 ECG/heart rate and 1 oxygen saturation

G0400 Home sleep test (HST) with type IV portable monitor, unattended; minimum of 3 channels

G0402 Initial preventive physical examination; face-to-face visit, services limited to new beneficiary during the first 12 months of Medicare enrollment

G0403 Electrocardiogram, routine ECG with 12 leads; performed as a screening for the initial preventive physical examination with interpretation and report

G0404 Electrocardiogram, routine ECG with 12 leads; tracing only, without interpretation and report, performed as a screening for the initial preventive physical examination

G0405 Electrocardiogram, routine ECG with 12 leads; interpretation and report only, performed as a screening for the initial preventive physical examination

G0406 Follow-up inpatient telehealth consultation, limited, physicians typically spend 15 minutes communicating with the patient via telehealth

G0407 Follow-up inpatient telehealth consultation, intermediate, physicians typically spend 25 minutes communicating with the patient via telehealth

G0408 Follow-up inpatient telehealth consultation, complex, physicians typically spend 35 minutes or more communicating with the patient via telehealth

G0409 Social work and psychological services, directly relating to and/or furthering the patient's rehabilitation goals, each 15 minutes, face-to-face; individual (services provided by a CORF qualified social worker or psychologist in a CORF)

G0410 Group psychotherapy other than of a multiple family group, in a partial hospitalization setting, approximately 45 to 50 minutes

G0411 Interactive group psychotherapy, in a partial hospitalization setting, approximately 45 to 50 minutes

G0412 Open treatment of iliac spine(s), tuberosity avulsion, or iliac wing fracture(s), unilateral or bilateral for pelvic bone fracture patterns which do not disrupt the pelvic ring, includes internal fixation, when performed

G0413 Percutaneous skeletal fixation of posterior pelvic bone fracture and/or dislocation, for fracture patterns which disrupt the pelvic ring, unilateral or bilateral, (includes ilium, sacroiliac joint and/or sacrum)

G0414 Open treatment of anterior pelvic bone fracture and/or dislocation for fracture patterns which disrupt the pelvic ring, unilateral or bilateral, includes internal fixation when performed (includes pubic symphysis and/or superior/inferior rami)

G0415 Open treatment of posterior pelvic bone fracture and/or dislocation, for fracture patterns which disrupt the pelvic ring, unilateral or bilateral, includes internal fixation, when performed (includes ilium, sacroiliac joint and/or sacrum)

G0416 Surgical pathology, gross and microscopic examination for prostate needle saturation biopsy sampling, 1-20 specimens

G0417 Surgical pathology, gross and microscopic examination for prostate needle saturation biopsy sampling, 21-40 specimens

G0418 Surgical pathology, gross and microscopic examination for prostate needle saturation biopsy sampling, 41-60 specimens

G0419 Surgical pathology, gross and microscopic examination for prostate needle saturation biopsy sampling, greater than 60 specimens

G3001 Administration and supply of tositumomab, 450 mg

PHYSICIAN QUALITY REPORTING INDICATOR CODE (PQRI)

Physician Quality Reporting Indicator Codes (PQRI) are to be used for the physician Quality Reporting Indicator Code (PQRI) program in which CMS seeks to analyze the quality of care provided to Medicare beneficiaries. Reporting of these codes is voluntary. Physicians should not charge for these codes. Unless otherwise indicated, report these codes in addition to office visit, home visit, nursing facility, and domiciliary evaluation and management codes. For additional information, please visit the following website: http://www.cms.hhs.gov/providers/PQRI

G8006 Acute myocardial infarction: patient documented to have received aspirin at arrival

G8007 Acute myocardial infarction: patient not documented to have received aspirin at arrival

G8008 Clinician documented that acute myocardial infarction patient was not an eligible candidate to receive aspirin at arrival measure

G8009 Acute myocardial infarction: patient documented to have received beta-blocker at arrival

G8010 Acute myocardial infarction: patient not documented to have received beta-blocker at arrival

G8011 Clinician documented that acute myocardial infarction patient was not an eligible candidate for beta-blocker at arrival measure

G8012 Pneumonia: patient documented to have received antibiotic within 4 hours of presentation

G8013 Pneumonia: patient not documented to have received antibiotic within 4 hours of presentation

G8014 Clinician documented that pneumonia patient was not an eligible candidate for antibiotic within 4 hours of presentation measure

G8015 Diabetic patient with most recent hemoglobin A1c level (within the last 6 months) documented as greater than 9%

G8016 Diabetic patient with most recent hemoglobin A1c level (within the last 6 months) documented as less than or equal to 9%

G8017 Clinician documented that diabetic patient was not eligible candidate for hemoglobin A1c measure

G8018 Clinician has not provided care for the diabetic patient for the required time for hemoglobin A1c measure (6 months)

G8019 Diabetic patient with most recent low-density lipoprotein (within the last 12 months) documented as greater than or equal to 100 mg/dl

G8020 Diabetic patient with most recent low-density lipoprotein (within the last 12 months) documented as less than 100 mg/dl

G8021 Clinician documented that diabetic patient was not eligible candidate for low-density lipoprotein measure

G8022 Clinician has not provided care for the diabetic patient for the required time for low-density lipoprotein measure (12 months)

G8023 Diabetic patient with most recent blood pressure (within the last 6 months) documented as equal to or greater than 140 systolic or equal to or greater than 80 mm Hg diastolic

G8024 Diabetic patient with most recent blood pressure (within the last 6 months) documented as less than 140 systolic and less than 80 diastolic

G8025 Clinician documented that the diabetic patient was not eligible candidate for blood pressure measure

G8026 Clinician has not provided care for the diabetic patient for the required time for blood pressure measure (within the last 6 months)

G8027 Heart failure patient with left ventricular systolic dysfunction (LVSD) documented to be on either angiotensin-converting enzyme-inhibitor or angiotensin-receptor blocker (ACE-1 or ARB) therapy

G8028 Heart failure patient with left ventricular systolic dysfunction (LVSD) not documented to be on either angiotensin-converting enzyme-inhibitor or angiotensin-receptor blocker (ACE-1 or ARB) therapy

G8029 Clinician documented that heart failure patient was not an eligible candidate for either angiotensin-converting enzyme-inhibitor or angiotensin-receptor blocker (ACE-1 or ARB) therapy measure

G8030 Heart failure patient with left ventricular systolic dysfunction (LVSD) documented to be on beta-blocker therapy

G8031 Heart failure patient with left ventricular systolic dysfunction (LVSD) not documented to be on beta-blocker therapy

G8032 Clinician documented that heart failure patient was not eligible candidate for beta-blocker therapy measure

G8033 Prior myocardial infarction, coronary artery disease patient documented to be on beta-blocker therapy

G8034 Prior myocardial infarction, coronary artery disease patient not documented to be on beta-blocker therapy

G8035 Clinician documented that prior myocardial infarction, coronary artery disease patient was not eligible candidate for beta-blocker therapy measure

G8036 Coronary artery disease patient documented to be on antiplatelet therapy

G8037 Coronary artery disease patient not documented to be on antiplatelet therapy

G8038 Clinician documented that coronary artery disease patient was not eligible candidate for antiplatelet therapy measure

G8039 Coronary artery disease patient with low-density lipoprotein documented to be greater than 100 mg/dl

G8040 Coronary artery disease patient with low-density lipoprotein documented to be less than or equal to 100 mg/dl

G8041 Clinician documented that coronary artery disease patient was not eligible candidate for low-density lipoprotein measure

G8051 Patient (female) documented to have been assessed for osteoporosis

G8052 Patient (female) not documented to have been assessed for osteoporosis

G8053 Clinician documented that (female) patient was not an eligible candidate for osteoporosis assessment measure

G8054 Patient not documented for the assessment for falls within last 12 months

G8055 Patient documented for the assessment for falls within last 12 months

G8056 Clinician documented that patient was not an eligible candidate for the falls assessment measure within the last 12 months

G8057 Patient documented to have received hearing assessment

G8058 Patient not documented to have received hearing assessment

G8059 Clinician documented that patient was not an eligible candidate for hearing assessment measure

G8060 Patient documented for the assessment of urinary incontinence

G8061 Patient not documented for the assessment of urinary incontinence

G8062 Clinician documented that patient was not an eligible candidate for urinary incontinence assessment measure

G8075 ESRD patient with documented dialysis dose of URR greater than or equal to 65% (or Kt/ V greater than or equal to 1.2)

G8076 ESRD patient with documented dialysis dose of URR less than 65% (or Kt/V less than 1.2)

G8077 Clinician documented that ESRD patient was not an eligible candidate for URR or Kt/V measure

G8078 ESRD patient with documented hematocrit greater than or equal to 33 (or hemoglobin greater than or equal to 11)

G8079 ESRD patient with documented hematocrit less than 33 (or hemoglobin less than 11)

G8080 Clinician documented that ESRD patient was not an eligible candidate for hematocrit (hemoglobin) measure

G8081 ESRD patient requiring hemodialysis vascular access documented to have received autogenous AV fistula

G8082 ESRD patient requiring hemodialysis documented to have received vascular access other than autogenous AV fistula

G8085 ESRD patient requiring hemodialysis vascular access was not an eligible candidate for autogenous AV fistula

G8093 Newly diagnosed chronic obstructive pulmonary disease (COPD) patient documented to have received smoking cessation intervention, within 3 months of diagnosis

G8094 Newly diagnosed chronic obstructive pulmonary disease (COPD) patient not documented to have received smoking cessation intervention, within 3 months of diagnosis

G8099 Osteoporosis patient documented to have been prescribed calcium and vitamin D supplements

G8100 Clinician documented that osteoporosis patient was not an eligible candidate for calcium and vitamin D supplement measure

G8103 Newly diagnosed osteoporosis patients documented to have been treated with antiresorptive therapy and/or PTH within 3 months of diagnosis

G8104 Clinician documented that newly diagnosed osteoporosis patient was not an eligible candidate for antiresorptive therapy and/or PTH treatment measure within 3 months of diagnosis

G8106 Within 6 months of suffering a nontraumatic fracture, female patient 65 years of age or older documented to have undergone bone mineral density testing or to have been prescribed a drug to treat or prevent osteoporosis

G8107 Clinician documented that female patient 65 years of age or older who suffered a nontraumatic fracture within the last 6 months was not an eligible candidate for measure to test bone mineral density or drug to treat or prevent osteoporosis

G8108 Patient documented to have received influenza vaccination during influenza season

G8109 Patient not documented to have received influenza vaccination during influenza season

G8110 Clinician documented that patient was not an eligible candidate for influenza vaccination measure

G8111 Patient (female) documented to have received a mammogram during the measurement year or prior year to the measurement year

G8112 Patient (female) not documented to have received a mammogram during the measurement year or prior year to the measurement year

G8113 Clinician documented that female patient was not an eligible candidate for mammography measure

G8114 Clinician did not provide care to patient for the required time of mammography measure (i.e., measurement year or prior year)

G8115 Patient documented to have received pneumococcal vaccination

G8116 Patient not documented to have received pneumococcal vaccination

G8117 Clinician documented that patient was not an eligible candidate for pneumococcal vaccination measure

G8126 Patient documented as being treated with antidepressant medication during the entire 12 week acute treatment phase

G8127 Patient not documented as being treated with antidepressant medication during the entire 12 weeks acute treatment phase

G8128 Clinician documented that patient was not an eligible candidate for antidepressant medication during the entire 12 week acute treatment phase measure

G8129 Patient documented as being treated with antidepressant medication for at least 6 months continuous treatment phase

G8130 Patient not documented as being treated with antidepressant medication for at least 6 months continuous treatment phase

G8131 Clinician documented that patient was not an eligible candidate for antidepressant medication for continuous treatment phase

G8152 Patient documented to have received antibiotic prophylaxis one hour prior to incision time (2 hours for vancomycin)

G8153 Patient not documented to have received antibiotic prophylaxis one hour prior to incision time (2 hours for vancomycin)

G8154 Clinician documented that patient was not an eligible candidate for antibiotic prophylaxis one hour prior to incision time (2 hours for vancomycin) measure

G8155 Patient with documented receipt of thromboembolism prophylaxis

G8156 Patient without documented receipt of thromboembolism prophylaxis

G8157 Clinician documented that patient was not an eligible candidate for thromboembolism prophylaxis measure

G8159 Patient documented to have received coronary artery bypass graft without use of internal mammary artery

G8162 Patient with isolated coronary artery bypass graft not documented to have received preoperative beta-blockade

G8164 Patient with isolated coronary artery bypass graft documented to have prolonged intubation

G8165 Patient with isolated coronary artery bypass graft not documented to have prolonged intubation

G8166 Patient with isolated coronary artery bypass graft documented to have required surgical re-exploration

G8167 Patient with isolated coronary artery bypass graft did not require surgical re-exploration

G8170 Patient with isolated coronary artery bypass graft documented to have been discharged on aspirin or clopidogrel

G8171 Patient with isolated coronary artery bypass graft not documented to have been discharged on aspirin or clopidogrel

G8172 Clinician documented that patient with isolated coronary artery bypass graft was not an eligible candidate for antiplatelet therapy at discharge measure

G8182 Clinician has not provided care for the cardiac patient for the required time for low-density lipoprotein measure (6 months)

G8183 Patient with heart failure and atrial fibrillation documented to be on warfarin therapy

G8184 Clinician documented that patient with heart failure and atrial fibrillation was not an eligible candidate for warfarin therapy measure

G8185 Patients diagnosed with symptomatic osteoarthritis with documented annual assessment of function and pain

G8186 Clinician documented that symptomatic osteoarthritis patient was not an eligible candidate for annual assessment of function and pain measure

G8193 Clinician did not document that an order for prophylactic antibiotic to be given within one hour (if vancomycin, 2 hours) prior to surgical incision (or start of procedure when no incision is required) was given

G8196 Clinician did not document a prophylactic antibiotic was administered within one hour (if vancomycin, 2 hours) prior to surgical incision (or start of procedure when no incision is required)

G8200 Order for cefazolin or cefuroxime for antimicrobial prophylaxis not documented

G8204 Clinician did not document an order was given to discontinue prophylactic antibiotics within 24 hours of surgical end time

G8209 Clinician did not document an order was given to discontinue prophylactic antibiotics within 48 hours of surgical end time

G8214 Clinician did not document an order was given for appropriate venous thromboembolism (VTE) prophylaxis to be given within 24 hrs prior to incision time or 24 hours after surgery end time

G8217 Patient not documented to have received DVT prophylaxis by end of hospital day 2

G8219 Patient documented to have received DVT prophylaxis by end of hospital day 2

G8220 Patient not documented to have received DVT prophylaxis by end of hospital day 2

G8221 Clinician documented that patient was not an eligible candidate for DVT prophylaxis by the end of hospital day 2, including physician documentation that patient is ambulatory

G8223 Patient not documented to have received prescription for antiplatelet therapy at discharge

G8226 Patient not documented to have received prescription for anticoagulant therapy at discharge

G8231 Patient not documented to have received T-PA or not documented to have been considered a candidate for T-PA administration

G8234 Patient not documented to have received dysphagia screening

G8238 Patient not documented to have received order for or consideration for rehabilitation services

G8240 Internal carotid stenosis patient in the 30-99% range, and no documentation of reference to measurements of distal internal carotid diameter as the denominator for stenosis measurement

G8243 Patient not documented to have received CT or MRI and the presence or absence of hemorrhage, mass lesion and acute infarction not documented in the final report

G8246 Patient was not an eligible candidate for medical history review with assessment of new or changing moles

G8248 Patient with at least one alarm symptom not documented to have had upper endoscopy or referral for upper endoscopy

G8251 Patient not documented to have received an esophageal biopsy when suspicion of Barrett's esophagus is indicated in the endoscopy report

G8254 Patient with no documentation order for barium swallow test

G8257 Clinician has not documented reconciliation of discharge medications with current medication list in medical record

G8260 Patient not documented to have surrogate decision maker or advance care plan in medical record

G8263 Patient not documented to have been assessed for presence or absence of urinary incontinence

G8266 Patient not documented to have received characterization of urinary incontinence

G8268 Patient not documented to have received plan of care for urinary incontinence

G8271 Patient with no documentation of screening for fall risks (2 or more falls in the past year or any fall with injury in the past year)

G8274 Clinician has not documented presence or absence of alarm symptoms

G8276 Patient not documented to have received medical history with assessment of new or changing moles

G8279 Patient not documented to have received a complete physical skin exam

G8282 Patient not documented to have received counseling to perform a self-examination

G8285 Patient not documented to have received pharmacologic therapy

G8289 Patient with no documentation of calcium and vitamin D use or counseling regarding both calcium and vitamin D use, or exercise

G8293 COPD patient without spirometry results documented

G8296 COPD patient not documented to have inhaled bronchodilator therapy prescribed

G8298 Patient documented to have received optic nerve head evaluation

G8299 Patient not documented to have received optic nerve head evaluation

G8302 Patient documented to have a specific target intraocular pressure range goal

G8303 Patient not documented to have a specific target intraocular pressure range goal

G8304 Clinician documented that patient was not an eligible candidate for a specific target intraocular pressure range goal

G8305 Clinician has not provided care for the primary open-angle glaucoma patient for the required time for treatment range goal documentation measurement

G8306 Primary open-angle glaucoma patient with intraocular pressure above the target range goal documented to have received plan of care

G8307 Primary open-angle glaucoma patient with intraocular pressure at or below goal, no plan of care necessary

G8308 Primary open-angle glaucoma patient with intraocular pressure above the target range goal, and not documented to have received plan of care during the reporting year

G8310 Patient not documented to have been prescribed/recommended at least one antioxidant vitamin or mineral supplement during the reporting year

G8314 Patient not documented to have received macular exam with documentation of presence or absence of macular thickening or hemorrhage and no documentation of Level of macular degeneration severity

G8318 Patient documented not to have visual functional status assessed

G8322 Patient not documented to have had presurgical axial length, corneal power measurement and method of intraocular lens power calculation

G8326 Patient not documented to have received fundus evaluation within 6 months prior to cataract surgery

G8330 Patient not documented to have received dilated macular or fundus exam with level of severity of retinopathy and the presence or absence of macular edema not documented

G8334 Documentation of findings of macular or fundus exam not communicated to the physician managing the patient's ongoing diabetes care

G8338 Clinician has not documented that communication was sent to the physician managing ongoing care of patient that a fracture occurred and that the patient was or should be tested or treated for osteoporosis

G8341 Patient not documented to have had central DEXA measurement or pharmacologic therapy

G8345 Patient not documented to have had central DEXA measurement ordered or performed or pharmacologic therapy

G8351 Patient not documented to have had ECG

G8354 Patient not documented to have received or taken aspirin 24 hours before emergency department arrival or during emergency department stay

G8357 Patient not documented to have had ECG

G8360 Patient not documented to have vital signs recorded and reviewed

G8362 Patient not documented to have oxygen saturation assessed

G8365 Patient not documented to have mental status assessed

G8367 Patient not documented to have appropriate empiric antibiotic prescribed

G8370 Asthma patients with numeric frequency of symptoms or patient completion of an asthma assessment tool/survey/questionnaire not documented

G8371 Chemotherapy documented as not received or prescribed for Stage III colon cancer patients

G8372 Chemotherapy documented as received or prescribed for Stage III colon cancer patients

G8373 Chemotherapy plan documented prior to chemotherapy administration

G8374 Chemotherapy plan not documented prior to chemotherapy administration

G8375 Chronic lymphocytic leukemia (CLL) patient with no documentation of baseline flow cytometry performed

G8376 Clinician documentation that breast cancer patient was not eligible for tamoxifen or aromatase inhibitor therapy measure

G8377 Clinician documentation that colon cancer patient is not eligible for chemotherapy measure

G8378 Clinician documentation that patient was not an eligible candidate for radiation therapy measure

G8379 Documentation of radiation therapy recommended within 12 months of first office visit

G8380 For patients with ER or PR positive, Stage IC-III breast cancer, clinician did not document that the patient received or was prescribed tamoxifen or aromatase inhibitor

G8381 For patients with ER or PR positive, Stage IC-III breast cancer, clinician documented or prescribed that the patient is receiving tamoxifen or aromatase inhibitor

G8382 Multiple myeloma patients with no documentation of prescribed or received intravenous bisphosphonate therapy

G8383 No documentation of radiation therapy recommended within 12 months of first office visit

G8384 Baseline cytogenetic testing not performed in patients with myelodysplastic syndrome (MDS) or acute leukemias

G8385 Diabetic patients with no documentation of hemoglobin A1c level (within the last 12 months)

G8386 Diabetic patients with no documentation of low-density lipoprotein (within the last 12 months)

G8387 ESRD patient with a hematocrit or hemoglobin not documented

G8388 ESRD patient with URR or Kt/V value not documented, but otherwise eligible for measure

G8389 Myelodysplastic syndrome (MDS) patients with no documentation of iron stores prior to receiving erythropoietin therapy

G8390 Diabetic patients with no documentation of blood pressure measurement (within the last 12 months)

G8391 Patients with persistent asthma, no documentation of preferred long-term control medication or acceptable alternative treatment prescribed

G8395 Left ventricular ejection fraction (LVEF) >= 40% or documentation as normal or mildly depressed left ventricular systolic function

G8396 Left ventricular ejection fraction (LVEF) not performed or documented

G8397 Dilated macular or fundus exam performed, including documentation of the presence or absence of macular edema and level of severity of retinopathy

G8398 Dilated macular or fundus exam not performed

G8399 Patient with central dual-energy x-ray absorptiometry (DXA) results documented or ordered or pharmacologic therapy (other than minerals/vitamins) for osteoporosis prescribed

G8400 Patient with central dual-energy x-ray absorptiometry (DXA) results not documented or not ordered or pharmacologic therapy (other than minerals/vitamins) for osteoporosis not prescribed

G8401 Clinician documented that patient was not an eligible candidate for screening or therapy for osteoporosis for women measure

G8402 Tobacco (smoke) use cessation intervention, counseling

G8403 Tobacco (smoke) use cessation intervention not counseled

G8404 Lower extremity neurological exam performed and documented

G8405 Lower extremity neurological exam not performed

G8406 Clinician documented that patient was not an eligible candidate for lower extremity neurological exam measure

G8407 ABI measured and documented

G8408 ABI measurement was not obtained

G8409 Clinician documented that patient was not an eligible candidate for ABI measurement measure

G8410 Footwear evaluation performed and documented

G8415 Footwear evaluation was not performed

G8416 Clinician documented that patient was not an eligible candidate for footwear evaluation measure

G8417 Calculated BMI above the upper parameter and a follow-up plan was documented in the medical record

G8418 Calculated BMI below the lower parameter and a follow-up plan was documented in the medical record

G8419 Calculated BMI outside normal parameters, no follow-up plan was documented in the medical record

G8420 Calculated BMI within normal parameters and documented

G8421 BMI not calculated

G8422 Patient not eligible for BMI calculation

G8423 Documented that patient was screened and either influenza vaccination status is current or patient was counseled

G8424 Influenza vaccine status was not screened

G8425 Influenza vaccine status screened, patient not current and counseling was not provided

G8426 Documented that patient was not appropriate for screening and/or counseling about the influenza vaccine (e.g., allergy to eggs)

G8427 List of current medications with dosages (includes prescription, over-the-counter, herbals, vitamin/mineral/dietary nutritional supplements) and verification with the patient or authorized representative documented by the provider

G8428 Provider documentation of current medications with dosages (includes prescription, over-the-counter, herbals, vitamin/mineral/dietary nutritional supplements) without documented patient verification

G8429 Incomplete or no provider documentation that patient's current medications with dosages (includes prescription, over-the-counter, herbals, vitamin/mineral/dietary nutritional supplements were assessed

G8430 Provider documentation that patient is not eligible for medication assessment

G8431 Positive screen for clinical depression using a standardized tool and a follow-up plan documented

G8432 No documentation of clinical depression screening using a standardized tool

G8433 Screening for clinical depression using a standardized tool not documented, patient not eligible/appropriate

G8434 Documentation of cognitive impairment screening using a standardized tool

G8435 No documentation of cognitive impairment screening using a standardized tool

G8436 Patient not eligible/not appropriate for cognitive impairment screening

G8437 Documentation of clinician and patient involvement with the development of a plan of care including signature by the practitioner/therapist and either a co-signature by the patient or documented verbal agreement obtained from the patient or, when necessary, an authorized representative

G8438 No documentation of clinician and patient involvement with the development of a plan of care including signature by the practitioner/therapist and either a co-signature by the patient or documented verbal agreement obtained from the patient or, when necessary, an authorized representative

G8439 Documentation that patient is not eligible for co-developing a plan of care including signature by the practitioner/therapist and either a co-signature by the patient or documented verbal agreement obtained from the patient or, when necessary, an authorized representative

G8440 Documentation of pain assessment (including location, intensity and description) prior to initiation of treatment or documentation of the absence of pain as a result of assessment through discussion with the patient including the use of a standardized tool and a follow-up plan is documented

G8441 No documentation of pain assessment (including location, intensity and description) prior to initiation of treatment

G8442 Documentation that patient is not eligible for pain assessment

G8443 All prescriptions created during the encounter were generated using a qualified e-prescribing system

G8445 No prescriptions were generated during the encounter, provider does have access to a qualified e-prescribing system

G8446 Provider does have access to a qualified e-prescribing system and some or all of the prescriptions generated during the encounter were printed or phoned in as required by state or Federal law or regulations, patient request or pharmacy system being unable to receive electronic transmission; or because they were for narcotics or other controlled substances

G8447 Patient encounter was documented using a CCHIT certified EHR

G8448 Patient encounter was documented using a qualified (non-CCHIT certified) EHR

G8449 Patient encounter was not documented using an EMR due to system reasons such as, the system being inoperable at the time of the visit; use of this code implies that an EMR is in place and generally available

G8450 Beta-blocker therapy prescribed for patients with left ventricular ejection fraction (LVEF) <40% or documentation as moderately or severely depressed left ventricular systolic function

G8451 Clinician documented patient with left ventricular ejection fraction (LVEF) <40% or documentation as moderately or severely depressed left ventricular systolic function was not eligible candidate for beta-blocker therapy

G8452 Beta-blocker therapy not prescribed for patients with left ventricular ejection fraction (LVEF) <40% or documentation as moderately or severely depressed left ventricular systolic function

G8453 Tobacco use cessation intervention, counseling

G8454 Tobacco use cessation intervention not counseled, reason not specified

G8455 Current tobacco smoker

G8456 Current smokeless tobacco user

G8457 Current tobacco nonuser

G8458 Clinician documented that patient is not an eligible candidate for genotype testing; patient not receiving antiviral treatment for hepatitis C

G8459 Clinician documented that patient is receiving antiviral treatment for hepatitis C

G8460 Clinician documented that patient is not an eligible candidate for quantitative RNA testing at week 12; patient not receiving antiviral treatment for hepatitis C

G8461 Patient receiving antiviral treatment for hepatitis C

G8462 Clinician documented that patient is not an eligible candidate for counseling regarding contraception prior to antiviral treatment; patient not receiving antiviral treatment for hepatitis C

G8463 Patient receiving antiviral treatment for hepatitis C documented

G8464 Clinician documented that prostate cancer patient is not an eligible candidate for adjuvant hormonal therapy; low or intermediate risk of recurrence or risk of recurrence not determined

G8465 High risk of recurrence of prostate cancer

G8466 Clinician documented that patient is not an eligible candidate for suicide risk assessment; major depressive disorder, in remission

G8467 Documentation of new diagnosis of initial or recurrent episode of major depressive disorder

G8468 Angiotensin converting enzyme (ACE) inhibitor or angiotensin receptor blocker (ARB) therapy prescribed for patients with a left ventricular ejection fraction (LVEF) <40% or documentation of moderately or severely depressed left ventricular systolic function

G8469 Clinician documented that patient with a left ventricular ejection fraction (LVEF) <40% or documentation of moderately or severely depressed left ventricular systolic function was not an eligible candidate for angiotensin converting enzyme (ACE) inhibitor or angiotensin receptor blocker (ARB) therapy

G8470 Patient with left ventricular ejection fraction (LVEF) >=40% or documentation as normal or mildly depressed left ventricular systolic function

G8471 Left ventricular ejection fraction (LVEF) was not performed or documented

G8472 Angiotensin converting enzyme (ACE) inhibitor or angiotensin receptor blocker (ARB) therapy not prescribed for patients with a left ventricular ejection fraction (LVEF) <40% or documentation of moderately or severely depressed left ventricular systolic function, reason not specified

G8473 Angiotensin converting enzyme (ACE) inhibitor or angiotensin receptor blocker (ARB) therapy prescribed

G8474 Angiotensin converting enzyme (ACE) inhibitor or angiotensin receptor blocker (ARB) therapy not prescribed for reasons documented by the clinician

G8475 Angiotensin converting enzyme (ACE) inhibitor or angiotensin receptor blocker (ARB) therapy not prescribed, reason not specified

G8476 Most recent blood pressure has a systolic measurement of <130 mm/Hg and a diastolic measurement of <80 mm/Hg

G8477 Most recent blood pressure has a systolic measurement of >=130 mm/Hg and/or a diastolic measurement of >=80 mm/Hg

G8478 Blood pressure measurement not performed or documented, reason not specified

G8479 Clinician prescribed angiotensin converting enzyme (ACE) inhibitor or angiotensin receptor blocker (ARB) therapy

G8480 Clinician documented that patient was not an eligible candidate for angiotensin converting enzyme (ACE) inhibitor or angiotensin receptor blocker (ARB) therapy

G8481 Clinician did not prescribe angiotensin converting enzyme (ACE) inhibitor or angiotensin receptor blocker (ARB) therapy, reason not specified

G8482 Influenza immunization was ordered or administered

G8483 Influenza immunization was not ordered or administered for reasons documented by clinician

G8484 Influenza immunization was not ordered or administered, reason not specified

G8485 I intend to report the diabetes mellitus measures group

G8486 I intend to report the preventive care measures group

G8487 I intend to report the chronic kidney disease (CKD) measures group

G8488 Clinician intends to report the ESRD measure group

G8489 I intend to report the coronary artery disease (CAD) measures group

G8490 I intend to report the rheumatoid arthritis measures group

G8491 I intend to report the HIV/AIDS measures group

G8492 I intend to report the perioperative care measures group

G8493 I intend to report the back pain measures group

G8494 All quality actions for the applicable measures in the diabetes mellitus measures group have been performed for this patient

G8495 All quality actions for the applicable measures in the CKD measures group have been performed for this patient

G8496 All quality actions for the applicable measures in the preventive care measures group have been performed for this patient

G8497 All quality actions for the applicable measures in the coronary artery bypass graft (CABG) measures group have been performed for this patient

G8498 All quality actions for the applicable measures in the coronary artery disease (CAD) measures group have been performed for this patient

G8499 All quality actions for the applicable measures in the rheumatoid arthritis measures group have been performed for this patient

G8500 All quality actions for the applicable measures in the HIV/AIDS measures group have been performed for this patient

G8501 All quality actions for the applicable measures in the perioperative care measures group have been performed for this patient

G8502 All quality actions for the applicable measures in the back pain measures group have been performed for this patient

G8503 Documentation that prophylactic antibiotic was given within one hour (if fluoroquinolone or vancomycin, two hours) prior to surgical incision (or start of procedure when no incision is required)

G8504 Documentation of order for prophylactic antibiotics to be given within one hour (if fluoroquinolone or vancomycin, two hours) prior to surgical incision (or start of procedure when no incision is required)

G8505 Documentation that prophylactic antibiotic was not given within one hour (if fluoroquinolone or vancomycin, two hours) prior to surgical incision (or start of procedure when no incision is required), reason not specified

G8506 Patient receiving angiotensin converting enzyme (ACE) inhibitor or angiotensin receptor blocker (ARB) therapy

G8507 Provider documentation that patient is not eligible for patient verification of current medications

G8508 Documentation of pain assessment (including location, intensity and description) prior to initiation of treatment or documentation of the absence of pain as a result of assessment through discussion with the patient including the use of a standardized tool; no documentation of a follow-up plan, patient not eligible

G8509 Documentation of pain assessment (including location, intensity and description) prior to initiation of treatment or documentation of the absence of pain as a result of assessment through discussion with the patient including the use of a standardized tool; no documentation of a follow-up plan, reason not specified

G8510 Negative screen for clinical depression using a standardized tool, patient not eligible/appropriate for follow-up plan documented

G8511 Screen for clinical depression using a standardized tool documented, follow up plan not documented, reason not specified

G8512 Pain severity quantified; pain present

G8513 ABI measured and documented

G8514 Clinician documented that patient was not an eligible candidate for ABI measurement measure

G8515 ABI measurement was not obtained

G8516 Patient screened for future falls risk; documentation of two or more falls in the past year or any fall with injury in the past year

G8517 Patient screened for future fall risk; documentation of no falls in the past year or only one fall without injury in the past year

G8518 Clinical stage prior to surgery for lung cancer and esophageal cancer resection was recorded

G8519 Clinician documented that patient was not eligible for clinical stage prior to surgery for lung cancer and esophageal cancer resection measure

G8520 Clinician stage prior to surgery for lung cancer and esophageal cancer resection was not recorded, reason not specified

G8521 Antiplatelet therapy received (ASA [81-325 mg/day] and/or clopidogrel [75 mg/day]) within 48 hours of the initiation of surgery and at discharge

G8522 Clinician documented that patient was not an eligible candidate for antiplatelet therapy

G8523 Antiplatelet therapy not received 48 hours prior to CEA and at discharge, reason not specified

G8524 Patch closure used for patient undergoing conventional CEA

G8525 Clinician documented that patient did not receive conventional CEA

G8526 Patch closure not used for patient undergoing conventional CEA, reason not specified

G8527 Documentation of order for cefazolin or cefuroxime for antimicrobial prophylaxis

G8528 Clinician documented that patient was ineligible for prophylactic antibiotic selection measure

G8529 Order for cefazolin or cefuroxime for antimicrobial prophylaxis not documented, reason not specified

G8530 Autogenous AV fistula received

G8531 Clinician documented that patient was not an eligible candidate for autogenous AV fistula

G8532 Clinician documented that patient received vascular access other than autogenous AV fistula, reason not specified

G8533 Participation by a physician or other clinician in systematic clinical database registry that includes consensus-endorsed quality measures

G8534 Documentation of an elder maltreatment screen and follow-up plan

G8535 No documentation of an elder maltreatment screen, patient not eligible

G8536 No documentation of an elder maltreatment screen, reason not specified

G8537 Elder maltreatment screen documented, follow-up plan not documented, patient not eligible

G8538 Elder maltreatment screen documented, follow-up plan not documented, reason not specified

G8539 Documentation of a current functional outcome assessment using a standardized tool and care plan based on identified deficiencies

G8540 Documentation that the patient is not eligible for a functional outcome assessment using a standardized tool

G8541 No documentation of a current functional outcome assessment using a standardized tool, reason not specified

G8542 Documentation of a current functional outcome assessment using a standardized tool; no documentation of a care plan, patient not eligible

G8543 Documentation of a current functional outcome assessment using a standardized tool; no documentation of a care plan, reason not specified

G8544 I intend to report the coronary artery bypass graft (CABG) measures group

G9001 Coordinated care fee, initial rate

G9002 Coordinated care fee, maintenance rate

G9003 Coordinated care fee, risk adjusted high, initial

G9004 Coordinated care fee, risk adjusted low, initial

G9005 Coordinated care fee, risk adjusted maintenance

G9006 Coordinated care fee, home monitoring

G9007 Coordinated care fee, scheduled team conference

G9008 Coordinated care fee, physician coordinated care oversight services

G9009 Coordinated care fee, risk adjusted maintenance, Level 3

G9010 Coordinated care fee, risk adjusted maintenance, Level 4

G9011 Coordinated care fee, risk adjusted maintenance, Level 5

G9012 Other specified case management service not elsewhere classified

G9013 ESRD demo basic bundle Level I

G9014 ESRD demo expanded bundle including venous access and related services

G9016 Smoking cessation counseling, individual, in the absence of or in addition to any other evaluation and management service, per session (6-10 minutes) [demo project code only]

G9017 Amantadine HCl, oral, per 100 mg (for use in a Medicare-approved demonstration project)

G9018 Zanamivir, inhalation powder, administered through inhaler, generic, per 10 mg (for use in a Medicare-approved demonstration project)

G9019 Oseltamivir phosphate, oral, generic, per 75 mg (for use in a Medicare-approved demonstration project)

G9020 Rimantadine HCl, oral, per 100 mg (for use in a Medicare-approved demonstration project)

G9033 Amantadine HCl, oral brand, per 100 mg (for use in a Medicare-approved demonstration project)

G9034 Zanamivir, inhalation powder, administered through inhaler, brand name, per 10 mg (for use in a Medicare-approved demonstration project)

G9035 Oseltamivir phosphate, oral, brand name, per 75 mg (for use in a Medicare-approved demonstration project)

G9036 Rimantadine HCl, oral, brand name, per 100 mg (for use in a Medicare-approved demonstration project)

G9041 Rehabilitation services for low vision by qualified occupational therapist, direct one-on-one contact, each 15 minutes

G9042 Rehabilitation services for low vision by certified orientation and mobility specialists, direct one-on-one contact, each 15 minutes

G9043 Rehabilitation services for low vision by certified low vision rehabilitation therapist, direct one-on-one contact, each 15 minutes

G9044 Rehabilitation services for low vision by certified low vision rehabilitation teacher, direct one-on-one contact, each 15 minutes

G9050 Oncology; primary focus of visit; work-up, evaluation, or staging at the time of cancer diagnosis or recurrence (for use in a Medicare-approved demonstration project)

G9051 Oncology; primary focus of visit; treatment decision-making after disease is staged or restaged, discussion of treatment options, supervising/coordinating active cancer-directed therapy or managing consequences of cancer-directed therapy (for use in a Medicare-approved demonstration project)

G9052 Oncology; primary focus of visit; surveillance for disease recurrence for patient who has completed definitive cancer-directed therapy and currently lacks evidence of recurrent disease; cancer-directed therapy might be considered in the future (for use in a Medicare-approved demonstration project)

G9053 Oncology; primary focus of visit; expectant management of patient with evidence of cancer for whom no cancer-directed therapy is being administered or arranged at present; cancer-directed therapy might be considered in the future (for use in a Medicare-approved demonstration project)

G9054 Oncology; primary focus of visit; supervising, coordinating or managing care of patient with terminal cancer or for whom other medical illness prevents further cancer treatment; includes symptom management, end-of-life care planning, management of palliative therapies (for use in a Medicare-approved demonstration project)

G9055 Oncology; primary focus of visit; other, unspecified service not otherwise listed (for use in a Medicare-approved demonstration project)

G9056 Oncology; practice guidelines; management adheres to guidelines (for use in a Medicare-approved demonstration project)

G9057 Oncology; practice guidelines; management differs from guidelines as a result of patient enrollment in an institutional review board-approved clinical trial (for use in a Medicare-approved demonstration project)

G9058 Oncology; practice guidelines; management differs from guidelines because the treating physician disagrees with guideline recommendations (for use in a Medicare-approved demonstration project)

G9059 Oncology; practice guidelines; management differs from guidelines because the patient, after being offered treatment consistent with guidelines, has opted for alternative treatment or management, including no treatment (for use in a Medicare-approved demonstration project)

G9060 Oncology; practice guidelines; management differs from guidelines for reason(s) associated with patient comorbid illness or performance status not factored into guidelines (for use in a Medicare-approved demonstration project)

G9061 Oncology; practice guidelines; patient's condition not addressed by available guidelines (for use in a Medicare-approved demonstration project)

G9062 Oncology; practice guidelines; management differs from guidelines for other reason(s) not listed (for use in a Medicare-approved demonstration project)

G9063 Oncology; disease status; limited to nonsmall cell lung cancer; extent of disease initially established as Stage I (prior to neoadjuvant therapy, if any) with no evidence of disease progression, recurrence, or metastases (for use in a Medicare-approved demonstration project)

G9064 Oncology; disease status; limited to nonsmall cell lung cancer; extent of disease initially established as Stage II (prior to neoadjuvant therapy, if any) with no evidence of disease progression, recurrence, or metastases (for use in a Medicare-approved demonstration project)

G9065 Oncology; disease status; limited to nonsmall cell lung cancer; extent of disease initially established as Stage III a (prior to neoadjuvant therapy, if any) with no evidence of disease progression, recurrence, or metastases (for use in a Medicare-approved demonstration project)

G9066 Oncology; disease status; limited to nonsmall cell lung cancer; Stage III B-IV at diagnosis, metastatic, locally recurrent, or progressive (for use in a Medicare-approved demonstration project)

G9067 Oncology; disease status; limited to nonsmall cell lung cancer; extent of disease unknown, staging in progress, or not listed (for use in a Medicare-approved demonstration project)

G9068 Oncology; disease status; limited to small cell and combined small cell/nonsmall cell; extent of disease initially established as limited with no evidence of disease progression, recurrence, or metastases (for use in a Medicare-approved demonstration project)

G9069 Oncology; disease status; small cell lung cancer, limited to small cell and combined small cell/nonsmall cell; extensive Stage at diagnosis, metastatic, locally recurrent, or progressive (for use in a Medicare-approved demonstration project)

G9070 Oncology; disease status; small cell lung cancer, limited to small cell and combined small cell/nonsmall; extent of disease unknown, staging in progress, or not listed (for use in a Medicare-approved demonstration project)

G9071 Oncology; disease status; invasive female breast cancer (does not include ductal carcinoma in situ); adenocarcinoma as predominant cell type; stage I or stage IIA-IIB; or T3, N1, M0; and ER and/or PR positive; with no evidence of disease progression, recurrence, or metastases (for use in a Medicare-approved demonstration project)

G9072 Oncology; disease status; invasive female breast cancer (does not include ductal carcinoma in situ); adenocarcinoma as predominant cell type; stage I, or stage IIA-IIB; or T3, N1, M0; and ER and PR negative; with no evidence of disease progression, recurrence, or metastases (for use in a Medicare-approved demonstration project)

G9073 Oncology; disease status; invasive female breast cancer (does not include ductal carcinoma in situ); adenocarcinoma as predominant cell type; stage IIIA-IIIB; and not T3, N1, M0; and ER and/or PR positive; with no evidence of disease progression, recurrence, or metastases (for use in a Medicare-approved demonstration project)

G9074 Oncology; disease status; invasive female breast cancer (does not include ductal carcinoma in situ); adenocarcinoma as predominant cell type; stage IIIA-IIIB; and not T3, N1, M0; and ER and PR negative; with no evidence of disease progression, recurrence, or metastases (for use in a Medicare-approved demonstration project)

G9075 Oncology; disease status; invasive female breast cancer (does not include ductal carcinoma in situ); adenocarcinoma as predominant cell type; M1 at diagnosis, metastatic locally recurrent, or progressive (for use in a Medicare-approved demonstration project)

G9077 Oncology; disease status; prostate cancer, limited to adenocarcinoma as predominant cell type; T1-T2C and Gleason 2-7 and PSA < or equal to 20 at diagnosis with no evidence of disease progression, recurrence, or metastases (for use in a Medicare-approved demonstration project)

G9078 Oncology; disease status; prostate cancer, limited to adenocarcinoma as predominant cell type; T2 or T3a Gleason 8-10 or PSA >20 at diagnosis with no evidence of disease progression, recurrence, or metastases (for use in a Medicare-approved demonstration project)

G9079 Oncology; disease status; prostate cancer, limited to adenocarcinoma as predominant cell type; T3B-T4, any N; any T, N1 at diagnosis with no evidence of disease progression, recurrence, or metastases (for use in a Medicare-approved demonstration project)

G9080 Oncology; disease status; prostate cancer, limited to adenocarcinoma; after initial treatment with rising PSA or failure of PSA decline (for use in a Medicare-approved demonstration project)

G9083 Oncology; disease status; prostate cancer, limited to adenocarcinoma; extent of disease unknown, staging in progress, or not listed (for use in a Medicare-approved demonstration project)

G9084 Oncology; disease status; colon cancer, limited to invasive cancer, adenocarcinoma as predominant cell type; extent of disease initially established as T1-3, N0, M0 with no evidence of disease progression, recurrence or metastases (for use in a Medicare-approved demonstration project)

G9085 Oncology; disease status; colon cancer, limited to invasive cancer, adenocarcinoma as predominant cell type; extent of disease initially established as T4, N0, M0 with no evidence of disease progression, recurrence, or metastases (for use in a Medicare-approved demonstration project)

G9086 Oncology; disease status; colon cancer, limited to invasive cancer, adenocarcinoma as predominant cell type; extent of disease initially established as T1-4, N1-2, M0 with no evidence of disease progression, recurrence, or metastases (for use in a Medicare-approved demonstration project)

G9087 Oncology; disease status; colon cancer, limited to invasive cancer, adenocarcinoma as predominant cell type; M1 at diagnosis, metastatic locally recurrent, or progressive with current clinical, radiologic, or biochemical evidence of disease (for use in a Medicare-approved demonstration project)

G9088 Oncology; disease status; colon cancer, limited to invasive cancer, adenocarcinoma as predominant cell type; M1 at diagnosis, metastatic, locally recurrent, or progressive without current clinical, radiologic, or biochemical evidence of disease (for use in a Medicare-approved demonstration project)

G9089 Oncology; disease status; colon cancer, limited to invasive cancer, adenocarcinoma as predominant cell type; extent of disease unknown, staging in progress or not listed (for use in a Medicare-approved demonstration project)

G9090 Oncology; disease status; rectal cancer, limited to invasive cancer, adenocarcinoma as predominant cell type; extent of disease initially established as T1-2, N0, M0 (prior to neoadjuvant therapy, if any) with no evidence of disease progression, recurrence, or metastases (for use in a Medicare-approved demonstration project)

G9091 Oncology; disease status; rectal cancer, limited to invasive cancer, adenocarcinoma as predominant cell type; extent of disease initially established as T3, N0, M0 (prior to neoadjuvant therapy, if any) with no evidence of disease progression, recurrence, or metastases (for use in a Medicare-approved demonstration project)

G9092 Oncology; disease status; rectal cancer, limited to invasive cancer, adenocarcinoma as predominant cell type; extent of disease initially established as T1-3, N1-2, M0 (prior to neoadjuvant therapy, if any) with no evidence of disease progression, recurrence or metastases (for use in a Medicare-approved demonstration project)

G9093 Oncology; disease status; rectal cancer, limited to invasive cancer, adenocarcinoma as predominant cell type; extent of disease initially established as T4, any N, M0 (prior to neoadjuvant therapy, if any) with no evidence of disease progression, recurrence, or metastases (for use in a Medicare-approved demonstration project)

G9094 Oncology; disease status; rectal cancer, limited to invasive cancer, adenocarcinoma as predominant cell type; M1 at diagnosis, metastatic, locally recurrent, or progressive (for use in a Medicare-approved demonstration project)

G9095 Oncology; disease status; rectal cancer, limited to invasive cancer, adenocarcinoma as predominant cell type; extent of disease unknown, staging in progress or not listed (for use in a Medicare-approved demonstration project)

G9096 Oncology; disease status; esophageal cancer, limited to adenocarcinoma or squamous cell carcinoma as predominant cell type; extent of disease initially established as T1-T3, N0-N1 or NX (prior to neoadjuvant therapy, if any) with no evidence of disease progression, recurrence, or metastases (for use in a Medicare-approved demonstration project)

G9097 Oncology; disease status; esophageal cancer, limited to adenocarcinoma or squamous cell carcinoma as predominant cell type; extent of disease initially established as T4, any N, M0 (prior to neoadjuvant therapy, if any) with no evidence of disease progression, recurrence, or metastases (for use in a Medicare-approved demonstration project)

G9098 Oncology; disease status; esophageal cancer, limited to adenocarcinoma or squamous cell carcinoma as predominant cell type; M1 at diagnosis, metastatic, locally recurrent, or progressive (for use in a Medicare-approved demonstration project)

G9099 Oncology; disease status; esophageal cancer, limited to adenocarcinoma or squamous cell carcinoma as predominant cell type; extent of disease unknown, staging in progress, or not listed (for use in a Medicare-approved demonstration project)

G9100 Oncology; disease status; gastric cancer, limited to adenocarcinoma as predominant cell type; post R0 resection (with or without neoadjuvant therapy) with no evidence of disease recurrence, progression, or metastases (for use in a Medicare-approved demonstration project)

G9101 Oncology; disease status; gastric cancer, limited to adenocarcinoma as predominant cell type; post R1 or R2 resection (with or without neoadjuvant therapy) with no evidence of disease progression, or metastases (for use in a Medicare-approved demonstration project)

G9102 Oncology; disease status; gastric cancer, limited to adenocarcinoma as predominant cell type; clinical or pathologic M0, unresectable with no evidence of disease progression, or metastases (for use in a Medicare-approved demonstration project)

G9103 Oncology; disease status; gastric cancer, limited to adenocarcinoma as predominant cell type; clinical or pathologic M1 at diagnosis, metastatic, locally recurrent, or progressive (for use in a Medicare-approved demonstration project)

G9104 Oncology; disease status; gastric cancer, limited to adenocarcinoma as predominant cell type; extent of disease unknown, staging in progress, or not listed (for use in a Medicare-approved demonstration project)

G9105 Oncology; disease status; pancreatic cancer, limited to adenocarcinoma as predominant cell type; post R0 resection without evidence of disease progression, recurrence, or metastases (for use in a Medicare-approved demonstration project)

G9106 Oncology; disease status; pancreatic cancer, limited to adenocarcinoma; post R1 or R2 resection with no evidence of disease progression, or metastases (for use in a Medicare-approved demonstration project)

G9107 Oncology; disease status; pancreatic cancer, limited to adenocarcinoma; unresectable at diagnosis, M1 at diagnosis, metastatic, locally recurrent, or progressive (for use in a Medicare-approved demonstration project)

G9108 Oncology; disease status; pancreatic cancer, limited to adenocarcinoma; extent of disease unknown, staging in progress, or not listed (for use in a Medicare-approved demonstration project)

G9109 Oncology; disease status; head and neck cancer, limited to cancers of oral cavity, pharynx and larynx with squamous cell as predominant cell type; extent of disease initially established as T1-T2 and N0, M0 (prior to neoadjuvant therapy, if any) with no evidence of disease progression, recurrence, or metastases (for use in a Medicare-approved demonstration project)

G9110 Oncology; disease status; head and neck cancer, limited to cancers of oral cavity, pharynx and larynx with squamous cell as predominant cell type; extent of disease initially established as T3-4 and/or N1-3, M0 (prior to neoadjuvant therapy, if any) with no evidence of disease progression, recurrence, or metastases (for use in a Medicare-approved demonstration project)

G9111 Oncology; disease status; head and neck cancer, limited to cancers of oral cavity, pharynx and larynx with squamous cell as predominant cell type; M1 at diagnosis, metastatic, locally recurrent, or progressive (for use in a Medicare-approved demonstration project)

G9112 Oncology; disease status; head and neck cancer, limited to cancers of oral cavity, pharynx and larynx with squamous cell as predominant cell type; extent of disease unknown, staging in progress, or not listed (for use in a Medicare-approved demonstration project)

G9113 Oncology; disease status; ovarian cancer, limited to epithelial cancer; pathologic stage 1A-B (Grade 1) without evidence of disease progression, recurrence, or metastases (for use in a Medicare-approved demonstration project)

G9114 Oncology; disease status; ovarian cancer, limited to epithelial cancer; pathologic stage IA-B (grade 2-3); or stage IC (all grades); or stage II; without evidence of disease progression, recurrence, or metastases (for use in a Medicare-approved demonstration project)

G9115 Oncology; disease status; ovarian cancer, limited to epithelial cancer; pathologic stage III-IV; without evidence of progression, recurrence, or metastases (for use in a Medicare-approved demonstration project)

G9116 Oncology; disease status; ovarian cancer, limited to epithelial cancer; evidence of disease progression, or recurrence, and/or platinum resistance (for use in a Medicare-approved demonstration project)

G9117 Oncology; disease status; ovarian cancer, limited to epithelial cancer; extent of disease unknown, staging in progress, or not listed (for use in a Medicare-approved demonstration project)

G9123 Oncology; disease status; chronic myelogenous leukemia, limited to Philadelphia chromosome positive and/or BCR-ABL positive; chronic phase not in hematologic, cytogenetic, or molecular remission (for use in a Medicare-approved demonstration project)

G9124 Oncology; disease status; chronic myelogenous leukemia, limited to Philadelphia chromosome positive and /or BCR-ABL positive; accelerated phase not in hematologic cytogenetic, or molecular remission (for use in a Medicare-approved demonstration project)

G9125 Oncology; disease status; chronic myelogenous leukemia, limited to Philadelphia chromosome positive and/or BCR-ABL positive; blast phase not in hematologic, cytogenetic, or molecular remission (for use in a Medicare-approved demonstration project)

G9126 Oncology; disease status; chronic myelogenous leukemia, limited to Philadelphia chromosome positive and/or BCR-ABL positive; in hematologic, cytogenetic, or molecular remission (for use in a Medicare-approved demonstration project)

G9128 Oncology; disease status; limited to multiple myeloma, systemic disease; smoldering, stage I (for use in a Medicare-approved demonstration project)

G9129 Oncology; disease status; limited to multiple myeloma, systemic disease; stage II or higher (for use in a Medicare-approved demonstration project)

G9130 Oncology; disease status; limited to multiple myeloma, systemic disease; extent of disease unknown, staging in progress, or not listed (for use in a Medicare-approved demonstration project)

G9131 Oncology; disease status; invasive female breast cancer (does not include ductal carcinoma in situ); adenocarcinoma as predominant cell type; extent of disease unknown, staging in progress, or not listed (for use in a Medicare-approved demonstration project)

G9132 Oncology; disease status; prostate cancer, limited to adenocarcinoma; hormone-refractory/androgen-independent (e.g., rising PSA on antiandrogen therapy or postorchiectomy); clinical metastases (for use in a Medicare-approved demonstration project)

G9133 Oncology; disease status; prostate cancer, limited to adenocarcinoma; hormone-responsive; clinical metastases or M1 at diagnosis (for use in a Medicare-approved demonstration project)

G9134 Oncology; disease status; non-Hodgkin's lymphoma, any cellular classification; Stage I, II at diagnosis, not relapsed, not refractory (for use in a Medicare-approved demonstration project)

G9135 Oncology; disease status; non-Hodgkin's lymphoma, any cellular classification; Stage III, IV, not relapsed, not refractory (for use in a Medicare-approved demonstration project)

G9136 Oncology; disease status; non-Hodgkin's lymphoma, transformed from original cellular diagnosis to a second cellular classification (for use in a medicare-approved demonstration project)

G9137 Oncology; disease status; non-Hodgkin's lymphoma, any cellular classification; relapsed/refractory (for use in a medicare-approved demonstration project)

G9138 Oncology; disease status; non-Hodgkin's lymphoma, any cellular classification; diagnostic evaluation, stage not determined, evaluation of possible relapse or nonresponse to therapy, or not listed (for use in a Medicare-approved demonstration project)

G9139 Oncology; disease status; chronic myelogenous leukemia, limited to Philadelphia chromosome positive and/or BCR-ABL positive; extent of disease unknown, staging in progress, not listed (for use in a Medicare-approved demonstration project)

G9140 Frontier extended stay clinic demonstration; for a patient stay in a clinic approved for the CMS demonstration project; the following measures should be present: the stay must be equal to or greater than 4 hours; weather or other conditions must prevent transfer or the case falls into a category of monitoring and observation cases that are permitted by the rules of the demonstration; there is a maximum frontier extended stay clinic (FESC) visit of 48 hours, except in the case when weather or other conditions prevent transfer; payment is made on each period up to 4 hours, after the first 4 hours

ALCOHOL AND DRUG ABUSE TREATMENT SERVICES H0001-H2037

The H codes are used by those state Medicaid agencies that are mandated by state law to establish separate codes for identifying mental health services that include alcohol and drug treatment services.

H0001 Alcohol and/or drug assessment

H0002 Behavioral health screening to determine eligibility for admission to treatment program

H0003 Alcohol and/or drug screening; laboratory analysis of specimens for presence of alcohol and/or drugs

H0004 Behavioral health counseling and therapy, per 15 minutes

H0005 Alcohol and/or drug services; group counseling by a clinician

H0006 Alcohol and/or drug services; case management

H0007 Alcohol and/or drug services; crisis intervention (outpatient)

H0008 Alcohol and/or drug services; subacute detoxification (hospital inpatient)

H0009 Alcohol and/or drug services; acute detoxification (hospital inpatient)

H0010 Alcohol and/or drug services; subacute detoxification (residential addiction program inpatient)

H0011 Alcohol and/or drug services; acute detoxification (residential addiction program inpatient)

H0012 Alcohol and/or drug services; subacute detoxification (residential addiction program outpatient)

H0013 Alcohol and/or drug services; acute detoxification (residential addiction program outpatient)

H0014 Alcohol and/or drug services; ambulatory detoxification

H0015 Alcohol and/or drug services; intensive outpatient (treatment program that operates at least 3 hours/day and at least 3 days/week and is based on an individualized treatment plan), including assessment, counseling; crisis intervention, and activity therapies or education

H0016 Alcohol and/or drug services; medical/somatic (medical intervention in ambulatory setting)

H0017 Behavioral health; residential (hospital residential treatment program), without room and board, per diem

H0018 Behavioral health; short-term residential (nonhospital residential treatment program), without room and board, per diem

H0019 Behavioral health; long-term residential (nonmedical, nonacute care in a residential treatment program where stay is typically longer than 30 days), without room and board, per diem

H0020 Alcohol and/or drug services; methadone administration and/or service (provision of the drug by a licensed program)

H0021 Alcohol and/or drug training service (for staff and personnel not employed by providers)

H0022 Alcohol and/or drug intervention service (planned facilitation)

H0023 Behavioral health outreach service (planned approach to reach a targeted population)

H0024 Behavioral health prevention information dissemination service (one-way direct or nondirect contact with service audiences to affect knowledge and attitude)

H0025 Behavioral health prevention education service (delivery of services with target population to affect knowledge, attitude and/or behavior)

H0026 Alcohol and/or drug prevention process service, community-based (delivery of services to develop skills of impactors)

H0027 Alcohol and/or drug prevention environmental service (broad range of external activities geared toward modifying systems in order to mainstream prevention through policy and law)

H0028 Alcohol and/or drug prevention problem identification and referral service (e.g., student assistance and employee assistance programs), does not include assessment

H0029 Alcohol and/or drug prevention alternatives service (services for populations that exclude alcohol and other drug use e.g., alcohol free social events)

H0030 Behavioral health hotline service

H0031 Mental health assessment, by nonphysician

H0032 Mental health service plan development by nonphysician

H0033 Oral medication administration, direct observation

H0034 Medication training and support, per 15 minutes

H0035 Mental health partial hospitalization, treatment, less than 24 hours

H0036 Community psychiatric supportive treatment, face-to-face, per 15 minutes

H0037 Community psychiatric supportive treatment program, per diem

H0038 Self-help/peer services, per 15 minutes

H0039 Assertive community treatment, face-to-face, per 15 minutes

H0040 Assertive community treatment program, per diem

H0041 Foster care, child, nontherapeutic, per diem

H0042 Foster care, child, nontherapeutic, per month

H0043 Supported housing, per diem

H0044 Supported housing, per month

H0045 Respite care services, not in the home, per diem

H0046 Mental health services, not otherwise specified

H0047 Alcohol and/or other drug abuse services, not otherwise specified

H0048 Alcohol and/or other drug testing: collection and handling only, specimens other than blood

H0049 Alcohol and/or drug screening

H0050 Alcohol and/or drug services, brief intervention, per 15 minutes

H1000 Prenatal care, at-risk assessment

H1001 Prenatal care, at-risk enhanced service; antepartum management

H1002 Prenatal care, at risk enhanced service; care coordination

H1003 Prenatal care, at-risk enhanced service; education

H1004 Prenatal care, at-risk enhanced service; follow-up home visit

H1005 Prenatal care, at-risk enhanced service package (includes H1001–H1004)

H1010 Nonmedical family planning education, per session

H1011 Family assessment by licensed behavioral health professional for state defined purposes

H2000 Comprehensive multidisciplinary evaluation

H2001 Rehabilitation program, per 1/2 day

H2010 Comprehensive medication services, per 15 minutes

H2011 Crisis intervention service, per 15 minutes

H2012 Behavioral health day treatment, per hour

H2013 Psychiatric health facility service, per diem

H2014 Skills training and development, per 15 minutes

H2015 Comprehensive community support services, per 15 minutes

H2016 Comprehensive community support services, per diem

H2017 Psychosocial rehabilitation services, per 15 minutes

H2018 Psychosocial rehabilitation services, per diem

H2019 Therapeutic behavioral services, per 15 minutes

H2020 Therapeutic behavioral services, per diem

H2021 Community-based wrap-around services, per 15 minutes

H2022 Community-based wrap-around services, per diem

H2023 Supported employment, per 15 minutes

H2024 Supported employment, per diem

H2025 Ongoing support to maintain employment, per 15 minutes

H2026 Ongoing support to maintain employment, per diem

H2027 Psychoeducational service, per 15 minutes

H2028 Sexual offender treatment service, per 15 minutes

H2029 Sexual offender treatment service, per diem

H2030 Mental health clubhouse services, per 15 minutes

H2031 Mental health clubhouse services, per diem

H2032 Activity therapy, per 15 minutes

H2033 Multisystemic therapy for juveniles, per 15 minutes

H2034 Alcohol and/or drug abuse halfway house services, per diem

H2035 Alcohol and/or other drug treatment program, per hour

H2036 Alcohol and/or other drug treatment program, per diem

H2037 Developmental delay prevention activities, dependent child of client, per 15 minutes

DRUGS ADMINISTERED OTHER THAN ORAL METHOD J0000-J9999

J codes include drugs that ordinarily cannot be self-administered, chemotherapy drugs, immunosuppressive drugs, inhalation solutions, and other miscellaneous drugs and solutions.

J0120 **Injection, tetracycline, up to 250 mg**
MED: 100-2,15,50

J0128 **Injection, abarelix, 10 mg**
Use this code for Planaxis.

J0129 **Injection, abatacept, 10 mg**
Use this code for Orencia

J0130 **Injection abciximab, 10 mg**
Use this code for ReoPro.
MED: 100-2,15,50

J0132 **Injection, acetylcysteine, 100 mg**
Use this code for Acetadote.

J0133 **Injection, acyclovir, 5 mg**
Use this code for Zovirax

J0135 **Injection, adalimumab, 20 mg**
Use this code for Humira.

J0150 **Injection, adenosine for therapeutic use, 6 mg (not to be used to report any adenosine phosphate compounds, instead use A9270)**
Use this code for Adenocard.
MED: 100-2,15,50
AHA: 2Q,'02,10

J0152 **Injection, adenosine for diagnostic use, 30 mg (not to be used to report any adenosine phosphate compounds; instead use A9270)**
Use this code for Adenoscan.

J0170 **Injection, adrenalin, epinephrine, up to 1 ml ampule**
Use this code for Adrenalin Chloride, Epipen, Sus-Phrine.
MED: 100-2,15,50

J0180 **Injection, agalsidase beta, 1 mg**
Use this code for Fabrazyme.

J0190 **Injection, biperiden lactate, per 5 mg**
MED: 100-2,15,50

J0200 **Injection, alatrofloxacin mesylate, 100 mg**
MED: 100-2,15,50.5

J0205 **Injection, alglucerase, per 10 units**
Use this code for Ceredase.
MED: 100-2,15,50

J0207 **Injection, amifostine, 500 mg**
Use this code for Ethyol.
MED: 100-2,15,50

J0210 **Injection, methyldopate HCl, up to 250 mg**
Use this code for Aldomet.
MED: 100-2,15,50

J0215 **Injection, alefacept, 0.5 mg**
Use this for Amevive.

J0220 **Injection, alglucosidase alfa, 10 mg**
Use this code for Myozime

J0256 **Injection, alpha 1-proteinase inhibitor — human, 10 mg**
Use this code for Prolastin, Zemira.
MED: 100-2,15,50

J0270 **Injection, alprostadil, 1.25 mcg (code may be used for Medicare when drug administered under the direct supervision of a physician, not for use when drug is self-administered)**
Use this code for Alprostadil, Caverject, Edex, Prostin VR Pediatric.
MED: 100-2,15,50

J0275 **Alprostadil urethral suppository (code may be used for Medicare when drug administered under the direct supervision of a physician, not for use when drug is self-administered)**
Use this code for Muse.
MED: 100-2,15,50

J0278 **Injection, amikacin sulfate, 100 mg**
Use this code for Amikin.

J0280 **Injection, aminophyllin, up to 250 mg**
MED: 100-2,15,50

J0282 **Injection, amiodarone HCl, 30 mg**
Use this code for Cordarone IV.
MED: 100-2,15,50

J0285 **Injection, amphotericin B, 50 mg**
Use this for Abelcet, Amphocin, Fungizone
MED: 100-2,15,50

J0287 **Injection, amphotericin B lipid complex, 10 mg**
MED: 100-2,15,50

J0288 **Injection, amphotericin B cholesteryl sulfate complex, 10 mg**
Use this code for Amphotec.
MED: 100-2,15,50

J0289 **Injection, amphotericin B liposome, 10 mg**
Use this code for Ambisome.
MED: 100-2,15,50

J0290 **Injection, ampicillin sodium, 500 mg**
MED: 100-2,15,50

J0295 **Injection, ampicillin sodium/sulbactam sodium, per 1.5 g**
Use this code for Unasyn.
MED: 100-2,15,50

J0300 **Injection, amobarbital, up to 125 mg**
Use this code for Amytal.
MED: 100-2,15,50

J0330 **Injection, succinylcholine chloride, up to 20 mg**
Use this code for Anectine, Quelicin.
MED: 100-2,15,50

J0348 **Injection, anidulafungin, 1 mg**
Use this code for Eraxis.

J0350 **Injection, anistreplase, per 30 units**
Use this code for Eminase.
MED: 100-2,15,50

J0360 **Injection, hydralazine HCl, up to 20 mg**
MED: 100-2,15,50

J0364 **Injection, apomorphine HCl, 1 mg**
Use this code for Apokyn.

J0365 **Injection, aprotonin, 10,000 kiu**
Use this code for Trasylol.
MED: 100-2,15,50

J0380 **Injection, metaraminol bitartrate, per 10 mg**
Use this code for Aramine.
MED: 100-2,15,50

J0390 **Injection, chloroquine HCl, up to 250 mg**
Use this code for Aralen.
MED: 100-2,15,50

J0395 **Injection, arbutamine HCl, 1 mg**
MED: 100-2,15,50

J0400 Injection, aripiprazole, intramuscular, 0.25 mg
Use this code for Abilify.

J0456 Injection, azithromycin, 500 mg
Use this code for Zithromax.
MED: 100-2,15,50.5

J0460 Injection, atropine sulfate, up to 0.3 mg
Use this code for Atropen.
MED: 100-2,15,50

J0470 Injection, dimercaprol, per 100 mg
Use this code for BAL
MED: 100-2,15,50

J0475 Injection, baclofen, 10 mg
Use this code for Lioresal.
MED: 100-2,15,50

J0476 Injection, baclofen, 50 mcg for intrathecal trial
Use this code for Lioresal for intrathecal trial.
MED: 100-2,15,50

J0480 Injection, basiliximab, 20 mg
Use this code for Simulect.
MED: 100-2,15,50; 100-4,4,240

J0500 Injection, dicyclomine HCl, up to 20 mg
Use this code for Bentyl.
MED: 100-2,15,50

J0515 Injection, benztropine mesylate, per 1 mg
Use this code for Cogentin.
MED: 100-2,15,50

J0520 Injection, bethanechol chloride, Myotonachol or Urecholine, up to 5 mg
MED: 100-2,15,50

J0530 Injection, penicillin G benzathine and penicillin G procaine, up to 600,000 units
Use this code for Bicillin C-R.
MED: 100-2,15,50

J0540 Injection, penicillin G benzathine and penicillin G procaine, up to 1,200,000 units
Use this code for Bicillin C-R, Bicillin C-R 900/300.
MED: 100-2,15,50

J0550 Injection, penicillin G benzathine and penicillin G procaine, up to 2,400,000 units
Use this code for Bicillin C-R.
MED: 100-2,15,50

J0560 Injection, penicillin G benzathine, up to 600,000 units
Use this code for Bicillin L-A, Permapen.
MED: 100-2,15,50

J0570 Injection, penicillin G benzathine, up to 1,200,000 units
Use this code for Bicillin L-A, Permapen.
MED: 100-2,15,50

J0580 Injection, penicillin G benzathine, up to 2,400,000 units
Use this code for Bicillin L-A, Permapen.
MED: 100-2,15,50

J0583 Injection, bivalirudin, 1 mg
Use this code for Angiomax.

J0585 Botulinum toxin type A, per unit
Use this code for Botox.
MED: 100-2,15,50

J0587 Botulinum toxin type B, per 100 units
Use this code for Myobloc.
MED: 100-2,15,50
AHA: 2Q,'02,8

J0592 Injection, buprenorphine HCl, 0.1 mg
Use this code for Buprenex.
MED: 100-2,15,50

J0594 Injection, busulfan, 1 mg
Use this code for Busulfex.

J0595 Injection, butorphanol tartrate, 1 mg
Use this code for Stadol.

J0600 Injection, edetate calcium disodium, up to 1,000 mg
Use this code for Calcium Disodium Versenate, Calcium EDTA.
MED: 100-2,15,50

J0610 Injection, calcium gluconate, per 10 ml
MED: 100-2,15,50

J0620 Injection, calcium glycerophosphate and calcium lactate, per 10 ml
MED: 100-2,15,50

J0630 Injection, calcitonin salmon, up to 400 units
Use this code for Calcimar, Miacalcin.
MED: 100-2,15,50

J0636 Injection, calcitriol, 0.1 mcg
Use this code for Calcijex.
MED: 100-2,15,50

J0637 Injection, caspofungin acetate, 5 mg
Use this code for Cancidas.

J0640 Injection, leucovorin calcium, per 50 mg
MED: 100-2,15,50

J0641 Injection, levoleucovorin calcium, 0.5 mg
Use this code for Fusilev

J0670 Injection, mepivacaine HCl, per 10 ml
Use this code for Carbocaine, Polocaine, Isocaine HCl, Scandonest
MED: 100-2,15,50

J0690 Injection, cefazolin sodium, 500 mg
Use this code for Ancef, Kefzol
MED: 100-2,15,50

J0692 Injection, cefepime HCl, 500 mg
Use this code for Maxipime.

J0694 Injection, cefoxitin sodium, 1 g
MED: 100-2,15,50

J0696 Injection, ceftriaxone sodium, per 250 mg
Use this code for Rocephin.
MED: 100-2,15,50

J0697 Injection, sterile cefuroxime sodium, per 750 mg
Use this code for Zinacef.
MED: 100-2,15,50

J0698 Injection, cefotaxime sodium, per g
Use this code for Claforan.
MED: 100-2,15,50

J0702 Injection, betamethasone acetate 3 mg and betamethasone sodium phosphate 3 mg
Use this code for Celestone Soluspan.
MED: 100-2,15,50

J0704 Injection, betamethasone sodium phosphate, per 4 mg
MED: 100-2,15,50

J0706 Injection, caffeine citrate, 5 mg
Use this code for Cafcit.
AHA: 2Q,'02,8

J0710 Injection, cephapirin sodium, up to 1 g
MED: 100-2,15,50

J0713 **Injection, ceftazidime, per 500 mg**
Use this code for Ceptax, Fortaz, Tazicef

MED: 100-2,15,50

J0715 **Injection, ceftizoxime sodium, per 500 mg**
Use this code for Cefizox.

MED: 100-2,15,50

J0720 **Injection, chloramphenicol sodium succinate, up to 1 g**
Use this code for Chlormycetin.

MED: 100-2,15,50

J0725 **Injection, chorionic gonadotropin, per 1,000 USP units**

MED: 100-2,15,50

J0735 **Injection, clonidine HCl, 1 mg**
Use this code for Clorpres, Duraclon, Iopidine

MED: 100-2,15,50

J0740 **Injection, cidofovir, 375 mg**
Use this code for Vistide.

MED: 100-2,15,50

J0743 **Injection, cilastatin sodium; imipenem, per 250 mg**
Use this code for Primaxin I.M., Primaxin I.V.

MED: 100-2,15,50

J0744 **Injection, ciprofloxacin for intravenous infusion, 200 mg**
Use this code for Cipro.

J0745 **Injection, codeine phosphate, per 30 mg**

MED: 100-2,15,50

J0760 **Injection, colchicine, per 1 mg**

MED: 100-2,15,50

J0770 **Injection, colistimethate sodium, up to 150 mg**
Use this code for Coly-Mycin M.

MED: 100-2,15,50

J0780 **Injection, prochlorperazine, up to 10 mg**
Use this code for Compazine, Cotranzine, Compa-Z, Ultrazine-10.

MED: 100-2,15,50

J0795 **Injection, corticorelin ovine triflutate, 1 mcg**
Use this code for Acthrel.

MED: 100-2,15,50

J0800 **Injection, corticotropin, up to 40 units**
Use this code for H.P. Acthar gel

MED: 100-2,15,50

J0835 **Injection, cosyntropin, per 0.25 mg**
Use this code for Cortrosyn.

MED: 100-2,15,50

J0850 **Injection, cytomegalovirus immune globulin intravenous (human), per vial**
Use this code for Cytogam.

MED: 100-2,15,50; 100-4,4,240

J0878 **Injection, daptomycin, 1 mg**
Use this code for Cubicin.

J0881 **Injection, darbepoetin alfa, 1 mcg (non-ESRD use)**
Use this code for Aranesp.

MED: 100-2,6,10; 100-4,4,240

J0882 **Injection, darbepoetin alfa, 1 mcg (for ESRD on dialysis)**
Use this code for Aranesp.

MED: 100-2,6,10; 100-4,4,240

J0885 **Injection, epoetin alfa, (for non-ESRD use), 1000 units**
Use this code for Epogen/Procrit.

MED: 100-2,6,10; 100-2,15,50; 100-4,4,240

J0886 **Injection, epoetin alfa, 1000 units (for ESRD on dialysis)**
Use this code for Epogen/Procrit.

MED: 100-2,6,10; 100-4,4,240

J0894 **Injection, decitabine, 1 mg**
Use this code for Dacogen.

J0895 **Injection, deferoxamine mesylate, 500 mg**
Use this code for Desferal.

MED: 100-2,15,50

J0900 **Injection, testosterone enanthate and estradiol valerate, up to 1 cc**

MED: 100-2,15,50

J0945 **Injection, brompheniramine maleate, per 10 mg**

MED: 100-2,15,50

J0970 **Injection, estradiol valerate, up to 40 mg**
Use this code for Clinagen LA, Clinagen, LA-10, Clinagen LA-20, Clinagen LA-40, Delestrogen

MED: 100-2,15,50

J1000 **Injection, depo-estradiol cypionate, up to 5 mg**
Use this code for depGynogen, Depogen, Estradiol Cypionate

MED: 100-2,15,50

J1020 **Injection, methylprednisolone acetate, 20 mg**
Use this code for Depo-Medrol.

MED: 100-2,15,50; 100-4,4,240

J1030 **Injection, methylprednisolone acetate, 40 mg**
Use this code for DepoMedalone40, Depo-Medrol, Sano-Drol

MED: 100-2,15,50; 100-4,4,240

J1040 **Injection, methylprednisolone acetate, 80 mg**
Use this code for Cortimed, DepMedalone, DepoMedalone 80, Depo-Medrol, Duro Cort, Methylcotolone, Pri-Methylate, Sano-Drol

MED: 100-2,15,50; 100-4,4,240

J1051 **Injection, medroxyprogesterone acetate, 50 mg**
Use this code for Depo-Provera.

MED: 100-2,15,50

J1055 **Injection, medroxyprogesterone acetate for contraceptive use, 150 mg**
Use this code for Depo-Provera.

J1056 **Injection, medroxyprogesterone acetate/estradiol cypionate, 5 mg/25 mg**
Use this code for Lunelle monthly contraceptive.

J1060 **Injection, testosterone cypionate and estradiol cypionate, up to 1 ml**
Use this code for Depo-Testadiol, Duo-Span, Duo-Span II.

MED: 100-2,15,50

J1070 **Injection, testosterone cypionate, up to 100 mg**
Use this code for Depo Testosterone Cypionate

MED: 100-2,15,50

J1080 **Injection, testosterone cypionate, 1 cc, 200 mg**
Use this code for Depandrante, Depo-Testosterone, Virilon

MED: 100-2,15,50

J1094 **Injection, dexamethasone acetate, 1 mg**
Use this code for Cortastat LA, Dalalone L.A., Dexamethasone Acetate Anhydrous, Dexone LA.

MED: 100-2,15,50

J1100 **Injection, dexamethasone sodium phosphate, 1 mg**
Use this code for Cortastat, Dalalone, Decaject, Dexone, Solurex, Adrenocort, Primethasone, Dexasone, Dexim, Medidex, Spectro-Dex.

MED: 100-2,15,50

J1110 **Injection, dihydroergotamine mesylate, per 1 mg**
Use this code for D.H.E. 45.

MED: 100-2,15,50

J1120 **Injection, acetazolamide sodium, up to 500 mg**
Use this code for Diamox.
MED: 100-2,15,50

J1160 **Injection, digoxin, up to 0.5 mg**
Use this code for Lanoxin.
MED: 100-2,15,50

J1162 **Injection, digoxin immune fab (ovine), per vial**
Use this code for Digibind, Digifab.
MED: 100-2,15,50

J1165 **Injection, phenytoin sodium, per 50 mg**
Use this code for Dilantin.
MED: 100-2,15,50

J1170 **Injection, hydromorphone, up to 4 mg**
Use this code for Dilaudid, Dilaudid-HP.
MED: 100-2,15,50

J1180 **Injection, dyphylline, up to 500 mg**
MED: 100-2,15,50

J1190 **Injection, dexrazoxane HCl, per 250 mg**
Use this code for Totect, Zinecard.
MED: 100-2,15,50

J1200 **Injection, diphenhydramine HCl, up to 50 mg**
Use this code for Benadryl, Benahist 10, Benahist 50, Benoject-10, Benoject-50, Bena-D 10, Bena-D 50, Nordryl, Dihydrex, Dimine, Diphenacen-50, Hyrexin-50, Truxadryl, Wehdryl.
MED: 100-2,15,50
AHA: 1Q,'02,2

J1205 **Injection, chlorothiazide sodium, per 500 mg**
Use this code for Diuril Sodium.
MED: 100-2,15,50

J1212 **Injection, DMSO, dimethyl sulfoxide, 50%, 50 ml**
Use this code for Rimso 50. DMSO is covered only as a treatment of interstitial cystitis.
MED: 100-2,15,50; 100-3,230.12

J1230 **Injection, methadone HCl, up to 10 mg**
Use this code for Dolophine HCl.
MED: 100-2,15,50

J1240 **Injection, dimenhydrinate, up to 50 mg**
Use this code for Dramamine, Dinate, Dommanate, Dramanate, Dramilin, Dramocen, Dramoject, Dymenate, Hydrate, Marmine, Wehamine.
MED: 100-2,15,50

J1245 **Injection, dipyridamole, per 10 mg**
Use this code for Persantine IV.
MED: 100-2,15,50

J1250 **Injection, Dobutamine HCl, per 250 mg**
MED: 100-2,15,50

J1260 **Injection, dolasetron mesylate, 10 mg**
Use this code for Anzemet.
MED: 100-2,15,50

J1265 **Injection, dopamine HCl, 40 mg**

J1267 **Injection, doripenem, 10 mg**
Use this code for Doribax

J1270 **Injection, doxercalciferol, 1 mcg**
Use this code for Hectorol.

J1300 **Injection, eculizumab, 10 mg**
Use this code for Soliris.

J1320 **Injection, amitriptyline HCl, up to 20 mg**
Use this code for Elavil
MED: 100-2,15,50

J1324 **Injection, enfuvirtide, 1 mg**
Use this code for Fuzeon.

J1325 **Injection, epoprostenol, 0.5 mg**
Use this code for Flolan. See K0455 for infusion pump for epoprosterol.
MED: 100-2,15,50

J1327 **Injection, eptifibatide, 5 mg**
Use this code for Integrilin.
MED: 100-2,15,50

J1330 **Injection, ergonovine maleate, up to 0.2 mg**
Medicare jurisdiction: local contractor. Use this code for Ergotrate Maleate.
MED: 100-2,15,50

J1335 **Injection, ertapenem sodium, 500 mg**
Use this code for Invanz.

J1364 **Injection, erythromycin lactobionate, per 500 mg**
MED: 100-2,15,50

J1380 **Injection, estradiol valerate, up to 10 mg**
Use this code for Delestrogen, Dioval, Dioval XX, Dioval 40, Duragen-10, Duragen-20, Duragen-40, Estradiol L.A., Estradiol L.A. 20, Estradiol L.A. 40, Gynogen L.A. 10, Gynogen L.A. 20, Gynogen L.A. 40, Valergen 10, Valergen 20, Valergen 40, Estra-L 20, Estra-L 40, L.A.E. 20.
MED: 100-2,15,50

J1390 **Injection, estradiol valerate, up to 20 mg**
Use this code for Delestrogen, Dioval, Dioval XX, Dioval 40, Duragen-10, Duragen-20, Duragen-40, Estradiol L.A., Estradiol L.A. 20, Estradiol L.A. 40, Gynogen L.A. 10, Gynogen L.A. 20, Gynogen L.A. 40, Valergen 10, Valergen 20, Valergen 40, Estra-L 20, Estra-L 40, L.A.E. 20.
MED: 100-2,15,50

J1410 **Injection, estrogen conjugated, per 25 mg**
Use this code for Natural Estrogenic Substance, Premarin Intravenous, Primestrin Aqueous.
MED: 100-2,15,50

J1430 **Injection, ethanolamine oleate, 100 mg**
Use this code for Ethamiolin.
MED: 100-2,15,50

J1435 **Injection, estrone, per 1 mg**
Use this code for Estone Aqueous, Estragyn, Estro-A, Estrone, Estronol, Theelin Aqueous, Estone 5, Kestrone 5.
MED: 100-2,15,50

J1436 **Injection, etidronate disodium, per 300 mg**
Use this code for Didronel.
MED: 100-2,15,50

J1438 **Injection, etanercept, 25 mg (code may be used for Medicare when drug administered under the direct supervision of a physician, not for use when drug is self-administered)**
Use this code for Enbrel.
MED: 100-2,15,50

J1440 **Injection, filgrastim (G-CSF), 300 mcg**
Use this code for Neupogen.
MED: 100-2,15,50

J1441 **Injection, filgrastim (G-CSF), 480 mcg**
Use this code for Neupogen.
MED: 100-2,15,50

J1450 **Injection, fluconazole, 200 mg**
Use this code for Diflucan.
MED: 100-2,15,50.5

J1451 **Injection, fomepizole, 15 mg**
Use this code for Antizol.
MED: 100-2,15,50

J1452 Injection, fomivirsen sodium, intraocular, 1.65 mg
Use this code for Vitavene.
MED: 100-2,15,50.4.2

J1453 Injection, fosaprepitant, 1 mg
Use this code for Emend

J1455 Injection, foscarnet sodium, per 1,000 mg
Use this code for Foscavir.

J1457 Injection, gallium nitrate, 1 mg
Use this code for Ganite.

J1458 Injection, galsulfase, 1 mg
Use this code for Naglazyme.

J1459 Injection, immune globulin (Privigen), intravenous, nonlyophilized (e.g., liquid), 500 mg

J1460 Injection, gamma globulin, intramuscular, 1 cc
Use this code for GamaSTAN SD.
MED: 100-2,15,50

J1470 Injection, gamma globulin, intramuscular, 2 cc
Use this code for GamaSTAN SD.
MED: 100-2,15,50

J1480 Injection, gamma globulin, intramuscular, 3 cc
Use this code for GamaSTAN SD.
MED: 100-2,15,50

J1490 Injection, gamma globulin, intramuscular, 4 cc
Use this code for GamaSTAN SD.
MED: 100-2,15,50

J1500 Injection, gamma globulin, intramuscular, 5 cc
Use this code for GamaSTAN SD.
MED: 100-2,15,50

J1510 Injection, gamma globulin, intramuscular, 6 cc
Use this code for GamaSTAN SD.
MED: 100-2,15,50

J1520 Injection, gamma globulin, intramuscular, 7 cc
Use this code for GamaSTAN SD.
MED: 100-2,15,50

J1530 Injection, gamma globulin, intramuscular, 8 cc
Use this code for GamaSTAN SD.
MED: 100-2,15,50

J1540 Injection, gamma globulin, intramuscular, 9 cc
Use this code for GamaSTAN SD.
MED: 100-2,15,50

J1550 Injection, gamma globulin, intramuscular, 10 cc
Use this code for GamaSTAN SD.
MED: 100-2,15,50

J1560 Injection, gamma globulin, intramuscular, over 10 cc
Use this code for GamaSTAN SD.
MED: 100-2,15,50

J1561 Injection, immune globulin, (Gamunex), intravenous, nonlyophilized (e.g., liquid), 500 mg

J1562 Injection, immune globulin (Vivaglobin), 100 mg

J1565 Injection, respiratory syncytial virus immune globulin, intravenous, 50 mg
Use this code for Respigam.
MED: 100-2,15,50

J1566 Injection, immune globulin, intravenous, lyophilized (e.g., powder), not otherwise specified, 500 mg
Use this code for Carimune.
MED: 100-2,15,50

J1568 Injection, immune globulin, (Octagam), intravenous, nonlyophilized (e.g., liquid), 500 mg

J1569 Injection, immune globulin, (Gammagard liquid), intravenous, nonlyophilized, (e.g., liquid), 500 mg

J1570 Injection, ganciclovir sodium, 500 mg
Use this code for Cytovene.
MED: 100-2,15,50

J1571 Injection, hepatitis B immune globulin (Hepagam B), intramuscular, 0.5 ml

J1572 Injection, immune globulin, (Flebogamma/Flebogamma Dif), intravenous, nonlyophilized (e.g., liquid), 500 mg

J1573 Injection, hepatitis B immune globulin (Hepagam B), intravenous, 0.5 ml

J1580 Injection, garamycin, gentamicin, up to 80 mg
Use this code for Gentamicin Sulfate, Jenamicin.
MED: 100-2,15,50

J1590 Injection, gatifloxacin, 10 mg

J1595 Injection, glatiramer acetate, 20 mg
Use this code for Copaxone.
MED: 100-2,15,50

J1600 Injection, gold sodium thiomalate, up to 50 mg
Use this code for Myochrysine.
MED: 100-2,15,50

J1610 Injection, glucagon HCl, per 1 mg
Use this code for Glucagen.
MED: 100-2,15,50

J1620 Injection, gonadorelin HCl, per 100 mcg
Use this code for Factrel, Lutrepulse.
MED: 100-2,15,50

J1626 Injection, granisetron HCl, 100 mcg
Use this code for Kytril.
MED: 100-2,15,50

J1630 Injection, haloperidol, up to 5 mg
Use this code for Haldol.
MED: 100-2,15,50

J1631 Injection, haloperidol decanoate, per 50 mg
Use this code for Haldol Decanoate-50.
MED: 100-2,15,50

J1640 Injection, hemin, 1 mg
Use this code for Panhematin.
MED: 100-2,15,50

J1642 Injection, heparin sodium, (heparin lock flush), per 10 units
Use this code for Hep-Lock, Hep-Lock U/P, Hep-Pak, Lok-Pak.
MED: 100-2,15,50

J1644 Injection, Heparin sodium, per 1000 units
Use this code for Heparin Sodium, Liquaemin Sodium.
MED: 100-2,15,50

J1645 Injection, dalteparin sodium, per 2500 IU
Use this code for Fragmin.
MED: 100-2,15,50

J1650 Injection, enoxaparin sodium, 10 mg
Use this code for Lovenox.

J1652 Injection, fondaparinux sodium, 0.5 mg
Use this code for Atrixtra.
MED: 100-2,15,50

J1655 Injection, tinzaparin sodium, 1000 IU
Use this code for Innohep.

J1670 Injection, tetanus immune globulin, human, up to 250 units
Use this code for HyperTET SD.
MED: 100-2,15,50

J1675 Injection, histrelin acetate, 10 mcg
Use this code for Supprelin LA.
MED: 100-2,15,50

J1700 Injection, hydrocortisone acetate, up to 25 mg
Use this code for Hydrocortone Acetate.
MED: 100-2,15,50

J1710 Injection, hydrocortisone sodium phosphate, up to 50 mg
Use this code for Hydrocortone Phosphate.
MED: 100-2,15,50

J1720 Injection, hydrocortisone sodium succinate, up to 100 mg
Use this code for Solu-Cortef, A-Hydrocort.
MED: 100-2,15,50

J1730 Injection, diazoxide, up to 300 mg
MED: 100-2,15,50

J1740 Injection, ibandronate sodium, 1 mg
Use this code for Boniva.

J1742 Injection, ibutilide fumarate, 1 mg
Use this code for Corvert.
MED: 100-2,15,50

J1743 Injection, idursulfase, 1 mg
Use this code for Elaprase.

J1745 Injection infliximab, 10 mg
Use this code for Remicade.
MED: 100-2,15,50

J1750 Injection, iron dextran, 50 mg
Use this code for INFeD.

J1756 Injection, iron sucrose, 1 mg
Use this code for Venofer.

J1785 Injection, imiglucerase, per unit
Use this code for Cerezyme.
MED: 100-2,15,50

J1790 Injection, droperidol, up to 5 mg
Use this code for Inapsine.
MED: 100-2,15,50

J1800 Injection, propranolol HCl, up to 1 mg
Use this code for Inderal.
MED: 100-2,15,50

J1810 Injection, droperidol and fentanyl citrate, up to 2 ml ampule
MED: 100-2,15,50
AHA: 2Q,'02,8

J1815 Injection, insulin, per 5 units
Use this code for Humalog, Humulin, Iletin, Insulin Lispo, Novo Nordisk, NPH, Pork insulin, Regular insulin, Ultralente, Velosulin, Humulin R, Iletin II Regular Port, Insulin Purified Pork, Relion, Lente Iletin I, Novolin R, Humulin R U-500.
MED: 100-2,15,50; 100-3,280.14

J1817 Insulin for administration through DME (i.e., insulin pump) per 50 units
Use this code for Humalog, Humulin, Vesolin BR, Iletin II NPH Pork, Lantus, Lispro-PFC, Novolin, Novolog, Novolog Flexpen, Novolog Mix, Relion Novolin.

J1825 Injection, interferon beta-1a, 33 mcg
Use this code for Avonex, Rebif.

J1830 Injection interferon beta-1b, 0.25 mg (code may be used for Medicare when drug administered under the direct supervision of a physician, not for use when drug is self-administered)
Use this code for Betaseron.
MED: 100-2,15,50

J1835 Injection, itraconazole, 50 mg
Use this code for Sporonox IV.

J1840 Injection, kanamycin sulfate, up to 500 mg
Use this code for Kantrex
MED: 100-2,15,50

J1850 Injection, kanamycin sulfate, up to 75 mg
Use this code for Kantrex
MED: 100-2,15,50

J1885 Injection, ketorolac tromethamine, per 15 mg
MED: 100-2,15,50

J1890 Injection, cephalothin sodium, up to 1 g
MED: 100-2,15,50

J1930 Injection, lanreotide, 1 mg
Use this code for Somatuline

J1931 Injection, laronidase, 0.1 mg
Use this code for Aldurazyme.

J1940 Injection, furosemide, up to 20 mg
Use this code for Lasix
MED: 100-2,15,50

J1945 Injection, lepirudin, 50 mg
Use this code for Refludan.
This drug is used for patients with heparin induced thrombocytopenia.
MED: 100-2,15,50

J1950 Injection, leuprolide acetate (for depot suspension), per 3.75 mg
Use this code for Eliguard, Lupron, Lupron-3, Lupron-4, Lupron Depot.
MED: 100-2,15,50

J1953 Injection, levetiracetam, 10 mg
Use this code for Keppra

J1955 Injection, levocarnitine, per 1 g
Use this code for Carnitor
MED: 100-2,15,50

J1956 Injection, levofloxacin, 250 mg
Use this code for Levaquin.
MED: 100-2,15,50

J1960 Injection, levorphanol tartrate, up to 2 mg
Use this code for Levo-Dromoran.
MED: 100-2,15,50

J1980 Injection, hyoscyamine sulfate, up to 0.25 mg
Use this code for Levsin.
MED: 100-2,15,50

J1990 Injection, chlordiazepoxide HCl, up to 100 mg
Use this code for Librium.
MED: 100-2,15,50

J2001 Injection, lidocaine HCl for intravenous infusion, 10 mg
Use this code for Xylocaine.
MED: 100-2,15,50

J2010 Injection, lincomycin HCl, up to 300 mg
Use this code for Lincocin
MED: 100-2,15,50

J2020 Injection, linezolid, 200 mg
Use this code for Zyvok.
AHA: 2Q,'02,8

J2060 Injection, lorazepam, 2 mg
Use this code for Ativan.
MED: 100-2,15,50

J2150 Injection, mannitol, 25% in 50 ml
Use this code for Osmitrol.
MED: 100-2,15,50

J2170 Injection, mecasermin, 1 mg
Use this code for Iplex, Increlex.

J2175 Injection, meperidine HCl, per 100 mg
Use this code for Demerol.
MED: 100-2,15,50

J2180 Injection, meperidine and promethazine HCl, up to 50 mg
Use this code for Mepergan Injection.
MED: 100-2,15,50

J2185 Injection, meropenem, 100 mg
Use this code for Merrem

J2210 Injection, methylergonovine maleate, up to 0.2 mg
Use this code for Methergine.
MED: 100-2,15,50

J2248 Injection, micafungin sodium, 1 mg
Use this code for Mycamine.

J2250 Injection, midazolam HCl, per 1 mg
Use this code for Versed.
MED: 100-2,15,50

J2260 Injection, milrinone lactate, 5 mg
Use this code for Primacor.
MED: 100-2,15,50

J2270 Injection, morphine sulfate, up to 10 mg
Use this code for Depodur, Infumorph
MED: 100-2,15,50

J2271 Injection, morphine sulfate, 100 mg
Use this code for Depodur, Infumorph
MED: 100-2,15,50; 100-3,280.14

J2275 Injection, morphine sulfate (preservative-free sterile solution), per 10 mg
Use this code for Astramorph PF, Duramorph, Infumorph.
MED: 100-2,15,50; 100-3,280.14

J2278 Injection, ziconotide, 1 mcg
Use this code for Prialt

J2280 Injection, moxifloxacin, 100 mg
Use this code for Avelox.

J2300 Injection, nalbuphine HCl, per 10 mg
Use this code for Nubain.
MED: 100-2,15,50

J2310 Injection, naloxone HCl, per 1 mg
Use this code for Narcan.
MED: 100-2,15,50

J2315 Injection, naltrexone, depot form, 1 mg
Use this code for Vivitrol.

J2320 Injection, nandrolone decanoate, up to 50 mg
MED: 100-2,15,50

J2321 Injection, nandrolone decanoate, up to 100 mg
MED: 100-2,15,50

J2322 Injection, nandrolone decanoate, up to 200 mg
MED: 100-2,15,50

J2323 Injection, natalizumab, 1 mg
Use this code for Tysabri.

J2325 Injection, nesiritide, 0.1 mg
Use this code for Natrecor.
MED: 100-2,15,50

J2353 Injection, octreotide, depot form for intramuscular injection, 1 mg
Use this code for Sandostatin LAR.

J2354 Injection, octreotide, nondepot form for subcutaneous or intravenous injection, 25 mcg
Use this code for Sandostatin.

J2355 Injection, oprelvekin, 5 mg
Use this code for Neumega.
MED: 100-2,15,50

J2357 Injection, omalizumab, 5 mg
Use this code for Xolair.

J2360 Injection, orphenadrine citrate, up to 60 mg
Use this code for Norflex
MED: 100-2,15,50

J2370 Injection, phenylephrine HCl, up to 1 ml
MED: 100-2,15,50

J2400 Injection, chloroprocaine HCl, per 30 ml
Use this code for Nesacaine, Nesacaine-MPF.
MED: 100-2,15,50

J2405 Injection, ondansetron HCl, per 1 mg
Use this code for Zofran.
MED: 100-2,15,50

J2410 Injection, oxymorphone HCl, up to 1 mg
Use this code for Numorphan, Oxymorphone HCl.
MED: 100-2,15,50

J2425 Injection, palifermin, 50 mcg
Use this code for Kepivance.

J2430 Injection, pamidronate disodium, per 30 mg
Use this code for Aredia
MED: 100-2,15,50

J2440 Injection, papaverine HCl, up to 60 mg
MED: 100-2,15,50

J2460 Injection, oxytetracycline HCl, up to 50 mg
Use this code for Terramycin IM.
MED: 100-2,15,50

J2469 Injection, palonosetron HCl, 25 mcg
Use this code for Aloxi.

J2501 Injection, paricalcitol, 1 mcg
Use this code For Zemplar.
MED: 100-2,15,50

J2503 Injection, pegaptanib sodium, 0.3 mg
Use this code for Mucagen.

J2504 Injection, pegademase bovine, 25 IU
Use this code for Adagen.
MED: 100-2,15,50

J2505 Injection, pegfilgrastim, 6 mg
Use this code for Neulasta.

J2510 Injection, penicillin G procaine, aqueous, up to 600,000 units
Use this code for Wycillin, Duracillin A.S., Pfizerpen A.S., Crysticillin 300 A.S., Crysticillin 600 A.S.
MED: 100-2,15,50

J2513 Injection, pentastarch, 10% solution, 100 ml
MED: 100-2,15,50

J2515 Injection, pentobarbital sodium, per 50 mg
Use this code for Nembutal Sodium Solution.
MED: 100-2,15,50

J2540 Injection, penicillin G potassium, up to 600,000 units
Use this code for Pfizerpen.
MED: 100-2,15,50

J2543 Injection, piperacillin sodium/tazobactam sodium, 1 g/0.125 g (1.125 g)
Use this code for Zosyn.
MED: 100-2,15,50

J2545 Pentamidine isethionate, inhalation solution, FDA-approved final product, noncompounded, administered through DME, unit dose form, per 300 mg
Use this code for Nebupent, Pentam 300

J2550 Injection, promethazine HCl, up to 50 mg
Use this code for Phenergan
MED: 100-2,15,50

J2560 Injection, phenobarbital sodium, up to 120 mg
MED: 100-2,15,50

J2590 Injection, oxytocin, up to 10 units
Use this code for Pitocin, Syntocinon.
MED: 100-2,15,50

J2597 Injection, desmopressin acetate, per 1 mcg
Use this code for DDAVP.
MED: 100-2,15,50

J2650 Injection, prednisolone acetate, up to 1 ml
MED: 100-2,15,50; 100-4,4,240

J2670 Injection, tolazoline HCl, up to 25 mg
MED: 100-2,15,50

J2675 Injection, progesterone, per 50 mg
Use this code for Gesterone, Gestrin.
MED: 100-2,15,50

J2680 Injection, fluphenazine decanoate, up to 25 mg
MED: 100-2,15,50

J2690 Injection, procainamide HCl, up to 1 g
Use this code for Pronestyl.
MED: 100-2,15,50

J2700 Injection, oxacillin sodium, up to 250 mg
Use this code for Bactocill
MED: 100-2,15,50

J2710 Injection, neostigmine methylsulfate, up to 0.5 mg
Use this code for Prostigmin.
MED: 100-2,15,50

J2720 Injection, protamine sulfate, per 10 mg
MED: 100-2,15,50

J2724 Injection, protein C concentrate, intravenous, human, 10 IU

J2725 Injection, protirelin, per 250 mcg
Use this code for Thyrel TRH
MED: 100-2,15,50

J2730 Injection, pralidoxime chloride, up to 1 g
Use this code for Protopam Chloride.
MED: 100-2,15,50

J2760 Injection, phentolamine mesylate, up to 5 mg
Use this code for Regitine.
MED: 100-2,15,50

J2765 Injection, metoclopramide HCl, up to 10 mg
Use this code for Reglan
MED: 100-2,15,50

J2770 Injection, quinupristin/dalfopristin, 500 mg (150/350)
Use this code for Synercid.
MED: 100-2,15,50

J2778 Injection, ranibizumab, 0.1 mg
Use this code for Lucentis.

J2780 Injection, ranitidine HCl, 25 mg
Use this code for Zantac.
MED: 100-2,15,50

J2783 Injection, rasburicase, 0.5 mg
Use this code for Elitek.

J2785 Injection, regadenoson, 0.1 mg
Use this code for Lexiscan

J2788 Injection, Rho D immune globulin, human, minidose, 50 mcg (250 i.u.)
Use this code for RhoGam, MiCRhoGAM.
MED: 100-2,15,50

J2790 Injection, Rho D immune globulin, human, full dose, 300 mcg (1500 i.u.)
Use this code for RhoGam, Rhophylac.
MED: 100-2,15,50

J2791 Injection, Rho(D) immune globulin (human), (Rhophylac), intramuscular or intravenous, 100 IU
Use this for HypRho SD, WINRho SDF.

J2792 Injection, Rho D immune globulin, intravenous, human, solvent detergent, 100 IU
MED: 100-2,15,50

J2794 Injection, risperidone, long acting, 0.5 mg
Use this code for Risperidal Consta Long Acting.

J2795 Injection, ropivacaine HCl, 1 mg
Use this code for Naropin.

J2800 Injection, methocarbamol, up to 10 ml
Use this code for Robaxin
MED: 100-2,15,50

J2805 Injection, sincalide, 5 mcg
Use this code for Kinevac.

J2810 Injection, theophylline, per 40 mg
MED: 100-2,15,50

J2820 Injection, sargramostim (GM-CSF), 50 mcg
Use this code for Leukine
MED: 100-2,15,50

J2850 Injection, secretin, synthetic, human, 1 mcg
MED: 100-2,15,50

J2910 Injection, aurothioglucose, up to 50 mg
Use this code for Solganal.
MED: 100-2,15,50

J2916 Injection, sodium ferric gluconate complex in sucrose injection, 12.5 mg
MED: 100-2,15,50.2

J2920 Injection, methylprednisolone sodium succinate, up to 40 mg
Use this code for Solu-Medrol, A-methaPred.
MED: 100-2,15,50; 100-4,4,240

J2930 Injection, methylprednisolone sodium succinate, up to 125 mg
Use this code for Solu-Medrol, A-methaPred.
MED: 100-2,15,50; 100-4,4,240

J2940 Injection, somatrem, 1 mg
Use this code for Protropin.
MED: 100-2,15,50
AHA: 2Q,'02,8

J2941 Injection, somatropin, 1 mg
Use this code for Humatrope, Genotropin Nutropin, Biotropin, Genotropin, Genotropin Miniquick, Norditropin, Nutropin, Nutropin AQ, Saizen, Saizen Somatropin RDNA Origin, Serostim, Serostim RDNA Origin, Zorbtive.
MED: 100-2,15,50
AHA: 2Q,'02,8

J2950 Injection, promazine HCl, up to 25 mg
Use this code for Sparine, Prozine-50.
MED: 100-2,15,50

J2993 Injection, reteplase, 18.1 mg
Use this code for Retavase
MED: 100-2,15,50

J2995 Injection, streptokinase, per 250,000 IU
Use this code for Streptase
MED: 100-2,15,50

J2997 Injection, alteplase recombinant, 1 mg
Use this code for Activase, Cathflo.
MED: 100-2,15,50

J3000 Injection, streptomycin, up to 1 g
Use this code for Streptomycin Sulfate.
MED: 100-2,15,50

J3010 Injection, fentanyl citrate, 0.1 mg
Use this code for Sublimaze.
MED: 100-2,15,50

J3030 Injection, sumatriptan succinate, 6 mg (code may be used for Medicare when drug administered under the direct supervision of a physician, not for use when drug is self-administered)
Use this code for Imitrex.
MED: 100-2,15,50

J3070 Injection, pentazocine, 30 mg
Use this code for Talwin.
MED: 100-2,15,50

J3101 Injection, tenecteplase, 1 mg
Use this code for TNKase.

J3105 Injection, terbutaline sulfate, up to 1 mg
For terbutaline in inhalation solution, see K0525 and K0526.
MED: 100-2,15,50

J3110 Injection, teriparatide, 10 mcg
Use this code for Forteo.

J3120 Injection, testosterone enanthate, up to 100 mg
Use this code for Delatestryl.
MED: 100-2,15,50

J3130 Injection, testosterone enanthate, up to 200 mg
Use this code for Delatestryl.
MED: 100-2,15,50

J3140 Injection, testosterone suspension, up to 50 mg
MED: 100-2,15,50

J3150 Injection, testosterone propionate, up to 100 mg
MED: 100-2,15,50

J3230 Injection, chlorpromazine HCl, up to 50 mg
Use this code for Thorazine.
MED: 100-2,15,50

J3240 Injection, thyrotropin alpha, 0.9 mg, provided in 1.1 mg vial
Use this code for Thyrogen.
MED: 100-2,15,50

J3243 Injection, tigecycline, 1 mg
Use this code for Tygacil.

J3246 Injection, tirofiban HCl, 0.25 mg
Use this code for Aggrastat.

J3250 Injection, trimethobenzamide HCl, up to 200 mg
Use this code for Tigan, Tiject-20, Arrestin.
MED: 100-2,15,50

J3260 Injection, tobramycin sulfate, up to 80 mg
Use this code for Nebcin.
MED: 100-2,15,50

J3265 Injection, torsemide, 10 mg/ml
Use this code for Demadex, Torsemide.
MED: 100-2,15,50

J3280 Injection, thiethylperazine maleate, up to 10 mg
MED: 100-2,15,50

J3285 Injection, treprostinil, 1 mg
Use this code for Remodulin.

J3300 Injection, triamcinolone acetonide, preservative free, 1 mg
Use this code for TRIVARIS.

J3301 Injection, triamcinolone acetonide, not otherwise specified, 10 mg
Use this code for Kenalog-10, Kenalog-40, Tri-Kort, Kenaject-40, Cenacort A-40, Triam-A, Trilog.
MED: 100-2,15,50

J3302 Injection, triamcinolone diacetate, per 5 mg
Use this code for Aristocort, Aristocort Intralesional, Aristocort Forte, Amcort, Trilone, Cenacort Forte.
MED: 100-2,15,50

J3303 Injection, triamcinolone hexacetonide, per 5 mg
Use this code for Aristospan Intralesional, Aristospan Intra-articular.
MED: 100-2,15,50

J3305 Injection, trimetrexate glucuronate, per 25 mg
Use this code for Neutrexin.
MED: 100-2,15,50

J3310 Injection, perphenazine, up to 5 mg
Use this code for Trilafon.
MED: 100-2,15,50

J3315 Injection, triptorelin pamoate, 3.75 mg
Use this code for Trelstar Depot, Trelstar Depot Plus Debioclip Kit, Trelstar LA.
MED: 100-2,15,50

J3320 Injection, spectinomycin dihydrochloride, up to 2 g
Use this code for Trobicin.
MED: 100-2,15,50

J3350 Injection, urea, up to 40 g
MED: 100-2,15,50

J3355 Injection, urofollitropin, 75 IU
Use this code for Metrodin, Bravelle, Fertinex.
MED: 100-2,15,50

J3360 Injection, diazepam, up to 5 mg
Use this code for Diastat, Dizac, Valium.
MED: 100-2,15,50

J3364 Injection, urokinase, 5,000 IU vial
Use this code for Kinlytic
MED: 100-2,15,50

J3365 Injection, IV, urokinase, 250,000 IU vial
Use this code for Kinlytic
MED: 100-2,15,50

J3370 Injection, vancomycin HCl, 500 mg
Use this code for Vancocin.
MED: 100-2,15,50; 100-3,280.14

J3396 **Injection, verteporfin, 0.1 mg**
Use this code for Visudyne.
MED: 100-3,80.2; 100-3,80.3

J3400 **Injection, triflupromazine HCl, up to 20 mg**
MED: 100-2,15,50

J3410 **Injection, hydroxyzine HCl, up to 25 mg**
Use this code for Vistaril, Vistaject-25, Hyzine, Hyzine-50.
MED: 100-2,15,50

J3411 **Injection, thiamine HCl, 100 mg**

J3415 **Injection, pyridoxine HCl, 100 mg**

J3420 **Injection, vitamin B-12 cyanocobalamin, up to 1,000 mcg**
Use this code for Sytobex, Redisol, Rubramin PC, Betalin 12, Berubigen, Cobex, Cobal, Crystal B12, Cyano, Cyanocobalamin, Hydroxocobalamin, Hydroxycobal, Nutri-Twelve.
MED: 100-2,15,50; 100-3,150.6

J3430 **Injection, phytonadione (vitamin K), per 1 mg**
Use this code for AquaMephyton, Konakion, Menadione, Phytonadione.
MED: 100-2,15,50

J3465 **Injection, voriconazole, 10 mg**
MED: 100-2,15,50

J3470 **Injection, hyaluronidase, up to 150 units**
MED: 100-2,15,50

J3471 **Injection, hyaluronidase, ovine, preservative free, per 1 USP unit (up to 999 USP units)**

J3472 **Injection, hyaluronidase, ovine, preservative free, per 1,000 USP units**

J3473 **Injection, hyaluronidase, recombinant, 1 USP unit**

J3475 **Injection, magnesium sulfate, per 500 mg**
Use this code for Mag Sul, Sulfa Mag.
MED: 100-2,15,50

J3480 **Injection, potassium chloride, per 2 mEq**
MED: 100-2,15,50

J3485 **Injection, zidovudine, 10 mg**
Use this code for Retrovir, Zidovudine.
MED: 100-2,15,50

J3486 **Injection, ziprasidone mesylate, 10 mg**
Use this code for Geodon.

J3487 **Injection, zoledronic acid (Zometa), 1 mg**

J3488 **Injection, zoledronic acid (Reclast), 1 mg**

J3490 **Unclassified drugs**
MED: 100-2,15,50

J3520 **Edetate disodium, per 150 mg**
Use this code for Endrate, Disotate, Meritate, Chealamide, E.D.T.A. This drug is used in chelation therapy, a treatment for atherosclerosis that is not covered by Medicare.
MED: 100-3,20.21; 100-3,20.22

J3530 **Nasal vaccine inhalation**
MED: 100-2,15,50

J3535 **Drug administered through a metered dose inhaler**
MED: 100-2,15,50

J3570 **Laetrile, amygdalin, vitamin B-17**
The FDA has found Laetrile to have no safe or effective therapeutic purpose.
MED: 100-3,30.7

J3590 **Unclassified biologics**

MISCELLANEOUS DRUGS AND SOLUTIONS

J7030 **Infusion, normal saline solution, 1,000 cc**
MED: 100-2,15,50

J7040 **Infusion, normal saline solution, sterile (500 ml=1 unit)**
MED: 100-2,15,50

J7042 **5% dextrose/normal saline (500 ml = 1 unit)**
MED: 100-2,15,50

J7050 **Infusion, normal saline solution, 250 cc**
MED: 100-2,15,50

J7060 **5% dextrose/water (500 ml = 1 unit)**
MED: 100-2,15,50

J7070 **Infusion, D-5-W, 1,000 cc**
MED: 100-2,15,50

J7100 **Infusion, dextran 40, 500 ml**
Use this code for Gentran, 10% LMD, Rheomacrodex.
MED: 100-2,15,50

J7110 **Infusion, dextran 75, 500 ml**
Use this code for Gentran 75.
MED: 100-2,15,50

J7120 **Ringers lactate infusion, up to 1,000 cc**
MED: 100-2,15,50

J7130 **Hypertonic saline solution, 50 or 100 mEq, 20 cc vial**
MED: 100-2,15,50

J7186 **Injection, antihemophilic factor VIII/von Willebrand factor complex (human), per factor VIII i.u.**
Use this code for Alphanate.

J7187 **Injection, von Willebrand factor complex (Humate-P), per IU vWF-RCO**

J7189 **Factor VIIa (antihemophilic factor, recombinant), per 1 mcg**
MED: 100-1,1,10.1; 100-2,6,10; 100-2,15,50; 100-4,3,20.7.3

J7190 **Factor VIII (antihemophilic factor, human) per IU**
Use this code for Koate-DVI, Monarc-M, Monoclate-P.
MED: 100-1,1,10.1; 100-2,6,10; 100-2,15,50; 100-4,3,20.7.3; 100-4,4,240; 100-4,17,80.4

J7191 **Factor VIII (antihemophilic factor (porcine)), per IU**
MED: 100-1,1,10.1; 100-2,6,10; 100-2,15,50; 100-4,3,20.7.3; 100-4,4,240; 100-4,17,80.4

J7192 **Factor VIII (antihemophilic factor, recombinant) per IU**
Use this code for Recombinate, Kogenate FS, Helixate FX, Advate rAHF-PFM, Antihemophilic Factor Human Method M Monoclonal Purified, Refacto.
MED: 100-1,1,10.1; 100-2,6,10; 100-2,15,50; 100-4,3,20.7.3; 100-4,4,240; 100-4,17,80.4

J7193 **Factor IX (antihemophilic factor, purified, nonrecombinant) per IU**
Use this code for AlphaNine SD, Mononine.
MED: 100-1,1,10.1; 100-2,6,10; 100-2,15,50; 100-4,3,20.7.3; 100-4,4,240; 100-4,17,80.4
AHA: 2Q,'02,8

J7194 **Factor IX complex, per IU**
Use this code for Konyne-80, Profilnine SD, Proplex T, Proplex T, Bebulin VH, factor IX+ complex, Profilnine SD.
MED: 100-1,1,10.1; 100-2,6,10; 100-2,15,50; 100-4,3,20.7.3; 100-4,4,240; 100-4,17,80.4

J7195 **Factor IX (antihemophilic factor, recombinant) per IU**
Use this code for Benefix.
MED: 100-1,1,10.1; 100-2,6,10; 100-2,15,50; 100-4,3,20.7.3; 100-4,4,240; 100-4,17,80.4
AHA: 2Q,'02,8

J7197 **Antithrombin III (human), per IU**
Use this code for Thrombate III, ATnativ.
MED: 100-2,15,50

J7198 **Antiinhibitor, per IU**
Medicare jurisdiction: local contractor. Use this code for Autoplex T, Feiba VH AICC.

J7199 **Hemophilia clotting factor, not otherwise classified**
Medicare jurisdiction: local contractor.

J7300 **Intrauterine copper contraceptive**
Use this code for Paragard T380A.

J7302 Levonorgestrel-releasing intrauterine contraceptive system, 52 mg
Use this code for Mirena.

J7303 Contraceptive supply, hormone containing vaginal ring, each
Use this code for Nuvaring Vaginal Ring.

J7304 Contraceptive supply, hormone containing patch, each

J7306 Levonorgestrel (contraceptive) implant system, including implants and supplies
Use this code for Norplant II.

J7307 Etonogestrel (contraceptive) implant system, including implant and supplies
Use this code for Implanon.

J7308 Aminolevulinic acid HCl for topical administration, 20%, single unit dosage form (354 mg)

J7310 Ganciclovir, 4.5 mg, long-acting implant
Use this code for Vitrasert.
MED: 100-2,15,50

J7311 Fluocinolone acetonide, intravitreal implant
Use this code for Retisert.

J7321 Hyaluronan or derivative, Hyalgan or Supartz, for intra-articular injection, per dose

J7322 Hyaluronan or derivative, Synvisc, for intra-articular injection, per dose

J7323 Hyaluronan or derivative, Euflexxa, for intra-articular injection, per dose

J7324 Hyaluronan or derivative, Orthovisc, for intra-articular injection, per dose

J7330 Autologous cultured chondrocytes, implant
Medicare jurisdiction: local contractor. Use this code for Carticel.

J7500 Azathioprine, oral, 50 mg
Use this code for Azasan, Imuran.
MED: 100-2,15,50.5; 100-4,4,240; 100-4,17,80.3

J7501 Azathioprine, parenteral, 100 mg
MED: 100-2,6,10; 100-2,15,50; 100-4,4,240; 100-4,17,80.3

J7502 Cyclosporine, oral, 100 mg
Use this code for Neoral, Sandimmune, Gengraf, Sangcya
MED: 100-2,15,50.5; 100-4,4,240; 100-4,17,80.3

J7504 Lymphocyte immune globulin, antithymocyte globulin, equine, parenteral, 250 mg
Use this code for Atgam.
MED: 100-2,6,10; 100-2,15,50; 100-3,260.7; 100-4,4,240; 100-4,17,80.3

J7505 Muromonab-CD3, parenteral, 5 mg
Use this code for Orthoclone OKT3.
MED: 100-2,6,10; 100-2,15,50; 100-4,4,240; 100-4,17,80.3

J7506 Prednisone, oral, per 5 mg
Use this code for Deltasone, Liquid Pred Syrup, Levoxyl, Predone, Prednicot, Sterapred.
MED: 100-2,15,50.5; 100-4,4,240; 100-4,17,80.3

J7507 Tacrolimus, oral, per 1 mg
Use this code for Prograf.
MED: 100-2,15,50.5; 100-4,4,240; 100-4,17,80.3

J7509 Methylprednisolone, oral, per 4 mg
Use this code for Medrol, Methylpred.
MED: 100-2,15,50.5; 100-4,4,240; 100-4,17,80.3

J7510 Prednisolone, oral, per 5 mg
Use this code for Delta-Cortef, Cotolone, Pediapred, Prednoral, Prelone.
MED: 100-2,15,50.5; 100-4,4,240; 100-4,17,80.3

J7511 Lymphocyte immune globulin, antithymocyte globulin, rabbit, parenteral, 25 mg
Use this code for Thymoglobulin.
MED: 100-2,6,10; 100-4,4,240; 100-4,17,80.3
AHA: 2Q,'02,8

J7513 Daclizumab, parenteral, 25 mg
Use this code for Zenapax.
MED: 100-2,6,10; 100-2,15,50.5; 100-4,4,240; 100-4,17,80.3

J7515 Cyclosporine, oral, 25 mg
Use this code for Neoral, Sandimmune, Gengraf, Sangcya.
MED: 100-4,4,240; 100-4,17,80.3

J7516 Cyclosporine, parenteral, 250 mg
Use this code for Neoral, Sandimmune, Gengraf, Sangcya.
MED: 100-2,6,10; 100-4,4,240; 100-4,17,80.3

J7517 Mycophenolate mofetil, oral, 250 mg
Use this code for CellCept.
MED: 100-4,4,240; 100-4,17,80.3

J7518 Mycophenolic acid, oral, 180 mg
Use this code for Myfortic Delayed Release.
MED: 100-4,4,240; 100-4,17,80.3.1

J7520 Sirolimus, oral, 1 mg
Use this code for Rapamune.
MED: 100-2,15,50.5; 100-4,4,240; 100-4,17,80.3

J7525 Tacrolimus, parenteral, 5 mg
Use this code for Prograf.
MED: 100-2,6,10; 100-2,15,50.5; 100-4,4,240; 100-4,17,80.3

J7599 Immunosuppressive drug, not otherwise classified
Determine if an alternative HCPCS Level II or a CPT code better describes the service being reported. This code should be used only if a more specific code is unavailable.
MED: 100-2,6,10; 100-2,15,50.5; 100-4,4,240; 100-4,17,80.3

INHALATION SOLUTIONS

J7604 Acetylcysteine, inhalation solution, compounded product, administered through DME, unit dose form, per g

J7605 Arformoterol, inhalation solution, FDA approved final product, noncompounded, administered through DME, unit dose form, 15 mcg

J7606 Formoterol fumarate, inhalation solution, FDA approved final product, noncompounded, administered through DME, unit dose form, 20 mcg
Use this code for Perforomist.

J7607 Levalbuterol, inhalation solution, compounded product, administered through DME, concentrated form, 0.5 mg

J7608 Acetylcysteine, inhalation solution, FDA-approved final product, noncompounded, administered through DME, unit dose form, per g
Use this code for Acetadote, Mucomyst, Mucosil.
MED: 100-2,15,110.3

J7609 Albuterol, inhalation solution, compounded product, administered through DME, unit dose, 1 mg

J7610 Albuterol, inhalation solution, compounded product, administered through DME, concentrated form, 1 mg

J7611 Albuterol, inhalation solution, FDA-approved final product, noncompounded, administered through DME, concentrated form, 1 mg
Use this code for Accuneb, Proventil, Respirol, Ventolin.
MED: 100-2,15,110.3

J7612 Levalbuterol, inhalation solution, FDA-approved final product, noncompounded, administered through DME, concentrated form, 0.5 mg
Use this code for Xopenex HFA.
MED: 100-2,15,110.3

J7613 Albuterol, inhalation solution, FDA-approved final product, noncompounded, administered through DME, unit dose, 1 mg
Use this code for Accuneb, Proventil, Respirol, Ventolin.
MED: 100-2,15,110.3

J7614 Levalbuterol, inhalation solution, FDA-approved final product, noncompounded, administered through DME, unit dose, 0.5 mg
Use this code for Xopenex.
MED: 100-2,15,110.3

J7615 Levalbuterol, inhalation solution, compounded product, administered through DME, unit dose, 0.5 mg

J7620 Albuterol, up to 2.5 mg and ipratropium bromide, up to 0.5 mg, FDA-approved final product, noncompounded, administered through DME
MED: 100-2,15,110.3

J7622 Beclomethasone, inhalation solution, compounded product, administered through DME, unit dose form, per mg
Use this code for Beclovent, Beconase.

J7624 Betamethasone, inhalation solution, compounded product, administered through DME, unit dose form, per mg

J7626 Budesonide, inhalation solution, FDA-approved final product, noncompounded, administered through DME, unit dose form, up to 0.5 mg
Use this code for Pulmicort, Pulmicort Flexhaler, Pulmicort Respules, Vanceril.

J7627 Budesonide, inhalation solution, compounded product, administered through DME, unit dose form, up to 0.5 mg

J7628 Bitolterol mesylate, inhalation solution, compounded product, administered through DME, concentrated form, per mg
MED: 100-2,15,110.3

J7629 Bitolterol mesylate, inhalation solution, compounded product, administered through DME, unit dose form, per mg
MED: 100-2,15,110.3

J7631 Cromolyn sodium, inhalation solution, FDA-approved final product, noncompounded, administered through DME, unit dose form, per 10 mg
Use this code for Intal, Nasalcrom
MED: 100-2,15,110.3

J7632 Cromolyn sodium, inhalation solution, compounded product, administered through DME, unit dose form, per 10 mg

J7633 Budesonide, inhalation solution, FDA-approved final product, noncompounded, administered through DME, concentrated form, per 0.25 mg
Use this code for Pulmicort, Pulmicort Flexhaler, Pulmicort Respules, Vanceril

J7634 Budesonide, inhalation solution, compounded product, administered through DME, concentrated form, per 0.25 mg

J7635 Atropine, inhalation solution, compounded product, administered through DME, concentrated form, per mg
MED: 100-2,15,110.3

J7636 Atropine, inhalation solution, compounded product, administered through DME, unit dose form, per mg
MED: 100-2,15,110.3

J7637 Dexamethasone, inhalation solution, compounded product, administered through DME, concentrated form, per mg
MED: 100-2,15,110.3

J7638 Dexamethasone, inhalation solution, compounded product, administered through DME, unit dose form, per mg
MED: 100-2,15,110.3

J7639 Dornase alfa, inhalation solution, FDA-approved final product, noncompounded, administered through DME, unit dose form, per mg
Use this code for Pulmozyme.
MED: 100-2,15,110.3

J7640 Formoterol, inhalation solution, compounded product, administered through DME, unit dose form, 12 mcg

J7641 Flunisolide, inhalation solution, compounded product, administered through DME, unit dose, per mg
Use this code for Aerobid, Flunisolide.

J7642 Glycopyrrolate, inhalation solution, compounded product, administered through DME, concentrated form, per mg
MED: 100-2,15,110.3

J7643 Glycopyrrolate, inhalation solution, compounded product, administered through DME, unit dose form, per mg
MED: 100-2,15,110.3

J7644 Ipratropium bromide, inhalation solution, FDA-approved final product, noncompounded, administered through DME, unit dose form, per mg
Use this code for Atrovent.
MED: 100-2,15,110.3

J7645 Ipratropium bromide, inhalation solution, compounded product, administered through DME, unit dose form, per mg

J7647 Isoetharine HCl, inhalation solution, compounded product, administered through DME, concentrated form, per mg

J7648 Isoetharine HCl, inhalation solution, FDA-approved final product, noncompounded, administered through DME, concentrated form, per mg
Use this code for Beta-2.
MED: 100-2,15,110.3

J7649 Isoetharine HCl, inhalation solution, FDA-approved final product, noncompounded, administered through DME, unit dose form, per mg
MED: 100-2,15,110.3

J7650 Isoetharine HCl, inhalation solution, compounded product, administered through DME, unit dose form, per mg

J7657 Isoproterenol HCl, inhalation solution, compounded product, administered through DME, concentrated form, per mg

J7658 Isoproterenol HCl, inhalation solution, FDA-approved final product, noncompounded, administered through DME, concentrated form, per mg
Use this code for Isuprel HCl.
MED: 100-2,15,110.3

J7659 Isoproterenol HCl, inhalation solution, FDA-approved final product, noncompounded, administered through DME, unit dose form, per mg
Use this code for Isuprel HCl
MED: 100-2,15,110.3

J7660 Isoproterenol HCl, inhalation solution, compounded product, administered through DME, unit dose form, per mg

J7667 Metaproterenol sulfate, inhalation solution, compounded product, concentrated form, per 10 mg

J7668 Metaproterenol sulfate, inhalation solution, FDA-approved final product, noncompounded, administered through DME, concentrated form, per 10 mg
Use this code for Alupent
MED: 100-2,15,110.3

J7669 **Metaproterenol sulfate, inhalation solution, FDA-approved final product, noncompounded, administered through DME, unit dose form, per 10 mg**
Use this code for Alupent.
MED: 100-2,15,110.3

J7670 **Metaproterenol sulfate, inhalation solution, compounded product, administered through DME, unit dose form, per 10 mg**

J7674 **Methacholine chloride administered as inhalation solution through a nebulizer, per 1 mg**

J7676 **Pentamidine isethionate, inhalation solution, compounded product, administered through DME, unit dose form, per 300 mg**

J7680 **Terbutaline sulfate, inhalation solution, compounded product, administered through DME, concentrated form, per mg**
Use this code for Brethine.
MED: 100-2,15,110.3

J7681 **Terbutaline sulfate, inhalation solution, compounded product, administered through DME, unit dose form, per mg**
Use this code for Brethine.
MED: 100-2,15,110.3

J7682 **Tobramycin, inhalation solution, FDA-approved final product, noncompounded, unit dose form, administered through DME, per 300 mg**
Use this code for Tobi.
MED: 100-2,15,110.3

J7683 **Triamcinolone, inhalation solution, compounded product, administered through DME, concentrated form, per mg**
Use this code for Azmacort.
MED: 100-2,15,110.3

J7684 **Triamcinolone, inhalation solution, compounded product, administered through DME, unit dose form, per mg**
Use this code for Azmacort.
MED: 100-2,15,110.3

J7685 **Tobramycin, inhalation solution, compounded product, administered through DME, unit dose form, per 300 mg**

J7699 **NOC drugs, inhalation solution administered through DME**
MED: 100-2,15,110.3

J7799 **NOC drugs, other than inhalation drugs, administered through DME**
MED: 100-2,15,110.3

J8498 **Antiemetic drug, rectal/suppository, not otherwise specified**

J8499 **Prescription drug, oral, nonchemotherapeutic, NOS**
MED: 100-2,15,50

J8501 **Aprepitant, oral, 5 mg**
Use this code for Emend.
MED: 100-4,4,240; 100-4,17,80.2; 100-4,17,80.2.1; 100-4,17,80.2.4

J8510 **Busulfan; oral, 2 mg**
Use this code for Busulfex, Myleran.
MED: 100-2,15,50.5; 100-4,4,240; 100-4,17,80.1.1

J8515 **Cabergoline, oral, 0.25 mg**
Use this code for Dostinex.
MED: 100-2,15,50.5; 100-4,4,240

J8520 **Capecitabine, oral, 150 mg**
Use this code for Xeloda.
MED: 100-2,15,50.5; 100-4,4,240; 100-4,17,80.1.1

J8521 **Capecitabine, oral, 500 mg**
Use this code for Xeloda.
MED: 100-2,15,50.5; 100-4,4,240; 100-4,17,80.1.1

J8530 **Cyclophosphamide; oral, 25 mg**
Use this code for Cytoxan.
MED: 100-2,15,50.5; 100-4,4,240; 100-4,17,80.1.1

J8540 **Dexamethasone, oral, 0.25 mg**
Use this code for Decadron.

J8560 **Etoposide; oral, 50 mg**
Use this code for VePesid.
MED: 100-2,15,50.5; 100-4,4,240; 100-4,17,80.1.1

J8565 **Gefitinib, oral, 250 mg**
Use this code for Iressa.
MED: 100-4,4,240; 100-4,17,80.1.1

J8597 **Antiemetic drug, oral, not otherwise specified**

J8600 **Melphalan; oral, 2 mg**
Use this code for Alkeran.
MED: 100-2,15,50.5; 100-4,4,240; 100-4,17,80.1.1

J8610 **Methotrexate; oral, 2.5 mg**
Use this code for Trexall.
Methotrexate is an anti-metabolite used in the treatment of certain neoplastic diseases, severe psoriasis, and adult rheumatoid arthritis.
MED: 100-2,15,50.5; 100-4,4,240; 100-4,17,80.1.1

J8650 **Nabilone, oral, 1 mg**
Use this code for Cesamet

J8700 **Temozolomide, oral, 5 mg**
Use this code for Temodar.
MED: 100-2,15,50.5; 100-4,4,240

J8705 **Topotecan, oral, 0.25 mg**
Use this code for Hycamtin.

J8999 **Prescription drug, oral, chemotherapeutic, NOS**
Determine if an alternative HCPCS Level II or a CPT code better describes the service being reported. This code should be used only if a more specific code is unavailable.
MED: 100-2,15,50.5; 100-4,4,240; 100-4,17,80.1.1; 100-4,17,80.1.2

CHEMOTHERAPY DRUGS J9000-J9999

These codes cover the cost of the chemotherapy drug only, not the administration.

J9000 **Injection, doxorubicin HCl, 10 mg**
Use this code for Adriamycin PFS, Adriamycin RDF, Rubex.
MED: 100-2,15,50; 100-4,17,80.2

J9001 **Injection, doxorubicin HCl, all lipid formulations, 10 mg**
Use this code for Doxil.
MED: 100-2,15,50; 100-4,17,80.2

J9010 **Injection, alemtuzumab, 10 mg**
Use this code for Campath.

J9015 **Injection, aldesleukin, per single use vial**
Use this code for Proleukin, IL-2, Interleukin.
MED: 100-2,15,50

J9017 **Injection, arsenic trioxide, 1 mg**
Use this code for Trisenox.
AHA: 2Q,'02,8

J9020 **Injection, asparaginase, 10,000 units**
Use this code for Elspar.
MED: 100-2,15,50

J9025 **Injection, azacitidine, 1 mg**
Use this code for Vidaza.

J9027 **Injection, clofarabine, 1 mg**
Use this code for Clolar.

J9031 **BCG (intravesical) per instillation**
Use this code for Tice BCG, PACIS BCG, TheraCys.
MED: 100-2,15,50

J9033 **Injection, bendamustine HCl, 1 mg**
Use this code for TREANDA.

J9035 Injection, bevacizumab, 10 mg
Use this code for Avastin.

J9040 Injection, bleomycin sulfate, 15 units
Use this code for Blenoxane.
MED: 100-2,15,50

J9041 Injection, bortezomib, 0.1 mg
Use this code for Velcade.

J9045 Injection, carboplatin, 50 mg
Use this code for Paraplatin, Platinol AQ.
MED: 100-2,15,50

J9050 Injection, carmustine, 100 mg
Use this code for BiCNU.
MED: 100-2,15,50; 100-4,17,80.2

J9055 Injection, cetuximab, 10 mg
Use this code for Erbitux.

J9060 Cisplatin, powder or solution, per 10 mg
Use this code for Plantinol AQ.
MED: 100-2,15,50; 100-4,17,80.2

J9062 Cisplatin, 50 mg
Use this code for Plantinol AQ.
MED: 100-2,15,50; 100-4,17,80.2

J9065 Injection, cladribine, per 1 mg
Use this code for Leustatin.
MED: 100-2,15,50

J9070 Cyclophosphamide, 100 mg
Use this code for Endoxan-Asta.
MED: 100-2,15,50; 100-4,17,80.2

J9080 Cyclophosphamide, 200 mg
Use this code for Cytoxan, Neosar.
MED: 100-2,15,50; 100-4,17,80.2

J9090 Cyclophosphamide, 500 mg
Use this code for Cytoxan, Neosar.
MED: 100-2,15,50; 100-4,17,80.2

J9091 Cyclophosphamide, 1 g
Use this code for Cytoxan, Neosar.
MED: 100-2,15,50; 100-4,17,80.2

J9092 Cyclophosphamide, 2 g
Use this code for Cytoxan, Neosar.
MED: 100-2,15,50; 100-4,17,80.2

J9093 Cyclophosphamide, lyophilized, 100 mg
Use this code for Cytoxan Lyophilized.
MED: 100-2,15,50; 100-4,17,80.2

J9094 Cyclophosphamide, lyophilized, 200 mg
Use this code for Cytoxan Lyophilized.
MED: 100-2,15,50; 100-4,17,80.2

J9095 Cyclophosphamide, lyophilized, 500 mg
Use this code for Cytoxan Lyophilized.
MED: 100-2,15,50; 100-4,17,80.2

J9096 Cyclophosphamide, lyophilized, 1 g
Use this code for Cytoxan Lyophilized.
MED: 100-2,15,50; 100-4,17,80.2

J9097 Cyclophosphamide, lyophilized, 2 g
Use this code for Cytoxan Lyophilized.
MED: 100-2,15,50; 100-4,17,80.2

J9098 Injection, cytarabine liposome, 10 mg
Use this code for Depocyt.

J9100 Injection, cytarabine, 100 mg
Use this code for Cytosar-U, Ara-C, Tarabin CFS.
MED: 100-2,15,50

J9110 Injection cytarabine 500 mg
Use this code for Cytosar-U.
MED: 100-2,15,50

J9120 Injection, dactinomycin, 0.5 mg
Use this code for Cosmegen.
MED: 100-2,15,50

J9130 Dacarbazine, 100 mg
Use this code for DTIC-Dome.
MED: 100-2,15,50; 100-4,17,80.2

J9140 Dacarbazine, 200 mg
Use this code for DTIC-Dome.
MED: 100-2,15,50; 100-4,17,80.2

J9150 Injection, daunorubicin, 10 mg
Use this code for Cerubidine.
MED: 100-2,15,50

J9151 Injection, daunorubicin citrate, liposomal formulation, 10 mg
Use this code for Daunoxome.
MED: 100-2,15,50

J9160 Injection, denileukin diftitox, 300 mcg
Use this code for Ontak.

J9165 Injection, diethylstilbestrol diphosphate, 250 mg
MED: 100-2,15,50

J9170 Injection, docetaxel, 20 mg
Use this code for Taxotere.
MED: 100-2,15,50

J9175 Injection, Elliotts' B solution, 1 ml
MED: 100-2,15,50

J9178 Injection, epirubicin HCl, 2 mg
Use this code for Ellence.
MED: 100-4,17,80.2

J9181 Injection, etoposide, 10 mg
Use this code for VePesid, Toposar.
MED: 100-2,15,50

J9185 Injection, fludarabine phosphate, 50 mg
Use this code for Fludara.
MED: 100-2,15,50

J9190 Injection, fluorouracil, 500 mg
Use this code for Adrucil.
MED: 100-2,15,50

J9200 Injection, floxuridine, 500 mg
Use this code for FUDR.
MED: 100-2,15,50

J9201 Injection, gemcitabine HCl, 200 mg
Use this code for Gemzar.
MED: 100-2,15,50

J9202 Goserelin acetate implant, per 3.6 mg
Use this code for Zoladex.
MED: 100-2,15,50

J9206 Injection, irinotecan, 20 mg
Use this code for Camptosar.
MED: 100-2,15,50

J9207 Injection, ixabepilone, 1 mg
Use this code for IXEMPRA.

J9208 **Injection, ifosfamide, 1 g**
Use this code for IFEX, Mitoxana.
MED: 100-2,15,50

J9209 **Injection, mesna, 200 mg**
Use this code for Mesnex.
MED: 100-2,15,50

J9211 **Injection, idarubicin HCl, 5 mg**
Use this code for Idamycin.
MED: 100-2,15,50

J9212 **Injection, interferon alfacon-1, recombinant, 1 mcg**
Use this code for Infergen.
MED: 100-2,15,50

J9213 **Injection, interferon, alfa-2a, recombinant, 3 million units**
Use this code for Roferon-A.
MED: 100-2,15,50

J9214 **Injection, interferon, alfa-2b, recombinant, 1 million units**
Use this code for Intron A, Rebetron Kit.
MED: 100-2,15,50

J9215 **Injection, interferon, alfa-N3, (human leukocyte derived), 250,000 IU**
Use this code for Alferon N.
MED: 100-2,15,50

J9216 **Injection, interferon, gamma-1b, 3 million units**
Use this code for Actimmune.
MED: 100-2,15,50

J9217 **Leuprolide acetate (for depot suspension), 7.5 mg**
Use this code for Lupron Depot, Eligard.
MED: 100-2,15,50

J9218 **Leuprolide acetate, per 1 mg**
Use this code for Lupron.
MED: 100-2,15,50

J9219 **Leuprolide acetate implant, 65 mg**
Use this code for Lupron Implant.
MED: 100-2,15,50
AHA: 4Q,'01,5

J9225 **Histrelin implant (Vantas), 50 mg**
MED: 100-2,15,50

J9226 **Histrelin implant (Supprelin LA), 50 mg**

J9230 **Injection, mechlorethamine HCl, (nitrogen mustard), 10 mg**
Use this code for Mustargen.
MED: 100-2,15,50; 100-4,17,80.2

J9245 **Injection, melphalan HCl, 50 mg**
Use this code for Alkeran, L-phenylalanine mustard.
MED: 100-2,15,50

J9250 **Methotrexate sodium, 5 mg**
Use this code for Folex, Folex PFS, Methotrexate LPF.
MED: 100-2,15,50

J9260 **Methotrexate sodium, 50 mg**
Use this code for Folex, Folex PFS, Methotrexate LPF.
MED: 100-2,15,50

J9261 **Injection, nelarabine, 50 mg**
Use this code for Arranon

J9263 **Injection, oxaliplatin, 0.5 mg**
Use this code for Eloxatin.

J9264 **Injection, paclitaxel protein-bound particles, 1 mg**
Use this code for Abraxane.

J9265 **Injection, paclitaxel, 30 mg**
Use this code for Taxol, Nov-Onxol.
MED: 100-2,15,50

J9266 **Injection, pegaspargase, per single dose vial**
Use this code for Oncaspar.
MED: 100-2,15,50
AHA: 2Q,'02,8

J9268 **Injection, pentostatin, 10 mg**
Use this code for Nipent.
MED: 100-2,15,50

J9270 **Injection, plicamycin, 2.5 mg**
Use this code for Mithacin.
MED: 100-2,15,50

J9280 **Mitomycin, 5 mg**
Use this code for Mutamycin.
MED: 100-2,15,50

J9290 **Mitomycin, 20 mg**
Use this code for Mutamycin.
MED: 100-2,15,50

J9291 **Mitomycin, 40 mg**
Use this code for Mutamycin.
MED: 100-2,15,50

J9293 **Injection, mitoxantrone HCl, per 5 mg**
Use this code for Navantrone.
MED: 100-2,15,50

J9300 **Injection, gemtuzumab ozogamicin, 5 mg**
Use this code for Mylotarg.
AHA: 2Q,'02,8

J9303 **Injection, panitumumab, 10 mg**
Use this code for Vectibix.

J9305 **Injection, pemetrexed, 10 mg**
Use this code for Alimta.

J9310 **Injection, rituximab, 100 mg**
Use this code for RituXan.
MED: 100-2,15,50

J9320 **Injection, streptozocin, 1 g**
Use this code for Zanosar.
MED: 100-2,15,50; 100-4,17,80.2

J9330 **Injection, temsirolimus, 1 mg**
Use this code for TORISEL.

J9340 **Injection, thiotepa, 15 mg**
Use this code for Thioplex.
MED: 100-2,15,50

J9350 **Injection, topotecan, 4 mg**
Use this code for Hycamtin.
MED: 100-2,15,50

J9355 **Injection, trastuzumab, 10 mg**
Use this code for Herceptin.

J9357 **Injection, valrubicin, intravesical, 200 mg**
Use this code for Valstar.
MED: 100-2,15,50

J9360 **Injection, vinblastine sulfate, 1 mg**
Use this code for Velban.
MED: 100-2,15,50

J9370 **Vincristine sulfate, 1 mg**
Use this code for Oncovin, Vincasar PFS.
MED: 100-2,15,50

J9375 **Vincristine sulfate, 2 mg**
Use this code for Oncovin, Vincasar PFS.
MED: 100-2,15,50

J9380 **Vincristine sulfate, 5 mg**
Use this code for Oncovin.
MED: 100-2,15,50

J9390 **Injection, vinorelbine tartrate, 10 mg**
Use this code for Navelbine.
MED: 100-2,15,50

J9395 **Injection, fulvestrant, 25 mg**
Use this code for Fastodex.

J9600 **Injection, porfimer sodium, 75 mg**
Use this code for Photofrin.
MED: 100-2,15,50

J9999 **Not otherwise classified, antineoplastic drugs**
Determine if an alternative HCPCS Level II or a CPT code better describes the service being reported. This code should be used only if a more specific code is unavailable.
MED: 100-2,15,50; 100-3,110.2

TEMPORARY CODES K0000-K9999

The K codes were established for use by the DME Medicare Administrative Contractors (DME MACs). The K codes are developed when the currently existing permanent national codes for supplies and certain product categories do not include the codes needed to implement a DME MAC medical review policy.

K CODES ASSIGNED TO DURABLE MEDICAL EQUIPMENT ADMINISTRATIVE CONTRACTORS (DME MACS)

WHEELCHAIR AND WHEELCHAIR ACCESSORIES

K0001 Standard wheelchair

K0002 Standard hemi (low seat) wheelchair

K0003 Lightweight wheelchair

K0004 High strength, lightweight wheelchair

K0005 Ultralightweight wheelchair

K0006 Heavy-duty wheelchair

K0007 Extra heavy-duty wheelchair

K0009 Other manual wheelchair/base

K0010 Standard-weight frame motorized/power wheelchair

K0011 Standard-weight frame motorized/power wheelchair with programmable control parameters for speed adjustment, tremor dampening, acceleration control and braking

K0012 Lightweight portable motorized/power wheelchair

K0014 Other motorized/power wheelchair base

K0015 Detachable, nonadjustable height armrest, each

K0017 Detachable, adjustable height armrest, base, each

K0018 Detachable, adjustable height armrest, upper portion, each

K0019 Arm pad, each

K0020 Fixed, adjustable height armrest, pair

K0037 High mount flip-up footrest, each

K0038 Leg strap, each

K0039 Leg strap, H style, each

K0040 Adjustable angle footplate, each

K0041 Large size footplate, each

K0042 Standard size footplate, each

K0043 Footrest, lower extension tube, each

K0044 Footrest, upper hanger bracket, each

K0045 Footrest, complete assembly

K0046 Elevating legrest, lower extension tube, each

K0047 Elevating legrest, upper hanger bracket, each

K0050 Ratchet assembly

K0051 Cam release assembly, footrest or legrest, each

K0052 Swingaway, detachable footrests, each

K0053 Elevating footrests, articulating (telescoping), each

K0056 Seat height less than 17 in or equal to or greater than 21 in for a high-strength, lightweight, or ultralightweight wheelchair

K0065 Spoke protectors, each

K0069 Rear wheel assembly, complete, with solid tire, spokes or molded, each

K0070 Rear wheel assembly, complete, with pneumatic tire, spokes or molded, each

K0071 Front caster assembly, complete, with pneumatic tire, each

K0072 Front caster assembly, complete, with semipneumatic tire, each

K0073 Caster pin lock, each

K0077 Front caster assembly, complete, with solid tire, each

K0098 Drive belt for power wheelchair

K0105 IV hanger, each

K0108 Wheelchair component or accessory, not otherwise specified

K0195 Elevating legrests, pair (for use with capped rental wheelchair base)

MED: 100-3,230.10

K0455 Infusion pump used for uninterrupted parenteral administration of medication, (e.g., epoprostenol or treprostinol)

MED: 100-3,280.14

K0462 Temporary replacement for patient-owned equipment being repaired, any type

MED: 100-4,20,40.1

K0552 Supplies for external drug infusion pump, syringe type cartridge, sterile, each

MED: 100-3,280.14

K0601 Replacement battery for external infusion pump owned by patient, silver oxide, 1.5 volt, each

AHA: 2Q,'03,7

K0602 Replacement battery for external infusion pump owned by patient, silver oxide, 3 volt, each

AHA: 2Q,'03,7

K0603 Replacement battery for external infusion pump owned by patient, alkaline, 1.5 volt, each

AHA: 2Q,'03,7

K0604 Replacement battery for external infusion pump owned by patient, lithium, 3.6 volt, each

AHA: 2Q,'03,7

K0605 Replacement battery for external infusion pump owned by patient, lithium, 4.5 volt, each

AHA: 2Q,'03,7

K0606 Automatic external defibrillator, with integrated electrocardiogram analysis, garment type

AHA: 4Q,'03,4

K0607 Replacement battery for automated external defibrillator, garment type only, each

AHA: 4Q,'03,4

K0608 Replacement garment for use with automated external defibrillator, each

AHA: 4Q,'03,4

K0609 Replacement electrodes for use with automated external defibrillator, garment type only, each

AHA: 4Q,'03,4

K0669 Wheelchair accessory, wheelchair seat or back cushion, does not meet specific code criteria or no written coding verification from DME PDAC

K0672 Addition to lower extremity orthotic, removable soft interface, all components, replacement only, each

K0730 Controlled dose inhalation drug delivery system

K0733 Power wheelchair accessory, 12 to 24 amp hour sealed lead acid battery, each (e.g., gel cell, absorbed glassmat)

K0734 Skin protection wheelchair seat cushion, adjustable, width less than 22 in, any depth

K0735 Skin protection wheelchair seat cushion, adjustable, width 22 in or greater, any depth

K0736 Skin protection and positioning wheelchair seat cushion, adjustable, width less than 22 in, any depth

K0737 Skin protection and positioning wheelchair seat cushion, adjustable, width 22 in or greater, any depth

K0738 Portable gaseous oxygen system, rental; home compressor used to fill portable oxygen cylinders; includes portable containers, regulator, flowmeter, humidifier, cannula or mask, and tubing

K0800 Power operated vehicle, group 1 standard, patient weight capacity up to and including 300 pounds

K0801 Power operated vehicle, group 1 heavy-duty, patient weight capacity 301 to 450 pounds

K0802 Power operated vehicle, group 1 very heavy-duty, patient weight capacity 451 to 600 pounds

K0806 Power operated vehicle, group 2 standard, patient weight capacity up to and including 300 pounds

K0807 Power operated vehicle, group 2 heavy-duty, patient weight capacity 301 to 450 pounds

K0808 Power operated vehicle, group 2 very heavy-duty, patient weight capacity 451 to 600 pounds

K0812 Power operated vehicle, not otherwise classified

K0813 Power wheelchair, group 1 standard, portable, sling/solid seat and back, patient weight capacity up to and including 300 pounds

K0814 Power wheelchair, group 1 standard, portable, captain's chair, patient weight capacity up to and including 300 pounds

K0815 Power wheelchair, group 1 standard, sling/solid seat and back, patient weight capacity up to and including 300 pounds

K0816 Power wheelchair, group 1 standard, captain's chair, patient weight capacity up to and including 300 pounds

K0820 Power wheelchair, group 2 standard, portable, sling/solid seat/back, patient weight capacity up to and including 300 pounds

K0821 Power wheelchair, group 2 standard, portable, captain's chair, patient weight capacity up to and including 300 pounds

K0822 Power wheelchair, group 2 standard, sling/solid seat/back, patient weight capacity up to and including 300 pounds

K0823 Power wheelchair, group 2 standard, captain's chair, patient weight capacity up to and including 300 pounds

K0824 Power wheelchair, group 2 heavy-duty, sling/solid seat/back, patient weight capacity 301 to 450 pounds

K0825 Power wheelchair, group 2 heavy-duty, captain's chair, patient weight capacity 301 to 450 pounds

K0826 Power wheelchair, group 2 very heavy-duty, sling/solid seat/back, patient weight capacity 451 to 600 pounds

K0827 Power wheelchair, group 2 very heavy-duty, captain's chair, patient weight capacity 451 to 600 pounds

K0828 Power wheelchair, group 2 extra heavy-duty, sling/solid seat/back, patient weight capacity 601 pounds or more

K0829 Power wheelchair, group 2 extra heavy-duty, captain's chair, patient weight 601 pounds or more

K0830 Power wheelchair, group 2 standard, seat elevator, sling/solid seat/back, patient weight capacity up to and including 300 pounds

K0831 Power wheelchair, group 2 standard, seat elevator, captain's chair, patient weight capacity up to and including 300 pounds

K0835 Power wheelchair, group 2 standard, single power option, sling/solid seat/back, patient weight capacity up to and including 300 pounds

K0836 Power wheelchair, group 2 standard, single power option, captain's chair, patient weight capacity up to and including 300 pounds

K0837 Power wheelchair, group 2 heavy-duty, single power option, sling/solid seat/back, patient weight capacity 301 to 450 pounds

K0838 Power wheelchair, group 2 heavy-duty, single power option, captain's chair, patient weight capacity 301 to 450 pounds

K0839 Power wheelchair, group 2 very heavy-duty, single power option sling/solid seat/back, patient weight capacity 451 to 600 pounds

K0840 Power wheelchair, group 2 extra heavy-duty, single power option, sling/solid seat/back, patient weight capacity 601 pounds or more

K0841 Power wheelchair, group 2 standard, multiple power option, sling/solid seat/back, patient weight capacity up to and including 300 pounds

K0842 Power wheelchair, group 2 standard, multiple power option, captain's chair, patient weight capacity up to and including 300 pounds

K0843 Power wheelchair, group 2 heavy-duty, multiple power option, sling/solid seat/back, patient weight capacity 301 to 450 pounds

K0848 Power wheelchair, group 3 standard, sling/solid seat/back, patient weight capacity up to and including 300 pounds

K0849 Power wheelchair, group 3 standard, captain's chair, patient weight capacity up to and including 300 pounds

K0850 Power wheelchair, group 3 heavy-duty, sling/solid seat/back, patient weight capacity 301 to 450 pounds

K0851 Power wheelchair, group 3 heavy-duty, captain's chair, patient weight capacity 301 to 450 pounds

K0852 Power wheelchair, group 3 very heavy-duty, sling/solid seat/back, patient weight capacity 451 to 600 pounds

K0853 Power wheelchair, group 3 very heavy-duty, captain's chair, patient weight capacity 451 to 600 pounds

K0854 Power wheelchair, group 3 extra heavy-duty, sling/solid seat/back, patient weight capacity 601 pounds or more

K0855 Power wheelchair, group 3 extra heavy duty, captain's chair, patient weight capacity 601 pounds or more

K0856 Power wheelchair, group 3 standard, single power option, sling/solid seat/back, patient weight capacity up to and including 300 pounds

K0857 Power wheelchair, group 3 standard, single power option, captain's chair, patient weight capacity up to and including 300 pounds

K0858 Power wheelchair, group 3 heavy-duty, single power option, sling/solid seat/back, patient weight 301 to 450 pounds

K0859 Power wheelchair, group 3 heavy-duty, single power option, captain's chair, patient weight capacity 301 to 450 pounds

K0860 Power wheelchair, group 3 very heavy-duty, single power option, sling/solid seat/back, patient weight capacity 451 to 600 pounds

K0861 Power wheelchair, group 3 standard, multiple power option, sling/solid seat/back, patient weight capacity up to and including 300 pounds

K0862 Power wheelchair, group 3 heavy-duty, multiple power option, sling/solid seat/back, patient weight capacity 301 to 450 pounds

K0863 Power wheelchair, group 3 very heavy-duty, multiple power option, sling/solid seat/back, patient weight capacity 451 to 600 pounds

K0864 Power wheelchair, group 3 extra heavy-duty, multiple power option, sling/solid seat/back, patient weight capacity 601 pounds or more

K0868 Power wheelchair, group 4 standard, sling/solid seat/back, patient weight capacity up to and including 300 pounds

K0869 Power wheelchair, group 4 standard, captain's chair, patient weight capacity up to and including 300 pounds

K0870 Power wheelchair, group 4 heavy-duty, sling/solid seat/back, patient weight capacity 301 to 450 pounds

K0871 Power wheelchair, group 4 very heavy-duty, sling/solid seat/back, patient weight capacity 451 to 600 pounds

K0877 Power wheelchair, group 4 standard, single power option, sling/solid seat/back, patient weight capacity up to and including 300 pounds

K0878 Power wheelchair, group 4 standard, single power option, captain's chair, patient weight capacity up to and including 300 pounds

K0879 Power wheelchair, group 4 heavy-duty, single power option, sling/solid seat/back, patient weight capacity 301 to 450 pounds

K0880 Power wheelchair, group 4 very heavy-duty, single power option, sling/solid seat/back, patient weight 451 to 600 pounds

K0884 Power wheelchair, group 4 standard, multiple power option, sling/solid seat/back, patient weight capacity up to and including 300 pounds

K0885 Power wheelchair, group 4 standard, multiple power option, captain's chair, patient weight capacity up to and including 300 pounds

K0886 Power wheelchair, group 4 heavy-duty, multiple power option, sling/solid seat/back, patient weight capacity 301 to 450 pounds

K0890 Power wheelchair, group 5 pediatric, single power option, sling/solid seat/back, patient weight capacity up to and including 125 pounds

K0891 Power wheelchair, group 5 pediatric, multiple power option, sling/solid seat/back, patient weight capacity up to and including 125 pounds

K0898 Power wheelchair, not otherwise classified

K0899 Power mobility device, not coded by DME PDAC or does not meet criteria

ORTHOTIC PROCEDURES AND DEVICES L0000-L4999

L codes include orthotic and prosthetic procedures and devices, as well as scoliosis equipment, orthopedic shoes, and prosthetic implants.

ORTHOTIC DEVICES - SPINAL

CERVICAL

L0112 **Cranial cervical orthotic, congenital torticollis type, with or without soft interface material, adjustable range of motion joint, custom fabricated**

L0113 **Cranial cervical orthotic, torticollis type, with or without joint, with or without soft interface material, prefabricated, includes fitting and adjustment**

L0120 **Cervical, flexible, nonadjustable (foam collar)**

L0130 **Cervical, flexible, thermoplastic collar, molded to patient**

L0140 **Cervical, semi-rigid, adjustable (plastic collar)**

L0150 **Cervical, semi-rigid, adjustable molded chin cup (plastic collar with mandibular/occipital piece)**

L0160 **Cervical, semi-rigid, wire frame occipital/mandibular support**

L0170 **Cervical, collar, molded to patient model**

L0172 **Cervical, collar, semi-rigid thermoplastic foam, 2 piece**

L0174 **Cervical, collar, semi-rigid, thermoplastic foam, 2 piece with thoracic extension**

MULTIPLE POST COLLAR

L0180 **Cervical, multiple post collar, occipital/mandibular supports, adjustable**

L0190 **Cervical, multiple post collar, occipital/mandibular supports, adjustable cervical bars (SOMI, Guilford, Taylor types)**

L0200 **Cervical, multiple post collar, occipital/mandibular supports, adjustable cervical bars, and thoracic extension**

THORACIC

L0210 **Thoracic, rib belt**

L0220 **Thoracic, rib belt, custom fabricated**

L0430 **Spinal orthotic, anterior-posterior-lateral control, with interface material, custom fitted (DeWall Posture Protector only)**

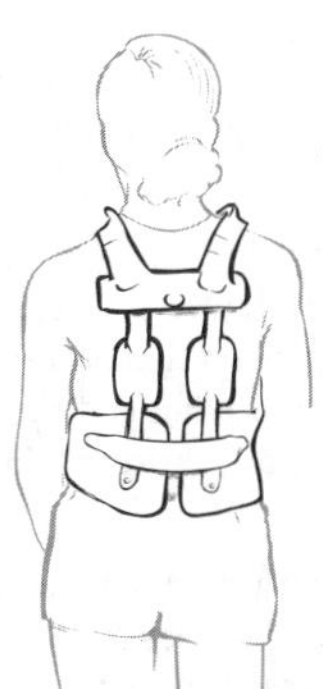

TLSO brace with adjustable straps and pads (L0450). The model at right and similar devices such as the Boston brace are molded polymer over foam and may be bivalve (front and back components)

Thoracic lumbar sacral orthosis (TLSO)

L0450 **Thoracic-lumbar-sacral orthotic (TLSO), flexible, provides trunk support, upper thoracic region, produces intracavitary pressure to reduce load on the intervertebral disks with rigid stays or panel(s), includes shoulder straps and closures, prefabricated, includes fitting and adjustment**

L0452 **Thoracic-lumbar-sacral orthotic (TLSO), flexible, provides trunk support, upper thoracic region, produces intracavitary pressure to reduce load on the intervertebral disks with rigid stays or panel(s), includes shoulder straps and closures, custom fabricated**

L0454 **Thoracic-lumbar-sacral orthotic (TLSO) flexible, provides trunk support, extends from sacrococcygeal junction to above T-9 vertebra, restricts gross trunk motion in the sagittal plane, produces intracavitary pressure to reduce load on the intervertebral disks with rigid stays or panel(s), includes shoulder straps and closures, prefabricated, includes fitting and adjustment**

L0456 **Thoracic-lumbar-sacral orthotic (TLSO), flexible, provides trunk support, thoracic region, rigid posterior panel and soft anterior apron, extends from the sacrococcygeal junction and terminates just inferior to the scapular spine, restricts gross trunk motion in the sagittal plane, produces intracavitary pressure to reduce load on the intervertebral disks, includes straps and closures, prefabricated, includes fitting and adjustment**

L0458 **Thoracic-lumbar-sacral orthotic (TLSO), triplanar control, modular segmented spinal system, 2 rigid plastic shells, posterior extends from the sacrococcygeal junction and terminates just inferior to the scapular spine, anterior extends from the symphysis pubis to the xiphoid, soft liner, restricts gross trunk motion in the sagittal, coronal, and transverse planes, lateral strength is provided by overlapping plastic and stabilizing closures, includes straps and closures, prefabricated, includes fitting and adjustment**

L0460 **Thoracic-lumbar-sacral orthotic (TLSO), triplanar control, modular segmented spinal system, 2 rigid plastic shells, posterior extends from the sacrococcygeal junction and terminates just inferior to the scapular spine, anterior extends from the symphysis pubis to the sternal notch, soft liner, restricts gross trunk motion in the sagittal, coronal, and transverse planes, lateral strength is provided by overlapping plastic and stabilizing closures, includes straps and closures, prefabricated, includes fitting and adjustment**

L0462 **Thoracic-lumbar-sacral orthotic (TLSO), triplanar control, modular segmented spinal system, 3 rigid plastic shells, posterior extends from the sacrococcygeal junction and terminates just inferior to the scapular spine, anterior extends from the symphysis pubis to the sternal notch, soft liner, restricts gross trunk motion in the sagittal, coronal, and transverse planes, lateral strength is provided by overlapping plastic and stabilizing closures, includes straps and closures, prefabricated, includes fitting and adjustment**

L0464 **Thoracic-lumbar-sacral orthotic (TLSO), triplanar control, modular segmented spinal system, 4 rigid plastic shells, posterior extends from sacrococcygeal junction and terminates just inferior to scapular spine, anterior extends from symphysis pubis to the sternal notch, soft liner, restricts gross trunk motion in sagittal, coronal, and transverse planes, lateral strength is provided by overlapping plastic and stabilizing closures, includes straps and closures, prefabricated, includes fitting and adjustment**

L0466 **Thoracic-lumbar-sacral orthotic (TLSO), sagittal control, rigid posterior frame and flexible soft anterior apron with straps, closures and padding, restricts gross trunk motion in sagittal plane, produces intracavitary pressure to reduce load on intervertebral disks, includes fitting and shaping the frame, prefabricated, includes fitting and adjustment**

L0468 **Thoracic-lumbar-sacral orthotic (TLSO), sagittal-coronal control, rigid posterior frame and flexible soft anterior apron with straps, closures and padding, extends from sacrococcygeal junction over scapulae, lateral strength provided by pelvic, thoracic, and lateral frame pieces, restricts gross trunk motion in sagittal, and coronal planes, produces intracavitary pressure to reduce load on intervertebral disks, includes fitting and shaping the frame, prefabricated, includes fitting and adjustment**

L0470 **Thoracic-lumbar-sacral orthotic (TLSO), triplanar control, rigid posterior frame and flexible soft anterior apron with straps, closures and padding, extends from sacrococcygeal junction to scapula, lateral strength provided by pelvic, thoracic, and lateral frame pieces, rotational strength provided by subclavicular extensions, restricts gross trunk motion in sagittal, coronal, and transverse planes, produces intracavitary pressure to reduce load on the intervertebral disks, includes fitting and shaping the frame, prefabricated, includes fitting and adjustment**

L0472 Thoracic-lumbar-sacral orthotic (TLSO), triplanar control, hyperextension, rigid anterior and lateral frame extends from symphysis pubis to sternal notch with 2 anterior components (one pubic and one sternal), posterior and lateral pads with straps and closures, limits spinal flexion, restricts gross trunk motion in sagittal, coronal, and transverse planes, includes fitting and shaping the frame, prefabricated, includes fitting and adjustment

L0480 Thoracic-lumbar-sacral orthotic (TLSO), triplanar control, 1 piece rigid plastic shell without interface liner, with multiple straps and closures, posterior extends from sacrococcygeal junction and terminates just inferior to scapular spine, anterior extends from symphysis pubis to sternal notch, anterior or posterior opening, restricts gross trunk motion in sagittal, coronal, and transverse planes, includes a carved plaster or CAD-CAM model, custom fabricated

L0482 Thoracic-lumbar-sacral orthotic (TLSO), triplanar control, 1 piece rigid plastic shell with interface liner, multiple straps and closures, posterior extends from sacrococcygeal junction and terminates just inferior to scapular spine, anterior extends from symphysis pubis to sternal notch, anterior or posterior opening, restricts gross trunk motion in sagittal, coronal, and transverse planes, includes a carved plaster or CAD-CAM model, custom fabricated

L0484 Thoracic-lumbar-sacral orthotic TLSO, triplanar control, 2 piece rigid plastic shell without interface liner, with multiple straps and closures, posterior extends from sacrococcygeal junction and terminates just inferior to scapular spine, anterior extends from symphysis pubis to sternal notch, lateral strength is enhanced by overlapping plastic, restricts gross trunk motion in the sagittal, coronal, and transverse planes, includes a carved plaster or CAD-CAM model, custom fabricated

L0486 Thoracic-lumbar-sacral orthotic (TLSO), triplanar control, 2 piece rigid plastic shell with interface liner, multiple straps and closures, posterior extends from sacrococcygeal junction and terminates just inferior to scapular spine, anterior extends from symphysis pubis to sternal notch, lateral strength is enhanced by overlapping plastic, restricts gross trunk motion in the sagittal, coronal, and transverse planes, includes a carved plaster or CAD-CAM model, custom fabricated

L0488 Thoracic-lumbar-sacral orthotic (TLSO), triplanar control, 1 piece rigid plastic shell with interface liner, multiple straps and closures, posterior extends from sacrococcygeal junction and terminates just inferior to scapular spine, anterior extends from symphysis pubis to sternal notch, anterior or posterior opening, restricts gross trunk motion in sagittal, coronal, and transverse planes, prefabricated, includes fitting and adjustment

L0490 Thoracic-lumbar-sacral orthotic (TLSO), sagittal-coronal control, 1 piece rigid plastic shell, with overlapping reinforced anterior, with multiple straps and closures, posterior extends from sacrococcygeal junction and terminates at or before the T-9 vertebra, anterior extends from symphysis pubis to xiphoid, anterior opening, restricts gross trunk motion in sagittal and coronal planes, prefabricated, includes fitting and adjustment

L0491 Thoracic-lumbar-sacral orthotic (TLSO), sagittal-coronal control, modular segmented spinal system, 2 rigid plastic shells, posterior extends from the sacrococcygeal junction and terminates just inferior to the scapular spine, anterior extends from the symphysis pubis to the xiphoid, soft liner, restricts gross trunk motion in the sagittal and coronal planes, lateral strength is provided by overlapping plastic and stabilizing closures, includes straps and closures, prefabricated, includes fitting and adjustment

L0492 Thoracic-lumbar-sacral orthotic (TLSO), sagittal-coronal control, modular segmented spinal system, 3 rigid plastic shells, posterior extends from the sacrococcygeal junction and terminates just inferior to the scapular spine, anterior extends from the symphysis pubis to the xiphoid, soft liner, restricts gross trunk motion in the sagittal and coronal planes, lateral strength is provided by overlapping plastic and stabilizing closures, includes straps and closures, prefabricated, includes fitting and adjustment

CERVICAL-THORACIC-LUMBAR-SACRAL ORTHOTIC (CTLSO)

L0621 Sacroiliac orthotic, flexible, provides pelvic-sacral support, reduces motion about the sacroiliac joint, includes straps, closures, may include pendulous abdomen design, prefabricated, includes fitting and adjustment

L0622 Sacroiliac orthotic, flexible, provides pelvic-sacral support, reduces motion about the sacroiliac joint, includes straps, closures, may include pendulous abdomen design, custom fabricated

L0623 Sacroiliac orthotic, provides pelvic-sacral support, with rigid or semi-rigid panels over the sacrum and abdomen, reduces motion about the sacroiliac joint, includes straps, closures, may include pendulous abdomen design, prefabricated, includes fitting and adjustment

L0624 Sacroiliac orthotic, provides pelvic-sacral support, with rigid or semi-rigid panels placed over the sacrum and abdomen, reduces motion about the sacroiliac joint, includes straps, closures, may include pendulous abdomen design, custom fabricated

L0625 Lumbar orthotic, flexible, provides lumbar support, posterior extends from L-1 to below L-5 vertebra, produces intracavitary pressure to reduce load on the intervertebral discs, includes straps, closures, may include pendulous abdomen design, shoulder straps, stays, prefabricated, includes fitting and adjustment

L0626 Lumbar orthotic, sagittal control, with rigid posterior panel(s), posterior extends from L-1 to below L-5 vertebra, produces intracavitary pressure to reduce load on the intervertebral discs, includes straps, closures, may include padding, stays, shoulder straps, pendulous abdomen design, prefabricated, includes fitting and adjustment

L0627 Lumbar orthotic, sagittal control, with rigid anterior and posterior panels, posterior extends from L-1 to below L-5 vertebra, produces intracavitary pressure to reduce load on the intervertebral discs, includes straps, closures, may include padding, shoulder straps, pendulous abdomen design, prefabricated, includes fitting and adjustment

L0628 Lumbar-sacral orthotic, flexible, provides lumbo-sacral support, posterior extends from sacrococcygeal junction to T-9 vertebra, produces intracavitary pressure to reduce load on the intervertebral discs, includes straps, closures, may include stays, shoulder straps, pendulous abdomen design, prefabricated, includes fitting and adjustment

L0629 Lumbar-sacral orthotic, flexible, provides lumbo-sacral support, posterior extends from sacrococcygeal junction to T-9 vertebra, produces intracavitary pressure to reduce load on the intervertebral discs, includes straps, closures, may include stays, shoulder straps, pendulous abdomen design, custom fabricated

L0630 Lumbar-sacral orthotic, sagittal control, with rigid posterior panel(s), posterior extends from sacrococcygeal junction to T-9 vertebra, produces intracavitary pressure to reduce load on the intervertebral discs, includes straps, closures, may include padding, stays, shoulder straps, pendulous abdomen design, prefabricated, includes fitting and adjustment

L0631 Lumbar-sacral orthotic, sagittal control, with rigid anterior and posterior panels, posterior extends from sacrococcygeal junction to T-9 vertebra, produces intracavitary pressure to reduce load on the intervertebral discs, includes straps, closures, may include padding, shoulder straps, pendulous abdomen design, prefabricated, includes fitting and adjustment

L0632 Lumbar-sacral orthotic (LSO), sagittal control, with rigid anterior and posterior panels, posterior extends from sacrococcygeal junction to T-9 vertebra, produces intracavitary pressure to reduce load on the intervertebral discs, includes straps, closures, may include padding, shoulder straps, pendulous abdomen design, custom fabricated

L0633 Lumbar-sacral orthotic (LSO), sagittal-coronal control, with rigid posterior frame/panel(s), posterior extends from sacrococcygeal junction to T-9 vertebra, lateral strength provided by rigid lateral frame/panels, produces intracavitary pressure to reduce load on intervertebral discs, includes straps, closures, may include padding, stays, shoulder straps, pendulous abdomen design, prefabricated, includes fitting and adjustment

L0634 Lumbar-sacral orthotic (LSO), sagittal-coronal control, with rigid posterior frame/panel(s), posterior extends from sacrococcygeal junction to T-9 vertebra, lateral strength provided by rigid lateral frame/panel(s), produces intracavitary pressure to reduce load on intervertebral discs, includes straps, closures, may include padding, stays, shoulder straps, pendulous abdomen design, custom fabricated

L0635 Lumbar-sacral orthotic (LSO), sagittal-coronal control, lumbar flexion, rigid posterior frame/panel(s), lateral articulating design to flex the lumbar spine, posterior extends from sacrococcygeal junction to T-9 vertebra, lateral strength provided by rigid lateral frame/panel(s), produces intracavitary pressure to reduce load on intervertebral discs, includes straps, closures, may include padding, anterior panel, pendulous abdomen design, prefabricated, includes fitting and adjustment

L0636 Lumbar-sacral orthotic (LSO), sagittal-coronal control, lumbar flexion, rigid posterior frame/panels, lateral articulating design to flex the lumbar spine, posterior extends from sacrococcygeal junction to T-9 vertebra, lateral strength provided by rigid lateral frame/panels, produces intracavitary pressure to reduce load on intervertebral discs, includes straps, closures, may include padding, anterior panel, pendulous abdomen design, custom fabricated

L0637 Lumbar-sacral orthotic (LSO), sagittal-coronal control, with rigid anterior and posterior frame/panels, posterior extends from sacrococcygeal junction to T-9 vertebra, lateral strength provided by rigid lateral frame/panels, produces intracavitary pressure to reduce load on intervertebral discs, includes straps, closures, may include padding, shoulder straps, pendulous abdomen design, prefabricated, includes fitting and adjustment

L0638 Lumbar-sacral orthotic (LSO), sagittal-coronal control, with rigid anterior and posterior frame/panels, posterior extends from sacrococcygeal junction to T-9 vertebra, lateral strength provided by rigid lateral frame/panels, produces intracavitary pressure to reduce load on intervertebral discs, includes straps, closures, may include padding, shoulder straps, pendulous abdomen design, custom fabricated

L0639 Lumbar-sacral orthotic (LSO), sagittal-coronal control, rigid shell(s)/panel(s), posterior extends from sacrococcygeal junction to T-9 vertebra, anterior extends from symphysis pubis to xyphoid, produces intracavitary pressure to reduce load on the intervertebral discs, overall strength is provided by overlapping rigid material and stabilizing closures, includes straps, closures, may include soft interface, pendulous abdomen design, prefabricated, includes fitting and adjustment

L0640 Lumbar-sacral orthotic (LSO), sagittal-coronal control, rigid shell(s)/panel(s), posterior extends from sacrococcygeal junction to T-9 vertebra, anterior extends from symphysis pubis to xyphoid, produces intracavitary pressure to reduce load on the intervertebral discs, overall strength is provided by overlapping rigid material and stabilizing closures, includes straps, closures, may include soft interface, pendulous abdomen design, custom fabricated

ANTERIOR-POSTERIOR-LATERAL CONTROL

L0700 Cervical-thoracic-lumbar-sacral orthosis (CTLSO), anterior-posterior-lateral control, molded to patient model, (Minerva type)

L0710 Cervical-thoracic-lumbar-sacral orthotic (CTLSO), anterior-posterior-lateral-control, molded to patient model, with interface material, (Minerva type)

HALO PROCEDURE

L0810 Halo procedure, cervical halo incorporated into jacket vest

L0820 Halo procedure, cervical halo incorporated into plaster body jacket

L0830 Halo procedure, cervical halo incorporated into Milwaukee type orthotic

L0859 Addition to halo procedure, magnetic resonance image compatible systems, rings and pins, any material

L0861 Addition to halo procedure, replacement liner/interface material

ADDITIONS TO SPINAL ORTHOTIC

L0970 Thoracic-lumbar-sacral orthotic (TLSO), corset front

L0972 Lumbar-sacral orthotic (LSO), corset front

L0974 Thoracic-lumbar-sacral orthotic (TLSO), full corset

L0976 Lumbar-sacral orthotic (LSO), full corset

L0978 Axillary crutch extension

L0980 Peroneal straps, pair

L0982 Stocking supporter grips, set of 4

L0984 Protective body sock, each

L0999 Addition to spinal orthotic, not otherwise specified

Determine if an alternative HCPCS Level II or a CPT code better describes the service being reported. This code should be used only if a more specific code is unavailable.

ORTHOTIC DEVICES - SCOLIOSIS PROCEDURES

The orthotic care of scoliosis differs from other orthotic care in that the treatment is more dynamic in nature and uses continual modification of the orthosis to the patient's changing condition. This coding structure uses the proper names - or eponyms - of the procedures because they have historic and universal acceptance in the profession. It should be recognized that variations to the basic procedures described by the founders/developers are accepted in various medical and orthotic practices throughout the country. All procedures include model of patient when indicated.

CERVICAL-THORACIC-LUMBAR-SACRAL ORTHOTIC (CTLSO)

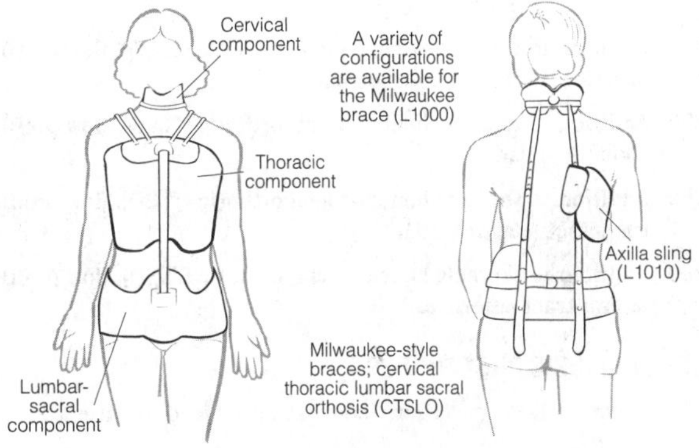

L1000 Cervical-thoracic-lumbar-sacral orthotic (CTLSO) (Milwaukee), inclusive of furnishing initial orthotic, including model

L1001 Cervical-thoracic-lumbar-sacral orthotic (CTLSO), immobilizer, infant size, prefabricated, includes fitting and adjustment

L1005 Tension based scoliosis orthotic and accessory pads, includes fitting and adjustment

L1010 Addition to cervical-thoracic-lumbar-sacral orthotic (CTLSO) or scoliosis orthotic, axilla sling

L1020 Addition to cervical-thoracic-lumbar-sacral orthotic (CTLSO) or scoliosis orthotic, kyphosis pad

L1025 Addition to cervical-thoracic-lumbar-sacral orthotic (CTLSO) or scoliosis orthotic, kyphosis pad, floating

L1030 Addition to cervical-thoracic-lumbar-sacral orthotic (CTLSO) or scoliosis orthotic, lumbar bolster pad

L1040 Addition to cervical-thoracic-lumbar-sacral orthotic (CTLSO) or scoliosis orthotic, lumbar or lumbar rib pad

L1050 Addition to cervical-thoracic-lumbar-sacral orthotic (CTLSO) or scoliosis orthotic, sternal pad

L1060 Addition to cervical-thoracic-lumbar-sacral orthotic (CTLSO) or scoliosis orthotic, thoracic pad

L1070 Addition to cervical-thoracic-lumbar-sacral orthotic (CTLSO) or scoliosis orthotic, trapezius sling

L1080 Addition to cervical-thoracic-lumbar-sacral orthotic (CTLSO) or scoliosis orthotic, outrigger

L1085 Addition to cervical-thoracic-lumbar-sacral orthotic (CTLSO) or scoliosis orthotic, outrigger, bilateral with vertical extensions

L1090 Addition to cervical-thoracic-lumbar-sacral orthotic (CTLSO) or scoliosis orthotic, lumbar sling

L1100 Addition to cervical-thoracic-lumbar-sacral orthotic (CTLSO) or scoliosis orthotic, ring flange, plastic or leather

L1110 Addition to cervical-thoracic-lumbar-sacral orthotic (CTLSO) or scoliosis orthotic, ring flange, plastic or leather, molded to patient model

L1120 Addition to cervical-thoracic-lumbar-sacral orthotic (CTLSO), scoliosis orthotic, cover for upright, each

THORACIC-LUMBAR-SACRAL ORTHOSIS (TLSO) (LOW PROFILE)

L1200 Thoracic-lumbar-sacral orthotic (TLSO), inclusive of furnishing initial orthotic only

L1210 Addition to thoracic-lumbar-sacral orthotic (TLSO), (low profile), lateral thoracic extension

L1220 Addition to thoracic-lumbar-sacral orthotic (TLSO), (low profile), anterior thoracic extension

L1230 Addition to thoracic-lumbar-sacral orthotic (TLSO), (low profile), Milwaukee type superstructure

L1240 Addition to thoracic-lumbar-sacral orthotic (TLSO), (low profile), lumbar derotation pad

L1250 Addition to thoracic-lumbar-sacral orthotic (TLSO), (low profile), anterior ASIS pad

L1260 Addition to thoracic-lumbar-sacral orthotic (TLSO), (low profile), anterior thoracic derotation pad

L1270 Addition to thoracic-lumbar-sacral orthotic (TLSO), (low profile), abdominal pad

L1280 Addition to thoracic-lumbar-sacral orthotic (TLSO), (low profile), rib gusset (elastic), each

L1290 Addition to thoracic-lumbar-sacral orthotic (TLSO), (low profile), lateral trochanteric pad

OTHER SCOLIOSIS PROCEDURES

L1300 Other scoliosis procedure, body jacket molded to patient model

L1310 Other scoliosis procedure, postoperative body jacket

L1499 Spinal orthotic, not otherwise specified

Determine if an alternative HCPCS Level II or a CPT code better describes the service being reported. This code should be used only if a more specific code is unavailable.

THORACIC-HIP-KNEE-ANKLE ORTHOTIC (THKAO)

L1500 Thoracic-hip-knee-ankle orthotic (THKAO), mobility frame (Newington, Parapodium types)

L1510 Thoracic-hip-knee-ankle orthotic (THKAO), standing frame, with or without tray and accessories

L1520 Thoracic-hip-knee-ankle orthotic (THKAO), swivel walker

ORTHOTIC DEVICES - LOWER LIMB

The procedures in L1600-L2999 are considered as "base" or "basic procedures" and may be modified by listing procedure from the "additions" sections and adding them to the base procedures.

HIP ORTHOTIC (HO) - FLEXIBLE

L1600 Hip orthotic (HO), abduction control of hip joints, flexible, Frejka type with cover, prefabricated, includes fitting and adjustment

L1610 Hip orthotic (HO), abduction control of hip joints, flexible, (Frejka cover only), prefabricated, includes fitting and adjustment

L1620 Hip orthosis (HO), abduction control of hip joints, flexible, (Pavlik harness), prefabricated, includes fitting and adjustment

L1630 Hip orthotic (HO), abduction control of hip joints, semi-flexible (Von Rosen type), custom fabricated

L1640 Hip orthotic (HO), abduction control of hip joints, static, pelvic band or spreader bar, thigh cuffs, custom fabricated

L1650 Hip orthotic (HO), abduction control of hip joints, static, adjustable, (Ilfled type), prefabricated, includes fitting and adjustment

L1652 Hip orthotic, bilateral thigh cuffs with adjustable abductor spreader bar, adult size, prefabricated, includes fitting and adjustment, any type

L1660 Hip orthotic (HO), abduction control of hip joints, static, plastic, prefabricated, includes fitting and adjustment

L1680 Hip orthotic (HO), abduction control of hip joints, dynamic, pelvic control, adjustable hip motion control, thigh cuffs (Rancho hip action type), custom fabricated

L1685 Hip orthosis (HO), abduction control of hip joint, postoperative hip abduction type, custom fabricated

L1686 Hip orthotic (HO), abduction control of hip joint, postoperative hip abduction type, prefabricated, includes fitting and adjustment

L1690 Combination, bilateral, lumbo-sacral, hip, femur orthotic providing adduction and internal rotation control, prefabricated, includes fitting and adjustment

LEGG PERTHES

L1700 Legg Perthes orthotic, (Toronto type), custom fabricated

L1710 Legg Perthes orthotic, (Newington type), custom fabricated

L1720 Legg Perthes orthotic, trilateral, (Tachdijan type), custom fabricated

L1730 Legg Perthes orthotic, (Scottish Rite type), custom fabricated

L1755 Legg Perthes orthotic, (Patten bottom type), custom fabricated

KNEE ORTHOTIC (KO)

L1800 Knee orthotic (KO), elastic with stays, prefabricated, includes fitting and adjustment

L1810 Knee orthotic (KO), elastic with joints, prefabricated, includes fitting and adjustment

L1815 Knee orthotic (KO), elastic or other elastic type material with condylar pad(s), prefabricated, includes fitting and adjustment

L1820 Knee orthotic, elastic with condylar pads and joints, with or without patellar control, prefabricated, includes fitting and adjustment

L1825 Knee orthotic (KO), elastic knee cap, prefabricated, includes fitting and adjustment

L1830 Knee orthotic (KO), immobilizer, canvas longitudinal, prefabricated, includes fitting and adjustment

L1831 Knee orthotic, locking knee joint(s), positional orthotic, prefabricated, includes fitting and adjustment

L1832 Knee orthotic, adjustable knee joints (unicentric or polycentric), positional orthotic, rigid support, prefabricated, includes fitting and adjustment

L1834 Knee orthotic (KO), without knee joint, rigid, custom fabricated

L1836 Knee orthotic, rigid, without joint(s), includes soft interface material, prefabricated, includes fitting and adjustment

L1840 Knee orthotic (KO), derotation, medial-lateral, anterior cruciate ligament, custom fabricated

L1843 Knee orthotic (KO), single upright, thigh and calf, with adjustable flexion and extension joint (unicentric or polycentric), medial-lateral and rotation control, with or without varus/valgus adjustment, prefabricated, includes fitting and adjustment

L1844 Knee orthotic (KO), single upright, thigh and calf, with adjustable flexion and extension joint (unicentric or polycentric), medial-lateral and rotation control, with or without varus/valgus adjustment, custom fabricated

L1845 Knee orthotic, double upright, thigh and calf, with adjustable flexion and extension joint (unicentric or polycentric), medial-lateral and rotation control, with or without varus/valgus adjustment, prefabricated, includes fitting and adjustment

L1846 Knee orthotic, double upright, thigh and calf, with adjustable flexion and extension joint (unicentric or polycentric), medial-lateral and rotation control, with or without varus/valgus adjustment, custom fabricated

L1847 Knee orthotic (KO), double upright with adjustable joint, with inflatable air support chamber(s), prefabricated, includes fitting and adjustment

L1850 Knee orthotic (KO), Swedish type, prefabricated, includes fitting and adjustment

L1860 Knee orthotic (KO), modification of supracondylar prosthetic socket, custom fabricated (SK)

ANKLE-FOOT ORTHOTIC (AFO)

L1900 Ankle-foot orthotic (AFO), spring wire, dorsiflexion assist calf band, custom fabricated

L1901 Ankle orthotic, elastic, prefabricated, includes fitting and adjustment (e.g., neoprene, Lycra)

L1902 Ankle-foot orthotic (AFO), ankle gauntlet, prefabricated, includes fitting and adjustment

L1904 Ankle-foot orthotic (AFO), molded ankle gauntlet, custom fabricated

L1906 Ankle-foot orthosis (AFO), multiligamentus ankle support, prefabricated, includes fitting and adjustment

L1907 AFO, supramalleolar with straps, with or without interface/pads, custom fabricated

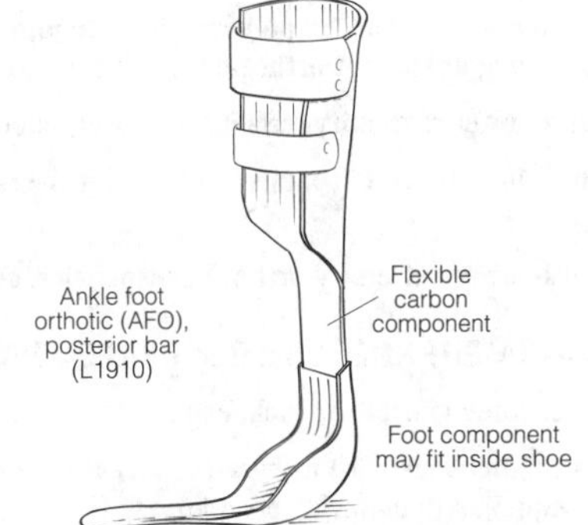

L1910 Ankle-foot orthotic (AFO), posterior, single bar, clasp attachment to shoe counter, prefabricated, includes fitting and adjustment

L1920 Ankle-foot orthotic (AFO), single upright with static or adjustable stop (Phelps or Perlstein type), custom fabricated

L1930 Ankle-foot orthotic (AFO), plastic or other material, prefabricated, includes fitting and adjustment

L1932 AFO, rigid anterior tibial section, total carbon fiber or equal material, prefabricated, includes fitting and adjustment

L1940 Ankle-foot orthotic (AFO), plastic or other material, custom fabricated

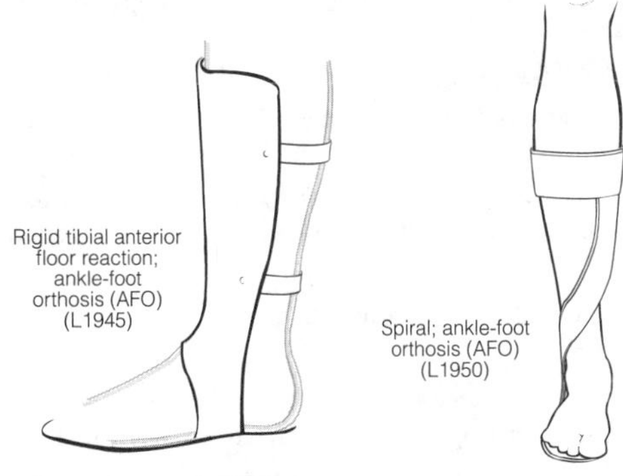

L1945 Ankle-foot orthotic (AFO), plastic, rigid anterior tibial section (floor reaction), custom fabricated

L1950 Ankle-foot orthotic (AFO), spiral, (Institute of Rehabilitative Medicine type), plastic, custom fabricated

L1951 Ankle-foot orthotic (AFO), spiral, (Institute of rehabilitative Medicine type), plastic or other material, prefabricated, includes fitting and adjustment

L1960 Ankle-foot orthotic (AFO), posterior solid ankle, plastic, custom fabricated

L1970 Ankle-foot orthotic (AFO), plastic with ankle joint, custom fabricated

L1971 Ankle-foot orthotic (AFO), plastic or other material with ankle joint, prefabricated, includes fitting and adjustment

L1980 Ankle-foot orthotic (AFO), single upright free plantar dorsiflexion, solid stirrup, calf band/cuff (single bar 'BK' orthotic), custom fabricated

L1990 Ankle-foot orthotic (AFO), double upright free plantar dorsiflexion, solid stirrup, calf band/cuff (double bar 'BK' orthotic), custom fabricated

KNEE-ANKLE-FOOT ORTHOTIC (KAFO) - OR ANY COMBINATION

L2000 Knee-ankle-foot orthotic (KAFO), single upright, free knee, free ankle, solid stirrup, thigh and calf bands/cuffs (single bar 'AK' orthotic), custom fabricated

L2005 Knee-ankle-foot orthotic (KAFO), any material, single or double upright, stance control, automatic lock and swing phase release, mechanical activation, includes ankle joint, any type, custom fabricated

L2010 Knee-ankle-foot orthotic (KAFO), single upright, free ankle, solid stirrup, thigh and calf bands/cuffs (single bar 'AK' orthotic), without knee joint, custom fabricated

L2020 Knee-ankle-foot orthotic (KAFO), double upright, free ankle, solid stirrup, thigh and calf bands/cuffs (double bar 'AK' orthotic), custom fabricated

L2030 Knee-ankle-foot orthotic (KAFO), double upright, free ankle, solid stirrup, thigh and calf bands/cuffs, (double bar 'AK' orthotic), without knee joint, custom fabricated

L2034 Knee-ankle-foot orthotic (KAFO), full plastic, single upright, with or without free motion knee, medial-lateral rotation control, with or without free motion ankle, custom fabricated

L2035 Knee-ankle-foot orthotic (KAFO), full plastic, static (pediatric size), without free motion ankle, prefabricated, includes fitting and adjustment

L2036 Knee-ankle-foot orthotic (KAFO), full plastic, double upright, with or without free motion knee, with or without free motion ankle, custom fabricated

L2037 Knee-ankle-foot orthotic (KAFO), full plastic, single upright, with or without free motion knee, with or without free motion ankle, custom fabricated

L2038 Knee-ankle-foot orthotic (KAFO), full plastic, with or without free motion knee, multi-axis ankle, custom fabricated

TORSION CONTROL: HIP-KNEE-ANKLE-FOOT ORTHOTIC (HKAFO)

L2040 Hip-knee-ankle-foot orthotic (HKAFO), torsion control, bilateral rotation straps, pelvic band/belt, custom fabricated

L2050 Hip-knee-ankle-foot orthotic (HKAFO), torsion control, bilateral torsion cables, hip joint, pelvic band/belt, custom fabricated

L2060 Hip-knee-ankle-foot orthotic (HKAFO), torsion control, bilateral torsion cables, ball bearing hip joint, pelvic band/ belt, custom fabricated

L2070 Hip-knee-ankle-foot orthotic (HKAFO), torsion control, unilateral rotation straps, pelvic band/belt, custom fabricated

L2080 Hip-knee-ankle-foot orthotic (HKAFO), torsion control, unilateral torsion cable, hip joint, pelvic band/belt, custom fabricated

L2090 Hip-knee-ankle-foot orthotic (HKAFO), torsion control, unilateral torsion cable, ball bearing hip joint, pelvic band/ belt, custom fabricated

L2106 Ankle-foot orthotic (AFO), fracture orthotic, tibial fracture cast orthotic, thermoplastic type casting material, custom fabricated

L2108 Ankle-foot orthotic (AFO), fracture orthotic, tibial fracture cast orthotic, custom fabricated

L2112 Ankle-foot orthotic (AFO), fracture orthotic, tibial fracture orthotic, soft, prefabricated, includes fitting and adjustment

L2114 Ankle-foot orthosis (AFO), fracture orthosis, tibial fracture orthosis, semi-rigid, prefabricated, includes fitting and adjustment

L2116 Ankle-foot orthotic (AFO), fracture orthotic, tibial fracture orthotic, rigid, prefabricated, includes fitting and adjustment

L2126 Knee-ankle-foot orthotic (KAFO), fracture orthotic, femoral fracture cast orthotic, thermoplastic type casting material, custom fabricated

L2128 Knee-ankle-foot orthotic (KAFO), fracture orthotic, femoral fracture cast orthotic, custom fabricated

L2132 Knee-ankle-foot orthotic (KAFO), fracture orthotic, femoral fracture cast orthotic, soft, prefabricated, includes fitting and adjustment

L2134 Knee-ankle-foot orthotic (KAFO), fracture orthotic, femoral fracture cast orthotic, semi-rigid, prefabricated, includes fitting and adjustment

L2136 KAFO, fracture orthotic, femoral fracture cast orthotic, rigid, prefabricated, includes fitting and adjustment

ADDITIONS TO FRACTURE ORTHOTIC

L2180 Addition to lower extremity fracture orthotic, plastic shoe insert with ankle joints

L2182 Addition to lower extremity fracture orthotic, drop lock knee joint

L2184 Addition to lower extremity fracture orthotic, limited motion knee joint

L2186 Addition to lower extremity fracture orthotic, adjustable motion knee joint, Lerman type

L2188 Addition to lower extremity fracture orthotic, quadrilateral brim

L2190 Addition to lower extremity fracture orthotic, waist belt

L2192 Addition to lower extremity fracture orthotic, hip joint, pelvic band, thigh flange, and pelvic belt

ADDITIONS TO LOWER EXTREMITY ORTHOTIC: SHOE-ANKLE-SHIN-KNEE

L2200 Addition to lower extremity, limited ankle motion, each joint

L2210 Addition to lower extremity, dorsiflexion assist (plantar flexion resist), each joint

L2220 Addition to lower extremity, dorsiflexion and plantar flexion assist/resist, each joint

L2230 Addition to lower extremity, split flat caliper stirrups and plate attachment

L2232 Addition to lower extremity orthotic, rocker bottom for total contact ankle-foot orthotic (AFO), for custom fabricated orthotic only

L2240 Addition to lower extremity, round caliper and plate attachment

L2250 Addition to lower extremity, foot plate, molded to patient model, stirrup attachment

L2260 Addition to lower extremity, reinforced solid stirrup (Scott-Craig type)

L2265 Addition to lower extremity, long tongue stirrup

L2270 Addition to lower extremity, varus/valgus correction (T) strap, padded/lined or malleolus pad

L2275 Addition to lower extremity, varus/valgus correction, plastic modification, padded/lined

L2280 Addition to lower extremity, molded inner boot

L2300 Addition to lower extremity, abduction bar (bilateral hip involvement), jointed, adjustable

L2310 Addition to lower extremity, abduction bar, straight

L2320 Addition to lower extremity, nonmolded lacer, for custom fabricated orthotic only

L2330 Addition to lower extremity, lacer molded to patient model, for custom fabricated orthotic only

L2335 Addition to lower extremity, anterior swing band

L2340 Addition to lower extremity, pretibial shell, molded to patient model

L2350 Addition to lower extremity, prosthetic type, (BK) socket, molded to patient model, (used for PTB, AFO orthoses)

L2360 Addition to lower extremity, extended steel shank

L2370 Addition to lower extremity, Patten bottom

L2375 Addition to lower extremity, torsion control, ankle joint and half solid stirrup

L2380 Addition to lower extremity, torsion control, straight knee joint, each joint

L2385 Addition to lower extremity, straight knee joint, heavy-duty, each joint

L2387 Addition to lower extremity, polycentric knee joint, for custom fabricated knee-ankle-foot orthotic(KAFO), each joint

L2390 Addition to lower extremity, offset knee joint, each joint

L2395 Addition to lower extremity, offset knee joint, heavy-duty, each joint

L2397 Addition to lower extremity orthotic, suspension sleeve

ADDITIONS TO STRAIGHT KNEE OR OFFSET KNEE JOINTS

L2405 Addition to knee joint, drop lock, each

L2415 Addition to knee lock with integrated release mechanism (bail, cable, or equal), any material, each joint

L2425 Addition to knee joint, disc or dial lock for adjustable knee flexion, each joint

L2430 Addition to knee joint, ratchet lock for active and progressive knee extension, each joint

L2492 Addition to knee joint, lift loop for drop lock ring

ADDITIONS: THIGH/WEIGHT BEARING - GLUTEAL/ISCHIAL WEIGHT BEARING

L2500 Addition to lower extremity, thigh/weight bearing, gluteal/ischial weight bearing, ring

L2510 Addition to lower extremity, thigh/weight bearing, quadri-lateral brim, molded to patient model

L2520 Addition to lower extremity, thigh/weight bearing, quadri-lateral brim, custom fitted

L2525 Addition to lower extremity, thigh/weight bearing, ischial containment/narrow M-L brim molded to patient model

L2526 Addition to lower extremity, thigh/weight bearing, ischial containment/narrow M-L brim, custom fitted

L2530 Addition to lower extremity, thigh/weight bearing, lacer, nonmolded

L2540 Addition to lower extremity, thigh/weight bearing, lacer, molded to patient model

L2550 Addition to lower extremity, thigh/weight bearing, high roll cuff

ADDITIONS: PELVIC AND THORACIC CONTROL

L2570 Addition to lower extremity, pelvic control, hip joint, Clevis type, 2-position joint, each

L2580 Addition to lower extremity, pelvic control, pelvic sling

L2600 Addition to lower extremity, pelvic control, hip joint, Clevis type, or thrust bearing, free, each

L2610 Addition to lower extremity, pelvic control, hip joint, Clevis or thrust bearing, lock, each

L2620 Addition to lower extremity, pelvic control, hip joint, heavy-duty, each

L2622 Addition to lower extremity, pelvic control, hip joint, adjustable flexion, each

L2624 Addition to lower extremity, pelvic control, hip joint, adjustable flexion, extension, abduction control, each

L2627 Addition to lower extremity, pelvic control, plastic, molded to patient model, reciprocating hip joint and cables

L2628 Addition to lower extremity, pelvic control, metal frame, reciprocating hip joint and cables

L2630 Addition to lower extremity, pelvic control, band and belt, unilateral

L2640 Addition to lower extremity, pelvic control, band and belt, bilateral

L2650 Addition to lower extremity, pelvic and thoracic control, gluteal pad, each

L2660 Addition to lower extremity, thoracic control, thoracic band

L2670 Addition to lower extremity, thoracic control, paraspinal uprights

L2680 Addition to lower extremity, thoracic control, lateral support uprights

ADDITIONS: GENERAL

L2750 Addition to lower extremity orthotic, plating chrome or nickel, per bar

L2755 Addition to lower extremity orthotic, high strength, lightweight material, all hybrid lamination/prepreg composite, per segment, for custom fabricated orthotic only

L2760 Addition to lower extremity orthotic, extension, per extension, per bar (for lineal adjustment for growth)

L2768 Orthotic side bar disconnect device, per bar

L2770 Addition to lower extremity orthotic, any material, per bar or joint

L2780 Addition to lower extremity orthotic, noncorrosive finish, per bar

L2785 Addition to lower extremity orthotic, drop lock retainer, each

L2795 Addition to lower extremity orthotic, knee control, full kneecap

L2800 Addition to lower extremity orthotic, knee control, knee cap, medial or lateral pull, for use with custom fabricated orthotic only

L2810 Addition to lower extremity orthotic, knee control, condylar pad

L2820 Addition to lower extremity orthotic, soft interface for molded plastic, below knee section

L2830 Addition to lower extremity orthotic, soft interface for molded plastic, above knee section

L2840 Addition to lower extremity orthotic, tibial length sock, fracture or equal, each

L2850 Addition to lower extremity orthotic, femoral length sock, fracture or equal, each

L2999 Lower extremity orthoses, not otherwise specified
Determine if an alternative HCPCS Level II or a CPT code better describes the service being reported. This code should be used only if a more specific code is unavailable.

ORTHOPEDIC SHOES

INSERTS

L3000 Foot insert, removable, molded to patient model, UCB type, Berkeley shell, each
MED: 100-2,15,290

L3001 Foot, insert, removable, molded to patient model, Spenco, each
MED: 100-2,15,290

L3002 Foot insert, removable, molded to patient model, Plastazote or equal, each
MED: 100-2,15,290

L3003 Foot insert, removable, molded to patient model, silicone gel, each
MED: 100-2,15,290

L3010 Foot insert, removable, molded to patient model, longitudinal arch support, each
MED: 100-2,15,290

L3020 Foot insert, removable, molded to patient model, longitudinal/metatarsal support, each
MED: 100-2,15,290

L3030 Foot insert, removable, formed to patient foot, each
MED: 100-2,15,290

L3031 Foot, insert/plate, removable, addition to lower extremity orthotic, high strength, lightweight material, all hybrid lamination/prepreg composite, each

ARCH SUPPORT, REMOVABLE, PREMOLDED

L3040 Foot, arch support, removable, premolded, longitudinal, each
MED: 100-2,15,290

L3050 Foot, arch support, removable, premolded, metatarsal, each
MED: 100-2,15,290

L3060 Foot, arch support, removable, premolded, longitudinal/metatarsal, each
MED: 100-2,15,290

ARCH SUPPORT, NONREMOVABLE, ATTACHED TO SHOE

L3070 Foot, arch support, nonremovable, attached to shoe, longitudinal, each
MED: 100-2,15,290

L3080 Foot, arch support, nonremovable, attached to shoe, metatarsal, each
MED: 100-2,15,290

L3090 Foot, arch support, nonremovable, attached to shoe, longitudinal/metatarsal, each
MED: 100-2,15,290

L3100 Hallus-valgus night dynamic splint
MED: 100-2,15,290; 100-4,4,240

ABDUCTION AND ROTATION BARS

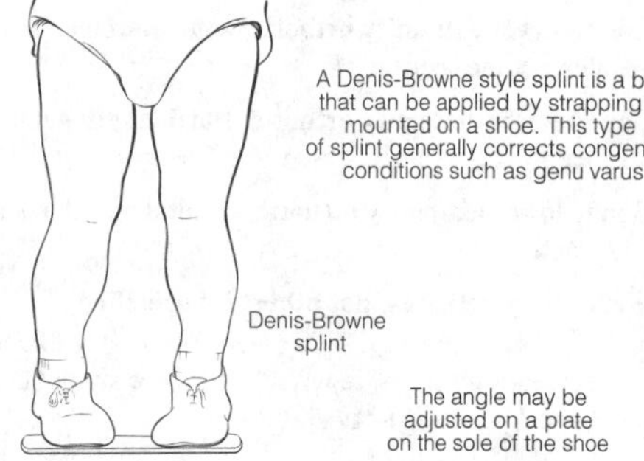

A Denis-Browne style splint is a bar that can be applied by strapping or mounted on a shoe. This type of splint generally corrects congenital conditions such as genu varus
Denis-Browne splint
The angle may be adjusted on a plate on the sole of the shoe

L3140 Foot, abduction rotation bar, including shoes
MED: 100-2,15,290

L3150 Foot, abduction rotation bar, without shoes
MED: 100-2,15,290

L3160 Foot, adjustable shoe-styled positioning device

L3170 Foot, plastic, silicone or equal, heel stabilizer, each
MED: 100-2,15,290

ORTHOPEDIC FOOTWEAR

L3201 Orthopedic shoe, Oxford with supinator or pronator, infant
MED: 100-2,15,290

L3202 Orthopedic shoe, Oxford with supinator or pronator, child
MED: 100-2,15,290

L3203 Orthopedic shoe, Oxford with supinator or pronator, junior
MED: 100-2,15,290

L3204 Orthopedic shoe, hightop with supinator or pronator, infant
MED: 100-2,15,290

L3206 Orthopedic shoe, hightop with supinator or pronator, child
MED: 100-2,15,290

L3207 Orthopedic shoe, hightop with supinator or pronator, junior
MED: 100-2,15,290

L3208 Surgical boot, each, infant
MED: 100-2,15,100

L3209 Surgical boot, each, child
MED: 100-2,15,100

L3211 Surgical boot, each, junior
MED: 100-2,15,100

L3212 Benesch boot, pair, infant
MED: 100-2,15,100

L3213 Benesch boot, pair, child
MED: 100-2,15,100

L3214 Benesch boot, pair, junior
MED: 100-2,15,100

L3215 Orthopedic footwear, ladies shoe, oxford, each

L3216 Orthopedic footwear, ladies shoe, depth inlay, each

L3217 Orthopedic footwear, ladies shoe, hightop, depth inlay, each

L3219 Orthopedic footwear, mens shoe, oxford, each

L3221 Orthopedic footwear, mens shoe, depth inlay, each

L3222 Orthopedic footwear, mens shoe, hightop, depth inlay, each

L3224 Orthopedic footwear, woman's shoe, oxford, used as an integral part of a brace (orthotic)
MED: 100-2,15,290

L3225 Orthopedic footwear, man's shoe, oxford, used as an integral part of a brace (orthotic)
MED: 100-2,15,290

L3230 Orthopedic footwear, custom shoe, depth inlay, each
MED: 100-2,15,290

L3250 Orthopedic footwear, custom molded shoe, removable inner mold, prosthetic shoe, each
MED: 100-2,15,290

L3251 Foot, shoe molded to patient model, silicone shoe, each
MED: 100-2,15,290

L3252 Foot, shoe molded to patient model, Plastazote (or similar), custom fabricated, each
MED: 100-2,15,290

L3253 Foot, molded shoe, Plastazote (or similar), custom fitted, each
MED: 100-2,15,290

L3254 Nonstandard size or width
MED: 100-2,15,290

L3255 Nonstandard size or length
MED: 100-2,15,290

L3257 Orthopedic footwear, additional charge for split size
MED: 100-2,15,290

L3260 Surgical boot/shoe, each
MED: 100-2,15,100

L3265 Plastazote sandal, each

SHOE MODIFICATION - LIFTS

L3300 Lift, elevation, heel, tapered to metatarsals, per in
MED: 100-2,15,290

L3310 Lift, elevation, heel and sole, neoprene, per in
MED: 100-2,15,290

L3320 Lift, elevation, heel and sole, cork, per in
MED: 100-2,15,290

L3330 Lift, elevation, metal extension (skate)
MED: 100-2,15,290

L3332 Lift, elevation, inside shoe, tapered, up to one-half in
MED: 100-2,15,290

L3334 Lift, elevation, heel, per in
MED: 100-2,15,290

SHOE MODIFICATION - WEDGES

L3340 Heel wedge, SACH
MED: 100-2,15,290

L3350 Heel wedge
MED: 100-2,15,290

L3360 Sole wedge, outside sole
MED: 100-2,15,290

L3370 Sole wedge, between sole
MED: 100-2,15,290

L3380 Clubfoot wedge
MED: 100-2,15,290

L3390 Outflare wedge
MED: 100-2,15,290

L3400 Metatarsal bar wedge, rocker
MED: 100-2,15,290

L3410 Metatarsal bar wedge, between sole
MED: 100-2,15,290

L3420 Full sole and heel wedge, between sole
MED: 100-2,15,290

SHOE MODIFICATIONS - HEELS

L3430 Heel, counter, plastic reinforced
MED: 100-2,15,290

L3440 Heel, counter, leather reinforced
MED: 100-2,15,290

L3450 Heel, SACH cushion type
MED: 100-2,15,290

L3455 Heel, new leather, standard
MED: 100-2,15,290

L3460 Heel, new rubber, standard
MED: 100-2,15,290

L3465 Heel, Thomas with wedge
MED: 100-2,15,290

L3470 Heel, Thomas extended to ball
MED: 100-2,15,290

L3480 Heel, pad and depression for spur
MED: 100-2,15,290

L3485 Heel, pad, removable for spur
MED: 100-2,15,290

MISCELLANEOUS SHOE ADDITIONS

L3500 Orthopedic shoe addition, insole, leather
MED: 100-2,15,290

L3510 Orthopedic shoe addition, insole, rubber
MED: 100-2,15,290

L3520 Orthopedic shoe addition, insole, felt covered with leather
MED: 100-2,15,290

L3530 Orthopedic shoe addition, sole, half
MED: 100-2,15,290

L3540 Orthopedic shoe addition, sole, full
MED: 100-2,15,290

L3550 Orthopedic shoe addition, toe tap, standard
MED: 100-2,15,290

L3560 Orthopedic shoe addition, toe tap, horseshoe
MED: 100-2,15,290

L3570 Orthopedic shoe addition, special extension to instep (leather with eyelets)
MED: 100-2,15,290

L3580 Orthopedic shoe addition, convert instep to Velcro closure
MED: 100-2,15,290

L3590 Orthopedic shoe addition, convert firm shoe counter to soft counter
MED: 100-2,15,290

L3595 Orthopedic shoe addition, March bar
MED: 100-2,15,290

TRANSFER OR REPLACEMENT

L3600 Transfer of an orthotic from one shoe to another, caliper plate, existing
MED: 100-2,15,290

L3610 Transfer of an orthotic from one shoe to another, caliper plate, new
MED: 100-2,15,290

L3620 Transfer of an orthotic from one shoe to another, solid stirrup, existing
MED: 100-2,15,290

L3630 Transfer of an orthotic from one shoe to another, solid stirrup, new
MED: 100-2,15,290

L3640 Transfer of an orthotic from one shoe to another, Dennis Browne splint (Riveton), both shoes
MED: 100-2,15,290

L3649 Orthopedic shoe, modification, addition or transfer, not otherwise specified
Determine if an alternative HCPCS Level II or a CPT code better describes the service being reported. This code should be used only if a more specific code is unavailable.
MED: 100-2,15,290

ORTHOTIC DEVICES - UPPER LIMB

The procedures in this section are considered as "base" or "basic procedures" and may be modified by listing procedures from the "additions" sections and adding them to the base procedure.

SHOULDER ORTHOTIC (SO)

L3650 Shoulder orthotic (SO), figure of eight design abduction restrainer, prefabricated, includes fitting and adjustment

L3651 Shoulder orthotic (SO), single shoulder, elastic, prefabricated, includes fitting and adjustment (e.g., neoprene, Lycra)

L3652 Shoulder orthotic (SO), double shoulder, elastic, prefabricated, includes fitting and adjustment (e.g., neoprene, Lycra)

L3660 Shoulder orthotic (SO), figure of eight design abduction restrainer, canvas and webbing, prefabricated, includes fitting and adjustment

L3670 Shoulder orthotic (SO), acromio/clavicular (canvas and webbing type), prefabricated, includes fitting and adjustment

L3671 Shoulder orthotic (SO), shoulder cap design, without joints, may include soft interface, straps, custom fabricated, includes fitting and adjustment

L3672 Shoulder orthotic (SO), abduction positioning (airplane design), thoracic component and support bar, without joints, may inlcude soft interface, straps, custom fabricated, includes fitting and adjustment

L3673 Shoulder orthotic (SO), abduction positioning (airplane design), thoracic component and support bar, includes nontorsion joint/turnbuckle, may include soft interface, straps, custom fabricated, includes fitting and adjustment

L3675 Shoulder orthotic (SO), vest type abduction restrainer, canvas webbing type or equal, prefabricated, includes fitting and adjustment

L3677 Shoulder orthotic (SO), hard plastic, shoulder stabilizer, prefabricated, includes fitting and adjustment
MED: 100-2,15,120

ELBOW ORTHOTIC (EO)

L3700 Elbow orthotic (EO), elastic with stays, prefabricated, includes fitting and adjustment

L3701 Elbow orthotic (EO), elastic, prefabricated, includes fitting and adjustment (e.g., neoprene, Lycra)

L3702 Elbow orthotic (EO), without joints, may include soft interface, straps, custom fabricated, includes fitting and adjustment

L3710 Elbow orthotic (EO), elastic with metal joints, prefabricated, includes fitting and adjustment

L3720 Elbow orthotic (EO), double upright with forearm/arm cuffs, free motion, custom fabricated

L3730 Elbow orthotic (EO), double upright with forearm/arm cuffs, extension/ flexion assist, custom fabricated

L3740 Elbow orthotic (EO), double upright with forearm/arm cuffs, adjustable position lock with active control, custom fabricated

L3760 Elbow orthotic (EO), with adjustable position locking joint(s), prefabricated, includes fitting and adjustments, any type

L3762 Elbow orthotic (EO), rigid, without joints, includes soft interface material, prefabricated, includes fitting and adjustment

L3763 Elbow-wrist-hand orthotic (EWHO), rigid, without joints, may include soft interface, straps, custom fabricated, includes fitting and adjustment

L3764 Elbow-wrist-hand orthotic (EWHO), includes one or more nontorsion joints, elastic bands, turnbuckles, may include soft interface, straps, custom fabricated, includes fitting and adjustment

L3765 Elbow-wrist-hand-finger orthotic (EWHFO), rigid, without joints, may include soft interface, straps, custom fabricated, includes fitting and adjustment

L3766 Elbow-wrist-hand-finger orthotic, includes one or more nontorsion joints, elastic bands (EWHFO), turnbuckles, may include soft interface, straps, custom fabricated, includes fitting and adjustment

WRIST-HAND-FINGER ORTHOTIC (WHFO)

L3806 Wrist-hand-finger orthotic (WHFO), includes one or more nontorsion joint(s), turnbuckles, elastic bands/springs, may include soft interface material, straps, custom fabricated, includes fitting and adjustment

L3807 Wrist-hand-finger orthotic (WHFO), without joint(s), prefabricated, includes fitting and adjustments, any type

L3808 Wrist-hand-finger orthotic (WHFO), rigid without joints, may include soft interface material; straps, custom fabricated, includes fitting and adjustment

ADDITIONS

DYNAMIC FLEXOR HINGE, RECIPROCAL WRIST EXTENSION/FLEXION, FINGER FLEXION/EXTENSION

L3900 Wrist-hand-finger orthotic (WHFO), dynamic flexor hinge, reciprocal wrist extension/ flexion, finger flexion/extension, wrist or finger driven, custom fabricated

L3901 Wrist-hand-finger orthotic (WHFO), dynamic flexor hinge, reciprocal wrist extension/ flexion, finger flexion/extension, cable driven, custom fabricated

EXTERNAL POWER

L3904 Wrist-hand-finger orthotic (WHFO), external powered, electric, custom fabricated

OTHER - CUSTOM FITTED

L3905 Wrist-hand orthotic (WHO), includes one or more nontorsion joints, elastic bands, turnbuckles, may include soft interface, straps, custom fabricated, includes fitting and adjustment

L3906 Wrist-hand orthosis (WHO), without joints, may include soft interface, straps, custom fabricated, includes fitting and adjustment

L3908 Wrist-hand orthotic (WHO), wrist extension control cock-up, nonmolded, prefabricated, includes fitting and adjustment

L3909 Wrist orthotic (WO), elastic, prefabricated, includes fitting and adjustment (e.g., neoprene, Lycra)

L3911 Wrist hand finger orthotic (WHFO), elastic, prefabricated, includes fitting and adjustment (e.g., neoprene, Lycra)

L3912 Hand-finger orthotic (HFO), flexion glove with elastic finger control, prefabricated, includes fitting and adjustment

L3913 Hand finger orthotic (HFO), without joints, may include soft interface, straps, custom fabricated, includes fitting and adjustment

L3915 Wrist hand orthotic (WHO), includes one or more nontorsion joint(s), elastic bands, turnbuckles, may include soft interface, straps, prefabricated, includes fitting and adjustment

L3917 Hand orthotic (HO), metacarpal fracture orthotic, prefabricated, includes fitting and adjustment

L3919 Hand orthotic (HO), without joints, may include soft interface, straps, custom fabricated, includes fitting and adjustment

L3921 Hand finger orthotic (HFO), includes one or more nontorsion joints, elastic bands, turnbuckles, may include soft interface, straps, custom fabricated, includes fitting and adjustment

L3923 Hand finger orthotic (HFO), without joints, may include soft interface, straps, prefabricated, includes fitting and adjustment

L3925 Finger orthotic (FO), proximal interphalangeal (PIP)/distal interphalangeal (DIP), nontorsion joint/spring, extension/flexion, may include soft interface material, prefabricated, includes fitting and adjustment

L3927 Finger orthotic (FO), proximal interphalangeal (PIP)/distal interphalangeal (DIP), without joint/spring, extension/flexion (e.g., static or ring type), may include soft interface material, prefabricated, includes fitting and adjustment

L3929 Hand-finger orthotic (HFO), includes one or more nontorsion joint(s), turnbuckles, elastic bands/springs, may include soft interface material, straps, prefabricated, includes fitting and adjustment

L3931 Wrist-hand-finger orthotic (WHFO), includes one or more nontorsion joint(s), turnbuckles, elastic bands/springs, may include soft interface material, straps, prefabricated, includes fitting and adjustment

L3933 Finger orthotic (FO), without joints, may include soft interface, custom fabricated, includes fitting and adjustment

L3935 Finger orthotic, nontorsion joint, may include soft interface, custom fabricated, includes fitting and adjustment

L3956 Addition of joint to upper extremity orthotic, any material; per joint

SHOULDER-ELBOW-WRIST-HAND ORTHOTIC (SEWHO)

ABDUCTION POSITION, CUSTOM FITTED

L3960 Shoulder-elbow-wrist-hand orthotic (SEWHO), abduction positioning, airplane design, prefabricated, includes fitting and adjustment

L3961 Shoulder elbow wrist hand orthotic (SEWHO), shoulder cap design, without joints, may include soft interface, straps, custom fabricated, includes fitting and adjustment

L3962 Shoulder-elbow-wrist-hand orthotic (SEWHO), abduction positioning, Erb's palsy design, prefabricated, includes fitting and adjustment

L3964 Shoulder-elbow orthotic (SEO), mobile arm support attached to wheelchair, balanced, adjustable, prefabricated, includes fitting and adjustment

L3965 Shoulder-elbow orthotic (SEO), mobile arm support attached to wheelchair, balanced, adjustable Rancho type, prefabricated, includes fitting and adjustment

L3966 Shoulder-elbow orthotic (SEO), mobile arm support attached to wheelchair, balanced, reclining, prefabricated, includes fitting and adjustment

L3967 Shoulder-elbow-wrist-hand orthotic (SEWHO), abduction positioning (airplane design), thoracic component and support bar, without joints, may include soft interface, straps, custom fabricated, includes fitting and adjustment

L3968 Shoulder-elbow orthotic (SEO), mobile arm support attached to wheelchair, balanced, friction arm support (friction dampening to proximal and distal joints), prefabricated, includes fitting and adjustment

L3969 Shoulder-elbow orthotic (SEO), mobile arm support, monosuspension arm and hand support, overhead elbow forearm hand sling support, yoke type suspension support, prefabricated, includes fitting and adjustment

ADDITIONS TO MOBILE ARM SUPPORTS

L3970 Shoulder-elbow orthotic (SEO), addition to mobile arm support, elevating proximal arm

L3971 Shoulder-elbow-wrist-hand orthotic (SEWHO), shoulder cap design, includes one or more nontorsion joints, elastic bands, turnbuckles, may include soft interface, straps, custom fabricated, includes fitting and adjustment

L3972 Shoulder-elbow orthotic (SEO), addition to mobile arm support, offset or lateral rocker arm with elastic balance control

L3973 Shoulder-elbow-wrist-hand orthotic (SEWHO), abduction positioning (airplane design), thoracic component and support bar, includes one or more nontorsion joints, elastic bands, turnbuckles, may include soft interface, straps, custom fabricated, includes fitting and adjustment

L3974 Shoulder-elbow orthotic (SEO), addition to mobile arm support, supinator

L3975 Shoulder-elbow-wrist-hand-finger orthotic (SEWHO), shoulder cap design, without joints, may include soft interface, straps, custom fabricated, includes fitting and adjustment

L3976 Shoulder-elbow-wrist-hand-finger orthotic (SEWHO), abduction positioning (airplane design), thoracic component and support bar, without joints, may include soft interface, straps, custom fabricated, includes fitting and adjustment

L3977 Shoulder-elbow-wrist-hand-finger orthotic (SEWHO), shoulder cap design, includes one or more nontorsion joints, elastic bands, turnbuckles, may include soft interface, straps, custom fabricated, includes fitting and adjustment

L3978 Shoulder-elbow-wrist-hand-finger orthotic (SEWHO), abduction positioning (airplane design), thoracic component and support bar, includes one or more nontorsion joints, elastic bands, turnbuckles, may include soft interface, straps, custom fabricated, includes fitting and adjustment

FRACTURE ORTHOTIC

L3980 Upper extremity fracture orthotic, humeral, prefabricated, includes fitting and adjustment

L3982 Upper extremity fracture orthotic, radius/ulnar, prefabricated, includes fitting and adjustment

L3984 Upper extremity fracture orthotic, wrist, prefabricated, includes fitting and adjustment

L3995 Addition to upper extremity orthotic, sock, fracture or equal, each

L3999 Upper limb orthosis, not otherwise specified

SPECIFIC REPAIR

L4000 Replace girdle for spinal orthotic (cervical-thoracic-lumbar-sacral orthotic (CTLSO) or spinal orthotic SO)

L4002 Replacement strap, any orthotic, includes all components, any length, any type

L4010 Replace trilateral socket brim

L4020 Replace quadrilateral socket brim, molded to patient model

L4030 Replace quadrilateral socket brim, custom fitted

L4040 Replace molded thigh lacer, for custom fabricated orthotic only

L4045 Replace nonmolded thigh lacer, for custom fabricated orthotic only

L4050 Replace molded calf lacer, for custom fabricated orthotic only

L4055 Replace nonmolded calf lacer, for custom fabricated orthotic only

L4060 Replace high roll cuff

L4070 Replace proximal and distal upright for KAFO

L4080 Replace metal bands KAFO, proximal thigh

L4090 Replace metal bands KAFO-AFO, calf or distal thigh

L4100 Replace leather cuff KAFO, proximal thigh

L4110 Replace leather cuff KAFO-AFO, calf or distal thigh

L4130 Replace pretibial shell

REPAIRS

L4205 Repair of orthotic device, labor component, per 15 minutes
MED: 100-2,15,110.2

L4210 Repair of orthotic device, repair or replace minor parts
MED: 100-2,15,110.2; 100-2,15,120

L4350 Ankle control orthotic, stirrup style, rigid, includes any type interface (e.g., pneumatic, gel), prefabricated, includes fitting and adjustment

L4360 Walking boot, pneumatic and/or vacuum, with or without joints, with or without interface material, prefabricated, includes fitting and adjustment

L4370 Pneumatic full leg splint, prefabricated, includes fitting and adjustment
MED: 100-4,4,240

L4380 Pneumatic knee splint, prefabricated, includes fitting and adjustment
MED: 100-4,4,240

L4386 Walking boot, nonpneumatic, with or without joints, with or without interface material, prefabricated, includes fitting and adjustment

L4392 Replacement, soft interface material, static AFO

L4394 Replace soft interface material, foot drop splint

L4396 Static ankle-foot orthotic (AFO), including soft interface material, adjustable for fit, for positioning, pressure reduction, may be used for minimal ambulation, prefabricated, includes fitting and adjustment

L4398 Foot drop splint, recumbent positioning device, prefabricated, includes fitting and adjustment
MED: 100-4,4,240

PROSTHETIC PROCEDURES L5000-L9999

LOWER LIMB

The procedures in this section are considered as "base" or "basic procedures" and may be modified by listing items/procedures or special materials from the "additions" sections and adding them to the base procedure.

PARTIAL FOOT

L5000 Partial foot, shoe insert with longitudinal arch, toe filler
MED: 100-2,15,290; 100-4,3,10.4

L5010 Partial foot, molded socket, ankle height, with toe filler
MED: 100-2,15,290; 100-4,3,10.4

L5020 Partial foot, molded socket, tibial tubercle height, with toe filler
MED: 100-2,15,290; 100-4,3,10.4

ANKLE

L5050 Ankle, Symes, molded socket, SACH foot
MED: 100-4,3,10.4

L5060 Ankle, Symes, metal frame, molded leather socket, articulated ankle/foot

MED: 100-4,3,10.4

BELOW KNEE

L5100 Below knee, molded socket, shin, SACH foot

MED: 100-4,3,10.4

L5105 Below knee, plastic socket, joints and thigh lacer, SACH foot

MED: 100-4,3,10.4

KNEE DISARTICULATION

L5150 Knee disarticulation (or through knee), molded socket, external knee joints, shin, SACH foot

MED: 100-4,3,10.4

L5160 Knee disarticulation (or through knee), molded socket, bent knee configuration, external knee joints, shin, SACH foot

MED: 100-4,3,10.4

ABOVE KNEE

L5200 Above knee, molded socket, single axis constant friction knee, shin, SACH foot

MED: 100-4,3,10.4

L5210 Above knee, short prosthesis, no knee joint (stubbies), with foot blocks, no ankle joints, each

MED: 100-4,3,10.4

L5220 Above knee, short prosthesis, no knee joint (stubbies), with articulated ankle/foot, dynamically aligned, each

MED: 100-4,3,10.4

L5230 Above knee, for proximal femoral focal deficiency, constant friction knee, shin, SACH foot

MED: 100-4,3,10.4

HIP DISARTICULATION

L5250 Hip disarticulation, Canadian type; molded socket, hip joint, single axis constant friction knee, shin, SACH foot

MED: 100-4,3,10.4

L5270 Hip disarticulation, tilt table type; molded socket, locking hip joint, single axis constant friction knee, shin, SACH foot

MED: 100-4,3,10.4

HEMIPELVECTOMY

L5280 Hemipelvectomy, Canadian type; molded socket, hip joint, single axis constant friction knee, shin, SACH foot

MED: 100-4,3,10.4

L5301 Below knee, molded socket, shin, SACH foot, endoskeletal system

MED: 100-4,3,10.4

L5311 Knee disarticulation (or through knee), molded socket, external knee joints, shin, SACH foot, endoskeletal system

MED: 100-4,3,10.4

L5321 Above knee, molded socket, open end, SACH foot, endoskeletal system, single axis knee

MED: 100-4,3,10.4

L5331 Hip disarticulation, Canadian type, molded socket, endoskeletal system, hip joint, single axis knee, SACH foot

MED: 100-4,3,10.4

L5341 Hemipelvectomy, Canadian type, molded socket, endoskeletal system, hip joint, single axis knee, SACH foot

MED: 100-4,3,10.4

IMMEDIATE POSTSURGICAL OR EARLY FITTING PROCEDURES

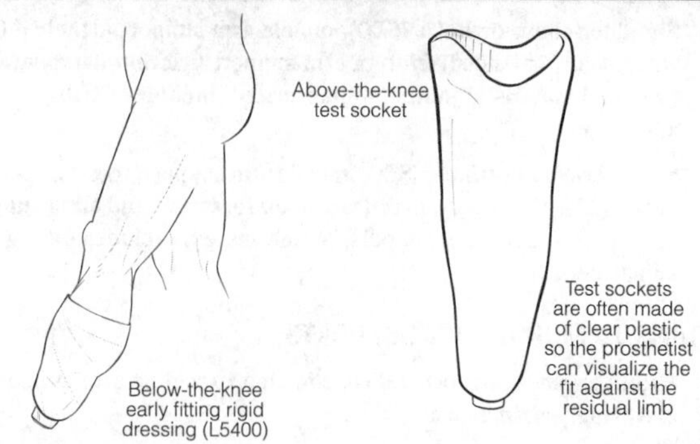
Above-the-knee test socket
Test sockets are often made of clear plastic so the prosthetist can visualize the fit against the residual limb
Below-the-knee early fitting rigid dressing (L5400)

L5400 Immediate postsurgical or early fitting, application of initial rigid dressing, including fitting, alignment, suspension, and one cast change, below knee

L5410 Immediate postsurgical or early fitting, application of initial rigid dressing, including fitting, alignment and suspension, below knee, each additional cast change and realignment

L5420 Immediate postsurgical or early fitting, application of initial rigid dressing, including fitting, alignment and suspension and one cast change AK or knee disarticulation

L5430 Immediate postsurgical or early fitting, application of initial rigid dressing, including fitting, alignment and suspension, AK or knee disarticulation, each additional cast change and realignment

L5450 Immediate postsurgical or early fitting, application of nonweight bearing rigid dressing, below knee

L5460 Immediate postsurgical or early fitting, application of nonweight bearing rigid dressing, above knee

INITIAL PROSTHESIS

L5500 Initial, below knee PTB type socket, nonalignable system, pylon, no cover, SACH foot, plaster socket, direct formed

MED: 100-4,3,10.4

L5505 Initial, above knee, knee disarticulation, ischial level socket, nonalignable system, pylon, no cover, SACH foot, plaster socket, direct formed

MED: 100-4,3,10.4

PREPARATORY PROSTHESIS

L5510 Preparatory, below knee PTB type socket, nonalignable system, pylon, no cover, SACH foot, plaster socket, molded to model

L5520 Preparatory, below knee PTB type socket, nonalignable system, pylon, no cover, SACH foot, thermoplastic or equal, direct formed

L5530 Preparatory, below knee PTB type socket, nonalignable system, pylon, no cover, SACH foot, thermoplastic or equal, molded to model

L5535 Preparatory, below knee PTB type socket, nonalignable system, pylon, no cover, SACH foot, prefabricated, adjustable open end socket

L5540 Preparatory, below knee PTB type socket, nonalignable system, pylon, no cover, SACH foot, laminated socket, molded to model

L5560 Preparatory, above knee, knee disarticulation, ischial level socket, nonalignable system, pylon, no cover, SACH foot, plaster socket, molded to model

L5570 Preparatory, above knee — knee disarticulation, ischial level socket, nonalignable system, pylon, no cover, SACH foot, thermoplastic or equal, direct formed

L5580 Preparatory, above knee, knee disarticulation, ischial level socket, nonalignable system, pylon, no cover, SACH foot, thermoplastic or equal, molded to model

L5585 Preparatory, above knee — knee disarticulation, ischial level socket, nonalignable system, pylon, no cover, SACH foot, prefabricated adjustable open end socket

L5590 Preparatory, above knee, knee disarticulation, ischial level socket, nonalignable system, pylon, no cover, SACH foot, laminated socket, molded to model

L5595 Preparatory, hip disarticulation/hemipelvectomy, pylon, no cover, SACH foot, thermoplastic or equal, molded to patient model

L5600 Preparatory, hip disarticulation/hemipelvectomy, pylon, no cover, SACH foot, laminated socket, molded to patient model

ADDITIONS: LOWER EXTREMITY

L5610 Addition to lower extremity, endoskeletal system, above knee, hydracadence system

L5611 Addition to lower extremity, endoskeletal system, above knee, knee disarticulation, 4-bar linkage, with friction swing phase control

L5613 Addition to lower extremity, endoskeletal system, above knee, knee disarticulation, 4-bar linkage, with hydraulic swing phase control

L5614 Addition to lower extremity, exoskeletal system, above knee-knee disarticulation, 4 bar linkage, with pneumatic swing phase control

L5616 Addition to lower extremity, endoskeletal system, above knee, universal multiplex system, friction swing phase control

L5617 Addition to lower extremity, quick change self-aligning unit, above knee or below knee, each

ADDITIONS: TEST SOCKETS

L5618 Addition to lower extremity, test socket, Symes

L5620 Addition to lower extremity, test socket, below knee

L5622 Addition to lower extremity, test socket, knee disarticulation

L5624 Addition to lower extremity, test socket, above knee

L5626 Addition to lower extremity, test socket, hip disarticulation

L5628 Addition to lower extremity, test socket, hemipelvectomy

L5629 Addition to lower extremity, below knee, acrylic socket

ADDITIONS: SOCKET VARIATIONS

L5630 Addition to lower extremity, Symes type, expandable wall socket

L5631 Addition to lower extremity, above knee or knee disarticulation, acrylic socket

L5632 Addition to lower extremity, Symes type, PTB brim design socket

L5634 Addition to lower extremity, Symes type, posterior opening (Canadian) socket

L5636 Addition to lower extremity, Symes type, medial opening socket

L5637 Addition to lower extremity, below knee, total contact

L5638 Addition to lower extremity, below knee, leather socket

L5639 Addition to lower extremity, below knee, wood socket

L5640 Addition to lower extremity, knee disarticulation, leather socket

L5642 Addition to lower extremity, above knee, leather socket

L5643 Addition to lower extremity, hip disarticulation, flexible inner socket, external frame

L5644 Addition to lower extremity, above knee, wood socket

L5645 Addition to lower extremity, below knee, flexible inner socket, external frame

L5646 Addition to lower extremity, below knee, air, fluid, gel or equal, cushion socket

L5647 Addition to lower extremity, below knee, suction socket

L5648 Addition to lower extremity, above knee, air, fluid, gel or equal, cushion socket

L5649 Addition to lower extremity, ischial containment/narrow M-L socket

L5650 Additions to lower extremity, total contact, above knee or knee disarticulation socket

L5651 Addition to lower extremity, above knee, flexible inner socket, external frame

L5652 Addition to lower extremity, suction suspension, above knee or knee disarticulation socket

L5653 Addition to lower extremity, knee disarticulation, expandable wall socket

ADDITIONS: SOCKET INSERT AND SUSPENSION

L5654 Addition to lower extremity, socket insert, Symes, (Kemblo, Pelite, Aliplast, Plastazote) or equal

L5655 Addition to lower extremity, socket insert, below knee (Kemblo, Pelite, Aliplast, Plastazote or equal)

L5656 Addition to lower extremity, socket insert, knee disarticulation (Kemblo, Pelite, Aliplast, Plastazote or equal)

L5658 Addition to lower extremity, socket insert, above knee (Kemblo, Pelite, Aliplast, Plastazote or equal)

L5661 Addition to lower extremity, socket insert, multidurometer Symes

L5665 Addition to lower extremity, socket insert, multidurometer, below knee

L5666 Addition to lower extremity, below knee, cuff suspension

L5668 Addition to lower extremity, below knee, molded distal cushion

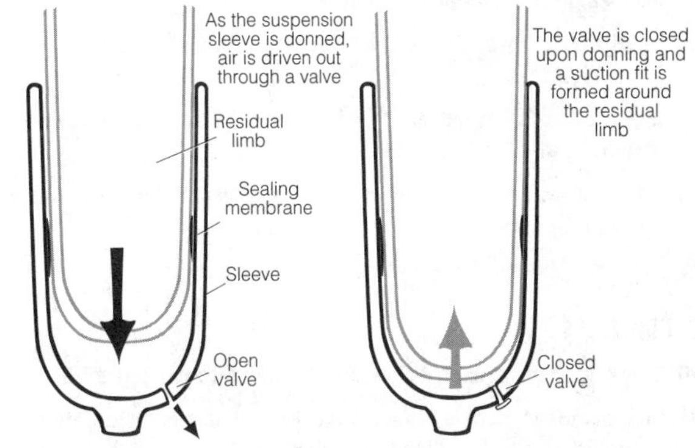
As the suspension sleeve is donned, air is driven out through a valve
Residual limb
Sealing membrane
Sleeve
Open valve
The valve is closed upon donning and a suction fit is formed around the residual limb
Closed valve

L5670 Addition to lower extremity, below knee, molded supracondylar suspension (PTS or similar)

L5671 Addition to lower extremity, below knee / above knee suspension locking mechanism (shuttle, lanyard, or equal), excludes socket insert

L5672 Addition to lower extremity, below knee, removable medial brim suspension

L5673 Addition to lower extremity, below knee/above knee, custom fabricated from existing mold or prefabricated, socket insert, silicone gel, elastomeric or equal, for use with locking mechanism

L5676 Additions to lower extremity, below knee, knee joints, single axis, pair

L5677 Additions to lower extremity, below knee, knee joints, polycentric, pair

L5678 Additions to lower extremity, below knee, joint covers, pair

L5679 Addition to lower extremity, below knee/above knee, custom fabricated from existing mold or prefabricated, socket insert, silicone gel, elastomeric or equal, not for use with locking mechanism

L5680 Addition to lower extremity, below knee, thigh lacer, nonmolded

L5681 Addition to lower extremity, below knee/above knee, custom fabricated socket insert for congenital or atypical traumatic amputee, silicone gel, elastomeric or equal, for use with or without locking mechanism, initial only (for other than initial, use code L5673 or L5679)

L5682 Addition to lower extremity, below knee, thigh lacer, gluteal/ischial, molded

L5683 Addition to lower extremity, below knee/above knee, custom fabricated socket insert for other than congenital or atypical traumatic amputee, silicone gel, elastomeric or equal, for use with or without locking mechanism, initial only (for other than initial, use code L5673 or L5679)

L5684 Addition to lower extremity, below knee, fork strap

L5685 Addition to lower extremity prosthesis, below knee, suspension/sealing sleeve, with or without valve, any material, each

L5686 Addition to lower extremity, below knee, back check (extension control)

L5688 Addition to lower extremity, below knee, waist belt, webbing

L5690 Addition to lower extremity, below knee, waist belt, padded and lined

L5692 Addition to lower extremity, above knee, pelvic control belt, light

L5694 Addition to lower extremity, above knee, pelvic control belt, padded and lined

L5695 Addition to lower extremity, above knee, pelvic control, sleeve suspension, neoprene or equal, each

L5696 Addition to lower extremity, above knee or knee disarticulation, pelvic joint

L5697 Addition to lower extremity, above knee or knee disarticulation, pelvic band

L5698 Addition to lower extremity, above knee or knee disarticulation, Silesian bandage

L5699 All lower extremity prostheses, shoulder harness

REPLACEMENTS

L5700 Replacement, socket, below knee, molded to patient model

L5701 Replacement, socket, above knee/knee disarticulation, including attachment plate, molded to patient model

L5702 Replacement, socket, hip disarticulation, including hip joint, molded to patient model

L5703 Ankle, Symes, molded to patient model, socket without solid ankle cushion heel (SACH) foot, replacement only

L5704 Custom shaped protective cover, below knee

L5705 Custom shaped protective cover, above knee

L5706 Custom shaped protective cover, knee disarticulation

L5707 Custom shaped protective cover, hip disarticulation

ADDITIONS: EXOSKELETAL KNEE-SHIN SYSTEM

L5710 Addition, exoskeletal knee-shin system, single axis, manual lock

L5711 Additions exoskeletal knee-shin system, single axis, manual lock, ultra-light material

L5712 Addition, exoskeletal knee-shin system, single axis, friction swing and stance phase control (safety knee)

L5714 Addition, exoskeletal knee-shin system, single axis, variable friction swing phase control

L5716 Addition, exoskeletal knee-shin system, polycentric, mechanical stance phase lock

L5718 Addition, exoskeletal knee-shin system, polycentric, friction swing and stance phase control

L5722 Addition, exoskeletal knee-shin system, single axis, pneumatic swing, friction stance phase control

L5724 Addition, exoskeletal knee-shin system, single axis, fluid swing phase control

L5726 Addition, exoskeletal knee/shin system, single axis, external joints, fluid swing phase control

L5728 Addition, exoskeletal knee-shin system, single axis, fluid swing and stance phase control

L5780 Addition, exoskeletal knee-shin system, single axis, pneumatic/hydra pneumatic swing phase control

L5781 Addition to lower limb prosthesis, vacuum pump, residual limb volume management and moisture evacuation system

L5782 Addition to lower limb prosthesis, vacuum pump, residual limb volume management and moisture evacuation system, heavy-duty

COMPONENT MODIFICATION

L5785 Addition, exoskeletal system, below knee, ultra-light material (titanium, carbon fiber or equal)

L5790 Addition, exoskeletal system, above knee, ultra-light material (titanium, carbon fiber or equal)

L5795 Addition, exoskeletal system, hip disarticulation, ultra-light material (titanium, carbon fiber or equal)

ADDITIONS: ENDOSKELETAL KNEE-SHIN SYSTEM

L5810 Addition, endoskeletal knee-shin system, single axis, manual lock

L5811 Addition, endoskeletal knee-shin system, single axis, manual lock, ultra-light material

L5812 Addition, endoskeletal knee-shin system, single axis, friction swing and stance phase control (safety knee)

L5814 Addition, endoskeletal knee-shin system, polycentric, hydraulic swing phase control, mechanical stance phase lock

L5816 Addition, endoskeletal knee-shin system, polycentric, mechanical stance phase lock

L5818 Addition, endoskeletal knee/shin system, polycentric, friction swing and stance phase control

L5822 Addition, endoskeletal knee-shin system, single axis, pneumatic swing, friction stance phase control

L5824 Addition, endoskeletal knee-shin system, single axis, fluid swing phase control

L5826 Addition, endoskeletal knee-shin system, single axis, hydraulic swing phase control, with miniature high activity frame

L5828 Addition, endoskeletal knee-shin system, single axis, fluid swing and stance phase control

L5830 Addition, endoskeletal knee/shin system, single axis, pneumatic/swing phase control

L5840 Addition, endoskeletal knee/shin system, 4-bar linkage or multiaxial, pneumatic swing phase control

L5845 Addition, endoskeletal knee/shin system, stance flexion feature, adjustable

L5848 Addition to endoskeletal knee-shin system, fluid stance extension, dampening feature, with or without adjustability

L5850 Addition, endoskeletal system, above knee or hip disarticulation, knee extension assist

L5855 Addition, endoskeletal system, hip disarticulation, mechanical hip extension assist

L5856 Addition to lower extremity prosthesis, endoskeletal knee-shin system, microprocessor control feature, swing and stance phase, includes electronic sensor(s), any type

L5857 Addition to lower extremity prosthesis, endoskeletal knee-shin system, microprocessor control feature, swing phase only, includes electronic sensor(s), any type

L5858 Addition to lower extremity prosthesis, endoskeletal knee shin system, microprocessor control feature, stance phase only, includes electronic sensor(s), any type

L5910 Addition, endoskeletal system, below knee, alignable system

L5920 Addition, endoskeletal system, above knee or hip disarticulation, alignable system

L5925 Addition, endoskeletal system, above knee, knee disarticulation or hip disarticulation, manual lock

L5930 Addition, endoskeletal system, high activity knee control frame

L5940 Addition, endoskeletal system, below knee, ultra-light material (titanium, carbon fiber or equal)

L5950 Addition, endoskeletal system, above knee, ultra-light material (titanium, carbon fiber or equal)

L5960 Addition, endoskeletal system, hip disarticulation, ultra-light material (titanium, carbon fiber or equal)

L5962 Addition, endoskeletal system, below knee, flexible protective outer surface covering system

L5964 Addition, endoskeletal system, above knee, flexible protective outer surface covering system

L5966 Addition, endoskeletal system, hip disarticulation, flexible protective outer surface covering system

L5968 Addition to lower limb prosthesis, multiaxial ankle with swing phase active dorsiflexion feature

L5970 All lower extremity prostheses, foot, external keel, SACH foot

L5971 All lower extremity prosthesis, solid ankle cushion heel (SACH) foot, replacement only

L5972 All lower extremity prostheses, flexible keel foot (SAFE, STEN, Bock Dynamic or equal)

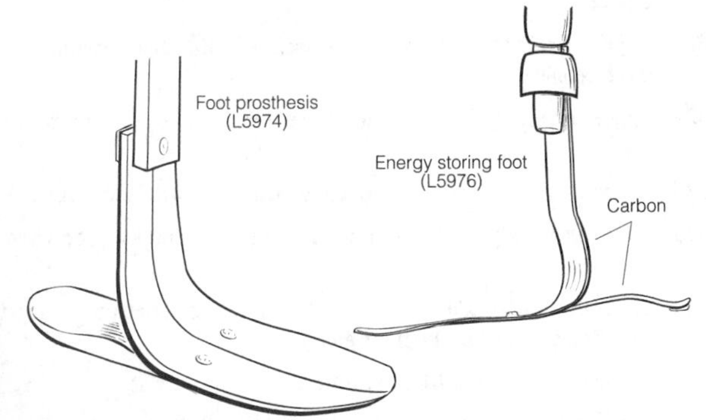

L5974 All lower extremity prostheses, foot, single axis ankle/foot

L5975 All lower extremity prosthesis, combination single axis ankle and flexible keel foot

L5976 All lower extremity prostheses, energy storing foot (Seattle Carbon Copy II or equal)

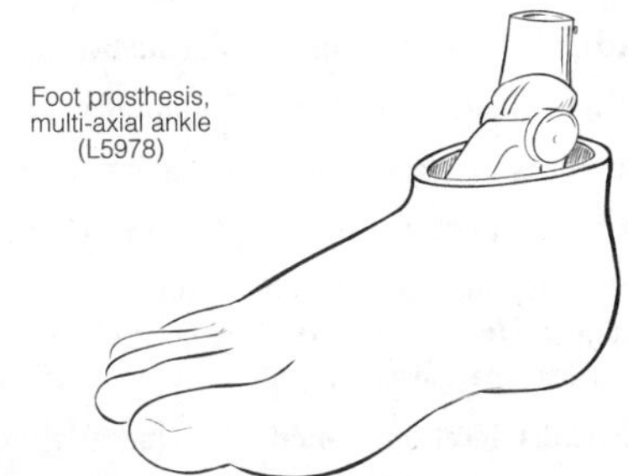

L5978 All lower extremity prostheses, foot, multiaxial ankle/foot

L5979 All lower extremity prostheses, multiaxial ankle, dynamic response foot, one piece system

L5980 All lower extremity prostheses, flex-foot system

L5981 All lower extremity prostheses, flex-walk system or equal

L5982 All exoskeletal lower extremity prostheses, axial rotation unit

L5984 All endoskeletal lower extremity prosthesis, axial rotation unit, with or without adjustability

L5985 All endoskeletal lower extremity prostheses, dynamic prosthetic pylon

L5986 All lower extremity prostheses, multiaxial rotation unit (MCP or equal)

L5987 All lower extremity prosthesis, shank foot system with vertical loading pylon

L5988 Addition to lower limb prosthesis, vertical shock reducing pylon feature

L5990 Addition to lower extremity prosthesis, user adjustable heel height

L5999 Lower extremity prosthesis, not otherwise specified
Determine if an alternative HCPCS Level II or a CPT code better describes the service being reported. This code should be used only if a more specific code is unavailable.

UPPER LIMB

The procedures in L6000-L6590 are considered as "base" or "basic procedures" and may be modified by listing procedures from the "addition" sections. The base procedures include only standard friction wrist and control cable system unless otherwise specified.

PARTIAL HAND

L6000 Partial hand, Robin-Aids, thumb remaining (or equal)

L6010 Partial hand, Robin-Aids, little and/or ring finger remaining (or equal)

L6020 Partial hand, Robin-Aids, no finger remaining (or equal)

L6025 Transcarpal/metacarpal or partial hand disarticulation prosthesis, external power, self-suspended, inner socket with removable forearm section, electrodes and cables, 2 batteries, charger, myoelectric control of terminal device

WRIST DISARTICULATION

L6050 Wrist disarticulation, molded socket, flexible elbow hinges, triceps pad

L6055 Wrist disarticulation, molded socket with expandable interface, flexible elbow hinges, triceps pad

BELOW ELBOW

L6100 Below elbow, molded socket, flexible elbow hinge, triceps pad

L6110 Below elbow, molded socket (Muenster or Northwestern suspension types)

L6120 Below elbow, molded double wall split socket, step-up hinges, half cuff

L6130 Below elbow, molded double wall split socket, stump activated locking hinge, half cuff

ELBOW DISARTICULATION

L6200 Elbow disarticulation, molded socket, outside locking hinge, forearm

L6205 Elbow disarticulation, molded socket with expandable interface, outside locking hinges, forearm

ABOVE ELBOW

L6250 Above elbow, molded double wall socket, internal locking elbow, forearm

SHOULDER DISARTICULATION

L6300 Shoulder disarticulation, molded socket, shoulder bulkhead, humeral section, internal locking elbow, forearm

L6310 Shoulder disarticulation, passive restoration (complete prosthesis)

L6320 Shoulder disarticulation, passive restoration (shoulder cap only)

INTERSCAPULAR THORACIC

L6350 Interscapular thoracic, molded socket, shoulder bulkhead, humeral section, internal locking elbow, forearm

L6360 Interscapular thoracic, passive restoration (complete prosthesis)

L6370 Interscapular thoracic, passive restoration (shoulder cap only)

IMMEDIATE AND EARLY POSTSURGICAL PROCEDURES

L6380 Immediate postsurgical or early fitting, application of initial rigid dressing, including fitting alignment and suspension of components, and one cast change, wrist disarticulation or below elbow

L6382 Immediate postsurgical or early fitting, application of initial rigid dressing including fitting alignment and suspension of components, and one cast change, elbow disarticulation or above elbow

L6384 Immediate postsurgical or early fitting, application of initial rigid dressing including fitting alignment and suspension of components, and one cast change, shoulder disarticulation or interscapular thoracic

L6386 Immediate postsurgical or early fitting, each additional cast change and realignment

L6388 Immediate postsurgical or early fitting, application of rigid dressing only

ENDOSKELETAL: BELOW ELBOW

L6400 Below elbow, molded socket, endoskeletal system, including soft prosthetic tissue shaping

ENDOSKELETAL: ELBOW DISARTICULATION

L6450 Elbow disarticulation, molded socket, endoskeletal system, including soft prosthetic tissue shaping

ENDOSKELETAL: ABOVE ELBOW

L6500 Above elbow, molded socket, endoskeletal system, including soft prosthetic tissue shaping

ENDOSKELETAL: SHOULDER DISARTICULATION

L6550 Shoulder disarticulation, molded socket, endoskeletal system, including soft prosthetic tissue shaping

ENDOSKELETAL: INTERSCAPULAR THORACIC

L6570 Interscapular thoracic, molded socket, endoskeletal system, including soft prosthetic tissue shaping

L6580 Preparatory, wrist disarticulation or below elbow, single wall plastic socket, friction wrist, flexible elbow hinges, figure of eight harness, humeral cuff, Bowden cable control, USMC or equal pylon, no cover, molded to patient model

L6582 Preparatory, wrist disarticulation or below elbow, single wall socket, friction wrist, flexible elbow hinges, figure of eight harness, humeral cuff, Bowden cable control, USMC or equal pylon, no cover, direct formed

L6584 Preparatory, elbow disarticulation or above elbow, single wall plastic socket, friction wrist, locking elbow, figure of eight harness, fair lead cable control, USMC or equal pylon, no cover, molded to patient model

L6586 Preparatory, elbow disarticulation or above elbow, single wall socket, friction wrist, locking elbow, figure of eight harness, fair lead cable control, USMC or equal pylon, no cover, direct formed

L6588 Preparatory, shoulder disarticulation or interscapular thoracic, single wall plastic socket, shoulder joint, locking elbow, friction wrist, chest strap, fair lead cable control, USMC or equal pylon, no cover, molded to patient model

L6590 Preparatory, shoulder disarticulation or interscapular thoracic, single wall socket, shoulder joint, locking elbow, friction wrist, chest strap, fair lead cable control, USMC or equal pylon, no cover, direct formed

ADDITIONS: UPPER LIMB

The following procedures/modifications/components may be added to other base procedures. The items in this section should reflect the additional complexity of each modification procedure, in addition to the base procedure, at the time of the original order.

L6600 Upper extremity additions, polycentric hinge, pair

L6605 Upper extremity additions, single pivot hinge, pair

L6610 Upper extremity additions, flexible metal hinge, pair

L6611 Addition to upper extremity prosthesis, external powered, additional switch, any type

L6615 Upper extremity addition, disconnect locking wrist unit

L6616 Upper extremity addition, additional disconnect insert for locking wrist unit, each

L6620 Upper extremity addition, flexion/extension wrist unit, with or without friction

L6621 Upper extremity prosthesis addition, flexion/extension wrist with or without friction, for use with external powered terminal device

L6623 Upper extremity addition, spring assisted rotational wrist unit with latch release

L6624 Upper extremity addition, flexion/extension and rotation wrist unit

L6625 Upper extremity addition, rotation wrist unit with cable lock

L6628 Upper extremity addition, quick disconnect hook adapter, Otto Bock or equal

L6629 Upper extremity addition, quick disconnect lamination collar with coupling piece, Otto Bock or equal

L6630 Upper extremity addition, stainless steel, any wrist

L6632 Upper extremity addition, latex suspension sleeve, each

L6635 Upper extremity addition, lift assist for elbow

L6637 Upper extremity addition, nudge control elbow lock

L6638 Upper extremity addition to prosthesis, electric locking feature, only for use with manually powered elbow

L6639 Upper extremity addition, heavy-duty feature, any elbow

L6640 Upper extremity additions, shoulder abduction joint, pair

L6641 Upper extremity addition, excursion amplifier, pulley type

L6642 Upper extremity addition, excursion amplifier, lever type

L6645 Upper extremity addition, shoulder flexion-abduction joint, each

L6646 Upper extremity addition, shoulder joint, multipositional locking, flexion, adjustable abduction friction control, for use with body powered or external powered system

L6647 Upper extremity addition, shoulder lock mechanism, body powered actuator

L6648 Upper extremity addition, shoulder lock mechanism, external powered actuator

L6650 Upper extremity addition, shoulder universal joint, each

L6655 Upper extremity addition, standard control cable, extra

L6660 Upper extremity addition, heavy-duty control cable

L6665 Upper extremity addition, Teflon, or equal, cable lining

L6670 Upper extremity addition, hook to hand, cable adapter

L6672 Upper extremity addition, harness, chest or shoulder, saddle type

L6675 Upper extremity addition, harness, (e.g., figure of eight type), single cable design

L6676 Upper extremity addition, harness, (e.g., figure of eight type), dual cable design

L6677 Upper extremity addition, harness, triple control, simultaneous operation of terminal device and elbow

L6680 Upper extremity addition, test socket, wrist disarticulation or below elbow

L6682 Upper extremity addition, test socket, elbow disarticulation or above elbow

L6684 Upper extremity addition, test socket, shoulder disarticulation or interscapular thoracic

L6686 Upper extremity addition, suction socket

L6687 Upper extremity addition, frame type socket, below elbow or wrist disarticulation

L6688 Upper extremity addition, frame type socket, above elbow or elbow disarticulation

L6689 Upper extremity addition, frame type socket, shoulder disarticulation

L6690 Upper extremity addition, frame type socket, interscapular-thoracic

L6691 Upper extremity addition, removable insert, each

L6692 Upper extremity addition, silicone gel insert or equal, each

L6693 Upper extremity addition, locking elbow, forearm counterbalance

L6694 Addition to upper extremity prosthesis, below elbow/above elbow, custom fabricated from existing mold or prefabricated, socket insert, silicone gel, elastomeric or equal, for use with locking mechanism

L6695 Addition to upper extremity prosthesis, below elbow/above elbow, custom fabricated from existing mold or prefabricated, socket insert, silicone gel, elastomeric or equal, not for use with locking mechanism

L6696 Addition to upper extremity prosthesis, below elbow/above elbow, custom fabricated socket insert for congenital or atypical traumatic amputee, silicone gel, elastomeric or equal, for use with or without locking mechanism, initial only (for other than initial, use code L6694 or L6695)

L6697 Addition to upper extremity prosthesis, below elbow/above elbow, custom fabricated socket insert for other than congenital or atypical traumatic amputee, silicone gel, elastomeric or equal, for use with or without locking mechanism, initial only (for other than initial, use code L6694 or L6695)

L6698 Addition to upper extremity prosthesis, below elbow/above elbow, lock mechanism, excludes socket insert

TERMINAL DEVICES

HOOKS AND HANDS

L6703 Terminal device, passive hand/mitt, any material, any size

L6704 Terminal device, sport/recreational/work attachment, any material, any size

L6706 Terminal device, hook, mechanical, voluntary opening, any material, any size, lined or unlined

L6707 Terminal device, hook, mechanical, voluntary closing, any material, any size, lined or unlined

L6708 Terminal device, hand, mechanical, voluntary opening, any material, any size

L6709 Terminal device, hand, mechanical, voluntary closing, any material, any size

L6711 Terminal device, hook, mechanical, voluntary opening, any material, any size, lined or unlined, pediatric

L6712 Terminal device, hook, mechanical, voluntary closing, any material, any size, lined or unlined, pediatric

L6713 Terminal device, hand, mechanical, voluntary opening, any material, any size, pediatric

L6714 Terminal device, hand, mechanical, voluntary closing, any material, any size, pediatric

L6721 Terminal device, hook or hand, heavy-duty, mechanical, voluntary opening, any material, any size, lined or unlined

L6722 Terminal device, hook or hand, heavy-duty, mechanical, voluntary closing, any material, any size, lined or unlined

L6805 Addition to terminal device, modifier wrist unit
MED: 100-2,15,120; 100-4,3,10.4

L6810 Addition to terminal device, precision pinch device
MED: 100-2,15,120; 100-4,3,10.4

L6881 Automatic grasp feature, addition to upper limb electric prosthetic terminal device

L6882 Microprocessor control feature, addition to upper limb prosthetic terminal device
MED: 100-2,15,120; 100-4,3,10.4

L6883 Replacement socket, below elbow/wrist disarticulation, molded to patient model, for use with or without external power

L6884 Replacement socket, above elbow/elbow disarticulation, molded to patient model, for use with or without external power

L6885 Replacement socket, shoulder disarticulation/interscapular thoracic, molded to patient model, for use with or without external power

GLOVES FOR ABOVE HANDS

L6890 Addition to upper extremity prosthesis, glove for terminal device, any material, prefabricated, includes fitting and adjustment

L6895 Addition to upper extremity prosthesis, glove for terminal device, any material, custom fabricated

HAND RESTORATION

L6900 Hand restoration (casts, shading and measurements included), partial hand, with glove, thumb or one finger remaining

L6905 Hand restoration (casts, shading and measurements included), partial hand, with glove, multiple fingers remaining

L6910 Hand restoration (casts, shading and measurements included), partial hand, with glove, no fingers remaining

L6915 Hand restoration (shading and measurements included), replacement glove for above

EXTERNAL POWER

BASE DEVICES

L6920 Wrist disarticulation, external power, self-suspended inner socket, removable forearm shell, Otto Bock or equal switch, cables, 2 batteries and 1 charger, switch control of terminal device

L6925 Wrist disarticulation, external power, self-suspended inner socket, removable forearm shell, Otto Bock or equal electrodes, cables, 2 batteries and one charger, myoelectronic control of terminal device

L6930 Below elbow, external power, self-suspended inner socket, removable forearm shell, Otto Bock or equal switch, cables, 2 batteries and one charger, switch control of terminal device

L6935 Below elbow, external power, self-suspended inner socket, removable forearm shell, Otto Bock or equal electrodes, cables, 2 batteries and one charger, myoelectronic control of terminal device

L6940 Elbow disarticulation, external power, molded inner socket, removable humeral shell, outside locking hinges, forearm, Otto Bock or equal switch, cables, 2 batteries and one charger, switch control of terminal device

L6945 Elbow disarticulation, external power, molded inner socket, removable humeral shell, outside locking hinges, forearm, Otto Bock or equal electrodes, cables, 2 batteries and one charger, myoelectronic control of terminal device

L6950 Above elbow, external power, molded inner socket, removable humeral shell, internal locking elbow, forearm, Otto Bock or equal switch, cables, 2 batteries and one charger, switch control of terminal device

L6955 Above elbow, external power, molded inner socket, removable humeral shell, internal locking elbow, forearm, Otto Bock or equal electrodes, cables, 2 batteries and one charger, myoelectronic control of terminal device

L6960 Shoulder disarticulation, external power, molded inner socket, removable shoulder shell, shoulder bulkhead, humeral section, mechanical elbow, forearm, Otto Bock or equal switch, cables, 2 batteries and one charger, switch control of terminal device

L6965 Shoulder disarticulation, external power, molded inner socket, removable shoulder shell, shoulder bulkhead, humeral section, mechanical elbow, forearm, Otto Bock or equal electrodes, cables, 2 batteries and one charger, myoelectronic control of terminal device

L6970 Interscapular-thoracic, external power, molded inner socket, removable shoulder shell, shoulder bulkhead, humeral section, mechanical elbow, forearm, Otto Bock or equal switch, cables, 2 batteries and one charger, switch control of terminal device

L6975 Interscapular-thoracic, external power, molded inner socket, removable shoulder shell, shoulder bulkhead, humeral section, mechanical elbow, forearm, Otto Bock or equal electrodes, cables, 2 batteries and one charger, myoelectronic control of terminal device

L7007 Electric hand, switch or myoelectric controlled, adult

L7008 Electric hand, switch or myoelectric, controlled, pediatric

L7009 Electric hook, switch or myoelectric controlled, adult

L7040 Prehensile actuator, switch controlled

L7045 Electric hook, switch or myoelectric controlled, pediatric

ELBOW

L7170 Electronic elbow, Hosmer or equal, switch controlled

L7180 Electronic elbow, microprocessor sequential control of elbow and terminal device

L7181 Electronic elbow, microprocessor simultaneous control of elbow and terminal device

L7185 Electronic elbow, adolescent, Variety Village or equal, switch controlled

L7186 Electronic elbow, child, Variety Village or equal, switch controlled

L7190 Electronic elbow, adolescent, Variety Village or equal, myoelectronically controlled

L7191 Electronic elbow, child, Variety Village or equal, myoelectronically controlled

L7260 Electronic wrist rotator, Otto Bock or equal

L7261 Electronic wrist rotator, for Utah arm

L7266 Servo control, Steeper or equal

L7272 Analogue control, UNB or equal

L7274 Proportional control, 6–12 volt, Liberty, Utah or equal

BATTERY COMPONENTS

L7360 Six volt battery, each

L7362 Battery charger, 6 volt, each

L7364 Twelve volt battery, each

L7366 Battery charger, twelve volt, each

L7367 Lithium ion battery, replacement

L7368 Lithium ion battery charger

L7400 Addition to upper extremity prosthesis, below elbow/wrist disarticulation, ultralight material (titanium, carbon fiber or equal)

L7401 Addition to upper extremity prosthesis, above elbow disarticulation, ultralight material (titanium, carbon fiber or equal)

L7402 Addition to upper extremity prosthesis, shoulder disarticulation/interscapular thoracic, ultralight material (titanium, carbon fiber or equal)

L7403 Addition to upper extremity prosthesis, below elbow/wrist disarticulation, acrylic material

L7404 Addition to upper extremity prosthesis, above elbow disarticulation, acrylic material

L7405 Addition to upper extremity prosthesis, shoulder disarticulation/interscapular thoracic, acrylic material

L7499 Upper extremity prosthesis, not otherwise specified

REPAIRS

L7500 Repair of prosthetic device, hourly rate (excludes V5335 repair of oral or laryngeal prosthesis or artificial larynx)
Medicare jurisdiction: local contractor if repair of implanted prosthetic device.

MED: 100-2,15,110.2; 100-2,15,120; 100-4,32,100

L7510 Repair of prosthetic device, repair or replace minor parts
Medicare jurisdiction: local contractor if repair of implanted prosthetic device.

MED: 100-2,15,110.2; 100-2,15,120; 100-4,32,100

L7520 Repair prosthetic device, labor component, per 15 minutes
Medicare jurisdiction: local contractor if repair of implanted prosthetic device.

L7600 Prosthetic donning sleeve, any material, each

TERMINAL DEVICES

GENERAL

L7900 Male vacuum erection system

PROSTHESIS

L8000 Breast prosthesis, mastectomy bra

MED: 100-2,15,120

L8001 Breast prosthesis, mastectomy bra, with integrated breast prosthesis form, unilateral

MED: 100-2,15,120

L8002 Breast prosthesis, mastectomy bra, with integrated breast prosthesis form, bilateral
MED: 100-2,15,120

L8010 Breast prosthesis, mastectomy sleeve
MED: 100-2,15,120

L8015 External breast prosthesis garment, with mastectomy form, postmastectomy
MED: 100-2,15,120

L8020 Breast prosthesis, mastectomy form
MED: 100-2,15,120

L8030 Breast prosthesis, silicone or equal
MED: 100-2,15,120

L8035 Custom breast prosthesis, post mastectomy, molded to patient model
MED: 100-2,15,120

L8039 Breast prosthesis, not otherwise specified

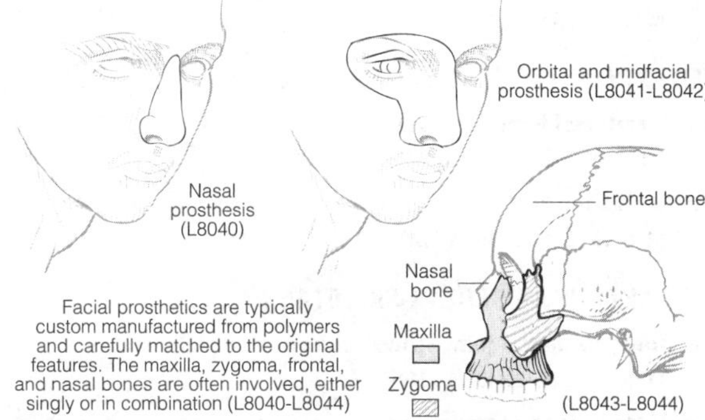

Facial prosthetics are typically custom manufactured from polymers and carefully matched to the original features. The maxilla, zygoma, frontal, and nasal bones are often involved, either singly or in combination (L8040-L8044)

L8040 Nasal prosthesis, provided by a nonphysician

L8041 Midfacial prosthesis, provided by a nonphysician

L8042 Orbital prosthesis, provided by a nonphysician

L8043 Upper facial prosthesis, provided by a nonphysician

L8044 Hemi-facial prosthesis, provided by a nonphysician

L8045 Auricular prosthesis, provided by a nonphysician

L8046 Partial facial prosthesis, provided by a nonphysician

L8047 Nasal septal prosthesis, provided by a nonphysician

L8048 Unspecified maxillofacial prosthesis, by report, provided by a nonphysician

L8049 Repair or modification of maxillofacial prosthesis, labor component, 15 minute increments, provided by a nonphysician

TRUSSES

L8300 Truss, single with standard pad
MED: 100-2,15,120; 100-3,280.11; 100-3,280.12; 100-4,4,240

L8310 Truss, double with standard pads
MED: 100-2,15,120; 100-3,280.11; 100-3,280.12; 100-4,4,240

L8320 Truss, addition to standard pad, water pad
MED: 100-2,15,120; 100-3,280.11; 100-3,280.12; 100-4,4,240

L8330 Truss, addition to standard pad, scrotal pad
MED: 100-2,15,120; 100-3,280.11; 100-3,280.12; 100-4,4,240

PROSTHETIC SOCKS

L8400 Prosthetic sheath, below knee, each
MED: 100-2,15,120

L8410 Prosthetic sheath, above knee, each
MED: 100-2,15,120

L8415 Prosthetic sheath, upper limb, each
MED: 100-2,15,120

L8417 Prosthetic sheath/sock, including a gel cushion layer, below knee or above knee, each

L8420 Prosthetic sock, multiple ply, below knee, each
MED: 100-2,15,120

L8430 Prosthetic sock, multiple ply, above knee, each
MED: 100-2,15,120

L8435 Prosthetic sock, multiple ply, upper limb, each
MED: 100-2,15,120

L8440 Prosthetic shrinker, below knee, each
MED: 100-2,15,120

L8460 Prosthetic shrinker, above knee, each
MED: 100-2,15,120

L8465 Prosthetic shrinker, upper limb, each
MED: 100-2,15,120

L8470 Prosthetic sock, single ply, fitting, below knee, each
MED: 100-2,15,120

L8480 Prosthetic sock, single ply, fitting, above knee, each
MED: 100-2,15,120

L8485 Prosthetic sock, single ply, fitting, upper limb, each
MED: 100-2,15,120

L8499 Unlisted procedure for miscellaneous prosthetic services
Determine if an alternative HCPCS Level II or a CPT code better describes the service being reported. This code should be used only if a more specific code is unavailable.

PROSTHETIC IMPLANTS

INTEGUMENTARY SYSTEM

L8500 Artificial larynx, any type
MED: 100-2,15,120; 100-3,50.2; 100-4,4,240

L8501 Tracheostomy speaking valve
MED: 100-3,50.4

L8505 Artificial larynx replacement battery/accessory, any type

L8507 Tracheo-esophageal voice prosthesis, patient inserted, any type, each

L8509 Tracheo-esophageal voice prosthesis, inserted by a licensed health care provider, any type

L8510 Voice amplifier
MED: 100-3,50.2

L8511 Insert for indwelling tracheoesophageal prosthesis, with or without valve, replacement only, each

L8512 Gelatin capsules or equivalent, for use with tracheoesophageal voice prosthesis, replacement only, per 10

L8513 Cleaning device used with tracheoesophageal voice prosthesis, pipet, brush, or equal, replacement only, each

L8514 Tracheoesophageal puncture dilator, replacement only, each

L8515 Gelatin capsule, application device for use with tracheoesophageal voice prosthesis, each

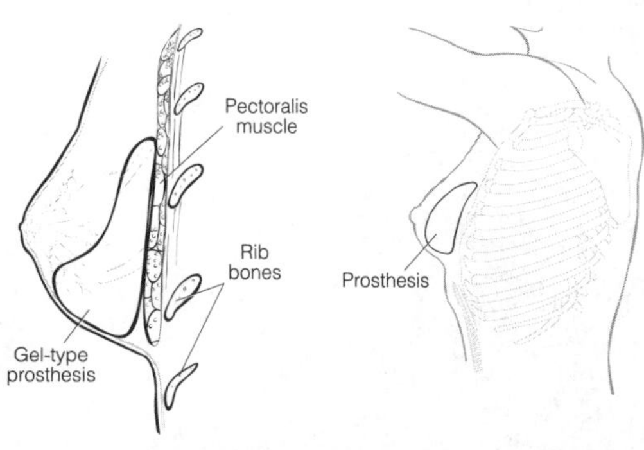

L8600 **Implantable breast prosthesis, silicone or equal**
Medicare covers implants inserted in post-mastectomy reconstruction in a breast cancer patient. Always report concurrent to the implant procedure.

MED: 100-2,15,120; 100-3,140.2; 100-4,4,240

L8603 **Injectable bulking agent, collagen implant, urinary tract, 2.5 ml syringe, includes shipping and necessary supplies**
Medicare covers up to five separate collagen implant treatments in patients with intrinsic sphincter deficiency. Who have passed a collagen sensitivity test.

MED: 100-3,230.10

L8604 **Injectable bulking agent, dextranomer/hyaluronic acid copolymer implant, urinary tract, 1 ml, includes shipping and necessary supplies**

L8606 **Injectable bulking agent, synthetic implant, urinary tract, 1 ml syringe, includes shipping and necessary supplies**
MED: 100-3,230.10

L8609 **Artificial cornea**

HEAD: SKULL, FACIAL BONES, AND TEMPOROMANDIBULAR JOINT

L8610 **Ocular implant**
MED: 100-2,15,120; 100-4,4,240

L8612 **Aqueous shunt**
MED: 100-2,15,120; 100-4,4,240

L8613 **Ossicula implant**
MED: 100-2,15,120; 100-4,4,240

L8614 **Cochlear device, includes all internal and external components**
A cochlear implant is covered by Medicare when the patient has bilateral sensorineural deafness.

MED: 100-2,15,120; 100-3,50.3; 100-4,4,240; 100-4,32,100
AHA: 4Q,'03,8; 3Q,'02,5

L8615 **Headset/headpiece for use with cochlear implant device, replacement**

L8616 **Microphone for use with cochlear implant device, replacement**

L8617 **Transmitting coil for use with cochlear implant device, replacement**

L8618 **Transmitter cable for use with cochlear implant device, replacement**

L8619 **Cochlear implant external speech processor, replacement**
Medicare jurisdiction: local contractor.

MED: 100-3,50.3; 100-4,32,100

L8621 **Zinc air battery for use with cochlear implant device, replacement, each**

L8622 **Alkaline battery for use with cochlear implant device, any size, replacement, each**

L8623 **Lithium ion battery for use with cochlear implant device speech processor, other than ear level, replacement, each**

L8624 **Lithium ion battery for use with cochlear implant device speech processor, ear level, replacement, each**

UPPER EXTREMITY

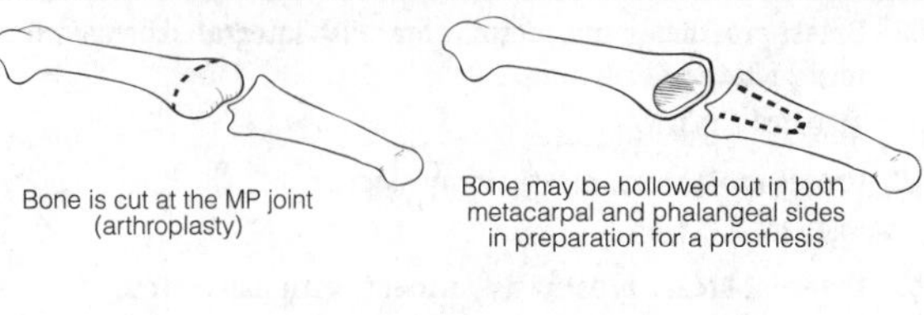

Bone is cut at the MP joint (arthroplasty)
Bone may be hollowed out in both metacarpal and phalangeal sides in preparation for a prosthesis

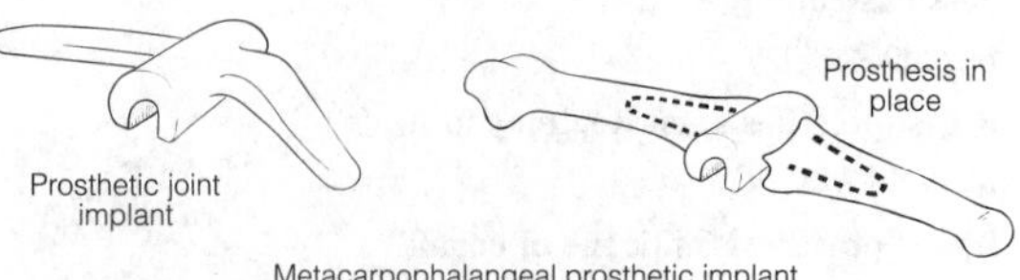

Metacarpophalangeal prosthetic implant

L8630 **Metacarpophalangeal joint implant**
MED: 100-2,15,120; 100-4,4,240

L8631 **Metacarpal phalangeal joint replacement, 2 or more pieces, metal (e.g., stainless steel or cobalt chrome), ceramic-like material (e.g., pyrocarbon), for surgical implantation (all sizes, includes entire system)**
MED: 100-2,15,120; 100-4,4,240

LOWER EXTREMITY - JOINT: KNEE, ANKLE, TOE

L8641 **Metatarsal joint implant**
MED: 100-2,15,120; 100-4,4,240

L8642 **Hallux implant**
MED: 100-2,15,120; 100-4,4,240

MISCELLANEOUS MUSCULAR-SKELETAL

L8658 **Interphalangeal joint spacer, silicone or equal, each**
MED: 100-2,15,120; 100-4,4,240

L8659 **Interphalangeal finger joint replacement, 2 or more pieces, metal (e.g., stainless steel or cobalt chrome), ceramic-like material (e.g., pyrocarbon) for surgical implantation, any size**
MED: 100-2,15,120; 100-4,4,240

CARDIOVASCULAR SYSTEM

L8670 **Vascular graft material, synthetic, implant**
MED: 100-2,15,120; 100-4,4,240

GENERAL

L8680 **Implantable neurostimulator electrode, each**
MED: 100-4,32,50

L8681 **Patient programmer (external) for use with implantable programmable neurostimulator pulse generator, replacement only**

L8682 **Implantable neurostimulator radiofrequency receiver**

L8683 **Radiofrequency transmitter (external) for use with implantable neurostimulator radiofrequency receiver**

L8684 **Radiofrequency transmitter (external) for use with implantable sacral root neurostimulator receiver for bowel and bladder management, replacement**

L8685 **Implantable neurostimulator pulse generator, single array, rechargeable, includes extension**
MED: 100-4,32,50

L8686 **Implantable neurostimulator pulse generator, single array, nonrechargeable, includes extension**
MED: 100-4,32,50

L8687 **Implantable neurostimulator pulse generator, dual array, rechargeable, includes extension**
MED: 100-4,32,50

L8688 **Implantable neurostimulator pulse generator, dual array, nonrechargeable, includes extension**
MED: 100-4,32,50

L8689 External recharging system for battery (internal) for use with implantable neurostimulator, replacement only

L8690 Auditory osseointegrated device, includes all internal and external components

L8691 Auditory osseointegrated device, external sound processor, replacement

L8695 External recharging system for battery (external) for use with implantable neurostimulator, replacement only

L8699 Prosthetic implant, not otherwise specified
Determine if an alternative HCPCS Level II or a CPT code better describes the service being reported. This code should be used only if a more specific code is unavailable.

L9900 Orthotic and prosthetic supply, accessory, and/or service component of another HCPCS L code

MEDICAL SERVICES M0000-M0301

OTHER MEDICAL SERVICES

M codes include office services, cellular therapy, prolotherapy, intragastric hypothermia, IV chelation therapy, and fabric wrapping of an abdominal aneurysm.

M0064 **Brief office visit for the sole purpose of monitoring or changing drug prescriptions used in the treatment of mental psychoneurotic and personality disorders**

MED: 100-4,12,210.1

M0075 Cellular therapy

The therapeutic efficacy of injecting foreign proteins has not been established.

MED: 100-3,30.8

M0076 Prolotherapy

The therapeutic efficacy of prolotherapy and joint sclerotherapy has not been established.

MED: 100-3,150.7

M0100 Intragastric hypothermia using gastric freezing

Code with caution: This procedure is considered obsolete.

MED: 100-3,100.6

CARDIOVASCULAR SERVICES

M0300 IV chelation therapy (chemical endarterectomy)

Chelation therapy is considered experimental in the United States.

MED: 100-3,20.21

M0301 Fabric wrapping of abdominal aneurysm

Code with caution: This procedure has largely been replaced with more effective treatment modalities. Submit documentation.

MED: 100-3,20.23

PATHOLOGY AND LABORATORY SERVICES P0000-P9999

P codes include chemistry, toxicology, and microbiology tests, screening Papanicolaou procedures, and various blood products.

CHEMISTRY AND TOXICOLOGY TESTS

P2028 Cephalin floculation, blood
Code with caution: This test is considered obsolete. Submit documentation.
MED: 100-3,300.1

P2029 Congo red, blood
Code with caution: This test is considered obsolete. Submit documentation.
MED: 100-3,300.1

P2031 Hair analysis (excluding arsenic)
MED: 100-3,190.6

P2033 Thymol turbidity, blood
Code with caution: This test is considered obsolete. Submit documentation.
MED: 100-3,300.1

P2038 Mucoprotein, blood (seromucoid) (medical necessity procedure)
Code with caution: This test is considered obsolete. Submit documentation.
MED: 100-3,300.1

PATHOLOGY SCREENING TESTS

P3000 Screening Papanicolaou smear, cervical or vaginal, up to 3 smears, by technician under physician supervision
One Pap test is covered by Medicare every two years, unless the physician suspects cervical abnormalities and shortens the interval. See also G0123-G0124.
MED: 100-2,6,10; 100-3,190.2; 100-4,4,240

P3001 Screening Papanicolaou smear, cervical or vaginal, up to 3 smears, requiring interpretation by physician
One Pap test is covered by Medicare every two years, unless the physician suspects cervical abnormalities and shortens the interval. See also G0123-G0124.
MED: 100-2,6,10; 100-3,190.2; 100-4,4,240

MICROBIOLOGY TESTS

P7001 Culture, bacterial, urine; quantitative, sensitivity study

MISCELLANEOUS

P9010 Blood (whole), for transfusion, per unit
MED: 100-1,3,20.5; 100-2,1,10; 100-4,3,40.2.2

P9011 Blood, split unit
MED: 100-1,3,20.5; 100-2,1,10; 100-4,3,40.2.2

P9012 Cryoprecipitate, each unit
MED: 100-1,3,20.5; 100-2,1,10; 100-4,3,40.2.2

P9016 Red blood cells, leukocytes reduced, each unit
MED: 100-1,3,20.5; 100-2,1,10; 100-4,3,40.2.2

P9017 Fresh frozen plasma (single donor), frozen within 8 hours of collection, each unit
MED: 100-1,3,20.5; 100-2,1,10; 100-4,3,40.2.2

P9019 Platelets, each unit
MED: 100-1,3,20.5; 100-2,1,10; 100-4,3,40.2.2

P9020 Platelet rich plasma, each unit
MED: 100-1,3,20.5; 100-4,3,40.2.2

P9021 Red blood cells, each unit
MED: 100-1,3,20.5; 100-2,1,10; 100-4,3,40.2.2

P9022 Red blood cells, washed, each unit
MED: 100-1,3,20.5; 100-2,1,10; 100-4,3,40.2.2

P9023 Plasma, pooled multiple donor, solvent/detergent treated, frozen, each unit
MED: 100-1,3,20.5; 100-2,1,10; 100-4,3,40.2.2

P9031 Platelets, leukocytes reduced, each unit
MED: 100-1,3,20.5; 100-1,3,20.5.2; 100-1,3,20.5.3; 100-2,1,10; 100-4,3,40.2.2

P9032 Platelets, irradiated, each unit
MED: 100-1,3,20.5; 100-1,3,20.5.2; 100-1,3,20.5.3; 100-2,1,10; 100-4,3,40.2.2

P9033 Platelets, leukocytes reduced, irradiated, each unit
MED: 100-1,3,20.5; 100-1,3,20.5.2; 100-1,3,20.5.3; 100-2,1,10; 100-4,3,40.2.2

P9034 Platelets, pheresis, each unit
MED: 100-1,3,20.5; 100-1,3,20.5.2; 100-1,3,20.5.3; 100-2,1,10; 100-4,3,40.2.2

P9035 Platelets, pheresis, leukocytes reduced, each unit
MED: 100-1,3,20.5; 100-1,3,20.5.2; 100-1,3,20.5.3; 100-2,1,10; 100-4,3,40.2.2

P9036 Platelets, pheresis, irradiated, each unit
MED: 100-1,3,20.5; 100-1,3,20.5.2; 100-1,3,20.5.3; 100-2,1,10; 100-4,3,40.2.2

P9037 Platelets, pheresis, leukocytes reduced, irradiated, each unit
MED: 100-1,3,20.5; 100-1,3,20.5.2; 100-1,3,20.5.3; 100-2,1,10; 100-4,3,40.2.2

P9038 Red blood cells, irradiated, each unit
MED: 100-1,3,20.5; 100-1,3,20.5.2; 100-1,3,20.5.3; 100-2,1,10; 100-4,3,40.2.2

P9039 Red blood cells, deglycerolized, each unit
MED: 100-1,3,20.5; 100-1,3,20.5.2; 100-1,3,20.5.3; 100-2,1,10; 100-4,3,40.2.2

P9040 Red blood cells, leukocytes reduced, irradiated, each unit
MED: 100-1,3,20.5; 100-1,3,20.5.2; 100-1,3,20.5.3; 100-2,1,10; 100-4,3,40.2.2

P9041 Infusion, albumin (human), 5%, 50 ml
Not considered a blood product for OPPS effective July 1, 2005.
MED: 100-2,1,10; 100-4,3,40.2.2

P9043 Infusion, plasma protein fraction (human), 5%, 50 ml
MED: 100-1,3,20.5; 100-2,1,10; 100-4,3,40.2.2

P9044 Plasma, cryoprecipitate reduced, each unit
MED: 100-1,3,20.5; 100-2,1,10; 100-4,3,40.2.2

P9045 Infusion, albumin (human), 5%, 250 ml
Not considered a blood product for OPPS effective July 1, 2005.
MED: 100-2,1,10; 100-4,3,40.2.2

P9046 Infusion, albumin (human), 25%, 20 ml
Not considered a blood product for OPPS effective July 1, 2005.
MED: 100-2,1,10; 100-4,3,40.2.2

P9047 Infusion, albumin (human), 25%, 50 ml
Not considered a blood product for OPPS effective July 1, 2005.
MED: 100-2,1,10; 100-4,3,40.2.2

P9048 Infusion, plasma protein fraction (human), 5%, 250 ml
MED: 100-2,1,10; 100-4,3,40.2.2

P9050 Granulocytes, pheresis, each unit
MED: 100-2,1,10; 100-4,3,40.2.2

P9051 Whole blood or red blood cells, leukocytes reduced, CMV-negative, each unit
MED: 100-2,1,10; 100-4,3,40.2.2

P9052 Platelets, HLA-matched leukocytes reduced, apheresis/pheresis, each unit
MED: 100-2,1,10; 100-4,3,40.2.2

P9053 Platelets, pheresis, leukocytes reduced, CMV-negative, irradiated, each unit
MED: 100-2,1,10; 100-4,3,40.2.2

P9054 Whole blood or red blood cells, leukocytes reduced, frozen, deglycerol, washed, each unit
MED: 100-2,1,10; 100-4,3,40.2.2

P9055 Platelets, leukocytes reduced, CMV-negative, apheresis/pheresis, each unit
MED: 100-2,1,10; 100-4,3,40.2.2

P9056 Whole blood, leukocytes reduced, irradiated, each unit
MED: 100-2,1,10; 100-4,3,40.2.2

P9057 Red blood cells, frozen/deglycerolized/washed, leukocytes reduced, irradiated, each unit
MED: 100-2,1,10; 100-4,3,40.2.2

P9058 Red blood cells, leukocytes reduced, CMV-negative, irradiated, each unit
MED: 100-2,1,10; 100-4,3,40.2.2

P9059 Fresh frozen plasma between 8-24 hours of collection, each unit
MED: 100-2,1,10; 100-4,3,40.2.2

P9060 Fresh frozen plasma, donor retested, each unit
MED: 100-2,1,10; 100-4,3,40.2.2

P9603 Travel allowance, one way in connection with medically necessary laboratory specimen collection drawn from homebound or nursing homebound patient; prorated miles actually travelled.
MED: 100-4,16,60

P9604 Travel allowance, one way in connection with medically necessary laboratory specimen collection drawn from homebound or nursing homebound patient; prorated trip charge
MED: 100-4,16,60

P9612 Catheterization for collection of specimen, single patient, all places of service
MED: 100-4,16,60

P9615 Catheterization for collection of specimen(s) (multiple patients)
MED: 100-4,16,60

Q CODES (TEMPORARY) Q0000-Q9999

New temporary Q codes to pay health care providers for the supplies used in creating casts were established to replace the removal of the practice expense for all HCPCS codes, including the CPT codes for fracture management and for casts and splints. Coders should continue to use the appropriate CPT code to report the work and practice expenses involved with creating the cast or splint; the temporary Q codes replace less specific coding for the casting and splinting supplies.

Q0035 **Cardiokymography**
Covered only in conjunction with electrocardiographic stress testing in male patients with atypical angina or nonischemic chest pain, or female patients with angina.
MED: 100-3,20.24

Q0081 **Infusion therapy, using other than chemotherapeutic drugs, per visit**
MED: 100-3,280.14
AHA: 1Q,'02,7; 4Q,'02,7

Q0083 **Chemotherapy administration by other than infusion technique only (e.g., subcutaneous, intramuscular, push), per visit**

Q0084 **Chemotherapy administration by infusion technique only, per visit**
MED: 100-3,280.14

Q0085 **Chemotherapy administration by both infusion technique and other technique(s) (e.g., subcutaneous, intramuscular, push), per visit**

Q0091 **Screening Papanicolaou smear; obtaining, preparing and conveyance of cervical or vaginal smear to laboratory**
One pap test is covered by Medicare every two years for low risk patients and every one year for high risk patients. Q0091 can be reported with an E/M code when a separately identifiable E/M service is provided.
MED: 100-3, 190.2
MED: 100-3,190.2
AHA: 4Q,'02,8

Q0092 **Set-up portable x-ray equipment**

Q0111 **Wet mounts, including preparations of vaginal, cervical or skin specimens**

Q0112 **All potassium hydroxide (KOH) preparations**

Q0113 **Pinworm examinations**

Q0114 **Fern test**

Q0115 **Postcoital direct, qualitative examinations of vaginal or cervical mucous**

Q0144 **Azithromycin dihydrate, oral, capsules/powder, 1 g**
Use this code for Zithromax, Zithromax Z-PAK.

Q0163 **Diphenhydramine HCl, 50 mg, oral, FDA approved prescription antiemetic, for use as a complete therapeutic substitute for an IV antiemetic at time of chemotherapy treatment not to exceed a 48-hour dosage regimen**
See also J1200. Medicare covers at the time of chemotherapy if regimen doesn't exceed 48 hours. Submit on the same claim as the chemotherapy. Use this code for Truxadryl.
MED: 100-2,6,10; 100-4,4,240; 100-4,17,80.2
AHA: 1Q,'02,2

Q0164 **Prochlorperazine maleate, 5 mg, oral, FDA approved prescription antiemetic, for use as a complete therapeutic substitute for an IV antiemetic at the time of chemotherapy treatment, not to exceed a 48-hour dosage regimen**
Medicare covers at the time of chemotherapy if regimen doesn't exceed 48 hours. Submit on the same claim as the chemotherapy. Use this code for Compazine.
MED: 100-2,6,10; 100-4,4,240; 100-4,17,80.2

Q0165 **Prochlorperazine maleate, 10 mg, oral, FDA approved prescription antiemetic, for use as a complete therapeutic substitute for an IV antiemetic at the time of chemotherapy treatment, not to exceed a 48-hour dosage regimen**
Medicare covers at the time of chemotherapy if regimen doesn't exceed 48 hours. Submit on the same claim as the chemotherapy. Use this code for Compazine.
MED: 100-2,6,10; 100-4,4,240; 100-4,17,80.2

Q0166 **Granisetron HCl, 1 mg, oral, FDA approved prescription antiemetic, for use as a complete therapeutic substitute for an IV antiemetic at the time of chemotherapy treatment, not to exceed a 24-hour dosage regimen**
Medicare covers at the time of chemotherapy if regimen doesn't exceed 48 hours. Submit on the same claim as the chemotherapy. Use this code for Kytril.
MED: 100-2,6,10; 100-4,4,240; 100-4,17,80.2

Q0167 **Dronabinol, 2.5 mg, oral, FDA approved prescription antiemetic, for use as a complete therapeutic substitute for an IV antiemetic at the time of chemotherapy treatment, not to exceed a 48-hour dosage regimen**
Medicare covers at the time of chemotherapy if regimen doesn't exceed 48 hours. Submit on the same claim as the chemotherapy. Use this code for Marinol.
MED: 100-2,6,10; 100-4,4,240; 100-4,17,80.2

Q0168 **Dronabinol, 5 mg, oral, FDA approved prescription antiemetic, for use as a complete therapeutic substitute for an IV antiemetic at the time of chemotherapy treatment, not to exceed a 48-hour dosage regimen**
Use this code for Marinol.
MED: 100-2,6,10; 100-4,4,240; 100-4,17,80.2

Q0169 **Promethazine HCl, 12.5 mg, oral, FDA approved prescription antiemetic, for use as a complete therapeutic substitute for an IV antiemetic at the time of chemotherapy treatment, not to exceed a 48-hour dosage regimen**
Medicare covers at the time of chemotherapy if regimen doesn't exceed 48 hours. Submit on the same claim as the chemotherapy. Use this code for Phenergan, Amergan.
MED: 100-2,6,10; 100-4,4,240; 100-4,17,80.2

Q0170 **Promethazine HCl, 25 mg, oral, FDA approved prescription antiemetic, for use as a complete therapeutic substitute for an IV antiemetic at the time of chemotherapy treatment, not to exceed a 48-hour dosage regimen**
Medicare covers at the time of chemotherapy if regimen doesn't exceed 48 hours. Submit on the same claim as the chemotherapy. Use this code for Phenergan, Amergan.
MED: 100-2,6,10; 100-4,4,240; 100-4,17,80.2

Q0171 **Chlorpromazine HCl, 10 mg, oral, FDA approved prescription antiemetic, for use as a complete therapeutic substitute for an IV antiemetic at the time of chemotherapy treatment, not to exceed a 48-hour dosage regimen**
Medicare covers at the time of chemotherapy if regimen doesn't exceed 48 hours. Submit on the same claim as the chemotherapy. Use this code for Thorazine.
MED: 100-2,6,10; 100-4,4,240; 100-4,17,80.2

Q0172 **Chlorpromazine HCl, 25 mg, oral, FDA approved prescription antiemetic, for use as a complete therapeutic substitute for an IV antiemetic at the time of chemotherapy treatment, not to exceed a 48-hour dosage regimen**
Medicare covers at the time of chemotherapy if regimen doesn't exceed 48 hours. Submit on the same claim as the chemotherapy. Use this code for Thorazine.
MED: 100-2,6,10; 100-4,4,240; 100-4,17,80.2

Q0173 Trimethobenzamide HCl, 250 mg, oral, FDA approved prescription antiemetic, for use as a complete therapeutic substitute for an IV antiemetic at the time of chemotherapy treatment, not to exceed a 48-hour dosage regimen
Medicare covers at the time of chemotherapy if regimen doesn't exceed 48 hours. Submit on the same claim as the chemotherapy. Use this code for Tebamide, T-Gen, Ticon, Tigan, Triban, Thimazide.
MED: 100-2,6,10; 100-4,4,240; 100-4,17,80.2

Q0174 Thiethylperazine maleate, 10 mg, oral, FDA approved prescription antiemetic, for use as a complete therapeutic substitute for an IV antiemetic at the time of chemotherapy treatment, not to exceed a 48-hour dosage regimen
Medicare covers at the time of chemotherapy if regimen doesn't exceed 48 hours. Submit on the same claim as the chemotherapy. Use this code for Torecan.
MED: 100-2,6,10; 100-4,4,240; 100-4,17,80.2

Q0175 Perphenazine, 4 mg, oral, FDA approved prescription antiemetic, for use as a complete therapeutic substitute for an IV antiemetic at the time of chemotherapy treatment, not to exceed a 48 hour dosage regimen
Medicare covers at the time of chemotherapy if regimen doesn't exceed 48 hours. Submit on the same claim as the chemotherapy. Use this code for Trilifon.
MED: 100-2,6,10; 100-4,4,240; 100-4,17,80.2

Q0176 Perphenazine, 8 mg, oral, FDA approved prescription antiemetic, for use as a complete therapeutic substitute for an IV antiemetic at the time of chemotherapy treatment, not to exceed a 48 hour dosage regimen
Medicare covers at the time of chemotherapy if regimen doesn't exceed 48 hours. Submit on the same claim as the chemotherapy. Use this code for Trilifon.
MED: 100-2,6,10; 100-4,4,240; 100-4,17,80.2

Q0177 Hydroxyzine pamoate, 25 mg, oral, FDA approved prescription antiemetic, for use as a complete therapeutic substitute for an IV antiemetic at the time of chemotherapy treatment, not to exceed a 48-hour dosage regimen
Medicare covers at the time of chemotherapy if regimen doesn't exceed 48 hours. Submit on the same claim as the chemotherapy. Use this code for Vistaril.
MED: 100-2,6,10; 100-4,4,240; 100-4,17,80.2

Q0178 Hydroxyzine pamoate, 50 mg, oral, FDA approved prescription antiemetic, for use as a complete therapeutic substitute for an IV antiemetic at the time of chemotherapy treatment, not to exceed a 48-hour dosage regimen
Medicare covers at the time of chemotherapy if regimen doesn't exceed 48 hours. Submit on the same claim as the chemotherapy.
MED: 100-2,6,10; 100-4,4,240; 100-4,17,80.2

Q0179 Ondansetron HCl 8 mg, oral, FDA approved prescription antiemetic, for use as a complete therapeutic substitute for an IV antiemetic at the time of chemotherapy treatment, not to exceed a 48-hour dosage regimen
Medicare covers at the time of chemotherapy if regimen doesn't exceed 48 hours. Submit on the same claim as the chemotherapy. Use this code for Zofran.
MED: 100-2,6,10; 100-4,4,240; 100-4,17,80.2

Q0180 Dolasetron mesylate, 100 mg, oral, FDA approved prescription antiemetic, for use as a complete therapeutic substitute for an IV antiemetic at the time of chemotherapy treatment, not to exceed a 24-hour dosage regimen
Medicare covers at the time of chemotherapy if regimen doesn't exceed 24 hours. Submit on the same claim as the chemotherapy. Use this code for Anzemet.
MED: 100-2,6,10; 100-4,4,240; 100-4,17,80.2

Q0181 Unspecified oral dosage form, FDA approved prescription antiemetic, for use as a complete therapeutic substitute for an IV antiemetic at the time of chemotherapy treatment, not to exceed a 48-hour dosage regimen
Medicare covers at the time of chemotherapy if regimen doesn't exceed 48-hours. Submit on the same claim as the chemotherapy.
MED: 100-2,6,10; 100-4,4,240; 100-4,17,80.2

Q0480 Driver for use with pneumatic ventricular assist device, replacement only
AHA: 3Q,'05,2

Q0481 Microprocessor control unit for use with electric ventricular assist device, replacement only
AHA: 3Q,'05,2

Q0482 Microprocessor control unit for use with electric/pneumatic combination ventricular assist device, replacement only
AHA: 3Q,'05,2

Q0483 Monitor/display module for use with electric ventricular assist device, replacement only
AHA: 3Q,'05,2

Q0484 Monitor/display module for use with electric or electric/pneumatic ventricular assist device, replacement only
AHA: 3Q,'05,2

Q0485 Monitor control cable for use with electric ventricular assist device, replacement only
AHA: 3Q,'05,2

Q0486 Monitor control cable for use with electric/pneumatic ventricular assist device, replacement only
AHA: 3Q,'05,2

Q0487 Leads (pneumatic/electrical) for use with any type electric/pneumatic ventricular assist device, replacement only
AHA: 3Q,'05,2

Q0488 Power pack base for use with electric ventricular assist device, replacement only
AHA: 3Q,'05,2

Q0489 Power pack base for use with electric/pneumatic ventricular assist device, replacement only
AHA: 3Q,'05,2

Q0490 Emergency power source for use with electric ventricular assist device, replacement only
AHA: 3Q,'05,2

Q0491 Emergency power source for use with electric/pneumatic ventricular assist device, replacement only
AHA: 3Q,'05,2

Q0492 Emergency power supply cable for use with electric ventricular assist device, replacement only
AHA: 3Q,'05,2

Q0493 Emergency power supply cable for use with electric/pneumatic ventricular assist device, replacement only
AHA: 3Q,'05,2

Q0494 Emergency hand pump for use with electric or electric/pneumatic ventricular assist device, replacement only
AHA: 3Q,'05,2

Q0495 Battery/power pack charger for use with electric or electric/pneumatic ventricular assist device, replacement only
AHA: 3Q,'05,2

Q0496 Battery for use with electric or electric/pneumatic ventricular assist device, replacement only
AHA: 3Q,'05,2

Q0497 Battery clips for use with electric or electric/pneumatic ventricular assist device, replacement only
AHA: 3Q,'05,2

Q0498 Holster for use with electric or electric/pneumatic ventricular assist device, replacement only
AHA: 3Q,'05,2

Q0499 Belt/vest for use with electric or electric/pneumatic ventricular assist device, replacement only
AHA: 3Q,'05,2

Q0500 Filters for use with electric or electric/pneumatic ventricular assist device, replacement only
The base unit for this code is for each filter.
AHA: 3Q,'05,2

Q0501 Shower cover for use with electric or electric/pneumatic ventricular assist device, replacement only
AHA: 3Q,'05,2

Q0502 Mobility cart for pneumatic ventricular assist device, replacement only
AHA: 3Q,'05,2

Q0503 Battery for pneumatic ventricular assist device, replacement only, each
AHA: 3Q,'05,2

Q0504 Power adapter for pneumatic ventricular assist device, replacement only, vehicle type
AHA: 3Q,'05,2

Q0505 Miscellaneous supply or accessory for use with ventricular assist device
AHA: 3Q,'05,2

Q0510 Pharmacy supply fee for initial immunosuppressive drug(s), first month following transplant
MED: 100-4,4,240

Q0511 Pharmacy supply fee for oral anticancer, oral antiemetic, or immunosuppressive drug(s); for the first prescription in a 30-day period
MED: 100-4,4,240

Q0512 Pharmacy supply fee for oral anticancer, oral antiemetic, or immunosuppressive drug(s); for a subsequent prescription in a 30-day period
MED: 100-4,4,240

Q0513 Pharmacy dispensing fee for inhalation drug(s); per 30 days

Q0514 Pharmacy dispensing fee for inhalation drug(s); per 90 days

Q0515 Injection, sermorelin acetate, 1 mcg
MED: 100-2,15,50

Q1003 New technology, intraocular lens, category 3 (reduced spherical aberration)

Q1004 New technology intraocular lens category 4 as defined in Federal Register notice

Q1005 New technology intraocular lens category 5 as defined in Federal Register notice

Q2004 Irrigation solution for treatment of bladder calculi, for example renacidin, per 500 ml
MED: 100-2,15,50

Q2009 Injection, fosphenytoin, 50 mg
Use this code for Cerebyx.

Q2017 Injection, teniposide, 50 mg
Use this code for Vumon.
MED: 100-2,15,50

Q3001 Radioelements for brachytherapy, any type, each

Q3014 Telehealth originating site facility fee

Q3025 Injection, interferon beta-1a, 11 mcg for intramuscular use
Use this code for Avonex, Rebif. See also J1825.
MED: 100-2,15,50

Q3026 Injection, interferon beta-1a, 11 mcg for subcutaneous use
Use this code for Avonex, Rebif. See also J1825.

Q3031 Collagen skin test
MED: 100-3,230.10

Q4001 Casting supplies, body cast adult, with or without head, plaster
MED: 100-4,4,240; 100-4,20,170

Q4002 Cast supplies, body cast adult, with or without head, fiberglass
MED: 100-4,4,240; 100-4,20,170

Q4003 Cast supplies, shoulder cast, adult (11 years +), plaster
MED: 100-4,4,240; 100-4,20,170

Q4004 Cast supplies, shoulder cast, adult (11 years +), fiberglass
MED: 100-4,4,240; 100-4,20,170

Q4005 Cast supplies, long arm cast, adult (11 years +), plaster
MED: 100-4,4,240; 100-4,20,170

Q4006 Cast supplies, long arm cast, adult (11 years +), fiberglass
MED: 100-4,4,240; 100-4,20,170

Q4007 Cast supplies, long arm cast, pediatric (0–10 years), plaster
MED: 100-4,4,240; 100-4,20,170

Q4008 Cast supplies, long arm cast, pediatric (0–10 years), fiberglass
MED: 100-4,4,240; 100-4,20,170

Q4009 Cast supplies, short arm cast, adult (11 years +), plaster
MED: 100-4,4,240; 100-4,20,170

Q4010 Cast supplies, short arm cast, adult (11 years +), fiberglass
MED: 100-4,4,240; 100-4,20,170

Q4011 Cast supplies, short arm cast, pediatric (0–10 years), plaster
MED: 100-4,4,240; 100-4,20,170

Q4012 Cast supplies, short arm cast, pediatric (0–10 years), fiberglass
MED: 100-4,4,240; 100-4,20,170

Q4013 Cast supplies, gauntlet cast (includes lower forearm and hand), adult (11 years +), plaster
MED: 100-4,4,240; 100-4,20,170

Q4014 Cast supplies, gauntlet cast (includes lower forearm and hand), adult (11 years +), fiberglass
MED: 100-4,4,240; 100-4,20,170

Q4015 Cast supplies, gauntlet cast (includes lower forearm and hand), pediatric (0–10 years), plaster
MED: 100-4,4,240; 100-4,20,170

Q4016 Cast supplies, gauntlet cast (includes lower forearm and hand), pediatric (0–10 years), fiberglass
MED: 100-4,4,240; 100-4,20,170

Q4017 Cast supplies, long arm splint, adult (11 years +), plaster
MED: 100-4,4,240; 100-4,20,170

Q4018 Cast supplies, long arm splint, adult (11 years +), fiberglass
MED: 100-4,4,240; 100-4,20,170

Q4019 Cast supplies, long arm splint, pediatric (0–10 years), plaster
MED: 100-4,4,240; 100-4,20,170

Q4020 Cast supplies, long arm splint, pediatric (0–10 years), fiberglass
MED: 100-4,4,240; 100-4,20,170

Q4021 Cast supplies, short arm splint, adult (11 years +), plaster
MED: 100-4,4,240; 100-4,20,170

Q4022 Cast supplies, short arm splint, adult (11 years +), fiberglass
MED: 100-4,4,240; 100-4,20,170

Q4023 Cast supplies, short arm splint, pediatric (0–10 years), plaster
MED: 100-4,4,240; 100-4,20,170

Q4024 Cast supplies, short arm splint, pediatric (0–10 years), fiberglass
MED: 100-4,4,240; 100-4,20,170

Q4025 Cast supplies, hip spica (one or both legs), adult (11 years +), plaster
MED: 100-4,4,240; 100-4,20,170

Q4026 Cast supplies, hip spica (one or both legs), adult (11 years +), fiberglass
MED: 100-4,4,240; 100-4,20,170

Q4027 Cast supplies, hip spica (one or both legs), pediatric (0–10 years), plaster
MED: 100-4,4,240; 100-4,20,170

Q4028 Cast supplies, hip spica (one or both legs), pediatric (0–10 years), fiberglass
MED: 100-4,4,240; 100-4,20,170

Q4029 Cast supplies, long leg cast, adult (11 years +), plaster
MED: 100-4,4,240; 100-4,20,170

Q4030 Cast supplies, long leg cast, adult (11 years +), fiberglass
MED: 100-4,4,240; 100-4,20,170

Q4031 Cast supplies, long leg cast, pediatric (0–10 years), plaster
MED: 100-4,4,240; 100-4,20,170

Q4032 Cast supplies, long leg cast, pediatric (0–10 years), fiberglass
MED: 100-4,4,240; 100-4,20,170

Q4033 Cast supplies, long leg cylinder cast, adult (11 years +), plaster
MED: 100-4,4,240; 100-4,20,170

Q4034 Cast supplies, long leg cylinder cast, adult (11 years +), fiberglass
MED: 100-4,4,240; 100-4,20,170

Q4035 Cast supplies, long leg cylinder cast, pediatric (0–10 years), plaster
MED: 100-4,4,240; 100-4,20,170

Q4036 Cast supplies, long leg cylinder cast, pediatric (0–10 years), fiberglass
MED: 100-4,4,240; 100-4,20,170

Q4037 Cast supplies, short leg cast, adult (11 years +), plaster
MED: 100-4,4,240; 100-4,20,170

Q4038 Cast supplies, short leg cast, adult (11 years +), fiberglass
MED: 100-4,4,240; 100-4,20,170

Q4039 Cast supplies, short leg cast, pediatric (0–10 years), plaster
MED: 100-4,4,240; 100-4,20,170

Q4040 Cast supplies, short leg cast, pediatric (0–10 years), fiberglass
MED: 100-4,4,240; 100-4,20,170

Q4041 Cast supplies, long leg splint, adult (11 years +), plaster
MED: 100-4,4,240; 100-4,20,170

Q4042 Cast supplies, long leg splint, adult (11 years +), fiberglass
MED: 100-4,4,240; 100-4,20,170

Q4043 Cast supplies, long leg splint, pediatric (0–10 years), plaster
MED: 100-4,4,240; 100-4,20,170

Q4044 Cast supplies, long leg splint, pediatric (0–10 years), fiberglass
MED: 100-4,4,240; 100-4,20,170

Q4045 Cast supplies, short leg splint, adult (11 years +), plaster
MED: 100-4,4,240; 100-4,20,170

Q4046 Cast supplies, short leg splint, adult (11 years +), fiberglass
MED: 100-4,4,240; 100-4,20,170

Q4047 Cast supplies, short leg splint, pediatric (0–10 years), plaster
MED: 100-4,4,240; 100-4,20,170

Q4048 Cast supplies, short leg splint, pediatric (0–10 years), fiberglass
MED: 100-4,4,240; 100-4,20,170

Q4049 Finger splint, static
MED: 100-4,4,240; 100-4,20,170

Q4050 Cast supplies, for unlisted types and materials of casts
MED: 100-4,4,240; 100-4,20,170

Q4051 Splint supplies, miscellaneous (includes thermoplastics, strapping, fasteners, padding and other supplies)
MED: 100-4,4,240; 100-4,20,170

Q4080 Iloprost, inhalation solution, FDA-approved final product, noncompounded, administered through DME, unit dose form, 20 mcg
AHA: 3Q,'05,7

Q4081 Injection, epoetin alfa, 100 units (for ESRD on dialysis)

Q4082 Drug or biological, not otherwise classified, Part B drug competitive acquisition program (CAP)

Q4100 Skin substitute, not otherwise specified

Q4101 Skin substitute, Apligraf, per sq cm

Q4102 Skin substitute, Oasis wound matrix, per sq cm

Q4103 Skin substitute, Oasis burn matrix, per sq cm

Q4104 Skin substitute, Integra bilayer matrix wound dressing (BMWD), per sq cm

Q4105 Skin substitute, Integra dermal regeneration template (DRT), per sq cm

Q4106 Skin substitute, Dermagraft, per sq cm

Q4107 Skin substitute, GRAFTJACKET, per sq cm

Q4108 Skin substitute, Integra matrix, per sq cm

Q4109 Skin substitute, TissueMend, per sq cm

Q4110 Skin substitute, PriMatrix, per sq cm

Q4111 Skin substitute, GammaGraft, per sq cm

Q4112 Allograft, Cymetra, injectable, 1 cc

Q4113 Allograft, GRAFTJACKET express, injectable, 1cc

Q4114 Integra flowable wound matrix, injectable, 1 cc

Q5001 Hospice care provided in patient's home/residence

Q5002 Hospice care provided in assisted living facility

Q5003 Hospice care provided in nursing long-term care facility (LTC) or nonskilled nursing facility (NF)

Q5004 Hospice care provided in skilled nursing facility (SNF)

Q5005 Hospice care provided in inpatient hospital

Q5006 Hospice care provided in inpatient hospice facility

Q5007 Hospice care provided in long-term care facility

Q5008 Hospice care provided in inpatient psychiatric facility

Q5009 Hospice care provided in place not otherwise specified (NOS)

Q9951 Low osmolar contrast material, 400 or greater mg/ml iodine concentration, per ml

Q9953 Injection, iron-based magnetic resonance contrast agent, per ml

Q9954 Oral magnetic resonance contrast agent, per 100 ml

Q9955 Injection, perflexane lipid microspheres, per ml

Q9956 Injection, octafluoropropane microspheres, per ml

Q9957 Injection, perflutren lipid microspheres, per ml

Q9958 High osmolar contrast material, up to 149 mg/ml iodine concentration, per ml
AHA: 3Q,'05,7

Q9959 High osmolar contrast material, 150–199 mg/ml iodine concentration, per ml
AHA: 3Q,'05,7

Q9960 High osmolar contrast material, 200–249 mg/ml iodine concentration, per ml
AHA: 3Q,'05,7

Q9961 High osmolar contrast material, 250–299 mg/ml iodine concentration, per ml
AHA: 3Q,'05,7

Q9962 High osmolar contrast material, 300–349 mg/ml iodine concentration, per ml
AHA: 3Q,'05,7

Q9963 High osmolar contrast material, 350–399 mg/ml iodine concentration, per ml
AHA: 3Q,'05,7

Q9964 **High osmolar contrast material, 400 or greater mg/ml iodine concentration, per ml**

AHA: 3Q,'05,7

Q9965 **Low osmolar contrast material, 100–199 mg/ml iodine concentration, per ml**

Use this code for Omnipaque 140, Omnipaque 180, Optiray 160, Optiray 140.

Q9966 **Low osmolar contrast material, 200–299 mg/ml iodine concentration, per ml**

Use this code for Omnipaque 240, Optiray 240.

Q9967 **Low osmolar contrast material, 300–399 mg/ml iodine concentration, per ml**

Use this code for Omnipaque 300, Omnipaque 350, Optiray, Optiray 300, Optiray 320, Oxilan 300, Oxilan 350.

DIAGNOSTIC RADIOLOGY SERVICES R0000-R5999

R codes are used for the transportation of portable x-ray and/or EKG equipment.

R0070 Transportation of portable x-ray equipment and personnel to home or nursing home, per trip to facility or location, one patient seen
Only a single, reasonable transportation charge is allowed for each trip the portable x-ray supplier makes to a location. When more than one patient is x-rayed at the same location, prorate the single allowable transport charge among all patients.

R0075 Transportation of portable x-ray equipment and personnel to home or nursing home, per trip to facility or location, more than one patient seen
Only a single, reasonable transportation charge is allowed for each trip the portable x-ray supplier makes to a location. When more than one patient is x-rayed at the same location, prorate the single allowable transport charge among all patients.

R0076 Transportation of portable EKG to facility or location, per patient
Only a single, reasonable transportation charge is allowed for each trip the portable EKG supplier makes to a location. When more than one patient is tested at the same location, prorate the single allowable transport charge among all patients.

MED: 100-1,5,90.2; 100-3,20.15

TEMPORARY NATIONAL CODES (NON-MEDICARE) S0000-S9999

The S codes are used by the Blue Cross/Blue Shield Association (BCBSA) and the Health Insurance Association of America (HIAA) to report drugs, services, and supplies for which there are no national codes but for which codes are needed by the private sector to implement policies, programs, or claims processing. They are for the purpose of meeting the particular needs of the private sector. These codes are also used by the Medicaid program, but they are not payable by Medicare.

S0012 Butorphanol tartrate, nasal spray, 25 mg
Use this code for Stadol NS.

S0014 Tacrine HCl, 10 mg
Use this code for Cognex.

S0017 Injection, aminocaproic acid, 5 g
Use this code for Amicar.

S0020 Injection, bupivicaine HCl, 30 ml
Use this code for Marcaine, Sensorcaine.

S0021 Injection, cefoperazone sodium, 1 g
Use this code for Cefobid.

S0023 Injection, cimetidine HCl, 300 mg
Use this code for Tagamet HCl.

S0028 Injection, famotidine, 20 mg
Use this code for Pepcid.

S0030 Injection, metronidazole, 500 mg
Use this code for Flagyl IV RTU.

S0032 Injection, nafcillin sodium, 2 g
Use this code for Nallpen, Unipen.

S0034 Injection, ofloxacin, 400 mg
Use this code for Floxin IV.

S0039 Injection, sulfamethoxazole and trimethoprim, 10 ml
Use this code for Bactrim IV, Septra IV, SMZ-TMP, Sulfutrim.

S0040 Injection, ticarcillin disodium and clavulanate potassium, 3.1 g
Use this code for Timentin.

S0073 Injection, aztreonam, 500 mg
Use this code for Azactam.

S0074 Injection, cefotetan disodium, 500 mg
Use this code for Cefotan.

S0077 Injection, clindamycin phosphate, 300 mg
Use this code for Cleocin Phosphate.

S0078 Injection, fosphenytoin sodium, 750 mg
Use this code for Cerebryx.

S0080 Injection, pentamidine isethionate, 300 mg
Use this code for NebuPent, Pentam 300, Pentacarinat. See also code J2545.

S0081 Injection, piperacillin sodium, 500 mg
Use this code for Pipracil.

S0088 Imatinib, 100 mg
Use this code for Gleevec.

S0090 Sildenafil citrate, 25 mg
Use this code for Viagra.

S0091 Granisetron HCl, 1 mg (for circumstances falling under the Medicare statute, use Q0166)
Use this code for Kytril.

S0092 Injection, hydromorphone HCl, 250 mg (loading dose for infusion pump)
Use this code for Dilaudid, Hydromophone. See also J1170.

S0093 Injection, morphine sulfate, 500 mg (loading dose for infusion pump)
Use this code for Duramorph, MS Contin, Morphine Sulfate. See also J2270, J2271, J2275.

S0104 Zidovudine, oral, 100 mg
See also J3485 for Retrovir.

S0106 Bupropion HCl sustained release tablet, 150 mg, per bottle of 60 tablets
Use this code for Wellbutrin SR tablets.

S0108 Mercaptopurine, oral, 50 mg
Use this code for Purinethol oral.

S0109 Methadone, oral, 5 mg
Use this code for Dolophine.

S0117 Tretinoin, topical, 5 g

S0122 Injection, menotropins, 75 IU
Use this code for Humegon, Pergonal, Repronex.

S0126 Injection, follitropin alfa, 75 IU
Use this code for Gonal-F.

S0128 Injection, follitropin beta, 75 IU
Use this code for Follistim.

S0132 Injection, ganirelix acetate, 250 mcg
Use this code for Antagon.

S0136 Clozapine, 25 mg
Use this code for Clozaril.

S0137 Didanosine (ddI), 25 mg
Use this code for Videx.

S0138 Finasteride, 5 mg
Use this code for Propecia (oral), Proscar (oral).

S0139 Minoxidil, 10 mg
Use this code for Loniten (oral).

S0140 Saquinavir, 200 mg
Use this code for Fortovase (oral), Invirase (oral).

S0142 Colistimethate sodium, inhalation solution administered through DME, concentrated form, per mg

S0145 Injection, pegylated interferon alfa-2a, 180 mcg per ml
Use this code for Pegasys.

S0146 Injection, pegylated interferon alfa-2b, 10 mcg per 0.5 ml

S0155 Sterile dilutant for epoprostenol, 50 ml
Use this code for Flolan.

S0156 Exemestane, 25 mg
Use this code for Aromasin.

S0157 Becaplermin gel 0.01%, 0.5 gm
Use this code for Regraex Gel.

S0160 Dextroamphetamine sulfate, 5 mg

S0161 Calcitrol, 0.25 mg

S0162 Injection, efalizumab, 125 mg
Use this code for Raptiva.

S0164 Injection, pantoprazole sodium, 40 mg
Use this code for Protonix IV.

S0166 Injection, olanzapine, 2.5 mg
Use this code for Zyprexa.

S0170 Anastrozole, oral, 1 mg
Use this code for Arimidex.

S0171 Injection, bumetanide, 0.5 mg
Use this code for Bumex.

S0172 Chlorambucil, oral, 2 mg
Use this code for Leukeran.

S0174 Dolasetron mesylate, oral 50 mg (for circumstances falling under the Medicare statute, use Q0180)
Use this code for Anzemet.

S0175 Flutamide, oral, 125 mg
Use this code for Eulexin.

S0176 Hydroxyurea, oral, 500 mg
Use this code for Droxia, Hydrea, Mylocel.

S0177 Levamisole HCl, oral, 50 mg
Use this code for Ergamisol.

S0178 Lomustine, oral, 10 mg
Use this code for Ceenu.

MED: 100-4,17,80.2

S0179 Megestrol acetate, oral, 20 mg
Use this code for Megace.

S0181 Ondansetron HCl, oral, 4 mg (for circumstances falling under the Medicare statute, use Q0179)
Use this code for Zofran.

S0182 Procarbazine HCl, oral, 50 mg
Use this code for Matulane.

S0183 Prochlorperazine maleate, oral, 5 mg (for circumstances falling under the Medicare statute, use Q0164-Q0165)
Use this code for Compazine.

S0187 Tamoxifen citrate, oral, 10 mg
Use this code for Nolvadex.

S0189 Testosterone pellet, 75 mg

S0190 Mifepristone, oral, 200 mg
Use this code for Mifoprex 200 mg oral.

S0191 Misoprostol, oral, 200 mcg

S0194 Dialysis/stress vitamin supplement, oral, 100 capsules

S0195 Pneumococcal conjugate vaccine, polyvalent, intramuscular, for children from 5 years to 9 years of age who have not previously received the vaccine
Use this code for Pneumovax II.

S0196 Injectable poly-l-lactic acid, restorative implant, 1 ml, face (deep dermis, subcutaneous layers)

S0197 Prenatal vitamins, 30-day supply

S0199 Medically induced abortion by oral ingestion of medication including all associated services and supplies (e.g., patient counseling, office visits, confirmation of pregnancy by HCG, ultrasound to confirm duration of pregnancy, ultrasound to confirm completion of abortion) except drugs

S0201 Partial hospitalization services, less than 24 hours, per diem

S0207 Paramedic intercept, nonhospital-based ALS service (nonvoluntary), nontransport

S0208 Paramedic intercept, hospital-based ALS service (nonvoluntary), nontransport

S0209 Wheelchair van, mileage, per mile

S0215 Nonemergency transportation; mileage, per mile
See also codes A0021-A0999 for transportation.

S0220 Medical conference by a physician with interdisciplinary team of health professionals or representatives of community agencies to coordinate activities of patient care (patient is present); approximately 30 minutes

S0221 Medical conference by a physician with interdisciplinary team of health professionals or representatives of community agencies to coordinate activities of patient care (patient is present); approximately 60 minutes

S0250 Comprehensive geriatric assessment and treatment planning performed by assessment team

S0255 Hospice referral visit (advising patient and family of care options) performed by nurse, social worker, or other designated staff

S0257 Counseling and discussion regarding advance directives or end of life care planning and decisions, with patient and/or surrogate (list separately in addition to code for appropriate evaluation and management service)

S0260 History and physical (outpatient or office) related to surgical procedure (list separately in addition to code for appropriate evaluation and management service)

S0265 Genetic counseling, under physician supervision, each 15 minutes

S0270 Physician management of patient home care, standard monthly case rate (per 30 days)

S0271 Physician management of patient home care, hospice monthly case rate (per 30 days)

S0272 Physician management of patient home care, episodic care monthly case rate (per 30 days)

S0273 Physician visit at member's home, outside of a capitation arrangement

S0274 Nurse practitioner visit at member's home, outside of a capitation arrangement

S0302 Completed early periodic screening diagnosis and treatment (EPSDT) service (list in addition to code for appropriate evaluation and management service)

S0310 Hospitalist services (list separately in addition to code for appropriate evaluation and management service)

S0315 Disease management program; initial assessment and initiation of the program

S0316 Disease management program, follow-up/reassessment

S0317 Disease management program; per diem

S0320 Telephone calls by a registered nurse to a disease management program member for monitoring purposes; per month

S0340 Lifestyle modification program for management of coronary artery disease, including all supportive services; first quarter/stage

S0341 Lifestyle modification program for management of coronary artery disease, including all supportive services; second or third quarter/stage

S0342 Lifestyle modification program for management of coronary artery disease, including all supportive services; 4th quarter / stage

S0345 Electrocardiographic monitoring utilizing a home computerized telemetry station with automatic activation and real-time notification of monitoring station, 24-hour attended monitoring, including recording, monitoring, receipt of transmissions, analysis, and physician review and interpretation; per 24-hour period

S0346 Electrocardiographic monitoring utilizing a home computerized telemetry station with automatic activation and real-time notification of monitoring station, 24-hour attended monitoring, including recording, monitoring, receipt of transmissions, and analysis; per 24-hour period

S0347 Electrocardiographic monitoring utilizing a home computerized telemetry station with automatic activation and real-time notification of monitoring station, 24-hour attended monitoring, including physician review and interpretation; 24-hour period

S0390 Routine foot care; removal and/or trimming of corns, calluses and/or nails and preventive maintenance in specific medical conditions (e.g., diabetes), per visit

S0395 Impression casting of a foot performed by a practitioner other than the manufacturer of the orthotic

S0400 Global fee for extracorporeal shock wave lithotripsy treatment of kidney stone(s)

S0500 Disposable contact lens, per lens

S0504 Single vision prescription lens (safety, athletic, or sunglass), per lens

S0506 Bifocal vision prescription lens (safety, athletic, or sunglass), per lens

S0508 Trifocal vision prescription lens (safety, athletic, or sunglass), per lens

S0510 Nonprescription lens (safety, athletic, or sunglass), per lens

S0512 Daily wear specialty contact lens, per lens

S0514 Color contact lens, per lens

S0515 Scleral lens, liquid bandage device, per lens

S0516 Safety eyeglass frames

S0518 Sunglasses frames

S0580 Polycarbonate lens (list this code in addition to the basic code for the lens)

S0581 Nonstandard lens (list this code in addition to the basic code for the lens)

S0590 Integral lens service, miscellaneous services reported separately

S0592 Comprehensive contact lens evaluation

S0595 Dispensing new spectacle lenses for patient supplied frame

S0601 Screening proctoscopy
MED: 100-4,4,240

S0605 Digital rectal examination, annual

S0610 Annual gynecological examination, new patient
MED: 100-4,4,240

S0612 Annual gynecological examination, established patient
MED: 100-4,4,240

S0613 Annual gynecological examination; clinical breast examination without pelvic evaluation

S0618 Audiometry for hearing aid evaluation to determine the level and degree of hearing loss

S0620 Routine ophthalmological examination including refraction; new patient

S0621 Routine ophthalmological examination including refraction; established patient

S0622 Physical exam for college, new or established patient (list separately in addition to appropriate evaluation and management code)

S0625 Retinal telescreening by digital imaging of multiple different fundus areas to screen for vision-threatening conditions, including imaging, interpretation and report

S0630 Removal of sutures; by a physician other than the physician who originally closed the wound

S0800 Laser in situ keratomileusis (LASIK)

S0810 Photorefractive keratectomy (PRK)

S0812 Phototherapeutic keratectomy (PTK)

S1001 Deluxe item, patient aware (list in addition to code for basic item)
MED: 100-2,1,10.1.4

S1002 Customized item (list in addition to code for basic item)

S1015 IV tubing extension set

S1016 Non-PVC (polyvinyl chloride) intravenous administration set, for use with drugs that are not stable in PVC e.g., Paclitaxel

S1030 Continuous noninvasive glucose monitoring device, purchase (for physician interpretation of data, use CPT code)

S1031 Continuous noninvasive glucose monitoring device, rental, including sensor, sensor replacement, and download to monitor (for physician interpretation of data, use CPT code)

S1040 Cranial remolding orthotic, pediatric, rigid, with soft interface material, custom fabricated, includes fitting and adjustment(s)

S2053 Transplantation of small intestine and liver allografts

S2054 Transplantation of multivisceral organs

S2055 Harvesting of donor multivisceral organs, with preparation and maintenance of allografts; from cadaver donor

S2060 Lobar lung transplantation

S2061 Donor lobectomy (lung) for transplantation, living donor

S2065 Simultaneous pancreas kidney transplantation

S2066 Breast reconstruction with gluteal artery perforator (GAP) flap, including harvesting of the flap, microvascular transfer, closure of donor site and shaping the flap into a breast, unilateral

S2067 Breast reconstruction of a single breast with "stacked" deep inferior epigastric perforator (DIEP) flap(s) and/or gluteal artery perforator (GAP) flap(s), including harvesting of the flap(s), microvascular transfer, closure of donor site(s) and shaping the flap into a breast, unilateral

S2068 Breast reconstruction with deep inferior epigastric perforator (DIEP) flap or superficial inferior epigastric artery (SIEA) flap, including harvesting of the flap, microvascular transfer, closure of donor site and shaping the flap into a breast, unilateral

S2070 Cystourethroscopy, with ureteroscopy and/or pyeloscopy; with endoscopic laser treatment of ureteral calculi (includes ureteral catheterization)

S2079 Laparoscopic esophagomyotomy (Heller type)

S2080 Laser-assisted uvulopalatoplasty (LAUP)

S2083 Adjustment of gastric band diameter via subcutaneous port by injection or aspiration of saline

S2095 Transcatheter occlusion or embolization for tumor destruction, percutaneous, any method, using yttrium-90 microspheres

S2102 Islet cell tissue transplant from pancreas; allogeneic

S2103 Adrenal tissue transplant to brain

S2107 Adoptive immunotherapy i.e. development of specific antitumor reactivity (e.g., tumor-infiltrating lymphocyte therapy) per course of treatment

S2112 Arthroscopy, knee, surgical for harvesting of cartilage (chondrocyte cells)

S2115 Osteotomy, periacetabular, with internal fixation

S2117 Arthroereisis, subtalar

S2118 Metal-on-metal total hip resurfacing, including acetabular and femoral components

S2120 Low density lipoprotein (LDL) apheresis using heparin-induced extracorporeal LDL precipitation

S2140 Cord blood harvesting for transplantation, allogeneic

S2142 Cord blood-derived stem-cell transplantation, allogeneic

S2150 Bone marrow or blood-derived stem cells (peripheral or umbilical), allogeneic or autologous, harvesting, transplantation, and related complications including pheresis and cell preparation/storage; marrow ablative therapy; drugs, supplies, hospitalization with outpatient follow-up; medical/surgical, diagnostic, emergency, and rehabilitative services; and the number of days of pre- and posttransplant care in the global definition

S2152 Solid organ(s), complete or segmental, single organ or combination of organs; deceased or living donor (s), procurement, transplantation, and related complications; including: drugs; supplies; hospitalization with outpatient follow-up; medical/surgical, diagnostic, emergency, and rehabilitative services, and the number of days of pre and posttransplant care in the global definition

S2202 Echosclerotherapy

S2205 Minimally invasive direct coronary artery bypass surgery involving mini-thoracotomy or mini-sternotomy surgery, performed under direct vision; using arterial graft(s), single coronary arterial graft

S2206 Minimally invasive direct coronary artery bypass surgery involving mini-thoracotomy or mini-sternotomy surgery, performed under direct vision; using arterial graft(s), 2 coronary arterial grafts

S2207 Minimally invasive direct coronary artery bypass surgery involving mini-thoracotomy or mini-sternotomy surgery, performed under direct vision; using venous graft only, single coronary venous graft

S2208 Minimally invasive direct coronary artery bypass surgery involving mini-thoracotomy or mini-sternotomy surgery, performed under direct vision; using single arterial and venous graft(s), single venous graft

S2209 Minimally invasive direct coronary artery bypass surgery involving mini-thoracotomy or mini-sternotomy surgery, performed under direct vision; using 2 arterial grafts and single venous graft

S2225 Myringotomy, laser-assisted

S2230 Implantation of magnetic component of semi-implantable hearing device on ossicles in middle ear

S2235 Implantation of auditory brain stem implant

S2260 Induced abortion, 17 to 24 weeks

S2265 Induced abortion, 25 to 28 weeks

S2266 Induced abortion, 29 to 31 weeks

S2267 Induced abortion, 32 weeks or greater

S2270 Insertion of vaginal cylinder for application of radiation source or clinical brachytherapy (report separately in addition to radiation source delivery)

S2300 Arthroscopy, shoulder, surgical; with thermally-induced capsulorrhaphy

S2325 Hip core decompression

S2340 Chemodenervation of abductor muscle(s) of vocal cord

S2341 Chemodenervation of adductor muscle(s) of vocal cord

S2342 Nasal endoscopy for postoperative debridement following functional endoscopic sinus surgery, nasal and/or sinus cavity(s), unilateral or bilateral

S2344 Nasal/sinus endoscopy, surgical; with enlargement of sinus ostium opening using inflatable device (i.e., balloon sinuplasty)

S2348 Decompression procedure, percutaneous, of nucleus pulposus of intervertebral disc, using radiofrequency energy, single or multiple levels, lumbar

S2350 Diskectomy, anterior, with decompression of spinal cord and/or nerve root(s), including osteophytectomy; lumbar, single interspace

S2351 Diskectomy, anterior, with decompression of spinal cord and/or nerve root(s), including osteophytectomy; lumbar, each additional interspace (list separately in addition to code for primary procedure)

S2360 Percutaneous vertebroplasty, one vertebral body, unilateral or bilateral injection; cervical

S2361 Each additional cervical vertebral body (list separately in addition to code for primary procedure)

S2400 Repair, congenital diaphragmatic hernia in the fetus using temporary tracheal occlusion, procedure performed in utero

S2401 Repair, urinary tract obstruction in the fetus, procedure performed in utero

S2402 Repair, congenital cystic adenomatoid malformation in the fetus, procedure performed in utero

S2403 Repair, extralobar pulmonary sequestration in the fetus, procedure performed in utero

S2404 Repair, myelomeningocele in the fetus, procedure performed in utero

S2405 Repair of sacrococcygeal teratoma in the fetus, procedure performed in utero

S2409 Repair, congenital malformation of fetus, procedure performed in utero, not otherwise classified

S2411 Fetoscopic laser therapy for treatment of twin-to-twin transfusion syndrome

S2900 Surgical techniques requiring use of robotic surgical system (list separately in addition to code for primary procedure)

S3000 Diabetic indicator; retinal eye exam, dilated, bilateral

S3005 Performance measurement, evaluation of patient self assessment, depression

S3600 STAT laboratory request (situations other than S3601)

S3601 Emergency STAT laboratory charge for patient who is homebound or residing in a nursing facility

S3620 Newborn metabolic screening panel, includes test kit, postage and the laboratory tests specified by the state for inclusion in this panel (e.g., galactose; hemoglobin, electrophoresis; hydroxyprogesterone, 17-d; phenylanine (PKU); and thyroxine, total)

S3625 Maternal serum triple marker screen including alpha-fetoprotein (AFP), estriol, and human chorionic gonadotropin (HCG)

S3626 Maternal serum quadruple marker screen including alpha-fetoprotein (AFP), estriol, human chorionic gonadotropin hCG) and inhibin A

S3628 Placental alpha microglobulin-1 rapid immunoassay for detection of rupture of fetal membranes

S3630 Eosinophil count, blood, direct

S3645 HIV-1 antibody testing of oral mucosal transudate

S3650 Saliva test, hormone level; during menopause

S3652 Saliva test, hormone level; to assess preterm labor risk

S3655 Antisperm antibodies test (immunobead)

S3708 Gastrointestinal fat absorption study

S3711 Circulating tumor cell test

S3800 Genetic testing for amyotrophic lateral sclerosis (ALS)

S3818 Complete gene sequence analysis; BRCA1 gene

S3819 Complete gene sequence analysis; BRCA2 gene

S3820 Complete BRCA1 and BRCA2 gene sequence analysis for susceptibility to breast and ovarian cancer

S3822 Single mutation analysis (in individual with a known BRCA1 or BRCA2 mutation in the family) for susceptibility to breast and ovarian cancer

S3823 Three-mutation BRCA1 and BRCA2 analysis for susceptibility to breast and ovarian cancer in Ashkenazi individuals

S3828 Complete gene sequence analysis; MLH1 gene

S3829 Complete gene sequence analysis; MLH2 gene

S3830 Complete MLH1 and MLH2 gene sequence analysis for hereditary nonpolyposis colorectal cancer (HNPCC) genetic testing

S3831 Single-mutation analysis (in individual with a known MLH1 and MLH2 mutation in the family) for hereditary nonpolyposis colorectal cancer (HNPCC) genetic testing

S3833 Complete APC gene sequence analysis for susceptibility to familial adenomatous polyposis (FAP) and attenuated fap

S3834 Single-mutation analysis (in individual with a known APC mutation in the family) for susceptibility to familial adenomatous polyposis (FAP) and attenuated FAP

S3835 Complete gene sequence analysis for cystic fibrosis genetic testing

S3837 Complete gene sequence analysis for hemochromatosis genetic testing

S3840 DNA analysis for germline mutations of the RET proto-oncogene for susceptibility to multiple endocrine neoplasia type 2

S3841 Genetic testing for retinoblastoma

S3842 Genetic testing for Von Hippel-Lindau disease

S3843 DNA analysis of the F5 gene for susceptibility to factor V Leiden thrombophilia

S3844 DNA analysis of the connexin 26 gene (GJB2) for susceptibility to congenital, profound deafness

S3845 Genetic testing for alpha-thalassemia

S3846 Genetic testing for hemoglobin E beta-thalassemia

S3847 Genetic testing for Tay-Sachs disease

S3848 Genetic testing for Gaucher disease

S3849 Genetic testing for Niemann-Pick disease

S3850 Genetic testing for sickle cell anemia

S3851 Genetic testing for Canavan disease

S3852 DNA analysis for APOE epsilon 4 allele for susceptibility to Alzheimer's disease

S3853 Genetic testing for myotonic muscular dystrophy

S3854 Gene expression profiling panel for use in the management of breast cancer treatment

S3855 Genetic testing for detection of mutations in the presenilin - 1 gene

S3860 Genetic testing, comprehensive cardiac ion channel analysis, for variants in 5 major cardiac ion channel genes for individuals with high index of suspicion for familial long QT syndrome (LQTS) or related syndromes

S3861 Genetic testing, sodium channel, voltage-gated, type V, alpha subunit (SCN5A) and variants for suspected Brugada Syndrome

S3862 Genetic testing, family-specific ion channel analysis, for blood-relatives of individuals (index case) who have previously tested positive for a genetic variant of a cardiac ion channel syndrome using either one of the above test configurations or confirmed results from another laboratory

S3890 DNA analysis, fecal, for colorectal cancer screening

S3900 Surface electromyography (EMG)

S3902 Ballistocardiogram

S3904 Masters 2 step

S3905 Noninvasive electrodiagnostic testing with automatic computerized hand-held device to stimulate and measure neuromuscular signals in diagnosing and evaluating systemic and entrapment neuropathies

S4005 Interim labor facility global (labor occurring but not resulting in delivery)

S4011 In vitro fertilization; including but not limited to identification and incubation of mature oocytes, fertilization with sperm, incubation of embryo(s), and subsequent visualization for determination of development

S4013 Complete cycle, gamete intrafallopian transfer (GIFT), case rate

S4014 Complete cycle, zygote intrafallopian transfer (ZIFT), case rate

S4015 Complete in vitro fertilization cycle, not otherwise specified, case rate

S4016 Frozen in vitro fertilization cycle, case rate

S4017 Incomplete cycle, treatment cancelled prior to stimulation, case rate

S4018 Frozen embryo transfer procedure cancelled before transfer, case rate

S4020 In vitro fertilization procedure cancelled before aspiration, case rate

S4021 In vitro fertilization procedure cancelled after aspiration, case rate

S4022 Assisted oocyte fertilization, case rate

S4023 Donor egg cycle, incomplete, case rate

S4025 Donor services for in vitro fertilization (sperm or embryo), case rate

S4026 Procurement of donor sperm from sperm bank

S4027 Storage of previously frozen embryos

S4028 Microsurgical epididymal sperm aspiration (MESA)

S4030 Sperm procurement and cryopreservation services; initial visit

S4031 Sperm procurement and cryopreservation services; subsequent visit

S4035 Stimulated intrauterine insemination (IUI), case rate

S4037 Cryopreserved embryo transfer, case rate

S4040 Monitoring and storage of cryopreserved embryos, per 30 days

S4042 Management of ovulation induction (interpretation of diagnostic tests and studies, nonface-to-face medical management of the patient), per cycle

S4981 Insertion of levonorgestrel-releasing intrauterine system

S4989 Contraceptive intrauterine device (e.g., Progestacert IUD), including implants and supplies

S4990 Nicotine patches, legend

S4991 Nicotine patches, nonlegend

S4993 Contraceptive pills for birth control

S4995 Smoking cessation gum

S5000 Prescription drug, generic

S5001 Prescription drug, brand name

S5010 5% dextrose and 0.45% normal saline, 1000 ml

S5011 5% dextrose in lactated ringer's, 1000 ml

S5012 5% dextrose with potassium chloride, 1000 ml

S5013 5% dextrose/0.45% normal saline with potassium chloride and magnesium sulfate, 1000 ml

S5014 5% dextrose/0.45% normal saline with potassium chloride and magnesium sulfate, 1500 ml

S5035 Home infusion therapy, routine service of infusion device (e.g., pump maintenance)

S5036 Home infusion therapy, repair of infusion device (e.g., pump repair)

S5100 Day care services, adult; per 15 minutes

S5101 Day care services, adult; per half day

S5102 Day care services, adult; per diem

S5105 Day care services, center-based; services not included in program fee, per diem

S5108 Home care training to home care client, per 15 minutes

S5109 Home care training to home care client, per session

S5110 Home care training, family; per 15 minutes

S5111 Home care training, family; per session

S5115 Home care training, nonfamily; per 15 minutes

S5116 Home care training, nonfamily; per session

S5120 Chore services; per 15 minutes

S5121 Chore services; per diem

S5125 Attendant care services; per 15 minutes

S5126 Attendant care services; per diem

S5130 Homemaker service, NOS; per 15 minutes

S5131 Homemaker service, NOS; per diem

S5135 Companion care, adult (e.g., IADL/ADL); per 15 minutes

S5136 Companion care, adult (e.g., IADL/ADL); per diem

S5140 Foster care, adult; per diem

S5141 Foster care, adult; per month

S5145 Foster care, therapeutic, child; per diem

S5146 Foster care, therapeutic, child; per month

S5150 Unskilled respite care, not hospice; per 15 minutes

S5151 Unskilled respite care, not hospice; per diem

S5160 Emergency response system; installation and testing

S5161 Emergency response system; service fee, per month (excludes installation and testing)

S5162 Emergency response system; purchase only

S5165 Home modifications; per service

S5170 Home delivered meals, including preparation; per meal

S5175 Laundry service, external, professional; per order

S5180 Home health respiratory therapy, initial evaluation

S5181 Home health respiratory therapy, NOS, per diem

S5185 Medication reminder service, nonface-to-face; per month

S5190 Wellness assessment, performed by nonphysician

S5199 Personal care item, NOS, each

S5497 Home infusion therapy, catheter care/maintenance, not otherwise classified; includes administrative services, professional pharmacy services, care coordination, and all necessary supplies and equipment (drugs and nursing visits coded separately), per diem

S5498 Home infusion therapy, catheter care/maintenance, simple (single lumen), includes administrative services, professional pharmacy services, care coordination and all necessary supplies and equipment, (drugs and nursing visits coded separately), per diem

S5501 Home infusion therapy, catheter care/maintenance, complex (more than one lumen), includes administrative services, professional pharmacy services, care coordination, and all necessary supplies and equipment (drugs and nursing visits coded separately), per diem

S5502 Home infusion therapy, catheter care/maintenance, implanted access device, includes administrative services, professional pharmacy services, care coordination and all necessary supplies and equipment (drugs and nursing visits coded separately), per diem (use this code for interim maintenance of vascular access not currently in use)

S5517 Home infusion therapy, all supplies necessary for restoration of catheter patency or declotting

S5518 Home infusion therapy, all supplies necessary for catheter repair

S5520 Home infusion therapy, all supplies (including catheter) necessary for a peripherally inserted central venous catheter (PICC) line insertion

S5521 Home infusion therapy, all supplies (including catheter) necessary for a midline catheter insertion

S5522 Home infusion therapy, insertion of peripherally inserted central venous catheter (PICC), nursing services only (no supplies or catheter included)

S5523 Home infusion therapy, insertion of midline venous catheter, nursing services only (no supplies or catheter included)

S5550 Insulin, rapid onset, 5 units

S5551 Insulin, most rapid onset (Lispro or Aspart); 5 units

S5552 Insulin, intermediate acting (NPH or LENTE); 5 units

S5553 Insulin, long acting; 5 units

S5560 Insulin delivery device, reusable pen; 1.5 ml size

S5561 Insulin delivery device, reusable pen; 3 ml size

S5565 Insulin cartridge for use in insulin delivery device other than pump; 150 units

S5566 Insulin cartridge for use in insulin delivery device other than pump; 300 units

S5570 Insulin delivery device, disposable pen (including insulin); 1.5 ml size

S5571 Insulin delivery device, disposable pen (including insulin); 3 ml size

S8030 Scleral application of tantalum ring(s) for localization of lesions for proton beam therapy

S8035 Magnetic source imaging

S8037 Magnetic resonance cholangiopancreatography (MRCP)

S8040 Topographic brain mapping

S8042 Magnetic resonance imaging (MRI), low-field

S8049 Intraoperative radiation therapy (single administration)

S8055 Ultrasound guidance for multifetal pregnancy reduction(s), technical component (only to be used when the physician doing the reduction procedure does not perform the ultrasound, guidance is included in the CPT code for multifetal pregnancy reduction (59866)

S8080 Scintimammography (radioimmunoscintigraphy of the breast), unilateral, including supply of radiopharmaceutical

S8085 Fluorine-18 fluorodeoxyglucose (F-18 FDG) imaging using dual-head coincidence detection system (nondedicated PET scan)

S8092 Electron beam computed tomography (also known as ultrafast CT, cine CT)

S8096 Portable peak flow meter

S8097 Asthma kit (including but not limited to portable peak expiratory flow meter, instructional video, brochure, and/or spacer)

S8100 Holding chamber or spacer for use with an inhaler or nebulizer; without mask

S8101 Holding chamber or spacer for use with an inhaler or nebulizer; with mask

S8110 Peak expiratory flow rate (physician services)

S8120 Oxygen contents, gaseous, 1 unit equals 1 cubic foot

S8121 Oxygen contents, liquid, 1 unit equals 1 pound

S8185 Flutter device

S8186 Swivel adaptor

S8189 Tracheostomy supply, not otherwise classified

S8190 Electronic spirometer (or microspirometer)

S8210 Mucus trap

S8262 Mandibular orthopedic repositioning device, each

S8265 Haberman feeder for cleft lip/palate

S8270 Enuresis alarm, using auditory buzzer and/or vibration device

S8301 Infection control supplies, not otherwise specified

S8415 Supplies for home delivery of infant

S8420 Gradient pressure aid (sleeve and glove combination), custom made

S8421 Gradient pressure aid (sleeve and glove combination), ready made

S8422 Gradient pressure aid (sleeve), custom made, medium weight

S8423 Gradient pressure aid (sleeve), custom made, heavy weight

S8424 Gradient pressure aid (sleeve), ready made

S8425 Gradient pressure aid (glove), custom made, medium weight

S8426 Gradient pressure aid (glove), custom made, heavy weight

S8427 Gradient pressure aid (glove), ready made

S8428 Gradient pressure aid (gauntlet), ready made

S8429 Gradient pressure exterior wrap

S8430 Padding for compression bandage, roll

S8431 Compression bandage, roll

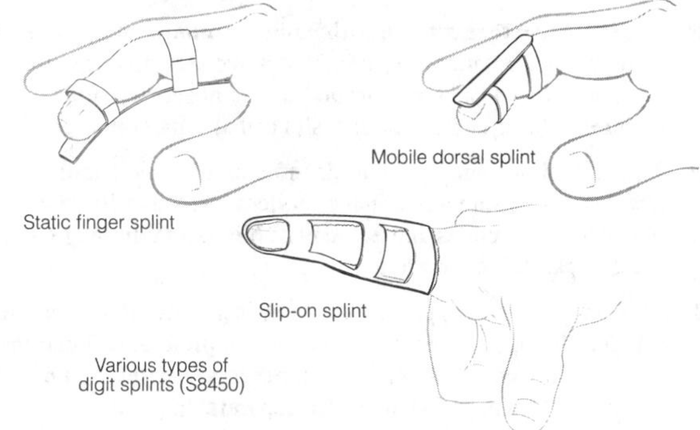

Various types of digit splints (S8450)

S8450 Splint, prefabricated, digit (specify digit by use of modifier)

S8451 Splint, prefabricated, wrist or ankle

S8452 Splint, prefabricated, elbow

S8460 Camisole, postmastectomy

S8490 Insulin syringes (100 syringes, any size)

S8940 Equestrian/hippotherapy, per session

S8948 Application of a modality (requiring constant provider attendance) to one or more areas; low-level laser; each 15 minutes

S8950 Complex lymphedema therapy, each 15 minutes

S8990 Physical or manipulative therapy performed for maintenance rather than restoration

S8999 Resuscitation bag (for use by patient on artificial respiration during power failure or other catastrophic event)

S9001 Home uterine monitor with or without associated nursing services

S9007 Ultrafiltration monitor

S9015 Automated EEG monitoring

S9024 Paranasal sinus ultrasound

S9025 Omnicardiogram/cardiointegram

S9034 Extracorporeal shockwave lithotripsy for gall stones (if performed with ERCP, use 43265)

S9055 Procuren or other growth factor preparation to promote wound healing

S9056 Coma stimulation per diem

S9061 Home administration of aerosolized drug therapy (e.g., Pentamidine); administrative services, professional pharmacy services, care coordination, all necessary supplies and equipment (drugs and nursing visits coded separately), per diem

S9075 Smoking cessation treatment

S9083 Global fee urgent care centers

S9088 Services provided in an urgent care center (list in addition to code for service)

S9090 Vertebral axial decompression, per session

S9097 Home visit for wound care

S9098 Home visit, phototherapy services (e.g., Bili-lite), including equipment rental, nursing services, blood draw, supplies, and other services, per diem

S9109 Congestive heart failure telemonitoring, equipment rental, including telescale, computer system and software, telephone connections, and maintenance, per month

S9117 Back school, per visit

S9122 Home health aide or certified nurse assistant, providing care in the home; per hour

S9123 Nursing care, in the home; by registered nurse, per hour (use for general nursing care only, not to be used when CPT codes 99500-99602 can be used)

S9124 Nursing care, in the home; by licensed practical nurse, per hour

S9125 Respite care, in the home, per diem

S9126 Hospice care, in the home, per diem

S9127 Social work visit, in the home, per diem

S9128 Speech therapy, in the home, per diem

S9129 Occupational therapy, in the home, per diem

S9131 Physical therapy; in the home, per diem

S9140 Diabetic management program, follow-up visit to non-MD provider

S9141 Diabetic management program, follow-up visit to MD provider

S9145 Insulin pump initiation, instruction in initial use of pump (pump not included)

S9150 Evaluation by ocularist

S9152 Speech therapy, re-evaluation

S9208 Home management of preterm labor, including administrative services, professional pharmacy services, care coordination, and all necessary supplies or equipment (drugs and nursing visits coded separately), per diem (do not use this code with any home infusion per diem code)

S9209 Home management of preterm premature rupture of membranes (PPROM), including administrative services, professional pharmacy services, care coordination, and all necessary supplies or equipment (drugs and nursing visits coded separately), per diem (do not use this code with any home infusion per diem code)

S9211 Home management of gestational hypertension, includes administrative services, professional pharmacy services, care coordination and all necessary supplies and equipment (drugs and nursing visits coded separately); per diem (do not use this code with any home infusion per diem code)

S9212 Home management of postpartum hypertension, includes administrative services, professional pharmacy services, care coordination, and all necessary supplies and equipment (drugs and nursing visits coded separately), per diem (do not use this code with any home infusion per diem code)

S9213 Home management of preeclampsia, includes administrative services, professional pharmacy services, care coordination, and all necessary supplies and equipment (drugs and nursing services coded separately); per diem (do not use this code with any home infusion per diem code)

S9214 Home management of gestational diabetes, includes administrative services, professional pharmacy services, care coordination, and all necessary supplies and equipment (drugs and nursing visits coded separately); per diem (do not use this code with any home infusion per diem code)

S9325 Home infusion therapy, pain management infusion; administrative services, professional pharmacy services, care coordination, and all necessary supplies and equipment, (drugs and nursing visits coded separately), per diem (do not use this code with S9326, S9327 or S9328)

S9326 Home infusion therapy, continuous (24 hours or more) pain management infusion; administrative services, professional pharmacy services, care coordination and all necessary supplies and equipment (drugs and nursing visits coded separately), per diem

S9327 Home infusion therapy, intermittent (less than 24 hours) pain management infusion; administrative services, professional pharmacy services, care coordination, and all necessary supplies and equipment (drugs and nursing visits coded separately), per diem

S9328 Home infusion therapy, implanted pump pain management infusion; administrative services, professional pharmacy services, care coordination, and all necessary supplies and equipment (drugs and nursing visits coded separately), per diem

S9329 Home infusion therapy, chemotherapy infusion; administrative services, professional pharmacy services, care coordination, and all necessary supplies and equipment (drugs and nursing visits coded separately), per diem (do not use this code with S9330 or S9331)

S9330 Home infusion therapy, continuous (24 hours or more) chemotherapy infusion; administrative services, professional pharmacy services, care coordination, and all necessary supplies and equipment (drugs and nursing visits coded separately), per diem

S9331 Home infusion therapy, intermittent (less than 24 hours) chemotherapy infusion; administrative services, professional pharmacy services, care coordination, and all necessary supplies and equipment (drugs and nursing visits coded separately), per diem

S9335 Home therapy, hemodialysis; administrative services, professional pharmacy services, care coordination, and all necessary supplies and equipment (drugs and nursing services coded separately), per diem

S9336 Home infusion therapy, continuous anticoagulant infusion therapy (e.g., Heparin), administrative services, professional pharmacy services, care coordination and all necessary supplies and equipment (drugs and nursing visits coded separately), per diem

S9338 Home infusion therapy, immunotherapy, administrative services, professional pharmacy services, care coordination, and all necessary supplies and equipment (drugs and nursing visits coded separately), per diem

S9339 Home therapy; peritoneal dialysis, administrative services, professional pharmacy services, care coordination and all necessary supplies and equipment (drugs and nursing visits coded separately), per diem

S9340 Home therapy; enteral nutrition; administrative services, professional pharmacy services, care coordination, and all necessary supplies and equipment (enteral formula and nursing visits coded separately), per diem

S9341 Home therapy; enteral nutrition via gravity; administrative services, professional pharmacy services, care coordination, and all necessary supplies and equipment (enteral formula and nursing visits coded separately), per diem

S9342 Home therapy; enteral nutrition via pump; administrative services, professional pharmacy services, care coordination, and all necessary supplies and equipment (enteral formula and nursing visits coded separately), per diem

S9343 Home therapy; enteral nutrition via bolus; administrative services, professional pharmacy services, care coordination, and all necessary supplies and equipment (enteral formula and nursing visits coded separately), per diem

S9345 Home infusion therapy, antihemophilic agent infusion therapy (e.g., factor VIII); administrative services, professional pharmacy services, care coordination, and all necessary supplies and equipment (drugs and nursing visits coded separately), per diem

S9346 Home infusion therapy, alpha-1-proteinase inhibitor (e.g., Prolastin); administrative services, professional pharmacy services, care coordination, and all necessary supplies and equipment (drugs and nursing visits coded separately), per diem

S9347 Home infusion therapy, uninterrupted, long-term, controlled rate intravenous or subcutaneous infusion therapy (e.g., epoprostenol); administrative services, professional pharmacy services, care coordination, and all necessary supplies and equipment (drugs and nursing visits coded separately), per diem

S9348 Home infusion therapy, sympathomimetic/inotropic agent infusion therapy (e.g., Dobutamine); administrative services, professional pharmacy services, care coordination, all necessary supplies and equipment (drugs and nursing visits coded separately), per diem

S9349 Home infusion therapy, tocolytic infusion therapy; administrative services, professional pharmacy services, care coordination, and all necessary supplies and equipment (drugs and nursing visits coded separately), per diem

S9351 Home infusion therapy, continuous or intermittent antiemetic infusion therapy; administrative services, professional pharmacy services, care coordination, and all necessary supplies and equipment (drugs and visits coded separately), per diem

S9353 Home infusion therapy, continuous insulin infusion therapy; administrative services, professional pharmacy services, care coordination, and all necessary supplies and equipment (drugs and nursing visits coded separately), per diem

S9355 Home infusion therapy, chelation therapy; administrative services, professional pharmacy services, care coordination, and all necessary supplies and equipment (drugs and nursing visits coded separately), per diem

S9357 Home infusion therapy, enzyme replacement intravenous therapy; (e.g., Imiglucerase); administrative services, professional pharmacy services, care coordination, and all necessary supplies and equipment (drugs and nursing visits coded separately), per diem

S9359 Home infusion therapy, antitumor necrosis factor intravenous therapy; (e.g., Infliximab); administrative services, professional pharmacy services, care coordination, and all necessary supplies and equipment (drugs and nursing visits coded separately), per diem

S9361 Home infusion therapy, diuretic intravenous therapy; administrative services, professional pharmacy services, care coordination, and all necessary supplies and equipment (drugs and nursing visits coded separately), per diem

S9363 Home infusion therapy, antispasmotic therapy; administrative services, professional pharmacy services, care coordination, and all necessary supplies and equipment (drugs and nursing visits coded separately), per diem

S9364 Home infusion therapy, total parenteral nutrition (TPN); administrative services, professional pharmacy services, care coordination, and all necessary supplies and equipment including standard TPN formula (lipids, specialty amino acid formulas, drugs other than in standard formula and nursing visits coded separately), per diem (do not use with home infusion codes S9365–S9368 using daily volume scales)

S9365 Home infusion therapy, total parenteral nutrition (TPN); 1 liter per day, administrative services, professional pharmacy services, care coordination, and all necessary supplies and equipment including standard TPN formula (lipids, specialty amino acid formulas, drugs other than in standard formula and nursing visits coded separately), per diem

S9366 Home infusion therapy, total parenteral nutrition (TPN); more than 1 liter but no more than 2 liters per day, administrative services, professional pharmacy services, care coordination, and all necessary supplies and equipment including standard TPN formula (lipids, specialty amino acid formulas, drugs other than in standard formula and nursing visits coded separately), per diem

S9367 Home infusion therapy, total parenteral nutrition (TPN); more than 2 liters but no more than 3 liters per day, administrative services, professional pharmacy services, care coordination, and all necessary supplies and equipment including standard TPN formula (lipids, specialty amino acid formulas, drugs other than in standard formula and nursing visits coded separately), per diem

S9368 Home infusion therapy, total parenteral nutrition (TPN); more than 3 liters per day, administrative services, professional pharmacy services, care coordination, and all necessary supplies and equipment including standard TPN formula (lipids, specialty amino acid formulas, drugs other than in standard formula and nursing visits coded separately), per diem

S9370 Home therapy, intermittent antiemetic injection therapy; administrative services, professional pharmacy services, care coordination, and all necessary supplies and equipment (drugs and nursing visits coded separately), per diem

S9372 Home therapy; intermittent anticoagulant injection therapy (e.g., Heparin); administrative services, professional pharmacy services, care coordination, and all necessary supplies and equipment (drugs and nursing visits coded separately), per diem (do not use this code for flushing of infusion devices with Heparin to maintain patency)

S9373 Home infusion therapy, hydration therapy; administrative services, professional pharmacy services, care coordination, and all necessary supplies and equipment (drugs and nursing visits coded separately), per diem (do not use with hydration therapy codes S9374–S9377 using daily volume scales)

S9374 Home infusion therapy, hydration therapy; 1 liter per day, administrative services, professional pharmacy services, care coordination, and all necessary supplies and equipment (drugs and nursing visits coded separately), per diem

S9375 Home infusion therapy, hydration therapy; more than 1 liter but no more than 2 liters per day, administrative services, professional pharmacy services, care coordination, and all necessary supplies and equipment (drugs and nursing visits coded separately), per diem

S9376 Home infusion therapy, hydration therapy; more than 2 liters but no more than 3 liters per day, administrative services, professional pharmacy services, care coordination, and all necessary supplies and equipment (drugs and nursing visits coded separately), per diem

S9377 Home infusion therapy, hydration therapy; more than 3 liters per day, administrative services, professional pharmacy services, care coordination, and all necessary supplies (drugs and nursing visits coded separately), per diem

S9379 Home infusion therapy, infusion therapy, not otherwise classified; administrative services, professional pharmacy services, care coordination, and all necessary supplies and equipment (drugs and nursing visits coded separately), per diem

S9381 Delivery or service to high risk areas requiring escort or extra protection, per visit

S9401 Anticoagulation clinic, inclusive of all services except laboratory tests, per session

S9430 Pharmacy compounding and dispensing services

S9433 Medical food nutritionally complete, administered orally, providing 100% of nutritional intake

S9434 Modified solid food supplements for inborn errors of metabolism

S9435 Medical foods for inborn errors of metabolism

S9436 Childbirth preparation/Lamaze classes, nonphysician provider, per session

S9437 Childbirth refresher classes, nonphysician provider, per session

S9438 Cesarean birth classes, nonphysician provider, per session

S9439 VBAC (vaginal birth after cesarean) classes, nonphysician provider, per session

S9441 Asthma education, nonphysician provider, per session

S9442 Birthing classes, nonphysician provider, per session

S9443 Lactation classes, nonphysician provider, per session

S9444 Parenting classes, nonphysician provider, per session

S9445 Patient education, not otherwise classified, nonphysician provider, individual, per session

S9446 Patient education, not otherwise classified, nonphysician provider, group, per session

S9447 Infant safety (including CPR) classes, nonphysician provider, per session

S9449 Weight management classes, nonphysician provider, per session

S9451 Exercise classes, nonphysician provider, per session

S9452 Nutrition classes, nonphysician provider, per session

S9453 Smoking cessation classes, nonphysician provider, per session

S9454 Stress management classes, nonphysician provider, per session

S9455 Diabetic management program, group session

S9460 Diabetic management program, nurse visit

S9465 Diabetic management program, dietitian visit

S9470 Nutritional counseling, dietitian visit

S9472 Cardiac rehabilitation program, nonphysician provider, per diem

S9473 Pulmonary rehabilitation program, nonphysician provider, per diem

S9474 Enterostomal therapy by a registered nurse certified in enterostomal therapy, per diem

S9475 Ambulatory setting substance abuse treatment or detoxification services, per diem

S9476 Vestibular rehabilitation program, nonphysician provider, per diem

S9480 Intensive outpatient psychiatric services, per diem

S9482 Family stabilization services, per 15 minutes

S9484 Crisis intervention mental health services, per hour

S9485 Crisis intervention mental health services, per diem

S9490 Home infusion therapy, corticosteroid infusion; administrative services, professional pharmacy services, care coordination, and all necessary supplies and equipment (drugs and nursing visits coded separately), per diem

S9494 Home infusion therapy, antibiotic, antiviral, or antifungal therapy; administrative services, professional pharmacy services, care coordination, and all necessary supplies and equipment (drugs and nursing visits coded separately, per diem) (do not use this code with home infusion codes for hourly dosing schedules S9497–S9504)

S9497 Home infusion therapy, antibiotic, antiviral, or antifungal therapy; once every 3 hours; administrative services, professional pharmacy services, care coordination, and all necessary supplies and equipment (drugs and nursing visits coded separately), per diem

S9500 Home infusion therapy, antibiotic, antiviral, or antifungal therapy; once every 24 hours; administrative services, professional pharmacy services, care coordination, and all necessary supplies and equipment (drugs and nursing visits coded separately), per diem

S9501 Home infusion therapy, antibiotic, antiviral, or antifungal therapy; once every 12 hours; administrative services, professional pharmacy services, care coordination, and all necessary supplies and equipment (drugs and nursing visits coded separately), per diem

S9502 Home infusion therapy, antibiotic, antiviral, or antifungal therapy; once every 8 hours, administrative services, professional pharmacy services, care coordination, and all necessary supplies and equipment (drugs and nursing visits coded separately), per diem

S9503 Home infusion therapy, antibiotic, antiviral, or antifungal; once every 6 hours; administrative services, professional pharmacy services, care coordination, and all necessary supplies and equipment (drugs and nursing visits coded separately), per diem

S9504 Home infusion therapy, antibiotic, antiviral, or antifungal; once every 4 hours; administrative services, professional pharmacy services, care coordination, and all necessary supplies and equipment (drugs and nursing visits coded separately), per diem

S9529 Routine venipuncture for collection of specimen(s), single homebound, nursing home, or skilled nursing facility patient

S9537 Home therapy; hematopoietic hormone injection therapy (e.g., erythropoietin, G-CSF, GM-CSF); administrative services, professional pharmacy services, care coordination, and all necessary supplies and equipment (drugs and nursing visits coded separately), per diem

S9538 Home transfusion of blood product(s); administrative services, professional pharmacy services, care coordination and all necessary supplies and equipment (blood products, drugs, and nursing visits coded separately), per diem

S9542 Home injectable therapy, not otherwise classified, including administrative services, professional pharmacy services, care coordination, and all necessary supplies and equipment (drugs and nursing visits coded separately), per diem

S9558 Home injectable therapy; growth hormone, including administrative services, professional pharmacy services, care coordination, and all necessary supplies and equipment (drugs and nursing visits coded separately), per diem

S9559 Home injectable therapy, interferon, including administrative services, professional pharmacy services, care coordination, and all necessary supplies and equipment (drugs and nursing visits coded separately), per diem

S9560 Home injectable therapy; hormonal therapy (e.g., leuprolide, goserelin), including administrative services, professional pharmacy services, care coordination, and all necessary supplies and equipment (drugs and nursing visits coded separately), per diem

S9562 Home injectable therapy, palivizumab, including administrative services, professional pharmacy services, care coordination, and all necessary supplies and equipment (drugs and nursing visits coded separately), per diem

S9590 Home therapy, irrigation therapy (e.g., sterile irrigation of an organ or anatomical cavity); including administrative services, professional pharmacy services, care coordination, and all necessary supplies and equipment (drugs and nursing visits coded separately), per diem

S9810 Home therapy; professional pharmacy services for provision of infusion, specialty drug administration, and/or disease state management, not otherwise classified, per hour (do not use this code with any per diem code)

S9900 Services by authorized Christian Science practitioner for the process of healing, per diem; not to be used for rest or study; excludes in-patient services

S9970 Health club membership, annual

S9975 Transplant related lodging, meals and transportation, per diem

S9976 Lodging, per diem, not otherwise classified

S9977 Meals, per diem, not otherwise specified

S9981 Medical records copying fee, administrative

S9982 Medical records copying fee, per page

S9986 Not medically necessary service (patient is aware that service not medically necessary)

S9988 Services provided as part of a Phase I clinical trial

S9989 Services provided outside of the United States of America (list in addition to code(s) for services(s))

S9990 Services provided as part of a Phase II clinical trial

S9991 Services provided as part of a Phase III clinical trial

S9992 Transportation costs to and from trial location and local transportation costs (e.g., fares for taxicab or bus) for clinical trial participant and one caregiver/companion

S9994 Lodging costs (e.g., hotel charges) for clinical trial participant and one caregiver/companion

S9996 Meals for clinical trial participant and one caregiver/companion

S9999 Sales tax

NATIONAL T CODES ESTABLISHED FOR STATE MEDICAID AGENCIES T1000-T9999

The T codes are designed for use by Medicaid state agencies to establish codes for items for which there are no permanent national codes but for which codes are necessary to administer the Medicaid program (T codes are not accepted by Medicare but can be used by private insurers). This range of codes describes nursing and home health-related services, substance abuse treatment, and certain training-related procedures.

T1000 Private duty/independent nursing service(s), licensed, up to 15 minutes

T1001 Nursing assessment/evaluation

T1002 RN services, up to 15 minutes

T1003 LPN/LVN services, up to 15 minutes

T1004 Services of a qualified nursing aide, up to 15 minutes

T1005 Respite care services, up to 15 minutes

T1006 Alcohol and/or substance abuse services, family/couple counseling

T1007 Alcohol and/or substance abuse services, treatment plan development and/or modification

T1009 Child sitting services for children of the individual receiving alcohol and/or substance abuse services

T1010 Meals for individuals receiving alcohol and/or substance abuse services (when meals not included in the program)

T1012 Alcohol and/or substance abuse services, skills development

T1013 Sign language or oral interpretive services, per 15 minutes

T1014 Telehealth transmission, per minute, professional services bill separately

T1015 Clinic visit/encounter, all-inclusive

T1016 Case management, each 15 minutes

T1017 Targeted case management, each 15 minutes

T1018 School-based individualized education program (IEP) services, bundled

T1019 Personal care services, per 15 minutes, not for an inpatient or resident of a hospital, nursing facility, ICF/MR or IMD, part of the individualized plan of treatment (code may not be used to identify services provided by home health aide or certified nurse assistant)

T1020 Personal care services, per diem, not for an inpatient or resident of a hospital, nursing facility, ICF/MR or IMD, part of the individualized plan of treatment (code may not be used to identify services provided by home health aide or certified nurse assistant)

T1021 Home health aide or certified nurse assistant, per visit

T1022 Contracted home health agency services, all services provided under contract, per day

T1023 Screening to determine the appropriateness of consideration of an individual for participation in a specified program, project or treatment protocol, per encounter

T1024 Evaluation and treatment by an integrated, specialty team contracted to provide coordinated care to multiple or severely handicapped children, per encounter

T1025 Intensive, extended multidisciplinary services provided in a clinic setting to children with complex medical, physical, mental and psychosocial impairments, per diem

T1026 Intensive, extended multidisciplinary services provided in a clinic setting to children with complex medical, physical, medical and psychosocial impairments, per hour

T1027 Family training and counseling for child development, per 15 minutes

T1028 Assessment of home, physical and family environment, to determine suitability to meet patient's medical needs

T1029 Comprehensive environmental lead investigation, not including laboratory analysis, per dwelling

T1030 Nursing care, in the home, by registered nurse, per diem

T1031 Nursing care, in the home, by licensed practical nurse, per diem

T1502 Administration of oral, intramuscular and/or subcutaneous medication by health care agency/professional, per visit

T1503 Administration of medication, other than oral and/or injectable, by a health care agency/professional, per visit

T1999 Miscellaneous therapeutic items and supplies, retail purchases, not otherwise classified; identify product in "remarks"

T2001 Nonemergency transportation; patient attendant/escort

T2002 Nonemergency transportation; per diem

T2003 Nonemergency transportation; encounter/trip

T2004 Nonemergency transport; commercial carrier, multipass

T2005 Nonemergency transportation; stretcher van

T2007 Transportation waiting time, air ambulance and nonemergency vehicle, one-half (1/2) hour increments

T2010 Preadmission screening and resident review (PASRR) level I identification screening, per screen

T2011 Preadmission screening and resident review (PASRR) level II evaluation, per evaluation

T2012 Habilitation, educational; waiver, per diem

T2013 Habilitation, educational, waiver; per hour

T2014 Habilitation, prevocational, waiver; per diem

T2015 Habilitation, prevocational, waiver; per hour

T2016 Habilitation, residential, waiver; per diem

T2017 Habilitation, residential, waiver; 15 minutes

T2018 Habilitation, supported employment, waiver; per diem

T2019 Habilitation, supported employment, waiver; per 15 minutes

T2020 Day habilitation, waiver; per diem

T2021 Day habilitation, waiver; per 15 minutes

T2022 Case management, per month

T2023 Targeted case management; per month

T2024 Service assessment/plan of care development, waiver

T2025 Waiver services; not otherwise specified (NOS)

T2026 Specialized childcare, waiver; per diem

T2027 Specialized childcare, waiver; per 15 minutes

T2028 Specialized supply, not otherwise specified, waiver

T2029 Specialized medical equipment, not otherwise specified, waiver

T2030 Assisted living, waiver; per month

T2031 Assisted living; waiver, per diem

T2032 Residential care, not otherwise specified (NOS), waiver; per month

T2033 Residential care, not otherwise specified (NOS), waiver; per diem

T2034 Crisis intervention, waiver; per diem

T2035 Utility services to support medical equipment and assistive technology/devices, waiver

T2036 Therapeutic camping, overnight, waiver; each session

T2037 Therapeutic camping, day, waiver; each session

T2038 Community transition, waiver; per service

T2039 Vehicle modifications, waiver; per service

T2040 Financial management, self-directed, waiver; per 15 minutes

T2041 Supports brokerage, self-directed, waiver; per 15 minutes

T2042 Hospice routine home care; per diem

T2043 Hospice continuous home care; per hour

T2044 Hospice inpatient respite care; per diem

T2045 Hospice general inpatient care; per diem

T2046 Hospice long-term care, room and board only; per diem

T2048 Behavioral health; long-term care residential (nonacute care in a residential treatment program where stay is typically longer than 30 days), with room and board, per diem

T2049 Nonemergency transportation; stretcher van, mileage; per mile

T2101 Human breast milk processing, storage and distribution only

T4521 Adult sized disposable incontinence product, brief/diaper, small, each

MED: 100-3,230.10

T4522 Adult sized disposable incontinence product, brief/diaper, medium, each

MED: 100-3,230.10

T4523 Adult sized disposable incontinence product, brief/diaper, large, each

MED: 100-3,230.10

T4524 Adult sized disposable incontinence product, brief/diaper, extra large, each

MED: 100-3,230.10

T4525 Adult sized disposable incontinence product, protective underwear/pull-on, small size, each

MED: 100-3,230.10

T4526 Adult sized disposable incontinence product, protective underwear/pull-on, medium size, each

MED: 100-3,230.10

T4527 Adult sized disposable incontinence product, protective underwear/pull-on, large size, each

MED: 100-3,230.10

T4528 Adult sized disposable incontinence product, protective underwear/pull-on, extra large size, each

MED: 100-3,230.10

T4529 Pediatric sized disposable incontinence product, brief/diaper, small/medium size, each

MED: 100-3,230.10

T4530 Pediatric sized disposable incontinence product, brief/diaper, large size, each

MED: 100-3,230.10

T4531 Pediatric sized disposable incontinence product, protective underwear/pull-on, small/medium size, each

MED: 100-3,230.10

T4532 Pediatric sized disposable incontinence product, protective underwear/pull-on, large size, each

MED: 100-3,230.10

T4533 Youth sized disposable incontinence product, brief/diaper, each

MED: 100-3,230.10

T4534 Youth sized disposable incontinence product, protective underwear/pull-on, each

MED: 100-3,230.10

T4535 Disposable liner/shield/guard/pad/undergarment, for incontinence, each

MED: 100-3,230.10

T4536 Incontinence product, protective underwear/pull-on, reusable, any size, each

MED: 100-3,230.10

T4537 Incontinence product, protective underpad, reusable, bed size, each

MED: 100-3,230.10

T4538 Diaper service, reusable diaper, each diaper

MED: 100-3,230.10

T4539 Incontinence product, diaper/brief, reusable, any size, each

MED: 100-3,230.10

T4540 Incontinence product, protective underpad, reusable, chair size, each

MED: 100-3,230.10

T4541 Incontinence product, disposable underpad, large, each

T4542 Incontinence product, disposable underpad, small size, each

T4543 Disposable incontinence product, brief/diaper, bariatric, each

T5001 Positioning seat for persons with special orthopedic needs

T5999 Supply, not otherwise specified

VISION SERVICES V0000-V2999

These V codes include vision-related supplies, including spectacles, lenses, contact lenses, prostheses, intraocular lenses, and miscellaneous lenses.

FRAMES

V2020 Frames, purchases
MED: 100-2,15,120; 100-4,3,10.4

V2025 Deluxe frame
MED: 100-4,1,30.3.5

SPECTACLE LENSES

See S0500-S0592 for temporary vision codes.

SINGLE VISION, GLASS, OR PLASTIC

Monofocal spectacles (V2100-V2114)

Trifocal spectacles (V2300-V2314)

Low vision aids mounted to spectacles (V2610)

Telescopic or other compound lens fitted on spectacles as a low vision aid (V2615)

V2100 Sphere, single vision, plano to plus or minus 4.00, per lens

V2101 Sphere, single vision, plus or minus 4.12 to plus or minus 7.00d, per lens

V2102 Sphere, single vision, plus or minus 7.12 to plus or minus 20.00d, per lens

V2103 Spherocylinder, single vision, plano to plus or minus 4.00d sphere, 0.12 to 2.00d cylinder, per lens

V2104 Spherocylinder, single vision, plano to plus or minus 4.00d sphere, 2.12 to 4.00d cylinder, per lens

V2105 Spherocylinder, single vision, plano to plus or minus 4.00d sphere, 4.25 to 6.00d cylinder, per lens

V2106 Spherocylinder, single vision, plano to plus or minus 4.00d sphere, over 6.00d cylinder, per lens

V2107 Spherocylinder, single vision, plus or minus 4.25 to plus or minus 7.00 sphere, 0.12 to 2.00d cylinder, per lens

V2108 Spherocylinder, single vision, plus or minus 4.25d to plus or minus 7.00d sphere, 2.12 to 4.00d cylinder, per lens

V2109 Spherocylinder, single vision, plus or minus 4.25 to plus or minus 7.00d sphere, 4.25 to 6.00d cylinder, per lens

V2110 Spherocylinder, single vision, plus or minus 4.25 to 7.00d sphere, over 6.00d cylinder, per lens

V2111 Spherocylinder, single vision, plus or minus 7.25 to plus or minus 12.00d sphere, 0.25 to 2.25d cylinder, per lens

V2112 Spherocylinder, single vision, plus or minus 7.25 to plus or minus 12.00d sphere, 2.25d to 4.00d cylinder, per lens

V2113 Spherocylinder, single vision, plus or minus 7.25 to plus or minus 12.00d sphere, 4.25 to 6.00d cylinder, per lens

V2114 Spherocylinder, single vision, sphere over plus or minus 12.00d, per lens

V2115 Lenticular (myodisc), per lens, single vision

V2118 Aniseikonic lens, single vision

V2121 Lenticular lens, per lens, single
MED: 100-2,15,120; 100-4,3,10.4

V2199 Not otherwise classified, single vision lens

BIFOCAL, GLASS, OR PLASTIC

V2200 Sphere, bifocal, plano to plus or minus 4.00d, per lens

V2201 Sphere, bifocal, plus or minus 4.12 to plus or minus 7.00d, per lens

V2202 Sphere, bifocal, plus or minus 7.12 to plus or minus 20.00d, per lens

V2203 Spherocylinder, bifocal, plano to plus or minus 4.00d sphere, 0.12 to 2.00d cylinder, per lens

V2204 Spherocylinder, bifocal, plano to plus or minus 4.00d sphere, 2.12 to 4.00d cylinder, per lens

V2205 Spherocylinder, bifocal, plano to plus or minus 4.00d sphere, 4.25 to 6.00d cylinder, per lens

V2206 Spherocylinder, bifocal, plano to plus or minus 4.00d sphere, over 6.00d cylinder, per lens

V2207 Spherocylinder, bifocal, plus or minus 4.25 to plus or minus 7.00d sphere, 0.12 to 2.00d cylinder, per lens

V2208 Spherocylinder, bifocal, plus or minus 4.25 to plus or minus 7.00d sphere, 2.12 to 4.00d cylinder, per lens

V2209 Spherocylinder, bifocal, plus or minus 4.25 to plus or minus 7.00d sphere, 4.25 to 6.00d cylinder, per lens

V2210 Spherocylinder, bifocal, plus or minus 4.25 to plus or minus 7.00d sphere, over 6.00d cylinder, per lens

V2211 Spherocylinder, bifocal, plus or minus 7.25 to plus or minus 12.00d sphere, 0.25 to 2.25d cylinder, per lens

V2212 Spherocylinder, bifocal, plus or minus 7.25 to plus or minus 12.00d sphere, 2.25 to 4.00d cylinder, per lens

V2213 Spherocylinder, bifocal, plus or minus 7.25 to plus or minus 12.00d sphere, 4.25 to 6.00d cylinder, per lens

V2214 Spherocylinder, bifocal, sphere over plus or minus 12.00d, per lens

V2215 Lenticular (myodisc), per lens, bifocal

V2218 Aniseikonic, per lens, bifocal

V2219 Bifocal seg width over 28mm

V2220 Bifocal add over 3.25d

V2221 Lenticular lens, per lens, bifocal
MED: 100-2,15,120; 100-4,3,10.4

V2299 Specialty bifocal (by report)
Pertinent documentation to evaluate medical appropriateness should be included when this code is reported.

TRIFOCAL, GLASS, OR PLASTIC

V2300 Sphere, trifocal, plano to plus or minus 4.00d, per lens

V2301 Sphere, trifocal, plus or minus 4.12 to plus or minus 7.00d per lens

V2302 Sphere, trifocal, plus or minus 7.12 to plus or minus 20.00, per lens

V2303 Spherocylinder, trifocal, plano to plus or minus 4.00d sphere, 0.12 to 2.00d cylinder, per lens

V2304 Spherocylinder, trifocal, plano to plus or minus 4.00d sphere, 2.25 to 4.00d cylinder, per lens

V2305 Spherocylinder, trifocal, plano to plus or minus 4.00d sphere, 4.25 to 6.00 cylinder, per lens

V2306 Spherocylinder, trifocal, plano to plus or minus 4.00d sphere, over 6.00d cylinder, per lens

V2307 Spherocylinder, trifocal, plus or minus 4.25 to plus or minus 7.00d sphere, 0.12 to 2.00d cylinder, per lens

V2308 Spherocylinder, trifocal, plus or minus 4.25 to plus or minus 7.00d sphere, 2.12 to 4.00d cylinder, per lens

V2309 Spherocylinder, trifocal, plus or minus 4.25 to plus or minus 7.00d sphere, 4.25 to 6.00d cylinder, per lens

V2310 Spherocylinder, trifocal, plus or minus 4.25 to plus or minus 7.00d sphere, over 6.00d cylinder, per lens

V2311 Spherocylinder, trifocal, plus or minus 7.25 to plus or minus 12.00d sphere, 0.25 to 2.25d cylinder, per lens

V2312 Spherocylinder, trifocal, plus or minus 7.25 to plus or minus 12.00d sphere, 2.25 to 4.00d cylinder, per lens

V2313 Spherocylinder, trifocal, plus or minus 7.25 to plus or minus 12.00d sphere, 4.25 to 6.00d cylinder, per lens

V2314 Spherocylinder, trifocal, sphere over plus or minus 12.00d, per lens

V2315 Lenticular, (myodisc), per lens, trifocal

V2318 Aniseikonic lens, trifocal

V2319 Trifocal seg width over 28 mm

V2320 Trifocal add over 3.25d

V2321 Lenticular lens, per lens, trifocal

MED: 100-2,15,120; 100-4,3,10.4

V2399 Specialty trifocal (by report)

Pertinent documentation to evaluate medical appropriateness should be included when this code is reported.

VARIABLE ASPHERICITY LENS, GLASS, OR PLASTIC

V2410 Variable asphericity lens, single vision, full field, glass or plastic, per lens

V2430 Variable asphericity lens, bifocal, full field, glass or plastic, per lens

V2499 Variable sphericity lens, other type

CONTACT LENS

If procedure code 92391 or 92396 is reported, recode with specific lens type listed below (per lens).

V2500 Contact lens, PMMA, spherical, per lens

V2501 Contact lens, PMMA, toric or prism ballast, per lens

V2502 Contact lens PMMA, bifocal, per lens

V2503 Contact lens, PMMA, color vision deficiency, per lens

V2510 Contact lens, gas permeable, spherical, per lens

V2511 Contact lens, gas permeable, toric, prism ballast, per lens

V2512 Contact lens, gas permeable, bifocal, per lens

V2513 Contact lens, gas permeable, extended wear, per lens

V2520 Contact lens, hydrophilic, spherical, per lens

Hydrophilic contact lenses are covered by Medicare only for aphakic patients. Local contractor if incident to physician services.

MED: 100-3,80.1; 100-3,80.4

V2521 Contact lens, hydrophilic, toric, or prism ballast, per lens

Hydrophilic contact lenses are covered by Medicare only for aphakic patients. Local contractor if incident to physician services.

MED: 100-3,80.1; 100-3,80.4

V2522 Contact lens, hydrophilic, bifocal, per lens

Hydrophilic contact lenses are covered by Medicare only for aphakic patients. Local contractor if incident to physician services.

MED: 100-3,80.1; 100-3,80.4

V2523 Contact lens, hydrophilic, extended wear, per lens

Hydrophilic contact lenses are covered by Medicare only for aphakic patients.

MED: 100-3,80.1; 100-3,80.4

V2530 Contact lens, scleral, gas impermeable, per lens (for contact lens modification, see 92325)

V2531 Contact lens, scleral, gas permeable, per lens (for contact lens modification, see 92325)

MED: 100-3,80.5

V2599 Contact lens, other type

Local contractor if incident to physician services.

VISION AIDS

V2600 Hand held low vision aids and other nonspectacle mounted aids

V2610 Single lens spectacle mounted low vision aids

V2615 Telescopic and other compound lens system, including distance vision telescopic, near vision telescopes and compound microscopic lens system

PROSTHETIC EYE

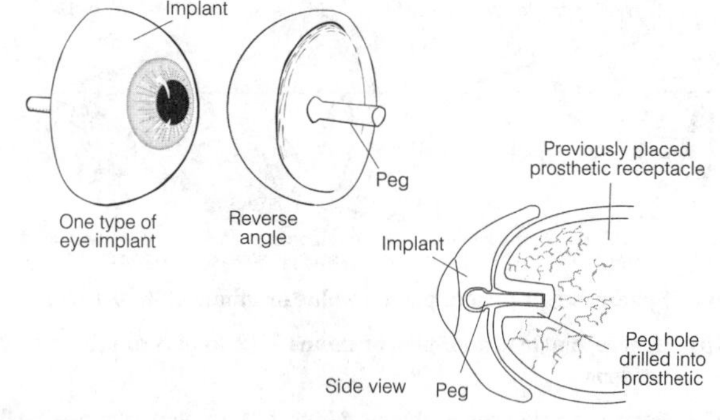

V2623 Prosthetic eye, plastic, custom

MED: 100-2,15,120; 100-4,3,10.4

V2624 Polishing/resurfacing of ocular prosthesis

V2625 Enlargement of ocular prosthesis

V2626 Reduction of ocular prosthesis

V2627 Scleral cover shell

A scleral shell covers the cornea and the anterior sclera. Medicare covers a scleral shell when it is prescribed as an artificial support to a shrunken and sightless eye or as a barrier in the treatment of severe dry eye.

MED: 100-3,80.5

V2628 Fabrication and fitting of ocular conformer

V2629 Prosthetic eye, other type

INTRAOCULAR LENSES

V2630 Anterior chamber intraocular lens

The IOL must be FDA-approved for reimbursement. Medicare payment for an IOL is included in the payment for ASC facility services. Medicare jurisdiction: local contractor.

MED: 100-2,15,120; 100-4,3,10.4

V2631 Iris supported intraocular lens

The IOL must be FDA-approved for reimbursement. Medicare payment for an IOL is included in the payment for ASC facility services. Medicare jurisdiction: local contractor.

MED: 100-2,15,120; 100-4,3,10.4

V2632 Posterior chamber intraocular lens
The IOL must be FDA-approved for reimbursement. Medicare payment for an IOL is included in the payment for ASC facility services. Medicare jurisdiction: local contractor.
MED: 100-2,15,120; 100-4,3,10.4

MISCELLANEOUS

V2700 Balance lens, per lens

V2702 Deluxe lens feature
MED: 100-2,15,120; 100-4,3,10.4

V2710 Slab off prism, glass or plastic, per lens

V2715 Prism, per lens

V2718 Press-on lens, Fresnel prism, per lens

V2730 Special base curve, glass or plastic, per lens

V2744 Tint, photochromatic, per lens
MED: 100-2,15,120; 100-4,3,10.4

V2745 Addition to lens; tint, any color, solid, gradient or equal, excludes photochromatic, any lens material, per lens
MED: 100-2,15,120; 100-4,3,10.4

V2750 Antireflective coating, per lens
MED: 100-2,15,120; 100-4,3,10.4

V2755 U-V lens, per lens
MED: 100-2,15,120; 100-4,3,10.4

V2756 Eye glass case

V2760 Scratch resistant coating, per lens

V2761 Mirror coating, any type, solid, gradient or equal, any lens material, per lens
MED: 100-2,15,120; 100-4,3,10.4

V2762 Polarization, any lens material, per lens
MED: 100-2,15,120; 100-4,3,10.4

V2770 Occluder lens, per lens

V2780 Oversize lens, per lens

V2781 Progressive lens, per lens

V2782 Lens, index 1.54 to 1.65 plastic or 1.60 to 1.79 glass, excludes polycarbonate, per lens
MED: 100-2,15,120; 100-4,3,10.4

V2783 Lens, index greater than or equal to 1.66 plastic or greater than or equal to 1.80 glass, excludes polycarbonate, per lens
MED: 100-2,15,120; 100-4,3,10.4

V2784 Lens, polycarbonate or equal, any index, per lens
MED: 100-2,15,120; 100-4,3,10.4

V2785 Processing, preserving and transporting corneal tissue
Medicare jurisdiction: local contractor.

V2786 Specialty occupational multifocal lens, per lens
MED: 100-2,15,120; 100-4,3,10.4

V2787 Astigmatism correcting function of intraocular lens

V2788 Presbyopia correcting function of intraocular lens

V2790 Amniotic membrane for surgical reconstruction, per procedure
Medicare jurisdiction: local contractor.

V2797 Vision supply, accessory and/or service component of another HCPCS vision code

V2799 Vision service, miscellaneous
Determine if an alternative HCPCS Level II or a CPT code better describes the service being reported. This code should be used only if a more specific code is unavailable.

HEARING SERVICES V5000-V5999

This range of codes describes hearing tests and related supplies and equipment, speech-language pathology screenings, and repair of augmentative communicative system.

V5008 Hearing screening
MED: 100-2,16,90

V5010 Assessment for hearing aid

V5011 Fitting/orientation/checking of hearing aid

V5014 Repair/modification of a hearing aid

V5020 Conformity evaluation

V5030 Hearing aid, monaural, body worn, air conduction

V5040 Hearing aid, monaural, body worn, bone conduction

V5050 Hearing aid, monaural, in the ear

V5060 Hearing aid, monaural, behind the ear

V5070 Glasses, air conduction

V5080 Glasses, bone conduction

V5090 Dispensing fee, unspecified hearing aid

V5095 Semi-implantable middle ear hearing prosthesis

V5100 Hearing aid, bilateral, body worn

V5110 Dispensing fee, bilateral

V5120 Binaural, body

V5130 Binaural, in the ear

V5140 Binaural, behind the ear

V5150 Binaural, glasses

V5160 Dispensing fee, binaural

V5170 Hearing aid, CROS, in the ear

V5180 Hearing aid, CROS, behind the ear

V5190 Hearing aid, CROS, glasses

V5200 Dispensing fee, CROS

V5210 Hearing aid, BICROS, in the ear

V5220 Hearing aid, BICROS, behind the ear

V5230 Hearing aid, BICROS, glasses

V5240 Dispensing fee, BICROS

V5241 Dispensing fee, monaural hearing aid, any type

V5242 Hearing aid, analog, monaural, CIC (completely in the ear canal)

V5243 Hearing aid, analog, monaural, ITC (in the canal)

V5244 Hearing aid, digitally programmable analog, monaural, CIC

V5245 Hearing aid, digitally programmable, analog, monaural, ITC

V5246 Hearing aid, digitally programmable analog, monaural, ITE (in the ear)

V5247 Hearing aid, digitally programmable analog, monaural, BTE (behind the ear)

V5248 Hearing aid, analog, binaural, CIC

V5249 Hearing aid, analog, binaural, ITC

V5250 Hearing aid, digitally programmable analog, binaural, CIC

V5251 Hearing aid, digitally programmable analog, binaural, ITC

V5252 Hearing aid, digitally programmable, binaural, ITE

V5253 Hearing aid, digitally programmable, binaural, BTE

V5254 Hearing aid, digital, monaural, CIC

V5255 Hearing aid, digital, monaural, ITC

V5256 Hearing aid, digital, monaural, ITE

V5257 Hearing aid, digital, monaural, BTE

V5258 Hearing aid, digital, binaural, CIC

V5259 Hearing aid, digital, binaural, ITC

V5260 Hearing aid, digital, binaural, ITE

V5261 Hearing aid, digital, binaural, BTE

V5262 Hearing aid, disposable, any type, monaural

V5263 Hearing aid, disposable, any type, binaural

V5264 Ear mold/insert, not disposable, any type

V5265 Ear mold/insert, disposable, any type

V5266 Battery for use in hearing device

V5267 Hearing aid supplies/accessories

V5268 Assistive listening device, telephone amplifier, any type

V5269 Assistive listening device, alerting, any type

V5270 Assistive listening device, television amplifier, any type

V5271 Assistive listening device, television caption decoder

V5272 Assistive listening device, TDD

V5273 Assistive listening device, for use with cochlear implant

V5274 Assistive listening device, not otherwise specified

V5275 Ear impression, each

V5298 Hearing aid, not otherwise classified

V5299 Hearing service, miscellaneous
Determine if an alternative HCPCS Level II or a CPT code better describes the service being reported. This code should be used only if a more specific code is unavailable.

MED: 100-2,16,90

SPEECH-LANGUAGE PATHOLOGY SERVICES

V5336 Repair/modification of augmentative communicative system or device (excludes adaptive hearing aid)
Medicare jurisdiction: DME regional contractor.

V5362 Speech screening

V5363 Language screening

V5364 Dysphagia screening

APPENDIX 1 — TABLE OF DRUGS

Introduction and Directions

The HCPCS 2009 Table of Drugs is designed to quickly and easily direct the user to drug names and their corresponding codes. Both generic and brand or trade names are alphabetically listed in the "Drug Name" column of the table. The associated A, C, J, K, Q, or S code is given only for the generic name of the drug.

The "Unit Per" column lists the stated amount for the referenced generic drug as provided by CMS. "Up to" listings are inclusive of all quantities up to and including the listed amount. All other listings are for the amount of the drug as listed. The editors recognize that the availability of some drugs in the quantities listed is dependent on many variables beyond the control of the clinical ordering clerk. The availability in your area of regularly used drugs in the most cost-effective quantities should be relayed to your third-party payers.

The "Route of Administration" column addresses the most common methods of delivering the referenced generic drug as described in current pharmaceutical literature. The official definitions for Level II drug codes generally describe administration other than by oral method. Therefore, with a handful of exceptions, oral-delivered options for most drugs are omitted from the Route of Administration column.

Intravenous administration includes all methods, such as gravity infusion, injections, and timed pushes. When several routes of administration are listed, the first listing is simply the first, or most common, method as described in current reference literature. The "VAR" posting denotes various routes of administration and is used for drugs that are commonly administered into joints, cavities, tissues, or topical applications, in addition to other parenteral administrations. Listings posted with "OTH" alert the user to other administration methods, such as suppositories or catheter injections.

Please be reminded that the Table of Drugs, as well as all HCPCS Level II national definitions and listings, constitutes a post-treatment medical reference for billing purposes only. Although the editors have exercised all normal precautions to ensure the accuracy of the table and related material, the use of any of this information to select medical treatment is entirely inappropriate. Do not code directly from the table of drugs. Refer to the tabular section for complete information.

See Appendix 3 for abbreviations.

Drug Name	Unit Per	Route	Code
10% LMD	500 ML	IV	J7100
5% DEXTROSE/NORMAL SALINE	5%	VAR	J7042
5% DEXTROSE/WATER	500 ML	IV	J7060
ABARELIX	10 MG	IM	J0128
ABATACEPT	10 MG	IV	J0129
ABCIXIMAB	10 MG	IV	J0130
ABELCET	50 MG	IV	J0285
ABILIFY	0.25 MG	IM	J0400
ABRAXANE	1 MG	IV	J9264
ACCELULAR PERICARDIAL TISSUE MATRIX NONHUMAN	SQ CM	OTH	C9354
ACCUNEB NONCOMPOUNDED, CONCENTRATED	1 MG	INH	J7611
ACCUNEB NONCOMPOUNDED, UNIT DOSE	1 MG	INH	J7613
ACETADOTE	1 G	INH	J7608
ACETADOTE	100 MG	IV	J0132
ACETAZOLAMIDE SODIUM	500 MG	IM, IV	J1120
ACETYLCYSTEINE COMPOUNDED	PER G	INH	J7604
ACETYLCYSTEINE NONCOMPOUNDED	1 G	INH	J7608
ACTHREL	1 MCG	IV	J0795
ACTIMMUNE	0.25 MG	SC	J1830
ACTIMMUNE	3 MU	SC	J9216
ACTIVASE	1 MG	IV	J2997
ACUTECT	DOSE	IV	A9504
ACYCLOVIR	5 MG	IV	J0133
ADAGEN	25 IU	IM	J2504
ADALIMUMAB	20 MG	SC	J0135
ADBEON	4 MG	IM, IV	J0704
ADENOCARD	6 MG	IV	J0150
ADENOSCAN	30 MG	IV	J0152
ADENOSINE	30 MG	IV	J0152
ADENOSINE	6 MG	IV	J0150
ADRENALIN	1 MG	IM, IV, SC	J0170
ADRENALIN CHLORIDE	1 MG	IM, IV, SC	J0170
ADRENOCORT	1 MG	IM, IV, OTH	J1100
ADRIAMYCIN	10 MG	IV	J9000
ADRUCIL	500 MG	IV	J9190
AEROBID	1 MG	INH	J7641
AGALSIDASE BETA	1 MG	IV	J0180
AGGRASTAT	12.5 MG	IM, IV	J3246
A-HYDROCORT	100 MG	IV, IM, SC	J1720
ALATROFLOXACIN MESYLATE	100 MG	IV	J0200
ALBUTEROL AND IPRATROPIUM BROMIDE NONCOMPOUNDED	2.5MG/0.5 MG	INH	J7620
ALBUTEROL COMPOUNDED, CONCENTRATED	1 MG	INH	J7610
ALBUTEROL COMPOUNDED, UNIT DOSE	1 MG	INH	J7609
ALBUTEROL NONCOMPOUNDED, UNIT DOSE	PER 1 MG	INH	J7613
ALBUTEROL, NONCOMPOUNDED, CONCENTRATED FORM	PER 1 MG	INH	J7611
ALDESLEUKIN	1 VIAL	IV	J9015
ALDURAZYME	0.1 MG	IV	J1931
ALEFACEPT	0.5 MG	IV, IM	J0215
ALEMTUZUMAB	10 MG	IV	J9010
ALFERON N	250,000 IU	IM	J9215
ALGLUCERASE	10 U	IV	J0205
ALGLUCOSIDASE ALFA	10 MG	IV	J0220
ALIMTA	10 MG	IV	J9305
ALKERAN	2 MG	ORAL	J8600
ALKERAN	50 MG	IV	J9245
ALLOGRAFT, CYMETRA	1 CC	INJ	Q4112
ALLOGRAFT, GRAFTJACKET EXPRESS	1 CC	INJ	Q4113
ALOXI	25 MCG	IV	J2469
ALPHA 1 - PROTEINASE INHIBITOR — HUMAN	10 MG	IV	J0256
ALPHANATE	PER FACTOR IU	IV	J7186
ALPHANINE SD	1 IU	IV	J7193
ALPROSTADIL	1.25 MCG	INJ	J0270
ALPROSTADIL	EA	OTH	J0275
ALTEPLASE RECOMBINANT	1 MG	IV	J2997
ALUPENT, NONCOMPOUNDED, CONCENTRATED	10 MG	INH	J7668
ALUPENT, NONCOMPOUNDED, UNIT DOSE	10 MG	INH	J7669
AMANTADINE HYDROCHLORIDE (BRAND NAME)	100 MG	ORAL	G9033
AMANTADINE HYDROCHLORIDE (GENERIC)	100 MG	ORAL	G9017
AMBISOME	10 MG	IV	J0289
AMCORT	5 MG	IM	J3302
AMERGAN	12.5 MG	ORAL	Q0169

Drug Name	Unit Per	Route	Code
A-METHAPRED	125 MG	IM, IV	J2930
A-METHAPRED	40 MG	IM, IV	J2920
AMEVIVE	0.5 MG	IV, IM	J0215
AMICAR	5 G	IV	S0017
AMIFOSTINE	500 MG	IV	J0207
AMIKACIN SULFATE	100 MG	IM, IV	J0278
AMINOCAPRIOC ACID	5 G	IV	S0017
AMINOPHYLLINE	250 MG	IV	J0280
AMIODARONE HCL	30 MG	IV	J0282
AMITRIPTYLINE HCL	20 MG	IM	J1320
AMMONIA N-13	DOSE	IV	A9526
AMOBARBITAL	125 MG	IM, IV	J0300
AMPHOCIN	50 MG	IV	J0285
AMPHOTEC	10 MG	IV	J0287
AMPHOTERICIN B	50 MG	IV	J0285
AMPHOTERICIN B CHOLESTERYL SULFATE COMPLEX	10 MG	IV	J0288
AMPHOTERICIN B LIPID COMPLEX	10 MG	IV	J0287
AMPHOTERICIN B LIPOSOME	10 MG	IV	J0289
AMPICILLIN SODIUM	500 MG	IM, IV	J0290
AMPICILLIN SODIUM/SULBACTAM SODIUM	1.5 G	IM, IV	J0295
AMYTAL	125 MG	IM, IV	J0300
ANASTROZOLE	1 MG	ORAL	S0170
ANCEF	500 MG	IV, IM	J0690
AN-DTPA DIAGNOSTIC	UP TO 25 MCI	IV	A9539
AN-DTPA THERAPEUTIC	UP TO 25 MCI	IV	A9567
ANECTINE	20 MG	IM, IV	J0330
ANGIOMAX	1 MG	IV	J0583
ANIDULAFUNGIN	1 MG	IV	J0348
ANISTREPLASE	30 U	IV	J0350
ANTAGON	250 MCG	SC	S0132
ANTIHEMOPHILIC FACTOR HUMAN METHOD M MONOCLONAL PURIFIED	1 IU	IV	J7192
ANTIHEMOPHILIC FACTOR PORCINE	1 IU	IV	J7191
ANTIHEMOPHILIC FACTOR VIII/VON WILLEBRAND FACTOR COMPLEX, HUMAN	PER FACTOR VIII IU	IV	J7186
ANTI-INHIBITOR	1 IU	IV	J7198
ANTITHROMBIN III	1 IU	IV	J7195
ANTI-THYMOCYTE GLOBULIN,EQUINE	250 MG	OTH	J7504
ANTIZOL	15 MG	IV	J1451
ANZEMET	10 MG	IV	J1260
ANZEMET	100 MG	ORAL	Q0180
APLIGRAF	SQ CM	OTH	Q4101
APOKYN	1 MG	SC	J0364
APOMORPHINE HYDROCHLORIDE	1 MG	SC	J0364
APREPITANT, ORAL, 5 MG	5 MG	ORAL	J8501
APROTININ	10,000 KIU	IV	J0365
AQUAMEPHYTON	1 MG	IM, SC, IV	J3430
ARA-C	100 MG	SC, IV	J9100
ARAMINE	10 MG	IV, IM, SC	J0380
ARANESP, ESRD USE	1 MCG	SC, IV	J0882
ARANESP, NON-ESRD USE	1 MCG	SC, IV	J0881
ARBUTAMINE HCL	1 MG	IV	J0395
AREDIA	30 MG	IV	J2430
ARFORMOTEROL	15 MCG	INH	J7605
ARIMIDEX	1 MG	ORAL	S0170
ARIPIPRAZOLE	0.25 MG	IM	J0400
ARISTOCORT	5 MG	IM	J3302
ARISTOCORTE FORTE	5 MG	IM	J3302
ARISTOCORTE INTRALESIONAL	5 MG	OTH	J3302
ARISTOSPAN	5 MG	VAR	J3303
ARIXTRA	0.5 MG	SC	J1652
AROMASIN	25 MG	ORAL	S0156
ARRANON	50 MG	IV	J9261
ARRESTIN	200 MG	IM	J3250
ARSENIC TRIOXIDE	1 MG	IV	J9017
ASPARAGINASE	10,000 U	VAR	J9020
ASTRAMORPH PF	10 MG	IM, IV, SC	J2275
ATGAM	250 MG	OTH	J7504
ATIVAN	2 MG	IM, IV	J2060
ATOPICLAIR	ANY SIZE	OTH	A6250
ATROPEN	0.3 MG	IV, IM, SC	J0460
ATROPINE SULFATE	0.3 MG	IV, IM, SC	J0460
ATROPINE, COMPOUNDED, CONCENTRATED	I MG	INH	J7635
ATROPINE, COMPOUNDED, UNIT DOSE	1 MG	INH	J7636
ATROVENT, NONCOMPOUNDED, UNIT DOSE	1 MG	INH	J7644
AUROTHIOGLUCOSE	50 MG	IM	J2910
AUTOPLEX T	1 IU	IV	J7198
AVASTIN	10 MG	IV	J9035
AVELOX	100 MG	IV	J2280
AVONEX	11 MCG	IM	Q3025
AVONEX	33 MCG	IM	J1825
AZACITIDINE	1 MG	SC	J9025
AZACTAM	500 MG	IV	S0073
AZASAN	50 MG	ORAL	J7500
AZATHIOPRINE	100 MG	OTH	J7501
AZATHIOPRINE	50 MG	ORAL	J7500
AZITHROMYCIN	500 MG	IV	J0456
AZMACORT	PER MG	INH	J7684
AZMACORT CONCENTRATED	PER MG	INH	J7683
AZTREONAM	500 MG	IV	S0073
BACLOFEN	10 MG	IT	J0475
BACLOFEN	50 MCG	OTH	J0476
BACTOCILL	250 MG	IM, IV	J2700
BACTRIM IV	10 ML	IV	S0039
BAL	100 MG	IM	J0470
BASILIXIMAB	20 MG	IV	J0480
BAYRHO-D	300 MCG	IM	J2790
BCG VACCINE LIVE	VIAL	IV	J9031
BEBULIN VH	1 IU	IV	J7194
BECAPLERMIN GEL 0.01%	0.5 G	OTH	S0157
BECLOMETHASONE COMPOUNDED	1 MG	INH	J7622
BECLOVENT COMPOUNDED	1 MG	INH	J7622
BECONASE COMPOUNDED	1 MG	INH	J7622
BENA-D 10	50 MG	IV, IM	J1200

Drug Name	Unit Per	Route	Code
BENA-D 50	50 MG	IV, IM	J1200
BENADRYL	50 MG	IV, IM	J1200
BENAHIST 10	50 MG	IV, IM	J1200
BENAHIST 50	50 MG	IV, IM	J1200
BENDAMUSTINE HCL	1 MG	IV	J9033
BENEFIX	1 IU	IV	J7195
BENOJECT-10	50 MG	IV, IM	J1200
BENOJECT-50	50 MG	IV, IM	J1200
BENTYL	20 MG	IM	J0500
BENZTROPINE MESYLATE	1 MG	IM, IV	J0515
BERUBIGEN	1,000 MCG	SC, IM	J3420
BETA-2	1 MG	INH	J7648
BETALIN 12	1,000 MCG	SC, IM	J3420
BETAMETHASONE ACETATE AND BETAMETHASONE SODIUM PHOSPHATE	3 MG, OF EACH	IM	J0702
BETAMETHASONE COMPOUNDED, UNIT DOSE	1 MG	INH	J7624
BETAMETHASONE SODIUM PHOSPHATE	4 MG	IM, IV	J0704
BETASERON	0.25 MG	SC	J1830
BETHANECHOL CHLORIDE, MYOTONACHOL OR URECHOLINE	5 MG	SC	J0520
BEVACIZUMAB	10 MG	IV	J9035
BEXXAR THERAPEUTIC	TX DOSE	IV	A9545
BICILLIN CR	1,200,000 U	IM	J0540
BICILLIN CR	600,000 U	IM	J0530
BICILLIN CR 900/300	1,200,000 U	IM, IV	J0540
BICILLIN CR 900/300	2,400,000 U	IM, IV	J0550
BICILLIN LA	1,200,000 U	IM	J0570
BICILLIN LA	600,000 U	IM	J0560
BICILLIN LA	2,400,000 U	INJ	J0580
BICNU	100 MG	IV	J9050
BIOCLATE	1 IU	IV	J7192
BIOTROPIN	1 MG	SC	J2941
BITOLTEROL MESYLATE, COMPOUNDED CONCENTRATED	PER MG	INH	J7628
BITOLTEROL MESYLATE, COMPOUNDED UNIT DOSE	PER MG	INH	J7629
BIVALIRUDIN	1 MG	IV	J0583
BLENOXANE	15 U	IM, IV, SC	J9040
BLEOMYCIN LYOPHILLIZED	15 U	IM, IV, SC	J9040
BLEOMYCIN SULFATE	15 U	IM, IV, SC	J9040
BONIVA	1 MG	IV	J1740
BORTEZOMIB	0.1 MG	IV	J9041
BOTOX	1 U	IM	J0585
BOTULINUM TOXIN TYPE A	1 U	OTH	J0585
BOTULINUM TOXIN TYPE B	100 U	OTH	J0587
BRAVELLE	75 IU	SC, IM	J3355
BRETHINE	PER MG	INH	J7681
BRETHINE CONCENTRATED	PER MG	INH	J7680
BRICANYL	PER MG	INH	J7681
BRICANYL CONCENTRATED	PER MG	INH	J7680
BROM-A-COT	10 MG	IM, SC, IV	J0945
BROMPHENIRAMINE MALEATE	10 MG	IM, SC, IV	J0945
BUDESONIDE COMPOUNDED, CONCETRATED	0.25 MG	INH	J7634
BUDESONIDE, COMPOUNDED, UNIT DOSE	0.5 MG	INH	J7627
BUDESONIDE, NONCOMPOUNDED, CONCENTRATED	0.25 MG	INH	J7633
BUDESONIDE, NONCOMPOUNDED, UNIT DOSE	0.5 MG	INH	J7626
BUMETANIDE	0.5 MG	IM, IV	S0171
BUPIVACAINE HCL	30 ML	OTH	S0020
BUPRENEX	0.1 MG	IM, IV	J0592
BUPRENORPHINE HCL	0.1 MG	IM, IV	J0592
BUPROPION HCL	150 MG	ORAL	S0106
BUSULFAN	1 MG	IV	J0594
BUSULFAN	2 MG	OTH	J8510
BUSULFEX	1 MG	IV	J0594
BUSULFEX	2 MG	ORAL	J8510
BUTORPHANOL TARTRATE	2 MG	IM, IV	J0595
BUTORPHANOL TARTRATE	25 MG	OTH	S0012
CABERGOLINE	0.25 MG	ORAL	J8515
CAFCIT	5 MG	IV	J0706
CAFFEINE CITRATE	5 MG	IV	J0706
CALCIJEX	0.1 MCG	IM	J0636
CALCIMAR	UP TO 400 U	SC, IM	J0630
CALCITONIN SALMON	400 U	SC, IM	J0630
CALCITRIOL	0.1 MCG	IM	J0636
CALCITROL	0.25 MG	IM	S0161
CALCIUM DISODIUM VERSENATE	1,000 MG	IV, SC, IM	J0600
CALCIUM GLUCONATE	10 ML	IV	J0610
CALCIUM GLYCEROPHOSPHATE AND CALCIUM LACTATE	10 ML	IM, SC	J0620
CAMPATH	10 MG	IV	J9010
CAMPTOSAR	20 MG	IV	J9206
CANCIDAS	5 MG	IV	J0637
CAPECITABINE	150 MG	ORAL	J8520
CAPROMAB PENDETIDE	DOSE	IV	A9507
CARBOCAINE	10 ML	VAR	J0670
CARBOPLATIN	50 MG	IV	J9045
CARDIOGEN 82	60 MCI	IV	A9555
CARDIOLITE	DOSE	IV	A9500
CARIMUNE	500 MG	IV	J1566
CARMUSTINE	100 MG	IV	J9050
CARNITOR	1 G	IV	J1955
CARTICEL		OTH	J7330
CASPOFUNGIN ACETATE	5 MG	IV	J0637
CATAPRES	1 MG	OTH	J0735
CATHFLO	1 MG	IV	J2997
CAVERJECT	1.25 MCG	VAR	J0270
CEA SCAN	UP TO 45 MCI	IV	A9568
CEENU	10 MG	ORAL	S0178
CEFEPIME HCL	500 MG	IV	J0692
CEFIZOX	500 MG	IV, IM	J0715
CEFOBID	1 G	IV	S0021
CEFOPERAZONE SODIUM	1 G	IV	S0021
CEFOTAN	500 MG	IM, IV	S0074
CEFOTAXIME SODIUM	1 GM	IV, IM	J0698
CEFOTETAN DISODIUM	500 MG	IM. IV	S0074
CEFOXITIN SODIUM	1 GM	IV, IM	J0694

Drug Name	Unit Per	Route	Code
CEFTAZIDIME	500 MG	IM, IV	J0713
CEFTIZOXIME SODIUM	500 MG	IV, IM	J0715
CEFTRIAXONE	250 MG	IV, IM	J0696
CEFTRIAXONE SODIUM	250 MG	IV, IM	J0696
CEFUROXIME	750 MG	IM, IV	J0697
CEFUROXIME SODIUM STERILE	750 MG	IM, IV	J0697
CELESTONE SOLUSPAN	3 MG	IM	J0702
CELLCEPT	250 MG	ORAL	J7517
CENACORT A-40	10 MG	IM	J3301
CENACORT FORTE	5 MG	IM	J3302
CEPHAPIRIN SODIUM	1 G	IV	J0710
CEPTAZ	500 MG	IM, IV	J0713
CEREBRYX	50 MG	IM, IV	Q2009
CEREBRYX	750 MG	IM, IV	S0078
CEREDASE	10 U	IV	J0205
CERETEC	DOSE	IV	A9521
CERETEC	PER STUDY DOSE	IV	A9569
CEREZYME	1 U	IV	J1785
CERUBIDINE	10 MG	IV	J9150
CESAMET	1 MG	ORAL	J8650
CETUXIMAB	10 MG	IV	J9055
CHEALAMIDE	150 MG	IV	J3520
CHLORAMBUCIL	2 MG	ORAL	S0172
CHLORAMPHENICOL SODIUM SUCCINATE	1 G	IV	J0720
CHLORDIAZEPOXIDE HCL	100 MG	IM, IV	J1990
CHLOROMYCETIN	1 G	IV	J0720
CHLOROPROCAINE HCL	30 ML	VAR	J2400
CHLOROTHIAZIDE SODIUM	500 MG	IV	J1205
CHLORPROMAZINE HCL	10 MG	ORAL	Q0171
CHLORPROMAZINE HCL	50 MG	IM, IV	J3230
CHLORPROMAZINE HCL	25 MG	ORAL	Q0172
CHOLETEC	UP TO 35 MCI	IV	A9537
CHORIONIC GONADOTROPIN	1,000 USP U	IM	J0725
CHROMIC PHOSPHATE P32	1 MCI	IV	A9564
CHROMITOPE SODIUM	250 UCI	IV	A9553
CHROMIUM CR-51 SODIUM IOTHALAMATE, DIAGNOSTIC	10 UCI	IV	A9553
CIDOFOVIR	375 MG	IV	J0740
CILASTATIN SODIUM	250 MG	IV, IM	J0743
CIMETIDINE HCL	300 MG	IM, IV	S0023
CIPRO	200 MG	IV	J0744
CIPROFLOXACIN FOR INTRAVENOUS INFUSION	200 MG	IV	J0744
CIS-MDP	30 MCI	IV	A9503
CISPLATIN	10 MG	IV	J9060
CIS-PYRO	UP TO 25 MCI	IV	A9538
CLADRIBINE	1 MG	IV	J9065
CLAFORAN	1 GM	IV, IM	J0698
CLEOCIN PHOSPHATE	300 MG	IV	S0077
CLEVIDIPINE BUTYRATE	1 MG	IV	C9248
CLEVIPREX	1 MG	IV	C9248
CLINAGEN LA	UP TO 40 MG	IM	J0970
CLINDAMYCIN PHOSPHATE	300 MG	IV	S0077
CLOFARABINE	1 MG	IV	J9027
CLOLAR	1 MG	IV	J9027
CLONIDINE HCL	1 MG	OTH	J0735
CLOSTRIDIUM BOTULINUM TOXIN	1 U	OTH	J0585
CLOZAPINE	25 MG	ORAL	S0136
CLOZARIL	25 MG	ORAL	S0136
COBAL	1,000 MCG	IM, SC	J3420
COBALT CO-57 CYNOCOBALAMIN, DIAGNOSTIC	1 UCI	ORAL	A9559
COBATOPE 57	1 UCI	ORAL	A9559
COBEX	1,000 MCG	SC, IM	J3420
CODEINE PHOSPHATE	30 MG	IM, IV, SC	J0745
COGENTIN	1 MG	IM, IV	J0515
COGNEX	10 MG	ORAL	S0014
COLCHICINE	1 MG	IV	J0760
COLHIST	10 MG	IM, SC, IV	J0945
COLISTIMETHATE SODIUM	150 MG	IM, IV	J0770
COLISTIMETHATE SODIUM	PER MG	INH	S0142
COLLAGEN BASED WOUND FILLER DRY FOAM	1 GM	OTH	A6010
COLLAGEN NERVE CUFF	0.5 CM LENGTH	OTH	C9355
COLLAGEN BASED WOUND FILLER, GEL/PASTE	1 GM	OTH	A6011
COLY-MYCIN M	150 MG	IM, IV	J0770
COMPAZINE	10 MG	IM, IV	J0780
COMPAZINE	5 MG	ORAL	S0183
COMPAZINE	10 MG	ORAL	Q0165
COMPAZINE	5 MG	ORAL	Q0164
CONTRACEPTIVE SUPPLY, HORMONE CONTAINING PATCH	EACH	OTH	J7304
COPAXONE	20 MG	SC	J1595
COPPER T MODEL TCU380A IUD COPPER WIRE/COPPER COLLAR	EA	OTH	J7300
CORDARONE	30 MG	IV	J0282
CORTASTAT	1 MG	IM, IV, OTH	J1100
CORTASTAT LA	1 MG	IM	J1094
CORTICORELIN OVINE TRIFLUTATE	1 MCG	IV	J0795
CORTICOTROPIN	40 U	IV, IM, SC	J0800
CORTIMED	80 MG	IM	J1040
CORTROSYN	0.25 MG	IM, IV	J0835
CORVERT	1 MG	IV	J1742
COSMEGEN	0.5 MG	IV	J9120
COSYNTROPIN	0.25 MG	IM, IV	J0835
COTOLONE	5 MG	ORAL	J7510
CROMOLYN SODIUM COMPOUNDED	PER 10 MG	INH	J7632
CROMOLYN SODIUM NONCOMPOUNDED	10 MG	INH	J7631
CRYSTAL B12	1,000 MCG	IM, SC	J3420
CRYSTICILLIN 300 A.S.	600,000 UNITS	IM, IV	J2510
CRYSTICILLIN 600 A.S.	600,000 UNITS	IM, IV	J2510
CUBICIN	1 MG	IV	J0878
CYANO	1,000 MCG	IM, SC	J3420
CYANOCOBALAMIN	1,000 MCG	IM, SC	J3420
CYANOCOBALAMIN COBALT 58/57	1 UCI	IV	A9546
CYANOCOBALAMIN COBALT CO-57	1 UCI	ORAL	A9559
CYCLOPHOSPHAMIDE	1 G	IV	J9091

Drug Name	Unit Per	Route	Code
CYCLOPHOSPHAMIDE	200 MG	IV	J9080
CYCLOPHOSPHAMIDE	25 MG	ORAL	J8530
CYCLOPHOSPHAMIDE	500 MG	IV	J9090
CYCLOPHOSPHAMIDE	2 G	IV	J9092
CYCLOPHOSPHAMIDE	100 MG	IV	J9070
CYCLOPHOSPHAMIDE LYOPHILIZED	1 G	IV	J9096
CYCLOPHOSPHAMIDE LYOPHILIZED	2 G	IV	J9097
CYCLOPHOSPHAMIDE LYOPHILIZED	500 MG	IV	J9095
CYCLOPHOSPHAMIDE LYOPHILIZED	100 MG	IV	J9093
CYCLOPHOSPHAMIDE LYOPHILIZED	200 MG	IV	J9094
CYCLOSPORINE	100 MG	ORAL	J7502
CYCLOSPORINE	25 MG	ORAL	J7515
CYCLOSPORINE	250 MG	IV	J7516
CYMETRA	1 CC	INJ	Q4112
CYTARABINE	100 MG	SC, IV	J9100
CYTARABINE	500 MG	SC, IV	J9110
CYTARABINE LIPOSOME	10 MG	IT	J9098
CYTOGAM	VIAL	IV	J0850
CYTOMEGALOVIRUS IMMUNE GLOB	VIAL	IV	J0850
CYTOSAR-U	100 MG	SC, IV	J9100
CYTOSAR-U	500 MG	SC, IV	J9110
CYTOTEC	200 MCG	ORAL	S0191
CYTOVENE	500 MG	IV	J1570
CYTOXAN	1 G	IV	J9091
CYTOXAN	100 MG	IV	J9070
CYTOXAN	500 MG	IV	J9090
CYTOXAN	200 MG	IV	J9080
CYTOXAN	2 G	IV	J9092
CYTOXAN	25 MG	ORAL	J8530
CYTOXAN LYOPHILIZED	1 G	IV	J9096
CYTOXAN LYOPHILIZED	500 MG	IV	J9095
CYTOXAN LYOPHILIZED	2 G	IV	J9097
CYTOXAN LYOPHILIZED	200 MG	IV	J9094
CYTOXAN LYOPHILIZED	100 MG	IV	J9093
D.H.E. 45	1 MG	IM, IV	J1110
DACARBAZINE	100 MG	IV	J9130
DACARBAZINE	200 MG	IV	J9140
DACLIZUMAB	25 MG	OTH	J7513
DACOGEN	1 MG	IV	J0894
DACTINOMYCIN	0.5 MG	IV	J9120
DALALONE	1 MG	IM, IV, OTH	J1100
DALALONE LA	1 MG	IM	J1094
DALTEPARIN SODIUM	2,500 IU	SC	J1645
DAPTOMYCIN	1 MG	IV	J0878
DARBEPOETIN ALFA, ESRD USE	1 MCG	SC, IV	J0882
DARBEPOETIN ALFA, NON-ESRD USE	1 MCG	SC, IV	J0881
DAUNORUBICIN	10 MG	IV	J9150
DAUNORUBICIN CITRATE, LIPOOSOMAL FORMULATION	10 MG	IV	J9151
DAUNOXOME	10 MG	IV	J9151
DDAVP	1 MCG	IV, SC	J2597
DECADRON	0.25 MG	ORAL	J8540
DECAJECT	1 MG	IM, IV, OTH	J1100
DECITABINE	1 MG	IV	J0894
DECOLONE-50	50 MG	IM	J2320
DEFEROXAMINE MESYLATE	500 MG	IM, SC, IV	J0895
DELATESTRYL	100 MG	IM	J3120
DELATESTRYL	200 MG	IM	J3130
DELESTROGEN	10 MG	IM	J1380
DELESTROGEN	20 MG	IM	J1390
DELESTROGEN	UP TO 40 MG	IM	J0970
DELTA-CORTEF	5 MG	ORAL	J7510
DELTASONE	5 MG	ORAL	J7506
DELTASONE	5 MG	OTH	J7506
DEMADEX	10 MG	IV	J3265
DEMEROL	100 MG	IM, IV, SC	J2175
DENILEUKIN DIFTITOX	300 MCG	IV	J9160
DEPANDRATE	1 CC, 200 MG	IM	J1080
DEPANDROGYN	1 ML	IM	J1060
DEPGYNOGEN	UP TO 5 MG	IM	J1000
DEPHENACEN-50	50 MG	IM, IV	J1200
DEPMEDALONE	40 MG	IM	J1030
DEPMEDALONE	80 MG	IM	J1040
DEPOCYT	10 MG	IT	J9098
DEPODUR	UP TO 10 MG	IV	J2270
DEPODUR	UP TO 10 MG	IV	J2271
DEPO-ESTRADIOL CYPIONATE	UP TO 5 MG	IM	J1000
DEPOGEN	UP TO 5 MG	IM	J1000
DEPO-MEDROL	20 MG	IM	J1020
DEPO-MEDROL	40 MG	IM	J1030
DEPO-MEDROL	80 MG	IM	J1040
DEPO-PROVERA	150 MG	IM	J1055
DEPO-PROVERA	50 MG	IM	J1051
DEPO-TESTADIOL	1 ML	IM	J1060
DEPO-TESTOSTERONE	1 CC, 200 MG	IM	J1080
DEPO-TESTOSTERONE	UP TO 100 MG	IM	J1070
DEPO-TESTOSTERONE CYPIONATE	UP TO 100 MG	IM	J1070
DEPTESTROGEN	UP TO 100 MG	IM	J1070
DERMAGRAFT	SQ CM	OTH	Q4106
DERMAL SUBSTITUTE, NATIVE, NONDENATURED	0.5 SQ CM	OTH	C9358
DERMAL SUBSTITUTE, NATIVE, NONDENTURED COLLAGEN	0.5 SQ CM	OTH	C9358
DESFERAL	500 MG	IM, SC, IV	J0895
DESMOPRESSIN ACETATE	1 MCG	IV, SC	J2597
DEXAMETHASONE	0.25 MG	ORAL	J8540
DEXAMETHASONE ACETATE	1 MG	IM	J1094
DEXAMETHASONE ACETATE ANHYDROUS	1 MG	IM	J1094
DEXAMETHASONE SODIUM PHOSPHATE	1 MG	IM, IV, OTH	J1100
DEXAMETHASONE, COMPOUNDED, CONCENTRATED	PER MG	INH	J7637
DEXAMETHASONE, COMPOUNDED, UNIT DOSE	PER MG	INH	J7638
DEXASONE	1 MG	IM, IV, OTH	J1100
DEXEDRINE	5 MG	ORAL	S0160
DEXIM	1 MG	IM, IV, OTH	J1100
DEXONE	0.25 MG	ORAL	J8540

Drug Name	Unit Per	Route	Code
DEXONE	1 MG	IM, IV, OTH	J1100
DEXONE LA	1 MG	IM	J1094
DEXRAZOXANE	250 MG	IV	J1190
DEXRAZOXANE HYDROCHLORIDE	250 MG	IV	J1190
DEXTRAN 40	500 ML	IV	J7100
DEXTROAMPHETAMINE SULFATE	5 MG	ORAL	S0160
DEXTROSE	500 ML	IV	J7060
DEXTROSE, STERILE WATER, AND/OR DEXTROSE DILUENT/FLUSH	10 ML	VAR	A4216
DEXTROSE/SODIUM CHLORIDE	5%	VAR	J7042
DEXTROSE/THEOPHYLLINE	40 MG	IV	J2810
DEXTROSTAT	5 MG	ORAL	S0160
DIALYSIS/STRESS VITAMINS	100 CAPS	ORAL	S0194
DIAMOX	500 MG	IM, IV	J1120
DIASTAT	5 MG	IV, IM	J3360
DIAZEPAM	5 MG	IV, IM	J3360
DIAZOXIDE	300 MG	IV	J1730
DICYCLOMINE HCL	20 MG	IM	J0500
DIDANOSINE (DDI)	25 MG	ORAL	S0137
DIDRONEL	300 MG	IV	J1436
DIETHYLSTILBESTROL DIPHOSPHATE	250 MG	INJ	J9165
DIFLUCAN	200 MG	IV	J1450
DIGIBIND	VIAL	IV	J1162
DIGIFAB	VIAL	IV	J1162
DIGOXIN	0.5 MG	IM, IV	J1160
DIGOXIN IMMUNE FAB	VIAL	IV	J1162
DIHYDROERGOTAMINE MESYLATE	1 MG	IM, IV	J1110
DILANTIN	50 MG	IM, IV	J1165
DILAUDID	250 MG	OTH	S0092
DILAUDID	4 MG	SC, IM, IV	J1170
DIMENHYDRINATE	50 MG	IM, IV	J1240
DIMERCAPROL	100 MG	IM	J0470
DIMINE	50 MG	IV, IM	J1200
DINATE	50 MG	IM, IV	J1240
DIOVAL	10 MG	IM	J1380
DIOVAL	20 MG	IM	J1390
DIOVAL 40	10 MG	IM	J1380
DIOVAL 40	20 MG	IM	J1390
DIOVAL XX	10 MG	IM	J1380
DIOVAL XX	20 MG	IM	J1390
DIPHENHYDRAMINE HCL	50 MG	IV, IM	J1200
DIPHENHYDRAMINE HCL	50 MG	ORAL	Q0163
DIPYRIDAMOLE	10 MG	IV	J1245
DISOTATE	150 MG	IV	J3520
DIURIL	500 MG	IV	J1205
DIURIL SODIUM	500 MG	IV	J1205
DIZAC	5 MG	IV, IM	J3360
DMSO, DIMETHYL SULFOXIDE	50%, 50 ML	OTH	J1212
DOBUTAMINE HCL	250 MG	IV	J1250
DOCETAXEL	20 MG	IV	J9170
DOLASETRON MESYLATE	10 MG	IV	J1260
DOLASETRON MESYLATE	50 MG	ORAL	S0174
DOLASETRON MESYLATE	100 MG	ORAL	Q0180
DOLOPHINE	5 MG	ORAL	S0109
DOLOPHINE HCL	10 MG	IM, SC	J1230
DOMMANATE	50 MG	IM, IV	J1240
DOPAMINE HCL	40 MG	IV	J1265
DORIBAX	10 MG	IV	J1267
DORIPENEM	10 MG	IV	J1267
DORNASE ALPHA, NONCOMPOUNDED, UNIT DOSE	PER MG	INH	J7639
DOSTINEX	0.25 MG	ORAL	J8515
DOXERCALCIFEROL	1 MG	IV	J1270
DOXIL	10 MG	IV	J9001
DOXORUBICIN HCL	10 MG	IV	J9000
DOXORUBICIN HCL, ALL LIPID FORMULATIONS	10 MG	IV	J9001
DRAMAMINE	50 MG	IM, IV	J1240
DRAMILIN	50 MG	IM, IV	J1240
DRAMOCEN	50 MG	IM, IV	J1240
DRAMOJECT	50 MG	IM, IV	J1240
DRAXIMAGE MDP-10	30 MCI	IV	A9503
DRAXIMAGE MDP-25	30 MCI	IV	A9503
DRONABINAL	2.5 MG	ORAL	Q0167
DRONABINAL	5 MG	ORAL	Q0168
DROPERIDOL	5 MG	IM, IV	J1790
DROPERIDOL AND FENTANYL CITRATE	2 ML	IM, IV	J1810
DROXIA	500 MG	ORAL	S0176
DTIC-DOME	100 MG	IV	J9130
DTIC-DOME	200 MG	IV	J9140
DTPA	UP TO 25 MCI	IV	A9539
DTPA	UP TO 25 MCI	INH	A9567
DUO-SPAN	1 ML	IM	J1060
DUO-SPAN II	1 ML	IM	J1060
DURACILLIN A.S.	600,000 UNITS	IM, IV	J2510
DURACLON	1 MG	OTH	J0735
DURAGEN-10	10 MG	IM	J1380
DURAGEN-10	20 MG	IM	J1390
DURAGEN-20	10 MG	IM	J1380
DURAGEN-20	20 MG	IM	J1390
DURAGEN-40	10 MG	IM	J1380
DURAGEN-40	20 MG	IM	J1390
DURAMORPH	10 MG	IM, IV, SC	J2275
DURAMORPH	500 MG	OTH	S0093
DURO CORT	80 MG	IM	J1040
DYMENATE	50 MG	IM, IV	J1240
DYPHYLLINE	500 MG	IM	J1180
E.D.T.A	150 MG	IV	J3520
ECHOCARDIOGRAM IMAGE ENHANCER	1 ML	IV	Q9955
ECHOCARDIOGRAM IMAGE ENHANCER	1 ML	INJ	Q9956
ECULIZUMAB	10 MG	IV	J1300
EDETATE CALCIUM DISODIUM	1,000 MG	IV, SC, IM	J0600
EDETATE DISODIUM	150 MG	IV	J3520
EDEX	1.25 MCG	VAR	J0270
EFALIZUMAB	125 MG	SC	S0162
ELAPRASE	1 MG	IV	J1743

Drug Name	Unit Per	Route	Code
ELAVIL	20 MG	IM	J1320
ELIGARD	7.5 MG	IM	J9217
ELIGARD	PER 3.75 MG	SC	J1950
ELITEK	50 MCG	IM	J2783
ELLENCE	2 MG	IV	J9178
ELLIOTTS B SOLUTION	1 ML	IV, IT	J9175
ELOXATIN	0.5 MG	IV	J9263
ELSPAR	10,000 U	VAR	J9020
EMEND	5 MG	ORAL	J8501
EMEND	1 MG	IV	J1453
EMINASE	30 U	IV	J0350
ENBREL	25 MG	IM, IV	J1438
ENDOXAN-ASTA	1 G	IV	J9091
ENDOXAN-ASTA	200 MG	IV	J9080
ENDOXAN-ASTA	100 MG	IV	J9070
ENDOXAN-ASTA	500 MG	IV	J9090
ENDRATE	150 MG	IV	J3520
ENFUVIRTIDE	1 MG	SC	J1324
ENOXAPARIN SODIUM	10 MG	SC	J1650
EOVIST	1 ML	IV	C9246
EPINEPHRINE	1 MG	IM, IV, SC, VAR	J0170
EPIPEN	0.3 MG	IM	J0170
EPIRUBICIN HCL	2 MG	IV	J9178
EPOETIN ALFA, ESRD USE	1,000 U	SC, IV	J0886
EPOETIN ALFA, NON-ESRD USE	1,000 U	SC, IV	J0885
EPOGEN/ESRD	1,000 U	SC, IV	J0886
EPOGEN/NON-ESRD	1,000 U	SC, IV	J0885
EPOPROSTENOL	0.5 MG	IV	J1325
EPOPROSTENOL STERILE DILUTANT	50 ML	IV	S0155
EPTIFIBATIDE	5 MG	IM, IV	J1327
ERAXIS	1 MG	IV	J0348
ERBITUX	10 MG	IV	J9055
ERGAMISOL	50 MG	ORAL	S0177
ERGONOVINE MALEATE	0.2 MG	IM, IV	J1330
ERTAPENEM SODIUM	500 MG	IM, IV	J1335
ERYTHROCIN LACTOBIONATE	500 MG	IV	J1364
ESTONE AQUEOUS	1 MG	IM, IV	J1435
ESTRADIOL CYPIONATE	UP TO 5 MG	IM	J1000
ESTRADIOL L.A.	10 MG	IM	J1380
ESTRADIOL L.A.	20 MG	IM	J1390
ESTRADIOL L.A. 20	10 MG	IM	J1380
ESTRADIOL L.A. 20	20 MG	IM	J1390
ESTRADIOL L.A. 40	10 MG	IM	J1380
ESTRADIOL L.A. 40	20 MG	IM	J1390
ESTRADIOL VALERATE	10 MG	IM	J1380
ESTRADIOL VALERATE	UP TO 40 MG	IM	J0970
ESTRADIOL VALERATE	20 MG	IM	J1390
ESTRAGYN	1 MG	IV, IM	J1435
ESTRA-L 20	10 MG	IM	J1380
ESTRA-L 20	20 MG	IM	J1390
ESTRA-L 40	10 MG	IM	J1380
ESTRA-L 40	20 MG	IM	J1390
ESTRO-A	1 MG	IV, IM	J1435
ESTROGEN CONJUGATED	25 MG	IV, IM	J1410
ESTRONE	1 MG	IV, IM	J1435
ESTRONOL	1 MG	IM, IV	J1435
ETANERCEPT	25 MG	IM, IV	J1438
ETHAMOLIN	100 MG	IV	J1430
ETHANOLAMINE OLEATE	100 MG	IV	J1430
ETHYOL	500 MG	IV	J0207
ETIDRONATE DISODIUM	300 MG	IV	J1436
ETONOGESTREL	PER IMPLANT	OTH	J7307
ETOPOSIDE	10 MG	IV	J9181
ETOPOSIDE	50 MG	ORAL	J8560
EUFLEXXA	PER DOSE	OTH	J7323
EULEXIN	125 MG	ORAL	S0175
EXAMETAZIME LABELED AUTOLOGOUS WHITE BLOOD CELLS, TECHNETIUM TC-99M	PER STUDY DOSE	IV	A9569
EXMESTANE	25 MG	ORAL	S0156
FABRAZYME	1 MG	IV	J0180
FACTOR IX NON-RECOMBINANT	1 IU	IV	J7193
FACTOR IX RECOMBINANT	1 IU	IV	J7195
FACTOR IX+ COMPLEX	1 IU	IV	J7194
FACTOR VIIA RECOMBINANT	1 MCG	IV	J7189
FACTOR VIII PORCINE	1 IU	IV	J7191
FACTOR VIII RECOMBINANT	1 IU	IV	J7192
FACTOR VIII, HUMAN	1 IU	IV	J7190
FACTREL	100 MCG	SC, IV	J1620
FAMOTIDINE	20 MG	IV	S0028
FASLODEX	25 MG	IM	J9395
FDG	STUDY DOSE		A9552
FEIBA-VH AICC	1 IU	IV	J7198
FENTANYL CITRATE	0.1 MG	IM, IV	J3010
FERIDEX IV	1 ML	IV	Q9953
FERRLECIT	12.5 MG	IV	J2916
FERTINEX	75 IU	SC	J3355
FILGRASTIM	300 MCG	SC, IV	J1440
FILGRASTIM	480 MCG	SC, IV	J1441
FINASTERIDE	5 MG	ORAL	S0138
FLAGYL	500 MG	IV	S0030
FLEBOGAMMA	500 MG	IV	J1572
FLEXON	60 MG	IV, IM	J2360
FLOLAN	0.5 MG	IV	J1325
FLOXIN IV	400 MG	IV	S0034
FLOXURIDINE	500 MG	IV	J9200
FLUCONAZOLE	200 MG	IV	J1450
FLUDARA	50 MG	IV	J9185
FLUDARABINE PHOSPHATE	50 MG	IV	J9185
FLUDEOXYGLUCOSE F18	STUDY DOSE	IV	A9552
FLUNISOLIDE, COMPOUNDED, UNIT DOSE	1 MG	INH	J7641
FLUOCINOLONE ACETONIDE INTRAVITREAL	IMPLANT	OTH	J7311
FLUORODEOXYGLUCOSE F-18 FDG, DIAGNOSTIC	45 MCI	IV	A9552
FLUOROURACIL	500 MG	IV	J9190
FLUPHENAZINE DECANOATE	25 MG	SC, IM	J2680
FLUTAMIDE	125 MG	ORAL	S0175

Drug Name	Unit Per	Route	Code
FOLEX	5 MG	IV, IM, IT, IA	J9250
FOLEX	50 MG	IV, IM, IT, IA	J9260
FOLEX PFS	5 MG	IV, IM, IT, IA	J9250
FOLEX PFS	50 MG	IV, IM, IT, IA	J9260
FOLLISTIM	75 IU	SC, IM	S0128
FOLLITROPIN ALFA	75 IU	SC	S0126
FOLLITROPIN BETA	75 IU	SC, IM	S0128
FOMEPIZOLE	15 MG	IV	J1451
FOMIVIRSEN SODIUM	1.65 MG	OTH	J1452
FONDAPARINUX SODIUM	0.5 MG	SC	J1652
FORMOTEROL FUMERATE NONCOMPOUNDED UNIT DOSE FORM	20 MCG	INH	J7606
FORMOTEROL, COMPOUNDED, UNIT DOSE	12 MCG	INH	J7640
FORTAZ	500 MG	IM, IV	J0713
FORTEO	10 MCG	SC	J3110
FORTOVASE	200 MG	ORAL	S0140
FOSAPREPITANT	1 MG	IV	J1453
FOSCARNET SODIUM	1,000 MG	IV	J1455
FOSCAVIR	1,000 MG	IV	J1455
FOSPHENYTOIN	50 MG	IM, IV	Q2009
FOSPHENYTOIN SODIUM	750 MG	IM, IV	S0078
FRAGMIN	2,500 IU	SC	J1645
FUDR	500 MG	IV	J9200
FULVESTRANT	25 MG	IM	J9395
FUNGIZONE	50 MG	IV	J0285
FUROSEMIDE	20 MG	IM, IV	J1940
FUSILEV	0.5 MG	IV	J0641
FUZEON	1 MG	SC	J1324
GADOBENATE DIMEGLUMINE (MULTIHANCE MULTIPACK)	PER ML	IV	A9577
GADOTERIDOL (PROHANCE MULTIPACK)	PER ML	IV	A9576
GADOXETATE DISODIUM	1 ML	IV	C9246
GALLIUM GA-67	1 MCI	IV	A9556
GALLIUM NITRATE	1 MG	IV	J1457
GALSULFASE	1 MG	IV	J1458
GAMASTAN	1 CC	IM	J1460
GAMASTAN	2 CC	IM	J1470
GAMASTAN	5 CC	IM	J1500
GAMASTAN	6 CC	IM	J1510
GAMASTAN	4 CC	IM	J1490
GAMASTAN	3 CC	IM	J1480
GAMASTAN	7 CC	IM	J1520
GAMASTAN	9 CC	IM	J1540
GAMASTAN	OVER 10 CC	IM	J1560
GAMASTAN	10 CC	IM	J1550
GAMASTAN	8 CC	IM	J1530
GAMASTAN SD	1 CC	IM	J1460
GAMASTAN SD	OVER 10 CC	IM	J1560
GAMASTAN SD	10 CC	IM	J1550
GAMASTAN SD	9 CC	IM	J1540
GAMASTAN SD	4 CC	IM	J1490
GAMASTAN SD	5 CC	IM	J1500
GAMASTAN SD	6 CC	IM	J1510
GAMASTAN SD	8 CC	IM	J1530
GAMASTAN SD	7 CC	IM	J1520
GAMASTAN SD	3 CC	IM	J1480
GAMASTAN SD	2 CC	IM	J1470
GAMMA GLOBULIN	1 CC	IM	J1460
GAMMA GLOBULIN	2 CC	IM	J1470
GAMMA GLOBULIN	3 CC	IM	J1480
GAMMA GLOBULIN	5 CC	IM	J1500
GAMMA GLOBULIN	OVER 10 CC	IM	J1560
GAMMA GLOBULIN	10 CC	IM	J1550
GAMMA GLOBULIN	9 CC	IM	J1540
GAMMA GLOBULIN	8 CC	IM	J1530
GAMMA GLOBULIN	7 CC	IM	J1520
GAMMA GLOBULIN	6 CC	IM	J1510
GAMMA GLOBULIN	4 CC	IM	J1490
GAMMAGARD	500 MG	IV	J1569
GAMMAGARD S/D	500 MG	IV	J1566
GAMMAGRAFT	SQ CM	OTH	Q4111
GAMUNEX	500 MG	IV	J1561
GANCICLOVIR	4.5 MG	OTH	J7310
GANCICLOVIR SODIUM	500 MG	IV	J1570
GANIRELIX ACETATE	250 MCG	SC	S0132
GANITE	1 MG	IV	J1457
GANITE	PER MCI	IV	A9556
GARAMYCIN	80 MG	IM, IV	J1580
GASTROCROM	10 MG	INH	J7631
GASTROMARK	1 ML	ORAL	Q9954
GATIFLOXACIN	10 MG	IV	J1590
GEFITINIB	250 MG	ORAL	J8565
GEMCITABINE HCL	200 MG	IV	J9201
GEMTUZUMAB	5 MG	IV	J9300
GEMZAR	200 MG	IV	J9201
GENGRAF	100 MG	ORAL	J7502
GENGRAF	25 MG	ORAL	J7515
GENOTROPIN	1 MG	SC	J2941
GENOTROPIN MINIQUICK	1 MG	SC	J2941
GENOTROPIN NUTROPIN	1 MG	SC	J2941
GENTAMICIN	80 MG	IM, IV	J1580
GENTRAN	500 ML	IV	J7100
GENTRAN 75	500 ML	IV	J7110
GEODON	10 MG	IM	J3486
GEREF	1MCG	SC	Q0515
GLATIRAMER ACETATE	20 MG	SC	J1595
GLEEVEC	100 MG	ORAL	S0088
GLOFIL-125	10 UCI	IV	A9554
GLUCAGEN	1 MG	SC, IM, IV	J1610
GLUCAGON	1 MG	SC, IM, IV	J1610
GLUCOTOPE	STUDY DOSE	IV	A9552
GLYCOPYRROLATE, COMPOUNDED CONCENTRATED	PER MG	INH	J7642
GLYCOPYRROLATE, COMPOUNDED, UNIT DOSE	1 MG	INH	J7643
GOLD SODIUM THIOMALATE	50 MG	IM	J1600
GONADORELIN HCL	100 MCG	SC, IV	J1620
GONAL-F	75 IU	SC	S0126

APPENDIX 1 — TABLE OF DRUGS

Drug Name	Unit Per	Route	Code
GOSERELIN ACETATE	3.6 MG	SC	J9202
GRAFTJACKET	SQ CM	OTH	Q4107
GRAFTJACKET EXPRESS	1 CC	INJ	Q4113
GRANISETRON HCL	1 MG	ORAL	Q0166
GRANISETRON HCL	1 MG	IV	S0091
GRANISETRON HCL	100 MCG	IV	J1626
GYNOGEN L.A. 10	10 MG	IM	J1380
GYNOGEN L.A. 10	20 MG	IM	J1390
GYNOGEN L.A. 20	10 MG	IM	J1380
GYNOGEN L.A. 20	20 MG	IM	J1390
GYNOGEN L.A. 40	10 MG	IM	J1380
GYNOGEN L.A. 40	20 MG	IM	J1390
GYNOGEN LA	20 MG	IM	J1390
H.P. ACTHAR GEL	UP TO 40 UNITS	OTH	J0800
HALDOL	5 MG	IM, IV	J1630
HALDOL DECANOATE	50 MG	IM	J1631
HALOPERIDOL	5 MG	IM, IV	J1630
HECTOROL	1 MG	IV	J1270
HELIXATE FS	1 IU	IV	J7192
HEMIN	1 MG	IV	J1640
HEMOFIL-M	1 IU	IV	J7190
HEP LOCK	10 U	IV	J1642
HEPAGAM B	0.5 ML	IM	J1571
HEPAGAM B	0.5 ML	IV	J1571
HEPARIN SODIUM	1,000 U	IV, SC	J1644
HEPARIN SODIUM	10 U	IV	J1642
HEPATOLITE	UP TO 15 MCI	IV	A9510
HEP-PAK	10 UNITS	IV	J1642
HERCEPTIN	10 MG	IV	J9355
HEXADROL	0.25 MG	ORAL	J8540
HIGH OSMOLAR CONTRAST MATERIAL, UP TO 149 MG/ML IODINE CONCENTRATION	1 ML	IV	Q9958
HIGH OSMOLAR CONTRAST MATERIAL, UP TO 150-199 MG/ML IODINE CONCENTRATION	1 ML	IV	Q9959
HIGH OSMOLAR CONTRAST MATERIAL, UP TO 200-249 MG/ML IODINE CONCENTRATION	1 ML	IV	Q9960
HIGH OSMOLAR CONTRAST MATERIAL, UP TO 250-299 MG/ML IODINE CONCENTRATION	1 ML	IV	Q9961
HIGH OSMOLAR CONTRAST MATERIAL, UP TO 300-349 MG/ML IODINE CONCENTRATION	1 ML	IV	Q9962
HIGH OSMOLAR CONTRAST MATERIAL, UP TO 350-399 MG/ML IODINE CONCENTRATION	1 ML	IV	Q9963
HIGH OSMOLAR CONTRAST MATERIAL, UP TO 400 OR GREATER MG/ML IODINE CONCENTRATION	1 ML	IV	Q9964
HISTERLIN IMPLANT	50 MG	OTH	J9225
HISTRELIN ACETATE	10 MG	INJ	J1675
HUMALOG	5 U	SC	J1815
HUMALOG	5 U	SC	S5551
HUMALOG	50 U	SC	J1817
HUMATE-P	1 IU	IV	J7187
HUMATROPE	1 MG	SC	J2941
HUMIRA	20 MG	SC	J0135
HUMULIN	5 U	SC	J1815
HUMULIN	50 U	SC	J1817
HUMULIN R	5 U	SC	J1815
HUMULIN R U-500	5 U	SC	J1815
HYALGAN	DOSE	OTH	J7321
HYALURONAN, EUFLEXXA	PER DOSE	OTH	J7323
HYALURONAN, HYALGAN OR SUPARTZ	PER DOSE	OTH	J7321
HYALURONAN, ORTHOVISC	PER DOSE	OTH	J7324
HYALURONAN, SYNVISC	PER DOSE	OTH	J7322
HYALURONIDASE	150 UNITS	VAR	J3470
HYALURONIDASE RECOMBINANT	1 USP UNIT	SC	J3473
HYALURONIDASE, OVINE, PRESERVATIVE FREE	1 USP	OTH	J3471
HYALURONIDASE, OVINE, PRESERVATIVE FREE	1000 USP	OTH	J3472
HYCAMTIN	4 MG	IV	J9350
HYCAMTIN	0.25 MG	ORAL	J8705
HYCAMTIN	0.25 MG	ORAL	J8705
HYDRALAZINE HCL	20 MG	IV, IM	J0360
HYDRATE	50 MG	IM, IV	J1240
HYDREA	500 MG	ORAL	S0176
HYDROCORTISONE ACETATE	25 MG	IV, IM, SC	J1700
HYDROCORTISONE SODIUM PHOSPHATE	50 MG	IV, IM, SC	J1710
HYDROCORTISONE SODIUM SUCCINATE	100 MG	IV, IM, SC	J1720
HYDROCORTONE PHOSPHATE	50 MG	SC, IM, IV	J1710
HYDROMORPHONE HCL	4 MG	SC, IM, IV	J1170
HYDROMORPHONE HYDROCHLORIDE	250 MG	OTH	S0092
HYDROXOCOBALAMIN	1,000 MCG	IM, SC	J3420
HYDROXYCOBAL	1,000 MCG	IM, SC	J3420
HYDROXYUREA	500 MG	ORAL	S0176
HYDROXYZINE HCL	25 MG	IM	J3410
HYDROXYZINE PAMOATE	25 MG	ORAL	Q0177
HYDROXYZINE PAMOATE	50 MG	ORAL	Q0178
HYOSCYAMINE SULFATE	0.25 MG	SC, IM, IV	J1980
HYPERTET SD	UP TO 250 MG	IM	J1670
HYREXIN	50 MG	IV, IM	J1200
HYZINE	25 MG	IM	J3410
HYZINE-50	25 MG	IM	J3410
I-131 TOSITUMOMAB DIAGNOSTIC	DOSE	IV	A9544
I-131 TOSITUMOMAB THERAPEUTIC	DOSE	IV	A9545
IBANDRONATE SODIUM	1 MG	IV	J1740
IBRITUMOMAB TUXETAN	5 MCI	IV	A9542
IBUTILIDE FUMARATE	1 MG	IV	J1742
IDAMYCIN	5 MG	IV	J9211
IDAMYCIN PFS	5 MG	IV	J9211
IDARUBICIN HCL	5 MG	IV	J9211
IDURSULFASE	1 MG	IV	J1743
IFEX	1 G	IV	J9208
IFOSFAMIDE	1 G	IV	J9208
IL-2	1 VIAL	IV	J9015
ILETIN	5 UNITS	SC	J1815
ILETIN II NPH PORK	50 U	SC	J1817

Drug Name	Unit Per	Route	Code
ILETIN II REGULAR PORK	5 U	SC	**J1815**
ILOPROST INHALATION SOLUTION	20 UCI	INH	**Q4080**
IMAGENT	1 ML	IV	**Q9955**
IMATINIB	100 MG	ORAL	**S0088**
IMIGLUCERASE	1 U	IV	**J1785**
IMITREX	6 MG	SC	**J3030**
IMMUNE GLOBULIN (FLEBOGAMMA, FLEBOGAMMA DIF	500 MG	IV	**J1572**
IMMUNE GLOBULIN (GAMMAGARD LIQUID)	500 MG	IV	**J1569**
IMMUNE GLOBULIN (GAMUNEX)	500 MG	IV	**J1561**
IMMUNE GLOBULIN (OCTAGAM)	500 MG	IV	**J1568**
IMMUNE GLOBULIN (PRIVIGEN) NONLYOPHILIZED	500 MG	IV	**J1459**
IMMUNE GLOBULIN (RHOPHYLAC)	100 IU	IM, IV	**J2791**
IMMUNE GLOBULIN LYOPHILIZED	500 MG	IV	**J1566**
IMMUNE GLOBULIN SUBCUTANEOUS	100 MG	SC	**J1562**
IMPLANON	PER IMPLANT	OTH	**J7307**
IMURAN	50 MG	ORAL	**J7500**
IN-111 SATUMOMAB PENDETIDE	DOSE	IV	**A4642**
INAPSINE	5 MG	IM, IV	**J1790**
INDERAL	1 MG	IV	**J1800**
INDIUM IN-111 IBRITUMOMAB TIUXETAN, DIAGNOSTIC	5 MCI	IV	**A9542**
INDIUM IN-111 LABELED AUTOLOGOUS PLATELETS	PER STUDY DOSAGE	IV	**A9571**
INDIUM IN-111 LABELED AUTOLOGOUS WHITE BLOOD CELLS	PER STUDY DOSE	IV	**A9570**
INDIUM IN-111 OXYQUINOLINE	0.5 MCI	IV	**A9547**
INDIUM IN-111PENTETREOTIDE	PER STUDY DOSE	IV	**A9572**
INDURSALFASE	1 MG	IV	**J1743**
INFED	50 MG	IM, IV	**J1750**
INFERGEN	1 MCG	SC	**J9212**
INFLIXIMAB	100 MG	IV	**J1745**
INFUMORPH	10 MG	IM, IV, SC	**J2270**
INFUMORPH	10 MG	OTH	**J2275**
INFUMORPH PRESERVATIVE FREE	100 MG	IM, IV, SC	**J2271**
INNOHEP	1,000 IU	SC	**J1655**
INSULIN	5 U	SC	**J1815**
INSULIN	50 U	SC	**J1817**
INSULIN LISPRO	5 U	SC	**J1815**
INSULIN LISPRO	5 U	SC	**S5551**
INSULIN PURIFIED REGULAR PORK	5 U	SC	**J1815**
INTAL	10 MG	INH	**J7631**
INTEGRA BILAYER MATRIX DRESSING	SQ CM	OTH	**Q4104**
INTEGRA DERMAL REGENERATION TEMPLATE	SQ CM	OTH	**Q4105**
INTEGRA FLOWABLE WOUND MATRIC	1 CC	INJ	**Q4114**
INTEGRA FLOWABLE WOUND MATRIX	1 CC	INJ	**Q4114**
INTEGRA MATRIX	PER SQ. CM.	OTH	**J7347**
INTEGRA MATRIX	SQ CM	OTH	**Q4108**
INTEGRA MOZAIK OSTEOCONDUCTIVE SCAFFOLD PUTTY	0.5 CC	OTH	**C9359**
INTEGRA MOZAIK OSTEOCONDUCTIVE SCAFFOLD PUTTY	0.5 CC	OTH	**C9359**
INTEGRA OS OSTEOCONDUCTIVE SCAFFOLD PUTTY	0.5 CC	OTH	**C9359**
INTEGRA OS OSTEOCONDUCTIVE SCAFFOLD PUTTY	0.5 CC	OTH	**C9359**
INTEGRILIN	5 MG	IM, IV	**J1327**
INTERFERON ALFA-2A	3,000,000 U	SC, IM	**J9213**
INTERFERON ALFA-2B	1,000,000 U	SC, IM	**J9214**
INTERFERON ALFACON-1	1 MCG	SC	**J9212**
INTERFERON ALFA-N3	250,000 IU	IM	**J9215**
INTERFERON BETA-1A	11 MCG	IM	**Q3025**
INTERFERON BETA-1A	33 MCG	IM	**J1825**
INTERFERON BETA-1A	11 MCG	SC	**Q3026**
INTERFERON BETA-1B	0.25 MG	SC	**J1830**
INTERFERON, ALFA-2A, RECOMBINANT	3,000,000 U	SC, IM	**J9213**
INTERFERON, ALFA-2B, RECOMBINANT	1,000,000 U	SC, IM	**J9214**
INTERFERON, ALFA-N3, (HUMAN LEUKOCYTE DERIVED)	250,000 IU	IM	**J9215**
INTERFERON, GAMMA 1-B	3,000,000 U	SC	**J9216**
INTERLUEKIN	1 VIAL	IV	**J9015**
INTRON A	1,000,000 U	SC, IM	**J9214**
INVANZ	500 MG	IM, IV	**J1335**
INVIRASE	200 MG	ORAL	**S0140**
IOBENGUANE SULFATE I-131	0.5 MCI	IV	**A9508**
IOBENGUANE, I-123, DIAGNOSTIC	PER STUDY DOSE UP TO 10 MCI	IV	**C9247**
IODINE I-123 SODIUM IODIDE	PER MCI	IV	**A9509**
IODINE I-123 SODIUM IODIDE CAPSULE(S), DIAGNOSTIC	100 UCI	ORAL	**A9516**
IODINE I-125 SERUM ALBUMIN, DIAGNOSTIC	10 UCI	IV	**A9554**
IODINE I-125 SODIUM IOTHALAMATE, DIAGNOSTIC	10 UCI	IV	**A9554**
IODINE I-125, SODIUM IODIDE SOLUTION, THERAPEUTIC	1 UCI	ORAL	**A9527**
IODINE I-131 IODINATED SERIUM ALBUMIN, DIAGNOSTIC	PER 5 UCI	ORAL	**A9524**
IODINE I-131 SERUM ALBUMIN, DIAGNOSTIC	5 UCI	IV	**A9532**
IODINE I-131 SODIUM IODIDE CAPSULE(S), DIAGNOSTIC	1 MCI	ORAL	**A9528**
IODINE I-131 SODIUM IODIDE CAPSULE(S), THERAPEUTIC	1 MCI	ORAL	**A9517**
IODINE I-131 SODIUM IODIDE SOLUTION, DIAGNOSTIC	1 MCI	ORAL	**A9529**
IODINE I-131 SODIUM IODIDE SOLUTION, THERAPEUTIC	1 MCI	ORAL	**A9530**
IODINE I-131 SODIUM IODIDE, DIAGNOSTIC	100 UCI	IV	**A9531**
IODINE I-131 TOSITUMOMAB, DIAGNOSTIC	STUDY DOSE	IV	**A9544**
IODINE I-131 TOSITUMOMAB, THERAPEUTIC	STUDY DOSE	IV	**A9545**
IODOTOPE THERAPEUTIC CAPSULE(S)	1 MCI	ORAL	**A9517**
IODOTOPE THERAPEUTIC SOLUTION	1 MCI	ORAL	**A9530**
ION-BASED MAGNETIC RESONANCE CONTRAST AGENT	1 ML	IV	**Q9953**

Drug Name	Unit Per	Route	Code
IOTHALAMATE SODIUM I-125	STUDY DOSE	IV	A9554
IPLEX	1 MG	SC	J2170
IPRATROPIUM BROMIDE, NONCOMPOUNDED, UNIT DOSE	1 MG	INH	J7644
IPTRATROPIUM BROMIDE COMPOUNDED, UNIT DOSE	1 MG	INH	J7645
IRESSA	250 MG	ORAL	J8565
IRINOTECAN	20 MG	IV	J9206
IRON DEXTRAN, 50 MG	50 MG	IM, IV	J1750
IRON SUCROSE	1 MG	IV	J1756
ISOCAINE	10 ML	VAR	J0670
ISOETHARINE HCL COMPOUNDED, CONCENTRATED	1 MG	INH	J7647
ISOETHARINE HCL NONCOMPOUNDED, CONCENTRATED	1 MG	INH	J7650
ISOETHARINE HCL, NONCOMPOUNDED CONCENTRATED	PER MG	INH	J7648
ISOETHARINE HCL, NONCOMPOUNDED, UNIT DOSE	1 MG	INH	J7649
ISOJEX	5 MCI	IV	A9532
ISOPROTERENOL HCL COMPOUNDED, CONCENTRATED	1 MG	INH	J7657
ISOPROTERENOL HCL COMPOUNDED, UNIT DOSE	1 MG	INH	J7660
ISOPROTERENOL HCL, NONCOMPOUNDED CONCENTRATED	1 MG	INH	J7658
ISOPROTERNOL HCL, NONCOMPOUNDED, UNIT DOSE	PER MG	INH	J7659
ITRACONAZOLE	50 MG	IV	J1835
IVEEGAM	500 MG	IV	J1566
IXABEPILONE	1 MG	IV	J9207
IXEMPRA	1 MG	IV	J9207
KANAMYCIN	500 MG	IM, IV	J1840
KANTREX	500 MG	IM, IV	J1840
KANTREX	75 MG	IM, IV	J1850
KEFZOL	500 MG	IV, IM	J0690
KENAJECT-40	10 MG	IM	J3301
KENALOG-10	10 MG	IM	J3301
KENALOG-40	10 MG	IM	J3301
KEPIVANCE	50 MCG	IV	J2425
KEPIVANCE	60 MCG	IV	J2425
KEPPRA	10 MG	IV	J1953
KESTRONE	1 MG	IV, IM	J1435
KETOROLAC TROMETHAMINE	15 MG	IM, IV	J1885
KINEVAC	5 MCG	IV	J2805
KOATE-DVI	1 IU	IV	J7190
KOGENATE FS	1 IU	IV	J7192
KONAKION	1 MG	SC, IM, IV	J3430
KONYNE 80	1 IU	IV	J7194
KYTRIL	1 MG	ORAL	Q0166
KYTRIL	1 MG	IV	S0091
KYTRIL	100 MCG	IV	J1626
L.A.E. 20	10 MG	IM	J1380
L.A.E. 20	20 MG	IM	J1390
LANOXIN	0.5 MG	IM, IV	J1160
LANREOTIDE	1 MG	SC	J1930
LANTUS	50 U	SC	J1817
LARONIDASE	0.1 MG	IV	J1931
LASIX	20 MG	IM, IV	J1940
LENTE ILETIN I	5 U	SC	J1815
LEPIRUDIN	50 MG	IV	J1945
LEUCOVORIN CALCIUM	50 MG	IM, IV	J0640
LEUKERAN	2 MG	ORAL	S0172
LEUKINE	50 MCG	IV	J2820
LEUPROLIDE ACETATE	1 MG	IM	J9218
LEUPROLIDE ACETATE	7.5 MG	IM	J9217
LEUPROLIDE ACETATE (FOR DEPOT SUSPENSION)	3.75 MG	IM	J1950
LEUPROLIDE ACETATE DEPOT	7.5 MG	IM	J9217
LEUPROLIDE ACETATE IMPLANT	65 MG	OTH	J9219
LEUSTATIN	1 MG	IV	J9065
LEVABUTEROL COMPOUNDED, UNIT DOSE	1 MG	INH	J7615
LEVABUTEROL, COMPOUNDED, CONCENTRATED	0.5 MG	INH	J7607
LEVALBUTEROL NONCOMPOUNDED, CONCENTRATED FORM	0.5 MG	INH	J7612
LEVALBUTEROL, NONCOMPOUNDED, CONCENTRATED FORM	PER 0.5 MG	INH	J7612
LEVALBUTEROL, NONCOMPOUNDED, UNIT DOSE	PER 0.5 MG	INH	J7614
LEVAMISOLE HCL	50 MG	ORAL	S0177
LEVAQUIN	250 MG	IV	J1956
LEVETIRACETAM	10 MG	IV	J1953
LEVOCARNITINE	1 G	IV	J1955
LEVOFLOXACIN	250 MG	IV	J1956
LEVOLEUCOVORIN CALCIUM	0.5 MG	IV	J0641
LEVONORGESTREL	52 MG	OTH	J7302
LEVORPHANOL TARTRATE	2 MG	SC, IV, IM	J1960
LEVOXYL	5 MG	ORAL	J7506
LEVSIN	0.25 MG	SC, IM, IV	J1980
LEVULAN KERASTICK	SINGLE UNIT DOSE (354 MG)	OTH	J7308
LEXISCAN	0.1 MG	IV	J2785
LIBRIUM	100 MG	IM, IV	J1990
LIDOCAINE HCL	10 MG	IV	J2001
LINCOCIN HCL	300 MG	IV	J2010
LINCOMYCIN HCL	300 MG	IM, IV	J2010
LINEZOLID	200 MG	IV	J2020
LIORESAL	10 MG	IT	J0475
LIORESAL INTRATHECAL REFILL	50 MCG	IT	J0476
LIQUAEMIN SODIUM	1,000 UNITS	SC, IV	J1644
LIQUID PRED SYRUP	5 MG	OTH	J7506
LISPRO-PFC	50 U	SC	J1817
LOK-PAK	10 UNITS	IV	J1642
LOMUSTINE	10 MG	ORAL	S0178
LONITEN	10 MG	ORAL	S0139
LORAZEPAM	2 MG	IM, IV	J2060
LOVENOX	10 MG	SC	J1650
LOW OSMOLAR CONTRAST MATERIAL, 100-199 MG/ML IODINE CONCENTRATIONS	PER ML	IV	Q9965

Drug Name	Unit Per	Route	Code
LOW OSMOLAR CONTRAST MATERIAL, 200-299 MG/ML IODINE CONCENTRATION	PER ML	IV	Q9966
LOW OSMOLAR CONTRAST MATERIAL, 300-399 MG/ML IODINE CONCENTRATION	PER ML	IV	Q9967
LOW OSMOLAR CONTRAST MATERIAL, 400 OR GREATER MG/ML IODINE CONCENTRATION	1 ML	IV	Q9951
L-PHENYLALANINE MUSTARD	50 MG	IV	J9245
LUCENTIS	0.1 MG	IV	J2778
LUNELLE	5 MG/25 MG	IM	J1056
LUPRON	1 MG	IM	J9218
LUPRON	PER 3.75 MG	SC	J1950
LUPRON	7.5 MG	IM	J9217
LUPRON DEPOT	3.75 MG	IM	J1950
LUPRON DEPOT	7.5 MG	IM	J9217
LUPRON IMPLANT	65 MG	OTH	J9219
LUPRON-3	PER 3.75 MG	SC	J1950
LUPRON-4	PER 3.75 MG	SC	J1950
LUTREPULSE	100 MCG	SC, IV	J1620
LYMPHOCYTE IMMUNE GLOBULIN, ANTITHYMOCYTE GLOBULIN, EQUINE	250 MG	OTH	J7504
LYMPHOCYTE IMMUNE GLOBULIN, ANTITHYMOCYTE GLOBULIN, RABBIT	25 MG	OTH	J7511
MACUGEN	0.3 MG	OTH	J2503
MAGNAVIST	UP TO 25 MCI	INH	A9567
MAGNESIUM SULFATE	500 MG	IV	J3475
MAGNETIC RESONANCE CONTRAST AGENT	1 ML	ORAL	Q9954
MAGNEVIST	UP TO 25 MCI	IV	A9539
MAGROTEC	10 MCI	IV	A9540
MANNITOL	25% IN 50 ML	IV	J2150
MARCAINE HCL	30 ML	VAR	S0020
MARINOL	2.5 MG	ORAL	Q0167
MARINOL	5 MG	ORAL	Q0168
MARMINE	50 MG	IM, IV	J1240
MATULANE	50 MG	ORAL	S0182
MAXIPIME	500 MG	IV	J0692
MDP-BRACCO	30 MCI	IV	A9503
MECASERMIN	1 MG	SC	J2170
MECHLORETHAMINE HYDROCHLORIDE (NITROGEN MUSTARD)	10 MG	IV	J9230
MEDIDEX	1 MG	IM, IV, OTH	J1100
MEDROL	4 MG	ORAL	J7509
MEDROXYPROGESTERONE ACETATE	150 MG	IM	J1055
MEDROXYPROGESTERONE ACETATE	50 MG	IM	J1051
MEDROXYPROGESTERONE ACETATE/ESTRADIOL CYPIONATE	5 MG/25 MG	IM	J1056
MEFOXIN	1 G	IV	J0694
MEGACE	20 MG	ORAL	S0179
MEGESTROL ACETATE	20 MG	ORAL	S0179
MELPHALAN HCL	2 MG	ORAL	J8600
MELPHALAN HCL	50 MG	IV	J9245
MENADIONE	1 MG	IM, SC, IV	J3430
MENOTROPINS	75 IU	SC, IM, IV	S0122
MEPERGAN	50 MG	IM, IV	J2180
MEPERIDINE AND PROMETHAZINE HCL	50 MG	IM, IV	J2180
MEPERIDINE HCL	100 MG	IM, IV, SC	J2175
MEPIVACAINE HCL	10 ML	VAR	J0670
MERCAPTOPURINE	50 MG	ORAL	S0108
MERITATE	150 MG	IV	J3520
MEROPENEM	100 MG	IV	J2185
MERREM	100 MG	IV	J2185
MESNA	200 MG	IV	J9209
MESNEX	200 MG	IV	J9209
METAPROTERENOL SULFATE COMPOUNDED, UNIT DOSE	10 MG	INH	J7670
METAPROTERENOL SULFATE, NONCOMPOUNDED, CONCENTRATED	10 MG	INH	J7668
METAPROTERENOL SULFATE, NONCOMPOUNDED, UNIT DOSE	10 MG	INH	J7669
METARAMINOL BITARTRATE	10 MG	IV, IM, SC	J0380
METASTRON STRONTIUM 89 CHLORIDE	1 MCI	IV	A9600
METATRACE	STUDY DOSE	IV	A9552
METHACHOLINE CHLORIDE	1 MG	INH	J7674
METHADONE	5 MG	ORAL	S0109
METHADONE HCL	10 MG	IM, SC	J1230
METHAPREL, COMPOUNDED, UNIT DOSE	10 MG	INH	J7670
METHAPREL, NONCOMPOUNDED, CONCENTRATED	10 MG	INH	J7668
METHAPREL, NONCOMPOUNDED, UNIT DOSE	10 MG	INH	J7669
METHERGINE	0.2 MG	IM, IV	J2210
METHOTREXATE	5 MG	IV, IM, IT, IA	J9250
METHOTREXATE	50 MG	IV, IM, IT, IA	J9260
METHOTREXATE LPF	5 MG	IV, IM, IT, IA	J9250
METHOTREXATE LPF	50 MG	IV, IM, IT, IA	J9260
METHOTREXATE SODIUM	2.5 MG	ORAL	J8610
METHOTREXATE SODIUM	5 MG	IV, IM, IT, IA	J9250
METHOTREXATE SODIUM	50 MG	IV, IM, IT, IA	J9260
METHYLCOTOLONE	80 MG	IM	J1040
METHYLDOPA HCL	250 MG	IV	J0210
METHYLDOPATE HCL	5 MG	IV	J0210
METHYLENE BLUE	1 ML	IV	A9535
METHYLERGONOVINE MALEATE	0.2 MG	IM, IV	J2210
METHYLPRED	4 MG	ORAL	J7509
METHYLPREDNISOLONE	125 MG	IM, IV	J2930
METHYLPREDNISOLONE	4 MG	ORAL	J7509
METHYLPREDNISOLONE	UP TO 40 MG	IM, IV	J2920
METHYLPREDNISOLONE ACETATE	20 MG	IM	J1020
METHYLPREDNISOLONE ACETATE	40 MG	IM	J1030
METHYLPREDNISOLONE ACETATE	80 MG	IM	J1040
METOCLOPRAMIDE	10 MG	IV	J2765
METRONIDAZOLE	500 MG	IV	S0030
MIACALCIN	400 U	SC, IM	J0630
MIBG	0.5 MCI	IV	A9508
MICAFUNGIN SODIUM	1 MG	IV	J2248
MICRHOGAM	50 MCG	IV	J2788

Drug Name	Unit Per	Route	Code
MICROPOROUS COLLAGEN IMPLANTABLE SLIT TUBE	1 CM LENGTH	OTH	C9353
MICROPOROUS COLLAGEN IMPLANTABLE TUBE	1 CM LENGTH	OTH	C9352
MIDAZOLAM HCI	1 MG	IM, IV	J2250
MIFEPRISTONE	200 MG	ORAL	S0190
MILRINONE LACTATE	5 MG	IV	J2260
MINOXIDIL	10 MG	ORAL	S0139
MIRENA	52 MG	OTH	J7302
MISOPROSTOL	200 MG	ORAL	S0191
MITHRACIN	2.5 MG	IV	J9270
MITOMYCIN	20 MG	IV	J9290
MITOMYCIN	5 MG	IV	J9280
MITOMYCIN	40 MG	IV	J9291
MITOXANA	1 G	IV	J9208
MITOXANTRONE HYDROCHLORIDE	5 MG	IV	J9293
MONARC-M	1 IU	IV	J7190
MONOCLATE-P	1 IU	IV	J7190
MONONINE	1 IU	IV	J7193
MONOPUR	75 IU	SC, IM	S0122
MORPHINE SULFATE	10 MG	IM, IV, SC	J2270
MORPHINE SULFATE	500 MG	OTH	S0093
MORPHINE SULFATE	100 MG	IM, IV, SC	J2271
MORPHINE SULFATE, PRESERVATIVE FREE, STERILE SOLUTION	10 MG	IM, IV, SC	J2275
MOXIFLOXACIN	100 MG	IV	J2280
MPI INDIUM DTPA	0.5 MCI	IV	A9548
MS CONTIN	500 MG	OTH	S0093
MUCOMYST	1 G	INH	J7608
MUCOSIL	1 G	INH	J7608
MULTIHANCE	1 ML	IV	A9577
MULTIHANCE MULTIPACK	1 ML	IV	A9578
MUROMONAB-CD3	5 MG	OTH	J7505
MUSE	EA	OTH	J0275
MUSTARGEN	10 MG	IV	J9230
MUTAMYCIN	20 MG	IV	J9290
MUTAMYCIN	5 MG	IV	J9280
MUTAMYCIN	40 MG	IV	J9291
MYCAMINE	1 MG	IV	J2248
MYCOPHENOLATE MOFETIL	250 MG	ORAL	J7517
MYCOPHENOLIC ACID	180 MG	ORAL	J7518
MYFORTIC DELAYED RELEASE	180 MG	ORAL	J7518
MYLERAN	2 MG	ORAL	J8510
MYLOCEL	500 MG	ORAL	S0176
MYLOTARG	5 MG	IV	J9300
MYOBLOC	100 U	IM	J0587
MYOCHRYSINE	50 MG	IM	J1600
NABILONE	1 MG	ORAL	J8650
NAFCILLIN SODIUM	2 GM	IM, IV	S0032
NAGLAZYME	1 MG	IV	J1458
NALBUPHINE HCL	10 MG	IM, IV, SC	J2300
NALLPEN	2 GM	IM, IV	S0032
NALOXONE HCL	1 MG	IM, IV, SC	J2310
NALTREXONE, DEPOT FORM	1 MG	IM	J2315
NANDROLONE DECANOATE	100 MG	IM	J2321
NANDROLONE DECANOATE	200 MG	IM	J2322
NANDROLONE DECANOATE	50 MG	IM	J2320
NARCAN	1 MG	IM, IV, SC	J2310
NAROPIN	1 MG	VAR	J2795
NASAHIST B	10 MG	IM	J0945
NASALCROM	10 MG	INH	J7631
NATALIZUMAB	1 MG	IV	J2323
NATRECOR	0.1 MG	IV	J2325
NATURAL ESTROGENIC SUBSTANCE	1 MG	IM, IV	J1410
NAVELBINE	10 MG	IV	J9390
ND-STAT	10 MG	IM, SC, IV	J0945
NEBCIN	80 MG	IM, IV	J3260
NEBUPENT	300 MG	INH	J2545
NEBUPENT	300 MG	IM, IV	S0080
NELARABINE	50 MG	IV	J9261
NEMBUTAL SODIUM	50 MG	IM, IV, OTH	J2515
NEORAL	25 MG	ORAL	J7515
NEORAL	250 MG	ORAL	J7516
NEOSAR	1 G	IV	J9091
NEOSAR	2 G	IV	J9092
NEOSAR	200 MG	IV	J9080
NEOSAR	100 MG	IV	J9070
NEOSAR	500 MG	IV	J9090
NEOSCAN	1 MCI	IV	A9556
NEOSTIGMINE METHYLSULFATE	250 MG	IM, IV	J2710
NEOTECT	STUDY DOSE	IV	A9536
NESACAINE	30 ML	VAR	J2400
NESACAINE-MPF	30 ML	VAR	J2400
NESIRITIDE	0.1 MG	IV	J2325
NEULASTA	6 MG	SC, SQ	J2505
NEUMEGA	5 MG	SC	J2355
NEUPOGEN	300 MCG	SC, IV	J1440
NEUPOGEN	480 MCG	SC, IV	J1441
NEURAGEN NERVE GUIDE	1 CM LENGTH	OTH	C9352
NEUROLITE	25 MCI	IV	A9557
NEUROMATRIX	0.5 CM LENGTH	OTH	C9355
NEUROWRAP NERVE PROTECTOR	1 CM LENGTH	OTH	C9353
NEUTREXIN	25 MG	IV	J3305
NEUTROSPEC	25 MCI	IV	A9566
NIPENT	10 MG	IV	J9268
NITROGEN MUSTARD	10 MG	IV	J9230
NITROGEN N-13 AMMONIA, DIAGNOSTIC	STUDY DOSE, UP TO 40 MCI	INJ	A9526
NOC DRUGS, INHALATION SOLUTION ADMINISTERED THROUGH DME	1 EA		J7699
NOLVADEX	10 MG	ORAL	S0187
NOLVADEX	10 MG	ORAL	S0187
NORDITROPIN	1 MG	SC	J2941
NORDYL	50 MG	IV, IM	J1200
NORFLEX	60 MG	IV, IM	J2360
NORPLANT II	PER IMPLANT	OTH	J7306

Drug Name	Unit Per	Route	Code
NOT OTHERWISE CLASSIFIED, ANTINEOPLASTIC DRUGS			J9999
NOVANTRONE	5 MG	IV	J9293
NOVAREL	1,000 USP U	IM	J0725
NOVASTAN	5 MG	IV	C9121
NOVO NORDISK	5 UNITS	SC	J1815
NOVOLIN	50 U	SC	J1817
NOVOLIN R	5 U	SC	J1815
NOVOLOG	50 U	SC	J1817
NOV-ONXOL	30 MG	IV	J9265
NOVOSEVEN	1 MCG	IV	J7189
NPH	5 UNITS	SC	J1815
NPLATE	10 MCG	SC	C9245
NUBAIN	10 MG	IM, IV, SC	J2300
NUMORPHAN	1 MG	IV, SC, IM	J2410
NUTRI-TWELVE	1,000 MCG	IM, SC	J3420
NUTROPIN	1 MG	SC	J2941
NUTROPIN A.Q.	1 MG	SC	J2941
NUVARING VAGINAL RING	EA	OTH	J7303
OASIS BURN MATRIX	SQ CM	OTH	Q4103
OASIS WOUND MATRIX	SQ CM	OTH	Q4102
OCTAFLUOROPROPANE UCISPHERES	1 ML	IV	Q9956
OCTAGAM	500 MG	IV	J1568
OCTREOSCAN	1 MCI	IV	A9572
OCTREOTIDE ACETATE DEPOT	1 MG	IM	J2353
OCTREOTIDE, NON-DEPOT FORM	25 MCG	SC, IV	J2354
OFLOXACIN	400 MG	IV	S0034
OLANZAPINE	2.5 MG	IM	S0166
OMALIZUMAB	5 MG	SC	J2357
OMNIPAQUE 140	PER ML	IV	Q9965
OMNIPAQUE 180	PER ML	IV	Q9965
OMNIPAQUE 240	PER ML	IV	Q9966
OMNIPAQUE 300	PER ML	IV	Q9966
OMNIPAQUE 350	PER ML	IV	Q9967
OMNISCAN	PER ML	IV	A9579
ONCASPAR	VIAL	IM, IV	J9266
ONCOSCINT	DOSE	IV	A4642
ONDANSETRON HCL	4 MG	ORAL	S0181
ONDANSETRON HCL	8 MG	ORAL	Q0179
ONDANSETRON HYDROCHLORIDE	1 MG	IV	J2405
ONTAK	300 MCG	IV	J9160
ONXOL	30 MG	IV	J9265
OPRELVEKIN	5 MG	SC	J2355
OPTIRAY	PER ML	IV	Q9967
OPTIRAY 160	PER ML	IV	Q9965
OPTIRAY 240	PER ML	IV	Q9966
OPTIRAY 300	PER ML	IV	Q9967
OPTIRAY 320	PER ML	IV	Q9967
OPTISON	1 ML	IV	Q9957
ORAL MAGNETIC RESONANCE CONTRAST AGENT, PER 100 ML	100 ML	ORAL	Q9954
ORENCIA	10 MG	IV	J0129
ORPHENADRINE CITRATE	60 MG	IV, IM	J2360
ORTHOCLONE OKT3	5 MG	OTH	J7505
ORTHOVISC	PER DOSE	OTH	J7324
OSELTAMIVIR PHOSPHATE (BRAND NAME)	75 MG	ORAL	G9035
OSELTAMIVIR PHOSPHATE (GENERIC)	75 MG	ORAL	G9019
OSMITROL	25% IN 50 ML	IV	J2150
OSTREOSCAN	UP TO 6 MCI	IV	A9572
OXACILLIN SODIUM	250 MG	IM, IV	J2700
OXALIPLATIN	0.5 MG	IV	J9263
OXILAN 300	PER ML	IV	Q9967
OXILAN 350	PER ML	IV	Q9967
OXYMORPHONE HCL	1 MG	IV, SC, IM	J2410
OXYTETRACYCLINE HCL	50 MG	IM	J2460
OXYTOCIN	10 U	IV, IM	J2590
PACIS BCG	VIAL	OTH	J9031
PACLITAXEL	30 MG	IV	J9265
PACLITAXEL PROTEIN-BOUND PARTICLES	1 MG	IV	J9264
PALIFERMIN	50 MCG	IV	J2425
PALONOSETRON HCL	25 MCG	IV	J2469
PAMIDRONATE DISODIUM	30 MG	IV	J2430
PANHEMATIN	1 MG	IV	J1640
PANITUMUMAB	10 MG	IV	J9303
PANTOPRAZOLE SODIUM	40 MG	IV	S0164
PANTOPRAZOLE SODIUM	VIAL	IV	C9113
PAPAVERINE HCL	60 MG	IV, IM	J2440
PARAGARD T380A	EA	OTH	J7300
PARAPLANTIN	50 MG	IV	J9045
PARICALCITOL	1 MCG	IV, IM	J2501
PEDIAPRED	5 MG	ORAL	J7510
PEGADEMASE BOVINE	25 IU	IM	J2504
PEGAPTANIB SODIUM	0.3 MG	OTH	J2503
PEGASPARGASE	VIAL	IM, IV	J9266
PEGASYS	10 MCG	SC	S0146
PEGFILGRASTIM	6 MG	SC	J2505
PEGINTERFERON ALFA-2A	180 MCG	SC	S0145
PEG-INTRON	10 MCG	SC	S0146
PEG-INTRON	180 MCG	SC	S0145
PEGYLATED INTERFERON ALFA-2A	180 MCG	SC	S0145
PEGYLATED INTERFERON ALFA-2B	10 MCG	SC	S0146
PEMETREXED	10 MG	IV	J9305
PEN G BENZ/PEN G PROCAINE	600,000 U	IM	J0530
PENICILLIN G BENZATHINE	1,200,000 U	IM	J0570
PENICILLIN G BENZATHINE	600,000 U	IM	J0560
PENICILLIN G BENZATHINE	2,400,000 U	IM	J0580
PENICILLIN G BENZATHINE AND PENICILLIN G PROCAINE	1,200,000 U	IM	J0540
PENICILLIN G POTASSIUM	600,000 U	IM, IV	J2540
PENICILLIN G PROCAINE	600,000 U	IM, IV	J2510
PENTACARINAT	300 MG	INH	S0080
PENTAM	300 MG	IM, IV	J2545
PENTAM 300	300 MG	IM, IV	S0080
PENTAMIDINE ISETHIONATE	300 MG	IM, IV	S0080
PENTAMIDINE ISETHIONATE COMPOUNDED	PER 300 MG	INH	J7676

APPENDIX 1 — TABLE OF DRUGS

Drug Name	Unit Per	Route	Code
PENTAMIDINE ISETHIONATE NONCOMPOUNDED	300 MG	INH	J2545
PENTASPAN	100 ML	IV	J2513
PENTASTARCH 10% SOLUTION	100 ML	IV	J2513
PENTATE CALCIUM TRISODIUM	UP TO 25 MCI	IV	A9539
PENTATE CALCIUM TRISODIUM	UP TO 25 MCI	INH	A9567
PENTATE ZINC TRISODIUM	UP TO 25 MCI	IV	A9539
PENTATE ZINC TRISODIUM	UP TO 25 MCI	INH	A9567
PENTAZOCINE	30 MG	IM, SC, IV	J3070
PENTOBARBITAL SODIUM	50 MG	IM, IV, OTH	J2515
PENTOSTATIN	10 MG	IV	J9268
PEPCID	20 MG	IV	S0028
PERFLEXANE LIPID UCISPHERE	1 ML	IV	Q9955
PERFLUTREN LIPID UCISPHERE	1 ML	IV	Q9957
PERFOROMIST	20 MCG	INH	J7606
PERMAPEN	>1,200,000 U	IM	J0570
PERMAPEN	600,000	IM	J0560
PERMAPEN	> 2,400,000 U	IM	J0580
PERPHENAZINE	4 MG	ORAL	Q0175
PERPHENAZINE	5 MG	IM, IV	J3310
PERSANTINE	10 MG	IV	J1245
PFIZERPEN A.S.	600,000 U	IM, IV	J2510
PHENERGAN	12.5 MG	ORAL	Q0169
PHENERGAN	50 MG	IM, IV	J2550
PHENOBARBITAL SODIUM	120 MG	IM, IV	J2560
PHENTOLAMINE MESYLATE	5 MG	IM, IV	J2760
PHENYLEPHRINE HCL	1 ML	SC, IM, IV	J2370
PHENYTOIN SODIUM	50 MG	IM, IV	J1165
PHOSPHOCOL	1 MCI	IV	A9563
PHOSPHOTEC	25 MCI	IV	A9538
PHOTOFRIN	75 MG	IV	J9600
PHYTONADIONE	1 MG	IM, SC, IV	J3430
PIPERACILLIN SODIUM	500 MG	IM, IV	S0081
PIPERACILLIN SODIUM/TAZOBACTAM SODIUM	1 G/1.125 GM	IV	J2543
PITOCIN	10 U	IV, IM	J2590
PLATINOL AQ	10 MG	IV	J9060
PLATINOL AQ	50 MG	IV	J9062
PLENAXIS	10 MG	IM	J0128
PLICAMYCIN	2.5 MG	IV	J9270
PNEUMOCOCCAL CONJUGATE	EA	IM	S0195
PNEUMOVAX II	EA	IM	S0195
POLOCAINE	10 ML	VAR	J0670
POLYGAM	500 MG	IV	J1566
POLYGAM S/D	500 MG	IV	J1566
POLY-L-LACTIC ACID	1 ML	SC	S0196
PORFIMER SODIUM	75 MG	IV	J9600
PORK INSULIN	5 U	SC	J1815
POROUS PURIFIED COLLAGEN MATRIX BONE VOID FILLER	0.5 CC	OTH	C9359
POROUS PURIFIED COLLAGEN MATRIX BONE VOID FILLER	0.5 CC	OTH	C9359
POTASSIUM CHLORIDE	2 MEQ	IV	J3480
PRALIDOXIME CHLORIDE	1 MG	IV, IM, SC	J2730
PREDNICOT	5 ML	ORAL	J7506
PREDNISOLONE	5 MG	ORAL	J7510

Drug Name	Unit Per	Route	Code
PREDNISOLONE ACETATE	1 ML	IM	J2650
PREDNISONE	5 MG	ORAL	J7506
PREDNORAL	5 MG	ORAL	J7510
PREDONE	5 MG	ORAL	J7506
PREGNYL	1,000 USP U	IM	J0725
PRELONE	5 MG	ORAL	J7510
PREMARIN	25 MG	IV, IM	J1410
PRENATAL VITAMINS	30 TABS	ORAL	S0197
PRIALT	1 MCG	OTH	J2278
PRIMACOR	5 MG	IV	J2260
PRIMATRIX	SQ CM	OTH	Q4110
PRIMAXIN	250 MG	IV, IM	J0743
PRIMESTRIN AQUEOUS	1 MG	IM, IV	J1410
PRIMETHASONE	1 MG	IM, IV, OTH	J1100
PRI-METHYLATE	80 MG	IM	J1040
PRIVIGEN	500 MG	IV	J1459
PROCAINAMIDE HCL	1 G	IM, IV	J2690
PROCARBAZINE HCL	50 MG	ORAL	S0182
PROCHLOPERAZINE MALEATE	5 MG	ORAL	S0183
PROCHLORPERAZINE	10 MG	IM, IV	J0780
PROCHLORPERAZINE MALEATE	10 MG	ORAL	Q0165
PROCHLORPERAZINE MALEATE	5 MG	ORAL	Q0164
PROCRIT, ESRD USE	1,000 U	SC, IV	J0886
PROCRIT, NON-ESRD USE	1,000 U	SC, IV	J0885
PROFILNINE HEAT-TREATED	1 IU	IV	J7194
PROFILNINE SD	1 IU	IV	J7194
PROFONIX	VIAL	INJ	C9113
PROGESTERONE	50 MG	IM	J2675
PROGRAF	1 MG	ORAL	J7507
PROGRAF	5 MG	OTH	J7525
PROHANCE	1 ML	IV	5005F
PROLASTIN	10 MG	IV	J0256
PROLEUKIN	1 VIAL	VAR	J9015
PROLIXIN DECANOATE	25 MG	SC, IM	J2680
PROMAZINE HCL	25 MG	IM	J2950
PROMETHAZINE HCL	12.5 MG	ORAL	Q0169
PROMETHAZINE HCL	50 MG	IM, IV	J2550
PRONESTYL	1 G	IM, IV	J2690
PROPECIA	5 MG	ORAL	S0138
PROPLEX SX-T	1 IU	IV	J7194
PROPLEX T	1 IU	IV	J7194
PROPRANOLOL HCL	1 MG	IV	J1800
PROREX	50 MG	IM, IV	J2550
PROSCAR	5 MG	ORAL	S0138
PROSTASCINT	DOSE	IV	A9507
PROSTIGMIN	0.5 MG	IM, IV	J2710
PROSTIN VR	1.25 MCG	INJ	J0270
PROTAMINE SULFATE	10 MG	IV	J2720
PROTEIN C CONCENTRATE	10 IU	IV	J2724
PROTEINASE INHIBITOR (HUMAN)	10 MG	IV	J0256
PROTIRELIN	250 MCG	IV	J2725
PROTONIX IV	40 MG	IV	S0164
PROTONIX IV	VIAL	IV	C9113
PROTOPAM CHLORIDE	1 G	SC, IM, IV	J2730

Drug Name	Unit Per	Route	Code
PROTROPIN	1 MG	SC, IM	J2940
PROVENTIL NONCOMPOUNDED, CONCENTRATED	1 MG	INH	J7611
PROVENTIL NONCOMPOUNDED, UNIT DOSE	1 MG	INH	J7613
PROVOCHOLINE POWDER	1 MG	INH	J7674
PROZINE-50	25 MG	IM	J2950
PULMICORT	0.25 MG	INH	J7633
PULMICORT RESPULES	0.5 MG	INH	J7627
PULMICORT RESPULES NONCOMPOUNDED, CONCETRATED	0.25 MG	INH	J7626
PULMOZYME	1 MG	INH	J7639
PURINETHOL	50 MG	ORAL	S0108
PYRIDOXINE HCL	100 MG	INJ	J3415
QUADRAMET	50 MCI	IV	A9605
QUELICIN	20 MG	IM, IV	J0330
QUINUPRISTIN/DALFOPRISTIN	500 MG	IV	J2770
RANIBIZUMAB	0.5 MG	OTH	J2778
RANITIDINE HCL	25 MG	INJ	J2780
RAPAMUNE	1 MG	ORAL	J7520
RAPTIVA	125 MG	SC	S0162
RASBURICASE	50 MCG	IM	J2783
REBETRON KIT	1,000,000 U	SC, IM	J9214
REBIF	11 MCG	SC	Q3026
REBIF	33 MCG	SC	J1825
RECLAST	1 MG	IV	J3488
RECOMBINATE	1 IU	IV	J7192
REDISOL	1,000 MCG	SC. IM	J3420
REFACTO	1 IU	IV	J7192
REFLUDAN	50 MG	IM, IV	J1945
REGADENOSON	0.1 MG	IV	J2785
REGITINE	5 MG	IM, IV	J2760
REGLAN	10 MG	IV	J2765
REGRANEX GEL	0.5 G	OTH	S0157
REGULAR INSULIN	5 UNITS	SC	J1815
RELAXIN	10 ML	IV, IM	J2800
RELION	5 U	SC	J1815
RELION NOVOLIN	50 U	SC	J1817
REMICADE	10 MG	IV	J1745
REMODULIN	1 MG	SC	J3285
REODULIN	1 MG	SC	J3285
REOPRO	10 MG	IV	J0130
REPRONEX	75 IU	SC, IM, IV	S0122
RESP SYNCYTIAL VIR IMMUNE GLOB	50 MG	IV	J1565
RESPIGAM	50 MG	IV	J1565
RESPIROL NONCOMPOUNDED, CONCENTRATED	1 MG	INH	J7611
RESPIROL NONCOMPOUNDED, UNIT DOSE	1 MG	INH	J7613
RETAVASE	18.1 MG	IV	J2993
RETEPLASE	18.1 MG	IV	J2993
RETISERT	IMPLANT	OTH	J7311
RETROVIR	10 MG	IV	J3485
RETROVIR	100 MG	ORAL	S0104
RHEOMACRODEX	500 ML	IV	J7100
RHEUMATREX DOSE PACK	2.5 MG	ORAL	J8610
RHO D IMMUNE GLOBULIN	300 MCG	IV	J2790
RHO D IMMUNE GLOBULIN (RHOPHYLAC)	100 IU	IM, IV	J2791
RHO D IMMUNE GLOBULIN MINIDOSE	50 MCG	IM	J2788
RHO D IMMUNE GLOBULIN SOLVENT DETERGENT	100 IU	IV	J2792
RHOGAM	300 MCG	IM	J2790
RHOGAM	50 MCG	IM	J2788
RHOPHYLAC	100 IU	IM, IV	J2791
RIMANTADINE HYDROCHLORIDE	100 MG	ORAL	G9036
RIMANTADINE HYDROCHLORIDE (GENERIC)	100 MG	ORAL	G9020
RIMSO 50	50 ML	IV	J1212
RINGERS LACTATE INFUSION	1,000 ML	VAR	J7120
RISPERDAL COSTA LONG ACTING	0.5 MG	IM	J2794
RISPERIDONE, LONG ACTING	0.5 MG	IM	J2794
RITUXAN	100 MG	IV	J9310
RITUXIMAB	100 MG	IV	J9310
ROBAXIN	10 ML	IV, IM	J2800
ROCEPHIN	250 MG	IV, IM	J0696
ROFERON-A	3,000,000 U	SC, IM	J9213
ROMIPLOSTIM	10 MCG	SC	C9245
ROPIVACAINE HYDROCHLORIDE	1 MG	VAR	J2795
RUBEX	10 MG	IV	J9000
RUBIDIUM RB-82	60 MCI	IV	A9555
RUBRAMIN PC	1,000 MCG	SC, IM	J3420
RUBRATOPE 57	1 MCI	ORAL	A9559
SAIZEN	1 MG	SC	J2941
SAIZEN SOMATROPIN RDNA ORIGIN	1 MG	SC	J2941
SALINE OR STERILE WATER, METERED DOSE DISPENSER	10 ML	INH	A4218
SALINE, STERILE WATER, AND/OR DEXTROSE DILUENT/FLUSH	10 ML	VAR	A4216
SALINE/STERILE WATER	500 ML	VAR	A4217
SAMARIUM LEXIDRONAMM	50 MCI	IV	A9605
SANDIMMUNE	100 MG	ORAL	J7502
SANDIMMUNE	25 MG	ORAL	J7515
SANDIMMUNE	250 MG	IV	J7516
SANDOSTATIN	25 MCG	SC, IV	J2354
SANDOSTATIN LAR	1 MG	IM	J2353
SANGCYA	100 MG	ORAL	J7502
SANO-DROL	40 MG	IM	J1030
SANO-DROL	80 MG	IM	J1040
SAQUINAVIR	200 MG	ORAL	S0140
SARGRAMOSTIM (GM-CSF)	50 MCG	IV	J2820
SCANDONEST	PER 10 ML	IV	J0670
SECREFLO	1 MCG	IV	J2850
SECRETIN, SYNTHETIC, HUMAN	1 MCG	IV	J2850
SENSORCAINE	30 ML	VAR	S0020
SEPTRA IV	10 ML	IV	S0039
SERMORELIN ACETATE	1 MCG	IV	Q0515
SEROSTIM	1 MG	SC	J2941
SEROSTIM RDNA ORIGIN	1 MG	SC	J2941
SILDENAFIL CITRATE	25 MG	ORAL	S0090

Drug Name	Unit Per	Route	Code
SIMULECT	20 MG	IV	J0480
SINCALIDE	5 MCG	IV	J2805
SIROLIMUS	1 MG	ORAL	J7520
SKIN SUBSTITUTE, APLIGRAF	SQ CM	OTH	Q4101
SKIN SUBSTITUTE, DERMAGRAFT	SQ CM	OTH	Q4106
SKIN SUBSTITUTE, GAMMAGRAFT	SQ CM	OTH	Q4111
SKIN SUBSTITUTE, GRAFTJACKET	SQ CM	OTH	Q4107
SKIN SUBSTITUTE, INTEGRA BILAYER MATRIX WOUND DRESSING	SQ CM	OTH	Q4104
SKIN SUBSTITUTE, INTEGRA DERMAL REGENERATION TEMPLATE	SQ CM	OTH	Q4105
SKIN SUBSTITUTE, INTEGRA MATRIX	SQ CM	OTH	Q4108
SKIN SUBSTITUTE, OASIS BURN MATRIX	SQ CM	OTH	Q4103
SKIN SUBSTITUTE, OASIS WOUND MATRIX	SQ CM	OTH	Q4102
SKIN SUBSTITUTE, PRIMATRIX	SQ CM	OTH	Q4110
SKIN SUBSTITUTE, TISSUEMEND	SQ CM	OTH	Q4109
SMZ-TMP	10 ML	IV	S0039
SODIUM FERRIC GLUCONATE COMPLEX IN SUCROSE	12.5 MG	IV	J2916
SODIUM FLUORIDE F-18, DIAGNOSTIC	STUDY DOSE UP TO 30 MCI	IV	A9580
SODIUM IODIDE I-131 CAPSULE DIAGNOSTIC	1 MCI	ORAL	A9528
SODIUM IODIDE I-131 CAPSULE THERAPEUTIC	1 MCI	ORAL	A9517
SODIUM IODIDE I-131 SOLUTION THERAPEUTIC	1 MCI	ORAL	A9530
SODIUM PHOSPHATE P32	1 MCI	IV	A9563
SOLGANAL	50 MG	IM	J2910
SOLIRIS	10 MG	IV	J1300
SOLTAMOX	10 MG	ORAL	S0187
SOLU-CORTEF	100 MG	IV, IM, SC	J1720
SOLU-MEDROL	125 MG	IM, IV	J2930
SOLU-MEDROL	40 MG	IM, IV	J2920
SOLUREX	1 MG	IM, IV, OTH	J1100
SOMATREM	1 MG	SC, IM	J2940
SOMATROPIN	1 MG	SC	J2941
SOMATULINE	1 MG	SC	J1930
SPECTINOMYCIN DIHYDROCHLORIDE	2 G	IM	J3320
SPECTRO-DEX	1 MG	IM, IV, OTH	J1100
SPORANOX	50 MG	IV	J1835
STADOL	1 MG	IM, IV	J0595
STADOL NS	25 MG	OTH	S0012
STERAPRED	5 MG	ORAL	J7506
STERILE WATER OR SALINE, METERED DOSE DISPENSER	10 ML	INH	A4218
STERILE WATER, SALINE, AND/OR DEXTROSE DILUENT/FLUSH	10 ML	VAR	A4216
STERILE WATER/SALINE	500 ML	VAR	A4217
STREPTASE	250,000 IU	IV	J2995
STREPTOKINASE	250,000 IU	IV	J2995
STREPTOMYCIN	1 G	IM	J3000
STREPTOZOCIN	1 GM	IV	J9320
STRONTIUM 89 CHLORIDE	1 MCI	IV	A9600

Drug Name	Unit Per	Route	Code
SUBLIMAZE	0.1 MG	IM, IV	J3010
SUCCINYLCHOLINE CHLORIDE	20 MG	IM, IV	J0330
SULFAMETHOXAZOLE AND TRIMETHOPRIM	10 ML	IV	S0039
SULFAMETHOXAZOLE-TRIMETHOPRIM	400-80 MG	ORAL	J8499
SULFUTRIM	10 ML	IV	S0039
SUMATRIPTAN SUCCINATE	6 MG	SC	J3030
SUPARTZ	PER DOSE	OTH	J7321
SUPPRELIN LA	10 MCG	OTH	J1675
SURGIMEND COLLAGEN MATRIX	0.5 SQ CM	OTH	C9358
SUS-PHRINE	UP TO 1 ML	VAR	J0170
SYNERCID	500 MG	IV	J2770
SYNTOCINON	10 UNITS	IV	J2590
SYNVISC	PER DOSE	OTH	J7322
SYTOBEX	1,000 MCG	SC, IM	J3420
TACRINE HCL	10 MG	ORAL	S0014
TACROLIMUS	1 MG	ORAL	J7507
TACROLIMUS	5 MG	OTH	J7525
TAGAMET HCL	300 MG	IM, IV	S0023
TALWIN	30 MG	IM, SC, IV	J3070
TAMOXIFEN CITRATE	10 MG	ORAL	S0187
TAXOL	30 MG	IV	J9265
TAXOTERE	20 MG	IV	J9170
TAZICEF	500 MG	IM, IV	J0713
TEBAMIDE	250 MG	ORAL	Q0173
TEBOROXIME TECHNETIUM TC 99	PER STUDY DOSE	IV	A9501
TEBOROXIME, TECHNETIUM	PER STUDY DOSE	IV	A9501
TECHNEPLEX	25 MCI	IV	A9539
TECHNESCAN	UP TO 30 MCI	IV	A9561
TECHNESCAN FANOLESOMAB	STUDY DOSE	IV	A9566
TECHNESCAN MAA	10 MCI	IV	A9540
TECHNESCAN MAG3	STUDY DOSE	IV	A9562
TECHNESCAN PYP	25 MCI	IV	A9538
TECHNESCAN PYP KIT	UP TO 25 MCI	IV	A9538
TECHNETIUM SESTAMBI	40 MCI	IV	A9500
TECHNETIUM TC 99M APCITIDE	20 MCI	IV	A9504
TECHNETIUM TC 99M ARCITUMOMAB, DIAGNOSTIC	45 MCI	IV	A9568
TECHNETIUM TC 99M BICISATE	25 MCI	IV	A9557
TECHNETIUM TC 99M DEPREOTIDE	35 MCI	IV	A9536
TECHNETIUM TC 99M EXAMETAZIME	25 MCI	IV	A9521
TECHNETIUM TC 99M FANOLESOMAB	25 MCI	IV	A9566
TECHNETIUM TC 99M LABELED RED BLOOD CELLS	30 MCI	IV	A9560
TECHNETIUM TC 99M MACROAGGREGATED ALBUMIN	10 MCI	IV	A9540
TECHNETIUM TC 99M MDI-MDP	30 MCI	IV	A9503
TECHNETIUM TC 99M MEBROFENIN	15 MCI	IV	A9537
TECHNETIUM TC 99M MEDRONATE	30 MCI	IV	A9503
TECHNETIUM TC 99M MERTIATIDE	15 MCI	IV	A9562
TECHNETIUM TC 99M OXIDRONATE	30 MCI	IV	A9561
TECHNETIUM TC 99M PENTETATE	75 MCI	INH	A9539
TECHNETIUM TC 99M PENTETATE	25 MCI	IV	A9539

Drug Name	Unit Per	Route	Code
TECHNETIUM TC 99M PYROPHOSPHATE	25 MCI	IV	A9538
TECHNETIUM TC 99M SODIUM GLUCEPATATE	25 MCI	IV	A9550
TECHNETIUM TC 99M SUCCIMER	10 MCI	IV	A9551
TECHNETIUM TC 99M SULFUR COLLOID	20 MCI	IV	A9541
TECHNETIUM TC 99M TETROFOSMIN, DIAGNOSTIC	STUDY DOSE	IV	A9502
TECHNETIUM TC-99M EXAMETAZIME LABELED AUTOLOGOUS WHITE BLOOD CELLS	PER STUDY DOSE	IV	A9569
TECHNETIUM TC-99M TEBOROXIME	PER STUDY DOSE	IV	A9501
TECHNILITE	PER MCI	IV	A9512
TEMODAR	100 MG	ORAL	J8700
TEMOZOLOMIDE	100 MG	ORAL	J8700
TEMSIROLIMUS	1 MG	IV	J9330
TENDON, POROUS MATRIX	1 SQ CM	OTH	C9356
TENDON, POROUS MATRIX CROSS-LINKED AND GLYCOSAMINOGLYCAN MATRIX	SQ CM	OTH	C9356
TENECTEPLASE	1 MG	IV	J3101
TENIPOSIDE	50 MG	IV	Q2017
TENOGLIDE TENDON PROTECTOR	1 SQ CM	OTH	C9356
TENOGLIDE TENDON PROTECTOR SHEET	SQ CM	OTH	C9356
TEQUIN	10 MG	IV	J1590
TERBUTALINE SULFATE	1 MG	SC, IV	J3105
TERBUTALINE SULFATE, COMPOUNDED, CONCENTRATED	1 MG	INH	J7680
TERBUTALINE SULFATE, COMPOUNDED, UNIT DOSE	1 MG	INH	J7681
TERIPARATIDE	10 MCG	SC	J3110
TERRAMYCIN	50 MG	IM	J2460
TESTERONE	50 MG	IM	J3140
TESTOSTERONE CYPIONATE	1 CC, 200 MG	IM	J1080
TESTOSTERONE CYPIONATE	UP TO 100 MG	IM	J1070
TESTOSTERONE CYPIONATE & ESTRADIOL CYPIONATE	1 ML	IM	J1060
TESTOSTERONE ENANTHATE	100 MG	IM	J3120
TESTOSTERONE ENANTHATE	200 MG	IM	J3130
TESTOSTERONE ENANTHATE & ESTRADIOL VALERATE	UP TO 1 CC	IM	J0900
TESTOSTERONE PELLET	75 MG	OTH	S0189
TESTOSTERONE PROPIONATE	100 MG	IM	J3150
TESTOSTERONE SUSPENSION	50 MG	IM	J3140
TESTRO AQ	50 MG	IM	J3140
TETANUS IMMUNE GLOBULIN	250 U	IM	J1670
TETRACYCLINE HCL	250 MG	IV	J0120
T-GEN	250 MG	ORAL	Q0173
THALLOUS CHLORIDE	1 MCI	IV	A9505
THALLOUS CHLORIDE TL-201	1 MCI	IV	A9505
THALLOUS CHLORIDE USP	1 MCI	IV	A9505
THEELIN AQUEOUS	1 MG	IM, IV	J1435
THEOPHYLLINE	40 MG	IV	J2810
THERACYS	VIAL	IV	J9031
THIAMINE HCL	100 MG	INJ	J3411
THIETHYLPERAZINE MALEATE	10 MG	IM	J3280
THIETHYLPERAZINE MALEATE	10 MG	ORAL	Q0174
THIMAZIDE	250 MG	ORAL	Q0173
THIOTEPA	15 MG	IV	J9340
THORAZINE	10 MG	ORAL	Q0171
THORAZINE	25 MG	ORAL	Q0172
THORAZINE	50 MG	IM, IV	J3230
THROMBATE III	1 IU	IV	J7197
THYMOGLOBULIN	25 MG	OTH	J7511
THYROGEN	0.9 MG	IM, SC	J3240
THYROTROPIN ALPHA	0.9 MG	IM, SC	J3240
TICARCILLIN DISODIUM AND CLAVULANATE	3.1 G	IV	S0040
TICE BCG	VIAL	OTH	J9031
TICON	250 MG	IM	Q0173
TIGAN	200 MG	IM	J3250
TIGECYCLINE	1 MG	IV	J3243
TIJECT-20	200 MG	IM	J3250
TIMENTIN	3.1 G	IV	S0040
TINZAPARIN	1,000 IU	SC	J1655
TIROFIBAN HCL	0.25 MG	IM, IV	J3246
TISSUEMEND	SQ CM	OTH	Q4109
TNKASE	1 MG	IV	J3101
TOBI	300 MG	INH	J7682
TOBRAMYCIN COMPOUNDED, UNIT DOSE	300 MG	INH	J7685
TOBRAMYCIN SULFATE	80 MG	IM, IV	J3260
TOBRAMYCIN, NONCOMPOUNDED, UNIT DOSE	300 MG	INH	J7682
TOLAZOLINE HCL	25 MG	IV	J2670
TOPOSAR	10 MG	IV	J9181
TOPOTECAN	4 MG	IV	J9350
TOPOTECAN	0.25 MG	ORAL	J8705
TORECAN	10 MG	ORAL	Q0174
TORISEL	1 MG	IV	J9330
TORISEL	1 MG	IV	J9330
TORNALATE	PER MG	INH	J7629
TORNALATE CONCENTRATE	PER MG	INH	J7628
TORSEMIDE	10 MG	IV	J3265
TOSITUMOMAB DIAGNOSTIC	DOSE	IV	A9544
TOSITUMOMAB THERAPEUTIC	DOSE	IV	A9545
TOTECT	PER 250 MG	IV	J1190
TRASTUZUMAB	10 MG	IV	J9355
TRASYLOL	10,000 KIU	IV	J0365
TREANDA	1 MG	IV	J9033
TRELSTAR DEPOT	3.75 MG	IM	J3315
TRELSTAR DEPOT PLUS DEBIOCLIP KIT	3.75 MG	IM	J3315
TRELSTAR LA	3.75 MG	IM	J3315
TREPROSTINIL	1 MG	SC	J3285
TRETINOIN	5 G	OTH	S0117
TRIAM-A	10 MG	IM	J3301
TRIAMCINOLONE ACETONIDE	10 MG	IM	J3301
TRIAMCINOLONE ACETONIDE, PRESERVATIVE FREE	1 MG	INJ	J3300
TRIAMCINOLONE DIACETATE	5 MG	IM	J3302
TRIAMCINOLONE HEXACETONIDE	5 MG	VAR	J3303

Drug Name	Unit Per	Route	Code
TRIAMCINOLONE, COMPOUNDED, CONCENTRATED	1 MG	INH	J7683
TRIAMCINOLONE, COMPOUNDED, UNIT DOSE	1 MG	INH	J7684
TRIBAN	250 MG	ORAL	Q0173
TRI-KORT	10 MG	IM	J3301
TRILIFON	4 MG	ORAL	Q0175
TRILOG	10 MG	IM	J3301
TRILONE	5 MG	IM	J3302
TRIMETHOBENZAMIDE HCL	200 MG	IM	J3250
TRIMETHOBENZAMIDE HCL	250 MG	ORAL	Q0173
TRIMETREXATE GLUCURONATE	25 MG	IV	J3305
TRIPTORELIN PAMOATE	3.75 MG	IM	J3315
TRISENOX	1 MG	IV	J9017
TRIVARIS	1 MG	VAR	J3300
TROBICIN	2 G	IM	J3320
TRUXADRYL	50 MG	IV, IM	J1200
TYGACIL	1 MG	IV	J3243
TYPE A BOTOX	1 U	OTH	J0585
TYSABRI	1 MG	IV	J2323
ULTRALENTE	5 U	SC	J1815
ULTRATAG	30 MCI	IV	A9560
ULTRA-TECHNEKOW	PER MCI	IV	A9512
UNASYN	1.5 G	IM, IV	J0295
UNCLASSIFIED BIOLOGICS			J3590
UREA	40 G	IV	J3350
UROFOLLITROPIN	75 IU	SC, IM	J3355
UROKINASE	250,000 IU	IV	J3365
UROKINASE	5,000 IU	IV	J3364
VALERGEN	10 MG	IM	J1380
VALERGEN	20 MG	IM	J1390
VALIUM	5 MG	IV, IM	J3360
VALRUBICIN INTRAVESICAL	200 MG	OTH	J9357
VALSTAR	200 MG	OTH	J9357
VANCOCIN	500 MG	IM, IV	J3370
VANCOMYCIN HCL	500 MG	IV, IM	J3370
VANTAS	50 MG	OTH	J9225
VECTIBIX	10 MG	IV	J9303
VELCADE	0.1 MG	IV	J9041
VELOSULIN	5 U	SC	J1815
VELOSULIN BR	5 U	SC	J1815
VENOFER	1 MG	IV	J1756
VENTOLIN NONCOMPOUNDED, CONCENTRATED	1 MG	INH	J7611
VENTOLIN NONCOMPOUNDED, UNIT DOSE	1 MG	INH	J7613
VEPESID	10 MG	IV	J9181
VEPESID	50 MG	ORAL	J8560
VERITAS	SQ CM	OTH	C9354
VERSED	1 MG	IM, IV	J2250
VERTEPORFIN	0.1 MG	IV	J3396
VFEND	200 MG	IV	J3465
VIAGRA	25 MG	ORAL	S0090
VIDAZA	1 MG	SC	J9025
VIDEX	25 MG	ORAL	S0137
VINBLASTINE SULFATE	1 MG	IV	J9360
VINCRISTINE SULFATE	1 MG	IV	J9370
VINCRISTINE SULFATE	2 MG	IV	J9375
VINORELBINE TARTRATE	10 MG	IV	J9390
VIRILON	1 CC, 200 MG	IM	J1080
VISTAJECT-25	25 MG	IM	J3410
VISTARIL	25 MG	IM	J3410
VISTARIL	25 MG	ORAL	Q0177
VISTIDE	375 MG	IV	J0740
VISUDYNE	0.1 MG	IV	J3396
VITAMIN B-12 CYANOCOBALAMIN	1,000 MCG	IM, SC	J3420
VITRASE	1 USP	OTH	J3471
VITRASE	1,000 USP	OTH	J3472
VITRASERT	4.5 MG	OTH	J7310
VITRAVENE	1.65 MG	OTH	J1452
VIVITROL	1 MG	IM	J2315
VON WILLEBAND FACTOR VIII COMPLEX, HUMAN	PER FACTOR VIII IU	IV	J7186
VON WILLEBRAND FACTOR COMPLEX, HUMATE-P	IU	IV	J7187
VORICONAZOLE	200 MG	IV	J3465
VUMON	50 MG	IV	Q2017
WEHAMINE	50 MG	IM, IV	J1240
WEHDRYL	50 MG	IM, IV	J1200
WELBUTRIN SR	150 MG	ORAL	S0106
WINRHO SDF	100 IU	IV	J2792
WYCILLIN	600,000 U	IM, IV	J2510
XELODA	150 MG	ORAL	J8520
XELODA	500 MG	ORAL	J8521
XENON XE-133	10 MCI	OTH	A9558
XOLAIR	5 MG	SC	J2357
XYLOCAINE	10 MG	IV	J2001
YTTRIUM 90 IBRITUMOMAB TIUXETAN	TX DOSE	IV	A9543
ZANAMIVIR (BRAND NAME)	10 MG	INH	G9034
ZANAMIVIR (GENERIC)	10 MG	INH	G9018
ZANOSAR	1 GM	IV	J9320
ZANTAC	25 MG	INJ	J2780
ZEMAIRA	10 MG	IV	J0256
ZEMPLAR	1 MCG	IV, IM	J2501
ZENAPAX	25 MG	OTH	J7513
ZEVALIN	UP TO 5 MCI	IV	A9542
ZEVALIN DIAGNOSTIC	TX DOSE	IV	A9542
ZEVALIN THERAPEUTIC	TX DOSE	IV	A9543
ZICONOTIDE	1 MCG	IT	J2278
ZIDOVUDINE	10 MG	IV	J3485
ZIDOVUDINE	100 MG	ORAL	S0104
ZINACEFT	PER 750 MG	IM, IV	J0697
ZINECARD	250 MG	IV	J1190
ZIPRASIDONE MESYLATE	10 MG	IM	J3486
ZITHROMAX	1 G	ORAL	Q0144
ZITHROMAX	500 MG	IV	J0456
ZOFRAN	1 MG	IV	J2405
ZOFRAN	8 MG	ORAL	Q0179
ZOFRAN	4 MG	ORAL	S0181
ZOLADEX	3.6 MG	SC	J9202

Drug Name	Unit Per	Route	Code
ZOLEDRONIC ACID	1 MG	IV	J3487
ZOLEDRONIC ACID (RECLAST)	1 MG	IV	J3488
ZOMETA	1 MG	IV	J3487
ZORBTIVE	1 MG	SC	J2941
ZOSYN	1 G/1.125 GM	IV	J2543
ZOVIRAX	5 MG	IV	J0133
ZYPREXA	2.5 MG	IM	S0166
ZYVOX	200 MG	IV	J2020

NOT OTHERWISE CLASSIFIED DRUGS

Drug Name	Unit Per	Route	Code
ALFENTANIL	500 MCG	IV	J3490
ALLOPURINOL SODIUM	500 MG	IV	J3490
AMINOCAPROIC ACID	250 MG	IV	J3490
ARGININE HYDROCHLORIDE	300 ML	IV	J3490
ASCORBIC ACID	250 MG	IV	J3490
ATROPINE SULFATE/EDROPHONIUM CHLORIDE	10 MG	IV	J3490
AZTREONAM	500 MG	IV	J3490
BUMETANIDE	0.25 MG	IM, IV	J3490
BUPIVACAINE, 0.25%	1 ML	OTH	J3490
BUPIVACAINE, 0.50%	1 ML	OTH	J3490
BUPIVACAINE, 0.75%	1 ML	OTH	J3490
CALCIUM CHLORIDE	100 MG	IV	J3490
CIMETIDINE HCL	150 MG	IM, IV	J3490
CLAVULANTE POTASSIUM/TICARCILLIN DISODIUM	0.1-3 GM	IV	J3490
CLINDAMYCIN PHOSPHATE	150 MG	IV	J3490
COPPER SULFATE	0.4 MG	INJ	J3490
DEXTROSE 50%	50 ML	IV	J3490
DILTIAZEM HCL	5 MG	IV	J3490
DILTIAZEM HCL	5 MG	IV	J3490
DOXAPRAM HCL	20 MG	IV	J3490
DOXYCYCLINE HYCLATE	100 MG	INJ	J3490
EDROPHONIUM CHLORIDE	10 MG	IM, IV	J3490
ENALAPRILAT	1.25 MG	IV	J3490
ESMOLOL HCL	10 MG	IV	J3490
ESOMEPRAZOLE SODIUM	20 MG	IV	J3490
ETOMIDATE	2 MG	IV	J3490
FAMOTIDINE	10 MG	IV	J3490
FLUMAZENIL	0.1 MG	IV	J3490
FOLIC ACID	5 MG	SC, IM, IV	J3490
GLYCOPYRROLATE	0.2 MG	IM, IV	J3490
IXABEPILONE	1 MG	IV	J3490
KETAMINE HCL	10 MG	IM, IV	J3490
LABETALOL HCL	5 MG	INJ	J3490
LEVETIRACETAM (KEPPRA INTRAVENOUS)	10 MG	IV	J3490
LIDOCAINE	1 ML	VAR	J3490
METOPROLOL TARTRATE	1 MG	IV	J3490
METRONIDAZOLE INJ	500 MG	IV	J3490
MORRHUATE SODIUM	50 MG	OTH	J3490
NAFCILLIN SODIUM	1 GM	IM, IV	J3490
NALMEFENE HCL	10 MCG	IV	J3490
NITROGLYCERIN	5 MG	IV	J3490
OLANZAPINE	0.5 MG	IM	J3490
POTASSIUM ACETATE	2 MEQ	IV	J3490
POTASSIUM POSPHATE	3 MMOL	IV	J3490
PROPOFOL	10 MG	IV	J3490
PROTONIX	40 MG	IV	J3490
RIFAMPIN	600 MG	IV	J3490
SARRACENIA PURPURA	1 ML	INJ	J3490
SODIUM ACETATE	2 MEQ		J3490
SODIUM BICARBONATE, 8.4%	50 ML	IV	J3490
SODIUM CHLORIDE, HYPERTONIC	250 CC	IV	J3490
SODIUM THIOSULFATE	100 MG	IV	J3490
SURGIMEND	0.5 SQ CM	OTH	J3490
TEMSIROLIMUS	1 MG	IV	J9330
VALPROATE SODIUM	100 MG	IV	J3490

APPENDIX 2 — MODIFIERS

A modifier is a two-position alpha or numeric code that is added to the end of a CPT code to clarify the services being billed. Modifiers provide a means by which a service can be altered without changing the procedure code. They add more information, such as the anatomical site, to the code. In addition, they help to eliminate the appearance of duplicate billing and unbundling. Modifiers are used to increase accuracy in reimbursement, coding consistency, editing, and to capture payment data.

A1 Dressing for one wound

A2 Dressing for 2 wounds

A3 Dressing for 3 wounds

A4 Dressing for 4 wounds

A5 Dressing for 5 wounds

A6 Dressing for 6 wounds

A7 Dressing for 7 wounds

A8 Dressing for 8 wounds

A9 Dressing for 9 or more wounds

AA Anesthesia services performed personally by anesthesiologist

AD Medical supervision by a physician: more than 4 concurrent anesthesia procedures

AE Registered dietician

AF Specialty physician

AG Primary physician

AH Clinical psychologist

AJ Clinical social worker

AK Non participating physician

AM Physician, team member service

AP Determination of refractive state was not performed in the course of diagnostic ophthalmological examination

AQ Physician providing a service in an unlisted health professional shortage area (HPSA)

AR Physician provider services in a physician scarcity area

AS Physician assistant, nurse practitioner, or clinical nurse specialist services for assistant at surgery

AT Acute treatment (this modifier should be used when reporting service 98940, 98941, 98942)

AU Item furnished in conjunction with a urological, ostomy, or tracheostomy supply

AV Item furnished in conjunction with a prosthetic device, prosthetic or orthotic

AW Item furnished in conjunction with a surgical dressing

AX Item furnished in conjunction with dialysis services

BA Item furnished in conjunction with parenteral enteral nutrition (PEN) services

BL Special acquisition of blood and blood products

BO Orally administered nutrition, not by feeding tube

BP The beneficiary has been informed of the purchase and rental options and has elected to purchase the item

BR The beneficiary has been informed of the purchase and rental options and has elected to rent the item

BU The beneficiary has been informed of the purchase and rental options and after 30 days has not informed the supplier of his/her decision

CA Procedure payable only in the inpatient setting when performed emergently on an outpatient who expires prior to admission

CB Service ordered by a renal dialysis facility (RDF) physician as part of the ESRD beneficiary's dialysis benefit, is not part of the composite rate, and is separately reimbursable

CC Procedure code change (use CC when the procedure code submitted was changed either for administrative reasons or because an incorrect code was filed)

CD AMCC test has been ordered by an ESRD facility or MCP physician that is part of the composite rate and is not separately billable

CE AMCC test has been ordered by an ESRD facility or MCP physician that is a composite rate test but is beyond the normal frequency covered under the rate and is separately reimbursable based on medical necessity

CF AMCC test has been ordered by an ESRD facility or MCP physician that is not part of the composite rate and is separately billable

CG Policy criteria applied

CR Catastrophe/Disaster related

E1 Upper left, eyelid

E2 Lower left, eyelid

E3 Upper right, eyelid

E4 Lower right, eyelid

EA Erythropoetic stimulating agent (ESA) administered to treat anemia due to anticancer chemotherapy

EB Erythropoetic stimulating agent (ESA) administered to treat anemia due to anticancer radiotherapy

EC Erythropoetic stimulating agent (ESA) administered to treat anemia not due to anticancer radiotherapy or anticancer chemotherapy

ED Hematocrit level has exceeded 39% (or hemoglobin level has exceeded 13.0 G/dl) for 3 or more consecutive billing cycles immediately prior to and including the current cycle

EE Hematocrit level has not exceeded 39% (or hemoglobin level has not exceeded 13.0 G/dl) for 3 or more consecutive billing cycles immediately prior to and including the current cycle

EJ Subsequent claims for a defined course of therapy, e.g., EPO, sodium hyaluronate, infliximab

EM Emergency reserve supply (for ESRD benefit only)

EP Service provided as part of Medicaid early periodic screening diagnosis and treatment (EPSDT) program

ET Emergency services

EY No physician or other licensed health care provider order for this item or service

F1 Left hand, 2nd digit

F2 Left hand, third digit

F3 Left hand, 4th digit

F4 Left hand, fifth digit

F5 Right hand, thumb

F6 Right hand, 2nd digit

F7 Right hand, third digit

F8 Right hand, 4th digit

F9 Right hand, 5th digit

FA Left hand, thumb

FB Item provided without cost to provider, supplier or practitioner, or full credit received for replaced device (examples, but not limited to, covered under warranty, replaced due to defect, free samples)

FC Partial credit received for replaced device

FP Service provided as part of family planning program

G1 Most recent URR reading of less than 60

G2 Most recent URR reading of 60 to 64.9

G3 Most recent URR reading of 65 to 69.9

G4 Most recent URR reading of 70 to 74.9

G5 Most recent URR reading of 75 or greater

G6 ESRD patient for whom less than 6 dialysis sessions have been provided in a month

G7 Pregnancy resulted from rape or incest or pregnancy certified by physician as life threatening

G8 Monitored anesthesia care (MAC) for deep complex, complicated, or markedly invasive surgical procedure

G9	Monitored anesthesia care for patient who has history of severe cardiopulmonary condition
GA	Waiver of liability statement on file
GB	Claim being resubmitted for payment because it is no longer covered under a global payment demonstration
GC	This service has been performed in part by a resident under the direction of a teaching physician
GD	Units of service exceeds medically unlikely edit value and represents reasonable and necessary services
GE	This service has been performed by a resident without the presence of a teaching physician under the primary care exception
GF	Nonphysician (e.g., nurse practitioner (NP), certified registered nurse anesthetist (CRNA), certified registered nurse (CRN), clinical nurse specialist (CNS), physician assistant (PA)) services in a critical access hospital
GG	Performance and payment of a screening mammogram and diagnostic mammogram on the same patient, same day
GH	Diagnostic mammogram converted from screening mammogram on same day
GJ	Opt out physician or practitioner emergency or urgent service
GK	Reasonable and necessary item/service associated with GA or GZ modifier
GL	Medically unnecessary upgrade provided instead of nonupgraded item, no charge, no advance beneficiary notice (ABN)
GM	Multiple patients on one ambulance trip
GN	Services delivered under an outpatient speech language pathology plan of care
GO	Services delivered under an outpatient occupational therapy plan of care
GP	Services delivered under an outpatient physical therapy plan of care
GQ	Via asynchronous telecommunications system
GR	This service was performed in whole or in part by a resident in a department of veterans affairs medical center or clinic, supervised in accordance with VA policy
GS	Dosage of EPO or darbepoetin alfa has been reduced and maintained in response to hematocrit or hemoglobin level
GT	Via interactive audio and video telecommunication systems
GV	Attending physician not employed or paid under arrangement by the patient's hospice provider
GW	Service not related to the hospice patient's terminal condition
GY	Item or service statutorily excluded, does not meet the definition of any Medicare benefit or for non-Medicare insurers, is not a contract benefit
GZ	Item or service expected to be denied as not reasonable and necessary
H9	Court-ordered
HA	Child/adolescent program
HB	Adult program, nongeriatric
HC	Adult program, geriatric
HD	Pregnant/parenting women's program
HE	Mental health program
HF	Substance abuse program
HG	Opioid addiction treatment program
HH	Integrated mental health/substance abuse program
HI	Integrated mental health and mental retardation/developmental disabilities program
HJ	Employee assistance program
HK	Specialized mental health programs for high-risk populations
HL	Intern
HM	Less than bachelor degree level
HN	Bachelors degree level
HO	Masters degree level
HP	Doctoral level
HQ	Group setting
HR	Family/couple with client present
HS	Family/couple without client present
HT	Multi-disciplinary team
HU	Funded by child welfare agency
HV	Funded state addictions agency
HW	Funded by state mental health agency
HX	Funded by county/local agency
HY	Funded by juvenile justice agency
HZ	Funded by criminal justice agency
J1	Competitive acquisition program no-pay submission for a prescription number
J2	Competitive acquisition program, restocking of emergency drugs after emergency administration
J3	Competitive acquisition program (CAP), drug not available through CAP as written, reimbursed under average sales price methodology
JA	Administered intravenously
JB	Administered subcutaneously
JC	Skin substitute used as a graft
JD	Skin substitute not used as a graft
JW	Drug amount discarded/not administered to any patient
K0	Lower extremity prosthesis functional level 0—does not have the ability or potential to ambulate or transfer safely with or without assistance and a prosthesis does not enhance their quality of life or mobility
K1	Lower extremity prosthesis functional level 1 - has the ability or potential to use a prosthesis for transfers or ambulation on level surfaces at fixed cadence, typical of the limited and unlimited household ambulator.
K2	Lower extremity prosthesis functional level 2 - has the ability or potential for ambulation with the ability to traverse low level environmental barriers such as curbs, stairs or uneven surfaces. typical of the limited community ambulator.
K3	Lower extremity prosthesis functional level 3—has the ability or potential for ambulation with variable cadence, typical of the community ambulator who has the ability to traverse most environmental barriers and may have vocational, therapeutic, or exercise activity that demands prosthetic utilization beyond simple locomotion
K4	Lower extremity prosthesis functional level 4 - has the ability or potential for prosthetic ambulation that exceeds the basic ambulation skills, exhibiting high impact, stress, or energy levels, typical of the prosthetic demands of the child, active adult, or athlete.
KA	Add on option/accessory for wheelchair
KB	Beneficiary requested upgrade for ABN, more than 4 modifiers identified on claim
KC	Replacement of special power wheelchair interface
KD	Drug or biological infused through DME
KE	Bid under round one of the DMEPOS competitive bidding program for use with noncompetitive bid base equipment
KF	Item designated by FDA as class III device
KG	DMEPOS item subject to DMEPOS competitive bidding program number 1
KH	DMEPOS item, initial claim, purchase or first month rental
KI	DMEPOS item, 2nd or 3rd month rental
KJ	DMEPOS item, parenteral enteral nutrition (PEN) pump or capped rental, months 4 to 15
KK	DMEPOS item subject to DMEPOS competitive bidding program number 2
KL	DMEPOS item delivered via mail
KM	Replacement of facial prosthesis including new impression/moulage

KN	Replacement of facial prosthesis using previous master model
KO	Single drug unit dose formulation
KP	First drug of a multiple drug unit dose formulation
KQ	Second or subsequent drug of a multiple drug unit dose formulation
KR	Rental item, billing for partial month
KS	Glucose monitor supply for diabetic beneficiary not treated with insulin
KT	Beneficiary resides in a competitive bidding area and travels outside that competitive bidding area and receives a competitive bid item.
KU	DMEPOS item subject to DMEPOS competitive bidding program number 3
KV	DMEPOS item subject to DMEPOS competitive bidding program that is furnished as part of a professional service
KW	DMEPOS item subject to DMEPOS competitive bidding program number 4
KX	Requirements specified in the medical policy have been met
KY	DMEPOS item subject to DMEPOS competitive bidding program number 5
KZ	New coverage not implemented by managed care
LC	Left circumflex coronary artery
LD	Left anterior descending coronary artery
LL	Lease/rental (use the LL modifier when DME equipment rental is to be applied against the purchase price)
LR	Laboratory round trip
LS	FDA-monitored intraocular lens implant
LT	Left side (used to identify procedures performed on the left side of the body)
M2	Medicare secondary payer (MSP)
MS	Six month maintenance and servicing fee for reasonable and necessary parts and labor which are not covered under any manufacturer or supplier warranty
NR	New when rented (use the NR modifier when DME which was new at the time of rental is subsequently purchased)
NU	New equipment
P1	A normal healthy patient
P2	A patient with mild systemic disease
P3	A patient with severe systemic disease
P4	A patient with severe systemic disease that is a constant threat to life
P5	A moribund patient who is not expected to survive without the operation
P6	A declared brain-dead patient whose organs are being removed for donor purposes
PL	Progressive addition lenses
PR	Ambulance transportation from physician's office (includes HMO non-hospital facility, clinic, etc.)to residence
Q0	Investigational clinical service provided in a clinical research study that is in an approved clinical research study
Q1	Routine clinical service provided in a clinical research study that is in an approved clinical research study
Q2	HCFA/ORD demonstration project procedure/service
Q3	Live kidney donor surgery and related services
Q4	Service for ordering/referring physician qualifies as a service exemption
Q5	Service furnished by a substitute physician under a reciprocal billing arrangement
Q6	Service furnished by a locum tenens physician
Q7	One Class A finding
Q8	Two Class B findings
Q9	One class B and 2 class C findings
QB	Physician providing service in a rural HPSA
QC	Single channel monitoring
QD	Recording and storage in solid state memory by a digital recorder
QE	Prescribed amount of oxygen is less than 1 liter per minute (LPM)
QF	Prescribed amount of oxygen exceeds 4 liters per minute (LPM) and portable oxygen is prescribed
QG	Prescribed amount of oxygen is greater than 4 liters per minute (LPM)
QH	Oxygen conserving device is being used with an oxygen delivery system
QJ	Services/items provided to a prisoner or patient in state or local custody, however the state or local government, as applicable, meets the requirements in 42 CFR 411.4(B)
QK	Medical direction of 2, 3, or 4 concurrent anesthesia procedures involving qualified individuals
QL	Patient pronounced dead after ambulance called
QM	Ambulance service provided under arrangement by a provider of services
QN	Ambulance service furnished directly by a provider of services
QP	Documentation is on file showing that the laboratory test(s) was ordered individually or ordered as a CPT-recognized panel other than automated profile codes 80002-80019, G0058, G0059, and G0060
QQ	Claim submitted with a written statement of intent
QS	Monitored anesthesia care service
QT	Recording and storage on tape by an analog tape recorder
QU	Physician providing service in an urban HPSA
QW	CLIA waived test
QX	CRNA service: with medical direction by a physician
QY	Medical direction of one certified registered nurse anesthetist (CRNA) by an anesthesiologist
QZ	CRNA service: without medical direction by a physician
RA	Replacement of a DME item
RB	Replacement of a part of DME furnished as part of a repair
RC	Right coronary artery
RD	Drug provided to beneficiary, but not administered "incident-to"
RE	Furnished in full compliance with FDA-mandated risk evaluation and mitigation strategy (REMS)
RR	Rental (use the RR modifier when DME is to be rented)
RT	Right side (used to identify procedures performed on the right side of the body)
SA	Nurse practitioner rendering service in collaboration with a physician
SB	Nurse midwife
SC	Medically necessary service or supply
SD	Services provided by registered nurse with specialized, highly technical home infusion training
SE	State and/or federally-funded programs/services
SF	Second opinion ordered by a professional review organization (PRO) per section 9401, p.l. 99-272 (100% reimbursement - no Medicare deductible or coinsurance)
SG	Ambulatory surgical center (ASC) facility service
SH	Second concurrently administered infusion therapy
SJ	Third or more concurrently administered infusion therapy
SK	Member of high risk population (use only with codes for immunization)
SL	State supplied vaccine
SM	Second surgical opinion
SN	Third surgical opinion
SQ	Item ordered by home health
SS	Home infusion services provided in the infusion suite of the IV therapy provider

ST Related to trauma or injury

SU Procedure performed in physician's office (to denote use of facility and equipment)

SV Pharmaceuticals delivered to patient's home but not utilized

SW Services provided by a certified diabetic educator

SY Persons who are in close contact with member of high-risk population (use only with codes for immunization)

T1 Left foot, 2nd digit

T2 Left foot, 3rd digit

T3 Left foot, 4th digit

T4 Left foot, 5th digit

T5 Right foot, great toe

T6 Right foot, 2nd digit

T7 Right foot, 3rd digit

T8 Right foot, 4th digit

T9 Right foot, 5th digit

TA Left foot, great toe

TC Technical component. Under certain circumstances, a charge may be made for the technical component alone. Under those circumstances the technical component charge is identified by adding modifier 'TC' to the usual procedure number. Technical component charges are institutional charges and not billed separately by physicians. However, portable x-ray suppliers only bill for technical component and should utilize modifier TC. The charge data from portable x-ray suppliers will then be used to build customary and prevailing profiles.

TD RN

TE LPN/LVN

TF Intermediate level of care

TG Complex/high tech level of care

TH Obstetrical treatment/services, prenatal or postpartum

TJ Program group, child and/or adolescent

TK Extra patient or passenger, nonambulance

TL Early intervention/individualized family service plan (IFSP)

TM Individualized education program (IEP)

TN Rural/outside providers' customary service area

TP Medical transport, unloaded vehicle

TQ Basic life support (BSL) transport by a volunteer ambulance provider

TR School-based individualized education program (IEP) services provided outside the public school district responsible for the student

TS Follow-up service

TT Individualized service provided to more than one patient in same setting

TU Special payment rate, overtime

TV Special payment rates, holidays/weekends

TW Back-up equipment

U1 Medicaid level of care 1, as defined by each state

U2 Medicaid level of care 2, as defined by each state

U3 Medicaid level of care 3, as defined by each state

U4 Medicaid level of care 4, as defined by each state

U5 Medicaid level of care 5, as defined by each state

U6 Medicaid level of care 6, as defined by each state

U7 Medicaid level of care 7, as defined by each state

U8 Medicaid level of care 8, as defined by each state

U9 Medicaid level of care 9, as defined by each state

UA Medicaid level of care 10, as defined by each state

UB Medicaid level of care 11, as defined by each state

UC Medicaid level of care 12, as defined by each state

UD Medicaid level of care 13, as defined by each state

UE Used durable medical equipment

UF Services provided in the morning

UG Services provided in the afternoon

UH Services provided in the evening

UJ Services provided at night

UK Services provided on behalf of the client to someone other than the client (collateral relationship)

UN Two patients served

UP Three patients served

UQ Four patients served

UR Five patients served

US Six or more patients served

VP Aphakic patient

APPENDIX 3 — ABBREVIATIONS AND ACRONYMS

HCPCS Abbreviations and Acronyms

The following abbreviations and acronyms are used in the HCPCS descriptions:

/	or
<	less than
<=	less than equal to
>	greater than
>=	greater than equal to
AC	alternating current
AFO	ankle-foot orthosis
AICC	anti-inhibitor coagulant complex
AK	above the knee
AKA	above knee amputation
ALS	advanced life support
AMP	ampule
ART	artery
ART	Arterial
ASC	ambulatory surgery center
ATT	attached
A-V	Arteriovenous
AVF	arteriovenous fistula
BICROS	bilateral routing of signals
BK	below the knee
BLS	basic life support
BMI	body mass index
BP	blood pressure
BTE	behind the ear (hearing aid)
CAPD	continuous ambulatory peritoneal dialysis
Carb	carbohydrate
CBC	complete blood count
cc	cubic centimeter
CCPD	continuous cycling peritoneal analysis
CHF	congestive heart failure
CIC	completely in the canal (hearing aid)
CIM	Coverage Issue Manual
Clsd	closed
cm	centimeter
CMN	certificate of medical necessity
CMS	Centers for Medicare and Medicaid Services
CMV	Cytomegalovirus
Conc	concentrate
Conc	concentrated
Cont	continuous
CP	clinical psychologist
CPAP	continuous positive airway pressure
CPT	Current Procedural Terminology
CRF	chronic renal failure
CRNA	certified registered nurse anesthetist
CROS	contralateral routing of signals
CSW	clinical social worker
CT	computed tomography
CTLSO	cervical-thoracic-lumbar-sacral orthosis
cu	cubic
DC	direct current
DI	diurnal rhythm
Dx	diagnosis
DLI	donor leukocyte infusion
DME	durable medical equipment
DME MAC	durable medical equipment Medicare administrative contractor
DMEPOS	Durable Medical Equipment, Prosthestics, Orthotics and Other Supplies
DMERC	durable medical equipment regional carrier
DR	diagnostic radiology
DX	diagnostic
e.g.	for example
Ea	each
ECF	extended care facility
EEG	electroencephalogram
EKG	electrocardiogram
EMG	electromyography
EO	elbow orthosis
EP	electrophysiologic
EPO	epoetin alfa
EPSDT	early periodic screening, diagnosis and treatment
ESRD	end-stage renal disease
Ex	extended
Exper	experimental
Ext	external
F	french
FDA	Food and Drug Administration
FDG-PET	Positron emission with tomography with 18 fluorodeoxyglucose
Fem	female
FO	finger orthosis
FPD	fixed partial denture
Fr	french
ft	foot
G-CSF	filgrastim (granulocyte colony-stimulating factor)
gm	gram (g)
H20	water
HCl	hydrochloric acid, hydrochloride
HCPCS	Healthcare Common Procedural Coding System
HCT	hematocrit
HFO	hand-finger orthosis
HHA	home health agency
HI	high
HI-LO	high-low
HIT	home infusion therapy
HKAFO	hip-knee-ankle foot orthosis
HLA	human leukocyte antigen
HMES	heat and moisture exchange system
HNPCC	hereditary non-polyposis colorectal cancer
HO	hip orthosis
HPSA	health professional shortage area
HST	home sleep test
IA	intra-arterial administration
ip	interphalangeal
I-131	Iodine 131
ICF	intermediate care facility
ICU	intensive care facility
IM	intramuscular
in	inch
INF	infusion
INH	inhalation solution
INJ	injection
IOL	intraocular lens
IPD	intermittent peritoneal dialysis
IPPB	intermittent positive pressure breathing
IT	intrathecal administration
ITC	in the canal (hearing aid)
ITE	in the ear (hearing aid)

IU	international units
IV	intravenous
IVF	in vitro fertilization
KAFO	knee-ankle-foot orthosis
KO	knee orthosis
KOH	potassium hydroxide
L	left
LASIK	laser in situ keratomileusis
LAUP	laser assisted uvulopalatoplasty
lbs	pounds
LDL	low density lipoprotein
Lo	low
LPM	liters per minute
LPN/LVN	Licensed Practical Nurse/Licensed Vocational Nurse
LSO	lumbar-sacral orthosis
MAC	Medicare administrative contractor
mp	metacarpophalangeal
mcg	microgram
mCi	millicurie
MCM	Medicare Carriers Manual
MCP	metacarparpophalangeal joint
MCP	monthly capitation payment
mEq	milliequivalent
MESA	microsurgical epididymal sperm aspiration
mg	milligram
mgs	milligrams
MHT	megahertz
ml	milliliter
mm	millimeter
mmHg	millimeters of Mercury
MRA	magnetic resonance angiography
MRI	magnetic resonance imaging
NA	sodium
NCI	National Cancer Institute
NEC	not elsewhere classified
NG	nasogastric
NH	nursing home
NMES	neuromuscular electrical stimulation
NOC	not otherwise classified
NOS	not otherwise specified
O2	oxygen
OBRA	Omnibus Budget Reconciliation Act
OMT	osteopathic manipulation therapy
OPPS	outpatient prospective payment system
ORAL	oral administration
OSA	obstructive sleep apnea
Ost	ostomy
OTH	other routes of administration
oz	ounce
PA	physician's assistant
PAR	parenteral
PCA	patient controlled analgesia
PCH	pouch
PEN	parenteral and enteral nutrition
PENS	percutaneous electrical nerve stimulation
PET	positron emission tomography
PHP	pre-paid health plan
PHP	physician hospital plan
PI	paramedic intercept
PICC	peripherally inserted central venous catheter
PKR	photorefractive keratotomy
Pow	powder
PRK	photoreactive keratectomy
PRO	peer review organization
PSA	prostate specific antigen
PTB	patellar tendon bearing
PTK	phototherapeutic keratectomy
PVC	polyvinyl chloride
R	right
Repl	replace
RN	registered nurse
RP	retrograde pyelogram
Rx	prescription
SACH	solid ankle, cushion heel
SC	subcutaneous
SCT	specialty care transport
SEO	shoulder-elbow orthosis
SEWHO	shoulder-elbow-wrist-hand orthosis
SEXA	single energy x-ray absorptiometry
SGD	speech generating device
SGD	sinus rhythm
SM	samarium
SNCT	sensory nerve conduction test
SNF	skilled nursing facility
SO	sacroilliac othrosis
SO	shoulder orthosis
Sol	solution
SQ	square
SR	screen
ST	standard
ST	sustained release
Syr	syrup
TABS	tablets
Tc	Technetium
Tc 99m	technetium isotope
TENS	transcutaneous electrical nerve stimulator
THKAO	thoracic-hip-knee-ankle orthosis
TLSO	thoracic-lumbar-sacral-orthosis
TM	temporomandibular
TMJ	temporomandibular joint
TPN	total parenteral nutrition
U	unit
uCi	microcurie
VAR	various routes of administration
w	with
w/	with
w/o	with or without
WAK	wearable artificial kidney
wc	wheelchair
WHFO	wrist-hand-finger orthotic
Wk	week
w/o	without
Xe	xenon (isotope mass of xenon 133)

APPENDIX 4 — PUB 100 REFERENCES

The Centers for Medicare and Medicaid Services restructured its paper-based manual system as a web-based system on October 1, 2003. Called the online CMS manual system, it combines all of the various program instructions into internet-only manuals (IOMs), which are used by all CMS programs and contractors. Complete versions of all of the manuals can be found at http://www.cms.hhs.gov/manuals.

Effective September 30, 2003, the former method of publishing program memoranda (PMs) to communicate program instructions was replaced by the following four templates:

- One-time notification
- Manual revisions
- Business requirements
- Confidential requirements

The web-based system has been organized by functional area (e.g., eligibility, entitlement, claims processing, benefit policy, program integrity) in an effort to eliminate redundancy within the manuals, simplify updating, and make CMS program instructions available more quickly. The web-based system contains the functional areas included below:

Pub. 100	Introduction
Pub. 100-1	Medicare General Information, Eligibility, and Entitlement Manual
Pub. 100-2	Medicare Benefit Policy Manual
Pub. 100-3	Medicare National Coverage Determinations Manual
Pub. 100-4	Medicare Claims Processing Manual
Pub. 100-5	Medicare Secondary Payer Manual
Pub. 100-6	Medicare Financial Management Manual
Pub. 100-7	State Operations Manual
Pub. 100-8	Medicare Program Integrity Manual
Pub. 100-9	Medicare Contractor Beneficiary and Provider Communications Manual
Pub. 100-10	Quality Improvement Organization Manual
Pub. 100-11	Reserved
Pub. 100-12	State Medicaid Manual (under development)
Pub. 100-13	Medicaid State Children's Health Insurance Program (under development)
Pub. 100-14	Medicare ESRD Network Organizations Manual
Pub. 100-15	State Buy-In Manual
Pub. 100-16	Medicare Managed Care Manual
Pub. 100-17	CMS/Business Partners Systems Security Manual
Pub. 100-18	Reserved
Pub. 100-19	Demonstrations
Pub. 100-20	One-Time Notification
Pub. 100-21	Recurring Update Notification

A brief description of the Medicare manuals primarily used for *CPC Expert* follows:

The **National Coverage Determinations Manual** (NCD), is organized according to categories such as diagnostic services, supplies, and medical procedures. The table of contents lists each category and subject within that category. Revision transmittals identify any new or background material, recap the changes, and provide an effective date for the change.

When complete, the manual will contain two chapters. Chapter 1 currently includes a description of CMS's national coverage determinations. When available, chapter 2 will contain a list of HCPCS codes related to each coverage determination. The manual is organized in accordance with CPT category sequences.

The **Medicare Benefit Policy Manual** contains Medicare general coverage instructions that are not national coverage determinations. As a general rule, in the past these instructions have been found in chapter II of the **Medicare Carriers Manual**, the **Medicare Intermediary Manual**, other provider manuals, and program memoranda.

The **Medicare Claims Processing Manual** contains instructions for processing claims for contractors and providers.

The **Medicare Program Integrity Manual** communicates the priorities and standards for the Medicare integrity programs.

100-1,1,10.1

Hospital Insurance (Part A) for Inpatient Hospital, Hospice, Home Health and Skilled Nursing Facility (SNF) Services - A Brief Description

Hospital insurance is designed to help patients defray the expenses incurred by hospitalization and related care. In addition to inpatient hospital benefits, hospital insurance covers post hospital extended care in SNFs and post hospital care furnished by a home health agency in the patient's home. Blood clotting factors, for hemophilia patients competent to use such factors to control bleeding without medical or other supervision, and items related to the administration of such factors, are also a Part A benefit for beneficiaries in a covered Part A stay. The purpose of these additional benefits is to provide continued treatment after hospitalization and to encourage the appropriate use of more economical alternatives to inpatient hospital care. Program payments for services rendered to beneficiaries by providers (i.e., hospitals, SNFs, and home health agencies) are generally made to the provider. In each benefit period, payment may be made for up to 90 inpatient hospital days, and 100 days of post hospital extended care services .Hospices also provide Part A hospital insurance services such as short-term inpatient care. In order to be eligible to elect hospice care under Medicare, an individual must be entitled to Part A of Medicare and be certified as being terminally ill. An individual is considered to be terminally ill if the individual has a medical prognosis that his or her life expectancy is 6 months or less if the illness runs its normal course.

100-1,3,20.5

Blood Deductibles (Part A and Part B)

Program payment may not be made for the first 3 pints of whole blood or equivalent units of packed red cells received under Part A and Part B combined in a calendar year. However, blood processing (e.g., administration, storage) is not subject to the deductible.

The blood deductibles are in addition to any other applicable deductible and coinsurance amounts for which the patient is responsible.

The deductible applies only to the first 3 pints of blood furnished in a calendar year, even if more than one provider furnished blood.

100-1,3,20.5.2

Part B Blood Deductible

Blood is furnished on an outpatient basis or is subject to the Part B blood deductible and is counted toward the combined limit. It should be noted that payment for blood may be made to the hospital under Part B only for blood furnished in an outpatient setting. Blood is not covered for inpatient Part B services.

100-1,3,20.5.3

Items Subject to Blood Deductibles

The blood deductibles apply only to whole blood and packed red cells. The term whole blood means human blood from which none of the liquid or cellular components have been removed. Where packed red cells are furnished, a unit of packed red cells is considered equivalent to a pint of whole blood. Other components of blood such as platelets, fibrinogen, plasma, gamma globulin, and serum albumin are not subject to the blood deductible. However, these components of blood are covered as biologicals.

Refer to Pub. 100-04, Medicare Claims Processing Manual, chapter 4, Sec.231 regarding billing for blood and blood products under the Hospital Outpatient Prospective Payment System (OPPS).

100-1,5,90.2

Laboratory Defined

Laboratory means a facility for the biological, microbiological, serological, chemical, immuno-hematological, hematological, biophysical, cytological, pathological, or other examination of materials derived from the human body for the purpose of providing information for the diagnosis, prevention, or treatment of any disease or impairment of, or the assessment of the health of, human beings. These examinations also include procedures to determine, measure, or otherwise describe the presence or absence of various substances or organisms in the body. Facilities only collecting or preparing specimens (or both) or only serving as a mailing service and not performing testing are not considered laboratories.

100-2,1,10

Covered Inpatient Hospital Services Covered Under Part A

A3-3101, HO-210

Patients covered under hospital insurance are entitled to have payment made on their behalf for inpatient hospital services. (Inpatient hospital services do not include extended care services provided by hospitals pursuant to swing bed approvals. See Pub. 100-1, Chapter 8, Sec.10.1, "Hospital Providers of Extended Care Services."). However, both inpatient hospital and inpatient SNF benefits are provided under Part A - Hospital Insurance Benefits for the Aged and Disabled, of Title XVIII).

Additional information concerning the following topics can be found in the following manual chapters:

- Benefit periods is found in Chapter 3, "Duration of Covered Inpatient Services";
- Copayment days is found in Chapter 2, "Duration of Covered Inpatient Services";
- Lifetime reserve days is found in Chapter 5, "Lifetime Reserve Days";
- Related payment information is housed in the Provider Reimbursement Manual.

Blood must be furnished on a day which counts as a day of inpatient hospital services to be covered as a Part A service and to count toward the blood deductible. Thus, blood is not covered under Part A and does not count toward the Part A blood deductible when furnished to an inpatient after the inpatient has exhausted all benefit days in a benefit period, or where the individual has elected not to use lifetime reserve days. However, where the patient is discharged on their first day of entitlement or on the hospital's first day of participation, the hospital is permitted to submit a billing form with no accommodation charge, but with ancillary charges including blood.

The records for all Medicare hospital inpatient discharges are maintained in CMS for statistical analysis and use in determining future PPS DRG classifications and rates.

Non-PPS hospitals do not pay for noncovered services generally excluded from coverage in the Medicare Program. This may result in denial of a part of the billed charges or in denial of the entire admission, depending upon circumstance. In PPS hospitals, the following are also possible:

1. In appropriately admitted cases where a noncovered procedure was performed, denied services may result in payment of a different DRG (i.e., one which excludes payment for the noncovered procedure); or
2. In appropriately admitted cases that become cost outlier cases, denied services may lead to denial of some or all of an outlier payment.

The following examples illustrate this principle. If care is noncovered because a patient does not need to be hospitalized, the intermediary denies the admission and makes no Part A (i.e., PPS) payment unless paid under limitation on liability. Under limitation on liability, Medicare payment may be made when the provider and the beneficiary were not aware the services were not necessary and could not reasonably be expected to know that he services were not necessary. For detailed instructions, see the Medicare Claims Processing Manual, Chapter 30,"Limitation on Liability." If a patient is appropriately hospitalized but receives (beyond routine services) only noncovered care, the admission is denied.

NOTE: The intermediary does not deny an admission that includes covered care, even if noncovered care was also rendered. Under PPS, Medicare assumes that it is paying for only the covered care rendered whenever covered services needed to treat and/or diagnose the illness were in fact provided.

If a noncovered procedure is provided along with covered nonroutine care, a DRG change rather than an admission denial might occur. If noncovered procedures are elevating costs into the cost outlier category, outlier payment is denied in whole or in part.

When the hospital is included in PPS, most of the subsequent discussion regarding coverage of inpatient hospital services is relevant only in the context of determining the appropriateness of admissions, which DRG, if any, to pay, and the appropriateness of payment for any outlier cases.

If a patient receives items or services in excess of, or more expensive than, those for which payment can be made, payment is made only for the covered items or services or for only the appropriate prospective payment amount. This provision applies not only to inpatient services, but also to all hospital services under Parts A and B of the program. If the items or services were requested by the patient, the hospital may charge him the difference between the amount customarily charged for the services requested and the amount customarily charged for covered services.

An inpatient is a person who has been admitted to a hospital for bed occupancy for purposes of receiving inpatient hospital services. Generally, a patient is considered an inpatient if formally admitted as inpatient with the expectation that he or she will remain at least overnight and occupy a bed even though it later develops that the patient can be discharged or transferred to another hospital and not actually use a hospital bed overnight.

The physician or other practitioner responsible for a patient's care at the hospital is also responsible for deciding whether the patient should be admitted as an inpatient. Physicians should use a 24-hour period as a benchmark, i.e., they should order admission for patients who are expected to need hospital care for 24 hours or more, and treat other patients on an outpatient basis. However, the decision to admit a patient is a complex medical judgment which can be made only after the physician has considered a number of factors, including the patient's medical history and current medical needs, the types of facilities available to inpatients and to outpatients, the hospital's by-laws and admissions policies, and the relative appropriateness of treatment in each setting. Factors to be considered when making the decision to admit include such things as:

The severity of the signs and symptoms exhibited by the patient;

The medical predictability of something adverse happening to the patient;

The need for diagnostic studies that appropriately are outpatient services (i.e., their performance does not ordinarily require the patient to remain at the hospital for 24 hours or more) to assist in assessing whether the patient should be admitted; and

The availability of diagnostic procedures at the time when and at the location where the patient presents.

Admissions of particular patients are not covered or noncovered solely on the basis of the length of time the patient actually spends in the hospital. In certain specific situations coverage of services on an inpatient or outpatient basis is determined by the following rules:

Minor Surgery or Other Treatment - When patients with known diagnoses enter a hospital for a specific minor surgical procedure or other treatment that is expected to keep them in the hospital for only a few hours (less than 24), they are considered outpatients for coverage purposes regardless of: the hour they came to the hospital, whether they used a bed, and whether they remained in the hospital past midnight.

Renal Dialysis - Renal dialysis treatments are usually covered only as outpatient services but may under certain circumstances be covered as inpatient services depending on the patient's condition. Patients staying at home, who are ambulatory, whose conditions are stable and who come to the hospital for routine chronic dialysis treatments, and not for a diagnostic workup or a change in therapy, are considered outpatients. On the other hand, patients undergoing short-term dialysis until their kidneys recover from an acute illness (acute dialysis), or persons with borderline renal failure who develop acute renal failure every time they have an illness and require dialysis (episodic dialysis) are usually inpatients. A patient may begin dialysis as an inpatient and then progress to an outpatient status.

Under original Medicare, the Quality Improvement Organization (QIO), for each hospital is responsible for deciding, during review of inpatient admissions on a case-by-case basis, whether the admission was medically necessary. Medicare law authorizes the QIO to make these judgments, and the judgments are binding for purposes of Medicare coverage. In making these judgments, however, QIOs consider only the medical evidence which was available to the physician at the time an admission decision had to be made. They do not take into account other information (e.g., test results) which became available only after admission, except in cases where considering the post-admission information would support a finding that an admission was medically necessary.

Refer to Parts 4 and 7 of the QIO Manual with regard to initial determinations for these services. The QIO will review the swing bed services in these PPS hospitals as well.

NOTE: When patients requiring extended care services are admitted to beds in a hospital, they are considered inpatients of the hospital. In such cases, the services furnished in the hospital will not be considered extended care services, and payment may not be made under the program for such services unless the services are extended care services furnished pursuant to a swing bed agreement granted to the hospital by the Secretary of Health and Human Services.

100-2,1,10.1.4

Charges for Deluxe Private Room

A3-3101.1.D, HO-210.1.D

Beneficiaries found to need a private room (either because they need isolation for medical reasons or because they need immediate admission when no other accommodations are available) may be assigned to any of the provider's private rooms. They do not have the right to insist on the private room of their choice, but their preferences should be given the same consideration as if they were paying all provider charges themselves. The program does not, under any circumstances, pay for personal comfort items. Thus, the program does not pay for deluxe accommodations and/or services. These would include a suite, or a room substantially more spacious than is required for treatment, or specially equipped or decorated, or serviced for the comfort and convenience of persons willing to pay a differential for such amenities. If the beneficiary (or representative) requests such deluxe accommodations, the provider should advise that there will be a charge, not covered by Medicare, of a specified amount per day (not exceeding the differential defined in the next sentence); and may charge the beneficiary that amount for each day he/she occupies the deluxe accommodations. The maximum amount the provider may charge the beneficiary for such accommodations is the differential between the most prevalent private room rate at the time of admission and the customary charge for the room occupied. Beneficiaries may not be charged this differential if they (or their representative) do not request the deluxe accommodations.

The beneficiary may not be charged such a differential in private room rates if that differential is based on factors other than personal comfort items. Such factors might include differences between older and newer wings, proximity to lounge, elevators or nursing stations, desirable view, etc. Such rooms are standard 1-bed units and not deluxe rooms for purposes of these instructions, even though the provider may call them deluxe and have a higher customary charge for them. No additional charge may be imposed upon the beneficiary who is assigned to a room that may be somewhat more desirable because of these factors.

100-2,1,40

Supplies, Appliances, and Equipment

Supplies, appliances, and equipment, which are ordinarily furnished by the hospital for the care and treatment of the beneficiary solely during the inpatient hospital stay, are covered inpatient hospital services.

Under certain circumstances, supplies, appliances, and equipment used during the beneficiary's inpatient stay are covered under Part A even though the supplies, appliances and equipment leave the hospital with the patient upon discharge. These are circumstances in which it would be unreasonable or impossible from a medical standpoint to limit the patient's use of the item to the periods during which the individual is an inpatient. Examples of items covered under this rule are:

- Items permanently installed in or attached to the patient's body while an inpatient, such as cardiac valves, cardiac pacemakers, and artificial limbs; and
- Items which are temporarily installed in or attached to the patient's body while an inpatient, and which are also necessary to permit or facilitate the patient's release from the hospital, such as tracheotomy or drainage tubes.

Hospital "admission packs" containing primarily toilet articles, such as soap, toothbrushes, toothpaste, and combs, are covered under Part A if routinely furnished by the hospital to all its inpatients. If not routinely furnished to all patients, the packs are not covered. In that situation, the hospital may charge beneficiaries for the pack, but only if they request it with knowledge of what they are requesting and what the charge to them will be.

Supplies, appliances, and equipment furnished to an inpatient for use only outside the hospital are not, in general, covered as inpatient hospital services. However, a temporary or disposable item, which is medically necessary to permit or facilitate the patient's departure from the hospital and is required until the patient can obtain a continuing supply, is covered as an inpatient hospital service.

Oxygen furnished to hospital inpatients is covered under Part A as an inpatient supply.

100-2,10,20

Coverage Guidelines for Ambulance Service Claims

B3-2125

Payment may be made for expenses incurred by a patient for ambulance service provided conditions l, 2, and 3 in the left-hand column have been met. The right-hand column indicates the documentation needed to establish that the condition has been met.

Conditions	Review Action
1. Patient was transported by an approved supplier of ambulance services.	1. Ambulance supplier is listed in the table of approved ambulance companies (§10.1.3)
2. The patient was suffering from an illness or injury, which contraindicated transportation by other means. (§10.2)	2. (a) The contractor presumes the requirement was met if the submitted documentation indicates that the patient: • Was transported in an emergency situation, e.g., as a result of an accident, injury or acute illness, or • Needed to be restrained to prevent injury to the beneficiary or others; or • Was unconscious or in shock; or • Required oxygen or other emergency treatment during transport to the nearest appropriate facility; or • Exhibits signs and symptoms of acute respiratory distress or cardiac distress such as shortness of breath or chest pain; or • Exhibits signs and symptoms that indicate the possibility of acute stroke; or • Had to remain immobile because of a fracture that had not been set or the possibility of a fracture; or • Was experiencing severe hemorrhage; or • Could be moved only by stretcher; or • Was bed-confined before and after the ambulance trip. (b) In the absence of any of the conditions listed in (a)above additional documentation should be obtained to establish medical need where the evidence indicates the existence of the circumstances listed below: (i) Patient's condition would not ordinarily require movement by stretcher, or (ii) The individual was not admitted as a hospital inpatient (except in accident cases), or (iii) The ambulance was used solely because other means of transportation were unavailable, or (iv) The individual merely needed assistance in getting from his room or home to a vehicle. (c) Where the information indicates a situation not listed in 2(a) or 2(b) above, refer the case to your supervisor.
3. The patient was transported from and to points listed below.	3. Claims should show the ZIP code of the point of pickup
(a) From patient's residence (or other place where need arose) to hospital or skilled nursing facility.	(a) i. Condition met if trip began within the institution's service area as shown in the carrier's locality guide ii. Condition met where the trip began outside the institution's service area if the institution was the nearest one with appropriate facilities.

NOTE: A patient's residence is the place where he or she makes his/her home and dwells permanently, or for an extended period of time. A skilled nursing facility is one, which is listed in the Directory of Medical Facilities as a participating SNF or as an institution which meets §1861(j)(1) of the Act.

NOTE: A claim for ambulance service to a participating hospital or skilled nursing facility should not be denied on the grounds that there is a nearer nonparticipating institution having appropriate facilities.

Conditions	Review Action
(b) Skilled nursing facility to a hospital or hospital to a skilled nursing facility.	(b) (i) Condition met if the ZIP code of the pickup point is within the service area of the destination as shown in the carrier's locality guide. (ii) Condition met where the ZIP code of the pickup point is outside the service area of the destination if the destination institution was the nearest appropriate facility.
(c) Hospital to hospital or skilled nursing facility to skilled nursing facility.	(c) Condition met if the discharging institution was not an appropriate facility and the admitting institution was the nearest appropriate facility.
(d) From a hospital or skilled nursing facility to patient's residence.	(d) (i) Condition met if patient's residence is within the institution's service area as shown in the carrier's locality guide. (ii) Condition met where the patient's residence is outside the institution's service area if the institution was the nearest appropriate facility.
(e) Round trip for hospital or participating skilled nursing facility inpatients to the nearest hospital or nonhospital treatment facility.	(e) Condition met if the reasonable and necessary diagnostic or therapeutic service required by patient's condition is not available at the institution where the beneficiary is an inpatient.

NOTE: Ambulance service to a physician's office or a physician-directed clinic is not covered. See §10.3.7 above, where a stop is made at a physician's office en route to a hospital and §10.3.3 for additional exceptions.)

4. Ambulance services involving hospital admissions in Canada or Mexico are covered (Medicare Claims Processing Manual, Chapter 1, "General Billing Requirements, " §§10.1.3.) if the following conditions are met:	(a) The foreign hospitalization has been determined to be covered; and (b) The ambulance service meets the coverage requirements set forth in §§10-10.3. If the foreign hospitalization has been determined to be covered on the basis of emergency services (See the Medicare Claims Processing Manual, Chapter 1, "General Billing Requirements," §10.1.3), the necessity requirement (§10.2) and the destination requirement (§10.3) are considered met.
5. The carrier will make partial payment for otherwise covered ambulance service, which exceeded limits defined in item	(a) From the pickup point to the nearest appropriate facility, or (b) From the nearest appropriate facility to the beneficiary's residence where he or she is being returned home from a distant institution.
6. The carrier will base the payment on the amount payable had the patient been transported:	

100-2,13,30

Rural Health Clinic and Federally Qualified Health Center Service Defined

Payments for covered RHC/FQHC services furnished to Medicare beneficiaries are made on the basis of an all-inclusive rate per covered visit (except for pneumococcal and influenza vaccines and their administration, which is paid at 100 percent of reasonable cost). The term "visit" is defined as a face-to-face encounter between the patient and a physician, physician assistant, nurse practitioner, certified nurse midwife, visiting nurse, clinical psychologist, or clinical social worker during which an RHC/FQHC service is rendered. As a result of section 5114 of the Deficit Reduction Act of 2005 (DRA), the FQHC definition of a face-to-face encounter is expanded to include encounters with qualified practitioners of Outpatient Diabetes Self-Management Training Services (DSMT) and medical nutrition therapy (MNT) services when the FQHC meets all relevant program requirements for the provision of such services.

Encounters with (1) more than one health professional; and (2) multiple encounters with the same health professional which take place on the same day and at a single location, constitute a single visit. An exception occurs in cases in which the patient, subsequent to the first encounter, suffers an illness or injury requiring additional diagnosis or treatment.

100-2,15,100

Surgical Dressings, Splints, Casts, and Other Devices Used for Reductions of Fractures and Dislocations

B3-2079, A3-3110.3, HO-228.3

Surgical dressings are limited to primary and secondary dressings required for the treatment of a wound caused by, or treated by, a surgical procedure that has been performed by a physician or other health care professional to the extent permissible under State law. In addition, surgical dressings required after debridement of a wound are also covered, irrespective of the type of debridement, as long as the debridement was reasonable and necessary and was performed by a health care professional acting within the scope of his/her legal authority when performing this function. Surgical dressings are covered for as long as they are medically necessary. Primary dressings are therapeutic or protective coverings applied directly to wounds or lesions either on the skin or caused by an opening to the skin. Secondary dressing materials that serve a therapeutic or protective function and that are needed to secure a primary dressing are also covered. Items such as adhesive tape, roll gauze, bandages, and disposable compression material are examples of secondary dressings. Elastic stockings, support hose, foot coverings, leotards, knee supports, surgical leggings, gauntlets, and pressure garments for the arms and hands are examples of items that are not ordinarily covered as surgical dressings. Some items, such as transparent film, may be used as a primary or secondary dressing. If a physician, certified nurse midwife, physician assistant, nurse practitioner, or clinical nurse specialist applies surgical dressings as part of a professional service that is billed to Medicare, the surgical dressings are considered incident to the professional services of the health care practitioner. (See Sec. 60.1, 180, 190, 200, and 210.) When surgical dressings are not covered incident to the services of a health care practitioner and are obtained by the patient from a supplier (e.g., a drugstore, physician, or other health care practitioner that qualifies as a supplier) on an order from a physician or other health care professional authorized under State law or regulation to make such an order, the surgical dressings are covered separately under Part B. Splints and casts, and other devices used for reductions of fractures and dislocations are covered under Part B of Medicare. This includes dental splints.

100-2,15,110

Durable Medical Equipment - General

B3-2100, A3-3113, HO-235, HHA-220

Expenses incurred by a beneficiary for the rental or purchases of durable medical equipment (DME) are reimbursable if the following three requirements are met:

- The equipment meets the definition of DME (Sec.110.1);
- The equipment is necessary and reasonable for the treatment of the patient's illness or injury or to improve the functioning of his or her malformed body member (Sec.110.1); and
- The equipment is used in the patient's home. The decision whether to rent or purchase an item of equipment generally resides with the beneficiary, but the decision on how to pay rests with CMS. For some DME, program payment policy calls for lump sum payments and in others for periodic payment. Where covered DME is furnished to a beneficiary by a supplier of services other than a provider of services, the DMERC makes the reimbursement. If a provider of services furnishes the equipment, the intermediary makes the reimbursement. The payment method is identified in the annual fee schedule update furnished by CMS. The CMS issues quarterly updates to a fee schedule file that contains rates by HCPCS code and also identifies the classification of the HCPCS code within the following categories. Category Code Definition IN Inexpensive and Other Routinely Purchased Items FS Frequently Serviced Items CR Capped Rental Items OX Oxygen and Oxygen Equipment OS Ostomy, Tracheostomy & Urological Items SD Surgical Dressings PO Prosthetics & Orthotics SU Supplies TE Transcutaneous Electrical Nerve Stimulators The DMERCs, carriers, and intermediaries, where appropriate, use the CMS files to determine payment rules. See the Medicare Claims Processing Manual, Chapter 20, "Durable Medical Equipment, Surgical Dressings and Casts, Orthotics and Artificial Limbs, and Prosthetic Devices," for a detailed description of payment rules for each classification. Payment may also be made for repairs, maintenance, and delivery of equipment and for expendable and nonreusable items essential to the effective use of the equipment subject to the conditions in Sec.110.2. See the Medicare Benefit Policy Manual, Chapter 11, "End Stage Renal Disease," for hemodialysis equipment and supplies.

100-2,15,110.1

Definition of Durable Medical Equipment

B3-2100.1, A3-3113.1, HO-235.1, HHA-220.1, B3-2100.2, A3-3113.2, HO-235.2, HHA-220.2

- Durable medical equipment is equipment which:
- Can withstand repeated use;
- Is primarily and customarily used to serve a medical purpose;
- Generally is not useful to a person in the absence of an illness or injury; and

- Is appropriate for use in the home.

All requirements of the definition must be met before an item can be considered to be durable medical equipment. The following describes the underlying policies for determining whether an item meets the definition of DME and may be covered.

A. Durability

An item is considered durable if it can withstand repeated use, i.e., the type of item that could normally be rented. Medical supplies of an expendable nature, such as incontinent pads, lambs wool pads, catheters, ace bandages, elastic stockings, surgical facemasks, irrigating kits, sheets, and bags are not considered "durable" within the meaning of the definition. There are other items that, although durable in nature, may fall into other coverage categories such as supplies, braces, prosthetic devices, artificial arms, legs, and eyes.

B. Medical Equipment

Medical equipment is equipment primarily and customarily used for medical purposes and is not generally useful in the absence of illness or injury. In most instances, no development will be needed to determine whether a specific item of equipment is medical in nature. However, some cases will require development to determine whether the item constitutes medical equipment. This development would include the advice of local medical organizations (hospitals, medical schools, medical societies) and specialists in the field of physical medicine and rehabilitation. If the equipment is new on the market, it may be necessary, prior to seeking professional advice, to obtain information from the supplier or manufacturer explaining the design, purpose, effectiveness and method of using the equipment in the home as well as the results of any tests or clinical studies that have been conducted.

1. Equipment Presumptively
   Medicalltems such as hospital beds, wheelchairs, hemodialysis equipment, iron lungs, respirators, intermittent positive pressure breathing machines, medical regulators, oxygen tents, crutches, canes, trapeze bars, walkers, inhalators, nebulizers, commodes, suction machines, and traction equipment presumptively constitute medical equipment. (Although hemodialysis equipment is covered as a prosthetic device (Sec.120), it also meets the definition of DME, and reimbursement for the rental or purchase of such equipment for use in the beneficiary's home will be made only under the provisions for payment applicable to DME. See the Medicare Benefit Policy Manual, Chapter 11, "End Stage Renal Disease," Sec.30.1, for coverage of home use of hemodialysis.) NOTE: There is a wide variety in types of respirators and suction machines. The DMERC's medical staff should determine whether the apparatus specified in the claim is appropriate for home use.

2. Equipment Presumptively Nonmedical
   Equipment which is primarily and customarily used for a nonmedical purpose may not be considered "medical" equipment for which payment can be made under the medical insurance program. This is true even though the item has some remote medically related use. For example, in the case of a cardiac patient, an air conditioner might possibly be used to lower room temperature to reduce fluid loss in the patient and to restore an environment conducive to maintenance of the proper fluid balance. Nevertheless, because the primary and customary use of an air conditioner is a nonmedical one, the air conditioner cannot be deemed to be medical equipment for which payment can be made. Other devices and equipment used for environmental control or to enhance the environmental setting in which the beneficiary is placed are not considered covered DME. These include, for example, room heaters, humidifiers, dehumidifiers, and electric air cleaners. Equipment which basically serves comfort or convenience functions or is primarily for the convenience of a person caring for the patient, such as elevators, stairway elevators, and posture chairs, do not constitute medical equipment. Similarly, physical fitness equipment (such as an exercycle), first-aid or precautionary-type equipment (such as preset portable oxygen units), self-help devices (such as safety grab bars), and training equipment (such as Braille training texts) are considered nonmedical in nature.

3. Special Exception Items
   Specified items of equipment may be covered under certain conditions even though they do not meet the definition of DME because they are not primarily and customarily used to serve a medical purpose and/or are generally useful in the absence of illness or injury. These items would be covered when it is clearly established that they serve a therapeutic purpose in an individual case and would include:

a. Gel pads and pressure and water mattresses (which generally serve a preventive purpose) when prescribed for a patient who had bed sores or there is medical evidence indicating that they are highly susceptible to such ulceration; and

b. Heat lamps for a medical rather than a soothing or cosmetic purpose, e.g., where the need for heat therapy has been established.

In establishing medical necessity for the above items, the evidence must show that the item is included in the physician's course of treatment and a physician is supervising its use.

NOTE: The above items represent special exceptions and no extension of coverage to other items should be inferred

C. Necessary and Reasonable

Although an item may be classified as DME, it may not be covered in every instance. Coverage in a particular case is subject to the requirement that the equipment be necessary and reasonable for treatment of an illness or injury, or to improve the functioning of a malformed body member. These considerations will bar payment for equipment which cannot reasonably be expected to perform a therapeutic function in an individual case or will permit only partial therapeutic function in an individual case or will permit only partial payment when the type of equipment furnished substantially exceeds that required for the treatment of the illness or injury involved. See the Medicare Claims Processing Manual, Chapter 1, "General Billing Requirements;" Sec.60, regarding the rules for providing advance beneficiary notices (ABNs) that advise beneficiaries, before items or services actually are furnished, when Medicare is likely to deny payment for them. ABNs allow beneficiaries to make an informed consumer decision about receiving items or services for which they may have to pay out-of-pocket and to be more active participants in their own health care treatment decisions.

1. Necessity for the Equipment
   Equipment is necessary when it can be expected to make a meaningful contribution to the treatment of the patient's illness or injury or to the improvement of his or her malformed body member. In most cases the physician's prescription for the equipment and other medical information available to the DMERC will be sufficient to establish that the equipment serves this purpose.

2. Reasonableness of the Equipment
   Even though an item of DME may serve a useful medical purpose, the DMERC or intermediary must also consider to what extent, if any, it would be reasonable for the Medicare program to pay for the item prescribed. The following considerations should enter into the determination of reasonableness:

1. Would the expense of the item to the program be clearly disproportionate to the therapeutic benefits which could ordinarily be derived from use of the equipment?

2. Is the item substantially more costly than a medically appropriate and realistically feasible alternative pattern of care?

3. Does the item serve essentially the same purpose as equipment already available to the beneficiary?

3. Payment Consistent With What is Necessary and Reasonable
   Where a claim is filed for equipment containing features of an aesthetic nature or features of a medical nature which are not required by the patient's condition or where there exists a reasonably feasible and medically appropriate alternative pattern of care which is less costly than the equipment furnished, the amount payable is based on the rate for the equipment or alternative treatment which meets the patient's medical needs. The acceptance of an assignment binds the supplier-assignee to accept the payment for the medically required equipment or service as the full charge and the supplier-assignee cannot charge the beneficiary the differential attributable to the equipment actually furnished.

4. Establishing the Period of Medical Necessity
   Generally, the period of time an item of durable medical equipment will be considered to be medically necessary is based on the physician's estimate of the time that his or her patient will need the equipment. See the Medicare Program Integrity Manual, Chapters 5 and 6, for medical review guideline

D. Definition of a Beneficiary's Home

For purposes of rental and purchase of DME a beneficiary's home may be his/her own dwelling, an apartment, a relative's home, a home for the aged, or some other type of institution. However, an institution may not be considered a beneficiary's home if it:

- Meets at least the basic requirement in the definition of a hospital, i.e., it is primarily engaged in providing by or under the supervision of physicians, to inpatients, diagnostic and therapeutic services for medical diagnosis, treatment, and care of injured, disabled, and sick persons, or rehabilitation services for the rehabilitation of injured, disabled, or sick persons; or
- Meets at least the basic requirement in the definition of a skilled nursing facility, i.e., it is primarily engaged in providing to inpatients skilled nursing care and related services for patients who require medical or nursing care, or rehabilitation services for the rehabilitation of injured, disabled, or sick persons.

Thus, if an individual is a patient in an institution or distinct part of an institution which provides the services described in the bullets above, the individual is not entitled to have separate Part B payment made for rental or purchase of DME. This is because such an institution may not be considered the individual's home. The same concept applies even if the patient resides in a bed or portion of the institution not certified for Medicare.

If the patient is at home for part of a month and, for part of the same month is in an institution that cannot qualify as his or her home, or is outside the U.S., monthly payments may be made for the entire month. Similarly, if DME is returned to the provider before the end of a payment month because the beneficiary died in that month or because the equipment became unnecessary in that month, payment may be made for the entire month.

100-2,15,110.2

Repairs, Maintenance, Replacement, and Delivery

Under the circumstances specified below, payment may be made for repair, maintenance, and replacement of medically required DME, including equipment which had been in use before the user enrolled in Part B of the program. However, do not pay for repair, maintenance, or replacement of equipment in the frequent and substantial servicing or oxygen equipment payment categories. In addition, payments for repair and maintenance may not include payment for parts and labor covered under a manufacturer's or supplier's warranty.

A. Repairs

To repair means to fix or mend and to put the equipment back in good condition after damage or wear. Repairs to equipment which a beneficiary owns are covered when necessary to make the equipment serviceable. However, do not pay for repair of previously denied equipment or equipment in the frequent and substantial servicing or oxygen equipment payment categories. If the expense for repairs exceeds the estimated expense of purchasing or renting another item of equipment for the remaining period of medical need, no payment can be made for the amount of the excess. (See subsection C where claims for repairs suggest malicious damage or culpable neglect.) Since renters of equipment recover from the rental charge the expenses they incur in maintaining in working order the equipment they rent out, separately itemized charges for repair of rented equipment are not covered. This includes items in the frequent and substantial servicing, oxygen equipment, capped rental, and inexpensive or routinely purchased payment categories which are being rented. A new Certificate of Medical Necessity (CMN) and/or physician's order is not needed for repairs. For replacement items, see Subsection C below.

B. Maintenance

Routine periodic servicing, such as testing, cleaning, regulating, and checking of the beneficiary's equipment, is not covered. The owner is expected to perform such routine maintenance rather than a retailer or some other person who charges the beneficiary. Normally, purchasers of DME are given operating manuals which describe the type of servicing an owner may perform to properly maintain the equipment. It is reasonable to expect that beneficiaries will perform this maintenance. Thus, hiring a third party to do such work is for the convenience of the beneficiary and is not covered. However, more extensive maintenance which, based on the manufacturers' recommendations, is to be performed by authorized technicians, is covered as repairs for medically necessary equipment which a beneficiary owns. This might include, for example, breaking down sealed components and performing tests which require specialized testing equipment not available to the beneficiary. Do not pay for maintenance of purchased items that require frequent and substantial servicing or oxygen equipment. Since renters of equipment recover from the rental charge the expenses they incur in maintaining in working order the equipment they rent out, separately itemized charges for maintenance of rented equipment are generally not covered. Payment may not be made for maintenance of rented equipment other than the maintenance and servicing fee established for capped rental items. For capped rental items which have reached the 15-month rental cap, contractors pay claims for maintenance and servicing fees after 6 months have passed from the end of the final paid rental month or from the end of the period the item is no longer covered under the supplier's or manufacturer's warranty, whichever is later. See the Medicare Claims Processing Manual, Chapter 20, "Durable Medical Equipment, Prosthetics and Orthotics, and Supplies (DMEPOS)," for additional instruction and an example. A new CMN and/or physician's order is not needed for covered maintenance.

C. Replacement

Replacement refers to the provision of an identical or nearly identical item. Situations involving the provision of a different item because of a change in medical condition are not addressed in this section.

Equipment which the beneficiary owns or is a capped rental item may be replaced in cases of loss or irreparable damage. Irreparable damage refers to a specific accident or to a natural disaster (e.g., fire, flood). A physician's order and/or new Certificate of Medical Necessity (CMN), when required, is needed to reaffirm the medical necessity of the item.

Irreparable wear refers to deterioration sustained from day-to-day usage over time and a specific event cannot be identified. Replacement of equipment due to irreparable wear takes into consideration the reasonable useful lifetime of the equipment. If the item of equipment has been in continuous use by the patient on either a rental or purchase basis for the equipment's useful lifetime, the beneficiary may elect to obtain a new piece of equipment. Replacement may be reimbursed when a new physician order and/or new CMN, when required, is needed to reaffirm the medical necessity of the item.

The reasonable useful lifetime of durable medical equipment is determined through program instructions. In the absence of program instructions, carriers may determine the reasonable useful lifetime of equipment, but in no case can it be less than 5 years. Computation of the useful lifetime is based on when the equipment is delivered to the beneficiary, not the age of the equipment. Replacement due to wear is not covered during the reasonable useful lifetime of the equipment. During the reasonable useful lifetime, Medicare does cover repair up to the cost of replacement (but not actual replacement) for medically necessary equipment owned by the beneficiary. (See subsection A.)

Charges for the replacement of oxygen equipment, items that require frequent and substantial servicing or inexpensive or routinely purchased items which are being rented are not covered. Cases suggesting malicious damage, culpable neglect, or wrongful disposition of equipment should be investigated and denied where the DMERC determines that it is unreasonable to make program payment under the circumstances. DMERCs refer such cases to the program integrity specialist in the RO.

D. Delivery

Payment for delivery of DME whether rented or purchased is generally included in the fee schedule allowance for the item. See Pub. 100-04, Medicare Claims Processing Manual, Chapter 20, "Durable Medical Equipment, Prosthetics and Orthotics, and Supplies (DMEPOS)," for the rules that apply to making reimbursement for exceptional cases.

100-2,15,110.3

Coverage of Supplies and Accessories

B3-2100.5, A3-3113.4, HO-235.4, HHA-220.5 B3-2100.5, A3-3113.4, HO-235.4, HHA-220.5

Payment may be made for supplies, e.g., oxygen, that are necessary for the effective use of durable medical equipment. Such supplies include those drugs and biologicals which must be put directly into the equipment in order to achieve the therapeutic benefit of the durable medical equipment or to assure the proper functioning of the equipment, e.g., tumor chemotherapy agents used with an infusion pump or heparin used with a home dialysis system. However, the coverage of such drugs or biologicals does not preclude the need for a determination that the drug or biological itself is reasonable and necessary for treatment of the illness or injury or to improve the functioning of a malformed body member. In the case of prescription drugs, other than oxygen, used in conjunction with durable medical equipment, prosthetic, orthotics, and supplies (DMEPOS) or prosthetic devices, the entity that dispenses the drug must furnish it directly to the patient for whom a prescription is written. The entity that dispenses the drugs must have a Medicare supplier number, must possess a current license to dispense prescription drugs in the State in which the drug is dispensed, and must bill and receive payment in its own name. A supplier that is not the entity that dispenses the drugs cannot purchase the drugs used in conjunction with DME for resale to the beneficiary. Reimbursement may be made for replacement of essential accessories such as hoses, tubes, mouthpieces, etc., for necessary DME, only if the beneficiary owns or is purchasing the equipment.Payment may be made for supplies, e.g., oxygen, that are necessary for the effective use of durable medical equipment. Such supplies include those drugs and biologicals which must be put directly into the equipment in order to achieve the therapeutic benefit of the durable medical equipment or to assure the proper functioning of the equipment, e.g., tumor chemotherapy agents used with an infusion pump or heparin used with a home dialysis system. However, the coverage of such drugs or biologicals does not preclude the need for a determination that the drug or biological itself is reasonable and necessary for treatment of the illness or injury or to improve the functioning of a malformed body member. In the case of prescription drugs, other than oxygen, used in conjunction with durable medical equipment, prosthetic, orthotics, and supplies (DMEPOS) or prosthetic devices, the entity that dispenses the drug must furnish it directly to the patient for whom a prescription is written. The entity that dispenses the drugs must have a Medicare supplier number, must possess a current license to dispense prescription drugs in the State in which the drug is dispensed, and must bill and receive payment in its own name. A supplier that is not the entity that dispenses the drugs cannot purchase the drugs used in conjunction with DME for resale to the beneficiary. Reimbursement may be made for replacement of essential accessories such as hoses, tubes, mouthpieces, etc., for necessary DME, only if the beneficiary owns or is purchasing the equipment.

100-2,15,120

Prosthetic Devices

B3-2130, A3-3110.4, HO-228.4, A3-3111, HO-229

A. General

Prosthetic devices (other than dental) which replace all or part of an internal body organ (including contiguous tissue), or replace all or part of the function of a permanently inoperative or malfunctioning internal body organ are covered when furnished on a physician's order. This does not require a determination that there is no possibility that the patient's condition may improve sometime in the future. If the medical record, including the judgment of the attending physician, indicates the condition is of long and indefinite duration, the test of permanence is considered met. (Such a device may also be covered under Sec.60.l as a supply when furnished incident to a physician's service.)

Examples of prosthetic devices include artificial limbs, parenteral and enteral (PEN) nutrition, cardiac pacemakers, prosthetic lenses (see subsection B), breast prostheses (including a surgical brassiere) for postmastectomy patients, maxillofacial devices, and devices which replace all or part of the ear or nose. A urinary collection and retention system with or without a tube is a prosthetic device replacing bladder function in case of permanent urinary incontinence. The foley catheter is also considered a prosthetic device when ordered for a patient with permanent urinary incontinence. However, chucks, diapers, rubber sheets, etc., are supplies that are not covered under this provision. Although hemodialysis equipment is a prosthetic device, payment for the rental or purchase of such equipment in the home is made only for use under the provisions for payment applicable to durable medical equipment.

An exception is that if payment cannot be made on an inpatient's behalf under Part A, hemodialysis equipment, supplies, and services required by such patient could be covered under Part B as a prosthetic device, which replaces the function of a kidney. See the Medicare Benefit Policy Manual, Chapter 11, "End Stage Renal Disease," for payment for hemodialysis equipment used in the home. See the Medicare Benefit Policy Manual, Chapter 1, "Inpatient Hospital Services," Sec.10, for additional instructions on hospitalization for renal dialysis.

NOTE: Medicare does not cover a prosthetic device dispensed to a patient prior to the time at which the patient undergoes the procedure that makes necessary the use of the device. For example, the carrier does not make a separate Part B payment for an intraocular lens (IOL) or pacemaker that a physician, during an office visit prior to the actual surgery, dispenses to the patient for his or her use. Dispensing a prosthetic device in this manner raises health and safety issues. Moreover, the need for the device cannot be clearly established until the procedure that makes its use possible is successfully performed. Therefore, dispensing a prosthetic device in this manner is not considered reasonable and necessary for the treatment of the patient's condition.

Colostomy (and other ostomy) bags and necessary accouterments required for attachment are covered as prosthetic devices. This coverage also includes irrigation and flushing equipment and other items and supplies directly related to ostomy care, whether the attachment of a bag is required.

Accessories and/or supplies which are used directly with an enteral or parenteral device to achieve the therapeutic benefit of the prosthesis or to assure the proper functioning of the device may also be covered under the prosthetic device benefit subject to the additional guidelines in the Medicare National Coverage Determinations Manual.

Covered items include catheters, filters, extension tubing, infusion bottles, pumps (either food or infusion), intravenous (I.V.) pole, needles, syringes, dressings, tape, Heparin Sodium (parenteral only), volumetric monitors (parenteral only), and parenteral and enteral nutrient solutions. Baby food and other regular grocery products that can be blenderized and used with the enteral system are not covered. Note that some of these items, e.g., a food pump and an I.V. pole, qualify as DME. Although coverage of the enteral and parenteral nutritional therapy systems is provided on the basis of the prosthetic device benefit, the payment rules relating to lump sum or monthly payment for DME apply to such items.

The coverage of prosthetic devices includes replacement of and repairs to such devices as explained in subsection D.

Finally, the Benefits Improvement and Protection Act of 2000 amended Sec.1834(h)(1) of the Act by adding a provision (1834 (h)(1)(G)(i)) that requires Medicare payment to be made for the replacement of prosthetic devices which are artificial limbs, or for the replacement of any part of such devices, without regard to continuous use or useful lifetime restrictions if an ordering physician determines that the replacement device, or replacement part of such a device, is necessary.

Payment may be made for the replacement of a prosthetic device that is an artificial limb, or replacement part of a device if the ordering physician determines that the replacement device or part is necessary because of any of the following:

1. A change in the physiological condition of the patient;
2. An irreparable change in the condition of the device, or in a part of the device; or
3. The condition of the device, or the part of the device, requires repairs and the cost of such repairs would be more than 60 percent of the cost of a replacement device, or, as the case may be, of the part being replaced.

This provision is effective for items replaced on or after April 1, 2001. It supersedes any rule that that provided a 5-year or other replacement rule with regard to prosthetic devices.

B. Prosthetic Lenses

The term "internal body organ" includes the lens of an eye. Prostheses replacing the lens of an eye include post-surgical lenses customarily used during convalescence from eye surgery in which the lens of the eye was removed. In addition, permanent lenses are also covered when required by an individual lacking the organic lens of the eye because of surgical removal or congenital absence. Prosthetic lenses obtained on or after the beneficiary's date of entitlement to supplementary medical insurance benefits may be covered even though the surgical removal of the crystalline lens occurred before entitlement.

1. Prosthetic Cataract Lenses
   One of the following prosthetic lenses or combinations of prosthetic lenses furnished by a physician (see Sec.30.4 for coverage of prosthetic lenses prescribed by a doctor of optometry) may be covered when determined to be reasonable and necessary to restore essentially the vision provided by the crystalline lens of the eye:

- Prosthetic bifocal lenses in frames;
- Prosthetic lenses in frames for far vision, and prosthetic lenses in frames for near vision; or
- When a prosthetic contact lens(es) for far vision is prescribed (including cases of binocular and monocular aphakia), make payment for the contact lens(es) and prosthetic lenses in frames for near vision to be worn at the same time as the contact lens(es), and prosthetic lenses in frames to be worn when the contacts have been removed.

Lenses which have ultraviolet absorbing or reflecting properties may be covered, in lieu of payment for regular (untinted) lenses, if it has been determined that such lenses are medically reasonable and necessary for the individual patient. Medicare does not cover cataract sunglasses obtained in addition to the regular (untinted) prosthetic lenses since the sunglasses duplicate the restoration of vision function performed by the regular prosthetic lenses.

2. Payment for Intraocular Lenses (IOLs) Furnished in Ambulatory Surgical Centers (ASCs)
   Effective for services furnished on or after March 12, 1990, payment for intraocular lenses (IOLs) inserted during or subsequent to cataract surgery in a Medicare certified ASC is included with the payment for facility services that are furnished in connection with the covered surgery. Refer to the Medicare Claims Processing Manual, Chapter 14, "Ambulatory Surgical Centers," for more information.
3. Limitation on Coverage of Conventional Lenses One pair of conventional eyeglasses or conventional contact lenses furnished after each cataract surgery with insertion of an IOL is covered.

C. Dentures

Dentures are excluded from coverage. However, when a denture or a portion of the denture is an integral part (built-in) of a covered prosthesis (e.g., an obturator to fill an opening in the palate), it is covered as part of that prosthesis.

D. Supplies, Repairs, Adjustments, and Replacement

Supplies are covered that are necessary for the effective use of a prosthetic device (e.g., the batteries needed to operate an artificial larynx). Adjustment of prosthetic devices required by wear or by a change in the patient's condition is covered when ordered by a physician. General provisions relating to the repair and replacement of durable medical equipment in Sec.110.2 for the repair and replacement of prosthetic devices are applicable. (See the Medicare Benefit Policy Manual, Chapter 16, "General Exclusions from Coverage," Sec.40.4, for payment for devices replaced under a warranty.) Replacement of conventional eyeglasses or contact lenses furnished in accordance with Sec.120.B.3 is not covered. Necessary supplies, adjustments, repairs, and replacements are covered even when the device had been in use before the user enrolled in Part B of the program, so long as the device continues to be medically required.

100-2,15,130

Leg, Arm, Back, and Neck Braces, Trusses, and Artificial Legs, Arms, and Eyes

B3-2133, A3-3110.5, HO-228.5, AB-01-06 dated 1/18/01

These appliances are covered under Part B when furnished incident to physicians' services or on a physician's order. A brace includes rigid and semi-rigid devices which are used for the purpose of supporting a weak or deformed body member or restricting or eliminating motion in a diseased or injured part of the body. Elastic stockings, garter belts, and similar devices do not come within the scope of the definition of a brace. Back braces include, but are not limited to, special corsets, e.g., sacroiliac, sacrolumbar, dorsolumbar corsets, and belts. A terminal device (e.g., hand or hook) is covered under this provision whether an artificial limb is required by the patient. Stump stockings and harnesses (including replacements) are also covered when these appliances are essential to the effective use of the artificial limb.

Adjustments to an artificial limb or other appliance required by wear or by a change in the patient's condition are covered when ordered by a physician.

Adjustments, repairs and replacements are covered even when the item had been in use before the user enrolled in Part B of the program so long as the device continues to be medically required.

100-2,15,140

Therapeutic Shoes for Individuals with Diabetes

B3-2134

Coverage of therapeutic shoes (depth or custom-molded) along with inserts for individuals with diabetes is available as of May 1, 1993. These diabetic shoes are covered if the requirements as specified in this section concerning certification and prescription are fulfilled. In addition, this benefit provides for a pair of diabetic shoes even if only one foot suffers from diabetic foot disease. Each shoe is equally equipped so that the affected limb, as well as the remaining limb, is protected. Claims for therapeutic shoes for diabetics are processed by the Durable Medical Equipment Regional Carriers (DMERCs). Therapeutic shoes for diabetics are not DME and are not considered DME nor orthotics, but a separate category of coverage under Medicare Part B. (See Sec.1861(s)(12) and Sec.1833(o) of the Act.)

A. Definitions

The following items may be covered under the diabetic shoe benefit:

1. Custom-Molded ShoesCustom-molded shoes are shoes that:

- Are constructed over a positive model of the patient's foot;
- Are made from leather or other suitable material of equal quality;
- Have removable inserts that can be altered or replaced as the patient's condition warrants; and
- Have some form of shoe closure.

2. Depth Shoes

   Depth shoes are shoes that:

- Have a full length, heel-to-toe filler that, when removed, provides a minimum of 3/16 inch of additional depth used to accommodate custom-molded or customized inserts;
- Are made from leather or other suitable material of equal quality;
- Have some form of shoe closure; and
- Are available in full and half sizes with a minimum of three widths so that the sole is graded to the size and width of the upper portions of the shoes according to the American standard last sizing schedule or its equivalent. (The American standard last sizing schedule is the numerical shoe sizing system used for shoes sold in the United States.)

3. Inserts

   Inserts are total contact, multiple density, removable inlays that are directly molded to the patient's foot or a model of the patient's foot and that are made of a suitable material with regard to the patient's condition.

B. Coverage

1. Limitations

   For each individual, coverage of the footwear and inserts is limited to one of the following within one calendar year:

- No more than one pair of custom-molded shoes (including inserts provided with such shoes) and two additional pairs of inserts; or
- No more than one pair of depth shoes and three pairs of inserts (not including the noncustomized removable inserts provided with such shoes).

2. Coverage of Diabetic Shoes and Brace

   Orthopedic shoes, as stated in the Medicare Claims Processing Manual, Chapter 20, "Durable Medical Equipment, Surgical Dressings and Casts, Orthotics and Artificial Limbs, and Prosthetic Devices," generally are not covered. This exclusion does not apply to orthopedic shoes that are an integral part of a leg brace. In situations in which an individual qualifies for both diabetic shoes and a leg brace, these items are covered separately. Thus, the diabetic shoes may be covered if the requirements for this section are met, while the brace may be covered if the requirements of Sec.130 are met.

3. Substitution of Modifications for Inserts

   An individual may substitute modification(s) of custom-molded or depth shoes instead of obtaining a pair(s) of inserts in any combination. Payment for the modification(s) may not exceed the limit set for the inserts for which the individual is entitled. The following is a list of the most common shoe modifications available, but it is not meant as an exhaustive list of the modifications available for diabetic shoes:

Rigid Rocker Bottoms - These are exterior elevations with apex positions for 51 percent to 75 percent distance measured from the back end of the heel. The apex is a narrowed or pointed end of an anatomical structure. The apex must be positioned behind the metatarsal heads and tapered off sharply to the front tip of the sole. Apex height helps to eliminate pressure at the metatarsal heads. Rigidity is ensured by the steel in the shoe. The heel of the shoe tapers off in the back in order to cause the heel to strike in the middle of the heel;

- Roller Bottoms (Sole or Bar) - These are the same as rocker bottoms, but the heel is tapered from the apex to the front tip of the sole;
- Metatarsal Bars- An exterior bar is placed behind the metatarsal heads in order to remove pressure from the metatarsal heads. The bars are of various shapes, heights, and construction depending on the exact purpose;
- Wedges (Posting) - Wedges are either of hind foot, fore foot, or both and may be in the middle or to the side. The function is to shift or transfer weight bearing upon standing or during ambulation to the opposite side for added support, stabilization, equalized weight distribution, or balance; and
- Offset Heels- This is a heel flanged at its base either in the middle, to the side, or a combination, that is then extended upward to the shoe in order to stabilize extreme positions of the hind foot. Other modifications to diabetic shoes include, but are not limited to flared heels, Velcro closures, and inserts for missing toes.

4. Separate Inserts Inserts may be covered and dispensed independently of diabetic shoes if the supplier of the shoes verifies in writing that the patient has appropriate footwear into which the insert can be placed. This footwear must meet the definitions found above for depth shoes and custom-molded shoes.

C. Certification

The need for diabetic shoes must be certified by a physician who is a doctor of medicine or a doctor of osteopathy and who is responsible for diagnosing and treating the patient's diabetic systemic condition through a comprehensive plan of care. This managing physician must:

- Document in the patient's medical record that the patient has diabetes;
- Certify that the patient is being treated under a comprehensive plan of care for diabetes, and that the patient needs diabetic shoes; and
- Document in the patient's record that the patient has one or more of the following conditions:
- Peripheral neuropathy with evidence of callus formation;
  - History of pre-ulcerative calluses;
  - History of previous ulceration;
  - Foot deformity;
  - Previous amputation of the foot or part of the foot; or
  - Poor circulation.

D. Prescription

Following certification by the physician managing the patient's systemic diabetic condition, a podiatrist or other qualified physician who is knowledgeable in the fitting of diabetic shoes and inserts may prescribe the particular type of footwear necessary.

E. Furnishing

Footwear The footwear must be fitted and furnished by a podiatrist or other qualified individual such as a pedorthist, an orthotist, or a prosthetist. The certifying physician may not furnish the diabetic shoes unless the certifying physician is the only qualified individual in the area. It is left to the discretion of each carrier to determine the meaning of "in the area."

100-2,15,150

Dental Services

B3-2136

As indicated under the general exclusions from coverage, items and services in connection with the care, treatment, filling, removal, or replacement of teeth or structures directly supporting the teeth are not covered. "Structures directly supporting the teeth" means the periodontium, which includes the gingivae, dentogingival junction, periodontal membrane, cementum of the teeth, and alveolar process.

In addition to the following, see Pub 100-01, the Medicare General Information, Eligibility, and Entitlement Manual, Chapter 5, Definitions and Pub 3, the Medicare National Coverage Determinations Manual for specific services which may be covered when furnished by a dentist. If an otherwise noncovered procedure or service is performed by a dentist as incident to and as an integral part of a covered procedure or service performed by the dentist, the total service performed by the dentist on such an occasion is covered.

EXAMPLE 1: The reconstruction of a ridge performed primarily to prepare the mouth for dentures is a noncovered procedure. However, when the reconstruction of a ridge is performed as a result of and at the same time as the surgical removal of a tumor (for other than dental purposes), the totality of surgical procedures is a covered service.

EXAMPLE 2: Medicare makes payment for the wiring of teeth when this is done in connection with the reduction of a jaw fracture.

The extraction of teeth to prepare the jaw for radiation treatment of neoplastic disease is also covered. This is an exception to the requirement that to be covered, a noncovered procedure or service performed by a dentist must be an incident to and an integral part of a covered procedure or service performed by the dentist. Ordinarily, the dentist extracts the patient's teeth, but another physician, e.g., a radiologist, administers the radiation treatments.

When an excluded service is the primary procedure involved, it is not covered, regardless of its complexity or difficulty. For example, the extraction of an impacted tooth is not covered. Similarly, an alveoplasty (the surgical improvement of the shape and condition of the alveolar process) and a frenectomy are excluded from coverage when either of these procedures is performed in connection with an excluded service, e.g., the preparation of the mouth for dentures. In a like manner, the removal of a torus palatinus (a bony protuberance of the hard palate) may be a covered service. However, with rare exception, this surgery is performed in connection with an excluded service, i.e., the preparation of the mouth for dentures. Under such circumstances, Medicare does not pay for this procedure.

Dental splints used to treat a dental condition are excluded from coverage under 1862(a)(12) of the Act. On the other hand, if the treatment is determined to be a covered medical condition (i.e., dislocated upper/lower jaw joints), then the splint can be covered.

Whether such services as the administration of anesthesia, diagnostic x-rays, and other related procedures are covered depends upon whether the primary procedure being performed by the dentist is itself covered. Thus, an x-ray taken in connection with the reduction of a fracture of the jaw or facial bone is covered. However, a single x-ray or x-ray survey taken in connection with the care or treatment of teeth or the periodontium is not covered.

Medicare makes payment for a covered dental procedure no matter where the service is performed. The hospitalization or nonhospitalization of a patient has no direct bearing on the coverage or exclusion of a given dental procedure.

Payment may also be made for services and supplies furnished incident to covered dental services. For example, the services of a dental technician or nurse who is under the direct supervision of the dentist or physician are covered if the services are included in the dentist's or physician's bill.

100-2,15,230

Practice of Physical Therapy, Occupational Therapy, and Speech-Language Pathology

A. Group Therapy Services.

Contractors pay for outpatient physical therapy services (which includes outpatient speech-language pathology services) and outpatient occupational therapy services provided simultaneously to two or more individuals by a practitioner as group therapy services (97150). The individuals can be, but need not be performing the same activity. The physician or therapist involved in group therapy services must be in constant attendance, but one-on-one patient contact is not required.

B. Therapy Students

1. General
   Only the services of the therapist can be billed and paid under Medicare Part B. The services performed by a student are not reimbursed even if provided under "line of sight" supervision of the therapist; however, the presence of the student "in the room" does not make the service unbillable. Pay for the direct (one-to-one) patient contact services of the physician or therapist provided to Medicare Part B patients. Group therapy services performed by a therapist or physician may be billed when a student is also present "in the room".

EXAMPLES:

Therapists may bill and be paid for the provision of services in the following scenarios:

- The qualified practitioner is present and in the room for the entire session. The student participates in the delivery of services when the qualified practitioner is directing the service, making the skilled judgment, and is responsible for the assessment and treatment.
- The qualified practitioner is present in the room guiding the student in service delivery when the therapy student and the therapy assistant student are participating in the provision of services, and the practitioner is not engaged in treating another patient or doing other tasks at the same time
- The qualified practitioner is responsible for the services and as such, signs all documentation. (A student may, of course, also sign but it is not necessary since the Part B payment is for the clinician's service, not for the student's services).

2. Therapy Assistants as Clinical Instructors
   Physical therapist assistants and occupational therapy assistants are not precluded from serving as clinical instructors for therapy students, while providing services within their scope of work and performed under the direction and supervision of a licensed physical or occupational therapist to a Medicare beneficiary.
3. Services Provided Under Part A and Part B
   The payment methodologies for Part A and B therapy services rendered by a student are different. Under the MPFS (Medicare Part B), Medicare pays for services provided by physicians and practitioners that are specifically authorized by statute. Students do not meet the definition of practitioners under Medicare Part B. Under SNF PPS, payments are based upon the case mix or Resource Utilization Group (RUG) category that describes the patient. In the rehabilitation groups, the number of therapy minutes delivered to the patient determines the RUG category. Payment levels for each category are based upon the costs of caring for patients in each group rather than providing pecific payment for each therapy service as is done in Medicare Part B.

100-2,15,280.1

Glaucoma Screening

A. Conditions of Coverage

The regulations implementing the Benefits Improvements and Protection Act of 2000, Sec.102, provide for annual coverage for glaucoma screening for beneficiaries in the following high risk categories:

- Individuals with diabetes mellitus;
- Individuals with a family history of glaucoma; or
- African-Americans age 50 and over. In addition, beginning with dates of service on or after January 1, 2006, 42 CFR 410.23(a)(2), revised, the definition of an eligible beneficiary in a high-risk category is expanded to include:
- Hispanic-Americans age 65 and over.

Medicare will pay for glaucoma screening examinations where they are furnished by or under the direct supervision in the office setting of an ophthalmologist or optometrist, who is legally authorized to perform the services under State law. Screening for glaucoma is defined to include:

- A dilated eye examination with an intraocular pressure measurement; and
- A direct ophthalmoscopy examination, or a slit-lamp biomicroscopic examination.

Payment may be made for a glaucoma screening examination that is performed on an eligible beneficiary after at least 11 months have passed following the month in which the last covered glaucoma screening examination was performed.

The following HCPCS codes apply for glaucoma screening:

G0117 Glaucoma screening for high-risk patients furnished by an optometrist or ophthalmologist; and

G0118 Glaucoma screening for high-risk patients furnished under the direct supervision of an optometrist or ophthalmologist.

The type of service for the above G codes is: TOS Q.

For providers who bill intermediaries, applicable types of bill for screening glaucoma services are 13X, 22X, 23X, 71X, 73X, 75X, and 85X. The following revenue codes should be reported when billing for screening glaucoma services:

- Comprehensive outpatient rehabilitation facilities (CORFs), critical access hospitals (CAHs), skilled nursing facilities (SNFs), independent and provider-based RHCs and free standing and provider-based FQHCs bill for this service under revenue code 770. CAHs electing the optional method of payment for outpatient services report this service under revenue codes 96X, 97X, or 98X.
- Hospital outpatient departments bill for this service under any valid/appropriate revenue code. They are not required to report revenue code 770.

B. Calculating the Frequency

Once a beneficiary has received a covered glaucoma screening procedure, the beneficiary may receive another procedure after 11 full months have passed. To determine the 11-month period, start the count beginning with the month after the month in which the previous covered screening procedure was performed.

C. Diagnosis Coding Requirements

Providers bill glaucoma screening using screening ("V") code V80.1 (Special Screening for Neurological, Eye, and Ear Diseases, Glaucoma). Claims submitted without a screening diagnosis code may be returned to the provider as unprocessable.

D. Payment Methodology

1. Carriers
   Contractors pay for glaucoma screening based on the Medicare physician fee schedule. Deductible and coinsurance apply. Claims from physicians or other providers where assignment was not taken are subject to the Medicare limiting charge (refer to the Medicare Claims Processing Manual, Chapter 12, "Physician/Non-physician Practitioners," for more information about the Medicare limiting charge).

2. Intermediaries
   Payment is made for the facility expense as follows:

- Independent and provider-based RHC/free standing and provider-based FQHC - payment is made under the all inclusive rate for the screening glaucoma service based on the visit furnished to the RHC/FQHC patient;
- CAH - payment is made on a reasonable cost basis unless the CAH has elected the optional method of payment for outpatient services in which case, procedures outlined in the Medicare Claims Processing Manual, Chapter 3, Sec.30.1.1, should be followed;
- CORF - payment is made under the Medicare physician fee schedule;
- Hospital outpatient department - payment is made under outpatient prospective payment system (OPPS);
- Hospital inpatient Part B - payment is made under OPPS;
- SNF outpatient - payment is made under the Medicare physician fee schedule (MPFS); and
- SNF inpatient Part B - payment is made under MPFS. Deductible and coinsurance apply.

E. Special Billing Instructions for RHCs and FQHCs

Screening glaucoma services are considered RHC/FQHC services. RHCs and FQHCs bill the contractor under bill type 71X or 73X along with revenue code 770 and HCPCS codes G0117 or G0118 and RHC/FQHC revenue code 520 or 521 to report the related visit. Reporting of revenue code 770 and HCPCS codes G0117 and G0118 in addition to revenue code 520 or 521 is required for this service in order for CWF to perform frequency editing.

Payment should not be made for a screening glaucoma service unless the claim also contains a visit code for the service. Therefore, the contractor installs an edit in its system to assure payment is not made for revenue code 770 unless the claim also contains a visit revenue code (520 or 521).

100-2,15,290

Foot Care

A. Treatment of Subluxation of Foot

Subluxations of the foot are defined as partial dislocations or displacements of joint surfaces, tendons ligaments, or muscles of the foot. Surgical or nonsurgical treatments undertaken for the sole purpose of correcting a subluxated structure in the foot as an isolated entity are not covered.

However, medical or surgical treatment of subluxation of the ankle joint (talo-crural joint) is covered. In addition, reasonable and necessary medical or surgical services, diagnosis, or treatment for medical conditions that have resulted from or are associated with partial displacement of structures is covered. For example, if a patient has osteoarthritis that has resulted in a partial displacement of joints in the foot, and the primary treatment is for the osteoarthritis, coverage is provided.

B. Exclusions from Coverage

The following foot care services are generally excluded from coverage under both Part A and Part B. (See Sec.290.F and Sec.290.G for instructions on applying foot care exclusions.)

1. Treatment of Flat Foot
   The term "flat foot" is defined as a condition in which one or more arches of the foot have flattened out. Services or devices directed toward the care or correction of such conditions, including the prescription of supportive devices, are not covered.

2. Routine Foot Care
   Except as provided above, routine foot care is excluded from coverage. Services that normally are considered routine and not covered by Medicare include the following:

- The cutting or removal of corns and calluses;
- The trimming, cutting, clipping, or debriding of nails; and
- Other hygienic and preventive maintenance care, such as cleaning and soaking the feet, the use of skin creams to maintain skin tone of either ambulatory or bedfast patients, and any other service performed in the absence of localized illness, injury, or symptoms involving the foot.

3. Supportive Devices for Feet
   Orthopedic shoes and other supportive devices for the feet generally are not covered. However, this exclusion does not apply to such a shoe if it is an integral part of a leg brace, and its expense is included as part of the cost of the brace. Also, this exclusion does not apply to therapeutic shoes furnished to diabetics.

C. Exceptions to Routine Foot Care Exclusion

1. Necessary and Integral Part of Otherwise Covered Services
   In certain circumstances, services ordinarily considered to be routine may be covered if they are performed as a necessary and integral part of otherwise covered services, such as diagnosis and treatment of ulcers, wounds, or infections.

2. Treatment of Warts on Foot
   The treatment of warts (including plantar warts) on the foot is covered to the same extent as services provided for the treatment of warts located elsewhere on the body.

3. Presence of Systemic Condition
   The presence of a systemic condition such as metabolic, neurologic, or peripheral vascular disease may require scrupulous foot care by a professional that in the absence of such condition(s) would be considered routine (and, therefore, excluded from coverage). Accordingly, foot care that would otherwise be considered routine may be covered when systemic condition(s) result in severe circulatory embarrassment or areas of diminished sensation in the individual's legs or feet. (See subsection A.)

   In these instances, certain foot care procedures that otherwise are considered routine (e.g., cutting or removing corns and calluses, or trimming, cutting, clipping, or debriding nails) may pose a hazard when performed by a nonprofessional person on patients with such systemic conditions. (See Sec.290.G for procedural instructions.)

4. Mycotic Nails
   In the absence of a systemic condition, treatment of mycotic nails may be covered. The treatment of mycotic nails for an ambulatory patient is covered only when the physician attending the patient's mycotic condition documents that (1) there is clinical evidence of mycosis of the toenail, and (2) the patient has marked limitation of ambulation, pain, or secondary infection resulting from the thickening and dystrophy of the infected toenail plate.

   The treatment of mycotic nails for a nonambulatory patient is covered only when the physician attending the patient's mycotic condition documents that (1) there is clinical evidence of mycosis of the toenail, and (2) the patient suffers from pain or secondary infection resulting from the thickening and dystrophy of the infected toenail plate.

   For the purpose of these requirements, documentation means any written information that is required by the carrier in order for services to be covered. Thus, the information submitted with claims must be substantiated by information found in the patient's medical record. Any information, including that contained in a form letter, used for documentation purposes is subject to carrier verification in order to ensure that the information adequately justifies coverage of the treatment of mycotic nails.

D. Systemic Conditions That Might Justify Coverage

Although not intended as a comprehensive list, the following metabolic, neurologic, and peripheral vascular diseases (with synonyms in parentheses) most commonly represent the underlying conditions that might justify coverage for routine foot care.

- Diabetes mellitus *
- Arteriosclerosis obliterans (A.S.O., arteriosclerosis of the extremities, occlusive peripheral arteriosclerosis)
- Buerger's disease (thromboangiitis obliterans)
- Chronic thrombophlebitis *
- Peripheral neuropathies involving the feet -
- Associated with malnutrition and vitamin deficiency *
  - Malnutrition (general, pellagra)
  - Alcoholism
  - Malabsorption (celiac disease, tropical sprue)
  - Pernicious anemia
- Associated with carcinoma *
- Associated with diabetes mellitus *
- Associated with drugs and toxins *
- Associated with multiple sclerosis *
- Associated with uremia (chronic renal disease) *
- Associated with traumatic injury
- Associated with leprosy or neurosyphilis

- Associated with hereditary disorders
- Hereditary sensory radicular neuropathy
- Angiokeratoma corporis diffusum (Fabry's)
- Amyloid neuropathy

When the patient's condition is one of those designated by an asterisk (*), routine procedures are covered only if the patient is under the active care of a doctor of medicine or osteopathy who documents the condition.

E. Supportive Devices for Feet

Orthopedic shoes and other supportive devices for the feet generally are not covered. However, this exclusion does not apply to such a shoe if it is an integral part of a leg brace, and its expense is included as part of the cost of the brace. Also, this exclusion does not apply to therapeutic shoes furnished to diabetics.

F. Presumption of Coverage

In evaluating whether the routine services can be reimbursed, a presumption of coverage may be made where the evidence available discloses certain physical and/or clinical findings consistent with the diagnosis and indicative of severe peripheral involvement. For purposes of applying this presumption the following findings are pertinent:

Class A Findings

Nontraumatic amputation of foot or integral skeletal portion thereof.

Class B Findings

Absent posterior tibial pulse;

Advanced trophic changes as: hair growth (decrease or absence) nail changes (thickening) pigmentary changes (discoloration) skin texture (thin, shiny) skin color (rubor or redness) (Three required); and

Absent dorsalis pedis pulse.

Class C Findings

Claudication;

Temperature changes (e.g., cold feet);

Edema;

Paresthesias (abnormal spontaneous sensations in the feet); and

Burning.

The presumption of coverage may be applied when the physician rendering the routine foot care has identified:

1. A Class A finding;
2. Two of the Class B findings; or
3. One Class B and two Class C findings.

Cases evidencing findings falling short of these alternatives may involve podiatric treatment that may constitute covered care and should be reviewed by the intermediary's medical staff and developed as necessary.

For purposes of applying the coverage presumption where the routine services have been rendered by a podiatrist, the contractor may deem the active care requirement met if the claim or other evidence available discloses that the patient has seen an M.D. or D.O. for treatment and/or evaluation of the complicating disease process during the 6-month period prior to the rendition of the routine-type services. The intermediary may also accept the podiatrist's statement that the diagnosing and treating M.D. or D.O. also concurs with the podiatrist's findings as to the severity of the peripheral involvement indicated.

Services ordinarily considered routine might also be covered if they are performed as a necessary and integral part of otherwise covered services, such as diagnosis and treatment of diabetic ulcers, wounds, and infections.

G. Application of Foot Care Exclusions to Physician's Services

The exclusion of foot care is determined by the nature of the service. Thus, payment for an excluded service should be denied whether performed by a podiatrist, osteopath, or a doctor of medicine, and without regard to the difficulty or complexity of the procedure.

When an itemized bill shows both covered services and noncovered services not integrally related to the covered service, the portion of charges attributable to the noncovered services should be denied. (For example, if an itemized bill shows surgery for an ingrown toenail and also removal of calluses not necessary for the performance of toe surgery, any additional charge attributable to removal of the calluses should be denied.)

In reviewing claims involving foot care, the carrier should be alert to the following exceptional situations:

1. Payment may be made for incidental noncovered services performed as a necessary and integral part of, and secondary to, a covered procedure. For example, if trimming of toenails is required for application of a cast to a fractured foot, the carrier need not allocate and deny a portion of the charge for the trimming of the nails. However, a separately itemized charge for such excluded service should be disallowed. When the primary procedure is covered the administration of anesthesia necessary for the performance of such procedure is also covered.
2. Payment may be made for initial diagnostic services performed in connection with a specific symptom or complaint if it seems likely that its treatment would be covered even though the resulting diagnosis may be one requiring only noncovered care.

The name of the M.D. or D.O. who diagnosed the complicating condition must be submitted with the claim. In those cases, where active care is required, the approximate date the beneficiary was last seen by such physician must also be indicated.

NOTE: Section 939 of P.L. 96-499 removed "warts" from the routine foot care exclusion effective July 1, 1981.

Relatively few claims for routine-type care are anticipated considering the severity of conditions contemplated as the basis for this exception. Claims for this type of foot care should not be paid in the absence of convincing evidence that nonprofessional performance of the service would have been hazardous for the beneficiary because of an underlying systemic disease. The mere statement of a diagnosis such as those mentioned in Sec.D above does not of itself indicate the severity of the condition. Where development is indicated to verify diagnosis and/or severity the carrier should follow existing claims processing practices which may include review of carrier's history and medical consultation as well as physician contacts.

The rules in Sec.290.F concerning presumption of coverage also apply.

Codes and policies for routine foot care and supportive devices for the feet are not exclusively for the use of podiatrists. These codes must be used to report foot care services regardless of the specialty of the physician who furnishes the services. Carriers must instruct physicians to use the most appropriate code available when billing for routine foot care.

100-2,15,290

Foot Care

Subluxations of the foot are defined as partial dislocations or displacements of joint surfaces, tendons ligaments, or muscles of the foot. Surgical or nonsurgical treatments undertaken for the sole purpose of correcting a subluxated structure in the foot as an isolated entity are not covered.

However, medical or surgical treatment of subluxation of the ankle joint (talo-crural joint) is covered. In addition, reasonable and necessary medical or surgical services, diagnosis, or treatment for medical conditions that have resulted from or are associated with partial displacement of structures is covered. For example, if a patient has osteoarthritis that has resulted in a partial displacement of joints in the foot, and the primary treatment is for the osteoarthritis, coverage is provided.

B. Exclusions from Coverage

The following foot care services are generally excluded from coverage under both Part A and Part B. (See Sec.290.F and Sec.290.G for instructions on applying foot care exclusions.)

1. Treatment of Flat Foot The term "flat foot" is defined as a condition in which one or more arches of the foot have flattened out. Services or devices directed toward the care or correction of such conditions, including the prescription of supportive devices, are not covered.
2. Routine Foot Care Except as provided above, routine foot care is excluded from coverage. Services that normally are considered routine and not covered by Medicare include the following: The cutting or removal of corns and calluses; The trimming, cutting, clipping, or debriding of nails; and Other hygienic and preventive maintenance care, such as cleaning and soaking the feet, the use of skin creams to maintain skin tone of either ambulatory or bedfast patients, and any other service performed in the absence of localized illness, injury, or symptoms involving the foot.
3. Supportive Devices for Feet Orthopedic shoes and other supportive devices for the feet generally are not covered.

However, this exclusion does not apply to such a shoe if it is an integral part of a leg brace, and its expense is included as part of the cost of the brace. Also, this exclusion does not apply to therapeutic shoes furnished to diabetics.

C. Exceptions to Routine Foot Care Exclusion

1. Necessary and Integral Part of Otherwise Covered Services In certain circumstances, services ordinarily considered to be routine may be covered if they are performed as a

necessary and integral part of otherwise covered services, such as diagnosis and treatment of ulcers, wounds, or infections.

2. Treatment of Warts on Foot The treatment of warts (including plantar warts) on the foot is covered to the same extent as services provided for the treatment of warts located elsewhere on the body.

3. Presence of Systemic Condition The presence of a systemic condition such as metabolic, neurologic, or peripheral vascular disease may require scrupulous foot care by a professional that in the absence of such condition(s) would be considered routine (and, therefore, excluded from coverage).

Accordingly, foot care that would otherwise be considered routine may be covered when systemic condition(s) result in severe circulatory embarrassment or areas of diminished sensation in the individual's legs or feet. (See subsection A.) In these instances, certain foot care procedures that otherwise are considered routine (e.g., cutting or removing corns and calluses, or trimming, cutting, clipping, or debriding nails) may pose a hazard when performed by a nonprofessional person on patients with such systemic conditions. (See Sec.290.G for procedural instructions.) 4. Mycotic Nails In the absence of a systemic condition, treatment of mycotic nails may be covered.

The treatment of mycotic nails for an ambulatory patient is covered only when the physician attending the patient's mycotic condition documents that (1) there is clinical evidence of mycosis of the toenail, and (2) the patient has marked limitation of ambulation, pain, or secondary infection resulting from the thickening and dystrophy of the infected toenail plate.

The treatment of mycotic nails for a nonambulatory patient is covered only when the physician attending the patient's mycotic condition documents that (1) there is clinical evidence of mycosis of the toenail, and (2) the patient suffers from pain or secondary infection resulting from the thickening and dystrophy of the infected toenail plate.

For the purpose of these requirements, documentation means any written information that is required by the carrier in order for services to be covered. Thus, the information submitted with claims must be substantiated by information found in the patient's medical record. Any information, including that contained in a form letter, used for documentation purposes is subject to carrier verification in order to ensure that the information adequately justifies coverage of the treatment of mycotic nails.

D. Systemic Conditions That Might Justify Coverage

Although not intended as a comprehensive list, the following metabolic, neurologic, and peripheral vascular diseases (with synonyms in parentheses) most commonly represent the underlying conditions that might justify coverage for routine foot care.

Diabetes mellitus * Arteriosclerosis obliterans (A.S.O., arteriosclerosis of the extremities, occlusive peripheral arteriosclerosis) Buerger's disease (thromboangiitis obliterans) Chronic thrombophlebitis * Peripheral neuropathies involving the feet - Associated with malnutrition and vitamin deficiency * Malnutrition (general, pellagra) Alcoholism Malabsorption (celiac disease, tropical sprue) Pernicious anemia Associated with carcinoma * Associated with diabetes mellitus * Associated with drugs and toxins * Associated with multiple sclerosis * Associated with uremia (chronic renal disease) * Associated with traumatic injury Associated with leprosy or neurosyphilis Associated with hereditary disorders Hereditary sensory radicular neuropathy Angiokeratoma corporis diffusum (Fabry's) Amyloid neuropathy When the patient's condition is one of those designated by an asterisk (*), routine procedures are covered only if the patient is under the active care of a doctor of medicine or osteopathy who documents the condition.

E. Supportive Devices for Feet

Orthopedic shoes and other supportive devices for the feet generally are not covered.However, this exclusion does not apply to such a shoe if it is an integral part of a leg brace, and its expense is included as part of the cost of the brace. Also, this exclusion does not apply to therapeutic shoes furnished to diabetics.

F. Presumption of Coverage

In evaluating whether the routine services can be reimbursed, a presumption of coverage may be made where the evidence available discloses certain physical and/or clinical findings consistent with the diagnosis and indicative of severe peripheral involvement. For purposes of applying this presumption the following findings are pertinent:

Class A Findings

Nontraumatic amputation of foot or integral skeletal portion thereof.

Class B Findings

Absent posterior tibial pulse; Advanced trophic changes as: hair growth (decrease or absence) nail changes (thickening) pigmentary changes (discoloration) skin texture (thin, shiny) skin color (rubor or redness) (Three required);

and Absent dorsalis pedis pulse.

Class C Findings

Claudication;

Temperature changes (e.g., cold feet);

Edema;

Paresthesias (abnormal spontaneous sensations in the feet); and

Burning.

The presumption of coverage may be applied when the physician rendering the routine foot care has identified:

1. A Class A finding;
2. Two of the Class B findings; or
3. One Class B and two Class C findings.

Cases evidencing findings falling short of these alternatives may involve podiatric treatment that may constitute covered care and should be reviewed by the intermediary's medical staff and developed as necessary.

For purposes of applying the coverage presumption where the routine services have been rendered by a podiatrist, the contractor may deem the active care requirement met if the claim or other evidence available discloses that the patient has seen an M.D. or D.O. for treatment and/or evaluation of the complicating disease process during the 6-month period prior to the rendition of the routine-type services. The intermediary may also accept the podiatrist's statement that the diagnosing and treating M.D. or D.O. also concurs with the podiatrist's findings as to the severity of the peripheral involvement indicated.

Services ordinarily considered routine might also be covered if they are performed as a necessary and integral part of otherwise covered services, such as diagnosis and treatment of diabetic ulcers, wounds, and infections.

G. Application of Foot Care Exclusions to Physician's Services

The exclusion of foot care is determined by the nature of the service. Thus, payment for an excluded service should be denied whether performed by a podiatrist, osteopath, or a doctor of medicine, and without regard to the difficulty or complexity of the procedure.

When an itemized bill shows both covered services and noncovered services not integrally related to the covered service, the portion of charges attributable to the noncovered services should be denied. (For example, if an itemized bill shows surgery for an ingrown toenail and also removal of calluses not necessary for the performance of toe surgery, any additional charge attributable to removal of the calluses should be denied.) In reviewing claims involving foot care, the carrier should be alert to the following exceptional situations:

1. Payment may be made for incidental noncovered services performed as a necessary and integral part of, and secondary to, a covered procedure. For example, if trimming of toenails is required for application of a cast to a fractured foot, the carrier need not allocate and deny a portion of the charge for the trimming of the nails. However, a separately itemized charge for such excluded service should be disallowed. When the primary procedure is covered the administration of anesthesia necessary for the performance of such procedure is also covered.
2. Payment may be made for initial diagnostic services performed in connection with a specific symptom or complaint if it seems likely that its treatment would be covered even though the resulting diagnosis may be one requiring only noncovered care.

The name of the M.D. or D.O. who diagnosed the complicating condition must be submitted with the claim. In those cases, where active care is required, the approximate date the beneficiary was last seen by such physician must also be indicated.

NOTE: Section 939 of P.L. 96-499 removed "warts" from the routine foot care exclusion effective July 1, 1981.

Relatively few claims for routine-type care are anticipated considering the severity of conditions contemplated as the basis for this exception. Claims for this type of foot care should not be paid in the absence of convincing evidence that nonprofessional performance of the service would have been hazardous for the beneficiary because of an underlying systemic disease. The mere statement of a diagnosis such as those mentioned in Sec.D above does not of itself indicate the severity of the condition. Where development is indicated to verify diagnosis and/or severity the carrier should follow existing claims processing practices, which may include review of carrier's history and medical consultation as well as physician contacts.

The rules in Sec.290.F concerning presumption of coverage also apply.

Codes and policies for routine foot care and supportive devices for the feet are not exclusively for the use of podiatrists. These codes must be used to report foot care services regardless of the specialty of the physician who furnishes the services. Carriers must instruct physicians to use the most appropriate code available when billing for routine foot care.

100-2,15,300

Diabetes Self-Management Training Services

Section 4105 of the Balanced Budget Act of 1997 permits Medicare coverage of diabetes self-management training (DSMT) services when these services are furnished by a certified provider who meets certain quality standards. This program is intended to educate beneficiaries in the successful self-management of diabetes. The program includes instructions in self-monitoring of blood glucose; education about diet and exercise; an insulin treatment plan developed specifically for the patient who is insulin-dependent; and motivation for patients to use the skills for self-management.

Diabetes self-management training services may be covered by Medicare only if the treating physician or treating qualified non-physician practitioner who is managing the beneficiary's diabetic condition certifies that such services are needed. The referring physician or qualified non-physician practitioner must maintain the plan of care in the beneficiary's medical record and documentation substantiating the need for training on an individual basis when group training is typically covered, if so ordered. The order must also include a statement signed by the physician that the service is needed as well as the following:

- The number of initial or follow-up hours ordered (the physician can order less than 10 hours of training);
- The topics to be covered in training (initial training hours can be used for the full initial training program or specific areas such as nutrition or insulin training); and
- A determination that the beneficiary should receive individual or group training.

The provider of the service must maintain documentation in a file that includes the original order from the physician and any special conditions noted by the physician.

When the training under the order is changed, the training order/referral must be signed by the physician or qualified non-physician practitioner treating the beneficiary and maintained in the beneficiary's file in the DSMT's program records.

NOTE: All entities billing for DSMT under the fee-for-service payment system or other payment systems must meet all national coverage requirements.

100-2,15,300.2

Certified Providers

A designated certified provider bills for DSMT provided by an accredited DSMT program. Certified providers must submit a copy of their accreditation certificate to the contractor. The statute states that a "certified provider" is a physician or other individual or entity designated by the Secretary that, in addition to providing outpatient self-management training services, provides other items and services for which payment may be made under title XVIII, and meets certain quality standards. The CMS is designating all providers and suppliers that bill Medicare for other individual services such as hospital outpatient departments, renal dialysis facilities, physicians and durable medical equipment suppliers as certified. All suppliers/providers who may bill for other Medicare services or items and who represent a DSMT program that is accredited as meeting quality standards can bill and receive payment for the entire DSMT program. Registered dietitians are eligible to bill on behalf of an entire DSMT program on or after January 1, 2002, as long as the provider has obtained a Medicare provider number. A dietitian may not be the sole provider of the DSMT service.

The CMS will not reimburse services on a fee-for-service basis rendered to a beneficiary under Part A.

NOTE: While separate payment is not made for this service to Rural Health Clinics (RHCs), the service is covered but is considered included in the all-inclusive encounter rate. Effective January 1, 2006, payment for DSMT provided in a Federally Qualified Health Clinic (FQHC) that meets all of the requirements identified in Pub. 100-04, chapter 18, section 120 may be made in addition to one other visit the beneficiary had during the same day.

All DSMT programs must be accredited as meeting quality standards by a CMS approved national accreditation organization. Currently, CMS recognizes the American Diabetes Association and the Indian Health Service as approved national accreditation organizations. Programs without accreditation by a CMS-approved national accreditation organization are not covered. Certified providers may be asked to submit updated accreditation documents at any time or to submit outcome data to an organization designated by CMS.

Enrollment of DMEPOS Suppliers The DMEPOS suppliers are reimbursed for diabetes training through local carriers. In order to file claims for DSMT, a DMEPOS supplier must be enrolled in the Medicare program with the National Supplier Clearinghouse (NSC). The supplier must also meet the quality standards of a CMS-approved national accreditation organization as stated above. DMEPOS suppliers must obtain a provider number from the local carrier in order to bill for DSMT.

The carrier requires a completed Form CMS-855, along with an accreditation certificate as part of the provider application process. After it has been determined that the quality standards are met, a billing number is assigned to the supplier. Once a supplier has received a provider identification (PIN) number, the supplier can begin receiving reimbursement for this service.

Carriers should contact the National Supplier Clearinghouse (NSC) according to the instruction in Pub 100-08, the Medicare Program Integrity Manual, Chapter 10, "Healthcare Provider/Supplier Enrollment," to verify an applicant is currently enrolled and eligible to receive direct payment from the Medicare program.

The applicant is assigned specialty 87.

Any DMEPOS supplier that has its billing privileges deactivated or revoked by the NSC will also have the billing number deactivated by the carrier.

100-2,15,300.3

Frequency of Training

A - Initial Training

The initial year for DSMT is the 12 month period following the initial date.

Medicare will cover initial training that meets the following conditions:

- Is furnished to a beneficiary who has not previously received initial or follow-up training under HCPCS codes G0108 or G0109;
- Is furnished within a continuous 12-month period;
- Does not exceed a total of 10 hours* (the 10 hours of training can be done in any combination of 1/2 hour increments);
- With the exception of 1 hour of individual training, training is usually furnished in a group setting, which can contain other patients besides Medicare beneficiaries, and;
- One hour of individual training may be used for any part of the training including insulin training.

* When a claim contains a DSMT HCPCS code and the associated units cause the total time for the DSMT initial year to exceed '10' hours, a CWF error will set.

B - Follow-Up Training

Medicare covers follow-up training under the following conditions:

- No more than 2 hours individual or group training per beneficiary per year;
- Group training consists of 2 to 20 individuals who need not all be Medicare beneficiaries;
- Follow-up training for subsequent years is based on a 12 month calendar after completion of the full 10 hours of initial training;
- Follow-up training is furnished in increments of no less than one-half hour*; and
- The physician (or qualified non-physician practitioner) treating the beneficiary must document in the beneficiary's medical record that the beneficiary is a diabetic.

*When a claim contains a DSMT HCPCS code and the associated units cause the total time for any follow-up year to exceed 2 hours, a CWF error will set.

100-2,15,300.4

Coverage Requirements for Individual Training

Medicare covers training on an individual basis for a Medicare beneficiary under any of the following conditions:

- No group session is available within 2 months of the date the training is ordered;
- The beneficiary's physician (or qualified non-physician practitioner) documents in the beneficiary's medical record that the beneficiary has special needs resulting from conditions, such as severe vision, hearing or language limitations or other such special conditions as identified by the treating physician or non-physician practitioner, that will hinder effective participation in a group training session; or
- The physician orders additional insulin training.

The need for individual training must be identified by the physician or non-physician practitioner in the referral.

NOTE: If individual training has been provided to a Medicare beneficiary and subsequently the carrier or intermediary determines that training should have been provided in a group, carriers and intermediaries down-code the reimbursement from individual to the group level and provider education would be the appropriate actions instead of denying the service as billed.

100-2,15,50

Drugs and Biologicals

B3-2049, A3-3112.4.B, HO-230.4.B

The Medicare program provides limited benefits for outpatient drugs. The program covers drugs that are furnished "incident to" a physician's service provided that the drugs are not usually self-administered by the patients who take them.

Generally, drugs and biologicals are covered only if all of the following requirements are met:

- They meet the definition of drugs or biologicals (see Sec.50.1);
- They are of the type that are not usually self-administered. (see Sec.50.2);
- They meet all the general requirements for coverage of items as incident to a physician's services (see Sec.Sec.50.1 and 50.3);
- They are reasonable and necessary for the diagnosis or treatment of the illness or injury for which they are administered according to accepted standards of medical practice (see Sec.50.4);
- They are not excluded as noncovered immunizations (see Sec.50.4.4.2); and
- They have not been determined by the FDA to be less than effective. (See Sec.Sec.50.4.4).

Medicare Part B does generally not cover drugs that can be self-administered, such as those in pill form, or are used for self-injection. However, the statute provides for the coverage of some self-administered drugs. Examples of self-administered drugs that are covered include blood-clotting factors, drugs used in immunosuppressive therapy, erythropoietin for dialysis patients, osteoporosis drugs for certain homebound patients, and certain oral cancer drugs. (See Sec.110.3 for coverage of drugs, which are necessary to the effective use of Durable Medical Equipment (DME) or prosthetic devices.)

100-2,15,50.2

Determining Self-Administration of Drug or Biological

AB-02-072, AB-02-139, B3-2049.2

The Medicare program provides limited benefits for outpatient prescription drugs. The program covers drugs that are furnished "incident to" a physician's service provided that the drugs are not usually self-administered by the patients who take them. Section 112 of the Benefits, Improvements & Protection Act of 2000 (BIPA) amended sections 1861(s)(2)(A) and 1861(s)(2)(B) of the Act to redefine this exclusion. The prior statutory language referred to those drugs "which cannot be self-administered." Implementation of the BIPA provision requires interpretation of the phrase "not usually self-administered by the patient".

A. Policy

Fiscal intermediaries and carriers are instructed to follow the instructions below when applying the exclusion for drugs that are usually self-administered by the patient. Each individual contractor must make its own individual determination on each drug. Contractors must continue to apply the policy that not only the drug is medically reasonable and necessary for any individual claim, but also that the route of administration is medically reasonable and necessary. That is, if a drug is available in both oral and injectable forms, the injectable form of the drug must be medically reasonable and necessary as compared to using the oral form.

For certain injectable drugs, it will be apparent due to the nature of the condition(s) for which they are administered or the usual course of treatment for those conditions, they are, or are not, usually self-administered. For example, an injectable drug used to treat migraine headaches is usually self-administered. On the other hand, an injectable drug, administered at the same time as chemotherapy, used to treat anemia secondary to chemotherapy is not usually self-administered.

B. Administered

The term "administered" refers only to the physical process by which the drug enters the patient's body. It does not refer to whether the process is supervised by a medical professional (for example, to observe proper technique or side-effects of the drug). Only injectable (including intravenous) drugs are eligible for inclusion under the "incident to" benefit. Other routes of administration including, but not limited to, oral drugs, suppositories, topical medications are all considered to be usually self-administered by the patient.

C. Usually

For the purposes of applying this exclusion, the term "usually" means more than 50 percent of the time for all Medicare beneficiaries who use the drug. Therefore, if a drug is self-administered by more than 50 percent of Medicare beneficiaries, the drug is excluded from coverage and the contractor may not make any Medicare payment for it. In arriving at a single determination as to whether a drug is usually self-administered, contractors should make a separate determination for each indication for a drug as to whether that drug is usually self-administered.

After determining whether a drug is usually self-administered for each indication, contractors should determine the relative contribution of each indication to total use of the drug (i.e., weighted average) in order to make an overall determination as to whether the drug is usually self-administered. For example, if a drug has three indications, is not self-administered for the first indication, but is self administered for the second and third indications, and the first indication makes up 40 percent of total usage, the second indication makes up 30 percent of total usage, and the third indication makes up 30 percent of total usage, then the drug would be considered usually self-administered.

Reliable statistical information on the extent of self-administration by the patient may not always be available. Consequently, CMS offers the following guidance for each contractor's consideration in making this determination in the absence of such data:

1. Absent evidence to the contrary, presume that drugs delivered intravenously are not usually self-administered by the patient.
2. Absent evidence to the contrary, presume that drugs delivered by intramuscular injection are not usually self-administered by the patient. (Avonex, for example, is delivered by intramuscular injection, not usually self-administered by the patient.) The contractor may consider the depth and nature of the particular intramuscular injection in applying this presumption. In applying this presumption, contractors should examine the use of the particular drug and consider the following factors:
3. Absent evidence to the contrary, presume that drugs delivered by subcutaneous injection are self-administered by the patient. However, contractors should examine the use of the particular drug and consider the following factors:
   A. Acute Condition - Is the condition for which the drug is used an acute condition? If so, it is less likely that a patient would self-administer the drug. If the condition were longer term, it would be more likely that the patient would self-administer the drug.

   B. Frequency of Administration - How often is the injection given? For example, if the drug is administered once per month, it is less likely to be self-administered by the patient. However, if it is administered once or more per week, it is likely that the drug is self-administered by the patient. In some instances, carriers may have provided payment for one or perhaps several doses of a drug that would otherwise not be paid for because the drug is usually self-administered. Carriers may have exercised this discretion for limited coverage, for example, during a brief time when the patient is being trained under the supervision of a physician in the proper technique for self-administration. Medicare will no longer pay for such doses. In addition, contractors may no longer pay for any drug when it is administered on an outpatient emergency basis, if the drug is excluded because it is usually self-administered by the patient.

D. Definition of Acute Condition

For the purposes of determining whether a drug is usually self-administered, an acute condition means a condition that begins over a short time period, is likely to be of short duration and/or the expected course of treatment is for a short, finite interval. A course of treatment consisting of scheduled injections lasting less than two weeks, regardless of frequency or route of administration, is considered acute. Evidence to support this may include Food and Drug administration (FDA) approval language, package inserts, drug compendia, and other information.

E. By the Patient

The term "by the patient" means Medicare beneficiaries as a collective whole. The carrier includes only the patients themselves and not other individuals (that is, spouses, friends, or other care-givers are not considered the patient). The determination is based on whether the drug is self-administered by the patient a majority of the time that the drug is used on an outpatient basis by Medicare beneficiaries for medically necessary indications.

The carrier ignores all instances when the drug is administered on an inpatient basis. The carrier makes this determination on a drug-by-drug basis, not on a beneficiary-by-beneficiary basis. In evaluating whether beneficiaries as a collective whole self-administer, individual beneficiaries who do not have the capacity to self-administer any drug due to a condition other than the condition for which they are taking the drug in question are not considered. For example, an individual afflicted with paraplegia or advanced dementia would not have the capacity to self-administer any injectable drug, so such individuals would not be included in the population upon which the determination for self-administration by the patient was based. Note that some individuals afflicted with a less severe stage of an otherwise debilitating condition would be included in the population upon which the determination for "self-administered by the patient" was based; for example, an early onset of dementia.

F. Evidentiary Criteria

Contractors are only required to consider the following types of evidence: peer reviewed medical literature, standards of medical practice, evidence-based practice guidelines, FDA approved label, and package inserts. Contractors may also consider other evidence submitted by interested individuals or groups subject to their judgment.

Contractors should also use these evidentiary criteria when reviewing requests for making a determination as to whether a drug is usually self-administered, and requests for reconsideration of a pending or published determination.

Please note that prior to the August 1, 2002, one of the principal factors used to determine whether a drug was subject to the self-administered exclusion was whether the FDA label contained instructions for self-administration. However, CMS notes that under the new standard, the fact that the FDA label includes instructions for self-administration is not, by itself, a determining factor that a drug is subject to this exclusion.

G. Provider Notice of Noncovered Drugs

Contractors must describe on their Web site the process they will use to determine whether a drug is usually self-administered and thus does not meet the "incident to" benefit category. Contractors must publish a list of the injectable drugs that are subject to the self-administered exclusion on their Web site, including the data and rationale that led to the determination. Contractors will report the workload associated with developing new coverage statements in CAFM 21208.

Contractors must provide notice 45 days prior to the date that these drugs will not be covered. During the 45-day time period, contractors will maintain existing medical review and payment procedures. After the 45-day notice, contractors may deny payment for the drugs subject to the notice.

Contractors must not develop local medical review policies (LMRPs) for this purpose because further elaboration to describe drugs that do not meet the ‚Äòincident to' and the ‚Äònot usually self-administered' provisions of the statute are unnecessary. Current LMRPs based solely on these provisions must be withdrawn. LMRPs that address the self-administered exclusion and other information may be reissued absent the self-administered drug exclusion material. Contractors will report this workload in CAFM 21206. However, contractors may continue to use and write LMRPs to describe reasonable and necessary uses of drugs that are not usually self-administered. H. Conferences Between Contractors Contractors' Medical Directors may meet and discuss whether a drug is usually self-administered without reaching a formal consensus. Each contractor uses its discretion as to whether or not it will participate in such discussions. Each contractor must make its own individual determinations, except that fiscal intermediaries may, at their discretion, follow the determinations of the local carrier with respect to the self-administered exclusion.

I. Beneficiary Appeals

If a beneficiary's claim for a particular drug is denied because the drug is subject to the "self-administered drug" exclusion, the beneficiary may appeal the denial. Because it is a "benefit category" denial and not a denial based on medical necessity, an Advance Beneficiary Notice (ABN) is not required. A "benefit category" denial (i.e., a denial based on the fact that there is no benefit category under which the drug may be covered) does not trigger the financial liability protection provisions of Limitation On Liability (under Sec.1879 of the Act). Therefore, physicians or providers may charge the beneficiary for an excluded drug.

J. Provider and Physician Appeals

A physician accepting assignment may appeal a denial under the provisions found in Chapter 29 of the Medicare Claims Processing Manual.

K. Reasonable and Necessary

Carriers and fiscal intermediaries will make the determination of reasonable and necessary with respect to the medical appropriateness of a drug to treat the patient's condition. Contractors will continue to make the determination of whether the intravenous or injection form of a drug is appropriate as opposed to the oral form. Contractors will also continue to make the determination as to whether a physician's office visit was reasonable and necessary. However, contractors should not make a determination of whether it was reasonable and necessary for the patient to choose to have his or her drug administered in the physician's office or outpatient hospital setting. That is, while a physician's office visit may not be reasonable and necessary in a specific situation, in such a case an injection service would be payable.

L. Reporting Requirements

Each carrier and intermediary must report to CMS, every September 1 and March 1, its complete list of injectable drugs that the contractor has determined are excluded when furnished incident to a physician's service on the basis that the drug is usually self-administered. The CMS anticipates that contractors will review injectable drugs on a rolling basis and publish their list of excluded drugs as it is developed. For example, contractors should not wait to publish this list until every drug has been reviewed.

Contractors must send their exclusion list to the following e-mail address: drugdata@cms.hhs.gov a template that CMS will provide separately, consisting of the following data elements in order:

1. Carrier Name
2. State
3. Carrier ID#
4. HCPCS
5. Descriptor
6. Effective Date of Exclusion
7. End Date of Exclusion
8. Comments

Any exclusion list not provided in the CMS mandated format will be returned for correction. To view the presently mandated CMS format for this report, open the file located at: http://cms.hhs.gov/manuals/pm_trans/AB02_139a

100-2,15,50.4.2

Unlabeled Use of Drug

B3-2049.3

An unlabeled use of a drug is a use that is not included as an indication on the drug's label as approved by the FDA. FDA approved drugs used for indications other than what is indicated on the official label may be covered under Medicare if the carrier determines the use to be medically accepted, taking into consideration the major drug compendia, authoritative medical literature and/or accepted standards of medical practice. In the case of drugs used in an anti-cancer chemotherapeutic regimen, unlabeled uses are covered for a medically accepted indication as defined in Sec.50.5. These decisions are made by the contractor on a case-by-case basis.

100-2,15,50.5

Self-Administered Drugs and Biologicals

B3-2049.5

Medicare Part B does not cover drugs that are usually self-administered by the patient unless the statute provides for such coverage. The statute explicitly provides coverage, for blood clotting factors, drugs used in immunosuppressive therapy, erythropoietin for dialysis patients, certain oral anti-cancer drugs and anti-emetics used in certain situations.

100-2,16,10

General Exclusions From Coverage

A3-3150, HO-260, HHA-232, B3-2300

No payment can be made under either the hospital insurance or supplementary medical insurance program for certain items and services, when the following conditions exist:

- Not reasonable and necessary (Sec.20);
- No legal obligation to pay for or provide (Sec.40);
- Paid for by a governmental entity (Sec.50);
- Not provided within United States (Sec.60);
- Resulting from war (Sec.70);
- Personal comfort (Sec.80);
- Routine services and appliances (Sec.90);
- Custodial care (Sec.110);
- Cosmetic surgery (Sec.120);
- Charges by immediate relatives or members of household (Sec.130);
- Dental services (Sec.140);
- Paid or expected to be paid under workers' compensation (Sec.150);
- Nonphysician services provided to a hospital inpatient that were not provided directly or arranged for by the hospital (Sec.170);
- Services Related to and Required as a Result of Services Which are not Covered Under Medicare (Sec.180);
- Excluded foot care services and supportive devices for feet (Sec.30); or
- Excluded investigational devices (See Chapter 14, Sec.30).

100-2,16,140

Dental Services Exclusion

A3-3162, HO-260.13, B3-2336

Items and services in connection with the care, treatment, filling, removal, or replacement of teeth, or structures directly supporting the teeth are not covered. Structures directly supporting the teeth mean the periodontium, which includes the gingivae, dentogingival junction, periodontal membrane, cementum, and alveolar process. However, payment may be made for certain other services of a dentist. (See the Medicare Benefit Policy Manual, Chapter 15, "Covered Medical and Other Health Services," Sec.150.)

The hospitalization or nonhospitalization of a patient has no direct bearing on the coverage or exclusion of a given dental procedure.

When an excluded service is the primary procedure involved, it is not covered regardless of its complexity or difficulty. For example, the extraction of an impacted tooth is not covered. Similarly, an alveoplasty (the surgical improvement of the shape and condition of the alveolar process) and a frenectomy are excluded from coverage when either of these procedures is performed in connection with an excluded service, e.g., the preparation of the mouth for dentures. In like manner, the removal of the torus palatinus (a bony protuberance of the hard palate) could be a covered service. However, with rare exception, this surgery is performed in connection with an excluded service, i.e., the preparation of the mouth for dentures. Under such circumstances, reimbursement is not made for this purpose.

The extraction of teeth to prepare the jaw for radiation treatments of neoplastic disease is also covered. This is an exception to the requirement that to be covered, a noncovered procedure or service performed by a dentist must be an incident to and an integral part of a covered procedure or service performed by the dentist. Ordinarily, the dentist extracts the patient's teeth, but another physician, e.g., a radiologist, administers the radiation treatments.

Whether such services as the administration of anesthesia, diagnostic x-rays, and other related procedures are covered depends upon whether the primary procedure being performed by the dentist is covered. Thus, an x-ray taken in connection with the reduction of a fracture of the jaw or facial bone is covered. However, a single x-ray or xray survey taken in connection with the care or treatment of teeth or the periodontium is not covered.

See also the Medicare Benefit Policy Manual, Chapter 1, "Inpatient Hospital Services, Sec.70, and Chapter 15, "Covered Medical and Other Health Services," Sec.150 for additional information on dental services.

100-2,16,20

Services Not Reasonable and Necessary

A3-3151, HO-260.1, B3-2303, AB-00-52 - 6/00

Items and services which are not reasonable and necessary for the diagnosis or treatment of illness or injury or to improve the functioning of a malformed body member are not covered, e.g., payment cannot be made for the rental of a special hospital bed to be used by the patient in their home unless it was a reasonable and necessary part of the patient's treatment. See also Sec.80.

A health care item or service for the purpose of causing, or assisting to cause, the death of any individual (assisted suicide) is not covered. This prohibition does not apply to the provision of an item or service for the purpose of alleviating pain or discomfort, even if such use may increase the risk of death, so long as the item or service is not furnished for the specific purpose of causing death.

100-2,16,90

Routine Services and Appliances

A3-3157, HO-260.7, B3-2320, R-1797A3 - 5/00

Routine physical checkups; eyeglasses, contact lenses, and eye examinations for the purpose of prescribing, fitting, or changing eyeglasses; eye refractions by whatever practitioner and for whatever purpose performed; hearing aids and examinations for hearing aids; and immunizations are not covered.

The routine physical checkup exclusion applies to (a) examinations performed without relationship to treatment or diagnosis for a specific illness, symptom, complaint, or injury; and (b) examinations required by third parties such as insurance companies business establishments, or Government agencies.

If the claim is for a diagnostic test or examination performed solely for the purpose of establishing a claim under title IV of Public Law 91-173, "Black Lung Benefits," the service is not covered under Medicare and the claimant should be advised to contact their Social Security office regarding the filing of a claim for reimbursement under the "Black Lung" program.

The exclusions apply to eyeglasses or contact lenses, and eye examinations for the purpose of prescribing, fitting, or changing eyeglasses or contact lenses for refractive errors. The exclusions do not apply to physicians' services (and services incident to a physicians' service) performed in conjunction with an eye disease, as for example, glaucoma or cataracts, or to post-surgical prosthetic lenses which are customarily used during convalescence from eye surgery in which the lens of the eye was removed, or to permanent prosthetic lenses required by an individual lacking the organic lens of the eye whether by surgical removal or congenital disease. Such prosthetic lens is a replacement for an internal body organ - the lens of the eye. (See the Medicare Benefit Policy Manual, Chapter 15, "Covered Medical and Other Health Services," Sec.120). Expenses for all refractive procedures, whether performed by an ophthalmologist (or any other physician) or an optometrist and without regard to the reason for performance of the refraction, are excluded from coverage.

A. Immunizations

Vaccinations or inoculations are excluded as immunizations unless they are either

Directly related to the treatment of an injury or direct exposure to a disease or condition, such as antirabies treatment, tetanus antitoxin or booster vaccine, botulin antitoxin, antivenin sera, or immune globulin. (In the absence of injury or direct exposure, preventive immunization (vaccination or inoculation) against such diseases as smallpox, polio, diphtheria, etc., is not covered.); or

Specifically covered by statute, as described in the Medicare Benefit Policy Manual, Chapter 15, "Covered Medical and Other Health Services," Sec.50.

B. Antigens

Prior to the Omnibus Reconciliation Act of 1980, a physician who prepared an antigen for a patient could not be reimbursed for that service unless the physician also administered the antigen to the patient. Effective January 1, 1981, payment may be made for a reasonable supply of antigens that have been prepared for a particular patient even though they have not been administered to the patient by the same physician who prepared them if:

The antigens are prepared by a physician who is a doctor of medicine or osteopathy, and "The physician who prepared the antigens has examined the patient and has determined a plan of treatment and a dosage regimen.

A reasonable supply of antigens is considered to be not more than a 12-week supply of antigens that has been prepared for a particular patient at any one time. The purpose of the reasonable supply limitation is to assure that the antigens retain their potency and effectiveness over the period in which they are to be administered to the patient. (See the Medicare Benefit Policy Manual, Chapter 15, "Covered Medical and Other Health Services," Sec.50.4.4.2)

100-2,6,10

Medical and Other Health Services Furnished to Inpatients of Participating Hospitals

Payment may be made under Part B for physician services and for the nonphysician medical and other health services listed below when furnished by a participating hospital (either directly or under arrangements) to an inpatient of the hospital, but only if payment for these services cannot be made under Part A.

In PPS hospitals, this means that Part B payment could be made for these services if:

- No Part A prospective payment is made at all for the hospital stay because of patient exhaustion of benefit days before admission;
- The admission was disapproved as not reasonable and necessary (and waiver of liability payment was not made);
- The day or days of the otherwise covered stay during which the services were provided were not reasonable and necessary (and no payment was made under waiver of liability);
- The patient was not otherwise eligible for or entitled to coverage under Part A (See the Medicare Benefit Policy Manual, Chapter 1, Sec.150, for services received as a result of noncovered services); or
- No Part A day outlier payment is made (for discharges before October 1997) for one or more outlier days due to patient exhaustion of benefit days after admission but before the case's arrival at outlier status, or because outlier days are otherwise not covered and waiver of liability payment is not made.

However, if only day outlier payment is denied under Part A (discharges before October 1997), Part B payment may be made for only the services covered under Part B and furnished on the denied outlier days.

In non-PPS hospitals, Part B payment may be made for services on any day for which Part A payment is denied (i.e., benefit days are exhausted; services are not at the hospital level of care; or patient is not otherwise eligible or entitled to payment under Part A).

Services payable are:

- Diagnostic x-ray tests, diagnostic laboratory tests, and other diagnostic tests;
- X-ray, radium, and radioactive isotope therapy, including materials and services of technicians;
- Surgical dressings, and splints, casts, and other devices used for reduction of fractures and dislocations;
- Prosthetic devices (other than dental) which replace all or part of an internal body organ (including contiguous tissue), or all or part of the function of a permanently inoperative or malfunctioning internal body organ, including replacement or repairs of such devices;
- Leg, arm, back, and neck braces, trusses, and artificial legs, arms, and eyes including adjustments, repairs, and replacements required because of breakage, wear, loss, or a change in the patient's physical condition;

- Outpatient physical therapy, outpatient speech-language pathology services, and outpatient occupational therapy (see the Medicare Benefit Policy Manual, Chapter 15, "Covered Medical and Other Health Services," Sec.Sec.220 and 230);
- Screening mammography services;
- Screening pap smears;
- Influenza, pneumococcal pneumonia, and hepatitis B vaccines;
- Colorectal screening;
- Bone mass measurements;
- Diabetes self-management;
- Prostate screening;
- Ambulance services;
- Hemophilia clotting factors for hemophilia patients competent to use these factors without supervision);
- Immunosuppressive drugs;
- Oral anti-cancer drugs;
- Oral drug prescribed for use as an acute anti-emetic used as part of an anti-cancer chemotherapeutic regimen; and
- Epoetin Alfa (EPO).

Coverage rules for these services are described in the Medicare Benefit Policy Manual, Chapters: 11, "End Stage Renal Disease (ESRD);" 14, "Medical Devices;" or 15, "Medical and Other Health Services."

For services to be covered under Part A or Part B, a hospital must furnish nonphysician services to its inpatients directly or under arrangements. A nonphysician service is one which does not meet the criteria defining physicians' services specifically provided for in regulation at 42 CFR 415.102. Services "incident to" physicians' services (except for the services of nurse anesthetists employed by anesthesiologists) are nonphysician services for purposes of this provision. This provision is applicable to all hospitals participating in Medicare, including those paid under alternative arrangements such as State cost control systems, and to emergency hospital services furnished by nonparticipating hospitals.

In all hospitals, every service provided to a hospital inpatient other than those listed in the next paragraph must be treated as an inpatient hospital service to be paid for under Part A, if Part A coverage is available and the beneficiary is entitled to Part A. This is because every hospital must provide directly or arrange for any nonphysician service rendered to its inpatients, and a hospital can be paid under Part B for a service provided in this manner only if Part A coverage does not exist.

These services, when provided to a hospital inpatient, may be covered under Part B, even though the patient has Part A coverage for the hospital stay. This is because these services are covered under Part B and not covered under Part A. They are:

- Physicians' services (including the services of residents and interns in unapproved teaching programs);
- Influenza vaccine;
- Pneumoccocal vaccine and its administration;
- Hepatitis B vaccine and its administration;
- Screening mammography services;
- Screening pap smears and pelvic exams;
- Colorectal screening;
- Bone mass measurements;
- Diabetes self management training services; and
- Prostate screening.

However, note that in order to have any Medicare coverage at all (Part A or Part B), any nonphysician service rendered to a hospital inpatient must be provided directly or arranged for by the hospital.

100-2,6,20.6

Outpatient Observation Services

A. Outpatient Observation Services Defined

Observation care is a well-defined set of specific, clinically appropriate services, which include ongoing short term treatment, assessment, and reassessment before a decision can be made regarding whether patients will require further treatment as hospital inpatients or if they are able to be discharged from the hospital. Observation status is commonly assigned to patients who present to the emergency department and who then require a significant period of treatment or monitoring in order to make a decision concerning their admission or discharge.

Observation services are covered only when provided by the order of a physician or another individual authorized by State licensure law and hospital staff bylaws to admit patients to the hospital or to order outpatient tests. In the majority of cases, the decision whether to discharge a patient from the hospital following resolution of the reason for the observation care or to admit the patient as an inpatient can be made in less than 48 hours, usually in less than 24 hours. In only rare and exceptional cases do reasonable and necessary outpatient observation services span more than 48 hours.

Hospitals may bill for patients who are directly admitted to the hospital for outpatient observation services. A "direct admission" occurs when a physician in the community refers a patient to the hospital for observation, bypassing the clinic or emergency department (ED). Effective for services furnished on or after January 1, 2003, hospitals may bill for patients directly admitted for observation services.

See, the Medicare Claims Processing Manual, Pub. 100-04, chapter 4, section 290, at http://www.cms.hhs.gov/manuals/downloads/clm104c04.pdf for billing and payment instructions for outpatient observation services.

B. Coverage of Outpatient Observation Services

When a physician orders that a patient be placed under observation care, the patient's status is that of an outpatient. The purpose of observation is to determine the need for further treatment or for inpatient admission. Thus, a patient receiving observation services may improve and be released, or be admitted as an inpatient (see Pub. 100-02, Medicare Benefit Policy Manual, Chapter 1, Section 10 "Covered Inpatient Hospital Services Covered Under Part A" at http://www.cms.hhs.gov/manuals/Downloads/bp102c01.pdf). For more information on correct reporting of observation services, see the Medicare Claims Processing Manual, Pub. 100-04, chapter 4, section 290.2.2.)

All hospital observation services, regardless of the duration of the observation care, that are medically reasonable and necessary are covered by Medicare. Observation services are reported using HCPCS code G0378 (Hospital observation service, per hour). Beginning January 1, 2008, HCPCS code G0378 for hourly observation services is assigned status indicator N, signifying that its payment is always packaged. No separate payment is made for observation services reported with HCPCS code G0378. In most circumstances, observation services are supportive and ancillary to the other separately payable services provided to a patient. In certain circumstances when observation care is billed in conjunction with a high level clinic visit (Level 5), high level emergency department visit (Level 4 or 5), critical care services, or direct admission to observation as an integral part of a patient's extended encounter of care, payment may be made for the entire extended care encounter through one of two composite APCs when certain criteria are met. For information about billing and payment methodology for observation services in years prior to CY 2008, see the Medicare Claims Processing Manual, Pub. 100-04, chapter 4, sections 290.3-290.4. For information about payment for extended assessment and management under composite APCs, see section 290.5.

Payment for all reasonable and necessary observation services is packaged into the payments for other separately payable services provided to the patient in the same encounter. Observation services that are packaged through assignment of status indicator N are covered OPPS services. Since the payment for these services is included in the APC payment for other separately payable services on the claim, hospitals must not bill Medicare beneficiaries directly for the packaged services.

C. Services Not Covered by Medicare and Notification to the Beneficiary

In making the determination whether an ABN can be used to shift liability to a beneficiary for the cost of non-covered items or services related to an encounter that includes observation care, the provider should follow a two step process. First, the provider must decide whether the item or service meets either the definition of observation care or would be otherwise covered. If the item or service does not meet the definitional requirements of any Medicare-covered benefit under Part B, then the item or service is not covered by Medicare and an ABN is not required to shift the liability to the beneficiary. However, the provider may choose to provide voluntary notification for these items or services.

Second, if the item or service meets the definition of observation services or would be otherwise covered, then the provider must decide whether the item or service is "reasonable and necessary" for the beneficiary on the occasion in question, or if the item or service exceeds any frequency limitation for the particular benefit or falls outside of a timeframe for receipt of a particular benefit. In these cases, the ABN would be used to shift the liability to the beneficiary (see the Medicare Claims Processing Manual; Pub. 100-04, Chapter 30, "Financial Liability Protections," Section 20, at http://www.cms.hhs.gov/manuals/downloads/clm104c30.pdf for information regarding Limitation On Liability (LOL) Under Sec.1879 Where Medicare Claims Are Disallowed).

If an ABN is not issued to the beneficiary, the provider may be held liable for the cost of the item or service unless the provider/supplier is able to demonstrate that they did not know and could not have reasonably been expected to know that Medicare would not pay for the item or service.

100-3,240.4

NCD for Continuous Positive Airway Pressure (CPAP) Therapy For Obstructive Sleep Apnea (OSA) (240.4)

B. Nationally Covered Indications

Effective for claims with dates of service on and after March 13, 2008, the Centers for Medicare & Medicaid Services (CMS) determines that CPAP therapy when used in adult patients with OSA is considered reasonable and necessary under the following situations:

1. The use of CPAP is covered under Medicare when used in adult patients with OSA. Coverage of CPAP is initially limited to a 12-week period to identify beneficiaries diagnosed with OSA as subsequently described who benefit from CPAP. CPAP is subsequently covered only for those beneficiaries diagnosed with OSA who benefit from CPAP during this 12-week period.
2. The provider of CPAP must conduct education of the beneficiary prior to the use of the CPAP device to ensure that the beneficiary has been educated in the proper use of the device. A caregiver, for example a family member, may be compensatory, if consistently available in the beneficiary's home and willing and able to safely operate the CPAP device.
3. A positive diagnosis of OSA for the coverage of CPAP must include a clinical evaluation and a positive:
   a. attended PSG performed in a sleep laboratory; or
   b. unattended HST with a Type II home sleep monitoring device; or
   c. unattended HST with a Type III home sleep monitoring device; or
   d. unattended HST with a Type IV home sleep monitoring device that measures at least 3 channels.
4. The sleep test must have been previously ordered by the beneficiaryÔø¾s treating physician and furnished under appropriate physician supervision.
5. An initial 12-week period of CPAP is covered in adult patients with OSA if either of the following criterion using the AHI or RDI are met:
   a. AHI or RDI greater than or equal to 15 events per hour, or
   b. AHI or RDI greater than or equal to 5 events and less than or equal to 14 events per hour with documented symptoms of excessive daytime sleepiness, impaired cognition, mood disorders or insomnia, or documented hypertension, ischemic heart disease, or history of stroke.
6. The AHI or RDI is calculated on the average number of events of per hour. If the AHI or RDI is calculated based on less than 2 hours of continuous recorded sleep, the total number of recorded events to calculate the AHI or RDI during sleep testing must be at a minimum the number of events that would have been required in a 2-hour period.
7. Apnea is defined as a cessation of airflow for at least 10 seconds. Hypopnea is defined as an abnormal respiratory event lasting at least 10 seconds with at least a 30% reduction in thoracoabdominal movement or airflow as compared to baseline, and with at least a 4% oxygen desaturation.
8. Coverage with Evidence Development (CED): Medicare provides the following limited coverage for CPAP in adult beneficiaries who do not qualify for CPAP coverage based on criteria 1-7 above. A clinical study seeking Medicare payment for CPAP provided to a beneficiary who is an enrolled subject in that study must address one or more of the following questions
   a. In Medicare-aged subjects with clinically identified risk factors for OSA, how does the diagnostic accuracy of a clinical trial of CPAP compare with PSG and Type II, III & IV HST in identifying subjects with OSA who will respond to CPAP?
   b. In Medicare-aged subjects with clinically identified risk factors for OSA who have not undergone confirmatory testing with PSG or Type II, III & IV HST, does CPAP cause clinically meaningful harm?

The study must meet the following additional standards:

c. The principal purpose of the research study is to test whether a particular intervention potentially improves the participantsÔø¾ health outcomes.

d. The research study is well-supported by available scientific and medical information or it is intended to clarify or establish the health outcomes of interventions already in common clinical use.

e. The research study does not unjustifiably duplicate existing studies.

f. The research study design is appropriate to answer the research question being asked in the study.

g. The research study is sponsored by an organization or individual capable of executing the proposed study successfully.

h. The research study is in compliance with all applicable Federal regulations concerning the protection of human subjects found at 45 CFR Part 46. If a study is Food and Drug Administration-regulated, it also must be in compliance with 21 CFR Parts 50 and 56.

i. All aspects of the research study are conducted according to the appropriate standards of scientific integrity.

j. The research study has a written protocol that clearly addresses, or incorporates by reference, the Medicare standards.

k. The clinical research study is not designed to exclusively test toxicity or disease pathophysiology in healthy individuals. Trials of all medical technologies measuring therapeutic outcomes as one of the objectives meet this standard only if the disease or condition being studied is life-threatening as defined in 21 CFR Ôø¾ 312.81(a) and the patient has no other viable treatment options.

l. The clinical research study is registered on the ClinicalTrials.gov Web site by the principal sponsor/investigator prior to the enrollment of the first study subject.

m. The research study protocol specifies the method and timing of public release of all pre-specified outcomes to be measured, including release of outcomes if outcomes are negative or study is terminated early. The results must be made public within 24 months of the end of data collection. If a report is planned for publication in a peer-reviewed journal, then that initial release may be an abstract that meets the requirements of the International Committee of Medical Journal Editors. However, a full report of the outcomes must be made public no later than 3 years after the end of data collection.

n. The research study protocol must explicitly discuss subpopulations affected by the treatment under investigation, particularly traditionally underrepresented groups in clinical studies, how the inclusion and exclusion criteria affect enrollment of these populations, and a plan for the retention and reporting of said populations in the trial. If the inclusion and exclusion criteria are expected to have a negative effect on the recruitment or retention of underrepresented populations, the protocol must discuss why these criteria are necessary.

o. The research study protocol explicitly discusses how the results are or are not expected to be generalizable to the Medicare population to infer whether Medicare patients may benefit from the intervention. Separate discussions in the protocol may be necessary for populations eligible for Medicare due to age, disability, or Medicaid eligibility.

C. Nationally Non-covered Indications

Effective for claims with dates of services on and after March 13, 2008, other diagnostic tests for the diagnosis of OSA, other than those noted above for prescribing CPAP, are not sufficient for the coverage of CPAP.

D. Other

N/A

(This NCD last reviewed March

100-4,1,10.1.4.1

Physician and Ambulance Services Furnished in Connection With Covered Foreign Inpatient Hospital Services

Payment is made for necessary physician and ambulance services that meet the other coverage requirements of the Medicare program, and are furnished in connection with and during a period of covered foreign hospitalization.

A. Coverage of Physician and Ambulance Services Furnished Outside the U.S.

Where inpatient services in a foreign hospital are covered, payment may also be made for

- Physicians' services furnished to the beneficiary while he/she is an inpatient,
- Physicians' services furnished to the beneficiary outside the hospital on the day of his/her admission as an inpatient, provided the services were for the same condition for which the beneficiary was hospitalized (including the services of a Canadian ship‚Äôs physician who furnishes emergency services in Canadian waters on the day the patient is admitted to a Canadian hospital for a covered emergency stay and,
- Ambulance services, where necessary, for the trip to the hospital in conjunction with the beneficiary's admission as an inpatient. Return trips from a foreign hospital are not covered.

In cases involving foreign ambulance services, the general requirements in Chapter 15 are also applicable, subject to the following special rules:

- If the foreign hospitalization was determined to be covered on the basis of emergency services, the medical necessity requirements outlined in Chapter 15 are considered met.
- The definition of:

- physician
- for purposes of coverage of services furnished outside the U.S., is expanded to include a foreign practitioner, provided the practitioner is legally licensed to practice in the country in which the services are furnished.

- Only the enrollee can file for Part B benefits; the assignment method may not be used.
- Where the enrollee is deceased, the rules for settling Part B underpayments are applicable. Payment is made to the foreign physician or foreign ambulance company on an unpaid bill provided the physician or ambulance company accepts the payment as the full charge for the service, or payment an be made to a person who has agreed to assume legal liability to pay the physician or supplier. Where the bill is paid, payment may be made in accordance with Medicare regulations. The regular deductible and coinsurance requirements apply to physicians' and ambulance service

100-4,1,30.3.5

Effect of Assignment Upon Purchase of Cataract Glasses FromParticipating Physician or Supplier on Claims Submitted to Carriers

B3-3045.4

A pair of cataract glasses is comprised of two distinct products: a professional product (the prescribed lenses) and a retail commercial product (the frames). The frames serve not only as a holder of lenses but also as an article of personal apparel. As such, they are usually selected on the basis of personal taste and style. Although Medicare will pay only for standard frames, most patients want deluxe frames. Participating physicians and suppliers cannot profitably furnish such deluxe frames unless they can make an extra (noncovered) charge for the frames even though they accept assignment.

Therefore, a participating physician or supplier (whether an ophthalmologist, optometrist, or optician) who accepts assignment on cataract glasses with deluxe frames may charge the Medicare patient the difference between his/her usual charge to private pay patients for glasses with standard frames and his/her usual charge to such patients for glasses with deluxe frames, in addition to the applicable deductible and coinsurance on glasses with standard frames, if all of the following requirements are met:

A. The participating physician or supplier has standard frames available, offers them for saleto the patient, and issues and ABN to the patient that explains the price and other differences between standard and deluxe frames. Refer to Chapter 30.

B. The participating physician or supplier obtains from the patient (or his/her representative) and keeps on file the following signed and dated statement:

____

Name of Patient Medicare Claim Number

Having been informed that an extra charge is being made by the physician or supplier for deluxe frames, that this extra charge is not covered by Medicare, and that standard frames are available for purchase from the physician or supplier at no extra charge, I have chosen to purchase deluxe frames. ______________

Signature Date

C. The participating physician or supplier itemizes on his/her claim his/her actual charge for the lenses, his/her actual charge for the standard frames, and his/her actual extra charge for the deluxe frames (charge differential). Once the assigned claim for deluxe frames has been processed, the carrier will follow the ABN instructions as described in Sec.60.

100-4,11,30.3

Data Required on Claim to FI

See Pub. 100-02, Chapter 9, Secs.10 & 20.2 for coverage requirements for Hospice benefits. This section addresses only the submittal of claims. See section 20, of this chapter for information on Notice of Election (NOE) transaction types (81A,C,E and 82A,C,E).

Before billing, the hospice must submit an admission notice to the FI (see section 20). The Social Security Act at Sec.1862 (a)(22) requires that all claims for Medicare payment must be submitted in an electronic form specified by the Secretary of Health and Human Services, unless an exception described at Sec.1862 (h) applies. The electronic form required for billing hospice services is the ANSI X12N 837 Institutional claim transaction. Since the data structure of the 837 transaction is difficult to express in narrative form and to provide assistance to small providers excepted from the electronic claim requirement, the instructions below are given relative to the data element names on the UB-04 (Form CMS-1450) hardcopy form. Each data element name is shown in bold type. Information regarding the form locator numbers that correspond to these data element names and a table to crosswalk UB-04 form locators to the 837 transaction is found in Chapter 25.

Because claim formats serve the needs of many payers, some data elements may not be needed by a particular payer. Detailed information is given only for items required for Medicare hospice claims. Items not listed need not be completed although hospices may complete them when billing multiple payers.

Provider Name, Address, and Telephone Number The hospice enters this information for their agency.

Type of Bill This three-digit alphanumeric code gives three specific pieces of information. The first digit identifies the type of facility. The second classifies the type of care. The third indicates the sequence of this bill in this particular benefit period. It is referred to as a "frequency" code.

Code Structure

1st Digit - Type of Facility
8 - Special facility (Hospice)

2nd Digit - Classification (Special Facility Only)
1 - Hospice (Nonhospital based)
2 - Hospice (Hospital based)

3rd Digit Frequency	Definition
0 - Nonpayment/Zero Claims	Used when no payment from Medicare is anticipated.
I - Admit Through Discharge Claim	This code is used for a bill encompassing an entire course of hospice treatment for which the provider expects payment from the payer, i.e., no further bills will be submitted for this patient.
2 - Interim - First Claim	This code is used for the first of an expected series of payment bills for a hospice course of treatment.
3 - Interim - Continuing Claim	This code is used when a payment bill for a hospice course of treatment has already been submitted and further bills are expected to be submitted.
4 - Interim - Last Claim	This code is used for a payment bill that is the last of a series for a hospice course of treatment. The "Through" date of this bill (FL 6) is the discharge date, transfer date, or date of death.
5 - Late Charges	Use this code for late charges that need to be billed. Late charges can be submitted only for revenue codes not on the original bill. For additional information on late charge bills see Chapter 3.
7 - Replacement of Prior Claim	This code is used by the provider when it wants to correct (other than late charges) a previously submitted bill. This is the code used on the corrected or "new" bill. For additional information on replacement bills see Chapter 3.
8 - Void/Cancel of a Prior Claim	This code is used to cancel a previously processed claim. For additional information on void/cancel bills see Chapter 3.

Statement Covers Period (From-Through)

The hospice shows the beginning and ending dates of the period covered by this bill in numeric fields (MM-DD-YY). The hospice does not show days before the patient's entitlement began. Since the 12-month hospice "cap period" (see Sec.80.2) ends each year on October 31, hospices must submit separate bills for October and November.

Patient Name/Identifier

The hospice enters the beneficiary's name exactly as it appears on the Medicare card.

Patient Address

Patient Birth date

Patient Sex

The hospice enters the appropriate address, date of birth and gender information describing the beneficiary.

Admission/Start of Care Date

The hospice enters the admission date, which must be the same date as the effective date of the hospice election or change of election. The date of admission may not precede the physician's certification by more than 2 calendar days.

The admission date stays the same on all continuing claims for the same hospice election.

The hospice enters the month, day, and year numerically as MM-DD-YY.

Patient Discharge Status

This code indicates the patient's status as of the "Through" date (FL 6) of the billing period. The hospice enters the most appropriate NUBC approved code.

The codes most commonly used on hospice claims include:

01 Discharged to home or self care

30 Still patient 40 Expired at home

41 Expired in a medical facility, such as a hospital, SNF, ICF or freestanding hospice

42 Expired - place unknown

50 Discharged/Transferred to Hospice - home

51 Discharged/Transferred to Hospice - medical facility

Condition Codes

The hospice enters any appropriate NUBC approved code(s) identifying conditions related to this bill that may affect processing.

Codes listed below are only those most frequently applicable to hospice claims. For a complete list of codes, see Chapter 25.

07	Treatment of Non-terminal Condition for Hospice	Code indicates the patient has elected hospice care but the provider is not treating the terminal condition, and is, therefore, requesting regular Medicare payment.
20	Beneficiary Requested Billing	Code indicates the provider realizes the services on this bill are at a noncovered level of care or otherwise excluded from coverage, but the beneficiary has requested a formal determination.
21	Billing for Denial Notice	Code indicates the provider realizes services are at a noncovered level of care or excluded, but requests a denial notice from Medicare in order to bill Medicaid or other insurers.

Occurrence Codes and Dates

The hospice enters any appropriate NUBC approved code(s) and associated date(s) defining specific event(s) relating to this billing period. Event codes are two numeric digits, and dates are six numeric digits (MM-DD-YY). If there are more occurrences than there are spaces on the form, use FL 36 (occurrence span) to record additional occurrences and dates.

Codes listed below are only those most frequently applicable to hospice claims. For a complete list of codes, see Chapter 25.

Code	Title	Definition
23	Cancellation of Hospice Election Period (FI USE Only)	Code indicates date on which a hospice period of election is cancelled by an FI as opposed to revocation by the beneficiary.
24	Date Insurance Denied	Code indicates the date of receipt of a denial of coverage by a higher priority payer.
27	Date of Hospice Certification or Re-Certification	Code indicates the date of certification or re-certification of the hospice benefit period, beginning with the first 2 initial benefit periods of 90 days each and the subsequent 60-day benefit periods. Note regarding transfers from one hospice to another hospice: If a patient is in the first certification period when they transfer to another hospice, the receiving hospice would use the same certification date as the previous hospice until the next certification period. However, if they were in the next certification at the time of transfer, then they would enter that date in the Occurrence Code 27 and date.
42	Date of Termination of Hospice Benefit	Enter code to indicate the date on which beneficiary terminated his/her election to receive hospice benefits. This code can be used only when the beneficiary has revoked the benefit, has been decertified or discharged. It cannot be used in transfer situations.

Occurrence Span Code and Dates

The hospice enters any appropriate NUBC approved code(s) and associated beginning and ending date(s) defining a specific event relating to this billing period are shown. Event codes are two alphanumeric digits and dates are shown numerically as MM-DD-YY.

Codes listed below are only those most frequently applicable to hospice claims. For a complete list of codes, see Chapter 25.

Code	Title	Definition
M2	Dates of Inpatient Respite Care	Code indicates From/Through dates of a period of inpatient respite care for hospice patients to differentiate separate respite periods of less than 5 days each. M2 is used when respite care is provided more than once during a benefit period.
77	Provider Liability -Utilization Charged	Code indicates From/Through dates for a period of non-covered hospice care for which the provider accepts payment liability (other than for medical necessity or custodial care).

Hospices must use occurrence span code 77 to identify days of care that are not covered by Medicare due to untimely physician recertification. This is particularly important when the non-covered days fall at the beginning of a billing period.

Value Codes and Amounts

The hospice enters any appropriate NUBC approved code(s) and the associated value amounts identifying numeric information related to this bill that may affect processing.

The most commonly used value codes on hospice claims are value codes 61 and G8, which are used to report the location of the site of hospice services. Otherwise, value codes are commonly used only to indicate Medicare is secondary to another payer. For detailed information on reporting Medicare secondary payer information, see the Medicare Secondary Payer Manual.

Code	Title	Definition
61	Place of Residence where Service is Furnished (Routine Home Care and Continuous Home Care)	MSA or Core-Based Statistical Area (CBSA) number (or rural State code) of the location where the hospice service is delivered. A residence can be an inpatient facility if an individual uses that facility as a place of residence. It is the level of care that is required and not the location where hospice services are provided that determines payment. In other words, if an individual resides in a freestanding hospice facility and requires routine home care, then claims are submitted for routine home care. Hospices must report value code 61 when billing revenue codes 0651 and 0652.

Code	Title	Definition
G8	Facility where Inpatient Hospice Service is Delivered (General Inpatient and Inpatient Respite Care).	MSA or Core Based Statistical Area (CBSA) number (or rural State code) of the facility where inpatient hospice services are delivered. Hospices must report value code G8 when billing revenue codes 0655 and 0656.

If hospice services are provided to the beneficiary in more than one CBSA area during the billing period, the hospice reports the CBSA that applies at the end of the billing period. This applies for either routine home care and continuous home care (e.g., the beneficiary's residence changes between locations in different CBSAs) or for general inpatient and inpatient respite care (e.g., the beneficiary is served in inpatient facilities in different CBSAs).

Revenue Codes

The hospice assigns a revenue code for each type of service provided and enter the appropriate four-digit numeric revenue code to explain each charge.

For claims with dates of service before July 1, 2008, hospices only reported the revenue codes in the table below. Effective on claims with dates of service on or after January 1, 2008, additional revenue codes will be reported describing the visits provided under each level of care. However, Medicare payment will continue to be reflected only on claim lines with the revenue codes in this table.

Code	Description	Standard Abbreviation
0651*	Routine Home Care	RTN Home
0652*	Continuous Home Care	CTNS Home A minimum of 8 hours of primarily nursing care within a 24-hour period. The 8-hours of care does not need to be continuous within the 24-hour period, but a need for an aggregate of 8 hours of primarily nursing care is required. Nursing care must be provided by a registered nurse or a licensed practical nurse. If skilled intervention is required for less than 8 aggregate hours (or less than 32 units) within a 24 hour period, then the care rendered would be covered as a routine home care day. Services provided by a nurse practitioner as the attending physician are not included in the CHC computation nor is care that is not directly related to the crisis included in the computation. CHC billing should reflect direct patient care during a period of crisis and should not reflect time related to staff working hours, time taken for meal breaks, time used for educating staff, time used to report etc.
0655***	Inpatient Respite Care	IP Respite
0656***	General Inpatient Care	GNL IP
0657**	Physician Services	PHY SER (must be accompanied by a physician procedure code)

* Reporting of value code 61 is required with these revenue codes.

**Reporting of modifier GV is required with

this revenue code when billing physician services performed by a nurse practitioner.

***Reporting of value code G8 is required with these revenue codes.

NOTE: Hospices use revenue code 0657 to identify hospice charges for services furnished to patients by physician or nurse practitioner employees, or physicians or nurse practitioners receiving compensation from the hospice. Physician services performed by a nurse practitioner require the addition of the modifier GV in conjunction with revenue code 0657. Procedure codes are required in order for the FI to determine the reimbursement rate for the physician services. Appropriate procedure codes are available from the FI.

Effective on claims with dates of service on or after July 1, 2008, hospices must report the number of visits that were provided to the beneficiary in the course of delivering the hospice levels of care billed with the codes above. Charges for these codes will be reported on the appropriate level of care line. Total number of patient care visits is to be reported by the discipline (registered nurse, nurse practitioner, licensed nurse, home health aide (also known as a hospice aide), social worker, physician or nurse practitioner serving as the beneficiary's attending physician) for each week at each location of service. If visits are provided in multiple sites, a separate line for each site and for each discipline will be required. The total number of visits does not imply the total number of activities or interventions provided. If patient care visits in a particular discipline are not provided under a given level of care or service location, do not report a line for the corresponding revenue code.

To constitute a visit, the discipline, (as defined above) must have provided care to the beneficiary. Services provided by a social worker to the beneficiary's family also constitute a visit. For example, phone calls, documentation in the medical/clinical record, interdisciplinary group meetings, obtaining physician orders, rounds in a facility or any other activity that is not related to the provision of items or services to a beneficiary, do not count towards a visit to be placed on the claim. In addition, the visit must be reasonable and necessary for the palliation and management of the terminal illness and related conditions as described in the patient's plan of care.

Example 1: Week 1: A visit by the RN was made to the beneficiary's home on Monday and Wednesday where the nurse assessed the patient, verified effect of pain medications, provided patient teaching, obtained vital signs and documented in the medical record. A

home health aide assisted the patient with a bath on Tuesday and Thursday. There were no social work or physician visits. Thus for that week there were 2 visits provided by the nurse and 2 by the home health aide. Since there were no visits by the social worker or by the physician, there would not be any line items for each of those disciplines.

Example 2: If a hospice patient is receiving routine home care while residing in a nursing home, the hospice would record visits for all of its physicians, nurses, social workers, and home health aides who visit the patient to provide care for the palliation and management of the terminal illness and related conditions, as described in the patient's plan of care. In this example the nursing home is acting as the patient's home. Only the patient care provided by the hospice staff constitutes a visit.

Hospices must enter the following revenue codes, when applicable: 055X Skilled Nursing

Required detail: The earliest date of service this discipline was provided during the delivery of each level of care in each service location, service units which represent the number of visits provided in that location, and a charge amount.

- 056X Medical Social Services

Required detail: The earliest date of service this discipline was provided during the delivery of each level of care in each service location, service units which represent the number of visits provided in that location, and a charge amount.

- 057X Home Health Aide

Required detail: The earliest date of service this discipline was provided during the delivery of each level of care in each service location, service units which represent the number of visits provided in that location, and a charge amount.

Hospices should follow NUBC coding guidelines for the use of the appropriate fourth position (the "X") when reporting these revenue codes.

Visits by registered nurses, licensed vocational nurses and nurse practitioners (unless the nurse practitioner is acting as the beneficiary's attending physician) are reported under revenue code 055X.

All visits to provide care related to the palliation and management of the terminal illness or related conditions, whether provided by hospice employees or provided under arrangement, must be reported. The one exception is related to General Inpatient Care. CMS is not requiring hospices to report visit data at this time for visits made by non-hospice staff providing General Inpatient Care in contract facilities. However, General Inpatient Care visits related to the palliation and management of the terminal illness or related conditions provided by hospice staff in contract facilities must be reported , and all General Inpatient Care visits related to the palliation and management of the terminal illness or related conditions provided in hospice-owned facilities must be reported.

HCPCS/Accommodation Rates/HIPPS Rate Codes

For services provided on or before December 31, 2006, HCPCS codes are required only to report procedures on service lines for attending physician services (revenue 657). Level of care revenue codes (651, 652, 655 or 656) do not require HCPCS coding.

For services provided on or after January 1, 2007, hospices must also report a HCPCS code along with each level of care revenue code (651, 652, 655 and 656) to identify the type of service location where that level of care was provided.

The following HCPCS codes will be used to report the type of service location for hospice services:

HCPCS Code	Definition
Q5001	HOSPICE CARE PROVIDED IN PATIENT'S HOME/RESIDENCE
Q5002	HOSPICE CARE PROVIDED IN ASSISTED LIVING FACILITY
Q5003	HOSPICE CARE PROVIDED IN NURSING LONG TERM CARE FACILITY (LTC) OR NON-SKILLED NURSING FACILITY (NF)
Q5004	HOSPICE CARE PROVIDED IN SKILLED NURSING FACILITY (SNF)
Q5005	HOSPICE CARE PROVIDED IN INPATIENT HOSPITAL
Q5006	HOSPICE CARE PROVIDED IN INPATIENT HOSPICE FACILITY
Q5007	HOSPICE CARE PROVIDED IN LONG TERM CARE HOSPITAL (LTCH)
Q5008	HOSPICE CARE PROVIDED IN INPATIENT PSYCHIATRIC FACILITY
Q5009	HOSPICE CARE PROVIDED IN PLACE NOT OTHERWISE SPECIFIED (NOS)

If care is rendered at multiple locations, each location is to be identified on the claim with a corresponding HCPCS code. For example, routine home care may be provided for a portion of the billing period in the patient's residence and another portion in an assisted living facility. In this case, report one revenue code 651 line with HCPCS code Q5001 and the number of days of routine home care provided in the residence and another revenue code 651 line with HCPCS code Q5002 and the number of days of routine home care provided in the assisted living facility.

- Q5003 is to be used for skilled nursing facility residents in a non Medicare covered stay and nursing facility residents.
- Q5004 is to be used for skilled nursing facility residents in a Medicare covered stay.

These service location HCPCS codes are not required on revenue code lines describing the visits provided under each level of care (e.g. 055X, 056X, 057X).

Service Date The HIPAA standard 837 Institutional claim format requires line item dates of service for all outpatient claims. Medicare classifies hospice claims as outpatient claims (see Chapter 1, Sec.60.4). For services provided on or before December 31, 2006, CMS allows hospices to satisfy the line item date of service requirement by placing any valid date within the FL 6 Statement Covers Period dates on line items on hospice claims.

For services provided on or after January 1, 2007, service date reporting requirements will vary between continuous home care lines (revenue code 652) and other revenue code lines.

Revenue code 652 - report a separately dated line item for each day that continuous home care is provided, reporting the number of hours, or parts of hours rounded to 15-minute increments, of continuous home care that was provided on that date.

Other payment revenue codes - report a separate line for each level of care provided at each service location type, as described in the instructions for HCPCS coding reported above. Hospices report the earliest date that each level of care was provided at each service location. Attending physician services should be individually dated, reporting the date that each HCPCS code billed was delivered.

Non-payment service revenue codes - report dates as described in the table above under Revenue Codes.

Service Units

The hospice enters the number of units for each type of service. Units are measured in days for revenue codes 651, 655, and 656, in hours for revenue code 652, and in procedures for revenue code 657. For services provided on or after January 1, 2007, hours for revenue code 652 are reported in 15-minute increments. For services provided on or after January 1, 2008, units for visit discipline revenue codes are measured by the number of visits.

Total Charges

The hospice enters the total charge for the service described on each revenue code line. This information is being collected for purposes of research and will not affect the amount of reimbursement.

Payer Name

The hospice identifies the appropriate payer(s) for the claim.

National Provider Identifier - Billing Provider

The hospice enters its own National Provider Identifier (NPI).

Principal Diagnosis Code

The hospice enters diagnosis coding as required by ICD-9-CM Coding Guidelines. Hospices may not report V-codes as the primary diagnosis on hospice claims. The principal diagnosis code describes the terminal illness of the hospice patient and V-codes do not describe terminal conditions.

Other Diagnosis Codes

The hospice enters diagnosis coding as required by ICD-9-CM Coding Guidelines.

Attending Provider Name and Identifiers

The hospice enters the National Provider Identifier (NPI) and name of the physician currently responsible for certifying the terminal illness, and signing the individual's plan of care for medical care and treatment.

Other Provider Name and Identifiers

If the attending physician is a nurse practitioner, the hospice enters the NPI and name of the nurse practitioner.

100-4,11,40.1.3.1

Care Plan Oversight

Care plan oversight (CPO) exists where there is physician supervision of patients under care of hospices that require complex and multidisciplinary care modalities involving regular physician development and/or revision of care plans. Implicit in the concept of CPO is the expectation that the physician has coordinated an aspect of the patient's care with the hospice during the month for which CPO services were billed.

For a physician or NP employed by or under arrangement with a hospice agency, CPO functions are incorporated and are part of the hospice per diem payment and as such may not be separately billed.

For information on separately billable CPO services by the attending physician or nurse practitioner see Chapter 12, 180 of this manual.

100-4,12,180

Care Plan Oversight Services

The Medicare Benefit Policy Manual, Chapter 15, contains requirements for coverage for medical and other health services including those of physicians and non-physician practitioners.

Care plan oversight (CPO) is the physician supervision of a patient receiving complex and/or multidisciplinary care as part of Medicare-covered services provided by a participating home health agency or Medicare approved hospice.

CPO services require complex or multidisciplinary care modalities involving: Regular physician development and/or revision of care plans; Review of subsequent reports of patient status; Review of related laboratory and other studies; Communication with other health professionals not employed in the same practice who are involved in the patient's care; Integration of new information into the medical treatment plan; and/or Adjustment of medical therapy.

The CPO services require recurrent physician supervision of a patient involving 30 or more minutes of the physician's time per month. Services not countable toward the 30 minutes threshold that must be provided in order to bill for CPO include, but are not limited to: Time associated with discussions with the patient, his or her family or friends to adjust medication or treatment; Time spent by staff getting or filing charts; Travel time; and/or Physician's time spent telephoning prescriptions into the pharmacist unless the telephone conversation involves discussions of pharmaceutical therapies.

Implicit in the concept of CPO is the expectation that the physician has coordinated an aspect of the patient's care with the home health agency or hospice during the month for which CPO services were billed. The physician who bills for CPO must be the same physician who signs the plan of care.

Nurse practitioners, physician assistants, and clinical nurse specialists, practicing within the scope of State law, may bill for care plan oversight. These non-physician practitioners must have been providing ongoing care for the beneficiary through evaluation and management services. These non-physician practitioners may not bill for CPO if they have been involved only with the delivery of the Medicare-covered home health or hospice service.

A. Home Health CPO

Non-physician practitioners can perform CPO only if the physician signing the plan of care provides regular ongoing care under the same plan of care as does the NPP billing for CPO and either: The physician and NPP are part of the same group practice; or If the NPP is a nurse practitioner or clinical nurse specialist, the physician signing the plan of care also has a collaborative agreement with the NPP; or If the NPP is a physician assistant, the physician signing the plan of care is also the physician who provides general supervision of physician assistant services for the practice.

Billing may be made for care plan oversight services furnished by an NPP when: The NPP providing the care plan oversight has seen and examined the patient; The NPP providing care plan oversight is not functioning as a consultant whose participation is limited to a single medical condition rather than multidisciplinary coordination of care; and The NPP providing care plan oversight integrates his or her care with that of the physician who signed the plan of care.

NPPs may not certify the beneficiary for home health care.

B. Hospice CPO

The attending physician or nurse practitioner (who has been designated as the attending physician) may bill for hospice CPO when they are acting as an "attending physician".

An "attending physician" is one who has been identified by the individual, at the time he/she elects hospice coverage, as having the most significant role in the determination and delivery of their medical care. They are not employed nor paid by the hospice. The care plan oversight services are billed using Form CMS-1500 or electronic equivalent.

For additional information on hospice CPO, see Chapter 11, 40.1.3.1 of this manual.

100-4,12,180.1

Care Plan Oversight Billing Requirements

A. Codes for Which Separate Payment May Be Made

Effective January 1, 1995, separate payment may be made for CPO oversight services for 30 minutes or more if the requirements specified in the Medicare Benefits Policy Manual, Chapter 15 are met.

Providers billing for CPO must submit the claim with no other services billed on that claim and may bill only after the end of the month in which the CPO services were rendered. CPO services may not be billed across calendar months and should be submitted (and paid) only for one unit of service.

Physicians may bill and be paid separately for CPO services only if all the criteria in the Medicare Benefit Policy Manual, Chapter 15 are met.

B. Physician Certification and Recertification of Home Health Plans of Care

Effective 2001, two new HCPCS codes for the certification and recertification and development of plans of care for Medicare-covered home health services were created.

See the Medicare General Information, Eligibility, and Entitlement Manual, Pub. 100-01, Chapter 4, "Physician Certification and Recertification of Services," 10-60, and the Medicare Benefit Policy Manual, Pub. 100-02, Chapter 7, "Home Health Services", 30.

The home health agency certification code can be billed only when the patient has not received Medicare-covered home health services for at least 60 days. The home health agency recertification code is used after a patient has received services for at least 60 days (or one certification period) when the physician signs the certification after the initial certification period. The home health agency recertification code will be reported only once every 60 days, except in the rare situation when the patient starts a new episode before 60 days elapses and requires a new plan of care to start a new episode.

C. Provider Number of Home Health Agency (HHA) or Hospice

For claims for CPO submitted on or after January 1, 1997, physicians must enter on the Medicare claim form the 6-character Medicare provider number of the HHA or hospice providing Medicare-covered services to the beneficiary for the period during which CPO services was furnished and for which the physician signed the plan of care. Physicians are responsible for obtaining the HHA or hospice Medicare provider numbers.

Additionally, physicians should provide their UPIN to the HHA or hospice furnishing services to their patient.

NOTE: There is currently no place on the HIPAA standard ASC X12N 837 professional format to specifically include the HHA or hospice provider number required for a care plan oversight claim. For this reason, the requirement to include the HHA or hospice provider number on a care plan oversight claim is temporarily waived until a new version of this electronic standard format is adopted under HIPAA and includes a place to provide the HHA and hospice provider numbers for care plan oversight claims.

100-4,12,190.3

List of Medicare Telehealth Services

The use of a telecommunications system may substitute for a face-to-face, "hands on" encounter for consultation, office visits, individual psychotherapy, pharmacologic management, psychiatric diagnostic interview examination, end stage renal disease related services, and individual medical nutrition therapy. These services and corresponding current procedure terminology (CPT) or Healthcare Common Procedure Coding System (HCPCS) codes are listed below.

Consultations (CPT codes 99241 - 99275) - Effective October 1, 2001 - December 31, 2005; Consultations (CPT codes 99241 - 99255) - Effective January 1, 2006; Office or other outpatient visits (CPT codes 99201 - 99215); Individual psychotherapy (CPT codes 90804 - 90809); Pharmacologic management (CPT code 90862); and Psychiatric diagnostic interview examination (CPT code 90801) - Effective March 1, 2003.

End Stage Renal Disease (ESRD) related services (HCPCS codes G0308, G0309, G0311, G0312, G0314, G0315, G0317, and G0318) - Effective January 1, 2005.

Individual Medical Nutrition Therapy (HCPCS codes G0270, 97802, and 97803) (Effective January 1, 2006).

Neurobehavioral status exam (CPT code 96116) (Effective January 1, 2008).

100-4,12,190.7

Contractor Editing of Telehealth Claims

Medicare telehealth services (as listed in section 190.3) are billed with either the "GT" or "GQ" modifier. The contractor shall approve covered telehealth services if the physician or practitioner is licensed under State law to provide the service. Contractors must familiarize themselves with licensure provisions of States for which they process claims and disallow telehealth services furnished by physicians or practitioners who are not authorized to furnish the applicable telehealth service under State law. For example, if a nurse practitioner is not licensed to provide individual psychotherapy under State law, he or she would not be permitted to receive payment for individual psychotherapy under Medicare. The contractor shall install edits to ensure that only properly licensed physicians and practitioners are paid for covered telehealth services.

If a contractor receives claims for professional telehealth services coded with the "GQ" modifier (representing "via asynchronous telecommunications system"), it shall approve/pay for these services only if the physician or practitioner is affiliated with a Federal telemedicine demonstration conducted in Alaska or Hawaii. The contractor may require the physician or practitioner at the distant site to document his or her participation in a Federal telemedicine demonstration program conducted in Alaska or Hawaii prior to paying for telehealth services provided via asynchronous, store and forward technologies.

If a contractor denies telehealth services because the physician or practitioner may not bill for them, the contractor uses MSN message 21.18: "This item or service is not covered when performed or ordered by this practitioner." The contractor uses remittance advice message 52 when denying the claim based upon MSN message 21.18.

If a service is billed with one of the telehealth modifiers and the procedure code is not designated as a covered telehealth service, the contractor denies the service using MSN message 9.4: "This item or service was denied because information required to make payment was incorrect." The remittance advice message depends on what is incorrect, e.g., B18 if procedure code or modifier is incorrect, 125 for submission billing errors, 4-12 for difference inconsistencies. The contractor uses B18 as the explanation for the denial of the claim.

The only claims from institutional facilities that FIs shall pay for telehealth services at the distant site, except for MNT services, are for physician or practitioner services when the distant site is located in a CAH that has elected Method II, and the physician or practitioner has reassigned his/her benefits to the CAH. The CAH bills its regular FI for the professional services provided at the distant site via a telecommunications system, in any of the revenue codes 096x, 097x or 098x. All requirements for billing distant site telehealth services apply.

Claims from hospitals or CAHs for MNT services are submitted to the hospital's or CAH's regular FI. Payment is based on the non-facility amount on the Medicare Physician Fee Schedule for the particular HCPCS codes.

100-4,12,210.1

Application of Limitation

B3-2472 - 2472.5

A. Status of Patient

The limitation is applicable to expenses incurred in connection with the treatment of an individual who is not an inpatient of a hospital. Thus, the limitation applies to mental health services furnished to a person in a physician's office, in the patient's home, in a skilled nursing facility, as an outpatient, and so forth. The term "hospital" in this context means an institution, which is primarily engaged in providing to inpatients, by or under the supervision of physician(s): Diagnostic and therapeutic services for medical diagnosis, treatment and care of injured, disabled, or sick persons; Rehabilitation services for injured, disabled, or sick persons; or Psychiatric services for the diagnosis and treatment of mentally ill patients.

B. Disorders Subject to Limitation

The term "mental, psychoneurotic, and personality disorders" is defined as the specific psychiatric conditions described in the American Psychiatric Association's (APA) "Diagnostic and Statistical Manual of Mental Disorders, Third Edition - Revised (DSMIII- R)." When the treatment services rendered are both for a psychiatric condition as defined in the DSM-III-R and one or more nonpsychiatric conditions, separate the expenses for the psychiatric aspects of treatment from the expenses for the nonpsychiatric aspects of treatment. However, in any case in which the psychiatric treatment component is not readily distinguishable from the nonpsychiatric treatment component, all of the expenses are allocated to whichever component constitutes the primary diagnosis.

1. Diagnosis Clearly Meets Definition - If the primary diagnosis reported for a particular service is the same as or equivalent to a condition described in the APA's DSM-III-R, the expense for the service is subject to the limitation except as described in subsection D.
2. Diagnosis Does Not Clearly Meet Definition - When it is not clear whether the primary diagnosis reported meets the definition of mental, psychoneurotic, and personality disorders, it may be necessary to contact the practitioner to clarify the diagnosis. In deciding whether contact is necessary in a given case, give consideration to such factors as the type of services rendered, the diagnosis, and the individual's previous utilization history.

C. Services Subject to Limitation

Carriers apply the limitation to claims for professional services that represent mental health treatment furnished to individuals who are not hospital inpatients by physicians, clinical psychologists, clinical social workers, and other allied health professionals.

Items and supplies furnished by physicians or other mental health practitioners in connection with treatment are also subject to the limitation. (The limitation also applies to CORF claims processed by intermediaries.) Carriers apply the limitation only to treatment services. It does not apply to diagnostic services as described in subsection D. Testing services performed to evaluate a patient's progress during treatment are considered part of treatment and are subject to the limitation.

D. Services Not Subject to Limitation

1. Diagnosis of Alzheimer's Disease or Related Disorder - When the primary diagnosis reported for a particular service is Alzheimer's Disease (coded 331.0 in the "International Classification of Diseases, 9th Revision") or Alzheimer's or other disorders coded 290.XX in the APA's DSM-III-R, carriers look to the nature of the service that has been rendered in determining whether it is subject to the limitation. Typically, treatment provided to a patient with a diagnosis of Alzheimer's Disease or a related disorder represents medical management of the patient's condition (rather than psychiatric treatment) and is not subject to the limitation. However, when the primary treatment rendered to a patient with such a diagnosis is psychotherapy, it is subject to the limitation.
2. Brief Office Visits for Monitoring or Changing Drug Prescriptions - Brief office visits for the sole purpose of monitoring or changing drug prescriptions used in the treatment of mental, psychoneurotic and personality disorders are not subject to the limitation. These visits are reported using HCPCS code M0064 (brief office visit for the sole purpose of monitoring or changing drug prescriptions used in the treatment of mental, psychoneurotic, and personality disorders). Claims where the diagnosis reported is a mental, psychoneurotic, or personality disorder (other than a diagnosis specified in subsection A) are subject to the limitation except for the procedure identified by HCPCS code M0064.
3. Diagnostic Services - Carriers do not apply the limitation to tests and evaluations performed to establish or confirm the patient's diagnosis. Diagnostic services include psychiatric or psychological tests and interpretations, diagnostic consultations, and initial evaluations.

   An initial visit to a practitioner for professional services often combines diagnostic evaluation and the start of therapy. Such a visit is neither solely diagnostic nor solely therapeutic. Therefore, carriers deem the initial visit to be diagnostic so that the limitation does not apply. Separating diagnostic and therapeutic components of a visit is not administratively feasible, unless the practitioner already has separately identified them on the bill. Determining the entire visit to be therapeutic is not justifiable since some diagnostic work must be done before even a tentative diagnosis can be made and certainly before therapy can be instituted. Moreover, the patient should not be disadvantaged because therapeutic as well as diagnostic services were provided in the initial visit. In the rare cases where a practitioner's diagnostic services take more than one visit, carriers do not apply the limitation to the additional visits. However, it is expected such cases are few. Therefore, when a practitioner bills for more than one visit for professional diagnostic services, carriers request documentation to justify the reason for more than one diagnostic visit.
4. Partial Hospitalization Services Not Directly Provided by Physician - The limitation does not apply to partial hospitalization services that are not directly provided by a physician. These services are billed by hospitals and community mental health centers (CMHCs) to intermediaries.

E. Computation of Limitation

Carriers determine the Medicare allowed payment amount for services subject to the limitation.

They:

- Multiply this amount by 0.625;
- Subtract any unsatisfied deductible; and,
- Multiply the remainder by 0.8 to obtain the amount of Medicare payment.

The beneficiary is responsible for the difference between the amount paid by Medicare and the full allowed amount.

EXAMPLE A:

A beneficiary is referred to a Medicare participating psychiatrist who performs a diagnostic evaluation that costs $350. Those services are not subject to the limitation, and they satisfy the deductible. The psychiatrist then conducts 10 weekly therapy sessions for which he/she charges $125 each. The Medicare allowed amount is $90 each, for a total of $900.

Apply the limitation by multiplying 0.625 times $900, which equals $562.50.

Apply regular 20 percent coinsurance by multiplying 0.8 times $562.50, which equals $450 (the amount of Medicare payment).

The beneficiary is responsible for $450 (the difference between Medicare payment and the allowed amount).

EXAMPLE B:

A beneficiary was an inpatient of a psychiatric hospital and was discharged on January 1, 1992. During his/her inpatient stay he/she was diagnosed and therapy was begun under a treatment team that included a clinical psychologist. He/she received post-discharge therapy from the psychologist for 12 sessions, at which point the psychologist administered testing that showed the patient had recovered sufficiently to warrant termination of therapy. The allowed amount for the therapy sessions was $80 each, and the amount for the testing was $125, for a total of $1085. All services in 1992 were subject to the limitation, since the diagnosis had been completed in the hospital and the subsequent testing was a part of therapy.

Apply the limitation by multiplying 0.625 times $1085, which gives $678.13.

Since the deductible must be met for 1992, subtract $100 from $678.13, for a remainder of $578.13.

Determine Medicare payment by multiplying the remainder by 0.8, which equals $462.50.

The beneficiary is responsible for $622.50.

100-4,12,30.4

Cardiovascular System (Codes 92950-93799)

A. Echocardiography Contrast Agents

Effective October 1, 2000, physicians may separately bill for contrast agents used in echocardiography. Physicians should use HCPCS Code A9700 (Supply of Injectable Contrast Material for Use in Echocardiography, per study). The type of service code is 9. This code will be carrier-priced.

B. Electronic Analyses of Implantable Cardioverter-defibrillators and Pacemakers

The CPT codes 93731, 93734, 93741 and 93743 are used to report electronic analyses of single or dual chamber pacemakers and single or dual chamber implantable cardioverterdefibrillators. In the office, a physician uses a device called a programmer to obtain information about the status and performance of the device and to evaluate the patient's cardiac rhythm and response to the implanted device. Advances in information technology now enable physicians to evaluate patients with implanted cardiac devices without requiring the patient to be present in the physician's office. Using a manufacturer's specific monitor/transmitter, a patient can send complete device data and specific cardiac data to a distant receiving station or secure Internet server. The electronic analysis of cardiac device data that is remotely obtained provides immediate and long-term data on the device and clinical data on the patient's cardiac functioning equivalent to that obtained during an in-office evaluation. Physicians should report the electronic analysis of an implanted cardiac device using remotely obtained data as described above with CPT code 93731, 93734, 93741 or 93743, depending on the type of cardiac device implanted in the patient.

100-4,12,60

Payment for Pathology Services

B3-15020, AB-01-47 (CR1499)

A. General Payment Rule

Payment may be made under the fee schedule for the professional component of physician laboratory or physician pathology services furnished to hospital inpatients or outpatients by hospital physicians or by independent laboratories, if they qualify as the reassignee for the physician service.. Payment may be made under the fee schedule, as noted below, for the technical component (TC) of pathology services furnished by an independent laboratory to hospital inpatients or outpatients. Payment may be made under the fee schedule for the technical component of physician pathology services furnished by an independent laboratory, or a hospital if it is acting as an independent laboratory, to non-hospital patients. The Medicare physician fee schedule identifies those physician laboratory or physician pathology services that have a technical component service.

CMS published a final regulation in 1999 that would no longer allow independent laboratories to bill under the physician fee schedule for the TC of physician pathology services. The implementation of this regulation was delayed by Section 542 of the Benefits and Improvement and Protection Act of 2000 (BIPA). Section 542 allows the Medicare carrier to continue to pay for the TC of physician pathology services when an independent laboratory furnishes this service to an inpatient or outpatient of a covered hospital. This provision is applicable to TC services furnished in 2001, 2002, 2003, 2004, 2005 or 2006.

For this provision, a covered hospital is a hospital that had an arrangement with an independent laboratory that was in effect as of July 22, 1999, under which a laboratory furnished the TC of physician pathology services to fee-for-service Medicare beneficiaries who were hospital inpatients or outpatients, and submitted claims for payment for the TC to a carrier. The TC could have been submitted separately or combined with the professional component and reported as a combined service.

The term, fee-for-service Medicare beneficiary, means an individual who:

- Is entitled to benefits under Part A or enrolled under Part B of title XVIII or both; and
- Is not enrolled in any of the following: A Medicare + Choice plan under Part C of such title; a plan offered by an eligible organization under 1876 of the Social Security Act; a program of all-inclusive care for the elderly under 1894; or a social health maintenance organization demonstration project established under Section 4108 of the Omnibus Budget Reconciliation Act of 1987.

In implementing Section 542, the carriers should consider as independent laboratories those entities that it has previously recognized as independent laboratories. An independent laboratory that has acquired another independent laboratory that had an arrangement of July 22, 1999, with a covered hospital, can bill the TC of physician pathology services for that hospital's inpatients and outpatients under the physician fee schedule.

An independent laboratory that furnishes the TC of physician pathology services to inpatients or outpatients of a hospital that is not a covered hospital may not bill the carrier for the TC of physician pathology services during the time 542 is in effect.

If the arrangement between the independent laboratory and the covered hospital limited the provision of TC physician pathology services to certain situations or at particular times, then the independent laboratory can bill the carrier only for these limited services.

The carrier shall require independent laboratories that had an arrangement, on or prior to July 22, 1999 with a covered hospital, to bill for the technical component of physician pathology services to provide a copy of this agreement, or other documentation substantiating that an arrangement was in effect between the hospital and the independent laboratory as of this date. The independent laboratory must submit this documentation for each covered hospital that the independent laboratory services.

See Chapter 16 for additional instruction on laboratory services including clinical diagnostic laboratory services.

Physician laboratory and pathology services are limited to:

- Surgical pathology services;
- Specific cytopathology, hematology and blood banking services that have been identified to require performance by a physician and are listed below;
- Clinical consultation services that meet the requirements in subsection D below; and
- Clinical laboratory interpretation services that meet the requirements and which are specifically listed in subsection E below.

B. Surgical Pathology Services

Surgical pathology services include the gross and microscopic examination of organ tissue performed by a physician, except for autopsies, which are not covered by Medicare. Surgical pathology services paid under the physician fee schedule are reported under the following CPT codes:

88300, 88302, 88304, 88305, 88307, 88309, 88311, 88312, 88313, 88314, 88318, 88319, 88321, 88323, 88325, 88329, 88331, 88332, 88342, 88346, 88347, 88348, 88349, 88355, 88356, 88358, 88361, 88362, 88365, 88380.

Depending upon circumstances and the billing entity, the carriers may pay professional component, technical component or both.

C. Specific Hematology, Cytopathology and Blood Banking Services

Cytopathology services include the examination of cells from fluids, washings, brushings or smears, but generally excluding hematology. Examining cervical and vaginal smears are the most common service in cytopathology. Cervical and vaginal smears do not require interpretation by a physician unless the results are or appear to be abnormal. In such cases, a physician personally conducts a separate microscopic evaluation to determine the nature of an abnormality. This microscopic evaluation ordinarily does require performance by a physician. When medically necessary and when furnished by a physician, it is paid under the fee schedule.

These codes include 88104, 88106, 88107, 88108, 88112, 88125, 88141, 88160, 88161, 88162, 88172, 88173, 88180, 88182.

For services furnished prior to January 1, 1999, carriers pay separately under the physician fee schedule for the interpretation of an abnormal pap smear furnished to a hospital inpatient by a physician. They must pay under the clinical laboratory fee schedule for pap smears furnished in all other situations. This policy also applies to screening pap smears requiring a physician interpretation. For services furnished on or after January 1, 1999, carriers allow separate payment for a physician's interpretation of a pap smear to any patient (i.e., hospital or non-hospital) as long as: (1) the laboratory's screening personnel suspect an abnormality; and (2) the physician reviews and interprets the pap smear.

This policy also applies to screening pap smears requiring a physician interpretation and described in the National Coverage Determination Manual and Chapter 18. These services are reported under codes P3000 or P3001.

Physician hematology services include microscopic evaluation of bone marrow aspirations and biopsies. It also includes those limited number of peripheral blood smears which need to be referred to a physician to evaluate the nature of an apparent abnormality identified by the technologist. These codes include 85060, 38220, 85097, and 38221.

Carriers pay the professional component for the interpretation of an abnormal blood smear (code 85060) furnished to a hospital inpatient by a hospital physician or an independent laboratory.

For the other listed hematology codes, payment may be made for the professional component if the service is furnished to a patient by a hospital physician or independent laboratory. In addition, payment may be made for these services furnished to patients by an independent laboratory.

Codes 38220 and 85097 represent professional-only component services and have no technical component values.

Blood banking services of hematologists and pathologists are paid under the physician fee schedule when analyses are performed on donor and/or patient blood to determine compatible donor units for transfusion where cross matching is difficult or where contamination with transmissible disease of donor is suspected.

The blood banking codes are 86077, 86078, and 86079 and represent professional component only services. These codes do not have a technical component.

D. Clinical Consultation Services

- Clinical consultations are paid under the physician fee schedule only if they:
- Are requested by the patient's attending physician;
- Relate to a test result that lies outside the clinically significant normal or expected range in view of the condition of the patient;
- Result in a written narrative report included in the patient's medical record; and
- Require the exercise of medical judgment by the consultant physician.

Clinical consultations are professional component services only. There is no technical component. The clinical consultation codes are 80500 and 80502.

Routine conversations held between a laboratory director and an attending physician about test orders or results do not qualify as consultations unless all four requirements are met. Laboratory personnel, including the director, may from time to time contact attending physicians to report test results or to suggest additional testing or be contacted by attending physicians on similar matters. These contacts do not constitute clinical consultations. However, if in the course of such a contact, the attending physician requests a consultation from the pathologist, and if that consultation meets the other criteria and is properly documented, it is paid under the fee schedule.

EXAMPLE: A pathologist telephones a surgeon about a patient's suitability for surgery based on the results of clinical laboratory test results. During the course of their conversation, the surgeon ask the pathologist whether, based on test results, patient history and medical records, the patient is a candidate for surgery. The surgeon's request requires the pathologist to render a medical judgment and provide a consultation. The athologist follows up his/her oral advice with a written report and the surgeon notes in the patient's medical record that he/she requested a consultation. This consultation is paid under the fee schedule.

In any case, if the information could ordinarily be furnished by a nonphysician laboratory specialist, the service of the physician is not a consultation payable under the fee schedule.

See the Program Integrity Manual for guidelines for related data analysis to identify inappropriate patterns of billing for consultations.

E. Clinical Laboratory Interpretation Services

Only clinical laboratory interpretation services listed below and which meet the criteria in subsections D.1, D.3, and D.4 for clinical consultations and, as a result, are billable under the fee schedule. These services are reported under the clinical laboratory code with modifier 26. These services can be paid under the physician fee schedule if they are furnished to a patient by a hospital pathologist or an independent laboratory. Note that a hospital's standing order policy can be used as a substitute for the individual request by the patient's attending physician. Carriers are not allowed to revise CMS's list to accommodate local medical practice. The CMS periodically reviews this list and adds or deletes clinical laboratory codes as warranted.

Clinical Laboratory Interpretation Services

Code	Definition
83020	Hemoglobin; electrophoresis
83912	Nucleic acid probe, with electrophoresis, with examination and report
84165	Protein, total, serum; electrophoretic fractionation and quantitation
84181	Protein; Western Blot with interpretation and report, blood or other body fluid
84182	Protein; Western Blot, with interpretation and report, blood or other body fluid, immunological probe for band identification; each
85390	Fibrinolysin; screening
85576	Platelet; aggregation (in vitro), any agent
86255	Fluorescent antibody; screen
86256	Fluorescent antibody; titer
86320	Immunoelectrophoresis; serum, each specimen
86325	Immunoelectrophoresis; other fluids (e.g.urine) with concentration, each specimen
86327	Immunoelectrophoresis; crossed (2 dimensional assay)
86334	Immunofixation electrophoresis
87164	Dark field examination, any source (e.g. penile, vaginal, oral, skin); includes specimen collection
87207	Smear, primary source, with interpretation; special stain for inclusion bodies or intracellular parasites (e.g. malaria, kala azar, herpes)
88371	Protein analysis of tissue by Western Blot, with interpretation and report.
88372	Protein analysis of tissue by Western Blot, immunological probe for band identification, each
89060	Crystal identification by light microscopy with or without polarizing lens analysis, any body fluid (except urine)

100-4,13,140

Bone Mass Measurements (BMMs)

Sections H1861(s)(15)H and H(rr)(1)H of the Social Security Act (the Act) (as added by 4106 of the Balanced Budget Act (BBA) of 1997) standardize Medicare coverage of medically necessary bone mass measurements by providing for uniform coverage under Medicare Part B. This coverage is effective for claims with dates of service furnished on or after July 1, l998.

Effective for dates of service on and after January 1, 2007, the CY 2007 Physician Fee Schedule final rule expanded the number of beneficiaries qualifying for BMM by reducing the dosage requirement for glucocorticoid (steroid) therapy from 7.5 mg of prednisone per day to 5.0 mg. It also changed the definition of BMM by removing coverage for a single-photon absorptiometry as it is not considered reasonable and necessary under section 1862 (a)(1)(A) of the Act. Finally, it required that in the case of monitoring and confirmatory baseline BMMs, they be performed with a dual-energy xray absorptiometry (axial) test.

Conditions of Coverage for BMMs are located in Pub.100-02, Medicare Benefit Policy Manual, chapter 15.

100-4,13,40.1.2

HCPCS Coding Requirements

Providers must report HCPCS codes when submitting claims for MRA of the chest, abdomen, head, neck or peripheral vessels of lower extremities. The following HCPCS codes should be used to report these services:

MRA of head	70544, 70544-26, 70544-TC
MRA of head	70545, 70545-26, 70545-TC
MRA of head	70546, 70546-26, 70546-TC
MRA of neck	70547, 70547-26, 70547-TC
MRA of neck	70548, 70548-26, 70548-TC
MRA of neck	70549, 70549-26, 70549-TC
MRA of chest	71555, 71555-26, 71555-TC
MRA of pelvis	72198, 72198-26, 72198-TC
MRA of abdomen (dates of service on or after July 1, 2003) - see below.	74185, 74185-26, 74185-TC
MRA of peripheral vessels of lower extremities	73725, 73725-26, 73725-TC

Hospitals subject to OPPS should report the following C codes in place of the above HCPCS codes as follows:

- MRA of chest 71555: C8909 - C8911
- MRA of abdomen 74185: C8900 - C8902
- MRA of peripheral vessels of lower extremities 73725: C8912 - C8914

For claims with dates of service on or after July 1, 2003, coverage under this benefit has been expanded for the use of MRA for diagnosing pathology in the renal or aortoiliac arteries. The following HCPCS code should be used to report this expanded coverage of MRA:

- MRA, pelvis, with or without contrast material(s) 72198, 72198-26, 72198-TC

Hospitals subject to OPPS report the following C codes in place of HCPCS code 72198:

- MRA, pelvis, with or without contrast material(s) 72198: C8918 - C8920

Providers utilizing the UB-92 flat file, use record type 61, HCPCS code (Field No. 6) to report HCPCS/CPT code. Providers utilizing the hard copy UB-92, report the HCPCS/CPT code in FL 44 "HCPCS/Rates." Providers utilizing the Medicare A 837 Health Care Claim version 3051 implementations 3A.01 and 1A.C1, report the HCPCS/CPT in 2-395-SV202-02.

100-4,13,60.14

Billing Requirements for PET Scans for Non-Covered Indications

For services performed on or after January 28, 2005, contractors shall accept claims with the following HCPCS code for non-covered PET indications:

- - G0235: PET imaging, any site not otherwise specified

Short Descriptor: PET not otherwise specified

Type of Service: 4

NOTE:This code is for a non-covered service.

100-4,13,60.3

PET Scan Qualifying Conditions and HCPCS Code Chart

Below is a summary of all covered PET scan conditions, with effective dates.

NOTE: The G codes below except those a # can be used to bill for PET Scan services through January 27, 2005. Effective for dates of service on or after January 28, 2005, providers must bill for PET Scan services using the appropriate CPT codes. See section 60.3.1. The G codes with a # can continue to be used for billing after January 28, 2005 and these remain non-covered by Medicare. (NOTE: PET Scanners must be FDA-approved.)

Conditions	Coverage Effective Date	****HCPCS/CPT
*Myocardial perfusion imaging (following previous PET G0030-G0047) single study, rest or stress (exercise and/or pharmacologic)	3/14/95	G0030
*Myocardial perfusion imaging (following previous PET G0030-G0047) multiple studies, rest or stress (exercise and/or pharmacologic)	3/14/95	G0031
*Myocardial perfusion imaging (following rest SPECT, 78464); single study, rest or stress (exercise and/or pharmacologic)	3/14/95	G0032
*Myocardial perfusion imaging (following rest SPECT 78464); multiple studies, rest or stress (exercise and/or pharmacologic)	3/14/95	G0033
*Myocardial perfusion (following stress SPECT 78465); single study, rest or stress (exercise and/or pharmacologic)	3/14/95	G0034
*Myocardial Perfusion Imaging (following stress SPECT 78465); multiple studies, rest or stress (exercise and/or pharmacologic)	3/14/95	G0035

Conditions	Coverage Effective Date	****HCPCS/CPT
*Myocardial Perfusion Imaging (following coronary angiography 93510-93529); single study, rest or stress (exercise and/or pharmacologic)	3/14/95	G0036
*Myocardial Perfusion Imaging, (following coronary angiography), 93510-93529); multiple studies, rest or stress (exercise and/or pharmacologic)	3/14/95	G0037
*Myocardial Perfusion Imaging (following stress planar myocardial perfusion, 78460); single study, rest or stress (exercise and/or pharmacologic)	3/14/95	G0038
*Myocardial Perfusion Imaging (following stress planar myocardial perfusion, 78460); multiple studies, rest or stress (exercise and/or pharmacologic)	3/14/95	G0039
*Myocardial Perfusion Imaging (following stress echocardiogram 93350); single study, rest or stress (exercise and/or pharmacologic)	3/14/95	G0040
*Myocardial Perfusion Imaging (following stress echocardiogram, 93350); multiple studies, rest or stress (exercise and/or pharmacologic)	3/14/95	G0041
*Myocardial Perfusion Imaging (following stress nuclear ventriculogram 78481 or 78483); single study, rest or stress (exercise and/or pharmacologic)	3/14/95	G0042
*Myocardial Perfusion Imaging (following stress nuclear ventriculogram 78481 or 78483); multiple studies, rest or stress (exercise and/or pharmacologic)	3/14/95	G0043
*Myocardial Perfusion Imaging (following stress ECG, 93000); single study, rest or stress (exercise and/or pharmacologic)	3/14/95	G0044
*Myocardial perfusion (following stress ECG, 93000), multiple studies; rest or stress (exercise and/or pharmacologic)	3/14/95	G0045
*Myocardial perfusion (following stress ECG, 93015), single study; rest or stress (exercise and/or pharmacologic)	3/14/95	G0046
*Myocardial perfusion (following stress ECG, 93015); multiple studies, rest or stress (exercise and/or pharmacologic)	3/14/95	G0047
PET imaging regional or whole body; single pulmonary nodule	1/1/98	G0125
Lung cancer, non-small cell (PET imaging whole body) Diagnosis, Initial Staging, Restaging	7/1/01	G0210 G0211 G0212
Colorectal cancer (PET imaging whole body) Diagnosis, Initial Staging, Restaging	7/1/01	G0213 G0214 G0215
Melanoma (PET imaging whole body) Diagnosis, Initial Staging, Restaging	7/1/01	G0216 G0217 G0218
Melanoma for non-covered indications Lymphoma (PET imaging whole body)	7/1/01	#G0219
Diagnosis, Initial Staging, Restaging	7/1/01	G0220 G0221 G0222
Head and neck cancer; excluding thyroid and CNS cancers (PET imaging whole body or regional) Diagnosis, Initial Staging, Restaging	7/1/01	G0223 G0224 G0225

100-4,13,60.3.1

Appropriate CPT Codes Effective for PET Scans for Services Performed on or After January 28, 2005

NOTE: All PET scan services require the use of a radiopharmaceutical diagnostic imaging agent (tracer). The applicable tracer code should be billed when billing for a PET scan service. See section 60.3.2 below for applicable tracer codes.

CPT Code	Description
78459	Myocardial imaging, positron emission tomography (PET), metabolic evaluation
78491	Myocardial imaging, positron emission tomography (PET), perfusion, single study at rest or stress
78492	Myocardial imaging, positron emission tomography (PET), perfusion, multiple studies at rest and/or stress
78608	Brain imaging, positron emission tomography (PET); metabolic evaluation
78811	Tumor imaging, positron emission tomography (PET); limited area (eg, chest, head/neck)
78812	Tumor imaging, positron emission tomography (PET); skull base to mid-thigh
78813	Tumor imaging, positron emission tomography (PET); whole body
78814	Tumor imaging, positron emission tomography (PET) with concurrently acquired computed tomography (CT) for attenuation correction and anatomical localization; limited area (eg, chest, head/neck)
78815	Tumor imaging, positron emission tomography (PET) with concurrently acquired computed tomography (CT) for attenuation correction and anatomical localization; skull base to mid-thigh
78816	Tumor imaging, positron emission tomography (PET) with concurrently acquired computed tomography (CT) for attenuation correction and anatomical localization; whole body

100-4,13,60.3.2

Tracer Codes Required for PET Scans

The following tracer codes are applicable only to CPT 78491 and 78492. They can not be reported with any other code.

Institutional providers billing the fiscal intermediary.

HCPCS	Description
*A9555	Rubidium Rb-82, Diagnostic, Per study dose, Up To 60 Millicuries
* Q3000 (Deleted effective 12/31/05)	Supply of Radiopharmaceutical Diagnostic Imaging Agent, Rubidium Rb-82, per dose
A9526	Nitrogen N-13 Ammonia, Diagnostic, Per study dose, Up To 40 Millicuries

NOTE: For claims with dates of service prior to 1/01/06, providers report Q3000 for supply of radiopharmaceutical diagnostic imaging agent, Rubidium Rb-82. For claims with dates of service 1/01/06 and later, providers report A9555 for radiopharmaceutical diagnostic imaging agent, Rubidium Rb-82 in place of Q3000.

Physicians / practitioners billing the carrier:

HCPCS	Description
*A4641	Supply of Radiopharmaceutical Diagnostic Imaging Agent, Not Otherwise Classified
A9526	Nitrogen N-13 Ammonia, Diagnostic, Per study dose, Up To 40 Millicuries
A9555	Rubidium Rb-82, Diagnostic, Per study dose, Up To 60 Millicuries

*NOTE: Effective January 1, 2008, tracer code A4641 is not applicable for PET Scans.

The following tracer codes are applicable only to CPT 78459, 78608, 78811-78816. They can not be reported with any other code:

Institutional providers billing the fiscal intermediary:

HCPCS	Description
* A9552	Fluorodeoxyglucose F18, FDG, Diagnostic, Per study dose, Up to 45 Millicuries

* C1775 (Deleted effective 12/31/05)	Supply of Radiopharmaceutical Diagnostic Imaging Agent, Fluorodeoxyglucose F18, (2-Deoxy-2-18F Fluoro-D-Glucose), Per dose (4-40 Mci/Ml)
**A4641	Supply of Radiopharmaceutical Diagnostic Imaging Agent, Not Otherwise Classified

* NOTE: For claims with dates of service prior to 1/01/06, OPPS hospitals report C1775 for supply of radiopharmaceutical diagnostic imaging agent, Fluorodeoxyglucose F18. For claims with dates of service 1/01/06 and later, providers report A9552 for radiopharmaceutical diagnostic imaging agent, Fluorodeoxyglucose F18 in place of C1775.

** NOTE: Effective January 1, 2008, tracer code A4641 is not applicable for PET Scans.

Physicians / practitioners billing the carrier:

HCPCS	Description
A9552	Fluorodeoxyglucose F18, FDG, Diagnostic, Per study dose, Up to 45 Millicuries
*A4641	Supply of Radiopharmaceutical Diagnostic Imaging Agent, Not Otherwise Classified

*NOTE: Effective January 1, 2008, tracer code A4641 is not applicable for PET Scans.

100-4,13,60.7.1

Darbepoetin Alfa (Aranesp) Facility Billing Requirements

Revenue code 0636 is used to report Aranesp.

The HCPCS code for aranesp must be included: HCPCS HCPCS Description Dates of Service Q4054 Injection, darbepoetin alfa, 1mcg (for ESRD on Dialysis) 1/1/2004 through 12/31/2005 J0882 Injection, darbepoetin alfa, 1mcg (for ESRD on Dialysis) 1/1/2006 to present The hematocrit reading taken prior to the last administration of Aranesp during the billing period must also be reported on the UB-92/Form CMS-1450 with value code 49. For claims with dates of service on or after April 1, 2006, a hemoglobin reading may be reported on Aranesp claims using value code 48.

Effective January 1, 2006 the definition of value code 48 and 49 used to report the hemoglobin and hematocrit readings are changed to indicate the patient's most recent reading taken before the start of the billing period.

To report a hematocrit or hemoglobin reading for a new patient on or after January 1, 2006, the provider should report the reading that prompted the treatment of darbepoetin alfa. The provider may use results documented on form CMS 2728 or the patient's medical records from a transferring facility.

The payment allowance for Aranesp is the only allowance for the drug and its administration when used for ESRD patients. Effective January 1, 2005, the cost of supplies to administer Aranesp may be billed to the FI. HCPCS A4657 and Revenue Code 270 should be used to capture the charges for syringes used in the administration of Aranesp. The maximum number of administrations of Aranesp for a billing cycle is 5 times in 30/ 31days.

100-4,16,10

Background

B3-2070, B3-2070.1, B3-4110.3, B3-5114

Diagnostic X-ray, laboratory, and other diagnostic tests, including materials and the services of technicians, are covered under the Medicare program. Some clinical laboratory procedures or tests require Food and Drug Administration (FDA) approval before coverage is provided.

A diagnostic laboratory test is considered a laboratory service for billing purposes, regardless of whether it is performed in:

- A physician's office, by an independent laboratory;
- By a hospital laboratory for its outpatients or nonpatients;
- In a rural health clinic; or
- In an HMO or Health Care Prepayment Plan (HCPP) for a patient who is not a member.

When a hospital laboratory performs laboratory tests for nonhospital patients, the laboratory is functioning as an independent laboratory, and still bills the fiscal intermediary (FI). Also, when physicians and laboratories perform the same test, whether manually or with automated equipment, the services are deemed similar. Laboratory services furnished by an independent laboratory are covered under SMI if the laboratory is an approved Independent Clinical Laboratory. However, as is the case of all diagnostic services, in order to be covered these services must be related to a patient's illness or injury (or symptom or complaint) and ordered by a physician. A small number of laboratory tests can be covered as a preventive screening service.

See the Medicare Benefit Policy Manual, Chapter 15, for detailed coverage requirements.

See the Medicare Program Integrity Manual, Chapter 10, for laboratory/supplier enrollment guidelines.

See the Medicare State Operations Manual for laboratory/supplier certification requirements.

100-4,16,60.2

Travel Allowance

In addition to a specimen collection fee allowed under Sec.60.1, Medicare, under Part B, covers a specimen collection fee and travel allowance for a laboratory technician to draw a specimen from either a nursing home patient or homebound patient under Sec.1833(h)(3) of the Act and payment is made based on the clinical laboratory fee schedule. The travel allowance is intended to cover the estimated travel costs of collecting a specimen and to reflect the technician's salary and travel costs.

The additional allowance can be made only where a specimen collection fee is also payable, i.e., no travel allowance is made where the technician merely performs a messenger service to pick up a specimen drawn by a physician or nursing home personnel. The travel allowance may not be paid to a physician unless the trip to the home, or to the nursing home was solely for the purpose of drawing a specimen. Otherwise travel costs are considered to be associated with the other purposes of the trip. The travel allowance is not distributed by CMS. Instead, the carrier must calculate the travel allowance for each claim using the following rules for the particular Code. The following HCPCS codes are used for travel allowances:

- Per Mile Travel Allowance (P9603)
- The minimum "per mile travel allowance" is $1.035. The per mile travel allowance is to be used in situations where the average trip to patients' homes is longer than 20 miles round trip, and is to be pro-rated in situations where specimens are drawn or picked up from non-Medicare patients in the same trip. - one way, in connection with medically necessary laboratory specimen collection drawn from homebound or nursing home bound patient; prorated miles actually traveled (carrier allowance on per mile basis); or
- The per mile allowance was computed using the Federal mileage rate plus an additional 45 cents a mile to cover the technician's time and travel costs. Contractors have the option of establishing a higher per mile rate in excess of the minimum (1.035 cents a mile in CY 2008) if local conditions warrant it. The minimum mileage rate will be reviewed and updated in conjunction with the clinical lab fee schedule as needed. At no time will the laboratory be allowed to bill for more miles than are reasonable or for miles not actually traveled by the laboratory technician.

Example 1: In CY 2008, a laboratory technician travels 60 miles round trip from a lab in a city to a remote rural location, and back to the lab to draw a single Medicare patient's blood. The total reimbursement would be $62.10 (60 miles x 1.035 cents a mile), plus the specimen collection fee.

Example 2: In CY 2008, a laboratory technician travels 40 miles from the lab to a

Medicare patient's home to draw blood, and then travels an additional 10 miles to a non-Medicare patient's home and then travels 30 miles to return to the lab. The total miles traveled would be 80 miles. The claim submitted would be for one half of the miles traveled or $41.40 (40 x 1.035), plus the specimen collection fee.

Flat Rate (P9604)

The CMS will pay a minimum of $9.55 one way flat rate travel allowance. The flat rate travel allowance is to be used in areas where average trips are less than 20 miles round trip. The flat rate travel fee is to be pro-rated for more than one blood drawn at the same address, and for stops at the homes of Medicare and non-Medicare patients. The laboratory does the pro-ration when the claim is submitted based on the number of patients seen on that trip. The specimen collection fee will be paid for each patient encounter.

This rate is based on an assumption that a trip is an average of 15 minutes and up to 10 miles one way. It uses the Federal mileage rate and a laboratory technician's time of $17.66 an hour, including overhead. Contractors have the option of establishing a flat rate in excess of the minimum of $9.55, if local conditions warrant it. The minimum national flat rate will be reviewed and updated in conjunction with the clinical laboratory fee schedule, as necessitated by adjustments in the Federal travel allowance and salaries.

The claimant identifies round trip travel by use of the LR modifier

Example 3: A laboratory technician travels from the laboratory to a single Medicare patient's home and returns to the laboratory without making any other stops. The flat rate would be calculated as follows: 2 x $9.55 for a total trip reimbursement of $19.10, plus the specimen collection fee.

Example 4: A laboratory technician travels from the laboratory to the homes of five patients to draw blood, four of the patients are Medicare patients and one is not. An additional flat rate would be charged to cover the 5 stops and the return trip to the lab (6 x $9.55 = $57.30). Each of the claims submitted would be for $11.46 ($57.30 /5 = $11.46). Since one of the patients is non-

Medicare, four claims would be submitted for $11.46 each, plus the specimen collection fee for each.

Example 5: A laboratory technician travels from a laboratory to a nursing home and draws blood from 5 patients and returns to the laboratory. Four of the patients are on Medicare and one is not. The $9.55 flat rate is multiplied by two to cover the return trip to the laboratory (2 x $9.55 = $19.10) and then divided by five (1/5 of $19.10 = $3.82).

Since one of the patients is non-Medicare, four claims would be submitted for $3.82 each, plus the specimen collection fee.

If a carrier determines that it results in equitable payment, the carrier may extend the former payment allowances for additional travel (such as to a distant rural nursing home) to all circumstances where travel is required. This might be appropriate, for example, if the carrier's former payment allowance was on a per mile basis. Otherwise, it should establish an appropriate allowance and inform the suppliers in its service area. If a carrier decides to establish a new allowance, one method is to consider developing a travel allowance consisting of:

- The current Federal mileage allowance for operating personal automobiles, plus a personnel allowance per mile to cover personnel costs based upon an estimate of average hourly wages and average driving speed.

Carriers must prorate travel allowance amounts claimed by suppliers by the number of patients (including Medicare and non-Medicare patients) from whom specimens were drawn on a given trip.

The carrier may determine that payment in addition to the routine travel allowance determined under this section is appropriate if:

- The patient from whom the specimen must be collected is in a nursing home or is homebound; and
- The clinical laboratory tests are needed on an emergency basis outside the general business hours of the laboratory making the collection.

Subsequent updated travel allowance amounts will be issued by CMS via Recurring Update Notification (RUN) on an annual basis.

100-4,18,10.2.1

Healthcare Common Procedure Coding System (HCPCS) andDiagnosis Codes

Vaccines and their administration are reported using separate codes. The following codes are for reporting the vaccines only.

HCPCS	Definition
90655	Influenza virus vaccine, split virus, preservative free, for children 6-35 months of age, for intramuscular use;
90656	Influenza virus vaccine, split virus, preservative free, for use in individuals 3 years and above, for intramuscular use;
90657	Influenza virus vaccine, split virus, for children 6-35 months of age, for intramuscular use;
90658	Influenza virus vaccine, split virus, for use in individuals 3 years of age and above, for intramuscular use;
90659	Influenza virus vaccine, whole virus, for intramuscular or jet injection use (Discontinued December 31, 2003);
90660	Influenza virus vaccine, live, for intranasal use;
90669	Pneumococcal conjugate vaccine, polyvalent, for children under 5 years, for intramuscular use
90732	Pneumococcal polysaccharide vaccine, 23-valent, adult or immunosuppressed patient dosage, for use in individuals 2 years or older, for subcutaneous or intramuscular use;
90740	Hepatitis B vaccine, dialysis or immunosuppressed patient dosage (3 dose schedule), for intramuscular use;
90743	Hepatitis B vaccine, adolescent (2 dose schedule), for intramuscular use;
90744	Hepatitis B vaccine, pediatric/adolescent dosage (3 dose schedule), for intramuscular use;
90746	Hepatitis B vaccine, adult dosage, for intramuscular use; and
90747	Hepatitis B vaccine, dialysis or immunosuppressed patient dosage (4 dose schedule), for intramuscular use.

The following codes are for reporting administration of the vaccines only. The administration of the vaccines is billed using:

HCPCS	Defintion
G0008	Administration of influenza virus vaccine;
G0009	Administration of pneumococcal vaccine; and
*G0010	Administration of hepatitis B vaccine.
*90471	Immunization administration. (For OPPS hospitals billing for the hepatitis B vaccine administration)
*90472	Each additional vaccine. (For OPPS hospitals billing for the hepatitis B vaccine administration)

* NOTE: For claims with dates of service prior to January 1, 2006, OPPS and non-OPPS hospitals report G0010 for Hepatitis B vaccine administration. For claims with dates of service January 1, 2006 and later, OPPS hospitals report 90471 or 90472 for hepatitis B vaccine administration as appropriate in place of G0010.

One of the following diagnosis codes must be reported as appropriate. If the sole purpose for the visit is to receive a vaccine or if a vaccine is the only service billed on a claim the applicable following diagnosis code may be used.

Diagnosis Code	Description
V03.82	Pneumococcus
V04.81**	Influenza
V06.6***	Pneumococcus and Influenza
V05.3	Hepatitis B

**Effective for influenza virus claims with dates of service October 1, 2003 and later.

***Effective October 1, 2006, providers may report diagnosis code V06.6 on claims for pneumococcus and/or influenza virus vaccines when the purpose of the visit was to receive both vaccines.

If a diagnosis code for pneumococcus, hepatitis B, or influenza virus vaccination is not reported on a claim, contractors may not enter the diagnosis on the claim. Contractors must follow current resolution processes for claims with missing diagnosis codes.

If the diagnosis code and the narrative description are correct, but the HCPCS code is incorrect, the carrier or intermediary may correct the HCPCS code and pay the claim. For example, if the reported diagnosis code is V04.81 and the narrative description (if annotated on the claim) says "flu shot" but the HCPCS code is incorrect, contractors may change the HCPCS code and pay for the flu vaccine. Effective October 1, 2006, carriers/AB MACs should follow the instructions in Pub. 100-04, Chapter 1, Section 80.3.2.1.1 (Carrier Data Element Requirements) for claims submitted without a HCPCS code.

Claims for Hepatitis B vaccinations must report the I.D. Number of referring physician. In addition, if a doctor of medicine or osteopathy does not order the influenza virus vaccine, the intermediary claims require:

UPIN code SLF000 to be reported on claims submitted prior to the date when Medicare will no longer accept identifiers other than NPIs, or

The provider's own NPI to be reported in the NPI field for the attending physician on claims submitted when NPI requirements are implemented.

100-4,18,10.2.2.1

FI Payment for Pneumococcal Pneumonia Virus, InfluenzaVirus, and Hepatitis B Virus Vaccines and Their Administration

Payment for Vaccines

Payment for all of these vaccines is on a reasonable cost basis for hospitals, home health agencies (HHAs), skilled nursing facilities (SNFs), critical access hospitals (CAHs), and hospital-based renal dialysis facilities (RDFs). Payment for comprehensive outpatient rehabilitation facilities (CORFs), Indian Health Service hospitals (IHS), IHS CAHs and independent RDFs is based on 95 percent of the average wholesale price (AWP). Section 10.2.4 of this chapter contains information on payment of these vaccines when provided by RDFs or hospices. See Sec.10.2.2.2 for payment to independent and provider- based Rural Health Centers and Federally Qualified Health Clinics.

Payment for these vaccines is as follows:

Facility	Type of Bill	Payment
Hospitals, other than Indian Health Service (IHS) Hospitals and Critical Access Hospitals (CAHs)	12x, 13x	Reasonable cost
IHS Hospitals	12x, 13x, 83x	95% of AWP
IHS CAHs	85x	95% of AWP
CAHs	85x	Reasonable cost
Method I and Method II		
Skilled Nursing Facilities	22x, 23x	Reasonable cost
Home Health Agencies	34x	Reasonable cost
Comprehensive Outpatient Rehabilitation Facilities	75x	95% of the AWP
Independent Renal Dialysis Facilities	72x	95% of the AWP
Hospital-based Renal Dialysis Facilities	72x	Reasonable cost

Payment for Vaccine Administration

Payment for the administration of Influenza Virus and PPV vaccines is as follows:

Facility	Type of Bill	Payment
Hospitals, other than IHS Hospitals and CAHs	12x, 13x	Outpatient Prospective Payment System (OPPS) for hospitals subject to OPPS Reasonable cost for hospitals not subject to OPPS
IHS Hospitals	12x, 13x, 83x	MPFS as indicated in guidelines below.
IHS CAHs	85x	MPFS as indicated in guidelines below.
CAHs	85x	Reasonable cost
Method I and II		
Skilled Nursing Facilities	22x, 23x	MPFS as indicated in the guidelines below
Home Health Agencies	34x	OPPS
Comprehensive Outpatient Rehabilitation Facilities	75x	MPFS as indicated in the guidelines below
Independent RDFs	72x	MPFS as indicated in the guidelines below
Hospital-based RDFs	72x	Reasonable cost

Guidelines for pricing PPV and Influenza vaccine administration under the MPFS.

Make reimbursement based on the rate in the MPFS associated with the CPT code 90782 or 90471 as follows:

HCPCS code	Effective prior to March 1, 2003	Effective on and after March 1, 2003
G0008	90782	90471
G0009	90782	90471

See Sec.10.2.2.2 for payment to independent and provider based Rural Health Centers and Federally Qualified Health Clinics.

Payment for the administration of Hepatitis B vaccine is as follows:

Facility	Type of Bill	Payment
Hospitals other than IHS hospitals and CAHs	12x, 13x	Outpatient Prospective Payment System (OPPS) for hospitals subject to OPPS Reasonable cost for hospitals not subject to OPPS
IHS Hospitals	12x, 13x, 83x	MPFS as indicated in the guidelines below
CAHs	85x	Reasonable cost
Method I and II		
IHS CAHs	85x	MPFS as indicated in guidelines below.
Skilled Nursing Facilities	22x, 23x	MPFS as indicated in the chart below
Home Health Agencies	34x	OPPS
Comprehensive Outpatient Rehabilitation Facilities	75x	MPFS as indicated in the guidelines below
Independent RDFs	72x	MPFS as indicated in the chart below
Hospital-based RDFs	72x	Reasonable cost

Guidelines for pricing Hepatitis B vaccine administration under the MPFS.

Make reimbursement based on the rate in the MPFS associated with the CPT code 90782 or 90471 as follows:

HCPCS code	Effective prior to March 1, 2003	Effective on and after March 1, 2003
G0010	90782	90471

See Sec.10.2.2.2 for payment to independent and provider based Rural Health Centers and Federally Qualified Health Clinics.

100-4,18,10.2.2.1

FI/AB MAC Payment for Pneumococcal Pneumonia Virus, Influenza Virus, and Hepatitis B Virus Vaccines and Their Administration

Payment for Vaccines

Payment for all of these vaccines is on a reasonable cost basis for hospitals, home health agencies (HHAs), skilled nursing facilities (SNFs), critical access hospitals (CAHs), and hospital-based renal dialysis facilities (RDFs). Payment for comprehensive outpatient rehabilitation facilities (CORFs), Indian Health Service hospitals (IHS), IHS CAHs and independent RDFs is based on 95 percent of the average wholesale price (AWP). Section 10.2.4 of this chapter contains information on payment of these vaccines when provided by RDFs or hospices. See Sec.10.2.2.2 for payment to independent and provider- based Rural Health Centers and Federally Qualified Health Clinics.

Payment for these vaccines is as follows:

Facility	Type of Bill	Payment
Hospitals, other than Indian Health Service (IHS) Hospitals and Critical Access Hospitals (CAHs)	12x, 13x	Reasonable cost
IHS Hospitals	12x, 13x, 83x	95% of AWP
IHS CAHs	85x	95% of AWP
CAHs	85x	Reasonable cost
Method I and Method II		
Skilled Nursing Facilities	22x, 23x	Reasonable cost
Home Health Agencies	34x	Reasonable cost
Comprehensive Outpatient Rehabilitation Facilities	75x	95% of the AWP
Independent Renal Dialysis Facilities	72x	95% of the AWP
Hospital-based Renal Dialysis	72x	Reasonable cost

Facilities

Payment for Vaccine Administration

Payment for the administration of influenza virus and pneumococcal vaccines is as follows:

Facility	Type of Bill	Payment
Hospitals, other than IHS Hospitals and CAHs	12x, 13x	Outpatient Prospective Payment System (OPPS) for hospitals subject to OPPS
Reasonable cost for hospitals not subject to OPPS IHS Hospitals	12x, 13x, 83x	MPFS as indicated in guidelines below.
IHS CAHs	85x	MPFS as indicated in guidelines below.
CAHs Method I and II	85x	Reasonable cost
Skilled Nursing Facilities	22x, 23x	MPFS as indicated in the guidelines below

Facility	Type of Bill	Payment
Home Health Agencies	34x	OPPS
Comprehensive Outpatient Rehabilitation Facilities	75x	MPFS as indicated in the guidelines below
Independent RDFs	72x	MPFS as indicated in the guidelines below
Hospital-based RDFs	72x	Reasonable cost

Guidelines for pricing pneumococcal and influenza virus vaccine administration under the MPFS.

Make reimbursement based on the rate in the MPFS associated with the CPT code 90782 or 90471 as follows:

HCPCS code	Effective prior to March 1, 2003	Effective on and after March 1, 2003
G0008	90782	90471
G0009	90782	90471

See Sec.10.2.2.2 for payment to independent and provider based Rural Health Centers and Federally Qualified Health Clinics.

Payment for the administration of hepatitis B vaccine is as follows:

Facility	Type of Bill	Payment
Hospitals other than IHS hospitals and CAHs	12x, 13x	Outpatient Prospective Payment System (OPPS) for hospitals subject to OPPS
Reasonable cost for hospitals not subject to OPPS IHS Hospitals	12x, 13x, 83x	MPFS as indicated in the guidelines below
CAHs	85x	Reasonable cost
Method I and II		
IHS CAHs	85x	MPFS as indicated in guidelines below.
Skilled Nursing Facilities	22x, 23x	MPFS as indicated in the chart below
Home Health Agencies	34x	OPPS
Comprehensive Outpatient Rehabilitation Facilities	75x	MPFS as indicated in the guidelines below
Independent RDFs	72x	MPFS as indicated in the chart below
Hospital-based RDFs	72x	Reasonable cost

Guidelines for pricing hepatitis B vaccine administration under the MPFS.

Make reimbursement based on the rate in the MPFS associated with the CPT code 90782 or 90471 as follows:

HCPCS code	Effective prior to March 1, 2003	Effective on and after March 1, 2003
G0010	90782	90471

See Sec.10.2.2.2 for payment to independent and provider based Rural Health Centers and Federally Qualified Health Clinics.

100-4,18,10.2.5.2

Carrier/AB MAC Payment Requirements

Payment for pneumococcal, influenza virus, and hepatitis B vaccines follows the same standard rules that are applicable to any injectable drug or biological. (See chapter 17 for procedures for determining the payment rates for pneumococcal and influenza virus vaccines.) Effective for claims with dates of service on or after February 1, 2001, Sec.114, of the Benefits Improvement and Protection Act of 2000 mandated that all drugs and biologicals be paid based on mandatory assignment. Therefore, all providers of influenza virus and pneumococcal vaccines must accept assignment for the vaccine.

Prior to March 1, 2003, the administration of pneumococcal, influenza virus, and hepatitis B vaccines, (HCPCS codes G0008, G0009, and G0010), though not reimbursed directly through the MPFS, were reimbursed at the same rate as HCPCS code 90782 on the MPFS for the year that corresponded to the date of service of the claim.

Prior to March 1, 2003, HCPCS codes G0008, G0009, and G0010 are reimbursed at the same rate as HCPCS code 90471. Assignment for the administration is not mandatory, but is applicable should the provider be enrolled as a provider type "Mass Immunization Roster Biller," submits roster bills, or participates in the centralized billing program.

Carriers/AB MACs may not apply the limiting charge provision for pneumococcal, influenza virus vaccine, or hepatitis B vaccine and their administration in accordance with Secs.1833(a)(1) and 1833(a)(10)(A) of the Social Security Act (the Act.) The administration of the influenza virus vaccine is covered in the influenza virus vaccine benefit under Sec.1861(s)(10)(A) of the Act, rather than under the physicians' services benefit. Therefore, it is not eligible for the 10 percent Health Professional Shortage Area (HPSA) incentive payment or the 5 percent Physician Scarcity Area (PSA) incentive payment.

No Legal Obligation to Pay Nongovernmental entities that provide immunizations free of charge to all patients, regardless of their ability to pay, must provide the immunizations free of charge to Medicare beneficiaries and may not bill Medicare. (See Pub. 100-02, Medicare Benefit Policy Manual, chapter 16.) Thus, for example, Medicare may not pay for influenza virus vaccinations administered to Medicare beneficiaries if a physician provides free vaccinations to all non-Medicare patients or where an employer offers free vaccinations to its employees. Physicians also may not charge Medicare beneficiaries more for a vaccine than they would charge non-Medicare patients. (See Sec.1128(b)(6)(A) of the Act.)

When an employer offers free vaccinations to its employees, it must also offer the free vaccination to an employee who is also a Medicare beneficiary. It does not have to offer free vaccinations to its non-Medicare employees.

Nongovernmental entities that do not charge patients who are unable to pay or reduce their charges for patients of limited means, yet expect to be paid if the patient has health insurance coverage for the services provided, may bill Medicare and expect payment.

Governmental entities (such as PHCs) may bill Medicare for pneumococcal, hepatitis B, and influenza virus vaccines administered to Medicare beneficiaries when services are rendered free of charge to non-Medicare beneficiaries.

100-4,18,10.3.1.1

Centralized Billing for Influenza Virus and Pneumococcal Vaccines to Medicare Carriers/AB MACs

The CMS currently authorizes a limited number of providers to centrally bill for influenza virus and pneumococcal immunization claims. Centralized billing is an optional program available to providers who qualify to enroll with Medicare as the

provider type "Mass Immunization Roster Biller," as well as to other individuals and entities that qualify to enroll as regular Medicare providers. Centralized billers must roster bill, must accept assignment, and must bill electronically.

To qualify for centralized billing, a mass immunizer must be operating in at least three payment localities for which there are three different contractors processing claims. Individuals and entities providing the vaccine and administration must be properly licensed in the State in which the immunizations are given and the contractor must verify this through the enrollment process.

Centralized billers must send all claims for influenza virus and pneumococcal immunizations to a single contractor for payment, regardless of the jurisdiction in which the vaccination was administered. (This does not include claims for the Railroad Retirement Board, United Mine Workers or Indian Health Services. These claims must continue to go to the appropriate processing entity.) Payment is made based on the payment locality where the service was provided. This process is only available for claims for the influenza virus and pneumococcal vaccines and their administration. The general coverage and coding rules still apply to these claims.

This section applies only to those individuals and entities that provide mass immunization services for influenza virus and pneumococcal vaccinations and that have been authorized by CMS to centrally bill. All other providers, including those individuals and entities that provide mass immunization services that are not authorized to centrally bill, must continue to bill for these claims to their regular carrier/AB MAC per the instructions in Sec.10.3.1 of this chapter.

The claims processing instructions in this section apply only to the designated processing contractor. However, all carriers/AB MACs must follow the instructions in Sec.10.3.1.1.J, below, "Provider Education Instructions for All Carriers/AB MACs." A. Processing Contractor Trailblazers Health Enterprises is designated as the sole contractor for the payment of influenza virus and pneumococcal claims for centralized billers from October 1, 2000, through the length of the contract. The CMS central office will notify centralized billers of the appropriate contractor to bill when they receive their notification of acceptance into the centralized billing program.

B. Request for Approval

Approval to participate in the CMS centralized billing program is a two part approval process. Individuals and corporations who wish to enroll as a CMS mass immunizer centralized biller must send their request in writing. CMS will complete Part 1 of the approval process by reviewing preliminary demographic information included in the request for participation letter. Completion of Part 1 is not approval to set up vaccination clinics, vaccinate beneficiaries, and bill Medicare for reimbursement. All new participants must complete Part 2 of the approval process (Form CMS-855 Application) before they may set up vaccination clinics, vaccinate Medicare beneficiaries, and bill Medicare for reimbursement. If an individual or entity's request is approved for centralized billing, the approval is limited to 12 months from September to August 31 of the next year. It is the responsibility of the centralized biller to reapply for approval each year. The designated contractor shall provide in writing to CMS and approved centralized billers notification of completion and approval of Part 2 of the approval process. The designated contractor may not process claims for any centralized biller who has not completed Parts 1 and 2 of the approval process. If claims are submitted by a provider who has not received approval of Parts 1 and 2 of the approval process to participate as a centralized biller, the contractor must return the claims to the provider to submit to the local carrier/AB MAC for payment.

C. Notification of Provider Participation to the Processing Contractor

Before September 1 of every year, CMS will provide the designated contractor with the names of the entities that are authorized to participate in centralized billing for the 12 month period beginning September 1 and ending August 31 of the next year.

D. Enrollment

Though centralized billers may already have a Medicare provider number, for purposes of centralized billing, they must also obtain a provider number from the processing contractor for centralized billing through completion of the Form CMS-855 (Provider Enrollment Application). Providers/suppliers are encouraged to apply to enroll as a centralized biller early as possible. Applicants who have not completed the entire enrollment process and received approval from CMS and the designated contractor to participate as a Medicare mass immunizer centralized biller will not be allowed to submit claims to Medicare for reimbursement.

Whether an entity enrolls as a provider type "Mass Immunization Roster Biller" or some other type of provider, all normal enrollment processes and procedures must be followed. Authorization from CMS to participate in centralized billing is dependent upon the entity's ability to qualify as some type of Medicare provider. In addition, as under normal enrollment procedures, the contractor must verify that the entity is fully qualified and certified per State requirements in each State in which they plan to operate.

The contractor will activate the provider number for the 12-month period from September 1 through August 31 of the following year. If the provider is authorized to participate in the centralized billing program the next year, the contractor will extend the activation of the provider number for another year. The entity need not re-enroll with the contractor every year. However, should there be changes in the States in which the entity plans to operate, the contractor will need to verify that the entity meets all State certification and licensure requirements in those new States.

E. Electronic Submission of Claims on Roster Bills

Centralized billers must agree to submit their claims on roster bills in an Electronic Media Claims standard format using the appropriate version of American National Standards Institute (ANSI) format. Contractors should refer to the appropriate ANSI Implementation Guide to determine the correct location for this information on electronic claims. The processing contractor must provide instructions on acceptable roster billing formats to the approved centralized billers. Paper claims will not be accepted.

F. Required Information on Roster Bills for Centralized Billing

In addition to the roster billing instructions found in Sec.10.3.1 of this chapter, centralized billers must complete on the electronic format the area that corresponds to Item 32 and 33 on Form CMS 1500 (08-05). The contractor must use the ZIP Code in Item 32 to determine the payment locality for the claim. Item 33 must be completed to report the provider of service/supplier's billing name, address, ZIP Code, and telephone number. In addition, the NPI of the billing provider or group must be appropriately reported.

For electronic claims, the name, address, and ZIP Code of the facility are reported in:

- The HIPAA compliant ANSI X12N 837: Claim level loop 2310D NM101=FA. When implemented, the facility (e.g., hospitals) NPI will be captured in the loop 2310D NM109 (NM108=XX) if one is available. Prior to NPI, enter the tax information in loop 2310D NM109 (NM108=24 or 34) and enter the Medicare legacy facility identifier in loop 2310D REF02 (REF01=1C). Report the address, city, state, and ZIP Code in loop 2310D N301 and N401, N402, and N403. Facility data is not required to be reported at the line level for centralized billing.

G. Payment Rates and Mandatory Assignment

The payment rates for the administration of the vaccinations are based on the Medicare Physician Fee Schedule (MPFS) for the appropriate year. Payment made through the MPFS is based on geographic locality. Therefore, payments vary based on the geographic locality where the service was performed.

The HCPCS codes G0008 and G0009 for the administration of the vaccines are not paid on the MPFS. However, prior to March 1, 2003, they must be paid at the same rate as HCPCS code 90782, which is on the MPFS. The designated contractor must pay per the correct MPFS file for each calendar year based on the date of service of the claim. Beginning March 1, 2003, HCPCS codes G0008, G0009, and G0010 are to be reimbursed at the same rate as HCPCS code 90471.

In order to pay claims correctly for centralized billers, the designated contractor must have the correct name and address, including ZIP Code, of the entity where the service was provided.

The following remittance advice and Medicare Summary Notice (MSN) messages apply:

- Claim adjustment reason code 16, "Claim/service lacks information which is needed for adjudication. At least one Remark Code must be provided (may be comprised of either the Remittance Advice Remark Code or NCPDP Reject Reason Code.)" and Remittance advice remark code MA114, "Missing/incomplete/invalid information on where the services were furnished." and MSN 9.4 - "This item or service was denied because information required to make payment was incorrect." The payment rates for the vaccines must be determined by the standard method used by Medicare for reimbursement of drugs and biologicals. (See chapter 17 for procedures for determining the payment rates for vaccines.) Effective for claims with dates of service on or after February 1, 2001, Sec.114, of the Benefits Improvement and Protection Act of 2000 mandated that all drugs and biologicals be paid based on mandatory assignment. Therefore, all providers of influenza virus and pneumococcal vaccines must accept assignment for the vaccine. In addition, as a requirement for both centralized billing and roster billing, providers must agree to accept assignment for the administration of the vaccines as well. This means that they must agree to accept the amount that Medicare pays for the vaccine and the administration. Also, since there is no coinsurance or deductible for the influenza virus and pneumococcal benefit, accepting assignment means that Medicare beneficiaries cannot be charged for the vaccination.

H. Common Working File Information

To identify these claims and to enable central office data collection on the project, special processing number 39 has been assigned. The number should be entered on the HUBC claim record to CWF in the field titled Demonstration Number.

I. Provider Education Instructions for the Processing Contractor

The processing contractor must fully educate the centralized billers on the processes for centralized billing as well as for roster billing. General information on influenza virus and pneumococcal coverage and billing instructions is available on the CMS Web site for providers.

J. Provider Education Instructions for All Carriers/AB MACs

By April 1 of every year, all carriers/AB MACs must publish in their bulletins and put on their Web sites the following notification to providers. Questions from interested providers should be forwarded to the central office address below. Carriers/AB MACs must enter the name of the assigned processing contractor where noted before sending.

NOTIFICATION TO PROVIDERS

Centralized billing is a process in which a provider, who provides mass immunization services for influenza virus and pneumococcal pneumonia virus (PPV) immunizations, can send all claims to a single contractor for payment regardless of the geographic locality in which the vaccination was administered. (This does not include claims for the Railroad Retirement Board, United Mine Workers or Indian Health Services. These claims must continue to go to the appropriate processing entity.) This process is only available for claims for the influenza virus and pneumococcal vaccines and their administration. The administration of the vaccinations is reimbursed at the assigned rate based on the Medicare physician fee schedule for the appropriate locality. The vaccines are reimbursed at the assigned rate using the Medicare standard method for reimbursement of drugs and biologicals.

Individuals and entities interested in centralized billing must contact CMS central office, in writing, at the following address by June 1 of the year they wish to begin centrally billing.

Center for Medicare & Medicaid Services Division of Practitioner Claims Processing Provider Billing and Education Group 7500 Security Boulevard Mail Stop C4-10-07 Baltimore, Maryland 21244 By agreeing to participate in the centralized billing program, providers agree to abide by the following criteria.

CRITERIA FOR CENTRALIZED BILLING

To qualify for centralized billing, an individual or entity providing mass immunization services for influenza virus and pneumococcal vaccinations must provide these services in at least three payment localities for which there are at least three different contractors processing claims.

Individuals and entities providing the vaccine and administration must be properly licensed in the State in which the immunizations are given.

Centralized billers must agree to accept assignment (i.e., they must agree to accept the amount that Medicare pays for the vaccine and the administration).

NOTE: The practice of requiring a beneficiary to pay for the vaccination upfront and to file their own claim for reimbursement is inappropriate. All Medicare providers are required to file claims on behalf of the beneficiary per Sec.1848(g)(4)(A) of the Social Security Act and centralized billers may not collect any payment.

The contractor assigned to process the claims for centralized billing is chosen at the discretion of CMS based on such considerations as workload, user-friendly software developed by the contractor for billing claims, and overall performance. The assigned contractor for this year is [Fill in name of contractor.]

The payment rates for the administration of the vaccinations are based on the Medicare physician fee schedule (MPFS) for the appropriate year. Payment made through the MPFS is based on geographic locality. Therefore, payments received may vary based on the geographic locality where the service was performed. Payment is made at the assigned rate.

The payment rates for the vaccines are determined by the standard method used by Medicare for reimbursement of drugs and biologicals. Payment is made at the assigned rate.

Centralized billers must submit their claims on roster bills in an approved Electronic Media Claims standard format. Paper claims will not be accepted.

Centralized billers must obtain certain information for each beneficiary including name, health insurance number, date of birth, sex, and signature. [Fill in name of contractor] must be contacted prior to the season for exact requirements. The responsibility lies with the centralized biller to submit correct beneficiary Medicare information (including the beneficiary's Medicare Health Insurance Claim Number) as the contractor will not be able to process incomplete or incorrect claims.

Centralized billers must obtain an address for each beneficiary so that a Medicare Summary Notice (MSN) can be sent to the beneficiary by the contractor. Beneficiaries are sometimes confused when they receive an MSN from a contractor other than the contractor that normally processes their claims which results in unnecessary beneficiary inquiries to the Medicare contractor. Therefore, centralized billers must provide every beneficiary receiving an influenza virus or pneumococcal vaccination with the name of the processing contractor. This notification must be in writing, in the form of a brochure or handout, and must be provided to each beneficiary at the time he or she receives the vaccination.

Centralized billers must retain roster bills with beneficiary signatures at their permanent location for a time period consistent with Medicare regulations. [Fill in name of contractor] can provide this information.

Though centralized billers may already have a Medicare provider number, for purposes of centralized billing, they must also obtain a provider number from [Fill in name of contractor]. This can be done by completing the Form CMS-855 (Provider Enrollment Application), which can be obtained from [Fill in name of contractor].

If an individual or entity's request for centralized billing is approved, the approval is limited to the 12 month period from September 1 through August 31 of the following year. It is the responsibility of the centralized biller to reapply to CMS CO for approval each year by June 1. Claims will not be processed for any centralized biller without permission from CMS.

Each year the centralized biller must contact [Fill in name of contractor] to verify understanding of the coverage policy for the administration of the pneumococcal vaccine, and for a copy of the warning language that is required on the roster bill.

The centralized biller is responsible for providing the beneficiary with a record of the pneumococcal vaccination.

The information in items 1 through 8 below must be included with the individual or entity's annual request to participate in centralized billing:

1. Estimates for the number of beneficiaries who will receive influenza virus vaccinations;
2. Estimates for the number of beneficiaries who will receive pneumococcal vaccinations;
3. The approximate dates for when the vaccinations will be given;
4. A list of the States in which influenza virus and pneumococcal clinics will be held;
5. The type of services generally provided by the corporation (e.g., ambulance, home health, or visiting nurse);
6. Whether the nurses who will administer the influenza virus and pneumococcal vaccinations are employees of the corporation or will be hired by the corporation specifically for the purpose of administering influenza virus and pneumococcal vaccinations;
7. Names and addresses of all entities operating under the corporation's application;
8. Contact information for designated contact person for centralized billing program.

100-4,18,10.4.1

In order to prevent duplicate payment by the same FI/AB MAC, CWF edits by line item on the FI/AB MAC number, the beneficiary Health Insurance Claim (HIC) number, and the date of service, the influenza virus procedure codes 90657, 90658, or 90659, the pneumonia procedure code 90732, and the administration codes G0008 or G0009.

If CWF receives a claim with either HCPCS codes 90657, 90658 or 90659, and it already has on record a claim with the same HIC number, same FI/AB MAC number, same date of service, and any one of those HCPCS codes, the second claim submitted to CWF rejects.

If CWF receives a claim with HCPCS code 90732 and it already has on record a claim with the same HIC number, same FI/AB MAC number, same date of service, and the same HCPCS code, the second claim submitted to CWF rejects when all four items match.

If CWF receives a claim with HCPCS administration codes G0008 or G0009 and it already has on record a claim with the same HIC number, same FI/AB MAC number, same date of service, and same procedure code, CWF rejects the second claim submitted when all four items match.

CWF returns to the FI/AB MAC a reject code "7262" for this edit. FIs/AB MACs must deny the second claim and use the same messages they currently use for the denial of duplicate claims.

100-4,18,120.1

Coding and Payment of DSMT Services

The following HCPCS codes are used to report DSMT: G0108 - Diabetes outpatient self-management training services, individual, per 30 minutes.

G0109 - Diabetes outpatient self-management training services, group session (2 or more), per 30 minutes.

The type of service for these codes is 1.

Type of Facility	Payment Method	Type of Bill
Physician (billed to the carrier)	MPFS	NA
Hospitals subject to OPPS	MPFS	12X, 13X
Method I and Method II Critical Access Hospitals (CAHs) (technical services)	101% of reasonable cost	12X and 85X
Indian Health Service (IHS) providers billing hospital outpatient Part B	OMB-approved outpatient per visit all inclusive rate (AIR)	13X
IHS providers billing inpatient Part B	All-inclusive inpatient ancillary per diem rate	12X
IHS CAHs billing outpatient Part B	101% of the all-inclusive facility specific per visit rate	85X
IHS CAHs billing inpatient Part B	101% of the all-inclusive facility specific per diem rate	12X
FQHCs*	All-inclusive encounter rate with other qualified services. Separate visit payment available with HCPCS.	73X
Skilled Nursing Facilities **	MPFS non-facility rate	22X, 23X
Maryland Hospitals under jurisdiction of the Health Services Cost Review Commission (HSCRC)	94% of provider submitted charges in accordance with the terms of the Maryland Waiver	12X, 13X
Home Health Agencies (can be billed only if the service is provided outside of the treatment plan)	MPFS non-facility rate	34X

* Effective January 1, 2006, payment for DSMT provided in an FQHC that meets all of the requirements as above, may be made in addition to one other visit the beneficiary had during the same day, if this qualifying visit is billed on TOB 73X, with HCPCS G0108 or G0109, and revenue codes 0520, 0521, 0522, 0524, 0525, 0527, 0528, or 0900.

** The SNF consolidated billing provision allows separate part B payment for training services for beneficiaries that are in skilled Part A SNF stays, however, the SNF must submit these services on a 22 bill type. Training services provided by other provider types must be reimbursed by X the SNF.

NOTE: An ESRD facility is a reasonable site for this service, however, because it is required to provide dietician and nutritional services as part of the care covered in the composite rate, ESRD facilities are not allowed to bill for it separately and do not receive separate reimbursement. Likewise, an RHC is a reasonable site for this service, however it must be provided in an RHC with other qualifying services and paid at the all-inclusive encounter rate.

Deductible and co-insurance apply.

100-4,18,20.4

Billing Requirements - FI/A/B MAC Claims

Contractors use the weekly-updated MQSA file to verify that the billing facility is certified by the FDA to perform mammography services, and has the appropriate certification to perform the type of mammogram billed (film and/or digital). (See Sec.20.1.) FIs/A/B MACs use the provider number submitted on the claim to identify the facility and use the MQSA data file to verify the facility's certification(s). FIs/A/B MACs complete the following activities in processing mammography claims:

If the provider number on the claim does not correspond with a certified mammography facility on the MQSA file, then intermediaries/A/B MACs deny the claim.

When a film mammography HCPCS code is on a claim, the claim is checked for a "1" film indicator.

If a film mammography HCPCS code comes in on a claim and the facility is certified for film mammography, the claim is paid if all other relevant Medicare criteria are met.

If a film mammography HCPCS code is on a claim and the facility is certified for digital mammography only, the claim is denied.

When a digital mammography HCPCS code is on a claim, the claim is checked for "2" digital indicator.

If a digital mammography HCPCS code is on a claim and the facility is certified for digital mammography, the claim is paid if all other relevant Medicare criteria are met.

If a digital mammography HCPCS code is on a claim and the facility is certified for film mammography only, the claim is denied.

NOTE: The Common Working File (CWF) no longer receives the mammography file for editing purposes.

Except as provided in the following sections for RHCs and FQHCs, the following procedures apply to billing for screening mammographies: The technical component portion of the screening mammography is billed on Form CMS-1450 under bill type 12X, 13X, 14X**, 22X, 23X or 85X using revenue code 0403 and HCPCS code 77057* (76092*).

The technical component portion of the diagnostic mammography is billed on Form CMS-1450 under bill type 12X, 13X, 14X**, 22X, 23X or 85X using revenue code 0401 and HCPCS code 77055* (76090*), 77056* (76091*), G0204 and G0206.

Separate bills are required for claims for screening mammographies with dates of service prior to January 1, 2002. Providers include on the bill only charges for the screening mammography. Separate bills are not required for claims for screening mammographies with dates of service on or after January 1, 2002.

See separate instructions below for rural health clinics (RHCs) and federally qualified health centers (FQHCs).

* For claims with dates of service prior to January 1, 2007, providers report CPT codes 76090, 76091, and 76092. For claims with dates of service January 1, 2007 and later, providers report CPT codes 77055, 77056, and 77057 respectively.

** For claims with dates of service April 1, 2005 and later, hospitals bill for all mammography services under the 13X type of bill or for dates of service April 1, 2007 and later, 12X or 13X as appropriate. The 14X type of bill is no longer applicable. Appropriate bill types for providers other than hospitals are 22X, 23X, and 85X.

In cases where screening mammography services are self-referred and as a result an attending physician NPI is not available, the provider shall duplicate their facility NPI in the attending physician identifier field on the claim.

100-4,18,60.1

Payment

Payment (contractor) is under the MPFS except as follows:

- Fecal occult blood tests (82270* (G0107*) and G0328) are paid under the clinical diagnostic lab fee schedule except reasonable cost is paid to all non-OPPS hospitals, including CAHs, but not IHS hospitals billing on TOB 83x. IHS hospitals billing on TOB 83x are paid the ASC payment amount. Other IHS hospitals (billing on TOB 13x) are paid the OMB approved AIR, or the facility specific per visit amount as applicable. Deductible and coinsurance do not apply for these tests. See section A below for payment to Maryland waiver on TOB 13X. Payment from all hospitals for non-patient laboratory specimens on TOB 14X will be based on the clinical diagnostic fee schedule, including CAHs and Maryland waiver hospitals

Flexible sigmoidoscopy (code G0104) is paid under OPPS for hospital outpatient departments and on a reasonable cost basis for CAHs; or current payment methodologies for hospitals not subject to OPPS.

Colonoscopies (G0105 and G0121) and barium enemas (G0106 and G0120) are paid under OPPS for hospital outpatient departments and on a reasonable costs basis for CAHs or current payment methodologies for hospitals not subject to OPPS. Also colonoscopies may be done in an Ambulatory Surgical Center (ASC) and when done in an ASC the ASC rate applies. The ASC rate is the same for diagnostic and screening colonoscopies. The ASC rate is paid to IHS hospitals when the service is billed on TOB 83x.

Prior to January 1, 2007, deductible and coinsurance apply to HCPCS codes G0104, G0105, G0106, G0120, and G0121. Beginning with services provided on or after January 1, 2007, Section 5113 of the Deficit Reduction Act of 2005 waives the requirement of the annual Part B deductible for these screening services. Coinsurance still applies. Coinsurance and deductible applies to the diagnostic colorectal service codes listed below.

The following screening codes must be paid at rates consistent with the diagnostic codes indicated.

Screening Code	Diagnostic Code
G0104	45330
G0105 and G0121	45378
G0106 and G0120	74280

A. Special Payment Instructions for TOB 13X Maryland Waiver Hospitals

For hospitals in Maryland under the jurisdiction of the Health Services Cost Review Commission, screening colorectal services HCPCS codes G0104, G0105, G0106, 82270* (G0107*), G0120, G0121 and G0328 are paid according to the terms of the waiver, that is 94% of submitted charges minus any unmet existing deductible, co-insurance and non-covered charges. Maryland Hospitals bill TOB 13X for outpatient colorectal cancer screenings.

B. Special Payment Instructions for Non-Patient Laboratory Specimen (TOB 14X) for all hospitals

Payment for colorectal cancer screenings (82270* (G0107*) and G0328) to a hospital for a non-patient laboratory specimen (TOB 14X), is the lesser of the actual charge, the fee schedule amount, or the National Limitation Amount (NLA), (including CAHs and Maryland Waiver hospitals). Part B deductible and coinsurance do not apply.

*NOTE: For claims with dates of service prior to January 1, 2007, physicians, suppliers, and providers report HCPCS code G0107. Effective January 1, 2007, code G0107 is discontinued and replaced with CPT code 82270.

100-4,18,60.2

HCPCS Codes, Frequency Requirements, and Age Requirements (If Applicable)

Effective for services furnished on or after January 1, 1998, the following codes are used for colorectal cancer screening services:

- 82270* (G0107*) - Colorectal cancer screening; fecal-occult blood tests, 1-3 simultaneous determinations;
- G0104 - Colorectal cancer screening; flexible sigmoidoscopy;
- G0105 - Colorectal cancer screening; colonoscopy on individual at high risk;
- G0106 - Colorectal cancer screening; barium enema; as an alternative to G0104, screening sigmoidoscopy;
- G0120 - Colorectal cancer screening; barium enema; as an alternative to G0105, screening colonoscopy.

Effective for services furnished on or after July 1, 2001, the following codes are used for colorectal cancer screening services:

- G0121 - Colorectal cancer screening; colonoscopy on individual not meeting criteria for high risk. Note that the description for this code has been revised to remove the term "noncovered."
- G0122 - Colorectal cancer screening; barium enema (noncovered).

Effective for services furnished on or after January 1, 2004, the following code is used for colorectal cancer screening services as an alternative to 82270* (G0107*):

- G0328 - Colorectal cancer screening; immunoassay, fecal-occult blood test, 1-3 simultaneous determinations

*NOTE: For claims with dates of service prior to January 1, 2007, physicians, suppliers, and providers report HCPCS code G0107. Effective January 1, 2007, code G0107 is discontinued and replaced with CPT code 82270.

- G0104 - Colorectal Cancer Screening; Flexible Sigmoidoscopy

Screening flexible sigmoidoscopies (code G0104) may be paid for beneficiaries who have attained age 50, when performed by a doctor of medicine or osteopathy at the frequencies noted below.

For claims with dates of service on or after January 1, 2002, contractors pay for screening flexible sigmoidoscopies (code G0104) for beneficiaries who have attained age 50 when these services were performed by a doctor of medicine or osteopathy, or by a physician assistant, nurse practitioner, or clinical nurse specialist (as defined in Sec.1861(aa)(5) of the Act and in the Code of Federal Regulations at42 CFR 410.74,410.75, and410.76) at the frequencies noted above. For claims with dates of service prior to January 1, 2002, contractors pay for these services under the conditions noted only when a doctor of medicine or osteopathy performs them.

For services furnished from January 1, 1998, through June 30, 2001, inclusive:

- Once every 48 months (i.e., at least 47 months have passed following the month in which the last covered screening flexible sigmoidoscopy was done).
- For services furnished on or after July 1, 2001:
- Once every 48 months as calculated above unless the beneficiary does not meet the criteria for high risk of developing colorectal cancer (refer to Sec.60.3 of this chapter) and he/she has had a screening colonoscopy (code G0121) within the preceding 10 years. If such a beneficiary has had a screening colonoscopy within the preceding 10 years, then he or she can have covered a screening flexible sigmoidoscopy only after at least 119 months have passed following the month that he/she received the screening colonoscopy (code G0121).

NOTE:If during the course of a screening flexible sigmoidoscopy a lesion or growth is detected which results in a biopsy or removal of the growth; the appropriate diagnostic procedure classified as a flexible sigmoidoscopy with biopsy or removal should be billed and paid rather than code G0104.

G0105 - Colorectal Cancer Screening; Colonoscopy on Individual at High Risk

Screening colonoscopies (code G0105) may be paid when performed by a doctor of medicine or osteopathy at a frequency of once every 24 months for beneficiaries at high risk for developing colorectal cancer (i.e., at least 23 months have passed following the month in which the last covered G0105 screening colonoscopy was performed). Refer to Sec.60.3of this chapter for the criteria to use in determining whether or not an individual is at high risk for developing colorectal cancer.

NOTE:If during the course of the screening colonoscopy, a lesion or growth is detected which results in a biopsy or removal of the growth, the appropriate diagnostic procedure classified as a colonoscopy with biopsy or removal should be billed and paid rather than code G0105.

A. Colonoscopy Cannot be Completed Because of Extenuating Circumstances

1. FIs

   When a covered colonoscopy is attempted but cannot be completed because of extenuating circumstances, Medicare will pay for the interrupted colonoscopy as long as the coverage conditions are met for the incomplete procedure. However, the frequency standards associated with screening colonoscopies will not be applied by CWF. When a covered colonoscopy is next attempted and completed, Medicare will pay for that colonoscopy according to its payment methodology for this procedure as long as coverage conditions are met, and the frequency standards will be applied by CWF. This policy is applied to both screening and diagnostic colonoscopies.

   When submitting a facility claim for the interrupted colonoscopy, providers are to suffix the colonoscopy HCPCS codes with a modifier of "-73" or" -74" as appropriate to indicate that the procedure was interrupted. Payment for covered incomplete screening colonoscopies shall be consistent with payment methodologies currently in place for complete screening colonoscopies, including those contained in42 CFR 419.44(b). In situations where a critical access hospital (CAH) has elected payment Method II for CAH patients, payment shall be consistent with payment methodologies currently in place as outlined in Chapter 3. As such, instruct CAHs that elect Method II payment to use modifier "-53" to identify an incomplete screening colonoscopy (physician professional service(s) billed in revenue code 096X, 097X, and/or 098X). Such CAHs will also bill the technical or facility component of the interrupted colonoscopy in revenue code 075X (or other appropriate revenue code) using the "-73" or "-74" modifier as appropriate.

Note that Medicare would expect the provider to maintain adequate information in the patient's medical record in case it is needed by the contractor to document the incomplete procedure.

2. Carriers

   When a covered colonoscopy is attempted but cannot be completed because of extenuating circumstances (see Chapter 12), Medicare will pay for the interrupted colonoscopy at a rate consistent with that of a flexible sigmoidoscopy as long as coverage conditions are met for the incomplete procedure. When a covered colonoscopy is next attempted and completed, Medicare will pay for that colonoscopy according to its payment methodology for this procedure as long as coverage conditions are met. This policy is applied to both screening and diagnostic colonoscopies.

   When submitting a claim for the interrupted colonoscopy, professional providers are to suffix the colonoscopy code with a modifier of "-53" to indicate that the procedure was interrupted. When submitting a claim for the facility fee associated with this procedure, Ambulatory Surgical Centers (ASCs) are to suffix the colonoscopy code with "-73" or "-74" as appropriate. Payment for covered screening colonoscopies, including that for the associated ASC facility fee when applicable, shall be consistent with payment for diagnostic colonoscopies, whether the procedure is complete or incomplete.

Note that Medicare would expect the provider to maintain adequate information in the patient's medical record in case it is needed by the contractor to document the incomplete procedure.

- G0106 - Colorectal Cancer Screening; Barium Enema; as an Alternative to G0104, Screening Sigmoidoscopy

Screening barium enema examinations may be paid as an alternative to a screening sigmoidoscopy (code G0104). The same frequency parameters for screening sigmoidoscopies (see those codes above) apply. In the case of an individual aged 50 or over, payment may be made for a screening barium enema examination (code G0106) performed after at least 47 months have passed following the month in which the last screening barium enema or screening flexible sigmoidoscopy was performed. For example, the beneficiary received a screening barium enema examination as an alternative to a screening flexible sigmoidoscopy in January 1999. Start counts beginning February 1999. The beneficiary is eligible for another screening barium enema in January 2003. The screening barium enema must be ordered in writing after a determination that the test is the appropriate screening test. Generally, it is expected that this will be a screening double contrast enema unless the individual is unable to withstand such an exam. This means that in the case of a particular individual, the attending physician must determine that the estimated screening potential for the barium enema is equal to or greater than the screening potential that has been estimated for a screening flexible sigmoidoscopy for the same individual. The screening single contrast barium enema also requires a written order from the beneficiary's attending physician in the same manner as described above for the screening double contrast barium enema examination.

- 82270* (G0107*) - Colorectal Cancer Screening; Fecal-Occult Blood Test, 1-3 Simultaneous Determinations

Effective for services furnished on or after January 1, 1998, screening FOBT (code 82270* (G0107*) may be paid for beneficiaries who have attained age 50, and at a frequency of once every 12 months (i.e., at least 11 months have passed following the month in which the last covered screening FOBT was performed). This screening FOBT means a guaiac-based test for peroxidase activity, in which the beneficiary completes it by taking samples from two different sites of three consecutive stools. This screening requires a written order from the beneficiary's attending physician. (The term "attending physician" is defined to mean a doctor of medicine or osteopathy (as defined in Sec.1861(r)(1)of the Act) who is fully knowledgeable about the beneficiary's medical condition, and who would be responsible for using the results of any examination performed in the overall management of the beneficiary's specific medical problem.)

Effective for services furnished on or after January 1, 2004, payment may be made for a immunoassay-based FOBT (G0328, described below) as an alternative to the guaiacbased FOBT, 82270* (G0107*). Medicare will pay for only one covered FOBT per year, either 82270* (G0107*) or G0328, but not both.

*NOTE: For claims with dates of service prior to January 1, 2007, physicians, suppliers, and providers report HCPCS code G0107. Effective January 1, 2007, code G0107 is discontinued and replaced with CPT code 82270.

- G0328 - Colorectal Cancer Screening; Immunoassay, Fecal-Occult Blood Test, 1-3 Simultaneous Determinations

Effective for services furnished on or after January 1, 2004, screening FOBT, (code G0328) may be paid as an alternative to 82270* (G0107*) for beneficiaries who have attained age 50. Medicare will pay for a covered FOBT (either 82270* (G0107*) or G0328, but not both) at a frequency of once every 12 months (i.e., at least 11 months have passed following the month in which the last covered screening FOBT was performed). Screening FOBT, immunoassay, includes the use of a spatula to collect the appropriate number of samples or the use of a special brush for the collection of samples, as determined by the individual manufacturer's instructions. This screening requires a written order from the beneficiary's attending physician. (The term "attending physician" is defined to mean a doctor of medicine or osteopathy (as defined in Sec.1861(r)(1) of the Act) who is fully knowledgeable about the beneficiary's medical condition, and who would be responsible for using the results of any examination performed in the overall management of the beneficiary's specific medical problem.)

- G0120 - Colorectal Cancer Screening; Barium Enema; as an Alternative to or G0105, Screening Colonoscopy

Screening barium enema examinations may be paid as an alternative to a screening colonoscopy (code G0105) examination. The same frequency parameters for screening colonoscopies (see those codes above) apply. In the case of an individual who is at high risk for colorectal cancer, payment may be made for a screening barium enema examination (code G0120) performed after at least 23 months have passed following the month in which the last screening barium enema or the last screening colonoscopy was performed. For example, a beneficiary at high risk for developing colorectal cancer received a screening barium enema examination (code G0120) as an alternative to a screening colonoscopy (code G0105) in January 2000. Start counts beginning February 2000. The beneficiary is eligible for another screening barium enema examination (code G0120) in January 2002. The screening barium enema must be ordered in writing after a determination that the test is the appropriate screening test. Generally, it is expected that this will be a screening double contrast enema unless the individual is unable to withstand such an exam. This means that in the case of a particular individual, the attending physician must determine that the estimated screening potential for the barium enema is equal to or greater than the screening potential that has been estimated for a screening colonoscopy, for the same individual. The screening single contrast barium enema also requires a written order from the beneficiary's attending physician in the same manner as described above for the screening double contrast barium enema examination.

- G0121 - Colorectal Screening; Colonoscopy on Individual Not Meeting Criteria for High Risk - Applicable On and After July 1, 2001

Effective for services furnished on or after July 1, 2001, screening colonoscopies (code G0121) performed on individuals not meeting the criteria for being at high risk for developing colorectal cancer (refer to Sec.60.3 of this chapter) may be paid under the following conditions:

- At a frequency of once every 10 years (i.e., at least 119 months have passed following the month in which the last covered G0121 screening colonoscopy was performed.)

If the individual would otherwise qualify to have covered a G0121 screening colonoscopy based on the above but has had a covered screening flexible sigmoidoscopy (code G0104), then he or she may have covered a G0121 screening colonoscopy only after at least 47 months have passed following the month in which the last covered G0104 flexible sigmoidoscopy was performed.

NOTE:If during the course of the screening colonoscopy, a lesion or growth is detected which results in a biopsy or removal of the growth, the appropriate diagnostic procedure classified as a colonoscopy with biopsy or removal should be billed and paid rather than code G0121.

- G0122 - Colorectal Cancer Screening; Barium Enema

The code is not covered by Medicare.

100-4,18,60.6

Billing Requirements for Claims Submitted to FIs

Follow the general bill review instructions in Chapter 25. Hospitals use the ANSI X12N 837I to bill the FI or on the hardcopy Form CMS-1450. Hospitals bill revenue codes and HCPCS codes as follows:

Screening Test/Procedure	Revenue Code	HCPCS Code	TOB
Fecal Occult blood test	030X	82270*** (G0107***), G0328	13X, 14X**, 22X, 23X, 83X, 85X
Barium enema	032X	G0106, G0120, G0122	13X, 22X, 23X, 85X****
Flexible Sigmoidoscopy	*	G0104	13X, 22X, 23X, 83X, 85X****
Colonoscopy-high risk	*	G0105, G0121	13X, 22X, 23X, 83X, 85X****

* The appropriate revenue code when reporting any other surgical procedure.

** 14X is only applicable for non-patient laboratory specimens.

*** For claims with dates of service prior to January 1, 2007, physicians, suppliers, and providers report HCPCS code G0107. Effective January 1, 2007, code G0107, is discontinued and replaced with CPT code 82270.

**** CAHs that elect Method II bill revenue code 096X, 097X, and/or 098X for professional services and 075X (or other appropriate revenue code) for the technical or facility component.

A Special Billing Instructions for Hospital Inpatients

When these tests/procedures are provided to inpatients of a hospital, they are covered under this benefit. However, the provider bills on bill type 13X using the discharge date of the hospital stay to avoid editing in the Common Working File (CWF) as a result of the hospital bundling rules.

100-4,20,100.2.2

Evidence of Medical Necessity for Parenteral and Enteral Nutrition (PEN) Therapy

The PEN coverage is determined by information provided by the treating physician and the PEN supplier. A completed certification of medical necessity (CMN) must accompany and support initial claims for PEN to establish whether coverage criteria are met and to ensure that the PEN therapy provided is consistent with the attending or ordering physician's prescription.

Contractors ensure that the CMN contains pertinent information from the treating physician. Uniform specific medical data facilitate the review and promote consistency in coverage determinations and timelier claims processing.The medical and prescription information on a PEN CMN can be most appropriatelycompleted by the treating physician or from information in the patient's records by an employee of the physician for the physician's review and signature.

Although PEN suppliers sometimes may assist in providing the PEN services, they cannot complete the CMN since they do not have the same access to patient information needed to properly enter medical or prescription information. Contractors use appropriate professional relations issuances, training sessions, and meetings to ensure that all persons and PEN suppliers are aware of this limitation of their role. When properly completed, the PEN CMN includes the elements of a prescription as well as other data needed to determine whether Medicare coverage is possible. This practice will facilitate prompt delivery of PEN services and timely submittal of the related claim.

100-4,20,160.1

Billing for Total Parenteral Nutrition and Enteral NutritionFurnished to Part B Inpatients

A3-3660.6, SNF-544, SNF-559, SNF-260.4, SNF-261, HHA-403, HO-438, HO-229

Inpatient Part A hospital or SNF care includes total parenteral nutrition (TPN) systems and enteral nutrition (EN).

For inpatients for whom Part A benefits are not payable (e.g., benefits are exhausted or the beneficiary is entitled to Part B only), total parenteral nutrition (TPN) systems and enteral nutrition (EN) delivery systems are covered by Medicare as prosthetic devices when the coverage criteria are met. When these criteria are met, the medical equipment and medical supplies (together with nutrients) being used comprise covered prosthetic devices for coverage purposes rather than durable medical equipment. However, reimbursement rules relating to DME continue to apply to such items.

When a facility supplies TPN or EN systems that meet the criteria for coverage as a prosthetic device to an inpatient whose care is not covered under Part A, the facility must bill one of the DMERCs. Additionally, HHAs, SNFs, and hospitals that provide PEN supplies, equipment and nutrients as a prosthetic device under Part B must use the CMS-1500 or the related NSF or ANSI ASC X12N 837 format to bill the appropriate DMERC. The DMERC is determined according to the residence of the beneficiary. Refer to Sec.10 for jurisdiction descriptions.

FIs return claims containing PEN charges for Part B services where the bill type is 12x, 13x, 22x, 23x, 32x, 33x, or 34x with instructions to the provider to bill the DMERC.

100-4,3,10.4

Payment of Nonphysician Services for Inpatients

All items and nonphysician services furnished to inpatients must be furnished directly by the hospital or billed through the hospital under arrangements. This provision applies to all hospitals, regardless of whether they are subject to PPS.

Other Medical Items, Supplies, and Services the following medical items, supplies, and services furnished to inpatients are covered under Part A. Consequently, they are covered by the prospective payment rate or reimbursed as reasonable costs under Part A to hospitals excluded from PPS.

- Laboratory services (excluding anatomic pathology services and certain clinical pathology services);

- Pacemakers and other prosthetic devices including lenses, and artificial limbs, knees, and hips;
- Radiology services including computed tomography (CT) scans furnished to inpatients by a physician's office, other hospital, or radiology clinic;
- Total parenteral nutrition (TPN) services; and
- Transportation, including transportation by ambulance, to and from another hospital or freestanding facility to receive specialized diagnostic or therapeutic services not available at the facility where the patient is an inpatient.

The hospital must include the cost of these services in the appropriate ancillary service cost center, i.e., in the cost of the diagnostic or therapeutic service. It must not show them separately under revenue code 0540.

EXCEPTIONS

Pneumococcal Vaccine -is payable under Part B only and is billed by the hospital on the Form CMS-1450.

Ambulance Service For purposes of this section "hospital inpatient" means beneficiary who has been formally admitted it does not include a beneficiary who is in the process of being transferred from one hospital to another. Where the patient is transferred from one hospital to another, and is admitted as an inpatient to the second, the ambulance service is payable under only Part B. If transportation is by a hospital owned and operated ambulance, the hospital bills separately on Form CMS-1450 as appropriate. Similarly, if the hospital arranges for the ambulance transportation with an ambulance operator, including paying the ambulance operator, it bills separately. However, if the hospital does not assume any financial responsibility, the billing is to the carrier by the ambulance operator or beneficiary, as appropriate, if an ambulance is used for the transportation of a hospital inpatient to another facility for diagnostic tests or special treatment the ambulance trip is considered part of the DRG, and not separately billable, if the resident hospital is under PPS.

Part B Inpatient Services Where Part A benefits are not payable, payment maybe made to the hospital under Part B for certain medical and other health services. See Chapter 4 for a description of Part B inpatient services.

Anesthetist Services "Incident to" Physician Services

If a physician's practice was to employ anesthetists and to bill on a reasonable charge basis for these services and that practice was in effect as of the last day of the hospital's most recent 12-month cost reporting period ending before September 30, 1983, the physician may continue that practice through cost reporting periods beginning October 1, 1984. However, if the physician chooses to continue this practice, the hospital may not add costs of the anesthetist's service to its base period costs for purposes of its transition payment rates. If it is the existing or new practice of the physician to employ certified registered nurse anesthetists (CRNAs) and other qualified anesthetists and include charges for their services in the physician bills for anesthesiology services for the hospital's cost report periods beginning on or after October 1, 1984, and before October 1, 1987, the physician may continue to do so.

B. Exceptions/Waivers

These provisions were waived before cost reporting periods beginning on or after October1, 1986, under certain circumstances. The basic criteria for waiver was that services furnished by outside suppliers are so extensive that a sudden change in billing practices would threaten the stability of patient care. Specific criteria for waiver and processing procedures are in Sec.2804 of the Provider Reimbursement Manual (CMS Pub. 15-1).

100-4,3,20.7.3

Payment for Blood Clotting Factor Administered to Hemophilia Patients

Section 6011 of Public Law (P.L.) 101-239 amended Sec.1886(a)(4) of the Social Security Act (the Act) to provide that prospective payment system (PPS) hospitals receive anadditional payment for the costs of administering blood clotting factor to Medicare hemophiliacs who are hospital inpatients. Section 6011(b) of P.L. 101.239 specified that the payment be based on a predetermined price per unit of clotting factor multiplied by the number of units provided. This add-on payment originally was effective for blood clotting factors furnished on or after June 19, 1990, and before December 19, 1991. Section 13505 of P. L. 103-66 amended Sec.6011 (d) of P.L. 101-239 to extend the period covered by the add-on payment for blood clotting factors administered to Medicare inpatients with hemophilia through September 30, 1994. Section 4452 of P.L. 105-33 amended Sec.6011(d) of P.L. 101-239 to reinstate the add-on payment for the costs of administering blood clotting factor to Medicare beneficiaries who have hemophilia and who are hospital inpatients for discharges occurring on or after October 1, 1998.

Local carriers shall process non-institutional blood clotting factor claims.

The FIs shall process institutional blood clotting factor claims payable under either Part A or Part B.

A. Inpatient Bills

Under the Inpatient Prospective Payment System (PPS), hospitals receive a special add-on payment for the costs of furnishing blood clotting factors to Medicare beneficiaries with hemophilia, admitted as inpatients of PPS hospitals. The clotting factor add-on payment is calculated using the number of units (as defined in the HCPCS code long descriptor) billed by the provider under special instructions for units of service.

The PPS Pricer software does not calculate the payment amount. The Fiscal Intermediary Standard System (FISS) calculates the payment amount and subtracts the charges from those submitted to Pricer so that the clotting factor charges are not included in cost outlier computations.

Blood clotting factors not paid on a cost or PPS basis are priced as a drug/biological under the Medicare Part B Drug Pricing File effective for the specific date of service. As of January 1, 2005, the average sales price (ASP) plus 6 percent shall be used.

If a beneficiary is in a covered Part A stay in a PPS hospital, the clotting factors are paid in addition to the DRG/HIPPS payment (For FY 2004, this payment is based on 95 percent of average wholesale price.) For a SNF subject to SNF/PPS, the payment is bundled into the SNF/PPS rate.

For SNF inpatient Part A, there is no add-on payment for blood clotting factors.

The codes for blood-clotting factors are found on the Medicare Part B Drug Pricing File. This file is distributed on a quarterly basis.

For discharges occurring on or after October 1, 2000, and before December 31, 2005, report HCPCS Q0187 based on 1 billing unit per 1.2 mg. Effective January 1, 2006, HCPCS code J7189 replaces Q0187 and is defined as 1 billing unit per 1 microgram (mcg).

The examples below include the HCPCS code and indicate the dosage amount specified in the descriptor of that code. Facilities use the units field as a multiplier to arrive at the dosage amount.

EXAMPLE 1

HCPCS Drug Dosage

J7189 Factor VIIa 1 mcg

Actual dosage: 13,365 mcg

On the bill, the facility shows J7189 and 13,365 in the units field (13,365 mcg divided by 1 mcg = 13,365 units).

NOTE:The process for dealing with one international unit (IU) is the same as the process of dealing with one microgram.

EXAMPLE 2

HCPCS Drug Dosage

J9355 Trastuzumab 10 mg

Actual dosage: 140 mg

On the bill, the facility shows J9355 and 14 in the units field (140 mg divided by 10mg = 14 units). When the dosage amount is greater than the amount indicated for the HCPCS code, the facility rounds up to determine units. When the dosage amount is less than the amount indicated for the HCPCS code, use 1 as the unit of measure.

EXAMPLE 3

HCPCS Drug Dosage

J3100 Tenecteplase 50 mg

Actual Dosage: 40 mg

The provider would bill for 1 unit, even though less than 1 full unit was furnished.

At times, the facility provides less than the amount provided in a single use vial and there is waste, i.e.; some drugs may be available only in packaged amounts that exceed the needs of an individual patient. Once the drug is reconstituted in the hospital's pharmacy, it may have a limited shelf life. Since an individual patient may receive less than the fully reconstituted amount, we encourage hospitals to schedule patients in such a way that the hospital can use the drug most efficiently. However, if the hospital must discard the remainder of a vial after administering part of it to a Medicare patient, the provider may bill for the amount of drug discarded plus the amount administered.

Example 1:

Drug X is available only in a 100-unit size. A hospital schedules three Medicare patients to receive drug X on the same day within the designated shelf life of the product. An appropriate hospital staff member administers 30 units to each patient. The remaining 10 units are billed to Medicare on the account of the last patient. Therefore, 30 units are billed on behalf of the first patient seen and 30 units are billed on behalf of the second patient seen. Forty units are billed on behalf of the last patient seen because the hospital had to discard 10 units at that point.

Example 2:

An appropriate hospital staff member must administer 30 units of drug X to a Medicare patient, and it is not practical to schedule another patient who requires the same drug. For example, the hospital has only one patient who requires drug X, or the hospital sees the patient for the first time and did not know the patient's condition. The hospital bills for 100 units on behalf of the patient, and Medicare pays for 100 units.

When the number of units of blood clotting factor administered to hemophiliac inpatients exceeds 99,999, the hospital reports the excess as a second line for revenue code 0636 and repeats the HCPCS code. One hundred thousand fifty (100,050) units are reported on one line as 99,999, and another line shows 1,051.

Revenue Code 0636 is used. It requires HCPCS. Some other inpatient drugs continue to be billed without HCPCS codes under pharmacy.

No changes in beneficiary notices are required. Coverage is applicable to hospital Part A claims only. Coverage is also applicable to inpatient Part B services in SNFs and all types of hospitals, including CAHs. Separate payment is not made to SNFs for beneficiaries in an inpatient Part A stay.

B. FI Action

The FI is responsible for the following:

- It accepts HCPCS codes for inpatient services;
- It edits to require HCPCS codes with Revenue Code 0636. Multiple iterations of the revenue code are possible with the same or different HCPCS codes. It does not edit units except to ensure a numeric value;
- It reduces charges forwarded to Pricer by the charges for hemophilia clotting factors in revenue code 0636. It retains the charges and revenue and HCPCS codes for CWF; and
- It modifies data entry screens to accept HCPCS codes for hospital (including CAH) swing bed, and SNF inpatient claims (bill types 11X, 12X, 18x, 21x and, 22x).

The September 1, 1993, IPPS final rule (58 FR 46304) states that payment will be made for the blood clotting factor only if an ICD-9-CM diagnosis code for hemophilia is included on the bill.

Since inpatient blood-clotting factors are covered only for beneficiaries with hemophilia, the FI must ensure that one of the following hemophilia diagnosis codes is listed on the bill before payment is made:

- 286.0 Congenital factor VIII disorder
- 286.1 Congenital factor IX disorder
- 286.2 Congenital factor IX disorder
- 286.3 Congenital deficiency of other clotting factor
- 286.4 von Willebrands' disease

Effective for discharges on or after August 1, 2001, payment may also be made if one of the following diagnosis codes is reported:

- 286.5 Hemorrhagic disorder due to circulating anticoagulants
- 286.7 Acquired coagulation factor deficiency

C. Part A Remittance Advice

1. X12.835 Ver. 003030M

   For remittance reporting PIP and/or non-PIP payments, the Hemophilia Add on will be reported in a claims level 2-090-CAS segment (CAS is the element identifier) exhibiting an "OA" Group Code and adjustment reason code "97" (payment is included in the allowance for the basic service/ procedure) followed by the associated dollar amount (POSITIVE) and units of service. For this version of the 835, "OA" group coded line level CAS segments are informational and are not included in the balancing routine. The Hemophilia Add On amount will always be included in the 2-010-CLP04 Claim Payment Amount.

   For remittance reporting PIP payments, the Hemophilia Add On will also be reported in the provider level adjustment (element identifier PLB) segment with the provider level adjustment reason code "CA" (Manual claims adjustment) followed by the associated dollar amount (NEGATIVE).

NOTE: A data maintenance request will be submitted to ANSI ASC X12 for a new PLB adjustment reason code specifically for PIP payment Hemophilia Add On situations for future use. However, continue to use adjustment reason code "CA" until further notice.

The FIs enter MA103 (Hemophilia Add On) in an open MIA (element identifier) remark code data element. This will alert the provider that the reason code 97 and PLB code "CA" adjustments are related to the Hemophilia Add On.

2. X12.835 Ver. 003051

   For remittances reporting PIP and/or non-PIP payments, Hemophilia Add On information will be reported in the claim level 2-062-AMT and 2-064-QTY segments. The 2-062-AMT01 element will carry a "ZK" (Federal Medicare claim MANDATE - Category 1) qualifier code followed by the total claim level Hemophilia Add On amount (POSITIVE). The 2-064QTY01 element will carry a "FL" (Units) qualifier code followed by the number of units approved for the Hemophilia Add On for the claim. The Hemophilia Add On amount will always be included in the 2-010-CLP04 Claim Payment Amount.

NOTE: A data maintenance request will be submitted to ANSI ASC X12 for a new AMT qualifier code specifically for the Hemophilia Add On for future use. However, continue to use adjustment reason code "ZK" until further notice.

For remittances reporting PIP payments, the Hemophilia Add On will be reported in the provider level adjustment PLB segment with the provider level adjustment reason "ZZ" followed by the associated dollar amount (NEGATIVE).

NOTE: A data maintenance request will be submitted to ANSI ASC X12 for a new PLB, adjustment reason code specifically for the Hemophilia Add On for future use. However, continue to use PLB adjustment reason code "ZZ" until further notice. The FIs enter MA103 (Hemophilia Add On) in an open MIA remark code data element. This will alert the provider that the ZK, FL and ZZ entries are related to the Hemophilia Add On. (Effective with version 4010 of the 835, report ZK in lieu of FL in the QTY segment.)

3. Standard Hard Copy Remittance Advice

   For paper remittances reporting non-PIP payments involving Hemophilia Add On, add a "Hemophilia Add On" category to the end of the "Pass Thru Amounts" listings in the "Summary" section of the paper remittance. Enter the total of the Hemophilia Add On amounts due for the claims covered by this remittance next to the Hemophilia Add On heading.

   The FIs add the Remark Code "MA103" (Hemophilia Add On) to the remittance advice under the REM column for those claims that qualify for Hemophilia Add On payments.

   This will be the full extent of Hemophilia Add On reporting on paper remittance notices; providers wishing more detailed information must subscribe to the Medicare Part A specifications for the ANSI ASC X12N 835, where additional information is available.

See chapter 22, for detailed instructions and definitions.

100-4,3,40.2.2

Charges to Beneficiaries for Part A Services

The hospital submits a bill even where the patient is responsible for a deductible which covers the entire amount of the charges for non-PPS hospitals, or in PPS hospitals, where the DRG payment amount will be less than the deductible.

A hospital receiving payment for a covered hospital stay (or PPS hospital that includes at least one covered day, or one treated as covered under guarantee of payment or limitation on liability) may charge the beneficiary, or other person, for items and services furnished during the stay only as described in subsections A through H. If limitation of liability applies, a beneficiary's liability for payment is governed by the limitation on liability notification rules in Chapter 30 of this manual. For related notices for inpatient hospitals, see CMS Transmittal 594, Change Request3903, dated June 24, 2005.

A. Deductible and Coinsurance

The hospital may charge the beneficiary or other person for applicable deductible and coinsurance amounts. The deductible is satisfied only by charges for covered services. The FI deducts the deductible and coinsurance first from the PPS payment. Where the deductible exceeds the PPS amount, the excess will be applied to a subsequent payment to the hospital. (See Chapter 3 of the Medicare General Information, Eligibility, and Entitlement Manual for specific policies.)

B. Blood Deductible

The Part A blood deductible provision applies to whole blood and red blood cells, and reporting of the number of pints is applicable to both PPS and non-PPS hospitals. (See Chapter 3 of the Medicare General Information, Eligibility, and Entitlement Manual for specific policies.) Hospitals shall report charges for red blood cells using revenue code 381, and charges for whole blood using revenue code 382.

C. Inpatient Care No Longer Required

The hospital may charge for services that are not reasonable and necessary or that constitute custodial care. Notification may be required under limitation of liability. See CMS Transmittal 594,

Change Request3903, dated June 24, 2005, section V. of the attachment, for specific notification requirements. Note this transmittal will be placed in Chapter 30 of this manual at a future point. Chapter 1, section 150 of this manual also contains related billing information in addition to that provided below.

In general, after proper notification has occurred, and assuming an expedited decision is received from a Quality Improvement Organization (QIO), the following entries are required on the bill the hospital prepares:

- Occurrence code 3l (and date) to indicate the date the hospital notified the patient in accordance with the first bullet above;
- Occurrence span code 76 (and dates) to indicate the period of noncovered care for which it is charging the beneficiary;
- Occurrence span code 77 (and dates) to indicate the period of noncovered care for which the provider is liable, when it is aware of this prior to billing; and
- Value code 3l (and amount) to indicate the amount of charges it may bill the beneficiary for days for which inpatient care was no longer required. They are included as noncovered charges on the bill.

D. Change in the Beneficiary's Condition

If the beneficiary remains in the hospital after receiving notice as described in subsection C, and the hospital, the physician who concurred in the hospital's determination, or the QIO, subsequently determines that the beneficiary again requires inpatient hospital care, the hospital may not charge the beneficiary or other person for services furnished after the beneficiary again required inpatient hospital care until proper notification occurs (see subsection C).

If a patient who needs only a SNF level of care remains in the hospital after the SNF bed becomes available, and the bed ceases to be available, the hospital may continue to charge the beneficiary. It need not provide the beneficiary with another notice when the patient chose not to be discharged to the SNF bed.

E. Admission Denied

If the entire hospital admission is determined to be not reasonable or necessary, limitation of liability may apply. See 2005 CMS transmittal 594, section V. of the attachment, for specific notification requirements.

NOTE: This transmittal will be placed in Chapter 30 of this manual at a future point.

In such cases the following entries are required on the bill:

- Occurrence code 3l (and date) to indicate the date the hospital notified the beneficiary.
- Occurrence span code 76 (and dates) to indicate the period of noncovered care for which the hospital is charging the beneficiary.
- Occurrence span code 77 (and dates) to indicate any period of noncovered care for which the provider is liable (e.g., the period between issuing the notice and the time it may charge the beneficiary) when the provider is aware of this prior to billing.
- Value code 3l (and amount) to indicate the amount of charges the hospital may bill the beneficiary for hospitalization that was not necessary or reasonable. They are included as noncovered charges on the bill.

F. Procedures, Studies and Courses of Treatment That Are Not Reasonable or Necessary

If diagnostic procedures, studies, therapeutic studies and courses of treatment are excluded from coverage as not reasonable and necessary (even though the beneficiary requires inpatient hospital care) the hospital may charge the beneficiary or other person for the services or care according the procedures given in CMS Transmittal 594, Change Request3903, dated June 24, 2005.

The following bill entries apply to these circumstances:

- Occurrence code 32 (and date) to indicate the date the hospital provided the notice to the beneficiary.
- Value code 3l (and amount) to indicate the amount of such charges to be billed to the beneficiary. They are included as noncovered charges on the bill.

G. Nonentitlement Days and Days after Benefits Exhausted

If a hospital stay exceeds the day outlier threshold, the hospital may charge for some, or all, of the days on which the patient is not entitled to Medicare Part A, or after the Part A benefits are exhausted (i.e., the hospital may charge its customary charges for services furnished on those days). It may charge the beneficiary for the lesser of:

- The number of days on which the patient was not entitled to benefits or after the benefits were exhausted; or
- The number of outlier days. (Day outliers were discontinued at the end of FY 1997.)

If the number of outlier days exceeds the number of days on which the patient was not entitled to benefits, or after benefits were exhausted, the hospital may charge for all days on which the patient was not entitled to benefits or after benefits were exhausted. If the number of days on which the beneficiary was not entitled to benefits, or after benefits were exhausted, exceeds the number of outlier days, the hospital determines the days for which it may charge by starting with the last day of the stay (i.e., the day before the day of discharge) and identifying and counting off in reverse order, days on which the patient was not entitled to benefits or after the benefits were exhausted, until the number of days counted off equals the number of outlier days. The days counted off are the days for which the hospital may charge.

H. Contractual Exclusions

In addition to receiving the basic prospective payment, the hospital may charge the beneficiary for any services that are excluded from coverage for reasons other than, or in addition to, absence of medical necessity, provision of custodial care, non-entitlement to Part A, or exhaustion of benefits. For example, it may charge for most cosmetic and dental surgery.

I. Private Room Care

Payment for medically necessary private room care is included in the prospective payment. Where the beneficiary requests private room accommodations, the hospital must inform the beneficiary of the additional charge. (See the Medicare Benefit Policy Manual, Chapter 1.) When the beneficiary accepts the liability, the hospital will supply the service, and bill the beneficiary directly. If the beneficiary believes the private room was medically necessary, the beneficiary has a right to a determination and may initiate a Part A appeal.

J. Deluxe Item or Service

Where a beneficiary requests a deluxe item or service, i.e., an item or service which is more expensive than is medically required for the beneficiary's condition, the hospital may collect the additional charge if it informs the beneficiary of the additional charge. That charge is the difference between the customary charge for the item or service most commonly furnished by the hospital to private pay patients with the beneficiary's condition, and the charge for the more expensive item or service requested. If the beneficiary believes that the more expensive item or service was medically necessary, the beneficiary has a right to a determination and may initiate a Part A appeal.

K - Inpatient Acute Care Hospital Admission Followed By a Death or Discharge Prior To Room Assignment

A patient of an acute care hospital is considered an inpatient upon issuance of written doctor's orders to that effect. If a patient either dies or is discharged prior to being assigned and/or occupying a room, a hospital may enter an appropriate room and board charge on the claim. If a patient leaves of their own volition prior to being assigned and/or occupying a room, a hospital may enter an appropriate room and board charge on the claim as well as a patient status code 07 which indicates they left against medical advice. A hospital is not required to enter a room and board charge, but failure to do so may have a minimal impact on future DRG weight calculations.

100-4,3,40.3

Outpatient Services Treated as Inpatient Services

A3-3610.3, HO-415.6, HO-400D, A-03-008, A-03-013, A-03-054

A. Outpatient Services Followed by Admission Before Midnight of the Following Day (Effective For Services Furnished Before October 1, 1991)

When a beneficiary receives outpatient hospital services during the day immediately preceding the hospital admission, the outpatient hospital services are treated as inpatient services if the beneficiary has Part A coverage. Hospitals and FIs apply this provision only when the beneficiary is admitted to the hospital before midnight of the day following receipt of outpatient services. The day on which the patient is formally admitted as an inpatient is counted as the first inpatient day.

When this provision applies, services are included in the applicable PPS payment and not billed separately. When this provision applies to hospitals and units excluded from the hospital PPS, services are shown on the bill and included in the Part A payment. See Chapter 1 for FI requirements for detecting duplicate claims in such cases.

B. Preadmission Diagnostic Services (Effective for Services Furnished On or After January 1, 1991)

Diagnostic services (including clinical diagnostic laboratory tests) provided to a beneficiary by the admitting hospital, or by an entity wholly owned or wholly operated by the admitting hospital (or by another entity under arrangements with the admitting hospital), within 3 days prior to and including the date of the beneficiary's admission are deemed to be inpatient services and included in the inpatient payment, unless there is no Part A coverage. For example, if a patient is admitted on a Wednesday, outpatient services provided by the hospital on Sunday, Monday, Tuesday, or Wednesday are included in the inpatient Part A payment.

This provision does not apply to ambulance services and maintenance renal dialysis services (see the Medicare Benefit Policy Manual, Chapters 10 and 11, respectively). Additionally, Part A services furnished by skilled nursing facilities, home health agencies, and hospices are excluded from the payment window provisions.

For services provided before October 31, 1994, this provision applies to both hospitals subject to the hospital inpatient prospective payment system (IPPS) as well as those hospitals and units excluded from IPPS.

For services provided on or after October 31, 1994, for hospitals and units excluded from IPPS, this provision applies only to services furnished within one day prior to and including the date of the beneficiary's admission. The hospitals and units that are excluded from IPPS are: psychiatric hospitals and units; inpatient rehabilitation facilities (IRF) and units; long-term care hospitals (LTCH); children's hospitals; and cancer hospitals.

Critical access hospitals (CAHs) are not subject to the 3-day (nor 1-day) DRG payment window.

An entity is considered to be "wholly owned or operated" by the hospital if the hospital is the sole owner or operator. A hospital need not exercise administrative control over a facility in order to operate it. A hospital is considered the sole operator of the facility if the hospital has exclusive responsibility for implementing facility policies (i.e., conducting or overseeing the facility's routine operations), regardless of whether it also has the authority to make the policies.

For this provision, diagnostic services are defined by the presence on the bill of the following revenue and/or CPT codes:

- 0254 - Drugs incident to other diagnostic services
- 0255 - Drugs incident to radiology
- 030X - Laboratory
- 031X - Laboratory pathological
- 032X - Radiology diagnostic
- 0341, 0343 - Nuclear medicine, diagnostic/Diagnostic Radiopharmaceuticals
- 035X - CT scan
- 0371 - Anesthesia incident to Radiology
- 0372 - Anesthesia incident to other diagnostic services
- 040X - Other imaging services
- 046X - Pulmonary function
- 0471 - Audiology diagnostic
- 0481, 0489- Cardiology, Cardiac Catheter Lab/Other Cardiology with CPT codes 93501, 93503, 93505, 93508, 93510, 93526, 93541, 93542, 93543, 93544, 93556, 93561, or 93562 diagnostic
- 0482- Cardiology, Stress Test
- 0483- Cardiology, Echocardiology
- 053X - Osteopathic services
- 061X - MRT
- 062X - Medical/surgical supplies, incident to radiology or other diagnostic services
- 073X - EKG/ECG
- 074X - EEG
- 0918- Testing- Behavioral Health
- 092X - Other diagnostic services

The CWF rejects services furnished January 1, 1991, or later when outpatient bills for diagnostic services with through dates or last date of service (occurrence span code 72) fall on the day of admission or any of the 3 days immediately prior to admission to an IPPS or IPPS-excluded hospital. This reject applies to the bill in process, regardless of whether the outpatient or inpatient bill is processed first. Hospitals must analyze the two bills and report appropriate corrections. For services on or after October 31, 1994, for hospitals and units excluded from IPPS, CWF will reject outpatient diagnostic bills that occur on the day of or one day before admission. For IPPS hospitals, CWF will continue to reject outpatient diagnostic bills for services that occur on the day of or any of the 3 days prior to admission. Effective for dates of service on or after July 1, 2008, CWF will reject diagnostic services when the line item date of service (LIDOS) falls on the day of admission or any of the 3 days immediately prior to an admission to an IPPS hospital or on the day of admission or one day prior to admission for hospitals excluded from IPPS.

Hospitals in Maryland that are under the jurisdiction of the Health Services Cost Review Commission are subject to the 3-day payment window.

C. Other Preadmission Services (Effective for Services Furnished On or After October 1, 1991)

Nondiagnostic outpatient services that are related to a patient's hospital admission and that are provided by the hospital, or by an entity wholly owned or wholly operated by the admitting hospital (or by another entity under arrangements with the admitting hospital), to the patient during the 3 days immediately preceding and including the date of the patient's admission are deemed to be inpatient services and are included in the inpatient payment. Effective March 13, 1998, we defined nondiagnostic preadmission services as being related to the admission only when there is an exact match (for all digits) between the ICD-9-CM principal diagnosis code assigned for both the preadmission services and the inpatient stay. Thus, whenever Part A covers an admission, the hospital may bill nondiagnostic preadmission services to Part B as outpatient services only if they are not related to the admission. The FI shall assume, in the absence of evidence to the contrary, that such bills are not admission related and, therefore, are not deemed to be inpatient (Part A) services. If there are both diagnostic and nondiagnostic preadmission services and the nondiagnostic services are unrelated to the admission, the hospital may separately bill the nondiagnostic preadmission services to Part B. This provision applies only when the patient has Part A coverage. This provision does not apply to ambulance services and maintenance renal dialysis. Additionally, Part A services furnished by skilled nursing facilities, home health agencies, and hospices are excluded from the payment window provisions.

For services provided before October 31, 1994, this provision applies to both hospitals subject to IPPS as well as those hospitals and units excluded from IPPS (see section B above).

For services provided on or after October 31, 1994, for hospitals and units excluded from IPPS, this provision applies only to services furnished within one day prior to and including the date of the beneficiary's admission.

Critical access hospitals (CAHs) are not subject to the 3-day (nor 1-day) DRG payment window.

Hospitals in Maryland that are under the jurisdiction of the Health Services Cost Review Commission are subject to the 3-day payment window.

Effective for dates of service on or after July 1, 2008, CWF will reject therapeutic services when the line item date of service (LIDOS) falls on the day of admission or any of the 3 days immediately prior to an admission to an IPPS hospital or on the day of admission or one day prior to admission for hospitals excluded from IPPS.

100-4,32,100

Billing Requirements for Expanded Coverage of Cochlear Implantation

Effective for dates of services on and after April 4, 2005, the Centers for Medicare & Medicaid Services (CMS) has expanded the coverage for cochlear implantation to cover moderate-to-profound hearing loss in individuals with hearing test scores equal to or less than 40% correct in the best aided listening condition on tape-recorded tests of open-set sentence recognition and who demonstrate limited benefit from amplification. (See Publication 100-03, chapter 1, section 50.3, for specific coverage criteria).

In addition CMS is covering cochlear implantation for individuals with open-set sentence recognition test scores of greater than 40% to less than or equal to 60% correct but only when the provider is participating in, and patients are enrolled in, either:

- A Food and Drug Administration (FDA)-approved category B investigational device exemption (IDE) clinical trial; or
- A trial under the CMS clinical trial policy (see Pub. 100-03, section 310.1); or
- A prospective, controlled comparative trial approved by CMS as consistent with the evidentiary requirements for national coverage analyses and meeting specific quality standards.

100-4,32,50

Deep Brain Stimulation for Essential Tremor and Parkinson‚Äôs Disease

Deep brain stimulation (DBS) refers to high-frequency electrical stimulation of anatomic regions deep within the brain utilizing neurosurgically implanted electrodes. These DBS electrodes are stereotactically placed within targeted nuclei on one (unilateral) or both (bilateral) sides of the brain. There are currently three targets for DBS -- the thalamic ventralis intermedius nucleus (VIM), subthalamic nucleus (STN) and globus pallidus interna (GPi).

Essential tremor (ET) is a progressive, disabling tremor most often affecting the hands. ET may also affect the head, voice and legs. The precise pathogenesis of ET is unknown. While it may start at any age, ET usually peaks within the second and sixth decades. Beta-adrenergic blockers and anticonvulsant medications are usually the first line treatments for reducing the severity of tremor. Many patients, however, do not adequately respond or cannot tolerate these medications. In these medically refractory ET patients, thalamic VIM DBS may be helpful for symptomatic relief of tremor.

Parkinson's disease (PD) is an age-related progressive neurodegenerative disorder involving the loss of dopaminergic cells in the substantia nigra of the midbrain. The disease is characterized by tremor, rigidity, bradykinesia and progressive postural instability. Dopaminergic medication is typically used as a first line treatment for reducing the primary symptoms of PD. However, after prolonged use, medication can become less effective and can produce significant adverse events such as dyskinesias and other motor function complications. For patients who become unresponsive to medical treatments and/or have intolerable side effects from medications, DBS for symptom relief may be considere

100-4,4,160

Clinic and Emergency Visits

CMS has acknowledged from the beginning of the OPPS that CMS believes that CPT Evaluation and Management (E/M) codes were designed to reflect the activities of physicians and do not describe well the range and mix of services provided by hospitals during visits of clinic and emergency department patients. While awaiting the development of a national set of facility-specific codes and guidelines, providers should continue to apply their current internal guidelines to the existing CPT codes. Each hospital's internal guidelines should follow the intent of the CPT code descriptors, in that the guidelines should be designed to reasonably relate the intensity of hospital resources to the different levels of effort represented by the codes. Hospitals should ensure that their guidelines accurately reflect resource distinctions between the five levels of codes.

Effective January 1, 2007, CMS is distinguishing between two types of emergency departments: Type A emergency departments and Type B emergency departments.

A Type A emergency department is defined as an emergency department that is available 24 hours a day, 7 days a week and is either licensed by the State in which it is located under applicable State law as an emergency room or emergency department or it is held out to the public (by name, posted signs, advertising, or other means) as a place that provides care for emergency medical conditions on an urgent basis without requiring a previously scheduled appointment.

A Type B emergency department is defined as an emergency department that meets the definition of a "dedicated emergency department" as defined in 42 CFR 489.24 under the EMTALA regulations. It must meet at least one of the following requirements: (1) It is licensed by the State in which it is located under applicable State law as an emergency room or emergency department; (2) It is held out to the public (by name, posted signs, advertising, or other means) as a place that provides care for emergency medical conditions on an urgent basis without requiring a previously scheduled appointment; or (3) During the calendar year immediately preceding the calendar year in which a determination under 42 CFR 489.24 is being made, based on a representative sample of patient visits that occurred during that calendar year, it provides at least one-third of all of its outpatient visits for the treatment of emergency medical conditions on an urgent basis without requiring a previously-scheduled appointment.

Hospitals must bill for visits provided in Type A emergency departments using CPT emergency department E/M codes. Hospitals must bill for visits provided in Type B emergency departments using the G-codes that describe visits provided in Type B emergency departments.

Hospitals that will be billing the new Type B ED visit codes may need to update their internal guidelines to report these codes.

Emergency department and clinic visits are paid in some cases separately and in other cases as part of a composite APC payment. See section 10.2.1 of this chapter for further details.

100-4,4,160.1

Critical Care Services

Beginning January 1, 2007, critical care services will be paid at two levels, depending on the presence or absence of trauma activation. Providers will receive one payment rate for critical care without trauma activation and will receive additional payment when critical care is associated with trauma activation.

To determine whether trauma activation occurs, follow the National Uniform Billing Committee (NUBC) guidelines in the Claims Processing Manual, Pub 100-04, Chapter 25, Sec.75.4 related to the reporting of the trauma revenue codes in the 68x series. The revenue code series 68x can be used only by trauma centers/hospitals as licensed or designated by the state or local government authority authorized to do so, or as verified by the American College of Surgeons. Different subcategory revenue codes are reported by designated Level 1-4 hospital trauma centers. Only patients for whom there has been prehospital notification based on triage information from prehospital caregivers, who meet either local, state or American College of Surgeons field triage criteria, or are delivered by inter-hospital transfers, and are given the appropriate team response can be billed a trauma activation charge.

When critical care services are provided without trauma activation, the hospital may bill CPT code 99291, Critical care, evaluation and management of the critically ill or critically injured patient; first 30-74 minutes (and 99292, if appropriate). If trauma activation occurs under the circumstances described by the NUBC guidelines that would permit reporting a charge under 68x, the hospital may also bill one unit of code G0390, which describes trauma activation associated with hospital critical care services. Revenue code 68x must be reported on the same date of service. The OCE will edit to ensure that G0390 appears with revenue code 68x on the same date of service and that only one unit of G0390 is billed. CMS believes that trauma activation is a one-time occurrence in association with critical care services, and therefore, CMS will only pay for one unit of G0390 per day.

The CPT code 99291 is defined by CPT as the first 30-74 minutes of critical care. This 30 minute minimum has always applied under the OPPS. The CPT code 99292, Critical care, evaluation and management of the critically ill or critically injured patient; each additional 30 minutes, remains a packaged service under the OPPS, so that hospitals do not have the ongoing administrative burden of reporting precisely the time for each critical service provided. As the CPT guidelines indicate, hospitals that provide less than 30 minutes of critical care should bill for a visit, typically an emergency department visit, at a level consistent with their own internal guidelines.

Under the OPPS, the time that can be reported as critical care is the time spent by a physician and/or hospital staff engaged in active face-to-face critical care of a critically ill or critically injured patient. If the physician and hospital staff or multiple hospital staff members are simultaneously engaged in this active face-to-face care, the time involved can only be counted once.

In CY 2007 hospitals may continue to report a charge with RC 68x without any HCPCS code when trauma team activation occurs. In order to receive additional payment when critical care services are associated with trauma activation, the hospital must report G0390 on the same date of service as RC 68x, in addition to CPT code 99291 (or 99292, if appropriate.)

In CY 2007 hospitals should continue to report 99291 (and 99292 as appropriate) for critical care services furnished without trauma team activation. CPT 99291 maps to APC 0617 (Critical Care). (CPT 99292 is packaged and not paid separately, but should be reported if provided.)

Critical care services are paid in some cases separately and in other cases as part of a composite APC payment. See Section 10.2.1 of this chapter for further details.

100-4,4,200.1

Billing for Corneal Tissue

Corneal tissue will be paid on a cost basis, not under OPPS. To receive cost based reimbursement hospitals must bill charges for corneal tissue using HCPCS code V2785.

100-4,4,200.3.4

Billing for Linear Accelerator (Robotic Image-Guided and Non-Robotic Image-Guided) SRS Planning and Delivery

Effective for services furnished on or after January 1, 2006, hospitals must bill using existing CPT codes that most accurately describe the service furnished for both robotic and non-robotic image-guided SRS planning. For robotic image-guided SRS delivery, hospitals must bill using HCPCS code G0039 for the first session and HCPCS code G0340 for the second through the fifth sessions. For non-robotic image-guided SRS delivery, hospitals must bill G0173 for delivery if the delivery occurs in one session, and G0251 for delivery per session (not to exceed five sessions) if delivery occurs during multiple sessions.

Linear Accelerator-Based Robotic Image-Guided SRS Planning Use existing CPT codes Delivery G0339 (complete, 1P st P session) G0340 (2P nd P - 5P th P session) Linear Accelerator-Based Non-Robotic Image-Guided SRS Planning Use existing CPT codes Delivery G0173 (single session) G0251 (multiple) G0173 Linear accelerator based stereotactic radiosurgery, delivery including collimator changes and custom plugging, complete course of treatment in one session, all lesions.

- G0251 Linear accelerator based stereotactic radiosurgery, delivery including collimator changes and custom plugging, fractionated treatment, all lesions, per session, maximum 5 sessions per course of treatment.
- G0339 Image-guided robotic linear accelerator-based stereotactic radiosurgery, complete course of therapy in one session or first session of fractionated treatment.
- G0340 Image-guided robotic linear accelerator-based stereotactic radiosurgery, delivery including collimator changes and custom plugging, fractionated treatment, all lesions, per session, second through fifth sessions, maximum five sessions per course of treatment.

100-4,4,200.4

Billing for Amniotic Membrane

Hospitals should report HCPCS code V2790 (Amniotic membrane for surgical reconstruction, per procedure) to report amniotic membrane tissue when the tissue is used. A specific procedure code associated with use of amniotic membrane tissue is CPT code 65780 (Ocular surface reconstruction; amniotic membrane transplantation).

Payment for the amniotic membrane tissue is packaged into payment for CPT code 65780 or other procedures with which the amniotic membrane is used.

100-4,4,200.6

Billing and Payment for Alcohol and/or Substance Abuse Assessment and Intervention Services

For CY 2008, the CPT Editorial Panel has created two new Category I CPT codes for reporting alcohol and/or substance abuse screening and intervention services. They are CPT code 99408 (Alcohol and/or substance (other than tobacco) abuse structured screening (e.g., AUDIT, DAST), and brief intervention (SBI) services; 15 to 30 minutes); and CPT code 99409 (Alcohol and/or substance (other than tobacco) abuse structured screening (e.g., AUDIT, DAST), and brief intervention (SBI) services; greater than 30 minutes). However, screening services are not covered by Medicare without specific statutory authority, such as has been provided for mammography, diabetes, and colorectal cancer screening. Therefore, beginning January 1, 2008, the OPPS recognizes two parallel G-codes (HCPCS codes G0396 and G0397) to allow for appropriate reporting and payment of alcohol and substance abuse structured assessment and intervention services that are not provided as screening services, but that are performed in the context of the diagnosis or treatment of illness or injury.

Contractors shall make payment under the OPPS for HCPCS code G0396 (Alcohol and/or substance (other than tobacco) abuse structured assessment (e.g., AUDIT, DAST) and brief intervention, 15 to 30 minutes) and HCPCS code G0397, (Alcohol and/or substance(other than tobacco) abuse structured assessment (e.g., AUDIT, DAST) and intervention greater than 30 minutes), only when reasonable and necessary (i.e., when the service is provided to evaluate patients with signs/symptoms of illness or injury) as per section 1862(a)(1)(A) of the Act.

HCPCS codes G0396 and G0397 are to be used for structured alcohol and/or substance (other than tobacco) abuse assessment and intervention services that are distinct from other clinic and emergency department visit services performed during the same encounter. Hospital resources expended performing services described by HCPCS codes G0396 and G0397 may not be counted as resources for determining the level of a visit service and vice versa (i.e., hospitals may not double count the same facility resources in order to reach a higher level clinic or emergency department visit). However, alcohol and/or substance structured assessment or intervention services lasting less than 15 minutes should not be reported using these HCPCS codes, but the hospital resources expended should be included in determining the level of the visit service reported.

100-4,4,200.7.2

Cardiac Echocardiography With Contrast

Hospitals are instructed to bill for echocardiograms with contrast using the applicable HCPCS code(s) included in Table 200.7.2 below. Hospitals should also report the appropriate units of the HCPCS codes for the contrast agents used in the performance of the echocardiograms.

Table 200.7.2 - HCPCS Codes For Echocardiograms With Contrast HCPCS Long Descriptor C8921 Transthoracic echocardiography with contrast for congenital cardiac anomalies; complete C8922 Transthoracic echocardiography with contrast for congenital cardiac anomalies; follow-up or limited study C8923 Transthoracic echocardiography with contrast, realtime with image documentation (2D) with or without HCPCS Long Descriptor M-mode recording; complete C8924 Transthoracic echocardiography with contrast, realtime with image documentation (2D) with or without M-mode recording; follow-up or limited study C8925 Transesophageal echocardiography (TEE) with contrast, real time with image documentation (2D) (with or without M-mode recording); including probe placement, image acquisition, interpretation and report C8926 Transesophageal echocardiography (TEE) with contrast for congenital cardiac anomalies; including probe placement, image acquisition, interpretation and report C8927 Transesophageal echocardiography (TEE) with contrast for monitoring purposes, including probe placement, real time 2-dimensional image acquisition and interpretation leading to ongoing (continuous) assessment of (dynamically changing) cardiac pumping function and to therapeutic measures on an immediate time basis C8928 Transthoracic echocardiography with contrast, realtime with image documentation (2D), with or without M-mode recording, during rest and cardiovascular stress test using treadmill, bicycle exercise and/or pharmacologically induced stress, with interpretation and report

100-4,4,230.2.1

Administration of Drugs Via Implantable or Portable Pumps

for Implantable or Portable Pumps 2005 CPT Final CY 2006 OPPS 2005 CPT 2005 Description Code Description SI APC n/a n/a C8957 Intravenous infusion for therapy/diagnosis; initiation of prolonged infusion (more than 8 hours), requiring use of portable or implantable pump S 0120 96414 Chemotherapy administration, intravenous; infusion technique, initiation of prolonged infusion (more than 8 hours), requiring the use of a portable or implantable pump 96416 Chemotherapy administration, intravenous infusion technique; initiation of prolonged chemotherapy infusion (more than 8 hours), requiring use of portable or implantable pump S 0117 96425 Chemotherapy administration, infusion technique, initiation of prolonged infusion (more than 8 hours), requiring the use of a portable or implantable pump) 96425 Chemotherapy administration, intra-arterial; infusion technique, initiation of prolonged infusion (more than 8 hours), requiring the use of a portable or implantable pump S 0117 96520 Refilling and maintenance of portable pump 96521 Refilling and maintenance of portable pump T 0125 2005 CPT Final CY 2006 OPPS 2005 CPT 2005 Description Code Description SI APC 96530 Refilling and maintenance of implantable pump or reservoir for drug delivery, systemic [e.g. Intravenous, intra-arterial] 96522 Refilling and maintenance of implantable pump or reservoir for drug delivery, systemic (e.g., intravenous, intra-arterial) T 0125 n/a n/a 96523 Irrigation of implanted venous access device for drug delivery systems N - Hospitals are to report HCPCS code C8957 and CPT codes 96416 and 96425 to indicate the initiation of a prolonged infusion that requires the use of an implantable or portable pump. CPT codes 96521, 92522, and 96523 should be used by hospitals to indicate refilling and maintenance of drug delivery systems or irrigation of implanted venous access devices for such systems, and may be reported for the servicing of devices used for therapeutic drugs other than chemotherapy.

100-4,4,230.2.3

Non-Chemotherapy Drug Administration

Table 5: CY 2006 OPPS Non-Chemotherapy Drug Administration -Intravenous Infusion Technique

2005 CPT	Final CY 2006 OPPS	2005 CPT	2005 Description	Code	Description	SI	APC
90780	Intravenous infusion for therapy/diagnosis, administered by physician or under direct supervision of physician; up to one hour\	C8950	Intravenous infusion for therapy/diagnosis; up to 1 hour	S	0120		
90781	Intravenous infusion for therapy/diagnosis, administered by physician or under direct supervision of physician; each additional hour, up to eight (8) hours (List separately in addition to code for primary procedure)	C8951	Intravenous infusion for therapy/diagnosis; each additional hour (List separately in addition to C8950)	N	-	n/a	n/a
		C8957	Intravenous infusion for therapy/diagnosis; initiation of prolonged infusion (more than 8 hours), requiring use of portable or implantable pump	S	120		

Hospitals are to report HCPCS code C8950 to indicate an infusion of drugs other than anti-neoplastic drugs furnished on or after January 1, 2006 (except as noted at 230.2.2(A) above). HCPCS code C8951 should be used to report all additional infusion hours, with no limit on the number of hours billed per line. Medically necessary separate therapeutic or diagnostic hydration services should be reported with C8950 and C8951, as these are considered intravenous infusions for therapy/diagnosis.

HCPCS codes C8950 and C8951 should not be reported when the infusion is a necessary and integral part of a separately payable OPPS procedure.

When more than one nonchemotherapy drug is infused, hospitals are to code HCPCS codes C8950 and C8951 (if necessary) to report the total duration of an infusion, regardless of the number of substances or drugs infused. Hospitals are reminded to bill separately for each drug infused, in addition to the drug administration services.

The OCE pays one APC for each encounter reported by HCPCS code C8950, and only pays one APC for C8950 per day (unless Modifier 59 is used). Payment for additional hours of infusion reported by HCPCS code C8951 is packaged into the payment for the initial infusion. While no separate payment will be made for units of HCPCS code C8951, hospitals are instructed to report all codes that appropriately describe the services provided and the corresponding charges so that CMS may capture specific historical hospital cost data for future payment rate setting activities.

OCE logic assumes that all services for non-chemotherapy infusions billed on the same date of service were provided during the same encounter. Where a beneficiary makes two separate visits to the hospital for non-chemotherapy infusions in the same day, hospitals are to report modifier 59 for non-chemotherapy infusion codes during the second encounter that were also furnished in the first encounter. The OCE identifies modifier 59 and pays up to a maximum number of units per day, as listed in Table 1.

EXAMPLE 1

A beneficiary receives infused drugs that are not anti-neoplastic drugs (including hydrating solutions) for 2 hours. The hospital reports one unit of HCPCS code C8950 and one unit of HCPCS code C8951. The OCE will pay one unit of APC 0120. Payment for the unit of HCPCS code C8951 is packaged into the payment for one unit of APC 0120. (NOTE: See 230.1 for drug billing instructions.)

EXAMPLE 2

A beneficiary receives infused drugs that are not anti-neoplastic drugs (including hydrating solutions) for 12 hours. The hospital reports one unit of HCPCS code C8950 and eleven units of HCPCS code C8951. The OCE will pay one unit of APC 0120. Payment for the 11 units of HCPCS code C8951 is packaged into the payment for one unit of APC 0120. (NOTE: See 230.1 for drug billing instructions.)

EXAMPLE 3

A beneficiary experiences multiple attempts to initiate an intravenous infusion before a successful infusion is started 20 minutes after the first attempt. Once started, the infusion lasts one hour. The hospital reports one unit of HCPCS code C8950 to identify the 1 hour of infusion time. The 20 minutes spent prior to the infusion attempting to establish an IV line are not separately billable in the OPPS. The OCE pays one unit of APC 0120. (NOTE: See 230.1 for drug billing instructions.)

B. Administration of Non-Chemotherapy Drugs by a Route Other Than Intravenous Infusion

Table 6: CY 2006 OPPS Non-Chemotherapy Drug Administration -Route Other Than Intravenous Infusion

2005 CPT	Final CY 2006 OPPS	2005 CPT	2005 Description	Code	Description	SI	APC
90784	Therapeutic, prophylactic or diagnostic injection (specify material injected); intravenous	C8952	Therapeutic, prophylactic or diagnostic injection; intravenous push	X	0359		
90782	Therapeutic, prophylactic or diagnostic injection (specify material injected); subcutaneous or intramuscular	90772	Therapeutic, prophylactic or diagnostic injection (specify substance or drug); subcutaneous or intramuscular	X	0353		
90783	Therapeutic, prophylactic or diagnostic injection (specify material injected); intra-arterial	90773	Therapeutic, prophylactic or diagnostic injection (specify substance or drug); intra-arterial	X	0359		
90779	Unlisted therapeutic, prophylactic or diagnostic intravenous or intra-arterial, injection or infusion	90779	Unlisted therapeutic, prophylactic or diagnostic intravenous or intra-arterial injection or infusion	X	0352		

100-4,4,231.4

Billing for Split Unit of Blood

HCPCS code P9011 was created to identify situations where one unit of blood or a blood product is split and some portion of the unit is transfused to one patient and the other portions are transfused to other patients or to the same patient at other times. When a patient receives a transfusion of a split unit of blood or blood product, OPPS providers should bill P9011 for the blood product transfused, as well as CPT 86985 (Splitting, blood products) for each splitting procedure performed to prepare the blood product for a specific patient.

Providers should bill split units of packed red cells and whole blood using Revenue Code 389 (Other blood), and should not use Revenue Codes 381 (Packed red cells) or 382 (Whole blood). Providers should bill split units of other blood products using the applicable revenue codes for the blood product type, such as 383 (Plasma) or 384 (Platelets), rather than 389. Reporting revenue codes according to these specifications will ensure the Medicare beneficiary's blood deductible is applied correctly.

EXAMPLE: OPPS provider splits off a 100cc aliquot from a 250 cc unit of leukocytereduced red blood cells for a transfusion to Patient X. The hospital then splits off an 80cc aliquot of the remaining unit for a transfusion to Patient Y. At a later time, the remaining 70cc from the unit is transfused to Patient Z.

In billing for the services for Patient X and Patient Y, the OPPS provider should report the charges by billing P9011 and 86985 in addition to the CPT code for the transfusion service, because a specific splitting service was required to prepare a split unit for transfusion to each of those patients. However, the OPPS provider should report only P9011 and the CPT code for the transfusion service for Patient Z because no additional splitting was necessary to prepare the split unit for transfusion to Patient Z. The OPPS provider should bill Revenue Code 0389 for each split unit of the leukocyte-reduced red blood cells that was transfused.

100-4,4,240

Inpatient Part B Hospital Services

Inpatient Part B services which are paid under OPPS include:

- Diagnostic x-ray tests, and other diagnostic tests (excluding clinical diagnostic laboratory tests);
- X-ray, radium, and radioactive isotope therapy, including materials and services of technicians;
- Surgical dressings applied during an encounter at the hospital and splints, casts, and other devices used for reduction of fractures and dislocations (splints and casts, etc., include dental splints);
- Implantable prosthetic devices;
- Hepatitis B vaccine and its administration, and certain preventive screening services (pelvic exams, screening sigmoidoscopies, screening colonoscopies, bone mass measurements, and prostate screening.)
  - Bone Mass measurements;
  - Prostate screening;
  - Immunosuppressive drugs;
  - Oral anti-cancer drugs;
  - Oral drug prescribed for use as an acute anti-emetic used as part of an anti-cancer chemotherapeutic regimen; and
  - Epoetin Alfa (EPO)

NOTE: Payment for some of these services is packaged into the payment rate of other separately payable services.

Inpatient Part B services paid under other payment methods include:

- Clinical diagnostic laboratory tests, prosthetic devices other than implantable ones and other than dental which replace all or part of an internal body organ (including contiguous tissue), or all or part of the function of a permanently inoperative or malfunctioning internal body organ, including replacement or repairs of such devices;
- Leg, arm, back and neck braces; trusses and artificial legs; arms and eyes including adjustments, repairs, and replacements required because of breakage, wear, loss, or a change in the patient's physical condition; take home surgical dressings; outpatient physical therapy; outpatient occupational therapy; and outpatient speech-language pathology services;
- Ambulance services;
- Screening pap smears, screening colorectal tests, and screening mammography;
- Influenza virus vaccine and its administration, pneumococcal vaccine and its administration;
- Diabetes self-management;
- Hemophilia clotting factors for hemophilia patients competent to use these factors without supervision).

See Chapter 6 of the Medicare Benefit Policy Manual for a discussion of the circumstances under which the above services may be covered as Part B Inpatient services.

100-4,4,290.1

Observation Services Overview

Observation care is a well-defined set of specific, clinically appropriate services, which include ongoing short term treatment, assessment, and reassessment, that are furnished while a decision is being made regarding whether patients will require further treatment as hospital inpatients or if they are able to be discharged from the hospital. Observation status is commonly assigned to patients who present to the emergency department and who then require a significant period of treatment or monitoring in order to make a decision concerning their admission or discharge. Observation services are covered only when provided by the order of a physician or another individual authorized by State licensure law and hospital staff bylaws to admit patients to the hospital or to order outpatient services.

Observation services must also be reasonable and necessary to be covered by Medicare. In only rare and exceptional cases do reasonable and necessary outpatient observation services span more than 48 hours. In the majority of cases, the decision whether to discharge a patient from the hospital following resolution of the reason for the observation care or to admit the patient as an inpatient can be made in less than 48 hours, usually in less than 24 hours.

100-4,4,290.2.2

Reporting Hours of Observation

Observation time begins at the clock time documented in the patient's medical record, which coincides with the time the patient is placed in a bed for the purpose of initiating observation care in accordance with a physician's order. Hospitals should round to the nearest hour. For example, a patient who was placed in an observation bed at 3:03 p.m. according to the nurses' notes and discharged to home at 9:45 p.m. should have a "7" placed in the units field of the reported observation HCPCS code.

General standing orders for observation services following all outpatient surgery are not recognized. Hospitals should not report as observation care, services that are part of another Part B service, such as postoperative monitoring during a standard recovery period (e.g., 4-6 hours), which should be billed as recovery room services. Similarly, in the case of patients who undergo diagnostic testing in a hospital outpatient department, routine preparation services furnished prior to the testing and recovery afterwards are included in the payments for those diagnostic services. Observation services should not be billed concurrently with diagnostic or therapeutic services for which active monitoring is a part of the procedure (e.g., colonoscopy, chemotherapy). In situations where such a procedure interrupts observation services, hospitals would record for each period of observation services the beginning and ending times during the hospital outpatient encounter and add the length of time for the periods of observation services together to reach the total number of units reported on the claim for the hourly observation services HCPCS code G0378 (Hospital observation service, per hour).

Observation time ends when all medically necessary services related to observation care are completed. For example, this could be before discharge when the need for observation has ended, but other medically necessary services not meeting the definition of observation care are provided (in which case, the additional medically necessary services would be billed separately or included as part of the emergency department or clinic visit). Alternatively, the end time of observation services may coincide with the time the patient is actually discharged from the hospital or admitted as an inpatient.

Observation time may include medically necessary services and follow-up care provided after the time that the physician writes the discharge order, but before the patient is discharged. However, reported observation time would not include the time patients remain in the observation area after treatment is finished for reasons such as waiting for transportation home.

If a period of observation spans more than 1 calendar day, all of the hours for the entire period of observation must be included on a single line and the date of service for that line is the date that observation care begins.

100-4,4,290.5.1

Billing and Payment for Observation Services Beginning January 1, 2008

Observation services are reported using HCPCS code G0378 (Hospital observation service, per hour). Beginning January 1, 2008, HCPCS code G0378 for hourly observation services is assigned status indicator N, signifying that its payment is always packaged. No separate payment is made for observation services reported with HCPCS code G0378, and APC 0339 is deleted as of January 1, 2008. In most circumstances, observation services are supportive and ancillary to the other services provided to a patient. In certain circumstances when observation care is billed in conjunction with a high level clinic visit (Level 5), high level emergency department visit (Level 4 or 5), critical care services, or direct admission as an integral part of a patient's extended encounter of care, payment may be made for the entire extended care encounter through one of two composite APCs when certain criteria are met. For information about payment for extended assessment and management composite APCs, see Sec.10.2.1 (Composite APCs) of this chapter.

APC 8002 (Level I Extended Assessment and Management Composite) describes an encounter for care provided to a patient that includes a high level (Level 5) clinic visit or direct admission to observation in conjunction with observation services of substantial duration (8 or more hours). APC 8003 (Level II Extended Assessment and Management Composite) describes an encounter for care provided to a patient that includes a high level (Level 4 or 5) emergency department visit or critical care services in conjunction with observation services of substantial duration. There is no limitation on diagnosis for payment of these composite APCs; however, composite APC payment will not be made when observation services are reported in association with a surgical procedure (T status procedure) or the hours of observation care reported are less than 8. The I/OCE evaluates every claim received to determine if payment through a composite APC is appropriate. If payment through a composite APC is inappropriate, the I/OCE, in conjunction with the Pricer, determines the appropriate status indicator, APC, and payment for every code on a claim.

All of the following requirements must be met in order for a hospital to receive an APC payment for an extended assessment and management composite APC:

1. Observation Time
   a. Observation time must be documented in the medical record.
   b. A beneficiary's time in observation (and hospital billing) begins with the beneficiary's admission to an observation bed.
   c. A beneficiary's time in observation (and hospital billing) ends when all clinical or medical interventions have been completed, including follow-up care furnished by hospital staff and physicians that may take place after a physician has ordered the patient be released or admitted as an inpatient.
   d. The number of units reported with HCPCS code G0378 must equal or exceed 8 hours.
2. Additional Hospital Services
   a. The claim for observation services must include one of the following services in addition to the reported observation services. The additional services listed below must have a line item date of service on the same day or the day before the date reported for observation: An emergency department visit (CPT code 99284 or 99285) or A clinic visit (CPT code 99205 or 99215); or Critical care (CPT code 99291); or Direct admission to observation reported with HCPCS code G0379 (APC 0604) must be reported on the same date of service as the date reported for observation services.
   b. No procedure with a T status indicator can be reported on the same day or day before observation care is provided.
3. Physician Evaluation
   a. The beneficiary must be in the care of a physician during the period of observation, as documented in the medical record by admission, discharge, and other appropriate progress notes that are timed, written, and signed by the physician.
   b. The medical record must include documentation that the physician explicitly assessed patient risk to determine that the beneficiary would benefit from observation care.

Criteria 1 and 3 related to observation care beginning and ending time and physician evaluation apply regardless of whether the hospital believes that observation services will be packaged or will meet the criteria for extended assessment and management composite payment.

Only observation services that are billed on a 13X bill type may be considered for a composite APC payment.

Non-repetitive services provided on the same day as either direct admission to observation care or observation services must be reported on the same claim because the OCE claim-by-claim logic cannot function properly unless all services related to the episode of observation care, including hospital clinic visits, emergency department visits, critical care services, and T status procedures, are reported on the same claim.

Additional guidance can be found in Change Request 4047, Transmittal 763, issued on November 25, 2005.

If a claim for services providing during an extended assessment and management encounter including observation care does not meet all of the requirements listed above, then the usual APC logic will apply to separately payable items and services on the claim; the special logic for direct admission will apply, and payment for the observation care will be packaged into payments for other separately payable services provided to the beneficiary in the same encounter.

100-4,5,10.2

A. Financial Limitation Prior to the Balanced Budget Refinement Act (BBRA)

Section 4541(a)(2) of the Balanced Budget Act (BBA) (P.L. 105-33) of 1997, which added ¬ß1834(k)(5) to the Act, required payment under a prospective payment system for outpatient rehabilitation services (except those furnished by or under arrangements with a hospital). Outpatient rehabilitation services include the following services:

- Physical therapy (which includes outpatient speech-language pathology); and
- Occupational therapy.

Section 4541(c) of the BBA required application of a financial limitation to all outpatient rehabilitation services (except those furnished by or under arrangements with a hospital). In 1999, an annual per beneficiary limit of $1,500 applied to all outpatient physical therapy services (including speech-language pathology services). A separate limit applied to all occupational therapy services. The limit is based on incurred expenses and includes applicable deductible and coinsurance. The BBA provided that the limits be indexed by the Medicare Economic Index (MEI) each year beginning in 2002.

The limitation is based on therapy services the Medicare beneficiary receives, not the type of practitioner who provides the service. Physical therapists, speech-language pathologists, occupational therapists as well as physicians and certain nonphysician practitioners could render a therapy service.

As a transitional measure, effective in 1999, providers/suppliers were instructed to keep track of the allowed incurred expenses. This process was put in place to assure providers/suppliers did not bill Medicare for patients who exceeded the annual limitations for physical therapy, and for occupational therapy services rendered by individual providers/suppliers. In 2003 and later, the limitation was applied through CMS systems.

B. Moratoria and Exceptions for Therapy Claims

Section 221 of the BBRA of 1999 placed a 2-year moratorium on the application of the financial limitation for claims for therapy services with dates of service January 1, 2000, through December 31, 2001.

Section 421 of the Medicare, Medicaid, and SCHIP Benefits Improvement and Protection Act (BIPA) of 2000, extended the moratorium on application of the financial limitation to claims for outpatient rehabilitation services with dates of service January 1, 2002, through December 31, 2002. Therefore, the moratorium was for a 3-year period and applied to outpatient rehabilitation claims with dates of service January 1, 2000, through December 31, 2002.

In 2003, there was not a moratorium on therapy caps. Implementation was delayed until September 1, 2003. Therapy caps were in effect for services rendered on September 1, 2003 through December 7, 2003.

Congress re-enacted a moratorium on financial limitations on outpatient therapy services on December 8, 2003 that extended through December 31, 2005. Caps were implemented again on January 1, 2006 and policies were modified to allow exceptions as directed by the Deficit Reduction Act of 2005 only for calendar year 2006. The Tax Relief and Health Care Act of 2006 extended the cap exceptions process through calendar year 2007. The Medicare, Medicaid, and SCHIP Extension Act of 2007 extended the cap exceptions process for services furnished through June 30, 2008.

Future exceptions. The cap exception for therapy services billed by outpatient hospitals was part of the original legislation and applies as long as caps are in effect. Exceptions to caps based on the medical necessity of the service are in effect only when Congress legislates the exceptions, as they did for 2007. References to the exceptions process in subsection C of this section apply only when the exceptions are in effect.

C. Application of Financial Limitations

Financial limitations on outpatient therapy services, as described above, began for therapy services rendered on or after on January 1, 2006. See C 1 to C 7 of this section when exceptions to therapy caps apply. The limits were $1740 in 2006 and $1780 in 2007. For 2008, the annual limit on the allowed amount for outpatient physical therapy and speech-language pathology combined is $1810; the limit for occupational therapy is $1810. Limits apply to outpatient Part B therapy services from all settings except outpatient hospital (place of service code 22 on carrier claims) and hospital emergency room (place of service code 23 on carrier claims). These excluded hospital services are reported on types of bill 12x or 13x on intermediary claims.

Contractors apply the financial limitations to the Medicare Physician Fee Schedule (MPFS) amount (or the amount charged if it is smaller) for therapy services for each beneficiary.

As with any Medicare payment, beneficiaries pay the coinsurance (20 percent) and any deductible that may apply. Medicare will pay the remaining 80 percent of the limit after the deductible is met. These amounts will change each calendar year. Medicare Contractors shall publish the financial limitation amount in educational articles. It is also available at 1-800-Medicare.

Medicare shall apply these financial limitations in order, according to the dates when the claims were received. When limitations apply, the Common Working File (CWF) tracks the limits. Shared System Maintainers are not responsible for tracking the dollar amounts of incurred expenses of rehabilitation services for each therapy limit.

In processing claims where Medicare is the secondary payer, the shared system takes the lowest secondary payment amount from MSPPAY and sends this amount on to CWF as the amount applied to therapy limits.

1. Exceptions to Therapy Caps - General

   The Tax Relief and Health Care Act of 2006 directed CMS to extend a process to allow for exceptions to the caps for services received in CY2007 in cases where continued therapy services are medically necessary. The following policies concerning exceptions to caps due to medical necessity apply only when the exceptions process is in effect. With the exception of the use of the KX modifier, the guidance in this section concerning medical necessity applies as well to services provided before caps are reached.

   Instructions for contractors to manage automatic process for exceptions will be found in the Program Integrity Manual, chapter 3, section 3.4.1.2. Provider and supplier information concerning exceptions is in this manual and in IOM Pub. 100-02, chapter 15, section 220.3. Exceptions shall be identified by a modifier on the claim and supported by documentation.

   Since the providers and suppliers will take an active role in obtaining an exception for a beneficiary, this manual section is written to address them as well as Medicare contractors.

   The beneficiary may qualify for use of the cap exceptions at any time during the episode when documented medically necessary services exceed caps. All covered and medically necessary services qualify for exceptions to caps.

   In 2006, the Exception Processes fell into two categories, Automatic Process Exceptions, and Manual Process Exceptions. Beginning January 1, 2007, there is no manual process for exceptions. All services that require exceptions to caps shall be processed using the automatic process. All requests for exception are in the form of a KX modifier added to claim lines. (See subsection C6 for use of the KX modifier.)

   Use of the automatic process for exceptions increases the responsibility of the provider/supplier for determining and documenting that services are appropriate.

   Also, use of the automatic process for exception does not exempt services from manual or other medical review processes as described in 100-08, Chapter 3, Section 3.4.1.1.1. Rather, atypical use of the automatic exception process may invite contractor scrutiny. Particular care should be taken to document improvement and avoid billing for services that do not meet the requirements for skilled services, or for services which are maintenance rather than rehabilitative treatment (See Pub. 100-02, chapter 15, sections 220.2, 220.3, and 230).

   The KX modifier, described in subsection C6, is added to claim lines to indicate that the clinician attests that services are medically necessary and justification is documented in the medical record.

2. Automatic Process Exceptions

   The term "automatic process exceptions" indicates that the claims processing for the exception is automatic, and not that the exception is automatic. An exception may be made when the patient‚Äôs condition is justified by documentation indicating that the beneficiary requires continued skilled therapy, i.e., therapy beyond the amount payable under the therapy cap, to achieve their prior functional status or maximum expected functional status within a reasonable amount of time.

   No special documentation is submitted to the contractor for automatic process exceptions. The clinician is responsible for consulting guidance in the Medicare manuals and in the professional literature to determine if the beneficiary may qualify for the automatic process exception when documentation justifies medically necessary services above the caps. The clinician's opinion is not binding on the Medicare contractor who makes the final determination concerning whether the claim is payable.

   Documentation justifying the services shall be submitted in response to any Additional Documentation Request (ADR) for claims that are selected for medical review. Follow the documentation requirements in Pub. 100-02, chapter 15, section 220.3. If medical records are requested for review, clinicians may include, at their discretion, a summary that specifically addresses the justification for therapy cap exception.

   In making a decision about whether to utilize the automatic process exception, clinicians shall consider, for example, whether services are appropriate to--

- The patient's condition including the diagnosis, complexities and severity (A list of the excepted evaluation codes are in C.2.a. A list of the ICD-9 codes for conditions and complexities that might qualify a beneficiary for exception to caps is in 10.2 C3. The list is a guideline and neither assures that services on the list will be excepted nor limits provision of covered and medically necessary services for conditions not on the list);
- The services provided including their type, frequency and duration;

- The interaction of current active conditions and complexities that directly and significantly influence the treatment such that it causes services to exceed caps.

In addition, the following should be considered before using the automatic exception process:

a. Exceptions for Services

Evaluation. The CMS will except therapy evaluations from caps after the therapy caps are reached when evaluation is necessary, e.g., to determine if the current status of the beneficiary requires therapy services. For example, the following evaluation procedures may be appropriate:

92506, 92597, 92607, 92608, 92610, 92611, 92612, 92614, 92616, 96105, 97001, 97002, 97003, 97004.

These codes will continue to be reported as outpatient therapy procedures as described in the Claims Processing Manual, Chapter 5, Section 20(B) "Applicable Outpatient Rehabilitation HCPCS Codes." They are not diagnostic tests. Definition of evaluations and documentation is found in Pub 100-02, sections 220 and 230.

Other Services. There are a number of sources that suggest the amount of certain services that may be typical, either per service, per episode, per condition, or per discipline. For example, see the CSC- Utilization and Edit Report, 2006, Appendices at www.cms.hhs.gov/TherapyServices (Studies and Reports). Professional literature and guidelines from professional associations also provide a basis on which to estimate whether the type, frequency and intensity of services are appropriate to an individual. Clinicians and contractors should utilize available evidence related to the patient's condition to justify provision of medically necessary services to individual beneficiaries, especially when they exceed caps. Contractors shall not limit medically necessary services that are justified by scientific research applicable to the beneficiary. Neither contractors nor clinicians shall utilize professional literature and scientific reports to justify payment for continued services after an individual's goals have been met earlier than is typical. Conversely, professional literature and scientific reports shall not be used as justification to deny payment to patients whose needs are greater than is typical or when the patient,Âôs condition is not represented by the literature.

b. Exceptions for Conditions or Complexities Identified by ICD-9 codes.

Clinicians may utilize the automatic process for exception for any diagnosis for which they can justify services exceeding the cap. Based upon analysis of claims data, research and evidence based practice guidelines, CMS has identified conditions and complexities represented by ICD-9 codes that may be more likely than others to require therapy services that exceed therapy caps. This list appears in 10.2 C3. Clinicians may use the automatic process of exception for beneficiaries who do not have a condition or complexity on this list when they justify the provision of therapy services that exceed caps for that patient's condition.

NOT ALL patients who have a condition or complexity on the list are "automatically" excepted from therapy caps. See Pub. 100-02, chapter 15, section 230.3 for documenting the patient's condition and complexities. Contractors may scrutinize claims from providers whose services exceed caps more frequently than is typical.

Regardless of the condition, the patient must also meet other requirements for coverage. For example, the patient must require skilled treatment for a covered, medically necessary service; the services must be appropriate in type, frequency and duration for the patient's condition and service must be documented appropriately. Guidelines for utilization of therapy services may be found in Medicare manuals, Local Coverage Determinations of Medicare contractors, and professional guidelines issued by associations and states.

Bill the most relevant diagnosis. As always, when billing for therapy services, the ICD-9 code that best relates to the reason for the treatment shall be on the claim, unless there is a compelling reason. For example, when a patient with diabetes is being treated for gait training due to amputation, the preferred diagnosis is abnormality of gait (which characterizes the treatment). Where it is possible in accordance with State and local laws and the contractors Local Coverage Determinations, avoid using vague or general diagnoses. When a claim includes several types of services, or where the physician/NPP must supply the diagnosis, it may not be possible to use the most relevant therapy code in the primary position. In that case, the relevant code should, if possible, be on the claim in another position.

Codes representing the medical condition that caused the treatment are used when there is no code representing the treatment. Complicating conditions are preferably used in non-primary positions on the claim and are billed in the primary position only in the rare circumstance that there is no more relevant code.

The condition or complexity that caused treatment to exceed caps must be related to the therapy goals and must either be the condition that is being treated or a complexity that directly and significantly impacts the rate of recovery of the condition being treated such that it is appropriate to exceed the caps. Codes marked as complexities represented by ICD-9 codes on the list below are unlikely to require therapy services that would exceed the caps unless they occur in a patient who also has another condition (either listed or not listed). Therefore, documentation for an exception should indicate how the complexity (or combination of complexities) directly and significantly affects treatment for a therapy condition. For example, if the condition underlying the reason for therapy is V43.64, hip replacement, the treatment may have a goal to ambulate 60' with stand-by assistance and a KX modifier may be appropriate for gait training (assuming the severity of the patient is such that the services exceed the cap). Alternatively, it would not be appropriate to use the KX modifier for a patient who recovered from hip replacement last year and is being treated this year for a sprain of a severity which does not justify extensive therapy exceeding caps.

3. ICD-9 Codes That are Likely to Qualify for the Automatic Process Therapy Cap Exception Based Upon Clinical Condition or Complexity

When using this table, refer to the ICD-9 code book for coding instructions. Some contractors' Local Coverage Determinations do not allow the use of some of the codes on this list in the primary diagnosis position on a claim. If the contractor has determined that these codes do not characterize patients who require medically necessary services, providers/suppliers may not use these codes, but must utilize a billable diagnosis code allowed by their contractor to describe the patient's condition. Contractors shall not apply therapy caps to services based on the patient's condition, but only on the medical necessity of the service for the condition. If a service would be payable before the cap is reached and is still medically necessary after the cap is reached, that service is excepted. Providers/suppliers may use the automatic process for exception for medically necessary services when the patient has a billable condition that is not on the list below. The diagnosis on the list below may be put in a secondary position on the claim and/or in the medical records, as the contractor directs.

When two codes are listed in the left cell in a row, all the codes between them are also eligible for exception. If one code is in the cell, only that one code is likely to qualify for exception. The descriptions in the table are not always identical to those in the ICD-9 code book, but may be summaries. Contact your contractor for interpretation if you are not sure that a condition or complexity is applicable for automatic process exception.

It is very important to recognize that most of the conditions on this list would not ordinarily result in services exceeding the cap. Use the KX modifier only in cases where the condition of the individual patient is such that services are APPROPRIATELY provided in an episode that exceeds the cap. In most cases, the severity of the condition, comorbidities, or complexities will contribute to the necessity of services exceeding the cap, and these should be documented. Routine use of the KX modifier for all patients with these conditions will likely show up on data analysis as aberrant and invite inquiry. Be sure that documentation is sufficiently detailed to support the use of the modifier.

The following ICD-9 codes describe the conditions (etiology or underlying medical conditions) that may result in excepted conditions (marked X) and complexities (marked *) that MIGHT cause medically necessary therapy services to qualify for the automatic process exception for each discipline separately. When the field corresponding to the therapy discipline treating and the diagnosis code is marked with a dash (,Äì) services by that discipline are not appropriate for that diagnosis and, therefore, services do not qualify for exception to caps.

These codes are grouped only to facilitate reference to them. The codes may be used only when the code is applicable to the condition being actively treated. For example, an exception should not be claimed for a diagnosis of hip replacement when the service provided is for an unrelated dysphagia.

ICD-9 Cluster	ICD-9 (Cluster) Description	PT	OT	SLP
V43.61-V43.69	Joint Replacement	X	X	--
V45.4	Arthrodesis Status	*	*	--
V45.81-V45.82 and V45.89	Other Postprocedural Status	*	*	--
V49-61-V49.67	Upper Limb Amputation Status	X	X	--
V49.71-V49.77	Lower Limb Amputation Status	X	X	--
V54.10-V54.29	Aftercare for Healing Traumatic or Pathologic Fracture	X	X	--
V58.71-V58.78	Aftercare Following Surgery to Specified Body Systems, Not Elsewhere Classified	*	*	*
244.0-244.9	Acquired Hypothyroidism	*	*	*

X Automatic (only ICD-9 needed on claim)

* Complexity (requires another ICD-9 on claim)

-- Does not serve as qualifying ICD-9 on claim

ICD-9 Cluster	ICD-9 (Cluster) Description	PT	OT	SLP
250.00-251.9	Diabetes Mellitus and Other Disorders of Pancreatic Internal Secretion	*	*	*
276.0-276.9	Disorders of Fluid, Electrolyte, and Acid-Base Balance	*	*	*
278.00-278.01	Obesity and Morbid Obesity	*	*	*
280.0-289.9	Diseases of the blood and blood-forming organs	*	*	*
290.0-290.43	Dementias	*	*	*
294.0-294.9	Persistent Mental Disorders due to Conditions Classified Elsewhere	*	*	*
295.00-299.91	Other Psychoses	*	*	*
300.00-300.9	Anxiety, Disassociative and Somatoform Disorders	*	*	*
310.0-310.9	Specific Nonpsychotic Mental Disorders due to Brain Damage	*	*	*
311	Depressive Disorder, Not Elsewhere Classified	*	*	*
315.00-315.9	Specific delays in Development	*	*	*
317	Mild Mental Retardation	*	*	*
320.0-326	Inflammatory Diseases of the Central Nervous System	*	*	*
330.0-337.9	Hereditary and Degenerative Diseases of the Central Nervous System	X	X	X
340-345.91 and 348.0-349.9	Other Disorders of the Central Nervous System	X	X	X
353.0-359.9	Disorders of the Peripheral Nervous system	X	X	--
365.00-365.9	Glaucoma	*	*	*
369.00-369.9	Blindness and Low Vision	*	*	*
386.00-386.9	Vertiginous Syndromes and Other Disorders of Vestibular System	*	*	*
389.00-389.9	Hearing Loss	*	*	*
401.0-405.99	Hypertensive Disease	*	*	*
410.00-414.9	Ischemic Heart Disease	*	*	*
415.0-417.9	Diseases of Pulmonary Circulation	*	*	*
420.0-429.9	Other Forms of Heart Disease	*	*	*
430-438.9	Cerebrovascular Disease	X	X	X
440.0-448.9	Diseases of Arteries, Arterioles, and Capillaries	*	*	*
451.0-453.9 and 456.0-459.9	Diseases of Veins and Lymphatics, and Other Diseases of Circulatory System	*	*	*
465.0-466.19	Acute Respiratory Infections	*	*	*
478.30-478.5	Paralysis, Polyps, or Other Diseases of Vocal Cords	*	*	*
480.0-486	Pneumonia	*	*	*
490-496	Chronic Obstructive Pulmonary Disease and Allied Conditions	*	*	*
507.0-507.8	Pneumonitis due to solids and liquids	*	*	*
510.0-519.9	Other Diseases of Respiratory System	*	*	*
560.0-560.9	Intestinal Obstruction Without Mention of Hernia	*	*	*
578.0-578.9	Gastrointestinal Hemorrhage	*	*	*
584.5-586	Renal Failure and Chronic Kidney Disease	*	*	*
590.00-599.9	Other Diseases of Urinary System	*	*	*
682.0-682.8	Other Cellulitis and Abscess	*	*	--
707.00-707.9	Chronic Ulcer of Skin	*	*	--
710.0-710.9	Diffuse Diseases of Connective Tissue	*	*	*

X Automatic (only ICD-9 needed on claim)

* Complexity (requires another ICD-9 on claim)

-- Does not serve as qualifying ICD-9 on claim

ICD-9 Cluster	ICD-9 (Cluster) Description	PT	OT	SLP
711.00-711.99	Arthropathy Associated with Infections	*	*	--
712.10-713.8	Crystal Arthropathies and Arthropathy Associated with Other Disorders Classified Elsewhere	*	*	--
714.0-714.9	Rheumatoid Arthritis and Other Inflammatory Polyarthropathies	*	*	--
715.00-715.98	Osteoarthrosis and Allied Disorders (Complexity except as listed below)	*	*	--
715.09	Osteoarthritis and allied disorders, multiple sites	X	X	--
715.11	Osteoarthritis, localized, primary, shoulder region	X	X	--
715.15	Osteoarthritis, localized, primary, pelvic region and thigh	X	X	--
715.16	Osteoarthritis, localized, primary, lower leg	X	X	--
715.91	Osteoarthritis, unspecified id gen. or local, shoulder	X	X	--
715.96	Osteoarthritis, unspecified if gen. or local, lower leg	X	X	--
716.00-716.99	Other and Unspecified Arthropathies	*	*	--
717.0-717.9	Internal Derangement of Knee	*	*	--
718.00-718.99	Other Derangement of Joint (Complexity except as listed below)	*	*	--
718.49	Contracture of Joint, Multiple Sites	X	X	--
719.00-719.99	Other and Unspecified Disorders of Joint (Complexity except as listed below)	*	*	--
719.7	Difficulty Walking	X	X	--
720.0-724.9	Dorsopathies	*	*	--
725-729.9	Rheumatism, Excluding Back (Complexity except as listed below)	*	*	--
726.10-726.19	Rotator Cuff Disorder and Allied Syndromes	X	X	--
727.61-727.62	Rupture of Tendon, Nontraumatic	X	X	--
730.00-739.9	Osteopathies, Chondropathies, and Acquired Musculoskeletal Deformities (Complexity except as listed below)	*	*	--
733.00	Osteoporosis	X	X	--
741.00-742.9 and 745.0-748.9 and 754.0-756.9	Congenital Anomalies	*	*	*
780.31-780.39	Convulsions	*	*	*
780.71-780.79	Malaise and Fatigue	*	*	*
780.93	Memory Loss	*	*	*
781.0-781.99	Symptoms Involving Nervous and Musculoskeletal System (Complexity except as listed below)	*	*	*
781.2	Abnormality of Gait	X	X	--
781.3	Lack of Coordination	X	X	--
783.0-783.9	Symptoms Concerning Nutrition, Metabolism, and Development	*	*	*
784.3-784.69	Aphasia, Voice and Other Speech Disturbance, Other Symbolic Dysfunction	*	*	X
785.4	Gangrene	*	*	--
786.00-786.9	Symptoms involving Respiratory System and Other Chest Symptoms	*	*	*
787.2	Dysphagia	*	*	X
800.00-828.1	Fractures (Complexity except as listed below)	*	*	--

X Automatic (only ICD-9 needed on claim)

* Complexity (requires another ICD-9 on claim)

-- Does not serve as qualifying ICD-9 on claim

ICD-9 Cluster	ICD-9 (Cluster) Description	PT	OT	SLP
806.00-806.9	Fracture of Vertebral Column With Spinal Cord Injury	X	X	--
810.11-810.13	Fracture of Clavicle	X	X	--
811.00-811.19	Fracture of Scapula	X	X	--
812.00-812.59	Fracture of Humerus	X	X	--
813.00-813.93	Fracture of Radius and Ulna	X	X	--
820.00-820.9	Fracture of Neck of Femue	X	X	--
821.00-821.39	Fracture of Other and Unspecified Parts of Femur	X	X	--
828.0-828.1	Multiple Fractures Involving Both Lower Limbs, Lower with Upper Limb, and Lower Limb(s) with Rib(s) and Sternum	X	X	--
830.0-839.9	Dislocations	X	X	--
840.0-848.8	Sprains and Strains of Joints and Adjacent Muscles	*	*	--
851.00-854.19	Intracranial Injury, excluding those with Skull Fracture	X	X	X
888.00-884.2	Open Wound of Upper Limb	*	*	--
885.0-887.7	Traumatic Amputation, Thumb(s), Finger(s), Arm and Hand (complete)(partial)	X	X	--
890.0-894.2	Open Wound Lower Limb	*	*	--
895.0-897.7	Traumatic Amputation, Toe(s), Foot/Feet, Leg(s) (complete) (partial)			
905.0-905.9	Late Effects of Musculoskeletal and Connective Tissue Injuries	*	*	*
907.0-907.9	Late Effect of Injuries to the Nervous System	*	*	*
941.00-949.5	Burns	*	*	*
952.00-952.9	Spinal Cord Injury Without Evidence of Spinal Bone Injury	X	X	X
953.0-953.8	Injury to Nerve Roots and Spinal Plexus	X	X*	
959.01	Head Injury, Unspecified	X	X	X

X Automatic (only ICD-9 needed on claim)

* Complexity (requires another ICD-9 on claim)

-- Does not serve as qualifying ICD-9 on claim

100-4,8,60.4.1

Epoetin Alfa (EPO) Facility Billing Requirements

Revenue codes required for reporting EPO:

Revenue Codes Dates of Service	Bill Type 72x	Bill Type 12x	Bill type 13x	Bill type 85x
0634 - administrations under 10,000 units	1/1/04 - present	4/1/06 - present	1/1/04 - present	1/1/04 - present

Revenue Codes Dates of Service	Bill Type 72x	Bill Type 12x	Bill type 13x	Bill type 85x
0635 - administrations of 10,000 units or more	1/1/04 - present	4/1/06 - present	1/1/04 - present	1/1/04 - prese
0636 - detailed drug coding	N/A	1/1/04 - 3/31/06	N/A	

N/A For additional hospital billing instructions related to bill types 12x, 13x and 85x see also sections 60.4.3.1 and 60.4.3.2 of this chapter.

The HCPCS code for EPO must be included:

HCPCS	HCPCS Description	Dates of Service
Q4055	Injection, Epoetin alfa, 1,000 units (for ESRD on Dialysis)	1/1/2004 through 12/31/2005
J0886	Injection, Epoetin alfa, 1,000 units (for ESRD on Dialysis)	1/1/2006 through 12/31/2006
Q4081	1 Injection, Epoetin alfa, 100	1/1/2007 to present

The number of units of EPO administered during the billing period is reported with value code 68 Medicare no longer requires value code 68 for claims with dates of service on or after January 1 2008. Each administration of epoetin alfa (EPO) is reported on a separate line item with the units reported used as a multiplier by the dosage description in the HCPCS to arrive at the dosage per administration.

Append the GS modifier to report a line item that represents an administration of EPO at the reduced dosage following existing instructions in section 60.4 of this chapter. The hematocrit reading taken prior to the last administration of EPO during the billing period must also be reported on the UB-92/Form CMS-1450 with value code 49. Effective January 1, 2006 the definition of value code 49 used to report the hematocrit reading is changed to indicate the patient's most recent hematocrit reading taken before the start of the billing period.

The hemoglobin reading taken during the billing period must be reported on the UB- 92/Form CMS-1450 with value code 48. Effective January 1, 2006 the definition of value code 48 used for the hemoglobin reading is changed to indicate the patient's most recent hemoglobin reading taken before the start of the billing period.

To report a hemoglobin or hematocrit reading for a new patient on or after January 1, 2006, the provider should report the reading that prompted the treatment of epoetin alfa. The provider may use results documented on form CMS 2728 or the patient's medical records from a transferring facility.

The maximum number of administrations of EPO for a billing cycle is 13 times in 30 days and 14 times in 31 days.

ICD-9-CM Self Test Answer Key

PART I ICD-9-CM DIAGNOSIS

1. Code assignment:

   066.41 West Nile fever with encephalitis

   No additional code is necessary for describing the encephalomyelitis.

2. Code assignment:

   070.51 Acute hepatitis C without mention of hepatic coma

3. Code assignment:

   046.11 Variant Creutzfeld-Jakob disease

   294.10 Dementia in conditions classified elsewhere with behavioral disturbances

4. Code assignment:

   051.02 Vaccinia not from vaccination

   692.9 Contact dermatitis and other eczema, unspecified

5. Code assignment: 193 Malignant neoplasm of thyroid gland

   258.02 Multiple endocrine neoplasia type IIA

   252.02 Secondary hyperparathyroidism, non-renal

   405.99 Secondary hypertension, unspecified V18.11 Family history of multiple endocrine neoplasia [MEN] syndrome

6. Code assignment:

   288.66 Bandemia

7. Code assignment:

   347.00 Narcolepsy without cataplexy

8. Code assignment:

   380.03 Chondritis of pinna

   041.7 Bacterial infection in conditions classified elsewhere, pseudomonas

9. Code assignment:

   434.91 Cerebral artery occlusion, unspecified, with cerebral infarction

10. Code assignment:

    453.41 Venous embolism and thrombosis of deep vessels of proximal lower extremity

11. Code assignment:

    209.17 Malignant carcinoid tumor of the rectum

    259.2 Carcinoid syndrome

12. Code assignment:

    491.22 Obstructive chronic bronchitis with acute bronchitis

13. Code assignment:

    521.01 Dental caries limited to enamel

    521.07 Dental caries of smooth surface

14. Code assignment:

    523.21 Gingival recession, minimal

15. Code assignment:

    996.82 Complications of transplanted organ, liver

    238.77 Post-transplant lymphoproliferative disorder

16. Code assignment:

    644.21 Early onset of delivery, delivered

    651.01 Multiple gestation, twins, delivered

    651.71 Multiple gestation following elective fetal reduction, delivered

    642.41 Mild pre-eclampsia, delivered V27.2 Outcome of delivery; twins, both liveborn

17. Code assignment:

    249.60 Secondary diabetes mellitus with neurological manifestation

    357.4 Polyneuropathy in other diseases classified elsewhere

    E932.0 Drugs, medicinal and biological substances causing adverse effects in therapeutic use; adrenal cortical steroids

18. Code assignment:

    796.2 Elevated blood pressure reading without diagnosis of hypertension

    272.9 Unspecified disorder of lipoid metabolism

    278.02 Overweight V85.23 Body mass index 27.0–27.9, adult

19. Code assignment:

    287.32 Evans' syndrome

20. Code assignment:

    250.50 Diabetes mellitus with ophthalmic manifestations, type II or unspecified type, not stated as uncontrolled

    362.07 Diabetic retinal edema

    362.06 Severe nonproliferative diabetic retinopathy

21. Code assignment:

    403.91 Hypertensive kidney disease, unspecified, with chronic kidney disease

    585.4 Chronic kidney disease, Stage IV (severe)

22. Code assignment:

    530.86 Infection of esophagostomy

    038.11 Staphylococcus aureus septicemia

    335.20 Amyotrophic lateral sclerosis

23. Code assignment:

    482.41 Methicillin resistant pneumonia due to Staphylococcus aureus

24. Code assignment:

    618.01 Cystocele, midline

    788.38 Overflow incontinence

25. Code assignment:

    202.80 Other lymphoma, unspecified site, extranodal and solid organ sites

    511.81 Malignant pleural effusion

26. Code assignment:
    558.42 Eosinophilic colitis

27. Code assignment:
    999.31 Infection due to central venous catheter
    038.11 Staphylococcus aureus septicemia

28. Code assignment:
    999.39 Infection following other infusion, injection, transfusion or vaccination

29. Code assignment:
    569.44 Dysplasia of anus
    V08 Asymptomatic human immunodeficiency virus [HIV] infection status

30. Coding scenario:
    707.05 Pressure ulcer, buttock
    707.23 Pressure ulcer, stage III
    290.40 Vascular dementia, uncomplicated

31. Code assignment:
    518.7 Transfusion related acute lung injury (TRALI)
    285.9 Anemia, unspecified

32. Code assignment:
    695.11 Erythema multiform minor
    695.51 Exfoliation due to erythematous condition involving 10-19 percent of body surface
    382.9 Unspecified otitis media,
    E930.0 Drugs, medicinal and biological substances causing adverse effects in therapeutic use, Penicillins

33. Code assignment:
    377.43 Optic nerve hypoplasia

34. Code assignment:
    053.14 Herpes zoster with other nervous system complications, herpes

35. Code assignment:
    692.6 Contact dermatitis and other eczema
    372.04 Pseudomembranous conjunctivitis
    462 Acute pharyngitis
    E928.6 Environmental exposure to harmful algae and toxins

PART II ICD-9-CM PROCEDURE CODING

1. Code assignment:
    414.00 Coronary atherosclerosis of unspecified type of vessel, native or graft
    414.3 Coronary atherosclerosis due to lipid rich plaque
    38.23 Intravascular spectroscopy

2. Code assignment:
    038.40 Gram negative septicemia
    995.92 Systemic inflammatory response syndrome due to infectious process with organ dysfunction
    785.52 Septic shock
    518.81 Acute respiratory failure
    96.71 Continuous mechanical ventilation for less than 96 consecutive hours
    00.17 Infusion of vasopressor agent

3. Code assignment:
    410.01 Acute myocardial infarction, of anterolateral wall, initial episode of care
    00.66 Percutaneous transluminal coronary angioplasty [PTCA] or coronary atherectomy
    36.07 Insertion of drug-eluting coronary artery stent(s)
    00.40 Procedure on single vessel
    00.45 Insertion of single vascular stent
    37.22 Left heart cardiac catheterization
    00.24 Intravascular imaging of coronary vessel
    99.10 Injection or infusion of thrombolytic agent

4. Code assignment:
    820.09 Transcervical fracture of neck of femur, closed, other
    E880.9 Fall on or from other stairs or steps E849.0 Place of occurrence, home
    81.51 Total hip replacement
    00.31 Computer assisted surgery with CT/CTA

5. Code assignment:
    433.10 Occlusion and stenosis of precerebral arteries, carotid, without mention of cerebral infarction
    00.61 Percutaneous angioplasty or atherectomy of precerebral (extracranial) vessel(s)
    00.63 Percutaneous insertion of carotid artery stent(s)
    00.40 Procedure on single vessel
    00.45 Insertion of single vascular stent
    99.10 Injection or infusion of thrombolytic agent

6. Code assignment:
    492.8 Other emphysema
    33.72 Endoscopic pulmonary airway flow measurement

7. Code assignment:
    780.57 Other and unspecified sleep apnea
    401.9 Hypertension NOS
    29.4 Plastic repair on pharynx
    27.64 Insertion of palatal implant

8. Code assignment;
    402.01 Malignant hypertensive heart disease with heart failure
    37.66 Insertion of implantable heart assist system
    428.0 Congestive heart failure, unspecified

9. Code assignment:
    553.1 Umbilical hernia without mention of obstruction or gangrene
    53.42 Laparoscopic repair of umbilical hernia with graft or prosthesis

10. Code assignment:
    - 736.81 Unequal leg length (acquired)
    - 905.4 Late effect of fracture of lower extremity
    - 78.35 Limb lengthening procedure, femur
    - 84.53 Implantation of internal limb lengthening device with kinetic distraction

11. Part 1 Code assignment:
    - 85.21 Local excision of lesion of breast
    - 92.41 Intra-operative radiation therapy

12. Code assignment:
    - 191.8 Malignant neoplasm of brain, other parts of brain
    - 174.9 Malignant neoplasm of female breast, unspecified
    - 00.19 Disruption of blood brain barrier via infusion [BBBD]
    - 99.25 Chemotherapy

13. Code assignment:
    - 745.69 Valgus deformities of feet; other
    - 343.9 Cerebral palsy, NOS
    - 81.18 Subtalar joint arthroereisis

14. Code assignment:
    - 823.00 Closed fracture, upper end, tibia alone
    - 79.06 Closed reduction of fracture without internal fixation, tibia and fibula
    - 78.17 Application of external fixation device, tibia and fibula
    - 84.72 Application of external fixator device, ring system

15. Code assignment:
    - 722.52 Degeneration of lumbar or lumbosacral intervertebral disc
    - 80.53 Repair of the anulus fibrosus with graft or prosthesis

16. Code assignment:
    - 153.8 Malignant neoplasm of other specified sites of large intestine
    - 45.82 Open total intra-abdominal colectomy

17. Code assignment:
    - 571.9 Other chronic nonalcoholic liver disease
    - 50.13 Transjugular liver biopsy

18. Code assignment:
    - 434.01 Cerebral thrombosis
    - 39.74 Endovascular removal of obstruction from head and neck vessel(s)
    - 00.40 Procedure on single vessel

19. Code assignment:
    - 996.46 Articular bearing surface wear of prosthetic joint V43.64 Organ or tissue replaced by other means; hip
    - 00.71 Revision of hip replacement, acetabular component only
    - 00.77 Hip bearing surface, ceramic-on-polyethylene

20. Code assignment:
    - 414.01 Coronary atherosclerosis of native coronary artery
    - 413.9 Other and unspecified angina pectoris
    - 00.66 Percutaneous transluminal coronary angioplasty [PTCA]
    - 36.07 Insertion of drug-eluting coronary artery stent(s)
    - 00.40 Procedure on single vessel
    - 00.47 Insertion of three vascular stents
    - 00.44 Procedure on bifurcated vessel

HCPCS Self Test Answer Key

1. b. A0380-SH, *BLS mileage (per mile)—from the scene of an accident to the hospital.*

2. a. B4168, 2 units, *Parenteral nutrition solution: amino acid, 3.5% (500 ml = 1 unit) –home mix*

3. d. D1110, Prophylaxis-adult

4. c. J0696, 2 units, *Injection, ceftriaxone sodium, per 250 mg*

5. a. M0064 *Brief office visit for the sole purpose of monitoring or changing drug prescriptions used in the treatment of mental psychoneurotic and personality disorders*

6. d. Healthcare Common Procedure Coding System

   The term HCPCS (pronounced "hick-picks") is most accurately used as the acronym for the entire two level coding system.

7. b. CPT codes

   HCPCS level I is the American Medical Associations (AMA) *Physicians' Current Procedural Terminology*

8. Level II HCPCS refers to:

   a. HCPCS alphanumeric codes

   HCPCS is commonly used to specifically identify HCPCS level II national codes

9. b. Code from index

   Codes should never be assigned directly from the index. Once locating the term in the index, refer to the tabular section of the book to verify the code.

10. d. Dental codes

11. a. A4550 *Surgical tray*

12 c. J0540 *Injection, penicillin G benzathine and pencillin procaine, up to 1, 200,000 units*

13. b. G0008 *Administration of influenza virus vaccine*

14. b. J1569 x 2 *Injection, immune globulin, (Gammagard liquid), intravenous, non-lyophilized, (e.g., liquid), 500 mg*

    This code is per 500 mg and should be reported with two units to report 1,000 mg.

15. d. J1885, 2 units, *Injection, ketorlac tromethamine, per 15 mg*

16. d. D2140 *Amalgam-one surface, primary or permanent*

17. d. a and b

18. a. J3488 x 5 *Injection, zoledronic acid, (Reclast), 1 mg*

    This code is per milligram and should be reported with five units for 5 mg.

19. a. A6532-RT *Gradient compression stocking, below knee, 40-50 mm Hg, each, right side*

    Code A6532-RT describes gradient compression stocking 40–50 mm Hg. The code is for each stocking. RT modifier is for the right side.

20. d. G0379 *Direct admission of patient for hospital observation care*

    Code G0379 is for a direct admission to the hospital's observation unit.

21. d. A8001 *Helmet, protective, hard, prefabricated, includes all components and accessories. A8001 includes the helmet and the chin strap.*

22. d. Q5001, *Hospice care provided in patient's home residence.*

23. b. J1953, 50 units, Injection levetiracetam (Keppra), per 10 mg

24. c. G8494 All quality actions for the applicable measures in the diabetes mellitus measures group have been performed for this patient.

    Reporting this code is voluntary. It should be reported in addition to the code for the office visit.

Notes

Notes

Notes

Notes